German
Dictionary
Plus Grammar

HarperResource
An Imprint of HarperCollins*Publishers*

third edition 2004

© HarperCollins Publishers 1997, 1999, 2004

HarperCollins Publishers
Westerhill Road, Bishopbriggs, Glasgow G64 2QT
Great Britain

www.collinsdictionaries.com

Collins® and Bank of English® are registered trademarks of
HarperCollins Publishers Limited

Collins is an imprint of HarperCollins Publishers

ISBN 0-00-712628-X

HarperCollins Publishers, Inc.
10 East 53rd Street, New York, NY 10022

ISBN 0-06-057577-8

Library of Congress Cataloging-in-Publication Data
has been applied for

www.harpercollins.com

First HarperCollins edition published 1998

HarperCollins books may be purchased for educational, business, or sales
promotional use. For information, please write to: Special Markets Department,
HarperCollins Publishers Inc., 10 East 53rd Street, New York, NY 10022

A catalogue record for this book is available from the British Library

Dictionary text typeset by Morton Word Processing Ltd, Scarborough
Grammar text typeset by Carol MacLeod

Printed in Italy by Legoprint S.P.A.

INHALT		CONTENTS	

Dagmar Förtsch, Hildegard Pesch, Veronika Schnorr, Gisela Moohan
Ulrike Seeberger, Elspeth Anderson, Val McNulty
Eva Vennebusch, Horst Kopleck, Robin Sawers, Ilse MacLean, Beate Wengel

editorial staff
Vivian Marr, Nicola Cooke, Joyce Littlejohn, Christine Bahr, Maree Airlie,
Carol MacLeod, Anne Lindsay, Megan Thomson, Caitlin McMahon

computing staff
Stewart Russell, André Gautier, Raymund Carrick

series editor
Lorna Sinclair

INTRODUCTION

You may be starting to learn German, or you may wish to extend your knowledge of the language. Perhaps you want to read and study German books, newspapers and magazines, or perhaps simply have a conversation with German speakers. Whatever the reason, whether you're a student, a tourist or want to use German for business, this is the ideal book to help you understand and communicate. This modern, user-friendly dictionary gives priority to everyday vocabulary and the language of current affairs, business and tourism. As in all Collins dictionaries, the emphasis is firmly placed on contemporary language and expressions.

HOW TO USE THE DICTIONARY

You will find below an outline of the way in which information is presented in your dictionary. Our aim is to give you the maximum amount of information whilst still providing a text which is clear and user-friendly.

Entries

A typical entry in your dictionary will be made up of the following elements:

Phonetic transcription

Phonetics appear in square brackets immediately after the headword. They are shown using the International Phonetic Alphabet (IPA), and a complete list of the symbols used in this system can be found on pages x and xi.

Grammatical information

All words belong to one of the following parts of speech: noun, verb, adjective, adverb, pronoun, article, conjunction, preposition, exclamation, abbreviation. Nouns can be singular or plural and, in German, masculine, feminine or neuter. Verbs can be transitive, intransitive, reflexive or impersonal. Parts of speech appear in *italics* immediately after the phonetic spelling of the headword. The gender of the translation appears in *italics* immediately following the key element of the translation.

Often a word can have more than one part of speech. Just as the English word **next** can be an adjective or an adverb, the German word **gut** can be an adjective ("good") or an adverb ("well"). In the same way the verb **to walk** is sometimes transitive, i.e. it takes an object ("to walk the dog") and sometimes intransitive, i.e. it doesn't take an object ("to walk to school"). To help you find the meaning you are looking for quickly and for clarity of presentation, the different part of speech categories are separated by a black lozenge ♦.

Meaning divisions

Most words have more than one meaning. Take, for example, **punch** which can be, amongst other things, a blow with the fist or an object used for making holes. Other words are translated differently depending on the context in which they are used. The intransitive verb **to recede**, for example, can be translated by "zurückgehen" or "verschwinden" depending on *what* is receding. To help you select the most appropriate translation in every context, entries are divided according to meaning. Each different meaning is introduced by an "indicator" in *italics* and in brackets. Thus, the examples given above will be shown as follows:

> **punch** n (*blow*) Schlag m; (*tool*) Locher m
> **recede** vi (*tide*) zurückgehen; (*lights etc*) verschwinden

Likewise, some words can have a different meaning when used to talk about a specific subject area or field. For example, **bishop**, which in a religious context means a high-ranking clergyman, is also the name of a chess piece. To show English speakers which translation to use, we have added "subject field labels" in capitals and in brackets, in this case (*REL*) and (*CHESS*):

bishop *n* (*REL*) Bischof *m*; (*CHESS*) Läufer *m*

Field labels are often shortened to save space. You will find a complete list of abbreviations used in the dictionary on pages vi to viii.

Translations

Most English words have a direct translation in German and vice versa, as shown in the examples given above. Sometimes, however, no exact equivalent exists in the target language. In such cases we have given an approximate equivalent, indicated by the sign ≈. Such is the case of **high school**, the German equivalent of which is "Oberschule *f*". This is not an exact translation since the systems of the two countries in question are quite different:

high school *n* ≈ Oberschule *f*

On occasion it is impossible to find even an approximate equivalent. This may be the case, for example, with the names of culinary specialities like this German cake:

Streuselkuchen *m cake with crumble topping*

Here the translation (which doesn't exist) is replaced by an explanation. For increased clarity the explanation, or "gloss", is shown in *italics*.

Register

In English you instinctively know when to say **I'm broke** *or* **I'm a bit short of cash** and when to say **I don't have any money**. When you are trying to understand someone who is speaking German, however, or when you yourself try to speak German, it is especially important to know what is polite and what is less so. To help you with this, we have added the register labels (*umg*) and (*inf*) to colloquial or offensive expressions. Those expressions which are particularly vulgar are also given an exclamation mark (*umg!*) or (*inf!*), warning you to use them with extreme care. Please note that the register labels (*umg*) and (*inf*) are not repeated in the target language when the register of the translation matches that of the word or phrase being translated.

Keywords

Words labelled in the text as *KEYWORDS*, such as **be** and **do** or their German equivalents **sein** and **machen**, have been given special treatment because they form the basic elements of the language. This extra help will ensure that you know how to use these complex words with confidence.

Cultural information

Entries which appear separated from the main text by a line above and below them explain aspects of culture in German- and English-speaking countries. Subject areas covered include politics, education, media and national festivals, for example **Bundestag**, **Abitur**, **BBC** and **Hallowe'en**.

German Spelling Reform

The German spelling reform has been fully implemented in this dictionary. All headwords on the German-English side which are affected by the spelling changes are marked with ▲, but old spellings which are markedly different from the new ones and have a different alphabetical position are still listed and are cross-referenced to the new spellings. The old spellings are marked with △.

ABKÜRZUNGEN

ABBREVIATIONS

Abkürzung	**abk, abbr**	abbreviation
Adjektiv	**adj**	adjective
Verwaltung	ADMIN	administration
Adverb	**adv**	adverb
Agrarwirtschaft	AGR	agriculture
Akkusativ	**akk, acc**	accusative
Anatomie	ANAT	anatomy
Architektur	ARCHIT	architecture
Artikel	**art**	article
Kunst	ART	
Astrologie	ASTROL	astrology
Astronomie	ASTRON	astronomy
attributiv	**attrib**	attributive
Kraftfahrzeugwesen	AUT	automobiles
Hilfsverb	**aux**	auxiliary
Luftfahrt	AVIAT	aviation
Bergbau	BERGB	mining
besonders	**bes**	especially
Biologie	BIOL	biology
Botanik	BOT	botany
britisch	BRIT	British
Kartenspiel	CARDS	
Chemie	CHEM	chemistry
Film	CINE	cinema
Handel	COMM	commerce
Komparativ	**comp**	comparative
Computerwesen	COMPUT	computers
Konjunktion	**conj**	conjunction
Bauwesen	CONSTR	building
zusammengesetztes Wort	**cpd**	compound
Kochen und Backen	CULIN	cooking
Dativ	**dat**	dative
bestimmt	**def**	definite
diminutiv	**dimin**	diminutive
dekliniert	**dekl**	declined
kirchlich	ECCL	ecclesiastical
Volkswirtschaft	ECON	economics
Eisenbahnwesen	EISENB	railways
Elektrizität	**ELEK, ELEC**	electricity
besonders	**esp**	especially
und so weiter	**etc**	et cetera
etwas	**etw**	something
Euphemismus	**euph**	euphemism
Ausruf	**excl**	exclamation
Femininum	**f**	feminine
übertragen	**fig**	figurative
Film	FILM	cinema
Finanzwesen	FIN	finance
formell	**form**	formal
'phrasal verb', bei dem Partikel und Verb nicht getrennt werden können	**fus**	fused: phrasal verb where the particle cannot be separated from the verb
gehoben	**geh**	elevated
Genitiv	**gen**	genitive
Geografie	GEOG	geography

ABKÜRZUNGEN

ABBREVIATIONS

Geologie	*GEOL*	geology
Geometrie	*GEOM*	geometry
Grammatik	*GRAM*	grammar
Geschichte	*HIST*	history
scherzhaft	*hum*	humorous
Imperfekt	*imperf*	imperfect
unpersönlich	*impers*	impersonal
unbestimmt	*indef*	indefinite
umgangssprachlich	*inf*	informal
untrennbares Verb	*insep*	inseparable
Interjektion	*interj*	interjection
interrogativ	*interrog*	interrogative
unveränderlich	*inv*	invariable
unregelmäßig	*irreg*	irregular
jemand	*jd*	somebody
jemandem	*jdm*	(to) somebody
jemanden	*jdn*	somebody
jemandes	*jds*	somebody's
Rechtswesen	*JUR*	law
Kartenspiel	*KARTEN*	cards
Kochen und Backen	*KOCH*	cooking
Komparativ	*komp*	comparative
Konjunktion	*konj*	conjunction
Rechtswesen	*LAW*	
Sprachwissenschaft	*LING*	linguistics
wörtlich	*lit*	literal
literarisch	*liter*	literary
Literatur	*LITER*	literature
Maskulinum	*m*	masculine
Mathematik	*MATH*	mathematics
Medizin	*MED*	medicine
Meteorologie	*MET*	meteorology
Militärwesen	*MIL*	military
Bergbau	*MIN*	mining
Musik	*MUS*	music
Substantiv	*n*	noun
nautisch	*NAUT*	nautical
Nominativ	*nom*	nominative
Norddeutschland	*NORDD*	North German
Neutrum	*nt*	neuter
Zahlwort	*num*	numeral
Objekt	*obj*	object
oder	*od*	or
veraltet	*old*	
sich	*o.s.*	oneself
Österreich	*ÖSTERR*	Austria
Parlament	*PARL*	parliament
pejorativ	*pej*	pejorative
Person/persönlich	*pers*	person/personal
Pharmazie	*PHARM*	pharmacy
Fotografie	*PHOT*	photography
Physik	*PHYS*	physics
Physiologie	*PHYSIOL*	physiology
Plural	*pl*	plural
Politik	*POL*	politics

ABKÜRZUNGEN   ABBREVIATIONS

possessiv	**poss**	possessive
Partizip Perfekt	**pp**	past participle
Präfix	**präf, pref**	prefix
Präposition	**präp, prep**	preposition
Präsens	**präs, pres**	present
Pronomen	**pron**	pronoun
Psychologie	**PSYCH**	psychology
Imperfekt	**pt**	past tense
Radio	**RADIO**	radio
Eisenbahnwesen	**RAIL**	railways
Relativ-	**rel**	relative
Religion	**REL**	religion
Rundfunk	**RUNDF**	broadcasting
jemand (-en, -em)	**sb**	somebody
Schulwesen	**SCH**	school
Naturwissenschaft	**SCI**	science
Schulwesen	**SCOL**	school
schottisch	**SCOT**	Scottish
Singular	**sing**	singular
Skisport	**SKI**	skiing
etwas	**sth**	something
Süddeutschland	**SÜDD**	South German
Suffix	**suff**	suffix
Superlativ	**superl**	superlative
Technik	**TECH**	technology
Nachrichtentechnik	**TEL**	telecommunications
Theater	**THEAT**	theatre
Fernsehen	**TV**	television
Typografie	**TYP**	typography
umgangssprachlich	**umg**	colloquial
Universität	**UNIV**	university
unpersönlich	**unpers**	impersonal
unregelmäßig	**unreg**	irregular
untrennbar	**untr**	inseparable
unveränderlich	**unver**	invariable
(nord)amerikanisch	**US**	(North) American
gewöhnlich	**usu**	usually
und so weiter	**usw**	et cetera
Verb	**vb**	verb
intransitives Verb	**vi**	intransitive verb
reflexives Verb	**vr**	reflexive verb
transitives Verb	**vt**	transitive verb
Wirtschaft	**WIRTS**	economy
Zoologie	**ZOOL**	zoology
zusammengesetztes Wort	**zW**	compound
zwischen zwei Sprechern	**-**	change of speaker
ungefähre Entsprechung	**≈**	cultural equivalent
eingetragenes Warenzeichen	**®**	registered trademark

GERMAN NOUN ENDINGS

After many noun entries on the German-English side of the dictionary, you will find two pieces of grammatical information, separated by commas, to help you with the declension of the noun, e.g. -, -n or -(e)s, -e.

The first item shows you the genitive singular form, and the second gives the plural form. The hyphen stands for the word itself and the other letters are endings. Sometimes an umlaut is shown over the hyphen, which means an umlaut must be placed on the vowel of the word, e.g.:

dictionary entry	genitive singular	plural
Mann *m* **-(e)s, ¨er**	**Mannes** *or* **Manns**	**Männer**
Jacht *f* **-, -en**	**Jacht**	**Jachten**

This information is not given when the noun has one of the regular German noun endings below, and you should refer to this table in such cases.

Similarly, genitive and plural endings are not shown when the German entry is a compound consisting of two or more words which are to be found elsewhere in the dictionary, since the compound form takes the endings of the LAST word of which it is formed, e.g.:

for **Nebenstraße**	*see* **Straße**
for **Schneeball**	*see* **Ball**

Regular German Noun Endings

nom		gen	pl
-ant	*m*	-anten	-anten
-anz	*f*	-anz	-anzen
-ar	*m*	-ar(e)s	-are
-chen	*nt*	-chens	-chen
-ei	*f*	-ei	-eien
-elle	*f*	-elle	-ellen
-ent	*m*	-enten	-enten
-enz	*f*	-enz	-enzen
-ette	*f*	-ette	-etten
-eur	*m*	-eurs	-eure
-euse	*f*	-euse	-eusen
-heit	*f*	-heit	-heiten
-ie	*f*	-ie	-ien
-ik	*f*	-ik	-iken
-in	*f*	-in	-innen
-ine	*f*	-ine	-inen
-ion	*f*	-ion	-ionen
-ist	*m*	-isten	-isten
-ium	*nt*	-iums	-ien
-ius	*m*	-ius	-iusse
-ive	*f*	-ive	-iven
-keit	*f*	-keit	-keiten
-lein	*nt*	-leins	-lein
-ling	*m*	-lings	-linge
-ment	*nt*	-ments	-mente
-mus	*m*	-mus	-men
-schaft	*f*	-schaft	-schaften
-tät	*f*	-tät	-täten
-tor	*m*	-tors	-toren
-ung	*f*	-ung	-ungen
-ur	*f*	-ur	-uren

PHONETIC SYMBOLS   LAUTSCHRIFT

NB: All vowels sounds are
approximate only.

NB: Alle Vokallaute sind nur
ungefähre Entsprechungen.

Vowels   Vokale

matt	[a]	
Fahne	[aː]	
Vater	[ər]	
	[ɑː]	calm, part
	[æ]	sat
Rendezvous	[ã]	
Chance	[aː]	
	[ãː]	clientele
Etage	[e]	
Seele, Mehl	[eː]	
Wäsche, Bett	[ɛ]	egg
zählen	[ɛː]	
Teint	[ɛ̃ː]	
mache	[ə]	above
	[əː]	burn, earn
Kiste	[ɪ]	pit, awfully
Vitamin	[i]	
Ziel	[iː]	peat
Oase	[o]	
oben	[oː]	
Champignon	[õ]	
Salon	[õː]	
Most	[ɔ]	cot
	[ɔː]	born, jaw
ökonomisch	[ø]	
blöd	[øː]	
Göttin	[œ]	
	[ʌ]	hut
zuletzt	[u]	put
Mut	[uː]	pool
Mutter	[ʊ]	
Physik	[y]	
Kübel	[yː]	
Sünde	[ʏ]	

Diphthongs

St<u>y</u>ling	[ai]	
w<u>ei</u>t	[aɪ]	b<u>uy</u>, d<u>ie</u>, m<u>y</u>
umb<u>au</u>en	[au]	h<u>ou</u>se, n<u>ow</u>
H<u>au</u>s	[aʊ]	
	[eɪ]	p<u>ay</u>, m<u>a</u>te
	[ɛə]	p<u>ai</u>r, m<u>a</u>re
	[əu]	n<u>o</u>, b<u>oa</u>t
	[ɪə]	m<u>e</u>re, sh<u>ea</u>r
H<u>eu</u>, H<u>äu</u>ser	[ɔɣ]	
	[ɔɪ]	b<u>oy</u>, c<u>oi</u>n
	[uə]	t<u>ou</u>r, p<u>oo</u>r

Diphthonge

Consonants

<u>B</u>all	[b]	<u>b</u>all
mi<u>ch</u>	[ç]	
	[tʃ]	<u>ch</u>ild
<u>f</u>ern	[f]	<u>f</u>ield
gern	[g]	good
<u>H</u>and	[h]	<u>h</u>and
<u>j</u>a	[j]	<u>y</u>et, mill<u>i</u>on
	[dʒ]	<u>j</u>ust
<u>K</u>ind	[k]	<u>k</u>ind, <u>c</u>atch
<u>l</u>inks, Pu<u>l</u>t	[l]	<u>l</u>eft, litt<u>l</u>e
<u>m</u>att	[m]	<u>m</u>at
<u>N</u>est	[n]	<u>n</u>est
la<u>ng</u>	[ŋ]	lo<u>ng</u>
<u>P</u>aar	[p]	<u>p</u>ut
<u>r</u>ennen	[r]	<u>r</u>un
fa<u>s</u>t, fa<u>ss</u>en	[s]	<u>s</u>it
<u>Ch</u>ef, <u>S</u>tein, <u>Sch</u>lag	[ʃ]	<u>sh</u>all
<u>T</u>afel	[t]	<u>t</u>ab
	[θ]	<u>th</u>ing
	[ð]	<u>th</u>is
<u>w</u>er	[v]	<u>v</u>ery
	[w]	<u>w</u>et
Lo<u>ch</u>	[x]	lo<u>ch</u>
fi<u>x</u>	[ks]	bo<u>x</u>
<u>s</u>ingen	[z]	pod<u>s</u>, <u>z</u>ip
<u>Z</u>ahn	[ts]	
<u>g</u>enieren	[ʒ]	mea<u>s</u>ure

Konsonanten

Other signs

glottal stop	|	Knacklaut
main stress	[']	Hauptton
long vowel	[:]	Längezeichen

Andere Zeichen

GERMAN IRREGULAR VERBS

* with 'sein'

Infinitive	Present Indicative 2nd pers sing ♦ 3rd pers sing	Imperfect Indicative	Past Participle
aufschrecken*	schrickst auf ♦ schrickt auf	schrak od schreckte auf	aufgeschreckt
ausbedingen	bedingst aus ♦ bedingt aus	bedang od bedingte aus	ausbedungen
backen	bäckst ♦ bäckt	backte od buk	gebacken
befehlen	befiehlst ♦ befiehlt	befahl	befohlen
beginnen	beginnst ♦ beginnt	begann	begonnen
beißen	beißt ♦ beißt	biß	gebissen
bergen	birgst ♦ birgt	barg	geborgen
bersten*	birst ♦ birst	barst	geborsten
bescheißen	bescheißt ♦ bescheißt	beschiss	beschissen
bewegen	bewegst ♦ bewegt	bewog	bewogen
biegen	biegst ♦ biegt	bog	gebogen
bieten	bietest ♦ bietet	bot	geboten
binden	bindest ♦ bindet	band	gebunden
bitten	bittest ♦ bittet	bat	gebeten
blasen	bläst ♦ bläst	blies	geblasen
bleiben*	bleibst ♦ bleibt	blieb	geblieben
braten	brätst ♦ brät	briet	gebraten
brechen*	brichst ♦ bricht	brach	gebrochen
brennen	brennst ♦ brennt	brannte	gebrannt
bringen	bringst ♦ bringt	brachte	gebracht
denken	denkst ♦ denkt	dachte	gedacht
dreschen	drisch(e)st ♦ drischt	drosch	gedroschen
dringen*	dringst ♦ dringt	drang	gedrungen
dürfen	darfst ♦ darf	durfte	gedurft
empfangen	empfängst ♦ empfängt	empfing	empfangen
empfehlen	empfiehlst ♦ empfiehlt	empfahl	empfohlen
erbleichen*	erbleichst ♦ erbleicht	erbleichte	erblichen
erlöschen*	erlischst ♦ erlischt	erlosch	erloschen
erschrecken*	erschrickst ♦ erschrickt	erschrak	erschrocken
essen	isst ♦ isst	aß	gegessen
fahren*	fährst ♦ fährt	fuhr	gefahren
fallen*	fällst ♦ fällt	fiel	gefallen
fangen	fängst ♦ fängt	fing	gefangen
fechten	fichtst ♦ ficht	focht	gefochten
finden	findest ♦ findet	fand	gefunden
flechten	flichtst ♦ flicht	flocht	geflochten
fliegen*	fliegst ♦ fliegt	flog	geflogen
fliehen*	fliehst ♦ flieht	floh	geflohen
fließen*	fließt ♦ fließt	floss	geflossen
fressen	frisst ♦ frisst	fraß	gefressen
frieren	frierst ♦ friert	fror	gefroren
gären*	gärst ♦ gärt	gor	gegoren
gebären	gebierst ♦ gebiert	gebar	geboren
geben	gibst ♦ gibt	gab	gegeben
gedeihen*	gedeihst ♦ gedeiht	gedieh	gediehen
gehen*	gehst ♦ geht	ging	gegangen
gelingen*	- ♦ gelingt	gelang	gelungen
gelten	giltst ♦ gilt	galt	gegolten
genesen*	gene(se)st ♦ genest	genas	genesen
genießen	genießt ♦ genießt	genoss	genossen
geraten*	gerätst ♦ gerät	geriet	geraten
geschehen*	- ♦ geschieht	geschah	geschehen
gewinnen	gewinnst ♦ gewinnt	gewann	gewonnen
gießen	gießt ♦ gießt	goss	gegossen
gleichen	gleichst ♦ gleicht	glich	geglichen
gleiten*	gleitest ♦ gleitet	glitt	geglitten
glimmen	glimmst ♦ glimmt	glomm	geglommen

Infinitive	Present Indicative 2nd pers sing ♦ 3rd pers sing	Imperfect Indicative	Past Participle
graben	gräbst ♦ gräbt	grub	gegraben
greifen	greifst ♦ greift	griff	gegriffen
haben	hast ♦ hat	hatte	gehabt
halten	hältst ♦ hält	hielt	gehalten
hängen	hängst ♦ hängt	hing	gehangen
hauen	haust ♦ haut	hieb	gehauen
heben	hebst ♦ hebt	hob	gehoben
heißen	heißt ♦ heißt	hieß	geheißen
helfen	hilfst ♦ hilft	half	geholfen
kennen	kennst ♦ kennt	kannte	gekannt
klimmen*	klimmst ♦ klimmt	klomm	geklommen
klingen	klingst ♦ klingt	klang	geklungen
kneifen	kneifst ♦ kneift	kniff	gekniffen
kommen*	kommst ♦ kommt	kam	gekommen
können	kannst ♦ kann	konnte	gekonnt
kriechen*	kriechst ♦ kriecht	kroch	gekrochen
laden	lädst ♦ lädt	lud	geladen
lassen	lässt ♦ lässt	ließ	gelassen
laufen*	läufst ♦ läuft	lief	gelaufen
leiden	leidest ♦ leidet	litt	gelitten
leihen	leihst ♦ leiht	lieh	geliehen
lesen	liest ♦ liest	las	gelesen
liegen	liegst ♦ liegt	lag	gelegen
lügen	lügst ♦ lügt	log	gelogen
mahlen	mahlst ♦ mahlt	mahlte	gemahlen
meiden	meidest ♦ meidet	mied	gemieden
melken	milkst ♦ milkt	molk	gemolken
messen	misst ♦ misst	maß	gemessen
misslingen*	- ♦ misslingt	misslang	misslungen
mögen	magst ♦ mag	mochte	gemocht
müssen	musst ♦ muss	musste	gemusst
nehmen	nimmst ♦ nimmt	nahm	genommen
nennen	nennst ♦ nennt	nannte	genannt
pfeifen	pfeifst ♦ pfeift	pfiff	gepfiffen
preisen	preist ♦ preist	pries	gepriesen
quellen*	quillst ♦ quillt	quoll	gequollen
raten	rätst ♦ rät	riet	geraten
reiben	reibst ♦ reibt	rieb	gerieben
reißen*	reißt ♦ reißt	riss	gerissen
reiten*	reitest ♦ reitet	ritt	geritten
rennen*	rennst ♦ rennt	rannte	gerannt
riechen	riechst ♦ riecht	roch	gerochen
ringen	ringst ♦ ringt	rang	gerungen
rinnen*	rinnst ♦ rinnt	rann	geronnen
rufen	rufst ♦ ruft	rief	gerufen
salzen	salzt ♦ salzt	salzte	gesalzen
saufen	säufst ♦ säuft	soff	gesoffen
saugen	saugst ♦ saugt	sog	gesogen od gesaugt
schaffen	schaffst ♦ schafft	schuf	geschaffen
schallen	schallst ♦ schallt	scholl	geschollen
scheiden*	scheidest ♦ scheidet	schied	geschieden
scheinen	scheinst ♦ scheint	schien	geschienen
scheißen	scheißt ♦ scheißt	schiss	geschissen
schelten	schiltst ♦ schilt	schalt	gescholten
scheren	scherst ♦ schert	schor	geschoren
schieben	schiebst ♦ schiebt	schob	geschoben
schießen	schießt ♦ schießt	schoss	geschossen
schinden	schindest ♦ schindet	schindete	geschunden
schlafen	schläfst ♦ schläft	schlief	geschlafen
schlagen	schlägst ♦ schlägt	schlug	geschlagen
schleichen*	schleichst ♦ schleicht	schlich	geschlichen
schleifen	schleifst ♦ schleift	schliff	geschliffen
schließen	schließt ♦ schließt	schloss	geschlossen
schlingen	schlingst ♦ schlingt	schlang	geschlungen
schmeißen	schmeißt ♦ schmeißt	schmiss	geschmissen
schmelzen*	schmilzt ♦ schmilzt	schmolz	geschmolzen

Infinitive	Present Indicative 2nd pers sing ♦ 3rd pers sing	Imperfect Indicative	Past Participle
schneiden	schneidest ♦ schneidet	schnitt	geschnitten
schreiben	schreibst ♦ schreibt	schrieb	geschrieben
schreien	schreist ♦ schreit	schrie	geschrie(e)n
schreiten	schreitest ♦ schreitet	schritt	geschritten
schweigen	schweigst ♦ schweigt	schwieg	geschwiegen
schwellen*	schwillst ♦ schwillt	schwoll	geschwollen
schwimmen*	schwimmst ♦ schwimmt	schwamm	geschwommen
schwinden*	schwindest ♦ schwindet	schwand	geschwunden
schwingen	schwingst ♦ schwingt	schwang	geschwungen
schwören	schwörst ♦ schwört	schwor	geschworen
sehen	siehst ♦ sieht	sah	gesehen
sein*	bist ♦ ist	war	gewesen
senden	sendest ♦ sendet	sandte	gesandt
singen	singst ♦ singt	sang	gesungen
sinken*	sinkst ♦ sinkt	sank	gesunken
sinnen	sinnst ♦ sinnt	sann	gesonnen
sitzen	sitzt ♦ sitzt	saß	gesessen
sollen	sollst ♦ soll	sollte	gesollt
speien	speist ♦ speit	spie	gespie(e)n
spinnen	spinnst ♦ spinnt	spann	gesponnen
sprechen	sprichst ♦ spricht	sprach	gesprochen
sprießen*	sprießt ♦ sprießt	spross	gesprossen
springen*	springst ♦ springt	sprang	gesprungen
stechen	stichst ♦ sticht	stach	gestochen
stecken	steckst ♦ steckt	steckte od stak	gesteckt
stehen	stehst ♦ steht	stand	gestanden
stehlen	stiehlst ♦ stiehlt	stahl	gestohlen
steigen*	steigst ♦ steigt	stieg	gestiegen
sterben*	stirbst ♦ stirbt	starb	gestorben
stinken	stinkst ♦ stinkt	stank	gestunken
stoßen	stößt ♦ stößt	stieß	gestoßen
streichen	streichst ♦ streicht	strich	gestrichen
streiten	streitest ♦ streitet	stritt	gestritten
tragen	trägst ♦ trägt	trug	getragen
treffen	triffst ♦ trifft	traf	getroffen
treiben*	treibst ♦ treibt	trieb	getrieben
treten*	trittst ♦ tritt	trat	getreten
trinken	trinkst ♦ trinkt	trank	getrunken
trügen	trügst ♦ trügt	trog	getrogen
tun	tust ♦ tut	tat	getan
verderben	verdirbst ♦ verdirbt	verdarb	verdorben
verdrießen	verdrießt ♦ verdrießt	verdross	verdrossen
vergessen	vergisst ♦ vergisst	vergaß	vergessen
verlieren	verlierst ♦ verliert	verlor	verloren
verschleißen	verschleißt ♦ verschleisst	verschliss	verschlissen
wachsen*	wächst ♦ wächst	wuchs	gewachsen
wägen	wägst ♦ wägt	wog	gewogen
waschen	wäschst ♦ wäscht	wusch	gewaschen
weben	webst ♦ webt	webte od wob	gewoben
weichen*	weichst ♦ weicht	wich	gewichen
weisen	weist ♦ weist	wies	gewiesen
wenden	wendest ♦ wendet	wendete	gewendet
werben	wirbst ♦ wirbt	warb	geworben
werden*	wirst ♦ wird	wurde	geworden
werfen	wirfst ♦ wirft	warf	geworfen
wiegen	wiegst ♦ wiegt	wog	gewogen
winden	windest ♦ windet	wand	gewunden
wissen	weißt ♦ weiß	wusste	gewusst
wollen	willst ♦ will	wollte	gewollt
wringen	wringst ♦ wringt	wrang	gewrungen
zeihen	zeihst ♦ zeiht	zieh	geziehen
ziehen*	ziehst ♦ zieht	zog	gezogen
zwingen	zwingst ♦ zwingt	zwang	gezwungen

A, a

A¹, a [aː] *nt* A, a; **~ wie Anton** ≈ A for Andrew, A for Able (*US*); **das ~ und O** the be-all and end-all; (*eines Wissensgebietes*) the basics *pl*; **wer ~ sagt, muss auch B sagen** in for a penny, in for a pound.

A² *f abk* (= *Autobahn*) ≈ M (*BRIT*).

a. *abk* = **am**.

à [aː] *präp* (*bes COMM*) at.

AA *nt abk* (= *Auswärtiges Amt*) F.O. (*BRIT*).

Aachen ['aːxən] (**-s**) *nt* Aachen.

Aal [aːl] (**-(e)s, -e**) *m* eel.

aalen ['aːlən] (*umg*) *vr*: **sich in der Sonne ~** to bask in the sun.

a. a. O. *abk* (= *am angegebenen od angeführten Ort*) loc. cit.

Aas [aːs] (**-es, -e** *od* **Äser**) *nt* carrion; **~geier** *m* vulture.

═══════════ *SCHLÜSSELWORT*

ab [ap] *präp +dat* from; **~ Werk** (*COMM*) ex works; **Kinder ~ 12 Jahren** children from the age of 12; **~ morgen** from tomorrow; **~ sofort** as of now.

♦ *adv* **1** off; **links ~** to the left; **der Knopf ist ~** the button has come off; **~ nach Hause!** off home with you!; **~ durch die Mitte!** (*umg*) beat it!

2 (*zeitlich*): **von da ~** from then on; **von heute ~** from today, as of today.

3 (*auf Fahrplänen*): **München ~ 12.20** leaving Munich 12.20.

4: **~ und zu** *od* **an** now and then *od* again.

---

abändern ['apɛndərn] *vt*: **~ (in +*akk*)** to alter (to); (*Gesetzentwurf*) to amend (to); (*Strafe, Urteil*) to revise (to).

Abänderung *f* alteration; amendment; revision.

Abänderungsantrag *m* (*PARL*) proposed amendment.

abarbeiten ['apˌarbaɪtən] *vr* to slave away.

Abart ['apˌaːrt] *f* (*BIOL*) variety.

abartig *adj* abnormal.

Abb. *abk* (= *Abbildung*) illus.

Abbau ['apbaʊ] (**-(e)s**) *m* (+*gen*) dismantling; (*Verminderung*) reduction (in); (*Verfall*) decline (in); (*MIN*) mining; (*über Tage*) quarrying; (*CHEM*) decomposition.

abbaubar *adj*: **biologisch ~** biodegradable.

abbauen *vt* to dismantle; (*verringern*) to reduce; (*MIN*) to mine; to quarry; (*CHEM*) to break down; **Arbeitsplätze ~** to make job cuts.

Abbaurechte *pl* mineral rights *pl*.

abbeißen ['apbaɪsən] *unreg vt* to bite off.

abbekommen ['apbəkɔmən] *unreg vt*: **etwas ~** to get some (of it); (*beschädigt werden*) to get damaged; (*verletzt werden*) to get hurt.

abberufen ['apbəruːfən] *unreg vt* to recall.

Abberufung *f* recall.

abbestellen ['apbəʃtɛlən] *vt* to cancel.

abbezahlen ['apbətsaːlən] *vt* to pay off.

abbiegen ['apbiːgən] *unreg vi* to turn off; (*Straße*) to bend ♦ *vt* to bend; (*verhindern*) to ward off.

Abbiegespur *f* turning lane.

Abbild ['apbɪlt] *nt* portrayal; (*einer Person*) image, likeness; **a~en** ['apbɪldən] *vt* to portray; **~ung** *f* illustration; (*Schaubild*) diagram.

abbinden ['apbɪndən] *unreg vt* (*MED: Arm, Bein etc*) to ligature.

Abbitte ['apbɪtə] *f*: **~ leisten** *od* **tun (bei)** to make one's apologies (to).

abblasen ['apblaːzən] *unreg vt* to blow off; (*fig: umg*) to call off.

abblättern ['apblɛtərn] *vi* (*Putz, Farbe*) to flake (off).

abblenden ['apblɛndən] *vt* (*AUT*) to dip (*BRIT*), dim (*US*) ♦ *vi* to dip (*BRIT*) *od* dim (*US*) one's headlights.

Abblendlicht ['apblɛntlɪçt] *nt* dipped (*BRIT*) *od* dimmed (*US*) headlights *pl*.

abblitzen ['apblɪtsən] (*umg*) *vi*: **jdn ~ lassen** to send sb packing.

abbrechen ['apbrɛçən] *unreg vt* to break off; (*Gebäude*) to pull down; (*Zelt*) to take down; (*aufhören*) to stop; (*COMPUT*) to abort ♦ *vi* to break off; to stop; **sich** *dat* **einen** ~ (*umg*: *sich sehr anstrengen*) to bust a gut.

abbrennen ['apbrɛnən] *unreg vt* to burn off; (*Feuerwerk*) to let off ♦ *vi* (*Hilfsverb sein*) to burn down; **abgebrannt sein** (*umg*) to be broke.

abbringen ['apbrɪŋən] *unreg vt*: **jdn von etw** ~ to dissuade sb from sth; **jdn vom Weg** ~ to divert sb; **ich bringe den Verschluss nicht ab** (*umg*) I can't get the top off.

abbröckeln ['apbrœkəln] *vi* to crumble off *od* away; (*BÖRSE: Preise*) to ease.

Abbruch ['apbrʊx] *m* (*von Verhandlungen etc*) breaking off; (*von Haus*) demolition; (*COMPUT*) abort; **jdm/etw** ~ **tun** to harm sb/sth; ~**arbeiten** *pl* demolition work *sing*; **a**~**reif** *adj* only fit for demolition.

abbrühen ['apbry:ən] *vt* to scald.

abbuchen ['apbu:xən] *vt* to debit; (*durch Dauerauftrag*): ~ **(von)** to pay by standing order (from).

abbürsten ['apbyrstən] *vt* to brush off.

abbüßen ['apby:sən] *vt* (*Strafe*) to serve.

ABC-Waffen *pl abk* (= *atomare, biologische und chemische Waffen*) ABC weapons (= atomic, biological and chemical weapons).

abdampfen ['apdampfən] *vi* (*fig: umg: losgehen/-fahren*) to hit the road.

abdanken ['apdaŋkən] *vi* to resign; (*König*) to abdicate.

Abdankung *f* resignation; abdication.

abdecken ['apdɛkən] *vt* to uncover; (*Tisch*) to clear; (*Loch*) to cover.

abdichten ['apdɪçtən] *vt* to seal; (*NAUT*) to caulk.

abdrängen ['apdrɛŋən] *vt* to push off.

abdrehen ['apdre:ən] *vt* (*Gas*) to turn off; (*Licht*) to switch off; (*Film*) to shoot ♦ *vi* (*Schiff*) to change course; **jdm den Hals** ~ **to** wring sb's neck.

abdriften ['apdrɪftən] *vi* to drift (away).

abdrosseln ['apdrɔsəln] *vt* to throttle; (*AUT*) to stall; (*Produktion*) to cut back.

Abdruck ['apdrʊk] *m* (*Nachdrucken*) reprinting; (*Gedrucktes*) reprint; (*Gips*~, *Wachs*~) impression; (*Finger*~) print; **a**~**en** *vt* to print.

abdrücken ['apdrykən] *vt* to make an impression of; (*Waffe*) to fire; (*umg: Person*) to hug, squeeze ♦ *vr* to leave imprints; (*abstoßen*) to push o.s. away; **jdm die Luft** ~ to squeeze all the breath out of sb.

abebben ['apɛbən] *vi* to ebb away.

Abend ['a:bənt] (-**s**, -**e**) *m* evening; **gegen** ~ towards (the) evening; **den ganzen** ~ **(über)** the whole evening; **zu** ~ **essen** to have dinner *od* supper; **heute** ~ this evening; ~**anzug** *m* dinner jacket (*BRIT*), tuxedo (*US*); ~**brot** *nt* supper; ~**essen** *nt* supper; **a**~**füllend** *adj* taking up the whole evening;

~**gymnasium** *nt* night school; ~**kasse** *f* (*THEAT*) box office; ~**kleid** *nt* evening gown; ~**kurs** *m* evening classes *pl*; ~**land** *nt* West; **a**~**lich** *adj* evening; ~**mahl** *nt* Holy Communion; ~**rot** *nt* sunset.

abends *adv* in the evening.

Abend- *zW*: ~**vorstellung** *f* evening performance; ~**zeitung** *f* evening paper.

Abenteuer ['a:bəntɔyər] (-**s**, -) *nt* adventure; (*Liebes*~) affair; **a**~**lich** *adj* adventurous; ~**spielplatz** *m* adventure playground.

Abenteurer (-**s**, -) *m* adventurer; ~**in** *f* adventuress.

aber ['a:bər] *konj* but; (*jedoch*) however ♦ *adv*: **oder** ~ or else; **bist du** ~ **braun!** aren't you brown!; **das ist** ~ **schön** that's really nice; **nun ist** ~ **Schluss!** now that's enough!; **A**~ *nt* but.

Aberglaube ['a:bərglaubə] *m* superstition.

abergläubisch ['a:bərglɔybɪʃ] *adj* superstitious.

aberkennen ['ap|ɛrkɛnən] *unreg vt*: **jdm etw** ~ to deprive sb of sth, take sth (away) from sb.

Aberkennung *f* taking away.

abermalig *adj* repeated.

abermals *adv* once again.

Abertausend▲, **abertausend**▲ ['a:bərtauznt] *indef pron*: **Tausend und** ~, **tausend und a**~ thousands upon thousands.

Abf. *abk* (= *Abfahrt*) dep.

abfahren ['apfa:rən] *unreg vi* to leave, depart ♦ *vt* to take *od* cart away; (*Film*) to start; (*FILM, TV: Kamera*) to roll; (*Strecke*) to drive; (*Reifen*) to wear; (*Fahrkarte*) to use; **der Zug ist abgefahren** (*lit*) the train has left; (*fig*) we've/you've *etc* missed the boat; **der Zug fährt um 8.00 von Bremen ab** the train leaves Bremen at 8 o'clock; **jdn** ~ **lassen** (*umg: abweisen*) to tell sb to get lost; **auf jdn** ~ (*umg*) to really go for sb.

Abfahrt ['apfa:rt] *f* departure; (*Autobahn*~) exit; (*SKI*) descent; (*Piste*) run; **Vorsicht bei der** ~ **des Zuges!** stand clear, the train is about to leave!

Abfahrts- *zW*: ~**lauf** *m* (*SKI*) downhill; ~**tag** *m* day of departure; ~**zeit** *f* departure time.

Abfall ['apfal] *m* waste; (*von Speisen etc*) rubbish (*BRIT*), garbage (*US*); (*Neigung*) slope; (*Verschlechterung*) decline; ~**eimer** *m* rubbish bin (*BRIT*), garbage can (*US*).

abfallen *unreg vi* (*lit, fig*) to fall *od* drop off; (*POL, vom Glauben*) to break away; (*sich neigen*) to fall *od* drop away; **wie viel fällt bei dem Geschäft für mich ab?** (*umg*) how much do I get out of the deal?

abfällig ['apfɛlɪç] *adj* disparaging, deprecatory.

Abfallprodukt *nt* (*lit, fig*) waste product.

abfangen ['apfaŋən] *unreg vt* to intercept;

(*Person*) to catch; (*unter Kontrolle bringen*) to check; (*Aufprall*) to absorb; (*Kunden*) to lure away.

Abfangjäger *m* (*MIL*) interceptor.

abfärben ['apfɛrbən] *vi* (*lit*) to lose its colour; (*Wäsche*) to run; (*fig*) to rub off.

abfassen ['apfasən] *vt* to write, draft.

abfeiern ['apfaiərn] (*umg*) *vt*: **Überstunden** ~ to take time off in lieu of overtime pay.

abfertigen ['apfɛrtɪɡən] *vt* to prepare for dispatch, process; (*an der Grenze*) to clear; (*Kundschaft*) to attend to; **jdn kurz** ~ to give sb short shrift.

Abfertigung *f* preparing for dispatch, processing; clearance; (*Bedienung: von Kunden*) service; (: *von Antragstellern*): ~ **von** dealing with.

abfeuern ['apfɔyərn] *vt* to fire.

abfinden ['apfɪndən] *unreg vt* to pay off ♦ *vr* to come to terms; **sich mit jdm** ~/**nicht** ~ to put up with/not to get on with sb; **er konnte sich nie damit** ~, **dass** ... he could never accept the fact that ...

Abfindung *f* (*von Gläubigern*) payment; (*Geld*) sum in settlement.

abflachen ['apflaxən] *vt* to level (off), flatten (out) ♦ *vi* (*fig: sinken*) to decline.

abflauen ['apflauən] *vi* (*Wind, Erregung*) to die away, subside; (*Nachfrage, Geschäft*) to fall *od* drop off.

abfliegen ['apfli:ɡən] *unreg vi* to take off ♦ *vt* (*Gebiet*) to fly over.

abfließen ['apfli:sən] *unreg vi* to drain away; **ins Ausland** ~ (*Geld*) to flow out of the country.

Abflug ['apflu:k] *m* departure; (*Start*) take-off; ~**zeit** *f* departure time.

Abfluss▲ ['apflʊs] *m* draining away; (*Öffnung*) outlet; ~**rohr** *nt* drainpipe; (*von sanitären Anlagen*) wastepipe.

abfragen ['apfra:ɡən] *vt* to test; (*COMPUT*) to call up; **jdn etw** ~ to question sb on sth.

abfrieren ['apfri:rən] *unreg vi*: **ihm sind die Füße abgefroren** his feet got frostbitten, he got frostbite in his feet.

Abfuhr ['apfu:r] (-, -en) *f* removal; (*fig*) snub, rebuff; **sich** *dat* **eine** ~ **holen** to meet with a rebuff.

abführen ['apfy:rən] *vt* to lead away; (*Gelder, Steuern*) to pay ♦ *vi* (*MED*) to have a laxative effect.

Abführmittel *nt* laxative, purgative.

Abfüllanlage *f* bottling plant.

abfüllen ['apfʏlən] *vt* to draw off; (*in Flaschen*) to bottle.

Abgabe ['apga:bə] *f* handing in; (*von Ball*) pass; (*Steuer*) tax; (*einer Erklärung*) giving.

abgabenfrei *adj* tax-free.

abgabenpflichtig *adj* liable to tax.

Abgabetermin *m* closing date; (*für*

Dissertation etc) submission date.

Abgang ['apgaŋ] *m* (*von Schule*) leaving; (*THEAT*) exit; (*MED: Ausscheiden*) passing; (: *Fehlgeburt*) miscarriage; (*Abfahrt*) departure; (*der Post, von Waren*) dispatch.

Abgangszeugnis *nt* leaving certificate.

Abgas ['apga:s] *nt* waste gas; (*AUT*) exhaust.

ABGB *nt abk* (*ÖSTERR*: = *Allgemeines Bürgerliches Gesetzbuch*) Civil Code in Austria.

abgeben ['apge:bən] *unreg vt* (*Gegenstand*) to hand *od* give in; (*Ball*) to pass; (*Wärme*) to give off; (*Amt*) to hand over; (*Schuss*) to fire; (*Erklärung, Urteil*) to give; (*darstellen*) to make ♦ *vr*: **sich mit jdm/etw** ~ to associate with sb/bother with sth; „**Kinderwagen abzugeben**" "pram for sale"; **jdm etw** ~ (*überlassen*) to let sb have sth.

abgebrannt ['apgəbrant] (*umg*) *adj* broke.

abgebrüht ['apgəbry:t] (*umg*) *adj* (*skrupellos*) hard-boiled, hardened.

abgedroschen ['apgədrɔʃən] *adj* trite; (*Witz*) corny.

abgefahren ['apgəfa:rən] *pp von* **abfahren**.

abgefeimt ['apgəfaimt] *adj* cunning.

abgegeben ['apgəge:bən] *pp von* **abgeben**.

abgegriffen ['apgəgrɪfən] *adj* (*Buch*) well-thumbed; (*Redensart*) trite.

abgehackt ['apgəhakt] *adj* clipped.

abgehalftert ['apgəhalftərt] *adj* (*fig: umg*) run-down, dead beat.

abgehangen ['apgəhaŋən] *pp von* **abhängen** ♦ *adj*: (**gut**) ~ (*Fleisch*) well-hung.

abgehärtet ['apgəhɛrtət] *adj* tough, hardy; (*fig*) hardened.

abgehen ['apge:ən] *unreg vi* to go away, leave; (*THEAT*) to exit; (*POST*) to go; (*MED*) to be passed; (*sterben*) to die; (*Knopf etc*) to come off; (*abgezogen werden*) to be taken off; (*Straße*) to branch off; (*abweichen*): **von einer Forderung** ~ to give up a demand ♦ *vt* (*Strecke*) to go *od* walk along; (*MIL: Gelände*) to patrol; **von seiner Meinung** ~ to change one's opinion; **davon gehen 5% ab** 5% is taken off that; **etw geht jdm ab** (*fehlt*) sb lacks sth.

abgekämpft ['apgəkɛmpft] *adj* exhausted.

abgekartet ['apgəkartət] *adj*: **ein** ~**es Spiel** a rigged job.

abgeklärt ['apgəklɛ:rt] *adj* serene, tranquil.

abgelegen ['apgəle:ɡən] *adj* remote.

abgelten ['apgɛltən] *unreg vt* (*Ansprüche*) to satisfy.

abgemacht ['apgəmaxt] *adj* fixed; ~! done!

abgemagert ['apgəma:ɡərt] *adj* (*sehr dünn*) thin; (*ausgemergelt*) emaciated.

abgeneigt ['apgənaikt] *adj* averse.

abgenutzt ['apgənʊtst] *adj* worn, shabby; (*Reifen*) worn; (*fig: Klischees*) well-worn.

Abgeordnete(r) ['apgəˈɔrdnətə(r)] *f(m)* elected

representative; (*von Parlament*) member of parliament.

Abgesandte(r) ['apgəzantə(r)] *f(m)* delegate; (*POL*) envoy.

abgeschieden ['apgəʃiːdən] *adv* (*einsam*): ~ **leben/wohnen** to live in seclusion.

abgeschlagen ['apgəʃlaːgən] *adj* (*besiegt*) defeated; (*erschöpft*) exhausted, worn-out.

abgeschlossen ['apgəʃlɔsən] *pp von* **abschließen ♦** *adj attrib* (*Wohnung*) self-contained.

abgeschmackt ['apgəʃmakt] *adj* tasteless; **A~heit** *f* lack of taste; (*Bemerkung*) tasteless remark.

abgesehen ['apgəzeːən] *adj*: **es auf jdn/etw** ~ **haben** to be after sb/sth; ~ **von ...** apart from ...

abgespannt ['apgəʃpant] *adj* tired out.

abgestanden ['apgəʃtandən] *adj* stale; (*Bier*) flat.

abgestorben ['apgəʃtɔrbən] *adj* numb; (*BIOL, MED*) dead.

abgestumpft ['apgəʃtumpft] *adj* (*gefühllos*: *Person*) insensitive; (*Gefühle, Gewissen*) dulled.

abgetakelt ['apgətaːkəlt] *adj* (*fig*) decrepit, past it.

abgetan ['apgətaːn] *adj*: **damit ist die Sache** ~ that settles the matter.

abgetragen ['apgətraːgən] *adj* worn.

abgewinnen ['apgəvɪnən] *unreg vt*: **jdm Geld** ~ to win money from sb; **einer Sache etw/ Geschmack** ~ to get sth/pleasure from sth.

abgewogen ['apgəvoːgən] *adj* (*Urteil, Worte*) balanced.

abgewöhnen ['apgəvøːnən] *vt*: **jdm/sich etw** ~ to cure sb of sth/give sth up.

abgießen ['apgiːsən] *unreg vt* (*Flüssigkeit*) to pour off.

Abglanz ['apglants] *m* (*auch fig*) reflection.

abgleiten ['apglaɪtən] *unreg vi* to slip, slide.

Abgott ['apgɔt] *m* idol.

abgöttisch ['apgœtɪʃ] *adj*: ~ **lieben** to idolize.

abgrasen ['apgraːzən] *vt* (*Feld*) to graze; (*umg*: *Thema*) to do to death.

abgrenzen ['apgrɛntsən] *vt* (*lit, fig*) to mark off; (*Gelände*) to fence off **♦** *vr*: **sich** ~ **(gegen)** to dis(as)sociate o.s. (from).

Abgrund ['apgrunt] *m* (*lit, fig*) abyss.

abgründig ['apgryndɪç] *adj* unfathomable; (*Lächeln*) cryptic.

abgrundtief *adj* (*Hass, Verachtung*) profound.

abgucken ['apgukən] *vt, vi* to copy.

Abguss▲ ['apgus] *m* (*KUNST, METALLURGIE*: *Vorgang*) casting; (: *Form*) cast.

abhaben ['aphaːbən] *unreg* (*umg*) *vt* (*abbekommen*): **willst du ein Stück ~?** do you want a bit?

abhacken ['aphakən] *vt* to chop off.

abhaken ['aphaːkən] *vt* to tick off (*BRIT*),

check off (*US*).

abhalten ['aphaltən] *unreg vt* (*Versammlung*) to hold; **jdn von etw** ~ (*fern halten*) to keep sb away from sth; (*hindern*) to keep sb from sth.

abhandeln ['aphandəln] *vt* (*Thema*) to deal with; **jdm die Waren/10 Euro** ~ to do a deal with sb for the goods/beat sb down 10 euros.

abhanden [ap'handən] *adj*: ~ **kommen** to get lost.

Abhandlung ['aphandluŋ] *f* treatise, discourse.

Abhang ['aphaŋ] *m* slope.

abhängen ['aphɛŋən] *unreg vt* (*Bild*) to take down; (*Anhänger*) to uncouple; (*Verfolger*) to shake off **♦** *vi* (*Fleisch*) to hang; **von jdm/etw** ~ to depend on sb/sth; **das hängt ganz davon ab** it all depends; **er hat abgehängt** (*TEL*: *umg*) he hung up (on me *etc*).

abhängig ['aphɛŋɪç] *adj*: ~ **(von)** dependent (on); **A~keit** *f*: **A~keit (von)** dependence (on).

abhärten ['aphɛrtən] *vt* to toughen up **♦** *vr* to toughen (o.s.) up; **sich gegen etw** ~ to harden o.s. to sth.

abhauen ['aphauən] *unreg vt* to cut off; (*Baum*) to cut down **♦** *vi* (*umg*) to clear off *od* out; **hau ab!** beat it!

abheben ['apheːbən] *unreg vt* to lift (up); (*Karten*) to cut; (*Masche*) to slip; (*Geld*) to withdraw, take out **♦** *vi* (*Flugzeug*) to take off; (*Rakete*) to lift off; (*KARTEN*) to cut **♦** *vr*: **sich** ~ **von** to stand out from, contrast with.

abheften ['aphɛftən] *vt* (*Rechnungen etc*) to file away; (*NÄHEN*) to tack, baste.

abhelfen ['aphɛlfən] *unreg vi* +*dat* to remedy.

abhetzen ['aphɛtsən] *vr* to wear *od* tire o.s. out.

Abhilfe ['aphɪlfə] *f* remedy; ~ **schaffen** to put things right.

Abholmarkt *m* cash and carry.

abholen ['aphoːlən] *vt* (*Gegenstand*) to fetch, collect; (*Person*) to call for; (*am Bahnhof etc*) to pick up, meet.

abholzen ['aphɔltsən] *vt* (*Wald*) to clear, deforest.

abhorchen ['aphɔrçən] *vt* (*MED*) to listen to, sound.

abhören ['aphøːrən] *vt* (*Vokabeln*) to test; (*Telefongespräch*) to tap; (*Tonband etc*) to listen to; **abgehört werden** (*umg*) to be bugged.

Abhörgerät *nt* bug.

abhungern ['aphuŋərn] *vr*: **sich** *dat* **10 Kilo** ~ to lose 10 kilos by going on a starvation diet.

Abi ['abi] (*-s, -s*) *nt* (*SCH*: *umg*) = **Abitur**.

Abitur [abi'tuːr] (*-s, -e*) *nt* German school-leaving examination, ≈ A-levels *pl* (*BRIT*); **(das)** ~ **machen** to take one's school-leaving exam *od* A-levels.

ABITUR

The **Abitur** is the German school-leaving examination which is taken at the age of 18 or 19 by pupils at a **Gymnasium**. It is taken in four subjects and is necessary for entry to a university education.

Abiturient(in) [abituri'ɛnt(ɪn)] m(f) candidate for school-leaving certificate.
abkämmen ['apkɛmən] vt (Gegend) to comb, scour.
abkanzeln ['apkantsəln] (umg) vt: **jdn** ~ to give sb a dressing-down.
abkapseln ['apkapsəln] vr to shut od cut o.s. off.
abkarten ['apkartən] (umg) vt: **die Sache war von vornherein abgekartet** the whole thing was a put-up job.
abkaufen ['apkaʊfən] vt: **jdm etw** ~ to buy sth from sb.
abkehren ['apkeːrən] vt (Blick) to avert, turn away ♦ vr to turn away.
abklappern ['apklapərn] (umg) vt (Kunden) to call on; (: Läden, Straße): ~ **(nach)** to scour (for), comb (for).
abklären ['apklɛːrən] vt (klarstellen) to clear up, clarify ♦ vr (sich setzen) to clarify.
Abklatsch ['apklatʃ] (-es, -e) m (fig) (poor) copy.
abklemmen ['apklɛmən] vt (Leitung) to clamp.
abklingen ['apklɪŋən] unreg vi to die away; (RUNDF) to fade out.
abknallen ['apknalən] (umg) vt to shoot down.
abknöpfen ['apknœpfən] vt to unbutton; **jdm etw** ~ (umg) to get sth off sb.
abkochen ['apkɔxən] vt to boil; (keimfrei machen) to sterilize (by boiling).
abkommandieren ['apkɔmandiːrən] vt (MIL: zu Einheit) to post; (zu bestimmtem Dienst): ~ **zu** to detail for.
abkommen ['apkɔmən] unreg vi to get away; **(vom Thema)** ~ to get off the subject, digress; **von der Straße/einem Plan** ~ to leave the road/give up a plan.
Abkommen (-s, -) nt agreement.
abkömmlich ['apkœmlɪç] adj available, free.
Abkömmling m (Nachkomme) descendant; (fig) adherent.
abkönnen ['apkœnən] unreg (umg) vt (mögen): **das kann ich nicht ab** I can't stand it.
abkratzen ['apkratsən] vt to scrape off ♦ vi (umg) to kick the bucket.
abkriegen ['apkriːgən] (umg) vt = abbekommen.
abkühlen ['apkyːlən] vt to cool down ♦ vr (Mensch) to cool down od off; (Wetter) to get cool; (Zuneigung) to cool.
Abkunft ['apkʊnft] (-) f origin, birth.
abkürzen ['apkʏrtsən] vt to shorten; (Wort) to

abbreviate; **den Weg** ~ to take a short cut.
Abkürzung f abbreviation; short cut.
abladen ['aplaːdən] unreg vi to unload ♦ vt to unload; (fig: umg): **seinen Ärger (bei jdm)** ~ to vent one's anger (on sb).
Ablage ['aplaːgə] f place to keep/put sth; (Aktenordnung) filing; (für Akten) tray.
ablagern ['aplaːgərn] vt to deposit ♦ vr to be deposited ♦ vi to mature.
Ablagerung f (abgelagerter Stoff) deposit.
ablassen ['aplasən] unreg vt (Wasser, Dampf) to let out od off; (vom Preis) to knock off ♦ vi: **von etw** ~ to give sth up, abandon sth.
Ablauf m (Abfluss) drain; (von Ereignissen) course; (einer Frist, Zeit) expiry (BRIT), expiration (US); **nach** ~ **des Jahres/dieser Zeit** at the end of the year/this time.
ablaufen ['aplaʊfən] unreg vi (abfließen) to drain away; (Ereignisse) to happen; (Frist, Zeit, Pass) to expire ♦ vt (Sohlen) to wear (down od out); ~ **lassen** (abspulen, abspielen: Platte, Tonband) to play; (Film) to run; **sich** dat **die Beine** od **Hacken nach etw** ~ (umg) to walk one's legs off looking for sth; **jdm den Rang** ~ to steal a march on sb.
Ableben ['apleːbən] nt (form) demise (form).
ablegen ['apleːgən] vt to put od lay down; (Kleider) to take off; (Gewohnheit) to get rid of; (Prüfung) to take, sit (BRIT); (Zeugnis) to give; (Schriftwechsel) to file (away); (nicht mehr tragen: Kleidung) to discard, cast off; (Schwur, Eid) to swear ♦ vi (Schiff) to cast off.
Ableger (-s, -) m layer; (fig) branch, offshoot.
ablehnen ['apleːnən] vt to reject; (missbilligen) to disapprove of; (Einladung) to decline, refuse ♦ vi to decline, refuse.
Ablehnung f rejection; refusal; **auf** ~ **stoßen** to meet with disapproval.
ableisten ['aplaɪstən] vt (form: Zeit) to serve.
ableiten ['aplaɪtən] vt (Wasser) to divert; (deduzieren) to deduce; (Wort) to derive.
Ableitung f diversion; deduction; derivation; (Wort) derivative.
ablenken ['aplɛŋkən] vt to turn away, deflect; (zerstreuen) to distract ♦ vi to change the subject; **das lenkt ab** (zerstreut) it takes your mind off things; (stört) it's distracting.
Ablenkung f deflection; distraction.
Ablenkungsmanöver nt diversionary tactic; (um vom Thema abzulenken) red herring.
ablesen ['apleːzən] unreg vt to read; **jdm jeden Wunsch von den Augen** ~ to anticipate sb's every wish.
ableugnen ['aplɔʏgnən] vt to deny.
ablichten ['aplɪçtən] vt to photocopy; (fotografieren) to photograph.
abliefern ['apliːfərn] vt to deliver; **etw bei jdm/einer Dienststelle** ~ to hand sth over to sb/in at an office.
Ablieferung f delivery.

abliegen ['apliːgən] *unreg vi* to be some distance away; (*fig*) to be far removed.

ablisten ['aplɪstən] *vt*: **jdm etw** ~ to trick *od* con sb out of sth.

ablösen ['apløːzən] *vt* (*abtrennen*) to take off, remove; (*in Amt*) to take over from; (*FIN: Schuld, Hypothek*) to pay off, redeem; (*Methode, System*) to supersede ♦ *vr* (*auch*: **einander** ~) to take turns; (*Fahrer, Kollegen, Wachen*) to relieve each other.

Ablösung *f* removal; relieving.

abluchsen ['apluksən] (*umg*) *vt*: **jdm etw** ~ to get *od* wangle sth out of sb.

Abluft *f* (*TECH*) used air.

ABM *pl abk* (= *Arbeitsbeschaffungsmaßnahmen*) *job-creation scheme*.

abmachen ['apmaxən] *vt* to take off; (*vereinbaren*) to agree; **etw mit sich allein** ~ to sort sth out for o.s.

Abmachung *f* agreement.

abmagern ['apmaːgərn] *vi* to get thinner, become emaciated.

Abmagerungskur *f* diet; **eine** ~ **machen** to go on a diet.

Abmarsch ['apmarʃ] *m* departure; **a~bereit** *adj* ready to start.

abmarschieren ['apmarʃiːrən] *vi* to march off.

abmelden ['apmɛldən] *vt* (*Auto*) to take off the road; (*Telefon*) to have disconnected; (*COMPUT*) to log off ♦ *vr* to give notice of one's departure; (*im Hotel*) to check out; **ein Kind von einer Schule** ~ to take a child away from a school; **er/sie ist bei mir abgemeldet** (*umg*) I don't want anything to do with him/her; **jdn bei der Polizei** ~ to register sb's departure with the police.

abmessen ['apmɛsən] *unreg vt* to measure.

Abmessung *f* measurement; (*Ausmaß*) dimension.

abmontieren ['apmɔntiːrən] *vt* to take off; (*Maschine*) to dismantle.

ABM-Stelle *f temporary post created as part of a job creation scheme*.

abmühen ['apmyːən] *vr* to wear o.s. out.

abnabeln ['apnaːbəln] *vt*: **jdn** ~ (*auch fig*) to cut sb's umbilical cord.

abnagen ['apnaːgən] *vt* to gnaw off; (*Knochen*) to gnaw.

Abnäher ['apnɛːər] (**-s**, **-**) *m* dart.

Abnahme ['apnaːmə] *f* (+*gen*) removal; (*COMM*) buying; (*Verringerung*) decrease (in).

abnehmen ['apneːmən] *unreg vt* to take off, remove; (*Führerschein*) to take away; (*Prüfung*) to hold; (*Maschen*) to decrease; (*Hörer*) to lift, pick up; (*begutachten: Gebäude, Auto*) to inspect ♦ *vi* to decrease; (*schlanker werden*) to lose weight; **jdm etw** ~ (*Geld*) to get sth out of sb; (*kaufen: auch umg: glauben*) to buy sth from sb; **kann ich dir etwas** ~? (*tragen*) can I take something for

you?; **jdm Arbeit** ~ to take work off sb's shoulders; **jdm ein Versprechen** ~ to make sb promise sth.

Abnehmer (**-s**, **-**) *m* purchaser, customer; **viele/wenige** ~ **finden** (*COMM*) to sell well/badly.

Abneigung ['apnaɪgʊŋ] *f* aversion, dislike.

abnorm [ap'nɔrm] *adj* abnormal.

abnötigen ['apnøːtɪgən] *vt*: **jdm etw/Respekt** ~ to force sth from sb/gain sb's respect.

abnutzen ['apnʊtsən] *vt* to wear out.

Abnutzung *f* wear (and tear).

Abo ['abo] (**-s**, **-s**) (*umg*) *nt* = **Abonnement**.

Abonnement [abɔn(ə)'mãː] (**-s**, **-s** *od* **-e**) *nt* subscription; (*Theater*~) season ticket.

Abonnent(in) [abɔ'nɛnt(ɪn)] *m(f)* subscriber.

abonnieren [abɔ'niːrən] *vt* to subscribe to.

abordnen ['apɔrdnən] *vt* to delegate.

Abordnung *f* delegation.

Abort [a'bɔrt] (**-(e)s**, **-e**) *m* (*veraltet*) lavatory.

abpacken ['appakən] *vt* to pack.

abpassen ['appasən] *vt* (*Person, Gelegenheit*) to wait for; (*warten auf*) to catch; (*jdm auflauern*) to waylay; **etw gut** ~ to time sth well.

abpausen ['appaʊzən] *vt* to make a tracing of.

abpfeifen ['appfaɪfən] *unreg vt, vi* (*SPORT*): (**das Spiel**) ~ to blow the whistle (for the end of the game).

Abpfiff ['appfɪf] *m* final whistle.

abplagen ['applaːgən] *vr* to struggle (away).

Abprall ['appral] *m* rebound; (*von Kugel*) ricochet.

abprallen ['appralən] *vi* to bounce off; to ricochet; **an jdm** ~ (*fig*) to make no impression on sb.

abputzen ['appʊtsən] *vt* to clean; (*Nase etc*) to wipe.

abquälen ['apkvɛːlən] *vr* to struggle (away).

abrackern ['aprakərn] (*umg*) *vr* to slave away.

abraten [apraːtən] *unreg vi*: **jdm von etw** ~ to advise sb against sth, warn sb against sth.

abräumen ['aprɔʏmən] *vt* to clear up *od* away; (*Tisch*) to clear ♦ *vi* to clear up *od* away.

abreagieren ['apreagiːrən] *vt*: **seinen Zorn (an jdm/etw)** ~ to work one's anger off (on sb/sth) ♦ *vr* to calm down; **seinen Ärger an anderen** ~ to take it out on others.

abrechnen ['aprɛçnən] *vt* to deduct, take off ♦ *vi* (*lit*) to settle up; (*fig*) to get even; **darf ich** ~? would you like your bill (*BRIT*) *od* check (*US*) now?

Abrechnung *f* settlement; (*Rechnung*) bill; (*Aufstellung*) statement; (*Bilanz*) balancing; (*fig: Rache*) revenge; **in** ~ **stellen** (*form: Abzug*) to deduct; ~ **über** +*akk* bill/statement for.

Abrechnungszeitraum *m* accounting period.

Abrede ['apreːdə] *f*: **etw in** ~ **stellen** to deny

od dispute sth.

abregen ['apreːgən] (*umg*) *vr* to calm *od* cool down.

abreiben ['apraɪbən] *unreg vt* to rub off; (*säubern*) to wipe; **jdn mit einem Handtuch ~** to towel sb down.

Abreibung (*umg*) *f* (*Prügel*) hiding, thrashing.

Abreise ['apraɪzə] *f* departure.

abreisen *vi* to leave, set off.

abreißen ['apraɪsən] *unreg vt* (*Haus*) to tear down; (*Blatt*) to tear off ♦ *vi*: **den Kontakt nicht ~ lassen** to stay in touch.

abrichten ['apriçtən] *vt* to train.

abriegeln ['apriːgəln] *vt* (*Tür*) to bolt; (*Straße, Gebiet*) to seal off.

abringen ['aprɪŋən] *unreg vt*: **sich** *dat* **ein Lächeln ~** to force a smile.

Abriss▲ ['aprɪs] (**-es, -e**) *m* (*Übersicht*) outline; (*Abbruch*) demolition.

abrollen ['aprɔlən] *vt* (*abwickeln*) to unwind ♦ *vi* (*vonstatten gehen: Programm*) to run; (: *Veranstaltung*) to go off; (: *Ereignisse*) to unfold.

Abruf ['apruːf] *m*: **auf ~** on call.

abrufen *unreg vt* (*Mensch*) to call away; (*COMM: Ware*) to request delivery of; (*COMPUT*) to recall, retrieve.

abrunden ['aprʊndən] *vt* to round off.

abrüsten ['aprʏstən] *vi* to disarm.

Abrüstung *f* disarmament.

abrutschen ['aprʊtʃən] *vi* to slip; (*AVIAT*) to sideslip.

Abs. *abk* = **Absender**; (= *Absatz*) par., para.

absacken ['apzakən] *vi* (*sinken*) to sink; (*Boden, Gebäude*) to subside.

Absage ['apzaːgə] (**-, -n**) *f* refusal; (*auf Einladung*) negative reply.

absagen *vt* to cancel, call off; (*Einladung*) to turn down ♦ *vi* to cry off; (*ablehnen*) to decline; **jdm ~** to tell sb that one can't come.

absägen ['apzɛːgən] *vt* to saw off.

absahnen ['apzaːnən] *vt* (*lit*) to skim; **das beste für sich ~** (*fig*) to take the cream.

Absatz ['apzats] *m* (*COMM*) sales *pl*; (*JUR*) section; (*Bodensatz*) deposit; (*neuer Abschnitt*) paragraph; (*Treppen~*) landing; (*Schuh~*) heel; **~flaute** *f* slump in the market; **~förderung** *f* sales promotion; **~gebiet** *nt* (*COMM*) market; sales territory; **~prognose** *f* sales forecast; **~schwierigkeiten** *pl* sales problems *pl*; **~ziffern** *pl* sales figures *pl*.

absaufen ['apzaʊfən] *unreg* (*umg*) *vi* (*ertrinken*) to drown; (: *Motor*) to flood; (: *Schiff etc*) to go down.

absaugen ['apzaʊgən] *vt* (*Flüssigkeit*) to suck out *od* off; (*Teppich, Sofa*) to hoover ®, vacuum.

abschaben ['apʃaːbən] *vt* to scrape off;

(*Möhren*) to scrape.

abschaffen ['apʃafən] *vt* to abolish, do away with.

Abschaffung *f* abolition.

abschalten ['apʃaltən] *vt*, *vi* (*lit*: *umg*) to switch off.

abschattieren ['apʃatiːrən] *vt* to shade.

abschätzen ['apʃɛtsən] *vt* to estimate; (*Lage*) to assess; (*Person*) to size up.

abschätzig ['apʃɛtsɪç] *adj* disparaging, derogatory.

Abschaum ['apʃaʊm] (**-(e)s**) *m* scum.

Abscheu ['apʃɔy] (**-(e)s**) *m* loathing, repugnance; **~erregend** repulsive, loathsome; **a~lich** *adj* abominable.

abschicken ['apʃɪkən] *vt* to send off.

abschieben ['apʃiːbən] *unreg vt* to push away; (*Person*) to pack off; (*ausweisen: Ausländer*) to deport; (*fig: Verantwortung, Schuld*): **~ (auf +***akk***)** to shift (onto).

Abschied ['apʃiːt] (**-(e)s, -e**) *m* parting; (*von Armee*) discharge; (**von jdm**) **~ nehmen** to say goodbye (to sb), take one's leave (of sb); **seinen ~ nehmen** (*MIL*) to apply for discharge; **zum ~** on parting.

Abschiedsbrief *m* farewell letter.

Abschiedsfeier *f* farewell party.

abschießen ['apʃiːsən] *unreg vt* (*Flugzeug*) to shoot down; (*Geschoss*) to fire; (*umg: Minister*) to get rid of.

abschirmen ['apʃɪrmən] *vt* to screen; (*schützen*) to protect ♦ *vr* (*sich isolieren*): **sich ~ (gegen)** to cut o.s. off (from).

abschlaffen ['apʃlafən] (*umg*) *vi* to flag.

abschlagen ['apʃlaːgən] *unreg vt* (*abhacken, COMM*) to knock off; (*ablehnen*) to refuse; (*MIL*) to repel.

abschlägig ['apʃlɛːgɪç] *adj* negative; **jdn/etw ~ bescheiden** (*form*) to turn sb/sth down.

Abschlagszahlung *f* interim payment.

abschleifen ['apʃlaɪfən] *unreg vt* to grind down; (*Holzboden*) to sand (down) ♦ *vr* to wear off.

Abschleppdienst *m* (*AUT*) breakdown service (*BRIT*), towing company (*US*).

abschleppen ['apʃlɛpən] *vt* to (take in) tow.

Abschleppseil *nt* towrope.

abschließen ['apʃliːsən] *unreg vt* (*Tür*) to lock; (*beenden*) to conclude, finish; (*Vertrag, Handel*) to conclude; (*Versicherung*) to take out; (*Wette*) to place ♦ *vr* (*sich isolieren*) to cut o.s. off; **mit abgeschlossenem Studium** with a degree; **mit der Vergangenheit ~** to break with the past.

abschließend *adj* concluding ♦ *adv* in conclusion, finally.

Abschluss▲ ['apʃlʊs] *m* (*Beendigung*) close, conclusion; (*COMM: Bilanz*) balancing; (*von Vertrag, Handel*) conclusion; **zum ~** in conclusion; **~feier** *f* (*SCH*) school-leavers' ceremony; **~prüfer** *m* accountant; **~prüfung**

f (*SCH*) final examination; (*UNIV*) finals *pl*; **~rechnung** *f* final account; **~zeugnis** *nt* (*SCH*) leaving certificate, diploma (*US*).

abschmecken ['apʃmɛkən] *vt* (*kosten*) to taste; (*würzen*) to season.

abschmieren ['apʃmiːrən] *vt* (*AUT*) to grease, lubricate.

abschminken ['apʃmɪŋkən] *vr*: **sich ~** to remove one's make-up.

abschmirgeln ['apʃmɪrgəln] *vt* to sand down.

abschnallen ['apʃnalən] *vr* to unfasten one's seat belt ♦ *vi* (*umg: nicht mehr folgen können*) to give up; (: *fassungslos sein*) to be staggered.

abschneiden ['apʃnaɪdən] *unreg vt* to cut off ♦ *vi* to do, come off; **bei etw gut/schlecht ~** (*umg*) to come off well/badly in sth.

Abschnitt ['apʃnɪt] *m* section; (*MIL*) sector; (*Kontroll~*) counterfoil (*BRIT*), stub (*US*); (*MATH*) segment; (*Zeit~*) period.

abschnüren ['apʃnyːrən] *vt* to constrict.

abschöpfen ['apʃœpfən] *vt* to skim off.

abschrauben ['apʃraʊbən] *vt* to unscrew.

abschrecken ['apʃrɛkən] *vt* to deter, put off; (*mit kaltem Wasser*) to plunge into cold water.

abschreckend *adj* deterrent; **~es Beispiel** warning; **eine ~e Wirkung haben, ~ wirken** to act as a deterrent.

abschreiben ['apʃraɪbən] *unreg vt* to copy; (*verloren geben*) to write off; (*COMM*) to deduct; **er ist bei mir abgeschrieben** I'm finished with him.

Abschreibung *f* (*COMM*) deduction; (*Wertverminderung*) depreciation.

Abschrift ['apʃrɪft] *f* copy.

abschuften ['apʃʊftən] (*umg*) *vr* to slog one's guts out (*umg*).

abschürfen ['apʃyrfən] *vt* to graze.

Abschuss▲ ['apʃʊs] *m* (*eines Geschützes*) firing; (*Herunterschießen*) shooting down; (*Tötung*) shooting.

abschüssig ['apʃysɪç] *adj* steep.

Abschussliste▲ *f*: **er steht auf der ~** (*umg*) his days are numbered.

Abschussrampe▲ *f* launch(ing) pad.

abschütteln ['apʃʏtəln] *vt* to shake off.

abschütten ['apʃʏtən] *vt* (*Flüssigkeit etc*) to pour off.

abschwächen ['apʃvɛçən] *vt* to lessen; (*Behauptung, Kritik*) to tone down ♦ *vr* to lessen.

abschweifen ['apʃvaɪfən] *vi* to wander; (*Redner*) to digress.

Abschweifung *f* digression.

abschwellen ['apʃvɛlən] *unreg vi* (*Geschwulst*) to go down; (*Lärm*) to die down.

abschwenken ['apʃvɛŋkən] *vi* to turn away.

abschwören ['apʃvøːrən] *unreg vi* +*dat* to renounce.

absehbar ['apzeːbaːr] *adj* foreseeable; **in ~er Zeit** in the foreseeable future; **das Ende ist ~** the end is in sight.

absehen *unreg vt* (*Ende, Folgen*) to foresee ♦ *vi*: **von etw ~** to refrain from sth; (*nicht berücksichtigen*) to leave sth out of consideration; **jdm etw ~** (*erlernen*) to copy sth from sb.

abseilen ['apzaɪlən] *vt* to lower down on a rope ♦ *vr* (*Bergsteiger*) to abseil (down).

Abseits ['apzaɪts] *nt* (*SPORT*) offside; **im ~ stehen** to be offside; **im ~ leben** (*fig*) to live in the shadows.

abseits *adv* out of the way ♦ *präp* +*gen* away from.

absenden ['apzɛndən] *unreg vt* to send off, dispatch.

Absender *m* sender.

Absendung *f* dispatch.

absetzbar ['apzɛtsbaːr] *adj* (*Beamter*) dismissible; (*Waren*) saleable; (*von Steuer*) deductible.

absetzen ['apzɛtsən] *vt* (*niederstellen, aussteigen lassen*) to put down; (*abnehmen; auch Theaterstück*) to take off; (*COMM: verkaufen*) to sell; (*FIN: abziehen*) to deduct; (*entlassen*) to dismiss; (*König*) to depose; (*streichen*) to drop; (*Fußballspiel, Termin*) to cancel; (*hervorheben*) to pick out ♦ *vi*: **er trank das Glas aus, ohne abzusetzen** he emptied his glass in one ♦ *vr* (*sich entfernen*) to clear off; (*sich ablagern*) to be deposited; **das kann man ~** that is tax-deductible.

Absetzung *f* (*FIN: Abzug*) deduction; (*Entlassung*) dismissal; (*von König*) deposing; (*Streichung*) dropping.

absichern ['apzɪçərn] *vt* to make safe; (*schützen*) to safeguard ♦ *vr* to protect o.s.

Absicht ['apzɪçt] *f* intention; **mit ~** on purpose; **a~lich** *adj* intentional, deliberate.

absichtslos *adj* unintentional.

absinken ['apzɪŋkən] *unreg vi* to sink; (*Temperatur, Geschwindigkeit*) to decrease.

absitzen ['apzɪtsən] *unreg vi* to dismount ♦ *vt* (*Strafe*) to serve.

absolut [apzoˈluːt] *adj* absolute.

Absolutheitsanspruch *m* claim to absolute right.

Absolutismus [apzoluˈtɪsmʊs] *m* absolutism.

Absolvent(in) *m(f)*: **die ~en eines Lehrgangs** the students who have completed a course.

absolvieren [apzɔlˈviːrən] *vt* (*SCH*) to complete.

absonderlich [apˈzɔndərlɪç] *adj* odd, strange.

absondern *vt* to separate; (*ausscheiden*) to give off, secrete ♦ *vr* to cut o.s. off.

Absonderung *f* separation; (*MED*) secretion.

absorbieren [apzɔrˈbiːrən] *vt* (*lit, fig*) to absorb.

abspalten ['apʃpaltən] *vt* to split off.

Abspannung ['apʃpanʊŋ] f (Ermüdung) exhaustion.

absparen ['apʃpaːrən] vt: **sich** dat **etw** ~ to scrimp and save for sth.

abspecken ['apʃpɛkən] (umg) vt to shed ♦ vi to lose weight.

abspeisen ['apʃpaɪzən] vt (fig) to fob off.

abspenstig ['apʃpɛnstɪç] adj: (jdm) ~ **machen** to lure away (from sb).

absperren ['apʃpɛrən] vt to block od close off; (Tür) to lock.

Absperrung f (Vorgang) blocking od closing off; (Sperre) barricade.

abspielen ['apʃpiːlən] vt (Platte, Tonband) to play; (SPORT: Ball) to pass ♦ vr to happen; **vom Blatt** ~ (MUS) to sight-read.

absplittern ['apʃplɪtərn] vt, vi to chip off.

Absprache ['apʃpraːxə] f arrangement; **ohne vorherige** ~ without prior consultation.

absprechen ['apʃprɛçən] unreg vt (vereinbaren) to arrange ♦ vr: **die beiden hatten sich vorher abgesprochen** they had agreed on what to do/say etc in advance; **jdm etw** ~ to deny sb sth; (in Abrede stellen: Begabung) to dispute sb's sth.

abspringen ['apʃprɪŋən] unreg vi to jump down/off; (Farbe, Lack) to flake off; (AVIAT) to bale out; (sich distanzieren) to back out.

Absprung ['apʃprʊŋ] m jump; **den** ~ **schaffen** (fig) to make the break (umg).

abspulen ['apʃpuːlən] vt (Kabel, Garn) to unwind.

abspülen ['apʃpyːlən] vt to rinse; **Geschirr** ~ to wash up (BRIT), do the dishes.

abstammen ['apʃtamən] vi to be descended; (Wort) to be derived.

Abstammung f descent; derivation; **französischer** ~ of French extraction od descent.

Abstand ['apʃtant] m distance; (zeitlich) interval; **davon** ~ **nehmen, etw zu tun** to refrain from doing sth; ~ **halten** (AUT) to keep one's distance; ~ **von etw gewinnen** (fig) to distance o.s. from sth; **mit großem** ~ **führen** to lead by a wide margin; **mit** ~ **der Beste** by far the best.

Abstandssumme f compensation.

abstatten ['apʃtatən] vt (form: Dank) to give; (: Besuch) to pay.

abstauben ['apʃtaʊbən] vt, vi to dust; (umg: mitgehen lassen) to help oneself to, pinch; **(den Ball)** ~ (SPORT) to tuck the ball away.

Abstauber(in) ['apʃtaʊbər(ɪn)] (-s, -) (umg) m(f) (Person) somebody on the make.

abstechen ['apʃtɛçən] unreg vt to cut; (Tier) to cut the throat of ♦ vi: ~ **gegen** od **von** to contrast with.

Abstecher (-s, -) m detour.

abstecken ['apʃtɛkən] vt (Fläche) to mark out; (Saum) to pin.

abstehen ['apʃteːən] unreg vi (Ohren, Haare) to stick out; (entfernt sein) to stand away.

Absteige f cheap hotel.

absteigen ['apʃtaɪgən] unreg vi (vom Rad etc) to get off, dismount; **in einem Gasthof** ~ to put up at an inn; **(in die zweite Liga)** ~ to be relegated (to the second division); **auf dem** ~**den Ast sein** (umg) to be going downhill, be on the decline.

abstellen ['apʃtɛlən] vt (niederstellen) to put down; (entfernt stellen) to pull out; (hinstellen: Auto) to park; (ausschalten) to turn od switch off; (Missstand, Unsitte) to stop; (abkommandieren) to order off; (ausrichten): ~ **auf** +akk to gear to; **das lässt sich nicht/ lässt sich** ~ nothing/something can be done about that.

Abstellgleis nt siding; **jdn aufs** ~ **schieben** (fig) to cast sb aside.

Abstellraum m storeroom.

abstempeln ['apʃtɛmpəln] vt to stamp; (fig): ~ **zu** od **als** to brand as.

absterben ['apʃtɛrbən] unreg vi to die; (Körperteil) to go numb.

Abstieg ['apʃtiːk] (-(e)s, -e) m descent; (SPORT) relegation; (fig) decline.

abstimmen ['apʃtɪmən] vi to vote ♦ vt: ~ **(auf** +akk**) (**Instrument**)** to tune (to); (Interessen) to match (with); (Termine, Ziele) to fit in (with) ♦ vr to agree.

Abstimmung f vote; (geheime ~) ballot.

abstinent [apstiˈnɛnt] adj (von Alkohol) teetotal.

Abstinenz [apstiˈnɛnts] f teetotalism.

Abstinenzler(in) (-s, -) m(f) teetotaller.

abstoßen ['apʃtoːsən] unreg vt to push off od away; (anekeln) to repel; (COMM: Ware, Aktien) to sell off.

abstoßend adj repulsive.

abstottern ['apʃtɔtərn] (umg) vt to pay off in instalments.

abstrahieren [apstraˈhiːrən] vt, vi to abstract.

abstrakt [apˈstrakt] adj abstract ♦ adv abstractly, in the abstract.

Abstraktion [apstraktsiˈoːn] f abstraction.

Abstraktum [apˈstraktʊm] (-s, **Abstrakta**) nt abstract concept; (GRAM) abstract noun.

abstrampeln ['apʃtrampəln] vr (fig: umg) to sweat (away).

abstreifen ['apʃtraɪfən] vt (abtreten: Schuhe, Füße) to wipe; (abziehen: Schmuck) to take off, slip off.

abstreiten ['apʃtraɪtən] unreg vt to deny.

Abstrich ['apʃtrɪç] m (Abzug) cut; (MED) smear; ~**e machen** to lower one's sights.

abstufen ['apʃtuːfən] vt (Hang) to terrace; (Farben) to shade; (Gehälter) to grade.

abstumpfen ['apʃtʊmpfən] vt (lit, fig) to dull, blunt ♦ vi to become dulled.

Absturz ['apʃtʊrts] m fall; (AVIAT) crash.

abstürzen ['apʃtʏrtsən] vi to fall; (AVIAT) to crash.

absuchen ['apzuːxən] vt to scour, search.

absurd [ap'zʊrt] adj absurd.

Abszess▲ [aps'tsɛs] (-es, -e) m abscess.

Abt [apt] (-(e)s, ⁼e) m abbot.

Abt. abk (= Abteilung) dept.

abtasten ['aptastən] vt to feel, probe; (ELEK) to scan; (bei Durchsuchung): ~ (auf +akk) to frisk (for).

abtauen ['aptauən] vt, vi to thaw; (Kühlschrank) to defrost.

Abtei [ap'taɪ] (-, -en) f abbey.

Abteil [ap'taɪl] (-(e)s, -e) nt compartment.

abteilen ['aptaɪlən] vt to divide up; (abtrennen) to divide off.

Abteilung f (in Firma, Kaufhaus) department; (MIL) unit; (in Krankenhaus, JUR) section.

Abteilungsleiter(in) m(f) head of department; (in Kaufhaus) department manager(ess).

abtelefonieren ['aptelefoniːrən] (umg) vi to telephone to say one can't make it.

Äbtissin [ɛp'tɪsɪn] f abbess.

abtönen ['aptøːnən] vt (PHOT) to tone down.

abtöten ['aptøːtən] vt (lit, fig) to destroy, kill (off); (Nerv) to deaden.

abtragen ['aptraːgən] unreg vt (Hügel, Erde) to level down; (Essen) to clear away; (Kleider) to wear out; (Schulden) to pay off.

abträglich ['aptrɛːklɪç] adj (+dat) harmful (to).

Abtragung f (GEOL) erosion.

Abtransport (-(e)s, -e) m transportation; (aus Katastrophengebiet) evacuation.

abtransportieren ['aptranspɔrtiːrən] vt to transport; to evacuate.

abtreiben ['aptraɪbən] unreg vt (Boot, Flugzeug) to drive off course; (Kind) to abort ♦ vi to be driven off course; (Frau) to have an abortion.

Abtreibung f abortion.

Abtreibungsparagraf▲ m abortion law.

Abtreibungsversuch m attempted abortion.

abtrennen ['aptrɛnən] vt (lostrennen) to detach; (entfernen) to take off; (abteilen) to separate off.

abtreten ['aptreːtən] unreg vt to wear out; (überlassen) to hand over, cede; (Rechte, Ansprüche) to transfer ♦ vi to go off; (zurücktreten) to step down; sich dat die Füße ~ to wipe one's feet; ~! (MIL) dismiss!

Abtritt ['aptrɪt] m (Rücktritt) resignation.

abtrocknen ['aptrɔknən] vt to dry ♦ vi to do the drying-up.

abtropfen ['aptrɔpfən] vi: etw ~ lassen to let sth drain.

abtrünnig ['aptrʏnɪç] adj renegade.

abtun ['aptuːn] unreg vt to take off; (fig) to dismiss; etw kurz ~ to brush sth aside.

aburteilen ['apˌʊrtaɪlən] vt to condemn.

abverlangen ['apfɛrlaŋən] vt: jdm etw ~ to demand sth from sb.

abwägen ['apvɛːgən] unreg vt to weigh up.

abwählen ['apvɛːlən] vt to vote out (of office); (SCH: Fach) to give up.

abwälzen ['apvɛltsən] vt: ~ (auf +akk) (Schuld, Verantwortung) to shift (onto); (Arbeit) to unload (onto); (Kosten) to pass on (to).

abwandeln ['apvandəln] vt to adapt.

abwandern ['apvandərn] vi to move away.

Abwärme ['apvɛrmə] f waste heat.

abwarten ['apvartən] vt to wait for ♦ vi to wait; das Gewitter ~ to wait till the storm is over; ~ und Tee trinken (umg) to wait and see; eine ~de Haltung einnehmen to play a waiting game.

abwärts ['apvɛrts] adv down; mit ihm/dem Land geht es ~ he/the country is going downhill.

Abwasch ['apvaʃ] (-(e)s) m washing-up; du kannst das auch machen, das ist (dann) ein ~ (umg) you could do that as well and kill two birds with one stone.

abwaschen unreg vt (Schmutz) to wash off; (Geschirr) to wash (up).

Abwasser ['apvasər] (-s, -wässer) nt sewage; ~aufbereitung f sewage treatment; ~kanal m sewer.

abwechseln ['apvɛksəln] vi, vr to alternate; (Personen) to take turns.

abwechselnd adj alternate.

Abwechslung f change; (Zerstreuung) diversion; für ~ sorgen to provide entertainment.

abwechslungsreich adj varied.

Abweg ['apveːk] m: auf ~e geraten/führen to go/lead astray.

abwegig ['apveːgɪç] adj wrong; (Verdacht) groundless.

Abwehr ['apveːr] (-) f defence; (Schutz) protection; (~dienst) counter-intelligence (service); auf ~ stoßen to be repulsed; a~en vt to ward off; (Ball) to stop; a~ende Geste dismissive gesture; ~reaktion f (PSYCH) defence (BRIT) od defense (US) reaction; ~stoff m antibody.

abweichen ['apvaɪçən] unreg vi to deviate; (Meinung) to differ; vom rechten Weg ~ (fig) to wander off the straight and narrow.

abweichend adj deviant; differing.

Abweichler (-s, -) m (POL) maverick.

Abweichung f (zeitlich, zahlenmäßig) allowance; (~ zulässige ~ (TECH) tolerance.

abweisen ['apvaɪzən] unreg vt to turn away; (Antrag) to turn down; er lässt sich nicht ~ he won't take no for an answer.

abweisend adj (Haltung) cold.

abwenden ['apvɛndən] unreg vt to avert ♦ vr to turn away.

abwerben ['apvɛrbən] unreg vt: (jdm) ~ to woo

away (from sb).

abwerfen ['apvɛrfən] *unreg vt* to throw off; (*Profit*) to yield; (*aus Flugzeug*) to drop; (*Spielkarte*) to discard.

abwerten ['apvɛrtən] *vt* (*FIN*) to devalue.

abwertend *adj* pejorative.

Abwertung *f* devaluation.

abwesend ['apveːzənt] *adj* absent; (*zerstreut*) far away.

Abwesenheit ['apveːzənhaɪt] *f* absence; **durch ~ glänzen** (*ironisch*) to be conspicuous by one's absence.

abwickeln ['apvɪkəln] *vt* to unwind; (*Geschäft*) to transact, conclude; (*fig: erledigen*) to deal with.

Abwicklungskosten ['apvɪklʊŋskɔstən] *pl* transaction costs *pl*.

abwiegen ['apviːɡən] *unreg vt* to weigh out.

abwimmeln ['apvɪməln] (*umg*) *vt* (*Person*) to get rid of; (: *Auftrag*) to get out of.

abwinken ['apvɪŋkən] *vi* to wave it/him *etc* aside; (*fig: ablehnen*) to say no.

abwirtschaften ['apvɪrtʃaftən] *vi* to go downhill.

abwischen ['apvɪʃən] *vt* to wipe off *od* away; (*putzen*) to wipe.

abwracken ['apvrakən] *vt* (*Schiff*) to break (up); **ein abgewrackter Mensch** a wreck (of a person).

Abwurf ['apvʊrf] *m* throwing off; (*von Bomben etc*) dropping; (*von Reiter, SPORT*) throw.

abwürgen ['apvʏrɡən] (*umg*) *vt* to scotch; (*Motor*) to stall; **etw von vornherein ~** to nip sth in the bud.

abzahlen ['aptsaːlən] *vt* to pay off.

abzählen ['aptsɛːlən] *vt* to count (up); **abgezähltes Fahrgeld** exact fare.

Abzählreim ['aptsɛːlraɪm] *m* counting rhyme (*e.g. eeny meeny miney mo*).

Abzahlung *f* repayment; **auf ~ kaufen** to buy on hire purchase (*BRIT*) *od* the installment plan (*US*).

abzapfen ['aptsapfən] *vt* to draw off; **jdm Blut ~** to take blood from sb.

abzäunen ['aptsɔynən] *vt* to fence off.

Abzeichen ['aptsaɪçən] *nt* badge; (*Orden*) decoration.

abzeichnen ['aptsaɪçnən] *vt* to draw, copy; (*unterschreiben*) to initial ♦ *vr* to stand out; (*fig: bevorstehen*) to loom.

Abziehbild *nt* transfer.

abziehen ['aptsiːən] *unreg vt* to take off; (*Tier*) to skin; (*Bett*) to strip; (*Truppen*) to withdraw; (*subtrahieren*) to take away, subtract; (*kopieren*) to run off; (*Schlüssel*) to take out, remove ♦ *vi* to go away; (*Truppen*) to withdraw; (*abdrücken*) to pull the trigger, fire.

abzielen ['aptsiːlən] *vi*: ~ **auf** +*akk* to be aimed at.

Abzug ['aptsuːk] *m* departure; (*von Truppen*) withdrawal; (*Kopie*) copy; (*Subtraktion*) subtraction; (*Betrag*) deduction; (*Rauch~*) flue; (*von Waffen*) trigger; (*Rabatt*) discount; (*Korrekturfahne*) proof; (*PHOT*) print; **jdm freien ~ gewähren** to grant sb safe passage.

abzüglich ['aptsyːklɪç] *präp* +*gen* less.

abzweigen ['aptsvaɪɡən] *vi* to branch off ♦ *vt* to set aside.

Abzweigung *f* junction.

Accessoires [akseso'aːrs] *pl* accessories *pl*.

ach [ax] *interj* oh; ~ **so!** I see!; **mit A~ und Krach** by the skin of one's teeth; ~ **was** *od* **wo, das ist doch nicht so schlimm!** come on now, it's not that bad!

Achillesferse [a'xɪlɛsfɛrzə] *f* Achilles heel.

Achse ['aksə] *f* (-, -n) *f* axis; (*AUT*) axle; **auf ~ sein** (*umg*) to be on the move.

Achsel ['aksəl] (-, -n) *f* shoulder; ~höhle *f* armpit; ~zucken *nt* shrug (of one's shoulders).

Achsenbruch *m* (*AUT*) broken axle.

Achsenkreuz *nt* coordinate system.

Acht¹ [axt] (-, -en) *f* eight; (*beim Eislaufen etc*) figure (of) eight.

Acht² (-) *f* attention; **hab ~** (*MIL*) attention!; ~ **geben (auf** +*akk*) to take care (of); (*aufmerksam sein*) to pay attention (to); **sich in ~ nehmen (vor** +*dat*) to be careful (of), watch out (for); **etw außer ~ lassen** to disregard sth.

acht *num* eight; ~ **Tage** a week.

achtbar *adj* worthy.

achte(r, s) *adj* eighth.

Achteck *nt* octagon.

Achtel *nt* eighth; ~**note** *f* quaver, eighth note (*US*).

achten *vt* to respect ♦ *vi*: ~ **(auf** +*akk*) to pay attention (to); **darauf ~, dass ...** to be careful that ...

ächten ['ɛçtən] *vt* to outlaw, ban.

Achterbahn *f* roller coaster.

Achterdeck *nt* (*NAUT*) afterdeck.

achtfach *adj* eightfold.

achtlos *adj* careless; **viele gehen ~ daran vorbei** many people just pass by without noticing.

achtmal *adv* eight times.

achtsam *adj* attentive.

Achtstundentag *m* eight-hour day.

Achtung ['axtʊŋ] *f* attention; (*Ehrfurcht*) respect ♦ *interj* look out!; (*MIL*) attention!; **alle ~!** good for you/him *etc*!; ~, **fertig, los!** ready, steady, go!; „~ **Hochspannung!"** "danger, high voltage"; „~ **Lebensgefahr/ Stufe!"** "danger/mind the step!".

Achtungserfolg *m* reasonable success.

achtzehn *num* eighteen.

achtzig *num* eighty; **A~er(in)** (-s, -) *m(f)* octogenarian.

ächzen ['ɛçtsən] *vi*: ~ **(vor** +*dat*) to groan (with).

Acker ['akər] **(-s,** ˝-) *m* field; ~**bau** *m* agriculture; ~**bau und Viehzucht** farming.

ackern *vi* to plough; (*umg*) to slog away.

a conto [a 'kɔnto] *adv* (*COMM*) on account.

A. D. *abk* (= *Anno Domini*) A.D.

a. D. *abk* = **außer Dienst**.

a. d. *abk* = **an der** (*bei Ortsnamen*).

ad absurdum [at ap'zurdum] *adv*: ~ **führen** (*Argument etc*) to reduce to absurdity.

ADAC (-) *m abk* (= *Allgemeiner Deutscher Automobilclub*) German motoring organization, ≈ AA (*BRIT*), AAA (*US*).

ad acta [at 'akta] *adv*: etw ~ **legen** (*fig*) to consider sth finished; (*Frage, Problem*) to consider sth closed.

Adam ['a:dam] *m*: **bei** ~ **und Eva anfangen** (*umg*) to start right from scratch *od* from square one.

adaptieren [adap'ti:rən] *vt* to adapt.

adäquat [adɛ'kva:t] *adj* (*Belohnung, Übersetzung*) adequate; (*Stellung, Verhalten*) suitable.

addieren [a'di:rən] *vt* to add (up).

Addis Abeba ['adɪs'a:beba] (-, -s) *nt* Addis Ababa.

Addition [aditsi'o:n] *f* addition.

ade *interj* bye!

Adel ['a:dəl] **(-s)** *m* nobility; ~ **verpflichtet** noblesse oblige.

adelig *adj* noble.

Adelsstand *m* nobility.

Ader ['a:dər] (-, -n) *f* vein; (*fig: Veranlagung*) bent.

Adhäsionsverschluss▲ [athɛzi'o:nsfɛrʃlʊs] *m* adhesive seal.

Adjektiv ['atjɛkti:f] **(-s, -e)** *nt* adjective.

Adler ['a:dlər] **(-s, -)** *m* eagle.

adlig *adj* = **adelig**.

Admiral [atmi'ra:l] **(-s, -e)** *m* admiral.

Admiralität *f* admiralty.

adoptieren [adɔp'ti:rən] *vt* to adopt.

Adoption [adɔptsi'o:n] *f* adoption.

Adoptiveltern *pl* adoptive parents *pl*.

Adoptivkind *nt* adopted child.

Adr. *abk* (= *Adresse*) add.

Adressant [adrɛ'sant] *m* sender.

Adressat [adrɛ'sa:t] **(-en, -en)** *m* addressee.

Adressbuch▲ *nt* directory; (*privat*) address book.

Adresse [a'drɛsə] (-, -n) *f* (*auch COMPUT*) address; **an der falschen** ~ **sein** (*umg*) to have gone/come to the wrong person; **absolute** ~ absolute address; **relative** ~ relative address.

adressieren [adrɛ'si:rən] *vt*: ~ **(an** +*akk*) to address (to).

Adria ['a:dria] (-) *f* Adriatic Sea.

Adriatisches Meer [adri'a:tɪʃəs me:r] *nt* (*form*) Adriatic Sea.

Advent [at'vɛnt] **(-(e)s, -e)** *m* Advent; **der erste/zweite** ~ the first/second Sunday in Advent.

Advents- *zW*: ~**kalender** *m* Advent calendar; ~**kranz** *m* Advent wreath.

Adverb [at'vɛrp] *nt* adverb.

adverbial [atverbi'a:l] *adj* adverbial.

aero- [aero] *präf* aero-.

Aerobic [ae'ro:bik] **(-s)** *nt* aerobics *sing*.

Affäre [a'fɛ:rə] (-, -n) *f* affair; **sich aus der** ~ **ziehen** (*umg*) to get (o.s.) out of it.

Affe ['afə] **(-n, -n)** *m* monkey; (*umg: Kerl*) berk (*BRIT*).

Affekt **(-(e)s, -e)** *m*: **im** ~ **handeln** to act in the heat of the moment.

affektiert [afɛk'ti:rt] *adj* affected.

Affen- *zW*: **a**~**artig** *adj* like a monkey; **mit a**~**artiger Geschwindigkeit** (*umg*) like a flash; **a**~**geil** (*umg*) *adj* magic, fantastic; ~**hitze** (*umg*) *f* incredible heat; ~**liebe** *f*: ~**liebe (zu)** blind adoration (of); ~**schande** (*umg*) *f* crying shame; ~**tempo** (*umg*) *nt*: **in od mit einem** ~**tempo** at breakneck speed; ~**theater** (*umg*) *nt*: **ein** ~**theater aufführen** to make a fuss.

affig ['afɪç] *adj* affected.

Afghane [af'ga:nə] **(-n, -n)** *m* Afghan.

Afghanin [af'ga:nɪn] *f* Afghan.

afghanisch *adj* Afghan.

Afghanistan [af'ga:nɪsta:n] **(-s)** *nt* Afghanistan.

Afrika ['a:frika] **(-s)** *nt* Africa.

Afrikaans [afri'ka:ns] (-) *nt* Afrikaans.

Afrikaner(in) [afri'ka:nər(ɪn)] **(-s, -)** *m(f)* African.

afrikanisch *adj* African.

afroamerikanisch ['a:fro|ameri'ka:nɪʃ] *adj* Afro-American.

After ['aftər] **(-s, -)** *m* anus.

AG (-) *f abk* (= *Aktiengesellschaft*) ≈ plc (*BRIT*), corp., inc. (*US*).

Ägäis [ɛ'gɛ:ɪs] (-) *f* Aegean (Sea).

Ägäisches Meer *nt* Aegean Sea.

Agent(in) [a'gɛnt(ɪn)] *m(f)* agent.

Agententätigkeit *f* espionage.

Agentur [agɛn'tu:r] *f* agency; ~**bericht** *m* (news) agency report.

Aggregat [agre'ga:t] **(-(e)s, -e)** *nt* aggregate; (*TECH*) unit; ~**zustand** *m* (*PHYS*) state.

Aggression [agrɛsi'o:n] *f* aggression.

aggressiv [agrɛ'si:f] *adj* aggressive.

Aggressivität [agrɛsivi'tɛ:t] *f* aggressiveness.

Aggressor [a'grɛso:r] **(-s, -en)** *m* aggressor.

Agitation [agitatsi'o:n] *f* agitation.

Agrarpolitik *f* agricultural policy.

Agrarstaat *m* agrarian state.

AGV *f abk* (= *Arbeitsgemeinschaft der Verbraucherverbände*) *consumer groups' association*.

Ägypten [ɛ'gʏptən] (**-s**) *nt* Egypt.
Ägypter(in) (**-s**, **-**) *m(f)* Egyptian.
ägyptisch *adj* Egyptian.
aha [a'haː] *interj* aha!
Aha-Erlebnis *nt* sudden insight.
ahd. *abk* (= *althochdeutsch*) OHG.
Ahn [aːn] (**-en**, **-en**) *m* forebear.
ahnden ['aːndən] *vt* (*geh: Freveltat, Verbrechen*)
   to avenge; (*Übertretung, Verstoß*) to punish.
ähneln ['ɛːnəln] *vi* +*dat* to be like, resemble
   ♦ *vr* to be alike *od* similar.
ahnen ['aːnən] *vt* to suspect; (*Tod, Gefahr*) to
   have a presentiment of; **nichts Böses** ~ to
   be unsuspecting; **du ahnst es nicht!** you
   have no idea!; **davon habe ich nichts geahnt**
   I didn't have the slightest inkling of it.
Ahnenforschung *f* genealogy.
ähnlich ['ɛːnlɪç] *adj* (+*dat*) similar (to); **das sieht
   ihm (ganz)** ~! (*umg*) that's just like him!,
   that's him all over!; **Ä~keit** *f* similarity.
Ahnung ['aːnʊŋ] *f* idea, suspicion; (*Vorgefühl*)
   presentiment.
ahnungslos *adj* unsuspecting.
Ahorn ['aːhɔrn] (**-s**, **-e**) *m* maple.
Ähre ['ɛːrə] (**-**, **-n**) *f* ear.
Aids [eːdz] (**-**) *nt* Aids.
Airbag ['ɛːbɛːg] (**-s**, **-s**) *m* (*AUT*) airbag.
Akademie [akade'miː] *f* academy.
Akademiker(in) [aka'deːmikər(ɪn)] (**-s**, **-**) *m(f)*
   university graduate.
akademisch *adj* academic.
Akazie [a'kaːtsiə] (**-**, **-n**) *f* acacia.
Akk. *abk* = **Akkusativ**.
akklimatisieren [aklimati'ziːrən] *vr* to become
   acclimatized.
Akkord [a'kɔrt] (**-(e)s**, **-e**) *m* (*MUS*) chord; **im**
   ~ **arbeiten** to do piecework; ~**arbeit** *f*
   piecework.
Akkordeon [a'kɔrdeɔn] (**-s**, **-s**) *nt* accordion.
Akkordlohn *m* piece wages *pl*, piece rate.
Akkreditiv [akredi'tiːf] (**-s**, **-e**) *nt* (*COMM*)
   letter of credit.
Akku ['aku] (**-s**, **-s**) (*umg*) *m* (*Akkumulator*)
   battery.
akkurat [aku'raːt] *adj* precise; (*sorgfältig*)
   meticulous.
Akkusativ ['akuzatiːf] (**-s**, **-e**) *m* accusative
   (case); ~**objekt** *nt* accusative *od* direct
   object.
Akne ['aknə] (**-**, **-n**) *f* acne.
Akribie [akri'biː] *f* (*geh*) meticulousness.
Akrobat(in) [akro'baːt(ɪn)] (**-en**, **-en**) *m(f)*
   acrobat.
Akt [akt] (**-(e)s**, **-e**) *m* act; (*KUNST*) nude.
Akte ['aktə] (**-**, **-n**) *f* file; **etw zu den** ~**n legen**
   (*lit, fig*) to file sth away.
Akten- *zW:* ~**deckel** *m* folder; ~**koffer** *m*
   attaché case; **a~kundig** *adj* on record;
   ~**notiz** *f* memo(randum); ~**ordner** *m* file;
   ~**schrank** *m* filing cabinet; ~**tasche** *f*

briefcase; ~**zeichen** *nt* reference.
Aktie ['aktsiə] (**-**, **-n**) *f* share; **wie stehen die**
   ~**n?** (*hum: umg*) how are things?
Aktien- *zW:* ~**bank** *f* joint-stock bank;
   ~**emission** *f* share issue; ~**gesellschaft** *f*
   joint-stock company; ~**index** *m* share index;
   ~**kapital** *nt* share capital; ~**kurs** *m* share
   price.
Aktion [aktsi'oːn] *f* campaign; (*Polizei*~,
   Such~) action.
Aktionär(in) [aktsio'nɛːr(ɪn)] (**-s**, **-e**) *m(f)*
   shareholder.
Aktionismus [aktsio'nɪsmʊs] *m* (*POL*)
   actionism.
Aktionsradius [aktsi'oːnzraːdiʊs] (**-**, **-ien**) *m*
   (*AVIAT, NAUT*) range; (*fig: Wirkungsbereich*)
   scope.
aktiv [ak'tiːf] *adj* active; (*MIL*) regular; **A~** (**-s**)
   nt (*GRAM*) active (voice).
Aktiva [ak'tiːva] *pl* assets *pl*.
aktivieren [akti'viːrən] *vt* to activate; (*fig:
   Arbeit, Kampagne*) to step up; (*Mitarbeiter*) to
   get moving.
Aktivität [aktivi'tɛːt] *f* activity.
Aktivposten *m* (*lit, fig*) asset.
Aktivsaldo *m* (*COMM*) credit balance.
Aktivurlaub *m* activity holiday.
aktualisieren [aktuali'ziːrən] *vt* (*COMPUT*) to
   update.
Aktualität [aktuali'tɛːt] *f* topicality; (*einer
   Mode*) up-to-dateness.
aktuell [aktu'ɛl] *adj* topical; up-to-date; **eine**
   ~**e Sendung** (*RUNDF, TV*) a current affairs
   programme.
Akupunktur [akupuŋk'tuːər] *f* acupuncture.
Akustik [a'kʊstɪk] *f* acoustics *pl*.
akustisch [a'kʊstɪʃ] *adj* acoustic; **ich habe dich
   rein** ~ **nicht verstanden** I simply didn't
   catch what you said (properly).
akut [a'kuːt] *adj* acute; (*Frage*) pressing,
   urgent.
AKW *nt abk* = **Atomkraftwerk**.
Akzent [ak'tsɛnt] (**-(e)s**, **-e**) *m* accent;
   (*Betonung*) stress; ~**e setzen** (*fig*) to bring
   out *od* emphasize the main points;
   ~**verschiebung** *f* (*fig*) shift of emphasis.
Akzept (**-(e)s**, **-e**) *nt* (*COMM: Wechsel*)
   acceptance.
akzeptabel [aktsɛp'taːbl] *adj* acceptable.
akzeptieren [aktsɛp'tiːrən] *vt* to accept.
AL *f abk* (= *Alternative Liste*) *siehe* **alternativ**.
Alarm [a'larm] (**-(e)s**, **-e**) *m* alarm; (*Zustand*)
   alert; ~ **schlagen** to give *od* raise the alarm;
   ~**anlage** *f* alarm system; **a~bereit** *adj*
   standing by; ~**bereitschaft** *f* stand-by.
alarmieren [alar'miːrən] *vt* to alarm.
Alaska [a'laska] (**-s**) *nt* Alaska.
Albaner(in) [al'baːnər(ɪn)] (**-s**, **-**) *m(f)* Albanian.
Albanien [al'baːniən] (**-s**) *nt* Albania.
albanisch *adj* Albanian.

albern ['albərn] *adj* silly.
Albtraum▲ ['alptraʊm] *m* nightmare.
Album ['albʊm] **(-s, Alben)** *nt* album.
Aleuten [ale'uːtən] *pl* Aleutian Islands *pl.*
Alge ['algə] **(-, -n)** *f* alga.
Algebra ['algebra] **(-)** *f* algebra.
Algerien [al'geːriən] **(-s)** *nt* Algeria.
Algerier(in) **(-s, -)** *m(f)* Algerian.
algerisch [al'geːrɪʃ] *adj* Algerian.
Algier ['alʒiːər] **(-s)** *nt* Algiers.
ALGOL ['algɔl] **(-(s))** *nt* (*COMPUT*) ALGOL.
Algorithmus [algo'rɪtmʊs] *m* algorithm.
alias ['aːlias] *adv* alias.
Alibi ['aːlibi] **(-s, -s)** *nt* alibi.
Alimente [ali'mɛntə] *pl* alimony *sing.*
Alkohol ['alkohɔl] **(-s, -e)** *m* alcohol; **unter ~ stehen** to be under the influence (of alcohol); **a~arm** *adj* low alcohol; **a~frei** *adj* non-alcoholic; **~gehalt** *m* proof.
Alkoholika [alko'hoːlika] *pl* alcoholic drinks *pl*, liquor (*US*).
Alkoholiker(in) [alko'hoːlikər(ɪn)] **(-s, -)** *m(f)* alcoholic.
alkoholisch *adj* alcoholic.
Alkoholverbot *nt* ban on alcohol.
All [al] **(-s)** *nt* universe; (*RAUMFAHRT*) space; (*außerhalb unseres Sternsystems*) outer space.
allabendlich *adj* every evening.
allbekannt *adj* universally known.
alle *adj siehe* **alle(r, s)**.
alledem ['alədeːm] *pron*: **bei/trotz** *etc* **~** with/in spite of *etc* all that; **zu ~** moreover.
Allee [a'leː] **(-, -n)** *f* avenue.
allein [a'laɪn] *adj*, *adv* alone; (*ohne Hilfe*) on one's own, by oneself ♦ *konj* (*geh*) but, only; **von ~** by oneself/itself; **nicht ~** (*nicht nur*) not only; **~ schon der Gedanke** the very *od* mere thought ..., the thought alone ...; **~ erziehend** single-parent; **~ stehend** single; **A~erziehende(r)** *f(m)* single parent; **A~gang** *m*: **im A~gang** on one's own; **A~herrscher(in)** *m(f)* autocrat; **A~hersteller(in)** *m(f)* sole manufacturer.
alleinig [a'laɪnɪç] *adj* sole.
allein- *zW*: **A~sein** *nt* being on one's own; (*Einsamkeit*) loneliness; **A~unterhalter(in)** *m(f)* solo entertainer; **A~vertretung** *f* (*COMM*) sole agency; **A~vertretungsvertrag** *m* (*COMM*) exclusive agency agreement.
allemal ['aləˈmaːl] *adv* (*jedes Mal*) always; (*ohne weiteres*) with no bother; *siehe auch* **Mal**.
allenfalls ['alənˈfals] *adv* at all events; (*höchstens*) at most.

──────────── *SCHLÜSSELWORT*

alle(r, s) *adj* **1** (*sämtliche*) all; **wir ~** all of us; **~ Kinder waren da** all the children were there; **~ Kinder mögen ...** all children like ...; **~ beide** both of us/them; **sie kamen ~** they all came; **~s Gute** all the best; **~s in**

~m all in all; **vor ~m** above all; **das ist ~s andere als ...** that's anything but ...; **es hat ~s keinen Sinn mehr** nothing makes sense any more; **was habt ihr ~s gemacht?** what did you get up to?
2 (*mit Zeit- oder Maßangaben*) every; **~ vier Jahre** every four years; **~ fünf Meter** every five metres.
♦ *pron* everything; **~s was er sagt** everything he says, all that he says; **trotz ~m** in spite of everything.
♦ *adv* (*zu Ende, aufgebraucht*) finished; **die Milch ist ~** the milk's all gone, there's no milk left; **etw ~ machen** to finish sth up.

allerbeste(r, s) ['alərˈbɛstə(r, s)] *adj* very best.
allerdings ['alərˈdɪŋs] *adv* (*zwar*) admittedly; (*gewiss*) certainly.
Allergie [alerˈgiː] *f* allergy.
allergisch [a'lɛrgɪʃ] *adj* allergic; **auf etw** *akk* **~ reagieren** to be allergic to sth.
allerhand (*umg*) *adj inv* all sorts of; **das ist doch ~!** that's a bit much!; **~!** (*lobend*) good show!
Allerheiligen *nt* All Saints' Day.

ALLERHEILIGEN

Allerheiligen (*All Saints' Day*) is a public holiday in Germany and in Austria. It is a day in honour of all the saints. **Allerseelen** (*All Souls' Day*) is celebrated on November 2nd in the Roman Catholic Church. It is customary to visit cemeteries and place lighted candles on the graves of deceased relatives and friends.

---

aller- *zW*: **~höchste(r, s)** *adj* very highest; **es wird ~höchste Zeit, dass ...** it's really high time that ...; **~höchstens** *adv* at the very most; **~lei** *adj inv* all sorts of; **~letzte(r, s)** *adj* very last; **der/das ist das A~letzte** (*umg*) he's/it's the absolute end!; **~neu(e)ste(r, s)** *adj* very latest; **~seits** *adv* on all sides; **prost ~seits!** cheers everyone!
Allerseelen **(-s)** *nt* All Soul's Day; *siehe auch* **Allerheiligen**.
Allerwelts- *in zW* (*Durchschnitts-*) common; (*nichts sagend*) commonplace.
allerwenigste(r, s) *adj* very least; **die ~n Menschen wissen das** very few people know that.
Allerwerteste(r) *m* (*hum*) posterior (*hum*).
alles *pron* everything; *siehe auch* **alle(r, s)**.
allesamt *adv* all (of them/us *etc*).
Alleskleber **(-s, -)** *m* all-purpose adhesive.
Allgäu ['algɔy] *nt part of the alpine region of Bavaria.*
allgegenwärtig *adj* omnipresent, ubiquitous.
allgemein ['algəmaɪn] *adj* general ♦ *adv*: **es ist ~ üblich** it's the general rule; **~ gültig**

generally accepted; ~ **verständlich** generally intelligible; **im A~** in general; **im ~en Interesse** in the common interest; **auf ~en Wunsch** by popular request; **A~bildung** f general od all-round education; **A~heit** f (Menschen) general public; **Allgemeinheiten** pl (Redensarten) general remarks pl; **A~wissen** nt general knowledge.

Allheilmittel [al'haɪlmɪtəl] nt cure-all, panacea (bes fig).

Alliierte(r) [ali'iːrtə(r)] f(m) ally.

all- zW: **~jährlich** adj annual; **~mächtig** adj all-powerful, omnipotent; **~mählich** adv gradually; **es wird ~mählich Zeit** (umg) it's about time; **A~radantrieb** m all-wheel drive; **~seitig** adj (allgemein) general; (ausnahmslos) universal; **A~tag** m everyday life; **~täglich** adj daily; (gewöhnlich) commonplace; **~tags** adv on weekdays.

Allüren [a'lyːrən] pl odd behaviour (BRIT) od behavior (US) sing; (eines Stars etc) airs and graces pl.

all- zW: **~wissend** adj omniscient; **~zu** adv all too; **~zu gern** (mögen) only too much; (bereitwillig) only too willingly; **~zu oft** all too often; **~zu viel** too much.

Allzweck- ['altsvɛk-] in zW all-purpose.

Alm [alm] (-, -en) f alpine pasture.

Almosen ['almoːzən] (-s, -) nt alms pl.

Alpen ['alpən] pl Alps pl; **~blume** f alpine flower; **~veilchen** nt cyclamen; **~vorland** nt foothills pl of the Alps.

Alphabet [alfa'beːt] (-(e)s, -e) nt alphabet.

alphabetisch adj alphabetical.

alphanumerisch [alfanu'meːrɪʃ] adj (COMPUT) alphanumeric.

Alptraum ['alptraʊm] m = **Albtraum**.

════════════ *SCHLÜSSELWORT*

als [als] konj **1** (zeitlich) when; (gleichzeitig) as; **damals ~ ...** ... (in the days) when ...; **gerade ~ ... just as ...**

2 (in der Eigenschaft) than; **~ Antwort** as an answer; **~ Kind** as a child.

3 (bei Vergleichen) than; **ich kam später ~ er** I came later than he (did) od later than him; **lieber ... ~ ...** rather ... than ...; **alles andere ~** anything but; **nichts ~ Ärger** nothing but trouble; **so viel/so weit ~ möglich** (bei Vergleichen) as much/far as possible.

4: ~ ob/wenn as if.

alsbaldig [als'baldɪç] konj: „**zum ~en Verbrauch bestimmt**" "for immediate use only".

also ['alzoː] konj so; (folglich) therefore; **~ wie ich schon sagte** well (then), as I said before; **ich komme ~ morgen** so I'll come tomorrow; **~ gut** od **schön**! okay then; **~, so was!** well really!; **na ~**! there you are then!

Alt [alt] (-s, -e) m (MUS) alto.

alt adj old; **ich bin nicht mehr der A~e** I am not the man I was; **alles beim A~en lassen** to leave everything as it was; **ich werde heute nicht ~ (werden)** (umg) I won't last long today/tonight etc; **~ aussehen** (fig: umg) to be in a pickle.

Altar [al'taːr] (-(e)s, -äre) m altar.

alt- zW: **A~bau** m old building; **A~bauwohnung** f flat (BRIT) od apartment (US) in an old building; **~bekannt** adj well-known; **~bewährt** adj (Methode etc) well-tried; (Tradition etc) long-standing; **A~bier** nt top-fermented German dark beer; **~eingesessen** adj old-established; **A~eisen** nt scrap iron.

Altenheim nt old people's home.

Altenteil ['altəntaɪl] nt: **sich aufs ~ setzen** od **zurückziehen** (fig) to retire from public life.

Alter ['altər] (-s, -) nt age; (hohes) old age; **er ist in deinem ~** he's your age; **im ~ von** at the age of.

älter ['ɛltər] adj (comp) older; (Bruder, Schwester) elder; (nicht mehr jung) elderly.

altern ['altərn] vi to grow old, age.

Alternativ- [altɛrna'tiːf] in zW alternative.

alternativ adj: **A~e Liste** electoral pact between the Greens and alternative parties; **~ leben** to live an alternative way of life.

Alternative [altɛrna'tiːvə] f alternative.

Alternativ- zW: **~medizin** f alternative medicine; **~szene** f alternative scene; **~technologie** f alternative technology.

alters ['altərs] adv (geh): **von** od **seit ~ (her)** from time immemorial.

Alters- zW: **a~bedingt** adj related to a particular age; caused by old age; **~grenze** f age limit; **flexible ~grenze** flexible retirement age; **~heim** nt old people's home; **~rente** f old age pension; **~ruhegeld** nt retirement benefit; **a~schwach** adj (Mensch) old and infirm; (Auto, Möbel) decrepit; **~versorgung** f provision for old age.

Altertum ['altərtuːm] nt antiquity.

altertümlich adj (aus dem Altertum) ancient; (veraltet) antiquated.

alt- zW: **~gedient** adj long-serving; **A~glas** nt used glass (for recycling), scrap glass; **A~glascontainer** m bottle bank; **~hergebracht** adj traditional; **A~herrenmannschaft** f (SPORT) team of players over thirty; **~klug** adj precocious; **A~lasten** pl legacy sing of dangerous waste; **A~material** nt scrap; **A~metall** nt scrap metal; **~modisch** adj old-fashioned; **A~papier** nt waste paper; **A~stadt** f old town.

Altstimme f alto.

Altwarenhändler m second-hand dealer.

Altweibersommer m Indian summer.

Alu ['a:lu] (*umg*) *abk* = **Arbeitslosen-unterstützung**; **Aluminium**.

Alufolie ['a:lufo:liə] *f* tinfoil.

Aluminium [alu'mi:niʊm] (**-s**) *nt* aluminium, aluminum (*US*); ~**folie** *f* tinfoil.

Alzheimerkrankheit ['altshaɪmər'kraŋkhaɪt] *f* Alzheimer's disease.

am [am] = **an dem**; ~ **Sterben** on the point of dying; ~ **15. März** on March 15th; ~ **letzten Sonntag** last Sunday; ~ **Morgen/Abend** in the morning/evening; ~ **besten/schönsten** best/most beautiful.

Amalgam [amal'ga:m] (**-s**, **-e**) *nt* amalgam.

Amateur [ama'tø:r] *m* amateur.

Amazonas [ama'tso:nas] (**-**) *m* Amazon (river).

Ambiente [ambi'ɛntə] (**-**) *nt* ambience.

Ambition [ambitsi'o:n] *f*: ~**en auf etw** *akk* **haben** to have ambitions of getting sth.

Amboss▲ ['ambɔs] (**-es**, **-e**) *m* anvil.

ambulant [ambu'lant] *adj* outpatient.

Ameise ['a:maɪzə] (**-**, **-n**) *f* ant.

Ameisenhaufen *m* anthill.

Amerika [a'me:rika] (**-s**) *nt* America.

Amerikaner [ameri'ka:nər] (**-s**, **-**) *m* American; (*Gebäck*) *flat iced cake*; ~**in** *f* American.

amerikanisch *adj* American.

Ami ['ami] (**-s**, **-s**) (*umg*) *m* Yank; (*Soldat*) GI.

Amme ['amə] (**-**, **-n**) *f* (*veraltet*) foster mother; (*Nährmutter*) wet nurse.

Ammenmärchen ['amənmɛ:rçən] *nt* fairy tale *od* story.

Amok ['a:mɔk] *m*: ~ **laufen** to run amok *od* amuck.

Amortisation [amɔrtizatsi'o:n] *f* amortization.

amortisieren [amɔrti'zi:rən] *vr* to pay for itself.

Ampel ['ampəl] (**-**, **-n**) *f* traffic lights *pl*.

amphibisch [am'fi:bɪʃ] *adj* amphibious.

Ampulle [am'pʊlə] (**-**, **-n**) *f* (*Behälter*) ampoule.

amputieren [ampu'ti:rən] *vt* to amputate.

Amsel ['amzəl] (**-**, **-n**) *f* blackbird.

Amsterdam [amstər'dam] *nt* (**-s**) Amsterdam.

Amt [amt] (**-(e)s**, **⁻er**) *nt* office; (*Pflicht*) duty; (*TEL*) exchange; **zum zuständigen** ~ **gehen** to go to the relevant authority; **von** ~**s wegen** (*auf behördliche Anordnung hin*) officially.

amtieren [am'ti:rən] *vi* to hold office; (*fungieren*): **als ...** ~ to act as ...

amtierend *adj* incumbent.

amtlich *adj* official; ~**es Kennzeichen** registration (number), license number (*US*).

Amtmann (**-(e)s**, *pl* **-männer** *od* **-leute**) *m* senior civil servant.

Amtmännin *f* senior civil servant.

Amts- *zW*: ~**arzt** *m* medical officer; **a**~**ärztlich** *adj*: **a**~**ärztlich untersucht werden** to have an official medical examination; ~**deutsch(e)** *nt* officialese; ~**eid** *m*: **den** ~**eid ablegen** to be sworn in, take the oath of office; ~**geheimnis** *nt* (*geheime Sache*) official secret; (*Schweigepflicht*) official secrecy; ~**gericht** *nt* county (*BRIT*) *od* district (*US*) court; ~**missbrauch▲** *m* abuse of one's position; ~**periode** *f* term of office; ~**person** *f* official; ~**richter** *m* district judge; ~**schimmel** *m* (*hum*) officialdom; ~**sprache** *f* official language; ~**stunden** *pl* office hours *pl*; ~**träger** *m* office bearer; ~**weg** *m*: **auf dem** ~**weg** through official channels; ~**zeit** *f* period of office.

amüsant [amy'zant] *adj* amusing.

Amüsement [amyzə'mãː] *nt* amusement.

amüsieren [amy'zi:rən] *vt* to amuse ♦ *vr* to enjoy o.s.; **sich über etw** *akk* ~ to find sth funny; (*unfreundlich*) to make fun of sth.

═══════════════════ SCHLÜSSELWORT

an [an] *präp* +*dat* **1** (*räumlich: wo?*) at; (*auf, bei*) on; (*nahe bei*) near; ~ **diesem Ort** at this place; ~ **der Wand** on the wall; **zu nahe** ~ **etw** too near to sth; **unten am Fluss** down by the river; **Köln liegt am Rhein** Cologne is on the Rhine; ~ **der gleichen Stelle** at *od* on the same spot; **jdn** ~ **der Hand nehmen** to take sb by the hand; **sie wohnen Tür** ~ **Tür** they live next door to one another; **es** ~ **der Leber** *etc* **haben** (*umg*) to have liver *etc* trouble.

2 (*zeitlich: wann?*) on; ~ **diesem Tag** on this day; ~ **Ostern** at Easter.

3: **arm** ~ **Fett** low in fat; **jung** ~ **Jahren sein** to be young in years; ~ **der ganzen Sache ist nichts** there is nothing in it; ~ **etw sterben** to die of sth; ~ **(und für) sich** actually.

♦ *präp* +*akk* **1** (*räumlich: wohin?*) to; **er ging** ~**s Fenster** he went (over) to the window; **etw** ~ **die Wand hängen/schreiben** to hang/write sth on the wall; ~ **die Arbeit gehen** to get down to work.

2 (*zeitlich: woran?*): ~ **etw denken** to think of sth.

3 (*gerichtet an*) to; **ein Gruß/eine Frage** ~ **dich** greetings/a question to you.

♦ *adv* **1** (*ungefähr*) about; ~ **die hundert** *od* **Hundert** about a hundred; ~ **die 10 Euro** around 10 euros.

2 (*auf Fahrplänen*): **Frankfurt** ~ **18.30** arriving Frankfurt 18.30.

3 (*ab*): **von dort/heute** ~ from there/today onwards.

4 (*angeschaltet, angezogen*) on; ~ **sein** (*umg*) to be on; **das Licht ist** ~ the light is on; **ohne etwas** ~ with nothing on; *siehe auch* **am**.

analog [ana'lo:k] *adj* analogous.

Analogie [analo'gi:] *f* analogy.

Analogrechner [ana'lo:krɛçnər] *m* analog

computer.

Analphabet(in) [an|alfa'be:t(ɪn)] **(-en, -en)** *m(f)* illiterate (person).

Analyse [ana'ly:zə] **(-, -n)** *f* analysis.

analysieren [analy'zi:rən] *vt* to analyse (*BRIT*), analyze (*US*).

Anämie [anɛ'mi:] **(-, -n)** *f* anaemia (*BRIT*), anemia (*US*).

Ananas ['ananas] **(-, - od -se)** *f* pineapple.

Anarchie [anar'çi:] *f* anarchy.

anarchisch [a'narçɪʃ] *adj* anarchic.

Anarchist(in) [anar'çɪst(ɪn)] *m(f)* **(-en, -en)** anarchist.

Anästhesist(in) [an|ɛste'zɪst(ɪn)] **(-en, -en)** *m(f)* anaesthetist (*BRIT*), anesthesiologist (*US*).

Anatomie [anato'mi:] *f* anatomy.

anbahnen ['anba:nən] *vr* to open up; (*sich andeuten*) to be in the offing; (*Unangenehmes*) to be looming ♦ *vt* to initiate.

Anbahnung *f* initiation.

anbändeln ['anbɛndəln] (*umg*) *vi* to flirt.

Anbau ['anbau] *m* (*AGR*) cultivation; (*Gebäude*) extension.

anbauen *vt* (*AGR*) to cultivate; (*Gebäudeteil*) to build on.

Anbaugebiet *nt:* **ein gutes ~ für etw** a good area for growing sth.

Anbaumöbel *pl* unit furniture *sing*.

anbehalten ['anbəhaltən] *unreg vt* to keep on.

anbei [an'bai] *adv* enclosed (*form*); **~ schicken wir Ihnen** ... please find enclosed ...

anbeißen ['anbaisən] *unreg vt* to bite into ♦ *vi* (*lit*) to bite; (*fig*) to swallow the bait; **zum A~ aussehen** (*umg*) to look good enough to eat.

anbelangen ['anbəlaŋən] *vt* to concern; **was mich anbelangt** as far as I am concerned.

anberaumen ['anbəraumən] *vt* (*form*) to fix, arrange.

anbeten ['anbe:tən] *vt* to worship.

Anbetracht ['anbətraxt] *m:* **in ~** *+gen* in view of.

Anbetung *f* worship.

anbiedern ['anbi:dərn] (*pej*) *vr:* **sich ~ (bei)** to curry favour (with).

anbieten ['anbi:tən] *unreg vt* to offer ♦ *vr* to volunteer; **das bietet sich als Lösung an** that would provide a solution.

anbinden ['anbɪndən] *unreg vt* to tie up; (*verbinden*) to connect.

Anblick ['anblɪk] *m* sight.

anblicken *vt* to look at.

anbraten ['anbra:tən] *unreg vt* (*Fleisch*) to brown.

anbrechen ['anbrɛçən] *unreg vt* to start; (*Vorräte*) to break into ♦ *vi* to start; (*Tag*) to break; (*Nacht*) to fall.

anbrennen ['anbrɛnən] *unreg vi* to catch fire;

(*KOCH*) to burn.

anbringen ['anbrɪŋən] *unreg vt* to bring; (*Ware*) to sell; (*festmachen*) to fasten; (*Telefon etc*) to install.

Anbruch ['anbrʊx] *m* beginning; **~ des Tages** dawn; **~ der Nacht** nightfall.

anbrüllen ['anbrʏlən] *vt* to roar at.

Andacht ['andaxt] **(-, -en)** *f* devotion; (*Versenkung*) rapt interest; (*Gottesdienst*) prayers *pl*; (*Ehrfurcht*) reverence.

andächtig ['andɛçtɪç] *adj* devout.

andauern ['andauərn] *vi* to last, go on.

andauernd *adj* continual.

Anden ['andən] *pl:* **die ~** the Andes *pl*.

Andenken ['andɛŋkən] **(-s, -)** *nt* memory; (*Reise~*) souvenir; (*Erinnerungsstück*): **ein ~ (an** +*akk*) a memento (of), a keepsake (from).

andere(r, s) *adj* other; (*verschieden*) different; **am ~n Tage** the next day; **ein ~s Mal** another time; **kein ~r** nobody else; **alles ~ als zufrieden** anything but pleased, far from pleased; **von etwas ~m sprechen** to talk about something else; **es blieb mir nichts ~s übrig als selbst hinzugehen** I had no alternative but to go myself; **unter ~m** among other things; **von einem Tag zum ~n** overnight; **sie hat einen ~n** she has someone else.

andererseits *adv* on the other hand.

andermal *adv:* **ein ~** some other time.

ändern ['ɛndərn] *vt* to alter, change ♦ *vr* to change.

andernfalls *adv* otherwise.

andernorts ['andərn'ɔrts] *adv* elsewhere.

anders *adv:* **~ (als)** differently (from); **wer ~?** who else?; **niemand ~** no-one else; **wie nicht ~ zu erwarten** as was to be expected; **wie könnte es ~ sein?** how could it be otherwise?; **ich kann nicht ~** (*kann es nicht lassen*) I can't help it; (*muss leider*) I have no choice; **~ ausgedrückt** to put it another way; **~ Denkende(r)** dissident, dissenter; **~ lautende Berichte** reports to the contrary; **jemand/irgendwo ~** somebody/somewhere else; **~ aussehen/klingen** to look/sound different.

andersartig *adj* different.

Andersdenkende(r) *f(m)* dissident, dissenter.

anderseits ['andər'zaits] *adv* = **andererseits**.

anders- *zW:* **~farbig** *adj* of a different colour; **~gläubig** *adj* of a different faith; **~herum** *adv* the other way round; **~wo** *adv* elsewhere; **~woher** *adv* from elsewhere; **~wohin** *adv* elsewhere.

anderthalb ['andərt'halp] *adj* one and a half.

Änderung ['ɛndərʊŋ] *f* alteration, change.

Änderungsantrag ['ɛndərʊŋs|antra:k] *m* (*PARL*) amendment.

anderweitig ['andər'vaɪtɪç] *adj* other ♦ *adv* otherwise; (*anderswo*) elsewhere.

andeuten ['andɔʏtən] *vt* to indicate; (*Wink geben*) to hint at.

Andeutung *f* indication; hint.

andeutungsweise *adv* (*als Anspielung, Anzeichen*) by way of a hint; (*als flüchtiger Hinweis*) in passing.

andichten ['andɪçtən] *vt*: **jdm etw ~** (*umg*: *Fähigkeiten*) to credit sb with sth.

Andorra [an'dɔra] (**-s**) *nt* Andorra.

Andorraner(in) [andɔ'ra:nər(ɪn)] *m(f)* Andorran.

Andrang ['andraŋ] *m* crush.

andrehen ['andre:ən] *vt* to turn *od* switch on; **jdm etw ~** (*umg*) to unload sth onto sb.

androhen ['andro:ən] *vt*: **jdm etw ~ to** threaten sb with sth.

Androhung *f*: **unter ~ von Gewalt** with the threat of violence.

anecken ['an|ɛkən] (*umg*) *vi*: **(bei jdm/allen) ~** to rub (sb/everyone) up the wrong way.

aneignen ['an|aɪgnən] *vt*: **sich** *dat* **etw ~** to acquire sth; (*widerrechtlich*) to appropriate sth; (*sich mit etw vertraut machen*) to learn sth.

aneinander [an|aɪ'nandər] *adv* at/on/to *etc* one another *od* each other; **~ fügen** to put together; **~ geraten** to clash; **~ legen** to put together.

anekeln ['an|e:kəln] *vt* to disgust.

Anemone [ane'mo:nə] (**-, -n**) *f* anemone.

anerkannt ['an|ɛrkant] *adj* recognized, acknowledged.

anerkennen ['an|ɛrkɛnən] *unreg vt* to recognize, acknowledge; (*würdigen*) to appreciate; **das muss man ~** (*zugeben*) you can't argue with that; (*würdigen*) one has to appreciate that.

anerkennend *adj* appreciative.

anerkennenswert *adj* praiseworthy.

Anerkennung *f* recognition, acknowledgement; appreciation.

anerzogen ['an|ɛrtso:gən] *adj* acquired.

anfachen ['anfaxən] *vt* (*lit*) to fan into flame; (*fig*) to kindle.

anfahren ['anfa:rən] *unreg vt* to deliver; (*fahren gegen*) to hit; (*Hafen*) to put into; (*umg*) to bawl at ♦ *vi* to drive up; (*losfahren*) to drive off.

Anfahrt ['anfa:rt] *f* (*~sweg, ~szeit*) journey; (*Zufahrt*) approach.

Anfall ['anfal] *m* (*MED*) attack; **in einem ~ von** (*fig*) in a fit of.

anfallen *unreg vt* to attack ♦ *vi* (*Arbeit*) to come up; (*Produkt, Nebenprodukte*) to be obtained; (*Zinsen*) to accrue; (*sich anhäufen*) to accumulate; **die ~den Kosten/Reparaturen** the costs/repairs incurred.

anfällig ['anfɛlɪç] *adj* delicate; **~ für etw** prone to sth.

Anfang ['anfaŋ] (**-(e)s, -fänge**) *m* beginning, start; **von ~ an** right from the beginning; **zu ~** at the beginning; **~ fünfzig** in one's early fifties; **~ Mai/1994** at the beginning of May/1994.

anfangen ['anfaŋən] *unreg vt* to begin, start; (*machen*) to do ♦ *vi* to begin, start; **damit kann ich nichts ~** (*nützt mir nichts*) that's no good to me; (*verstehe ich nicht*) it doesn't mean a thing to me; **mit dir ist heute (aber) gar nichts anzufangen!** you're no fun at all today!; **bei einer Firma ~** to start working for a firm.

Anfänger(in) ['anfɛŋər(ɪn)] (**-s, -**) *m(f)* beginner.

anfänglich ['anfɛŋlɪç] *adj* initial.

anfangs *adv* at first; **wie ich schon ~ erwähnte** as I mentioned at the beginning; **A~buchstabe** *m* initial *od* first letter; **A~gehalt** *nt* starting salary; **A~stadium** *nt* initial stages *pl*.

anfassen ['anfasən] *vt* to handle; (*berühren*) to touch ♦ *vi* to lend a hand ♦ *vr* to feel.

anfechtbar ['anfɛçtba:r] *adj* contestable.

anfechten ['anfɛçtən] *unreg vt* to dispute; (*Meinung, Aussage*) to challenge; (*Urteil*) to appeal against; (*beunruhigen*) to trouble.

anfeinden ['anfaɪndən] *vt* to treat with hostility.

anfertigen ['anfɛrtɪgən] *vt* to make.

anfeuchten ['anfɔʏçtən] *vt* to moisten.

anfeuern ['anfɔʏərn] *vt* (*fig*) to spur on.

anflehen ['anfle:ən] *vt* to implore.

anfliegen ['anfli:gən] *unreg vt* to fly to ♦ *vi* to fly up.

Anflug ['anflu:k] *m* (*AVIAT*) approach; (*Spur*) trace.

anfordern ['anfɔrdərn] *vt* to demand; (*COMM*) to requisition.

Anforderung *f* (*+gen*) demand (for); (*COMM*) requisition.

Anfrage ['anfra:gə] *f* inquiry; (*PARL*) question.

anfragen ['anfra:gən] *vi* to inquire.

anfreunden ['anfrɔʏndən] *vr* to make friends; **sich mit etw ~** (*fig*) to get to like sth.

anfügen ['anfy:gən] *vt* to add; (*beifügen*) to enclose.

anfühlen ['anfy:lən] *vt, vr* to feel.

anführen ['anfy:rən] *vt* to lead; (*zitieren*) to quote; (*umg*: *betrügen*) to lead up the garden path.

Anführer(in) (**-s, -**) *m(f)* leader.

Anführung *f* leadership; (*Zitat*) quotation.

Anführungszeichen *pl* quotation marks *pl*, inverted commas *pl* (*BRIT*).

Angabe ['anga:bə] *f* statement; (*TECH*) specification; (*umg*: *Prahlerei*) boasting; (*SPORT*) service; **Angaben** *pl* (*Auskunft*) particulars *pl*; **ohne ~ von Gründen** without giving any reasons; ~n zur Person (form) personal details od particulars.

angeben ['angeːbən] unreg vt to give; (anzeigen) to inform on; (bestimmen) to set ♦ vi (umg) to boast; (SPORT) to serve.

Angeber(in) (-s, -) (umg) m(f) show-off.

Angeberei [angeːbəˈraɪ] (umg) f showing off.

angeblich ['angeːplɪç] adj alleged.

angeboren ['angəboːrən] adj (+dat) inborn, innate (in); (MED, fig): ~ (bei) congenital (to).

Angebot ['angəboːt] nt offer; (COMM): ~ (an +dat) supply (of); im ~ (umg) on special offer.

angeboten ['angəboːtən] pp von anbieten.

Angebotspreis m offer price.

angebracht ['angəbraxt] adj appropriate.

angebrannt ['angəbrant] adv: es riecht hier so ~ there's a smell of burning here.

angebrochen ['angəbrɔxən] adj (Packung, Flasche) open(ed); was machen wir mit dem ~en Abend? (umg) what shall we do with the rest of the evening?

angebunden ['angəbundən] adj: kurz ~ sein (umg) to be abrupt od curt.

angefangen pp von anfangen.

angegeben pp von angeben.

angegossen ['angəgɔsən] adj: wie ~ sitzen to fit like a glove.

angegriffen ['angəgrɪfən] adj: er wirkt ~ he looks as if he's under a lot of strain.

angehalten ['angəhaltən] pp von anhalten ♦ adj: ~ sein, etw zu tun to be required od obliged to do sth.

angehaucht ['angəhauxt] adj: links/rechts ~ sein to have left-/right-wing tendencies od leanings.

angeheiratet ['angəhaɪratət] adj related by marriage.

angeheitert ['angəhaɪtərt] adj tipsy.

angehen ['angeːən] unreg vt to concern; (angreifen) to attack; (bitten): jdn ~ (um) to approach sb (for) ♦ vi (Feuer) to light; (umg: beginnen) to begin; das geht ihn gar nichts an that's none of his business; gegen jdn ~ (entgegentreten) to fight sb; gegen etw ~ (entgegentreten) to fight sth; (Missstände, Zustände) to take measures against sth.

angehend adj prospective; (Musiker, Künstler) budding.

angehören ['angəhøːrən] vi +dat to belong to.

Angehörige(r) f(m) relative.

Angeklagte(r) ['angəklaːktə(r)] f(m) accused, defendant.

angeknackst ['angəknakst] (umg) adj (Mensch) uptight; (: Selbstbewusstsein) weakened.

angekommen ['angəkɔmən] pp von ankommen.

Angel ['angəl] (-, -n) f fishing rod; (Tür~) hinge; die Welt aus den ~n heben (fig) to turn the

world upside down.

Angelegenheit ['angələːgənhaɪt] f affair, matter.

angelernt ['angəlɛrnt] adj (Arbeiter) semi-skilled.

Angelhaken m fish hook.

angeln ['angəln] vt to catch ♦ vi to fish; A~ (-s) nt angling, fishing.

Angelpunkt m crucial od central point; (Frage) key od central issue.

Angelrute f fishing rod.

Angelsachse ['angəlzaksə] (-n, -n) m Anglo-Saxon.

Angelsächsin ['angəlzɛksɪn] f Anglo-Saxon.

angelsächsisch ['angəlzɛksɪʃ] adj Anglo-Saxon.

Angelschein m fishing permit.

angemessen ['angəmɛsən] adj appropriate, suitable; eine der Leistung ~e Bezahlung payment commensurate with the input.

angenehm ['angəneːm] adj pleasant; ~! (bei Vorstellung) pleased to meet you; das A~e mit dem Nützlichen verbinden to combine business with pleasure.

angenommen ['angənɔmən] pp von annehmen ♦ adj assumed; (Kind) adopted; ~, wir ... assuming we ...

angepasst▲ ['angəpast] adj conformist.

angerufen ['angəruːfən] pp von anrufen.

angesäuselt ['angəzɔyzəlt] adj tipsy, merry.

angeschlagen ['angəʃlaːgən] (umg) adj (Mensch, Aussehen, Nerven) shattered; (: Gesundheit) poor.

angeschlossen ['angəʃlɔsən] adj (+dat) affiliated (to od with), associated (with).

angeschmiert ['angəʃmiːrt] (umg) adj in trouble; der/die A~e sein to have been had.

angeschrieben ['angəʃriːbən] (umg) adj: bei jdm gut/schlecht ~ sein to be in sb's good/bad books.

angesehen ['angəzeːən] pp von ansehen ♦ adj respected.

Angesicht ['angəzɪçt] nt (geh) face.

angesichts ['angəzɪçts] präp +gen in view of, considering.

angespannt ['angəʃpant] adj (Aufmerksamkeit) close; (Nerven, Lage) tense, strained; (COMM: Markt) tight, overstretched; (Arbeit) hard.

Angest. abk = Angestellte(r).

angestammt ['angəʃtamt] adj (überkommen) traditional; (ererbt: Rechte) hereditary; (: Besitz) inherited.

Angestellte(r) ['angəʃtɛltə(r)] f(m) employee; (Büro~) white-collar worker.

angestrengt ['angəʃtrɛŋt] adv as hard as one can.

angetan ['angətaːn] adj: von jdm/etw ~ sein to be taken with sb/sth; es jdm ~ haben to appeal to sb.

angetrunken ['angətrʊŋkən] adj inebriated.

angewiesen ['angəviːzən] adj: **auf jdn/etw ~ sein** to be dependent on sb/sth; **auf sich selbst ~ sein** to be left to one's own devices.

angewöhnen ['angəvøːnən] vt: **jdm/sich etw ~** to accustom sb/become accustomed to sth.

Angewohnheit ['angəvoːnhaɪt] f habit.

angewurzelt ['angəvʊrtsəlt] adj: **wie ~ dastehen** to be rooted to the spot.

angiften ['angɪftən] (pej: umg) vt to snap at.

angleichen ['anglaɪçən] unreg vt, vr to adjust.

Angler ['anlər] (-s, -) m angler.

angliedern ['angliːdərn] vt: **~ (an +akk)** (Verein, Partei) to affiliate (to od with); (Land) to annex (to).

Anglist(in) [an'glɪst(ɪn)] (-en, -en) m(f) English specialist; (Student) English student; (Professor etc) English lecturer/professor.

Angola [an'goːla] (-s) nt Angola.

angolanisch [ango'laːnɪʃ] adj Angolan.

angreifen ['angraɪfən] unreg vt to attack; (anfassen) to touch; (Arbeit) to tackle; (beschädigen) to damage.

Angreifer(in) (-s, -) m(f) attacker.

angrenzen ['angrɛntsən] vi: **an etw** akk **~** border on sth, adjoin sth.

Angriff ['angrɪf] m attack; **etw in ~ nehmen** to make a start on sth.

Angriffsfläche f: **jdm/etw eine ~ bieten** (lit, fig) to provide sb/sth with a target.

angriffslustig adj aggressive.

Angst [anst] (-, ̈-e) f fear; **~ haben (vor** +dat**)** to be afraid od scared (of); **~ um jdn/etw haben** to be worried about sb/sth; **jdm ~ einflößen** od **einjagen** to frighten sb; **jdm ~ machen** to scare sb; **nur keine ~!** don't be scared; **a~** adj: **jdm ist a~** sb is afraid od scared; **a~frei** adj free of fear; **~hase** (umg) m chicken, scaredy-cat.

ängstigen ['ɛŋstɪgən] vt to frighten ♦ vr: **sich ~ (vor** +dat od **um)** to worry (o.s.) (about).

ängstlich adj nervous; (besorgt) worried; (schüchtern) timid; **Ä~keit** f nervousness.

Angstschweiß m: **mir brach der ~ aus** I broke out in a cold sweat.

angurten ['angʊrtən] vt, vr = **anschnallen**.

Anh. abk (= Anhang) app.

anhaben ['anhaːbən] unreg vt to have on; **er kann mir nichts ~** he can't hurt me.

anhaften ['anhaftən] vi (lit): **~ (an** +dat**)** to stick (to); (fig): **~ +dat** to stick to, stay with.

anhalten ['anhaltən] unreg vt to stop ♦ vi to stop; (andauern) to persist; (werben): **um die Hand eines Mädchens ~** to ask for a girl's hand in marriage; **(jdm) etw ~** to hold sth up (against sb); **jdn zur Arbeit/Höflichkeit ~** to get sb to work/teach sb to be polite.

anhaltend adj persistent.

Anhalter(in) (-s, -) m(f) hitch-hiker; **per ~ fahren** to hitch-hike.

Anhaltspunkt m clue.

anhand [an'hant] präp +gen with; **~ eines Beispiels** by means of an example.

Anhang ['anhaŋ] m appendix; (Leute) family; (Anhängerschaft) supporters pl.

anhängen ['anhɛŋən] unreg vt to hang up; (Wagen) to couple up; (Zusatz) to add (on); (COMPUT) to append; **sich an jdn ~** to attach o.s. to sb; **jdm etw ~** (umg: nachsagen, anlasten) to blame sb for sth, blame sth on sb; (: Verdacht, Schuld) to pin sth on sb.

Anhänger (-s, -) m supporter; (AUT) trailer; (am Koffer) tag; (Schmuck) pendant; **~schaft** f supporters pl.

Anhängeschloss▲ nt padlock.

anhängig adj (JUR) sub judice; **etw ~ machen** to start legal proceedings over sth.

anhänglich adj devoted; **A~keit** f devotion.

Anhängsel (-s, -) nt appendage.

anhauen ['anhaʊən] (umg) vt (ansprechen): **jdn ~ (um)** to accost sb (for).

anhäufen ['anhɔʏfən] vt to accumulate, amass ♦ vr to accrue.

Anhäufung ['anhɔʏfʊŋ] f accumulation.

anheben ['anheːbən] unreg vt to lift up; (Preise) to raise.

anheim [an'haɪm] adv: **jdm etw ~ stellen** to leave sth up to sb.

anheimelnd ['anhaɪməlnt] adj comfortable, cosy.

anheizen ['anhaɪtsən] vt (Ofen) to light; (fig: umg: Wirtschaft) to stimulate; (verschlimmern: Krise) to aggravate.

anheuern ['anhɔʏərn] vt, vi (NAUT, fig) to sign on od up.

Anhieb ['anhiːb] m: **auf ~** straight off, first go; **es klappte auf ~** it was an immediate success.

anhimmeln ['anhɪməln] (umg) vt to idolize, worship.

Anhöhe ['anhøːə] f hill.

anhören ['anhøːrən] vt to listen to; (anmerken) to hear ♦ vr to sound.

Anhörung f hearing.

Animierdame [ani'miːrdamə] f nightclub/bar hostess.

animieren [ani'miːrən] vt to encourage, urge on.

Anis [a'niːs] (-es, -e) m aniseed.

Ank. abk (= Ankunft) arr.

ankämpfen ['ankɛmpfən] vi: **gegen etw ~** to fight (against) sth; (gegen Wind, Strömung) to battle against sth.

Ankara ['aŋkara] (-s) nt Ankara.

Ankauf ['ankaʊf] m: **~ und Verkauf von ...** we buy and sell ...; **a~en** vt to purchase, buy.

Anker ['aŋkər] (-s, -) m anchor; **vor ~ gehen** to drop anchor.

ankern vt, vi to anchor.

Ankerplatz *m* anchorage.

Anklage ['ankla:gǝ] *f* accusation; (*JUR*) charge; **gegen jdn ~ erheben** (*JUR*) to bring *od* prefer charges against sb; **~bank** *f* dock.

anklagen ['ankla:gǝn] *vt* to accuse; **jdn (eines Verbrechens) ~** (*JUR*) to charge sb (with a crime).

Anklagepunkt *m* charge.

Ankläger(in) ['anklɛ:gǝr(ɪn)] **(-s, -)** *m(f)* accuser.

Anklageschrift *f* indictment.

anklammern ['anklamǝrn] *vt* to clip, staple ♦ *vr*: **sich an etw** *akk od dat* **~** to cling to sth.

Anklang ['anklaŋ] *m*: **bei jdm ~ finden** to meet with sb's approval.

ankleben ['ankle:bǝn] *vt*: „**Plakate ~ verboten!**" "stick no bills".

Ankleidekabine *f* changing cubicle.

ankleiden ['anklaɪdǝn] *vt, vr* to dress.

anklingen ['anklɪŋǝn] *vi* (*angeschnitten werden*) to be touched (up)on; (*erinnern*): **~ an** +*akk* to be reminiscent of.

anklopfen ['anklɔpfǝn] *vi* to knock.

anknipsen ['anknɪpsǝn] *vt* to switch on; (*Schalter*) to flick.

anknüpfen ['anknypfǝn] *vt* to fasten *od* tie on; (*Beziehungen*) to establish; (*Gespräch*) to start up ♦ *vi* (*anschließen*): **~ an** +*akk* to refer to.

Anknüpfungspunkt *m* link.

ankommen ['ankɔmǝn] *unreg vi* to arrive; (*näher kommen*) to approach; (*Anklang finden*): **bei jdm (gut) ~** to go down well with sb ♦ *vi unpers*: **er ließ es auf einen Streit/einen Versuch ~** he was prepared to argue about it/to give it a try; **es kommt darauf an** it depends; (*wichtig sein*) that is what matters; **es kommt auf ihn an** it depends on him; **es darauf ~ lassen** to let things take their course; **gegen jdn/etw ~** to cope with sb/sth; **damit kommst du bei ihm nicht an!** you won't get anywhere with him like that.

ankreiden ['ankraɪdǝn] *vt* (*fig*): **jdm etw (dick** *od* **übel) ~** to hold sth against sb.

ankreuzen ['ankrɔʏtsǝn] *vt* to mark with a cross.

ankündigen ['ankʏndɪgǝn] *vt* to announce.

Ankündigung *f* announcement.

Ankunft ['ankʊnft] **(-, -künfte)** *f* arrival.

Ankunftszeit *f* time of arrival.

ankurbeln ['ankʊrbǝln] *vt* (*AUT*) to crank; (*fig*) to boost.

Anl. *abk* (= *Anlage*) enc(l).

anlachen ['anlaxǝn] *vt* to smile at; **sich** *dat* **jdn ~** (*umg*) to pick sb up.

Anlage ['anla:gǝ] *f* disposition; (*Begabung*) talent; (*Park*) gardens *pl*; (*Beilage*) enclosure; (*TECH*) plant; (*Einrichtung: MIL, ELEK*) installation(s *pl*); (*Sport~ etc*) facilities *pl*; (*umg: Stereo~*) (stereo) system; (*FIN*)

investment; (*Entwurf*) layout; **als ~** *od* **in der ~ erhalten Sie ...** please find enclosed ...; **~berater(in)** *m(f)* investment consultant; **~kapital** *nt* fixed capital.

Anlagenabschreibung *f* capital allowance.

Anlagevermögen *nt* capital assets *pl*, fixed assets *pl*.

anlangen ['anlaŋǝn] *vi* (*ankommen*) to arrive.

Anlass▲ ['anlas] **(-es, -lässe)** *m*: **~ (zu)** cause (for); (*Ereignis*) occasion; **aus ~** +*gen* on the occasion of; **~ zu etw geben** to give rise to sth; **beim geringsten/bei jedem ~** for the slightest reason/at every opportunity; **etw zum ~ nehmen** to take the opportunity of sth.

anlassen *unreg vt* to leave on; (*Motor*) to start ♦ *vr* (*umg*) to start off.

Anlasser **(-s, -)** *m* (*AUT*) starter.

anlässlich▲ ['anlɛslɪç] *präp* +*gen* on the occasion of.

anlasten ['anlastǝn] *vt*: **jdm etw ~** to blame sb for sth.

Anlauf ['anlaʊf] *m* run-up; (*fig: Versuch*) attempt, try.

anlaufen *unreg vi* to begin; (*Film*) to be showing; (*SPORT*) to run up; (*Fenster*) to mist up; (*Metall*) to tarnish ♦ *vt* to call at; **rot ~** to turn *od* go red; **gegen etw ~** to run into *od* up against sth; **angelaufen kommen** to come running up.

Anlauf- *zW*: **~stelle** *f* place to go (with one's problems); **~zeit** *f* (*fig*) time to get going *od* started.

anläuten ['anlɔʏtǝn] *vi* to ring.

anlegen ['anle:gǝn] *vt* to put; (*anziehen*) to put on; (*gestalten*) to lay out; (*Kartei, Akte*) to start; (*COMPUT: Datei*) to create; (*Geld*) to invest ♦ *vi* to dock; (*NAUT*) to berth; **etw an etw** *akk* **~** to put sth against *od* on sth; **ein Gewehr ~ (auf** +*akk*) to aim a weapon (at); **es auf etw** *akk* **~** to be out for sth/to do sth; **strengere Maßstäbe ~ (bei)** to lay down *od* impose stricter standards (in); **sich mit jdm ~** (*umg*) to quarrel with sb.

Anlegeplatz *m* landing place.

Anleger(in) **(-s, -)** *m(f)* (*FIN*) investor.

Anlegestelle *f* landing place.

anlehnen ['anle:nǝn] *vt* to lean; (*Tür*) to leave ajar; **(sich) an etw** *akk* **~** to lean on *od* against sth.

Anlehnung *f* (*Imitation*): **in ~ an jdn/etw** following sb/sth.

Anlehnungsbedürfnis *nt* need of loving care.

anleiern ['anlaɪǝrn] (*umg*) *vt* to get going.

Anleihe ['anlaɪǝ] **(-, -n)** *f* (*FIN*) loan; (*Wertpapier*) bond.

anleiten ['anlaɪtǝn] *vt* to instruct.

Anleitung *f* instructions *pl*.

anlernen ['anlɛrnǝn] *vt* to teach, instruct.

anlesen ['anleːzən] *unreg vt* (*aneignen*): **sich** *dat* **etw** ~ to learn sth by reading.

Anliegen ['anliːgən] (**-s**, -) *nt* matter; (*Wunsch*) wish.

anliegen *unreg vi* (*Kleidung*) to cling.

anliegend *adj* adjacent; (*beigefügt*) enclosed.

Anlieger (**-s**, -) *m* resident; ~ **frei** no thoroughfare - residents only.

anlocken ['anlɔkən] *vt* to attract; (*Tiere*) to lure.

anlügen ['anlyːgən] *unreg vt* to lie to.

Anm. *abk* (= *Anmerkung*) n.

anmachen ['anmaxən] *vt* to attach; (*Elektrisches*) to put on; (*Salat*) to dress; **jdn** ~ (*umg*) to try and pick sb up.

anmalen ['anmaːlən] *vt* to paint ♦ *vr* (*pej*: *schminken*) to paint one's face *od* o.s.

Anmarsch ['anmarʃ] *m*: **im** ~ **sein** to be advancing; (*hum*) to be on the way; **im** ~ **sein auf** +*akk* to be advancing on.

anmaßen ['anmaːsən] *vt*: **sich** *dat* **etw** ~ to lay claim to sth.

anmaßend *adj* arrogant.

Anmaßung *f* presumption.

Anmeldeformular ['anmɛldəfɔrmulaːr] *nt* registration form.

anmelden *vt* to announce; (*geltend machen*: *Recht, Ansprüche, zu Steuerzwecken*) to declare; (*COMPUT*) to log on ♦ *vr* (*sich ankündigen*) to make an appointment; (*polizeilich, für Kurs etc*) to register; **ein Gespräch nach Deutschland** ~ (*TEL*) to book a call to Germany.

Anmeldung *f* announcement; appointment; registration; **nur nach vorheriger** ~ by appointment only.

anmerken ['anmɛrkən] *vt* to observe; (*anstreichen*) to mark; **jdm seine Verlegenheit** *etc* ~ to notice sb's embarrassment *etc*; **sich** *dat* **nichts** ~ **lassen** not to give anything away.

Anmerkung *f* note.

Anmut ['anmuːt] (-) *f* grace.

anmuten *vt* (*geh*): **jdn** ~ to appear *od* seem to sb.

anmutig *adj* charming.

annähen ['annɛːən] *vt* to sew on.

annähern ['annɛːərn] *vr* to get closer.

annähernd *adj* approximate; **nicht** ~ **so viel** not nearly as much.

Annäherung *f* approach.

Annäherungsversuch *m* advances *pl*.

Annahme ['annaːmə] (-, **-n**) *f* acceptance; (*Vermutung*) assumption; ~**stelle** *f* counter; (*für Reparaturen*) reception; ~**verweigerung** *f* refusal.

annehmbar ['annɛːmbaːr] *adj* acceptable.

annehmen *unreg vt* to accept; (*Namen*) to take; (*Kind*) to adopt; (*vermuten*) to suppose, assume ♦ *vr* (+*gen*) to take care (of); **jdn an**

Kindes statt ~ to adopt sb; **angenommen, das ist so** assuming that is so.

Annehmlichkeit *f* comfort.

annektieren [anɛk'tiːrən] *vt* to annex.

anno ['ano] *adj*: **von** ~ **dazumal** (*umg*) from the year dot.

Annonce [a'nõːsə] (-, **-n**) *f* advertisement.

annoncieren [anõ'siːrən] *vt, vi* to advertise.

annullieren [anʊ'liːrən] *vt* to annul.

Anode [a'noːdə] (-, **-n**) *f* anode.

anöden ['anǀøːdən] (*umg*) *vt* to bore stiff.

anomal [ano'maːl] *adj* (*regelwidrig*) unusual, abnormal; (*nicht normal*) strange, odd.

anonym [ano'nyːm] *adj* anonymous.

Anorak ['anorak] (**-s**, -**s**) *m* anorak.

anordnen ['anǀɔrdnən] *vt* to arrange; (*befehlen*) to order.

Anordnung *f* arrangement; order; ~**en treffen** to give orders.

anorganisch ['anǀɔrgaːnɪʃ] *adj* (*CHEM*) inorganic.

anpacken ['anpakən] *vt* to grasp; (*fig*) to tackle; **mit** ~ to lend a hand.

anpassen ['anpasən] *vt* (*Kleidung*) to fit; (*fig*) to adapt ♦ *vr* to adapt.

Anpassung *f* fitting; adaptation.

Anpassungsdruck *m* pressure to conform (*to society*).

anpassungsfähig *adj* adaptable.

anpeilen ['anpaɪlən] *vt* (*mit Radar, Funk etc*) to take a bearing on; **etw** ~ (*fig*: *umg*) to have one's sights on sth.

Anpfiff ['anpfɪf] *m* (*SPORT*) (starting) whistle; (*Spielbeginn: Fußball etc*) kick-off; **einen** ~ **bekommen** (*umg*) to get a rocket (*BRIT*).

anpöbeln ['anpøːbəln] *vt* to abuse; (*umg*) to pester.

Anprall ['anpral] *m*: ~ **gegen** *od* **an** +*akk* impact on *od* against.

anprangern ['anpraŋərn] *vt* to denounce.

anpreisen ['anpraɪzən] *unreg vt* to extol; **sich** ~ (**als**) to sell o.s. (as); **etw** ~ to extol (the virtues of) sth; **seine Waren** ~ to cry one's wares.

Anprobe ['anproːbə] *f* trying on.

anprobieren ['anproːbiːrən] *vt* to try on.

anpumpen ['anpʊmpən] (*umg*) *vt* to borrow from.

anquatschen ['ankvatʃən] (*umg*) *vt* to speak to; (: *Mädchen*) to try to pick up.

Anrainer ['anraɪnər] (**-s**, -) *m* neighbour (*BRIT*), neighbor (*US*).

anranzen ['anrantsən] (*umg*) *vt*: **jdn** ~ to tick sb off.

anraten ['anraːtən] *unreg vt* to recommend; **auf A**~ **des Arztes** *etc* on the doctor's *etc* advice *od* recommendation.

anrechnen ['anrɛçnən] *vt* to charge; (*fig*) to count; **jdm etw hoch** ~ to think highly of sb for sth.

Anrecht ['anrɛçt] *nt*: ~ **auf** +*akk* right (to); **ein** ~ **auf etw haben** to be entitled to sth, have a right to sth.

Anrede ['anre:də] *f* form of address.

anreden *vt* to address.

anregen ['anre:gən] *vt* to stimulate; **angeregte Unterhaltung** lively discussion.

anregend *adj* stimulating.

Anregung *f* stimulation; (*Vorschlag*) suggestion.

anreichern ['anraɪçərn] *vt* to enrich.

Anreise ['anraɪzə] *f* journey there/here.

anreisen *vi* to arrive.

anreißen ['anraɪsən] *unreg vt* (*kurz zur Sprache bringen*) to touch on.

Anreiz ['anraɪts] *m* incentive.

anrempeln ['anrɛmpəln] *vt* (*anstoßen*) to bump into; (*absichtlich*) to jostle.

anrennen ['anrɛnən] *unreg vi*: **gegen etw** ~ (*gegen Wind etc*) to run against sth; (*MIL*) to storm sth.

Anrichte ['anrɪçtə] (-, -n) *f* sideboard.

anrichten *vt* to serve up; **Unheil** ~ to make mischief; **da hast du aber etwas angerichtet!** (*umg: verursacht*) you've started something there all right!; (: *angestellt*) you've really made a mess there!

anrüchig ['anrʏçɪç] *adj* dubious.

anrücken ['anrʏkən] *vi* to approach; (*MIL*) to advance.

Anruf ['anru:f] *m* call; ~**beantworter** *m* (telephone) answering machine, answerphone.

anrufen *unreg vt* to call out to; (*bitten*) to call on; (*TEL*) to ring up, phone, call.

anrühren ['anry:rən] *vt* to touch; (*mischen*) to mix.

ans [ans] = **an das**.

Ansage ['anza:gə] *f* announcement.

ansagen *vt* to announce ♦ *vr* to say one will come.

Ansager(in) (-s, -) *m(f)* announcer.

ansammeln ['anzaməln] *vt* to collect ♦ *vr* to accumulate; (*fig: Wut, Druck*) to build up.

Ansammlung *f* collection; (*Leute*) crowd.

ansässig ['anzɛsɪç] *adj* resident.

Ansatz ['anzats] *m* start; (*Haar~*) hairline; (*Hals~*) base; (*Verlängerungsstück*) extension; (*Veranschlagung*) estimate; **die ersten Ansätze zu etw** the beginnings of sth; ~**punkt** *m* starting point; ~**stück** *nt* (*TECH*) attachment.

anschaffen ['anʃafən] *vt* to buy, purchase ♦ *vi*: ~ **gehen** (*umg: durch Prostitution*) to be on the game; **sich** *dat* **Kinder** ~ (*umg*) to have children.

Anschaffung *f* purchase.

anschalten ['anʃaltən] *vt* to switch on.

anschauen ['anʃauən] *vt* to look at.

anschaulich *adj* illustrative.

Anschauung *f* (*Meinung*) view; **aus eigener** ~ from one's own experience.

Anschauungsmaterial *nt* illustrative material.

Anschein ['anʃaɪn] *m* appearance; **allem** ~ **nach** to all appearances; **den** ~ **haben** to seem, appear.

anscheinend *adj* apparent.

anschieben ['anʃi:bən] *unreg vt* (*Fahrzeug*) to push.

Anschiss▲ ['anʃɪs] (*umg*) *m*: **einen** ~ **bekommen** to get a telling-off *od* ticking-off (*bes BRIT*).

Anschlag ['anʃla:k] *m* notice; (*Attentat*) attack; (*COMM*) estimate; (*auf Klavier*) touch; (*auf Schreibmaschine*) keystroke; **einem** ~ **zum Opfer fallen** to be assassinated; **ein Gewehr im** ~ **haben** (*MIL*) to have a rifle at the ready; ~**brett** *nt* notice board (*BRIT*), bulletin board (*US*).

anschlagen ['anʃla:gən] *unreg vt* to put up; (*beschädigen*) to chip; (*Akkord*) to strike; (*Kosten*) to estimate ♦ *vi* to hit; (*wirken*) to have an effect; (*Glocke*) to ring; (*Hund*) to bark; **einen anderen Ton** ~ (*fig*) to change one's tune; **an etw** *akk* ~ to hit against sth.

anschlagfrei *adj*: ~**er Drucker** non-impact printer.

Anschlagzettel *m* notice.

anschleppen ['anʃlɛpən] (*umg*) *vt* (*unerwünscht mitbringen*) to bring along.

anschließen ['anʃli:sən] *unreg vt* to connect up; (*Sender*) to link up; (*in Steckdose*) to plug in; (*fig: hinzufügen*) to add ♦ *vi*: **an etw** *akk* ~ (*zeitlich*) to follow sth ♦ *vr*: **sich jdm/etw** ~ to join sb/sth; (*beipflichten*) to agree with sb/sth; **sich an etw** *akk* ~ (*angrenzen*) to adjoin sth.

anschließend *adj* adjacent; (*zeitlich*) subsequent ♦ *adv* afterwards; ~ **an** +*akk* following.

Anschluss▲ ['anʃlʊs] *m* (*ELEK, EISENB, TEL*) connection; (*weiterer Apparat*) extension; (*von Wasser etc*) supply; (*COMPUT*) port; **im** ~ **an** +*akk* following; ~ **finden** to make friends; ~ **bekommen** to get through; **kein** ~ **unter dieser Nummer** number unobtainable; **den** ~ **verpassen** (*EISENB etc*) to miss one's connection; (*fig*) to miss the boat.

anschmiegen ['anʃmi:gən] *vr*: **sich an jdn/etw** ~ (*Kind, Hund*) to snuggle *od* nestle up to *od* against sb/sth.

anschmiegsam ['anʃmi:kza:m] *adj* affectionate.

anschmieren ['anʃmi:rən] *vt* to smear; (*umg*) to take in.

anschnallen ['anʃnalən] *vt* to buckle on ♦ *vr* to fasten one's seat belt.

Anschnallpflicht *f*: **für Kinder besteht** ~

children must wear seat belts.
anschnauzen ['anʃnautsən] (*umg*) *vt* to yell at.
anschneiden ['anʃnaɪdən] *unreg vt* to cut into; (*Thema*) to introduce.
Anschnitt ['anʃnɪt] *m* first slice.
anschreiben ['anʃraɪbən] *unreg vt* to write (up); (*COMM*) to charge up; (*benachrichtigen*) to write to; **bei jdm gut/schlecht angeschrieben sein** to be well/badly thought of by sb, be in sb's good/bad books.
anschreien ['anʃraɪən] *unreg vt* to shout at.
Anschrift ['anʃrɪft] *f* address.
Anschriftenliste *f* mailing list.
Anschuldigung ['anʃʊldɪgʊŋ] *f* accusation.
anschwärzen ['anʃvɛrtsən] *vt* (*fig: umg*): **jdn ~ (bei)** to blacken sb's name (with).
anschwellen ['anʃvɛlən] *unreg vi* to swell (up).
anschwemmen ['anʃvɛmən] *vt* to wash ashore.
anschwindeln ['anʃvɪndəln] (*umg*) *vt* to lie to.
ansehen ['anzeːən] *unreg vt* to look at; **jdm etw ~** to see sth (from sb's face); **jdn/etw als etw ~** to look on sb/sth as sth; **~ für** to consider; (**sich** *dat*) **etw ~** to (have a) look at sth; (*Fernsehsendung*) to watch sth; (*Film, Stück, Sportveranstaltung*) to see sth; **etw (mit) ~** to watch sth, see sth happening.
Ansehen (**-s**) *nt* respect; (*Ruf*) reputation; **ohne ~ der Person** (*JUR*) without respect of person.
ansehnlich ['anzeːnlɪç] *adj* fine-looking; (*beträchtlich*) considerable.
anseilen ['anzaɪlən] *vt*: **jdn/sich ~** to rope sb/o.s. up.
an sein▲ ['anzaɪn] *siehe* **an**.
ansetzen ['anzɛtsən] *vt* (*festlegen*) to fix; (*entwickeln*) to develop; (*Fett*) to put on; (*Blätter*) to grow; (*zubereiten*) to prepare ♦ *vi* (*anfangen*) to start, begin; (*Entwicklung*) to set in; (*dick werden*) to put on weight ♦ *vr* (*Rost etc*) to start to develop; **~ an** +*akk* (*anfügen*) to fit on to; (*anlegen, an Mund etc*) to put to; **zu etw ~** to prepare to do sth; **jdn/etw auf jdn/etw ~** to set sb/sth on sb/sth.
Ansicht ['anzɪçt] *f* (*Anblick*) sight; (*Meinung*) view, opinion; **zur ~** on approval; **meiner ~ nach** in my opinion.
Ansichtskarte *f* picture postcard.
Ansichtssache *f* matter of opinion.
ansiedeln ['anziːdəln] *vt* to settle; (*Tierart*) to introduce ♦ *vr* to settle; (*Industrie etc*) to get established.
ansonsten [an'zɔnstən] *adv* otherwise.
anspannen ['anʃpanən] *vt* to harness; (*Muskel*) to strain.
Anspannung *f* strain.
Anspiel ['anʃpiːl] *nt* (*SPORT*) start of play.
anspielen *vt* (*SPORT*) to play the ball *etc* to ♦ *vi*: **auf etw** *akk* **~** to refer *od* allude to sth.

Anspielung *f*: **~ (auf** +*akk*) reference (to), allusion (to).
Ansporn ['anʃpɔrn] (**-(e)s**) *m* incentive.
Ansprache ['anʃpraːxə] *f* (*Rede*) address.
ansprechen ['anʃprɛçən] *unreg vt* to speak to; (*bitten, gefallen*) to appeal to; (*Eindruck machen auf*) to make an impression on ♦ *vi*: **~ auf** +*akk* (*Patient*) to respond (to); (*Messgerät*) to react (to); **jdn auf etw** *akk* **(hin) ~** to ask sb about sth.
ansprechend *adj* attractive.
Ansprechpartner *m* contact.
anspringen ['anʃprɪŋən] *unreg vi* (*AUT*) to start ♦ *vt* (*anfallen*) to jump; (*Raubtier*) to pounce (up)on; (*Hund: hochspringen*) to jump up at.
Anspruch ['anʃprʊx] (**-s, -sprüche**) *m* (*Recht*): **~ (auf** +*akk*) claim (to); **den Ansprüchen gerecht werden** to meet the requirements; **hohe Ansprüche stellen/haben** to demand/ expect a lot; **jdn/etw in ~ nehmen** to occupy sb/take up sth.
anspruchslos *adj* undemanding.
anspruchsvoll *adj* demanding; (*COMM*) upmarket.
anspucken ['anʃpʊkən] *vt* to spit at.
anstacheln ['anʃtaxəln] *vt* to spur on.
Anstalt ['anʃtalt] (**-, -en**) *f* institution; **~en machen, etw zu tun** to prepare to do sth.
Anstand ['anʃtant] *m* decency; (*Manieren*) (good) manners *pl*.
anständig ['anʃtɛndɪç] *adj* decent; (*umg*) proper; (*groß*) considerable; **A~keit** *f* propriety, decency.
anstandshalber ['anʃtantshalbər] *adv* out of politeness.
anstandslos *adv* without any ado.
anstarren ['anʃtarən] *vt* to stare at.
anstatt [an'ʃtat] *präp* +*gen* instead of ♦ *konj*: **~ etw zu tun** instead of doing sth.
anstauen ['anʃtauən] *vr* to accumulate; (*Blut in Adern etc*) to congest; (*fig: Gefühle*) to build up.
anstechen ['anʃtɛçən] *unreg vt* to prick; (*Fass*) to tap.
anstecken ['anʃtɛkən] *vt* to pin on; (*Ring*) to put *od* slip on; (*MED*) to infect; (*Pfeife*) to light; (*Haus*) to set fire to ♦ *vr*: **ich habe mich bei ihm angesteckt** I caught it from him ♦ *vi* (*fig*) to be infectious.
ansteckend *adj* infectious.
Ansteckung *f* infection.
anstehen ['anʃteːən] *unreg vi* to queue (up) (*BRIT*), line up (*US*); (*Verhandlungspunkt*) to be on the agenda.
ansteigen ['anʃtaɪgən] *unreg vi* to rise; (*Straße*) to climb.
anstelle, an Stelle [an'ʃtɛlə] *präp* +*gen* in place of.
anstellen ['anʃtɛlən] *vt* (*einschalten*) to turn on; (*Arbeit geben*) to employ; (*umg: Unfug*

treiben) to get up to; (: *machen*) to do ♦ *vr* to queue (up) (*BRIT*), line up (*US*); (*umg*) to act; (: *sich zieren*) to make a fuss, act up.

Anstellung *f* employment; (*Posten*) post, position; ~ **auf Lebenszeit** tenure.

ansteuern ['anʃtɔʏərn] *vt* to make *od* steer *od* head for.

Anstich ['anʃtɪç] *m* (*von Fass*) tapping, broaching.

Anstieg ['anʃtiːk] (-(e)s, -e) *m* climb; (*fig: von Preisen etc*) increase.

anstiften ['anʃtɪftən] *vt* (*Unglück*) to cause; **jdn zu etw** ~ to put sb up to sth.

Anstifter (-s, -) *m* instigator.

Anstiftung *f* (*von Tat*) instigation; (*von Mensch*): ~ (**zu**) incitement (to).

anstimmen ['anʃtɪmən] *vt* (*Lied*) to strike up (with); (*Geschrei*) to set up ♦ *vi* to strike up.

Anstoß ['anʃtoːs] *m* impetus; (*Ärgernis*) offence (*BRIT*), offense (*US*); (*SPORT*) kick-off; **der erste** ~ the initiative; **ein Stein des** ~**es** (*umstrittene Sache*) a bone of contention; ~ **nehmen an** +*dat* to take offence at.

anstoßen *unreg vt* to push; (*mit Fuß*) to kick ♦ *vi* to knock, bump; (*mit der Zunge*) to lisp; (*mit Gläsern*) to drink a toast; **an etw** *akk* ~ (*angrenzen*) to adjoin sth; ~ **auf** +*akk* to drink (a toast) to.

anstößig ['anʃtøːsɪç] *adj* offensive, indecent; **A**~**keit** *f* indecency, offensiveness.

anstrahlen ['anʃtraːlən] *vt* to floodlight; (*strahlend ansehen*) to beam at.

anstreben ['anʃtreːbən] *vt* to strive for.

anstreichen ['anʃtraɪçən] *unreg vt* to paint; (**jdm**) **etw als Fehler** ~ to mark sth wrong.

Anstreicher(in) (-s, -) *m(f)* painter.

anstrengen ['anʃtrɛŋən] *vt* to strain; (*strapazieren: jdn*) to tire out; (: *Patienten*) to fatigue; (*JUR*) to bring ♦ *vr* to make an effort; **eine Klage** ~ (**gegen**) (*JUR*) to initiate *od* institute proceedings (against).

anstrengend *adj* tiring.

Anstrengung *f* effort.

Anstrich ['anʃtrɪç] *m* coat of paint.

Ansturm ['anʃtʊrm] *m* rush; (*MIL*) attack.

Ansuchen ['anzuːxən] (-s, -) *nt* request.

ansuchen ['anzuːxən] *vi*: **um etw** ~ to apply for sth.

Antagonismus [antago'nɪsmʊs] *m* antagonism.

antanzen ['antantsən] (*umg*) *vi* to turn *od* show up.

Antarktis [ant'|arktɪs] (-) *f* Antarctic.

antarktisch *adj* Antarctic.

antasten ['antastən] *vt* to touch; (*Recht*) to infringe upon; (*Ehre*) to question.

Anteil ['antaɪl] (-s, -e) *m* share; (*Mitgefühl*) sympathy; ~ **nehmen an** +*dat* to share in; (*sich interessieren*) to take an interest in; ~ **an etw** *dat* **haben** (*beitragen*) to contribute

to sth; (*teilnehmen*) to take part in sth.

anteilig *adj* proportionate, proportional.

anteilmäßig *adj* pro rata.

Anteilnahme (-) *f* sympathy.

Antenne [an'tɛnə] (-, -n) *f* aerial; (*ZOOL*) antenna; **eine/keine** ~ **für etw haben** (*fig: umg*) to have a/no feeling for sth.

Anthrazit [antra'tsiːt] (-s, -e) *m* anthracite.

Anthropologie [antropolo'giː] (-) *f* anthropology.

Anti- ['anti] *in zW* anti; ~**alkoholiker** *m* teetotaller; **a**~**autoritär** *adj* anti-authoritarian; ~**babypille** *f* (contraceptive) pill; ~**biotikum** (-s, -ka) *nt* antibiotic; ~**held** *m* antihero.

antik [an'tiːk] *adj* antique.

Antike (-, -n) *f* (*Zeitalter*) ancient world; (*Kunstgegenstand*) antique.

Antikörper *m* antibody.

Antillen [an'tɪlən] *pl* Antilles *pl*.

Antilope [anti'loːpə] (-, -n) *f* antelope.

Antipathie [antipa'tiː] *f* antipathy.

antippen ['antɪpən] *vt* to tap; (*Pedal, Bremse*) to touch; (*fig: Thema*) to touch on.

Antiquariat [antikvari'aːt] (-(e)s, -e) *nt* secondhand bookshop; **modernes** ~ remainder bookshop/department.

antiquiert [anti'kviːrt] (*pej*) *adj* antiquated.

Antiquitäten [antikvi'tɛːtən] *pl* antiques *pl*; ~**handel** *m* antique business; ~**händler(in)** *m(f)* antique dealer.

Antisemitismus [antizemi'tɪsmʊs] *m* anti-semitism.

antiseptisch [anti'zɛptɪʃ] *adj* antiseptic.

Antlitz ['antlɪts] (-es, -e) *nt* (*liter*) countenance (*liter*), face.

antörnen ['antœrnən] (*umg*) *vt* (*Drogen, Musik*) to turn on ♦ *vi*: ... **törnt an** ... turns you on.

Antrag ['antraːk] (-(e)s, -träge) *m* proposal; (*PARL*) motion; (*Gesuch*) application; **einen** ~ **auf etw** *akk* **stellen** to make an application for sth; (*JUR etc*) to file a petition/claim for sth.

Antragsformular *nt* application form.

Antragsgegner(in) *m(f)* (*JUR*) respondent.

Antragsteller(in) (-s, -) *m(f)* claimant; (*für Kredit etc*) applicant.

antreffen ['antrɛfən] *unreg vt* to meet.

antreiben ['antraɪbən] *unreg vt* to drive on; (*Motor*) to drive; (*anschwemmen*) to wash up ♦ *vi* to be washed up; **jdn zur Eile/Arbeit** ~ to urge sb to hurry up/to work.

Antreiber (-s, -) (*pej*) *m* slave-driver (*pej*).

antreten ['antreːtən] *unreg vt* (*Amt*) to take up; (*Erbschaft*) to come into; (*Beweis*) to offer; (*Reise*) to start, begin ♦ *vi* (*MIL*) to fall in; (*SPORT*) to line up; (*zum Dienst*) to report; **gegen jdn** ~ to play/fight against sb.

Antrieb ['antriːp] *m* (*lit, fig*) drive; **aus eigenem** ~ of one's own accord.

Antriebskraft *f* (*TECH*) power.
antrinken ['antrɪŋkən] *unreg vt* (*Flasche, Glas*) to start to drink from; **sich** *dat* **Mut/einen Rausch** ~ to give o.s. Dutch courage/get drunk; **angetrunken sein** to be tipsy.
Antritt ['antrɪt] *m* beginning, commencement; (*eines Amts*) taking up.
antun ['antuːn] *unreg vt*: **jdm etw** ~ to do sth to sb; **sich** *dat* **Zwang** ~ to force o.s.
anturnen ['antœrnən] (*umg*) *vt* = **antörnen.**
Antwerpen [ant'vɛrpən] (**-s**) *nt* Antwerp.
Antwort ['antvɔrt] (**-**, **-en**) *f* answer, reply; **um** ~ **wird gebeten** RSVP.
antworten *vi* to answer, reply.
anvertrauen ['anfertrauən] *vt*: **jdm etw** ~ to entrust sb with sth; **sich jdm** ~ to confide in sb.
anvisieren ['anviziːrən] *vt* (*fig*) to set one's sights on.
anwachsen ['anvaksən] *unreg vi* to grow; (*Pflanze*) to take root.
Anwalt ['anvalt] (**-(e)s**, **-wälte**) *m* solicitor; lawyer; (*fig: Fürsprecher*) advocate; (: *der Armen etc*) champion.
Anwältin ['anvɛltɪn] *f siehe* **Anwalt.**
Anwalts- *zW*: **~honorar** *nt* retainer, retaining fee; **~kammer** *f professional association of lawyers*, ≈ Law Society (*BRIT*); **~kosten** *pl* legal expenses *pl*.
Anwandlung ['anvandlʊŋ] *f* caprice; **eine** ~ **von etw** a fit of sth.
anwärmen ['anvɛrmən] *vt* to warm up.
Anwärter(in) ['anvɛrtər(ɪn)] *m(f)* candidate.
anweisen ['anvaɪzən] *unreg vt* to instruct; (*zuteilen*) to assign.
Anweisung *f* instruction; (*COMM*) remittance; (*Post~, Zahlungs~*) money order.
anwendbar ['anvɛntbaːr] *adj* practicable, applicable.
anwenden ['anvɛndən] *unreg vt* to use, employ; (*Gesetz, Regel*) to apply.
Anwenderprogramm *nt* (*COMPUT*) application program.
Anwendersoftware *f* application package.
Anwendung *f* use; application.
anwerfen ['anvɛrfən] *unreg vt* (*TECH*) to start up.
anwesend ['anveːzənt] *adj* present; **die A~en** those present.
Anwesenheit *f* presence.
Anwesenheitsliste *f* attendance register.
anwidern ['anviːdərn] *vt* to disgust.
Anwohner(in) ['anvoːnər(ɪn)] (**-s**, **-**) *m(f)* resident.
Anwuchs ['anvuːks] *m* growth.
Anzahl ['antsaːl] *f*: ~ (**an** +*dat*) number (of).
anzahlen *vt* to pay on account.
Anzahlung *f* deposit, payment on account.
anzapfen ['antsapfən] *vt* to tap.
Anzeichen ['antsaɪçən] *nt* sign, indication; **alle**

~ **deuten darauf hin, dass** ... all the signs are that ...
Anzeige ['antsaɪgə] (**-**, **-n**) *f* (*Zeitungs~*) announcement; (*Werbung*) advertisement; (*COMPUT*) display; (*bei Polizei*) report; **gegen jdn** ~ **erstatten** to report sb (to the police).
anzeigen *vt* (*zu erkennen geben*) to show; (*bekannt geben*) to announce; (*bei Polizei*) to report.
Anzeigenteil *m* advertisements *pl*.
anzeigepflichtig *adj* notifiable.
Anzeiger *m* indicator.
anzetteln ['antsɛtəln] (*umg*) *vt* to instigate.
anziehen ['antsiːən] *unreg vt* to attract; (*Kleidung*) to put on; (*Mensch*) to dress; (*Schraube, Seil*) to pull tight; (*Knie*) to draw up; (*Feuchtigkeit*) to absorb ♦ *vr* to get dressed.
anziehend *adj* attractive.
Anziehung *f* (*Reiz*) attraction.
Anziehungskraft *f* power of attraction; (*PHYS*) force of gravitation.
Anzug ['antsuːk] *m* suit; **im** ~ **sein** to be approaching.
anzüglich ['antsyːklɪç] *adj* personal; (*anstößig*) offensive; **A~keit** *f* offensiveness; (*Bemerkung*) personal remark.
anzünden ['antsyndən] *vt* to light.
Anzünder *m* lighter.
anzweifeln ['antsvaɪfəln] *vt* to doubt.
AOK (**-**) *f abk* (= *Allgemeine Ortskrankenkasse*) *siehe* **Ortskrankenkasse.**

> **AOK**
>
> The **AOK** (*Allgemeine Ortskrankenkasse*) forms part of a compulsory medical insurance scheme for people who are not members of a private scheme. In every large town there is an independently run **AOK** office. Foreign nationals may also receive help from these offices if they fall ill while in Germany.

APA *f abk* (= *Austria Presse-Agentur*) *Austrian news agency*.
apart [a'part] *adj* distinctive.
Apartheid [a'paːrthaɪt] *f* apartheid.
Apartment [a'partmənt] (**-s**, **-s**) *nt* flat (*BRIT*), apartment (*bes US*).
Apathie [apa'tiː] *f* apathy.
apathisch [a'paːtɪʃ] *adj* apathetic.
Apenninen [apɛ'niːnən] *pl* Apennines *pl*.
Apfel ['apfəl] (**-s**, **-̈**) *m* apple; **in den sauren** ~ **beißen** (*fig: umg*) to swallow the bitter pill; **für einen** ~ **und ein Ei kaufen** (*umg*) to buy sth dirt cheap *od* for a song; **~mus** *nt* apple purée; (*als Beilage*) apple sauce; **~saft** *m* apple juice.
Apfelsine [apfəl'ziːnə] (**-**, **-n**) *f* orange.
Apfeltasche *f* apple turnover.

Apfelwein *m* strong cider.
apl. *abk* = außerplanmäßig.
APO, Apo ['a:po] (-) *f abk*
(= *außerparlamentarische Opposition*)
extraparliamentary opposition.

APO

The **APO** was an extraparliamentary opposition
group formed in West Germany in the late 1960s
by those who felt that their interests were not
being sufficiently represented in parliament. It was
disbanded in the 1970s. Some of its members then
formed the RAF, a terrorist organisation. Some
formed the Green Party (**die Grünen**).

---

apolitisch ['apoli:tɪʃ] *adj* non-political,
apolitical.
Apostel [a'pɔstəl] (-s, -) *m* apostle.
Apostroph [apo'stro:f] (-s, -e) *m* apostrophe.
Apotheke [apo'te:kə] (-, -n) *f* chemist's (shop)
(BRIT), drugstore (US).

APOTHEKE

The **Apotheke** is a pharmacy where prescribed
drugs and other medicines only available on
prescription are sold. It also sells toiletries. The
pharmacist is qualified to give advice on
medicines and treatment.

Apotheker(in) (-s, -) *m(f)* pharmacist,
(dispensing) chemist (BRIT), druggist (US).
Appalachen [apa'laxən] *pl* Appalachian
Mountains *pl*.
Apparat [apa'ra:t] (-(e)s, -e) *m* piece of
apparatus; (Foto~) camera; (Telefon)
telephone; (RUNDF, TV) set; (Verwaltungs~,
Partei~) machinery, apparatus; **am** ~ on the
phone; (als Antwort) speaking; **am** ~ **bleiben**
to hold the line.
Apparatur [apara'tu:r] *f* apparatus.
Appartement [apart(ə)'mã:] (-s, -s) *nt* flat
(BRIT), apartment (bes US).
Appell [a'pɛl] (-s, -e) *m* (MIL) muster, parade;
(fig) appeal; **zum** ~ **antreten** to line up for
roll call.
appellieren [apɛ'li:rən] *vi:* ~ **(an** +akk) to
appeal (to).
Appetit [ape'ti:t] (-(e)s, -e) *m* appetite; **guten**
~! enjoy your meal; **a~lich** *adj* appetizing;
~**losigkeit** *f* lack of appetite.
Applaus [ap'laus] (-es, -e) *m* applause.
Appretur [apre'tu:r] *f* finish;
(Wasserundurchlässigkeit) waterproofing.
approbiert [apro'bi:rt] *adj* (Arzt) registered,
certified.
Apr. *abk* (= *April*) Apr.
Aprikose [apri'ko:zə] (-, -n) *f* apricot.
April [a'prɪl] (-(s), -e) (pl selten) *m* April; **jdn in**

den ~ **schicken** to make an April fool of sb;
siehe auch September; ~**wetter** *nt* April
showers *pl*.
apropos [apro'po:] *adv* by the way, that
reminds me.
Aquaplaning [akva'pla:nɪŋ] (-(s)) *nt*
aquaplaning.
Aquarell [akva'rɛl] (-s, -e) *nt* watercolour
(BRIT), watercolor (US).
Aquarium [a'kva:rium] *nt* aquarium.
Äquator [ɛ'kva:tɔr] (-s) *m* equator.
Äquivalent [ɛkviva'lɛnt] (-(e)s, -e) *nt*
equivalent.
Ar [a:r] (-s, -e) *nt od m* (Maß) are (100 m²).
Ära ['ɛːra] (-, Ären) *f* era.
Araber(in) ['a:rabər(ɪn)] (-s, -) *m(f)* Arab.
Arabien [a'ra:biən] (-s) *nt* Arabia.
arabisch *adj* Arab; (Arabien betreffend)
Arabian; (Sprache) Arabic; **A~er Golf**
Arabian Gulf; **A~es Meer** Arabian Sea; **A~e**
Wüste Arabian Desert.
Arbeit ['arbaɪt] (-, -en) *f* work *no art*; (Stelle)
job; (Erzeugnis) piece of work;
(wissenschaftliche) dissertation; (Klassen~)
test; **Tag der** ~ Labour (BRIT) od Labor (US)
Day; **sich an die** ~ **machen, an die** ~ **gehen**
to get down to work, start working; **jdm**
~ **machen** (Mühe) to put sb to trouble; **das**
war eine ~ that was a hard job.
arbeiten *vi* to work ♦ *vt* to make ♦ *vr:* **sich**
nach oben/an die Spitze ~ (fig) to work
one's way up/to the top.
Arbeiter(in) (-s, -) *m(f)* worker; (ungelernt)
labourer (BRIT), laborer (US).
Arbeiter- *zW:* ~**familie** *f* working-class family;
~**kind** *nt* child from a working-class family;
~**mitbestimmung** *f* employee participation;
~**schaft** *f* workers *pl*, labour (BRIT) od labor
(US) force; ~**selbstkontrolle** *f* workers'
control; ~**-und-Bauern-Staat** *m* (DDR)
workers' and peasants' state; ~**wohlfahrt** *f*
workers' welfare association.
Arbeit- *zW:* ~**geber** (-s, -) *m* employer;
~**nehmer** (-s, -) *m* employee; **a~sam** *adj*
industrious.
Arbeits- *in zW* labour (BRIT), labor (US); ~**amt**
nt employment exchange, Job Centre (BRIT);
~**aufwand** *m* expenditure of energy;
(INDUSTRIE) use of labour (BRIT) od labor
(US); ~**bedingungen** *pl* working conditions
pl; ~**beschaffung** *f* (~platzbeschaffung) job
creation; ~**erlaubnis** *f* work permit; **a~fähig**
adj fit for work, able-bodied; ~**gang** *m*
operation; ~**gemeinschaft** *f* study group;
~**gericht** *nt* industrial tribunal; **a~intensiv**
adj labour-intensive (BRIT), labor-intensive
(US); ~**konflikt** *m* industrial dispute; ~**kraft** *f*
worker; ~**kräfte** *pl* workers *pl*, labour (BRIT),
labor (US); **a~los** *adj* unemployed, out-of-
work; ~**losengeld** *nt* unemployment benefit;

~**losenhilfe** *f* supplementary benefit;
~**losenunterstützung** *f* unemployment
benefit; ~**losenversicherung** *f compulsory
insurance against unemployment*;
~**losigkeit** *f* unemployment; ~**markt** *m* job
market; ~**moral** *f* attitude to work; (*in
Betrieb*) work climate; ~**niederlegung** *f*
walkout; ~**platte** *f* (*Küche*) work-top, work
surface; ~**platz** *m* place of work; (*Stelle*) job;
~**platzrechner** *m* (*COMPUT*) work station;
~**recht** *nt* industrial law; **a**~**scheu** *adj*
workshy; ~**schutz** *m maintenance of health
and safety standards at work*; ~**tag** *m*
work(ing) day; ~**teilung** *f* division of labour
(*BRIT*) *od* labor (*US*); ~**tier** *nt* (*fig: umg*)
glutton for work, workaholic; **a**~**unfähig** *adj*
unfit for work; ~**unfall** *m* industrial
accident; ~**verhältnis** *nt* employee-employer
relationship; ~**vermittlung** *f* (*Amt*)
employment exchange; (*privat*) employment
agency; ~**vertrag** *m* contract of
employment; ~**zeit** *f* working hours *pl*;
~**zeitkonto** *nt* record of hours worked;
~**zeitverkürzung** *f* reduction in working
hours; ~**zimmer** *nt* study.
Archäologe [arçeo'lo:gə] (**-n, -n**) *m*
arch(a)eologist.
Archäologin [arçeo'lo:gɪn] *f* arch(a)eologist.
Arche ['arçə] (**-, -n**) *f*: **die ~ Noah** Noah's Ark.
Architekt(in) [arçi'tɛkt(ɪn)] (**-en, -en**) *m(f)*
architect.
architektonisch [arçitɛk'to:nɪʃ] *adj*
architectural.
Architektur [arçitɛk'tu:r] *f* architecture.
Archiv [ar'çi:f] (**-s, -e**) *nt* archive.

ARD

*The **ARD** (Arbeitsgemeinschaft der öffentlich-
rechtlichen Rundfunkanstalten der Bundesrepublik
Deutschland) is the name of the German
broadcasting corporation founded as a result of
several mergers after 1945. It is financed by
licence fees and advertising and transmits the First
Programme nationwide as well as the Third and
other regional programmes. News and
educational programmes make up about a third of
its transmissions.*

Arena [a're:na] (**-, Arenen**) *f* (*lit, fig*) arena;
(*Zirkus~, Stierkampf~*) ring.
arg [ark] *adj* bad, awful ♦ *adv* awfully, very; **es
zu ~ treiben** to go too far.
Argentinien [argɛn'ti:niən] (**-s**) *nt* Argentina,
the Argentine.
Argentinier(in) (**-s, -**) *m(f)* Argentine,
Argentinian (*BRIT*), Argentinean (*US*).
argentinisch [argɛn'ti:nɪʃ] *adj* Argentine,
Argentinian (*BRIT*), Argentinean (*US*).
Ärger ['ɛrgər] (**-s**) *m* (*Wut*) anger;

(*Unannehmlichkeit*) trouble; **jdm ~ machen**
od **bereiten** to cause sb a lot of trouble *od*
bother; **ä~lich** *adj* (*zornig*) angry; (*lästig*)
annoying, aggravating.
ärgern *vt* to annoy ♦ *vr* to get annoyed.
Ärgernis (**-ses, -se**) *nt* annoyance; (*Anstoß*)
offence (*BRIT*), offense (*US*), outrage;
öffentliches ~ erregen to be a public
nuisance.
arg- *zW*: ~**listig** *adj* cunning, insidious; ~**listige
Täuschung** fraud; ~**los** *adj* guileless,
innocent; **A**~**losigkeit** *f* guilelessness,
innocence.
Argument [argu'mɛnt] *nt* argument.
argumentieren [argumɛn'ti:rən] *vi* to argue.
Argusauge ['argʊs|aʊgə] *nt* (*geh*): **mit ~n**
eagle-eyed.
Argwohn *m* suspicion.
argwöhnisch *adj* suspicious.
Arie ['a:riə] *f* aria.
Aristokrat(in) [arɪsto'kra:t(ɪn)] (**-en, -en**) *m(f)*
aristocrat.
Aristokratie [arɪstokra:'ti:] *f* aristocracy.
aristokratisch *adj* aristocratic.
arithmetisch [arɪt'me:tɪʃ] *adj* arithmetical;
~**es Mittel** arithmetic mean.
Arkaden [ar'ka:dən] *pl* (*Bogengang*) arcade
sing.
Arktis ['arktɪs] (**-**) *f* Arctic.
arktisch *adj* Arctic.
arm [arm] *adj* poor; **~ dran sein** (*umg*) to have
a hard time of it.
Arm (**-(e)s, -e**) *m* arm; (*Fluss~*) branch; **jdn auf
den ~ nehmen** (*fig: umg*) to pull sb's leg;
jdm unter die ~e greifen (*fig*) to help sb out;
einen langen/den längeren ~ haben (*fig*) to
have a lot of/more pull (*umg*) *od* influence.
Armatur [arma'tu:r] *f* (*ELEK*) armature.
Armaturenbrett *nt* instrument panel; (*AUT*)
dashboard.
Armband *nt* bracelet; ~**uhr** *f* (wrist) watch.
Arme(r) *f(m)* poor man/woman; **die ~n** the
poor.
Armee [ar'me:] (**-, -n**) *f* army; ~**korps** *nt* army
corps.
Ärmel ['ɛrməl] (**-s, -**) *m* sleeve; **etw aus dem
~ schütteln** (*fig*) to produce sth just like
that.
Ärmelkanal *m* (English) Channel.
Armenien [ar'me:niən] (**-s**) *nt* Armenia.
Armenier(in) [ar'me:niər(ɪn)] (**-s, -**) *m(f)*
Armenian.
armenisch [ar'me:nɪʃ] *adj* Armenian.
Armenrecht *nt* (*JUR*) legal aid.
Armer *m siehe* **Arme(r)**.
Armlehne *f* armrest.
Armleuchter (*pej: umg*) *m* (*Dummkopf*) twit
(*BRIT*), fool.
ärmlich ['ɛrmlıç] *adj* poor; **aus ~en
Verhältnissen** from a poor family.

armselig *adj* wretched, miserable; (*Mitleid erregend*) pathetic, pitiful.

Armut ['armuːt] (-) *f* poverty.

Armutsgrenze *f* poverty line.

Armutszeugnis *nt* (*fig*): **jdm/sich ein ~ ausstellen** to show sb's/one's shortcomings.

Aroma [a'roːma] (-s, **Aromen**) *nt* aroma; **~therapie** *f* aromatherapy.

aromatisch [aro'maːtɪʃ] *adj* aromatic.

arrangieren [arãː'ʒiːrən] *vt* to arrange ♦ *vr* to come to an arrangement.

Arrest [a'rɛst] (-(e)s, -e) *m* detention.

arretieren [are'tiːrən] *vt* (*TECH*) to lock (in place).

arrogant [aro'gant] *adj* arrogant.

Arroganz *f* arrogance.

Arsch [arʃ] (-es, ⸚e) (*umg!*) *m* arse (*!*); **leck mich am ~!** (*lass mich in Ruhe*) get stuffed! (*!*), fuck off! (*!*); **am ~ der Welt** (*umg*) in the back of beyond; **~kriecher** (*umg!*) *m* arse licker (*!*), crawler; **~loch** (*umg!*) *nt* (*Mensch*) bastard (*!*).

Arsen [ar'zeːn] (-s) *nt* arsenic.

Art [aːrt] (-, -en) *f* (*Weise*) way; (*Sorte*) kind, sort; (*BIOL*) species; **eine ~ (von) Frucht** a kind of fruit; **Häuser aller ~** houses of all kinds; **einzig in seiner ~ sein** to be the only one of its kind, be unique; **auf diese ~ und Weise** in this way; **das ist doch keine ~!** that's no way to behave!; **es ist nicht seine ~, das zu tun** it's not like him to do that; **ich mache das auf meine ~** I do that my (own) way; **Schnitzel nach ~ des Hauses** chef's special escalope.

arten *vi*: **nach jdm ~** to take after sb; **der Mensch ist so geartet, dass ...** human nature is such that ...

Artenschutz *m* protection of endangered species.

Arterie [ar'teːriə] *f* artery.

Arterienverkalkung *f* arteriosclerosis.

Artgenosse ['aːrtgənɔsə] *m* animal/plant of the same species; (*Mensch*) person of the same type.

Arthritis [ar'triːtɪs] (-, -ritiden) *f* arthritis.

artig ['aːrtɪç] *adj* good, well-behaved.

Artikel [ar'tiːkəl] (-s, -) *m* article.

Artillerie [artɪlə'riː] *f* artillery.

Artischocke [arti'ʃɔkə] (-, -n) *f* artichoke.

Artistik [ar'tɪstɪk] (-) *f* artistry; (*Zirkus-/Varieteekunst*) circus/variety performing.

Arznei [aːrts'naɪ] *f* medicine; **~mittel** *nt* medicine, medicament.

Arzt [aːrtst] (-es, ⸚e) *m* doctor; **praktischer ~** general practitioner, GP.

Ärztekammer *f* ≈ General Medical Council (*BRIT*), State Medical Board of Registration (*US*).

Arzthelferin *f* doctor's assistant.

Ärztin ['ɛːrtstɪn] *f* woman doctor; *siehe auch* **Arzt.**

ärztlich ['ɛːrtstlɪç] *adj* medical.

Arztpraxis *f* doctor's practice; (*Räume*) doctor's surgery (*BRIT*) od office (*US*).

As [as] (-ses, -se) *nt* (*MUS*) A flat; *siehe auch* **Ass.**

Asbest [as'bɛst] (-(e)s, -e) *m* asbestos.

Asche ['aʃə] (-, -n) *f* ash.

Aschen- *zW*: **~bahn** *f* cinder track; **~becher** *m* ashtray; **~brödel** *nt* (*LITER, fig*) Cinderella; **~puttel** *nt* (*LITER, fig*) Cinderella.

Aschermittwoch *m* Ash Wednesday.

Aserbaidschan [azɛrbaɪ'dʒaːn] (-s) *nt* Azerbaijan.

aserbaidschanisch *adj* Azerbaijani.

Asiat(in) [azi'aːt(ɪn)] (-en, -en) *m(f)* Asian.

asiatisch *adj* Asian, Asiatic.

Asien ['aːziən] (-s) *nt* Asia.

asozial ['azotsiaːl] *adj* antisocial; (*Familie*) asocial.

Asoziale(r) (*pej*) *dekl wie adj f(m)* antisocial person; **Asoziale** *pl* antisocial elements.

Aspekt [as'pɛkt] (-(e)s, -e) *m* aspect.

Asphalt [as'falt] (-(e)s, -e) *m* asphalt.

asphaltieren [asfal'tiːrən] *vt* to asphalt.

Asphaltstraße *f* asphalt road.

Ass▲ [as] (-es, -e) *nt* ace.

aß *etc* [aːs] *vb siehe* **essen.**

Ass. *abk* = **Assessor.**

Assekurant(in) [aseku'rant(ɪn)] (-en, -en) *m(f)* underwriter.

Assemblersprache [ə'sɛmblərʃpraːxə] *f* (*COMPUT*) assembly language.

Assessor(in) [a'sɛsɔr, -'soːrɪn] (-s, -en) *m(f)* graduate civil servant who has completed his/her traineeship.

Assistent(in) [asɪs'tɛnt(ɪn)] *m(f)* assistant.

Assistenzarzt [asɪs'tɛntsaːrtst] *m* houseman (*BRIT*), intern (*US*).

Assoziation [asotsiatsi'oːn] *f* association.

assoziieren [asotsi'iːrən] *vt* (*geh*) to associate.

Ast [ast] (-(e)s, ⸚e) *m* branch; **sich** *dat* **einen ~ lachen** (*umg*) to double up (with laughter).

AStA ['asta] (-(s), -(s)) *m abk* (= *Allgemeiner Studentenausschuss*) students' association.

Aster ['astər] (-, -n) *f* aster.

ästhetisch [ɛs'teːtɪʃ] *adj* aesthetic (*BRIT*), esthetic (*US*).

Asthma ['astma] (-s) *nt* asthma.

Asthmatiker(in) [ast'maːtikər(ɪn)] (-s, -) *m(f)* asthmatic.

astrein ['astraɪn] *adj* (*fig: umg: moralisch einwandfrei*) straight, on the level; (: *echt*) genuine; (*prima*) fantastic.

Astrologe [astro'loːgə] (-n, -n) *m* astrologer.

Astrologie [astrolo'giː] *f* astrology.

Astrologin *f* astrologer.

Astronaut(in) [astro'naʊt(ɪn)] (-en, -en) *m(f)* astronaut.

Astronautik *f* astronautics.
Astronom(in) [astro'no:m(ɪn)] (**-en, -en**) *m(f)* astronomer.
Astronomie [astrono'mi:] *f* astronomy.
ASU *f abk* (= *Arbeitsgemeinschaft selbstständiger Unternehmer*) association of private traders; (= *Abgassonderuntersuchung*) exhaust emission test.
ASW *f abk* (= *außersinnliche Wahrnehmung*) ESP.
Asyl [a'zy:l] (**-s, -e**) *nt* asylum; (*Heim*) home; (*Obdachlosen~*) shelter.
Asylant(in) [azy'lant(ɪn)] (**-en, -en**) *m(f)* person seeking (political) asylum.
Asylrecht *nt* (*POL*) right of (political) asylum.
A.T. *abk* (= *Altes Testament*) O.T.
Atelier [atəli'e:] (**-s, -s**) *nt* studio.
Atem ['a:təm] (**-s**) *m* breath; **den ~ anhalten** to hold one's breath; **außer ~** out of breath; **jdn in ~ halten** to keep sb in suspense *od* on tenterhooks; **das verschlug mir den ~** it took my breath away; **einen langen/den längeren ~ haben** to have a lot of staying power; **a~beraubend** *adj* breathtaking; **a~los** *adj* breathless; **~pause** *f* breather; **~wege** *pl* (*ANAT*) respiratory tract; **~zug** *m* breath.
Atheismus [ate'ɪsmʊs] *m* atheism.
Atheist(in) *m(f)* atheist; **a~isch** *adj* atheistic.
Athen [a'te:n] (**-s**) *nt* Athens.
Athener(in) (**-s, -**) *m(f)* Athenian.
Äther ['ɛ:tər] (**-s, -**) *m* ether.
Äthiopien [ɛti'o:piən] (**-s**) *nt* Ethiopia.
Äthiopier(in) (**-s, -**) *m(f)* Ethiopian.
äthiopisch *adj* Ethiopian.
Athlet(in) [at'le:t(ɪn)] (**-en, -en**) *m(f)* athlete.
Athletik *f* athletics *sing*.
Atlanten *pl von* **Atlas.**
Atlantik [at'lantɪk] (**-s**) *m* Atlantic.
atlantisch *adj* Atlantic; **der A~e Ozean** the Atlantic Ocean.
Atlas ['atlas] (**- *od* -ses, -se** *od* **Atlanten**) *m* atlas; **~gebirge** *nt* Atlas Mountains *pl*.
atmen ['a:tmən] *vt, vi* to breathe.
Atmosphäre [atmo'sfɛ:rə] (**-, -n**) *f* atmosphere.
atmosphärisch *adj* atmospheric.
Atmung ['a:tmʊŋ] *f* respiration.
Ätna ['ɛ:tna] (**-(s)**) *m* Etna.
Atom [a'to:m] (**-s, -e**) *nt* atom.
atomar [ato'ma:r] *adj* atomic, nuclear; (*Drohung*) nuclear.
Atom- *zW:* **~bombe** *f* atom bomb; **~energie** *f* nuclear *od* atomic energy; **~gegner** *m:* **~gegner sein** to be antinuclear; **~kern** *m* atomic nucleus; **~kraft** *f* nuclear power; **~kraftwerk** *nt* nuclear power station; **~krieg** *m* nuclear *od* atomic war; **~lobby** *f* nuclear lobby; **~macht** *f* nuclear *od* atomic power; **~meiler** *m* nuclear reactor; **~müll** *m* nuclear waste; **~physik** *f* nuclear physics *sing*; **~pilz**

m mushroom cloud; **~sperrvertrag** *m* (*POL*) nuclear non-proliferation treaty; **~sprengkopf** *m* nuclear *od* atomic warhead; **~strom** *m* electricity generated by nuclear power; **~test** *m* nuclear test; **~testgelände** *nt* nuclear testing range; **~waffen** *pl* nuclear *od* atomic weapons *pl*; **a~waffenfrei** *adj* (*Zone*) nuclear-free; **~wirtschaft** *f* nuclear industry; **~zeitalter** *nt* atomic age.
Attacke [a'takə] (**-, -n**) *f* (*Angriff*) attack.
Attentat [atɛn'ta:t] (**-(e)s, -e**) *nt*: **~ (auf** +*akk*) (attempted) assassination (of).
Attentäter(in) [atɛn'tɛ:tər(ɪn)] (**-s, -**) *m(f)* (would-be) assassin.
Attest [a'tɛst] (**-(e)s, -e**) *nt* certificate.
Attraktion [atraktsi'o:n] *f* attraction.
attraktiv [atrak'ti:f] *adj* attractive.
Attrappe [a'trapə] (**-, -n**) *f* dummy; **bei ihr ist alles ~** everything about her is false.
Attribut [atri'bu:t] (**-(e)s, -e**) *nt* (*GRAM*) attribute.
ätzen ['ɛtsən] *vi* to be caustic.
ätzend *adj* (*lit: Säure*) corrosive; (*Geruch*) pungent; (*fig: umg: furchtbar*) dreadful, horrible; (: *toll*) magic.

auch [aʊx] *adv* **1** (*ebenfalls*) also, too, as well; **das ist ~ schön** that's nice too *od* as well; **er kommt - ich ~** he's coming - so am I, me too; **~ nicht** not ... either; **ich ~ nicht** nor I, me neither; **oder ~** or; **~ das noch!** not that as well!; **nicht nur ..., sondern ~** ... not only ... but also ...

2 (*selbst, sogar*) even; **~ wenn das Wetter schlecht ist** even if the weather is bad; **ohne ~ nur zu fragen** without even asking.

3 (*wirklich*) really; **du siehst müde aus - bin ich ~** you look tired - (so) I am; **so sieht es ~ aus** (and) that's what it looks like.

4 (**~ immer**): **wer ~** whoever; **was ~** whatever; **wozu ~?** (*emphatisch*) whatever for?; **wie dem ~ sei** be that as it may; **wie sehr er sich ~ bemühte** however much he tried.

Audienz [aʊdi'ɛnts] (**-, -en**) *f* (*bei Papst, König etc*) audience.
Audimax [aʊdi'maks] *nt* (*UNIV: umg*) main lecture hall.
audiovisuell [aʊdiovizu'ɛl] *adj* audiovisual.
Auditorium [aʊdi'to:riʊm] *nt* (*Hörsaal*) lecture hall; (*geh: Zuhörerschaft*) audience.

auf [aʊf] *präp* +*dat* (*wo?*) on; **~ dem Tisch** on the table; **~ der Reise** on the way; **~ der Post/ dem Fest** at the post office/party; **~ der Straße** on the road; **~ dem Land/der ganzen Welt** in the country/the whole world; **was**

hat es damit ~ sich? what does it mean?
♦ *präp +akk* **1** (*wohin?*) on(to); ~ **den Tisch**
on(to) the table; ~ **die Post gehen** to go to
the post office; ~ **das Land** into the country;
etw ~ **einen Zettel schreiben** to write sth on
a piece of paper; ~ **eine Tasse Kaffee/eine
Zigarette(nlänge)** for a cup of coffee/a
smoke; **die Nacht (von Montag)** ~ **Dienstag**
Monday night; ~ **einen Polizisten kommen
1.000 Bürger** there is one policeman to
every 1,000 citizens.
2: ~ **Deutsch** in German; ~ **Lebenszeit** for
my/his lifetime; **bis** ~ **ihn** except for him;
~ **einmal** at once; ~ **seinen Vorschlag (hin)**
at his suggestion.
♦ *adv* **1** (*offen*) open; ~ **sein** to be open; **das
Fenster ist** ~ the window is open.
2 (*hinauf*) up; ~ **und ab** up and down; ~ **und
davon** up and away; ~**!** (*los!*) come on!; **von
klein** ~ from childhood onwards.
3 (*aufgestanden*) up; ~ **sein** (*Person*) to be up;
ist er schon ~**?** is he up yet?
♦ *konj:* ~ **dass** (so) that.

aufarbeiten ['auf|arbaɪtən] *vt* (*erledigen:
Korrespondenz etc*) to catch up with.
aufatmen ['auf|aːtmən] *vi* to heave a sigh of
relief.
aufbahren ['aufbaːrən] *vt* to lay out.
Aufbau ['aufbau] *m* (*Bauen*) building,
construction; (*Struktur*) structure;
(*aufgebautes Teil*) superstructure.
aufbauen ['aufbauən] *vt* to erect, build (up);
(*Existenz*) to make; (*gestalten*) to construct;
(*gründen*): ~ (**auf** +*dat*) to found (on), base
(on) ♦ *vr:* **sich vor jdm** ~ to draw o.s. up to
one's full height in front of sb.
aufbäumen ['aufbɔʏmən] *vr* to rear; (*fig*) to
revolt, rebel.
aufbauschen ['aufbauʃən] *vt* to puff out; (*fig*)
to exaggerate.
aufbegehren ['aufbəgeːrən] *vi* (*geh*) to rebel.
aufbehalten ['aufbəhaltən] *unreg vt* to keep on.
aufbekommen ['aufbəkɔmən] *unreg* (*umg*) *vt*
(*öffnen*) to get open; (: *Hausaufgaben*) to be
given.
aufbereiten ['aufbəraɪtən] *vt* to process;
(*Trinkwasser*) to purify; (*Text etc*) to work up.
Aufbereitungsanlage *f* processing plant.
aufbessern ['aufbɛsərn] *vt* (*Gehalt*) to
increase.
aufbewahren ['aufbəvaːrən] *vt* to keep;
(*Gepäck*) to put in the left-luggage office.
Aufbewahrung *f* (safe)keeping; (*Gepäck~*)
left-luggage office (*BRIT*), baggage check
(*US*); **jdm etw zur** ~ **geben** to give sb sth for
safekeeping.
Aufbewahrungsort *m* storage place.
aufbieten ['aufbiːtən] *unreg vt* (*Kraft*) to
summon (up); (*Armee, Polizei*) to mobilize.

Aufbietung *f:* **unter** ~ **aller Kräfte ...**
summoning (up) all his/her *etc* strength ...
aufbinden ['aufbɪndən] *unreg vt:* **lass dir doch
so etwas nicht** ~ (*fig*) don't fall for that.
aufblähen ['aufblɛːən] *vr* to blow out; (*Segel*)
to billow out; (*MED*) to become swollen; (*fig:
pej*) to puff o.s. up.
aufblasen ['aufblaːzən] *unreg vt* to blow up,
inflate ♦ *vr* (*umg*) to become big-headed.
aufbleiben ['aufblaɪbən] *unreg vi* (*Laden*) to
remain open; (*Person*) to stay up.
aufblenden ['aufblɛndən] *vt* (*Scheinwerfer*) to
turn on full beam.
aufblicken ['aufblɪkən] *vi* to look up; ~ **zu** (*lit*)
to look up at; (*fig*) to look up to.
aufblühen ['aufblyːən] *vi* to blossom; (*fig*) to
blossom, flourish.
aufblühend *adj* (*COMM*) booming.
aufbocken ['aufbɔkən] *vt* (*Auto*) to jack up.
aufbrauchen ['aufbrauxən] *vt* to use up.
aufbrausen ['aufbrauzən] *vi* (*fig*) to flare up.
aufbrausend *adj* hot-tempered.
aufbrechen ['aufbrɛçən] *unreg vt* to break
open, to prise (*BRIT*) *od* pry (*US*) open ♦ *vi* to
burst open; (*gehen*) to start, set off.
aufbringen ['aufbrɪŋən] *unreg vt* (*öffnen*) to
open; (*in Mode*) to bring into fashion;
(*beschaffen*) to procure; (*FIN*) to raise;
(*ärgern*) to irritate; **Verständnis für etw** ~ to
be able to understand sth.
Aufbruch ['aufbrʊx] *m* departure.
aufbrühen ['aufbryːən] *vt* (*Tee*) to make.
aufbrummen ['aufbrʊmən] (*umg*) *vt:* **jdm die
Kosten** ~ to land sb with the costs.
aufbürden ['aufbyrdən] *vt:* **jdm etw** ~ to
burden sb with sth.
aufdecken ['aufdɛkən] *vt* to uncover;
(*Spielkarten*) to show.
aufdrängen ['aufdrɛŋən] *vt:* **jdm etw** ~ to
force sth on sb ♦ *vr:* **sich jdm** ~ to intrude on
sb.
aufdrehen ['aufdreːən] *vt* (*Wasserhahn etc*) to
turn on; (*Ventil*) to open; (*Schraubverschluss*)
to unscrew; (*Radio etc*) to turn up; (*Haar*) to
put in rollers.
aufdringlich ['aufdrɪŋlɪç] *adj* pushy;
(*Benehmen*) obtrusive; (*Parfüm*) powerful.
aufeinander [auf|aɪˈnandər] *adv* on top of one
another; (*schießen*) at each other; (*warten*)
for one another; (*vertrauen*) each other;
~ **folgen** to follow one another; ~ **folgend**
consecutive; ~ **legen** to lay on top of one
another; ~ **prallen** (*Autos etc*) to collide;
(*Truppen, Meinungen*) to clash; **A~folge** *f*
succession, series.
Aufenthalt ['auf|ɛnthalt] *m* stay; (*Verzögerung*)
delay; (*EISENB: Halten*) stop; (*Ort*) haunt.
Aufenthalts- *zW:* ~**erlaubnis** *f*,
~**genehmigung** *f* residence permit; ~**raum**
m day room; (*in Betrieb*) recreation room.

Spelling Reform: ▲ *new spelling* △ *old spelling (to be phased out)*

auferlegen ['aʊf|ɛrle:gən] *vt*: **(jdm)** ~ to impose (upon sb).

auferstehen ['aʊf|ɛrʃte:ən] *unreg vi untr* to rise from the dead.

Auferstehung *f* resurrection.

aufessen ['aʊf|ɛsən] *unreg vt* to eat up.

auffahren ['aʊffa:rən] *unreg vi* (*herankommen*) to draw up; (*hochfahren*) to jump up; (*wütend werden*) to flare up; (*in den Himmel*) to ascend ♦ *vt* (*Kanonen, Geschütz*) to bring up; ~ **auf** +*akk* (*Auto*) to run *od* crash into.

auffahrend *adj* hot-tempered.

Auffahrt *f* (*Haus*~) drive; (*Autobahn*~) slip road (*BRIT*), entrance ramp (*US*).

Auffahrunfall *m* pile-up.

auffallen ['aʊffalən] *unreg vi* to be noticeable; **angenehm/unangenehm** ~ to make a good/ bad impression; **jdm** ~ (*bemerkt werden*) to strike sb.

auffallend *adj* striking.

auffällig ['aʊffɛlɪç] *adj* conspicuous, striking.

auffangen ['aʊffaŋən] *unreg vt* to catch; (*Funkspruch*) to intercept; (*Preise*) to peg; (*abfangen: Aufprall etc*) to cushion, absorb.

Auffanglager *nt* reception camp.

auffassen ['aʊffasən] *vt* to understand, comprehend; (*auslegen*) to see, view.

Auffassung *f* (*Meinung*) opinion; (*Auslegung*) view, conception; (*auch*: ~**sgabe**) grasp.

auffindbar ['aʊffɪntba:r] *adj* to be found.

aufflammen ['aʊfflamən] *vi* (*lit, fig: Feuer, Unruhen etc*) to flare up.

auffliegen ['aʊffli:gən] *unreg vi* to fly up; (*umg: Rauschgiftring etc*) to be busted.

auffordern ['aʊffɔrdərn] *vt* to challenge; (*befehlen*) to call upon, order; (*bitten*) to ask.

Aufforderung *f* (*Befehl*) order; (*Einladung*) invitation.

aufforsten ['aʊffɔrstən] *vt* (*Gebiet*) to reafforest; (*Wald*) to restock.

auffrischen ['aʊffrɪʃən] *vt* to freshen up; (*Kenntnisse*) to brush up; (*Erinnerungen*) to reawaken ♦ *vi* (*Wind*) to freshen.

aufführen ['aʊffy:rən] *vt* (*THEAT*) to perform; (*in einem Verzeichnis*) to list, specify ♦ *vr* (*sich benehmen*) to behave; **einzeln** ~ to itemize.

Aufführung *f* (*THEAT*) performance; (*Liste*) specification.

auffüllen ['aʊffʏlən] *vt* to fill up; (*Vorräte*) to replenish; (*Öl*) to top up.

Aufgabe ['aʊfga:bə] (-, **-n**) *f* task; (*SCH*) exercise; (*Haus*~) homework; (*Verzicht*) giving up; (*von Gepäck*) registration; (*von Post*) posting; (*von Inserat*) insertion; **sich** *dat* **etw zur** ~ **machen** to make sth one's job *od* business.

aufgabeln ['aʊfga:bəln] *vt* (*fig: umg: jdn*) to pick up; (: *Sache*) to get hold of.

Aufgabenbereich *m* area of responsibility.

Aufgang ['aʊfgaŋ] *m* ascent; (*Sonnen*~) rise;

(*Treppe*) staircase.

aufgeben ['aʊfge:bən] *unreg vt* (*verzichten auf*) to give up; (*Paket*) to send, post; (*Gepäck*) to register; (*Bestellung*) to give; (*Inserat*) to insert; (*Rätsel, Problem*) to set ♦ *vi* to give up.

aufgeblasen ['aʊfgəbla:zən] *adj* (*fig*) puffed up, self-important.

Aufgebot ['aʊfgəbo:t] *nt* supply; (*von Kräften*) utilization; (*Ehe*~) banns *pl*.

aufgedonnert ['aʊfgədɔnərt] (*pej: umg*) *adj* tarted up.

aufgedreht ['aʊfgədre:t] (*umg*) *adj* excited.

aufgedunsen ['aʊfgedʊnzən] *adj* swollen, puffed up.

aufgegeben ['aʊfgəge:bən] *pp von* **aufgeben**.

aufgehen ['aʊfge:ən] *unreg vi* (*Sonne, Teig*) to rise; (*sich öffnen*) to open; (*THEAT: Vorhang*) to go up; (*Knopf, Knoten etc*) to come undone; (*klar werden*) to become clear; (*MATH*) to come out exactly; ~ **(in** +*dat*) (*sich widmen*) to be absorbed (in); **in Rauch/Flammen** ~ to go up in smoke/flames.

aufgeilen ['aʊfgaɪlən] (*umg*) *vt* to turn on ♦ *vr* to be turned on.

aufgeklärt ['aʊfgəkle:rt] *adj* enlightened; (*sexuell*) knowing the facts of life.

aufgekratzt ['aʊfgəkratst] (*umg*) *adj* in high spirits, full of beans.

aufgelaufen ['aʊfgəlaʊfən] *adj*: ~**e Zinsen** ♦ *pl* accrued interest *sing*.

Aufgeld *nt* premium.

aufgelegt ['aʊfgəle:kt] *adj*: **gut/schlecht** ~ **sein** to be in a good/bad mood; **zu etw** ~ **sein** to be in the mood for sth.

aufgenommen ['aʊfgənɔmən] *pp von* **aufnehmen**.

aufgeregt ['aʊfgəre:kt] *adj* excited.

aufgeschlossen ['aʊfgəʃlɔsən] *adj* open, open-minded.

aufgeschmissen ['aʊfgəʃmɪsən] (*umg*) *adj* in a fix, stuck.

aufgeschrieben ['aʊfgəʃri:bən] *pp von* **aufschreiben**.

aufgestanden ['aʊfgəʃtandən] *pp von* **aufstehen**.

aufgetakelt ['aʊfgəta:kəlt] *adj* (*fig: umg*) dressed up to the nines.

aufgeweckt ['aʊfgəvɛkt] *adj* bright, intelligent.

aufgießen ['aʊfgi:sən] *unreg vt* (*Wasser*) to pour over; (*Tee*) to infuse.

aufgliedern ['aʊfgli:dərn] *vr*: **sich** ~ **(in** +*akk*) to (sub)divide (into), break down (into).

aufgreifen ['aʊfgraɪfən] *unreg vt* (*Thema*) to take up; (*Verdächtige*) to pick up, seize.

aufgrund, auf Grund [aʊf'grʊnt] *präp* +*gen*: ~ **von** on the basis of; (*wegen*) because of.

Aufgussbeutel▲ ['aʊfgʊsbɔʏtəl] *m* sachet (containing coffee/herbs *etc*) for brewing; (*Teebeutel*) tea bag.

aufhaben ['aʊfhaːbən] unreg vt (Hut etc) to have on; (Arbeit) to have to do.

aufhalsen ['aʊfhalzən] (umg) vt: **jdm etw** ~ to saddle od lumber sb with sth.

aufhalten ['aʊfhaltən] unreg vt (Person) to detain; (Entwicklung) to check; (Tür, Hand) to hold open; (Augen) to keep open ♦ vr (wohnen) to live; (bleiben) to stay; **jdn (bei etw)** ~ (abhalten, stören) to hold od keep sb back (from sth); **sich über etw/jdn** ~ to go on about sth/sb; **sich mit etw** ~ to waste time over sth; **sich bei etw** ~ (sich befassen) to dwell on sth.

aufhängen ['aʊfhɛŋən] unreg vt (Wäsche) to hang up; (Menschen) to hang ♦ vr to hang o.s.

Aufhänger (-s, -) m (am Mantel) hook; (fig) peg.

Aufhängung f (TECH) suspension.

aufheben ['aʊfheːbən] unreg vt (hochheben) to raise, lift; (Sitzung) to wind up; (Urteil) to annul; (Gesetz) to repeal, abolish; (aufbewahren) to keep; (ausgleichen) to offset, make up for ♦ vr to cancel itself out; **viel A~(s) machen (von)** to make a fuss (about); **bei jdm gut aufgehoben sein** to be well looked after at sb's.

aufheitern ['aʊfhaɪtərn] vt, vr (Himmel, Miene) to brighten; (Mensch) to cheer up.

Aufheiterungen pl (MET) bright periods pl.

aufheizen ['aʊfhaɪtsən] vt: **die Stimmung** ~ to stir up feelings.

aufhelfen ['aʊfhɛlfən] unreg vi (lit: beim Aufstehen): **jdm** ~ to help sb up.

aufhellen ['aʊfhɛlən] vt, vr to clear up; (Farbe, Haare) to lighten.

aufhetzen ['aʊfhɛtsən] vt to stir up.

aufheulen ['aʊfhɔʏlən] vi to howl; (Sirene) to (start to) wail; (Motor) to (give a) roar.

aufholen ['aʊfhoːlən] vt to make up ♦ vi to catch up.

aufhorchen ['aʊfhɔrçən] vi to prick up one's ears.

aufhören ['aʊfhøːrən] vi to stop; ~, **etw zu tun** to stop doing sth.

aufkaufen ['aʊfkaʊfən] vt to buy up.

aufklappen ['aʊfklapən] vt to open; (Verdeck) to fold back.

aufklären ['aʊfklɛːrən] vt (Geheimnis etc) to clear up; (Person) to enlighten; (sexuell) to tell the facts of life to; (MIL) to reconnoitre ♦ vr to clear up.

Aufklärung f (von Geheimnis) clearing up; (Unterrichtung, Zeitalter) enlightenment; (sexuell) sex education; (MIL, AVIAT) reconnaissance.

Aufklärungsarbeit f educational work.

aufkleben ['aʊfkleːbən] vt to stick on.

Aufkleber (-s, -) m sticker.

aufknöpfen ['aʊfknœpfən] vt to unbutton.

aufkochen ['aʊfkɔxən] vt to bring to the boil.

aufkommen ['aʊfkɔmən] unreg vi (Wind) to come up; (Zweifel, Gefühl) to arise; (Mode) to start; **für jdn/etw** ~ to be liable od responsible for sb/sth; **für den Schaden** ~ to pay for the damage; **endlich kam Stimmung auf** at last things livened up.

aufkreuzen ['aʊfkrɔʏtsən] (umg) vi (erscheinen) to turn od show up.

aufkündigen ['aʊfkʏndɪgən] vt (Vertrag etc) to terminate.

aufladen ['aʊflaːdən] unreg vt to load ♦ vr (Batterie etc) to be charged; (neu ~) to be recharged; **jdm/sich etw** ~ (fig) to saddle sb/o.s. with sth.

Auflage ['aʊflaːgə] f edition; (Zeitung) circulation; (Bedingung) condition; **jdm etw zur** ~ **machen** to make sth a condition for sb.

Auflage(n)höhe f (von Buch) number of copies published; (von Zeitung) circulation.

auflassen ['aʊflasən] unreg (umg) vt (offen) to leave open; (: aufgesetzt) to leave on; **die Kinder länger** ~ to let the children stay up (longer).

auflauern ['aʊflaʊərn] vi: **jdn** ~ to lie in wait for sb.

Auflauf ['aʊflaʊf] m (KOCH) pudding; (Menschen~) crowd.

auflaufen unreg vi (auf Grund laufen: Schiff) to run aground; **jdn** ~ **lassen** (umg) to drop sb in it.

Auflaufform f (KOCH) ovenproof dish.

aufleben ['aʊfleːbən] vi to revive.

auflegen ['aʊfleːgən] vt to put on; (Hörer) to put down; (TYP) to print ♦ vi (TEL) to hang up.

auflehnen ['aʊfleːnən] vt to lean on ♦ vr to rebel.

Auflehnung f rebellion.

auflesen ['aʊfleːzən] unreg vt to pick up.

aufleuchten ['aʊflɔʏçtən] vi to light up.

aufliegen ['aʊfliːgən] unreg vi to lie on; (COMM) to be available.

auflisten ['aʊflɪstən] vt (auch COMPUT) to list.

auflockern ['aʊflɔkərn] vt to loosen; (fig: Eintönigkeit etc) to liven up; (entspannen, zwangloser machen) to make relaxed; (Atmosphäre) to make more relaxed, ease.

auflösen ['aʊfløːzən] vt to dissolve; (Missverständnis) to sort out; (Konto) to close; (Firma) to wind up; (Haushalt) to break up; **in Tränen aufgelöst sein** to be in tears.

Auflösung f dissolving; (fig) solution; (Bildschirm) resolution.

aufmachen ['aʊfmaxən] vt to open; (Kleidung) to undo; (zurechtmachen) to do up ♦ vr to set out.

Aufmacher m (PRESSE) lead.

Aufmachung f (Kleidung) outfit, get-up; (Gestaltung) format.

aufmerksam ['aʊfmɛrkzaːm] *adj* attentive; **auf etw** *akk* ~ **werden** to become aware of sth; **jdn auf etw** *akk* ~ **machen** to point sth out to sb; **(das ist) sehr** ~ **von Ihnen** (*zuvorkommend*) (that's) most kind of you; **A~keit** *f* attention, attentiveness; (*Geschenk*) token (gift).

aufmöbeln ['aʊfmøːbəln] (*umg*) *vt* (*Gegenstand*) to do up; (: *beleben*) to buck up, pep up.

aufmucken ['aʊfmʊkən] (*umg*) *vi*: ~ **gegen** to protest at *od* against.

aufmuntern ['aʊfmʊntərn] *vt* (*ermutigen*) to encourage; (*erheitern*) to cheer up.

aufmüpfig ['aʊfmʏpfɪç] (*umg*) *adj* rebellious.

Aufnahme ['aʊfnaːmə] (-, **-n**) *f* reception; (*Beginn*) beginning; (*in Verein etc*) admission; (*in Liste etc*) inclusion; (*Notieren*) taking down; (*PHOT*) shot; (*auf Tonband etc*) recording; ~**antrag** *m* application for membership *od* admission; **a~fähig** *adj* receptive; ~**leiter** *m* (*FILM*) production manager; (*RUNDF, TV*) producer; ~**prüfung** *f* entrance test; ~**stopp** *m* (*für Flüchtlinge etc*) freeze on immigration.

aufnehmen ['aʊfneːmən] *unreg vt* to receive; (*hochheben*) to pick up; (*beginnen*) to take up; (*in Verein etc*) to admit; (*in Liste etc*) to include; (*fassen*) to hold; (*begreifen*) to take in, grasp; (*beim Stricken*: *Maschen*) to increase, make; (*notieren*) to take down; (*fotografieren*) to photograph; (*auf Tonband, Platte*) to record; (*FIN*: *leihen*) to take out; **es mit jdm** ~ **können** to be able to compete with sb.

aufnötigen ['aʊfnøːtɪgən] *vt*: **jdm etw** ~ to force sth on sb.

aufoktroyieren ['aʊfʔɔktroajiːrən] *vt*: **jdm etw** ~ (*geh*) to impose *od* force sth on sb.

aufopfern ['aʊfʔɔpfərn] *vt* to sacrifice ♦ *vr* to sacrifice o.s.

aufopfernd *adj* selfless.

aufpassen ['aʊfpasən] *vi* (*aufmerksam sein*) to pay attention; **auf jdn/etw** ~ to look after *od* watch sb/sth; **aufgepasst!** look out!

Aufpasser(in) (-s, -) *m(f)* (*pej*) *m(f)* (*Aufseher, Spitzel*) spy, watchdog; (*Beobachter*) supervisor; (*Wächter*) guard.

aufpflanzen ['aʊfpflantsən] *vr*: **sich vor jdm** ~ to plant o.s. in front of sb.

aufplatzen ['aʊfplatsən] *vi* to burst open.

aufplustern ['aʊfpluːstərn] *vr* (*Vogel*) to ruffle (up) its feathers; (*Mensch*) to puff o.s. up.

aufprägen ['aʊfprɛːgən] *vt*: **jdm/etw seinen Stempel** ~ (*fig*) to leave one's mark on sb/sth.

Aufprall ['aʊfpral] (-(e)s, **-e**) *m* impact.

aufprallen *vi* to hit, strike.

Aufpreis ['aʊfpraɪs] *m* extra charge.

aufpumpen ['aʊfpʊmpən] *vt* to pump up.

aufputschen ['aʊfpʊtʃən] *vt* (*aufhetzen*) to inflame; (*erregen*) to stimulate.

Aufputschmittel *nt* stimulant.

aufraffen ['aʊfrafən] *vr* to rouse o.s.

aufräumen ['aʊfrɔymən] *vt, vi* (*Dinge*) to clear away; (*Zimmer*) to tidy up.

Aufräumungsarbeiten *pl* clearing-up operations *pl*.

aufrecht ['aʊfrɛçt] *adj* (*lit, fig*) upright.

aufrechterhalten *unreg vt* to maintain.

aufregen ['aʊfreːgən] *vt* to excite; (*ärgerlich machen*) to irritate, annoy; (*nervös machen*) to make nervous; (*beunruhigen*) to disturb ♦ *vr* to get excited.

aufregend *adj* exciting.

Aufregung *f* excitement.

aufreiben ['aʊfraɪbən] *unreg vt* (*Haut*) to rub raw; (*erschöpfen*) to exhaust; (*MIL*: *völlig vernichten*) to wipe out, annihilate.

aufreibend *adj* strenuous.

aufreihen ['aʊfraɪən] *vt* (*in Linie*) to line up; (*Perlen*) to string.

aufreißen ['aʊfraɪsən] *unreg vt* (*Umschlag*) to tear open; (*Augen*) to open wide; (*Tür*) to throw open; (*Straße*) to take up; (*umg*: *Mädchen*) to pick up.

Aufreißer (-s, -) *m* (*Person*) smooth operator.

aufreizen ['aʊfraɪtsən] *vt* to incite, stir up.

aufreizend *adj* exciting, stimulating.

aufrichten ['aʊfrɪçtən] *vt* to put up, erect; (*moralisch*) to console ♦ *vr* to rise; (*moralisch*): **sich** ~ **(an** +*dat*) to take heart (from); **sich im Bett** ~ to sit up in bed.

aufrichtig ['aʊfrɪçtɪç] *adj* sincere; honest; **A~keit** *f* sincerity.

aufrollen ['aʊfrɔlən] *vt* (*zusammenrollen*) to roll up; (*Kabel*) to coil *od* wind up; **einen Fall/Prozess wieder** ~ to reopen a case/trial.

aufrücken ['aʊfrʏkən] *vi* to move up; (*beruflich*) to be promoted.

Aufruf ['aʊfruːf] *m* summons; (*zur Hilfe*) call; (*des Namens*) calling out.

aufrufen *unreg vt* (*Namen*) to call out; (*auffordern*): **jdn** ~ **(zu)** to call upon sb (for); **einen Schüler** ~ to ask a pupil (to answer) a question.

Aufruhr ['aʊfruːr] (-(e)s, **-e**) *m* uprising, revolt; **in** ~ **sein** to be in uproar.

Aufrührer(in) (-s, -) *m(f)* rabble-rouser.

aufrührerisch ['aʊfryːrərɪʃ] *adj* rebellious.

aufrunden ['aʊfrʊndən] *vt* (*Summe*) to round up.

aufrüsten ['aʊfrʏstən] *vt, vi* to arm.

Aufrüstung *f* rearmament.

aufrütteln ['aʊfrʏtəln] *vt* (*lit, fig*) to shake up.

aufs [aʊfs] = **auf das**.

aufsagen ['aʊfzaːgən] *vt* (*Gedicht*) to recite; (*geh*: *Freundschaft*) to put an end to.

aufsammeln ['aʊfzaməln] *vt* to gather up.

aufsässig ['aʊfzɛsɪç] *adj* rebellious.

Aufsatz ['aʊfzats] *m* (*Geschriebenes*) essay, composition; (*auf Schrank etc*) top.

aufsaugen ['aʊfzaʊɡən] *unreg vt* to soak up.

aufschauen ['aʊfʃaʊən] *vi* to look up.

aufscheuchen ['aʊfʃɔʏçən] *vt* to scare, startle.

aufschichten ['aʊfʃɪçtən] *vt* to stack, pile up.

aufschieben ['aʊfʃiːbən] *unreg vt* to push open; (*verzögern*) to put off, postpone.

Aufschlag ['aʊfʃlaːk] *m* (*Ärmel~*) cuff; (*Jacken~*) lapel; (*Hosen~*) turn-up (*BRIT*), cuff (*US*); (*Aufprall*) impact; (*Preis~*) surcharge; (*TENNIS*) service.

aufschlagen ['aʊfʃlaːɡən] *unreg vt* (*öffnen*) to open; (*verwunden*) to cut; (*hochschlagen*) to turn up; (*aufbauen: Zelt, Lager*) to pitch, erect; (*Wohnsitz*) to take up ♦ *vi* (*aufprallen*) to hit; (*teurer werden*) to go up; (*TENNIS*) to serve; **schlagt Seite 111 auf** open your books at page 111.

aufschließen ['aʊfʃliːsən] *unreg vt* to open up, unlock ♦ *vi* (*aufrücken*) to close up.

Aufschluss▲ ['aʊfʃlʊs] *m* information.

aufschlüsseln ['aʊfʃlʏsəln] *vt*: ~ **(nach)** to break down (into); (*klassifizieren*) to classify (according to).

aufschlussreich▲ *adj* informative, illuminating.

aufschnappen ['aʊfʃnapən] *vt* (*umg*) to pick up ♦ *vi* to fly open.

aufschneiden ['aʊfʃnaɪdən] *unreg vt* to cut open; (*Brot*) to cut up; (*MED: Geschwür*) to lance ♦ *vi* (*umg*) to brag.

Aufschneider (*-s, -*) *m* boaster, braggart.

Aufschnitt ['aʊfʃnɪt] *m* (slices of) cold meat.

aufschnüren ['aʊfʃnyːrən] *vt* to unlace; (*Paket*) to untie.

aufschrauben ['aʊfʃraʊbən] *vt* (*fest~*) to screw on; (*lösen*) to unscrew.

aufschrecken ['aʊfʃrɛkən] *vt* to startle ♦ *vi* (*unreg*) to start up.

Aufschrei ['aʊfʃraɪ] *m* cry.

aufschreiben ['aʊfʃraɪbən] *unreg vt* to write down.

aufschreien *unreg vi* to cry out.

Aufschrift ['aʊfʃrɪft] *f* (*Inschrift*) inscription; (*Etikett*) label.

Aufschub ['aʊfʃuːp] (*-(e)s, -schübe*) *m* delay, postponement; **jdm** ~ **gewähren** to grant sb an extension.

aufschürfen ['aʊfʃʏrfən] *vt*: **sich** *dat* **die Haut/ das Knie** ~ to graze *od* scrape o.s./one's knee.

aufschütten ['aʊfʃʏtən] *vt* (*Flüssigkeit*) to pour on; (*Kohle*) to put on (the fire); (*Damm, Deich*) to throw up; **Kaffee** ~ to make coffee.

aufschwatzen ['aʊfʃvatsən] (*umg*) *vt*: **jdm etw** ~ to talk sb into (getting/having *etc*) sth.

Aufschwung ['aʊfʃvʊŋ] *m* (*Elan*) boost; (*wirtschaftlich*) upturn, boom; (*SPORT: an*

Gerät) mount.

aufsehen ['aʊfzeːən] *unreg vi* to look up; ~ **zu** (*lit*) to look up at; (*fig*) to look up to; **A~** (*-s*) *nt* sensation, stir; **A~ erregend** sensational.

Aufseher(in) (*-s, -*) *m(f)* guard; (*im Betrieb*) supervisor; (*Museums~*) attendant; (*Park~*) keeper.

auf sein▲ ['aʊfzaɪn] *siehe* **auf**.

aufseiten▲, auf Seiten▲ [aʊf'zaɪtn] *präp +gen*: ~ **von** on the part of.

aufsetzen ['aʊfzɛtsən] *vt* to put on; (*Flugzeug*) to put down; (*Dokument*) to draw up ♦ *vr* to sit upright ♦ *vi* (*Flugzeug*) to touch down.

Aufsicht ['aʊfzɪçt] *f* supervision; **die** ~ **haben** to be in charge; **bei einer Prüfung** ~ **führen** to invigilate (*BRIT*) *od* supervise an exam.

Aufsichtsrat *m* board (of directors).

aufsitzen ['aʊfzɪtsən] *unreg vi* (*aufgerichtet sitzen*) to sit up; (*aufs Pferd, Motorrad*) to mount, get on; (*Schiff*) to run aground; **jdn** ~ **lassen** (*umg*) to stand sb up; **jdm** ~ (*umg*) to be taken in by sb.

aufspalten ['aʊfʃpaltən] *vt* to split.

aufspannen ['aʊfʃpanən] *vt* (*Netz, Sprungtuch*) to stretch *od* spread out; (*Schirm*) to put up, open.

aufsparen ['aʊfʃpaːrən] *vt* to save (up).

aufsperren ['aʊfʃpɛrən] *vt* to unlock; (*Mund*) to open wide; **die Ohren** ~ (*umg*) to prick up one's ears.

aufspielen ['aʊfʃpiːlən] *vr* to show off; **sich als etw** ~ to try to come on as sth.

aufspießen ['aʊfʃpiːsən] *vt* to spear.

aufspringen ['aʊfʃprɪŋən] *unreg vi* (*hochspringen*) to jump up; (*sich öffnen*) to spring open; (*Hände, Lippen*) to become chapped; ~ **auf** *+akk* to jump onto.

aufspüren ['aʊfʃpyːrən] *vt* to track down, trace.

aufstacheln ['aʊfʃtaxəln] *vt* to incite.

aufstampfen ['aʊfʃtampfən] *vi*: **mit dem Fuß** ~ to stamp one's foot.

Aufstand ['aʊfʃtant] *m* insurrection, rebellion.

aufständisch ['aʊfʃtɛndɪʃ] *adj* rebellious, mutinous.

aufstauen ['aʊfʃtaʊən] *vr* to collect; (*fig: Ärger*) to be bottled up.

aufstechen ['aʊfʃtɛçən] *unreg vt* to prick open, puncture.

aufstecken ['aʊfʃtɛkən] *vt* to stick on; (*mit Nadeln*) to pin up; (*umg*) to give up.

aufstehen ['aʊfʃteːən] *unreg vi* to get up; (*Tür*) to be open; **da musst du früher** *od* **eher** ~**!** (*fig: umg*) you'll have to do better than that!

aufsteigen ['aʊfʃtaɪɡən] *unreg vi* (*hochsteigen*) to climb; (*Rauch*) to rise; ~ **auf** *+akk* to get onto; **in jdm** ~ (*Hass, Verdacht, Erinnerung etc*) to well up in sb.

Aufsteiger (*-s, -*) *m* (*SPORT*) promoted team;

(sozialer) ~ social climber.
aufstellen ['aʊfʃtɛlən] vt *(aufrecht stellen)* to put up; *(Maschine)* to install; *(aufreihen)* to line up; *(Kandidaten)* to nominate; *(Forderung, Behauptung)* to put forward; *(formulieren: Programm etc)* to draw up; *(leisten: Rekord)* to set up.
Aufstellung f *(SPORT)* line-up; *(Liste)* list.
Aufstieg ['aʊfʃtiːk] (-(e)s, -e) m *(auf Berg)* ascent; *(Fortschritt)* rise; *(beruflich, SPORT)* promotion.
Aufstiegschance f prospect of promotion.
aufstöbern ['aʊfʃtøːbərn] vt *(Wild)* to start, flush; *(umg: entdecken)* to run to earth.
aufstocken ['aʊfʃtɔkən] vt *(Vorräte)* to build up.
aufstoßen ['aʊfʃtoːsən] unreg vt to push open ♦ vi to belch.
aufstrebend ['aʊfʃtreːbənd] adj ambitious; *(Land)* striving for progress.
Aufstrich ['aʊfʃtrɪç] m spread.
aufstülpen ['aʊfʃtʏlpən] vt *(Ärmel)* to turn up; *(Hut)* to put on.
aufstützen ['aʊfʃtʏtsən] vt *(Körperteil)* to prop, lean; *(Person)* to prop up ♦ vr: **sich** ~ **auf** +akk to lean on.
aufsuchen ['aʊfzuːxən] vt *(besuchen)* to visit; *(konsultieren)* to consult.
auftakeln ['aʊftaːkəln] vt *(NAUT)* to rig (out) ♦ vr *(pej: umg)* to deck o.s. out.
Auftakt ['aʊftakt] m *(MUS)* upbeat; *(fig)* prelude.
auftanken ['aʊftaŋkən] vi to get petrol *(BRIT)* od gas *(US)* ♦ vt to refuel.
auftauchen ['aʊftaʊxən] vi to appear; *(gefunden werden, kommen)* to turn up; *(aus Wasser etc)* to emerge; *(U-Boot)* to surface; *(Zweifel)* to arise.
auftauen ['aʊftaʊən] vt to thaw ♦ vi to thaw; *(fig)* to relax.
aufteilen ['aʊftaɪlən] vt to divide up; *(Raum)* to partition.
Aufteilung f division; partition.
auftischen ['aʊftɪʃən] vt to serve (up); *(fig)* to tell.
Auftr. abk = **Auftrag**.
Auftrag ['aʊftraːk] (-(e)s, -träge) m order; *(Anweisung)* commission; *(Aufgabe)* mission; **etw in** ~ **geben (bei)** to order/commission sth (from); **im** ~ **von** on behalf of; **im** ~ od **i. A. J. Burnett** pp J. Burnett.
auftragen ['aʊftraːgən] unreg vt *(Essen)* to serve; *(Farbe)* to put on; *(Kleidung)* to wear out ♦ vi *(dick machen)*: **die Jacke trägt auf** the jacket makes one look fat; **jdm etw** ~ to tell sb sth; **dick** ~ *(umg)* to exaggerate.
Auftraggeber(in) (-s, -) m(f) client; *(COMM)* customer.
Auftragsbestätigung f confirmation of order.

auftreiben ['aʊftraɪbən] unreg *(umg)* vt *(beschaffen)* to raise.
auftrennen ['aʊftrɛnən] vt to undo.
auftreten ['aʊftreːtən] unreg vt to kick open ♦ vi to appear; *(mit Füßen)* to tread; *(sich verhalten)* to behave; *(fig: eintreten)* to occur; *(Schwierigkeiten etc)* to arise; **als Vermittler** etc ~ to act as intermediary etc; **geschlossen** ~ to put up a united front.
Auftreten (-s) nt *(Vorkommen)* appearance; *(Benehmen)* behaviour *(BRIT)*, behavior *(US)*.
Auftrieb ['aʊftriːp] m *(PHYS)* buoyancy, lift; *(fig)* impetus.
Auftritt ['aʊftrɪt] m *(des Schauspielers)* entrance; *(lit, fig: Szene)* scene.
auftrumpfen ['aʊftrʊmpfən] vi to show how good one is; *(mit Bemerkung)* to crow.
auftun ['aʊftuːn] unreg vt to open ♦ vr to open up.
auftürmen ['aʊftʏrmən] vr *(Gebirge etc)* to tower up; *(Schwierigkeiten)* to pile od mount up.
aufwachen ['aʊfvaxən] vi to wake up.
aufwachsen ['aʊfvaksən] unreg vi to grow up.
Aufwand ['aʊfvant] (-(e)s) m expenditure; *(Kosten)* expense; *(Luxus)* show; **bitte, keinen** ~! please don't go out of your way.
aufwändig ▲ ['aʊfvɛndɪç] adj, adv costly.
Aufwandsentschädigung f expense allowance.
aufwärmen ['aʊfvɛrmən] vt to warm up; *(alte Geschichten)* to rake up.
aufwarten ['aʊfvartən] vi *(zu bieten haben)*: **mit etw** ~ to offer sth.
aufwärts ['aʊfvɛrts] adv upwards; ~ **gehen** to look up; **A~entwicklung** f upward trend.
aufwecken ['aʊfvɛkən] vt to wake(n) up.
aufweichen ['aʊfvaɪçən] vt to soften; *(Brot)* to soak.
aufweisen ['aʊfvaɪzən] unreg vt to show.
aufwenden ['aʊfvɛndən] unreg vt to expend; *(Geld)* to spend; *(Sorgfalt)* to devote.
aufwendig adj = **aufwändig**.
aufwerfen ['aʊfvɛrfən] unreg vt *(Fenster etc)* to throw open; *(Probleme)* to throw up, raise ♦ vr: **sich zu etw** ~ to make o.s. out to be sth.
aufwerten ['aʊfvɛrtən] vt *(FIN)* to revalue; *(fig)* to raise in value.
Aufwertung f revaluation.
aufwickeln ['aʊfvɪkəln] vt *(aufrollen)* to roll up; *(umg: Haar)* to put in curlers; *(lösen)* to untie.
aufwiegeln ['aʊfviːgəln] vt to stir up, incite.
aufwiegen ['aʊfviːgən] unreg vt to make up for.
Aufwind ['aʊfvɪnt] m up-current; **neuen** ~ **bekommen** *(fig)* to get new impetus.
aufwirbeln ['aʊfvɪrbəln] vt to whirl up; **Staub** ~ *(fig)* to create a stir.
aufwischen ['aʊfvɪʃən] vt to wipe up.
aufwühlen ['aʊfvyːlən] vt *(lit: Erde, Meer)* to

churn (up); (*Gefühle*) to stir.
aufzählen ['aʊftsɛːlən] *vt* to count out.
aufzeichnen ['aʊftsaɪçnən] *vt* to sketch;
(*schriftlich*) to jot down; (*auf Band*) to record.
Aufzeichnung *f* (*schriftlich*) note; (*Tonband~*, *Film~*) recording.
aufzeigen ['aʊftsaɪgən] *vt* to show, demonstrate.
aufziehen ['aʊftsiːən] *unreg vt* (*hochziehen*) to raise, draw up; (*öffnen*) to pull open;
(: *Reißverschluss*) to undo; (*Gardinen*) to draw (back); (*Uhr*) to wind; (*großziehen*: *Kinder*) to raise, bring up; (*Tiere*) to rear; (*umg*: *necken*) to tease; (: *veranstalten*) to set up;
(: *Fest*) to arrange ♦ *vi* (*Gewitter, Wolken*) to gather.
Aufzucht ['aʊftsʊxt] *f* (*das Großziehen*) rearing, raising.
Aufzug ['aʊftsuːk] *m* (*Fahrstuhl*) lift (*BRIT*), elevator (*US*); (*Aufmarsch*) procession, parade; (*Kleidung*) get-up; (*THEAT*) act.
aufzwingen ['aʊftsvɪŋən] *unreg vt*: **jdm etw ~** to force sth upon sb.
Aug. *abk* (= *August*) Aug.
Augapfel ['aʊkˌapfəl] *m* eyeball; (*fig*) apple of one's eye.
Auge ['aʊgə] (**-s, -n**) *nt* eye; (*Fett~*) globule of fat; **unter vier ~n** in private; **vor aller ~n** in front of everybody, for all to see; **jdn/etw mit anderen ~n (an)sehen** to see sb/sth in a different light; **ich habe kein ~ zugetan** I didn't sleep a wink; **ein ~/beide ~n zudrücken** (*umg*) to turn a blind eye; **jdn/ etw aus den ~n verlieren** to lose sight of sb/ sth; (*fig*) to lose touch with sb/sth; **etw ins ~ fassen** to contemplate sth; **das kann leicht ins ~ gehen** (*fig: umg*) it might easily go wrong.
Augenarzt *m* eye specialist, ophthalmologist.
Augenblick *m* moment; **im ~** at the moment; **im ersten ~** for a moment; **a~lich** *adj* (*sofort*) instantaneous; (*gegenwärtig*) present.
Augen- *zW*: **~braue** *f* eyebrow; **~höhe** *f*: **in ~höhe** at eye level; **~merk** *nt*
(*Aufmerksamkeit*) attention; **~schein** *m*: **jdn/ etw in ~schein nehmen** to have a close look at sb/sth; **a~scheinlich** *adj* obvious; **~weide** *f* sight for sore eyes; **~wischerei** *f* (*fig*) eye-wash; **~zeuge** *m* eye witness; **~zeugin** *f* eye witness.
August [aʊˈgʊst] (**-(e)s** *od* **-, -e**) (*pl selten*) *m* August; *siehe auch* **September**.
Auktion [aʊktsiˈoːn] *f* auction.
Auktionator [aʊktsioˈnaːtɔr] *m* auction-eer.
Aula ['aʊla] (**-, Aulen** *od* **-s**) *f* assembly hall.
Aus [aʊs] (**-**) *nt* (*SPORT*) outfield; **ins ~ gehen** to go out.

aus [aʊs] *präp* +*dat* **1** (*räumlich*) out of; (*von ... her*) from; **er ist ~ Berlin** he's from Berlin;
~ dem Fenster out of the window.
2 (*gemacht/hergestellt ~*) made of; **ein Herz ~ Stein** a heart of stone.
3 (*auf Ursache deutend*) out of; **~ Mitleid** out of sympathy; **~ Erfahrung** from experience;
~ Spaß for fun.
4: **~ ihr wird nie etwas** she'll never get anywhere.
♦ *adv* **1** (*zu Ende*) finished, over; **~ sein** to be over; **es ist ~ mit ihm** he is finished, he has had it; **~ und vorbei** over and done with.
2 (*ausgeschaltet, ausgezogen*) off; **~ sein** to be out; **Licht ~!** lights out!
3 (*in Verbindung mit von*): **von Rom ~** from Rome; **von Fenster ~** out of the window;
von sich ~ (*selbständig*) of one's own accord; **von mir ~** as far as I'm concerned.
4 ~ und ein gehen to come and go; (*bei jdm*) to visit frequently; **weder ~ noch ein wissen** to be at one's wits' end; **auf etw** *akk* **~ sein** to be after sth.

ausarbeiten ['aʊsˌarbaɪtən] *vt* to work out.
ausarten ['aʊsˌartən] *vi* to degenerate; (*Kind*) to become overexcited.
ausatmen ['aʊsˌaːtmən] *vi* to breathe out.
ausbaden ['aʊsbaːdən] (*umg*) *vt*: **etw ~ müssen** to carry the can for sth.
Ausbau ['aʊsbaʊ] *m* extension, expansion; removal.
ausbauen *vt* to extend, expand;
(*herausnehmen*) to take out, remove.
ausbaufähig *adj* (*fig*) worth developing.
ausbedingen ['aʊsbədɪŋən] *unreg vt*: **sich** *dat* **etw ~** to insist on sth.
ausbeißen ['aʊsbaɪsən] *unreg vr*: **sich** *dat* **an etw** *dat* **die Zähne ~** (*fig*) to have a tough time of it with sth.
ausbessern ['aʊsbɛsərn] *vt* to mend, repair.
Ausbesserungsarbeiten *pl* repair work *sing*.
ausbeulen ['aʊsbɔylən] *vt* to beat out.
Ausbeute ['aʊsbɔytə] *f* yield; (*Gewinn*) profit, gain; (*Fische*) catch.
ausbeuten *vt* to exploit; (*MIN*) to work.
ausbezahlen ['aʊsbətsaːlən] *vt* (*Geld*) to pay out.
ausbilden ['aʊsbɪldən] *vt* to educate; (*Lehrling, Soldat*) to instruct, train; (*Fähigkeiten*) to develop; (*Geschmack*) to cultivate.
Ausbilder(in) (**-s, -**) *m(f)* instructor, instructress.
Ausbildung *f* education; training, instruction; development; cultivation; **er ist noch in der ~** he's still a trainee; he hasn't finished his education.
Ausbildungs- *zW*: **~förderung** *f* (provision of)

grants for students and trainees;
(*Stipendium*) grant; ~**platz** *m* (*Stelle*) training
vacancy.

ausbitten ['aʊsbɪtən] *unreg vt*: **sich** *dat* **etw** ~
(*geh*: *erbitten*) to ask for sth; (*verlangen*) to
insist on sth.

ausblasen ['aʊsblaːzən] *unreg vt* to blow out;
(*Ei*) to blow.

ausbleiben ['aʊsblaɪbən] *unreg vi* (*Personen*) to
stay away, not come; (*Ereignisse*) to fail to
happen, not happen; **es konnte nicht** ~, **dass**
... it was inevitable that ...

ausblenden ['aʊsblɛndən] *vt, vi* (*TV etc*) to fade
out.

Ausblick ['aʊsblɪk] *m* (*lit, fig*) prospect,
outlook, view.

ausbomben ['aʊsbɔmbən] *vt* to bomb out.

ausbooten ['aʊsboːtən] (*umg*) *vt* (*jdn*) to kick
od boot out.

ausbrechen ['aʊsbrɛçən] *unreg vi* to break out
♦ *vt* to break off; **in Tränen/Gelächter** ~ to
burst into tears/out laughing.

Ausbrecher(in) (-**s**, -) (*umg*) *m(f)* (*Gefangener*)
escaped prisoner, escapee.

ausbreiten ['aʊsbraɪtən] *vt* to spread (out);
(*Arme*) to stretch out ♦ *vr* to spread; **sich**
über ein Thema ~ to expand *od* enlarge on a
topic.

ausbrennen ['aʊsbrɛnən] *unreg vt* to scorch;
(*Wunde*) to cauterize ♦ *vi* to burn out.

ausbringen ['aʊsbrɪŋən] *unreg vt* (*ein Hoch*) to
propose.

Ausbruch ['aʊsbrʊx] *m* outbreak; (*von Vulkan*)
eruption; (*Gefühls~*) outburst; (*von*
Gefangenen) escape.

ausbrüten ['aʊsbryːtən] *vt* (*lit, fig*) to hatch.

Ausbuchtung ['aʊsbʊxtʊŋ] *f* bulge; (*Küste*)
cove.

ausbügeln ['aʊsbyːgəln] *vt* to iron out; (*umg*:
Fehler, Verlust) to make good.

ausbuhen ['aʊsbuːən] *vt* to boo.

Ausbund ['aʊsbʊnt] *m*: **ein** ~ **an** *od* **von**
Tugend/Sparsamkeit a paragon of virtue/a
model of thrift.

ausbürgern ['aʊsbyrgərn] *vt* to expatriate.

ausbürsten ['aʊsbyrstən] *vt* to brush out.

Ausdauer ['aʊsdaʊər] *f* stamina;
(*Beharrlichkeit*) perseverance.

ausdauernd *adj* persevering.

ausdehnen ['aʊsdeːnən] *vt, vr* (*räumlich*) to
expand; (*zeitlich, auch Gummi*) to stretch;
(*Nebel, fig*: *Macht*) to extend.

ausdenken ['aʊsdɛŋkən] *unreg vt* (*zu Ende*
denken) to think through; **sich** *dat* **etw** ~ to
think sth up; **das ist nicht auszudenken**
(*unvorstellbar*) it's inconceivable.

ausdiskutieren ['aʊsdɪskutiːrən] *vt* to talk out.

ausdrehen ['aʊsdreːən] *vt* to turn *od* switch
off.

Ausdruck ['aʊsdrʊk] (-**s**, -**drücke**) *m*

expression, phrase; (*Kundgabe, Gesichts~*)
expression; (*Fach~*) term; (*COMPUT*) hard
copy; **mit dem** ~ **des Bedauerns** (*form*)
expressing regret.

ausdrucken *vt* (*Text*) to print out.

ausdrücken ['aʊsdrʏkən] *vt* (*auch vr*:
formulieren, zeigen) to express; (*Zigarette*) to
put out; (*Zitrone*) to squeeze.

ausdrücklich *adj* express, explicit.

Ausdrucks- *zW*: ~**fähigkeit** *f* expressiveness;
(*Gewandtheit*) articulateness; **a~los** *adj*
expressionless, blank; **a~voll** *adj*
expressive; ~**weise** *f* mode of expression.

Ausdünstung ['aʊsdʏnstʊŋ] *f* (*Dampf*) vapour
(*BRIT*), vapor (*US*); (*Geruch*) smell.

auseinander [aʊs|aɪ'nandər] *adv* (*getrennt*)
apart; **weit** ~ far apart; ~ **bringen** to
separate; ~ **fallen** to fall apart; ~ **gehen**
(*Menschen*) to separate; (*Meinungen*) to
differ; (*Gegenstand*) to fall apart; (*umg: dick*
werden) to put on weight; ~ **halten** to tell
apart; ~ **klaffen** to gape open; (*fig*:
Meinungen) to be far apart, diverge (wildly);
~ **laufen** (*umg: sich trennen*) to break up;
(*Menge*) to disperse; **sich** ~ **leben** to drift
apart; ~ **nehmen** to take to pieces,
dismantle; ~ **schreiben** to write as separate
words; ~ **setzen** (*erklären*) to set forth,
explain; **sich** ~ **setzen** (*sich verständigen*) to
come to terms, settle; (*sich befassen*) to
concern o.s.; **sich mit jdm** ~ **setzen** to talk
with sb; (*sich streiten*) to argue with sb;
A~setzung *f* argument.

auserkoren ['aʊs|ɛrkoːrən] *adj* (*liter*) chosen,
selected.

auserlesen ['aʊs|ɛrleːzən] *adj* select, choice.

ausersehen ['aʊs|ɛrzeːən] *unreg vt* (*geh*): **dazu**
~ **sein, etw zu tun** to be chosen to do sth.

ausfahrbar *adj* extendable; (*Antenne*,
Fahrgestell) retractable.

ausfahren ['aʊsfaːrən] *unreg vi* to drive out;
(*NAUT*) to put out (to sea) ♦ *vt* to take out;
(*AUT*) to drive flat out; (*ausliefern: Waren*) to
deliver; **ausgefahrene Wege** rutted roads.

Ausfahrt *f* (*des Zuges etc*) leaving, departure;
(*Autobahn~, Garagen~*) exit, way out;
(*Spazierfahrt*) drive, excursion.

Ausfall ['aʊsfal] *m* loss; (*Nichtstattfinden*)
cancellation; (*das Versagen: TECH, MED*)
failure; (*von Motor*) breakdown;
(*Produktionsstörung*) stoppage; (*MIL*) sortie;
(*Fechten*) lunge; (*radioaktiv*) fallout.

ausfallen ['aʊsfalən] *unreg vi* (*Zähne, Haare*) to
fall *od* come out; (*nicht stattfinden*) to be
cancelled; (*wegbleiben*) to be omitted;
(*Person*) to drop out; (*Lohn*) to be stopped;
(*nicht funktionieren*) to break down; (*Resultat*
haben) to turn out; **wie ist das Spiel**
ausgefallen? what was the result of the
game?; **die Schule fällt morgen aus** there's

no school tomorrow.

ausfallend *adj* impertinent.

Ausfallstraße *f* arterial road.

Ausfallzeit *f* (*Maschine*) downtime.

ausfegen ['aʊsfeːgən] *vt* to sweep out.

ausfeilen ['aʊsfaɪlən] *vt* to file out; (*Stil*) to polish up.

ausfertigen ['aʊsfɛrtɪgən] *vt* (*form*) to draw up; (*Rechnung*) to make out; **doppelt** ~ to duplicate.

Ausfertigung *f* (*form*) drawing up; making out; (*Exemplar*) copy; **in doppelter/dreifacher** ~ in duplicate/triplicate.

ausfindig ['aʊsfɪndɪç] *adj*: ~ **machen** to discover.

ausfliegen ['aʊsfliːgən] *unreg vi* to fly away ♦ *vt* to fly out; **sie sind ausgeflogen** (*umg*) they're out.

ausfließen ['aʊsfliːsən] *unreg vi*: ~ **(aus)** (*herausfließen*) to flow out (of); (*auslaufen*: *Öl etc*) to leak (out of); (*Eiter etc*) to be discharged (from).

ausflippen ['aʊsflɪpən] (*umg*) *vi* to freak out.

Ausflucht ['aʊsflʊxt] (-, -flüchte) *f* excuse.

Ausflug ['aʊsfluːk] *m* excursion, outing.

Ausflügler(in) ['aʊsflyːklər(ɪn)] (-s, -) *m(f)* tripper (*BRIT*), excursionist (*US*).

Ausfluss▲ ['aʊsflʊs] *m* outlet; (*MED*) discharge.

ausfragen ['aʊsfraːgən] *vt* to interrogate, question.

ausfransen ['aʊsfranzən] *vi* to fray.

ausfressen ['aʊsfrɛsən] *unreg* (*umg*) *vt* (*anstellen*) to be up to.

Ausfuhr ['aʊsfuːr] (-, -en) *f* export, exportation; (*Ware*) export ♦ *in zW* export.

ausführbar ['aʊsfyːrbaːr] *adj* feasible; (*COMM*) exportable.

ausführen ['aʊsfyːrən] *vt* (*verwirklichen*) to carry out; (*Person*) to take out; (*Hund*) to take for a walk; (*COMM*) to export; (*erklären*) to give details of; **die ~de Gewalt** (*POL*) the executive.

Ausfuhrgenehmigung *f* export licence.

ausführlich *adj* detailed ♦ *adv* in detail; **A~keit** *f* detail.

Ausführung *f* execution, performance; (*von Waren*) design; (*von Thema*) exposition; (*Durchführung*) completion; (*Herstellungsart*) version; (*Erklärung*) explanation.

Ausfuhrzoll *m* export duty.

ausfüllen ['aʊsfylən] *vt* to fill up; (*Fragebogen etc*) to fill in; (*Beruf*) to be fulfilling for; **jdn** **(ganz)** ~ (*Zeit in Anspruch nehmen*) to take (all) sb's time.

Ausg. *abk* (= *Ausgabe*) ed.

Ausgabe ['aʊsgaːbə] *f* (*Geld*) expenditure, outlay; (*Aushändigung*) giving out; (*Schalter*) counter; (*Ausführung*) version; (*Buch*) edition; (*Nummer*) issue.

Ausgang ['aʊsgaŋ] *m* way out, exit; (*Ende*) end; (~*punkt*) starting point; (*Ergebnis*) result; (*Ausgehtag*) free time, time off; **ein Unfall mit tödlichem** ~ a fatal accident; **kein** ~ no exit.

Ausgangs- *zW*: ~**basis** *f* starting point; ~**punkt** *m* starting point; ~**sperre** *f* curfew.

ausgeben ['aʊsgeːbən] *unreg vt* (*Geld*) to spend; (*austeilen*) to issue, distribute; (*COMPUT*) to output ♦ *vr*: **sich für etw/jdn** ~ to pass o.s. off as sth/sb; **ich gebe heute Abend einen aus** (*umg*) it's my treat this evening.

ausgebeult ['aʊsgəbɔʏlt] *adj* (*Kleidung*) baggy; (*Hut*) battered.

ausgebucht ['aʊsgəbuːxt] *adj* fully booked.

Ausgeburt ['aʊsgəbuːrt] *(pej) f* (*der Fantasie etc*) monstrous product *od* invention.

ausgedehnt ['aʊsgədeːnt] *adj* (*breit, groß, fig*: *weitreichend*) extensive; (*Spaziergang*) long; (*zeitlich*) lengthy.

ausgedient ['aʊsgədiːnt] *adj* (*Soldat*) discharged; (*verbraucht*) no longer in use; ~ **haben** to have come to the end of its useful life.

ausgefallen ['aʊsgəfalən] *adj* (*ungewöhnlich*) exceptional.

ausgefuchst ['aʊsgəfʊkst] (*umg*) *adj* clever; (: *listig*) crafty.

ausgegangen ['aʊsgəgaŋən] *pp von* **ausgehen**.

ausgeglichen ['aʊsgəglɪçən] *adj* (well-)balanced; **A~heit** *f* balance; (*von Mensch*) even-temperedness.

Ausgehanzug *m* good suit.

ausgehen ['aʊsgeːən] *unreg vi* (*auch Feuer, Ofen, Licht*) to go out; (*zu Ende gehen*) to come to an end; (*Benzin*) to run out; (*Haare, Zähne*) to fall *od* come out; (*Strom*) to go off; (*Resultat haben*) to turn out; (*spazieren gehen*) to go (out) for a walk; (*abgeschickt werden*: *Post*) to be sent off; **mir ging das Benzin aus** I ran out of petrol (*BRIT*) *od* gas (*US*); **auf etw** *akk* ~ to aim at sth; **von etw** ~ (*wegführen*) to lead away from sth; (*herrühren*) to come from sth; (*zugrunde legen*) to proceed from sth; **wir können davon** ~, **dass ...** we can proceed from the assumption that ..., we can take as our starting point that ...; **leer** ~ to get nothing; **schlecht** ~ to turn out badly.

ausgehungert ['aʊsgəhʊŋərt] *adj* starved; (*abgezehrt*: *Mensch etc*) emaciated.

Ausgehverbot *nt* curfew.

ausgeklügelt ['aʊsgəklyːgəlt] *adj* ingenious.

ausgekocht ['aʊsgəkɔxt] *(pej: umg) adj* (*durchtrieben*) cunning; (*fig*) out-and-out.

ausgelassen ['aʊsgəlasən] *adj* boisterous, high-spirited, exuberant; **A~heit** *f* boisterousness, high spirits *pl*, exuberance.

ausgelastet ['aʊsgəlastət] *adj* fully occupied.

ausgeleiert ['aʊsgəlaɪərt] *adj* worn; (*Gummiband*) stretched.

ausgelernt ['ausgəlɛrnt] *adj* trained, qualified.

ausgemacht ['ausgəmaxt] *adj* settled; (*umg*: *Dummkopf etc*) out-and-out, downright; **es gilt als ~, dass ...** it is settled that ...; **es war eine ~e Sache, dass ...** it was a foregone conclusion that ...

ausgemergelt ['ausgəmɛrgəlt] *adj* (*Gesicht*) emaciated, gaunt.

ausgenommen ['ausgənɔmən] *konj* except; **Anwesende sind ~** present company excepted.

ausgepowert ['ausgəpo:vərt] *adj*: **~ sein** (*umg*) to be tired, be exhausted.

ausgeprägt ['ausgəprɛːkt] *adj* prominent; (*Eigenschaft*) distinct.

ausgerechnet ['ausgərɛçnət] *adv* just, precisely; **~ du** you of all people; **~ heute** today of all days.

ausgeschlossen ['ausgəʃlɔsən] *pp von* **ausschließen** ♦ *adj* (*unmöglich*) impossible, out of the question; **es ist nicht ~, dass ...** it cannot be ruled out that ...

ausgeschnitten ['ausgəʃnɪtən] *adj* (*Kleid*) low-necked.

ausgesehen ['ausgəzeːən] *pp von* **aussehen**.

ausgesprochen ['ausgəʃprɔxən] *adj* (*Faulheit, Lüge etc*) out-and-out; (*unverkennbar*) marked ♦ *adv* decidedly.

ausgestorben ['ausgəʃtɔrbən] *adj* (*Tierart*) extinct; (*fig*) deserted.

ausgewogen ['ausgəvoːgən] *adj* balanced; (*Maß*) equal.

ausgezeichnet ['ausgətsaiçnət] *adj* excellent.

ausgiebig ['ausgiːbɪç] *adj* (*Gebrauch*) full, good; (*Essen*) generous, lavish; **~ schlafen** to have a good sleep.

ausgießen ['ausgiːsən] *unreg vt* (*aus einem Behälter*) to pour out; (*Behälter*) to empty; (*weggießen*) to pour away.

Ausgleich ['ausglaiç] (*-(e)s, -e*) *m* balance; (*von Fehler, Mangel*) compensation; (*SPORT*): **den ~ erzielen** to equalize; **zum ~ +gen** in order to offset sth; **das ist ein guter ~** (*entspannend*) that's very relaxing.

ausgleichen ['ausglaiçən] *unreg vt* to balance (out); (*Konflikte*) to reconcile; (*Höhe*) to even up ♦ *vi* (*SPORT*) to equalize; **~de Gerechtigkeit** poetic justice.

Ausgleichssport *m* keep-fit activity.

Ausgleichstor *nt* equalizer.

ausgraben ['ausgraːbən] *unreg vt* to dig up; (*Leichen*) to exhume; (*fig*) to unearth.

Ausgrabung *f* excavation.

ausgrenzen ['ausgrɛntsən] *vt* to shut out, separate.

Ausgrenzung *f* shut-out, separation.

Ausguck ['ausgʊk] *m* look-out.

Ausguss▲ ['ausgʊs] *m* (*Spüle*) sink; (*Abfluss*) outlet; (*Tülle*) spout.

aushaben ['aushaːbən] *unreg* (*umg*) *vt*
(*Kleidung*) to have taken off; (*Buch*) to have finished.

aushalten ['aushaltən] *unreg vt* to bear, stand; (*umg*: *Geliebte*) to keep ♦ *vi* to hold out; **das ist nicht zum A~** that is unbearable; **sich von jdm ~ lassen** to be kept by sb.

aushandeln ['aushandəln] *vt* to negotiate.

aushändigen ['aushɛndɪgən] *vt*: **jdm etw ~ to** hand sth over to sb.

Aushang ['aushaŋ] *m* notice.

aushängen ['aushɛŋən] *unreg vt* (*Meldung*) to put up; (*Fenster*) to take off its hinges ♦ *vi* to be displayed ♦ *vr* to hang out.

Aushängeschild *nt* (shop) sign; (*fig*): **als ~ für etw dienen** to promote sth.

ausharren ['ausharən] *vi* to hold out.

aushäusig ['aushɔyzɪç] *adj* gallivanting around, on the tiles.

ausheben ['aushɛːbən] *unreg vt* (*Erde*) to lift out; (*Grube*) to hollow out; (*Tür*) to take off its hinges; (*Diebesnest*) to clear out; (*MIL*) to enlist.

aushecken ['aushɛkən] (*umg*) *vt* to concoct, think up.

aushelfen ['aushɛlfən] *unreg vi*: **jdm ~** to help sb out.

Aushilfe ['aushilfə] *f* help, assistance; (*Person*) (temporary) worker.

Aushilfs- *zW*: **~kraft** *f* temporary worker; **~lehrer(in)** *m(f)* supply teacher; **a~weise** *adv* temporarily, as a stopgap.

aushöhlen ['aushøːlən] *vt* to hollow out; (*fig*: *untergraben*) to undermine.

ausholen ['aushoːlən] *vi* to swing one's arm back; (*zur Ohrfeige*) to raise one's hand; (*beim Gehen*) to take long strides; **zum Gegenschlag ~** (*lit, fig*) to prepare for a counter-attack.

aushorchen ['aushɔrçən] *vt* to sound out, pump.

aushungern ['aushʊŋərn] *vt* to starve out.

auskennen ['auskɛnən] *unreg vr* to know a lot; (*an einem Ort*) to know one's way about; (*in Fragen etc*) to be knowledgeable; **man kennt sich bei ihm nie aus** you never know where you are with him.

auskippen ['auskɪpən] *vt* to empty.

ausklammern ['ausklamərn] *vt* (*Thema*) to exclude, leave out.

Ausklang ['ausklaŋ] *m* (*geh*) end.

ausklappbar ['ausklapbaːr] *adj*: **dieser Tisch ist ~** this table can be opened out.

auskleiden ['ausklaidən] *vr* (*geh*) to undress ♦ *vt* (*Wand*) to line.

ausklingen ['ausklɪŋən] *unreg vi* to end; (*Ton, Lied*) to die away; (*Fest*) to come to an end.

ausklinken ['ausklɪŋkən] *vt* (*Bomben*) to release ♦ *vi* (*umg*) to flip one's lid.

ausklopfen ['ausklɔpfən] *vt* (*Teppich*) to beat; (*Pfeife*) to knock out.

auskochen ['aʊskɔxən] *vt* to boil; (*MED*) to sterilize.

auskommen ['aʊskɔmən] *unreg vi*: **mit jdm ~** to get on with sb; **mit etw ~** to get by with sth; **A~ (-s)** *nt*: **sein A~ haben** to get by; **mit ihr ist kein A~** she's impossible to get on with.

auskosten ['aʊskɔstən] *vt* to enjoy to the full.

auskramen ['aʊskraːmən] (*umg*) *vt* to dig out, unearth; (*fig*: *alte Geschichten etc*) to bring up.

auskratzen ['aʊskratsən] *vt* (*auch MED*) to scrape out.

auskugeln ['aʊskuːgəln] *vr*: **sich** *dat* **den Arm ~** to dislocate one's arm.

auskundschaften ['aʊskʊntʃaftən] *vt* to spy out; (*Gebiet*) to reconnoitre (*BRIT*), reconnoiter (*US*).

Auskunft ['aʊskʊnft] **(-, -künfte)** *f* information; (*nähere*) details *pl*, particulars *pl*; (*Stelle*) information office; (*TEL*) inquiries; **jdm ~ erteilen** to give sb information.

auskuppeln ['aʊskʊpəln] *vi* to disengage the clutch.

auskurieren ['aʊskuriːrən] (*umg*) *vt* to cure.

auslachen ['aʊslaxən] *vt* to laugh at, mock.

ausladen ['aʊslaːdən] *unreg vt* to unload; (*umg*: *Gäste*) to cancel an invitation to ♦ *vi* (*Äste*) to spread.

ausladend *adj* (*Gebärden, Bewegung*) sweeping.

Auslage ['aʊslaːgə] *f* shop window (display).

Auslagen *pl* outlay *sing*, expenditure *sing*.

Ausland ['aʊslant] *nt* foreign countries *pl*; **im ~** abroad; **ins ~** abroad.

Ausländer(in) ['aʊslɛndər(ɪn)] **(-s, -)** *m(f)* foreigner.

Ausländerfeindlichkeit *f* hostility to foreigners, xenophobia.

ausländisch *adj* foreign.

Auslands- *zW*: **~aufenthalt** *m* stay abroad; **~gespräch** *nt* international call; **~korrespondent(in)** *m(f)* foreign correspondent; **~reise** *f* trip abroad; **~schutzbrief** *m* international travel cover; **~vertretung** *f* agency abroad; (*von Firma*) foreign branch.

auslassen ['aʊslasən] *unreg vt* to leave out; (*Wort etc*) to omit; (*Fett*) to melt; (*Kleidungsstück*) to let out ♦ *vr*: **sich über etw** *akk* **~** to speak one's mind about sth; **seine Wut** *etc* **an jdm ~** to vent one's rage *etc* on sb.

Auslassung *f* omission.

Auslassungszeichen *nt* apostrophe.

auslasten ['aʊslastən] *vt* (*Fahrzeug*) to make full use of; (*Maschine*) to use to capacity; (*jdn*) to occupy fully.

Auslauf ['aʊslaʊf] *m* (*für Tiere*) run; (*Ausfluss*) outflow, outlet.

auslaufen *unreg vi* to run out; (*Behälter*) to leak; (*NAUT*) to put out (to sea); (*langsam aufhören*) to run down.

Ausläufer ['aʊslɔyfər] *m* (*von Gebirge*) spur; (*Pflanze*) runner; (*MET*: *von Hoch*) ridge; (: *von Tief*) trough.

ausleeren ['aʊsleːrən] *vt* to empty.

auslegen ['aʊsleːgən] *vt* (*Waren*) to lay out; (*Köder*) to put down; (*Geld*) to lend; (*bedecken*) to cover; (*Text etc*) to interpret.

Ausleger (-s, -) *m* (*von Kran etc*) jib, boom.

Auslegung *f* interpretation.

Ausleihe ['aʊslaɪə] **(-, -n)** *f* issuing; (*Stelle*) issue desk.

ausleihen ['aʊslaɪən] *unreg vt* (*verleihen*) to lend; **sich** *dat* **etw ~** to borrow sth.

auslernen ['aʊslɛrnən] *vi* (*Lehrling*) to finish one's apprenticeship; **man lernt nie aus** (*Sprichwort*) you live and learn.

Auslese ['aʊsleːzə] **(-, -n)** *f* selection; (*Elite*) elite; (*Wein*) choice wine.

auslesen ['aʊsleːzən] *unreg vt* to select; (*umg*: *zu Ende lesen*) to finish.

ausliefern ['aʊsliːfərn] *vt* to hand over; (*COMM*) to deliver ♦ *vr*: **sich jdm ~** to give o.s. up to sb; **(an** +*akk*) to deliver (up) (to), hand over (to); (*an anderen Staat*) to extradite (to); **jdm/etw ausgeliefert sein** to be at the mercy of sb/sth.

Auslieferungsabkommen *nt* extradition treaty.

ausliegen ['aʊsliːgən] *unreg vi* (*zur Ansicht*) to be displayed; (*Zeitschriften etc*) to be available (to the public); (*Liste*) to be up.

auslöschen ['aʊslœʃən] *vt* to extinguish; (*fig*) to wipe out, obliterate.

auslosen ['aʊsloːzən] *vt* to draw lots for.

auslösen ['aʊsløːzən] *vt* (*Explosion, Schuss*) to set off; (*hervorrufen*) to cause, produce; (*Gefangene*) to ransom; (*Pfand*) to redeem.

Auslöser (-s, -) *m* trigger; (*PHOT*) release; (*Anlass*) cause.

ausloten ['aʊsloːtən] *vt* (*NAUT*: *Tiefe*) to sound; (*fig geh*) to plumb.

ausmachen ['aʊsmaxən] *vt* (*Licht, Radio*) to turn off; (*Feuer*) to put out; (*entdecken*) to make out; (*vereinbaren*) to agree; (*beilegen*) to settle; (*Anteil darstellen, betragen*) to represent; (*bedeuten*) to matter; **das macht ihm nichts aus** it doesn't matter to him; **macht es Ihnen etwas aus, wenn ...?** would you mind if ...?

ausmalen ['aʊsmaːlən] *vt* to paint; (*fig*) to describe; **sich** *dat* **etw ~** to imagine sth.

Ausmaß ['aʊsmaːs] *nt* dimension; (*fig*) scale.

ausmerzen ['aʊsmɛrtsən] *vt* to eliminate.

ausmessen ['aʊsmɛsən] *unreg vt* to measure.

ausmisten ['aʊsmɪstən] *vt* (*Stall*) to muck out; (*fig*: *umg*: *Schrank etc*) to tidy out; (: *Zimmer*) to clean out.

ausmustern ['aʊsmʊstərn] *vt* (*Maschine, Fahrzeug etc*) to take out of service; (*MIL: entlassen*) to invalid out.

Ausnahme ['aʊsnaːmə] (*-, -n*) *f* exception; **eine ~ machen** to make an exception; **~erscheinung** *f* exception, one-off example; **~fall** *m* exceptional case; **~zustand** *m* state of emergency.

ausnahmslos *adv* without exception.

ausnahmsweise *adv* by way of exception, for once.

ausnehmen ['aʊsneːmən] *unreg vt* to take out, remove; (*Tier*) to gut; (*Nest*) to rob; (*umg: Geld abnehmen*) to clean out; (*ausschließen*) to make an exception of ♦ *vr* to look, appear.

ausnehmend *adj* exceptional.

ausnüchtern ['aʊsnʏçtərn] *vt, vi* to sober up.

Ausnüchterungszelle *f* drying-out cell.

ausnutzen ['aʊsnʊtsən] *vt* (*Zeit, Gelegenheit*) to use, turn to good account; (*Einfluss*) to use; (*Mensch, Gutmütigkeit*) to exploit.

auspacken ['aʊspakən] *vt* to unpack ♦ *vi* (*umg: alles sagen*) to talk.

auspfeifen ['aʊspfaɪfən] *unreg vt* to hiss/boo at.

ausplaudern ['aʊsplaʊdərn] *vt* (*Geheimnis*) to blab.

ausposaunen ['aʊspozaʊnən] (*umg*) *vt* to tell the world about.

ausprägen ['aʊsprɛːgən] *vr* (*Begabung, Charaktereigenschaft*) to reveal *od* show itself.

auspressen ['aʊspresən] *vt* (*Saft, Schwamm etc*) to squeeze out; (*Zitrone etc*) to squeeze.

ausprobieren ['aʊsprobiːrən] *vt* to try (out).

Auspuff ['aʊspʊf] (*-(e)s, -e*) *m* (*TECH*) exhaust; **~rohr** *nt* exhaust (pipe); **~topf** *m* (*AUT*) silencer (*BRIT*), muffler (*US*).

ausquartieren ['aʊskvartiːrən] *vt* to move out.

ausquetschen ['aʊskvɛtʃən] *vt* (*Zitrone etc*) to squeeze; (*umg: ausfragen*) to grill; (: *aus Neugier*) to pump.

ausradieren ['aʊsradiːrən] *vt* to erase, rub out.

ausrangieren ['aʊsrãʒiːrən] (*umg*) *vt* to chuck out; (*Maschine, Auto*) to scrap.

ausrauben ['aʊsraʊbən] *vt* to rob.

ausräumen ['aʊsrɔʏmən] *vt* (*Dinge*) to clear away; (*Schrank, Zimmer*) to empty; (*Bedenken*) to put aside.

ausrechnen ['aʊsrɛçnən] *vt* to calculate, reckon.

Ausrechnung *f* calculation, reckoning.

Ausrede ['aʊsreːdə] *f* excuse.

ausreden ['aʊsreːdən] *vi* to have one's say ♦ *vt*: **jdm etw ~** to talk sb out of sth; **er hat mich nicht mal ~ lassen** he didn't even let me finish (speaking).

ausreichen ['aʊsraɪçən] *vi* to suffice, be enough.

ausreichend *adj* sufficient, adequate; (*SCH*) adequate.

Ausreise ['aʊsraɪzə] *f* departure; **bei der ~** when leaving the country; **~erlaubnis** *f* exit visa.

ausreisen ['aʊsraɪzən] *vi* to leave the country.

ausreißen ['aʊsraɪsən] *unreg vt* to tear *od* pull out ♦ *vi* (*Riss bekommen*) to tear; (*umg*) to make off, scram; **er hat sich** *dat* **kein Bein ausgerissen** (*umg*) he didn't exactly overstrain himself.

ausrenken ['aʊsrɛŋkən] *vt* to dislocate.

ausrichten ['aʊsrɪçtən] *vt* (*Botschaft*) to deliver; (*Gruß*) to pass on; (*Hochzeit etc*) to arrange; (*in gerade Linie bringen*) to get in a straight line; (*angleichen*) to bring into line; (*TYP etc*) to justify; **etwas/nichts bei jdm ~** to get somewhere/nowhere with sb; **jdm etw ~** to take a message for sb; **ich werde es ihm ~** I'll tell him.

ausrotten ['aʊsrɔtən] *vt* to stamp out, exterminate.

ausrücken ['aʊsrʏkən] *vi* (*MIL*) to move off; (*Feuerwehr, Polizei*) to be called out; (*umg: weglaufen*) to run away.

Ausruf ['aʊsruːf] *m* (*Schrei*) cry, exclamation; (*Verkünden*) proclamation.

ausrufen *unreg vt* to cry out, exclaim; to call out; **jdn ~ (lassen)** (*über Lautsprecher etc*) to page sb.

Ausrufezeichen *nt* exclamation mark.

ausruhen ['aʊsruːən] *vt, vi, vr* to rest.

ausrüsten ['aʊsrʏstən] *vt* to equip, fit out.

Ausrüstung *f* equipment.

ausrutschen ['aʊsrʊtʃən] *vi* to slip.

Ausrutscher (*-s, -*) (*umg*) *m* (*lit, fig*) slip.

Aussage ['aʊszaːgə] (*-, -n*) *f* (*JUR*) statement; **der Angeklagte/Zeuge verweigerte die ~** the accused/witness refused to give evidence.

aussagekräftig *adj* expressive, full of expression.

aussagen ['aʊszaːgən] *vt* to say, state ♦ *vi* (*JUR*) to give evidence.

Aussatz ['aʊszats] (*-es*) *m* (*MED*) leprosy.

aussaugen ['aʊszaʊgən] *vt* (*Saft etc*) to suck out; (*Wunde*) to suck the poison out of; (*fig: ausbeuten*) to drain dry.

ausschalten ['aʊsʃaltən] *vt* to switch off; (*fig*) to eliminate.

Ausschank ['aʊsʃaŋk] (*-(e)s, -schänke*) *m* dispensing, giving out; (*COMM*) selling; (*Theke*) bar.

Ausschankerlaubnis *f* licence (*BRIT*), license (*US*).

Ausschau ['aʊsʃaʊ] *f*: **~ halten (nach)** to look out (for), watch (for).

ausschauen *vi*: **~ (nach)** to look out (for), be on the look-out (for).

ausscheiden ['aʊsʃaɪdən] *unreg vt* (*aussondern*) to take out; (*MED*) to excrete ♦ *vi* (*aus*) to leave; (*aus einem Amt*) to retire (from);

(*SPORT*) to be eliminated (from), be knocked out (of); **er scheidet für den Posten aus** he can't be considered for the job.

Ausscheidung *f* (*Aussondern*) removal; (*MED*) excretion; (*SPORT*) elimination.

ausschenken ['aʊsʃɛŋkən] *vt* to pour out; (*am Ausschank*) to serve.

ausscheren ['aʊsʃeːrən] *vi* (*Fahrzeug*) to leave the line *od* convoy; (*zum Überholen*) to pull out.

ausschildern ['aʊsʃɪldərn] *vt* to signpost.

ausschimpfen ['aʊsʃɪmpfən] *vt* to scold, tell off.

ausschlachten ['aʊsʃlaxtən] *vt* (*Auto*) to cannibalize; (*fig*) to make a meal of.

ausschlafen ['aʊsʃlaːfən] *unreg vi, vr* to sleep late ♦ *vt* to sleep off; **ich bin nicht ausgeschlafen** I didn't have *od* get enough sleep.

Ausschlag ['aʊsʃlaːk] *m* (*MED*) rash; (*Pendel~*) swing; (*von Nadel*) deflection; **den ~ geben** (*fig*) to tip the balance.

ausschlagen ['aʊsʃlaːgən] *unreg vt* to knock out; (*auskleiden*) to deck out; (*verweigern*) to decline ♦ *vi* (*Pferd*) to kick out; (*BOT*) to sprout; (*Zeiger*) to be deflected.

ausschlaggebend *adj* decisive.

ausschließen ['aʊsʃliːsən] *unreg vt* to shut *od* lock out; (*SPORT*) to disqualify; (*Fehler, Möglichkeit etc*) to rule out; (*fig*) to exclude; **ich will mich nicht ~** myself not excepted.

ausschließlich *adj* exclusive ♦ *adv* exclusively ♦ *präp +gen* excluding, exclusive of.

ausschlüpfen ['aʊsʃlʏpfən] *vi* to slip out; (*aus Ei, Puppe*) to hatch out.

Ausschluss▲ ['aʊsʃlʊs] *m* exclusion; **unter ~ der Öffentlichkeit stattfinden** to be closed to the public; (*JUR*) to be held in camera.

ausschmücken ['aʊsʃmʏkən] *vt* to decorate; (*fig*) to embellish.

ausschneiden ['aʊsʃnaɪdən] *unreg vt* to cut out; (*Büsche*) to trim.

Ausschnitt ['aʊsʃnɪt] *m* (*Teil*) section; (*von Kleid*) neckline; (*Zeitungs~*) cutting (*BRIT*), clipping (*US*); (*aus Film etc*) excerpt.

ausschöpfen ['aʊsʃœpfən] *vt* to ladle out; (*fig*) to exhaust; **Wasser** *etc* **aus etw ~** to ladle water *etc* out of sth.

ausschreiben ['aʊsʃraɪbən] *unreg vt* (*ganz schreiben*) to write out (in full); (*Scheck, Rechnung etc*) to write (out); (*Stelle, Wettbewerb etc*) to announce, advertise.

Ausschreibung *f* (*Bekanntmachung: von Wahlen*) calling; (: *von Stelle*) advertising.

Ausschreitung ['aʊsʃraɪtʊŋ] *f* excess.

Ausschuss▲ ['aʊsʃʊs] *m* committee, board; (*Abfall*) waste, scraps *pl*; (*COMM: auch:* **~ware**) reject.

ausschütten ['aʊsʃʏtən] *vt* to pour out; (*Eimer*)

to empty; (*Geld*) to pay ♦ *vr* to shake (with laughter).

Ausschüttung *f* (*FIN*) distribution.

ausschwärmen ['aʊsʃvɛrmən] *vi* (*Bienen, Menschen*) to swarm out; (*MIL*) to fan out.

ausschweifend ['aʊsʃvaɪfənt] *adj* (*Leben*) dissipated, debauched; (*Fantasie*) extravagant.

Ausschweifung *f* excess.

ausschweigen ['aʊsʃvaɪgən] *unreg vr* to keep silent.

ausschwitzen ['aʊsʃvɪtsən] *vt* to sweat out.

aussehen ['aʊszeːən] *unreg vi* to look; **gut ~** to look good/well; **wie siehts aus?** (*umg: wie stehts?*) how's things?; **das sieht nach nichts aus** that doesn't look anything special; **es sieht nach Regen aus** it looks like rain; **es sieht schlecht aus** things look bad; **A~ (-s)** *nt* appearance.

aus sein▲ ['aʊssaɪn] *siehe* **aus**.

außen ['aʊsən] *adv* outside; (*nach ~*) outwards; **~ ist es rot** it's red (on the) outside.

Außen- *zW:* **~antenne** *f* outside aerial; **~arbeiten** *pl* work *sing* on the exterior; **~aufnahme** *f* outdoor shot; **~bezirk** *m* outlying district; **~bordmotor** *m* outboard motor.

aussenden ['aʊszɛndən] *unreg vt* to send out, emit.

Außen- *zW:* **~dienst** *m* outside *od* field service; (*von Diplomat*) foreign service; **~handel** *m* foreign trade; **~minister** *m* foreign minister; **~ministerium** *nt* foreign office; **~politik** *f* foreign policy; **~seite** *f* outside; **~seiter(in)** (**-s, -**) *m(f)* outsider; **~spiegel** *m* (*AUT*) outside mirror; **~stände** *pl* (*bes COMM*) outstanding debts *pl*, arrears *pl*; **~stehende(r)** *f(m)* outsider; **~stelle** *f* branch; **~welt** *f* outside world.

außer ['aʊsər] *präp +dat* (*räumlich*) out of; (*abgesehen von*) except ♦ *konj* (*ausgenommen*) except; **~ Gefahr sein** to be out of danger; **~ Zweifel** beyond any doubt; **~ Betrieb** out of order; **~ sich** *dat* **sein/ geraten** to be beside o.s.; **~ Dienst** retired; **~ Landes** abroad; **~ wenn** unless; **~ dass** except; **~amtlich** *adj* unofficial, private.

außerdem *konj* besides, in addition ♦ *adv* anyway.

außerdienstlich *adj* private.

äußere(r, s) ['ɔysərə(r,s)] *adj* outer, external; **Ä~(s)** *nt* exterior; (*fig: Aussehen*) outward appearance.

außer- *zW:* **~ehelich** *adj* extramarital; **~gewöhnlich** *adj* unusual; **~halb** *präp +gen* outside ♦ *adv* outside; **~irdisch** *adj* extraterrestrial; **A~kraftsetzung** *f* repeal.

äußerlich *adj* external; **rein ~ betrachtet** on the face of it; **Ä~keit** *f* (*fig*) triviality; (*Oberflächlichkeit*) superficiality; (*Formalität*) formality.

äußern *vt* to utter, express; (*zeigen*) to show ♦ *vr* to give one's opinion; (*sich zeigen*) to show itself.

außer- *zW*: **~ordentlich** *adj* extraordinary; **~planmäßig** *adj* unscheduled; **~sinnlich** *adj*: **~sinnliche Wahrnehmung** extrasensory perception.

äußerst ['ɔysərst] *adv* extremely, most.

außerstande, außer Stande▲ [ausər'ʃtandə] *adv* (*nicht in der Lage*) not in a position; (*nicht fähig*) unable.

Äußerste(s) *nt*: **bis zum ~n gehen** to go to extremes.

äußerste(r, s) *adj* utmost; (*räumlich*) farthest; (*Termin*) last possible; (*Preis*) highest; **mein ~s Angebot** my final offer.

äußerstenfalls *adv* if the worst comes to the worst.

Äußerung *f* (*Bemerkung*) remark, comment; (*Behauptung*) statement; (*Zeichen*) expression.

aussetzen ['auszɛtsən] *vt* (*Kind, Tier*) to abandon; (*Boote*) to lower; (*Belohnung*) to offer; (*Urteil, Verfahren*) to postpone ♦ *vi* (*aufhören*) to stop; (*Pause machen*) to have a break; **jdn/sich einer Sache** *dat* ~ to lay sb/ o.s. open to sth; **jdm/etw ausgesetzt sein** to be exposed to sb/sth; **was haben Sie daran auszusetzen?** what's your objection to it?; **an jdm/etw etwas ~** to find fault with sb/sth.

Aussicht ['auszɪçt] *f* view; (*in Zukunft*) prospect; **in ~ sein** to be in view; **etw in ~ haben** to have sth in view; **jdm etw in ~ stellen** to promise sb sth.

Aussichts- *zW*: **a~los** *adj* hopeless; **~punkt** *m* viewpoint; **a~reich** *adj* promising; **~turm** *m* observation tower.

Aussiedler(in) ['auszi:dlər(ɪn)] **(-s, -)** *m(f)* (*Auswanderer*) emigrant.

AUSSIEDLER

Aussiedler *are people of German origin from East and South-East Europe who have resettled in Germany. Many come from the former Soviet Union. They are given free German language tuition and receive financial help. The number of* **Aussiedler** *increased dramatically in the early 1990s.*

---

aussöhnen ['auszø:nən] *vt* to reconcile ♦ *vr* (*einander*) to become reconciled; **sich mit jdm/etw ~** to reconcile o.s. with sb/to sth.

Aussöhnung *f* reconciliation.

aussondern ['auszɔndərn] *vt* to separate off, select.

aussorgen ['auszɔrgən] *vi*: **ausgesorgt haben** to have no more money worries.

aussortieren ['auszɔrti:rən] *vt* to sort out.

ausspannen ['ausʃpanən] *vt* to spread *od* stretch out; (*Pferd*) to unharness; (*umg: Mädchen*): **jdm jdn ~** to steal sb from sb ♦ *vi* to relax.

aussparen ['ausʃpa:rən] *vt* to leave open.

aussperren ['ausʃpɛrən] *vt* to lock out.

Aussperrung *f* (*INDUSTRIE*) lock-out.

ausspielen ['ausʃpi:lən] *vt* (*Karte*) to lead; (*Geldprämie*) to offer as a prize ♦ *vi* (*KARTEN*) to lead; **ausgespielt haben** to be finished; **jdn gegen jdn ~** to play sb off against sb.

Ausspielung *f* (*im Lotto*) draw.

ausspionieren ['ausʃpioni:rən] *vt* (*Pläne etc*) to spy out; (*Person*) to spy on.

Aussprache ['ausʃpra:xə] *f* pronunciation; (*Unterredung*) (frank) discussion.

aussprechen ['ausʃprɛçən] *unreg vt* to pronounce; (*zu Ende sprechen*) to speak; (*äußern*) to say, express ♦ *vr* (*sich äußern*): **sich ~ (über +akk)** to speak (about); (*sich anvertrauen*) to unburden o.s. (about *od* on); (*diskutieren*) to discuss ♦ *vi* (*zu Ende sprechen*) to finish speaking; **der Regierung das Vertrauen ~** to pass a vote of confidence in the government.

Ausspruch ['ausʃprʊx] *m* remark; (*geflügeltes Wort*) saying.

ausspucken ['ausʃpʊkən] *vt* to spit out ♦ *vi* to spit.

ausspülen ['ausʃpy:lən] *vt* to wash out; (*Mund*) to rinse.

ausstaffieren ['ausʃtafi:rən] *vt* to equip, kit out; (*Zimmer*) to furnish.

Ausstand ['ausʃtant] *m* strike; **in den ~ treten** to go on strike; **seinen ~ geben** to hold a leaving party.

ausstatten ['ausʃtatən] *vt* (*Zimmer etc*) to furnish; **jdn mit etw ~** to equip sb *od* kit sb out with sth.

Ausstattung *f* (*Ausstatten*) provision; (*Kleidung*) outfit; (*Aussteuer*) dowry; (*Aufmachung*) make-up; (*Einrichtung*) furnishing.

ausstechen ['ausʃtɛçən] *unreg vt* (*Torf, Kekse*) to cut out; (*Augen*) to gouge out; (*übertreffen*) to outshine.

ausstehen ['ausʃte:ən] *unreg vt* to stand, endure ♦ *vi* (*noch nicht da sein*) to be outstanding.

aussteigen ['ausʃtaigən] *unreg vi* to get out, alight; **alles ~!** (*von Schaffner*) all change!; **aus der Gesellschaft ~** to drop out (of society).

Aussteiger(in) (*umg*) *m(f)* dropout.

ausstellen ['ausʃtɛlən] *vt* to exhibit, display; (*umg: ausschalten*) to switch off; (*Rechnung etc*) to make out; (*Pass, Zeugnis*) to issue.

Aussteller(in) *m(f)* (*auf Messe*) exhibitor; (*von Scheck*) drawer.

Ausstellung *f* exhibition; (*FIN*) drawing up; (*einer Rechnung*) making out; (*eines Passes etc*) issuing.

Ausstellungsdatum *nt* date of issue.

Ausstellungsstück *nt* (*in Ausstellung*) exhibit; (*in Schaufenster etc*) display item.

aussterben ['aʊsʃtɛrbən] *unreg vi* to die out; **A~** *nt* extinction.

Aussteuer ['aʊsʃtɔyər] *f* dowry.

aussteuern ['aʊsʃtɔyərn] *vt* (*Verstärker*) to adjust.

Ausstieg ['aʊsʃtiːk] (-(e)s, -e) *m* (*Ausgang*) exit; **~ aus der Atomenergie** abandonment of nuclear energy.

ausstopfen ['aʊsʃtɔpfən] *vt* to stuff.

ausstoßen ['aʊsʃtoːsən] *unreg vt* (*Luft, Rauch*) to give off, emit; (*aus Verein etc*) to expel, exclude; (*herstellen: Teile, Stückzahl*) to turn out, produce.

ausstrahlen ['aʊsʃtraːlən] *vt, vi* to radiate; (*RUNDF*) to broadcast.

Ausstrahlung *f* radiation; (*fig*) charisma.

ausstrecken ['aʊsʃtrɛkən] *vt, vr* to stretch out.

ausstreichen ['aʊsʃtraɪçən] *unreg vt* to cross out; (*glätten*) to smooth out.

ausstreuen ['aʊsʃtrɔyən] *vt* to scatter; (*fig: Gerücht*) to spread.

ausströmen ['aʊsʃtrøːmən] *vi* (*Gas*) to pour out, escape ♦ *vt* to give off; (*fig*) to radiate.

aussuchen ['aʊszuːxən] *vt* to select, pick out.

Austausch ['aʊstaʊʃ] *m* exchange; **a~bar** *adj* exchangeable.

austauschen *vt* to exchange, swop.

Austauschmotor *m* replacement engine; (*gebraucht*) factory-reconditioned engine.

Austauschstudent(in) *m(f)* exchange student.

austeilen ['aʊstaɪlən] *vt* to distribute, give out.

Auster ['aʊstər] (-, -n) *f* oyster.

austoben ['aʊstoːbən] *vr* (*Kind*) to run wild; (*Erwachsene*) to let off steam; (*sich müde machen*) to tire o.s. out.

austragen ['aʊstraːgən] *unreg vt* (*Post*) to deliver; (*Streit etc*) to decide; (*Wettkämpfe*) to hold; **ein Kind ~** (*nicht abtreiben*) to have a child.

Austräger ['aʊstrɛːgər] *m* delivery boy; (*Zeitungs~*) newspaper boy.

Austragungsort *m* (*SPORT*) venue.

Australien [aʊsˈtraːliən] (-s) *nt* Australia.

Australier(in) (-s, -) *m(f)* Australian.

australisch *adj* Australian.

austreiben ['aʊstraɪbən] *unreg vt* to drive out, expel; (*Teufel etc*) to exorcize; **jdm etw ~** to cure sb of sth; (*bes durch Schläge*) to knock sth out of sb.

austreten ['aʊstreːtən] *unreg vi* (*zur Toilette*) to be excused ♦ *vt* (*Feuer*) to tread out, trample; (*Schuhe*) to wear out; (*Treppe*) to

wear down; **aus etw ~** to leave sth.

austricksen ['aʊstrɪksən] (*umg*) *vt* (*SPORT, fig*) to trick.

austrinken ['aʊstrɪŋkən] *unreg vt* (*Glas*) to drain; (*Getränk*) to drink up ♦ *vi* to finish one's drink, drink up.

Austritt ['aʊstrɪt] *m* emission; (*aus Verein, Partei etc*) retirement, withdrawal.

austrocknen ['aʊstrɔknən] *vt, vi* to dry up.

austüfteln ['aʊstyftəln] (*umg*) *vt* to work out; (*ersinnen*) to think up.

ausüben ['aʊsʔyːbən] *vt* (*Beruf*) to practise (*BRIT*), practice (*US*), carry out; (*innehaben: Amt*) to hold; (*Funktion*) to perform; (*Einfluss*) to exert; **einen Reiz auf jdn ~** to hold an attraction for sb; **eine Wirkung auf jdn ~** to have an effect on sb.

Ausübung *f* practice, exercise; **in ~ seines Dienstes/seiner Pflicht** (*form*) in the execution of his duty.

ausufern ['aʊsʔuːfərn] *vi* (*fig*) to get out of hand; (*Konflikt etc*): **~ (zu)** to escalate (into).

Ausverkauf ['aʊsfɛrkaʊf] *m* sale; (*fig: Verrat*) sell-out.

ausverkaufen *vt* to sell out; (*Geschäft*) to sell up.

ausverkauft *adj* (*Karten, Artikel*) sold out; (*THEAT: Haus*) full.

auswachsen ['aʊsvaksən] *unreg vi*: **das ist (ja) zum A~** (*umg*) it's enough to drive you mad.

Auswahl ['aʊsvaːl] *f*: **eine ~ (an +dat)** a selection (of), a choice (of).

auswählen ['aʊsvɛːlən] *vt* to select, choose.

Auswahlmöglichkeit *f* choice.

Auswanderer ['aʊsvandərər] (-s, -) *m* emigrant.

Auswanderin ['aʊsvandərɪn] *f* emigrant.

auswandern *vi* to emigrate.

Auswanderung *f* emigration.

auswärtig ['aʊsvɛrtɪç] *adj* (*nicht am/vom Ort*) out-of-town; (*ausländisch*) foreign; **das A~e Amt** the Foreign Office (*BRIT*), the State Department (*US*).

auswärts ['aʊsverts] *adv* outside; (*nach außen*) outwards; **~ essen** to eat out; **A~spiel** *nt* away game.

auswaschen ['aʊsvaʃən] *unreg vt* to wash out; (*spülen*) to rinse (out).

auswechseln ['aʊsvɛksəln] *vt* to change, substitute.

Ausweg ['aʊsveːk] *m* way out; **der letzte ~** the last resort; **a~los** *adj* hopeless.

ausweichen ['aʊsvaɪçən] *unreg vi*: **jdm/etw ~** (*lit*) to move aside or make way for sb/sth; (*fig*) to sidestep sb/sth; **jdm/einer Begegnung ~** to avoid sb/a meeting.

ausweichend *adj* evasive.

Ausweichmanöver *nt* evasive action.

ausweinen ['aʊsvaɪnən] *vr* to have a (good) cry.

Ausweis ['aʊsvaɪs] (**-es, -e**) *m* identity card; passport; (*Mitglieds~, Bibliotheks~ etc*) card; **~, bitte** your papers, please.

ausweisen ['aʊsvaɪzən] *unreg vt* to expel, banish ♦ *vr* to prove one's identity.

Ausweis- *zW:* **~karte** *f* identity papers *pl*; **~kontrolle** *f* identity check; **~papiere** *pl* identity papers *pl*.

Ausweisung *f* expulsion.

ausweiten ['aʊsvaɪtən] *vt* to stretch.

auswendig ['aʊsvɛndɪç] *adv* by heart; **~ lernen** to learn by heart.

auswerfen ['aʊsvɛrfən] *unreg vt* (*Anker, Netz*) to cast.

auswerten ['aʊsvɛrtən] *vt* to evaluate.

Auswertung *f* evaluation, analysis; (*Nutzung*) utilization.

auswickeln ['aʊsvɪkəln] *vt* (*Paket, Bonbon etc*) to unwrap.

auswirken ['aʊsvɪrkən] *vr* to have an effect.

Auswirkung *f* effect.

auswischen ['aʊsvɪʃən] *vt* to wipe out; **jdm eins ~** (*umg*) to put one over on sb.

Auswuchs ['aʊsvuːks] *m* (out)growth; (*fig*) product; (*Missstand, Übersteigerung*) excess.

auswuchten ['aʊsvʊxtən] *vt* (*AUT*) to balance.

auszacken ['aʊstsakən] *vt* (*Stoff etc*) to pink.

auszahlen ['aʊstsaːlən] *vt* (*Lohn, Summe*) to pay out; (*Arbeiter*) to pay off; (*Miterben*) to buy out ♦ *vr* (*sich lohnen*) to pay.

auszählen ['aʊstsɛːlən] *vt* (*Stimmen*) to count; (*BOXEN*) to count out.

auszeichnen ['aʊstsaɪçnən] *vt* to honour (*BRIT*), honor (*US*); (*MIL*) to decorate; (*COMM*) to price ♦ *vr* to distinguish o.s.; **der Wagen zeichnet sich durch ... aus** one of the car's main features is ...

Auszeichnung *f* distinction; (*COMM*) pricing; (*Ehrung*) awarding of decoration; (*Ehre*) honour (*BRIT*), honor (*US*); (*Orden*) decoration; **mit ~** with distinction.

ausziehen ['aʊstsiːən] *unreg vt* (*Kleidung*) to take off; (*Haare, Zähne, Tisch etc*) to pull out ♦ *vr* to undress ♦ *vi* (*aufbrechen*) to leave; (*aus Wohnung*) to move out.

Auszubildende(r) ['aʊstsʊbɪldəndə(r)] *f(m)* trainee; (*als Handwerker*) apprentice.

Auszug ['aʊstsuːk] *m* (*aus Wohnung*) removal; (*aus Buch etc*) extract; (*Konto~*) statement; (*Ausmarsch*) departure.

autark [aʊ'tark] *adj* self-sufficient (*auch fig*); (*COMM*) autarkical.

Auto ['aʊto] (**-s, -s**) *nt* (motor-)car, automobile (*US*); **mit dem ~ fahren** to go by car; **~ fahren** to drive.

Autoatlas *m* road atlas.

Autobahn *f* motorway (*BRIT*), expressway (*US*).

Autobahndreieck *nt* motorway (*BRIT*) *od* expressway (*US*) junction.

Autobahnkreuz *nt* motorway (*BRIT*) *od* expressway (*US*) intersection.

Autobahnzubringer *m* motorway feeder *od* access road.

Autobiografie▲ [aʊtobiogra'fiː] *f* autobiography.

Auto- *zW:* **~bombe** *f* car bomb; **~bus** *m* bus; (*Reisebus*) coach (*BRIT*), bus (*US*); **~fähre** *f* car ferry; **~fahrer(in)** *m(f)* motorist, driver; **~fahrt** *f* drive; **~friedhof** (*umg*) *m* car dump.

autogen [aʊto'geːn] *adj* autogenous; **~es Training** (*PSYCH*) relaxation through self-hypnosis.

Autogramm [aʊto'gram] *nt* autograph.

Automat (**-en, -en**) *m* machine.

Automatik [aʊto'maːtɪk] *f* automatic mechanism (*auch fig*); (*Gesamtanlage*) automatic system; (*AUT*) automatic transmission.

automatisch *adj* automatic.

Automatisierung [aʊtomati'ziːrʊŋ] *f* automation.

Automobilausstellung [aʊtomo'biːlaʊsʃtɛlʊŋ] *f* motor show.

autonom [aʊto'noːm] *adj* autonomous.

Autopsie [aʊtɔ'psiː] *f* post-mortem, autopsy.

Autor ['aʊtɔr] (**-s, -en**) *m* author.

Auto- *zW:* **~radio** *nt* car radio; **~reifen** *m* car tyre (*BRIT*) *od* tire (*US*); **~reisezug** *m* motorail train; **~rennen** *nt* motor race; (*Sportart*) motor racing.

Autorin [aʊ'toːrɪn] *f* authoress.

autoritär [aʊtori'tɛːr] *adj* authoritarian.

Autorität *f* authority.

Auto- *zW:* **~schalter** *m* drive-in bank (counter); **~telefon** *nt* car phone; **~unfall** *m* car *od* motor accident; **~verleih** *m*, **~vermietung** *f* car hire (*BRIT*) *od* rental (*US*).

AvD (**-**) *m abk* (= *Automobilclub von Deutschland*) *German motoring organization,* ≈ AA (*BRIT*), AAA (*US*).

Axt [akst] (**-, ̈e**) *f* axe (*BRIT*), ax (*US*).

AZ, Az. *abk* (= *Aktenzeichen*) ref.

Azoren [a'tsoːrən] *pl* (*GEOG*) Azores *pl*.

Azteke [ats'teːkə] (**-n, -n**) *m* Aztec.

Azubi [a'tsu:bi] (-s, -s) (*umg*) *f(m)* *abk*
= **Auszubildende(r)**.

B, b

B¹, b [be:] *nt* (*letter*) B, b; ~ **wie Bertha** ≈ B
for Benjamin, B for Baker (*US*); **B-Dur/b-
Moll** (the key of) B flat major/minor.
B² [be:] *f abk* = **Bundesstraße**.
Baby ['be:bi] (-s, -s) *nt* baby; ~**ausstattung** *f*
layette; ~**klappe** *f anonymous drop-off point
for unwanted babies;* ~**raum** *m* (*Flughafen
etc*) nursing room; **b~sitten** *vi* to babysit;
~**sitter** ['be:bisɪtər] (-s, -) *m* baby-sitter;
~**speck** (*umg*) *m* puppy fat.
Bach [bax] (-(e)s, ⁻e) *m* stream, brook.
Backblech *nt* baking tray.
Backbord (-(e)s, -e) *nt* (*NAUT*) port.
Backe (-, -n) *f* cheek.
backen ['bakən] *unreg vt, vi* to bake; **frisch/
knusprig gebackenes Brot** fresh/crusty
bread.
Backenbart *m* sideboards *pl*.
Backenzahn *m* molar.
Bäcker(in) ['bɛkər(ɪn)] (-s, -) *m(f)* baker.
Bäckerei [bɛkə'raɪ] *f* bakery; (*Bäckerladen*)
baker's (shop).
Bäckerjunge *m* (*Lehrling*) baker's apprentice.
Back- *zW:* ~**fisch** *m* fried fish; (*veraltet*)
teenager; ~**form** *f* baking tin (*BRIT*) *od* pan
(*US*); ~**hähnchen** *nt* fried chicken in
breadcrumbs; ~**obst** *nt* dried fruit; ~**ofen** *m*
oven; ~**pflaume** *f* prune; ~**pulver** *nt* baking
powder; ~**stein** *m* brick.
bäckt [bɛkt] *vb siehe* **backen**.
Bad [ba:t] (-(e)s, ⁻er) *nt* bath; (*Schwimmen*)
bathing; (*Ort*) spa.
Bade- *zW:* ~**anstalt** *f* swimming pool; ~**anzug**
m bathing suit; ~**hose** *f* bathing *od*
swimming trunks *pl*; ~**kappe** *f* bathing cap;
~**mantel** *m* bath(ing) robe; ~**meister** *m*
swimming pool attendant.
baden ['ba:dən] *vi* to bathe, have a bath ♦ *vt* to
bath; ~ **gehen** (*fig: umg*) to come a cropper.
Baden-Württemberg ['ba:dən'vyrtəmbɛrk] *nt*
Baden-Württemberg.
Bade- *zW:* ~**ort** *m* spa; ~**sachen** *pl* swimming
things *pl*; ~**tuch** *nt* bath towel; ~**wanne** *f*
bath(tub); ~**zimmer** *nt* bathroom.
baff [baf] *adj:* ~ **sein** (*umg*) to be
flabbergasted.
BAföG, Bafög [ba:føk] *nt abk*
(= *Bundesausbildungsförderungsgesetz*).

BAG (-) *nt abk* (= *Bundesarbeitsgericht*) German
industrial tribunal.
Bagatelle [baga'tɛlə] (-, -n) *f* trifle.
Bagdad ['bakdat] (-s) *nt* Baghdad.
Bagger ['bagər] (-s, -) *m* excavator; (*NAUT*)
dredger.
baggern *vt, vi* to excavate; (*NAUT*) to dredge.
Baggersee *m* (flooded) gravel pit.
Bahamas [ba'ha:mas] *pl:* **die** ~ the Bahamas
pl.
Bahn [ba:n] (-, -en) *f* railway (*BRIT*), railroad
(*US*); (*Weg*) road, way; (*Spur*) lane; (*Renn~*)
track; (*ASTRON*) orbit; (*Stoff~*) length; **mit
der** ~ by train *od* rail/tram; **frei** ~ (*COMM*)
carriage free to station of destination;
jdm/etw die ~ **ebnen** (*fig*) to clear the way
for sb/sth; **von der rechten** ~ **abkommen** to
stray from the straight and narrow; **jdn aus
der** ~ **werfen** (*fig*) to shatter sb; ~**beamte(r)**
m railway (*BRIT*) *od* railroad (*US*) official;
b~brechend *adj* pioneering; ~**brecher(in)** (-s,
-) *m(f)* pioneer; ~**damm** *m* railway
embankment.
bahnen *vt:* **sich einen Weg** ~ to clear a way.
Bahnfahrt *f* railway (*BRIT*) *od* railroad (*US*)
journey.
Bahnhof *m* station; **auf dem** ~ at the station;
ich verstehe nur ~ (*hum: umg*) it's all Greek
to me.
Bahnhofshalle *f* station concourse.
Bahnhofsmission *f charitable organization
for helping rail travellers.*

Bahnhofswirtschaft *f* station restaurant.
Bahn- *zW:* **b~lagernd** *adj* (*COMM*) to be
collected from the station; ~**linie** *f* (railway
(*BRIT*) *od* railroad (*US*)) line; ~**schranke** *f*
level (*BRIT*) *od* grade (*US*) crossing barrier;
~**steig** *m* platform; ~**steigkarte** *f* platform
ticket; ~**strecke** *f* railway (*BRIT*) *od* railroad
(*US*) line; ~**übergang** *m* level (*BRIT*) *od* grade
(*US*) crossing; **beschrankter** ~**übergang**
crossing with gates; **unbeschrankter**

~**übergang** unguarded crossing; ~**wärter** *m* signalman.

Bahrain [ba'raɪn] (**-s**) *nt* Bahrain.

Bahre ['baːrə] (**-**, **-n**) *f* stretcher.

Baiser [bɛ'zeː] (**-s**, **-s**) *nt* meringue.

Baisse ['bɛːsə] (**-**, **-n**) *f* (*Börse*) fall; (*plötzlich*) slump.

Bajonett [bajo'nɛt] (**-(e)s**, **-e**) *nt* bayonet.

Bakelit ® [bake'liːt] (**-s**) *nt* Bakelite ®.

Bakterien [bak'teːriən] *pl* bacteria *pl*.

Balance [ba'lãːsə] (**-**, **-n**) *f* balance, equilibrium.

balancieren *vt, vi* to balance.

bald [balt] *adv* (*zeitlich*) soon; (*beinahe*) almost; ~ ... ~ ... now ... now ...; ~ **darauf** soon afterwards; **bis** ~! see you soon.

baldig ['baldɪç] *adj* early, speedy.

baldmöglichst *adv* as soon as possible.

Baldrian ['baldriaːn] (**-s**, **-e**) *m* valerian.

Balearen [bale'aːrən] *pl*: **die** ~ the Balearics *pl*.

Balg [balk] (**-(e)s**, **⁻er**) (*pej: umg*) *m od nt* (*Kind*) brat.

balgen ['balgən] *vr*: **sich** ~ (**um**) to scrap (over).

Balkan ['balkaːn] *m*: **der** ~ the Balkans *pl*.

Balken ['balkən] (**-s**, **-**) *m* beam; (*Trag~*) girder; (*Stütz~*) prop.

Balkon [bal'kõː] (**-s**, **-s** *od* **-e**) *m* balcony; (*THEAT*) (dress) circle.

Ball [bal] (**-(e)s**, **⁻e**) *m* ball; (*Tanz*) dance, ball.

Ballade [ba'laːdə] (**-**, **-n**) *f* ballad.

Ballast ['balast] (**-(e)s**, **-e**) *m* ballast; (*fig*) weight, burden; ~**stoffe** *pl* (*MED*) roughage *sing*.

Ballen ['balən] (**-s**, **-**) *m* bale; (*ANAT*) ball.

ballen *vt* (*formen*) to make into a ball; (*Faust*) to clench ♦ *vr* to build up; (*Menschen*) to gather.

ballern ['balərn] (*umg*) *vi* to shoot, fire.

Ballett [ba'lɛt] (**-(e)s**, **-e**) *nt* ballet; ~**tänzer(in)** ▲ *m(f)* ballet dancer.

Ballistik [ba'lɪstɪk] *f* ballistics *sing*.

Balljunge *m* ball boy.

Ballkleid *nt* evening dress.

Ballon [ba'lõː] (**-s**, **-s** *od* **-e**) *m* balloon.

Ballspiel *nt* ball game.

Ballung ['balʊŋ] *f* concentration; (*von Energie*) build-up.

Ballungs- *zW*: ~**gebiet** *nt*, ~**raum** *m* conurbation; ~**zentrum** *nt* centre (*BRIT*) *od* center (*US*) (*of population, industry etc*).

Balsam ['balzaːm] (**-s**, **-e**) *m* balsam; (*fig*) balm.

Balte ['baltə] (**-n**, **-n**) *m* Balt; **er ist** ~ he comes from the Baltic.

Baltikum ['baltikʊm] (**-s**) *nt*: **das** ~ the Baltic States *pl*.

Baltin ['baltɪn] *f siehe* **Balte**.

baltisch *adj* Baltic *attrib*.

Balz [balts] (**-**, **-en**) *f* (*Paarungsspiel*) courtship

display; (*Paarungszeit*) mating season.

Bambus ['bambʊs] (**-ses**, **-se**) *m* bamboo; ~**rohr** *nt* bamboo cane.

Bammel ['baməl] (**-s**) (*umg*) *m*: (**einen**) ~ **vor jdm/etw haben** to be scared of sb/sth.

banal [ba'naːl] *adj* banal.

Banalität [banali'tɛːt] *f* banality.

Banane [ba'naːnə] (**-**, **-n**) *f* banana.

Bananenschale *f* banana skin.

Bananenstecker *m* jack plug.

Banause [ba'naʊzə] (**-n**, **-n**) *m* philistine.

Band¹ [bant] (**-(e)s**, **⁻e**) *m* (*Buchband*) volume; **das spricht Bände** that speaks volumes.

Band² (**-(e)s**, **⁻er**) *nt* (*Stoff~*) ribbon, tape; (*Fließ~*) production line; (*Fass~*) hoop; (*Ziel~*, *Ton~*) tape; (*ANAT*) ligament; **etw auf** ~ **aufnehmen** to tape sth; **am laufenden** ~ (*umg*) non-stop.

Band³ (**-(e)s**, **-e**) *nt* (*Freundschafts~ etc*) bond.

Band⁴ [bɛnt] (**-**, **-s**) *f* band, group.

band *etc* [bant] *vb siehe* **binden**.

Bandage [ban'daːʒə] (**-**, **-n**) *f* bandage.

bandagieren *vt* to bandage.

Bandbreite *f* (*von Meinungen etc*) range.

Bande ['bandə] (**-**, **-n**) *f* band; (*Straßen~*) gang.

bändigen ['bɛndɪgən] *vt* (*Tier*) to tame; (*Trieb, Leidenschaft*) to control, restrain.

Bandit [ban'diːt] (**-en**, **-en**) *m* bandit.

Band- *zW*: ~**maß** *nt* tape measure; ~**nudeln** *pl* tagliatelle *pl*; ~**säge** *f* band saw; ~**scheibe** *f* (*ANAT*) disc; ~**scheibenschaden** *m* slipped disc; ~**wurm** *m* tapeworm.

bange ['baŋə] *adj* scared; (*besorgt*) anxious; **jdm wird es** ~ sb is becoming scared; **jdm B**~ **machen** to scare sb; **B**~**macher** (**-s**, **-**) *m* scaremonger.

bangen *vi*: **um jdn/etw** ~ to be anxious *od* worried about sb/sth.

Bangkok ['baŋkɔk] (**-s**) *nt* Bangkok.

Bangladesch [baŋgla'dɛʃ] (**-s**) *nt* Bangladesh.

Banjo ['banjo, 'bɛndʒo] (**-s**, **-s**) *nt* banjo.

Bank¹ [baŋk] (**-**, **⁻e**) *f* (*Sitz~*) bench; (*Sand~ etc*) (sand)bank, (sand)bar; **etw auf die lange** ~ **schieben** (*umg*) to put sth off.

Bank² (**-**, **-en**) *f* (*Geld~*) bank; **bei der** ~ at the bank; **Geld auf der** ~ **haben** to have money in the bank; ~**anweisung** *f* banker's order; ~**automat** *m* cash dispenser; ~**beamte(r)** *m* bank clerk; ~**einlage** *f* (bank) deposit.

Bankett [baŋ'kɛt] (**-(e)s**, **-e**) *nt* (*Essen*) banquet; (*Straßenrand*) verge (*BRIT*), shoulder (*US*).

Bank- *zW*: ~**fach** *nt* (*Schließfach*) safe-deposit box; ~**gebühr** *f* bank charge; ~**geheimnis** *nt* confidentiality in banking.

Bankier [baŋki'eː] (**-s**, **-s**) *m* banker.

Bank- *zW*: ~**konto** *nt* bank account; ~**leitzahl** *f* bank code number; ~**note** *f* banknote; ~**raub** *m* bank robbery.

bankrott [baŋ'krɔt] *adj* bankrupt; **B**~ (**-(e)s**, **-e**)

m bankruptcy; **B~ machen** to go bankrupt;
den B~ anmelden *od* **erklären** to declare o.s.
bankrupt; **B~erklärung** *f* (*lit*) declaration of
bankruptcy; (*fig: umg*) declaration of
failure.

Banküberfall *m* bank raid.

Bann [ban] (**-(e)s, -e**) *m* (*HIST*) ban; (*Kirchen~*)
excommunication; (*fig: Zauber*) spell; **b~en**
vt (*Geister*) to exorcize; (*Gefahr*) to avert;
(*bezaubern*) to enchant; (*HIST*) to banish.

Banner (**-s, -**) *nt* banner, flag.

Bar [baːr] (**-, -s**) *f* bar.

bar *adj* (*+gen*) (*unbedeckt*) bare; (*frei von*)
lacking (in); (*offenkundig*) utter, sheer; **~e(s)
Geld** cash; **etw (in) ~ bezahlen** to pay sth
(in) cash; **etw für ~e Münze nehmen** (*fig*) to
take sth at face value; **~ aller Hoffnung**
(*liter*) devoid of hope, completely without
hope.

Bär [bɛːr] (**-en, -en**) *m* bear; **jdm einen ~en
aufbinden** (*umg*) to have sb on.

Baracke [baˈrakə] (**-, -n**) *f* hut.

barbarisch [barˈbaːrɪʃ] *adj* barbaric,
barbarous.

Barbestand *m* money in hand.

Bardame *f* barmaid.

Bärenhunger (*umg*) *m*: **einen ~ haben** to be
famished.

bärenstark (*umg*) *adj* strapping, strong as an
ox; (*fig*) terrific.

barfuß *adj* barefoot.

barg *etc* [bark] *vb siehe* **bergen**.

Bargeld *nt* cash, ready money.

bargeldlos *adj* non-cash; **~er
Zahlungsverkehr** non-cash *od* credit
transactions *pl*.

barhäuptig *adj* bareheaded.

Barhocker *m* bar stool.

Bariton [ˈbaːritɔn] *m* baritone.

Barkauf *m* cash purchase.

Barkeeper [ˈbaːrkiːpər] (**-s, -**) *m* barman,
bartender.

Barkredit *m* cash loan.

Barmann (**-(e)s, *pl* -männer**) *m* barman.

barmherzig [barmˈhɛrtsɪç] *adj* merciful,
compassionate; **B~keit** *f* mercy,
compassion.

Barock [baˈrɔk] (**-s** *od* **-**) *nt od m* baroque.

Barometer [baroˈmeːtər] (**-s, -**) *nt* barometer;
das ~ steht auf Sturm (*fig*) there's a storm
brewing.

Baron [baˈroːn] (**-s, -e**) *m* baron.

Baronesse [baroˈnɛsə] (**-, -n**) *f* baroness.

Baronin *f* baroness.

Barren [ˈbarən] (**-s, -**) *m* parallel bars *pl*;
(*Gold~*) ingot.

Barriere [bariˈɛːrə] (**-, -n**) *f* barrier.

Barrikade [bariˈkaːdə] (**-, -n**) *f* barricade.

Barsch [barʃ] (**-(e)s, -e**) *m* perch.

barsch [barʃ] *adj* brusque, gruff; **jdn**

~ anfahren to snap at sb.

Barschaft *f* ready money.

Barscheck *m* open *od* uncrossed cheque
(*BRIT*), open check (*US*).

barst *etc* [barst] *vb siehe* **bersten**.

Bart [baːrt] (**-(e)s, ¨e**) *m* beard; (*Schlüssel~*)
bit.

bärtig [ˈbɛːrtɪç] *adj* bearded.

Barvermögen *nt* liquid assets *pl*.

Barzahlung *f* cash payment.

Basar [baˈzaːr] (**-s, -e**) *m* bazaar.

Base [ˈbaːzə] (**-, -n**) *f* (*CHEM*) base; (*Kusine*)
cousin.

Basel [ˈbaːzəl] (**-s**) *nt* Basle.

Basen *pl von* **Base, Basis**.

basieren [baˈziːrən] *vt* to base ♦ *vi* to be based.

Basilikum [baˈziːlikʊm] (**-s**) *nt* basil.

Basis [ˈbaːzɪs] (**-, *pl* Basen**) *f* basis; (*ARCHIT,
MIL, MATH*) base; **~ und Überbau** (*POL,
SOZIOLOGIE*) foundation and
superstructure; **die ~** (*umg*) the grass roots.

basisch [ˈbaːzɪʃ] *adj* (*CHEM*) alkaline.

Basisgruppe *f* action group.

Baske [ˈbaskə] (**-n, -n**) *m* Basque.

Baskenland *nt* Basque region.

Baskenmütze *f* beret.

Baskin *f* Basque.

Bass▲ [bas] (**-es, ¨e**) *m* bass.

Bassin [baˈsɛː] (**-s, -s**) *nt* pool.

Bassist [baˈsɪst] *m* bass.

Bassschlüssel▲ *m* bass clef.

Bassstimme▲ *f* bass voice.

Bast [bast] (**-(e)s, -e**) *m* raffia.

basta [ˈbasta] *interj*: **(und damit) ~!** (and)
that's that!

basteln [ˈbastəln] *vt* to make ♦ *vi* to do
handicrafts; **an etw** *dat* **~** (*an etw herum~*) to
tinker with sth.

Bastler [ˈbastlər] (**-s, -**) *m* do-it-yourselfer;
(*handwerklich*) handicrafts enthusiast.

BAT *m abk* (= *Bundesangestelltentarif*) *German
salary scale for employees*.

bat *etc* [baːt] *vb siehe* **bitten**.

Bataillon [batalˈjoːn] (**-s, -e**) *nt* battalion.

Batist [baˈtɪst] (**-(e)s, -e**) *m* batiste.

Batterie [batəˈriː] *f* battery.

Bau [bau] (**-(e)s**) *m* (**~en**) building,
construction; (*Auf~*) structure; (*Körper~*)
frame; (*~stelle*) building site; (*pl* **~e:** *Tier~*)
hole, burrow; (: *MIN*) working(s); (*pl* **~ten:**
Gebäude) building; **sich im ~ befinden** to be
under construction; **~arbeiten** *pl* (*Straßen~*)
roadworks *pl* (*BRIT*), roadwork *sing* (*US*);
building *od* construction work *sing*;
~arbeiter *m* building worker.

Bauch [baux] (**-(e)s, Bäuche**) *m* belly; (*ANAT*)
stomach, abdomen; **sich** *dat* (**vor Lachen) den
~ halten** (*umg*) to split one's sides
(laughing); **mit etw auf den ~ fallen** (*umg*)
to come a cropper with sth; **~ansatz** *m*

beginning of a paunch; ~**fell** nt peritoneum.
bauchig adj bulging.
Bauch- zW: ~**landung** f: eine ~**landung machen** (fig) to experience a failure, to flop; ~**muskel** m abdominal muscle; ~**nabel** m navel, belly-button (umg); ~**redner** m ventriloquist; ~**schmerzen** pl stomachache sing; ~**speicheldrüse** f pancreas; ~**tanz** m belly dance; belly dancing; ~**weh** nt stomachache.
Baudrate [baut'ra:tə] f (COMPUT) baud rate.
bauen ['bauən] vt to build; (TECH) to construct; (umg: verursachen: Unfall) to cause ♦ vi to build; **auf jdn/etw** ~ to depend od count upon sb/sth; **da hast du Mist gebaut** (umg) you really messed that up.
Bauer[1] ['bauər] (-n od -s, -n) m farmer; (SCHACH) pawn.
Bauer[2] (-s, -) nt od m (Vogel~) cage.
Bäuerchen ['bɔyərçən] nt (Kindersprache) burp.
Bäuerin ['bɔyərɪn] f farmer; (Frau des Bauern) farmer's wife.
bäuerlich adj rustic.
Bauern- zW: ~**brot** nt black bread; ~**fängerei** f deception, confidence trick(s); ~**frühstück** nt bacon and potato omelette (BRIT) od omelet (US); ~**haus** nt farmhouse; ~**hof** m farm; ~**schaft** f farming community; ~**schläue** f native cunning, craftiness, shrewdness.
Bau- zW: b~**fällig** adj dilapidated; ~**fälligkeit** f dilapidation; ~**firma** f construction firm; ~**führer** m site foreman; ~**gelände** nt building site; ~**genehmigung** f building permit; ~**gerüst** nt scaffolding; ~**herr** m client (of construction firm); ~**ingenieur** m civil engineer.
Bauj. abk = **Baujahr.**
Bau- zW: ~**jahr** nt year of construction; (von Auto) year of manufacture; ~**kasten** m box of bricks; ~**klötzchen** nt (building) block; ~**kosten** pl construction costs pl; ~**land** nt building land; ~**leute** pl building workers pl; b~**lich** adj structural; ~**löwe** m building speculator; ~**lücke** f undeveloped building plot.
Baum [baum] (-(e)s, pl **Bäume**) m tree; **heute könnte ich Bäume ausreißen** I feel full of energy today.
Baumarkt m DIY superstore.
baumeln ['bauməln] vi to dangle.
bäumen ['bɔymən] vr to rear (up).
Baum- zW: ~**grenze** f tree line; ~**schule** f nursery; ~**stamm** m tree trunk; ~**stumpf** m tree stump; ~**wolle** f cotton.
Bau- zW: ~**plan** m architect's plan; ~**platz** m building site; ~**sachverständige(r)** f(m) quantity surveyor; ~**satz** m construction kit.
Bausch [bauʃ] (-(e)s, pl **Bäusche**) m (Watte~)

ball, wad; **in** ~ **und Bogen** (fig) lock, stock, and barrel.
bauschen vt, vi, vr to puff out.
bauschig adj baggy, wide.
Bau- zW: **b~sparen** vi untr to save with a building society (BRIT) od a building and loan association (US); ~**sparkasse** f building society (BRIT), building and loan association (US); ~**sparvertrag** m savings contract with a building society (BRIT) od building and loan association (US); ~**stein** m building stone, freestone; ~**stelle** f building site; ~**stil** m architectural style; b~**technisch** adj in accordance with building od construction methods; ~**teil** nt prefabricated part (of building); ~**ten** pl von **Bau**; ~**unternehmer** m contractor, builder; ~**weise** f (method of) construction; ~**werk** nt building; ~**zaun** m hoarding.
b. a. w. abk (= bis auf weiteres) until further notice.
Bayer(in) ['baiər(ɪn)] (-n, -n) m(f) Bavarian.
bay(e)risch adj Bavarian.
Bayern nt Bavaria.
Bazillus [ba'tsɪlus] (-, pl **Bazillen**) m bacillus.
Bd. abk (= Band) vol.
Bde. abk (= Bände) vols.
beabsichtigen [bə'|apzɪçtɪgən] vt to intend.
beachten [bə'|axtən] vt to take note of; (Vorschrift) to obey; (Vorfahrt) to observe.
beachtenswert adj noteworthy.
beachtlich adj considerable.
Beachtung f notice, attention, observation; **jdm keine** ~ **schenken** to take no notice of sb.
Beamte(r) [bə'|amtə(r)] (-n, -n) m official; (Staats~) civil servant; (Bank~ etc) employee.
Beamtenlaufbahn f: **die** ~ **einschlagen** to enter the civil service.
Beamtenverhältnis nt: **im** ~ **stehen** to be a civil servant.
beamtet adj (form) appointed on a permanent basis (by the state).
Beamtin f siehe **Beamte(r)**.
beängstigend [bə'|ɛŋstɪgənt] adj alarming.
beanspruchen [bə'|anʃpruxən] vt to claim; (Zeit, Platz) to take up, occupy; **jdn** ~ to take up sb's time; **etw stark** ~ to put sth under a lot of stress.
beanstanden [bə'|anʃtandən] vt to complain about, object to; (Rechnung) to query.
Beanstandung f complaint.
beantragen [bə'|antra:gən] vt to apply for, ask for.
beantworten [bə'|antvɔrtən] vt to answer.
Beantwortung f reply.
bearbeiten [bə'|arbaitən] vt to work; (Material) to process; (Thema) to deal with; (Land) to cultivate; (CHEM) to treat; (Buch) to revise;

(*umg: beeinflussen wollen*) to work on.

Bearbeitung *f* processing; cultivation; treatment; revision; **die ~ meines Antrags hat lange gedauert** it took a long time to deal with my claim.

Bearbeitungsgebühr *f* handling charge.

beatmen [bə'|aːtmən] *vt*: **jdn künstlich ~ to** give sb artificial respiration.

Beatmung [bə'|aːtmʊŋ] *f* respiration.

beaufsichtigen [bə'|aʊfzɪçtɪgən] *vt* to supervise.

Beaufsichtigung *f* supervision.

beauftragen [bə'|aʊftraːgən] *vt* to instruct; **jdn mit etw ~** to entrust sb with sth.

Beauftragte(r) *f(m)* representative.

bebauen [bə'baʊən] *vt* to build on; (*AGR*) to cultivate.

beben ['beːbən] *vi* to tremble, shake; **B~** (**-s** -) *nt* earthquake.

bebildern [bə'bɪldərn] *vt* to illustrate.

Becher ['bɛçər] (**-s,** -) *m* mug; (*ohne Henkel*) tumbler.

bechern ['bɛçərn] (*umg*) *vi* (*trinken*) to have a few (drinks).

Becken ['bɛkən] (**-s,** -) *nt* basin; (*MUS*) cymbal; (*ANAT*) pelvis.

Bedacht [bə'daxt] *m*: **mit ~** (*vorsichtig*) prudently, carefully; (*absichtlich*) deliberately.

bedacht *adj* thoughtful, careful; **auf etw** *akk* **~ sein** to be concerned about sth.

bedächtig [bə'dɛçtɪç] *adj* (*umsichtig*) thoughtful, reflective; (*langsam*) slow, deliberate.

bedanken [bə'daŋkən] *vr*: **sich (bei jdm) ~** to say thank you (to sb); **ich bedanke mich herzlich** thank you very much.

Bedarf [bə'darf] (**-(e)s**) *m* need; (*~smenge*) requirements *pl*; (*COMM*) demand; supply; **alles für den häuslichen ~** all household requirements; **je nach ~** according to demand; **bei ~** if necessary; **~ an etw** *dat* **haben** to be in need of sth.

Bedarfs- *zW*: **~artikel** *m* requisite; **~deckung** *f* satisfaction of sb's needs; **~fall** *m* case of need; **~haltestelle** *f* request stop.

bedauerlich [bə'daʊərlɪç] *adj* regrettable.

bedauern [bə'daʊərn] *vt* to be sorry for; (*bemitleiden*) to pity; **wir ~, Ihnen mitteilen zu müssen, ...** we regret to have to inform you ...; **B~** (**-s**) *nt* regret.

bedauernswert *adj* (*Zustände*) regrettable; (*Mensch*) pitiable, unfortunate.

bedecken [bə'dɛkən] *vt* to cover.

bedeckt *adj* covered; (*Himmel*) overcast.

bedenken [bə'dɛŋkən] *unreg vt* to think over, consider; **ich gebe zu ~, dass ...** (*geh*) I would ask you to consider that ...; **B~** (**-s, -)** *nt* (*Überlegen*) consideration; (*Zweifel*) doubt; (*Skrupel*) scruple; **mir kommen B~** I am

having second thoughts.

bedenklich *adj* doubtful; (*bedrohlich*) dangerous, risky.

Bedenkzeit *f* time to consider; **zwei Tage ~** two days to think about it.

bedeuten [bə'dɔytən] *vt* to mean; to signify; (*wichtig sein*) to be of importance; **das bedeutet nichts Gutes** that means trouble.

bedeutend *adj* important; (*beträchtlich*) considerable.

bedeutsam *adj* significant; (*viel sagend*) meaningful.

Bedeutung *f* meaning; significance; (*Wichtigkeit*) importance.

bedeutungslos *adj* insignificant, unimportant.

bedeutungsvoll *adj* momentous, significant.

bedienen [bə'diːnən] *vt* to serve; (*Maschine*) to work, operate ♦ *vr* (*beim Essen*) to help o.s.; (*gebrauchen*): **sich jds/einer Sache ~** to make use of sb/sth; **werden Sie schon bedient?** are you being served?; **damit sind Sie sehr gut bedient** that should serve you very well; **ich bin bedient!** (*umg*) I've had enough.

Bedienung *f* service; (*Kellner etc*) waiter/ waitress; (*Zuschlag*) service (charge); (*von Maschinen*) operation.

Bedienungsanleitung *f* operating instructions *pl*.

bedingen [bə'dɪŋən] *vt* (*voraussetzen*) to demand, involve; (*verursachen*) to cause, occasion.

bedingt *adj* limited; (*Straferlass*) conditional; (*Reflex*) conditioned; **(nur) ~ gelten** to be (only) partially valid; **~ geeignet** suitable up to a point.

Bedingung *f* condition; (*Voraussetzung*) stipulation; **mit** *od* **unter der ~, dass ...** on condition that ...; **zu günstigen ~en** (*COMM*) on favourable (*BRIT*) *od* favorable (*US*) terms.

Bedingungsform *f* (*GRAM*) conditional.

bedingungslos *adj* unconditional.

bedrängen [bə'drɛŋən] *vt* to pester, harass.

Bedrängnis [bə'drɛŋnɪs] *f* (*seelisch*) distress, torment.

Bedrängung *f* trouble.

bedrohen [bə'droːən] *vt* to threaten.

bedrohlich *adj* ominous, threatening.

Bedrohung *f* threat, menace.

bedrucken [bə'drʊkən] *vt* to print on.

bedrücken [bədrykən] *vt* to oppress, trouble.

bedürfen [bə'dyrfən] *unreg vi +gen* (*geh*) to need, require; **ohne dass es eines Hinweises bedurft hätte, ...** without having to be asked ...

Bedürfnis [bə'dyrfnɪs] (**-ses, -se**) *nt* need; **das ~ nach etw haben** to need sth; **~anstalt** *f* (*form*) public convenience (*BRIT*), comfort station (*US*); **b~los** *adj* frugal, modest.

Spelling Reform: ▲ *new spelling* △ *old spelling* (to be phased out)

bedürftig *adj* in need, poor, needy.

Beefsteak [ˈbiːfsteːk] (**-s, -s**) *nt* steak; **deutsches** ~ hamburger.

beehren [bəˈ|eːrən] *vt* (*geh*) to honour (*BRIT*), honor (*US*); **wir** ~ **uns ...** we have pleasure in ...

beeilen [bəˈ|aɪlən] *vr* to hurry.

beeindrucken [bəˈ|aɪndrʊkən] *vt* to impress, make an impression on.

beeinflussen [bəˈ|aɪnflʊsən] *vt* to influence.

Beeinflussung *f* influence.

beeinträchtigen [bəˈ|aɪntrɛçtɪgən] *vt* to affect adversely; (*Sehvermögen*) to impair; (*Freiheit*) to infringe upon.

beend(ig)en [bəˈ|ɛnd(ɪg)ən] *vt* to end, finish, terminate.

Beend(ig)ung *f* end(ing), finish(ing).

beengen [bəˈ|ɛŋən] *vt* to cramp; (*fig*) to hamper, inhibit; ~**de Kleidung** restricting clothing.

beengt *adj* cramped; (*fig*) stifled.

beerben [bəˈ|ɛrbən] *vt* to inherit from.

beerdigen [bəˈ|eːrdɪgən] *vt* to bury.

Beerdigung *f* funeral, burial.

Beerdigungsunternehmer *m* undertaker.

Beere [ˈbeːrə] (**-, -n**) *f* berry; (*Trauben~*) grape.

Beerenauslese *f* wine made from specially selected grapes.

Beet [beːt] (**-(e)s, -e**) *nt* (*Blumen~*) bed.

befähigen [bəˈfɛːɪgən] *vt* to enable.

befähigt *adj* (*begabt*) talented; (*fähig*): ~ (**für**) capable (of).

Befähigung *f* capability; (*Begabung*) talent, aptitude; **die** ~ **zum Richteramt** the qualifications to become a judge.

befahl *etc* [bəˈfaːl] *vb siehe* **befehlen**.

befahrbar [bəˈfaːrbaːr] *adj* passable; (*NAUT*) navigable; **nicht** ~ **sein** (*Straße, Weg*) to be closed (to traffic); (*wegen Schnee etc*) to be impassable.

befahren [bəˈfaːrən] *unreg vt* to use, drive over; (*NAUT*) to navigate ♦ *adj* used.

befallen [bəˈfalən] *unreg vt* to come over.

befangen [bəˈfaŋən] *adj* (*schüchtern*) shy, self-conscious; (*voreingenommen*) bias(s)ed; **B~heit** *f* shyness; bias.

befassen [bəˈfasən] *vr* to concern o.s.

Befehl [bəˈfeːl] (**-(e)s, -e**) *m* command, order; (*COMPUT*) command; **auf** ~ **handeln** to act under orders; **zu** ~, **Herr Hauptmann!** (*MIL*) yes, sir; **den** ~ **haben od führen (über** +*akk*) to be in command (of).

befehlen *unreg vt* to order ♦ *vi* to give orders; **jdm etw** ~ to order sb to do sth; **du hast mir gar nichts zu** ~ I won't take orders from you.

befehligen *vt* to be in command of.

Befehls- *zW*: ~**empfänger** *m* subordinate; ~**form** *f* (*GRAM*) imperative; ~**haber** (**-s, -**) *m* commanding officer; ~**notstand** *m* (*JUR*) obligation to obey orders; ~**verweigerung** *f* insubordination.

befestigen [bəˈfɛstɪgən] *vt* to fasten; (*stärken*) to strengthen; (*MIL*) to fortify; ~ **an** +*dat* to fasten to.

Befestigung *f* fastening; strengthening; (*MIL*) fortification.

Befestigungsanlage *f* fortification.

befeuchten [bəˈfɔʏçtən] *vt* to damp(en), moisten.

befinden [bəˈfɪndən] *unreg vr* to be; (*sich fühlen*) to feel ♦ *vt*: **jdn/etw für** *od* **als etw** ~ to deem sb/sth to be sth ♦ *vi*: ~ (**über** +*akk*) to decide (on), adjudicate (on).

Befinden (**-s**) *nt* health, condition; (*Meinung*) view, opinion.

beflecken [bəˈflɛkən] *vt* (*lit*) to stain; (*fig geh*: *Ruf, Ehre*) to besmirch.

befliegen [bəˈfliːgən] *unreg vt* (*Strecke*) to fly.

beflügeln [bəˈflyːgəln] *vt* (*geh*) to inspire.

befohlen [bəˈfoːlən] *pp von* **befehlen**.

befolgen [bəˈfɔlgən] *vt* to comply with, follow.

befördern [bəˈfœrdərn] *vt* (*senden*) to transport, send; (*beruflich*) to promote; **etw mit der Post/per Bahn** ~ to send sth by post/by rail.

Beförderung *f* transport; promotion.

Beförderungskosten *pl* transport costs *pl*.

befragen [bəˈfraːgən] *vt* to question; (*um Stellungnahme bitten*): ~ (**über** +*akk*) to consult (about).

Befragung *f* poll.

befreien [bəˈfraɪən] *vt* to set free; (*erlassen*) to exempt.

Befreier(in) (**-s, -**) *m(f)* liberator.

befreit *adj* (*erleichtert*) relieved.

Befreiung *f* liberation, release; (*Erlassen*) exemption.

Befreiungs- *zW*: ~**bewegung** *f* liberation movement; ~**kampf** *m* struggle for liberation; ~**versuch** *m* escape attempt.

befremden [bəˈfrɛmdən] *vt* to surprise; (*unangenehm*) to disturb; **B~** (**-s**) *nt* surprise, astonishment.

befreunden [bəˈfrɔʏndən] *vr* to make friends; (*mit Idee etc*) to acquaint o.s.

befreundet *adj* friendly; **wir sind schon lange (miteinander)** ~ we have been friends for a long time.

befriedigen [bəˈfriːdɪgən] *vt* to satisfy.

befriedigend *adj* satisfactory.

Befriedigung *f* satisfaction, gratification.

befristet [bəˈfrɪstət] *adj* limited; (*Arbeitsverhältnis, Anstellung*) temporary.

befruchten [bəˈfrʊxtən] *vt* to fertilize; (*fig*) to stimulate.

Befruchtung *f*: **künstliche** ~ artificial insemination.

Befugnis [bəˈfuːknɪs] (**-, -se**) *f* authorization, powers *pl*.

befugt *adj* authorized, entitled.

befühlen [bə'fy:lən] *vt* to feel, touch.

Befund [bə'fʊnt] **(-(e)s, -e)** *m* findings *pl*; (*MED*) diagnosis; **ohne** ~ (*MED*) (results) negative.

befürchten [bə'fyrçtən] *vt* to fear.

Befürchtung *f* fear, apprehension.

befürworten [bə'fy:rvɔrtən] *vt* to support, speak in favour (*BRIT*) *od* favor (*US*) of.

Befürworter(in) **(-s, -)** *m(f)* supporter, advocate.

Befürwortung *f* support(ing), favouring (*BRIT*), favoring (*US*).

begabt [bə'ga:pt] *adj* gifted.

Begabung [bə'ga:bʊŋ] *f* talent, gift.

begann *etc* [bə'gan] *vb siehe* **beginnen**.

begatten [bə'gatən] *vr* to mate ♦ *vt* to mate *od* pair (with).

begeben [bə'ge:bən] *unreg vr* (*gehen*) to proceed; (*geschehen*) to occur; **sich** ~ **nach** *od* **zu** to proceed to(wards); **sich in ärztliche Behandlung** ~ to undergo medical treatment; **sich in Gefahr** ~ to expose o.s. to danger; **B~heit** *f* occurrence.

begegnen [bə'ge:gnən] *vi*: **jdm** ~ to meet sb; (*behandeln*) to treat; **Blicke** ~ **sich** eyes meet.

Begegnung *f* meeting; (*SPORT*) match.

begehen [bə'ge:ən] *unreg vt* (*Straftat*) to commit; (*Weg etc*) to use, negotiate; (*geh: feiern*) to celebrate.

begehren [bə'ge:rən] *vt* to desire.

begehrenswert *adj* desirable.

begehrt *adj* in demand; (*Junggeselle*) eligible.

begeistern [bə'gaɪstərn] *vt* to fill with enthusiasm; (*inspirieren*) to inspire ♦ *vr*: **sich für etw** ~ to get enthusiastic about sth; **er ist für nichts zu** ~ he's not interested in doing anything.

begeistert *adj* enthusiastic.

Begeisterung *f* enthusiasm.

Begierde [bə'gi:rdə] **(-, -n)** *f* desire, passion.

begierig [bə'gi:rɪç] *adj* eager, keen; (*voll Verlangen*) hungry, greedy.

begießen [bə'gi:sən] *unreg vt* to water; (*mit Fett: Braten etc*) to baste; (*mit Alkohol*) to drink to.

Beginn [bə'gɪn] **(-(e)s)** *m* beginning; **zu** ~ at the beginning.

beginnen *unreg vt, vi* to start, begin.

beglaubigen [bə'glaʊbɪgən] *vt* to countersign; (*Abschrift*) to authenticate; (*Echtheit, Übersetzung*) to certify.

Beglaubigung *f* countersignature.

Beglaubigungsschreiben *nt* credentials *pl*.

begleichen [bə'glaɪçən] *unreg vt* to settle, pay; **mit Ihnen habe ich noch eine Rechnung zu** ~ (*fig*) I've a score to settle with you.

begleiten [bə'glaɪtən] *vt* to accompany; (*MIL*) to escort.

Begleiter(in) **(-s, -)** *m(f)* companion; (*zum Schutz*) escort; (*MUS*) accompanist.

Begleit- *zW*: ~**erscheinung** *f* side effect; ~**musik** *f* accompaniment; ~**papiere** *pl* (*COMM*) accompanying documents *pl*; ~**schiff** *nt* escort vessel; ~**schreiben** *nt* covering letter; ~**umstände** *pl* attendant circumstances.

Begleitung *f* company; (*MIL*) escort; (*MUS*) accompaniment.

beglücken [bə'glʏkən] *vt* to make happy, delight.

beglückwünschen [bə'glʏkvʏnʃən] *vt*: ~ **(zu)** to congratulate (on).

begnadet [bə'gna:dət] *adj* gifted.

begnadigen [bə'gna:dɪgən] *vt* to pardon.

Begnadigung *f* pardon.

begnügen [bə'gny:gən] *vr*: **sich** ~ **mit** to be satisfied with, content o.s. with.

Begonie [bə'go:niə] *f* begonia.

begonnen [bə'gɔnən] *pp von* **beginnen**.

begossen [bə'gɔsən] *pp von* **begießen** ♦ *adj*: **er stand da wie ein** ~**er Pudel** (*umg*) he looked so sheepish.

begraben [bə'gra:bən] *unreg vt* to bury; (*aufgeben: Hoffnung*) to abandon; (*beenden: Streit etc*) to end; **dort möchte ich nicht** ~ **sein** (*umg*) I wouldn't like to be stuck in that hole.

Begräbnis [bə'grɛ:pnɪs] **(-ses, -se)** *nt* burial, funeral.

begradigen [bə'gra:dɪgən] *vt* to straighten (out).

begreifen [bə'graɪfən] *unreg vt* to understand, comprehend.

begreiflich [bə'graɪflɪç] *adj* understandable; **ich kann mich ihm nicht** ~ **machen** I can't make myself clear to him.

begrenzen [bə'grɛntsən] *vt* (*beschränken*): ~ **(auf** +*akk*) to restrict (to), limit (to).

Begrenztheit [bə'grɛntsthaɪt] *f* limitation, restriction; (*fig*) narrowness.

Begriff [bə'grɪf] **(-(e)s, -e)** *m* concept, idea; **im** ~ **sein, etw zu tun** to be about to do sth; **sein Name ist mir ein/kein** ~ his name means something/doesn't mean anything to me; **du machst dir keinen** ~ **(davon)** you've no idea; **für meine** ~**e** in my opinion; **schwer von** ~ (*umg*) slow on the uptake.

Begriffsbestimmung *f* definition.

begriffsstutzig *adj* slow-witted, dense.

begrub *etc* [bə'gru:p] *vb siehe* **begraben**.

begründen [bə'grʏndən] *vt* (*Gründe geben*) to justify; **etw näher** ~ to give specific reasons for sth.

Begründer(in) **(-s, -)** *m(f)* founder.

begründet *adj* well-founded, justified; **sachlich** ~ founded on fact.

Begründung *f* justification, reason.

begrünen [bə'gry:nən] *vt* to plant with greenery.

begrüßen [bə'gryːsən] *vt* to greet, welcome.
begrüßenswert *adj* welcome.
Begrüßung *f* greeting, welcome.
begünstigen [bə'gʏnstɪgən] *vt* (*Person*) to favour (*BRIT*), favor (*US*); (*Sache*) to further, promote.
Begünstigte(r) *f(m)* beneficiary.
begutachten [bə'guːt|axtən] *vt* to assess; (*umg: ansehen*) to have a look at.
begütert [bə'gyːtərt] *adj* wealthy, well-to-do.
begütigend *adj* (*Worte etc*) soothing; ~ **auf jdn einreden** to calm sb down.
behaart [bə'haːrt] *adj* hairy.
behäbig [bə'hɛːbɪç] *adj* (*dick*) portly, stout; (*geruhsam*) comfortable.
behaftet [bə'haftət] *adj*: **mit etw ~ sein** to be afflicted by sth.
behagen [bə'haːgən] *vi*: **das behagt ihm nicht** he does not like it; **B~** (**-s**) *nt* comfort, ease; **mit B~ essen** to eat with relish.
behaglich [bə'haːklɪç] *adj* comfortable, cosy; **B~keit** *f* comfort, cosiness.
behält [bə'hɛlt] *vb siehe* **behalten**.
behalten [bə'haltən] *unreg vt* to keep, retain; (*im Gedächtnis*) to remember; ~ **Sie (doch) Platz!** please don't get up!
Behälter [bə'hɛltər] (**-s, -**) *m* container, receptacle.
behämmert [bə'hɛmərt] (*umg*) *adj* screwy, crazy.
behandeln [bə'handəln] *vt* to treat; (*Thema*) to deal with; (*Maschine*) to handle; **der ~de Arzt** the doctor in attendance.
Behändigkeit▲ [bə'hɛndɪçkaɪt] *f* agility, quickness.
Behandlung *f* treatment; (*von Maschine*) handling.
behängen [bə'hɛŋən] *vt* to decorate.
beharren [bə'harən] *vi*: **auf etw** *dat* ~ to stick *od* keep to sth.
beharrlich [bə'harlɪç] *adj* (*ausdauernd*) steadfast, unwavering; (*hartnäckig*) tenacious, dogged; **B~keit** *f* steadfastness; tenacity.
behaupten [bə'haʊptən] *vt* to claim, assert, maintain; (*sein Recht*) to defend ♦ *vr* to assert o.s.; **von jdm ~, dass ...** to say (of sb) that ...; **sich auf dem Markt ~** to establish itself on the market.
Behauptung *f* claim, assertion.
Behausung [bə'haʊzʊŋ] *f* dwelling, abode; (*armselig*) hovel.
beheben [bə'heːbən] *unreg vt* (*beseitigen*) to remove; (*Missstände*) to remedy; (*Schaden*) to repair; (*Störung*) to clear.
beheimatet [bə'haɪmaːtət] *adj*: ~ (**in** +*dat*) domiciled (at/in); (*Tier, Pflanze*) native (to).
beheizen [bə'haɪtsən] *vt* to heat.
Behelf [bə'hɛlf] (**-(e)s, -e**) *m* expedient, makeshift; **b~en** *unreg vr*: **sich mit etw b~en**

to make do with sth.
behelfsmäßig *adj* improvised, makeshift; (*vorübergehend*) temporary.
behelligen [bə'hɛlɪgən] *vt* to trouble, bother.
Behendigkeit△ [bə'hɛndɪçkaɪt] *f siehe* **Behändigkeit.**
beherbergen [bə'hɛrbɛrgən] *vt* (*lit, fig*) to house.
beherrschen [bə'hɛrʃən] *vt* (*Volk*) to rule, govern; (*Situation*) to control; (*Sprache, Gefühle*) to master ♦ *vr* to control o.s.
beherrscht *adj* controlled; **B~heit** *f* self-control.
Beherrschung *f* rule; control; mastery; **die ~ verlieren** to lose one's temper.
beherzigen [bə'hɛrtsɪgən] *vt* to take to heart.
beherzt *adj* spirited, brave.
behielt *etc* [bə'hiːlt] *vb siehe* **behalten.**
behilflich [bə'hɪlflɪç] *adj* helpful; **jdm ~ sein** (**bei**) to help sb (with).
behindern [bə'hɪndərn] *vt* to hinder, impede.
Behinderte(r) *f(m)* disabled person.
Behinderung *f* hindrance; (*Körperbehinderung*) handicap.
Behörde [bə'høːrdə] (**-, -n**) *f* authorities *pl*; (*Amtsgebäude*) office(s *pl*).
behördlich [bə'høːrtlɪç] *adj* official.
behüten [bə'hyːtən] *vt* to guard; **jdn vor etw** *dat* ~ to preserve sb from sth.
behütet *adj* (*Jugend etc*) sheltered.
behutsam [bə'huːtzaːm] *adj* cautious, careful; **man muss es ihr ~ beibringen** it will have to be broken to her gently; **B~keit** *f* caution, carefulness.

===================== *SCHLÜSSELWORT*

bei [baɪ] *präp* +*dat* **1** (*nahe* ~) near; (*zum Aufenthalt*) at, with; (*unter, zwischen*) among; ~ **München** near Munich; ~ **uns** at our place; ~**m Friseur** at the hairdresser's; ~ **seinen Eltern wohnen** to live with one's parents; ~ **einer Firma arbeiten** to work for a firm; **etw** ~ **sich haben** to have sth on one; **jdn** ~ **sich haben** to have sb with one; ~ **Goethe** in Goethe; ~**m Militär** in the army.
2 (*zeitlich*) at, on; (*während*) during; (*Zustand, Umstand*) in; ~ **Nacht** at night; ~ **Nebel** in fog; ~ **Regen** if it rains; ~ **solcher Hitze** in such heat; ~ **meiner Ankunft** on my arrival; ~ **der Arbeit** when I'm *etc* working; ~**m Fahren** while driving; ~ **offenem Fenster schlafen** to sleep with the window open; ~ **Feuer Scheibe einschlagen** in case of fire break glass; ~ **seinem Talent** with his talent.

beibehalten ['baɪbəhaltən] *unreg vt* to keep, retain.
Beibehaltung *f* keeping, retaining.

Beiblatt ['baɪblat] *nt* supplement.
beibringen ['baɪbrɪŋən] *unreg vt* (*Beweis, Zeugen*) to bring forward; (*Gründe*) to adduce; **jdm etw** ~ (*zufügen*) to inflict sth on sb; (*zu verstehen geben*) to make sb understand sth; (*lehren*) to teach sb sth.
Beichte ['baɪçtə] *f* confession.
beichten *vt* to confess ♦ *vi* to go to confession.
Beichtgeheimnis *nt* secret of the confessional.
Beichtstuhl *m* confessional.
beide ['baɪdə] *pron, adj* both; **meine** ~**n Brüder** my two brothers, both my brothers; **die ersten** ~**n** the first two; **wir** ~ we two; **einer von** ~**n** one of the two; **alles** ~**s** both (of them); ~ **Mal** both times.
beider- *zW:* ~**lei** *adj inv* of both; ~**seitig** *adj* mutual, reciprocal; ~**seits** *adv* mutually ♦ *präp +gen* on both sides of.
beidhändig ['baɪthɛndɪç] *adj* ambidextrous.
beidrehen ['baɪdreːən] *vi* to heave to.
beidseitig ['baɪtzaɪtɪç] *adj* (*auf beiden Seiten*) on both sides.
beieinander [baɪʔaɪˈnandər] *adv* together; **gut** ~ **sein** (*umg: gesundheitlich*) to be in good shape; (*: geistig*) to be all there.
Beifahrer(in) ['baɪfaːrər(ɪn)] (**-s, -**) *m(f)* passenger; ~**airbag** *m* (*AUT*) passenger airbag; ~**sitz** *m* passenger seat.
Beifall ['baɪfal] (**-(e)s**) *m* applause; (*Zustimmung*) approval; ~ **heischend** fishing for applause/approval.
beifällig ['baɪfɛlɪç] *adj* approving; (*Kommentar*) favourable (*BRIT*), favorable (*US*).
Beifilm ['baɪfɪlm] *m* supporting film.
beifügen ['baɪfyːgən] *vt* to enclose.
Beigabe ['baɪgaːbə] *f* addition.
beige ['beːʒ] *adj* beige.
beigeben ['baɪgeːbən] *unreg vt* (*zufügen*) to add; (*mitgeben*) to give ♦ *vi*: **klein** ~ (*nachgeben*) to climb down.
Beigeschmack ['baɪgəʃmak] *m* aftertaste.
Beihilfe ['baɪhɪlfə] *f* aid, assistance; (*Studienbeihilfe*) grant; (*JUR*) aiding and abetting; **wegen** ~ **zum Mord** (*JUR*) because of being an accessory to the murder.
beikommen ['baɪkɔmən] *unreg vi +dat* to get at; (*einem Problem*) to deal with.
Beil [baɪl] (**-(e)s, -e**) *nt* axe (*BRIT*), ax (*US*), hatchet.
Beilage ['baɪlaːgə] *f* (*Buch*~ *etc*) supplement; (*KOCH*) accompanying vegetables; (*getrennt serviert*) side dish etc.
beiläufig ['baɪlɔyfɪç] *adj* casual, incidental ♦ *adv* casually, by the way.
beilegen ['baɪleːgən] *vt* (*hinzufügen*) to enclose, add; (*beimessen*) to attribute, ascribe; (*Streit*) to settle.
beileibe [baɪˈlaɪbə] *adv*: ~ **nicht** by no means.

Beileid ['baɪlaɪt] *nt* condolence, sympathy; **herzliches** ~ deepest sympathy.
beiliegend ['baɪliːgənt] *adj* (*COMM*) enclosed.
beim [baɪm] = **bei dem**.
beimessen ['baɪmɛsən] *unreg vt* to attribute, ascribe.
Bein [baɪn] (**-(e)s, -e**) *nt* leg; **jdm ein** ~ **stellen** (*lit, fig*) to trip sb up; **wir sollten uns auf die** ~**e machen** (*umg*) we ought to be making tracks; **jdm** ~**e machen** (*umg: antreiben*) to make sb get a move on; **die** ~**e in die Hand nehmen** (*umg*) to take to one's heels; **sich** *dat* **die** ~**e in den Bauch stehen** (*umg*) to stand about until one is fit to drop; **etw auf die** ~**e stellen** (*fig*) to get sth off the ground.
beinah(e) [baɪˈnaː(ə)] *adv* almost, nearly.
Beinbruch *m* fracture of the leg; **das ist kein** ~ (*fig: umg*) it could be worse.
beinhalten [bəˈʔɪnhaltən] *vt* to contain.
beipflichten ['baɪpflɪçtən] *vi*: **jdm/etw** ~ to agree with sb/sth.
Beiprogramm ['baɪprogram] *nt* supporting programme (*BRIT*) *od* program (*US*).
Beirat ['baɪraːt] *m* advisory council; (*Eltern*~) parents' council.
beirren [bəˈʔɪrən] *vt* to confuse, muddle; **sich nicht** ~ **lassen** not to let o.s. be confused.
Beirut [baɪˈruːt] (**-s**) *nt* Beirut.
beisammen [baɪˈzamən] *adv* together; ~**haben** *unreg vt*: **er hat (sie) nicht alle** ~ (*umg*) he's not all there; **B**~**sein** (**-s**) *nt* get-together.
Beischlaf ['baɪʃlaːf] *m* (*JUR*) sexual intercourse.
Beisein ['baɪzaɪn] (**-s**) *nt* presence.
beiseite [baɪˈzaɪtə] *adv* to one side, aside; (*stehen*) on one side, aside; **Spaß** ~! joking apart!; **etw** ~ **legen** (*sparen*) to put sth by; **jdn/etw** ~ **schaffen** to get rid of sb/sth.
beisetzen ['baɪzɛtsən] *vt* to bury.
Beisetzung *f* funeral.
Beisitzer(in) ['baɪzɪtsər(ɪn)] (**-s, -**) *m(f)* (*JUR*) assessor; (*bei Prüfung*) observer.
Beispiel ['baɪʃpiːl] (**-(e)s, -e**) *nt* example; **mit gutem** ~ **vorangehen** to set a good example; **sich** *dat* **an jdm ein** ~ **nehmen** to take sb as an example; **zum** ~ for example; **b**~**haft** *adj* exemplary; **b**~**los** *adj* unprecedented.
beispielsweise *adv* for instance, for example.
beispringen ['baɪʃprɪŋən] *unreg vi +dat* to come to the aid of.
beißen ['baɪsən] *unreg vt, vi* to bite; (*stechen: Rauch, Säure*) to burn ♦ *vr* (*Farben*) to clash.
beißend *adj* biting, caustic; (*Geruch*) pungent, sharp; (*fig*) sarcastic.
Beißzange ['baɪstsangə] *f* pliers *pl*.
Beistand ['baɪʃtant] (**-(e)s, ⁼e**) *m* support, help; (*JUR*) adviser; **jdm** ~ **leisten** to give sb assistance/one's support.
beistehen ['baɪʃteːən] *unreg vi*: **jdm** ~ to stand

Beistelltisch ['baɪʃtɛltɪʃ] m occasional table.
beisteuern ['baɪʃtɔʏərn] vt to contribute.
beistimmen ['baɪʃtɪmən] vi +dat to agree with.
Beistrich ['baɪʃtrɪç] m comma.
Beitrag ['baɪtraːk] (-(e)s, ⁼e) m contribution; (Zahlung) fee, subscription; (Versicherungs~) premium; **einen ~ zu etw leisten** to make a contribution to sth.
beitragen ['baɪtraːgən] unreg vt, vi: **~ (zu)** to contribute (to); (mithelfen) to help (with).
Beitrags- zW: **b~frei** adj non-contributory; **b~pflichtig** adj contributory; **b~pflichtig sein** (Mensch) to have to pay contributions; **~zahlende(r)** f(m) fee-paying member.
beitreten ['baɪtreːtən] unreg vi +dat to join.
Beitritt ['baɪtrɪt] m joining; membership.
Beitrittserklärung f declaration of membership.
Beiwagen ['baɪvaːgən] m (Motorrad~) sidecar; (Straßenbahn~) extra carriage.
beiwohnen ['baɪvoːnən] vi (geh): **einer Sache** dat ~ to attend od be present at sth.
Beiwort ['baɪvɔrt] nt adjective.
Beize ['baɪtsə] (-, -n) f (Holz~) stain; (KOCH) marinade.
beizeiten [baɪ'tsaɪtən] adv in time.
bejahen [bə'jaːən] vt (Frage) to say yes to, answer in the affirmative; (gutheißen) to agree with.
bejahrt [bə'jaːrt] adj elderly, advanced in years.
bejammern [bə'jamərn] vt to lament, bewail.
bejammernswert adj lamentable.
bekakeln [bə'kaːkəln] (umg) vt to discuss.
bekam etc [bə'kam] vb siehe **bekommen**.
bekämpfen [bə'kɛmpfən] vt (Gegner) to fight; (Seuche) to combat ♦ vr to fight.
Bekämpfung f: **~ (+gen)** fight (against), struggle (against).
bekannt [bə'kant] adj (well-)known; (nicht fremd) familiar; **~ geben** to announce publicly; **mit jdm ~ sein** to know sb; **~ machen** to announce; **jdn jdm ~ machen** to introduce sb to sb; **sich mit etw ~ machen** to familiarize o.s. with sth; **das ist mir ~** I know that; **es/sie kommt mir ~ vor** it/she seems familiar; **durch etw ~ werden** to become famous because of sth.
Bekannte(r) f(m) friend, acquaintance.
Bekanntenkreis m circle of friends.
bekanntermaßen adv as is known.
bekannt- zW: **B~gabe** f announcement; **B~heitsgrad** m degree of fame; **~lich** adv as is well known, as you know; **B~machung** f publication; (Anschlag etc) announcement; **B~schaft** f acquaintance.
bekehren [bə'keːrən] vt to convert ♦ vr to be od become converted.

Bekehrung f conversion.
bekennen [bə'kɛnən] unreg vt to confess; (Glauben) to profess ♦ vr: **sich zu jdm/etw ~** to declare one's support for sb/sth; **Farbe ~** (umg) to show where one stands.
Bekenntnis [bə'kɛntnɪs] (-ses, -se) nt admission, confession; (Religion) confession, denomination; **ein ~ zur Demokratie ablegen** to declare one's belief in democracy; **~schule** f denominational school.
beklagen [bə'klaːgən] vt to deplore, lament ♦ vr to complain.
beklagenswert adj lamentable, pathetic; (Mensch) pitiful; (Zustand) deplorable; (Unfall) terrible.
beklatschen [bə'klatʃən] vt to applaud, clap.
bekleben [bə'kleːbən] vt: **etw mit Bildern ~** to stick pictures onto sth.
bekleckern [bə'klɛkərn] (umg) vt to stain.
bekleiden [bə'klaɪdən] vt to clothe; (Amt) to occupy, fill.
Bekleidung f clothing; (form: eines Amtes) tenure.
Bekleidungsindustrie f clothing industry, rag trade (umg).
beklemmen [bə'klɛmən] vt to oppress.
Beklemmung f oppressiveness; (Gefühl der Angst) feeling of apprehension.
beklommen [bə'klɔmən] adj anxious, uneasy; **B~heit** f anxiety, uneasiness.
bekloppt [bə'klɔpt] (umg) adj (Mensch) crazy; (: Sache) lousy.
beknackt [bə'knakt] (umg) adj = **bekloppt**.
beknien [bə'kniːən] (umg) vt (jdn) to beg.
bekommen [bə'kɔmən] unreg vt to get, receive; (Kind) to have; (Zug) to catch, get ♦ vi: **jdm ~** to agree with sb; **es mit jdm zu tun ~** to get into trouble with sb; **wohl bekomms!** your health!
bekömmlich [bə'kœmlɪç] adj easily digestible.
beköstigen [bə'kœstɪgən] vt to cater for.
bekräftigen [bə'krɛftɪgən] vt to confirm, corroborate.
Bekräftigung f corroboration.
bekreuzigen [bə'krɔʏtsɪgən] vr to cross o.s.
bekritteln [bə'krɪtəln] vt to criticize, pick holes in.
bekümmern [bə'kʏmərn] vt to worry, trouble.
bekunden [bə'kʊndən] vt (sagen) to state; (zeigen) to show.
belächeln [bə'lɛçəln] vt to laugh at.
beladen [bə'laːdən] unreg vt to load.
Belag [bə'laːk] (-(e)s, ⁼e) m covering, coating; (Brot~) spread; (auf Pizza, Brot) topping; (auf Tortenboden, zwischen Brotscheiben) filling; (Zahn~) tartar; (auf Zunge) fur; (Brems~) lining.
belagern [bə'laːgərn] vt to besiege.
Belagerung f siege.

Belagerungszustand m state of siege.
belämmert▲ [bəˈlɛmt] (umg) adj sheepish.
Belang [bəˈlaŋ] (-(e)s) m importance.
Belange pl interests pl, concerns pl.
belangen vt (JUR) to take to court.
belanglos adj trivial, unimportant.
Belanglosigkeit f triviality.
belassen [bəˈlasən] unreg vt (in Zustand, Glauben) to leave; (in Stellung) to retain; **es dabei ~** to leave it at that.
Belastbarkeit f (von Brücke, Aufzug) load-bearing capacity; (von Menschen, Nerven) ability to take stress.
belasten [bəˈlastən] vt (lit) to burden; (fig: bedrücken) to trouble, worry; (COMM: Konto) to debit; (JUR) to incriminate ♦ vr to weigh o.s. down; (JUR) to incriminate o.s.; **etw (mit einer Hypothek) ~** to mortgage sth.
belastend adj (JUR) incriminating.
belästigen [bəˈlɛstɪɡən] vt to annoy, pester.
Belästigung f annoyance, pestering; (körperlich) molesting.
Belastung [bəˈlastʊŋ] f (lit) load; (fig: Sorge etc) weight; (COMM) charge, debit(ing); (mit Hypothek): **~** (+gen) mortgage (on); (JUR) incriminating evidence.
Belastungs- zW: **~material** nt (JUR) incriminating evidence; **~probe** f capacity test; (fig) test; **~zeuge** m witness for the prosecution.
belaubt [bəˈlaʊpt] adj: **dicht ~ sein** to have thick foliage.
belaufen [bəˈlaʊfən] unreg vr: **sich ~ auf** +akk to amount to.
belauschen [bəˈlaʊʃən] vt to eavesdrop on.
beleben [bəˈleːbən] vt (anregen) to liven up; (Konjunktur, jds Hoffnungen) to stimulate.
belebt [bəˈleːpt] adj (Straße) crowded.
Beleg [bəˈleːk] (-(e)s, -e) m (COMM) receipt; (Beweis) documentary evidence, proof; (Beispiel) example.
belegen [bəˈleːɡən] vt to cover; (Kuchen, Brot) to spread; (Platz) to reserve, book; (Kurs, Vorlesung) to register for; (beweisen) to verify, prove.
Belegschaft f personnel, staff.
belegt adj (Zunge) furred; (Stimme) hoarse; (Zimmer) occupied; **~e Brote** open sandwiches.
belehren [bəˈleːrən] vt to instruct, teach; **jdn eines Besseren ~** to teach sb better; **er ist nicht zu ~** he won't be told.
Belehrung f instruction.
beleibt [bəˈlaɪpt] adj stout, corpulent.
beleidigen [bəˈlaɪdɪɡən] vt to insult; to offend.
beleidigt adj insulted; (gekränkt) offended; **die ~e Leberwurst spielen** (umg) to be in a huff.
Beleidigung f insult; (JUR) slander; (: schriftlich) libel.
beleihen [bəˈlaɪən] unreg vt (COMM) to lend

money on.
belemmert△ [bəˈlɛmərt] (umg) adj siehe **belämmert**.
belesen [bəˈleːzən] adj well-read.
beleuchten [bəˈlɔʏçtən] vt to light, illuminate; (fig) to throw light on.
Beleuchter(in) (-s, -) m(f) lighting technician.
Beleuchtung f lighting, illumination.
beleumdet [bəˈlɔʏmdət] adj: **gut/schlecht ~ sein** to have a good/bad reputation.
beleumundet [bəˈlɔʏmʊndət] adj = **beleumdet**.
Belgien [ˈbɛlɡiən] (-s) nt Belgium.
Belgier(in) (-s, -) m(f) Belgian.
belgisch adj Belgian.
Belgrad [ˈbɛlɡraːt] (-s) nt Belgrade.
belichten [bəˈlɪçtən] vt to expose.
Belichtung f exposure.
Belichtungsmesser m exposure meter.
Belieben [bəˈliːbən] nt: **(ganz) nach ~** (just) as you wish.
belieben vi unpers (geh): **wie es Ihnen beliebt** as you wish.
beliebig [bəˈliːbɪç] adj any you like, as you like; **~ viel** as much as you like; **in ~er Reihenfolge** in any order whatever; **ein ~es Thema** any subject you like od want.
beliebt [bəˈliːpt] adj popular; **sich bei jdm ~ machen** to make o.s. popular with sb; **B~heit** f popularity.
beliefern [bəˈliːfərn] vt to supply.
Belize [bɛˈliːz] (-s) nt Belize.
bellen [ˈbɛlən] vi to bark.
Belletristik [bɛleˈtrɪstɪk] f fiction and poetry.
belohnen [bəˈloːnən] vt to reward.
Belohnung f reward.
Belüftung [bəˈlʏftʊŋ] f ventilation.
belügen [bəˈlyːɡən] unreg vt to lie to, deceive.
belustigen [bəˈlʊstɪɡən] vt to amuse.
Belustigung f amusement.
bemächtigen [bəˈmɛçtɪɡən] vr: **sich einer Sache** gen **~** to take possession of sth, seize sth.
bemalen [bəˈmaːlən] vt to paint ♦ vr (pej: schminken) to put on one's war paint (umg).
bemängeln [bəˈmɛŋəln] vt to criticize.
bemannen [bəˈmanən] vt to man.
Bemannung f manning; (NAUT, AVIAT etc) crew.
bemänteln [bəˈmɛntəln] vt to cloak, hide.
bemerkbar adj perceptible, noticeable; **sich ~ machen** (Person) to make od get o.s. noticed; (Unruhe) to become noticeable.
bemerken [bəˈmɛrkən] vt (wahrnehmen) to notice, observe; (sagen) to say, mention; **nebenbei bemerkt** by the way.
bemerkenswert adj remarkable, noteworthy.
Bemerkung f remark, comment; (schriftlich) comment, note.
bemitleiden [bəˈmɪtlaɪdən] vt to pity.

bemittelt [bəˈmɪtəlt] *adj* well-to-do, well-off.
bemühen [bəˈmyːən] *vr* to take trouble; **sich um eine Stelle ~** to try to get a job.
bemüht *adj*: **(darum) ~ sein, etw zu tun** to endeavour (*BRIT*) *od* endeavor (*US*) *od* be at pains to do sth.
Bemühung *f* trouble, pains *pl*, effort.
bemüßigt [bəˈmyːsɪçt] *adj*: **sich ~ fühlen/ sehen** (*geh*) to feel called upon.
bemuttern [bəˈmʊtərn] *vt* to mother.
benachbart [bəˈnaxbaːrt] *adj* neighbouring (*BRIT*), neighboring (*US*).
benachrichtigen [bəˈnaːxrɪçtɪgən] *vt* to inform.
Benachrichtigung *f* notification.
benachteiligen [bəˈnaːxtaɪlɪgən] *vt* to (put at a) disadvantage, victimize.
benehmen [bəˈneːmən] *unreg vr* to behave; **B~ (-s)** *nt* behaviour (*BRIT*), behavior (*US*); **kein B~ haben** not to know how to behave.
beneiden [bəˈnaɪdən] *vt* to envy.
beneidenswert *adj* enviable.
Beneluxländer [ˈbeːnelʊkslɛndər] *pl* Benelux (countries *pl*).
Beneluxstaaten *pl* Benelux (countries *pl*).
benennen [bəˈnɛnən] *unreg vt* to name.
Bengel [ˈbɛŋəl] **(-s, -)** *m* (little) rascal *od* rogue.
Benimm [bəˈnɪm] **(-s)** (*umg*) *m* manners *pl*.
Benin [beˈniːn] **(-s)** *nt* Benin.
benommen [bəˈnɔmən] *adj* dazed.
benoten [bəˈnoːtən] *vt* to mark.
benötigen [bəˈnøːtɪgən] *vt* to need.
benutzen [bəˈnʊtsən] *vt* to use.
benützen [bəˈnʏtsən] *vt* to use.
Benutzer(in) **(-s, -)** *m(f)* user; **b~freundlich** *adj* user-friendly.
benutzerdefiniert *adj* (*COMPUT*) user-defined.
Benutzung *f* utilization, use; **jdm etw zur ~ überlassen** to put sth at sb's disposal.
Benzin [bɛntˈsiːn] **(-s, -e)** *nt* (*AUT*) petrol (*BRIT*), gas(oline) (*US*); **~einspritzanlage** *f* (*AUT*) fuel injection system; **~kanister** *m* petrol (*BRIT*) *od* gas (*US*) can; **~tank** *m* petrol (*BRIT*) *od* gas (*US*) tank; **~uhr** *f* petrol (*BRIT*) *od* gas (*US*) gauge.
beobachten [bəˈoːbaxtən] *vt* to observe.
Beobachter(in) **(-s, -)** *m(f)* observer; (*eines Unfalls*) witness; (*PRESSE, TV*) correspondent.
Beobachtung *f* observation.
beordern [bəˈɔrdərn] *vt*: **jdn zu sich ~** to send for sb.
bepacken [bəˈpakən] *vt* to load, pack.
bepflanzen [bəˈpflantsən] *vt* to plant.
bequatschen [bəˈkvatʃən] (*umg*) *vt* (*überreden*) to persuade; **etw ~** to talk sth over.
bequem [bəˈkveːm] *adj* comfortable; (*Ausrede*) convenient; (*Person*) lazy, indolent.

bequemen [bəˈkveːmən] *vr*: **sich ~, etw zu tun** to condescend to do sth.
Bequemlichkeit *f* convenience, comfort; (*Faulheit*) laziness, indolence.
Ber. *abk* = **Bericht; Beruf.**
berät [bəˈrɛːt] *vb siehe* **beraten.**
beraten [bəˈraːtən] *unreg vt* to advise; (*besprechen*) to discuss, debate ♦ *vr* to consult; **gut/schlecht ~ sein** to be well/ill advised; **sich ~ lassen** to get advice.
beratend *adj* consultative; **jdm ~ zur Seite stehen** to act in an advisory capacity to sb.
Berater(in) **(-s, -)** *m(f)* adviser; **~vertrag** *m* consultancy contract.
beratschlagen [bəˈraːtʃlaːgən] *vi* to deliberate, confer ♦ *vt* to deliberate on, confer about.
Beratung *f* advice; (*Besprechung*) consultation.
Beratungsstelle *f* advice centre (*BRIT*) *od* center (*US*).
berauben [bəˈraʊbən] *vt* to rob.
berauschen [bəˈraʊʃən] *vt* (*lit, fig*) to intoxicate.
berauschend *adj*: **das war nicht sehr ~** (*ironisch*) that wasn't very exciting.
berechenbar [bəˈrɛçənbaːr] *adj* calculable; (*Verhalten*) predictable.
berechnen [bəˈrɛçnən] *vt* to calculate; (*COMM: anrechnen*) to charge.
berechnend *adj* (*Mensch*) calculating, scheming.
Berechnung *f* calculation; (*COMM*) charge.
berechtigen [bəˈrɛçtɪgən] *vt* to entitle; (*bevollmächtigen*) to authorize; (*fig*) to justify.
berechtigt [bəˈrɛçtɪçt] *adj* justifiable, justified.
Berechtigung *f* authorization; (*fig*) justification.
bereden [bəˈreːdən] *vt* (*besprechen*) to discuss; (*überreden*) to persuade ♦ *vr* to discuss.
beredt [bəˈreːt] *adj* eloquent.
Bereich [bəˈraɪç] **(-(e)s, -e)** *m* (*Bezirk*) area; (*Ressort, Gebiet*) sphere; **im ~ des Möglichen liegen** to be within the bounds of possibility.
bereichern [bəˈraɪçərn] *vt* to enrich ♦ *vr* to get rich; **sich auf Kosten anderer ~** to feather one's nest at the expense of other people.
Bereifung [bəˈraɪfʊŋ] *f* (set of) tyres (*BRIT*) *od* tires (*US*) *pl*; (*Vorgang*) fitting with tyres (*BRIT*) *od* tires (*US*).
bereinigen [bəˈraɪnɪgən] *vt* to settle.
bereisen [bəˈraɪzən] *vt* to travel through; (*COMM: Gebiet*) to travel, cover.
bereit [bəˈraɪt] *adj* ready, prepared; **zu etw ~ sein** to be ready for sth; **sich ~ erklären** to declare o.s. willing.
bereiten *vt* to prepare, make ready; (*Kummer, Freude*) to cause; **einer Sache** *dat* **ein Ende ~**

to put an end to sth.

bereit- zW: **~halten** unreg vt to keep in readiness; **~legen** vt to lay out; **~machen** vt, vr to prepare, get ready.

bereits adv already.

bereit- zW: **B~schaft** f readiness; (Polizei) alert; **in B~schaft sein** to be on the alert od on stand-by; **B~schaftsarzt** m doctor on call; (im Krankenhaus) duty doctor; **B~schaftsdienst** m emergency service; **~stehen** unreg vi (Person) to be prepared; (Ding) to be ready; **~stellen** vt (Kisten, Pakete etc) to put ready; (Geld etc) to make available; (Truppen, Maschinen) to put at the ready.

Bereitung f preparation.

bereitwillig adj willing, ready; **B~keit** f willingness, readiness.

bereuen [bə'rɔyən] vt to regret.

Berg [bɛrk] (-(e)s, -e) m mountain; (kleiner) hill; **mit etw hinterm ~ halten** (fig) to keep quiet about sth; **über alle ~e sein** to be miles away; **da stehen einem ja die Haare zu ~e** it's enough to make your hair stand on end; **b~ab** adv downhill; **b~an** adv uphill; **~arbeiter** m miner; **b~auf** adv uphill; **~bahn** f mountain railway (BRIT) od railroad (US); **~bau** m mining.

bergen ['bɛrgən] unreg vt (retten) to rescue; (Ladung) to salvage; (enthalten) to contain.

Bergführer m mountain guide.

Berggipfel m mountain top, peak, summit.

bergig ['bɛrgɪç] adj mountainous, hilly.

Berg- zW: **~kamm** m crest, ridge; **~kette** f mountain range; **~kristall** m rock crystal; **~mann** (-(e)s, pl **~leute**) m miner; **~not** f: **in ~not sein/geraten** to be in/get into difficulties while climbing; **~predigt** f (REL) Sermon on the Mount; **~rettungsdienst** m mountain rescue service; **~rutsch** m landslide; **~schuh** m walking boot; **~steigen** nt mountaineering; **~steiger(in)** m(f) mountaineer, climber; **~-und-Tal-Bahn** f big dipper, roller-coaster.

Bergung ['bɛrgʊŋ] f (von Menschen) rescue; (von Material) recovery; (NAUT) salvage.

Bergwacht f mountain rescue service.

Bergwerk nt mine.

Bericht [bə'rɪçt] (-(e)s, -e) m report, account; **b~en** vt, vi to report; **~erstatter** (-s, -) m reporter, (newspaper) correspondent; **~erstattung** f reporting.

berichtigen [bə'rɪçtɪgən] vt to correct.

Berichtigung f correction.

berieseln [bə'ri:zəln] vt to spray with water.

Berieselung f watering; **die dauernde ~ mit Musik ...** (fig) the constant stream of music ...

Berieselungsanlage f sprinkler (system).

Beringmeer ['be:rɪŋme:r] nt Bering Sea.

beritten [bə'rɪtən] adj mounted.

Berlin [bɛr'li:n] (-s) nt Berlin.

Berliner[1] adj attrib Berlin.

Berliner[2] (-s, -) m (Person) Berliner; (KOCH) jam doughnut.

Berlinerin f Berliner.

berlinerisch (umg) adj (Dialekt) Berlin attr.

Bermudas [bɛr'mu:das] pl: **auf den ~ in** Bermuda.

Bern [bɛrn] (-s) nt Berne.

Bernhardiner [bɛrnhar'di:nər] (-s, -) m Saint Bernard (dog).

Bernstein ['bɛrnʃtain] m amber.

bersten ['bɛrstən] unreg vi to burst, split.

berüchtigt [bə'rʏçtɪçt] adj notorious, infamous.

berücksichtigen [bə'rʏkzɪçtɪgən] vt to consider, bear in mind.

Berücksichtigung f consideration; **in od unter ~ der Tatsache, dass ...** in view of the fact that ...

Beruf [bə'ru:f] (-(e)s, -e) m occupation, profession; (Gewerbe) trade; **was sind Sie von ~?** what is your occupation etc?, what do you do for a living?; **seinen ~ verfehlt haben** to have missed one's vocation.

berufen unreg vt (in Amt): **jdn in etw akk ~ to** appoint sb to sth ♦ vr: **sich auf jdn/etw ~ to** refer od appeal to sb/sth ♦ adj competent, qualified; (ausersehen): **zu etw ~ sein** to have a vocation for sth.

beruflich adj professional; **er ist ~ viel unterwegs** he is away a lot on business.

Berufs- zW: **~ausbildung** f vocational od professional training; **b~bedingt** adj occupational; **~berater** m careers adviser; **~beratung** f vocational guidance; **~bezeichnung** f job description; **~erfahrung** f (professional) experience; **~feuerwehr** f fire service; **~geheimnis** nt professional secret; **~krankheit** f occupational disease; **~kriminalität** f professional crime; **~leben** nt professional life; **im ~leben stehen** to be working od in employment; **b~mäßig** adj professional; **~risiko** nt occupational hazard; **~schule** f vocational od trade school; **~soldat** m professional soldier, regular; **~sportler** m professional (sportsman); **b~tätig** adj employed; **b~unfähig** adj unable to work (at one's profession); **~unfall** m occupational accident; **~verbot** nt: **jdm ~verbot erteilen** to ban sb from his/her profession; (einem Arzt, Anwalt) to strike sb off; **~verkehr** m commuter traffic; **~wahl** f choice of a job.

Berufung f vocation, calling; (Ernennung) appointment; (JUR) appeal; **~ einlegen to** appeal; **unter ~ auf etw akk** (form) with reference to sth.

Berufungsgericht nt appeal court, court of

appeal.

beruhen [bə'ruːən] *vi:* **auf etw** *dat* ~ **to be** based on sth; **etw auf sich** ~ **lassen** to leave sth at that; **das beruht auf Gegenseitigkeit** the feeling is mutual.

beruhigen [bə'ruːɪgən] *vt* to calm, pacify, soothe ♦ *vr (Mensch)* to calm (o.s.) down; *(Situation)* to calm down.

beruhigend *adj (Gefühl, Wissen)* reassuring; *(Worte)* comforting; *(Mittel)* tranquillizing.

Beruhigung *f* reassurance; *(der Nerven)* calming; **zu jds** ~ to reassure sb.

Beruhigungsmittel *nt* sedative.

Beruhigungspille *f* tranquillizer.

berühmt [bə'ryːmt] *adj* famous; **das war nicht** ~ *(umg)* it was nothing to write home about; **~-berüchtigt** *adj* infamous, notorious; **B~heit** *f (Ruf)* fame; *(Mensch)* celebrity.

berühren [bə'ryːrən] *vt* to touch; *(gefühlsmäßig bewegen)* to affect; *(flüchtig erwähnen)* to mention, touch on ♦ *vr* to meet, touch; **von etw peinlich berührt sein** to be embarrassed by sth.

Berührung *f* contact.

Berührungspunkt *m* point of contact.

bes. *abk (= besonders)* esp.

besagen [bə'zaːgən] *vt* to mean.

besagt *adj (form: Tag etc)* in question.

besaiten [bə'zaɪtən] *vt:* **neu** ~ *(Instrument)* to restring.

besänftigen [bə'zɛnftɪgən] *vt* to soothe, calm.

besänftigend *adj* soothing.

Besänftigung *f* soothing, calming.

besaß *etc* [bə'zaːs] *vb siehe* **besitzen**.

besät [bə'zɛːt] *adj* covered; *(mit Blättern etc)* strewn.

Besatz [bə'zats] **(-es, -̈e)** *m* trimming, edging.

Besatzung *f* garrison; *(NAUT, AVIAT)* crew.

Besatzungsmacht *f* occupying power.

Besatzungszone *f* occupied zone.

besaufen [bə'zaʊfən] *unreg (umg) vr* to get drunk od stoned.

beschädigen [bə'ʃɛːdɪgən] *vt* to damage.

Beschädigung *f* damage; *(Stelle)* damaged spot.

beschaffen [bə'ʃafən] *vt* to get, acquire ♦ *adj* constituted; **so** ~ **sein** to be the same as ...; **B~heit** *f* constitution, nature; **je nach B~heit der Lage** according to the situation.

Beschaffung *f* acquisition.

beschäftigen [bə'ʃɛftɪgən] *vt* to occupy; *(beruflich)* to employ; *(innerlich)*: **jdn** ~ to be on sb's mind ♦ *vr* to occupy od concern o.s.

beschäftigt *adj* busy, occupied; *(angestellt)*: **(bei einer Firma)** ~ employed (by a firm).

Beschäftigung *f (Beruf)* employment; *(Tätigkeit)* occupation; *(geistige ~)* preoccupation; **einer** ~ **nachgehen** *(form)* to be employed.

Beschäftigungsprogramm *nt* employment

scheme.

Beschäftigungstherapie *f* occupational therapy.

beschämen [bə'ʃɛːmən] *vt* to put to shame.

beschämend *adj* shameful; *(Hilfsbereitschaft)* shaming.

beschämt *adj* ashamed.

beschatten [bə'ʃatən] *vt* to shade; *(Verdächtige)* to shadow.

beschaulich [bə'ʃaʊlɪç] *adj* contemplative; *(Leben, Abend)* quiet, tranquil.

Bescheid [bə'ʃaɪt] **(-(e)s, -e)** *m* information; *(Weisung)* directions *pl;* ~ **wissen (über** +*akk)* to be well-informed (about); **ich weiß** ~ I know; **jdm** ~ **geben** *od* **sagen** to let sb know; **jdm ordentlich** ~ **sagen** *(umg)* to tell sb where to go.

bescheiden [bə'ʃaɪdən] *unreg vr* to content o.s. ♦ *vt:* **etw abschlägig** ~ *(form)* to turn sth down ♦ *adj* modest; **B~heit** *f* modesty.

bescheinen [bə'ʃaɪnən] *unreg vt* to shine on.

bescheinigen [bə'ʃaɪnɪgən] *vt* to certify; *(bestätigen)* to acknowledge; **hiermit wird bescheinigt, dass ...** this is to certify that ...

Bescheinigung *f* certificate; *(Quittung)* receipt.

bescheißen [bə'ʃaɪsən] *unreg (umg!) vt* to cheat.

beschenken [bə'ʃɛŋkən] *vt* to give presents to.

bescheren [bə'ʃeːrən] *vt:* **jdm etw** ~ to give sb sth as a present; **jdn** ~ to give presents to sb.

Bescherung *f* giving of presents; *(umg)* mess; **da haben wir die** ~! *(umg)* what did I tell you!

bescheuert [bə'ʃɔʏərt] *(umg) adj* stupid.

beschichten [bə'ʃɪçtən] *vt (TECH)* to coat, cover.

beschießen [bə'ʃiːsən] *unreg vt* to shoot *od* fire at.

beschildern [bə'ʃɪldərn] *vt* to signpost.

beschimpfen [bə'ʃɪmpfən] *vt* to abuse.

Beschimpfung *f* abuse, insult.

beschirmen [bə'ʃɪrmən] *vt (geh: beschützen)* to shield.

Beschiss▲ [bə'ʃɪs] **(-es)** *(umg) m:* **das ist** ~ that is a cheat.

beschiss *etc*▲ *vb siehe* **bescheißen**.

beschissen *pp von* **bescheißen** ♦ *adj (umg!)* bloody awful, lousy.

Beschlag [bə'ʃlaːk] **(-(e)s, -̈e)** *m (Metallband)* fitting; *(auf Fenster)* condensation; *(auf Metall)* tarnish; finish; *(Hufeisen)* horseshoe; **jdn/etw in** ~ **nehmen** *od* **mit** ~ **belegen** to monopolize sb/sth.

beschlagen [bə'ʃlaːgən] *unreg vt* to cover; *(Pferd)* to shoe; *(Fenster, Metall)* to cover ♦ *vi, vr (Fenster etc)* to mist over; ~ **sein (in** *od* **auf** +*dat)* to be well versed (in).

beschlagnahmen vt to seize, confiscate.

Beschlagnahmung f confiscation.

beschleunigen [bə'ʃlɔynɪgən] vt to accelerate, speed up ♦ vi (AUT) to accelerate.

Beschleunigung f acceleration.

beschließen [bə'ʃliːsən] unreg vt to decide on; (beenden) to end, close.

beschlossen [bə'ʃlɔsən] pp von **beschließen** ♦ adj (entschieden) decided, agreed; **das ist ~e Sache** that's been settled.

Beschluss▲ [bə'ʃlʊs] (-es, ⁻e) m decision, conclusion; (Ende) close, end; **einen ~ fassen** to pass a resolution.

beschlussfähig▲ adj: **~ sein** to have a quorum.

beschmieren [bə'ʃmiːrən] vt (Wand) to bedaub.

beschmutzen [bə'ʃmʊtsən] vt to dirty, soil.

beschneiden [bə'ʃnaɪdən] unreg vt to cut; (stutzen) to trim; (: Strauch) to prune; (REL) to circumcise.

beschnuppern [bə'ʃnʊpərn] vr (Hunde) to sniff each other; (fig: umg) to size each other up.

beschönigen [bə'ʃøːnɪgən] vt to gloss over; **~der Ausdruck** euphemism.

beschränken [bə'ʃrɛŋkən] vt, vr: (sich) ~ (auf +akk) to limit od restrict (o.s.) (to).

beschrankt [bə'ʃraŋkt] adj (Bahnübergang) with barrier.

beschränkt [bə'ʃrɛŋkt] adj confined, narrow; (Mensch) limited, narrow-minded; (pej: geistig) dim; **Gesellschaft mit ~er Haftung** limited company (BRIT), corporation (US); **B~heit** f narrowness.

Beschränkung f limitation.

beschreiben [bə'ʃraɪbən] unreg vt to describe; (Papier) to write on.

Beschreibung f description.

beschrieb etc [bə'ʃriːp] vb siehe **beschreiben**.

beschrieben [bə'ʃriːbən] pp von **beschreiben**.

beschriften [bə'ʃrɪftən] vt to mark, label.

Beschriftung f lettering.

beschuldigen [bə'ʃʊldɪgən] vt to accuse.

Beschuldigung f accusation.

beschummeln [bə'ʃʊməln] (umg) vt, vi to cheat.

Beschuss▲ [bə'ʃʊs] m: **jdn/etw unter ~ nehmen** (MIL) to (start to) bombard od shell sb/sth; (fig) to attack sb/sth; **unter ~ geraten** (lit, fig) to come into the firing line.

beschützen [bə'ʃʏtsən] vt: **~ (vor +dat)** to protect (from).

Beschützer(in) (-s, -) m(f) protector.

Beschützung f protection.

beschwatzen [bə'ʃvatsən] (umg) vt (überreden) to talk over.

Beschwerde [bə'ʃveːrdə] (-, -n) f complaint; (Mühe) hardship; (INDUSTRIE) grievance;

Beschwerden pl (Leiden) trouble; **~ einlegen** (form) to lodge a complaint; **b~frei** adj fit and healthy; **~frist** f (JUR) period of time during which an appeal may be lodged.

beschweren [bə'ʃveːrən] vt to weight down; (fig) to burden ♦ vr to complain.

beschwerlich adj tiring, exhausting.

beschwichtigen [bə'ʃvɪçtɪgən] vt to soothe, pacify.

Beschwichtigung f soothing, calming.

beschwindeln [bə'ʃvɪndəln] vt (betrügen) to cheat; (belügen) to fib to.

beschwingt [bə'ʃvɪŋt] adj cheery, in high spirits.

beschwipst [bə'ʃvɪpst] adj tipsy.

beschwören [bə'ʃvøːrən] unreg vt (Aussage) to swear to; (anflehen) to implore; (Geister) to conjure up.

beseelen [bə'zeːlən] vt to inspire.

besehen [bə'zeːən] unreg vt to look at; **genau ~** to examine closely.

beseitigen [bə'zaɪtɪgən] vt to remove.

Beseitigung f removal.

Besen ['beːzən] (-s, -) m broom; (pej: umg: Frau) old bag; **ich fresse einen ~, wenn das stimmt** (umg) if that's right, I'll eat my hat; **~stiel** m broomstick.

besessen [bə'zɛsən] adj possessed; (von einer Idee etc): **~ (von)** obsessed (with).

besetzen [bə'zɛtsən] vt (Haus, Land) to occupy; (Platz) to take, fill; (Posten) to fill; (Rolle) to cast; (mit Edelsteinen) to set.

besetzt adj full; (TEL) engaged, busy; (Platz) taken; (WC) engaged; **B~zeichen** nt engaged tone (BRIT), busy signal (US).

Besetzung f occupation; (von Stelle) filling; (von Rolle) casting; (die Schauspieler) cast; **zweite ~** (THEAT) understudy.

besichtigen [bə'zɪçtɪgən] vt to visit, look at.

Besichtigung f visit.

besiedeln vt: **dicht/dünn besiedelt** densely/thinly populated.

Besied(e)lung [bə'ziːd(ə)lʊŋ] f population.

besiegeln [bə'ziːgəln] vt to seal.

besiegen [bə'ziːgən] vt to defeat, overcome.

Besiegte(r) [bə'ziːktə(r)] f(m) loser.

besinnen [bə'zɪnən] unreg vr (nachdenken) to think, reflect; (erinnern) to remember; **sich anders ~** to change one's mind.

besinnlich adj contemplative.

Besinnung f consciousness; **bei/ohne ~ sein** to be conscious/unconscious; **zur ~ kommen** to recover consciousness; (fig) to come to one's senses.

besinnungslos adj unconscious; (fig) blind.

Besitz [bə'zɪts] (-es) m possession; (Eigentum) property; **~anspruch** m claim of ownership; (JUR) title; **b~anzeigend** adj (GRAM) possessive.

besitzen unreg vt to possess, own; (Eigenschaft)

to have.

Besitzer(in) (-s, -) *m(f)* owner, proprietor.

Besitz- *zW:* **~ergreifung** *f* seizure; **~nahme** *f* seizure; **~tum** *nt* (*Grundbesitz*) estate(s *pl*), property; **~urkunde** *f* title deeds *pl*.

besoffen [bə'zɔfən] (*umg*) *adj* sozzled.

besohlen [bə'zo:lən] *vt* to sole.

Besoldung [bə'zɔldʊŋ] *f* salary, pay.

besondere(r, s) [bə'zɔndərə(r, s)] *adj* special; (*eigen*) particular; (*gesondert*) separate; (*eigentümlich*) peculiar.

Besonderheit *f* peculiarity.

besonders *adv* especially, particularly; (*getrennt*) separately; **das Essen/der Film war nicht ~** the food/film was nothing special *od* out of the ordinary; **wie gehts dir? - nicht ~** how are you? - not too hot.

besonnen [bə'zɔnən] *adj* sensible, level-headed; **B~heit** *f* level-headedness.

besorgen [bə'zɔrgən] *vt* (*beschaffen*) to acquire; (*kaufen*) to purchase; (*erledigen: Geschäfte*) to deal with; (*sich kümmern um*) to take care of; **es jdm ~** (*umg*) to sort sb out.

Besorgnis (-, -se) *f* anxiety, concern; **~ erregend** alarming, worrying.

besorgt [bə'zɔrkt] *adj* anxious, worried; **B~heit** *f* anxiety, worry.

Besorgung *f* acquisition; (*Kauf*) purchase; (*Einkauf*): **~en machen** to do some shopping.

bespannen [bə'ʃpanən] *vt* (*mit Saiten, Fäden*) to string.

bespielbar *adj* (*Rasen etc*) playable.

bespielen [bə'ʃpi:lən] *vt* (*Tonband, Kassette*) to make a recording on.

bespitzeln [bə'ʃpɪtsəln] *vt* to spy on.

besprechen [bə'ʃprɛçən] *unreg vt* to discuss; (*Tonband etc*) to record, speak onto; (*Buch*) to review ♦ *vr* to discuss, consult.

Besprechung *f* meeting, discussion; (*von Buch*) review.

bespringen [bə'ʃprɪŋən] *unreg vt* (*Tier*) to mount, cover.

bespritzen [bə'ʃprɪtsən] *vt* to spray; (*beschmutzen*) to spatter.

besser ['bɛsər] *adj* better; **nur ein ~er ...** just a glorified ...; **~e Leute** a better class of people; **es geht ihm ~** he feels better; **~ stehen** (*umg*) to be better off.

bessern *vt* to make better, improve ♦ *vr* to improve; (*Mensch*) to reform.

Besserung *f* improvement; **auf dem Weg(e) der ~ sein** to be getting better, be improving; **gute ~!** get well soon!

Besserwisser(in) (-s, -) *m(f)* know-all (*BRIT*), know-it-all (*US*).

Bestand [bə'ʃtant] (-(e)s, ⁻e) *m* (*Fortbestehen*) duration, continuance; (*Kassenbestand*) amount, balance; (*Vorrat*) stock; **eiserner ~** iron rations *pl*; **~ haben, von ~ sein** to last long, endure.

bestand *etc vb siehe* **bestehen**.

bestanden *pp von* **bestehen** ♦ *adj*: **nach ~er Prüfung** after passing the exam.

beständig [bə'ʃtɛndɪç] *adj* (*ausdauernd*) constant (*auch fig*); (*Wetter*) settled; (*Stoffe*) resistant; (*Klagen etc*) continual.

Bestandsaufnahme *f* stocktaking.

Bestandsüberwachung *f* stock control, inventory control.

Bestandteil *m* part, component; (*Zutat*) ingredient; **sich in seine ~e auflösen** to fall to pieces.

bestärken [bə'ʃtɛrkən] *vt*: **jdn in etw** *dat* **~ to** strengthen *od* confirm sb in sth.

bestätigen [bə'ʃtɛ:tɪgən] *vt* to confirm; (*anerkennen, COMM*) to acknowledge; **jdn (im Amt) ~** to confirm sb's appointment.

Bestätigung *f* confirmation; acknowledgement.

bestatten [bə'ʃtatən] *vt* to bury.

Bestatter (-s, -) *m* undertaker.

Bestattung *f* funeral.

Bestattungsinstitut *nt* undertaker's (*BRIT*), mortician's (*US*).

bestäuben [bə'ʃtɔybən] *vt* to powder, dust; (*Pflanze*) to pollinate.

beste(r, s) ['bɛstə(r, s)] *adj* best; **sie singt am ~n** she sings best; **so ist es am ~n** it's best that way; **am ~n gehst du gleich** you'd better go at once; **jdn zum B~n haben** to pull sb's leg; **einen Witz etc zum B~n geben** to tell a joke *etc*; **aufs ~** *od* **B~** in the best possible way; **zu jds B~n** for the benefit of sb; **es steht nicht zum B~n** it does not look too promising.

bestechen [bə'ʃtɛçən] *unreg vt* to bribe ♦ *vi* (*Eindruck machen*): **(durch etw) ~** to be impressive (because of sth).

bestechend *adj* (*Schönheit, Eindruck*) captivating; (*Angebot*) tempting.

bestechlich *adj* corruptible; **B~keit** *f* corruptibility.

Bestechung *f* bribery, corruption.

Bestechungsgelder *pl* bribe *sing*.

Bestechungsversuch *m* attempted bribery.

Besteck [bə'ʃtɛk] (-(e)s, -e) *nt* knife, fork and spoon, cutlery; (*MED*) set of instruments; **~kasten** *m* cutlery canteen.

bestehen [bə'ʃte:ən] *unreg vi* to exist; (*andauern*) to last ♦ *vt* (*Probe, Prüfung*) to pass; (*Kampf*) to win; **~ bleiben** to last, endure; (*Frage, Hoffnung*) to remain; **die Schwierigkeit/das Problem besteht darin, dass ...** the difficulty/problem lies in the fact that ..., the difficulty/problem is that ...; **~ auf** +*dat* to insist on; **~ aus** to consist of; **B~** *nt*: **seit B~ der Firma** ever since the firm came into existence *od* has existed.

bestehlen [bə'ʃte:lən] *unreg vt* to rob.

besteigen [bə'ʃtaɪgən] *unreg vt* to climb,

ascend; (*Pferd*) to mount; (*Thron*) to ascend.

Bestellbuch *nt* order book.

bestellen [bəˈʃtɛlən] *vt* to order; (*kommen lassen*) to arrange to see; (*nominieren*) to name; (*Acker*) to cultivate; (*Grüße, Auftrag*) to pass on; **wie bestellt und nicht abgeholt** (*hum: umg*) like orphan Annie; **er hat nicht viel/nichts zu** ~ he doesn't have much/any say here; **ich bin für 10 Uhr bestellt** I have an appointment for *od* at 10 o'clock; **es ist schlecht um ihn bestellt** (*fig*) he is in a bad way.

Bestell- *zW:* ~**formular** *nt* purchase order; ~**nummer** *f* order number; ~**schein** *m* order coupon.

Bestellung *f* (*COMM*) order; (*Bestellen*) ordering; (*Ernennung*) nomination, appointment.

bestenfalls [ˈbɛstənˈfals] *adv* at best.

bestens [ˈbɛstəns] *adv* very well.

besteuern [bəˈʃtɔʏərn] *vt* to tax.

bestialisch [bɛstiˈaːlɪʃ] (*umg*) *adj* awful, beastly.

besticken [bəˈʃtɪkən] *vt* to embroider.

Bestie [ˈbɛstiə] *f* (*lit, fig*) beast.

bestimmen [bəˈʃtɪmən] *vt* (*Regeln*) to lay down; (*Tag, Ort*) to fix; (*prägen*) to characterize; (*ausersehen*) to mean; (*ernennen*) to appoint; (*definieren*) to define; (*veranlassen*) to induce ♦ *vi:* **du hast hier nicht zu** ~ you don't make the decisions here; **er kann über sein Geld allein** ~ it is up to him what he does with his money.

bestimmend *adj* (*Faktor, Einfluss*) determining, decisive.

bestimmt *adj* (*entschlossen*) firm; (*gewiss*) certain, definite; (*Artikel*) definite ♦ *adv* (*gewiss*) definitely, for sure; **suchen Sie etwas B~es?** are you looking for anything in particular?; **B~heit** *f* certainty; **in** *od* **mit aller B~heit** quite categorically.

Bestimmung *f* (*Verordnung*) regulation; (*Festsetzen*) determining; (*Verwendungszweck*) purpose; (*Schicksal*) fate; (*Definition*) definition.

Bestimmungs- *zW:* ~**bahnhof** *m* (*EISENB*) destination; **b~gemäß** *adj* as agreed; ~**hafen** *m* (port of) destination; ~**ort** *m* destination.

Bestleistung *f* best performance.

bestmöglich *adj* best possible.

Best.-Nr. *abk* = **Bestellnummer**.

bestrafen [bəˈʃtraːfən] *vt* to punish.

Bestrafung *f* punishment.

bestrahlen [bəˈʃtraːlən] *vt* to shine on; (*MED*) to treat with X-rays.

Bestrahlung *f* (*MED*) X-ray treatment, radiotherapy.

Bestreben [bəˈʃtreːbən] (**-s**) *nt* endeavour (*BRIT*), endeavor (*US*), effort.

bestrebt [bəˈʃtreːpt] *adj:* ~ **sein, etw zu tun** to endeavour (*BRIT*) *od* endeavor (*US*) to do sth.

Bestrebung [bəˈʃtreːbʊŋ] *f* = **Bestreben**.

bestreichen [bəˈʃtraɪçən] *unreg vt* (*Brot*) to spread.

bestreiken [bəˈʃtraɪkən] *vt* (*INDUSTRIE*) to black; **die Fabrik wird zur Zeit bestreikt** there's a strike on in the factory at the moment.

bestreiten [bəˈʃtraɪtən] *unreg vt* (*abstreiten*) to dispute; (*finanzieren*) to pay for, finance; **er hat das ganze Gespräch allein bestritten** he did all the talking.

bestreuen [bəˈʃtrɔʏən] *vt* to sprinkle, dust; (*Straße*) to (spread with) grit.

Bestseller [ˈbɛstsɛlər] (**-s, -**) *m* best-seller.

bestürmen [bəˈʃtʏrmən] *vt* (*mit Fragen, Bitten etc*) to overwhelm, swamp.

bestürzen [bəˈʃtʏrtsən] *vt* to dismay.

bestürzt *adj* dismayed.

Bestürzung *f* consternation.

Bestzeit *f* (*bes SPORT*) best time.

Besuch [bəˈzuːx] (**-(e)s, -e**) *m* visit; (*Person*) visitor; **einen** ~ **bei jdm machen** to pay sb a visit *od* call; ~ **haben** to have visitors; **bei jdm auf** *od* **zu** ~ **sein** to be visiting sb.

besuchen *vt* to visit; (*SCH etc*) to attend; **gut besucht** well-attended.

Besucher(in) (**-s, -**) *m(f)* visitor, guest.

Besuchserlaubnis *f* permission to visit.

Besuchszeit *f* visiting hours *pl*.

besudeln [bəˈzuːdəln] *vt* (*Wände*) to smear; (*fig: Namen, Ehre*) to sully.

betagt [bəˈtaːkt] *adj* aged.

betasten [bəˈtastən] *vt* to touch, feel.

betätigen [bəˈtɛːtɪgən] *vt* (*bedienen*) to work, operate ♦ *vr* to involve o.s.; **sich politisch** ~ to be involved in politics; **sich als etw** ~ to work as sth.

Betätigung *f* activity; (*beruflich*) occupation; (*TECH*) operation.

betäuben [bəˈtɔʏbən] *vt* to stun; (*fig: Gewissen*) to still; (*MED*) to anaesthetize (*BRIT*), anesthetize (*US*); **ein** ~**der Duft** an overpowering smell.

Betäubung *f* (*Narkose*): **örtliche** ~ local anaesthetic (*BRIT*) *od* anesthetic (*US*).

Betäubungsmittel *nt* anaesthetic (*BRIT*), anesthetic (*US*).

Bete [ˈbeːtə] (**-, -n**) *f:* **Rote** ~ beetroot (*BRIT*), beet (*US*).

beteiligen [bəˈtaɪlɪgən] *vr:* **sich (an etw** *dat*) ~ to take part (in sth), participate (in sth); (*an Geschäft: finanziell*) to have a share (in sth) ♦ *vt:* **jdn (an etw** *dat*) ~ to give sb a share *od* interest (in sth); **sich an den Unkosten** ~ to contribute to the expenses.

Beteiligung *f* participation; (*Anteil*) share, interest; (*Besucherzahl*) attendance.

Beteiligungsgesellschaft *f* associated

company.
beten ['be:tən] *vi* to pray ♦ *vt* (*Rosenkranz*) to say.
beteuern [bə'tɔʏərn] *vt* to assert; (*Unschuld*) to protest; **jdm etw ~** to assure sb of sth.
Beteuerung *f* assertion; protestation; assurance.
Beton [be'tõː] (**-s, -s**) *m* concrete.
betonen [bə'toːnən] *vt* to stress.
betonieren [beto'niːrən] *vt* to concrete.
Betonmischmaschine *f* concrete mixer.
betont [bə'toːnt] *adj* (*Höflichkeit*) emphatic, deliberate; (*Kühle, Sachlichkeit*) pointed.
Betonung *f* stress, emphasis.
betören [bə'tøːrən] *vt* to beguile.
Betr. *abk* = **Betreff**.
betr. *abk* (= *betreffend, betreffs*) re.
Betracht [bə'traxt] *m*: **in ~ kommen** to be concerned *od* relevant; **nicht in ~ kommen** to be out of the question; **etw in ~ ziehen** to consider sth; **außer ~ bleiben** not to be considered.
betrachten *vt* to look at; (*fig*) to consider, look at.
Betrachter(in) (**-s, -**) *m(f)* onlooker.
beträchtlich [bə'trɛçtlɪç] *adj* considerable.
Betrachtung *f* (*Ansehen*) examination; (*Erwägung*) consideration; **über etw** *akk* **~en anstellen** to reflect on *od* contemplate sth.
betraf *etc* [bə'traːf] *vb siehe* **betreffen**.
Betrag [bə'traːk] (**-(e)s, ̈-e**) *m* amount, sum; **~ erhalten** (*COMM*) sum received.
betragen [bə'traːgən] *unreg vt* to amount to ♦ *vr* to behave.
Betragen (**-s**) *nt* behaviour (*BRIT*), behavior (*US*); (*bes in Zeugnis*) conduct.
beträgt [bə'trɛːkt] *vb siehe* **betragen**.
betrat *etc* [bə'traːt] *vb siehe* **betreten**.
betrauen [bə'trauən] *vt*: **jdn mit etw ~** to entrust sb with sth.
betrauern [bə'trauərn] *vt* to mourn.
beträufeln [bə'trɔʏfəln] *vt*: **den Fisch mit Zitrone ~** to sprinkle lemon juice on the fish.
Betreff *m*: **~: Ihr Schreiben vom ...** re *od* reference your letter of ...
betreffen [bə'trɛfən] *unreg vt* to concern, affect; **was mich betrifft** as for me.
betreffend *adj* relevant, in question.
betreffs [bə'trɛfs] *präp +gen* concerning, regarding.
betreiben [bə'traibən] *unreg vt* (*ausüben*) to practise (*BRIT*), practice (*US*); (*Politik*) to follow; (*Studien*) to pursue; (*vorantreiben*) to push ahead; (*TECH: antreiben*) to drive; **auf jds B~** *akk* **hin** (*form*) at sb's instigation.
betreten [bə'treːtən] *unreg vt* to enter; (*Bühne etc*) to step onto ♦ *adj* embarrassed; **„B~ verboten"** "keep off/out".
betreuen [bə'trɔʏən] *vt* to look after.

Betreuer(in) (**-s, -**) *m(f)* carer; (*Kinderbetreuer*) child-minder.
Betreuung *f*: **er wurde mit der ~ der Gruppe beauftragt** he was put in charge of the group.
Betrieb (**-(e)s, -e**) *m* (*Firma*) firm, concern; (*Anlage*) plant; (*Tätigkeit*) operation; (*Treiben*) bustle; (*Verkehr*) traffic; **außer ~ sein** to be out of order; **in ~ sein** to be in operation; **eine Maschine in/außer ~ setzen** to start a machine up/stop a machine; **eine Maschine/Fabrik in ~ nehmen** to put a machine/factory into operation; **in den Geschäften herrscht großer ~** the shops are very busy; **er hält den ganzen ~ auf** (*umg*) he's holding everything up.
betrieb *etc* [bə'triːp] *vb siehe* **betreiben**.
betrieben [bə'triːbən] *pp von* **betreiben**.
betrieblich *adj* company *attr* ♦ *adv* (*regeln*) within the company.
Betriebs- *zW*: **~anleitung** *f* operating instructions *pl*; **~ausflug** *m* firm's outing; **~ausgaben** *pl* revenue expenditure *sing*; **b~eigen** *adj* company *attr*; **~erlaubnis** *f* operating permission/licence (*BRIT*) *od* license (*US*); **b~fähig** *adj* in working order; **~ferien** *pl* company holidays *pl* (*BRIT*) *od* vacation *sing* (*US*); **~führung** *f* management; **~geheimnis** *nt* trade secret; **~kapital** *nt* capital employed; **~klima** *nt* (working) atmosphere; **~kosten** *pl* running costs; **~leitung** *f* management; **~rat** *m* workers' council; **~rente** *f* company pension; **b~sicher** *adj* safe, reliable; **~stoff** *m* fuel; **~störung** *f* breakdown; **~system** *nt* (*COMPUT*) operating system; **~unfall** *m* industrial accident; **~wirt** *m* management expert; **~wirtschaft** *f* business management.
betrifft [bə'trɪft] *vb siehe* **betreffen**.
betrinken [bə'trɪŋkən] *unreg vr* to get drunk.
betritt [bə'trɪt] *vb siehe* **betreten**.
betroffen [bə'trɔfən] *pp von* **betreffen** ♦ *adj* (*bestürzt*) amazed, perplexed; **von etw ~ werden** *od* **sein** to be affected by sth.
betrüben [bə'tryːbən] *vt* to grieve.
betrübt [bə'tryːpt] *adj* sorrowful, grieved.
Betrug (**-(e)s**) *m* deception; (*JUR*) fraud.
betrug *etc* [bə'truːk] *vb siehe* **betragen**.
betrügen [bə'tryːgən] *unreg vt* to cheat; (*JUR*) to defraud; (*Ehepartner*) to be unfaithful to ♦ *vr* to deceive o.s.
Betrüger(in) (**-s, -**) *m(f)* cheat, deceiver.
betrügerisch *adj* deceitful; (*JUR*) fraudulent; **in ~er Absicht** with intent to defraud.
betrunken [bə'trʊŋkən] *adj* drunk.
Betrunkene(r) *f(m)* drunk.
Bett [bɛt] (**-(e)s, -en**) *nt* bed; **im ~** in bed; **ins od zu ~ gehen** to go to bed; **~bezug** *m* duvet cover; **~decke** *f* blanket; (*Daunenbettdecke*) quilt; (*Überwurf*) bedspread.

bettelarm ['bɛtəl|arm] *adj* very poor, destitute.
Bettelei [bɛtə'laɪ] *f* begging.
Bettelmönch *m* mendicant *od* begging monk.
betteln *vi* to beg.
betten *vt* to make a bed for.
Bett- *zW:* ~**hupferl** (*SÜDD*) *nt* bedtime sweet; **b~lägerig** *adj* bedridden; ~**laken** *nt* sheet; ~**lektüre** *f* bedtime reading.
Bettler(in) ['bɛtlər(ɪn)] (-**s**, -) *m(f)* beggar.
Bett- *zW:* ~**nässer** (-**s**, -) *m* bedwetter; ~**schwere** (*umg*) *f:* **die nötige** ~**schwere haben/bekommen** to be/get tired enough to sleep; ~**tuch▲** *nt* sheet; ~**vorleger** *m* bedside rug; ~**wäsche** *f* bedclothes *pl*, bedding; ~**zeug** *nt* = **Bettwäsche.**
betucht [bə'tuːxt] (*umg*) *adj* well-to-do.
betulich [bə'tuːlɪç] *adj* (*übertrieben besorgt*) fussing *attr*; (*Redeweise*) twee.
betupfen [bə'tʊpfən] *vt* to dab; (*MED*) to swab.
Beugehaft ['bɔʏgəhaft] *f* (*JUR*) coercive detention.
beugen ['bɔʏgən] *vt* to bend; (*GRAM*) to inflect ♦ *vr* (+*dat*) (*sich fügen*) to bow (to).
Beule ['bɔʏlə] (-, -**n**) *f* bump.
beunruhigen [bə'|ʊnruːɪgən] *vt* to disturb, alarm ♦ *vr* to become worried.
Beunruhigung *f* worry, alarm.
beurkunden [bə'|uːrkʊndən] *vt* to attest, verify.
beurlauben [bə'|uːrlaʊbən] *vt* to give leave *od* holiday to (*BRIT*), grant vacation to (*US*); **beurlaubt sein** to have leave of absence; (*suspendiert sein*) to have been relieved of one's duties.
beurteilen [bə'|ʊrtaɪlən] *vt* to judge; (*Buch etc*) to review.
Beurteilung *f* judgement; (*von Buch etc*) review; (*Note*) mark.
Beute ['bɔʏtə] (-) *f* booty, loot; (*von Raubtieren etc*) prey.
Beutel (-**s**, -) *m* bag; (*Geld*~) purse; (*Tabaks*~) pouch.
bevölkern [bə'fœlkərn] *vt* to populate.
Bevölkerung *f* population.
Bevölkerungs- *zW:* ~**explosion** *f* population explosion; ~**schicht** *f* social stratum; ~**statistik** *f* vital statistics *pl*.
bevollmächtigen [bə'fɔlmɛçtɪgən] *vt* to authorize.
Bevollmächtigte(r) *f(m)* authorized agent.
Bevollmächtigung *f* authorization.
bevor [bə'foːr] *konj* before; ~**munden** *vt untr* to dominate; ~**stehen** *unreg vi:* (**jdm**) ~**stehen** to be in store (for sb); ~**stehend** *adj* imminent, approaching; ~**zugen** *vt untr* to prefer; ~**zugt** [bə'foːrtsuːkt] *adv:* **etw** ~**zugt abfertigen** *etc* to give sth priority; **B~zugung** *f* preference.
bewachen [bə'vaxən] *vt* to watch, guard.

bewachsen [bə'vaksən] *adj* overgrown.
Bewachung *f* (*Bewachen*) guarding; (*Leute*) guard, watch.
bewaffnen [bə'vafnən] *vt* to arm.
Bewaffnung *f* (*Vorgang*) arming; (*Ausrüstung*) armament, arms *pl*.
bewahren [bə'vaːrən] *vt* to keep; **jdn vor jdm/ etw** ~ to save sb from sb/sth; (**Gott**) **bewahre!** (*umg*) heaven *od* God forbid!
bewähren [bə'vɛːrən] *vr* to prove o.s.; (*Maschine*) to prove its worth.
bewahrheiten [bə'vaːrhaɪtən] *vr* to come true.
bewährt *adj* reliable.
Bewährung *f* (*JUR*) probation; **ein Jahr Gefängnis mit** ~ a suspended sentence of one year with probation.
Bewährungs- *zW:* ~**frist** *f* (period of) probation; ~**helfer** *m* probation officer; ~**probe** *f:* **etw einer** ~**probe** *dat* **unterziehen** to put sth to the test.
bewaldet [bə'valdət] *adj* wooded.
bewältigen [bə'vɛltɪgən] *vt* to overcome; (*Arbeit*) to finish; (*Portion*) to manage; (*Schwierigkeiten*) to cope with.
bewandert [bə'vandərt] *adj* expert, knowledgeable.
Bewandtnis [bə'vantnɪs] *f:* **damit hat es folgende** ~ the fact of the matter is this.
bewarb *etc* [bə'varp] *vb siehe* **bewerben.**
bewässern [bə'vɛsərn] *vt* to irrigate.
Bewässerung *f* irrigation.
bewegen [bə'veːgən] *vt, vr* to move; **der Preis bewegt sich um die 50 Euro** the price is about 50 euros; **jdn zu etw** ~ to induce sb to do sth.
Beweggrund *m* motive.
beweglich *adj* movable, mobile; (*flink*) quick.
bewegt [bə'veːkt] *adj* (*Leben*) eventful; (*Meer*) rough; (*ergriffen*) touched.
Bewegung *f* movement, motion; (*innere*) emotion; (*körperlich*) exercise; **sich** *dat* ~ **machen** to take exercise.
Bewegungsfreiheit *f* freedom of movement; (*fig*) freedom of action.
bewegungslos *adj* motionless.
Beweis [bə'vaɪs] (-**es**, -**e**) *m* proof; (*Zeichen*) sign; ~**aufnahme** *f* (*JUR*) taking *od* hearing of evidence; **b~bar** *adj* provable.
beweisen *unreg vt* to prove; (*zeigen*) to show; **was zu** ~ **war** QED.
Beweis- *zW:* ~**führung** *f* reasoning; (*JUR*) presentation of one's case; ~**kraft** *f* weight, conclusiveness; **b~kräftig** *adj* convincing, conclusive; ~**last** *f* (*JUR*) onus, burden of proof; ~**mittel** *nt* evidence; ~**not** *f* (*JUR*) lack of evidence; ~**stück** *nt* exhibit.
bewenden [bə'vɛndən] *vi:* **etw dabei** ~ **lassen** to leave sth at that.
bewerben [bə'vɛrbən] *unreg vr:* **sich** ~ (**um**) to apply (for).

Bewerber(in) (-s, -) *m(f)* applicant.
Bewerbung *f* application.
Bewerbungsunterlagen *pl* application documents.
bewerkstelligen [bə'vɛrkʃtɛlɪgən] *vt* to manage, accomplish.
bewerten [bə've:rtən] *vt* to assess.
bewies *etc* [bə'vi:s] *vb siehe* **beweisen**.
bewiesen [bə'vi:zən] *pp von* **beweisen**.
bewilligen [bə'vɪlɪgən] *vt* to grant, allow.
Bewilligung *f* granting.
bewirbt [bə'vɪrpt] *vb siehe* **bewerben**.
bewirken [bə'vɪrkən] *vt* to cause, bring about.
bewirten [bə'vɪrtən] *vt* to entertain.
bewirtschaften [bə'vɪrtʃaftən] *vt* to manage.
Bewirtung *f* hospitality; **die ~ so vieler Gäste** catering for so many guests.
bewog *etc* [bə'vo:k] *vb siehe* **bewegen**.
bewogen [bə'vo:gən] *pp von* **bewegen**.
bewohnbar *adj* inhabitable.
bewohnen [bə'vo:nən] *vt* to inhabit, live in.
Bewohner(in) (-s, -) *m(f)* inhabitant; (*von Haus*) resident.
bewölkt [bə'vœlkt] *adj* cloudy, overcast.
Bewölkung *f* clouds *pl*.
Bewölkungsauflockerung *f* break-up of the cloud.
beworben [bə'vɔrbən] *pp von* **bewerben**.
Bewunderer(in) (-s, -) *m(f)* admirer.
bewundern [bə'vʊndərn] *vt* to admire.
bewundernswert *adj* admirable, wonderful.
Bewunderung *f* admiration.
bewusst▲ [bə'vʊst] *adj* conscious; (*absichtlich*) deliberate; **jdm etw ~ machen** to make sb conscious of sth; **sich** *dat* **etw ~ machen** to realize sth; **sich** *dat* **einer Sache** *gen* **~ sein** to be aware of sth; **~los** *adj* unconscious; **B~losigkeit** *f* unconsciousness; **bis zur B~losigkeit** (*umg*) ad nauseam; **B~sein** *nt* consciousness; **bei B~sein** conscious; **im B~sein, dass ...** in the knowledge that ...
Bewusstseins-▲ *zW:* **~bildung** *f* (*POL*) shaping of political ideas; **b~erweiternd** *adj:* **b~erweiternde Drogen** mind-expanding drugs; **~erweiterung** *f* consciousness raising.
Bez. *abk* = **Bezirk**.
bez. *abk* (= *bezüglich*) re.
bezahlen [bə'tsa:lən] *vt* to pay (for); **es macht sich bezahlt** it will pay.
Bezahlfernsehen *nt* pay TV.
Bezahlung *f* payment; **ohne/gegen** *od* **für ~** without/for payment.
bezaubern [bə'tsaubərn] *vt* to enchant, charm.
bezeichnen [bə'tsaɪçnən] *vt* (*kennzeichnen*) to mark; (*nennen*) to call; (*beschreiben*) to describe; (*zeigen*) to show, indicate.
bezeichnend *adj:* **~ (für)** characteristic (of), typical (of).
Bezeichnung *f* (*Zeichen*) mark, sign;

(*Beschreibung*) description; (*Ausdruck*) expression, term.
bezeugen [bə'tsɔygən] *vt* to testify to.
bezichtigen [bə'tsɪçtɪgən] *vt* (+*gen*) to accuse (of).
Bezichtigung *f* accusation.
beziehen [bə'tsi:ən] *unreg vt* (*mit Überzug*) to cover; (*Haus, Position*) to move into; (*Standpunkt*) to take up; (*erhalten*) to receive; (*Zeitung*) to subscribe to, take ♦ *vr* (*Himmel*) to cloud over; **die Betten frisch ~** to change the beds; **etw auf jdn/etw ~** to relate sth to sb/sth; **sich ~ auf** +*akk* to refer to.
Beziehung *f* (*Verbindung*) connection; (*Zusammenhang*) relation; (*Verhältnis*) relationship; (*Hinsicht*) respect; **diplomatische ~en** diplomatic relations; **seine ~en spielen lassen** to pull strings; **in jeder ~** in every respect; **~en haben** (*vorteilhaft*) to have connections *od* contacts.
Beziehungskiste (*umg*) *f* relationship.
beziehungsweise *adv* or; (*genauer gesagt*) that is, or rather; (*im anderen Fall*) and ... respectively.
beziffern [bə'tsɪfərn] *vt* (*angeben*): **~ auf** +*akk* *od* **mit** to estimate at.
Bezirk [bə'tsɪrk] (-(e)s, -e) *m* district.
bezirzen [bə'tsɪrtsən] (*umg*) *vt* to bewitch.
bezogen [bə'tso:gən] *pp von* **beziehen**.
Bezogene(r) [bə'tso:gənə(r)] *f(m)* (*von Scheck etc*) drawee.
Bezug [bə'tsu:k] (-(e)s, ¨e) *m* (*Hülle*) covering; (*COMM*) ordering; (*Gehalt*) income, salary; (*Beziehung*): **~ (zu)** relationship (to); **in ~ auf** +*akk* with reference to; **mit** *od* **unter ~ auf** +*akk* regarding; (*form*) with reference to; **~ nehmen auf** +*akk* to refer to.
bezüglich [bə'tsy:klɪç] *präp* +*gen* concerning, referring to ♦ *adj* concerning; (*GRAM*) relative.
Bezugnahme *f:* **~ (auf** +*akk*) reference (to).
Bezugs- *zW:* **~person** *f:* **die wichtigste ~person des Kleinkindes** the person to whom the small child relates most closely; **~preis** *m* retail price; **~quelle** *f* source of supply.
bezuschussen [bə'tsu:ʃusən] *vt* to subsidize.
bezwecken [bə'tsvɛkən] *vt* to aim at.
bezweifeln [bə'tsvaɪfəln] *vt* to doubt.
bezwingen [bə'tsvɪŋən] *unreg vt* to conquer; (*Feind*) to defeat, overcome.
bezwungen [bə'tsvʊŋən] *pp von* **bezwingen**.
Bf. *abk* = **Bahnhof; Brief**.
BfA (-) *f abk* (= *Bundesversicherungsanstalt für Angestellte*) *Federal insurance company for employees.*
BfV (-) *nt abk* (= *Bundesamt für Verfassungsschutz*) *Federal Office for Protection of the Constitution.*
BG (-) *f abk* (= *Berufsgenossenschaft*) *professional association.*

BGB (-) *nt abk* (= *Bürgerliches Gesetzbuch*) *siehe* **bürgerlich**.

BGH (-) *m abk* (= *Bundesgerichtshof*) *Federal Supreme Court*.

BGS (-) *m abk* = **Bundesgrenzschutz**.

BH (-s, -(s)) *m abk* (= *Büstenhalter*) bra.

Bhf. *abk* = **Bahnhof**.

BI *f abk* = **Bürgerinitiative**.

Biathlon ['biːatlɔn] (-s, -s) *nt* biathlon.

bibbern ['bɪbərn] (*umg*) *vi* (*vor Kälte*) to shiver.

Bibel ['biːbəl] (-, -n) *f* Bible.

bibelfest *adj* well versed in the Bible.

Biber ['biːbər] (-s, -) *m* beaver.

Biberbetttuch▲ *nt* flannelette sheet.

Bibliografie▲ [bibliogra'fiː] *f* bibliography.

Bibliothek [biblio'teːk] (-, -en) *f* (*auch* *COMPUT*) library.

Bibliothekar(in) [bibliote'kaːr(ɪn)] (-s, -e) *m(f)* librarian.

biblisch ['biːblɪʃ] *adj* biblical.

bieder ['biːdər] *adj* upright, worthy; (*pej*) conventional; (*Kleid etc*) plain.

Biedermann (-(e)s, *pl* **-männer**) (*pej*) *m* (*geh*) petty bourgeois.

biegbar ['biːkbaːr] *adj* flexible.

Biege *f:* **die ~ machen** (*umg*) to buzz off, split.

biegen ['biːgən] *unreg vt, vr* to bend ♦ *vi* to turn; **sich vor Lachen ~** (*fig*) to double up with laughter; **auf B~ oder Brechen** (*umg*) by hook or by crook.

biegsam ['biːkzaːm] *adj* supple.

Biegung *f* bend, curve.

Biene ['biːnə] (-, -n) *f* bee; (*veraltet: umg: Mädchen*) bird (*BRIT*), chick (*bes US*).

Bienen- *zW:* **~honig** *m* honey; **~korb** *m* beehive; **~stich** *m* (*KOCH*) sugar-and-almond coated cake filled with custard or cream; **~stock** *m* beehive; **~wachs** *nt* beeswax.

Bier [biːr] (-(e)s, -e) *nt* beer; **zwei ~, bitte!** two beers, please.

Bier- *zW:* **~bauch** (*umg*) *m* beer belly; **~brauer** *m* brewer; **~deckel** *m* beer mat; **~filz** *m* beer mat; **~krug** *m* beer mug; **~schinken** *m* ham sausage; **~seidel** *nt* beer mug; **~wurst** *f* ham sausage.

Biest [biːst] (-(e)s, -er) (*pej: umg*) *nt* (*Mensch*) (little) wretch; (*Frau*) bitch (*!*).

biestig *adj* beastly.

bieten ['biːtən] *unreg vt* to offer; (*bei Versteigerung*) to bid ♦ *vr* (*Gelegenheit*): **sich jdm ~** to present itself to sb; **sich dat etw ~ lassen** to put up with sth.

Bigamie [biga'miː] *f* bigamy.

Bikini [bi'kiːni] (-s, -s) *m* bikini.

Bilanz [bi'lants] *f* balance; (*fig*) outcome; **eine ~ aufstellen** to draw up a balance sheet; **~ ziehen (aus)** to take stock (of); **~prüfer** *m* auditor.

bilateral ['biːlateraːl] *adj* bilateral; **~er Handel** bilateral trade; **~es Abkommen** bilateral agreement.

Bild [bɪlt] (-(e)s, -er) *nt* (*lit, fig*) picture; photo; (*Spiegel~*) reflection; (*fig: Vorstellung*) image, picture; **ein ~ machen** to take a photo *od* picture; **im ~e sein (über** +*akk*) to be in the picture (about); **~auflösung** *f* (*TV, COMPUT*) resolution; **~band** *m* illustrated book; **~bericht** *m* pictorial report; **~beschreibung** *f* (*SCH*) description of a picture.

bilden ['bɪldən] *vt* to form; (*erziehen*) to educate; (*ausmachen*) to constitute ♦ *vr* to arise; (*durch Lesen etc*) to improve one's mind; (*erziehen*) to educate o.s.

bildend *adj:* **die ~e Kunst** art.

Bilderbuch *nt* picture book.

Bilderrahmen *m* picture frame.

Bild- *zW:* **~fläche** *f* screen; (*fig*) scene; **von der ~fläche verschwinden** (*fig: umg*) to disappear (from the scene); **b~haft** *adj* (*Sprache*) vivid; **~hauer** *m* sculptor; **b~hübsch** *adj* lovely, pretty as a picture; **b~lich** *adj* figurative; pictorial; **sich dat etw b~lich vorstellen** to picture sth in one's mind's eye.

Bildnis ['bɪltnɪs] *nt* (*liter*) portrait.

Bild- *zW:* **~platte** *f* videodisc; **~röhre** *f* (*TV*) cathode ray tube; **~schirm** *m* (*TV, COMPUT*) screen; **~schirmgerät** *nt* (*COMPUT*) visual display unit, VDU; **~schirmschoner** (-s, -) *m* (*COMPUT*) screen saver; **~schirmtext** *m* teletext; ≈ Ceefax ®, Oracle ®; **b~schön** *adj* lovely.

Bildtelefon *nt* videophone.

Bildung ['bɪlduŋ] *f* formation; (*Wissen, Benehmen*) education.

Bildungs- *zW:* **~gang** *m* school (and university/college) career; **~gut** *nt* cultural heritage; **~lücke** *f* gap in one's education; **~politik** *f* educational policy; **~roman** *m* (*LITER*) Bildungsroman, *novel relating hero's intellectual/spiritual development*; **~urlaub** *m* educational holiday; **~weg** *m:* **auf dem zweiten ~weg** through night school/ the Open University *etc*; **~wesen** *nt* education system.

Bildweite *f* (*PHOT*) distance.

Bildzuschrift *f* reply enclosing photograph.

Billard ['bɪljart] (-s, -e) *nt* billiards; **~ball** *m* billiard ball; **~kugel** *f* billiard ball.

billig ['bɪlɪç] *adj* cheap; (*gerecht*) fair, reasonable; **~e Handelsflagge** flag of convenience; **~es Geld** cheap/easy money.

billigen ['bɪlɪgən] *vt* to approve of; **etw stillschweigend ~** to condone sth.

billigerweise *adv* (*veraltet*) in all fairness, reasonably.

Billigladen *m* discount store.

Billigpreis *m* low price.

Billigung *f* approval.

Billion [bɪliˈoːn] f billion (*BRIT*), trillion (*US*).
bimmeln [ˈbɪməln] vi to tinkle.
Bimsstein [ˈbɪmsʃtaɪn] m pumice stone.
bin [bɪn] vb siehe **sein**.
binär [biˈnɛːr] adj binary; **B~zahl** f binary number.
Binde [ˈbɪndə] (-, -n) f bandage; (*Armbinde*) band; (*MED*) sanitary towel (*BRIT*) od napkin (*US*); **sich** dat **einen hinter die ~ gießen** od **kippen** (umg) to put a few drinks away.
Binde- zW: **~glied** nt connecting link; **~hautentzündung** f conjunctivitis; **~mittel** nt binder.
binden unreg vt to bind, tie ♦ vr (*sich verpflichten*): **sich ~ (an** +akk) to commit o.s. (to).
bindend adj binding; (*Zusage*) definite; **~ für** binding on.
Bindestrich m hyphen.
Bindewort nt conjunction.
Bindfaden m string; **es regnet Bindfäden** (umg) it's sheeting down.
Bindung f bond, tie; (*SKI*) binding.
binnen [ˈbɪnən] präp (+dat od gen) within; **B~hafen** m inland harbour (*BRIT*) od harbor (*US*); **B~handel** m internal trade; **B~markt** m home market; **Europäischer B~markt** single European market.
Binse [ˈbɪnzə] (-, -n) f rush, reed; **in die ~n gehen** (fig: umg) to be a wash-out.
Binsenwahrheit f truism.
Biografie▲ [biograˈfiː] f biography.
Bioladen [ˈbiolaːdən] m health food shop (*BRIT*) od store (*US*).

BIOLADEN

A **Bioladen** is a shop which specializes in selling environmentally-friendly products such as phosphate-free washing powders, recycled paper and organically-grown vegetables.

Biologe [bioˈloːgə] (-n, -n) m biologist.
Biologie [bioloˈgiː] f biology.
Biologin f biologist.
biologisch [bioˈloːgɪʃ] adj biological; **~e Vielfalt** biodiversity; **~e Uhr** biological clock.
Bio- [bio-] zW: **~sphäre** f biosphere; **~technik** [bioˈtɛçnɪk] f biotechnology; **~terrorismus** m bioterrorism; **~treibstoff** [ˈbiːotraɪpʃtɔf] m biofuel.
birgt [bɪrkt] vb siehe **bergen**.
Birke [ˈbɪrkə] (-, -n) f birch.
Birma [ˈbɪrma] (-s) nt Burma.
Birnbaum m pear tree.
Birne [ˈbɪrnə] (-, -n) f pear; (*ELEK*) (light) bulb.
birst [bɪrst] vb siehe **bersten**.

bis [bɪs] präp +akk ♦ adv **1** (*zeitlich*) till, until; (**~** *spätestens*) by; **Sie haben ~ Dienstag Zeit** you have until od till Tuesday; **~ zum Wochenende** up to od until the weekend; (*spätestens*) by the weekend; **~ Dienstag muss es fertig sein** it must be ready by Tuesday; **~ wann ist das fertig?** when will that be finished?; **~ auf weiteres** until further notice; **~ in die Nacht** into the night; **~ bald!/gleich!** see you later/soon.
2 (*räumlich*) (up) to; **ich fahre ~ Köln** I'm going as far as Cologne; **~ an unser Grundstück** (right od up) to our plot; **~ hierher** this far; **~ zur Straße kommen** to get as far as the road.
3 (*bei Zahlen, Angaben*) up to; **~ zu** up to; **Gefängnis ~ zu 8 Jahren** a maximum of 8 years' imprisonment.
4 ~ auf etw akk (*außer*) except sth; (*einschließlich*) including sth.
♦ konj **1** (*mit Zahlen*) to; **10 ~ 20** 10 to 20.
2 (*zeitlich*) till, until; **~ es dunkel wird** till od until it gets dark; **von ... ~ ...** from ... to ...

Bisamratte [ˈbiːzamratə] f muskrat (beaver).
Bischof [ˈbɪʃɔf] (-s, ⸚e) m bishop.
bischöflich [ˈbɪʃøːflɪç] adj episcopal.
bisexuell [bizɛksuˈɛl] adj bisexual.
bisher [bɪsˈheːr] adv till now, hitherto.
bisherig [bɪsˈheːrɪç] adj till now.
Biskaya [bɪsˈkaːya] f: **Golf von ~** Bay of Biscay.
Biskuit [bɪsˈkviːt] (-(e)s, -s od -e) m od nt biscuit; **~gebäck** nt sponge cake(s); **~teig** m sponge mixture.
bislang [bɪsˈlaŋ] adv hitherto.
Biss▲ (-es, -e) m bite.
biss etc▲ [bɪs] vb siehe **beißen**.
bisschen▲ [ˈbɪsçən] adj, adv bit.
Bissen [ˈbɪsən] (-s, -) m bite, morsel; **sich** dat **jeden ~ vom** od **am Munde absparen** to watch every penny one spends.
bissig [ˈbɪsɪç] adj (*Hund*) snappy; vicious; (*Bemerkung*) cutting, biting; „**Vorsicht, ~er Hund**" "beware of the dog".
bist [bɪst] vb siehe **sein**.
Bistum [ˈbɪstuːm] nt bishopric.
bisweilen [bɪsˈvaɪlən] adv at times, occasionally.
Bit [bɪt] (-(s), -(s)) nt (*COMPUT*) bit.
Bittbrief m petition.
Bitte [ˈbɪtə] (-, -n) f request; **auf seine ~ hin** at his request; **b~** interj please; (*als Antwort auf Dank*) you're welcome; **wie b~?** (I beg your) pardon?; **b~ schön!** it was a pleasure; **b~ schön?** (*in Geschäft*) can I help you?; **na b~!** there you are!
bitten unreg vt to ask ♦ vi (*einladen*): **ich lasse ~**

bittend – blicken

would you ask him/her *etc* to come in now?; ~ **um** to ask for; **aber ich bitte dich!** not at all; **ich bitte darum** (*form*) if you wouldn't mind; **ich muss doch (sehr)** ~! well I must say!

bittend *adj* pleading, imploring.

bitter ['bɪtər] *adj* bitter; (*Schokolade*) plain; **etw** ~ **nötig haben** to be in dire need of sth; ~**böse** *adj* very angry; ~**ernst** *adj*: **damit ist es mir** ~**ernst** I am deadly serious *od* in deadly earnest; **B**~**keit** *f* bitterness; ~**lich** *adj* bitter ♦ *adv* bitterly.

Bittsteller(in) (-s, -) *m(f)* petitioner.

Biwak ['biːvak] (-s, -s *od* -e) *nt* bivouac.

Bj. *abk* = **Baujahr**.

Blabla [blaˈblaː] (-s) (*umg*) *nt* waffle.

blähen ['blɛːən] *vt, vr* to swell, blow out ♦ *vi* (*Speisen*) to cause flatulence *od* wind.

Blähungen *pl* (*MED*) wind *sing*.

blamabel [blaˈmaːbəl] *adj* disgraceful.

Blamage [blaˈmaːʒə] (-, -n) *f* disgrace.

blamieren [blaˈmiːrən] *vr* to make a fool of o.s., disgrace o.s. ♦ *vt* to let down, disgrace.

blank [blaŋk] *adj* bright; (*unbedeckt*) bare; (*sauber*) clean, polished; (*umg: ohne Geld*) broke; (*offensichtlich*) blatant.

blanko ['blaŋko] *adv* blank; **B**~**scheck** *m* blank cheque (*BRIT*) *od* check (*US*); **B**~**vollmacht** *f* carte blanche.

Bläschen ['blɛːsçən] *nt* bubble; (*MED*) small blister.

Blase ['blaːzə] (-, -n) *f* bubble; (*MED*) blister; (*ANAT*) bladder.

Blasebalg *m* bellows *pl*.

blasen *unreg vt, vi* to blow; **zum Aufbruch** ~ (*fig*) to say it's time to go.

Blasenentzündung *f* cystitis.

Bläser(in) ['blɛːzər(ɪn)] (-s, -) *m(f)* (*MUS*) wind player; **die** ~ the wind (section).

blasiert [blaˈziːrt] (*pej*) *adj* (*geh*) blasé.

Blas- *zW*: ~**instrument** *nt* wind instrument; ~**kapelle** *f* brass band; ~**musik** *f* brass band music.

blass▲ [blas] *adj* pale; (*Ausdruck*) weak, insipid; (*fig: Ahnung, Vorstellung*) faint, vague; ~ **vor Neid werden** to go green with envy.

Blässe ['blɛsə] (-) *f* paleness, pallor.

Blatt [blat] (-(e)s, ⁻er) *nt* leaf; (*von Papier*) sheet; (*Zeitung*) newspaper; (*KARTEN*) hand; **vom** ~ **singen/spielen** to sight-read; **kein** ~ **vor den Mund nehmen** not to mince one's words.

blättern ['blɛtərn] *vi*: **in etw** *dat* ~ to leaf through sth.

Blätterteig *m* flaky *od* puff pastry.

Blattlaus *f* greenfly, aphid.

blau [blau] *adj* blue; (*umg*) drunk, stoned; (*KOCH*) boiled; (*Auge*) black; ~**er Fleck** bruise; **mit einem** ~**en Auge davonkommen**

(*fig*) to get off lightly; ~**er Brief** (*SCH*) *letter telling parents a child may have to repeat a year*; **er wird sein** ~**es Wunder erleben** (*umg*) he won't know what's hit him; ~**äugig** *adj* blue-eyed; **B**~**beere** *f* bilberry.

Blaue *nt*: **Fahrt ins** ~ mystery tour; **das** ~ **vom Himmel (herunter) lügen** (*umg*) to tell a pack of lies.

blau- *zW*: **B**~**helm** (*umg*) *m* UN Soldier; **B**~**kraut** *nt* red cabbage; **B**~**licht** *nt* flashing blue light; ~**machen** (*umg*) *vi* to skive off work; **B**~**pause** *f* blueprint; **B**~**säure** *f* prussic acid; **B**~**strumpf** *m* (*fig*) bluestocking.

Blech [blɛç] (-(e)s, -e) *nt* tin, sheet metal; (*Back*~) baking tray; ~ **reden** (*umg*) to talk rubbish *od* nonsense; ~**bläser** *pl* the brass (section); ~**büchse** *f* tin, can; ~**dose** *f* tin, can.

blechen (*umg*) *vt, vi* to pay.

Blechschaden *m* (*AUT*) damage to bodywork.

Blechtrommel *f* tin drum.

blecken ['blɛkən] *vt*: **die Zähne** ~ to bare *od* show one's teeth.

Blei [blai] (-(e)s, -e) *nt* lead.

Bleibe (-, -n) *f* roof over one's head.

bleiben *unreg vi* to stay, remain; **bitte,** ~ **Sie doch sitzen** please don't get up; **wo bleibst du so lange?** (*umg*) what's keeping you?; **das bleibt unter uns** (*fig*) that's (just) between ourselves; ~ **lassen** (*aufgeben*) to give up; **etw** ~ **lassen** (*unterlassen*) to give sth a miss.

bleich [blaiç] *adj* faded, pale; ~**en** *vt* to bleach; **B**~**gesicht** (*umg*) *nt* (*blasser Mensch*) pasty-face.

bleiern *adj* leaden.

Blei- *zW*: **b**~**frei** *adj* lead-free; ~**gießen** *nt New Year's Eve fortune-telling using lead shapes*; **b**~**haltig** *adj*: **b**~**haltig sein** to contain lead; ~**stift** *m* pencil; ~**stiftabsatz** *m* stiletto heel (*BRIT*), spike heel (*US*); ~**stiftspitzer** *m* pencil sharpener; ~**vergiftung** *f* lead poisoning.

Blende ['blɛndə] (-, -n) *f* (*PHOT*) aperture; (: *Einstellungsposition*) f-stop.

blenden *vt* to blind, dazzle; (*fig*) to hoodwink.

blendend (*umg*) *adj* grand; ~ **aussehen** to look smashing.

Blender (-s, -) *m* con-man.

blendfrei ['blɛntfrai] *adj* (*Glas*) non-reflective.

Blick [blɪk] (-(e)s, -e) *m* (*kurz*) glance, glimpse; (*Anschauen*) look, gaze; (*Aussicht*) view; **Liebe auf den ersten** ~ love at first sight; **den** ~ **senken** to look down; **den bösen** ~ **haben** to have the evil eye; **einen (guten)** ~ **für etw haben** to have an eye for sth; **mit einem** ~ at a glance.

blicken *vi* to look; **das lässt tief** ~ that's very revealing; **sich** ~ **lassen** to put in an appearance.

Blick- *zW:* ~**fang** *m* eye-catcher; ~**feld** *nt* range of vision (*auch fig*); ~**kontakt** *m* visual contact; ~**punkt** *m:* **im** ~**punkt der Öffentlichkeit stehen** to be in the public eye.

blieb *etc* [bli:p] *vb siehe* **bleiben**.

blies *etc* [bli:s] *vb siehe* **blasen**.

blind [blɪnt] *adj* blind; (*Glas etc*) dull; (*Alarm*) false; ~**er Passagier** stowaway; ~ **schreiben** to touch type.

Blinddarm *m* appendix; ~**entzündung** *f* appendicitis.

Blindekuh [ˈblɪndəku:] *f:* ~ **spielen** to play blind man's buff.

Blindenhund *m* guide dog.

Blindenschrift *f* braille.

Blind- *zW:* ~**gänger** *m* (*MIL, fig*) dud; ~**heit** *f* blindness; **mit** ~**heit geschlagen sein** (*fig*) to be blind; **b**~**lings** *adv* blindly; ~**schleiche** *f* slow worm.

blinken [ˈblɪŋkən] *vi* to twinkle, sparkle; (*Licht*) to flash, signal; (*AUT*) to indicate ♦ *vt* to flash, signal.

Blinker (**-s, -**) *m* (*AUT*) indicator.

Blinklicht *nt* (*AUT*) indicator.

blinzeln [ˈblɪntsəln] *vi* to blink, wink.

Blitz [blɪts] (**-es, -e**) *m* (flash of) lightning; **wie ein** ~ **aus heiterem Himmel** (*fig*) like a bolt from the blue; ~**ableiter** *m* lightning conductor; (*fig*) vent *od* safety valve for feelings; **b**~**en** *vi* (*aufleuchten*) to glint, shine; **es b**~**t** (*MET*) there's a flash of lightning; ~**gerät** *nt* (*PHOT*) flash(gun); ~**licht** *nt* flashlight; **b**~**sauber** *adj* spick and span; **b**~**schnell** *adj, adv* as quick as a flash; ~**würfel** *m* (*PHOT*) flashcube.

Block [blɔk] (**-(e)s, ⁻e**) *m* (*lit, fig*) block; (*von Papier*) pad; (*POL: Staaten*~) bloc; (*Fraktion*) faction.

Blockade [blɔˈka:də] (**-, -n**) *f* blockade.

Block- *zW:* ~**buchstabe** *m* block letter *od* capital; ~**flöte** *f* recorder; **b**~**frei** *adj* (*POL*) non-aligned; ~**haus** *nt* log cabin; ~**hütte** *f* log cabin.

blockieren [blɔˈki:rən] *vt* to block ♦ *vi* (*Räder*) to jam.

Block- *zW:* ~**schokolade** *f* cooking chocolate; ~**schrift** *f* block letters *pl*; ~**stunde** *f* double period.

blöd [blø:t] *adj* silly, stupid.

blödeln [ˈblø:dəln] (*umg*) *vi* to fool around.

Blödheit *f* stupidity.

Blödian [ˈblø:dian] (**-(e)s, -e**) (*umg*) *m* idiot.

blöd- *zW:* **B**~**mann** (**-(e)s,** *pl* **-männer**) (*umg*) *m* idiot; **B**~**sinn** *m* nonsense; ~**sinnig** *adj* silly, idiotic.

blöken [ˈblø:kən] *vi* (*Schaf*) to bleat.

blond [blɔnt] *adj* blond(e), fair-haired.

Blondine [blɔnˈdi:nə] *f* blonde.

bloß [blo:s] *adj* **1** (*unbedeckt*) bare; (*nackt*) naked; **mit der** ~**en Hand** with one's bare hand; **mit** ~**em Auge** with the naked eye. **2** (*alleinig: nur*) mere; **der** ~**e Gedanke** the very thought; ~**er Neid** sheer envy.
♦ *adv* only, merely; **lass das** ~**!** just don't do that!; **wie ist das** ~ **passiert?** how on earth did that happen?

Blöße [ˈblø:sə] (**-, -n**) *f* bareness; nakedness; (*fig*) weakness; **sich** *dat* **eine** ~ **geben** (*fig*) to lay o.s. open to attack.

bloßlegen *vt* to expose.

bloßstellen *vt* to show up.

blühen [ˈbly:ən] *vi* (*lit*) to bloom, be in bloom; (*fig*) to flourish; (*umg: bevorstehen*): **(jdm)** ~ to be in store (for sb).

blühend *adj:* **wie das** ~**e Leben aussehen** to look the very picture of health.

Blume [ˈblu:mə] (**-, -n**) *f* flower; (*von Wein*) bouquet; **jdm etw durch die** ~ **sagen** to say sth in a roundabout way to sb.

Blumen- *zW:* ~**geschäft** *nt* flower shop, florist's; ~**kasten** *m* window box; ~**kohl** *m* cauliflower; ~**strauß** *m* bouquet, bunch of flowers; ~**topf** *m* flowerpot; ~**zwiebel** *f* bulb.

Bluse [ˈblu:zə] (**-, -n**) *f* blouse.

Blut [blu:t] (**-(e)s**) *nt* (*lit, fig*) blood; **(nur) ruhig** ~ keep your shirt on (*umg*); **jdn/sich bis aufs** ~ **bekämpfen** to fight sb/fight bitterly; **b**~**arm** *adj* anaemic (*BRIT*), anemic (*US*); (*fig*) penniless; ~**bahn** *f* bloodstream; ~**bank** *f* blood bank; **b**~**befleckt** *adj* bloodstained; ~**bild** *nt* blood count; ~**buche** *f* copper beech; ~**druck** *m* blood pressure.

Blüte [ˈbly:tə] (**-, -n**) *f* blossom; (*fig*) prime.

Blutegel [ˈblu:tˌe:gəl] *m* leech.

bluten *vi* to bleed.

Blütenstaub *m* pollen.

Bluter (**-s, -**) *m* (*MED*) haemophiliac (*BRIT*), hemophiliac (*US*).

Bluterguss▲ *m* haemorrhage (*BRIT*), hemorrhage (*US*); (*auf Haut*) bruise.

Blütezeit *f* flowering period; (*fig*) prime.

Blutgerinnsel *nt* blood clot.

Blutgruppe *f* blood group.

blutig *adj* bloody; (*umg: Anfänger*) absolute; (*: Ernst*) deadly.

Blut- *zW:* **b**~**jung** *adj* very young; ~**konserve** *f* unit *od* pint of stored blood; ~**körperchen** *nt* blood corpuscle; ~**probe** *f* blood test; **b**~**rünstig** *adj* bloodthirsty; ~**schande** *f* incest; ~**senkung** *f* (*MED*): **eine** ~**senkung machen** to test the sedimentation rate of the blood; ~**spender** *m* blood donor; **b**~**stillend** *adj* styptic; ~**sturz** *m* haemorrhage (*BRIT*), hemorrhage (*US*).

blutsverwandt *adj* related by blood.

Blutübertragung *f* blood transfusion.

Blutung *f* bleeding, haemorrhage (*BRIT*), hemorrhage (*US*).

Blut- *zW:* **b~unterlaufen** *adj* suffused with blood; (*Augen*) bloodshot; **~vergießen** *nt* bloodshed; **~vergiftung** *f* blood poisoning; **~wurst** *f* black pudding; **~zuckerspiegel** *m* blood sugar level.

BLZ *abk* = **Bankleitzahl.**

BMX-Rad *nt* BMX.

BND (**-s**, -) *m abk* = **Bundesnachrichtendienst.**

Bö (**-**, **-en**) *f* squall.

Boccia ['bɔtʃa] *nt od f* bowls *sing.*

Bock [bɔk] (**-(e)s**, **ᵘe**) *m* buck, ram; (*Gestell*) trestle, support; (*SPORT*) buck; **alter ~** (*umg*) old goat; **den ~ zum Gärtner machen** (*fig*) to choose the worst possible person for the job; **einen ~ schießen** (*fig: umg*) to (make a) boob; **~ haben, etw zu tun** (*umg: Lust*) to fancy doing sth.

Bockbier *nt* bock (beer) (*type of strong beer*).

bocken ['bɔkən] (*umg*) *vi* (*Auto, Mensch*) to play up.

Bocksbeutel *m* wide, rounded (dumpy) bottle containing Franconian wine.

Bockshorn *nt:* **sich von jdm ins ~ jagen lassen** to let sb upset one.

Bocksprung *m* leapfrog; (*SPORT*) vault.

Bockwurst *f* bockwurst (*large frankfurter*).

Boden ['boːdən] (**-s**, **ᵘ**) *m* ground; (*Fuß~*) floor; (*Meeres~, Fass~*) bottom; (*Speicher*) attic; **den ~ unter den Füßen verlieren** (*lit*) to lose one's footing; (*fig: in Diskussion*) to get out of one's depth; **ich hätte (vor Scham) im ~ versinken können** (*fig*) I was so ashamed, I wished the ground would swallow me up; **am ~ zerstört sein** (*umg*) to be shattered; **etw aus dem ~ stampfen** (*fig*) to conjure sth up out of nothing; (*Häuser*) to build overnight; **auf dem ~ der Tatsachen bleiben** (*fig: Grundlage*) to stick to the facts; **zu ~ fallen** to fall to the ground; **festen ~ unter den Füßen haben** to be on firm ground, be on terra firma; **~kontrolle** *f* (*RAUMFAHRT*) ground control; **b~los** *adj* bottomless; (*umg*) incredible; **~personal** *nt* (*AVIAT*) ground personnel *pl*, ground staff; **~satz** *m* dregs *pl*, sediment; **~schätze** *pl* mineral wealth *sing.*

Bodensee ['boːdənzeː] *m:* **der ~** Lake Constance.

Bodenturnen *nt* floor exercises *pl.*

Böe (**-**, **-n**) *f* squall.

bog *etc* [boːk] *vb siehe* **biegen.**

Bogen ['boːgən] (**-s**, -) *m* (*Biegung*) curve; (*ARCHIT*) arch; (*Waffe, MUS*) bow; (*Papier*) sheet; **den ~ heraushaben** (*umg*) to have got the hang of it; **einen großen ~ um jdn/etw machen** (*meiden*) to give sb/sth a wide berth; **jdn in hohem ~ hinauswerfen** (*umg*) to fling sb out; **~gang** *m* arcade; **~schütze** *m* archer.

Bohle ['boːlə] (**-**, **-n**) *f* plank.

Böhme ['bøːmə] (**-n**, **-n**) *m* Bohemian.

Böhmen (**-s**) *nt* Bohemia.

Böhmin *f* Bohemian woman.

böhmisch ['bøːmɪʃ] *adj* Bohemian; **das sind für mich ~e Dörfer** (*umg*) that's all Greek to me.

Bohne ['boːnə] (**-**, **-n**) *f* bean; **blaue ~** (*umg*) bullet; **nicht die ~** not one little bit.

Bohnen- *zW:* **~kaffee** *m* real coffee; **~stange** *f* (*fig: umg*) beanpole; **~stroh** *nt:* **dumm wie ~stroh** (*umg*) (as) thick as two (short) planks.

bohnern *vt* to wax, polish.

Bohnerwachs *nt* floor polish.

bohren ['boːrən] *vt* to bore; (*Loch*) to drill ♦ *vi* to drill; (*fig: drängen*) to keep on; (*peinigen: Schmerz, Zweifel etc*) to gnaw; **nach Öl/Wasser ~** drill for oil/water; **in der Nase ~** to pick one's nose.

Bohrer (**-s**, -) *m* drill.

Bohr- *zW:* **~insel** *f* oil rig; **~maschine** *f* drill; **~turm** *m* derrick.

Boiler ['bɔylər] (**-s**, -) *m* water heater.

Boje ['boːjə] (**-**, **-n**) *f* buoy.

Bolivianer(in) [boliviˈaːnər(ɪn)] (**-s**, -) *m(f)* Bolivian.

Bolivien [boˈliːviən] *nt* Bolivia.

bolivisch [boˈliːvɪʃ] *adj* Bolivian.

Bollwerk ['bɔlvɛrk] *nt* (*lit, fig*) bulwark.

Bolschewismus [bɔlʃeˈvɪsmʊs] (**-**) *m* Bolshevism.

Bolzen ['bɔltsən] (**-s**, -) *m* bolt.

bombardieren [bɔmbarˈdiːrən] *vt* to bombard; (*aus der Luft*) to bomb.

Bombe ['bɔmbə] (**-**, **-n**) *f* bomb; **wie eine ~ einschlagen** to come as a (real) bombshell.

Bomben- *zW:* **~alarm** *m* bomb scare; **~angriff** *m* bombing raid; **~anschlag** *m* bomb attack; **~erfolg** (*umg*) *m* huge success; **~geschäft** (*umg*) *nt:* **ein ~geschäft machen** to do a roaring trade; **b~sicher** (*umg*) *adj* dead certain.

bombig (*umg*) *adj* great, super.

Bon [bɔŋ] (**-s**, **-s**) *m* voucher; (*Kassenzettel*) receipt.

Bonbon [bõˈbõː] (**-s**, **-s**) *nt od m* sweet.

Bonn [bɔn] (**-s**) *nt* Bonn.

Bonze ['bɔntsə] (**-n**, **-n**) *m* big shot (*umg*).

Bonzenviertel (*umg*) *nt* posh quarter (*of town*).

Boot [boːt] (**-(e)s**, **-e**) *nt* boat.

Bord [bɔrt] (**-(e)s**, **-e**) *m* (*AVIAT, NAUT*) board ♦ *nt* (*Brett*) shelf; **über ~ gehen** to go overboard; (*fig*) to go by the board; **an ~** on board.

Bordell [bɔrˈdɛl] (**-s**, **-e**) *nt* brothel.

Bordfunkanlage *f* radio.

Bordstein *m* kerb(stone) (*BRIT*), curb(-

stone) (*US*).

borgen ['bɔrgən] *vt* to borrow; **jdm etw ~ to** lend sb sth.

Borneo ['bɔrneo] **(-s)** *nt* Borneo.

borniert [bɔr'niːrt] *adj* narrow-minded.

Börse ['bœːrzə] **(-, -n)** *f* stock exchange; (*Geld~*) purse.

Börsen- *zW*: **~makler** *m* stockbroker; **b~notiert** *adj*: **b~notierte Firma** listed company; **~notierung** *f* quotation (on the stock exchange).

Borste ['bɔrstə] **(-, -n)** *f* bristle.

Borte ['bɔrtə] **(-, -n)** *f* edging; (*Band*) trimming.

bös [bøːs] *adj* = **böse**; **~artig** *adj* malicious; (*MED*) malignant.

Böschung ['bœʃʊŋ] *f* slope; (*Ufer~ etc*) embankment.

böse ['bøːzə] *adj* bad, evil; (*zornig*) angry; **das war nicht ~ gemeint** I/he *etc* didn't mean it nastily.

Bösewicht (*umg*) *m* baddy.

boshaft ['boːshaft] *adj* malicious, spiteful.

Bosheit *f* malice, spite.

Bosnien ['bɔsniən] **(-s)** *nt* Bosnia.

Bosnien-Herzegowina ['bɔsniənhɛrtsə'goːviːna] **(-s)** *nt* Bosnia-Herzegovina.

Bosnier(in) **(-s, -)** *m(f)* Bosnian.

bosnisch *adj* Bosnian.

Boss▲ [bɔs] **(-es, -e)** (*umg*) *m* boss.

böswillig ['bøːsvɪlɪç] *adj* malicious.

bot *etc* [boːt] *vb siehe* **bieten**.

Botanik [bo'taːnɪk] *f* botany.

botanisch [bo'taːnɪʃ] *adj* botanical.

Bote ['boːtə] **(-n, -n)** *m* messenger.

Botengang *m* errand.

Botenjunge *m* errand boy.

Botin ['boːtɪn] *f* messenger.

Botschaft *f* message, news; (*POL*) embassy; **die Frohe ~** the Gospel; **~er (-s, -)** *m* ambassador.

Botswana [bɔ'tsvaːna] **(-s)** *nt* Botswana.

Bottich ['bɔtɪç] **(-(e)s, -e)** *m* vat, tub.

Bouillon [bʊ'ljõː] **(-, -s)** *f* consommé.

Boulevard- [bulə'vaːr] *zW*: **~blatt** (*umg*) *nt* tabloid; **~presse** *f* tabloid press; **~stück** *nt* light play/comedy.

Boutique [bu'tiːk] **(-, -n)** *f* boutique.

Bowle ['boːlə] **(-, -n)** *f* punch.

Bowlingbahn ['boːlɪŋbaːn] *f* bowling alley.

Box [bɔks] *f* (*Lautsprecher~*) speaker.

boxen *vi* to box.

Boxer **(-s, -)** *m* boxer.

Boxhandschuh *m* boxing glove.

Boxkampf *m* boxing match.

Boykott [bɔy'kɔt] **(-(e)s, -s)** *m* boycott.

boykottieren [bɔykɔ'tiːrən] *vt* to boycott.

BR *abk* (= *Bayerischer Rundfunk*) *German radio station.*

brach *etc* [braːx] *vb siehe* **brechen**.

brachial [braxi'aːl] *adj*: **mit ~er Gewalt** by brute force.

brachliegen ['braːxliːgən] *unreg vi* (*lit, fig*) to lie fallow.

brachte *etc* ['braxtə] *vb siehe* **bringen**.

Branche ['brãːʃə] **(-, -n)** *f* line of business.

Branchenführer(in) *m(f)* market leader.

Branchenverzeichnis *nt* trade directory.

Brand [brant] **(-(e)s, ⁻e)** *m* fire; (*MED*) gangrene.

Brandanschlag *m* arson attack.

branden ['brandən] *vi* to surge; (*Meer*) to break.

Brandenburg ['brandənbʊrk] **(-s)** *nt* Brandenburg.

Brandherd *m* source of the fire.

brandmarken *vt* to brand; (*fig*) to stigmatize.

brandneu (*umg*) *adj* brand-new.

Brand- *zW*: **~salbe** *f* ointment for burns; **~satz** *m* incendiary device; **~stifter** *m* arsonist, fire-raiser; **~stiftung** *f* arson.

Brandung *f* surf.

Brandwunde *f* burn.

brannte *etc* ['brantə] *vb siehe* **brennen**.

Branntwein ['brantvain] *m* brandy; **~steuer** *f* tax on spirits.

Brasilianer(in) [brazili'aːnər(ın)] **(-s, -)** *m(f)* Brazilian.

brasilianisch *adj* Brazilian.

Brasilien [bra'ziːliən] *nt* Brazil.

brät [brɛt] *vb siehe* **braten**.

Bratapfel *m* baked apple.

braten ['braːtən] *unreg vt* to roast; (*in Pfanne*) to fry; **B~ (-s, -)** (*umg*) *m* roast, joint; **den B~ riechen** (*umg*) to smell a rat, suss something.

Brat- *zW*: **~hähnchen** *nt* (*SÜDD, ÖSTERR*) roast chicken; **~hendl** *nt* roast chicken; **~huhn** *nt* roast chicken; **~kartoffeln** *pl* fried/roast potatoes *pl*; **~pfanne** *f* frying pan; **~rost** *m* grill.

Bratsche ['braːtʃə] **(-, -n)** *f* viola.

Bratspieß *m* spit.

Bratwurst *f* grilled sausage.

Brauch [braux] **(-(e)s, *pl* Bräuche)** *m* custom.

brauchbar *adj* usable, serviceable; (*Person*) capable.

brauchen *vt* (*bedürfen*) to need; (*müssen*) to have to; (*verwenden*) to use; **wie lange braucht man, um ...?** how long does it take to ...?

Brauchtum *nt* customs *pl*, traditions *pl*.

Braue ['brauə] **(-, -n)** *f* brow.

brauen ['brauən] *vt* to brew.

Brauerei [brauə'rai] *f* brewery.

braun [braun] *adj* brown; (*von Sonne*) tanned; **~ gebrannt** tanned; (*pej*) Nazi.

Bräune ['brɔynə] **(-, -n)** *f* brownness; (*Sonnen~*) tan.

bräunen *vt* to make brown; (*Sonne*) to tan.

Braunkohle f brown coal.
Braunschweig ['braʊnʃvaɪk] (-s) nt Brunswick.
Brause ['braʊzə] (-, -n) f shower; (von Gießkanne) rose; (Getränk) lemonade.
brausen vi to roar; (auch vr: duschen) to take a shower.
Brausepulver nt lemonade powder.
Brausetablette f lemonade tablet.
Braut [braʊt] (-, pl **Bräute**) f bride; (Verlobte) fiancée.
Bräutigam ['brɔʏtɪgam] (-s, -e) m bridegroom; (Verlobter) fiancé.
Braut- zW: ~**jungfer** f bridesmaid; ~**kleid** nt wedding dress; ~**paar** nt bride and bridegroom, bridal pair.
brav [braːf] adj (artig) good; (ehrenhaft) worthy, honest; (bieder: Frisur, Kleid) plain; **sei schön** ~! be a good boy/girl.
BRD (-) f abk (= Bundesrepublik Deutschland) FRG; **die alte** ~ former West Germany.

> **BRD**
>
> The **BRD** (Bundesrepublik Deutschland) is the official name for the Federal Republic of Germany. It comprises 16 **Länder** (see **Land**). It was the name given to the former West Germany as opposed to East Germany (the **DDR**). The two Germanies were reunited on 3rd October 1990.

Brechbohne f French bean.
Brecheisen nt crowbar.
brechen unreg vt, vi to break; (Licht) to refract; (speien) to vomit; **die Ehe** ~ to commit adultery; **mir bricht das Herz** it breaks my heart; ~**d voll sein** to be full to bursting.
Brechmittel nt: **er/das ist das reinste** ~ (umg) he/it makes me feel ill.
Brechreiz m nausea.
Brechung f (des Lichts) refraction.
Brei [braɪ] (-(e)s, -e) m (Masse) pulp; (KOCH) gruel; (Hafer~) porridge (BRIT), oatmeal (US); (für Kinder, Kranke) mash; **um den heißen** ~ **herumreden** (umg) to beat about the bush.
breit [braɪt] adj broad; (bei Maßangabe) wide; **die** ~**e Masse** the masses pl ♦ adv: **ein** ~ **gefächertes Angebot** a wide range; **sich** ~ **machen** to spread o.s. out; ~ **treten** (umg) to go on about; ~**beinig** adj with one's legs apart.
Breite (-, -n) f breadth; (bei Maßangabe) width; (GEOG) latitude.
breiten vt: **etw über etw** akk ~ to spread sth over sth.
Breitengrad m degree of latitude.
Breitensport m popular sport.
breit- zW: ~**schlagen** unreg (umg) vt: **sich** ~**schlagen lassen** to let o.s. be talked round;

~**schult(e)rig** adj broad-shouldered; **B**~**wandfilm** m wide-screen film.
Bremen ['breːmən] (-s) nt Bremen.
Bremsbelag m brake lining.
Bremse ['brɛmzə] (-, -n) f brake; (ZOOL) horsefly.
bremsen vi to brake, apply the brakes ♦ vt (Auto) to brake; (fig) to slow down ♦ vr: **ich kann mich** ~ (umg) not likely!
Brems- zW: ~**flüssigkeit** f brake fluid; ~**licht** nt brake light; ~**pedal** nt brake pedal; ~**schuh** m brake shoe; ~**spur** f tyre (BRIT) od tire (US) marks pl; ~**weg** m braking distance.
brennbar adj inflammable; **leicht** ~ highly inflammable.
Brennelement nt fuel element.
brennen ['brɛnən] unreg vi to burn, be on fire; (Licht, Kerze etc) to burn ♦ vt (Holz etc) to burn; (Ziegel, Ton) to fire; (Kaffee) to roast; (Branntwein) to distil; **wo brennts denn?** (fig: umg) what's the panic?; **darauf** ~, **etw zu tun** to be dying to do sth.
Brenn- zW: ~**material** nt fuel; ~**nessel** ▲ f nettle; ~**ofen** m kiln; ~**punkt** m (MATH, OPTIK) focus; ~**spiritus** m methylated spirits pl; ~**stoff** m liquid fuel.
brenzlig ['brɛntslɪç] adj smelling of burning, burnt; (fig) precarious.
Bresche ['brɛʃə] (-, -n) f: **in die** ~ **springen** (fig) to step into the breach.
Bretagne [bre'tanjə] f: **die** ~ Brittany.
Bretone [bre'toːnə] (-n, -n) m Breton.
Bretonin [bre'toːnɪn] f Breton.
Brett [brɛt] (-(e)s, -er) nt board, plank; (Bord) shelf; (Spiel~) board; **Bretter** pl (SKI) skis pl; (THEAT) boards pl; **schwarzes** ~ notice board; **er hat ein** ~ **vor dem Kopf** (umg) he's really thick.
brettern (umg) vi to speed.
Bretterzaun m wooden fence.
Brezel ['breːtsəl] (-, -n) f pretzel.
bricht [brɪçt] vb siehe **brechen**.
Brief [briːf] (-(e)s, -e) m letter; ~**beschwerer** (-s, -) m paperweight; ~**drucksache** f circular; ~**freund(in)** m(f) pen friend, pen-pal; ~**kasten** m letter box; (COMPUT) mailbox; ~**kopf** m letterhead; **b**~**lich** adj, adv by letter; ~**marke** f postage stamp; ~**öffner** m letter opener; ~**papier** nt notepaper; ~**qualität** f (COMPUT) letter quality; ~**tasche** f wallet; ~**taube** f carrier pigeon; ~**träger** m postman; ~**umschlag** m envelope; ~**wahl** f postal vote; ~**wechsel** m correspondence.
briet etc [briːt] vb siehe **braten**.
Brigade [bri'gaːdə] (-, -n) f (MIL) brigade; (DDR) (work) team od group.
Brikett [bri'kɛt] (-s, -s) nt briquette.
brillant [brɪl'jant] adj (fig) sparkling, brilliant; **B**~ (-en, -en) m brilliant, diamond.
Brille ['brɪlə] (-, -n) f spectacles pl; (Schutz~)

goggles *pl*; (*Toiletten~*) (toilet) seat.

Brillenschlange *f* (*hum*) four-eyes.

Brillenträger(in) *m(f)*: **er ist** ~ he wears glasses.

bringen ['brɪŋən] *unreg vt* to bring; (*mitnehmen, begleiten*) to take; (*einbringen: Profit*) to bring in; (*veröffentlichen*) to publish; (*THEAT, FILM*) to show; (*RUNDF, TV*) to broadcast; (*in einen Zustand versetzen*) to get; (*umg: tun können*) to manage; **jdn dazu** ~, **etw zu tun** to make sb do sth; **jdn zum Lachen/Weinen** ~ to make sb laugh/cry; **es weit** ~ to do very well, get far; **jdn nach Hause** ~ to take sb home; **jdn um etw** ~ to make sb lose sth; **jdn auf eine Idee** ~ to give sb an idea.

brisant [bri'zant] *adj* (*fig*) controversial.

Brisanz [bri'zants] *f* (*fig*) controversial nature.

Brise ['briːzə] (-, -n) *f* breeze.

Brite ['briːtə] (-n, -n) *m* Briton, Britisher (*US*); **die ~n** the British.

Britin *f* Briton, Britisher (*US*).

britisch ['briːtɪʃ] *adj* British; **die B~en Inseln** the British Isles.

bröckelig ['brœkəlɪç] *adj* crumbly.

Brocken ['brɔkən] (-s, -) *m* piece, bit; (*Felsbrocken*) lump of rock; **ein paar** ~ **Spanisch** a smattering of Spanish; **ein harter** ~ (*umg*) a tough nut to crack.

brodeln ['broːdəln] *vi* to bubble.

Brokat [bro'kaːt] (-(e)s, -e) *m* brocade.

Brokkoli ['brɔkoli] *pl* broccoli.

Brombeere ['brɔmbeːrə] *f* blackberry, bramble (*BRIT*).

bronchial [brɔnçi'aːl] *adj* bronchial.

Bronchien ['brɔnçiən] *pl* bronchial tubes *pl*.

Bronchitis [brɔn'çiːtɪs] (-, -tiden) *f* bronchitis.

Bronze ['brõːsə] (-, -n) *f* bronze.

Brosame ['broːzaːmə] (-, -n) *f* crumb.

Brosche ['brɔʃə] (-, -n) *f* brooch.

Broschüre [brɔ'ʃyːrə] (-, -n) *f* pamphlet.

Brot [broːt] (-(e)s, -e) *nt* bread; (*~laib*) loaf; **das ist ein hartes** ~ (*fig*) that's a hard way to earn one's living.

Brötchen ['brøːtçən] *nt* roll; **kleine** ~ **backen** (*fig*) to set one's sights lower; **~geber** *m* (*hum*) employer, provider (*hum*).

brotlos ['broːtloːs] *adj* (*Person*) unemployed; (*Arbeit etc*) unprofitable.

Brotzeit (*SÜDD*) *f* (*Pause*) ≈ tea break.

browsen ['brauzən] *vi* (*COMPUT*) to browse.

BRT *abk* (= *Bruttoregistertonne*) GRT.

Bruch [brux] (-(e)s, ⁻e) *m* breakage; (*zerbrochene Stelle*) break; (*fig*) split, breach; (*MED: Eingeweide~*) rupture, hernia; (*Bein~ etc*) fracture; (*MATH*) fraction; **zu** ~ **gehen** to get broken; **sich einen** ~ **heben** to rupture o.s.; **~bude** (*umg*) *f* shack.

brüchig ['brʏçɪç] *adj* brittle, fragile.

Bruch- *zW*: **~landung** *f* crash landing; **~schaden** *m* breakage; **~stelle** *f* break; (*von*

Knochen) fracture; **~strich** *m* (*MATH*) line; **~stück** *nt* fragment; **~teil** *m* fraction.

Brücke ['brʏkə] (-, -n) *f* bridge; (*Teppich*) rug; (*Turnen*) crab.

Bruder ['bruːdər] (-s, ⁻) *m* brother; **unter Brüdern** (*umg*) between friends.

brüderlich *adj* brotherly; **B~keit** *f* fraternity.

Brudermord *m* fratricide.

Brüderschaft *f* brotherhood, fellowship; ~ **trinken** to agree to use the familiar "du" (*over a drink*).

Brühe ['bryːə] (-, -n) *f* broth, stock; (*pej*) muck.

brühwarm ['bryː'varm] (*umg*) *adj*: **er hat das sofort** ~ **weitererzählt** he promptly spread it around.

Brühwürfel *m* stock cube (*BRIT*), bouillon cube (*US*).

brüllen ['brʏlən] *vi* to bellow, roar.

Brummbär *m* grumbler.

brummeln ['brʊməln] *vt, vi* to mumble.

brummen *vi* (*Bär, Mensch etc*) to growl; (*Insekt, Radio*) to buzz; (*Motor*) to roar; (*murren*) to grumble ♦ *vt* to growl; **jdm brummt der Kopf** sb's head is buzzing.

Brummer ['brʊmər] (-s, -) (*umg*) *m* (*Lastwagen*) juggernaut.

brummig (*umg*) *adj* grumpy.

Brummschädel (*umg*) *m* thick head.

brünett [brʏ'nɛt] *adj* brunette, brown-haired.

Brunnen ['brʊnən] (-s, -) *m* fountain; (*tief*) well; (*natürlich*) spring; **~kresse** *f* watercress.

Brunst [brʊnst] *f* (*von männlichen Tieren*) rut; (*von weiblichen Tieren*) heat; **~zeit** *f* rutting season.

brüsk [brʏsk] *adj* abrupt, brusque.

brüskieren [brʏs'kiːrən] *vt* to snub.

Brüssel ['brʏsəl] (-s) *nt* Brussels.

Brust [brʊst] (-, ⁻e) *f* breast; (*Männer~*) chest; **einem Kind die** ~ **geben** to breast-feed (*BRIT*) *od* nurse (*US*) a baby.

brüsten ['brʏstən] *vr* to boast.

Brust- *zW*: **~fellentzündung** *f* pleurisy; **~kasten** *m* chest; **~korb** *m* (*ANAT*) thorax; **~schwimmen** *nt* breast-stroke; **~ton** *m*: **im ~ton der Überzeugung** in a tone of utter conviction.

Brüstung ['brʏstʊŋ] *f* parapet.

Brustwarze *f* nipple.

Brut [bruːt] (-, -en) *f* brood; (*Brüten*) hatching.

brutal [bru'taːl] *adj* brutal; **B~ität** *f* brutality.

Brutapparat *m* incubator.

brüten ['bryːtən] *vi* (*auch fig*) to brood; **~de Hitze** oppressive *od* stifling heat.

Brüter (-s, -) *m* (*TECH*): **schneller** ~ fast-breeder (reactor).

Brutkasten *m* incubator.

Brutstätte *f* (*+gen*) (*lit, fig*) breeding ground (for).

brutto ['brʊto] *adv* gross; **B~einkommen** *nt*

gross salary; **B~gehalt** nt gross salary;
B~gewicht nt gross weight; **B~gewinn** m
gross profit; **B~inlandsprodukt** nt gross
domestic product; **B~lohn** m gross wages pl;
B~sozialprodukt nt gross national product.
brutzeln ['brʊtsəln] (umg) vi to sizzle away
♦ vt to fry (up).
Btx abk = **Bildschirmtext**.
Bub [buːp] (-en, -en) m boy, lad.
Bube ['buːbə] (-n, -n) m (Schurke) rogue;
(KARTEN) jack.
Bubikopf m bobbed hair.
Buch [buːx] (-(e)s, ⁻er) nt book; (COMM)
account book; **er redet wie ein ~** (umg) he
never stops talking; **ein ~ mit sieben
Siegeln** (fig) a closed book; **über etw** akk
~ führen to keep a record of sth; **zu ~(e)
schlagen** to make a significant difference,
tip the balance; **~binder** m bookbinder;
~drucker m printer.
Buche (-, -n) f beech tree.
buchen vt to book; (Betrag) to enter; **etw als
Erfolg ~** to put sth down as a success.
Bücherbord ['byːçər-] nt bookshelf.
Bücherbrett nt bookshelf.
Bücherei [byːçə'raɪ] f library.
Bücherregal nt bookshelves pl, bookcase.
Bücherschrank m bookcase.
Bücherwurm (umg) m bookworm.
Buchfink ['buːxfɪŋk] m chaffinch.
Buch- zW: **~führung** f book-keeping,
accounting; **~halter(in)** (-s, -) m(f) book-
keeper; **~handel** m book trade; **im ~handel
erhältlich** available in bookshops;
~händler(in) m(f) bookseller; **~handlung** f
bookshop; **~prüfung** f audit; **~rücken** m
spine.
Büchse ['byksə] (-, -n) f tin, can; (Holz~) box;
(Gewehr) rifle.
Büchsenfleisch nt tinned meat.
Büchsenöffner m tin od can opener.
Buchstabe (-ns, -n) m letter (of the
alphabet).
buchstabieren [buːxʃta'biːrən] vt to spell.
buchstäblich ['buːxʃtɛːplɪç] adj literal.
Buchstütze f book end.
Bucht ['bʊxt] (-, -en) f bay.
Buchung ['buːxʊŋ] f booking; (COMM)
entry.
Buchweizen m buckwheat.
Buchwert m book value.
Buckel ['bʊkəl] (-s, -) m hump; **er kann mir den
~ runterrutschen** (umg) he can (go and) take
a running jump.
buckeln (pej) vi to bow and scrape.
bücken ['bykən] vr to bend; **sich nach etw ~** to
bend down od stoop to pick sth up.
Bückling ['byklɪŋ] m (Fisch) kipper;
(Verbeugung) bow.
Budapest ['buːdapɛst] (-s) nt Budapest.

buddeln ['bʊdəln] (umg) vi to dig.
Bude ['buːdə] (-, -n) f booth, stall; (umg) digs pl
(BRIT) od place (US); **jdm die ~ einrennen**
(umg) to pester sb; **Leben in die ~ bringen** to
liven up the place.
Budget [by'dʒeː] (-s, -s) nt budget.
Büfett [by'fɛt] (-s, -s) nt (Anrichte) sideboard;
(Geschirrschrank) dresser; **kaltes ~** cold
buffet.
Büffel ['byfəl] (-s, -) m buffalo.
büffeln ['byfəln] (umg) vi to swot, cram ♦ vt
(Lernstoff) to swot up.
Bug [buːk] (-(e)s, -e) m (NAUT) bow; (AVIAT)
nose.
Bügel ['byːɡəl] (-s, -) m (Kleider~) hanger;
(Steig~) stirrup; (Brillen~) arm; **~brett** nt
ironing board; **~eisen** nt iron; **~falte** f
crease; **b~frei** adj non-iron; (Hemd)
drip-dry.
bügeln vt, vi to iron.
Buhmann ['buːman] (umg) m bogeyman.
Bühne ['byːnə] (-, -n) f stage.
Bühnenbild nt set, scenery.
Buhruf ['buːruːf] m boo.
buk etc [buːk] vb (veraltet) siehe **backen**.
Bukarest ['buːkarɛst] (-s) nt Bucharest.
Bulette [bu'lɛtə] f meatball.
Bulgare [bʊl'ɡaːrə] (-n, -n) m Bulgarian.
Bulgarien (-s) nt Bulgaria.
Bulgarin f Bulgarian.
bulgarisch adj Bulgarian.
Bulimie [buli'miː] f (MED) bulimia.
Bull- zW: **~auge** nt (NAUT) porthole; **~dogge** f
bulldog; **~dozer** ['bʊldoːzər] (-s, -) m
bulldozer.
Bulle (-n, -n) m bull; **die ~n** (pej: umg) the fuzz
sing, the cops.
Bullenhitze (umg) f sweltering heat.
Bummel ['bʊməl] (-s, -) m stroll;
(Schaufenster~) window-shopping
(expedition).
Bummelant [bʊmə'lant] m slowcoach.
Bummelei [bʊmə'laɪ] f wandering; dawdling;
skiving.
bummeln vi to wander, stroll; (trödeln) to
dawdle; (faulenzen) to skive (BRIT), loaf
around.
Bummelstreik m go-slow (BRIT), slowdown
(US).
Bummelzug m slow train.
Bummler(in) ['bʊmlər(ɪn)] (-s, -) m(f)
(langsamer Mensch) dawdler (BRIT),
slowpoke (US); (Faulenzer) idler, loafer.
bumsen ['bʊmzən] vi (schlagen) to thump;
(prallen, stoßen) to bump, bang; (umg:
koitieren) to bonk, have it off (BRIT).
Bund¹ [bʊnt] (-(e)s, ⁻e) m (Freundschafts~ etc)
bond; (Organisation) union; (POL)
confederacy; (Hosen~, Rock~) waistband;
den ~ fürs Leben schließen to take the

marriage vows.
Bund² [bʊnt] (**-(e)s, -e**) *nt* bunch; (*Stroh~*)
bundle.
Bündchen ['bʏntçən] *nt* ribbing; (*Ärmel~*)
cuff.
Bündel (**-s, -**) *nt* bundle, bale.
bündeln *vt* to bundle.
Bundes- ['bʊndəs] *in zW* Federal; **~bahn** *f*: **die
Deutsche ~bahn** German Federal Railways
pl; **~bank** *f* Federal Bank, Bundesbank;
~bürger *m* German citizen; (*vor 1990*) West
German citizen; **~gebiet** *nt* Federal
territory; **~gerichtshof** *m* Federal Supreme
Court; **~grenzschutz** *m* Federal Border
Guard; **~hauptstadt** *f* Federal capital;
~haushalt *m* (*POL*) National Budget;
~kanzler *m* Federal Chancellor.

BUNDESKANZLER

*The **Bundeskanzler**, head of the German
government, is elected for 4 years and determines
government guidelines. He is formally proposed
by the **Bundespräsident** but needs a majority in
parliament to be elected to office.*

Bundes- *zW*: **~land** *nt* state, Land; **~liga** *f*
(*SPORT*) national league; **~ministerium** *nt*
Federal Ministry; **~nachrichtendienst** *m*
Federal Intelligence Service; **~post** *f*
(*früher*): **die (Deutsche) ~post** the (German)
Federal Post (Office).

BUNDESPRÄSIDENT

*The **Bundespräsident** is the head of state of the
Federal Republic of Germany who is elected every
5 years by the members of the **Bundestag** and
by delegates of the Landtage (regional
parliaments). His role is that of a figurehead who
represents Germany at home and abroad. He can
only be elected twice.*

BUNDESRAT

*The **Bundesrat** is the Upper House of the
German Parliament whose 68 members are not
elected but determined by the parliaments of the
individual **Länder**. Its most important function is
the approval of federal laws which concern
jurisdiction of the Länder. It can raise objections to
all other laws but can be outvoted by the
Bundestag.*

Bundes- *zw*: **~rechnungshof** *m* Federal Audit
Office; **~regierung** *f* Federal Government;
~republik *f* Federal Republic (of Germany);
~staat *m* Federal state; **~straße** *f* Federal
Highway, main road.

BUNDESTAG

*The **Bundestag** is the Lower House of the
German Parliament, elected by the people. There
are 646 MP's, half of them elected directly from
the first vote (**Erststimme**), and half from the
regional list of parliamentary candidates resulting
from the second vote (**Zweitstimme**), and giving
proportional representation to the parties. The
Bundestag exercises parliamentary control over
the government.*

Bundes- *zW*: **~tagsabgeordnete(r)** *f(m)*
member of the German Parliament;
~tagswahl *f* (Federal) parliamentary
elections *pl*; **~verfassungsgericht** *nt* Federal
Constitutional Court; **~wehr** *f* German *od*
(*vor 1990*) West German Armed Forces *pl*.

BUNDESWEHR

*The **Bundeswehr** is the name for the German
armed forces. It was established in 1955, first of all
for volunteers, but since 1956 there has been
compulsory military service for all able-bodied
young men of 18 (see **Wehrdienst**). In peacetime
the Defence Minister is the head of the
Bundeswehr, but in wartime, the **Bundeskanzler**
takes over. The Bundeswehr comes under the
jurisdiction of NATO.*

Bundfaltenhose *f* pleated trousers *pl*.
Bundhose *f* knee breeches *pl*.
bündig ['bʏndɪç] *adj* (*kurz*) concise.
Bündnis ['bʏntnɪs] (**-ses, -se**) *nt* alliance.
Bunker ['bʊŋkər] (**-s, -**) *m* bunker;
(*Luftschutzbunker*) air-raid shelter.
bunt [bʊnt] *adj* coloured (*BRIT*), colored
(*US*); (*gemischt*) mixed; **jdm wird es zu ~**
it's getting too much for sb; **B~stift** *m*
coloured (*BRIT*) *od* colored (*US*) pencil,
crayon.
Bürde ['bʏrdə] (**-, -n**) *f* (*lit, fig*) burden.
Burg [bʊrk] (**-, -en**) *f* castle, fort.
Bürge ['bʏrgə] (**-n, -n**) *m* guarantor.
bürgen *vi* to vouch; **für jdn ~** (*fig*) to vouch
for sb; (*FIN*) to stand surety for sb.
Bürger(in) (**-s, -**) *m(f)* citizen; member of the
middle class; **~initiative** *f* citizen's
initiative; **~krieg** *m* civil war; **b~lich** *adj*
(*Rechte*) civil; (*Klasse*) middle-class; (*pej*)
bourgeois; **b~liches Gesetzbuch** Civil Code;
~meister *m* mayor; **~recht** *nt* civil rights *pl*;
~rechtler(in) *m(f)* civil rights campaigner;
~schaft *f* population, citizens *pl*; **~schreck** *m*
bogey of the middle classes; **~steig** *m*
pavement (*BRIT*), sidewalk (*US*); **~tum** *nt*
citizens *pl*; **~wehr** *f* vigilantes *pl*.
Burgfriede(n) *m* (*fig*) truce.

Bürgin f guarantor.
Bürgschaft f surety; ~ **leisten** to give security.
Burgund [bur'gunt] (-(s)) nt Burgundy.
Burgunder (-s, -) m (Wein) burgundy.
Büro [by'ro:] (-s, -s) nt office; ~**angestellte(r)** f(m) office worker; ~**klammer** f paper clip; ~**kraft** f (office) clerk.
Bürokrat [byro'kra:t] (-en, -en) m bureaucrat.
Bürokratie [byrokra'ti:] f bureaucracy.
bürokratisch adj bureaucratic.
Bürokratismus m red tape.
Büroschluss▲ m office closing time.
Bursch ['burʃ(ə)] (-en, -en) m = Bursche.
Bursche (-n, -n) m lad, fellow; (Diener) servant.
Burschenschaft f student fraternity.
burschikos [burʃi'ko:s] adj (jungenhaft) (tom)boyish; (unbekümmert) casual.
Bürste ['byrstə] (-, -n) f brush.
bürsten vt to brush.
Bus [bus] (-ses, -se) m bus.
Busch [buʃ] (-(e)s, ̈-e) m bush, shrub; **bei jdm auf den** ~ **klopfen** (umg) to sound sb out.
Büschel ['byʃəl] (-s, -) nt tuft.
buschig adj bushy.
Busen ['bu:zən] (-s, -) m bosom; (Meer~) inlet, bay; ~**freund(in)** m(f) bosom friend.
Bushaltestelle f bus stop.
Bussard ['busart] (-s, -e) m buzzard.
Buße ['bu:sə] (-, -n) f atonement, penance; (Geld) fine.
büßen ['by:sən] vi to do penance, atone ♦ vt to atone for.
Bußgeld nt fine.
Buß- und Bettag m day of prayer and repentance.
Büste ['bystə] (-, -n) f bust.
Büstenhalter m bra.
Butan [bu'ta:n] (-s) nt butane.
Büttenrede ['bytənre:də] f carnival speech.
Butter ['butər] (-) f butter; **alles (ist) in** ~ (umg) everything is fine od hunky-dory; ~**berg** (umg) m butter mountain; ~**blume** f buttercup; ~**brot** nt (piece of) bread and butter; ~**brotpapier** nt greaseproof paper; ~**cremetorte** f gateau with buttercream filling; ~**dose** f butter dish; ~**keks** m ≈ Rich Tea ® biscuit; ~**milch** f buttermilk; **b**~**weich** adj soft as butter; (fig: umg) soft.
Butzen ['butsən] (-s, -) m core.
BVG nt abk (= Betriebsverfassungsgesetz) ≈ Industrial Relations Act; = Bundesverfassungsgericht.
b. w. abk (= bitte wenden) p.t.o.
Byte [bait] (-s, -s) nt (COMPUT) byte.
Bz. abk = Bezirk.
bzgl. abk (= bezüglich) re.
bzw. abk = beziehungsweise.

C, c

C1, c [tse:] nt C, c; ~ **wie Cäsar** ≈ C for Charlie.
C2 [tse:] abk (= Celsius) C.
ca. [ka] abk (= circa) approx.
Cabriolet [kabrio'le:] (-s, -s) nt (AUT) convertible.
Café [ka'fe:] (-s, -s) nt café.
Cafeteria [kafete'ri:a] (-, -s) f cafeteria.
cal abk (= Kalorie) cal.
Calais [ka'lɛ:] (-') nt: **die Straße von** ~ the Straits of Dover.
Callcenter ['kɔ:lsɛntər] nt call centre (BRIT) or center (US).
Camcorder (-s, -) m camcorder.
campen ['kɛmpən] vi to camp.
Camper(in) (-s, -) m(f) camper.
Camping ['kɛmpɪŋ] (-s) nt camping; ~**bus** m camper; ~**platz** m camp(ing) site.
Caravan ['karavan] (-s, -s) m caravan.
Cäsium ['tsɛ:zɪʊm] nt = Zäsium.
ccm abk (= Kubikzentimeter) cm³.
CD f abk (= Compact Disc) CD; ~**-Brenner** m CD burner; ~**-ROM** (-, -s) f CD-ROM; ~**-Spieler** m CD player.
CDU [tse:de:'u:] (-) f abk (= Christlich-Demokratische Union (Deutschlands)) Christian Democratic Union.

CDU

The **CDU** *(Christlich-Demokratische Union) is a Christian and conservative political party founded in 1945. It operates in all the* **Länder** *apart from Bavaria where its sister party the* **CSU** *is active. In the* **Bundestag** *the two parties form a coalition. It is the second largest party in Germany after the* **SPD,** *the Social Democratic Party.*

Celli pl von **Cello.**
Cellist(in) [tʃɛ'lɪst(ɪn)] m(f) cellist.
Cello ['tʃɛlo] (-s, -s od **Celli**) nt cello.
Celsius ['tsɛlzius] m Celsius.
Cent [(t)sɛnt] (-s, -s) m cent.
Ces [tsɛs] (-, -) nt (MUS) C flat.
ces [tsɛs] (-, -) nt (MUS) C flat.
Ceylon ['tsailɔn] (-s) nt Ceylon.
Chamäleon [ka'mɛ:leɔn] (-s, -s) nt chameleon.
Champagner [ʃam'panjər] (-s, -) m champagne.
Champignon ['ʃampɪnjõ] (-s, -s) m button

mushroom.
Chance ['ʃãːs(ə)] (-, -n) *f* chance, opportunity.
Chancengleichheit *f* equality of
opportunity.
Chaos ['kaːɔs] (-) *nt* chaos.
Chaot(in) [ka'oːt(ɪn)] (-en, -en) *m(f)* (*POL: pej*)
anarchist (*pej*).
chaotisch [ka'oːtɪʃ] *adj* chaotic.
Charakter [ka'raktər] (-s, -e) *m* character;
c~fest *adj* of firm character.
charakterisieren [karakteri'ziːrən] *vt* to
characterize.
Charakteristik [karakte'rɪstɪk] *f*
characterization.
charakteristisch [karakte'rɪstɪʃ] *adj*: ~ (für)
characteristic (of), typical (of).
Charakter- *zW*: c~los *adj* unprincipled;
~losigkeit *f* lack of principle; ~schwäche *f*
weakness of character; ~stärke *f* strength
of character; ~zug *m* characteristic, trait.
charmant [ʃar'mant] *adj* charming.
Charme [ʃarm] (-s) *m* charm.
Charta ['karta] (-, -s) *f* charter.
Charterflug ['tʃartərfluːk] *m* charter flight.
Chartermaschine ['tʃartərmaʃiːnə] *f* charter
plane.
chartern ['tʃartərn] *vt* to charter.
Chassis [ʃa'siː] (-, -) *nt* chassis.
Chauffeur [ʃɔ'føːr] *m* chauffeur.
Chaussee [ʃo'seː] (-, -n) *f* (*veraltet*) high road.
Chauvi ['ʃovi] (-s, -s) (*umg*) *m* male
chauvinist.
Chauvinismus [ʃovi'nɪsmʊs] *m* chauvinism.
Chauvinist [ʃovi'nɪst] *m* chauvinist.
checken ['tʃɛkən] *vt* (*überprüfen*) to check;
(*umg: verstehen*) to get.
Chef(in) [ʃɛf(ɪn)] (-s, -s) *m(f)* head; (*umg*) boss;
~arzt *m* senior consultant; ~etage *f*
executive floor; ~redakteur *m* editor-in-
chief; ~sekretärin *f* personal assistant/
secretary; ~visite *f* (*MED*) consultant's
round.
Chemie [çe'miː] (-) *f* chemistry; ~faser *f* man-
made fibre (*BRIT*) *od* fiber (*US*).
Chemikalie [çemi'kaːliə] *f* chemical.
Chemiker(in) ['çeːmikər(ɪn)] (-s, -) *m(f)*
(industrial) chemist.
chemisch ['çeːmɪʃ] *adj* chemical; ~e
Reinigung dry cleaning.
Chemotherapie [çemotera'piː] *f*
chemotherapy.
Chicorée [ʃiko'reː] (-s) *f od m* chicory.
Chiffre ['ʃɪfrə] (-, -n) *f* (*Geheimzeichen*) cipher;
(*in Zeitung*) box number.
Chiffriermaschine [ʃɪ'friːrmaʃiːnə] *f* cipher
machine.
Chile ['tʃiːlə] (-s) *nt* Chile.
Chilene [tʃi'leːnə] (-n, -n) *m* Chilean.
Chilenin [tʃi'leːnɪn] *f* Chilean.
chilenisch *adj* Chilean.

China ['çiːna] (-s) *nt* China.
Chinakohl *m* Chinese leaves *pl*.
Chinese [çi'neːzə] (-n, -n) *m* Chinaman,
Chinese.
Chinesin *f* Chinese woman.
chinesisch *adj* Chinese.
Chinin [çi'niːn] (-s) *nt* quinine.
Chipkarte ['tʃɪpkartə] *f* smart card.
Chips [tʃɪps] *pl* crisps *pl* (*BRIT*), chips *pl* (*US*).
Chirurg(in) [çi'rʊrg(ɪn)] (-en, -en) *m(f)* surgeon.
Chirurgie [çirʊr'giː] *f* surgery.
chirurgisch *adj* surgical; ein ~er Eingriff
surgery.
Chlor [kloːr] (-s) *nt* chlorine.
Chloroform [kloro'fɔrm] (-s) *nt* chloroform.
chloroformieren [klorofor'miːrən] *vt* to
chloroform.
Chlorophyll [kloro'fʏl] (-s) *nt* chlorophyll.
Cholera ['koːlera] (-) *f* cholera.
Choleriker(in) [ko'leːrikər(ɪn)] (-s, -) *m(f)* hot-
tempered person.
cholerisch [ko'leːrɪʃ] *adj* choleric.
Cholesterin [kolɛste'riːn] (-s) *nt* cholesterol;
~spiegel [kolɛste'riːnʃpiɡəl] *m* cholesterol
level.
Chor [koːr] (-(e)s, ̈-e) *m* choir; (*Musikstück,
THEAT*) chorus.
Choral [ko'raːl] (-s, -äle) *m* chorale.
Choreograf(in)▲ [koreo'graːf(ɪn)] (-en, -en)
m(f) choreographer.
Choreografie▲ [koreogra'fiː] *f* choreography.
Chorgestühl *nt* choir stalls *pl*.
Chorknabe *m* choirboy.
Chose ['ʃoːzə] (-, -n) (*umg*) *f* (*Angelegenheit*)
thing.
Chr. *abk* = Christus, Chronik.
Christ [krɪst] (-en, -en) *m* Christian; ~baum *m*
Christmas tree.
Christenheit *f* Christendom.
Christentum (-s) *nt* Christianity.
Christin *f* Christian.
Christkind *nt* ≈ Father Christmas; (*Jesus*)
baby Jesus.
christlich *adj* Christian; C~er Verein Junger
Männer Young Men's Christian Association.
Christus (Christi) *m* Christ; Christi
Himmelfahrt Ascension Day.
Chrom [kroːm] (-s) *nt* (*CHEM*) chromium;
chrome.
Chromosom [kromo'zoːm] (-s, -en) *nt* (*BIOL*)
chromosome.
Chronik ['kroːnɪk] *f* chronicle.
chronisch *adj* chronic.
Chronologie [kronolo'giː] *f* chronology.
chronologisch *adj* chronological.
Chrysantheme [kryzan'teːmə] (-, -n) *f*
chrysanthemum.
CIA ['siːar'eɪ] (-) *f od m abk* (= *Central Intelligence
Agency*) CIA.
circa ['tsɪrka] *adv* (round) about.

Cis [tsɪs] (-, -) *nt* (*MUS*) C sharp.
cis [tsɪs] (-, -) *nt* (*MUS*) C sharp.
City ['sɪti] (-, -s) *f* city centre (*BRIT*); **in der ~** in
the city centre (*BRIT*), downtown (*US*); **die
~ von Berlin** the (city) centre of Berlin
(*BRIT*), downtown Berlin (*US*).
clean [kliːn] *adj* (*DROGEN: umg*) off drugs.
clever ['klɛvər] *adj* clever; (*gerissen*) crafty.
Clique ['klɪkə] (-, -n) *f* set, crowd.
Clou [kluː] (-s, -s) *m* (*von Geschichte*) (whole)
point; (*von Show*) highlight, high spot.
Clown [klaʊn] (-s, -s) *m* clown.
cm *abk* (= *Zentimeter*) cm.
Cockpit ['kɔkpɪt] (-s, -s) *nt* cockpit.
Cocktail ['kɔkteːl] (-s, -s) *m* cocktail.
Cola ['koːla] (-(s), -s) *nt od f* Coke ®.
Comicheft ['kɔmɪkhɛft] *nt* comic.
Computer [kɔm'pjuːtər] (-s, -) *m* computer;
c~gesteuert *adj* computer-controlled;
c~gestützt *adj* computer-based;
c~gestütztes Design computer-aided
design; **~kriminalität** *f* computer crime;
~spiel *nt* computer game; **~technik** *f*
computer technology.
Conférencier [kõferãsi'eː] (-s, -s) *m* compère.
Container [kɔn'teːnər] (-s, -) *m* container;
~schiff *nt* container ship.
Contergankind [kɔntɛr'gankɪnt] (*umg*) *nt*
thalidomide child.
cool [kuːl] (*umg*) *adj* (*gefasst*) cool.
Cord [kɔrt] (-(e)s, -e *od* -s) *m* = **Kord.**
Cornichon [kɔrni'ʃõː] (-s, -s) *nt* gherkin.
Couch [kaʊtʃ] (-, -es *od* -en) *f* couch; **~garnitur**
['kaʊtʃgarni'tuːr] *f* three-piece suite.
Couleur [ku'løːr] (-s, -s) *f* (*geh*) kind, sort.
Coupé [ku'peː] (-s, -s) *nt* (*AUT*) coupé, sports
version.
Coupon [ku'põː] (-s, -s) *m* = **Kupon.**
Courage [ku'raːʒə] (-) *f* courage.
Cousin [ku'zɛ̃ː] (-s, -s) *m* cousin.
Cousine [ku'ziːnə] (-, -n) *f* cousin.
Crack [krɛk] (-) *nt* (*Droge*) crack.
Creme [krɛːm] (-, -s) *f* (*lit, fig*) cream; (*Schuh~*)
polish; (*KOCH*) mousse; **c~farben** *adj*
cream(-coloured (*BRIT*) *od* -colored (*US*)).
cremig ['kreːmɪç] *adj* creamy.
Crux [krʊks] (-) *f* (*Schwierigkeit*) trouble,
problem.
CSU [tseː'ɛs'uː] (-) *f abk* (= *Christlich-Soziale
Union*) Christian Social Union.

CSU

The **CSU** (Christlich-Soziale Union) is a party
founded in 1945 in Bavaria. Like its sister party the
CDU it is a Christian, right-wing party.

CT-Scanner [tseː'teːskɛnər] *m* CT scanner.
Curriculum [kʊ'riːkulʊm] (-s, -cula) *nt* (*geh*)
curriculum.

Curry ['kari] (-s) *m od nt* curry powder;
~pulver ['karipulfər] *nt* curry powder;
~wurst *f* curried sausage.
Cursor ['kɔːrsər] (-s) *m* (*COMPUT*) cursor;
~taste *f* cursor key.
Cutter(in) ['katər(ɪn)] (-s, -) *m(f)* (*FILM*) editor.
CVJM [tseːfaʊjɔt'ɛm] (-) *m abk* (= *Christlicher
Verein Junger Männer*) YMCA.

D, d

D, d [deː] *nt* D, d; **~ wie Dora** ≈ D for David,
D for Dog (*US*).
D. *abk* = **Doktor** (*der evangelischen Theologie*).

da [daː] *adv* **1** (*örtlich*) there; (*hier*) here;
~ draußen out there; **~ sein** to be there; **ein
Arzt, der immer für seine Patienten ~ ist** a
doctor who always has time for his
patients; **~ bin ich** here I am; **~ hast du dein
Geld** (there you are,) there's your money;
~, wo where; **ist noch Milch ~?** is there any
milk left?
2 (*zeitlich*) then; (*folglich*) so; **es war niemand
im Zimmer, ~ habe ich** ... there was nobody
in the room, so I ...
3: **~ haben wir Glück gehabt** we were lucky
there; **was gibts denn ~ zu lachen?** what's
so funny about that?; **~ kann man nichts
machen** there's nothing one can do (in a
case like that).
♦ *konj* (*weil*) as, since.

d. Ä. *abk* (= *der Ältere*) Sen., sen.
DAAD (-) *m abk* (= *Deutscher Akademischer
Austauschdienst*) German Academic
Exchange Service.
dabehalten *unreg vt* to keep.
dabei [da'baɪ] *adv* (*räumlich*) close to it; (*noch
dazu*) besides; (*zusammen mit*) with them/it
etc; (*zeitlich*) during this; (*obwohl doch*) but,
however; **~ sein** (*anwesend*) to be present;
(*beteiligt*) to be involved; **ich bin ~!** count
me in!; **was ist schon ~?** what of it?; **es ist
doch nichts ~, wenn** ... it doesn't matter if
...; **bleiben wir ~** let's leave it at that; **es soll
nicht ~ bleiben** this isn't the end of it; **es
bleibt ~** that's settled; **das Dumme/
Schwierige ~** the stupid/difficult part of it;
er war gerade ~ zu gehen he was just
leaving; **hast du ~ etwas gelernt?** did you
learn anything from it?; **~ darf man nicht**

vergessen, dass ... it shouldn't be forgotten that ...; **die ~ entstehenden Kosten** the expenses arising from this; **es kommt doch nichts ~ heraus** nothing will come of it; **ich finde gar nichts ~** I don't see any harm in it; **~stehen** *unreg vi* to stand around.

Dach [dax] (**-(e)s, ¨er**) *nt* roof; **unter ~ und Fach sein** (*abgeschlossen*) to be in the bag (*umg*); (*Vertrag, Geschäft*) to be signed and sealed; (*in Sicherheit*) to be safe; **jdm eins aufs ~ geben** (*umg: ausschimpfen*) to give sb a (good) talking to; **~boden** *m* attic, loft; **~decker** (**-s, -**) *m* slater, tiler; **~fenster** *nt* skylight; (*ausgestellt*) dormer window; **~first** *m* ridge of the roof; **~gepäckträger** *m* (*AUT*) roof rack; **~geschoss▲** *nt* attic storey (*BRIT*) *od* story (*US*); (*oberster Stock*) top floor *od* storey (*BRIT*) *od* story (*US*); **~luke** *f* skylight; **~pappe** *f* roofing felt; **~rinne** *f* gutter.

Dachs [daks] (**-es, -e**) *m* badger.

Dachschaden (*umg*) *m*: **einen ~ haben** to have a screw loose.

dachte *etc* ['daxtə] *vb siehe* **denken**.

Dach- *zW*: **~terrasse** *f* roof terrace; **~verband** *m* umbrella organization; **~ziegel** *m* roof tile.

Dackel ['dakəl] (**-s, -**) *m* dachshund.

dadurch [da'dʊrç] *adv* (*räumlich*) through it; (*durch diesen Umstand*) thereby, in that way; (*deshalb*) because of that, for that reason ♦ *konj*: **~, dass** because.

dafür [da'fyːr] *adv* for it; (*anstatt*) instead; (*zum Ausgleich*): **in Latein ist er schlecht, ~ kann er gut Fußball spielen** he's bad at Latin but he makes up for it at football; **er ist bekannt ~** he is well-known for that; **was bekomme ich ~?** what will I get for it?; **~ ist er immer zu haben** he never says no to that; **~ bin ich ja hier** that's what I'm here for; **er kann nichts ~ (, dass ...)** he can't help it (that ...); **D~halten** (**-s**) *nt* (*geh*): **nach meinem D~halten** in my opinion.

DAG *f abk* (= *Deutsche Angestellten-Gewerkschaft*) *Clerical and Administrative Workers' Union*.

dagegen [da'geːgən] *adv* against it; (*im Vergleich damit*) in comparison with it; (*bei Tausch*) for it ♦ *konj* however; **haben Sie etwas ~, wenn ich rauche?** do you mind if I smoke?; **ich habe nichts ~** I don't mind; **ich war ~** I was against it; **ich hätte nichts ~ (einzuwenden)** that's okay by me; **~ kann man nichts tun** one can't do anything about it; **~halten** *unreg vt* (*vergleichen*) to compare with it; (*entgegnen*) to put forward as an objection.

daheim [da'haɪm] *adv* at home; **bei uns ~** back home; **D~** (**-s**) *nt* home.

daher [da'heːr] *adv* (*räumlich*) from there; (*Ursache*) from that ♦ *konj* (*deshalb*) that's why; **das kommt ~, dass** ... that is because

...; **~ kommt er auch** that's where he comes from too; **~ die Schwierigkeiten** that's what is causing the difficulties; **~gelaufen** *adj*: **jeder ~gelaufene Kerl** any Tom, Dick or Harry; **~reden** *vi* to talk away ♦ *vt* to say without thinking.

dahin [da'hɪn] *adv* (*räumlich*) there; (*zeitlich*) then; (*vergangen*) gone; **ist es noch weit bis ~?** is there still far to go?; **~ gehend** on this matter; **das tendiert ~** it is tending towards that; **er bringt es noch ~, dass ich ...** he'll make me ...; **~gegen** *konj* on the other hand; **~gehen** *unreg vi* (*Zeit*) to pass; **~gestellt** *adv*: **~gestellt bleiben** to remain to be seen; **etw ~gestellt sein lassen** to leave sth open *od* undecided; **~schleppen** *vr* (*lit: sich fortbewegen*) to drag o.s. along; (*fig: Verhandlungen, Zeit*) to drag on; **~schmelzen** *vi* to be enthralled.

dahinten [da'hɪntən] *adv* over there.

dahinter [da'hɪntər] *adv* behind it; **sich ~ klemmen** *od* **knien** (*umg*) to put one's back into it; **~ kommen** (*umg*) to find out.

dahinvegetieren [da'hɪnvegeˈtiːrən] *vi* to vegetate.

Dahlie ['daːliə] (**-, -n**) *f* dahlia.

DAK (**-**) *f abk* (= *Deutsche Angestellten-Krankenkasse*) *health insurance company for employees*.

Dakar ['dakar] (**-s**) *nt* Dakar.

dalassen ['daːlasən] *unreg vt* to leave (behind).

dalli ['dali] (*umg*) *adv*: **~, ~!** on (*BRIT*) *od* at (*US*) the double!

damalig ['daːmaːlɪç] *adj* of that time, then.

damals ['daːmaːls] *adv* at that time, then.

Damaskus [da'maskʊs] *nt* Damascus.

Damast [da'mast] (**-(e)s, -e**) *m* damask.

Dame [da'mə] (**-, -n**) *f* lady; (*SCHACH, KARTEN*) queen; (*Spiel*) draughts (*BRIT*), checkers (*US*).

Damen- *zW*: **~besuch** *m* lady visitor *od* visitors; **~binde** *f* sanitary towel (*BRIT*) *od* napkin (*US*); **d~haft** *adj* ladylike; **~sattel** *m*: **im ~sattel reiten** to ride side-saddle; **~wahl** *f* ladies' excuse-me.

Damespiel *nt* draughts (*BRIT*), checkers (*US*).

damit [da'mɪt] *adv* with it; (*begründend*) by that ♦ *konj* in order that *od* to; **was meint er ~?** what does he mean by that?; **was soll ich ~?** what am I meant to do with that?; **muss er denn immer wieder ~ ankommen?** must he keep on about it?; **was ist ~?** what about it?; **genug ~!** that's enough!; **~ basta!** and that's that!; **~ eilt es nicht** there's no hurry.

dämlich ['dɛːmlɪç] (*umg*) *adj* silly, stupid.

Damm [dam] (**-(e)s, ¨e**) *m* dyke (*BRIT*), dike (*US*); (*Stau~*) dam; (*Hafen~*) mole; (*Bahn~, Straßen~*) embankment.

dämmen ['dɛmən] *vt* (*Wasser*) to dam up; (*Schmerzen*) to keep back.

dämmerig *adj* dim, faint.
Dämmerlicht *nt* twilight; (*abends*) dusk; (*Halbdunkel*) half-light.
dämmern ['dɛmərn] *vi* (*Tag*) to dawn; (*Abend*) to fall; **es dämmerte ihm, dass ...** (*umg*) it dawned on him that ...
Dämmerung *f* twilight; (*Morgen~*) dawn; (*Abend~*) dusk.
Dämmerzustand *m* (*Halbschlaf*) dozy state; (*Bewusstseinstrübung*) semi-conscious state.
Dämmung *f* insulation.
Dämon ['dɛːmɔn] (-s, -en) *m* demon.
dämonisch [dɛ'moːnɪʃ] *adj* demonic.
Dampf [dampf] (-(e)s, ⁼e) *m* steam; (*Dunst*) vapour (*BRIT*), vapor (*US*); **jdm ~ machen** (*umg*) to make sb get a move on; **~ ablassen** (*lit, fig*) to let off steam; **d~en** *vi* to steam.
dämpfen ['dɛmpfən] *vt* (*KOCH*) to steam; (*bügeln*) to iron with a damp cloth; (*mit Dampfbügeleisen*) to steam iron; (*fig*) to dampen, subdue.
Dampfer ['dampfər] (-s, -) *m* steamer; **auf dem falschen ~ sein** (*fig*) to have got the wrong idea.
Dämpfer (-s, -) *m* (*MUS: bei Klavier*) damper; (*bei Geige, Trompete*) mute; **er hat einen ~ bekommen** (*fig*) it dampened his spirits.
Dampf- *zW:* **~kochtopf** *m* pressure cooker; **~maschine** *f* steam engine; **~schiff** *nt* steamship; **~walze** *f* steamroller.
Damwild ['damvɪlt] *nt* fallow deer.
danach [da'naːx] *adv* after that; (*zeitlich*) afterwards; (*gemäß*) accordingly; (*laut diesem*) according to which *od* that; **mir war nicht ~** (**zumute** *od* **zu Mute**) I didn't feel like it; **er griff schnell ~** he grabbed at it; **~ kann man nicht gehen** you can't go by that; **er sieht ~ aus** he looks it.
Däne ['dɛːnə] (-n, -n) *m* Dane, Danish man/ boy.
daneben [da'neːbən] *adv* beside it; (*im Vergleich*) in comparison; **~ sein** (*umg: verwirrt sein*) to be completely confused; **~benehmen** *unreg vr* to misbehave; **~gehen** *unreg vi* to miss; (*Plan*) to fail; **~greifen** *unreg vi* to miss; (*fig: mit Schätzung etc*) to be wide of the mark.
Dänemark ['dɛːnəmark] (-s) *nt* Denmark.
Dänin ['dɛːnɪn] *f* Dane, Danish woman *od* girl.
dänisch *adj* Danish.
Dank [daŋk] (-(e)s) *m* thanks *pl*; **vielen** *od* **schönen ~** many thanks; **jdm ~ sagen** to thank sb; **mit (bestem) ~ zurück!** many thanks for the loan; **d~** *präp* (+*dat od gen*) thanks to; **d~bar** *adj* grateful; (*Aufgabe*) rewarding; (*haltbar*) hard-wearing; **~barkeit** *f* gratitude.
danke *interj* thank you, thanks.
danken *vi* +*dat* to thank; **nichts zu ~!** don't mention it; **~d erhalten/ablehnen** to

receive/decline with thanks.
dankenswert *adj* (*Arbeit*) worthwhile; rewarding; (*Bemühung*) kind.
Dank- *zW:* **~gottesdienst** *m* service of thanksgiving; **d~sagen** *vi* to express one's thanks; **~schreiben** *nt* letter of thanks.
dann [dan] *adv* then; **~ und wann** now and then; **~ eben nicht** well, in that case (there's no more to be said); **erst ~, wenn ...** only when ...; **~ erst recht nicht!** in that case no way (*umg*).
dannen ['danən] *adv:* **von ~** (*liter: weg*) away.
daran [da'ran] *adv* on it; (*stoßen*) against it; **es liegt ~, dass ...** the cause of it is that ...; **gut/schlecht ~ sein** to be well/badly off; **das Beste/Dümmste ~** the best/stupidest thing about it; **ich war nahe ~, zu ...** I was on the point of ...; **im Anschluss ~** (*zeitlich: danach anschließend*) following that *od* this; **wir können nichts ~ machen** we can't do anything about it; **es ist nichts ~** (*ist nicht fundiert*) there's nothing in it; (*ist nichts Besonderes*) it's nothing special; **er ist ~ gestorben** he died from *od* of it; **~gehen** *unreg vi* to start; **~machen** (*umg*) *vr:* **sich ~machen, etw zu tun** to set about doing sth; **~setzen** *vt* to stake; **er hat alles ~gesetzt, von Glasgow wegzukommen** he has done his utmost to get away from Glasgow.
darauf [da'rauf] *adv* (*räumlich*) on it; (*zielgerichtet*) towards it; (*danach*) afterwards; **~ legen** to lay *od* put on top; **es kommt ganz ~ an, ob ...** it depends whether ...; **seine Behauptungen stützen sich ~, dass ...** his claims are based on the supposition that ...; **wie kommst du ~?** what makes you think that?; **die Tage ~** the days following *od* thereafter; **am Tag ~** the next day; **~ folgend** (*Tag, Jahr*) next, following; **~hin** *adv* (*im Hinblick ~*) in this respect; (*aus diesem Grund*) as a result; **wir müssen es ~hin prüfen, ob ...** we must test it to see whether ...
daraus [da'raus] *adv* from it; **was ist ~ geworden?** what became of it?; **~ geht hervor, dass ...** this means that ...
darbieten ['daːrbiːtən] *vt* (*vortragen: Lehrstoff*) to present ♦ *vr* to present itself.
Darbietung *f* performance.
Dardanellen [darda'nɛlən] *pl* Dardanelles *pl*.
darein- *präf* = **drein-**.
Daressalam [darɛsa'laːm] *nt* Dar-es-Salaam.
darf [darf] *vb siehe* **dürfen**.
darin [da'rɪn] *adv* in (there), in it; **der Unterschied liegt ~, dass ...** the difference is that ...
darlegen ['daːrleːgən] *vt* to explain, expound, set forth.
Darlegung *f* explanation.
Darleh(e)n (-s, -) *nt* loan.

Darm [darm] (-(e)s, ⁻e) *m* intestine; (*Wurst~*) skin; **~ausgang** *m* anus; **~grippe** *f* gastric influenza; **~saite** *f* gut string.

darstellen ['da:rʃtɛlən] *vt* (*abbilden, bedeuten*) to represent; (*THEAT*) to act; (*beschreiben*) to describe ♦ *vr* to appear to be.

Darsteller(in) (-s, -) *m(f)* actor, actress.

darstellerisch *adj*: **eine ~e Höchstleistung** a magnificent piece of acting.

Darstellung *f* portrayal, depiction.

darüber [da'ry:bər] *adv* (*räumlich*) over/above it; (*fahren*) over it; (*mehr*) more; (*währenddessen*) meanwhile; (*sprechen, streiten*) about it; **~ hinweg sein** (*fig*) to have got over it; **~ hinaus** over and above that; **~ geht nichts** there's nothing like it; **seine Gedanken ~** his thoughts about *od* on it; **~ liegen** (*fig*) to be higher.

darum [da'rʊm] *adv* (*räumlich*) round it ♦ *konj* that's why; **~ herum** round about (it); **er bittet ~** he is pleading for it; **es geht ~, dass ...** the thing is that ...; **~ geht es mir/geht es mir nicht** that's my point/that's not the point for me; **er würde viel ~ geben, wenn ...** he would give a lot to ...; *siehe auch* **drum**.

darunter [da'rʊntər] *adv* (*räumlich*) under it; (*dazwischen*) among them; (*weniger*) less; **ein Stockwerk ~** one floor below (it); **was verstehen Sie ~?** what do you understand by that?; **~ kann ich mir nichts vorstellen** that doesn't mean anything to me; **~ fallen** to be included; **~ mischen** (*Mehl*) to mix in; **sich ~ mischen** to mingle; **~ setzen** (*Unterschrift*) to put to it.

das [das] *pron* that ♦ *def art* the; *siehe auch* **der**; **~ heißt** that is; **~ und ~** such and such.

Dasein ['da:zaɪn] (-s) *nt* (*Leben*) life; (*Anwesenheit*) presence; (*Bestehen*) existence.

da sein▲ *unreg vi siehe* **da**.

Daseinsberechtigung *f* right to exist.

Daseinskampf *m* struggle for survival.

dass▲ [das] *konj* that.

dasselbe [das'zɛlbə] *nt pron* the same.

dastehen ['da:ʃte:ən] *unreg vi* to stand there; (*fig*): **gut/schlecht ~** to be in a good/bad position; **allein ~** to be on one's own.

Dat. *abk* = **Dativ**.

Datei [da'taɪ] *f* (*COMPUT*) file; **~manager** *m* file manager; **~name** *m* file name; **~verwaltung** *f* file management.

Daten ['da:tən] *pl* (*COMPUT*) data; (*Angaben*) data *pl*, particulars; *siehe auch* **Datum**; **~autobahn** *f* information (super)highway; **~bank** *f* data base; **~erfassung** *f* data capture; **~müll** *m* (*aus dem Internet*) Internet buildup; (*auf Festplatte*) hard disk clutter; **~netz** *nt* data network; **~satz** *m* record; **~schutz** *m* data protection; **~sichtgerät** *nt* visual display unit, VDU; **~träger** *m* data

carrier; **~übertragung** *f* data transmission; **~verarbeitung** *f* data processing; **~verarbeitungsanlage** *f* data processing equipment, DP equipment.

datieren [da'ti:rən] *vt* to date.

Dativ ['da:ti:f] (-s, -e) *m* dative; **~objekt** *nt* (*GRAM*) indirect object.

dato ['da:to] *adv*: **bis ~** (*COMM*: *umg*) to date.

Dattel ['datəl] (-, -n) *f* date.

Datum ['da:tʊm] (-s, **Daten**) *nt* date; **das heutige ~** today's date.

Datumsgrenze *f* (*GEOG*) (international) date line.

Dauer ['daʊər] (-, -n) *f* duration; (*gewisse Zeitspanne*) length; (*Bestand, Fortbestehen*) permanence; **es war nur von kurzer ~** it didn't last long; **auf die ~** in the long run; (*auf längere Zeit*) indefinitely; **~auftrag** *m* standing order; **d~haft** *adj* lasting, durable; **~haftigkeit** *f* durability; **~karte** *f* season ticket; **~lauf** *m* long-distance run.

dauern *vi* to last; **es hat sehr lang gedauert, bis er ...** it took him a long time to ...

dauernd *adj* constant.

Dauer- *zW*: **~obst** *nt* fruit suitable for storing; **~redner** (*pej*) *m* long-winded speaker; **~regen** *m* continuous rain; **~schlaf** *m* prolonged sleep; **~stellung** *f* permanent position; **~welle** *f* perm, permanent wave; **~wurst** *f* German salami; **~zustand** *m* permanent condition.

Daumen ['daʊmən] (-s, -) *m* thumb; **jdm die ~ drücken** *od* **halten** to keep one's fingers crossed for sb; **über den ~ peilen** to guess roughly; **~lutscher** *m* thumb-sucker.

Daune ['daʊnə] (-, -n) *f* down.

Daunendecke *f* eiderdown duvet.

davon [da'fɔn] *adv* of it; (*räumlich*) away; (*weg von*) away from it; (*Grund*) because of it; (*mit Passiv*) by it; **das kommt ~!** that's what you get; **~ abgesehen** apart from that; **wenn wir einmal ~ absehen, dass ...** if for once we overlook the fact that ...; **~ sprechen/wissen** to talk/know of *od* about it; **was habe ich ~?** what's the point?; **~ betroffen werden** to be affected by it; **~gehen** *unreg vi* to leave, go away; **~kommen** *unreg vi* to escape; **~lassen** *unreg vt*: **die Finger ~lassen** (*umg*) to keep one's hands *od* fingers off (it); **~laufen** *unreg vi* to run away; **~machen** *vr* to make off; **~tragen** *unreg vt* to carry off; (*Verletzung*) to receive.

davor [da'fo:r] *adv* (*räumlich*) in front of it, (*zeitlich*) before (that); **~ warnen** to warn about it.

dazu [da'tsu:] *adv* (*legen, stellen*) by it; (*essen*) with it; **und ~ noch** and in addition; **ein Beispiel/seine Gedanken ~** one example for/his thoughts on this; **wie komme ich denn ~?** why should I?; **... aber ich bin nicht**

~ **gekommen** ... but I didn't get around to it; **das Recht** ~ the right to do it; ~ **bereit sein, etw zu tun** to be prepared to do sth; ~ **fähig sein** to be capable of it; **sich** ~ **äußern** to say something on it; ~**gehören** *vi* to belong to it; **das gehört** ~ (*versteht sich von selbst*) it's all part of it; **es gehört schon einiges** ~, **das zu tun** it takes a lot to do that; ~**gehörig** *adj* appropriate; ~**kommen** *unreg vi* (*Ereignisse*) to happen too; (*an einen Ort*) to come along; **kommt noch etwas** ~? will there be anything else?; ~**lernen** *vt*: **schon wieder was** ~**gelernt!** you learn something (new) every day!; ~**mal** ['da:tsuma:l] *adv* in those days; ~**tun** *unreg vt* to add; **er hat es ohne dein D~tun geschafft** he managed it without your doing *etc* anything.

dazwischen [da'tsvɪʃən] *adv* in between; (*zusammen mit*) among them; **der Unterschied** ~ the difference between them; ~**fahren** *unreg vi* (*eingreifen*) to intervene; ~**funken** (*umg*) *vi* (*eingreifen*) to put one's oar in; ~**kommen** *unreg vi* (*hineingeraten*) to get caught in it; **es ist etwas** ~**gekommen** something (has) cropped up; ~**reden** *vi* (*unterbrechen*) to interrupt; (*sich einmischen*) to interfere; ~**treten** *unreg vi* to intervene.

DB *f abk* (= *Deutsche Bahn*) German railways.

DBP *f abk* (*früher*) = **Deutsche Bundespost**.

DDR (-) *f abk* (*früher.* = *Deutsche Demokratische Republik*) GDR.

DDR

The **DDR** *(Deutsche Demokratische Republik) was the name by which the former Communist German Democratic Republic was known. It was founded in 1949 from the Soviet-occupied zone. After the building of the Berlin Wall in 1961 it was virtually sealed off from the West until mass demonstrations and demands for reform forced the opening of the borders in 1989. It then merged in 1990 with the* **BRD**.

DDT ® *nt abk* DDT.

Dealer(in) ['di:lər(ɪn)] (**-s, -**) (*umg*) *m(f)* pusher.

Debatte [de'batə] (**-, -n**) *f* debate; **das steht hier nicht zur** ~ that's not the issue.

debattieren [deba'ti:rən] *vt* to debate.

Debet ['de:bɛt] (**-s, -s**) *nt* (*FIN*) debits *pl*.

Debüt [de'by:] (**-s, -s**) *nt* debut.

dechiffrieren [deʃɪ'fri:rən] *vt* to decode; (*Text*) to decipher.

Deck [dɛk] (**-(e)s, -s** *od* **-e**) *nt* deck; **an** ~ **gehen** to go on deck.

Deckbett *nt* feather quilt.

Deckblatt *nt* (*Schutzblatt*) cover.

Decke (**-, -n**) *f* cover; (*Bett*~) blanket; (*Tisch*~) tablecloth; (*Zimmer*~) ceiling; **unter einer**

~ **stecken** to be hand in glove; **an die** ~ **gehen** to hit the roof; **mir fällt die** ~ **auf den Kopf** (*fig*) I feel really claustrophobic.

Deckel (**-s, -**) *m* lid; **du kriegst gleich eins auf den** ~ (*umg*) you're going to catch it.

decken *vt* to cover ♦ *vr* to coincide ♦ *vi* to lay the table; **mein Bedarf ist gedeckt** I have all I need; (*fig*) I've had enough; **sich an einen gedeckten Tisch setzen** (*fig*) to be handed everything on a plate.

Deckmantel *m*: **unter dem** ~ **von** under the guise of.

Deckname *m* assumed name.

Deckung *f* (*das Schützen*) covering; (*Schutz*) cover; (*SPORT*) defence (*BRIT*), defense (*US*); (*Übereinstimmen*) agreement; **zur** ~ **seiner Schulden** to meet his debts.

deckungsgleich *adj* congruent.

Decoder *m* (*TV*) decoder.

de facto [de: 'fakto] *adv* de facto.

Defekt [de'fɛkt] (**-(e)s, -e**) *m* fault, defect; **d~** *adj* faulty.

defensiv [defɛn'si:f] *adj* defensive.

Defensive *f*: **jdn in die** ~ **drängen** to force sb onto the defensive.

definieren [defi'ni:rən] *vt* to define.

Definition [definitsi'o:n] *f* definition.

definitiv [defini'ti:f] *adj* definite.

Defizit ['de:fitsɪt] (**-s, -e**) *nt* deficit.

defizitär [defitsi'tɛ:r] *adj*: **eine ~e Haushaltspolitik führen** to follow an economic policy which can only lead to deficit.

Deflation [deflatsi'o:n] *f* (*ECON*) deflation.

deflationär [deflatsio'nɛ:r] *adj* deflationary.

deftig ['dɛftɪç] *adj* (*Essen*) large; (*Witz*) coarse.

Degen ['de:gən] (**-s, -**) *m* sword.

degenerieren [degene'ri:rən] *vi* to degenerate.

degradieren [degra'di:rən] *vt* to degrade.

dehnbar ['de:nba:r] *adj* elastic; (*fig: Begriff*) loose; **D~keit** *f* elasticity; looseness.

dehnen *vt, vr* to stretch.

Dehnung *f* stretching.

Deich [daɪç] (**-(e)s, -e**) *m* dyke (*BRIT*), dike (*US*).

Deichsel ['daɪksəl] (**-, -n**) *f* shaft.

deichseln *vt* (*fig: umg*) to wangle.

dein [daɪn] *pron* your; (*adjektivisch*): **herzliche Grüße, ~e Elke** with best wishes, yours *od* (*herzlicher*) love, Elke.

deine(r, s) *poss pron* yours.

deiner *gen von* **du** *pron* of you.

deinerseits *adv* on your part.

deinesgleichen *pron* people like you.

deinetwegen ['daɪnət've:gən] *adv* (*für dich*) for your sake; (*wegen dir*) on your account.

deinetwillen ['daɪnət'vɪlən] *adv*: **um** ~ = **deinetwegen**.

deinige *pron*: **der/die/das** ~ *od* **D~** yours.

dekadent [deka'dɛnt] *adj* decadent.

Dekadenz *f* decadence.

Dekan [de'ka:n] (**-s, -e**) *m* dean.

deklassieren [dekla'si:rən] *vt* (*SOZIOLOGIE: herabsetzen*) to downgrade; (*SPORT: übertreffen*) to outclass.

Deklination [deklinatsi'o:n] *f* declension.

deklinieren [dekli'ni:rən] *vt* to decline.

Dekolletee▲, **Dekolleté** [dekɔl'te:] (**-s, -s**) *nt* low neckline.

dekomprimieren *vt* (*COMPUT*) to decompress.

Dekor [de'ko:r] (**-s, -s** *od* **-e**) *m od nt* decoration.

Dekorateur(in) [dekora'tø:r(ɪn)] *m(f)* window dresser.

Dekoration [dekoratsi'o:n] *f* decoration; (*in Laden*) window dressing.

dekorativ [dekora'ti:f] *adj* decorative.

dekorieren [deko'ri:rən] *vt* to decorate; (*Schaufenster*) to dress.

Dekostoff ['de:kɔʃtɔf] *m* (*TEXTIL*) furnishing fabric.

Dekret [de'kre:t] (**-(e)s, -e**) *nt* decree.

Delegation [delegatsi'o:n] *f* delegation.

delegieren [dele'gi:rən] *vt*: ~ (**an** +*akk*) to delegate (to).

Delegierte(r) *f(m)* delegate.

Delfin▲ [dɛl'fi:n] (**-s, -e**) *m* dolphin.

Delfinschwimmen▲ *nt* butterfly (stroke).

Delhi ['de:lɪ] (**-s**) *nt* Delhi.

delikat [deli'ka:t] *adj* (*zart, heikel*) delicate; (*köstlich*) delicious.

Delikatesse [delika'tɛsə] (**-, -n**) *f* delicacy.

Delikatessengeschäft *nt* delicatessen (shop).

Delikt [de'lɪkt] (**-(e)s, -e**) *nt* (*JUR*) offence (*BRIT*), offense (*US*).

Delinquent [delɪŋ'kvɛnt] *m* (*geh*) offender.

Delirium [de'li:rium] *nt*: **im** ~ **sein** to be delirious; (*umg: betrunken*) to be paralytic.

Delle ['dɛlə] (**-, -n**) (*umg*) *f* dent.

Delphin *etc* [dɛl'fi:n] (**-s, -e**) *m* = **Delfin** *etc*.

Delta ['dɛlta] (**-s, -s**) *nt* delta.

dem [de(:)m] *art dat von* **der, das; wie** ~ **auch sei** be that as it may.

Demagoge [dema'go:gə] (**-n, -n**) *m* demagogue.

Demarkationslinie [demarkatsi'o:nzli:niə] *f* demarcation line.

Dementi [de'mɛnti] (**-s, -s**) *nt* denial.

dementieren [demɛn'ti:rən] *vt* to deny.

dem- *zW*: **~entsprechend** *adj* appropriate ♦ *adv* correspondingly; (*demnach*) accordingly; **~gemäß** *adv* accordingly; **~nach** *adv* accordingly; **~nächst** *adv* shortly.

Demo ['de:mo] (**-s, -s**) (*umg*) *f* demo.

Demografie▲ [demogra'fi:] *f* demography.

Demokrat(in) [demo'kra:t(ɪn)] (**-en, -en**) *m(f)* democrat.

Demokratie [demokra'ti:] *f* democracy; **~verständnis** *nt* understanding of (the meaning of) democracy.

demokratisch *adj* democratic.

demokratisieren [demokrati'zi:rən] *vt* to democratize.

demolieren [demo'li:rən] *vt* to demolish.

Demonstrant(in) [demɔn'strant(ɪn)] *m(f)* demonstrator.

Demonstration [demɔnstratsi'o:n] *f* demonstration.

demonstrativ [demɔnstra'ti:f] *adj* demonstrative; (*Protest*) pointed.

demonstrieren [demɔn'stri:rən] *vt, vi* to demonstrate.

Demontage [demɔn'ta:ʒə] (**-, -n**) *f* (*lit, fig*) dismantling.

demontieren [demɔn'ti:rən] *vt* (*lit, fig*) to dismantle; (*Räder*) to take off.

demoralisieren [demorali'zi:rən] *vt* to demoralize.

Demoskopie [demosko'pi:] *f* public opinion research.

demselben *dat von* **derselbe, dasselbe**.

Demut ['de:mu:t] (**-**) *f* humility.

demütig ['de:my:tɪç] *adj* humble.

demütigen ['de:my:tɪgən] *vt* to humiliate.

Demütigung *f* humiliation.

demzufolge ['de:mtsu'fɔlgə] *adv* accordingly.

den [de(:)n] *art akk von* **der**.

denen ['de:nən] *pron dat pl von* **der, die, das**.

Denk- *zW*: **~anstoß** *m*: **jdm ~anstöße geben** to give sb food for thought; **~art** *f* mentality; **d~bar** *adj* conceivable.

denken ['dɛŋkən] *unreg vi* to think ♦ *vt*: **für jdn/ etw gedacht sein** to be intended *od* meant for sb/sth ♦ *vr* (*vorstellen*): **das kann ich mir** ~ I can imagine; (*beabsichtigen*): **sich** *dat* **etw bei etw** ~ to mean sth by sth; **wo** ~ **Sie hin!** what an idea!; **ich denke schon** I think so; **an jdn/etw** ~ to think of sb/sth; **daran ist gar nicht zu** ~ that's (quite) out of the question; **ich denke nicht daran, das zu tun** there's no way I'm going to do that (*umg*).

Denken (**-s**) *nt* thinking.

Denker(in) (**-s, -**) *m(f)* thinker; **das Volk der Dichter und** ~ the nation of poets and philosophers.

Denk- *zW*: **~fähigkeit** *f* intelligence; **d~faul** *adj* mentally lazy; **~fehler** *m* logical error; **~horizont** *m* mental horizon.

Denkmal (**-s, ⁻er**) *nt* monument; **~schutz** *m*: **etw unter ~schutz stellen** to classify sth as a historical monument.

Denk- *zW*: **~pause** *f*: **eine ~pause einlegen** to have a break to think things over; **~schrift** *f* memorandum; **~vermögen** *nt* intellectual capacity; **d~würdig** *adj* memorable; **~zettel** *m*: **jdm einen ~zettel verpassen** to teach sb a lesson.

denn [dɛn] *konj* for; (*konzessiv*): **es sei** ~, (**dass**) unless ♦ *adv* then; (*nach Komparativ*) than.

dennoch ['dɛnnɔx] *konj* nevertheless ♦ *adv*: **und** ~, ... and yet ...

denselben *akk von* **derselbe** ♦ *dat von* **dieselben**.
Denunziant(in) [denʊntsi'ant(ɪn)] *m(f)* informer.
denunzieren [denʊn'tsiːrən] *vt* to inform against.
Deospray ['deːoʃpreɪ] *nt od m* deodorant spray.
Depesche [de'pɛʃə] (-, -n) *f* dispatch.
deplatziert▲ [depla'tsiːrt] *adj* out of place.
Deponent(in) [depo'nɛnt(ɪn)] *m(f)* depositor.
Deponie *f* dump, disposal site.
deponieren [depo'niːrən] *vt* (*COMM*) to deposit.
deportieren [depɔr'tiːrən] *vt* to deport.
Depot [de'poː] (-s, -s) *nt* warehouse; (*Bus~, EISENB*) depot; (*Bank~*) strongroom (*BRIT*), safe (*US*).
Depp [dɛp] (-en, -en) *m* (*Dialekt: pej*) twit.
Depression [deprɛsi'oːn] *f* depression.
depressiv *adj* depressive; (*FIN*) depressed.
deprimieren [depri'miːrən] *vt* to depress.

SCHLÜSSELWORT

der [de(ː)r] (*f* **die**, *nt* **das**) (*gen* **des, der, des**, *dat* **dem, der, dem**) *def art* the; ~ **Rhein** the Rhine; ~ **Klaus** (*umg*) Klaus; **die Frau** (*im allgemeinen*) women; ~ **Tod/das Leben** death/life; ~ **Fuß des Berges** the foot of the hill; **gib es** ~ **Frau** give it to the woman; **er hat sich** *dat* **die Hand verletzt** he has hurt his hand.
♦ *rel pron* (*bei Menschen*) who, that; (*bei Tieren, Sachen*) which, that; ~ **Mann, den ich gesehen habe** the man who *od* whom *od* that I saw.
♦ *demon pron* he/she/it; (*jener, dieser*) that; (*pl*) those; ~**/die war es** it was him/her; ~ **mit** ~ **Brille** the one with the glasses; **ich will den (da)** I want that one.

derart ['deːr'aːrt] *adv* (*Art und Weise*) in such a way; (*Ausmaß: vor adj*) so; (: *vor vb*) so much.
derartig *adj* such, this sort of.
derb [dɛrp] *adj* sturdy; (*Kost*) solid; (*grob*) coarse; **D~heit** *f* sturdiness; solidity; coarseness.
deren ['deːrən] *rel pron* (*gen sing von die*) whose; (*von Sachen*) of which; (*gen pl von der, die, das*) their; whose; of whom.
derentwillen ['deːrənt'vɪlən] *adv*: **um** ~ (*rel*) for whose sake; (*von Sachen*) for the sake of which.
dergestalt *adv* (*geh*): ~, **dass** ... in such a way that ...
der- *zW*: ~**gleichen** *pron* such; (*substantivisch*): **er tat nichts** ~**gleichen** he did nothing of the kind; **und** ~**gleichen (mehr)** and suchlike; ~**jenige** *pron* he; she; it; (*rel*) the one (who); that (which); ~**maßen** *adv* to such an extent, so; ~**selbe** *m pron* the same; ~**weil(en)** *adv* in the meantime; ~**zeit** *adv* (*jetzt*) at present, at

the moment; ~**zeitig** *adj* present, current; (*damalig*) then.
des [dɛs] *art gen von* **der**.
Des [dɛs] (-) *nt* (*MUS: auch:* **d~**) D flat.
Deserteur [dezɛr'tøːr] *m* deserter.
desertieren [dezɛr'tiːrən] *vi* to desert.
desgl. *abk* = **desgleichen**.
desgleichen ['dɛs'glaɪçən] *pron* the same.
deshalb ['dɛs'halp] *adv, konj* therefore, that's why.
Design [di'zaɪn] (-s, -s) *nt* design.
designiert [dezi'gniːrt] *adj attrib*: **der** ~**e Vorsitzende/Nachfolger** the chairman designate/prospective successor.
Desinfektion [dɛzɪnfɛktsi'oːn] *f* disinfection.
Desinfektionsmittel *nt* disinfectant.
desinfizieren [dɛzɪnfi'tsiːrən] *vt* to disinfect.
Desinteresse [dɛs|ɪntə'rɛsə] (-s) *nt*: ~ **(an** +*dat*) lack of interest (in).
desinteressiert [dɛs|ɪntərɛ'siːrt] *adj* uninterested.
desselben *gen von* **derselbe, dasselbe**.
dessen ['dɛsən] *pron gen von* **der, das**; ~ **ungeachtet** nevertheless, regardless.
Dessert [dɛ'seːr] (-s, -s) *nt* dessert.
Dessin [dɛ'sɛ̃ː] (-s, -s) *nt* pattern, design.
Destillation [dɛstɪlatsi'oːn] *f* distillation.
destillieren [dɛstɪ'liːrən] *vt* to distil.
desto ['dɛsto] *adv* all *od* so much the; ~ **besser** all the better.
destruktiv [dɛstrʊk'tiːf] *adj* destructive.
deswegen ['dɛs've:gən] *konj* therefore, hence.
Detail [de'taɪ] (-s, -s) *nt* detail.
detaillieren [deta'jiːrən] *vt* to specify, give details of.
Detektiv [detɛk'tiːf] (-s, -e) *m* detective.
Detektor [de'tɛktɔr] *m* (*TECH*) detector.
Detonation [detonatsi'oːn] *f* explosion, blast.
Deut *m*: **(um) keinen** ~ not one iota *od* jot.
deuten ['dɔytən] *vt* to interpret; (*Zukunft*) to read ♦ *vi*: ~ **(auf** +*akk*) to point (to *od* at).
deutlich *adj* clear; (*Unterschied*) distinct; **jdm etw** ~ **zu verstehen geben** to make sth perfectly clear *od* plain to sb; **D~keit** *f* clarity; distinctness.
deutsch [dɔytʃ] *adj* German; ~**e Schrift** Gothic script; **auf D~** in German; **auf gut D~** (**gesagt**) (*fig: umg*) ≈ in plain English; **D~e Demokratische Republik** (*HIST*) German Democratic Republic.
Deutsche(r) *f(m)*: **er ist** ~**r** he is (a) German.
Deutschland *nt* Germany; ~**lied** *nt* German national anthem; ~**politik** *f* home *od* domestic policy; (*von fremdem Staat*) policy towards Germany.
deutschsprachig *adj* (*Bevölkerung, Gebiete*) German-speaking; (*Zeitung, Ausgabe*) German-language; (*Literatur*) German.
deutschstämmig *adj* of German origin.
Deutung *f* interpretation.

Devise [de'vi:zə] (-, -n) *f* motto, device;
Devisen *pl (FIN)* foreign currency *od*
exchange.
Devisenausgleich *m* foreign exchange
offset.
Devisenkontrolle *f* exchange control.
Dez. *abk (= Dezember)* Dec.
Dezember [de'tsɛmbər] (-(s), -) *m* December;
siehe auch **September.**
dezent [de'tsɛnt] *adj* discreet.
Dezentralisation [detsɛntralizatsi'o:n] *f*
decentralization.
Dezernat [detser'na:t] (-(e)s, -e) *nt*
(VERWALTUNG) department.
Dezibel [detsi'bɛl] (-s, -) *nt* decibel.
dezidiert [detsi'di:rt] *adj* firm, determined.
dezimal [detsi'ma:l] *adj* decimal; **D~bruch** *m*
decimal (fraction); **D~system** *nt* decimal
system.
dezimieren [detsi'mi:rən] *vt (fig)* to decimate
♦ *vr* to be decimated.
DFB *m abk (= Deutscher Fußball-Bund)* German
Football Association.
DFG *f abk (= Deutsche Forschungsgemeinschaft)*
German Research Council.
DGB *m abk (= Deutscher Gewerkschaftsbund)* ≈
TUC.
dgl. *abk* = **dergleichen.**
d. h. *abk (= das heißt)* i.e.
Di. *abk* = **Dienstag.**
Dia ['di:a] (-s, -s) *nt* = **Diapositiv.**
Diabetes [dia'be:tɛs] (-, -) *m (MED)* diabetes.
Diabetiker(in) [dia'be:tikər(ɪn)] (-s, -) *m(f)*
diabetic.
Diagnose [dia'gno:zə] (-, -n) *f* diagnosis.
diagnostizieren [diagnɔsti'tsi:rən] *vt, vi (MED,
fig)* to diagnose.
diagonal [diago'na:l] *adj* diagonal.
Diagonale (-, -n) *f* diagonal.
Diagramm [dia'gram] *nt* diagram.
Diakonie [diako'ni:] *f (REL)* social welfare
work.
Dialekt [dia'lɛkt] (-(e)s, -e) *m* dialect;
~ausdruck *m* dialect expression *od* word;
d~frei *adj* without an accent.
dialektisch *adj* dialectal; *(Logik)* dialectical.
Dialog [dia'lo:k] (-(e)s, -e) *m* dialogue.
Diamant [dia'mant] *m* diamond.
Diapositiv [diapozi'ti:f] (-s, -e) *nt (PHOT)* slide,
transparency.
Diaprojektor *m* slide projector.
Diät [di'ɛ:t] (-) *f* diet; **Diäten** *pl (POL)* allowance
sing; **~ essen** to eat according to a diet;
(nach einer) ~ leben to be on a special diet.
dich [dɪç] *akk von* **du** ♦ *pron* you ♦ *refl pron*
yourself.
dicht [dɪçt] *adj* dense; *(Nebel)* thick; *(Gewebe)*
close; *(undurchlässig)* (water)tight; *(fig)*
concise; *(umg: zu)* shut, closed ♦ *adv:* **~ an/
bei** close to; **er ist nicht ganz ~** *(umg)* he's

crackers; **~ machen** to make watertight/
airtight; **~ hintereinander** right behind one
another; **~ bevölkert** densely *od* heavily
populated.
Dichte (-, -n) *f* density; thickness; closeness;
*(water)*tightness; *(fig)* conciseness.
dichten *vt (dicht machen)* to make watertight;
to seal; *(NAUT)* to caulk; *(LITER)* to compose,
write ♦ *vi (LITER)* to compose, write.
Dichter(in) (-s, -) *m(f)* poet; *(Autor)* writer;
d~isch *adj* poetical; **d~ische Freiheit** poetic
licence *(BRIT) od* license *(US).*
dichthalten *unreg (umg) vi* to keep one's
mouth shut.
dichtmachen *(umg) vt (Geschäft)* to wind up
♦ *vi (Person)* to close one's mind.
Dichtung *f (TECH)* washer; *(AUT)* gasket;
(Gedichte) poetry; *(Prosa)* (piece of) writing;
~ und Wahrheit *(fig)* fact and fantasy.
dick [dɪk] *adj* thick; *(fett)* fat; **durch ~ und
dünn** through thick and thin; **D~darm** *m*
(ANAT) colon.
Dicke (-, -n) *f* thickness; fatness.
dickfellig *adj* thick-skinned.
dickflüssig *adj* viscous.
Dickicht (-s, -e) *nt* thicket.
dick- *zW:* **D~kopf** *m* mule; **D~milch** *f* soured
milk; **D~schädel** *m* = **Dickkopf.**
die [di:] *def art* the; *siehe auch* **der.**
Dieb(in) [di:p, 'di:bɪn] (-(e)s, -e) *m(f)* thief;
haltet den ~! stop thief!; **d~isch** *adj*
thieving; *(umg)* immense; **~stahl** *m* theft;
d~stahlsicher *adj* theft-proof.
diejenige ['di:je:nɪgə] *pron siehe* **derjenige.**
Diele ['di:lə] (-, -n) *f (Brett)* board; *(Flur)* hall,
lobby; *(Eis~)* ice-cream parlour *(BRIT) od*
parlor *(US).*
dienen ['di:nən] *vi:* **(jdm) ~** to serve (sb);
womit kann ich Ihnen ~? what can I do for
you?; *(in Geschäft)* can I help you?
Diener (-s, -) *m* servant; *(umg: Verbeugung)*
bow; **~in** *f* (maid)servant.
dienern *vi (fig):* **~ (vor** +dat) to bow and
scrape (to).
Dienerschaft *f* servants *pl.*
dienlich *adj* useful, helpful.
Dienst [di:nst] (-(e)s, -e) *m* service; *(Arbeit,
Arbeitszeit)* work; **~ am Kunden** customer
service; **jdm zu ~en stehen** to be at sb's
disposal; **außer ~** retired; **~ haben** to be on
duty; **~ habend** *(Arzt, Offizier)* on duty;
~ tuend on duty; **der öffentliche ~** the civil
service.
Dienstag *m* Tuesday; **am ~** on Tuesday; **~ in
acht Tagen** *od* **in einer Woche** a week on
Tuesday, Tuesday week; **~ vor einer Woche**
od **acht Tagen** a week (ago) last Tuesday.
dienstags *adv* on Tuesdays.
Dienst- *zW:* **~alter** *nt* length of service;
d~beflissen *adj* zealous; **~bote** *m* servant;

~**boteneingang** m tradesmen's od service entrance; **d~eifrig** adj zealous; **d~frei** adj off duty; ~**gebrauch** m (MIL, VERWALTUNG): **nur für den ~gebrauch** for official use only; ~**geheimnis** nt professional secret; ~**gespräch** nt business call; ~**grad** m rank; ~**leistung** f service; ~**leistungsbetrieb** m service industry business; ~**leistungsgewerbe** nt service industries pl; **d~lich** adj official; (Angelegenheiten) business attrib; ~**mädchen** nt domestic servant; ~**plan** m duty rota; ~**reise** f business trip; ~**stelle** f office; ~**vorschrift** f service regulations pl; ~**wagen** m (von Beamten) official car; ~**weg** m official channels pl; ~**zeit** f office hours pl; (MIL) period of service.

diesbezüglich adj (Frage) on this matter.
diese(r, s) pron this (one) ♦ adj this; ~ **Nacht** tonight.
Diesel ['di:zəl] (-s) m (Kraftstoff) diesel fuel; ~**öl** ['di:zələ:l] nt diesel oil.
dieselbe [di:'zɛlbə] f pron the same.
dieselben [di:'zɛlbən] pl pron the same.
diesig adj drizzly.
dies- zW: ~**jährig** adj this year's; ~**mal** adv this time; **D~seits** (-) nt this life; ~**seits** präp +gen on this side.
Dietrich ['di:trɪç] (-s, -e) m picklock.
Diffamierungskampagne
[dɪfa'mi:rʊŋskampanjə] f smear campaign.
differential etc [dɪferɛntsi'a:l] adj = **differenzial** etc.
Differenz [dɪfe'rɛnts] f difference; ~**betrag m** difference, balance.
differenzial▲ [dɪferɛntsi'a:l] adj differential; **D~getriebe** nt differential gear; **D~rechnung** f differential calculus.
differenzieren [dɪferɛn'tsi:rən] vt to make distinctions in ♦ vi: ~ **(bei)** to make distinctions (in).
differenziert adj complex.
diffus [dɪ'fu:s] adj (Gedanken etc) confused.
Digital- [digi'ta:l-] zW: ~**anzeige** f digital display; ~**fernsehen** nt digital TV; ~**rechner** m digital computer; ~**uhr** f digital watch.
Diktafon▲, **Diktaphon** [dɪkta'fo:n] nt dictaphone ®.
Diktat [dɪk'ta:t] (-(e)s, -e) nt dictation; (fig: Gebot) dictate; (POL) diktat, dictate.
Diktator [dɪk'ta:tɔr] m dictator; **d~isch** [-a'tɔ:rɪʃ] adj dictatorial.
Diktatur [dɪkta'tu:r] f dictatorship.
diktieren [dɪk'ti:rən] vt to dictate.
Diktion [dɪktsi'o:n] f style.
Dilemma [di'lɛma] (-s, -s od -ta) nt dilemma.
Dilettant [dilɛ'tant] m dilettante, amateur; **d~isch** adj dilettante.
Dimension [dimɛnzi'o:n] f dimension.
DIN f abk (= Deutsche Industrie-Norm) German

Industrial Standard; ~ **A4** A4.
Ding [dɪŋ] (-(e)s, -e) nt thing; object; **das ist ein ~ der Unmöglichkeit** that is totally impossible; **guter ~e sein** to be in good spirits; **so wie die ~e liegen, nach Lage der ~e** as things are; **es müsste nicht mit rechten ~en zugehen, wenn** ... it would be more than a little strange if ...; **ein krummes ~ drehen** to commit a crime; **to do something wrong**; **d~fest** adj: **jdn d~fest machen** to arrest sb; **d~lich** adj real, concrete.
Dings (-) (umg) nt thingummyjig (BRIT).
Dingsbums ['dɪŋsbʊms] (-) (umg) nt thingummybob (BRIT).
Dingsda (-) (umg) nt thingummyjig (BRIT).
Dinosaurier [dino'zauriər] m dinosaur.
Diözese [diø'tse:zə] (-, -n) f diocese.
Diphtherie [dɪfte'ri:] f diphtheria.
Dipl.-Ing. abk = Diplomingenieur.
Diplom [di'plo:m] (-(e)s, -e) nt diploma; (Hochschulabschluss) degree; ~**arbeit** f dissertation.
Diplomat [diplo'ma:t] (-en, -en) m diplomat.
Diplomatie [diploma'ti:] f diplomacy.
diplomatisch [diplo'ma:tɪʃ] adj diplomatic.
Diplomingenieur m academically qualified engineer.
dir [di:r] dat von **du** ♦ pron (to) you.
direkt [di'rɛkt] adj direct; ~ **fragen** to ask outright od straight out.
Direktion [dirɛktsi'o:n] f management; (Büro) manager's office.
Direktmandat nt (POL) direct mandate.
Direktor(in) m(f) director; (von Hochschule) principal; (von Schule) principal, head (teacher) (BRIT).
Direktorium [direk'to:riʊm] nt board of directors.
Direktübertragung f live broadcast.
Direktverkauf m direct selling.
Dirigent(in) [diri'gɛnt(ɪn)] m(f) conductor.
dirigieren [diri'gi:rən] vt to direct; (MUS) to conduct.
Dirne ['dɪrnə] (-, -n) f prostitute.
Dis [dɪs] (-, -) nt (MUS) D sharp.
dis [dɪs] (-, -) nt (MUS) D sharp.
Disharmonie [dɪsharmo'ni:] f (lit, fig) discord.
Diskette [dɪs'kɛtə] f disk, diskette.
Diskettenlaufwerk nt disk drive.
Disko ['dɪsko] (-, -s) f disco.
Diskont [dɪs'kɔnt] (-s, -e) m discount; ~**satz** m rate of discount.
Diskothek [dɪsko'te:k] (-, -en) f disco(theque).
diskreditieren [dɪskredi'ti:rən] vt (geh) to discredit.
Diskrepanz [dɪskre'pants] f discrepancy.
diskret [dɪs'kre:t] adj discreet.
Diskretion [dɪskretsi'o:n] f discretion; **strengste ~ wahren** to preserve the

strictest confidence.
diskriminieren [dɪskrimi'niːrən] *vt* to
discriminate against.
Diskriminierung *f*: ~ **(von)** discrimination
(against).
Diskussion [dɪskʊsi'oːn] *f* discussion; **zur**
~ **stehen** to be under discussion.
Diskussionsbeitrag *m* contribution to the
discussion.
Diskuswerfen ['dɪskʊsvɛrfən] *nt* throwing the
discus.
diskutabel [dɪsku'taːbəl] *adj* debatable.
diskutieren [dɪsku'tiːrən] *vt, vi* to discuss;
darüber lässt sich ~ that sounds like
something we could talk about.
disponieren [dɪspo'niːrən] *vi* (*geh: planen*) to
make arrangements.
Disposition [dɪspozitsi'oːn] *f* (*geh: Verfügung*):
jdm zur *od* **zu jds** ~ **stehen** to be at sb's
disposal.
disqualifizieren [dɪskvalifi'tsiːrən] *vt* to
disqualify.
dissen ['dɪsən] (*umg*) *vt* to slag off (*BRIT*) to
diss (*esp US*).
Dissertation [dɪsɛrtatsi'oːn] *f* dissertation;
doctoral thesis.
Dissident(in) [dɪsi'dɛnt(ɪn)] *m(f)* dissident.
Distanz [dɪs'tants] *f* distance; (*fig: Abstand,
Entfernung*) detachment; (*Zurückhaltung*)
reserve.
distanzieren [dɪstan'tsiːrən] *vr*: **sich von jdm/
etw** ~ to dissociate o.s. from sb/sth.
distanziert *adj* (*Verhalten*) distant.
Distel ['dɪstəl] (*-, -n*) *f* thistle.
Disziplin [dɪstsi'pliːn] (*-, -en*) *f* discipline.
Disziplinarverfahren [dɪstsipli'narfɛrfaːrən] *nt*
disciplinary proceedings *pl*.
dito ['diːto] *adv* (*COMM, hum*) ditto.
Diva ['diːva] (*-, -s*) *f* star; (*FILM*) screen
goddess.
divers [di'vɛrs] *adj* various.
Diverses *pl* sundries *pl*; „~~"
"miscellaneous".
Dividende [divi'dɛndə] (*-, -n*) *f* dividend.
dividieren [divi'diːrən] *vt*: ~ **(durch)** to divide
(by).
d. J. *abk* (= *der Jüngere*) jun.
Djakarta [dʒa'karta] *nt* Jakarta.
DJH *nt abk* (= *Deutsches Jugendherbergswerk*)
German Youth Hostel Association.
DKP *f abk* (= *Deutsche Kommunistische Partei*)
German Communist Party.
DLV *m abk* (= *Deutscher Leichtathletik-Verband*)
German track and field association.
DM *f abk* (*HIST* = *Deutsche Mark*) DM.
d. M. *abk* (= *dieses Monats*) inst.
D-Mark ['deːmark] (*-, -*) *f* (*HIST*) deutschmark.
DNS *f abk* (= *Desoxyribo(se)nukleinsäure*)
DNA.
Do. *abk* = *Donnerstag*.

doch [dɔx] *adv* **1** (*dennoch*) after all; (*sowieso*)
anyway; **er kam** ~ **noch** he came after all;
du weißt es ja ~ **besser** you know more
about it (than I do) anyway; **es war** ~ **ganz
interessant** it was actually quite interesting;
und ~, ... and yet ...
2 (*als bejahende Antwort*) yes I do/it does *etc*;
das ist nicht wahr - ~! that's not true - yes it
is!
3 (*auffordernd*): **komm** ~ do come; **lass ihn** ~
just leave him; **nicht** ~! oh no!
4: **sie ist** ~ **noch so jung** but she's still so
young; **Sie wissen** ~, **wie das ist** you know
how it is(, don't you?); **wenn** ~ if only.
♦ *konj* (*aber*) but; (*trotzdem*) all the same; **und**
~ **hat er es getan** but still he did it.

Docht [dɔxt] (*-(e)s, -e*) *m* wick.
Dock [dɔk] (*-s, -s* *od* *-e*) *nt* dock; ~**gebühren** *pl*
dock dues *pl*.
Dogge ['dɔgə] (*-, -n*) *f* bulldog; **Deutsche** ~
Great Dane.
Dogma ['dɔgma] (*-s, -men*) *nt* dogma.
dogmatisch [dɔ'gmaːtɪʃ] *adj* dogmatic.
Dohle ['doːlə] (*-, -n*) *f* jackdaw.
Doktor ['dɔktɔr] (*-s, -en*) *m* doctor; **den**
~ **machen** (*umg*) to do a doctorate *od* Ph.D.
Doktorand(in) [dɔktɔ'rant (-dɪn)] (*-en, -en*)
m(f) Ph.D. student.
Doktor- *zW*: ~**arbeit** *f* doctoral thesis; ~**titel** *m*
doctorate; ~**vater** *m* supervisor.
doktrinär [dɔktri'nɛːr] *adj* doctrinal; (*stur*)
doctrinaire.
Dokument [doku'mɛnt] *nt* document.
Dokumentar- *zW*: ~**bericht** *m* documentary;
~**film** *m* documentary (film); **d~isch** *adj*
documentary; ~**spiel** *nt* docudrama.
dokumentieren [dokumɛn'tiːrən] *vt* to
document; (*fig: zu erkennen geben*) to reveal,
show.
Dolch [dɔlç] (*-(e)s, -e*) *m* dagger; ~**stoß** *m* (*bes
fig*) stab.
dolmetschen ['dɔlmɛtʃən] *vt, vi* to interpret.
Dolmetscher(in) [dɔlmɛtʃər(ɪn)] (*-s, -*) *m(f)* interpreter.
Dolomiten [dolo'miːtən] *pl* (*GEOG*): **die** ~ the
Dolomites *pl*.
Dom [doːm] (*-(e)s, -e*) *m* cathedral.
Domäne [do'mɛːnə] (*-, -n*) *f* (*fig*) domain,
province.
dominieren [domi'niːrən] *vt* to dominate ♦ *vi*
to predominate.
Dominikanische Republik
[domini'kaːnɪʃərepu'bliːk] *f* Dominican
Republic.
Dompfaff ['dɔmpfaf] (*-en, -en*) *m* bullfinch.
Dompteur [dɔmp'tøːr] *m* (*Zirkus*) trainer.
Dompteuse [dɔmp'tøːzə] *f* (*Zirkus*) trainer.
Donau ['doːnaʊ] *f*: **die** ~ the Danube.

Donner ['dɔnər] (-s, -) *m* thunder; **wie vom ~ gerührt** (*fig*) thunderstruck.

donnern *vi unpers* to thunder ♦ *vt* (*umg*) to slam, crash.

Donnerschlag *m* thunderclap.

Donnerstag *m* Thursday; *siehe auch* **Dienstag**.

Donnerwetter *nt* thunderstorm; (*fig*) dressing-down ♦ *interj* good heavens!; (*anerkennend*) my word!

doof [do:f] (*umg*) *adj* daft, stupid.

Dopingkontrolle ['dɔpɪŋkɔntrɔlə] *f* (*SPORT*) dope check.

Doppel ['dɔpəl] (-s, -) *nt* duplicate; (*SPORT*) doubles; **~band** *m* (*von doppeltem Umfang*) double-sized volume; (*zwei Bände*) two volumes *pl*; **~bett** *nt* double bed; **d~bödig** *adj* (*fig*) ambiguous; **d~deutig** *adj* ambiguous; **~fenster** *nt* double glazing; **~gänger(in)** (-s, -) *m(f)* double; **~korn** *m* type of schnapps; **~punkt** *m* colon; **d~seitig** *adj* (*auch COMPUT*: *Diskette*) double-sided; (*Lungenentzündung*) double; **d~seitige Anzeige** double-page advertisement; **d~sinnig** *adj* ambiguous; **~stecker** *m* two-way adaptor; **~stunde** *f* (*SCH*) double period.

doppelt *adj* double; (*COMM*: *Buchführung*) double-entry; (*Staatsbürgerschaft*) dual ♦ *adv*: **die Karte habe ich ~** I have two of these cards; **~ gemoppelt** (*umg*) saying the same thing twice over; **in ~er Ausführung** in duplicate.

Doppel- *zW*: **~verdiener** *pl* two-income family; **~zentner** *m* 100 kilograms; **~zimmer** *nt* double room.

Dorf [dɔrf] (-(e)s, -̈er) *nt* village; **~bewohner** *m* villager.

dörflich ['dœrflɪç] *adj* village *attrib*.

Dorn¹ [dɔrn] (-(e)s, -en) *m* (*BOT*) thorn; **das ist mir ein ~ im Auge** (*fig*) it's a thorn in my flesh.

Dorn² [dɔrn] (-(e)s, -e) *m* (*Schnallen~*) tongue, pin.

dornig *adj* thorny.

Dornröschen *nt* Sleeping Beauty.

dörren ['dœrən] *vt* to dry.

Dörrobst ['dœro:pst] *nt* dried fruit.

dort [dɔrt] *adv* there; **~ drüben** over there; **~her** *adv* from there; **~hin** *adv* (to) there.

dortig *adj* of that place; in that town.

Dose ['do:zə] (-, -n) *f* box; (*Blech~*) tin, can; **in ~n** (*Konserven*) canned, tinned (*BRIT*).

Dosen *pl von* **Dose**, **Dosis**.

dösen ['dø:zən] (*umg*) *vi* to doze.

Dosenmilch *f* evaporated milk.

Dosenöffner *m* tin (*BRIT*) *od* can opener.

Dosenpfand *nt* deposit on drink cans; (*allgemein: Einwegpfand*) deposit on drink cans and disposable bottles.

dosieren [do'zi:rən] *vt* (*lit, fig*) to measure out.

Dosis ['do:zɪs] (-, **Dosen**) *f* dose.

Dotierung [do'ti:rʊŋ] *f* endowment; (*von Posten*) remuneration.

Dotter ['dɔtər] (-s, -) *m* egg yolk.

Double ['du:bəl] (-s, -s) *nt* (*FILM etc*) stand-in.

downloaden ['daunlo:dən] *vti* (*COMPUT*) to download.

Down-Syndrom *nt no pl* (*MED*) Down's Syndrome.

Doz. *abk =* **Dozent(in)**.

Dozent(in) [do'tsɛnt(ɪn)] (-en, -en) *m(f)*: **~ (für)** lecturer (in), professor (of) (*US*).

dpa (-) *f abk* (= *Deutsche Presse-Agentur*) German Press Agency.

Dr. *abk =* **Doktor**.

Drache ['draxə] (-n, -n) *m* (*Tier*) dragon.

Drachen (-s, -) *m* kite; **einen ~ steigen lassen** to fly a kite; **d~fliegen** *vi* to hang-glide; **~fliegen** *nt* (*SPORT*) hang-gliding.

Dragee, Dragée [dra'ʒe:] (-s, -s) *nt* (*PHARM*) dragee, sugar-coated pill.

Draht [dra:t] (-(e)s, -̈e) *m* wire; **auf ~ sein** to be on the ball; **~esel** *m* (*hum*) trusty bicycle; **~gitter** *nt* wire grating; **d~los** *adj* cordless; (*Telefon*) mobile; **~seil** *nt* cable; **Nerven wie ~seile** (*umg*) nerves of steel; **~seilbahn** *f* cable railway; **~zange** *f* pliers *pl*; **~zieher(in)** *m(f)* (*fig*) wire-puller.

Drall *m* (*fig: Hang*) tendency; **einen ~ nach links haben** (*AUT*) to pull to the left.

drall [dral] *adj* strapping; (*Frau*) buxom.

Drama ['dra:ma] (-s, **Dramen**) *nt* drama.

Dramatiker(in) [dra'ma:tikər(ɪn)] (-s, -) *m(f)* dramatist.

dramatisch [dra'ma:tɪʃ] *adj* dramatic.

Dramaturg(in) [drama'tʊrk (-gɪn)] (-en, -en) *m(f)* artistic director; (*TV*) drama producer.

dran [dran] (*umg*) *adv* (*an der Reihe*): **jetzt bist du ~** it's your turn now; **früh/spät ~ sein** to be early/late; **ich weiß nicht, wie ich (bei ihm) ~ bin** I don't know where I stand (with him); *siehe auch* **daran**; **~bleiben** *unreg* (*umg*) *vi* to stay close; (*am Apparat*) to hang on.

Drang (-(e)s, -̈e) *m* (*Trieb*) urge, yearning; (*Druck*) pressure; **~ nach** urge *od* yearning for.

drang *etc* [dran] *vb siehe* **dringen**.

drängeln ['drɛŋəln] *vt, vi* to push, jostle.

drängen ['drɛŋən] *vt* (*schieben*) to push, press; (*antreiben*) to urge ♦ *vi* (*eilig sein*) to be urgent; (*Zeit*) to press; **auf etw akk ~** to press for sth.

drangsalieren [draŋza'li:rən] *vt* to pester, plague.

dranhalten (*umg*) *vr* to get a move on.

drankommen (*umg*) *unreg vi* (*an die Reihe kommen*) to have one's turn; (*SCH: beim Melden*) to be called; (*Frage, Aufgabe etc*) to come up.

drannehmen (*umg*) *unreg vt* (*Schüler*) to ask.

drastisch ['drastɪʃ] *adj* drastic.

drauf [drauf] (*umg*) *adv*: **~ und dran sein, etw zu tun** to be on the point of doing sth; *siehe* *auch* **darauf; D~gänger (-s, -)** *m* daredevil; **~gehen** *unreg vi* (*verbraucht werden*) to be used up; (*kaputtgehen*) to be smashed up; **~haben** (*umg*) *unreg vt*: **etw ~haben** (*können*) to be able to do sth just like that; (*Kenntnisse*) to be well up on sth; **~zahlen** *vi* (*fig: Einbußen erleiden*) to pay the price.

draußen ['drausən] *adv* outside, out-of-doors.

Drechsler(in) ['drɛkslər(ɪn)] **(-s, -)** *m(f)* (wood) turner.

Dreck [drɛk] **(-(e)s)** *m* mud, dirt; **~ am Stecken haben** (*fig*) to have a skeleton in the cupboard; **das geht ihn einen ~ an** (*umg*) that's none of his business.

dreckig *adj* dirty, filthy; **es geht mir ~** (*umg*) I'm in a bad way.

Dreckskerl (*umg!*) *m* dirty swine (*!*).

Dreh [dre:] *m*: **den ~ raushaben** *od* **weghaben** (*umg*) to have got the hang of it.

Dreh- *zW*: **~achse** *f* axis of rotation; **~arbeiten** *pl* (*FILM*) shooting *sing*; **~bank** *f* lathe; **d~bar** *adj* revolving; **~buch** *nt* (*FILM*) script.

drehen *vt* to turn, rotate; (*Zigaretten*) to roll; (*Film*) to shoot ♦ *vi* to turn, rotate ♦ *vr* to turn; (*handeln von*): **sich um etw ~** to be about sth; **ein Ding ~** (*umg*) to play a prank.

Dreher(in) (-s, -) *m(f)* lathe operator.

Dreh- *zW*: **~orgel** *f* barrel organ; **~ort** *m* (*FILM*) location; **~scheibe** *f* (*EISENB*) turntable; **~tür** *f* revolving door.

Drehung *f* (*Rotation*) rotation; (*Um~, Wendung*) turn.

Dreh- *zW*: **~wurm** (*umg*) *m*: **einen ~wurm haben/bekommen** to be/become dizzy; **~zahl** *f* rate of revolution; **~zahlmesser** *m* rev(olution) counter.

drei [draɪ] *num* three; **~ viertel** three quarters; **aller guten Dinge sind ~!** (*Sprichwort*) all good things come in threes!; (*nach zwei missglückten Versuchen*) third time lucky!; **D~eck** *nt* triangle; **~eckig** *adj* triangular; **D~ecksverhältnis** *nt* eternal triangle; **~einhalb** *num* three and a half; **D~einigkeit** [-'aɪnɪçkaɪt] *f* Trinity.

dreierlei *adj inv* of three kinds.

drei- *zW*: **~fach** *adj* triple, treble ♦ *adv* three times; **die ~fache Menge** three times the amount; **D~faltigkeit** *f* trinity; **D~fuß** *m* tripod; (*Schemel*) three-legged stool; **D~gangschaltung** *f* three-speed gear; **~hundert** *num* three hundred; **D~käsehoch** (*umg*) *m* tiny tot; **D~königsfest** *nt* Epiphany; **~mal** *adv* three times, thrice; **~malig** *adj* three times.

dreinblicken ['draɪnblɪkən] *vi*: **traurig** *etc* **~** to look sad *etc*.

dreinreden ['draɪnre:dən] *vi*: **jdm ~** (*dazwischenreden*) to interrupt sb; (*sich einmischen*) to interfere with sb.

Dreirad *nt* tricycle.

Dreisprung *m* triple jump.

dreißig ['draɪsɪç] *num* thirty.

dreist [draɪst] *adj* bold, audacious.

Dreistigkeit *f* boldness, audacity.

drei- *zW*: **~viertelstunde** *f* three-quarters of an hour; **D~vierteltakt** *m*: **im D~vierteltakt** in three-four time; **~zehn** *num* thirteen; **jetzt schlägt's ~zehn!** (*umg*) that's a bit much.

dreschen ['drɛʃən] *unreg vt* to thresh; **Skat ~** (*umg*) to play skat.

Dresden ['dre:sdən] **(-s)** *nt* Dresden.

dressieren [drɛ'si:rən] *vt* to train.

Dressur [drɛ'su:r] *f* training; (*für ~reiten*) dressage.

Dr. h. c. *abk* (= *Doktor honoris causa*) honorary doctor.

driften ['drɪftən] *vi* (*NAUT, fig*) to drift.

Drillbohrer *m* light drill.

drillen ['drɪlən] *vt* (*bohren*) to drill, bore; (*MIL*) to drill; (*fig*) to train; **auf etw** *akk* **gedrillt sein** (*fig: umg*) to be practised (*BRIT*) *od* practiced (*US*) at doing sth.

Drilling *m* triplet.

drin [drɪn] (*umg*) *adv*: **bis jetzt ist noch alles ~** everything is still quite open; *siehe auch* **darin**.

dringen ['drɪŋən] *unreg vi* (*Wasser, Licht, Kälte*): **~ (durch/in** *+akk*) to penetrate (through/into); **auf etw** *akk* **~** to insist on sth; **in jdn ~** (*geh*) to entreat sb.

dringend ['drɪŋənt] *adj* urgent; **~ empfehlen** to recommend strongly.

dringlich ['drɪŋlɪç] *adj* = **dringend**.

Dringlichkeit *f* urgency.

Dringlichkeitsstufe *f* priority; **~ 1** top priority.

drinnen ['drɪnən] *adv* inside, indoors.

drinstecken ['drɪnʃtɛkən] (*umg*) *vi*: **da steckt eine Menge Arbeit drin** a lot of work has gone into it.

drischt [drɪʃt] *vb siehe* **dreschen**.

dritt *adv*: **wir kommen zu ~** three of us are coming together.

dritte(r, s) *adj* third; **D~ Welt** Third World; **im Beisein D~r** in the presence of a third party.

Drittel (-s, -) *nt* third.

drittens *adv* thirdly.

drittklassig *adj* third-rate, third-class.

Dr. jur. *abk* (= *Doktor der Rechtswissenschaften*) ≈ L.L.D.

DRK (-) *nt abk* (= *Deutsches Rotes Kreuz*) ≈ R.C.

Dr. med. *abk* (= *Doktor der Medizin*) ≈ M.D.

droben ['dro:bən] *adv* above, up there.

Droge ['dro:gə] **(-, -n)** *f* drug.

dröge ['drø:gə] (*NORDD*) *adj* boring.

Drogen- *zW*: **d~abhängig** *adj* addicted to drugs; **~händler(in)** *m(f)* peddler, pusher; **d~süchtig** *adj* addicted to drugs.

Drogerie [drogə'ri:] *f* chemist's shop (*BRIT*),

drugstore (*US*).

DROGERIE

The **Drogerie** *as opposed to the* **Apotheke** *sells medicines not requiring a prescription. It tends to be cheaper and also sells cosmetics, perfume and toiletries.*

Drogist(in) [dro'gɪst(ɪn)] *m(f)* pharmacist, chemist (*BRIT*).
Drohbrief *m* threatening letter.
drohen ['droːən] *vi:* (**jdm**) ~ to threaten (sb).
Drohgebärde *f* (*lit, fig*) threatening gesture.
Drohne ['droːnə] (**-, -n**) *f* drone.
dröhnen ['drøːnən] *vi* (*Motor*) to roar; (*Stimme, Musik*) to ring, resound.
Drohung ['droːʊŋ] *f* threat.
drollig ['drɔlɪç] *adj* droll.
Drops [drɔps] (**-, -**) *m od nt* fruit drop.
drosch *etc* [drɔʃ] *vb siehe* **dreschen**.
Droschke ['drɔʃkə] (**-, -n**) *f* cab.
Droschkenkutscher *m* cabman.
Drossel ['drɔsəl] (**-, -n**) *f* thrush.
drosseln ['drɔsəln] *vt* (*Motor etc*) to throttle; (*Heizung*) to turn down; (*Strom, Tempo, Produktion etc*) to cut down.
Dr. phil. *abk* (= *Doktor der Geisteswissenschaften*) ≈ Ph.D.
Dr. theol. *abk* (= *Doktor der Theologie*) ≈ D.D.
drüben ['dryːbən] *adv* over there, on the other side.
drüber ['dryːbər] (*umg*) *adv* = **darüber**.
Druck [drʊk] (**-(e)s, -e**) *m* (*PHYS, Zwang*) pressure; (*TYP: Vorgang*) printing; (: *Produkt*) print; (*fig: Belastung*) burden, weight; ~ **hinter etw** *akk* **machen** to put some pressure on sth; ~**buchstabe** *m* block letter; **in** ~**buchstaben schreiben** to print.
Drückeberger ['drʏkəbɛrgər] (**-s, -**) *m* shirker, dodger.
drucken ['drʊkən] *vt, vi* (*TYP, COMPUT*) to print.
drücken ['drʏkən] *vt* (*Knopf, Hand*) to press; (*zu eng sein*) to pinch; (*fig: Preise*) to keep down; (: *belasten*) to oppress, weigh down ♦ *vi* to press; to pinch ♦ *vr:* **sich vor etw** *dat* ~ **to get out of (doing) sth; jdm etw in die Hand** ~ **to press sth into sb's hand.
drückend *adj* oppressive; (*Last, Steuern*) heavy; (*Armut*) grinding; (*Wetter, Hitze*) oppressive, close.
Drucker (**-s, -**) *m* printer.
Drücker (**-s, -**) *m* button; (*Tür~*) handle; (*Gewehr~*) trigger; **am** ~ **sein** *od* **sitzen** (*fig: umg*) to be the key person; **auf den letzten** ~ (*fig: umg*) at the last minute.
Druckerei [drʊkəˈraɪ] *f* printing works, press.
Druckerschwärze *f* printer's ink.
Druck- *zW:* ~**fahne** *f* galley(-proof); ~**fehler** *m*

misprint; ~**knopf** *m* press stud (*BRIT*), snap fastener; ~**kopf** *m* printhead; ~**luft** *f* compressed air; ~**mittel** *nt* leverage; **d~reif** *adj* ready for printing, passed for press; (*fig*) polished; ~**sache** *f* printed matter; ~**schrift** *f* printing; (*gedrucktes Werk*) pamphlet; ~**taste** *f* push button; ~**welle** *f* shock wave.
drum [drʊm] (*umg*) *adv* around; **mit allem D~ und Dran** with all the bits and pieces *pl*; (*Mahlzeit*) with all the trimmings *pl*.
Drumherum *nt* trappings *pl*.
drunten ['drʊntən] *adv* below, down there.
Drüse ['dryːzə] (**-, -n**) *f* gland.
DSB (**-**) *m abk* (= *Deutscher Sportbund*) *German Sports Association*.
Dschungel ['dʒʊŋəl] (**-s, -**) *m* jungle.
DSD *nt abk* (= *Duales System Deutschland*) *German waste collection and recycling service.*

DSD

The **DSD** *(Duales System Deutschland) is a scheme introduced in Germany for separating domestic refuse into two types so as to reduce environmental damage. Normal refuse is disposed of in the usual way by burning or dumping at land-fill sites; packets and containers with a green spot* (**grüner Punkt**) *imprinted on them are kept separate and are then collected for recycling.*

---

dt. *abk* = **deutsch**.
DTC (**-**) *m abk* (= *Deutscher Touring-Automobil-Club*) *German motoring organization*.
DTP (**-**) *nt abk* (= *Desktop publishing*) DTP.
Dtzd. *abk* (= *Dutzend*) doz.
du [duː] *pron* you; **mit jdm per** ~ **sein** to be on familiar terms with sb; **D~** *nt:* **jdm das D~ anbieten** to suggest that sb uses "du", suggest that sb uses the familiar form of address.
Dübel ['dyːbəl] (**-s, -**) *m* plug; (*Holz~*) dowel.
dübeln ['dyːbəln] *vt, vi* to plug.
Dublin ['dablɪn] *nt* Dublin.
ducken ['dʊkən] *vt* (*Kopf*) to duck; (*fig*) to take down a peg or two ♦ *vr* to duck.
Duckmäuser ['dʊkmɔʏzər] (**-s, -**) *m* yes-man.
Dudelsack ['duːdəlzak] *m* bagpipes *pl*.
Duell [du'ɛl] (**-s, -e**) *nt* duel.
Duett [du'ɛt] (**-(e)s, -e**) *nt* duet.
Duft [dʊft] (**-(e)s, -e**) *m* scent, odour (*BRIT*), odor (*US*); **d~en** *vi* to smell, be fragrant.
duftig *adj* (*Stoff, Kleid*) delicate, diaphanous; (*Muster*) fine.
Duftnote *f* (*von Parfüm*) scent.
dulden ['dʊldən] *vt* to suffer; (*zulassen*) to tolerate ♦ *vi* to suffer.
duldsam *adj* tolerant.
dumm [dʊm] *adj* stupid; **das wird mir zu** ~ that's just too much; **der D~e sein** to be the

loser; der ~e August (*umg*) the clown; **du willst mich wohl für** ~ **verkaufen** you must think I'm stupid; **sich** ~ **und dämlich reden** (*umg*) to talk till one is blue in the face; **so etwas D~es** how stupid; what a nuisance; ~**dreist** *adj* impudent.

dummerweise *adv* stupidly.

Dummheit *f* stupidity; (*Tat*) blunder, stupid mistake.

Dummkopf *m* blockhead.

dumpf [dʊmpf] *adj* (*Ton*) hollow, dull; (*Luft*) close; (*Erinnerung, Schmerz*) vague; **D~heit** *f* hollowness, dullness; closeness; vagueness.

dumpfig *adj* musty.

Dumpingpreis ['dampɪŋpraɪs] *m* give-away price.

Düne ['dy:nə] (-, -n) *f* dune.

Dung [dʊŋ] (-(e)s) *m* manure.

düngen ['dyŋən] *vt* to fertilize.

Dünger (-s, -) *m* fertilizer; (*Dung*) manure.

dunkel ['dʊŋkəl] *adj* dark; (*Stimme*) deep; (*Ahnung*) vague; (*rätselhaft*) obscure; (*verdächtig*) dubious, shady; **im D~n tappen** (*fig*) to grope in the dark.

Dünkel ['dyŋkəl] (-s) *m* self-conceit; **d~haft** *adj* conceited.

Dunkelheit *f* darkness; (*fig*) obscurity; **bei Einbruch der** ~ at nightfall.

Dunkelkammer *f* (*PHOT*) dark room.

dunkeln *vi unpers* to grow dark.

Dunkelziffer *f* estimated number of unnotified cases.

dünn [dyn] *adj* thin ♦ *adv*: ~ **gesät** scarce; **D~darm** *m* small intestine; ~**flüssig** *adj* watery, thin; **D~heit** *f* thinness; **D~schiss**▲ (*umg*) *m* the runs.

Dunst [dʊnst] (-es, ̈-e) *m* vapour (*BRIT*), vapor (*US*); (*Wetter*) haze; ~**abzugshaube** *f* extractor hood.

dünsten ['dynstən] *vt* to steam.

Dunstglocke *f* haze; (*Smog*) pall of smog.

dunstig ['dʊnstɪç] *adj* vaporous; (*Wetter*) hazy, misty.

düpieren [dy'pi:rən] *vt* to dupe.

Duplikat [dupli'ka:t] (-(e)s, -e) *nt* duplicate.

Dur [du:r] (-, -) *nt* (*MUS*) major.

=========== *SCHLÜSSELWORT*

durch [dʊrç] *präp +akk* **1** (*hindurch*) through; ~ **den Urwald** through the jungle; ~ **die ganze Welt reisen** to travel all over the world.

2 (*mittels*) through, by (means of); (*aufgrund*) due to, owing to; **Tod** ~ **Herzschlag/den Strang** death from a heart attack/by hanging; ~ **die Post** by post; ~ **seine Bemühungen** through his efforts.

♦ *adj* **1** (*hin-*) through; **die ganze Nacht** ~ all through the night; **den Sommer** ~ during the summer; **8 Uhr** ~ past 8 o'clock; ~ **und**

~ **completely; das geht mir** ~ **und** ~ that goes right through me.

2 (*KOCH: umg: durchgebraten*) done; (**gut**) ~ well-done.

durcharbeiten *vt, vi* to work through ♦ *vr*: **sich durch etw** ~ to work one's way through sth.

durchatmen *vi* to breathe deeply.

durchaus [dʊrç'aʊs] *adv* completely; (*unbedingt*) definitely; ~ **nicht** (*in verneinten Sätzen: als Verstärkung*) by no means; (: *als Antwort*) not at all; **das lässt sich** ~ **machen** that sounds feasible; **ich bin** ~ **Ihrer Meinung** I quite *od* absolutely agree with you.

durchbeißen *unreg vt* to bite through ♦ *vr* (*fig*) to battle on.

durchblättern *vt* to leaf through.

Durchblick ['dʊrçblɪk] *m* view; (*fig*) comprehension; **den** ~ **haben** (*fig: umg*) to know what's what.

durchblicken *vi* to look through; (*umg*: *verstehen*): (**bei etw**) ~ to understand (sth); **etw** ~ **lassen** (*fig*) to hint at sth.

Durchblutung [dʊrç'blu:tʊŋ] *f* circulation (of blood).

durchbohren *vt untr* to bore through, pierce.

durchboxen ['dʊrçbɔksən] *vr* (*fig: umg*): **sich (durch etw)** ~ to fight one's way through (sth).

durchbrechen¹ ['dʊrçbrɛçən] *unreg vt, vi* to break.

durchbrechen² [dʊrç'brɛçən] *unreg vt untr* (*Schranken*) to break through.

durchbrennen *unreg vi* (*Draht, Sicherung*) to burn through; (*umg*) to run away.

durchbringen *unreg vt* to get through; (*Geld*) to squander ♦ *vr* to make a living.

Durchbruch ['dʊrçbrʊx] *m* (*Öffnung*) opening; (*MIL*) breach; (*von Gefühlen etc*) eruption; (*der Zähne*) cutting; (*fig*) breakthrough; **zum** ~ **kommen** to break through.

durchdacht [dʊrç'daxt] *adj* well thought-out.

durchdenken *unreg vt untr* to think out.

durch- *zW*: ~**diskutieren** *vt* to talk over, discuss; ~**drängen** *vr* to force one's way through; ~**drehen** *vt* (*Fleisch*) to mince ♦ *vi* (*umg*) to crack up.

durchdringen¹ ['dʊrçdrɪŋən] *unreg vi* to penetrate, get through.

durchdringen² [dʊrç'drɪŋən] *unreg vt untr* to penetrate.

durchdringend *adj* piercing; (*Kälte, Wind*) biting; (*Geruch*) pungent.

durchdrücken ['dʊrçdrykən] *vt* (*durch Presse*) to press through; (*Creme, Teig*) to pipe; (*fig: Gesetz, Reformen etc*) to push through; (*seinen Willen*) to get; (*Knie, Kreuz etc*) to straighten.

durcheinander [dʊrçˌaɪˈnandər] *adv* in a mess, in confusion; (*verwirrt*) confused; ~ **trinken** to mix one's drinks; ~ **bringen** to mess up; (*verwirren*) to confuse; ~ **reden** to talk at the same time; ~ **werfen** to muddle up; **D~** (**-s**) *nt* (*Verwirrung*) confusion; (*Unordnung*) mess.

durch- *zW*: ~**fahren** *unreg vi*: **er ist bei Rot** ~**gefahren** he jumped the lights ♦ *vt*: **die Nacht** ~**fahren** to travel through the night; **D~fahrt** *f* transit; (*Verkehr*) thoroughfare; **D~fahrt bitte freihalten!** please keep access free; **D~fahrt verboten!** no through road; **D~fall** *m* (*MED*) diarrhoea (*BRIT*), diarrhea (*US*); ~**fallen** *unreg vi* to fall through; (*in Prüfung*) to fail; ~**finden** *unreg vr* to find one's way through; ~**fliegen** *unreg* (*umg*) *vi* (*in Prüfung*): (**durch etw** *od* **in etw** *dat*) ~**fliegen** to fail (sth); **D~flug** *m*: **Passagiere auf dem D~flug** transit passengers.

durchforschen *vt untr* to explore.

durchforsten [dʊrçˈfɔrstən] *vt untr* (*fig: Akten etc*) to go through.

durchfragen *vr* to find one's way by asking.

durchfressen *unreg vr* to eat one's way through.

durchführbar *adj* feasible, practicable.

durchführen [ˈdʊrçfyːrən] *vt* to carry out; (*Gesetz*) to implement; (*Kursus*) to run.

Durchführung *f* execution, performance.

Durchgang [ˈdʊrçgaŋ] *m* passage(way); (*bei Produktion, Versuch*) run; (*SPORT*) round; (*bei Wahl*) ballot; ~ **verboten** no thoroughfare.

durchgängig [ˈdʊrçgɛŋɪç] *adj* universal, general.

Durchgangs- *zW*: ~**handel** *m* transit trade; ~**lager** *nt* transit camp; ~**stadium** *nt* transitory stage; ~**verkehr** *m* through traffic.

durchgeben [ˈdʊrçgeːbən] *unreg vt* (*RUNDF, TV*: *Hinweis, Wetter*) to give; (*Lottozahlen*) to announce.

durchgefroren [ˈdʊrçgəfroːrən] *adj* (*See*) completely frozen; (*Mensch*) frozen stiff.

durchgehen [ˈdʊrçgeːən] *unreg vt* (*behandeln*) to go over *od* through ♦ *vi* to go through; (*ausreißen: Pferd*) to break loose; (*Mensch*) to run away; **mein Temperament ging mit mir durch** my temper got the better of me; **jdm etw** ~ **lassen** to let sb get away with sth.

durchgehend *adj* (*Zug*) through; (*Öffnungszeiten*) continuous.

durchgeschwitzt [ˈdʊrçgəʃvɪtst] *adj* soaked in sweat.

durch- *zW*: ~**greifen** *unreg vi* to take strong action; ~**halten** *unreg vi* to last out ♦ *vt* to keep up; **D~haltevermögen** *nt* staying power; ~**hängen** *unreg vi* (*lit, fig*) to sag; ~**hecheln** (*umg*) *vt* to gossip about; ~**kommen** *unreg vi* to get through; (*überleben*) to pull through.

durchkreuzen *vt untr* to thwart, frustrate.

durchlassen *unreg vt* (*Person*) to let through; (*Wasser*) to let in.

durchlässig *adj* leaky.

Durchlaucht [ˈdʊrçlaʊxt] (**-, -en**) *f*: (**Euer**) ~ Your Highness.

Durchlauf [ˈdʊrçlaʊf] *m* (*COMPUT*) run.

durchlaufen *unreg vt untr* (*Schule, Phase*) to go through.

Durchlauferhitzer (**-s, -**) *m* continuous-flow water heater.

Durchlaufzeit *f* (*COMPUT*) length of the run.

durch- *zW*: ~**leben** *vt untr* (*Zeit*) to live *od* go through; (*Jugend, Gefühl*) to experience; ~**lesen** *unreg vt* to read through; ~**leuchten** *vt untr* to X-ray; ~**löchern** *vt untr* to perforate; (*mit Löchern*) to punch holes in; (*mit Kugeln*) to riddle; ~**machen** *vt* to go through; **die Nacht** ~**machen** to make a night of it.

Durchmarsch *m* march through.

Durchmesser (**-s, -**) *m* diameter.

durchnässen *vt untr* to soak (through).

durch- *zW*: ~**nehmen** *unreg vt* to go over; ~**nummerieren**▲ *vt* to number consecutively; ~**organisieren** *vt* to organize down to the last detail; ~**pausen** *vt* to trace; ~**peitschen** *vt* (*lit*) to whip soundly; (*fig: Gesetzentwurf, Reform*) to force through.

durchqueren [dʊrçˈkveːrən] *vt untr* to cross.

durch- *zW*: ~**rechnen** *vt* to calculate; ~**regnen** *vi unpers*: **es regnet durchs Dach** ~ the rain is coming through the roof; **D~reiche** (**-, -n**) *f* (serving) hatch, pass-through (*US*); **D~reise** *f* transit; **auf der D~reise** passing through; (*Güter*) in transit; **D~reisevisum** *nt* transit visa; ~**ringen** *unreg vr* to make up one's mind finally; ~**rosten** *vi* to rust through; ~**rutschen** *vi*: (**durch etw**) ~**rutschen** (*lit*) to slip through (sth); (*bei Prüfung*) to scrape through (sth).

durchs [dʊrçs] = **durch das**.

Durchsage [ˈdʊrçzaːgə] *f* intercom *od* radio announcement.

Durchsatz [ˈdʊrçzats] *m* (*COMPUT, Produktion*) throughput.

durchschauen[1] [ˈdʊrçʃaʊən] *vt, vi* (*lit*) to look *od* see through.

durchschauen[2] [dʊrçˈʃaʊən] *vt untr* (*Person, Lüge*) to see through.

durchscheinen [ˈdʊrçʃaɪnən] *unreg vi* to shine through.

durchscheinend *adj* translucent.

durchschlafen [ˈdʊrçʃlaːfən] *unreg vi* to sleep through.

Durchschlag [ˈdʊrçʃlaːk] *m* (*Doppel*) carbon copy; (*Sieb*) strainer.

durchschlagen *unreg vt* (*entzweischlagen*) to split (in two); (*sieben*) to sieve ♦ *vi* (*zum Vorschein kommen*) to emerge, come out ♦ *vr* to get by.

durchschlagend *adj* resounding; **(eine) ~e Wirkung haben** to be totally effective.
Durchschlagpapier *nt* flimsy; (*Kohlepapier*) carbon paper.
Durchschlagskraft *f* (*von Geschoss*) penetration; (*fig: von Argument*) decisiveness.
durch- *zW:* **~schlängeln** *vr* (*durch etw: Mensch*) to thread one's way through; **~schlüpfen** *vi* to slip through; **~schneiden** *unreg vt* to cut through.
Durchschnitt ['dʊrçʃnɪt] *m* (*Mittelwert*) average; **über/unter dem ~** above/below average; **im ~** on average; **d~lich** *adj* average ♦ *adv* on average; **d~lich begabt/ groß** *etc* of average ability/height *etc*.
Durchschnitts- *zW:* **~geschwindigkeit** *f* average speed; **~mensch** *m* average man, man in the street; **~wert** *m* average.
durch- *zW:* **D~schrift** *f* copy; **D~schuss ▲** *m* (*Loch*) bullet hole; **~schwimmen** *unreg vt untr* to swim across; **~segeln** (*umg*) *vi* (*nicht bestehen*): **durch** *od* **bei etw ~segeln** to fail *od* flunk (*umg*) (sth); **~sehen** *unreg vt* to look through.
durchsetzen¹ ['dʊrçzɛtsən] *vt* to enforce ♦ *vr* (*Erfolg haben*) to succeed; (*sich behaupten*) to get one's way; **seinen Kopf ~** to get one's own way.
durchsetzen² [dʊrç'zɛtsən] *vt untr* to mix.
Durchsicht ['dʊrçzɪçt] *f* looking through, checking.
durchsichtig *adj* transparent; **D~keit** *f* transparency.
durch- *zW:* **~sickern** *vi* to seep through; (*fig*) to leak out; **~sieben** *vt* to sieve; **~sitzen** *unreg vt* (*Sessel etc*) to wear out (the seat of); **~spielen** *vt* to go *od* run through; **~sprechen** *unreg vt* to talk over; **~stehen** *unreg vt* to live through; **D~stehvermögen** *nt* endurance, staying power; **~stellen** *vt* (*TEL*) to put through; **~stöbern** [-'ʃtøːbərn] *vt untr* to ransack, search through; **~stoßen** *unreg vt, vi* to break through (*auch MIL*); **~streichen** *unreg vt* to cross out; **~stylen** *vt* to ponce up (*umg*); **~suchen** *vt untr* to search; **D~suchung** *f* search; **D~suchungsbefehl** *m* search warrant; **~trainieren** *vt* (*Sportler, Körper*): **gut ~trainiert** in superb condition; **~tränken** *vt untr* to soak; **~treten** *unreg vt* (*Pedal*) to step on; (*Starter*) to kick; **~trieben** *adj* cunning, wily; **~wachsen** *adj* (*lit: Speck*) streaky; (*fig: mittelmäßig*) so-so.
Durchwahl ['dʊrçvaːl] *f* (*TEL*) direct dialling; (*bei Firma*) extension.
durch- *zW:* **~weg** *adv* throughout, completely; **~wursteln** (*umg*) *vr* to muddle through; **~zählen** *vt* to count ♦ *vi* to count *od* number off; **~zechen** *vt untr:* **eine ~zechte Nacht** a night of drinking; **~ziehen** *unreg vt* (*Faden*) to

draw through ♦ *vi* to pass through; **eine Sache ~ziehen** to finish off sth; **~zucken** *vt untr* to shoot *od* flash through; **D~zug** *m* (*Luft*) draught (*BRIT*), draft (*US*); (*von Truppen, Vögeln*) passage; **~zwängen** *vt, vr* to squeeze *od* force through.

═══════════════ *SCHLÜSSELWORT*

dürfen ['dʏrfən] *unreg vi* **1** (*Erlaubnis haben*) to be allowed to; **ich darf das** I'm allowed to (do that); **darf ich?** may I?; **darf ich ins Kino?** can *od* may I go to the cinema?; **es darf geraucht werden** you may smoke.
2 (*in Verneinungen*): **er darf das nicht** he's not allowed to (do that); **das darf nicht geschehen** that must not happen; **da darf sie sich nicht wundern** that shouldn't surprise her; **das darf doch nicht wahr sein!** that can't be true!
3 (*in Höflichkeitsformeln*): **darf ich Sie bitten, das zu tun?** may *od* could I ask you to do that?; **wir freuen uns, Ihnen mitteilen zu ~** we are pleased to be able to tell you; **was darf es sein?** what can I get for you?
4 (*können*): **das ~ Sie mir glauben** you can believe me.
5 (*Möglichkeit*): **das dürfte genug sein** that should be enough; **es dürfte Ihnen bekannte sein, dass ...** as you will probably know ...

durfte *etc* ['dʊrftə] *vb siehe* **dürfen.**
dürftig ['dʏrftɪç] *adj* (*ärmlich*) needy, poor; (*unzulänglich*) inadequate.
dürr [dʏr] *adj* dried-up; (*Land*) arid; (*mager*) skinny.
Dürre (-, -n) *f* aridity; (*Zeit*) drought.
Durst [dʊrst] (-(e)s) *m* thirst; **~ haben** to be thirsty; **einen über den ~ getrunken haben** (*umg*) to have had one too many.
durstig *adj* thirsty.
Durststrecke *f* hard times *pl.*
Dusche ['dʊʃə] (-, -n) *f* shower; **das war eine kalte ~** (*fig*) that really brought him/her *etc* down with a bump.
duschen *vi, vr* to have a shower.
Duschgelegenheit *f* shower facilities *pl.*
Düse ['dyːzə] (-, -n) *f* nozzle; (*Flugzeug~*) jet.
Dusel ['duːzəl] (*umg*) *m:* **da hat er (einen) ~ gehabt** he was lucky.
Düsen- *zW:* **~antrieb** *m* jet propulsion; **~flugzeug** *nt* jet (plane); **~jäger** *m* jet fighter.
Dussel ['dʊsəl] (-s, -) (*umg*) *m* twit, berk.
Düsseldorf ['dʏsəldɔrf] *nt* Dusseldorf.
dusselig ['dʊsəlɪç], **dusslig ▲** ['dʊslɪç] (*umg*) *adj* stupid.
düster ['dyːstər] *adj* dark; (*Gedanken, Zukunft*) gloomy; **D~keit** *f* darkness, gloom; gloominess.
Dutzend ['dʊtsənt] (-s, -e) *nt* dozen; **~(e)** *od*

d~(e) Mal a dozen times; **~ware** (*pej*) *f* (cheap) mass-produced item; **d~weise** *adv* by the dozen.

duzen ['du:tsən] *vt* to address with the familiar "du" form ♦ *vr* to address each other with the familiar "du" form; *siehe auch* **siezen**

DUZEN/SIEZEN

There are two different forms of address in German: du and Sie. Duzen means addressing someone as 'du' and siezen means addressing someone as 'Sie'. 'Du' is used to address children, family and close friends. Students almost always use 'du' to each other. Sie is used for all grown-ups and older teenagers.

Duzfreund *m* good friend.
DVD (-, -s) *f abk* (= *Digital Versatile Disk*) DVD.
Dynamik [dy'na:mɪk] *f* (*PHYS*) dynamics; (*fig: Schwung*) momentum; (*von Mensch*) dynamism.
dynamisch [dy'na:mɪʃ] *adj* (*lit, fig*) dynamic; (*renten~*) index-linked.
Dynamit [dyna'mi:t] (-**s**) *nt* dynamite.
Dynamo [dy'na:mo] (-**s, -s**) *m* dynamo.
dz *abk* = **Doppelzentner**.
D-Zug ['de:tsu:k] *m* through train; **ein alter Mann ist doch kein ~** (*umg*) I am going as fast as I can.

E, e

E¹, e [e:] *nt* E, e; **~ wie Emil** ≈ E for Edward, E for Easy (*US*).
E² [e:] *abk* = **Eilzug; Europastraße**.
Ebbe ['ɛbə] (-, -**n**) *f* low tide; **~ und Flut** ebb and flow.
eben ['e:bən] *adj* level; (*glatt*) smooth ♦ *adv* just; (*bestätigend*) exactly; **das ist ~ so** that's just the way it is; **mein Bleistift war doch ~ noch da** my pencil was there (just) a minute ago; **~ deswegen** just because of that.
Ebenbild *nt*: **das genaue ~ seines Vaters** the spitting image of his father.
ebenbürtig *adj*: **jdm ~ sein** to be sb's peer.
Ebene (-, -**n**) *f* plain; (*MATH, PHYS*) plane; (*fig*) level.
eben- *zW*: **~erdig** *adj* at ground level; **~falls** *adv* likewise; **E~heit** *f* levelness; (*Glätte*)

smoothness; **E~holz** *nt* ebony; **~so** *adv* just as; **~so gut** just as well; **~so oft** just as often; **~so viel** just as much; **~so weit** just as far; **~so wenig** just as little.
Eber ['e:bər] (-**s, -**) *m* boar.
Eberesche *f* mountain ash, rowan.
ebnen ['e:bnən] *vt* to level; **jdm den Weg ~** (*fig*) to smooth the way for sb.
Echo ['ɛço] (-**s, -s**) *nt* echo; (**bei jdm**) **ein lebhaftes ~ finden** (*fig*) to meet with a lively response (from sb).
Echolot ['ɛço:lo:t] *nt* (*NAUT*) echo-sounder, sonar.
Echse ['ɛksə] (-, -**n**) *f* (*ZOOL*) lizard.
echt [ɛçt] *adj* genuine; (*typisch*) typical; **ich hab ~ keine Zeit** (*umg*) I really don't have any time; **E~heit** *f* genuineness.
Eckball ['ɛkbal] *m* corner (kick).
Ecke ['ɛkə] (-, -**n**) *f* corner; (*MATH*) angle; **gleich um die ~** just around the corner; **an allen ~n und Enden sparen** (*umg*) to pinch and scrape; **jdn um die ~ bringen** (*umg*) to bump sb off; **mit jdm um ein paar ~n herum verwandt sein** (*umg*) to be distantly related to sb, be sb's second cousin twice removed (*hum*).
eckig *adj* angular.
Eckzahn *m* eye tooth.
Eckzins *m* (*FIN*) minimum lending rate.
Ecstasy ['ɛkstəsɪ] *nt* (*Droge*) ecstasy.
Ecuador [ekua'do:r] (-**s**) *nt* Ecuador.
edel ['e:dəl] *adj* noble; **E~ganove** *m* gentleman criminal; **E~gas** *nt* rare gas; **E~metall** *nt* rare metal; **E~stein** *m* precious stone.
Edinburg(h) ['e:dɪnburk] *nt* Edinburgh.
EDV (-) *f abk* (= *elektronische Datenverarbeitung*) EDP.
EEG (-) *nt abk* (= *Elektroenzephalogramm*) EEG.
Efeu ['e:fɔy] (-**s**) *m* ivy.
Effeff [ɛf'|ɛf] (-) (*umg*) *nt*: **etw aus dem ~ können** to be able to do sth standing on one's head.
Effekt [ɛ'fɛkt] (-(**e**)**s, -e**) *m* effect.
Effekten [ɛ'fɛktən] *pl* stocks *pl*; **~börse** *f* Stock Exchange.
Effekthascherei [ɛfɛktha∫ə'raɪ] *f* sensationalism.
effektiv [ɛfɛk'ti:f] *adj* effective, actual.
Effet [ɛ'fe:] (-**s**) *m* spin.
EG (-) *f abk* (= *Europäische Gemeinschaft*) EC.
egal [e'ga:l] *adj* all the same; **das ist mir ganz ~** it's all the same to me.
egalitär [egali'tɛ:r] *adj* (*geh*) egalitarian.
Egge ['ɛgə] (-, -**n**) *f* (*AGR*) harrow.
Egoismus [ego'ɪsmʊs] *m* selfishness, egoism.
Egoist(in) *m(f)* egoist; **e~isch** *adj* selfish, egoistic.
egozentrisch [ego'tsɛntrɪʃ] *adj* egocentric, self-centred (*BRIT*), self-centered (*US*).

Spelling Reform: ▲ *new spelling* △ *old spelling (to be phased out)*

eh [eː] *adv:* **seit ~ und je** for ages, since the year dot (*umg*); **ich komme ~ nicht dazu** I won't get around to it anyway.

e. h. *abk* = **ehrenhalber**.

Ehe ['eːə] (-, -n) *f* marriage; **die ~ eingehen** (*form*) to enter into matrimony; **sie leben in wilder ~** (*veraltet*) they are living in sin.

ehe *konj* before.

Ehe- *zW:* **~brecher** (-s, -) *m* adulterer; **~brecherin** *f* adulteress; **~bruch** *m* adultery; **~frau** *f* wife; **~leute** *pl* married couple *pl*; **e~lich** *adj* matrimonial; (*Kind*) legitimate.

ehemalig *adj* former.

ehemals *adv* formerly.

Ehe- *zW:* **~mann** *m* married man; (*Partner*) husband; **~paar** *nt* married couple; **~partner** *m* husband; **~partnerin** *f* wife.

eher ['eːər] *adv* (*früher*) sooner; (*lieber*) rather, sooner; (*mehr*) more; **nicht ~ als** not before; **umso ~, als** the more so because.

Ehe- *zW:* **~ring** *m* wedding ring; **~scheidung** *f* divorce; **~schließung** *f* marriage; **~stand** *m:* **in den ~stand treten** (*form*) to enter into matrimony.

eheste(r, s) ['eːəstə(r, s)] *adj* (*früheste*) first, earliest; **am ~n** (*am liebsten*) soonest; (*meist*) most; (*am wahrscheinlichsten*) most probably.

Ehevermittlung *f* (*Büro*) marriage bureau.

Eheversprechen *nt* (*JUR*) promise to marry.

ehrbar ['eːrbaːr] *adj* honourable (*BRIT*), honorable (*US*), respectable.

Ehre (-, -n) *f* honour (*BRIT*), honor (*US*); **etw in ~n halten** to treasure *od* cherish sth.

ehren *vt* to honour (*BRIT*), honor (*US*).

Ehren- *zW:* **e~amtlich** *adj* honorary; **~bürgerrecht** *nt:* **die Stadt verlieh ihr das ~bürgerrecht** she was given the freedom of the city; **~gast** *m* guest of honour (*BRIT*) *od* honor (*US*); **e~haft** *adj* honourable (*BRIT*), honorable (*US*); **e~halber** *adv:* **er wurde e~halber zum Vorsitzenden auf Lebenszeit ernannt** he was made honorary president for life; **~mann** *m* man of honour (*BRIT*) *od* honor (*US*); **~mitglied** *nt* honorary member; **~platz** *m* place of honour (*BRIT*) *od* honor (*US*); **~rechte** *pl* civic rights *pl*; **e~rührig** *adj* defamatory; **~runde** *f* lap of honour (*BRIT*) *od* honor (*US*); **~sache** *f* point of honour (*BRIT*) *od* honor (*US*); **~sache!** (*umg*) you can count on me; **~tag** *m* (*Geburtstag*) birthday; (*großer Tag*) big day; **e~voll** *adj* honourable (*BRIT*), honorable (*US*); **~wort** *nt* word of honour (*BRIT*) *od* honor (*US*); **Urlaub auf ~wort** parole.

Ehr- *zW:* **e~erbietig** *adj* respectful; **~furcht** *f* awe, deep respect; **~furcht gebietend** awesome; (*Stimme*) authoritative; **~gefühl** *nt* sense of honour (*BRIT*) *od* honor (*US*); **~geiz** *m* ambition; **e~geizig** *adj* ambitious; **e~lich** *adj* honest; **e~lich verdientes Geld** hard-

earned money; **e~lich gesagt ...** quite frankly *od* honestly ...; **~lichkeit** *f* honesty; **e~los** *adj* dishonourable (*BRIT*), dishonorable (*US*).

Ehrung *f* honour(ing) (*BRIT*), honor(ing) (*US*).

ehrwürdig *adj* venerable.

Ei [aɪ] (-(e)s, -er) *nt* egg; **Eier** *pl* (*umg!: Hoden*) balls *pl* (!); **jdn wie ein rohes ~ behandeln** (*fig*) to handle sb with kid gloves; **wie aus dem ~ gepellt aussehen** (*umg*) to look spruce.

ei *interj* well, well; (*beschwichtigend*) now, now.

Eibe ['aɪbə] (-, -n) *f* (*BOT*) yew.

Eichamt ['aɪç|amt] *nt* Office of Weights and Measures.

Eiche (-, -n) *f* oak (tree).

Eichel (-, -n) *f* acorn; (*KARTEN*) club; (*ANAT*) glans.

eichen *vt* to calibrate.

Eichhörnchen *nt* squirrel.

Eichmaß *nt* standard.

Eichung *f* standardization.

Eid ['aɪt] (-(e)s, -e) *m* oath; **eine Erklärung an ~es statt abgeben** (*JUR*) to make a solemn declaration.

Eidechse ['aɪdɛksə] (-, -n) *f* lizard.

eidesstattlich *adj:* **~e Erklärung** affidavit.

Eid- *zW:* **~genosse** *m* Swiss; **~genossenschaft** *f:* **Schweizerische ~genossenschaft** Swiss Confederation; **e~lich** *adj* (sworn) upon oath.

Eidotter *nt* egg yolk.

Eier- *zW:* **~becher** *m* egg cup; **~kuchen** *m* pancake; (*Omelett*) omelette (*BRIT*), omelet (*US*); **~likör** *m* advocaat.

eiern ['aɪərn] (*umg*) *vi* to wobble.

Eier- *zW:* **~schale** *f* eggshell; **~stock** *m* ovary; **~uhr** *f* egg timer.

Eifel ['aɪfəl] (-) *f* Eifel (Mountains).

Eifer ['aɪfər] (-s) *m* zeal, enthusiasm; **mit großem ~ bei der Sache sein** to put one's heart into it; **im ~ des Gefechts** (*fig*) in the heat of the moment; **~sucht** *f* jealousy; **e~süchtig** *adj:* **e~süchtig (auf +akk)** jealous (of).

eifrig ['aɪfrɪç] *adj* zealous, enthusiastic.

Eigelb ['aɪgɛlp] (-(e)s, -e *od* -) *nt* egg yolk.

eigen ['aɪgən] *adj* own; (*~artig*) peculiar; (*ordentlich*) particular; (*übergenau*) fussy; **ich möchte kurz in ~er Sache sprechen** I would like to say something on my own account; **mit dem ihm ~en Lächeln** with that smile peculiar to him; **sich** *dat* **etw zu E~ machen** to make sth one's own; **E~art** *f* (*Besonderheit*) peculiarity; (*Eigenschaft*) characteristic; **~artig** *adj* peculiar; **E~bau** *m:* **er fährt ein Fahrrad Marke E~bau** (*hum: umg*) he rides a home-made bike; **E~bedarf** *m* one's own requirements *pl*; **E~brötler(in)** (-s, -) *m(f)* loner, lone wolf; (*komischer Kauz*) oddball (*umg*); **E~gewicht** *nt* dead weight; **~händig**

adj with one's own hand; **E~heim** *nt* owner-occupied house; **E~heit** *f* peculiarity; **E~initiative** *f* initiative of one's own; **E~kapital** *nt* personal capital; (*von Firma*) company capital; **E~lob** *nt* self-praise; **~mächtig** *adj* high-handed; (*~verantwortlich*) taken/done *etc* on one's own authority; (*unbefugt*) unauthorized; **E~name** *m* proper name; **E~nutz** *m* self-interest.

eigens *adv* expressly, on purpose.

eigen- *zW:* **E~schaft** *f* quality, property, attribute; **E~schaftswort** *nt* adjective; **E~sinn** *m* obstinacy; **~sinnig** *adj* obstinate; **~ständig** *adj* independent; **E~ständigkeit** *f* independence.

eigentlich *adj* actual, real ♦ *adv* actually, really; **was willst du ~ hier?** what do you want here anyway?

eigen- *zW:* **E~tor** *nt* own goal; **E~tum** *nt* property; **E~tümer(in)** (**-s, -**) *m(f)* owner, proprietor; **~tümlich** *adj* peculiar; **E~tümlichkeit** *f* peculiarity.

Eigentumsdelikt *nt* (*JUR: Diebstahl*) theft.

Eigentumswohnung *f* freehold flat.

eigenwillig *adj* with a mind of one's own.

eignen ['aɪɡnən] *vr* to be suited.

Eignung *f* suitability.

Eignungsprüfung *f* aptitude test.

Eignungstest (**-(e)s, -s** *od* **-e**) *m* aptitude test.

Eilbote *m* courier; **per** *od* **durch ~n** express.

Eilbrief *m* express letter.

Eile (**-**) *f* haste; **es hat keine ~** there's no hurry.

Eileiter ['aɪlaɪtər] *m* (*ANAT*) Fallopian tube.

eilen *vi* (*Mensch*) to hurry; (*dringend sein*) to be urgent.

eilends *adv* hastily.

Eilgut *nt* express goods *pl*, fast freight (*US*).

eilig *adj* hasty, hurried; (*dringlich*) urgent; **es ~ haben** to be in a hurry.

Eil- *zW:* **~tempo** *nt:* **etw im ~tempo machen** to do sth in a rush; **~zug** *m* fast stopping train; **~zustellung** *f* special delivery.

Eimer ['aɪmər] (**-s, -**) *m* bucket, pail; **im ~ sein** (*umg*) to be up the spout.

ein(e) ['aɪn(ə)] *num* one ♦ *indef art* a, an ♦ *adv:* **nicht ~ noch aus wissen** not to know what to do; **E~/Aus** (*an Geräten*) on/off; **er ist ihr E~ und Alles** he means everything to her; **er geht bei uns ~ und aus** he is always round at our place.

einander [aɪ'nandər] *pron* one another, each other.

einarbeiten ['aɪnʔarbaɪtən] *vr:* **sich (in etw** *akk*) **~** to familiarize o.s. (with sth).

Einarbeitungszeit *f* training period.

einarmig ['aɪnʔarmɪç] *adj* one-armed.

einäschern ['aɪnʔɛʃərn] *vt* (*Leichnam*) to cremate; (*Stadt etc*) to reduce to ashes.

einatmen ['aɪnʔaːtmən] *vt, vi* to inhale, breathe in.

einäugig ['aɪnʔɔʏɡɪç] *adj* one-eyed.

Einbahnstraße ['aɪnbaːnʃtrasə] *f* one-way street.

Einband ['aɪnbant] *m* binding, cover.

einbändig ['aɪnbɛndɪç] *adj* one-volume.

einbauen ['aɪnbauən] *vt* to build in; (*Motor*) to install, fit.

Einbau- *zW:* **~küche** *f* (fully-)fitted kitchen; **~möbel** *pl* built-in furniture *sing*; **~schrank** *m* fitted cupboard.

einbegriffen ['aɪnbəɡrɪfən] *adj* included, inclusive.

einbehalten ['aɪnbəhaltən] *unreg vt* to keep back.

einberufen *unreg vt* to convene; (*MIL*) to call up (*BRIT*), draft (*US*).

Einberufung *f* convocation; call-up (*BRIT*), draft (*US*).

Einberufungsbefehl *m,*
Einberufungsbescheid *m* (*MIL*) call-up (*BRIT*) *od* draft (*US*) papers *pl*.

einbetten ['aɪnbɛtən] *vt* to embed.

Einbettzimmer *nt* single room.

einbeziehen ['aɪnbətsiːən] *unreg vt* to include.

einbiegen ['aɪnbiːɡən] *unreg vi* to turn.

einbilden ['aɪnbɪldən] *vr:* **sich** *dat* **etw ~** to imagine sth; **sich** *dat* **viel auf etw** *akk* **~** (*stolz sein*) to be conceited about sth.

Einbildung *f* imagination; (*Dünkel*) conceit.

Einbildungskraft *f* imagination.

einbinden ['aɪnbɪndən] *unreg vt* to bind (up).

einbläuen▲ ['aɪnblɔʏən] (*umg*) *vt:* **jdm etw ~** to hammer sth into sb.

einblenden ['aɪnblɛndən] *vt* to fade in.

Einblick ['aɪnblɪk] *m* insight; **~ in die Akten nehmen** to examine the files; **jdm ~ in etw** *akk* **gewähren** to allow sb to look at sth.

einbrechen ['aɪnbrɛçən] *unreg vi* (*einstürzen*) to fall in; (*Einbruch verüben*) to break in; **bei ~der Dunkelheit** at nightfall.

Einbrecher (**-s, -**) *m* burglar.

einbringen ['aɪnbrɪŋən] *unreg vt* to bring in; (*Geld, Vorteil*) to yield; (*mitbringen*) to contribute; **das bringt nichts ein** (*fig*) it's not worth it.

einbrocken ['aɪnbrɔkən] (*umg*) *vt:* **jdm/sich etwas ~** to land sb/o.s. in it.

Einbruch ['aɪnbrʊx] *m* (*Haus~*) break-in, burglary; (*des Winters*) onset; (*Einsturz, FIN*) collapse; (*MIL: in Front*) breakthrough; **bei ~ der Nacht** at nightfall.

einbruchssicher *adj* burglar-proof.

Einbuchtung ['aɪnbʊxtʊŋ] *f* indentation; (*Bucht*) inlet, bay.

einbürgern ['aɪnbʏrɡərn] *vt* to naturalize ♦ *vr* to become adopted; **das hat sich so eingebürgert** that's become a custom.

Einbürgerung *f* naturalization.

Einbuße ['aɪnbuːsə] *f* loss, forfeiture.

einbüßen ['aɪnbyːsən] *vt* to lose, forfeit.

einchecken ['aɪntʃɛkən] *vt, vi* to check in.

eincremen ['aɪnkreːmən] *vt* to put cream on.

eindämmen ['aɪndɛmən] *vt* (*Fluss*) to dam; (*fig*) to check, contain.

eindecken ['aɪndɛkən] *vr:* **sich ~ (mit)** to lay in stocks (of) ♦ *vt* (*umg: überhäufen*): **mit Arbeit eingedeckt sein** to be inundated with work.

eindeutig ['aɪndɔytɪç] *adj* unequivocal.

eindeutschen ['aɪndɔytʃən] *vt* (*Fremdwort*) to Germanize.

eindösen ['aɪndøːzən] (*umg*) *vi* to doze off.

eindringen ['aɪndrɪŋən] *unreg vi:* **~ (in** +akk**)** to force one's way in(to); (*in Haus*) to break in(to); (*in Land*) to invade; (*Gas, Wasser*) to penetrate; **auf jdn ~** (*mit Bitten*) to pester sb.

eindringlich *adj* forcible, urgent; **ich habe ihn ~ gebeten** ... I urged him ...

Eindringling *m* intruder.

Eindruck ['aɪndrʊk] *m* impression.

eindrücken ['aɪndrykən] *vt* to press in.

eindrucksfähig *adj* impressionable.

eindrucksvoll *adj* impressive.

eine(r, s) *pron* one; (*jemand*) someone; **wie kann ~r nur so dumm sein!** how could anybody be so stupid!; **es kam ~s zum anderen** it was (just) one thing after another; **sich** *dat* **~n genehmigen** (*umg*) to have a quick one.

einebnen ['aɪnˌeːbnən] *vt* (*lit*) to level (off); (*fig*) to level out.

Einehe ['aɪnˌeːə] *f* monogamy.

eineiig ['aɪnˌaɪç] *adj* (*Zwillinge*) identical.

eineinhalb ['aɪnˌaɪnˈhalp] *num* one and a half.

einengen ['aɪnˌɛŋən] *vt* to confine, restrict.

Einer ['aɪnər] (-) *m* (*MATH*) unit; (*Ruderboot*) single scull.

Einerlei ['aɪnərˈlaɪ] (-s) *nt* monotony; **e~** *adj* (*gleichartig*) the same kind of; **es ist mir e~** it is all the same to me.

einerseits *adv* on the one hand.

einfach ['aɪnfax] *adj* simple; (*nicht mehrfach*) single ♦ *adv* simply; **E~heit** *f* simplicity.

einfädeln ['aɪnfɛːdəln] *vt* (*Nadel*) to thread; (*fig*) to contrive.

einfahren ['aɪnfaːrən] *unreg vt* to bring in; (*Barriere*) to knock down; (*Auto*) to run in ♦ *vi* to drive in; (*Zug*) to pull in; (*MIN*) to go down.

Einfahrt *f* (*Vorgang*) driving in; pulling in; (*MIN*) descent; (*Ort*) entrance; (*von Autobahn*) slip road (*BRIT*), entrance ramp (*US*).

Einfall ['aɪnfal] *m* (*Idee*) idea, notion; (*Licht~*) incidence; (*MIL*) raid.

einfallen *unreg vi* (*einstürzen*) to fall in, collapse; (*Licht*) to fall; (*MIL*) to raid; (*einstimmen*): **~ (in** +akk**)** to join in (with); **etw fällt jdm ein** sth occurs to sb; **das fällt mir gar nicht ein!** I wouldn't dream of it;

sich *dat* **etwas ~ lassen** to have a good idea; **dabei fällt mir mein Onkel ein, der ...** that reminds me of my uncle who ...; **es fällt mir jetzt nicht ein** I can't think of it *od* it won't come to me at the moment.

einfallslos *adj* unimaginative.

einfallsreich *adj* imaginative.

einfältig ['aɪnfɛltɪç] *adj* simple(-minded).

Einfaltspinsel ['aɪnfaltspɪnzəl] (*umg*) *m* simpleton.

Einfamilienhaus [aɪnfaˈmiːliənhaʊs] *nt* detached house.

einfangen ['aɪnfaŋən] *unreg vt* to catch.

einfarbig ['aɪnfarbɪç] *adj* all one colour (*BRIT*) *od* color (*US*); (*Stoff etc*) self-coloured (*BRIT*), self-colored (*US*).

einfassen ['aɪnfasən] *vt* (*Edelstein*) to set; (*Beet, Stoff*) to edge.

Einfassung *f* setting; border.

einfetten ['aɪnfɛtən] *vt* to grease.

einfinden ['aɪnfɪndən] *unreg vr* to come, turn up.

einfliegen ['aɪnfliːgən] *unreg vt* to fly in.

einfließen ['aɪnfliːsən] *unreg vi* to flow in.

einflößen ['aɪnfløːsən] *vt:* **jdm etw ~** (*lit*) to give sb sth; (*fig*) to instil sth into sb.

Einfluss▲ ['aɪnflʊs] *m* influence; **~ nehmen** to bring an influence to bear; **~bereich** *m* sphere of influence; **e~reich** *adj* influential.

einflüstern ['aɪnflystərn] *vt:* **jdm etw ~** to whisper sth to sb; (*fig*) to insinuate sth to sb.

einförmig ['aɪnfœrmɪç] *adj* uniform; (*eintönig*) monotonous; **E~keit** *f* uniformity; monotony.

einfrieren ['aɪnfriːrən] *unreg vi* to freeze (in) ♦ *vt* to freeze; (*POL: Beziehungen*) to suspend.

einfügen ['aɪnfyːgən] *vt* to fit in; (*zusätzlich*) to add; (*COMPUT*) to insert.

einfühlen ['aɪnfyːlən] *vr:* **sich in jdn ~** to empathize with sb.

einfühlsam ['aɪnfyːlzaːm] *adj* sensitive.

Einfühlungsvermögen *nt* empathy; **mit großem ~** with a great deal of sensitivity.

Einfuhr ['aɪnfuːr] (-) *f* import; **~artikel** *m* imported article.

einführen ['aɪnfyːrən] *vt* to bring in; (*Mensch, Sitten*) to introduce; (*Ware*) to import; **jdn in sein Amt ~** to install sb (in office).

Einfuhr- *zW:* **~genehmigung** *f* import permit; **~kontingent** *nt* import quota; **~sperre** *f* ban on imports; **~stopp** *m* ban on imports.

Einführung *f* introduction.

Einführungspreis *m* introductory price.

Einfuhrzoll *m* import duty.

einfüllen ['aɪnfʏlən] *vt* to pour in.

Eingabe ['aɪngaːbə] *f* petition; (*Daten~*) input; **~/Ausgabe** (*COMPUT*) input/output.

Eingang ['aɪngaŋ] *m* entrance; (*COMM: Ankunft*) arrival; (*Sendung*) post; **wir bestätigen den ~ Ihres Schreibens vom ...**

we acknowledge receipt of your letter of the ...

eingängig ['aɪngɛŋɪç] *adj* catchy.

eingangs *adv* at the outset ♦ *präp +gen* at the outset of.

Eingangs- *zW*: ~**bestätigung** *f* acknowledgement of receipt; ~**halle** *f* entrance hall; ~**stempel** *m* (*COMM*) receipt stamp.

eingeben ['aɪnge:bən] *unreg vt* (*Arznei*) to give; (*Daten etc*) to enter; (*Gedanken*) to inspire.

eingebettet ['aɪngəbɛtət] *adj*: **in** *od* **zwischen Hügeln** ~ nestling among the hills.

eingebildet ['aɪngəbɪldət] *adj* imaginary; (*eitel*) conceited; ~**er Kranker** hypochondriac.

Eingeborene(r) ['aɪngəbo:rənə(r)] *f(m)* native.

Eingebung *f* inspiration.

eingedenk ['aɪngədɛŋk] *präp +gen* bearing in mind.

eingefahren ['aɪngəfa:rən] *adj* (*Verhaltensweise*) well-worn.

eingefallen ['aɪngəfalən] *adj* (*Gesicht*) gaunt.

eingefleischt ['aɪngəflaɪʃt] *adj* inveterate; ~**er Junggeselle** confirmed bachelor.

eingefroren ['aɪngəfro:rən] *adj* frozen.

eingehen ['aɪnge:ən] *unreg vi* (*Aufnahme finden*) to come in; (*Sendung, Geld*) to be received; (*Tier, Pflanze*) to die; (*Firma*) to fold; (*schrumpfen*) to shrink ♦ *vt* (*abmachen*) to enter into; (*Wette*) to make; **auf etw** *akk* ~ to go into sth; **auf jdn** ~ to respond to sb; **jdm** ~ (*verständlich sein*) to be comprehensible to sb; **auf einen Vorschlag/Plan** ~ (*zustimmen*) to go along with a suggestion/plan; **bei dieser Hitze/Kälte geht man ja ein!** (*umg*) this heat/cold is just too much.

eingehend *adj* in-depth, thorough.

eingekeilt ['aɪngəkaɪlt] *adj* hemmed in; (*fig*) trapped.

eingekesselt ['aɪngəkɛsəlt] *adj*: ~ **sein** to be encircled *od* surrounded.

Eingemachte(s) ['aɪngəma:xtə(s)] *nt* preserves *pl*.

eingemeinden ['aɪngəmaɪndən] *vt* to incorporate.

eingenommen ['aɪngənɔmən] *adj*: ~ **(von)** fond (of), partial (to); ~ **(gegen)** prejudiced (against).

eingeschnappt ['aɪngəʃnapt] (*umg*) *adj* cross; ~ **sein** to be in a huff.

eingeschrieben ['aɪngəʃri:bən] *adj* registered.

eingeschworen ['aɪngəʃvo:rən] *adj* confirmed; (*Gemeinschaft*) close.

eingesessen ['aɪngəzɛsən] *adj* old-established.

eingespannt ['aɪngəʃpant] *adj* busy.

eingespielt ['aɪngəʃpi:lt] *adj*: **aufeinander** ~ **sein** to be in tune with each other.

Eingeständnis ['aɪngəʃtɛntnɪs] *nt* admission, confession.

eingestehen ['aɪngəʃte:ən] *unreg vt* to confess.

eingestellt ['aɪngəʃtɛlt] *adj*: **ich bin im Moment nicht auf Besuch** ~ I'm not prepared for visitors.

eingetragen ['aɪngətra:gən] *adj* (*COMM*) registered; ~**er Gesellschaftssitz** registered office; ~**es Warenzeichen** registered trademark.

Eingeweide ['aɪngəvaɪdə] (-**s**, -) *nt* innards *pl*, intestines *pl*.

Eingeweihte(r) ['aɪngəvaɪtə(r)] *f(m)* initiate.

eingewöhnen ['aɪngəvø:nən] *vr*: **sich** ~ **(in** +*dat*) to settle down (in).

eingezahlt ['aɪngətsa:lt] *adj*: ~**es Kapital** paid-up capital.

eingießen ['aɪngi:sən] *unreg vt* to pour (out).

eingleisig ['aɪnglaɪzɪç] *adj* single-track; **er denkt sehr** ~ (*fig*) he's completely single-minded.

eingliedern ['aɪngli:dərn] *vt*: ~ **(in** +*akk*) to integrate (into) ♦ *vr*: **sich** ~ **(in** +*akk*) to integrate o.s. (into).

eingraben ['aɪngra:bən] *unreg vt* to dig in ♦ *vr* to dig o.s. in; **dieses Erlebnis hat sich seinem Gedächtnis eingegraben** this experience has engraved itself on his memory.

eingreifen ['aɪngraɪfən] *unreg vi* to intervene, interfere; (*Zahnrad*) to mesh.

Eingreiftruppe *f* (*MIL*) strike force.

eingrenzen ['aɪngrɛntsən] *vt* to enclose; (*fig: Problem*) to delimit.

Eingriff ['aɪngrɪf] *m* intervention, interference; (*Operation*) operation.

einhaken ['aɪnha:kən] *vt* to hook in ♦ *vr*: **sich bei jdm** ~ to link arms with sb ♦ *vi* (*sich einmischen*) to intervene.

Einhalt ['aɪnhalt] *m*: ~ **gebieten** +*dat* to put a stop to.

einhalten *unreg vt* (*Regel*) to keep ♦ *vi* to stop.

einhämmern ['aɪnhɛmərn] *vt*: **jdm etw** ~ (*fig*) to hammer sth into sb.

einhandeln ['aɪnhandəln] *vt*: **etw gegen** *od* **für etw** ~ to trade sth for sth.

einhändig ['aɪnhɛndɪç] *adj* one-handed.

einhändigen ['aɪnhɛndɪgən] *vt* to hand in.

einhängen ['aɪnhɛŋən] *vt* to hang; (*Telefon: auch vi*) to hang up; **sich bei jdm** ~ to link arms with sb.

einheimisch ['aɪnhaɪmɪʃ] *adj* native.

Einheimische(r) *f(m)* local.

einheimsen ['aɪnhaɪmzən] (*umg*) *vt* to bring home.

einheiraten ['aɪnhaɪra:tən] *vi*: **in einen Betrieb** ~ to marry into a business.

Einheit ['aɪnhaɪt] *f* unity; (*Maß, MIL*) unit; **eine geschlossene** ~ **bilden** to form an integrated whole; **e~lich** *adj* uniform.

Einheits- *zW*: ~**front** *f* (*POL*) united front; ~**liste** *f* (*POL*) single *od* unified list of candidates; ~**preis** *m* uniform price.

einheizen ['aɪnhaɪtsən] *vi*: **jdm (tüchtig)** ~

(*umg*: *die Meinung sagen*) to make things hot for sb.

einhellig ['aɪnhɛlɪç] *adj* unanimous ♦ *adv* unanimously.

einholen ['aɪnhoːlən] *vt* (*Tau*) to haul in; (*Fahne, Segel*) to lower; (*Vorsprung aufholen*) to catch up with; (*Verspätung*) to make up; (*Rat, Erlaubnis*) to ask ♦ *vi* (*einkaufen*) to buy, shop.

Einhorn ['aɪnhɔrn] *nt* unicorn.

einhüllen ['aɪnhʏlən] *vt* to wrap up.

einhundert ['aɪn'hʊndərt] *num* one hundred.

einig ['aɪnɪç] *adj* (*vereint*) united; **sich** *dat* **~ sein** to be in agreement; **~ gehen** to agree; **~ werden** to agree.

einige(r, s) *adj, pron* some ♦ *pl* some; (*mehrere*) several; **mit Ausnahme ~r weniger** with a few exceptions; **vor ~n Tagen** the other day, a few days ago; **dazu ist noch ~s zu sagen** there are still one or two things to say about that; **~ Mal** a few times.

einigen *vt* to unite ♦ *vr*: **sich (auf etw** *akk*) **~** to agree (on sth).

einigermaßen *adv* somewhat; (*leidlich*) reasonably.

einiges *pron siehe* **einige(r, s)**.

Einigkeit *f* unity; (*Übereinstimmung*) agreement.

Einigung *f* agreement; (*Ver~*) unification.

einimpfen ['aɪn|ɪmpfən] *vt*: **jdm etw ~** to inoculate sb with sth; (*fig*) to impress sth upon sb.

einjagen ['aɪnjaːgən] *vt*: **jdm Furcht/einen Schrecken ~** to give sb a fright.

einjährig ['aɪnjɛːrɪç] *adj* of *od* for one year; (*Alter*) one-year-old; (*Pflanze*) annual.

einkalkulieren ['aɪnkalkuliːrən] *vt* to take into account, allow for.

einkassieren ['aɪnkasiːrən] *vt* (*Geld, Schulden*) to collect.

Einkauf ['aɪnkauf] *m* purchase; (*COMM*: *Abteilung*) purchasing (department).

einkaufen *vt* to buy ♦ *vi* to shop; **~ gehen** to go shopping.

Einkäufer(in) ['aɪnkɔyfər(ɪn)] *m(f)* (*COMM*) buyer.

Einkaufs- *zW*: **~bummel** *m*: **einen ~bummel machen** to go on a shopping spree; **~korb** *m* shopping basket; **~leiter(in)** *m(f)* (*COMM*) chief buyer; **~netz** *nt* string bag; **~preis** *m* cost price, wholesale price; **~wagen** *m* trolley (*BRIT*), cart (*US*); **~zentrum** *nt* shopping centre.

einkehren ['aɪnkeːrən] *vi* (*geh*: *Ruhe, Frühling*) to come; **in einem Gasthof ~** to (make a) stop at an inn.

einkerben ['aɪnkɛrbən] *vt* to notch.

einklagen ['aɪnklaːgən] *vt* (*Schulden*) to sue for (the recovery of).

einklammern ['aɪnklamərn] *vt* to put in

brackets, bracket.

Einklang ['aɪnklaŋ] *m* harmony.

einkleiden ['aɪnklaɪdən] *vt* to clothe; (*fig*) to express.

einklemmen ['aɪnklɛmən] *vt* to jam.

einknicken ['aɪnknɪkən] *vt* to bend in; (*Papier*) to fold ♦ *vi* (*Knie*) to give way.

einkochen ['aɪnkɔxən] *vt* to boil down; (*Obst*) to preserve, bottle.

Einkommen ['aɪnkɔmən] (**-s, -**) *nt* income.

einkommensschwach *adj* low-income *attrib*.

einkommensstark *adj* high-income *attrib*.

Einkommen(s)steuer *f* income tax; **~erklärung** *f* income tax return.

Einkommensverhältnisse *pl* (level of) income *sing*.

einkreisen ['aɪnkraɪzən] *vt* to encircle.

einkriegen ['aɪnkriːgən] (*umg*) *vr*: **sie konnte sich gar nicht mehr darüber ~, dass ...** she couldn't get over the fact that ...

Einkünfte ['aɪnkʏnftə] *pl* income *sing*, revenue *sing*.

einladen ['aɪnlaːdən] *unreg vt* (*Person*) to invite; (*Gegenstände*) to load; **jdn ins Kino ~** to take sb to the cinema.

Einladung *f* invitation.

Einlage ['aɪnlaːgə] *f* (*Programm~*) interlude; (*Spar~*) deposit; (*FIN*: *Kapital~*) investment; (*Schuh~*) insole; (*Fußstütze*) support; (*Zahn~*) temporary filling; (*KOCH*) noodles, vegetables etc (*in clear soup*).

einlagern ['aɪnlaːgərn] *vt* to store.

Einlass▲ ['aɪnlas] (**-es, ̈-e**) *m* admission; **jdm ~ gewähren** to admit sb.

einlassen *unreg vt* to let in; (*einsetzen*) to set in ♦ *vr*: **sich mit jdm/auf etw** *akk* **~** to get involved with sb/sth; **sich auf einen Kompromiss ~** to agree to a compromise; **ich lasse mich auf keine Diskussion ein** I'm not having any discussion about it.

Einlauf ['aɪnlauf] *m* arrival; (*von Pferden*) finish; (*MED*) enema.

einlaufen *unreg vi* to arrive, come in; (*SPORT*) to finish; (*Wasser*) to run in; (*Stoff*) to shrink ♦ *vt* (*Schuhe*) to break in ♦ *vr* (*SPORT*) to warm up; (*Motor, Maschine*) to run in; **jdm das Haus ~** to invade sb's house; **in den Hafen ~** to enter the harbour.

einläuten ['aɪnlɔytən] *vt* (*neues Jahr*) to ring in; (*SPORT*: *Runde*) to sound the bell for.

einleben ['aɪnleːbən] *vr* to settle down.

Einlegearbeit *f* inlay.

einlegen ['aɪnleːgən] *vt* (*einfügen*: *Blatt, Sohle*) to insert; (*KOCH*) to pickle; (*in Holz etc*) to inlay; (*Geld*) to deposit; (*Pause*) to have; (*Protest*) to make; (*Veto*) to use; (*Berufung*) to lodge; **ein gutes Wort bei jdm ~** to put in a good word for sb.

Einlegesohle *f* insole.

einleiten ['aɪnlaɪtən] *vt* to introduce, start;

(*Geburt*) to induce.
Einleitung *f* introduction; induction.
einlenken ['aınlɛŋkən] *vi* (*fig*) to yield, give
way.
einlesen ['aınleːzən] *unreg vr*: **sich in ein Gebiet**
~ to get into a subject ♦ *vt*: **etw in etw** +*akk*
~ (*Daten*) to feed sth into sth.
einleuchten ['aınlɔyçtən] *vi*: (**jdm**) ~ to be
clear *od* evident (to sb).
einleuchtend *adj* clear.
einliefern ['aınliːfərn] *vt*: ~ (**in** +*akk*) to take
(into); **jdn ins Krankenhaus** ~ to admit sb to
hospital.
Einlieferungsschein *m* certificate of
posting.
einlochen ['aınlɔxən] (*umg*) *vt* (*einsperren*) to
lock up.
einlösen ['aınløːzən] *vt* (*Scheck*) to cash;
(*Schuldschein, Pfand*) to redeem;
(*Versprechen*) to keep.
einmachen ['aınmaxən] *vt* to preserve.
Einmachglas *nt* bottling jar.
einmal ['aınmaːl] *adv* once; (*erstens*) first of
all, firstly; (*später*) one day; **nehmen wir**
~ **an** just let's suppose; **noch** ~ once more;
nicht ~ not even; **auf** ~ all at once; **es war** ~
once upon a time there was/were; ~ **ist**
keinmal (*Sprichwort*) once doesn't count;
waren Sie schon ~ **in Rom?** have you ever
been to Rome?
Einmaleins *nt* multiplication tables *pl*; (*fig*)
ABC, basics *pl*.
einmalig *adj* unique; (*einmal geschehend*)
single; (*prima*) fantastic.
Einmannbetrieb *m* one-man business.
Einmannbus *m* one-man-operated bus.
Einmarsch ['aınmarʃ] *m* entry; (*MIL*) invasion.
einmarschieren *vi* to march in.
einmengen ['aınmɛŋən] *vr*: **sich (in etw** +*akk*)
~ to interfere (with sth).
einmieten ['aınmiːtən] *vr*: **sich bei jdm** ~ to
take lodgings with sb.
einmischen ['aınmɪʃən] *vr*: **sich (in etw** +*akk*) ~
to interfere (with sth).
einmotten ['aınmɔtən] *vt* (*Kleider etc*) to put in
mothballs.
einmünden ['aınmyndən] *vi*: ~ **in** +*akk* (*subj*:
Fluss) to flow *od* run into, join; (: *Straße*: *in*
Platz) to run into; (: : *in andere Straße*) to run
into, join.
einmütig ['aınmyːtıç] *adj* unanimous.
einnähen ['aınnɛːən] *vt* (*enger machen*) to take
in.
Einnahme ['aınnaːmə] (-, -n) *f* (*Geld*) takings
pl, revenue; (*von Medizin*) taking; (*MIL*)
capture, taking; ~**n und Ausgaben** income
and expenditure; ~**quelle** *f* source of
income.
einnehmen ['aınneːmən] *unreg vt* to take;
(*Stellung, Raum*) to take up; ~ **für/gegen** to

persuade in favour of/against.
einnehmend *adj* charming.
einnicken ['aınnıkən] *vi* to nod off.
einnisten ['aınnıstən] *vr* to nest; (*fig*) to settle
o.s.
Einöde ['aın|øːdə] (-, -n) *f* desert, wilderness.
einordnen ['aın|ɔrdnən] *vt* to arrange, fit in
♦ *vr* to adapt; (*AUT*) to get in(to) lane.
einpacken ['aınpakən] *vt* to pack (up).
einparken ['aınparkən] *vt*, *vi* to park.
einpauken ['aınpaukən] (*umg*) *vt*: **jdm etw** ~
to drum sth into sb.
einpendeln ['aınpɛndəln] *vr* to even out.
einpennen ['aınpɛnən] (*umg*) *vi* to drop off.
einpferchen ['aınpfɛrçən] *vt* to pen in; (*fig*) to
coop up.
einpflanzen ['aınpflantsən] *vt* to plant; (*MED*)
to implant.
einplanen ['aınplaːnən] *vt* to plan for.
einprägen ['aınprɛːgən] *vt* to impress,
imprint; (*beibringen*): **jdm etw** ~ to impress
sth on sb; **sich** *dat* **etw** ~ to memorize sth.
einprägsam ['aınprɛːkzaːm] *adj* easy to
remember; (*Melodie*) catchy.
einprogrammieren ['aınprogramiːrən] *vt*
(*COMPUT*) to feed in.
einprügeln ['aınpryːgəln] (*umg*) *vt*: **jdm etw** ~
to din sth into sb.
einquartieren ['aınkvartiːrən] *vt* (*MIL*) to
billet; **Gäste bei Freunden** ~ to put visitors
up with friends.
einrahmen ['aınraːmən] *vt* to frame.
einrasten ['aınrastən] *vi* to engage.
einräumen ['aınrɔymən] *vt* (*ordnend*) to put
away; (*überlassen*: *Platz*) to give up;
(*zugestehen*) to admit, concede.
einrechnen ['aınrɛçnən] *vt* to include;
(*berücksichtigen*) to take into account.
einreden ['aınreːdən] *vt*: **jdm/sich etw** ~ to
talk sb/o.s. into believing sth ♦ *vi*: **auf jdn** ~
to keep on and on at sb.
Einreibemittel *nt* liniment.
einreiben ['aınraıbən] *unreg vt* to rub in.
einreichen ['aınraıçən] *vt* to hand in; (*Antrag*)
to submit.
einreihen ['aınraıən] *vt* (*einordnen, einfügen*) to
put in; (*klassifizieren*) to classify ♦ *vr* (*Auto*) to
get in lane; **etw in etw** *akk* ~ to put sth into
sth.
Einreise ['aınraızə] *f* entry; ~**bestimmungen** *pl*
entry regulations *pl*; ~**erlaubnis** *f* entry
permit; ~**genehmigung** *f* entry permit.
einreisen ['aınraızən] *vi*: **in ein Land** ~ to
enter a country.
Einreiseverbot *nt* refusal of entry.
Einreisevisum *nt* entry visa.
einreißen ['aınraısən] *unreg vt* (*Papier*) to tear;
(*Gebäude*) to pull down ♦ *vi* to tear;
(*Gewohnheit werden*) to catch on.
einrenken ['aınrɛŋkən] *vt* (*Gelenk, Knie*) to put

back in place; (*fig: umg*) to sort out ♦ *vr* (*fig: umg*) to sort itself out.

einrichten ['aɪnrɪçtən] *vt* (*Haus*) to furnish; (*schaffen*) to establish, set up; (*arrangieren*) to arrange; (*möglich machen*) to manage ♦ *vr* (*in Haus*) to furnish one's house; **sich ~ (auf** +*akk*) (*sich vorbereiten*) to prepare o.s. (for); (*sich anpassen*) to adapt (to).

Einrichtung *f* (*Wohnungs~*) furnishings *pl*; (*öffentliche Anstalt*) organization; (*Dienste*) service; (*Labor~ etc*) equipment; (*Gewohnheit*): **zur ständigen ~ werden** to become an institution.

Einrichtungsgegenstand *m* item of furniture.

einrosten ['aɪnrɔstən] *vi* to get rusty.

einrücken ['aɪnrykən] *vi* (*MIL: Soldat*) to join up; (: *in Land*) to move in ♦ *vt* (*Anzeige*) to insert; (*Zeile, Text*) to indent.

Eins [aɪns] (-, -en) *f* one; **e~** *num* one; **es ist mir alles e~** it's all one to me; **e~ zu e~** (*SPORT*) one all; **e~ a** (*umg*) first-rate.

einsalzen ['aɪnzaltsən] *vt* to salt.

einsam ['aɪnzaːm] *adj* lonely, solitary; **~e Klasse/Spitze** (*umg: hervorragend*) absolutely fantastic; **E~keit** *f* loneliness, solitude.

einsammeln ['aɪnzaməln] *vt* to collect.

Einsatz ['aɪnzats] *m* (*Teil*) insert; (*an Kleid*) insertion; (*Tisch~*) leaf; (*Verwendung*) use, employment; (*Spiel~*) stake; (*Risiko*) risk; (*MIL*) operation; (*MUS*) entry; **im ~** in action; **etw unter ~ seines Lebens tun** to risk one's life to do sth; **~befehl** *m* order to go into action; **e~bereit** *adj* ready for action; **~kommando** *nt* (*MIL*) task force.

einschalten ['aɪnʃaltən] *vt* (*ELEK*) to switch on; (*einfügen*) to insert; (*Pause*) to make; (*AUT: Gang*) to engage; (*Anwalt*) to bring in ♦ *vr* (*dazwischentreten*) to intervene.

Einschaltquote *f* (*TV*) viewing figures *pl*.

einschärfen ['aɪnʃɛrfən] *vt*: **jdm etw ~** to impress sth on sb.

einschätzen ['aɪnʃɛtsən] *vt* to estimate, assess ♦ *vr* to rate o.s.

einschenken ['aɪnʃɛŋkən] *vt* to pour out.

einscheren ['aɪnʃeːrən] *vi* to get back (into lane).

einschicken ['aɪnʃɪkən] *vt* to send in.

einschieben ['aɪnʃiːbən] *unreg vt* to push in; (*zusätzlich*) to insert; **eine Pause ~** to have a break.

einschiffen ['aɪnʃɪfən] *vt* to ship ♦ *vr* to embark, go on board.

einschl. *abk* (= *einschließlich*) inc.

einschlafen ['aɪnʃlaːfən] *unreg vi* to fall asleep, go to sleep; (*fig: Freundschaft*) to peter out.

einschläfern ['aɪnʃlɛːfərn] *vt* (*schläfrig machen*) to make sleepy; (*Gewissen*) to soothe; (*narkotisieren*) to give a soporific to; (*töten: Tier*) to put to sleep.

einschläfernd *adj* (*MED*) soporific; (*langweilig*) boring; (*Stimme*) lulling.

Einschlag ['aɪnʃlaːk] *m* impact; (*AUT*) lock; (*fig: Beimischung*) touch, hint.

einschlagen ['aɪnʃlaːgən] *unreg vt* to knock in; (*Fenster*) to smash, break; (*Zähne, Schädel*) to smash in; (*Steuer*) to turn; (*kürzer machen*) to take up; (*Ware*) to pack, wrap up; (*Weg, Richtung*) to take ♦ *vi* to hit; (*sich einigen*) to agree; (*Anklang finden*) to work, succeed; **es muss irgendwo eingeschlagen haben** something must have been struck by lightning; **gut ~** (*umg*) to go down well, be a big hit; **auf jdn ~** to hit sb.

einschlägig ['aɪnʃlɛːgɪç] *adj* relevant; **er ist ~ vorbestraft** (*JUR*) he has a previous conviction for a similar offence.

einschleichen ['aɪnʃlaɪçən] *unreg vr* (*in Haus, fig: Fehler*) to creep in, steal in; (*in Vertrauen*) to worm one's way in.

einschleppen ['aɪnʃlɛpən] *vt* (*fig: Krankheit etc*) to bring in.

einschleusen ['aɪnʃlɔyzən] *vt*: **~ (in** +*akk*) to smuggle in(to).

einschließen ['aɪnʃliːsən] *unreg vt* (*Kind*) to lock in; (*Häftling*) to lock up; (*Gegenstand*) to lock away; (*Bergleute*) to cut off; (*umgeben*) to surround; (*MIL*) to encircle; (*fig*) to include, comprise ♦ *vr* to lock o.s. in.

einschließlich *adv* inclusive ♦ *präp* +*gen* inclusive of, including.

einschmeicheln ['aɪnʃmaɪçəln] *vr*: **sich (bei jdm) ~** to ingratiate o.s. (with sb).

einschmuggeln ['aɪnʃmʊgəln] *vt*: **~ (in** +*akk*) to smuggle in(to).

einschnappen ['aɪnʃnapən] *vi* (*Tür*) to click to; (*fig*) to be touchy; **eingeschnappt sein** to be in a huff.

einschneidend ['aɪnʃnaɪdənt] *adj* incisive.

einschneien ['aɪnʃnaɪən] *vi*: **eingeschneit sein** to be snowed in.

Einschnitt ['aɪnʃnɪt] *m* (*MED*) incision; (*im Tal, Gebirge*) cleft; (*im Leben*) decisive point.

einschnüren ['aɪnʃnyːrən] *vt* (*einengen*) to cut into; **dieser Kragen schnürt mir den Hals ein** this collar is strangling me.

einschränken ['aɪnʃrɛŋkən] *vt* to limit, restrict; (*Kosten*) to cut down, reduce ♦ *vr* to cut down (on expenditure); **~d möchte ich sagen, dass ...** I'd like to qualify that by saying ...

einschränkend *adj* restrictive.

Einschränkung *f* restriction, limitation; reduction; (*von Behauptung*) qualification.

Einschreib(e)brief *m* registered (*BRIT*) *od* certified (*US*) letter.

einschreiben ['aɪnʃraɪbən] *unreg vt* to write in; (*POST*) to send by registered (*BRIT*) *od* certified (*US*) mail ♦ *vr* to register; (*UNIV*) to enrol; **E~** *nt* registered (*BRIT*) *od* certified

(*US*) letter.

einschreiten ['aɪnʃraɪtən] *unreg vi* to step in, intervene; ~ **gegen** to take action against.

Einschub ['aɪnʃuːp] (-(e)s, ⁻e) *m* insertion.

einschüchtern ['aɪnʃʏçtərn] *vt* to intimidate.

Einschüchterung ['aɪnʃʏçtəruŋ] *f* intimidation.

einschulen ['aɪnʃuːlən] *vt*: **eingeschult werden** (*Kind*) to start school.

einschweißen ['aɪnʃvaɪsən] *vt* (*in Plastik*) to shrink-wrap; (*TECH*): **etw in etw** *akk* ~ to weld sth into sth.

einschwenken ['aɪnʃvɛŋkən] *vi*: ~ **(in** +*akk*) to turn *od* swing in(to).

einsehen ['aɪnzeːən] *unreg vt* (*prüfen*) to inspect; (*Fehler etc*) to recognize; (*verstehen*) to see; **das sehe ich nicht ein** I don't see why; **E**~ (-**s**) *nt* understanding; **ein E**~ **haben** to show understanding.

einseifen ['aɪnzaɪfən] *vt* to soap, lather; (*fig: umg*) to take in, con.

einseitig ['aɪnzaɪtɪç] *adj* one-sided; (*POL*) unilateral; (*Ernährung*) unbalanced; (*Diskette*) single-sided; **E**~**keit** *f* one-sidedness.

einsenden ['aɪnzɛndən] *unreg vt* to send in.

Einsender(in) (-**s**, -) *m(f)* sender, contributor.

Einsendeschluss▲ *m* closing date (for entries).

Einsendung *f* sending in.

einsetzen ['aɪnzɛtsən] *vt* to put (in); (*in Amt*) to appoint, install; (*Geld*) to stake; (*verwenden*) to use; (*MIL*) to employ ♦ *vi* (*beginnen*) to set in; (*MUS*) to enter, come in ♦ *vr* to work hard; **sich für jdn/etw** ~ to support sb/sth; **ich werde mich dafür** ~, **dass** ... I will do what I can to see that ...

Einsicht ['aɪnzɪçt] *f* insight; (*in Akten*) look, inspection; **zu der** ~ **kommen, dass** ... to come to the conclusion that ...

einsichtig *adj* (*Mensch*) judicious; **jdm etw** ~ **machen** to make sb understand *od* see sth.

Einsichtnahme (-, -**n**) *f* (*form*) perusal; „**zur** ~" "for attention".

einsichtslos *adj* unreasonable.

einsichtsvoll *adj* understanding.

Einsiedler ['aɪnziːdlər] (-**s**, -) *m* hermit.

einsilbig ['aɪnzɪlbɪç] *adj* (*lit, fig*) monosyllabic; **E**~**keit** *f* (*fig*) taciturnity.

einsinken ['aɪnzɪŋkən] *unreg vi* to sink in.

Einsitzer ['aɪnzɪtsər] (-**s**, -) *m* single-seater.

einspannen ['aɪnʃpanən] *vt* (*Werkstück, Papier*) to put (in), insert; (*Pferde*) to harness; (*umg: Person*) to rope in; **jdn für seine Zwecke** ~ to use sb for one's own ends.

einsparen ['aɪnʃpaːrən] *vt* to save, economize on; (*Kosten*) to cut down on; (*Posten*) to eliminate.

Einsparung *f* saving.

einspeichern ['aɪnʃpaɪçərn] *vt*: **etw (in etw** +*akk*) ~ (*COMPUT*) to feed sth in(to sth).

einsperren ['aɪnʃpɛrən] *vt* to lock up.

einspielen ['aɪnʃpiːlən] *vr* (*SPORT*) to warm up ♦ *vt* (*Film: Geld*) to bring in; (*Instrument*) to play in; **sich aufeinander** ~ to become attuned to each other; **gut eingespielt** running smoothly.

einsprachig ['aɪnʃpraːxɪç] *adj* monolingual.

einspringen ['aɪnʃprɪŋən] *unreg vi* (*aushelfen*) to stand in; (*mit Geld*) to help out.

einspritzen ['aɪnʃprɪtsən] *vt* to inject.

Einspritzmotor *m* (*AUT*) injection engine.

Einspruch ['aɪnʃprʊx] *m* protest, objection; ~ **einlegen** (*JUR*) to file an objection.

Einspruchsfrist *f* (*JUR*) period for filing an objection.

Einspruchsrecht *nt* veto.

einspurig ['aɪnʃpuːrɪç] *adj* single-lane; (*EISENB*) single-track.

einst [aɪnst] *adv* once; (*zukünftig*) one *od* some day.

Einstand ['aɪnʃtant] *m* (*TENNIS*) deuce; (*Antritt*) entrance (to office); **er hat gestern seinen** ~ **gegeben** yesterday he celebrated starting his new job.

einstechen ['aɪnʃtɛçən] *unreg vt* to pierce.

einstecken ['aɪnʃtɛkən] *vt* to stick in, insert; (*Brief*) to post, mail (*US*); (*ELEK: Stecker*) to plug in; (*Geld*) to pocket; (*mitnehmen*) to take; (*überlegen sein*) to put in the shade; (*hinnehmen*) to swallow.

einstehen ['aɪnʃteːən] *unreg vi*: **für jdn** ~ to vouch for sb; **für etw** ~ to guarantee sth, vouch for sth; (*Ersatz leisten*) to make good sth.

einsteigen ['aɪnʃtaɪgən] *unreg vi* to get in *od* on; (*in Schiff*) to go on board; (*sich beteiligen*) to come in; (*hineinklettern*) to climb in; ~! (*EISENB etc*) all aboard!

Einsteiger (-**s**, -) (*umg*) *m* beginner.

einstellbar *adj* adjustable.

einstellen ['aɪnʃtɛlən] *vt* (*in Firma*) to employ, take on; (*aufhören*) to stop; (*Geräte*) to adjust; (*Kamera etc*) to focus; (*Sender, Radio*) to tune in to; (*unterstellen*) to put ♦ *vi* to take on staff/workers ♦ *vr* (*anfangen*) to set in; (*kommen*) to arrive; **Zahlungen** ~ to suspend payment; **etw auf etw** *akk* ~ to adjust sth to sth; to focus sth on sth; **sich auf jdn/etw** ~ to adapt to sb/prepare o.s. for sth.

einstellig *adj* (*Zahl*) single-digit.

Einstellplatz *m* (*auf Hof*) carport; (*in Großgarage*) (covered) parking space.

Einstellung *f* (*Aufhören*) suspension, cessation; (*von Gerät*) adjustment; (*von Kamera etc*) focusing; (*von Arbeiter etc*) appointment; (*Haltung*) attitude.

Einstellungsgespräch *nt* interview.

Einstellungsstopp *m* halt in recruitment.

Einstieg ['aɪnʃtiːk] (-(e)s, -e) *m* entry; *(fig)* approach; *(von Bus, Bahn)* door; **kein ~ exit** only.

einstig ['aɪnstɪç] *adj* former.

einstimmen ['aɪnʃtɪmən] *vi* to join in ♦ *vt* *(MUS)* to tune; *(in Stimmung bringen)* to put in the mood.

einstimmig *adj* unanimous; *(MUS)* for one voice; **E~keit** *f* unanimity.

einstmalig *adj* former.

einstmals *adv* once, formerly.

einstöckig ['aɪnʃtœkɪç] *adj* two-storeyed *(BRIT)*, two-storied *(US)*.

einstöpseln ['aɪnʃtœpsəln] *vt*: **etw (in etw** +akk**) ~** *(ELEK)* to plug sth in(to sth).

einstudieren ['aɪnʃtudiːrən] *vt* to study, rehearse.

einstufen ['aɪnʃtuːfən] *vt* to classify.

Einstufung *f*: **nach seiner ~ in eine höhere Gehaltsklasse** after he was put on a higher salary grade.

einstündig ['aɪnʃtyndɪç] *adj* one-hour *attrib.*

einstürmen ['aɪnʃtyrmən] *vi*: **auf jdn ~** to rush at sb; *(Eindrücke)* to overwhelm sb.

Einsturz ['aɪnʃtʊrts] *m* collapse.

einstürzen ['aɪnʃtʏrtsən] *vi* to fall in, collapse; **auf jdn ~** *(fig)* to overwhelm sb.

Einsturzgefahr *f* danger of collapse.

einstweilen *adv* meanwhile; *(vorläufig)* temporarily, for the time being.

einstweilig *adj* temporary; **~e Verfügung** *(JUR)* temporary *od* interim injunction.

eintägig ['aɪntɛːgɪç] *adj* one-day.

Eintagsfliege ['aɪntaːksfliːgə] *f* *(ZOOL)* mayfly; *(fig)* nine-day wonder.

eintauchen ['aɪntaʊxən] *vt* to immerse, dip in ♦ *vi* to dive.

eintauschen ['aɪntaʊʃən] *vt* to exchange.

eintausend ['aɪn'taʊzənt] *num* one thousand.

einteilen ['aɪntaɪlən] *vt* *(in Teile)* to divide (up); *(Menschen)* to assign.

einteilig *adj* one-piece.

eintönig ['aɪntøːnɪç] *adj* monotonous; **E~keit** *f* monotony.

Eintopf ['aɪntɔpf] *m* stew.

Eintopfgericht ['aɪntɔpfɡərɪçt] *nt* stew.

Eintracht ['aɪntraxt] (-) *f* concord, harmony.

einträchtig ['aɪntrɛçtɪç] *adj* harmonious.

Eintrag ['aɪntraːk] (-(e)s, -e) *m* entry; **amtlicher ~** entry in the register.

eintragen ['aɪntraːɡən] *unreg vt* *(in Buch)* to enter; *(Profit)* to yield ♦ *vr* to put one's name down; **jdm etw ~** to bring sb sth.

einträglich ['aɪntrɛːklɪç] *adj* profitable.

Eintragung *f*: **~ (in** +akk**)** entry (in).

eintreffen ['aɪntrɛfən] *unreg vi* to happen; *(ankommen)* to arrive; *(fig: wahr werden)* to come true.

eintreiben ['aɪntraɪbən] *unreg vt* *(Geldbeträge)* to collect.

eintreten ['aɪntreːtən] *unreg vi* *(hineingehen)* to enter; *(sich ereignen)* to occur ♦ *vt* *(Tür)* to kick open; **in etw** akk **~** to enter sth; *(in Klub, Partei)* to join sth; **für jdn/etw ~** to stand up for sb/sth.

eintrichtern ['aɪntrɪçtərn] *(umg)* *vt*: **jdm etw ~** to drum sth into sb.

Eintritt ['aɪntrɪt] *m* *(Betreten)* entrance; *(in Klub etc)* joining; **~ frei** admission free; **„~ verboten"** "no admittance"; **bei ~ der Dunkelheit** at nightfall.

Eintritts- *zW*: **~geld** *nt* admission charge; **~karte** *f* (admission) ticket; **~preis** *m* admission charge.

eintrocknen ['aɪntrɔknən] *vi* to dry up.

eintrudeln ['aɪntruːdəln] *(umg)* *vi* to drift in.

eintunken ['aɪntʊŋkən] *vt* *(Brot)*: **etw in etw** akk **~** to dunk sth in sth.

einüben ['aɪnˈyːbən] *vt* to practise *(BRIT)*, practice *(US)*, drill.

einverleiben ['aɪnfɛrlaɪbən] *vt* to incorporate; *(Gebiet)* to annex; **sich** dat **etw ~** *(fig: geistig)* to assimilate sth.

Einvernehmen ['aɪnfɛrneːmən] (-s, -) *nt* agreement, understanding.

einverstanden ['aɪnfɛrʃtandən] *interj* agreed ♦ *adj*: **~ sein** to agree, be agreed; **sich mit etw ~ erklären** to give one's agreement to sth.

Einverständnis ['aɪnfɛrʃtɛntnɪs] (-ses) *nt* understanding; *(gleiche Meinung)* agreement; **im ~ mit jdm handeln** to act with sb's consent.

Einwand ['aɪnvant] (-(e)s, -e) *m* objection; **einen ~ erheben** to raise an objection.

Einwanderer ['aɪnvandərər] *m* immigrant.

Einwanderin *f* immigrant.

einwandern *vi* to immigrate.

Einwanderung *f* immigration.

einwandfrei *adj* perfect; **etw ~ beweisen** to prove sth beyond doubt.

einwärts ['aɪnvɛrts] *adv* inwards.

Einwegflasche ['aɪnveːgflaʃə] *f* non-returnable bottle.

Einwegpfand *nt* deposit on drink cans and disposable bottles.

Einwegspritze *f* disposable (hypodermic) syringe.

einweichen ['aɪnvaɪçən] *vt* to soak.

einweihen ['aɪnvaɪən] *vt* *(Kirche)* to consecrate; *(Brücke)* to open; *(Gebäude)* to inaugurate; *(Person)*: **in etw** akk **~** to initiate in sth; **er ist eingeweiht** *(fig)* he knows all about it.

Einweihung *f* consecration; opening; inauguration; initiation.

einweisen ['aɪnvaɪzən] *unreg vt* *(in Amt)* to install; *(in Arbeit)* to introduce; *(in Anstalt)* to send; *(in Krankenhaus)*: **~ (in** +akk**)** to admit (to).

Einweisung *f* installation; introduction;

sending.

einwenden ['aɪnvɛndən] *unreg vt*: **etwas ~ gegen** to object to, oppose.

einwerfen ['aɪnvɛrfən] *unreg vt* to throw in; (*Brief*) to post; (*Geld*) to put in, insert; (*Fenster*) to smash; (*äußern*) to interpose.

einwickeln ['aɪnvɪkəln] *vt* to wrap up; (*fig: umg*) to outsmart.

einwilligen ['aɪnvɪlɪgən] *vi*: (**in etw** *akk*) **~** to consent (to sth), agree (to sth).

Einwilligung *f* consent.

einwirken ['aɪnvɪrkən] *vi*: **auf jdn/etw ~** to influence sb/sth.

Einwirkung *f* influence.

Einwohner(in) ['aɪnvoːnər(ɪn)] (**-s, -**) *m(f)* inhabitant; **~meldeamt** *nt* registration office; **sich beim ~meldeamt (an)melden** ≈ to register with the police; **~schaft** *f* population, inhabitants *pl*.

Einwurf ['aɪnvʊrf] *m* (*Öffnung*) slot; (*Einwand*) objection; (*SPORT*) throw-in.

Einzahl ['aɪntsaːl] *f* singular.

einzahlen *vt* to pay in.

Einzahlung *f* payment; (*auf Sparkonto*) deposit.

einzäunen ['aɪntsɔʏnən] *vt* to fence in.

einzeichnen ['aɪntsaɪçnən] *vt* to draw in.

Einzel ['aɪntsəl] (**-s, -**) *nt* (*TENNIS*) singles *pl*.

Einzel- *zW*: **~aufstellung** *f* (*COMM*) itemized list; **~bett** *nt* single bed; **~blattzuführung** *f* sheet feed; **~fall** *m* single instance, individual case; **~gänger(in)** *m(f)* loner; **~haft** *f* solitary confinement; **~handel** *m* retail trade; **im ~handel erhältlich** available retail; **~handelsgeschäft** *nt* retail outlet; **~handelspreis** *m* retail price; **~händler** *m* retailer; **~heit** *f* particular, detail; **~kind** *nt* only child.

Einzeller ['aɪntsɛlər] (**-s, -**) *m* (*BIOL*) single-celled organism.

einzeln *adj* single; (*von Paar*) odd ♦ *adv* singly; **~ angeben** to specify; **~e** some (people), a few (people); **der/die E~e** the individual; **das E~e** the particular; **ins E~e gehen** to go into detail(s); **etw im E~en besprechen** to discuss sth in detail; **~ aufführen** to list separately *od* individually; **bitte ~ eintreten** please come in one (person) at a time.

Einzelteil *nt* individual part; (*Ersatzteil*) spare part; **etw in seine ~e zerlegen** to take sth to pieces, dismantle sth.

Einzelzimmer *nt* single room.

einziehen ['aɪntsiːən] *unreg vt* to draw in, take in; (*Kopf*) to duck; (*Fühler, Antenne, Fahrgestell*) to retract; (*Steuern, Erkundigungen*) to collect; (*MIL*) to call up, draft (*US*); (*aus dem Verkehr ziehen*) to withdraw; (*konfiszieren*) to confiscate ♦ *vi* to move in; (*Friede, Ruhe*) to come; (*Flüssigkeit*): **~ (in** +*akk*) to soak in(to).

einzig ['aɪntsɪç] *adj* only; (*ohnegleichen*) unique ♦ *adv*: **~ und allein** solely; **das E~e** the only thing; **der/die E~e** the only one; **kein ~es Mal** not once, not one single time; **kein E~er** nobody, not a single person; **~artig** *adj* unique.

Einzug ['aɪntsuːk] *m* entry, moving in.

Einzugsauftrag *m* (*FIN*) direct debit.

Einzugsbereich *m* catchment area.

Einzugsverfahren *nt* (*FIN*) direct debit.

Eis [aɪs] (**-es, -**) *nt* ice; (*Speise~*) ice cream; **~ am Stiel** ice lolly (*BRIT*), popsicle ® (*US*); **~bahn** *f* ice *od* skating rink; **~bär** *m* polar bear; **~becher** *m* sundae; **~bein** *nt* pig's trotters *pl*; **~berg** *m* iceberg; **~beutel** *m* ice pack; **~café** *nt* = **Eisdiele**.

Eischnee ['aɪʃneː] *m* (*KOCH*) beaten white of egg.

Eisdecke *f* sheet of ice.

Eisdiele *f* ice-cream parlour (*BRIT*) *od* parlor (*US*).

Eisen ['aɪzən] (**-s, -**) *nt* iron; **zum alten ~ gehören** (*fig*) to be on the scrap heap.

Eisenbahn *f* railway, railroad (*US*); **es ist (aller)höchste ~** (*umg*) it's high time; **~er** (**-s, -**) *m* railwayman, railway employee, railroader (*US*); **~netz** *nt* rail network; **~schaffner** *m* railway guard, (railroad) conductor (*US*); **~überführung** *f* footbridge; **~übergang** *m* level crossing, grade crossing (*US*); **~wagen** *m* railway *od* railroad (*US*) carriage; **~waggon**, **~wagon▲** *m* (*Güterwagen*) goods wagon.

Eisen- *zW*: **~erz** *nt* iron ore; **e~haltig** *adj* containing iron; **~mangel** *m* iron deficiency; **~warenhandlung** *f* ironmonger's (*BRIT*), hardware store (*US*).

eisern ['aɪzərn] *adj* iron; (*Gesundheit*) robust; (*Energie*) unrelenting; (*Reserve*) emergency; **der E~e Vorhang** the Iron Curtain; **in etw** *dat* **~ sein** to be adamant about sth; **er ist ~ bei seinem Entschluss geblieben** he stuck firmly to his decision.

Eis- *zW*: **~fach** *nt* freezer compartment, icebox; **e~frei** *adj* clear of ice; **e~gekühlt** *adj* chilled; **~hockey** *nt* ice hockey.

eisig ['aɪzɪç] *adj* icy.

Eis- *zW*: **~kaffee** *m* iced coffee; **e~kalt** *adj* icy cold; **~kunstlauf** *m* figure skating; **~laufen** *nt* ice-skating; **~läufer** *m* ice-skater; **~meer** *nt*: **Nördliches/Südliches ~meer** Arctic/Antarctic Ocean; **~pickel** *m* ice-axe (*BRIT*), ice-ax (*US*).

Eisprung ['aɪʃprʊŋ] *m* ovulation.

Eis- *zW*: **~schießen** *nt* ≈ curling; **~scholle** *f* ice floe; **~schrank** *m* fridge, icebox (*US*); **~stadion** *nt* ice *od* skating rink; **~würfel** *m* ice cube; **~zapfen** *m* icicle; **~zeit** *f* Ice Age.

eitel ['aɪtəl] *adj* vain; **E~keit** *f* vanity.

Eiter ['aɪtər] (**-s**) *m* pus.

eiterig *adj* suppurating.
eitern *vi* to suppurate.
Ei- *zW:* ~**weiß** (-es, -e) *nt* white of an egg;
(*CHEM*) protein; ~**weißgehalt** *m* protein
content; ~**zelle** *f* ovum.
EKD *f abk* (= *Evangelische Kirche in Deutschland*)
German Protestant Church.
Ekel[1] ['e:kəl] (-s) *m* nausea, disgust; **vor jdm/**
etw einen ~ **haben** to loathe sb/sth;
~ **erregend** nauseating, disgusting.
Ekel[2] ['e:kəl] (-s, -) (*umg*) *nt* (*Mensch*)
nauseating person.
ekelhaft *adj*, **ekelig** *adj* nauseating,
disgusting.
ekeln *vt* to disgust ♦ *vr:* **sich vor etw** *dat* ~ to be
disgusted at sth; **es ekelt ihn** he is disgusted.
EKG (-) *nt abk* (= *Elektrokardiogramm*) ECG.
Eklat [e'kla:] (-s) *m* (*geh: Aufsehen*) sensation.
eklig *adj* nauseating, disgusting.
Ekstase [ɛk'sta:zə] (-, -n) *f* ecstasy; **jdn in**
~ **versetzen** to send sb into ecstasies.
Ekzem [ɛk'tse:m] (-s, -e) *nt* (*MED*) eczema.
Elan [e'lã:] (-s) *m* élan.
elastisch [e'lastıʃ] *adj* elastic.
Elastizität [elastitsi'tɛːt] *f* elasticity.
Elbe ['ɛlbə] *f* (*Fluss*) Elbe.
Elch [ɛlç] (-(e)s, -e) *m* elk.
Elefant [ele'fant] *m* elephant; **wie ein** ~ **im**
Porzellanladen (*umg*) like a bull in a china
shop.
elegant [ele'gant] *adj* elegant.
Eleganz [ele'gants] *f* elegance.
Elektrifizierung [elɛktrifi'tsi:rʊŋ] *f*
electrification.
Elektriker [e'lɛktrikər] (-s, -) *m* electrician.
elektrisch [e'lɛktrıʃ] *adj* electric.
elektrisieren [elɛktri'zi:rən] *vt* (*lit, fig*) to
electrify; (*Mensch*) to give an electric shock
to ♦ *vr* to get an electric shock.
Elektrizität [elɛktritsi'tɛːt] *f* electricity.
Elektrizitätswerk *nt* electric power station.
Elektroartikel [e'lɛktro|artıkəl] *m* electrical
appliance.
Elektrode [elɛk'tro:də] (-, -n) *f* electrode.
Elektro- *zW:* ~**gerät** *nt* electrical appliance;
~**herd** *m* electric cooker; ~**kardiogramm** *nt*
(*MED*) electrocardiogram.
Elektrolyse [elɛktro'ly:zə] (-, -n) *f* electrolysis.
Elektromotor *m* electric motor.
Elektron [e'lɛktrɔn] (-s, -en) *nt* electron.
Elektronen(ge)hirn *nt* electronic brain.
Elektronenrechner *m* computer.
Elektronik [elɛk'tro:nɪk] *f* electronics *sing*;
(*Teile*) electronics *pl*.
elektronisch *adj* electronic; ~**e Post**
electronic mail.
Elektro- *zW:* ~**rasierer** (-s, -) *m* electric razor;
~**schock** *m* (*MED*) electric shock,
electroshock; ~**techniker** *m* electrician;
(*Ingenieur*) electrical engineer.

Element [ele'mɛnt] (-s, -e) *nt* element; (*ELEK*)
cell, battery.
elementar [elemɛn'ta:r] *adj* elementary;
(*naturhaft*) elemental; **E~teilchen** *nt* (*PHYS*)
elementary particle.
Elend ['e:lɛnt] (-(e)s) *nt* misery; **da kann man**
das heulende ~ **kriegen** (*umg*) it's enough to
make you scream; **e~** *adj* miserable; **mir ist**
ganz e~ I feel really awful.
elendiglich ['e:lɛndıklıç] *adv* miserably;
~ **zugrunde** *od* **zu Grunde gehen** to come to
a wretched end.
Elendsviertel *nt* slum.
elf [ɛlf] *num* eleven; **E~** (-, en) *f* (*SPORT*)
eleven.
Elfe (-, -n) *f* elf.
Elfenbein *nt* ivory; ~**küste** *f* Ivory Coast.
Elfmeter *m* (*SPORT*) penalty (kick).
Elfmeterschießen *nt* (*SPORT*) penalty shoot-
out.
eliminieren [elimi'ni:rən] *vt* to eliminate.
elitär [eli'tɛːr] *adj* elitist ♦ *adv* in an elitist
fashion.
Elite [e'li:tə] (-, -n) *f* elite.
Elixier [elɪ'ksi:r] (-s, -e) *nt* elixir.
Ellbogen *m* = **Ellenbogen**.
Elle ['ɛlə] (-, -n) *f* ell; (*Maß*) ≈ yard.
Ellenbogen *m* elbow; **die** ~ **gebrauchen**
(*umg*) to be pushy; ~**freiheit** *f* (*fig*) elbow
room; ~**gesellschaft** *f* dog-eat-dog society.
Ellipse [ɛ'lıpsə] (-, -n) *f* ellipse.
E-Lok ['e:lɔk] (-) *f abk* (= *elektrische Lokomotive*)
electric locomotive *od* engine.
Elsass▲ ['ɛlzas] *nt:* **das** ~ Alsace.
Elsässer ['ɛlzɛsər] *adj* Alsatian.
Elsässer(in) (-s, -) *m(f)* Alsatian, inhabitant of
Alsace.
elsässisch *adj* Alsatian.
Elster ['ɛlstər] (-, -n) *f* magpie.
elterlich *adj* parental.
Eltern ['ɛltərn] *pl* parents *pl*; **nicht von**
schlechten ~ **sein** (*umg*) to be quite
something; ~**abend** *m* (*SCH*) parents'
evening; ~**haus** *nt* home; **e~los** *adj* orphaned;
~**sprechtag** *m* open day (for parents); ~**teil**
m parent.
Email [e'ma:j] (-s, -s) *nt* enamel.
E-Mail ['i:me:l] (-, -s) *f* E-mail, e-mail; ~-
Adresse *f* E-mail address.
e-mailen [i:me:lən] *vt* to e-mail.
emaillieren [ema'ji:rən] *vt* to enamel.
Emanze (-, -n) (*pej*) *f* women's libber (*umg*).
Emanzipation [emantsipatsi'o:n] *f*
emancipation.
emanzipieren [emantsi'pi:rən] *vt* to
emancipate.
Embargo [ɛm'bargo] (-s, -s) *nt* embargo.
Embryo ['ɛmbryo] (-s, -s *od* -nen) *m* embryo.
Embryonenforschung *f* embryo research.
Emigrant(in) [emi'grant(ın)] *m(f)* emigrant.

Emigration [emigratsi'o:n] *f* emigration.
emigrieren [emi'gri:rən] *vi* to emigrate.
Emissionen *npl* emissions *pl.*
Emissionskurs [emisi'o:nskʊrs] *m* (*Aktien*) issued price.
EMNID *m abk* (= *Erforschung, Meinung, Nachrichten, Informationsdienst*) *opinion poll organization.*
emotional [emotsio'na:l] *adj* emotional; (*Ausdrucksweise*) emotive.
emotionsgeladen [emotsi'o:nsgəla:dən] *adj* emotionally-charged.
Empf. *abk* = **Empfänger.**
empfahl *etc* [ɛm'pfa:l] *vb siehe* **empfehlen.**
empfand *etc* [ɛm'pfant] *vb siehe* **empfinden.**
Empfang [ɛm'pfaŋ] (**-(e)s, ̈-e**) *m* reception; (*Erhalten*) receipt; **in ~ nehmen** to receive; (**zahlbar**) **nach** *od* **bei ~** +*gen* (payable) on receipt (of).
empfangen *unreg vt* to receive ♦ *vi* (*schwanger werden*) to conceive.
Empfänger(in) [ɛm'pfɛŋər(ɪn)] (**-s, -**) *m(f)* receiver; (*COMM*) addressee, consignee; **~ unbekannt** (*auf Briefen*) not known at this address.
empfänglich *adj* receptive, susceptible.
Empfängnis (**-, -se**) *f* conception; **e~verhütend** *adj:* **e~verhütende Mittel** contraceptives *pl;* **~verhütung** *f* contraception.
Empfangs- *zW:* **~bestätigung** *f* (acknowledgement of) receipt; **~chef** *m* (*von Hotel*) head porter; **~dame** *f* receptionist; **~schein** *m* receipt; **~störung** *f* (*RUNDF, TV*) interference; **~zimmer** *nt* reception room.
empfehlen [ɛm'pfe:lən] *unreg vt* to recommend ♦ *vr* to take one's leave.
empfehlenswert *adj* recommendable.
Empfehlung *f* recommendation; **auf ~ von** on the recommendation of.
Empfehlungsschreiben *nt* letter of recommendation.
empfiehlt [ɛm'pfi:lt] *vb siehe* **empfehlen.**
empfinden [ɛm'pfɪndən] *unreg vt* to feel; **etw als Beleidigung ~** to find sth insulting; **E~** (**-s**) *nt:* **meinem E~ nach** to my mind.
empfindlich *adj* sensitive; (*Stelle*) sore; (*reizbar*) touchy; **deine Kritik hat ihn ~ getroffen** your criticism cut him to the quick; **E~keit** *f* sensitiveness; (*Reizbarkeit*) touchiness.
empfindsam *adj* sentimental; (*Mensch*) sensitive.
Empfindung *f* feeling, sentiment.
empfindungslos *adj* unfeeling, insensitive.
empfing *etc* [ɛm'pfɪŋ] *vb siehe* **empfangen.**
empfohlen [ɛm'pfo:lən] *pp von* **empfehlen** ♦ *adj:* **~er Einzelhandelspreis** recommended retail price.
empfunden [ɛm'pfʊndən] *pp von* **empfinden.**

empor [ɛm'po:r] *adv* up, upwards.
emporarbeiten *vr* (*geh*) to work one's way up.
Empore [ɛm'po:rə] (**-, -n**) *f* (*ARCHIT*) gallery.
empören [ɛm'po:rən] *vt* to make indignant; to shock ♦ *vr* to become indignant.
empörend *adj* outrageous.
emporkommen *unreg vi* to rise; (*vorankommen*) to succeed.
Emporkömmling *m* upstart, parvenu.
empört *adj:* **~ (über** +*akk*) indignant (at), outraged (at).
Empörung *f* indignation.
emsig ['ɛmzɪç] *adj* diligent, busy.
End- ['ɛnt] *in zW* final; **~auswertung** *f* final analysis; **~bahnhof** *m* terminus; **~betrag** *m* final amount.
Ende ['ɛndə] (**-s, -n**) *nt* end; **am ~** at the end; (*schließlich*) in the end; **am ~ sein** to be at the end of one's tether; **~ Dezember** at the end of December; **zu ~ sein** to be finished; **zu ~ gehen** to come to an end; **zu ~ führen** to finish (off); **letzten ~s** in the end, at the end of the day; **ein böses ~ nehmen** to come to a bad end; **ich bin mit meiner Weisheit am ~** I'm at my wits' end; **er wohnt am ~ der Welt** (*umg*) he lives at the back of beyond.
Endeffekt *m:* **im ~** (*umg*) when it comes down to it.
enden *vi* to end.
Endergebnis *nt* final result.
endgültig *adj* final, definite.
Endivie [ɛn'di:viə] *f* endive.
End- *zW:* **~lager** *nt* permanent waste disposal site; **~lagerung** *f* permanent disposal; **e~lich** *adj* final; (*MATH*) finite ♦ *adv* finally; **e~lich!** at last!; **hör e~lich damit auf!** will you stop that!; **e~los** *adj* endless; **~lospapier** *nt* continuous paper; **~produkt** *nt* end *od* final product; **~spiel** *nt* final(s); **~spurt** *m* (*SPORT*) final spurt; **~station** *f* terminus.
Endung *f* ending.
Endverbraucher *m* consumer, end-user.
Energie [enɛr'gi:] *f* energy; **~aufwand** *m* energy expenditure; **~bedarf** *m* energy requirement; **~einsparung** *f* energy saving; **~gewinnung** *f* generation of energy; **e~los** *adj* lacking in energy, weak; **~quelle** *f* source of energy; **~versorgung** *f* supply of energy; **~wirtschaft** *f* energy industry.
energisch [e'nɛrgɪʃ] *adj* energetic; **~ durchgreifen** to take vigorous *od* firm action.
eng [ɛŋ] *adj* narrow; (*Kleidung*) tight; (*fig: Horizont*) narrow, limited; (*Freundschaft, Verhältnis*) close; **~ an etw** *dat* close to sth; **in die ~ere Wahl kommen** to be short-listed (*BRIT*).
Engadin ['ɛŋgadi:n] (**-s**) *nt:* **das ~** the Engadine.

Engagement [āgaʒə'mãː] (**-s, -s**) *nt*
engagement; (*Verpflichtung*) commitment.
engagieren [āga'ʒiːrən] *vt* to engage ♦ *vr* to
commit o.s.; **ein engagierter Schriftsteller** a
committed writer.
Enge ['εŋə] (**-, -n**) *f* (*lit, fig*) narrowness;
(*Land~*) defile; (*Meer~*) straits *pl*; **jdn in die**
~ treiben to drive sb into a corner.
Engel ['εŋəl] (**-s, -**) *m* angel; **e~haft** *adj* angelic;
~macher(in) (**-s, -**) (*umg*) *m(f)* backstreet
abortionist.
Engelsgeduld *f*: **sie hat eine ~** she has the
patience of a saint.
Engelszungen *pl*: **(wie) mit ~ reden** to use
all one's own powers of persuasion.
engherzig *adj* petty.
engl. *abk* = **englisch**.
England ['εŋlant] *nt* England.
Engländer ['εŋlεndər] (**-s, -**) *m* Englishman;
English boy; **die Engländer** *pl* the English,
the Britishers (*US*); **~in** *f* Englishwoman;
English girl.
englisch ['εŋlıʃ] *adj* English.
engmaschig ['εŋmaʃıç] *adj* close-meshed.
Engpass▲ *m* defile, pass; (*fig: Verkehr*)
bottleneck.
en gros [ã'gro] *adv* wholesale.
engstirnig ['εŋʃtırnıç] *adj* narrow-minded.
Enkel ['εŋkəl] (**-s, -**) *m* grandson; **~in** *f*
granddaughter; **~kind** *nt* grandchild.
en masse [ã'mas] *adv* en masse.
enorm [e'nɔrm] *adj* enormous; (*umg: herrlich,*
kolossal) tremendous.
en passant [ãpa'sã] *adv* en passant, in
passing.
Ensemble [ã'sãbəl] (**-s, -s**) *nt* ensemble.
entarten [εnt'|aːrtən] *vi* to degenerate.
entbehren [εnt'beːrən] *vt* to do without,
dispense with.
entbehrlich *adj* superfluous.
Entbehrung *f* privation; **~en auf sich** *akk*
nehmen to make sacrifices.
entbinden [εnt'bındən] *unreg vt* (*+gen*) to
release (from); (*MED*) to deliver ♦ *vi* (*MED*)
to give birth.
Entbindung *f* release; (*MED*) delivery, birth.
Entbindungsheim *nt* maternity hospital.
Entbindungsstation *f* maternity ward.
entblößen [εnt'bløːsən] *vt* to denude,
uncover; (*berauben*): **einer Sache** *gen*
entblößt deprived of sth.
entbrennen [εnt'brεnən] *unreg vi* (*liter: Kampf,*
Streit) to flare up; (: *Liebe*) to be aroused.
entdecken [εnt'dεkən] *vt* to discover; **jdm etw**
~ to disclose sth to sb.
Entdecker(in) (**-s, -**) *m(f)* discoverer.
Entdeckung *f* discovery.
Ente ['εntə] (**-, -n**) *f* duck; (*fig*) canard, false
report; (*AUT*) Citroën 2CV, deux-chevaux.
entehren [εnt'|eːrən] *vt* to dishonour (*BRIT*),

dishonor (*US*), disgrace.
enteignen [εnt'|aıgnən] *vt* to expropriate;
(*Besitzer*) to dispossess.
enteisen [εnt'|aızən] *vt* to de-ice; (*Kühlschrank*)
to defrost.
enterben [εnt'|εrbən] *vt* to disinherit.
Enterhaken ['εntərhaːkən] *m* grappling iron
od hook.
entfachen [εnt'faxən] *vt* to kindle.
entfallen [εnt'falən] *unreg vi* to drop, fall;
(*wegfallen*) to be dropped; **jdm ~** (*vergessen*)
to slip sb's memory; **auf jdn ~** to be allotted
to sb.
entfalten [εnt'faltən] *vt* to unfold; (*Talente*) to
develop ♦ *vr* to open; (*Mensch*) to develop
one's potential.
Entfaltung *f* unfolding; (*von Talenten*)
development.
entfernen [εnt'fεrnən] *vt* to remove;
(*hinauswerfen*) to expel ♦ *vr* to go away,
retire, withdraw.
entfernt *adj* distant ♦ *adv*: **nicht im E~esten!**
not in the slightest!; **weit davon ~ sein, etw**
zu tun to be far from doing sth.
Entfernung *f* distance; (*Wegschaffen*)
removal; **unerlaubte ~ von der Truppe**
absence without leave.
Entfernungsmesser *m* (*PHOT*) rangefinder.
entfesseln [εnt'fεsəln] *vt* (*fig*) to arouse.
entfetten [εnt'fεtən] *vt* to take the fat from.
entflammen [εnt'flamən] *vt* (*fig*) to (a)rouse
♦ *vi* to burst into flames; (*fig: Streit*) to flare
up; (: *Leidenschaft*) to be (a)roused *od*
inflamed.
entfremden [εnt'frεmdən] *vt* to estrange,
alienate.
Entfremdung *f* estrangement, alienation.
entfrosten [εnt'frɔstən] *vt* to defrost.
Entfroster (**-s, -**) *m* (*AUT*) defroster.
entführen [εnt'fyːrən] *vt* to abduct, kidnap;
(*Flugzeug*) to hijack.
Entführer (**-s, -**) *m* kidnapper (*BRIT*), kidnaper
(*US*); hijacker.
Entführung *f* abduction, kidnapping (*BRIT*),
kidnaping (*US*); hijacking.
entgegen [εnt'geːgən] *präp +dat* contrary to,
against ♦ *adv* towards; **~bringen** *unreg vt* to
bring; (*fig*): **jdm etw ~bringen** to show sb
sth; **~ gehen** *unreg vi +dat* to go to meet, go
towards; **Schwierigkeiten ~gehen** to be
heading for difficulties; **~gesetzt** *adj*
opposite; (*widersprechend*) opposed; **~halten**
unreg vt (*fig*): **einer Sache** *dat* **~halten, dass ...**
to object to sth that ...; **E~kommen** *nt*
obligingness; **~kommen** *unreg vi +dat* to come
towards, approach; (*fig*): **jdm ~kommen** to
accommodate sb; **das kommt unseren**
Plänen sehr ~ that fits in very well with our
plans; **~kommend** *adj* obliging; **~laufen** *unreg*
vi +dat to run towards *od* to meet; (*fig*) to run

counter to; **E~nahme** *f* (*form: Empfang*) receipt; (*Annahme*) acceptance; **~nehmen** *unreg vt* to receive, accept; **~sehen** *unreg vi* +*dat* to await; **~setzen** *vt* to oppose; **dem habe ich ~zusetzen, dass ...** against that I'd like to say that ...; **jdm/etw Widerstand ~setzen** to put up resistance to sb/sth; **~stehen** *unreg vi*: **dem steht nichts ~** there's no objection to that; **~treten** *unreg vi* +*dat* (*lit*) to step up to; (*fig*) to oppose, counter; **~wirken** *vi* +*dat* to counteract.

entgegnen [ɛnt'geːgnən] *vt* to reply, retort. **Entgegnung** *f* reply, retort.

entgehen [ɛnt'geːən] *unreg vi* (*fig*): **jdm ~** to escape sb's notice; **sich** *dat* **etw ~ lassen** to miss sth.

entgeistert [ɛnt'gaɪstərt] *adj* thunderstruck.

Entgelt [ɛnt'gɛlt] (**-(e)s, -e**) *nt* remuneration.

entgelten *unreg vt*: **jdm etw ~** to repay sb for sth.

entgleisen [ɛnt'glaɪzən] *vi* (*EISENB*) to be derailed; (*fig: Person*) to misbehave; **~ lassen** to derail.

Entgleisung *f* derailment; (*fig*) faux pas, gaffe.

entgleiten [ɛnt'glaɪtən] *unreg vi*: **jdm ~** to slip from sb's hand.

entgräten [ɛnt'grɛːtən] *vt* to fillet, bone.

Enthaarungsmittel [ɛnt'haːrʊŋsmɪtəl] *nt* depilatory.

enthält [ɛnt'hɛlt] *vb siehe* **enthalten**.

enthalten [ɛnt'haltən] *unreg vt* to contain ♦ *vr* +*gen* to abstain from, refrain from; **sich (der Stimme) ~** to abstain.

enthaltsam [ɛnt'haltzaːm] *adj* abstinent, abstemious; **E~keit** *f* abstinence.

enthärten [ɛnt'hɛrtən] *vt* (*Wasser*) to soften; (*Metall*) to anneal.

enthaupten [ɛnt'haʊptən] *vt* to decapitate; (*als Hinrichtung*) to behead.

enthäuten [ɛnt'hɔytən] *vt* to skin.

entheben [ɛnt'heːbən] *unreg vt*: **jdn einer Sache** *gen* **~** to relieve sb of sth.

enthemmen [ɛnt'hɛmən] *vt*: **jdn ~** to free sb from his/her inhibitions.

enthielt *etc* [ɛnt'hiːlt] *vb siehe* **enthalten**.

enthüllen [ɛnt'hylən] *vt* to reveal, unveil.

Enthüllung *f* revelation; (*von Skandal*) exposure.

Enthusiasmus [ɛntuzi'asmʊs] *m* enthusiasm.

entjungfern [ɛnt'jʊŋfərn] *vt* to deflower.

entkalken [ɛnt'kalkən] *vt* to decalcify.

entkernen [ɛnt'kɛrnən] *vt* (*Kernobst*) to core; (*Steinobst*) to stone.

entkleiden [ɛnt'klaɪdən] *vt, vr* (*geh*) to undress.

entkommen [ɛnt'kɔmən] *unreg vi* to get away, escape; **jdm/etw** *od* **aus etw ~** to get away *od* escape from sb/sth.

entkorken [ɛnt'kɔrkən] *vt* to uncork.

entkräften [ɛnt'krɛftən] *vt* to weaken, exhaust; (*Argument*) to refute.

entkrampfen [ɛnt'krampfən] *vt* (*fig*) to relax, ease.

entladen [ɛnt'laːdən] *unreg vt* to unload; (*ELEK*) to discharge ♦ *vr* (*ELEK, Gewehr*) to discharge; (*Ärger etc*) to vent itself.

entlang [ɛnt'laŋ] *präp* (+*akk od dat*) along ♦ *adv* along; **~ dem Fluss, den Fluss ~** along the river; **hier ~** this way; **~gehen** *unreg vi* to walk along.

entlarven [ɛnt'larfən] *vt* to unmask, expose.

entlassen [ɛnt'lasən] *unreg vt* to discharge; (*Arbeiter*) to dismiss; (*nach Stellenabbau*) to make redundant.

entlässt [ɛnt'lɛst] *vb siehe* **entlassen**.

Entlassung *f* discharge; dismissal; **es gab 20 ~en** there were 20 redundancies.

Entlassungszeugnis *nt* (*SCH*) school-leaving certificate.

entlasten [ɛnt'lastən] *vt* to relieve; (*Arbeit abnehmen*) to take some of the load off; (*Angeklagte*) to exonerate; (*Konto*) to clear.

Entlastung *f* relief; (*COMM*) crediting.

Entlastungszeuge *m* defence (*BRIT*) *od* defense (*US*) witness.

Entlastungszug *m* relief train.

entledigen [ɛnt'leːdɪgən] *vr*: **sich jds/einer Sache ~** to rid o.s. of sb/sth.

entleeren [ɛnt'leːrən] *vt* to empty; (*Darm*) to evacuate.

entlegen [ɛnt'leːgən] *adj* remote.

entließ *etc* [ɛnt'liːs] *vb siehe* **entlassen**.

entlocken [ɛnt'lɔkən] *vt*: **jdm etw ~** to elicit sth from sb.

entlohnen *vt* to pay; (*fig*) to reward.

entlüften [ɛnt'lyftən] *vt* to ventilate.

entmachten [ɛnt'maxtən] *vt* to deprive of power.

entmenscht [ɛnt'mɛnʃt] *adj* inhuman, bestial.

entmilitarisiert [ɛntmilitari'ziːrt] *adj* demilitarized.

entmündigen [ɛnt'mʏndɪgən] *vt* to certify; (*JUR*) to (legally) incapacitate, declare incapable of managing one's own affairs.

entmutigen [ɛnt'muːtɪgən] *vt* to discourage.

Entnahme [ɛnt'naːmə] (**-, -n**) *f* removal, withdrawal.

Entnazifizierung [ɛntnatsifi'tsiːrʊŋ] *f* denazification.

entnehmen [ɛnt'neːmən] *unreg vt* +*dat* to take out of, take from; (*folgern*) to infer from; **wie ich Ihren Worten entnehme, ...** I gather from what you say that ...

entpuppen [ɛnt'pʊpən] *vr* (*fig*) to reveal o.s., turn out; **sich als etw ~** to turn out to be sth.

entrahmen [ɛnt'raːmən] *vt* to skim.

entreißen [ɛnt'raɪsən] *unreg vt*: **jdm etw ~** to snatch sth (away) from sb.

entrichten [ɛnt'rɪçtən] *vt* (*form*) to pay.

entrosten [ɛnt'rɔstən] *vt* to derust.

entrüsten [ɛnt'rʏstən] *vt* to incense, outrage ♦ *vr* to be filled with indignation.

entrüstet *adj* indignant, outraged.

Entrüstung *f* indignation.

Entsafter [ɛnt'zaftər] (**-s, -**) *m* juice extractor.

entsagen [ɛnt'za:gən] *vi* +*dat* to renounce.

entschädigen [ɛnt'ʃɛ:dɪgən] *vt* to compensate.

Entschädigung *f* compensation.

entschärfen [ɛnt'ʃɛrfən] *vt* to defuse; (*Kritik*) to tone down.

Entscheid [ɛnt'ʃaɪt] (**-(e)s, -e**) *m* (*form*) decision.

entscheiden *unreg vt, vi, vr* to decide; **darüber habe ich nicht zu** ~ that is not for me to decide; **sich für jdn/etw** ~ to decide in favour of sb/sth; to decide on sb/sth.

entscheidend *adj* decisive; (*Stimme*) casting; **das E~e** the decisive *od* deciding factor.

Entscheidung *f* decision; **wie ist die** ~ **ausgefallen?** which way did the decision go?

Entscheidungs- *zW:* ~**befugnis** *f* decision-making powers *pl;* **e~fähig** *adj* capable of deciding; ~**spiel** *nt* play-off; ~**träger** *m* decision-maker.

entschied *etc* [ɛnt'ʃi:t] *vb siehe* **entscheiden.**

entschieden [ɛnt'ʃi:dən] *pp von* **entscheiden** ♦ *adj* decided; (*entschlossen*) resolute; **das geht** ~ **zu weit** that's definitely going too far; **E~heit** *f* firmness, determination.

entschlacken [ɛnt'ʃlakən] *vt* (*MED: Körper*) to purify.

entschließen [ɛnt'ʃli:sən] *unreg vr* to decide; **sich zu nichts** ~ **können** to be unable to make up one's mind; **kurz entschlossen** straight away.

Entschließungsantrag *m* (*POL*) resolution proposal.

entschloss *etc*▲ [ɛnt'ʃlɔs] *vb siehe* **entschließen.**

entschlossen [ɛnt'ʃlɔsən] *pp von* **entschließen** ♦ *adj* determined, resolute; **E~heit** *f* determination.

entschlüpfen [ɛnt'ʃlʏpfən] *vi* to escape, slip away; (*fig: Wort etc*) to slip out.

Entschluss▲ [ɛnt'ʃlʊs] *m* decision; **aus eigenem** ~ **handeln** to act on one's own initiative; **es ist mein fester** ~ it is my firm intention.

entschlüsseln [ɛnt'ʃlʏsəln] *vt* to decipher; (*Funkspruch*) to decode.

entschlussfreudig▲ *adj* decisive.

Entschlusskraft▲ *f* determination, decisiveness.

entschuldbar [ɛnt'ʃʊltba:r] *adj* excusable.

entschuldigen [ɛnt'ʃʊldɪgən] *vt* to excuse ♦ *vr* to apologize ♦ *vi:* ~ **Sie (bitte)!** excuse me; (*Verzeihung*) sorry; **jdn bei jdm** ~ to make sb's excuses *od* apologies to sb; **sich**

~ **lassen** to send one's apologies.

entschuldigend *adj* apologetic.

Entschuldigung *f* apology; (*Grund*) excuse; **jdn um** ~ **bitten** to apologize to sb; ~**!** excuse me; (*Verzeihung*) sorry.

entschwefeln [ɛnt'ʃvɛ:fəln] *vt* to desulphurize.

Entschwefelungsanlage *f* desulphurization plant.

entschwinden [ɛnt'ʃvɪndən] *unreg vi* to disappear.

entsetzen [ɛnt'zɛtsən] *vt* to horrify ♦ *vr* to be horrified *od* appalled; **E~** (**-s**) *nt* horror, dismay.

entsetzlich *adj* dreadful, appalling.

entsetzt *adj* horrified.

entsichern [ɛnt'zɪçərn] *vt* to release the safety catch of.

entsinnen [ɛnt'zɪnən] *unreg vr* +*gen* to remember.

entsorgen [ɛnt'zɔrgən] *vt:* **eine Stadt** ~ to dispose of a town's refuse and sewage.

Entsorgung *f* waste disposal; (*von Chemikalien*) disposal.

entspannen [ɛnt'ʃpanən] *vt, vr* (*Körper*) to relax; (*POL: Lage*) to ease.

Entspannung *f* relaxation, rest; (*POL*) détente.

Entspannungspolitik *f* policy of détente.

Entspannungsübungen *pl* relaxation exercises *pl.*

entspr. *abk* = **entsprechend.**

entsprach *etc* [ɛnt'ʃprax] *vb siehe* **entsprechen.**

entsprechen [ɛnt'ʃprɛçən] *unreg vi* +*dat* to correspond to; (*Anforderungen, Wünschen*) to meet, comply with.

entsprechend *adj* appropriate ♦ *adv* accordingly ♦ *präp* +*dat:* **er wird seiner Leistung** ~ **bezahlt** he is paid according to output.

entspricht [ɛnt'ʃprɪçt] *vb siehe* **entsprechen.**

entspringen [ɛnt'ʃprɪŋən] *unreg vi* (+*dat*) to spring (from).

entsprochen [ɛnt'ʃprɔxən] *pp von* **entsprechen.**

entstaatlichen [ɛnt'ʃta:tlɪçən] *vt* to denationalize.

entstammen [ɛnt'ʃtamən] *vi* +*dat* to stem *od* come from.

entstand *etc* [ɛnt'ʃtant] *vb siehe* **entstehen.**

entstanden [ɛnt'ʃtandən] *pp von* **entstehen.**

entstehen [ɛnt'ʃte:ən] *unreg vi:* ~ (**aus** *od* **durch**) to arise (from), result (from); **wir wollen nicht den Eindruck** ~ **lassen, ...** we don't want to give rise to the impression that ...; **für** ~**den** *od* **entstandenen Schaden** for damages incurred.

Entstehung *f* genesis, origin.

entstellen [ɛnt'ʃtɛlən] *vt* to disfigure; (*Wahrheit*) to distort.

Entstellung *f* distortion; disfigurement.

entstören [ɛnt'ʃtøːrən] *vt* (*RUNDF*) to eliminate interference from; (*AUT*) to suppress.

enttäuschen [ɛnt'tɔyʃən] *vt* to disappoint.

Enttäuschung *f* disappointment.

entwachsen [ɛnt'vaksən] *unreg vi* +*dat* to outgrow, grow out of; (*geh: herauswachsen aus*) to spring from.

entwaffnen [ɛnt'vafnən] *vt* (*lit, fig*) to disarm.

entwaffnend *adj* disarming.

Entwarnung [ɛnt'varnʊŋ] *f* all clear (signal).

entwässern [ɛnt'vɛsərn] *vt* to drain.

Entwässerung *f* drainage.

entweder [ɛnt'veːdər] *konj* either; ~ ... oder ... either ... or ...

entweichen [ɛnt'vaiçən] *unreg vi* to escape.

entweihen [ɛnt'vaiən] *unreg vi* to desecrate.

entwenden [ɛnt'vɛndən] *unreg vt* to purloin, steal.

entwerfen [ɛnt'vɛrfən] *unreg vt* (*Zeichnung*) to sketch; (*Modell*) to design; (*Vortrag, Gesetz etc*) to draft.

entwerten [ɛnt'veːrtən] *vt* to devalue; (*stempeln*) to cancel.

Entwerter (**-s**, **-**) *m* (ticket-)cancelling (*BRIT*) *od* canceling (*US*) machine.

entwickeln [ɛnt'vɪkəln] *vt* to develop (*auch PHOT*); (*Mut, Energie*) to show, display ♦ *vr* to develop.

Entwickler (**-s**, **-**) *m* developer.

Entwicklung [ɛnt'vɪklʊŋ] *f* development; (*PHOT*) developing; **in der ~** at the development stage; (*Jugendliche etc*) still developing.

Entwicklungs- *zW*: **~abschnitt** *m* stage of development; **~helfer(in)** *m(f)* VSO worker (*BRIT*), Peace Corps worker (*US*); **~hilfe** *f* aid for developing countries; **~jahre** *pl* adolescence *sing*; **~land** *nt* developing country; **~zeit** *f* period of development; (*PHOT*) developing time.

entwirren [ɛnt'vɪrən] *vt* to disentangle.

entwischen [ɛnt'vɪʃən] *vi* to escape.

entwöhnen [ɛnt'vøːnən] *vt* to wean; (*Süchtige*): (**einer Sache** *dat od* **von etw**) ~ to cure (of sth).

Entwöhnung *f* weaning; cure, curing.

entwürdigend [ɛnt'vʏrdɪgənt] *adj* degrading.

Entwurf [ɛnt'vʊrf] *m* outline, design; (*Vertrags~, Konzept*) draft.

entwurzeln [ɛnt'vʊrtsəln] *vt* to uproot.

entziehen [ɛnt'tsiːən] *unreg vt* (+*dat*) to withdraw (from), take away (from); (*Flüssigkeit*) to draw (from), extract (from) ♦ *vr* (+*dat*) to escape (from); (*jds Kenntnis*) to be outside *od* beyond; (*der Pflicht*) to shirk (from); **sich jds Blicken ~** to be hidden from sight.

Entziehung *f* withdrawal.

Entziehungsanstalt *f* drug addiction/

alcoholism treatment centre (*BRIT*) *od* center (*US*).

Entziehungskur *f* treatment for drug addiction/alcoholism.

entziffern [ɛnt'tsɪfərn] *vt* to decipher; (*Funkspruch*) to decode.

entzücken [ɛnt'tsʏkən] *vt* to delight; **E~** (**-s**) *nt* delight.

entzückend *adj* delightful, charming.

Entzug [ɛnt'tsuːk] (**-(e)s**) *m* (*einer Lizenz etc, MED*) withdrawal.

Entzugserscheinung *f* withdrawal symptom.

entzündbar *adj*: **leicht ~** highly inflammable; (*fig*) easily roused.

entzünden [ɛnt'tsʏndən] *vt* to light, set light to; (*fig, MED*) to inflame; (*Streit*) to spark off ♦ *vr* (*lit, fig*) to catch fire; (*Streit*) to start; (*MED*) to become inflamed.

Entzündung *f* (*MED*) inflammation.

entzwei [ɛnt'tsvai] *adv* in two; broken; **~brechen** *unreg vt, vi* to break in two.

entzweien *vt* to set at odds ♦ *vr* to fall out.

entzweigehen *unreg vi* to break (in two).

Enzian ['ɛntsiaːn] (**-s**, **-e**) *m* gentian.

Enzyklika [ɛn'tsyːklika] (**-**, **-liken**) *f* (*REL*) encyclical.

Enzyklopädie [ɛntsyklope'diː] *f* encyclop(a)edia.

Enzym [ɛn'tsyːm] (**-s**, **-e**) *nt* enzyme.

Epen *pl von* **Epos**.

Epidemie [epide'miː] *f* epidemic.

Epilepsie [epile'psiː] *f* epilepsy.

episch ['eːpɪʃ] *adj* epic.

Episode [epi'zoːdə] (**-**, **-n**) *f* episode.

Epoche [e'pɔxə] (**-**, **-n**) *f* epoch; **~ machend** epoch-making.

Epos ['eːpɔs] (**-**, **Epen**) *nt* epic (poem).

Equipe [e'kɪp] (**-**, **-n**) *f* team.

er [eːr] *pron* he; it.

erachten [ɛr'|axtən] *vt* (*geh*): ~ **für** *od* **als** to consider (to be); **meines E~s** in my opinion.

erarbeiten [ɛr'|arbaitən] *vt* to work for, acquire; (*Theorie*) to work out.

Erbanlage ['ɛrp|anlaːgə] *f* hereditary factor(s *pl*).

erbarmen [ɛr'barmən] *vr* (+*gen*) to have pity *od* mercy (on) ♦ *vt*: **er sieht zum E~ aus** he's a pitiful sight; **Herr, erbarme dich (unser)!** Lord, have mercy (upon us)!; **E~** (**-s**) *nt* pity.

erbärmlich [ɛr'bɛrmlɪç] *adj* wretched, pitiful; **E~keit** *f* wretchedness.

Erbarmungs- *zW*: **e~los** *adj* pitiless, merciless; **e~voll** *adj* compassionate; **e~würdig** *adj* pitiable, wretched.

erbauen [ɛr'bauən] *vt* to build, erect; (*fig*) to edify; **er ist von meinem Plan nicht besonders erbaut** (*umg*) he isn't particularly enthusiastic about my plan.

Erbauer (**-s**, **-**) *m* builder.

erbaulich *adj* edifying.

Erbauung *f* construction; (*fig*) edification.

erbberechtigt *adj* entitled to inherit.

erbbiologisch *adj*: ~es Gutachten (*JUR*) blood test (*to establish paternity*).

Erbe¹ ['ɛrbə] (-n, -n) *m* heir; **jdn zum** *od* **als** ~n einsetzen to make sb one's/sb's heir.

Erbe² ['ɛrbə] (-s) *nt* inheritance; (*fig*) heritage.

erben *vt* to inherit; (*umg: geschenkt bekommen*) to get, be given.

erbeuten [ɛrˈbɔytən] *vt* to carry off; (*MIL*) to capture.

Erb- *zW*: ~**faktor** *m* gene; ~**fehler** *m* hereditary defect; ~**feind** *m* traditional *od* arch enemy; ~**folge** *f* (line of) succession.

Erbin *f* heiress.

erbitten [ɛrˈbɪtən] *unreg vt* to ask for, request.

erbittern [ɛrˈbɪtɐn] *vt* to embitter; (*erzürnen*) to incense.

erbittert [ɛrˈbɪtɐt] *adj* (*Kampf*) fierce, bitter.

erblassen [ɛrˈblasən] *vi* to (turn) pale.

Erblasser(in) ['ɛrblasɐ(ɪn)] (-s, -) *m(f)* (*JUR*) person who leaves an inheritance.

erbleichen [ɛrˈblaɪçən] *unreg vi* to (turn) pale.

erblich ['ɛrplɪç] *adj* hereditary; **er/sie ist** ~ **(vor)belastet** it runs in the family.

erblichen *pp von* **erbleichen**.

erblicken [ɛrˈblɪkən] *vt* to see; (*erspähen*) to catch sight of.

erblinden [ɛrˈblɪndən] *vi* to go blind.

Erbmasse ['ɛrpmasə] *f* estate; (*BIOL*) genotype.

erbosen [ɛrˈboːzən] *vt* (*geh*) to anger ♦ *vr* to grow angry.

erbrechen [ɛrˈbrɛçən] *unreg vt, vr* to vomit.

Erbrecht *nt* hereditary right; (*Gesetze*) law of inheritance.

Erbschaft *f* inheritance, legacy.

Erbschaftssteuer *f* estate *od* death duties *pl*.

Erbschleicher(in) ['ɛrpʃlaɪçɐ(ɪn)] (-s, -) *m(f)* legacy-hunter.

Erbse ['ɛrpsə] (-, -n) *f* pea.

Erb- *zW*: ~**stück** *nt* heirloom; ~**sünde** *f* (*REL*) original sin; ~**teil** *nt* inherited trait; (*JUR*) (portion of) inheritance.

Erd- *zW*: ~**achse** *f* earth's axis; ~**apfel** (*ÖSTERR*) *m* potato; ~**atmosphäre** *f* earth's atmosphere; ~**bahn** *f* orbit of the earth; ~**beben** *nt* earthquake; ~**beere** *f* strawberry; ~**boden** *m* ground; **etw dem ~boden gleichmachen** to level sth, raze sth to the ground.

Erde (-, -n) *f* earth; **zu ebener** ~ at ground level; **auf der ganzen** ~ all over the world; **du wirst mich noch unter die** ~ **bringen** (*umg*) you'll be the death of me yet.

erden *vt* (*ELEK*) to earth.

erdenkbar [ɛrˈdɛŋkbaːr] *adj* conceivable; **sich** *dat* **alle** ~**e Mühe geben** to take the greatest (possible) pains.

erdenklich [ɛrˈdɛŋklɪç] *adj* = **erdenkbar**.

Erdg. *abk* = **Erdgeschoss**.

Erd- *zW*: ~**gas** *nt* natural gas; ~**geschoss**▲ *nt* ground floor (*BRIT*), first floor (*US*); ~**kunde** *f* geography; ~**nuss**▲ *f* peanut; ~**oberfläche** *f* surface of the earth; ~**öl** *nt* (mineral) oil; ~**ölfeld** *nt* oilfield; ~**ölindustrie** *f* oil industry; ~**reich** *nt* soil, earth.

erdreisten [ɛrˈdraɪstən] *vr* to dare, have the audacity (*to do sth*).

erdrosseln [ɛrˈdrɔsəln] *vt* to strangle, throttle.

erdrücken [ɛrˈdrykən] *vt* to crush; ~**de Übermacht/~des Beweismaterial** overwhelming superiority/evidence.

Erd- *zW*: ~**rutsch** *m* landslide; ~**stoß** *m* (seismic) shock; ~**teil** *m* continent.

erdulden [ɛrˈdʊldən] *vt* to endure, suffer.

ereifern [ɛrˈʔaɪfɐn] *vr* to get excited.

ereignen [ɛrˈʔaɪɡnən] *vr* to happen.

Ereignis [ɛrˈʔaɪɡnɪs] (-ses, -se) *nt* event; **e~los** *adj* uneventful; **e~reich** *adj* eventful.

Eremit [ere'miːt] (-en, -en) *m* hermit.

erfahren [ɛrˈfaːrən] *unreg vt* to learn, find out; (*erleben*) to experience ♦ *adj* experienced.

Erfahrung *f* experience; ~**en sammeln** to gain experience; **etw in** ~ **bringen** to learn *od* find out sth.

Erfahrungsaustausch *m* exchange of experiences.

erfahrungsgemäß *adv* according to experience.

erfand *etc* [ɛrˈfant] *vb siehe* **erfinden**.

erfassen [ɛrˈfasən] *vt* to seize; (*fig: einbeziehen*) to include, register; (*verstehen*) to grasp.

erfinden [ɛrˈfɪndən] *unreg vt* to invent; **frei erfunden** completely fictitious.

Erfinder(in) (-s, -) *m(f)* inventor; **e~isch** *adj* inventive.

Erfindung *f* invention.

Erfindungsgabe *f* inventiveness.

Erfolg [ɛrˈfɔlk] (-(e)s, -e) *m* success; (*Folge*) result; ~ **versprechend** promising; **viel** ~! good luck!

erfolgen [ɛrˈfɔlɡən] *vi* to follow; (*sich ergeben*) to result; (*stattfinden*) to take place; (*Zahlung*) to be effected; **nach erfolgter Zahlung** when payment has been made.

Erfolg- *zW*: **e~los** *adj* unsuccessful; ~**losigkeit** *f* lack of success; **e~reich** *adj* successful.

Erfolgserlebnis *nt* feeling of success, sense of achievement.

erforderlich *adj* requisite, necessary.

erfordern [ɛrˈfɔrdɐn] *vt* to require, demand.

Erfordernis (-ses, -se) *nt* requirement, prerequisite.

erforschen [ɛrˈfɔrʃən] *vt* (*Land*) to explore; (*Problem*) to investigate; (*Gewissen*) to search.

Erforscher(in) (-s, -) *m(f)* explorer;

investigator.

Erforschung f exploration; investigation; searching.

erfragen [ɛrˈfraːɡən] vt to inquire, ascertain.

erfreuen [ɛrˈfrɔʏən] vr: **sich ~ an** +dat to enjoy ♦ vt to delight; **sich einer Sache** gen ~ (geh) to enjoy sth; **sehr erfreut!** (form: bei Vorstellung) pleased to meet you!

erfreulich [ɛrˈfrɔʏlɪç] adj pleasing, gratifying.

erfreulicherweise adv happily, luckily.

erfrieren [ɛrˈfriːrən] unreg vi to freeze (to death); (Glieder) to get frostbitten; (Pflanzen) to be killed by frost.

erfrischen [ɛrˈfrɪʃən] vt to refresh.

Erfrischung f refreshment.

Erfrischungsraum m snack bar, cafeteria.

erfüllen [ɛrˈfʏlən] vt (Raum etc) to fill; (fig: Bitte etc) to fulfil (BRIT), fulfill (US) ♦ vr to come true; **ein erfülltes Leben** a full life.

Erfüllung f: **in ~ gehen** to be fulfilled.

erfunden [ɛrˈfʊndən] pp von **erfinden**.

ergab etc [ɛrˈɡaːp] vb siehe **ergeben**.

ergänzen [ɛrˈɡɛntsən] vt to supplement, complete ♦ vr to complement one another.

Ergänzung f completion; (Zusatz) supplement.

ergattern [ɛrˈɡatərn] (umg) vt to get hold of, hunt up.

ergaunern [ɛrˈɡaʊnərn] (umg) vt: **sich** dat **etw ~** to get hold of sth by underhand methods.

ergeben [ɛrˈɡeːbən] unreg vt to yield, produce ♦ vr to surrender; (folgen) to result ♦ adj devoted; (demütig) humble; **sich einer Sache** dat **~** (sich hingeben) to give o.s. up to sth, yield to sth; **es ergab sich, dass unsere Befürchtungen ...** it turned out that our fears ...; **dem Trunk ~** addicted to drink; **E~heit** f devotion; humility.

Ergebnis [ɛrˈɡeːpnɪs] (-ses, -se) nt result; **zu einem ~ kommen** to come to od reach a conclusion; **e~los** adj without result, fruitless; **e~los bleiben** od **verlaufen** to come to nothing.

ergehen [ɛrˈɡeːən] unreg vi (form) to be issued, go out ♦ vi unpers: **es ergeht ihm gut/schlecht** he's faring od getting on well/badly ♦ vr: **sich in etw** dat **~** to indulge in sth; **etw über sich** akk **~ lassen** to put up with sth; **sich (in langen Reden) über ein Thema ~** (fig) to hold forth at length on sth.

ergiebig [ɛrˈɡiːbɪç] adj productive.

ergo [ˈɛrɡo] konj therefore, ergo (liter, hum).

Ergonomie [ɛrɡonoˈmiː] f ergonomics pl.

ergötzen [ɛrˈɡœtsən] vt to amuse, delight.

ergrauen [ɛrˈɡraʊən] vi to turn od go grey (BRIT) od gray (US).

ergreifen [ɛrˈɡraɪfən] unreg vt (lit, fig) to seize; (Beruf) to take up; (Maßnahmen) to resort to; (rühren) to move; **er ergriff das Wort** he began to speak.

ergreifend adj moving, affecting.

ergriff etc [ɛrˈɡrɪf] vb siehe **ergreifen**.

ergriffen pp von **ergreifen** ♦ adj deeply moved.

Ergriffenheit f emotion.

ergründen [ɛrˈɡrʏndən] vt (Sinn etc) to fathom; (Ursache, Motive) to discover.

Erguss▲ [ɛrˈɡʊs] (-es, ⁼e) m discharge; (fig) outpouring, effusion.

erhaben [ɛrˈhaːbən] adj (lit) raised, embossed; (fig) exalted, lofty; **über etw** akk **~ sein** to be above sth.

Erhalt m: **bei** od **nach ~** on receipt.

erhält [ɛrˈhɛlt] vb siehe **erhalten**.

erhalten [ɛrˈhaltən] unreg vt to receive; (bewahren) to preserve, maintain; **das Wort ~** to receive permission to speak; **jdn am Leben ~** to keep sb alive; **gut ~** in good condition.

erhältlich [ɛrˈhɛltlɪç] adj obtainable, available.

Erhaltung f maintenance, preservation.

erhängen [ɛrˈhɛŋən] vt, vr to hang.

erhärten [ɛrˈhɛrtən] vt to harden; (These) to substantiate, corroborate.

erhaschen [ɛrˈhaʃən] vt to catch.

erheben [ɛrˈheːbən] unreg vt to raise; (Protest, Forderungen) to make; (Fakten) to ascertain ♦ vr to rise (up); **sich über etw** akk **~** to rise above sth.

erheblich [ɛrˈheːplɪç] adj considerable.

erheitern [ɛrˈhaɪtərn] vt to amuse, cheer (up).

Erheiterung f exhilaration; **zur allgemeinen ~** to everybody's amusement.

erhellen [ɛrˈhɛlən] vt (lit, fig) to illuminate; (Geheimnis) to shed light on ♦ vr (Fenster) to light up; (Himmel, Miene) to brighten (up); (Gesicht) to brighten up.

erhielt etc [ɛrˈhiːlt] vb siehe **erhalten**.

erhitzen [ɛrˈhɪtsən] vt to heat ♦ vr to heat up; (fig) to become heated od aroused.

erhoffen [ɛrˈhɔfən] vt to hope for; **was erhoffst du dir davon?** what do you hope to gain from it?

erhöhen [ɛrˈhøːən] vt to raise; (verstärken) to increase; **erhöhte Temperatur haben** to have a temperature.

Erhöhung f (Gehalt) increment.

erholen [ɛrˈhoːlən] vr to recover; (entspannen) to have a rest; (fig: Preise, Aktien) to rally, pick up.

erholsam adj restful.

Erholung f recovery; relaxation, rest.

erholungsbedürftig adj in need of a rest, run-down.

Erholungsgebiet nt holiday (BRIT) od vacation (US) area.

Erholungsheim nt convalescent home.

erhören [ɛrˈhøːrən] vt (Gebet etc) to hear; (Bitte etc) to yield to.

Erika [ˈeːrika] (-, **Eriken**) f heather.

erinnern [ɛrˈʔɪnərn] vt: **~ (an** +akk) to remind

(of) ♦ vr: **sich (an etw** akk**)** ~ to remember
(sth).

Erinnerung f memory; (Andenken) reminder;
Erinnerungen pl (Lebens~) reminiscences pl;
(LITER) memoirs pl; **jdn/etw in guter**
~ **behalten** to have pleasant memories of
sb/sth.

Erinnerungsschreiben nt (COMM) reminder.

Erinnerungstafel f commemorative plaque.

Eritrea [eri'tre:a] **(-s)** nt Eritrea.

erkalten [ɛr'kaltən] vi to go cold, cool (down).

erkälten [ɛr'kɛltən] vr to catch cold; **sich** dat
die Blase ~ to catch a chill in one's bladder.

erkältet adj with a cold; ~ **sein** to have a cold.

Erkältung f cold.

erkämpfen [ɛr'kɛmpfən] vt to win, secure.

erkannt [ɛr'kant] pp von **erkennen**.

erkannte etc vb siehe **erkennen**.

erkennbar adj recognizable.

erkennen [ɛr'kɛnən] unreg vt to recognize;
(sehen, verstehen) to see; **jdm zu** ~ **geben,**
dass ... to give sb to understand that ...

erkenntlich adj: **sich** ~ **zeigen** to show one's
appreciation; **E~keit** f gratitude; (Geschenk)
token of one's gratitude.

Erkenntnis (-, -se) f knowledge; (das
Erkennen) recognition; (Einsicht) insight; **zur**
~ **kommen** to realize.

Erkennung f recognition.

Erkennungsdienst m police records
department.

Erkennungsmarke f identity disc.

Erker ['ɛrkər] **(-s, -)** m bay; ~**fenster** nt bay
window.

erklärbar adj explicable.

erklären [ɛr'klɛːrən] vt to explain; (Rücktritt) to
announce; (Politiker, Pressesprecher etc) to
say; **ich kann mir nicht ~, warum** ... I can't
understand why ...

erklärlich adj explicable; (verständlich)
understandable.

erklärt adj attrib (Gegner etc) professed,
avowed; (Favorit, Liebling) acknowledged.

Erklärung f explanation; (Aussage)
declaration.

erklecklich [ɛr'klɛklɪç] adj considerable.

erklimmen [ɛr'klɪmən] unreg vt to climb to.

erklingen [ɛr'klɪŋən] unreg vi to resound, ring
out.

erklomm etc [ɛr'klɔm] vb siehe **erklimmen**.

erklommen pp von **erklimmen**.

erkranken [ɛr'kraŋkən] vi: ~ **(an** +dat**)** to be
taken ill (with); (Organ, Pflanze, Tier) to
become diseased (with).

Erkrankung f illness.

erkunden [ɛr'kʊndən] vt to find out, ascertain;
(bes MIL) to reconnoitre (BRIT), reconnoiter
(US).

erkundigen vr: **sich** ~ **(nach)** to inquire
(about); **ich werde mich** ~ I'll find out.

Erkundigung f inquiry; ~**en einholen** to
make inquiries.

Erkundung f (MIL) reconnaissance, scouting.

erlahmen [ɛr'laːmən] vi to tire; (nachlassen) to
flag, wane.

erlangen [ɛr'laŋən] vt to attain, achieve.

Erlass▲ [ɛr'las] **(-es, -e)** m decree; (Aufhebung)
remission.

erlassen unreg vt (Verfügung) to issue; (Gesetz)
to enact; (Strafe) to remit; **jdm etw** ~ **to**
release sb from sth.

erlauben [ɛr'laʊbən] vt to allow, permit ♦ vr:
sich dat **etw** ~ (Zigarette, Pause) to permit o.s.
sth; (Bemerkung, Verschlag) to venture sth;
(sich leisten) to afford sth; **jdm etw** ~ **to**
allow od permit sb (to do) sth; ~ **Sie?** may
I?; ~ **Sie mal!** do you mind!; **was** ~ **Sie sich**
(eigentlich)! how dare you!

Erlaubnis [ɛr'laʊpnɪs] **(-, -se)** f permission.

erläutern [ɛr'lɔʏtərn] vt to explain.

Erläuterung f explanation; **zur** ~ **in**
explanation.

Erle ['ɛrlə] **(-, -n)** f alder.

erleben [ɛr'leːbən] vt to experience; (Zeit) to
live through; (mit~) to witness; (noch mit~)
to live to see; **so wütend habe ich ihn noch**
nie erlebt I've never seen od known him so
furious.

Erlebnis [ɛr'leːpnɪs] **(-ses, -se)** nt experience.

erledigen [ɛr'leːdɪgən] vt to take care of, deal
with; (Antrag etc) to process; (umg:
erschöpfen) to wear out; (ruinieren) to finish;
(umbringen) to do in ♦ vr: **das hat sich**
erledigt that's all settled; **das ist erledigt**
that's taken care of, that's been done; **ich**
habe noch einiges in der Stadt zu ~ I've still
got a few things to do in town.

erledigt (umg) adj (erschöpft) shattered, done
in; (: ruiniert) finished, ruined.

erlegen [ɛr'leːgən] vt to kill.

erleichtern [ɛr'laɪçtərn] vt to make easier; (fig:
Last) to lighten; (lindern, beruhigen) to
relieve.

erleichtert adj relieved; ~ **aufatmen** to
breathe a sigh of relief.

Erleichterung f facilitation; lightening;
relief.

erleiden [ɛr'laɪdən] unreg vt to suffer, endure.

erlernbar adj learnable.

erlernen [ɛr'lɛrnən] vt to learn, acquire.

erlesen [ɛr'leːzən] adj select, choice.

erleuchten [ɛr'lɔʏçtən] vt to illuminate; (fig) to
inspire.

Erleuchtung f (Einfall) inspiration.

erliegen [ɛr'liːgən] unreg vi +dat (lit, fig) to
succumb to; (einem Irrtum) to be the victim
of; **zum E~ kommen** to come to a standstill.

erlischt [ɛr'lɪʃt] vb siehe **erlöschen**.

erlogen [ɛr'loːgən] adj untrue, made-up.

Erlös [ɛr'løːs] **(-es, -e)** m proceeds pl.

erlosch etc [ɛr'lɔʃ] vb siehe **erlöschen**.

erlöschen [ɛr'lœʃən] unreg vi (Feuer) to go out; (Interesse) to cease, die; (Vertrag, Recht) to expire; **ein erloschener Vulkan** an extinct volcano.

erlösen [ɛr'løːzən] vt to redeem, save.

Erlöser (-s, -) m (REL) Redeemer; (Befreier) saviour (BRIT), savior (US).

Erlösung f release; (REL) redemption.

ermächtigen [ɛr'mɛçtɪgən] vt to authorize, empower.

Ermächtigung f authorization.

ermahnen [ɛr'maːnən] vt to admonish, exhort.

Ermahnung f admonition, exhortation.

Ermang(e)lung [ɛr'maŋəluŋ] f: **in ~** +gen because of the lack of.

ermäßigen [ɛr'mɛsɪgən] vt to reduce.

Ermäßigung f reduction.

ermessen [ɛr'mɛsən] unreg vt to estimate, gauge; **E~** (-s) nt estimation; discretion; **in jds E~** +dat **liegen** to lie within sb's discretion; **nach meinem E~** in my judgement.

Ermessensfrage f matter of discretion.

ermitteln [ɛr'mɪtəln] vt to determine; (Täter) to trace ♦ vi: **gegen jdn ~** to investigate sb.

Ermittlung [ɛr'mɪtluŋ] f determination; (Polizei~) investigation; **~en anstellen (über** +akk) to make inquiries (about).

Ermittlungsverfahren nt (JUR) preliminary proceedings pl.

ermöglichen [ɛr'møːklɪçən] vt (+dat) to make possible (for).

ermorden [ɛr'mɔrdən] vt to murder.

Ermordung f murder.

ermüden [ɛr'myːdən] vt to tire; (TECH) to fatigue ♦ vi to tire.

ermüdend adj tiring; (fig) wearisome.

Ermüdung f fatigue.

Ermüdungserscheinung f sign of fatigue.

ermuntern [ɛr'muntərn] vt to rouse; (ermutigen) to encourage; (beleben) to liven up; (aufmuntern) to cheer up.

ermutigen [ɛr'muːtɪgən] vt to encourage.

ernähren [ɛr'nɛːrən] vt to feed, nourish; (Familie) to support ♦ vr to support o.s., earn a living; **sich ~ von** to live on.

Ernährer(in) (-s, -) m(f) breadwinner.

Ernährung f nourishment; (MED) nutrition; (Unterhalt) maintenance.

ernennen [ɛr'nɛnən] unreg vt to appoint.

Ernennung f appointment.

erneuern [ɛr'nɔyərn] vt to renew; (restaurieren) to restore; (renovieren) to renovate.

Erneuerung f renewal; restoration; renovation.

erneut adj renewed, fresh ♦ adv once more.

erniedrigen [ɛr'niːdrɪgən] vt to humiliate, degrade.

Ernst [ɛrnst] (-es) m seriousness; **das ist mein**

~ I'm quite serious; **im ~** in earnest; **~ machen mit etw** to put sth into practice; **e~** adj serious ♦ adv: **es steht e~ um ihn** things don't look too good for him; **e~ gemeint** meant in earnest, serious; **~fall** m emergency; **e~haft** adj serious; **~haftigkeit** f seriousness; **e~lich** adj serious.

Ernte ['ɛrntə] (-, -n) f harvest; **~dankfest** nt harvest festival.

ernten vt to harvest; (Lob etc) to earn.

ernüchtern [ɛr'nyçtərn] vt to sober up; (fig) to bring down to earth.

Ernüchterung f sobering up; (fig) disillusionment.

Eroberer [ɛr'ʔobərər] (-s, -) m conqueror.

erobern vt to conquer.

Eroberung f conquest.

eröffnen [ɛr'ʔœfnən] vt to open ♦ vr to present itself; **jdm etw ~** (geh) to disclose sth to sb.

Eröffnung f opening.

Eröffnungsansprache f inaugural od opening address.

Eröffnungsfeier f opening ceremony.

erogen [ɛro'geːn] adj erogenous.

erörtern [ɛr'ʔœrtərn] vt to discuss (in detail).

Erörterung f discussion.

Erotik [e'roːtɪk] f eroticism.

erotisch adj erotic.

Erpel ['ɛrpəl] (-, -) m drake.

erpicht [ɛr'pɪçt] adj: **~ (auf** +akk) keen (on).

erpressen [ɛr'prɛsən] vt (Geld etc) to extort; (jdn) to blackmail.

Erpresser (-s, -) m blackmailer.

Erpressung f blackmail; extortion.

erproben [ɛr'proːbən] vt to test; **erprobt** tried and tested.

erraten [ɛr'raːtən] unreg vt to guess.

errechnen [ɛr'rɛçnən] vt to calculate, work out.

erregbar [ɛr're:kbaːr] adj excitable; (reizbar) irritable; **E~keit** f excitability; irritability.

erregen [ɛr're:gən] vt to excite; (sexuell) to arouse; (ärgern) to infuriate; (hervorrufen) to arouse, provoke ♦ vr to get excited od worked up.

Erreger (-s, -) m causative agent.

Erregtheit f excitement; (Beunruhigung) agitation.

Erregung f excitement; (sexuell) arousal.

erreichbar adj accessible, within reach.

erreichen [ɛr'raɪçən] vt to reach; (Zweck) to achieve; (Zug) to catch; **wann kann ich Sie morgen ~?** when can I get in touch with you tomorrow?; **vom Bahnhof leicht zu ~** within easy reach of the station.

errichten [ɛr'rɪçtən] vt to erect, put up; (gründen) to establish, set up.

erringen [ɛr'rɪŋən] unreg vt to gain, win.

erröten [ɛr'røːtən] vi to blush, flush.

Errungenschaft [ɛr'ruŋənʃaft] f achievement;

(*umg: Anschaffung*) acquisition.
Ersatz [ɛrˈzats] (**-es**) *m* substitute;
replacement; (*Schaden~*) compensation;
(*MIL*) reinforcements *pl*; **als ~ für jdn
einspringen** to stand in for sb;
~befriedigung *f* vicarious satisfaction;
~dienst *m* (*MIL*) alternative service; **~kasse**
f private health insurance; **~mann** *m*
replacement; (*SPORT*) substitute; **~mutter** *f*
substitute mother; **e~pflichtig** *adj* liable to
pay compensation; **~reifen** *m* (*AUT*) spare
tyre (*BRIT*) *od* tire (*US*); **~teil** *nt* spare (part);
e~weise *adv* as an alternative.
ersaufen [ɛrˈzaufən] *unreg* (*umg*) *vi* to drown.
ersäufen [ɛrˈzɔyfən] *vt* to drown.
erschaffen [ɛrˈʃafən] *unreg vt* to create.
erscheinen [ɛrˈʃainən] *unreg vi* to appear.
Erscheinung *f* appearance; (*Geist*)
apparition; (*Gegebenheit*) phenomenon;
(*Gestalt*) figure; **in ~ treten** (*Merkmale*) to
appear; (*Gefühle*) to show themselves.
Erscheinungsform *f* manifestation.
Erscheinungsjahr *nt* (*von Buch*) year of
publication.
erschien *etc* [ɛrˈʃiːn] *vb siehe* **erscheinen.**
erschienen *pp von* **erscheinen.**
erschießen [ɛrˈʃiːsən] *unreg vt* to shoot (dead).
erschlaffen [ɛrˈʃlafən] *vi* to go limp; (*Mensch*)
to become exhausted.
erschlagen [ɛrˈʃlaːgən] *unreg vt* to strike dead
♦ *adj* (*umg: todmüde*) worn out, dead beat
(*umg*).
erschleichen [ɛrˈʃlaiçən] *unreg vt* to obtain by
stealth *od* dubious methods.
erschließen [ɛrˈʃliːsən] *unreg vt* (*Gebiet,
Absatzmarkt*) to develop, open up;
(*Bodenschätze*) to tap.
erschlossen [ɛrˈʃlɔsən] *adj* (*Gebiet*) developed.
erschöpfen [ɛrˈʃœpfən] *vt* to exhaust.
erschöpfend *adj* exhaustive, thorough.
erschöpft *adj* exhausted.
Erschöpfung *f* exhaustion.
erschossen [ɛrˈʃɔsən] (*umg*) *adj:* (**völlig**)
~ sein to be whacked, be dead (beat).
erschrak *etc* [ɛrˈʃraːk] *vb siehe* **erschrecken².**
erschrecken¹ [ɛrˈʃrɛkən] *vt* to startle,
frighten.
erschrecken² [ɛrˈʃrɛkən] *unreg vi* to be
frightened *od* startled.
erschreckend *adj* alarming, frightening.
erschrickt [ɛrˈʃrɪkt] *vb siehe* **erschrecken².**
erschrocken [ɛrˈʃrɔkən] *pp von* **erschrecken²**
♦ *adj* frightened, startled.
erschüttern [ɛrˈʃʏtərn] *vt* to shake; (*ergreifen*)
to move deeply; **ihn kann nichts ~** he
always keeps his cool (*umg*).
erschütternd *adj* shattering.
Erschütterung *f* (*des Bodens*) tremor; (*tiefe
Ergriffenheit*) shock.
erschweren [ɛrˈʃveːrən] *vt* to complicate; **~de**

Umstände (*JUR*) aggravating
circumstances; **es kommt noch ~d hinzu,
dass ...** to compound matters ...
erschwindeln [ɛrˈʃvɪndəln] *vt* to obtain by
fraud.
erschwinglich *adj* affordable.
ersehen [ɛrˈzeːən] *unreg vt:* **aus etw ~, dass ...**
to gather from sth that ...
ersehnt [ɛrˈzeːnt] *adj* longed-for.
ersetzbar *adj* replaceable.
ersetzen [ɛrˈzɛtsən] *vt* to replace; **jdm
Unkosten** *etc* **~** to pay sb's expenses *etc*.
ersichtlich [ɛrˈzɪçtlɪç] *adj* evident, obvious.
ersparen [ɛrˈʃpaːrən] *vt* (*Ärger etc*) to spare;
(*Geld*) to save; **ihr blieb auch nichts erspart**
she was spared nothing.
Ersparnis (**-, -se**) *f* saving.
ersprießlich [ɛrˈʃpriːslɪç] *adj* profitable,
useful; (*angenehm*) pleasant.

===================================== *SCHLÜSSELWORT*

erst [eːrst] *adv* **1** first; **mach ~ (ein)mal die
Arbeit fertig** finish your work first; **wenn du
das ~ (ein)mal hinter dir hast** once you've
got that behind you.
2 (*nicht früher als, nur*) only; (*nicht bis*) not
till; **~ gestern** only yesterday; **~ morgen**
not until tomorrow; **~ als** only when, not
until; **wir fahren ~ später** we're not going
until later; **er ist (gerade) ~ angekommen**
he's only just arrived.
3: wäre er doch ~ zurück! if only he were
back!; **da fange ich ~ gar nicht an** I simply
won't bother to begin; **jetzt ~ recht!** that
just makes me all the more determined; **da
gings ~ richtig los** then things really got
going.

erstarren [ɛrˈʃtarən] *vi* to stiffen; (*vor Furcht*)
to grow rigid; (*Materie*) to solidify.
erstatten [ɛrˈʃtatən] *vt* (*Unkosten*) to refund;
Anzeige gegen jdn ~ to report sb; **Bericht ~**
to make a report.
Erstattung *f* (*von Unkosten*) reimbursement.
Erstaufführung [ˈeːrstǀauffyːrʊŋ] *f* first
performance.
erstaunen [ɛrˈʃtaunən] *vt* to astonish ♦ *vi* to be
astonished; **E~ (-s)** *nt* astonishment.
erstaunlich *adj* astonishing.
Erstausgabe *f* first edition.
erstbeste(r, s) *adj* first that comes along.
erste(r, s) *adj* first; **als E~s** first of all; **in ~r
Linie** first and foremost; **fürs E~** for the
time being; **~ Hilfe** first aid; **das ~ Mal** the
first time.
erstechen [ɛrˈʃtɛçən] *unreg vt* to stab (to
death).
erstehen [ɛrˈʃteːən] *unreg vt* to buy ♦ *vi* to
(a)rise.
ersteigen [ɛrˈʃtaigən] *unreg vt* to climb,

ascend.

ersteigern [εr'ʃtaɪgərn] *vt* to buy at an auction.

erstellen [εr'ʃtεlən] *vt* to erect, build.

erstens *adv* firstly, in the first place.

erstere(r, s) *pron* (the) former; **der/die/das E~** the former.

ersticken [εr'ʃtɪkən] *vt* (*lit, fig*) to stifle; (*Mensch*) to suffocate; (*Flammen*) to smother ♦ *vi* (*Mensch*) to suffocate; (*Feuer*) to be smothered; **mit erstickter Stimme** in a choked voice; **in Arbeit ~** to be snowed under with work.

Erstickung *f* suffocation.

erst- *zW*: **~klassig** *adj* first-class; **E~kommunion** *f* first communion; **~malig** *adj* first; **~mals** *adv* for the first time; **~rangig** *adj* first-rate.

erstrebenswert [εr'ʃtre:bənsve:rt] *adj* desirable, worthwhile.

erstrecken [εr'ʃtrεkən] *vr* to extend, stretch.

Erststimme *f* first vote.

ERSTSTIMME/ZWEITSTIMME

The **Erststimme** and **Zweitstimme** (first and second vote) system is used to elect MPs to the **Bundestag**. Each elector is given two votes. The first is to choose a candidate in his constituency; the candidate with the most votes is elected MP. The second is to choose a party. All the second votes in each **Land** are counted and a proportionate number of MPs from each party is sent to the **Bundestag**.

Ersttagsbrief *m* first-day cover.

Ersttagsstempel *m* first-day (date) stamp.

erstunken [εr'ʃtʊŋkən] *adj*: **das ist ~ und erlogen** (*umg*) that's a pack of lies.

Erstwähler (-s, -) *m* first-time voter.

ersuchen [εr'zu:xən] *vt* to request.

ertappen [εr'tapən] *vt* to catch, detect.

erteilen [εr'taɪlən] *vt* to give.

ertönen [εr'tø:nən] *vi* to sound, ring out.

Ertrag [εr'tra:k] (**-(e)s, ⁼e**) *m* yield; (*Gewinn*) proceeds *pl*.

ertragen *unreg vt* to bear, stand.

erträglich [εr'trε:klɪç] *adj* tolerable, bearable.

ertragreich *adj* (*Geschäft*) profitable, lucrative.

ertrank *etc* [εr'traŋk] *vb siehe* **ertrinken**.

ertränken [εr'trεŋkən] *vt* to drown.

erträumen [εr'trɔʏmən] *vt*: **sich** *dat* **etw ~** to dream of sth, imagine sth.

ertrinken [εr'trɪŋkən] *unreg vi* to drown; **E~ (-s)** *nt* drowning.

ertrunken [εr'trʊŋkən] *pp von* **ertrinken**.

erübrigen [εr'|y:brɪgən] *vt* to spare ♦ *vr* to be unnecessary.

erwachen [εr'vaxən] *vi* to awake; **ein böses E~** (*fig*) a rude awakening.

erwachsen [εr'vaksən] *adj* grown-up; *unreg* ♦ *vi*: **daraus erwuchsen ihm Unannehmlichkeiten** that caused him some trouble.

Erwachsene(r) *f(m)* adult.

Erwachsenenbildung *f* adult education.

erwägen [εr'vε:gən] *unreg vt* to consider.

Erwägung *f* consideration; **etw in ~ ziehen** to take sth into consideration.

erwähnen [εr'vε:nən] *vt* to mention.

erwähnenswert *adj* worth mentioning.

Erwähnung *f* mention.

erwarb *etc* [εr'varp] *vb siehe* **erwerben**.

erwärmen [εr'vεrmən] *vt* to warm, heat ♦ *vr* to get warm, warm up; **sich ~ für** to warm to.

erwarten [εr'vartən] *vt* to expect; (*warten auf*) to wait for; **etw kaum ~ können** to hardly be able to wait for sth.

Erwartung *f* expectation; **in ~ Ihrer baldigen Antwort** (*form*) in anticipation of your early reply.

erwartungsgemäß *adv* as expected.

erwartungsvoll *adj* expectant.

erwecken [εr'vεkən] *vt* to rouse, awake; **den Anschein ~** to give the impression; **etw zu neuem Leben ~** to resurrect sth.

erwehren [εr'veːrən] *vr* +*gen* (*geh*) to fend off, ward off; (*des Lachens etc*) to refrain from.

erweichen [εr'vaɪçən] *vt* to soften; **sich nicht ~ lassen** to be unmoved.

erweisen [εr'vaɪzən] *unreg vt* to prove ♦ *vr*: **sich ~ als** to prove to be; **jdm einen Gefallen/ Dienst ~** to do sb a favour/service; **sich jdm gegenüber dankbar ~** to show one's gratitude to sb.

erweitern [εr'vaɪtərn] *vt, vr* to widen, enlarge; (*Geschäft*) to expand; (*MED*) to dilate; (*fig: Kenntnisse*) to broaden; (*Macht*) to extend.

Erweiterung *f* expansion.

Erwerb [εr'vεrp] (**-(e)s, -e**) *m* acquisition; (*Beruf*) trade.

erwerben [εr'vεrbən] *unreg vt* to acquire; **er hat sich** *dat* **große Verdienste um die Firma erworben** he has done great service for the firm.

Erwerbs- *zW*: **e~fähig** *adj* (*form*) capable of gainful employment; **~gesellschaft** *f* acquisitive society; **e~los** *adj* unemployed; **~quelle** *f* source of income; **e~tätig** *adj* (gainfully) employed; **e~unfähig** *adj* unable to work.

erwidern [εr'vi:dərn] *vt* to reply; (*vergelten*) to return.

Erwiderung *f*: **in ~ Ihres Schreibens vom ...** (*form*) in reply to your letter of the ...

erwiesen [εr'vi:zən] *adj* proven.

erwirbt [εr'vɪrpt] *vb siehe* **erwerben**.

erwirtschaften [εr'vɪrtʃaftən] *vt* (*Gewinn etc*) to make by good management.

erwischen [εr'vɪʃən] (*umg*) *vt* to catch, get;

ihn hats erwischt! (*umg: verliebt*) he's got it bad; (: *krank*) he's got it; **kalt** ~ (*umg*) to catch off-balance.

erworben [ɛr'vɔrbən] *pp von* erwerben.

erwünscht [ɛr'vynʃt] *adj* desired.

erwürgen [ɛr'vyrgən] *vt* to strangle.

Erz [eːrts] (**-es, -e**) *nt* ore.

erzählen [ɛr'tsɛːlən] *vt, vi* to tell; **dem werd ich was** ~! (*umg*) I'll have something to say to him; ~**de Dichtung** narrative fiction.

Erzähler(in) (**-s, -**) *m(f)* narrator.

Erzählung *f* story, tale.

Erzbischof *m* archbishop.

Erzengel *m* archangel.

erzeugen [ɛr'tsɔygən] *vt* to produce; (*Strom*) to generate.

Erzeuger (**-s, -**) *m* producer; ~**preis** *m* manufacturer's price.

Erzeugnis (**-ses, -se**) *nt* product, produce.

Erzeugung *f* production; generation.

Erzfeind *m* arch enemy.

erziehbar *adj*: **ein Heim für schwer** ~**e Kinder** a home for difficult children.

erziehen [ɛr'tsiːən] *unreg vt* to bring up; (*bilden*) to educate, train.

Erzieher(in) (**-s, -**) *m(f)* educator; (*in Kindergarten*) nursery school teacher.

Erziehung *f* bringing up; (*Bildung*) education.

Erziehungs- *zW*: ~**berechtigte(r)** *f(m)* parent, legal guardian; ~**geld** *nt* payment for new parents; ~**heim** *nt* community home; ~**urlaub** *m* leave for a new parent.

erzielen [ɛr'tsiːlən] *vt* to achieve, obtain; (*Tor*) to score.

erzkonservativ ['ɛrtskɔnzɛrva'tiːf] *adj* ultraconservative.

erzog *etc* [ɛr'tsoːk] *vb siehe* erziehen.

erzogen [ɛr'tsoːgən] *pp von* erziehen.

erzürnen [ɛr'tsyrnən] *vt* (*geh*) to anger, incense.

erzwingen [ɛr'tsviŋən] *unreg vt* to force, obtain by force.

Es [ɛs] (**-**) *nt* (*MUS: Dur*) E flat.

es [ɛs] *nom, akk pron* it.

Esche ['ɛʃə] (**-, -n**) *f* ash.

Esel ['eːzəl] (**-s, -**) *m* donkey, ass; **ich** ~! (*umg*) silly me!

Eselsbrücke *f* (*Gedächtnishilfe*) mnemonic, aide-mémoire.

Eselsohr *nt* dog-ear.

Eskalation [ɛskalatsi'oːn] *f* escalation.

eskalieren [ɛska'liːrən] *vt, vi* to escalate.

Eskimo ['ɛskimo] (**-s, -s**) *m* eskimo.

Eskorte [ɛs'kɔrtə] (**-, -n**) *f* (*MIL*) escort.

eskortieren [ɛskɔr'tiːrən] *vt* (*geh*) to escort.

Espenlaub ['ɛspənlaup] *nt*: **zittern wie** ~ to shake like a leaf.

essbar▲ ['ɛsbaːr] *adj* eatable, edible.

Essecke▲ *f* dining area.

essen ['ɛsən] *unreg vt, vi* to eat; ~ **gehen**

(*auswärts*) to eat out; ~ **Sie gern Äpfel?** do you like apples?; **E**~ (**-s, -**) *nt* (*Mahlzeit*) meal; (*Nahrung*) food; **E**~ **auf Rädern** meals on wheels.

Essens- *zW*: ~**ausgabe** *f* serving of meals; (*Stelle*) serving counter; ~**marke** *f* meal voucher; ~**zeit** *f* mealtime.

Essgeschirr▲ *nt* dinner service.

Essig ['ɛsɪç] (**-s, -e**) *m* vinegar; **damit ist es** ~ (*umg*) it's all off; ~**gurke** *f* gherkin.

Esskastanie▲ *f* sweet chestnut.

Essl.▲ *abk* (= *Esslöffel*) tbsp.

Ess-▲ *zW*: ~**löffel** *m* tablespoon; ~**tisch** *m* dining table; ~**waren** *pl* foodstuffs *pl*; ~**zimmer** *nt* dining room.

Establishment [ɪs'tæblɪʃmənt] (**-s, -s**) *nt* establishment.

Este ['eːstə] (**-n, -n**) *m*, Estin *f* Estonian.

Estland ['eːstlant] *nt* Estonia.

estnisch ['eːstnɪʃ] *adj* Estonian.

Estragon ['ɛstragɔn] (**-s**) *m* tarragon.

Estrich ['ɛstrɪç] (**-s, -e**) *m* stone/clay *etc* floor.

etablieren [eta'bliːrən] *vr* to establish o.s.; (*COMM*) to set up.

Etage [e'taːʒə] (**-, -n**) *f* floor, storey (*BRIT*), story (*US*).

Etagenbetten *pl* bunk beds *pl*.

Etagenwohnung *f* flat (*BRIT*), apartment (*US*).

Etappe [e'tapə] (**-, -n**) *f* stage.

etappenweise *adv* step by step, stage by stage.

Etat [e'taː] (**-s, -s**) *m* budget; ~**jahr** *nt* financial year; ~**posten** *m* budget item.

etc *abk* (= *et cetera*) etc.

etepetete [eːtəpe'teːtə] (*umg*) *adj* fussy.

Ethik ['eːtɪk] *f* ethics *sing*.

ethisch ['eːtɪʃ] *adj* ethical.

ethnisch ['ɛtnɪʃ] *adj* ethnic; ~**e Säuberung** ethnic cleansing.

Etikett [eti'kɛt] (**-(e)s, -e**) *nt* (*lit, fig*) label.

Etikette *f* etiquette, manners *pl*.

Etikettenschwindel *m* (*POL*): **es ist reinster** ~, **wenn ...** it is just playing *od* juggling with names if ...

etikettieren [etikɛ'tiːrən] *vt* to label.

etliche(r, s) ['ɛtlɪçə(r, s)] *adj* quite a lot of ◆ *pron pl* some, quite a few; ~**s** quite a lot.

Etüde [e'tyːdə] (**-, -n**) *f* (*MUS*) étude.

Etui [ɛt'viː] (**-s, -s**) *nt* case.

etwa ['ɛtva] *adv* (*ungefähr*) about; (*vielleicht*) perhaps; (*beispielsweise*) for instance; (*entrüstet, erstaunt*): **hast du** ~ **schon wieder kein Geld dabei?** don't tell me you haven't got any money again! ◆ *adv* (*zur Bestätigung*): **Sie kommen doch, oder** ~ **nicht?** you are coming, aren't you?; **nicht** ~ by no means; **willst du** ~ **schon gehen?** (surely) you don't want to go already?

etwaig ['ɛtvaɪç] *adj* possible.

etwas *pron* something; (*fragend, verneinend*) anything; (*ein wenig*) a little ♦ *adv* a little; **er kann ~** he's good; **E~** *nt*: **das gewisse E~** that certain something.

Etymologie [etymolo'giː] *f* etymology.

EU (-) *f abk* (= *Europäische Union*) EU.

euch [ɔyç] *pron* (*akk von ihr*) you; yourselves; (*dat von ihr*) (to/for) you ♦ *refl pron* yourselves.

euer ['ɔyər] *pron gen von* **ihr** of you ♦ *adj* your.

EU-Erweiterung [eː'luː-] *f* enlargement of the EU.

Eule ['ɔylə] (-, -n) *f* owl.

Euphemismus [ɔyfe'mɪsmʊs] *m* euphemism.

Eurasien [ɔy'raːziən] *nt* Eurasia.

Euratom [ɔyra'toːm] *f abk* (= *Europäische Atomgemeinschaft*) Euratom.

eure(r, s) ['ɔyrə(r, s)] *pron* yours.

eurerseits *adv* on your part.

euresgleichen *pron* people like you.

euretwegen ['ɔyrət'veːgən] *adv* (*für euch*) for your sakes; (*wegen euch*) on your account.

euretwillen ['ɔyrət'vɪlən] *adv*: **um ~ =** euretwegen.

eurige *pron*: **der/die/das ~** *od* **E~** (*geh*) yours.

Euro ['ɔyro] (-, -s) *m* (*FIN*) euro.

Eurokrat [ɔyro'kraːt] (-en, -en) *m* eurocrat.

Europa [ɔy'roːpa] (-s) *nt* Europe.

Europäer(in) [ɔyro'pɛːər(ɪn)] (-s, -) *m(f)* European.

europäisch *adj* European; **das E~e Parlament** the European Parliament; **E~e Union** European Union; **E~e (Wirtschafts)gemeinschaft** European (Economic) Community, Common Market.

Europa- *zW*: **~meister** *m* European champion; **~rat** *m* Council of Europe; **~straße** *f* Euroroute.

Euroscheck [ɔyro'ʃɛk] *m* Eurocheque.

Euter ['ɔytər] (-s, -) *nt* udder.

Euthanasie [ɔytana'ziː] *f* euthanasia.

E. V., e. V. *abk* (= *eingetragener Verein*) registered association.

ev. *abk* = **evangelisch**.

evakuieren [evaku'iːrən] *vt* to evacuate.

evangelisch [evaŋ'geːlɪʃ] *adj* Protestant.

Evangelium [evaŋ'geːlium] *nt* Gospel.

Evaskostüm *nt*: **im ~** in her birthday suit.

eventuell [eventu'ɛl] *adj* possible ♦ *adv* possibly, perhaps.

Evolution [evolutsi'oːn] *f* evolution.

Evolutionstheorie *f* theory of evolution.

evtl. *abk* = **eventuell**.

EWG [eːveː'geː] (-) *f abk* (*früher*: = *Europäische Wirtschaftsgemeinschaft*) EEC.

ewig ['eːvɪç] *adj* eternal ♦ *adv*: **auf ~** forever; **ich habe Sie ~ lange nicht gesehen** (*umg*) I haven't seen you for ages; **E~keit** *f* eternity; **bis in alle E~keit** forever.

EWS (-) *nt abk* (= *Europäisches Währungssystem*) EMS.

EWU (-) *f abk* (= *Europäische Währungsunion*) EMU.

ex [ɛks] (*umg*) *adv*: **etw ~ trinken** to drink sth down in one.

exakt [ɛ'ksakt] *adj* exact.

exaltiert [ɛksal'tiːrt] *adj* exaggerated, effusive.

Examen [ɛ'ksaːmən] (-s, - *od* **Examina**) *nt* examination.

Examensarbeit *f* dissertation.

Exekutionskommando [ɛksekutsi'oːnskɔmando] *nt* firing squad.

Exekutive [ɛkseku'tiːvə] *f* executive.

Exempel [ɛ'ksɛmpəl] (-s, -) *nt* example; **die Probe aufs ~ machen** to put it to the test.

Exemplar [ɛksɛm'plaːr] (-s, -e) *nt* specimen; (*Buch~*) copy; **e~isch** *adj* exemplary.

exerzieren [ɛksɛr'tsiːrən] *vi* to drill.

Exhibitionist [ɛkshibitsio'nɪst] *m* exhibitionist.

Exil [ɛ'ksiːl] (-s, -e) *nt* exile.

existentiell [ɛksɪstɛntsi'ɛl] *adj* = **existentiell**.

Existenz [ɛksɪs'tɛnts] *f* existence; (*Unterhalt*) livelihood, living; (*pej: Mensch*) character; **~berechtigung** *f* right to exist; **~grundlage** *f* basis of one's livelihood.

existenziell ▲ [ɛksɪstɛntsi'ɛl] *adj*: **von ~er Bedeutung** of vital significance.

Existenzkampf *m* struggle for existence.

Existenzminimum (-s, -ma) *nt* subsistence level.

existieren [ɛksɪs'tiːrən] *vi* to exist.

exkl. *abk* = **exklusive**.

exklusiv [ɛksklu'ziːf] *adj* exclusive; **E~bericht** *m* (*PRESSE*) exclusive report.

exklusive [ɛksklu'ziːvə] *präp +gen* exclusive of, not including ♦ *adv* exclusive of, excluding.

Exkursion [ɛkskʊrzi'oːn] *f* (*study*) trip.

Exmatrikulation [ɛksmatrikulatsi'oːn] *f* (*UNIV*): **bei seiner ~** when he left university.

exorzieren [ɛksɔr'tsiːrən] *vt* to exorcize.

exotisch [ɛ'ksoːtɪʃ] *adj* exotic.

expandieren [ɛkspan'diːrən] *vi* (*ECON*) to expand.

Expansion [ɛkspanzi'oːn] *f* expansion.

expansiv [ɛkspan'ziːf] *adj* expansionist; (*Wirtschaftszweige*) expanding.

Expedition [ɛkspeditsi'oːn] *f* expedition; (*COMM*) forwarding department.

Experiment [ɛksperi'mɛnt] *nt* experiment.

experimentell [ɛksperimɛn'tɛl] *adj* experimental.

experimentieren [ɛksperimɛn'tiːrən] *vi* to experiment.

Experte [ɛks'pɛrtə] (-n, -n) *m* expert, specialist.

Expertin [ɛks'pɛrtɪn] *f* expert, specialist.

explodieren [ɛksplo'diːrən] *vi* to explode.

Explosion [ɛksplozi'oːn] *f* explosion.

explosiv [ɛksplo'ziːf] *adj* explosive.
Exponent [ɛkspo'nɛnt] *m* exponent.
exponieren [ɛkspo'niːrən] *vt*: **an exponierter Stelle stehen** to be in an exposed position.
Export [ɛks'pɔrt] (-(e)s, -e) *m* export.
Exportartikel *m* export.
Exporteur [ɛkspɔr'tøːr] *m* exporter.
Exporthandel *m* export trade.
Exporthaus *nt* export house.
exportieren [ɛkspɔr'tiːrən] *vt* to export.
Exportkaufmann *m* exporter.
Exportland *nt* exporting country.
Exportvertreter *m* export agent.
Expressgut▲ [ɛks'prɛsgut] *nt* express goods *pl od* freight.
Expressionismus [ɛksprɛsio'nɪsmʊs] *m* expressionism.
Expresszug▲ *m* express (train).
extra ['ɛkstra] *adj inv* (*umg: gesondert*) separate; (*besondere*) extra ♦ *adv* (*gesondert*) separately; (*speziell*) specially; (*absichtlich*) on purpose; (*vor Adjektiven, zusätzlich*) extra; **E~** (-s, -s) *nt* extra; **E~ausgabe** *f* special edition; **E~blatt** *nt* special edition.
Extrakt [ɛks'trakt] (-(e)s, -e) *m* extract.
Extratour *f* (*fig: umg*): **sich** *dat* **~en leisten** to do one's own thing.
extravagant [ɛkstrava'gant] *adj* extravagant; (*Kleidung*) flamboyant.
Extrawurst (*umg*) *f* (*Sonderwunsch*): **er will immer eine ~ (gebraten haben)** he always wants something different.
Extrem [ɛks'treːm] (-s, -e) *nt* extreme; **e~** *adj* extreme; **~fall** *m* extreme (case).
Extremist(in) *m(f)* extremist.
Extremistenerlass▲ [ɛkstre'mɪstən|ɛrlas] *m law(s) governing extremism.*
extremistisch [ɛkstre'mɪstɪʃ] *adj* (*POL*) extremist.
Extremitäten [ɛkstremi'tɛːtən] *pl* extremities *pl*.
extrovertiert [ɛkstrover'tiːrt] *adj* extrovert.
Exzellenz [ɛkstsɛ'lɛnts] *f* excellency.
exzentrisch [ɛks'tsɛntrɪʃ] *adj* eccentric.
Exzess▲ [ɛks'tsɛs] (-es, -e) *m* excess.

F, f

F, f¹ [ɛf] (-, -) *nt* F, f; **~ wie Friedrich** ≈ F for Frederick, F for Fox (*US*); **nach Schema F** (*umg*) in the usual old way.
f² *abk* (= *feminin*) fem.
Fa. *abk* (= *Firma*) co.
Fabel ['faːbəl] (-, -n) *f* fable; **f~haft** *adj* fabulous, marvellous (*BRIT*), marvelous (*US*).
Fabrik [fa'briːk] *f* factory; **~anlage** *f* plant; (*Gelände*) factory premises *pl*.
Fabrikant [fabri'kant] *m* (*Hersteller*) manufacturer; (*Besitzer*) industrialist.
Fabrikarbeiter(in) *m(f)* factory worker.
Fabrikat [fabri'kaːt] (-(e)s, -e) *nt* product; (*Marke*) make.
Fabrikation [fabriːkatsi'oːn] *f* manufacture, production.
Fabrikbesitzer *m* factory owner.
Fabrikgelände *nt* factory site.
fabrizieren [fabri'tsiːrən] *vt* (*geistiges Produkt*) to produce; (*Geschichte*) to concoct, fabricate.
Fach [fax] (-(e)s, ¨er) *nt* compartment; (*in Schrank, Regal etc*) shelf; (*Sachgebiet*) subject; **ein Mann/eine Frau vom ~** an expert; **~arbeiter** *m* skilled worker; **~arzt** *m* (medical) specialist; **~ausdruck** *m* technical term; **~bereich** *m* (special) field; (*UNIV*) school, faculty; **~buch** *nt* reference book.
Fächer ['fɛçər] (-s, -) *m* fan.
Fach- *zW*: **~frau** *f* expert; **~gebiet** *nt* (special) field; **~geschäft** *nt* specialist shop (*BRIT*) *od* store (*US*); **~händler** *m* stockist; **~hochschule** *f* college; **~idiot** (*umg*) *m* narrow-minded specialist; **~kraft** *f* qualified employee; **~kreise** *pl*: **in ~kreisen** among experts; **f~kundig** *adj* expert, specialist; **~lehrer** *m* specialist subject teacher; **f~lich** *adj* technical; (*beruflich*) professional; **~mann** (-(e)s, *pl* **~leute**) *m* expert; **f~männisch** *adj* professional; **~richtung** *f* subject area; **~schule** *f* technical college; **f~simpeln** *vi* to talk shop; **f~spezifisch** *adj* technical; **~verband** *m* trade association; **~welt** *f* profession; **~werk** *nt* timber frame; **~werkhaus** *nt* half-timbered house.
Fackel ['fakəl] (-, -n) *f* torch.
fackeln (*umg*) *vi* to dither.
Fackelzug *m* torchlight procession.
fad(e) *adj* insipid; (*langweilig*) dull; (*Essen*)

tasteless.
Faden ['faːdən] (-s, ⸚) m thread; **der rote ~**
(fig) the central theme; **alle Fäden laufen
hier zusammen** this is the nerve centre
(BRIT) od center (US) of the whole thing;
~nudeln pl vermicelli sing; **f~scheinig** adj (lit,
fig) threadbare.
Fagott [fa'gɔt] (-(e)s, -e) nt bassoon.
fähig ['fɛːɪç] adj: **~ (zu** od +gen) capable (of);
able (to); **zu allem ~ sein** to be capable of
anything; **F~keit** f ability.
Fähnchen ['fɛːnçən] nt pennon, streamer.
fahnden ['faːndən] vi: **~ nach** to search for.
Fahndung f search.
Fahndungsliste f list of wanted criminals,
wanted list.
Fahne ['faːnə] (-, -n) f flag; standard; **mit
fliegenden ~n zu jdm/etw überlaufen** to go
over to sb/sth; **eine ~ haben** (umg) to smell
of drink.
Fahnenflucht f desertion.
Fahrausweis m (form) ticket.
Fahrbahn f carriageway (BRIT), roadway.
fahrbar adj: **~er Untersatz** (hum) wheels pl.
Fähre ['fɛːrə] (-, -n) f ferry.
fahren ['faːrən] unreg vt to drive; (Rad) to ride;
(befördern) to drive, take; (Rennen) to drive
in ♦ vi (sich bewegen) to go; (Schiff) to sail;
(ab~) to leave; **mit dem Auto/Zug ~** to go od
travel by car/train; **mit dem Aufzug ~** to
take the lift, ride the elevator (US); **links/
rechts ~** to drive on the left/right; **gegen
einen Baum ~** to drive od go into a tree; **die
U-Bahn fährt alle fünf Minuten** the
underground goes od runs every five
minutes; **mit der Hand ~ über** +akk to pass
one's hand over; **(bei etw) gut/schlecht ~**
(zurechtkommen) to do well/badly (with sth);
was ist (denn) in dich gefahren? what's got
(BRIT) od gotten (US) into you?; **einen
~ lassen** (umg) to fart (!).
fahrend adj: **~es Volk** travelling people.
Fahrer(in) ['faːrər(ɪn)] (-s, -) m(f) driver;
~flucht f hit-and-run driving.
Fahr- zW: **~gast** m passenger; **~geld** nt fare;
~gelegenheit f transport; **~gestell** nt
chassis; (AVIAT) undercarriage.
fahrig ['faːrɪç] adj nervous; (unkonzentriert)
distracted.
Fahr- zW: **~karte** f ticket; **~kartenausgabe** f
ticket office; **~kartenautomat** m ticket
machine; **~kartenschalter** m ticket office.
fahrlässig adj negligent; **~e Tötung**
manslaughter; **F~keit** f negligence.
Fahr- zW: **~lehrer** m driving instructor; **~plan**
m timetable; **f~planmäßig** adj (EISENB)
scheduled; **~praxis** f driving experience;
~preis m fare; **~prüfung** f driving test; **~rad**
nt bicycle; **~radweg** m cycle path; **~rinne** f
(NAUT) shipping channel, fairway; **~schein**

m ticket; **~schule** f driving school; **~schüler**
m learner (driver); **~spur** f lane; **~stuhl** m
lift (BRIT), elevator (US); **~stunde** f driving
lesson.
Fahrt [faːrt] (-, -en) f journey; (kurz) trip;
(AUT) drive; (Geschwindigkeit) speed; **gute
~!** safe journey!; **volle ~ voraus!** (NAUT)
full speed ahead!
fährt [fɛːrt] vb siehe **fahren.**
fahrtauglich ['faːrtaʊklɪç] adj fit to drive.
Fährte ['fɛːrtə] (-, -n) f track, trail; **jdn auf eine
falsche ~ locken** (fig) to put sb off the scent.
Fahrtenschreiber m tachograph.
Fahrtkosten pl travelling expenses pl.
Fahrtrichtung f course, direction.
Fahr- zW: **f~tüchtig** ['faːrtʏçtɪç] adj fit to drive;
~verhalten nt (von Fahrer) behaviour (BRIT)
od behavior (US) behind the wheel; (von
Wagen) road performance; **~zeug** nt vehicle;
~zeughalter (-s, -) m owner of a vehicle;
~zeugpapiere pl vehicle documents pl.
Faible ['fɛːbl] (-s, -s) nt (geh) liking;
(Schwäche) weakness; (Vorliebe) penchant.
fair [fɛːr] adj fair.
Fäkalien [fɛ'kaːliən] pl faeces pl.
Faksimile [fak'ziːmile] (-s, -s) nt facsimile.
faktisch ['faktɪʃ] adj actual.
Faktor m factor.
Faktum (-s, -ten) nt fact.
fakturieren [faktu'riːrən] vt (COMM) to
invoice.
Fakultät [fakʊl'tɛːt] f faculty.
Falke ['falkə] (-n, -n) m falcon.
Falklandinseln ['falklant'ɪnzəln] pl Falkland
Islands, Falklands.
Fall [fal] (-(e)s, ⸚e) m (Sturz) fall; (Sachverhalt,
JUR, GRAM) case; **auf jeden ~, auf alle Fälle**
in any case; (bestimmt) definitely; **gesetzt
den ~** assuming (that); **jds ~ sein** (umg) to
be sb's cup of tea; **klarer ~!** (umg) sure
thing!, you bet!; **das mache ich auf keinen ~**
there's no way I'm going to do that.
Falle (-, -n) f trap; (umg: Bett) bed; **jdm eine
~ stellen** to set a trap for sb.
fallen unreg vi to fall; (im Krieg) to fall, be
killed; **etw ~ lassen** to drop sth;
(Bemerkung) to make sth; (Plan) to abandon
sth, to drop sth.
fällen ['fɛlən] vt (Baum) to fell; (Urteil) to pass.
fällig ['fɛlɪç] adj due; (Wechsel) mature(d);
längst ~ long overdue; **F~keit** f (COMM)
maturity.
Fallobst nt fallen fruit, windfall.
falls adv in case, if.
Fall- zW: **~schirm** m parachute; **~schirmjäger**
m paratrooper; **~schirmspringer(in)** m(f)
parachutist; **~schirmtruppe** f paratroops pl;
~strick m (fig) trap, snare; **~studie** f case
study.
fällt [fɛlt] vb siehe **fallen.**

Falltür f trap door.
fallweise adj from case to case.
falsch [falʃ] adj false; (unrichtig) wrong;
~ **liegen (bei** od **in** +dat) (umg) to be wrong
(about); ~ **liegen mit** to be wrong in; **ein ~es
Spiel (mit jdm) treiben** to play (sb) false;
etw ~ verstehen to misunderstand sth, get
sth wrong.
fälschen ['fɛlʃən] vt to forge.
Fälscher(in) (-s, -) m(f) forger.
Falschgeld nt counterfeit money.
Falschheit f falsity, falseness; (Unrichtigkeit)
wrongness.
fälschlich adj false.
fälschlicherweise adv mistakenly.
Falschmeldung f (PRESSE) false report.
Fälschung f forgery.
fälschungssicher adj forgery-proof.
Faltblatt nt leaflet; (in Zeitschrift etc) insert.
Fältchen ['fɛltçən] nt crease, wrinkle.
Falte ['faltə] (-, -n) f (Knick) fold, crease;
(Haut~) wrinkle; (Rock~) pleat.
falten vt to fold; (Stirn) to wrinkle.
faltenlos adj without folds; without wrinkles.
Faltenrock m pleated skirt.
Falter ['faltər] (-s, -) m (Tag~) butterfly;
(Nacht~) moth.
faltig ['faltıç] adj (Haut) wrinkled; (Rock usw)
creased.
falzen ['faltsən] vt (Papierbogen) to fold.
Fam. abk = **Familie**.
familiär [famili'ɛːr] adj familiar.
Familie [fa'miːliə] f family; ~ **Otto Francke**
(als Anschrift) Mr. & Mrs. Otto Francke and
family; **zur ~ gehören** to be one of the
family.
Familien- zW: ~**anschluss**▲ m: **Unterkunft mit
~anschluss** accommodation where one is
treated as one of the family; ~**kreis** m
family circle; ~**mitglied** nt member of the
family; ~**name** m surname; ~**packung** f
family(-size) pack; ~**planung** f family
planning; ~**stand** m marital status; ~**vater** m
head of the family; ~**verhältnisse** pl family
circumstances pl.
Fanatiker(in) [fa'naːtikər(ın)] (-s, -) m(f)
fanatic.
fanatisch adj fanatical.
Fanatismus [fana'tısmʊs] m fanaticism.
fand etc [fant] vb siehe **finden**.
Fang [faŋ] (-(e)s, ⁻e) m catch; (Jagen) hunting;
(Kralle) talon, claw.
fangen unreg vt to catch ♦ vr to get caught;
(Flugzeug) to level out; (Mensch: nicht fallen)
to steady o.s.; (fig) to compose o.s.; (in
Leistung) to get back on form.
Fangfrage f catch od trick question.
Fanggründe pl fishing grounds pl.
fängt [fɛŋkt] vb siehe **fangen**.
Fantasie▲ [fanta'ziː] f imagination; **in seiner**

~ in his mind; ~**gebilde** nt (Einbildung)
figment of the imagination; **f~los** adj
unimaginative.
fantasieren▲ [fanta'ziːrən] vi to fantasize;
(MED) to be delirious.
fantasievoll▲ adj imaginative.
Fantast▲ [fan'tast] (-en, -en) m dreamer.
fantastisch▲ adj fantastic.
Farb- zW: ~**abzug** m coloured (BRIT) od
colored (US) print; ~**aufnahme** f colour
(BRIT) od color (US) photograph; ~**band** nt
typewriter ribbon.
Farbe ['farbə] (-, -n) f colour (BRIT), color
(US); (zum Malen etc) paint; (Stoff~) dye;
(KARTEN) suit.
farbecht ['farp|ɛçt] adj colourfast (BRIT),
colorfast (US).
färben ['fɛrbən] vt to colour (BRIT), color (US);
(Stoff, Haar) to dye.
farben- zW: ~**blind** adj colour-blind (BRIT),
color-blind (US); ~**froh** adj colourful (BRIT),
colorful (US); ~**prächtig** adj colourful (BRIT),
colorful (US).
Farbfernsehen nt colour (BRIT) od color (US)
television.
Farbfilm m colour (BRIT) od color (US) film.
Farbfoto nt colour (BRIT) od color (US) photo.
farbig adj coloured (BRIT), colored (US).
Farbige(r) f(m) coloured (BRIT) od colored (US)
person.
Farb- zW: ~**kasten** m paintbox; **f~los** adj
colourless (BRIT), colorless (US); ~**stift** m
coloured (BRIT) od colored (US) pencil;
~**stoff** m dye; (Lebensmittel~) (artificial)
colouring (BRIT) od coloring (US); ~**ton** m
hue, tone.
Färbung ['fɛrbʊŋ] f colouring (BRIT), coloring
(US); (Tendenz) bias.
Farn [farn] (-(e)s, -e) m fern; (Adler~) bracken.
Farnkraut [farn] nt = **Farn**.
Färöer [fɛ'røːər] pl Faeroe Islands pl.
Fasan [fa'zaːn] (-(e)s, -e(n)) m pheasant.
Fasching ['faʃıŋ] (-s, -e od -s) m carnival.
Faschismus [fa'ʃısmʊs] m fascism.
Faschist(in) m(f) fascist.
faschistisch [fa'ʃıstıʃ] adj fascist.
faseln ['faːzəln] vi to talk nonsense, drivel.
Faser ['faːzər] (-, -n) f fibre.
Fass▲ [fas] (-es, ⁻er) nt vat, barrel; (für Öl)
drum; **Bier vom ~** draught beer; **ein ~ ohne
Boden** (fig) a bottomless pit.
Fassade [fa'saːdə] f (lit, fig) façade.
fassbar▲ adj comprehensible.
Fassbier▲ nt draught beer.
fassen ['fasən] vt (ergreifen) to grasp, take;
(inhaltlich) to hold; (Entschluss etc) to take;
(verstehen) to understand; (Ring etc) to set;
(formulieren) to formulate, phrase ♦ vr to
calm down; **nicht zu ~** unbelievable; **sich
kurz ~** to be brief.

fasslich – Feier

fasslich ['faslıç] adj comprehensible.
Fasson [fa'sõ:] (-, -s) f style; (Art und Weise) way; **aus der ~ geraten** (lit) to lose its shape.
Fassung ['fasuŋ] f (Umrahmung) mounting; (Lampen~) socket; (Wortlaut) version; (Beherrschung) composure; **jdn aus der ~ bringen** to upset sb; **völlig außer ~ geraten** to lose all self-control.
fassungslos adj speechless.
Fassungsvermögen nt capacity; (Verständnis) comprehension.
fast [fast] adv almost, nearly; **~ nie** hardly ever.
fasten ['fastən] vi to fast; **F~** (-s) nt fasting; **F~zeit** f Lent.
Fastnacht f Shrovetide carnival.
faszinieren [fastsi'ni:rən] vt to fascinate.
fatal [fa'ta:l] adj fatal; (peinlich) embarrassing.
fauchen ['fauxən] vt, vi to hiss.
faul [faul] adj rotten; (Person) lazy; (Ausreden) lame; **daran ist etwas ~** there's something fishy about it.
faulen vi to rot.
faulenzen ['faulɛntsən] vi to idle.
Faulenzer(in) (-s, -) m(f) idler, loafer.
Faulheit f laziness.
faulig adj putrid.
Fäulnis ['fɔylnıs] (-) f decay, putrefaction.
Faulpelz (umg) m lazybones sing.
Faust ['faust] (-, Fäuste) f fist; **das passt wie die ~ aufs Auge** (passt nicht) it's all wrong; **auf eigene ~** (fig) on one's own initiative.
Fäustchen ['fɔystçən] nt: **sich** dat **ins ~ lachen** to laugh up one's sleeve.
faustdick (umg) adj: **er hat es ~ hinter den Ohren** he's a crafty one.
Fausthandschuh m mitten.
Faustregel f rule of thumb.
Favorit(in) [favo'ri:t(ın)] (-en, -en) m(f) favourite (BRIT), favorite (US).
Fax [faks] (-, -e) nt fax; **f~en** vt to fax.
Faxen ['faksən] pl: **~ machen** to fool around.
Fazit ['fa:tsıt] (-s, -s od -e) nt: **wenn wir aus diesen vier Jahren das ~ ziehen** if we take stock of these four years.
FCKW (-s, -s) m abk (= Fluorchlorkohlenwasserstoff) CFC.
FdH (umg) abk (= Friss die Hälfte) eat less.
FDP, F.D.P. f abk (= Freie Demokratische Partei) Free Democratic Party.

> **FDP**
>
> The **FDP** (Freie Demokratische Partei) was founded in 1948 and is Germany's centre party. It is a liberal party which has formed governing coalitions with both the **SPD** and the **CDU/CSU** at times, both in the regions and in the **Bundestag**.

Feb. abk (= Februar) Feb.
Februar ['fe:brua:r] (-(s), -e) (pl selten) m February; siehe auch **September**.
fechten ['fɛçtən] unreg vi to fence.
Feder ['fe:dər] (-, -n) f feather; (Schreib~) pen nib; (TECH) spring; **in den ~n liegen** (umg) to be/stay in bed; **~ball** m shuttlecock; **~ballspiel** nt badminton; **~bett** nt continental quilt; **f~führend** adj (Behörde): **f~führend (für)** in overall charge (of); **~halter** m pen; **f~leicht** adj light as a feather; **~lesen** nt: **nicht viel ~lesens mit jdm/etw machen** to make short work of sb/sth.
federn vi (nachgeben) to be springy; (sich bewegen) to bounce ♦ vt to spring.
Federung f suspension.
Federvieh nt poultry.
Federweiße(r) m new wine.
Federzeichnung f pen-and-ink drawing.
Fee [fe:] (-, -n) f fairy.
feenhaft ['fe:ənhaft] adj (liter) fairylike.
Fegefeuer ['fe:gəfɔyər] nt purgatory.
fegen ['fe:gən] vt to sweep.
fehl [fe:l] adj: **~ am Platz** od **Ort** out of place; **F~anzeige** (umg) f dead loss.
fehlen vi to be wanting od missing; (abwesend sein) to be absent ♦ vi unpers: **es fehlte nicht viel und ich hätte ihn verprügelt** I almost hit him; **etw fehlt jdm** sb lacks sth; **du fehlst mir** I miss you; **was fehlt ihm?** what's wrong with him?; **der/das hat mir gerade noch gefehlt!** (ironisch) he/that was all I needed; **weit gefehlt!** (fig) you're way out! (umg); (ganz im Gegenteil) far from it!; **mir ~ die Worte** words fail me; **wo fehlt es?** what's the trouble?, what's up? (umg).
Fehlentscheidung f wrong decision.
Fehlentwicklung f mistake.
Fehler (-s, -) m mistake, error; (Mangel, Schwäche) fault; **ihr ist ein ~ unterlaufen** she's made a mistake; **~beseitigung** f (COMPUT) debugging; **f~frei** adj faultless; without any mistakes; **f~haft** adj incorrect; faulty; **f~los** adj = **fehlerfrei**; **~meldung** f (COMPUT) error message; **~suchprogramm** nt (COMPUT) debugger.
fehl- zW: **F~geburt** f miscarriage; **~gehen** unreg vi to go astray; **F~griff** m blunder; **F~konstruktion** f: **eine F~konstruktion sein** to be badly designed; **F~leistung** f: **freudsche F~leistung** Freudian slip; **F~schlag** m failure; **~schlagen** unreg vi to fail; **F~schluss ▲** m wrong conclusion; **F~start** m (SPORT) false start; **F~tritt** m false move; (fig) blunder, slip; (: Affäre) indiscretion; **F~urteil** nt miscarriage of justice; **F~zündung** f (AUT) misfire, backfire.
Feier ['faıər] (-, -n) f celebration; **~abend** m

time to stop work; **~abend machen** to stop, knock off; **was machst du am ~abend?** what are you doing after work?; **jetzt ist ~abend!** that's enough!

feierlich *adj* solemn; **das ist ja nicht mehr ~** (*umg*) that's beyond a joke; **F~keit** *f* solemnity; **Feierlichkeiten** *pl* festivities *pl*.

feiern *vt, vi* to celebrate.

Feiertag *m* holiday.

feig *adj* cowardly.

Feige ['faɪɡə] (-, -n) *f* fig.

feige *adj* cowardly.

Feigheit *f* cowardice.

Feigling *m* coward.

Feile ['faɪlə] (-, -n) *f* file.

feilen *vt, vi* to file.

feilschen ['faɪlʃən] *vi* to haggle.

fein [faɪn] *adj* fine; (*vornehm*) refined; (*Gehör etc*) keen; **~!** great!; **er ist ~ raus** (*umg*) he's sitting pretty; **sich ~ machen** to get all dressed up.

Feind(in) [faɪnt, 'faɪndɪn] (-(e)s, -e) *m(f)* enemy; **~bild** *nt* concept of an/the enemy; **f~lich** *adj* hostile; **~schaft** *f* enmity; **f~selig** *adj* hostile; **~seligkeit** *f* hostility.

Fein- *zW*: **f~fühlend** *adj* sensitive; **f~fühlig** *adj* sensitive; **~gefühl** *nt* delicacy, tact; **~heit** *f* fineness; refinement; keenness; **~kostgeschäft** *nt* delicatessen (shop), deli; **~schmecker** (-s, -) *m* gourmet; **~waschmittel** *nt* mild(-action) detergent.

feist [faɪst] *adj* fat.

feixen ['faɪksən] (*umg*) *vi* to smirk.

Feld [fɛlt] (-(e)s, -er) *nt* field; (*SCHACH*) square; (*SPORT*) pitch; **Argumente ins ~ führen** to bring arguments to bear; **das ~ räumen** (*fig*) to bow out; **~arbeit** *f* (*AGR*) work in the fields; (*GEOG etc*) fieldwork; **~blume** *f* wild flower; **~herr** *m* commander; **~jäger** *pl* (*MIL*) the military police; **~lazarett** *nt* (*MIL*) field hospital; **~salat** *m* lamb's lettuce; **~stecher** *m* (pair of) binoculars *pl od* field glasses *pl*.

Feld-Wald-und-Wiesen- (*umg*) *in zW* common-or-garden.

Feld- *zW*: **~webel** (-s, -) *m* sergeant; **~weg** *m* path; **~zug** *m* (*lit, fig*) campaign.

Felge ['fɛlɡə] (-, -n) *f* (wheel) rim.

Felgenbremse *f* caliper brake.

Fell [fɛl] (-(e)s, -e) *nt* fur; coat; (*von Schaf*) fleece; (*von toten Tieren*) skin; **ein dickes ~ haben** to be thick-skinned, have a thick skin; **ihm sind die ~e weggeschwommen** (*fig*) all his hopes were dashed.

Fels [fɛls] (-en, -en) *m* = **Felsen.**

Felsen ['fɛlzən] (-s, -) *m* rock; (*Klippe*) cliff; **f~fest** *adj* firm.

felsig *adj* rocky.

Felsspalte *f* crevice.

Felsvorsprung *m* ledge.

feminin [femi'niːn] *adj* feminine; (*pej*)

effeminate.

Feministin [femi'nɪstɪn] *f* feminist.

Fenchel ['fɛnçəl] (-s) *m* fennel.

Fenster ['fɛnstər] (-s, -) *nt* window; **weg vom ~** (*umg*) out of the game, finished; **~brett** *nt* windowsill; **~laden** *m* shutter; **~leder** *nt* chamois, shammy (leather); **~platz** *m* window seat; **~putzer** (-s, -) *m* window cleaner; **~scheibe** *f* windowpane; **~sims** *m* windowsill.

Ferien ['feːriən] *pl* holidays *pl*, vacation (*US*); **die großen ~** the summer holidays (*BRIT*), the long vacation (*US UNIV*); **~ haben** to be on holiday; **~kurs** *m* holiday course; **~reise** *f* holiday; **~wohnung** *f* holiday flat (*BRIT*), vacation apartment (*US*); **~zeit** *f* holiday period.

Ferkel ['fɛrkəl] (-s, -) *nt* piglet.

fern [fɛrn] *adj, adv* far-off, distant; **~ von hier** a long way (away) from here; **~ halten** to keep away; **jdm ~ liegen** to be far from sb's mind; **F~amt** *nt* (*TEL*) exchange; **F~bedienung** *f* remote control; **~bleiben** *unreg vi*: **~bleiben (von** *od +dat*) to stay away (from).

Ferne (-, -n) *f* distance.

ferner *adj, adv* further; (*weiterhin*) in future; **unter „~ liefen" rangieren** (*umg*) to be an also-ran.

fern- *zW*: **F~fahrer** *m* long-distance lorry (*BRIT*) *od* truck driver; **F~flug** *m* long-distance flight; **F~gespräch** *nt* long-distance call (*BRIT*), toll call (*US*); **~gesteuert** *adj* remote-controlled; (*Rakete*) guided; **F~glas** *nt* binoculars *pl*; **~kopie** *f* fax; **~kopierer** *m* fax machine; **F~kurs(us)** *m* correspondence course; **F~lenkung** *f* remote control; **F~licht** *nt* **mit F~licht fahren** to drive on full beam.

Fernmelde- *in zW* telecommunications; (*MIL*) signals.

fern- *zW*: **F~ost: aus/in F~ost** from/in the Far East; **~östlich** *adj* Far Eastern *attrib*; **F~rohr** *nt* telescope; **F~schreiben** *nt* telex; **F~schreiber** *m* teleprinter; **~schriftlich** *adj* by telex.

Fernsehapparat *m* television (set).

fernsehen ['fɛrnzeːən] *unreg vi* to watch television; **F~** (-s) *nt* television; **im F~** on television.

Fernseher (-s, -) *m* television (set).

Fernseh- *zW*: **~gebühr** *f* television licence (*BRIT*) *od* license (*US*) fee; **~gerät** *nt* television set; **~programm** *nt* (*Kanal*) channel, station (*US*); (*Sendung*) programme (*BRIT*), program (*US*); (*~zeitschrift*) (television) programme (*BRIT*) *od* program (*US*) guide; **~sendung** *f* television programme (*BRIT*) *od* program (*US*); **~überwachungsanlage** *f* closed-circuit television; **~zuschauer** *m* (television)

viewer.
Fern- *zW*: ~**sprecher** *m* telephone;
  ~**sprechzelle** *f* telephone box (*BRIT*) *od* booth
  (*US*); ~**steuerung** *f* remote control.
Fernstudium *nt* multimedia course, ≈ Open
  University course (*BRIT*).

> **FERNSTUDIUM**
>
> **Fernstudium** *is a distance-learning degree
> course where students do not go to university but
> receive their tuition by letter, television or radio
> programmes. There is no personal contact
> between student and lecturer. The first*
> **Fernstudium** *was founded in 1974. Students are
> free to practise their career or to bring up a family
> at the same time as studying.*

Fernverkehr *m* long-distance traffic.
Fernweh *nt* wanderlust.
Ferse ['fɛrzə] (-, -n) *f* heel.
Fersengeld *nt*: ~ **geben** to take to one's
  heels.
fertig ['fɛrtɪç] *adj* (*bereit*) ready; (*beendet*)
  finished; (*gebrauchs*~) ready-made;
  ~ **ausgebildet** fully qualified; **mit jdm/etw**
  ~ **werden** to cope with sb/sth; **mit den
  Nerven** ~ **sein** to be at the end of one's
  tether; ~ **bringen** (*fähig sein*) to manage, be
  capable of; (*beenden*) to finish; ~ **essen/
  lesen** to finish eating/reading; ~ **machen**
  (*beenden*) to finish; (*umg: Person*) to finish;
  (: *körperlich*) to exhaust; (: *moralisch*) to get
  down; **sich** ~ **machen** to get ready; ~ **stellen**
  to complete; **F~bau** *m* prefab(ricated
  house).
fertigen ['fɛrtɪɡən] *vt* to manufacture.
Fertig- *zW*: ~**gericht** *nt* ready-to-serve meal;
  ~**haus** *nt* prefab(ricated house); ~**keit** *f* skill.
Fertigung *f* production.
Fertigungs- *in zW* production; ~**straße** *f*
  production line.
Fertigware *f* finished product.
fesch [fɛʃ] (*umg*) *adj* (*modisch*) smart;
  (: *hübsch*) attractive.
Fessel ['fɛsəl] (-, -n) *f* fetter.
fesseln *vt* to bind; (*mit F*~) to fetter; (*fig*) to
  grip; **ans Bett gefesselt** (*fig*) confined to bed.
fesselnd *adj* gripping.
Fest [fɛst] (-(e)s, -e) *nt* (*Feier*) celebration;
  (*Party*) party; **man soll die ~e feiern wie sie
  fallen** (*Sprichwort*) make hay while the sun
  shines.
fest *adj* firm; (*Nahrung*) solid; (*Gehalt*) regular;
  (*Gewebe, Schuhe*) strong, sturdy; (*Freund(in)*)
  steady ♦ *adv* (*schlafen*) soundly; ~ **angestellt**
  employed on a permanent basis;
  ~ **entschlossen sein** to be absolutely
  determined; ~ **umrissen** clearcut; ~**e
  Kosten** (*COMM*) fixed costs *pl*.

Festbeleuchtung *f* illumination.
festbinden *unreg vt* to tie, fasten.
festbleiben *unreg vi* to stand firm.
Festessen *nt* banquet.
festfahren *unreg vr* to get stuck.
festhalten *unreg vt* to seize, hold fast;
  (*Ereignis*) to record ♦ *vr*: **sich** ~ (**an** +*dat*) to
  hold on (to).
festigen *vt* to strengthen.
Festigkeit *f* strength.
fest- *zW*: ~**klammern** *vr*: **sich** ~**klammern** (**an**
  +*dat*) to cling on (to); ~**klemmen** *vt* to wedge
  fast; **F~komma** *nt* (*COMPUT*) fixed point;
  F~land *nt* mainland; ~**legen** *vt* to fix ♦ *vr* to
  commit o.s.; **jdn auf etw** *akk* ~**legen**
  (~*nageln*) to tie sb (down) to sth;
  (*verpflichten*) to commit sb to sth.
festlich *adj* festive.
fest- *zW*: ~**liegen** *unreg vi* (*FIN: Geld*) to be tied
  up; ~**machen** *vt* to fasten; (*Termin etc*) to fix;
  ~**nageln** *vt*: **jdn** ~**nageln** (**auf** +*akk*) (*fig*: *umg*)
  to pin sb down (to); **F~nahme** (-, -n) *f*
  capture; ~**nehmen** *unreg vt* to capture,
  arrest; **F~platte** *f* (*COMPUT*) hard disk;
  F~preis *m* (*COMM*) fixed price.
Festrede *f* speech, address.
festschnallen *vt* to strap down ♦ *vr* to fasten
  one's seat belt.
festsetzen *vt* to fix, settle.
Festspiel *nt* festival.
fest- *zW*: ~**stehen** *unreg vi* to be certain;
  ~**stellbar** *adj* (*herauszufinden*) ascertainable;
  ~**stellen** *vt* to establish; (*sagen*) to remark;
  (*TECH*) to lock (fast); **F~stellung** *f*: **die
  F~stellung machen, dass** ... to realize that
  ...; (*bemerken*) to remark *od* observe that ...;
  F~tag *m* holiday.
Festung *f* fortress.
festverzinslich *adj* fixed-interest *attrib*.
Festwertspeicher *m* (*COMPUT*) read-only
  memory.
Festzelt *nt* marquee.
Fête ['fɛːtə] (-, -n) *f* party.
Fett [fɛt] (-(e)s, -e) *nt* fat, grease; **f~** *adj* fat;
  (*Essen etc*) greasy; **f~ gedruckt** bold-type;
  f~arm *adj* low fat; **f~en** *vt* to grease; ~**fleck** *m*
  grease spot *od* stain; **f~frei** *adj* fat-free;
  ~**gehalt** *m* fat content; **f~ig** *adj* greasy, fatty;
  ~**näpfchen** *nt*: **ins ~näpfchen treten** to put
  one's foot in it; ~**polster** *nt* (*hum*: *umg*):
  ~**polster haben** to be well-padded.
Fetzen ['fɛtsən] (-s, -) *m* scrap; ..., **dass die
  ~ fliegen** (*umg*) ... like mad.
feucht [fɔʏçt] *adj* damp; (*Luft*) humid;
  ~**fröhlich** *adj* (*hum*) boozy.
Feuchtigkeit *f* dampness; humidity.
Feuchtigkeitscreme *f* moisturizer.
feudal [fɔʏ'daːl] *adj* (*POL, HIST*) feudal; (*umg*)
  plush.
Feuer ['fɔʏər] (-s, -) *nt* fire; (*zum Rauchen*) a

light; (*fig*: *Schwung*) spirit; **für jdn durchs ~ gehen** to go through fire and water for sb; **~ und Flamme (für etw) sein** (*umg*) to be dead keen (on sth); **~ für etw/jdn fangen** (*fig*) to develop a great interest in sth/sb; **~alarm** *m* fire alarm; **~eifer** *m* zeal; **f~fest** *adj* fireproof; **~gefahr** *f* danger of fire; **bei ~gefahr** in the event of fire; **f~gefährlich** *adj* inflammable; **~leiter** *f* fire escape ladder; **~löscher** (**-s,** -) *m* fire extinguisher; **~melder** (**-s,** -) *m* fire alarm.

feuern *vt, vi* (*lit, fig*) to fire.

Feuer- *zW*: **f~polizeilich** *adj* (*Bestimmungen*) laid down by the fire authorities; **~probe** *f* acid test; **f~rot** *adj* fiery red.

Feuersbrunst *f* (*geh*) conflagration.

Feuer- *zW*: **~schlucker** *m* fire-eater; **~schutz** *m* (*Vorbeugung*) fire prevention; (*MIL: Deckung*) covering fire; **f~sicher** *adj* fireproof; **~stein** *m* flint; **~stelle** *f* fireplace; **~treppe** *f* fire escape; **~versicherung** *f* fire insurance; **~waffe** *f* firearm; **~wehr** *f* fire brigade; **~wehrauto** *nt* fire engine; **~werk** *nt* fireworks *pl*; **~werkskörper** *m* firework; **~zangenbowle** *f* red wine punch containing rum which has been flamed off; **~zeug** *nt* (cigarette) lighter.

Feuilleton [fœjə'tõː] (**-s,** -s) *nt* (*PRESSE*) feature section; (*Artikel*) feature (article).

feurig ['fɔʏrɪç] *adj* fiery.

Fiche [fiːʃ] (**-s,** -s) *m od nt* (micro)fiche.

ficht [fɪçt] *vb siehe* **fechten**.

Fichte ['fɪçtə] (**-,** -n) *f* spruce.

ficken ['fɪkən] (*umg!*) *vt, vi* to fuck (!).

fick(e)rig ['fɪk(ə)rɪç] (*umg*) *adj* fidgety.

fidel [fi'deːl] (*umg*) *adj* jolly.

Fidschiinseln ['fɪdʒiˌɪnzəln] *pl* Fiji Islands.

Fieber ['fiːbər] (**-s,** -) *nt* fever, temperature; (*Krankheit*) fever; **~ haben** to have a temperature; **f~haft** *adj* feverish; **~messer** *m* thermometer; **~thermometer** *nt* thermometer.

fiel *etc* [fiːl] *vb siehe* **fallen**.

fies [fiːs] (*umg*) *adj* nasty.

Figur [fi'guːr] (**-,** -en) *f* figure; (*Schach~*) chessman, chess piece; **eine gute/ schlechte/traurige ~ abgeben** to cut a good/ poor/sorry figure.

fiktiv [fɪk'tiːf] *adj* fictitious.

Filet [fi'leː] (**-s,** -s) *nt* (*KOCH*) fillet; (*Rinder~*) fillet steak; (*zum Braten*) piece of sirloin *od* tenderloin (*US*).

Filiale [fili'aːlə] (**-,** -n) *f* (*COMM*) branch.

Filipino [fili'piːno] (**-s,** -s) *m* Filipino.

Film [fɪlm] (**-(e)s,** -e) *m* film, movie (*bes US*); **da ist bei mir der ~ gerissen** (*umg*) I had a mental blackout; **~aufnahme** *f* shooting.

Filmemacher(in) *m(f)* film-maker.

filmen *vt, vi* to film.

Film- *zW*: **~festspiele** *pl* film festival *sing*;

~kamera *f* cine-camera; **~riss**▲ (*umg*) *m* mental blackout; **~schauspieler(in)** *m(f)* film *od* movie (*bes US*) actor, film *od* movie actress; **~verleih** *m* film distributors *pl*; **~vorführgerät** *nt* cine-projector.

Filter ['fɪltər] (**-s,** -) *m* filter; **~kaffee** *m* filter *od* drip (*US*) coffee; **~mundstück** *nt* filter tip.

filtern *vt* to filter.

Filterpapier *nt* filter paper.

Filterzigarette *f* tipped cigarette.

Filz [fɪlts] (**-es,** -e) *m* felt.

filzen *vt* (*umg*) to frisk ♦ *vi* (*Wolle*) to mat.

Filzstift *m* felt-tip (pen).

Fimmel ['fɪməl] (**-s,** -) (*umg*) *m*: **du hast wohl einen ~!** you're crazy!

Finale [fi'naːlə] (**-s,** -(s)) *nt* finale; (*SPORT*) final(s *pl*).

Finanz [fi'nants] *f* finance; **Finanzen** *pl* finances *pl*; **das übersteigt meine ~en** that's beyond my means; **~amt** *nt* ≈ Inland Revenue Office (*BRIT*), Internal Revenue Office (*US*); **~beamte(r)** *f(m)* revenue officer.

finanziell [finantsi'ɛl] *adj* financial.

finanzieren [finan'tsiːrən] *vt* to finance, to fund.

Finanzierung *f* financing, funding.

Finanz- *zW*: **~minister** *m* ≈ Chancellor of the Exchequer (*BRIT*), Minister of Finance; **f~schwach** *adj* financially weak; **~wesen** *nt* financial system; **~wirtschaft** *f* public finances *pl*.

finden ['fɪndən] *unreg vt* to find; (*meinen*) to think ♦ *vr* to be (found); (*sich fassen*) to compose o.s. ♦ *vi*: **ich finde schon allein hinaus** I can see myself out; **ich finde nichts dabei, wenn …** I don't see what's wrong if …; **das wird sich ~** things will work out.

Finder(in) (**-s,** -) *m(f)* finder; **~lohn** *m* reward (for the finder).

findig *adj* resourceful.

fing *etc* [fɪŋ] *vb siehe* **fangen**.

Finger ['fɪŋər] (**-s,** -) *m* finger; **mit ~n auf jdn zeigen** (*fig*) to look askance at sb; **das kann sich jeder an den (fünf) ~n abzählen** (*umg*) it sticks out a mile; **sich** *dat* **etw aus den ~n saugen** to conjure sth up; **lange ~ machen** (*umg*) to be light-fingered; **~abdruck** *m* fingerprint; **~handschuh** *m* glove; **~hut** *m* thimble; (*BOT*) foxglove; **~nagel** *m* fingernail; **~ring** *m* ring; **~spitze** *f* fingertip; **~spitzengefühl** *nt* sensitivity; **~zeig** (**-(e)s,** -e) *m* hint, pointer.

fingieren [fɪŋ'giːrən] *vt* to feign.

fingiert *adj* made-up, fictitious.

Fink ['fɪŋk] (**-en,** -en) *m* finch.

Finne ['fɪnə] (**-n,** -n) *m* Finn.

Finnin ['fɪnɪn] *f* Finn.

finnisch *adj* Finnish.

Finnland *nt* Finland.

finster ['fɪnstər] *adj* dark, gloomy; (*verdächtig*)

dubious; (*verdrossen*) grim; (*Gedanke*) dark;
jdn ~ ansehen to give sb a black look; **F~nis**
(-) *f* darkness, gloom.

Finte ['fɪntə] (-, -n) *f* feint, trick.

Firlefanz ['fɪrləfants] (*umg*) *m* (*Kram*) frippery;
(*Albernheit*): **mach keinen** ~ don't clown
around.

firm [fɪrm] *adj* well-up.

Firma (-, -men) *f* firm; **die** ~ **dankt** (*hum*)
much obliged (to you).

Firmen- *zW:* ~**inhaber** *m* proprietor (*of firm*);
~**register** *nt* register of companies; ~**schild**
nt (shop) sign; ~**übernahme** *f* takeover;
~**wagen** *m* company car; ~**zeichen** *nt*
trademark.

Firmung *f* (*REL*) confirmation.

Firnis ['fɪrnɪs] (-ses, -se) *m* varnish.

Fis [fɪs] (-, -) *nt* (*MUS*) F sharp.

Fisch [fɪʃ] (-(e)s, -e) *m* fish; **Fische** *pl* (*ASTROL*)
Pisces *sing*; **das sind kleine ~e** (*fig: umg*)
that's child's play.

fischen *vt, vi* to fish.

Fischer (-s, -) *m* fisherman.

Fischerei [fɪʃəˈraɪ] *f* fishing, fishery.

Fisch- *zW:* ~**fang** *m* fishing; ~**geschäft** *nt*
fishmonger's (shop); ~**gräte** *f* fishbone;
~**gründe** *pl* fishing grounds *pl*, fisheries *pl*;
~**stäbchen** *nt* fish finger (*BRIT*), fish stick
(*US*); ~**zucht** *f* fish-farming; ~**zug** *m* catch of
fish.

Fisimatenten [fizimaˈtɛntən] (*umg*) *pl*
(*Ausflüchte*) excuses *pl*; (*Umstände*) fuss *sing*.

Fiskus ['fɪskʊs] *m* (*fig: Staatskasse*) Treasury.

fit [fɪt] *adj* fit.

Fitness ['fɪtnəs] *nt* fitness.

Fittich ['fɪtɪç] (-(e)s, -e) *m* (*liter*): **jdn unter**
seine ~e nehmen (*hum*) to take sb under
one's wing.

fix [fɪks] *adj* (*flink*) quick; (*Person*) alert, smart;
~**e Idee** obsession, idée fixe; ~ **und fertig**
finished; (*erschöpft*) done in; **jdn ~ und fertig**
machen (*nervös machen*) to drive sb mad.

fixen (*umg*) *vi* (*Drogen spritzen*) to fix.

Fixer(in) ['fɪksər(ɪn)] (*umg*) *m(f)* junkie (*inf*);
~**stube** (*umg*) *f* junkies' centre (*inf*).

fixieren [fɪˈksiːrən] *vt* to fix; (*anstarren*) to stare
at; **er ist zu stark auf seine Mutter fixiert**
(*PSYCH*) he has a mother fixation.

Fixkosten *pl* (*COMM*) fixed costs *pl*.

FKK *abk* = Freikörperkultur.

flach [flax] *adj* flat; (*Gefäß*) shallow; **auf dem**
~**en Land** in the middle of the country.

Fläche ['flɛçə] (-, -n) *f* area; (*Ober~*) surface.

Flächeninhalt *m* surface area.

Flach- *zW:* **f~fallen** *unreg* (*umg*) *vi* to fall
through; ~**heit** *f* flatness; shallowness;
~**land** *nt* lowland; **f~liegen** *unreg* (*umg*) *vi* to
be laid up; ~**mann** (-(e)s, *pl* -**männer**) (*umg*)
m hip flask.

flachsen ['flaksən] (*umg*) *vi* to kid around.

flackern ['flakərn] *vi* to flare, flicker.

Fladen ['flaːdən] (-s, -) *m* (*KOCH*) round flat
dough-cake; (*umg: Kuh~*) cowpat.

Flagge ['flagə] (-, -n) *f* flag; ~ **zeigen** (*fig*) to
nail one's colours to the mast.

flaggen *vi* to fly flags *od* a flag.

flagrant [flaˈgrant] *adj* flagrant; **in ~i** red-
handed.

Flak [flak] (-s, -) *f* (= Flug(zeug)abwehrkanone)
anti-aircraft gun; (*Einheit*) anti-aircraft unit.

flambieren [flamˈbiːrən] *vt* (*KOCH*) to flambé.

Flame ['flaːmə] (-n, -n) *m* Fleming.

Flämin ['flɛːmɪn] *f* Fleming.

flämisch ['flɛːmɪʃ] *adj* Flemish.

Flamme ['flamə] (-, -n) *f* flame; **in ~n stehen/**
aufgehen to be in/go up in flames.

Flandern ['flandərn] *nt* Flanders *sing*.

Flanell [flaˈnɛl] (-s, -e) *m* flannel.

Flanke ['flaŋkə] (-, -n) *f* flank; (*SPORT: Seite*)
wing.

Flasche ['flaʃə] (-, -n) *f* bottle; (*umg: Versager*)
wash-out; **zur ~ greifen** (*fig*) to hit the bottle.

Flaschen- *zW:* ~**bier** *nt* bottled beer; ~**öffner** *m*
bottle opener; ~**wein** *m* bottled wine; ~**zug**
m pulley.

flatterhaft *adj* flighty, fickle.

flattern ['flatərn] *vi* to flutter.

flau [flaʊ] *adj* (*Brise, COMM*) slack; **jdm ist**
~ **(im Magen)** sb feels queasy.

Flaum [flaʊm] (-(e)s) *m* (*Feder*) down.

flauschig ['flaʊʃɪç] *adj* fluffy.

Flausen ['flaʊzən] *pl* silly ideas *pl*; (*Ausflüchte*)
weak excuses *pl*.

Flaute ['flaʊtə] (-, -n) *f* calm; (*COMM*)
recession.

Flechte ['flɛçtə] (-, -n) *f* (*MED*) dry scab; (*BOT*)
lichen.

flechten *unreg vt* to plait; (*Kranz*) to twine.

Fleck [flɛk] (-(e)s, -e) *m* (*Schmutz~*) stain;
(*Farb~*) patch; (*Stelle*) spot; **nicht vom**
~ **kommen** (*lit, fig*) not to get any further;
sich nicht vom ~ rühren not to budge; **vom**
~ **weg** straight away.

Fleckchen *nt*: **ein schönes ~ (Erde)** a lovely
little spot.

Flecken (-s, -) *m* = Fleck; **f~los** *adj* spotless;
~**mittel** *nt* stain remover; ~**wasser** *nt* stain
remover.

fleckig *adj* marked; (*schmutzig*) stained.

Fledermaus ['fleːdərmaʊs] *f* bat.

Flegel ['fleːgəl] (-s, -) *m* flail; (*Person*) lout;
f~haft *adj* loutish, unmannerly; ~**jahre** *pl*
adolescence *sing*.

flegeln *vr* to loll, sprawl.

flehen ['fleːən] *vi* (*geh*) to implore.

flehentlich *adj* imploring.

Fleisch ['flaɪʃ] (-(e)s) *nt* flesh; (*Essen*) meat;
sich auf od akk ins eigene ~ schneiden to cut
off one's nose to spite one's face (*Sprichwort*);
es ist mir in ~ und Blut übergegangen it has

become second nature to me; ~**brühe** _f_ meat
stock.

Fleischer (-s, -) _m_ butcher.

Fleischerei [flaɪʃə'raɪ] _f_ butcher's (shop).

fleischig _adj_ fleshy.

Fleisch- _zW_: ~**käse** _m_ meat loaf; **f~lich** _adj_
carnal; ~**pastete** _f_ meat pie; ~**salat** _m_ diced
meat salad with mayonnaise; ~**vergiftung** _f_
food poisoning (_from meat_); ~**wolf** _m_ mincer;
~**wunde** _f_ flesh wound; ~**wurst** _f_ pork
sausage.

Fleiß ['flaɪs] (-es) _m_ diligence, industry; **ohne**
~ **kein Preis** (_Sprichwort_) success never
comes easily.

fleißig _adj_ diligent, industrious; ~ **studieren/**
arbeiten to study/work hard.

flektieren [flɛk'tiːrən] _vt_ to inflect.

flennen ['flɛnən] (_umg_) _vi_ to cry, blubber.

fletschen ['flɛtʃən] _vt_ (_Zähne_) to show.

Fleurop ® ['flɔʏrɔp] _f_ ≈ Interflora ®.

flexibel [flɛ'ksiːbəl] _adj_ flexible.

Flexibilität [flɛksibili'tɛːt] _f_ flexibility.

flicht [flɪçt] _vb siehe_ **flechten**.

Flicken ['flɪkən] (-s, -) _m_ patch.

flicken _vt_ to mend.

Flickschusterei ['flɪkʃuːstəraɪ] _f_: **das ist** ~
that's a patch-up job.

Flieder ['fliːdər] (-s, -) _m_ lilac.

Fliege ['fliːgə] (-, -n) _f_ fly; (_Schlips_) bow tie;
zwei ~**n mit einer Klappe schlagen**
(_Sprichwort_) to kill two birds with one stone;
ihn stört die ~ **an der Wand** every little
thing irritates him.

fliegen _unreg vt, vi_ to fly; **auf jdn/etw** ~ (_umg_)
to be mad about sb/sth; **aus der Kurve** ~ to
skid off the bend; **aus der Firma** ~ (_umg_) to
get the sack.

fliegend _adj attrib_ flying; ~**e Hitze** hot flushes
_pl_.

Fliegengewicht _nt_ (_SPORT, fig_) flyweight.

Fliegenklatsche ['fliːgənklatʃə] _f_ fly-swat.

Fliegenpilz _m_ fly agaric.

Flieger (-s, -) _m_ flier, airman; ~**alarm** _m_ air-
raid warning.

fliehen ['fliːən] _unreg vi_ to flee.

Fliehkraft ['fliːkraft] _f_ centrifugal force.

Fliese ['fliːzə] (-, -n) _f_ tile.

Fließband ['fliːsbant] _nt_ assembly _od_
production line; **am** ~ **arbeiten** to work on
the assembly _od_ production line; ~**arbeit** _f_
production-line work; ~**produktion** _f_
assembly-line production.

fließen _unreg vi_ to flow.

fließend _adj_ flowing; (_Rede, Deutsch_) fluent;
(_Übergang_) smooth.

Fließ- _zW_: ~**heck** _nt_ fastback; ~**komma** _nt_
(_COMPUT_) ≈ floating point; ~**papier** _nt_
blotting paper (_BRIT_), fleece paper (_US_).

Flimmerkasten (_umg_) _m_ (_Fernsehen_) box.

Flimmerkiste (_umg_) _f_ (_Fernsehen_) box.

flimmern ['flɪmərn] _vi_ to glimmer; **es flimmert**
mir vor den Augen my head's swimming.

flink [flɪŋk] _adj_ nimble, lively; **mit etw** ~ **bei**
der Hand sein to be quick (off the mark)
with sth; **F~heit** _f_ nimbleness, liveliness.

Flinte ['flɪntə] (-, -n) _f_ shotgun; **die** ~ **ins Korn**
werfen to throw in the sponge.

Flirt [flœrt] (-s, -s) _m_ flirtation; **einen** ~ (**mit**
jdm) **haben** flirt (with sb).

flirten ['flɪrtən] _vi_ to flirt.

Flittchen (_pej_: _umg_) _nt_ floozy.

Flitter (-s, -) _m_ (~**schmuck**) sequins _pl_.

Flitterwochen _pl_ honeymoon _sing_.

flitzen ['flɪtsən] _vi_ to flit.

Flitzer (-s, -) (_umg_) _m_ (_Auto_) sporty car.

floaten ['floːtən] _vt, vi_ (_FIN_) to float.

flocht _etc_ [flɔxt] _vb siehe_ **flechten**.

Flocke ['flɔkə] (-, -n) _f_ flake.

flockig _adj_ flaky.

flog _etc_ [floːk] _vb siehe_ **fliegen**.

Floh [floː] (-(e)s, ̈-e) _m_ flea; **jdm einen** ~ **ins**
Ohr setzen (_umg_) to put an idea into sb's
head.

floh _etc vb siehe_ **fliehen**.

Flohmarkt _m_ flea market.

Flora ['floːra] (-, -ren) _f_ flora.

Florenz [flo'rɛnts] _nt_ Florence.

florieren [flo'riːrən] _vi_ to flourish.

Florist(in) _m(f)_ florist.

Floskel ['flɔskəl] (-, -n) _f_ set phrase; **f~haft** _adj_
cliché-ridden, stereotyped.

Floß [floːs] (-es, ̈-e) _nt_ raft.

floss _etc_▲ [flɔs] _vb siehe_ **fließen**.

Flosse ['flɔsə] (-, -n) _f_ fin; (_Taucher~_) flipper;
(_umg_: _Hand_) paw.

Flöte ['fløːtə] (-, -n) _f_ flute; (_Block~_) recorder.

flöten gehen▲ ['fløːtəngeːən] (_umg_) _unreg vi_ to
go for a burton.

Flötist(in) [fløːtɪst(ɪn)] _m(f)_ flautist, flutist (_bes_
_US_).

flott [flɔt] _adj_ lively; (_elegant_) smart; (_NAUT_)
afloat.

Flotte (-, -n) _f_ fleet.

Flottenstützpunkt _m_ naval base.

flottmachen _vt_ (_Schiff_) to float off; (_Auto,_
Fahrrad etc) to put back on the road.

Flöz [fløːts] (-es, -e) _nt_ layer, seam.

Fluch [fluːx] (-(e)s, ̈-e) _m_ curse; **f~en** _vi_ to
curse, swear.

Flucht [fluxt] (-, -en) _f_ flight; (_Fenster~_) row;
(_Reihe_) range; (_Zimmer~_) suite; (_geglückt_)
flight, escape; **jdn/etw in die** ~ **schlagen** to
put sb/sth to flight.

fluchtartig _adj_ hasty.

flüchten ['flʏçtən] _vi_ to flee ♦ _vr_ to take refuge.

Fluchthilfe _f_: ~ **leisten** to aid an escape.

flüchtig _adj_ fugitive; (_CHEM_) volatile;
(_oberflächlich_) cursory; (_eilig_) fleeting; ~**er**
Speicher (_COMPUT_) volatile memory; **jdn**
~ **kennen** to have met sb briefly; **F~keit** _f_

transitoriness; volatility; cursoriness;
F~**keitsfehler** *m* careless slip.
Flüchtling *m* refugee.
Flüchtlingslager *nt* refugee camp.
Flucht- *zW:* ~**versuch** *m* escape attempt;
~**weg** *m* escape route.
Flug [flu:k] (-(e)s, ¨e) *m* flight; **im** ~ airborne,
in flight; **wie im** ~(e) (*fig*) in a flash;
~**abwehr** *f* anti-aircraft defence; ~**bahn** *f*
flight path; (*Kreisbahn*) orbit; ~**begleiter(in)**
m(f) (*AVIAT*) flight attendant; ~**blatt** *nt*
pamphlet.
Flügel ['fly:gəl] (-s, -) *m* wing; (*MUS*) grand
piano; ~**tür** *f* double door.
flugfähig *adj* able to fly; (*Flugzeug: in Ordnung*)
airworthy.
Fluggast *m* airline passenger.
flügge ['flygə] *adj* (fully-)fledged; ~ **werden**
(*lit*) to be able to fly; (*fig*) to leave the nest.
Flug- *zW:* ~**geschwindigkeit** *f* flying *od* air
speed; ~**gesellschaft** *f* airline (company);
~**hafen** *m* airport; ~**höhe** *f* altitude (of
flight); ~**lotse** *m* air traffic *od* flight
controller; ~**plan** *m* flight schedule; ~**platz**
m airport; (*klein*) airfield; ~**reise** *f* flight.
flugs [fluks] *adv* speedily.
Flug- *zW:* ~**sand** *m* drifting sand; ~**schein** *m*
pilot's licence (*BRIT*) *od* license (*US*);
~**schreiber** *m* flight recorder; ~**schrift** *f*
pamphlet; ~**steig** *m* gate; ~**strecke** *f* air
route; ~**verkehr** *m* air traffic; ~**wesen** *nt*
aviation.
Flugzeug (-(e)s, -e) *nt* plane, aeroplane (*BRIT*),
airplane (*US*); ~**entführung** *f* hijacking of a
plane; ~**halle** *f* hangar; ~**träger** *m* aircraft
carrier.
fluktuieren [fluktu'i:rən] *vi* to fluctuate.
Flunder ['flundər] (-, -n) *f* flounder.
flunkern ['fluŋkərn] *vi* to fib, tell stories.
Fluor ['flu:ɔr] (-s) *nt* fluorine.
Flur[1] [flu:r] (-(e)s, -e) *m* hall; (*Treppen*~)
staircase.
Flur[2] [flu:r] (-, -en) *f* (*geh*) open fields *pl*; **allein
auf weiter** ~ **stehen** (*fig*) to be out on a limb.
Fluss▲ [flus] (-es, ¨e) *m* river; (*Fließen*) flow;
im ~ **sein** (*fig*) to be in a state of flux; **etw in**
~ *akk* **bringen** to get sth moving;
f~ab(wärts) *adv* downstream; **f~auf(wärts)**
adv upstream; ~**diagramm** *nt* flow chart.
flüssig ['flysɪç] *adj* liquid; (*Stil*) flowing; ~**es
Vermögen** (*COMM*) liquid assets *pl*;
~ **machen** (*Geld*) to make available; **F~keit** *f*
liquid; (*Zustand*) liquidity.
Flussmündung▲ *f* estuary.
Flusspferd▲ *nt* hippopotamus.
flüstern ['flystərn] *vt, vi* to whisper.
Flüsterpropaganda *f* whispering campaign.
Flut [flu:t] (-, -en) *f* (*lit, fig*) flood; (*Gezeiten*)
high tide; **f~en** *vi* to flood; ~**licht** *nt*
floodlight.

flutschen ['flutʃən] (*umg*) *vi* (*rutschen*) to
slide; (: *funktionieren*) to go well.
Flutwelle *f* tidal wave.
fl. W. *abk* (= *fließendes Wasser*) running water.
focht *etc* [fɔxt] *vb siehe* **fechten**.
föderativ [fødera'ti:f] *adj* federal.
Fohlen ['fo:lən] (-s, -) *nt* foal.
Föhn [fø:n] (-(e)s, -e) *m* foehn, *warm dry
alpine wind*; (*Haartrockner*) hairdryer.
föhnen▲ *vt* to blow-dry.
Föhre ['fø:rə] (-, -n) *f* Scots pine.
Folge ['fɔlgə] (-, -n) *f* series, sequence;
(*Fortsetzung*) instalment (*BRIT*), installment
(*US*); (*TV, RUNDF*) episode; (*Auswirkung*)
result; **in rascher** ~ in quick succession; **etw
zur** ~ **haben** to result in sth; ~**n haben** to
have consequences; **einer Sache** *dat*
~ **leisten** to comply with sth; ~**erscheinung** *f*
result, consequence.
folgen *vi* +*dat* to follow ♦ *vi* (*gehorchen*) to
obey; **jdm** ~ **können** (*fig*) to follow *od*
understand sb; **daraus folgt, dass** ... it
follows from this that ...
folgend *adj* following; **im F~en** in the
following; (*schriftlich*) below.
folgendermaßen ['fɔlgəndər'ma:sən] *adv* as
follows, in the following way.
folgenreich *adj* momentous.
folgenschwer *adj* momentous.
folgerichtig *adj* logical.
folgern *vt:* ~ (**aus**) to conclude (from).
Folgerung *f* conclusion.
folgewidrig *adj* illogical.
folglich ['fɔlklɪç] *adv* consequently.
folgsam ['fɔlkza:m] *adj* obedient.
Folie ['fo:liə] (-, -n) *f* foil.
Folienschweißgerät *nt* shrink-wrap
machine.
Folklore ['fɔlklo:ər] (-) *f* folklore.
Folter ['fɔltər] (-, -n) *f* torture; (*Gerät*) rack;
jdn auf die ~ **spannen** (*fig*) to keep sb on
tenterhooks.
foltern *vt* to torture.
Fön ® [fø:n] (-(e)s, -e) *m* hairdryer.
Fonds [fõ:] (-, -) *m* (*lit, fig*) fund; (*FIN:
Schuldverschreibung*) government bond.
fönen△ *vt siehe* **föhnen**.
Fono-▲, **fono-**▲ *in zW* = **Phono-**, **phono-**.
Fontäne [fɔn'tɛ:nə] (-, -n) *f* fountain.
foppen ['fɔpən] *vt* to tease.
forcieren [fɔr'si:rən] *vt* to push; (*Tempo*) to
force; (*Konsum, Produktion*) to push *od* force
up.
Förderband ['fœrdərbant] *nt* conveyor belt.
Förderer (-s, -) *m* patron.
Fördergebiet *nt* development area.
Förderin *f* patroness.
Förderkorb *m* pit cage.
Förderleistung *f* (*MIN*) output.
förderlich *adj* beneficial.

fordern ['fɔrdərn] *vt* to demand; (*fig: kosten: Opfer*) to claim; (*: heraus~*) to challenge.

fördern ['fœrdərn] *vt* to promote; (*unterstützen*) to help; (*Kohle*) to extract; (*finanziell: Projekt*) to sponsor; (*jds Talent, Neigung*) to encourage, foster.

Förderplattform *f* production platform.

Förderstufe *f* (*SCH*) *first stage of secondary school where abilities are judged.*

Förderturm *m* (*MIN*) winding tower; (*auf Bohrstelle*) derrick.

Forderung ['fɔrdəruŋ] *f* demand.

Förderung ['fœrdəruŋ] *f* promotion; help; extraction.

Forelle [fo'rɛlə] *f* trout.

Form [fɔrm] (-, -en) *f* shape; (*Gestaltung*) form; (*Guss~*) mould; (*Back~*) baking tin; **in ~ von** in the shape of; **in ~ sein** to be in good form *od* shape; **die ~ wahren** to observe the proprieties; **in aller ~** formally.

formal [fɔr'maːl] *adj* formal; (*Besitzer, Grund*) technical.

formalisieren [fɔrmali'ziːrən] *vt* to formalize.

Formalität [fɔrmalı'tɛːt] *f* formality; **alle ~en erledigen** to go through all the formalities.

Format [fɔr'maːt] (-(e)s, -e) *nt* format; (*fig*) quality.

formatieren [fɔrma'tiːrən] *vt* (*Text, Diskette*) to format.

Formation [fɔrmatsi'oːn] *f* formation.

formbar *adj* malleable.

Formblatt *nt* form.

Formel (-, -n) *f* formula; (*von Eid etc*) wording; (*Floskel*) set phrase; **f~haft** *adj* (*Sprache, Stil*) stereotyped.

formell [fɔr'mɛl] *adj* formal.

formen *vt* to form, shape.

Formfehler *m* faux pas, gaffe; (*JUR*) irregularity.

formieren [fɔr'miːrən] *vt* to form ♦ *vr* to form up.

förmlich ['fœrmlıç] *adj* formal; (*umg*) real; **F~keit** *f* formality.

formlos *adj* shapeless; (*Benehmen etc*) informal; (*Antrag*) unaccompanied by a form *od* any forms.

Formsache *f* formality.

Formular [fɔrmu'laːr] (-s, -e) *nt* form.

formulieren [fɔrmu'liːrən] *vt* to formulate.

Formulierung *f* wording.

formvollendet *adj* perfect; (*Vase etc*) perfectly formed.

forsch [fɔrʃ] *adj* energetic, vigorous.

forschen [fɔrʃən] *vi* to search; (*wissenschaftlich*) to (do) research; **~ nach** to search for.

forschend *adj* searching.

Forscher (-s, -) *m* research scientist; (*Natur~*) explorer.

Forschung ['fɔrʃuŋ] *f* research; **~ und Lehre** research and teaching; **~ und Entwicklung** research and development.

Forschungsreise *f* scientific expedition.

Forst [fɔrst] (-(e)s, -e) *m* forest; **~arbeiter** *m* forestry worker.

Förster ['fœrstər] (-s, -) *m* forester; (*für Wild*) gamekeeper.

Forstwesen *nt* forestry.

Forstwirtschaft *f* forestry.

fort [fɔrt] *adv* away; (*verschwunden*) gone; (*vorwärts*) on; **und so ~** and so on; **in einem ~** incessantly; **~bestehen** *unreg vi* to continue to exist; **~bewegen** *vt, vr* to move away; **~bilden** *vr* to continue one's education; **F~bildung** *f* further education; **~bleiben** *unreg vi* to stay away; **~bringen** *unreg vt* to take away; **F~dauer** *f* continuance; **~dauernd** *adj* continuing; (*in der Vergangenheit*) continued ♦ *adv* constantly, continuously; **~fahren** *unreg vi* to depart; (*~setzen*) to go on, continue; **~führen** *vt* to continue, carry on; **F~gang** *m* (*Verlauf*) progress; (*Weggang*): **F~gang (aus)** departure (from); **~gehen** *unreg vi* to go away; **~geschritten** *adj* advanced; **~kommen** *unreg vi* to get on; (*wegkommen*) to get away; **~können** *unreg vi* to be able to get away; **~lassen** *vt* (*auslassen*) to leave out, omit; (*weggehen lassen*): **jdn ~lassen** to let sb go; **~laufend** *adj*: **~laufend nummeriert** consecutively numbered; **~müssen** *unreg vi* to have to go; **~pflanzen** *vr* to reproduce; **F~pflanzung** *f* reproduction.

FORTRAN ['fɔrtran] *nt* FORTRAN.

Forts. *abk* = **Fortsetzung**.

fortschaffen *vt* to remove.

fortschreiten *unreg vi* to advance.

Fortschritt ['fɔrtʃrıt] *m* advance; **~e machen** to make progress; **dem ~ dienen** to further progress; **f~lich** *adj* progressive.

fortschrittsgläubig *adj* believing in progress.

fort- *zW*: **~setzen** *vt* to continue; **F~setzung** *f* continuation; (*folgender Teil*) instalment (*BRIT*), installment (*US*); **F~setzung folgt** to be continued; **F~setzungsroman** *m* serialized novel; **~während** *adj* incessant, continual; **~wirken** *vi* to continue to have an effect; **~ziehen** *unreg vt* to pull away ♦ *vi* to move on; (*umziehen*) to move away.

Foto ['foːto] (-s, -s) *nt* photo(graph); **ein ~ machen** to take a photo(graph); **~album** *nt* photograph album; **~apparat** *m* camera; **~graf(in)** (-en, -en) *m(f)* photographer; **~grafie** *f* photography; (*Bild*) photograph; **f~grafieren** *vt* to photograph ♦ *vi* to take photographs; **~kopie** *f* photocopy; **f~kopieren** *vt* to photocopy; **~kopierer** *m* photocopier; **~kopiergerät** *nt* photocopier.

Foul [faʊl] (-s, -s) *nt* foul.

Foyer [foa'je:] (**-s, -s**) nt foyer; (in Hotel) lobby, foyer.

FPÖ (-) f abk (= Freiheitliche Partei Österreichs) Austrian Freedom Party.

Fr. abk (= Frau) Mrs, Ms.

Fracht [fraxt] (**-, -en**) f freight; (NAUT) cargo; (Preis) carriage; ~ **zahlt Empfänger** (COMM) carriage forward; ~**brief** m consignment note, waybill.

Frachter (**-s, -**) m freighter.

Fracht- zW: **f~frei** adj (COMM) carriage paid od free; ~**gut** nt freight; ~**kosten** pl (COMM) freight charges pl.

Frack [frak] (**-(e)s, ̈e**) m tails pl, tail coat.

Frage ['fra:gə] (**-, -n**) f question; **jdm eine** ~ **stellen** to ask sb a question, put a question to sb; **das ist gar keine ~, das steht außer ~** there's no question about it; siehe auch **infrage**; ~**bogen** m questionnaire.

fragen vt, vi to ask ♦ vr to wonder; **nach Arbeit/Post** ~ to ask whether there is/was any work/mail; **da fragst du mich zu viel** (umg) I really couldn't say; **nach jdm** (umg) ~ to ask for sb; (nach jds Befinden) to ask after sb; **ohne lange zu** ~ without asking a lot of questions.

Fragerei [fra:gə'raı] f questions pl.

Fragestunde f (PARL) question time.

Fragezeichen nt question mark.

fraglich adj questionable, doubtful; (betreffend) in question.

fraglos adv unquestionably.

Fragment [fra'gmɛnt] nt fragment.

fragmentarisch [fragmɛn'ta:rıʃ] adj fragmentary.

fragwürdig ['fra:kvʏrdıç] adj questionable, dubious.

Fraktion [fraktsi'o:n] f parliamentary party.

Fraktionsvorsitzende(r) f(m) (POL) party whip.

Fraktionszwang m requirement to obey the party whip.

frank [fraŋk] adj frank, candid.

Franken[1] ['fraŋkən] nt Franconia.

Franken[2] ['fraŋkən] (**-, -**) m: **(Schweizer)** ~ (Swiss) Franc.

Frankfurt ['fraŋkfurt] (**-s**) nt Frankfurt.

Frankfurter(in) m(f) native of Frankfurt ♦ adj Frankfurt; ~ **Würstchen** pl frankfurters.

frankieren [fraŋ'ki:rən] vt to stamp, frank.

Frankiermaschine f franking machine.

fränkisch ['fraŋkıʃ] adj Franconian.

franko adv carriage paid; (POST) post-paid.

Frankreich ['fraŋkraıç] (**-s**) nt France.

Franse ['franzə] (**-, -n**) f fringe.

fransen vi to fray.

franz. abk = **französisch**.

Franzbranntwein m alcoholic liniment.

Franzose [fran'tso:zə] (**-n, -n**) m Frenchman; French boy.

Französin [fran'tsø:zın] f Frenchwoman; French girl.

französisch adj French; ~**es Bett** double bed.

Fräse ['frɛ:zə] (**-, -n**) f (Werkzeug) milling cutter; (für Holz) moulding cutter.

Fraß (**-es, -e**) (pej: umg) m (Essen) muck.

fraß etc [fra:s] vb siehe **fressen**.

Fratze ['fratsə] (**-, -n**) f grimace; **eine** ~ **schneiden** to pull od make a face.

Frau [frau] (**-, -en**) f woman; (Ehe~) wife; (Anrede) Mrs, Ms; ~ **Doktor** Doctor.

Frauen- zW: ~**arzt** m gynaecologist (BRIT), gynecologist (US); ~**bewegung** f feminist movement; **f~feindlich** adj anti-women, misogynous; ~**haus** nt women's refuge; ~**quote** f recommended proportion of women (employed); ~**rechtlerin** f feminist; ~**zentrum** nt women's advice centre; ~**zimmer** (pej) nt female, broad (US).

Fräulein ['frɔʏlaın] nt young lady; (Anrede) Miss; (Verkäuferin) assistant (BRIT), sales clerk (US); (Kellnerin) waitress.

fraulich ['fraʊlıç] adj womanly.

frech [frɛç] adj cheeky, impudent; ~ **wie Oskar sein** (umg) to be a little monkey; **F~dachs** m cheeky monkey; **F~heit** f cheek, impudence; **sich** dat **(einige) F~heiten erlauben** to be a bit cheeky (bes BRIT) od fresh (bes US).

Fregatte [fre'gatə] (**-, -n**) f frigate.

frei [fraı] adj free; (Stelle) vacant; (Mitarbeiter) freelance; (Geld) available; (unbekleidet) bare; **aus ~en Stücken** od ~**em Willen** of one's own free will; ~ **nach ...** based on ...; **für etw ~e Fahrt geben** (fig) to give sth the go-ahead; **der Film ist ~ ab 16 (Jahren)** the film may be seen by people of 16 years (of age) and over; **unter ~em Himmel** in the open (air); **morgen/Mittwoch ist ~** tomorrow/Wednesday is a holiday; „**Zimmer ~**" "vacancies"; **auf ~er Strecke** (EISENB) between stations; (AUT) on the road; ~**er Wettbewerb** fair/open competition; ~ **Haus** (COMM) carriage paid; ~ **Schiff** (COMM) free on board; ~**e Marktwirtschaft** free market economy; **von etw ~ sein** to be free of sth; **im F~en** in the open air; ~ **sprechen** to talk without notes; **F~bad** nt open-air swimming pool; ~**bekommen** unreg vt: **jdn/einen Tag ~bekommen** to get sb freed/get a day off; ~**beruflich** adj self-employed; **F~betrag** m tax allowance;

Freier (**-s, -**) m suitor.

Frei- zW: ~**exemplar** nt free copy; **f~geben** unreg vt: **etw zum Verkauf f~geben** to allow sth to be sold on the open market; **f~gebig** adj generous; ~**gebigkeit** f generosity; ~**hafen** m free port; **f~halten** unreg vt to keep free; (bezahlen) to pay for; ~**handel** m free trade; ~**handelszone** f free trade area;

f~händig *adv* (*fahren*) with no hands.
Freiheit *f* freedom; **sich** *dat* **die ~ nehmen,
etw zu tun** to take the liberty of doing sth;
f~lich *adj* liberal; (*Verfassung*) based on the
principle of liberty; (*Demokratie*) free.
Freiheits- *zW*: **~beraubung** *f* (*JUR*) wrongful
deprivation of personal liberty; **~drang** *m*
urge/desire for freedom; **~kampf** *m* fight
for freedom; **~kämpfer(in)** *m(f)* freedom
fighter; **~rechte** *pl* civil liberties *pl*; **~strafe** *f*
prison sentence.
frei- *zW*: **~heraus** *adv* frankly; **F~karte** *f* free
ticket; **~kaufen** *vt*: **jdn/sich ~kaufen** to buy
sb's/one's freedom; **~kommen** *unreg vi* to get
free; **F~körperkultur** *f* nudism; **~lassen** *unreg
vt* to (set) free; **F~lauf** *m* freewheeling;
~laufend *adj* (*Hühner*) free-range; **~legen** *vt*
to expose; **~lich** *adv* certainly, admittedly; **ja
~lich!** yes of course; **F~lichtbühne** *f* open-
air theatre; **~machen** *vt* (*POST*) to frank ♦ *vr*
to arrange to be free; **Tage ~machen** to
take days off; **sich ~machen** (*beim Arzt*) to
take one's clothes off, strip; **F~maurer** *m*
Mason, Freemason.
freimütig ['fraimy:tɪç] *adj* frank, honest.
Frei- *zW*: **f~nehmen▲** *vt*: **sich** *dat* **einen Tag
f~nehmen** to take a day off; **~raum** *m*:
~raum (zu) (*fig*) freedom (for); **f~schaffend**
adj attrib freelance; **~schärler (-s, -)** *m*
guerrilla; **f~schwimmen** *vr* (*fig*) to learn to
stand on one's own two feet; **f~setzen** *vt*
(*Energien*) to release; **f~sinnig** *adj* liberal;
f~sprechanlage *f* hands-free (headset); (*im
Auto*) hands-free (car kit); **f~sprechen** *unreg
vt*: **f~sprechen (von)** to acquit (of); **~spruch**
m acquittal; **f~stehen** *unreg vi*: **es steht dir f~,
das zu tun** you are free to do so; **das steht
Ihnen völlig f~** that is completely up to you;
f~stellen *vt*: **jdm etw f~stellen** to leave sth
(up) to sb; **~stoß** *m* free kick; **~stunde** *f*
free hour; (*SCH*) free period.
Freitag *m* Friday; *siehe auch* **Dienstag**.
freitags *adv* on Fridays.
Frei- *zW*: **~tod** *m* suicide; **~übungen** *pl*
(physical) exercises *pl*; **~umschlag** *m* reply-
paid envelope; **~wild** *nt* (*fig*) fair game;
f~willig *adj* voluntary; **~willige(r)** *f(m)*
volunteer; **~zeichen** *nt* (*TEL*) ringing tone;
~zeit *f* spare *od* free time; **~zeitgestaltung** *f*
organization of one's leisure time; **f~zügig**
adj liberal, broad-minded; (*mit Geld*)
generous.
fremd [frɛmt] *adj* (*unvertraut*) strange;
(*ausländisch*) foreign; (*nicht eigen*) someone
else's; **etw ist jdm ~** sth is foreign to sb; **ich
bin hier ~** I'm a stranger here; **sich ~ fühlen**
to feel like a stranger; **~artig** *adj* strange.
Fremde (-) *f* (*liter*): **die ~** foreign parts *pl*.
Fremde(r) *f(m)* stranger; (*Ausländer*)
foreigner.

Fremden- *zW*: **~führer** *m* (tourist) guide;
(*Buch*) guide (book); **~legion** *f* foreign
legion; **~verkehr** *m* tourism; **~zimmer** *nt*
guest room.
fremd- *zW*: **~gehen** *unreg* (*umg*) *vi* to be
unfaithful; **F~kapital** *nt* loan capital;
F~körper *m* foreign body; **~ländisch** *adj*
foreign; **F~ling** *m* stranger; **F~sprache** *f*
foreign language;
F~sprachenkorrespondentin *f* bilingual
secretary; **~sprachig** *adj attrib* foreign-
language; **F~wort** *nt* foreign word.
frenetisch [fre'ne:tɪʃ] *adj* frenetic.
Frequenz [fre'kvɛnts] *f* (*RUNDF*) frequency.
Fresse (-, -n) (*umg!*) *f* (*Mund*) gob; (*Gesicht*)
mug.
fressen ['frɛsən] *unreg vt, vi* to eat ♦ *vr*: **sich voll
od satt ~** to gorge o.s.; **einen Narren an
jdm/etw gefressen haben** to dote on sb/sth.
Freude ['frɔydə] (-, -n) *f* joy, delight; **~ an etw**
dat **haben** to get *od* derive pleasure from
sth; **jdm eine ~ machen** *od* **bereiten** to make
sb happy.
Freudenhaus *nt* (*veraltet*) house of ill repute.
Freudentanz *m*: **einen ~ aufführen** to dance
with joy.
freudestrahlend *adj* beaming with delight.
freudig *adj* joyful, happy.
freudlos *adj* joyless.
freuen ['frɔyən] *vt unpers* to make happy *od*
pleased ♦ *vr* to be glad *od* happy; **sich auf
etw** *akk* **~** to look forward to sth; **sich über
etw** *akk* **~** to be pleased about sth; **sich zu
früh ~** to get one's hopes up too soon.
Freund ['frɔynt] (-(e)s, -e) *m* friend;
(*Liebhaber*) boyfriend; **ich bin kein ~ von so
etwas** I'm not one for that sort of thing; **~in**
f friend; (*Liebhaberin*) girlfriend; **f~lich** *adj*
kind, friendly; **bitte recht f~lich!** smile
please!; **würden Sie bitte so f~lich sein und
das tun?** would you be so kind as to do
that?; **f~licherweise** *adv* kindly; **~lichkeit** *f*
friendliness, kindness; **~schaft** *f* friendship;
f~schaftlich *adj* friendly.
Frevel ['fre:fəl] (-s, -) *m*: **~ (an +dat)** crime *od*
offence (against); **f~haft** *adj* wicked.
Frieden ['fri:dən] (-s, -) *m* peace; **im ~** in
peacetime; **~ schließen** to make one's
peace; (*POL*) to make peace; **um des lieben
~s willen** (*umg*) for the sake of peace and
quiet; **ich traue dem ~ nicht** (*umg*)
something (fishy) is going on.
Friedens- *zW*: **~bewegung** *f* peace movement;
~richter *m* justice of the peace; **~schluss▲**
m peace agreement; **~truppe** *f* peacekeeping force; **~verhandlungen** *pl* peace
negotiations *pl*; **~vertrag** *m* peace treaty;
~zeit *f* peacetime.
fried- *zW*: **~fertig** *adj* peaceable; **F~hof** *m*
cemetery; **~lich** *adj* peaceful; **etw auf**

~**lichem Wege lösen** to solve sth by peaceful means.

frieren ['fri:rən] *unreg vi* to freeze ♦ *vt unpers* to freeze ♦ *vi unpers*: **heute Nacht hat es gefroren** it was below freezing last night; **ich friere, es friert mich** I am freezing, I'm cold; **wie ein Schneider** ~ (*umg*) to be *od* get frozen to the marrow.

Fries [fri:s] (**-es, -e**) *m* (*ARCHIT*) frieze.

Friese ['fri:zə] (**-n, -n**) *m* Fri(e)sian.

Friesin ['fri:zɪn] *f* Fri(e)sian.

frigid(e) *adj* frigid.

Frikadelle [frika'dɛlə] *f* meatball.

frisch [frɪʃ] *adj* fresh; (*lebhaft*) lively; ~ **gestrichen!** wet paint!; **sich** ~ **machen** to freshen (o.s.) up; **jdn auf** ~**er Tat ertappen** to catch sb red-handed *od* in the act.

Frische (**-**) *f* freshness; liveliness; **in alter** ~ (*umg*) as always.

Frischhaltebeutel *m* airtight bag.

Frischhaltefolie *f* clingfilm.

frischweg *adv* (*munter*) straight out.

Friseur [fri'zø:r] *m* hairdresser.

Friseuse [fri'zø:zə] *f* hairdresser.

frisieren [fri'zi:rən] *vt* (*Haar*) to do; (*fig: Abrechnung*) to fiddle, doctor ♦ *vr* to do one's hair; **jdn** ~, **jdm das Haar** ~ to do sb's hair.

Frisiersalon *m* hairdressing salon.

Frisiertisch *m* dressing table.

Frisör [fri'zø:r] (**-s, -e**) *m* hairdresser.

frisst▲ [frɪst] *vb siehe* **fressen**.

Frist [frɪst] (**-, -en**) *f* period; (*Termin*) deadline; **eine** ~ **einhalten/verstreichen lassen** to meet a deadline/let a deadline pass; (*bei Rechnung*) to pay/not to pay within the period stipulated; **jdm eine** ~ **von vier Tagen geben** to give sb four days' grace.

fristen *vt* (*Dasein*) to lead; (*kümmerlich*) to eke out.

Fristenlösung *f* abortion law (*permitting abortion in the first three months*).

fristgerecht *adj* within the period stipulated.

fristlos *adj* (*Entlassung*) instant.

Frisur [fri'zu:r] *f* hairdo, hairstyle.

Fritteuse▲ [fri'tø:zə] (**-, -n**) *f* chip pan (*BRIT*), deep fat fryer.

frittieren▲ [fri'ti:rən] *vt* to deep fry.

frivol [fri'vo:l] *adj* frivolous.

Frl. *abk* (= *Fräulein*) Miss.

froh [fro:] *adj* happy, cheerful; **ich bin** ~, **dass** ... I'm glad that ...

fröhlich ['frø:lɪç] *adj* merry, happy; **F**~**keit** *f* merriment, gaiety.

frohlocken *vi* (*geh*) to rejoice; (*pej*) to gloat.

Frohsinn *m* cheerfulness.

fromm [frɔm] *adj* pious, good; (*Wunsch*) idle.

Frömmelei [frœmə'lai] *f* false piety.

Frömmigkeit *f* piety.

frönen ['frø:nən] *vi* +*dat* to indulge in.

Fronleichnam [fro:n'laiçna:m] (**-(e)s**) *m*

Corpus Christi.

Front [frɔnt] (**-, -en**) *f* front; **klare** ~**en schaffen** (*fig*) to clarify the position.

frontal [frɔn'ta:l] *adj* frontal; **F**~**angriff** *m* frontal attack.

fror *etc* [fro:r] *vb siehe* **frieren**.

Frosch [frɔʃ] (**-(e)s, ¨e**) *m* frog; (*Feuerwerk*) squib; **sei kein** ~! (*umg*) be a sport!; ~**mann** *m* frogman; ~**perspektive** *f*: **etw aus der** ~**perspektive sehen** to get a worm's-eye view of sth; ~**schenkel** *m* frog's leg.

Frost [frɔst] (**-(e)s, ¨e**) *m* frost; **f**~**beständig** *adj* frost-resistant; ~**beule** *f* chilblain.

frösteln ['frœstəln] *vi* to shiver.

frostig *adj* frosty.

Frostschutzmittel *nt* anti-freeze.

Frottee [frɔ'te:] (**-(s), -s**) *nt od m* towelling.

frottieren [frɔ'ti:rən] *vt* to rub, towel.

Frottierhandtuch *nt* towel.

Frottiertuch *nt* towel.

frotzeln ['frɔtsəln] (*umg*) *vt, vi* to tease.

Frucht [fruxt] (**-, ¨e**) *f* (*lit, fig*) fruit; (*Getreide*) corn; (*Embryo*) foetus; **f**~**bar** *adj* fruitful, fertile; ~**barkeit** *f* fertility; ~**becher** *m* fruit sundae.

Früchtchen ['fryçtçən] (*umg*) *nt* (*Tunichtgut*) good-for-nothing.

fruchten *vi* to be of use.

fruchtlos *adj* fruitless.

Fruchtsaft *m* fruit juice.

früh [fry:] *adj, adv* early; **heute** ~ this morning; **von** ~ **auf** from an early age; **F**~**aufsteher** (**-s, -**) *m* early riser; **F**~**dienst** *m*: **F**~**dienst haben** to be on early shift.

Frühe (**-**) *f* early morning; **in aller** ~ at the crack of dawn.

früher *adj* earlier; (*ehemalig*) former ♦ *adv* formerly; ~ **war das anders** that used to be different; ~ **oder später** sooner or later.

frühestens *adv* at the earliest.

Frühgeburt *f* premature birth; (*Kind*) premature baby.

Frühjahr *nt* spring.

Frühjahrsmüdigkeit *f* springtime lethargy.

Frühjahrsputz *m* spring-cleaning.

Frühling *m* spring; **im** ~ in spring.

früh- *zW*: ~**reif** *adj* precocious; **F**~**rentner** *m* person who has retired early; **F**~**schicht** *f* early shift; **F**~**schoppen** *m* morning/lunchtime drink; **F**~**sport** *m* early morning exercise; **F**~**stück** *nt* breakfast; ~**stücken** *vi* to (have) breakfast; **F**~**warnsystem** *nt* early warning system; ~**zeitig** *adj* early; (*vorzeitig*) premature.

Frust (**-(e)s**) (*umg*) *m* frustration.

frustrieren [frus'tri:rən] *vt* to frustrate.

frz. *abk* = **französisch**.

FSV *abk* (= *Fußball-Sportverein*) F.C.

FU (**-**) *f abk* (= *Freie Universität Berlin*) *Berlin University*.

Fuchs [fʊks] (**-es**, **ⁱe**) *m* fox.
fuchsen (*umg*) *vt* to rile, annoy ♦ *vr* to be annoyed.
Füchsin ['fʏksın] *f* vixen.
fuchsteufelswild *adj* hopping mad.
Fuchtel ['fʊxtl] (**-**, **-n**) *f* (*fig: umg*): **unter jds ~** under sb's control *od* thumb.
fuchteln ['fʊxtəln] *vi* to gesticulate wildly.
Fuge ['fuːɡə] (**-**, **-n**) *f* joint; (*MUS*) fugue.
fügen ['fyːɡən] *vt* to place, join ♦ *vr unpers* to happen ♦ *vr*: **sich ~** (**in** +*akk*) to be obedient (to); (*anpassen*) to adapt o.s. (to).
fügsam ['fyːkzaːm] *adj* obedient.
fühlbar *adj* perceptible, noticeable.
fühlen ['fyːlən] *vt*, *vi*, *vr* to feel.
Fühler (**-s**, **-**) *m* feeler.
Fühlung *f*: **mit jdm in ~ bleiben/stehen** to stay/be in contact *od* touch with sb.
fuhr *etc* [fuːr] *vb siehe* **fahren**.
Fuhre (**-**, **-n**) *f* (*Ladung*) load.
führen ['fyːrən] *vt* to lead; (*Geschäft*) to run; (*Name*) to bear; (*Buch*) to keep; (*im Angebot haben*) to stock ♦ *vi* to lead ♦ *vr* to behave; **was führt Sie zu mir?** (*form*) what brings you to me?; **Geld/die Papiere bei sich ~** (*form*) to carry money/one's papers on one's person; **das führt zu nichts** that will come to nothing.
Führer(in) ['fyːrər(ın)] (**-s**, **-**) *m(f)* leader; (*Fremden~*) guide; **~haus** *nt* cab; **~schein** *m* driving licence (*BRIT*), driver's license (*US*); **den ~schein machen** (*AUT*) to learn to drive; (*die Prüfung ablegen*) to take one's (driving) test; **~scheinentzug** *m* disqualification from driving.
Fuhrmann ['fuːrman] (**-(e)s**, *pl* **-leute**) *m* carter.
Führung ['fyːrʊŋ] *f* leadership; (*eines Unternehmens*) management; (*MIL*) command; (*Benehmen*) conduct; (*Museums~*) conducted tour.
Führungs- *zW*: **~kraft** *f* executive; **~stab** *m* (*MIL*) command; (*COMM*) top management; **~stil** *m* management style; **~zeugnis** *nt* certificate of good conduct.
Fuhrunternehmen *nt* haulage business.
Fuhrwerk *nt* cart.
Fülle ['fʏlə] (**-**) *f* wealth, abundance.
Füllen (**-s**, **-**) *nt* foal.
füllen *vt* to fill; (*KOCH*) to stuff ♦ *vr* to fill (up).
Füller (**-s**, **-**) *m* fountain pen.
Füllfederhalter *m* fountain pen.
Füllgewicht *nt* (*COMM*) weight at time of packing; (*auf Dosen*) net weight.
füllig ['fʏlıç] *adj* (*Mensch*) corpulent, portly; (*Figur*) ample.
Füllung *f* filling; (*Holz~*) panel.
fummeln ['fʊməln] (*umg*) *vi* to fumble.
Fund [fʊnt] (**-(e)s**, **-e**) *m* find.
Fundament [fʊndaˈmɛnt] *nt* foundation.

fundamental *adj* fundamental.
Fundamentalismus *m* fundamentalism.
Fundbüro *nt* lost property office, lost and found (*US*).
Fundgrube *f* (*fig*) treasure trove.
fundieren [fʊnˈdiːrən] *vt* to back up.
fundiert *adj* sound.
fündig ['fʏndıç] *adj* (*MIN*) rich; **~ werden** to make a strike; (*fig*) to strike it lucky.
Fundsachen *pl* lost property *sing*.
fünf [fʏnf] *num* five; **seine ~ Sinne beisammen haben** to have all one's wits about one; **~(e) gerade sein lassen** (*umg*) to turn a blind eye; **~hundert** *num* five hundred; **~jährig** *adj* (*Frist, Plan*) five-year; (*Kind*) five-year-old; **F~kampf** *m* pentathlon.
Fünfprozentklausel *f* (*PARL*) *clause debarring parties with less than 5% of the vote from Parliament.*

FÜNFPROZENTKLAUSEL

The **Fünfprozentklausel** *is a rule in German Federal elections whereby only those parties who collect at least 5% of the second vote (***Zweitstimme***) receive a parliamentary seat. This is to avoid the parliament being made up of a large number of very small parties which, in the Weimar Republic, led to political instability.*

Fünftagewoche *f* five-day week.
fünfte(r, s) *adj* fifth.
Fünftel (**-s**, **-**) *nt* fifth.
fünfzehn *num* fifteen.
fünfzig *num* fifty.
fungieren [fʊŋˈɡiːrən] *vi* to function; (*Person*) to act.
Funk [fʊŋk] (**-s**) *m* radio, wireless (*BRIT old*); **~ausstellung** *f* radio and television exhibition.
Funke (**-ns**, **-n**) *m* (*lit, fig*) spark.
funkeln *vi* to sparkle.
funkelnagelneu (*umg*) *adj* brand-new.
Funken (**-s**, **-**) *m* = **Funke**.
funken *vt* to radio.
Funker (**-s**, **-**) *m* radio operator.
Funk- *zW*: **~gerät** *nt* radio set; **~haus** *nt* broadcasting centre; **~kolleg** *nt* educational radio broadcasts *pl*; **~rufempfänger** *m* (*TELEC*) pager, paging device; **~spot** *m* advertisement on the radio; **~sprechgerät** *nt* radio telephone; **~spruch** *m* radio signal; **~station** *f* radio station; **~stille** *f* (*fig*) ominous silence; **~streife** *f* police radio patrol; **~taxi** *nt* radio taxi; **~telefon** *nt* cell phone; **~telefonnetz** *nt* radio telephone network.
Funktion [fʊŋktsiˈoːn] *f* function; **in ~ treten/sein** to come into/be in operation.
Funktionär(in) [fʊŋktsioˈnɛːr(ın)] (**-s**, **-e**) *m(f)*

functionary, official.

funktionieren [foŋktsio'ni:rən] *vi* to work, function.

Funktions- *zW:* **f~fähig** *adj* working; **~taste** *f* (*COMPUT*) function key; **f~tüchtig** *adj* in working order.

Funzel [funtsəl] (**-, -n**) (*umg*) *f* dim lamp.

für [fy:r] *präp* +*akk* for; **was ~** what kind *od* sort of; **~s Erste** for the moment; **was Sie da sagen, hat etwas ~ sich** there's something in what you're saying; **Tag ~ Tag** day after day; **Schritt ~ Schritt** step by step; **das F~ und Wider** the pros and cons *pl*; **F~bitte** *f* intercession.

Furche ['furçə] (**-, -n**) *f* furrow.

furchen *vt* to furrow.

Furcht [furçt] (**-**) *f* fear; **f~bar** *adj* terrible, awful.

fürchten ['fyrçtən] *vt* to be afraid of, fear ♦ *vr:* **sich ~ (vor** +*dat*) to be afraid (of).

fürchterlich *adj* awful.

furchtlos *adj* fearless.

furchtsam *adj* timorous.

füreinander [fy:r|aı'nandər] *adv* for each other.

Furie ['fu:riə] (**-, -n**) *f* (*MYTHOLOGIE*) fury; (*fig*) hellcat.

Furnier [fur'ni:r] (**-s, -e**) *nt* veneer.

Furore [fu'ro:rə] *f od nt:* **~ machen** (*umg*) to cause a sensation.

fürs [fy:rs] = **für das**.

Fürsorge ['fy:rzɔrgə] *f* care; (*Sozial~*) welfare; **von der ~ leben** to live on social security (*BRIT*) *od* welfare (*US*); **~amt** *nt* welfare office.

Fürsorger(in) (**-s, -**) *m(f)* welfare worker.

Fürsorgeunterstützung *f* social security (*BRIT*), welfare benefit (*US*).

fürsorglich *adj* caring.

Fürsprache *f* recommendation; (*um Gnade*) intercession.

Fürsprecher *m* advocate.

Fürst [fyrst] (**-en, -en**) *m* prince.

Fürstentum *nt* principality.

Fürstin *f* princess.

fürstlich *adj* princely.

Furt [furt] (**-, -en**) *f* ford.

Furunkel [fu'ruŋkəl] (**-s, -**) *nt od m* boil.

Fürwort ['fy:rvɔrt] *nt* pronoun.

furzen ['furtsən] (*umg!*) *vi* to fart (!).

Fusion [fuzi'o:n] *f* amalgamation; (*von Unternehmen*) merger; (*von Atomkernen, Zellen*) fusion.

fusionieren [fuzio'ni:rən] *vt* to amalgamate.

Fuß [fu:s] (**-es, -̈e**) *m* foot; (*von Glas, Säule etc*) base; (*von Möbel*) leg; **zu ~** on foot; **bei ~!** heel!; **jdm etw vor die Füße werfen** (*lit*) to throw sth at sb; (*fig*) to tell sb to keep sth; **(festen) ~ fassen** (*lit, fig*) to gain a foothold; (*sich niederlassen*) to settle down; **mit jdm**

auf gutem ~ stehen to be on good terms with sb; **auf großem ~ leben** to live the high life.

Fußball *m* football; **~platz** *m* football pitch; **~spiel** *nt* football match; **~spieler** *m* footballer (*BRIT*), football player (*US*); **~toto** *m od nt* football pools *pl*.

Fußboden *m* floor; **~heizung** *f* underfloor heating.

Fußbremse *f* (*AUT*) foot brake.

fusselig ['fusəlıç] *adj:* **sich** *dat* **den Mund ~ reden** (*umg*) to talk till one is blue in the face.

fusseln ['fusəln] *vi* (*Stoff, Kleid etc*) to go bobbly (*umg*).

fußen *vi:* **~ auf** +*dat* to rest on, be based on.

Fuß- *zW:* **~ende** *nt* foot; **~gänger(in)** (**-s, -**) *m(f)* pedestrian; **~gängerüberführung** *f* pedestrian bridge; **~gängerzone** *f* pedestrian precinct; **~leiste** *f* skirting board (*BRIT*), baseboard (*US*); **~nagel** *m* toenail; **~note** *f* footnote; **~pfleger** *m* chiropodist; **~pilz** *m* (*MED*) athlete's foot; **~spur** *f* footprint; **~stapfen** (**-s, -**) *m:* **in jds ~stapfen treten** (*fig*) to follow in sb's footsteps; **~tritt** *m* kick; (*Spur*) footstep; **~volk** *nt* (*fig*): **das ~volk** the rank and file; **~weg** *m* footpath.

futsch [futʃ] (*umg*) *adj* (*weg*) gone, vanished.

Futter ['futər] (**-s, -**) *nt* fodder, feed; (*Stoff*) lining.

Futteral [futə'ra:l] (**-s, -e**) *nt* case.

futtern ['futərn] *vi* (*hum: umg*) to stuff o.s. ♦ *vt* to scoff.

füttern ['fytərn] *vt* to feed; (*Kleidung*) to line; **„F~ verboten"** "do not feed the animals".

Futur [fu'tu:r] (**-s, -e**) *nt* future.

G, g

G, g¹ [ge:] *nt* G, g; **~ wie Gustav** ≈ G for George.

g² *abk* (*ÖSTERR*) = **Groschen**; (= *Gramm*) g.

gab *etc* [ga:p] *vb siehe* **geben**.

Gabe ['ga:bə] (**-, -n**) *f* gift.

Gabel ['ga:bəl] (**-, -n**) *f* fork; (*TEL*) rest, cradle; **~frühstück** *nt* mid-morning light lunch; **~stapler** (**-s, -**) *m* fork-lift truck.

gabeln *vr* to fork.

Gabelung *f* fork.

Gabentisch ['ga:bəntıʃ] *m* table for *Christmas or birthday presents*.

Gabun [ga'bu:n] *nt* Gabon.

gackern ['gakərn] *vi* to cackle.

gaffen ['gafən] *vi* to gape.
Gag [gɛk] (**-s, -s**) *m* (*Film~*) gag; (*Werbe~*) gimmick.
Gage ['gaːʒə] (**-, -n**) *f* fee.
gähnen ['gɛːnən] *vi* to yawn; ~**de Leere** total emptiness.
GAL (**-**) *f abk* (= *Grün-Alternative Liste*) *electoral pact of Greens and alternative parties.*
Gala ['gala] (**-**) *f* formal dress.
galant [ga'lant] *adj* gallant, courteous.
Galavorstellung *f* (*THEAT*) gala performance.
Galerie [galə'riː] *f* gallery.
Galgen ['galgən] (**-s, -**) *m* gallows *pl*; ~**frist** *f* respite; ~**humor** *m* macabre humour (*BRIT*) *od* humor (*US*); ~**strick** (*umg*) *m*, ~**vogel** (*umg*) *m* gallows bird.
Galionsfigur [gali'oːnsfiguːr] *f* figurehead.
gälisch ['gɛːlɪʃ] *adj* Gaelic.
Galle ['galə] (**-, -n**) *f* gall; (*Organ*) gall bladder; **jdm kommt die ~ hoch** sb's blood begins to boil.
Galopp [ga'lɔp] (**-s, -s** *od* **-e**) *m* gallop; **im ~** (*lit*) at a gallop; (*fig*) at top speed.
galoppieren [galo'piːrən] *vi* to gallop.
galt *etc* [galt] *vb siehe* **gelten**.
galvanisieren [galvani'ziːrən] *vt* to galvanize.
Gamasche [ga'maʃə] (**-, -n**) *f* gaiter; (*kurz*) spat.
Gameboy ® ['gɛːmbɔy] *m* (*COMPUT*) games console.
Gammastrahlen ['gamaʃtraːlən] *pl* gamma rays *pl*.
gamm(e)lig ['gam(ə)lɪç] (*umg*) *adj* (*Kleidung*) tatty.
gammeln ['gaməln] (*umg*) *vi* to loaf about.
Gammler(in) ['gamlər(ɪn)] (**-s, -**) *m(f)* dropout.
Gämse▲ ['gɛmzə] (**-, -n**) *f* chamois.
Gang[1] [gaŋ] (**-(e)s, ⁻e**) *m* walk; (*Boten~*) errand; (*~art*) gait; (*Abschnitt eines Vorgangs*) operation; (*Essens~, Ablauf*) course; (*Flur etc*) corridor; (*Durch~*) passage; (*AUT, TECH*) gear; (*THEAT, AVIAT, in Kirche*) aisle; **den ersten ~ einlegen** to engage first (gear); **einen ~ machen/tun** to go on an errand/for a walk; **den ~ nach Canossa antreten** (*fig*) to eat humble pie; **seinen gewohnten ~ gehen** (*fig*) to run its usual course; **in ~ bringen** to start up; (*fig*) to get off the ground; **in ~ sein** to be in operation; (*fig*) to be under way.
Gang[2] [gɛŋ] (**-, -s**) *f* gang.
gang *adj*: ~ **und gäbe** usual, normal.
Gangart *f* way of walking, walk, gait; (*von Pferd*) gait; **eine härtere ~ einschlagen** (*fig*) to apply harder tactics.
gangbar *adj* passable; (*Methode*) practicable.
Gängelband ['gɛŋəlbant] *nt*: **jdn am ~ halten** (*fig*) to spoon-feed sb.
gängeln *vt* to spoonfeed; **jdn ~** to treat sb

like a child.
gängig ['gɛŋɪç] *adj* common, current; (*Ware*) in demand, selling well.
Gangschaltung *f* gears *pl*.
Gangway ['gæŋweɪ] *f* (*NAUT*) gangway; (*AVIAT*) steps *pl*.
Ganove [ga'noːvə] (**-n, -n**) (*umg*) *m* crook.
Gans [gans] (**-, ⁻e**) *f* goose.
Gänse- *zW:* ~**blümchen** *nt* daisy; ~**braten** *m* roast goose; ~**füßchen** (*umg*) *pl* inverted commas *pl* (*BRIT*), quotes *pl*; ~**haut** *f* goose pimples *pl*; ~**marsch** *m*: **im ~marsch** in single file.
Gänserich (**-s, -e**) *m* gander.
ganz [gants] *adj* whole; (*vollständig*) complete ♦ *adv* quite; (*völlig*) completely; (*sehr*) really; (*genau*) exactly; ~ **Europa** all Europe; **im (Großen und) G~en genommen** on the whole, all in all; **etw wieder ~ machen** to mend sth; **sein ~es Geld** all his money; ~ **gewiss!** absolutely; **ein ~ klein wenig** just a tiny bit; **das mag ich ~ besonders gern(e)** I'm particularly fond of that; **sie ist ~ die Mutter** she's just *od* exactly like her mother; ~ **und gar nicht** not at all.
Ganze(s) *nt*: **es geht ums ~** everything's at stake; **aufs ~ gehen** to go for the lot.
Ganzheitsmethode ['gantshaɪtsmetoːdə] *f* (*SCH*) look-and-say method.
gänzlich ['gɛntslɪç] *adj* complete, entire ♦ *adv* completely, entirely.
ganztägig ['gantstɛːgɪç] *adj* all-day *attrib*.
ganztags *adv* (*arbeiten*) full time.
gar [gaːr] *adj* cooked, done ♦ *adv* quite; ~ **nicht/nichts/keiner** not/nothing/nobody at all; ~ **nicht schlecht** not bad at all; ~ **kein Grund** no reason whatsoever *od* at all; **er wäre ~ zu gern noch länger geblieben** he would really have liked to stay longer.
Garage [ga'raːʒə] (**-, -n**) *f* garage.
Garantie [garan'tiː] *f* guarantee; **das fällt noch unter die ~** that's covered by the guarantee.
garantieren *vt* to guarantee.
garantiert *adv* guaranteed; (*umg*) I bet.
Garantieschein *m* guarantee.
Garaus ['gaːraus] (*umg*) *m*: **jdm den ~ machen** to do sb in.
Garbe ['garbə] (**-, -n**) *f* sheaf; (*MIL*) burst of fire.
Garde ['gardə] (**-, -n**) *f* guard(s); **die alte ~** the old guard.
Garderobe [gardə'roːbə] (**-, -n**) *f* wardrobe; (*Abgabe*) cloakroom (*BRIT*), checkroom (*US*); (*Kleiderablage*) hall stand; (*THEAT: Umkleideraum*) dressing room.
Garderobenfrau *f* cloakroom attendant.
Garderobenständer *m* hall stand.
Gardine [gar'diːnə] (**-, -n**) *f* curtain.
Gardinenpredigt (*umg*) *f*: **jdm eine ~ halten** to give sb a talking-to.

Gardinenstange *f* curtain rail; (*zum Ziehen*) curtain rod.
garen ['ga:rən] *vt, vi* (*KOCH*) to cook.
gären ['gɛ:rən] *unreg vi* to ferment.
Garn [garn] (**-(e)s, -e**) *nt* thread; (*Häkel~, fig*) yarn.
Garnele [gar'ne:lə] (**-, -n**) *f* shrimp, prawn.
garnieren [gar'ni:rən] *vt* to decorate; (*Speisen*) to garnish.
Garnison [garni'zo:n] (**-, -en**) *f* garrison.
Garnitur [garni'tu:r] *f* (*Satz*) set; (*Unterwäsche*) set of (matching) underwear; **erste ~** (*fig*) top rank; **zweite ~** second rate.
garstig ['garstɪç] *adj* nasty, horrid.
Garten ['gartən] (**-s, ⸚**) *m* garden; **~arbeit** *f* gardening; **~bau** *m* horticulture; **~fest** *nt* garden party; **~gerät** *nt* gardening tool; **~haus** *nt* summerhouse; **~kresse** *f* cress; **~laube** *f* (*~häuschen*) summerhouse; **~lokal** *nt* beer garden; **~schere** *f* pruning shears *pl*; **~tür** *f* garden gate; **~zaun** *m* garden fence; **~zwerg** *m* garden gnome; (*pej: umg*) squirt.
Gärtner(in) ['gɛrtnər(ɪn)] (**-s, -**) *m(f)* gardener.
Gärtnerei [gɛrtnə'raɪ] *f* nursery; (*Gemüse~*) market garden (*BRIT*), truck farm (*US*).
gärtnern *vi* to garden.
Gärung ['gɛ:rʊŋ] *f* fermentation.
Gas [ga:s] (**-es, -e**) *nt* gas; **~ geben** (*AUT*) to accelerate, step on the gas.
Gascogne [gas'kɔnjə] *f* Gascony.
Gas- *zW:* **~flasche** *f* bottle of gas, gas canister; **g~förmig** *adj* gaseous; **~hahn** *m* gas tap; **~herd** *m* gas cooker; **~kocher** *m* gas cooker; **~leitung** *f* gas pipeline; **~maske** *f* gas mask; **~pedal** *nt* accelerator, gas pedal (*US*); **~pistole** *f* gas pistol.
Gasse ['gasə] (**-, -n**) *f* lane, alley.
Gassenhauer (**-s, -**) (*veraltet: umg*) *m* popular melody.
Gassenjunge *m* street urchin.
Gast [gast] (**-es, ⸚e**) *m* guest; **bei jdm zu ~ sein** to be sb's guest(s); **~arbeiter** *m* foreign worker.
Gäste- *zW:* **~bett** *nt* spare bed; **~buch** *nt* visitors' book; **~zimmer** *nt* guest room.
Gast- *zW:* **g~freundlich** *adj* hospitable; **~freundlichkeit** *f* hospitality; **~freundschaft** *f* hospitality; **~geber(in)** (**-s, -**) *m(f)* host(ess); **~haus** *nt* hotel, inn; **~hof** *m* hotel, inn; **~hörer(in)** *m(f)* (*UNIV*) observer, auditor (*US*).
gastieren [gas'ti:rən] *vi* (*THEAT*) to (appear as a) guest.
Gast- *zW:* **~land** *nt* host country; **g~lich** *adj* hospitable; **~lichkeit** *f* hospitality; **~rolle** *f* (*THEAT*) guest role; **eine ~rolle spielen** to make a guest appearance.
Gastronomie [gastrono'mi:] *f* (*form: Gaststättengewerbe*) catering trade.
gastronomisch [gastro'no:mɪʃ] *adj*

gastronomic(al).
Gast- *zW:* **~spiel** *nt* (*SPORT*) away game; **ein ~spiel geben** (*THEAT*) to give a guest performance; (*fig*) to put in a brief appearance; **~stätte** *f* restaurant; (*Trinklokal*) pub; **~wirt** *m* innkeeper; **~wirtschaft** *f* hotel, inn; **~zimmer** *nt* guest room.
Gas- *zW:* **~vergiftung** *f* gas poisoning; **~versorgung** *f* (*System*) gas supply; **~werk** *nt* gasworks *sing od pl*; **~zähler** *m* gas meter.
Gatte ['gatə] (**-n, -n**) *m* (*form*) husband, spouse; **die ~n** husband and wife.
Gatter ['gatər] (**-s, -**) *nt* grating; (*Tür*) gate.
Gattin *f* (*form*) wife, spouse.
Gattung ['gatʊŋ] *f* (*BIOL*) genus; (*Sorte*) kind.
GAU [gaʊ] *m abk* (= *größter anzunehmender Unfall*) MCA, maximum credible accident.
Gaudi ['gaʊdi] (*SÜDD, ÖSTERR: umg*) *nt od f* fun.
Gaukler ['gaʊklər] (**-s, -**) *m* (*liter*) travelling entertainer; (*Zauberkünstler*) conjurer, magician.
Gaul [gaʊl] (**-(e)s, Gäule**) (*pej*) *m* nag.
Gaumen ['gaʊmən] (**-s, -**) *m* palate.
Gauner ['gaʊnər] (**-s, -**) *m* rogue.
Gaunerei [gaʊnə'raɪ] *f* swindle.
Gaunersprache *f* underworld jargon.
Gaze ['ga:zə] (**-, -n**) *f* gauze.
Geäst [gə'ɛst] *nt* branches *pl*.
geb. *abk* = **geboren**.
Gebäck [gə'bɛk] (**-(e)s, -e**) *nt* (*Kekse*) biscuits *pl* (*BRIT*), cookies *pl* (*US*); (*Teilchen*) pastries *pl*.
gebacken [gə'bakən] *pp von* **backen**.
Gebälk [gə'bɛlk] (**-(e)s**) *nt* timberwork.
gebannt [gə'bant] *adj* spellbound.
gebar *etc* [gə'ba:r] *vb siehe* **gebären**.
Gebärde [gə'bɛ:rdə] (**-, -n**) *f* gesture.
gebärden *vr* to behave.
Gebaren [gə'ba:rən] (**-s**) *nt* behaviour (*BRIT*), behavior (*US*); (*Geschäfts~*) conduct.
gebären [gə'bɛ:rən] *unreg vt* to give birth to.
Gebärmutter *f* uterus, womb.
Gebäude [gə'bɔydə] (**-s, -**) *nt* building; **~komplex** *m* (building) complex; **~reinigung** *f* (*das Reinigen*) commercial cleaning; (*Firma*) cleaning contractors *pl*.
Gebein [gə'baɪn] (**-(e)s, -e**) *nt* bones *pl*.
Gebell [gə'bɛl] (**-(e)s**) *nt* barking.
geben ['ge:bən] *unreg vt, vi* to give; (*Karten*) to deal ♦ *vt unpers:* **es gibt** there is/are; there will be ♦ *vr* (*sich verhalten*) to behave, act; (*aufhören*) to abate; **jdm etw ~** to give sb sth *od* sth to sb; **in die Post ~** to post; **das gibt keinen Sinn** that doesn't make sense; **er gibt Englisch** he teaches English; **viel/nicht viel auf etw** *akk* **~** to set great store/not much store by sth; **etw von sich ~** (*Laute etc*) to utter; **ein Wort gab das andere** one angry word led to another; **ein gutes Beispiel ~** to

set a good example; ~ **Sie mir bitte Herrn Braun** (*TEL*) can I speak to Mr Braun please?; **ein Auto in Reparatur** ~ to have a car repaired; **was gibts?** what's the matter?, what's up?; **was gibts zum Mittagessen?** what's for lunch?; **das gibts doch nicht!** that's impossible!; **sich geschlagen** ~ to admit defeat; **das wird sich schon** ~ that'll soon sort itself out.

Gebet [gə'beːt] (**-(e)s, -e**) *nt* prayer; **jdn ins** ~ **nehmen** (*fig*) to take sb to task.

gebeten [gə'beːtən] *pp von* **bitten**.

gebeugt [gə'bɔykt] *adj* (*Haltung*) stooped; (*Kopf*) bowed; (*Schultern*) sloping.

gebiert [gə'biːrt] *vb siehe* **gebären**.

Gebiet [gə'biːt] (**-(e)s, -e**) *nt* area; (*Hoheits~*) territory; (*fig*) field.

gebieten *unreg vt* to command, demand.

Gebieter (**-s, -**) *m* master; (*Herrscher*) ruler; ~**in** *f* mistress; **g~isch** *adj* imperious.

Gebietshoheit *f* territorial sovereignty.

Gebilde [gə'bɪldə] (**-s, -**) *nt* object, structure.

gebildet *adj* cultured, educated.

Gebimmel [gə'bɪməl] (**-s**) *nt* (continual) ringing.

Gebirge [gə'bɪrgə] (**-s, -**) *nt* mountains *pl*.

gebirgig *adj* mountainous.

Gebirgs- *zW:* ~**bahn** *f railway crossing a mountain range;* ~**kette** *f,* ~**zug** *m* mountain range.

Gebiss▲ [gə'bɪs] (**-es, -e**) *nt* teeth *pl*; (*künstlich*) dentures *pl*.

gebissen *pp von* **beißen**.

Gebläse [gə'blɛːzə] (**-s, -**) *nt* fan, blower.

geblasen [gə'blaːzən] *pp von* **blasen**.

geblichen [gə'blɪçən] *pp von* **bleichen**.

geblieben [gə'bliːbən] *pp von* **bleiben**.

geblümt [gə'blyːmt] *adj* flowered; (*Stil*) flowery.

Geblüt [gə'blyːt] (**-(e)s**) *nt* blood, race.

gebogen [gə'boːgən] *pp von* **biegen**.

geboren [gə'boːrən] *pp von* **gebären** ♦ *adj* born; (*Frau*) née; **wo sind Sie** ~? where were you born?

geborgen [gə'bɔrgən] *pp von* **bergen** ♦ *adj* secure, safe.

geborsten [gə'bɔrstən] *pp von* **bersten**.

Gebot (**-(e)s, -e**) *nt* (*Gesetz*) law; (*REL*) commandment; (*bei Auktion*) bid; **das** ~ **der Stunde** the needs of the moment.

gebot *etc* [gə'boːt] *vb siehe* **gebieten**.

geboten [gə'boːtən] *pp von* **bieten, gebieten** ♦ *adj* (*geh: ratsam*) advisable; (*: notwendig*) necessary; (*: dringend* ~) imperative.

Gebr. *abk* (= *Gebrüder*) Bros., bros.

gebracht [gə'braxt] *pp von* **bringen**.

gebrannt [gə'brant] *pp von* **brennen** ♦ *adj*: **ein** ~**es Kind scheut das Feuer** (*Sprichwort*) once bitten twice shy (*Sprichwort*).

gebraten [gə'braːtən] *pp von* **braten**.

Gebräu [gə'brɔy] (**-(e)s, -e**) *nt* brew, concoction.

Gebrauch [gə'braʊx] (**-(e)s, Gebräuche**) *m* use; (*Sitte*) custom; **zum äußerlichen/innerlichen** ~ for external use/to be taken internally.

gebrauchen *vt* to use; **er/das ist zu nichts zu** ~ he's/that's (of) no use to anybody.

gebräuchlich [gə'brɔyçlɪç] *adj* usual, customary.

Gebrauchs- *zW:* ~**anweisung** *f* directions *pl* for use; ~**artikel** *m* article of everyday use; **g~fertig** *adj* ready for use; ~**gegenstand** *m* commodity.

gebraucht [gə'braʊxt] *adj* used; **G~wagen** *m* second-hand *od* used car.

gebrechlich [gə'brɛçlɪç] *adj* frail; **G~keit** *f* frailty.

gebrochen [gə'brɔxən] *pp von* **brechen**.

Gebrüder [gə'bryːdər] *pl* brothers *pl*.

Gebrüll [gə'brʏl] (**-(e)s**) *nt* (*von Mensch*) yelling; (*von Löwe*) roar.

gebückt [gə'bʏkt] *adj*: **eine** ~**e Haltung** a stoop.

Gebühr [gə'byːr] (**-, -en**) *f* charge; (*Post~*) postage *no pl*; (*Honorar*) fee; **zu ermäßigter** ~ at a reduced rate; ~ **(be)zahlt Empfänger** postage to be paid by addressee; **nach** ~ suitably; **über** ~ excessively.

gebühren *vi* (*geh*): **jdm** ~ to be sb's due *od* due to sb ♦ *vr* to be fitting.

gebührend *adj* (*verdient*) due; (*angemessen*) suitable.

Gebühren- *zW:* ~**einheit** *f* (*TEL*) tariff unit; ~**erlass**▲ *m* remission of fees; ~**ermäßigung** *f* reduction of fees; **g~frei** *adj* free of charge; **g~pflichtig** *adj* subject to charges; **g~pflichtige Verwarnung** (*JUR*) fine.

gebunden [gə'bʊndən] *pp von* **binden** ♦ *adj*: **vertraglich** ~ **sein** to be bound by contract.

Geburt [gə'buːrt] (**-, -en**) *f* birth; **das war eine schwere** ~! (*fig: umg*) that took some doing.

Geburten- *zW:* ~**kontrolle** *f* birth control; ~**regelung** *f* birth control; ~**rückgang** *m* drop in the birth rate; **g~schwach** *adj* (*Jahrgang*) with a low birth rate; ~**ziffer** *f* birth rate.

gebürtig [gə'bʏrtɪç] *adj* born in, native of; ~**e Schweizerin** native of Switzerland, Swiss-born woman.

Geburts- *zW:* ~**anzeige** *f* birth notice; ~**datum** *nt* date of birth; ~**fehler** *m* congenital defect; ~**helfer** *m* (*Arzt*) obstetrician; ~**helferin** *f* (*Ärztin*) obstetrician; (*Hebamme*) midwife; ~**hilfe** *f* (*als Fach*) obstetrics *sing*; (*von Hebamme*) midwifery; ~**jahr** *nt* year of birth; ~**ort** *m* birthplace; ~**tag** *m* birthday; **herzlichen Glückwunsch zum** ~**tag!** happy birthday!, many happy returns (of the day)!; ~**urkunde** *f* birth certificate.

Gebüsch [gə'bʏʃ] (**-(e)s, -e**) *nt* bushes *pl*.

gedacht [gə'daxt] *pp von* **denken, gedenken**.

gedachte *etc vb siehe* **gedenken**.

Gedächtnis [gə'dɛçtnɪs] (**-ses, -se**) *nt* memory; **wenn mich mein ~ nicht trügt** if my memory serves me right; **~feier** *f* commemoration; **~hilfe** *f* memory aid, mnemonic; **~schwund** *m* loss of memory; **~verlust** *m* amnesia.

gedämpft [gə'dɛmpft] *adj* (*Geräusch*) muffled; (*Farben, Instrument, Stimmung*) muted; (*Licht, Freude*) subdued.

Gedanke [gə'daŋkə] (**-ns, -n**) *m* thought; (*Idee, Plan, Einfall*) idea; (*Konzept*) concept; **sich über etw** *akk* **~n machen** to think about sth; **jdn auf andere ~n bringen** to make sb think about other things; **etw ganz in ~n** *dat* **tun** to do sth without thinking; **auf einen ~n kommen** to have *od* get an idea.

Gedanken- *zW*: **~austausch** *m* exchange of ideas; **~freiheit** *f* freedom of thought; **g~los** *adj* thoughtless; **~losigkeit** *f* thoughtlessness; **~sprung** *m* mental leap; **~strich** *m* dash; **~übertragung** *f* thought transference, telepathy; **g~verloren** *adj* lost in thought; **g~voll** *adj* thoughtful.

Gedärme [gə'dɛrmə] *pl* intestines *pl*.

Gedeck [gə'dɛk] (**-(e)s, -e**) *nt* cover(ing); (*Menü*) set meal; **ein ~ auflegen** to lay a place.

gedeckt *adj* (*Farbe*) muted.

Gedeih *m*: **auf ~ und Verderb** for better or for worse.

gedeihen [gə'daɪən] *unreg vi* to thrive, prosper; **die Sache ist so weit gediehen, dass** ... the matter has reached the point *od* stage where ...

gedenken [gə'dɛŋkən] *unreg vi +gen* (*geh: denken an*) to remember; (*beabsichtigen*) to intend; **G~** *nt*: **zum G~ an jdn** in memory *od* remembrance of sb.

Gedenk- *zW*: **~feier** *f* commemoration; **~minute** *f* minute's silence; **~stätte** *f* memorial; **~tag** *m* remembrance day.

Gedicht [gə'dɪçt] (**-(e)s, -e**) *nt* poem.

gediegen [gə'diːgən] *adj* (*good*) quality; (*Mensch*) reliable; (*rechtschaffen*) honest; **G~heit** *f* quality; reliability; honesty.

gedieh *etc* [gə'diː] *vb siehe* **gedeihen**.

gediehen *pp von* **gedeihen**.

gedr. *abk* = **gedruckt**.

Gedränge [gə'drɛŋə] (**-s**) *nt* crush, crowd; **ins ~ kommen** (*fig*) to get into difficulties.

gedrängt *adj* compressed; **~ voll** packed.

gedroschen [gə'drɔʃən] *pp von* **dreschen**.

gedruckt [gə'drʊkt] *adj* printed; **lügen wie ~** (*umg*) to lie left, right and centre.

gedrungen [gə'drʊŋən] *pp von* **dringen ♦** *adj* thickset, stocky.

Geduld [gə'dʊlt] (**-**) *f* patience; **mir reißt die ~, ich verliere die ~** my patience is wearing thin, I'm losing my patience.

gedulden [gə'dʊldən] *vr* to be patient.

geduldig *adj* patient.

Geduldsprobe *f* trial of (one's) patience.

gedungen [gə'dʊŋən] (*pej*) *adj* (*geh: Mörder*) hired.

gedunsen [gə'dʊnzən] *adj* bloated.

gedurft [gə'dʊrft] *pp von* **dürfen**.

geehrt [gə'|eːrt] *adj*: **Sehr ~e Damen und Herren!** Ladies and Gentlemen!; (*in Briefen*) Dear Sir or Madam.

geeignet [gə'|aɪgnət] *adj* suitable; **im ~en Augenblick** at the right moment.

Gefahr [gə'faːr] (**-, -en**) *f* danger; **~ laufen, etw zu tun** to run the risk of doing sth; **auf eigene ~** at one's own risk; **außer ~** (*nicht gefährdet*) not in danger; (*nicht mehr gefährdet*) out of danger; (*Patienten*) off the danger list.

gefährden [gə'fɛːrdən] *vt* to endanger.

gefahren [gə'faːrən] *pp von* **fahren**.

Gefahren- *zW*: **~quelle** *f* source of danger; **~schwelle** *f* threshold of danger; **~stelle** *f* danger spot; **~zulage** *f* danger money.

gefährlich [gə'fɛːrlɪç] *adj* dangerous.

Gefährte [gə'fɛːrtə] (**-n, -n**) *m* companion.

Gefährtin [gə'fɛːrtɪn] *f* companion.

Gefälle [gə'fɛlə] (**-s, -**) *nt* (*von Land, Straße*) slope; (*Neigungsgrad*) gradient; **starkes ~!** steep hill.

Gefallen¹ [gə'falən] (**-s, -**) *m* favour; **jdm etw zu ~ tun** to do sth to please sb.

Gefallen² [gə'falən] (**-s**) *nt* pleasure; **an etw** *dat* **~ finden** to derive pleasure from sth; **an jdm ~ finden** to take to sb.

gefallen *pp von* **fallen, gefallen ♦** *vi* (*unreg*): **jdm ~** to please sb; **er/es gefällt mir** I like him/it; **das gefällt mir an ihm** that's one thing I like about him; **sich** *dat* **etw ~ lassen** to put up with sth.

Gefallene(r) *m* soldier killed in action.

gefällig [gə'fɛlɪç] *adj* (*hilfsbereit*) obliging; (*erfreulich*) pleasant; **sonst noch etwas ~?** (*veraltet, ironisch*) will there be anything else?; **G~keit** *f* favour (*BRIT*), favor (*US*); helpfulness; **etw aus G~keit tun** to do sth as a favour (*BRIT*) *od* favor (*US*).

gefälligst (*umg*) *adv* kindly; **sei ~ still!** will you kindly keep your mouth shut!

gefällt [gə'fɛlt] *vb siehe* **gefallen**.

gefangen [gə'faŋən] *pp von* **fangen ♦** *adj* captured; (*fig*) captivated; **~ halten** to keep prisoner; **~ nehmen** to capture.

Gefangene(r) *f(m)* prisoner, captive.

Gefangenenlager *nt* prisoner-of-war camp.

Gefangen- *zW*: **~nahme** (**-, -n**) *f* capture; **~schaft** *f* captivity.

Gefängnis [gə'fɛŋnɪs] (**-ses, -se**) *nt* prison; **zwei Jahre ~ bekommen** to get two years' imprisonment; **~strafe** *f* prison sentence; **~wärter** *m* prison warder (*BRIT*) *od* guard.

gefärbt [gəˈfɛrpt] *adj* (*fig: Bericht*) biased; (*Lebensmittel*) coloured (*BRIT*), colored (*US*).

Gefasel [gəˈfaːzəl] (**-s**) *nt* twaddle, drivel.

Gefäß [gəˈfɛːs] (**-es, -e**) *nt* vessel (*auch ANAT*), container.

gefasst▲ [gəˈfast] *adj* composed, calm; **auf etw** *akk* **~ sein** to be prepared *od* ready for sth; **er kann sich auf etwas ~ machen** (*umg*) I'll give him something to think about.

Gefecht [gəˈfɛçt] (**-(e)s, -e**) *nt* fight; (*MIL*) engagement; **jdn/etw außer ~ setzen** (*lit, fig*) to put sb/sth out of action.

gefedert [gəˈfeːdərt] *adj* (*Matratze*) sprung.

gefeiert [gəˈfaiərt] *adj* celebrated.

gefeit [gəˈfait] *adj*: **gegen etw ~ sein** to be immune to sth.

gefestigt [gəˈfɛstiçt] *adj* (*Charakter*) steadfast.

Gefieder [gəˈfiːdər] (**-s, -**) *nt* plumage, feathers *pl*.

gefiedert *adj* feathered.

gefiel *etc* [gəˈfiːl] *vb siehe* **gefallen**.

Geflecht [gəˈflɛçt] (**-(e)s, -e**) *nt* (*lit, fig*) network.

gefleckt [gəˈflɛkt] *adj* spotted; (*Blume, Vogel*) speckled.

Geflimmer [gəˈflimər] (**-s**) *nt* shimmering; (*FILM, TV*) flicker(ing).

geflissentlich [gəˈflisəntliç] *adj* intentional ♦ *adv* intentionally.

geflochten [gəˈflɔxtən] *pp von* **flechten**.

geflogen [gəˈfloːgən] *pp von* **fliegen**.

geflohen [gəˈfloːən] *pp von* **fliehen**.

geflossen [gəˈflɔsən] *pp von* **fließen**.

Geflügel [gəˈflyːgəl] (**-s**) *nt* poultry.

geflügelt *adj*: **~e Worte** familiar quotations.

Geflüster [gəˈflystər] (**-s**) *nt* whispering.

gefochten [gəˈfɔxtən] *pp von* **fechten**.

Gefolge [gəˈfɔlgə] (**-s, -**) *nt* retinue.

Gefolgschaft [gəˈfɔlkʃaft] *f* following.

Gefolgsmann (**-(e)s**, *pl* **-leute**) *m* follower.

gefragt [geˈfraːkt] *adj* in demand.

gefräßig [gəˈfrɛːsiç] *adj* voracious.

Gefreite(r) [gəˈfraitə(r)] *m* (*MIL*) lance corporal (*BRIT*), private first class (*US*); (*NAUT*) able seaman (*BRIT*), seaman apprentice (*US*); (*AVIAT*) aircraftman (*BRIT*), airman first class (*US*).

gefressen [gəˈfrɛsən] *pp von* **fressen** ♦ *adj*: **den hab(e) ich ~** (*umg*) I'm sick of him.

gefrieren [gəˈfriːrən] *unreg vi* to freeze.

Gefrier- *zW*: **~fach** *nt* freezer compartment; **~fleisch** *nt* frozen meat; **g~getrocknet** *adj* freeze-dried; **~punkt** *m* freezing point; **~schutzmittel** *nt* antifreeze; **~truhe** *f* deep-freeze.

gefror *etc* [gəˈfroːr] *vb siehe* **gefrieren**.

gefroren *pp von* **frieren, gefrieren**.

Gefüge [gəˈfyːgə] (**-s, -**) *nt* structure.

gefügig *adj* submissive; (*gehorsam*) obedient.

Gefühl [gəˈfyːl] (**-(e)s, -e**) *nt* feeling; **etw im ~ haben** to have a feel for sth; **g~los** *adj* unfeeling; (*Glieder*) numb.

Gefühls- *zW*: **g~betont** *adj* emotional; **~duselei** [-duːzəˈlai] (*pej*) *f* mawkishness; **~leben** *nt* emotional life; **g~mäßig** *adj* instinctive; **~mensch** *m* emotional person.

gefühlvoll *adj* (*empfindsam*) sensitive; (*ausdrucksvoll*) expressive; (*liebevoll*) loving.

gefüllt [gəˈfylt] *adj* (*KOCH*) stuffed; (*Pralinen*) with soft centres.

gefunden [gəˈfʊndən] *pp von* **finden** ♦ *adj*: **das war ein ~es Fressen für ihn** that was handing it to him on a plate.

gegangen [gəˈgaŋən] *pp von* **gehen**.

gegeben [gəˈgeːbən] *pp von* **geben** ♦ *adj* given; **zu ~er Zeit** in due course.

gegebenenfalls [gəˈgeːbənənfals] *adv* if need be.

═══════════════════ *SCHLÜSSELWORT*

gegen [ˈgeːgən] *präp +akk* **1** against; **nichts ~ jdn haben** to have nothing against sb; **X ~ Y** (*SPORT, JUR*) X versus Y; **ein Mittel ~ Schnupfen** something for colds.

2 (*in Richtung auf*) towards; **~ Osten** to(wards) the east; **~ Abend** towards evening; **~ einen Baum fahren** to drive into a tree.

3 (*ungefähr*) round about; **~ 3 Uhr** around 3 o'clock.

4 (*gegenüber*) towards; (*ungefähr*) around; **gerecht ~ alle** fair to all.

5 (*im Austausch für*) for; **~ bar** for cash; **~ Quittung** against a receipt.

6 (*verglichen mit*) compared with.

─────────────────────────

Gegen- *zW*: **~angriff** *m* counter-attack; **~besuch** *m* return visit; **~beweis** *m* counter-evidence.

Gegend [ˈgeːgənt] (**-, -en**) *f* area, district.

Gegen- *zW*: **~darstellung** *f* (*PRESSE*) reply; **g~einander** *adv* against one another; **~fahrbahn** *f* opposite carriageway; **~frage** *f* counterquestion; **~gewicht** *nt* counterbalance; **~gift** *nt* antidote; **~kandidat** *m* rival candidate; **g~läufig** *adj* contrary; **~leistung** *f* service in return; **~lichtaufnahme** *f* back lit photograph; **~liebe** *f* requited love; (*fig: Zustimmung*) approval; **~maßnahme** *f* countermeasure; **~mittel** *nt*: **~mittel (gegen)** (*MED*) antidote (to); **~probe** *f* cross-check.

Gegensatz (**-es, -̈e**) *m* contrast; **Gegensätze überbrücken** to overcome differences.

gegensätzlich *adj* contrary, opposite; (*widersprüchlich*) contradictory.

Gegen- *zW*: **~schlag** *m* counter-attack; **~seite** *f* opposite side; (*Rückseite*) reverse; **g~seitig** *adj* mutual, reciprocal; **sich g~seitig helfen** to help each other; **in g~seitigem**

Einverständnis by mutual agreement; **~seitigkeit** *f* reciprocity; **~spieler** *m* opponent; **~sprechanlage** *f* (two-way) intercom; **~stand** *m* object; **g~ständlich** *adj* objective, concrete; (*KUNST*) representational; **g~standslos** *adj* (*überflüssig*) irrelevant; (*grundlos*) groundless; **~stimme** *f* vote against; **~stoß** *m* counterblow; **~stück** *nt* counterpart; **~teil** *nt* opposite; **im ~teil** on the contrary; **das ~teil bewirken** to have the opposite effect; (*Mensch*) to achieve the exact opposite; **ganz im ~teil** quite the reverse; **ins ~teil umschlagen** to swing to the other extreme; **g~teilig** *adj* opposite, contrary; **ich habe nichts ~teiliges gehört** I've heard nothing to the contrary.

gegenüber [ge:gən'|y:bər] *präp +dat* opposite; (*zu*) to(wards); (*in Bezug auf*) with regard to; (*im Vergleich zu*) in comparison with; (*angesichts*) in the face of ♦ *adv* opposite; **mir ~ hat er das nicht geäußert** he didn't say that to me; **G~** (**-s, -**) *nt* person opposite; (*bei Kampf*) opponent; (*bei Diskussion*) opposite number; **~liegen** *unreg vr* to face each other; **~stehen** *unreg vr* to be opposed (to each other); **~stellen** *vt* to confront; (*fig*) to contrast; **G~stellung** *f* confrontation; (*fig*) contrast; (*: Vergleich*) comparison; **~treten** *unreg vi +dat* to face.

Gegen- *zW:* **~veranstaltung** *f* counter-meeting; **~verkehr** *m* oncoming traffic; **~vorschlag** *m* counterproposal.

Gegenwart ['ge:gənvart] *f* present; **in ~ von** in the presence of.

gegenwärtig *adj* present ♦ *adv* at present; **das ist mir nicht mehr ~** that has slipped my mind.

gegenwartsbezogen *adj* (*Roman etc*) relevant to present times.

Gegen- *zW:* **~wert** *m* equivalent; **~wind** *m* headwind; **~wirkung** *f* reaction; **g~zeichnen** *vt* to countersign; **~zug** *m* countermove; (*EISENB*) corresponding train in the other direction.

gegessen [gə'gɛsən] *pp von* **essen**.

geglichen [gə'glɪçən] *pp von* **gleichen**.

gegliedert [gə'gli:dərt] *adj* jointed; (*fig*) structured.

geglitten [gə'glɪtən] *pp von* **gleiten**.

geglommen [gə'glɔmən] *pp von* **glimmen**.

geglückt [gə'glʏkt] *adj* (*Feier*) successful; (*Überraschung*) real.

Gegner(in) ['ge:gnər(ɪn)] (**-s, -**) *m(f)* opponent; **g~isch** *adj* opposing; **~schaft** *f* opposition.

gegolten [gə'gɔltən] *pp von* **gelten**.

gegoren [gə'go:rən] *pp von* **gären**.

gegossen [gə'gɔsən] *pp von* **gießen**.

gegr. *abk* (= *gegründet*) estab.

gegraben [gə'gra:bən] *pp von* **graben**.

gegriffen [gə'grɪfən] *pp von* **greifen**.

Gehabe [gə'ha:bə] (**-s**) (*umg*) *nt* affected behaviour (*BRIT*) *od* behavior (*US*).

gehabt [gə'ha:pt] *pp von* **haben**.

Gehackte(s) [ge'haktə(s)] *nt* mince(d meat) (*BRIT*), ground meat (*US*).

Gehalt¹ [gə'halt] (**-(e)s, -e**) *m* content.

Gehalt² [gə'halt] (**-(e)s, -̈er**) *nt* salary.

gehalten [gə'haltən] *pp von* **halten** ♦ *adj:* **~ sein, etw zu tun** (*form*) to be required to do sth.

Gehalts- *zW:* **~abrechnung** *f* salary statement; **~empfänger** *m* salary earner; **~erhöhung** *f* salary increase; **~klasse** *f* salary bracket; **~konto** *nt* current account (*BRIT*), checking account (*US*); **~zulage** *f* salary increment.

gehaltvoll [gə'haltfɔl] *adj* (*Speise, Buch*) substantial.

gehandikapt [gə'hɛndikɛpt] *adj* handicapped.

gehangen [gə'haŋən] *pp von* **hängen**.

geharnischt [gə'harnɪʃt] *adj* (*fig*) forceful, sharp.

gehässig [gə'hɛsɪç] *adj* spiteful, nasty; **G~keit** *f* spite(fulness).

gehäuft [gə'hɔyft] *adj* (*Löffel*) heaped.

Gehäuse [gə'hɔyzə] (**-s, -**) *nt* case; (*Radio~, Uhr~*) casing; (*von Apfel etc*) core.

gehbehindert ['ge:bəhɪndərt] *adj* disabled.

Gehege [gə'he:gə] (**-s, -**) *nt* enclosure, preserve; **jdm ins ~ kommen** (*fig*) to poach on sb's preserve.

geheim [gə'haim] *adj* secret; (*Dokumente*) classified; **streng ~** top secret; **~ halten** to keep secret; **G~dienst** *m* secret service, intelligence service; **G~fach** *nt* secret compartment.

Geheimnis (**-ses, -se**) *nt* secret; (*rätselhaftes ~*) mystery; **~krämer** *m* mystery-monger; **g~voll** *adj* mysterious.

Geheim- *zW:* **~nummer** *f* (*TEL*) secret number; **~polizei** *f* secret police; **~rat** *m* privy councillor; **~ratsecken** *pl:* **er hat ~ratsecken** he is going bald at the temples; **~schrift** *f* code, secret writing; **~tipp ▲** *m* (personal) tip.

Geheiß [gə'hais] (**-es**) *nt* (*geh*) command; **auf jds ~** *akk* at sb's bidding.

geheißen [gə'haisən] *pp von* **heißen**.

gehemmt [gə'hɛmt] *adj* inhibited.

gehen ['ge:ən] *unreg vi* (*auch Auto, Uhr*) to go; (*zu Fuß ~*) to walk; (*funktionieren*) to work; (*Teig*) to rise ♦ *vi* to go; to walk ♦ *vi unpers:* **wie geht es dir?** how are you *od* things?; **~ nach** (*Fenster*) to face; **in sich** *akk* **~** to think things over; **nach etw ~** (*urteilen*) to go by sth; **sich ~ lassen** to lose one's self-control; (*nachlässig sein*) to let o.s. go; **wie viele Leute ~ in deinen Wagen?** how many people can you get in your car?; **nichts geht über** *+akk* ... there's nothing to beat ..., there's nothing better than ...; **schwimmen/ schlafen** ~ to go swimming/to bed; **in die tausende** *od* **Tausende** ~ to run into (the) thousands; **mir/ihm geht es gut** I'm/he's (doing) fine; **geht das?** is that possible?; **gehts noch?** can you manage?; **es geht** not too bad, O.K.; **das geht nicht** that's not on; **es geht um etw** it concerns sth, it's about sth; **lass es dir gut** ~ look after yourself, take care of yourself; **so geht das, das geht so** that/this is how it's done; **darum geht es (mir) nicht** that's not the point; (*spielt keine Rolle*) that's not important to me; **morgen geht es nicht** tomorrow's no good; **wenn es nach mir ginge** ... if it were *od* was up to me ...

gehetzt [gə'hɛtst] *adj* harassed.

geheuer [gə'hɔyər] *adj*: **nicht** ~ eerie; (*fragwürdig*) dubious.

Geheul [gə'hɔyl] (-(e)s) *nt* howling.

Gehilfe [gə'hɪlfə] (-n, -n) *m* assistant.

Gehilfin [gə'hɪlfɪn] *f* assistant.

Gehirn [gə'hɪrn] (-(e)s, -e) *nt* brain; ~**erschütterung** *f* concussion; ~**schlag** *m* stroke; ~**wäsche** *f* brainwashing.

gehoben [gə'hoːbən] *pp von* **heben** ♦ *adj*: ~**er Dienst** *professional and executive levels of the civil service.*

geholfen [gə'hɔlfən] *pp von* **helfen**.

Gehör [gə'høːr] (-(e)s) *nt* hearing; **musikalisches** ~ ear; **absolutes** ~ perfect pitch; ~ **finden** to gain a hearing; **jdm** ~ **schenken** to give sb a hearing.

gehorchen [gə'hɔrçən] *vi +dat* to obey.

gehören [gə'høːrən] *vi* to belong ♦ *vr unpers* to be right *od* proper; **das gehört nicht zur Sache** that's irrelevant; **dazu gehört (schon) einiges** *od* **etwas** that takes some doing (*umg*); **er gehört ins Bett** he should be in bed.

gehörig *adj* proper; ~ **zu** *od +dat* (*geh*) belonging to.

gehörlos *adj* (*form*) deaf.

gehorsam [gə'hoːrzaːm] *adj* obedient; **G**~ (-s) *m* obedience.

Gehörsinn *m* sense of hearing.

Gehsteig ['geːʃtaɪk] *m*, **Gehweg** ['geːvɛk] *m* pavement (*BRIT*), sidewalk (*US*).

Geier ['gaɪər] (-s, -) *m* vulture; **weiß der** ~! (*umg*) God knows.

geifern ['gaɪfərn] *vi* to slaver; (*fig*) to be bursting with venom.

Geige ['gaɪgə] (-, -n) *f* violin; **die erste/zweite** ~ **spielen** (*lit*) to play first/second violin; (*fig*) to call the tune/play second fiddle.

Geiger(in) (-s, -) *m(f)* violinist.

Geigerzähler *m* geiger counter.

geil [gaɪl] *adj* randy (*BRIT*), horny (*US*); (*pej*: *lüstern*) lecherous; (*umg*: *gut*) fantastic.

Geisel ['gaɪzəl] (-, -n) *f* hostage; ~**nahme** (-) *f* taking of hostages.

Geißel ['gaɪsəl] (-, -n) *f* scourge, whip.

geißeln *vt* to scourge.

Geist [gaɪst] (-(e)s, -er) *m* spirit; (*Gespenst*) ghost; (*Verstand*) mind; **von allen guten** ~**ern verlassen sein** (*umg*) to have taken leave of one's senses; **hier scheiden sich die** ~**er** this is the parting of the ways; **den** *od* **seinen** ~ **aufgeben** to give up the ghost.

Geister- *zW*: ~**fahrer** (*umg*) *m* ghost-driver (*US*), *person driving in the wrong direction*; **g**~**haft** *adj* ghostly; ~**hand** *f*: **wie von** ~**hand** as if by magic.

Geistes- *zW*: **g**~**abwesend** *adj* absent-minded; ~**akrobat** *m* mental acrobat; ~**blitz** *m* brain wave; ~**gegenwart** *f* presence of mind; **g**~**gegenwärtig** *adj* quick-witted; **g**~**gestört** *adj* mentally disturbed; (*stärker*) (mentally) deranged; ~**haltung** *f* mental attitude; **g**~**krank** *adj* mentally ill; ~**kranke(r)** *f(m)* mentally ill person; ~**krankheit** *f* mental illness; ~**störung** *f* mental disturbance; ~**verfassung** *f* frame of mind; ~**wissenschaften** *pl* arts (subjects) *pl*; ~**zustand** *m* state of mind; **jdn auf seinen** ~**zustand untersuchen** to give sb a psychiatric examination.

geistig *adj* intellectual; (*PSYCH*) mental; (*Getränke*) alcoholic; ~ **behindert** mentally handicapped; ~**-seelisch** mental and spiritual.

geistlich *adj* spiritual; (*religiös*) religious; **G**~**e(r)** *m* clergyman; **G**~**keit** *f* clergy.

geist- *zW*: ~**los** *adj* uninspired, dull; ~**reich** *adj* intelligent; (*witzig*) witty; ~**tötend** *adj* soul-destroying; ~**voll** *adj* intellectual; (*weise*) wise.

Geiz [gaɪts] (-es) *m* miserliness, meanness; **g**~**en** *vi* to be miserly; ~**hals** *m* miser.

geizig *adj* miserly, mean.

Geizkragen *m* miser.

gekannt [gə'kant] *pp von* **kennen**.

Gekicher [gə'kɪçər] (-s) *nt* giggling.

Geklapper [gə'klapər] (-s) *nt* rattling.

Geklimper [gə'klɪmpər] (-s) (*umg*) *nt* (*Klavier*~) tinkling; (: *stümperhaft*) plonking; (*von Geld*) jingling.

geklungen [gə'kluŋən] *pp von* **klingen**.

geknickt [gə'knɪkt] *adj* (*fig*) dejected.

gekniffen [gə'knɪfən] *pp von* **kneifen**.

gekommen [gə'kɔmən] *pp von* **kommen**.

gekonnt [gə'kɔnt] *pp von* **können** ♦ *adj* skilful (*BRIT*), skillful (*US*).

Gekritzel [gə'krɪtsəl] (-s) *nt* scrawl, scribble.

gekrochen [gə'krɔxən] *pp von* **kriechen**.

gekünstelt [gə'kʏnstəlt] *adj* artificial; (*Sprache, Benehmen*) affected.

Gel [geːl] (-s, -e) *nt* gel.

Gelaber(e) [gə'laːbər(ə)] (-s) (*umg*) *nt* prattle.

Gelächter [gə'lɛçtər] (-s, -) *nt* laughter; **in** ~ **ausbrechen** to burst out laughing.

gelackmeiert [gə'lakmaɪɐt] (*umg*) *adj* conned.
geladen [ge'la:dən] *pp von* **laden** ♦ *adj* loaded;
(*ELEK*) live; (*fig*) furious.
Gelage [gə'la:gə] (**-s**, **-**) *nt* feast, banquet.
gelagert [gə'la:gɐt] *adj*: **in anders/ähnlich**
~**en Fällen** in different/similar cases.
gelähmt [gə'lɛ:mt] *adj* paralysed.
Gelände [gə'lɛndə] (**-s**, **-**) *nt* land, terrain; (*von
Fabrik, Sport*~) grounds *pl*; (*Bau*~) site;
~**fahrzeug** *nt* cross-country vehicle;
g~**gängig** *adj* able to go cross-country; ~**lauf**
m cross-country race.
Geländer [gə'lɛndɐr] (**-s**, **-**) *nt* railing;
(*Treppen*~) banister(s).
gelang *etc vb siehe* **gelingen**.
gelangen [gə'laŋən] *vi*: ~ **an** +*akk od* **zu** to
reach; (*erwerben*) to attain; **in jds Besitz** *akk*
~ to come into sb's possession; **in die
richtigen/falschen Hände** ~ to fall into the
right/wrong hands.
gelangweilt *adj* bored.
gelassen [gə'lasən] *pp von* **lassen** ♦ *adj* calm;
(*gefasst*) composed; **G**~**heit** *f* calmness;
composure.
Gelatine [ʒela'ti:nə] *f* gelatine.
gelaufen [gə'laʊfən] *pp von* **laufen**.
geläufig [gə'lɔyfɪç] *adj* (*üblich*) common; **das
ist mir nicht** ~ I'm not familiar with that;
G~**keit** *f* commonness; familiarity.
gelaunt [gə'laʊnt] *adj*: **schlecht/gut** ~ in a
bad/good mood; **wie ist er** ~**?** what sort of
mood is he in?
Geläut [gə'lɔyt] (**-(e)s**) *nt* ringing; (*Läutwerk*)
chime.
Geläute (**-s**) *nt* ringing.
gelb [gɛlp] *adj* yellow; (*Ampellicht*) amber
(*BRIT*), yellow (*US*); **g**~**e Seiten** Yellow
Pages; ~**lich** *adj* yellowish.
Gelbsucht *f* jaundice.
Geld [gɛlt] (**-(e)s**, **-er**) *nt* money; **etw zu**
~ **machen** to sell sth off; **er hat** ~ **wie Heu**
(*umg*) he's stinking rich; **am** ~ **hängen** *od*
kleben to be tight with money; **staatliche/
öffentliche** ~**er** state/public funds *pl od*
money; ~**adel** *m*: **der** ~**adel** the moneyed
aristocracy; (*hum: die Reichen*) the rich;
~**anlage** *f* investment; ~**automat** *m* cash
dispenser; ~**automatenkarte** *f* cash card;
~**beutel** *m* purse; ~**börse** *f* purse; ~**einwurf**
m slot; ~**geber** (**-s**, **-**) *m* financial backer;
g~**gierig** *adj* avaricious; ~**institut** *nt* financial
institution; ~**mittel** *pl* capital *sing*, means *pl*;
~**quelle** *f* source of income; ~**schein** *m*
banknote; ~**schrank** *m* safe, strongbox;
~**strafe** *f* fine; ~**stück** *nt* coin; ~**verlegenheit**
f: **in** ~**verlegenheit sein/kommen** to be/run
short of money; ~**verleiher** *m* moneylender;
~**wäsche** *f* money-laundering; ~**wechsel** *m*
exchange (of money); „**e**~**wechsel**"
"bureau de change"; ~**wert** *m* cash value;

(*FIN*: *Kaufkraft*) currency value.
geleckt [gə'lɛkt] *adj*: **wie** ~ **aussehen** to be
neat and tidy.
Gelee [ʒe'le:] (**-s**, **-s**) *nt od m* jelly.
gelegen [gə'le:gən] *pp von* **liegen** ♦ *adj* situated;
(*passend*) convenient, opportune; **etw
kommt jdm** ~ sth is convenient for sb; **mir
ist viel/nichts daran** ~ (*wichtig*) it matters a
great deal/doesn't matter to me.
Gelegenheit [gə'le:gənhaɪt] *f* opportunity;
(*Anlass*) occasion; **bei** ~ some time (or
other); **bei jeder** ~ at every opportunity.
Gelegenheits- *zW*: ~**arbeit** *f* casual work;
~**arbeiter** *m* casual worker; ~**kauf** *m*
bargain.
gelegentlich [gə'le:gəntlɪç] *adj* occasional
♦ *adv* occasionally; (*bei Gelegenheit*) some
time (or other) ♦ *präp* +*gen* on the occasion
of.
gelehrig [gə'le:rɪç] *adj* quick to learn.
gelehrt *adj* learned; **G**~**e(r)** *f(m)* scholar;
G~**heit** *f* scholarliness.
Geleise [gə'laɪzə] (**-s**, **-**) *nt* = **Gleis**.
Geleit [gə'laɪt] (**-(e)s**, **-e**) *nt* escort; **freies** *od*
sicheres ~ safe conduct; **g**~**en** *vt* to escort;
~**schutz** *m* escort.
Gelenk [gə'lɛŋk] (**-(e)s**, **-e**) *nt* joint.
gelenkig *adj* supple.
gelernt [gə'lɛrnt] *adj* skilled.
gelesen [gə'le:zən] *pp von* **lesen**.
Geliebte *f* sweetheart; (*Liebhaberin*) mistress.
Geliebte(r) *m* sweetheart; (*Liebhaber*) lover.
geliefert [gə'li:fɐt] *adj*: **ich bin** ~ (*umg*) I've
had it.
geliehen [gə'li:ən] *pp von* **leihen**.
gelind [gə'lɪnt] *adj* = **gelinde**.
gelinde [gə'lɪndə] *adj* (*geh*) mild; ~ **gesagt** to
put it mildly.
gelingen [gə'lɪŋən] *unreg vi* to succeed; **die
Arbeit gelingt mir nicht** I'm not doing very
well with this work; **es ist mir gelungen, etw
zu tun** I succeeded in doing sth; **G**~ *nt* (*geh*:
Glück) success; (: *erfolgreiches Ergebnis*)
successful outcome.
gelitten [gə'lɪtən] *pp von* **leiden**.
gellen ['gɛlən] *vi* to shrill.
gellend *adj* shrill, piercing.
geloben [gə'lo:bən] *vt, vi* to vow, swear; **das
Gelobte Land** (*REL*) the Promised Land.
gelogen [gə'lo:gən] *pp von* **lügen**.
gelten ['gɛltən] *unreg vt* (*wert sein*) to be worth
♦ *vi* (*gültig sein*) to be valid; (*erlaubt sein*) to
be allowed ♦ *vb unpers* (*geh*): **es gilt, etw zu
tun** it is necessary to do sth; **was gilt die
Wette?** do you want a bet?; **das gilt nicht!**
that doesn't count!; (*nicht erlaubt*) that's not
allowed; **etw gilt bei jdm viel/wenig** sb
values sth highly/doesn't value sth very
highly; **jdm viel/wenig** ~ to mean a lot/not
mean much to sb; **jdm** ~ (*gemünzt sein auf*)

to be meant for *od* aimed at sb; **etw ~ lassen** to accept sth; **für diesmal lasse ichs ~** I'll let it go this time; **als** *od* **für etw ~** to be considered to be sth; **jdm** *od* **für jdn ~** (*betreffen*) to apply to sb.

geltend *adj* (*Preise*) current; (*Gesetz*) in force; (*Meinung*) prevailing; **etw ~ machen** to assert sth; **sich ~ machen** to make itself/o.s. felt; **einen Einwand ~ machen** to raise an objection.

Geltung ['gɛltʊŋ] *f*: **~ haben** to have validity; **sich/etw** *dat* **~ verschaffen** to establish o.s./ sth; **etw zur ~ bringen** to show sth to its best advantage; **zur ~ kommen** to be seen/ heard *etc* to its best advantage.

Geltungsbedürfnis *nt* desire for admiration.

geltungssüchtig *adj* craving admiration.

Gelübde [gə'lypdə] (**-s, -**) *nt* vow.

gelungen [gə'lʊŋən] *pp von* **gelingen** ♦ *adj* successful.

Gem. *abk* = **Gemeinde.**

gemächlich [gə'mɛːçlɪç] *adj* leisurely.

gemacht [gə'maːxt] *adj* (*gewollt, gekünstelt*) false, contrived; **ein ~er Mann sein** to be made.

Gemahl [gə'maːl] (**-(e)s, -e**) *m* (*geh, form*) spouse, husband.

gemahlen [gə'maːlən] *pp von* **mahlen.**

Gemahlin *f* (*geh, form*) spouse, wife.

Gemälde [gə'mɛːldə] (**-s, -**) *nt* picture, painting.

gemasert [gə'maːzərt] *adj* (*Holz*) grained.

gemäß [gə'mɛːs] *präp +dat* in accordance with ♦ *adj +dat* appropriate to.

gemäßigt *adj* moderate; (*Klima*) temperate.

Gemauschel [gə'maʊʃəl] (**-s**) (*umg*) *nt* scheming.

Gemecker [gə'mɛkər] (**-s**) *nt* (*von Ziegen*) bleating; (*umg: Nörgelei*) moaning.

gemein [gə'maɪn] *adj* common; (*niederträchtig*) mean; **etw ~ haben (mit)** to have sth in common (with).

Gemeinde [gə'maɪndə] (**-, -n**) *f* district; (*Bewohner*) community; (*Pfarr~*) parish; (*Kirchen~*) congregation; **~abgaben** *pl* rates and local taxes *pl*; **~ordnung** *f* by(e) laws *pl*, ordinances *pl* (*US*); **~rat** *m* district council; (*Mitglied*) district councillor; **~schwester** *f* district nurse (*BRIT*); **~steuer** *f* local rates *pl*; **~verwaltung** *f* local administration; **~vorstand** *m* local council; **~wahl** *f* local election.

Gemein- *zW*: **~eigentum** *nt* common property; **g~gefährlich** *adj* dangerous to the public; **~gut** *nt* public property; **~heit** *f* (*Niedertracht*) meanness; **das war eine ~heit** that was a mean thing to do/to say; **g~hin** *adv* generally; **~kosten** *pl* overheads *pl*; **~nutz** *m* public good; **g~nützig** *adj* of benefit to the public; (*wohltätig*) charitable; **~platz** *m* commonplace, platitude; **g~sam** *adj* joint, common (*auch MATH*) ♦ *adv* together; **g~same Sache mit jdm machen** to be in cahoots with sb; **der ~same Markt** the Common Market; **g~sames Konto** joint account; **etw g~sam haben** to have sth in common; **~samkeit** *f* common ground; **~schaft** *f* community; **in ~schaft mit** jointly *od* together with; **eheliche ~schaft** (*JUR*) matrimony; **~schaft Unabhängiger Staaten** Commonwealth of Independent States; **g~schaftlich** *adj* = **gemeinsam**; **~schaftsantenne** *f* party aerial (*BRIT*) *od* antenna (*US*); **~schaftsarbeit** *f* teamwork; **~schaftsbesitz** *m* collective ownership; **~schaftserziehung** *f* coeducation; **~schaftskunde** *f* social studies *pl*; **~schaftsraum** *m* common room; **~sinn** *m* public spirit; **g~verständlich** *adj* generally comprehensible; **~wesen** *nt* community; **~wohl** *nt* common good.

Gemenge [gə'mɛŋə] (**-s, -**) *nt* mixture; (*Hand~*) scuffle.

gemessen [gə'mɛsən] *pp von* **messen** ♦ *adj* measured.

Gemetzel [gə'mɛtsəl] (**-s, -**) *nt* slaughter, carnage.

gemieden [gə'miːdən] *pp von* **meiden.**

Gemisch [gə'mɪʃ] (**-es, -e**) *nt* mixture.

gemischt *adj* mixed.

gemocht [gə'mɔxt] *pp von* **mögen.**

gemolken [gə'mɔlkən] *pp von* **melken.**

Gemse △ ['gɛmzə] (**-, -n**) *f siehe* **Gämse.**

Gemunkel [gə'mʊŋkəl] (**-s**) *nt* gossip.

Gemurmel [gə'mʊrməl] (**-s**) *nt* murmur(ing).

Gemüse [gə'myːzə] (**-s, -**) *nt* vegetables *pl*; **~garten** *m* vegetable garden; **~händler** *m* greengrocer (*BRIT*), vegetable dealer (*US*); **~platte** *f* (*KOCH*): **eine ~platte** assorted vegetables.

gemusst ▲ [gə'mʊst] *pp von* **müssen.**

gemustert [gə'mʊstərt] *adj* patterned.

Gemüt [gə'myːt] (**-(e)s, -er**) *nt* disposition, nature; (*fig: Mensch*) person; **sich** *dat* **etw zu ~e führen** (*umg*) to indulge in sth; **die ~er erregen** to arouse strong feelings; **wir müssen warten, bis sich die ~er beruhigt haben** we must wait until feelings have cooled down.

gemütlich *adj* comfortable, cosy; (*Person*) good-natured; **wir verbrachten einen ~en Abend** we spent a very pleasant evening; **G~keit** *f* comfortableness, cosiness, amiability.

Gemüts- *zW*: **~bewegung** *f* emotion; **g~krank** *adj* emotionally disturbed; **~mensch** *m* sentimental person; **~ruhe** *f* composure; **in aller ~ruhe** (*umg*) (as) cool as a cucumber; (*gemächlich*) at a leisurely pace; **~zustand** *m* state of mind.

gemütvoll *adj* warm, tender.

Gen [geːn] (**-s, -e**) *nt* gene.

Gen. *abk* = **Genossenschaft**; (= *Genitiv*) gen.

gen. *abk* (= *genannt*) named, called.

genannt [gə'nant] *pp von* **nennen.**

genas *etc* [gə'naːs] *vb siehe* **genesen.**

genau [gə'nau] *adj* exact, precise ♦ *adv* exactly, precisely; **etw** ~ **nehmen** to take sth seriously; ~ **genommen** strictly speaking; **G~eres** further details *pl*; **etw** ~ **wissen** to know sth for certain; ~ **auf die Minute, auf die Minute** ~ exactly on time.

Genauigkeit *f* exactness, accuracy.

genauso [gə'nauzoː] *adv* (*vor Adjektiv*) just as; (*allein stehend*) just *od* exactly the same.

genehm [gə'neːm] *adj* agreeable, acceptable.

genehmigen *vt* to approve, authorize; **sich** *dat* **etw** ~ to indulge in sth.

Genehmigung *f* approval, authorization.

geneigt [gə'naikt] *adj* (*geh*) well-disposed, willing; ~ **sein, etw zu tun** to be inclined to do sth.

Genera *pl von* **Genus.**

General [gene'raːl] (**-s, -e** *od* **-̈e**) *m* general; ~**direktor** *m* chairman (*BRIT*), president (*US*); ~**konsulat** *nt* consulate general; ~**probe** *f* dress rehearsal; ~**sekretär** *m* secretary-general; ~**stabskarte** *f* ordnance survey map; ~**streik** *m* general strike; **g~überholen** *vt* to overhaul thoroughly; ~**vertretung** *f* sole agency.

Generation [generatsi'oːn] *f* generation.

Generationskonflikt *m* generation gap.

Generator [gene'raːtɔr] *m* generator, dynamo.

generell [genə'rɛl] *adj* general.

genesen [ge'neːzən] *unreg vi* (*geh*) to convalesce, recover.

Genesende(r) *f(m)* convalescent.

Genesung *f* recovery, convalescence.

Genetik [ge'neːtɪk] *f* genetics.

genetisch [ge'neːtɪʃ] *adj* genetic.

Genf ['gɛnf] (**-s**) *nt* Geneva.

Genfer *adj attrib*: **der** ~ **See** Lake Geneva; **die** ~ **Konvention** the Geneva Convention.

genial [geni'aːl] *adj* brilliant.

Genialität [geniali'tɛːt] *f* brilliance, genius.

Genick [gə'nɪk] (**-(e)s, -e**) *nt* (back of the) neck; **jdm/etw das** ~ **brechen** (*fig*) to finish sb/sth; ~**starre** *f* stiff neck.

Genie [ʒe'niː] (**-s, -s**) *nt* genius.

genieren [ʒe'niːrən] *vr* to be embarrassed ♦ *vt* to bother; **geniert es Sie, wenn ...?** do you mind if ...?

genießbar *adj* edible; (*trinkbar*) drinkable.

genießen [gə'niːsən] *unreg vt* to enjoy; (*essen*) to eat; (*trinken*) to drink; **er ist heute nicht zu** ~ (*umg*) he is unbearable today.

Genießer(in) (**-s, -**) *m(f)* connoisseur; (*des Lebens*) pleasure-lover; **g~isch** *adj* appreciative ♦ *adv* with relish.

Genitalien [geni'taːliən] *pl* genitals *pl*.

Genitiv ['geːnitiːf] *m* genitive.

Genmais *m* GM maize.

genmanipuliert *adj* genetically modified.

genommen [gə'nɔmən] *pp von* **nehmen.**

genoss *etc*▲ [gə'nɔs] *vb siehe* **genießen.**

Genosse [gə'nɔsə] (**-n, -n**) *m* comrade (*bes POL*), companion.

genossen *pp von* **genießen.**

Genossenschaft *f* cooperative (association).

Genossin [gə'nɔsɪn] *f* comrade (*bes POL*), companion.

genötigt [gə'nøːtɪçt] *adj*: **sich** ~ **sehen, etw zu tun** to feel obliged to do sth.

Genre [ʒãːrə] (**-s, -s**) *nt* genre.

Gent [gɛnt] (**-s**) *nt* Ghent.

Gentechnik *f*, **Gentechnologie** *f* gene technology.

Genua ['geːnua] (**-s**) *nt* Genoa.

genug [gə'nuːk] *adv* enough; **jetzt ist(s) aber** ~**!** that's enough!

Genüge [gə'nyːgə] *f*: **jdm/etw** ~ **tun** *od* **leisten** to satisfy sb/sth; **etw zur** ~ **kennen** to know sth well enough; (*abwertender*) to know sth only too well.

genügen *vi* to be enough; (*den Anforderungen etc*) to satisfy; **jdm** ~ to be enough for sb.

genügend *adj* enough, sufficient; (*befriedigend*) satisfactory.

genügsam [gə'nyːkzaːm] *adj* modest, easily satisfied; **G~keit** *f* moderation.

Genugtuung [gə'nuːktuːʊŋ] *f* satisfaction.

Genus ['geːnʊs] (**-, Genera**) *nt* (*GRAM*) gender.

Genuss▲ [gə'nʊs] (**-es, -̈e**) *m* pleasure; (*Zusichnehmen*) consumption; **etw mit** ~ **essen** to eat sth with relish; **in den** ~ **von etw kommen** to receive the benefit of sth.

genüsslich▲ [gə'nʏslɪç] *adv* with relish.

Genussmittel▲ *pl* (semi-)luxury items *pl*.

geöffnet [gə'œfnət] *adj* open.

Geograf▲ [geo'graːf] (**-en, -en**) *m* geographer.

Geografie▲ [geogra'fiː] *f* geography.

Geografin▲ *f* geographer.

geografisch▲ *adj* geographical.

Geologe [geo'loːgə] (**-n, -n**) *m* geologist.

Geologie [geolo'giː] *f* geology.

Geologin *f* geologist.

Geometrie [geome'triː] *f* geometry.

geordnet [gə'ɔrdnət] *adj*: **in** ~**en Verhältnissen leben** to live a well-ordered life.

Georgien [ge'ɔrgiən] (**-s**) *nt* Georgia.

Gepäck [gə'pɛk] (**-(e)s**) *nt* luggage, baggage; **mit leichtem** ~ **reisen** to travel light; ~**abfertigung** *f* luggage desk/office; ~**annahme** *f* (*Bahnhof*) baggage office; (*Flughafen*) baggage check-in; ~**aufbewahrung** *f* left-luggage office (*BRIT*), baggage check (*US*); ~**ausgabe** *f* (*Bahnhof*) baggage office; (*Flughafen*) baggage reclaim; ~**netz** *nt* luggage rack; ~**schein** *m* luggage *od* baggage ticket; ~**stück** *nt* piece of baggage; ~**träger** *m* porter; (*Fahrrad*) carrier; ~**wagen** *m* luggage van (*BRIT*), baggage car (*US*).

Gepard ['geːpart] (**-(e)s, -e**) *m* cheetah.

gepfeffert [gə'pfɛfərt] (*umg*) *adj* (*Preise*) steep; (*Fragen, Prüfung*) tough; (*Kritik*) biting.

gepfiffen [gə'pfɪfən] *pp von* **pfeifen**.

gepflegt [gə'pfleːkt] *adj* well-groomed; (*Park etc*) well looked after; (*Atmosphäre*) sophisticated; (*Ausdrucksweise, Sprache*) cultured.

Gepflogenheit [gə'pfloːgənhaɪt] *f* (*geh*) custom.

Geplapper [gə'plapər] (**-s**) *nt* chatter.

Geplauder [gə'plaʊdər] (**-s**) *nt* chat(ting).

Gepolter [gə'pɔltər] (**-s**) *nt* din.

gepr. *abk* (= *geprüft*) tested.

gepriesen [gə'priːzən] *pp von* **preisen**.

gequält [gə'kvɛːlt] *adj* (*Lächeln*) forced; (*Miene, Ausdruck*) pained; (*Gesang, Stimme*) strained.

Gequatsche [gə'kvatʃə] (**-s**) (*pej: umg*) *nt* gabbing; (*Blödsinn*) twaddle.

gequollen [gə'kvɔlən] *pp von* **quellen**.

Gerade [gə'raːdə] (**-n, -n**) *f* straight line.

═══════════════════ *SCHLÜSSELWORT*

gerade [gə'raːdə] *adj* straight; (*aufrecht*) upright; **eine ~ Zahl** an even number.
♦ *adv* **1** (*genau*) just, exactly; (*speziell*) especially; ~ **deshalb** that's just *od* exactly why; **das ist es ja ~!** that's just it; ~ **du** you especially; **warum ~ ich?** why me (of all people)?; **jetzt ~ nicht!** not now!; ~ **neben** right next to; **nicht ~ schön** not exactly beautiful; ~ **biegen** to straighten out; ~ **stehen** (*aufrecht*) to stand up straight.
2 (*eben, soeben*) just; **er wollte ~ aufstehen** he was just about to get up; **da wir ~ von Geld sprechen** ... talking of money ...; ~ **erst** only just; ~ **noch** (only) just.

gerade- *zW:* ~**aus** *adv* straight ahead; ~**biegen** *unreg vt* (*fig*) to straighten out; ~**heraus** *adv* straight out, bluntly.

gerädert [gə'rɛːdərt] *adj:* **wie ~ sein, sich wie ~ fühlen** to be *od* feel (absolutely) whacked (*umg*).

geradeso *adv* just so; ~ **dumm** *etc* just as stupid *etc*; ~ **wie** just as.

geradestehen *unreg vi:* **für jdn/etw ~** (*fig*) to answer *od* be answerable for sb/sth.

geradezu *adv* (*beinahe*) virtually, almost.

geradlinig *adj* straight.

gerammelt [gə'raməlt] *adv:* ~ **voll** (*umg*) (jam-)packed.

Geranie [gɛ'raːniə] *f* geranium.

gerannt [gə'rant] *pp von* **rennen**.

Gerät [gə'rɛːt] (**-(e)s, -e**) *nt* device; (*Apparat*) gadget; (*elektrisches ~*) appliance;

(*Werkzeug*) tool; (*SPORT*) apparatus; (*Zubehör*) equipment *no pl*.

gerät [gə'rɛːt] *vb siehe* **geraten**.

geraten [gə'raːtən] *unreg pp von* **raten, geraten**
♦ *vi* (*gedeihen*) to thrive; (*gelingen*): (**jdm**) ~ to turn out well (for sb); (*zufällig gelangen*): ~ **in** +*akk* to get into; **gut/schlecht** ~ to turn out well/badly; **an jdn** ~ to come across sb; **an den Richtigen/Falschen** ~ to come to the right/wrong person; **in Angst** ~ to get frightened; **nach jdm** ~ to take after sb.

Geräteturnen *nt* apparatus gymnastics.

Geratewohl [gəraːtə'voːl] *nt:* **aufs ~** on the off chance; (*bei Wahl*) at random.

geraum [gə'raʊm] *adj:* **seit ~er Zeit** for some considerable time.

geräumig [gə'rɔymɪç] *adj* roomy.

Geräusch [gə'rɔyʃ] (**-(e)s, -e**) *nt* sound; (*unangenehm*) noise; **g~arm** *adj* quiet; ~**kulisse** *f* background noise; (*FILM, RUNDF, TV*) sound effects *pl*; **g~los** *adj* silent; ~**pegel** *m* sound level; **g~voll** *adj* noisy.

gerben ['gɛrbən] *vt* to tan.

Gerber (**-s, -**) *m* tanner.

Gerberei [gɛrbə'raɪ] *f* tannery.

gerecht [gə'rɛçt] *adj* just, fair; **jdm/etw ~ werden** to do justice to sb/sth; ~**fertigt** *adj* justified.

Gerechtigkeit *f* justice, fairness.

Gerechtigkeits- *zW:* ~**fanatiker** *m* justice fanatic; ~**gefühl** *nt* sense of justice; ~**sinn** *m* sense of justice.

Gerede [gə'reːdə] (**-s**) *nt* talk; (*Klatsch*) gossip.

geregelt [gə'reːgəlt] *adj* (*Arbeit, Mahlzeiten*) regular; (*Leben*) well-ordered.

gereizt [gə'raɪtst] *adj* irritable; **G~heit** *f* irritation.

Gericht [gə'rɪçt] (**-(e)s, -e**) *nt* court; (*Essen*) dish; **jdn/einen Fall vor ~ bringen** to take sb/a case to court; **mit jdm ins ~ gehen** (*fig*) to judge sb harshly; **über jdn zu ~ sitzen** to sit in judgement on sb; **das Jüngste ~** the Last Judgement; **g~lich** *adj* judicial, legal
♦ *adv* judicially, legally; **ein g~liches Nachspiel haben** to finish up in court; **g~lich gegen jdn vorgehen** to take legal proceedings against sb.

Gerichts- *zW:* ~**akten** *pl* court records *pl*; ~**barkeit** *f* jurisdiction; ~**hof** *m* court (of law); ~**kosten** *pl* (legal) costs *pl*; **g~medizinisch** *adj* forensic medical *attrib*; ~**saal** *m* courtroom; ~**stand** *m* court of jurisdiction; ~**verfahren** *nt* legal proceedings *pl*; ~**verhandlung** *f* court proceedings *pl*; ~**vollzieher** *m* bailiff.

gerieben [gə'riːbən] *pp von* **reiben** ♦ *adj* grated; (*umg: schlau*) smart, wily.

geriet *etc* [gə'riːt] *vb siehe* **geraten**.

gering [gə'rɪŋ] *adj* slight, small; (*niedrig*) low; (*Zeit*) short ♦ *adv:* ~ **achten** to think little of;

~**fügig** adj slight, trivial; ~ **Beschäftigte** ≈ part-time workers pl; ~**schätzig** adj disparaging; **G**~**schätzung** f disdain.
geringste(r, s) adj slightest, least; **nicht im G**~**n** not in the least od slightest.
gerinnen [gə'rɪnən] unreg vi to congeal; (Blut) to clot; (Milch) to curdle.
Gerinnsel [gə'rɪnzəl] (-s, -) nt clot.
Gerippe [gə'rɪpə] (-s, -) nt skeleton.
gerissen [gə'rɪsən] pp von **reißen** ♦ adj wily, smart.
geritten [gə'rɪtən] pp von **reiten**.
geritzt [gə'rɪtst] (umg) adj: **die Sache ist** ~ everything's fixed up od settled.
Germanist(in) [gɛrma'nɪst(ɪn)] m(f) Germanist, German specialist; (Student) German student.
Germanistik f German (studies pl).
gern [gɛrn] adv willingly, gladly; **(aber)** ~! of course!; ~ **haben,** ~ **mögen** to like; **etw** ~ **tun** to like doing sth; ~ **geschehen!** you're welcome!, not at all!; **ein** ~ **gesehener Gast** a welcome visitor; **ich hätte** od **möchte** ~ ... I would like ...; **du kannst mich mal** ~ **haben!** (umg) (you can) go to hell!
gerne ['gɛrnə] adv = **gern**.
Gernegroß (-, -e) m show-off.
gerochen [gə'rɔxən] pp von **riechen**.
Geröll [gə'rœl] (-(e)s, -e) nt scree.
geronnen [gə'rɔnən] pp von **rinnen, gerinnen**.
Gerste ['gɛrstə] (-, -n) f barley.
Gerstenkorn nt (im Auge) stye.
Gerte ['gɛrtə] (-, -n) f switch, rod.
gertenschlank adj willowy.
Geruch [gə'rʊx] (-(e)s, ̈e) m smell, odour (BRIT), odor (US); **g**~**los** adj odourless (BRIT), odorless (US).
Geruchssinn m sense of smell.
Gerücht [gə'rʏçt] (-(e)s, -e) nt rumour (BRIT), rumor (US).
geruchtilgend adj deodorant.
gerufen [gə'ru:fən] pp von **rufen**.
geruhen [gə'ru:ən] vi to deign.
geruhsam [gə'ru:za:m] adj peaceful; (Spaziergang etc) leisurely.
Gerümpel [gə'rʏmpəl] (-s) nt junk.
gerungen [gə'rʊŋən] pp von **ringen**.
Gerüst [gə'rʏst] (-(e)s, -e) nt (Bau~) scaffold(ing); (fig) framework.
Ges. abk (= Gesellschaft) Co., co.
gesalzen [gə'zaltsən] pp von **salzen** ♦ adj (fig: umg: Preis, Rechnung) steep, stiff.
gesamt [gə'zamt] adj whole, entire; (Kosten) total; (Werke) complete; **im G**~**en** all in all; **G**~**auflage** f gross circulation; **G**~**ausgabe** f complete edition; **G**~**betrag** m total (amount); ~**deutsch** adj all-German; **G**~**eindruck** m general impression; **G**~**heit** f totality, whole.

Gesamthochschule f polytechnic (BRIT).

Gesamt- zW: ~**masse** f (COMM) total assets pl; ~**nachfrage** f (COMM) composite demand; ~**schaden** m total damage.
Gesamtschule f ≈ comprehensive school.

Gesamtwertung f (SPORT) overall placings pl.
gesandt pp von **senden**.
Gesandte(r) [gə'zantə(r)] f(m) envoy.
Gesandtschaft [gə'zantʃaft] f legation.
Gesang [gə'zaŋ] (-(e)s, ̈e) m song; (Singen) singing; ~**buch** nt (REL) hymn book.
Gesäß [gə'zɛːs] (-es, -e) nt seat, bottom.
gesättigt [gə'zɛtɪçt] adj (CHEM) saturated.
gesch. abk (= geschieden) div.
Geschädigte(r) [gə'ʃɛːdɪçtə(r)] f(m) victim.
geschaffen [gə'ʃafən] pp von **schaffen**.
Geschäft [gə'ʃɛft] (-(e)s, -e) nt business; (Laden) shop; (~sabschluss) deal; **mit jdm ins** ~ **kommen** to do business with sb; **dabei hat er ein** ~ **gemacht** he made a profit by it; **im** ~ at work; (im Laden) in the shop; **sein** ~ **verrichten** to do one's business (euph).
Geschäftemacher m wheeler-dealer.
geschäftig adj active, busy; (pej) officious.
geschäftlich adj commercial ♦ adv on business; ~ **unterwegs** away on business.
Geschäfts- zW: ~**abschluss**▲ m business deal od transaction; ~**aufgabe** f closure of a/the business; ~**auflösung** f closure of a/the business; ~**bedingungen** pl terms of business; ~**bereich** m (PARL) responsibilities pl; **Minister ohne** ~**bereich** minister without portfolio; ~**bericht** m financial report;

~**computer** *m* business computer; ~**essen** *nt* business lunch; ~**führer** *m* manager; (*Klub*) secretary; ~**geheimnis** *nt* trade secret; ~**inhaber** *m* owner; ~**jahr** *nt* financial year; ~**lage** *f* business conditions *pl*; ~**leitung** *f* management; ~**mann** (-(e)s, *pl* -leute) *m* businessman; **g**~**mäßig** *adj* businesslike; ~**ordnung** *f* standing orders *pl*; **eine Frage zur** ~**ordnung** a question on a point of order; ~**partner** *m* partner; ~**reise** *f* business trip; ~**schluss**▲ *m* closing time; ~**sinn** *m* business sense; ~**stelle** *f* office(s *pl*), place of business; **g**~**tüchtig** *adj* business-minded; ~**viertel** *nt* shopping centre (*BRIT*) *od* center (*US*); (*Banken etc*) business quarter, commercial district; ~**wagen** *m* company car; ~**wesen** *nt* business; ~**zeit** *f* business hours *pl*; ~**zweig** *m* branch (of a business).
geschah *etc* [gə'ʃaː] *vb siehe* **geschehen**.
geschehen [gə'ʃeːən] *unreg vi* to happen; **das geschieht ihm (ganz) recht** it serves him (jolly well (*umg*)) right; **was soll mit ihm/damit** ~**?** what is to be done with him/it?; **es war um ihn** ~ that was the end of him.
gescheit [gə'ʃait] *adj* clever; (*vernünftig*) sensible.
Geschenk [gə'ʃɛŋk] (-(e)s, -e) *nt* present, gift; ~**artikel** *m* gift; ~**gutschein** *m* gift voucher; ~**packung** *f* gift pack; ~**sendung** *f* gift parcel.
Geschichte [gə'ʃɪçtə] (-, -n) *f* story; (*Sache*) affair; (*Historie*) history.
Geschichtenerzähler *m* storyteller.
geschichtlich *adj* historical; (*bedeutungsvoll*) historic.
Geschichtsfälschung *f* falsification of history.
Geschichtsschreiber *m* historian.
Geschick [gə'ʃɪk] (-(e)s, -e) *nt* skill; (*geh*: *Schicksal*) fate.
Geschicklichkeit *f* skill, dexterity.
Geschicklichkeitsspiel *nt* game of skill.
geschickt *adj* skilful (*BRIT*), skillful (*US*); (*taktisch*) clever; (*beweglich*) agile.
geschieden [gə'ʃiːdən] *pp von* **scheiden** ♦ *adj* divorced.
geschieht [gə'ʃiːt] *vb siehe* **geschehen**.
geschienen [gə'ʃiːnən] *pp von* **scheinen**.
Geschirr [gə'ʃɪr] (-(e)s, -e) *nt* crockery; (*Küchen*~) pots and pans *pl*; (*Pferde*~) harness; ~**spülmaschine** *f* dishwasher; ~**tuch** *nt* tea towel (*BRIT*), dishtowel (*US*).
geschissen [gə'ʃɪsən] *pp von* **scheißen**.
geschlafen [gə'ʃlaːfən] *pp von* **schlafen**.
geschlagen [gə'ʃlaːgən] *pp von* **schlagen**.
geschlaucht [gə'ʃlauxt] *adv*: ~ **sein** (*umg*) to be exhausted *od* knackered.
Geschlecht [gə'ʃlɛçt] (-(e)s, -er) *nt* sex; (*GRAM*) gender; (*Gattung*) race; (*Abstammung*) lineage; **g**~**lich** *adj* sexual.

Geschlechts- *zW*: ~**krankheit** *f* sexually-transmitted disease; **g**~**reif** *adj* sexually mature; **g**~**spezifisch** *adj* (*SOZIOLOGIE*) sex-specific; ~**teil** *nt od m* genitals *pl*; ~**verkehr** *m* sexual intercourse; ~**wort** *nt* (*GRAM*) article.
geschlichen [gə'ʃlɪçən] *pp von* **schleichen**.
geschliffen [gə'ʃlɪfən] *pp von* **schleifen**.
geschlossen [gə'ʃlɔsən] *pp von* **schließen** ♦ *adj*: ~**e Gesellschaft** (*Fest*) private party ♦ *adv*: ~ **hinter jdm stehen** to stand solidly behind sb; ~**e Ortschaft** built-up area.
geschlungen [gə'ʃlʊŋən] *pp von* **schlingen**.
Geschmack [gə'ʃmak] (-(e)s, ⁻e) *m* taste; **nach jds** ~ to sb's taste; ~ **an etw** *dat* **finden** to (come to) like sth; **je nach** ~ to one's own taste; **er hat einen guten** ~ (*fig*) he has good taste; **g**~**los** *adj* tasteless; (*fig*) in bad taste.
Geschmacks- *zW*: ~**sache** *f* matter of taste; ~**sinn** *m* sense of taste; ~**verirrung** *f*: **unter** ~**verirrung leiden** (*ironisch*) to have no taste.
geschmackvoll *adj* tasteful.
Geschmeide [gə'ʃmaidə] (-s, -) *nt* jewellery (*BRIT*), jewelry (*US*).
geschmeidig *adj* supple; (*formbar*) malleable.
Geschmeiß *nt* vermin *pl*.
Geschmiere [gə'ʃmiːrə] (-s) *nt* scrawl; (*Bild*) daub.
geschmissen [gə'ʃmɪsən] *pp von* **schmeißen**.
geschmolzen [gə'ʃmɔltsən] *pp von* **schmelzen**.
Geschnetzelte(s) [gə'ʃnɛtsəltə(s)] *nt* (*KOCH*) *meat cut into strips and stewed to produce a thick sauce.*
geschnitten [gə'ʃnɪtən] *pp von* **schneiden**.
geschoben [gə'ʃoːbən] *pp von* **schieben**.
geschollen [gə'ʃɔlən] *pp von* **schallen**.
gescholten [gə'ʃɔltən] *pp von* **schelten**.
Geschöpf [gə'ʃœpf] (-(e)s, -e) *nt* creature.
geschoren▲ [gə'ʃoːrən] *pp von* **scheren**.
Geschoss▲ [gə'ʃɔs] (-es, -e) *nt*, **Geschoß** [gə'ʃoːs] (-sses, -sse) (*ÖSTERR*) *nt* (*MIL*) projectile; (*Rakete*) missile; (*Stockwerk*) floor.
geschossen [gə'ʃɔsən] *pp von* **schießen**.
geschraubt [gə'ʃraupt] *adj* stilted, artificial.
Geschrei [gə'ʃrai] (-s) *nt* cries *pl*, shouting; (*fig*: *Aufheben*) noise, fuss.
geschrieben [gə'ʃriːbən] *pp von* **schreiben**.
geschrie(e)n [gə'ʃriː(ə)n] *pp von* **schreien**.
geschritten [gə'ʃrɪtən] *pp von* **schreiten**.
geschunden [gə'ʃʊndən] *pp von* **schinden**.
Geschütz [gə'ʃyts] (-es, -e) *nt* gun, piece of artillery; **ein schweres** ~ **auffahren** (*fig*) to bring out the big guns; ~**feuer** *nt* artillery fire, gunfire.
geschützt *adj* protected; (*Winkel, Ecke*) sheltered.
Geschw. *abk* = **Geschwister**.
Geschwader [gə'ʃvaːdər] (-s, -) *nt* (*NAUT*) squadron; (*AVIAT*) group.

Geschwafel [gə'ʃvaːfəl] **(-s)** *nt* silly talk.
Geschwätz [gə'ʃvɛts] **(-es)** *nt* chatter; (*Klatsch*) gossip.
geschwätzig *adj* talkative; **G~keit** *f* talkativeness.
geschweige [gə'ʃvaɪgə] *adv:* ~ **(denn)** let alone, not to mention.
geschwiegen [gə'ʃviːgən] *pp von* **schweigen**.
geschwind [gə'ʃvɪnt] *adj* quick, swift.
Geschwindigkeit [gə'ʃvɪndɪçkaɪt] *f* speed, velocity.
Geschwindigkeits- *zW:* **~begrenzung** *f*, **~beschränkung** *f* speed limit; **~messer** *m* (*AUT*) speedometer; **~überschreitung** *f* speeding.
Geschwister [gə'ʃvɪstər] *pl* brothers and sisters *pl*.
geschwollen [gə'ʃvɔlən] *pp von* **schwellen** ♦ *adj* pompous.
geschwommen [gə'ʃvɔmən] *pp von* **schwimmen**.
geschworen [gə'ʃvoːrən] *pp von* **schwören**.
Geschworene(r) *f(m)* juror; **die Geschworenen** *pl* the jury.
Geschwulst [gə'ʃvʊlst] **(-, ̈-e)** *f* growth, tumour.
geschwunden [gə'ʃvʊndən] *pp von* **schwinden**.
geschwungen [gə'ʃvʊŋən] *pp von* **schwingen** ♦ *adj* curved.
Geschwür [gə'ʃvyːr] **(-(e)s, -e)** *nt* ulcer; (*Furunkel*) boil.
gesehen [gə'zeːən] *pp von* **sehen**.
Geselle [gə'zɛlə] **(-n, -n)** *m* fellow; (*Handwerks~*) journeyman.
gesellen *vr:* **sich zu jdm** ~ to join sb.
Gesellenbrief *m* articles *pl*.
Gesellenprüfung *f* examination to become a journeyman.
gesellig *adj* sociable; **~es Beisammensein** get-together; **G~keit** *f* sociability.
Gesellschaft *f* society; (*Begleitung, COMM*) company; (*Abend~ etc*) party; (*pej*) crowd (*umg*); (*Kreis von Menschen*) group of people; **in schlechte** ~ **geraten** to get into bad company; **geschlossene** ~ private party; **jdm** ~ **leisten** to keep sb company.
Gesellschafter(in) **(-s, -)** *m(f)* shareholder; (*Partner*) partner.
gesellschaftlich *adj* social.
Gesellschafts- *zW:* **~anzug** *m* evening dress; **g~fähig** *adj* socially acceptable; **~ordnung** *f* social structure; **~reise** *f* group tour; **~schicht** *f* social stratum; **~system** *nt* social system.
gesessen [gə'zɛsən] *pp von* **sitzen**.
Gesetz [gə'zɛts] **(-es, -e)** *nt* law; (*PARL*) act; (*Satzung, Regel*) rule; **vor dem** ~ in (the eyes of the) law; **nach dem** ~ under the law; **das oberste** ~ **(der Wirtschaft** *etc*) the golden rule (of industry *etc*); **~blatt** *nt* law gazette;

~buch *nt* statute book; **~entwurf** *m* bill.
Gesetzeshüter *m* (*ironisch*) guardian of the law.
Gesetzesvorlage *f* bill.
Gesetz- *zW:* **g~gebend** *adj* legislative; **~geber** **(-s, -)** *m* legislator; **~gebung** *f* legislation; **g~lich** *adj* legal, lawful; **~lichkeit** *f* legality, lawfulness; **g~los** *adj* lawless; **g~mäßig** *adj* lawful.
gesetzt *adj* (*Mensch*) sedate ♦ *konj:* ~ **den Fall** ... assuming (that) ...
gesetzwidrig *adj* illegal; (*unrechtmäßig*) unlawful.
ges. gesch. *abk* (= *gesetzlich geschützt*) reg.
Gesicht [gə'zɪçt] **(-(e)s, -er)** *nt* face; **das zweite** ~ second sight; **das ist mir nie zu** ~ **gekommen** I've never laid eyes on that; **jdn zu** ~ **bekommen** to clap eyes on sb; **jdm etw ins** ~ **sagen** to tell sb sth to his face; **sein wahres** ~ **zeigen** to show (o.s. in) one's true colours; **jdm wie aus dem** ~ **geschnitten sein** to be the spitting image of sb.
Gesichts- *zW:* **~ausdruck** *m* (facial) expression; **~farbe** *f* complexion; **~packung** *f* face pack; **~punkt** *m* point of view; **~wasser** *nt* face lotion; **~züge** *pl* features *pl*.
Gesindel [gə'zɪndəl] **(-s)** *nt* rabble.
gesinnt [gə'zɪnt] *adj* disposed, minded.
Gesinnung [gə'zɪnʊŋ] *f* disposition; (*Ansicht*) views *pl*.
Gesinnungs- *zW:* **~genosse** *m* like-minded person; **~losigkeit** *f* lack of conviction; **~schnüffelei** (*pej*) *f:* **~schnüffelei betreiben** to pry into people's political convictions; **~wandel** *m* change of opinion.
gesittet [gə'zɪtət] *adj* well-mannered.
gesoffen [gə'zɔfən] *pp von* **saufen**.
gesogen [gə'zoːgən] *pp von* **saugen**.
gesollt [gə'zɔlt] *pp von* **sollen**.
gesondert [gə'zɔndərt] *adj* separate.
gesonnen [gə'zɔnən] *pp von* **sinnen**.
gespalten [gə'ʃpaltən] *adj* (*Bewusstsein*) split; (*Lippe*) cleft.
Gespann [gə'ʃpan] **(-(e)s, -e)** *nt* team; (*umg*) couple.
gespannt *adj* tense, strained; (*neugierig*) curious; (*begierig*) eager; **ich bin** ~, **ob I** wonder if *od* whether; **auf etw/jdn** ~ **sein** to look forward to sth/to meeting sb; **ich bin** ~ **wie ein Flitzebogen** (*hum: umg*) I'm on tenterhooks.
Gespenst [gə'ʃpɛnst] **(-(e)s, -er)** *nt* ghost; (*fig: Gefahr*) spectre (*BRIT*), specter (*US*); **~er sehen** (*fig: umg*) to imagine things.
gespensterhaft, gespenstisch *adj* ghostly.
gespie(e)n [gə'ʃpiː(ə)n] *pp von* **speien**.
gespielt [gə'ʃpiːlt] *adj* feigned.
gesponnen [gə'ʃpɔnən] *pp von* **spinnen**.
Gespött [gə'ʃpœt] **(-(e)s)** *nt* mockery; **zum**

~ werden to become a laughing stock.

Gespräch [gə'ʃprɛːç] **(-(e)s, -e)** *nt* conversation; (*Diskussion*) discussion; (*Anruf*) call; **zum ~ werden** to become a topic of conversation; **ein ~ unter vier Augen** a confidential *od* private talk; **mit jdm ins ~ kommen** to get into conversation with sb; (*fig*) to establish a dialogue with sb.

gesprächig *adj* talkative; **G~keit** *f* talkativeness.

Gesprächs- *zW*: **~einheit** *f* (*TEL*) unit; **~gegenstand** *m* topic; **~partner** *m*: **mein ~partner bei den Verhandlungen** my opposite number at the talks; **~stoff** *m* topics *pl*; **~thema** *nt* subject *od* topic (of conversation).

gesprochen [gə'ʃprɔxən] *pp von* **sprechen**.

gesprossen [gə'ʃprɔsən] *pp von* **sprießen**.

gesprungen [gə'ʃpruŋən] *pp von* **springen**.

Gespür [gə'ʃpyːr] **(-s)** *nt* feeling.

gest. *abk* (= *gestorben*) dec.

Gestalt [gə'ʃtalt] **(-, -en)** *f* form, shape; (*Person*) figure; (*LITER: pej: Mensch*) character; **in ~ von** in the form of; **~ annehmen** to take shape.

gestalten *vt* (*formen*) to shape, form; (*organisieren*) to arrange, organize ♦ *vr*: **sich ~ (zu)** to turn out (to be); **etw interessanter** *etc* **~** to make sth more interesting *etc*.

Gestaltung *f* formation; organization.

gestanden [gəʃtandən] *pp von* **stehen, gestehen**.

geständig [gə'ʃtɛndiç] *adj*: **~ sein** to have confessed.

Geständnis [gə'ʃtɛntnɪs] **(-ses, -se)** *nt* confession.

Gestank [gə'ʃtaŋk] **(-(e)s)** *m* stench.

gestatten [gə'ʃtatən] *vt* to permit, allow; **~ Sie?** may I?; **sich** *dat* **~, etw zu tun** to take the liberty of doing sth.

Geste ['gɛstə] **(-, -n)** *f* gesture.

Gesteck [gə'ʃtɛk] **(-(e)s, -e)** *nt* flower arrangement.

gestehen [gə'ʃteːən] *unreg vt* to confess; **offen gestanden** quite frankly.

Gestein [gə'ʃtain] **(-(e)s, -e)** *nt* rock.

Gestell [gə'ʃtɛl] **(-(e)s, -e)** *nt* stand; (*Regal*) shelf; (*Bett~, Brillen~*) frame.

gestellt *adj* (*unecht*) posed.

gestern ['gɛstərn] *adv* yesterday; **~ Abend/ Morgen** yesterday evening/morning; **er ist nicht von ~** (*umg*) he wasn't born yesterday.

gestiefelt [gə'ʃtiːfəlt] *adj*: **der G~e Kater** Puss-in-Boots.

gestiegen [gə'ʃtiːgən] *pp von* **steigen**.

Gestik **(-)** *f* gestures *pl*.

gestikulieren [gɛstiku'liːrən] *vi* to gesticulate.

Gestirn [gə'ʃtɪrn] **(-(e)s, -e)** *nt* star.

gestoben [gə'ʃtoːbən] *pp von* **stieben**.

Gestöber [gə'ʃtøːbər] **(-s, -)** *nt* flurry; (*länger*) blizzard.

gestochen [gə'ʃtɔxən] *pp von* **stechen** ♦ *adj* (*Handschrift*) clear, neat.

gestohlen [gə'ʃtoːlən] *pp von* **stehlen** ♦ *adj*: **der/das kann mir ~ bleiben** (*umg*) he/it can go hang.

gestorben [gə'ʃtɔrbən] *pp von* **sterben**.

gestört [gə'ʃtøːrt] *adj* disturbed; (*Rundfunkempfang*) poor, with a lot of interference.

gestoßen [gə'ʃtoːsən] *pp von* **stoßen**.

Gestotter [gə'ʃtɔtər] **(-s)** *nt* stuttering, stammering.

Gesträuch [gə'ʃtrɔyç] **(-(e)s, -e)** *nt* shrubbery, bushes *pl*.

gestreift [gə'ʃtraift] *adj* striped.

gestrichen [gə'ʃtriçən] *pp von* **streichen** ♦ *adj*: **~ voll** (*genau voll*) level; (*sehr voll*) full to the brim; **ein ~er Teelöffel voll** a level teaspoon(ful).

gestrig ['gɛstriç] *adj* yesterday's.

gestritten [gə'ʃtritən] *pp von* **streiten**.

Gestrüpp [gə'ʃtryp] **(-(e)s, -e)** *nt* undergrowth.

gestunken [gə'ʃtuŋkən] *pp von* **stinken**.

Gestüt [gə'ʃtyːt] **(-(e)s, -e)** *nt* stud farm.

Gesuch [gə'zuːx] **(-(e)s, -e)** *nt* petition; (*Antrag*) application.

gesucht *adj* (*begehrt*) sought after.

gesund [gə'zunt] *adj* healthy; **wieder ~ werden** to get better; **~ und munter** hale and hearty; **G~heit** *f* health; (*Sportlichkeit, fig*) healthiness; **G~heit!** bless you!; **bei guter G~heit** in good health; **~heitlich** *adj* health *attrib*, physical ♦ *adv* physically; **wie geht es Ihnen ~heitlich?** how's your health?

Gesundheits- *zW*: **~amt** *nt* public health department; **~apostel** *m* (*ironisch*) health freak (*umg*); **~farm** *f* health farm; **~fürsorge** *f* health care; **~reform** *f* health service reforms *pl*; **~risiko** *nt* health hazard; **g~schädlich** *adj* unhealthy; **~wesen** *nt* health service; **~zeugnis** *nt* health certificate; **~zustand** *m* state of health.

gesundschreiben▲ *unreg vt*: **jdn ~** to certify sb (as) fit.

gesungen [gə'zuŋən] *pp von* **singen**.

gesunken [gə'zuŋkən] *pp von* **sinken**.

getan [gə'taːn] *pp von* **tun** ♦ *adj*: **nach ~er Arbeit** when the day's work is done.

Getier [gə'tiːər] **(-(e)s, -e)** *nt* (*Tiere, bes Insekten*) creatures *pl*; (*einzelnes*) creature.

Getöse [gə'tøːzə] **(-s)** *nt* din, racket.

getragen [gə'traːgən] *pp von* **tragen**.

Getränk [gə'trɛŋk] **(-(e)s, -e)** *nt* drink.

Getränkeautomat *m* drinks machine *od* dispenser.

Getränkekarte *f* (*in Café*) list of beverages; (*in Restaurant*) wine list.

getrauen [gə'trauən] *vr* to dare.

Getreide [gə'traɪdə] (-s, -) nt cereal, grain; ~**speicher** m granary.

getrennt [gə'trɛnt] adj separate; ~ **leben** to be separated, live apart.

getreten [gə'tre:tən] pp von **treten**.

getreu [gə'trɔy] adj faithful.

Getriebe [gə'tri:bə] (-s, -) nt (Leute) bustle; (AUT) gearbox.

getrieben pp von **treiben**.

Getriebeöl nt transmission oil.

getroffen [gə'trɔfən] pp von **treffen**.

getrogen [gə'tro:gən] pp von **trügen**.

getrost [gə'tro:st] adv confidently; ~ **sterben** to die in peace; **du kannst dich ~ auf ihn verlassen** you need have no fears about relying on him.

getrunken [gə'truŋkən] pp von **trinken**.

Getto ['gɛto] (-s, -s) nt ghetto.

Getue [gə'tu:ə] (-s) nt fuss.

Getümmel [gə'tʏml] (-s) nt turmoil.

geübt [gə'y:pt] adj experienced.

GEW (-) f abk (= Gewerkschaft Erziehung und Wissenschaft) union of employees in education and science.

Gew. abk = **Gewerkschaft**.

Gewächs [gə'vɛks] (-es, -e) nt growth; (Pflanze) plant.

gewachsen [gə'vaksən] pp von **wachsen ♦** adj: **jdm/etw ~ sein** to be sb's equal/equal to sth.

Gewächshaus nt greenhouse.

gewagt [gə'va:kt] adj daring, risky.

gewählt [gə'vɛ:lt] adj (Sprache) refined, elegant.

gewahr [gə'va:r] adj: **eine od einer Sache** gen ~ **werden** to become aware of sth.

Gewähr [gə'vɛ:r] (-) f guarantee; **keine ~ übernehmen für** to accept no responsibility for; **die Angabe erfolgt ohne ~** this information is supplied without liability.

gewähren vt to grant; (geben) to provide; **jdn ~ lassen** not to stop sb.

gewährleisten vt to guarantee.

Gewahrsam [gə'va:rza:m] (-s, -e) m safekeeping; (Polizei~) custody.

Gewährsmann m informant, source.

Gewährung f granting.

Gewalt [gə'valt] (-, -en) f power; (große Kraft) force; (~taten) violence; **mit aller ~** with all one's might; **die ausübende/ gesetzgebende/richterliche ~** the executive/legislature/judiciary; **elterliche ~** parental authority; **höhere ~** acts/an act of God; ~**anwendung** f use of force.

Gewaltenteilung f separation of powers.

Gewaltherrschaft f tyranny.

gewaltig adj tremendous; (Irrtum) huge; **sich ~ irren** to be very much mistaken.

Gewalt- zW: **g~los** adj non-violent ♦ adv without force/violence; ~**marsch** m forced march; ~**monopol** nt monopoly on the use of force; **g~sam** adj forcible; **g~tätig** adj violent; ~**verbrechen** nt crime of violence; ~**verzicht** m non-aggression.

Gewand [gə'vant] (-(e)s, ̈er) nt garment.

gewandt [gə'vant] pp von **wenden ♦** adj deft, skilful (BRIT), skillful (US); (erfahren) experienced; **G~heit** f dexterity, skill.

gewann etc [gə'van] vb siehe **gewinnen**.

gewaschen [gə'vaʃən] pp von **waschen**.

Gewässer [gə'vɛsər] (-s, -) nt waters pl.

Gewebe [gə've:bə] (-s, -) nt (Stoff) fabric; (BIOL) tissue.

Gewehr [gə've:r] (-(e)s, -e) nt (Flinte) rifle; (Schrotbüchse) shotgun; ~**lauf** m rifle barrel; barrel of a shotgun.

Geweih [gə'vaɪ] (-(e)s, -e) nt antlers pl.

Gewerbe [gə'vɛrbə] (-s, -) nt trade, occupation; **Handel und ~** trade and industry; ~ **treibend** carrying on a trade; **fahrendes ~** mobile trade; ~**aufsichtsamt** nt ≈ factory inspectorate; ~**schein** m trading licence; ~**schule** f technical school.

gewerblich adj industrial.

gewerbsmäßig adj professional.

Gewerbszweig m line of trade.

Gewerkschaft [gə'vɛrkʃaft] f trade od labor (US) union.

Gewerkschaft(l)er(in) m(f) trade od labor (US) unionist.

gewerkschaftlich adj: **wir haben uns ~ organisiert** we organized ourselves into a union.

Gewerkschaftsbund m federation of trade od labor (US) unions, ≈ Trades Union Congress (BRIT), Federation of Labor (US).

gewesen [gə've:zən] pp von **sein**.

gewichen [gə'vɪçən] pp von **weichen**.

Gewicht [gə'vɪçt] (-(e)s, -e) nt weight; (fig) importance.

gewichten vt to evaluate.

Gewichtheben (-s) nt (SPORT) weight-lifting.

gewichtig adj weighty.

Gewichtsklasse f (SPORT) weight (category).

gewieft [gə'vi:ft] (umg) adj shrewd, cunning.

gewiesen [gə'vi:zən] pp von **weisen**.

gewillt [gə'vɪlt] adj willing, prepared.

Gewimmel [gə'vɪml] (-s) nt swarm; (Menge) crush.

Gewinde [gə'vɪndə] (-s, -) nt (Kranz) wreath; (von Schraube) thread.

Gewinn [gə'vɪn] (-(e)s, -e) m profit; (bei Spiel) winnings pl; ~ **bringend** profitable; **etw mit ~ verkaufen** to sell sth at a profit; **aus etw ~ schlagen** (umg) to make a profit out of sth; ~**anteil** m (COMM) dividend; ~**ausschüttung** f prize draw; ~**beteiligung** f profit-sharing; **g~bringend** adj profitable;

~**chancen** *pl* (*beim Wetten*) odds *pl*.

gewinnen *unreg vt* to win; (*erwerben*) to gain; (*Kohle, Öl*) to extract ♦ *vi* to win; (*profitieren*) to gain; **jdn (für etw)** ~ to win sb over (to sth); **an etw** *dat* ~ to gain in sth.

gewinnend *adj* winning, attractive.

Gewinner(in) (-s, -) *m(f)* winner.

Gewinn- *zW*: ~**nummer**▲ *f* winning number; ~**spanne** *f* profit margin; ~**sucht** *f* love of gain; ~**- und Verlustrechnung** *f* profit and loss account.

Gewinnung *f* (*von Kohle etc*) mining; (*von Zucker etc*) extraction.

Gewinnwarnung *f* (*COMM*) profit warning.

Gewirr [gə'vɪr] (-(e)s, -e) *nt* tangle; (*von Straßen*) maze.

gewiss▲ [gə'vɪs] *adj* certain ♦ *adv* certainly; **in gewissem Maße** to a certain extent.

Gewissen [gə'vɪsən] (-s, -) *nt* conscience; **jdm ins** ~ **reden** to have a serious talk with sb; **g~haft** *adj* conscientious; ~**haftigkeit** *f* conscientiousness; **g~los** *adj* unscrupulous.

Gewissens- *zW*: ~**bisse** *pl* pangs of conscience *pl*, qualms *pl*; ~**frage** *f* matter of conscience; ~**freiheit** *f* freedom of conscience; ~**konflikt** *m* moral conflict.

gewissermaßen [gəvɪsər'ma:sən] *adv* more or less, in a way.

Gewissheit▲ *f* certainty; **sich** *dat* ~ **verschaffen** to find out for certain.

gewisslich▲ *adv* surely.

Gewitter [gə'vɪtər] (-s, -) *nt* thunderstorm.

gewittern *vi unpers*: **es gewittert** there's a thunderstorm.

gewitterschwül *adj* sultry and thundery.

Gewitterwolke *f* thundercloud; (*fig: umg*) storm cloud.

gewitzt [gə'vɪtst] *adj* shrewd, cunning.

gewoben [gə'vo:bən] *pp von* **weben**.

gewogen [gə'vo:gən] *pp von* **wiegen** ♦ *adj* (+*dat*) well-disposed (towards).

gewöhnen [gə'vø:nən] *vt*: **jdn an etw** *akk* ~ to accustom sb to sth; (*erziehen zu*) to teach sb sth ♦ *vr*: **sich an etw** *akk* ~ to get used *od* accustomed to sth.

Gewohnheit [gə'vo:nhaɪt] *f* habit; (*Brauch*) custom; **aus** ~ from habit; **zur** ~ **werden** to become a habit; **sich** *dat* **etw zur** ~ **machen** to make a habit of sth.

Gewohnheits- *in zW* habitual; ~**mensch** *m* creature of habit; ~**recht** *nt* common law; ~**tier** (*umg*) *nt* creature of habit.

gewöhnlich [gə'vø:nlɪç] *adj* usual; (*durchschnittlich*) ordinary; (*pej*) common; **wie** ~ as usual.

gewohnt [gə'vo:nt] *adj* usual; **etw** ~ **sein** to be used to sth.

Gewöhnung *f*: ~ **(an** +*akk*) getting accustomed (to); (*das Angewöhnen*) training (in).

Gewölbe [gə'vœlbə] (-s, -) *nt* vault.

gewollt [gə'vɔlt] *pp von* **wollen** ♦ *adj* forced, artificial.

gewonnen [gə'vɔnən] *pp von* **gewinnen**.

geworben [gə'vɔrbən] *pp von* **werben**.

geworden [gə'vɔrdən] *pp von* **werden**.

geworfen [gə'vɔrfən] *pp von* **werfen**.

gewrungen [gə'vrʊŋən] *pp von* **wringen**.

Gewühl [gə'vy:l] (-(e)s) *nt* throng.

gewunden [gə'vʊndən] *pp von* **winden**.

gewunken [gə'vʊŋkən] *pp von* **winken**.

Gewürz [gə'vʏrts] (-es, -e) *nt* spice; (*Pfeffer, Salz*) seasoning; ~**gurke** *f* pickled gherkin; ~**nelke** *f* clove.

gewusst▲ [gə'vʊst] *pp von* **wissen**.

gez. *abk* (= *gezeichnet*) signed.

gezackt [gə'tsakt] *adj* (*Fels*) jagged; (*Blatt*) serrated.

gezähnt [gə'tsɛ:nt] *adj* serrated, toothed.

gezeichnet [gə'tsaɪçnət] *adj* marked.

Gezeiten [gə'tsaɪtən] *pl* tides *pl*.

Gezeter [gə'tse:tər] (-s) *nt* nagging.

gezielt [gə'tsi:lt] *adj* (*Frage, Maßnahme*) specific; (*Hilfe*) well-directed; (*Kritik*) pointed.

geziemen [gə'tsi:mən] *vr unpers* to be fitting.

geziemend *adj* proper.

geziert [gə'tsi:rt] *adj* affected; **G~heit** *f* affectation.

gezogen [gə'tso:gən] *pp von* **ziehen**.

Gezwitscher [gə'tsvɪtʃər] (-s) *nt* twitter(ing), chirping.

gezwungen [gə'tsvʊŋən] *pp von* **zwingen** ♦ *adj* forced; (*Atmosphäre*) strained.

gezwungenermaßen *adv* of necessity; **etw** ~ **tun** to be forced to do sth, do sth of necessity.

GG *abk* = **Grundgesetz**.

ggf. *abk* = **gegebenenfalls**.

Ghetto ['gɛto] (-s, -s) *nt* ghetto.

Ghettoblaster ['gɛtobla:stər] (-s, -s) *m* ghettoblaster.

Gibraltar [gi'braltar] (-s) *nt* Gibraltar.

gibst [gi:pst] *vb siehe* **geben**.

gibt *vb siehe* **geben**.

Gicht [gɪçt] (-) *f* gout; **g~isch** *adj* gouty.

Giebel ['gi:bəl] (-s, -) *m* gable; ~**dach** *nt* gable(d) roof; ~**fenster** *nt* gable window.

Gier [gi:r] (-) *f* greed.

gierig *adj* greedy.

Gießbach *m* torrent.

gießen [gi:sən] *unreg vt* to pour; (*Blumen*) to water; (*Metall*) to cast; (*Wachs*) to mould ♦ *vi unpers*: **es gießt in Strömen** it's pouring down.

Gießerei [gi:sə'raɪ] *f* foundry.

Gießkanne *f* watering can.

Gift [gɪft] (-(e)s, -e) *nt* poison; **das ist** ~ **für ihn** (*umg*) that is very bad for him; **darauf kannst du** ~ **nehmen** (*umg*) you can bet your life on it; **g~grün** adj bilious green.

giftig adj poisonous; (fig: boshaft) venomous.

Gift- zW: **~müll** m toxic waste; **~pilz** m poisonous toadstool; **~stoff** m toxic substance; **~wolke** f poisonous cloud; **~zahn** m fang; **~zwerg** (umg) m spiteful little devil.

Gigabyte ['gɪgabaɪt] nt (COMPUT) gigabyte.

Gilde ['gɪldə] (-, -n) f guild.

gilt [gɪlt] vb siehe **gelten**.

ging etc [gɪŋ] vb siehe **gehen**.

Ginseng ['gɪnzɛŋ] (-s, -s) m ginseng.

Ginster ['gɪnstər] (-s, -) m broom.

Gipfel ['gɪpfəl] (-s, -) m summit, peak; (fig) height; **das ist der ~**! (umg) that's the limit!; **~konferenz** f (POL) summit conference.

gipfeln vi to culminate.

Gipfeltreffen nt summit (meeting).

Gips [gɪps] (-es, -e) m plaster; (MED) plaster (of Paris); **~abdruck** m plaster cast; **~bein** (umg) nt leg in plaster; **g~en** vt to plaster; **~figur** f plaster figure; **~verband** m plaster (cast).

Giraffe [gi'rafə] (-, -n) f giraffe.

Girlande [gɪr'landə] (-, -n) f garland.

Giro ['ʒiːro] (-s, -s) nt giro; **~konto** nt current account (BRIT), checking account (US).

girren ['gɪrən] vi to coo.

Gis [gɪs] (-, -) nt (MUS) G sharp.

Gischt [gɪʃt] (-(e)s, -e) m od f spray, foam.

Gitarre [gi'tarə] (-, -n) f guitar.

Gitter ['gɪtər] (-s, -) nt grating, bars pl; (für Pflanzen) trellis; (Zaun) railing(s); **~bett** nt cot (BRIT), crib (US); **~fenster** nt barred window; **~zaun** m railing(s).

Glacéhandschuh, Glaceehandschuh▲ [gla'seːhantʃuː] m kid glove.

Gladiole [gladi'oːlə] (-, -n) f gladiolus.

Glanz [glants] (-es) m shine, lustre (BRIT), luster (US); (fig) splendour (BRIT), splendor (US); **~abzug** m (PHOT) glossy od gloss print.

glänzen ['glɛntsən] vi to shine (also fig), gleam.

glänzend adj shining; (fig) brilliant; **wir haben uns ~ amüsiert** we had a marvellous od great time.

Glanz- zW: **~lack** m gloss (paint); **~leistung** f brilliant achievement; **g~los** adj dull; **~stück** nt pièce de résistance; **~zeit** f heyday.

Glas [glaːs] (-es, ̈-er) nt glass; (Brillen~) lens sing; **zwei ~ Wein** two glasses of wine; **~bläser** m glass blower; **~er** (-s, -) m glazier; **~faser** f fibreglass (BRIT), fiberglass (US); **~faserkabel** nt optical fibre (BRIT) od fiber (US) cable.

Glasgow ['glaːsgoʊ] nt Glasgow.

glasieren [gla'ziːrən] vt to glaze.

glasig adj glassy; (Zwiebeln) transparent.

glasklar adj crystal clear.

Glasscheibe f pane.

Glasur [gla'zuːr] f glaze; (KOCH) icing,

frosting (bes US).

glatt [glat] adj smooth; (rutschig) slippery; (Absage) flat; (Lüge) downright; (Haar) straight; (MED: Bruch) clean; (pej: allzu gewandt) smooth, slick ♦ adv: **~ gehen** to go smoothly; **~ rasiert** (Mann, Kinn) clean-shaven; **~ streichen** to smooth out.

Glätte ['glɛtə] (-, -n) f smoothness; slipperiness.

Glatteis nt (black) ice; **„Vorsicht ~!"** "danger, black ice!"; **jdn aufs ~ führen** (fig) to take sb for a ride.

glätten vt to smooth out.

Glatze ['glatsə] (-, -n) f bald head; **eine ~ bekommen** to go bald.

glatzköpfig adj bald.

Glaube ['glaubə] (-ns, -n) m: **~ (an +akk)** faith (in); (Überzeugung) belief (in); **den ~n an jdn/etw verlieren** to lose faith in sb/sth.

glauben vt, vi to believe; (meinen) to think; **jdm ~** to believe sb; **~ an +akk** to believe in; **jdm (etw) aufs Wort ~** to take sb's word (for sth); **wers glaubt, wird selig** (ironisch) a likely story.

Glaubens- zW: **~bekenntnis** nt creed; **~freiheit** f religious freedom; **~gemeinschaft** f religious sect; (christliche) denomination.

glaubhaft ['glaubhaft] adj credible; **jdm etw ~ machen** to satisfy sb of sth.

Glaubhaftigkeit f credibility.

gläubig ['glɔʏbɪç] adj (REL) devout; (vertrauensvoll) trustful; **G~e(r)** f(m) believer; **die Gläubigen** pl the faithful.

Gläubiger(in) (-s, -) m(f) creditor.

glaubwürdig ['glaubvyrdɪç] adj credible; (Mensch) trustworthy; **G~keit** f credibility; trustworthiness.

gleich [glaɪç] adj equal; (identisch) (the) same, identical ♦ adv equally; (sofort) straight away; (bald) in a minute; (räumlich): **~ hinter dem Haus** just behind the house; (zeitlich): **~ am Anfang** at the very beginning; **es ist mir ~** it's all the same to me; **zu ~en Teilen** in equal parts; **das ~e, aber nicht dasselbe Auto** a similar car, but not the same one; **ganz ~ wer/was** etc no matter who/what etc; **2 mal 2 ~ 4** 2 times 2 is od equals 4; **bis ~!** see you soon!; **wie war doch ~ Ihr Name?** what was your name again?; **es ist ~ drei Uhr** it's very nearly three o'clock; **~ bleibend** constant; **bei ~ bleibendem Gehalt** when one's salary stays the same; **~ gesinnt** like-minded; **~ lautend** identical; **sie sind ~ groß** they are the same size; **~ nach/an** right after/at; **~altrig** adj of the same age; **~artig** adj similar; **~bedeutend** adj synonymous; **~berechtigt** adj with equal rights; **G~berechtigung** f equal rights pl.

gleichen unreg vi: **jdm/etw ~** to be like sb/sth

♦ *vr* to be alike.
gleichermaßen *adv* equally.
gleich- *zW*: ~**falls** *adv* likewise; **danke** ~**falls!** the same to you; **G**~**förmigkeit** *f* uniformity; ~**gestellt** *adj*: **rechtlich** ~**gestellt** equal in law; **G**~**gewicht** *nt* equilibrium, balance; **jdm aus dem G**~**gewicht bringen** to throw sb off balance; ~**gültig** *adj* indifferent; (*unbedeutend*) unimportant; **G**~**gültigkeit** *f* indifference; **G**~**heit** *f* equality; (*Identität*) identity; (*INDUSTRIE*) parity; **G**~**heitsprinzip** *nt* principle of equality; **G**~**heitszeichen** *nt* (*MATH*) equals sign; ~**kommen** *unreg vi +dat* to be equal to; **G**~**macherei** *f* egalitarianism, levelling down (*pej*); ~**mäßig** *adj* even, equal; **G**~**mut** *m* equanimity.
Gleichnis (-ses, -se) *nt* parable.
gleich- *zW*: ~**rangig** *adj* (*Probleme etc*) equally important; ~**rangig** (**mit**) (*Beamte etc*) equal in rank (to), at the same level (as); ~**sam** *adv* as it were; ~**schalten** (*pej*) *vt* to bring into line; **G**~**schritt** *m*: **im G**~**schritt, marsch!** forward march!; ~**sehen** *unreg vi*: **jdm** ~**sehen** to be *od* look like sb; ~**stellen** *vt* (*rechtlich etc*) to treat as equal; **G**~**strom** *m* (*ELEK*) direct current; ~**tun** *unreg vi*: **es jdm** ~**tun** to match sb.
Gleichung *f* equation.
gleich- *zW*: ~**viel** *adv* no matter; ~**wertig** *adj* of the same value; (*Leistung, Qualität*) equal; (*Gegner*) evenly matched; ~**wohl** *adv* (*geh*) nevertheless; ~**zeitig** *adj* simultaneous.
Gleis [glaɪs] (-es, -e) *nt* track, rails *pl*; (*am Bahnhof*) platform (*BRIT*), track (*US*).
gleißend ['glaɪsənt] *adj* glistening, gleaming.
gleiten *unreg vi* to glide; (*rutschen*) to slide.
gleitend ['glaɪtənt] *adj*: ~**e Arbeitszeit** flexible working hours *pl*, flex(i)time.
Gleit- *zW*: ~**flug** *m* glide; ~**klausel** *f* (*COMM*) escalator clause; ~**komma** *nt* floating point; ~**zeit** *f* flex(i)time.
Gletscher ['glɛtʃər] (-s, -) *m* glacier; ~**spalte** *f* crevasse.
glich *etc* [glɪç] *vb siehe* **gleichen**.
Glied [gliːt] (-(e)s, -er) *nt* member; (*Arm, Bein*) limb; (*Penis*) penis; (*von Kette*) link; (*MIL*) rank(s); **der Schreck steckt ihr noch in den** ~**ern** she is still shaking with the shock.
gliedern *vt* to organize, structure.
Gliederreißen *nt* rheumatic pains *pl*.
Gliederschmerz *m* rheumatic pains *pl*.
Gliederung *f* structure, organization.
Gliedmaßen *pl* limbs *pl*.
glimmen ['glɪmən] *unreg vi* to glow.
Glimmer (-s, -) *m* (*MINERAL*) mica.
Glimmstengel (*umg*) *m* fag (*BRIT*), butt (*US*).
glimpflich ['glɪmpflɪç] *adj* mild, lenient; ~ **davonkommen** to get off lightly.
glitschig ['glɪtʃɪç] (*umg*) *adj* slippery, slippy.
glitt *etc* [glɪt] *vb siehe* **gleiten**.

glitzern ['glɪtsərn] *vi* to glitter; (*Stern*) to twinkle.
global [glo'baːl] *adj* (*weltweit*) global, worldwide; (*ungefähr, pauschal*) general.
Globus ['gloːbʊs] (- *od* -ses, **Globen** *od* -se) *m* globe.
Glöckchen ['glœkçən] *nt* (little) bell.
Glocke ['glɔkə] (-, -n) *f* bell; **etw an die große** ~ **hängen** (*fig*) to shout sth from the rooftops.
Glocken- *zW*: ~**geläut** *nt* peal of bells; ~**schlag** *m* stroke (of the bell); (*von Uhr*) chime; ~**spiel** *nt* chime(s); (*MUS*) glockenspiel; ~**turm** *m* belfry, bell-tower.
glomm *etc* [glɔm] *vb siehe* **glimmen**.
Glorie ['gloːriə] *f* glory; (*von Heiligen*) halo.
glorreich ['gloːrraɪç] *adj* glorious.
Glossar [glɔ'saːr] (-s, -e) *nt* glossary.
Glosse ['glɔsə] (-, -n) *f* comment.
Glotze (-, -n) (*umg*) *f* gogglebox (*BRIT*), TV set.
glotzen ['glɔtsən] (*umg*) *vi* to stare.
Glück [glʏk] (-(e)s) *nt* luck, fortune; (*Freude*) happiness; ~ **haben** to be lucky; **viel** ~ good luck; **zum** ~ fortunately; **ein** ~! how lucky!, what a stroke of luck!; **auf gut** ~ (*aufs Geratewohl*) on the off-chance; (*unvorbereitet*) trusting to luck; (*wahllos*) at random; **sie weiß noch nichts von ihrem** ~ (*ironisch*) she doesn't know anything about it yet; **er kann von** ~ **sagen, dass ...** he can count himself lucky that ...; ~**auf** *nt*: „~**auf"** (*Bergleute*) (cry of) "good luck".
Glucke (-, -n) *f* (*Bruthenne*) broody hen; (*mit Jungen*) mother hen.
glücken *vi* to succeed; **es glückte ihm, es zu bekommen** he succeeded in getting it.
gluckern ['glʊkərn] *vi* to glug.
glücklich *adj* fortunate; (*froh*) happy ♦ *adv* happily; (*umg*: *endlich, zu guter Letzt*) finally, eventually.
glücklicherweise *adv* fortunately.
glücklos *adj* luckless.
Glücksbringer (-s, -) *m* lucky charm.
glückselig [glʏk'zeːlɪç] *adj* blissful.
Glücks- *zW*: ~**fall** *m* stroke of luck; ~**kind** *nt* lucky person; ~**pilz** *m* lucky beggar (*umg*); ~**sache** *f* matter of luck; ~**spiel** *nt* game of chance; ~**stern** *m* lucky star; ~**strähne** *f* lucky streak.
glückstrahlend *adj* radiant (with happiness).
Glückszahl *f* lucky number.
Glückwunsch *m*: ~ **(zu)** congratulations *pl* (on), best wishes *pl* (on).
Glühbirne *f* light bulb.
glühen ['glyːən] *vi* to glow.
glühend *adj* glowing; (*heiß* ~: *Metall*) red-hot; (*Hitze*) blazing; (*fig*: *leidenschaftlich*) ardent; (: *Hass*) burning; (*Wangen*) flushed, burning.
Glüh- *zW*: ~**faden** *m* (*ELEK*) filament; ~**wein** *m*

mulled wine; ~**würmchen** *nt* glow-worm.

Glut [gluːt] (-, -en) *f* (*Röte*) glow; (*Feuers*~) fire; (*Hitze*) heat; (*fig*) ardour (*BRIT*), ardor (*US*).

GmbH (-, -s) *f abk* (= *Gesellschaft mit beschränkter Haftung*) ≈ Ltd. (*BRIT*), plc (*BRIT*), Inc. (*US*).

Gnade ['gnaːdə] (-, -n) *f* (*Gunst*) favour (*BRIT*), favor (*US*); (*Erbarmen*) mercy; (*Milde*) clemency; ~ **vor Recht ergehen lassen** to temper justice with mercy.

gnaden *vi*: (**dann**) **gnade dir Gott!** (then) God help you *od* heaven have mercy on you!

Gnaden- *zW*: ~**brot** *nt*: **jdm/einem Tier das** ~**brot geben** to keep sb/an animal in his/her/its old age; ~**frist** *f* reprieve; ~**gesuch** *nt* petition for clemency; **g**~**los** *adj* merciless; ~**stoß** *m* coup de grâce.

gnädig ['gnɛːdɪç] *adj* gracious; (*voll Erbarmen*) merciful; ~**e Frau** (*form*) madam, ma'am.

Gockel ['gɔkəl] (-s, -) *m* (*bes SÜDD*) cock.

Gold [gɔlt] (-(e)s) *nt* gold; **nicht mit** ~ **zu bezahlen** *od* **aufzuwiegen sein** to be worth one's weight in gold; **g**~**en** *adj* golden; **g**~**ene Worte** words of wisdom; **der Tanz ums** ~**ene Kalb** (*fig*) the worship of Mammon; ~**fisch** *m* goldfish; ~**grube** *f* gold mine; ~**hamster** *m* (golden) hamster.

goldig ['gɔldɪç] *adj* (*fig: umg*) sweet, cute.

Gold- *zW*: ~**regen** *m* laburnum; (*fig*) riches *pl*; **g**~**richtig** (*umg*) *adj* dead right; ~**schmied** *m* goldsmith; ~**schnitt** *m* gilt edging; ~**standard** *m* gold standard; ~**stück** *nt* piece of gold; (*fig: umg*) treasure; ~**waage** *f*: **jedes Wort auf die** ~**waage legen** (*fig*) to weigh one's words; ~**währung** *f* gold standard.

Golf[1] [gɔlf] (-(e)s, -e) *m* gulf; **der (Persische)** ~ the Gulf.

Golf[2] [gɔlf] (-s) *nt* golf; ~**platz** *m* golf course; ~**schläger** *m* golf club; ~**spieler** *m* golfer.

Golfstaaten *pl*: **die** ~ the Gulf States *pl*.

Golfstrom *m* (*GEOG*) Gulf Stream.

Gondel ['gɔndəl] (-, -n) *f* gondola; (*von Seilbahn*) cable car.

gondeln (*umg*) *vi*: **durch die Welt** ~ to go globetrotting.

Gong [gɔŋ] (-s, -s) *m* gong; (*bei Boxkampf etc*) bell.

gönnen ['gœnən] *vt*: **jdm etw** ~ not to begrudge sb sth; **sich** *dat* **etw** ~ to allow o.s. sth.

Gönner (-s, -) *m* patron; **g**~**haft** *adj* patronizing; ~**in** *f* patroness; ~**miene** *f* patronizing air.

gor *etc* [goːr] *vb siehe* **gären**.

Gorilla [go'rɪla] (-s, -s) *m* gorilla; (*umg: Leibwächter*) heavy.

goss *etc*▲ [gɔs] *vb siehe* **gießen**.

Gosse ['gɔsə] (-, -n) *f* gutter.

Gote ['goːtə] (-n, -n) *m* Goth.

Gotik ['goːtɪk] *f* (*KUNST*) Gothic (style); (*Epoche*) Gothic period.

Gotin ['goːtɪn] *f* Goth.

Gott [gɔt] (-es, ¨er) *m* god; (*als Name*) God; **um** ~**es Willen!** for heaven's sake!; ~ **sei Dank!** thank God!; **grüß** ~! (*bes SÜDD, ÖSTERR*) hello, good morning/afternoon/evening; **den lieben** ~ **einen guten Mann sein lassen** (*umg*) to take things as they come; **ein Bild für die Götter** (*hum: umg*) a sight for sore eyes; **das wissen die Götter** (*umg*) God (only) knows; **über** ~ **und die Welt reden** (*fig*) to talk about everything under the sun; **wie** ~ **in Frankreich leben** (*umg*) to be in clover.

Götterspeise *f* (*KOCH*) jelly (*BRIT*), jello (*US*).

Gottes- *zW*: ~**dienst** *m* service; **g**~**fürchtig** *adj* god-fearing; ~**haus** *nt* place of worship; ~**krieger(in)** *m(f)* religious terrorist; ~**lästerung** *f* blasphemy.

Gottheit *f* deity.

Göttin ['gœtɪn] *f* goddess.

göttlich *adj* divine.

Gott- *zW*: **g**~**lob** *interj* thank heavens!; **g**~**los** *adj* godless; **g**~**verdammt** *adj* goddamn(ed); **g**~**verlassen** *adj* godforsaken; ~**vertrauen** *nt* trust in God.

Götze ['gœtsə] (-n, -n) *m* idol.

Grab [graːp] (-(e)s, ¨er) *nt* grave.

grabbeln ['grabəln] (*NORDD: umg*) *vt* to rummage.

Graben ['graːbən] (-s, ¨) *m* ditch; (*MIL*) trench.

graben *unreg vt* to dig.

Grabesstille *f* (*liter*) deathly hush.

Grab- *zW*: ~**mal** *nt* monument; (*~stein*) gravestone; ~**rede** *f* funeral oration; ~**stein** *m* gravestone.

gräbt *vb siehe* **graben**.

Gracht [graxt] (-, -en) *f* canal.

Grad [graːt] (-(e)s, -e) *m* degree; **im höchsten** ~(**e**) extremely; **Verbrennungen ersten** ~**es** (*MED*) first-degree burns; ~**einteilung** *f* graduation; **g**~**linig** *adj* straight; **g**~**weise** *adv* gradually.

Graf [graːf] (-en, -en) *m* count, earl (*BRIT*).

Grafik ['graːfɪk] (-, -en) *f* (*COMPUT, TECH*) graphics; (*ART*) graphic arts *pl*.

Grafiker(in) ['graːfɪkər(ɪn)] (-s, -) *m(f)* graphic artist; (*Illustrator*) illustrator.

Gräfin ['grɛːfɪn] *f* countess.

grafisch *adj* ['graːfɪʃ] ♦ *adj* graphic; ~**e Darstellung** graph.

Grafschaft *f* county.

Grahambrot ['graːhambroːt] *nt* type of wholemeal (*BRIT*) *od* whole-wheat (*US*) bread.

Gralshüter ['graːlzhyːtər] (-s, -) *m* (*fig*) guardian.

Gram [graːm] (-(e)s) *m* (*geh*) grief, sorrow.

grämen ['grɛːmən] *vr* to grieve; **sich zu Tode**

~ to die of grief *od* sorrow.
Gramm [gram] (**-s, -e**) *nt* gram(me).
Grammatik [gra'matɪk] *f* grammar.
grammatisch *adj* grammatical.
Grammofon▲, Grammophon [gramo'fo:n] (**-s, -e**) *nt* gramophone.
Granat [gra'na:t] (**-(e)s, -e**) *m* (*Stein*) garnet; **~apfel** *m* pomegranate.
Granate (**-, -n**) *f* (*MIL*) shell; (*Hand~*) grenade.
grandios [gran'dio:s] *adj* magnificent, superb.
Granit [gra'ni:t] (**-s, -e**) *m* granite; **auf ~ beißen (bei …)** to bang one's head against a brick wall (with …).
grantig ['grantɪç] (*umg*) *adj* grumpy.
Graphik *etc* ['gra:fɪk] = **Grafik** *etc.*
grapschen ['grapʃən] (*umg*) *vt, vi* to grab; (**sich** *dat*) **etw ~** to grab sth.
Gras [gra:s] (**-es, -er**) *nt* grass; (*auch umg: Marihuana*) grass; **über etw** *akk* **~ wachsen lassen** (*fig*) to let the dust settle on sth; **g~en** *vi* to graze; **~halm** *m* blade of grass.
grasig *adj* grassy.
Grasnarbe *f* turf.
grassieren [gra'si:rən] *vi* to be rampant, rage.
grässlich▲ ['grɛslɪç] *adj* horrible.
Grat [gra:t] (**-(e)s, -e**) *m* ridge.
Gräte ['grɛːtə] (**-, -n**) *f* fish-bone.
Gratifikation [gratifikatsi'o:n] *f* bonus.
gratis ['gra:tɪs] *adj, adv* free (of charge); **G~probe** *f* free sample.
Grätsche ['grɛːtʃə] (**-, -n**) *f* (*SPORT*) straddle.
Gratulant(in) [gratu'lant(ɪn)] *m(f)* well-wisher.
Gratulation [gratulatsi'o:n] *f* congratulation(s).
gratulieren [gratu'li:rən] *vi*: **jdm (zu etw) ~** to congratulate sb (on sth); (**ich) gratuliere!** congratulations!
Gratwanderung *f* (*fig*) tightrope walk.
grau [grau] *adj* grey (*BRIT*), gray (*US*); **der ~e Alltag** drab reality; **~ meliert** grey-flecked (*BRIT*), gray-flecked (*US*); **G~brot** *nt* = **Mischbrot**.
Gräuel▲ ['grɔʏəl] (**-s, -**) *m* horror; (*~tat*) atrocity; **etw ist jdm ein ~** sb loathes sth; **~propaganda** *f* atrocity propaganda; **~tat** *f* atrocity.
Grauen (**-s**) *nt* horror.
grauen *vi* (*Tag*) to dawn ♦ *vi unpers*: **es graut jdm vor etw** sb dreads sth, sb is afraid of sth ♦ *vr*: **sich ~ vor** to dread.
grauenhaft, grauenvoll *adj* horrible.
grauhaarig *adj* grey-haired (*BRIT*), gray-haired (*US*).
gräulich▲ ['grɔʏlɪç] *adj* horrible.
Graupelregen ['graupəlre:gən] *m* sleet.
Graupelschauer *m* sleet.
Graupen ['graupən] *pl* pearl barley *sing.*
grausam ['grauza:m] *adj* cruel; **G~keit** *f* cruelty.
Grausen ['grauzən] (**-s**) *nt* horror; **da kann**

man das kalte ~ kriegen (*umg*) it's enough to give you the creeps.
grausen *vb* = **grauen**.
Grauzone *f* (*fig*) grey (*BRIT*) *od* gray (*US*) area.
gravieren [gra'vi:rən] *vt* to engrave.
gravierend *adj* grave.
Grazie ['gra:tsiə] *f* grace.
graziös [gratsi'øːs] *adj* graceful.
Greencard ['gri:nka:əd] (**-, -s**) *f* green card.
greifbar *adj* tangible, concrete; **in ~er Nähe** within reach.
greifen ['graɪfən] *unreg* *vt* (*nehmen*) to grasp; (*grapschen*) to seize, grab ♦ *vi* (*nicht rutschen, einrasten*) to grip; **nach etw ~** to reach for sth; **um sich ~** (*fig*) to spread; **zu etw ~** (*fig*) to turn to sth; **diese Zahl ist zu niedrig gegriffen** (*fig*) this figure is too low; **aus dem Leben gegriffen** taken from life.
Greifer (**-s, -**) *m* (*TECH*) grab.
Greifvogel *m* bird of prey.
Greis [graɪs] (**-es, -e**) *m* old man.
Greisenalter *nt* old age.
greisenhaft *adj* very old.
Greisin ['graɪzɪn] *f* old woman.
grell [grɛl] *adj* harsh.
Gremium ['gre:miʊm] *nt* body; (*Ausschuss*) committee.
Grenadier [grena'di:ər] (**-s, -e**) *m* (*MIL: Infanterist*) infantryman.
Grenzbeamte(r) *m* frontier official.
Grenze (**-, -n**) *f* border; (*zwischen Grundstücken, fig*) boundary; (*Staats~*) frontier; (*Schranke*) limit; **über die ~ gehen/fahren** to cross the border; **hart an der ~ des Erlaubten** bordering on the limits of what is permitted.
grenzen *vi*: **~ an** +*akk* to border on.
grenzenlos *adj* boundless.
Grenz- *zW*: **~fall** *m* borderline case; **~gänger** *m* (*Arbeiter*) international commuter (*across a local border*); **~gebiet** *nt* (*lit, fig*) border area; **~kosten** *pl* marginal cost *sing*; **~linie** *f* boundary; **~übergang** *m* frontier crossing; **~wert** *m* limit; **~zwischenfall** *m* border incident.
Gretchenfrage ['gre:tçənfra:gə] *f* (*fig*) crunch question, sixty-four-thousand-dollar question (*umg*).
Greuel *etc* △ ['grɔʏəl] *siehe* **Gräuel**.
greulich △ ['grɔʏlɪç] *siehe* **gräulich**.
Grieche ['gri:çə] (**-n, -n**) *m* Greek.
Griechenland *nt* Greece.
Griechin ['gri:çɪn] *f* Greek.
griechisch *adj* Greek.
griesgrämig ['gri:sgrɛ:mɪç] *adj* grumpy.
Grieß [gri:s] (**-es, -e**) *m* (*KOCH*) semolina; **~brei** *m* cooked semolina.
Griff [grɪf] (**-(e)s, -e**) *m* grip; (*Vorrichtung*) handle; (*das Greifen*): **der ~ nach etw**

reaching for sth; **jdn/etw in den ~ bekommen** (*fig*) to gain control of sb/sth; **etw in den ~ bekommen** (*geistig*) to get a grasp of sth.

griff *etc vb siehe* **greifen**.

griffbereit *adj* handy.

Griffel ['grɪfəl] (**-s, -**) *m* slate pencil; (*BOT*) style.

griffig ['grɪfɪç] *adj* (*Fahrbahn etc*) that has a good grip; (*fig*: *Ausdruck*) useful, handy.

Grill [grɪl] (**-s, -s**) *m* grill; (*AUT*) grille.

Grille ['grɪlə] (**-, -n**) *f* cricket; (*fig*) whim.

grillen *vt* to grill.

Grimasse [gri'masə] (**-, -n**) *f* grimace; **~n schneiden** to make faces.

grimmig *adj* furious; (*heftig*) fierce, severe.

grinsen ['grɪnzən] *vi* to grin; (*höhnisch*) to smirk.

Grippe ['grɪpə] (**-, -n**) *f* influenza, flu.

Grips [grɪps] (**-es, -e**) (*umg*) *m* sense.

grob [gro:p] *adj* coarse, gross; (*Fehler, Verstoß*) gross; (*brutal, derb*) rough; (*unhöflich*) ill-mannered; **~ geschätzt** at a rough estimate; **G~heit** *f* coarseness; (*Beschimpfung*) coarse expression.

Grobian ['gro:bia:n] (**-s, -e**) *m* ruffian.

grobknochig *adj* large-boned.

groggy ['grɔgɪ] *adj* (*BOXEN*) groggy; (*umg*: *erschöpft*) bushed.

grölen ['grø:lən] (*pej*) *vt, vi* to bawl.

Groll [grɔl] (**-(e)s**) *m* resentment; **g~en** *vi* (*Donner*) to rumble; **g~en (mit** *od* **+dat)** to bear ill will (towards).

Grönland ['grø:nlant] (**-s**) *nt* Greenland.

Grönländer(in) (**-s, -**) *m(f)* Greenlander.

Groschen ['grɔʃən] (**-s, -**) (*umg*) *m* 10-pfennig piece; (*ÖSTERR*) groschen; (*fig*) penny, cent (*US*); **~roman** (*pej*) *m* cheap *od* dime (*US*) novel.

groß [gro:s] *adj* big, large; (*hoch*) tall; (*Freude, Werk*) great ♦ *adv* greatly; **im G~en und Ganzen** on the whole; **wie ~ bist du?** how tall are you?; **die G~en** (*Erwachsene*) the grown-ups; **mit etw ~ geworden sein** to have grown up with sth; **die G~en Seen** the Great Lakes *pl*; **~en Hunger haben** to be very hungry; **~e Mode sein** to be all the fashion; **~ angelegt** large-scale, on a large scale; **~ und breit** (*fig: umg*) at great *od* enormous length; **~ geschrieben werden** (*umg*) to be stressed; **G~alarm** *m* red alert; **~artig** *adj* great, splendid; **G~aufnahme** *f* (*FILM*) close-up; **G~britannien** (**-s**) *nt* (Great) Britain; **g~buchstabe** *m* capital (letter).

Größe ['grø:sə] (**-, -n**) *f* size; (*Länge*) height; (*fig*) greatness; **eine unbekannte ~** (*lit, fig*) an unknown quantity.

Groß- *zW*: **~einkauf** *m* bulk purchase; **~einsatz** *m*: **~einsatz der Polizei** *etc* large-

scale operation by the police *etc*; **~eltern** *pl* grandparents *pl*.

Größenordnung *f* scale; (*Größe*) magnitude; (*MATH*) order (of magnitude).

großenteils *adv* for the most part.

Größen- *zW*: **~unterschied** *m* difference in size; **~wahn** *m*, **~wahnsinn** *m* megalomania, delusions *pl* of grandeur.

Groß- *zW*: **~format** *nt* large size; **~handel** *m* wholesale trade; **~handelspreisindex** *m* wholesale-price index; **~händler** *m* wholesaler; **g~herzig** *adj* generous; **~hirn** *nt* cerebrum; **g~industrielle(r)** *f(m)* major industrialist; **g~kotzig** (*umg*) *adj* show-offish, bragging; **~kundgebung** *f* mass rally; **~macht** *f* great power; **~maul** *m* braggart; **~mut** (**-**) *f* magnanimity; **g~mütig** *adj* magnanimous; **~mutter** *f* grandmother; **~raum** *m*: **der ~raum München** the Munich area *od* conurbation, Greater Munich; **~raumbüro** *nt* open-plan office; **~rechner** *m* mainframe; **~reinemachen** *nt* thorough cleaning, ≈ spring cleaning; **g~schreiben** *unreg vt*: **ein Wort g~schreiben** to write a word with a capital; **~schreibung** *f* capitalization; **g~spurig** *adj* pompous; **~stadt** *f* city.

größte(r, s) [grø:stə(r, s)] *adj superl von* **groß**.

größtenteils *adv* for the most part.

Groß- *zW*: **~tuer** (**-s, -**) *m* boaster; **g~tun** *unreg vi* to boast; **~vater** *m* grandfather; **~verbraucher** *m* (*COMM*) heavy user; **~verdiener** *m* big earner; **~wild** *nt* big game; **g~ziehen** *unreg vt* to raise; **g~zügig** *adj* generous; (*Planung*) on a large scale.

grotesk [gro'tɛsk] *adj* grotesque.

Grotte ['grɔtə] (**-, -n**) *f* grotto.

grub *etc* [gru:p] *vb siehe* **graben**.

Grübchen ['gry:pçən] *nt* dimple.

Grube ['gru:bə] (**-, -n**) *f* pit; (*Bergwerk*) mine.

grübeln ['gry:bəln] *vi* to brood.

Grubenarbeiter *m* miner.

Grubengas *nt* firedamp.

Grübler ['gry:blər] (**-s, -**) *m* brooder; **g~isch** *adj* brooding, pensive.

Gruft [gruft] (**-, ⁻e**) *f* tomb, vault.

grün [gry:n] *adj* green; (*ökologisch*) green; (*POL*): **die G~en** the Greens; **~e Minna** (*umg*) Black Maria (*BRIT*), paddy wagon (*US*); **~e Welle** phased traffic lights; **~e Versicherungskarte** (*AUT*) green card; **sich ~ und blau** *od* **gelb ärgern** (*umg*) to be furious; **auf keinen ~en Zweig kommen** (*fig: umg*) to get nowhere; **jdm ~es Licht geben** to give sb the green light; **G~anlage** *f* park.

Grund [grunt] (**-(e)s, ⁻e**) *m* ground; (*von See, Gefäß*) bottom; (*fig*) reason; **von ~ auf** entirely, completely; **aus gesundheitlichen** *etc* **Gründen** for health *etc* reasons; **im ~e genommen** basically; **ich habe ~ zu der**

Annahme, dass ... I have reason to believe that ...; **einer Sache** *dat* **auf den ~ gehen** (*fig*) to get to the bottom of sth; **in ~ und Boden** (*fig*) utterly, thoroughly; *siehe auch* **aufgrund, zugrunde,** **~ausbildung** *f* basic training; **~bedeutung** *f* basic meaning; **~bedingung** *f* fundamental condition; **~begriff** *m* basic concept; **~besitz** *m* land(ed property), real estate; **~buch** *nt* land register; **g~ehrlich** *adj* thoroughly honest.

gründen [grʏndən] *vt* to found ♦ *vr*: **sich ~ auf** *+akk* to be based on; **~ auf** *+akk* to base on.

Gründer(in) (**-s, -**) *m(f)* founder.

Grund- *zW*: **g~falsch** *adj* utterly wrong; **~gebühr** *f* basic charge; **~gedanke** *m* basic idea; **~gesetz** *nt* constitution.

Grundierung [grʊn'diːrʊŋ] *f* (*Farbe*) primer.

Grund- [zl]: **~kapital** *nt* nominal capital; **~kurs** *m* basic course; **~lage** *f* foundation; **jeder ~lage** *gen* **entbehren** to be completely unfounded; **g~legend** *adj* fundamental.

gründlich *adj* thorough; **jdm ~ die Meinung sagen** to give sb a piece of one's mind.

Grund- *zW*: **g~los** *adj* (*fig*) groundless; **~mauer** *f* foundation wall; **~nahrungsmittel** *nt* basic food(stuff).

Gründonnerstag *m* Maundy Thursday.

Grund- *zW*: **~ordnung** *f*: **die freiheitlich-demokratische ~ordnung** (*BRD POL*) *the German constitution based on democratic liberty*; **~rechenart** *f* basic arithmetical operation; **~recht** *nt* basic *od* constitutional right; **~regel** *f* basic *od* ground rule; **~riss**▲ *m* plan; (*fig*) outline; **~satz** *m* principle; **g~sätzlich** *adj* fundamental; (*Frage*) of principle ♦ *adv* fundamentally; (*prinzipiell*) on principle; **das ist g~sätzlich verboten** it is absolutely forbidden; **~satzurteil** *nt* *judgement that establishes a principle.*

Grundschule *f* primary (*BRIT*) *od* elementary school.

Grund- *zW*: **~stein** *m* foundation stone; **~steuer** *f* rates *pl*; **~stück** *nt* plot (of land); (*Anwesen*) estate; **~stücksmakler** *m* estate agent (*BRIT*), realtor (*US*); **~stufe** *f* first stage; (*SCH*) ≈ junior (*BRIT*) *od* grade (*US*) school.

Gründung *f* foundation.

Gründungsurkunde *f* (*COMM*) certificate of incorporation.

Gründungsversammlung *f* (*Aktiengesellschaft*) statutory meeting.

Grund- *zW*: **g~verschieden** *adj* utterly different; **~wasser** *nt* ground water; **~wasserspiegel** *m* water table, ground-water level; **~zug** *m* characteristic; **etw in seinen ~zügen darstellen** to outline (the essentials of) sth.

Grüne (**-n**) *nt*: **im ~n** in the open air; **ins ~ fahren** to go to the country.

Grüne(r) *f(m)* (*POL*) Ecologist, Green; **die Grünen** *pl* (*als Partei*) the Greens.

Grün- *zW*: **~kohl** *m* kale; **~schnabel** *m* greenhorn; **~span** *m* verdigris; **~streifen** *m* central reservation.

grunzen ['grʊntsən] *vi* to grunt.

Gruppe ['grʊpə] (**-, -n**) *f* group.

Gruppen- *zW*: **~arbeit** *f* teamwork; **~dynamik** *f* group dynamics *pl*; **~therapie** *f* group therapy; **g~weise** *adv* in groups.

gruppieren [grʊ'piːrən] *vt*, *vr* to group.

gruselig *adj* creepy.

gruseln ['gruːzəln] *vi unpers*: **es gruselt jdm vor etw** sth gives sb the creeps ♦ *vr* to have the creeps.

Gruß [gruːs] (**-es, -̈e**) *m* greeting; (*MIL*) salute; **viele Grüße** best wishes; **Grüße an** *+akk* regards to; **einen (schönen) ~ an Ihre Frau!** (*geh*) my regards to your wife; **mit freundlichen Grüßen** (*als Briefformel*) Yours sincerely.

grüßen ['gryːsən] *vt* to greet; (*MIL*) to salute; **jdn von jdm ~** to give sb sb's regards; **jdn ~ lassen** to send sb one's regards.

Grütze ['grʏtsə] (**-, -n**) *f* (*Brei*) gruel; **rote ~** (type of) red fruit jelly.

Guatemala [guate'maːla] (**-s**) *nt* Guatemala.

Guayana [gua'jaːna] (**-s**) *nt* Guyana.

gucken ['gʊkən] *vi* to look.

Guckloch nt peephole.
Guinea [gi'ne:a] (-s) nt Guinea.
Gulasch ['gu:laʃ] (-(e)s, -e) nt goulash;
~**kanone** f (MIL: umg) field kitchen.
gültig ['gʏltɪç] adj valid; ~ **werden** to become
valid; (Gesetz, Vertrag) to come into effect;
(Münze) to become legal tender; **G~keit** f
validity; **G~keitsdauer** f period of validity.
Gummi ['gʊmi] (-s, -s) nt od m rubber; (~harze)
gum; (umg: Kondom) rubber, Durex ®;
(~band) rubber od elastic band; (Hosen~)
elastic; ~**band** nt rubber od elastic band;
~**bärchen** nt jelly baby; ~**geschoss**▲ nt
rubber bullet; ~**knüppel** m rubber
truncheon; ~**paragraf**▲ m ambiguous od
meaningless law od statute; ~**stiefel** m
rubber boot, wellington (boot) (BRIT);
~**strumpf** m elastic stocking; ~**zelle** f padded
cell.
Gunst [gʊnst] (-) f favour (BRIT), favor (US);
siehe auch **zugunsten**.
günstig ['gʏnstɪç] adj favourable (BRIT),
favorable (US); (Angebot, Preis etc)
reasonable, good; **bei** ~**er Witterung**
weather permitting; **im** ~**sten Fall(e)** with
luck.
Gurgel ['gʊrgəl] (-, -n) f throat.
gurgeln vi to gurgle; (im Rachen) to gargle.
Gurke ['gʊrkə] (-, -n) f cucumber; **saure** ~
pickled cucumber, gherkin.
Gurt [gʊrt] (-(e)s, -e) m belt.
Gurtanlegepflicht f (form) obligation to
wear a safety belt in vehicles.
Gürtel ['gʏrtəl] (-s, -) m belt; (GEOG) zone;
~**reifen** m radial tyre; ~**rose** f shingles sing od
pl.
GUS [ge:|u:'|ɛs] f abk (= Gemeinschaft
Unabhängiger Staaten) CIS.
Guss▲ [gʊs] (-es, ¨e) m casting; (Regen~)
downpour; (KOCH) glazing; ~**eisen** nt cast
iron.
Gut [gu:t] (-(e)s, ¨er) nt (Besitz) possession;
(Landgut) estate; **Güter** pl (Waren) goods pl.

===================== *SCHLÜSSELWORT*

gut adj good; **das ist** ~ **gegen** od **für** (umg)
Husten it's good for coughs; **sei so** ~ **(und)
gib mir das** would you mind giving me that;
dafür ist er sich zu ~ he wouldn't stoop to
that sort of thing; **das ist ja alles** ~ **und
schön, aber** ... that's all very well but ...; **du
bist** ~! (umg) you're a fine one!; **alles G~e**
all the best; **also** ~ all right then.
♦ adv well; ~ **gehen** to work, come off; **es
geht jdm** ~ sb's doing fine; **das ist noch
einmal** ~ **gegangen** it turned out all right;
~ **gehend** thriving; ~ **gelaunt** cheerful, in a
good mood; ~ **gemeint** well meant; **du hast
es** ~! you've got it made!; ~ **situiert** well-
off; **jdm** ~ **tun** to do sb good; ~ **unterrichtet**

well-informed; ~**, aber** ... OK, but ...; **(na)** ~**,
ich komme** all right, I'll come; ~ **drei
Stunden** a good three hours; **das kann**
~ **sein** that may well be; ~ **und gern** easily;
lass es ~ **sein** that'll do.

Gut- zW: ~**achten** (-s, -) nt report; ~**achter** (-s,
-) m expert; ~**achterkommission** f quango;
g~artig adj good-natured; (MED) benign;
g~bürgerlich adj (Küche) (good) plain;
~**dünken** nt: **nach** ~**dünken** at one's
discretion.
Güte ['gy:tə] (-) f goodness, kindness; (Qualität)
quality; **ach du liebe** od **meine** ~! (umg)
goodness me!; ~**klasse** f (COMM) grade;
~**klasseneinteilung** f (COMM) grading.
Güter- zW: ~**abfertigung** f (EISENB) goods
office; ~**bahnhof** m goods station;
~**trennung** f (JUR) separation of property;
~**verkehr** m freight traffic; ~**wagen** m goods
waggon (BRIT), freight car (US); ~**zug** m
goods train (BRIT), freight train (US).
Gütesiegel nt (COMM) stamp of quality.
gut- zW: ~**gläubig** adj trusting; **G~haben** (-s)
nt credit; ~**haben** unreg vt: **20 Mark (bei jdm)**
~**haben** to be in credit (with sb) to the tune
of 20 marks; ~**heißen** unreg vt to approve
(of); ~**herzig** adj kind(-hearted).
gütig ['gy:tɪç] adj kind.
gütlich ['gy:tlɪç] adj amicable.
gut- zW: ~**machen** vt (in Ordnung bringen:
Fehler) to put right, correct; (Schaden) to
make good; ~**mütig** adj good-natured;
G~mütigkeit f good nature.
Gutsbesitzer(in) m(f) landowner.
Gut- zW: ~**schein** m voucher; **g~schreiben**
unreg vt to credit; ~**schrift** f credit.
Gutsherr m squire.
Gutshof m estate.
gutwillig adj willing.
Gymnasiallehrer(in) [gʏmnazi'a:lle:rər(ɪn)]
m(f) ≈ grammar school teacher (BRIT), high
school teacher (US).
Gymnasium [gʏm'na:ziʊm] nt ≈ grammar
school (BRIT), high school (US).

GYMNASIUM

The **Gymnasium** *is a selective secondary school.
There are nine years of study at a* **Gymnasium**
leading to the **Abitur** *which gives access to
higher education. Pupils who successfully
complete six years automatically gain the*
mittlere Reife*.*

Gymnastik [gʏm'nastɪk] f exercises pl, keep-
fit; ~ **machen** to do keep-fit (exercises)/
gymnastics.
Gynäkologe [gʏnɛko'lo:gə] (-n, -n) m
gynaecologist (BRIT), gynecologist (US).

Gynäkologin [gynɛko'loːgɪn] *f* gynaecologist (*BRIT*), gynecologist (*US*).

H, h

H, h [haː] *nt* H, h; ~ **wie Heinrich** ≈ H for Harry, H for How (*US*); (*MUS*) B.

ha *abk* = **Hektar**.

Haag [haːk] (**-s**) *m*: **Den ~** The Hague.

Haar [haːr] (**-(e)s, -e**) *nt* hair; **um ein ~** nearly; **~e auf den Zähnen haben** to be a tough customer; **sich die ~e raufen** (*umg*) to tear one's hair; **sich** *dat* **in die ~e kriegen** (*umg*) to quarrel; **das ist an den ~en herbeigezogen** that's rather far-fetched; **~ansatz** *m* hairline; **~bürste** *f* hairbrush.

haaren *vi, vr* to lose hair.

Haaresbreite *f*: **um ~** by a hair's-breadth.

Haarfestiger (**-s, -**) *m* setting lotion.

haargenau *adv* precisely.

haarig *adj* hairy; (*fig*) nasty.

Haar- *zW*: **~klammer** *f*, **~klemme** *f* hair grip (*BRIT*), barrette (*US*); **h~klein** *adv* in minute detail; **h~los** *adj* hairless; **~nadel** *f* hairpin; **h~scharf** *adv* (*beobachten*) very sharply; (*verfehlen*) by a hair's breadth; **~schnitt** *m* haircut; **~schopf** *m* head of hair; **~sieb** *nt* fine sieve; **~spalterei** *f* hair-splitting; **~spange** *f* hair slide; **h~sträubend** *adj* hair-raising; **~teil** *nt* hairpiece; **~waschmittel** *nt* shampoo; **~wasser** *nt* hair lotion.

Hab [haːp] *nt*: **~ und Gut** possessions *pl*, belongings *pl*, worldly goods *pl*.

Habe ['haːbə] (**-**) *f* property.

haben ['haːbən] *unreg vt, Hilfsverb* to have ♦ *vr unpers*: **und damit hat es sich** (*umg*) and that's that; **Hunger/Angst ~** to be hungry/afraid; **da hast du 10 Mark** there's 10 Marks; **die ~s (ja)** (*umg*) they can afford it; **Ferien ~** to be on holiday; **es am Herzen ~** (*umg*) to have heart trouble; **sie ist noch zu ~** (*umg: nicht verheiratet*) she's still single; **für etw zu ~ sein** to be keen on sth; **sie werden schon merken, was sie an ihm ~** they'll see how valuable he is; **haste was, biste was** (*Sprichwort*) money brings status; **wie gehabt!** some things don't change; **das hast du jetzt davon** now see what's happened; **woher hast du das?** where did you get that from?; **was hast du denn?** what's the matter (with you)?; **ich habe zu tun** I'm busy.

Haben (**-s, -**) *nt* (*COMM*) credit.

Habenseite *f* (*COMM*) credit side.

Habgier *f* avarice.

habgierig *adj* avaricious.

habhaft *adj*: **jds/einer Sache ~ werden** (*geh*) to get hold of sb/sth.

Habicht ['haːbɪçt] (**-(e)s, -e**) *m* hawk.

Habilitation [habilitatsi'oːn] *f* (*Lehrberechtigung*) postdoctoral lecturing qualification.

Habseligkeiten ['haːpzeːlɪçkaɪtən] *pl* belongings *pl*.

Habsucht ['haːpzʊxt] *f* greed.

Hachse ['haksə] (**-, -n**) *f* (*KOCH*) knuckle.

Hackbraten *m* meat loaf.

Hackbrett *nt* chopping board; (*MUS*) dulcimer.

Hacke ['hakə] (**-, -n**) *f* hoe; (*Ferse*) heel.

hacken *vt* to hack, chop; (*Erde*) to hoe.

Hacker ['hakər] (**-s, -**) *m* (*COMPUT*) hacker.

Hackfleisch *nt* mince, minced meat, ground meat (*US*).

Hackordnung *f* (*lit, fig*) pecking order.

Häcksel ['hɛksəl] (**-s**) *m od nt* chopped straw, chaff.

hadern ['haːdərn] *vi* (*geh*): **~ mit** to quarrel with; (*unzufrieden sein*) to be at odds with.

Hafen ['haːfən] (**-s, ⸚**) *m* harbour, harbor (*US*), port; (*fig*) haven; **~anlagen** *pl* docks *pl*; **~arbeiter** *m* docker; **~damm** *m* jetty, mole; **~gebühren** *pl* harbo(u)r dues *pl*; **~stadt** *f* port.

Hafer ['haːfər] (**-s, -**) *m* oats *pl*; **ihn sticht der ~** (*umg*) he is feeling his oats; **~brei** *m* porridge (*BRIT*), oatmeal (*US*); **~flocken** *pl* rolled oats *pl* (*BRIT*), oatmeal (*US*); **~schleim** *m* gruel.

Haff [haf] (**-s, -s od -e**) *nt* lagoon.

Haft [haft] (**-**) *f* custody; **~anstalt** *f* detention centre (*BRIT*) *od* center (*US*); **h~bar** *adj* liable, responsible; **~befehl** *m* warrant (for arrest); **einen ~befehl gegen jdn ausstellen** to issue a warrant for sb's arrest.

haften *vi* to stick, cling; **~ für** to be liable *od* responsible for; **für Garderobe kann nicht gehaftet werden** all articles are left at owner's risk; **~ bleiben (an** +*dat*) to stick (to).

Häftling ['hɛftlɪŋ] *m* prisoner.

Haft- *zW*: **~pflicht** *f* liability; **~pflichtversicherung** *f* third party insurance; **~richter** *m* magistrate.

Haftschalen *pl* contact lenses *pl*.

Haftung *f* liability.

Hagebutte ['haːgəbʊtə] (**-, -n**) *f* rose hip.

Hagedorn *m* hawthorn.

Hagel ['haːgəl] (**-s**) *m* hail; **~korn** *nt* hailstone; (*MED*) eye cyst.

hageln *vi unpers* to hail.

Hagelschauer *m* (short) hailstorm.

hager ['haːgər] *adj* gaunt.

Häher ['hɛːər] (**-s, -**) *m* jay.

Hahn [haːn] (-(e)s, ⁻e) *m* cock; (*Wasser~*) tap, faucet (*US*); (*Abzug*) trigger; ~ **im Korb sein** (*umg*) to be cock of the walk; **danach kräht kein** ~ **mehr** (*umg*) no one cares two hoots about that any more.

Hähnchen ['hɛɪnçən] *nt* cockerel; (*KOCH*) chicken.

Hai(fisch) ['haɪ(fɪʃ)] (-(e)s, -e) *m* shark.

Haiti [ha'iːti] (-s) *nt* Haiti.

Häkchen ['hɛːkçən] *nt* small hook.

Häkelarbeit *f* crochet work.

häkeln ['hɛːkəln] *vt* to crochet.

Häkelnadel *f* crochet hook.

Haken ['haːkən] (-s, -) *m* hook; (*fig*) catch; **einen** ~ **schlagen** to dart sideways; **~kreuz** *nt* swastika; **~nase** *f* hooked nose.

halb [halp] *adj* half ♦ *adv* (*beinahe*) almost; ~ **eins** half past twelve; ~ **offen** half-open; **ein ~es Dutzend** half a dozen; **nichts H~es und nichts Ganzes** neither one thing nor the other; **(noch) ein ~es Kind sein** to be scarcely more than a child; **das ist** ~ **so schlimm** it's not as bad as all that; **mit jdm** ~**e-~e machen** (*umg*) to go halves with sb.

halb- *zW*: **H~blut** *nt* (*Tier*) crossbreed; **H~bruder** *m* half-brother; **H~dunkel** *nt* semi-darkness.

halber ['halbər] *präp +gen* (*wegen*) on account of; (*für*) for the sake of.

Halb- *zW*: **h~fett** *adj* medium fat; **~finale** *nt* semi-final; **~heit** *f* half-measure; **h~herzig** *adj* half-hearted.

halbieren [hal'biːrən] *vt* to halve.

Halb- *zW*: **~insel** *f* peninsula; **h~jährlich** *adj* half-yearly; **~kreis** *m* semicircle; **~kugel** *f* hemisphere; **h~lang** *adj*: **nun mach mal h~lang!** (*umg*) now wait a minute!; **h~laut** *adv* in an undertone; **~leiter** *m* (*PHYS*) semiconductor; **h~mast** *adv* at half-mast; **~mond** *m* half-moon; (*fig*) crescent; **~pension** *f* half-board (*BRIT*), European plan (*US*); **~schuh** *m* shoe; **~schwester** *f* half-sister; **h~seiden** *adj* (*lit*) fifty per cent silk; (*fig*: *Dame*) fast; (: *homosexuell*) gay; **h~seitig** *adj* (*Anzeige*) half-page; **~starke(r)** *f(m)* hooligan, rowdy; **h~tags** *adv*: **h~tags arbeiten** to work part-time; **~tagsarbeit** *f* part-time work; **~tagskraft** *f* part-time worker; **~ton** *m* half-tone; (*MUS*) semitone; **h~trocken** *adj* medium-dry; **~waise** *f* child/ person who has lost one parent; **h~wegs** *adv* half-way; **h~wegs besser** more or less better; **~welt** *f* demimonde; **~wertzeit** *f* half-life; **~wüchsige(r)** *f(m)* adolescent; **~zeit** *f* (*SPORT*) half; (*Pause*) half-time.

Halde ['haldə] *f* tip; (*Schlacken~*) slag heap.

half *etc* [half] *vb siehe* **helfen**.

Hälfte ['hɛlftə] (-, -n) *f* half; **um die** ~ **steigen** to increase by half.

Halfter¹ ['halftər] (-s, -) *m od nt* (*für Tiere*)

halter.

Halfter² ['halftər] (-, -n *od* -s, -) *f od nt* (*Pistolen~*) holster.

Hall [hal] (-(e)s, -e) *m* sound.

Halle ['halə] (-, -n) *f* hall; (*AVIAT*) hangar.

hallen *vi* to echo, resound.

Hallen- *in zW* indoor; **~bad** *nt* indoor swimming pool.

hallo [ha'loː] *interj* hallo.

Halluzination [halutsinatsi'oːn] *f* hallucination.

Halm ['halm] (-(e)s, -e) *m* blade, stalk.

Hals [hals] (-es, ⁻e) *m* neck; (*Kehle*) throat; **sich** *dat* **nach jdm/etw den** ~ **verrenken** (*umg*) to crane one's neck to see sb/sth; **jdm um den** ~ **fallen** to fling one's arms around sb's neck; **aus vollem** ~**(e)** at the top of one's voice; ~ **über Kopf** in a rush; **jdn auf dem** *od* **am** ~ **haben** (*umg*) to be lumbered *od* saddled with sb; **das hängt mir zum** ~ **raus** (*umg*) I'm sick and tired of it; **sie hat es in den falschen** ~ **bekommen** (*falsch verstehen*) she took it wrongly; **~abschneider** (*pej*: *umg*) *m* shark; **~band** *nt* (*Hundehalsband*) collar; **h~brecherisch** *adj* (*Tempo*) breakneck; (*Fahrt*) hair-raising; **~kette** *f* necklace; **~krause** *f* ruff; **~-Nasen-Ohren-Arzt** *m* ear, nose and throat specialist; **~schlagader** *f* carotid artery; **~schmerzen** *pl* sore throat *sing*; **h~starrig** *adj* stubborn, obstinate; **~tuch** *nt* scarf; **~- und Beinbruch** *interj* good luck; **~weh** *nt* sore throat; **~wirbel** *m* cervical vertebra.

Halt [halt] (-(e)s, -e) *m* stop; (*fester ~*) hold; (*innerer ~*) stability; ~**!, h~!** stop!, halt!; ~ **machen** to stop.

hält [hɛlt] *vb siehe* **halten**.

Halt- *zW*: **h~bar** *adj* durable; (*Lebensmittel*) non-perishable; (*MIL, fig*) tenable; **h~bar bis 6.11.** use by 6 Nov.; **~barkeit** *f* durability; (non-)perishability; tenability; (*von Lebensmitteln*) shelf life; **~barkeitsdatum** *nt* best-before date.

halten ['haltən] *unreg vt* to keep; (*fest~*) to hold ♦ *vi* to hold; (*frisch bleiben*) to keep; (*stoppen*) to stop ♦ *vr* (*frisch bleiben*) to keep; (*sich behaupten*) to hold out; **den Mund** ~ (*umg*) to keep one's mouth shut; ~ **für** to regard as; ~ **von** to think of; **das kannst du** ~ **wie du willst** that's completely up to you; **der Film hält nicht, was er verspricht** the film doesn't live up to expectations; **davon halt(e) ich nichts** I don't think much of it; **zu jdm** ~ to stand *od* stick by sb; **an sich** *akk* ~ to restrain o.s.; **auf sich** *akk* ~ (*auf Äußeres achten*) to take a pride in o.s.; **er hat sich gut gehalten** (*umg*) he's well-preserved; **sich an ein Versprechen** ~ to keep a promise; **sich rechts/links** ~ to keep to the right/left.

Halter ['haltər] (-s, -) *m* (*Halterung*) holder.

Haltestelle *f* stop.
Halteverbot *nt*: **absolutes** ~ no stopping; **eingeschränktes** ~ no waiting; **hier ist** ~ you cannot stop here.
haltlos *adj* unstable.
Haltlosigkeit *f* instability.
Haltung *f* posture; (*fig*) attitude; (*Selbstbeherrschung*) composure; ~ **bewahren** to keep one's composure.
Halunke [haˈlʊŋkə] (**-n, -n**) *m* rascal.
Hamburg [ˈhamburk] (**-s**) *nt* Hamburg.
Hamburger (**-s, -**) *m* (*KOCH*) burger, hamburger.
Hamburger(in) (**-s, -**) *m(f)* native of Hamburg.
Hameln [ˈhaːməln] *nt* Hamelin.
hämisch [ˈhɛːmɪʃ] *adj* malicious.
Hammel [ˈhaməl] (**-s,** *≐ od* **-**) *m* wether; ~**fleisch** *nt* mutton; ~**keule** *f* leg of mutton.
Hammelsprung *m* (*PARL*) division.
Hammer [ˈhamər] (**-s,** *≐*) *m* hammer; **das ist ein** ~**!** (*umg: unerhört*) that's absurd!
hämmern [ˈhɛmərn] *vt, vi* to hammer.
Hammondorgel [ˈhæməndˌɔrgəl] *f* electric organ.
Hämorrhoiden [hɛmɔroˈiːdən],
Hämorriden▲ [hɛmɔˈriːdən] *pl* piles *pl*, haemorrhoids *pl* (*BRIT*), hemorrhoids *pl* (*US*).
Hampelmann [ˈhampəlman] *m* (*lit, fig*) puppet.
Hamster [ˈhamstər] (**-s, -**) *m* hamster.
Hamsterei [hamstəˈraɪ] *f* hoarding.
Hamsterer (**-s, -**) *m* hoarder.
hamstern *vi* to hoard.
Hand [hant] (**-,** *≐***e**) *f* hand; **etw zur** ~ **haben** to have sth to hand; (*Ausrede, Erklärung*) to have sth ready; **jdm zur** ~ **gehen** to lend sb a helping hand; **zu Händen von jdm** for the attention of sb; **in festen Händen sein** to be spoken for; **die** ~ **für jdn ins Feuer legen** to vouch for sb; **hinter vorgehaltener** ~ on the quiet; ~ **aufs Herz** cross your heart; **jdn auf Händen tragen** to cherish sb; **bei etw die** *od* **seine** ~ **im Spiel haben** to have a hand in sth; **eine** ~ **wäscht die andere** (*Sprichwort*) if you scratch my back I'll scratch yours; **das hat weder** ~ **noch Fuß** that doesn't make sense; **das liegt auf der** ~ (*umg*) that's obvious; **unter der** ~ secretly; (*verkaufen*) privately; *siehe auch* **anhand**; ~**arbeit** *f* manual work; (*Nadelarbeit*) needlework; ~**arbeiter** *m* manual worker; ~**ball** *m* handball; ~**besen** *m* brush; ~**betrieb** *m*: **mit** ~**betrieb** hand-operated; ~**bewegung** *f* gesture; ~**bibliothek** *f* (*in Bibliothek*) reference section; (*auf Schreibtisch*) reference books *pl*; ~**bremse** *f* handbrake; ~**buch** *nt* handbook, manual.
Händedruck *m* handshake.
Händeklatschen *nt* clapping, applause.
Handel[1] [ˈhandəl] (**-s**) *m* trade; (*Geschäft*)

transaction; **im** ~ **sein** to be on the market; (**mit jdm**) ~ **treiben** to trade (with sb); **etw in den** ~ **bringen/aus dem** ~ **ziehen** to put sth on/take sth off the market.
Handel[2] (**-s,** *≐*) *m* quarrel.
handeln [ˈhandəln] *vi* to trade; (*tätig werden*) to act ♦ *vr unpers*: **sich** ~ **um** to be a question of, be about; ~ **von** to be about; **ich lasse mit mir** ~ I'm open to persuasion; (*in Bezug auf Preis*) I'm open to offers.
Handeln (**-s**) *nt* action.
handelnd *adj*: **die** ~**en Personen in einem Drama** the characters in a drama.
Handels- *zW*: ~**bank** *f* merchant bank (*BRIT*), commercial bank; ~**bilanz** *f* balance of trade; **aktive/passive** ~**bilanz** balance of trade surplus/deficit; ~**delegation** *f* trade mission; **h**~**einig** *adj*: **mit jdm h**~**einig werden** to conclude a deal with sb; ~**gesellschaft** *f* commercial company; ~**kammer** *f* chamber of commerce; ~**klasse** *f* grade; ~**marine** *f* merchant navy; ~**marke** *f* trade name; ~**name** *m* trade name; ~**recht** *nt* commercial law; ~**register** *nt* register of companies; ~**reisende(r)** *f(m)* = Handlungsreisende(r) commercial traveller; ~**sanktionen** *pl* trade sanctions *pl*; ~**schule** *f* business school; ~**spanne** *f* gross margin, mark-up; ~**sperre** *f* trade embargo; **h**~**üblich** *adj* customary; ~**vertreter** *m* sales representative; ~**vertretung** *f* trade mission; ~**ware** *f* commodity.
händeringend [ˈhɛndərɪŋənd] *adv* wringing one's hands; (*fig*) imploringly.
Hand- *zW*: ~**feger** (**-s, -**) *m* brush; ~**fertigkeit** *f* dexterity; **h**~**fest** *adj* hefty; ~**fläche** *f* palm *od* flat (of one's hand); **h**~**gearbeitet** *adj* handmade; ~**gelenk** *nt* wrist; **aus dem** ~**gelenk** (*umg: ohne Mühe*) effortlessly; (: *improvisiert*) off the cuff; ~**gemenge** *nt* scuffle; ~**gepäck** *nt* hand baggage *od* luggage; **h**~**geschrieben** *adj* handwritten; ~**granate** *f* hand grenade; **h**~**greiflich** *adj* palpable; **h**~**greiflich werden** to become violent; ~**griff** *m* flick of the wrist; ~**habe** *f*: **ich habe gegen ihn keine** ~**habe** (*fig*) I have no hold on him; **h**~**haben** *unreg vt untr* to handle; ~**karren** *m* handcart; ~**käse** *m* *strong-smelling, round German cheese*; ~**kuss▲** *m* kiss on the hand; ~**langer** (**-s, -**) *m* odd-job man, handyman; (*fig: Untergeordneter*) dogsbody.
Händler [ˈhɛndlər] (**-s, -**) *m* trader, dealer.
handlich [ˈhantlɪç] *adj* handy.
Handlung [ˈhandlʊŋ] *f* action; (*Tat*) act; (*in Buch*) plot; (*Geschäft*) shop.
Handlungs- *zW*: ~**ablauf** *m* plot; ~**bevollmächtigte(r)** *f(m)* authorized agent; **h**~**fähig** *adj* (*Regierung*) able to act; (*JUR*) empowered to act; ~**freiheit** *f* freedom of

action; **h~orientiert** *adj* action-orientated; **~reisende(r)** *f(m)* commercial traveller (*BRIT*), traveling salesman (*US*); **~vollmacht** *f* proxy; **~weise** *f* manner of dealing.

Hand- *zW*: **~pflege** *f* manicure; **~schelle** *f* handcuff; **~schlag** *m* handshake; **keinen ~schlag tun** not to do a stroke (of work); **~schrift** *f* handwriting; (*Text*) manuscript; **h~schriftlich** *adj* handwritten ♦ *adv* (*korrigieren, einfügen*) by hand; **~schuh** *m* glove; **~schuhfach** *nt* (*AUT*) glove compartment; **~tasche** *f* handbag (*BRIT*), pocket book (*US*), purse (*US*); **~tuch** *nt* towel; **~umdrehen** *nt*: **im ~umdrehen** (*fig*) in the twinkling of an eye.

Handwerk *nt* trade, craft; **jdm das ~ legen** (*fig*) to put a stop to sb's game.

Handwerker (**-s, -**) *m* craftsman, artisan; **wir haben seit Wochen die ~ im Haus** we've had workmen in the house for weeks.

Handwerkskammer *f* trade corporation.

Handwerkszeug *nt* tools *pl*.

Handwörterbuch *nt* concise dictionary.

Handy ['hɛndi] (**-s, -s**) *nt* (*TEL*) mobile (phone).

Handzeichen *nt* signal; (*Geste*) sign; (*bei Abstimmung*) show of hands.

Handzettel *m* leaflet, handbill.

Hanf [hanf] (**-(e)s**) *m* hemp.

Hang [haŋ] (**-(e)s, ¨e**) *m* inclination; (*Ab~*) slope.

Hänge- ['hɛŋə] *in zW* hanging; **~brücke** *f* suspension bridge; **~matte** *f* hammock.

Hängen ['hɛŋən] *nt*: **mit ~ und Würgen** (*umg*) by the skin of one's teeth.

hängen *unreg vi* to hang ♦ *vt*: **~ (an** +*akk*) to hang (on(to)); **an jdm ~** (*fig*) to be attached to sb; **~ bleiben** to be caught; (*fig*) to remain, stick; **~ bleiben an** +*dat* to catch *od* get caught on; **es bleibt ja doch alles an mir ~** (*fig*: *umg*) in the end it's all down to me anyhow; **~ lassen** (*vergessen*) to leave behind; **sich ~ lassen** to let o.s. go; **den Kopf ~ lassen** (*fig*) to be downcast; **die ganze Sache hängt an ihm** it all depends on him; **sich ~ an** +*akk* to hang on to, cling to.

hängend *adj*: **mit ~er Zunge kam er angelaufen** (*fig*) he came running up panting.

Hängeschloss▲ *nt* padlock.

Hanglage *f*: **in ~** situated on a slope.

Hannover [ha'noːfər] (**-s**) *nt* Hanover.

Hannoveraner(in) [hanovə'raːnər(ɪn)] (**-s, -**) *m(f)* Hanoverian.

hänseln ['hɛnzəln] *vt* to tease.

Hansestadt ['hanzəʃtat] *f* Hanseatic *od* Hanse town.

Hanswurst [hans'vʊrst] (**-(e)s, -e** *od* **-würste**) *m* clown.

Hantel ['hantəl] (**-, -n**) *f* (*SPORT*) dumb-bell.

hantieren [han'tiːrən] *vi* to work, be busy; **mit**

etw ~ to handle sth.

hapern ['haːpərn] *vi unpers*: **es hapert an etw** *dat* there is a lack of sth.

Happen ['hapən] (**-s, -**) *m* mouthful.

happig ['hapɪç] (*umg*) *adj* steep.

Hardware ['haːdwɛə] (**-, -s**) *f* hardware.

Harfe ['harfə] (**-, -n**) *f* harp.

Harke ['harkə] (**-, -n**) *f* rake.

harken *vt, vi* to rake.

harmlos ['harmloːs] *adj* harmless.

Harmlosigkeit *f* harmlessness.

Harmonie [harmo'niː] *f* harmony.

harmonieren *vi* to harmonize.

Harmonika [har'moːnika] (**-, -s**) *f* (*Zieh~*) concertina.

harmonisch [har'moːnɪʃ] *adj* harmonious.

Harmonium [har'moːniʊm] (**-s, -nien** *od* **-s**) *nt* harmonium.

Harn ['harn] (**-(e)s, -e**) *m* urine; **~blase** *f* bladder.

Harnisch ['harnɪʃ] (**-(e)s, -e**) *m* armour, armor (*US*); **jdn in ~ bringen** to infuriate sb; **in ~ geraten** to become angry.

Harpune [har'puːnə] (**-, -n**) *f* harpoon.

harren ['harən] *vi*: **~ auf** +*akk* to wait for.

Harsch [harʃ] (**-(e)s**) *m* frozen snow.

harschig *adj* (*Schnee*) frozen.

hart [hart] *adj* hard; (*fig*) harsh ♦ *adv*: **das ist ~ an der Grenze** that's almost going too far; **~e Währung** hard currency; **~ bleiben** to stand firm; **~ gekocht** hard-boiled; **~ gesotten** (*Ei*) hard-boiled; **es geht ~ auf ~** it's a tough fight.

Härte ['hɛrtə] (**-, -n**) *f* hardness; (*fig*) harshness; **soziale ~n** social hardships; **~fall** *m* case of hardship; (*umg*: *Mensch*) hardship case; **~klausel** *f* hardship clause.

härten *vt, vr* to harden.

hart- *zW*: **H~faserplatte** *f* hardboard, fiberboard (*US*); **~gesotten** *adj* (*Kerl*) tough, hard-boiled; **~herzig** *adj* hard-hearted; **~näckig** *adj* stubborn; **H~näckigkeit** *f* stubbornness.

Harz¹ [haːrts] (**-es, -e**) *nt* resin.

Harz² (**-es**) *m* (*GEOG*) Harz Mountains *pl*.

Haschee [ha'ʃeː] (**-s, -s**) *nt* hash.

haschen ['haʃən] *vt* to catch, snatch ♦ *vi* (*umg*) to smoke hash.

Haschisch ['haʃɪʃ] (**-**) *nt* hashish.

Hase ['haːzə] (**-n, -n**) *m* hare; **falscher ~** (*KOCH*) meat loaf; **wissen, wie der ~ läuft** (*fig*: *umg*) to know which way the wind blows; **mein Name ist ~(, ich weiß von nichts)** I don't know anything about anything.

Haselnuss▲ ['haːzəlnʊs] *f* hazelnut.

Hasenfuß *m* coward.

Hasenscharte *f* harelip.

Haspel (**-, -n**) *f* reel, bobbin; (*Winde*) winch.

Hass▲ [has] (**-es**) *m* hate, hatred; **einen ~ (auf**

jdn) haben (*umg: Wut*) to be really mad (with sb).

hassen ['hasən] *vt* to hate; **etw ~ wie die Pest** (*umg*) to detest sth.

hassenswert *adj* hateful.

hässlich▲ ['hɛslɪç] *adj* ugly; (*gemein*) nasty; **H~keit** *f* ugliness; nastiness.

Hassliebe▲ *f* love-hate relationship.

Hast [hast] (-) *f* haste.

hast *vb siehe* **haben.**

hasten *vi, vr* to rush.

hastig *adj* hasty.

hat [hat] *vb siehe* **haben.**

hätscheln ['hɛtʃəln] *vt* to pamper; (*zärtlich*) to cuddle.

hatte *etc* ['hatə] *vb siehe* **haben.**

hätte *etc* ['hɛtə] *vb siehe* **haben.**

Haube ['haubə] (-, -n) *f* hood; (*Mütze*) cap; (*AUT*) bonnet (*BRIT*), hood (*US*); **unter der ~ sein/unter die ~ kommen** (*hum*) to be/get married.

Hauch [haux] (-(e)s, -e) *m* breath; (*Luft~*) breeze; (*fig*) trace; **h~dünn** *adj* extremely thin; (*Scheiben*) wafer-thin; (*fig: Mehrheit*) extremely narrow; **h~en** *vi* to breathe; **h~fein** *adj* very fine.

Haue ['hauə] (-, -n) *f* hoe; (*Pickel*) pick; (*umg*) hiding.

hauen *unreg vt* to hew, cut; (*umg*) to thrash.

Hauer ['hauər] (-s, -) *m* (*MIN*) face-worker.

Häufchen ['hɔyfçən] *nt:* **ein ~ Unglück** *od* **Elend** a picture of misery.

Haufen ['haufən] (-s, -) *m* heap; (*Leute*) crowd; **ein ~ (Bücher)** (*umg*) loads *od* a lot (of books); **auf einem ~** in one heap; **etw über den ~ werfen** (*umg: verwerfen*) to chuck sth out; **jdn über den ~ rennen** *od* **fahren** *etc* (*umg*) to knock sb down.

häufen ['hɔyfən] *vt* to pile up ♦ *vr* to accumulate.

haufenweise *adv* in heaps; in droves; **etw ~ haben** to have piles of sth.

häufig ['hɔyfɪç] *adj* frequent ♦ *adv* frequently; **H~keit** *f* frequency.

Haupt [haupt] (-(e)s, Häupter) *nt* head; (*Ober~*) chief ♦ *in zW* main; **~akteur** *m* (*lit, fig*) leading light; (*pej*) main figure; **~aktionär** *m* major shareholder; **~bahnhof** *m* central station; **h~beruflich** *adv* as one's main occupation; **~buch** *nt* (*COMM*) ledger; **~darsteller(in)** *m(f)* leading actor, leading actress; **~eingang** *m* main entrance; **~fach** *nt* (*SCH, UNIV*) main subject, major (*US*); **etw im ~fach studieren** to study sth as one's main subject, major in sth (*US*); **~film** *m* main film; (*umg*) main course; **~geschäftsstelle** *f* head office; **~geschäftszeit** *f* peak (shopping) period; **~gewinn** *m* first prize; **einer der ~gewinne** one of the main prizes; **~leitung** *f* mains *pl*.

Häuptling ['hɔyptlɪŋ] *m* chief(tain).

Haupt- *zW:* **~mahlzeit** *f* main meal; **~mann** (-(e)s, *pl* -leute) *m* (*MIL*) captain; **~nahrungsmittel** *nt* staple food; **~person** *f* (*im Roman usw*) main character; (*fig*) central figure; **~postamt** *nt* main post office; **~quartier** *nt* headquarters *pl*; **~rolle** *f* leading part; **~sache** *f* main thing; **in der ~sache** in the main, mainly; **h~sächlich** *adj* chief ♦ *adv* chiefly; **~saison** *f* peak *od* high season; **~satz** *m* main clause; **~schlagader** *f* aorta; **~schlüssel** *m* master key.

Hauptschule *f* ≈ secondary modern (school) (*BRIT*), junior high (school) (*US*).

Haupt- *zW:* **~sendezeit** *f* (*TV*) prime time; **~stadt** *f* capital; **~straße** *f* main street; **~verkehrsstraße** *f* (*in Stadt*) main street; (*Durchgangsstraße*) main thoroughfare; (*zwischen Städten*) main highway, trunk road (*BRIT*); **~verkehrszeit** *f* rush hour; **~versammlung** *f* general meeting; **~wohnsitz** *m* main place of residence; **~wort** *nt* noun.

hau ruck ['hau 'ruk] *interj* heave-ho.

Haus [haus] (-es, Häuser) *nt* house; **nach ~e** home; **zu ~e** at home; **fühl dich wie zu ~e!** make yourself at home!; **ein Freund des ~es** a friend of the family; **~ halten** (*sparen*) to economize; **wir liefern frei ~** (*COMM*) we offer free delivery; **das erste ~ am Platze** (*Hotel*) the best hotel in town; *siehe auch* **nachhause, zuhause;** **~angestellte** *f* domestic servant; **~arbeit** *f* housework; (*SCH*) homework; **~arrest** *m* (*im Internat*) detention; (*JUR*) house arrest; **~arzt** *m* family doctor; **~aufgabe** *f* (*SCH*) homework; **~besetzung** *f* squat; **~besitzer** *m* house-owner; **~besuch** *m* home visit; (*von Arzt*) house call.

Häuschen ['hɔysçən] *nt:* **ganz aus dem ~ sein** (*fig: umg*) to be out of one's mind (with excitement/fear *etc*).

Hauseigentümer *m* house-owner.

hausen ['hauzən] *vi* to live (in poverty); (*pej*) to wreak havoc.

Häuser- *zW:* **~block** *m* block (of houses); **~makler** *m* estate agent (*BRIT*), real estate agent (*US*); **~reihe** *f*, **~zeile** *f* row of houses; (*aneinander gebaut*) terrace (*BRIT*).

Haus- *zW:* **~frau** *f* housewife; **~freund** *m* family friend; (*umg*) lover; **~friedensbruch** *m* (*JUR*) trespass (*in sb's house*); **~gebrauch** *m:* **für den ~gebrauch** (*Gerät*) for domestic *od*

household use; **h~gemacht** adj home-made;
~gemeinschaft f household (community);
~halt m household; (POL) budget; **h~halten**
unreg vi (old) to keep house; (sparen) to
economize; **~hälterin** f housekeeper.

Haushalts- zW: **~auflösung** f dissolution of
the household; **~buch** nt housekeeping book;
~debatte f (PARL) budget debate; **~geld** nt
housekeeping (money); **~gerät** nt domestic
appliance; **~hilfe** f domestic od home help;
~jahr nt (POL, WIRTS) financial od fiscal
year; **~periode** f budget period; **~plan** m
budget.

Haus- zW: **~haltung** f housekeeping; **~herr** m
host; (Vermieter) landlord; **h~hoch** adv:
h~hoch verlieren to lose by a mile.

hausieren [hauˈziːrən] vi to peddle.

Hausierer (-s, -) m pedlar (BRIT), peddler (US).

hausintern [ˈhausˌɪntɛrn] adj internal
company attrib.

häuslich [ˈhɔyslɪç] adj domestic; **sich irgendwo
~ einrichten** od **niederlassen** to settle in
somewhere; **H~keit** f domesticity.

Hausmacherart [ˈhausmaxərˌaːrt] f: **Wurst** etc
nach ~ home-made-style sausage etc.

Haus- zW: **~mann** (-(e)s, pl **-männer**) m (den
Haushalt versorgender Mann) househusband;
~marke f (eigene Marke) own brand;
(bevorzugte Marke) favourite (BRIT) od
favorite (US) brand; **~meister** m caretaker,
janitor; **~mittel** nt household remedy;
~nummer f house number; **~ordnung** f
house rules pl; **~putz** m house cleaning;
~ratversicherung f (household) contents
insurance; **~schlüssel** m front-door key;
~schuh m slipper; **~schwamm** m dry rot.

Hausse [ˈhoːsə] (-, -n) f (WIRTS) boom;
(BÖRSE) bull market; **~ an** +dat boom in.

Haus- zW: **~segen** m: **bei ihnen hängt der
~segen schief** (hum) they're a bit short on
domestic bliss; **~stand** m: **einen ~stand
gründen** to set up house od home;
~(durch)suchung f police raid;
~(durch)suchungsbefehl m search warrant;
~tier nt domestic animal; **~tür** f front door;
~verbot nt: **jdm ~verbot erteilen** to ban sb
from the house; **~verwalter** m property
manager; **~verwaltung** f property
management; **~wirt** m landlord; **~wirtschaft**
f domestic science; **~-zu-~-Verkauf** m door-
to-door selling.

Haut [haut] (-, **Häute**) f skin; (Tier~) hide; **mit
~ und Haar(en)** (umg) completely; **aus der
~ fahren** (umg) to go through the roof;
~arzt m skin specialist, dermatologist.

häuten [ˈhɔytən] vt to skin ♦ vr to shed one's
skin.

hauteng adj skintight.

Hautfarbe f complexion.

Hautkrebs m (MED) skin cancer.

Havanna [haˈvana] (-s) nt Havana.

Havel [ˈhaːfəl] (-) f (Fluss) Havel.

Haxe [ˈhaksə] (-, -n) f = **Hachse**.

Hbf. abk = **Hauptbahnhof**.

H-Bombe [ˈhaːbɔmbə] f abk H-bomb.

Hebamme [ˈheːpˌamə] f midwife.

Hebel [ˈheːbəl] (-s, -) m lever; **alle ~ in
Bewegung setzen** (umg) to move heaven
and earth; **am längeren ~ sitzen** (umg) to
have the whip hand.

heben [ˈheːbən] unreg vt to raise, lift; (steigern)
to increase; **einen ~ gehen** (umg) to go for a
drink.

Hebräer(in) [heˈbrɛːər(ɪn)] (-s, -) m(f) Hebrew.

hebräisch [heˈbrɛːɪʃ] adj Hebrew.

Hebriden [heˈbriːdən] pl: **die ~** the Hebrides
pl.

hecheln [ˈhɛçəln] vi (Hund) to pant.

Hecht [hɛçt] (-(e)s, -e) m pike; **~sprung** m
(beim Schwimmen) racing dive; (beim
Turnen) forward dive; (FUSSBALL: umg)
dive.

Heck [hɛk] (-(e)s, -e) nt stern; (von Auto) rear.

Hecke [ˈhɛkə] (-, -n) f hedge.

Heckenrose f dog rose.

Heckenschütze m sniper.

Heck- zW: **~fenster** nt (AUT) rear window;
~klappe f tailgate; **~motor** m rear engine.

heda [ˈheːda] interj hey there.

Heer [heːr] (-(e)s, -e) nt army.

Hefe [ˈheːfə] (-, -n) f yeast.

Heft [hɛft] (-(e)s, -e) nt exercise book;
(Zeitschrift) number; (von Messer) haft; **jdm
das ~ aus der Hand nehmen** (fig) to seize
control od power from sb.

Heftchen nt (Fahrkarten~) book of tickets;
(Briefmarken~) book of stamps.

heften vt: **~ (an** +akk) to fasten (to); (nähen) to
tack (on (to)); (mit Heftmaschine) to staple od
fasten (on) ♦ vr: **sich an jds Fersen** od **Sohlen
~** (fig) to dog sb's heels.

Hefter (-s, -) m folder.

heftig adj fierce, violent; **H~keit** f fierceness,
violence.

Heft- zW: **~klammer** f staple; **~maschine** f
stapling machine; **~pflaster** nt sticking
plaster; **~zwecke** f drawing pin (BRIT),
thumb tack (US).

hegen [ˈheːgən] vt to nurse; (fig) to harbour
(BRIT), harbor (US), foster.

Hehl [heːl] m od nt: **kein(en) ~ aus etw machen**
to make no secret of sth.

Hehler (-s, -) m receiver (of stolen goods),
fence.

Heide¹ [ˈhaɪdə] (-, -n) f heath, moor; (~kraut)
heather.

Heide² [ˈhaɪdə] (-n, -n) m heathen, pagan.

Heidekraut nt heather.

Heidelbeere f bilberry.

Heiden- zW: **~angst** (umg) f: **eine ~angst vor**

etw/jdm haben to be scared stiff of sth/sb;
~**arbeit** (*umg*) *f* real slog; **h~mäßig** (*umg*) *adj*
terrific; ~**tum** *nt* paganism.
Heidin *f* heathen, pagan.
heidnisch ['haɪdnɪʃ] *adj* heathen, pagan.
heikel ['haɪkəl] *adj* awkward, thorny;
(*wählerisch*) fussy.
Heil [haɪl] (**-(e)s**) *nt* well-being; (*Seelen~*)
salvation ♦ *interj* hail; **Ski/Petri ~!** good
skiing/fishing!
heil *adj* in one piece, intact; **mit ~er Haut
davonkommen** to escape unscathed; **die ~e
Welt** an ideal world (*without problems etc*).
Heiland (**-(e)s, -e**) *m* saviour (*BRIT*), savior
(*US*).
Heil- *zW*: ~**anstalt** *f* nursing home; (*für Sucht-
oder Geisteskranke*) home; ~**bad** *nt* (*Bad*)
medicinal bath; (*Ort*) spa; **h~bar** *adj* curable.
Heilbutt ['haɪlbʊt] (**-s, -e**) *m* halibut.
heilen *vt* to cure ♦ *vi* to heal; **als geheilt
entlassen werden** to be discharged with a
clean bill of health.
heilfroh *adj* very relieved.
Heilgymnastin *f* physiotherapist.
heilig ['haɪlɪç] *adj* holy; **jdm ~ sein** (*lit, fig*) to
be sacred to sb; **jdn ~ sprechen** to canonize;
die H~e Schrift the Holy Scriptures *pl*; **es ist
mein ~er Ernst** I am deadly serious;
H~abend *m* Christmas Eve.
Heilige(r) *f(m)* saint.
heiligen *vt* to sanctify, hallow; **der Zweck
heiligt die Mittel** the end justifies the means.
Heiligenschein *m* halo.
Heiligkeit *f* holiness.
Heiligtum *nt* shrine; (*Gegenstand*) relic.
Heilkunde *f* medicine.
heillos *adj* unholy; (*Schreck*) terrible.
Heil- *zW*: ~**mittel** *nt* remedy; ~**praktiker(in)** (**-s,
-**) *m(f)* non-medical practitioner; **h~sam** *adj*
(*fig*) salutary.
Heilsarmee *f* Salvation Army.
Heilung *f* cure.
heim [haɪm] *adv* home.
Heim (**-(e)s, -e**) *nt* home; (*Wohn~*) hostel.
Heimarbeit *f* (*INDUSTRIE*) homework,
outwork.
Heimat ['haɪmaːt] (**-, -en**) *f* home (town/
country *etc*); ~**film** *m* sentimental film in
idealized regional setting; ~**kunde** *f* (*SCH*)
local history; ~**land** *nt* homeland; **h~lich** *adj*
native, home *attrib*; (*Gefühle*) nostalgic;
h~los *adj* homeless; ~**museum** *nt* local
history museum; ~**ort** *m* home town *od* area;
~**vertriebene(r)** *f(m)* displaced person.
heimbegleiten *vt* to accompany home.
Heimchen *nt*: ~ **(am Herd)** (*pej: Frau*)
housewife.
Heimcomputer *m* home computer.
heimelig ['haɪməlɪç] *adj* homely.
Heim- *zW*: **h~fahren** *unreg vi* to drive *od* go

home; ~**fahrt** *f* journey home; ~**gang** *m*
return home; (*Tod*) decease; **h~gehen** *unreg
vi* to go home; (*sterben*) to pass away; **h~isch**
adj (*gebürtig*) native; **sich h~isch fühlen** to
feel at home; ~**kehr** (**-, -en**) *f* homecoming;
h~kehren *vi* to return home; ~**kind** *nt* child
brought up in a home; **h~kommen** *unreg vi* to
come home; ~**leiter** *m* warden of a home/
hostel.
heimlich *adj* secret ♦ *adv*: ~, **still und leise**
(*umg*) quietly, on the quiet; **H~keit** *f*
secrecy; **H~tuerei** *f* secrecy.
Heim- *zW*: ~**reise** *f* journey home; ~**spiel** *nt*
home game; **h~suchen** *vt* to afflict; (*Geist*) to
haunt; **h~tückisch** *adj* malicious; **h~wärts**
adv homewards; ~**weg** *m* way home; ~**weh** *nt*
homesickness; ~**weh haben** to be homesick;
~**werker** *m* handyman; **h~zahlen** *vt*: **jdm etw
h~zahlen** to pay back sb for sth.
Heini ['haɪni] (**-s, -s**) *m*: **blöder ~** (*umg*) silly
idiot.
Heirat ['haɪraːt] (**-, -en**) *f* marriage; **h~en** *vt, vi*
to marry.
Heirats- *zW*: ~**antrag** *m* proposal (of
marriage); ~**anzeige** *f* (*Annonce*)
advertisement for a marriage partner;
~**schwindler** *m person who makes a
marriage proposal under false pretences*;
~**urkunde** *f* marriage certificate.
heiser ['haɪzər] *adj* hoarse; **H~keit** *f*
hoarseness.
heiß [haɪs] *adj* hot; (*Thema*) hotly disputed;
(*Diskussion, Kampf*) heated, fierce; (*Begierde,
Liebe, Wunsch*) burning; **es wird nichts so
~ gegessen, wie es gekocht wird**
(*Sprichwort*) things are never as bad as they
seem; ~**er Draht** hot line; ~**es Eisen** (*fig:
umg*) hot potato; ~**es Geld** hot money;
~ **ersehnt** longed for; ~ **umstritten** hotly
debated; **jdn/etw ~ und innig lieben** to love
sb/sth madly; ~**blütig** *adj* hot-blooded.
heißen ['haɪsən] *unreg vi* to be called;
(*bedeuten*) to mean ♦ *vt* to command;
(*nennen*) to name ♦ *vi unpers*: **es heißt hier ...**
it says here ...; **es heißt, dass ...** they say
that ...; **wie ~ Sie?** what's your name?; ...
und wie sie alle ~ ... and the rest of them;
das will schon etwas ~ that's quite
something; **jdn willkommen ~** to bid sb
welcome; **das heißt** that is; (*mit anderen
Worten*) that is to say.
Heiß- *zW*: ~**hunger** *m* ravenous hunger;
h~laufen *unreg vi, vr* to overheat; ~**luft** *f* hot
air; ~**wasserbereiter** *m* water heater.
heiter ['haɪtər] *adj* cheerful; (*Wetter*) bright;
aus ~em Himmel (*fig*) out of the blue;
H~keit *f* cheerfulness; (*Belustigung*)
amusement.
heizbar *adj* heated; (*Raum*) with heating;
leicht ~ easily heated.

Heizdecke *f* electric blanket.
heizen *vt* to heat.
Heizer (-s, -) *m* stoker.
Heiz- *zW*: ~**gerät** *nt* heater; ~**körper** *m* radiator; ~**öl** *nt* fuel oil; ~**sonne** *f* electric fire.
Heizung *f* heating.
Heizungsanlage *f* heating system.
Hektar [hɛk'taːr] (-s, -e) *nt od m* hectare.
Hektik [['hɛktɪk]] *f* hectic rush; (*von Leben etc*) hectic pace.
hektisch ['hɛktɪʃ] *adj* hectic.
Hektoliter [hɛktoˈliːtər] *m od nt* hectolitre (*BRIT*), hectoliter (*US*).
Held [hɛlt] (-en, -en) *m* hero; **h~enhaft** ['hɛldənhaft] *adj* heroic; ~**in** *f* heroine.
helfen ['hɛlfən] *unreg vi* to help; (*nützen*) to be of use ♦ *vb unpers*: **es hilft nichts, du musst ...** it's no use, you'll have to ...; **jdm (bei etw)** ~ to help sb (with sth); **sich** *dat* **zu** ~ **wissen** to be resourceful; **er weiß sich** *dat* **nicht mehr zu** ~ he's at his wits' end.
Helfer(in) (-s, -) *m(f)* helper, assistant.
Helfershelfer *m* accomplice.
Helgoland ['hɛlgolant] (-s) *nt* Heligoland.
hell [hɛl] *adj* clear; (*Licht, Himmel*) bright; (*Farbe*) light; ~**es Bier** ≈ lager; **von etw** ~ **begeistert sein** to be very enthusiastic about sth; **es wird** ~ it's getting light; ~**blau** *adj* light blue; ~**blond** *adj* ash-blond.
Helle (-) *f* clearness; brightness.
Heller (-s, -) *m* farthing; **auf** ~ **und Pfennig** (down) to the last penny.
hellhörig *adj* keen of hearing; (*Wand*) poorly soundproofed.
hellicht△ ['hɛllɪçt] *adj siehe* **helllicht**.
Helligkeit *f* clearness; brightness; lightness.
helllicht▲ ['hɛllɪçt] *adj*: **am** ~**en Tage** in broad daylight.
hell- *zW*: ~**sehen** *vi*: ~**sehen können** to be clairvoyant; **H~seher(in)** *m(f)* clairvoyant; ~**wach** *adj* wide-awake.
Helm ['hɛlm] (-(e)s, -e) *m* helmet.
Helsinki ['hɛlzɪŋki] (-s) *nt* Helsinki.
Hemd [hɛmt] (-(e)s, -en) *nt* shirt; (*Unter~*) vest; ~**bluse** *f* blouse.
Hemdenknopf *m* shirt button.
hemdsärmelig *adj* shirt-sleeved; (*fig: umg: salopp*) pally; (*Ausdrucksweise*) casual.
Hemisphäre [hemiˈsfɛːrə] *f* hemisphere.
hemmen ['hɛmən] *vt* to check, hold up; **gehemmt sein** to be inhibited.
Hemmschuh *m* (*fig*) impediment.
Hemmung *f* check; (*PSYCH*) inhibition; (*Bedenken*) scruple.
hemmungslos *adj* unrestrained, without restraint.
Hengst [hɛŋst] (-es, -e) *m* stallion.
Henkel ['hɛŋkəl] (-s, -) *m* handle; ~**krug** *m* jug; ~**mann** (*umg*) *m* (*Gefäß*) canteen.

henken ['hɛŋkən] *vt* to hang.
Henker (-s, -) *m* hangman.
Henne ['hɛnə] (-, -n) *f* hen.
Hepatitis [hepaˈtiːtɪs] *f* (-, **Hepatitiden**) hepatitis.

═══════════════════ *SCHLÜSSELWORT*

her [heːr] *adv* **1** (*Richtung*): **komm** ~ **zu mir** come here (to me); **von England** ~ from England; **von weit** ~ from a long way away; ~ **damit!** hand it over!; **wo bist du** ~? where do you come from?; **wo hat er das** ~? where did he get that from?; **hinter jdm/etw** ~ **sein** to be after sb/sth.
2 (*Blickpunkt*): **von der Form** ~ as far as the form is concerned.
3 (*zeitlich*): **das ist 5 Jahre** ~ that was 5 years ago; **ich kenne ihn von früher** ~ I know him from before.

herab [hɛˈrap] *adv* down, downward(s); ~**hängen** *unreg vi* to hang down; ~**lassen** *unreg vt* to let down ♦ *vr* to condescend; ~**lassend** *adj* condescending; **H~lassung** *f* condescension; ~**sehen** *unreg vi*: ~**sehen (auf** +*akk*) to look down (on); ~**setzen** *vt* to lower, reduce; (*fig*) to belittle, disparage; **zu stark** ~**gesetzten Preisen** at greatly reduced prices; **H~setzung** *f* reduction; disparagement; ~**stürzen** *vi* to fall off; (*Felsbrocken*) to fall down; **von etw** ~**stürzen** to fall off sth; to fall down from sth; ~**würdigen** *vt* to belittle, disparage.
heran [hɛˈran] *adv*: **näher** ~! come closer!; ~ **zu mir!** come up to me!; ~**bilden** *vt* to train; ~**bringen** *unreg vt*: ~**bringen (an** +*akk*) to bring up (to); ~**fahren** *unreg vi*: ~**fahren (an** +*akk*) to drive up (to); ~**gehen** *unreg vi*: **an etw** *akk* ~**gehen** (*an Problem, Aufgabe*) to tackle sth; ~**kommen** *unreg vi*: (**an jdn/etw**) ~**kommen** to approach (sb/sth), come near ((to) sb/sth); **er lässt alle Probleme an sich** ~**kommen** he always adopts a wait-and-see attitude; ~**machen** *vr*: **sich an jdn** ~**machen** to make up to sb; (*umg*) to approach sb; ~**wachsen** *unreg vi* to grow up; **H~wachsende(r)** *f(m)* adolescent; ~**winken** *vt* to beckon over; (*Taxi*) to hail; ~**ziehen** *unreg vt* to pull nearer; (*aufziehen*) to raise; (*ausbilden*) to train; (*zu Hilfe holen*) to call in; (*Literatur*) to consult; **etw zum Vergleich** ~**ziehen** to use sth by way of comparison; **jdn zu etw** ~**ziehen** to call upon sb to help in sth.
herauf [hɛˈrauf] *adv* up, upward(s); up here; ~**beschwören** *unreg vt* to conjure up, evoke; ~**bringen** *unreg vt* to bring up; ~**setzen** *vt* to increase; ~**ziehen** *unreg vt* to draw *od* pull up ♦ *vi* to approach; (*Sturm*) to gather.
heraus [hɛˈraus] *adv* out; **nach vorn** ~ **wohnen**

to live at the front (of the house); **aus dem Gröbsten ~ sein** to be over the worst; **~ mit der Sprache!** out with it!; **~arbeiten** vt to work out; **~bekommen** unreg vt to get out; (fig) to find od figure out; (Wechselgeld) to get back; **~bringen** unreg vt to bring out; (Geheimnis) to elicit; **jdn/etw ganz groß ~bringen** (umg) to give sb/sth a big build-up; **aus ihm war kein Wort ~zubringen** they couldn't get a single word out of him; **~finden** unreg vt to find out; **~fordern** vt to challenge; (provozieren) to provoke; **H~forderung** f challenge; provocation; **~geben** unreg vt to give up, surrender; (Geld) to give back; (Buch) to edit; (veröffentlichen) to publish ♦ vi (Wechselgeld geben): **können Sie (mir) ~geben?** can you give me change?; **H~geber (-s, -)** m editor; (Verleger) publisher; **~gehen** unreg vi: **aus sich ~gehen** to come out of one's shell; **~halten** unreg vr: **sich aus etw ~halten** to keep out of sth; **~hängen** unreg vt, vi to hang out; **~holen** vt: **~holen (aus)** to get out (of); **~hören** vt (wahrnehmen) to hear; (fühlen): **~hören (aus)** to detect (in); **~kehren** vt (fig): **den Vorgesetzten ~kehren** to act the boss; **~kommen** unreg vi to come out; **dabei kommt nichts ~** nothing will come of it; **er kam aus dem Staunen nicht ~** he couldn't get over his astonishment; **es kommt auf dasselbe ~** it comes (down) to the same thing; **~nehmen** unreg vt to take out; **sich** dat **Freiheiten ~nehmen** to take liberties; **Sie nehmen sich zu viel ~** you're going too far; **~putzen** vt: **sich ~putzen** to get dressed up; **~reden** vr to talk one's way out of it (umg); **~reißen** unreg vt to tear out; (Zahn, Baum) to pull out; **~rücken** vt (Geld) to fork out, hand over; **mit etw ~rücken** (fig) to come out with sth; **~rutschen** vi to slip out; **~schlagen** unreg vt to knock out; (fig) to obtain; **~stellen** vr: **sich ~stellen (als)** to turn out (to be); **das muss sich erst ~stellen** that remains to be seen; **~strecken** vt to stick out; **~suchen** vt: **sich** dat **jdn/etw ~suchen** to pick out sb/sth; **~treten** unreg vi: **~treten (aus)** to come out (of); **~wachsen** unreg vi: **~wachsen aus** to grow out of; **~winden** unreg vr (fig): **sich aus etw ~winden** to wriggle out of sth; **~wollen** vi: **nicht mit etw ~wollen** (umg: sagen wollen) to not want to come out with sth; **~ziehen** unreg vt to pull out, extract.

herb [hɛrp] adj (slightly) bitter, acid; (Wein) dry; (fig: schmerzlich) bitter; (: streng) stern, austere.

herbei [hɛr'baɪ] adv (over) here; **~führen** vt to bring about; **~schaffen** vt to procure; **~sehnen** vt to long for.

herbemühen ['hɛːrbəmyːən] vr to take the trouble to come.

Herberge ['hɛrbɛrgə] (-, -n) f (Jugend~ etc) hostel.
Herbergsmutter f warden.
Herbergsvater m warden.
herbitten unreg vt to ask to come (here).
herbringen unreg vt to bring here.
Herbst [hɛrpst] (-(e)s, -e) m autumn, fall (US); **im ~** in autumn, in the fall (US); **h~lich** adj autumnal.
Herd [heːrt] (-(e)s, -e) m cooker; (fig, MED) focus, centre (BRIT), center (US).
Herde ['heːrdə] (-, -n) f herd; (Schaf~) flock.
Herdentrieb m (lit, fig: pej) herd instinct.
Herdplatte f (von Elektroherd) hotplate.
herein [hɛ'raɪn] adv in (here), here; **~!** come in!; **~bitten** unreg vt to ask in; **~brechen** unreg vi to set in; **~bringen** unreg vt to bring in; **~dürfen** unreg vi to have permission to enter; **H~fall** m letdown; **~fallen** unreg vi to be caught, be taken in; **~fallen auf** +akk to fall for; **~kommen** unreg vi to come in; **~lassen** unreg vt to admit; **~legen** vt: **jdn ~legen** to take sb in; **~platzen** vi to burst in; **~schneien** (umg) vi to drop in; **~spazieren** vi: **~spaziert!** come right in!
her- zW: **H~fahrt** f journey here; **~fallen** unreg vi: **~fallen über** +akk to fall upon; **H~gang** m course of events, circumstances pl; **~geben** unreg vt to give, hand (over); **sich zu etw ~geben** to lend one's name to sth; **das Thema gibt viel/nichts ~** there's a lot/ nothing to this topic; **~gebracht** adj: **in ~gebrachter Weise** in the traditional way; **~gehen** unreg vi: **hinter jdm ~gehen** to follow sb; **es geht hoch ~** there are a lot of goings-on; **~haben** unreg (umg) vt: **wo hat er das ~?** where did he get that from?; **~halten** unreg vt to hold out; **~halten müssen** (umg) to have to suffer; **~hören** vi to listen; **hör mal ~!** listen here!
Hering ['heːrɪŋ] (-s, -e) m herring; (Zeltpflock) (tent) peg.
herkommen unreg vi to come; **komm mal her!** come here!
herkömmlich adj traditional.
Herkunft (-, -künfte) f origin.
Herkunftsland nt (COMM) country of origin.
her- zW: **~laufen** unreg vi: **~laufen hinter** +dat to run after; **~leiten** vr to derive; **~machen** vr: **sich ~machen über** +akk to set about od upon ♦ vt (umg): **viel ~machen** to look impressive.
Hermelin [hɛrmə'liːn] (-s, -e) m od nt ermine.
hermetisch [hɛr'meːtɪʃ] adj hermetic; **~ abgeriegelt** completely sealed off.
her- zW: **~nach** adv afterwards; **~nehmen** unreg vt: **wo soll ich das ~nehmen?** where am I supposed to get that from?; **~nieder** adv down.
Heroin [hero'iːn] (-s) nt heroin; **h~süchtig** adj addicted to heroin; **~süchtige(r)** f(m) heroin

addict.

heroisch [he'ro:ɪʃ] *adj* heroic.

Herold ['he:rɔlt] (-(e)s, -e) *m* herald.

Herpes [['hɛrpes]] *m* (-) (*MED*) herpes.

Herr [hɛr] (-(e)n, -en) *m* master; (*Mann*) gentleman; (*adliger, REL*) Lord; (*vor Namen*) Mr.; **mein ~**! sir!; **meine ~en**! gentlemen!; **Lieber ~ A, Sehr geehrter ~ A** (*in Brief*) Dear Mr. A; **„~en"** (*Toilette*) "gentlemen" (*BRIT*), "men's room" (*US*); **die ~en der Schöpfung** (*hum: Männer*) the gentlemen.

Herrchen (*umg*) *nt* (*von Hund*) master.

Herren- *zW:* **~bekanntschaft** *f* gentleman friend; **~bekleidung** *f* menswear; **~besuch** *m* gentleman visitor *od* visitors; **~doppel** *nt* men's doubles; **~einzel** *nt* men's singles; **~haus** *nt* mansion; **h~los** *adj* ownerless; **~magazin** *nt* men's magazine.

Herrgott *m:* **~ noch mal!** (*umg*) damn it all!

Herrgottsfrühe *f:* **in aller ~** (*umg*) at the crack of dawn.

herrichten ['he:rrɪçtən] *vt* to prepare.

Herrin *f* mistress.

herrisch *adj* domineering.

herrje [hɛr'je:] *interj* goodness gracious!

herrjemine [hɛr'je:mine] *interj* goodness gracious!

herrlich *adj* marvellous (*BRIT*), marvelous (*US*), splendid; **H~keit** *f* splendour (*BRIT*), splendor (*US*), magnificence.

Herrschaft *f* power, rule; (*Herr und Herrin*) master and mistress; **meine ~en!** ladies and gentlemen!

herrschen ['hɛrʃən] *vi* to rule; (*bestehen*) to prevail, be; **hier ~ ja Zustände!** things are in a pretty state round here!

Herrscher(in) (-s, -) *m(f)* ruler.

Herrschsucht *f* domineeringness.

her- *zW:* **~rühren** *vi* to arise, originate; **~sagen** *vt* to recite; **~sehen** *unreg vi:* **hinter jdm/etw ~sehen** to follow sb/sth with one's eyes; **~ sein▲** *siehe* **her.**

her- *zW:* **~stammen** *vi* to descend *od* come from; **~stellen** *vt* to make, manufacture; (*zustande bringen*) to establish; **H~steller** (-s, -) *m* manufacturer; **H~stellung** *f* manufacture; **H~stellungskosten** *pl* manufacturing costs *pl*; **~tragen** *unreg vt:* **etw hinter jdm ~tragen** to carry sth behind sb.

herüber [hɛ'ry:bər] *adv* over (here), across.

herum [hɛ'rʊm] *adv* about, (a)round; **um etw ~** around sth; **~ärgern** *vr:* **sich ~ärgern (mit)** to get annoyed (with); **~blättern** *vi:* **~blättern** in +*dat* to browse *od* flick through; **~doktern** (*umg*) *vi* to fiddle *od* tinker about; **~drehen** *vt:* **jdm das Wort im Mund ~drehen** to twist sb's words; **~drücken** *vr* (*vermeiden*): **sich um etw ~drücken** to dodge sth; **~fahren** *unreg vi* to travel around; (*mit Auto*) to drive around; (*sich rasch umdrehen*) to spin

(a)round; **~führen** *vt* to show around; **~gammeln** (*umg*) *vi* to bum around; **~gehen** *unreg vi* (**~spazieren**) to walk about; **um etw ~gehen** to walk *od* go round sth; **etw ~gehen lassen** to circulate sth; **~hacken** *vi* (*fig: umg*): **auf jdm ~hacken** to pick on sb; **~irren** *vi* to wander about; **~kommen** *unreg* (*umg*) *vi:* **um etw ~kommen** to get out of sth; **er ist viel ~gekommen** he has been around a lot; **~kriegen** *vt* to bring *od* talk round; **~lungern** *vi* to lounge about; (*umg*) to hang around; **~quälen** *vr:* **sich mit Rheuma ~quälen** to be plagued by rheumatism; **~reißen** *unreg vt* to swing around (hard); **~schlagen** *unreg vr:* **sich mit etw ~schlagen** (*umg*) to tussle with sth; **~schleppen** *vt:* **etw mit sich ~schleppen** (*Sorge, Problem*) to be troubled by sth; (*Krankheit*) to have sth; **~sprechen** *unreg vr* to get around, be spread; **~stochern** (*umg*) *vi:* **im Essen ~stochern** to pick at one's food; **~treiben** *unreg vi, vr* to drift about; **H~treiber(in)** (-s, -) (*pej*) *m(f)* tramp; **~ziehen** *unreg vi, vr* to wander about.

herunter [hɛ'rʊntər] *adv* downward(s), down (there); **mit den Nerven/der Gesundheit ~ sein** (*umg*) to be at the end of one's tether/be run-down; **~fahren** *unreg vti* (*COMPUT, TECH*) to shut down; **~gekommen** *adj* run-down; **~handeln** (*umg*) *vt* (*Preis*) to beat down; **~hängen** *unreg vi* to hang down; **~holen** *vt* to bring down; **~kommen** *unreg vi* to come down; (*fig*) to come down in the world; **~leiern** (*umg*) *vt* to reel off; **~machen** *vt* to take down; (*schlecht machen*) to run down, knock; **~putzen** (*umg*) *vt:* **jdn ~putzen** to tear sb off a strip; **~spielen** *vt* to play down; **~wirtschaften** (*umg*) *vt* to bring to the brink of ruin.

hervor [hɛr'fo:r] *adv* out, forth; **~brechen** *unreg vi* to burst forth, break out; **~bringen** *unreg vt* to produce; (*Wort*) to utter; **~gehen** *unreg vi* to emerge, result; **daraus geht ~, dass ...** from this it follows that ...; **~heben** *unreg vt* to stress; (*als Kontrast*) to set off; **~ragend** *adj* excellent; (*lit*) projecting; **~rufen** *unreg vt* to cause, give rise to; **~stechen** *unreg vi* (*lit, fig*) to stand out; **~stoßen** *unreg vt* (*Worte*) to gasp (out); **~treten** *unreg vi* to come out; **~tun** *unreg vr* to distinguish o.s.; (*umg: sich wichtig tun*) to show off; **sich mit etw ~tun** to show off sth.

Herz [hɛrts] (-ens, -en) *nt* heart; (*KARTEN: Farbe*) hearts *pl*; **mit ganzem ~en** wholeheartedly; **etw auf dem ~en haben** to have sth on one's mind; **sich** *dat* **etw zu ~en nehmen** to take sth to heart; **du sprichst mir aus dem ~en** that's just what I feel; **es liegt mir am ~en** I am very concerned about it; **seinem ~en Luft machen** to give vent to one's feelings; **sein ~ an jdn/etw hängen** to commit o.s. heart and soul to sb/sth; **ein**

~ **und eine Seele sein** to be the best of friends; **jdn/etw auf ~ und Nieren prüfen** to examine sb/sth very thoroughly; **~anfall** *m* heart attack; **~beschwerden** *pl* heart trouble *sing.*

herzen *vt* to caress, embrace.

Herzenslust *f*: **nach ~** to one's heart's content.

Herz- *zW*: **h~ergreifend** *adj* heart-rending; **h~erweichend** *adj* heartrending; **~fehler** *m* heart defect; **h~haft** *adj* hearty.

herziehen ['hɛːrtsiːən] *vi*: **über jdn/etw ~** (*umg*) to pull sb/sth to pieces (*fig*).

Herz- *zW*: **~infarkt** *m* heart attack; **~klappe** *f* (heart) valve; **~klopfen** *nt* palpitation; **h~krank** *adj* suffering from a heart condition.

herzlich *adj* cordial ♦ *adv* (*sehr*): ~ **gern!** with the greatest of pleasure!; **~en Glückwunsch** congratulations *pl*; **~e Grüße** best wishes; **H~keit** *f* cordiality.

herzlos *adj* heartless; **H~igkeit** *f* heartlessness.

Herzog ['hɛrtsoːk] (**-(e)s, ̈-e**) *m* duke; **~in** *f* duchess; **h~lich** *adj* ducal; **~tum** *nt* duchy.

Herz- *zW*: **~schlag** *m* heartbeat; (*MED*) heart attack; **~schrittmacher** *m* pacemaker; **h~zerreißend** *adj* heartrending.

Hesse ['hɛsə] (**-n, -n**) *m* Hessian.

Hessen ['hɛsən] (**-s**) *nt* Hesse.

Hessin *f* Hessian.

hessisch *adj* Hessian.

heterogen [hetero'geːn] *adj* heterogeneous.

heterosexuell [heterozɛksu'ɛl] *adj* heterosexual.

Hetze ['hɛtsə] *f* (*Eile*) rush.

hetzen *vt* to hunt; (*verfolgen*) to chase ♦ *vi* (*eilen*) to rush; **jdn/etw auf jdn/etw ~** to set sb/sth on sb/sth; **~ gegen** to stir up feeling against; **~ zu** to agitate for.

Hetzerei [hɛtsə'raɪ] *f* agitation; (*Eile*) rush.

Hetzkampagne ['hɛtskampanjə] *f* smear campaign.

Heu [hɔy] (**-(e)s**) *nt* hay; **~boden** *m* hayloft.

Heuchelei [hɔyçə'laɪ] *f* hypocrisy.

heucheln ['hɔyçəln] *vt* to pretend, feign ♦ *vi* to be hypocritical.

Heuchler(in) [hɔyçlər(ɪn)] (**-s, -**) *m(f)* hypocrite; **h~isch** *adj* hypocritical.

Heuer ['hɔyər] (**-, -n**) *f* (*NAUT*) pay.

heuer *adv* this year.

heuern ['hɔyərn] *vt* to sign on, hire.

Heugabel *f* pitchfork.

Heuhaufen *m* haystack.

heulen ['hɔylən] *vi* to howl; (*weinen*) to cry; **das ~de Elend bekommen** to get the blues.

heurig ['hɔyrɪç] *adj* this year's.

Heuschnupfen *m* hay fever.

Heuschrecke *f* grasshopper; (*in heißen Ländern*) locust.

heute ['hɔytə] *adv* today; **~ Abend/früh** this evening/morning; **~ Morgen** this morning; **~ in einer Woche** a week today, today week; **von ~ auf morgen** (*fig: plötzlich*) overnight, from one day to the next; **das H~** today.

heutig ['hɔytɪç] *adj* today's; **unser ~es Schreiben** (*COMM*) our letter of today('s date).

heutzutage ['hɔyttsutaːgə] *adv* nowadays.

Hexe ['hɛksə] (**-, -n**) *f* witch.

hexen *vi* to practise witchcraft; **ich kann doch nicht ~** I can't work miracles.

Hexen- *zW*: **~häuschen** *nt* gingerbread house; **~kessel** *m* (*lit, fig*) cauldron; **~meister** *m* wizard; **~schuss▲** *m* lumbago.

Hexerei [hɛksə'raɪ] *f* witchcraft.

HG *f abk* = **Handelsgesellschaft**.

Hg. *abk* (= *Herausgeber*) ed.

hg. *abk* (= *herausgegeben*) ed.

HGB (**-**) *nt abk* (= *Handelsgesetzbuch*) *statutes of commercial law*.

Hieb (**-(e)s, -e**) *m* blow; (*Wunde*) cut, gash; (*Stichelei*) cutting remark; **~e bekommen** to get a thrashing.

hieb *etc* [hiːp] *vb* (*veraltet*) *siehe* **hauen**.

hieb- und stichfest *adj* (*fig*) watertight.

hielt *etc* [hiːlt] *vb siehe* **halten**.

hier [hiːr] *adv* here; **~ behalten** to keep here; **~ bleiben** to stay here; **~ lassen** to leave here; **~ spricht Dr. Müller** (*TEL*) this is Dr Müller (speaking); **er ist von ~** he's a local (man).

Hierarchie [hierar'çiː] *f* hierarchy.

hier- *zW*: **~auf** *adv* thereupon; (*danach*) after that; **~aus** *adv*: **~aus folgt, dass ...** from this it follows that ...; **~bei** *adv* (*bei dieser Gelegenheit*) on this occasion; **~durch** *adv* by this means; (*örtlich*) through here; **~her** *adv* this way, here; **~her gehören** to belong here; (*fig: relevant sein*) to be relevant; **~mit** *adv* hereby; **~mit erkläre ich ...** (*form*) I hereby declare ...; **~nach** *adv* hereafter; **~von** *adv* about this, hereof; **~von abgesehen** apart from this; **~zu** *adv* (*dafür*) for this; (*dazu*) with this; (*außerdem*) in addition to this, moreover; (*zu diesem Punkt*) about this; **~zulande, ~ zu Lande** *adv* in this country.

hiesig ['hiːzɪç] *adj* of this place, local.

hieß *etc* [hiːs] *vb siehe* **heißen**.

Hi-Fi-Anlage ['haɪfianlaːgə] *f* hi-fi set *od* system.

Hightechindustrie▲ ['haɪtɛkɪndus'triː] *f* high tech *od* hi-tech industry.

Hilfe ['hɪlfə] (**-, -n**) *f* help; (*für Notleidende*) aid; **erste ~** first aid; **jdm ~ leisten** to help sb; **~!** help!; **~leistung** *f*: **unterlassene ~leistung** (*JUR*) denial of assistance; **~stellung** *f* (*SPORT, fig*) support.

Hilf- *zW*: **h~los** *adj* helpless; **~losigkeit** *f* helplessness; **h~reich** adj helpful.

Hilfs- zW: **~aktion** f relief action, relief measures pl; **~arbeiter** m labourer (BRIT), laborer (US); **h~bedürftig** adj needy; **h~bereit** adj ready to help; **~kraft** f assistant, helper; **~mittel** nt aid; **~schule** f school for backward children; **~zeitwort** nt auxiliary verb.

hilft [hɪlft] vb siehe **helfen**.

Himalaja [hi'maːlaja] (**-s**) m: **der** ~ the Himalayas pl.

Himbeere ['hɪmbeːrə] (**-**, **-n**) f raspberry.

Himmel ['hɪməl] (**-s**, **-**) m sky; (REL, liter) heaven; **um ~s willen** (umg) for Heaven's sake; **zwischen** ~ **und Erde** in midair; **h~angst** adj: **es ist mir h~angst** I'm scared to death; **~bett** nt four-poster bed; **h~blau** adj sky-blue.

Himmelfahrt f Ascension.

Himmelfahrtskommando nt (MIL: umg) suicide squad; (Unternehmen) suicide mission.

Himmelreich nt (REL) Kingdom of Heaven.

himmelschreiend adj outrageous.

Himmelsrichtung f direction; **die vier ~en** the four points of the compass.

himmelweit adj: **ein ~er Unterschied** a world of difference.

himmlisch ['hɪmlɪʃ] adj heavenly.

========= *SCHLÜSSELWORT*

hin [hɪn] adv **1** (Richtung): ~ **und zurück** there and back; **einmal London** ~ **und zurück** a return to London (BRIT), a roundtrip ticket to London (US); ~ **und her** to and fro; **etw** ~ **und her überlegen** to turn sth over and over in one's mind; **bis zur Mauer** ~ up to the wall; **wo ist er** ~? where has he gone?; **nichts wie** ~! (umg) let's go then!; **nach außen** ~ (fig) outwardly; **Geld ~, Geld her** money or no money.

2 (auf … ~): **auf meine Bitte** ~ at my request; **auf seinen Rat** ~ on the basis of his advice; **auf meinen Brief** ~ on the strength of my letter.

3: ~ **sein** (umg: kaputt sein) to have had it; (Ruhe) to be gone; **mein Glück ist** ~ my happiness has gone; ~ **und wieder** (every) now and again.

hinab [hɪ'nap] adv down; **~gehen** unreg vi to go down; **~sehen** unreg vi to look down.

hinarbeiten ['hɪnarbaɪtən] vi: **auf etw** akk ~ (auf Ziel) to work towards sth.

hinauf [hɪ'nauf] adv up; **~arbeiten** vr to work one's way up; **~steigen** unreg vi to climb.

hinaus [hɪ'naus] adv out; **hinten/vorn** ~ at the back/front; **darüber** ~ over and above this; **auf Jahre** ~ for years to come; **~befördern** vt to kick od throw out; **~fliegen** unreg (umg)

vi to be kicked out; **~führen** vi: **über etw** akk **~führen** (lit, fig) to go beyond sth; **~gehen** unreg vi to go out; **~gehen über** +akk to exceed; **~laufen** unreg vi to run out; **~laufen auf** +akk to come to, amount to; **~schieben** unreg vt to put off, postpone; **~schießen** unreg vi: **über das Ziel ~schießen** (fig) to overshoot the mark; **~wachsen** unreg vi: **er wuchs über sich selbst** ~ he surpassed himself; **~werfen** unreg vt to throw out; **~wollen** vi to want to go out; **hoch ~wollen** to aim high; **~wollen auf** +akk to drive at, get at; **~ziehen** unreg vt to draw out ◆ vr to be protracted; **~zögern** vt to delay, put off ◆ vr to be delayed, be put off.

hinbekommen unreg (umg) vt: **das hast du gut** ~ you've made a good job of it.

hinblättern (umg) vt (Geld) to fork out.

Hinblick ['hɪnblɪk] m: **in od im** ~ **auf** +akk in view of.

hinderlich ['hɪndərlɪç] adj awkward; **jds Karriere** dat ~ **sein** to be a hindrance to sb's career.

hindern vt to hinder, hamper; **jdn an etw** dat ~ to prevent sb from doing sth.

Hindernis (**-ses**, **-se**) nt obstacle; **~lauf** m, **~rennen** nt steeplechase.

Hinderungsgrund m obstacle.

hindeuten ['hɪndɔytən] vi: ~ **auf** +akk to point to.

Hinduismus [hɪndu'ɪsmʊs] m Hinduism.

hindurch [hɪn'dʊrç] adv through; across; (zeitlich) over.

hindürfen [hɪn'dʏrfən] unreg vi: ~ (zu) to be allowed to go there.

hinein [hɪ'naɪn] adv in; **bis tief in die Nacht** ~ well into the night; **~fallen** unreg vi to fall in; **~fallen in** +akk to fall into; **~finden** unreg vr (fig: sich vertraut machen) to find one's feet; (sich abfinden) to come to terms with it; **~gehen** unreg vi to go in; **~gehen in** +akk to go into, enter; **~geraten** unreg vi: **~geraten in** +akk to get into; **~knien** vr (fig: umg): **sich in etw** akk **~knien** to get into sth; **~lesen** unreg vt: **etw in etw** akk **~lesen** to read sth into sth; **~passen** vi to fit in; **~passen in** +akk to fit into; **~prügeln** vt: **etw in jdn ~prügeln** to cudgel sth into sb; **~reden** vi: **jdm ~reden** to interfere in sb's affairs; **~stecken** vt: **Geld/Arbeit in etw** akk **~stecken** to put money/some work into sth; **~steigern** vr to get worked up; **~versetzen** vr: **sich in jdn ~versetzen** to put o.s. in sb's position; **~ziehen** unreg vt: **~ziehen (in** +akk) to pull in (to); **jdn in etw ~ziehen** (in Konflikt, Gespräch) to draw sb into sth.

hin- zW: **~fahren** unreg vi to go; to drive ◆ vt to take; to drive; **H~fahrt** f journey there; **~fallen** unreg vi to fall down; **~fällig** adj frail, decrepit; (Regel etc) unnecessary; **~fliegen**

unreg vi to fly there; (*umg:* ~*fallen*) to fall over; **H~flug** *m* outward flight.

hing *etc* [hɪŋ] *vb siehe* **hängen.**

hin- *zW:* **H~gabe** *f* devotion; **mit H~gabe tanzen/singen** *etc* (*fig*) to dance/sing *etc* with abandon; ~**geben** *unreg vr +dat* to give o.s. up to, devote o.s. to; ~**gebungsvoll** ['hɪŋgeːbʊŋsfɔl] *adv* (*begeistert*) with abandon; (*lauschen*) raptly.

hingegen [hɪn'geːgən] *konj* however.

hin- *zW:* ~**gehen** *unreg vi* to go; (*Zeit*) to pass; **gehst du auch ~?** are you going too?; ~**gerissen** *adj:* ~**gerissen sein** to be enraptured; ~**- und hergerissen sein** (*fig*) to be torn; **ich bin ganz ~- und hergerissen** (*ironisch*) that's absolutely great; ~**halten** *unreg vt* to hold out; (*warten lassen*) to put off, stall; **H~haltetaktik** *f* stalling *od* delaying tactics *pl.*

hinhauen ['hɪnhauən] *unreg* (*umg*) *vi* (*klappen*) to work; (*ausreichen*) to do.

hinhören ['hɪnhøːrən] *vi* to listen.

hinken ['hɪŋkən] *vi* to limp; (*Vergleich*) to be unconvincing.

hin- *zW:* ~**kommen** *unreg* (*umg*) *vi* (*auskommen*) to manage; (: *ausreichen, stimmen*) to be right; ~**länglich** *adj* adequate ♦ *adv* adequately; ~**legen** *vt* to put down ♦ *vr* to lie down; **sich der Länge nach ~legen** (*umg*) to fall flat; ~**nehmen** *unreg vt* (*fig*) to put up with, take; ~**reichen** *vi* to be adequate ♦ *vt:* **jdm etw ~reichen** to hand sb sth; ~**reichend** *adj* adequate; (*genug*) sufficient; **H~reise** *f* journey out; ~**reißen** *unreg vt* to carry away, enrapture; **sich ~reißen lassen, etw zu tun** to get carried away and do sth; ~**reißend** *adj* (*Landschaft, Anblick*) enchanting; (*Schönheit, Mensch*) captivating; ~**richten** *vt* to execute; **H~richtung** *f* execution; ~**sehen** *unreg vi:* **bei genauerem H~sehen** on closer inspection.

hin sein▲ ['hɪnzaɪn] *siehe* **hin.**

hin- *zW:* ~**setzen** *vr* to sit down; **H~sicht** *f:* **in mancher** *od* **gewisser H~sicht** in some respects *od* ways; ~**sichtlich** *präp +gen* with regard to; ~**sollen** (*umg*) *vi:* **wo soll ich/das Buch ~?** where do I/does the book go?; **H~spiel** *nt* (*SPORT*) first leg; ~**stellen** *vt* to put (down) ♦ *vr* to place o.s.

hintanstellen [hɪnt'|anʃtɛlən] *vt* (*fig*) to ignore.

hinten ['hɪntən] *adv* behind; (*rückwärtig*) at the back; ~ **und vorn** (*fig: betrügen*) left, right and centre; **das reicht ~ und vorn nicht** that's nowhere near enough; ~**dran** (*umg*) *adv* at the back; ~**herum** *adv* round the back; (*fig*) secretly.

hinter ['hɪntər] *präp* (+*dat od akk*) behind; (: *nach*) after; ~ **jdm her sein** to be after sb; ~ **die Wahrheit kommen** to get to the truth; **sich ~ jdn stellen** (*fig*) to support sb; **etw ~ sich** *dat* **haben** (*zurückgelegt haben*) to have

got through sth; **sie hat viel ~ sich** she has been through a lot; **H~achse** *f* rear axle; **H~bänkler (-s, -)** *m* (*POL: pej*) backbencher; **H~bein** *nt* hind leg; **sich auf die H~beine stellen** to get tough; **H~bliebene(r)** *f(m)* surviving relative; ~**drein** *adv* afterwards.

hintere(r, s) *adj* rear, back.

hinter- *zW:* ~**einander** *adv* one after the other; **zwei Tage ~einander** two days running; ~**fotzig** (*umg*) *adj* underhanded; ~**fragen** *vt untr* to analyse; **H~gedanke** *m* ulterior motive; ~**gehen** *unreg vt untr* to deceive; **H~grund** *m* background; ~**gründig** *adj* cryptic, enigmatic; **H~grundprogramm** *nt* (*COMPUT*) background program; **H~halt** *m* ambush; **etw im H~halt haben** to have sth in reserve; ~**hältig** *adj* underhand, sneaky; ~**her** *adv* afterwards, after; **er ist ~her, dass** ... (*fig*) he sees to it that ...; **H~hof** *m* back yard; **H~kopf** *m* back of one's head; **H~land** *nt* hinterland; ~**lassen** *unreg vt untr* to leave; **H~lassenschaft** *f* (testator's) estate; ~**legen** *vt untr* to deposit; **H~legungsstelle** *f* depository; **H~list** *f* cunning, trickery; (*Handlung*) trick, dodge; ~**listig** *adj* cunning, crafty; **H~mann (-(e)s,** *pl* **-männer)** *m* person behind; **die H~männer des Skandals** the men behind the scandal.

Hintern ['hɪntərn] **(-s, -)** (*umg*) *m* bottom, backside; **jdm den ~ versohlen** to smack sb's bottom.

hinter- *zW:* **H~rad** *nt* back wheel; **H~radantrieb** *m* (*AUT*) rear-wheel drive; ~**rücks** *adv* from behind; **H~teil** *nt* behind; **H~treffen** *nt:* **ins H~treffen kommen** to lose ground; ~**treiben** *unreg vt untr* to prevent, frustrate; **H~treppe** *f* back stairs *pl*; **H~tür** *f* back door; (*fig: Ausweg*) escape, loophole; **H~wäldler (-s, -)** (*umg*) *m* backwoodsman, hillbilly (*bes US*); ~**ziehen** *unreg vt untr* (*Steuern*) to evade (paying).

hintun ['hɪntuːn] *unreg* (*umg*) *vt:* **ich weiß nicht, wo ich ihn ~ soll** (*fig*) I can't (quite) place him.

hinüber [hɪ'nyːbər] *adv* across, over; ~**gehen** *unreg vi* to go over *od* across.

hinunter [hɪ'nʊntər] *adv* down; ~**bringen** *unreg vt* to take down; ~**schlucken** *vt* (*lit, fig*) to swallow; ~**spülen** *vt* to flush away; (*Essen, Tablette*) to wash down; (*fig: Ärger*) to soothe; ~**steigen** *unreg vi* to descend.

Hinweg ['hɪnveːk] *m* journey out.

hinweg- [hɪn'vɛk] *zW:* ~**gehen** *unreg vi:* **über etw** *akk* ~**gehen** (*fig*) to pass over sth; ~**helfen** *unreg vi:* **jdm über etw** *akk* ~**helfen** to help sb to get over sth; ~**kommen** *unreg vi* (*fig*): **über etw** *akk* ~**kommen** to get over sth; ~**sehen** *unreg vi:* **darüber ~sehen, dass** ... to overlook the fact that ...; ~**setzen** *vr:* **sich ~setzen über** +*akk* to disregard.

Hinweis ['hɪnvaɪs] (-es, -e) m (Andeutung) hint; (Anweisung) instruction; (Verweis) reference; **sachdienliche** ~**e** relevant information.

hinweisen unreg vi: ~ **auf** +akk to point to; (verweisen) to refer to; **darauf** ~, **dass** ... to point out that ...; (anzeigen) to indicate that ...

Hinweisschild nt sign.

Hinweistafel f sign.

hinwerfen unreg vt to throw down; **eine hingeworfene Bemerkung** a casual remark.

hinwirken vi: **auf etw** akk ~ to work towards sth.

Hinz [hɪnts] m: ~ **und Kunz** (umg) every Tom, Dick and Harry.

hinziehen unreg vr (fig) to drag on.

hinzielen vi: ~ **auf** +akk to aim at.

hinzu [hɪn'tsuː] adv in addition; ~**fügen** vt to add; **H~fügung** f: **unter H~fügung von etw** (form) by adding sth; ~**kommen** unreg vi: **es kommt noch** ~, **dass** ... there is also the fact that ...; ~**ziehen** unreg vt to consult.

Hiobsbotschaft ['hiːɔpsboːtʃaft] f bad news.

Hirn [hɪrn] (-(e)s, -e) nt brain(s); ~**gespinst** (-(e)s, -e) nt fantasy; ~**hautentzündung** f (MED) meningitis; **h~tot** adj braindead; **h~verbrannt** adj (umg) harebrained.

Hirsch [hɪrʃ] (-(e)s, -e) m stag.

Hirse ['hɪrzə] (-, -n) f millet.

Hirt ['hɪrt] (-en, -en) m, **Hirte** (-n, -n) m herdsman; (Schaf~, fig) shepherd.

Hirtin f herdswoman; (Schaf~) shepherdess.

hissen ['hɪsən] vt to hoist.

Historiker [hɪs'toːrikər] (-s, -) m historian.

historisch [hɪs'toːrɪʃ] adj historical.

Hit [hɪt] (-s, -s) m (MUS, fig: umg) hit; ~**parade** f hit parade.

Hitze ['hɪtsə] (-) f heat; **h~beständig** adj heat-resistant; **h~frei** adj: **h~frei haben** to have time off school/work because of excessive heat; ~**welle** f heat wave.

hitzig adj hot-tempered; (Debatte) heated.

Hitz- zW: ~**kopf** m hothead; **h~köpfig** adj fiery, hot-headed; ~**schlag** m heatstroke.

HIV-negativ adj HIV-negative.

HIV-positiv adj HIV-positive.

hl. abk = heilig.

H-Milch ['haːmɪlç] f long-life milk, UHT milk.

HNO-Arzt m ENT specialist.

hob etc [hoːp] vb siehe **heben**.

Hobby ['hɔbi] (-s, -s) nt hobby.

Hobel ['hoːbəl] (-s, -) m plane; ~**bank** f carpenter's bench.

hobeln vt, vi to plane.

Hobelspäne pl wood shavings pl.

hoch [hoːx] (attrib hohe(r, s)) adj high ♦ adv: ~ **achten** to respect; ~ **begabt** extremely gifted; ~ **dotiert** highly paid; ~ **empfindlich** highly sensitive; (Film) high-speed;

~ **entwickelt** (Kultur, Land) highly developed; (Geräte, Methoden) sophisticated; ~ **gestellt** (fig: Persönlichkeit) high-ranking; **wenn es** ~ **kommt** (umg) at (the) most, at the outside; **das ist mir zu** ~ (umg) that's above my head; **ein hohes Tier** (umg) a big fish; **es ging** ~ **her** (umg) we/they etc had a whale of a time; ~ **und heilig versprechen** to promise faithfully.

Hoch (-s, -s) nt (Ruf) cheer; (MET, fig) high.

hoch- zW: **H~achtung** f respect, esteem; **mit vorzüglicher H~achtung** (form: Briefschluss) yours faithfully; ~**achtungsvoll** adv yours faithfully; ~**aktuell** adj highly topical; **H~amt** nt high mass; ~**arbeiten** vr to work one's way up; ~**betagt** adj very old, aged; **H~betrieb** m intense activity; (COMM) peak time; **H~betrieb haben** to be at one's od its busiest; ~**bringen** unreg vt to bring up; **H~burg** f stronghold; **H~deutsch** nt High German; **H~druck** m high pressure; **H~ebene** f plateau; ~**erfreut** adj highly delighted; ~**fahren** unreg vi (erschreckt) to jump ♦ vt (COMPUT, TECH) to start up; ~**fliegend** adj ambitious; (fig) high-flown; **H~form** f top form; **H~gebirge** nt high mountains pl; **H~gefühl** nt elation; ~**gehen** unreg (umg) vi (explodieren) to blow up; (Bombe) to go off; **H~genuss▲** m great od special treat; (großes Vergnügen) great pleasure; ~**geschlossen** adj (Kleid etc) high-necked; **H~glanz** m high polish; (PHOT) gloss; ~**gradig** adj intense, extreme; ~**halten** unreg vt to hold up; (fig) to uphold, cherish; **H~haus** nt multi-storey building; ~**heben** unreg vt to lift (up); ~**kant** adv: **jdn** ~**kant hinauswerfen** (fig: umg) to chuck sb out on his/her ear; ~**kommen** unreg vi (nach oben) to come up; (fig: gesund werden) to get back on one's feet; (beruflich, gesellschaftlich) to come up in the world; **H~konjunktur** f boom; ~**krempeln** vt to roll up; **H~land** nt highlands pl; ~**leben** vi: **jdn** ~**leben lassen** to give sb three cheers; **H~leistungssport** m competitive sport; ~**modern** adj very modern, ultra-modern; **H~mut** m pride; ~**mütig** adj proud, haughty; ~**näsig** adj stuck-up, snooty; ~**nehmen** unreg vt to pick up; **jdn** ~**nehmen** (umg: verspotten) to pull sb's leg; **H~ofen** m blast furnace; ~**prozentig** adj (Alkohol) strong; **H~rechnung** f projected result; **H~saison** f high season; **H~schätzung** f high esteem.

Hochschulabschluss▲ m degree.

Hochschulbildung f higher education.

Hochschule f college; (Universität) university.

Hochschulreife f: **er hat (die)** ~ ≈ he's got his A-levels (BRIT), he's graduated from high school (US).

hoch- zW: ~**schwanger** adj heavily pregnant,

well advanced in pregnancy; **H~seefischerei**
f deep-sea fishing; **H~sitz** *m* (*Jagd*) (raised)
hide; **H~sommer** *m* middle of summer;
H~spannung *f* high tension; **~spielen** *vt* (*fig*)
to blow up; **H~sprache** *f* standard language;
~springen *unreg vi* to jump up; **H~sprung** *m*
high jump.

höchst [høːçst] *adv* highly, extremely.

Hochstapler ['hoːxstaːplər] (**-s, -**) *m* swindler.

höchste(r, s) *adj* highest; (*äußerste*) extreme;
die ~ Instanz (*JUR*) the supreme court of
appeal.

höchstens *adv* at the most.

Höchstgeschwindigkeit *f* maximum speed.

Höchstgrenze *f* upper limit.

Hochstimmung *f* high spirits *pl*.

Höchst- *zW*: **~leistung** *f* best performance;
(*bei Produktion*) maximum output;
h~persönlich *adv* personally, in person;
~preis *m* maximum price; **~stand** *m* peak;
h~wahrscheinlich *adv* most probably.

Hoch- *zW*: **~technologie** *f* high technology;
h~technologisch *adj* high-tech;
~temperaturreaktor *m* high-temperature
reactor; **~tour** *f*: **auf ~touren laufen** *od*
arbeiten to be working flat out; **h~trabend**
adj pompous; **~- und Tiefbau** *m* structural
and civil engineering; **~verrat** *m* high
treason; **~wasser** *nt* high water;
(*Überschwemmung*) floods *pl*; **h~wertig** *adj*
high-class, first-rate; **~würden** *m* Reverend;
~zahl *f* (*MATH*) exponent.

Hochzeit ['hɔxtsaɪt] (**-, -en**) *f* wedding; **man
kann nicht auf zwei ~en tanzen** (*Sprichwort*)
you can't have your cake and eat it.

Hochzeitsreise *f* honeymoon.

Hochzeitstag *m* wedding day; (*Jahrestag*)
wedding anniversary.

hochziehen *unreg vt* (*Rollladen, Hose*) to pull
up; (*Brauen*) to raise.

Hocke ['hɔkə] (**-, -n**) *f* squatting position;
(*beim Turnen*) squat vault; (*beim Skilaufen*)
crouch.

hocken ['hɔkən] *vi, vr* to squat, crouch.

Hocker (**-s, -**) *m* stool.

Höcker ['hœkər] (**-s, -**) *m* hump.

Hockey ['hɔki] (**-s**) *nt* hockey.

Hoden [['hoːdən]] (**-s, -**) *m* testicle.

Hodensack *m* scrotum.

Hof [hoːf] (**-(e)s, ̈-e**) *m* (*Hinter~*) yard;
(*Bauern~*) farm; (*Königs~*) court; **einem
Mädchen den ~ machen** (*veraltet*) to court a
girl.

hoffen ['hɔfən] *vi*: **~ (auf** +*akk*) to hope (for).

hoffentlich *adv* I hope, hopefully.

Hoffnung ['hɔfnʊŋ] *f* hope; **jdm ~en machen**
to raise sb's hopes; **sich** *dat* **~en machen** to
have hopes; **sich** *dat* **keine ~en machen** not
to hold out any hope(s).

Hoffnungs- *zW*: **h~los** *adj* hopeless; **~losigkeit**
f hopelessness; **~schimmer** *m* glimmer of
hope; **h~voll** *adj* hopeful.

höflich ['høːflɪç] *adj* courteous, polite; **H~keit** *f*
courtesy, politeness.

hohe(r, s) ['hoːə(r, s)] *adj siehe* **hoch**.

Höhe ['høːə] (**-, -n**) *f* height; (*An~*) hill; **nicht
auf der ~ sein** (*fig: umg*) to feel below par;
ein Scheck in ~ von ... a cheque (*BRIT*) *od*
check (*US*) for the amount of ...; **das ist doch
die ~** (*fig: umg*) that's the limit; **er geht
immer gleich in die ~** (*umg*) he always flares
up; **auf der ~ der Zeit sein** to be up-to-date.

Hoheit ['hoːhaɪt] *f* (*POL*) sovereignty; (*Titel*)
Highness.

Hoheits- *zW*: **~gebiet** *nt* sovereign territory;
~gewalt *f* (national) jurisdiction;
~gewässer *nt* territorial waters *pl*; **~zeichen**
nt national emblem.

Höhen- *zW*: **~angabe** *f* altitude reading; (*auf
Karte*) height marking; **~flug** *m*: **geistiger
~flug** intellectual flight; **~lage** *f* altitude;
~luft *f* mountain air; **~messer** *m* altimeter;
~sonne *f* sun lamp; **~unterschied** *m*
difference in altitude; **~zug** *m* mountain
chain.

Höhepunkt *m* climax; (*des Lebens*) high
point.

höher *adj, adv* higher.

hohl [hoːl] *adj* hollow; (*umg: dumm*)
hollow(-headed).

Höhle ['høːlə] (**-, -n**) *f* cave; hole; (*Mund~*)
cavity; (*fig, ZOOL*) den.

Hohl- *zW*: **~heit** *f* hollowness; **~kreuz** *nt* (*MED*)
hollow back; **~maß** *nt* measure of volume;
~raum *m* hollow space; (*Gebäude*) cavity;
~saum *m* hemstitch; **~spiegel** *m* concave
mirror.

Hohn [hoːn] (**-(e)s**) *m* scorn; **das ist der reinste
~** it's sheer mockery.

höhnen ['høːnən] *vt* to taunt, scoff at.

höhnisch *adj* scornful, taunting.

Hokuspokus [hoːkʊs'poːkʊs] (**-**) *m*
(*Zauberformel*) hey presto; (*fig: Täuschung*)
hocus-pocus.

hold [hɔlt] *adj* charming, sweet.

holen ['hoːlən] *vt* to get, fetch; (*Atem*) to take;
jdn/etw ~ lassen to send for sb/sth; **sich** *dat*
eine Erkältung ~ to catch a cold.

Holland ['hɔlant] (**-s**) *nt* Holland.

Holländer ['hɔlɛndər] (**-s, -**) *m* Dutchman.

Holländerin *f* Dutchwoman, Dutch girl.

holländisch *adj* Dutch.

Hölle ['hœlə] (**-, -n**) *f* hell; **ich werde ihm die
~ heiß machen** (*umg*) I'll give him hell.

Höllenangst *f*: **eine ~ haben** to be scared to
death.

Höllenlärm *m* infernal noise (*umg*).

höllisch ['hœlɪʃ] *adj* hellish, infernal.

Hologramm [holo'gram] (**-s, -e**) *nt* hologram.

holperig ['hɔlpərɪç] *adj* rough, bumpy.

holpern ['hɔlpərn] *vi* to jolt.

Holunder [ho'lʊndər] **(-s, -)** *m* elder.

Holz [hɔlts] **(-es, ⁻er)** *nt* wood; **aus** ~ **made of wood, wooden; aus einem anderen/ demselben** ~ **geschnitzt sein** (*fig*) to be cast in a different/the same mould; **gut** ~**!** (*Kegeln*) have a good game!; ~**bläser** *m* woodwind player.

hölzern ['hœltsərn] *adj* (*lit, fig*) wooden.

Holz- *zW:* ~**fäller (-s, -)** *m* lumberjack, woodcutter; ~**faserplatte** *f* (wood) fibreboard (*BRIT*) *od* fiberboard (*US*); **h**~**frei** *adj* (*Papier*) wood-free.

holzig *adj* woody.

Holz- *zW:* ~**klotz** *m* wooden block; ~**kohle** *f* charcoal; ~**kopf** *m* (*fig: umg*) blockhead, numbskull; ~**scheit** *nt* log; ~**schuh** *m* clog; ~**weg** *m* (*fig*) wrong track; ~**wolle** *f* fine wood shavings *pl*; ~**wurm** *m* woodworm.

Homecomputer ['hoʊmkɔmˈpjuːtər] **(-s, -)** *m* home computer.

Homepage ['hoʊmˈpaːgə] *nt* (*COMPUT*) home page.

Homoehe ['hoːmoˌleːə] *f* (*umg*) gay marriage.

homogen [homoˈgeːn] *adj* homogenous.

Homöopath [homøoˈpaːt] **(-en, -en)** *m* homeopath.

Homöopathie [homøopaˈtiː] *f* homeopathy, homeopathic medicine.

homosexuell [homozɛksuˈɛl] *adj* homosexual.

Honduras [hɔnˈduːras] **(-)** *nt* Honduras.

Hongkong [hɔŋˈkɔŋ] **(-s)** *nt* Hong Kong.

Honig ['hoːnɪç] **(-s, -e)** *m* honey; ~**lecken** *nt* (*fig*): **das ist kein** ~**lecken** it's no picnic; ~**melone** *f* honeydew melon; ~**wabe** *f* honeycomb.

Honorar [honoˈraːr] **(-s, -e)** *nt* fee.

Honoratioren [honoratsiˈoːrən] *pl* dignitaries.

honorieren [honoˈriːrən] *vt* to remunerate; (*Scheck*) to honour (*BRIT*), honor (*US*).

Hopfen ['hɔpfən] **(-s, -)** *m* hops *pl*; **bei ihm ist** ~ **und Malz verloren** (*umg*) he's a dead loss.

hoppla ['hɔpla] *interj* whoops.

hopsen ['hɔpsən] *vi* to hop.

hörbar *adj* audible.

horch [hɔrç] *interj* listen.

horchen *vi* to listen; (*pej*) to eavesdrop.

Horcher (-s, -) *m* listener; eavesdropper.

Horde ['hɔrdə] **(-, -n)** *f* horde.

hören ['høːrən] *vt, vi* to hear; **auf jdn/etw** ~ to listen to sb/sth; **ich lasse von mir** ~ I'll be in touch; **etwas/nichts von sich** ~ **lassen** to get/not to get in touch; **H**~ *nt*: **es verging ihm H**~ **und Sehen** (*umg*) he didn't know whether he was coming or going.

Hörensagen *nt*: **vom** ~ from hearsay.

Hörer (-s, -) *m* (*RUNDF*) listener; (*UNIV*) student; (*Telefon*~) receiver.

Hörfunk *m* radio.

Hörgerät *nt* hearing aid.

hörig ['høːrɪç] *adj*: **sie ist ihm (sexuell)** ~ he has (sexual) power over her.

Horizont [horiˈtsɔnt] **(-(e)s, -e)** *m* horizon; **das geht über meinen** ~ (*fig*) that is beyond me.

horizontal [horitsoˈtaːl] *adj* horizontal.

Hormon [hɔrˈmoːn] **(-s, -e)** *nt* hormone.

Hörmuschel *f* (*TEL*) earpiece.

Horn [hɔrn] **(-(e)s, ⁻er)** *nt* horn; **ins gleiche** *od* **in jds** ~ **blasen** to chime in; **sich** *dat* **die Hörner abstoßen** (*umg*) to sow one's wild oats; ~**brille** *f* horn-rimmed spectacles *pl*.

Hörnchen ['hœrnçən] *nt* (*Gebäck*) croissant.

Hornhaut *f* horny skin; (*des Auges*) cornea.

Hornisse [hɔrˈnɪsə] **(-, -n)** *f* hornet.

Hornochs(e) *m* (*fig: umg*) blockhead, idiot.

Horoskop [horoˈskoːp] **(-s, -e)** *nt* horoscope.

Hör- *zW:* ~**rohr** *nt* ear trumpet; (*MED*) stethoscope; ~**saal** *m* lecture room; ~**spiel** *nt* radio play.

Hort [hɔrt] **(-(e)s, -e)** *m* hoard; (*SCH*) nursery school; **h**~**en** *vt* to hoard.

Hörweite *f*: **in/außer** ~ within/out of hearing *od* earshot.

Hose ['hoːzə] **(-, -n)** *f* trousers *pl*, pants *pl* (*US*); **in die** ~ **gehen** (*umg*) to be a complete flop.

Hosen- *zW:* ~**anzug** *m* trouser suit, pantsuit (*US*); ~**boden** *m*: **sich auf den** ~**boden setzen** (*umg*) to get stuck in; ~**rock** *m* culottes *pl*; ~**tasche** *f* trouser pocket; ~**träger** *pl* braces *pl* (*BRIT*), suspenders *pl* (*US*).

Hostie ['hɔstiə] *f* (*REL*) host.

Hotel [ho'tɛl] **(-s, -s)** *nt* hotel; ~**fach** *nt* hotel management; ~ **garni** *nt* bed and breakfast hotel.

Hotelier [hoteliˈeː] **(-s, -s)** *m* hotelier.

Hr. *abk* (= *Herr*) Mr.

Hrsg. *abk* (= *Herausgeber*) ed.

hrsg. *abk* (= *herausgegeben*) ed.

HTML *abk* (= *Hyper Text Markup Language*) HTML.

Hub [huːp] **(-(e)s, ⁻e)** *m* lift; (*TECH*) stroke.

hüben ['hyːbən] *adv* on this side, over here; ~ **und drüben** on both sides.

Hubraum *m* (*AUT*) cubic capacity.

hübsch [hypʃ] *adj* pretty, nice; **immer** ~ **langsam!** (*umg*) nice and easy.

Hubschrauber (-s, -) *m* helicopter.

Hucke ['hʊkə] **(-, -n)** *f*: **jdm die** ~ **voll hauen** (*umg*) to give sb a good hiding.

huckepack ['hʊkəpak] *adv* piggy-back, pick-a-back.

hudeln ['huːdəln] *vi* to be sloppy.

Huf ['huːf] **(-(e)s, -e)** *m* hoof; ~**eisen** *nt* horseshoe; ~**nagel** *m* horseshoe nail.

Hüfte ['hyftə] **(-, -n)** *f* hip.

Hüftgürtel *m* girdle.

Hüfthalter *m* girdle.

Huftier *nt* hoofed animal, ungulate.

Hügel ['hyːgəl] **(-s, -)** *m* hill.

hüg(e)lig *adj* hilly.

Huhn [huːn] (-(e)s, ⁻er) *nt* hen; (*KOCH*) chicken; **da lachen ja die Hühner** (*umg*) it's enough to make a cat laugh; **er sah aus wie ein gerupftes ~** (*umg*) he looked as if he'd been dragged through a hedge backwards.

Hühnchen ['hyːnçən] *nt* young chicken; **mit jdm ein ~ zu rupfen haben** (*umg*) to have a bone to pick with sb.

Hühner- *zW:* **~auge** *nt* corn; **~brühe** *f* chicken broth; **~klein** *nt* (*KOCH*) chicken trimmings *pl*.

Huld [hʊlt] (-) *f* favour (*BRIT*), favor (*US*).

huldigen ['hʊldɪgən] *vi:* **jdm ~** to pay homage to sb.

Huldigung *f* homage.

Hülle ['hylə] (-, -n) *f* cover(ing); (*Zellophan~*) wrapping; **in ~ und Fülle** galore; **die ~n fallen lassen** (*fig*) to strip off.

hüllen *vt:* **~ (in** +*akk*) to cover (with); to wrap (in).

Hülse ['hylzə] (-, -n) *f* husk, shell.

Hülsenfrucht *f* pulse.

human [huˈmaːn] *adj* humane.

humanistisch [humaˈnɪstɪʃ] *adj:* **~es Gymnasium** *secondary school with bias on Latin and Greek*.

humanitär [humaniˈtɛːr] *adj* humanitarian.

Humanität *f* humanity.

Humanmedizin *f* (human) medicine.

Hummel ['hʊməl] (-, -n) *f* bumblebee.

Hummer ['hʊmər] (-s, -) *m* lobster.

Humor [huˈmoːr] (-s, -e) *m* humour (*BRIT*), humor (*US*); **~ haben** to have a sense of humo(u)r; **~ist(in)** *m(f)* humorist; **h~istisch** *adj* humorous; **h~voll** *adj* humorous.

humpeln ['hʊmpəln] *vi* to hobble.

Humpen ['hʊmpən] (-s, -) *m* tankard.

Humus ['huːmʊs] (-) *m* humus.

Hund [hʊnt] (-(e)s, -e) *m* dog; **auf den ~ kommen, vor die ~e gehen** (*fig: umg*) to go to the dogs; **~e, die bellen, beißen nicht** (*Sprichwort*) empty vessels make most noise (*Sprichwort*); **er ist bekannt wie ein bunter ~** (*umg*) everybody knows him.

Hunde- *zW:* **h~elend** (*umg*) *adj:* **mir ist h~elend** I feel lousy; **~hütte** *f* (dog) kennel; **~kuchen** *m* dog biscuit; **~marke** *f* dog licence disc, dog tag (*US*); **h~müde** (*umg*) *adj* dog-tired.

hundert ['hʊndərt] *num* hundred; **H~** (-s, -e) *nt* hundred; **~e** *od* **H~e von Menschen** hundreds of people.

Hunderter (-s, -) *m* hundred; (*umg: Geldschein*) hundred (euro/pound/dollar *etc* note).

hundert- *zW:* **H~jahrfeier** *f* centenary; **H~meterlauf** *m* (*SPORT*): **der/ein H~meterlauf** the/a hundred metres (*BRIT*) *od* meters (*US*) *sing*; **~prozentig** *adj, adv* one hundred per cent.

hundertste(r, s) *adj* hundredth; **von H~n ins**

Tausendste kommen (*fig*) to get carried away.

Hundesteuer *f* dog licence (*BRIT*) *od* license (*US*) fee.

Hundewetter (*umg*) *nt* filthy weather.

Hündin ['hyndɪn] *f* bitch.

Hüne ['hyːnə] (-n, -n) *m:* **ein ~ von Mensch** a giant of a man.

Hünengrab *nt* megalithic tomb.

Hunger ['hʊŋər] (-s) *m* hunger; **~ haben** to be hungry; **ich sterbe vor ~** (*umg*) I'm starving; **~lohn** *m* starvation wages *pl*.

hungern *vi* to starve.

Hungersnot *f* famine.

Hungerstreik *m* hunger strike.

Hungertuch *nt:* **am ~ nagen** (*fig*) to be starving.

hungrig ['hʊŋrɪç] *adj* hungry.

Hunsrück ['hʊnsryk] *m* Hunsruck (Mountains *pl*).

Hupe ['huːpə] (-, -n) *f* horn.

hupen *vi* to hoot, sound one's horn.

hupfen ['huːpfən] *vi* to hop, jump; **das ist gehupft wie gesprungen** (*umg*) it's six of one and half a dozen of the other.

hüpfen ['hypfən] *vi* = **hupfen**.

Hupkonzert (*umg*) *nt* hooting (of car horns).

Hürde ['hyrdə] (-, -n) *f* hurdle; (*für Schafe*) pen.

Hürdenlauf *m* hurdling.

Hure ['huːrə] (-, -n) *f* whore.

Hurensohn (*pej: umg!*) *m* bastard (!), son of a bitch (!).

hurra [hʊˈraː] *interj* hurray, hurrah.

hurtig ['hʊrtɪç] *adj* brisk, quick ♦ *adv* briskly, quickly.

huschen ['hʊʃən] *vi* to flit, scurry.

Husten ['huːstən] (-s) *m* cough; **h~** *vi* to cough; **auf etw** *akk* **h~** (*umg*) not to give a damn for sth; **~anfall** *m* coughing fit; **~bonbon** *m od nt* cough drop; **~saft** *m* cough mixture.

Hut¹ [huːt] (-(e)s, ⁻e) *m* hat; **unter einen ~ bringen** (*umg*) to reconcile; (*Termine etc*) to fit in.

Hut² [huːt] (-) *f* care; **auf der ~ sein** to be on one's guard.

hüten ['hyːtən] *vt* to guard ♦ *vr* to watch out; **das Bett/Haus ~** to stay in bed/indoors; **sich ~ zu** to take care not to; **sich ~ vor** +*dat* to beware of; **ich werde mich ~!** not likely!

Hutschnur *f:* **das geht mir über die ~** (*umg*) that's going too far.

Hütte ['hytə] (-, -n) *f* hut; (*Holz~, Block~*) cabin; (*Eisen~*) forge; (*umg: Wohnung*) pad; (*TECH: Hüttenwerk*) iron and steel works.

Hüttenindustrie *f* iron and steel industry.

Hüttenkäse *m* cottage cheese.

Hüttenwerk *nt* iron and steel works.

hutzelig ['hʊtsəlɪç] *adj* shrivelled.

Hyäne [hyˈɛːnə] (-, -n) *f* hyena.

Hyazinthe [hyaˈtsɪntə] (-, -n) *f* hyacinth.

Hyazinthe [hya'tsɪntə] (-, -n) *f* hyacinth.
Hydrant [hy'drant] *m* hydrant.
hydraulisch [hy'draʊlɪʃ] *adj* hydraulic.
Hydrierung [hy'driːrʊŋ] *f* hydrogenation.
Hygiene [hygi'eːnə] (-) *f* hygiene.
hygienisch [hygi'eːnɪʃ] *adj* hygienic.
Hymne ['hymnə] (-, -n) *f* hymn, anthem.
hyper- ['hypɛr] *präf* hyper-.
Hypnose [hyp'noːzə] (-, -n) *f* hypnosis.
hypnotisch *adj* hypnotic.
Hypnotiseur [hypnoti'zøːr] *m* hypnotist.
hypnotisieren [hypnoti|zi:rən] *vt* to hypnotize.
Hypotenuse [hypote'nuːzə] (-, -n) *f* hypotenuse.
Hypothek [hypo'teːk] (-, -en) *f* mortgage; **eine ~ aufnehmen** to raise a mortgage; **etw mit einer ~ belasten** to mortgage sth.
Hypothese [hypo'teːzə] (-, -n) *f* hypothesis.
hypothetisch [hypo'teːtɪʃ] *adj* hypothetical.
Hysterie [hyste'riː] *f* hysteria.
hysterisch [hys'teːrɪʃ] *adj* hysterical; **einen ~en Anfall bekommen** (*fig*) to have hysterics.

I, i

I, i [iː] *nt* I, i; ~ **wie Ida** ≈ I for Isaac, I for Item (*US*); **das Tüpfelchen auf dem i** (*fig*) the final touch.
i. *abk* = **in; im.**
i. A. *abk* (= *im Auftrag*) p.p.
iberisch [i'beːrɪʃ] *adj* Iberian; **die I~e Halbinsel** the Iberian Peninsula.
IC (-) *m abk* = **Intercity-Zug.**
ICE *m abk* (= *Intercity-Expresszug*) inter-city train.
ich [ɪç] *pron* I; ~ **bins!** it's me!; **I~** (-(**s)**, **-(s)**) *nt* self; (*PSYCH*) ego; **I~form** *f* first person; **I~roman▲** *m* novel in the first person.
Ideal [ide'aːl] (-s, -e) *nt* ideal; **i~** *adj* ideal; **~fall** *m*: **im ~fall** ideally.
Idealismus [idea'lɪsmʊs] *m* idealism.
Idealist(in) *m(f)* idealist.
idealistisch *adj* idealistic.
Idealvorstellung *f* ideal.
Idee [i'deː] (-, -n) *f* idea; (*ein wenig*) shade, trifle; **jdn auf die ~ bringen, etw zu tun** to give sb the idea of doing sth.
ideell [ide'ɛl] *adj* ideal.
identifizieren [idɛntifi'tsiːrən] *vt* to identify.
identisch [i'dɛntɪʃ] *adj* identical.
Identität [idɛnti'tɛːt] *f* identity.
Ideologe [ideo'loːgə] (-n, -n) *m* ideologist.

Ideologie [ideolo'giː] *f* ideology.
Ideologin [ideo'loːgɪn] *f* ideologist.
ideologisch [ideo'loːgɪʃ] *adj* ideological.
idiomatisch [idio'maːtɪʃ] *adj* idiomatic.
Idiot [idi'oːt] (-en, -en) *m* idiot.
Idiotenhügel *m* (*hum*: *umg*) beginners' *od* nursery slope.
idiotensicher (*umg*) *adj* foolproof.
Idiotin *f* idiot.
idiotisch *adj* idiotic.
Idol [i'doːl] *nt* (-s, -e) idol.
idyllisch [i'dylɪʃ] *adj* idyllic.
IG *f abk* (= *Industriegewerkschaft*) industrial trade union.
IGB (-) *m abk* (= *Internationaler Gewerkschaftsbund*) International Trades Union Congress.
Igel ['iːgəl] (-s, -) *m* hedgehog.
igitt(igitt) [i'gɪt(i'gɪt)] *interj* ugh!
Iglu ['iːglu] (-s, -s) *m od nt* igloo.
Ignorant [ɪgno'rant] (-en, -en) *m* ignoramus.
ignorieren [ɪgno'riːrən] *vt* to ignore.
IHK *f abk* = **Industrie- und Handelskammer.**
ihm [iːm] *dat von er, es pers pron* (to) him, (to) it; **es ist ~ nicht gut** he doesn't feel well.
ihn [iːn] *akk von er pers pron* him; (*bei Tieren, Dingen*) it.
ihnen ['iːnən] *dat pl von sie pers pron* (to) them; (*nach Präpositionen*) them.
Ihnen *dat von Sie pers pron* (to) you; (*nach Präpositionen*) you.

═══════════ *SCHLÜSSELWORT*

ihr [iːr] *pron* **1** (*nom pl*) you; ~ **seid es** it's you.
2 (*dat von sie*) (to) her; (*bei Tieren, Dingen*) (to) it; **gib es** ~ give it to her; **er steht neben** ~ he is standing beside her.
♦ *poss pron* **1** (*sing*) her; (: *bei Tieren, Dingen*) its; ~ **Mann** her husband.
2 (*pl*) their; **die Bäume und ~e Blätter** the trees and their leaves.

Ihr *poss pron* your.
Ihre(r, s) *poss pron* yours; **tun Sie das** ~ (*geh*) you do your bit.
ihre(r, s) *poss pron* hers; (*eines Tieres*) its; (*von mehreren*) theirs; **sie taten das** ~ *od* **I~** (*geh*) they did their bit.
ihrer ['iːrər] *gen von sie pers pron* (*sing*) of her; (*pl*) of them.
Ihrer *gen von Sie pers pron* of you.
ihrerseits *adv* for your part.
ihrerseits *adv* for her/their part.
ihresgleichen *pron* people like her/them; (*von Dingen*) others like it; **eine Frechheit, die ~ sucht!** an incredible cheek!
ihretwegen *adv* (*für sie*) for her/its/their sake; (*wegen ihr, ihnen*) on her/its/their account; **sie sagte,** ~ **könnten wir gehen** she said that, as far as she was concerned, we

could go.

ihretwillen *adv*: um ~ for her/its/their sake.

ihrige ['iːrɪgə] *pron*: **der/die/das** ~ *od* l~ hers; its; theirs.

i. J. *abk* (= *im Jahre*) in (the year).

Ikone [i'koːnə] (-, -n) *f* icon.

IKRK *nt abk* (= *Internationales Komitee vom Roten Kreuz*) ICRC.

illegal ['ɪlegaːl] *adj* illegal.

illegitim ['ɪlegitiːm] *adj* illegitimate.

Illusion [ɪluzi'oːn] *f* illusion; **sich** *dat* ~**en machen** to delude o.s.

illusorisch [ɪlu'zoːrɪʃ] *adj* illusory.

Illustration [ɪlʊstratsi'oːn] *f* illustration.

illustrieren [ɪlʊs'triːrən] *vt* to illustrate.

Illustrierte (-n, -n) *f* picture magazine.

Iltis ['ɪltɪs] (-ses, -se) *m* polecat.

im [ɪm] = in dem *präp*: **etw** ~ **Liegen/Stehen tun** do sth lying down/standing up.

Image ['ɪmɪtʃ] (-(s), -s) *nt* image; ~**pflege** ['ɪmɪtʃpfleːgə] (*umg*) *f* image-building.

imaginär [imagi'nɛːr] *adj* imaginary.

Imbiss▲ ['ɪmbɪs] (-es, -e) *m* snack; ~**halle** *f* snack bar; ~**stube** *f* snack bar.

imitieren [imi'tiːrən] *vt* to imitate.

Imker ['ɪmkər] (-s, -) *m* beekeeper.

immanent [ima'nɛnt] *adj* inherent, intrinsic.

Immatrikulation [ɪmatrikulatsi'oːn] *f* (*UNIV*) registration.

immatrikulieren [ɪmatriku'liːrən] *vi, vr* to register.

immer ['ɪmər] *adv* always; ~ **wieder** again and again; **etw** ~ **wieder tun** to keep on doing sth; ~ **noch** still; ~ **noch nicht** still not; **für** ~ forever; ~ **wenn ich** ... every time I ...; ~ **schöner** more and more beautiful; ~ **trauriger** sadder and sadder; **was/wer (auch)** ~ whatever/whoever; ~**hin** *adv* all the same; ~**zu** *adv* all the time.

Immigrant(in) [ɪmi'grant(ɪn)] *m(f)* immigrant.

Immobilien [ɪmo'biːliən] *pl* real property (*BRIT*), real estate (*US*); (*in Zeitungsannoncen*) property *sing*; ~**händler**, ~**makler** *m* estate agent (*BRIT*), realtor (*US*).

immun [ɪ'muːn] *adj* immune.

immunisieren [ɪmuni'ziːrən] *vt* to immunize.

Immunität [ɪmuːni'tɛːt] *f* immunity.

Immunschwäche *f* immunodeficiency.

Immunsystem *nt* immune system.

imperativ ['ɪmperatiːf] *adj*: ~**es Mandat** imperative mandate.

Imperativ (-s, -e) *m* imperative.

Imperfekt ['ɪmpɛrfɛkt] (-s, -e) *nt* imperfect (tense).

Imperialismus [ɪmperia'lɪsmʊs] *m* imperialism.

Imperialist [ɪmperia'lɪst] *m* imperialist; **i~isch** *adj* imperialistic.

impfen ['ɪmpfən] *vt* to vaccinate.

Impf- *zW*: ~**pass▲** *m* vaccination card;

~**schutz** *m* protection given by vaccination; ~**stoff** *m* vaccine; ~**ung** *f* vaccination; ~**zwang** *m* compulsory vaccination.

implizieren [ɪmpli'tsiːrən] *vt* to imply.

imponieren [ɪmpo'niːrən] *vi +dat* to impress.

Import [ɪm'pɔrt] (-(e)s, -e) *m* import.

Importeur [ɪmpɔr'tøːr] (-s, -e) *m* importer.

importieren [ɪmpɔr'tiːrən] *vt* to import.

imposant [ɪmpo'zant] *adj* imposing.

impotent ['ɪmpotɛnt] *adj* impotent.

Impotenz ['ɪmpotɛnts] *f* impotence.

imprägnieren [ɪmprɛ'gniːrən] *vt* to (water)proof.

Impressionismus [ɪmpresio'nɪsmʊs] *m* impressionism.

Impressum [ɪm'prɛsʊm] (-s, -ssen) *nt* imprint; (*von Zeitung*) masthead.

Improvisation [ɪmprovizatsi'oːn] *f* improvisation.

improvisieren [ɪmprovi'ziːrən] *vt, vi* to improvise.

Impuls [ɪm'pʊls] (-es, -e) *m* impulse; **etw aus einem** ~ **heraus tun** to do sth on impulse.

impulsiv [ɪmpʊl'ziːf] *adj* impulsive.

imstande, im Stande▲ [ɪm'ʃtandə] *adj*: ~ **sein** to be in a position; (*fähig*) to be able; **er ist zu allem** ~ he's capable of anything.

══════════════ *SCHLÜSSELWORT*

in [ɪn] *präp +akk* **1** (*räumlich: wohin*) in, into; ~ **die Stadt** into town; ~ **die Schule gehen** to go to school; ~ **die hunderte** *od* **Hunderte gehen** to run into (the) hundreds.

2 (*zeitlich*): **bis** ~**s 20. Jahrhundert** into *od* up to the 20th century.

♦ *präp +dat* **1** (*räumlich: wo*) in; ~ **der Stadt** in town; ~ **der Schule sein** to be at school; **es** ~ **sich haben** (*umg: Text*) to be tough; (: *Drink*) to have quite a kick.

2 (*zeitlich: wann*): ~ **diesem Jahr** this year; (*in jenem Jahr*) in that year; **heute** ~ **zwei Wochen** two weeks today.

inaktiv ['ɪnaktiːf] *adj* inactive; (*Mitglied*) nonactive.

Inangriffnahme [ɪn'|angrɪfnaːmə] (-, -n) *f* (*form*) commencement.

Inanspruchnahme [ɪn'|anʃprʊxnaːmə] (-, -n) *f*: ~ **(+gen)** demands *pl* (on); **im Falle einer** ~ **der Arbeitslosenunterstützung** (*form*) where unemployment benefit has been sought.

Inbegriff ['ɪnbəgrɪf] *m* embodiment, personification.

inbegriffen *adv* included.

Inbetriebnahme [ɪnbə'triːpnaːmə] (-, -n) *f* (*form*) commissioning; (*von Gebäude, U-Bahn etc*) inauguration.

inbrünstig ['ɪnbrʏnstɪç] *adj* ardent.

indem [ɪn'deːm] *konj* while; ~ **man etw macht**

(dadurch) by doing sth.

Inder(in) ['ɪndər(ɪn)] **(-s, -)** *m(f)* Indian.

indes(sen) [ɪn'dɛs(ən)] *adv* meanwhile ♦ *konj* while.

Index ['ɪndɛks] **(-(es), -e** *od* **Indizes)** *m*: **auf dem ~ stehen** *(fig)* to be banned; **~zahl** *f* index number.

Indianer(in) [ɪndi'aːnər(ɪn)] **(-s, -)** *m(f)* (Red *od* American) Indian.

indianisch *adj* (Red *od* American) Indian.

Indien ['ɪndiən] **(-s)** *nt* India.

indigniert [ɪndɪ'gniːrt] *adj* indignant.

Indikation [ɪndɪkatsi'oːn] *f*: **medizinische/ soziale ~** medical/social grounds *pl* for the termination of pregnancy.

Indikativ ['ɪndɪkatiːf] **(-s, -e)** *m* indicative.

indirekt ['ɪndɪrɛkt] *adj* indirect; **~e Steuer** indirect tax.

indisch ['ɪndɪʃ] *adj* Indian; **I~er Ozean** Indian Ocean.

indiskret ['ɪndɪskreːt] *adj* indiscreet.

Indiskretion [ɪndɪskretsi'oːn] *f* indiscretion.

indiskutabel ['ɪndɪskutaːbəl] *adj* out of the question.

indisponiert ['ɪndɪsponiːrt] *adj* (*geh*) indisposed.

Individualist [ɪndividua'lɪst] *m* individualist.

Individualität [ɪndividuali'tɛt] *f* individuality.

individuell [ɪndividu'ɛl] *adj* individual; **etw ~ gestalten** to give sth a personal note.

Individuum [ɪndi'viːduʊm] **(-s, -duen)** *nt* individual.

Indiz [ɪn'diːts] **(-es, -ien)** *nt* (*JUR*) clue; **~ (für)** sign (of).

Indizes ['ɪndiːtseːz] *pl von* **Index**.

Indizienbeweis *m* circumstantial evidence.

indizieren [ɪndi'tsiːrən] *vt, vi* (*COMPUT*) to index.

Indochina ['ɪndo'çiːna] **(-s)** *nt* Indochina.

indogermanisch ['ɪndoger'maːnɪʃ] *adj* Indo-Germanic, Indo-European.

indoktrinieren [ɪndɔktri'niːrən] *vt* to indoctrinate.

Indonesien [ɪndo'neːziən] **(-s)** *nt* Indonesia.

Indonesier(in) **(-s, -)** *m(f)* Indonesian.

indonesisch [ɪndo'neːzɪʃ] *adj* Indonesian.

Indossament [ɪndɔsa'mɛnt] *nt* (*COMM*) endorsement.

Indossant [ɪndɔ'sant] *m* endorser.

Indossat [ɪndɔ'saːt] **(-en, -en)** *m* endorsee.

indossieren *vt* to endorse.

industrialisieren [ɪndʊstriali'ziːrən] *vt* to industrialize.

Industrialisierung *f* industrialization.

Industrie [ɪndʊs'triː] *f* industry; **in der ~ arbeiten** to be in industry; **~gebiet** *nt* industrial area; **~gelände** *nt* industrial *od* trading estate; **~kaufmann** *m* industrial manager.

industriell [ɪndʊstri'ɛl] *adj* industrial; **~e**

Revolution industrial revolution.

Industrielle(r) *f(m)* industrialist.

Industrie- *zW*: **~staat** *m* industrial nation; **~- und Handelskammer** *f* chamber of industry and commerce; **~zweig** *m* branch of industry.

ineinander [ɪnʔaɪ'nandər] *adv* in(to) one another *od* each other; **~ übergehen** to merge (into each other); **~ greifen** (*lit*) to interlock; (*Zahnräder*) to mesh; (*fig: Ereignisse etc*) to overlap.

Infanterie [ɪnfantə'riː] *f* infantry.

Infarkt [ɪn'farkt] **(-(e)s, -e)** *m* coronary (thrombosis).

Infektion [ɪnfɛktsi'oːn] *f* infection.

Infektionsherd *m* focus of infection.

Infektionskrankheit *f* infectious disease.

Infinitiv ['ɪnfinitiːf] **(-s, -e)** *m* infinitive.

infizieren [ɪnfi'tsiːrən] *vt* to infect ♦ *vr*: **sich (bei jdm) ~** to be infected (by sb).

in flagranti [ɪn fla'granti] *adv* in the act, red-handed.

Inflation [ɪnflatsi'oːn] *f* inflation.

inflationär [ɪnflatsio'nɛːr] *adj* inflationary.

Inflationsrate *f* rate of inflation.

inflatorisch [ɪnfla'toːrɪʃ] *adj* inflationary.

Info ['ɪnfo] **(-s, -s)** (*umg*) *nt* (information) leaflet.

infolge [ɪn'fɔlgə] *präp +gen* as a result of, owing to; **~dessen** *adv* consequently.

Informatik [ɪnfɔr'maːtɪk] *f* information studies *pl*.

Informatiker(in) **(-s, -)** *m(f)* computer scientist.

Information [ɪnfɔrmatsi'oːn] *f* information *no pl*; **Informationen** *pl* (*COMPUT*) data; **zu Ihrer ~** for your information.

Informationsabruf *m* (*COMPUT*) information retrieval.

Informationstechnik *f* information technology.

informativ [ɪnfɔrma'tiːf] *adj* informative.

informieren [ɪnfɔr'miːrən] *vt*: **~ (über +akk)** to inform (about) ♦ *vr*: **sich ~ (über +akk)** to find out (about).

Infotelefon *nt* information line.

infrage▲, in Frage [ɪn'fraːgə] *adv*: **etw ~ stellen** to question sth; **~ kommend** possible; (*Bewerber*) worth considering; **nicht ~ kommen** to be out of the question.

Infrastruktur ['ɪnfraʃtrʊktuːr] *f* infrastructure.

Infusion [ɪnfuzi'oːn] *f* infusion.

Ing. *abk* = **Ingenieur**.

Ingenieur [ɪnʒeni'øːr] *m* engineer; **~schule** *f* school of engineering.

Ingwer ['ɪŋvər] **(-s)** *m* ginger.

Inh. *abk* (= *Inhaber(in)*) prop.; (= *Inhalt*) cont.

Inhaber(in) ['ɪnhaːbər(ɪn)] **(-s, -)** *m(f)* owner; (*COMM*) proprietor; (*Haus~*) occupier;

(*Lizenz~*) licensee, holder; (*FIN*) bearer.
inhaftieren [ɪnhaf'ti:rən] *vt* to take into custody.
inhalieren [ɪnha'li:rən] *vt, vi* to inhale.
Inhalt ['ɪnhalt] (-(e)s, -e) *m* contents *pl*; (*eines Buchs etc*) content; (*MATH: Flächen*) area; (: *Raum~*) volume; **i~lich** *adj* as regards content.
Inhalts- *zW*: **~angabe** *f* summary; **~los** *adj* empty; **~reich** *adj* full; **~verzeichnis** *nt* table of contents; (*COMPUT*) directory.
inhuman ['ɪnhuma:n] *adj* inhuman.
initialisieren [ɪnitsia:li'zi:rən] *vt* (*COMPUT*) to initialize.
Initialisierung *f* (*COMPUT*) initialization.
Initiative [initsia'ti:və] *f* initiative; **die ~ ergreifen** to take the initiative.
Initiator(in) [initsi'a:tɔr, -'to:rɪn] *m(f)* (*geh*) initiator.
Injektion [ɪnjɛktsi'o:n] *f* injection.
injizieren [ɪnji'tsi:rən] *vt* to inject; **jdm etw ~** to inject sb with sth.
Inka ['ɪŋka] (-(s), -s) *f(m)* Inca.
Inkaufnahme [ɪn'kaufna:mə] *f* (*form*): **unter ~ finanzieller Verluste** accepting the inevitable financial losses.
inkl. *abk* (= *inklusive*) inc.
inklusive [ɪnklu'zi:və] *präp +gen* inclusive of
♦ *adv* inclusive.
Inklusivpreis *m* all-in rate.
inkognito [ɪn'kɔgnito] *adv* incognito.
inkonsequent ['ɪnkɔnzekvɛnt] *adj* inconsistent.
inkorrekt ['ɪnkɔrɛkt] *adj* incorrect.
In-Kraft-Treten▲ [ɪn'krafttre:tən] (-s) *nt* coming into force.
Inkubationszeit [ɪnkubatsi'o:nstsaɪt] *f* (*MED*) incubation period.
Inland ['ɪnlant] (-(e)s) *nt* (*GEOG*) inland; (*POL, COMM*) home (country); **im ~ und Ausland** at home and abroad; **~flug** *m* domestic flight.
Inlandsporto *nt* inland postage.
inmitten [ɪn'mɪtən] *präp +gen* in the middle of; **~ von** amongst.
innehaben ['ɪnəha:bən] *unreg vt* to hold.
innehalten ['ɪnəhaltən] *unreg vi* to pause, stop.
innen ['ɪnən] *adv* inside; **nach ~** inwards; **von ~** from the inside; **I~architekt** *m* interior designer; **I~aufnahme** *f* indoor photograph; **I~bahn** *f* (*SPORT*) inside lane; **I~dienst** *m*: **im I~dienst sein** to work in the office; **I~einrichtung** *f* (interior) furnishings *pl*; **I~leben** *nt* (*seelisch*) emotional life; (*umg: körperlich*) insides *pl*; **I~minister** *m* minister of the interior, Home Secretary (*BRIT*); **I~politik** *f* domestic policy; **~politisch** *adj* relating to domestic policy, domestic; **I~stadt** *f* town *od* city centre (*BRIT*) *od* center (*US*).

innerbetrieblich *adj* in-house; **etw ~ regeln** to settle sth within the company.
innerdeutsch *adj*: **~e(r) Handel** domestic trade in Germany.
Innere(s) *nt* inside; (*Mitte*) centre (*BRIT*), center (*US*); (*fig*) heart.
innere(r, s) *adj* inner; (*im Körper, inländisch*) internal.
Innereien [ɪnə'raɪən] *pl* innards *pl*.
inner- *zW*: **~halb** *adv* within; (*räumlich*) inside ♦ *prep +dat* within; inside; **~lich** *adj* internal; (*geistig*) inward; **I~lichkeit** *f* (*LITER*) inwardness; **~parteilich** *adj*: **~parteiliche Demokratie** democracy (with)in the party structure.
Innerste(s) *nt* heart; **bis ins ~ getroffen** hurt to the quick.
innerste(r, s) *adj* innermost.
innewohnen ['ɪnəvo:nən] *vi +dat* (*geh*) to be inherent in.
innig ['ɪnɪç] *adj* profound; (*Freundschaft*) intimate; **mein ~ster Wunsch** my dearest wish.
Innung ['ɪnʊŋ] *f* (trade) guild; **du blamierst die ganze ~** (*hum: umg*) you are letting the whole side down.
inoffiziell ['ɪn|ofitsiɛl] *adj* unofficial.
ins [ɪns] = **in das**.
Insasse ['ɪnzasə] (-n, -n) *m*, **Insassin** *f* (*einer Anstalt*) inmate; (*AUT*) passenger.
insbesondere [ɪnsbə'zɔndərə] *adv* (e)specially.
Inschrift ['ɪnʃrɪft] *f* inscription.
Insekt [ɪn'zɛkt] (-(e)s, -en) *nt* insect.
Insektenvertilgungsmittel *nt* insecticide.
Insel ['ɪnzəl] (-, -n) *f* island.
Inserat [ɪnze'ra:t] (-(e)s, -e) *nt* advertisement.
Inserent [ɪnze'rɛnt] *m* advertiser.
inserieren [ɪnze'ri:rən] *vt, vi* to advertise.
insgeheim [ɪnsgə'haɪm] *adv* secretly.
insgesamt [ɪnsgə'zamt] *adv* altogether, all in all.
Insiderhandel *m* insider dealing *od* trading.
insofern [ɪnzo'fɛrn] *adv* in this respect ♦ *konj* if; (*deshalb*) (and) so; **~ als** in so far as.
insolvent ['ɪnzɔlvɛnt] *adj* bankrupt, insolvent.
Insolvenz *f* (*COMM*) insolvency.
insoweit *adv, konj* = **insofern**.
in spe [ɪn'ʃpe:] (*umg*) *adj*: **unser Schwiegersohn ~** our son-in-law to be, our future son-in-law.
Inspektion [ɪnspɛktsi'o:n] *f* inspection; (*AUT*) service.
Inspektor(in) [ɪn'spɛktɔr, -'to:rɪn] (-s, -en) *m(f)* inspector.
Inspiration [ɪnspiratsi'o:n] *f* inspiration.
inspirieren [ɪnspi'ri:rən] *vt* to inspire; **sich von etw ~ lassen** to get one's inspiration from sth.
inspizieren [ɪnspi'tsi:rən] *vt* to inspect.

Installateur [ɪnstalaˈtøːr] *m* plumber; (*Elektro~*) electrician.

installieren [ɪnstaˈliːrən] *vt* to install (*auch fig, COMPUT*).

Instandhaltung [ɪnˈʃtanthaltʊŋ] *f* maintenance.

inständig [ɪnˈʃtɛndɪç] *adj* urgent; ~ **bitten** to beg.

Instandsetzung *f* overhaul; (*eines Gebäudes*) restoration.

Instanz [ɪnˈstants] *f* authority; (*JUR*) court; **Verhandlung in erster/zweiter** ~ first/second court case.

Instanzenweg *m* official channels *pl.*

Instinkt [ɪnˈstɪŋkt] (-(e)s, -e) *m* instinct.

instinktiv [ɪnstɪŋkˈtiːf] *adj* instinctive.

Institut [ɪnstiˈtuːt] (-(e)s, -e) *nt* institute.

Institution [ɪnstitutsiˈoːn] *f* institution.

Instrument [ɪnstruˈmɛnt] *nt* instrument.

Insulin [ɪnzuˈliːn] (-s) *nt* insulin.

inszenieren [ɪnstseˈniːrən] *vt* to direct; (*fig*) to stage-manage.

Inszenierung *f* production.

intakt [ɪnˈtakt] *adj* intact.

Integralrechnung [ɪnteˈɡraːlrɛçnʊŋ] *f* integral calculus.

Integration [ɪntegratsiˈoːn] *f* integration.

integrieren [ɪnteˈɡriːrən] *vt* to integrate; **integrierte Gesamtschule** comprehensive school (*BRIT*).

Integrität [ɪntegriˈtɛːt] *f* integrity.

Intellekt [ɪnteˈlɛkt] (-(e)s) *m* intellect.

intellektuell [ɪntelɛktuˈɛl] *adj* intellectual.

Intellektuelle(r) *f(m)* intellectual.

intelligent [ɪnteliˈɡɛnt] *adj* intelligent.

Intelligenz [ɪnteliˈɡɛnts] *f* intelligence; (*Leute*) intelligentsia *pl*; ~**quotient** *m* IQ, intelligence quotient.

Intendant [ɪntɛnˈdant] *m* director.

Intensität [ɪntɛnziˈtɛːt] *f* intensity.

intensiv [ɪntɛnˈziːf] *adj* intensive.

intensivieren [ɪntɛnziˈviːrən] *vt* to intensify.

Intensivkurs *m* intensive course.

Intensivstation *f* intensive care unit.

interaktiv *adj* (*COMPUT*) interactive.

Intercityzug [ɪntərˈsɪtitsuːk] *m* inter-city train.

interessant [ɪntɛrɛˈsant] *adj* interesting; **sich** ~ **machen** to attract attention.

interessanterweise *adv* interestingly enough.

Interesse [ɪnteˈrɛsə] (-s, -n) *nt* interest; ~ **haben an** +*dat* to be interested in.

Interessengebiet *nt* field of interest.

Interessengegensatz *m* clash of interests.

Interessent(in) [ɪntɛrɛˈsɛnt(ɪn)] *m(f)* interested party; **es haben sich mehrere ~en gemeldet** several people have shown interest.

Interessenvertretung *f* representation of

interests; (*Personen*) group representing (one's) interests.

interessieren [ɪntɛrɛˈsiːrən] *vt*: **jdn (für etw** *od* **an etw** *dat*) ~ to interest sb (in sth) ♦ *vr*: **sich** ~ **für** to be interested in.

interessiert *adj*: **politisch** ~ interested in politics.

Interkontinentalrakete [ɪntərkɔntinɛnˈtaːlrakeːtə] *f* intercontinental missile.

intern [ɪnˈtɛrn] *adj* internal.

Internat [ɪntɛrˈnaːt] (-(e)s, -e) *nt* boarding school.

international [ɪntɛrnatsioˈnaːl] *adj* international.

Internatsschüler(in) *m(f)* boarder.

Internet [ˈɪntɛrnɛt] (-s) *nt*: **das** ~ the Internet; ~**-Café** *nt* Internet café.

internieren [ɪntɛrˈniːrən] *vt* to intern.

Internierungslager *nt* internment camp.

Internist(in) *m(f)* internist.

Interpol [ˈɪntɛrpoːl] (-) *f abk* (= *Internationale Polizei*) Interpol.

Interpret [ɪntɛrˈpreːt] (-en, -en) *m*: **Lieder verschiedener ~en** songs by various singers.

Interpretation [ɪntɛrpretatsiˈoːn] *f* interpretation.

interpretieren [ɪntɛrpreˈtiːrən] *vt* to interpret.

Interpretin *f siehe* **Interpret**.

Interpunktion [ɪntɛrpʊŋktsiˈoːn] *f* punctuation.

Intervall [ɪntɛrˈval] (-s, -e) *nt* interval.

intervenieren [ɪntɛrveˈniːrən] *vi* to intervene.

Interview [ɪntərˈvjuː] (-s, -s) *nt* interview; **i~en** [-ˈvjuːən] *vt* to interview.

intim [ɪnˈtiːm] *adj* intimate; **I~bereich** *m* (*ANAT*) genital area.

Intimität [ɪntimiˈtɛːt] *f* intimacy.

Intimsphäre *f*: **jds** ~ **verletzen** to invade sb's privacy.

intolerant [ˈɪntolerant] *adj* intolerant.

intransitiv [ˈɪntranzitiːf] *adj* (*GRAM*) intransitive.

Intrige [ɪnˈtriːɡə] (-, -n) *f* intrigue, plot.

intrinsisch [ɪnˈtrɪnzɪʃ] *adj*: ~**er Wert** intrinsic value.

introvertiert [ɪntrovɛrˈtiːrt] *adj*: ~ **sein** to be an introvert.

intuitiv [ɪntuiˈtiːf] *adj* intuitive.

intus [ˈɪntus] *adj*: **etw** ~ **haben** (*umg: Wissen*) to have got sth into one's head; (*Essen, Trinken*) to have got sth down one (*umg*).

Invalide [ɪnvaˈliːdə] (-n, -n) *m* disabled person, invalid.

Invalidenrente *f* disability pension.

Invasion [ɪnvaziˈoːn] *f* invasion.

Inventar [ɪnvɛnˈtaːr] (-s, -e) *nt* inventory; (*COMM*) assets and liabilities *pl.*

Inventur [ɪnvɛnˈtuːr] *f* stocktaking; ~ **machen**

to stocktake.
investieren [ɪnvɛs'tiːrən] *vt* to invest.
investiert *adj:* ~**es Kapital** capital employed.
Investition [ɪnvɛstitsi'oːn] *f* investment.
Investitionszulage *f* investment grant.
Investmentgesellschaft
[ɪn'vɛstməntɡəzɛlʃaft] *f* unit trust.
inwiefern [ɪnvi'fɛrn] *adv* how far, to what
extent.
inwieweit [ɪnvi'vaɪt] *adv* how far, to what
extent.
Inzest [ɪn'tsɛst] (**-(e)s, -e**) *m* incest *no pl.*
inzwischen [ɪn'tsvɪʃən] *adv* meanwhile.
IOK *nt abk* (= *Internationales Olympisches
Komitee*) IOC.
Ion [i'oːn] (**-s, -en**) *nt* ion.
ionisch [i'oːnɪʃ] *adj* Ionian; I~**es Meer** Ionian
Sea.
IP *abk* (*COMPUT:* = *Internet Protocol*) IP.
IQ *m abk* (= *Intelligenzquotient*) IQ.
i. R. *abk* (= *im Ruhestand*) retd.
IRA *f abk* (= *Irisch-Republikanische Armee*) IRA.
Irak [i'raːk] (**-s**) *m:* (**der**) ~ Iraq.
Iraker(in) (**-s, -**) *m(f)* Iraqi.
irakisch *adj* Iraqi.
Iran [i'raːn] (**-s**) *m:* (**der**) ~ Iran.
Iraner(in) (**-s, -**) *m(f)* Iranian.
iranisch *adj* Iranian.
irdisch ['ɪrdɪʃ] *adj* earthly; **den Weg alles
Irdischen gehen** to go the way of all flesh.
Ire ['iːrə] (**-n, -n**) *m* Irishman; **die** ~**n** the Irish.
irgend ['ɪrɡənt] *adv* at all; **wann/was/wer** ~
whenever/whatever/whoever; ~**ein(e, s)** *adj*
some, any; **haben Sie (sonst) noch** ~**einen
Wunsch?** is there anything else you would
like?; ~**eine(r, s)** *pron* (*Person*) somebody;
(*Ding*) something; (*fragend, verneinend*)
anybody/anything; **ich will nicht bloß**
~**ein(e)s** I don't want any old one; ~**einmal**
adv sometime or other; (*fragend*) ever;
~**etwas▲** *pron* something; (*fragend,
verneinend*) anything; ~**jemand▲** *pron*
somebody; (*fragend, verneinend*) anybody;
~**wann** *adv* sometime; (*fragend, verneinend*)
somebody; (*fragend, verneinend*) anybody;
~**wie** *adv* somehow; ~**wo** *adv* somewhere
(*BRIT*), someplace (*US*); (*fragend, verneinend,
bedingend*) anywhere (*BRIT*), any place (*US*);
~**wohin** *adv* somewhere (*BRIT*), someplace
(*US*); (*fragend, verneinend, bedingend*)
anywhere (*BRIT*), any place (*US*).
Irin ['iːrɪn] *f* Irishwoman; Irish girl.
Iris ['iːrɪs] (**-, -**) *f* iris.
irisch *adj* Irish; **Irische See** Irish Sea.
IRK *nt abk* (= *Internationales Rotes Kreuz*) IRC.
Irland ['ɪrlant] (**-s**) *nt* Ireland; (*Republik* ~)
Eire.
Irländer ['ɪrlɛndər(ɪn)] (**-s, -**) *m* = **Ire;** ~**in** *f*
= **Irin.**
Ironie [iro'niː] *f* irony.

ironisch [i'roːnɪʃ] *adj* ironic(al).
irre ['ɪrə] *adj* crazy, mad; ~ **gut** (*umg*) way out
(*umg*); **I~(r)** *f(m)* lunatic; ~**führen** *vt* to
mislead; **I~führung** *f* fraud.
irrelevant ['ɪrelevant] *adj:* ~ (**für**) irrelevant
(for *od* to).
irremachen *vt* to confuse.
irren *vi* to be mistaken; (*umher*~) to wander,
stray ♦ *vr* to be mistaken; **jeder kann sich
mal** ~ anyone can make a mistake;
I~anstalt *f* (*veraltet*) lunatic asylum; **I~haus**
nt: **hier geht es zu wie im I~haus** (*umg*) this
place is an absolute madhouse.
Irrfahrt ['ɪrfaːrt] *f* wandering.
irrig ['ɪrɪç] *adj* incorrect, wrong.
irritieren [ɪri'tiːrən] *vt* (*verwirren*) to confuse,
muddle; (*ärgern*) to irritate.
Irr- *zW:* ~**licht** *nt* will-o'-the-wisp; ~**sinn** *m*
madness; **so ein** ~**sinn, das zu tun** what a
crazy thing to do!; **i~sinnig** *adj* mad, crazy;
(*umg*) terrific; **i~sinnig komisch** incredibly
funny; ~**tum** (**-s, -tümer**) *m* mistake, error;
im ~**tum sein** to be wrong *od* mistaken;
~**tum!** wrong!; **i~tümlich** *adj* mistaken.
ISBN *f abk* (= *Internationale
Standardbuchnummer*) ISBN.
Ischias ['ɪʃias] (**-**) *m od nt* sciatica.
Islam ['ɪslam] (**-s**) *m* Islam.
islamisch [ɪs'laːmɪʃ] *adj* Islamic.
Island ['iːslant] (**-s**) *nt* Iceland.
Isländer(in) ['iːslɛndər(ɪn)] (**-s, -**) *m(f)*
Icelander.
isländisch *adj* Icelandic.
Isolation [izolatsi'oːn] *f* isolation; (*ELEK*)
insulation; (*von Häftlingen*) solitary
confinement.
Isolator [izo'laːtɔr] *m* insulator.
Isolierband *nt* insulating tape.
isolieren [izo'liːrən] *vt* to isolate; (*ELEK*) to
insulate.
Isolierstation *f* (*MED*) isolation ward.
Isolierung *f* isolation; (*ELEK*) insulation.
Israel ['ɪsraeːl] (**-s**) *nt* Israel.
Israeli[1] [ɪsra'eːli] (**-(s), -s**) *m* Israeli.
Israeli[2] [ɪsra'eːli] (**-, -(s)**) *f* Israeli.
israelisch *adj* Israeli.
isst▲ [ɪst] *vb siehe* **essen.**
ist [ɪst] *vb siehe* **sein.**
Istanbul ['ɪstambuːl] (**-s**) *nt* Istanbul.
Istbestand▲ *m* (*Geld*) cash in hand; (*Waren*)
actual stock.
Italien [i'taːliən] (**-s**) *nt* Italy.
Italiener(in) [itali'eːnər(ɪn)] (**-s, -**) *m(f)* Italian.
italienisch *adj* Italian; **die** ~**e Schweiz**
Italian-speaking Switzerland.
i. V., I. V. *abk* (= *in Vertretung*) on behalf of;
(= *in Vollmacht*) by proxy.
IWF *m abk* (= *Internationaler Währungsfonds*)
IMF.

J, j

J, j [jɔt] *nt* J, j; ~ **wie Julius** ≈ J for Jack, J for Jig (*US*).

ja [ja:] *adv* **1** yes; **haben Sie das gesehen? - ~** did you see it? - yes(, I did); **ich glaube ~** (yes) I think so; **zu allem J~ und Amen** *od* **~ und amen sagen** (*umg*) to accept everything without question.

2 (*fragend*) really; **ich habe gekündigt - ~?** I've quit - have you?; **du kommst, ~?** you're coming, aren't you?

3: sei ~ vorsichtig do be careful; **Sie wissen ~, dass** ... as you know, ...; **tu das ~ nicht!** don't do that!; **sie ist ~ erst fünf** (after all) she's only five; **Sie wissen ~, wie das so ist** you know how it is; **ich habe es ~ gewusst** I just knew it; **~, also** ... well you see ...

Jacht [jaxt] (-, **-en**) *f* yacht.
Jacke ['jakə] (-, **-n**) *f* jacket; (*Woll~*) cardigan.
Jacketkrone ['dʒɛ'kɪtkro:nə] *f* (*Zahnkrone*) jacket crown.
Jackett [ʒa'kɛt] (-**s**, **-s** *od* **-e**) *nt* jacket.
Jagd [ja:kt] (-, **-en**) *f* hunt; (*Jagen*) hunting; **~beute** *f* kill; **~flugzeug** *nt* fighter; **~gewehr** *nt* sporting gun; **~hund** *m* hunting dog; **~schein** *m* hunting licence (*BRIT*) *od* license (*US*); **~wurst** *f* smoked sausage.
jagen ['ja:gən] *vi* to hunt; (*eilen*) to race ♦ *vt* to hunt; (*weg~*) to drive (off); (*verfolgen*) to chase; **mit diesem Essen kannst du mich ~** (*umg*) I wouldn't touch that food with a barge pole (*BRIT*) *od* ten-foot pole (*US*).
Jäger ['jɛ:gər] (-**s**, -) *m* hunter; **~in** *f* huntress, huntswoman; **~latein** (*umg*) *nt* hunters' tales *pl*; **~schnitzel** *nt* (*KOCH*) cutlet served with mushroom sauce.
jäh [jɛ:] *adj* abrupt, sudden; (*steil*) steep, precipitous; **~lings** *adv* abruptly.
Jahr [ja:r] (-(**e**)**s**, **-e**) *nt* year; **im ~(e) 1066** (the year) 1066; **die sechziger ~e** the sixties *pl*; **mit dreißig ~en** at the age of thirty; **in den besten ~en sein** to be in the prime of (one's) life; **nach ~ und Tag** after (many) years; **zwischen den ~en** (*umg*) between Christmas and New Year; **j~aus** *adv*: **j~aus, j~ein** year in, year out; **~buch** *nt* annual, year book.
jahrelang *adv* for years.

Jahres- *zW*: **~abonnement** *nt* annual subscription; **~abschluss▲** *m* end of the year; (*COMM*) annual statement of account; **~beitrag** *m* annual subscription; **~bericht** *m* annual report; **~hauptversammlung** *f* (*COMM*) annual general meeting, AGM; **~karte** *f* annual season ticket; **~tag** *m* anniversary; **~umsatz** *m* (*COMM*) yearly turnover; **~wechsel** *m* turn of the year; **~zahl** *f* date, year; **~zeit** *f* season.
Jahr- *zW*: **~gang** *m* age group; (*von Wein*) vintage; **er ist ~gang 1950** he was born in 1950; **~hundert** *nt* century; **~hundertfeier** *f* centenary; **~hundertwende** *f* turn of the century.
jährlich ['jɛ:rlɪç] *adj*, *adv* yearly; **zweimal ~** twice a year.
Jahr- *zW*: **~markt** *m* fair; **~tausend** *nt* millennium; **~zehnt** *nt* decade.
Jähzorn ['jɛ:tsɔrn] *m* hot temper.
jähzornig *adj* hot-tempered.
Jalousie [ʒalu'zi:] *f* venetian blind.
Jamaika [ja'maɪka] (-**s**) *nt* Jamaica.
Jammer ['jamər] (-**s**) *m* misery; **es ist ein ~, dass** ... it is a crying shame that ...
jämmerlich ['jɛmərlɪç] *adj* wretched, pathetic; **J~keit** *f* wretchedness.
jammern *vi* to wail ♦ *vt unpers*: **es jammert mich** it makes me feel sorry.
jammerschade *adj*: **es ist ~** it is a crying shame.
Jan. *abk* (= *Januar*) Jan.
Januar ['janua:r] (-**s**, **-e**) (*pl selten*) *m* January; *siehe auch* **September**.
Japan ['ja:pan] (-**s**) *nt* Japan.
Japaner(in) [ja'pa:nər(ɪn)] (-**s**, -) *m(f)* Japanese.
japanisch *adj* Japanese.
Jargon [ʒar'gõ:] (-**s**, **-s**) *m* jargon.
Jasager ['ja:za:gər] (-**s**, -) (*pej*) *m* yes man.
Jastimme *f* vote in favour (*BRIT*) *od* favor (*US*) (of).
jäten ['jɛ:tən] *vt*, *vi* to weed.
Jauche ['jauxə] *f* liquid manure; **~grube** *f* cesspool, cesspit.
jauchzen ['jauxtsən] *vi* to rejoice, shout (with joy).
Jauchzer (-**s**, -) *m* shout of joy.
jaulen ['jaulən] *vi* to howl.
Jause ['jauzə] (*ÖSTERR*) *f* snack.
jawohl *adv* yes (of course).
Jawort *nt* consent; **jdm das ~ geben** to consent to marry sb; (*bei Trauung*) to say "I do".
Jazz [dʒæz] (-) *m* jazz; **~keller** *m* jazz club.

je [je:] *adv* **1** (*jemals*) ever; **hast du so was ~ gesehen?** did you ever see anything like it?

2 (*jeweils*) every, each; **sie zahlten ~ 15 Euro** they paid 15 euros each.
♦ *konj* **1**: **~ nach** depending on; **~ nachdem** it depends; **~ nachdem, ob** ... depending on whether ...
2: **~ eher, desto** *od* **umso besser** the sooner the better; **~ länger, ~ lieber** the longer the better.

Jeans [dʒiːnz] *pl* jeans *pl*; **~anzug** *m* denim suit.

jede(r, s) ['jeːdə(r, s)] *adj* (*einzeln*) each; (*von zweien*) either; (**~ von allen**) every ♦ *indef pron* (*einzeln*) each (one); (**~ von allen**) everyone, everybody; **ohne ~ Anstrengung** without any effort; **~r Zweite** every other (one); **~s Mal** every time, each time.

jedenfalls *adv* in any case.

jedermann *pron* everyone; **das ist nicht ~s Sache** it's not everyone's cup of tea.

jederzeit *adv* at any time.

jedoch [je'dɔx] *adv* however.

jeher ['jeːheːr] *adv*: **von ~** all along.

jein [jaɪn] *adv* (*hum*) yes no.

jemals ['jeːmaːls] *adv* ever.

jemand ['jeːmant] *indef pron* someone, somebody; (*bei Fragen, bedingenden Sätzen, Negation*) anyone, anybody.

Jemen ['jeːmən] (**-s**) *m* Yemen.

Jemenit(in) [jeme'niːt(ɪn)] (**-en, -en**) *m(f)* Yemeni.

jemenitisch *adj* Yemeni.

Jenaer Glas ® ['jeːnaərglaːs] *nt* heatproof glass, ≈ Pyrex ®.

jene(r, s) ['jeːnə(r, s)] *adj* that; (*pl*) those ♦ *pron* that one; (*pl*) those; (*der Vorherige, die Vorherigen*) the former.

jenseits ['jeːnzaɪts] *adv* on the other side ♦ *präp* +*gen* on the other side of, beyond; **J~** *nt*: **das J~** the hereafter, the beyond; **jdn ins J~ befördern** (*umg*) to send sb to kingdom come.

Jesus ['jeːzʊs] (**Jesu**) *m* Jesus; **~ Christus** Jesus Christ.

jetten ['dʒɛtən] (*umg*) *vi* to jet (*inf*).

jetzig ['jɛtsɪç] *adj* present.

jetzt [jɛtst] *adv* now; **~ gleich** right now.

jeweilig *adj* respective; **die ~e Regierung** the government of the day.

jeweils *adv*: **~ zwei zusammen** two at a time; **zu ~ 10 Euro** at 10 euros each; **~ das Erste** the first each time; **~ am Monatsletzten** on the last day of each month.

Jg. *abk* = **Jahrgang**.

Jh. *abk* (= *Jahrhundert*) cent.

jiddisch ['jɪdɪʃ] *adj* Yiddish.

Job [dʒɔp] (**-s, -s**) (*umg*) *m* job.

jobben ['dʒɔbən] (*umg*) *vi* to work, have a job.

Joch [jɔx] (**-(e)s, -e**) *nt* yoke.

Jochbein *nt* cheekbone.

Jockei, Jockey ['dʒɔke] (**-s, -s**) *m* jockey.

Jod [joːt] (**-(e)s**) *nt* iodine.

jodeln ['joːdəln] *vi* to yodel.

joggen ['dʒɔgən] *vi* to jog.

Joghurt, Jogurt▲ ['joːgʊrt] (**-s, -s**) *m* *od* *nt* yog(h)urt.

Johannisbeere [jo'hanɪsbeːrə] *f*: **rote ~** redcurrant; **schwarze ~** blackcurrant.

johlen ['joːlən] *vi* to yell.

Joint [dʒɔɪnt] (**-s, -s**) (*umg*) *m* joint.

Jointventure▲, **Joint Venture**▲ ['dʒɔɪntventʃəʳ] (**-, -s**) *nt* joint venture.

Jolle ['jɔlə] (**-, -n**) *f* dinghy.

Jongleur [ʒõ'gløːr] (**-s, -e**) *m* juggler.

jonglieren [ʒõ'gliːrən] *vi* to juggle.

Joppe ['jɔpə] (**-, -n**) *f* jacket.

Jordanien [jɔr'daːniən] (**-s**) *nt* Jordan.

Jordanier(in) (**-s, -**) *m(f)* Jordanian.

jordanisch *adj* Jordanian.

Journalismus [ʒʊrna'lɪsmʊs] *m* journalism.

Journalist(in) [ʒʊrna'lɪst(ɪn)] *m(f)* journalist; **j~isch** *adj* journalistic.

Jubel ['juːbəl] (**-s**) *m* rejoicing; **~, Trubel, Heiterkeit** laughter and merriment; **~jahr** *nt*: **alle ~jahre (einmal)** (*umg*) once in a blue moon; **j~n** *vi* to rejoice.

Jubilar(in) [jubi'laːr(ɪn)] (**-s, -e**) *m(f)* person celebrating an anniversary.

Jubiläum [jubi'lɛːʊm] (**-s, Jubiläen**) *nt* jubilee; (*Jahrestag*) anniversary.

jucken ['jʊkən] *vi* to itch ♦ *vt*: **es juckt mich am Arm** my arm is itching; **das juckt mich** that's itchy; **das juckt mich doch nicht** (*umg*) I don't care.

Juckpulver *nt* itching powder.

Juckreiz *m* itch.

Judaslohn ['juːdasloːn] (*liter*) blood money.

Jude ['juːdə] (**-n, -n**) *m* Jew.

Juden- *zW*: **~stern** *m* star of David; **~tum** (**-s**) *nt* (*die Juden*) Jewry; **~verfolgung** *f* persecution of the Jews.

Jüdin ['jyːdɪn] *f* Jewess.

jüdisch *adj* Jewish.

Judo ['juːdo] (**-(s)**) *nt* judo.

Jugend ['juːgənt] (**-**) *f* youth; **~amt** *nt* youth welfare department; **j~frei** *adj* suitable for young people; (*FILM*) U(-certificate), G (*US*); **~herberge** *f* youth hostel; **~hilfe** *f* youth welfare scheme; **~kriminalität** *f* juvenile crime; **j~lich** *adj* youthful; **~liche(r)** *f(m)* teenager, young person; **~liebe** *f* (*Geliebte(r)*) love of one's youth; **~richter** *m* juvenile court judge; **~schutz** *m* protection of children and young people; **~stil** *m* (*KUNST*) Art Nouveau; **~strafanstalt** *f* youth custody centre (*BRIT*); **~sünde** *f* youthful misdeed; **~zentrum** *nt* youth centre (*BRIT*) *od* center (*US*).

Jugoslawe [jugo'slaːvə] (**-n, -n**) *m* Yugoslav.

Jugoslawien [jugo'slaːviən] (**-s**) *nt*

Yugoslavia.
Jugoslawin [jugo'sla:vɪn] f Yugoslav.
jugoslawisch adj Yugoslav(ian).
Juli ['ju:li] (-(s), -s) (pl selten) m July; siehe auch September.
jun. abk (= junior) jun.
jung [jʊŋ] adj young.
Junge (-n, -n) m boy, lad ♦ nt young animal; (pl) young pl.
Jünger ['jʏŋər] (-s, -) m disciple.
jünger adj younger.
Jungfer (-, -n) f: alte ~ old maid.
Jungfernfahrt f maiden voyage.
Jung- zW: ~**frau** f virgin; (ASTROL) Virgo; ~**geselle** m bachelor; ~**gesellin** f bachelor girl; (älter) single woman.
Jüngling ['jʏŋlɪŋ] m youth.
Jungsozialist m (BRD POL) Young Socialist.
jüngst [jʏŋst] adv lately, recently.
jüngste(r, s) adj youngest; (neueste) latest; das J~ Gericht the Last Judgement; der J~ Tag Doomsday, the Day of Judgement.
Jungwähler(in) m(f) young voter.
Juni ['ju:ni] (-(s), -s) (pl selten) m June; siehe auch September.
Junior ['ju:niɔr] (-s, -en) m junior.
Junta ['xʊnta] (-, -ten) f (POL) junta.
jur. abk = juristisch.
Jura ['ju:ra] no art (UNIV) law.
Jurist(in) [ju'rɪst(ɪn)] m(f) jurist, lawyer; (Student) law student; j~**isch** adj legal.
Juso ['ju:zo] (-s, -s) m abk = Jungsozialist.
just [jʊst] adv just.
Justiz [jʊs'ti:ts] (-) f justice; ~**beamte(r)** m judicial officer; ~**irrtum** m miscarriage of justice; ~**minister** m minister of justice; ~**mord** m judicial murder.
Juwel [ju've:l] (-s, -en) m od nt jewel.
Juwelier [juve'li:r] (-s, -e) m jeweller (BRIT), jeweler (US); ~**geschäft** nt jeweller's (BRIT) od jeweler's (US) (shop).
Jux [jʊks] (-es, -e) m joke, lark; **etw aus** ~ **tun/sagen** (umg) to do/say sth in fun.
jwd [jɔtveː'deː] adv (hum) in the back of beyond.

K, k

K, k [ka:] nt K, k; ~ **wie Kaufmann** ≈ K for King.
Kabarett [kaba'rɛt] (-s, -e od -s) nt cabaret; ~**ist(in)** [kabarɛ'tɪst(ɪn)] m(f) cabaret artiste.
Kabel ['ka:bəl] (-s, -) nt (ELEK) wire; (stark) cable; ~**anschluss▲** m: ~**anschluss haben** to have cable television; ~**fernsehen** nt cable television.
Kabeljau ['ka:bəljaʊ] (-s, -e od -s) m cod.
kabeln vt, vi to cable.
Kabelsalat (umg) m tangle of cable.
Kabine [ka'bi:nə] f cabin; (Zelle) cubicle.
Kabinett [kabi'nɛt] (-s, -e) nt (POL) cabinet; (kleines Zimmer) small room ♦ m high-quality German white wine.
Kabriolett [kabrio'lɛt] (-s, -s) nt (AUT) convertible.
Kachel ['kaxəl] (-, -n) f tile.
kacheln vt to tile.
Kachelofen m tiled stove.
Kacke ['kakə] (-, -n) (umg!) f crap (!).
Kadaver [ka'da:vər] (-s, -) m carcass.
Kader ['ka:dər] (-s, -) m (MIL, POL) cadre; (SPORT) squad; (DDR, SCHWEIZ: Fachleute) group of specialists; ~**schmiede** f (POL: umg) institution for the training of cadre personnel.
Kadett [ka'dɛt] (-en, -en) m cadet.
Käfer ['kɛ:fər] (-s, -) m beetle.
Kaff [kaf] (-s, -s) (umg) nt dump, hole.
Kaffee ['kafe] (-s, -s) m coffee; **zwei** ~**, bitte!** two coffees, please; **das ist kalter** ~ (umg) that's old hat; ~**kanne** f coffeepot; ~**klatsch** m, ~**kränzchen** nt coffee circle; ~**löffel** m coffee spoon; ~**maschine** f coffee maker; ~**mühle** f coffee grinder; ~**satz** m coffee grounds pl; ~**tante** f (hum) coffee addict; (in Café) old biddy; ~**wärmer** m cosy (for coffeepot).
Käfig ['kɛ:fɪç] (-s, -e) m cage.
kahl [ka:l] adj bald; ~ **fressen** to strip bare; ~ **geschoren** shaven, shorn; **K~heit** f baldness; ~**köpfig** adj bald-headed; **K~schlag** m (in Wald) clearing.
Kahn [ka:n] (-(e)s, ̈-e) m boat, barge.
Kai [kai] (-s, -e od -s) m quay.
Kairo ['kairo] (-s) nt Cairo.
Kaiser ['kaizər] (-s, -) m emperor; ~**in** f empress; **k~lich** adj imperial; ~**reich** nt empire; ~**schmarren** ['kaizərʃmarən] m

(KOCH) sugared, cut-up pancake with raisins; **~schnitt** m *(MED)* Caesarean *(BRIT)* od Cesarean *(US)* (section).

Kajak ['ka:jak] (-s, -s) m or nt kayak.

Kajüte [ka'jy:tə] (-, -n) f cabin.

Kakao [ka'ka:o] (-s, -s) m cocoa; **jdn durch den ~ ziehen** *(umg: veralbern)* to make fun of sb; (: *boshaft reden*) to run sb down.

Kakerlak ['ka:kərlak] (-en, -en) m cockroach.

Kaktee [kak'te:ə] (-, -n) f cactus.

Kaktus ['kaktʊs] (-, -se) m cactus.

Kalabrien [ka'la:briən] (-s) nt Calabria.

Kalauer ['ka:laʊər] (-s, -) m corny joke; *(Wortspiel)* corny pun.

Kalb [kalp] (-(e)s, -̈er) nt calf; **k~en** ['kalbən] vi to calve; **~fleisch** nt veal.

Kalbsleder nt calf(skin).

Kalender [ka'lɛndər] (-s, -) m calendar; *(Taschen~)* diary.

Kali ['ka:li] (-s, -s) nt potash.

Kaliber [ka'li:bər] (-s, -) nt *(lit, fig)* calibre *(BRIT)*, caliber *(US)*.

Kalifornien [kali'fɔrniən] (-s) nt California.

Kalk [kalk] (-(e)s, -e) m lime; *(BIOL)* calcium; **~stein** m limestone.

Kalkül [kal'ky:l] (-s, -e) m od nt *(geh)* calculation.

Kalkulation [kalkulatsi'o:n] f calculation.

Kalkulator [kalku'la:tɔr] m cost accountant.

kalkulieren [kalku'li:rən] vt to calculate.

kalkuliert adj: **~es Risiko** calculated risk.

Kalkutta [kal'kʊta] (-s) nt Calcutta.

Kalorie [kalo'ri:] (-, -n) f calorie.

kalorienarm adj low-calorie.

kalt [kalt] adj cold; **mir ist (es) ~** I am cold; **~e Platte** cold meat; **der K~e Krieg** the Cold War; **etw ~ stellen** to chill, to put sth to chill; **die Wohnung kostet ~ 980 DM** the flat costs 980 DM without heating; **~ bleiben** to be unmoved; **~ lächeln** *(ironisch)* cool as you please; **~blütig** adj cold-blooded; *(ruhig)* cool; **K~blütigkeit** f cold-bloodedness; coolness.

Kälte ['kɛltə] (-) f coldness; *(Wetter)* cold; **~einbruch** m cold spell; **~grad** m degree of frost od below zero; **~welle** f cold spell.

kalt- zW: **~herzig** adj cold-hearted; **~machen** *(umg)* vt to do in; **K~miete** f rent exclusive of heating; **K~schale** f *(KOCH)* cold sweet soup; **~schnäuzig** adj cold, unfeeling; **~stellen** vt *(fig)* to leave out in the cold.

Kalzium ['kaltsiʊm] (-s) nt calcium.

kam etc [ka:m] vb siehe **kommen**.

Kambodscha [kam'bɔdʒa] nt Cambodia.

Kamel [ka'me:l] (-(e)s, -e) m camel.

Kamera ['kamera] (-, -s) f camera; **~rekorder** m camcorder.

Kamerad(in) [kamə'ra:t,-'ra:dɪn] (-en, -en) m(f) comrade, friend; **~schaft** f comradeship; **k~schaftlich** adj comradely.

Kameraführung f camera work.

Kameramann (-(e)s, pl -männer) m cameraman.

Kamerun ['kaməru:n] (-s) nt Cameroon.

Kamille [ka'mɪlə] (-, -n) f camomile.

Kamillentee m camomile tea.

Kamin [ka'mi:n] (-s, -e) m *(außen)* chimney; *(innen)* fireside; *(Feuerstelle)* fireplace; **~feger** (-s, -) m chimney sweep; **~kehrer** (-s, -) m chimney sweep.

Kamm [kam] (-(e)s, -̈e) m comb; *(Berg~)* ridge; *(Hahnen~)* crest; **alle/alles über einen ~ scheren** *(fig)* to lump everyone/everything together.

kämmen ['kɛmən] vt to comb.

Kammer ['kamər] (-, -n) f chamber; *(Zimmer)* small bedroom; **~diener** m valet; **~jäger** m *(Schädlingsbekämpfer)* pest controller; **~musik** f chamber music; **~zofe** f chambermaid.

Kammstück nt *(KOCH)* shoulder.

Kampagne [kam'panjə] (-, -n) f campaign.

Kampf [kampf] (-(e)s, -̈e) m fight, battle; *(Wettbewerb)* contest; *(fig: Anstrengung)* struggle; **jdm/etw den ~ ansagen** *(fig)* to declare war on sb/sth; **k~bereit** adj ready for action.

kämpfen ['kɛmpfən] vi to fight; **ich habe lange mit mir ~ müssen, ehe ...** I had a long battle with myself before ...

Kampfer ['kampfər] (-s) m camphor.

Kämpfer(in) (-s, -) m(f) fighter, combatant.

Kampf- zW: **~flugzeug** nt fighter (aircraft); **~geist** m fighting spirit; **~handlung** f action; **~kunst** f martial arts pl; **k~los** adj without a fight; **k~lustig** adj pugnacious; **~platz** m battlefield; *(SPORT)* arena, stadium; **~richter** m *(SPORT)* referee; **~sport** m martial art.

Kampuchea [kampu'tʃe:a] (-s) nt Kampuchea.

Kanada ['kanada] (-s) nt Canada.

Kanadier(in) [ka'na:diər(ɪn)] (-s, -) m(f) Canadian.

kanadisch [ka'na:dɪʃ] adj Canadian.

Kanal [ka'na:l] (-s, Kanäle) m *(Fluss)* canal; *(Rinne)* channel; *(für Abfluss)* drain; **der ~** *(auch: der Ärmelkanal)* the (English) Channel.

Kanalinseln pl Channel Islands pl.

Kanalisation [kanalizatsi'o:n] f sewage system.

kanalisieren [kanali'zi:rən] vt to provide with a sewage system; *(fig: Energie etc)* to channel.

Kanaltunnel m Channel Tunnel.

Kanarienvogel [ka'na:riənfo:gəl] m canary.

Kanarische Inseln [ka'na:rɪʃə'ɪnzəln] pl Canary Islands pl, Canaries pl.

Kandare [kan'da:rə] (-, -n) f: **jdn an die ~ nehmen** *(fig)* to take sb in hand.

Kandidat(in) [kandi'da:t(ɪn)] (-en, -en) m(f)

candidate; **jdn als ~en aufstellen** to nominate sb.

Kandidatur [kandida'tu:r] f candidature, candidacy.

kandidieren [kandi'di:rən] vi (POL) to stand, run.

kandiert [kan'di:rt] adj (Frucht) candied.

Kandis(zucker) ['kandɪs(tsʊkər)] (-) m rock candy.

Känguru▲ ['kɛŋguru] (-s, -s) nt kangaroo.

Kaninchen [ka'ni:nçən] nt rabbit.

Kanister [ka'nɪstər] (-s, -) m can, canister.

kann [kan] vb siehe **können**.

Kännchen ['kɛnçən] nt pot; (für Milch) jug.

Kanne ['kanə] (-, -n) f (Krug) jug; (Kaffee~) pot; (Milch~) churn; (Gieß~) watering can.

Kannibale [kani'ba:lə] (-n, -n) m cannibal.

kannte etc ['kantə] vb siehe **kennen**.

Kanon ['ka:nɔn] (-s, -s) m canon.

Kanone [ka'no:nə] (-, -n) f gun; (HIST) cannon; (fig: Mensch) ace; **das ist unter aller ~** (umg) that defies description.

Kanonenfutter (umg) nt cannon fodder.

Kant. abk = **Kanton**.

Kantate [kan'ta:tə] (-, -n) f cantata.

Kante ['kantə] (-, -n) f edge; **Geld auf die hohe ~ legen** (umg) to put money by.

kantig ['kantɪç] adj (Holz) edged; (Gesicht) angular.

Kantine [kan'ti:nə] f canteen.

Kanton [kan'to:n] (-s, -e) m canton.

Kantor ['kantɔr] m choirmaster.

Kanu ['ka:nu] (-s, -s) nt canoe.

Kanzel ['kantsəl] (-, -n) f pulpit; (AVIAT) cockpit.

Kanzlei [kants'lai] f chancery; (Büro) chambers pl.

Kanzler ['kantslər] (-s, -) m chancellor.

Kap [kap] (-s, -s) nt cape; **das ~ der guten Hoffnung** the Cape of Good Hope.

Kapazität [kapatsi'tɛ:t] f capacity; (Fachmann) authority.

Kapelle [ka'pɛlə] f (Gebäude) chapel; (MUS) band.

Kapellmeister(in) m(f) director of music; (MIL, von Tanzkapelle etc) bandmaster, bandleader.

Kaper ['ka:pər] (-, -n) f caper.

kapern vt to capture.

kapieren [ka'pi:rən] (umg) vt, vi to understand.

Kapital [kapi'ta:l] (-s, -e od -ien) nt capital; **aus etw ~ schlagen** (pej: lit, fig) to make capital out of sth; **~anlage** f investment; **~aufwand** m capital expenditure; **~ertrag** m capital gains pl; **~ertragssteuer** f capital gains tax; **~flucht** f flight of capital; **~gesellschaft** f (COMM) joint-stock company; **~güter** pl capital goods pl; **k~intensiv** adj capital-intensive.

Kapitalismus [kapita'lɪsmʊs] m capitalism.

Kapitalist [kapita'lɪst] m capitalist.

kapitalistisch adj capitalist.

Kapital- zW: **k~kräftig** adj wealthy; **~markt** m money market; **k~schwach** adj financially weak; **k~stark** adj financially strong; **~verbrechen** nt serious crime; (mit Todesstrafe) capital crime.

Kapitän [kapi'tɛ:n] (-s, -e) m captain.

Kapitel [ka'pɪtəl] (-s, -) nt chapter; **ein trauriges ~** (Angelegenheit) a sad story.

Kapitulation [kapitulatsi'o:n] f capitulation.

kapitulieren [kapitu'li:rən] vi to capitulate.

Kaplan [ka'pla:n] (-s, **Kapläne**) m chaplain.

Kappe ['kapə] (-, -n) f cap; (Kapuze) hood; **das nehme ich auf meine ~** (fig: umg) I'll take the responsibility for that.

kappen vt to cut.

Kapsel ['kapsəl] (-, -n) f capsule.

Kapstadt ['kapʃtat] nt Cape Town.

kaputt [ka'pʊt] (umg) adj smashed, broken; (Person) exhausted, knackered; **der Fernseher ist ~** the TV's not working; **ein ~er Typ** a bum; **~gehen** unreg vi to break; (Schuhe) to fall apart; (Firma) to go bust; (Stoff) to wear out; (sterben) to cop it (umg); **~lachen** vr to laugh o.s. silly; **~machen** vt to break; (Mensch) to exhaust, wear out; **~schlagen** unreg vt to smash.

Kapuze [ka'pu:tsə] (-, -n) f hood.

Karabiner [kara'bi:nər] (-s, -) m (Gewehr) carbine.

Karacho [ka'raxo] (-s) nt: **mit ~** (umg) hell for leather.

Karaffe [ka'rafə] (-, -n) f carafe; (geschliffen) decanter.

Karambolage [karambo'la:ʒə] (-, -n) f (Zusammenstoß) crash.

Karamell▲ [kara'mɛl] (-s) m caramel; **~bonbon** m od nt toffee.

Karat [ka'ra:t] (-(e)s, -e) nt carat.

Karate (-s) nt karate.

Karawane [kara'va:nə] (-, -n) f caravan.

Kardinal [kardi'na:l] (-s, **Kardinäle**) m cardinal; **~fehler** m cardinal error; **~zahl** f cardinal number.

Karenzzeit [ka'rɛntstsait] f waiting period.

Karfreitag [ka:r'fraita:k] m Good Friday.

karg [kark] adj scanty, poor; (Mahlzeit) meagre (BRIT), meager (US); **etw ~ bemessen** to be mean with sth; **K~heit** f poverty, scantiness; meagreness (BRIT), meagerness (US).

kärglich ['kɛrklɪç] adj poor, scanty.

Kargo ['kargo] (-s, -s) m (COMM) cargo.

Karibik [ka'ri:bɪk] (-) f: **die ~** the Caribbean.

karibisch adj Caribbean; **das K~e Meer** the Caribbean Sea.

kariert [ka'ri:rt] adj (Stoff) checked (BRIT), checkered (US); (Papier) squared; **~ reden** (umg) to talk rubbish od nonsense.

Karies ['ka:riɛs] (-) f caries.

Karikatur [karika'tuːr] *f* caricature; **~ist(in)** [karikatu:'rɪst(ɪn)] *m(f)* cartoonist.
karikieren [kari'kiːrən] *vt* to caricature.
karitativ [karita'tiːf] *adj* charitable.
Karneval ['karnəval] **(-s, -e** *od* **-s)** *m* carnival.

KARNEVAL

Karneval *is the name given to the days immediately before Lent when people gather to sing, dance, eat, drink and generally make merry before the fasting begins.* **Rosenmontag,** *the day before Shrove Tuesday, is the most important day of* **Karneval** *on the Rhine. Most firms take a day's holiday on that day to enjoy the parades and revelry. In South Germany* **Karneval** *is called "Fasching".*

Karnickel [kar'nɪkəl] **(-s, -)** *(umg)* *nt* rabbit.
Kärnten ['kɛrntən] **(-s)** *nt* Carinthia.
Karo ['kaːro] **(-s, -s)** *nt* square; *(KARTEN)* diamonds; **~-As** *nt* ace of diamonds.
Karosse [ka'rɔsə] **(-, -n)** *f* coach, carriage.
Karosserie [karɔsə'riː] *f (AUT)* body(work).
Karotte [ka'rɔtə] **(-, -n)** *f* carrot.
Karpaten [kar'paːtən] *pl* Carpathians *pl.*
Karpfen ['karpfən] **(-s, -)** *m* carp.
Karre ['karə] **(-, -n)** *f* = **Karren.**
Karree [ka:'reː] **(-s, -s)** *nt*: **einmal ums ~ gehen** *(umg)* to walk around the block.
karren ['karən] *vt* to cart, transport; **K~ (-s, -)** *m* cart, barrow; **den K~ aus dem Dreck ziehen** *(umg)* to get things sorted out.
Karriere [kari'ɛːrə] **(-, -n)** *f* career; **~ machen** to get on, get to the top; **~macher(in)** *m(f)* careerist.
Karsamstag [ka:r'zamsta:k] *m* Easter Saturday.
Karst [karst] **(-s, -e)** *m (GEOG, GEOL)* karst, *barren landscape.*
Karte ['kartə] **(-, -n)** *f* card; *(Land~)* map; *(Speise~)* menu; *(Eintritts~, Fahr~)* ticket; **mit offenen ~n spielen** *(fig)* to put one's cards on the table; **alles auf eine ~ setzen** to put all one's eggs in one basket.
Kartei [kar'taɪ] *f* card index; **~karte** *f* index card; **~leiche** *(umg)* *f* sleeping *od* non-active member; **~schrank** *m* filing cabinet.
Kartell [kar'tɛl] **(-s, -e)** *nt* cartel; **~amt** *nt* monopolies commission; **~gesetzgebung** *f* anti-trust legislation.
Karten- *zW*: **~haus** *nt (lit, fig)* house of cards; **~legen** *nt* fortune-telling *(using cards)*; **~spiel** *nt* card game; *(Karten)* pack *(BRIT)* *od* deck *(US)* of cards; **~telefon** *nt* cardphone; **~vorverkauf** *m* advance sale of tickets.
Kartoffel [kar'tɔfəl] **(-, -n)** *f* potato; **~brei** *m* mashed potatoes *pl*; **~chips** *pl* potato crisps *pl (BRIT)*, potato chips *pl (US)*; **~püree** *nt* mashed potatoes *pl*; **~salat** *m* potato salad.
Karton [kar'tõː] **(-s, -s)** *m* cardboard;

(Schachtel) cardboard box.
kartoniert [karto'niːrt] *adj* hardback.
Karussell [karu'sɛl] **(-s, -s)** *nt* roundabout *(BRIT)*, merry-go-round.
Karwoche ['kaːrvɔxə] *f* Holy Week.
Karzinom [kartsi'noːm] **(-s, -e)** *nt (MED)* carcinoma.
Kasachstan [kazaxs'taːn] **(-s)** *nt (GEOG)* Kazakhstan.
Kaschemme [ka'ʃɛmə] **(-, -n)** *f* dive.
kaschieren [ka'ʃiːrən] *vt* to conceal, cover up.
Kaschmir ['kaʃmiːr] **(-s)** *nt (GEOG)* Kashmir.
Käse ['kɛːzə] **(-s, -)** *m* cheese; *(umg: Unsinn)* rubbish, twaddle; **~blatt** *(umg)* *nt* (local) rag; **~glocke** *f* cheese cover; **~kuchen** *m* cheesecake.
Kaserne [ka'zɛrnə] **(-, -n)** *f* barracks *pl.*
Kasernenhof *m* parade ground.
käsig ['kɛːzɪç] *adj (fig: umg: Gesicht, Haut)* pasty, pale; *(vor Schreck)* white; *(lit)* cheesy.
Kasino [ka'ziːno] **(-s, -s)** *nt* club; *(MIL)* officers' mess; *(Spiel~)* casino.
Kaskoversicherung ['kaskofɛrziçərʊŋ] *f (AUT: Teil~)* ≈ third party, fire and theft insurance; *(: Voll~)* fully comprehensive insurance.
Kasper ['kaspər] **(-s, -)** *m* Punch; *(fig)* clown.
Kasperl(e)theater ['kaspərl(ə)tea:tər] *nt* Punch and Judy (show).
Kaspisches Meer ['kaspɪʃəs'meːr] *nt* Caspian Sea.
Kasse ['kasə] **(-, -n)** *f (Geldkasten)* cashbox; *(in Geschäft)* till, cash register; *(Kino~, Theater~ etc)* box office; *(Kranken~)* health insurance; *(Spar~)* savings bank; **die ~ führen** to be in charge of the money; **jdn zur ~ bitten** to ask sb to pay up; **~ machen** to count the money; **getrennte ~ führen** to pay separately; **an der ~** *(in Geschäft)* at the (cash) desk; **gut bei ~ sein** to be in the money.
Kasseler ['kasələr] **(-s, -)** *nt lightly smoked pork loin.*
Kassen- *zW*: **~arzt** *m* ≈ National Health doctor *(BRIT)*, panel doctor *(US)*; **~bestand** *m* cash balance; **~führer** *m (COMM)* cashier; **~patient** *m* ≈ National Health patient *(BRIT)*; **~prüfung** *f* audit; **~schlager** *(umg)* *m (THEAT etc)* box-office hit; *(: Ware)* big seller; **~sturz** *m*: **~sturz machen** to check one's money; **~wart** *m (von Klub etc)* treasurer; **~zettel** *m* sales slip.
Kasserolle [kasə'rɔlə] **(-, -n)** *f* casserole.
Kassette [ka'sɛtə] *f* small box; *(Tonband, PHOT)* cassette; *(COMPUT)* cartridge, cassette; *(Bücher~)* case.
Kassettenrekorder (-s, -) *m* cassette recorder.
Kassiber [ka'siːbər] **(-s, -)** *m (in Gefängnis)* secret message.

kassieren [ka'siːrən] vt (Gelder etc) to collect; (umg: wegnehmen) to take (away) ♦ vi: **darf ich ~?** would you like to pay now?
Kassierer(in) [ka'siːrər(ın)] (-s, -) m(f) cashier; (von Klub) treasurer.
Kastanie [kas'taːniə] f chestnut.
Kastanienbaum m chestnut tree.
Kästchen ['kɛstçən] nt small box, casket.
Kaste ['kastə] (-, -n) f caste.
Kasten ['kastən] (-s, ⸚) m box (auch SPORT), case; (Truhe) chest; **er hat was auf dem ~** (umg) he's brainy; **~form** f (KOCH) (square) baking tin (BRIT) od pan (US); **~wagen** m van.
kastrieren [kas'triːrən] vt to castrate.
Kat (-, -s) m abk (AUT) = **Katalysator**.
katalanisch [kata'laːnıʃ] adj Catalan.
Katalog [kata'loːk] (-(e)s, -e) m catalogue (BRIT), catalog (US).
katalogisieren [katalogi'ziːrən] vt to catalogue (BRIT), catalog (US).
Katalysator [kataly'zaːtor] m (lit, fig) catalyst; (AUT) catalytic converter; **~-Auto** vehicle fitted with a catalytic converter.
Katapult [kata'pult] (-(e)s, -e) nt or m catapult.
katapultieren [katapul'tiːrən] vt to catapult ♦ vr to catapult o.s.; (Pilot) to eject.
Katar ['kaːtar] nt Qatar.
Katarr▲, **Katarrh** [ka'tar] (-s, -e) m catarrh.
Katasteramt [ka'tastəramt] nt land registry.
katastrophal [katastro'faːl] adj catastrophic.
Katastrophe [kata'stroːfə] (-, -n) f catastrophe, disaster.
Katastrophen- zW: **~alarm** m emergency alert; **~gebiet** nt disaster area; **~medizin** f medical treatment in disasters; **~schutz** m disaster control.
Katechismus [katɛ'çısmʊs] m catechism.
Kategorie [katego'riː] f category.
kategorisch [kate'goːrıʃ] adj categorical.
kategorisieren [kategori'ziːrən] vt to categorize.
Kater ['kaːtər] (-s, -) m tomcat; (umg) hangover; **~frühstück** nt breakfast (of pickled herring etc) to cure a hangover.
kath. abk = **katholisch**.
Katheder [ka'teːdər] (-s, -) nt (SCH) teacher's desk; (UNIV) lectern.
Kathedrale [kate'draːlə] (-, -n) f cathedral.
Katheter [ka'teːtər] (-s, -) m (MED) catheter.
Kat(h)ode [ka'toːdə] (-, -n) f cathode.
Katholik(in) [kato'liːk(ın)] (-en, -en) m(f) Catholic.
katholisch [ka'toːlıʃ] adj Catholic.
Katholizismus [katoli'tsısmʊs] m Catholicism.
katzbuckeln ['katsbʊkəln] (pej: umg) vi to bow and scrape.
Kätzchen ['kɛtsçən] nt kitten.
Katze ['katsə] (-, -n) f cat; **die ~ im Sack kaufen** to buy a pig in a poke; **für die Katz** (umg) in vain, for nothing.

Katzen- zW: **~auge** nt cat's-eye (BRIT); (am Fahrrad) rear light; **~jammer** (umg) m hangover; **~musik** f (fig) caterwauling; **~sprung** (umg) m stone's throw, short distance; **~tür** f cat flap; **~wäsche** f a lick and a promise.
Kauderwelsch ['kaʊdərvɛlʃ] (-(s)) nt jargon; (umg) double Dutch (BRIT).
kauen ['kaʊən] vt, vi to chew.
kauern ['kaʊərn] vi to crouch.
Kauf [kaʊf] (-(e)s, **Käufe**) m purchase, buy; (~en) buying; **ein guter ~** a bargain; **etw in ~ nehmen** to put up with sth.
kaufen vt to buy; **dafür kann ich mir nichts ~** (ironisch) what use is that to me!
Käufer(in) ['kɔyfər(ın)] (-s, -) m(f) buyer.
Kauf- zW: **~frau** f businesswoman; (Einzelhandelskauffrau) shopkeeper; **~haus** nt department store; **~kraft** f purchasing power; **~laden** m shop, store.
käuflich ['kɔyflıç] adj purchasable, for sale; (pej) venal ♦ adv: **~ erwerben** to purchase.
Kauf- zW: **~lust** f desire to buy things; (BÖRSE) buying; **k~lustig** adj interested in buying; **~mann** (-(e)s, pl **-leute**) m businessman; (Einzelhandelskaufmann) shopkeeper; **k~männisch** adj commercial; **k~männischer Angestellter** clerk; **~preis** m purchase price; ♦ adj: **k~süchtig sein** to be a shopaholic (inf); **~vertrag** m bill of sale; **~willige(r)** f(m) potential buyer; **~zwang** m: **kein/ohne ~zwang** no/without obligation.
Kaugummi ['kaʊgʊmi] m chewing gum.
Kaukasus ['kaʊkazʊs] m: **der ~** the Caucasus.
Kaulquappe ['kaʊlkvapə] (-, -n) f tadpole.
kaum [kaʊm] adv hardly, scarcely; **wohl ~, ich glaube ~** I hardly think so.
Kausalzusammenhang [kaʊ'zaːltsuzamənhaŋ] m causal connection.
Kaution [kaʊtsi'oːn] f deposit; (JUR) bail.
Kautschuk ['kaʊtʃʊk] (-s, -e) m India rubber.
Kauz [kaʊts] (-es, **Käuze**) m owl; (fig) queer fellow.
Kavalier [kava'liːr] (-s, -e) m gentleman.
Kavaliersdelikt nt peccadillo.
Kavallerie [kavalə'riː] f cavalry.
Kavallerist [kavalə'rıst] m cavalryman.
Kaviar ['kaːviar] m caviar.
KB nt abk (= Kilobyte) KB, kbyte.
Kcal abk (= Kilokalorie) kcal.
keck [kɛk] adj daring, bold; **K~heit** f daring, boldness.
Kegel ['keːgəl] (-s, -) m skittle; (MATH) cone; **~bahn** f skittle alley, bowling alley; **k~förmig** adj conical.
kegeln vi to play skittles.
Kehle ['keːlə] (-, -n) f throat; **er hat das in die falsche ~ bekommen** (lit) it went down the wrong way; (fig) he took it the wrong way;

aus voller ~ at the top of one's voice.

Kehl- *zW:* ~**kopf** *m* larynx; ~**kopfkrebs** *m* cancer of the throat; ~**laut** *m* guttural.

Kehre ['keːrə] (-, -n) *f* turn(ing), bend.

kehren *vt, vi* (*wenden*) to turn; (*mit Besen*) to sweep; **sich an etw** *dat* **nicht** ~ not to heed sth; **in sich** *akk* **gekehrt** (*versunken*) pensive; (*verschlossen*) introspective, introverted.

Kehricht (-s) *m* sweepings *pl*.

Kehr- *zW:* ~**maschine** *f* sweeper; ~**reim** *m* refrain; ~**seite** *f* reverse, other side; (*ungünstig*) wrong *od* bad side; **die ~seite der Medaille** the other side of the coin.

kehrtmachen *vi* to turn about, about-turn.

Kehrtwendung *f* about-turn.

keifen ['kaɪfən] *vi* to scold, nag.

Keil [kaɪl] (-(e)s, -e) *m* wedge; (*MIL*) arrowhead; **k~en** *vt* to wedge ♦ *vr* to fight.

Keilerei [kaɪlə'raɪ] (*umg*) *f* punch-up.

Keilriemen *m* (*AUT*) fan belt.

Keim [kaɪm] (-(e)s, -e) *m* bud; (*MED, fig*) germ; **etw im** ~ **ersticken** to nip sth in the bud.

keimen *vi* to germinate.

Keim- *zW:* **k~frei** *adj* sterile; **k~tötend** *adj* antiseptic, germicidal; ~**zelle** *f* (*fig*) nucleus.

kein(e) ['kaɪn(ə)] *pron* none ♦ *adj* no, not any; ~ **schlechte Idee** not a bad idea; ~ **Stunde/drei Monate** (*nicht einmal*) less than an hour/three months.

keine(r, s) *indef pron* no one, nobody; (*von Gegenstand*) none.

keinerlei ['kaɪnər'laɪ] *adj attrib* no ... whatever.

keinesfalls *adv* on no account.

keineswegs *adv* by no means.

keinmal *adv* not once.

Keks [keːks] (-es, -e) *m od nt* biscuit (*BRIT*), cookie (*US*).

Kelch [kɛlç] (-(e)s, -e) *m* cup, goblet, chalice.

Kelle ['kɛlə] (-, -n) *f* ladle; (*Maurer~*) trowel.

Keller ['kɛlər] (-s, -) *m* cellar; ~**assel** (-, -n) *f* woodlouse.

Kellerei [kɛlə'raɪ] *f* wine cellars *pl*; (*Firma*) wine producer.

Kellergeschoss▲ *nt* basement.

Kellerwohnung *f* basement flat (*BRIT*) *od* apartment (*US*).

Kellner(in) ['kɛlnər(ɪn)] (-s, -) *m(f)* waiter, waitress.

kellnern (*umg*) *vi* to work as a waiter/waitress (*BRIT*), wait on tables (*US*).

Kelte ['kɛltə] (-n, -n) *m* Celt.

Kelter (-, -n) *f* winepress; (*Obst~*) press.

keltern ['kɛltərn] *vt* to press.

Keltin ['kɛltɪn] *f* (female) Celt.

keltisch *adj* Celtic.

Kenia ['keːnia] (-s) *nt* Kenya.

kennen ['kɛnən] *unreg vt* to know; ~ **Sie sich schon?** do you know each other (already)?; **kennst du mich noch?** do you remember me?; ~ **lernen** to get to know; **sich** ~ **lernen**

to get to know each other; (*zum ersten Mal*) to meet.

Kenner(in) (-s, -) *m(f):* ~ (**von** *od +gen*) connoisseur (of); expert (on).

Kennkarte *f* identity card.

kenntlich *adj* distinguishable, discernible; **etw** ~ **machen** to mark sth.

Kenntnis (-, -se) *f* knowledge *no pl;* **etw zur** ~ **nehmen** to note sth; **von etw** ~ **nehmen** to take notice of sth; **jdn in** ~ **setzen** to inform sb; **über** ~**se von etw verfügen** to be knowledgeable about sth.

Kenn- *zW:* ~**wort** *nt* (*Chiffre*) code name; (*Losungswort*) password, code word; ~**zeichen** *nt* mark, characteristic; (**amtliches/polizeiliches**) ~**zeichen** (*AUT*) number plate (*BRIT*), license plate (*US*); **k~zeichnen** *vt untr* to characterize; **k~zeichnenderweise** *adv* characteristically; ~**ziffer** *f* (code) number; (*COMM*) reference number.

kentern ['kɛntərn] *vi* to capsize.

Keramik [ke'raːmɪk] (-, -en) *f* ceramics *pl*, pottery; (*Gegenstand*) piece of ceramic work *od* pottery.

Kerbe ['kɛrbə] (-, -n) *f* notch, groove.

Kerbel (-s, -) *m* chervil.

kerben *vt* to notch.

Kerbholz *nt:* **etw auf dem** ~ **haben** to have done sth wrong.

Kerker ['kɛrkər] (-s, -) *m* prison.

Kerl [kɛrl] (-s, -e) (*umg*) *m* chap, bloke (*BRIT*), guy; **du gemeiner** ~! you swine!

Kern [kɛrn] (-(e)s, -e) *m* (*Obst~*) pip, stone; (*Nuss~*) kernel; (*Atom~*) nucleus; (*fig*) heart, core; ~**energie** *f* nuclear energy; ~**fach** *nt* (*SCH*) core subject; ~**familie** *f* nuclear family; ~**forschung** *f* nuclear research; ~**frage** *f* central issue; ~**fusion** *f* nuclear fusion; ~**gehäuse** *nt* core; **k~gesund** *adj* thoroughly healthy, fit as a fiddle.

kernig *adj* robust; (*Ausspruch*) pithy.

Kern- *zW:* ~**kraftwerk** *nt* nuclear power station; **k~los** *adj* seedless, pipless; ~**physik** *f* nuclear physics *sing;* ~**reaktion** *f* nuclear reaction; ~**reaktor** *m* nuclear reactor; ~**schmelze** *f* meltdown; ~**seife** *f* washing soap; ~**spaltung** *f* nuclear fission; ~**stück** *nt* (*fig*) main item; (*von Theorie etc*) central part, core; ~**waffen** *pl* nuclear weapons *pl;* **k~waffenfrei** *adj* nuclear-free; ~**zeit** *f* core time.

Kerze ['kɛrtsə] (-, -n) *f* candle; (*Zünd~*) plug.

Kerzen- *zW:* **k~gerade** *adj* straight as a die; ~**halter** *m* candlestick; ~**ständer** *m* candleholder.

kess▲ [kɛs] *adj* saucy.

Kessel ['kɛsəl] (-s, -) *m* kettle; (*von Lokomotive etc*) boiler; (*Mulde*) basin; (*GEOG*) depression; (*MIL*) encirclement; ~**stein** *m*

scale, fur (*BRIT*); ~**treiben** nt (*fig*) witch-hunt.
Kette ['kɛtə] (-, -**n**) f chain; **jdn an die ~ legen**
(*fig*) to tie sb down.
ketten vt to chain.
Ketten- zW: ~**fahrzeug** nt tracked vehicle;
~**hund** m watchdog; ~**karussell** nt merry-go-
round (*with gondolas on chains*); ~**laden** m chain
store; ~**rauchen** nt chain smoking;
~**reaktion** f chain reaction.
Ketzer(in) ['kɛtsər(ɪn)] (-**s**, -) m(f) heretic; ~**ei**
[kɛtsə'raɪ] f heresy; **k~isch** adj heretical.
keuchen ['kɔʏçən] vi to pant, gasp.
Keuchhusten m whooping cough.
Keule ['kɔʏlə] (-, -**n**) f club; (*KOCH*) leg.
keusch [kɔʏʃ] adj chaste; **K~heit** f chastity.
Kfm. abk = **Kaufmann.**
kfm. abk = **kaufmännisch.**
Kfz (-(**s**), -(**s**)) f abk = **Kraftfahrzeug.**
KG (-, -**s**) f abk = **Kommanditgesellschaft.**
kg abk (= **Kilogramm**) kg.
kHz abk (= **Kilohertz**) kHz.
Kibbuz [kɪ'buːts] (-, **Kibbuzim** od -**e**) m
kibbutz.
kichern ['kɪçərn] vi to giggle.
kicken ['kɪkən] vt, vi (*Fußball*) to kick.
kidnappen ['kɪtnɛpən] vt to kidnap.
Kidnapper(in) (-**s**, -) m(f) kidnapper.
Kiebitz ['kiːbɪts] (-**es**, -**e**) m peewit.
Kiefer¹ ['kiːfər] (-**s**, -) m jaw.
Kiefer² ['kiːfər] (-, -**n**) f pine.
Kiefernholz nt pine(wood).
Kiefernzapfen m pine cone.
Kieferorthopäde m orthodontist.
Kieker ['kiːkər] (-**s**, -) m: **jdn auf dem ~ haben**
(*umg*) to have it in for sb.
Kiel [kiːl] (-(**e**)**s**, -**e**) m (*Feder~*) quill; (*NAUT*)
keel; ~**wasser** nt wake.
Kieme ['kiːmə] (-, -**n**) f gill.
Kies [kiːs] (-**es**, -**e**) m gravel; (*umg: Geld*)
money, dough.
Kiesel ['kiːzəl] (-**s**, -) m pebble; ~**stein** m
pebble.
Kiesgrube f gravel pit.
Kiesweg m gravel path.
Kiew ['kiːɛf] (-**s**) nt Kiev.
kiffen ['kɪfən] (*umg*) vt to smoke pot od grass.
Kilimandscharo [kiliman'dʒaːro] (-**s**) m
Kilimanjaro.
Killer(in) ['kɪlər(ɪn)] (-**s**, -) (*umg*) m killer,
murderer; (*gedungener*) hit man; ~**in** (*umg*) f
killer, female murderer, murderess.
Kilo ['kiːlo] (-**s**, -(**s**)) nt kilo; ~**byte** [kilo'baɪt] nt
(*COMPUT*) kilobyte; ~**gramm** [kilo'gram] nt
kilogram.
Kilometer [kilo'meːtər] m kilometre (*BRIT*),
kilometer (*US*); ~**fresser** (*umg*) m long-haul
driver; ~**geld** nt ≈ mileage (allowance);
~**stand** m ≈ mileage; ~**stein** m ≈ milestone;
~**zähler** m ≈ mileometer.
Kilowatt [kilo'vat] nt kilowatt.

Kimme ['kɪmə] (-, -**n**) f notch; (*Gewehr*) back
sight.
Kind [kɪnt] (-(**e**)**s**, -**er**) nt child; **sich freuen wie
ein ~** to be as pleased as Punch; **mit ~ und
Kegel** (*hum: umg*) with the whole family;
von ~ auf from childhood.
Kinderarzt m paediatrician (*BRIT*),
pediatrician (*US*).
Kinderbett nt cot (*BRIT*), crib (*US*).
Kinderei [kɪndə'raɪ] f childishness.
Kindererziehung f bringing up of children;
(*durch Schule*) education of children.
kinderfeindlich adj anti-children; (*Architektur,
Planung*) not catering for children.
Kinderfreibetrag m child allowance.
Kindergarten m nursery school.

Kinder- zW: ~**gärtner(in)** m(f) nursery-school
teacher; ~**geld** nt child benefit (*BRIT*); ~**heim**
nt children's home; ~**krankheit** f childhood
illness; ~**laden** m (alternative) playgroup;
~**lähmung** f polio(myelitis); **k~leicht** adj
childishly easy; **k~lieb** adj fond of children;
~**lied** nt nursery rhyme; **k~los** adj childless;
~**mädchen** nt nursemaid; ~**pflegerin** f child
minder; **k~reich** adj with a lot of children;
~**schuh** m: **es steckt noch in den ~schuhen**
(*fig*) it's still in its infancy; ~**spiel** nt child's
play; **ein ~spiel sein** to be a doddle; ~**stube**
f: **eine gute ~stube haben** to be well-
mannered; ~**tagesstätte** f day-nursery;
~**teller** m children's dish; ~**wagen** m pram
(*BRIT*), baby carriage (*US*); ~**zimmer** nt
child's/children's room; (*für Kleinkinder*)
nursery.
Kindes- zW: ~**alter** nt infancy; ~**beine** pl: **von
~beinen an** from early childhood;
~**misshandlung**▲ f child abuse.
Kind- zW: **k~gemäß** adj suitable for a child od
children; ~**heit** f childhood; **k~isch** adj
childish; **k~lich** adj childlike.
kindsköpfig adj childish.
Kinkerlitzchen ['kɪŋkərlɪtsçən] (*umg*) pl
knick-knacks pl.
Kinn [kɪn] (-(**e**)**s**, -**e**) nt chin; ~**haken** m
(*BOXEN*) uppercut; ~**lade** f jaw.
Kino ['kiːno] (-**s**, -**s**) nt cinema (*BRIT*), movies
(*US*); ~**besucher** m, ~**gänger** m cinema-goer
(*BRIT*), movie-goer (*US*); ~**programm** nt film
programme (*BRIT*), movie program (*US*).
Kiosk [ki'ɔsk] (-(**e**)**s**, -**e**) m kiosk.

Kippe ['kɪpə] (-, -n) *f* (*umg*) cigarette end; **auf der ~ stehen** (*fig*) to be touch and go.

kippen *vi* to topple over, overturn ♦ *vt* to tilt.

Kipper ['kɪpər] (-s, -) *m* (*AUT*) tipper, dump(er) truck.

Kippschalter *m* rocker switch.

Kirche ['kɪrçə] (-, -n) *f* church.

Kirchen- *zW*: **~chor** *m* church choir; **~diener** *m* churchwarden; **~fest** *nt* church festival; **~lied** *nt* hymn; **~schiff** *nt* (*Längsschiff*) nave; (*Querschiff*) transept; **~steuer** *f* church tax; **~tag** *m* church congress.

Kirch- *zW*: **~gänger(in)** (-s, -) *m(f)* churchgoer; **~hof** *m* churchyard; **k~lich** *adj* ecclesiastical; **~turm** *m* church tower, steeple; **~weih** *f* fair, kermis (*US*).

Kirgistan ['kɪrgistaːn] (-s) *nt* (*GEOG*) Kirghizia.

Kirmes ['kɪrmɛs] (-, -sen) *f* (*Dialekt*) fair, kermis (*US*).

Kirschbaum ['kɪrʃbaʊm] *m* cherry tree; (*Holz*) cherry (wood).

Kirsche ['kɪrʃə] (-, -n) *f* cherry; **mit ihm ist nicht gut ~n essen** (*fig*) it's best not to tangle with him.

Kirschtorte *f*: **Schwarzwälder ~** Black Forest Gateau.

Kirschwasser *nt* kirsch.

Kissen ['kɪsən] (-s, -) *nt* cushion; (*Kopf~*) pillow; **~bezug** *m* pillow case.

Kiste ['kɪstə] (-, -n) *f* box; (*Truhe*) chest; (*umg*: *Bett*) sack; (: *Fernsehen*) box (*BRIT*), tube (*US*).

Kita ['kɪta] *f abk* = **Kindertagesstätte**.

Kitsch [kɪtʃ] (-(e)s) *m* trash.

kitschig *adj* trashy.

Kitt [kɪt] (-(e)s, -e) *m* putty.

Kittchen (*umg*) *nt* clink.

Kittel (-s, -) *m* overall; (*von Arzt, Laborant etc*) (white) coat.

kitten *vt* to putty; (*fig*) to patch up.

Kitz [kɪts] (-es, -e) *nt* kid; (*Reh~*) fawn.

kitzelig ['kɪtsəlɪç] *adj* (*lit, fig*) ticklish.

kitzeln *vt, vi* to tickle.

Kiwi ['kiːvi] (-, -s) *f* kiwi fruit.

KKW (-, -s) *nt abk* = **Kernkraftwerk**.

Kl. *abk* (= *Klasse*) cl.

Klacks [klaks] (-es, -e) (*umg*) *m* (*von Kartoffelbrei, Sahne*) dollop; (*von Senf, Farbe etc*) blob.

Kladde ['kladə] (-, -n) *f* rough book; (*Block*) scribbling pad.

klaffen ['klafən] *vi* to gape.

kläffen ['klɛfən] *vi* to yelp.

Klage ['klaːgə] (-, -n) *f* complaint; (*JUR*) action; **eine ~ gegen jdn einreichen** *od* **erheben** to institute proceedings against sb; **~lied** *nt*: **ein ~lied über jdn/etw anstimmen** (*fig*) to complain about sb/sth; **~mauer** *f*: **die ~mauer** the Wailing Wall.

klagen *vi* (*weh~*) to lament, wail; (*sich beschweren*) to complain; (*JUR*) to take legal action; **jdm sein Leid/seine Not ~** to pour out one's sorrow/distress to sb.

Kläger(in) ['klɛːgər(ɪn)] (-s, -) *m(f)* (*JUR*: *im Zivilrecht*) plaintiff; (: *im Strafrecht*) prosecuting party; (: *in Scheidung*) petitioner.

Klageschrift *f* (*JUR*) charge; (*bei Scheidung*) petition.

kläglich ['klɛːklɪç] *adj* wretched.

Klamauk [kla'maʊk] (-s) (*umg*) *m* (*Alberei*) tomfoolery; (*im Theater*) slapstick.

Klamm [klam] (-, -en) *f* ravine.

klamm *adj* (*Finger*) numb; (*feucht*) damp.

Klammer ['klamər] (-, -n) *f* clamp; (*in Text*) bracket; (*Büro~*) clip; (*Wäsche~*) peg (*BRIT*), pin (*US*); (*Zahn~*) brace; **~ auf/zu** open/close brackets.

klammern *vr*: **sich ~ an** +*akk* to cling to.

klammheimlich [klam'haɪmlɪç] (*umg*) *adj* secret ♦ *adv* on the quiet.

Klamotte [kla'mɔtə] (-, -n) *f* (*pej*: *Film etc*) rubbishy old film *etc*; **Klamotten** *pl* (*umg*: *Kleider*) clothes *pl*; (: *Zeug*) stuff.

Klampfe ['klampfə] (-, -n) (*umg*) *f* guitar.

klang *etc* [klaŋ] *vb siehe* **klingen**.

Klang (-(e)s, ̈-e) *m* sound.

klangvoll *adj* sonorous.

Klappbett *nt* folding bed.

Klappe ['klapə] (-, -n) *f* valve; (*an Oboe etc*) key; (*FILM*) clapperboard; (*Ofen~*) damper; (*umg*: *Mund*) trap; **die ~ halten** to shut one's trap.

klappen *vi* (*Geräusch*) to click; (*Sitz etc*) to tip ♦ *vt* to tip ♦ *vi unpers* to work; **hat es mit den Karten/dem Job geklappt?** did you get the tickets/job O.K.?

Klappentext *m* blurb.

Klapper ['klapər] (-, -n) *f* rattle.

klapperig *adj* run-down, worn-out.

klappern *vi* to clatter, rattle.

Klapperschlange *f* rattlesnake.

Klapperstorch *m* stork; **er glaubt noch an den ~** he still thinks babies are found under the gooseberry bush.

Klapp- *zW*: **~messer** *nt* jackknife; **~rad** *nt* collapsible *od* folding bicycle; **~stuhl** *m* folding chair; **~tisch** *m* folding table.

Klaps [klaps] (-es, -e) *m* slap; **einen ~ haben** (*umg*) to have a screw loose; **k~en** *vt* to slap.

klar [klaːr] *adj* clear; (*NAUT*) ready to sail; (*MIL*) ready for action; **bei ~em Verstand sein** to be in full possession of one's faculties; **sich** *dat* **im K~en sein über** +*akk* to be clear about; **ins K~e kommen** to get clear; **~ sehen** to see clearly; **sich** *dat* **über etw** *akk* **~ werden** to get sth clear in one's mind.

Kläranlage *f* sewage plant; (*von Fabrik*)

purification plant.

Klare(r) (*umg*) *m* schnapps.

klären *vt* (*Flüssigkeit*) to purify; (*Probleme*) to clarify ♦ *vr* to clear (itself) up.

Klarheit *f* clarity; **sich** ~ **über etw** *akk* **verschaffen** to get sth straight.

Klarinette [klari'nɛtə] *f* clarinet.

klar- *zW*: ~**kommen** *unreg* (*umg*) *vi*: **mit jdm/ etw** ~**kommen** to be able to cope with sb/ sth; ~**legen** *vt* to clear up, explain; ~**machen** *vt* (*Schiff*) to get ready for sea; **jdm etw** ~**machen** to make sth clear to sb; **K~sichtfolie** *f* transparent film; ~**stellen** *vt* to clarify; **K~text** *m*: **im K~text** in clear; (*fig: umg*) ≈ in plain English.

Klärung ['klɛːrʊŋ] *f* purification; clarification.

Klasse ['klasə] (-, -n) *f* class; (*SCH*) class, form; (*auch*: **Steuer~**) bracket; (*Güter~*) grade.

klasse (*umg*) *adj* smashing.

Klassen- *zW*: ~**arbeit** *f* test; ~**bewusstsein**▲ *nt* class-consciousness; ~**buch** *nt* (*SCH*) (class) register; ~**gesellschaft** *f* class society; ~**kamerad(in)** *m(f)* classmate; ~**kampf** *m* class conflict; ~**lehrer(in)** *m(f)* class teacher; **k~los** *adj* classless; ~**sprecher(in)** *m(f)* class spokesperson; ~**ziel** *nt*: **das** ~**ziel nicht erreichen** (*SCH*) not to reach the required standard (for the year); (*fig*) not to make the grade; ~**zimmer** *nt* classroom.

klassifizieren [klasifi'tsiːrən] *vt* to classify.

Klassifizierung *f* classification.

Klassik ['klasɪk] *f* (*Zeit*) classical period; (*Stil*) classicism; ~**er** (-s, -) *m* classic.

klassisch *adj* (*lit, fig*) classical.

Klassizismus [klasi'tsɪsmʊs] *m* classicism.

Klatsch [klatʃ] (-(e)s, -e) *m* smack, crack; (*Gerede*) gossip; ~**base** *f* gossip(monger).

klatschen *vi* (*tratschen*) to gossip; (*Beifall spenden*) to applaud, to clap ♦ *vt*: **(jdm) Beifall** ~ to applaud *od* clap (sb).

Klatsch- *zW*: ~**mohn** *m* (corn) poppy; **k~nass**▲ *adj* soaking wet; ~**spalte** *f* gossip column; ~**tante** (*pej: umg*) *f* gossip(monger).

klauben ['klaubən] *vt* to pick.

Klaue ['klaʊə] (-, -n) *f* claw; (*umg: Schrift*) scrawl.

klauen *vt* to claw; (*umg*) to pinch.

Klause ['klaʊzə] (-, -n) *f* cell; (*von Mönch*) hermitage.

Klausel ['klaʊzəl] (-, -n) *f* clause; (*Vorbehalt*) proviso.

Klausur [klaʊ'zuːr] *f* seclusion; ~**arbeit** *f* examination paper.

Klaviatur [klavia'tuːr] *f* keyboard.

Klavier [kla'viːr] (-s, -e) *nt* piano; ~**auszug** *m* piano score.

Klebeband *nt* adhesive tape.

Klebemittel *nt* glue.

kleben ['kleːbən] *vt, vi*: ~ **(an** +*akk*) to stick (to);

jdm eine ~ (*umg*) to belt sb one.

Klebezettel *m* gummed label.

klebrig *adj* sticky.

Klebstoff *m* glue.

Klebstreifen *m* adhesive tape.

kleckern ['klɛkərn] *vi* to slobber.

Klecks [klɛks] (-es, -e) *m* blot, stain; **k~en** *vi* to blot; (*pej*) to daub.

Klee [kleː] (-s) *m* clover; **jdn/etw über den grünen** ~ **loben** (*fig*) to praise sb/sth to the skies; ~**blatt** *nt* cloverleaf; (*fig*) trio.

Kleid [klaɪt] (-(e)s, -er) *nt* garment; (*Frauen~*) dress; **Kleider** *pl* clothes *pl*.

kleiden ['klaɪdən] *vt* to clothe, dress ♦ *vr* to dress; **jdn** ~ to suit sb.

Kleider- *zW*: ~**bügel** *m* coat hanger; ~**bürste** *f* clothes brush; ~**schrank** *m* wardrobe; ~**ständer** *m* coat-stand.

kleidsam *adj* becoming.

Kleidung *f* clothing.

Kleidungsstück *nt* garment.

Kleie ['klaɪə] (-, -n) *f* bran.

klein [klaɪn] *adj* little, small; **haben Sie es nicht** ~**er?** haven't you got anything smaller?; **ein** ~**es Bier ein K~es** (*umg*) ≈ half a pint, a half; **von** ~ **an** *od* **auf** (*von Kindheit an*) from childhood; (*von Anfang an*) from the very beginning; **das** ~**ere Übel** the lesser evil; **sein Vater war (ein)** ~**er Beamter** his father was a minor civil servant; ~ **anfangen** to start off in a small way; ~ **geschrieben werden** (*umg*) to count for (very) little; **K~anzeige** *f* small ad (*BRIT*), want ad (*US*); **Kleinanzeigen** *pl* classified advertising *sing*; **K~arbeit** *f*: **in zäher/ mühseliger K~arbeit** with rigorous/ painstaking attention to detail; **K~asien** *nt* Asia Minor; **K~bürgertum** *nt* petite bourgeoisie; **K~bus** *m* minibus.

Kleine(r) *f(m)* little one.

klein- *zW*: **K~familie** *f* small family, nuclear family (*SOZIOLOGIE*); **K~format** *nt* small size; **im K~format** small-scale; **K~gedruckte(s)** *nt* small print; **K~geld** *nt* small change; **das nötige K~geld haben** (*fig*) to have the wherewithal (*umg*); ~**gläubig** *adj* of little faith; ~**hacken** *vt* to chop up; **K~holz** *nt* firewood; **K~holz aus jdm machen** to make mincemeat of sb.

Kleinigkeit *f* trifle; **wegen** *od* **bei jeder** ~ for the slightest reason; **eine** ~ **essen** to have a bite to eat.

klein- *zW*: ~**kariert** *adj*: ~**kariert denken** to think small; **K~kind** *nt* infant; **K~kram** *m* details *pl*; **K~kredit** *m* personal loan; ~**kriegen** (*umg*) *vt* (*gefügig machen*) to bring into line; (*unterkriegen*) to get down; (*körperlich*) to tire out; ~**laut** *adj* dejected, quiet; ~**lich** *adj* petty, paltry; **K~lichkeit** *f* pettiness, paltriness; ~**mütig** *adj* fa;nthearted.

Kleinod ['klaɪnoːt] **(-s, -odien)** *nt* gem.

klein- *zW:* **K~rechner** *m* minicomputer; **~schneiden** *unreg vt* to chop up; **~schreiben** *unreg vt:* **ein Wort ~schreiben** to write a word with a small initial letter; **K~schreibung** *f* use of small initial letters; **K~stadt** *f* small town; **~städtisch** *adj* provincial.

kleinstmöglich *adj* smallest possible.

Kleinwagen *m* small car.

Kleister ['klaɪstər] **(-s, -)** *m* paste.

kleistern *vt* to paste.

Klemme ['klɛmə] **(-, -n)** *f* clip; (*MED*) clamp; (*fig*) jam; **in der ~ sitzen** *od* **sein** (*fig: umg*) to be in a fix.

klemmen *vt* (*festhalten*) to jam; (*quetschen*) to pinch, nip ♦ *vr* to catch o.s.; (*sich hineinzwängen*) to squeeze o.s. ♦ *vi* (*Tür*) to stick, jam; **sich hinter jdn/etw ~** to get on to sb/get down to sth.

Klempner ['klɛmpnər] **(-s, -)** *m* plumber.

Kleptomanie [klɛptoma'niː] *f* kleptomania.

Kleriker ['kleːrikər] **(-s, -)** *m* cleric.

Klerus ['kleːrʊs] **(-)** *m* clergy.

Klette ['klɛtə] **(-, -n)** *f* burr; **sich wie eine ~ an jdn hängen** to cling to sb like a limpet.

Kletterer ['klɛtərər] **(-s, -)** *m* climber.

Klettergerüst *nt* climbing frame.

klettern *vi* to climb.

Kletterpflanze *f* creeper.

Kletterseil *nt* climbing rope.

Klettverschluss▲ *m* Velcro ® fastener.

klicken ['klɪkən] *vi* to click.

Klient(in) [kli'ɛnt(ɪn)] *m(f)* client.

Klima ['kliːma] **(-s, -s** *od* **-te)** *nt* climate; **~anlage** *f* air conditioning.

Klimaschutz *m* climate protection.

Klimaschutzabkommen *nt* agreement on climate control.

klimatisieren [klima'tiːzirən] *vt* to air-condition.

klimatisiert *adj* air-conditioned.

Klimawechsel *m* change of air.

Klimbim [klɪm'bɪm] **(-s)** (*umg*) *m* odds and ends *pl*.

klimpern ['klɪmpərn] *vi* to tinkle; (*auf Gitarre*) to strum.

Klinge ['klɪŋə] **(-, -n)** *f* blade, sword; **jdn über die ~ springen lassen** (*fig: umg*) to allow sb to run into trouble.

Klingel ['klɪŋəl] **(-, -n)** *f* bell; **~beutel** *m* collection bag; **~knopf** *m* bell push.

klingeln *vi* to ring; **es hat geklingelt** (*an Tür*) somebody just rang the doorbell, the doorbell just rang.

klingen ['klɪŋən] *unreg vi* to sound; (*Gläser*) to clink.

Klinik ['kliːnɪk] *f* clinic.

klinisch ['kliːnɪʃ] *adj* clinical.

Klinke ['klɪŋkə] **(-, -n)** *f* handle.

Klinker ['klɪŋkər] **(-s, -)** *m* clinker.

Klippe ['klɪpə] **(-, -n)** *f* cliff; (*im Meer*) reef; (*fig*) hurdle.

klippenreich *adj* rocky.

klipp und klar ['klɪp|ʊntklaːr] *adj* clear and concise.

Klips [klɪps] **(-es, -e)** *m* clip; (*Ohr~*) earring.

klirren ['klɪrən] *vi* to clank, jangle; (*Gläser*) to clink; **~de Kälte** biting cold.

Klischee [klɪ'ʃeː] **(-s, -s)** *nt* (*Druckplatte*) plate, block; (*fig*) cliché; **~vorstellung** *f* stereotyped idea.

Klitoris ['kliːtorɪs] **(-, -)** *f* clitoris.

Klo [kloː] **(-s, -s)** (*umg*) *nt* loo (*BRIT*), john (*US*).

Kloake [klo'aːkə] **(-, -n)** *f* sewer.

klobig ['kloːbɪç] *adj* clumsy.

Klon [kloːn] **(-s, -e)** *m* clone.

Klopapier (*umg*) *nt* toilet paper.

klopfen ['klɔpfən] *vi* to knock; (*Herz*) to thump ♦ *vt* to beat; **es klopft** somebody's knocking; **jdm auf die Finger ~** (*lit, fig*) to give sb a rap on the knuckles; **jdm auf die Schulter ~** to tap sb on the shoulder.

Klopfer **(-s, -)** *m* (*Teppich~*) beater; (*Tür~*) knocker.

Klöppel ['klœpəl] **(-s, -)** *m* (*von Glocke*) clapper.

klöppeln *vi* to make lace.

Klops [klɔps] **(-es, -e)** *m* meatball.

Klosett [klo'zɛt] **(-s, -e** *od* **-s)** *nt* lavatory, toilet; **~brille** *f* toilet seat; **~papier** *nt* toilet paper.

Kloß [kloːs] **(-es, ̈-e)** *m* (*Erd~*) clod; (*im Hals*) lump; (*KOCH*) dumpling.

Kloster ['kloːstər] **(-s, ̈-)** *nt* (*Männer~*) monastery; (*Frauen~*) convent; **ins ~ gehen** to become a monk/nun.

klösterlich ['kloːstərlɪç] *adj* monastic; convent.

Klotz [klɔts] **(-es, ̈-e)** *m* log; (*Hack~*) block; **jdm ein ~ am Bein sein** (*fig*) to be a millstone round sb's neck.

Klub [klʊp] **(-s, -s)** *m* club; **~jacke** *f* blazer; **~sessel** *m* easy chair.

Kluft [klʊft] **(-, ̈-e)** *f* cleft, gap; (*GEOG*) chasm; (*Uniform*) uniform; (*umg: Kleidung*) gear.

klug [kluːk] *adj* clever, intelligent; **ich werde daraus nicht ~** I can't make head or tail of it; **K~heit** *f* cleverness, intelligence; **K~scheißer** (*umg*) *m* smart-ass.

Klümpchen ['klʏmpçən] *nt* clot, blob.

klumpen ['klʊmpən] *vi* to go lumpy, clot.

Klumpen **(-s, -)** *m* (*KOCH*) lump; (*Erd~*) clod; (*Blut~*) clot; (*Gold~*) nugget.

Klumpfuß ['klʊmpfuːs] *m* club foot.

Klüngel ['klʏŋəl] **(-s, -)** (*umg*) *m* (*Clique*) clique.

Klunker ['klʊŋkər] **(-s, -)** (*umg*) *m* (*Schmuck*) rock(s *pl*).

km *abk* (= *Kilometer*) km.

km/h *abk* (= *Kilometer pro Stunde*) km/h.

knabbern ['knabərn] *vt, vi* to nibble; **an etw** *dat* **~** (*fig: umg*) to puzzle over sth.

Knabe ['knaːbə] **(-n, -n)** *m* boy.

knabenhaft *adj* boyish.
Knäckebrot ['knɛkəbroːt] *nt* crispbread.
knacken ['knakən] *vi* (*lit, fig*) to crack ♦ *vt* (*umg: Auto*) to break into.
knackfrisch (*umg*) *adj* oven-fresh, crispy-fresh.
knackig *adj* crisp.
Knacks [knaks] (**-es, -e**) *m*: **einen ~ weghaben** (*umg*) to be uptight about sth.
Knackwurst *f type of frankfurter.*
Knall [knal] (**-(e)s, -e**) *m* bang; (*Peitschen~*) crack; **~ auf Fall** (*umg*) just like that; **einen ~ haben** (*umg*) to be crazy *od* crackers; **~bonbon** *nt* cracker; **~effekt** *m* surprise effect, spectacular effect; **k~en** *vi* to bang; to crack ♦ *vt*: **jdm eine k~en** (*umg*) to clout sb; **~frosch** *m* jumping jack; **k~hart** (*umg*) *adj* really hard; (: *Worte*) hard-hitting; (: *Film*) brutal; (: *Porno*) hard-core; **~kopf** (*umg*) *m* dickhead; **k~rot** *adj* bright red.
knapp [knap] *adj* tight; (*Geld*) scarce; (*kurz*) short; (*Mehrheit, Sieg*) narrow; (*Sprache*) concise; **meine Zeit ist ~ bemessen** I am short of time; **mit ~er Not** only just; **jdn ~ halten (mit)** to keep sb short (of).
Knappe (**-n, -n**) *m* (*Edelmann*) young knight.
Knappheit *f* tightness; scarcity; conciseness.
Knarre ['knarə] (**-, -n**) (*umg*) *f* (*Gewehr*) shooter.
knarren *vi* to creak.
Knast [knast] (**-(e)s**) (*umg*) *m* clink, can (*US*).
Knatsch [knaːtʃ] (**-es**) (*umg*) *m* trouble.
knattern ['knatərn] *vi* to rattle; (*Maschinengewehr*) to chatter.
Knäuel ['knɔʏəl] (**-s, -**) *m od nt* (*Woll~*) ball; (*Menschen~*) knot.
Knauf [knauf] (**-(e)s, Knäufe**) *m* knob; (*Schwert~*) pommel.
Knauser ['knauzər] (**-s, -**) *m* miser.
knauserig *adj* miserly.
knausern *vi* to be mean.
knautschen ['knautʃən] *vt, vi* to crumple.
Knebel ['kneːbəl] (**-s, -**) *m* gag.
knebeln *vt* to gag; (*NAUT*) to fasten.
Knecht [knɛçt] (**-(e)s, -e**) *m* servant; (*auf Bauernhof*) farm labourer (*BRIT*) *od* laborer (*US*).
knechten *vt* to enslave.
Knechtschaft *f* servitude.
kneifen ['knaɪfən] *unreg vt* to pinch ♦ *vi* to pinch; (*sich drücken*) to back out; **vor etw** *dat* **~** to dodge sth.
Kneifzange *f* pliers *pl*; (*kleine*) pincers *pl*.
Kneipe ['knaɪpə] (**-, -n**) (*umg*) *f* pub (*BRIT*), bar, saloon (*US*).
Kneippkur ['knaɪpkuːr] *f* Kneipp cure, *type of hydropathic treatment combined with diet, rest etc.*
Knete ['kneːtə] (*umg*) *f* (*Geld*) dough.
kneten *vt* to knead; (*Wachs*) to mould (*BRIT*),

mold (*US*).
Knetgummi *m od nt* Plasticine ®.
Knetmasse *f* Plasticine ®.
Knick [knɪk] (**-(e)s, -e**) *m* (*Sprung*) crack; (*Kurve*) bend; (*Falte*) fold.
knicken *vt, vi* (*springen*) to crack; (*brechen*) to break; (*Papier*) to fold; **„nicht ~!"** "do not bend"; **geknickt sein** to be downcast.
Knicks [knɪks] (**-es, -e**) *m* curts(e)y; **k~en** *vi* to curts(e)y.
Knie [kniː] (**-s, -**) *nt* knee; **in die ~ gehen** to kneel; (*fig*) to be brought to one's knees; **~beuge** (**-, -n**) *f* knee bend; **~fall** *m* genuflection; **~gelenk** *nt* knee joint; **~kehle** *f* back of the knee.
knien *vi* to kneel ♦ *vr*: **sich in die Arbeit ~** (*fig*) to get down to (one's) work.
Kniescheibe *f* kneecap.
Kniestrumpf *m* knee-length sock.
kniff *etc* [knɪf] *vb siehe* **kneifen**.
Kniff (**-(e)s, -e**) *m* (*Zwicken*) pinch; (*Falte*) fold; (*fig*) trick, knack.
kniffelig *adj* tricky.
knipsen ['knɪpsən] *vt* (*Fahrkarte*) to punch; (*PHOT*) to take a snap of, snap ♦ *vi* (*PHOT*) to take snaps/a snap.
Knirps [knɪrps] (**-es, -e**) *m* little chap; (®: *Schirm*) telescopic umbrella.
knirschen ['knɪrʃən] *vi* to crunch; **mit den Zähnen ~** to grind one's teeth.
knistern ['knɪstərn] *vi* to crackle; (*Papier, Seide*) to rustle.
Knitterfalte *f* crease.
knitterfrei *adj* non-crease.
knittern *vi* to crease.
knobeln ['knoːbəln] *vi* (*würfeln*) to play dice; (*um eine Entscheidung*) to toss for it.
Knoblauch ['knoːblaux] (**-(e)s**) *m* garlic.
Knöchel ['knœçəl] (**-s, -**) *m* knuckle; (*Fuß~*) ankle.
Knochen ['knɔxən] (**-s, -**) *m* bone; **~arbeit** (*umg*) *f* hard work; **~bau** *m* bone structure; **~bruch** *m* fracture; **~gerüst** *nt* skeleton; **~mark** *nt* bone marrow.
knöchern ['knœçərn] *adj* bone.
knochig ['knɔxɪç] *adj* bony.
Knödel ['knøːdəl] (**-s, -**) *m* dumpling.
Knolle ['knɔlə] (**-, -n**) *f* bulb.
Knopf [knɔpf] (**-(e)s, ⁻e**) *m* button; **~druck** *m* touch of a button.
knöpfen ['knœpfən] *vt* to button.
Knopfloch *nt* buttonhole.
Knorpel ['knɔrpəl] (**-s, -**) *m* cartilage, gristle.
knorpelig *adj* gristly.
knorrig ['knɔrɪç] *adj* gnarled, knotted.
Knospe ['knɔspə] (**-, -n**) *f* bud.
knospen *vi* to bud.
knoten ['knoːtən] *vt* to knot; **K~** (**-s, -**) *m* knot; (*Haar*) bun; (*BOT*) node; (*MED*) lump.
Knotenpunkt *m* junction.

knuffen ['knʊfən] (*umg*) *vt* to cuff.
Knüller ['knʏlər] (**-s, -**) (*umg*) *m* hit; (*Reportage*) scoop.
knüpfen ['knʏpfən] *vt* to tie; (*Teppich*) to knot; (*Freundschaft*) to form.
Knüppel ['knʏpəl] (**-s, -**) *m* cudgel; (*Polizei~*) baton, truncheon; (*AVIAT*) (joy)stick; **jdm ~ zwischen die Beine werfen** (*fig*) to put a spoke in sb's wheel; **k~dick** (*umg*) *adj* very thick; (*fig*) thick and fast; **~schaltung** *f* (*AUT*) floor-mounted gear change.
knurren ['knʊrən] *vi* (*Hund*) to snarl, growl; (*Magen*) to rumble; (*Mensch*) to mutter.
knusp(e)rig ['knʊsp(ə)rɪç] *adj* crisp; (*Keks*) crunchy.
knutschen ['knuːtʃən] (*umg*) *vt* to snog with ♦ *vi, vr* to snog.
k. o. *adj* (*SPORT*) knocked out; (*fig: umg*) whacked.
Koalition [koalitsiˈoːn] *f* coalition.
Kobalt ['koːbalt] (**-s**) *nt* cobalt.
Kobold ['koːbɔlt] (**-(e)s, -e**) *m* imp.
Kobra ['koːbra] (**-, -s**) *f* cobra.
Koch [kɔx] (**-(e)s, ⁻e**) *m* cook; **~buch** *nt* cookery book, cookbook; **k~echt** *adj* (*Farbe*) fast.
kochen *vi* to cook; (*Wasser*) to boil ♦ *vt* (*Essen*) to cook; **er kochte vor Wut** (*umg*) he was seething; **etw auf kleiner Flamme ~** to simmer sth over a low heat.
Kocher (**-s, -**) *m* stove, cooker.
Köcher ['kœçər] (**-s, -**) *m* quiver.
Kochgelegenheit *f* cooking facilities *pl*.
Köchin ['kœçɪn] *f* cook.
Koch- *zW*: **~kunst** *f* cooking; **~löffel** *m* kitchen spoon; **~nische** *f* kitchenette; **~platte** *f* hotplate; **~salz** *nt* cooking salt; **~topf** *m* saucepan, pot; **~wäsche** *f* washing that can be boiled.
Kode [koːt] (**-s, -s**) *m* code.
Köder ['køːdər] (**-s, -**) *m* bait, lure.
ködern *vt* to lure, entice.
Koexistenz [koɛksɪsˈtɛnts] *f* coexistence.
Koffein [kɔfeˈiːn] (**-s**) *nt* caffeine; **k~frei** *adj* decaffeinated.
Koffer ['kɔfər] (**-s, -**) *m* suitcase; (*Schrank~*) trunk; **die ~ packen** (*lit, fig*) to pack one's bags; **~kuli** *m* (luggage) trolley (*BRIT*), cart (*US*); **~radio** *nt* portable radio; **~raum** *m* (*AUT*) boot (*BRIT*), trunk (*US*).
Kognak ['kɔnjak] (**-s, -s**) *m* brandy, cognac.
Kohl [koːl] (**-(e)s, -e**) *m* cabbage.
Kohldampf (*umg*) *m*: **~ haben** to be famished.
Kohle ['koːlə] (**-, -n**) *f* coal; (*Holz~*) charcoal; (*CHEM*) carbon; (*umg: Geld*): **die ~n stimmen** the money's right; **~hydrat** (**-(e)s, -e**) *nt* carbohydrate; **~kraftwerk** *nt* coal-fired power station.
kohlen ['koːlən] (*umg*) *vi* to tell white lies.

Kohlen- *zW*: **~bergwerk** *nt* coal mine, pit, colliery (*BRIT*); **~dioxid** (**-(e)s, -e**) *nt* carbon dioxide; **~grube** *f* coal mine, pit; **~händler** *m* coal merchant, coalman; **~säure** *f* carbon dioxide; **ein Getränk ohne ~säure** a non-fizzy *od* still drink; **~stoff** *m* carbon.
Kohlepapier *nt* carbon paper.
Köhler ['køːlər] (**-s, -**) *m* charcoal burner.
Kohlestift *m* charcoal pencil.
Kohlezeichnung *f* charcoal drawing.
Kohl- *zW*: **k~(pech)rabenschwarz** *adj* (*Haar*) jet-black; (*Nacht*) pitch-black; **~rübe** *f* turnip; **k~schwarz** *adj* coal-black.
Koitus ['koːitʊs] (**-, -** *od* **-se**) *m* coitus.
Koje ['koːjə] (**-, -n**) *f* cabin; (*Bett*) bunk.
Kokain [kokaˈiːn] (**-s**) *nt* cocaine.
kokett [koˈkɛt] *adj* coquettish, flirtatious.
kokettieren [kokeˈtiːrən] *vi* to flirt.
Kokosnuss▲ ['koːkɔsnʊs] *f* coconut.
Koks [koːks] (**-es, -e**) *m* coke.
Kolben ['kɔlbən] (**-s, -**) *m* (*Gewehr~*) butt; (*Keule*) club; (*CHEM*) flask; (*TECH*) piston; (*Mais~*) cob.
Kolchose [kɔlˈçoːzə] (**-, -n**) *f* collective farm.
Kolik ['koːlɪk] *f* colic, gripe.
Kollaborateur(in) [kɔlaboraˈtøːr(ɪn)] *m(f)* (*POL*) collaborator.
Kollaps [kɔˈlaps] (**-es, -e**) *m* collapse.
Kolleg [kɔˈleːk] (**-s, -s** *od* **-ien**) *nt* lecture course.
Kollege [kɔˈleːgə] (**-n, -n**) *m* colleague.
kollegial [kɔlegiˈaːl] *adj* cooperative.
Kollegin [kɔˈleːgɪn] *f* colleague.
Kollegium *nt* board; (*SCH*) staff.
Kollekte [kɔˈlɛktə] (**-, -n**) *f* (*REL*) collection.
Kollektion [kɔlɛktiˈoːn] *f* collection; (*Sortiment*) range.
kollektiv [kɔlɛkˈtiːf] *adj* collective.
Koller ['kɔlər] (**-s, -**) (*umg*) *m* (*Anfall*) funny mood; (*Wutanfall*) rage; (*Tropen~, Gefängnis~*) madness.
kollidieren [kɔliˈdiːrən] *vi* to collide; (*zeitlich*) to clash.
Kollier [kɔliˈeː] (**-s, -s**) *nt* necklet, necklace.
Kollision [kɔliziˈoːn] *f* collision; (*zeitlich*) clash.
Kollisionskurs *m*: **auf ~ gehen** (*fig*) to be heading for trouble.
Köln [kœln] (**-s**) *nt* Cologne.
Kölnischwasser *nt* eau de Cologne.
kolonial [koloniˈaːl] *adj* colonial; **K~macht** *f* colonial power; **K~warenhändler** *m* grocer.
Kolonie [koloˈniː] *f* colony.
kolonisieren [koloniˈziːrən] *vt* to colonize.
Kolonist(in) [koloˈnɪst(ɪn)] *m(f)* colonist.
Kolonne [koˈlɔnə] (**-, -n**) *f* column; (*von Fahrzeugen*) convoy.
Koloss▲ [koˈlɔs] (**-es, -e**) *m* colossus.
kolossal [kolɔˈsaːl] *adj* colossal.
Kolumbianer(in) [kolumbiˈaːnər(ɪn)] *m(f)* Columbian.

kolumbianisch *adj* Columbian.
Kolumbien [ko'lʊmbiən] (**-s**) *nt* Columbia.
Koma ['koːma] (**-s, -s** *od* **-ta**) *nt* (*MED*) coma.
Kombi ['kɔmbi] (**-s, -s**) *m* (*AUT*) estate (car) (*BRIT*), station wagon (*US*).
Kombination [kɔmbinatsi'oːn] *f* combination; (*Vermutung*) conjecture; (*Hemdhose*) combinations *pl*; (*AVIAT*) flying suit.
Kombinationsschloss▲ *nt* combination lock.
kombinieren [kɔmbi'niːrən] *vt* to combine ♦ *vi* to deduce, work out; (*vermuten*) to guess.
Kombiwagen *m* (*AUT*) estate (car) (*BRIT*), station wagon (*US*).
Kombizange *f* (pair of) pliers.
Komet [ko'meːt] (**-en, -en**) *m* comet.
kometenhaft *adj* (*fig: Aufstieg*) meteoric.
Komfort [kɔm'foːr] (**-s**) *m* luxury; (*von Möbel etc*) comfort; (*von Wohnung*) amenities *pl*; (*von Auto*) luxury features *pl*; (*von Gerät*) extras *pl*.
komfortabel [kɔmfɔr'taːbəl] *adj* comfortable.
Komik ['koːmɪk] *f* humour (*BRIT*), humor (*US*), comedy; **~er** (**-s, -**) *m* comedian.
komisch ['koːmɪʃ] *adj* funny; **mir ist so ~** (*umg*) I feel funny *od* strange *od* odd; **~erweise** ['koːmɪʃ'ər'vaizə] *adv* funnily enough.
Komitee [komi'teː] (**-s, -s**) *nt* committee.
Komm. *abk* (= *Kommission*) comm.
Komma ['kɔma] (**-s, -s** *od* **-ta**) *nt* comma; (*MATH*) decimal point; **fünf ~ drei** five point three.
Kommandant [koman'dant] *m* commander, commanding officer.
Kommandeur [koman'døːr] *m* commanding officer.
kommandieren [koman'diːrən] *vt* to command ♦ *vi* to command; (*Befehle geben*) to give orders.
Kommanditgesellschaft [koman'diːtɡəzelʃaft] *f* limited partnership.
Kommando [kɔ'mando] (**-s, -s**) *nt* command, order; (*Truppe*) detachment, squad; **auf ~** to order; **~brücke** *f* (*NAUT*) bridge; **~wirtschaft** *f* command economy.
kommen ['kɔmən] *unreg vi* to come; (*näher ~*) to approach; (*passieren*) to happen; (*gelangen, geraten*) to get; (*Blumen, Zähne, Tränen etc*) to appear; (*in die Schule, ins Gefängnis etc*) to go; **was kommt diese Woche im Kino?** what's on at the cinema this week? ♦ *vi unpers*: **es kam eins zum anderen** one thing led to another; **~ lassen** to send for; **in Bewegung ~** to start moving; **jdn besuchen ~** to come and visit sb; **das kommt davon!** see what happens?; **du kommst mir gerade recht** (*ironisch*) you're just what I need; **das kommt in den Schrank** that goes in the cupboard; **an etw** *akk* **~**

(*berühren*) to touch sth; (*sich verschaffen*) to get hold of sth; **auf etw** *akk* **~** (*sich erinnern*) to think of sth; (*sprechen über*) to get onto sth; **das kommt auf die Rechnung** that goes onto the bill; **hinter etw** *akk* **~** (*herausfinden*) to find sth out; **zu sich ~** to come round *od* to; **zu etw ~** to acquire sth; **um etw ~** to lose sth; **nichts auf jdn/etw ~ lassen** to have nothing said against sb/sth; **jdm frech ~** to get cheeky with sb; **auf jeden vierten kommt ein Platz** there's one place to every fourth person; **mit einem Anliegen ~** to have a request (to make); **wer kommt zuerst?** who's first?; **wer zuerst kommt, mahlt zuerst** (*Sprichwort*) first come first served; **unter ein Auto ~** to be run over by a car; **das kommt zusammen auf 20 DM** that comes to 20 marks altogether; **und so kam es, dass ...** and that is how it happened that ...; **daher kommt es, dass ...** that's why ...
Kommen (**-s**) *nt* coming.
kommend *adj* (*Jahr, Woche, Generation*) coming; (*Ereignisse, Mode*) future; (*Trend*) upcoming; (**am**) **~en Montag** next Monday.
Kommentar [kɔmɛn'taːr] *m* commentary; **kein ~** no comment; **k~los** *adj* without comment.
Kommentator [kɔmɛn'taːtɔr] *m* (*TV*) commentator.
kommentieren [kɔmɛn'tiːrən] *vt* to comment on; **kommentierte Ausgabe** annotated edition.
kommerziell [kɔmɛrtsi'ɛl] *adj* commercial.
Kommilitone [kɔmili'toːnə] (**-n, -n**) *m*, **Kommilitonin** *f* fellow student.
Kommiss▲ [kɔ'mɪs] (**-es**) *m* (life in the) army.
Kommissar [kɔmɪ'saːr] *m* police inspector.
Kommissbrot▲ *nt* army bread.
Kommission [kɔmɪsi'oːn] *f* (*COMM*) commission; (*Ausschuss*) committee; **in ~ geben** to give (to a dealer) for sale on commission.
Kommode [kɔ'moːdə] (**-, -n**) *f* (chest of) drawers.
kommunal [kɔmu'naːl] *adj* local; (*von Stadt*) municipal; **K~abgaben** *pl* local rates and taxes *pl*; **K~politik** *f* local government politics; **K~verwaltung** *f* local government; **K~wahlen** *pl* local (government) elections *pl*.
Kommune [kɔ'muːnə] (**-, -n**) *f* commune.
Kommunikation [kɔmunɪkatsi'oːn] *f* communication.
Kommunikee▲ [kɔmyni'keː] (**-s, -s**) *nt* = **Kommuniqué**.
Kommunion [kɔmuni'oːn] *f* communion.
Kommuniqué [kɔmyni'keː] (**-s, -s**) *nt* communiqué.
Kommunismus [kɔmu'nɪsmʊs] *m* communism.

Kommunist(in) [kɔmu'nɪst(ɪn)] *m(f)*
communist; **k~isch** *adj* communist.
kommunizieren [kɔmuni'tsiːrən] *vi* to
communicate; *(ECCL)* to receive
communion.
Komödiant [komødi'ant] *m* comedian; **~in** *f*
comedienne.
Komödie [ko'møːdiə] *f* comedy; **~ spielen** *(fig)*
to put on an act.
Kompagnon [kɔmpan'jõː] **(-s, -s)** *m (COMM)*
partner.
kompakt [kɔm'pakt] *adj* compact.
Kompaktanlage *f (RUNDF)* audio system.
Kompanie [kɔmpa'niː] *f* company.
Komparativ ['kɔmparatiːf] **(-s, -e)** *m*
comparative.
Kompass▲ ['kɔmpas] **(-es, -e)** *m* compass.
kompatibel [kɔmpa'tiːbəl] *adj (auch COMPUT)*
compatible.
Kompatibilität [kɔmpatibili'tɛːt] *f (auch
COMPUT)* compatibility.
kompensieren [kɔmpɛn'ziːrən] *vt* to
compensate for, offset.
kompetent [kɔmpe'tɛnt] *adj* competent.
Kompetenz *f* competence, authority;
~streitigkeiten *pl* dispute over respective
areas of responsibility.
komplett [kɔm'plɛt] *adj* complete.
komplex [kɔm'plɛks] *adj* complex; **K~ (-es, -e)**
m complex.
Komplikation [kɔmplikatsi'oːn] *f*
complication.
Kompliment [kɔmpli'mɛnt] *nt* compliment.
Komplize [kɔm'pliːtsə] **(-n, -n)** *m* accomplice.
komplizieren [kɔmpli'tsiːrən] *vt* to
complicate.
kompliziert *adj* complicated; *(MED: Bruch)*
compound.
Komplizin [kɔm'pliːtsɪn] *f* accomplice.
Komplott [kɔm'plɔt] **(-(e)s, -e)** *nt* plot.
komponieren [kɔmpo'niːrən] *vt* to compose.
Komponist(in) [kɔmpo'nɪst(ɪn)] *m(f)*
composer.
Komposition [kɔmpozitsi'oːn] *f* composition.
Kompost [kɔm'pɔst] **(-(e)s, -e)** *m* compost;
~haufen *m* compost heap.
Kompott [kɔm'pɔt] **(-(e)s, -e)** *nt* stewed fruit.
Kompresse [kɔm'prɛsə] **(-, -n)** *f* compress.
Kompressor [kɔm'prɛsɔr] *m* compressor.
Kompromiss▲ [kɔmpro'mɪs] **(-es, -e)** *m*
compromise; **einen ~ schließen** to
compromise; **k~bereit** *adj* willing to
compromise; **~lösung** *f* compromise
solution.
kompromittieren [kɔmprɔmɪ'tiːrən] *vt* to
compromise.
Kondensation [kɔndɛnzatsi'oːn] *f*
condensation.
Kondensator [kɔndɛn'zaːtɔr] *m* condenser.
kondensieren [kɔndɛn'ziːrən] *vt* to condense.

Kondensmilch *f* condensed milk.
Kondensstreifen *m* vapour *(BRIT)* od vapor
(US) trail.
Kondition [kɔnditsi'oːn] *f* condition, shape;
(Durchhaltevermögen) stamina.
Konditionalsatz [kɔnditsio'naːlzats] *m*
conditional clause.
Konditionstraining *nt* fitness training.
Konditor [kɔn'diːtɔr] *m* pastry-cook.
Konditorei [kɔndito'raɪ] *f* cake shop; *(mit Café)*
café.
kondolieren [kɔndo'liːrən] *vi*: **jdm ~** to
condole with sb, offer sb one's condolences.
Kondom [kɔn'doːm] **(-s, -e)** *m or nt* condom.
Konfektion [kɔnfɛktsi'oːn] *f* (production of)
ready-to-wear od off-the-peg clothing.
Konfektionsgröße *f* clothes size.
Konfektionskleidung *f* ready-to-wear od
off-the-peg clothing.
Konferenz [kɔnfe'rɛnts] *f* conference;
(Besprechung) meeting; **~schaltung** *f (TEL)*
conference circuit; *(RUNDF, TV)* television
od radio link-up.
konferieren [kɔnfe'riːrən] *vi* to confer; to have
a meeting.
Konfession [kɔnfɛsi'oːn] *f* religion; *(christlich)*
denomination; **k~ell** [-'nɛl] *adj*
denominational.
Konfessions- *zW*: **k~gebunden** *adj*
denominational; **k~los** *adj* non-
denominational; **~schule** *f* denominational
school.
Konfetti [kɔn'fɛti] **(-(s))** *nt* confetti.
Konfiguration [kɔnfiguratsi'oːn] *f (COMPUT)*
configuration.
Konfirmand(in) [kɔnfɪr'mant, -'mandɪn] *m(f)*
candidate for confirmation.
Konfirmation [kɔnfɪrmatsi'oːn] *f (ECCL)*
confirmation.
konfirmieren [kɔnfɪr'miːrən] *vt* to confirm.
konfiszieren [kɔnfɪs'tsiːrən] *vt* to confiscate.
Konfitüre [kɔnfi'tyːrə] **(-, -n)** *f* jam.
Konflikt [kɔn'flɪkt] **(-(e)s, -e)** *m* conflict; **~herd**
m (POL) centre *(BRIT)* od center *(US)* of
conflict; **~stoff** *m* cause of conflict.
konform [kɔn'fɔrm] *adj* concurring; **~ gehen**
to be in agreement.
Konfrontation [kɔnfrɔntatsi'oːn] *f*
confrontation.
konfrontieren [kɔnfrɔn'tiːrən] *vt* to confront.
konfus [kɔn'fuːs] *adj* confused.
Kongo ['kɔŋgo] **(-(s))** *m* Congo.
Kongress▲ [kɔn'grɛs] **(-es, -e)** *m* congress.
Kongruenz [kɔŋgru'ɛnts] *f* agreement,
congruence.
König ['køːnɪç] **(-(e)s, -e)** *m* king.
Königin ['køːnɪgɪn] *f* queen.
königlich *adj* royal ♦ *adv*: **sich ~ amüsieren**
(umg) to have the time of one's life.
Königreich *nt* kingdom.

Königtum ['køːnɪçtuːm] (-(e)s, -tümer) nt
kingship; (Reich) kingdom.
konisch ['koːnɪʃ] adj conical.
Konj. abk (= Konjunktiv) conj.
Konjugation [kɔnjugatsi'oːn] f conjugation.
konjugieren [kɔnju'giːrən] vt to conjugate.
Konjunktion [kɔnjʊŋktsi'oːn] f conjunction.
Konjunktiv ['kɔnjʊŋktiːf] (-s, -e) m
subjunctive.
Konjunktur [kɔnjʊŋk'tuːr] f economic
situation; (Hoch~) boom; **steigende/fallende**
~ upward/downward economic trend;
~**barometer** nt economic indicators pl; ~**loch**
nt temporary economic dip; ~**politik** f
policies aimed at preventing economic
fluctuations.
konkav [kɔn'kaːf] adj concave.
konkret [kɔn'kreːt] adj concrete.
Konkurrent(in) [kɔnkʊ'rɛnt(ɪn)] m(f)
competitor.
Konkurrenz [kɔnkʊ'rɛnts] f competition; **jdm**
~ **machen** (COMM, fig) to compete with sb;
k~fähig adj competitive; ~**kampf** m
competition; (umg) rat race.
konkurrieren [kɔnkʊ'riːrən] vi to compete.
Konkurs [kɔn'kʊrs] (-es, -e) m bankruptcy; **in**
~ **gehen** to go into receivership; ~ **machen**
(umg) to go bankrupt; ~**verfahren** nt
bankruptcy proceedings pl; ~**verwalter** m
receiver; (von Gläubigern bevollmächtigt)
trustee.

════════════ SCHLÜSSELWORT

können ['kœnən] (pt **konnte**, pp **gekonnt** od (als
Hilfsverb) **können**) vt, vi **1** to be able to; **ich**
kann es machen I can do it, I am able to do
it; **ich kann es nicht machen** I can't do it, I'm
not able to do it; **ich kann nicht ...** I can't ..., I
cannot ...; **was** ~ **Sie?** what can you do?; **ich**
kann nicht mehr I can't go on; **ich kann**
nichts dafür I can't help it; **du kannst mich**
(mal)! (umg) get lost!
2 (wissen, beherrschen) to know; ~ **Sie**
Deutsch? can you speak German?; **er kann**
gut Englisch he speaks English well; **sie**
kann keine Mathematik she can't do
mathematics.
3 (dürfen) to be allowed to; **kann ich gehen?**
can I go?; **könnte ich ...?** could I ...?; **kann ich**
mit? (umg) can I come with you?
4 (möglich sein): **Sie könnten Recht haben**
you may be right; **das kann sein** that's
possible; **kann sein** maybe.

Können (-s) nt ability.
Könner (-s, -) m expert.
Konnossement [kɔnɔsə'mɛnt] nt (Export) bill
of lading.
konnte etc ['kɔntə] vb siehe **können**.
konsequent [kɔnze'kvɛnt] adj consistent; **ein**

Ziel ~ **verfolgen** to pursue an objective
single-mindedly.
Konsequenz [kɔnze'kvɛnts] f consistency;
(Folgerung) conclusion; **die** ~**en tragen** to
take the consequences; **(aus etw) die** ~**en**
ziehen to take the appropriate steps.
konservativ [kɔnzɛrva'tiːf] adj conservative.
Konservatorium [kɔnzɛrva'toːriʊm] nt
academy of music, conservatory.
Konserve [kɔn'zɛrvə] (-, -n) f tinned (BRIT) od
canned food.
Konservenbüchse f, **Konservendose** f tin
(BRIT), can.
konservieren [kɔnzɛr'viːrən] vt to preserve.
Konservierung f preservation.
Konservierungsstoff m preservative.
Konsole [kɔnzoːlə] f games console.
konsolidiert [kɔnzoli'diːrt] adj consolidated.
Konsolidierung f consolidation.
Konsonant [kɔnzo'nant] m consonant.
Konsortium [kɔn'zɔrtsiʊm] nt consortium,
syndicate.
konspirativ [kɔnspira'tiːf] adj: ~**e Wohnung**
conspirators' hideaway.
konstant [kɔn'stant] adj constant.
Konstellation [kɔnstɛlatsi'oːn] f constellation;
(fig) line-up; (von Faktoren etc) combination.
Konstitution [kɔnstitutsi'oːn] f constitution.
konstitutionell [kɔnstitutsio'nɛl] adj
constitutional.
konstruieren [kɔnstru'iːrən] vt to construct.
Konstrukteur(in) [kɔnstrʊk'tøːr(ɪn)] m(f)
designer.
Konstruktion [kɔnstrʊktsi'on] f construction.
Konstruktionsfehler m (im Entwurf) design
fault; (im Aufbau) structural defect.
konstruktiv [kɔnstrʊk'tiːf] adj constructive.
Konsul ['kɔnzʊl] (-s, -n) m consul.
Konsulat [kɔnzʊ'laːt] (-(e)s, -e) nt consulate.
konsultieren [kɔnzʊl'tiːrən] vt to consult.
Konsum¹ [kɔn'zuːm] (-s) m consumption.
Konsum² ['kɔnzuːm] (-s, -s) m
(Genossenschaft) cooperative society;
(Laden) cooperative store, co-op (umg).
Konsumartikel m consumer article.
Konsument [kɔnzu'mɛnt] m consumer.
Konsumgesellschaft f consumer society.
konsumieren [kɔnzu'miːrən] vt to consume.
Konsumterror m pressures pl of a
materialistic society.
Konsumzwang m compulsion to buy.
Kontakt [kɔn'takt] (-(e)s, -e) m contact; **mit**
jdm ~ **aufnehmen** to get in touch with sb;
~**anzeige** f lonely hearts ad; **k~arm** adj
unsociable; **k~freudig** adj sociable.
kontaktieren [kɔntak'tiːrən] vt to contact.
Kontakt- zW: ~**linsen** pl contact lenses pl;
~**mann** (-(e)s, pl -**männer**) m (Agent) contact;
~**sperre** f ban on visits and letters (to a
prisoner).

Konterfei ['kɔntərfaɪ] (-s, -s) *nt* likeness, portrait.

kontern ['kɔntərn] *vt, vi* to counter.

Konterrevolution ['kɔntərrevolutsioːn] *f* counter-revolution.

Kontinent [kɔnti'nɛnt] *m* continent.

Kontingent [kɔntɪŋ'gɛnt] (-(e)s, -e) *nt* quota; (*Truppen~*) contingent.

kontinuierlich [kɔntinu'iːrlɪç] *adj* continuous.

Kontinuität [kɔntinui'tɛːt] *f* continuity.

Konto ['kɔnto] (-s, **Konten**) *nt* account; **das geht auf mein ~** (*umg: ich bin schuldig*) I am to blame for this; (*ich zahle*) this is on me (*umg*); **~auszug** *m* statement (of account); **~inhaber(in)** *m(f)* account holder.

Kontor [kɔn'toːr] (-s, -e) *nt* office.

Kontorist(in) [kɔnto'rɪst(ɪn)] *m(f)* clerk, office worker.

Kontostand *m* bank balance.

kontra ['kɔntra] *präp +akk* against; (*JUR*) versus.

Kontra (-s, -s) *nt* (*KARTEN*) double; **jdm ~ geben** (*fig*) to contradict sb.

Kontrabass▲ *m* double bass.

Kontrahent [-'hɛnt] *m* contracting party; (*Gegner*) opponent.

Kontrapunkt *m* counterpoint.

Kontrast [kɔn'trast] (-(e)s, -e) *m* contrast.

Kontrollabschnitt *m* (*COMM*) counterfoil, stub.

Kontrollampe△ [kɔn'trɔllampə] *f siehe* **Kontrolllampe**.

Kontrolle [kɔn'trɔlə] (-, -n) *f* control, supervision; (*Pass~*) passport control.

Kontrolleur [kɔntrɔ'løːr] *m* inspector.

kontrollieren [kɔntrɔ'liːrən] *vt* to control, supervise; (*nachprüfen*) to check.

Kontrolllampe▲ [kɔn'trɔllampə] *f* pilot lamp; (*AUT: für Ölstand etc*) warning light.

Kontrollturm *m* control tower.

Kontroverse [kɔntro'vɛrzə] (-, -n) *f* controversy.

Kontur [kɔn'tuːr] *f* contour.

Konvention [kɔnvɛntsi'oːn] *f* convention.

Konventionalstrafe [kɔnvɛntsio'naːlʃtraːfə] *f* penalty *od* fine (*for breach of contract*).

konventionell [kɔnvɛntsio'nɛl] *adj* conventional.

Konversation [kɔnvɛrzatsi'oːn] *f* conversation.

Konversationslexikon *nt* encyclopaedia.

konvex [kɔn'vɛks] *adj* convex.

Konvoi ['kɔnvɔy] (-s, -s) *m* convoy.

Konzentrat [kɔntsɛn'traːt] (-s, -e) *nt* concentrate.

Konzentration [kɔntsɛntratsi'oːn] *f* concentration.

Konzentrationsfähigkeit *f* power of concentration.

Konzentrationslager *nt* concentration camp.

konzentrieren [kɔntsɛn'triːrən] *vt, vr* to concentrate.

konzentriert *adj* concentrated ♦ *adv* (*zuhören, arbeiten*) intently.

Konzept [kɔn'tsɛpt] (-(e)s, -e) *nt* rough draft; (*Plan, Programm*) plan; (*Begriff, Vorstellung*) concept; **jdn aus dem ~ bringen** to confuse sb; **~papier** *nt* rough paper.

Konzern [kɔn'tsɛrn] (-s, -e) *m* combine.

Konzert [kɔn'tsɛrt] (-(e)s, -e) *nt* concert; (*Stück*) concerto; **~saal** *m* concert hall.

Konzession [kɔntsɛsi'oːn] *f* licence (*BRIT*), license (*US*); (*Zugeständnis*) concession; **die ~ entziehen** *+dat* (*COMM*) to disenfranchise.

Konzessionär [kɔntsɛsio'nɛːr] (-s, -e) *m* concessionaire.

konzessionieren [kɔntsɛsio'niːrən] *vt* to license.

Konzil [kɔn'tsiːl] (-s, -e *od* -ien) *nt* council.

konzipieren [kɔntsi'piːrən] *vt* to conceive; (*entwerfen*) to design.

kooperativ [koʔopera'tiːf] *adj* cooperative.

kooperieren [koʔope'riːrən] *vi* to cooperate.

koordinieren [koʔɔrdi'niːrən] *vt* to coordinate.

Kopenhagen [koːpən'haːgən] (-s) *nt* Copenhagen.

Kopf [kɔpf] (-(e)s, ⁻e) *m* head; **~ hoch!** chin up!; **~ an ~** shoulder to shoulder; (*SPORT*) neck and neck; **pro ~** per person *od* head; **~ oder Zahl?** heads or tails?; **jdm den ~ waschen** (*fig: umg*) to give sb a piece of one's mind; **jdm über den ~ wachsen** (*lit*) to outgrow sb; (*fig: Sorgen etc*) to be more than sb can cope with; **jdn vor den ~ stoßen** to antagonize sb; **sich** *dat* **an den ~ fassen** (*fig*) to be speechless; **sich** *dat* **über etw** *akk* **den ~ zerbrechen** to rack one's brains over sth; **sich** *dat* **etw durch den ~ gehen lassen** to think about sth; **sich** *dat* **etw aus dem ~ schlagen** to put sth out of one's mind; **... und wenn du dich auf den ~ stellst!** (*umg*) ... no matter what you say/do!; **er ist nicht auf den ~ gefallen** he's no fool; **~bahnhof** *m* terminus station; **~bedeckung** *f* headgear.

Köpfchen ['kœpfçən] *nt*: **~ haben** to be brainy.

köpfen ['kœpfən] *vt* to behead; (*Baum*) to lop; (*Ei*) to take the top off; (*Ball*) to head.

Kopf- *zW*: **~ende** *nt* head; **~haut** *f* scalp; **~hörer** *m* headphone; **~kissen** *nt* pillow; **k~lastig** *adj* (*fig*) completely rational; **k~los** *adj* panic-stricken; **~losigkeit** *f* panic; **k~rechnen** *vi* to do mental arithmetic; **~salat** *m* lettuce; **k~scheu** *adj*: **jdn k~scheu machen** to intimidate sb; **~schmerzen** *pl* headache *sing*; **~sprung** *m* header, dive; **~stand** *m* headstand; **~steinpflaster** *nt*: **eine Straße mit ~steinpflaster** a cobbled street; **~stütze** *f* headrest; (*im Auto*) head restraint;

~**tuch** nt headscarf; **k~über** adv head-first; ~**weh** nt headache; ~**zerbrechen** nt: **jdm** ~**zerbrechen machen** to give sb a lot of headaches.

Kopie [ko'piː] f copy.

kopieren [ko'piːrən] vt to copy.

Kopierer (-s, -) m (photo)copier.

Kopilot(in) ['koːpiloːt(ɪn)] m(f) co-pilot.

Koppel[1] ['kɔpəl] (-, -n) f (Weide) enclosure.

Koppel[2] ['kɔpəl] (-s, -) nt (Gürtel) belt.

koppeln vt to couple.

Koppelung f coupling.

Koppelungsmanöver nt docking manoeuvre (BRIT) od maneuver (US).

Koralle [ko'ralə] (-, -n) f coral.

Korallenkette f coral necklace.

Korallenriff nt coral reef.

Korb [kɔrp] (-(e)s, ̈-e) m basket; **jdm einen** ~ **geben** (fig) to turn sb down; ~**ball** m basketball.

Körbchen ['kœrpçən] nt (von Büstenhalter) cup.

Korbstuhl m wicker chair.

Kord [kɔrt] (-(e)s, -e) m corduroy.

Kordel ['kɔrdəl] (-, -n) f cord, string.

Korea [ko'reːa] (-s) nt Korea.

Koreaner(in) (-s, -) m(f) Korean.

Korfu ['kɔrfu] (-s) nt Corfu.

Korinthe [ko'rɪntə] (-, -n) f currant.

Korinthenkacker [ko'rɪntənkakər] (-s, -) (umg) m fusspot, hair-splitter.

Kork [kɔrk] (-(e)s, -e) m cork.

Korken (-s, -) m stopper, cork; ~**zieher** (-s, -) m corkscrew.

Korn[1] [kɔrn] (-(e)s, ̈-er) nt corn, grain.

Korn[2] [kɔrn] (-(e)s, -e) nt (Gewehr) sight; **etw aufs** ~ **nehmen** (fig: umg) to hit out at sth.

Korn[3] [kɔrn] (-, -s) m (Kornbranntwein) corn schnapps.

Kornblume f cornflower.

Körnchen ['kœrnçən] nt grain, granule.

körnig ['kœrnɪç] adj granular, grainy.

Kornkammer f granary.

Körnung ['kœrnʊŋ] f (TECH) grain size; (PHOT) granularity.

Körper ['kœrpər] (-s, -) m body; ~**bau** m build; **k~behindert** adj disabled; ~**geruch** m body odour (BRIT) od odor (US); ~**gewicht** nt weight; ~**größe** f height; ~**haltung** f carriage, deportment; **k~lich** adj physical; **k~liche Arbeit** manual work; ~**pflege** f personal hygiene; ~**schaft** f corporation; ~**schaft des öffentlichen Rechts** public corporation od body; ~**schaftssteuer** f corporation tax; ~**sprache** f body language; ~**teil** m part of the body; ~**verletzung** f (JUR): **schwere** ~**verletzung** grievous bodily harm.

Korps [koːr] (-, -) nt (MIL) corps; (UNIV) students' club.

korpulent [kɔrpu'lɛnt] adj corpulent.

korrekt [kɔ'rɛkt] adj correct; **K~heit** f correctness.

Korrektor(in) [kɔ'rɛktɔr, -'toːrɪn] (-s, -) m(f) proofreader.

Korrektur [kɔrɛk'tuːr] f (eines Textes) proofreading; (Text) proof; (SCH) marking, correction; **(bei etw)** ~ **lesen** to proofread (sth); ~**fahne** f (TYP) proof.

Korrespondent(in) [kɔrɛspɔn'dɛnt(ɪn)] m(f) correspondent.

Korrespondenz [kɔrɛspɔn'dɛnts] f correspondence; ~**qualität** f (Drucker) letter quality.

korrespondieren [kɔrɛspɔn'diːrən] vi to correspond.

Korridor ['kɔridoːr] (-s, -e) m corridor.

korrigieren [kɔri'giːrən] vt to correct; (Meinung, Einstellung) to change.

Korrosion [kɔrozi'oːn] f corrosion.

Korrosionsschutz m corrosion protection.

korrumpieren [kɔrʊm'piːrən] vt (auch COMPUT) to corrupt.

korrupt [kɔ'rʊpt] adj corrupt.

Korruption [kɔrʊptsi'oːn] f corruption.

Korsett [kɔr'zɛt] (-(e)s, -e) nt corset.

Korsika ['kɔrzika] (-s) nt Corsica.

Koseform ['koːzəfɔrm] f pet form.

kosen vt to caress ♦ vi to bill and coo.

Kosename m pet name.

Kosewort nt term of endearment.

Kosmetik [kɔs'meːtɪk] f cosmetics pl.

Kosmetikerin f beautician.

kosmetisch adj cosmetic; (Chirurgie) plastic.

kosmisch ['kɔsmɪʃ] adj cosmic.

Kosmonaut [kɔsmo'naut] (-en, -en) m cosmonaut.

Kosmopolit [kɔsmopo'liːt] (-en, -en) m cosmopolitan; **k~isch** [-po'liːtɪʃ] adj cosmopolitan.

Kosmos ['kɔsmɔs] (-) m cosmos.

Kost [kɔst] (-) f (Nahrung) food; (Verpflegung) board; ~ **und Logis** board and lodging.

kostbar adj precious; (teuer) costly, expensive; **K~keit** f preciousness; costliness, expensiveness; (Wertstück) treasure.

Kosten pl cost(s); (Ausgaben) expenses pl; **auf** ~ **von** at the expense of; **auf seine** ~ **kommen** (fig) to get one's money's worth.

kosten vt to cost; (versuchen) to taste ♦ vi to taste; **koste es, was es wolle** whatever the cost.

Kosten- zW: ~**anschlag** m estimate; **k~deckend** adj cost-effective; ~**erstattung** f reimbursement of expenses; ~**kontrolle** f cost control; **k~los** adj free (of charge); ~**-Nutzen-Analyse** f cost-benefit analysis; **k~pflichtig** adj: **ein Auto k~pflichtig abschleppen** to tow away a car at the owner's expense; ~**stelle** f (COMM) cost centre (*BRIT*) *od* center (*US*); ~**voranschlag** *m* (costs) estimate.

Kostgeld *nt* board.

köstlich ['kœstlıç] *adj* precious; (*Einfall*) delightful; (*Essen*) delicious; **sich ~ amüsieren** to have a marvellous time.

Kostprobe *f* taste; (*fig*) sample.

kostspielig *adj* expensive.

Kostüm [kɔs'tyːm] (**-s, -e**) *nt* costume; (*Damen~*) suit; ~**fest** *nt* fancy-dress party.

kostümieren [kɔsty'miːrən] *vt, vr* to dress up.

Kostümprobe *f* (*THEAT*) dress rehearsal.

Kostümverleih *m* costume agency.

Kot [koːt] (**-(e)s**) *m* excrement.

Kotelett [kɔtə'lɛt] (**-(e)s, -e** *od* **-s**) *nt* cutlet, chop.

Koteletten *pl* sideboards *pl* (*BRIT*), sideburns *pl* (*US*).

Köter ['køːtər] (**-s, -**) *m* cur.

Kotflügel *m* (*AUT*) wing.

kotzen ['kɔtsən] (*umg!*) *vi* to puke (*!*), throw up; **das ist zum K~** it makes you sick.

KP (**-, -s**) *f abk* (= *Kommunistische Partei*) C.P.

KPÖ (**-**) *f abk* (= *Kommunistische Partei Österreichs*) Austrian Communist Party.

Kr. *abk* = **Kreis**.

Krabbe ['krabə] (**-, -n**) *f* shrimp.

krabbeln *vi* to crawl.

Krach [krax] (**-(e)s, -s** *od* **-e**) *m* crash; (*andauernd*) noise; (*umg: Streit*) quarrel, argument; ~ **schlagen** to make a fuss; **k~en** *vi* to crash; (*beim Brechen*) to crack ♦ *vr* (*umg*) to argue, quarrel.

krächzen ['krɛçtsən] *vi* to croak.

Kräcker ['krɛkər] (**-s, -**) *m* (*KOCH*) cracker.

kraft [kraft] *präp +gen* by virtue of.

Kraft (**-, -̈e**) *f* strength; (*von Stimme, fig*) power, force; (*Arbeits~*) worker; **mit vereinten Kräften werden wir ...** if we combine our efforts we will ...; **nach (besten) Kräften** to the best of one's abilities; **außer ~ sein** (*JUR: Geltung*) to be no longer in force; **in ~ treten** to come into effect.

Kraft- *zW:* ~**aufwand** *m* effort; ~**ausdruck** *m* swearword; ~**brühe** *f* beef tea.

Kräfteverhältnis ['krɛftəferhɛltnıs] *nt* (*POL*) balance of power; (*von Mannschaften etc*) relative strength.

Kraftfahrer *m* motor driver.

Kraftfahrzeug *nt* motor vehicle; ~**brief** *m* (*AUT*) logbook (*BRIT*), motor-vehicle registration certificate (*US*); ~**schein** *m* (*AUT*) car licence (*BRIT*) *od* license (*US*); ~**steuer** *f* ≈ road tax.

kräftig ['krɛftıç] *adj* strong; (*Suppe, Essen*) nourishing; ~**en** ['krɛftıgən] *vt* to strengthen.

Kraft- *zW:* **k~los** *adj* weak; powerless; (*JUR*) invalid; ~**meierei** (*umg*) *f showing off of physical strength*; ~**probe** *f* trial of

strength; ~**rad** *nt* motorcycle; ~**stoff** *m* fuel; ~**training** *nt* weight training; **k~voll** *adj* vigorous; ~**wagen** *m* motor vehicle; ~**werk** *nt* power station; ~**werker** *m* power station worker.

Kragen ['kraːgən] (**-s, -**) *m* collar; **da ist mir der ~ geplatzt** (*umg*) I blew my top; **es geht ihm an den ~** (*umg*) he's in for it; ~**weite** *f* collar size; **das ist nicht meine ~weite** (*fig: umg*) that's not my cup of tea.

Krähe ['krɛːə] (**-, -n**) *f* crow.

krähen *vi* to crow.

krakeelen [kra'keːlən] (*umg*) *vi* to make a din.

krakelig ['kraːkəlıç] (*umg*) *adj* (*Schrift*) scrawly, spidery.

Kralle ['kralə] (**-, -n**) *f* claw; (*Vogel~*) talon.

krallen *vt* to clutch; (*krampfhaft*) to claw.

Kram [kraːm] (**-(e)s**) *m* stuff, rubbish; **den ~ hinschmeißen** (*umg*) to chuck the whole thing; **k~en** *vi* to rummage; ~**laden** (*pej*) *m* small shop.

Krampf [krampf] (**-(e)s, -̈e**) *m* cramp; (*zuckend*) spasm; (*Unsinn*) rubbish; ~**ader** *f* varicose vein; **k~haft** *adj* convulsive; (*fig: Versuche*) desperate.

Kran [kraːn] (**-(e)s, -̈e**) *m* crane; (*Wasser~*) tap (*BRIT*), faucet (*US*).

Kranich ['kraːnıç] (**-s, -e**) *m* (*ZOOL*) crane.

krank [kraŋk] *adj* ill, sick; **das macht mich ~!** (*umg*) it gets on my nerves!, it drives me round the bend!; **sich ~ stellen** to pretend to be ill, malinger.

Kranke(r) *f(m)* sick person, invalid; (*Patient*) patient.

kränkeln ['krɛŋkəln] *vi* to be in bad health.

kranken ['kraŋkən] *vi:* **an etw** *dat* ~ (*fig*) to suffer from sth.

kränken ['krɛŋkən] *vt* to hurt.

Kranken- *zW:* ~**bericht** *m* medical report; ~**besuch** *m* visit to a sick person; ~**geld** *nt* sick pay; ~**geschichte** *f* medical history; ~**gymnastik** *f* physiotherapy; ~**haus** *nt* hospital; ~**kasse** *f* health insurance; ~**pfleger** *m* orderly; (*mit Schwesternausbildung*) male nurse; ~**pflegerin** *f* nurse; ~**schein** *m* medical insurance certificate; ~**schwester** *f* nurse; ~**versicherung** *f* health insurance; ~**wagen** *m* ambulance.

krankfeiern (*umg*) *vi* to be off sick; (*vortäuschend*) to skive (*BRIT*).

krankhaft *adj* diseased; (*Angst etc*) morbid; **sein Geiz ist schon ~** his meanness is almost pathological.

Krankheit *f* illness; disease; **nach langer schwerer ~** after a long serious illness.

Krankheitserreger *m* disease-causing agent.

kränklich ['krɛŋklıç] *adj* sickly.

krankmelden▲ *vr* to let one's boss *etc* know that one is ill; (*telefonisch*) to phone in sick;

(*bes MIL*) to report sick.

krankschreiben▲ *unreg vt* to give sb a medical certificate; (*bes MIL*) to put sb on the sick list.

Kränkung *f* insult, offence (*BRIT*), offense (*US*).

Kranz [krants] (**-es, -̈e**) *m* wreath, garland.

Kränzchen ['krɛntsçən] *nt* small wreath; (*fig: Kaffee~*) coffee circle.

Krapfen ['krapfən] (**-s, -**) *m* fritter; (*Berliner*) doughnut (*BRIT*), donut (*US*).

krass▲ [kras] *adj* crass; (*Unterschied*) extreme.

Krater ['kraːtər] (**-s, -**) *m* crater.

Kratzbürste ['kratsbʏrstə] *f* (*fig*) crosspatch.

Krätze ['krɛtsə] *f* (*MED*) scabies *sing*.

kratzen ['kratsən] *vt, vi* to scratch; (*ab~*): **etw von etw ~** to scrape sth off sth.

Kratzer (**-s, -**) *m* scratch; (*Werkzeug*) scraper.

Kraul [kraʊl] (**-s**) *nt* (*auch: ~schwimmen*) crawl; **k~en** *vi* (*schwimmen*) to do the crawl ♦ *vt* (*streicheln*) to tickle.

kraus [kraʊs] *adj* crinkly; (*Haar*) frizzy; (*Stirn*) wrinkled.

Krause ['kraʊzə] (**-, -n**) *f* frill, ruffle.

kräuseln ['krɔyzəln] *vt* (*Haar*) to make frizzy; (*Stoff*) to gather; (*Stirn*) to wrinkle ♦ *vr* (*Haar*) to go frizzy; (*Stirn*) to wrinkle; (*Wasser*) to ripple.

Kraut [kraʊt] (**-(e)s, Kräuter**) *nt* plant; (*Gewürz*) herb; (*Gemüse*) cabbage; **dagegen ist kein ~ gewachsen** (*fig*) there's nothing anyone can do about that; **ins ~ schießen** (*lit*) to run to seed; (*fig*) to get out of control; **wie ~ und Rüben** (*umg*) extremely untidy.

Kräutertee ['krɔytərteː] *m* herb tea.

Krawall [kra'val] (**-s, -e**) *m* row, uproar.

Krawatte [kra'vatə] (**-, -n**) *f* tie.

kreativ [krea'tiːf] *adj* creative.

Kreativität [kreativi'tɛːt] *f* creativity.

Kreatur [krea'tuːr] *f* creature.

Krebs [kreːps] (**-es, -e**) *m* crab; (*MED*) cancer; (*ASTROL*) Cancer; **~ erregend** carcinogenic; **k~krank** *adj* suffering from cancer; **k~krank sein** to have cancer; **~kranke(r)** *f(m)* cancer victim; (*Patient*) cancer patient; **k~rot** *adj* red as a lobster.

Kredit [kre'diːt] (**-(e)s, -e**) *m* credit; (*Darlehen*) loan; (*fig*) standing; **~drosselung** *f* credit squeeze; **k~fähig** *adj* creditworthy; **~grenze** *f* credit limit; **~hai** (*umg*) *m* loan-shark; **~karte** *f* credit card; **~konto** *nt* credit account; **~politik** *f* lending policy; **k~würdig** *adj* creditworthy; **~würdigkeit** *f* creditworthiness, credit status.

Kreide ['kraɪdə] (**-, -n**) *f* chalk; **bei jdm (tief) in der ~ stehen** to be (deep) in debt to sb; **k~bleich** *adj* as white as a sheet.

Kreis [kraɪs] (**-es, -e**) *m* circle; (*Stadt~ etc*) district; **im ~ gehen** (*lit, fig*) to go round in circles; (**weite**) **~e ziehen** (*fig*) to have

(wide) repercussions; **weite ~e der Bevölkerung** wide sections of the population; **eine Feier im kleinen ~e** a celebration for a few close friends and relatives.

kreischen ['kraɪʃən] *vi* to shriek, screech.

Kreisel ['kraɪzəl] (**-s, -**) *m* top; (*Verkehrs~*) roundabout (*BRIT*), traffic circle (*US*).

kreisen ['kraɪzən] *vi* to spin; (*fig: Gedanken, Gespräch*): **~ um** to revolve around.

Kreis- *zW:* **k~förmig** *adj* circular; **~lauf** *m* (*MED*) circulation; (*fig: der Natur etc*) cycle; **~laufkollaps** *m* circulatory collapse; **~laufstörungen** *pl* circulation trouble *sing*; **~säge** *f* circular saw.

Kreißsaal ['kraɪszaːl] *m* delivery room.

Kreisstadt *f* ≈ county town.

Kreisverkehr *m* roundabout (*BRIT*), traffic circle (*US*).

Krematorium [krema'toːriʊm] *nt* crematorium.

Kreml ['kreːml] (**-s**) *m*: **der ~** the Kremlin.

Krempe ['krɛmpə] (**-, -n**) *f* brim.

Krempel (**-s**) (*umg*) *m* rubbish.

krepieren [kre'piːrən] (*umg*) *vi* (*sterben*) to die, kick the bucket.

Krepp [krɛp] (**-s, -s** *od* **-e**) *m* crêpe.

Krepppapier▲ *nt* crêpe paper.

Kreppsohle *f* crêpe sole.

Kresse ['krɛsə] (**-, -n**) *f* cress.

Kreta ['kreːta] (**-s**) *nt* Crete.

Kreter(in) [kreːtər(ɪn)] (**-s, -**) *m(f)* Cretan.

kretisch *adj* Cretan.

kreuz [krɔyts] *adj*: **~ und quer** all over.

Kreuz (**-es, -e**) *nt* cross; (*ANAT*) small of the back; (*KARTEN*) clubs; (*MUS*) sharp; (*Autobahn~*) intersection; **zu ~e kriechen** (*fig*) to eat humble pie, eat crow (*US*); **jdn aufs ~ legen** to throw sb on his back; (*fig: umg*) to take sb for a ride.

kreuzen *vt* to cross ♦ *vr* to cross; (*Meinungen etc*) to clash ♦ *vi* (*NAUT*) to cruise; **die Arme ~** to fold one's arms.

Kreuzer (**-s, -**) *m* (*Schiff*) cruiser.

Kreuz- *zW:* **~fahrt** *f* cruise; **~feuer** *nt* (*fig*): **im ~feuer stehen** to be caught in the crossfire; **~gang** *m* cloisters *pl*.

kreuzigen *vt* to crucify.

Kreuzigung *f* crucifixion.

Kreuzotter *f* adder.

Kreuzschmerzen *pl* backache *sing*.

Kreuzung *f* (*Verkehrs~*) crossing, junction; (*Züchtung*) cross.

Kreuz- *zW:* **k~unglücklich** *adj* absolutely miserable; **~verhör** *nt* cross-examination; **ins ~verhör nehmen** to cross-examine; **~weg** *m* crossroads; (*REL*) Way of the Cross; **~worträtsel** *nt* crossword puzzle; **~zeichen** *nt* sign of the cross; **~zug** *m* crusade.

kribb(e)lig ['krɪb(ə)lɪç] (*umg*) *adj* fidgety;

(*kribbelnd*) tingly.

kribbeln ['krɪbəln] *vi* (*jucken*) to itch; (*prickeln*) to tingle.

kriechen ['kriːçən] *unreg vi* to crawl, creep; (*pej*) to grovel, crawl.

Kriecher (-s, -) *m* crawler.

kriecherisch *adj* grovelling (*BRIT*), groveling (*US*).

Kriechspur *f* crawler lane (*BRIT*).

Kriechtier *nt* reptile.

Krieg [kriːk] (-(e)s, -e) *m* war; ~ **führen (mit** *od* **gegen)** to wage war (on).

kriegen ['kriːgən] (*umg*) *vt* to get.

Krieger (-s, -) *m* warrior; ~**denkmal** *nt* war memorial; **k**~**isch** *adj* warlike.

Kriegführung *f* warfare.

Kriegs- *zW*: ~**beil** *nt*: **das** ~**beil begraben** (*fig*) to bury the hatchet; ~**bemalung** *f* war paint; ~**dienstverweigerer** *m* conscientious objector; ~**erklärung** *f* declaration of war; ~**fuß** *m*: **mit jdm/etw auf** ~**fuß stehen** to be at loggerheads with sb/not to get on with sth; ~**gefangene(r)** *f(m)* prisoner of war; ~**gefangenschaft** *f* captivity; ~**gericht** *nt* court-martial; ~**rat** *m* council of war; ~**recht** *nt* (*MIL*) martial law; ~**schauplatz** *m* theatre (*BRIT*) *od* theater (*US*) of war; ~**schiff** *nt* warship; ~**schuld** *f* war guilt; ~**verbrecher** *m* war criminal; ~**versehrte(r)** *f(m)* person disabled in the war; ~**zustand** *m* state of war.

Krim [krɪm] *f*: **die** ~ the Crimea.

Krimi ['kriːmi] (-s, -s) (*umg*) *m* thriller.

kriminal [krimi'naːl] *adj* criminal; **K**~**beamte(r)** *m* detective; **K**~**film** *m* crime thriller *od* movie (*bes US*).

Kriminalität [kriminali'tɛːt] *f* criminality.

Kriminalpolizei *f* ≈ Criminal Investigation Department (*BRIT*), Federal Bureau of Investigation (*US*).

Kriminalroman *m* detective story.

kriminell [kriˈmiˈnɛl] *adj* criminal.

Kriminelle(r) *f(m)* criminal.

Krimskrams ['krɪmskrams] (-es) (*umg*) *m* odds and ends *pl*.

Kringel ['krɪŋəl] (-s, -) *m* (*der Schrift*) squiggle; (*KOCH*) ring.

kringelig *adj*: **sich** ~ **lachen** (*umg*) to kill o.s. laughing.

Kripo ['kriːpo] (-, -s) *f abk* (= *Kriminalpolizei*) ≈ CID (*BRIT*), FBI (*US*).

Krippe ['krɪpə] (-, -n) *f* manger, crib; (*Kinder*~) crèche.

Krippenspiel *nt* nativity play.

Krippentod *m* cot death.

Krise ['kriːzə] (-, -n) *f* crisis.

kriseln *vi*: **es kriselt** there's a crisis looming, there is trouble brewing.

Krisen- *zW*: **k**~**fest** *adj* stable; ~**herd** *m* flash point; trouble spot; ~**stab** *m* action *od* crisis committee.

Kristall[1] [krɪs'tal] (-s, -e) *m* crystal.

Kristall[2] (-s) *nt* (*Glas*) crystal; ~**zucker** *m* refined sugar crystals *pl*.

Kriterium [kri'teːrium] *nt* criterion.

Kritik [kri'tiːk] *f* criticism; (*Zeitungs*~) review, write-up; **an jdm/etw** ~ **üben** to criticize sb/sth; **unter aller** ~ **sein** (*umg*) to be beneath contempt.

Kritiker(in) ['kriːtikər(ɪn)] (-s, -) *m(f)* critic.

kritiklos *adj* uncritical.

kritisch ['kriːtɪʃ] *adj* critical.

kritisieren [kriti'ziːrən] *vt, vi* to criticize.

kritteln ['krɪtəln] *vi* to find fault, carp.

kritzeln ['krɪtsəln] *vt, vi* to scribble, scrawl.

Kroate [kro'aːtə] (-n, -n) *m* Croat.

Kroatien [kro'aːtsiən] (-s) *nt* Croatia.

Kroatin *f* Croat.

kroatisch *adj* Croatian.

kroch *etc* [krɔx] *vb siehe* **kriechen**.

Krokodil [kroko'diːl] (-s, -e) *nt* crocodile.

Krokodilstränen *pl* crocodile tears *pl*.

Krokus ['kroːkus] (-, - *od* -se) *m* crocus.

Krone ['kroːnə] (-, -n) *f* crown; (*Baum*~) top; **einen in der** ~ **haben** (*umg*) to be tipsy.

krönen ['krøːnən] *vt* to crown.

Kron- *zW*: ~**korken** *m* bottle top; ~**leuchter** *m* chandelier; ~**prinz** *m* crown prince.

Krönung ['krøːnʊŋ] *f* coronation.

Kronzeuge *m* (*JUR*) person who turns Queen's/King's (*BRIT*) *od* State's (*US*) evidence; (*Hauptzeuge*) principal witness.

Kropf [krɔpf] (-(e)s, ⸚e) *m* (*MED*) goitre (*BRIT*), goiter (*US*); (*von Vogel*) crop.

Krösus ['krøːzus] (-ses, -se) *m*: **ich bin doch kein** ~ (*umg*) I'm not made of money.

Kröte ['krøːtə] (-, -n) *f* toad; **Kröten** *pl* (*umg*: *Geld*) pennies *pl*.

Krs. *abk* = **Kreis**.

Krücke ['krʏkə] (-, -n) *f* crutch.

Krug [kruːk] (-(e)s, ⸚e) *m* jug; (*Bier*~) mug.

Krümel ['kryːməl] (-s, -) *m* crumb.

krümeln *vt, vi* to crumble.

krumm [krum] *adj* (*lit, fig*) crooked; (*kurvig*) curved; **jdm etw** ~ **nehmen** (*umg*) to take sth amiss; **keinen Finger** ~ **machen** (*umg*) not to lift a finger; **ein** ~**es Ding drehen** (*umg*) to do something crooked; ~**beinig** *adj* bandy-legged.

krümmen ['krʏmən] *vt* to bend ♦ *vr* to bend, curve.

krummlachen (*umg*) *vr* to laugh o.s. silly; **sich krumm- und schieflachen** to fall about laughing.

Krümmung *f* bend, curve.

Krüppel ['krʏpəl] (-s, -) *m* cripple.

Kruste ['krustə] (-, -n) *f* crust.

Kruzifix [krutsi'fɪks] (-es, -e) *nt* crucifix.

Kt. *abk* = **Kanton**.

Kto. *abk* (= *Konto*) a/c.

Kuba ['kuːba] (**-s**) nt Cuba.
Kubaner(in) [ku'baːnər(ın)] (**-s, -**) m(f) Cuban.
kubanisch [ku'baːnıʃ] adj Cuban.
Kübel ['kyːbəl] (**-s, -**) m tub; (Eimer) pail.
Kubik- [ku'biːk] in zW cubic; ~**meter** m cubic metre (BRIT) od meter (US).
Küche ['kʏçə] (**-, -n**) f kitchen; (Kochen) cooking, cuisine.
Kuchen ['kuːxən] (**-s, -**) m cake; ~**blech** nt baking tray; ~**form** f baking tin (BRIT) od pan (US); ~**gabel** f pastry fork.
Küchen- zW: ~**gerät** nt kitchen utensil; (elektrisch) kitchen appliance; ~**herd** m cooker, stove; ~**maschine** f food processor; ~**messer** nt kitchen knife; ~**schabe** f cockroach; ~**schrank** m kitchen cabinet.
Kuchenteig m cake mixture.
Kuckuck ['kʊkʊk] (**-s, -e**) m cuckoo; (umg: Siegel des Gerichtsvollziehers) bailiff's seal (for distraint of goods); **das weiß der** ~ heaven (only) knows.
Kuckucksuhr f cuckoo clock.
Kuddelmuddel ['kʊdəlmʊdəl] (**-s**) (umg) m od nt mess.
Kufe ['kuːfə] (**-, -n**) f (Fass~) vat; (Schlitten~) runner; (AVIAT) skid.
Kugel ['kuːgəl] (**-, -n**) f ball; (MATH) sphere; (MIL) bullet; (Erd~) globe; (SPORT) shot; **eine ruhige** ~ **schieben** (umg) to have a cushy number; k~**förmig** adj spherical; ~**kopf** m (Schreibmaschine) golf ball; ~**kopfschreibmaschine** f golf-ball typewriter; ~**lager** nt ball bearing.
kugeln vt to roll; (SPORT) to bowl ♦ vr (vor Lachen) to double up.
Kugel- zW: k~**rund** adj (Gegenstand) round; (umg: Person) tubby; ~**schreiber** m ball-point (pen), Biro ®; k~**sicher** adj bulletproof; ~**stoßen** (**-s**) nt shot put.
Kuh [kuː] (**-, -̈e**) f cow; ~**dorf** (pej: umg) nt one-horse town; ~**handel** (pej: umg) m horse-trading; ~**haut** f: **das geht auf keine** ~**haut** (fig: umg) that's absolutely incredible.
kühl [kyːl] adj (lit, fig) cool; **K**~**anlage** f refrigeration plant.
Kühle (**-**) f coolness.
kühlen vt to cool.
Kühler (**-s, -**) m (AUT) radiator; ~**haube** f (AUT) bonnet (BRIT), hood (US).
Kühl- zW: ~**flüssigkeit** f coolant; ~**haus** nt cold-storage depot; ~**raum** m cold-storage chamber; ~**schrank** m refrigerator; ~**tasche** f cool bag; ~**truhe** f freezer.
Kühlung f cooling.
Kühlwagen m (EISENB, Lastwagen) refrigerator van.
Kühlwasser nt coolant.
kühn [kyːn] adj bold, daring; **K**~**heit** f boldness.
Kuhstall m cow-shed.

k. u. k. abk (= kaiserlich und königlich) imperial and royal.
Küken ['kyːkən] (**-s, -**) nt chicken; (umg: Nesthäkchen) baby of the family.
kulant [ku'lant] adj obliging.
Kulanz [ku'lants] f accommodating attitude, generousness.
Kuli ['kuːli] (**-s, -s**) m coolie; (umg: Kugelschreiber) Biro ®.
kulinarisch [kuli'naːrıʃ] adj culinary.
Kulisse [ku'lısə] (**-, -n**) f scene.
Kulissenschieber(in) m(f) stagehand.
Kulleraugen ['kʊləraʊgən] (umg) pl wide eyes pl.
kullern ['kʊlərn] vi to roll.
Kult [kʊlt] (**-(e)s, -e**) m worship, cult; **mit etw** ~ **treiben** to make a cult out of sth.
kultivieren [kʊlti'viːrən] vt to cultivate.
kultiviert adj cultivated, refined.
Kultstätte f place of worship.
Kultur [kʊl'tuːr] f culture; (Lebensform) civilization; (des Bodens) cultivation; ~**banause** (umg) m philistine, low-brow; ~**betrieb** m culture industry; ~**beutel** m toilet bag (BRIT), washbag.
kulturell [kʊltu'rɛl] adj cultural.
Kulturfilm m documentary film.
Kulturhauptstadt f: **Europäische** ~ European City of Culture.
Kulturteil m (von Zeitung) arts section.
Kultusminister ['kʊltʊsmınıstər] m minister of education and the arts.
Kümmel ['kʏməl] (**-s, -**) m caraway seed; (Branntwein) kümmel.
Kummer ['kʊmər] (**-s**) m grief, sorrow.
kümmerlich ['kʏmərlıç] adj miserable, wretched.
kümmern vr: **sich um jdn** ~ to look after sb ♦ vt to concern; **sich um etw** ~ to see to sth; **das kümmert mich nicht** that doesn't worry me.
Kumpan(in) [kʊm'paːn(ın)] (**-s, -e**) m(f) mate; (pej) accomplice.
Kumpel ['kʊmpəl] (**-s, -**) (umg) m mate.
kündbar ['kʏntbaːr] adj redeemable, recallable; (Vertrag) terminable.
Kunde¹ ['kʊndə] (**-n, -n**) m customer.
Kunde² ['kʊndə] (**-, -n**) f (Botschaft) news.
Kunden- zW: ~**beratung** f customer advisory service; ~**dienst** m after-sales service; ~**fang** (pej) m: **auf** ~**fang sein** to be touting for customers; ~**fänger** m tout (umg); ~**konto** nt charge account; ~**kreis** m customers pl, clientele; ~**werbung** f publicity (aimed at attracting custom or customers).
Kund- zW: ~**gabe** f announcement; k~**geben** unreg vt to announce; ~**gebung** f announcement; (Versammlung) rally.
kundig adj expert, experienced.
kündigen ['kʏndıgən] vi to give in one's notice

♦ *vt* to cancel; **jdm ~** to give sb his notice; **zum 1. April ~** to give one's notice for April 1st; (*Mieter*) to give notice for April 1st; (*bei Mitgliedschaft*) to cancel one's membership as of April 1st; **(jdm) die Stellung ~** to give (sb) notice; **sie hat ihm die Freundschaft gekündigt** she has broken off their friendship.

Kündigung *f* notice.

Kündigungsfrist *f* period of notice.

Kündigungsschutz *m* protection against wrongful dismissal.

Kundin *f* customer.

Kundschaft *f* customers *pl*, clientele.

Kundschafter (**-s, -**) *m* spy; (*MIL*) scout.

künftig ['kʏnftɪç] *adj* future ♦ *adv* in future.

Kunst [kʊnst] (**-, ̈e**) *f* (*auch SCH*) art; (*Können*) skill; **das ist doch keine ~** it's easy; **mit seiner ~ am Ende sein** to be at one's wits' end; **das ist eine brotlose ~** there's no money in that; **~akademie** *f* academy of art; **~druck** *m* art print; **~dünger** *m* artificial manure; **~erziehung** *f* (*SCH*) art; **~faser** *f* synthetic fibre (*BRIT*) *od* fiber (*US*); **~fehler** *m* professional error; (*weniger ernst*) slip; **~fertigkeit** *f* skilfulness (*BRIT*), skillfulness (*US*); **~flieger** *m* stunt flyer; **k~gerecht** *adj* skilful (*BRIT*), skillful (*US*); **~geschichte** *f* history of art; **~gewerbe** *nt* arts and crafts *pl*; **~griff** *m* trick, knack; **~händler** *m* art dealer; **~harz** *nt* artificial resin; **~leder** *nt* artificial leather.

Künstler(in) ['kʏnstlər(ɪn)] (**-s, -**) *m(f)* artist; **k~isch** *adj* artistic; **~name** *m* pseudonym; (*von Schauspieler*) stage name; **~pech** (*umg*) *nt* hard luck.

künstlich ['kʏnstlɪç] *adj* artificial; **~e Intelligenz** (*COMPUT*) artificial intelligence; **sich ~ aufregen** (*umg*) to get all worked up about nothing.

Kunst- *zW*: **~sammler** *m* art collector; **~seide** *f* artificial silk; **~stoff** *m* synthetic material; **~stopfen** (**-s**) *nt* invisible mending; **~stück** *nt* trick; **das ist kein ~stück** (*fig*) there's nothing to it; **~turnen** *nt* gymnastics *sing*; **k~voll** *adj* artistic; **~werk** *nt* work of art.

kunterbunt ['kʊntərbʊnt] *adj* higgledy-piggledy.

Kupee [ku'pe:] (**-s, -s**) *nt* = **Coupé.**

Kupfer ['kʊpfər] (**-s, -**) *nt* copper; **~geld** *nt* coppers *pl*.

kupfern *adj* copper ♦ *vt* (*fig: umg*) to plagiarize, copy, imitate.

Kupferstich *m* copperplate engraving.

Kupon [ku'põ:, ku'pɔŋ] (**-s, -s**) *m* coupon, voucher; (*Stoff~*) length of cloth.

Kuppe ['kʊpə] (**-, -n**) *f* (*Berg~*) top; (*Finger~*) tip.

Kuppel (**-, -n**) *f* cupola, dome.

Kuppelei [kʊpə'laɪ] *f* (*JUR*) procuring.

kuppeln *vi* (*JUR*) to procure; (*AUT*) to operate *od* use the clutch ♦ *vt* to join.

Kuppler ['kʊplər] (**-s, -**) *m* procurer; **~in** *f* procuress.

Kupplung *f* (*auch TECH*) coupling; (*AUT etc*) clutch; **die ~ (durch)treten** to disengage the clutch.

Kur [ku:r] (**-, -en**) *f* (*im Kurort*) (health) cure, (course of) treatment; (*Schlankheitskur*) diet; **eine ~ machen** to take a cure (in a health resort).

Kür [ky:r] (**-, -en**) *f* (*SPORT*) free exercises *pl*.

Kuratorium [kura'to:riʊm] *nt* (*Vereinigung*) committee.

Kurbel ['kʊrbəl] (**-, -n**) *f* crank, winder; (*AUT*) starting handle; **~welle** *f* crankshaft.

Kürbis ['kʏrbɪs] (**-ses, -se**) *m* pumpkin; (*exotisch*) gourd.

Kurde ['kʊrdə] (**-n, -n**) *m*, **Kurdin** *f* Kurd.

Kurfürst ['ku:rfʏrst] *m* Elector, electoral prince.

Kurgast *m* visitor (to a health resort).

Kurier [ku'ri:r] (**-s, -e**) *m* courier, messenger.

kurieren [ku'ri:rən] *vt* to cure.

kurios [kuri'o:s] *adj* curious, odd.

Kuriosität [kuriozi'tɛːt] *f* curiosity.

Kur- *zW*: **~konzert** *nt* concert (*at a health resort*); **~ort** *m* health resort; **~pfuscher** *m* quack.

Kurs [kʊrs] (**-es, -e**) *m* course; (*FIN*) rate; **hoch im ~ stehen** (*fig*) to be highly thought of; **einen ~ besuchen** *od* **mitmachen** to attend a class; **harter/weicher ~** (*POL*) hard/soft line; **~änderung** *f* (*lit, fig*) change of course; **~buch** *nt* timetable.

Kürschner(in) ['kʏrʃnər(ɪn)] (**-s, -**) *m(f)* furrier.

kursieren [kʊr'zi:rən] *vi* to circulate.

kursiv *adv* in italics.

Kursnotierung *f* quotation.

Kursus ['kʊrzʊs] (**-, Kurse**) *m* course.

Kurswagen *m* (*EISENB*) through carriage.

Kurswert *m* (*FIN*) market value.

Kurtaxe *f* spa tax (*paid by visitors*).

Kurve ['kʊrvə] (**-, -n**) *f* curve; (*Straßen~*) bend; (*statistisch, Fieber~ etc*) graph; **die ~ nicht kriegen** (*umg*) to not get around to it.

kurvenreich *adj*: **„~e Strecke"** "bends".

kurvig *adj* (*Straße*) bendy.

kurz [kʊrts] *adj* short ♦ *adv*: **~ und bündig** concisely; **zu ~ kommen** to come off badly; **den Kürzeren ziehen** to get the worst of it; **~ und gut** in short; **über ~ oder lang** sooner or later; **eine Sache ~ abtun** to dismiss sth out of hand; **sich ~ fassen** to be brief; **~ gefasst** concise; **~ halten** to keep short; **~ treten** (*fig: umg*) to go easy; **darf ich mal ~ stören?** could I just interrupt for a moment?

Kurzarbeit *f* short-time work.

kurzärm(e)lig *adj* short-sleeved.
kurzatmig *adj* (*fig*) feeble, lame; (*MED*)
short-winded.
Kürze ['kyrtsə] (-, -n) *f* shortness, brevity.
kürzen *vt* to cut short; (*in der Länge*) to
shorten; (*Gehalt*) to reduce.
kurzerhand ['kurtsər'hant] *adv* without
further ado; (*entlassen*) on the spot.
kurz- *zW*: **K~fassung** *f* shortened version;
~fristig *adj* short-term; **~fristige
Verbindlichkeiten** current liabilities *pl*;
K~geschichte *f* short story; **~lebig** *adj* short-
lived.
kürzlich ['kyrtslıç] *adv* lately, recently.
Kurz- *zW*: **~meldung** *f* news flash; **~parker** *m*
short-stay parker; **~schluss▲** *m* (*ELEK*)
short circuit; **~schlusshandlung▲** *f* (*fig*)
rash action; **~schrift** *f* shorthand; **k~sichtig**
adj short-sighted; **~strecken-** *in zW* short-
range; **~streckenläufer(in)** *m(f)* sprinter;
k~um *adv* in a word.
Kürzung *f* cutback.
Kurz- *zW*: **~waren** *pl* haberdashery (*BRIT*),
notions *pl* (*US*); **~welle** *f* short wave
kuschelig *adj* cuddly.
kuscheln ['kuʃəln] *vr* to snuggle up.
kuschen ['kuʃən] *vi, vr* (*Hund etc*) to get down;
(*fig*) to knuckle under.
Kusine [ku'zi:nə] *f* cousin.
Kuss▲ [kus] (-es, ¨e) *m* kiss.
küssen ['kysən] *vt, vr* to kiss.
Küste ['kystə] (-, -n) *f* coast, shore.
Küsten- *zW*: **~gewässer** *pl* coastal waters *pl*;
~schiff *nt* coaster; **~wache** *f* coastguard
(station).
Küster ['kystər] (-s, -) *m* sexton, verger.
Kutsche ['kutʃə] (-, -n) *f* coach, carriage.
Kutscher (-s, -) *m* coachman.
kutschieren [ku'tʃiːrən] *vi*: **durch die Gegend
~** (*umg*) to drive around.
Kutte ['kutə] (-, -n) *f* cowl.
Kuvert [ku'vɛrt] (-s, -e *od* -s) *nt* envelope;
(*Gedeck*) cover.
KV *abk* (*MUS*: = *Köchelverzeichnis*): **~ 280** K.
(number) 280.
KW *abk* (= *Kurzwelle*) SW.
kW *abk* (= *Kilowatt*) kW.
Kybernetik [kybɛr'neːtɪk] *f* cybernetics *sing*.
kybernetisch [kybɛr'neːtɪʃ] *adj* cybernetic.
KZ (-s, -s) *nt abk* = **Konzentrationslager**.

L, l

L, l¹ [ɛl] *nt* L, l; **~ wie Ludwig** ≈ L for Lucy, L
for Love (*US*).
l² [ɛl] *abk* (= *Liter*) l.
laben ['laːbən] *vt* to refresh ♦ *vr* to refresh
o.s.; (*fig*): **sich an etw** *dat* **~** to relish sth.
labern ['laːbərn] (*umg*) *vi* to prattle (on) ♦ *vt* to
talk.
labil [la'biːl] *adj* (*physisch: Gesundheit*) delicate;
(: *Kreislauf*) poor; (*psychisch*) unstable.
Labor [la'boːr] (-s, -e *od* -s) *nt* lab(oratory).
Laborant(in) [labo'rant(ɪn)] *m(f)* lab(oratory)
assistant.
Laboratorium [labora'toːriʊm] *nt*
lab(oratory).
Labyrinth [laby'rɪnt] (-s, -e) *nt* labyrinth.
Lache ['laxə] (-, -n) *f* (*Wasser*) pool, puddle;
(*umg: Gelächter*) laugh.
lächeln ['lɛçəln] *vi* to smile; **L~** (-s) *nt* smile.
lachen ['laxən] *vi* to laugh; **mir ist nicht zum
L~** (**zumute** *od* **zu Mute**) I'm in no laughing
mood; **dass ich nicht lache!** (*umg*) don't
make me laugh!; **das wäre doch gelacht** it
would be ridiculous; **L~** *nt*: **dir wird das
L~ schon noch vergehen!** you'll soon be
laughing on the other side of your face.
Lacher (-s, -) *m*: **die ~ auf seiner Seite haben**
to have the last laugh.
lächerlich ['lɛçərlıç] *adj* ridiculous; **L~keit** *f*
absurdity.
Lach- *zW*: **~gas** *nt* laughing gas; **l~haft** *adj*
laughable; **~krampf** *m*: **einen ~krampf
bekommen** to go into fits of laughter.
Lachs [laks] (-es, -e) *m* salmon.
Lachsalve ['laxzalvə] *f* burst *od* roar of
laughter.
Lachsschinken *m* smoked, rolled fillet of
ham.
Lack [lak] (-(e)s, -e) *m* lacquer, varnish; (*von
Auto*) paint.
lackieren [la'kiːrən] *vt* to varnish; (*Auto*) to
spray.
Lackierer [la'kiːrər] (-s, -) *m* varnisher.
Lackleder *nt* patent leather.
Lackmus ['lakmus] (-) *m od nt* litmus.
Lade ['laːdə] (-, -n) *f* box, chest; **~baum** *m*
derrick; **~fähigkeit** *f* load capacity; **~fläche** *f*
load area; **~gewicht** *nt* tonnage; **~hemmung**
f: **das Gewehr hat ~hemmung** the gun is
jammed.
Laden ['laːdən] (-s, ¨) *m* shop; (*Fenster~*)

shutter; (*umg*: *Betrieb*) outfit; **der ~ läuft** (*umg*) business is good.

laden ['laːdən] *unreg vt* (*Lasten, COMPUT*) to load; (*JUR*) to summon; (*ein~*) to invite; **eine schwere Schuld auf sich** *akk* **~** to place o.s. under a heavy burden of guilt.

Laden- *zW:* **~aufsicht** *f* shopwalker (*BRIT*), floorwalker (*US*); **~besitzer** *m* shopkeeper; **~dieb** *m* shoplifter; **~diebstahl** *m* shoplifting; **~hüter** (**-s, -**) *m* unsaleable item; **~preis** *m* retail price; **~schluss▲** *m*, **~schlusszeit▲** *f* closing time; **~tisch** *m* counter.

Laderampe *f* loading ramp.

Laderaum *m* (*NAUT*) hold.

lädieren [lɛˈdiːrən] *vt* to damage.

lädt [lɛːt] *vb siehe* **laden**.

Ladung ['laːdʊŋ] *f* (*Last*) cargo, load; (*Beladen*) loading; (*JUR*) summons; (*Ein~*) invitation; (*Spreng~*) charge.

lag *etc* [laːk] *vb siehe* **liegen**.

Lage ['laːgə] (**-, -n**) *f* position, situation; (*Schicht*) layer; **in der ~ sein** to be in a position; **eine gute/ruhige ~ haben** to be in a good/peaceful location; **Herr der ~ sein** to be in control of the situation; **~bericht** *m* report; (*MIL*) situation report; **~beurteilung** *f* situation assessment.

lagenweise *adv* in layers.

Lager ['laːgər] (**-s, -**) *nt* camp; (*COMM*) warehouse; (*Schlaf~*) bed; (*von Tier*) lair; (*TECH*) bearing; **etw auf ~ haben** to have sth in stock; **~arbeiter** *m* storehand; **~bestand** *m* stocks *pl*; **~feuer** *nt* camp fire; **~geld** *nt* storage (charges *pl*); **~haus** *nt* warehouse, store.

Lagerist(in) [laːgəˈrɪst(ɪn)] *m(f)* storeman, storewoman.

lagern ['laːgərn] *vi* (*Dinge*) to be stored; (*Menschen*) to camp; (*auch vr: rasten*) to lie down ♦ *vt* to store; (*betten*) to lay down; (*Maschine*) to bed.

Lager- *zW:* **~raum** *m* storeroom; (*in Geschäft*) stockroom; **~schuppen** *m* store shed; **~stätte** *f* resting place.

Lagerung *f* storage.

Lagune [laˈguːnə] (**-, -n**) *f* lagoon.

lahm [laːm] *adj* lame; (*umg*: *langsam, langweilig*) dreary, dull; (*Geschäftsgang*) slow, sluggish; **eine ~e Ente sein** (*umg*) to have no zip; **~ legen** to paralyse (*BRIT*), paralyze (*US*); **~arschig** ['laːm|arʃɪç] (*umg*) *adj* bloody *od* damn (*!*) slow.

lahmen *vi* to be lame, limp.

lähmen ['lɛːmən] *vt* to paralyse (*BRIT*), paralyze (*US*).

Lähmung *f* paralysis.

Lahn [laːn] (**-**) *f* (*Fluss*) Lahn.

Laib [laɪp] (**-s, -e**) *m* loaf.

Laich [laɪç] (**-(e)s, -e**) *m* spawn; **l~en** *vi* to spawn.

Laie [ˈlaɪə] (**-n, -n**) *m* layman; (*fig, THEAT*) amateur.

laienhaft *adj* amateurish.

Lakai [laˈkaɪ] (**-en, -en**) *m* lackey.

Laken ['laːkən] (**-s, -**) *nt* sheet.

Lakritze [laˈkrɪtsə] (**-, -n**) *f* liquorice.

lala ['laˈla] (*umg*) *adv*: **so ~** so-so, not too bad.

lallen ['lalən] *vt, vi* to slur; (*Baby*) to babble.

Lama ['laːma] (**-s, -s**) *nt* llama.

Lamelle [laˈmɛlə] *f* lamella; (*ELEK*) lamina; (*TECH*) plate.

lamentieren [lamɛnˈtiːrən] *vi* to lament.

Lametta [laˈmɛta] (**-s**) *nt* tinsel.

Lamm [lam] (**-(e)s, ̈er**) *nt* lamb; **~fell** *nt* lambskin; **l~fromm** *adj* like a lamb; **~wolle** *f* lambswool.

Lampe ['lampə] (**-, -n**) *f* lamp.

Lampenfieber *nt* stage fright.

Lampenschirm *m* lampshade.

Lampion [lampiˈõː] (**-s, -s**) *m* Chinese lantern.

Land [lant] (**-(e)s, ̈er**) *nt* land; (*Nation, nicht Stadt*) country; (*Bundes~*) state; **auf dem ~(e)** in the country; **an ~ gehen** to go ashore; **endlich sehe ich ~** (*fig*) at last I can see the light at the end of the tunnel; **einen Auftrag an ~ ziehen** (*umg*) to land an order; **aus aller Herren Länder** from all over the world; *siehe auch* **hierzulande**.

LAND

A **Land** (*plural* **Länder**) *is a member state of the* **BRD**. *There are 16* **Länder**, *namely Baden-Württemberg, Bayern, Berlin, Brandenburg, Bremen, Hamburg, Hessen, Mecklenburg-Vorpommern, Niedersachsen, Nordrhein-Westfalen, Rheinland-Pfalz, Saarland, Sachsen, Sachsen-Anhalt, Schleswig-Holstein and Thüringen. Each* **Land** *has its own parliament and constitution.*

Landarbeiter *m* farm *od* agricultural worker.

Landbesitz *m* landed property.

Landbesitzer *m* landowner.

Landebahn *f* runway.

Landeerlaubnis *f* permission to land.

landeinwärts ['landˈ|aɪnvɛrts] *adv* inland.

landen ['landən] *vt, vi* to land; **mit deinen Komplimenten kannst du bei mir nicht ~** your compliments won't get you anywhere with me.

Ländereien [lɛndəˈraɪən] *pl* estates *pl*.

Länderspiel *nt* international (match).

Landes- *zW:* **~farben** *pl* national colours *pl* (*BRIT*) *od* colors *pl* (*US*); **~grenze** *f* (national) frontier; (*von Bundesland*) state boundary; **~innere(s)** *nt* inland region; **~kind** *nt* native *of a German state*; **~kunde** *f* regional studies *pl*; **~tracht** *f* national costume;

l~üblich *adj* customary; ~**verrat** *m* high treason; ~**verweisung** *f* banishment; ~**währung** *f* national currency; l~**weit** *adj* countrywide.

Landeverbot *nt* refusal of permission to land.

Land- *zW:* ~**flucht** *f* emigration to the cities; ~**gut** *nt* estate; ~**haus** *nt* country house; ~**karte** *f* map; ~**kreis** *m* administrative region; l~**läufig** *adj* customary.

ländlich ['lɛntlɪç] *adj* rural.

Land- *zW:* ~**rat** *m head of administration of a Landkreis;* ~**schaft** *f* countryside; (*KUNST*) landscape; **die politische** ~**schaft** the political scene; l~**schaftlich** *adj* scenic; (*Besonderheiten*) regional.

Landsmann (-(e)s, *pl* -**leute**) *m* compatriot, fellow countryman.

Landsmännin *f* compatriot, fellow countrywoman.

Land- *zW:* ~**straße** *f* country road; ~**streicher** (-**s**, -) *m* tramp; ~**strich** *m* region; ~**tag** *m* (*POL*) regional parliament.

Landung ['landʊŋ] *f* landing.

Landungs- *zW:* ~**boot** *nt* landing craft; ~**brücke** *f* jetty, pier; ~**stelle** *f* landing place.

Landurlaub *m* shore leave.

Landvermesser *m* surveyor.

landw. *abk* (= *landwirtschaftlich*) agricultural.

Land- *zW:* ~**wirt** *m* farmer; ~**wirtschaft** *f* agriculture; ~**wirtschaft betreiben** to farm; ~**zunge** *f* spit.

lang [laŋ] *adj* long; (*umg: Mensch*) tall ♦ *adv:* ~ **anhaltender Beifall** prolonged applause; ~ **ersehnt** longed-for; **hier wird mir die Zeit nicht** ~ I won't get bored here; **er machte ein** ~**es Gesicht** his face fell; ~ **und breit** at great length; ~**atmig** *adj* long-winded.

lange *adv* for a long time; (*dauern, brauchen*) a long time; ~ **nicht so** ... not nearly as ...; **wenn der das schafft, kannst du das schon** ~ if he can do it, you can do it easily.

Länge ['lɛŋə] (-, -**n**) *f* length; (*GEOG*) longitude; **etw der** ~ **nach falten** to fold sth lengthways; **etw in die** ~ **ziehen** to drag sth out (*umg*); **der** ~ **nach hinfallen** to fall flat (on one's face).

langen ['laŋən] *vi* (*ausreichen*) to do, suffice; (*fassen*): ~ **nach** to reach for; **es langt mir** I've had enough; **jdm eine** ~ (*umg*) to give sb a clip on the ear.

Längengrad *m* longitude.

Längenmaß *nt* linear measure.

Langeweile *f* boredom.

lang- *zW:* ~**fristig** *adj* long-term ♦ *adv* in the long term; (*planen*) for the long term; ~**fristige Verbindlichkeiten** long-term liabilities *pl*; ~**jährig** *adj* (*Freundschaft, Gewohnheit*) long-standing; (*Erfahrung, Verhandlungen*) many years of; (*Mitarbeiter*)

of many years' standing; **L**~**lauf** *m* (*SKI*) cross-country skiing; ~**lebig** *adj* long-lived; ~**lebige Gebrauchsgüter** consumer durables *pl.*

länglich *adj* longish.

Langmut *f* forbearance, patience.

langmütig *adj* forbearing.

längs [lɛŋs] *präp* (+*gen od dat*) along ♦ *adv* lengthways.

langsam *adj* slow; **immer schön** ~! (*umg*) easy does it!; **ich muss jetzt** ~ **gehen** I must be getting on my way; ~ (**aber sicher**) **reicht es mir** I've just about had enough; **L**~**keit** *f* slowness.

Langschläfer *m* late riser.

Langspielplatte *f* long-playing record.

längsseit(s) *adv* alongside ♦ *präp* +*gen* alongside.

längst [lɛŋst] *adv:* **das ist** ~ **fertig** that was finished a long time ago, that has been finished for a long time.

längste(r, s) *adj* longest.

Langstrecken- *in zW* long-distance; ~**flugzeug** *nt* long-range aircraft.

Languste [laŋ'gʊstə] (-, -**n**) *f* crayfish, crawfish (*US*).

lang- *zW:* ~**weilen** *vt untr* to bore ♦ *vr untr* to be *od* get bored; **L**~**weiler** (-**s**, -) *m* bore; ~**weilig** *adj* boring, tedious; **L**~**welle** *f* long wave; ~**wierig** *adj* lengthy, long-drawn-out.

Lanze ['lantsə] (-, -**n**) *f* lance.

Lanzette [lan'tsɛtə] *f* lancet.

Laos ['laːɔs] (-) *nt* Laos.

Laote [la'oːtə] (-**n**, -**n**,) *m*, **Laotin** *f* Laotian.

laotisch [la'oːtɪʃ] *adj* Laotian.

lapidar [lapi'daːr] *adj* terse, pithy.

Lappalie [la'paːliə] *f* trifle.

Lappe ['lapə] (-**n**, -**n**) *m* Lapp, Laplander.

Lappen (-**s**, -) *m* cloth, rag; (*ANAT*) lobe; **jdm durch die** ~ **gehen** (*umg*) to slip through sb's fingers.

läppern ['lɛpərn] (*umg*) *vr unpers:* **es läppert sich zusammen** it (all) mounts up.

Lappin ['lapɪn] *f* Lapp, Laplander.

läppisch ['lɛpɪʃ] *adj* foolish.

Lappland ['laplant] (-**s**) *nt* Lapland.

Lappländer(in) ['laplɛndər(ɪn)] (-**s**, -) *m(f)* Lapp, Laplander.

lappländisch *adj* Lapp.

Lapsus ['lapsʊs] (-, -) *m* slip.

Laptop ['lɛptɔp] (-**s**, -**s**) *m* laptop.

Lärche ['lɛrçə] (-, -**n**) *f* larch.

Lärm [lɛrm] (-(e)s) *m* noise; ~**belästigung** *f* noise nuisance; l~**en** *vi* to be noisy, make a noise.

Larve ['larfə] (-, -**n**) *f* mask; (*BIOL*) larva.

las *etc* [laːs] *vb siehe* **lesen**.

Lasagne [la'zanjə] *pl* lasagne *sing.*

lasch [laʃ] *adj* slack; (*Geschmack*) tasteless.

Lasche ['laʃə] (-, -**n**) *f* (*Schuh*~) tongue;

(*EISENB*) fishplate.
Laser ['le:zər] **(-s, -)** *m* laser; **~drucker** *m* laser printer.

SCHLÜSSELWORT

lassen ['lasən] (*pt* **ließ**, *pp* **gelassen** *od (als Hilfsverb)* **lassen**) *vt* **1** (*unter~*) to stop; (*momentan*) to leave; **lass das (sein)!** don't (do it)!; (*hör auf*) stop it!; **lass mich!** leave me alone!; ~ **wir das!** let's leave it; **er kann das Trinken nicht** ~ he can't stop drinking; **tu, was du nicht ~ kannst!** if you must, you must!
2 (*zurück~*) to leave; **etw ~, wie es ist** to leave sth (just) as it is.
3 (*erlauben*) to let, allow; **lass ihn doch** let him; **jdn ins Haus** ~ to let sb into the house; **das muss man ihr** ~ (*zugestehen*) you've got to grant her that.
♦ *vi*: **lass mal, ich mache das schon** leave it, I'll do it.
♦ *Hilfsverb* **1** (*veran~*): **etw machen** ~ to have *od* get sth done; **jdn etw machen** ~ to get sb to do sth; (*durch Befehl usw*) to make sb do sth; **er ließ mich warten** he kept me waiting; **mein Vater wollte mich studieren** ~ my father wanted me to study; **sich** *dat* **etw schicken** ~ to have sth sent (to one).
2 (*zu~*): **jdn etw wissen** ~ to let sb know sth; **das Licht brennen** ~ to leave the light on; **einen Bart wachsen** ~ to grow a beard; **lass es dir gut gehen!** take care of yourself!
3: lass uns gehen let's go.
♦ *vr*: **das lässt sich machen** that can be done; **es lässt sich schwer sagen** it's difficult to say.

lässig ['lɛsɪç] *adj* casual; **L~keit** *f* casualness.
lässlich▲ ['lɛslɪç] *adj* pardonable, venial.
lässt▲ [lɛst] *vb siehe* **lassen**.
Last [last] **(-, -en)** *f* load; (*Trag~*) burden; (*NAUT, AVIAT*) cargo; (*meist pl*: *Gebühr*) charge; **jdm zur ~ fallen** to be a burden to sb; **~auto** *nt* lorry (*BRIT*), truck.
lasten *vi*: ~ **auf** *+dat* to weigh on.
Lastenaufzug *m* hoist, goods lift (*BRIT*) *od* elevator (*US*).
Lastenausgleichsgesetz *nt law on financial compensation for losses suffered in WWII*.
Laster ['lastər] **(-s, -)** *nt* vice ♦ *m* (*umg*) lorry (*BRIT*), truck.
Lästerer ['lɛstərər] **(-s, -)** *m* mocker; (*Gottes~*) blasphemer.
lasterhaft *adj* immoral.
lästerlich *adj* scandalous.
lästern ['lɛstərn] *vt, vi* (*Gott*) to blaspheme; (*schlecht sprechen*) to mock.
Lästerung *f* jibe; (*Gottes~*) blasphemy.
lästig ['lɛstɪç] *adj* troublesome, tiresome; **(jdm) ~ werden** to become a nuisance (to sb); (*zum Ärgernis werden*) to get annoying (to sb).
Last- *zW*: **~kahn** *m* barge; **~kraftwagen** *m* heavy goods vehicle; **~schrift** *f* debiting; (*Eintrag*) debit item; **~tier** *nt* beast of burden; **~träger** *m* porter; **~wagen** *m* lorry (*BRIT*), truck; **~zug** *m* truck and trailer.
Latein [la'taɪn] **(-s)** *nt* Latin; **mit seinem ~ am Ende sein** (*fig*) to be stumped (*umg*); **~amerika** *nt* Latin America; **l~amerikanisch** *adj* Latin-American; **l~isch** *adj* Latin.
latent [la'tɛnt] *adj* latent.
Laterne [la'tɛrnə] **(-, -n)** *f* lantern; (*Straßen~*) lamp, light.
Laternenpfahl *m* lamppost.
Latinum [la'ti:nʊm] **(-s)** *nt*: **kleines/großes ~** ≈ Latin O-/A-level exams (*BRIT*).
Latrine [la'tri:nə] *f* latrine.
Latsche ['latʃə] **(-, -n)** *f* dwarf pine.
Latschen ['la:tʃən] (*umg*) *m* (*Hausschuh*) slipper; (*pej*: *Schuh*) worn-out shoe.
latschen (*umg*) *vi* (*gehen*) to wander, go; (*lässig*) to slouch.
Latte ['latə] **(-, -n)** *f* lath; (*SPORT*) goalpost; (*quer*) crossbar.
Lattenzaun *m* lattice fence.
Latz [lats] **(-es, ¨-e)** *m* bib; (*Hosen~*) front flap.
Lätzchen ['lɛtsçən] *nt* bib.
Latzhose *f* dungarees *pl*.
lau [laʊ] *adj* (*Nacht*) balmy; (*Wasser*) lukewarm; (*fig*: *Haltung*) half-hearted.
Laub [laʊp] **(-(e)s)** *nt* foliage; **~baum** *m* deciduous tree.
Laube ['laʊbə] **(-, -n)** *f* arbour (*BRIT*), arbor (*US*); (*Gartenhäuschen*) summerhouse.
Laub- *zW*: **~frosch** *m* tree frog; **~säge** *f* fretsaw; **~wald** *m* deciduous forest.
Lauch [laʊx] **(-(e)s, -e)** *m* leek.
Lauer ['laʊər] *f*: **auf der ~ sein** *od* **liegen** to lie in wait.
lauern *vi* to lie in wait; (*Gefahr*) to lurk.
Lauf [laʊf] **(-(e)s, Läufe)** *m* run; (*Wett~*) race; (*Entwicklung, ASTRON*) course; (*Gewehr~*) barrel; **im ~e des Gesprächs** during the conversation; **sie ließ ihren Gefühlen freien ~** she gave way to her feelings; **einer Sache** *dat* **ihren ~ lassen** to let sth take its course; **~bahn** *f* career; **eine ~bahn einschlagen** to embark on a career; **~bursche** *m* errand boy.
laufen ['laʊfən] *unreg vi* to run; (*umg*: *gehen*) to walk; (*Uhr*) to go; (*funktionieren*) to work; (*Elektrogerät*: *eingeschaltet sein*) to be on; (*gezeigt werden*: *Film, Stück*) to be on; (*Bewerbung, Antrag*) to be under consideration ♦ *vt* to run; **es lief mir eiskalt über den Rücken** a chill ran up my spine; **ihm läuft die Nase** he's got a runny nose; ~ **lassen** (*Person*) to let go; **die Dinge ~ lassen** to let things slide; **die Sache ist gelaufen** (*umg*) it's in the bag; **das Auto läuft**

auf meinen **Namen** the car is in my name;
Ski/Schlittschuh/Rollschuh etc ~ to ski/
skate/rollerskate etc.
laufend adj running; (Monat, Ausgaben)
current; **auf dem L~en sein/halten** to be/
keep up to date; **am ~en Band** (fig) continuously; **~e Nummer** serial number; (von
Konto) number; **~e Kosten** running costs pl.
Läufer ['lɔyfər] (-s, -) m (Teppich, SPORT)
runner; (Fußball) half-back; (Schach) bishop.
Lauferei [laufə'raɪ] (umg) f running about.
Läuferin f (SPORT) runner.
Lauf- zW: **l~fähig** adj (COMPUT): **das
Programm is unter Windows l~fähig** the
program can be run under Windows; **~feuer**
nt: **sich wie ein ~feuer verbreiten** to spread
like wildfire; **~kundschaft** f passing trade;
~masche f run, ladder (BRIT); **~pass▲** m:
jdm den ~pass geben (umg) to give sb his/
her marching orders; **~schritt** m: **im
~schritt** at a run; **~stall** m playpen; **~steg** m
catwalk.
läuft [lɔyft] vb siehe **laufen**.
Lauf- zW: **~werk** nt running gear; (COMPUT)
drive; **~zeit** f (von Wechsel, Vertrag) period of
validity; (von Maschine) life; **~zettel** m
circular.
Lauge ['laugə] (-, -n) f soapy water; (CHEM)
alkaline solution.
Laune ['launə] (-, -n) f mood, humour (BRIT),
humor (US); (Einfall) caprice; (schlechte ~)
temper.
launenhaft adj capricious, changeable.
launisch adj moody.
Laus [laus] (-, Läuse) f louse; **ihm ist (wohl)
eine ~ über die Leber gelaufen** (umg)
something's biting him; **~bub** m rascal, imp.
Lauschangriff m: ~ **(gegen)** bugging
operation (on).
lauschen ['lauʃən] vi to eavesdrop, listen in.
Lauscher(in) (-s, -) m(f) eavesdropper.
lauschig ['lauʃɪç] adj snug.
Lausejunge (umg) m little devil;
(wohlwollend) rascal.
lausen ['lauzən] vt to delouse.
lausig ['lauzɪç] (umg) adj lousy; (Kälte)
perishing ♦ adv awfully.
laut [laut] adj loud ♦ adv loudly; (lesen) aloud
♦ präp (+gen od dat) according to.
Laut (-(e)s, -e) m sound.
Laute ['lautə] (-, -n) f lute.
lauten ['lautən] vi to say; (Urteil) to be.
läuten ['lɔytən] vt, vi to ring, sound; **er hat
davon (etwas) ~ hören** (umg) he has heard
something about it.
lauter ['lautər] adj (Wasser) clear, pure;
(Wahrheit, Charakter) honest ♦ adj inv (Freude,
Dummheit etc) sheer ♦ adv (nur) nothing but,
only; **L~keit** f purity; honesty, integrity.
läutern ['lɔytərn] vt to purify.

laut- zW: **~hals** adv at the top of one's voice;
~los adj noiseless, silent; **~malend** adj
onomatopoeic; **L~schrift** f phonetics pl;
L~sprecher m loudspeaker;
L~sprecheranlage f: **öffentliche
L~sprecheranlage** public-address od PA
system; **L~sprecherwagen** m loudspeaker
van; **~stark** adj vociferous; **L~stärke** f
(RUNDF) volume.
lauwarm ['lauvarm] adj (lit, fig) lukewarm.
Lava ['la:va] (-, **Laven**) f lava.
Lavendel [la'vɛndəl] (-s, -) m lavender.
Lawine [la'vi:nə] f avalanche.
Lawinengefahr f danger of avalanches.
lax [laks] adj lax.
Lay-out▲, **Layout** ['le:aut] (-s, -s) nt layout.
Lazarett [latsa'rɛt] (-(e)s, -e) nt (MIL) hospital,
infirmary.
Ldkrs. abk = **Landkreis.**
leasen ['li:zən] vt to lease.
Leasing ['li:zɪŋ] (-s, -s) nt (COMM) leasing.
Lebehoch nt three cheers pl.
Lebemann (-(e)s, pl **-männer**) m man about
town.
Leben ['le:bən] (-s, -) nt life; **am ~ sein/
bleiben** to be/stay alive; **ums ~ kommen** to
die; **etw ins ~ rufen** to bring sth into being;
seines ~s nicht mehr sicher sein to fear for
one's life; **etw für sein ~ gern tun** to love
doing sth.
leben vt, vi to live.
lebend adj living; **~es Inventar** livestock.
lebendig [le'bɛndɪç] adj living, alive; (lebhaft)
lively; **L~keit** f liveliness.
Lebens- zW: **~abend** m old age; **~alter** nt age;
~anschauung f philosophy of life; **~art** f way
of life; **l~bejahend** adj positive; **~dauer** f life
(span); (von Maschine) life; **~erfahrung** f
experience of life; **~erwartung** f life
expectancy; **l~fähig** adj able to live; **l~froh**
adj full of the joys of life; **~gefahr** f:
~gefahr! danger!; **in ~gefahr** critically od
dangerously ill; **l~gefährlich** adj dangerous;
(Krankheit, Verletzung) critical; **~gefährte** m:
ihr ~gefährte the man she lives with;
~gefährtin f: **seine ~gefährtin** the woman he
lives with; **~größe** f: **in ~größe** life-size(d);
~haltungskosten pl cost of living sing;
~inhalt m purpose in life; **~jahr** nt year of
life; **~künstler** m master in the art of living;
~lage f situation in life; **l~länglich** adj
(Strafe) for life; **~lauf** m curriculum vitae,
CV; **l~lustig** adj cheerful, lively; **~mittel** pl
food sing; **~mittelgeschäft** nt grocer's;
~mittelvergiftung f food poisoning; **l~müde**
adj tired of life; **~partnerschaft** f long-term
relationship; **eingetragene ~partnerschaft**
registered partnership; **~qualität** f quality
of life; **~raum** m (POL) Lebensraum; (BIOL)
biosphere; **~retter** m lifesaver; **~standard** m

standard of living; **~stellung** f permanent post; **~stil** m life style; **~unterhalt** m livelihood; **~versicherung** f life insurance; **~wandel** m way of life; **~weise** f way of life, habits pl; **~weisheit** f maxim; (~erfahrung) wisdom; **~wichtig** adj vital; **~zeichen** nt sign of life; **~zeit** f lifetime; **Beamter auf ~zeit** permanent civil servant.

Leber ['le:bər] (-, -n) f liver; **frei** od **frisch von der ~ weg reden** (umg) to speak out frankly; **~fleck** m mole; **~käse** m ≈ meat loaf; **~tran** m cod-liver oil; **~wurst** f liver sausage.

Lebewesen nt creature.

Lebewohl nt farewell, goodbye.

leb- zW: **~haft** adj lively, vivacious; **L~haftigkeit** f liveliness, vivacity; **L~kuchen** m gingerbread; **~los** adj lifeless; **L~tag** m (fig): **das werde ich mein L~tag nicht vergessen** I'll never forget that as long as I live; **L~zeiten** pl: **zu jds L~zeiten** (Leben) in sb's lifetime.

lechzen ['lɛçtsən] vi: **nach etw ~** to long for sth.

leck [lɛk] adj leaky, leaking; **L~** (-(e)s, -e) nt leak.

lecken¹ vi (Loch haben) to leak.

lecken² vt, vi (schlecken) to lick.

lecker ['lɛkər] adj delicious, tasty; **L~bissen** m dainty morsel; **L~maul** nt: **ein L~maul sein** to enjoy one's food.

led. abk = **ledig**.

Leder ['le:dər] (-s, -) nt leather; (umg: Fußball) ball; **~hose** f leather trousers pl; (von Tracht) leather shorts pl.

ledern adj leather.

Lederwaren pl leather goods pl.

ledig ['le:dɪç] adj single; **einer Sache** gen **~ sein** to be free of sth; **~lich** adv merely, solely.

leer [le:r] adj empty; (Blick) vacant; **~ gefegt** (Straße) deserted; **~ stehend** empty.

Leere (-) f emptiness; **(eine) gähnende ~** a gaping void.

leeren vt to empty ♦ vr to become empty.

Leer- zW: **~gewicht** nt unladen weight; **~gut** nt empties pl; **~lauf** m (AUT) neutral; **~taste** f (Schreibmaschine) space-bar.

Leerung f emptying; (POST) collection.

legal [le'ga:l] adj legal, lawful.

legalisieren [legali'zi:rən] vt to legalize.

Legalität [legali'tɛ:t] f legality; **(etwas) außerhalb der ~** (euph) (slightly) outside the law.

Legasthenie [legaste'ni:] f dyslexia.

Legastheniker(in) [legas'te:nikər(ɪn)] (-s, -) m(f) dyslexic.

Legebatterie f laying battery.

legen ['le:gən] vt to lay, put, place; (Ei) to lay ♦ vr to lie down; (fig) to subside; **sich ins Bett ~** to go to bed.

Legende [le'gɛndə] (-, -n) f legend.

leger [le'ʒɛ:r] adj casual.

legieren [le'gi:rən] vt to alloy.

Legierung f alloy.

Legislative [legɪsla'ti:və] f legislature.

Legislaturperiode [legɪsla'tu:rperio:də] f parliamentary (BRIT) od congressional (US) term.

legitim [legi'ti:m] adj legitimate.

Legitimation [legiti:matsi'o:n] f legitimation.

legitimieren [legiti'mi:rən] vt to legitimate ♦ vr to prove one's identity.

Legitimität [legitimi'tɛ:t] f legitimacy.

Lehm [le:m] (-(e)s, -e) m loam.

lehmig adj loamy.

Lehne ['le:nə] (-, -n) f arm; (Rücken~) back.

lehnen vt, vr to lean.

Lehnstuhl m armchair.

Lehr- zW: **~amt** nt teaching profession; **~befähigung** f teaching qualification; **~brief** m indentures pl; **~buch** nt textbook.

Lehre ['le:rə] (-, -n) f teaching, doctrine; (beruflich) apprenticeship; (moralisch) lesson; (TECH) gauge; **bei jdm in die ~ gehen** to serve one's apprenticeship with sb.

lehren vt to teach.

Lehrer(in) (-s, -) m(f) teacher; **~ausbildung** f teacher training; **~kollegium** nt teaching staff; **~zimmer** nt staff room.

Lehr- zW: **~gang** m course; **~geld** nt: **~geld für etw zahlen müssen** (fig) to pay dearly for sth; **~jahre** pl apprenticeship sing; **~kraft** f (form) teacher; **~ling** m apprentice; trainee; **~mittel** nt teaching aid; **~plan** m syllabus; **~probe** f demonstration lesson, crit (umg); **l~reich** adj instructive; **~satz** m proposition; **~stelle** f apprenticeship; **~stuhl** m chair; **~zeit** f apprenticeship.

Leib [laip] (-(e)s, -er) m body; **halt ihn mir vom ~!** keep him away from me!; **etw am eigenen ~(e) spüren** to experience sth for o.s.

leiben ['laibən] vi: **wie er leibt und lebt** to a T (umg).

Leibes- zW: **~erziehung** f physical education; **~kräfte** pl: **aus ~kräften schreien** etc to shout etc with all one's might; **~übung** f physical exercise; **~visitation** f body search.

Leibgericht nt favourite (BRIT) od favorite (US) meal.

Leib- zW: **l~haftig** adj personified; (Teufel) incarnate; **l~lich** adj bodily; (Vater etc) natural; **~rente** f life annuity; **~wache** f bodyguard.

Leiche ['laiçə] (-, -n) f corpse; **er geht über ~n** (umg) he'd stick at nothing.

Leichen- zW: **~beschauer** (-s, -) m doctor conducting a post-mortem; **~halle** f mortuary; **~hemd** nt shroud; **~träger** m bearer; **~wagen** m hearse.

Leichnam ['laiçnɑːm] (-(e)s, -e) m corpse.

leicht [laiçt] adj light; (einfach) easy ♦ adv:
~ **zerbrechlich** very fragile; **jdm ~ fallen** to
be easy for sb; **es sich** dat ~ **machen** to
make things easy for o.s.; (nicht gewissenhaft
sein) to take the easy way out; ~ **nehmen** to
take lightly; ~ **verletzt** slightly injured;
nichts ~er als das! nothing (could be)
simpler!; **L~athletik** f athletics sing; **~fertig**
adj thoughtless; **~gläubig** adj gullible,
credulous; **L~gläubigkeit** f gullibility,
credulity; **~hin** adv lightly.
Leichtigkeit f easiness; **mit** ~ with ease.

leicht- zW: **~lebig** adj easy-going; **L~matrose**
m ordinary seaman; **L~metall** nt light alloy;
L~sinn m carelessness; **sträflicher L~sinn**
criminal negligence; **~sinnig** adj careless.

Leid [lait] (-(e)s) nt grief, sorrow; **jdm sein**
~ **klagen** to tell sb one's troubles; **es tut**
mir/ihm ~ I am/he is sorry; **es tut mir** ~
I am sorry for him/about it; **sie kann einem**
~ **tun** you can't help feeling sorry for her.

leid adj: **etw** ~ **haben** od **sein** to be tired of
sth.

leiden ['laidən] unreg vt to suffer; (erlauben) to
permit ♦ vi to suffer; **jdn/etw nicht**
~ **können** not to be able to stand sb/sth; **L~**
(-s, -) nt suffering; (Krankheit) complaint.
Leidenschaft f passion; **l~lich** adj passionate.
Leidens- zW: **~genosse** m, **~genossin** f fellow
sufferer; **~geschichte** f: **die ~geschichte**
(Christi) (REL) Christ's Passion.

leider ['laidər] adv unfortunately; **ja**, ~ yes,
I'm afraid so; ~ **nicht** I'm afraid not.
leidig ['laidiç] adj miserable, tiresome.
leidlich [laitliç] adj tolerable ♦ adv tolerably.
Leidtragende(r) f(m) bereaved;
(Benachteiligter) one who suffers.
Leidwesen nt: **zu jds** ~ to sb's dismay.
Leier ['laiər] (-, -n) f lyre; (fig) old story.
Leierkasten m barrel organ.
leiern vt (Kurbel) to turn; (umg: Gedicht) to
rattle off ♦ vi (drehen): ~ **an** +dat to crank.
Leiharbeit f subcontracted labour;
~arbeiter(in) m(f) subcontracted worker;
~bibliothek f, **~bücherei** f lending library.
leihen ['laiən] unreg vt to lend; **sich** dat **etw** ~ to
borrow sth.
Leih- zW: **~gabe** f loan; **~gebühr** f hire charge;
~haus nt pawnshop; **~mutter** f surrogate
mother; **~schein** m pawn ticket; (in der
Bibliothek) borrowing slip; **~unternehmen** nt
hire service; (Arbeitsmarkt) temp service;
~wagen m hired car (BRIT), rental car (US);
l~weise adv on loan.
Leim [laim] (-(e)s, -e) m glue; **jdm auf den**
~ **gehen** to be taken in by sb; **l~en** vt to
glue.
Leine ['lainə] (-, -n) f line, cord; (Hunde~)
leash, lead; ~ **ziehen** (umg) to clear out.

Leinen (-s, -) nt linen; (grob, segeltuchartig)
canvas; (als Bucheinband) cloth.
leinen adj linen.
Lein- zW: **~samen** m linseed; **~tuch** nt linen
cloth; (Bettuch) sheet; **~wand** f (KUNST)
canvas; (FILM) screen.
leise ['laizə] adj quiet; (sanft) soft, gentle; **mit**
~r Stimme in a low voice; **nicht die ~ste**
Ahnung haben not to have the slightest
(idea).
Leisetreter (pej: umg) m pussyfoot(er).
Leiste ['laistə] (-, -n) f ledge; (Zier~) strip;
(ANAT) groin.
leisten ['laistən] vt (Arbeit) to do; (Gesellschaft)
to keep; (Ersatz) to supply; (vollbringen) to
achieve; **sich** dat **etw** ~ to allow o.s. sth; (sich
gönnen) to treat o.s. to sth; **sich** dat **etw**
~ **können** to be able to afford sth.
Leistenbruch m (MED) hernia, rupture.
Leistung f performance; (gute) achievement;
(eines Motors) power; (von Krankenkasse etc)
benefit; (Zahlung) payment.
Leistungs- zW: **~abfall** m (in Bezug auf Qualität)
drop in performance; (in Bezug auf Quantität)
drop in productivity; **~beurteilung** f
performance appraisal; **~druck** m pressure;
l~fähig adj efficient; **~fähigkeit** f efficiency;
~gesellschaft f meritocracy; **~kurs** m (SCH)
set; **l~orientiert** adj performance-orientated;
~prinzip nt achievement principle; **~sport** m
competitive sport; **~zulage** f productivity
bonus.
Leitartikel m leader.
Leitbild nt model.
leiten ['laitən] vt to lead; (Firma) to manage;
(in eine Richtung) to direct; (ELEK) to
conduct; **sich von jdm/etw** ~ **lassen** (lit, fig)
to (let o.s.) be guided by sb/sth.
leitend adj leading; (Gedanke, Idee) dominant;
(Stellung, Position) managerial; (Ingenieur,
Beamter) in charge; (PHYS) conductive; **~er**
Angestellter executive.
Leiter[1] ['laitər] (-s, -) m leader, head; (ELEK)
conductor.
Leiter[2] ['laitər] (-, -n) f ladder.
Leiterin f leader, head.
Leiterplatte f (COMPUT) circuit board.
Leit- zW: **~faden** m guide; **~fähigkeit** f
conductivity; **~gedanke** m central idea;
~motiv nt leitmotiv; **~planke** f crash
barrier; **~spruch** m motto.
Leitung f (Führung) direction; (FILM, THEAT
etc) production; (von Firma) management;
directors pl; (Wasser~) pipe; (Kabel) cable;
eine lange ~ haben to be slow on the
uptake; **da ist jemand in der** ~ (umg) there's
somebody else on the line.
Leitungs- zW: **~draht** m wire; **~mast** m
telegraph pole; **~rohr** nt pipe; **~wasser** nt
tap water.

Leitwerk *nt* (*AVIAT*) tail unit.
Leitzins *m* (*FIN*) base rate.
Lektion [lɛktsi'oːn] *f* lesson; **jdm eine**
~ **erteilen** (*fig*) to teach sb a lesson.
Lektor(in) ['lɛktɔr, lɛk'toːrɪn] *m(f)* (*UNIV*)
lector; (*Verlag*) editor.
Lektüre [lɛk'tyːrə] (-, **-n**) *f* (*Lesen*) reading;
(*Lesestoff*) reading matter.
Lende ['lɛndə] (-, **-n**) *f* loin.
Lendenbraten *m* roast sirloin.
Lendenstück *nt* fillet.
lenkbar ['lɛŋkbaːr] *adj* (*Fahrzeug*) steerable;
(*Kind*) manageable.
lenken *vt* to steer; (*Kind*) to guide; (*Gespräch*)
to lead; ~ **auf** +*akk* (*Blick, Aufmerksamkeit*) to
direct at; (*Verdacht*) to throw on(to); (: *auf*
sich) to draw onto.
Lenkrad *nt* steering wheel.
Lenkstange *f* handlebars *pl*.
Lenkung *f* steering; (*Führung*) direction.
Lenz [lɛnts] (-es, -e) *m* (*liter*) spring; **sich** *dat*
einen (faulen) ~ **machen** (*umg*) to laze
about, swing the lead.
Leopard [leo'part] (-en, -en) *m* leopard.
Lepra ['leːpra] (-) *f* leprosy; ~**kranke(r)** *f(m)*
leper.
Lerche ['lɛrçə] (-, **-n**) *f* lark.
lernbegierig *adj* eager to learn.
lernbehindert *adj* educationally handicapped
(*BRIT*) *od* handicaped (*US*).
lernen *vt* to learn ♦ *vi*: **er lernt bei der Firma**
Braun he's training at Braun's.
Lernhilfe *f* educational aid.
lesbar ['leːsbaːr] *adj* legible.
Lesbierin ['lɛsbiərɪn] *f* lesbian.
lesbisch *adj* lesbian.
Lese ['leːzə] (-, **-n**) *f* (*Wein~*) harvest.
Lesebuch *nt* reading book, reader.
lesen *unreg vt* to read; (*ernten*) to gather, pick
♦ *vi* to read; ~/**schreiben** (*COMPUT*) to read/
write.
Leser(in) (-s, -) *m(f)* reader.
Leseratte ['leːzəratə] (*umg*) *f* bookworm.
Leser- *zW*: ~**brief** *m* reader's letter; „~**briefe**"
"letters to the editor"; ~**kreis** *m* readership;
l~lich *adj* legible.
Lese- *zW*: ~**saal** *m* reading room; ~**stoff** *m*
reading material; ~**zeichen** *nt* bookmark;
~**zirkel** *m* magazine club.
Lesotho [le'zoːto] (-s) *nt* Lesotho.
Lesung ['leːzʊŋ] *f* (*PARL*) reading; (*ECCL*)
lesson.
lethargisch [le'targɪʃ] *adj* (*MED, fig*) lethargic.
Lette ['lɛtə] (-n, **-n**) *m*, **Lettin** *f* Latvian.
lettisch *adj* Latvian.
Lettland ['lɛtlant] (-s) *nt* Latvia.
Letzt *f*: **zu guter** ~ finally, in the end.
letzte(r, s) ['lɛtstə(r, s)] *adj* last; (*neueste*)
latest; **der** ~ **Wille** the last will and
testament; **bis zum L~n** to the utmost; **zum**

~**n Mal** for the last time; **in** ~**r Zeit** recently.
Letzte(s) *nt*: **das ist ja das** ~! (*umg*) that
really is the limit!
letztens *adv* lately.
letztere(r, s) *adj* the latter.
letztlich *adv* in the end.
Leuchte ['lɔyçtə] (-, **-n**) *f* lamp, light; (*umg*:
Mensch) genius.
leuchten *vi* to shine, gleam.
Leuchter (-s, -) *m* candlestick.
Leucht- *zW*: ~**farbe** *f* fluorescent colour (*BRIT*)
od color (*US*); ~**feuer** *nt* beacon; ~**käfer** *m*
glow-worm; ~**kugel** *f* flare; ~**pistole** *f* flare
pistol; ~**rakete** *f* flare; ~**reklame** *f* neon sign;
~**röhre** *f* strip light; ~**turm** *m* lighthouse;
~**zifferblatt** *nt* luminous dial.
leugnen ['lɔygnən] *vt, vi* to deny.
Leugnung *f* denial.
Leukämie [lɔykɛ'miː] *f* leukaemia (*BRIT*),
leukemia (*US*).
Leukoplast ® [lɔyko'plast] (-(e)s, -e) *nt*
Elastoplast ®.
Leumund ['lɔymʊnt] (-(e)s, -e) *m* reputation.
Leumundszeugnis *nt* character reference.
Leute ['lɔytə] *pl* people *pl*; **kleine** ~ (*fig*)
ordinary people; **etw unter die** ~ **bringen**
(*umg*: *Gerücht etc*) to spread sth around.
Leutnant ['lɔytnant] (-s, **-s** *od* **-e**) *m* lieutenant.
leutselig ['lɔytzeːlɪç] *adj* affable; **L~keit** *f*
affability.
Leviten [le'viːtən] *pl*: **jdm die** ~ **lesen** (*umg*) to
haul sb over the coals.
lexikalisch [lɛksi'kaːlɪʃ] *adj* lexical.
Lexikografie▲ [lɛksikogra'fiː] *f* lexicography.
Lexikon ['lɛksikɔn] (-s, **Lexiken** *od* **Lexika**) *nt*
encyclopedia.
lfd. *abk* = **laufend**.
Libanese [liba'neːzə] (-n, **-n**) *m*, **Libanesin** *f*
Lebanese.
libanesisch *adj* Lebanese.
Libanon ['liːbanɔn] (-s) *m*: **der** ~ the Lebanon.
Libelle [li'bɛlə] (-, **-n**) *f* dragonfly; (*TECH*) spirit
level.
liberal [libe'raːl] *adj* liberal.
Liberale(r) *f(m)* (*POL*) Liberal.
Liberalisierung [liberali'ziːrʊŋ] *f*
liberalization.
Liberalismus [libera'lɪsmʊs] *m* liberalism.
Liberia [li'beːria] (-s) *nt* Liberia.
Liberianer(in) [liberi'aːnər(ɪn)] (-s, -) *m(f)*
Liberian.
liberianisch *adj* Liberian.
Libero ['liːbero] (-s, **-s**) *m* (*FUSSBALL*)
sweeper.
Libyen ['liːbyən] (-s) *nt* Libya.
Libyer(in) (-s, -) *m(f)* Libyan.
libysch *adj* Libyan.
Licht [lɪçt] (-(e)s, -er) *nt* light; ~ **machen**
(*anschalten*) to turn on a light; (*anzünden*) to
light a candle *etc*; **mir geht ein** ~ **auf** it's

dawned on me; **jdn hinters ~ führen** (*fig*) to lead sb up the garden path.

licht *adj* light, bright.

Licht- *zW*: **~bild** *nt* photograph; (*Dia*) slide; **~blick** *m* cheering prospect; **l~empfindlich** *adj* sensitive to light.

lichten ['lıçtən] *vt* to clear; (*Anker*) to weigh ♦ *vr* (*Nebel*) to clear; (*Haar*) to thin.

lichterloh ['lıçtər'loː] *adv*: **~ brennen** to blaze.

Licht- *zW*: **~geschwindigkeit** *f* speed of light; **~griffel** *m* (*COMPUT*) light pen; **~hupe** *f* flashing of headlights; **~jahr** *nt* light year; **~maschine** *f* dynamo; **~mess▲** (-) *f* Candlemas; **~pause** *f* photocopy; (*bei Blaupausverfahren*) blueprint; **~schalter** *m* light switch; **l~scheu** *adj* averse to light; (*fig: Gesindel*) shady.

Lichtung *f* clearing, glade.

Lid [liːt] (-(e)s, -er) *nt* eyelid; **~schatten** *m* eyeshadow.

lieb [liːp] *adj* dear; (**viele**) **~e Grüße, deine Silvia** love, Silvia; **L~e Anna, ~er Klaus!** ... Dear Anna and Klaus, ...; **am ~sten lese ich Kriminalromane** best of all I like detective novels; **den ~en langen Tag** (*umg*) all the livelong day; **sich bei jdm ~ Kind machen** (*pej*) to suck up to sb (*umg*); **~ gewinnen** to get fond of; **~ haben** (*weniger stark*) to be (very) fond of.

liebäugeln ['liːplɔygəln] *vi untr*: **mit dem Gedanken ~, etw zu tun** to toy with the idea of doing sth.

Liebe ['liːbə] (-, -n) *f* love; **l~bedürftig** *adj*: **l~bedürftig sein** to need love.

Liebelei *f* flirtation.

lieben ['liːbən] *vt* to love; (*weniger stark*) to like; **etw ~d gern tun** to love to do sth.

liebens- *zW*: **~wert** *adj* loveable; **~würdig** *adj* kind; **~würdigerweise** *adv* kindly; **L~würdigkeit** *f* kindness.

lieber ['liːbər] *adv* rather, preferably; **ich gehe ~ nicht** I'd rather not go; **ich trinke ~ Wein als Bier** I prefer wine to beer; **bleib ~ im Bett** you'd better stay in bed.

Liebes- *zW*: **~brief** *m* love letter; **~dienst** *m* good turn; **~kummer** *m*: **~kummer haben** to be lovesick; **~paar** *nt* courting couple, lovers *pl*; **~roman** *m* romantic novel.

liebevoll *adj* loving.

lieb- *zW*: **L~haber(in)** (-s, -) *m(f)* lover; (*Sammler*) collector; **L~haberei** *f* hobby; **~kosen** *vt untr* to caress; **~lich** *adj* lovely, charming; (*Duft, Wein*) sweet.

Liebling *m* darling.

Lieblings- *in zW* favourite (*BRIT*), favorite (*US*).

lieblos *adj* unloving.

Liebschaft *f* love affair.

Liechtenstein ['lıçtənʃtain] (-s) *nt* Liechtenstein.

Lied [liːt] (-(e)s, -er) *nt* song; (*ECCL*) hymn; **davon kann ich ein ~ singen** (*fig*) I could tell you a thing or two about that (*umg*).

Liederbuch *nt* songbook; (*REL*) hymn book.

liederlich ['liːdərlıç] *adj* slovenly; (*Lebenswandel*) loose, immoral; **L~keit** *f* slovenliness; immorality.

lief *etc* [liːf] *vb siehe* **laufen**.

Lieferant [liːfa'rant] *m* supplier.

Lieferanteneingang *m* tradesmen's entrance; (*von Warenhaus etc*) goods entrance.

lieferbar *adj* (*vorrätig*) available.

Lieferbedingungen *pl* terms of delivery.

Lieferfrist *f* delivery period.

liefern ['liːfərn] *vt* to deliver; (*versorgen mit*) to supply; (*Beweis*) to produce.

Lieferschein *m* delivery note.

Liefertermin *m* delivery date.

Lieferung *f* delivery; (*Versorgung*) supply.

Lieferwagen *m* (delivery) van, panel truck (*US*).

Lieferzeit *f* delivery period; **~ 6 Monate** delivery six months.

Liege ['liːgə] (-, -n) *f* bed; (*Camping~*) camp bed (*BRIT*), cot (*US*); **~geld** *nt* (*Hafen, Flughafen*) demurrage.

liegen ['liːgən] *unreg vi* to lie; (*sich befinden*) to be (situated); **mir liegt nichts/viel daran** it doesn't matter to me/it matters a lot to me; **es liegt bei Ihnen, ob** ... it rests with you whether ...; **Sprachen ~ mir nicht** languages are not my line; **woran liegt es?** what's the cause?; **so, wie die Dinge jetzt ~** as things stand at the moment; **an mir soll es nicht ~, wenn die Sache schief geht** it won't be my fault if things go wrong; **~ bleiben** (*Person*) to stay in bed; (*nicht aufstehen*) to stay lying down; (*Ding*) to be left (behind); (*nicht ausgeführt werden*) to be left (undone); **~ lassen** (*vergessen*) to leave behind; **L~schaft** *f* real estate.

Liege- *zW*: **~platz** *m* (*auf Schiff, in Zug etc*) berth; (*Ankerplatz*) moorings *pl*; **~sitz** *m* (*AUT*) reclining seat; **~stuhl** *m* deck chair; **~stütz** *m* (*SPORT*) press-up (*BRIT*), push-up (*US*); **~wagen** *m* (*EISENB*) couchette car; **~wiese** *f* lawn (*for sunbathing*).

lieh *etc* [liː] *vb siehe* **leihen**.

ließ *etc* [liːs] *vb siehe* **lassen**.

liest [liːst] *vb siehe* **lesen**.

Lift [lıft] (-(e)s, -e *od* -s) *m* lift.

Liga ['liːga] (-, **Ligen**) *f* (*SPORT*) league.

liieren [li'iːrən] *vt*: **liiert sein** (*Firmen etc*) to be working together; (*ein Verhältnis haben*) to have a relationship.

Likör [li'køːr] (-s, -e) *m* liqueur.

lila ['liːla] *adj inv* purple; **L~** (-s, -s) *nt* (*Farbe*) purple.

Lilie ['liːliə] *f* lily.

Liliputaner(in) [lilipu'ta:nər(ın)] **(-s, -)** *m(f)* midget.
Limit ['lımıt] **(-s, -s** *od* **-e)** *nt* limit; (*FIN*) ceiling.
Limonade [limo'na:də] **(-, -n)** *f* lemonade.
lind [lınt] *adj* gentle, mild.
Linde ['lındə] **(-, -n)** *f* lime tree, linden.
lindern ['lındərn] *vt* to alleviate, soothe.
Linderung *f* alleviation.
lindgrün *adj* lime green.
Lineal [line'a:l] **(-s, -e)** *nt* ruler.
linear [line'a:r] *adj* linear.
Linguist(in) [lıŋgu'ıst(ın)] *m(f)* linguist.
Linguistik *f* linguistics *sing*.
Linie ['li:niə] *f* line; **in erster** ~ first and foremost; **auf die** ~ **achten** to watch one's figure; **fahren Sie mit der** ~ **2** take the number 2 (bus *etc*).
Linien- *zW*: ~**blatt** *nt* ruled sheet; ~**bus** *m* service bus; ~**flug** *m* scheduled flight; ~**richter** *m* (*SPORT*) linesman; **l~treu** *adj* loyal to the (party) line.
linieren [li'ni:rən], **liniieren** [lini'i:rən] *vt* to line.
Link [lıŋk] **(-s, -s)** *m* (*COMPUT*) link.
Linke ['lıŋkə] **(-, -n)** *f* left side; left hand; (*POL*) left.
Linke(r) *f(m)* (*POL*) left-winger, leftie (*pej*).
linke(r, s) *adj* left; ~ **Masche** purl.
linkisch *adj* awkward, gauche.
links *adv* left; to *od* on the left; ~ **von mir** on *od* to my left; ~ **von der Mitte** left of centre; **jdn** ~ **liegen lassen** (*fig: umg*) to ignore sb; **das mache ich mit** ~ (*umg*) I can do that with my eyes shut; **L~abbieger** *m* motorist/ vehicle turning left; **L~außen (-s, -)** *m* (*SPORT*) outside left; **L~händer(in) (-s, -)** *m(f)* left-handed person; **L~kurve** *f* left-hand bend; ~**lastig** *adj*; ~**lastig sein** to list *od* lean to the left; ~**radikal** *adj* (*POL*) radically left-wing; **L~rutsch** *m* (*POL*) swing to the left; **L~steuerung** *f* (*AUT*) left-hand drive; **L~verkehr** *m* driving on the left.
Linse ['lınzə] **(-, -n)** *f* lentil; (*optisch*) lens.
linsen (*umg*) *vi* to peek.
Lippe ['lıpə] **(-, -n)** *f* lip.
Lippenbekenntnis *nt* lip service.
Lippenstift *m* lipstick.
Liquidation [likvidatsi'o:n] *f* liquidation.
Liquidationswert *m* break-up value.
Liquidator [likvi'da:tor] *m* liquidator.
liquid(e) [lik'vi:t, lik'vi:də] *adj* (*Firma*) solvent.
liquidieren [likvi'di:rən] *vt* to liquidate.
Liquidität [likvidi'tɛ:t] *f* liquidity.
lispeln ['lıspəln] *vi* to lisp.
Lissabon ['lısabɔn] *nt* Lisbon.
List [lıst] **(-, -en)** *f* cunning; (*Plan*) trick, ruse; **mit** ~ **und Tücke** (*umg*) with a lot of coaxing.
Liste ['lıstə] **(-, -n)** *f* list.

Listenplatz *m* (*POL*) place on the party list.
Listenpreis *m* list price.
listig *adj* cunning, sly.
Litanei [lita'naı] *f* litany.
Litauen ['li:tauən] **(-s)** *nt* Lithuania.
Litauer(in) **(-s, -)** *m(f)* Lithuanian.
litauisch *adj* Lithuanian.
Liter ['li:tər] **(-s, -)** *m od nt* litre (*BRIT*), liter (*US*).
literarisch [lıte'ra:rıʃ] *adj* literary.
Literatur [lıtera'tu:r] *f* literature; ~**preis** *m* award *od* prize for literature; ~**wissenschaft** *f* literary studies *pl*.
literweise ['li:tərvaizə] *adv* (*lit*) by the litre (*BRIT*) *od* liter (*US*); (*fig*) by the gallon.
Litfaßsäule ['lıtfaszɔylə] *f* advertising (*BRIT*) *od* advertizing (*US*) pillar.
Lithografie▲ [litogra'fi:] *f* lithography.
litt *etc* [lıt] *vb siehe* **leiden**.
Liturgie [litʊr'gi:] *f* liturgy.
liturgisch [li'tʊrgıʃ] *adj* liturgical.
Litze ['lıtsə] **(-, -n)** *f* braid; (*ELEK*) flex.
live [laıf] *adj, adv* (*RUNDF, TV*) live.
Livree [li'vre:] **(-, -n)** *f* livery.
Lizenz [li'tsɛnts] *f* licence (*BRIT*), license (*US*); ~**ausgabe** *f* licensed edition; ~**gebühr** *f* licence fee; (*im Verlagswesen*) royalty.
LKW, Lkw (-(s), -(s)) *m abk* = **Lastkraftwagen**.
l. M. *abk* (= *laufenden Monats*) inst.
Lob [lo:p] **(-(e)s)** *nt* praise.
Lobby ['lɔbi] **(-, -s)** *f* lobby.
loben ['lo:bən] *vt* to praise; **das lob ich mir** that's what I like (to see/hear *etc*).
lobenswert *adj* praiseworthy.
löblich ['lø:plıç] *adj* praiseworthy, laudable.
Loblied *nt*: **ein** ~ **auf jdn/etw singen** to sing sb's/sth's praises.
Lobrede *f* eulogy.
Loch [lɔx] **(-(e)s, ⁻er)** *nt* hole; **l~en** *vt* to punch holes in; ~**er (-s, -)** *m* punch.
löcherig ['lœçərıç] *adj* full of holes.
löchern (*umg*) *vt*: **jdn** ~ to pester sb with questions.
Loch- *zW*: ~**karte** *f* punch card; ~**streifen** *m* punch tape; ~**zange** *f* punch.
Locke ['lɔkə] **(-, -n)** *f* lock, curl.
locken *vt* to entice; (*Haare*) to curl.
lockend *adj* tempting.
Lockenwickler (-s, -) *m* curler.
locker ['lɔkər] *adj* loose; (*Kuchen, Schaum*) light; (*umg*) cool; ~**lassen** *unreg vi*: **nicht** ~**lassen** not to let up.
lockern *vt* to loosen ♦ *vr* (*Atmosphäre*) to get more relaxed.
Lockerungsübung *f* loosening-up exercise; (*zum Warmwerden*) limbering-up exercise.
lockig ['lɔkıç] *adj* curly.
Lockmittel *nt* lure.
Lockruf *m* call.
Lockung *f* enticement.

Lockvogel m decoy, bait; ~**angebot** nt (COMM) loss leader.

Lodenmantel ['lo:dənmantəl] m thick woollen coat.

lodern ['lo:dərn] vi to blaze.

Löffel ['lœfəl] (-s, -) m spoon.

löffeln vt to spoon.

löffelweise adv by the spoonful.

log etc [lo:k] vb siehe **lügen**.

Logarithmentafel [loga'rıtmənta:fəl] f log(arithm) tables pl.

Logarithmus [loga'rıtmʊs] m logarithm.

Loge ['lo:ʒə] (-, -n) f (THEAT) box; (Freimaurer~) (masonic) lodge; (Pförtner~) office.

logieren [lo'ʒi:rən] vi to lodge, stay.

Logik ['lo:gık] f logic.

Logis [lo'ʒi:] (-, -) nt: **Kost und** ~ board and lodging.

logisch ['lo:gıʃ] adj logical; (umg: selbstverständlich): **gehst du auch hin?** - ~ are you going too? - of course.

logo ['logo] (umg) interj obvious!

Logopäde [logo'pɛ:də] (-n, -n) m speech therapist.

Logopädin [logo'pɛ:dın] f speech therapist.

Lohn [lo:n] (-(e)s, ⁻e) m reward; (Arbeits~) pay, wages pl; ~**abrechnung** f wages slip; ~**ausfall** m loss of earnings; ~**büro** nt wages office; ~**diktat** nt wage dictate; ~**empfänger** m wage earner.

lohnen ['lo:nən] vt (liter): **jdm etw** ~ to reward sb for sth ♦ vr unpers to be worth it.

lohnend adj worthwhile.

Lohn- zW: ~**erhöhung** f wage increase, pay rise; ~**forderung** f wage claim; ~**fortzahlung** f continued payment of wages; ~**fortzahlungsgesetz** nt law on continued payment of wages; ~**gefälle** nt wage differential; ~**kosten** pl labour (BRIT) od labor (US) costs; ~**politik** f wages policy; ~**runde** f pay round; ~**steuer** f income tax; ~**steuerjahresausgleich** m income tax return; ~**steuerkarte** f (income) tax card; ~**stopp** m pay freeze; ~**streifen** m pay slip; ~**tüte** f pay packet.

Lok [lɔk] (-, -s) f abk (= Lokomotive) loco (umg).

lokal [lo'ka:l] adj local.

Lokal (-(e)s, -e) nt pub(lic house) (BRIT).

Lokalblatt (umg) nt local paper.

lokalisieren [lokali'zi:rən] vt to localize.

Lokalisierung f localization.

Lokalität [lokali'tɛ:t] f locality; (Raum) premises pl.

Lokal- zW: ~**presse** f local press; ~**teil** m (Zeitung) local section; ~**termin** m (JUR) visit to the scene of the crime.

Lokomotive [lokomo'ti:və] (-, -n) f locomotive.

Lokomotivführer m engine driver (BRIT),

engineer (US).

Lombardei [lɔmbar'daı] f Lombardy.

London ['lɔndɔn] (-s) nt London.

Londoner adj attrib London.

Londoner(in) (-s, -) m(f) Londoner.

Lorbeer ['lɔrbe:r] (-s, -en) m (lit, fig) laurel; ~**blatt** nt (KOCH) bay leaf.

Lore ['lo:rə] (-, -n) f (MIN) truck.

Los [lo:s] (-es, -e) nt (Schicksal) lot, fate; (in der Lotterie) lottery ticket; **das große** ~ **ziehen** (lit, fig) to hit the jackpot; **etw durch das** ~ **entscheiden** to decide sth by drawing lots.

los adj loose ♦ adv: ~! go on!; **etw** ~ **sein** to be rid of sth; **was ist** ~? what's the matter?; **dort ist nichts/viel** ~ there's nothing/a lot going on there; **ich bin mein ganzes Geld** ~ (umg) I'm cleaned out; **irgendwas ist mit ihm** ~ there's something wrong with him; **wir wollen früh** ~ we want to be off early; **nichts wie** ~! let's get going; ~**binden** unreg vt to untie; ~**brechen** unreg vi (Sturm, Gewitter) to break.

losch etc [lɔʃ] vb siehe **löschen**.

Löschblatt ['lœʃblat] nt sheet of blotting paper.

löschen ['lœʃən] vt (Feuer, Licht) to put out, extinguish; (Durst) to quench; (COMM) to cancel; (Tonband) to erase; (Fracht) to unload; (COMPUT) to delete; (Tinte) to blot ♦ vi (Feuerwehr) to put out a fire; (Papier) to blot.

Lösch- zW: ~**fahrzeug** nt fire engine; ~**gerät** nt fire extinguisher; ~**papier** nt blotting paper; ~**taste** f (COMPUT) delete key.

Löschung f extinguishing; (COMM) cancellation; (Fracht) unloading.

lose ['lo:zə] adj loose.

Lösegeld nt ransom.

losen ['lo:zən] vi to draw lots.

lösen ['lø:zən] vt to loosen; (Handbremse) to release; (Husten, Krampf) to ease; (Rätsel etc) to solve; (Verlobung) to call off; (CHEM) to dissolve; (Partnerschaft) to break up; (Fahrkarte) to buy ♦ vr (aufgehen) to come loose; (Schuss) to go off; (Zucker etc) to dissolve; (Problem, Schwierigkeit) to (re)solve itself.

los- zW: ~**fahren** unreg vi to leave; ~**gehen** unreg vi to set out; (anfangen) to start; (Bombe) to go off; **jetzt gehts** ~! here we go!; **nach hinten** ~**gehen** (umg) to backfire; **auf jdn** ~**gehen** to go for sb; ~**kaufen** vt (Gefangene, Geiseln) to pay ransom for; ~**kommen** unreg vi (sich befreien) to free o.s.; **von etw** ~**kommen** to get away from sth; ~**lassen** unreg vt (Seil etc) to let go of; **der Gedanke lässt mich nicht mehr** ~ the thought haunts me; ~**laufen** unreg vi to run off; ~**legen** (umg) vi: **nun leg mal** ~ **und erzähl(e)** ... now come on and tell me/us ...

löslich ['løːslɪç] *adj* soluble; **L~keit** *f* solubility.

loslösen *vt* to free ♦ *vr*: **sich (von etw)** ~ to detach o.s. (from sth).

losmachen *vt* to loosen; (*Boot*) to unmoor ♦ *vr* to get free.

Losnummer *f* ticket number.

los- *zW*: **~sagen** *vr*: **sich von jdm/etw ~sagen** to renounce sb/sth; **~schießen** *unreg vi*: **schieß ~!** (*fig: umg*) fire away!; **~schrauben** *vt* to unscrew; **~sprechen** *unreg vt* to absolve; **~stürzen** *vi*: **auf jdn/etw ~stürzen** to pounce on sb/sth.

Losung ['loːzʊŋ] *f* watchword, slogan.

Lösung ['løːzʊŋ] *f* (*Lockermachen*) loosening; (*eines Rätsels, CHEM*) solution.

Lösungsmittel *nt* solvent.

loswerden *unreg vt* to get rid of.

losziehen *unreg vi* (*sich aufmachen*) to set out; **gegen jdn** ~ (*fig*) to run sb down.

Lot [loːt] (**-(e)s, -e**) *nt* plumbline; (*MATH*) perpendicular; **im** ~ vertical; (*fig*) on an even keel; **die Sache ist wieder im** ~ things have been straightened out; **l~en** *vt* to plumb, sound.

löten ['løːtən] *vt* to solder.

Lothringen ['loːtrɪŋən] (**-s**) *nt* Lorraine.

Lötkolben *m* soldering iron.

Lotse ['loːtsə] (**-n, -n**) *m* pilot; (*AVIAT*) air traffic controller.

lotsen *vt* to pilot; (*umg*) to lure.

Lotterie [lɔtə'riː] *f* lottery.

Lotterleben ['lɔtərleːbən] (*umg*) *nt* dissolute life.

Lotto ['lɔto] (**-s, -s**) *nt* ≈ National Lottery.

Lottozahlen *pl* winning Lotto numbers *pl*.

Löwe ['løːvə] (**-n, -n**) *m* lion; (*ASTROL*) Leo.

Löwen- *zW*: **~anteil** *m* lion's share; **~maul** *nt*, **~mäulchen** *nt* antirrhinum, snapdragon; **~zahn** *m* dandelion.

Löwin ['løːvɪn] *f* lioness.

loyal [loa'jaːl] *adj* loyal.

Loyalität [loajali'tɛːt] *f* loyalty.

LP (**-, -s**) *f abk* (= *Langspielplatte*) LP.

LSD (**-(s)**) *nt abk* (= *Lysergsäurediäthylamid*) LSD.

lt. *abk* = **laut**.

Luchs [lʊks] (**-es, -e**) *m* lynx.

Lücke ['lʏkə] (**-, -n**) *f* gap; (*Gesetzes~*) loophole; (*in Versorgung*) break.

Lücken- *zW*: **~büßer** (**-s, -**) *m* stopgap; **l~haft** *adj* full of gaps; (*Versorgung*) deficient; **l~los** *adj* complete.

lud *etc* [luːt] *vb siehe* **laden**.

Luder ['luːdər] (**-s, -**) (*pej*) *nt* (*Frau*) hussy; (*bedauernswert*) poor wretch.

Luft [lʊft] (**-, ⁻e**) *f* air; (*Atem*) breath; **die** ~ **anhalten** (*lit*) to hold one's breath; **seinem Herzen** ~ **machen** to get everything off one's chest; **in der** ~ **liegen** to be in the air;

dicke ~ (*umg*) a bad atmosphere; (**frische**) ~ **schnappen** (*umg*) to get some fresh air; **in die** ~ **fliegen** (*umg*) to explode; **diese Behauptung ist aus der** ~ **gegriffen** this statement is (a) pure invention; **die** ~ **ist rein** (*umg*) the coast is clear; **jdn an die** (**frische**) ~ **setzen** (*umg*) to show sb the door; **er ist** ~ **für mich** I'm not speaking to him; **jdn wie** ~ **behandeln** to ignore sb; **~angriff** *m* air raid; **~aufnahme** *f* aerial photo; **~ballon** *m* balloon; **~blase** *f* air bubble; **~brücke** *f* airlift; **l~dicht** *adj* airtight; **~druck** *m* atmospheric pressure; **l~durchlässig** *adj* pervious to air.

lüften ['lʏftən] *vt* to air; (*Hut*) to lift, raise ♦ *vi* to let some air in.

Luft- *zW*: **~fahrt** *f* aviation; **~feuchtigkeit** *f* humidity; **~fracht** *f* air cargo; **l~gekühlt** *adj* air-cooled; **~gewehr** *nt* air rifle.

luftig *adj* (*Ort*) breezy; (*Raum*) airy; (*Kleider*) summery.

Luft- *zW*: **~kissenfahrzeug** *nt* hovercraft; **~krieg** *m* war in the air, aerial warfare; **~kurort** *m* health resort; **l~leer** *adj*: **l~leerer Raum** vacuum; **~linie** *f*: **in der ~linie** as the crow flies; **~loch** *nt* air hole; (*AVIAT*) air pocket; **~matratze** *f* Lilo ® (*BRIT*), air mattress; **~pirat** *m* hijacker; **~post** *f* airmail; **~pumpe** *f* (*für Fahrrad*) (bicycle) pump; **~raum** *m* air space; **~röhre** *f* (*ANAT*) windpipe; **~schlange** *f* streamer; **~schloss▲** *nt* (*fig*) castle in the air; **~schutz** *m* anti-aircraft defence (*BRIT*) *od* defense (*US*); **~schutzbunker** *m*, **~schutzkeller** *m* air-raid shelter; **~sprung** *m* (*fig*): **einen ~sprung machen** to jump for joy.

Lüftung ['lʏftʊŋ] *f* ventilation.

Luft- *zW*: **~veränderung** *f* change of air; **~verkehr** *m* air traffic; **~verschmutzung** *f* air pollution; **~waffe** *f* air force; **~weg** *m*: **etw auf dem ~weg befördern** to transport sth by air; **~zufuhr** *f* air supply; **~zug** *m* draught (*BRIT*), draft (*US*).

Lüge ['lyːgə] (**-, -n**) *f* lie; **jdn/etw ~n strafen** to give the lie to sb/sth.

lügen ['lyːgən] *unreg vi* to lie; **wie gedruckt** ~ (*umg*) to lie like mad.

Lügendetektor ['lyːgəndetɛktɔr] *m* lie detector.

Lügner(in) (**-s, -**) *m(f)* liar.

Luke ['luːkə] (**-, -n**) *f* hatch; (*Dach~*) skylight.

lukrativ [lukra'tiːf] *adj* lucrative.

Lümmel ['lʏməl] (**-s, -**) *m* lout.

lümmeln *vr* to lounge (about).

Lump [lʊmp] (**-en, -en**) *m* scamp, rascal.

lumpen ['lʊmpən] *vt*: **sich nicht ~ lassen** not to be mean.

Lumpen (**-s, -**) *m* rag.

Lumpensammler *m* rag and bone man.

lumpig ['lʊmpɪç] *adj* shabby; **~e 10 Euro** (*umg*)

10 measly euros.

Lüneburger Heide ['ly:nəbʊrgər 'haɪdə] *f* Lüneburg Heath.

Lunge ['lʊŋə] (-, -n) *f* lung.

Lungen- *zW*: **~entzündung** *f* pneumonia; **l~krank** *adj* suffering from a lung disease; **~krankheit** *f* lung disease.

lungern ['lʊŋərn] *vi* to hang about.

Lunte ['lʊntə] (-, -n) *f* fuse; **~ riechen** to smell a rat.

Lupe ['lu:pə] (-, -n) *f* magnifying glass; **unter die ~ nehmen** (*fig*) to scrutinize.

lupenrein *adj* (*lit: Edelstein*) flawless.

Lupine [lu'pi:nə] *f* lupin.

Lurch [lʊrç] (-(e)s, -e) *m* amphibian.

Lust [lʊst] (-, -̈e) *f* joy, delight; (*Neigung*) desire; (*sexuell*) lust (*pej*); **~ haben zu** *od* **auf etw** *akk*/**etw zu tun** to feel like sth/doing sth; **hast du ~?** how about it?; **er hat die ~ daran verloren** he has lost all interest in it; **je nach ~ und Laune** just depending on how I *od* you *etc* feel; **l~betont** *adj* pleasure-orientated.

lüstern ['lystərn] *adj* lustful, lecherous.

Lustgefühl *nt* pleasurable feeling.

Lustgewinn *m* pleasure.

lustig ['lʊstɪç] *adj* (*komisch*) amusing, funny; (*fröhlich*) cheerful; **sich über jdn/etw ~ machen** to make fun of sb/sth.

Lüstling *m* lecher.

Lust- *zW*: **l~los** *adj* unenthusiastic; **~mord** *m* sex(ual) murder; **~prinzip** *nt* (*PSYCH*) pleasure principle; **~spiel** *nt* comedy; **l~wandeln** *vi* to stroll about.

luth. *abk* = **lutherisch**.

Lutheraner(in) [lʊtə'ra:nər(ɪn)] *m(f)* Lutheran.

lutherisch ['lʊtərɪʃ] *adj* Lutheran.

lutschen ['lʊtʃən] *vt, vi* to suck; **am Daumen ~** to suck one's thumb.

Lutscher (-s, -) *m* lollipop.

Luxemburg ['lʊksəmbʊrk] (-s) *nt* Luxembourg.

Luxemburger(in) ['lʊksəmbʊrgər(ɪn)] (-s, -) *m(f)* citizen of Luxembourg, Luxembourger.

luxemburgisch *adj* Luxembourgian.

luxuriös [lʊksuri'ø:s] *adj* luxurious.

Luxus ['lʊksʊs] (-) *m* luxury; **~artikel** *pl* luxury goods *pl*; **~ausführung** *f* de luxe model; **~dampfer** *m* luxury cruise ship; **~hotel** *nt* luxury hotel; **~steuer** *f* tax on luxuries.

LVA (-) *f abk* (= *Landesversicherungsanstalt*) county insurance company.

LW *abk* (= *Langwelle*) LW.

Lycra ['ly:kra] (-(s)) *no pl nt* Lycra ®.

Lymphe ['lymfə] (-, -n) *f* lymph.

Lymphknoten *m* lymph(atic) gland.

lynchen ['lynçən] *vt* to lynch.

Lynchjustiz *f* lynch law.

Lyrik ['ly:rɪk] *f* lyric poetry; **~er(in)** (-s, -) *m(f)* lyric poet.

M, m

M, m¹ [ɛm] *nt* M, m; **~ wie Martha** ≈ M for Mary, M for Mike (*US*).

m² *abk* (= *Meter*) m; (= *männlich*) m.

M. *abk* = **Monat**.

MA. *abk* = **Mittelalter**.

Maat [ma:t] (-s, -e *od* -en) *m* (*NAUT*) (ship's) mate.

Machart *f* make.

machbar *adj* feasible.

Mache (-) (*umg*) *f* show, sham; **jdn in der ~ haben** to be having a go at sb.

SCHLÜSSELWORT

machen ['maxən] *vt* **1** to do; **was machst du da?** what are you doing there?; **das ist nicht zu ~** that can't be done; **was ~ Sie (beruflich)?** what do you do for a living?; **mach, dass du hier verschwindest!** (you just) get out of here!; **mit mir kann mans ja ~!** (*umg*) the things I put up with!; **das lässt er nicht mit sich ~** he won't stand for that; **eine Prüfung ~** to take an exam.

2 (*herstellen*) to make; **das Radio leiser ~** to turn the radio down; **aus Holz gemacht** made of wood; **das Essen ~** to get the meal; **Schluss ~** to finish (off).

3 (*verursachen, bewirken*) to make; **jdm Angst ~** to make sb afraid; **das macht die Kälte** it's the cold that does that.

4 (*aus~*) to matter; **das macht nichts** that doesn't matter; **die Kälte macht mir nichts** I don't mind the cold.

5 (*kosten: ergeben*) to be; **3 und 5 macht 8** 3 and 5 is *od* are 8; **was** *od* **wie viel macht das?** how much does that come to?

6: was macht die Arbeit? how's the work going?; **was macht dein Bruder?** how is your brother doing?; **das Auto ~ lassen** to have the car done; **machs gut!** take care!; (*viel Glück*) good luck!

♦ *vi*: **mach schnell!** hurry up!; **mach schon!** come on!; **jetzt macht sie auf große Dame** (*umg*) she's playing the lady now; **lass mich mal ~** (*umg*) let me do it; (*ich bringe das in Ordnung*) I'll deal with it; **groß/klein ~** (*umg: Notdurft*) to do a big/little job; **sich** *dat* **in die Hose ~** to wet o.s.; **ins Bett ~** to wet one's bed; **das macht müde** it makes you tired; **in etw** *dat* **~** to be *od* deal in sth.

♦ *vr* to come along (nicely); **sich an etw** *akk*

~ to set about sth; **sich verständlich** ~ to make o.s. understood; **sich** *dat* **viel aus jdm/ etw** ~ to like sb/sth; **mach dir nichts daraus** don't let it bother you; **sich auf den Weg** ~ to get going; **sich an etw** *akk* ~ to set about sth.

Machenschaften *pl* wheelings and dealings *pl*.
Macher (-s, -) (*umg*) *m* man of action.
Macho ['matʃo] (*umg*) *adj* macho.
Macho (-s, -s) (*umg*) *m* macho type.
Macht [maxt] (-, ⁻e) *f* power; **mit aller** ~ with all one's might; **an der** ~ sein to be in power; **alles in unserer** ~ **Stehende** everything in our power; ~**ergreifung** *f* seizure of power; ~**haber** (-s, -) *m* ruler.
mächtig ['mɛçtɪç] *adj* powerful, mighty; (*umg*: *ungeheuer*) enormous.
Macht- *zW:* **m**~**los** *adj* powerless; ~**probe** *f* trial of strength; ~**stellung** *f* position of power; ~**wort** *nt:* **ein** ~**wort sprechen** to lay down the law.
Machwerk *nt* work; (*schlechte Arbeit*) botched job.
Macke ['makə] (-, -n) (*umg*) *f* (*Tick, Knall*) quirk; (*Fehler*) fault.
Macker (-s, -) (*umg*) *m* fellow, guy.
MAD (-) *m abk* (= *Militärischer Abschirmdienst*) ≈ MI5 (*BRIT*), CIA (*US*).
Madagaskar [mada'gaskar] (-s) *nt* Madagascar.
Mädchen ['mɛːtçən] *nt* girl; **ein** ~ **für alles** (*umg*) a dogsbody; (*im Büro etc*) a girl Friday; **m**~**haft** *adj* girlish; ~**name** *m* maiden name.
Made ['maːdə] (-, -n) *f* maggot.
Madeira[1] [ma'deːra] (-s) *nt* (*GEOG*) Madeira.
Madeira[2] (-s, -s) *m* (*Wein*) Madeira.
Mädel ['mɛːdl] (-s, -(s)) *nt* (*Dialekt*) lass, girl.
madig ['maːdɪç] *adj* maggoty; **jdm etw** ~ **machen** to spoil sth for sb.
Madrid [ma'drɪt] (-s) *nt* Madrid.
mag [maːk] *vb siehe* **mögen**.
Mag. *abk* = **Magister**.
Magazin [maga'tsiːn] (-s, -e) *nt* (*Zeitschrift, am Gewehr*) magazine; (*Lager*) storeroom; (*Bibliotheks*~) stockroom.
Magd [maːkt] (-, ⁻e) *f* maid(servant).
Magen ['maːgən] (-s, - *od* ⁻) *m* stomach; **jdm auf den** ~ **schlagen** (*umg*) to upset sb's stomach; (*fig*) to upset sb; **sich** *dat* **den** ~ **verderben** to upset one's stomach; ~**bitter** *m* bitters *pl*; ~**geschwür** *nt* stomach ulcer; ~**schmerzen** *pl* stomach-ache *sing*; ~**verstimmung** *f* stomach upset.
mager ['maːgər] *adj* lean; (*dünn*) thin; **M**~**keit** *f* leanness; thinness; **M**~**milch** *f* skimmed milk; **M**~**quark** *m* low-fat soft cheese; **M**~**sucht** *f* (*MED*) anorexia; ~**süchtig** *adj* anorexic.

Magie [ma'giː] *f* magic.
Magier ['maːgiər] (-s, -) *m* magician.
magisch ['maːgɪʃ] *adj* magical.
Magister [ma'gɪstər] (-s, -) *m* (*UNIV*) M.A., Master of Arts.
Magistrat [magɪs'traːt] (-(e)s, -e) *m* municipal authorities *pl*.
Magnat [ma'gnaːt] (-en, -en) *m* magnate.
Magnet [ma'gneːt] (-s *od* -en, -en) *m* magnet; ~**bahn** *f* magnetic railway; ~**band** *nt* (*COMPUT*) magnetic tape; **m**~**isch** *adj* magnetic.
magnetisieren [magneti'ziːrən] *vt* to magnetize.
Magnetnadel *f* magnetic needle.
Magnettafel *f* magnetic board.
Mahagoni [maha'goːni] (-s) *nt* mahogany.
Mähdrescher (-s, -) *m* combine (harvester).
mähen ['mɛːən] *vt, vi* to mow.
Mahl [maːl] (-(e)s, -e) *nt* meal.
mahlen *unreg vt* to grind.
Mahlstein *m* grindstone.
Mahlzeit *f* meal ♦ *interj* enjoy your meal!
Mahnbrief *m* reminder.
Mähne ['mɛːnə] (-, -n) *f* mane.
mahnen ['maːnən] *vt* to remind; (*warnend*) to warn; (*wegen Schuld*) to demand payment from; **jdn zur Eile/Geduld** ~ (*auffordern*) to urge sb to hurry/be patient *etc.*
Mahn- *zW:* ~**gebühr** *f* reminder fee; ~**mal** *nt* memorial; ~**schreiben** *nt* reminder.
Mahnung *f* admonition, warning; (*Mahnbrief*) reminder.
Mähre ['mɛːrə] (-, -n) *f* mare.
Mähren ['mɛːrən] (-s) *nt* Moravia.
Mai [mai] (-(e)s, -e) (*pl selten*) *m* May; *siehe auch* **September**; ~**baum** *m* maypole; ~**bowle** *f* white wine punch (*flavoured with woodruff*); ~**glöckchen** *nt* lily of the valley; ~**käfer** *m* cockchafer.
Mail [meːl] (-, -s) *f* (*COMPUT*) e-mail.
Mailand ['mailant] (-s) *nt* Milan.
Main [main] (-(e)s) *m* (*Fluss*) Main.
Mais [mais] (-es, -e) *m* maize, corn (*US*); ~**kolben** *m* corncob.
Majestät [majɛs'tɛːt] *f* majesty.
majestätisch *adj* majestic.
Majestätsbeleidigung *f* lese-majesty.
Majonäse [majo'nɛːzə] (-, -n) *f* mayonnaise.
Major [ma'joːr] (-s, -e) *m* (*MIL*) major; (*AVIAT*) squadron leader.
Majoran [majo'raːn] (-s, -e) *m* marjoram.
makaber [ma'kaːbər] *adj* macabre.
Makedonien [make'doːniən] (-s) *nt* Macedonia.
makedonisch *adj* Macedonian.
Makel ['maːkəl] (-s, -) *m* blemish; (*moralisch*) stain; **ohne** ~ flawless; **m**~**los** *adj* immaculate, spotless.
mäkeln ['mɛːkəln] *vi* to find fault.

Make-up [meːk'|ap] **(-s, -s)** *nt* make-up; (*flüssig*) foundation.

Makkaroni [maka'roːni] *pl* macaroni *sing.*

Makler ['maːklər] **(-s, -)** *m* broker; (*Grundstücks~*) estate agent (*BRIT*), realtor (*US*); ~**gebühr** *f* broker's commission, brokerage.

Makrele [ma'kreːlə] **(-, -n)** *f* mackerel.

Makro- *in zW* macro-.

Makrone [ma'kroːnə] **(-, -n)** *f* macaroon.

Makroökonomie *f* macroeconomics *sing.*

Mal [maːl] **(-(e)s, -e)** *nt* mark, sign; (*Zeitpunkt*) time; **ein für alle** ~ once and for all; **mit einem** ~**(e)** all of a sudden; **das erste** ~ the first time; **jedes** ~ every time, each time; **zum letzten** ~ for the last time; **ein paar** ~ a few times.

mal *adv* times.

-mal *suff* -times.

Malaie [ma'laɪə] **(-n, -n)** *m*, **Malaiin** *f* Malay.

malaiisch *adj* Malayan.

Malawi [ma'laːvi] **(-s)** *nt* Malawi.

Malaysia [ma'laɪzia] **(-s)** *nt* Malaysia.

Malaysier(in) **(-s, -)** *m(f)* Malaysian.

malaysisch *adj* Malaysian.

Malediven [male'diːvən] *pl*: **die** ~ the Maldive Islands.

malen *vt, vi* to paint.

Maler **(-s, -)** *m* painter.

Malerei [maːlə'raɪ] *f* painting.

malerisch *adj* picturesque.

Malkasten *m* paintbox.

Mallorca [ma'jɔrka, ma'lɔrka] **(-s)** *nt* Majorca.

Mallorquiner(in) [majɔr'kiːnər(ɪn), malɔr'kiːnər(ɪn)] **(-s, -)** *m(f)* Majorcan.

mallorquinisch *adj* Majorcan.

malnehmen *unreg vt, vi* to multiply.

Malta ['malta] **(-s)** *nt* Malta.

Malteser(in) [mal'teːzər(ɪn)] **(-s, -)** *m(f)* Maltese.

Malteser-Hilfsdienst *m* ≈ St. John's Ambulance Brigade (*BRIT*).

maltesisch *adj* Maltese.

malträtieren [maltrɛ'tiːrən] *vt* to ill-treat, maltreat.

Malz [malts] **(-es)** *nt* malt; ~**bonbon** *nt or m* cough drop; ~**kaffee** *m coffee substitute made from malt barley.*

Mama ['mamaː] **(-, -s)** (*umg*) *f* mum(my) (*BRIT*), mom(my) (*US*).

Mami ['mami] **(-, -s)** *f* = **Mama.**

Mammografie▲ [mamɔgra'fiː] *f* (*MED*) mammography.

Mammut ['mamʊt] **(-s, -e od -s)** *nt* mammoth ♦ *in zW* mammoth, giant; ~**anlagen** *pl* (*INDUSTRIE*) mammoth plants.

mampfen ['mampfən] (*umg*) *vt, vi* to munch, chomp.

man [man] *pron* one, you, people *pl*; ~ **hat mir gesagt** ... I was told ...

managen ['mɛnɪdʒən] *vt* to manage; **ich manage das schon!** (*umg*) I'll fix it somehow!

Manager(in) **(-s, -)** *m(f)* manager.

manch [manç] *pron*: ~ **ein(e)** ... many a ...; ~ **eine(r)** many a person.

manche(r, s) *adj* many a; (*pl*) a number of ♦ *pron* some.

mancherlei [mançər'laɪ] *adj inv* various ♦ *pron* a variety of things.

manchmal *adv* sometimes.

Mandant(in) [man'dant(ɪn)] *m(f)* (*JUR*) client.

Mandarine [manda'riːnə] *f* mandarin, tangerine.

Mandat [man'daːt] **(-(e)s, -e)** *nt* mandate; **sein** ~ **niederlegen** (*PARL*) to resign one's seat.

Mandel ['mandəl] **(-, -n)** *f* almond; (*ANAT*) tonsil; ~**entzündung** *f* tonsillitis.

Mandschurei **(-)** [mandʒu'raɪ] *f*: **die** ~ Manchuria.

Manege [ma'nɛːʒə] **(-, -n)** *f* ring, arena.

Mangel¹ ['maŋəl] **(-, -n)** *f* mangle; **durch die** ~ **drehen** (*fig*: *umg*) to put through it; (*Prüfling etc*) to put through the mill.

Mangel² ['maŋəl] **(-s, ⁻)** *m* lack; (*Knappheit*) shortage; (*Fehler*) defect, fault; ~ **an** +*dat* shortage of.

Mängelbericht ['mɛŋəlbərɪçt] *m* list of faults.

Mangelerscheinung *f* deficiency symptom.

mangelhaft *adj* poor; (*fehlerhaft*) defective, faulty; (*Schulnote*) unsatisfactory.

mangeln *vi unpers*: **es mangelt jdm an etw** *dat* **sb lacks sth** ♦ *vt* (*Wäsche*) to mangle.

mangels *präp* +*gen* for lack of.

Mangelware *f* scarce commodity.

Manie [ma'niː] *f* mania.

Manier [ma'niːr] **(-)** *f* manner; (*Stil*) style; (*pej*) mannerism.

Manieren *pl* manners *pl*; (*pej*) mannerisms *pl*.

manieriert [mani'riːrt] *adj* mannered, affected.

manierlich *adj* well-mannered.

Manifest [mani'fɛst] **(-es, -e)** *nt* manifesto.

Maniküre [mani'kyːrə] **(-, -n)** *f* manicure.

maniküren *vt* to manicure.

Manipulation [manipulatsi'oːn] *f* manipulation; (*Trick*) manoeuvre (*BRIT*), maneuver (*US*).

manipulieren [manipu'liːrən] *vt* to manipulate.

Manko ['maŋko] **(-s, -s)** *nt* deficiency; (*COMM*) deficit.

Mann [man] **(-(e)s, ⁻er** *od* (*NAUT*) **Leute)** *m* man; (*Ehe~*) husband; (*NAUT*) hand; **pro** ~ per head; **mit** ~ **und Maus untergehen** to go down with all hands; (*Passagierschiff*) to go down with no survivors; **seinen** ~ **stehen** to hold one's own; **etw an den** ~ **bringen** (*umg*) to get rid of sth; **einen kleinen** ~ **im Ohr haben** (*hum*: *umg*) to be crazy.

Männchen ['mɛnçən] *nt* little man; (*Tier*)

male; ~ **machen** (*Hund*) to (sit up and) beg.

Mannequin [manə'kɛ̃ː] (**-s, -s**) *nt* fashion model.

Männersache ['mɛnərzaxə] *f* (*Angelegenheit*) man's business; (*Arbeit*) man's job.

mannigfaltig ['manıçfaltıç] *adj* various, varied; **M~keit** *f* variety.

männlich ['mɛnlıç] *adj* (*BIOL*) male; (*fig*, *GRAM*) masculine.

Mannsbild *nt* (*veraltet: pej*) fellow.

Mannschaft *f* (*SPORT, fig*) team; (*NAUT, AVIAT*) crew; (*MIL*) other ranks *pl.*

Mannschaftsgeist *m* team spirit.

Mannsleute (*umg*) *pl* menfolk *pl.*

Mannweib (*pej*) *nt* mannish woman.

Manometer [mano'meːtər] *nt* (*TECH*) pressure gauge; ~! (*umg*) wow!

Manöver [ma'nøːvər] (**-s, -**) *nt* manoeuvre (*BRIT*), maneuver (*US*).

manövrieren [manø'vriːrən] *vt, vi* to manoeuvre (*BRIT*), maneuver (*US*).

Mansarde [man'zardə] (**-, -n**) *f* attic.

Manschette [man'ʃɛtə] *f* cuff; (*Papier~*) paper frill; (*TECH*) sleeve.

Manschettenknopf *m* cufflink.

Mantel ['mantəl] (**-s, ̈-**) *m* coat; (*TECH*) casing, jacket; ~**tarif** *m* general terms of employment; ~**tarifvertrag** *m* general agreement on conditions of employment.

Manuskript [manu'skrıpt] (**-(e)s, -e**) *nt* manuscript.

Mappe ['mapə] (**-, -n**) *f* briefcase; (*Akten~*) folder.

Marathonlauf ['maːratɔnlaʊf] *m* marathon.

Märchen ['mɛːrçən] *nt* fairy tale; **m~haft** *adj* fabulous; ~**prinz** *m* prince charming.

Marder ['mardər] (**-s, -**) *m* marten.

Margarine [marga'riːnə] *f* margarine.

Marge ['marʒə] (**-, -n**) *f* (*COMM*) margin.

Maria [ma'riːa] (**-**) *f* Mary.

Marienbild *nt* picture of the Virgin Mary.

Marienkäfer *m* ladybird.

Marihuana [marihu'aːna] (**-s**) *nt* marijuana.

Marinade [mari'naːdə] (**-, -n**) *f* (*KOCH*) marinade; (*Soße*) mayonnaise-based sauce.

Marine [ma'riːnə] *f* navy; **m~blau** *adj* navy-blue.

marinieren [mari'niːrən] *vt* to marinate.

Marionette [mario'nɛtə] *f* puppet.

Mark¹ [mark] (**-, -**) *f* (*HIST: Geld*) mark.

Mark² (**-(e)s**) *nt* (*Knochen~*) marrow; **jdn bis ins ~ treffen** (*fig*) to cut sb to the quick; **jdm durch ~ und Bein gehen** to go right through sb.

markant [mar'kant] *adj* striking.

Marke ['markə] (**-, -n**) *f* mark; (*Warensorte*) brand; (*Fabrikat*) make; (*Rabatt~, Brief~*) stamp; (*Essen(s)~*) luncheon voucher; (*aus Metall etc*) token, disc.

Marken- *zW:* ~**artikel** *m* proprietary article;

~**butter** *f* best quality butter; ~**kleidung** *f* designer clothes; ~**zeichen** *nt* trademark.

Marketing ['markətıŋ] (**-s**) *nt* marketing.

markieren [mar'kiːrən] *vt* to mark; (*umg*) to act ♦ *vi* (*umg*) to act it.

Markierung *f* marking.

markig ['markıç] *adj* (*fig*) pithy.

Markise [mar'kiːzə] (**-, -n**) *f* awning.

Markstück *nt* one-mark piece.

Markt [markt] (**-(e)s, ̈-e**) *m* market; ~**analyse** *f* market analysis; ~**anteil** *m* market share; **m~fähig** *adj* marketable; ~**forschung** *f* market research; **m~gängig** *adj* marketable; **m~gerecht** *adj* geared to market requirements; ~**lücke** *f* gap in the market; ~**platz** *m* market place; ~**preis** *m* market price; ~**wert** *m* market value; ~**wirtschaft** *f* market economy; **m~wirtschaftlich** *adj* free enterprise.

Marmelade [marmə'laːdə] (**-, -n**) *f* jam.

Marmor ['marmɔr] (**-s, -e**) *m* marble.

marmorieren [marmo'riːrən] *vt* to marble.

Marmorkuchen *m* marble cake.

marmorn *adj* marble.

Marokkaner(in) [marɔ'kaːnər(ın)] (**-s, -**) *m(f)* Moroccan.

marokkanisch *adj* Moroccan.

Marokko [ma'rɔko] (**-s**) *nt* Morocco.

Marone [ma'roːnə] (**-, -n**) *f* chestnut.

Marotte [ma'rɔtə] (**-, -n**) *f* fad, quirk.

Marsch¹ [marʃ] (**-, -en**) *f* marsh.

Marsch² (**-(e)s, ̈-e**) *m* march; **jdm den ~ blasen** (*umg*) to give sb a rocket; **m~** *interj* march; **m~ ins Bett!** off to bed with you!

Marschbefehl *m* marching orders *pl.*

marschbereit *adj* ready to move.

marschieren [mar'ʃiːrən] *vi* to march.

Marschverpflegung *f* rations *pl*; (*MIL*) field rations *pl.*

Marseille [mar'sɛːj] (**-s**) *nt* Marseilles.

Marsmensch ['marsmɛnʃ] *m* Martian.

Marter ['martər] (**-, -n**) *f* torment.

martern *vt* to torture.

Martinshorn ['martiːnshɔrn] *nt* siren (*of police etc*).

Märtyrer(in) ['mɛrtyrər(ın)] (**-s, -**) *m(f)* martyr.

Martyrium [mar'tyːriʊm] *nt* (*fig*) ordeal.

Marxismus [mar'ksısmʊs] *m* Marxism.

März [mɛrts] (**-(es), -e**) (*pl selten*) *m* March; *siehe auch* **September**.

Marzipan [martsi'paːn] (**-s, -e**) *nt* marzipan.

Masche ['maʃə] (**-, -n**) *f* mesh; (*Strick~*) stitch; **das ist die neueste ~** that's the latest dodge; **durch die ~n schlüpfen** to slip through the net.

Maschendraht *m* wire mesh.

maschenfest *adj* runproof.

Maschine [ma'ʃiːnə] *f* machine; (*Motor*) engine; ~ **schreiben** to type.

maschinell [maʃi'nɛl] *adj* machine(-),

mechanical.

Maschinen- *zW:* **~ausfallzeit** *f* machine downtime; **~bauer** *m* mechanical engineer; **~führer** *m* machinist; **m~geschrieben** *adj* typewritten; **~gewehr** *nt* machine gun; **m~lesbar** *adj* (*COMPUT*) machine-readable; **~pistole** *f* submachine gun; **~raum** *m* plant room; (*NAUT*) engine room; **~saal** *m* machine shop; **~schaden** *m* mechanical fault; **~schlosser** *m* fitter; **~schrift** *f* typescript; **~sprache** *f* (*COMPUT*) machine language.

Maschinerie [maʃinəˈriː] *f* (*fig*) machinery.

Maschinist(in) [maʃiˈnɪst(ɪn)] *m(f)* engineer.

Maser [ˈmaːzər] (**-, -n**) *f* grain.

Masern *pl* (*MED*) measles *sing*.

Maserung *f* grain(ing).

Maske [ˈmaskə] (**-, -n**) *f* mask.

Maskenball *m* fancy-dress ball.

Maskenbildner(in) *m(f)* make-up artist.

Maskerade [maskəˈraːdə] *f* masquerade.

maskieren [masˈkiːrən] *vt* to mask; (*verkleiden*) to dress up ♦ *vr* to disguise o.s., dress up.

Maskottchen [masˈkɔtçən] *nt* (lucky) mascot.

Maskulinum [maskuˈliːnʊm] (**-s, Maskulina**) *nt* (*GRAM*) masculine noun.

Masochist [mazoˈxɪst] (**-en, -en**) *m* masochist.

Maß¹ [maːs] (**-es, -e**) *nt* measure; (*Mäßigung*) moderation; (*Grad*) degree, extent; **über alle ~en** (*liter*) extremely, beyond measure; **~ halten** to exercise moderation; **mit zweierlei ~ messen** (*fig*) to operate a double standard; **sich** *dat* **etw nach ~ anfertigen lassen** to have sth made to measure *od* order (*US*); **in besonderem ~e** especially; **das ~ ist voll** (*fig*) that's enough (of that).

Maß² (**-, -(e)**) *f* litre (*BRIT*) *od* liter (*US*) of beer.

maß *etc vb siehe* **messen**.

Massage [maˈsaːʒə] (**-, -n**) *f* massage.

Massaker [maˈsaːkər] (**-s, -**) *nt* massacre.

Maßanzug *m* made-to-measure suit.

Maßarbeit *f* (*fig*) neat piece of work.

Masse [ˈmasə] (**-, -n**) *f* mass; **eine ganze ~** (*umg*) a great deal.

Maßeinheit *f* unit of measurement.

Massen- *zW:* **~artikel** *m* mass-produced article; **~blatt** *nt* tabloid; **~grab** *nt* mass grave; **m~haft** *adj* masses of; **~medien** *pl* mass media *pl*; **~produktion** *f* mass production; **~veranstaltung** *f* mass meeting; **~vernichtungswaffen** *pl* weapons of mass destruction *od* extermination; **~ware** *f* mass-produced article; **m~weise** *adv* in huge numbers.

Masseur [maˈsøːr] *m* masseur.

Masseuse [maˈsøːzə] *f* masseuse.

Maß- *zW:* **m~gebend** *adj* authoritative; **m~gebende Kreise** influential circles; **m~geblich** *adj* definitive; **m~geschneidert**

adj (*Anzug*) made-to-measure, made-to-order (*US*), custom *attrib* (*US*).

massieren [maˈsiːrən] *vt* to massage; (*MIL*) to mass.

massig [ˈmasɪç] *adj* massive; (*umg*) a massive amount of.

mäßig [ˈmɛːsɪç] *adj* moderate; **~en** [ˈmɛːsɪgən] *vt* to restrain, moderate; **sein Tempo ~en** to slacken one's pace; **M~keit** *f* moderation.

massiv [maˈsiːf] *adj* solid; (*fig*) heavy, rough; **~ werden** (*umg*) to turn nasty; **M~** (**-s, -e**) *nt* massif.

Maß- *zW:* **~krug** *m* tankard; **m~los** *adj* (*Verschwendung, Essen, Trinken*) excessive, immoderate; (*Enttäuschung, Ärger etc*) extreme; **~nahme** (**-, -n**) *f* measure, step; **m~regeln** *vt untr* to reprimand.

Maßstab *m* rule, measure; (*fig*) standard; (*GEOG*) scale; **als ~ dienen** to serve as a model.

maßstab(s)getreu *adj* (true) to scale.

maßvoll *adj* moderate.

Mast [mast] (**-(e)s, -e(n)**) *m* mast; (*ELEK*) pylon.

Mastdarm *m* rectum.

mästen [ˈmɛstən] *vt* to fatten.

masturbieren [mastʊrˈbiːrən] *vi* to masturbate.

Material [materiˈaːl] (**-s, -ien**) *nt* material(s); **~fehler** *m* material defect.

Materialismus [materiaˈlɪsmʊs] *m* materialism.

Materialist(in) *m(f)* materialist; **m~isch** *adj* materialistic.

Materialkosten *pl* cost *sing* of materials.

Materialprüfung *f* material(s) control.

Materie [maˈteːriə] *f* matter, substance.

materiell [materiˈɛl] *adj* material.

Mathe [ˈmatə] (**-**) *f* (*SCH: umg*) maths (*BRIT*), math (*US*).

Mathematik [matemaˈtiːk] *f* mathematics *sing*; **~er(in)** [mateˈmaːtɪkər(ɪn)] (**-s, -**) *m(f)* mathematician.

mathematisch [mateˈmaːtɪʃ] *adj* mathematical.

Matjeshering [ˈmatjəsheːrɪŋ] (*umg*) *m* salted young herring.

Matratze [maˈtratsə] (**-, -n**) *f* mattress.

Matrixdrucker *m* dot-matrix printer.

Matrixzeichen *nt* matrix character.

Matrize [maˈtriːtsə] (**-, -n**) *f* matrix; (*zum Abziehen*) stencil.

Matrose [maˈtroːzə] (**-n, -n**) *m* sailor.

Matsch [matʃ] (**-(e)s**) *m* mud; (*Schnee~*) slush.

matschig *adj* muddy; slushy.

matt [mat] *adj* weak; (*glanzlos*) dull; (*PHOT*) matt; (*SCHACH*) mate; **jdn ~ setzen** (*auch fig*) to checkmate sb; **M~** (**-s, -s**) *nt* (*SCHACH*) checkmate.

Matte [ˈmatə] (**-, -n**) *f* mat; **auf der ~ stehen** (*am Arbeitsplatz etc*) to be in.

Mattigkeit *f* weakness; dullness.
Mattscheibe *f* (*TV*) screen; ~ **haben** (*umg*) to be not quite with it.
Matura [ma'tuːra] (-) (*ÖSTERR, SCHWEIZ*) *f* = **Abitur**.
Mätzchen ['mɛtsçən] (*umg*) *nt* antics *pl*; ~ **machen** to fool around.
mau [mau] (*umg*) *adj* poor, bad.
Mauer ['mauər] (-, -n) *f* wall; ~**blümchen** (*umg*) *nt* (*fig*) wallflower.
mauern *vi* to build, lay bricks ♦ *vt* to build.
Mauer- *zW*: ~**schwalbe** *f* swift; ~**segler** *m* swift; ~**werk** *nt* brickwork; (*Stein*) masonry.
Maul [maul] (-(e)s, **Mäuler**) *nt* mouth; **ein loses** *od* **lockeres** ~ **haben** (*umg: frech sein*) to be an impudent so-and-so; (: *indiskret sein*) to be a blabbermouth; **halts** ~! (*umg*) shut your face (*!*); **darüber werden sich die Leute das** ~ **zerreißen** (*umg*) that will start people's tongues wagging; **dem Volk** *od* **den Leuten aufs** ~ **schauen** (*umg*) to listen to what ordinary people say; **m**~**en** (*umg*) *vi* to grumble; ~**esel** *m* mule; ~**korb** *m* muzzle; ~**sperre** *f* lockjaw; ~**tier** *nt* mule; ~**- und Klauenseuche** *f* (*Tiere*) foot-and-mouth disease.
Maulwurf *m* mole.
Maulwurfshaufen *m* molehill.
Maurer ['maurər] (-s, -) *m* bricklayer; **pünktlich wie die** ~ (*hum*) super-punctual.
Mauretanien [maurə'taːniən] (-s) *nt* Mauritania.
Maus [maus] (-, **Mäuse**) *f* (*auch COMPUT*) mouse; **Mäuse** *pl* (*umg: Geld*) bread *sing*, dough *sing*.
mauscheln ['mauʃəln] (*umg*) *vt, vi* (*manipulieren*) to fiddle.
mäuschenstill ['mɔysçən'ʃtɪl] *adj* very quiet.
Mausefalle *f* mousetrap.
mausen *vt* (*umg*) to pinch ♦ *vi* to catch mice.
mausern *vr* to moult (*BRIT*), molt (*US*).
mausetot *adj* stone dead.
mausgesteuert *adj* (*COMPUT*) mouse-driven.
Mausklick [mausklɪk] *nt* (*COMPUT*) (mouse) click.
Maut [maut] (-, -en) *f* toll.
max. *abk* (= *maximal*) max.
maximal [maksi'maːl] *adj* maximum.
Maxime [ma'ksiːmə] (-, -n) *f* maxim.
maximieren [maksi'miːrən] *vt* to maximize.
Maximierung *f* (*WIRTS*) maximization.
Maximum ['maksimʊm] (-s, **Maxima**) *nt* maximum.
Mayonnaise [majɔ'nɛːzə] (-, -n) *f* mayonnaise.
Mazedonien [matse'doːniən] (-s) *nt* Macedonia.
Mäzen [mɛ'tseːn] (-s, -e) *m* (*gen*) patron, sponsor.
MdB *nt abk* (= *Mitglied des Bundestages*) *member of the Bundestag*, ≈ MP.

MdL *nt abk* (= *Mitglied des Landtages*) *member of the Landtag*.
m. E. *abk* (= *meines Erachtens*) in my opinion.
Mechanik [me'çaːnɪk] *f* mechanics *sing*; (*Getriebe*) mechanics *pl*; ~**er** (-s, -) *m* mechanic, engineer.
mechanisch *adj* mechanical.
Mechanisierung *f* mechanization.
Mechanismus [meça'nɪsmʊs] *m* mechanism.
meckern ['mɛkərn] *vi* to bleat; (*umg*) to moan.
Mecklenburg ['meːklənburk] (-s) *nt* Mecklenburg.
Mecklenburg-Vorpommern (-s) *nt* (state of) Mecklenburg-Vorpommern.
Medaille [me'daljə] (-, -n) *f* medal.
Medaillon [medal'jõː] (-s, -s) *nt* (*Schmuck*) locket.
Medien ['meːdiən] *pl* media *pl*; ~**forschung** *f* media research; ~**gesellschaft** *f* media society.
Medikament [medika'mɛnt] *nt* medicine.
Meditation [meditatsi'oːn] *f* meditation.
meditieren [medi'tiːrən] *vi* to meditate.
Medium ['meːdiʊm] *nt* medium.
Medizin [medi'tsiːn] (-, -en) *f* medicine.
Mediziner(in) (-s, -) *m(f)* doctor; (*UNIV*) medic (*umg*).
medizinisch *adj* medical; ~**-technische Assistentin** medical assistant.
Meer [meːr] (-(e)s, -e) *nt* sea; **am** ~(**e**) by the sea; **ans** ~ **fahren** to go to the sea(side); ~**busen** *m* bay, gulf; ~**enge** *f* straits *pl*.
Meeres- *zW*: ~**früchte** *pl* seafood; ~**klima** *nt* maritime climate; ~**spiegel** *m* sea level.
Meer- *zW*: ~**jungfrau** *f* mermaid; ~**rettich** *m* horseradish; ~**schweinchen** *nt* guinea pig; ~**wasser** *nt* sea water.
Mega-, mega- [mega-] *in zW* mega-; ~**byte** [mega'bait] *nt* megabyte; ~**fon▲, ~phon** [mega'foːn] (-s, -e) *nt* megaphone; ~**watt** [mega'vat] *nt* megawatt.
Mehl [meːl] (-(e)s, -e) *nt* flour.
mehlig *adj* floury.
Mehlschwitze *f* (*KOCH*) roux.
mehr [meːr] *adv* more; **nie** ~ never again, nevermore (*liter*); **es war niemand** ~ **da** there was no one left; **nicht** ~ **lange** not much longer; **M**~**aufwand** *m* additional expenditure; **M**~**belastung** *f* excess load; (*fig*) additional burden; ~**deutig** *adj* ambiguous.
mehrere *indef pron* several; (*verschiedene*) various; ~**s** several things.
mehrfach *adj* multiple; (*wiederholt*) repeated.
Mehrheit *f* majority.
Mehrheitsprinzip *nt* principle of majority rule.
Mehrheitswahlrecht *nt* first-past-the-post voting system.
mehr- *zW*: ~**jährig** *adj attrib* of several years;

M~kosten pl additional costs pl; **~malig** adj repeated; **~mals** adv repeatedly;
M~parteiensystem nt multi-party system;
M~platzsystem nt (COMPUT) multi-user system; **M~programmbetrieb** m (COMPUT) multiprogramming; **~sprachig** adj multilingual; **~stimmig** adj for several voices; **~stimmig singen** to harmonize; **M~wegflasche** f returnable bottle; **M~wertsteuer** f value added tax, VAT; **M~zahl** f majority; (GRAM) plural.

Mehrzweck- in zW multipurpose.

meiden ['maɪdən] unreg vt to avoid.

Meile ['maɪlə] (-, -n) f mile; **das riecht man drei ~n gegen den Wind** (umg) you can smell that a mile off.

Meilenstein m milestone.

meilenweit adj for miles.

mein [maɪn] pron my.

meine(r, s) poss pron mine.

Meineid ['maɪnʔaɪt] m perjury.

meinen ['maɪnən] vt to think; (sagen) to say; (sagen wollen) to mean ♦ vi to think; **wie Sie ~!** as you wish; **damit bin ich gemeint** that refers to me; **das will ich ~** I should think so.

meiner gen von ich ♦ pron of me.

meinerseits adv for my part.

meinesgleichen ['maɪnəs'glaɪçən] pron people like me.

meinetwegen ['maɪnət've:gən] adv (für mich) for my sake; (wegen mir) on my account; (von mir aus) as far as I'm concerned; (ich habe nichts dagegen) I don't care od mind.

meinetwillen ['maɪnət'vɪlən] adv: **um ~ = meinetwegen**.

meinige pron: **der/die/das ~** od **M~** mine.

meins [maɪns] pron mine.

Meinung ['maɪnʊŋ] f opinion; **meiner ~ nach** in my opinion; **einer ~ sein** to think the same; **jdm die ~ sagen** to give sb a piece of one's mind.

Meinungs- zW: **~austausch** m exchange of views; **~forscher(in)** m(f) pollster; **~forschungsinstitut** nt opinion research institute; **~freiheit** f freedom of speech; **~umfrage** f opinion poll; **~verschiedenheit** f difference of opinion.

Meise ['maɪzə] (-, -n) f tit(mouse); **eine ~ haben** (umg) to be crackers.

Meißel ['maɪsəl] (-s, -) m chisel.

meißeln vt to chisel.

meist [maɪst] adj most ♦ adv mostly; **M~begünstigungsklausel** f (COMM) most-favoured-nation clause; **~bietend** adj: **~bietend versteigern** to sell to the highest bidder.

meiste(r, s) superl von **viel**.

meistens adv mostly.

Meister ['maɪstər] (-s, -) m master; (SPORT)

champion; **seinen ~ machen** to take one's master craftsman's diploma; **es ist noch kein ~ vom Himmel gefallen** (Sprichwort) no one is born an expert; **~brief** m master craftsman's diploma; **m~haft** adj masterly.

Meisterin f (auf einem Gebiet) master, expert; (SPORT) (woman) champion.

meistern vt to master; **sein Leben ~** to come to grips with one's life.

Meister- zW: **~schaft** f mastery; (SPORT) championship; **~stück** nt masterpiece; **~werk** nt masterpiece.

meistgekauft adj attrib best-selling.

Mekka ['mɛka] (-s, -s) nt (GEOG, fig) Mecca.

Melancholie [melaŋko'li:] f melancholy.

melancholisch [melaŋ'ko:lɪʃ] adj melancholy.

Meldebehörde f registration authorities pl.

Meldefrist f registration period.

melden vt to report; (registrieren) to register ♦ vr to report; to register; (SCH) to put one's hand up; (freiwillig) to volunteer; (auf etw, am Telefon) to answer; **nichts zu ~ haben** (umg) to have no say; **wen darf ich ~?** who shall I say (is here)?; **sich ~ bei** to report to; to register with; **sich auf eine Anzeige ~** to answer an advertisement; **es meldet sich niemand** there's no answer; **sich zu Wort ~** to ask to speak.

Meldepflicht f obligation to register with the police.

Meldestelle f registration office.

Meldung ['mɛldʊŋ] f announcement; (Bericht) report.

meliert [me'li:rt] adj mottled, speckled.

melken ['mɛlkən] unreg vt to milk.

Melodie [melo'di:] f melody, tune.

melodisch [me'lo:dɪʃ] adj melodious, tuneful.

melodramatisch [melodra'ma:tɪʃ] adj (auch fig) melodramatic.

Melone [me'lo:nə] (-, -n) f melon; (Hut) bowler (hat).

Membran [mem'bra:n] (-, -en) f (TECH) diaphragm; (ANAT) membrane.

Memme ['mɛmə] (-, -n) (umg) f cissy, yellow-belly.

Memoiren [memo'a:rən] pl memoirs pl.

Menge ['mɛŋə] (-, -n) f quantity; (Menschen~) crowd; (große Anzahl) lot (of); **jede ~** (umg) masses pl, loads pl.

mengen vt to mix ♦ vr: **sich ~ in** +akk to meddle with.

Mengen- zW: **~einkauf** m bulk buying; **~lehre** f (MATH) set theory; **~rabatt** m bulk discount.

Menorca [me'nɔrka] (-s) nt Menorca.

Mensa ['mɛnza] (-, -s od **Mensen**) f (UNIV) refectory (BRIT), commons (US).

Mensch [mɛnʃ] (-en, -en) m human being, man; (Person) person; **kein ~** nobody; **ich bin auch nur ein ~!** I'm only human; **~ ärgere**

dich nicht *nt* (*Spiel*) ludo.
Menschen- *zW:* ~**alter** *nt* generation; ~**feind**
m misanthrope; **m~freundlich** *adj*
philanthropical; ~**gedenken** *nt*: **der kälteste**
Winter seit ~**gedenken** the coldest winter in
living memory; ~**handel** *m* slave trade;
(*JUR*) trafficking in human beings; ~**kenner**
m judge of human nature; ~**kenntnis** *f*
knowledge of human nature; **m~leer** *adj*
deserted; ~**liebe** *f* philanthropy; ~**masse** *f*
crowd (of people); ~**menge** *f* crowd (of
people); **m~möglich** *adj* humanly possible;
~**rechte** *pl* human rights *pl*; **m~scheu** *adj*
shy; ~**schlag** (*umg*) *m* kind of people; ~**seele**
f: **keine** ~**seele** (*fig*) not a soul.
Menschenskind *interj* good heavens!
Menschen- *zW:* **m~unwürdig** *adj* degrading;
~**verachtung** *f* contempt for human beings
od of mankind; ~**verstand** *m*: **gesunder**
~**verstand** common sense; ~**würde** *f* human
dignity; **m~würdig** *adj* (*Behandlung*)
humane; (*Unterkunft*) fit for human
habitation.
Mensch- *zW:* ~**heit** *f* humanity, mankind;
m~lich *adj* human; (*human*) humane;
~**lichkeit** *f* humanity.
Menstruation [mɛnstruatsiˈoːn] *f*
menstruation.
Mentalität [mɛntaliˈtɛːt] *f* mentality.
Menü [meˈnyː] (**-s, -s**) *nt* (*auch COMPUT*) menu;
m~gesteuert *adj* (*COMPUT*) menu-driven.
Merkblatt *nt* instruction sheet *od* leaflet.
merken [ˈmɛrkən] *vt* to notice; **sich** *dat* **etw** ~
to remember sth; **sich** *dat* **eine Autonummer**
~ to make a (mental) note of a licence
(*BRIT*) *od* license (*US*) number.
merklich *adj* noticeable.
Merkmal *nt* sign, characteristic.
merkwürdig *adj* odd.
meschugge [meˈʃʊgə] (*umg*) *adj* nuts,
meshuga (*US*).
Mess-▲ *zW:* ~**band** *nt* tape measure; **m~bar**
adj measurable; ~**becher** *m* measuring cup.
Messbuch▲ *nt* missal.
Messdiener▲ *m* (*REL*) server, acolyte (*form*).
Messe [ˈmɛsə] (**-, -n**) *f* fair; (*ECCL*) mass; (*MIL*)
mess; **auf der** ~ at the fair; ~**gelände** *nt*
exhibition centre (*BRIT*) *od* center (*US*).
messen *unreg vt* to measure ♦ *vr* to compete.
Messer (**-s, -**) *nt* knife; **auf des** ~**s Schneide**
stehen (*fig*) to hang in the balance; **jdm ins**
offene ~ **laufen** (*fig*) to walk into a trap;
m~scharf *adj* (*fig*): **m~scharf schließen** to
conclude with incredible logic (*ironisch*);
~**spitze** *f* knife point; (*in Rezept*) pinch;
~**stecherei** *f* knife fight.
Messestadt *f* (town with an) exhibition
centre (*BRIT*) *od* center (*US*).
Messestand *m* exhibition stand.
Messgerät▲ *nt* measuring device, gauge.

Messgewand▲ *nt* chasuble.
Messing [ˈmɛsɪŋ] (**-s**) *nt* brass.
Messstab▲ *m* (*AUT: Öl~ etc*) dipstick.
Messung *f* (*das Messen*) measuring; (*von*
Blutdruck) taking; (*Messergebnis*)
measurement.
Messwert▲ *m* measurement;
(*Ableseergebnis*) reading.
Metall [meˈtal] (**-s, -e**) *nt* metal; **die**
~ **verarbeitende Industrie** the metal-
processing industry; **m~en** *adj* metallic;
m~isch *adj* metallic.
Metallurgie [metalʊrˈgiː] *f* metallurgy.
Metapher [meˈtafər] (**-, -n**) *f* metaphor.
metaphorisch [metaˈfoːrɪʃ] *adj* metaphorical.
Metaphysik [metafyˈziːk] *f* metaphysics *sing*.
Metastase [metaˈstaːzə] (**-, -n**) *f* (*MED*)
secondary growth.
Meteor [meteˈoːr] (**-s, -e**) *m* meteor.
Meteorologe [meteoroˈloːgə] (**-n, -n**) *m*
meteorologist.
Meter [ˈmeːtər] (**-s, -**) *m od nt* metre (*BRIT*),
meter (*US*); **in 500** ~ **Höhe** at a height of 500
metres; ~**maß** *nt* tape measure; ~**ware** *f*
(*TEXTIL*) piece goods.
Methode [meˈtoːdə] (**-, -n**) *f* method.
Methodik [meˈtoːdɪk] *f* methodology.
methodisch [meˈtoːdɪʃ] *adj* methodical.
Metier [metiˈeː] (**-s, -s**) *nt* (*hum*) job, profession.
metrisch [ˈmeːtrɪʃ] *adj* metric, metrical.
Metropole [metroˈpoːlə] (**-, -n**) *f* metropolis.
Mettwurst [ˈmɛtvʊrst] *f* (smoked) sausage.
Metzger [ˈmɛtsgər] (**-s, -**) *m* butcher.
Metzgerei [mɛtsgəˈraɪ] *f* butcher's (shop).
Meuchelmord [ˈmɔʏçəlmɔrt] *m* assassination.
Meute [ˈmɔʏtə] (**-, -n**) *f* pack.
Meuterei [mɔʏtəˈraɪ] *f* mutiny.
meutern *vi* to mutiny.
Mexikaner(in) [mɛksiˈkaːnər(ɪn)] (**-s, -**) *m(f)*
Mexican.
mexikanisch *adj* Mexican.
Mexiko [ˈmɛksiko] (**-s**) *nt* Mexico.
MEZ *abk* (= *mitteleuropäische Zeit*) C.E.T.
MFG *abk* = **Mitfahrgelegenheit**.
MfG *abk* (= *Mit freundlichen Grüßen*) (with)
best wishes.
MG (**-(s), -(s)**) *nt abk* = **Maschinengewehr**.
mg *abk* (= *Milligramm*) mg.
mhd. *abk* (= *mittelhochdeutsch*) MHG.
MHz *abk* (= *Megahertz*) MHz.
Mi. *abk* = **Mittwoch**.
miauen [miˈaʊən] *vi* to miaow.
mich [mɪç] *akk von* **ich** ♦ *pron* me; (*reflexiv*)
myself.
mick(e)rig [ˈmɪk(ə)rɪç] (*umg*) *adj* pathetic;
(*altes Männchen*) puny.
mied *etc* [miːt] *vb siehe* **meiden**.
Miederwaren [ˈmiːdərvaːrən] *pl* corsetry *sing*.
Mief [miːf] (**-s**) (*umg*) *m* fug; (*muffig*) stale air;
(*Gestank*) stink, pong (*BRIT*).

miefig (*umg*) *adj* smelly, pongy (*BRIT*).
Miene ['mi:nə] (-, -n) *f* look, expression; **gute**
~ **zum bösen Spiel machen** to grin and bear
it.
Mienenspiel *nt* facial expressions *pl*.
mies [mi:s] (*umg*) *adj* lousy.
Miese ['mi:zə] (*umg*) *pl*: **in den** ~**n sein** to be
in the red.
Miesmacher(in) (*umg*) *m(f)* killjoy.
Mietauto *nt* hired car (*BRIT*), rental car (*US*).
Miete ['mi:tə] (-, -n) *f* rent; **zur** ~ **wohnen** to
live in rented accommodation *od*
accommodations (*US*).
mieten *vt* to rent; (*Auto*) to hire (*BRIT*), rent.
Mieter(in) (-s, -) *m(f)* tenant; ~**schutz** *m* rent
control.
Mietshaus *nt* tenement, block of flats (*BRIT*)
od apartments (*US*).
Miet- *zW*: ~**verhältnis** *nt* tenancy; ~**vertrag** *m*
tenancy agreement; ~**wagen** *m* = ~**auto**;
~**wucher** *m* the charging of exorbitant
rent(s).
Mieze ['mi:tsə] (-, -n) (*umg*) *f* (*Katze*) pussy;
(*Mädchen*) chick, bird (*BRIT*).
Migräne [mi'grɛ:nə] (-, -n) *f* migraine.
Mikado [mi'ka:do] (-s) *nt* (*Spiel*) pick-a-stick.
Mikro- ['mi:kro] *in zW* micro-.
Mikrobe [mi'kro:bə] (-, -n) *f* microbe.
Mikro- *zW*: ~**chip** *m* microchip; ~**computer** *m*
microcomputer; ~**fiche** *m od nt* microfiche;
~**film** *m* microfilm.
Mikrofon [mikro'fo:n] (-s, -e) *nt* microphone.
Mikroökonomie *f* microeconomics *pl*.
Mikrophon [mikro'fo:n] (-s, -e) *nt*
microphone.
Mikroprozessor (-s, -oren) *m*
microprocessor.
Mikroskop [mikro'sko:p] (-s, -e) *nt*
microscope; **m**~**isch** *adj* microscopic.
Mikrowelle ['mi:krovelə] *f* microwave.
Mikrowellenherd *m* microwave (oven).
Milbe ['milbə] (-, -n) *f* mite.
Milch [milç] (-) *f* milk; (*Fisch*~) milt, roe;
~**drüse** *f* mammary gland; ~**glas** *nt* frosted
glass.
milchig *adj* milky.
Milch- *zW*: ~**kaffee** *m* white coffee;
~**mixgetränk** *nt* milk shake; ~**pulver** *nt*
powdered milk; ~**straße** *f* Milky Way; ~**tüte**
f milk carton; ~**zahn** *m* milk tooth.
mild [milt] *adj* mild; (*Richter*) lenient;
(*freundlich*) kind, charitable.
Milde ['mildə] (-, -n) *f* mildness; leniency.
mildern *vt* to mitigate, soften; (*Schmerz*) to
alleviate; ~**de Umstände** extenuating
circumstances.
Milieu [mili'ø:] (-s, -s) *nt* background,
environment; **m**~**geschädigt** *adj*
maladjusted.
militant [mili'tant] *adj* militant.

Militär [mili'tɛ:r] (-s) *nt* military, army;
~**dienst** *m* military service; ~**gericht** *nt*
military court; **m**~**isch** *adj* military.
Militarismus [milita'rɪsmʊs] *m* militarism.
militaristisch *adj* militaristic.
Militärpflicht *f* (compulsory) military
service.
Mill. *abk* (= *Million(en)*) m.
Milli- *in zW* milli-.
Milliardär(in) [miliar'dɛ:r(in)] (-s, -e) *m(f)*
multimillionaire.
Milliarde [mi'liardə] (-, -n) *f* milliard, billion
(*bes US*).
Millimeter *m* millimetre (*BRIT*), millimeter
(*US*); ~**papier** *nt* graph paper.
Million [mili'o:n] (-, -en) *f* million.
Millionär(in) [milio'nɛ:r(in)] (-s, -e) *m(f)*
millionaire.
millionenschwer (*umg*) *adj* worth a few
million.
Milz [milts] (-, -en) *f* spleen.
Mimik ['mi:mik] *f* mime.
Mimose [mi'mo:zə] (-, -n) *f* mimosa; (*fig*)
sensitive person.
minder ['mindər] *adj* inferior ♦ *adv* less;
~**begabt** *adj* less able; ~**bemittelt** *adj*: **geistig**
~**bemittelt** (*ironisch*) intellectually
challenged.
Minderheit *f* minority.
Minderheitsbeteiligung *f* (*Aktien*) minority
interest.
Minderheitsregierung *f* minority
government.
minderjährig *adj* minor; **M**~**jährige(r)** *f(m)*
minor; **M**~**keit** *f* minority.
mindern *vt*, *vr* to decrease, diminish.
Minderung *f* decrease.
minder- *zW*: ~**wertig** *adj* inferior;
M~**wertigkeitsgefühl** *nt* inferiority complex;
M~**wertigkeitskomplex** (-es, -e) *m*
inferiority complex.
Mindestalter *nt* minimum age.
Mindestbetrag *m* minimum amount.
mindeste(r, s) *adj* least.
mindestens *adv* at least.
Mindest- *zW*: ~**lohn** *m* minimum wage; ~**maß**
nt minimum; ~**stand** *m* (*COMM*) minimum
stock; ~**umtausch** *m* minimum obligatory
exchange.
Mine ['mi:nə] (-, -n) *f* mine; (*Bleistift*~) lead;
(*Kugelschreiber*~) refill.
Minenfeld *nt* minefield.
Minensuchboot *nt* minesweeper.
Mineral [mine'ra:l] (-s, -e *od* -ien) *nt* mineral;
m~**isch** *adj* mineral; ~**ölsteuer** *f* tax on oil
and petrol (*BRIT*) *od* gasoline (*US*); ~**wasser**
nt mineral water.
Miniatur [minia'tu:r] *f* miniature.
Minigolf ['minigɔlf] *nt* miniature golf.
minimal [mini'ma:l] *adj* minimal.

Minimum ['mi:nimʊm] (**-s, Minima**) *nt* minimum.

Minirock ['minirɔk] *m* miniskirt.

Minister(in) [mi'nɪstər(ın)] (**-s, -**) *m(f)* (*POL*) minister.

ministeriell [mınısteri'ɛl] *adj* ministerial.

Ministerium [mınıs'te:riʊm] *nt* ministry.

Ministerpräsident(in) *m(f)* prime minister.

Minna ['mına] *f*: **jdn zur ~ machen** (*umg*) to give sb a piece of one's mind.

minus ['mi:nʊs] *adv* minus; **M~** (**-, -**) *nt* deficit; **M~pol** *m* negative pole; **M~zeichen** *nt* minus sign.

Minute [mi'nu:tə] (**-, -n**) *f* minute; **auf die ~ (genau** *od* **pünktlich)** (right) on the dot.

Minutenzeiger *m* minute hand.

Mio. *abk* (= *Million(en)*) m.

mir [mi:r] *dat von* **ich ♦** *pron* (to) me; **von ~ aus!** I don't mind; **wie du ~, so ich dir** (*Sprichwort*) tit for tat (*umg*); (*als Drohung*) I'll get my own back; **~ nichts, dir nichts** just like that.

Mirabelle [mira'bɛlə] *f* mirabelle, *small yellow plum*.

Misch- *zW*: **~batterie** *f* mixer tap; **~brot** *nt bread made from more than one kind of flour*; **~ehe** *f* mixed marriage.

mischen *vt* to mix; (*COMPUT: Datei, Text*) to merge; (*Karten*) to shuffle ♦ *vi* (*Karten*) to shuffle.

Misch- *zW*: **~konzern** *m* conglomerate; **~ling** *m* half-caste; **~masch** (*umg*) *m* hotchpotch; (*Essen*) concoction; **~pult** *nt* (*RUNDF, TV*) mixing panel.

Mischung *f* mixture.

Mischwald *m* mixed (deciduous and coniferous) woodland.

miserabel [mizə'ra:bəl] (*umg*) *adj* lousy; (*Gesundheit*) wretched; (*Benehmen*) dreadful.

Misere [mi'ze:rə] (**-, -n**) *f* (*von Leuten, Wirtschaft etc*) plight; (*von Hunger, Krieg etc*) misery, miseries *pl*.

Miss-▲ *zW*: **m~achten** *vt untr* to disregard; **~achtung** *f* disregard; **~behagen** *nt* uneasiness; (*~fallen*) discontent; **~bildung** *f* deformity; **m~billigen** *vt untr* to disapprove of; **~billigung** *f* disapproval; **~brauch** *m* abuse; (*falscher Gebrauch*) misuse; **m~brauchen** *vt untr* to abuse; to misuse; (*vergewaltigen*) to assault; **jdn zu** *od* **für etw m~brauchen** to use sb for *od* to do sth; **m~deuten** *vt untr* to misinterpret.

missen *vt* to do without; (*Erfahrung*) to miss.

Misserfolg▲ *m* failure.

Missernte▲ *f* crop failure.

Missetat ['mısəta:t] *f* misdeed.

Missetäter *m* criminal; (*umg*) scoundrel.

Miss-▲ *zW*: **m~fallen** *unreg vi untr*: **jdm m~fallen** to displease sb; **~fallen** (**-s**) *nt*

displeasure; **~geburt** *f* freak; (*fig*) failure; **~geschick** *nt* misfortune; **m~glücken** *vi untr* to fail; **jdm m~glückt etw** sb does not succeed with sth; **m~gönnen** *vt untr*: **jdm etw m~gönnen** to (be)grudge sb sth; **~griff** *m* mistake; **~gunst** *f* envy; **m~günstig** *adj* envious; **m~handeln** *vt untr* to ill-treat; **~handlung** *f* ill-treatment; **~helligkeit** *f*: **~helligkeiten haben** to be at variance.

Mission [mısi'o:n] *f* mission.

Missionar(in) [mısio'na:r(ın)] *m(f)* missionary.

Missklang▲ *m* discord.

Misskredit▲ *m* discredit.

misslang *etc▲* [mıs'laŋ] *vb siehe* **misslingen**.

missliebig▲ *adj* unpopular.

misslingen▲ [mıs'lıŋən] *unreg vi untr* to fail; **M~** (**-s**) *nt* failure.

misslungen▲ [mıs'lʊŋən] *pp von* **misslingen**.

Miss-▲ *zW*: **~mut** *m* bad temper; **m~mutig** *adj* cross; **m~raten** *unreg vi untr* to turn out badly ♦ *adj* ill-bred; **~stand** *m* deplorable state of affairs; **~stimmung** *f* discord; (*~mut*) ill feeling.

misst▲ *vb siehe* **messen**.

Miss-▲ *zW*: **m~trauen** *vi untr* to mistrust; **~trauen** (**-s**) *nt*: **~trauen (gegenüber)** distrust (of), suspicion (of); **~trauensantrag** *m* (*POL*) motion of no confidence; **~trauensvotum** *nt* (*POL*) vote of no confidence; **m~trauisch** *adj* distrustful, suspicious; **~verhältnis** *nt* disproportion; **m~verständlich** *adj* unclear; **~verständnis** *nt* misunderstanding; **m~verstehen** *unreg vt untr* to misunderstand.

Misswahl ['mısva:l] *f* beauty contest.

Misswirtschaft▲ *f* mismanagement.

Mist [mıst] *m* dung; (*umg*) rubbish; **~!** (*umg*) blast!; **das ist nicht auf seinem ~ gewachsen** (*umg*) he didn't think that up himself.

Mistel (**-, -n**) *f* mistletoe.

Mist- *zW*: **~gabel** *f* pitchfork (*used for shifting manure*); **~haufen** *m* dungheap; **~stück** (*umg!*) *nt*, **~vieh** (*umg!*) *nt* (*Mann*) bastard (*!*); (*Frau*) bitch (*!*).

mit [mıt] *präp +dat* with; (*mittels*) by ♦ *adv* along, too; **~ der Bahn** by train; **~ dem nächsten Flugzeug/Bus kommen** to come on the next plane/bus; **~ Bleistift schreiben** to write in pencil; **~ Verlust** at a loss; **er ist ~ der Beste in der Gruppe** he is among the best in the group; **wie wärs ~ einem Bier?** (*umg*) how about a beer?; **~ 10 Jahren** at the age of 10; **wollen Sie ~?** do you want to come along?

Mitarbeit ['mıt|arbaıt] *f* cooperation; **m~en** *vi*: **m~en (an +***dat*) to cooperate (on), collaborate (on).

Mitarbeiter(in) *m(f)* (*an Projekt*) collaborator; (*Kollege*) colleague; (*Angestellter*) member of staff ♦ *pl* staff; ~**stab** *m* staff.

mit- *zW:* ~**bekommen** *unreg vt* to get *od* be given; (*umg: verstehen*) to get; ~**bestimmen** *vi:* (**bei etw**) ~**bestimmen** to have a say (in sth) ♦ *vt* to have an influence on; **M**~**bestimmung** *f* participation in decision-making; (*POL*) determination; ~**bringen** *unreg vt* to bring along; **M**~**bringsel** ['mɪtbrɪŋzəl] (**-s, -**) *nt* (*Geschenk*) small present; (*Andenken*) souvenir; **M**~**bürger(in)** *m(f)* fellow citizen; ~**denken** *unreg vi* to follow; **du hast ja** ~**gedacht!** good thinking!; ~**dürfen** *unreg vi:* **wir durften nicht** ~ we weren't allowed to go along; **M**~**eigentümer** *m* joint owner.

miteinander [mɪt|aɪ'nandər] *adv* together, with one another.

miterleben *vt* to see, witness.

Mitesser ['mɪt|ɛsər] (**-s, -**) *m* blackhead.

mit- *zW:* ~**fahren** *unreg vi:* (**mit jdm**) ~**fahren** to go (with sb); (*auf Reise auch*) to go *od* travel (with sb); **M**~**fahrerzentrale** *f* agency for arranging lifts; **M**~**fahrgelegenheit** *f* lift; ~**fühlen** *vi:* ~ **jdm/etw** ~**fühlen** to sympathize with sb/sth; ~**fühlend** *adj* sympathetic; ~**führen** *vt* (*Papiere, Ware etc*) to carry (with one); (*Fluss*) to carry along; ~**geben** *unreg vt* to give; **M**~**gefühl** *nt* sympathy; ~**gehen** *unreg vi* to go *od* come along; **etw** ~**gehen lassen** (*umg*) to pinch sth; ~**genommen** *adj* done in, in a bad way; **M**~**gift** *f* dowry.

Mitglied ['mɪtgliːt] *nt* member.

Mitgliedsbeitrag *m* membership fee, subscription.

Mitgliedschaft *f* membership.

mit- *zW:* ~**haben** *unreg vt:* **etw** ~**haben** to have sth (with one); ~**halten** *unreg vi* to keep up; ~**helfen** *vi unreg* to help, lend a hand; **bei etw** ~**helfen** to help with sth; **M**~**hilfe** *f* help, assistance; ~**hören** *vt* to listen in to; ~**kommen** *unreg vi* to come along; (*verstehen*) to keep up, follow; **M**~**läufer** *m* hanger-on; (*POL*) fellow traveller.

Mitleid *nt* sympathy; (*Erbarmen*) compassion.

Mitleidenschaft *f:* **in** ~ **ziehen** to affect.

mitleidig *adj* sympathetic.

mitleidlos *adj* pitiless, merciless.

mit- *zW:* ~**machen** *vt* to join in, take part in; (*umg: einverstanden sein*): **da macht mein Chef nicht** ~ my boss won't go along with that; **M**~**mensch** *m* fellow man; ~**mischen** (*umg*) *vi* (*sich beteiligen*): ~**mischen (in** +*dat od* **bei**) to be involved (in); (*sich einmischen*) to interfere (in); ~**nehmen** *unreg vt* to take along *od* away; (*anstrengen*) to wear out, exhaust; ~**genommen aussehen** to look the worse for wear; ~**reden** *vi* (*Meinung äußern*): (**bei etw**) ~**reden** to join in (sth); (~*bestimmen*) to have a say (in sth) ♦ *vt:* **Sie**

haben hier nichts ~**zureden** this is none of your concern; ~**reißen** *vt unreg* to sweep away; (*fig: begeistern*) to carry away; ~**reißend** *adj* (*Rhythmus*) infectious; (*Reden*) rousing; (*Film, Fußballspiel*) thrilling, exciting.

mitsamt [mɪt'zamt] *präp* +*dat* together with.

mitschneiden *vt unreg* to record.

Mitschnitt ['mɪtʃnɪt] (**-(e)s, -e**) *m* recording.

mitschreiben *unreg vt* to write *od* take down ♦ *vi* to take notes.

Mitschuld *f* complicity.

mitschuldig *adj:* ~ (**an** +*dat*) implicated (in); (*an Unfall*) partly responsible (for).

Mitschuldige(r) *f(m)* accomplice.

mit- *zW:* **M**~**schüler(in)** *m(f)* schoolmate; ~**spielen** *vi* to join in, take part; **er hat ihr übel** *od* **hart** ~**gespielt** (*Schaden zufügen*) he has treated her badly; **M**~**spieler(in)** *m(f)* partner; **M**~**spracherecht** *nt* voice, say.

Mittag ['mɪtaːk] (**-(e)s, -e**) *m* midday, noon, lunchtime; **morgen** ~ tomorrow at lunchtime *od* noon; ~ **machen** to take one's lunch hour; (**zu**) ~ **essen** to have lunch; ~**essen** *nt* lunch, dinner.

mittags *adv* at lunchtime *od* noon.

Mittags- *zW:* ~**pause** *f* lunch break; ~**ruhe** *f* period of quiet (after lunch); (*in Geschäft*) midday closing; ~**schlaf** *m* early afternoon nap, siesta; ~**zeit** *f:* **während** *od* **in der** ~**zeit** at lunchtime.

Mittäter(in) ['mɪttɛːtər(ɪn)] *m(f)* accomplice.

Mitte ['mɪtə] (**-, -n**) *f* middle; **aus unserer** ~ from our midst.

mitteilen ['mɪttaɪlən] *vt:* **jdm etw** ~ to inform sb of sth, communicate sth to sb ♦ *vr:* **sich** (**jdm**) ~ to communicate (with sb).

mitteilsam *adj* communicative.

Mitteilung *f* communication; **jdm (eine)** ~ **von etw machen** (*form*) to inform sb of sth; (*bekannt geben*) to announce sth to sb.

Mitteilungsbedürfnis *nt* need to talk to other people.

Mittel ['mɪtəl] (**-s, -**) *nt* means; (*Methode*) method; (*MATH*) average; (*MED*) medicine; **kein** ~ **unversucht lassen** to try everything; **als letztes** ~ as a last resort; **ein** ~ **zum Zweck** a means to an end; ~**alter** *nt* Middle Ages *pl*; **m**~**alterlich** *adj* medieval; ~**amerika** *nt* Central America (and the Caribbean); **m**~**amerikanisch** *adj* Central American; **m**~**bar** *adj* indirect; ~**ding** *nt* (*Mischung*) cross; ~**europa** *nt* Central Europe; ~**europäer(in)** *m(f)* Central European; **m**~**europäisch** *adj* Central European; **m**~**fristig** *adj* (*Finanzplanung, Kredite*) medium-term; ~**gebirge** *nt* low mountain range; **m**~**groß** *adj* medium-sized; **m**~**los** *adj* without means; ~**maß** *nt:* **das (gesunde)** ~**maß** the happy medium; **m**~**mäßig** *adj* mediocre, middling; ~**mäßigkeit** *f* mediocrity; ~**meer** *nt* Mediterranean (Sea); **m~prächtig** *adj* not bad; ~**punkt** *m* centre (*BRIT*), center (*US*); **im ~punkt stehen** to be centre-stage.

mittels *präp +gen* by means of.

Mittelschicht *f* middle class.

Mittelsmann (-(e)s, *pl* **Mittelsmänner** *od* **Mittelsleute**) *m* intermediary.

Mittel- *zW:* ~**stand** *m* middle class; ~**streckenrakete** *f* medium-range missile; ~**streifen** *m* central reservation (*BRIT*), median strip (*US*); ~**stufe** *f* (*SCH*) middle school (*BRIT*), junior high (*US*); ~**stürmer** *m* centre forward; ~**weg** *m* middle course; ~**welle** *f* (*RUNDF*) medium wave; ~**wert** *m* average value, mean.

mitten ['mɪtən] *adv* in the middle; ~ **auf der Straße/in der Nacht** in the middle of the street/night; ~**drin** *adv* (right) in the middle of it; ~**durch** *adv* (right) through the middle.

Mitternacht ['mɪtɐrnaxt] *f* midnight.

mittlere(r, s) ['mɪtlərə(r, s)] *adj* middle; (*durchschnittlich*) medium, average; **der Mittlere Osten** the Middle East; **mittleres Management** middle management.

MITTLERE REIFE

The **mittlere Reife** *is the standard certificate achieved at a* **Realschule** *on successful completion of 6 years' education there. If a pupil at a* **Realschule** *attains good results in several subjects he or she is allowed to enter the the 11th class of a* **Gymnasium** *to study for the* **Abitur**.

---

mittlerweile ['mɪtlər'vaɪlə] *adv* meanwhile.

Mittwoch ['mɪtvɔx] (-(e)s, -e) *m* Wednesday; *siehe auch* **Dienstag**.

mittwochs *adv* on Wednesdays.

mitunter [mɪt'|ʊntər] *adv* occasionally, sometimes.

mit- *zW:* ~**verantwortlich** *adj* also responsible; ~**verdienen** *vi* (to go out to) work as well; **M~verfasser** *m* co-author; **M~verschulden** *nt* contributory negligence; ~**wirken** *vi:* (**bei etw**) ~**wirken** to contribute (to sth); (*THEAT*) to take part in (sth); **M~wirkende(r)** *f(m):* **die M~wirkenden** (*THEAT*) the cast; **M~wirkung** *f* contribution; participation; **unter M~wirkung von** with the help of; **M~wisser** (-s, -) *m:* **M~wisser (einer Sache** *gen*) **sein** to be in the know (about sth); **jdn zum M~wisser machen** to tell sb (all) about it.

Mixer ['mɪksər] (-s, -) *m* (*Bar~*) cocktail waiter; (*Küchen~*) blender; (*Rührmaschine*, *RUNDF*, *TV*) mixer.

ml *abk* (= *Milliliter*) ml.

mm *abk* (= *Millimeter*) mm.

Mnemonik [mne'mo:nɪk] *f* mnemonic.

Mo. *abk* = **Montag**.

mobben ['mɔbən] *vt* to bully (at work).

Mobbing ['mɔbɪŋ] (-s) *nt* workplace bullying.

Möbel ['møːbəl] (-s, -) *nt* (piece of) furniture; ~**packer** *m* removal man (*BRIT*), (furniture) mover (*US*); ~**wagen** *m* furniture *od* removal van (*BRIT*), moving van (*US*).

mobil [mo'biːl] *adj* mobile; (*MIL*) mobilized.

Mobilfunk *m* cellular telephone service.

Mobiliar [mobili'aːr] (-s, -e) *nt* movable assets *pl*.

mobilisieren [mobili'ziːrən] *vt* (*MIL*) to mobilize.

Mobilmachung *f* mobilization.

Mobiltelefon *nt* (*TELEC*) mobile phone.

möbl. *abk* = **möbliert**.

möblieren [mø'bliːrən] *vt* to furnish; **möbliert wohnen** to live in furnished accommodation.

mochte *etc* ['mɔxtə] *vb siehe* **mögen**.

Möchtegern- ['mœçtəgern] *in zW* (*ironisch*) would-be.

Modalität [modali'tɛːt] *f* (*von Plan, Vertrag etc*) arrangement.

Mode ['moːdə] (-, -n) *f* fashion; ~**farbe** *f* in colour (*BRIT*) *od* color (*US*); ~**heft** *nt* fashion magazine; ~**journal** *nt* fashion magazine.

Modell [mo'dɛl] (-s, -e) *nt* model; ~**eisenbahn** *f* model railway; (*als Spielzeug*) train set; ~**fall** *m* textbook case.

modellieren [modɛ'liːrən] *vt* to model.

Modellversuch *m* (*bes SCH*) pilot scheme.

Modem ['moːdɛm] (-s, -s) *nt* (*COMPUT*) modem.

Modenschau *f* fashion show.

Modepapst *m* high priest of fashion.

Moder ['moːdər] (-s) *m* mustiness; (*Schimmel*) mildew.

moderat [mode'raːt] *adj* moderate.

Moderator(in) [mode'raːtɔr, -a'toːrɪn] *m(f)* presenter.

moderieren [mode'riːrən] *vt, vi* (*RUNDF, TV*) to present.

modern [mo'dɛrn] *adj* modern; (*modisch*) fashionable.

modernisieren [moderni'ziːrən] *vt* to modernize.

Mode- *zW:* ~**schmuck** *m* fashion jewellery (*BRIT*) *od* jewelry (*US*); ~**schöpfer(in)** *m(f)* fashion designer; ~**wort** *nt* fashionable word.

modifizieren [modifi'tsiːrən] *vt* to modify.

modisch ['moːdɪʃ] *adj* fashionable.

Modul ['moːdʊl] (-s, -n) *nt* (*COMPUT*) module.

Modus ['moːdʊs] (-, **Modi**) *m* way; (*GRAM*) mood; (*COMPUT*) mode.

Mofa ['moːfa] (-s, -s) *nt* (= *Motorfahrrad*) small moped.

Mogadischu (-s) [moga'dɪʃu] *nt* Mogadishu.

mogeln ['moːgəln] (*umg*) *vi* to cheat.

===================== SCHLÜSSELWORT

mögen ['møːgən] (*pt* **mochte**, *pp* **gemocht** *od*
(als Hilfsverb) **mögen**) *vt, vi* to like; **magst du/**
mögen Sie ihn? do you like him?; **ich**
möchte ... I would like ..., I'd like ...; **er**
möchte in die Stadt he'd like to go into
town; **ich möchte nicht, dass du ...** I wouldn't
like you to ...; **ich mag nicht mehr** I've had
enough; *(bin am Ende)* I can't take any more;
man möchte meinen, dass ... you would
think that ...

♦ *Hilfsverb* to like to; *(wollen)* to want;
möchtest du etwas essen? would you like
something to eat?; **sie mag nicht bleiben** she
doesn't want to stay; **das mag wohl sein** that
may very well be; **was mag das heißen?**
what might that mean?; **Sie möchten zu**
Hause anrufen could you please call home?

möglich ['møːklɪç] *adj* possible; **er tat sein**
M~stes he did his utmost.

möglicherweise *adv* possibly.

Möglichkeit *f* possibility; **nach ~** if possible.

möglichst *adv* as ... as possible.

Mohammedaner(in) [mohame'daːnər(ɪn)] (**-s,**
-) *m(f)* Mohammedan, Muslim.

Mohikaner [mohi'kaːnər] (**-s, -**) *m*: **der letzte ~**
(hum: umg) the very last one.

Mohn [moːn] (**-(e)s, -e**) *m* (*~blume*) poppy;
(*~samen*) poppy seed.

Möhre ['møːrə] (**-, -n**) *f* carrot.

Mohrenkopf ['moːrənkɔpf] *m* chocolate-
covered marshmallow.

Mohrrübe *f* carrot.

mokieren [mo'kiːrən] *vr*: **sich über etw** *akk* **~**
to make fun of sth.

Mokka ['mɔka] (**-s**) *m* mocha, *strong coffee.*

Moldau ['mɔldaʊ] *f*: **die ~** the Vltava.

Moldawien [mɔl'daːviən] (**-s**) *nt* Moldavia.

moldawisch *adj* Moldavian.

Mole ['moːlə] (**-, -n**) *f (NAUT)* mole.

Molekül [mole'kyːl] (**-s, -e**) *nt* molecule.

molk *etc* [mɔlk] *vb siehe* **melken**.

Molkerei [mɔlkə'raɪ] *f* dairy; **~butter** *f* blended
butter.

Moll [mɔl] (**-, -**) *nt (MUS)* minor (key).

mollig *adj* cosy; *(dicklich)* plump.

Molotowcocktail ['moːlotɔfkɔkteːl] *m*
Molotov cocktail.

Moment [mo'mɛnt] (**-(e)s, -e**) *m* moment ♦ *nt*
factor, element; **im ~** at the moment;
~ mal! just a minute!; **im ersten ~** for a
moment.

momentan [momɛn'taːn] *adj* momentary ♦ *adv*
at the moment.

Monaco [mo'nako, 'moːnako] (**-s**) *nt* Monaco.

Monarch [mo'narç] (**-en, -en**) *m* monarch.

Monarchie [monar'çiː] *f* monarchy.

Monat ['moːnat] (**-(e)s, -e**) *m* month; **sie ist im**
sechsten **~ (schwanger)** she's five months
pregnant; **was verdient er im ~?** how much
does he earn a month?

monatelang *adv* for months.

monatlich *adj* monthly.

Monats- *zW*: **~blutung** *f* menstrual period;
~karte *f* monthly ticket; **~rate** *f* monthly
instalment (*BRIT*) *od* installment (*US*).

Mönch [mœnç] (**-(e)s, -e**) *m* monk.

Mond [moːnt] (**-(e)s, -e**) *m* moon; **auf** *od* **hinter**
dem ~ leben *(umg)* to be behind the times;
~fähre *f* lunar (excursion) module;
~finsternis *f* eclipse of the moon; **m~hell** *adj*
moonlit; **~landung** *f* moon landing; **~schein**
m moonlight; **~sonde** *f* moon probe.

Monegasse [mone'gasə] (**-n, -n**) *m*
Monegasque.

Monegassin [mone'gasɪn] *f* Monegasque.

monegassisch *adj* Monegasque.

Monetarismus [moneta'rɪsmʊs] *m (ECON)*
monetarism.

Monetarist *m* monetarist.

Moneten [mo'neːtən] *(umg)* *pl (Geld)* bread
sing, dough *sing*.

Mongole [mɔŋ'goːlə] (**-n, -n**) *m* Mongolian,
Mongol.

Mongolei [mɔŋgo'laɪ] *f*: **die ~** Mongolia.

Mongolin *f* Mongolian, Mongol.

mongolisch [mɔŋ'goːlɪʃ] *adj* Mongolian.

mongoloid [mɔŋgolo'iːt] *adj (MED)* mongoloid.

monieren [mo'niːrən] *vt* to complain about
♦ *vi* to complain.

Monitor ['moːnitɔr] *m (Bildschirm)* monitor.

Mono- [mono] *in zW* mono.

monogam [mono'gaːm] *adj* monogamous.

Monogamie [monoga'miː] *f* monogamy.

Monolog [mono'loːk] (**-s, -e**) *m* monologue.

Monopol (**-s, -e**) *nt* monopoly.

monopolisieren [monopoli'ziːrən] *vt* to
monopolize.

Monopolstellung *f* monopoly.

monoton [mono'toːn] *adj* monotonous.

Monotonie [monoto'niː] *f* monotony.

Monstrum ['mɔnstrʊm] (**-s, Monstren**) *nt (lit,*
fig) monster; **ein ~ von einem/einer ...** a
hulking great ...

Monsun [mɔn'zuːn] (**-s, -e**) *m* monsoon.

Montag ['moːntaːk] (**-(e)s, -e**) *m* Monday; *siehe*
auch **Dienstag**.

Montage [mɔn'taːʒə] (**-, -n**) *f (PHOT etc)*
montage; *(TECH)* assembly; *(Einbauen)*
fitting.

montags *adv* on Mondays.

Montanindustrie [mɔn'taːnɪndʊstriː] *f* coal
and steel industry.

Montblanc [mõ'blãː] *m* Mont Blanc.

Monte Carlo ['mɔntə 'karlo] (**-s**) *nt* Monte
Carlo.

Montenegro [mɔnte'neːgro] (**-s**) *nt*
Montenegro.

Monteur [mɔn'tøːr] *m* fitter, assembly man.
montieren [mɔn'tiːrən] *vt* to assemble, set up.
Montur [mɔn'tuːr] (*umg*) *f* (*Spezialkleidung*)
gear, rig-out.
Monument [monu'mɛnt] *nt* monument.
monumental [monumɛn'taːl] *adj* monumental.
Moor [moːr] (-(e)s, -e) *nt* moor; ~**bad** *nt* mud
bath.
Moos [moːs] (-es, -e) *nt* moss.
Moped ['moːpɛt] (-s, -s) *nt* moped.
Mops [mɔps] (-es, ⁻e) *m* (*Hund*) pug.
Moral [mo'raːl] (-, -en) *f* morality; (*einer
Geschichte*) moral; (*Disziplin: von Volk,
Soldaten*) morale; ~**apostel** *m* upholder of
moral standards; **m~isch** *adj* moral; **einen** *od*
den m~ischen haben (*umg*) to have (a fit of)
the blues.
Moräne [mo'rɛːnə] (-, -n) *f* moraine.
Morast [mo'rast] (-(e)s, -e) *m* morass, mire.
morastig *adj* boggy.
Mord [mɔrt] (-(e)s, -e) *m* murder; **dann gibt es
~ und Totschlag** (*umg*) there'll be hell to
pay; ~**anschlag** *m* murder attempt.
Mörder ['mœrdər] (-s, -) *m* murderer; ~**in** *f*
murderess.
mörderisch *adj* (*fig: schrecklich*) dreadful,
terrible; (*Preise*) exorbitant;
(*Konkurrenzkampf*) cut-throat ♦ *adv* (*umg:
entsetzlich*) dreadfully, terribly.
Mordkommission *f* murder squad.
Mords- *zW*: ~**ding** (*umg*) *nt* whopper; ~**glück**
(*umg*) *nt* amazing luck; ~**kerl** (*umg*) *m*
(*verwegen*) hell of a guy; **m~mäßig** (*umg*) *adj*
terrific, enormous; ~**schreck** (*umg*) *m*
terrible fright.
Mord- *zW*: ~**verdacht** *m* suspicion of murder;
~**versuch** *m* murder attempt; ~**waffe** *f*
murder weapon.
morgen ['mɔrgən] *adv* tomorrow; **bis ~!** see
you tomorrow!; **~ in acht Tagen** a week
(from) tomorrow; **~ um diese Zeit** this time
tomorrow; **~ früh** tomorrow morning; **M~**
(-s, -) *m* morning; (*Maß*) ≈ acre; **am M~** in
the morning; **guten M~!** good morning!
Morgen- *zW*: ~**grauen** *nt* dawn, daybreak;
~**mantel** *m* dressing gown; ~**rock** *m* dressing
gown; ~**rot** *nt*, ~**röte** *f* dawn.
morgens *adv* in the morning; **von ~ bis
abends** from morning to night.
Morgenstunde *f*: **Morgenstund(e) hat Gold
im Mund(e)** (*Sprichwort*) the early bird
catches the worm (*Sprichwort*).
morgig ['mɔrgɪç] *adj* tomorrow's; **der ~e Tag**
tomorrow.
Morphium ['mɔrfiʊm] *nt* morphine.
morsch [mɔrʃ] *adj* rotten.
Morsealphabet ['mɔrzə|alfabeːt] *nt* Morse
code.
morsen *vi* to send a message by Morse code.
Mörser ['mœrzər] (-s, -) *m* mortar (*auch MIL*).

Mörtel ['mœrtəl] (-s, -) *m* mortar.
Mosaik [moza'iːk] (-s, -en *od* -e) *nt* mosaic.
Mosambik [mosam'biːk] (-s) *nt* Mozambique.
Moschee [mɔ'ʃeː] (-, -n) *f* mosque.
Mosel¹ ['moːzəl] *f* (*GEOG*) Moselle.
Mosel² (-s, -) *m* (*auch*: ~**wein**) Moselle (wine).
mosern ['moːzərn] (*umg*) *vi* to gripe,
bellyache.
Moskau ['mɔskaʊ] (-s) *nt* Moscow.
Moskauer *adj* Moscow *attrib*.
Moskauer(in) (-s, -) *m(f)* Muscovite.
Moskito [mɔs'kiːto] (-s, -s) *m* mosquito.
Moslem ['mɔslɛm] (-s, -s) *m* Muslim.
moslemisch [mɔs'leːmɪʃ] *adj* Muslim.
Most [mɔst] (-(e)s, -e) *m* (*unfermented*) fruit
juice; (*Apfelwein*) cider.
Motel [mo'tɛl] (-s, -s) *nt* motel.
Motiv [mo'tiːf] (-s, -e) *nt* motive; (*MUS*) theme.
Motivation [motivatsi'oːn] *f* motivation.
motivieren [moti'viːrən] *vt* to motivate.
Motivierung *f* motivation.
Motor ['moːtɔr] (-s, -en) *m* engine; (*bes ELEK*)
motor; ~**boot** *nt* motorboat.
Motorenöl *nt* engine oil.
Motorhaube *f* (*AUT*) bonnet (*BRIT*), hood (*US*).
motorisch *adj* (*PHYSIOLOGIE*) motor *attrib*.
motorisieren [motori'ziːrən] *vt* to motorize.
Motor- *zW*: ~**rad** *nt* motorcycle; ~**radfahrer** *m*
motorcyclist; ~**roller** *m* motor scooter;
~**schaden** *m* engine trouble *od* failure;
~**sport** *m* motor sport.
Motte ['mɔtə] (-, -n) *f* moth.
Motten- *zW*: **m~fest** *adj* mothproof; ~**kiste** *f*:
etw aus der ~kiste hervorholen (*fig*) to dig
sth out; ~**kugel** *f* mothball.
Motto ['mɔto] (-s, -s) *nt* motto.
motzen ['mɔtsən] (*umg*) *vi* to grouse, beef.
Mountainbike *nt* mountain bike.
Möwe ['møːvə] (-, -n) *f* seagull.
MP (-) *f abk* = **Maschinenpistole**.
MP3 *abk* (*COMPUT*) MP3.
Mrd. *abk* = **Milliarde(n)**.
MS *abk* (= *Motorschiff*) motor vessel, MV;
(= *multiple Sklerose*) MS.
MTA (-, -s) *f abk* (= *medizinisch-technische
Assistentin*) medical assistant.
mtl. *abk* = **monatlich**.
Mucke ['mʊkə] (-, -n) *f* (*meist pl*) caprice; (*von
Ding*) snag, bug; **seine ~n haben** to be
temperamental.
Mücke ['mʏkə] (-, -n) *f* midge, gnat; **aus einer
~ einen Elefanten machen** (*umg*) to make a
mountain out of a molehill.
Muckefuck ['mʊkəfʊk] (-s) (*umg*) *m* coffee
substitute.
mucken *vi*: **ohne zu ~** without a murmur.
Mückenstich *m* midge *od* gnat bite.
Mucks [mʊks] (-es, e) *m*: **keinen ~ sagen** not
to make a sound; (*nicht widersprechen*) not to
say a word.

mucksen (*umg*) *vr* to budge; (*Laut geben*) to open one's mouth.
mucksmäuschenstill ['mʊksˈmɔysçənʃtɪl] (*umg*) *adj* (as) quiet as a mouse.
müde ['myːdə] *adj* tired; **nicht ~ werden, etw zu tun** never to tire of doing something.
Müdigkeit ['myːdɪçkaɪt] *f* tiredness; **nur keine ~ vorschützen!** (*umg*) don't (you) tell me you're tired.
Muff [mʊf] (**-(e)s, -e**) *m* (*Handwärmer*) muff.
Muffel (**-s, -**) (*umg*) *m* killjoy, sourpuss.
muffig *adj* (*Luft*) musty.
Mühe ['myːə] (**-, -n**) *f* trouble, pains *pl*; **mit Müh(e) und Not** with great difficulty; **sich** *dat* **~ geben** to go to a lot of trouble; **m~los** *adj* effortless, easy.
muhen ['muːən] *vi* to low, moo.
mühevoll *adj* laborious, arduous.
Mühle ['myːlə] (**-, -n**) *f* mill; (*Kaffee~*) grinder; (*~spiel*) nine men's morris.
Mühlrad *nt* millwheel.
Mühlstein *m* millstone.
Mühsal (**-, -e**) *f* tribulation.
mühsam *adj* arduous, troublesome ♦ *adv* with difficulty.
mühselig *adj* arduous, laborious.
Mulatte [muˈlatə] (**-, -n**) *m* mulatto.
Mulattin *f* mulatto.
Mulde ['mʊldə] (**-, -n**) *f* hollow, depression.
Mull [mʊl] (**-(e)s, -e**) *m* thin muslin.
Müll [myl] (**-(e)s**) *m* refuse, rubbish, garbage (*US*); **~abfuhr** *f* refuse *od* garbage (*US*) collection; (*Leute*) dustmen *pl* (*BRIT*), garbage collectors *pl* (*US*); **~abladeplatz** *m* rubbish dump; **~beutel** *m* bin liner (*BRIT*), trashcan liner (*US*).
Mullbinde *f* gauze bandage.
Mülldeponie *f* waste disposal site, rubbish tip.
Mülleimer *m* rubbish bin (*BRIT*), garbage can (*US*).
Müller (**-s, -**) *m* miller.
Müll- *zW*: **~halde** *f*, **~haufen** *m* rubbish *od* garbage (*US*) heap; **~mann** (**-(e)s**, *pl* **~männer**) (*umg*) *m* dustman (*BRIT*), garbage collector (*US*); **~sack** *m* rubbish *od* garbage (*US*) bag; **~schlucker** *m* waste (*BRIT*) *od* garbage (*US*) disposal unit; **~tonne** *f* dustbin (*BRIT*), trashcan (*US*); **~verbrennung** *f* rubbish *od* garbage (*US*) incineration; **~verbrennungsanlage** *f* incinerator, incinerating plant; **~wagen** *m* dustcart (*BRIT*), garbage truck (*US*).
mulmig ['mʊlmɪç] *adj* rotten; (*umg*) uncomfortable; **jdm ist ~** sb feels funny.
Multi ['mʊlti] (**-s, -s**) (*umg*) *m* multinational (organization).
multi- *in zW* multi; **~lateral** *adj*: **~lateraler Handel** multilateral trade; **~national** *adj* multinational; **~nationaler Konzern** multinational organization.
multiple Sklerose [mʊlˈtiːplə skleˈroːzə] *f* multiple sclerosis.
multiplizieren [mʊltipliˈtsiːrən] *vt* to multiply.
Mumie ['muːmiə] *f* (*Leiche*) mummy.
Mumm [mʊm] (**-s**) (*umg*) *m* gumption, nerve.
Mumps [mʊmps] (**-**) *m od f* mumps *sing*.
München ['mʏnçən] *nt* Munich.
Münch(e)ner(in) (**-s, -**) *m(f)* person from Munich.
Mund [mʊnt] (**-(e)s, ̈-er**) *m* mouth; **den ~ aufmachen** (*fig: seine Meinung sagen*) to speak up; **sie ist nicht auf den ~ gefallen** (*umg*) she's never at a loss for words; **~art** *f* dialect.
Mündel ['mʏndəl] (**-s, -**) *nt* (*JUR*) ward.
münden ['mʏndən] *vi*: **in etw** *akk* **~** to flow into sth.
Mund- *zW*: **m~faul** *adj* uncommunicative; **m~gerecht** *adj* bite-sized; **~geruch** *m* bad breath; **~harmonika** *f* mouth organ.
mündig ['mʏndɪç] *adj* of age; **M~keit** *f* majority.
mündlich ['mʏntlɪç] *adj* oral; **~e Prüfung** oral (exam); **~e Verhandlung** (*JUR*) hearing; **alles Weitere ~!** let's talk about it more when I see you.
Mund- *zW*: **~raub** *m* (*JUR*) theft of food for personal consumption; **~stück** *nt* mouthpiece; (*von Zigarette*) tip; **m~tot** *adj*: **jdn m~tot machen** to muzzle sb.
Mündung ['mʏndʊŋ] *f* estuary; (*von Fluss, Rohr etc*) mouth; (*Gewehr~*) muzzle.
Mund- *zW*: **~wasser** *nt* mouthwash; **~werk** *nt*: **ein großes ~werk haben** to have a big mouth; **~winkel** *m* corner of the mouth; **~-zu-~-Beatmung** *f* mouth-to-mouth resuscitation.
Munition [munitsiˈoːn] *f* ammunition.
Munitionslager *nt* ammunition dump.
munkeln ['mʊŋkəln] *vi* to whisper, mutter; **man munkelt, dass ...** there's a rumour (*BRIT*) *od* rumor (*US*) that ...
Münster ['mʏnstər] (**-s, -**) *nt* minster.
munter ['mʊntər] *adj* lively; (*wach*) awake; (*aufgestanden*) up and about; **M~keit** *f* liveliness.
Münzanstalt *f* mint.
Münzautomat *m* slot machine.
Münze ['mʏntsə] (**-, -n**) *f* coin.
münzen *vt* to coin, mint; **auf jdn gemünzt sein** to be aimed at sb.
Münzfernsprecher ['mʏntsfɛrnʃprɛçər] *m* callbox (*BRIT*), pay phone (*US*).
Münzwechsler *m* change machine.
mürb(e) ['mʏrb(ə)] *adj* (*Gestein*) crumbly; (*Holz*) rotten; (*Gebäck*) crisp; **jdn ~ machen** to wear sb down.
Mürb(e)teig *m* shortcrust pastry.
Murmel ['mʊrməl] (**-, -n**) *f* marble.

murmeln *vt, vi* to murmur, mutter.

Murmeltier ['mʊrməltiːr] *nt* marmot; **schlafen wie ein ~** to sleep like a log.

murren ['mʊrən] *vi* to grumble, grouse.

mürrisch ['myrɪʃ] *adj* sullen.

Mus [muːs] (**-es, -e**) *nt* purée.

Muschel ['mʊʃəl] (**-, -n**) *f* mussel; (*~schale*) shell; (*Telefon~*) receiver.

Muse ['muːzə] (**-, -n**) *f* muse.

Museum [mu'zeːʊm] (**-s, Museen**) *nt* museum.

museumsreif *adj*: **~ sein** to be almost a museum piece.

Musik [mu'ziːk] *f* music; (*Kapelle*) band.

musikalisch [muzi'kaːlɪʃ] *adj* musical.

Musikbox *f* jukebox.

Musiker(in) ['muːzikər(ɪn)] (**-s, -**) *m(f)* musician.

Musik- *zW*: **~hochschule** *f* music school; **~instrument** *nt* musical instrument; **~kapelle** *f* band; **~stück** *nt* piece of music; **~stunde** *f* music lesson.

musisch ['muːzɪʃ] *adj* artistic.

musizieren [muzi'tsiːrən] *vi* to make music.

Muskat [mʊs'kaːt] (**-(e)s, -e**) *m* nutmeg.

Muskel ['mʊskəl] (**-s, -n**) *m* muscle; **~dystrophie** *f* muscular dystrophy; **~kater** *m*: **einen ~kater haben** to be stiff; **~paket** (*umg*) *nt* muscleman; **~zerrung** (*umg*) *f* pulled muscle.

Muskulatur [mʊskula'tuːr] *f* muscular system.

muskulös [mʊsku'løːs] *adj* muscular.

Müsli ['myːsli] (**-s, -**) *nt* muesli.

Muss▲ [mʊs] (**-**) *nt* necessity, must.

muss▲ *vb siehe* **müssen**.

Muße ['muːsə] (**-**) *f* leisure.

═══════════ *SCHLÜSSELWORT*

müssen ['mʏsən] (*pt* **musste,** *pp* **gemusst** *od* (*als Hilfsverb*) **müssen**) *vi* **1** (*Zwang*) must (*nur im Präsens*), to have to; **ich muss es tun** I must do it, I have to do it; **ich musste es tun** I had to do it; **er muss es nicht tun** he doesn't have to do it; **muss ich?** must I?, do I have to?; **wann müsst ihr zur Schule?** when do you have to go to school?; **der Brief muss heute noch zur Post** the letter must be posted (*BRIT*) *od* mailed (*US*) today; **er hat gehen ~** he (has) had to go; **muss das sein?** is that really necessary?; **wenn es (unbedingt) sein muss** if it's absolutely necessary; **ich muss mal** (*umg*) I need to go to the loo (*BRIT*) *od* bathroom (*US*).

2 (*sollen*): **das musst du nicht tun!** you oughtn't to *od* shouldn't do that; **das müsstest du eigentlich wissen** you ought to *od* you should know that; **Sie hätten ihn fragen ~** you should have asked him.

3: es muss geregnet haben it must have rained; **es muss nicht wahr sein** it needn't be true.

Mussheirat▲ (*umg*) *f* shotgun wedding.

müßig ['myːsɪç] *adj* idle; **M~gang** *m* idleness.

musst▲ [mʊst] *vb siehe* **müssen**.

musste *etc▲* ['mʊstə] *vb siehe* **müssen**.

Muster ['mʊstər] (**-s, -**) *nt* model; (*Dessin*) pattern; (*Probe*) sample; **~ ohne Wert** free sample; **~beispiel** *nt* classic example; **m~gültig** *adj* exemplary; **m~haft** *adj* exemplary.

mustern *vt* (*betrachten, MIL*) to examine; (*Truppen*) to inspect.

Musterprozess▲ *m* test case.

Musterschüler *m* model pupil.

Musterung *f* (*von Stoff*) pattern; (*MIL*) inspection.

Mut [muːt] *m* courage; **nur ~!** cheer up!; **jdm ~ machen** to encourage sb; **~ fassen** to pluck up courage.

mutig *adj* courageous.

mutlos *adj* discouraged, despondent.

mutmaßen *vt untr* to conjecture ♦ *vi untr* to conjecture.

mutmaßlich ['muːtmaːslɪç] *adj* presumed ♦ *adv* probably.

Mutprobe *f* test of courage.

Mutter¹ ['mʊtər] (**-, -n**) *f* (*Schrauben~*) nut.

Mutter² ['mʊtər] (**-, ⁻**) *f* mother; **~freuden** *pl* the joys *pl* of motherhood; **~gesellschaft** *f* (*COMM*) parent company; **~kuchen** *m* (*ANAT*) placenta; **~land** *nt* mother country; **~leib** *m* womb.

mütterlich ['mʏtərlɪç] *adj* motherly.

mütterlicherseits *adv* on the mother's side.

Mutter- *zW*: **~liebe** *f* motherly love; **~mal** *nt* birthmark; **~milch** *f* mother's milk.

Mutterschaft *f* motherhood.

Mutterschaftsgeld *nt* maternity benefit.

Mutterschaftsurlaub *m* maternity leave.

Mutter- *zW*: **~schutz** *m* maternity regulations *pl*; **m~seelenallein** *adj* all alone; **~sprache** *f* native language; **~tag** *m* Mother's Day.

Mutti (**-, -s**) (*umg*) *f* mum(my) (*BRIT*), mom(my) (*US*).

mutwillig ['muːtvɪlɪç] *adj* deliberate.

Mütze ['mʏtsə] (**-, -n**) *f* cap.

MV *f abk* (= *Mitgliederversammlung*) general meeting.

MW *abk* (= *Mittelwelle*) MW.

MwSt, Mw.-St. *abk* (= *Mehrwertsteuer*) VAT.

mysteriös [mysteri'øːs] *adj* mysterious.

Mystik ['mʏstɪk] *f* mysticism.

Mystiker(in) (**-s, -**) *m(f)* mystic.

mystisch ['mʏstɪʃ] *adj* mystical; (*rätselhaft*) mysterious.

Mythologie [mytolo'giː] *f* mythology.

Mythos ['myːtɔs] (**-, Mythen**) *m* myth.

N, n

N¹, n [ɛn] *nt* N, n; ~ **wie Nordpol** ≈ N for Nellie, N for Nan (*US*).

N² [ɛn] *abk* (= *Norden*) N.

na [na] *interj* well; ~ **gut** (*umg*) all right, OK; ~ **also!** (well,) there you are (then)!; ~ **so was!** well, I never!; ~ **und?** so what?

Nabel ['naːbəl] (**-s, -**) *m* navel; **der** ~ **der Welt** (*fig*) the hub of the universe; ~**schnur** *f* umbilical cord.

========== *SCHLÜSSELWORT*

nach [naːx] *präp +dat* **1** (*örtlich*) to; ~ **Berlin** to Berlin; ~ **links/rechts** (to the) left/right; ~ **oben/hinten** up/back; **er ist schon** ~ **London abgefahren** he has already left for London.

2 (*zeitlich*) after; **einer** ~ **dem anderen** one after the other; ~ **Ihnen!** after you!; **zehn (Minuten)** ~ **drei** ten (minutes) past *od* after (*US*) three.

3 (*gemäß*) according to; ~ **dem Gesetz** according to the law; **die Uhr** ~ **dem Radio stellen** to put a clock right by the radio; **ihrer Sprache** ~ (**zu urteilen**) judging by her language; **dem Namen** ~ judging by his/her name; ~ **allem, was ich weiß** as far as I know.

♦ *adv*: **ihm** ~**!** after him!; ~ **und** ~ gradually, little by little; ~ **wie vor** still.

nachäffen ['naːxɛfən] *vt* to ape.

nachahmen ['naːxaːmən] *vt* to imitate.

nachahmenswert *adj* exemplary.

Nachahmung *f* imitation; **etw zur** ~ **empfehlen** to recommend sth as an example.

Nachbar(in) ['naxbaːr(ɪn)] (**-s, -n**) *m(f)* neighbour (*BRIT*), neighbor (*US*); ~**haus** *nt*: **im** ~**haus** next door; **n**~**lich** *adj* neighbourly (*BRIT*), neighborly (*US*); ~**schaft** *f* neighbourhood (*BRIT*), neighborhood (*US*); ~**staat** *m* neighbouring (*BRIT*) *od* neighboring (*US*) state.

nach- *zW*: **N**~**behandlung** *f* (*MED*) follow-up treatment; ~**bestellen** *vt* to order again; **N**~**bestellung** *f* (*COMM*) repeat order; ~**beten** (*pej: umg*) *vt* to repeat parrot-fashion; ~**bezahlen** *vt* to pay; (*später*) to pay later; ~**bilden** *vt* to copy; **N**~**bildung** *f* imitation, copy; ~**blicken** *vi* to look *od* gaze after; ~**datieren** *vt* to postdate.

nachdem [naːx'deːm] *konj* after; (*weil*) since; **je** ~ (**ob**) it depends (whether).

nach- *zW*: ~**denken** *unreg vi*: **über etw** *akk* ~**denken** to think about sth; **darüber darf man gar nicht** ~**denken** it doesn't bear thinking about; **N**~**denken** *nt* reflection, meditation; ~**denklich** *adj* thoughtful, pensive; ~**denklich gestimmt sein** to be in a thoughtful mood.

Nachdruck ['naːxdrʊk] *m* emphasis; (*TYP*) reprint, reproduction; **besonderen** ~ **darauf legen, dass ...** to stress *od* emphasize particularly that ...

nachdrücklich ['naːxdrʏklɪç] *adj* emphatic; ~ **auf etw** *dat* **bestehen** to insist firmly (up)on sth.

nacheifern ['naːxaɪfərn] *vi*: **jdm** ~ to emulate sb.

nacheinander [naːxaɪ'nandər] *adv* one after the other; **kurz** ~ shortly after each other; **drei Tage** ~ three days running, three days on the trot (*umg*).

nachempfinden ['naːxɛmpfɪndən] *unreg vt*: **jdm etw** ~ to feel sth with sb.

nacherzählen ['naːxɛrtsɛːlən] *vt* to retell.

Nacherzählung *f* reproduction (of a story).

Nachf. *abk* = **Nachfolger**.

Nachfahr ['naːxfaːr] (**-en, -en**) *m* descendant.

Nachfolge ['naːxfɔlgə] *f* succession; **die/jds** ~ **antreten** to succeed/succeed sb.

nachfolgen *vi* (*lit*): **jdm/etw** ~ to follow sb/sth.

nachfolgend *adj* following.

Nachfolger(in) (**-s, -**) *m(f)* successor.

nachforschen *vt, vi* to investigate.

Nachforschung *f* investigation; ~**en anstellen** to make enquiries.

Nachfrage ['naːxfraːgə] *f* inquiry; (*COMM*) demand; **es besteht eine rege** ~ (*COMM*) there is a great demand; **danke der** ~ (*form*) thank you for your concern; (*umg*) nice of you to ask; **n**~**mäßig** *adj* according to demand.

nachfragen *vi* to inquire.

nach- *zW*: ~**fühlen** *vt* = **nachempfinden**; ~**füllen** *vt* to refill; ~**geben** *unreg vi* to give way, yield.

Nachgebühr *f* surcharge; (*POST*) excess postage.

Nachgeburt *f* afterbirth.

nachgehen ['naːxgeːən] *unreg vi* (*+dat*) to follow; (*erforschen*) to inquire (into); (*Uhr*) to be slow; **einer geregelten Arbeit** ~ to have a steady job.

Nachgeschmack ['naːxgəʃmak] *m* aftertaste.

nachgiebig ['naːxgiːbɪç] *adj* soft, accommodating; **N**~**keit** *f* softness.

nachgrübeln ['naːxgryːbəln] *vi*: **über etw** *akk* ~ to think about sth; (*sich Gedanken machen*) to ponder on sth.

nachgucken ['na:xgʊkən] vt, vi = **nachsehen**.

nachhaken ['na:xha:kən] (umg) vi to dig deeper.

Nachhall ['na:xhal] m resonance.

nachhallen vi to resound.

nachhaltig ['na:xhaltɪç] adj lasting; (Widerstand) persistent.

nachhängen ['na:xhɛŋən] unreg vi: **seinen Erinnerungen ~** to lose o.s. in one's memories.

nachhause▲ adv (ÖSTERR, SCHWEIZ) home.

Nachhauseweg [na:x'hauzəve:k] m way home.

nachhelfen ['na:xhɛlfən] unreg vi: **jdm ~** to help od assist sb; **er hat dem Glück ein bisschen nachgeholfen** he engineered himself a little luck.

nachher [na:x'he:r] adv afterwards; **bis ~** see you later!

Nachhilfe ['na:xhɪlfə] f (auch: ~**unterricht**) extra (private) tuition.

Nachhinein▲ ['na:xhɪnaɪn] adv: **im ~** afterwards; (rückblickend) in retrospect.

Nachholbedarf m: **einen ~ an etw** dat **haben** to have a lot of sth to catch up on.

nachholen ['na:xho:lən] vt to catch up with; (Versäumtes) to make up for.

Nachkomme ['na:xkɔmə] (-n, -n) m descendant.

nachkommen unreg vi to follow; (einer Verpflichtung) to fulfil; **Sie können Ihr Gepäck ~ lassen** you can have your luggage sent on (after).

Nachkommenschaft f descendants pl.

Nachkriegs- ['na:xkri:ks] in zW postwar; ~**zeit** f postwar period.

Nach- zW: ~**lass▲** (-es, -lässe) m (COMM) discount, rebate; (Erbe) estate; **n~lassen** unreg vt (Strafe) to remit; (Summe) to take off; (Schulden) to cancel ♦ vi to decrease, ease off; (Sturm) to die down; (schlechter werden) to deteriorate; **er hat n~gelassen** he has got worse; **n~lässig** adj negligent, careless; ~**lässigkeit** f negligence, carelessness; ~**lasssteuer▲** f death duty; ~**lassverwalter▲** m executor.

nachlaufen ['na:xlaufən] unreg vi: **jdm ~** to run after od chase sb.

nachliefern ['na:xli:fərn] vt (später liefern) to deliver at a later date; (zuzüglich liefern) to make a further delivery of.

nachlösen ['na:xlø:zən] vi to pay on the train/ when one gets off; (zur Weiterfahrt) to pay the extra.

nachm. abk (= nachmittags) p.m.

nachmachen ['na:xmaxən] vt to imitate, copy; (fälschen) to counterfeit; **jdm etw ~** to copy sth from sb; **das soll erst mal einer ~!** I'd like to see anyone else do that!

Nachmieter(in) ['na:xmi:tər(ɪn)] m(f): **wir müssen einen ~ finden** we have to find someone to take over the flat etc.

Nachmittag ['na:xmɪta:k] m afternoon; **am ~** in the afternoon; **gestern/heute ~** yesterday/this afternoon.

nachmittags adv in the afternoon.

Nachmittagsvorstellung f matinée (performance).

Nachn. abk = **Nachnahme**.

Nachnahme (-, -n) f cash on delivery (BRIT), collect on delivery (US); **per ~** C.O.D.

Nachname m surname.

Nachporto nt excess postage.

nachprüfbar ['na:xpry:fba:r] adj verifiable.

nachprüfen ['na:xpry:fən] vt to check, verify.

nachrechnen ['na:xrɛçnən] vt to check.

Nachrede ['na:xre:də] f: **üble ~** (JUR) defamation of character.

nachreichen ['na:xraɪçən] vt to hand in later.

Nachricht ['na:xrɪçt] (-, -en) f (piece of) news sing; (Mitteilung) message.

Nachrichten pl news sing; ~**agentur** f news agency; ~**dienst** m (MIL) intelligence service; ~**satellit** m (tele)communications satellite; ~**sperre** f news blackout; ~**sprecher(in)** m(f) newsreader; ~**technik** f telecommunications sing.

nachrücken ['na:xrʏkən] vi to move up.

Nachruf ['na:xru:f] m obituary (notice).

nachrüsten ['na:xrʏstən] vt (Kraftwerk etc) to modernize; (Auto etc) to refit; (Waffen) to keep up to date ♦ vi (MIL) to deploy new arms.

nachsagen ['na:xza:gən] vt to repeat; **jdm etw ~** to say sth of sb; **das lasse ich mir nicht ~!** I'm not having that said of me!

Nachsaison ['na:xzɛzõ:] f off season.

nachschenken ['na:xʃɛŋkən] vt, vi: **darf ich Ihnen noch (etwas) ~?** may I top up your glass?

nachschicken ['na:xʃɪkən] vt to forward.

nachschlagen ['na:xʃla:gən] unreg vt to look up ♦ vi: **jdm ~** to take after sb.

Nachschlagewerk nt reference book.

Nachschlüssel m master key.

nachschmeißen ['na:xʃmaɪsən] unreg (umg) vt: **das ist ja nachgeschmissen!** it's a real bargain!

Nachschrift ['na:xʃrɪft] f postscript.

Nachschub ['na:xʃu:p] m supplies pl; (Truppen) reinforcements pl.

nachsehen ['na:xze:ən] unreg vt (prüfen) to check ♦ vi (erforschen) to look and see; **jdm etw ~** to forgive sb sth; **jdm ~** to gaze after sb.

Nachsehen nt: **das ~ haben** to be left empty-handed.

nachsenden ['na:xzɛndən] unreg vt to send on, forward.

Nachsicht ['na:xzɪçt] (-) f indulgence,

leniency.
nachsichtig *adj* indulgent, lenient.
Nachsilbe ['naːxzɪlbə] *f* suffix.
nachsitzen ['naːxzɪtsən] *unreg vi* (*SCH*) to be kept in.
Nachsorge ['naːxzɔrgə] *f* (*MED*) aftercare.
Nachspann ['naːxʃpan] *m* credits *pl*.
Nachspeise ['naːxʃpaɪzə] *f* dessert, sweet (*BRIT*).
Nachspiel ['naːxʃpiːl] *nt* epilogue; (*fig*) sequel.
nachspionieren ['naːxʃpioniːrən] (*umg*) *vi*: **jdm** ~ to spy on sb.
nachsprechen ['naːxʃprɛçən] *unreg vt*: (**jdm**) ~ to repeat (after sb).
nächst [nɛːçst] *präp +dat* (*räumlich*) next to; (*außer*) apart from; ~**beste(r, s)** *adj* first that comes along; (*zweitbeste*) next-best.
Nächste(r, s) *f(m)* neighbour (*BRIT*), neighbor (*US*).
nächste(r, s) *adj* next; (*nächstgelegen*) nearest; **aus** ~**r Nähe** from close by; (*betrachten*) at close quarters; **Ende** ~**n Monats** at the end of next month; **am** ~**n Tag** (the) next day; **bei** ~**r Gelegenheit** at the earliest opportunity; **in** ~**r Zeit** some time soon; **der** ~ **Angehörige** the next of kin.
nachstehen ['naːxʃteːən] *unreg vi*: **jdm in nichts** ~ to be sb's equal in every way.
nachstehend *adj attrib* following.
nachstellen ['naːxʃtɛlən] *vi*: **jdm** ~ to follow sb; (*aufdringlich umwerben*) to pester sb.
Nächstenliebe *f* love for one's fellow men.
nächstens *adv* shortly, soon.
nächstliegend *adj* (*lit*) nearest; (*fig*) obvious.
nächstmöglich *adj* next possible.
nachsuchen ['naːxzuːxən] *vi*: **um etw** ~ to ask *od* apply for sth.
Nacht [naxt] (-, ⁻e) *f* night; **gute** ~! good night!; **heute** ~ tonight; **in der** ~ at night; **in der** ~ **auf Dienstag** during Monday night; **in der** ~ **vom 12. zum 13. April** during the night of April 12th to 13th; **über** ~ (*auch fig*) overnight; **bei** ~ **und Nebel** (*umg*) at dead of night; **sich** *dat* **die** ~ **um die Ohren schlagen** (*umg*) to stay up all night; (*mit Feiern, arbeiten*) to make a night of it.
Nachtdienst *m* night duty.
Nachteil ['naːxtaɪl] *m* disadvantage; **im** ~ **sein** to be at a disadvantage.
nachteilig *adj* disadvantageous.
Nachtfalter *m* moth.
Nachthemd *nt* (*Herren*~) nightshirt; nightdress (*BRIT*), nightgown.
Nachtigall ['naxtɪgal] (-, -en) *f* nightingale.
Nachtisch ['naːxtɪʃ] *m* = **Nachspeise**.
Nachtleben *nt* night life.
nächtlich ['nɛçtlɪç] *adj* nightly.
Nacht- *zW*: ~**lokal** *nt* night club; ~**mensch** ['naxtmɛnʃ] *m* night person; ~**portier** *m* night

porter.
nach- *zW*: **N**~**trag** ['naːxtraːk] (-(e)s, -träge) *m* supplement; ~**tragen** *unreg vt* (*zufügen*) to add; **jdm etw** ~**tragen** to carry sth after sb; (*fig*) to hold sth against sb; ~**tragend** *adj* resentful; ~**träglich** *adj* later, subsequent; (*zusätzlich*) additional ♦ *adv* later, subsequently; (*zusätzlich*) additionally; ~**trauern** *vi*: **jdm/etw** ~**trauern** to mourn the loss of sb/sth.
Nachtruhe ['naːxtruːə] *f* sleep.
nachts *adv* by night.
Nachtschicht *f* night shift.
Nachtschwester *f* night nurse.
nachtsüber *adv* during the night.
Nacht- *zW*: ~**tarif** *m* off-peak tariff; ~**tisch** *m* bedside table; ~**topf** *m* chamber pot; ~**wache** *f* night watch; (*im Krankenhaus*) night duty; ~**wächter** *m* night watchman.
Nach- *zW*: ~**untersuchung** *f* checkup; **n**~**vollziehen** *unreg vt* to understand, comprehend; **n**~**wachsen** *unreg vi* to grow again; ~**wahl** *f* ≈ by-election (*bes BRIT*); ~**wehen** *pl* afterpains *pl*; (*fig*) aftereffects *pl*; **n**~**weinen** *vi +dat* to mourn ♦ *vt*: **dieser Sache** *dat* **weine ich keine Träne n**~ I won't shed any tears over that.
Nachweis ['naːxvaɪs] (-es, -e) *m* proof; **den** ~ **für etw erbringen** *od* **liefern** to furnish proof of sth; **n**~**bar** *adj* provable, demonstrable; **n**~**en** ['naːxvaɪzən] *unreg vt* to prove; **jdm etw n**~**en** to point sth out to sb; **n**~**lich** *adj* evident, demonstrable.
nach- *zW*: **N**~**welt** *f*: **die N**~**welt** posterity; ~**winken** *vi*: **jdm** ~**winken** to wave after sb; ~**wirken** *vi* to have aftereffects; **N**~**wirkung** *f* aftereffect; **N**~**wort** *nt* appendix; **N**~**wuchs** *m* offspring; (*beruflich etc*) new recruits *pl*; ~**zahlen** *vt, vi* to pay extra; ~**zählen** *vt* to count again; **N**~**zahlung** *f* additional payment; (*zurückdatiert*) back pay.
nachziehen ['naːxtsiːən] *unreg vt* (*Linie*) to go over; (*Lippen*) to paint; (*Augenbrauen*) to pencil in; (*hinterherziehen*): **etw** ~ to drag sth behind one.
Nachzügler (-s, -) *m* straggler.
Nackedei ['nakədaɪ] (-(e)s, -e *od* -s) *m* (*hum*: *umg*: *Kind*) little bare human.
Nacken ['nakən] (-s, -) *m* nape of the neck; **jdm im** ~ **sitzen** (*umg*) to breathe down sb's neck.
nackt [nakt] *adj* naked; (*Tatsachen*) plain, bare; **N**~**heit** *f* nakedness; **N**~**kultur** *f* nudism.
Nadel ['naːdəl] (-, -n) *f* needle; (*Steck*~) pin; ~**baum** *m* conifer; ~**kissen** *nt* pincushion; ~**öhr** *nt* eye of a needle; ~**wald** *m* coniferous forest.
Nagel ['naːgəl] (-s, ⁻) *m* nail; **sich** *dat* **etw unter den** ~ **reißen** (*umg*) to pinch sth; **etw an den** ~ **hängen** (*fig*) to chuck sth in (*umg*); **Nägel**

mit Köpfen machen (*umg*) to do the job properly; ~**bürste** *f* nailbrush; ~**feile** *f* nailfile; ~**haut** *f* cuticle; ~**lack** *m* nail varnish (*BRIT*) *od* polish; ~**lackentferner** (**-s,** -) *m* nail polish remover.

nageln *vt, vi* to nail.

nagelneu *adj* brand-new.

Nagelschere *f* nail scissors *pl*.

nagen ['na:gən] *vt, vi* to gnaw.

Nagetier ['na:gəti:r] *nt* rodent.

nah *adj* = **nahe**.

Nahaufnahme *f* close-up.

Nahe *f* (*Fluss*) Nahe.

nahe *adj* (*räumlich*) near(by); (*Verwandte*) near, close; (*Freunde*) close; (*zeitlich*) near, close ♦ *adv*: **von nah und fern** from near and far ♦ *präp* +*dat* near (to), close to; **von ~ at** close quarters; **der N~ Osten** the Middle East; **jdm etw ~ bringen** (*fig*) to bring sth home to sb; **jdm ~ gehen** to grieve sb; **jdm ~ kommen** to get close to sb; **jdm etw ~ legen** to suggest sth to sb; **~ liegen** to be obvious; **der Verdacht liegt ~, dass ...** it seems reasonable to suspect that ...; **~ liegend** obvious; **jdm ~ stehen** to be close to sb; **einer Sache ~ stehen** to sympathize with sth; **~ stehend** close; **jdm zu ~ treten** (*fig*) to offend sb; **mit jdm ~ verwandt sein** to be closely related to sb.

Nähe ['nɛ:ə] (-) *f* nearness, proximity; (*Umgebung*) vicinity; **in der ~** close by; at hand; **aus der ~** from close to.

nahebei *adv* nearby.

nahen *vi, vr* to approach, draw near.

nähen ['nɛ:ən] *vt, vi* to sew.

näher *adj* nearer; (*Erklärung, Erkundigung*) more detailed ♦ *adv* nearer; in greater detail; **~ kommen** to get closer; **ich kenne ihn nicht ~** I don't know him well.

Nähere(s) *nt* details *pl*, particulars *pl*.

Näherei [nɛ:ə'raɪ] *f* sewing, needlework.

Naherholungsgebiet *nt* recreational area (*close to a centre of population*).

Näherin *f* seamstress.

nähern *vr* to approach.

Näherungswert *m* approximate value.

nahezu *adv* nearly.

Nähgarn *nt* thread.

Nahkampf *m* hand-to-hand fighting.

Nähkasten *m* workbox, sewing basket.

nahm *etc* [na:m] *vb siehe* **nehmen**.

Nähmaschine *f* sewing machine.

Nähnadel *f* (sewing) needle.

Nahost [na:'ɔst] *m*: **aus ~** from the Middle East.

Nährboden *m* (*lit*) fertile soil; (*fig*) breeding ground.

nähren ['nɛ:rən] *vt* to feed ♦ *vr* (*Person*) to feed o.s.; (*Tier*) to feed; **er sieht gut genährt aus** he looks well fed.

Nährgehalt ['nɛ:rgəhalt] *m* nutritional value.

nahrhaft ['na:rhaft] *adj* (*Essen*) nourishing.

Nährstoffe *pl* nutrients *pl*.

Nahrung ['na:rʊŋ] *f* food; (*fig*) sustenance.

Nahrungs- *zW*: ~**aufnahme** *f*: **die ~aufnahme verweigern** to refuse food; ~**kette** *f* food chain; ~**mittel** *nt* food(stuff); ~**mittelindustrie** *f* food industry; ~**suche** *f* search for food.

Nährwert *m* nutritional value.

Naht [na:t] (-, **-̈e**) *f* seam; (*MED*) suture; (*TECH*) join; **aus allen Nähten platzen** (*umg*) to be bursting at the seams; **n~los** *adj* seamless; **n~los ineinander übergehen** to follow without a gap.

Nahverkehr *m* local traffic.

Nahverkehrszug *m* local train.

Nähzeug *nt* sewing kit, sewing things *pl*.

Nahziel *nt* immediate objective.

naiv [na'i:f] *adj* naïve.

Naivität [naivi'tɛ:t] *f* naïveté, naïvety.

Name ['na:mə] (**-ns, -n**) *m* name; **im ~n von** on behalf of; **dem ~n nach müsste sie Deutsche sein** judging by her name she must be German; **die Dinge beim ~n nennen** (*fig*) to call a spade a spade; **ich kenne das Stück nur dem ~n nach** I've heard of the play but that's all.

namens *adv* by the name of.

Namensänderung *f* change of name.

Namenstag *m* name day, saint's day.

NAMENSTAG

*In Catholic areas of Germany the **Namenstag** is often a more important celebration than a birthday. It is the day dedicated to the saint after whom a person is called, and on that day the person receives presents and invites relatives and friends round to celebrate.*

---

namentlich ['na:məntlɪç] *adj* by name ♦ *adv* particularly, especially.

namhaft ['na:mhaft] *adj* (*berühmt*) famed, renowned; (*beträchtlich*) considerable; **~ machen** to name, identify.

Namibia [na'mi:bia] *nt* Namibia.

nämlich ['nɛ:mlɪç] *adv* that is to say, namely; (*denn*) since; **der/die/das N~e** the same.

nannte *etc* ['nantə] *vb siehe* **nennen**.

nanu [na'nu:] *interj* well I never!

Napalm [na:palm] (**-s**) *nt* napalm.

Napf [napf] (**-(e)s, -̈e**) *m* bowl, dish; ~**kuchen** *m* ≈ ring-shaped pound cake.

Narbe ['narbə] (**-, -n**) *f* scar.

narbig ['narbɪç] *adj* scarred.

Narkose [nar'ko:zə] (**-, -n**) *f* anaesthetic (*BRIT*), anesthetic (*US*).

Narr [nar] (**-en, -en**) *m* fool; **jdn zum ~en halten** to make a fool of sb; **n~en** *vt* to fool.

Narrenfreiheit *f*: **sie hat bei ihm** ~ he gives her (a) free rein.
narrensicher *adj* foolproof.
Narrheit *f* foolishness.
Närrin ['nɛrɪn] *f* fool.
närrisch *adj* foolish, crazy; **die ~en Tage** *Fasching and the period leading up to it.*
Narzisse [nar'tsɪsə] (-, -n) *f* narcissus.
narzisstisch▲ [nar'tsɪstɪʃ] *adj* narcissistic.
NASA ['na:za] (-) *f abk* (= *National Aeronautics and Space Administration*) NASA.
naschen ['naʃən] *vt* to nibble; (*heimlich*) to eat secretly ♦ *vi* to nibble sweet things; ~ **von** *od an* +dat to nibble at.
naschhaft *adj* sweet-toothed.
Nase ['na:zə] (-, -n) *f* nose; **sich** *dat* **die** ~ **putzen** to wipe one's nose; (*sich schnäuzen*) to blow one's nose; **jdm auf der** ~ **herumtanzen** (*umg*) to play sb up; **jdm etw vor der** ~ **wegschnappen** (*umg*) to just beat sb to sth; **die** ~ **voll haben** (*umg*) to have had enough; **jdm etw auf die** ~ **binden** (*umg*) to tell sb all about sth; **(immer) der** ~ **nachgehen** (*umg*) to follow one's nose; **jdn an der** ~ **herumführen** (*als Täuschung*) to lead sb by the nose; (*als Scherz*) to pull sb's leg.
Nasen- *zW*: ~**bluten** (-s) *nt* nosebleed; ~**loch** *nt* nostril; ~**rücken** *m* bridge of the nose; ~**tropfen** *pl* nose drops *pl*.
naseweis *adj* pert, cheeky; (*neugierig*) nosey.
Nashorn ['na:shɔrn] *nt* rhinoceros.
nass▲ [nas] *adj* wet.
Nassauer ['nasauɔr] (-s, -) (*umg*) *m* scrounger.
Nässe ['nɛsə] (-) *f* wetness.
nässen *vt* to wet.
nasskalt▲ *adj* wet and cold.
Nassrasur▲ *f* wet shave.
Nation [natsi'o:n] *f* nation.
national [natsio'na:l] *adj* national; **N~elf** *f* international (football) team; **N~feiertag** *m* national holiday; **N~hymne** *f* national anthem.
nationalisieren [natsionali'zi:rən] *vt* to nationalize.
Nationalisierung *f* nationalization.
Nationalismus [natsiona'lɪsmʊs] *m* nationalism.
nationalistisch [natsiona'lɪstɪʃ] *adj* nationalistic.
Nationalität [natsionali'tɛ:t] *f* nationality.
National- *zW*: ~**mannschaft** *f* international team; ~**sozialismus** *m* National Socialism; ~**sozialist** *m* National Socialist.
NATO, Nato ['na:to] (-) *f abk*: **die** ~ NATO.
Natrium ['na:triʊm] (-s) *nt* sodium.
Natron ['na:trɔn] (-s) *nt* soda.
Natter ['natər] (-, -n) *f* adder.
Natur [na'tu:r] *f* nature; (*körperlich*) constitution; (*freies Land*) countryside; **das**

geht gegen meine ~ it goes against the grain.
Naturalien [natu'ra:liən] *pl* natural produce *sing*; **in** ~ in kind.
Naturalismus [natura'lɪsmʊs] *m* naturalism.
Naturell [natu'rɛl] (-s, -e) *nt* temperament, disposition.
Natur- *zW*: ~**erscheinung** *f* natural phenomenon *od* event; **n~farben** *adj* natural-coloured (*BRIT*) *od* -colored (*US*); ~**forscher** *m* natural scientist; ~**freak** (-s, -s) (*umg*) *m* back-to-nature freak; **n~gemäß** *adj* natural; ~**geschichte** *f* natural history; ~**gesetz** *nt* law of nature; **n~getreu** *adj* true to life; ~**heilverfahren** *nt* natural cure; ~**katastrophe** *f* natural disaster; ~**kostladen** *m* health food shop; ~**kunde** *f* natural history; ~**lehrpfad** *m* nature trail.
natürlich [na'ty:rlɪç] *adj* natural ♦ *adv* naturally; **eines ~en Todes sterben** to die of natural causes.
natürlicherweise [na'ty:rlɪçər'vaɪzə] *adv* naturally, of course.
Natürlichkeit *f* naturalness.
Natur- *zW*: ~**produkt** *nt* natural product; **n~rein** *adj* natural, pure; ~**schutz** *m*: **unter** ~**schutz stehen** to be legally protected; ~**schutzgebiet** *nt* nature reserve (*BRIT*), national park (*US*); ~**talent** *nt* natural prodigy; **n~verbunden** *adj* nature-loving; ~**wissenschaft** *f* natural science; ~**wissenschaftler** *m* scientist; ~**zustand** *m* natural state.
Nautik ['nautɪk] *f* nautical science, navigation.
nautisch ['nautɪʃ] *adj* nautical.
Navelorange ['na:vəlorã:ʒə] *f* navel orange.
Navigation [navigatsi'o:n] *f* navigation.
Navigationsfehler *m* navigational error.
Navigationsinstrumente *pl* navigation instruments *pl*.
Nazi ['na:tsi] (-s, -s) *m* Nazi.
NB *abk* (= *nota bene*) NB.
n. Br. *abk* (= *nördlicher Breite*) northern latitude.
NC *m abk* (= *numerus clausus*) *siehe* **Numerus**.
Nchf. *abk* = **Nachfolger**.
n. Chr. *abk* (= *nach Christus*) A.D.
NDR (-) *m abk* (= *Norddeutscher Rundfunk*) North German Radio.
Neapel [ne'a:pəl] (-s) *nt* Naples.
Neapolitaner(in) [neapoli'ta:nər(ɪn)] (-s, -) *m(f)* Neapolitan.
neapolitanisch [neapoli'ta:nɪʃ] *adj* Neapolitan.
Nebel ['ne:bəl] (-s, -) *m* fog, mist.
nebelig *adj* foggy, misty.
Nebel- *zW*: ~**leuchte** *f* (*AUT*) rear fog-light; ~**scheinwerfer** *m* fog-lamp; ~**schlussleuchte**▲ *f* (*AUT*) rear fog-light.
neben ['ne:bən] *präp* +akk next to ♦ *präp* +dat

next to; (*außer*) apart from, besides; ~**an** [neːbən|'an] *adv* next door; **N~anschluss▲** *m* (*TEL*) extension; **N~ausgaben** *pl* incidental expenses *pl*; ~**bei** [neːbən'baɪ] *adv* at the same time; (*außerdem*) additionally; (*beiläufig*) incidentally; ~**bei bemerkt** *od* **gesagt** by the way, incidentally; **N~beruf** *m* second occupation; **er ist im N~beruf ...** he has a second job as a ...; **N~beschäftigung** *f* sideline; (*Zweitberuf*) extra job; **N~buhler(in)** (**-s, -**) *m(f)* rival; ~**einander** [neːbən|aɪ'nandər] *adv* side by side; ~**einander legen** to put next to each other; **N~eingang** *m* side entrance; **N~einkünfte** *pl*, **N~einnahmen** *pl* supplementary income *sing*; **N~erscheinung** *f* side effect; **N~fach** *nt* subsidiary subject; **N~fluss▲** *m* tributary; **N~geräusch** *nt* (*RUNDF*) atmospherics *pl*, interference; **N~handlung** *f* (*LITER*) subplot; ~**her** [neːbən'heːr] *adv* (*zusätzlich*) besides; (*gleichzeitig*) at the same time; (*daneben*) alongside; ~**herfahren** *unreg vi* to drive alongside; **N~kläger** *m* (*JUR*) joint plaintiff; **N~kosten** *pl* extra charges *pl*, extras *pl*; **N~mann** (**-(e)s**, *pl* **-männer**) *m*: **Ihr N~mann** the person next to you; **N~produkt** *nt* by-product; **N~rolle** *f* minor part; **N~sache** *f* trifle, side issue; ~**sächlich** *adj* minor, peripheral; **N~saison** *f* low season; **N~satz** *m* (*GRAM*) subordinate clause; ~**stehend** *adj*: ~**stehende Abbildung** illustration opposite; **N~straße** *f* side street; **N~strecke** *f* (*EISENB*) branch *od* local line; **N~verdienst** *m* secondary income; **N~zimmer** *nt* adjoining room.

neblig ['neːblɪç] *adj* = **nebelig**.

nebst [neːpst] *präp +dat* together with.

Necessaire [nesɛ'sɛːr] (**-s, -s**) *nt* (*Näh~*) needlework box; (*Nagel~*) manicure case.

Neckar ['nɛkar] (**-s**) *m* (*Fluss*) Neckar.

necken ['nɛkən] *vt* to tease.

Neckerei [nɛkə'raɪ] *f* teasing.

neckisch *adj* coy; (*Einfall, Lied*) amusing.

nee [neː] (*umg*) *adv* no, nope.

Neffe ['nɛfə] (**-n, -n**) *m* nephew.

negativ ['neːgatiːf] *adj* negative; **N~** (**-s, -e**) *nt* (*PHOT*) negative.

Neger ['neːgər] (**-s, -**) *m* negro; ~**in** *f* negress; ~**kuss▲** *m* *chocolate-covered marshmallow*.

negieren [ne'giːrən] *vt* (*bestreiten*) to deny; (*verneinen*) to negate.

nehmen ['neːmən] *unreg vt, vi* to take; **etw zu sich ~** to take sth, partake of sth (*liter*); **jdm etw ~** to take sth (away) from sb; **sich ernst ~** to take o.s. seriously; ~ **Sie sich doch bitte** help yourself; **man nehme ...** (*KOCH*) take ...; **wie mans nimmt** depending on your point of view; **die Mauer nimmt einem die ganze Sicht** the wall blocks the whole view; **er ließ es sich** *dat* **nicht ~, es persönlich zu**

tun he insisted on doing it himself.

Nehrung ['neːrʊŋ] *f* (*GEOG*) spit (of land).

Neid [naɪt] (**-(e)s**) *m* envy.

Neider ['naɪdər] (**-s, -**) *m* envier.

Neidhammel (*umg*) *m* envious person.

neidisch *adj* envious, jealous.

Neige (**-, -n**) *f* (*geh: Ende*): **die Vorräte gehen zur ~** the provisions are fast becoming exhausted.

neigen ['naɪgən] *vt* to incline, lean; (*Kopf*) to bow ♦ *vi*: **zu etw ~** to tend to sth.

Neigung *f* (*des Geländes*) slope; (*Tendenz*) tendency, inclination; (*Vorliebe*) liking; (*Zuneigung*) affection.

Neigungswinkel *m* angle of inclination.

nein [naɪn] *adv* no.

Nelke ['nɛlkə] (**-, -n**) *f* carnation, pink; (*Gewürz~*) clove.

nennen ['nɛnən] *unreg vt* to name; (*mit Namen*) to call; **das nenne ich Mut!** that's what I call courage!

nennenswert *adj* worth mentioning.

Nenner (**-s, -**) *m* denominator; **etw auf einen ~ bringen** (*lit, fig*) to reduce sth to a common denominator.

Nennung *f* naming.

Nennwert *m* nominal value; (*COMM*) par.

Neon ['neːɔn] (**-s**) *nt* neon.

Neonazi [neo'naːtsi] *m* Neonazi.

Neon- *zW*: ~**licht** *nt* neon light; ~**reklame** *f* neon sign; ~**röhre** *f* neon tube.

Nepal ['neːpal] (**-s**) *nt* Nepal.

Nepp [nɛp] (**-s**) (*umg*) *m*: **der reinste ~** daylight robbery, a rip-off.

Nerv [nɛrf] (**-s, -en**) *m* nerve; **die ~en sind mit ihm durchgegangen** he lost control, he snapped (*umg*); **jdm auf die ~en gehen** to get on sb's nerves.

nerven (*umg*) *vt*: **jdn ~** to get on sb's nerves.

Nerven- *zW*: ~**aufreibend** *adj* nerve-racking; ~**bündel** *nt* bundle of nerves; ~**gas** *nt* (*MIL*) nerve gas; ~**heilanstalt** *f* mental hospital; ~**klinik** *f* psychiatric clinic; **n~krank** *adj* mentally ill; ~**säge** (*umg*) *f* pain (in the neck); ~**schwäche** *f* neurasthenia; ~**system** *nt* nervous system; ~**zusammenbruch** *m* nervous breakdown.

nervig ['nɛrvɪç] (*umg*) *adj* exasperating, annoying.

nervös [nɛr'vøːs] *adj* nervous.

Nervosität [nɛrvozi'tɛːt] *f* nervousness.

nervtötend *adj* nerve-racking; (*Arbeit*) soul-destroying.

Nerz [nɛrts] (**-es, -e**) *m* mink.

Nessel ['nɛsəl] (**-, -n**) *f* nettle; **sich in die ~n setzen** (*fig: umg*) to put o.s. in a spot.

Nessessär▲ [nɛsɛ'sɛːr] (**-s, -s**) *nt* = **Necessaire**.

Nest [nɛst] (**-(e)s, -er**) *nt* nest; (*umg: Ort*) dump; (*fig: Bett*) bed; (: *Schlupfwinkel*) hide-out, lair; **da hat er sich ins warme ~ gesetzt**

(*umg*) he's got it made; ~**beschmutzung**
(*pej*) *f* running-down (*umg*) *od* denigration (of
one's family/country).
nesteln *vi*: **an etw** +*dat* ~ to fumble *od* fiddle
about with sth.
Nesthäkchen ['nɛsthɛːkçən] *nt* baby of the
family.
nett [nɛt] *adj* nice; **sei so** ~ **und räum auf!**
would you mind clearing up?
netterweise ['nɛtər'vaɪzə] *adv* kindly.
netto *adv* net; **N~einkommen** *nt* net income;
N~gewicht *nt* net weight; **N~gewinn** *m* net
profit; **N~gewinnspanne** *f* net margin;
N~lohn *m* take-home pay.
Netz [nɛts] (**-es, -e**) *nt* net; (*Gepäck~*) rack;
(*Einkaufs~*) string bag; (*Spinnen~*) web;
(*System, auch COMPUT*) network; (*Strom~*)
mains *sing od pl*; **das soziale** ~ the social
security network; **jdm ins** ~ **gehen** (*fig*) to
fall into sb's trap; ~**anbieter** *m* (*COMPUT*)
Internet provider; ~**anschluss▲** *m* mains
connection; ~**betreiber** *m* (*COMPUT*)
Internet provider; ~**computer** *m* network
computer; ~**haut** *f* retina; ~**karte** *f* (*EISENB*)
runabout ticket (*BRIT*); ~**plantechnik** *f*
network analysis; ~**spannung** *f* mains
voltage; ~**zugang** *m* (*COMPUT*) network
access.
neu [nɔy] *adj* new; (*Sprache, Geschichte*)
modern; **der/die N~e** the new person, the
newcomer; **seit** ~**estem** (since) recently;
~ **schreiben** to rewrite, write again; **auf ein**
N~es! (*Aufmunterung*) let's try again; **was**
gibts N~es? (*umg*) what's the latest?; **von**
~**em** (*von vorn*) from the beginning; (*wieder*)
again; **sich** ~ **einkleiden** to buy o.s. a new
set of clothes; ~ **eröffnet** newly-opened;
(*wieder geöffnet*) reopened; **N~ankömmling**
m newcomer; **N~anschaffung** *f* new
purchase *od* acquisition; ~**artig** *adj* new kind
of; **N~auflage** *f* new edition; **N~ausgabe** *f*
new edition; **N~bau** (**-(e)s, -ten**) *m* new
building; **N~bauwohnung** *f* newly-built flat;
N~bearbeitung *f* revised edition; (*das*
Neubearbeiten) revision, reworking;
N~druck *m* reprint; **N~emission** *f* (*Aktien*)
new issue.
neuerdings *adv* (*kürzlich*) (since) recently;
(*von neuem*) again.
Neuerscheinung *f* (*Buch*) new publication;
(*Schallplatte*) new release.
Neuerung *f* innovation, new departure.
Neufassung *f* revised version.
Neufundland [nɔy'fʊntlant] *nt* Newfoundland;
Neufundländer(in) (**-s, -**) *m(f)*
Newfoundlander; **neufundländisch** *adj*
Newfoundland *attrib*.
neugeboren *adj* newborn; **sich wie** ~ **fühlen**
to feel (like) a new man/woman.
Neugier *f* curiosity.

Neugierde (**-**) *f*: **aus** ~ out of curiosity.
neugierig *adj* curious.
Neuguinea [nɔygi'neːa] (**-s**) *nt* New Guinea.
Neuheit *f* novelty; (*neuartige Ware*) new thing.
Neuigkeit *f* news *sing*.
neu- *zW*: **N~jahr** *nt* New Year; **N~land** *nt*
virgin land; (*fig*) new ground; ~**lich** *adv*
recently, the other day; **N~ling** *m* novice;
~**modisch** *adj* fashionable; (*pej*) newfangled;
~**mond** *m* new moon.
neun [nɔyn] *num* nine; **N~** (**-, -en**) *f* nine; **ach**
du grüne N~e! (*umg*) well I'm blowed!
neunmalklug *adj* (*ironisch*) smart-aleck *attrib*.
neunzehn *num* nineteen.
neunzig *num* ninety.
Neureg(e)lung *f* adjustment.
neureich *adj* nouveau riche; **N~e(r)** *f(m)*
nouveau riche.
Neurologie [nɔyrolo'giː] *f* neurology.
neurologisch [nɔyro'loːgɪʃ] *adj* neurological.
Neurose [nɔy'roːzə] (**-, -n**) *f* neurosis.
Neurotiker(in) [nɔy'roːtikər(ɪn)] (**-s, -**) *m(f)*
neurotic.
neurotisch *adj* neurotic.
Neu- *zW*: ~**schnee** *m* fresh snow; ~**seeland**
[nɔy'zeːlant] *nt* New Zealand; ~**seeländer(in)**
(**-s, -**) *m(f)* New Zealander; **n~seeländisch** *adj*
New Zealand *attrib*; **n~sprachlich** *adj*:
n~sprachliches Gymnasium grammar
school (*BRIT*) *od* high school (*bes US*)
stressing modern languages.
neutral [nɔy'traːl] *adj* neutral.
neutralisieren [nɔytrali'ziːrən] *vt* to
neutralize.
Neutralität [nɔytrali'tɛːt] *f* neutrality.
Neutron ['nɔytrɔn] (**-s, -en**) *nt* neutron.
Neutrum ['nɔytrʊm] (**-s, Neutra** *od* **Neutren**) *nt*
neuter.
Neu- *zW*: ~**wert** *m* purchase price; **n~wertig**
adj as new; ~**zeit** *f* modern age; **n~zeitlich** *adj*
modern, recent.
N. H. *abk* (= *Normalhöhenpunkt*) normal peak
(level).
nhd. *abk* (= *neuhochdeutsch*) NHG.
Nicaragua [nika'raːgua] (**-s**) *nt* Nicaragua;
~**ner(in)** [nikaragu'aːnər(ɪn)] (**-s, -**) *m(f)*
Nicaraguan; **n~nisch** [nikaragu'aːnɪʃ] *adj*
Nicaraguan.

═══════════ *SCHLÜSSELWORT*

nicht [nɪçt] *adv* **1** (*Verneinung*) not; **er ist es** ~
it's not him, it isn't him; ~ **rostend**
stainless; **er raucht** ~ (*gerade*) he isn't
smoking; (*gewöhnlich*) he doesn't smoke; **ich**
kann das ~ - **ich auch** ~ I can't do it -
neither *od* nor can I; **es regnet** ~ **mehr** it's
not raining any more; ~ **mehr als** no more
than.
2 (*Bitte, Verbot*): ~**!** don't!, no!; ~ **berühren!**
do not touch!; ~ **doch!** don't!

3 (*rhetorisch*): **du bist müde, ~ (wahr)?**
you're tired, aren't you?; **das ist schön,
~ (wahr)?** it's nice, isn't it?
4: was du ~ sagst! the things you say!
♦ *präf* non-.

Nicht- *zW*: **~achtung** *f* disregard;
~anerkennung *f* repudiation; **~angriffspakt**
m non-aggression pact.

Nichte ['nɪçtə] (**-, -n**) *f* niece.

Nicht- *zW*: **~einhaltung** *f* (+*gen*) non-
compliance (with); **~einmischung** *f* (*POL*)
nonintervention; **~gefallen** *nt*: **bei ~gefallen
(zurück)** if not satisfied (return).

nichtig ['nɪçtɪç] *adj* (*ungültig*) null, void;
(*wertlos*) futile; **N~keit** *f* nullity, invalidity;
(*Sinnlosigkeit*) futility.

Nichtraucher *m* nonsmoker; **ich bin ~** I don't
smoke.

nichts [nɪçts] *pron* nothing; **~ ahnend**
unsuspecting; **~ sagend** meaningless; **~ als**
nothing but; **~ da!** (*ausgeschlossen*) nothing
doing (*umg*); **~ wie raus/hin** *etc* (*umg*) let's
get out/over there *etc* (on the double); **für
~ und wieder ~** for nothing at all; **N~** (**-s**) *nt*
nothingness; (*pej*: *Person*) nonentity.

Nichtschwimmer (**-s, -**) *m* nonswimmer.

nichts- *zW*: **~destotrotz** *adv* notwithstanding
(*form*), nonetheless; **~destoweniger** *adv*
nevertheless; **N~nutz** (**-es, -e**) *m* good-for-
nothing; **~nutzig** *adj* worthless, useless;
N~tun (**-s**) *nt* idleness.

Nichtzutreffende(s) *nt*: **~s** *od* **nicht
Zutreffendes (bitte) streichen** (please) delete
as applicable.

Nickel ['nɪkəl] (**-s**) *nt* nickel; **~brille** *f* metal-
rimmed glasses *pl*.

nicken ['nɪkən] *vi* to nod.

Nickerchen ['nɪkərçən] *nt* nap; **ein ~ machen**
(*umg*) to have forty winks.

Nicki ['nɪki] (**-s, -s**) *m* velours pullover.

nie [niː] *adv* never; **~ wieder** *od* **mehr** never
again; **~ und nimmer** never ever; **fast ~**
hardly ever.

nieder ['niːdər] *adj* low; (*gering*) inferior ♦ *adv*
down; **~deutsch** *adj* (*LING*) Low-German;
N~gang *m* decline; **~gedrückt** *adj* depressed;
~gehen *unreg vi* to descend; (*AVIAT*) to come
down; (*Regen*) to fall; (*Boxer*) to go down;
~geschlagen *adj* depressed, dejected;
N~geschlagenheit *f* depression, dejection;
N~kunft *f* (*veraltet*) delivery, giving birth;
N~lage *f* defeat.

Niederlande ['niːdərlandə] *pl*: **die ~** the
Netherlands *pl*.

Niederländer(in) ['niːdərlɛndər(ɪn)] (**-s, -**) *m(f)*
Dutchman, Dutchwoman.

niederländisch *adj* Dutch, Netherlands *attrib*.

nieder- *zW*: **~lassen** *unreg vr* (*sich setzen*) to sit
down; (*an Ort*) to settle (down); (*Arzt,*

Rechtsanwalt) to set up in practice;
N~lassung *f* settlement; (*COMM*) branch;
~legen *vt* to lay down; (*Arbeit*) to stop; (*Amt*)
to resign; **~machen** *vt* to mow down;
N~österreich *nt* Lower Austria; **N~rhein** *m*
Lower Rhine; **~rheinisch** *adj* Lower Rhine
attrib; **N~sachsen** *nt* Lower Saxony;
N~schlag *m* (*CHEM*) precipitate; (*Bodensatz*)
sediment; (*MET*) precipitation (*form*),
rainfall; (*BOXEN*) knockdown; **radioaktiver
N~schlag** (radioactive) fallout; **~schlagen**
unreg vt (*Gegner*) to beat down; (*Gegenstand*)
to knock down; (*Augen*) to lower; (*JUR:
Prozess*) to dismiss; (*Aufstand*) to put down
♦ *vr* (*CHEM*) to precipitate; **sich in etw** *dat*
~schlagen (*Erfahrungen etc*) to find
expression in sth; **~schlagsfrei**
['niːdərʃlaːksfraɪ] *adj* dry, without
precipitation (*form*); **~schmetternd** *adj*
(*Nachricht, Ergebnis*) shattering; **~schreiben**
unreg vt to write down; **N~schrift** *f*
transcription; **~tourig** *adj* (*Motor*) low-
revving; **~trächtig** *adj* base, mean;
N~trächtigkeit *f* despicable *od* malicious
behaviour.

Niederung *f* (*GEOG*) depression.

niederwalzen ['niːdərvaltsən] *vt*: **jdn/etw ~**
(*umg*) to mow sb/sth down.

niederwerfen ['niːdərvɛrfən] *unreg vt* to throw
down; (*fig*) to overcome; (*Aufstand*) to
suppress.

niedlich ['niːtlɪç] *adj* sweet, nice, cute.

niedrig ['niːdrɪç] *adj* low; (*Stand*) lowly,
humble; (*Gesinnung*) mean.

niemals ['niːmaːls] *adv* never.

niemand ['niːmant] *pron* nobody, no-one.

Niemandsland ['niːmantslant] *nt* no-man's-
land.

Niere ['niːrə] (**-, -n**) *f* kidney; **künstliche ~**
kidney machine.

Nierenentzündung *f* kidney infection.

nieseln ['niːzəln] *vi* to drizzle.

Nieselregen *m* drizzle.

niesen ['niːzən] *vi* to sneeze.

Niespulver *nt* sneezing powder.

Niet [niːt] (**-(e)s, -e**) *m* (*TECH*) rivet.

Niete ['niːtə] (**-, -n**) *f* (*TECH*) rivet; (*Los*) blank;
(*Reinfall*) flop; (*Mensch*) failure.

nieten *vt* to rivet.

Nietenhose *f* (pair of) studded jeans *pl*.

niet- und nagelfest (*umg*) *adj* nailed down.

Niger¹ ['niːgər] (**-s**) *nt* (*Staat*) Niger.

Niger² ['niːgər] (**-s**) *m* (*Fluss*) Niger.

Nigeria [niˈgeːria] (**-s**) *nt* Nigeria; **~ner(in)**
[nigeriˈaːnər(ɪn)] *m(f)* Nigerian; **n~nisch**
[nigeːriˈaːnɪʃ] *adj* Nigerian.

Nihilismus [nihiˈlɪsmʊs] *m* nihilism.

Nihilist [nihiˈlɪst] *m* nihilist; **n~isch** *adj*
nihilistic.

Nikolaus ['niːkolaʊs] (**-, -e** *od* (*hum: umg*)

-läuse) *m* ≈ Santa Claus, Father Christmas.
Nikosia [niko'ziːa] (-s) *nt* Nicosia.
Nikotin [niko'tiːn] (-s) *nt* nicotine; **n~arm** *adj* low-nicotine.
Nil [niːl] (-s) *m* Nile; **~pferd** *nt* hippopotamus.
Nimbus ['nɪmbʊs] (-, -se) *m* (*Heiligenschein*) halo; (*fig*) aura.
nimmersatt ['nɪmərzat] *adj* insatiable; **N~** (-(e)s, -e) *m* glutton.
Nimmerwiedersehen (*umg*) *nt*: **auf ~!** I never want to see you again.
nimmt [nɪmt] *vb siehe* **nehmen**.
nippen ['nɪpən] *vt, vi* to sip.
Nippes ['nɪpəs] *pl* knick-knacks *pl*, bric-a-brac *sing*.
Nippsachen ['nɪpzaxən] *pl* knick-knacks *pl*.
nirgends ['nɪrgənts] *adv* nowhere; **überall und ~** here, there and everywhere.
nirgendwo ['nɪrgəntvo] *adv* = **nirgends**.
nirgendwohin *adv* nowhere.
Nische ['niːʃə] (-, -n) *f* niche.
nisten ['nɪstən] *vi* to nest.
Nitrat [ni'traːt] (-(e)s, -e) *nt* nitrate.
Niveau [ni'voː] (-s, -s) *nt* level; **diese Schule hat ein hohes ~** this school has high standards; **unter meinem ~** beneath me.
Nivellierung [nivɛ'liːrʊŋ] *f* (*Ausgleichung*) levelling out.
nix [nɪks] (*umg*) *pron* = **nichts**.
Nixe ['nɪksə] (-, -n) *f* water nymph.
Nizza ['nɪtsa] (-s) *nt* Nice.
n. J. *abk* (= *nächsten Jahres*) next year.
n. M. *abk* (= *nächsten Monats*) next month.
NN *abk* (= *Normalnull*) m.s.l.
N. N. *abk* = **NN**.
NO *abk* (= *Nordost*) NE.
no. *abk* (= *netto*) net.
nobel ['noːbəl] *adj* (*großzügig*) generous; (*elegant*) posh (*umg*).
Nobelpreis [no'bɛlpraɪs] *m* Nobel prize; **~träger(in)** *m(f)* Nobel prize winner.

=============== *SCHLÜSSELWORT*

noch [nɔx] *adv* **1** (*weiterhin*) still; **~ nicht** not yet; **~ nie** never (yet); **~ immer** *od* **immer ~** still; **bleiben Sie doch ~** stay a bit longer; **ich gehe kaum ~ aus** I hardly go out any more.
2 (*in Zukunft*) still, yet; (*irgendwann einmal*) one day; **das kann ~ passieren** that might still happen; **er wird ~ kommen** he'll come (yet); **das wirst du ~ bereuen** you'll come to regret it (one day).
3 (*nicht später als*): **~ vor einer Woche** only a week ago; **~ am selben Tag** the very same day; **~ im 19. Jahrhundert** as late as the 19th century; **~ heute** today.
4 (*zusätzlich*): **wer war ~ da?** who else was there?; **~ einmal** once more, again; **~ dreimal** three more times; **~ einer**

another one; **und es regnete auch ~** and on top of that it was raining.
5 (*bei Vergleichen*): **~ größer** even bigger; **das ist ~ besser** that's better still; **und wenn es ~ so schwer ist** however hard it is.
6: **Geld ~ und ~** heaps (and heaps) of money; **sie hat ~ und ~ versucht**, ... she tried again and again to ...
♦ *konj*: **weder A ~ B** neither A nor B.

nochmal(s) *adv* again, once more.
nochmalig *adj* repeated.
Nockenwelle ['nɔkənvɛlə] *f* camshaft.
NOK *nt abk* (= *Nationales Olympisches Komitee*) National Olympic Committee.
Nom. *abk* = **Nominativ**.
Nominalwert [nomi'naːlveːrt] *m* (*FIN*) nominal *od* par value.
Nominativ ['noːminatiːf] (-s, -e) *m* nominative.
nominell [nomi'nɛl] *adj* nominal.
nominieren [nomi'niːrən] *vt* to nominate.
Nonne ['nɔnə] (-, -n) *f* nun.
Nonnenkloster *nt* convent.
Nonplusultra [nɔnplʊs'|ʊltra] (-s) *nt* ultimate.
Nord [nɔrt] (-s) *m* north; **~afrika** ['nɔrt'|aːfrika] *nt* North Africa; **~amerika** *nt* North America; **n~amerikanisch** ['nɔrt|ameri'kaːnɪʃ] *adj* North American.
nordd. *abk* = **norddeutsch**.
norddeutsch *adj* North German.
Norddeutschland *nt* North(ern) Germany.
Norden ['nɔrdən] *m* north.
Nord- *zW*: **~england** *nt* the North of England; **~irland** *nt* Northern Ireland, Ulster; **n~isch** *adj* northern; **n~ische Kombination** (*SKI*) nordic combination; **~kap** *nt* North Cape; **~korea** ['nɔrtko'reːa] *nt* North Korea.
nördlich ['nœrtlɪç] *adj* northerly, northern ♦ *präp +gen* (to the) north of; **der ~ e Polarkreis** the Arctic Circle; **N~es Eismeer** Arctic Ocean; **~ von** north of.
Nord- *zW*: **~licht** *nt* northern lights *pl*, aurora borealis; **~-Ostsee-Kanal** *m* Kiel Canal; **~pol** *m* North Pole; **~polargebiet** *nt* Arctic (Zone).
Nordrhein-Westfalen ['nɔrtraɪnvɛst'faːlən] (-s) *nt* North Rhine-Westphalia.
Nordsee *f* North Sea.
nordwärts *adv* northwards.
Nörgelei [nœrgə'laɪ] *f* grumbling.
nörgeln *vi* to grumble.
Nörgler(in) (-s, -) *m(f)* grumbler.
Norm [nɔrm] (-, -en) *f* norm; (*Leistungssoll*) quota; (*Größenvorschrift*) standard (specification).
normal [nɔr'maːl] *adj* normal; **bist du noch ~?** (*umg*) have you gone mad?; **N~benzin** *nt* two-star petrol (*BRIT veraltet*), regular gas (*US*).
normalerweise *adv* normally.

Normalfall *m*: **im** ~ normally.
Normalgewicht *nt* normal weight; (*genormt*) standard weight.
normalisieren [nɔrmali'ziːrən] *vt* to normalize ♦ *vr* to return to normal.
Normalzeit *f* (*GEOG*) standard time.
Normandie [nɔrman'diː] *f* Normandy.
normen *vt* to standardize.
Norwegen ['nɔrveːgən] (**-s**) *nt* Norway.
Norweger(in) (**-s**, **-**) *m(f)* Norwegian.
norwegisch *adj* Norwegian.
Nostalgie [nɔstal'giː] *f* nostalgia.
Not [noːt] (**-**, **-̈e**) *f* need; (*Mangel*) want; (*Mühe*) trouble; (*Zwang*) necessity; ~ **leidend** needy; **zur** ~ if necessary; (*gerade noch*) just about; **wenn** ~ **am Mann ist** if you/they *etc* are short (*umg*); (*im Notfall*) in an emergency; **er hat seine liebe** ~ **mit ihr/ damit** he really has problems with her/it; **in seiner** ~ in his hour of need.
Notar(in) [no'taːr(ɪn)] (**-s**, **-e**) *m(f)* notary; **n~iell** *adj* notarial; **n~iell beglaubigt** attested by a notary.
Not- *zW*: ~**arzt** *m* doctor on emergency call; ~**ausgang** *m* emergency exit; ~**behelf** *m* stopgap; ~**bremse** *f* emergency brake; ~**dienst** *m*: ~**dienst haben** (*Apotheke*) to be open 24 hours; (*Arzt*) to be on call; **n~dürftig** *adj* scanty; (*behelfsmäßig*) makeshift; **sich n~dürftig verständigen können** to be able to communicate to some extent.
Note ['noːtə] (**-**, **-n**) *f* note; (*SCH*) mark (*BRIT*), grade (*US*); **Noten** *pl* (*MUS*) music *sing*; **eine persönliche** ~ a personal touch.
Noten- *zW*: ~**bank** *f* issuing bank; ~**blatt** *nt* sheet of music; ~**schlüssel** *m* clef; ~**ständer** *m* music stand.
Not- *zW*: ~**fall** *m* (case of) emergency; **n~falls** *adv* if need be; **n~gedrungen** *adj* necessary, unavoidable; **etw n~gedrungen machen** to be forced to do sth; ~**groschen** ['noːtgrɔʃən] *m* nest egg.
notieren [no'tiːrən] *vt* to note; (*COMM*) to quote.
Notierung *f* (*COMM*) quotation.
nötig ['nøːtɪç] *adj* necessary ♦ *adv* (*dringend*): **etw** ~ **brauchen** to need sth urgently; **etw** ~ **haben** to need sth; **das habe ich nicht** ~! I can do without that!
nötigen *vt* to compel, force; ~**falls** *adv* if necessary.
Nötigung *f* compulsion, coercion (*JUR*).
Notiz [no'tiːts] (**-**, **-en**) *f* note; (*Zeitungs*~) item; ~ **nehmen** to take notice; ~**block** *m* notepad; ~**buch** *nt* notebook; ~**zettel** *m* piece of paper.
Not- *zW*: ~**lage** *f* crisis, emergency; **n~landen** *vi* to make a forced *od* emergency landing; ~**landung** *f* forced *od* emergency landing; ~**lösung** *f* temporary solution; ~**lüge** *f* white lie.

notorisch [no'toːrɪʃ] *adj* notorious.
Not- *zW*: ~**ruf** *m* emergency call; ~**rufsäule** *f* emergency telephone; **n~schlachten** *vt* (*Tiere*) to destroy; ~**stand** *m* state of emergency; ~**standsgebiet** *nt* (*wirtschaftlich*) depressed area; (*bei Katastrophen*) disaster area; ~**standsgesetz** *nt* emergency law; ~**unterkunft** *f* emergency accommodation; ~**verband** *m* emergency dressing; ~**wehr** (**-**) *f* self-defence; **n~wendig** *adj* necessary; ~**wendigkeit** *f* necessity; ~**zucht** *f* rape.
Nov. *abk* (= *November*) Nov.
Novelle [no'vɛlə] (**-**, **-n**) *f* novella; (*JUR*) amendment.
November [no'vɛmbər] (**-(s)**, **-**) *m* November; *siehe auch* **September**.
Novum ['noːvʊm] (**-s**, **Nova**) *nt* novelty.
NPD (**-**) *f abk* (= *Nationaldemokratische Partei Deutschlands*) National Democratic Party.
Nr. *abk* (= *Nummer*) no.
NRW *abk* = **Nordrhein-Westfalen**.
NS *abk* = **Nachschrift**; **Nationalsozialismus**.
NS- *in zW* Nazi.
N. T. *abk* (= *Neues Testament*) N.T.
Nu [nuː] *m*: **im** ~ in an instant.
Nuance [ny'ãːsə] (**-**, **-n**) *f* nuance; (*Kleinigkeit*) shade.
nüchtern ['nʏçtərn] *adj* sober; (*Magen*) empty; (*Urteil*) prudent; **N~heit** *f* sobriety.
Nudel ['nuːdəl] (**-**, **-n**) *f* noodle; (*umg: Mensch: dick*) dumpling; (: : *komisch*) character; ~**holz** *nt* rolling pin.
Nugat ['nuːgat] (**-s**, **-s**) *m od nt* nougat.
nuklear [nukle'aːr] *adj attrib* nuclear.
null [nʊl] *num* zero; (*Fehler*) no; ~ **Uhr** midnight; **in** ~ **Komma nichts** (*umg*) in less than no time; **die Stunde** ~ the new starting point; **gleich** ~ **sein** to be absolutely nil; ~ **und nichtig** null and void; **N~** (**-**, **-en**) *f* nought, zero; (*pej: Mensch*) dead loss; ~**achtfünfzehn** (*umg*) *adj* run-of-the-mill; **N~diät** *f* starvation diet; **N~lösung** *f* (*POL*) zero option; **N~punkt** *m* zero; **auf dem N~punkt** at zero; **N~tarif** *m* (*für Verkehrsmittel*) free travel; **zum N~tarif** free of charge.
numerieren △ [nume'riːrən] *vt siehe* **nummerieren**.
numerisch [nu'meːrɪʃ] *adj* numerical; ~**es Tastenfeld** (*COMPUT*) numeric pad.
Numerus ['nuːmerʊs] (**-**, **Numeri**) *m* (*GRAM*) number; ~ **clausus** (*UNIV*) restricted entry.
Nummer ['nʊmər] (**-**, **-n**) *f* number; **auf** ~ **sicher** *od* **Sicher gehen** (*umg*) to play (it) safe.
nummerieren ▲ [nume'riːrən] *vt* to number.
Nummern- *zW*: ~**konto** *nt* numbered bank account; ~**scheibe** *f* telephone dial; ~**schild** *nt* (*AUT*) number *od* license (*US*) plate.

nun [nuːn] *adv* now ♦ *interj* well.
nur [nuːr] *adv* just, only; **nicht ~ ..., sondern
auch ...** not only ... but also ...; **alle, ~ ich
nicht** everyone but me; **ich hab das ~ so
gesagt** I was just talking.
Nürnberg ['nʏrnbɛrk] (**-s**) *nt* Nuremberg.
nuscheln ['nuʃəln] (*umg*) *vt, vi* to mutter,
mumble.
Nuss▲ [nʊs] (**-, ̈-e**) *f* nut; **eine doofe ~** (*umg*) a
stupid twit; **eine harte ~** a hard nut (to
crack); **~baum** *m* walnut tree; **~knacker** (**-s,
-**) *m* nutcracker.
Nüster ['nyːstər] (**-, -n**) *f* nostril.
Nutte ['nʊtə] (**-, -n**) *f* tart (*BRIT*), hooker (*US*).
nutz [nʊts] *adj* = **nütze**; **~bar** *adj*: **~bar machen**
to utilize; **N~barmachung** *f* utilization;
~bringend *adj* profitable; **etw ~bringend
anwenden** to use sth to good effect, put sth
to good use.
nütze ['nʏtsə] *adj*: **zu nichts ~ sein** to be
useless.
nutzen *vi* to be of use ♦ *vt*: (**zu etw**) **~** to use
(for sth); **was nutzt es?** what's the use?,
what use is it?; **N~** (**-s**) *m* usefulness;
(*Gewinn*) profit; **von N~** useful.
nützen *vt, vi* = **nutzen**.
Nutz- *zW*: **~fahrzeug** *nt farm od military
vehicle etc*; (*COMM*) commercial vehicle;
~fläche *f* us(e)able floor space; (*AGR*)
productive land; **~last** *f* maximum load,
payload.
nützlich ['nʏtslɪç] *adj* useful; **N~keit** *f*
usefulness.
Nutz- *zW*: **n~los** *adj* useless; (*unnötig*)
needless; **~losigkeit** *f* uselessness; **~nießer**
(**-s, -**) *m* beneficiary.
Nutzung *f* (*Gebrauch*) use; (*das Ausnutzen*)
exploitation.
NW *abk* (= *Nordwest*) NW.
Nylon ['naɪlɔn] (**-s**) *nt* nylon.
Nymphe ['nʏmfə] (**-, -n**) *f* nymph.

O, o

O¹, o [oː] *nt* O, o; **~ wie Otto** ≈ O for Olive, O
for Oboe (*US*).
O² [oː] *abk* (= *Osten*) E.
o. Ä. *abk* (= *oder Ähnliche(s)*) or similar.
Oase [oˈaːzə] (**-, -n**) *f* oasis.
OB (**-s, -s**) *m abk* = **Oberbürgermeister**.
ob [ɔp] *konj* if, whether; **~ das wohl wahr ist?**
can that be true?; **~ ich (nicht) lieber gehe?**
maybe I'd better go; (**so**) **tun als ~** (*umg*) to

pretend; **und ~!** you bet!
Obacht ['oːbaxt] *f*: **~ geben** to pay attention.
Obdach ['ɔpdax] (**-(e)s**) *nt* shelter, lodging;
o~los *adj* homeless; **~losenasyl** *nt* hostel *od*
shelter for the homeless; **~losenheim** *nt*
= **Obdachlosenasyl**; **~lose(r)** *f(m)* homeless
person.
Obduktion [ɔpdʊktsiˈoːn] *f* postmortem.
obduzieren [ɔpduˈtsiːrən] *vt* to do a
postmortem on.
O-Beine ['oːbaɪnə] *pl* bow *od* bandy legs *pl*.
oben ['oːbən] *adv* above; (*in Haus*) upstairs;
(*am oberen Ende*) at the top; **~ erwähnt,
~ genannt** above-mentioned; **nach ~** up;
von ~ down; **siehe ~** see above; **ganz ~**
right at the top; **~ ohne** topless; **die
Abbildung ~ links** *od* **links ~** the illustration
in the top left-hand corner; **jdn von ~ herab
behandeln** to treat sb condescendingly; **jdn
von ~ bis unten ansehen** to look sb up and
down; **Befehl von ~** orders from above; **die
da ~** (*umg*: *die Vorgesetzten*) the powers that
be; **~adv** at the top; **~'auf** *adv* up above, on
the top ♦ *adj* (*munter*) in form; **~'drein** *adv*
into the bargain; **~'hin** *adv* cursorily,
superficially.
Ober ['oːbər] (**-s, -**) *m* waiter.
Ober- *zW*: **~arm** *m* upper arm; **~arzt** *m* senior
physician; **~aufsicht** *f* supervision; **~bayern**
nt Upper Bavaria; **~befehl** *m* supreme
command; **~befehlshaber** *m* commander-in-
chief; **~begriff** *m* generic term; **~bekleidung**
f outer clothing; **~bett** *nt* quilt;
~bürgermeister *m* lord mayor; **~deck** *nt*
upper *od* top deck.
obere(r, s) *adj* upper; **die O~n** the bosses;
(*ECCL*) the superiors; **die ~n zehntausend**
(*umg*) high society.
Ober- *zW*: **~fläche** *f* surface; **o~flächlich** *adj*
superficial; **bei o~flächlicher Betrachtung** at
a quick glance; **jdn (nur) o~flächlich kennen**
to know sb (only) slightly; **~geschoss▲** *nt*
upper storey *od* story (*US*); **im zweiten
~geschoss** on the second floor (*BRIT*), on the
third floor (*US*); **o~halb** *adv* above ♦ *präp +gen*
above; **~hand** *f* (*fig*): **die ~hand gewinnen**
(**über** +*akk*) to get the upper hand (over);
~haupt *nt* head, chief; **~haus** *nt* (*BRIT POL*)
upper house, House of Lords; **~hemd** *nt*
shirt; **~herrschaft** *f* supremacy, sovereignty.
Oberin *f* matron; (*ECCL*) Mother Superior.
Ober- *zW*: **o~irdisch** *adj* above ground;
(*Leitung*) overhead; **~italien** *nt* Northern
Italy; **~kellner** *m* head waiter; **~kiefer** *m*
upper jaw; **~kommando** *nt* supreme
command; **~körper** *m* upper part of body;
~lauf *m*: **am ~lauf des Rheins** in the upper
reaches of the Rhine; **~leitung** *f* (*ELEK*)
overhead cable; **~licht** *nt* skylight; **~lippe** *f*
upper lip; **~österreich** *nt* Upper Austria;

~**prima** f (früher) final year of German secondary school; ~**schenkel** m thigh; ~**schicht** f upper classes pl; ~**schule** f grammar school (BRIT), high school (US); ~**schwester** f (MED) matron; ~**seite** f top (side); ~**sekunda** f (früher) seventh year of German secondary school.

Oberst ['o:bərst] (-en od -s, -en od -e) m colonel.

oberste(r, s) adj very top, topmost.

Ober- zW: ~**stübchen** (umg) nt: **er ist nicht ganz richtig im ~stübchen** he's not quite right up top; ~**stufe** f upper school; ~**teil** nt upper part; ~**tertia** f (früher) fifth year of German secondary school; ~**wasser** nt: ~**wasser haben/bekommen** to be/get on top (of things); ~**weite** f bust od chest measurement.

obgleich [ɔp'glaiç] konj although.

Obhut ['ɔphu:t] (-) f care, protection; **in jds ~** dat **sein** to be in sb's care.

obig ['o:biç] adj above.

Objekt [ɔp'jɛkt] (-(e)s, -e) nt object.

objektiv [ɔpjɛk'ti:f] adj objective.

Objektiv (-s, -e) nt lens sing.

Objektivität [ɔpjɛktivi'tɛ:t] f objectivity.

Oblate [o'bla:tə] (-, -n) f (Gebäck) wafer; (ECCL) host.

obligatorisch [obliga'to:rɪʃ] adj compulsory, obligatory.

Oboe [o'bo:ə] (-, -n) f oboe.

Obrigkeit ['o:briçkait] f (Behörden) authorities pl, administration; (Regierung) government.

Obrigkeitsdenken nt acceptance of authority.

obschon [ɔp'ʃo:n] konj although.

Observatorium [ɔpzɛrva'to:riʊm] nt observatory.

obskur [ɔps'ku:r] adj obscure; (verdächtig) dubious.

Obst [o:pst] (-(e)s) nt fruit; ~**bau** m fruit-growing; ~**baum** m fruit tree; ~**garten** m orchard; ~**händler** m fruiterer (BRIT), fruit merchant; ~**kuchen** m fruit tart; ~**saft** m fruit juice; ~**salat** m fruit salad.

obszön [ɔps'tsø:n] adj obscene.

Obszönität [ɔpstøni'tɛ:t] f obscenity.

Obus ['o:bus] (-ses, -se) (umg) m trolleybus.

obwohl [ɔp'vo:l] konj although.

Ochse ['ɔksə] (-n, -n) m ox; (umg: Dummkopf) twit; **er stand da wie der ~ vorm Berg** (umg) he stood there utterly bewildered.

ochsen (umg) vt, vi to cram, swot (BRIT).

Ochsenschwanzsuppe f oxtail soup.

Ochsenzunge f ox tongue.

Ocker ['ɔkər] (-s, -) m od nt ochre (BRIT), ocher (US).

öd [ø:t(ə)] adj = öde.

öde adj (Land) waste, barren; (fig) dull; ~ **und leer** dreary and desolate.

Öde (-, -n) f desert, waste(land); (fig) tedium.

oder ['o:dər] konj or; **entweder ... ~** either ... or; **du kommst doch, ~?** you're coming, aren't you?

Ofen ['o:fən] (-s, ⸚) m oven; (Heiz~) fire, heater; (Kohle~) stove; (Hoch~) furnace; (Herd) cooker, stove; **jetzt ist der ~ aus** (umg) that does it!; ~**rohr** nt stovepipe.

offen ['ɔfən] adj open; (aufrichtig) frank; (Stelle) vacant; (Bein) ulcerated; (Haare) loose; ~**er Wein** wine by the carafe od glass; **auf ~er Strecke** (Straße) on the open road; (EISENB) between stations; **Tag der ~en Tür** open day (BRIT), open house (US); ~**e Handelsgesellschaft** (COMM) general od ordinary (US) partnership; ~ **bleiben** (Fenster) to stay open; (Frage, Entscheidung) to remain open; ~ **halten** to keep open; ~ **lassen** to leave open; ~ **stehen** to be open; (Rechnung) to be unpaid; **es steht Ihnen ~, es zu tun** you are at liberty to do it; **die (ganze) Welt steht ihm ~** he has the (whole) world at his feet; **seine Meinung ~ sagen** to speak one's mind; **ein ~es Wort mit jdm reden** to have a frank talk with sb; ~ **gesagt** to be honest.

offenbar adj obvious; (vermutlich) apparently.

offenbaren [ɔfən'ba:rən] vt to reveal, manifest.

Offenbarung f (REL) revelation.

Offenbarungseid m (JUR) oath of disclosure.

Offen- zW: ~**heit** f candour (BRIT), candor (US), frankness; **o~herzig** adj candid, frank; (hum: Kleid) revealing; ~**herzigkeit** f frankness; **o~kundig** adj well-known; (klar) evident; **o~sichtlich** adj evident, obvious.

offensiv [ɔfɛn'zi:f] adj offensive.

Offensive (-, -n) f offensive.

öffentlich ['œfəntlɪç] adj public; **die ~e Hand** (central/local) government; **Anstalt des ~en Rechts** public institution; **Ausgaben der ~en Hand** public spending sing.

Öffentlichkeit f (Leute) public; (einer Versammlung etc) public nature; **in aller ~** in public; **an die ~ dringen** to reach the public ear; **unter Ausschluss der ~** in secret; (JUR) in camera.

Öffentlichkeitsarbeit f public relations work.

öffentlich-rechtlich adj attrib (under) public law.

offerieren [ɔfe'ri:rən] vt to offer.

Offerte [ɔ'fɛrtə] (-, -n) f offer.

offiziell [ɔfitsi'ɛl] adj official.

Offizier [ɔfi'tsi:r] (-s, -e) m officer.

Offizierskasino nt officers' mess.

öffnen ['œfnən] vt, vr to open; **jdm die Tür ~** to open the door for sb.

Öffner ['œfnər] (-s, -) m opener.

Öffnung ['œfnʊŋ] f opening.

Öffnungszeiten *pl* opening times *pl*.
Offsetdruck ['ɔfsɛtdrʊk] *m* offset (printing).
oft [ɔft] *adv* often.
öfter ['œftər] *adv* more often *od* frequently;
des Ö~en quite frequently; **~ mal was
Neues** (*umg*) variety is the spice of life
(*Sprichwort*).
öfters *adv* often, frequently.
oftmals *adv* often, frequently.
o. G. *abk* (= *ohne Gewähr*) without liability.
OHG *f abk* (= *offene Handelsgesellschaft*) *siehe*
offen.
ohne ['oːnə] *präp +akk, konj* without; **das
Darlehen ist ~ weiteres bewilligt worden**
the loan was granted without any problem;
**das kann man nicht ~ weiteres
voraussetzen** you can't just assume that
automatically; **das ist nicht ~** (*umg*) it's not
bad; **~ weiteres** without a second thought;
(*sofort*) immediately; **~dies** *adv* anyway;
~einander [oːnəˈaɪˈnandər] *adv* without each
other; **~gleichen** *adj* unsurpassed, without
equal; **~hin** *adv* anyway, in any case; **es ist
~hin schon spät** it's late enough already.
Ohnmacht ['oːnmaxt] *f* faint; (*fig*) impotence;
in ~ fallen to faint.
ohnmächtig ['oːnmɛçtɪç] *adj* in a faint,
unconscious; (*fig*) weak, impotent; **sie ist ~**
she has fainted; **~e Wut, ~er Zorn** helpless
rage; **einer Sache** *dat* **~ gegenüberstehen** to
be helpless in the face of sth.
Ohr [oːr] (**-(e)s, -en**) *nt* ear; (*Gehör*) hearing;
sich aufs ~ legen *od* **hauen** (*umg*) to kip
down; **jdm die ~en lang ziehen** (*umg*) to
tweak sb's ear(s); **jdm in den ~en liegen** to
keep on at sb; **jdn übers ~ hauen** (*umg*) to
pull a fast one on sb; **auf dem ~ bin ich taub**
(*fig*) nothing doing (*umg*); **schreib es dir
hinter die ~en** (*umg*) will you (finally) get
that into your (thick) head!; **bis über die** *od*
beide ~en verliebt sein to be head over
heels in love; **viel um die ~en haben** (*umg*)
to have a lot on (one's plate); **halt die ~en
steif!** keep a stiff upper lip!
Öhr [øːr] (**-(e)s, -e**) *nt* eye.
Ohren- *zW*: **~arzt** *m* ear specialist;
o~betäubend *adj* deafening; **~sausen** *nt*
(*MED*) buzzing in one's ears; **~schmalz** *nt*
earwax; **~schmerzen** *pl* earache *sing*;
~schützer (**-s, -**) *m* earmuff.
Ohr- *zW*: **~feige** *f* slap on the face; (*als Strafe*)
box on the ears; **o~feigen** *vt untr*: **jdn
o~feigen** to slap sb's face; to box sb's ears;
**ich könnte mich selbst o~feigen, dass ich
das gemacht habe** I could kick myself for
doing that; **~läppchen** *nt* ear lobe; **~ringe** *pl*
earrings *pl*; **~wurm** *m* earwig; (*MUS*) catchy
tune.
o. J. *abk* (= *ohne Jahr*) no year given.
okkupieren [ɔkuˈpiːrən] *vt* to occupy.

Öko- ['øko-] *in zW* eco-, ecological; **~laden**
['øːkolaːdən] *m* wholefood shop.
Ökologie [økoloˈgiː] *f* ecology.
ökologisch [økoˈloːgɪʃ] *adj* ecological,
environmental.
Ökonometrie [økonomeˈtriː] *f* econometrics
pl.
Ökonomie [økonoˈmiː] *f* economy; (*als
Wissenschaft*) economics *sing*.
ökonomisch [økoˈnoːmɪʃ] *adj* economical.
Ökopax [økoˈpaks] (**-en, -e**) (*umg*) *m*
environmentalist.
Ökosystem ['øːkozysteːm] *nt* ecosystem.
Okt. *abk* (= *Oktober*) Oct.
Oktan [ɔkˈtaːn] (**-s, -e**) *nt* octane; **~zahl** *f*
octane rating.
Oktave [ɔkˈtaːvə] (**-, -n**) *f* octave.
Oktober [ɔkˈtoːbər] (**-(s), -**) *m* October; *siehe
auch* **September**.

OKTOBERFEST

The annual October beer festival, the
Oktoberfest, *takes place in Munich on a huge
field where beer tents, roller coasters and many
other amusements are set up. People sit at long
wooden tables, drink beer from enormous litre
beer mugs, eat pretzels and listen to brass bands.
It is a great attraction for tourists and locals alike.*

ökumenisch [økuˈmeːnɪʃ] *adj* ecumenical.
Öl [øːl] (**-(e)s, -e**) *nt* oil; **auf ~ stoßen** to strike
oil.
Öl- *zW*: **~baum** *m* olive tree; **ö~en** *vt* to oil;
(*TECH*) to lubricate; **wie ein geölter Blitz**
(*umg*) like greased lightning; **~farbe** *f* oil
paint; **~feld** *nt* oilfield; **~film** *m* film of oil;
~heizung *f* oil-fired central heating.
ölig *adj* oily.
Oligopol [oligoˈpoːl] (**-s, -e**) *nt* oligopoly.
oliv [oˈliːf] *adj* olive-green.
Olive [oˈliːvə] (**-, -n**) *f* olive.
Olivenöl *nt* olive oil.
Öljacke *f* oilskin jacket.
oll [ɔl] (*umg*) *adj* old; **das sind ~e Kamellen**
that's old hat.
Öl- *zW*: **~messstab▲** *m* dipstick; **~pest** *f* oil
pollution; **~plattform** *f* oil rig; **~sardine** *f*
sardine; **~scheich** *m* oil sheik; **~stand** *m* oil
level; **~standanzeiger** *m* (*AUT*) oil level
indicator; **~tanker** *m* oil tanker; **~teppich** *m*
oil slick.
Ölung *f* oiling; (*ECCL*) anointment; **die Letzte
~** Extreme Unction.
Ölwanne *f* (*AUT*) sump (*BRIT*), oil pan (*US*).
Ölwechsel *m* oil change.
Olymp [oˈlʏmp] (**-s**) *m* (*Berg*) Mount Olympus.
Olympiade [olʏmpiˈaːdə] (**-, -n**) *f* Olympic
Games *pl*.
Olympiasieger(in) [oˈlʏmpiaziːgər(ɪn)] *m(f)*

Olympic champion.
olympisch [o'lɣmpɪʃ] *adj* Olympic.
Ölzeug *nt* oilskins *pl.*
Oma ['oːma] (-, -s) (*umg*) *f* granny.
Oman [o'maːn] (-s) *nt* Oman.
Omelett [ɔm(ə)'lɛt] (-(e)s, -s) *nt* omelette (*BRIT*), omelet (*US*).
Omelette [ɔm(ə)'lɛt] *f* = **Omelett**.
Omen ['oːmɛn] (-s, - *od* Omina) *nt* omen.
Omnibus ['ɔmnibʊs] *m* (omni)bus.
Onanie [ona'niː] *f* masturbation.
onanieren *vi* to masturbate.
ondulieren [ɔndu'liːrən] *vt*, *vi* to crimp.
Onkel ['ɔŋkəl] (-s, -) *m* uncle.
online ['ɔnlaɪn] *adj* (*COMPUT*) on-line.
Onlinedienst *m* (*COMPUT*) on-line service.
OP *m abk* = **Operationssaal**.
Opa ['oːpa] (-s, -s) (*umg*) *m* grandpa.
Opal [o'paːl] (-s, -e) *m* opal.
Oper ['oːpər] (-, -n) *f* opera; (*Opernhaus*) opera house.
Operation [operatsi'oːn] *f* operation.
Operationssaal *m* operating theatre (*BRIT*) *od* theater (*US*).
operativ [opəra'tiːf] *adv* (*MED*): **eine Geschwulst ~ entfernen** to remove a growth by surgery.
Operette [ope'rɛtə] *f* operetta.
operieren [ope'riːrən] *vt*, *vi* to operate; **sich ~ lassen** to have an operation.
Opern- *zW*: **~glas** *nt* opera glasses *pl*; **~haus** *nt* opera house; **~sänger(in)** *m(f)* opera singer.
Opfer ['ɔpfər] (-s, -) *nt* sacrifice; (*Mensch*) victim; **~bereitschaft** *f* readiness to make sacrifices.
opfern *vt* to sacrifice.
Opferstock *m* (*ECCL*) offertory box.
Opferung *f* sacrifice; (*ECCL*) offertory.
Opium ['oːpiʊm] (-s) *nt* opium.
opponieren [ɔpo'niːrən] *vi*: **gegen jdn/etw ~** to oppose sb/sth.
opportun [ɔpɔr'tuːn] *adj* opportune; **O~ismus** [-'nɪsmʊs] *m* opportunism; **O~ist(in)** [-'nɪst(ɪn)] *m(f)* opportunist.
Opposition [ɔpozitsi'oːn] *f* opposition.
oppositionell [ɔpozitsio'nɛl] *adj* opposing.
Oppositionsführer *m* leader of the opposition.
optieren [ɔp'tiːrən] *vi* (*POL*: *form*): **~ für** to opt for.
Optik ['ɔptɪk] *f* optics *sing*.
Optiker(in) (-s, -) *m(f)* optician.
optimal [ɔpti'maːl] *adj* optimal, optimum.
Optimismus [ɔpti'mɪsmʊs] *m* optimism.
Optimist(in) [ɔpti'mɪst(ɪn)] *m(f)* optimist; **o~isch** *adj* optimistic.
optisch ['ɔptɪʃ] *adj* optical; **~e Täuschung** optical illusion.
Orakel [o'raːkəl] (-s, -) *nt* oracle.
Orange [o'rãːʒə] (-, -n) *f* orange; **o~** *adj*

orange.
Orangeade [orã'ʒaːdə] (-, -n) *f* orangeade.
Orangeat [orã'ʒaːt] (-s, -e) *nt* candied peel.
Orangen- *zW*: **~marmelade** *f* marmalade; **~saft** *m* orange juice; **~schale** *f* orange peel.
Oratorium [ora'toːriʊm] *nt* (*MUS*) oratorio.
Orchester [ɔr'kɛstər] (-s, -) *nt* orchestra.
Orchidee [ɔrçi'deːə] (-, -n) *f* orchid.
Orden ['ɔrdən] (-s, -) *m* (*ECCL*) order; (*MIL*) decoration.
Ordensgemeinschaft *f* religious order.
Ordensschwester *f* nun.
ordentlich ['ɔrdəntlɪç] *adj* (*anständig*) decent, respectable; (*geordnet*) tidy, neat; (*umg*: *annehmbar*) not bad; (: *tüchtig*) real, proper; (*Leistung*) reasonable; **~es Mitglied** full member; **~er Professor** (full) professor; **eine ~e Tracht Prügel** a proper hiding; **~ arbeiten** to be a thorough and precise worker; **O~keit** *f* respectability; tidiness.
Order (-, -s *od* -n) *f* (*COMM*: *Auftrag*) order.
ordern *vt* (*COMM*) to order.
Ordinalzahl [ɔrdi'naːltsaːl] *f* ordinal number.
ordinär [ɔrdi'nɛːr] *adj* common, vulgar.
Ordinarius [ɔrdi'naːriʊs] (-, Ordinarien) *m* (*UNIV*): **~ (für)** professor (of).
ordnen ['ɔrdnən] *vt* to order, put in order.
Ordner (-s, -) *m* steward; (*COMM*) file.
Ordnung *f* order; (*Ordnen*) ordering; (*Geordnetsein*) tidiness; **geht in ~** (*umg*) that's all right *od* OK (*umg*); **~ schaffen, für ~ sorgen** to put things in order, tidy things up; **jdn zur ~ rufen** to call sb to order; **bei ihm muss alles seine ~ haben** (*räumlich*) he has to have everything in its proper place; (*zeitlich*) he has to do everything according to a fixed schedule; **das Kind braucht seine ~** the child needs a routine.
Ordnungs- *zW*: **~amt** *nt* ≈ town clerk's office; **o~gemäß** *adj* proper, according to the rules; **o~halber** *adv* as a matter of form; **~liebe** *f* tidiness, orderliness; **~strafe** *f* fine; **o~widrig** *adj* contrary to the rules, irregular; **~widrigkeit** *f* infringement (*of law or rule*); **~zahl** *f* ordinal number.
ORF (-) *m abk* = **Österreichischer Rundfunk**.
Organ [ɔr'gaːn] (-s, -e) *nt* organ; (*Stimme*) voice.
Organisation [ɔrganizatsi'oːn] *f* organization.
Organisationstalent *nt* organizing ability; (*Person*) good organizer.
Organisator [ɔrgani'zaːtɔr] *m* organizer.
organisch [ɔr'gaːnɪʃ] *adj* organic; (*Erkrankung, Leiden*) physical.
organisieren [ɔrgani'ziːrən] *vt* to organize, arrange; (*umg*: *beschaffen*) to acquire ♦ *vr* to organize.
Organismus [ɔrga'nɪsmʊs] *m* organism.
Organist [ɔrga'nɪst] *m* organist.
Organspender *m* donor (of an organ).

Organspenderausweis *m* donor card.
Organverpflanzung *f* transplantation (of an organ).
Orgasmus [ɔr'gasmʊs] *m* orgasm.
Orgel ['ɔrgəl] (**-, -n**) *f* organ; **~pfeife** *f* organ pipe; **wie die ~pfeifen stehen** to stand in order of height.
Orgie ['ɔrgiə] *f* orgy.
Orient ['oːriɛnt] (**-s**) *m* Orient, east; **der Vordere ~** the Near East.
Orientale [oːriɛn'taːlə] (**-n, -n**) *m* Oriental.
Orientalin [oːriɛn'taːlɪn] *f* Oriental.
orientalisch *adj* oriental.
orientieren [oːriɛn'tiːrən] *vt* (*örtlich*) to locate; (*fig*) to inform ♦ *vr* to find one's way *od* bearings; (*fig*) to inform o.s.
Orientierung [oːriɛn'tiːrʊŋ] *f* orientation; (*fig*) information; **die ~ verlieren** to lose one's bearings.
Orientierungssinn *m* sense of direction.

ORIENTIERUNGSSTUFE

The **Orientierungsstufe** *is the name given to the first two years spent in a* **Realschule** *or* **Gymnasium***, during which a child is assessed as to his or her suitability for the school. At the end of the two years it may be decided to transfer the child to a school more suited to his or her ability.*

---

original [origi'naːl] *adj* original; **~ Meißener Porzellan** genuine Meissen porcelain; **O~** (**-s, -e**) *nt* original; (*Mensch*) character; **O~ausgabe** *f* first edition; **O~fassung** *f* original version.
Originalität [originali'tɛːt] *f* originality.
Originalübertragung *f* live broadcast.
originell [origi'nɛl] *adj* original.
Orkan [ɔr'kaːn] (**-(e)s, -e**) *m* hurricane; **o~artig** *adj* (*Wind*) gale-force; (*Beifall*) thunderous.
Orkneyinseln ['ɔːknɪ|ɪnzəln] *pl* Orkney Islands *pl*, Orkneys *pl*.
Ornament [ɔrna'mɛnt] *nt* decoration, ornament.
ornamental [ɔrnamɛn'taːl] *adj* decorative, ornamental.
Ornithologe [ɔrnito'loːgə] (**-n, -n**) *m* ornithologist.
Ornithologin [ɔrnito'loːgɪn] *f* ornithologist.
Ort¹ [ɔrt] (**-(e)s, -e**) *m* place; **an ~ und Stelle** on the spot; **am ~** in the place; **am angegebenen ~** in the place quoted, loc. cit.; **~ der Handlung** (*THEAT*) scene of the action; **das ist höheren ~(e)s entschieden worden** (*hum: form*) the decision came from above.
Ort² [ɔrt] (**-(e)s, ⁻er**) *m:* **vor ~** at the (coal) face; (*auch fig*) on the spot.
Örtchen ['œrtçən] (*umg*) *nt* loo (*BRIT*), john (*US*).

orten *vt* to locate.
orthodox [ɔrto'dɔks] *adj* orthodox.
Orthografie▲ [ɔrtogra'fiː] *f* spelling, orthography.
orthografisch▲ [ɔrto'graːfɪʃ] *adj* orthographic.
Orthopäde [ɔrto'pɛːdə] (**-n, -n**) *m* orthopaedic (*BRIT*) *od* orthopedic (*US*) specialist, orthopaedist (*BRIT*), orthopedist (*US*).
Orthopädie [ɔrtope'diː] *f* orthopaedics *sing* (*BRIT*), orthopedics *sing* (*US*).
orthopädisch *adj* orthopaedic (*BRIT*), orthopedic (*US*).
örtlich ['œrtlɪç] *adj* local; **jdn ~ betäuben** to give sb a local anaesthetic (*BRIT*) *od* anesthetic (*US*); **Ö~keit** *f* locality; **sich mit den Ö~keiten vertraut machen** to get to know the place.
Ortsangabe *f* (name of the) town; **ohne ~** (*Buch*) no place of publication indicated.
ortsansässig *adj* local.
Ortschaft *f* village, small town; **geschlossene ~** built-up area.
Orts- *zW:* **o~fremd** *adj* nonlocal; **~fremde(r)** *f(m)* stranger; **~gespräch** *nt* local (phone) call; **~gruppe** *f* local branch *od* group; **~kenntnis** *f:* **(gute) ~kenntnisse haben** to know one's way around (well); **~krankenkasse** *f:* **Allgemeine ~krankenkasse** *compulsory medical insurance scheme;* **o~kundig** *adj* familiar with the place; **o~kundig sein** to know one's way around; **~name** *m* place name; **~netz** *nt* (*TEL*) local telephone exchange area; **~netzkennzahl** *f* (*TEL*) dialling (*BRIT*) *od* area (*US*) code; **~schild** *nt* place name sign; **~sinn** *m* sense of direction; **~tarif** *m* (*TEL*) charge for local calls; **~vorschriften** *pl* by(e)-laws *pl*; **~zeit** *f* local time; **~zuschlag** *m* (local) weighting allowance.
Ortung *f* locating.
öS. *abk* = **österreichischer Schilling.**
Öse ['øːzə] (**-, -n**) *f* loop; (*an Kleidung*) eye.
Oslo ['ɔslo] (**-s**) *nt* Oslo.
Ossi ['ɔsi] (**-s, -s**) (*umg*) *m* East German.

OSSI

Ossi *is a colloquial and rather derogatory word used to describe a German from the former* **DDR**.

öst. *abk* (= *österreichisch*) Aust.
Ost- *zW:* **~afrika** *nt* East Africa; **o~deutsch** *adj* East German; **~deutsche(r)** *f(m)* East German; **~deutschland** *nt* (*POL: früher*) East Germany; (*GEOG*) Eastern Germany.
Osten (**-s**) *m* east; **der Ferne ~** the Far East; **der Nahe ~** the Middle East, the Near East.
ostentativ [ɔstɛnta'tiːf] *adj* pointed, ostentatious.

Oster- *zW:* ~**ei** *nt* Easter egg; ~**fest** *nt* Easter; ~**glocke** *f* daffodil; ~**hase** *m* Easter bunny; ~**insel** *f* Easter Island; ~**marsch** *m* Easter demonstration; ~**montag** *m* Easter Monday.

Ostern (-s, -) *nt* Easter; **frohe** *od* **fröhliche ~**! Happy Easter!; **zu ~** at Easter.

Österreich ['ø:stəraıç] (-s) *nt* Austria.

Österreicher(in) (-s, -) *m(f)* Austrian.

österreichisch *adj* Austrian.

Ostersonntag *m* Easter Day *od* Sunday.

Osteuropa *nt* East(ern) Europe.

osteuropäisch *adj* East European.

östlich ['œstlıç] *adj* eastern, easterly.

Östrogen [œstro'ge:n] (-s, -e) *nt* oestrogen (*BRIT*), estrogen (*US*).

Ost- *zW:* ~**see** *f* Baltic Sea; **o~wärts** *adv* eastwards; ~**wind** *m* east wind.

oszillieren [ɔstsı'li:rən] *vi* to oscillate.

Otter¹ ['ɔtər] (-s, -) *m* otter.

Otter² ['ɔtər] (-, -n) *f* (*Schlange*) adder.

ÖTV (-) *f abk* (= *Gewerkschaft öffentliche Dienste, Transport und Verkehr*) ≈ Transport and General Workers' Union.

Ouvertüre [uvɛr'ty:rə] (-, -n) *f* overture.

oval [o'va:l] *adj* oval.

Ovation [ovatsi'o:n] *f* ovation.

Overall ['ouvərɔ:l] (-s, -s) *m* (*Schutzanzug*) overalls *pl*.

ÖVP (-) *f abk* (= *Österreichische Volkspartei*) Austrian People's Party.

Ovulation [ovulatsi'o:n] *f* ovulation.

Oxid, Oxyd [ɔ'ksy:t] (-(e)s, -e) *nt* oxide.

oxidieren, oxydieren [ɔksy'di:rən] *vt, vi* to oxidize.

Oxidierung, Oxydierung *f* oxidization.

Ozean ['o:tsea:n] (-s, -e) *m* ocean; ~**dampfer** *m* (ocean-going) liner.

Ozeanien [otse'a:niən] (-s) *nt* Oceania.

ozeanisch [otse'a:nıʃ] *adj* oceanic; (*Sprachen*) Oceanic.

Ozeanriese (*umg*) *m* ocean liner.

Ozon [o'tso:n] (-s) *nt* ozone; ~**loch** *nt* hole in the ozone layer; ~**schicht** *f* ozone layer.

P, p

P, p [pe:] *nt* P, p; **~ wie Peter** ≈ P for Peter.

P. *abk* = **Pastor; Pater.**

Paar [pa:r] (-(e)s, -e) *nt* pair; (*Liebes~*) couple.

paar *adj inv:* **ein ~** a few; (*zwei oder drei*) a couple of; **ein ~ Mal** a few times.

paaren *vt, vr* (*Tiere*) to mate, pair.

Paar- *zW:* ~**hufer** *pl* (*ZOOL*) cloven-hoofed

animals *pl*; ~**lauf** *m* pair skating.

Paarung *f* combination; (*von Tieren*) mating.

paarweise *adv* in pairs; in couples.

Pacht [paxt] (-, -en) *f* lease; (*Entgelt*) rent; **p~en** *vt* to lease; **du hast das Sofa doch nicht für dich gepachtet** (*umg*) don't hog the sofa.

Pächter(in) ['pɛçtər(ın)] (-s, -) *m(f)* leaseholder; tenant.

Pachtvertrag *m* lease.

Pack¹ [pak] (-(e)s, -e *od* ⁻e) *m* bundle, pack.

Pack² [pak] (-(e)s) (*pej*) *nt* mob, rabble.

Päckchen ['pɛkçən] *nt* small package; (*Zigaretten*) packet; (*Post~*) small parcel.

Packeis *nt* pack ice.

Packen (-s, -) *m* bundle; (*fig: Menge*) heaps (of); **p~** *vt, vi* (*auch COMPUT*) to pack; (*fassen*) to grasp, seize; (*umg: schaffen*) to manage; (*fig: fesseln*) to grip; **p~ wirs!** (*umg: gehen*) let's go.

Packer(in) (-s, -) *m(f)* packer.

Packesel *m* pack mule; (*fig*) packhorse.

Packpapier *nt* brown paper, wrapping paper.

Packung *f* packet; (*Pralinen~*) box; (*MED*) compress.

Packzettel *m* (*COMM*) packing slip.

Pädagoge [pɛda'go:gə] (-n, -n) *m* educationalist.

Pädagogik *f* education.

Pädagogin [pɛda'go:gın] *f* educationalist.

pädagogisch *adj* educational, pedagogical; ~**e Hochschule** college of education.

Paddel ['padəl] (-s, -) *nt* paddle; ~**boot** *nt* canoe.

paddeln *vi* to paddle.

pädophil [pɛdo'fi:l] *adj* paedophile (*BRIT*), pedophile (*US*).

Pädophilie [pɛdofı'li:] *f* paedophilia (*BRIT*), pedophilia (*US*).

paffen ['pafən] *vt, vi* to puff.

Page ['pa:ʒə] (-n, -n) *m* page(boy).

Pagenkopf *m* pageboy cut.

paginieren [pagi'ni:rən] *vt* to paginate.

Paginierung *f* pagination.

Paillette [paı'jɛtə] *f* sequin.

Paket [pa'ke:t] (-(e)s, -e) *nt* packet; (*Post~*) parcel; ~**annahme** *f* parcels office; ~**ausgabe** *f* parcels office; ~**karte** *f* dispatch note; ~**post** *f* parcel post; ~**schalter** *m* parcels counter.

Pakistan ['pa:kısta:n] (-s) *nt* Pakistan.

Pakistaner(in) [pakıs'ta:nər(ın)] (-s, -) *m(f)* Pakistani.

Pakistani [pakıs'ta:ni] (-(s), -(s)) *m* Pakistani.

pakistanisch *adj* Pakistani.

Pakt [pakt] (-(e)s, -e) *m* pact.

Paläontologie [palɛontolo'gi:] *f* palaeontology (*BRIT*), paleontology (*US*).

Palast [pa'last] (-es, **Paläste**) *m* palace.

Palästina [palɛ'sti:na] (-s) *nt* Palestine.

Palästinenser(in) [palɛsti'nɛnzər(ın)] (-s, -)

m(f) Palestinian.
palästinensisch *adj* Palestinian.
Palaver [pa'la:vər] (**-s, -**) *nt* (*auch fig: umg*) palaver.
Palette [pa'lɛtə] *f* palette; (*fig*) range; (*Lade~*) pallet.
Palme ['palmə] (**-, -n**) *f* palm (tree); **jdn auf die ~ bringen** (*umg*) to make sb see red.
Palmsonntag *m* Palm Sunday.
Pampelmuse ['pampəlmu:zə] (**-, -n**) *f* grapefruit.
pampig ['pampɪç] (*umg*) *adj* (*frech*) fresh.
Panama ['panama] (**-s**) *nt* Panama; **~kanal** *m* Panama Canal.
Panflöte ['pa:nflø:tə] *f* panpipes *pl*, Pan's pipes *pl*.
panieren [pa'ni:rən] *vt* (*KOCH*) to coat with egg and breadcrumbs.
Paniermehl [pa'ni:rme:l] *nt* breadcrumbs *pl*.
Panik ['pa:nɪk] *f* panic; **nur keine ~!** I don't panic!; **in ~ ausbrechen** to panic.
Panikkäufe *pl* panic buying *sing*; **~mache** (*umg*) *f* panicmongering.
panisch ['pa:nɪʃ] *adj* panic-stricken.
Panne ['panə] (**-, -n**) *f* (*AUT etc*) breakdown; (*Missgeschick*) slip; **uns ist eine ~ passiert** we've boobed (*BRIT*) (*umg*) *od* goofed (*US*) (*umg*).
Pannendienst *m* breakdown service.
Pannenhilfe *f* breakdown service.
Panorama [pano'ra:ma] (**-s, -men**) *nt* panorama.
panschen ['panʃən] *vi* to splash about ♦ *vt* to water down.
Panter▲, Panther ['pantər] (**-s, -**) *m* panther.
Pantoffel [pan'tɔfəl] (**-s, -n**) *m* slipper; **~held** (*umg*) *m* henpecked husband.
Pantomime [panto'mi:mə] (**-, -n**) *f* mime.
Panzer ['pantsər] (**-s, -**) *m* armour (*BRIT*), armor (*US*); (*fig*) shield; (*Platte*) armo(u)r plate; (*Fahrzeug*) tank; **~faust** *f* bazooka; **~glas** *nt* bulletproof glass; **~grenadier** *m* armoured (*BRIT*) *od* armored (*US*) infantryman.
panzern *vt* to armour (*BRIT*) *od* armor (*US*) plate ♦ *vr* (*fig*) to arm o.s.
Panzerschrank *m* strongbox.
Panzerwagen *m* armoured (*BRIT*) *od* armored (*US*) car.
Papa [pa'pa:] (**-s, -s**) (*umg*) *m* dad(dy), pa.
Papagei [papa'gaɪ] (**-s, -en**) *m* parrot.
Papier [pa'pi:r] (**-s, -e**) *nt* paper; (*Wert~*) share; **Papiere** *pl* (identity) papers *pl*; (*Urkunden*) documents *pl*; **seine ~e bekommen** (*entlassen werden*) to get one's cards; **~fabrik** *f* paper mill; **~geld** *nt* paper money; **~korb** *m* wastepaper basket; **~kram** (*umg*) *m* bumf (*BRIT*) (*umg*); **~krieg** *m* red tape; **~tüte** *f* paper bag; **~vorschub** *m* (*Drucker*) paper advance.

Pappbecher *m* paper cup.
Pappdeckel (**-, -n**) *m* cardboard.
Pappe ['papə] *f* cardboard; **das ist nicht von ~** (*umg*) that is really something.
Pappeinband *m* pasteboard.
Pappel (**-, -n**) *f* poplar.
pappen (*umg*) *vt, vi* to stick.
Pappenheimer *pl*: **ich kenne meine ~** (*umg*) I know you lot/that lot (inside out).
Pappenstiel (*umg*) *m*: **keinen ~ wert sein** not to be worth a thing; **für einen ~ bekommen** to get for a song.
papperlapapp [papərla'pap] *interj* rubbish!
pappig *adj* sticky.
Pappmaché, Pappmaschee▲ [papma'ʃe:] (**-s, -s**) *nt* papier-mâché.
Pappteller *m* paper plate.
Paprika ['paprika] (**-s, -s**) *m* (*Gewürz*) paprika; (*~schote*) pepper; **~schote** *f* pepper; **gefüllte ~schoten** stuffed peppers.
Papst [pa:pst] (**-(e)s, ⁻e**) *m* pope.
päpstlich ['pɛ:pstlɪç] *adj* papal; **~er als der Papst sein** to be more Catholic than the Pope.
Parabel [pa'ra:bəl] (**-, -n**) *f* parable; (*MATH*) parabola.
Parabolantenne [para'bo:l|antɛnə] *f* (*TV*) satellite dish.
Parade [pa'ra:də] (**-, -n**) *f* (*MIL*) parade, review; (*SPORT*) parry; **~beispiel** *nt* prime example; **~marsch** *m* march past; **~schritt** *m* goose step.
Paradies [para'di:s] (**-es, -e**) *nt* paradise; **p~isch** *adj* heavenly.
Paradox [para'dɔks] (**-es, -e**) *nt* paradox; **p~** *adj* paradoxical.
Paraffin [para'fi:n] (**-s, -e**) *nt* (*CHEM*: *~öl*) paraffin (*BRIT*), kerosene (*US*); (*~wachs*) paraffin wax.
Paragraf▲ [para'gra:f] (**-en, -en**) *m* paragraph; (*JUR*) section.
Paragrafenreiter▲ (*umg*) *m* pedant.
Paraguay [paragu'a:i] (**-s**) *nt* Paraguay.
Paraguayer(in) [para'gua:jər(ɪn)] (**-s, -**) *m(f)* Paraguayan.
paraguayisch *adj* Paraguayan.
parallel [para'le:l] *adj* parallel; **~ schalten** (*ELEK*) to connect in parallel.
Parallele (**-, -n**) *f* parallel.
Parameter [pa'ra:metər] *m* parameter.
paramilitärisch [paramili'tɛ:rɪʃ] *adj* paramilitary.
Paranuss▲ ['pa:ranʊs] *f* Brazil nut.
paraphieren [para'fi:rən] *vt* (*Vertrag*) to initial.
Parasit [para'zi:t] (**-en, -en**) *m* (*lit, fig*) parasite.
parat [pa'ra:t] *adj* ready.
Pärchen ['pɛ:rçən] *nt* couple.
Parcours [par'ku:r] (**-, -**) *m* showjumping course; (*Sportart*) showjumping.
Pardon [par'dõ:] (**-s**) (*umg*) *m od nt*: **~!**

(*Verzeihung*) sorry!; **kein ~ kennen** to be ruthless.

Parfüm [par'fy:m] **(-s, -s** *od* **-e)** *nt* perfume.

Parfümerie [parfymə'ri:] *f* perfumery.

Parfümflasche *f* scent bottle.

parfümieren [parfy'mi:rən] *vt* to scent, perfume.

parieren [pa'ri:rən] *vt* to parry ♦ *vi* (*umg*) to obey.

Paris [pa'ri:s] **(-)** *nt* Paris.

Pariser [pa'ri:zər] **(-s, -)** *m* Parisian; (*umg: Kondom*) rubber ♦ *adj attrib* Parisian, Paris *attrib*.

Pariserin *f* Parisian.

Parität [pari'tɛ:t] *f* parity; **p~isch** *adj*: **p~ische Mitbestimmung** equal representation.

Pariwert ['pa:rive:rt] *m* par value, parity.

Park [park] **(-s, -s)** *m* park.

Parka ['parka] **(-(s), -s)** *m* parka.

Parkanlage *f* park; (*um Gebäude*) grounds *pl*.

Parkbucht *f* parking bay.

parken *vt*, *vi* to park; „P~ **verboten!"** "No Parking".

Parkett [par'kɛt] **(-(e)s, -e)** *nt* parquet (floor); (*THEAT*) stalls *pl* (*BRIT*), orchestra (*US*).

Park- *zW*: **~haus** *nt* multistorey car park; **~lücke** *f* parking space; **~platz** *m* car park, parking lot (*US*); parking place; **~scheibe** *f* parking disc; **~uhr** *f* parking meter; **~verbot** *nt* parking ban.

Parlament [parla'mɛnt] *nt* parliament.

Parlamentarier [parlamɛn'ta:riər] **(-s, -)** *m* parliamentarian.

parlamentarisch *adj* parliamentary.

Parlaments- *zW*: **~ausschuss▲** *m* parliamentary committee; **~beschluss▲** *m* vote of parliament; **~ferien** *pl* recess *sing*; **~mitglied** *nt* Member of Parliament (*BRIT*), Congressman (*US*); **~sitzung** *f* sitting (of parliament).

Parodie [paro'di:] *f* parody.

parodieren *vt* to parody.

Parodontose [parodɔn'to:zə] **(-, -n)** *f* shrinking gums *pl*.

Parole [pa'ro:lə] **(-, -n)** *f* password; (*Wahlspruch*) motto.

Partei [par'tai] *f* party; (*im Mietshaus*) tenant, party (*form*); **für jdn ~ ergreifen** to take sb's side; **~buch** *nt* party membership book; **~führung** *f* party leadership; **~genosse** *m* party member; **p~isch** *adj* partial, bias(s)ed; **p~lich** *adj* party attrib; **~linie** *f* party line; **p~los** *adj* neutral; **~nahme (-, -n)** *f* partisanship; **p~politisch** *adj* party political; **~programm** *nt* (party) manifesto; **~tag** *m* party conference; **~vorsitzende(r)** *f(m)* party leader.

Parterre [par'tɛr] **(-s, -s)** *nt* ground floor; (*THEAT*) stalls *pl* (*BRIT*), orchestra (*US*).

Partie [par'ti:] *f* part; (*Spiel*) game; (*Ausflug*) outing; (*Mann, Frau*) catch; (*COMM*) lot; **mit von der ~ sein** to join in.

partiell [partsi'ɛl] *adj* partial.

Partikel [par'ti:kəl] **(-, -n)** *f* particle.

Partisan(in) [parti'za:n(ɪn)] **(-s** *od* **-en, -en)** *m(f)* partisan.

Partitur [parti'tu:r] *f* (*MUS*) score.

Partizip [parti'tsi:p] **(-s, -ien)** *nt* participle; **~ Präsens/Perfekt** (*GRAM*) present/past participle.

Partner(in) ['partnər(ɪn)] **(-s, -)** *m(f)* partner; **~schaft** *f* partnership; (*Städtepartnerschaft*) twinning; **p~schaftlich** *adj* as partners; **~stadt** *f* twin town (*BRIT*).

partout [par'tu:] *adv*: **er will ~ ins Kino gehen** he insists on going to the cinema.

Party ['pa:rti] **(-, -s)** *f* party.

Parzelle [par'tsɛlə] *f* plot, lot.

Pascha ['paʃa] **(-s, -s)** *m*: **wie ein ~** like Lord Muck (*BRIT*) (*umg*).

Pass▲ [pas] **(-es, -̈e)** *m* pass; (*Ausweis*) passport.

passabel [pa'sa:bəl] *adj* passable, reasonable.

Passage [pa'sa:ʒə] **(-, -n)** *f* passage; (*Ladenstraße*) arcade.

Passagier [pasa'ʒi:r] **(-s, -e)** *m* passenger; **~dampfer** *m* passenger steamer; **~flugzeug** *nt* airliner.

Passah(fest) ['pasa(fɛst)] *nt* (Feast of the) Passover.

Passamt▲ *nt* passport office.

Passant(in) [pa'sant(ɪn)] *m(f)* passer-by.

Passbild▲ *nt* passport photo(graph).

passé, passee▲ [pa'se:] *adj*: **diese Mode ist längst ~** this fashion went out long ago.

passen ['pasən] *vi* to fit; (*auf Frage, KARTEN*) to pass; **~ zu** (*Farbe etc*) to go with; **Sonntag passt uns nicht** Sunday is no good for us; **die Schuhe ~ (mir) gut** the shoes are a good fit (for me); **zu jdm ~** (*Mensch*) to suit sb; **das passt mir nicht** that doesn't suit me; **er passt nicht zu dir** he's not right for you; **das könnte dir so ~!** (*umg*) you'd like that, wouldn't you?

passend *adj* suitable; (*zusammen~*) matching; (*angebracht*) fitting; (*Zeit*) convenient; **haben Sie es ~?** (*Geld*) have you got the right money?

Passfoto▲ *nt* passport photo(graph).

passierbar [pa'si:rba:r] *adj* passable; (*Fluss, Kanal*) negotiable.

passieren *vt* to pass; (*durch Sieb*) to strain ♦ *vi* (*Hilfsverb sein*) to happen; **es ist ein Unfall passiert** there has been an accident.

Passierschein *m* pass, permit.

Passion [pasi'o:n] *f* passion.

passioniert [pasio'ni:rt] *adj* enthusiastic, passionate.

Passionsfrucht *f* passion fruit.

Passionsspiel *nt* Passion Play.

Passionszeit f Passiontide.

passiv ['pasi:f] adj passive; ~**es Rauchen** passive smoking; **P~** (**-s, -e**) nt passive.

Passiva [pa'si:va] pl (COMM) liabilities pl.

Passivität [pasivi'te:t] f passiveness.

Passivposten m (COMM) debit entry.

Pass-▲ zW: ~**kontrolle** f passport control; ~**stelle** f passport office; ~**straße** f (mountain) pass; ~**zwang** m requirement to carry a passport.

Paste ['pastə] (-, -n) f paste.

Pastell [pas'tɛl] (-(e)s, -e) nt pastel; ~**farbe** f pastel colour (BRIT) od color (US); **p~farben** adj pastel-colo(u)red.

Pastete [pas'te:tə] (-, -n) f pie; (Pastetchen) vol-au-vent; (: ungefüllt) vol-au-vent case.

pasteurisieren [pastøri'zi:rən] vt to pasteurize.

Pastor ['pastɔr] m vicar; pastor, minister.

Pate ['pa:tə] (-n, -n) m godfather; **bei etw ~ gestanden haben** (fig) to be the force behind sth.

Patenkind nt godchild.

Patenstadt f twin town (BRIT).

patent [pa'tɛnt] adj clever.

Patent (-(e)s, -e) nt patent; (MIL) commission; **etw als** od **zum ~ anmelden** to apply for a patent on sth.

Patentamt nt patent office.

patentieren [patɛn'ti:rən] vt to patent.

Patent- zW: ~**inhaber** m patentee; ~**lösung** f (fig) patent remedy; ~**schutz** m patent right; ~**urkunde** f letters patent pl.

Pater ['pa:tər] (-s, - od **Patres**) m Father.

Paternoster [patər'nɔstər] (-s, -) m (Aufzug) paternoster.

pathetisch [pa'te:tɪʃ] adj emotional.

Pathologe [pato'lo:gə] (-n, -n) m pathologist.

Pathologin [pato'lo:gɪn] f pathologist.

pathologisch adj pathological.

Pathos ['pa:tɔs] (-) nt pathos.

Patience [pasi'ã:s] (-, -n) f: ~**n legen** to play patience.

Patient(in) [patsi'ɛnt(ɪn)] m(f) patient.

Patin ['pa:tɪn] f godmother.

Patriarch [patri'arç] (-en, -en) m patriarch.

patriarchalisch [patriar'ça:lɪʃ] adj patriarchal.

Patriot(in) [patri'o:t(ɪn)] (-en, -en) m(f) patriot; **p~isch** adj patriotic.

Patriotismus [patrio'tɪsmʊs] m patriotism.

Patron [pa'tro:n] (-s, -e) m patron; (ECCL) patron saint.

Patrone (-, -n) f cartridge.

Patronenhülse f cartridge case.

Patronin f patroness; (ECCL) patron saint.

Patrouille [pa'trʊljə] (-, -n) f patrol.

patrouillieren [patrʊl'ji:rən] vi to patrol.

patsch [patʃ] interj splash!

Patsche (-, -n) (umg) f (Händchen) paw; (Fliegen~) swat; (Feuer~) beater;
(Bedrängnis) mess, jam.

patschen vi to smack, slap; (im Wasser) to splash.

patschnass▲ adj soaking wet.

Patt [pat] (-s, -s) nt (lit, fig) stalemate.

patzen ['patsən] (umg) vi to boob (BRIT), goof (US).

patzig ['patsɪç] (umg) adj cheeky, saucy.

Pauke ['paʊkə] (-, -n) f kettledrum; **auf die ~ hauen** to live it up; **mit ~n und Trompeten durchfallen** (umg) to fail dismally.

pauken vt, vi (SCH) to swot (BRIT), cram.

Pauker (-s, -) (umg) m teacher.

pausbäckig ['paʊsbɛkɪç] adj chubby-cheeked.

pauschal [paʊ'ʃa:l] adj (Kosten) inclusive; (einheitlich) flat-rate attrib; (Urteil) sweeping; **die Werkstatt berechnet ~ pro Inspektion 250 DM** the garage has a flat rate of 250 marks per service.

Pauschale (-, -n) f flat rate; (vorläufig geschätzter Betrag) estimated amount.

Pauschal- zW: ~**gebühr** f flat rate; ~**preis** m all-in price; ~**reise** f package tour; ~**summe** f lump sum; ~**versicherung** f comprehensive insurance.

Pause ['paʊzə] (-, -n) f break; (THEAT) interval; (das Innehalten) pause; (MUS) rest; (Kopie) tracing.

pausen vt to trace.

Pausen- zW: ~**brot** nt sandwich (to eat at break); ~**hof** m playground, schoolyard (US); **p~los** adj nonstop; ~**zeichen** nt (RUNDF) call sign; (MUS) rest.

pausieren [paʊ'si:rən] vi to make a break.

Pauspapier ['paʊspapi:r] nt tracing paper.

Pavian ['pa:via:n] (-s, -e) m baboon.

Pay-per-Click ['pe:pərklɪk] (-s) nt pay-per-click.

Pazifik [pa'tsi:fɪk] (-s) m Pacific.

pazifisch adj Pacific; **der P~e Ozean** the Pacific (Ocean).

Pazifist(in) [patsi'fɪst(ɪn)] m(f) pacifist; **p~isch** adj pacifist.

PC m abk (= Personalcomputer) PC.

PDA m abk (COMPUT: = personal digital assistant) PDA.

PDS f abk (= Partei des Demokratischen Sozialismus) German Socialist Party.

PDS

The **PDS** (Partei des Demokratischen Sozialismus) was founded in 1989 as the successor of the SED, the former East German Communist Party. Its aims are the establishment of a democratic socialist society and to hold a position in the German political scene left of the **SPD**.

Pech [pɛç] (-s, -e) nt pitch; (fig) bad luck; **~ haben** to be unlucky; **die beiden halten**

zusammen wie ~ und Schwefel (*umg*) the two are inseparable; ~ gehabt! tough! (*umg*); p~schwarz *adj* pitch-black; ~strähne (*umg*) *f* unlucky patch; ~vogel (*umg*) *m* unlucky person.

Pedal [pe'da:l] (-s, -e) *nt* pedal; in die ~e treten to pedal (hard).

Pedant [pe'dant] *m* pedant.

Pedanterie [pedantə'ri:] *f* pedantry.

pedantisch *adj* pedantic.

Peddigrohr ['pɛdıçro:r] *nt* cane.

Pediküre [pedi'ky:rə] (-, -n) *f* (*Fußpflege*) pedicure; (*Fußpflegerin*) chiropodist.

Pegel ['pe:gəl] (-s, -) *m* water gauge; (*Geräusch~*) noise level; ~stand *m* water level.

peilen ['paılən] *vt* to get a fix on; die Lage ~ (*umg*) to see how the land lies.

Pein [paın] (-) *f* agony, suffering.

peinigen *vt* to torture; (*plagen*) to torment.

peinlich *adj* (*unangenehm*) embarrassing, awkward, painful; (*genau*) painstaking; in seinem Zimmer herrschte ~e Ordnung his room was meticulously tidy; er vermied es ~st, davon zu sprechen he was at pains not to talk about it; P~keit *f* painfulness, awkwardness; (*Genauigkeit*) scrupulousness.

Peitsche ['paıtʃə] (-, -n) *f* whip.

peitschen *vt* to whip; (*Regen*) to lash.

Peitschenhieb *m* lash.

Pekinese [peki'ne:zə] (-n, -n) *m* Pekinese, peke (*umg*).

Peking ['pe:kıŋ] (-s) *nt* Peking.

Pelikan ['pe:lika:n] (-s, -e) *m* pelican.

Pelle ['pɛlə] (-, -n) *f* skin; der Chef sitzt mir auf der ~ (*umg*) I've got the boss on my back.

pellen *vt* to skin, peel.

Pellkartoffeln *pl* jacket potatoes *pl*.

Pelz [pɛlts] (-es, -e) *m* fur.

Pendel ['pɛndəl] (-s, -) *nt* pendulum.

pendeln *vi* (*schwingen*) to swing (to and fro); (*Zug, Fähre etc*) to shuttle; (*Mensch*) to commute; (*fig*) to fluctuate.

Pendelverkehr *m* shuttle service; (*Berufsverkehr*) commuter traffic.

Pendler(in) ['pɛndlər(ın)] (-s, -) *m(f)* commuter.

penetrant [pene'trant] *adj* sharp; (*Person*) pushing; das schmeckt/riecht ~ nach Knoblauch it has a very strong taste/smell of garlic.

penibel [pe'ni:bəl] *adj* pernickety (*BRIT*) (*umg*), persnickety (*US*) (*umg*), precise.

Penis ['pe:nıs] (-, -se) *m* penis.

Pennbruder ['pɛnbru:dər] (*umg*) *m* tramp (*BRIT*), hobo (*US*).

Penne (-, -n) (*umg*) *f* (*SCH*) school.

pennen (*umg*) *vi* to kip.

Penner (-s, -) (*pej: umg*) *m* tramp (*BRIT*), hobo (*US*).

Pension [pɛnzi'o:n] *f* (*Geld*) pension;

(*Ruhestand*) retirement; (*für Gäste*) boarding house, guesthouse; halbe/volle ~ half/full board; in ~ gehen to retire.

Pensionär(in) [pɛnzio'nɛ:r(ın)] (-s, -e) *m(f)* pensioner.

Pensionat (-(e)s, -e) *nt* boarding school.

pensionieren [pɛnzio'ni:rən] *vt* to pension (off); sich ~ lassen to retire.

pensioniert *adj* retired.

Pensionierung *f* retirement.

Pensions- *zW*: p~berechtigt *adj* entitled to a pension; ~gast *m* boarder, paying guest; p~reif (*umg*) *adj* ready for retirement.

Pensum ['pɛnzom] (-s, Pensen) *nt* quota; (*SCH*) curriculum.

Peperoni [pepe'ro:ni] *pl* chillies *pl*.

per [pɛr] *präp +akk* by, per; (*pro*) per; (*bis*) by; ~ Adresse (*COMM*) care of, c/o; mit jdm ~ du sein (*umg*) to be on first-name terms with sb.

Perfekt ['pɛrfɛkt] (-(e)s, -e) *nt* perfect.

perfekt [pɛr'fɛkt] *adj* perfect; (*abgemacht*) settled; die Sache ~ machen to clinch the deal; der Vertrag ist ~ the contract is all settled.

perfektionieren [pɛrfɛktsio'ni:rən] *vt* to perfect.

Perfektionismus [pɛrfɛktsio'nısmos] *m* perfectionism.

perforieren [pɛrfo'ri:rən] *vt* to perforate.

Pergament [pɛrga'mɛnt] *nt* parchment; ~papier *nt* greaseproof paper (*BRIT*), wax(ed) paper (*US*).

Pergola ['pɛrgola] (-, Pergolen) *f* pergola, arbour (*BRIT*), arbor (*US*).

Periode [peri'o:də] (-, -n) *f* period; 0,33 ~ 0.33 recurring.

periodisch [peri'o:dıʃ] *adj* periodic; (*dezimal*) recurring.

Peripherie [perife'ri:] *f* periphery; (*um Stadt*) outskirts *pl*; (*MATH*) circumference; ~gerät *nt* (*COMPUT*) peripheral.

Perle ['pɛrlə] (-, -n) *f* (*lit, fig*) pearl; (*Glas~, Holz~, Tropfen*) bead; (*veraltet: umg: Hausgehilfin*) maid.

perlen *vi* to sparkle; (*Tropfen*) to trickle.

Perlenkette *f* pearl necklace.

Perlhuhn *nt* guinea fowl.

Perlmutt ['pɛrlmot] (-s) *nt* mother-of-pearl.

Perlon ® ['pɛrlɔn] (-s) *nt* ≈ nylon.

Perlwein *m* sparkling wine.

perplex [pɛr'plɛks] *adj* dumbfounded.

Perser ['pɛrzər] (-s, -) *m* (*Person*) Persian; (*umg: Teppich*) Persian carpet.

Perserin *f* Persian.

Persianer [pɛrzi'a:nər] (-s, -) *m* Persian lamb (coat).

Persien ['pɛrziən] (-s) *nt* Persia.

Persiflage [pɛrzi'fla:ʒə] (-, -n) *f*: ~ (+*gen od auf* +*akk*) pastiche (of), satire (on).

persisch *adj* Persian; **P~er Golf** Persian Gulf.

Person [pɛr'zoːn] (-, -en) *f* person; (*pej: Frau*) female; **sie ist Köchin und Haushälterin in einer ~** she is cook and housekeeper rolled into one; **ich für meine ~** personally I.

Personal [pɛrzo'naːl] (-s) *nt* personnel; (*Bedienung*) servants *pl*; **~abbau** *m* staff cuts *pl*; **~akte** *f* personal file; **~angaben** *pl* particulars *pl*; **~ausweis** *m* identity card; **~bogen** *m* personal record; **~büro** *nt* personnel (department); **~chef** *m* personnel manager; **~computer** *m* personal computer.

Personalien [pɛrzo'naːliən] *pl* particulars *pl*.

Personalität [pɛrzonali'tɛːt] *f* personality.

Personal- *zW:* **~kosten** *pl* staff costs; **~mangel** *m* staff shortage; **~pronomen** *nt* personal pronoun; **~reduzierung** *f* staff reduction.

personell [pɛrzo'nɛl] *adj* staff *attrib*; **~e Veränderungen** changes in personnel.

Personen- *zW:* **~aufzug** *m* lift, elevator (*US*); **~beschreibung** *f* (personal) description; **~gedächtnis** *nt* memory for faces; **~gesellschaft** *f* partnership; **~kraftwagen** *m* private motorcar, automobile (*US*); **~kreis** *m* group of people; **~kult** *m* personality cult; **~nahverkehr** *m:* **öffentlicher ~nahverkehr** local public transport; **~schaden** *m* injury to persons; **~verkehr** *m* passenger services *pl*; **~waage** *f* scales *pl*; **~zug** *m* stopping train; passenger train.

personifizieren [pɛrzonifi'tsiːrən] *vt* to personify.

persönlich [pɛr'zøːnlɪç] *adj* personal ♦ *adv* in person; personally; (*auf Briefen*) private (and confidential); **~ haften** (*COMM*) to be personally liable; **P~keit** *f* personality; **P~keiten des öffentlichen Lebens** public figures.

Perspektive [pɛrspɛk'tiːvə] *f* perspective; **das eröffnet ganz neue ~n für uns** that opens new horizons for us.

Pers. Ref. *abk* (= *Persönlicher Referent*) personal representative.

Peru [pe'ruː] (-s) *nt* Peru.

Peruaner(in) [peru'aːnər(ɪn)] (-s, -) *m(f)* Peruvian.

peruanisch *adj* Peruvian.

Perücke [pe'rʏkə] (-, -n) *f* wig.

pervers [pɛr'vɛrs] *adj* perverse.

Perversität [pɛrvɛrzi'tɛːt] *f* perversity.

Pessar [pɛ'saːr] (-s, -e) *nt* pessary; (*zur Empfängnisverhütung*) cap, diaphragm.

Pessimismus [pɛsi'mɪsmʊs] *m* pessimism.

Pessimist(in) [pɛsi'mɪst(ɪn)] *m(f)* pessimist; **p~isch** *adj* pessimistic.

Pest [pɛst] (-) *f* plague; **jdn/etw wie die ~ hassen** (*umg*) to loathe (and detest) sb/sth.

Petersilie [petər'ziːliə] *f* parsley.

Petrochemie [petro:çe'miː] *f* petrochemistry.

Petrodollar [petro'dɔlar] *m* petrodollar.

Petroleum [pe'troːleʊm] (-s) *nt* paraffin (*BRIT*), kerosene (*US*).

petzen ['pɛtsən] (*umg*) *vi* to tell tales; **er petzt immer** he always tells.

Pf. *abk* = **Pfennig**.

Pfad [pfaːt] (-(e)s, -e) *m* path; **~finder** *m* Boy Scout; **er ist bei den ~findern** he's in the (Boy) Scouts; **~finderin** *f* Girl Guide.

Pfaffe ['pfafə] (-n, -n) (*pej*) *m* cleric, parson.

Pfahl [pfaːl] (-(e)s, ⁻e) *m* post, stake; **~bau** *m* pile dwelling.

Pfalz [pfalts] (-, -en) *f* (*GEOG*) Palatinate.

Pfälzer(in) ['pfɛltsər(ɪn)] (-s, -) *m(f)* person from the Palatinate.

pfälzisch *adj* Palatine, of the (Rhineland) Palatinate.

Pfand [pfant] (-(e)s, ⁻er) *nt* pledge, security; (*Flaschen~*) deposit; (*im Spiel*) forfeit; (*fig: der Liebe etc*) pledge; **~brief** *m* bond.

pfänden ['pfɛndən] *vt* to seize, impound.

Pfänderspiel *nt* game of forfeits.

Pfand- *zW:* **~haus** *nt* pawnshop; **~leiher** (-s, -) *m* pawnbroker; **~recht** *nt* lien; **~schein** *m* pawn ticket.

Pfändung ['pfɛndʊŋ] *f* seizure, distraint (*form*).

Pfanne ['pfanə] (-, -n) *f* (frying) pan; **jdn in die ~ hauen** (*umg*) to tear a strip off sb.

Pfannkuchen *m* pancake; (*Berliner*) doughnut (*BRIT*), donut (*US*).

Pfarrei [pfar'raɪ] *f* parish.

Pfarrer (-s, -) *m* priest; (*evangelisch*) vicar; (*von Freikirchen*) minister.

Pfarrhaus *nt* vicarage.

Pfau [pfaʊ] (-(e)s, -en) *m* peacock.

Pfauenauge *nt* peacock butterfly.

Pfd. *abk* (= *Pfund*) ≈ lb.

Pfeffer ['pfɛfər] (-s, -) *m* pepper; **er soll bleiben, wo der ~ wächst!** (*umg*) he can take a running jump!; **~korn** *nt* peppercorn; **~kuchen** *m* gingerbread; **~minz** (-es, -e) *nt* peppermint; **~minze** *f* peppermint (plant); **~mühle** *f* pepper mill.

pfeffern *vt* to pepper; (*umg: werfen*) to fling; **gepfefferte Preise/Witze** steep prices/spicy jokes.

Pfeife ['pfaɪfə] (-, -n) *f* whistle; (*Tabak~, Orgel~*) pipe; **nach jds ~ tanzen** to dance to sb's tune.

pfeifen *unreg vt, vi* to whistle; **auf dem letzten Loch ~** (*umg: erschöpft sein*) to be on one's last legs; (: *finanziell*) to be on one's beam ends; **ich pfeif(e) drauf!** (*umg*) I don't give a damn!; **P~stopfer** *m* tamper.

Pfeifer (-s, -) *m* piper.

Pfeifkonzert *nt* catcalls *pl*.

Pfeil [pfaɪl] (-(e)s, -e) *m* arrow.

Pfeiler ['pfaɪlər] (-s, -) *m* pillar, prop;

Pfennig – Phantom

(*Brücken~*) pier.

Pfennig ['pfɛnɪç] (-(e)s, -e) *m* pfennig (*hundredth part of a mark*); ~**absatz** *m* stiletto heel; ~**fuchser** (-s, -) (*umg*) *m* skinflint.

pferchen ['pfɛrçən] *vt* to cram, pack.

Pferd [pfeːrt] (-(e)s, -e) *nt* horse; **wie ein ~ arbeiten** (*umg*) to work like a Trojan; **mit ihm kann man ~e stehlen** (*umg*) he's a great sport; **auf das falsche/richtige ~ setzen** (*lit, fig*) to back the wrong/right horse.

Pferde- *zW:* ~**äpfel** *pl* horse droppings *pl od* dung *sing*; ~**fuß** *m*: **die Sache hat aber einen ~fuß** there's just one snag; ~**rennen** *nt* horse-race; (*Sportart*) horse-racing; ~**schwanz** *m* (*Frisur*) ponytail; ~**stall** *m* stable; ~**stärke** *f* horsepower.

Pfiff (-(e)s, -e) *m* whistle; (*Kniff*) trick.

pfiff *etc* [pfɪf] *vb siehe* **pfeifen.**

Pfifferling ['pfɪfərlɪŋ] *m* yellow chanterelle; **keinen ~ wert** not worth a thing.

pfiffig *adj* smart.

Pfingsten ['pfɪŋstən] (-, -) *nt* Whitsun.

Pfingstrose *f* peony.

Pfingstsonntag *m* Whit Sunday, Pentecost (*REL*).

Pfirsich ['pfɪrzɪç] (-s, -e) *m* peach.

Pflanze ['pflantsə] (-, -n) *f* plant.

pflanzen *vt* to plant ♦ *vr* (*umg*) to plonk o.s.

Pflanzenfett *nt* vegetable fat.

Pflanzenschutzmittel *nt* pesticide.

pflanzlich *adj* vegetable.

Pflanzung *f* plantation.

Pflaster ['pflastər] (-s, -) *nt* plaster; (*Straßen~*) pavement (*BRIT*), sidewalk (*US*); **ein teures ~** (*umg*) a pricey place; **ein heißes ~** a dangerous *od* unsafe place; **p~müde** *adj* dead on one's feet.

pflastern *vt* to pave.

Pflasterstein *m* paving stone.

Pflaume ['pflaʊmə] (-, -n) *f* plum; (*umg: Mensch*) twit (*BRIT*).

Pflaumenmus *nt* plum jam.

Pflege ['pfleːgə] (-, -n) *f* care; (*von Idee*) cultivation; (*Kranken~*) nursing; **jdn/etw in ~ nehmen** to look after sb/sth; **in ~ sein** (*Kind*) to be fostered out; **p~bedürftig** *adj* needing care; ~**eltern** *pl* foster parents *pl*; ~**fall** *m* case for nursing; ~**geld** *nt* (*für ~kinder*) boarding-out allowance; (*für Kranke*) attendance allowance; ~**heim** *nt* nursing home; ~**kind** *nt* foster child; **p~leicht** *adj* easy-care; ~**mutter** *f* foster mother.

pflegen *vt* to look after; (*Kranke*) to nurse; (*Beziehungen*) to foster ♦ *vi* (*gewöhnlich tun*): **sie pflegte zu sagen** she used to say.

Pfleger (-s, -) *m* (*im Krankenhaus*) orderly; (*vollqualifiziert*) male nurse; ~**in** *f* nurse.

Pflegesatz *m* hospital and nursing charges *pl*.

Pflegevater *m* foster father.

Pflegeversicherung *f* geriatric care insurance.

Pflicht [pflɪçt] (-, -en) *f* duty; (*SPORT*) compulsory section; **Rechte und ~en** rights and responsibilities; **p~bewusst**▲ *adj* conscientious; ~**bewusstsein**▲ *nt* sense of duty; ~**fach** *nt* (*SCH*) compulsory subject; ~**gefühl** *nt* sense of duty; **p~gemäß** *adj* dutiful; **p~vergessen** *adj* irresponsible; ~**versicherung** *f* compulsory insurance.

Pflock [pflɔk] (-(e)s, -̈e) *m* peg; (*für Tiere*) stake.

pflog *etc* [pfloːk] *vb* (*veraltet*) *siehe* **pflegen.**

pflücken ['pflʏkən] *vt* to pick.

Pflug [pfluːk] (-(e)s, -̈e) *m* plough (*BRIT*), plow (*US*).

pflügen ['pflyːgən] *vt* to plough (*BRIT*), plow (*US*).

Pflugschar *f* ploughshare (*BRIT*), plowshare (*US*).

Pforte ['pfɔrtə] (-, -n) *f* (*Tor*) gate.

Pförtner ['pfœrtnər] (-s, -) *m* porter, doorkeeper, doorman.

Pförtnerin *f* doorkeeper, porter.

Pfosten ['pfɔstən] (-s, -) *m* post; (*senkrechter Balken*) upright.

Pfote ['pfoːtə] (-, -n) *f* paw; (*umg: Schrift*) scrawl.

Pfropf [pfrɔpf] (-(e)s, -e) *m* (*Flaschen~*) stopper; (*Blut~*) clot.

Pfropfen (-s, -) *m* = **Pfropf.**

pfropfen *vt* (*stopfen*) to cram; (*Baum*) to graft; **gepfropft voll** crammed full.

pfui [pfʊɪ] *interj* ugh!; (*na na*) tut tut tut!; (*Buhruf*) boo!; ~ **Teufel!** (*umg*) ugh!, yuck!

Pfund [pfʊnt] (-(e)s, -e) *nt* (*Gewicht, FIN*) pound; **das ~ sinkt** sterling *od* the pound is falling.

pfundig (*umg*) *adj* great.

Pfundskerl ['pfʊntskɛrl] (*umg*) *m* great guy.

pfundweise *adv* by the pound.

pfuschen ['pfʊʃən] *vi* to bungle; (*einen Fehler machen*) to slip up.

Pfuscher(in) ['pfʊʃər(ɪn)] (-s, -) (*umg*) *m(f)* sloppy worker; (*Kur~*) quack.

Pfuscherei [pfʊʃə'raɪ] (*umg*) *f* sloppy work; (*Kur~*) quackery.

Pfütze ['pfʏtsə] (-, -n) *f* puddle.

PH (-, -s) *f abk* = **pädagogische Hochschule.**

Phänomen [fɛno'meːn] (-s, -e) *nt* phenomenon; **p~al** [-'naːl] *adj* phenomenal.

Phantasie *etc* [fanta'ziː] = **Fantasie** *etc.*

phantasieren [fanta'ziːrən] *vi* = **fantasieren.**

phantasievoll *adj* = **fantasievoll.**

Phantast [fan'tast] (-en, -en) *m* = **Fantast.**

phantastisch *adj* = **fantastisch.**

Phantom [fan'toːm] (-s, -e) *nt* (*Trugbild*) phantom; **einem ~ nachjagen** (*fig*) to tilt at windmills; ~**bild** *nt* Identikit ® picture.

Pharisäer [fari'zɛ:ər] (-s, -) m (lit, fig) pharisee.
Pharmazeut(in) [farma'tsɔyt(ın)] (-en, -en) m(f) pharmacist.
pharmazeutisch adj pharmaceutical.
Pharmazie f pharmacy, pharmaceutics sing.
Phase ['fa:zə] (-, -n) f phase.
Philanthrop [filan'tro:p] (-en, -en) m philanthropist; **p~isch** adj philanthropic.
Philharmoniker [fɪlhar'mo:nikər] (-s, -) m: **die ~** the philharmonic (orchestra) sing.
Philatelist(in) [filate'lıst(ın)] (-en, -en) m(f) philatelist.
Philippine [fɪlɪ'pi:nə] (-n, -n) m Filipino.
Philippinen pl Philippines pl, Philippine Islands pl.
Philippinin f Filipino.
philippinisch adj Filipino.
Philologe [filo'lo:gə] (-n, -n) m philologist.
Philologie [filolo'gi:] f philology.
Philologin f philologist.
Philosoph(in) [filo'zo:f(ın)] (-en, -en) m(f) philosopher.
Philosophie [filozo'fi:] f philosophy.
philosophieren [filozo'fi:rən] vi: **~ (über** +akk) to philosophize (about).
philosophisch adj philosophical.
Phlegma ['flɛgma] (-s) nt lethargy.
phlegmatisch [flɛ'gma:tıʃ] adj lethargic.
Phobie [fo'bi:] f: **~ (vor** +dat) phobia (about).
Phonetik [fo'ne:tık] f phonetics sing.
phonetisch adj phonetic.
Phonotypistin [fonoty'pıstın] f audiotypist.
Phosphat [fɔs'fa:t] (-(e)s, -e) nt phosphate.
Phosphor ['fɔsfɔr] (-s) m phosphorus.
phosphoreszieren [fɔsforɛs'tsi:rən] vt to phosphoresce.
Photo etc ['fo:to] = **Foto** etc.
Phrase ['fra:zə] (-, -n) f phrase; (pej) hollow phrase; **~n dreschen** (umg) to churn out one cliché after another.
pH-Wert [pe:'ha:ve:rt] m pH value.
Physik [fy'zi:k] f physics sing.
physikalisch [fyzi'ka:lıʃ] adj of physics.
Physiker(in) ['fy:zikər(ın)] (-s, -) m(f) physicist.
Physikum ['fy:zikʊm] (-s) nt (UNIV) preliminary examination in medicine.
Physiologe [fyzio'lo:gə] (-n, -n) m physiologist.
Physiologie [fyziolo'gi:] f physiology.
Physiologin f physiologist.
physisch ['fy:zıʃ] adj physical.
Pianist(in) [pia'nıst(ın)] m(f) pianist.
picheln ['pıçəln] (umg) vi to booze.
Pickel ['pıkəl] (-s, -) m pimple; (Werkzeug) pickaxe; (Berg~) ice axe.
pick(e)lig adj pimply.
picken ['pıkən] vt to peck ♦ vi: **~ (nach)** to peck (at).
Picknick ['pıknık] (-s, -e od -s) nt picnic;

~ machen to have a picnic.
piekfein ['pi:k'faın] (umg) adj posh.
Piemont [pie'mɔnt] (-s) nt Piedmont.
piepen ['pi:pən] vi to chirp; (Funkgerät etc) to bleep; **bei dir piepts wohl!** (umg) are you off your head?; **es war zum P~!** (umg) it was a scream!
piepsen ['pi:psən] vi = **piepen**.
Piepser (umg) m pager, paging device.
Piepsstimme f squeaky voice.
Piepton m bleep.
Pier [pi:ər] (-s, -s od -e) m jetty, pier.
piesacken ['pi:zakən] (umg) vt to torment.
Pietät [pie'tɛ:t] f piety; reverence; **p~los** adj impious, irreverent.
Pigment [pıg'mɛnt] (-(e)s, -e) nt pigment.
Pik [pi:k] (-s, -s) nt (KARTEN) spades; **einen ~ auf jdn haben** (umg) to have it in for sb.
pikant [pi'kant] adj spicy, piquant; (anzüglich) suggestive.
Pike (-, -n) f: **etw von der ~ auf lernen** (fig) to learn sth from the bottom up.
pikiert [pi'ki:rt] adj offended.
Pikkolo ['pıkolo] (-s, -s) m trainee waiter; (auch: **~flasche**) quarter bottle of champagne; (MUS: auch: **~flöte**) piccolo.
Piktogramm [pıkto'gram] nt pictogram.
Pilger(in) ['pılgər(ın)] (-s, -) m(f) pilgrim; **~fahrt** f pilgrimage.
pilgern vi to make a pilgrimage; (umg: gehen) to wend one's way.
Pille ['pılə] (-, -n) f pill.
Pilot(in) [pi'lo:t(ın)] (-en, -en) m(f) pilot; **~enschein** m pilot's licence (BRIT) od license (US).
Pils [pıls] (-, -) nt Pilsner (lager).
Pils(e)ner [pılz(ə)nər] (-s, -) nt Pilsner (lager).
Pilz [pılts] (-es, -e) m fungus; (essbar) mushroom; (giftig) toadstool; **wie ~e aus dem Boden schießen** (fig) to mushroom; **~krankheit** f fungal disease.
Pimmel ['pıməl] (-s, -) (umg) m (Penis) willie.
pingelig ['pıŋəlıç] (umg) adj fussy.
Pinguin ['pıŋgui:n] (-s, -e) m penguin.
Pinie ['pi:niə] f pine.
Pinkel (-s, -) (umg) m: **ein feiner** od **vornehmer ~** a swell, Lord Muck (BRIT) (umg).
pinkeln ['pıŋkəln] (umg) vi to pee.
Pinnwand ['pınvant] f pinboard.
Pinsel ['pınzəl] (-s, -) m paintbrush.
pinseln (umg) vt, vi to paint; (pej: malen) to daub.
Pinte ['pıntə] (-, -n) (umg) f (Lokal) boozer (BRIT).
Pinzette [pın'tsɛtə] f tweezers pl.
Pionier [pio'ni:r] (-s, -e) m pioneer; (MIL) sapper, engineer; **~arbeit** f pioneering work; **~unternehmen** nt pioneer company.
Pipi [pi'pi:] (-s, -s) nt od m (Kindersprache) wee(-wee).

Pirat [pi'ra:t] (**-en, -en**) *m* pirate.

Piratensender *m* pirate radio station.

Pirsch [pɪrʃ] (**-**) *f* stalking.

pissen ['pɪsən] (*umg!*) *vi* to (have a) piss (!); (*regnen*) to piss down (!).

Pistazie [pɪs'ta:tsiə] (**-, -n**) *f* pistachio.

Piste ['pɪstə] (**-, -n**) *f* (*SKI*) run, piste; (*AVIAT*) runway.

Pistole [pɪs'to:lə] (**-, -n**) *f* pistol; **wie aus der ~ geschossen** (*fig*) like a shot; **jdm die ~ auf die Brust setzen** (*fig*) to hold a pistol to sb's head.

pitsch(e)nass▲ ['pɪtʃ(ə)'nas] (*umg*) *adj* soaking (wet).

Pizza ['pɪtsa] (**-, -s**) *f* pizza.

PKW, Pkw (**-(s), -(s)**) *m abk* = **Personenkraftwagen**.

Pl. *abk* (= *Plural*) pl.; (= *Platz*) Sq.

Plackerei [plakə'raɪ] *f* drudgery.

plädieren [plɛ'di:rən] *vi* to plead.

Plädoyer [plɛdoa'je:] (**-s, -s**) *nt* speech for the defence; (*fig*) plea.

Plage ['pla:gə] (**-, -n**) *f* plague; (*Mühe*) nuisance; **~geist** *m* pest, nuisance.

plagen *vt* to torment ♦ *vr* to toil, slave.

Plagiat [plagi'a:t] (**-(e)s, -e**) *nt* plagiarism.

Plakat [pla'ka:t] (**-(e)s, -e**) *nt* poster; (*aus Pappe*) placard.

plakativ [plaka'ti:f] *adj* striking, bold.

Plakatwand *f* hoarding, billboard (*US*).

Plakette [pla'kɛtə] (**-, -n**) *f* (*Abzeichen*) badge; (*Münze*) commemorative coin; (*an Wänden*) plaque.

Plan [pla:n] (**-(e)s, ⁻e**) *m* plan; (*Karte*) map; **Pläne schmieden** to make plans; **nach ~ verlaufen** to go according to plan; **jdn auf den ~ rufen** (*fig*) to bring sb into the arena.

Plane (**-, -n**) *f* tarpaulin.

planen *vt* to plan; (*Mord etc*) to plot.

Planer(in) (**-s, -**) *m(f)* planner.

Planet [pla'ne:t] (**-en, -en**) *m* planet.

Planetenbahn *f* orbit (of a planet).

planieren [pla'ni:rən] *vt* to level off.

Planierraupe *f* bulldozer.

Planke ['plaŋkə] (**-, -n**) *f* plank.

Plänkelei [plɛŋkə'laɪ] *f* skirmish(ing).

plänkeln ['plɛŋkəln] *vi* to skirmish.

Plankton ['plaŋktɔn] (**-s**) *nt* plankton.

planlos *adj* (*Vorgehen*) unsystematic; (*Umherlaufen*) aimless.

planmäßig *adj* according to plan; (*methodisch*) systematic; (*EISENB*) scheduled.

Planschbecken, Plantschbecken▲ ['planʃbɛkən] *nt* paddling pool.

planschen, plantschen▲ *vi* to splash.

Plansoll *nt* output target.

Planstelle *f* post.

Plantage [plan'ta:ʒə] (**-, -n**) *f* plantation.

Planung *f* planning.

Planwagen *m* covered wagon.

Planwirtschaft *f* planned economy.

Plappermaul (*umg*) *nt* (*Kind*) chatterbox.

plappern ['plapərn] *vi* to chatter.

plärren ['plɛrən] *vi* (*Mensch*) to cry, whine; (*Radio*) to blare.

Plasma ['plasma] (**-s, Plasmen**) *nt* plasma.

Plastik¹ ['plastɪk] *f* sculpture.

Plastik² ['plastɪk] (**-s**) *nt* (*Kunststoff*) plastic; **~folie** *f* plastic film; **~geschoss▲** *nt* plastic bullet; **~tüte** *f* plastic bag.

Plastilin [plasti'li:n] (**-s**) *nt* Plasticine ®.

plastisch ['plastɪʃ] *adj* plastic; **stell dir das ~ vor!** just picture it!

Platane [pla'ta:nə] (**-, -n**) *f* plane (tree).

Platin ['pla:ti:n] (**-s**) *nt* platinum.

Platitüde△ [plati'ty:də] (**-, -n**) *f siehe* **Plattitüde**.

platonisch [pla'to:nɪʃ] *adj* platonic.

platsch [platʃ] *interj* splash!

platschen *vi* to splash.

plätschern ['plɛtʃərn] *vi* to babble.

platschnass▲ *adj* drenched.

platt [plat] *adj* flat; (*umg: überrascht*) flabbergasted; (*fig: geistlos*) flat, boring; **einen P~en haben** to have a flat (*umg*), have a flat tyre (*BRIT*) *od* tire (*US*).

plattdeutsch *adj* Low German.

Platte (**-, -n**) *f* (*Speisen~, PHOT, TECH*) plate; (*Stein~*) flag; (*Kachel*) tile; (*Schall~*) record; **kalte ~** cold dish; **die ~ kenne ich schon** (*umg*) I've heard all that before.

Plätteisen *nt* iron.

plätten *vt, vi* to iron.

Platten- *zW*: **~leger** (**-s, -**) *m* paver; **~spieler** *m* record player; **~teller** *m* turntable.

Plattform *f* platform; (*fig: Grundlage*) basis.

Plattfuß *m* flat foot; (*Reifen*) flat tyre (*BRIT*) *od* tire (*US*).

Plattitüde▲ [plati'ty:də] (**-, -n**) *f* platitude.

Platz [plats] (**-es, ⁻e**) *m* place; (*Sitz~*) seat; (*Raum*) space, room; (*in Stadt*) square; (*Sport~*) playing field; **~ machen** to get out of the way; **~ nehmen** to take a seat; **jdm ~ machen** to make room for sb; **~ sparend** space-saving; **auf ~ zwei** in second place; **fehl am ~e sein** to be out of place; **seinen ~ behaupten** to stand one's ground; **das erste Hotel am ~** the best hotel in town; **auf die Plätze, fertig, los!** (*beim Sport*) on your marks, get set, go!; **einen Spieler vom ~ stellen** *od* **verweisen** (*SPORT*) to send a player off; **~angst** *f* (*MED*) agoraphobia; (*umg*) claustrophobia; **~angst haben/bekommen** (*umg*) to feel/get claustrophobic; **~anweiser(in)** (**-s, -**) *m(f)* usher(ette).

Plätzchen ['plɛtsçən] *nt* spot; (*Gebäck*) biscuit.

platzen *vi* (*Hilfsverb sein*) to burst; (*Bombe*) to explode; (*Naht, Hose, Haut*) to split; (*umg: scheitern: Geschäft*) to fall through;

(: *Freundschaft*) to break up; (: *Theorie, Verschwörung*) to collapse; (: *Wechsel*) to bounce; **vor Wut** ~ (*umg*) to be bursting with anger.

platzieren▲ [pla'tsi:rən] *vt* to place ♦ *vr* (*SPORT*) to be placed; (*TENNIS*) to be seeded; (*umg: sich setzen, stellen*) to plant o.s.

Platz- *zW:* ~**karte** *f* seat reservation; ~**konzert** *nt* open-air concert; ~**mangel** *m* lack of space; ~**patrone** *f* blank cartridge; ~**regen** *m* downpour; ~**verweis** *m* sending-off; ~**wart** *m* (*SPORT*) groundsman (*BRIT*), groundskeeper (*US*); ~**wunde** *f* cut.

Plauderei [plaudə'raɪ] *f* chat, conversation.
plaudern ['plaudərn] *vi* to chat, talk.
Plausch [plauʃ] (-(e)s, -e) (*umg*) *m* chat.
plausibel [plau'zi:bəl] *adj* plausible.
Play-back▲, **Playback** ['pleɪbæk] (-s, -s) *nt* (*Verfahren: Schallplatte*) double-tracking; (*TV*) miming.
plazieren△ [pla'tsi:rən] *vt siehe* **platzieren**.
Plebejer(in) [ple'be:jər(ɪn)] (-s, -) *m(f)* plebeian.
plebejisch [ple'be:jɪʃ] *adj* plebeian.
pleite ['plaɪtə] (*umg*) *adj* broke; **P~** (-, -n) *f* bankruptcy; (*umg: Reinfall*) flop; **P~ machen** to go bust.
Pleitegeier (*umg*) *m* (*drohende Pleite*) vulture; (*Bankrotteur*) bankrupt.
plemplem [plɛm'plɛm] (*umg*) *adj* nuts.
Plenarsitzung [ple'na:rzɪtsuŋ] *f* plenary session.
Plenum ['ple:num] (-s, **Plenen**) *nt* plenum.
Pleuelstange ['plɔyəlʃtaŋə] *f* connecting rod.
Plissee [plɪ'se:] (-s, -s) *nt* pleat.
Plombe ['plɔmbə] (-, -n) *f* lead seal; (*Zahn~*) filling.
plombieren [plɔm'bi:rən] *vt* to seal; (*Zahn*) to fill.
Plotter ['plɔtər] (-s, -s) *m* (*COMPUT*) plotter.
plötzlich ['plœtslɪç] *adj* sudden ♦ *adv* suddenly; ~**er Kindstod** SIDS= sudden infant death syndrome.
Pluderhose ['plu:dərho:zə] *f* harem trousers *pl*.
plump [plump] *adj* clumsy; (*Hände*) coarse; (*Körper*) shapeless; ~**e Annäherungsversuche** very obvious advances.
plumpsen (*umg*) *vi* to plump down, fall.
Plumpsklo(sett) (*umg*) *nt* earth closet.
Plunder ['plundər] (-s) *m* junk, rubbish.
Plundergebäck *nt* flaky pastry.
plündern ['plʏndərn] *vt* to plunder; (*Stadt*) to sack ♦ *vi* to plunder.
Plünderung ['plʏndəruŋ] *f* plundering, sack, pillage.
Plural ['plu:ra:l] (-s, -e) *m* plural; **im** ~ **stehen** to be (in the) plural.
pluralistisch [plura'lɪstɪʃ] *adj* pluralistic.
plus [plus] *adv* plus; **mit** ~ **minus null**

abschließen (*COMM*) to break even; **P~** (-, -) *nt* plus; (*FIN*) profit; (*Vorteil*) advantage.
Plüsch [ply:ʃ] (-(e)s, -e) *m* plush; ~**tier** *nt* ≈ soft toy.
Plus- *zW:* ~**pol** *m* (*ELEK*) positive pole; ~**punkt** *m* (*SPORT*) point; (*fig*) point in sb's favour; ~**quamperfekt** *nt* pluperfect.
Plutonium [plu'to:niʊm] (-s) *nt* plutonium.
PLZ *abk* = **Postleitzahl**.
Pneu [pnɔy] (-s, -s) *m* *abk* (= *Pneumatik*) tyre (*BRIT*), tire (*US*).
Po [po:] (-s, -s) (*umg*) *m* bum (*BRIT*), fanny (*US*).
Pöbel ['pø:bəl] (-s) *m* mob, rabble.
Pöbelei [pø:bə'laɪ] *f* vulgarity.
pöbelhaft *adj* low, vulgar.
pochen ['pɔxən] *vi* to knock; (*Herz*) to pound; **auf etw** *akk* ~ (*fig*) to insist on sth.
Pocken ['pɔkən] *pl* smallpox *sing*.
Pocken(schutz)impfung *f* smallpox vaccination.
Podest [po'dɛst] (-(e)s, -e) *nt od m* (*Sockel, fig*) pedestal; (*Podium*) platform.
Podium ['po:diʊm] *nt* podium.
Podiumsdiskussion *f* panel discussion.
Poesie [poe'zi:] *f* poetry.
Poet [po'e:t] (-en, -en) *m* poet; **p~isch** *adj* poetic.
pofen ['po:fən] (*umg*) *vi* to kip (*BRIT*), doss.
Pointe [po'ɛ̃:tə] (-, -n) *f* point; (*eines Witzes*) punch line.
pointiert [poɛ̃'ti:rt] *adj* trenchant, pithy.
Pokal [po'ka:l] (-s, -e) *m* goblet; (*SPORT*) cup; ~**spiel** *nt* cup tie.
Pökelfleisch ['pø:kəlflaɪʃ] *nt* salt meat.
pökeln *vt* (*Fleisch, Fisch*) to pickle, salt.
Poker ['po:kər] (-s) *nt* poker.
pokern ['po:kərn] *vi* to play poker.
Pol [po:l] (-s, -e) *m* pole; **der ruhende** ~ (*fig*) the calming influence.
pol. *abk* = **politisch; polizeilich.**
polar [po'la:r] *adj* polar.
polarisieren [polari'zi:rən] *vt*, *vr* to polarize.
Polarkreis *m* polar circle; **nördlicher/ südlicher** ~ Arctic/Antarctic Circle.
Polarstern *m* Pole Star.
Pole [po:lə] (-n, -n) *m* Pole.
Polemik [po'le:mɪk] *f* polemics *sing*.
polemisch *adj* polemical.
polemisieren [polemi'zi:rən] *vi* to polemicize.
Polen ['po:lən] (-s) *nt* Poland.
Polente (-) (*veraltet: umg*) *f* cops *pl*.
Police [po'li:s(ə)] (-, -n) *f* insurance policy.
Polier [po'li:r] (-s, -e) *m* foreman.
polieren *vt* to polish.
Poliklinik [poli'kli:nɪk] *f* outpatients (department) *sing*.
Polin *f* Pole, Polish woman.
Politesse [poli'tɛsə] (-, -n) *f* (*Frau*) ≈ traffic warden (*BRIT*).

Politik [poli'tiːk] *f* politics *sing*; (*eine bestimmte*) policy; **in die ~ gehen** to go into politics; **eine ~ verfolgen** to pursue a policy.

Politiker(in) [po'liːtikər(ın)] (**-s, -**) *m(f)* politician.

politisch [po'liːtıʃ] *adj* political.

politisieren [politi'ziːrən] *vi* to talk politics ♦ *vt* to politicize; **jdn ~** to make sb politically aware.

Politur [poli'tuːr] *f* polish.

Polizei [poli'tsaı] *f* police; **~aufsicht** *f*: **unter ~aufsicht stehen** to have to report regularly to the police; **~beamte(r)** *m* police officer; **p~lich** *adj* police *attrib*; **sich p~lich melden** to register with the police; **p~liches Führungszeugnis** *certificate of "no criminal record" issued by the police*; **~präsidium** *nt* police headquarters *pl*; **~revier** *nt* police station; **~spitzel** *m* police spy, informer; **~staat** *m* police state; **~streife** *f* police patrol; **~stunde** *f* closing time; **~wache** *f* police station; **p~widrig** *adj* illegal.

Polizist(in) [poli'tsıst(ın)] (**-en, -en**) *m(f)* policeman/-woman.

Pollen ['polən] (**-s, -**) *m* pollen.

poln. *abk* = **polnisch**.

polnisch ['polnıʃ] *adj* Polish.

Polohemd ['poːlohɛmt] *nt* polo shirt.

Polster ['polstər] (**-s, -**) *nt* cushion; (*~ung*) upholstery; (*in Kleidung*) padding; (*fig: Geld*) reserves *pl*; **~er** (**-s, -**) *m* upholsterer; **~garnitur** *f* three-piece suite; **~möbel** *pl* upholstered furniture *sing*.

polstern *vt* to upholster; (*Kleidung*) to pad; **sie ist gut gepolstert** (*umg*) she's well padded; (: *finanziell*) she's not short of the odd penny.

Polsterung *f* upholstery.

Polterabend ['poltəraːbənt] *m* party on the eve of a wedding.

poltern *vi* (*Krach machen*) to crash; (*schimpfen*) to rant.

Polygamie [polyga'miː] *f* polygamy.

Polynesien [poly'neːziən] (**-s**) *nt* Polynesia.

Polynesier(in) [poly'neːziər(ın)] (**-s, -**) *m(f)* Polynesian.

polynesisch *adj* Polynesian.

Polyp [po'lyːp] (**-en, -en**) *m* polyp; (*umg*) cop; **Polypen** *pl* (*MED*) adenoids *pl*.

Polytechnikum [poly'tɛçnikum] (**-s, Polytechnika**) *nt* polytechnic, poly (*umg*).

Pomade [po'maːdə] *f* pomade.

Pommern ['pomərn] (**-s**) *nt* Pomerania.

Pommes frites [pom'frıt] *pl* chips *pl* (*BRIT*), French fried potatoes *pl* (*BRIT*), French fries *pl* (*US*).

Pomp [pomp] (**-(e)s**) *m* pomp.

pompös [pom'pøːs] *adj* grandiose.

Pontius ['pontsius] *m*: **von ~ zu Pilatus** from pillar to post.

Pony ['poni] (**-s, -s**) *m* (*Frisur*) fringe (*BRIT*), bangs *pl* (*US*) ♦ *nt* (*Pferd*) pony.

Pop [pop] (**-s**) *m* (*MUS*) pop; (*KUNST*) pop art.

Popelin [popə'liːn] (**-s, -e**) *m* poplin.

Popeline (**-, -n**) *f* poplin.

Popkonzert *nt* pop concert.

Popmusik *f* pop music.

Popo [po'poː] (**-s, -s**) (*umg*) *m* bottom, bum (*BRIT*).

populär [popu'lɛːr] *adj* popular.

Popularität [populari'tɛːt] *f* popularity.

populärwissenschaftlich *adj* popular science.

Pore ['poːrə] (**-, -n**) *f* pore.

Porno ['porno] (**-s**) *no pl* (*umg*) *m* porn.

Pornografie▲ [pornogra'fiː] *f* pornography.

pornografisch▲ [porno'graːfıʃ] *adj* pornographic.

porös [po'røːs] *adj* porous.

Porree ['porə] (**-s, -s**) *m* leek.

Portal [por'taːl] (**-s, -e**) *nt* portal.

Portefeuille [port(ə)'føːj] (**-s, -s**) *nt* (*POL, FIN*) portfolio.

Portemonnaie [portmo'neː] (**-s, -s**) *nt* purse.

Portier [porti'eː] (**-s, -s**) *m* porter; (*Pförtner*) porter, doorkeeper, doorman.

Portion [portsi'oːn] *f* portion, helping; (*umg: Anteil*) amount; **eine halbe ~** (*fig: umg: Person*) a half-pint; **eine ~ Kaffee** a pot of coffee.

Portmonee▲ [portmo'neː] (**-s, -s**) *nt* = **Portemonnaie**.

Porto ['porto] (**-s, -s** *od* **Porti**) *nt* postage; **~ zahlt Empfänger** postage paid; **p~frei** *adj* post-free, (postage) prepaid.

Porträt [por'trɛː] (**-s, -s**) *nt* portrait.

porträtieren [portrɛ'tiːrən] *vt* to paint (a portrait of); (*fig*) to portray.

Portugal ['portugal] (**-s**) *nt* Portugal.

Portugiese [portu'giːzə] (**-n, -n**) *m* Portuguese.

Portugiesin *f* Portuguese.

portugiesisch *adj* Portuguese.

Portwein ['portvaın] *m* port.

Porzellan [portsɛ'laːn] (**-s, -e**) *nt* china, porcelain; (*Geschirr*) china.

Posaune [po'zaunə] (**-, -n**) *f* trombone.

Pose ['poːzə] (**-, -n**) *f* pose.

posieren [po'ziːrən] *vi* to pose.

Position [pozitsi'oːn] *f* position; (*COMM: auf Liste*) item.

Positionslichter *pl* navigation lights *pl*.

positiv ['poːzitiːf] *adj* positive; **~ zu etw stehen** to be in favour (*BRIT*) *od* favor (*US*) of sth; **P~** (**-s, -e**) *nt* (*PHOT*) positive.

Positur [pozi'tuːr] *f* posture, attitude; **sich in ~ setzen** *od* **stellen** to adopt a posture.

Posse ['posə] (**-, -n**) *f* farce.

possessiv ['posɛsiːf] *adj* possessive; **P~** (**-s, -e**) *nt* possessive pronoun; **P~pronomen** (**-s, -e**) *nt* possessive pronoun.

possierlich [po'siːrlıç] *adj* funny.

Post [pɔst] (-, -en) f post (office); (*Briefe*) post, mail; **ist ~ für mich da?** are there any letters for me?; **mit getrennter ~** under separate cover; **etw auf die ~ geben** to post (*BRIT*) od mail sth; **auf die** od **zur ~ gehen** to go to the post office; **~amt** nt post office; **~anweisung** f postal order (*BRIT*), money order; **~bote** m postman (*BRIT*), mailman (*US*).

Posten (-s, -) m post, position; (*COMM*) item; (: *Warenmenge*) quantity, lot; (*auf Liste*) entry; (*MIL*) sentry; (*Streik~*) picket; **~ beziehen** to take up one's post; **nicht ganz auf dem ~ sein** (*nicht gesund sein*) to be off-colour (*BRIT*) od off-color (*US*).

Poster ['pɔstər] (-s, -(s)) nt poster.

Postf. abk (= *Postfach*) PO Box.

Post- zW: **~fach** nt post office box; **~karte** f postcard; **p~lagernd** adv poste restante; **~leitzahl** f postal code.

postmodern [pɔstmo'dɛrn] adj postmodern.

Post- zW: **~scheckkonto** nt Post Office Giro account (*BRIT*); **~sparbuch** nt post office savings book (*Brit*); **~sparkasse** f post office savings bank; **~stempel** m postmark; **p~wendend** adv by return (of post); **~wertzeichen** nt (*form*) postage stamp; **~wurfsendung** f direct mail advertising.

potent [po'tɛnt] adj potent; (*fig*) high-powered.

Potential [potɛntsi'a:l] (-s, -e) nt = **Potenzial**.

potentiell [potɛntsi'ɛl] adj = **potenziell**.

Potenz [po'tɛnts] f power; (*eines Mannes*) potency.

Potenzial▲ [potɛntsi'a:l] (-s, -e) nt potential.

potenziell▲ [potɛntsi'ɛl] adj potential.

potenzieren [potɛn'tsi:rən] vt (*MATH*) to raise to the power of.

Potpourri ['pɔtpʊri] (-s, -s) nt: **~ (aus)** (*MUS*) medley (of); (*fig*) assortment (of).

Pott [pɔt] (-(e)s, ⸚e) (*umg*) m pot; **p~hässlich**▲ (*umg*) adj ugly as sin.

pp., ppa. abk (= *per procura*) p.p.

Präambel [prɛ'|ambəl] (-, -n) f (+*gen*) preamble (to).

Pracht [praxt] (-) f splendour (*BRIT*), splendor (*US*), magnificence; **es ist eine wahre ~** it's (really) marvellous; **~exemplar** nt beauty (*umg*); (*fig: Mensch*) fine specimen.

prächtig ['prɛçtɪç] adj splendid.

Prachtstück nt showpiece.

prachtvoll adj splendid, magnificent.

prädestinieren [prɛdɛsti'ni:rən] vt to predestine.

Prädikat [prɛdi'ka:t] (-(e)s, -e) nt title; (*GRAM*) predicate; (*Zensur*) distinction; **Wein mit ~** special quality wine.

Prag [pra:k] (-s) nt Prague.

prägen ['prɛ:gən] vt to stamp; (*Münze*) to mint; (*Ausdruck*) to coin; (*Charakter*) to form;

(*kennzeichnen: Stadtbild*) to characterize; **das Erlebnis prägte ihn** the experience left its mark on him.

prägend adj having a forming od shaping influence.

pragmatisch [pra'gma:tɪʃ] adj pragmatic.

prägnant [prɛ'gnant] adj concise, terse.

Prägnanz f conciseness, terseness.

Prägung ['prɛ:gʊŋ] f minting; forming; (*Eigenart*) character, stamp.

prahlen ['pra:lən] vi to boast, brag.

Prahlerei [pra:lə'raɪ] f boasting.

prahlerisch adj boastful.

Praktik ['praktɪk] f practice.

praktikabel [praktɪ'ka:bəl] adj practicable.

Praktikant(in) [praktɪ'kant(ɪn)] m(f) trainee.

Praktikum (-s, **Praktika** od **Praktiken**) nt practical training.

praktisch ['praktɪʃ] adj practical, handy; **~er Arzt** general practitioner; **~es Beispiel** concrete example.

praktizieren [prakti'tsi:rən] vt, vi to practise (*BRIT*), practice (*US*).

Praline [pra'li:nə] f chocolate.

prall [pral] adj firmly rounded; (*Segel*) taut; (*Arme*) plump; (*Sonne*) blazing.

prallen vi to bounce, rebound; (*Sonne*) to blaze.

prallvoll adj full to bursting; (*Brieftasche*) bulging.

Prämie ['prɛ:miə] f premium; (*Belohnung*) award, prize.

prämienbegünstigt adj with benefit of premiums.

prämiensparen vi to save in a bonus scheme.

prämieren [prɛ'mi:rən] vt to give an award to.

Pranger ['praŋər] (-s, -) m (*HIST*) pillory; **jdn an den ~ stellen** (*fig*) to pillory sb.

Pranke ['praŋkə] (-, -n) f (*Tier~: umg: Hand*) paw.

Präparat [prɛpa'ra:t] (-(e)s, -e) nt (*BIOL*) preparation; (*MED*) medicine.

präparieren vt (*konservieren*) to preserve; (*MED: zerlegen*) to dissect.

Präposition [prɛpozitsi'o:n] f preposition.

Prärie [prɛ'ri:] f prairie.

Präs. abk = **Präsens**; **Präsident**.

Präsens ['prɛ:zɛns] (-) nt present tense.

präsent adj: **etw ~ haben** to have sth at hand.

präsentieren [prɛzɛn'ti:rən] vt to present.

Präsenzbibliothek f reference library.

Präservativ [prɛzɛrva'ti:f] (-s, -e) nt condom, sheath.

Präsident(in) [prɛzi'dɛnt(ɪn)] m(f) president; **~schaft** f presidency; **~schaftskandidat** m presidential candidate.

Präsidium [prɛ'zi:diʊm] nt presidency, chairmanship; (*Polizei~*) police headquarters pl.

prasseln ['prasəln] *vi* (*Feuer*) to crackle; (*Hagel*) to drum; (*Wörter*) to rain down.
prassen ['prasən] *vi* to live it up.
Präteritum [prɛ'teːritʊm] (**-s, Präterita**) *nt* preterite.
Pratze ['pratsə] (**-, -n**) *f* paw.
Präventiv- [prɛvɛn'tiːf] *in zW* preventive.
Praxis ['praksɪs] (**-, Praxen**) *f* practice; (*Erfahrung*) experience; (*Behandlungsraum*) surgery; (*von Anwalt*) office; **die ~ sieht anders aus** the reality is different; **ein Beispiel aus der ~** an example from real life.
Präzedenzfall [prɛtse'dɛntsfal] *m* precedent.
präzis [prɛ'tsiːs] *adj* precise.
Präzision [prɛtsizi'oːn] *f* precision.
PR-Chef *m* PR officer.
predigen ['preːdɪgən] *vt, vi* to preach.
Prediger (**-s, -**) *m* preacher.
Predigt ['preːdɪçt] (**-, -en**) *f* sermon.
Preis [prais] (**-es, -e**) *m* price; (*Sieges~*) prize; (*Auszeichnung*) award; **um keinen ~** not at any price; **um jeden ~** at all costs; **~angebot** *nt* quotation; **~ausschreiben** *nt* competition; **~bindung** *f* price-fixing; **~brecher** *m* (*Firma*) undercutter.
Preiselbeere *f* cranberry.
preisempfindlich *adj* price-sensitive.
preisen [praizən] *unreg vt* to praise; **sich glücklich ~** (*geh*) to count o.s. lucky.
Preis- *zW*: **~entwicklung** *f* price trend; **~erhöhung** *f* price increase; **~frage** *f* question of price; (*Wettbewerb*) prize question.
preisgeben *unreg vt* to abandon; (*opfern*) to sacrifice; (*zeigen*) to expose.
Preis- *zW*: **~gefälle** *nt* price gap; **p~gekrönt** *adj* prizewinning; **~gericht** *nt* jury; **p~günstig** *adj* inexpensive; **~index** *m* price index; **~krieg** *m* price war; **~lage** *f* price range; **p~lich** *adj* price *attr*, in price; **~liste** *f* price list, tariff; **~nachlass▲** *m* discount; **~schild** *nt* price tag; **~spanne** *f* price range; **~sturz** *m* slump; **~träger** *m* prizewinner; **p~wert** *adj* inexpensive.
prekär [pre'kɛːr] *adj* precarious.
Prellbock [prɛlbɔk] *m* buffers *pl*.
prellen *vt* to bruise; (*fig*) to cheat, swindle.
Prellung *f* bruise.
Premiere [prəmi'ɛːrə] (**-, -n**) *f* premiere.
Premierminister(in) [prəmi'eːmɪnɪstər(ɪn)] *m(f)* prime minister, premier.
Presse ['prɛsə] (**-, -n**) *f* press; **~agentur** *f* press *od* news agency; **~ausweis** *m* press pass; **~erklärung** *f* press release; **~freiheit** *f* freedom of the press; **~konferenz** *f* press conference; **~meldung** *f* press report.
pressen *vt* to press.
Presse- *zW*: **~sprecher(in)** *m(f)* spokesperson, press officer; **~stelle** *f* press office.

~verlautbarung *f* press release.
pressieren [prɛ'siːrən] *vi* to be in a hurry; **es pressiert** it's urgent.
Pressluft▲ ['prɛslʊft] *f* compressed air; **~bohrer** *m* pneumatic drill.
Prestige [prɛs'tiːʒə] (**-s**) *nt* prestige; **~verlust** *m* loss of prestige.
Preuße ['prɔysə] (**-n, -n**) *m* Prussian.
Preußen (**-s**) *nt* Prussia.
Preußin *f* Prussian.
preußisch *adj* Prussian.
prickeln ['prɪkəln] *vi* to tingle; (*kitzeln*) to tickle; (*Bläschen bilden*) to sparkle, bubble ♦ *vt* to tickle.
pries *etc* [priːs] *vb siehe* **preisen**.
Priester ['priːstər] (**-s, -**) *m* priest.
Priesterin *f* priestess.
Priesterweihe *f* ordination (to the priesthood).
Prima ['priːma] (**-, Primen**) *f* (*früher*) eighth and ninth year of German secondary school.
prima *adj inv* first-class, excellent.
primär [pri'mɛːr] *adj* primary; **P~daten** *pl* primary data *pl*.
Primel ['priːməl] (**-, -n**) *f* primrose.
primitiv [primi'tiːf] *adj* primitive.
Primzahl ['priːmtsaːl] *f* prime (number).
Prinz [prɪnts] (**-en, -en**) *m* prince.
Prinzessin [prɪn'tsɛsɪn] *f* princess.
Prinzip [prɪn'tsiːp] (**-s, -ien**) *nt* principle; **aus ~** on principle; **im ~** in principle.
prinzipiell [prɪntsi'piɛl] *adj* on principle.
prinzipienlos *adj* unprincipled.
Priorität [priori'tɛːt] *f* priority; **Prioritäten** *pl* (*COMM*) preference shares *pl*, preferred stock *sing* (*US*); **~en setzen** to establish one's priorities.
Prise ['priːzə] (**-, -n**) *f* pinch.
Prisma ['prɪsma] (**-s, Prismen**) *nt* prism.
privat [pri'vaːt] *adj* private; **jdn ~ sprechen** to speak to sb in private; **P~besitz** *m* private property; **P~dozent** *m* outside lecturer; **P~fernsehen** *nt* commercial television; **P~gespräch** *nt* private conversation; (*am Telefon*) private call.
privatisieren [privati'ziːrən] *vt* to privatize.
Privatschule *f* private school.
Privatwirtschaft *f* private sector.
Privileg [privi'leːk] (**-(e)s, -ien**) *nt* privilege.
Pro [proː] (**-**) *nt* pro.
pro *präp +akk* per; **~ Stück** each, apiece.
Probe ['proːbə] (**-, -n**) *f* test; (*Teststück*) sample; (*THEAT*) rehearsal; **jdn auf die ~ stellen** to put sb to the test; **er ist auf ~ angestellt** he's employed for a probationary period; **zur ~** to try out; **~bohrung** *f* (*Öl*) exploration well; **~exemplar** *nt* specimen copy; **~fahrt** *f* test drive; **~lauf** *m* trial run.
proben *vt* to try; (*THEAT*) to rehearse.

Probe- zW: **~stück** nt specimen; **p~weise** adv on approval; **~zeit** f probation period.

probieren [pro'biːrən] vt to try; (Wein, Speise) to taste, sample ♦ vi to try; to taste.

Problem [pro'bleːm] (**-s, -e**) nt problem; **vor einem ~ stehen** to be faced with a problem.

Problematik [proble'maːtɪk] f problem.

problematisch [proble'maːtɪʃ] adj problematic.

problemlos adj problem-free.

Problemstellung f way of looking at a problem.

Produkt [pro'dʊkt] (**-(e)s, -e**) nt product; (AGR) produce no pl.

Produktion [prodʊktsi'oːn] f production.

Produktionsleiter m production manager.

Produktionsstätte f (Halle) shop floor.

produktiv [prodʊk'tiːf] adj productive.

Produktivität [prodʊktivi'tɛːt] f productivity.

Produzent [produ'tsɛnt] m manufacturer; (FILM) producer.

produzieren [produ'tsiːrən] vt to produce ♦ vr to show off.

Prof. [prof] abk (= Professor) Prof.

profan [pro'faːn] adj (weltlich) secular, profane; (gewöhnlich) mundane.

professionell [profɛsio'nɛl] adj professional.

Professor(in) [pro'fɛsɔr, profɛ'soːrɪn] m(f) professor; (ÖSTERR: Gymnasiallehrer) grammar school teacher (BRIT), high school teacher (US).

Professur [profɛ'suːr] f: ~ (**für**) chair (of).

Profi ['proːfi] (**-s, -s**) m abk (= Professional) pro.

Profil [pro'fiːl] (**-s, -e**) nt profile; (fig) image; (Querschnitt) cross section; (Längsschnitt) vertical section; (von Reifen, Schuhsohle) tread.

profilieren [profi'liːrən] vr to create an image for o.s.

Profilsohle f sole with a tread.

Profit [pro'fiːt] (**-(e)s, -e**) m profit.

profitieren [profi'tiːrən] vi: ~ (**von**) to profit (from).

Profitmacherei (umg) f profiteering.

pro forma adv as a matter of form.

Pro-forma-Rechnung f pro forma invoice.

Prognose [pro'gnoːzə] (**-, -n**) f prediction, prognosis.

Programm [pro'gram] (**-s, -e**) nt programme (BRIT), program (US); (COMPUT) program; (TV: Sender) channel; (Kollektion) range; **nach ~** as planned; **p~gemäß** adj according to plan; **~fehler** m (COMPUT) bug; **~hinweis** m (RUNDF, TV) programme (BRIT) od program (US) announcement.

programmieren [progra'miːrən] vt to programme (BRIT), program (US); (COMPUT) to program; **auf etw** akk **programmiert sein** (fig) to be geared to sth.

Programmierer(in) (**-s, -**) m(f) programmer.

Programmiersprache f (COMPUT) programming language.

Programmierung f (COMPUT) programming.

Programmvorschau f preview; (FILM) trailer.

progressiv [progrɛ'siːf] adj progressive.

Projekt [pro'jɛkt] (**-(e)s, -e**) nt project.

Projektleiter(in) m(f) project manager(ess).

Projektor [pro'jɛktɔr] m projector.

projizieren [proji'tsiːrən] vt to project.

proklamieren [prokla'miːrən] vt to proclaim.

Pro-Kopf-Einkommen nt per capita income.

Prokura [pro'kuːra] (**-, Prokuren**) f (form) power of attorney.

Prokurist(in) [proku'rɪst(ɪn)] m(f) attorney.

Prolet [pro'leːt] (**-en, -en**) m prole, pleb.

Proletariat [proletari'aːt] (**-(e)s, -e**) nt proletariat.

Proletarier [prole'taːriər] (**-s, -**) m proletarian.

Prolog [pro'loːk] (**-(e)s, -e**) m prologue.

Promenade [promə'naːdə] (**-, -n**) f promenade.

Promenadenmischung f (hum) mongrel.

Promille [pro'mɪle] (**-(s), -**) (umg) nt alcohol level; **~grenze** f legal (alcohol) limit.

prominent [promi'nɛnt] adj prominent.

Prominenz [promi'nɛnts] f VIPs pl.

Promoter [pro'moːtər] (**-s, -**) m promoter.

Promotion [promotsi'oːn] f doctorate, Ph.D.

promovieren [promo'viːrən] vi to receive a doctorate etc.

prompt [prɔmpt] adj prompt.

Pronomen [pro'noːmɛn] (**-s, -**) nt pronoun.

Propaganda [propa'ganda] (**-**) f propaganda.

propagieren [propa'giːrən] vt to propagate.

Propangas [pro'paːngaːs] nt propane gas.

Propeller [pro'pɛlər] (**-s, -**) m propeller.

proper ['prɔpər] (umg) adj neat, tidy.

Prophet(in) [pro'feːt(ɪn)] (**-en, -en**) m(f) prophet(ess).

prophezeien [profe'tsaɪən] vt to prophesy.

Prophezeiung f prophecy.

prophylaktisch [profy'laktɪʃ] adj prophylactic (form), preventive.

Proportion [proportsi'oːn] f proportion.

proportional [proportsio'naːl] adj proportional; **P~schrift** f (COMPUT) proportional printing.

proportioniert [proportsio'niːrt] adj: **gut/ schlecht ~** well/badly proportioned.

Proporz [pro'pɔrts] (**-es, -e**) m proportional representation.

Prosa ['proːza] (**-**) f prose.

prosaisch [pro'zaːɪʃ] adj prosaic.

prosit ['proːzɪt] interj cheers!; ~ **Neujahr!** happy New Year!

Prospekt [pro'spɛkt] (**-(e)s, -e**) m leaflet, brochure.

prost [proːst] interj cheers!

Prostata ['prɔstata] (**-**) f prostate gland.

Prostituierte [prostitu'iːrtə] (**-n, -n**) f

Prostitution – Publikum

prostitute.
Prostitution [prostitutsi'o:n] *f* prostitution.
prot. [prot] *abk* = **protestantisch.**
Protektionismus [protɛktsio'nɪsmʊs] *m* protectionism.
Protektorat [protɛkto'ra:t] (-(e)s, -e) *nt* (*Schirmherrschaft*) patronage; (*Schutzgebiet*) protectorate.
Protest [pro'tɛst] (-(e)s, -e) *m* protest.
Protestant(in) [protɛs'tant(ɪn)] *m(f)* Protestant; **p~isch** *adj* Protestant.
Protestbewegung *f* protest movement.
protestieren [protɛs'ti:rən] *vi* to protest.
Protestkundgebung *f* (protest) rally.
Prothese [pro'te:zə] (-, -n) *f* artificial limb; (*Zahn~*) dentures *pl.*
Protokoll [proto'kɔl] (-s, -e) *nt* register; (*Niederschrift*) record; (*von Sitzung*) minutes *pl*; (*diplomatisch*) protocol; (*Polizei~*) statement; (*Strafzettel*) ticket; (**das**) **~ führen** (*bei Sitzung*) to take the minutes; (*bei Gericht*) to make a transcript of the proceedings; **etw zu ~ geben** to have sth put on record; (*bei Polizei*) to say sth in one's statement; **~führer** *m* secretary; (*JUR*) clerk (of the court).
protokollieren [protokɔ'li:rən] *vt* to take down; (*Bemerkung*) to enter in the minutes.
Proton ['pro:tɔn] (-s, -en) *nt* proton.
Prototyp *m* prototype.
Protz ['prɔts] (-es, -e) *m* swank; **p~en** *vi* to show off.
protzig *adj* ostentatious.
Proviant [provi'ant] (-s, -e) *m* provisions *pl*, supplies *pl.*
Provinz [pro'vɪnts] (-, -en) *f* province; **das ist finsterste ~** (*pej*) it's a cultural backwater.
provinziell [provɪn'tsiɛl] *adj* provincial.
Provision [provizi'o:n] *f* (*COMM*) commission.
provisorisch [provi'zo:rɪʃ] *adj* provisional.
Provisorium [provi'zo:riʊm] (-s, -ien) *nt* provisional arrangement.
Provokation [provokatsi'o:n] *f* provocation.
provokativ [provoka'ti:f] *adj* provocative, provoking.
provokatorisch [provoka'to:rɪʃ] *adj* provocative, provoking.
provozieren [provo'tsi:rən] *vt* to provoke.
Proz. *abk* (= *Prozent*) pc.
Prozedur [protse'du:r] *f* procedure; (*pej*) carry-on; **die ~ beim Zahnarzt** the ordeal at the dentist's.
Prozent [pro'tsɛnt] (-(e)s, -e) *nt* per cent, percentage; **~rechnung** *f* percentage calculation; **~satz** *m* percentage.
prozentual [protsɛntu'a:l] *adj* percentage *attrib.*
Prozess▲ [pro'tsɛs] (-es, -e) *m* trial, case; (*Vorgang*) process; **es zum ~ kommen lassen** to go to court; **mit jdm/etw kurzen**

~ machen (*fig: umg*) to make short work of sb/sth; **~anwalt** *m* barrister, counsel; **~führung** *f* handling of a case.
prozessieren [protsɛ'si:rən] *vi*: **~ (mit)** to bring an action (against), go to law (with *od* against).
Prozession [protsɛsi'o:n] *f* procession.
Prozesskosten▲ *pl* (legal) costs *pl.*
prüde ['pry:də] *adj* prudish.
Prüderie [pry:də'ri:] *f* prudery.
prüfen ['pry:fən] *vt* to examine, test; (*nach~*) to check; (*erwägen*) to consider; (*Geschäftsbücher*) to audit; (*mustern*) to scrutinize.
Prüfer(in) (-s, -) *m(f)* examiner.
Prüfling *m* examinee.
Prüfstein *m* touchstone.
Prüfung *f* (*SCH, UNIV*) examination, exam; (*Über~*) checking; **eine ~ machen** to take *od* sit (*BRIT*) an exam(ination); **durch eine ~ fallen** to fail an exam(ination).
Prüfungs- *zW*: **~ausschuss▲** *m* examining board; **~kommission** *f* examining board; **~ordnung** *f* exam(ination) regulations *pl.*
Prügel ['pry:gəl] (-s, -) *m* cudgel ♦ *pl* beating *sing.*
Prügelei [pry:gə'laɪ] *f* fight.
Prügelknabe *m* scapegoat.
prügeln *vt* to beat ♦ *vr* to fight.
Prügelstrafe *f* corporal punishment.
Prunk [prʊŋk] (-(e)s) *m* pomp, show; **p~voll** *adj* splendid, magnificent.
prusten ['pru:stən] (*umg*) *vi* to snort.
PS *abk* (= *Pferdestärke*) hp; (= *Postskript(um)*) PS.
Psalm [psalm] (-s, -en) *m* psalm.
pseudo- [psɔydo] *in zW* pseudo.
Psychiater [psy'çia:tər] (-s, -) *m* psychiatrist.
Psychiatrie [psyçia'tri:] *f* psychiatry.
psychiatrisch [psy'çia:trɪʃ] *adj* psychiatric; **~e Klinik** mental *od* psychiatric hospital.
psychisch ['psy:çɪʃ] *adj* psychological; **~ gestört** emotionally *od* psychologically disturbed.
Psychoanalyse [psyçoana'ly:zə] *f* psychoanalysis.
Psychologe [psyço'lo:gə] (-n, -n) *m* psychologist.
Psychologie *f* psychology.
Psychologin *f* psychologist.
psychologisch *adj* psychological.
Psychotherapie *f* psychotherapy.
PTT (*SCHWEIZ*) *abk* (= *Post, Telefon, Telegraf*) *postal and telecommunication services.*
Pubertät [puber'tɛ:t] *f* puberty.
publik [pu'bli:k] *adj*: **~ werden** to become public knowledge.
Publikum ['pu:blikʊm] (-s) *nt* audience; (*SPORT*) crowd; **das ~ in dieser Bar ist sehr gemischt** you get a very mixed group of

people using this bar.

Publikumserfolg *m* popular success.

Publikumsverkehr *m: „heute kein ~"* "closed today for public business".

publizieren [publi'tsiːrən] *vt* to publish.

Pudding ['pʊdɪŋ] (**-s, -e** *od* **-s**) *m* blancmange; **~pulver** *nt* custard powder.

Pudel ['puːdəl] (**-s, -**) *m* poodle; **das also ist des ~s Kern** (*fig*) that's what it's really all about.

pudelwohl (*umg*) *adj:* **sich ~ fühlen** to feel on top of the world.

Puder ['puːdər] (**-s, -**) *m* powder; **~dose** *f* powder compact.

pudern *vt* to powder.

Puderzucker *m* icing sugar (*BRIT*), confectioner's sugar (*US*).

Puertoricaner(in) [puɛrtori'kaːnər(ɪn)] (**-s, -**) *m(f)* Puerto Rican.

puertoricanisch *adj* Puerto Rican.

Puerto Rico [pu'ɛrto'riːko] (**-s**) *nt* Puerto Rico.

Puff¹ [puf] (**-(e)s, -e**) *m* (*Wäsche~*) linen basket; (*Sitz~*) pouf.

Puff² (**-(e)s, ⁻e**) (*umg*) *m* (*Stoß*) push.

Puff³ (**-s, -s**) (*umg*) *m od nt* (*Bordell*) brothel.

Puffer (**-s, -**) *m* (*auch COMPUT*) buffer; **~speicher** *m* (*COMPUT*) cache; **~staat** *m* buffer state; **~zone** *f* buffer zone.

Puffreis *m* puffed rice.

Pulle ['pʊlə] (**-, -n**) (*umg*) *f* bottle; **volle ~ fahren** (*umg*) to drive flat out.

Pulli ['pʊli] (**-s, -s**) (*umg*) *m* sweater, jumper (*BRIT*).

Pullover [pʊ'loːvər] (**-s, -**) *m* sweater, jumper (*BRIT*).

Pullunder [pʊ'lʊndər] (**-s, -**) *m* slipover.

Puls [pʊls] (**-es, -e**) *m* pulse; **~ader** *f* artery; **sich** *dat* **die ~ader(n) aufschneiden** to slash one's wrists.

pulsieren [pʊl'ziːrən] *vi* to throb, pulsate.

Pult [pʊlt] (**-(e)s, -e**) *nt* desk.

Pulver ['pʊlfər] (**-s, -**) *nt* powder; **~fass▲** *nt* powder keg; **(wie) auf einem ~fass sitzen** (*fig*) to be sitting on (top of) a volcano.

pulverig *adj* powdery.

pulverisieren [pʊlveri'ziːrən] *vt* to pulverize.

Pulverkaffee *m* instant coffee.

Pulverschnee *m* powdery snow.

pummelig ['pʊməlɪç] *adj* chubby.

Pump (**-(e)s**) (*umg*) *m:* **auf ~ kaufen** to buy on tick (*BRIT*) *od* credit.

Pumpe ['pʊmpə] (**-, -n**) *f* pump; (*umg: Herz*) ticker.

pumpen *vt* to pump; (*umg*) to lend; (: *entleihen*) to borrow.

Pumphose *f* knickerbockers *pl.*

puncto ['pʊŋkto] *präp +gen:* **in ~ X** where X is concerned.

Punkt [pʊŋkt] (**-(e)s, -e**) *m* point; (*bei Muster*) dot; (*Satzzeichen*) full stop, period (*bes US*); **~ 12 Uhr** at 12 o'clock on the dot; **nun mach aber mal einen ~!** (*umg*) come off it!; **p~gleich** *adj* (*SPORT*) level.

punktieren [pʊŋk'tiːrən] *vt* to dot; (*MED*) to aspirate.

pünktlich ['pʏŋktlɪç] *adj* punctual; **P~keit** *f* punctuality.

Punkt- *zW:* **~matrix** *f* dot matrix; **~richter** *m* (*SPORT*) judge; **~sieg** *m* victory on points; **~wertung** *f* points system; **~zahl** *f* score.

Punsch [pʊnʃ] (**-(e)s, -e**) *m* (hot) punch.

Pupille [pu'pɪlə] (**-, -n**) *f* (*im Auge*) pupil.

Puppe ['pʊpə] (**-, -n**) *f* doll; (*Marionette*) puppet; (*Insekten~*) pupa, chrysalis; (*Schaufenster~, MIL: Übungs~*) dummy; (*umg: Mädchen*) doll, bird (*bes BRIT*).

Puppen- *zW:* **~haus** *nt* doll's house, dollhouse (*US*); **~spieler** *m* puppeteer; **~stube** *f* (single-room) doll's house *od* dollhouse (*US*); **~theater** *nt* puppet theatre (*BRIT*) *od* theater (*US*); **~wagen** *m* doll's pram.

pupsen ['puːpsən] (*umg*) *vi* to make a rude noise/smell.

pur [puːr] *adj* pure; (*völlig*) sheer; (*Whisky*) neat.

Püree [py're:] (**-s, -s**) *nt* purée; (*Kartoffel~*) mashed potatoes *pl.*

Purpur ['pʊrpʊr] (**-s**) *m* crimson.

Purzelbaum ['pʊrtsəlbaʊm] *m* somersault.

purzeln *vi* to tumble.

Puste ['puːstə] (**-**) (*umg*) *f* puff; (*fig*) steam.

Pusteblume (*umg*) *f* dandelion.

Pustel ['pʊstəl] (**-, -n**) *f* pustule.

pusten ['puːstən] (*umg*) *vi* to puff, blow.

Pute ['puːtə] (**-, -n**) *f* turkey hen.

Puter (**-s, -**) *m* turkey cock; **p~rot** *adj* scarlet.

Putsch [pʊtʃ] (**-(e)s, -e**) *m* revolt, putsch; **p~en** *vi* to revolt; **~ist** *m* rebel; **~versuch** *m* attempted coup (d'état).

Putte ['pʊtə] (**-, -n**) *f* (*KUNST*) cherub.

Putz [pʊts] (**-es**) *m* (*Mörtel*) plaster, roughcast; **eine Mauer mit ~ verkleiden** to roughcast a wall.

putzen *vt* to clean; (*Nase*) to wipe, blow ♦ *vr* to clean o.s.; (*veraltet: sich schmücken*) to dress o.s. up.

Putzfrau *f* cleaning lady, charwoman (*BRIT*).

putzig *adj* quaint, funny.

Putzlappen *m* cloth.

putzmunter (*umg*) *adj* full of beans.

Putz- *zW:* **~tag** *m* cleaning day; **~teufel** (*umg*) *m* maniac for housework; **~zeug** *nt* cleaning things *pl.*

Puzzle ['pasəl] (**-s, -s**) *nt* jigsaw (puzzle).

PVC [peːfau'tseː] (**-(s)**) *nt abk* PVC.

Pygmäe [pʏ'gmɛːə] (**-n, -n**) *m* Pygmy.

Pyjama [pi'dʒaːma] (**-s, -s**) *m* pyjamas *pl* (*BRIT*), pajamas *pl* (*US*).

Pyramide [pyra'miːdə] (**-, -n**) *f* pyramid.

Pyrenäen [pyre'nɛːən] *pl:* **die ~** the Pyrenees

pl.
Python ['py:tɔn] (**-s, -s**) *m* python; ~**schlange** *f*
python.

Q, q

Q, q [ku:] *nt* Q, q; ~ **wie Quelle** ≈ Q for Queen.
qcm *abk* (= *Quadratzentimeter*) cm².
qkm *abk* (= *Quadratkilometer*) km².
qm *abk* (= *Quadratmeter*) m².
quabb(e)lig ['kvab(ə)lıç] *adj* wobbly; (*Frosch*)
slimy.
Quacksalber ['kvakzalbər] (**-s, -**) *m* quack
(doctor).
Quader ['kva:dər] (**-s, -**) *m* square stone block;
(*MATH*) cuboid.
Quadrat [kva'dra:t] (**-(e)s, -e**) *nt* square;
q~isch *adj* square; ~**latschen** *pl* (*hum: umg:*
Schuhe) clodhoppers *pl*; ~**meter** *m* square
metre (*BRIT*) *od* meter (*US*).
quadrieren [kva'dri:rən] *vt* to square.
quaken ['kva:kən] *vi* to croak; (*Ente*) to quack.
quäken ['kvɛ:kən] *vi* to screech.
quäkend *adj* screeching.
Quäker(in) (**-s, -**) *m(f)* Quaker.
Qual [kva:l] (**-, -en**) *f* pain, agony; (*seelisch*)
anguish; **er machte ihr das Leben zur** ~ he
made her life a misery.
quälen ['kvɛ:lən] *vt* to torment ♦ *vr* (*sich*
abmühen) to struggle; (*geistig*) to torment
o.s.; ~**de Ungewissheit** agonizing
uncertainty.
Quälerei [kvɛ:lə'raı] *f* torture, torment.
Quälgeist (*umg*) *m* pest.
Qualifikation [kvalifikatsi'o:n] *f* qualification.
qualifizieren [kvalifi'tsi:rən] *vt* to qualify;
(*einstufen*) to label ♦ *vr* to qualify.
qualifiziert *adj* (*Arbeiter, Nachwuchs*) qualified;
(*Arbeit*) professional; (*POL: Mehrheit*)
requisite.
Qualität [kvali'tɛ:t] *f* quality; **von**
ausgezeichneter ~ (of) top quality.
qualitativ [kvalita'ti:f] *adj* qualitative.
Qualitätskontrolle *f* quality control.
Qualitätsware *f* article of high quality.
Qualle ['kvalə] (**-, -n**) *f* jellyfish.
Qualm [kvalm] (**-(e)s**) *m* thick smoke.
qualmen *vt, vi* to smoke.
qualvoll ['kva:lfɔl] *adj* painful; (*Schmerzen*)
excruciating, agonizing.
Quantensprung *m* quantum leap.
Quantentheorie ['kvantənteori:] *f* quantum
theory.

Quantität [kvanti'tɛ:t] *f* quantity.
quantitativ [kvantita'ti:f] *adj* quantitative.
Quantum ['kvantʊm] (**-s, Quanten**) *nt*
quantity, amount.
Quarantäne [karan'tɛ:nə] (**-, -n**) *f* quarantine.
Quark¹ [kvark] (**-s**) *m* curd cheese, quark;
(*umg*) rubbish.
Quark² [kvark] (**-s, -s**) *nt* (*PHYS*) quark.
Quarta ['kvarta] (**-, Quarten**) *f* (*früher*) *third*
year of German secondary school.
Quartal [kvar'ta:l] (**-s, -e**) *nt* quarter (year);
Kündigung zum ~ quarterly notice date.
Quartett [kvar'tɛt] (**-(e)s, -e**) *nt* (*MUS*) quartet;
(*KARTEN*) set of four cards; (: *Spiel*) ≈
happy families.
Quartier [kvar'ti:r] (**-s, -e**) *nt* accommodation
(*BRIT*), accommodations *pl* (*US*); (*MIL*)
quarters *pl*; (*Stadt*~) district.
Quarz [kva:rts] (**-es, -e**) *m* quartz.
quasi ['kva:zi] *adv* virtually ♦ *präf* quasi.
quasseln ['kvasəln] (*umg*) *vi* to natter.
Quaste ['kvastə] (**-, -n**) *f* (*Troddel*) tassel; (*von*
Pinsel) bristles *pl*.
Quästur [kvɛs'tu:r] *f* (*UNIV*) bursary.
Quatsch [kvatʃ] (**-es**) (*umg*) *m* rubbish,
hogwash; **hört doch endlich auf mit dem** ~!
stop being so stupid!; ~ **machen** to mess
about.
quatschen *vi* to chat, natter.
Quatschkopf (*umg*) *m* (*pej: Schwätzer*)
windbag; (*Dummkopf*) twit (*BRIT*).
Quecksilber ['kvɛkzılbər] *nt* mercury.
Quelle ['kvɛlə] (**-, -n**) *f* spring; (*eines Flusses,*
COMPUT) source; **an der** ~ **sitzen** (*fig*) to be
well placed; **aus zuverlässiger** ~ from a
reliable source.
quellen *vi* (*hervor*~) to pour *od* gush forth;
(*schwellen*) to swell.
Quellenangabe *f* reference.
Quellsprache *f* source language.
Quengelei [kvɛŋə'laı] (*umg*) *f* whining.
quengelig (*umg*) *adj* whining.
quengeln (*umg*) *vi* to whine.
quer [kve:r] *adv* crossways, diagonally;
(*rechtwinklig*) at right angles; ~ **gestreift**
horizontally striped; **sich** ~ **legen** (*fig: umg*)
to be awkward; ~ **auf dem Bett** across the
bed; **Q~balken** *m* crossbeam; **Q~denker** *m*
maverick.
Quere ['kve:rə] (**-**) *f*: **jdm in die** ~ **kommen** to
cross sb's path.
quer- *zW*: ~**feldein** *adv* across country;
Q~feldeinrennen *nt* cross-country; (*mit*
Motorrädern) motocross; (*Radrennen*) cyclo-
cross; **Q~flöte** *f* flute; **Q~format** *nt* oblong
format; **Q~kopf** *m* awkward customer;
Q~schiff *nt* transept; **Q~schläger** (*umg*) *m*
ricochet; **Q~schnitt** *m* cross section;
~**schnittsgelähmt** *adj* paraplegic, paralysed
below the waist; **Q~schnittslähmung** *f*

paraplegia; **Q~straße** *f* intersecting road;
Q~strich *m* (horizontal) stroke *od* line;
Q~summe *f* (*MATH*) sum of digits of a
number; **Q~treiber** (**-s, -**) *m* obstructionist.
Querulant(in) [kveru'lant(ın)] (**-en, -en**) *m(f)*
grumbler.
Querverbindung *f* connection, link.
Querverweis *m* cross-reference.
quetschen ['kvɛtʃən] *vt* to squash, crush;
(*MED*) to bruise ♦ *vr* (*sich klemmen*) to be
caught; (*sich zwängen*) to squeeze (o.s.).
Quetschung *f* bruise, contusion (*form*).
Queue [kø:] (**-s, -s**) *nt* (*BILLIARD*) cue.
quicklebendig ['kvıkle'bɛndıç] (*umg*) *adj*
(*Kind*) lively, active; (*ältere Person*) spry.
quieken ['kvi:kən] *vi* to squeak.
quietschen ['kvi:tʃən] *vi* to squeak.
quietschvergnügt ['kvi:tʃfɛrgny:kt] (*umg*) *adj*
happy as a sandboy.
quillt [kvılt] *vb siehe* **quellen.**
Quinta ['kvınta] (**-, Quinten**) *f* (*früher*) second
year in German secondary school.
Quintessenz ['kvıntɛsɛnts] *f* quintessence.
Quintett [kvın'tɛt] (**-(e)s, -e**) *nt* quintet.
Quirl [kvırl] (**-(e)s, -e**) *m* whisk.
quirlig ['kvırlıç] *adj* lively, frisky.
quitt [kvıt] *adj* quits, even.
Quitte (**-, -n**) *f* quince.
quittieren [kvı'ti:rən] *vt* to give a receipt for;
(*Dienst*) to leave.
Quittung *f* receipt; **er hat seine ~ bekommen**
he's paid the penalty *od* price.
Quiz [kvıs] (**-, -**) *nt* quiz.
quoll *etc* [kvɔl] *vb siehe* **quellen.**
Quote ['kvo:tə] (**-, -n**) *f* proportion; (*Rate*) rate.
Quotenregelung *f* quota system (*for ensuring
adequate representation of women*).
Quotierung [kvo'ti:rʊŋ] *f* (*COMM*) quotation.

R, r

R¹, r *nt* R, r; **~ wie Richard** ≈ R for Robert, R
for Roger (*US*).
R², r *abk* (= *Radius*) r.
r. *abk* (= *rechts*) r.
Rabatt [ra'bat] (**-(e)s, -e**) *m* discount.
Rabatte (**-, -n**) *f* flower bed, border.
Rabattmarke *f* trading stamp.
Rabatz [ra'bats] (**-es**) (*umg*) *m* row, din.
Rabe ['ra:bə] (**-n, -n**) *m* raven.
Rabenmutter *f* bad mother.
rabenschwarz *adj* pitch-black.
rabiat [rabi'a:t] *adj* furious.

Rache ['raxə] (**-**) *f* revenge, vengeance.
Rachen (**-s, -**) *m* throat.
rächen ['rɛçən] *vt* to avenge, revenge ♦ *vr* to
take (one's) revenge; **das wird sich ~** you'll
pay for that.
Rachitis [ra'xi:tıs] (**-**) *f* rickets *sing.*
Rachsucht *f* vindictiveness.
rachsüchtig *adj* vindictive.
Racker ['rakər] (**-s, -**) *m* rascal, scamp.
Rad [ra:t] (**-(e)s, ̈-er**) *nt* wheel; (*Fahr~*) bike;
~ fahren to cycle; **unter die Räder kommen**
(*umg*) to fall into bad ways; **das fünfte ~ am
Wagen sein** (*umg*) to be in the way.
Radar ['ra:da:r] (**-s**) *m od nt* radar; **~falle** *f*
speed trap; **~kontrolle** *f* radar-controlled
speed check.
Radau [ra'dau] (**-s**) (*umg*) *m* row; **~ machen**
kick up a row; (*Unruhe stiften*) to cause
trouble.
Raddampfer *m* paddle steamer.
radebrechen ['ra:dəbrɛçən] *vi untr*: **Deutsch** *etc*
~ to speak broken German *etc*.
radeln *vi* (*Hilfsverb sein*) to cycle.
Rädelsführer ['rɛ:dəlsfy:rər] (**-s, -**) *m*
ringleader.
Rad- *zW*: **~fahrer** *m* cyclist; (*pej*: *umg*) crawler;
~fahrweg *m* cycle track *od* path.
radieren [ra'di:rən] *vt* to rub out, erase; (*ART*)
to etch.
Radiergummi *m* rubber (*BRIT*), eraser (*bes
US*).
Radierung *f* etching.
Radieschen [ra'di:sçən] *nt* radish.
radikal [radi'ka:l] *adj* radical; **~ gegen etw
vorgehen** to take radical steps against sth.
Radikale(r) *f(m)* radical.
Radikalisierung [radikali'zi:rʊŋ] *f*
radicalization.
Radikalkur (*umg*) *f* drastic remedy.
Radio ['ra:dio] (**-s, -s**) *nt* radio, wireless (*bes
BRIT*); **im ~** on the radio; **r~aktiv** *adj*
radioactive; **r~aktiver Niederschlag**
(radioactive) fallout; **~aktivität** *f*
radioactivity; **~apparat** *m* radio (set);
~rekorder *m* radio-cassette recorder.
Radium ['ra:diʊm] (**-s**) *nt* radium.
Radius ['ra:diʊs] (**-, Radien**) *m* radius.
Radkappe *f* (*AUT*) hub cap.
Radler(in) (**-s, -**) *m(f)* cyclist.
Rad- *zW*: **~rennbahn** *f* cycling (race)track;
~rennen *nt* cycle race; (*Sportart*) cycle
racing; **~sport** *m* cycling.
RAF (**-**) *f abk* (= *Rote Armee Fraktion*) Red Army
Faction.
raffen ['rafən] *vt* to snatch, pick up; (*Stoff*) to
gather (up); (*Geld*) to pile up, rake in; (*umg*:
verstehen) to catch on to.
Raffgier *f* greed, avarice.
Raffinade [rafi'na:də] *f* refined sugar.
Raffinesse [rafi'nɛsə] (**-**) *f* (*Feinheit*)

refinement; (*Schlauheit*) cunning.
raffinieren [rafi'ni:rən] *vt* to refine.
raffiniert *adj* crafty, cunning; (*Zucker*) refined.
Rage ['ra:ʒə] (-) *f* (*Wut*) rage, fury.
ragen ['ra:gən] *vi* to tower, rise.
Rahm [ra:m] (-s) *m* cream.
Rahmen (-s, -) *m* frame(work); **aus dem ~ fallen** to go too far; **im ~ des Möglichen** within the bounds of possibility; **r~** *vt* to frame; **~handlung** *f* (*LITER*) background story; **~plan** *m* outline plan; **~richtlinien** *pl* guidelines *pl*.
rahmig *adj* creamy.
räkeln ['rɛːkln] *vr* = **rekeln**.
Rakete [ra'ke:tə] (-, -n) *f* rocket; **ferngelenkte ~** guided missile.
Raketenstützpunkt *m* missile base.
Rallye ['rali] (-, -s) *f* rally.
rammdösig ['ramdøːzɪç] (*umg*) *adj* giddy, dizzy.
rammen ['ramən] *vt* to ram.
Rampe ['rampə] (-, -n) *f* ramp.
Rampenlicht *nt* (*THEAT*) footlights *pl*; **sie möchte immer im ~ stehen** (*fig*) she always wants to be in the limelight.
ramponieren [rampo'ni:rən] (*umg*) *vt* to damage.
Ramsch [ramʃ] (-(e)s, -e) *m* junk.
ran [ran] (*umg*) *adv* = **heran**.
Rand [rant] (-(e)s, ⁻er) *m* edge; (*von Brille, Tasse etc*) rim; (*Hut~*) brim; (*auf Papier*) margin; (*Schmutz~, unter Augen*) ring; (*fig*) verge, brink; **außer ~ und Band** wild; **am ~e bemerkt** mentioned in passing; **am ~e der Stadt** on the outskirts of the town; **etw am ~e miterleben** to experience sth from the sidelines.
randalieren [randa'li:rən] *vi* to (go on the) rampage.
Rand- *zW:* **~bemerkung** *f* marginal note; (*fig*) odd comment; **~erscheinung** *f* unimportant side effect, marginal phenomenon; **~figur** *f* minor figure; **~gebiet** *nt* (*GEOG*) fringe; (*POL*) border territory; (*fig*) subsidiary; **~streifen** *m* (*der Straße*) verge (*BRIT*), berm (*US*); (*der Autobahn*) hard shoulder (*BRIT*), shoulder (*US*); **r~voll** *adj* full to the brim.
rang *etc* [raŋ] *vb siehe* **ringen**.
Rang (-(e)s, ⁻e) *m* rank; (*Stand*) standing; (*Wert*) quality; (*THEAT*) circle; **ein Mann ohne ~ und Namen** a man without any standing; **erster/zweiter ~** dress/upper circle.
Rangabzeichen *nt* badge of rank.
Rangälteste(r) *m* senior officer.
rangeln ['raŋəln] (*umg*) *vi* to scrap; (*um Posten*): **~ (um)** to wrangle (for).
Rangfolge *f* order of rank (*bes MIL*).
Rangierbahnhof [rã'ʒi:rba:nhoːf] *m* marshalling yard.

rangieren *vt* (*EISENB*) to shunt, switch (*US*)
♦ *vi* to rank, be classed.
Rangiergleis *nt* siding.
Rangliste *f* (*SPORT*) ranking list, rankings *pl*.
Rangordnung *f* hierarchy; (*MIL*) rank.
Rangunterschied *m* social distinction; (*MIL*) difference in rank.
rank [raŋk] *adj:* **~ und schlank** (*liter*) slender and supple.
Ranke ['raŋkə] (-, -n) *f* tendril, shoot.
Ränke ['rɛŋkə] *pl* intrigues *pl*; **~schmied** *m* (*liter*) intriguer.
ranken ['raŋkən] *vr* to trail, grow; **sich um etw ~** to twine around sth.
ränkevoll *adj* scheming.
ranklotzen ['raŋklɔtsən] (*umg*) *vi* to put one's nose to the grindstone.
ranlassen *unreg* (*umg*) *vt:* **jdn ~** to let sb have a go.
rann *etc* [ran] *vb siehe* **rinnen**.
rannte *etc* ['rantə] *vb siehe* **rennen**.
Ranzen ['rantsən] (-s, -) *m* satchel; (*umg: Bauch*) belly, gut.
ranzig ['rantsɪç] *adj* rancid.
Rappe ['rapə] (-n, -n) *m* black horse.
Rappel ['rapəl] (-s, -) (*umg*) *m* (*Fimmel*) craze; (*Wutanfall*): **einen ~ kriegen** to throw a fit.
Rappen ['rapən] (-s, -) (*SCHWEIZ*) *m* (*Geld*) centime, rappen.
Raps [raps] (-es, -e) *m* (*BOT*) rape; **~öl** *nt* rapeseed oil.
rar [ra:r] *adj* rare; **sich ~ machen** (*umg*) to stay away.
Rarität [rari'tɛːt] *f* rarity; (*Sammelobjekt*) curio.
rasant [ra'zant] *adj* quick, rapid.
rasch [raʃ] *adj* quick.
rascheln *vi* to rustle.
rasen ['ra:zən] *vi* to rave; (*sich schnell bewegen*) to race.
Rasen (-s, -) *m* grass; (*gepflegt*) lawn.
rasend *adj* furious; **~e Kopfschmerzen** a splitting headache.
Rasen- *zW:* **~mäher** (-s, -) *m* lawnmower; **~mähmaschine** *f* lawnmower; **~platz** *m* lawn; **~sprenger** *m* (lawn) sprinkler.
Raserei [ra:zə'rai] *f* raving, ranting; (*Schnelle*) reckless speeding.
Rasier- *zW:* **~apparat** *m* shaver; **~creme** *f* shaving cream; **r~en** *vt, vr* to shave; **~klinge** *f* razor blade; **~messer** *nt* razor; **~pinsel** *m* shaving brush; **~seife** *f* shaving soap *od* stick; **~wasser** *nt* aftershave.
raspeln ['raspəln] *vt* to grate; (*Holz*) to rasp.
Rasse ['rasə] (-, -n) *f* race; (*Tier~*) breed; **~hund** *m* thoroughbred dog.
Rassel (-, -n) *f* rattle.
rasseln *vi* to rattle, clatter.
Rassenhass▲ *m* race *od* racial hatred.
Rassentrennung *f* racial segregation.

rassig ['rasıç] *adj* (*Pferd, Auto*) sleek; (*Frau*) vivacious; (*Wein*) spirited, lively.

Rassismus [ra'sısmʊs] (-) *m* racialism, racism.

rassistisch [ra'sıstıʃ] *adj* racialist, racist.

Rast [rast] (-, -en) *f* rest; **r~en** *vi* to rest.

Raster ['rastər] (-s, -) *m* (*ARCHIT*) grid; (*PHOT: Gitter*) screen; (*TV*) raster; (*fig*) framework.

Rast- *zW*: ~**haus** *nt* (*AUT*) service area, services *pl*; ~**hof** *m* (motorway) motel; (*mit Tankstelle*) service area (*with a motel*); **r~los** *adj* tireless; (*unruhig*) restless; ~**platz** *m* (*AUT*) lay-by (*BRIT*); ~**stätte** *f* service area, services *pl*.

Rasur [ra'zu:r] *f* shave; (*das Rasieren*) shaving.

Rat [ra:t] (-(e)s, -schläge) *m* (piece of) advice; **jdm mit** ~ **und Tat zur Seite stehen** to support sb in (both) word and deed; **sich** ~ **suchend an jdn wenden** to turn to sb for advice; (**sich** *dat*) **keinen** ~ **wissen** not to know what to do; *siehe auch* **zurate**.

rät [rɛ:t] *vb siehe* **raten**.

Rate (-, -n) *f* instalment (*BRIT*), installment (*US*); **auf** ~**n kaufen** to buy on hire purchase (*BRIT*) *od* on the installment plan (*US*); **in** ~**n zahlen** to pay in instalments (*BRIT*) *od* installments (*US*).

raten *unreg vt, vi* to guess; (*empfehlen*): **jdm** ~ to advise sb; **dreimal darfst du** ~ I'll give you three guesses (*auch ironisch*).

ratenweise *adv* by instalments (*BRIT*) *od* installments (*US*).

Ratenzahlung *f* hire purchase (*BRIT*), installment plan (*US*).

Ratespiel *nt* guessing game; (*TV*) quiz; (*: Beruferaten etc*) panel game.

Ratgeber (-s, -) *m* adviser.

Rathaus *nt* town hall; (*einer Großstadt*) city hall (*bes US*).

ratifizieren [ratifi'tsi:rən] *vt* to ratify.

Ratifizierung *f* ratification.

Ration [ratsi'o:n] *f* ration.

rational [ratsio'na:l] *adj* rational.

rationalisieren [ratsionali'zi:rən] *vt* to rationalize.

rationell [ratsio'nɛl] *adj* efficient.

rationieren [ratsio'ni:rən] *vt* to ration.

ratlos *adj* at a loss, helpless.

Ratlosigkeit *f* helplessness.

rätoromanisch [rɛtoro'ma:nıʃ] *adj* Rhaetian.

ratsam *adj* advisable.

Ratschlag *m* (piece of) advice.

Rätsel ['rɛ:tsəl] (-s, -) *nt* puzzle; (*Wort~*) riddle; **vor einem** ~ **stehen** to be baffled; **r~haft** *adj* mysterious; **es ist mir r~haft** it's a mystery to me; **r~n** *vi* to puzzle; ~**raten** *nt* guessing game.

Ratsherr *m* councillor (*BRIT*), councilor (*US*).

Ratskeller *m* town-hall restaurant.

Ratte ['ratə] (-, -n) *f* rat.

Rattenfänger (-s, -) *m* rat-catcher.

rattern ['ratərn] *vi* to rattle, clatter.

rau▲ [rau] *adj* rough, coarse; (*Wetter*) harsh; **in** ~**en Mengen** (*umg*) by the ton, galore.

Raub [raup] (-(e)s) *m* robbery; (*Beute*) loot, booty; ~**bau** *m* overexploitation; ~**druck** *m* pirate(d) edition.

raubeinig▲ *adj* rough-and-ready.

rauben ['raubən] *vt* to rob; (*jdn*) to kidnap, abduct.

Räuber ['rɔybər] (-s, -) *m* robber; **r~isch** *adj* thieving.

Raub- *zW*: ~**fisch** *m* predatory fish; **r~gierig** *adj* rapacious; ~**kassette** *f* pirate cassette; ~**mord** *m* robbery with murder; ~**tier** *nt* predator; ~**überfall** *m* robbery with violence; ~**vogel** *m* bird of prey.

Rauch [raux] (-(e)s) *m* smoke; ~**abzug** *m* smoke outlet.

rauchen *vt, vi* to smoke; **mir raucht der Kopf** (*fig*) my head's spinning; „**R~ verboten**" "no smoking".

Raucher(in) (-s, -) *m(f)* smoker; ~**abteil** *nt* (*EISENB*) smoker.

räuchern ['rɔyçərn] *vt* to smoke, cure.

Räucherspeck *m* ≈ smoked bacon.

Räucherstäbchen *nt* joss stick.

Rauch- *zW*: ~**fahne** *f* smoke trail; ~**fang** *m* chimney hood; ~**fleisch** *nt* smoked meat.

rauchig *adj* smoky.

Rauchschwaden *pl* drifts of smoke *pl*.

räudig ['rɔydıç] *adj* mangy.

rauf [rauf] (*umg*) *adv* = **herauf; hinauf**.

Raufasertapete▲ *f* woodchip paper.

Raufbold (-(e)s, -e) *m* thug, hooligan.

raufen *vt* (*Haare*) to pull out ♦ *vi, vr* to fight.

Rauferei [raufə'rai] *f* brawl, fight.

rauflustig *adj* ready for a fight, pugnacious.

rauh *etc* △ *siehe* **rau** *etc*.

rauhaarig▲ *adj* wire-haired; **R~reif** *m* hoarfrost.

Raum [raum] (-(e)s, Räume) *m* space; (*Zimmer, Platz*) room; (*Gebiet*) area; ~ **sparend** space-saving; **eine Frage im** ~ **stehen lassen** to leave a question unresolved; ~**ausstatter(in)** *m(f)* interior decorator.

räumen ['rɔymən] *vt* to clear; (*Wohnung, Platz*) to vacate, move out of; (*verlassen: Gebäude, Gebiet*) to evacuate; (*wegbringen*) to shift, move; (*in Schrank etc*) to put away.

Raum- *zW*: ~**fähre** *f* space shuttle; ~**fahrer** *m* astronaut; (*sowjetisch*) cosmonaut; ~**fahrt** *f* space travel.

Räumfahrzeug ['rɔymfa:rtsɔyk] *nt* bulldozer; (*für Schnee*) snow-clearer.

Rauminhalt *m* cubic capacity, volume.

Raumkapsel *f* space capsule.

räumlich ['rɔymlıç] *adj* spatial; **R~keiten** *pl* premises *pl*.

Raum- *zW*: ~**mangel** *m* lack of space; ~**maß**

nt unit of volume; cubic measurement;
~**meter** *m* cubic metre (*BRIT*) *od* meter (*US*);
~**not** *f* shortage of space; ~**ordnung** *f*
environmental planning; ~**pflegerin** *f*
cleaner; ~**schiff** *nt* spaceship; ~**schifffahrt**▲ *f*
space travel; ~**station** *f* space station;
~**transporter** *m* space shuttle.

Räumung ['rɔymʊŋ] *f* clearing (away); (*von
Haus etc*) vacating; (*wegen Gefahr*)
evacuation; (*unter Zwang*) eviction.

Räumungs- *zW:* ~**befehl** *m* eviction order;
~**klage** *f* action for eviction; ~**verkauf** *m*
clearance sale.

raunen ['raʊnən] *vt, vi* to whisper.

Raupe ['raʊpə] (-, -n) *f* caterpillar;
(*Raupenkette*) (caterpillar) track.

Raupenschlepper *m* caterpillar tractor.

Raureif▲ ['raʊraɪf] *m* hoarfrost.

raus [raʊs] (*umg*) *adv* = **heraus; hinaus**.

Rausch [raʊʃ] (-(e), *pl* **Räusche**) *m* intoxication;
einen ~ haben to be drunk.

rauschen *vi* (*Wasser*) to rush; (*Baum*) to rustle;
(*Radio etc*) to hiss; (*Mensch*) to sweep, sail.

rauschend *adj* (*Beifall*) thunderous; (*Fest*)
sumptuous.

Rauschgift *nt* drug; ~**handel** *m* drug traffic;
~**händler(in)** *m(f)* drug trafficker;
~**süchtige(r)** *f(m)* drug addict.

rausfliegen *unreg* (*umg*) *vi* to be chucked
out.

räuspern ['rɔyspərn] *vr* to clear one's throat.

Rausschmeißer ['raʊsʃmaɪsər] (-s, -) (*umg*) *m*
bouncer.

Raute ['raʊtə] (-, -n) *f* diamond; rhombus.

rautenförmig *adj* rhombic.

Razzia ['ratsia] (-, **Razzien**) *f* raid.

Reagenzglas [rea'gɛntsglaːs] *nt* test tube.

reagieren [rea'giːrən] *vi:* ~ (**auf** +*akk*) to react
(to).

Reaktion [reaktsi'oːn] *f* reaction.

reaktionär [reaktsio'nɛːr] *adj* reactionary.

Reaktionsfähigkeit *f* reactions *pl*.

Reaktionsgeschwindigkeit *f* speed of
reaction.

Reaktor [re'aktɔr] *m* reactor; ~**kern** *m*
reactor core; ~**unglück** *nt* nuclear
accident.

real [re'aːl] *adj* real, material; **R~einkommen**
nt real income.

realisierbar [reali'ziːrbaːr] *adj* practicable,
feasible.

Realismus [rea'lɪsmʊs] *m* realism.

Realist(in) [rea'lɪst(ɪn)] *m(f)* realist; **r~isch** *adj*
realistic.

Realität [reali'tɛːt] *f* reality; **Realitäten** *pl*
(*Gegebenheiten*) facts *pl*.

realitätsfremd *adj* out of touch with reality.

Realpolitik *f* political realism.

Realschule *f* ≈ middle school (*BRIT*), junior
high school (*US*).

Realzeit *f* real time.

Rebe ['reːbə] (-, -n) *f* vine.

Rebell(in) [re'bɛl(ɪn)] (-en, -en) *m(f)* rebel.

rebellieren [rebɛ'liːrən] *vi* to rebel.

Rebellion [rebɛli'oːn] *f* rebellion.

rebellisch [re'bɛlɪʃ] *adj* rebellious.

Rebensaft *m* wine.

Reb- [rɛp] *zW:* ~**huhn** *nt* partridge; ~**laus** *f* vine
pest; ~**stock** *m* vine.

Rechen ['rɛçən] (-s, -) *m* rake; **r~** *vt, vi* to rake.

Rechen- *zW:* ~**aufgabe** *f* sum, mathematical
problem; ~**fehler** *m* miscalculation;
~**maschine** *f* adding machine.

Rechenschaft *f* account; **jdm über etw** *akk* ~
ablegen to account for sth to sb; **jdn zur** ~
ziehen (für) to call sb to account (for *od* over);
jdm ~ **schulden** to be accountable to sb.

Rechenschaftsbericht *m* report.

Rechenschieber *m* slide rule.

Rechenzentrum *nt* computer centre (*BRIT*)
od center (*US*).

recherchieren [reʃɛr'ʃiːrən] *vt, vi* to
investigate.

rechnen ['rɛçnən] *vt, vi* to calculate;
(*veranschlagen*) to estimate, reckon; **jdn/etw
zu etw** ~ to count sb/sth among sth; ~ **mit**
to reckon with; ~ **auf** +*akk* to count on.

Rechnen *nt* arithmetic; (*bes SCH*) sums *pl*.

Rechner (-s, -) *m* calculator; (*COMPUT*)
computer; **r~fern** *adj* (*COMPUT*) remote;
r~isch *adj* arithmetical.

Rechnung *f* calculation(s); (*COMM*) bill
(*BRIT*), check (*US*); **auf eigene** ~ on one's
own account; **(jdm) etw in** ~ **stellen** to
charge (sb) for sth; **jdm/etw** ~ **tragen** to
take sb/sth into account.

Rechnungs- *zW:* ~**buch** *nt* account book; ~**hof**
m ≈ Auditor-General's office (*BRIT*), audit
division (*US*); ~**jahr** *nt* financial year;
~**prüfer** *m* auditor; ~**prüfung** *f* audit(ing).

recht [rɛçt] *adj* right ♦ *adv* (*vor Adjektiv*) really,
quite; **das ist mir** ~ that suits me; **jetzt erst**
~ now more than ever; **alles, was** ~ **ist**
(*empört*) fair's fair; (*anerkennend*) you can't
deny it; **nach dem R~en sehen** to see that
everything's O.K.; **R~ haben** to be right;
jdm R~ ~ **geben** to agree with sb, admit that
sb is right; **du kommst gerade** ~, **um ...**
you're just in time to ...; **gehe ich** ~ **in der**

Annahme, dass ...? am I correct in assuming that ...?; ~ **herzlichen Dank** thank you very much indeed.
Recht (-(e)s, -e) *nt* right; (*JUR*) law; ~ **sprechen** to administer justice; **mit** *od* **zu** ~ rightly, justly; **von** ~**s wegen** by rights; **zu seinem** ~ **kommen** (*lit*) to gain one's rights; (*fig*) to come into one's own; **gleiches** ~ **für alle!** equal rights for all!
Rechte *f* right (hand); (*POL*) Right.
Rechte(r, s) *f(m)* (*POL*) right-winger ♦ *nt* right thing; **etwas/nichts** ~**s** something/nothing proper.
rechte(r, s) *adj* right; (*POL*) right-wing.
recht- *zW*: **R**~**eck** (-(e)s, -e) *nt* rectangle; ~**eckig** *adj* rectangular; ~**fertigen** *vt untr* to justify ♦ *vr untr* to justify o.s.; **R**~**fertigung** *f* justification; ~**haberisch** *adj* dogmatic; ~**lich** *adj* legal, lawful; ~**lich nicht zulässig** not permissible in law, illegal; ~**mäßig** *adj* legal, lawful.
rechts [rɛçts] *adv* on *od* to the right; ~ **stehen** *od* **sein** (*POL*) to be right-wing; ~ **stricken** to knit (plain); **R**~**abbieger** (-s, -) *m*: **die Spur für R**~**abbieger** the right-hand turn-off lane; **R**~**anspruch** *m*: **einen R**~**anspruch auf etw** *akk* **haben** to be legally entitled to sth; **R**~**anwalt** *m*, **R**~**anwältin** *f* lawyer, barrister; **R**~**außen** (-, -) *m* (*SPORT*) outside right; **R**~**beistand** *m* legal adviser.
rechtschaffen *adj* upright.
Rechtschreibung *f* spelling.
Rechts- *zW*: ~**drehung** *f* clockwise rotation; ~**extremismus** *m* right-wing extremism; ~**extremist** *m* right-wing extremist; ~**fall** *m* (law) case; ~**frage** *f* legal question; **r**~**gültig** *adj* legally valid; ~**händer(in)** (-s, -) *m(f)* right-handed person; **r**~**kräftig** *adj* valid, legal; ~**kurve** *f* right-hand bend; ~**lage** *f* legal position; **r**~**lastig** *adj* listing to the right; (*fig*) leaning to the right; ~**pflege** *f* administration of justice; ~**pfleger** *m official with certain judicial powers.*
Rechtsprechung ['rɛçtʃprɛçʊŋ] *f* (*Gerichtsbarkeit*) jurisdiction; (*richterliche Tätigkeit*) dispensation of justice.
Rechts- *zW*: **r**~**radikal** *adj* (*POL*) extreme right-wing; ~**schutz** *m* legal protection; ~**spruch** *m* verdict; ~**staat** *m* state under the rule of law; ~**streit** *m* lawsuit; ~**titel** *m* title; **r**~**verbindlich** *adj* legally binding; ~**verkehr** *m* driving on the right; ~**weg** *m*: **der** ~**weg ist ausgeschlossen** ≈ the judges' decision is final; **r**~**widrig** *adj* illegal; ~**wissenschaft** *f* jurisprudence.
rechtwinklig *adj* right-angled.
rechtzeitig *adj* timely ♦ *adv* in time.
Reck [rɛk] (-(e)s, -e) *nt* horizontal bar.
recken *vt, vr* to stretch.
recyceln [riː'saɪkəln] *vt* to recycle.

Recycling [ri'saɪklɪŋ] (-s) *nt* recycling.
Red. *abk* = **Redaktion**; (= *Redakteur(in)*) ed.
Redakteur(in) [redak'tøːr(ɪn)] *m(f)* editor.
Redaktion [redaktsi'oːn] *f* editing; (*Leute*) editorial staff; (*Büro*) editorial office(s *pl*).
Redaktionsschluss▲ *m* time of going to press; (*Einsendeschluss*) copy deadline.
Rede ['reːdə] (-, -n) *f* speech; (*Gespräch*) talk; **jdn zur** ~ **stellen** to take sb to task; **eine** ~ **halten** to make a speech; **das ist nicht der** ~ **wert** it's not worth mentioning; **davon kann keine** ~ **sein** it's out of the question; ~**freiheit** *f* freedom of speech; **r**~**gewandt** *adj* eloquent.
Reden (-s) *nt* talking, speech.
reden *vi* to talk, speak ♦ *vt* to say; (*Unsinn etc*) to talk; **(viel) von sich** ~ **machen** to become (very much) a talking point; **darüber lässt sich** ~ that's a possibility; (*über Preis, Bedingungen*) I think we could discuss that; **er lässt mit sich** ~ he could be persuaded; (*in Bezug auf Preis*) he's open to offers; (*gesprächsbereit*) he's open to discussion.
Redensart *f* set phrase.
Redeschwall *m* torrent of words.
Redewendung *f* expression, idiom.
redlich ['reːtlɪç] *adj* honest; **R**~**keit** *f* honesty.
Redner(in) (-s, -) *m(f)* speaker, orator.
redselig ['reːtzeːlɪç] *adj* talkative, loquacious; **R**~**keit** *f* talkativeness, loquacity.
redundant [redʊn'dant] *adj* redundant.
Redundanz [redʊn'dants] (-) *f* redundancy.
reduzieren [redu'tsiːrən] *vt* to reduce.
Reduzierung *f* reduction.
Reede ['reːdə] (-, -n) *f* protected anchorage.
Reeder (-s, -) *m* shipowner.
Reederei [reːdə'raɪ] *f* shipping line *od* firm.
reell [re'ɛl] *adj* fair, honest; (*Preis*) fair; (*COMM: Geschäft*) sound; (*MATH*) real.
Reetdach ['reːtdax] *nt* thatched roof.
Ref. *abk* = **Referendar(in)**; **Referent(in)**.
Referat [refe'raːt] (-(e)s, -e) *nt* report; (*Vortrag*) paper; (*Gebiet*) section; (*VERWALTUNG: Ressort*) department; **ein** ~ **halten** to present a seminar paper.
Referendar(in) [referɛn'daːr(ɪn)] *m(f)* trainee (in civil service); (*Studien*~) trainee teacher; (*Gerichts*~) articled clerk.
Referendum [refe'rɛndʊm] (-s, **Referenden**) *nt* referendum.
Referent(in) [refe'rɛnt(ɪn)] *m(f)* speaker; (*Berichterstatter*) reporter; (*Sachbearbeiter*) expert.
Referenz [refe'rɛnts] *f* reference.
referieren [refe'riːrən] *vi*: ~ **über** +*akk* to speak *od* talk on.
reflektieren [reflɛk'tiːrən] *vt, vi* to reflect; ~ **auf** +*akk* to be interested in.
Reflex [re'flɛks] (-es, -e) *m* reflex; ~**bewegung** *f* reflex action.

reflexiv [reflɛˈksiːf] *adj* (*GRAM*) reflexive.
Reform [reˈfɔrm] (-, -en) *f* reform.
Reformation [refɔrmatsiˈoːn] *f* reformation.
Reformator [refɔrˈmaːtɔr] *m* reformer; **r~isch** *adj* reformatory, reforming.
reform- *zW*: **~bedürftig** *adj* in need of reform; **~freudig** *adj* avid for reform; **R~haus** *nt* health food shop.
reformieren [refɔrˈmiːrən] *vt* to reform.
Refrain [rəˈfrɛ:] (-s, -s) *m* refrain, chorus.
Reg. *abk* (= *Regierungs-*) gov.; (= *Register*) reg.
Regal [reˈgaːl] (-s, -e) *nt* (book)shelves *pl*, bookcase; (*TYP*) stand, rack.
Regatta [reˈgata] (-, **Regatten**) *f* regatta.
Reg.-Bez. *abk* = **Regierungsbezirk.**
rege [ˈreːgə] *adj* lively, active; (*Geschäft*) brisk.
Regel [ˈreːgəl] (-, -n) *f* rule; (*MED*) period; **in der ~** as a rule; **nach allen ~n der Kunst** (*fig*) thoroughly; **sich** *dat* **etw zur ~ machen** to make a habit of sth; **r~los** *adj* irregular, unsystematic; **r~mäßig** *adj* regular; **~mäßigkeit** *f* regularity.
regeln *vt* to regulate, control; (*Angelegenheit*) to settle ♦ *vr*: **sich von selbst ~** to take care of itself; **gesetzlich geregelt sein** to be laid down by law.
regelrecht *adj* proper, thorough.
Regelung *f* regulation; settlement.
regelwidrig *adj* irregular, against the rules.
regen [ˈreːgən] *vt* to move ♦ *vr* to move, stir.
Regen (-s, -) *m* rain; **vom ~ in die Traufe kommen** (*Sprichwort*) to jump out of the frying pan into the fire (*Sprichwort*).
Regenbogen *m* rainbow; **~haut** *f* (*ANAT*) iris; **~presse** *f* trashy magazines *pl*.
regenerieren [regeneˈriːrən] *vr* (*BIOL*) to regenerate; (*fig*) to revitalize *od* regenerate o.s. *od* itself; (*nach Anstrengung, Schock etc*) to recover.
Regen- *zW*: **~guss▲** *m* downpour; **~mantel** *m* raincoat, mac(kintosh); **~menge** *f* rainfall; **~schauer** *m* shower (of rain); **~schirm** *m* umbrella.
Regent(in) [reˈgɛnt(ɪn)] *m(f)* regent.
Regentag *m* rainy day.
Regentropfen *m* raindrop.
Regentschaft *f* regency.
Regen- *zW*: **~wald** *m* (*GEOG*) rain forest; **~wetter** *nt*: **er macht ein Gesicht wie drei** *od* **sieben Tage ~wetter** (*umg*) he's got a face as long as a month of Sundays; **~wurm** *m* earthworm; **~zeit** *f* rainy season, rains *pl*.
Regie [reˈʒiː] *f* (*FILM etc*) direction; (*THEAT*) production; **unter der ~ von** directed *od* produced by; **~anweisung** *f* (stage) direction.
regieren [reˈgiːrən] *vt, vi* to govern, rule.
Regierung *f* government; (*Monarchie*) reign; **an die ~ kommen** to come to power.

Regierungs- *zW*: **~bezirk** *m* ≈ county (*BRIT, US*), region (*SCOT*); **~erklärung** *f* inaugural speech; (*in Großbritannien*) Queen's/King's Speech; **~sprecher** *m* government spokesman; **~vorlage** *f* government bill; **~wechsel** *m* change of government; **~zeit** *f* period in government; (*von König*) reign.
Regiment [regiˈmɛnt] (-s, -er) *nt* regiment.
Region [regiˈoːn] *f* region.
Regionalplanung [regioˈnaːlplaːnʊŋ] *f* regional planning.
Regionalprogramm *nt* (*RUNDF, TV*) regional programme (*BRIT*) *od* program (*US*).
Regisseur(in) [reʒɪˈsøːr(ɪn)] *m(f)* director; (*THEAT*) (stage) producer.
Register [reˈgɪstər] (-s, -) *nt* register; (*in Buch*) table of contents, index; **alle ~ ziehen** (*fig*) to pull out all the stops; **~führer** *m* registrar.
Registratur [regɪstraˈtuːr] *f* registry, records office.
registrieren [regɪsˈtriːrən] *vt* to register; (*umg: zur Kenntnis nehmen*) to note.
Registrierkasse *f* cash register.
Regler [ˈreːglər] (-s, -) *m* regulator, governor.
reglos [ˈreːkloːs] *adj* motionless.
regnen [ˈreːgnən] *vi unpers* to rain ♦ *vt unpers*: **es regnet Glückwünsche** congratulations are pouring in; **es regnet in Strömen** it's pouring (with rain).
regnerisch *adj* rainy.
Regress▲ [reˈgrɛs] (-es, -e) *m* (*JUR*) recourse, redress; **~anspruch** *m* (*JUR*) claim for compensation.
regsam [ˈreːkzaːm] *adj* active.
regulär [reguˈlɛːr] *adj* regular.
regulieren [reguˈliːrən] *vt* to regulate; (*COMM*) to settle; **sich von selbst ~** to be self-regulating.
Regung [ˈreːgʊŋ] *f* motion; (*Gefühl*) feeling, impulse.
regungslos *adj* motionless.
Reh [reː] (-(e)s, -e) *nt* deer; (*weiblich*) roe deer.
rehabilitieren [rehabiliˈtiːrən] *vt* to rehabilitate; (*Ruf, Ehre*) to vindicate ♦ *vr* to rehabilitate (*form*) *od* vindicate o.s.
Rehabilitierung *f* rehabilitation.
Reh- *zW*: **~bock** *m* roebuck; **~braten** *m* roast venison; **~kalb** *nt* fawn; **~kitz** *nt* fawn.
Reibach [ˈraɪbax] (-s) *m*: **einen ~ machen** (*umg*) to make a killing.
Reibe [ˈraɪbə] (-, -n) *f* grater.
Reibeisen [ˈraɪpˌaɪzən] *nt* grater.
Reibekuchen *m* (*KOCH*) ≈ potato waffle.
reiben *unreg vt* to rub; (*KOCH*) to grate.
Reiberei [raɪbəˈraɪ] *f* friction *no pl*.
Reibfläche *f* rough surface.
Reibung *f* friction.
reibungslos *adj* smooth; **~ verlaufen** to go off smoothly.
Reich [raɪç] (-(e)s, -e) *nt* empire, kingdom; (*fig*)

realm; **das Dritte** ~ the Third Reich.
reich *adj* rich ♦ *adv*: **eine** ~ **ausgestattete Bibliothek** a well-stocked library.
reichen *vi* to reach; (*genügen*) to be enough *od* sufficient ♦ *vt* to hold out; (*geben*) to pass, hand; (*anbieten*) to offer; **so weit das Auge reicht** as far as the eye can see; **jdm** ~ (*genügen*) to be enough *od* sufficient for sb; **mir reichts!** I've had enough!
reich- *zW*: ~**haltig** *adj* ample, rich; ~**lich** *adj* ample, plenty of; **R~tum (-s, -tümer)** *m* wealth; **R~weite** *f* range; **jd ist in R~weite** sb is nearby.
reif [raɪf] *adj* ripe; (*Mensch, Urteil*) mature; **für etw** ~ **sein** (*umg*) to be ready for sth.
Reif¹ (-(e)s) *m* hoarfrost.
Reif² **(-(e)s, -e)** *m* (*Ring*) ring, hoop.
Reife (-) *f* ripeness; maturity; **mittlere** ~ (*SCH*) *first public examination in secondary school*, ≈ O-Levels *pl* (*BRIT*).
Reifen (-s, -) *m* ring, hoop; (*Fahrzeug~*) tyre (*BRIT*), tire (*US*).
reifen *vi* to mature; (*Obst*) to ripen.
Reifen- *zW*: ~**druck** *m* tyre (*BRIT*) *od* tire (*US*) pressure; ~**panne** *f* puncture, flat; ~**profil** *nt* tyre (*BRIT*) *od* tire (*US*) tread; ~**schaden** *m* puncture, flat.
Reifeprüfung *f* school-leaving exam.
Reifezeugnis *nt* school-leaving certificate.
reiflich ['raɪflɪç] *adj* thorough, careful.
Reihe ['raɪə] **(-, -n)** *f* row; (*von Tagen etc*: *umg*: *Anzahl*) series *sing*; **eine ganze** ~ **(von)** (*unbestimmte Anzahl*) a whole lot (of); **der** ~ **nach** in turn; **er ist an der** ~ it's his turn; **an die** ~ **kommen** to have one's turn; **außer der** ~ out of turn; (*ausnahmsweise*) out of the usual way of things; **aus der** ~ **tanzen** (*fig*: *umg*) to be different; (*gegen Konventionen verstoßen*) to step out of line; **ich kriege heute nichts auf die** ~ I can't get my act together today.
reihen *vt* to set in a row; to arrange in series; (*Perlen*) to string.
Reihen- *zW*: ~**folge** *f* sequence; **alphabetische** ~**folge** alphabetical order; ~**haus** *nt* terraced (*BRIT*) *od* row (*US*) house; ~**untersuchung** *f* mass screening; **r~weise** *adv* (*in Reihen*) in rows; (*fig*: *in großer Anzahl*) by the dozen.
Reiher (-s, -) *m* heron.
reihum [raɪˈʊm] *adv*: **etw** ~ **gehen lassen** to pass sth around.
Reim [raɪm] **(-(e)s, -e)** *m* rhyme; **sich** *dat* **einen** ~ **auf etw** *akk* **machen** (*umg*) to make sense of sth; **r~en** *vt* to rhyme.
rein¹ [raɪn] (*umg*) *adv* = **herein, hinein.**
rein² [raɪn] *adj* pure; (*sauber*) clean ♦ *adv* purely; ~ **waschen** to clear o.s.; **das ist die** ~**ste Freude/der** ~**ste Hohn** *etc* it's pure *od* sheer joy/mockery *etc*; **etw ins R~e**

schreiben to make a fair copy of sth; **etw ins R~e bringen** to clear sth up; ~**en Tisch machen** (*fig*) to get things straight; ~ **unmöglich** (*umg*: *ganz, völlig*) absolutely impossible.
Rein- *in zW* (*COMM*) net(t).
Rein(e)machefrau *f* cleaning lady, charwoman (*BRIT*).
rein(e)weg (*umg*) *adv* completely, absolutely.
rein- *zW*: **R~fall** (*umg*) *m* let-down; (*Misserfolg*) flop; ~**fallen** *vi*: **auf jdn/etw** ~**fallen** to be taken in by sb/sth; **R~gewinn** *m* net profit; **R~heit** *f* purity; cleanness.
reinigen ['raɪnɪgən] *vt* to clean; (*Wasser*) to purify.
Reiniger (-s, -) *m* cleaner.
Reinigung *f* cleaning; purification; (*Geschäft*) cleaner's; **chemische** ~ dry-cleaning; (*Geschäft*) dry-cleaner's.
Reinigungsmittel *nt* cleansing agent.
rein- *zW*: ~**lich** *adj* clean; **R~lichkeit** *f* cleanliness; ~**rassig** *adj* pedigree; ~**reiten** *unreg vt*: **jdn** ~**reiten** to get sb into a mess; **R~schrift** *f* fair copy; **R~vermögen** *nt* net assets *pl*.
Reis¹ [raɪs] **(-es, -e)** *m* rice.
Reis² [raɪs] **(-es, -er)** *nt* twig, sprig.
Reise ['raɪzə] **(-, -n)** *f* journey; (*Schiffs~*) voyage; **Reisen** *pl* travels *pl*; **gute** ~! bon voyage!, have a good journey!; **auf** ~**n sein** to be away (travelling (*BRIT*) *od* traveling (*US*)); **er ist viel auf** ~**n** he does a lot of travelling (*BRIT*) *od* traveling (*US*); ~**andenken** *nt* souvenir; ~**apotheke** *f* first-aid kit; ~**bericht** *m* account of one's journey; (*Buch*) travel story; (*Film*) travelogue (*BRIT*), travelog (*US*); ~**büro** *nt* travel agency; ~**diplomatie** *f* shuttle diplomacy; ~**erleichterungen** *pl* easing *sing* of travel restrictions; **r~fertig** *adj* ready to start; ~**fieber** *nt* (*fig*) travel nerves *pl*; ~**führer** *m* guide(book); (*Mensch*) (travel) guide; ~**gepäck** *nt* luggage; ~**gesellschaft** *f* party of travellers (*BRIT*) *od* travelers (*US*); ~**kosten** *pl* travelling (*BRIT*) *od* traveling (*US*) expenses *pl*; ~**leiter** *m* courier; ~**lektüre** *f* reading for the journey; ~**lust** *f* wanderlust.
reisen *vi* to travel; ~ **nach** to go to.
Reisende(r) *f(m)* traveller (*BRIT*), traveler (*US*).
Reise- *zW*: ~**pass▲** *m* passport; ~**pläne** *pl* plans *pl* for a *od* the journey; ~**proviant** *m* provisions *pl* for the journey; ~**route** *f* itinerary; ~**scheck** *m* traveller's cheque (*BRIT*), traveler's check (*US*); ~**schreibmaschine** *f* portable typewriter; ~**tasche** *f* travelling (*BRIT*) *od* traveling (*US*) bag *od* case; ~**veranstalter** *m* tour operator; ~**verkehr** *m* tourist *od* holiday traffic; ~**wetter** *nt* holiday weather; ~**ziel** *nt*

destination.

Reisig ['raɪzɪç] **(-s)** *nt* brushwood.

Reißaus *m*: ~ **nehmen** to run away, flee.

Reißbrett *nt* drawing board; ~**stift** *m* drawing pin (*BRIT*), thumbtack (*US*).

reißen ['raɪsən] *unreg vt* to tear; (*ziehen*) to pull, drag; (*Witz*) to crack ♦ *vi* to tear; to pull, drag; **etw an sich** ~ to snatch sth up; (*fig*) to take sth over; **sich um etw** ~ to scramble for sth; **wenn alle Stricke** ~ (*fig: umg*) if the worst comes to the worst; *siehe auch* **hingerissen**.

Reißen *nt* (*Gewichtheben: Disziplin*) snatch; (*umg: Glieder~*) ache.

reißend *adj* (*Fluss*) torrential; (*COMM*) rapid; ~**en Absatz finden** to sell like hot cakes (*umg*).

Reißer (-s, -) (*umg*) *m* thriller; **r~isch** *adj* sensational.

Reiß- *zW*: ~**leine** *f* (*AVIAT*) ripcord; ~**nagel** *m* drawing pin (*BRIT*), thumbtack (*US*); ~**schiene** *f* T-square; ~**verschluss** ▲ *m* zip (fastener) (*BRIT*), zipper (*US*); ~**wolf** *m* shredder; **durch den** ~**wolf geben** (*Dokumente*) to shred; ~**zeug** *nt* geometry set; ~**zwecke** *f* = **Reißnagel**.

reiten ['raɪtən] *unreg vt, vi* to ride.

Reiter (-s, -) *m* rider; (*MIL*) cavalryman, trooper.

Reiterei [raɪtə'raɪ] *f* cavalry.

Reiterin *f* rider.

Reit- *zW*: ~**hose** *f* riding breeches *pl*; ~**pferd** *nt* saddle horse; ~**schule** *f* riding school; ~**stiefel** *m* riding boot; ~**turnier** *nt* horse show; ~**weg** *m* bridle path; ~**zeug** *nt* riding outfit.

Reiz [raɪts] **(-es, -e)** *m* stimulus; (*angenehm*) charm; (*Verlockung*) attraction.

reizbar *adj* irritable; **R~keit** *f* irritability.

reizen *vt* to stimulate; (*unangenehm*) to irritate; (*verlocken*) to appeal to, attract; (*KARTEN*) to bid ♦ *vi*: **zum Widerspruch** ~ to invite contradiction.

reizend *adj* charming.

Reiz- *zW*: ~**gas** *nt* tear gas, CS gas; ~**husten** *m* chesty cough; **r~los** *adj* unattractive; **r~voll** *adj* attractive; ~**wäsche** *f* sexy underwear; ~**wort** *nt* emotive word.

rekapitulieren [rekapitu'liːrən] *vt* to recapitulate.

rekeln ['reːkəln] *vr* to stretch out; (*lümmeln*) to lounge *od* loll about.

Reklamation [reklamatsi'oːn] *f* complaint.

Reklame [re'klaːmə] **(-, -n)** *f* advertising; (*Anzeige*) advertisement; **mit etw** ~ **machen** (*pej*) to show off about sth; **für etw** ~ **machen** to advertise sth; ~**trommel** *f*: **die** ~**trommel für jdn/etw rühren** (*umg*) to beat the (big) drum for sb/sth; ~**wand** *f* notice (*BRIT*) *od* bulletin (*US*) board.

reklamieren [rekla'miːrən] *vi* to complain ♦ *vt* to complain about; (*zurückfordern*) to reclaim.

rekonstruieren [rekɔnstru'iːrən] *vt* to reconstruct.

Rekonvaleszenz [rekɔnvalɛs'tsɛnts] *f* convalescence.

Rekord [re'kɔrt] **(-(e)s, -e)** *m* record; ~**leistung** *f* record performance.

Rekrut [re'kruːt] **(-en, -en)** *m* recruit.

rekrutieren [rekru'tiːrən] *vt* to recruit ♦ *vr* to be recruited.

Rektor ['rɛktɔr] *m* (*UNIV*) rector, vice-chancellor; (*SCH*) head teacher (*BRIT*), principal (*US*).

Rektorat [rɛktɔ'raːt] **(-(e)s, -e)** *nt* rectorate, vice-chancellorship; headship (*BRIT*), principalship (*US*); (*Zimmer*) rector's *etc* office.

Rektorin [rɛk'toːrɪn] *f* (*SCH*) head teacher (*BRIT*), principal (*US*).

Rel. *abk* (= *Religion*) rel.

Relais [rə'lɛː] **(-, -)** *nt* relay.

Relation [relatsi'oːn] *f* relation.

relativ [rela'tiːf] *adj* relative.

Relativität [relativi'tɛːt] *f* relativity.

Relativpronomen *nt* (*GRAM*) relative pronoun.

relevant [rele'vant] *adj* relevant.

Relevanz *f* relevance.

Relief [reli'ɛf] **(-s, -s)** *nt* relief.

Religion [religi'oːn] *f* religion.

Religions- *zW*: ~**freiheit** *f* freedom of worship; ~**lehre** *f* religious education; ~**unterricht** *m* religious education.

religiös [religi'øːs] *adj* religious.

Relikt [re'lɪkt] **(-(e)s, -e)** *nt* relic.

Reling ['reːlɪŋ] **(-, -s)** *f* (*NAUT*) rail.

Reliquie [re'liːkviə] *f* relic.

Reminiszenz [reminɪs'tsɛnts] *f* reminiscence, recollection.

Remis [rə'miː] **(-, - od -en)** *nt* (*SCHACH, SPORT*) draw.

Remittende [remɪ'tɛndə] **(-, -n)** *f* (*COMM*) return.

Remittent *m* (*FIN*) payee.

remittieren *vt* (*COMM: Waren*) to return; (*Geld*) to remit.

Remmidemmi ['remi'dɛmi] **(-s)** (*umg*) *nt* (*Krach*) row, rumpus; (*Trubel*) rave-up.

Remoulade [remu'laːdə] **(-, -n)** *f* remoulade.

rempeln ['rɛmpəln] (*umg*) *vt* to jostle, elbow; (*SPORT*) to barge into; (*foulen*) to push.

Ren [reːn, rɛn] **(-s, -s od -e)** *nt* reindeer.

Renaissance [rənɛ'sãːs] **(-, -n)** *f* (*HIST*) renaissance; (*fig*) revival, rebirth.

Rendezvous [rãde'vuː] **(-, -)** *nt* rendezvous.

Rendite [rɛn'diːtə] **(-, -n)** *f* (*FIN*) yield, return on capital.

Rennbahn *f* racecourse; (*AUT*) circuit,

racetrack.

rennen ['rɛnən] *unreg vt, vi* to run, race; **um die Wette** ~ to have a race; **R~** (**-s, -**) *nt* running; (*Wettbewerb*) race; **das R~ machen** (*lit, fig*) to win (the race).

Renner (**-s, -**) (*umg*) *m* winner, worldbeater.

Renn- *zW:* ~**fahrer** *m* racing driver (*BRIT*), race car driver (*US*); ~**pferd** *nt* racehorse; ~**platz** *m* racecourse; ~**rad** *nt* racing cycle; ~**sport** *m* racing; ~**wagen** *m* racing car (*BRIT*), race car (*US*).

renommiert [renɔ'miːrt] *adj:* ~ (**wegen**) renowned (for), famous (for).

renovieren [reno'viːrən] *vt* to renovate.

Renovierung *f* renovation.

rentabel [rɛn'taːbəl] *adj* profitable, lucrative.

Rentabilität [rɛntabili'tɛːt] *f* profitability.

Rente ['rɛntə] (**-, -n**) *f* pension.

Renten- *zW:* ~**basis** *f* annuity basis; ~**empfänger** *m* pensioner; ~**papier** *nt* (*FIN*) fixed-interest security; ~**versicherung** *f* pension scheme.

Rentier ['rɛntiːr] *nt* reindeer.

rentieren [rɛn'tiːrən] *vi, vr* to pay, be profitable; **das rentiert (sich) nicht** it's not worth it.

Rentner(in) ['rɛntnər(ɪn)] (**-s, -**) *m(f)* pensioner.

Reparation [reparatsi'oːn] *f* reparation.

Reparatur [repara'tuːr] *f* repairing; repair; **etw in** ~ **geben** to have sth repaired; **r~bedürftig** *adj* in need of repair; ~**werkstatt** *f* repair shop; (*AUT*) garage.

reparieren [repa'riːrən] *vt* to repair.

Repertoire [reperto'aːr] (**-s, -s**) *nt* repertoire.

Reportage [repɔr'taːʒə] (**-, -n**) *f* report.

Reporter(in) [re'pɔrtər(ɪn)] (**-s, -**) *m(f)* reporter, commentator.

Repräsentant(in) [reprezɛn'tant(ɪn)] *m(f)* representative.

repräsentativ [reprezɛnta'tiːf] *adj* representative; (*Geschenk etc*) prestigious; **die ~en Pflichten eines Botschafters** the social duties of an ambassador.

repräsentieren [reprezɛn'tiːrən] *vt* to represent ♦ *vi* to perform official duties.

Repressalien [reprɛ'saːliən] *pl* reprisals *pl*.

reprivatisieren [reprivati'ziːrən] *vt* to denationalize.

Reprivatisierung *f* denationalization.

Reproduktion [reprodʊktsi'oːn] *f* reproduction.

reproduzieren [reprodu'tsiːrən] *vt* to reproduce.

Reptil [rɛp'tiːl] (**-s, -ien**) *nt* reptile.

Republik [repu'bliːk] *f* republic.

Republikaner [republi'kaːnər] (**-s, -**) *m* republican.

republikanisch *adj* republican.

Requisiten *pl* (*THEAT*) props *pl*, properties *pl* (*form*).

Reservat [rezɛr'vaːt] (**-(e)s, -e**) *nt* reservation.

Reserve [re'zɛrvə] (**-, -n**) *f* reserve; **jdn aus der** ~ **locken** to bring sb out of his/her shell; ~**rad** *nt* (*AUT*) spare wheel; ~**spieler** *m* reserve; ~**tank** *m* reserve tank.

reservieren [rezɛr'viːrən] *vt* to reserve.

reserviert *adj* (*Platz, Mensch*) reserved.

Reservist [rezɛr'vɪst] *m* reservist.

Reservoir [rezɛrvo'aːr] (**-s, -e**) *nt* reservoir.

Residenz [rezi'dɛnts] *f* residence, seat.

residieren [rezi'diːrən] *vi* to reside.

Resignation [rezɪgnatsi'oːn] *f* resignation.

resignieren [rezɪ'gniːrən] *vi* to resign.

resolut [rezo'luːt] *adj* resolute.

Resolution [rezolutsi'oːn] *f* resolution; (*Bittschrift*) petition.

Resonanz [rezo'nants] *f* (*lit, fig*) resonance; ~**boden** *m* sounding board; ~**kasten** *m* soundbox.

Resopal ® [rezo'paːl] (**-s**) *nt* Formica ®.

resozialisieren [rezotsiali'ziːrən] *vt* to rehabilitate.

Resozialisierung *f* rehabilitation.

Respekt [re'spɛkt] (**-(e)s**) *m* respect; (*Angst*) fear; **bei allem** ~ (**vor jdm/etw**) with all due respect (to sb/for sth).

respektabel [rɛspɛk'taːbəl] *adj* respectable.

respektieren [rɛspɛk'tiːrən] *vt* to respect.

respektlos *adj* disrespectful.

Respektsperson *f* person commanding respect.

respektvoll *adj* respectful.

Ressentiment [rɛsãti'mãː] (**-s, -s**) *nt* resentment.

Ressort [rɛ'soːr] (**-s, -s**) *nt* department; **in das** ~ **von jdm fallen** (*lit, fig*) to be sb's department.

Ressourcen [rɛ'sʊrsən] *pl* resources *pl*.

Rest [rɛst] (**-(e)s, -e**) *m* remainder, rest; (*Über~*) remains *pl*; **Reste** *pl* (*COMM*) remnants *pl*; **das hat mir den** ~ **gegeben** (*umg*) that finished me off.

Restaurant [rɛsto'rãː] (**-s, -s**) *nt* restaurant.

Restauration [rɛstauratsi'oːn] *f* restoration.

restaurieren [rɛstau'riːrən] *vt* to restore.

Restaurierung *f* restoration.

Rest- *zW:* ~**betrag** *m* remainder, outstanding sum; **r~lich** *adj* remaining; **r~los** *adj* complete; ~**posten** *m* (*COMM*) remaining stock.

Resultat [rezul'taːt] (**-(e)s, -e**) *nt* result.

Retorte [re'tɔrtə] (**-, -n**) *f* retort; **aus der** ~ (*umg*) synthetic.

Retortenbaby *nt* test-tube baby.

retour [re'tuːr] *adv* (*veraltet*) back.

Retouren *pl* (*Waren*) returns *pl*.

retten ['rɛtən] *vt* to save, rescue ♦ *vr* to escape; **bist du noch zu** ~? (*umg*) are you out of your mind?; **sich vor etw** *dat* **nicht mehr** ~ **können** (*fig*) to be swamped with sth.

Retter(in) (**-s, -**) *m(f)* rescuer, saviour (*BRIT*), savior (*US*).

Rettich ['rɛtɪç] (**-s, -e**) *m* radish.

Rettung *f* rescue; (*Hilfe*) help; **seine letzte ~** his last hope.

Rettungs- *zW:* **~aktion** *f* rescue operation; **~boot** *nt* lifeboat; **~dienst** *m* rescue service; **~gürtel** *m* lifebelt, life preserver (*US*); **r~los** *adj* hopeless; **~ring** *m* = **Rettungsgürtel**; **~schwimmer** *m* lifesaver; (*am Strand*) lifeguard; **~wagen** *m* ambulance.

Return-Taste [ri'tø:rntastə] *f* (*COMPUT*) return key.

retuschieren [retu'ʃiːrən] *vt* (*PHOT*) to retouch.

Reue ['rɔyə] (**-**) *f* remorse; (*Bedauern*) regret.

reuen *vt:* **es reut ihn** he regrets it, he is sorry about it.

reuig ['rɔyɪç] *adj* penitent.

reumütig *adj* remorseful; (*Sünder*) contrite.

Reuse ['rɔyzə] (**-, -n**) *f* fish trap.

Revanche [re'vãː∫ə] (**-, -n**) *f* revenge; (*SPORT*) return match.

revanchieren [revã'ʃiːrən] *vr* (*sich rächen*) to get one's own back, have one's revenge; (*erwidern*) to reciprocate, return the compliment.

Revers [re'vɛːr] (**-, -**) *nt or m* lapel.

revidieren [revi'diːrən] *vt* to revise; (*COMM*) to audit.

Revier [re'viːr] (**-s, -e**) *nt* district; (*MIN:* *Kohlen~*) (coal)mine; (*Jagd~*) preserve; (*Polizei~*) police station, station house (*US*); (*Dienstbereich*) beat (*BRIT*), precinct (*US*); (*MIL*) sick bay.

Revision [revizi'oːn] *f* revision; (*COMM*) auditing; (*JUR*) appeal.

Revisionsverhandlung *f* appeal hearing.

Revisor [re'viːzɔr] (**-s, -en**) *m* (*COMM*) auditor.

Revolte [re'vɔltə] (**-, -n**) *f* revolt.

Revolution [revolutsi'oːn] *f* revolution.

revolutionär [revolutsio'nɛːr] *adj* revolutionary.

Revolutionär(in) [revolutsio'nɛːr(ɪn)] (**-s, -e**) *m(f)* revolutionary.

revolutionieren [revolutsio'niːrən] *vt* to revolutionize.

Revoluzzer [revo'lutsər] (**-s, -**) (*pej*) *m* would-be revolutionary.

Revolver [re'vɔlvər] (**-s, -**) *m* revolver.

Revue [rə'vyː] (**-, -n**) *f:* **etw ~ passieren lassen** (*fig*) to pass sth in review.

Reykjavik ['raɪkjaviːk] (**-s**) *nt* Reykjavik.

Rezensent [retsɛn'zɛnt] *m* reviewer, critic.

rezensieren [retsɛn'ziːrən] *vt* to review.

Rezension *f* review.

Rezept [re'tsɛpt] (**-(e)s, -e**) *nt* (*KOCH*) recipe; (*MED*) prescription.

Rezeption [retsɛptsi'oːn] *f* (*von Hotel:* *Empfang*) reception.

rezeptpflichtig *adj* available only on prescription.

Rezession [retsɛsi'oːn] *f* (*FIN*) recession.

rezitieren [retsi'tiːrən] *vt* to recite.

R-Gespräch ['ɛrgəʃprɛːç] *nt* (*TEL*) reverse charge call (*BRIT*), collect call (*US*).

Rh *abk* (= *Rhesus(faktor) positiv*) Rh positive.

rh *abk* (= *Rhesus(faktor) negativ*) Rh negative.

Rhabarber [ra'barbər] (**-s**) *m* rhubarb.

Rhein [raɪn] (**-(e)s**) *m* Rhine.

rhein. *abk* = **rheinisch**.

Rheingau *m* wine-growing area along the Rhine.

Rheinhessen *nt* wine-growing area along the Rhine.

rheinisch *adj attrib* Rhenish, Rhineland.

Rheinland *nt* Rhineland.

Rheinländer(in) *m(f)* Rhinelander.

Rheinland-Pfalz *nt* Rhineland-Palatinate.

Rhesusfaktor ['reːzusfaktɔr] *m* rhesus factor.

Rhetorik [re'toːrɪk] *f* rhetoric.

rhetorisch [re'toːrɪʃ] *adj* rhetorical.

Rheuma ['rɔyma] (**-s**) *nt* rheumatism.

Rheumatismus [rɔyma'tɪsmʊs] *m* rheumatism.

Rhinozeros [ri'noːtserɔs] (**- od -ses, -se**) *nt* rhinoceros; (*umg: Dummkopf*) fool.

Rhld. *abk* = **Rheinland**.

Rhodesien [ro'deːziən] (**-s**) *nt* Rhodesia.

Rhodos ['roːdɔs] (**-**) *nt* Rhodes.

rhythmisch ['rytmɪʃ] *adj* rythmical.

Rhythmus *m* rhythm.

RIAS ['riːas] (**-**) *m abk* (= *Rundfunk im amerikanischen Sektor (Berlin)*) broadcasting station in the former American sector of Berlin.

Richtantenne ['rɪçt|antɛnə] (**-, -n**) *f* directional aerial (*bes BRIT*) *od* antenna.

richten ['rɪçtən] *vt* to direct; (*Waffe*) to aim; (*einstellen*) to adjust; (*instand setzen*) to repair; (*zurechtmachen*) to prepare, get ready; (*adressieren: Briefe, Anfragen*) to address; (*Bitten, Forderungen*) to make; (*in Ordnung bringen*) to do, fix; (*bestrafen*) to pass judgement on ♦ *vr:* **sich ~ nach** to go by; **~ an** +*akk* to direct at; (*fig*) to direct to; (*Briefe etc*) to address to; (*Bitten etc*) to make to; **~ auf** +*akk* to aim at; **wir ~ uns ganz nach unseren Kunden** we are guided entirely by our customers' wishes.

Richter(in) (**-s, -**) *m(f)* judge; **sich zum ~ machen** (*fig*) to set (o.s.) up in judgement; **r~lich** *adj* judicial.

Richtgeschwindigkeit *f* recommended speed.

richtig *adj* right, correct; (*echt*) proper ♦ *adv* correctly, right; (*umg: sehr*) really; **der/die R~e** the right one *od* person; **das R~e** the right thing; **die Uhr geht ~** the clock is

right; ~ **stellen** to correct; R~**keit** *f*
correctness; **das hat schon seine R~keit** it's
right enough; R~**stellung** *f* correction,
rectification.

Richt- *zW*: ~**linie** *f* guideline; ~**preis** *m*
recommended price; ~**schnur** *f* (*fig*:
Grundsatz) guiding principle.

Richtung *f* direction; (*Tendenz*) tendency,
orientation; **in jeder** ~ each way.

richtungweisend *adj*: ~ **sein** to point the
way (ahead).

rieb *etc* [riːp] *vb siehe* **reiben**.

riechen ['riːçən] *unreg vt, vi* to smell; **an etw** *dat*
~ to smell sth; **es riecht nach Gas** there's a
smell of gas; **ich kann das/ihn nicht** ~ (*umg*)
I can't stand it/him; **das konnte ich doch
nicht** ~! (*umg*) how was I (supposed to)
know?

Riecher (-s, -) *m*: **einen guten** *od* **den richtigen**
~ **für etw haben** (*umg*) to have a nose for
sth.

Ried [riːt] (-(e)s, -e) *nt* reed; (*Moor*) marsh.

rief *etc* [riːf] *vb siehe* **rufen**.

Riege ['riːgə] (-, -n) *f* team, squad.

Riegel ['riːgəl] (-s, -) *m* bolt, bar; **einer Sache**
dat **einen** ~ **vorschieben** (*fig*) to clamp down
on sth.

Riemen ['riːmən] (-s, -) *m* strap; (*Gürtel, TECH*)
belt; (*NAUT*) oar; **sich am** ~ **reißen** (*fig*: *umg*)
to get a grip on o.s.; ~**antrieb** *m* belt drive.

Riese ['riːzə] (-n, -n) *m* giant.

rieseln *vi* to trickle; (*Schnee*) to fall gently.

Riesen- *zW*: ~**erfolg** *m* enormous success;
~**gebirge** *nt* (*GEOG*) Sudeten Mountains *pl*;
r~groß *adj*, **r~haft** *adj* colossal, gigantic,
huge; ~**rad** *nt* big *od* Ferris wheel; ~**schritt**
m: **sich mit** ~**schritten nähern** (*fig*) to be
drawing on apace; ~**slalom** *m* (*SKI*) giant
slalom.

riesig ['riːzɪç] *adj* enormous, huge, vast.

Riesin *f* giantess.

riet *etc* [riːt] *vb siehe* **raten**.

Riff [rɪf] (-(e)s, -e) *nt* reef.

rigoros [rigo'roːs] *adj* rigorous.

Rille ['rɪlə] (-, -n) *f* groove.

Rind [rɪnt] (-(e)s, -er) *nt* ox; (*Kuh*) cow; (*KOCH*)
beef; **Rinder** *pl* cattle *pl*; **vom** ~ beef.

Rinde ['rɪndə] (-, -n) *f* rind; (*Baum*~) bark;
(*Brot*~) crust.

Rinderbraten *m* roast beef.

Rinderwahn ['rɪndərvaːn] *m* mad cow disease.

Rindfleisch *nt* beef.

Rindvieh *nt* cattle *pl*; (*umg*) blockhead, stupid
oaf.

Ring [rɪŋ] (-(e)s, -e) *m* ring; ~**buch** *nt* ring
binder.

ringeln ['rɪŋəln] *vt* (*Pflanze*) to (en)twine;
(*Schwanz etc*) to curl ♦ *vr* to go curly, curl;
(*Rauch*) to curl up(wards).

Ringelnatter *f* grass snake.

Ringeltaube *f* wood pigeon.

ringen *unreg vi* to wrestle; **nach** *od* **um etw** ~
(*streben*) to struggle for sth; R~ (-s) *nt*
wrestling.

Ringer (-s, -) *m* wrestler.

Ring- *zW*: ~**finger** *m* ring finger; **r~förmig** *adj*
ring-shaped; ~**kampf** *m* wrestling bout;
~**richter** *m* referee.

rings *adv*: ~ **um** round; ~**herum** *adv* round
about.

Ringstraße *f* ring road.

ringsum(her) [rɪŋs'ʊm, ˌrɪŋsʊm'heːr] *adv*
(*rundherum*) round about; (*überall*) all round.

Rinne ['rɪnə] (-, -n) *f* gutter, drain.

rinnen *unreg vi* to run, trickle.

Rinnsal (-s, -e) *nt* trickle of water.

Rinnstein *m* gutter.

Rippchen ['rɪpçən] *nt* small rib; cutlet.

Rippe ['rɪpə] (-, -n) *f* rib.

Rippen- *zW*: ~**fellentzündung** *f* pleurisy;
~**speer** *m od nt* (*KOCH*): **Kasseler** ~**speer**
slightly cured pork spare rib; ~**stoß** *m* dig
in the ribs.

Risiko ['riːziko] (-s, -s *od* Risiken) *nt* risk;
r~behaftet *adj* fraught with risk;
~**investition** *f* sunk cost.

riskant [rɪs'kant] *adj* risky, hazardous.

riskieren [rɪs'kiːrən] *vt* to risk.

riss *etc*▲ [rɪs] *vb siehe* **reißen**.

Riss▲ (-es, -e) *m* tear; (*in Mauer, Tasse etc*)
crack; (*in Haut*) scratch; (*TECH*) design.

rissig ['rɪsɪç] *adj* torn; cracked; scratched.

ritt *etc* [rɪt] *vb siehe* **reiten**.

Ritt (-(e)s, -e) *m* ride.

Ritter (-s, -) *m* knight; **jdn zum** ~ **schlagen** to
knight sb; **arme** ~ *pl* (*KOCH*) sweet French
toast, made with bread soaked in milk;
r~lich *adj* chivalrous; ~**schlag** *m* knighting;
~**tum** (-s) *nt* chivalry; ~**zeit** *f* age of
chivalry.

rittlings *adv* astride.

Ritual [ritu'aːl] (-s, -e *od* -ien) *nt* (*lit, fig*) ritual.

rituell [ritu'ɛl] *adj* ritual.

Ritus ['riːtʊs] (-, Riten) *m* rite.

Ritze ['rɪtsə] (-, -n) *f* crack, chink.

ritzen *vt* to scratch; **die Sache ist geritzt**
(*umg*) it's all fixed up.

Rivale [ri'vaːlə] (-n, -n) *m*, **Rivalin** *f* rival.

rivalisieren [rivali'ziːrən] *vi*: **mit jdm** ~ to
compete with sb.

Rivalität [rivali'tɛːt] *f* rivalry.

Riviera [rivi'eːra] (-) *f* Riviera.

Rizinusöl ['riːtsinʊsˌøːl] *nt* castor oil.

r.-k. *abk* (= *römisch-katholisch*) R.C.

Robbe ['rɔbə] (-, -n) *f* seal.

robben ['rɔbən] *vi* (*Hilfsverb sein*: *auch MIL*) to
crawl (*using elbows*).

Robbenfang *m* seal hunting.

Robe ['roːbə] (-, -n) *f* robe.

Roboter ['rɔbɔtər] (-s, -) *m* robot; ~**technik** *f*

robotics *sing.*
Robotik ['robotɪk] *f* robotics *sing.*
robust [ro'bʊst] *adj* (*Mensch, Gesundheit*) robust; (*Material*) tough.
roch *etc* [rɔx] *vb siehe* **riechen.**
Rochade [rɔ'xaːdə] (-, -n) *f* (*SCHACH*): **die kleine/große** ~ castling king's side/queen's side.
röcheln ['ʀœçəln] *vi* to wheeze; (*Sterbender*) to give the death rattle.
Rock¹ [rɔk] (-(e)s, ̈e) *m* skirt; (*Jackett*) jacket; (*Uniform*~) tunic.
Rock² [rɔk] (-(s), -(s)) *m* (*MUS*) rock; ~**musik** *f* rock music.
Rockzipfel *m*: **an Mutters** ~ **hängen** (*umg*) to cling to (one's) mother's skirts.
Rodel ['roːdəl] (-s, -) *m* toboggan; ~**bahn** *f* toboggan run.
rodeln *vi* to toboggan.
roden ['roːdən] *vt, vi* to clear.
Rogen ['roːgən] (-s, -) *m* roe.
Roggen ['rɔgən] (-s, -) *m* rye; ~**brot** *nt* rye bread; (*Vollkornbrot*) black bread.
roh [roː] *adj* raw; (*Mensch*) coarse, crude; ~**e Gewalt** brute force; **R**~**bau** *m* shell of a building; **R**~**eisen** *nt* pig iron; **R**~**fassung** *f* rough draft; **R**~**kost** *f* raw fruit and vegetables *pl*; **R**~**ling** *m* ruffian; **R**~**material** *nt* raw material; **R**~**öl** *nt* crude oil.
Rohr [roːr] (-(e)s, -e) *nt* pipe, tube; (*BOT*) cane; (*Schilf*) reed; (*Gewehr*~) barrel; ~**bruch** *m* burst pipe.
Röhre ['røːrə] (-, -n) *f* tube, pipe; (*RUNDF etc*) valve; (*Back*~) oven.
Rohr- *zW*: ~**geflecht** *nt* wickerwork; ~**leger** (-s, -) *m* plumber; ~**leitung** *f* pipeline; ~**post** *f* pneumatic post; ~**spatz** *m*: **schimpfen wie ein** ~**spatz** (*umg*) to curse and swear; ~**stock** *m* cane; ~**stuhl** *m* basket chair; ~**zucker** *m* cane sugar.
Rohseide *f* raw silk.
Rohstoff *m* raw material.
Rokoko ['rɔkoko] (-s) *nt* rococo.
Rolladen△ *m siehe* **Rollladen.**
Rollbahn *f* (*AVIAT*) runway.
Rolle ['rɔlə] (-, -n) *f* roll; (*THEAT, SOZIOLOGIE*) role; (*Garn*~ *etc*) reel, spool; (*Walze*) roller; (*Wäsche*~) mangle, wringer; **bei** *od* **in etw** *dat* **eine** ~ **spielen** to play a part in sth; **aus der** ~ **fallen** (*fig*) to forget o.s.; **keine** ~ **spielen** not to matter.
rollen *vi* to roll; (*AVIAT*) to taxi ♦ *vt* to roll; (*Wäsche*) to mangle, put through the wringer; **den Stein ins R**~ **bringen** (*fig*) to start the ball rolling.
Rollen- *zW*: ~**besetzung** *f* (*THEAT*) cast; ~**konflikt** *m* (*PSYCH*) role conflict; ~**spiel** *nt* role-play; ~**tausch** *m* exchange of roles; (*SOZIOLOGIE*) role reversal.
Roller (-s, -) *m* scooter; (*Welle*) roller.

Roll- *zW*: ~**feld** *nt* runway; ~**kragen** *m* roll *od* polo neck; ~**laden**▲ *m* shutter; ~**mops** *m* pickled herring.
Rollo ['rɔlo] (-, -s) *nt* (roller) blind.
Roll- *zW*: ~**schrank** *m* roll-fronted cupboard; ~**schuh** *m* roller skate; ~**schuhlaufen** *nt* roller skating; ~**splitt** *m* grit; ~**stuhl** *m* wheelchair; ~**treppe** *f* escalator.
Rom [roːm] (-s) *nt* Rome; **das sind Zustände wie im alten** ~ (*umg: unmoralisch*) it's disgraceful; (: *primitiv*) it's medieval (*umg*).
röm. *abk* = **römisch.**
Roman [ro'maːn] (-s, -e) *m* novel; (**jdm) einen ganzen** ~ **erzählen** (*umg*) to give (sb) a long rigmarole; ~**heft** *nt* pulp novel.
romanisch *adj* (*Volk, Sprache*) Romance; (*KUNST*) Romanesque.
Romanistik [roma'nɪstɪk] *f* (*UNIV*) Romance languages and literature.
Romanschreiber *m* novelist.
Romanschriftsteller *m* novelist.
Romantik [ro'mantɪk] *f* romanticism.
Romantiker(in) (-s, -) *m(f)* romanticist.
romantisch *adj* romantic.
Romanze [ro'mantsə] (-, -n) *f* romance.
Römer ['røːmər] (-s, -) *m* wineglass; (*Mensch*) Roman; ~**topf** ® *m* (*KOCH*) ≈ (chicken) brick.
römisch ['røːmɪʃ] *adj* Roman; ~-**katholisch** *adj* Roman Catholic.
röm.-kath. *abk* (= *römisch-katholisch*) R.C.
Rommé, Rommee▲ [rɔ'meː] (-s, -s) *nt* rummy.
röntgen ['rœntgən] *vt* to X-ray; **R**~**aufnahme** *f* X-ray; **R**~**bild** *nt* X-ray; **R**~**strahlen** *pl* X-rays *pl.*
rosa ['roːza] *adj inv* pink, rose(-coloured).
Rose ['roːzə] (-, -n) *f* rose.
Rosé [ro'zeː] (-s, -s) *m* rosé.
Rosenkohl *m* Brussels sprouts *pl.*
Rosenkranz *m* rosary.
Rosenmontag *m* Monday of Shrovetide; *siehe auch* **Karneval.**
Rosette [ro'zɛtə] *f* rosette.
rosig ['roːzɪç] *adj* rosy.
Rosine [ro'ziːnə] *f* raisin; (**große**) ~**n im Kopf haben** (*umg*) to have big ideas.
Rosmarin ['roːsmariːn] (-s) *m* rosemary.
Ross▲ [rɔs] (-es, -e) *nt* horse, steed; **auf dem hohen** ~ **sitzen** (*fig*) to be on one's high horse; ~**kastanie** *f* horse chestnut; ~**kur** (*umg*) *f* kill-or-cure remedy.
Rost [rɔst] (-(e)s, -e) *m* rust; (*Gitter*) grill, gridiron; (*Bett*~) springs *pl*; ~**braten** *m* roast(ed) meat, roast; ~**bratwurst** *f* grilled *od* barbecued sausage.
rosten *vi* to rust.
rösten ['røːstən] *vt* to roast; (*Brot*) to toast.
rostfrei *adj* (*Stahl*) stainless.
rostig *adj* rusty.

Röstkartoffeln *pl* fried potatoes *pl*.
Rostschutz *m* rustproofing.
rot [roːt] *adj* red; ~ **werden, einen ~en Kopf bekommen** to blush, go red; **die R~e Armee** the Red Army; **das R~e Kreuz** the Red Cross; **das R~e Meer** the Red Sea.
Rotation [rotatsi'oːn] *f* rotation.
rot- *zW:* ~**bäckig** *adj* red-cheeked; **R~barsch** *m* rosefish; ~**blond** *adj* strawberry blond.
Röte ['røːtə] (-) *f* redness.
Röteln *pl* German measles *sing*.
röten *vt, vr* to redden.
rothaarig *adj* red-haired.
rotieren [ro'tiːrən] *vi* to rotate.
Rot- *zW:* ~**käppchen** *nt* Little Red Riding Hood; ~**kehlchen** *nt* robin; ~**kohl** *m* red cabbage; ~**kraut** *nt* red cabbage; **r~sehen** (*umg*) *unreg vi* to see red, to become angry; ~**stift** *m* red pencil; ~**wein** *m* red wine.
Rotz [rɔts] (-es, -e) (*umg*) *m* snot; **r~frech** (*umg*) *adj* cocky; **r~näsig** (*umg*) *adj* snotty-nosed.
Rouge [ruːʒ] (-s, -s) *nt* rouge.
Roulade [ru'laːdə] (-, -n) *f* (*KOCH*) beef olive.
Roulett(e) [ru'lɛt(ə)] (-s, -s) *nt* roulette.
Route ['ruːtə] (-, -n) *f* route.
Routine [ru'tiːnə] *f* experience; (*Gewohnheit*) routine.
routiniert [ruti'niːɐt] *adj* experienced.
Rowdy ['raʊdɪ] (-s, -s) *m* hooligan; (*zerstörerisch*) vandal; (*lärmend*) rowdy (type).
Ruanda [ru'anda] *nt* Rwanda.
ruandisch *adj* Rwandan.
rubbeln ['rʊbəln] (*umg*) *vt, vi* to rub.
Rübe ['ryːbə] (-, -n) *f* turnip; **Gelbe ~** carrot; **Rote ~** beetroot (*BRIT*), beet (*US*).
Rübenzucker *m* beet sugar.
Rubin [ru'biːn] (-s, -e) *m* ruby.
Rubrik [ru'briːk] *f* heading; (*Spalte*) column.
Ruck [rʊk] (-(e)s, -e) *m* jerk, jolt; **sich** *dat* **einen ~ geben** (*fig: umg*) to make an effort.
ruck *adv:* **das geht ~, zuck** it won't take a second.
Rückantwort *f* reply, answer; **um ~ wird gebeten** please reply.
ruckartig *adj:* **er stand ~ auf** he shot to his feet.
Rück- *zW:* ~**besinnung** *f* recollection; **r~bezüglich** *adj* reflexive; ~**blende** *f* flashback; **r~blenden** *vi* to flash back; ~**blick** *m:* **im ~blick auf etw** *akk* looking back on sth; **r~blickend** *adj* retrospective ♦ *adv* in retrospect; **r~datieren** *vt* to backdate.
Rücken (-s, -) *m* back; (*Berg~*) ridge; **jdm in den ~ fallen** (*fig*) to stab sb in the back.
rücken *vt, vi* to move.
Rücken- *zW:* ~**deckung** *f* backing; ~**lage** *f* supine position; ~**lehne** *f* back (of chair); ~**mark** *nt* spinal cord; ~**schwimmen** *nt*

backstroke; ~**stärkung** *f* (*fig*) moral support; ~**wind** *m* following wind.
Rück- *zW:* ~**erstattung** *f* return, restitution; ~**fahrkarte** *f* return ticket (*BRIT*), round-trip ticket (*US*); ~**fahrt** *f* return journey; ~**fall** *m* relapse; **r~fällig** *adj* relapsed; **r~fällig werden** to relapse; ~**flug** *m* return flight; ~**frage** *f* question; **nach ~frage bei der zuständigen Behörde ...** after checking this with the appropriate authority ...; **r~fragen** *vi* to inquire; (*nachprüfen*) to check; ~**führung** *f* (*von Menschen*) repatriation, return; ~**gabe** *f* return; **gegen ~gabe** (+ *gen*) on return (of); ~**gang** *m* decline, fall; **r~gängig** *adj:* **etw r~gängig machen** (*widerrufen*) to undo sth; (*Bestellung*) to cancel sth; ~**gewinnung** *f* recovery; (*von Land, Gebiet*) reclaiming; (*aus verbrauchten Stoffen*) recycling.
Rückgrat *nt* spine, backbone.
Rück- *zW:* ~**griff** *m* recourse; ~**halt** *m* backing; (*Einschränkung*) reserve; **r~haltlos** *adj* unreserved; ~**hand** *f* (*SPORT*) backhand; **r~kaufbar** *adj* redeemable; ~**kehr** (-, -en) *f* return; ~**koppelung** *f* feedback; ~**lage** *f* reserve, savings *pl*; ~**lauf** *m* reverse running; (*beim Tonband*) rewind; (*von Maschinenteil*) return travel; **r~läufig** *adj* declining, falling; **eine r~läufige Entwicklung** a decline; ~**licht** *nt* rear light; **r~lings** *adv* from behind; (*rückwärts*) backwards; ~**meldung** *f* (*UNIV*) reregistration; ~**nahme** (-, -n) *f* taking back; ~**porto** *nt* return postage; ~**reise** *f* return journey; (*NAUT*) home voyage; ~**ruf** *m* recall.
Rucksack ['rʊkzak] *m* rucksack.
Rück- *zW:* ~**schau** *f* reflection; **r~schauend** *adj* = **rückblickend**; ~**schlag** *m* setback; ~**schluss**▲ *m* conclusion; ~**schritt** *m* retrogression; **r~schrittlich** *adj* reactionary; (*Entwicklung*) retrograde; ~**seite** *f* back; (*von Münze etc*) reverse; **siehe ~seite** see over(leaf); **r~setzen** *vt* (*COMPUT*) to reset.
Rücksicht *f* consideration; ~ **nehmen auf** +*akk* to show consideration for; ~**nahme** *f* consideration.
rücksichtslos *adj* inconsiderate; (*Fahren*) reckless; (*unbarmherzig*) ruthless.
Rücksichtslosigkeit *f* lack of consideration; (*beim Fahren*) recklessness; (*Unbarmherzigkeit*) ruthlessness.
rücksichtsvoll *adj* considerate.
Rück- *zW:* ~**sitz** *m* back seat; ~**spiegel** *m* (*AUT*) rear-view mirror; ~**spiel** *nt* return match; ~**sprache** *f* further discussion *od* talk; ~**sprache mit jdm nehmen** to confer with sb; ~**stand** *m* arrears *pl*; (*Verzug*) delay; **r~ständig** *adj* backward, out-of-date; (*Zahlungen*) in arrears; ~**stau** *m* (*AUT*)

tailback (*BRIT*), line of cars; ~**stoß** *m* recoil;
~**strahler** (**-s,** **-**) *m* rear reflector; ~**strom** *m*
(*von Menschen, Fahrzeugen*) return; ~**taste** *f*
(*an Schreibmaschine*) backspace key; ~**tritt** *m*
resignation; ~**trittbremse** *f* backpedal
brake; ~**trittsklausel** *f* (*Vertrag*) escape
clause; ~**vergütung** *f* repayment; (*COMM*)
refund; **r~versichern** *vt, vi* to reinsure ♦ *vr* to
check (up *od* back); ~**versicherung** *f*
reinsurance; **r~wärtig** *adj* rear; **r~wärts** *adv*
backward(s), back; ~**wärtsgang** *m* (*AUT*)
reverse gear; **im ~wärtsgang fahren** to
reverse; ~**weg** *m* return journey, way back;
r~wirkend *adj* retroactive; ~**wirkung** *f*
repercussion; **eine Zahlung mit ~wirkung
vom ...** a payment backdated to ...; **eine
Gesetzesänderung mit ~wirkung vom ...** an
amendment made retrospective to ...;
~**zahlung** *f* repayment; ~**zieher** (*umg*) *m*:
einen ~zieher machen to back out; ~**zug** *m*
retreat; ~**zugsgefecht** *nt* (*MIL, fig*) rearguard
action.

rüde ['ry:də] *adj* blunt, gruff.

Rüde (**-n, -n**) *m* male dog.

Rudel ['ru:dəl] (**-s, -**) *nt* pack; (*von Hirschen*)
herd.

Ruder ['ru:dər] (**-s, -**) *nt* oar; (*Steuer*) rudder;
das ~ fest in der Hand haben (*fig*) to be in
control of the situation; ~**boot** *nt* rowing
boat; ~**er** (**-s, -**) *m* rower, oarsman.

rudern *vt, vi* to row; **mit den Armen ~** (*fig*) to
flail one's arms about.

Ruf [ru:f] (**-(e)s, -e**) *m* call, cry; (*Ansehen*)
reputation; (*UNIV: Berufung*) offer of a chair.

rufen *unreg vt, vi* to call; (*aus~*) to cry; **um Hilfe
~** to call for help; **das kommt mir wie
gerufen** that's just what I needed.

Rüffel ['ryfəl] (**-s, -**) (*umg*) *m* telling-off,
ticking-off.

Ruf- *zW:* ~**mord** *m* character assassination;
~**name** *m* usual (first) name; ~**nummer** *f*
(tele)phone number; ~**säule** *f* (*für Taxi*)
telephone; (*an Autobahn*) emergency
telephone; ~**zeichen** *nt* (*RUNDF*) call sign;
(*TEL*) ringing tone.

Rüge ['ry:gə] (**-, -n**) *f* reprimand, rebuke.

rügen *vt* to reprimand.

Ruhe ['ru:ə] (**-**) *f* rest; (*Ungestörtheit*) peace,
quiet; (*Gelassenheit, Stille*) calm; (*Schweigen*)
silence; ~**!** be quiet!, silence!; **angenehme
~!** sleep well!; ~ **bewahren** to stay cool *od*
calm; **das lässt ihm keine ~** he can't stop
thinking about it; **sich zur ~ setzen** to
retire; **die ~ weghaben** (*umg*) to be
unflappable; **immer mit der ~** (*umg*) don't
panic; **die letzte ~ finden** (*liter*) to be laid to
rest; ~**lage** *f* (*von Mensch*) reclining position;
(*MED: bei Bruch*) immobile position; **r~los** *adj*
restless.

ruhen *vi* to rest; (*Verkehr*) to cease; (*Arbeit*) to

stop, cease; (*Waffen*) to be laid down;
(*begraben sein*) to lie, be buried.

Ruhe- *zW:* ~**pause** *f* break; ~**platz** *m* resting
place; ~**stand** *m* retirement; ~**stätte** *f*: **letzte
~stätte** final resting place; ~**störung** *f*
breach of the peace; ~**tag** *m* closing day.

ruhig ['ru:ɪç] *adj* quiet; (*bewegungslos*) still;
(*Hand*) steady; (*gelassen, friedlich*) calm;
(*Gewissen*) clear; **tu das ~** feel free to do
that; **etw ~ mit ansehen** (*gleichgültig*) to
stand by and watch sth; **du könntest ~ mal
etwas für mich tun!** it's about time you did
something for me!

Ruhm [ru:m] (**-(e)s**) *m* fame, glory.

rühmen ['ry:mən] *vt* to praise ♦ *vr* to boast.

rühmlich *adj* praiseworthy; (*Ausnahme*)
notable.

ruhmlos *adj* inglorious.

ruhmreich *adj* glorious.

Ruhr [ru:r] (**-**) *f* dysentery.

Rührei ['ry:r|aɪ] *nt* scrambled egg.

rühren *vt* (*lit, fig*) to move, stir (*auch KOCH*) ♦ *vr*
(*lit, fig*) to move, stir ♦ *vi*: ~ **von** to come *od*
stem from; ~ **an** +*akk* to touch; (*fig*) to touch
on.

rührend *adj* touching, moving; **das ist ~ von
Ihnen** that is sweet of you.

Ruhrgebiet *nt* Ruhr (area).

rührig *adj* active, lively.

rührselig *adj* sentimental, emotional.

Rührung *f* emotion.

Ruin [ru'i:n] (**-s**) *m* ruin; **vor dem ~ stehen** to
be on the brink *od* verge of ruin.

Ruine (**-, -n**) *f* (*lit, fig*) ruin.

ruinieren [rui'ni:rən] *vt* to ruin.

rülpsen ['rylpsən] *vi* to burp, belch.

Rum [rʊm] (**-s, -s**) *m* rum.

rum (*umg*) *adv* = **herum**.

Rumäne [ru'mɛ:nə] (**-n, -n**) *m* Romanian.

Rumänien (**-s**) *nt* Romania.

Rumänin *f* Romanian.

rumänisch *adj* Romanian.

rumfuhrwerken ['rʊmfu:rvɛrkən] (*umg*) *vt* to
bustle around.

Rummel ['rʊməl] (**-s**) (*umg*) *m* hurly-burly;
(*Jahrmarkt*) fair; ~**platz** *m* fairground, fair.

rumoren [ru'mo:rən] *vi* to be noisy, make a
noise.

Rumpelkammer ['rʊmpəlkamər] *f* junk room.

rumpeln *vi* to rumble; (*holpern*) to jolt.

Rumpf [rʊmpf] (**-(e)s, -̈e**) *m* trunk, torso;
(*AVIAT*) fuselage; (*NAUT*) hull.

rümpfen ['rympfən] *vt* (*Nase*) to turn up.

Rumtopf *m* soft fruit in rum.

rund [rʊnt] *adj* round ♦ *adv* (*etwa*) around;
~ **um etw** round sth; **jetzt gehts ~** (*umg*)
this is where the fun starts; **wenn er das
erfährt, gehts ~** (*umg*) there'll be a to-do
when he finds out; **R~bogen** *m* Norman *od*
Romanesque arch; **R~brief** *m* circular.

Runde ['rʊndə] (-, -n) f round; (in Rennen) lap; (Gesellschaft) circle; **die ~ machen** to do the rounds; (herumgegeben werden) to be passed round; **über die ~n kommen** (SPORT, fig) to pull through; **eine ~ spendieren** od **schmeißen** (umg: Getränke) to stand a round.

runden vt to make round ♦ vr (fig) to take shape.

rund- zW: **~erneuert** adj (Reifen) remoulded (BRIT), remolded (US); **R~fahrt** f (round) trip; **R~frage** f: **R~frage (unter** +dat) survey (of).

Rundfunk ['rʊntfʊŋk] (-(e)s) m broadcasting; (bes Hörfunk) radio; (~anstalt) broadcasting corporation; **im ~** on the radio; **~anstalt** f broadcasting corporation; **~empfang** m reception; **~gebühr** f licence (BRIT), license (US); **~gerät** nt radio set; **~sendung** f broadcast, radio programme (BRIT) od program (US).

Rund- zW: **~gang** m (Spaziergang) walk; (von Wachmann) rounds pl; (von Briefträger etc) round; (zur Besichtigung): **~gang (durch)** tour (of); **r~heraus** adv straight out, bluntly; **r~herum** adv all round; (fig: umg: völlig) totally; **r~lich** adj plump, rounded; **~reise** f round trip; **~schreiben** nt (COMM) circular; **r~um** adv all around; (fig) completely.

Rundung f curve, roundness.

rundweg adv straight out.

runter ['rʊntər] (umg) adv = herunter; hinunter; **~würgen** (umg) vt (Ärger) to swallow.

Runzel ['rʊntsəl] (-, -n) f wrinkle.

runz(e)lig adj wrinkled.

runzeln vt to wrinkle; **die Stirn ~** to frown.

Rüpel ['ry:pəl] (-s, -) m lout; **r~haft** adj loutish.

rupfen ['rʊpfən] vt to pluck.

Rupfen (-s, -) m sackcloth.

ruppig ['rʊpɪç] adj rough, gruff.

Rüsche ['ry:ʃə] (-, -n) f frill.

Ruß [ru:s] (-es) m soot.

Russe ['rʊsə] (-n, -n) m Russian.

Rüssel ['rʏsəl] (-s, -) m snout; (Elefanten~) trunk.

rußen vi to smoke; (Ofen) to be sooty.

rußig adj sooty.

Russin f Russian.

russisch adj Russian; **~e Eier** (KOCH) egg(s) mayonnaise.

Russland▲ (-s) nt Russia.

rüsten ['rʏstən] vt, vi, vr to prepare; (MIL) to arm.

rüstig ['rʏstɪç] adj sprightly, vigorous; **R~keit** f sprightliness, vigour (BRIT), vigor (US).

rustikal [rʊsti'ka:l] adj: **sich ~ einrichten** to furnish one's home in a rustic style.

Rüstung ['rʏstʊŋ] f preparation; (MIL) arming; (Ritter~) armour (BRIT), armor (US); (Waffen etc) armaments pl.

Rüstungs- zW: **~gegner** m opponent of the arms race; **~industrie** f armaments industry; **~kontrolle** f arms control; **~wettlauf** m arms race.

Rüstzeug nt tools pl; (fig) capacity.

Rute ['ru:tə] (-, -n) f rod, switch.

Rutsch [rʊtʃ] (-(e)s, -e) m slide; (Erd~) landslide; **guten ~!** (umg) have a good New Year!; **~bahn** f slide.

rutschen vi to slide; (aus~) to slip; **auf dem Stuhl hin und her ~** to fidget around on one's chair.

rutschfest adj non-slip.

rutschig adj slippery.

rütteln ['rʏtəln] vt, vi to shake, jolt; **daran ist nicht zu ~** (fig: umg: an Grundsätzen) there's no doubt about that.

Rüttelschwelle f (AUT) rumble strips pl.

S, s

S¹, s¹ [ɛs] nt S, s; **~ wie Samuel** ≈ S for Sugar.

S² [ɛs] abk (= Süden) S; (= Seite) p; (= Schilling) S.

s² abk (= Sekunde) sec.; (= siehe) v., vid.

Sa. abk = **Samstag.**

SA (-) f abk (= Sturmabteilung) SA.

s. a. abk (= siehe auch) see also.

Saal [za:l] (-(e)s, **Säle**) m hall; (für Sitzungen etc) room.

Saarland ['za:rlant] (-s) nt Saarland.

Saat [za:t] (-, -en) f seed; (Pflanzen) crop; (Säen) sowing; **~gut** nt seed(s pl).

Sabbat ['zabat] (-s, -e) m sabbath.

sabbern ['zabərn] (umg) vi to dribble.

Säbel ['zɛ:bəl] (-s, -) m sabre (BRIT), saber (US); **~rasseln** nt sabre-rattling.

Sabotage [zabo'ta:ʒə] (-, -n) f sabotage.

sabotieren [zabo'ti:rən] vt to sabotage.

Sa(c)charin [zaxa'ri:n] (-s) nt saccharin.

Sachanlagen ['zax|anla:gən] pl tangible assets pl.

Sachbearbeiter(in) m(f): **~ (für)** (Beamter) official in charge (of).

Sachbuch nt non-fiction book.

sachdienlich adj relevant, helpful.

Sache ['zaxə] (-, -n) f thing; (Angelegenheit) affair, business; (Frage) matter; (Pflicht) task; (Thema) subject; (JUR) case; (Aufgabe) job; (Ideal) cause; (umg: km/h): **mit 60/100 ~n** ≈ at 40/60 (mph); **ich habe mir die ~ anders vorgestellt** I had imagined things differently; **er versteht seine ~** he knows what he's doing; **das ist so eine ~** (umg) it's a bit tricky; **mach keine ~n!** (*umg*) don't be daft!; **bei der ~ bleiben** (*bei Diskussion*) to keep to the point; **bei der ~ sein** to be with it (*umg*); **das ist ~ der Polizei** this is a matter for the police; **zur ~** to the point; **das ist eine runde ~** that is well-balanced *od* rounded-off.

Sachertorte ['zaxərtɔrtə] *f* rich chocolate cake, sachertorte.

Sach- *zW:* **s~gemäß** *adj* appropriate, suitable; **~kenntnis** *f* (*in Bezug auf Wissensgebiet*) knowledge of the/his *etc* subject; (*in Bezug auf ~lage*) knowledge of the facts; **s~kundig** *adj* (well-)informed; **sich s~kundig machen** to inform oneself; **~lage** *f* situation, state of affairs; **~leistung** *f* payment in kind; **s~lich** *adj* matter-of-fact; (*Kritik etc*) objective; (*Irrtum, Angabe*) factual; **bleiben Sie bitte s~lich** don't get carried away (*umg*); (*nicht persönlich werden*) please stay objective.

sächlich ['zɛxlɪç] *adj* neuter.

Sachregister *nt* subject index.

Sachschaden *m* material damage.

Sachse ['zaksə] (**-n, -n**) *m* Saxon.

Sachsen (**-s**) *nt* Saxony; **~-Anhalt** (**-s**) *nt* Saxony Anhalt.

Sächsin ['zɛksɪn] *f* Saxon.

sächsisch ['zɛksɪʃ] *adj* Saxon.

sacht(e) *adv* softly, gently.

Sach- *zW:* **~verhalt** (**-(e)s, -e**) *m* facts *pl* (of the case); **s~verständig** *adj* (*Urteil*) expert; (*Publikum*) informed; **~verständige(r)** *f(m)* expert; **~zwang** *m* force of circumstances.

Sack [zak] (**-(e)s, ̈-e**) *m* sack; (*aus Papier, Plastik*) bag; (*ANAT, ZOOL*) sac; (*umg!: Hoden*) balls *pl* (!); (: *Kerl, Bursche*) bastard (!); **mit ~ und Pack** (*umg*) with bag and baggage.

sacken *vi* to sag, sink.

Sackgasse *f* cul-de-sac, dead-end street (*US*).

Sackhüpfen *nt* sack race.

Sadismus [za'dɪsmʊs] *m* sadism.

Sadist(in) [za'dɪst(ɪn)] *m(f)* sadist; **s~isch** *adj* sadistic.

Sadomasochismus [zadomazɔ'xɪsmʊs] *m* sadomasochism.

säen ['zɛːən] *vt, vi* to sow; **dünn gesät** (*fig*) thin on the ground, few and far between.

Safari [za'faːri] (**-, -s**) *f* safari.

Safe [zeːf] (**-s, -s**) *m od nt* safe.

Saft [zaft] (**-(e)s, ̈-e**) *m* juice; (*BOT*) sap; **ohne ~ und Kraft** (*fig*) wishy-washy (*umg*), effete.

saftig *adj* juicy; (*Grün*) lush; (*umg: Rechnung, Ohrfeige*) hefty; (*Brief, Antwort*) hard-hitting.

Saftladen (*pej: umg*) *m* rum joint.

saftlos *adj* dry.

Sage ['zaːgə] (**-, -n**) *f* saga.

Säge ['zɛːgə] (**-, -n**) *f* saw; **~blatt** *nt* saw blade; **~mehl** *nt* sawdust.

sagen ['zaːgən] *vt, vi:* (*jdm etw*) **~** to say (sth to sb), tell (sb sth); **unter uns gesagt**

between you and me (and the gatepost (*hum umg*)); **lass dir das gesagt sein** take it from me; **das hat nichts zu ~** that doesn't mean anything; **sagt dir der Name etwas?** does the name mean anything to you?; **das ist nicht gesagt** that's by no means certain; **sage und schreibe** (whether you) believe it or not.

sägen *vt, vi* to saw; (*hum: umg: schnarchen*) to snore, saw wood (*US*).

sagenhaft *adj* legendary; (*umg*) great, smashing.

sagenumwoben *adj* legendary.

Sägespäne *pl* wood shavings *pl*.

Sägewerk *nt* sawmill.

sah *etc* [zaː] *vb siehe* **sehen.**

Sahara [za'haːra] *f* Sahara (Desert).

Sahne ['zaːnə] (**-**) *f* cream.

Saison [zɛ'zõː] (**-, -s**) *f* season.

saisonal [zɛzo'naːl] *adj* seasonal.

Saisonarbeiter *m* seasonal worker.

saisonbedingt *adj* seasonal.

Saite ['zaɪtə] (**-, -n**) *f* string; **andere ~n aufziehen** (*umg*) to get tough.

Saiteninstrument *nt* string(ed) instrument.

Sakko ['zako] (**-s, -s**) *m od nt* jacket.

Sakrament [zakra'mɛnt] *nt* sacrament.

Sakristei [zakrɪs'taɪ] *f* sacristy.

Salami [za'laːmi] (**-, -s**) *f* salami.

Salat [za'laːt] (**-(e)s, -e**) *m* salad; (*Kopf~*) lettuce; **da haben wir den ~!** (*umg*) now we're in a fine mess; **~besteck** *nt* salad servers *pl*; **~platte** *f* salad; **~soße** *f* salad dressing.

Salbe ['zalbə] (**-, -n**) *f* ointment.

Salbei ['zalbaɪ] (**-s**) *m* sage.

salben *vt* to anoint.

Salbung *f* anointing.

salbungsvoll *adj* unctuous.

saldieren [zal'diːrən] *vt* (*COMM*) to balance.

Saldo ['zaldo] (**-s, Salden**) *m* balance; **~übertrag** *m* balance brought *od* carried forward; **~vortrag** *m* balance brought *od* carried forward.

Säle ['zɛːlə] *pl von* **Saal.**

Salmiak [zalmi'ak] (**-s**) *m* sal ammoniac; **~geist** *m* liquid ammonia.

Salmonellen [zalmo'nɛlən] *pl* salmonellae *pl*.

Salon [za'lõ, za'lõː] (**-s, -s**) *m* salon; **~löwe** *m* lounge lizard.

salopp [za'lɔp] *adj* casual; (*Manieren*) slovenly; (*Sprache*) slangy.

Salpeter [zal'peːtər] (**-s**) *m* saltpetre (*BRIT*), saltpeter (*US*); **~säure** *f* nitric acid.

Salto ['zalto] (**-s, -s od Salti**) *m* somersault.

Salut [za'luːt] (**-(e)s, -e**) *m* salute.

salutieren [zalu'tiːrən] *vi* to salute.

Salve ['zalvə] (**-, -n**) *f* salvo.

Salz [zalts] (**-es, -e**) *nt* salt; **s~arm** *adj* (*KOCH*) low-salt; **~bergwerk** *nt* salt mine.

salzen *unreg vt* to salt.

salzig *adj* salty.
Salz- *zW:* ~**kartoffeln** *pl* boiled potatoes *pl*; ~**säule** *f:* **zur** ~**säule erstarren** (*fig*) to stand (as though) rooted to the spot; ~**säure** *f* hydrochloric acid; ~**stange** *f* pretzel stick; ~**streuer** *m* salt cellar; ~**wasser** *nt* salt water.
Sambia ['zambia] (**-s**) *nt* Zambia.
sambisch *adj* Zambian.
Samen ['za:mən] (**-s, -**) *m* seed; (*ANAT*) sperm; ~**bank** *f* sperm bank; ~**handlung** *f* seed shop.
sämig ['zɛːmɪç] *adj* thick, creamy.
Sammel- *zW:* ~**anschluss**▲ *m* (*TEL*) private (branch) exchange; (*von Privathäusern*) party line; ~**antrag** *m* composite motion; ~**band** *m* anthology; ~**becken** *nt* reservoir; (*fig*): ~**becken (von)** melting pot (for); ~**begriff** *m* collective term; ~**bestellung** *f* collective order; ~**büchse** *f* collecting tin; ~**mappe** *f* folder.
sammeln *vt* to collect ♦ *vr* to assemble, gather; (*sich konzentrieren*) to collect one's thoughts.
Sammelname *m* collective term.
Sammelnummer *f* (*TEL*) private exchange number, switchboard number.
Sammelsurium [zaməl'zu:riʊm] *nt* hotchpotch (*BRIT*), hodgepodge (*US*).
Sammler(in) (**-s, -**) *m(f)* collector.
Sammlung ['zamlʊŋ] *f* collection; (*Konzentration*) composure.
Samstag ['zamsta:k] *m* Saturday; *siehe auch* **Dienstag**.
samstags *adv* (on) Saturdays.
samt [zamt] *präp +dat* (along) with, together with; ~ **und sonders** each and every one (of them); **S**~ (**-(e)s, -e**) *m* velvet; **in S**~ **und Seide** (*liter*) in silks and satins.
Samthandschuh *m:* **jdn mit** ~**en anfassen** (*umg*) to handle sb with kid gloves.
sämtlich ['zɛmtlɪç] *adj* (*alle*) all (the); (*vollständig*) complete; **Schillers** ~**e Werke** the complete works of Schiller.
Sanatorium [zana'to:riʊm] *nt* sanatorium (*BRIT*), sanitarium (*US*).
Sand [zant] (**-(e)s, -e**) *m* sand; **das/die gibts wie** ~ **am Meer** (*umg*) there are piles of it/ heaps of them; **im** ~**e verlaufen** to peter out.
Sandale [zan'da:lə] (**-, -n**) *f* sandal.
Sandbank *f* sandbank.
Sandelholz ['zandəlhɔlts] (**-es**) *nt* sandalwood.
sandig ['zandɪç] *adj* sandy.
Sand- *zW:* ~**kasten** *m* sandpit; ~**kastenspiele** *pl* (*MIL*) sand-table exercises *pl*; (*fig*) tactical manoeuvrings *pl* (*BRIT*) *od* maneuverings *pl* (*US*); ~**kuchen** *m* Madeira cake; ~**mann** *m*, ~**männchen** *nt* (*in Geschichten*) sandman; ~**papier** *nt* sandpaper; ~**stein** *m* sandstone; **s**~**strahlen** *vt, vi untr* to sandblast.
sandte *etc* ['zantə] *vb siehe* **senden**.
Sanduhr *f* hourglass; (*Eieruhr*) egg timer.

sanft [zanft] *adj* soft, gentle; ~**mütig** *adj* gentle, meek.
sang *etc* [zaŋ] *vb siehe* **singen**.
Sänger(in) ['zɛŋər(ɪn)] (**-s, -**) *m(f)* singer.
sang- und klanglos (*umg*) *adv* without any ado, quietly.
Sani ['zani] (**-s, -s**) (*umg*) *m* = **Sanitäter**.
sanieren [za'ni:rən] *vt* to redevelop; (*Betrieb*) to make financially sound; (*Haus*) to renovate ♦ *vr* to line one's pockets; (*Unternehmen*) to become financially sound.
Sanierung *f* redevelopment; renovation.
sanitär [zani'tɛːr] *adj* sanitary; ~**e Anlagen** sanitation *sing*.
Sanitäter [zani'tɛːtər] (**-s, -**) *m* first-aid attendant; (*in Krankenwagen*) ambulance man; (*MIL*) (medical) orderly.
Sanitätsauto *nt* ambulance.
sank *etc* [zaŋk] *vb siehe* **sinken**.
Sanktion [zaŋktsi'o:n] *f* sanction.
sanktionieren [zaŋktsio'ni:rən] *vt* to sanction.
sann *etc* [zan] *vb siehe* **sinnen**.
Saphir ['za:fi:r] (**-s, -e**) *m* sapphire.
Sarde ['zardə] (**-n, -n**) *m* Sardinian.
Sardelle [zar'dɛlə] *f* anchovy.
Sardine [zar'di:nə] *f* sardine.
Sardinien [zar'di:niən] (**-s**) *nt* Sardinia.
Sardinier(in) [zar'di:niər] (**-s, -**) *m(f)* Sardinian.
sardinisch *adj* Sardinian.
sardisch *adj* Sardinian.
Sarg [zark] (**-(e)s, ⸚e**) *m* coffin; ~**nagel** (*umg*) *m* (*Zigarette*) coffin nail.
Sarkasmus [zar'kasmʊs] *m* sarcasm.
sarkastisch [zar'kastɪʃ] *adj* sarcastic.
SARS, Sars [zars] *abk* (= *Schweres Akutes Respiratorisches Syndrom*) SARS.
saß *etc* [zas] *vb siehe* **sitzen**.
Satan ['za:tan] (**-s, -e**) *m* Satan; (*fig*) devil.
Satansbraten *m* (*hum: umg*) young devil.
Satellit [zatɛ'li:t] (**-en, -en**) *m* satellite.
Satelliten- *zW:* ~**antenne** *f* satellite dish; ~**fernsehen** *nt* satellite television; ~**foto** *nt* satellite picture; ~**schüssel** *f* satellite dish; ~**station** *f* space station.
Satin [za'tɛ̃:] (**-s, -s**) *m* satin.
Satire [za'ti:rə] (**-, -n**) *f:* ~ (**auf** *+akk*) satire (on).
Satiriker [za'ti:rikər] (**-s, -**) *m* satirist.
satirisch [za'ti:rɪʃ] *adj* satirical.
satt [zat] *adj* full; (*Farbe*) rich, deep; (*blasiert, übersättigt*) well-fed; (*selbstgefällig*) smug; **jdn/etw** ~ **sein** *od* **haben** to be fed-up with sb/sth; **sich** ~ **hören/sehen an** *+dat* to see/ hear enough of; **sich** ~ **essen** to eat one's fill; ~ **machen** to be filling.
Sattel ['zatəl] (**-s, ⸚**) *m* saddle; (*Berg*) ridge; **s**~**fest** *adj* (*fig*) proficient.
satteln *vt* to saddle.
Sattelschlepper *m* articulated lorry (*BRIT*), artic (*BRIT umg*), semitrailer (*US*), semi (*US umg*).

Satteltasche *f* saddlebag; (*Gepäcktasche am Fahrrad*) pannier.

sättigen ['zɛtɪgən] *vt* to satisfy; (*CHEM*) to saturate.

Sattler (-s, -) *m* saddler; (*Polsterer*) upholsterer.

Satz [zats] (-es, ⁼e) *m* (*GRAM*) sentence; (*Neben~, Adverbial~*) clause; (*Theorem*) theorem; (*der gesetzte Text*) type; (*MUS*) movement; (*COMPUT*) set; (*TENNIS, Briefmarken, Zusammengehöriges*) set; (*Kaffee~*) grounds *pl*; (*Boden~*) dregs *pl*; (*Spesen~*) allowance; (*COMM*) rate; (*Sprung*) jump; **~bau** *nt* sentence construction; **~gegenstand** *m* (*GRAM*) subject; **~lehre** *f* syntax; **~teil** *m* constituent (of a sentence).

Satzung *f* statute, rule; (*Firma*) (memorandum and) articles of association.

satzungsgemäß *adj* statutory.

Satzzeichen *nt* punctuation mark.

Sau [zaʊ] (-, **Säue**) *f* sow; (*umg*) dirty pig; **die ~ rauslassen** (*fig: umg*) to let it all hang out.

sauber ['zaʊbər] *adj* clean; (*anständig*) honest, upstanding; (*umg: großartig*) fantastic, great; (: *ironisch*) fine; **~ sein** (*Kind*) to be (potty-)trained; (*Hund etc*) to be house-trained; **~ halten** to keep clean; **~ machen** to clean; **S~keit** *f* cleanness; (*einer Person*) cleanliness.

säuberlich ['zɔʏbərlɪç] *adv* neatly.

säubern *vt* to clean; (*POL etc*) to purge.

Säuberung *f* cleaning; purge.

Säuberungsaktion *f* cleaning-up operation; (*POL*) purge.

saublöd (*umg*) *adj* bloody (*BRIT!*) *od* damn (*!*) stupid.

Saubohne *f* broad bean.

Sauce ['zoːsə] (-, -n) *f* = **Soße**.

Sauciere [zosiˈeːrə] (-, -n) *f* sauce boat.

Saudi- [zaʊdi-] *zW:* **~-Araber(in)** *m(f)* Saudi; **~-Arabien** (-s) *nt* Saudi Arabia; **s~-arabisch** *adj* Saudi(-Arabian).

sauer ['zaʊər] *adj* sour; (*CHEM*) acid; (*umg*) cross; **saurer Regen** acid rain; **~ werden** (*Milch, Sahne*) to go sour, turn; **jdm das Leben ~ machen** to make sb's life a misery; **S~braten** *m* braised beef (marinaded in vinegar), sauerbraten (*US*).

Sauerei [zaʊəˈraɪ] (*umg*) *f* rotten state of affairs, scandal; (*Schmutz etc*) mess; (*Unanständigkeit*) obscenity.

Sauerkirsche *f* sour cherry.

Sauerkraut (-(e)s) *nt* sauerkraut, pickled cabbage.

säuerlich ['zɔʏərlɪç] *adj* sourish, tart.

Sauer- *zW:* **~milch** *f* sour milk; **~stoff** *m* oxygen; **~stoffgerät** *nt* breathing apparatus; **~teig** *m* leaven.

saufen ['zaʊfən] *unreg* (*umg*) *vt, vi* to drink, booze; **wie ein Loch ~** (*umg*) to drink like a

fish.

Säufer(in) ['zɔʏfər(ɪn)] (-s, -) (*umg*) *m(f)* boozer, drunkard.

Sauferei [zaʊfəˈraɪ] *f* drinking, boozing; (*Saufgelage*) booze-up.

Saufgelage (*pej: umg*) *nt* drinking bout, booze-up.

säuft [zɔʏft] *vb siehe* **saufen**.

saugen ['zaʊgən] *unreg vt, vi* to suck.

säugen ['zɔʏgən] *vt* to suckle.

Sauger ['zaʊgər] (-s, -) *m* dummy (*BRIT*), pacifier (*US*); (*auf Flasche*) teat; (*Staub~*) vacuum cleaner, hoover ® (*BRIT*).

Säugetier *nt* mammal.

saugfähig *adj* absorbent.

Säugling *m* infant, baby.

Säuglingsschwester *f* infant nurse.

Sau- *zW:* **~haufen** (*umg*) *m* bunch of layabouts; **s~kalt** (*umg*) *adj* bloody (*BRIT!*) *od* damn (*!*) cold; **~klaue** (*umg*) *f* scrawl.

Säule ['zɔʏlə] (-, -n) *f* column, pillar.

Säulengang *m* arcade.

Saum [zaʊm] (-(e)s, **Säume**) *m* hem; (*Naht*) seam.

saumäßig (*umg*) *adj* lousy ♦ *adv* lousily.

säumen ['zɔʏmən] *vt* to hem; to seam ♦ *vi* to delay, hesitate.

säumig ['zɔʏmɪç] *adj* (*geh: Schuldner*) defaulting; (*Zahlung*) outstanding, overdue.

Sauna ['zaʊna] (-, -s) *f* sauna.

Säure ['zɔʏrə] (-, -n) *f* acid; (*Geschmack*) sourness, acidity; **s~beständig** *adj* acid-proof.

Saure-Gurken-Zeit▲ (-) *f* (*hum: umg*) bad time *od* period; (*in den Medien*) silly season.

säurehaltig *adj* acidic.

Saurier ['zaʊriər] (-s, -) *m* dinosaur.

Saus [zaʊs] (-es) *m*: **in ~ und Braus leben** to live like a lord.

säuseln ['zɔʏzəln] *vi* to murmur; (*Blätter*) to rustle ♦ *vt* to murmur.

sausen ['zaʊzən] *vi* to blow; (*umg: eilen*) to rush; (*Ohren*) to buzz; **etw ~ lassen** (*umg*) not to bother with sth.

Sau- *zW:* **~stall** (*umg*) *m* pigsty; **~wetter** *nt* bloody (*BRIT!*) *od* damn (*!*) awful weather; **s~wohl** (*umg*) *adj*: **ich fühle mich s~wohl** I feel bloody (*BRIT!*) *od* really good.

Saxofon▲, Saxophon [zaksoˈfoːn] (-s, -e) *nt* saxophone.

SB *abk* = **Selbstbedienung**.

S-Bahn *f abk* (= *Schnellbahn*) high-speed suburban railway or railroad (*US*).

SBB *abk* (= *Schweizerische Bundesbahnen*) Swiss Railways.

s. Br. *abk* (= *südlicher Breite*) southern latitude.

Schabe ['ʃaːbə] (-, -n) *f* cockroach.

schaben *vt* to scrape.

Schaber (-s, -) *m* scraper.

Schabernack (-(e)s, -e) *m* trick, prank.

schäbig ['ʃɛːbɪç] *adj* shabby; (*Mensch*) mean; **S~keit** *f* shabbiness.

Schablone [ʃa'bloːnə] (-, -n) *f* stencil; (*Muster*) pattern; (*fig*) convention.

schablonenhaft *adj* stereotyped, conventional.

Schach [ʃax] (-s, -s) *nt* chess; (*Stellung*) check; **im ~ stehen** to be in check; **jdn in ~ halten** (*fig*) to stall sb; **~brett** *nt* chessboard.

schachern (*pej*) *vi*: **um etw ~** to haggle over sth.

Schach- *zW*: **~figur** *f* chessman; **s~matt** *adj* checkmate; **jdn s~matt setzen** (*lit*) to (check)mate sb; (*fig*) to snooker sb (*umg*); **~partie** *f* game of chess; **~spiel** *nt* game of chess.

Schacht [ʃaxt] (-(e)s, ̈e) *m* shaft.

Schachtel (-, -n) *f* box; (*pej: Frau*) bag, cow (*BRIT*); **~satz** *m* complicated *od* multi-clause sentence.

Schachzug *m* (*auch fig*) move.

schade ['ʃaːdə] *adj* a pity *od* shame ♦ *interj* (what a) pity *od* shame; **sich** *dat* **für etw zu ~ sein** to consider o.s. too good for sth; **um sie ist es nicht ~** she's no great loss.

Schädel ['ʃɛːdəl] (-s, -) *m* skull; **einen dicken ~ haben** (*fig: umg*) to be stubborn; **~bruch** *m* fractured skull.

Schaden (-s, ̈) *m* damage; (*Verletzung*) injury; (*Nachteil*) disadvantage; **zu ~ kommen** to suffer; (*physisch*) to be injured; **jdm ~ zufügen** to harm sb.

schaden ['ʃaːdən] *vi* +*dat* to hurt; **einer Sache ~** to damage sth.

Schaden- *zW*: **~ersatz** *m* compensation, damages *pl*; **~ersatz leisten** to pay compensation; **~ersatzanspruch** *m* claim for compensation; **s~ersatzpflichtig** *adj* liable for damages; **~freiheitsrabatt** *m* (*Versicherung*) no-claim(s) bonus; **~freude** *f* malicious delight; **s~froh** *adj* gloating.

schadhaft ['ʃaːthaft] *adj* faulty, damaged.

schädigen ['ʃɛːdɪɡən] *vt* to damage; (*Person*) to do harm to, harm.

Schädigung *f* damage; harm.

schädlich *adj*: **~ (für)** harmful (to); **S~keit** *f* harmfulness.

Schädling *m* pest.

Schädlingsbekämpfungsmittel *nt* pesticide.

schadlos ['ʃaːtloːs] *adj*: **sich ~ halten an** +*dat* to take advantage of.

Schadstoff (-(e)s, -e) *m* pollutant; **s~arm** *adj* low in pollutants; **s~haltig** *adj* containing pollutants.

Schaf [ʃaːf] (-(e)s, -e) *nt* sheep; (*umg: Dummkopf*) twit (*BRIT*), dope; **~bock** *m* ram.

Schäfchen ['ʃɛːfçən] *nt* lamb; **sein ~ ins Trockene bringen** (*Sprichwort*) to see o.s. all right (*umg*); **~wolken** *pl* cirrus clouds *pl*.

Schäfer ['ʃɛːfər] (-s, -) *m* shepherd; **~hund** *m* Alsatian (dog) (*BRIT*), German shepherd (dog) (*US*); **~in** *f* shepherdess.

Schaffen ['ʃafən] (-s) *nt* (creative) activity.

schaffen¹ *unreg vt* to create; (*Platz*) to make; **sich** *dat* **etw ~** to get o.s. sth; **dafür ist er wie geschaffen** he's just made for it.

schaffen² ['ʃafən] *vt* (*erreichen*) to manage, do; (*erledigen*) to finish; (*Prüfung*) to pass; (*transportieren*) to take ♦ *vi* (*tun*) to do; (*umg: arbeiten*) to work; **das ist nicht zu ~** that can't be done; **das hat mich geschafft** it took it out of me; (*nervlich*) to get on top of me; **ich habe damit nichts zu ~** that has nothing to do with me; **jdm (schwer) zu ~ machen** (*zusetzen*) to cause sb (a lot of) trouble; (*bekümmern*) to worry sb (a lot); **sich** *dat* **an etw** *dat* **zu ~ machen** to busy o.s. with sth.

Schaffensdrang *m* energy; (*von Künstler*) creative urge.

Schaffenskraft *f* creativity.

Schaffner(in) ['ʃafnər(ɪn)] (-s, -) *m(f)* (*Bus~*) conductor, conductress; (*EISENB*) guard (*BRIT*), conductor (*US*).

Schaffung *f* creation.

Schafskäse *m* sheep's *od* ewe's milk cheese.

Schaft [ʃaft] (-(e)s, ̈e) *m* shaft; (*von Gewehr*) stock; (*von Stiefel*) leg; (*BOT*) stalk; (*von Baum*) tree trunk; **~stiefel** *m* high boot.

Schakal [ʃa'kaːl] (-s, -e) *m* jackal.

Schäker(in) ['ʃɛːkər(ɪn)] (-s, -) *m(f)* flirt; (*Witzbold*) joker.

schäkern *vi* to flirt; to joke.

Schal [ʃaːl] (-s, -s *od* -e) *m* scarf.

schal *adj* flat; (*fig*) insipid.

Schälchen ['ʃɛːlçən] *nt* bowl.

Schale ['ʃaːlə] (-, -n) *f* skin; (*abgeschält*) peel; (*Nuss~, Muschel~, Eier~*) shell; (*Geschirr*) dish, bowl; **sich in ~ werfen** (*umg*) to get dressed up.

schälen ['ʃɛːlən] *vt* to peel; to shell ♦ *vr* to peel.

Schalk [ʃalk] (-s, -e *od* ̈e) *m* (*veraltet*) joker.

Schall [ʃal] (-(e)s, -e) *m* sound; **Name ist ~ und Rauch** what's in a name?; **s~dämmend** *adj* sound-deadening; **~dämpfer** *m* (*AUT*) silencer (*BRIT*), muffler (*US*); **s~dicht** *adj* soundproof.

schallen *vi* to (re)sound.

schallend *adj* resounding, loud.

Schall- *zW*: **~geschwindigkeit** *f* speed of sound; **~grenze** *f* sound barrier; **~mauer** *f* sound barrier; **~platte** *f* record.

schalt *etc* [ʃalt] *vb siehe* **schelten**.

Schaltbild *nt* circuit diagram.

Schaltbrett *nt* switchboard.

schalten ['ʃaltən] *vt* to switch, turn ♦ *vi* (*AUT*) to change (gear); (*umg: begreifen*) to catch on; (*reagieren*) to react; **in Reihe/parallel ~** (*ELEK*) to connect in series/in parallel;

~ **und walten** to do as one pleases.
Schalter (-s, -) *m* counter; (*an Gerät*) switch; ~**beamte(r)** *m* counter clerk; ~**stunden** *pl* hours of business *pl*.
Schalt- *zW:* ~**hebel** *m* switch; (*AUT*) gear lever (*BRIT*), gearshift (*US*); ~**jahr** *nt* leap year; ~**knüppel** *m* (*AUT*) gear lever (*BRIT*), gearshift (*US*); (*AVIAT, COMPUT*) joystick; ~**kreis** *m* (switching) circuit; ~**plan** *m* circuit diagram; ~**pult** *nt* control desk; ~**stelle** *f* (*fig*) coordinating point; ~**uhr** *f* time switch.
Schaltung *f* switching; (*ELEK*) circuit; (*AUT*) gear change.
Scham [ʃaːm] (-) *f* shame; (~*gefühl*) modesty; (*Organe*) private parts *pl*.
schämen [ˈʃɛːmən] *vr* to be ashamed.
Scham- *zW:* ~**gefühl** *nt* sense of shame; ~**haare** *pl* pubic hair *sing*; **s**~**haft** *adj* modest; bashful; ~**lippen** *pl* labia *pl*, lips *pl* of the vulva; **s**~**los** *adj* shameless; (*unanständig*) indecent; (*Lüge*) brazen, barefaced.
Schampus [ˈʃampʊs] (-) *no pl* (*umg*) *m* champagne, champers (*BRIT*).
Schande [ˈʃandə] (-) *f* disgrace; **zu meiner** ~ **muss ich gestehen, dass** ... to my shame I have to admit that ...
schänden [ˈʃɛndən] *vt* to violate.
Schandfleck [ˈʃantflɛk] *m:* **er war der** ~ **der Familie** he was the disgrace of his family.
schändlich [ˈʃɛntlɪç] *adj* disgraceful, shameful; **S**~**keit** *f* disgracefulness, shamefulness.
Schandtat (*umg*) *f* escapade, shenanigan.
Schändung *f* violation, defilement.
Schänke▲ [ˈʃɛŋkə] (-, -n) *f* = **Schenke**.
Schank- *zW:* ~**erlaubnis** *f*, ~**konzession** *f* (publican's) licence (*BRIT*), excise license (*US*); ~**tisch** *m* bar.
Schanze [ˈʃantsə] (-, -n) *f* (*MIL*) fieldwork, earthworks *pl*; (*Sprung*~) ski jump.
Schar [ʃaːr] (-, -en) *f* band, company; (*Vögel*) flock; (*Menge*) crowd; **in** ~**en** in droves.
Scharade [ʃaˈraːdə] (-, -n) *f* charade.
scharen *vr* to assemble, rally.
scharenweise *adv* in droves.
scharf [ʃarf] *adj* sharp; (*Verstand, Augen*) keen; (*Kälte, Wind*) biting; (*Protest*) fierce; (*Ton*) piercing, shrill; (*Essen*) hot, spicy; (*Munition*) live; (*Maßnahmen*) severe; (*Bewachung*) close, tight; (*Geruch, Geschmack*) pungent, acrid; (*umg: geil*) randy (*BRIT*), horny; (*Film*) sexy, blue *attrib*; ~ **nachdenken** to think hard; ~ **aufpassen/ zuhören** to pay close attention/listen closely; **etw** ~ **einstellen** (*Bild, Diaprojektor etc*) to bring sth into focus; **mit** ~**em Blick** (*fig*) with penetrating insight; **auf etw** *akk* ~ **sein** (*umg*) to be keen on sth; ~**e Sachen** (*umg*) hard stuff.
Scharfblick *m* (*fig*) penetration.

Schärfe [ˈʃɛrfə] (-, -n) *f* sharpness; (*Strenge*) rigour (*BRIT*), rigor (*US*); (*an Kamera, Fernsehen*) focus.
schärfen *vt* to sharpen.
Schärfentiefe *f* (*PHOT*) depth of focus.
Scharf- *zW:* **s**~**machen** (*umg*) *vt* to stir up; ~**richter** *m* executioner; ~**schießen** *nt* shooting with live ammunition; ~**schütze** *m* marksman, sharpshooter; ~**sinn** *m* astuteness, shrewdness; **s**~**sinnig** *adj* astute, shrewd.
Scharlach [ˈʃarlax] (-s, -e) *m* scarlet; (*Krankheit*) scarlet fever; ~**fieber** *nt* scarlet fever.
Scharlatan [ˈʃarlatan] (-s, -e) *m* charlatan.
Scharmützel [ʃarˈmʏtsəl] (-s, -) *nt* skirmish.
Scharnier [ʃarˈniːr] (-s, -e) *nt* hinge.
Schärpe [ˈʃɛrpə] (-, -n) *f* sash.
scharren [ˈʃarən] *vt, vi* to scrape, scratch.
Scharte [ˈʃartə] (-, -n) *f* notch, nick; (*Berg*) wind gap.
schartig [ˈʃartɪç] *adj* jagged.
Schaschlik [ˈʃaʃlɪk] (-s, -s) *m od nt* (shish) kebab.
Schatten [ˈʃatən] (-s, -) *m* shadow; (*schattige Stelle*) shade; **jdn/etw in den** ~ **stellen** (*fig*) to put sb/sth in the shade; ~**bild** *nt* silhouette; **s**~**haft** *adj* shadowy.
Schattenmorelle (-, -n) *f* morello cherry.
Schatten- *zW:* ~**riss**▲ *m* silhouette; ~**seite** *f* shady side; (*von Planeten*) dark side; (*fig: Nachteil*) drawback; ~**wirtschaft** *f* black economy.
schattieren [ʃaˈtiːrən] *vt, vi* to shade.
Schattierung *f* shading.
schattig [ˈʃatɪç] *adj* shady.
Schatulle [ʃaˈtʊlə] (-, -n) *f* casket; (*Geld*~) coffer.
Schatz [ʃats] (-es, ¨e) *m* treasure; (*Person*) darling; ~**amt** *nt* treasury.
schätzbar [ˈʃɛtsbaːr] *adj* assessable.
Schätzchen *nt* darling, love.
schätzen *vt* (*ab*~) to estimate; (*Gegenstand*) to value; (*würdigen*) to value, esteem; (*vermuten*) to reckon; **etw zu** ~ **wissen** to appreciate sth; **sich glücklich** ~ to consider o.s. lucky; ~ **lernen** to learn to appreciate.
Schatzkammer *f* treasure chamber *od* vault.
Schatzmeister *m* treasurer.
Schätzung *f* estimate; estimation; valuation; **nach meiner** ~ ... I reckon that ...
schätzungsweise *adv* (*ungefähr*) approximately; (*so vermutet man*) it is thought.
Schätzwert *m* estimated value.
Schau [ʃaʊ] (-) *f* show; (*Ausstellung*) display, exhibition; **etw zur** ~ **stellen** to make a show of sth, show sth off; **eine** ~ **abziehen** (*umg*) to put on a show; ~**bild** *nt* diagram.
Schauder [ˈʃaʊdər] (-s, -) *m* shudder; (*wegen*

Kälte) shiver; **s~haft** *adj* horrible.
schaudern *vi* to shudder; (*wegen Kälte*) to shiver.
schauen ['ʃaʊən] *vi* to look; **da schau her!** well, well!
Schauer ['ʃaʊər] (**-s, -**) *m* (*Regen~*) shower; (*Schreck*) shudder; **~geschichte** *f* horror story; **s~lich** *adj* horrific, spine-chilling; **~märchen** (*umg*) *nt* horror story.
Schaufel ['ʃaʊfəl] (**-, -n**) *f* shovel; (*Kehricht~*) dustpan; (*von Turbine*) vane; (*NAUT*) paddle; (*TECH*) scoop.
schaufeln *vt* to shovel; (*Grab, Grube*) to dig ♦ *vi* to shovel.
Schaufenster *nt* shop window; **~auslage** *f* window display; **~bummel** *m* window-shopping (expedition); **~dekorateur(in)** *m(f)* window dresser; **~puppe** *f* display dummy.
Schaugeschäft *nt* show business.
Schaukasten *m* showcase.
Schaukel ['ʃaʊkəl] (**-, -n**) *f* swing.
schaukeln *vi* to swing, rock ♦ *vt* to rock; **wir werden das Kind** *od* **das schon** ~ (*fig: umg*) we'll manage it.
Schaukelpferd *nt* rocking horse.
Schaukelstuhl *m* rocking chair.
Schaulustige(r) ['ʃaʊlʊstɪɡə(r)] *f(m)* onlooker.
Schaum [ʃaʊm] (**-(e)s, Schäume**) *m* foam; (*Seifen~*) lather; (*von Getränken*) froth; (*von Bier*) head; **~bad** *nt* bubble bath.
schäumen ['ʃɔʏmən] *vi* to foam.
Schaumgummi *m* foam (rubber).
schaumig *adj* frothy, foamy.
Schaum- *zW*: **~krone** *f* whitecap; **~schläger** *m* (*fig*) windbag; **~schlägerei** *f* (*fig: umg*) hot air; **~stoff** *m* foam material; **~wein** *m* sparkling wine.
Schauplatz *m* scene.
Schauprozess▲ *m* show trial.
schaurig *adj* horrific, dreadful.
Schauspiel *nt* spectacle; (*THEAT*) play.
Schauspieler(in) *m(f)* actor, actress; **s~isch** *adj* (*Können, Leistung*) acting.
schauspielern *vi untr* to act.
Schauspielhaus *nt* playhouse, theatre (*BRIT*), theater (*US*).
Schauspielschule *f* drama school.
Schausteller ['ʃaʊʃtɛlər] (**-s, -**) *m* person who owns or runs a fairground ride/sideshow etc.
Scheck [ʃɛk] (**-s, -s**) *m* cheque (*BRIT*), check (*US*); **~buch** *nt*, **~heft** *nt* cheque book (*BRIT*), check book (*US*).
scheckig *adj* dappled, piebald.
Scheckkarte *f* cheque (*BRIT*) *od* check (*US*) card, banker's card.
scheel [ʃeːl] (*umg*) *adj* dirty; **jdn** ~ **ansehen** to give sb a dirty look.
scheffeln ['ʃɛfəln] *vt* to amass.
Scheibe ['ʃaɪbə] (**-, -n**) *f* disc (*BRIT*), disk (*US*);

(*Brot etc*) slice; (*Glas~*) pane; (*MIL*) target; (*Eishockey*) puck; (*Töpfer~*) wheel; (*umg: Schallplatte*) disc (*BRIT*), disk (*US*); **von ihm könntest du dir eine** ~ **abschneiden** (*fig: umg*) you could take a leaf out of his book.
Scheiben- *zW*: **~bremse** *f* (*AUT*) disc brake; **~kleister** *interj* (*euph: umg*) sugar!; **~waschanlage** *f* (*AUT*) windscreen (*BRIT*) *od* windshield (*US*) washers *pl*; **~wischer** *m* (*AUT*) windscreen (*BRIT*) *od* windshield (*US*) wiper.
Scheich [ʃaɪç] (**-s, -e** *od* **-s**) *m* sheik(h).
Scheide ['ʃaɪdə] (**-, -n**) *f* sheath; (*ANAT*) vagina.
scheiden *unreg vt* to separate; (*Ehe*) to dissolve ♦ *vi* to depart; (*sich trennen*) to part ♦ *vr* (*Wege*) to divide; (*Meinungen*) to diverge; **sich** ~ **lassen** to get a divorce; **von dem Moment an waren wir (zwei) geschiedene Leute** (*umg*) after that it was the parting of the ways for us; **aus dem Leben** ~ to depart this life.
Scheideweg *m* (*fig*) crossroads *sing*.
Scheidung *f* (*Ehe~*) divorce; **die** ~ **einreichen** to file a petition for divorce.
Scheidungsgrund *m* grounds *pl* for divorce.
Scheidungsklage *f* divorce suit.
Schein [ʃaɪn] (**-(e)s, -e**) *m* light; (*An~*) appearance; (*Geld~*) (bank)note; (*Bescheinigung*) certificate; **den** ~ **wahren** to keep up appearances; **etw zum** ~ **tun** to pretend to do sth, make a pretence (*BRIT*) *od* pretense (*US*) of doing sth; **s~bar** *adj* apparent.
scheinen *unreg vi* to shine; (*Anschein haben*) to seem.
Schein- *zW*: **s~heilig** *adj* hypocritical; **~tod** *m* apparent death; **~werfer** (**-s, -**) *m* floodlight; (*THEAT*) spotlight; (*Suchscheinwerfer*) searchlight; (*AUT*) headlight.
Scheiß [ʃaɪs] (**-, no pl**) (*umg*) *m* bullshit (!).
Scheiß- ['ʃaɪs-] (*umg*) in *zW* bloody (*BRIT*!); **~dreck** (*umg!*) *m* shit (!), crap (!); **das geht dich einen ~dreck an** it's got bugger-all to do with you (!).
Scheiße ['ʃaɪsə] (**-**) (*umg!*) *f* shit (!).
scheißegal (*umg!*) *adj*: **das ist mir doch ~!** I don't give a shit (!).
scheißen (*umg!*) *vi* to shit (!).
scheißfreundlich (*pej: umg*) *adj* as nice as pie (*ironisch*).
Scheißkerl (*umg!*) *m* bastard (!), son-of-a-bitch (*US!*).
Scheit [ʃaɪt] (**-(e)s, -e** *od* **-er**) *nt* log.
Scheitel ['ʃaɪtəl] (**-s, -**) *m* top; (*Haar*) parting (*BRIT*), part (*US*).
scheiteln *vt* to part.
Scheitelpunkt *m* zenith, apex.
Scheiterhaufen ['ʃaɪtərhaʊfən] *m* (funeral) pyre; (*HIST: zur Hinrichtung*) stake.

scheitern ['ʃaɪtərn] _vi_ to fail.
Schelle ['ʃɛlə] (-, -n) _f_ small bell.
schellen _vi_ to ring; **es hat geschellt** the bell has gone.
Schellfisch ['ʃɛlfɪʃ] _m_ haddock.
Schelm [ʃɛlm] (-(e)s, -e) _m_ rogue.
Schelmenroman _m_ picaresque novel.
schelmisch _adj_ mischievous, roguish.
Schelte ['ʃɛltə] (-, -n) _f_ scolding.
schelten _unreg vt_ to scold.
Schema ['ʃeːma] (-s, -s _od_ **-ta**) _nt_ scheme, plan; (_Darstellung_) schema; **nach ~ F** quite mechanically.
schematisch [ʃeˈmaːtɪʃ] _adj_ schematic; (_pej_) mechanical.
Schemel ['ʃeːməl] (-s, -) _m_ (foot)stool.
schemenhaft _adj_ shadowy.
Schenke (-, -n) _f_ tavern, inn.
Schenkel ['ʃɛŋkəl] (-s, -) _m_ thigh; (_MATH: von Winkel_) side.
schenken ['ʃɛŋkən] _vt_ (_lit, fig_) to give; (_Getränk_) to pour; **ich möchte nichts geschenkt haben!** (_lit_) I don't want any presents!; (_fig: bevorzugt werden_) I don't want any special treatment!; **sich** _dat_ **etw ~** (_umg_) to skip sth; **jdm etw ~** (_erlassen_) to let sb off sth; **ihm ist nie etwas geschenkt worden** (_fig_) he never had it easy; **das ist geschenkt!** (_billig_) that's a giveaway!; (_nichts wert_) that's worthless!
Schenkung _f_ gift.
Schenkungsurkunde _f_ deed of gift.
scheppern ['ʃɛpərn] (_umg_) _vi_ to clatter.
Scherbe ['ʃɛrbə] (-, -n) _f_ broken piece, fragment; (_archäologisch_) potsherd.
Schere ['ʃeːrə] (-, -n) _f_ scissors _pl_; (_groß_) shears _pl_; (_ZOOL_) pincer; (_von Hummer, Krebs etc_) pincer, claw; **eine ~** a pair of scissors.
scheren _unreg vt_ to cut; (_Schaf_) to shear; (_stören_) to bother ♦ _vr_ (_sich kümmern_) to care; **scher dich (zum Teufel)!** get lost!
Scherenschleifer (-s, -) _m_ knife grinder.
Scherenschnitt _m_ silhouette.
Schererei [ʃeːrəˈraɪ] (_umg_) _f_ bother, trouble.
Scherflein ['ʃɛrflaɪn] _nt_ mite, bit.
Scherz [ʃɛrts] (-es, -e) _m_ joke; fun; **s~en** _vi_ to joke; (_albern_) to banter; **~frage** _f_ conundrum; **s~haft** _adj_ joking, jocular.
Scheu [ʃɔy] (-) _f_ shyness; (_Ehrfurcht_) awe; (_Angst_): **~ (vor** +_dat_) fear (of).
scheu [ʃɔy] _adj_ shy.
Scheuche (-, -n) _f_ scarecrow.
scheuchen ['ʃɔyçən] _vt_ to scare (off).
scheuen _vr_: **sich ~ vor** +_dat_ to be afraid of, shrink from ♦ _vt_ to shun ♦ _vi_ (_Pferd_) to shy; **weder Mühe noch Kosten ~** to spare neither trouble nor expense.
Scheuer ['ʃɔyər] (-, -n) _f_ barn.
Scheuer- _zW_: **~bürste** _f_ scrubbing brush; **~lappen** _m_ floorcloth (_BRIT_), scrubbing rag

(_US_); **~leiste** _f_ skirting board.
scheuern _vt_ to scour; (_mit Bürste_) to scrub ♦ _vr_: **sich** _akk_ **(wund) ~** to chafe o.s.; **jdm eine ~** (_umg_) to clout sb one.
Scheuklappe _f_ blinker.
Scheune ['ʃɔynə] (-, -n) _f_ barn.
Scheunendrescher (-s, -) _m_: **er frisst wie ein ~** (_umg_) he eats like a horse.
Scheusal ['ʃɔyzaːl] (-s, -e) _nt_ monster.
scheußlich ['ʃɔyslɪç] _adj_ dreadful, frightful; **S~keit** _f_ dreadfulness.
Schi [ʃiː] _m_ = **Ski**.
Schicht [ʃɪçt] (-, -en) _f_ layer; (_Klasse_) class, level; (_in Fabrik etc_) shift; **~arbeit** _f_ shift work.
schichten _vt_ to layer, stack.
Schichtwechsel _m_ change of shifts.
schick [ʃɪk] _adj_ stylish, chic.
schicken _vt_ to send ♦ _vr_: **sich ~ (in** +_akk_) to resign o.s. (to) ♦ _vb unpers_ (_anständig sein_) to be fitting.
Schickeria [ʃɪkəˈriːa] _f_ (_ironisch_) in-people _pl_.
Schicki(micki) ['ʃɪkɪ('mɪkɪ)] (-s, -s) (_umg_) _m_ trendy.
schicklich _adj_ proper, fitting.
Schicksal (-s, -e) _nt_ fate.
schicksalhaft _adj_ fateful.
Schicksalsschlag _m_ great misfortune, blow.
Schickse ['ʃɪksə] (-, -n) (_umg_) _f_ floozy, shiksa (_US_).
Schiebedach _nt_ (_AUT_) sunroof, sunshine roof.
schieben ['ʃiːbən] _unreg vt_ (_auch Drogen_) to push; (_Schuld_) to put; (_umg: handeln mit_) to traffic in; **die Schuld auf jdn ~** to put the blame on (to) sb; **etw vor sich** _dat_ **her ~** (_fig_) to put sth off.
Schieber (-s, -) _m_ slide; (_Besteckteil_) pusher; (_Person_) profiteer; (_umg: Schwarzhändler_) black marketeer; (: _Waffen~_) gunrunner; (: _Drogen~_) pusher.
Schiebetür _f_ sliding door.
Schieblehre _f_ (_MATH_) calliper (_BRIT_) _od_ caliper (_US_) rule.
Schiebung _f_ fiddle; **das war doch ~** (_umg_) that was rigged _od_ a fix.
schied _etc_ [ʃiːt] _vb siehe_ **scheiden**.
Schieds- _zW_: **~gericht** _nt_ court of arbitration; **~mann** (-(e)s, _pl_ **-männer**) _m_ arbitrator; **~richter** _m_ referee, umpire; (_Schlichter_) arbitrator; **s~richtern** _vi untr_ to referee, umpire; to arbitrate; **~spruch** _m_ (arbitration) award; **~verfahren** _nt_ arbitration.
schief [ʃiːf] _adj_ crooked; (_Ebene_) sloping; (_Turm_) leaning; (_Winkel_) oblique; (_Blick_) wry; (_Vergleich_) distorted ♦ _adv_ crookedly; (_ansehen_) askance; **auf die ~e Bahn geraten** (_fig_) to leave the straight and narrow; **~ gehen** (_umg_) to go wrong; **es wird schon**

~ **gehen!** (*hum*) it'll be OK; ~ **liegen** (*umg*) to be wrong, be on the wrong track (*umg*); **etw ~ stellen** to slope sth.

Schiefer ['ʃiːfər] (**-s, -**) *m* slate; ~**dach** *nt* slate roof; ~**tafel** *f* (child's) slate.

schieflachen (*umg*) *vr* to kill o.s. laughing.

schielen ['ʃiːlən] *vi* to squint; **nach etw ~** (*fig*) to eye sth up.

schien *etc* [ʃiːn] *vb siehe* **scheinen**.

Schienbein *nt* shinbone.

Schiene ['ʃiːnə] *f* rail; (*MED*) splint.

schienen *vt* to put in splints.

Schienenbus *m* railcar.

Schienenstrang *m* (*EISENB etc*) (section of) track.

schier [ʃiːr] *adj* pure; (*fig*) sheer ♦ *adv* nearly, almost.

Schießbude *f* shooting gallery.

Schießbudenfigur (*umg*) *f* clown, ludicrous figure.

schießen ['ʃiːsən] *unreg vi* to shoot; (*Salat etc*) to run to seed ♦ *vt* to shoot; (*Ball*) to kick; (*Geschoss*) to fire; ~ **auf** +*akk* to shoot at; **aus dem Boden ~** (*lit, fig*) to spring *od* sprout up; **jdm durch den Kopf ~** (*fig*) to flash through sb's mind.

Schießerei [ʃiːsəˈraɪ] *f* shoot-out, gun battle.

Schieß- *zW:* ~**gewehr** *nt* (*hum*) gun; ~**hund** *m:* **wie ein** ~**hund aufpassen** (*umg*) to watch like a hawk; ~**platz** *m* firing range; ~**pulver** *nt* gunpowder; ~**scharte** *f* embrasure; ~**stand** *m* rifle *od* shooting range.

Schiff [ʃif] (**-(e)s, -e**) *nt* ship, vessel; (*Kirchen~*) nave.

Schiffahrt△ *f siehe* **Schifffahrt**.

Schiff- *zW:* **s~bar** *adj* navigable; ~**bau** *m* shipbuilding; ~**bruch** *m* shipwreck; ~**bruch erleiden** (*lit*) to be shipwrecked; (*fig*) to fail; (*Unternehmen*) to founder; **s~brüchig** *adj* shipwrecked.

Schiffchen *nt* small boat; (*WEBEN*) shuttle; (*Mütze*) forage cap.

Schiffer (**-s, -**) *m* boatman, sailor; (*von Lastkahn*) bargee.

Schiff- *zW:* ~**fahrt**▲ *f* shipping; (*Reise*) voyage; ~**fahrtslinie**▲ *f* shipping route; ~**schaukel** *f* swing boat.

Schiffs- *zW:* ~**junge** *m* cabin boy; ~**körper** *m* hull; ~**ladung** *f* cargo, shipload; ~**planke** *f* gangplank; ~**schraube** *f* ship's propeller.

Schiit [ʃiːit] (**-en, -en**) *m* Shiite; **s~isch** *adj* Shiite.

Schikane [ʃiˈkaːnə] (**-, -n**) *f* harassment; dirty trick; **mit allen** ~**n** with all the trimmings; **das hat er aus reiner** ~ **gemacht** he did it out of sheer bloody-mindedness.

schikanieren [ʃikaˈniːrən] *vt* to harass; (*Ehepartner*) to mess around; (*Mitschüler*) to bully.

schikanös [ʃikaˈnøːs] *adj* (*Mensch*) bloody-minded; (*Maßnahme etc*) harassing.

Schild¹ [ʃilt] (**-(e)s, -e**) *m* shield; (*Mützen~*) peak, visor; **etwas im** ~**e führen** to be up to something.

Schild² [ʃilt] (**-(e)s, -er**) *nt* sign; (*Namens~*) nameplate; (*an Monument, Haus, Grab*) plaque; (*Etikett*) label.

Schildbürger *m* duffer, blockhead.

Schilddrüse *f* thyroid gland.

schildern ['ʃildərn] *vt* to describe; (*Menschen etc*) to portray; (*skizzieren*) to outline.

Schilderung *f* description; portrayal.

Schildkröte *f* tortoise; (*Wasser~*) turtle.

Schildkrötensuppe *f* turtle soup.

Schilf [ʃilf] (**-(e)s, -e**) *nt*, ~**rohr** *nt* (*Pflanze*) reed; (*Material*) reeds *pl*, rushes *pl*.

Schillerlocke ['ʃilərlɔkə] *f* (*Gebäck*) cream horn; (*Räucherfisch*) strip of smoked rock salmon.

schillern ['ʃilərn] *vi* to shimmer.

schillernd *adj* iridescent; (*fig: Charakter*) enigmatic.

Schilling ['ʃiliŋ] (**-s, - od (Schillingstücke) -e**) (*ÖSTERR*) *m* schilling.

schilt [ʃilt] *vb siehe* **schelten**.

Schimmel ['ʃiməl] (**-s, -**) *m* mould (*BRIT*), mold (*US*); (*Pferd*) white horse.

schimm(e)lig *adj* mouldy (*BRIT*), moldy (*US*).

schimmeln *vi* to go mouldy (*BRIT*) *od* moldy (*US*).

Schimmer ['ʃimər] (**-s**) *m* glimmer; **keinen (blassen)** ~ **von etw haben** (*umg*) not to have the slightest idea about sth.

schimmern *vi* to glimmer; (*Seide, Perlen*) to shimmer.

Schimpanse [ʃimˈpanzə] (**-n, -n**) *m* chimpanzee.

Schimpf [ʃimpf] (**-(e)s, -e**) *m* disgrace; **mit** ~ **und Schande** in disgrace.

schimpfen *vi* (*sich beklagen*) to grumble; (*fluchen*) to curse.

Schimpfkanonade *f* barrage of abuse.

Schimpfwort *nt* term of abuse.

Schindel ['ʃindəl] (**-, -n**) *f* shingle.

schinden ['ʃindən] *unreg vt* to maltreat, drive too hard ♦ *vr:* **sich ~ (mit)** to sweat and strain (at), toil away (at); **Eindruck ~** (*umg*) to create an impression.

Schinder (**-s, -**) *m* knacker; (*fig*) slave driver.

Schinderei [ʃindəˈraɪ] *f* grind, drudgery.

Schindluder ['ʃintluːdər] *nt:* **mit etw ~ treiben** to muck *od* mess sth about; (*Vorrecht*) to abuse sth.

Schinken ['ʃiŋkən] (**-s, -**) *m* ham; (*gekocht und geräuchert*) gammon; (*pej: umg: Theaterstück etc*) hackneyed and clichéd play *etc*; ~**speck** *m* bacon.

Schippe ['ʃipə] (**-, -n**) *f* shovel; **jdn auf die** ~ **nehmen** (*fig: umg*) to pull sb's leg.

schippen *vt* to shovel.

Schirm [ʃɪrm] (-(e)s, -e) *m* (*Regen~*) umbrella; (*Sonnen~*) parasol, sunshade; (*Wand~, Bild~*) screen; (*Lampen~*) (lamp)shade; (*Mützen~*) peak; (*Pilz~*) cap; ~**bildaufnahme** *f* X-ray; ~**herr(in)** *m(f)* patron(ess); ~**herrschaft** *f* patronage; ~**mütze** *f* peaked cap; ~**ständer** *m* umbrella stand.
Schiss▲ *m:* ~ **haben** (*umg*) to be shit scared (!).
schiss *etc▲* [ʃɪs] *vb siehe* **scheißen.**
schizophren [ʃitso'freːn] *adj* schizophrenic.
Schizophrenie [ʃitsofre'niː] *f* schizophrenia.
schlabbern ['ʃlabərn] (*umg*) *vt, vi* to slurp.
Schlacht [ʃlaxt] (-, -en) *f* battle.
schlachten *vt* to slaughter, kill.
Schlachtenbummler (*umg*) *m* visiting football fan.
Schlachter (-s, -) *m* butcher.
Schlacht- *zW:* ~**feld** *nt* battlefield; ~**fest** *nt* *country feast at which freshly slaughtered meat is served*; ~**haus** *nt*, ~**hof** *m* slaughterhouse, abattoir (*BRIT*); ~**opfer** *nt* sacrifice; (*Mensch*) human sacrifice; ~**plan** *m* battle plan; (*fig*) plan of action; ~**ruf** *m* battle cry, war cry; ~**schiff** *nt* battleship; ~**vieh** *nt* animals *pl* kept for meat.
Schlacke ['ʃlakə] (-, -n) *f* slag.
schlackern (*umg*) *vi* to tremble; (*Kleidung*) to hang loosely, be baggy; **mit den Ohren** ~ (*fig*) to be (left) speechless.
Schlaf [ʃlaːf] (-(e)s) *m* sleep; **um seinen** ~ **kommen** *od* **gebracht werden** to lose sleep; ~**anzug** *m* pyjamas *pl* (*BRIT*), pajamas *pl* (*US*).
Schläfchen ['ʃlɛːfçən] *nt* nap.
Schläfe (-, -n) *f* (*ANAT*) temple.
schlafen *unreg vi* to sleep; (*umg: nicht aufpassen*) to be asleep; ~ **gehen** to go to bed; **bei jdm** ~ to stay overnight with sb; **S~gehen** *nt* going to bed.
Schlafenszeit *f* bedtime.
Schläfer(in) ['ʃlɛːfər(ɪn)] (-s, -) *m(f)* sleeper.
schlaff [ʃlaf] *adj* slack; (*Haut*) loose; (*Muskeln*) flabby; (*energielos*) limp; (*erschöpft*) exhausted; **S~heit** *f* slackness; looseness; flabbiness; limpness; exhaustion.
Schlafgelegenheit *f* place to sleep.
Schlafittchen [ʃla'fɪtçən] (*umg*) *nt:* **jdn am** *od* **beim** ~ **nehmen** to take sb by the scruff of the neck.
Schlaf- *zW:* ~**krankheit** *f* sleeping sickness; ~**lied** *nt* lullaby; **s~los** *adj* sleepless; ~**losigkeit** *f* sleeplessness, insomnia; ~**mittel** *nt* sleeping drug; (*fig, ironisch*) soporific; ~**mütze** (*umg*) *f* dope.
schläfrig ['ʃlɛːfrɪç] *adj* sleepy.
Schlaf- *zW:* ~**rock** *m* dressing gown; **Apfel im** ~**rock** baked apple in puff pastry; ~**saal** *m* dormitory; ~**sack** *m* sleeping bag.
schläft [ʃlɛːft] *vb siehe* **schlafen.**

Schlaf- *zW:* ~**tablette** *f* sleeping pill; **s~trunken** *adj* drowsy, half-asleep; ~**wagen** *m* sleeping car, sleeper; **s~wandeln** *vi untr* to sleepwalk; ~**wandler(in)** (-s, -) *m(f)* sleepwalker; ~**zimmer** *nt* bedroom.
Schlag [ʃlaːk] (-(e)s, ⸚e) *m* (*lit, fig*) blow; (*auch MED*) stroke; (*Puls~, Herz~*) beat; (*ELEK*) shock; (*Blitz~*) bolt, stroke; (*Glocken~*) chime; (*Autotür*) car door; (*umg: Portion*) helping; (: *Art*) kind, type; **Schläge** *pl* (*Tracht Prügel*) beating *sing*; ~ **acht Uhr** (*umg*) on the stroke of eight; **mit einem** ~ all at once; ~ **auf** ~ in rapid succession; **die haben keinen** ~ **getan** (*umg*) they haven't done a stroke (of work); **ich dachte, mich trifft der** ~ (*umg*) I was thunderstruck; **vom gleichen** ~ **sein** to be cast in the same mould (*BRIT*) *od* mold (*US*); (*pej*) to be tarred with the same brush; **ein** ~ **ins Wasser** (*umg*) a wash-out; ~**abtausch** *m* (*BOXEN*) exchange of blows; (*fig*) (verbal) exchange; ~**ader** *f* artery; ~**anfall** *m* stroke; **s~artig** *adj* sudden, without warning; ~**baum** *m* barrier; ~**bohrer** *m* percussion drill.
Schlägel▲ ['ʃlɛːgl] (-s, -) *m* drumstick; (*Hammer*) hammer.
schlagen ['ʃlaːgən] *unreg vt* to strike, hit; (*wiederholt* ~, *besiegen*) to beat; (*Glocke*) to ring; (*Stunde*) to strike; (*Kreis, Bogen*) to describe; (*Purzelbaum*) to do; (*Sahne*) to whip; (*Schlacht*) to fight; (*einwickeln*) to wrap ♦ *vi* to strike, hit; to beat; to ring; to strike ♦ *vr* to fight; **um sich** ~ to lash out; **ein Ei in die Pfanne** ~ to crack an egg into the pan; **eine geschlagene Stunde** a full hour; **na ja, ehe ich mich** ~ **lasse!** (*hum: umg*) I suppose you could twist my arm; **nach jdm** ~ (*fig*) to take after sb; **sich gut** ~ (*fig*) to do well; **sich nach links/Norden** ~ to strike out to the left/(for the) north; **sich auf jds Seite** *akk* ~ to side with sb; (*die Fronten wechseln*) to go over to sb.
schlagend *adj* (*Beweis*) convincing; ~**e Wetter** (*MIN*) firedamp.
Schlager ['ʃlaːgər] (-s, -) *m* (*MUS, fig*) hit.
Schläger ['ʃlɛːgər] (-s, -) *m* brawler; (*SPORT*) bat; (*TENNIS etc*) racket; (*GOLF*) club; (*Hockey~*) hockey stick.
Schlägerei [ʃlɛːgə'raɪ] *f* fight, punch-up.
Schlagersänger *m* pop singer.
Schlägertyp (*umg*) *m* thug.
Schlag- *zW:* **s~fertig** *adj* quick-witted; ~**fertigkeit** *f* ready wit, quickness of repartee; ~**instrument** *nt* percussion instrument; ~**kraft** *f* (*lit, fig*) power; (*MIL*) strike power; (*BOXEN*) punch(ing power); **s~kräftig** *adj* powerful; (*Beweise*) clear-cut; ~**loch** *nt* pothole; ~**obers** (-, -) (*ÖSTERR*) *nt*, ~**rahm** *m*, ~**sahne** *f* (whipped) cream; ~**seite** *f* (*NAUT*) list; ~**stock** *m* (*form*) truncheon

(*BRIT*), nightstick (*US*).

schlägt [ʃlɛːkt] *vb siehe* **schlagen**.

Schlag- *zW*: **~wort** *nt* slogan, catch phrase; **~zeile** *f* headline; **~zeilen machen** (*umg*) to hit the headlines; **~zeug** *nt* drums *pl*; (*in Orchester*) percussion; **~zeuger** (**-s, -**) *m* drummer; percussionist.

schlaksig ['ʃlaːksɪç] (*umg*) *adj* gangling, gawky.

Schlamassel [ʃla'masəl] (**-s, -**) (*umg*) *m* mess.

Schlamm [ʃlam] (**-(e)s, -e**) *m* mud.

schlammig *adj* muddy.

Schlampe ['ʃlampə] (**-, -n**) (*umg*) *f* slattern, slut.

schlampen (*umg*) *vi* to be sloppy.

Schlamperei [ʃlampə'raɪ] (*umg*) *f* disorder, untidiness; (*schlechte Arbeit*) sloppy work.

schlampig (*umg*) *adj* slovenly, sloppy.

schlang *etc* [ʃlaŋ] *vb siehe* **schlingen**.

Schlange ['ʃlaŋə] (**-, -n**) *f* snake; (*Menschen~*) queue (*US*), line (*US*); **~ stehen** to (form a) queue (*BRIT*), stand in line (*US*); **eine falsche ~** a snake in the grass.

schlängeln ['ʃlɛŋəln] *vr* to twist, wind; (*Fluss*) to meander.

Schlangen- *zW*: **~biss** ▲ *m* snake bite; **~gift** *nt* snake venom; **~linie** *f* wavy line.

schlank [ʃlaŋk] *adj* slim, slender; **S~heit** *f* slimness, slenderness; **S~heitskur** *f* diet.

schlapp [ʃlap] *adj* limp; (*locker*) slack; (*umg*: *energielos*) listless; (*nach Krankheit etc*) run-down.

Schlappe (**-, -n**) (*umg*) *f* setback.

Schlappen (**-s, -**) (*umg*) *m* slipper.

schlapp- *zW*: **S~heit** *f* limpness; slackness; **S~hut** *m* slouch hat; **~machen** (*umg*) *vi* to wilt, droop; **S~schwanz** (*pej: umg*) *m* weakling, softy.

Schlaraffenland [ʃla'rafənlant] *nt* land of milk and honey.

schlau [ʃlaʊ] *adj* crafty, cunning; **ich werde nicht ~ aus ihm** I don't know what to make of him; **S~berger** (**-s, -**) (*umg*) *m* clever Dick.

Schlauch [ʃlaʊx] (**-(e)s, Schläuche**) *m* hose; (*in Reifen*) inner tube; (*umg: Anstrengung*) grind; **auf dem ~ stehen** (*umg*) to be in a jam *od* fix; **~boot** *nt* rubber dinghy.

schlauchen (*umg*) *vt* to tell on, exhaust.

schlauchlos *adj* (*Reifen*) tubeless.

Schläue ['ʃlɔʏə] (**-**) *f* cunning.

Schlaufe ['ʃlaʊfə] (**-, -n**) *f* loop; (*Aufhänger*) hanger.

Schlauheit *f* cunning.

Schlaukopf *m* clever Dick.

Schlawiner [ʃla'viːnər] (**-s, -**) *m* (*hum: umg*) villain, rogue.

schlecht [ʃlɛçt] *adj* bad; (*ungenießbar*) bad, off (*BRIT*) ♦ *adv*: **jdm geht es ~** sb is in a bad way; **heute geht es ~** today is not very convenient; **~ machen** to run down,

denigrate; **er kann ~ Nein** *od* **nein sagen** he finds it hard to say no, he can't say no; **jdm ist ~** sb feels sick *od* ill; **~ und recht** after a fashion; **auf jdn ~ zu sprechen sein** not to have a good word to say for sb; **er hat nicht ~ gestaunt** (*umg*) he wasn't half surprised.

schlechterdings *adv* simply.

Schlecht- *zW*: **~heit** *f* badness; **s~hin** *adv* simply; **der Dramatiker s~hin** THE playwright.

Schlechtigkeit *f* badness; (*Tat*) bad deed.

schlecken ['ʃlɛkən] *vt, vi* to lick.

Schlegel ['ʃleːgəl] (**-s, -**) *m* (*KOCH*) leg; *siehe auch* **Schlägel**.

schleichen ['ʃlaɪçən] *unreg vi* to creep, crawl.

schleichend *adj* creeping; (*Krankheit, Gift*) insidious.

Schleichweg *m*: **auf ~en** (*fig*) on the quiet.

Schleichwerbung *f*: **eine ~** a plug.

Schleie ['ʃlaɪə] (**-, -n**) *f* tench.

Schleier ['ʃlaɪər] (**-s, -**) *m* veil; **~eule** *f* barn owl; **s~haft** (*umg*) *adj*: **jdm s~haft sein** to be a mystery to sb.

Schleife ['ʃlaɪfə] (**-, -n**) *f* (*auch COMPUT*) loop; (*Band*) bow; (*Kranz~*) ribbon.

schleifen¹ *vt* to drag; (*MIL: Festung*) to raze ♦ *vi* to drag; **die Kupplung ~ lassen** (*AUT*) to slip the clutch.

schleifen² *unreg vt* to grind; (*Edelstein*) to cut; (*MIL: Soldaten*) to drill.

Schleifmaschine *f* sander; (*in Fabrik*) grinding machine.

Schleifstein *m* grindstone.

Schleim [ʃlaɪm] (**-(e)s, -e**) *m* slime; (*MED*) mucus; (*KOCH*) gruel; **~haut** *f* mucous membrane.

schleimig *adj* slimy.

schlemmen ['ʃlɛmən] *vi* to feast.

Schlemmer(in) (**-s, -**) *m(f)* gourmet, bon vivant.

Schlemmerei [ʃlɛmə'raɪ] *f* feasting.

schlendern ['ʃlɛndərn] *vi* to stroll.

Schlendrian ['ʃlɛndriaːn] (**-(e)s**) *m* sloppy way of working.

Schlenker ['ʃlɛŋkər] (**-s, -**) *m* swerve.

schlenkern *vt, vi* to swing, dangle.

Schleppe ['ʃlɛpə] (**-, -n**) *f* train.

schleppen *vt* to drag; (*Auto, Schiff*) to tow; (*tragen*) to lug.

schleppend *adj* dragging; (*Bedienung, Abfertigung*) sluggish, slow.

Schlepper (**-s, -**) *m* tractor; (*Schiff*) tug.

Schleppkahn *m* (canal) barge.

Schlepptau *nt* towrope; **jdn ins ~ nehmen** (*fig*) to take sb in tow.

Schlesien ['ʃleːziən] (**-s**) *nt* Silesia.

Schlesier(in) (**-s, -**) *m(f)* Silesian.

schlesisch *adj* Silesian.

Schleswig-Holstein ['ʃleːsvɪç'hɔlʃtaɪn] (**-s**) *nt* Schleswig-Holstein.

Schleuder ['ʃlɔydər] (-, -n) f catapult; (Wäsche~) spin-dryer; (Zentrifuge) centrifuge; ~honig m extracted honey.

schleudern vt to hurl; (Wäsche) to spin-dry ♦ vi (AUT) to skid; **ins S~ kommen** (AUT) to go into a skid; (fig: umg) to run into trouble.

Schleuder- zW: ~**preis** m give-away price; ~**sitz** m (AVIAT) ejector seat; (fig) hot seat; ~**ware** f cut-price (BRIT) od cut-rate (US) goods pl.

schleunig ['ʃlɔyniç] adj prompt, speedy; (Schritte) quick.

schleunigst adv straight away.

Schleuse ['ʃlɔyzə] (-, -n) f lock; (Schleusentor) sluice.

schleusen vt (Schiffe) to pass through a lock, lock; (Wasser) to channel; (Menschen) to filter; (fig: heimlich) to smuggle.

Schlich (-(e)s, -e) m dodge, trick; **jdm auf die ~e kommen** to get wise to sb.

schlich etc [ʃliç] vb siehe **schleichen**.

schlicht [ʃliçt] adj simple, plain.

schlichten vt to smooth; (beilegen) to settle; (Streit: vermitteln) to mediate, arbitrate.

Schlichter(in) (-s, -) m(f) mediator, arbitrator.

Schlichtheit f simplicity, plainness.

Schlichtung f settlement; arbitration.

Schlick [ʃlɪk] (-(e)s, -e) m mud; (Öl~) slick.

schlief etc [ʃliːf] vb siehe **schlafen**.

Schließe ['ʃliːsə] (-, -n) f fastener.

schließen ['ʃliːsən] unreg vt to close, shut; (beenden) to close; (Freundschaft, Bündnis, Ehe) to enter into; (COMPUT: Datei) to close; (folgern): ~ **(aus)** to infer (from) ♦ vi, vr to close, shut; **auf etw** akk ~ **lassen** to suggest sth; **jdn/etw in sein Herz** ~ to take sb/sth to one's heart; **etw in sich** ~ to include sth; „geschlossen" "closed".

Schließfach nt locker.

schließlich adv finally; (~ **doch**) after all.

Schliff (-(e)s, -e) m cut(ting); (fig) polish; **einer Sache den letzten** ~ **geben** (fig) to put the finishing touch(es) to sth.

schliff etc [ʃlɪf] vb siehe **schleifen**.

schlimm [ʃlɪm] adj bad; **das war** ~ that was terrible; **das ist halb so** ~! that's not so bad!; ~**er** adj worse; ~**ste(r, s)** adj worst.

schlimmstenfalls adv at (the) worst.

Schlinge ['ʃlɪŋə] (-, -n) f loop; (an Galgen) noose; (Falle) snare; (MED) sling.

Schlingel (-s, -) m rascal.

schlingen unreg vt to wind ♦ vi (essen) to bolt one's food, gobble.

schlingern vi to roll.

Schlingpflanze f creeper.

Schlips [ʃlɪps] (-es, -e) m tie, necktie (US); **sich auf den** ~ **getreten fühlen** (fig: umg) to feel offended.

Schlitten ['ʃlɪtən] (-s, -) m sledge, sled; (Pferde~) sleigh; **mit jdm** ~ **fahren** (umg) to give sb a rough time; ~**bahn** f toboggan run; ~**fahren** (-s) nt tobogganing.

schlittern ['ʃlɪtərn] vi to slide; (Wagen) to skid.

Schlittschuh ['ʃlɪtʃuː] m skate; ~ **laufen** to skate; ~**bahn** f skating rink; ~**läufer** m skater.

Schlitz [ʃlɪts] (-es, -e) m slit; (für Münze) slot; (Hosen~) flies pl; **s~äugig** adj slant-eyed; **s~en** vt to slit; ~**ohr** nt (fig) sly fox.

schlohweiß ['ʃloːˈvaɪs] adj snow-white.

Schlokal nt gourmet restaurant.

Schloss▲ (-es, ⁻er) nt lock, padlock; (an Schmuck etc) clasp; (Bau) castle; (Palast) palace; **ins** ~ **fallen** to lock (itself).

schloss etc▲ [ʃlɔs] vb siehe **schließen**.

Schlosser ['ʃlɔsər] (-s, -) m (Auto~) fitter; (für Schlüssel etc) locksmith.

Schlosserei [ʃlɔsəˈraɪ] f metal(working) shop.

Schlosshund▲ m: **heulen wie ein** ~ to howl one's head off.

Schlot [ʃloːt] (-(e)s, -e) m chimney; (NAUT) funnel.

schlottern ['ʃlɔtərn] vi to shake; (vor Angst) to tremble; (Kleidung) to be baggy.

Schlucht [ʃluxt] (-, -en) f gorge, ravine.

schluchzen ['ʃluxtsən] vi to sob.

Schluck [ʃluk] (-(e)s, -e) m swallow; (größer) gulp; (kleiner) sip; (ein bisschen) drop.

Schluckauf (-s) m hiccups pl.

schlucken vt to swallow; (umg: Alkohol, Benzin) to guzzle; (: verschlingen) to swallow up ♦ vi to swallow.

Schlucker (-s, -) (umg) m: **armer** ~ poor devil.

Schluckimpfung f oral vaccination.

schlud(e)rig ['ʃluːdrɪç] (umg) adj slipshod.

schludern ['ʃluːdərn] (umg) vi to do slipshod work.

schlug etc [ʃluːk] vb siehe **schlagen**.

Schlummer ['ʃlumər] (-s) m slumber.

schlummern vi to slumber.

Schlund [ʃlunt] (-(e)s, ⁻e) m gullet; (fig) jaw.

schlüpfen ['ʃlʏpfən] vi to slip; (Vogel etc) to hatch (out).

Schlüpfer ['ʃlʏpfər] (-s, -) m panties pl, knickers pl.

Schlupfloch ['ʃlupflɔx] nt hole; (Versteck) hide-out; (fig) loophole.

schlüpfrig ['ʃlʏpfrɪç] adj slippery; (fig) lewd; **S~keit** f slipperiness; lewdness.

Schlupfwinkel m hiding place; (fig) quiet corner.

schlurfen ['ʃlurfən] vi to shuffle.

schlürfen ['ʃlʏrfən] vt, vi to slurp.

Schluss▲ [ʃlus] (-es, ⁻e) m end; (~folgerung) conclusion; **am** ~ at the end; ~ **für heute!** that'll do for today; ~ **jetzt!** that's enough now!; ~ **machen mit** to finish with.

Schlüssel ['ʃlʏsəl] (-s, -) m (lit, fig) key; (Schraub~) spanner, wrench; (MUS) clef;

~**bein** nt collarbone; ~**blume** f cowslip, primrose; ~**bund** m bunch of keys; ~**erlebnis** nt (PSYCH) crucial experience; ~**kind** nt latchkey child; ~**loch** nt keyhole; ~**position** f key position; ~**wort** nt safe combination; (COMPUT) keyword.

Schlussfolgerung▲ f conclusion, inference.

Schlussformel▲ f (in Brief) closing formula; (bei Vertrag) final clause.

schlüssig ['ʃlʏsɪç] adj conclusive; **sich** dat (über etw akk) ~ **sein** to have made up one's mind (about sth).

Schluss-▲ zW: ~**licht** nt rear light (BRIT), taillight (US); (fig) tail ender; ~**strich** m (fig) final stroke; **einen** ~**strich unter etw** akk **ziehen** to consider sth finished; ~**verkauf** m clearance sale; ~**wort** nt concluding words pl.

Schmach [ʃmaːx] (-) f disgrace, ignominy.

schmachten ['ʃmaxtən] vi to languish; **nach jdm** ~ to pine for sb.

schmächtig ['ʃmɛçtɪç] adj slight.

schmachvoll adj ignominious, humiliating.

schmackhaft ['ʃmakhaft] adj tasty; **jdm etw** ~ **machen** (fig) to make sth palatable to sb.

schmähen ['ʃmɛːən] vt to abuse, revile.

schmählich adj ignominious, shameful.

Schmähung f abuse.

schmal [ʃmaːl] adj narrow; (Person, Buch etc) slender, slim; (karg) meagre (BRIT), meager (US); ~**brüstig** adj narrow-chested.

schmälern ['ʃmɛːlərn] vt to diminish; (fig) to belittle.

Schmalfilm m cine (BRIT) od movie (US) film.

Schmalspur f narrow gauge.

Schmalspur- (pej) in zW small-time.

Schmalz [ʃmalts] (-es, -e) nt dripping; (Schweine~) lard; (fig) sentiment, schmaltz.

schmalzig adj (fig) schmaltzy, slushy.

schmarotzen [ʃmaˈrɔtsən] vi (BIOL) to be parasitic; (fig) to sponge.

Schmarotzer (-s, -) m (auch fig) parasite.

Schmarren ['ʃmarən] (-s, -) m (ÖSTERR) small pieces of pancake; (fig) rubbish, tripe.

schmatzen ['ʃmatsən] vi to eat noisily.

Schmaus [ʃmaʊs] (-es, Schmäuse) m feast; **s~en** vi to feast.

schmecken ['ʃmɛkən] vt, vi to taste; **es schmeckt ihm** he likes it; **schmeckt es Ihnen?** is it good?, are you enjoying your food od meal?; **das schmeckt nach mehr!** (umg) it's very moreish (hum); **es sich** ~ **lassen** to tuck in.

Schmeichelei [ʃmaɪçəˈlaɪ] f flattery.

schmeichelhaft ['ʃmaɪçəlhaft] adj flattering.

schmeicheln vi to flatter.

Schmeichler(in) (-s, -) m(f) flatterer.

schmeißen ['ʃmaɪsən] unreg (umg) vt to throw, chuck; (spendieren): **eine Runde** od **Lage** ~ to stand a round.

Schmeißfliege f bluebottle.

Schmelz [ʃmɛlts] (-es, -e) m enamel; (Glasur) glaze; (von Stimme) melodiousness; **s~bar** adj fusible.

schmelzen unreg vt to melt; (Erz) to smelt ♦ vi to melt.

Schmelz- zW: ~**hütte** f smelting works pl; ~**käse** m cheese spread; (in Scheiben) processed cheese; ~**ofen** m melting furnace; (für Erze) smelting furnace; ~**punkt** m melting point; ~**tiegel** m (lit, fig) melting pot; ~**wasser** nt melted snow.

Schmerbauch ['ʃmeːrbaʊx] (umg) m paunch, potbelly.

Schmerz [ʃmɛrts] (-es, -en) m pain; (Trauer) grief no pl; ~**en haben** to be in pain; **s~empfindlich** adj sensitive to pain.

schmerzen vt, vi to hurt.

Schmerzensgeld nt compensation.

Schmerz- zW: **s~haft** adj painful; **s~lich** adj painful; **s~lindernd** adj pain-relieving; **s~los** adj painless; ~**mittel** nt painkiller, analgesic; **s~stillend** adj pain-killing, analgesic; ~**tablette** f pain-killing tablet.

Schmetterling ['ʃmɛtərlɪŋ] m butterfly.

Schmetterlingsstil m (SCHWIMMEN) butterfly stroke.

schmettern ['ʃmɛtərn] vt to smash; (Melodie) to sing loudly, bellow out ♦ vi to smash (SPORT); (Trompete) to blare.

Schmied [ʃmiːt] (-(e)s, -e) m blacksmith.

Schmiede ['ʃmiːdə] (-, -n) f smithy, forge; ~**eisen** nt wrought iron.

schmieden vt to forge; (Pläne) to devise, concoct.

schmiegen ['ʃmiːgən] vt to press, nestle ♦ vr: **sich** ~ **an** +akk to cuddle up to, nestle up to.

schmiegsam ['ʃmiːkzaːm] adj flexible, pliable.

Schmiere ['ʃmiːrə] f grease; (THEAT) greasepaint, make-up; (pej: schlechtes Theater) fleapit; ~ **stehen** (umg) to be the look-out.

schmieren vt to smear; (ölen) to lubricate, grease; (bestechen) to bribe ♦ vi (schreiben) to scrawl; **es läuft wie geschmiert** it's going like clockwork; **jdm eine** ~ (umg) to clout sb one.

Schmierenkomödiant (pej) m ham (actor).

Schmier- zW: ~**fett** nt grease; ~**fink** m messy person; ~**geld** nt bribe; ~**heft** nt jotter.

schmierig adj greasy.

Schmiermittel nt lubricant.

Schmierseife f soft soap.

schmilzt [ʃmɪltst] vb siehe **schmelzen**.

Schminke ['ʃmɪŋkə] (-, -n) f make-up.

schminken vt, vr to make up.

schmirgeln ['ʃmɪrgəln] vt to sand (down).

Schmirgelpapier (-s) nt emery paper.

Schmiss▲ (-es, -e) m (Narbe) duelling (BRIT) od dueling (US) scar; (veraltet: Schwung) dash, élan.

schmiss *etc*▲ [ʃmɪs] *vb siehe* **schmeißen.**

Schmöker ['ʃmøːkər] (**-s, -**) (*umg*) *m* (trashy) old book.

schmökern *vi* to bury o.s. in a book; (*umg*) to browse.

schmollen ['ʃmɔlən] *vi* to pout; (*gekränkt*) to sulk.

schmollend *adj* sulky.

Schmollmund *m* pout.

schmolz *etc* [ʃmɔlts] *vb siehe* **schmelzen.**

Schmorbraten *m* stewed *od* braised meat.

schmoren ['ʃmoːrən] *vt* to braise.

Schmu [ʃmuː] (**-s**) (*umg*) *m* cheating.

Schmuck [ʃmʊk] (**-(e)s, -e**) *m* jewellery (*BRIT*), jewelry (*US*); (*Verzierung*) decoration.

schmücken ['ʃmʏkən] *vt* to decorate.

Schmuck- *zW*: **s~los** *adj* unadorned, plain; **~losigkeit** *f* simplicity; **~sachen** *pl* jewels *pl*, jewellery *sing* (*BRIT*), jewelry *sing* (*US*); **~stück** *nt* (*Ring etc*) piece of jewellery (*BRIT*) *od* jewelry (*US*); (*fig: Prachtstück*) gem.

schmudd(e)lig ['ʃmʊd(ə)lɪç] *adj* messy; (*schmutzig*) dirty; (*schmierig, unsauber*) filthy.

Schmuggel ['ʃmʊɡəl] (**-s**) *m* smuggling.

schmuggeln *vt, vi* to smuggle.

Schmuggelware *f* contraband.

Schmuggler(in) (**-s, -**) *m(f)* smuggler.

schmunzeln ['ʃmʊntsəln] *vi* to smile benignly.

schmusen ['ʃmuːzən] (*umg*) *vi* (*zärtlich sein*) to cuddle; **mit jdm ~** to cuddle sb.

Schmutz [ʃmʊts] (**-es**) *m* dirt; (*fig*) filth; **s~en** *vi* to get dirty; **~fink** *m* filthy creature; **~fleck** *m* stain.

schmutzig *adj* dirty; **~e Wäsche waschen** (*fig*) to wash one's dirty linen in public.

Schnabel ['ʃnaːbəl] (**-s, ⸚**) *m* beak, bill; (*Ausguss*) spout; (*umg: Mund*) mouth; **reden, wie einem der ~ gewachsen ist** to say exactly what comes into one's head; (*unaffektiert*) to talk naturally.

schnacken ['ʃnakən] (*NORDD: umg*) *vi* to chat.

Schnake ['ʃnaːkə] (**-, -n**) *f* crane fly; (*Stechmücke*) gnat.

Schnalle ['ʃnalə] (**-, -n**) *f* buckle; (*an Handtasche, Buch*) clasp.

schnallen *vt* to buckle.

schnalzen ['ʃnaltsən] *vi* to snap; (*mit Zunge*) to click.

Schnäppchen ['ʃnɛpçən] (*umg*) *nt* bargain, snip.

schnappen ['ʃnapən] *vt* to grab, catch; (*umg: ergreifen*) to snatch ♦ *vi* to snap.

Schnappschloss▲ *nt* spring lock.

Schnappschuss▲ *m* (*PHOT*) snapshot.

Schnaps [ʃnaps] (**-es, ⸚e**) *m* schnapps; (*umg: Branntwein*) spirits *pl*; **~idee** (*umg*) *f* crackpot idea; **~leiche** (*umg*) *f* drunk.

schnarchen ['ʃnarçən] *vi* to snore.

schnattern ['ʃnatərn] *vi* to chatter; (*zittern*) to shiver.

schnauben ['ʃnaʊbən] *vi* to snort ♦ *vr* to blow one's nose.

schnaufen ['ʃnaʊfən] *vi* to puff, pant.

Schnaufer (**-s, -**) (*umg*) *m* breath.

Schnauzbart ['ʃnaʊtsbaːrt] *m* moustache (*BRIT*), mustache (*US*).

Schnauze (**-, -n**) *f* snout, muzzle; (*Ausguss*) spout; (*umg*) gob; **auf die ~ fallen** (*fig*) to come a cropper (*umg*); **etw frei nach ~ machen** to do sth any old how.

schnäuzen▲ ['ʃnɔytsn] *vr* to blow one's nose.

Schnecke ['ʃnɛkə] (**-, -n**) *f* snail; (*Nackt~*) slug; (*KOCH: Gebäck*) ≈ Chelsea bun; **jdn zur ~ machen** (*umg*) to give sb a real bawling out.

Schneckenhaus *nt* snail's shell.

Schneckentempo (*umg*) *nt*: **im ~** at a snail's pace.

Schnee [ʃneː] (**-s**) *m* snow; (*Ei~*) beaten egg white; **~ von gestern** old hat; **water under the bridge**; **~ball** *m* snowball; **~besen** *m* (*KOCH*) whisk; **~fall** *m* snowfall; **~flocke** *f* snowflake; **~gestöber** *nt* snowstorm; **~glöckchen** *nt* snowdrop; **~grenze** *f* snowline; **~kette** *f* (*AUT*) snow chain; **~könig** *m*: **sich freuen wie ein ~könig** to be as pleased as Punch; **~mann** *m* snowman; **~pflug** *m* snowplough (*BRIT*), snowplow (*US*); **~regen** *m* sleet; **~schmelze** *f* thaw; **~treiben** *nt* driving snow; **~wehe** *f* snowdrift; **~wittchen** *nt* Snow White.

Schneid [ʃnaɪt] (**-(e)s**) (*umg*) *m* pluck.

Schneidbrenner (**-s, -**) *m* (*TECH*) oxyacetylene cutter.

Schneide ['ʃnaɪdə] (**-, -n**) *f* edge; (*Klinge*) blade.

schneiden *unreg vt* to cut; (*Film, Tonband*) to edit; (*kreuzen*) to cross, intersect ♦ *vr* to cut o.s.; (*umg: sich täuschen*): **da hat er sich aber geschnitten!** he's very much mistaken; **die Luft ist zum S~** (*fig: umg*) the air is very bad.

schneidend *adj* cutting.

Schneider (**-s, -**) *m* tailor; **frieren wie ein ~** (*umg*) to be frozen to the marrow; **aus dem ~ sein** (*fig*) to be out of the woods.

Schneiderei [ʃnaɪdəˈraɪ] *f* tailor's shop; (*einer Schneiderin*) dressmaker's shop.

Schneiderin *f* dressmaker.

schneidern *vt* to make ♦ *vi* to be a tailor.

Schneidersitz (**-es**) *m*: **im ~ sitzen** to sit cross-legged.

Schneidezahn *m* incisor.

schneidig *adj* dashing; (*mutig*) plucky.

schneien ['ʃnaɪən] *vi* to snow; **jdm ins Haus ~** (*umg: Besuch*) to drop in on sb; (: *Rechnung, Brief*) to come in the post (*BRIT*) *od* mail (*US*).

Schneise ['ʃnaɪzə] (**-, -n**) *f* (*Wald~*) clearing.

schnell [ʃnɛl] *adj* quick, fast ♦ *adv* quick(ly),

fast; **das ging** ~ that was quick; **S~boot** *nt* speedboat.

Schnelle (-) *f*: **etw auf die** ~ **machen** to do sth in a rush.

schnellen *vi* to shoot.

Schnellgericht *nt* (*JUR*) summary court; (*KOCH*) convenience food.

Schnellhefter *m* loose-leaf binder.

Schnelligkeit *f* speed.

Schnell- *zW*: ~**imbiss▲** *m* (*Essen*) (quick) snack; (*Raum*) snack bar; ~**kochtopf** *m* (*Dampfkochtopf*) pressure cooker; ~**reinigung** *f* express cleaner's.

schnellstens *adv* as quickly as possible.

Schnellstraße *f* expressway.

Schnellzug *m* fast *od* express train.

schneuzen△ [ʃnɔytsən] *vr siehe* **schnäuzen**.

Schnickschnack [ʃnɪkʃnak] (-(e)s) (*umg*) *m* twaddle.

Schnippchen [ʃnɪpçən] *nt*: **jdm ein** ~ **schlagen** to play a trick on sb.

schnippeln [ʃnɪpəln] (*umg*) *vt* to snip; (*mit Messer*) to hack ♦ *vi*: ~ **an** +*dat* to snip at; to hack at.

schnippen [ʃnɪpən] *vi*: **mit den Fingern** ~ to snap one's fingers.

schnippisch [ʃnɪpɪʃ] *adj* sharp-tongued.

Schnipsel [ʃnɪpsəl] (-s, -) (*umg*) *m od nt* scrap; (*Papier~*) scrap of paper.

Schnitt (-(e)s, -e) *m* cut(ting); (~*punkt*) intersection; (*Quer~*) (cross) section; (*Durch~*) average; (~*muster*) pattern; (*Ernte*) crop; (*an Buch*) edge; (*umg: Gewinn*) profit; ~: **L. Schwarz** (*FILM*) editor - L. Schwarz; **im** ~ **on average.**

schnitt *etc* [ʃnɪt] *vb siehe* **schneiden**.

Schnittblumen *pl* cut flowers *pl*.

Schnittbohnen *pl* French *od* green beans *pl*.

Schnitte (-, -n) *f* slice; (*belegt*) sandwich.

schnittfest *adj* (*Tomaten*) firm.

Schnittfläche *f* section.

schnittig [ʃnɪtɪç] *adj* smart; (*Auto, Formen*) stylish.

Schnitt- *zW*: ~**lauch** *m* chive; ~**muster** *nt* pattern; ~**punkt** *m* (point of) intersection; ~**stelle** *f* (*COMPUT*) interface; ~**wunde** *f* cut.

Schnitzarbeit *f* wood carving.

Schnitzel (-s, -) *nt* scrap; (*KOCH*) escalope; ~**jagd** *f* paperchase.

schnitzen [ʃnɪtsən] *vt* to carve.

Schnitzer (-s, -) *m* carver; (*umg*) blunder.

Schnitzerei [ʃnɪtsəˈrai] *f* wood carving.

schnodderig [ʃnɔdərɪç] (*umg*) *adj* snotty.

schnöde [ʃnøːdə] *adj* base, mean.

Schnorchel [ʃnɔrçəl] (-s, -) *m* snorkel.

schnorcheln *vi* to go snorkelling.

Schnörkel [ʃnœrkəl] (-s, -) *m* flourish; (*ARCHIT*) scroll.

schnorren [ʃnɔrən] *vt, vi* to cadge (*BRIT*).

Schnorrer (-s, -) (*umg*) *m* cadger (*BRIT*).

Schnösel [ʃnøːzəl] (-s, -) (*umg*) *m* snotty(-nosed) little upstart.

schnuckelig [ʃnʊkəlɪç] (*umg*) *adj* (*gemütlich*) snug, cosy; (*Person*) sweet.

schnüffeln [ʃnʏfəln] *vi* to sniff; (*fig: umg: spionieren*) to snoop around; **S~** *nt* (*von Klebstoff etc*) glue-sniffing *etc*.

Schnüffler(in) (-s, -) *m(f)* snooper.

Schnuller [ʃnʊlər] (-s, -) *m* dummy (*BRIT*), pacifier (*US*).

Schnulze [ʃnʊltsə] (-, -n) (*umg*) *f* schmaltzy film/book/song.

Schnupfen [ʃnʊpfən] (-s, -) *m* cold.

Schnupftabak *m* snuff.

schnuppe [ʃnʊpə] (*umg*) *adj*: **jdm** ~ **sein** to be all the same to sb.

schnuppern [ʃnʊpərn] *vi* to sniff.

Schnur [ʃnuːr] (-, ⁼e) *f* string; (*Kordel*) cord; (*ELEK*) flex.

Schnürchen [ʃnyːrçən] *nt*: **es läuft** *od* **klappt (alles) wie am** ~ everything's going like clockwork.

schnüren [ʃnyːrən] *vt* to tie.

schnurgerade *adj* straight (as a die *od* an arrow).

Schnurrbart [ʃnʊrbaːrt] *m* moustache (*BRIT*), mustache (*US*).

schnurren [ʃnʊrən] *vi* to purr; (*Kreisel*) to hum.

Schnürschuh *m* lace-up (shoe).

Schnürsenkel *m* shoelace.

schnurstracks *adv* straight (away); ~ **auf jdn/etw zugehen** to make a beeline for sb/sth (*umg*).

schob *etc* [ʃoːp] *vb siehe* **schieben**.

Schock [ʃɔk] (-(e)s, -e) *m* shock; **unter** ~ **stehen** to be in (a state of) shock.

schocken (*umg*) *vt* to shock.

Schocker (-s, -) (*umg*) *m* shocking film/novel, shocker.

schockieren *vt* to shock, outrage.

Schöffe [ʃœfə] (-n, -n) *m* lay magistrate.

Schöffengericht *nt* magistrates' court.

Schöffin *f* lay magistrate.

Schokolade [ʃokoˈlaːdə] (-, -n) *f* chocolate.

scholl *etc* [ʃɔl] *vb siehe* **schallen**.

Scholle [ʃɔlə] (-, -n) *f* clod; (*Eis~*) ice floe; (*Fisch*) plaice.

Scholli [ʃɔlɪ] (*umg*) *m*: **mein lieber** ~! (*drohend*) now look here!

═══════════════════════ *SCHLÜSSELWORT*

schon [ʃoːn] *adv* **1** (*bereits*) already; **er ist** ~ **da** he's there/here already, he's already there/ here; **ist er** ~ **da?** is he there/here yet?; **warst du** ~ **einmal dort?** have you ever been there?; **ich war** ~ **einmal dort** I've been there before; **das war** ~ **immer so** that has always been the case; **hast du** ~ **gehört?** have you heard?; ~ **1920** as early as 1920;

~ **vor 100 Jahren** as far back as 100 years ago; **er wollte** ~ **die Hoffnung aufgeben, als** ... he was just about to give up hope when ...; **wartest du** ~ **lange?** have you been waiting (for) long?; **wie** ~ **so oft** as so often (before); **was,** ~ **wieder?** what - again?

2 (*bestimmt*) all right; **du wirst** ~ **sehen** you'll see (all right); **das wird** ~ **noch gut gehen** that should turn out OK (in the end).

3 (*bloß*) just; **allein** ~ **das Gefühl** ... just the very feeling ...; ~ **der Gedanke** the mere *od* very thought; **wenn ich das** ~ **höre** I only have to hear that.

4 (*einschränkend*): **ja** ~, **aber** ... yes (well), but ...

5: das ist ~ **möglich** that's quite possible; ~ **gut** OK; **du weißt** ~ you know; **komm** ~ come on; **hör** ~ **auf damit!** will you stop that!; **was macht das** ~, **wenn** ...? what does it matter if ...?; **und wenn** ~! (*umg*) so what?

schön [ʃøːn] *adj* beautiful; (*Mann*) handsome; (*nett*) nice ♦ *adv*: **sich ganz** ~ **ärgern** to be very angry; **da hast du etwas S~es angerichtet** you've made a fine *od* nice mess; **sich** ~ **machen** to make o.s. look nice; ~**e Grüße** best wishes; ~**en Dank** (many) thanks; ~ **weich/warm** nice and soft/warm.

schonen [ˈʃoːnən] *vt* to look after; (*jds Nerven*) to spare; (*Gegner, Kind*) to be easy on; (*Teppich, Füße*) to save ♦ *vr* to take it easy.

schonend *adj* careful, gentle; **jdm etw** ~ **beibringen** to break sth to sb gently.

Schoner [ˈʃoːnər] (**-s, -**) *m* (*NAUT*) schooner; (*Sessel*~) cover.

Schönfärberei *f* (*fig*) glossing things over.

Schonfrist *f* period of grace.

Schöngeist *m* cultured person, aesthete (*BRIT*), esthete (*US*).

Schönheit *f* beauty.

Schönheits- *zW*: ~**fehler** *m* blemish, flaw; ~**operation** *f* cosmetic surgery; ~**wettbewerb** *m* beauty contest.

Schonkost (**-**) *f* light diet.

Schönschrift *f*: **in** ~ in one's best (hand)writing.

schöntun *unreg vi*: **jdm** ~ (*schmeicheln*) to flatter *od* soft-soap sb, play up to sb.

Schonung *f* good care; (*Nachsicht*) consideration; (*Forst*) plantation of young trees.

schonungslos *adj* ruthless, harsh.

Schonzeit *f* close season.

Schopf [ʃɔpf] (**-(e)s, ¨e**) *m*: **eine Gelegenheit beim** ~ **ergreifen** *od* **fassen** to seize *od* grasp an opportunity with both hands.

schöpfen [ˈʃœpfən] *vt* to scoop; (*Suppe*) to ladle; (*Mut*) to summon up; (*Luft*) to breathe in; (*Hoffnung*) to find.

Schöpfer (**-s, -**) *m* creator; (*Gott*) Creator;

(*umg*: *Schöpfkelle*) ladle; **s~isch** *adj* creative.

Schöpfkelle *f* ladle.

Schöpflöffel *m* skimmer, scoop.

Schöpfung *f* creation.

Schoppen [ˈʃɔpən] (**-s, -**) *m* (*Glas Wein*) glass of wine; ~**wein** *m* wine by the glass.

schor *etc* [ʃoːr] *vb siehe* **scheren**.

Schorf [ʃɔrf] (**-(e)s, -e**) *m* scab.

Schorle [ˈʃɔrlə] (**-, -n**) *f* spritzer, *wine and soda water or lemonade*.

Schornstein [ˈʃɔrnʃtaɪn] *m* chimney; (*NAUT*) funnel; ~**feger** (**-s, -**) *m* chimney sweep.

Schose [ˈʃoːzə] (**-, -n**) *f* = **Chose**.

Schoß (**-es, ¨e**) *m* lap; (*Rock*~) coat tail; **im** ~**e der Familie** in the bosom of one's family.

schoss *etc*▲ [ʃɔs] *vb siehe* **schießen**.

Schoßhund *m* lapdog.

Schössling▲ [ˈʃœslɪŋ] *m* (*BOT*) shoot.

Schote [ˈʃoːtə] (**-, -n**) *f* pod.

Schotte [ˈʃɔtə] (**-n, -n**) *m* Scot, Scotsman.

Schottenrock [ˈʃɔtənrɔk] *m* kilt; (*für Frauen*) tartan skirt.

Schotter [ˈʃɔtər] (**-s**) *m* gravel; (*im Straßenbau*) road metal; (*EISENB*) ballast.

Schottin [ˈʃɔtɪn] *f* Scot, Scotswoman.

schottisch [ˈʃɔtɪʃ] *adj* Scottish, Scots; **das** ~**e Hochland** the Scottish Highlands *pl*.

Schottland (**-s**) *nt* Scotland.

schraffieren [ʃraˈfiːrən] *vt* to hatch.

schräg [ʃrɛːk] *adj* slanting; (*schief, geneigt*) sloping; (*nicht gerade od parallel*) oblique ♦ *adv*: ~ **gedruckt** in italics; **etw** ~ **stellen** to put sth at an angle; ~ **gegenüber** diagonally opposite.

Schräge [ˈʃrɛːgə] (**-, -n**) *f* slant.

Schräg- *zW*: ~**kante** *f* bevelled (*BRIT*) *od* beveled (*US*) edge; ~**schrift** *f* italics *pl*; ~**streifen** *m* bias binding; ~**strich** *m* oblique stroke.

Schramme [ˈʃramə] (**-, -n**) *f* scratch.

schrammen *vt* to scratch.

Schrank [ʃraŋk] (**-(e)s, ¨e**) *m* cupboard (*BRIT*), closet (*US*); (*Kleider*~) wardrobe.

Schranke (**-, -n**) *f* barrier; (*fig*: *Grenze*) limit; (: *Hindernis*) barrier; **jdn in seine** ~**n (ver)weisen** (*fig*) to put sb in his place.

schrankenlos *adj* boundless; (*zügellos*) unrestrained.

Schrankenwärter *m* (*EISENB*) level-crossing (*BRIT*) *od* grade-crossing (*US*) attendant.

Schrankkoffer *m* wardrobe trunk.

Schrankwand *f* wall unit.

Schraube [ˈʃraubə] (**-, -n**) *f* screw.

schrauben *vt* to screw; **etw in die Höhe** ~ (*fig*: *Preise, Rekorde*) to push sth up; (: *Ansprüche*) to raise sth.

Schraubenschlüssel *m* spanner (*BRIT*), wrench (*US*).

Schraubenzieher (**-s, -**) *m* screwdriver.

Schraubstock [ˈʃraupʃtɔk] *m* (*TECH*) vice

(*BRIT*), vise (*US*).

Schrebergarten ['ʃreːbərgartən] *m* allotment (*BRIT*).

Schreck [ʃrɛk] (-(e)s, -e) *m* fright; **o ~ lass nach!** (*hum: umg*) for goodness' sake!

Schrecken (-s, -) *m* terror; (*Schreck*) fright; **s~** *vt* to frighten, scare ♦ *vi:* **aus dem Schlaf s~** to be startled out of one's sleep.

schreckensbleich *adj* as white as a sheet *od* ghost.

Schreckensherrschaft *f* (reign of) terror.

Schreck- *zW:* **~gespenst** *nt* nightmare; **s~haft** *adj* jumpy, easily frightened; **s~lich** *adj* terrible, dreadful; **s~lich gerne!** (*umg*) I'd absolutely love to; **~schraube** (*pej: umg*) *f* (old) battle-axe; **~schuss▲** *m* shot fired in the air; **~sekunde** *f* moment of shock.

Schrei [ʃraɪ] (-(e)s, -e) *m* scream; (*Ruf*) shout; **der letzte ~** (*umg*) the latest thing, all the rage.

Schreibbedarf *m* writing materials *pl*, stationery.

Schreibblock *m* writing pad.

schreiben ['ʃraɪbən] *unreg vt* to write; (*mit Schreibmaschine*) to type out; (*berichten: Zeitung etc*) to say; (*buchstabieren*) to spell ♦ *vi* to write; to type; to say; to spell ♦ *vr:* **wie schreibt sich das?** how is that spelt?; **S~** (-s, -) *nt* letter, communication.

Schreiber(in) (-s, -) *m(f)* writer; (*Büro~*) clerk.

Schreib- *zW:* **s~faul** *adj* lazy about writing letters; **~fehler** *m* spelling mistake; **~kraft** *f* typist; **~maschine** *f* typewriter; **~papier** *nt* notepaper; **~schrift** *f* running handwriting; (*TYP*) script; **~schutz** *m* (*COMPUT*) write-protect; **~stube** *f* orderly room; **~tisch** *m* desk; **~tischtäter** *m* wire *od* string puller.

Schreibung *f* spelling.

Schreib- *zW:* **~unterlage** *f* pad; **~waren** *pl* stationery *sing*; **~warengeschäft** *nt* stationer's (shop) (*BRIT*), stationery store (*US*); **~weise** *f* spelling; (*Stil*) style; **s~wütig** *adj* crazy about writing; **~zentrale** *f* typing pool; **~zeug** *nt* writing materials *pl*.

schreien ['ʃraɪən] *unreg vt, vi* to scream; (*rufen*) to shout; **es war zum S~** (*umg*) it was a scream *od* a hoot; **nach etw ~** (*fig*) to cry out for sth.

schreiend *adj* (*fig*) glaring; (*: Farbe*) loud.

Schreihals (*umg*) *m* (*Baby*) bawler; (*Unruhestifter*) noisy troublemaker.

Schreikrampf *m* screaming fit.

Schreiner ['ʃraɪnər] (-s, -) *m* joiner; (*Zimmermann*) carpenter; (*Möbel~*) cabinetmaker.

Schreinerei [ʃraɪnə'raɪ] *f* joiner's workshop.

schreiten ['ʃraɪtən] *unreg vi* to stride.

schrie *etc* [ʃriː] *vb siehe* **schreien**.

Schrieb (-(e)s, -e) (*umg*) *m* missive (*hum*).

schrieb *etc* [ʃriːp] *vb siehe* **schreiben**.

Schrift [ʃrɪft] (-, -en) *f* writing; (*Hand~*) handwriting; (*~art*) script; (*TYP*) typeface; (*Buch*) work; **~art** *f* (*Hand~*) script; (*TYP*) typeface; **~bild** *nt* script; (*COMPUT*) typeface; **~deutsch** *nt* written German; **~führer** *m* secretary; **s~lich** *adj* written ♦ *adv* in writing; **das kann ich Ihnen s~lich geben** (*fig: umg*) I can tell you that for free; **~probe** *f* (*Hand~*) specimen of one's handwriting; **~satz** *m* (*TYP*) fount (*BRIT*), font (*US*); **~setzer** *m* compositor; **~sprache** *f* written language.

Schriftsteller(in) (-s, -) *m(f)* writer; **s~isch** *adj* literary.

Schrift- *zW:* **~stück** *nt* document; **~verkehr** *m* correspondence; **~wechsel** *m* correspondence.

schrill [ʃrɪl] *adj* shrill; **~en** *vi* (*Stimme*) to sound shrilly; (*Telefon*) to ring shrilly.

Schritt (-(e)s, -e) *m* step; (*Gangart*) walk; (*Tempo*) pace; (*von Hose*) crotch, crutch (*BRIT*); **auf ~ und Tritt** (*lit, fig*) wherever *od* everywhere one goes; **„~ fahren"** "dead slow"; **mit zehn ~en Abstand** at a distance of ten paces; **den ersten ~ tun** (*fig*) to make the first move; (: *etw beginnen*) to take the first step.

schritt *etc* [ʃrɪt] *vb siehe* **schreiten**.

Schritt- *zW:* **~macher** *m* pacemaker; **~tempo▲** *nt:* **im ~tempo** at a walking pace; **s~weise** *adv* gradually, little by little.

schroff [ʃrɔf] *adj* steep; (*zackig*) jagged; (*fig*) brusque; (*ungeduldig*) abrupt.

schröpfen ['ʃrœpfən] *vt* (*fig*) to fleece.

Schrot [ʃroːt] (-(e)s, -e) *m od nt* (*Blei*) (small) shot; (*Getreide*) coarsely ground grain, groats *pl*; **~flinte** *f* shotgun.

Schrott [ʃrɔt] (-(e)s, -e) *m* scrap metal; **ein Auto zu ~ fahren** to write off a car; **~händler** *m* scrap merchant; **~haufen** *m* scrap heap; **s~reif** *adj* ready for the scrap heap; **~wert** *m* scrap value.

schrubben ['ʃrʊbən] *vt* to scrub.

Schrubber (-s, -) *m* scrubbing brush.

Schrulle ['ʃrʊlə] (-, -n) *f* eccentricity, quirk.

schrullig *adj* cranky.

schrumpfen ['ʃrʊmpfən] *vi* (*Hilfsverb sein*) to shrink; (*Apfel*) to shrivel; (*Leber, Niere*) to atrophy.

Schub [ʃuːp] (-(e)s, ̈-e) *m* (*Stoß*) push, shove; (*Gruppe, Anzahl*) batch; **~fach** *nt* drawer; **~karren** *m* wheelbarrow; **~lade** *f* drawer.

Schubs [ʃuːps] (-es, -e) (*umg*) *m* shove, push; **s~en** (*umg*) *vt, vi* to shove, push.

schüchtern ['ʃʏçtərn] *adj* shy; **S~heit** *f* shyness.

schuf *etc* [ʃuːf] *vb siehe* **schaffen**.

Schuft [ʃʊft] (-(e)s, -e) *m* scoundrel.

schuften (*umg*) *vi* to graft, slave away.

Schuh [ʃuː] (-(e)s, -e) m shoe; **jdm etw in die ~e schieben** (fig: umg) to put the blame for sth on sb; **wo drückt der ~?** (fig) what's troubling you?; ~**band** nt shoelace; ~**creme** f shoe polish; ~**größe** f shoe size; ~**löffel** m shoehorn; ~**macher** m shoemaker; ~**werk** nt footwear.

Schukosteckdose ® [ˈʃuːkoʃtɛkdoːzə] f safety socket.

Schukostecker ® m safety plug.

Schul- zW: ~**aufgaben** pl homework sing; ~**bank** f: **die ~bank drücken** (umg) to go to school; ~**behörde** f education authority; ~**besuch** m school attendance; ~**buch** nt schoolbook; ~**buchverlag** m educational publisher.

Schuld [ʃʊlt] (-, -en) f guilt; (FIN) debt; (Verschulden) fault; ~ **haben (an** +dat) to be to blame (for); **jdm (die) ~ geben, jdm die ~ zuschieben** to blame sb; **ich bin mir keiner ~ bewusst** I'm not aware of having done anything wrong; ~ **und Sühne** crime and punishment; **ich stehe tief in seiner ~** (fig) I'm deeply indebted to him; ~**en machen** to run up debts; siehe auch **zuschulden**; **s~ sein (an** +dat) to be to blame (for); **er ist s~** it's his fault.

schuldbewusst▲ adj (Mensch) feeling guilty; (Miene) guilty.

schulden [ˈʃʊldən] vt to owe.

schuldenfrei adj free from debt.

Schuldgefühl nt feeling of guilt.

schuldhaft adj (JUR) culpable.

Schuldienst (-(e)s) m (school)teaching.

schuldig adj guilty; (gebührend) due; **an etw** dat ~ **sein** to be guilty of sth; **jdm etw ~ sein** od **bleiben** to owe sb sth; **jdn ~ sprechen** to find sb guilty; ~ **geschieden sein** to be the guilty party in a divorce; **S~keit** f duty.

schuldlos adj innocent, blameless.

Schuldner(in) (-s, -) m(f) debtor.

Schuld- zW: ~**prinzip** nt (JUR) principle of the guilty party; ~**schein** m promissory note, IOU; ~**spruch** m verdict of guilty.

Schule [ˈʃuːlə] (-, -n) f school; **auf** od **in der ~** at school; **in die ~ kommen/gehen** to start school/go to school; ~ **machen** (fig) to become the accepted thing.

schulen vt to train, school.

Schüler(in) [ˈʃyːlər(ɪn)] (-s, -) m(f) pupil; ~**ausweis** m (school) student card; ~**lotse** m pupil acting as a road-crossing warden; ~**mitverwaltung** f school od student council.

Schul- zW: ~**ferien** pl school holidays pl (BRIT) od vacation sing (US); ~**fernsehen** nt schools' od educational television; **s~frei** adj: **die Kinder haben morgen s~frei** the children don't have to go to school tomorrow; ~**funk** m schools' broadcasts pl; ~**geld** nt school fees pl, tuition (US); ~**heft** nt exercise book;

~**hof** m playground, schoolyard.

schulisch [ˈʃuːlɪʃ] adj (Leistungen, Probleme) at school; (Angelegenheiten) school attrib.

Schul- zW: ~**jahr** nt school year; ~**junge** m schoolboy; ~**kind** nt schoolchild; ~**leiter** m headmaster (bes BRIT), principal; ~**leiterin** f headmistress (bes BRIT), principal; ~**mädchen** nt schoolgirl; ~**medizin** f orthodox medicine; **s~pflicht** f compulsory school attendance; **s~pflichtig** adj of school age; ~**reife** f: **die ~reife haben** to be ready to go to school; ~**schiff** nt (NAUT) training ship; ~**sprecher(in)** m(f) head boy/girl (BRIT); ~**stunde** f period, lesson; ~**tasche** f schoolbag.

Schulter [ˈʃʊltər] (-, -n) f shoulder; **auf die leichte ~ nehmen** to take lightly; ~**blatt** nt shoulder blade.

schultern vt to shoulder.

Schultüte f bag of sweets given to children on the first day at school.

Schulung f education, schooling.

Schul- zW: ~**verweigerer(in)** m(f) school refuser; ~**weg** m way to school; ~**wesen** nt educational system; ~**zeugnis** nt school report.

schummeln [ˈʃʊməln] (umg) vi: **(bei etw) ~** to cheat (at sth).

schummerig [ˈʃʊm(ə)rɪç] adj (Beleuchtung) dim; (Raum) dimly-lit.

Schund (-(e)s) m trash, garbage.

schund etc [ʃʊnt] vb siehe **schinden**.

Schundroman m trashy novel.

Schupo [ˈʃuːpo] (-s, -s) m abk (veraltet: = Schutzpolizist) cop.

Schuppe [ˈʃʊpə] (-, -n) f scale; **Schuppen** pl (Haarschuppen) dandruff.

Schuppen (-s, -) m shed; (umg: übles Lokal) dive; siehe auch **Schuppe**.

schuppen vt to scale ♦ vr to peel.

schuppig [ˈʃʊpɪç] adj scaly.

Schur [ʃuːr] (-, -en) f shearing.

Schüreisen nt poker.

schüren [ˈʃyːrən] vt to rake; (fig) to stir up.

schürfen [ˈʃʏrfən] vt, vi to scrape, scratch; (MIN) to prospect; to dig.

Schürfung f abrasion; (MIN) prospecting.

Schürhaken m poker.

Schurke [ˈʃʊrkə] (-s, -n) m rogue.

Schurwolle f: „**reine ~**" "pure new wool".

Schurz [ʃʊrts] (-es, -e) m apron.

Schürze [ˈʃʏrtsə] (-, -n) f apron.

Schürzenjäger (umg) m philanderer, one for the girls.

Schuss▲ [ʃʊs] (-es, ̈-e) m shot; (FUSSBALL) kick; (Spritzer: von Wein, Essig etc) dash; (WEBEN) weft; **(gut) in ~ sein** (umg) to be in good shape od nick; (Mensch) to be in form; **etw in ~ halten** to keep sth in good shape; **weitab vom ~ sein** (fig: umg) to be miles from where the action is; **der goldene ~** ≈ a lethal dose of a drug; **ein ~ in den Ofen** (*umg*) a complete waste of time, a failure; **~bereich** *m* effective range.

Schüssel ['fʏsəl] (-, -n) *f* bowl, basin; (*Servier~*, *umg*: *Satelliten~*) dish; (*Wasch~*) basin.

schusselig ['fʊsəlɪç] (*umg*) *adj* (*zerstreut*) scatterbrained, muddle-headed (*umg*).

Schuss-▲ *zW*: **~linie** *f* line of fire; **~verletzung** *f* bullet wound; **~waffe** *f* firearm; **~waffengebrauch** *m* (*form*) use of firearms; **~wechsel** *m* exchange of shots; **~weite** *f* range (of fire).

Schuster ['fuːstər] (-s, -) *m* cobbler, shoemaker.

Schutt [fʊt] (-(e)s) *m* rubbish; (*Bau~*) rubble; „**~ abladen verboten**" "no tipping"; **~abladeplatz** *m* refuse dump.

Schüttelfrost *m* shivering.

schütteln ['fʏtəln] *vt* to shake ♦ *vr* to shake o.s.; **sich vor Kälte ~** to shiver with cold; **sich vor Ekel ~** to shudder with *od* in disgust.

schütten ['fʏtən] *vt* to pour; (*Zucker, Kies etc*) to tip; (*ver~*) to spill ♦ *vi unpers* to pour (down).

schütter *adj* (*Haare*) sparse, thin.

Schutthalde *f* dump.

Schutthaufen *m* heap of rubble.

Schutz [fʊts] (-es) *m* protection; (*Unterschlupf*) shelter; **jdn in ~ nehmen** to stand up for sb; **~anzug** *m* overalls *pl*; **s~bedürftig** *adj* in need of protection; **~befohlene(r)** *f(m)* charge; **~blech** *nt* mudguard; **~brief** *m* (international) travel cover; **~brille** *f* goggles *pl*.

Schütze ['fʏtsə] (-n, -n) *m* gunman; (*Gewehr~*) rifleman; (*Scharf~, Sport~*) marksman; (*ASTROL*) Sagittarius.

schützen ['fʏtsən] *vt* to protect ♦ *vr* to protect o.s.; **(sich) ~ vor** +*dat od* **gegen** to protect (o.s.) from *od* against; **gesetzlich geschützt** registered; **urheberrechtlich geschützt** protected by copyright; **vor Nässe ~!** keep dry.

Schützenfest *nt fair featuring shooting matches.*

Schutzengel *m* guardian angel.

Schützen- *zW*: **~graben** *m* trench; **~hilfe** *f* (*fig*) support; **~verein** *m* shooting club.

Schutz- *zW*: **~gebiet** *nt* protectorate; (*Naturschutzgebiet*) reserve; **~gebühr** *f* (token) fee; **~haft** *f* protective custody; **~heilige(r)** *f(m)* patron saint; **~helm** *m* safety helmet; **~impfung** *f* immunization.

Schützling ['fʏtslɪŋ] *m* protégé; (*bes Kind*) charge.

Schutz- *zW*: **s~los** *adj* defenceless (*BRIT*), defenseless (*US*); **~mann** (-(e)s, *pl* **-leute** *od* **-männer**) *m* policeman; **~marke** *f* trademark;

~maßnahme *f* precaution; **~patron** *m* patron saint; **~schirm** *m* (*TECH*) protective screen; **~umschlag** *m* (book) jacket; **~verband** *m* (*MED*) protective bandage *od* dressing; **~vorrichtung** *f* safety device.

Schw. *abk* = **Schwester.**

schwabbelig ['fvab(ə)lɪç] (*umg*) *adj* (*Körperteil*) flabby; (: *Gelee*) wobbly.

Schwabe ['fvaːbə] (-n, -n) *m* Swabian.

Schwaben (-s) *nt* Swabia.

Schwäbin ['fvɛːbɪn] *f* Swabian.

schwäbisch ['fvɛːbɪʃ] *adj* Swabian.

schwach [fvax] *adj* weak, feeble; (*Gedächtnis, Gesundheit*) poor; (*Hoffnung*) faint; **~ werden** to weaken; **das ist ein ~es Bild** (*umg*) *od* **eine ~e Leistung** (*umg*) that's a poor show; **ein ~er Trost** cold *od* small comfort; **mach mich nicht ~!** (*umg*) don't say that!; **auf ~en Beinen** *od* **Füßen stehen** (*fig*) to be on shaky ground; (: *Theorie*) to be shaky.

Schwäche ['fvɛçə] (-, -n) *f* weakness.

schwächen *vt* to weaken.

schwach- *zW*: **S~heit** *f* weakness; **S~kopf** (*umg*) *m* dimwit, idiot; **~köpfig** *adj* silly, daft (*BRIT*).

schwächlich *adj* weakly, delicate.

Schwächling *m* weakling.

Schwach- *zW*: **~sinn** *m* (*MED*) mental deficiency, feeble-mindedness (*veraltet*); (*umg*: *Quatsch*) rubbish; (*fig*: *umg*: *unsinnige Tat*) idiocy; **s~sinnig** *adj* mentally deficient; (*Idee*) idiotic; **~stelle** *f* weak point; **~strom** *m* weak current.

Schwächung ['fvɛçʊŋ] *f* weakening.

Schwaden ['fvaːdən] (-s, -) *m* cloud.

schwafeln ['fvaːfəln] (*umg*) *vi* to blather, drivel; (*in einer Prüfung*) to waffle.

Schwager ['fvaːgər] (-s, **ⁱⁱ**) *m* brother-in-law.

Schwägerin ['fvɛːgərɪn] *f* sister-in-law.

Schwalbe ['fvalbə] (-, -n) *f* swallow.

Schwall [fval] (-(e)s, -e) *m* surge; (*Worte*) flood, torrent.

Schwamm (-(e)s, **ⁱⁱe**) *m* sponge; (*Pilz*) fungus; **~ drüber!** (*umg*) (let's) forget it!

schwamm *etc* [fvam] *vb siehe* **schwimmen.**

schwammig *adj* spongy; (*Gesicht*) puffy; (*vage: Begriff*) woolly (*BRIT*), wooly (*US*).

Schwan [fvaːn] (-(e)s, **ⁱⁱe**) *m* swan.

schwand *etc* [fvant] *vb siehe* **schwinden.**

schwanen *vi unpers*: **jdm schwant es** sb has a foreboding *od* forebodings; **jdm schwant etwas** sb senses something might happen.

schwang *etc* [fvaŋ] *vb siehe* **schwingen.**

schwanger ['fvaŋər] *adj* pregnant.

schwängern ['fvɛŋərn] *vt* to make pregnant.

Schwangerschaft *f* pregnancy.

Schwangerschaftsabbruch *m* termination of pregnancy, abortion.

Schwank [fvaŋk] (-(e)s, **ⁱⁱe**) *m* funny story; (*LITER*) merry *od* comical tale; (*THEAT*) farce.

schwanken *vi* to sway; (*taumeln*) to stagger, reel; (*Preise, Zahlen*) to fluctuate; (*zögern*) to hesitate; (*Überzeugung etc*) to begin to waver; **ins S~ kommen** (*Baum, Gebäude etc*) to start to sway; (*Preise, Kurs etc*) to start to fluctuate *od* vary.

Schwankung *f* fluctuation.

Schwanz [ʃvants] (**-es**, **ˆe**) *m* tail; (*umgl: Penis*) prick (*!*); **kein ~** (*umg*) not a (blessed) soul.

schwänzen ['ʃvɛntsən] (*umg*) *vt* (*Stunde, Vorlesung*) to skip ◆ *vi* to play truant.

Schwänzer ['ʃvɛntsər] (**-s**, **-**) (*umg*) *m* truant.

schwappen ['ʃvapən] *vi* (*über~*) to splash, slosh.

Schwarm [ʃvarm] (**-(e)s**, **ˆe**) *m* swarm; (*umg*) heart-throb, idol.

schwärmen ['ʃvɛrmən] *vi* to swarm; **~ für** to be mad *od* wild about.

Schwärmerei [ʃvɛrmaˈraɪ] *f* enthusiasm.

schwärmerisch *adj* impassioned, effusive.

Schwarte ['ʃvartə] (**-**, **-n**) *f* hard skin; (*Speck~*) rind; (*umg: Buch*) tome (*hum*).

Schwartenmagen (**-s**) *m* (*KOCH*) brawn.

schwarz [ʃvarts] *adj* black; (*umg: ungesetzlich*) illicit; (: *katholisch*) Catholic, Papist (*pej*); (*POL*) Christian Democrat; **ins S~e treffen** (*lit, fig*) to hit the bull's-eye; **das ~e Brett** the notice (*BRIT*) *od* bulletin (*US*) board; **~e Liste** blacklist; **~es Loch** black hole; **das S~e Meer** the Black Sea; **S~er Peter** (*KARTEN*) *children's card game*; **jdm den ~en Peter zuschieben** (*fig: die Verantwortung abschieben*) to pass the buck to sb (*umg*); **sich ~ ärgern** to get extremely annoyed; **~ malen** to be pessimistic (about); **~ sehen** (*umg*) to see the gloomy side of things; **dort wählen alle ~** they all vote conservative there; **in den ~en Zahlen** in the black; **S~arbeit** *f* illicit work, moonlighting; **S~arbeiter** *m* moonlighter; **S~brot** *nt* (*Pumpernickel*) black bread, pumpernickel; (*braun*) brown rye bread.

Schwärze ['ʃvɛrtsə] (**-**, **-n**) *f* blackness; (*Farbe*) blacking; (*Drucker~*) printer's ink.

Schwarze(r) *f(m)* (*Neger*) black; (*umg: Katholik*) Papist; (*POL: umg*) Christian Democrat.

schwärzen *vt* to blacken.

Schwarz- *zW*: **s~fahren** *unreg vi* to travel without paying; (*ohne Führerschein*) to drive without a licence (*BRIT*) *od* license (*US*); **~fahrer** *m* (*Bus etc*) fare dodger (*umg*); **~handel** *m* black market (trade); **~händler** *m* black-market operator; **s~hören** *vi* to listen to the radio without a licence (*BRIT*) *od* license (*US*).

schwärzlich ['ʃvɛrtslıç] *adj* blackish, darkish.

Schwarz- *zW*: **~markt** *m* black market;

s~sehen (*umg*) *vi unreg* (*TV*) to watch TV without a licence (*BRIT*) *od* license (*US*); **~seher** *m* pessimist; (*TV*) viewer without a licence (*BRIT*); **~wald** *m* Black Forest; **~wälder Kirschtorte** *f* Black Forest gâteau; **s~weiß, s~-weiß▲** *adj* black and white; **~weiß-** *in zW* black and white; **~wurzel** *f* (*KOCH*) salsify.

Schwatz [ʃvats] (**-es**, **-e**) *m* chat.

schwatzen ['ʃvatsən] *vi* to chat; (*schnell, unaufhörlich*) to chatter; (*über belanglose Dinge*) to prattle; (*Unsinn reden*) to blether (*umg*).

schwätzen ['ʃvɛtsən] *vi* = **schwatzen**.

Schwätzer(in) ['ʃvɛtsər(ın)] (**-s**, **-**) *m(f)* chatterbox; (*Schwafler*) gasbag (*umg*); (*Klatschbase*) gossip.

schwatzhaft *adj* talkative, gossipy.

Schwebe ['ʃveːbə] *f*: **in der ~** (*fig*) in abeyance; (*JUR, COMM*) pending.

Schwebebahn *f* overhead railway (*BRIT*) *od* railroad (*US*).

Schwebebalken *m* (*SPORT*) beam.

schweben *vi* to drift, float; (*hoch*) to soar; (*unentschieden sein*) to be in the balance; **es schwebte mir vor Augen** (*Bild*) I saw it in my mind's eye.

schwebend *adj* (*TECH, CHEM*) suspended; (*fig*) undecided, unresolved; **~es Verfahren** (*JUR*) pending case.

schwed. *abk* = **schwedisch**.

Schwede ['ʃveːdə] (**-n**, **-n**) *m* Swede.

Schweden (**-s**) *nt* Sweden.

Schwedin ['ʃveːdın] *f* Swede.

schwedisch *adj* Swedish.

Schwefel ['ʃveːfəl] (**-s**) *m* sulphur (*BRIT*), sulfur (*US*); **~dioxid** *nt* sulphur dioxide.

schwefelig *adj* sulphurous (*BRIT*), sulfurous (*US*).

Schwefelsäure *f* sulphuric (*BRIT*) *od* sulfuric (*US*) acid.

Schweif [ʃvaɪf] (**-(e)s**, **-e**) *m* tail.

schweifen *vi* to wander, roam.

Schweigegeld *nt* hush money.

Schweigeminute *f* one minute('s) silence.

schweigen ['ʃvaɪgən] *unreg vi* to be silent; (*still sein*) to keep quiet; **kannst du ~?** can you keep a secret?; **ganz zu ~ von ...** to say nothing of ...; **S~** (**-s**) *nt* silence.

schweigend *adj* silent.

Schweigepflicht *f* pledge of secrecy; (*von Anwalt etc*) requirement of confidentiality.

schweigsam ['ʃvaɪkzaːm] *adj* silent; (*als Charaktereigenschaft*) taciturn; **S~keit** *f* silence; taciturnity.

Schwein [ʃvaɪn] (**-(e)s**, **-e**) *nt* pig; (*fig: umg*) (good) luck; **kein ~** (*umg*) nobody, not a single person.

Schweine- *zW*: **~braten** *m* joint of pork; (*gekocht*) roast pork; **~fleisch** *nt* pork; **~geld**

(*umg*) *nt*: **ein ~geld** a packet; **~hund** (*umg*) *m* stinker, swine.

Schweinerei [ʃvaɪnə'raɪ] *f* mess; (*Gemeinheit*) dirty trick; **so eine ~!** (*umg*) how disgusting!

Schweineschmalz *nt* dripping; (*als Kochfett*) lard.

Schweinestall *m* pigsty.

schweinisch *adj* filthy.

Schweinsleder *nt* pigskin.

Schweinsohr *nt* pig's ear; (*Gebäck*) (kidney-shaped) pastry.

Schweiß [ʃvaɪs] (**-es**) *m* sweat, perspiration; **~band** *nt* sweatband.

Schweißbrenner (**-s, -**) *m* (*TECH*) welding torch.

schweißen *vt, vi* to weld.

Schweißer (**-s, -**) *m* welder.

Schweiß- *zW*: **~füße** *pl* sweaty feet *pl*; **~naht** *f* weld; **s~nass▲** *adj* sweaty.

Schweiz [ʃvaɪts] *f*: **die ~** Switzerland.

schweiz. *abk* = **schweizerisch**.

Schweizer ['ʃvaɪtsər] (**-s, -**) *m* Swiss ♦ *adj attrib* Swiss; **~deutsch** *nt* Swiss German; **~in** *f* Swiss; **s~isch** *adj* Swiss.

schwelen ['ʃveːlən] *vi* to smoulder (*BRIT*), smolder (*US*).

schwelgen ['ʃvɛlɡən] *vi* to indulge o.s.; **~ in** +*dat* to indulge in.

Schwelle ['ʃvɛlə] (**-, -n**) *f* (*auch fig*) threshold; (*EISENB*) sleeper (*BRIT*), tie (*US*).

schwellen *unreg vi* to swell.

Schwellenland *nt* threshold country.

Schwellung *f* swelling.

Schwemme ['ʃvɛmə] *f*: **eine ~ an** +*dat* a glut of.

schwemmen ['ʃvɛmən] *vt* (*treiben: Sand etc*) to wash.

Schwengel ['ʃvɛŋəl] (**-s, -**) *m* pump handle; (*Glocken~*) clapper.

Schwenk [ʃvɛŋk] (**-(e)s, -s**) *m* (*FILM*) pan, panning shot.

Schwenkarm *m* swivel arm.

schwenkbar *adj* swivel-mounted.

schwenken *vt* to swing; (*Kamera*) to pan; (*Fahne*) to wave; (*Kartoffeln*) to toss; (*abspülen*) to rinse ♦ *vi* to turn, swivel; (*MIL*) to wheel.

Schwenkung *f* turn; (*MIL*) wheel.

schwer [ʃveːr] *adj* heavy; (*schwierig*) difficult, hard; (*schlimm*) serious, bad ♦ *adv* (*sehr*) very (much); (*verletzt etc*) seriously, badly; **~ erziehbar** maladjusted; **jdm ~ fallen** to be difficult for sb; **jdm/sich etw ~ machen** to make sth difficult for sb/o.s.; **~ nehmen** to take to heart; **sich** *dat od akk* **~ tun** to have difficulties; **~ verdaulich** indigestible; (*fig*) heavy; **~ verdient** (*Geld*) hard-earned; **~ verletzt** seriously *od* badly injured; **~ verwundet** seriously wounded;

~ wiegend weighty, important; **~ erkältet sein** to have a heavy cold; **er lernt ~** he's a slow learner; **er ist ~ in Ordnung** (*umg*) he's a good bloke (*BRIT*) *od* guy; **~ hören** to be hard of hearing; **S~arbeiter** *m* labourer (*BRIT*), laborer (*US*); **S~behinderte(r)** *f(m)*, **S~beschädigte(r)** *f(m)* (*veraltet*) severely handicapped person.

Schwere (**-, -n**) *f* weight; heaviness; (*PHYS*) gravity; **s~los** *adj* weightless; **~losigkeit** *f* weightlessness.

schwer- *zW*: **~fällig** *adj* (*auch Stil*) ponderous; (*Gang*) clumsy, awkward; (*Verstand*) slow; **S~gewicht** *nt* heavyweight; (*fig*) emphasis; **~gewichtig** *adj* heavyweight; **~hörig** *adj* hard of hearing; **S~industrie** *f* heavy industry; **S~kraft** *f* gravity; **S~kranke(r)** *f(m)* person who is seriously ill; **~lich** *adv* hardly; **S~metall** *nt* heavy metal; **~mütig** *adj* melancholy; **S~punkt** *m* centre (*BRIT*) *od* center (*US*) of gravity; (*fig*) emphasis, crucial point; **S~punktstreik** *m* pinpoint strike; **~reich** (*umg*) *adj attrib* stinking rich.

Schwert [ʃveːrt] (**-(e)s, -er**) *nt* sword; **~lilie** *f* iris.

schwer- *zW*: **S~verbrecher** *m* criminal; **S~verletzte(r)** *f(m)* serious casualty; **~wiegend** *adj* weighty, important.

Schwester ['ʃvɛstər] (**-, -n**) *f* sister; (*MED*) nurse; **s~lich** *adj* sisterly.

schwieg *etc* [ʃviːk] *vb siehe* **schweigen**.

Schwieger- *zW*: **~eltern** *pl* parents-in-law *pl*; **~mutter** *f* mother-in-law; **~sohn** *m* son-in-law; **~tochter** *f* daughter-in-law; **~vater** *m* father-in-law.

Schwiele ['ʃviːlə] (**-, -n**) *f* callus.

schwierig ['ʃviːrɪç] *adj* difficult, hard; **S~keit** *f* difficulty; **S~keitsgrad** *m* degree of difficulty.

schwillt [ʃvɪlt] *vb siehe* **schwellen**.

Schwimmbad *nt* swimming baths *pl*.

Schwimmbecken *nt* swimming pool.

schwimmen *unreg vi* to swim; (*treiben, nicht sinken*) to float; (*fig: unsicher sein*) to be all at sea; **im Geld ~** (*umg*) to be rolling in money; **mir schwimmt es vor den Augen** I feel dizzy.

Schwimmer (**-s, -**) *m* swimmer; (*ANGELN*) float.

Schwimmerin *f* swimmer.

Schwimm- *zW*: **~flosse** *f* (*von Taucher*) flipper; **~haut** *f* (*ORNITHOLOGIE*) web; **~lehrer** *m* swimming instructor; **~sport** *m* swimming; **~weste** *f* life jacket.

Schwindel ['ʃvɪndəl] (**-s**) *m* dizziness; (*Betrug*) swindle, fraud; (*Zeug*) stuff; **in ~ erregender Höhe** at a dizzy height; **s~frei** *adj* free from giddiness.

schwindeln *vi* (*umg: lügen*) to fib; **mir schwindelt** I feel dizzy; **jdm schwindelt es**

sb feels dizzy.

schwinden ['ʃvɪndən] *unreg vi* to disappear; (*Kräfte*) to fade, fail; (*sich verringern*) to decrease.

Schwindler (**-s, -**) *m* swindler; (*Hochstapler*) con man, fraud; (*Lügner*) liar.

schwindlig *adj* dizzy; **mir ist ~** I feel dizzy.

Schwindsucht *f* (*veraltet*) consumption.

schwingen ['ʃvɪŋən] *unreg vt* to swing; (*Waffe etc*) to brandish ♦ *vi* to swing; (*vibrieren*) to vibrate; (*klingen*) to sound.

Schwinger (**-s, -**) *m* (*BOXEN*) swing.

Schwingtor *nt* up-and-over door.

Schwingtür *f* swing door(s *pl*) (*BRIT*), swinging door(s *pl*) (*US*).

Schwingung *f* vibration; (*PHYS*) oscillation.

Schwips [ʃvɪps] (**-es, -e**) *m*: **einen ~ haben** to be tipsy.

schwirren ['ʃvɪrən] *vi* to buzz.

Schwitze ['ʃvɪtsə] (**-, -n**) *f* (*KOCH*) roux.

schwitzen *vi* to sweat, perspire.

schwofen ['ʃvoːfən] (*umg*) *vi* to dance.

schwoll *etc* [ʃvɔl] *vb siehe* **schwellen.**

schwören ['ʃvøːrən] *unreg vt, vi* to swear; **auf jdn/etw ~** (*fig*) to swear by sb/sth.

schwul [ʃvuːl] (*umg*) *adj* gay, queer (*pej*).

schwül [ʃvyːl] *adj* sultry, close.

Schwule(r) (*umg*) *m* gay, queer (*pej*), fag (*US pej*).

Schwüle (**-**) *f* sultriness, closeness.

Schwulität [ʃvuliˈtɛːt] (*umg*) *f* trouble, difficulty.

Schwulst [ʃvʊlst] (**-(e)s**) *m* bombast.

schwülstig ['ʃvʏlstɪç] *adj* pompous.

Schwund [ʃvʊnt] (**-(e)s**) *m* (+*gen*) decrease (in), decline (in), dwindling (of); (*MED*) atrophy; (*Schrumpfen*) shrinkage.

Schwung [ʃvʊŋ] (**-(e)s, ¨e**) *m* swing; (*Triebkraft*) momentum; (*fig: Energie*) verve, energy; (*umg: Menge*) batch; **in ~ sein** (*fig*) to be in full swing; **~ in die Sache bringen** (*umg*) to liven things up; **s~haft** *adj* brisk, lively; **~rad** *nt* flywheel; **s~voll** *adj* vigorous.

Schwur (**-(e)s, ¨e**) *m* oath.

schwur *etc* [ʃvuːr] *vb siehe* **schwören.**

Schwurgericht *nt* court with a jury.

SDR (**-**) *m abk* (= *Süddeutscher Rundfunk*) South German Radio.

sechs [zɛks] *num* six; **S~eck** *nt* hexagon; **~hundert** *num* six hundred.

sechste(r, s) *adj* sixth.

Sechstel ['zɛkstəl] (**-s, -**) *nt* sixth.

sechzehn ['zɛçtseːn] *num* sixteen.

sechzig ['zɛçtsɪç] *num* sixty.

See[1] [zeː] (**-, -n**) *f* sea; **an der ~** by the sea, at the seaside; **in ~ stechen** to put to sea; **auf hoher ~** on the high seas.

See[2] [zeː] (**-s, -n**) *m* lake.

See- *zW*: **~bad** *nt* seaside resort; **~bär** *m* (*hum: umg*) seadog; (*ZOOL*) fur seal; **~fahrt** *f*

seafaring; (*Reise*) voyage; **s~fest** *adj* (*Mensch*) not subject to seasickness; **~gang** *m* (motion of the) sea; **~gras** *nt* seaweed; **~hund** *m* seal; **~igel** *m* sea urchin; **~karte** *f* chart; **s~krank** *adj* seasick; **~krankheit** *f* seasickness; **~lachs** *m* rock salmon.

Seele ['zeːlə] (**-, -n**) *f* soul; (*Mittelpunkt*) life and soul; **jdm aus der ~ sprechen** to express exactly what sb feels; **das liegt mir auf der ~** it weighs heavily on my mind; **eine ~ von Mensch** an absolute dear.

Seelen- *zW*: **~amt** *nt* (*REL*) requiem; **~friede(n)** *m* peace of mind; **~heil** *nt* salvation of one's soul; (*fig*) spiritual welfare; **~ruhe** *f*: **in aller ~ruhe** calmly; (*kaltblütig*) as cool as you please; **s~ruhig** *adv* calmly.

Seeleute ['zeːlɔʏtə] *pl* seamen *pl*.

Seel- *zW*: **s~isch** *adj* mental; (*REL*) spiritual; (*Belastung*) emotional; **~sorge** *f* pastoral duties *pl*; **~sorger** (**-s, -**) *m* clergyman.

See- *zW*: **~macht** *f* naval power; **~mann** (**-(e)s**, *pl* **-leute**) *m* seaman, sailor; **~meile** *f* nautical mile.

Seengebiet ['zeːəngəbiːt] *nt* lakeland district.

See- *zW*: **~not** *f*: **in ~not** (*Schiff etc*) in distress; **~pferd(chen)** *nt* sea horse; **~räuber** *m* pirate; **~recht** *nt* maritime law; **~rose** *f* waterlily; **~stern** *m* starfish; **~tang** *m* seaweed; **s~tüchtig** *adj* seaworthy; **~versicherung** *f* marine insurance; **~weg** *m* sea route; **auf dem ~weg** by sea; **~zunge** *f* sole.

Segel ['zeːgəl] (**-s, -**) *nt* sail; **mit vollen ~n** under full sail *od* canvas; (*fig*) with gusto; **die ~ streichen** (*fig*) to give in; **~boot** *nt* yacht; **~fliegen** (**-s**) *nt* gliding; **~flieger** *m* glider pilot; **~flugzeug** *nt* glider.

segeln *vt, vi* to sail; **durch eine Prüfung ~** (*umg*) to flop in an exam, fail (in) an exam.

Segel- *zW*: **~schiff** *nt* sailing vessel; **~sport** *m* sailing; **~tuch** *nt* canvas.

Segen ['zeːgən] (**-s, -**) *m* blessing.

segensreich *adj* beneficial.

Segler ['zeːglər] (**-s, -**) *m* sailor, yachtsman; (*Boot*) sailing boat.

Seglerin *f* yachtswoman.

segnen ['zeːgnən] *vt* to bless.

sehen ['zeːən] *unreg vt, vi* to see; (*in bestimmte Richtung*) to look; (*Fernsehsendung*) to watch; **sieht man das?** does it show?; **da sieht man(s) mal wieder!** that's typical!; **du siehst das nicht richtig** you've got it wrong; **so gesehen** looked at in this way; **sich ~ lassen** to put in an appearance, appear; **das neue Rathaus kann sich ~ lassen** the new town hall is certainly something to be proud of; **siehe oben/unten** see above/below; **da kann man mal ~** that just shows (you) *od* just goes to show (*umg*); **mal ~!** we'll see; **darauf**

~, **dass** ... to make sure (that) ...; **jdn kommen** ~ to see sb coming.
sehenswert *adj* worth seeing.
Sehenswürdigkeiten *pl* sights *pl* (of a town).
Seher (**-s**, **-**) *m* seer.
Sehfehler *m* sight defect.
Sehkraft *f* (eye)sight.
Sehne ['ze:nə] (**-**, **-n**) *f* sinew; (*an Bogen*) string.
sehnen *vr*: **sich** ~ **nach** to long *od* yearn for.
Sehnenscheidenentzündung *f* (*MED*) tendovaginitis.
Sehnerv *m* optic nerve.
sehnig *adj* sinewy.
sehnlich *adj* ardent.
Sehnsucht *f* longing.
sehnsüchtig *adj* longing; (*Erwartung*) eager.
sehnsuchtsvoll *adv* longingly, yearningly.
sehr [ze:r] *adv* (*vor adj, adv*) very; (*mit Verben*) a lot, (very) much; **zu** ~ too much; **er ist** ~ **dafür/dagegen** he is all for it/very much against it; **wie** ~ **er sich auch bemühte** ... however much he tried ...
Sehvermögen ['ze:fɛrmø:gən] (**-s**) *nt* powers *pl* of vision.
seicht [zaɪçt] *adj* (*lit, fig*) shallow.
seid [zaɪt] *vb siehe* **sein**.
Seide ['zaɪdə] (**-**, **-n**) *f* silk.
Seidel (**-s**, **-**) *nt* tankard, beer mug.
seiden *adj* silk; **S~papier** *nt* tissue paper.
seidig ['zaɪdɪç] *adj* silky.
Seife ['zaɪfə] (**-**, **-n**) *f* soap.
Seifen- *zW*: **~blase** *f* soap bubble; (*fig*) bubble; **~lauge** *f* soapsuds *pl*; **~schale** *f* soap dish; **~schaum** *m* lather.
seifig ['zaɪfɪç] *adj* soapy.
seihen ['zaɪən] *vt* to strain, filter.
Seil [zaɪl] (**-(e)s**, **-e**) *nt* rope; (*Kabel*) cable; **~bahn** *f* cable railway; **~hüpfen** (**-s**) *nt* skipping; **~springen** (**-s**) *nt* skipping; **~tänzer(in)** *m(f)* tightrope walker; **~zug** *m* tackle.

================= *SCHLÜSSELWORT*

sein [zaɪn] (*pt* **war**, *pp* **gewesen**) *vi* **1** to be; **ich bin** I am; **du bist** you are; **er/sie/es ist** he/she/it is; **wir sind/ihr seid/sie sind** we/you/they are; **wir waren** we were; **wir sind gewesen** we have been.
2: seien Sie nicht böse don't be angry; **sei so gut und** ... be so kind as to ...; **das wäre gut** that would *od* that'd be a good thing; **wenn ich Sie wäre** if I were *od* was you; **das wärs** that's all, that's it; **morgen bin ich in Rom** tomorrow I'll *od* I will *od* I shall be in Rome; **waren Sie mal in Rom?** have you ever been to Rome?
3: wie ist das zu verstehen? how is that to be understood?; **er ist nicht zu ersetzen** he cannot be replaced; **mit ihr ist nicht zu**

reden you can't talk to her.
4: mir ist kalt I'm cold; **mir ist, als hätte ich ihn früher schon einmal gesehen** I've a feeling I've seen him before; **was ist?** what's the matter?, what is it?; **ist was?** is something the matter?; **es sei denn(, dass** ...**)** unless ...; **wie dem auch sei** be that as it may; **wie wäre es mit** ...**?** how *od* what about ...?; **etw** ~ **lassen** (*aufhören*) to stop (doing) sth; (*nicht tun*) to drop sth, leave sth; **lass das** ~**!** stop that!; **es ist an dir, zu** ... it's up to you to ...; **was sind Sie (beruflich)?** what do you do?; **das kann schon** ~ that may well be.
♦ *pron* his; (*bei Dingen*) its.

Sein (**-s**) *nt*: ~ **oder Nichtsein** to be or not to be.
seine(r, s) *poss pron* his; its; **er ist gut** ~ **zwei Meter** (*umg*) he's a good two metres (*BRIT*) *od* meters (*US*); **die** ~**n** *od* **S~n** (*geh*) his family, his people; **jedem das** ~ *od* **S~** to each his own.
seiner *gen von* **er, es** ♦ *pron* of him; of it.
seinerseits *adv* for his part.
seinerzeit *adv* in those days, formerly.
seinesgleichen *pron* people like him.
seinetwegen *adv* (*für ihn*) for his sake; (*wegen ihm*) on his account; (*von ihm aus*) as far as he is concerned.
seinetwillen *adv*: **um** ~ = **seinetwegen**.
seinige *pron*: **der/die/das** ~ *od* **S~** his.
Seismograf▲ [zaɪsmo'gra:f] (**-en**, **-en**) *m* seismograph.
seit [zaɪt] *präp* +*dat* since; (*Zeitdauer*) for, in (*bes US*) ♦ *konj* since; **er ist** ~ **einer Woche hier** he has been here for a week; ~ **langem** for a long time; **~dem** *adv*, *konj* since.
Seite ['zaɪtə] (**-**, **-n**) *f* side; (*Buch*~) page; (*MIL*) flank; ~ **an** ~ side by side; **jdm zur** ~ **stehen** (*fig*) to stand by sb's side; **jdn zur** ~ **nehmen** to take sb aside *od* on one side; **auf der einen** ~ ..., **auf der anderen (**~**)** ... on the one hand ..., on the other (hand) ...; **einer Sache** *dat* **die beste** ~ **abgewinnen** to make the best *od* most of sth; *siehe auch* **aufseiten, vonseiten**.
Seiten- *zW*: **~airbag** *m* (*AUT*) side-impact airbag; **~ansicht** *f* side view; **~hieb** *m* (*fig*) passing shot, dig; **s~lang** *adj* several pages long, going on for pages; **~ruder** *nt* (*AVIAT*) rudder.
seitens *präp* +*gen* on the part of.
Seiten- *zW*: **~schiff** *nt* aisle; **~sprung** *m* extramarital escapade; **~stechen** *nt* (a) stitch; **~straße** *f* side road; **~streifen** *m* (*der Straße*) verge (*BRIT*), berm (*US*); (*der Autobahn*) hard shoulder (*BRIT*), shoulder (*US*); **s~verkehrt** *adj* the wrong way round; **~wagen** *m* sidecar; **~wind** *m* crosswind; **~zahl** *f* page number; (*Gesamtzahl*) number of pages.

seit- *zW*: **~her** [zaɪt'heːr] *adv, konj* since (then);
~lich *adv* on one/the side ♦ *adj* side *attrib*;
~wärts *adv* sideways.

sek, Sek. *abk* (= *Sekunde*) sec.

Sekretär [zekre'tɛːr] *m* secretary; (*Möbel*)
bureau.

Sekretariat [zekretari'aːt] (-(e)s, -e) *nt*
secretary's office, secretariat.

Sekretärin *f* secretary.

Sekt [zɛkt] (-(e)s, -e) *m* sparkling wine.

Sekte (-, -n) *f* sect.

Sektor ['zɛktɔr] *m* sector; (*Sachgebiet*) field.

Sekunda [ze'kunda] (-, **Sekunden**) *f* (*SCH*:
früher: *Unter~/Ober~*) sixth/seventh year of
German secondary school.

sekundär [zekʊn'dɛːr] *adj* secondary;
S~literatur *f* secondary literature.

Sekunde [ze'kunda] (-, -n) *f* second.

Sekunden- *zW*: **~kleber** *m* superglue;
~schnelle *f*: **in ~schnelle** in a matter of
seconds; **~zeiger** *m* second hand.

sel. *abk* = **selig**.

selber ['zɛlbər] *demon pron* = **selbst**; **S~machen**
nt do-it-yourself, DIY (*BRIT*); (*von Kleidern
etc*) making one's own.

Selbst [zɛlpst] (-) *nt* self.

━━━━━━━━━━━━━━━ *SCHLÜSSELWORT*

selbst [zɛlpst] *pron* **1**: **ich/er/wir ~** I myself/he
himself/we ourselves; **sie ist die Tugend ~**
she's virtue itself; **er braut sein Bier ~** he
brews his own beer; **das muss er ~ wissen**
it's up to him; **wie gehts? - gut, und ~?** how
are things? - fine, and yourself?
2 (*ohne Hilfe*) alone, on my/his/one's *etc* own;
von ~ by itself; **er kam von ~** he came of
his own accord; **~ ist der Mann/die Frau!**
self-reliance is the name of the game (*umg*);
~ gemacht home-made; **~ gestrickt** hand-
knitted; (*umg*: *Methode etc*) homespun,
amateurish; **~ verdientes Geld** money one
has earned o.s.
♦ *adv* even; **~ wenn** even if; **~ Gott** even
God (himself).

Selbstachtung *f* self-respect.

selbständig *etc* ['zɛlpʃtɛndɪç] *adj*
= **selbstständig** *etc*.

Selbst- *zW*: **~anzeige** *f*: **~anzeige erstatten** to
come forward oneself; **der Dieb hat ~an-
zeige erstattet** the thief has come forward;
~auslöser *m* (*PHOT*) delayed-action shutter
release; **~bedienung** *f* self-service; **~befrie-
digung** *f* masturbation; (*fig*) self-gratification;
~beherrschung *f* self-control; **~bestätigung** *f*
self-affirmation; **s~bewusst▲** *adj* self-
confident; (*selbstsicher*) self-assured;
~bewusstsein▲ *nt* self-confidence; **~bildnis**
nt self-portrait; **~erhaltung** *f* self-
preservation; **~erkenntnis** *f* self-knowledge;

~fahrer *m* (*AUT*): **Autovermietung für ~fahrer**
self-drive car hire (*BRIT*) *od* rental; **s~gefällig**
adj smug, self-satisfied; **s~gerecht** *adj* self-
righteous; **~gespräch** *nt* conversation with
o.s.; **s~gewiss▲** *adj* confident; **s~herrlich** *adj*
high-handed; (*selbstgerecht*) self-satisfied;
~hilfe *f* self-help; **zur ~hilfe greifen** to take
matters into one's own hands; **s~klebend** *adj*
self-adhesive; **~kostenpreis** *m* cost price;
s~los *adj* unselfish, selfless; **~mord** *m*
suicide; **~mörder(in)** *m(f)* (*Person*) suicide;
s~mörderisch *adj* suicidal; **s~sicher** *adj* self-
assured; **~sicherheit** *f* self-assurance;
s~ständig▲ ['zɛlpstʃtɛndɪç] *adj* independent;
sich ~ machen (*beruflich*) to set up on one's
own, start one's own business;
~ständigkeit▲ *f* independence; **~studium** *nt*
private study; **s~süchtig** *adj* selfish; **s~tätig**
adj automatic; **~überwindung** *f* willpower;
s~vergessen *adj* absent-minded; (*Blick*)
faraway; **s~verschuldet** *adj*: **wenn der Unfall
s~verschuldet ist** if there is personal
responsibility for the accident; **~versorger**
m: **~versorger sein** to be self-sufficient *od*
self-reliant; **Urlaub für ~versorger** self-
catering holiday.

selbstverständlich *adj* obvious ♦ *adv*
naturally; **ich halte das für ~** I take that for
granted.

Selbstverständlichkeit *f* (*Unbefangenheit*)
naturalness; (*natürliche Voraussetzung*)
matter of course.

Selbst- *zW*: **~verständnis** *nt*: **nach seinem
eigenen ~verständnis** as he sees himself;
~verteidigung *f* self-defence (*BRIT*), self-
defense (*US*); **~vertrauen** *nt* self-confidence;
~verwaltung *f* autonomy, self-government;
~wählferndienst *m* (*TEL*) automatic dialling
service, subscriber trunk dialling (*BRIT*),
STD (*BRIT*), direct distance dialing (*US*);
~wertgefühl *nt* feeling of one's own worth
od value, self-esteem; **s~zufrieden** *adj* self-
satisfied; **~zweck** *m* end in itself.

selig ['zeːlɪç] *adj* happy, blissful; (*REL*)
blessed; (*tot*) late; **S~keit** *f* bliss.

Sellerie ['zɛləriː] (-s, -(s) *od* -, -n) *m od f* celery.

selten ['zɛltən] *adj* rare ♦ *adv* seldom, rarely;
S~heit *f* rarity; **S~heitswert** (-(e)s) *m* rarity
value.

Selterswasser ['zɛltərsvasər] *nt* soda water.

seltsam ['zɛltzaːm] *adj* curious, strange.

seltsamerweise *adv* curiously, strangely.

Seltsamkeit *f* strangeness.

Semester [ze'mɛstər] (-s, -) *nt* semester; **ein
älteres ~** a senior student.

Semi- [zemi] *in zW* semi-.

Semikolon [-'koːlɔn] (-s, -s) *nt* semicolon.

Seminar [zemi'naːr] (-s, -e) *nt* seminary; (*Kurs*)
seminar; (*UNIV*: *Ort*) department building.

semitisch [ze'miːtɪʃ] *adj* Semitic.

Semmel ['zɛməl] (-, -n) *f* roll; ~**brösel(n)** *pl* breadcrumbs *pl*; ~**knödel** (*SÜDD, ÖSTERR*) *m* bread dumpling.

sen. *abk* (= *senior*) sen.

Senat [ze'naːt] (-(e)s, -e) *m* senate.

Sendebereich *m* transmission range.

Sendefolge *f* (*Serie*) series.

senden[1] *unreg vt* to send.

senden[2] *vt, vi* (*RUNDF, TV*) to transmit, broadcast.

Sendenetz *nt* network.

Sendepause *f* (*RUNDF, TV*) interval.

Sender (-s, -) *m* station; (*Anlage*) transmitter.

Sende- *zW:* ~**reihe** *f* series (of broadcasts); ~**schluss▲** *m* (*RUNDF, TV*) closedown; ~**station** *f* transmitting station; ~**stelle** *f* transmitting station; ~**zeit** *f* broadcasting time, air time.

Sendung ['zɛnduŋ] *f* consignment; (*Aufgabe*) mission; (*RUNDF, TV*) transmission; (*Programm*) programme (*BRIT*), program (*US*).

Senegal ['zeːnegal] (-s) *nt* Senegal.

Senf [zɛnf] (-(e)s, -e) *m* mustard; **seinen** ~ **dazugeben** (*umg*) to put one's oar in; ~**korn** *nt* mustard seed.

sengen ['zɛŋən] *vt* to singe ♦ *vi* to scorch.

senil [ze'niːl] (*pej*) *adj* senile.

Senior ['zeːnɪɔr] (-s, -en) *m* (*Rentner*) senior citizen; (*Geschäftspartner*) senior partner.

Seniorenpass▲ [zeni'oːrənpas] *m* senior citizen's travel pass (*BRIT*).

Senkblei ['zɛŋkblaɪ] *nt* plumb.

Senke (-, -n) *f* depression.

Senkel (-s, -) *m* (shoe)lace.

senken *vt* to lower; (*Kopf*) to bow; (*TECH*) to sink ♦ *vr* to sink; (*Stimme*) to drop.

Senk- *zW:* ~**fuß** *m* flat foot; ~**grube** *f* cesspit; **s**~**recht** *adj* vertical, perpendicular; ~**rechte** *f* perpendicular; ~**rechtstarter** *m* (*AVIAT*) vertical takeoff plane; (*fig: Person*) highflier.

Senner(in) ['zɛnər(ɪn)] (-s, -) *m(f)* (Alpine) dairyman, dairymaid.

Sensation [zɛnzatsi'oːn] *f* sensation.

sensationell [zɛnzatsio'nɛl] *adj* sensational.

Sensationsblatt *nt* sensational paper.

Sensationssucht *f* sensationalism.

Sense ['zɛnzə] (-, -n) *f* scythe; **dann ist** ~! (*umg*) that's the end!

sensibel [zɛn'ziːbəl] *adj* sensitive.

sensibilisieren [zɛnzibili'ziːrən] *vt* to sensitize.

Sensibilität [zɛnzibili'tɛːt] *f* sensitivity.

sentimental [zɛntimɛn'taːl] *adj* sentimental.

Sentimentalität [zɛntimɛntali'tɛːt] *f* sentimentality.

separat [zepa'raːt] *adj* separate; (*Wohnung, Zimmer*) self-contained.

Sept. *abk* (= *September*) Sept.

September [zɛp'tɛmbər] (-(s), -) *m*

September; **im** ~ in September; **im Monat** ~ in the month of September; **heute ist der zweite** ~ today is the second of September *od* September second (*US*); (*geschrieben*) today is 2nd September; **in diesem** ~ this September; **Anfang/Ende/Mitte** ~ at the beginning/end/in the middle of September.

septisch ['zɛptɪʃ] *adj* septic.

sequentiell [zekvɛntsi'ɛl] *adj* = **sequenziell**.

Sequenz [ze'kvɛnts] *f* sequence.

sequenziell▲ [zekvɛntsi'ɛl] *adj* (*COMPUT*) sequential; ~**er Zugriff** sequential access.

Serbe ['zɛrbə] (-n, -n) *m* Serbian.

Serbien (-s) *nt* Serbia.

Serbin *f* Serbian.

serbisch *adj* Serbian.

Serbokroatisch(e) *nt* Serbo-Croat.

Serie ['zeːriə] *f* series.

seriell [zeri'ɛl] *adj* (*COMPUT*) serial; ~**e Daten** serial data *pl*; ~**er Anschluss** serial port; ~**er Drucker** serial printer.

Serien- *zW:* ~**anfertigung** *f*, ~**herstellung** *f* series production; **s**~**mäßig** *adj* (*Ausstattung*) standard; (*Herstellung*) series *attrib* ♦ *adv* (*herstellen*) in series; ~**nummer** *f* serial number; **s**~**weise** *adv* in series.

seriös [zeri'øːs] *adj* serious; (*anständig*) respectable.

Serpentine [zɛrpɛn'tiːnə] *f* hairpin (bend).

Serum ['zeːrum] (-s, Seren) *nt* serum.

Service[1] [zɛr'viːs] (-(s), -) *nt* (*Gläser~*) set; (*Geschirr*) service.

Service[2] ['səːvɪs] (-, -s) *m* (*COMM, SPORT*) service.

servieren [zɛr'viːrən] *vt, vi* to serve.

Serviererin [zɛr'viːrərɪn] *f* waitress.

Servierwagen *m* trolley.

Serviette [zɛrvi'ɛtə] *f* napkin, serviette.

Servolenkung *f* power steering.

Servomotor *m* servo motor.

Servus ['zɛrvʊs] (*ÖSTERR, SÜDD*) *interj* hello; (*beim Abschied*) goodbye, so long (*umg*).

Sesam ['zeːzam] (-s, -s) *m* sesame.

Sessel ['zɛsəl] (-s, -) *m* armchair; ~**lift** *m* chairlift.

sesshaft▲ ['zɛshaft] *adj* settled; (*ansässig*) resident.

Set [zɛt] (-s, -s) *nt od m* set; (*Deckchen*) tablemat.

setzen ['zɛtsən] *vt* to put, place, set; (*Baum etc*) to plant; (*Segel, TYP*) to set ♦ *vr* (*Platz nehmen*) to sit down; (*Kaffee, Tee*) to settle ♦ *vi* to leap; (*wetten*) to bet; (*TYP*) to set; **jdm ein Denkmal** ~ to build a monument to sb; **sich zu jdm** ~ to sit with sb.

Setzer ['zɛtsər] (-s, -) *m* (*TYP*) typesetter.

Setzerei [zɛtsə'raɪ] *f* caseroom; (*Firma*) typesetting firm.

Setz- *zW:* ~**kasten** *m* (*TYP*) case; (*an Wand*) ornament shelf; ~**ling** *m* young plant;

~**maschine** *f* (*TYP*) typesetting machine.
Seuche ['zɔʏçə] (-, -n) *f* epidemic.
Seuchengebiet *nt* infected area.
seufzen ['zɔʏftsən] *vt, vi* to sigh.
Seufzer ['zɔʏftsər] (-s, -) *m* sigh.
Sex [zɛks] (-(es)) *m* sex.
Sexta ['zɛksta] (-, **Sexten**) *f* (*früher*) first year
of German secondary school.
Sexualerziehung [zɛksu'a:lɛrtsi:ʊŋ] *f* sex
education.
Sexualität [zɛksuali'tɛ:t] *f* sex, sexuality.
Sexual- *zW:* ~**kunde** [zɛksu'a:lkʊndə] *f* sex
education; ~**leben** *nt* sex life; ~**objekt** *nt* sex
object.
sexuell [zɛksu'ɛl] *adj* sexual.
Seychellen [ze'ʃɛlən] *pl* Seychelles *pl*.
sezieren [ze'tsi:rən] *vt* to dissect.
SFB (-) *m abk* (= *Sender Freies Berlin*) Radio
Free Berlin.
Sfr, sFr. *abk* (= *Schweizer Franken*) sfr.
Shampoo [ʃam'pu:] (-s, -s) *nt* shampoo.
Shetlandinseln ['ʃɛtlant|ɪnzəln] *pl* Shetland,
Shetland Isles *pl*.
Shorts [ʃɔrts] *pl* shorts *pl*.
Showmaster ['ʃouma:stər] (-s, -) *m* compère,
MC.
siamesisch [zia'me:zɪʃ] *adj:* ~**e Zwillinge**
Siamese twins.
Siamkatze *f* Siamese (cat).
Sibirien [zi'bi:riən] (-s) *nt* Siberia.
sibirisch *adj* Siberian.

══════════════════════ *SCHLÜSSELWORT*

sich [zɪç] *pron* **1** (*akk*): **er/sie/es** ... ~ he/she/it ...
himself/herself/itself; **sie** *pl*/**man** ... ~ they/
one ...themselves/oneself; **Sie** ... ~ you ...
yourself/yourselves *pl*; ~ **wiederholen** to
repeat oneself/itself.
2 (*dat*): **er/sie/es** ... ~ he/she/it ... to himself/
herself/itself; **sie** *pl*/**man** ... ~ they/one ... to
themselves/oneself; **Sie** ... ~ you ... to
yourself/yourselves *pl*; **sie hat** ~ **einen**
Pullover gekauft she bought herself a
jumper; ~ **die Haare waschen** to wash one's
hair.
3 (*mit Präposition*): **haben Sie Ihren Ausweis**
bei ~? do you have your pass on you?; **er**
hat nichts bei ~ he's got nothing on him; **sie**
bleiben gern unter ~ they keep themselves
to themselves.
4 (*einander*) each other, one another; **sie**
bekämpfen ~ they fight each other *od* one
another.
5: dieses Auto fährt ~ **gut** this car drives
well; **hier sitzt es** ~ **gut** it's good to sit here.

Sichel ['zɪçəl] (-, -n) *f* sickle; (*Mond*~)
crescent.
sicher ['zɪçər] *adj* safe; (*gewiss*) certain; (*Hand,*
Job) steady; (*zuverlässig*) secure, reliable;

(*selbst*~) confident; (*Stellung*) secure ♦ *adv*
(*natürlich*): **du hast dich** ~ **verrechnet** you
must have counted wrongly; **vor jdm/etw**
~ **sein** to be safe from sb/sth; **sich** *dat* **einer**
Sache/jds ~ **sein** to be sure of sth/sb; ~ **ist**
~ you can't be too sure.
sichergehen *unreg vi* to make sure.
Sicherheit ['zɪçərhaɪt] *f* safety; (*auch FIN*)
security; (*Gewissheit*) certainty; (*Selbst*~)
confidence; **die öffentliche** ~ public
security; ~ **im Straßenverkehr** road safety;
~ **leisten** (*COMM*) to offer security.
Sicherheits- *zW:* ~**abstand** *m* safe distance;
~**bestimmungen** *pl* safety regulations *pl*;
(*betrieblich, POL etc*) security controls *pl*;
~**einrichtungen** *pl* security equipment *sing*,
security devices *pl*; ~**glas** *nt* safety glass;
~**gurt** *m* seat belt; **s**~**halber** *adv* to be on the
safe side; ~**nadel** *f* safety pin; ~**rat** *m*
Security Council; ~**schloss**▲ *nt* safety lock;
~**spanne** *f* (*COMM*) margin of safety;
~**verschluss**▲ *m* safety clasp; ~**vorkehrung** *f*
safety precaution.
sicherlich *adv* certainly, surely.
sichern *vt* to secure; (*schützen*) to protect;
(*Bergsteiger etc*) to belay; (*Waffe*) to put the
safety catch on; (*COMPUT: Daten*) to back
up; **jdm/sich etw** ~ to secure sth for sb/for
o.s.
sicherstellen *vt* to impound; (*garantieren*) to
guarantee.
Sicherung *f* (*Sichern*) securing; (*Vorrichtung*)
safety device; (*an Waffen*) safety catch;
(*ELEK*) fuse; **da ist (bei) ihm die**
~ **durchgebrannt** (*fig: umg*) he blew a fuse.
Sicherungskopie *f* backup copy.
Sicht [zɪçt] (-) *f* sight; (*Aus*~) view; (*Sehweite*)
visibility; **auf** *od* **nach** ~ (*FIN*) at sight; **auf**
lange ~ on a long-term basis; **s**~**bar** *adj*
visible; ~**barkeit** *f* visibility.
sichten *vt* to sight; (*auswählen*) to sort out;
(*ordnen*) to sift through.
Sicht- *zW:* **s**~**lich** *adj* evident, obvious;
~**verhältnisse** *pl* visibility *sing*; ~**vermerk** *m*
visa; ~**weite** *f* visibility; **außer** ~**weite** out of
sight.
sickern ['zɪkərn] *vi* (*Hilfsverb sein*) to seep; (*in*
Tropfen) to drip.
Sie [zi:] *nom, akk pron* you.
sie *pron* (*sing: nom*) she; (: *akk*) her; (*pl: nom*)
they; (: *akk*) them.
Sieb [zi:p] (-(e)s, -e) *nt* sieve; (*KOCH*) strainer;
(*Gemüse*~) colander.
sieben[1] ['zi:bən] *vt* to sieve, sift; (*Flüssigkeit*)
to strain ♦ *vi:* **bei der Prüfung wird stark**
gesiebt (*fig: umg*) the exam will weed a lot
of people out.
sieben[2] ['zi:bən] *num* seven; **S**~**gebirge** *nt:*
das S~**gebirge** the Seven Mountains *pl* (*near*
Bonn); ~**hundert** *num* seven hundred;

S~meter *m* (*SPORT*) penalty; **S~sachen** *pl* belongings *pl*; **S~schläfer** *m* dormouse.

siebte(r, s) ['ziːptə(r, s)] *adj* seventh.

Siebtel (**-s, -**) *nt* seventh.

siebzehn ['ziːptseːn] *num* seventeen.

siebzig ['ziːptsɪç] *num* seventy.

siedeln ['ziːdəln] *vi* to settle.

sieden ['ziːdən] *vt, vi* to boil.

Siedepunkt *m* boiling point.

Siedler (**-s, -**) *m* settler.

Siedlung *f* settlement; (*Häuser~*) housing estate (*BRIT*) *od* development (*US*).

Sieg [ziːk] (**-(e)s, -e**) *m* victory.

Siegel ['ziːgəl] (**-s, -**) *nt* seal; **~lack** *m* sealing wax; **~ring** *m* signet ring.

siegen ['ziːgən] *vi* to be victorious; (*SPORT*) to win; **über jdn/etw ~** (*fig*) to triumph over sb/sth; (*in Wettkampf*) to beat sb/sth.

Sieger(in) (**-s, -**) *m(f)* victor; (*SPORT etc*) winner; **~ehrung** *f* (*SPORT*) presentation ceremony.

siegessicher *adj* sure of victory.

Siegeszug *m* triumphal procession.

siegreich *adj* victorious.

siehe ['ziːə] *Imperativ* see; (**~ da**) behold.

siehst [ziːst], **sieht** [ziːt] *vb siehe* **sehen**.

Siel [ziːl] (**-(e)s, -e**) *nt od m* (*Schleuse*) sluice; (*Abwasserkanal*) sewer.

siezen ['ziːtsən] *vt* to address as "Sie"; *siehe auch* **duzen**.

Signal [zɪ'gnaːl] (**-s, -e**) *nt* signal; **~anlage** *f* signals *pl*, set of signals.

signalisieren [zɪgnali'ziːrən] *vt* (*lit, fig*) to signal.

Signatur [zɪgna'tuːr] *f* signature; (*Bibliotheks~*) shelf mark.

Silbe ['zɪlbə] (**-, -n**) *f* syllable; **er hat es mit keiner ~ erwähnt** he didn't say a word about it.

Silber ['zɪlbər] (**-s**) *nt* silver; **~bergwerk** *nt* silver mine; **~blick** *m:* **einen ~blick haben** to have a slight squint; **~hochzeit** *f* silver wedding.

silbern *adj* silver.

Silberpapier *nt* silver paper.

Silhouette [zilu'ɛtə] *f* silhouette.

Silikonchip [zili'koːntʃɪp] *m* silicon chip.

Silo ['ziːlo] (**-s, -s**) *nt od m* silo.

Silvester [zɪl'vestər] (**-s, -**) *m or nt* New Year's Eve, Hogmanay (*SCOT*).

SILVESTER

Silvester *is the German name for New Year's Eve. Although not an official holiday, most businesses close early and shops shut at midday. Most Germans celebrate in the evening and at midnight they let off fireworks and rockets; the revelry usually lasts until the early hours of the morning.*

Simbabwe [zɪm'baːbvə] (**-s**) *nt* Zimbabwe.

simpel ['zɪmpəl] *adj* simple; **S~** (**-s, -**) (*umg*) *m* simpleton.

Sims [zɪms] (**-es, -e**) *nt od m* (*Kamin~*) mantelpiece; (*Fenster~*) (window)sill.

simsen ['zɪmzən] *vti* (*umg*) to text.

Simulant(in) [zimu'lant(ɪn)] (**-en, -en**) *m(f)* malingerer.

simulieren [zimu'liːrən] *vt* to simulate; (*vortäuschen*) to feign ♦ *vi* to feign illness.

simultan [zimʊl'taːn] *adj* simultaneous; **S~dolmetscher** *m* simultaneous interpreter.

sind [zɪnt] *vb siehe* **sein**.

Sinfonie [zɪnfo'niː] *f* symphony.

Singapur [zɪŋgapuːr] (**-s**) *nt* Singapore.

singen ['zɪŋən] *unreg vt, vi* to sing.

Single¹ ['sɪŋəl] (**-s, -s**) *m* (*Alleinlebender*) single person.

Single² ['sɪŋəl] (**-, -s**) *f* (*MUS*) single.

Singsang *m* (*Gesang*) monotonous singing.

Singstimme *f* vocal part.

Singular ['zɪŋgulaːr] *m* singular.

Singvogel ['zɪŋfoːgəl] *m* songbird.

sinken ['zɪŋkən] *unreg vi* to sink; (*Boden, Gebäude*) to subside; (*Fundament*) to settle; (*Preise etc*) to fall, go down; **den Mut/die Hoffnung ~ lassen** to lose courage/hope.

Sinn [zɪn] (**-(e)s, -e**) *m* mind; (*Wahrnehmungssinn*) sense; (*Bedeutung*) sense, meaning; **im ~e des Gesetzes** according to the spirit of the law; **~ für etw** sense of sth; **im ~e des Verstorbenen** in accordance with the wishes of the deceased; **von ~en sein** to be out of one's mind; **das ist nicht der ~ der Sache** that is not the point; **das hat keinen ~** there is no point in that; **~bild** *nt* symbol; **s~bildlich** *adj* symbolic.

sinnen *unreg vi* to ponder; **auf etw** *akk* **~** to contemplate sth; **über etw** *akk* **~** to reflect on sth.

Sinnenmensch *m* sensualist.

Sinnes- *zW:* **~organ** *nt* sense organ; **~täuschung** *f* illusion; **~wandel** *m* change of mind.

sinngemäß *adj* faithful; (*Wiedergabe*) in one's own words.

sinnig *adj* apt; (*ironisch*) clever.

Sinn- *zW:* **s~lich** *adj* sensual, sensuous; (*Wahrnehmung*) sensory; **~lichkeit** *f* sensuality; **s~los** *adj* senseless, meaningless; **s~los betrunken** blind drunk; **~losigkeit** *f* senselessness, meaninglessness; **s~verwandt** *adj* synonymous; **s~voll** *adj* meaningful; (*vernünftig*) sensible.

Sinologe [zino'loːgə] (**-n, -n**) *m* Sinologist.

Sinologin *f* Sinologist.

Sinologie [zinolo'giː] *f* Sinology.

Sintflut ['zɪntfluːt] *f* Flood; **nach uns die ~**

(*umg*) it doesn't matter what happens after we've gone; **s~artig** *adj*: **s~artige Regenfälle** torrential rain *sing*.

Sinus ['zi:nʊs] **(-, - *od* -se)** *m* (*ANAT*) sinus; (*MATH*) sine.

Siphon [zi'fõ:] **(-s, -s)** *m* siphon.

Sippe ['zɪpə] **(-, -n)** *f* (extended) family; (*umg*: *Verwandtschaft*) clan.

Sippschaft ['zɪpʃaft] (*pej*) *f* tribe; (*Bande*) gang.

Sirene [zi're:nə] **(-, -n)** *f* siren.

Sirup ['zi:rʊp] **(-s, -e)** *m* syrup.

Sit-in [sɪt'|ɪn] **(-(s), -s)** *nt*: **ein ~ machen** to stage a sit-in.

Sitte ['zɪtə] **(-, -n)** *f* custom; **Sitten** *pl* morals *pl*; **was sind denn das für ~n?** what sort of way is that to behave?

Sitten- *zW*: **~polizei** *f* vice squad; **~strolch** (*umg*) *m* sex fiend; **~wächter** *m* (*ironisch*) guardian of public morals; **s~widrig** *adj* (*form*) immoral.

Sittich ['zɪtɪç] **(-(e)s, -e)** *m* parakeet.

Sitt- *zW*: **s~lich** *adj* moral; **~lichkeit** *f* morality; **~lichkeitsverbrechen** *nt* sex offence (*BRIT*) *od* offense (*US*); **s~sam** *adj* modest, demure.

Situation [zituatsi'o:n] *f* situation.

situiert [zitu'i:rt] *adj*: **gut ~ sein** to be well off.

Sitz [zɪts] **(-es, -e)** *m* seat; (*von Firma, Verwaltung*) headquarters *pl*; **der Anzug hat einen guten ~** the suit sits well.

sitzen *unreg vi* to sit; (*Bemerkung, Schlag*) to strike home; (*Gelerntes*) to have sunk in; (*umg*: *im Gefängnis ~*) to be inside; **locker ~** to be loose; **einen ~ haben** (*umg*) to have had one too many; **er sitzt im Kultusministerium** (*umg*: *sein*) he's in the Ministry of Education; **~ bleiben** to remain seated; (*SCH*) to have to repeat a year; **auf etw** *dat* **~ bleiben** to be lumbered with sth; **~ lassen** (*SCH*) to keep down a year; (*Mädchen*) to jilt; (*Wartenden*) to stand up; **etw auf sich** *dat* **~ lassen** to take sth lying down.

sitzend *adj* (*Tätigkeit*) sedentary.

Sitz- *zW*: **~fleisch** (*umg*) *nt*: **~fleisch haben** to be able to sit still; **~gelegenheit** *f* seats *pl*; **~ordnung** *f* seating plan; **~platz** *m* seat; **~streik** *m* sit-down strike.

Sitzung *f* meeting.

Sizilianer(in) [zitsili'a:nər(ɪn)] **(-s, -)** *m(f)* Sicilian.

sizilianisch *adj* Sicilian.

Sizilien [zi'tsi:liən] **(-s)** *nt* Sicily.

Skala ['ska:la] **(-, Skalen)** *f* scale; (*fig*) range.

Skalpell [skal'pɛl] **(-s, -e)** *nt* scalpel.

skalpieren [skal'pi:rən] *vt* to scalp.

Skandal [skan'da:l] **(-s, -e)** *m* scandal.

skandalös [skanda'lø:s] *adj* scandalous.

Skandinavien [skandi'na:viən] **(-s)** *nt* Scandinavia.

Skandinavier(in) **(-s, -)** *m(f)* Scandinavian.

skandinavisch *adj* Scandinavian.

Skat [ska:t] **(-(e)s, -e *od* -s)** *m* (*KARTEN*) skat.

Skelett [ske'lɛt] **(-(e)s, -e)** *nt* skeleton.

Skepsis ['skɛpsɪs] **(-)** *f* scepticism (*BRIT*), skepticism (*US*).

skeptisch ['skɛptɪʃ] *adj* sceptical (*BRIT*), skeptical (*US*).

Ski [ʃi:] **(-s, -er)** *m* ski; **~ laufen** *od* **fahren** to ski; **~fahrer** *m* skier; **~hütte** *f* ski hut; **~läufer** *m* skier; **~lehrer** *m* ski instructor; **~lift** *m* ski lift; **~springen** *nt* ski jumping; **~stiefel** *m* ski boot; **~stock** *m* ski pole.

Skizze ['skɪtsə] **(-, -n)** *f* sketch.

skizzieren [skɪ'tsi:rən] *vt* to sketch; (*fig*: *Plan etc*) to outline ♦ *vi* to sketch.

Sklave ['skla:və] **(-n, -n)** *m* slave.

Sklaventreiber **(-s, -)** (*pej*) *m* slave-driver.

Sklaverei [skla:və'raɪ] *f* slavery.

Sklavin *f* slave.

sklavisch *adj* slavish.

Skonto ['skɔnto] **(-s, -s)** *nt od m* discount.

Skorbut [skɔr'bu:t] **(-(e)s)** *m* scurvy.

Skorpion [skɔrpi'o:n] **(-s, -e)** *m* scorpion; (*ASTROL*) Scorpio.

Skrupel ['skru:pəl] **(-s, -)** *m* scruple; **s~los** *adj* unscrupulous.

Skulptur [skʊlp'tu:r] *f* sculpture.

skurril [skʊ'ri:l] *adj* (*geh*) droll, comical.

Slalom ['sla:lɔm] **(-s, -s)** *m* slalom.

Slawe ['sla:və] **(-n, -n)** *m* Slav.

Slawin *f* Slav.

slawisch *adj* Slavonic, Slavic.

Slip [slɪp] **(-s, -s)** *m* (pair of) briefs *pl*.

Slowake [slo'va:kə] **(-n, -n)** *m* Slovak.

Slowakei [slova'kaɪ] *f* Slovakia.

Slowakin *f* Slovak.

Slowakisch [slo'va:kɪʃ] *nt* (*LING*) Slovak; **s~** *adj* Slovak.

Slowenien [slo've:niən] **(-s)** *nt* Slovenia.

slowenisch *adj* Slovene.

Smaragd [sma'rakt] **(-(e)s, -e)** *m* emerald.

Smoking ['smo:kɪŋ] **(-s, -s)** *m* dinner jacket (*BRIT*), tuxedo (*US*).

SMS **(-, -)** *f abk* (= *Short Message Service*) SMS; **~-Nachricht** *f* text message.

SMV **(-, -s)** *f abk* = **Schülermitverwaltung**.

Snob [snɔp] **(-s, -s)** *m* snob.

So. *abk* = **Sonntag**.

SO *abk* (= *Südost(en)*) SE.

═══════════════════════ *SCHLÜSSELWORT*

so [zo:] *adv* **1** (*so sehr*) so; **~ groß/schön** *etc* so big/nice *etc*; **~ groß/schön wie ...** as big/nice as ...; **das hat ihn ~ geärgert, dass ...** that annoyed him so much that ...
2 (*auf diese Weise*) like this; **~ genannt** so-called; **mach es nicht ~** don't do it like that; **~ oder ~** (in) one way or the other; **... oder ~ something** (like that); **und ~ weiter** and

so on; ~ **viel (wie)** as much as; **rede nicht**
~ **viel** don't talk so much; ~ **weit sein** to be
ready; ~ **weit wie** od **als möglich** as far as
possible; **ich bin** ~ **weit zufrieden** by and
large I'm quite satisfied; **es ist bald** ~ **weit**
it's nearly time; ~ **wenig (wie)** no more
(than), not any more (than); ~ **wenig wie**
möglich as little as possible; ~ **ein ... such a**
...; ~ **einer wie ich** somebody like me;
~ **(et)was** something like this/that; **na**
~ **was!** well I never!; **das ist gut** ~ that's
fine; **sie ist nun einmal** ~ that's just the way
she is; **das habe ich nur** ~ **gesagt** I didn't
really mean it.
3 (*umg: umsonst*): **ich habe es** ~ **bekommen**
I got it for nothing.
4 (*als Füllwort: nicht übersetzt*): ~ **mancher** a
number of people *pl*.
◆ *konj*: ~ **dass** so that; ~ **wie es jetzt ist** as
things are at the moment; *siehe auch* **sodass**.
◆ *interj*: ~**?** really?; ~**, das wärs** right, that's
it then.

s. o. *abk* (= *siehe oben*) see above.
sobald [zo'balt] *konj* as soon as.
Söckchen ['zœkçən] *nt* ankle sock.
Socke ['zɔkə] (**-, -n**) *f* sock; **sich auf die ~n**
machen (*umg*) to get going.
Sockel ['zɔkəl] (**-s, -**) *m* pedestal, base.
sodass▲ [zo'das] *konj* so that.
Sodawasser ['zo:davasər] *nt* soda water.
Sodbrennen ['zo:tbrɛnən] (**-s**) *nt* heartburn.
Sodomie [zodo'mi:] *f* bestiality.
soeben [zo'ʔe:bən] *adv* just (now).
Sofa ['zo:fa] (**-s, -s**) *nt* sofa.
Sofabett *nt* sofa bed, bed settee.
sofern [zo'fɛrn] *konj* if, provided (that).
soff *etc* [zɔf] *vb siehe* **saufen**.
sofort [zo'fɔrt] *adv* immediately, at once; **(ich)**
komme ~**!** (I'm) just coming!; **S~hilfe** *f*
emergency relief *od* aid; **S~hilfegesetz** *nt*
law on emergency aid.
sofortig *adj* immediate.
Sofortmaßnahme *f* immediate measure.
Softeis ['sɔft|aɪs] (**-es**) *nt* soft ice-cream.
Softie ['zɔfti:] (**-s, -s**) (*umg*) *m* softy.
Software ['zɔftweːər] (**-, -s**) *f* software;
s~kompatibel *adj* software compatible;
~**paket** *nt* software package.
Sog (**-(e)s, -e**) *m* suction; (*von Strudel*) vortex;
(*fig*) maelstrom.
sog *etc* [zo:k] *vb siehe* **saugen**.
sogar [zo'ga:r] *adv* even.
sogleich [zo'glaɪç] *adv* straight away, at once.
Sogwirkung *f* suction; (*fig*) knock-on effect.
Sohle ['zo:lə] (**-, -n**) *f* (*Fuß~*) sole; (*Tal~ etc*)
bottom; (*MIN*) level; **auf leisen** ~**n** (*fig*)
softly, noiselessly.
Sohn [zo:n] (**-(e)s, ~e**) *m* son.
Sojasoße ['zo:jazo:sə] *f* soy *od* soya sauce.

solang(e) *konj* as *od* so long as.
Solar- [zo'la:r] *in zW* solar; ~**energie** *f* solar
energy.
Solarium [zo'la:riʊm] *nt* solarium.
Solbad ['zo:lba:t] *nt* saltwater bath.
solch [zɔlç] *adj inv* such.
solche(r, s) *adj* such; **ein** ~**r Mensch** such a
person.
Sold [zɔlt] (**-(e)s, -e**) *m* pay.
Soldat [zɔl'da:t] (**-en, -en**) *m* soldier; **s~isch**
adj soldierly.
Söldner ['zœldnər] (**-s, -**) *m* mercenary.
Sole ['zo:lə] (**-, -n**) *f* brine, salt water.
Solei ['zo:laɪ] *nt* pickled egg.
Soli ['zo:li] *pl von* **Solo**.
solid(e) [zo'li:d(ə)] *adj* solid; (*Arbeit, Wissen*)
sound; (*Leben, Person*) staid, respectable.
solidarisch [zoli'da:rɪʃ] *adj in od* with
solidarity; **sich** ~ **erklären** to declare one's
solidarity.
solidarisieren [zolidari'zi:rən] *vr*: **sich** ~ **mit** to
show (one's) solidarity with.
Solidarität [zolidari'tɛ:t] *f* solidarity.
Solidaritätsstreik *m* sympathy strike.
Solist(in) [zo'lɪst(ɪn)] *m(f)* (*MUS*) soloist.
Soll [zɔl] (**-(s), -(s)**) *nt* (*FIN*) debit (side);
(*Arbeitsmenge*) quota, target; ~ **und Haben**
debit and credit.
soll *vb siehe* **sollen**.

═══════════════════════════ *SCHLÜSSELWORT*

sollen ['zɔlən] (*pt* **sollte**, *pp* **gesollt**) (*od* (*als*
Hilfsverb) **sollen**) *Hilfsverb* **1** (*Pflicht, Befehl*) be
supposed to; **du hättest nicht gehen** ~ you
shouldn't have gone, you oughtn't to have
gone; **er sollte eigentlich morgen kommen**
he was supposed to come tomorrow; **soll**
ich? shall I?; **soll ich dir helfen?** shall I help
you?; **sag ihm, er soll warten** tell him he's to
wait; **was soll ich machen?** what should I
do?; **mir soll es gleich sein** it's all the same
to me; **er sollte sie nie wiedersehen** he was
never to see her again.
2 (*Vermutung*): **sie soll verheiratet sein** she's
said to be married; **was soll das heißen?**
what's that supposed to mean?; **man sollte**
glauben, dass ... you would think that ...; **sollte**
das passieren, ... if that should happen ...
◆ *vt, vi*: **was soll das?** what's all this about *od* in
aid of?; **das sollst du nicht** you shouldn't do
that; **was solls?** what the hell!

sollte *etc* ['zɔltə] *vb siehe* **sollen**.
Solo ['zo:lo] (**-s, -s** *od* **Soli**) *nt* solo.
solo *adv* (*MUS*) solo; (*fig: umg*) on one's own,
alone.
solvent [zɔl'vɛnt] *adj* (*FIN*) solvent.
Solvenz [zɔl'vɛnts] *f* (*FIN*) solvency.
Somalia [zo'ma:lia] (**-s**) *nt* Somalia.
somit [zo'mɪt] *konj* and so, therefore.

Sommer ['zɔmər] **(-s, -)** *m* summer; ~ **wie Winter** all year round; ~**ferien** *pl* summer holidays *pl* (*BRIT*) *od* vacation *sing* (*US*); (*JUR*, *PARL*) summer recess *sing*; **s**~**lich** *adj* summer *attrib*; (*sommerartig*) summery; ~**loch** *nt* silly season; ~**reifen** *m* normal tyre (*BRIT*) *od* tire (*US*); ~**schlussverkauf**▲ *m* summer sale; ~**semester** *nt* (*UNIV*) summer semester (*bes US*); ≈ summer term (*BRIT*); ~**sprossen** *pl* freckles *pl*; ~**zeit** *f* summertime.

Sonate [zo'naːtə] **(-, -n)** *f* sonata.

Sonde ['zɔndə] **(-, -n)** *f* probe.

Sonder- ['zɔndər] *in zW* special; ~**anfertigung** *f* special model; ~**angebot** *nt* special offer; ~**ausgabe** *f* special edition; **s**~**bar** *adj* strange, odd; ~**beauftragte(r)** *f(m)* (*POL*) special emissary; ~**beitrag** *m* (special) feature; ~**fahrt** *f* special trip; ~**fall** *m* special case; **s**~**gleichen** *adj inv* without parallel, unparalleled; **eine Frechheit s**~**gleichen** the height of cheek; **s**~**lich** *adj* particular; (*außergewöhnlich*) remarkable; (*eigenartig*) peculiar; ~**ling** *m* eccentric; ~**marke** *f* special issue (stamp); ~**müll** *m* dangerous waste.

sondern *konj* but ♦ *vt* to separate; **nicht nur ...,** ~ **auch** not only ..., but also.

Sonder- *zW*: ~**preis** *m* special price; ~**regelung** *f* special provision; ~**schule** *f* special school; ~**vergünstigungen** *pl* perquisites *pl*, perks *pl* (*bes BRIT*); ~**wünsche** *pl* special requests *pl*; ~**zug** *m* special train.

sondieren [zɔn'diːrən] *vt* to suss out; (*Gelände*) to scout out.

Sonett [zo'nɛt] **(-(e)s, -e)** *nt* sonnet.

Sonnabend ['zɔn|aːbənt] *m* Saturday; *siehe auch* **Dienstag**.

Sonne ['zɔnə] **(-, -n)** *f* sun; **an die** ~ **gehen** to go out in the sun.

sonnen *vr* to sun o.s.; **sich in etw** (*dat*) ~ (*fig*) to bask in sth.

Sonnen- *zW*: ~**aufgang** *m* sunrise; **s**~**baden** *vi* to sunbathe; ~**blume** *f* sunflower; ~**brand** *m* sunburn; ~**brille** *f* sunglasses *pl*; ~**creme** *f* suntan lotion; ~**energie** *f* solar energy; ~**finsternis** *f* solar eclipse; ~**fleck** *m* sunspot; **s**~**gebräunt** *adj* suntanned; **s**~**klar** *adj* crystal-clear; ~**kollektor** *m* solar panel; ~**kraftwerk** *nt* solar power station; ~**milch** *f* suntan lotion; ~**öl** *nt* suntan oil; ~**schein** *m* sunshine; ~**schirm** *m* sunshade; ~**schutzmittel** *nt* sunscreen; ~**stich** *m* sunstroke; **du hast wohl einen** ~**stich!** (*hum*: *umg*) you must have been out in the sun too long!; ~**system** *nt* solar system; ~**uhr** *f* sundial; ~**untergang** *m* sunset; ~**wende** *f* solstice.

sonnig ['zɔnɪç] *adj* sunny.

Sonntag ['zɔntaːk] *m* Sunday; *siehe auch* **Dienstag**.

sonntäglich *adj attrib*: ~ **gekleidet** dressed in one's Sunday best.

sonntags *adv* (on) Sundays.

Sonntagsdienst *m*: ~ **haben** (*Apotheke*) to be open on Sundays.

Sonntagsfahrer (*pej*) *m* Sunday driver.

sonst [zɔnst] *adv* otherwise; (*mit pron, in Fragen*) else; (*zu anderer Zeit*) at other times; (*gewöhnlich*) usually, normally ♦ *konj* otherwise; **er denkt, er ist** ~ **wer** (*umg*) he thinks he's somebody special; ~ **gehts dir gut?** (*ironisch*: *umg*) are you feeling okay?; **wenn ich Ihnen** ~ **noch behilflich sein kann** if I can help you in any other way; ~ **noch etwas?** anything else?; ~ **nichts** nothing else; ~ **jemand** (*umg*) anybody (at all); **da kann ja** ~ **was passieren** (*umg*) anything could happen; ~ **wo** (*umg*) somewhere else; ~ **woher** (*umg*) from somewhere else; ~ **wohin** (*umg*) somewhere else.

sonstig *adj* other; „**S**~**es**" "other".

sooft [zo'|ɔft] *konj* whenever.

Sopran [zo'praːn] **(-s, -e)** *m* soprano (voice).

Sopranistin [zopra'nɪstɪn] *f* soprano (singer).

Sorge ['zɔrgə] **(-, -n)** *f* care, worry; **dafür** ~ **tragen, dass ...** (*geh*) to see to it that ...

sorgen *vi*: **für jdn** ~ to look after sb ♦ *vr*: **sich** ~ (**um**) to worry (about); **für etw** ~ to take care of *od* see to sth; **dafür** ~, **dass ...** to see to it that ...; **dafür ist gesorgt** that's taken care of.

Sorgen- *zW*: **s**~**frei** *adj* carefree; ~**kind** *nt* problem child; **s**~**voll** *adj* troubled, worried.

Sorgerecht **(-(e)s)** *nt* custody (of a child).

Sorgfalt ['zɔrkfalt] **(-)** *f* care(fulness); **viel** ~ **auf etw** *akk* **verwenden** to take a lot of care over sth.

sorgfältig *adj* careful.

sorglos *adj* careless; (*ohne Sorgen*) carefree.

sorgsam *adj* careful.

Sorte ['zɔrtə] **(-, -n)** *f* sort; (*Waren*~) brand; **Sorten** *pl* (*FIN*) foreign currency *sing*.

sortieren [zɔr'tiːrən] *vt* to sort (out); (*COMPUT*) to sort.

Sortiermaschine *f* sorting machine.

Sortiment [zɔrti'mɛnt] *nt* assortment.

SOS [ɛs|oː'|ɛs] *nt abk* SOS.

sosehr [zo'zeːr] *konj* as much as.

soso [zo'zoː] *interj*: ~**!** I see!; (*erstaunt*) well, well!; (*drohend*) well!

Soße ['zoːsə] **(-, -n)** *f* sauce; (*Braten*~) gravy.

Souffleur [zu'fløːr] *m* prompter.

Souffleuse [zu'fløːzə] *f* prompter.

soufflieren [zu'fliːrən] *vt, vi* to prompt.

soundso ['zoː|ʊnt'zoː] *adv*: ~ **lange** for such and such a time.

soundsovielte(r, s) *adj*: **am S**~**n** (*Datum*) on such and such a date.

Souterrain [zutɛ'rɛ̃] **(-s, -s)** *nt* basement.

Souvenir [zuvə'ni:r] (**-s, -s**) *nt* souvenir.
souverän [zuvə'rɛ:n] *adj* sovereign;
(*überlegen*) superior; (*fig*) supremely good.
soviel [zo'fi:l] *konj* as far as.
sowenig [zo've:nɪç] *konj* however little.
sowie [zo'vi:] *konj* (*sobald*) as soon as; (*ebenso*)
as well as.
sowieso [zovi'zo:] *adv* anyway.
Sowjetbürger *m* (*früher*) Soviet citizen.
sowjetisch [zɔ'vjɛtɪʃ] *adj* (*früher*) Soviet.
Sowjet- *zW* (*früher*): **~republik** *f* Soviet
Republic; **~russe** *m* Soviet Russian; **~union** *f*
Soviet Union.
sowohl [zo'vo:l] *konj*: **~ ... als** *od* **wie auch ...**
both ... and ...
soz. *abk* = **sozial; sozialistisch**.
sozial [zotsi'a:l] *adj* social; **~ eingestellt**
public-spirited; **~er Wohnungsbau** public-
sector housing (programme); **S~abbau** *m*
public-spending cuts *pl*; **S~abgaben** *pl*
National Insurance contributions *pl* (*BRIT*),
Social Security contributions *pl* (*US*); **S~amt**
nt (social) welfare office; **S~arbeiter** *m*
social worker; **S~beruf** *m* caring profession;
S~demokrat *m* social democrat; **S~hilfe** *f*
welfare (aid).
Sozialisation [zotsializatsi'o:n] *f* (*PSYCH*,
SOZIOLOGIE) socialization.
sozialisieren [zotsiali'zi:rən] *vt* to socialize.
Sozialismus [zotsia'lɪsmʊs] *m* socialism.
Sozialist(in) [zotsia'lɪst(ɪn)] *m(f)* socialist.
sozialistisch *adj* socialist.
Sozial- *zW*: **~kunde** *f* social studies *sing*;
~leistungen *pl* social security contributions
(*from the state and employer*); **~plan** *m*
redundancy payments scheme; **~politik** *f*
social welfare policy; **~produkt** *nt* (gross *od*
net) national product; **~staat** *m* welfare
state; **~versicherung** *f* national insurance
(*BRIT*), social security (*US*); **s~verträglich** *adj*
socially acceptable; **~wohnung** *f* ≈ council
flat (*BRIT*), state-subsidized apartment.

SOZIALWOHNUNG

A **Sozialwohnung** *is a council house or flat let
at a fairly low rent to people on low income. They
are built from public funds. People applying for a*
Sozialwohnung *have to prove their entitlement.*

Soziologe [zotsio'lo:gə] (**-n, -n**) *m* sociologist.
Soziologie [zotsiolo'gi:] *f* sociology.
Soziologin [zotsio'lo:gɪn] *f* sociologist.
soziologisch [zotsio'lo:gɪʃ] *adj* sociological.
Sozius ['zo:tsiʊs] (**-, -se**) *m* (*COMM*) partner;
(*Motorrad*) pillion rider; **~sitz** *m* pillion
(seat).
sozusagen [zotsu'za:gən] *adv* so to speak.
Spachtel ['ʃpaxtəl] (**-s, -**) *m* spatula.
spachteln *vt* (*Mauerfugen, Ritzen*) to fill (in)

♦ *vi* (*umg: essen*) to tuck in.
Spagat [ʃpa'ga:t] (**-s, -e**) *m od nt* splits *pl*.
Spagetti▲, Spaghetti [ʃpa'gɛti] *pl* spaghetti
sing.
spähen ['ʃpɛ:ən] *vi* to peep, peek.
Spalier [ʃpa'li:r] (**-s, -e**) *nt* (*Gerüst*) trellis;
(*Leute*) guard of honour (*BRIT*) *od* honor (*US*);
~ stehen, ein ~ bilden to form a guard of
honour (*BRIT*) *od* honor (*US*).
Spalt [ʃpalt] (**-(e)s, -e**) *m* crack; (*Tür~*) chink;
(*fig: Kluft*) split.
Spalte (**-, -n**) *f* crack, fissure; (*Gletscher~*)
crevasse; (*in Text*) column.
spalten *vt, vr* (*lit, fig*) to split.
Spaltung *f* splitting.
Span [ʃpa:n] (**-(e)s, -̈e**) *m* shaving.
Spanferkel *nt* sucking pig.
Spange ['ʃpaŋə] (**-, -n**) *f* clasp; (*Haar~*) hair
slide; (*Schnalle*) buckle; (*Arm~*) bangle.
Spaniel ['ʃpa:niəl] (**-s, -s**) *m* spaniel.
Spanien ['ʃpa:niən] (**-s**) *nt* Spain.
Spanier(in) (**-s, -**) *m(f)* Spaniard.
spanisch *adj* Spanish; **das kommt mir ~ vor**
(*umg*) that seems odd to me; **~e Wand**
(folding) screen.
Spann (**-(e)s, -e**) *m* instep.
spann *etc* [ʃpan] *vb siehe* **spinnen**.
Spannbeton (**-s**) *m* prestressed concrete.
Spanne (**-, -n**) *f* (*Zeit~*) space; (*Differenz*) gap;
siehe auch **Spann**.
spannen *vt* (*straffen*) to tighten, tauten;
(*befestigen*) to brace ♦ *vi* to be tight.
spannend *adj* exciting, gripping; **machs nicht
so ~!** (*umg*) don't keep me *etc* in suspense.
Spanner (**-s, -**) (*umg*) *m* (*Voyeur*) peeping
Tom.
Spannkraft *f* elasticity; (*fig*) energy.
Spannung *f* tension; (*ELEK*) voltage; (*fig*)
suspense; (*unangenehm*) tension.
Spannungsgebiet *nt* (*POL*) flashpoint, area
of tension.
Spannungsprüfer *m* voltage detector.
Spannweite *f* (*von Flügeln, AVIAT*)
(wing)span.
Spanplatte *f* chipboard.
Sparbuch *nt* savings book.
Sparbüchse *f* moneybox.
sparen ['ʃpa:rən] *vt, vi* to save; **sich** *dat* **etw ~**
to save o.s. sth; (*Bemerkung*) to keep sth to
o.s.; **mit etw ~** to be sparing with sth; **an
etw** *dat* **~** to economize on sth.
Sparer(in) (**-s, -**) *m(f)* (*bei Bank etc*) saver.
Sparflamme *f* low flame; **auf ~** (*fig: umg*) just
ticking over.
Spargel ['ʃpargəl] (**-s, -**) *m* asparagus.
Spar- *zW*: **~groschen** *m* nest egg; **~kasse** *f*
savings bank; **~konto** *nt* savings account.
spärlich ['ʃpɛ:rlɪç] *adj* meagre (*BRIT*), meager
(*US*); (*Bekleidung*) scanty; (*Beleuchtung*) poor.
Spar- *zW*: **~maßnahme** *f* economy measure;

~**packung** f economy size; **s~sam** adj
economical, thrifty; **s~sam im Verbrauch**
economical; ~**samkeit** f thrift, economizing;
~**schwein** nt piggy bank.
Sparte ['ʃpartə] (-, -n) f field; (COMM) line of
business; (PRESSE) column.
Sparvertrag m savings agreement.
Spaß [ʃpaːs] (-es, ⁀e) m joke; (Freude) fun;
~ **muss sein** there's no harm in a joke; **jdm**
~ **machen** to be fun (for sb); **s~en** vi to joke;
mit ihm ist nicht zu s~en you can't take
liberties with him.
spaßeshalber adv for the fun of it.
spaßig adj funny, droll.
Spaß- zW: ~**macher** m joker, funny man;
~**verderber** (-s, -) m spoilsport; ~**vogel** m
joker.
Spastiker(in) ['ʃpastikər(ɪn)] m(f) (MED)
spastic.
spät [ʃpɛːt] adj, adv late; **heute Abend wird es**
~ it'll be a late night tonight.
Spaten ['ʃpaːtən] (-s, -) m spade; ~**stich** m: **den**
ersten ~stich tun to turn the first sod.
Spätentwickler m late developer.
später adj, adv later; **an** ~ **denken** to think of
the future; **bis ~!** see you later!
spätestens adv at the latest.
Spätlese f late vintage.
Spatz [ʃpats] (-en, -en) m sparrow.
spazieren [ʃpa'tsiːrən] vi (Hilfsverb sein) to
stroll; ~ **fahren** to go for a drive; ~ **gehen** to
go for a walk.
Spazier- zW: ~**gang** m walk; **einen ~gang**
machen to go for a walk; ~**gänger(in)** m(f)
stroller; ~**stock** m walking stick; ~**weg** m
path, walk.
SPD (-) f abk (= Sozialdemokratische Partei
Deutschlands) German Social Democratic
Party.

SPD

The **SPD** (Sozialdemokratische Partei
Deutschlands), the German Social Democratic
Party, was newly formed in 1945. It is the largest
political party in Germany.

Specht [ʃpɛçt] (-(e)s, -e) m woodpecker.
Speck [ʃpɛk] (-(e)s, -e) m bacon; **mit ~ fängt**
man Mäuse (Sprichwort) you need a sprat to
catch a mackerel; **ran an den ~** (umg) let's
get stuck in.
Spediteur [ʃpedi'tøːr] m carrier; (Möbel~)
furniture remover.
Spedition [ʃpeditsi'oːn] f carriage; (~sfirma)
road haulage contractor; (Umzugsfirma)
removal (BRIT) od moving (US) firm.
Speer [ʃpeːr] (-(e)s, -e) m spear; (SPORT)
javelin; ~**werfen** nt: **das ~werfen** throwing
the javelin.

Speiche ['ʃpaɪçə] (-, -n) f spoke.
Speichel ['ʃpaɪçəl] (-s) m saliva, spit(tle);
~**lecker** (pej: umg) m bootlicker.
Speicher ['ʃpaɪçər] (-s, -) m storehouse;
(Dach~) attic, loft; (Korn~) granary;
(Wasser~) tank; (TECH) store; (COMPUT)
memory; ~**auszug** m (COMPUT) dump.
speichern vt (auch COMPUT) to store.
speien ['ʃpaɪən] unreg vt, vi to spit; (erbrechen)
to vomit; (Vulkan) to spew.
Speise ['ʃpaɪzə] (-, -n) f food; **kalte und warme**
~n hot and cold meals; ~**eis** nt ice-cream;
~**fett** nt cooking fat; ~**kammer** f larder,
pantry; ~**karte** f menu.
speisen vt to feed; to eat ♦ vi to dine.
Speise- zW: ~**öl** nt salad oil; (zum Braten)
cooking oil; ~**röhre** f (ANAT) gullet,
oesophagus (BRIT), esophagus (US); ~**saal** m
dining room; ~**wagen** m dining car; ~**zettel**
m menu.
Spektakel [ʃpɛk'taːkəl] (-s, -) m (umg: Lärm)
row ♦ nt (-s, -) spectacle.
spektakulär [ʃpɛktakuˈlɛːr] adj spectacular.
Spektrum ['ʃpɛktrʊm] (-s, -tren) nt spectrum.
Spekulant(in) [ʃpeku'lant(ɪn)] m(f) speculator.
Spekulation [ʃpekulatsi'oːn] f speculation.
Spekulatius [ʃpeku'laːtsiʊs] (-, -) m spiced
biscuit (BRIT) od cookie (US).
spekulieren [ʃpeku'liːrən] vi (fig) to speculate;
auf etw akk ~ to have hopes of sth.
Spelunke [ʃpe'lʊŋkə] (-, -n) f dive.
spendabel [ʃpɛn'daːbəl] (umg) adj generous,
open-handed.
Spende ['ʃpɛndə] (-, -n) f donation.
spenden vt to donate, give; **S~konto** nt
donations account; **S~waschanlage** f
donation-laundering organization.
Spender(in) (-s, -) m(f) donator; (MED) donor.
spendieren [ʃpɛn'diːrən] vt to pay for, buy;
jdm etw ~ to treat sb to sth, stand sb sth.
Sperling ['ʃpɛrlɪŋ] m sparrow.
Sperma ['ʃpɛrma] (-s, Spermen) nt sperm.
sperrangelweit ['ʃpɛr|aŋəl'vaɪt] adj wide-
open.
Sperrbezirk m no-go area.
Sperre (-, -n) f barrier; (Verbot) ban; (Polizei~)
roadblock.
sperren ['ʃpɛrən] vt to block; (COMM: Konto) to
freeze; (COMPUT: Daten) to disable; (SPORT)
to suspend, bar; (: vom Ball) to obstruct;
(einschließen) to lock; (verbieten) to ban ♦ vr
to baulk, jibe, jib.
Sperr- zW: ~**feuer** nt (MIL, fig) barrage; ~**frist** f
(auch JUR) waiting period; (SPORT) (period
of) suspension; ~**gebiet** nt prohibited area;
~**gut** nt bulky freight; ~**holz** nt plywood.
sperrig adj bulky.
Sperr- zW: ~**konto** nt blocked account; ~**müll**
m bulky refuse; ~**sitz** m (THEAT) stalls pl
(BRIT), orchestra (US); ~**stunde** f closing

time; ~**zeit** f closing time; ~**zone** f exclusion zone.

Spesen ['ʃpeːzən] pl expenses pl; ~**abrechnung** f expense account.

Spessart ['ʃpɛsart] (-s) m Spessart (Mountains pl).

Spezi ['ʃpeːtsi] (-s, -s) (umg) m pal, mate (BRIT).

Spezial- [ʃpetsi'aːl] in zW special; ~**ausbildung** f specialized training.

spezialisieren [ʃpetsiali'ziːrən] vr to specialize.

Spezialisierung f specialization.

Spezialist(in) [ʃpetsia'lɪst(ɪn)] m(f): ~ **(für)** specialist (in).

Spezialität [ʃpetsiali'tɛːt] f speciality (BRIT), specialty (US).

speziell [ʃpetsi'ɛl] adj special.

Spezifikation [ʃpetsifikatsi'oːn] f specification.

spezifisch [ʃpe'tsiːfɪʃ] adj specific.

Sphäre ['sfɛːrə] (-, -n) f sphere.

spicken ['ʃpɪkən] vt to lard ♦ vi (SCH) to copy, crib.

Spickzettel m (SCH: umg) crib.

spie etc [ʃpiː] vb siehe **speien**.

Spiegel ['ʃpiːgəl] (-s, -) m mirror; (Wasser~) level; (MIL) tab; ~**bild** nt reflection; **s~bildlich** adj reversed.

Spiegelei ['ʃpiːgəlˌaɪ] nt fried egg.

spiegeln vt to mirror, reflect ♦ vr to be reflected ♦ vi to gleam; (wider~) to be reflective.

Spiegelreflexkamera f reflex camera.

Spiegelschrift f mirror writing.

Spiegelung f reflection.

spiegelverkehrt adj in mirror image.

Spiel [ʃpiːl] (-(e)s, -e) nt game; (Schau~) play; (Tätigkeit) play(ing); (KARTEN) pack (BRIT), deck (US); (TECH) (free) play; **leichtes ~ (bei** od **mit jdm) haben** to have an easy job of it (with sb); **die Hand** od **Finger im ~ haben** to have a hand in affairs; **jdn/etw aus dem ~ lassen** to leave sb/sth out of it; **auf dem ~(e) stehen** to be at stake; ~**automat** m gambling machine; (zum Geldgewinnen) fruit machine (BRIT); ~**bank** f casino; ~**dose** f musical box (BRIT), music box (US).

spielen vt, vi to play; (um Geld) to gamble; (THEAT) to perform, act; **was wird hier gespielt?** (umg) what's going on here?

spielend adv easily.

Spieler(in) (-s, -) m(f) player; (um Geld) gambler.

Spielerei [ʃpiːlə'raɪ] f (Kinderspiel) child's play.

spielerisch adj playful; (Leichtigkeit) effortless; ~**es Können** skill as a player; (THEAT) acting ability.

Spiel- zW: ~**feld** nt pitch, field; ~**film** m feature film; ~**geld** nt (Einsatz) stake; (unechtes Geld)

toy money; ~**karte** f playing card; ~**konsole** f play console; ~**mannszug** m (brass) band; ~**plan** m (THEAT) programme (BRIT), program (US); ~**platz** m playground; ~**raum** m room to manoeuvre (BRIT) od maneuver (US), scope; ~**regel** f (lit, fig) rule of the game; ~**sachen** pl toys pl; ~**show** f gameshow; ~**stand** m score; ~**straße** f play street; ~**sucht** f addiction to gambling; ~**verderber** (-s, -) m spoilsport; ~**waren** pl toys pl; ~**zeit** f (Saison) season; (~dauer) playing time; ~**zeug** nt toy; (~sachen) toys pl.

Spieß [ʃpiːs] (-es, -e) m spear; (Brat~) spit; (MIL: umg) sarge; **den ~ umdrehen** (fig) to turn the tables; **wie am ~(e) schreien** (umg) to squeal like a stuck pig; ~**braten** m joint roasted on a spit.

Spießbürger (-s, -) m bourgeois.

Spießer (-s, -) m bourgeois.

Spikes [spaɪks] pl (SPORT) spikes pl; (AUT) studs pl; ~**reifen** m studded tyre (BRIT) od tire (US).

Spinat [ʃpi'naːt] (-(e)s, -e) m spinach.

Spind [ʃpɪnt] (-(e)s, -e) m od nt locker.

spindeldürr ['ʃpɪndəl'dʏr] (pej) adj spindly, thin as a rake.

Spinne ['ʃpɪnə] (-, -n) f spider; **s~feind** (umg) adj: **sich** od **einander** dat **s~feind sein** to be deadly enemies.

spinnen unreg vt to spin ♦ vi (umg) to talk rubbish; (verrückt) to be crazy od mad; **ich denk ich spinne** (umg) I don't believe it.

Spinnengewebe nt cobweb.

Spinner(in) (-s, -) m(f) (fig: umg) screwball, crackpot.

Spinnerei [ʃpɪnə'raɪ] f spinning mill.

Spinn- zW: ~**gewebe** nt cobweb; ~**rad** nt spinning wheel; ~**webe** f cobweb.

Spion [ʃpi'oːn] (-s, -e) m spy; (in Tür) spyhole.

Spionage [ʃpio'naːʒə] (-) f espionage; ~**abwehr** f counterintelligence; ~**satellit** m spy satellite.

spionieren [ʃpio'niːrən] vi to spy.

Spionin f (woman) spy.

Spirale [ʃpi'raːlə] (-, -n) f spiral; (MED) coil.

Spirituosen [ʃpiritu'oːzən] pl spirits pl.

Spiritus ['ʃpiːritus] (-, -se) m (methylated) spirits pl; ~**kocher** m spirit stove.

Spitz [ʃpɪts] (-es, -e) m (Hund) spitz.

spitz adj pointed; (Winkel) acute; (fig: Zunge) sharp; (: Bemerkung) caustic.

Spitz- zW: **s~bekommen** unreg vt: **etw s~bekommen** (umg) to get wise to sth; ~**bogen** m pointed arch; ~**bube** m rogue.

Spitze (-, -n) f point, tip; (Berg~) peak; (Bemerkung) taunt; (fig: Stichelei) dig; (erster Platz) lead, top; (meist pl: Gewebe) lace; (umg: prima) great; **etw auf die ~ treiben** to carry sth too far.

Spitzel (-s, -) m police informer.

spitzen *vt* to sharpen; (*Lippen, Mund*) to purse; (*lit, fig: Ohren*) to prick up.

Spitzen- *in zW* top; ~**leistung** *f* top performance; ~**lohn** *m* top wages *pl*; ~**marke** *f* brand leader; **s**~**mäßig** *adj* really great; ~**position** *f* leading position; ~**reiter** *m* (*SPORT*) leader; (*fig: Kandidat*) front runner; (*Ware*) top seller; (*Schlager*) number one; ~**sportler** *m* top-class sportsman; ~**verband** *m* leading organization.

Spitzer (-s, -) *m* sharpener.

spitzfindig *adj* (over)subtle.

Spitzmaus *f* shrew.

Spitzname *m* nickname.

Spleen [ʃpliːn] (-s, -e *od* -s) *m* (*Angewohnheit*) crazy habit; (*Idee*) crazy idea; (*Fimmel*) obsession.

Splitt [ʃplɪt] (-s, -e) *m* stone chippings *pl*; (*Streumittel*) grit.

Splitter (-s, -) *m* splinter; ~**gruppe** *f* (*POL*) splinter group; **s**~**nackt** *adj* stark naked.

SPÖ (-) *f abk* (= *Sozialistische Partei Österreichs*) Austrian Socialist Party.

sponsern [ʃpɔnzərn] *vt* to sponsor.

Sponsor [ʃpɔnzɔr] (-s, -en) *m* sponsor.

spontan [ʃpɔnˈtaːn] *adj* spontaneous.

sporadisch [ʃpoˈraːdɪʃ] *adj* sporadic.

Sporen [ʃpoːrən] *pl* (*auch BOT, ZOOL*) spurs *pl*.

Sport [ʃpɔrt] (-(e)s, -e) *m* sport; (*fig*) hobby; **treiben Sie** ~? do you do any sport?; ~**abzeichen** *nt* sports certificate; ~**artikel** *pl* sports equipment *sing*; ~**fest** *nt* sports gala; (*SCH*) sports day (*BRIT*); ~**geist** *m* sportsmanship; ~**halle** *f* sports hall; ~**klub** *m* sports club; ~**lehrer** *m* games *od* P.E. teacher.

Sportler(in) (-s, -) *m(f)* sportsman, sportswoman.

Sport- *zW:* **s**~**lich** *adj* sporting; (*Mensch*) sporty; (*durchtrainiert*) athletic; (*Kleidung*) smart but casual; ~**medizin** *f* sports medicine; ~**platz** *m* playing *od* sports field; ~**schuh** *m* sports shoe; (*sportlicher Schuh*) casual shoe.

Sportsfreund *m* (*fig: umg*) buddy.

Sport- *zW:* ~**verein** *m* sports club; ~**wagen** *m* sports car; ~**zeug** *nt* sports gear.

Spot [spɔt] (-s, -s) *m* commercial, advertisement.

Spott [ʃpɔt] (-(e)s) *m* mockery, ridicule; **s**~**billig** *adj* dirt-cheap; **s**~**en** *vi* to mock; **s**~**en über** *+akk* to mock (at), ridicule; **das s**~**et jeder Beschreibung** that simply defies description.

spöttisch [ʃpœtɪʃ] *adj* mocking.

Spottpreis *m* ridiculously low price.

sprach *etc* [ʃpraːx] *vb siehe* **sprechen.**

sprachbegabt *adj* good at languages.

Sprache (-, -n) *f* language; **heraus mit der** ~! (*umg*) come on, out with it!; **zur** ~ **kommen** to be mentioned; **in französischer** ~ in French.

Sprachenschule *f* language school.

Sprach- *zW:* ~**fehler** *m* speech defect; ~**fertigkeit** *f* fluency; ~**führer** *m* phrase book; ~**gebrauch** *m* (linguistic) usage; ~**gefühl** *nt* feeling for language; ~**kenntnisse** *pl:* **mit englischen** ~**kenntnissen** with a knowledge of English; ~**kurs** *m* language course; ~**labor** *nt* language laboratory; **s**~**lich** *adj* linguistic; **s**~**los** *adj* speechless; ~**rohr** *nt* megaphone; (*fig*) mouthpiece; ~**störung** *f* speech disorder; ~**wissenschaft** *f* linguistics *sing*.

sprang *etc* [ʃpraŋ] *vb siehe* **springen.**

Spray [spreː] (-s, -s) *m od nt* spray; ~**dose** *f* aerosol (can), spray.

sprayen *vt, vi* to spray.

Sprechanlage *f* intercom.

Sprechblase *f* speech balloon.

sprechen [ʃpreçən] *unreg vi* to speak, talk ♦ *vt* to say; (*Sprache*) to speak; (*Person*) to speak to; **mit jdm** ~ to speak *od* talk to sb; **das spricht für ihn** that's a point in his favour; **frei** ~ to extemporize; **nicht gut auf jdn zu** ~ **sein** to be on bad terms with sb; **es spricht vieles dafür, dass ...** there is every reason to believe that ...; **hier spricht man Spanisch** Spanish spoken; **wir** ~ **uns noch!** you haven't heard the last of this!

Sprecher(in) (-s, -) *m(f)* speaker; (*für Gruppe*) spokesman, spokeswoman; (*RUNDF, TV*) announcer.

Sprech- *zW:* ~**funkgerät** *nt* radio telephone; ~**rolle** *f* speaking part; ~**stunde** *f* consultation (hour); (*von Arzt*) (doctor's) surgery (*BRIT*); ~**stundenhilfe** *f* (doctor's) receptionist; ~**zimmer** *nt* consulting room, surgery (*BRIT*).

spreizen [ʃpraɪtsən] *vt* to spread ♦ *vr* to put on airs.

Sprengarbeiten *pl* blasting operations *pl*.

sprengen [ʃprɛŋən] *vt* to sprinkle; (*mit Sprengstoff*) to blow up; (*Gestein*) to blast; (*Versammlung*) to break up.

Spreng- *zW:* ~**kopf** *m* warhead; ~**ladung** *f* explosive charge; ~**satz** *m* explosive device; ~**stoff** *m* explosive(s *pl*); ~**stoffanschlag** *m* bomb attack.

Spreu [ʃprɔy] (-) *f* chaff.

spricht [ʃprɪçt] *vb siehe* **sprechen.**

Sprichwort *nt* proverb.

sprichwörtlich *adj* proverbial.

sprießen [ʃpriːsən] *vi* (*aus der Erde*) to spring up; (*Knospen*) to shoot.

Springbrunnen *m* fountain.

springen [ʃprɪŋən] *unreg vi* to jump, leap; (*Glas*) to crack; (*mit Kopfsprung*) to dive; **etw** ~ **lassen** (*umg*) to fork out sth.

springend *adj:* **der** ~**e Punkt** the crucial

point.

Springer (-s, -) m jumper; (*SCHACH*) knight.

Springreiten nt show jumping.

Springseil nt skipping rope.

Sprinkler ['ʃprɪŋklər] (-s, -) m sprinkler.

Sprit [ʃprɪt] (-(e)s, -e) (*umg*) m petrol (*BRIT*), gas(oline) (*US*), fuel.

Spritzbeutel m icing bag.

Spritze ['ʃprɪtsə] (-, -n) f syringe; (*Injektion*) injection; (*an Schlauch*) nozzle.

spritzen vt to spray; (*Wein*) to dilute with soda water/lemonade; (*MED*) to inject ♦ vi to splash; (*heißes Fett*) to spit; (*heraus~*) to spurt; (*aus einer Tube etc*) to squirt; (*MED*) to give injections.

Spritzer (-s, -) m (*Farb~, Wasser~*) splash.

Spritzpistole f spray gun.

Spritztour (*umg*) f spin.

spröde ['ʃprøːdə] adj brittle; (*Person*) reserved; (*Haut*) rough.

Spross▲ (-es, -e) m shoot.

spross etc▲ [ʃprɔs] vb siehe **sprießen**.

Sprosse ['ʃprɔsə] (-, -n) f rung.

Sprossenwand f (*SPORT*) wall bars pl.

Sprössling▲ ['ʃprœslɪŋ] m offspring no pl.

Spruch [ʃprʊx] (-(e)s, ⁻e) m saying, maxim; (*JUR*) judgement; **Sprüche klopfen** (*umg*) to talk fancy; **~band** nt banner.

Sprüchemacher ['ʃpryçəmaxər] (*umg*) m patter-merchant.

spruchreif adj: **die Sache ist noch nicht ~** it's not definite yet.

Sprudel ['ʃpruːdəl] (-s, -) m mineral water; (*süß*) lemonade.

sprudeln vi to bubble.

Sprüh- zW: **~dose** f aerosol (can); **s~en** vi to spray; (*fig*) to sparkle ♦ vt to spray; **~regen** m drizzle.

Sprung [ʃprʊŋ] (-(e)s, ⁻e) m jump; (*schwungvoll, fig: Gedanken~*) leap; (*Riss*) crack; **immer auf dem ~ sein** (*umg*) to be always on the go; **jdm auf die Sprünge helfen** (*wohlwollend*) to give sb a (helping) hand; **auf einen ~ bei jdm vorbeikommen** (*umg*) to drop in to see sb; **damit kann man keine großen Sprünge machen** (*umg*) you can't exactly live it up on that; **~brett** nt springboard; **~feder** f spring; **s~haft** adj erratic; (*Aufstieg*) rapid; **~schanze** f ski jump; **~turm** m diving platform.

Spucke ['ʃpʊkə] (-) f spit.

spucken vt, vi to spit; **in die Hände ~** (*fig*) to roll up one's sleeves.

Spucknapf m spittoon.

Spucktüte f sickbag.

Spuk [ʃpuːk] (-(e)s, -e) m haunting; (*fig*) nightmare; **s~en** vi to haunt; **hier s~t es** this place is haunted.

Spülbecken ['ʃpyːlbɛkən] nt sink.

Spule ['ʃpuːlə] (-, -n) f spool; (*ELEK*) coil.

Spüle ['ʃpyːlə] (-, -n) f (kitchen) sink.

spülen vt to rinse; (*Geschirr*) to wash, do; (*Toilette*) to flush ♦ vi to rinse; to wash up (*BRIT*), do the dishes; to flush; **etw an Land ~** to wash sth ashore.

Spül- zW: **~maschine** f dishwasher; **~mittel** nt washing-up liquid (*BRIT*), dish-washing liquid; **~stein** m sink.

Spülung f rinsing; (*Wasser~*) flush; (*MED*) irrigation.

Spund [ʃpʊnt] (-(e)s, -e) m: **junger ~** (*veraltet: umg*) young pup.

Spur [ʃpuːr] (-, -en) f trace; (*Fuß~, Rad~, Tonband~*) track; (*Fährte*) trail; (*Fahr~*) lane; **jdm auf die ~ kommen** to get onto sb; **(seine) ~en hinterlassen** (*fig*) to leave its mark; **keine ~** (*umg*) not/nothing at all.

spürbar adj noticeable, perceptible.

spuren (*umg*) vi to obey; (*sich fügen*) to toe the line.

spüren ['ʃpyːrən] vt to feel; **etw zu ~ bekommen** (*lit*) to feel sth; (*fig*) to feel the (full) force of sth.

Spurenelement nt trace element.

Spurensicherung f securing of evidence.

Spürhund m tracker dog; (*fig*) sleuth.

spurlos adv without (a) trace; **~ an jdm vorübergehen** to have no effect on sb.

Spurt [ʃpʊrt] (-(e)s, -s od -e) m spurt.

spurten vi (*Hilfsverb sein: SPORT*) to spurt; (*umg: rennen*) to sprint.

Squash [skvɔʃ] (-) nt (*SPORT*) squash.

sputen ['ʃpuːtən] vr to make haste.

SS (-) f abk (= *Schutzstaffel*) SS ♦ nt abk = **Sommersemester**.

s. S. abk (= *siehe Seite*) see p.

SSV abk = **Sommerschlussverkauf**.

st abk (= *Stunde*) h.

St. abk = **Stück** (= *Stunde*) h.; (= *Sankt*) St.

Staat [ʃtaːt] (-(e)s, -en) m state; (*Prunk*) show; (*Kleidung*) finery; **mit etw ~ machen** to show off od parade sth.

staatenlos adj stateless.

staatl. abk = **staatlich**.

staatlich adj state attrib; state-run ♦ adv: **~ geprüft** state-certified.

Staats- zW: **~affäre** f (*lit*) affair of state; (*fig*) major operation; **~angehörige(r)** f(m) national; **~angehörigkeit** f nationality; **~anleihe** f government bond; **~anwalt** m public prosecutor; **~bürger** m citizen; **~bürgerschaft** f nationality; **doppelte ~bürgerschaft** dual nationality; **~dienst** m civil service; **s~eigen** adj state-owned; **~eigentum** nt public ownership; **~examen** (*UNIV*) degree; **s~feindlich** adj subversive; **~geheimnis** nt (*lit, fig hum*) state secret; **~haushalt** m budget; **~kosten** pl public expenses pl; **~mann** (-(e)s, pl -männer) m statesman; **s~männisch** adj statesmanlike;

~oberhaupt *nt* head of state; **~schuld** *f* (*FIN*) national debt; **~sekretär** *m* secretary of state; **~streich** *m* coup (d'état); **~verschuldung** *f* national debt.

Stab [ʃtaːp] (-(e)s, ^=e) *m* rod; (*für ~hochsprung*) pole; (*für Staffellauf*) baton; (*Gitter~*) bar; (*Menschen*) staff; (*von Experten*) panel.

Stäbchen ['ʃtɛːpçən] *nt* (*Ess~*) chopstick.

Stabhochsprung *m* pole vault.

stabil [ʃtaˈbiːl] *adj* stable; (*Möbel*) sturdy.

Stabilisator [ʃtabiliˈzaːtɔr] *m* stabilizer.

stabilisieren [ʃtabiliˈziːrən] *vt* to stabilize.

Stabilisierung *f* stabilization.

Stabilität [ʃtabiliˈtɛːt] *f* stability.

Stabreim *m* alliteration.

Stabsarzt *m* (*MIL*) captain in the medical corps.

stach *etc* [ʃtaːx] *vb siehe* **stechen**.

Stachel ['ʃtaxəl] (-s, -n) *m* spike; (*von Tier*) spine; (*von Insekten*) sting; **~beere** *f* gooseberry; **~draht** *m* barbed wire.

stach(e)lig *adj* prickly.

Stachelschwein *nt* porcupine.

Stadion ['ʃtaːdiɔn] (-s, **Stadien**) *nt* stadium.

Stadium ['ʃtaːdiʊm] *nt* stage, phase.

Stadt [ʃtat] (-, ^=e) *f* town; (*Groß~*) city; (*~verwaltung*) (town/city) council; **~bad** *nt* municipal swimming baths *pl*; **s~bekannt** *adj* known all over town; **~bezirk** *m* municipal district.

Städtchen ['ʃtɛːtçən] *nt* small town.

Städtebau (-(e)s) *m* town planning.

Städter(in) (-s, -) *m(f)* town/city dweller, townie.

Stadtgespräch *nt*: (**das**) **~ sein** to be the talk of the town.

Stadtguerilla *f* urban guerrilla.

städtisch *adj* municipal; (*nicht ländlich*) urban.

Stadt- *zW*: **~kasse** *f* town/city treasury; **~kern** *m* = **Stadtzentrum**; **~kreis** *m* town/city borough; **~mauer** *f* city wall(s *pl*); **~mitte** *f* town/city centre (*BRIT*) *od* center (*US*); **~park** *m* municipal park; **~plan** *m* street map; **~rand** *m* outskirts *pl*; **~rat** *m* (*Behörde*) (town/city) council; **~streicher** *m* street vagrant; **~streicherin** *f* bag lady; **~teil** *m* district, part of town; **~verwaltung** *f* (*Behörde*) municipal authority; **~viertel** *nt* district *od* part of a town; **~zentrum** *nt* town/city centre (*BRIT*) *od* center (*US*).

Staffel ['ʃtafəl] (-, -n) *f* rung; (*SPORT*) relay (team); (*AVIAT*) squadron.

Staffelei [ʃtafəˈlai] *f* easel.

Staffellauf *m* relay race.

staffeln *vt* to graduate.

Staffelung *f* graduation.

Stagnation [ʃtagnatsiˈoːn] *f* stagnation.

stagnieren [ʃtaˈgniːrən] *vi* to stagnate.

Stahl (-(e)s, ^=e) *m* steel.

stahl *etc* [ʃtaːl] *vb siehe* **stehlen**.

Stahlhelm *m* steel helmet.

stak *etc* [ʃtaːk] *vb siehe* **stecken**.

Stall [ʃtal] (-(e)s, ^=e) *m* stable; (*Kaninchen~*) hutch; (*Schweine~*) sty; (*Hühner~*) henhouse.

Stallung *f* stables *pl*.

Stamm [ʃtam] (-(e)s, ^=e) *m* (*Baum~*) trunk; (*Menschen~*) tribe; (*GRAM*) stem; (*Bakterien~*) strain; **~aktie** *f* ordinary share, common stock (*US*); **~baum** *m* family tree; (*von Tier*) pedigree; **~buch** *nt* book of family events with legal documents.

stammeln *vt, vi* to stammer.

stammen *vi*: **~ von** *od* **aus** to come from.

Stamm- *zW*: **~form** *f* base form; **~gast** *m* regular (customer); **~halter** *m* son and heir.

stämmig ['ʃtɛmɪç] *adj* sturdy; (*Mensch*) stocky; **S~keit** *f* sturdiness; stockiness.

Stamm- *zW*: **~kapital** *nt* (*FIN*) ordinary share *od* common stock (*US*) capital; **~kunde** *m*, **~kundin** *f* regular (customer); **~lokal** *nt* favourite (*BRIT*) *od* favorite (*US*) café/ restaurant *etc*; (*Kneipe*) local (*BRIT*); **~platz** *m* usual seat; **~tisch** *m* (*Tisch in Gasthaus*) *table reserved for the regulars*; **~zelle** *f* stem cell; **embryonale ~zellen** embryonic stem cells.

stampfen ['ʃtampfən] *vi* to stamp; (*stapfen*) to tramp ♦ *vt* (*mit Stampfer*) to mash.

Stampfer (-s, -) *m* (*Stampfgerät*) masher.

Stand (-(e)s, ^=e) *m* position; (*Wasser~*, *Benzin~ etc*) level; (*Zähler~ etc*) reading; (*Stehen*) standing position; (*Zustand*) state; (*Spiel~*) score; (*Messe~ etc*) stand; (*Klasse*) class; (*Beruf*) profession; **bei jdm** *od* **gegen jdn einen schweren ~ haben** (*fig*) to have a hard time of it with sb; **etw auf den neuesten ~ bringen** to bring sth up to date; *siehe auch* **außerstande, imstande, zustande**.

stand *etc* [ʃtant] *vb siehe* **stehen**.

Standard ['ʃtandart] (-s, -s) *m* standard; **~ausführung** *f* standard design.

standardisieren [ʃtandardiˈziːrən] *vt* to standardize.

Standarte (-, -n) *f* (*MIL, POL*) standard.

Standbild *nt* statue.

Ständchen ['ʃtɛntçən] *nt* serenade.

Ständer (-s, -) *m* stand.

Standes- *zW*: **~amt** *nt* registry office (*BRIT*), city/county clerk's office (*US*); **s~amtlich** *adj*: **s~amtliche Trauung** registry office wedding (*BRIT*), civil marriage ceremony; **~beamte(r)** *m* registrar; **~bewusstsein▲** *nt* status consciousness; **~dünkel** *m* snobbery; **s~gemäß** *adj, adv* according to one's social position; **~unterschied** *m* social difference.

Stand- *zW*: **s~fest** *adj* (*Tisch, Leiter*) stable, steady; (*fig*) steadfast; **s~haft** *adj* steadfast; **~haftigkeit** *f* steadfastness; **s~halten** *unreg vi*: **(jdm/etw) s~halten** to stand firm (against sb/sth), resist (sb/sth).

ständig ['ʃtɛndɪç] *adj* permanent; (*ununterbrochen*) constant, continual.

Stand- *zW*: ~**licht** *nt* sidelights *pl* (*BRIT*), parking lights *pl* (*US*); ~**ort** *m* location; (*MIL*) garrison; ~**pauke** (*umg*) *f*: **jdm eine ~pauke halten** to give sb a lecture; ~**punkt** *m* standpoint; **s~rechtlich** *adj*: **s~rechtlich erschießen** to put before a firing squad; ~**spur** *f* (*AUT*) hard shoulder (*BRIT*), berm (*US*).

Stange ['ʃtaŋə] (-, -n) *f* stick; (*Stab*) pole; (*Quer~*) bar; (*Zigaretten*) carton; **von der ~** (*COMM*) off the peg (*BRIT*) *od* rack (*US*); **eine ~ Geld** quite a packet; **jdm die ~ halten** (*umg*) to stick up for sb; **bei der ~ bleiben** (*umg*) to stick at *od* to sth.

Stängel▲ ['ʃtɛŋl] (-s, -) *m* stalk; **vom ~ fallen** (*umg: überrascht sein*) to be staggered.

Stangenbohne *f* runner bean.

Stangenbrot *nt* French bread; (*Laib*) French stick (loaf).

stank *etc* [ʃtaŋk] *vb siehe* **stinken**.

stänkern ['ʃtɛŋkərn] (*umg*) *vi* to stir things up.

Stanniol [ʃtani'oːl] (-s, -e) *nt* tinfoil.

Stanze ['ʃtantsə] (-, -n) *f* stanza; (*TECH*) stamp.

stanzen *vt* to stamp; (*Löcher*) to punch.

Stapel ['ʃtaːpəl] (-s, -) *m* pile; (*NAUT*) stocks *pl*; ~**lauf** *m* launch.

stapeln *vt* to pile (up).

Stapelverarbeitung *f* (*COMPUT*) batch processing.

stapfen ['ʃtapfən] *vi* to trudge, plod.

Star¹ [ʃtaːr] (-(e)s, -e) *m* starling; **grauer/ grüner ~** (*MED*) cataract/glaucoma.

Star² [ʃtaːr] (-s, -s) *m* (*Film~ etc*) star.

starb *etc* [ʃtarp] *vb siehe* **sterben**.

stark [ʃtark] *adj* strong; (*heftig, groß*) heavy; (*Maßangabe*) thick; (*umg: hervorragend*) great ♦ *adv* very; (*beschädigt etc*) badly; (*vergrößert, verkleinert*) greatly; **das ist ein ~es Stück!** (*umg*) that's a bit much!; **sich für etw ~ machen** (*umg*) to stand up for sth; **er ist ~ erkältet** he has a bad cold.

Stärke ['ʃtɛrkə] (-, -n) *f* strength (*auch fig*); heaviness; thickness; (*von Mannschaft*) size; (*KOCH, Wäsche~*) starch; ~**mehl** *nt* (*KOCH*) thickening agent.

stärken *vt* (*lit, fig*) to strengthen; (*Wäsche*) to starch; (*Selbstbewusstsein*) to boost; (*Gesundheit*) to improve; (*erfrischen*) to fortify ♦ *vi* to be fortifying; ~**des Mittel** tonic.

Starkstrom *m* heavy current.

Stärkung ['ʃtɛrkʊŋ] *f* strengthening; (*Essen*) refreshment.

Stärkungsmittel *nt* tonic.

starr [ʃtar] *adj* stiff; (*unnachgiebig*) rigid; (*Blick*) staring.

starren *vi* to stare; ~ **vor** +*dat od* **von** (*voll von*) to be covered in; (*Waffen*) to be bristling with;

vor sich *akk* **hin** ~ to stare straight ahead.

starr- *zW*: **S~heit** *f* rigidity; ~**köpfig** *adj* stubborn; **S~sinn** *m* obstinacy.

Start [ʃtart] (-(e)s, -e) *m* start; (*AVIAT*) takeoff; ~**automatik** *f* (*AUT*) automatic choke; ~**bahn** *f* runway; **s~en** *vi* to start; (*AVIAT*) to take off ♦ *vt* to start; ~**er** (-s, -) *m* starter; ~**erlaubnis** *f* takeoff clearance; ~**hilfe** *f* (*AVIAT*) rocket-assisted takeoff; (*fig*) initial aid; **jdm ~hilfe geben** to help sb get off the ground; ~**hilfekabel** *nt* jump leads *pl* (*BRIT*), jumper cables *pl* (*US*); **s~klar** *adj* (*AVIAT*) clear for takeoff; (*SPORT*) ready to start; ~**kommando** *nt* (*SPORT*) starting signal; ~**zeichen** *nt* start signal.

Stasi ['ʃtaːzi] (-) (*umg*) *f abk* (*früher: = Staatssicherheitsdienst der DDR*) Stasi.

STASI

Stasi, an abbreviation of *Staatssicherheitsdienst*, the **DDR** *secret service, was founded in 1950 and disbanded in 1989. The* **Stasi** *organized an extensive spy network of full-time and part-time workers who often held positions of trust in both the* **DDR** *and the* **BRD**. *They held personal files on 6 million people.*

Station [ʃtatsi'oːn] *f* station; (*Kranken~*) hospital ward; (*Haltestelle*) stop; ~ **machen** to stop off.

stationär [ʃtatsio'nɛːr] *adj* stationary; (*MED*) in-patient *attrib*.

stationieren [ʃtatsio'niːrən] *vt* to station; (*Atomwaffen etc*) to deploy.

Stations- *zW*: ~**arzt** *m* ward doctor; ~**ärztin** *f* ward doctor; ~**vorsteher** *m* (*EISENB*) stationmaster.

statisch ['ʃtaːtɪʃ] *adj* static.

Statist(in) [ʃta'tɪst(ɪn)] *m(f)* (*FILM*) extra; (*THEAT*) supernumerary.

Statistik *f* statistic; (*Wissenschaft*) statistics *sing*.

Statistiker(in) (-s, -) *m(f)* statistician.

statistisch *adj* statistical.

Stativ [ʃta'tiːf] (-s, -e) *nt* tripod.

Statt [ʃtat] (-) *f* place.

statt *konj* instead of ♦ *präp* (+*dat od gen*) instead of; ~ **dessen** instead.

stattdessen▲ *adv* instead.

Stätte ['ʃtɛtə] (-, -n) *f* place.

statt- *zW*: ~**finden** *unreg vi* to take place; ~**haft** *adj* admissible; **S~halter** *m* governor; ~**lich** *adj* imposing, handsome; (*Bursche*) strapping; (*Sammlung*) impressive; (*Familie*) large; (*Summe*) handsome.

Statue ['ʃtaːtuə] (-, -n) *f* statue.

Statur [ʃta'tuːr] *f* build.

Status ['ʃtaːtos] (-, -) *m* status; ~**symbol** *nt* status symbol.

Statuten [ʃtaˈtuːtən] *pl* by(e)-law(s *pl*).

Stau [ʃtaʊ] **(-(e)s, -e)** *m* blockage; (*Verkehrs~*) (traffic) jam.

Staub [ʃtaʊp] **(-(e)s)** *m* dust; ~ **saugen** to vacuum; ~ **wischen** to dust; **sich aus dem** ~ **machen** (*umg*) to clear off.

stauben [ˈʃtaʊbən] *vi* to be dusty.

Staubfaden *m* (*BOT*) stamen.

staubig [ˈʃtaʊbɪç] *adj* dusty.

Staub- *zW*: ~**lappen** *m* duster; ~**lunge** *f* (*MED*) dust on the lung; **s~saugen** (*pp* **s~gesaugt**) *vi untr* to vacuum; ~**sauger** *m* vacuum cleaner; ~**tuch** *nt* duster.

Staudamm *m* dam.

Staude [ˈʃtaʊdə] **(-, -n)** *f* shrub.

stauen [ˈʃtaʊən] *vt* (*Wasser*) to dam up; (*Blut*) to stop the flow of ♦ *vr* (*Wasser*) to become dammed up; (*MED, Verkehr*) to become congested; (*Menschen*) to collect together; (*Gefühle*) to build up.

staunen [ˈʃtaʊnən] *vi* to be astonished; **da kann man nur noch** ~ it's just amazing; **S~ (-s)** *nt* amazement.

Stausee [ˈʃtaʊzeː] *m* reservoir; artificial lake.

Stauung [ˈʃtaʊʊŋ] *f* (*von Wasser*) damming-up; (*von Blut, Verkehr*) congestion.

Std. *abk* (= *Stunde*) h.

stdl. *abk* = **stündlich**.

Steak [ʃteːk] **(-s, -s)** *nt* steak.

Stechen [ˈʃtɛçən] **(-s, -)** *nt* (*SPORT*) play-off; (*Springreiten*) jump-off; (*Schmerz*) sharp pain.

stechen *unreg vt* (*mit Nadel etc*) to prick; (*mit Messer*) to stab; (*mit Finger*) to poke; (*Biene etc*) to sting; (*Mücke*) to bite; (*KARTEN*) to take; (*KUNST*) to engrave; (*Torf, Spargel*) to cut ♦ *vi* (*Sonne*) to beat down; (*mit Stechkarte*) to clock in ♦ *vr*: **sich** *akk od dat* **in den Finger** ~ to prick one's finger; **es sticht** it is prickly; **in See** ~ to put to sea.

stechend *adj* piercing, stabbing; (*Geruch*) pungent.

Stech- *zW*: ~**ginster** *m* gorse; ~**karte** *f* clocking-in card; ~**mücke** *f* gnat; ~**palme** *f* holly; ~**uhr** *f* time clock.

Steck- *zW*: ~**brief** *m* "wanted" poster; **s~brieflich** *adv*: **s~brieflich gesucht werden** to be wanted; ~**dose** *f* (wall) socket.

stecken [ˈʃtɛkən] *vt* to put; (*einführen*) to insert; (*Nadel*) to stick; (*Pflanzen*) to plant; (*beim Nähen*) to pin ♦ *vi* (*auch unreg*) to be; (*festsitzen*) to be stuck; (*Nadeln*) to stick; **etw in etw** *akk* ~ (*umg: Geld, Mühe*) to put sth into sth; (: *Zeit*) to devote sth to sth; **der Schlüssel steckt** the key is in the lock; **wo steckt er?** where has he got to?; **zeigen, was in einem steckt** to show what one is made of; ~ **bleiben** to get stuck; ~ **lassen** to leave in.

Steckenpferd *nt* hobbyhorse.

Stecker **(-s, -)** *m* (*ELEK*) plug.

Steck- *zW*: ~**nadel** *f* pin; ~**rübe** *f* swede, turnip; ~**schlüssel** *m* box spanner (*BRIT*) *od* wrench (*US*); ~**zwiebel** *f* bulb.

Steg [ʃteːk] **(-(e)s, -e)** *m* small bridge; (*Anlege~*) landing stage.

Stegreif *m*: **aus dem** ~ just like that.

Stehaufmännchen [ˈʃteː|aʊfmɛnçən] *nt* (*Spielzeug*) tumbler.

stehen [ˈʃteːən] *unreg vi* to stand; (*sich befinden*) to be; (*in Zeitung*) to say; (*angehalten haben*) to have stopped ♦ *vi unpers*: **es steht schlecht um** ... things are bad for ... ♦ *vr*: **sich gut/schlecht** ~ to be well-off/badly off; **zu jdm/etw** ~ to stand by sb/sth; **jdm** ~ to suit sb; **ich tue, was in meinen Kräften steht** I'll do everything I can; **es steht 2:1 für München** the score is 2-1 to Munich; **mit dem Dativ** ~ (*GRAM*) to take the dative; **auf Betrug steht eine Gefängnisstrafe** the penalty for fraud is imprisonment; **wie** ~ **Sie dazu?** what are your views on that?; **wie stehts?** how are things?; (*SPORT*) what's the score?; **wie steht es damit?** how about it?; ~ **bleiben** (*Uhr*) to stop; (*Zeit*) to stand still; (*Auto, Zug*) to stand; (*Fehler*) to stay as it is; (*Verkehr, Produktion etc*) to come to a standstill *od* stop; ~ **lassen** to leave; (*Bart*) to grow; **alles** ~ **und liegen lassen** to drop everything.

stehend *adj attrib* (*Fahrzeug*) stationary; (*Gewässer*) stagnant; (*ständig: Heer*) regular.

Stehlampe *f* standard lamp (*BRIT*), floor lamp (*US*).

stehlen [ˈʃteːlən] *unreg vt* to steal.

Stehplatz *m*: **ein** ~ **kostet 15 Euro** a standing ticket costs 15 euros.

Stehvermögen *nt* staying power, stamina.

Steiermark [ˈʃtaɪrmark] *f*: **die** ~ Styria.

steif [ʃtaɪf] *adj* stiff; ~ **und fest auf etw** *dat* **beharren** to insist stubbornly on sth.

Steifftier ® [ˈʃtaɪftiːr] *nt* soft toy animal.

Steifheit *f* stiffness.

Steigbügel [ˈʃtaɪkbyːgəl] *m* stirrup.

Steigeisen *nt* crampon.

steigen *unreg vi* to rise; (*klettern*) to climb ♦ *vt* (*Treppen, Stufen*) to climb (up); **das Blut stieg ihm in den Kopf** the blood rushed to his head; ~ **in** +*akk*/**auf** +*akk* to get in/on.

Steiger **(-s, -)** *m* (*MIN*) pit foreman.

steigern *vt* to raise; (*GRAM*) to compare ♦ *vi* (*Auktion*) to bid ♦ *vr* to increase.

Steigerung *f* raising; (*GRAM*) comparison.

Steigung *f* incline, gradient, rise.

steil [ʃtaɪl] *adj* steep; **S~hang** *m* steep slope; **S~pass ▲** *m* (*SPORT*) through ball.

Stein [ʃtaɪn] **(-(e)s, -e)** *m* stone; (*in Uhr*) jewel; **mir fällt ein** ~ **vom Herzen!** (*fig*) that's a load off my mind!; **bei jdm einen** ~ **im Brett haben** (*fig: umg*) to be well in with sb; **jdm**

~e in den Weg legen to make things difficult for sb; **~adler** *m* golden eagle; **s~alt** *adj* ancient; **~bock** *m* (*ASTROL*) Capricorn; **~bruch** *m* quarry.

steinern *adj* (made of) stone; (*fig*) stony.

Stein- *zW*: **~erweichen** *nt*: **zum ~erweichen weinen** to cry heartbreakingly; **~garten** *m* rockery; **~gut** *nt* stoneware; **s~hart** *adj* hard as stone.

steinig *adj* stony.

steinigen *vt* to stone.

Stein- *zW*: **~kohle** *f* mineral coal; **~metz (-es, -e)** *m* stonemason; **s~reich** (*umg*) *adj* stinking rich; **~schlag** *m*: „**Achtung ~schlag**" "danger - falling stones"; **~wurf** *m* (*fig*) stone's throw; **~zeit** *f* Stone Age.

Steiß [ʃtaɪs] **(-es, -e)** *m* rump; **~bein** *nt* (*ANAT*) coccyx.

Stelle [ʃtɛlə] **(-, -n)** *f* place; (*Arbeit*) post, job; (*Amt*) office; (*Abschnitt*) passage; (*Text~, bes beim Zitieren*) reference; **drei ~n hinter dem Komma** (*MATH*) three decimal places; **eine freie** *od* **offene ~** a vacancy; **an dieser ~** in this place, here; **an anderer ~** elsewhere; **nicht von der ~ kommen** not to make any progress; **auf der ~** (*fig: sofort*) on the spot; *siehe auch* **anstelle**.

stellen *vt* to put; (*Uhr etc*) to set; (*zur Verfügung ~*) to supply; (*fassen: Dieb*) to apprehend; (*Antrag, Forderung*) to make; (*Aufnahme*) to pose; (*arrangieren: Szene*) to arrange ♦ *vr* (*sich auf~*) to stand; (*sich einfinden*) to present o.s.; (*bei Polizei*) to give o.s. up; (*vorgeben*) to pretend (to be); **das Radio lauter/leiser ~** to turn the radio up/down; **auf sich** *akk* **selbst gestellt sein** (*fig*) to have to fend for o.s.; **sich hinter jdn/etw ~** (*fig*) to support sb/sth; **sich einer Herausforderung ~** to take up a challenge; **sich zu etw ~** to have an opinion of sth.

Stellen- *zW*: **~angebot** *nt* offer of a post; (*in Zeitung*): „**~angebote**" "vacancies"; **~anzeige** *f* job advertisement *od* ad (*umg*); **~gesuch** *nt* application for a post; „**~gesuche**" "situations wanted"; **~markt** *m* job market; (*in Zeitung*) appointments section; **~nachweis** *m* employment agency; **~vermittlung** *f* employment agency; **s~weise** *adv* in places; **~wert** *m* (*fig*) status.

Stellung *f* position; (*MIL*) line; **~ nehmen zu** to comment on.

Stellungnahme *f* comment.

stellungslos *adj* unemployed.

stellv. *abk* = **stellvertretend**.

Stell- *zW*: **s~vertretend** *adj* deputy *attrib*, acting *attrib*; **~vertreter** *m* (*von Amts wegen*) deputy, representative; **~werk** *nt* (*EISENB*) signal box.

Stelze [ʃtɛltsə] **(-, -n)** *f* stilt.

stelzen (*umg*) *vi* to stalk.

Stemmbogen *m* (*SKI*) stem turn.

Stemmeisen *nt* crowbar.

stemmen [ʃtɛmən] *vt* to lift (up); (*drücken*) to press; **sich ~ gegen** (*fig*) to resist, oppose.

Stempel [ʃtɛmpəl] **(-s, -)** *m* stamp; (*Post~*) postmark; (*TECH: Präge~*) die; (*BOT*) pistil; **~gebühr** *f* stamp duty; **~kissen** *nt* inkpad.

stempeln *vt* to stamp; (*Briefmarke*) to cancel ♦ *vi* (*umg: Stempeluhr betätigen*) to clock in/out; **~ gehen** (*umg*) to be *od* go on the dole (*BRIT*) *od* on welfare (*US*).

Stengel△ [ʃtɛŋəl] **(-s, -)** *m siehe* **Stängel**.

Steno [ʃteno] (*umg*) *f* shorthand; **~gramm** [-ˈɡram] *nt* text in shorthand; **~graf(in)**▲ [-ɡraːf(ɪn)] *m(f)* (*im Büro*) shorthand secretary; **~grafie**▲ [-ɡraˈfiː] *f* shorthand; **s~grafieren**▲ [-ɡraˈfiːrən] *vt, vi* to write (in) shorthand; **~typist(in)** [-tyˈpɪst(ɪn)] *m(f)* shorthand typist (*BRIT*), stenographer (*US*).

Steppdecke *f* quilt.

Steppe (-, -n) *f* steppe.

steppen [ʃtɛpən] *vt* to stitch ♦ *vi* to tap-dance.

Stepptanz▲ *m* tap-dance.

Sterbe- *zW*: **~bett** *nt* deathbed; **~fall** *m* death; **~hilfe** *f* euthanasia; **~kasse** *f* death benefit fund.

sterben [ʃtɛrbən] *unreg vi* to die; **an einer Krankheit/Verletzung ~** to die of an illness/from an injury; **er ist für mich gestorben** (*fig: umg*) he might as well be dead.

Sterben *nt*: **im ~ liegen** to be dying.

sterbenslangweilig (*umg*) *adj* deadly boring.

Sterbenswörtchen (*umg*) *nt*: **er hat kein ~ gesagt** he didn't say a word.

Sterbeurkunde *f* death certificate.

sterblich [ʃtɛrplɪç] *adj* mortal; **S~keit** *f* mortality; **S~keitsziffer** *f* death rate.

stereo- [ˈsteːreo] *in zW* stereo(-); **S~anlage** *f* stereo unit; **~typ** *adj* stereotyped.

steril [ʃteˈriːl] *adj* sterile.

sterilisieren [ʃterɪliˈziːrən] *vt* to sterilize.

Sterilisierung *f* sterilization.

Stern [ʃtɛrn] **(-(e)s, -e)** *m* star; **das steht (noch) in den ~en** (*fig*) it's in the lap of the gods; **~bild** *nt* constellation; **~chen** *nt* asterisk; **~enbanner** *nt* Stars and Stripes *sing*; **s~hagelvoll** (*umg*) *adj* legless; **~schnuppe (-, -n)** *f* meteor, falling star; **~stunde** *f* historic moment; **~warte** *f* observatory; **~zeichen** *nt* (*ASTROL*) sign of the zodiac.

stet [ʃteːt] *adj* steady.

Stethoskop [ʃtetoˈskoːp] **(-(e)s, -e)** *nt* stethoscope.

stetig *adj* constant, continual; (*MATH: Funktion*) continuous.

stets *adv* continually, always.

Steuer¹ [ˈʃtɔʏər] **(-s, -)** *nt* (*NAUT*) helm; (*~ruder*) rudder; (*AUT*) steering wheel; **am ~ sitzen** (*AUT*) to be at the wheel; (*AVIAT*) to be at the controls.

Steuer² (-, -n) f tax.
Steuer- zW: ~**befreiung** f tax exemption;
s~begünstigt adj (Investitionen, Hypothek)
tax-deductible; (Waren) taxed at a lower
rate; ~**berater(in)** m(f) tax consultant;
~**bescheid** m tax assessment; ~**bord** nt
starboard; ~**erhöhung** f tax increase;
~**erklärung** f tax return; **s~frei** adj tax-free;
~**freibetrag** m tax allowance;
~**hinterziehung** f tax evasion; ~**jahr** nt fiscal
od tax year; ~**karte** f tax notice; ~**klasse** f
tax group; ~**knüppel** m control column;
(AVIAT, COMPUT) joystick; **s~lich** adj tax
attrib; ~**mann** (-(e)s, pl -**männer** od -**leute**) m
helmsman.
steuern vt to steer; (Flugzeug) to pilot;
(Entwicklung, Tonstärke) to control ♦ vi to
steer; (in Flugzeug etc) to be at the controls;
(bei Entwicklung etc) to be in control.
Steuer- zW: ~**nummer** f ≈ National Insurance
Number (BRIT), Social Security Number
(US); ~**paradies** nt tax haven; **s~pflichtig** adj
taxable; (Person) liable to pay tax;
~**progression** f progressive taxation;
~**prüfung** f tax inspector's investigation;
~**rad** nt steering wheel; ~**rückvergütung** f
tax rebate; ~**senkung** f tax cut.
Steuerung f steering (auch AUT), piloting,
control; (Vorrichtung) controls pl;
automatische ~ (AVIAT) autopilot; (TECH)
automatic steering (device).
Steuer- zW: ~**vergünstigung** f tax relief;
~**zahler** m taxpayer; ~**zuschlag** m additional
tax.
Steward ['stjuːərt] (-s, -s) m steward.
Stewardess▲ ['stjuːərdɛs] (-, -en) f
stewardess.
StGB (-s) nt abk = **Strafgesetzbuch**.
stibitzen [ʃtiˈbɪtsən] (umg) vt to pilfer, pinch
(umg).
Stich [ʃtɪç] (-(e)s, -e) m (Insekten~) sting;
(Messer~) stab; (beim Nähen) stitch;
(Färbung) tinge; (KARTEN) trick; (ART)
engraving; (fig) pang; **ein ~ ins Rote** a tinge
of red; **einen ~ haben** (umg: Esswaren) to be
bad od off (BRIT); (: Mensch: verrückt sein) to
be nuts; **jdn im ~ lassen** to leave sb in the
lurch.
Stichel (-s, -) m engraving tool, style.
Stichelei [ʃtɪçəˈlaɪ] f jibe, taunt.
sticheln vi (fig) to jibe; (pej: umg) to make
snide remarks.
Stich- zW: ~**flamme** f tongue of flame;
s~haltig adj valid; (Beweis) conclusive;
~**probe** f spot check.
sticht [ʃtɪçt] vb siehe **stechen**.
Stichtag m qualifying date.
Stichwahl f final ballot.
Stichwort nt (pl -**worte**) cue; (: für Vortrag)
note; (pl -**wörter**) (in Wörterbuch) headword;

~**katalog** m classified catalogue (BRIT) od
catalog (US); ~**verzeichnis** nt index.
Stichwunde f stab wound.
sticken ['ʃtɪkən] vt, vi to embroider.
Stickerei [ʃtɪkəˈraɪ] f embroidery.
stickig adj stuffy, close.
Stickstoff (-(e)s) m nitrogen.
stieben ['ʃtiːbən] vi (geh: sprühen) to fly.
Stief- ['ʃtiːf] in zW step-.
Stiefel ['ʃtiːfəl] (-s, -) m boot; (Trinkgefäß)
large boot-shaped beer glass.
Stief- zW: ~**kind** nt stepchild; (fig) Cinderella;
~**mutter** f stepmother; ~**mütterchen** nt
pansy; **s~mütterlich** adj (fig): **jdn/etw
s~mütterlich behandeln** to pay little
attention to sb/sth; ~**vater** m stepfather.
stieg etc [ʃtiːk] vb siehe **steigen**.
Stiege ['ʃtiːgə] (-, -n) f staircase.
Stieglitz ['ʃtiːglɪts] (-es, -e) m goldfinch.
stiehlt [ʃtiːlt] vb siehe **stehlen**.
Stiel [ʃtiːl] (-(e)s, -e) m handle; (BOT) stalk.
Stielaugen pl (fig: umg): **er machte ~** his eyes
(nearly) popped out of his head.
Stier (-(e)s, -e) m bull; (ASTROL) Taurus.
stier [ʃtiːr] adj staring, fixed.
stieren vi to stare.
Stierkampf m bullfight.
stieß etc [ʃtiːs] vb siehe **stoßen**.
Stift [ʃtɪft] (-(e)s, -e) m peg; (Nagel) tack;
(Bunt~) crayon; (Blei~) pencil; (umg:
Lehrling) apprentice (boy).
stiften vt to found; (Unruhe) to cause;
(spenden) to contribute; **~ gehen** to hop it.
Stifter(in) (-s, -) m(f) founder.
Stiftung f donation; (Organisation) foundation.
Stiftzahn m post crown.
Stil [ʃtiːl] (-(e)s, -e) m style; (Eigenart) way,
manner; ~**blüte** f howler; ~**bruch** m stylistic
incongruity.
stilistisch [ʃtiˈlɪstɪʃ] adj stylistic.
still [ʃtɪl] adj quiet; (unbewegt) still; (heimlich)
secret; **ich dachte mir im S~en** I thought to
myself; **er ist ein ~es Wasser** he's a deep
one; ~**er Teilhaber** (COMM) sleeping (BRIT)
od silent (US) partner; **der S~e Ozean** the
Pacific (Ocean); **~ stehen** (unbewegt) to
stand still.
Stille (-, -n) f quietness; stillness; **in aller ~**
quietly.
Stilleben△ nt siehe **Stillleben**.
Stillegung△ f siehe **Stilllegung**.
stillen vt to stop; (befriedigen) to satisfy;
(Säugling) to breast-feed.
still- zW: ~**gestanden** interj attention!;
S~halteabkommen nt (FIN, fig) moratorium;
~**halten** unreg vi to keep still; **S~leben▲** nt
still life; ~**legen▲** vt to close down;
S~legung▲ f (Betrieb) shut-down, closure;
~**liegen▲** unreg vi (außer Betrieb sein) to be
shut down; (lahm gelegt sein) to be at a

standstill; **S~schweigen** *nt* silence;
~schweigen *unreg vi* to be silent;
~schweigend *ad* silent; (*Einverständnis*) tacit
♦ *adv* silently; tacitly; **S~stand** *m* standstill;
~stehen *unreg vi* to stand still.

Stilmöbel *pl* reproduction *od* (*antik*) period
furniture *sing*.

stilvoll *adj* stylish.

Stimm- *zW*: **~abgabe** *f* voting; **~bänder** *pl*
vocal cords *pl*; **s~berechtigt** *adj* entitled to
vote; **~bruch** *m*: **er ist im ~bruch** his voice is
breaking.

Stimme ['ʃtɪmə] (-, -n) *f* voice; (*Wahl~*) vote;
(*MUS: Rolle*) part; **mit leiser/lauter ~** in a
soft/loud voice; **seine ~ abgeben** to vote.

stimmen *vi* (*richtig sein*) to be right; (*wählen*)
to vote ♦ *vt* (*Instrument*) to tune; **stimmt so!**
that's all right; **für/gegen etw ~** to vote for/
against sth; **jdn traurig ~** to make sb feel
sad.

Stimmen- *zW*: **~gewirr** *nt* babble of voices;
~gleichheit *f* tied vote; **~mehrheit** *f* majority
(of votes).

Stimm- *zW*: **~enthaltung** *f* abstention; **~gabel**
f tuning fork; **s~haft** *adj* voiced.

stimmig *adj* harmonious.

Stimm- *zW*: **s~los** *adj* (*LING*) unvoiced; **~recht**
nt right to vote; **s~rechtslos** *adj*:
s~rechtslose Aktien "A" shares.

Stimmung *f* mood; (*Atmosphäre*)
atmosphere; (*Moral*) morale; **in ~ kommen**
to liven up; **~ gegen/für jdn/etw machen** to
stir up (public) opinion against/in favour of
sb/sth.

Stimmungs- *zW*: **~kanone** (*umg*) *f* life and
soul of the party; **~mache** (*pej*) *f* cheap
propaganda; **s~voll** *adj* (*Atmosphäre*)
enjoyable; (*Gedicht*) full of atmosphere.

Stimmzettel *m* ballot paper.

stinken ['ʃtɪŋkən] *unreg vi* to stink; **die Sache
stinkt mir** (*umg*) I'm fed-up to the back
teeth (with it).

Stink- *zW*: **s~faul** (*umg*) *adj* bone-lazy;
s~langweilig (*umg*) *adj* deadly boring; **~tier**
nt skunk; **~wut** (*umg*) *f*: **eine ~wut (auf jdn)
haben** to be livid (with sb).

Stipendium [ʃti'pɛndiʊm] *nt* grant; (*als
Auszeichnung*) scholarship.

Stippvisite ['ʃtɪpvi'zi:tə] (*umg*) *f* flying visit.

stirbt [ʃtɪrpt] *vb siehe* **sterben**.

Stirn [ʃtɪrn] (-, -en) *f* forehead, brow;
(*Frechheit*) impudence; **die ~ haben zu ... to
have the nerve to ...**; **~band** *nt* headband;
~höhle *f* sinus; **~runzeln** (-s) *nt* frown.

stob *etc* [ʃto:p] *vb siehe* **stieben**.

stöbern ['ʃtøbərn] *vi* to rummage.

stochern ['ʃtɔxərn] *vi* to poke (about).

Stock¹ [ʃtɔk] (-(e)s, ⸚e) *m* stick; (*Rohr~*) cane;
(*Zeige~*) pointer; (*BOT*) stock; **über ~ und
Stein** up hill and down dale.

Stock² [ʃtɔk] (-(e)s, - *od* -werke) *m* storey
(*BRIT*), story (*US*); **im ersten ~** on the first
(*BRIT*) *od* second (*US*) floor.

stock- *in zW* (*vor adj: umg*) completely.

Stöckelschuh ['ʃtœkəlʃu:] *m* stiletto-heeled
shoe.

stocken *vi* to stop, pause; (*Arbeit, Entwicklung*)
to make no progress; (*im Satz*) to break off;
(*Verkehr*) to be held up.

stockend *adj* halting.

stockfinster (*umg*) *adj* pitch-dark.

Stockholm ['ʃtɔkhɔlm] (-s) *nt* Stockholm.

stocksauer (*umg*) *adj* pissed-off (*!*).

stocktaub *adj* stone-deaf.

Stockung *f* stoppage.

Stockwerk *nt* storey (*BRIT*), story (*US*), floor.

Stoff [ʃtɔf] (-(e)s, -e) *m* (*Gewebe*) material,
cloth; (*Materie*) matter; (*von Buch etc*)
subject (matter); (*umg: Rauschgift*) dope.

Stoffel (-s, -) (*pej: umg*) *m* lout, boor.

Stoff- *zW*: **s~lich** *adj* with regard to subject
matter; **~rest** *m* remnant; **~tier** *nt* soft toy;
~wechsel *m* metabolism.

stöhnen ['ʃtønən] *vi* to groan.

stoisch ['ʃto:ɪʃ] *adj* stoical.

Stola ['ʃto:la] (-, Stolen) *f* stole.

Stollen ['ʃtɔlən] (-s, -) *m* (*MIN*) gallery; (*KOCH*)
stollen, *cake eaten at Christmas*; (*von
Schuhen*) stud.

stolpern ['ʃtɔlpərn] *vi* to stumble, trip; (*fig: zu
Fall kommen*) to come a cropper (*umg*).

stolz [ʃtɔlts] *adj* proud; (*imposant: Bauwerk*)
majestic; (*ironisch: Preis*) princely; **S~ (-es)**
m pride.

stolzieren [ʃtɔl'tsi:rən] *vi* to strut.

stopfen ['ʃtɔpfən] *vt* (*hinein~*) to stuff; (*voll ~*)
to fill (up); (*nähen*) to darn ♦ *vi* (*MED*) to
cause constipation; **jdm das Maul ~** (*umg*)
to silence sb.

Stopfgarn *nt* darning thread.

Stopp [ʃtɔp] (-s, -s) *m* stop, halt; (*Lohn~*)
freeze.

Stoppel ['ʃtɔpəl] (-, -n) *f* stubble.

stoppen *vt* to stop; (*mit Uhr*) to time ♦ *vi* to
stop.

Stoppschild *nt* stop sign.

Stoppuhr *f* stopwatch.

Stöpsel ['ʃtœpsəl] (-s, -) *m* plug; (*für Flaschen*)
stopper.

Stör [ʃtø:r] (-(e)s, -e) *m* sturgeon.

Störaktion *f* disruptive action.

störanfällig *adj* susceptible to interference
od breakdown.

Storch [ʃtɔrç] (-(e)s, ⸚e) *m* stork.

Store [ʃto:r] (-s, -s) *m* net curtain.

stören ['ʃtø:rən] *vt* to disturb; (*behindern,
RUNDF*) to interfere with ♦ *vr*: **sich an etw**
dat ~ to let sth bother one ♦ *vi* to get in the
way; **was mich an ihm/daran stört** what I
don't like about him/it; **stört es Sie, wenn**

ich rauche? do you mind if I smoke?; **ich möchte nicht** ~ I don't want to be in the way.

störend *adj* disturbing, annoying.

Störenfried (-(e)s, -e) *m* troublemaker.

Störfall *m* (*in Kraftwerk etc*) malfunction, accident.

stornieren [ʃtɔrˈniːrən] *vt* (*COMM: Auftrag*) to cancel; (: *Buchungsfehler*) to reverse.

Storno [ˈʃtɔrno] (-s) *m od nt* (*COMM: von Buchungsfehler*) reversal; (: *von Auftrag*) cancellation (*BRIT*), cancelation (*US*).

störrisch [ˈʃtœrɪʃ] *adj* stubborn, perverse.

Störsender *m* jammer, jamming transmitter.

Störung *f* disturbance; interference; (*TECH*) fault; (*MED*) disorder.

Störungsstelle *f* (*TEL*) faults service.

Stoß [ʃtoːs] (-es, ⁻e) *m* (*Schub*) push; (*leicht*) poke; (*Schlag*) blow; (*mit Schwert*) thrust; (*mit Ellbogen*) nudge; (*mit Fuß*) kick; (*Erd~*) shock; (*Haufen*) pile; **seinem Herzen einen** ~ **geben** to pluck up courage; ~**dämpfer** *m* shock absorber.

Stößel [ˈʃtøːsəl] (-s, -) *m* pestle; (*AUT: Ventil~*) tappet.

stoßen *unreg vt* (*mit Druck*) to shove, push; (*mit Schlag*) to knock, bump; (*mit Ellbogen*) to nudge; (*mit Fuß*) to kick; (*mit Schwert*) to thrust; (*an~: Kopf etc*) to bump; (*zerkleinern*) to pulverize ♦ *vr* to get a knock ♦ *vi:* ~ **an** *od* **auf** +*akk* to bump into; (*finden*) to come across; (*angrenzen*) to be next to; **sich** ~ **an** +*dat* (*fig*) to take exception to; **zu jdm** ~ to meet up with sb.

Stoßgebet *nt* quick prayer.

Stoßstange *f* (*AUT*) bumper.

stößt [ʃtøːst] *vb siehe* **stoßen**.

Stoß- *zW:* ~**verkehr** *m* rush-hour traffic; ~**zahn** *m* tusk; ~**zeit** *f* (*im Verkehr*) rush hour; (*in Geschäft etc*) peak period.

Stotterer (-s, -) *m* stutterer.

Stotterin *f* stutterer.

stottern [ˈʃtɔtərn] *vt, vi* to stutter.

Stövchen [ˈʃtøːfçən] *nt* (teapot- *etc*) warmer.

StPO *abk* = **Strafprozessordnung**.

Str. *abk* (= *Straße*) St.

stracks [ʃtraks] *adv* straight.

Straf- *zW:* ~**anstalt** *f* penal institution; ~**arbeit** *f* (*SCH*) lines *pl*, punishment exercise; ~**bank** *f* (*SPORT*) penalty bench; **s**~**bar** *adj* punishable; **sich s**~**bar machen** to commit an offence (*BRIT*) *od* offense (*US*); ~**barkeit** *f* criminal nature.

Strafe [ˈʃtraːfə] (-, -n) *f* punishment; (*JUR*) penalty; (*Gefängnis~*) sentence; (*Geld~*) fine; ... **bei** ~ **verboten** ... forbidden; **100 Dollar** ~ **zahlen** to pay a \$100 fine; **er hat seine** ~ **weg** (*umg*) he's had his punishment.

strafen *vt, vi* to punish; **mit etw gestraft sein**

to be cursed with sth.

strafend *adj attrib* punitive; (*Blick*) reproachful.

straff [ʃtraf] *adj* tight; (*streng*) strict; (*Stil etc*) concise; (*Haltung*) erect.

straffällig [ˈʃtraːfɛlɪç] *adj:* ~ **werden** to commit a criminal offence (*BRIT*) *od* offense (*US*).

straffen *vt* to tighten.

Straf- *zW:* **s**~**frei** *adj:* **s**~**frei ausgehen** to go unpunished; ~**gefangene(r)** *f(m)* prisoner, convict; ~**gesetzbuch** *nt* penal code; ~**kolonie** *f* penal colony.

sträflich [ˈʃtrɛːflɪç] *adj* criminal ♦ *adv* (*vernachlässigen etc*) criminally.

Sträfling *m* convict.

Straf- *zW:* ~**mandat** *nt* ticket; ~**maß** *nt* sentence; **s**~**mildernd** *adj* mitigating; ~**porto** *nt* excess postage (charge); ~**predigt** *f* severe lecture; ~**prozessordnung**▲ *f* code of criminal procedure; ~**raum** *m* (*SPORT*) penalty area; ~**recht** *nt* criminal law; **s**~**rechtlich** *adj* criminal; ~**stoß** *m* (*SPORT*) penalty (kick); ~**tat** *f* punishable act; **s**~**versetzen** *vt untr* (*Beamte*) to transfer for disciplinary reasons; ~**vollzug** *m* penal system; ~**zettel** (*umg*) *m* ticket.

Strahl [ʃtraːl] (-(e)s, -en) *m* ray, beam; (*Wasser~*) jet.

strahlen *vi* (*Kernreaktor*) to radiate; (*Sonne, Licht*) to shine; (*fig*) to beam.

Strahlenbehandlung *f* radiotherapy.

Strahlenbelastung *f* (effects of) radiation.

strahlend *adj* (*Wetter*) glorious; (*Lächeln, Schönheit*) radiant.

Strahlen- *zW:* ~**dosis** *f* radiation dose; **s**~**geschädigt** *adj* suffering from radiation damage; ~**opfer** *nt* victim of radiation; ~**schutz** *m* radiation protection; ~**therapie** *f* radiotherapy.

Strahlung *f* radiation.

Strähnchen [ˈʃtrɛːnçən] *pl* strands (of hair); (*gefärbt*) highlights.

Strähne [ˈʃtrɛːnə] (-, -n) *f* strand.

strähnig *adj* (*Haar*) straggly.

stramm [ʃtram] *adj* tight; (*Haltung*) erect; (*Mensch*) robust; ~**stehen** *unreg vi* (*MIL*) to stand to attention.

Strampelhöschen *nt* rompers *pl*.

strampeln [ˈʃtrampəln] *vi* to kick (about), fidget.

Strand [ʃtrant] (-(e)s, ⁻e) *m* shore; (*Meeres~*) beach; **am** ~ on the beach; ~**bad** *nt* open-air swimming pool; (*Badeort*) bathing resort.

stranden [ˈʃtrandən] *vi* to run aground; (*fig: Mensch*) to fail.

Strandgut *nt* flotsam and jetsam.

Strandkorb *m* beach chair.

Strang [ʃtraŋ] (-(e)s, ⁻e) *m* (*Nerven~, Muskel~*) cord; (*Schienen~*) track; **über die Stränge**

schlagen to run riot (*umg*); **an einem** ~ **ziehen** (*fig*) to act in concert.
strangulieren [ʃtraŋguˈliːrən] *vt* to strangle.
Strapaze [ʃtraˈpaːtsə] (-, -n) *f* strain.
strapazieren [ʃtrapaˈtsiːrən] *vt* (*Material*) to be hard on, punish; (*jdn*) to be a strain on; (*erschöpfen*) to wear out, exhaust.
strapazierfähig *adj* hard-wearing.
strapaziös [ʃtrapatsiˈøːs] *adj* exhausting, tough.
Straßburg [ˈʃtraːsburk] (-s) *nt* Strasbourg.
Straße [ˈʃtraːsə] (-, -n) *f* road; (*in Stadt, Dorf*) street; **auf der** ~ in the street; **auf der** ~ **liegen** (*fig: umg*) to be out of work; **auf die** ~ **gesetzt werden** (*umg*) to be turned out (onto the streets).
Straßen- *zW:* ~**bahn** *f* tram (*BRIT*), streetcar (*US*); ~**bauarbeiten** *pl* roadworks *pl* (*BRIT*), roadwork *sing* (*US*); ~**beleuchtung** *f* street lighting; ~**feger** (-s, -) *m* roadsweeper; ~**glätte** *f* slippery road surface; ~**junge** (*pej*) *m* street urchin; ~**karte** *f* road map; ~**kehrer** (-s, -) *m* roadsweeper; ~**kind** *nt* child of the streets; ~**kreuzer** (*umg*) *m* limousine; ~**mädchen** *nt* streetwalker; ~**rand** *m* road side; ~**sperre** *f* roadblock; ~**überführung** *f* footbridge; ~**verkehr** *m* road traffic; ~**verkehrsordnung** *f* Highway Code (*BRIT*); ~**zustandsbericht** *m* road report.
Stratege [ʃtraˈteːgə] (-n, -n) *m* strategist.
Strategie [ʃtrateˈɡiː] *f* strategy.
strategisch *adj* strategic.
Stratosphäre [ʃtratoˈsfɛːrə] (-) *f* stratosphere.
sträuben [ˈʃtrɔybən] *vt* to ruffle ♦ *vr* to bristle; (*Mensch*): **sich (gegen etw)** ~ to resist (sth).
Strauch [ʃtraʊx] (-(e)s, Sträucher) *m* bush, shrub.
straucheln [ˈʃtraʊxəln] *vi* to stumble, stagger.
Strauß[1] [ʃtraʊs] (-es, Sträuße) *m* (*Blumen*~) bouquet, bunch.
Strauß[2] [ʃtraʊs] (-es, -e) *m* ostrich.
Strebe [ˈʃtreːbə] (-, -n) *f* strut.
Strebebalken *m* buttress.
streben *vi* to strive, endeavour (*BRIT*), endeavor (*US*); ~ **nach** to strive for; ~ **zu** *od* **nach** (*sich bewegen*) to make for.
Strebepfeiler *m* buttress.
Streber (-s, -) *m* (*pej*) pushy person; (*SCH*) swot (*BRIT*).
strebsam *adj* industrious; **S**~**keit** *f* industry.
Strecke [ˈʃtrɛkə] (-, -n) *f* stretch; (*Entfernung*) distance; (*EISENB, MATH*) line; **auf der** ~ **Paris-Brüssel** on the way from Paris to Brussels; **auf der** ~ **bleiben** (*fig*) to fall by the wayside; **zur** ~ **bringen** (*Jagd*) to bag.
strecken *vt* to stretch; (*Waffen*) to lay down; (*KOCH*) to eke out ♦ *vr* to stretch (o.s.).
streckenweise *adv* in parts.
Streich [ʃtraɪç] (-(e)s, -e) *m* trick, prank; (*Hieb*) blow; **jdm einen** ~ **spielen** (*Person*) to play a trick on sb.
streicheln *vt* to stroke.
streichen *unreg vt* (*berühren*) to stroke; (*auftragen*) to spread; (*anmalen*) to paint; (*durch*~) to delete; (*nicht genehmigen*) to cancel; (*Schulden*) to write off; (*Zuschuss etc*) to cut ♦ *vi* (*berühren*) to brush past; (*schleichen*) to prowl; **etw glatt** ~ to smooth sth (out).
Streicher *pl* (*MUS*) strings *pl*.
Streich- *zW:* ~**holz** *nt* match; ~**holzschachtel** *f* matchbox; ~**instrument** *nt* string(ed) instrument; ~**käse** *m* cheese spread.
Streifband *nt* wrapper; ~**zeitung** *f* newspaper sent at printed paper rate.
streifen [ˈʃtraɪfən] *vt* (*leicht berühren*) to brush against, graze; (*Blick*) to skim over; (*Thema, Problem*) to touch on; (*ab*~) to take off ♦ *vi* (*gehen*) to roam.
Streifen (-s, -) *m* (*Linie*) stripe; (*Stück*) strip; (*Film*) film.
Streifendienst *m* patrol duty.
Streifenwagen *m* patrol car.
Streifschuss▲ *m* graze, grazing shot.
Streifzug *m* scouting trip; (*Bummel*) expedition; (*fig: kurzer Überblick*): ~ **(durch)** brief survey (of).
Streik [ʃtraɪk] (-(e)s, -s) *m* strike; **in den** ~ **treten** to come out on strike, strike; ~**brecher** *m* blackleg (*BRIT*), strikebreaker; **s**~**en** *vi* to strike; **der Computer s**~**t** the computer's packed up (*umg*), the computer's on the blink (*umg*); **da s**~**e ich** (*umg*) I refuse!; ~**kasse** *f* strike fund; ~**maßnahmen** *pl* industrial action *sing*; ~**posten** *m* (peaceful) picket.
Streit [ʃtraɪt] (-(e)s, -e) *m* argument; (*Auseinandersetzung*) dispute.
streiten *unreg vi, vr* to argue; to dispute; **darüber lässt sich** ~ that's debatable.
Streitfrage *f* point at issue.
Streitgespräch *nt* debate.
streitig *adj:* **jdm etw** ~ **machen** to dispute sb's right to sth; **S**~**keiten** *pl* quarrel *sing*, dispute *sing*.
Streit- *zW:* ~**kräfte** *pl* (*MIL*) armed forces *pl*; **s**~**lustig** *adj* quarrelsome; ~**punkt** *m* contentious issue; ~**sucht** *f* quarrelsomeness.
streng [ʃtrɛŋ] *adj* severe; (*Lehrer, Maßnahme*) strict; (*Geruch etc*) sharp; ~ **geheim** top-secret; ~ **genommen** strictly speaking; ~ **verboten!** strictly prohibited.
Strenge (-) *f* severity; strictness; sharpness.
strenggläubig *adj* strict.
strengstens *adv* strictly.
Stress▲ [ʃtrɛs] (-es, -e) *m* stress.
stressen *vt* to put under stress.
stressfrei▲ *adj* without stress.

Spelling Reform: ▲ *new spelling* △ *old spelling (to be phased out)*

stressig *adj* stressful.
Streu [ʃtrɔy] (-, -en) *f* litter, bed of straw.
streuen *vt* to strew, scatter, spread ♦ *vi* (*mit Streupulver*) to grit; (*mit Salz*) to put down salt.
Streuer (-s, -) *m* shaker; (*Salz~*) cellar; (*Pfeffer~*) pot.
Streufahrzeug *nt* gritter (*BRIT*), sander.
streunen *vi* to roam about; (*Hund, Katze*) to stray.
Streupulver (-s) *nt* grit *od* sand for road.
Streuselkuchen [ˈʃtrɔyzəlkuːxən] *m cake with crumble topping.*
Streuung *f* dispersion; (*Statistik*) mean variation; (*PHYS*) scattering.
Strich (-(e)s, -e) *m* (*Linie*) line; (*Feder~, Pinsel~*) stroke; (*von Geweben*) nap; (*von Fell*) pile; (*Quer~*) dash; (*Schräg~*) oblique, slash (*bes US*); **einen ~ machen durch** (*lit*) to cross out; (*fig*) to foil; **jdm einen ~ durch die Rechnung machen** to thwart *od* foil sb's plans; **einen ~ unter etw akk machen** (*fig*) to forget sth; **nach ~ und Faden** (*umg*) good and proper; **auf den ~ gehen** (*umg*) to walk the streets; **jdm gegen den ~ gehen** to rub sb up the wrong way.
strich *etc* [ʃtrɪç] *vb siehe* **streichen.**
Strichcode *m* = **Strichkode.**
Stricheinteilung *f* calibration.
stricheln [ˈʃtrɪçəln] *vt*: **eine gestrichelte Linie** a broken line.
Strich- *zW*: **~junge** (*umg*) *m* male prostitute; **~kode** *m* bar code (*BRIT*), universal product code (*US*); **~mädchen** *nt* streetwalker; **~punkt** *m* semicolon; **s~weise** *adv* here and there; **s~weise Regen** (*MET*) rain in places.
Strick [ʃtrɪk] (-(e)s, -e) *m* rope; **jdm aus etw einen ~ drehen** to use sth against sb.
stricken *vt, vi* to knit.
Strick- *zW*: **~jacke** *f* cardigan; **~leiter** *f* rope ladder; **~nadel** *f* knitting needle; **~waren** *pl* knitwear *sing*.
striegeln [ˈʃtriːgəln] (*umg*) *vr* to spruce o.s. up.
Strieme [ˈʃtriːmə] (-, -n) *f* weal.
strikt [strɪkt] *adj* strict.
Strippe [ˈʃtrɪpə] (-, -n) *f* (*TEL: umg*): **jdn an der ~ haben** to have sb on the line.
Stripper(in) (-s, -) *m(f)* stripper.
stritt *etc* [ʃtrɪt] *vb siehe* **streiten.**
strittig [ˈʃtrɪtɪç] *adj* disputed, in dispute.
Stroh [ʃtroː] (-(e)s) *nt* straw; **~blume** *f* everlasting flower; **~dach** *nt* thatched roof; **s~dumm** (*umg*) *adj* thick; **~feuer** *nt*: **ein ~feuer sein** (*fig*) to be a passing fancy; **~halm** *m* (drinking) straw; **~mann** (-(e)s, *pl* **-männer**) *m* (*COMM*) dummy; **~witwe** *f* grass widow; **~witwer** *m* grass widower.
Strolch [ʃtrɔlç] (-(e)s, -e) (*pej*) *m* rogue, rascal.
Strom [ʃtroːm] (-(e)s, ⁻e) *m* river; (*fig*) stream;

(*ELEK*) current; **unter ~ stehen** (*ELEK*) to be live; (*fig*) to be excited; **der Wein floss in Strömen** the wine flowed like water; **in Strömen regnen** to be pouring with rain; **s~abwärts** *adv* downstream; **~anschluss▲** *m*: **~anschluss haben** to be connected to the electricity mains; **s~aufwärts** *adv* upstream; **~ausfall** *m* power failure.
strömen [ˈʃtrøːmən] *vi* to stream, pour.
Strom- *zW*: **~kabel** *nt* electric cable; **~kreis** *m* (electrical) circuit; **s~linienförmig** *adj* streamlined; **~netz** *nt* power supply system; **~rechnung** *f* electricity bill; **~schnelle** *f* rapids *pl*; **~sperre** *f* power cut; **~stärke** *f* amperage.
Strömung [ˈʃtrøːmʊŋ] *f* current.
Stromzähler *m* electricity meter.
Strophe [ˈʃtroːfə] (-, -n) *f* verse.
strotzen [ˈʃtrɔtsən] *vi*: **~ vor** +*dat od* **von** to abound in, be full of.
Strudel [ˈʃtruːdəl] (-s, -) *m* whirlpool, vortex; (*KOCH*) strudel.
strudeln *vi* to swirl, eddy.
Struktur [ʃtrʊkˈtuːr] *f* structure.
strukturell [ʃtrʊktuˈrɛl] *adj* structural.
strukturieren [ʃtrʊktuˈriːrən] *vt* to structure.
Strumpf [ʃtrʊmpf] (-(e)s, ⁻e) *m* stocking; **~band** *nt* garter; **~halter** *m* suspender (*BRIT*), garter (*US*); **~hose** *f* (pair of) tights *pl* (*BRIT*) *od* pantihose *pl* (*US*).
Strunk [ʃtrʊŋk] (-(e)s, ⁻e) *m* stump.
struppig [ˈʃtrʊpɪç] *adj* shaggy, unkempt.
Stube [ˈʃtuːbə] (-, -n) *f* room; **die gute ~** (*veraltet*) the parlour (*BRIT*) *od* parlor (*US*).
Stuben- *zW*: **~arrest** *m* confinement to one's room; (*MIL*) confinement to quarters; **~fliege** *f* (common) housefly; **~hocker** (*umg*) *m* stay-at-home; **s~rein** *adj* house-trained.
Stuck [ʃtʊk] (-(e)s) *m* stucco.
Stück [ʃtʏk] (-(e)s, -e) *nt* piece; (*etwas*) bit; (*THEAT*) play; **am ~** in one piece; **das ist ein starkes ~!** (*umg*) that's a bit much!; **große ~e auf jdn halten** to think highly of sb; **~arbeit** *f* piecework.
Stuckateur▲ [ʃtʊkaˈtøːr] *m* (ornamental) plasterer.
Stück- *zW*: **~gut** *nt* (*EISENB*) parcel service; **~kosten** *pl* unit cost *sing*; **~lohn** *m* piecework rates *pl*; **s~weise** *adv* bit by bit, piecemeal; (*COMM*) individually; **~werk** *nt* bits and pieces *pl*.
Student(in) [ʃtuˈdɛnt(ɪn)] *m(f)* student.
Studenten- *zW*: **~ausweis** *m* student card; **~futter** *nt* nuts and raisins *pl*; **~werk** *nt* student administration; **~wohnheim** *nt* hall of residence (*BRIT*), dormitory (*US*).
studentisch *adj* student *attrib*.
Studie [ˈʃtuːdiə] *f* study.
Studien- *zW*: **~beratung** *f* course guidance service; **~buch** *nt* (*UNIV*) book in which the

courses one has attended are entered;
~**fahrt** f study trip; ~**platz** m university
place; ~**rat** m, ~**rätin** f teacher at a
secondary (*BRIT*) od high (*US*) school.
studieren [ʃtu'diːrən] vt, vi to study; **bei jdm ~**
to study under sb.
Studio ['ʃtuːdio] (**-s, -s**) nt studio.
Studium ['ʃtuːdiʊm] nt studies pl.
Stufe ['ʃtuːfə] (**-, -n**) f step; (*Entwicklungs~*)
stage; (*Niveau*) level.
Stufen- zW: ~**heck** nt (*AUT*) notchback; ~**leiter**
f (*fig*) ladder; **s~los** adj (*TECH*) infinitely
variable; **s~los verstellbar** continuously
adjustable; ~**plan** m graduated plan;
~**schnitt** m (*Frisur*) layered cut; **s~weise** adv
gradually.
Stuhl [ʃtuːl] (**-(e)s, ⁻e**) m chair; **zwischen zwei
Stühlen sitzen** (*fig*) to fall between two
stools.
Stuhlgang m bowel movement.
Stukkateur△ [ʃtʊka'tøːr] m siehe **Stuckateur**.
stülpen ['ʃtʏlpən] vt (*bedecken*) to put; **etw
über etw** akk ~ to put sth over sth; **den
Kragen nach oben** ~ to turn up one's collar.
stumm [ʃtʊm] adj silent; (*MED*) dumb.
Stummel (**-s, -**) m stump; (*Zigaretten~*) stub.
Stummfilm m silent film (*BRIT*) od movie
(*US*).
Stümper(in) ['ʃtʏmpər(ɪn)] (**-s, -**) m(f)
incompetent, duffer; **s~haft** adj bungling,
incompetent.
stümpern (*umg*) vi to bungle.
Stumpf [ʃtʊmpf] (**-(e)s, ⁻e**) m stump; **etw mit
~ und Stiel ausrotten** to eradicate sth root
and branch.
stumpf adj blunt; (*teilnahmslos, glanzlos*) dull;
(*Winkel*) obtuse.
Stumpfsinn (**-(e)s**) m tediousness.
stumpfsinnig adj dull.
Stunde ['ʃtʊndə] (**-, -n**) f hour; (*Augenblick,
Zeitpunkt*) time; (*SCH*) lesson, period (*BRIT*);
~ **um** ~ hour after hour; **80 Kilometer in der**
~ ≈ 50 miles per hour.
stunden vt: **jdm etw** ~ to give sb time to pay
sth.
Stunden- zW: ~**geschwindigkeit** f average
speed (per hour); ~**kilometer** pl kilometres
(*BRIT*) od kilometers (*US*) per hour; **s~lang**
adj for hours; ~**lohn** m hourly wage; ~**plan** m
timetable; **s~weise** adv by the hour;
(*stündlich*) every hour.
stündlich ['ʃtʏntlɪç] adj hourly.
Stunk [ʃtʊŋk] (**-s, no pl**) m: ~ **machen** (*umg*) to
kick up a stink.
stupide [ʃtu'piːdə] adj mindless.
Stups [ʃtʊps] (**-es, -e**) (*umg*) m push.
stupsen vt to nudge.
Stupsnase f snub nose.
stur [ʃtuːr] adj obstinate, stubborn; (*Nein,
Arbeiten*) dogged; **er fuhr** ~ **geradeaus** he

just carried straight on; **sich** ~ **stellen, auf**
~ **stellen** (*umg*) to dig one's heels in; **ein** ~**er
Bock** (*umg*) a pig-headed fellow.
Sturm [ʃtʊrm] (**-(e)s, ⁻e**) m storm; (*Wind*) gale;
(*MIL etc*) attack, assault; ~ **läuten** to keep
one's finger on the doorbell; **gegen etw**
~ **laufen** (*fig*) to be up in arms against sth.
stürmen ['ʃtʏrmən] vi (*Wind*) to blow hard, to
rage; (*rennen*) to storm ♦ vt (*MIL, fig*) to
storm ♦ vi unpers: **es stürmt** there's a gale
blowing.
Stürmer (**-s, -**) m (*SPORT*) forward.
sturmfrei adj (*MIL*) unassailable; **eine** ~**e
Bude** (*umg*) a room free from disturbance.
stürmisch adj stormy; (*fig*) tempestuous;
(*Entwicklung*) rapid; (*Liebhaber*) passionate;
(*Beifall*) tumultuous; **nicht so** ~ take it easy.
Sturm- zW: ~**schritt** m (*MIL, fig*): **im** ~**schritt** at
the double; ~**warnung** f gale warning;
~**wind** m gale.
Sturz [ʃtʊrts] (**-es, ⁻e**) m fall; (*POL*) overthrow;
(*in Temperatur, Preis*) drop.
stürzen ['ʃtʏrtsən] vt (*werfen*) to hurl; (*POL*) to
overthrow; (*umkehren*) to overturn ♦ vr to
rush; (*hinein~*) to plunge ♦ vi to fall; (*AVIAT*)
to dive; (*rennen*) to dash; **jdn ins Unglück** ~
to bring disaster upon sb; „**nicht** ~" "this
side up"; **sich auf jdn/etw** ~ to pounce on
sb/sth; **sich in Unkosten** ~ to go to great
expense.
Sturzflug m nose dive.
Sturzhelm m crash helmet.
Stuss▲ [ʃtʊs] (**-es**) (*umg*) m nonsense,
rubbish.
Stute ['ʃtuːtə] (**-, -n**) f mare.
Stuttgart ['ʃtʊtgart] (**-s**) nt Stuttgart.
Stützbalken m brace, joist.
Stütze ['ʃtʏtsə] (**-, -n**) f support; (*Hilfe*) help;
die ~**n der Gesellschaft** the pillars of
society.
stutzen ['ʃtʊtsən] vt to trim; (*Ohr, Schwanz*) to
dock; (*Flügel*) to clip ♦ vi to hesitate;
(*argwöhnisch werden*) to become suspicious.
stützen vt (*lit, fig*) to support; (*Ellbogen etc*) to
prop up ♦ vr: **sich auf jdn/etw** ~ (*lit*) to lean
on sb/sth; (*Beweise, Theorie*) to be based on
sb/sth.
stutzig adj perplexed, puzzled; (*misstrauisch*)
suspicious.
Stützmauer f supporting wall.
Stützpunkt m point of support; (*von Hebel*)
fulcrum; (*MIL, fig*) base.
Stützungskäufe pl (*FIN*) support buying sing.
StVO abk = **Straßenverkehrsordnung**.
stylen ['staɪlən] vt to style; (*Wohnung*) to
design.
Styling ['staɪlɪŋ] (**-s, no pl**) nt styling.
Styropor ® [ʃtyro'poːr] (**-s**) nt (expanded)
polystyrene.
s. u. abk (= siehe unten) see below.

Suaheli [zua'he:li] (-(s)) *nt* Swahili.
Subjekt [zʊp'jɛkt] (-(e)s, -e) *nt* subject; (*pej: Mensch*) character (*umg*).
subjektiv [zʊpjɛk'ti:f] *adj* subjective.
Subjektivität [zʊpjɛktivi'tɛ:t] *f* subjectivity.
Subkultur ['zʊpkʊltu:r] *f* subculture.
sublimieren [zubli'mi:rən] *vt* (*CHEM, PSYCH*) to sublimate.
Submissionsangebot [zʊpmɪsi'o:ns-|angəbo:t] *nt* sealed-bid tender.
Subroutine ['zʊpruti:nə] *f* (*COMPUT*) subroutine.
Subskription [zʊpskrɪptsi'o:n] *f* subscription.
Substantiv ['zʊpstanti:f] (-s, -e) *nt* noun.
Substanz [zʊp'stants] *f* substance; **von der ~ zehren** to live on one's capital.
subtil [zʊp'ti:l] *adj* subtle.
subtrahieren [zʊptra'hi:rən] *vt* to subtract.
subtropisch ['zʊptro:pɪʃ] *adj* subtropical.
Subunternehmer *m* subcontractor.
Subvention [zʊpvɛntsi'o:n] *f* subsidy.
subventionieren [zʊpvɛntsio'ni:rən] *vt* to subsidize.
subversiv [zʊpvɛr'zi:f] *adj* subversive.
Suchaktion *f* search.
Suchdienst *m* missing persons tracing service.
Suche (-, -n) *f* search.
suchen ['zu:xən] *vt* to look for, seek; (*versuchen*) to try ♦ *vi* to seek, search; **du hast hier nichts zu ~** you have no business being here; **nach Worten ~** to search for words; (*sprachlos sein*) to be at a loss for words; **such!** (*zu Hund*) seek!, find!; **~ und ersetzen** (*COMPUT*) search and replace.
Sucher (-s, -) *m* seeker, searcher; (*PHOT*) viewfinder.
Suchmaschine *f* (*COMPUT*) search engine.
Suchmeldung *f* missing *od* wanted person announcement.
Suchscheinwerfer *m* searchlight.
Sucht [zʊxt] (-, ⁻e) *f* mania; (*MED*) addiction; **~droge** *f* addictive drug; **s~erzeugend** *adj* addictive.
süchtig ['zʏçtɪç] *adj* addicted.
Süchtige(r) *f(m)* addict.
Süd [zy:t] (-(e)s) *m* south; **~afrika** *nt* South Africa; **~amerika** *nt* South America.
Sudan [zu'da:n] (-s) *m*: **der ~** the Sudan.
Sudanese [zuda'ne:zə] (-n, -n) *m* Sudanese.
Sudanesin *f* Sudanese.
südd. *abk* = **süddeutsch**.
süddeutsch *adj* South German.
Süddeutschland *nt* South(ern) Germany.
Süden ['zy:dən] (-s) *m* south.
Süd- *zW*: **~europa** *nt* Southern Europe; **~früchte** *pl* Mediterranean fruit; **~korea** *nt* South Korea; **s~ländisch** *adj* southern; (*italienisch, spanisch etc*) Latin; **s~lich** *adj* southern; **s~lich von** (to the) south of;

~ostasien *nt* South-East Asia; **~pol** *m* South Pole; **~polarmeer** *nt* Antarctic Ocean; **~see** *f* South Seas *pl*, South Pacific; **~tirol** *nt* South Tyrol; **s~wärts** *adv* southwards; **~westafrika** *nt* South West Africa, Namibia.
Sueskanal ['zu:ɛskana:l] (-s) *m* Suez Canal.
Suff [zʊf] *m*: **etw im ~ sagen** (*umg*) to say sth while under the influence.
süffig ['zʏfɪç] *adj* (*Wein*) very drinkable.
süffisant [zʏfi'zant] *adj* smug.
suggerieren [zʊge'ri:rən] *vt* to suggest.
Suggestivfrage [zʊgɛs'ti:ffra:gə] *f* leading question.
suhlen ['zu:lən] *vr* (*lit, fig*) to wallow.
Sühne ['zy:nə] (-, -n) *f* atonement, expiation.
sühnen *vt* to atone for, expiate.
Sühnetermin *m* (*JUR*) conciliatory hearing.
Suite ['svi:tə] *f* suite.
Sulfat [zʊl'fa:t] (-(e)s, -e) *nt* sulphate (*BRIT*), sulfate (*US*).
Sultan ['zʊltan] (-s, -e) *m* sultan.
Sultanine [zʊlta'ni:nə] *f* sultana.
Sülze ['zʏltsə] (-, -n) *f* brawn (*BRIT*), headcheese (*US*); (*Aspik*) aspic.
summarisch [zʊ'ma:rɪʃ] *adj* summary.
Sümmchen ['zʏmçən] *nt*: **ein hübsches ~** a tidy sum.
Summe (-, -n) *f* sum, total.
summen *vi* to buzz ♦ *vt* (*Lied*) to hum.
Summer (-s, -) *m* buzzer.
summieren [zʊ'mi:rən] *vt* to add up ♦ *vr* to mount up.
Sumpf [zʊmpf] (-(e)s, ⁻e) *m* swamp, marsh.
sumpfig *adj* marshy.
Sund [zʊnt] (-(e)s, -e) *m* sound, straits *pl*.
Sünde ['zʏndə] (-, -n) *f* sin.
Sünden- *zW*: **~bock** *m* (*fig*) scapegoat; **~fall** *m* (*REL*) Fall; **~register** *nt* (*fig*) list of sins.
Sünder(in) (-s, -) *m(f)* sinner.
sündhaft *adj* (*lit*) sinful; (*fig: umg: Preise*) wicked.
sündigen ['zʏndɪgən] *vi* to sin; (*hum*) to indulge; **~ an** +*dat* to sin against.
Super ['zu:pər] (-s) *nt* (*Benzin*) four-star (petrol) (*BRIT*), premium (*US*).
super (*umg*) *adj* super ♦ *adv* incredibly well.
Superlativ ['zu:pərlati:f] (-s, -e) *m* superlative.
Supermarkt *m* supermarket.
Superstar *m* superstar.
Suppe ['zʊpə] (-, -n) *f* soup; (*mit Einlage*) broth; (*klare Brühe*) bouillon; (*fig: umg: Nebel*) peasouper (*BRIT*), pea soup (*US*); **jdm die ~ versalzen** (*umg*) to put a spoke in sb's wheel.
Suppen- *zW*: **~fleisch** *nt* meat for making soup; **~grün** *nt* herbs and vegetables for making soup; **~kasper** (*umg*) *m* poor eater; **~teller** *m* soup plate.
Surfbrett ['zø:rfbrɛt] *nt* surfboard.
surfen ['zø:rfən] *vi* to surf.

Surfer(in) *m(f)* surfer.
Surrealismus [zʊrea'lɪsmʊs] *m* surrealism.
surren ['zʊrən] *vi* to buzz; (*Insekt*) to hum.
Surrogat [zʊro'gaːt] (-(e)s, -e) *nt* substitute, surrogate.
suspekt [zʊs'pɛkt] *adj* suspect.
suspendieren [zʊspɛn'diːrən] *vt*: ~ **(von)** to suspend (from).
Suspendierung *f* suspension.
süß [zyːs] *adj* sweet.
Süße (-) *f* sweetness.
süßen *vt* to sweeten.
Süßholz *nt*: ~ **raspeln** (*fig*) to turn on the blarney.
Süßigkeit *f* sweetness; (*Bonbon etc*) sweet (*BRIT*), candy (*US*).
süß- *zW*: ~**lich** *adj* sweetish; (*fig*) sugary; ~**sauer** *adj* sweet-and-sour; (*fig: gezwungen*: *Lächeln*) forced; (*Gurken etc*) pickled; (*Miene*) artificially friendly; **S~speise** *f* pudding, sweet (*BRIT*); **S~stoff** *m* sweetener; **S~waren** *pl* confectionery *sing*; **S~wasser** *nt* fresh water.
SV (-) *m abk* = **Sportverein**.
SW *abk* (= *Südwest(en)*) SW.
Swasiland ['svaːzilant] (-s) *nt* Swaziland.
SWF (-) *m abk* (*früher*: = *Südwestfunk*) *South West German Radio*.
Sylvester [zyl'vɛstər] (-s, -) *nt* = **Silvester**.
Symbol [zym'boːl] (-s, -e) *nt* symbol.
Symbolik *f* symbolism.
symbolisch *adj* symbolic(al).
symbolisieren [zymboli'ziːrən] *vt* to symbolize.
Symmetrie [zyme'triː] *f* symmetry; ~**achse** *f* symmetric axis.
symmetrisch [zy'meːtrɪʃ] *adj* symmetrical.
Sympathie [zympa'tiː] *f* liking; sympathy; **er hat sich** *dat* **alle ~(n) verscherzt** he has turned everyone against him; ~**kundgebung** *f* demonstration of support; ~**streik** *m* sympathy strike.
Sympathisant(in) *m(f)* sympathizer.
sympathisch [zym'paːtɪʃ] *adj* likeable, congenial; **er ist mir ~** I like him.
sympathisieren [zympati'ziːrən] *vi* to sympathize.
Symphonie [zymfo'niː] *f* = **Sinfonie**.
Symptom [zymp'toːm] (-s, -e) *nt* symptom.
symptomatisch [zympto'maːtɪʃ] *adj* symptomatic.
Synagoge [zyna'goːgə] (-, -n) *f* synagogue.
synchron [zyn'kroːn] *adj* synchronous; **S~getriebe** *nt* synchromesh gearbox (*BRIT*) *od* transmission (*US*).
synchronisieren [zynkroni'ziːrən] *vt* to synchronize; (*Film*) to dub.
Synchronschwimmen *nt* synchronized swimming.
Syndikat [zyndi'kaːt] (-(e)s, -e) *nt* combine, syndicate.
Syndrom [zyn'droːm] (-s, -e) *nt* syndrome.
Synkope [zyn'koːpə] (-, -n) *f* (*MUS*) syncopation.
Synode [zy'noːdə] (-, -n) *f* (*REL*) synod.
Synonym [zyno'nyːm] (-s, -e) *nt* synonym; **s~** *adj* synonymous.
Syntax ['zyntaks] (-, -en) *f* syntax.
Synthese [zyn'teːzə] (-, -n) *f* synthesis.
synthetisch *adj* synthetic.
Syphilis ['zyːfilɪs] (-) *f* syphilis.
Syrer(in) ['zyːrər(ɪn)] (-s, -) *m(f)* Syrian.
Syrien (-s) *nt* Syria.
syrisch *adj* Syrian.
System [zys'teːm] (-s, -e) *nt* system; ~**analyse** *f* systems analysis; ~**analytiker(in)** *m(f)* systems analyst.
Systematik *f* system.
systematisch [zyste'maːtɪʃ] *adj* systematic.
systematisieren [zystemati'ziːrən] *vt* to systematize.
System- *zW*: ~**kritiker** *m* critic of the system; ~**platte** *f* (*COMPUT*) system disk; ~**zwang** *m* obligation to conform (to the system).
Szenarium [stse'naːriʊm] *nt* scenario.
Szene ['stseːnə] (-, -n) *f* scene; **sich in der ~ auskennen** (*umg*) to know the scene; **sich in ~ setzen** to play to the gallery.
Szenenwechsel *m* scene change.
Szenerie [stsenə'riː] *f* scenery.

T, t

T, t[1] [teː] *nt* T, t; ~ **wie Theodor** ≈ T for Tommy.
t[2] *abk* (= *Tonne*) t.
Tabak ['taːbak] (-s, -e) *m* tobacco; ~**laden** *m* tobacconist's (*BRIT*), tobacco store (*US*).
tabellarisch [tabɛ'laːrɪʃ] *adj* tabular.
Tabelle (-, -n) *f* table.
Tabellenführer *m* (*SPORT*) top of the table, league leader.
Tabernakel [taber'naːkəl] (-s, -) *nt* tabernacle.
Tabl. *abk* = **Tablette(n)**.
Tablett (-(e)s, -s *od* -e) *nt* tray.
Tablette [ta'blɛtə] (-, -n) *f* tablet, pill.
Tabu [ta'buː] (-s, -s) *nt* taboo.
tabuisieren [tabui'ziːrən] *vt* to make taboo.
Tabulator [tabu'laːtɔr] *m* tabulator, tab (*umg*).
tabulieren *vt* to tab.
Tacho ['taxo] (-s, -s) (*umg*) *m* speedo (*BRIT*).
Tachometer [taxo'meːtər] (-s, -) *m* (*AUT*) speedometer.

Tadel ['taːdəl] (**-s, -**) *m* censure, scolding; (*Fehler*) fault; (*Makel*) blemish; **t~los** *adj* faultless, irreproachable.

tadeln *vt* to scold.

tadelnswert *adj* blameworthy.

Tadschikistan [taˈdʒiːkistaːn] (**-s**) *nt* Tajikistan.

Tafel ['taːfəl] (**-, -n**) *f* (*form: festlicher Speisetisch, MATH*) table; (*Festmahl*) meal; (*Anschlag~*) board; (*Wand~*) blackboard; (*Schiefer~*) slate; (*Gedenk~*) plaque; (*Illustration*) plate; (*Schalt~*) panel; (*Schokoladen~ etc*) bar; **t~fertig** *adj* ready to serve.

täfeln ['tɛːfəln] *vt* to panel.

Tafelöl *nt* cooking oil; salad oil.

Täfelung *f* panelling (*BRIT*), paneling (*US*).

Tafelwasser *nt* table water.

Taft [taft] (**-(e)s, -e**) *m* taffeta.

Tag [taːk] (**-(e)s, -e**) *m* day; (*Tageslicht*) daylight; **am ~** during the day; **für** *od* **auf ein paar ~e** for a few days; **in den ~ hinein leben** to take each day as it comes; **bei ~(e)** (*ankommen*) while it's light; (*arbeiten, reisen*) during the day; **unter ~e** (*MIN*) underground; **über ~e** (*MIN*) on the surface; **an den ~ kommen** to come to light; **er legte großes Interesse an den ~** he showed great interest; **auf den ~ (genau)** to the day; **auf seine alten ~e** at his age; **guten ~!** good morning/afternoon!; *siehe auch* **zutage**; **t~aus** *adv*: **t~aus, t~ein** day in, day out; **~dienst** *m* day duty.

Tage- *zW*: **~bau** *m* (*MIN*) open-cast mining; **~buch** *nt* diary; **~dieb** *m* idler; **~geld** *nt* daily allowance; **t~lang** *adv* for days.

tagen *vi* to sit, meet ♦ *vi unpers*: **es tagt** dawn is breaking.

Tages- *zW*: **~ablauf** *m* daily routine; **~anbruch** *m* dawn; **~ausflug** *m* day trip; **~decke** *f* bedspread; **~fahrt** *f* day trip; **~karte** *f* (*Eintrittskarte*) day ticket; (*Speisekarte*) menu of the day; **~kasse** *f* (*COMM*) day's takings *pl*; (*THEAT*) box office; **~licht** *nt* daylight; **~mutter** *f* child minder; **~ordnung** *f* agenda; **an der ~ordnung sein** (*fig*) to be the order of the day; **~rückfahrkarte** *f* day return (ticket); **~satz** *m* daily rate; **~schau** *f* (*TV*) television news (programme (*BRIT*) *od* program (*US*)); **~stätte** *f* day nursery (*BRIT*), daycare center (*US*); **~wert** *m* (*FIN*) present value; **~zeit** *f* time of day; **zu jeder ~- und Nachtzeit** at all hours of the day and night; **~zeitung** *f* daily (paper).

tägl. *abk* = **täglich**.

täglich ['tɛːklɪç] *adj, adv* daily; **einmal ~** once a day.

tags [taːks] *adv*: **~ darauf** *od* **danach** the next *od* following day; **~über** *adv* during the day.

tagtäglich *adj* daily ♦ *adv* every (single) day.

Tagung *f* conference.

Tagungsort *m* venue (of a conference).

Tahiti [taˈhiːti] (**-s**) *nt* Tahiti.

Taifun [taɪˈfuːn] (**-s, -e**) *m* typhoon.

Taille ['taljə] (**-, -n**) *f* waist.

tailliert [taˈjiːrt] *adj* waisted, gathered at the waist.

Taiwan ['taɪvan] (**-s**) *nt* Taiwan.

Takel ['taːkəl] (**-s, -**) *nt* tackle.

takeln ['taːkəln] *vt* to rig.

Takt [takt] (**-(e)s, -e**) *m* tact; (*MUS*) time; **~gefühl** *nt* tact.

Taktik *f* tactics *pl*.

Taktiker(in) *m(f)* tactician.

taktisch *adj* tactical.

Takt- *zW*: **t~los** *adj* tactless; **~losigkeit** *f* tactlessness; **~stock** *m* (conductor's) baton; **~strich** *m* (*MUS*) bar (line); **t~voll** *adj* tactful.

Tal [taːl] (**-(e)s, ̈-er**) *nt* valley.

Talar [taˈlaːr] (**-s, -e**) *m* (*JUR*) robe; (*UNIV*) gown.

Talbrücke *f* bridge over a valley.

Talent [taˈlɛnt] (**-(e)s, -e**) *nt* talent.

talentiert [talɛnˈtiːrt] *adj* talented, gifted.

Talfahrt *f* descent; (*fig*) decline.

Talg [talk] (**-(e)s, -e**) *m* tallow.

Talgdrüse *f* sebaceous gland.

Talisman ['taːlɪsman] (**-s, -e**) *m* talisman.

Tal- *zW*: **~sohle** *f* bottom of a valley; **~sperre** *f* dam; **t~wärts** *adv* down to the valley.

Tamburin [tambuˈriːn] (**-s, -e**) *nt* tambourine.

Tamile [taˈmiːlə] (**-n, -n**) *m*, **Tamilin** *f* Tamil.

tamilisch *adj* Tamil.

Tampon ['tampɔn] (**-s, -s**) *m* tampon.

Tamtam [tam'tam] (**-s, -s**) *nt* (*MUS*) tomtom; (*umg: Wirbel*) fuss, ballyhoo; (*Lärm*) din.

Tang [taŋ] (**-(e)s, -e**) *m* seaweed.

Tangente [taŋˈgɛntə] (**-, -n**) *f* tangent.

Tanger ['taŋər] (**-s**) *nt* Tangier(s).

tangieren [taŋˈgiːrən] *vt* (*Problem*) to touch on; (*fig*) to affect.

Tank [taŋk] (**-s, -s**) *m* tank.

tanken *vt* (*Wagen etc*) to fill up with petrol (*BRIT*) *od* gas (*US*); (*Benzin etc*) to fill up with; (*AVIAT*) to (re)fuel; (*umg: frische Luft, neue Kräfte*) to get ♦ *vi* to fill up (with petrol *od* gas); to (re)fuel.

Tanker (**-s, -**) *m* tanker.

Tank- *zW*: **~laster** *m* tanker; **~schiff** *nt* tanker; **~stelle** *f* petrol (*BRIT*) *od* gas (*US*) station; **~uhr** *f* fuel gauge; **~verschluss▲** *m* fuel cap; **~wart** *m* petrol pump (*BRIT*) *od* gas station (*US*) attendant.

Tanne ['tanə] (**-, -n**) *f* fir.

Tannenbaum *m* fir tree.

Tannenzapfen *m* fir cone.

Tansania [tanˈzaːnia] (**-s**) *nt* Tanzania.

Tante ['tantə] (**-, -n**) *f* aunt; **~-Emma-Laden** (*umg*) *m* corner shop.

Tantieme [tãtiˈeːmə] (**-, -n**) *f* fee; (*für Künstler*

etc) royalty.
Tanz [tants] (**-es, ⁻e**) *m* dance.
tänzeln ['tɛntsəln] *vi* to dance along.
tanzen *vt, vi* to dance.
Tänzer(in) (**-s, -**) *m(f)* dancer.
Tanz- *zW:* ~**fläche** *f* (dance) floor; ~**lokal** *nt* café/restaurant with dancing; ~**schule** *f* dancing school.
Tapet [ta'peːt] (*umg*) *nt:* **etw aufs** ~ **bringen** to bring sth up.
Tapete [ta'peːtə] (**-, -n**) *f* wallpaper.
Tapetenwechsel *m* (*fig*) change of scenery.
tapezieren [tape'tsiːrən] *vt* to (wall)paper.
Tapezierer (**-s, -**) *m* (interior) decorator.
tapfer ['tapfər] *adj* brave; **sich** ~ **schlagen** (*umg*) to put on a brave show; **T~keit** *f* courage, bravery.
tappen ['tapən] *vi* to walk uncertainly *od* clumsily; **im Dunkeln** ~ (*fig*) to grope in the dark.
täppisch ['tɛpɪʃ] *adj* clumsy.
Tara ['taːra] (**-, Taren**) *f* tare.
Tarantel [ta'rantəl] (**-, -n**) *f*: **wie von der** ~ **gestochen** as if stung by a bee.
Tarif [ta'riːf] (**-s, -e**) *m* tariff, (scale of) fares/charges; **nach/über/unter** ~ **bezahlen** to pay according to/above/below the (union) rate(s); ~**autonomie** *f* free collective bargaining; ~**gruppe** *f* grade; **t~lich** *adj* agreed, union; ~**lohn** *m* standard wage rate; ~**ordnung** *f* wage *od* salary scale; ~**partner** *m*: **die** ~**partner** union and management; ~**vereinbarung** *f* labour (*BRIT*) *od* labor (*US*) agreement; ~**verhandlungen** *pl* collective bargaining *sing*; ~**vertrag** *m* pay agreement.
tarnen ['tarnən] *vt* to camouflage; (*Person, Absicht*) to disguise.
Tarnfarbe *f* camouflage paint.
Tarnmanöver *nt* (*lit, fig*) feint, covering ploy.
Tarnung *f* camouflaging; disguising.
Tarock [ta'rɔk] (**-s, s**) *m od nt* tarot.
Tasche ['taʃə] (**-, -n**) *f* pocket; (*Hand~*) handbag; **in die eigene** ~ **wirtschaften** to line one's own pockets; **jdm auf der** ~ **liegen** (*umg*) to live off sb.
Taschen- *zW:* ~**buch** *nt* paperback; ~**dieb** *m* pickpocket; ~**geld** *nt* pocket money; ~**lampe** *f* (electric) torch, flashlight (*US*); ~**messer** *nt* penknife; ~**rechner** *m* pocket calculator; ~**spieler** *m* conjurer; ~**tuch** *nt* handkerchief.
Tasmanien [tas'maːniən] (**-s**) *nt* Tasmania.
Tasse ['tasə] (**-, -n**) *f* cup; **er hat nicht alle** ~**n im Schrank** (*umg*) he's not all there.
Tastatur [tasta'tuːr] *f* keyboard.
Taste ['tastə] (**-, -n**) *f* push-button control; (*an Schreibmaschine*) key.
tasten *vt* to feel, touch; (*drücken*) to press ♦ *vi* to feel, grope ♦ *vr* to feel one's way.
Tastentelefon *nt* push-button telephone.
Tastsinn *m* sense of touch.

Tat (**-, -en**) *f* act, deed, action; **in der** ~ indeed, as a matter of fact; **etw in die** ~ **umsetzen** to put sth into action.
tat *etc* [taːt] *vb siehe* **tun**.
Tatbestand *m* facts *pl* of the case.
Tatendrang *m* energy.
tatenlos *adj* inactive.
Täter(in) ['tɛːtər(ɪn)] (**-s, -**) *m(f)* perpetrator, culprit; ~**schaft** *f* guilt.
tätig *adj* active; ~**er Teilhaber** active partner; **in einer Firma** ~ **sein** to work for a firm.
tätigen *vt* (*COMM*) to conclude; (*geh: Einkäufe, Anruf*) to make.
Tätigkeit *f* activity; (*Beruf*) occupation.
Tätigkeitsbereich *m* field of activity.
tatkräftig *adj* energetic; (*Hilfe*) active.
tätlich *adj* violent; **T~keit** *f* violence; **es kam zu T~keiten** there were violent scenes.
Tatort (**-(e)s, -e**) *m* scene of the crime.
tätowieren [tɛto'viːrən] *vt* to tattoo.
Tätowierung *f* tattooing; (*Ergebnis*) tattoo.
Tatsache *f* fact; **jdn vor vollendete** ~**n stellen** to present sb with a fait accompli.
Tatsachenbericht *m* documentary (report).
tatsächlich *adj* actual ♦ *adv* really.
tatverdächtig *adj* suspected.
Tatze ['tatsə] (**-, -n**) *f* paw.
Tau¹ [tau] (**-(e)s, -e**) *nt* rope.
Tau² (**-(e)s**) *m* dew.
taub [taup] *adj* deaf; (*Nuss*) hollow; **sich** ~ **stellen** to pretend not to hear.
Taube ['taubə] (**-, -n**) *f* (*ZOOL*) pigeon; (*fig*) dove.
Taubenschlag *m* dovecote; **hier geht es zu wie im** ~ (*fig: umg*) it's like Waterloo Station here (*BRIT*), it's like Grand Central Station here (*US*).
Taubheit *f* deafness.
taubstumm *adj* deaf-mute.
tauchen ['tauxən] *vt* to dip ♦ *vi* to dive; (*NAUT*) to submerge.
Taucher (**-s, -**) *m* diver; ~**anzug** *m* diving suit.
Tauchsieder (**-s, -**) *m* portable immersion heater.
Tauchstation *f*: **auf** ~ **gehen** (*U-Boot*) to dive.
tauen ['tauən] *vt, vi* to thaw ♦ *vi unpers:* **es taut** it's thawing.
Taufbecken *nt* font.
Taufe ['taufə] (**-, -n**) *f* baptism.
taufen *vt* to baptize; (*nennen*) to christen.
Tauf- *zW:* ~**name** *m* Christian name; ~**pate** *m* godfather; ~**patin** *f* godmother; ~**schein** *m* certificate of baptism.
taugen ['taugən] *vi* to be of use; ~ **für** to do *od* be good for; **nicht** ~ to be no good *od* useless.
Taugenichts (**-es, -e**) *m* good-for-nothing.
tauglich ['tauklɪç] *adj* suitable; (*MIL*) fit (for service); **T~keit** *f* suitability; fitness.
Taumel ['tauməl] (**-s**) *m* dizziness; (*fig*) frenzy.

taumelig *adj* giddy, reeling.

taumeln *vi* to reel, stagger.

Taunus ['taunʊs] (-) *m* Taunus (Mountains *pl*).

Tausch [tauʃ] (-(e)s, -e) *m* exchange; **einen guten/schlechten ~ machen** to get a good/bad deal.

tauschen *vt* to exchange, swap ♦ *vi*: **ich möchte nicht mit ihm ~** I wouldn't like to be in his place.

täuschen ['tɔʏʃən] *vt* to deceive ♦ *vi* to be deceptive ♦ *vr* to be wrong; **wenn mich nicht alles täuscht** unless I'm completely wrong.

täuschend *adj* deceptive.

Tauschhandel *m* barter.

Täuschung *f* deception; (*optisch*) illusion.

Täuschungsmanöver *nt* (*SPORT*) feint; (*fig*) ploy.

tausend ['tauzənt] *num* a *od* one thousand; **T~** (-, -en) *f* (*Zahl*) thousand.

Tausender (-s, -) *m* (*Geldschein*) thousand.

Tausendfüßler (-s, -) *m* centipede.

Tau- *zW*: **~tropfen** *m* dew drop; **~wetter** *nt* thaw; **~ziehen** *nt* tug-of-war.

Taxe ['taksə] (-, -n) *f* taxi, cab.

Taxi ['taksi] (-(s), -(s)) *nt* taxi, cab.

taxieren [ta'ksiːrən] *vt* (*Preis, Wert*) to estimate; (*Haus, Gemälde*) to value; (*mustern*) to look up and down.

Taxi- *zW*: **~fahrer** *m* taxi driver; **~stand** *m* taxi rank (*BRIT*) *od* stand (*US*).

Tb, Tbc *f abk* (= *Tuberkulose*) TB.

Teamarbeit ['tiːmˌarbaɪt] *f* teamwork.

Technik ['tɛçnɪk] *f* technology; (*Methode, Kunstfertigkeit*) technique.

Techniker(in) (-s -) *m(f)* technician.

technisch *adj* technical; **~e Hochschule** ≈ polytechnic.

Technologie [tɛçnolo'giː] *f* technology.

technologisch [tɛçno'loːgɪʃ] *adj* technological.

Techtelmechtel [tɛçtəl'mɛçtəl] (-s, -) (*umg*) *nt* (*Liebschaft*) affair, carry-on.

TEE *abk* (= *Trans-Europ-Express*) Trans-Europe-Express.

Tee [teː] (-s, -s) *m* tea; **~beutel** *m* tea bag; **~kanne** *f* teapot; **~licht** *nt* night-light; **~löffel** *m* teaspoon; **~mischung** *f* blend of tea.

Teer [teːr] (-(e)s, -e) *m* tar; **t~en** *vt* to tar.

Teesieb *nt* tea strainer.

Teewagen *m* tea trolley.

Teflon ® ['teflon] (-s) *nt* Teflon ®.

Teheran ['teːhəraːn] (-s) *nt* Teheran.

Teich [taɪç] (-(e)s, -e) *m* pond.

Teig [taɪk] (-(e)s, -e) *m* dough.

teigig ['taɪgɪç] *adj* doughy.

Teigwaren *pl* pasta *sing*.

Teil [taɪl] (-(e)s, -e) *m od nt* part; (*Anteil*) share ♦ *nt* (*Bestand~*) component, part; (*Ersatz~*) spare (part); **zum ~** partly; **ich für mein(en) ~ ...** I, for my part ...; **sich** *dat* **sein ~ denken**

(*umg*) to draw one's own conclusions; **er hat sein(en) ~ dazu beigetragen** he did his bit *od* share; **t~bar** *adj* divisible; **~betrag** *m* instalment (*BRIT*), installment (*US*); **~chen** *nt* (atomic) particle.

teilen *vt* to divide; (*mit jdm*) to share ♦ *vr* to divide; (*in Gruppen*) to split up.

Teil- *zW*: **t~entrahmt** *adj* semi-skimmed; **~gebiet** *nt* (*Bereich*) branch; (*räumlich*) area; **t~haben** *unreg vi*: **an etw** *dat* **t~haben** to share in sth; **~haber** (-s, -) *m* partner; **~kaskoversicherung** *f* third party, fire and theft insurance.

Teilnahme (-, -n) *f* participation; (*Mitleid*) sympathy; **jdm seine herzliche ~ aussprechen** to offer sb one's heartfelt sympathy.

teilnahmslos *adj* disinterested, apathetic.

teilnehmen *unreg vi*: **an etw** *dat* **~** to take part in sth.

Teilnehmer(in) (-s, -) *m(f)* participant.

teils *adv* partly.

Teilschaden *m* partial loss.

Teilstrecke *f* stage; (*von Straße*) stretch; (*bei Bus etc*) fare stage.

Teilung *f* division.

Teil- *zW*: **t~weise** *adv* partially, in part; **~zahlung** *f* payment by instalments (*BRIT*) *od* installments (*US*); **~zeitarbeit** *f* part-time job *od* work.

Teint [tɛː] (-s, -s) *m* complexion.

Telearbeit ['teːlearbaɪt] *f* teleworking.

Telebanking ['teːlebɛŋkɪŋ] (-s) *nt* telebanking.

Telebrief ['teːlebriːf] *m* facsimile, fax.

Telefax ['teːlefaks] (-) *nt* telefax.

Telefon [tele'foːn] (-s, -e) *nt* (tele)phone; **ans ~ gehen** to answer the phone; **~amt** *nt* telephone exchange; **~anruf** *m* (tele)phone call.

Telefonat [telefo'naːt] (-(e)s, -e) *nt* (tele)phone call.

Telefon- *zW*: **~buch** *nt* (tele)phone directory; **~gebühr** *f* call charge; (*Grundgebühr*) (tele)phone rental; **~gespräch** *nt* (tele)phone call; **~häuschen** (*umg*) *nt* = **Telefonzelle**.

telefonieren [telefo'niːrən] *vi* to (tele)phone; **bei jdm ~** to use sb's phone; **mit jdm ~** to speak to sb on the phone.

telefonisch [tele'foːnɪʃ] *adj* telephone; (*Benachrichtigung*) by telephone; **ich bin ~ zu erreichen** I can be reached by phone.

Telefonist(in) [telefo'nɪst(ɪn)] *m(f)* telephonist.

Telefon- *zW*: **~karte** *f* phone card; **~nummer** *f* (tele)phone number; **~seelsorge** *f*: **die ~seelsorge** ≈ the Samaritans; **~verbindung** *f* telephone connection; **~zelle** *f* telephone box (*BRIT*) *od* booth (*US*), callbox (*BRIT*); **~zentrale** *f* telephone exchange.

Telegraf [tele'graːf] (-en, -en) *m* telegraph.

Telegrafenleitung *f* telegraph line.

Telegrafenmast *m* telegraph pole.
Telegrafie [telegra'fiː] *f* telegraphy.
telegrafieren [telegra'fiːrən] *vt, vi* to telegraph, cable, wire.
telegrafisch [tele'graːfɪʃ] *adj* telegraphic; **jdm ~ Geld überweisen** to cable sb money.
Telegramm [tele'gram] (-s, -e) *nt* telegram, cable; **~adresse** *f* telegram address; **~formular** *nt* telegram form.
Telekolleg ['teːləkɔleːk] *nt* ≈ Open University (*BRIT*).
Teleobjektiv ['teːləʔɔpjɛktiːf] *nt* telephoto lens.
Telepathie [telepa'tiː] *f* telepathy.
telepathisch [tele'paːtɪʃ] *adj* telepathic.
Teleskop [tele'skoːp] (-s, -e) *nt* telescope.
Telespiel *nt* video game.
Telex ['teːlɛks] (-, -(e)) *nt* telex.
Teller ['tɛlər] (-s, -) *m* plate.
Tempel ['tɛmpəl] (-s, -) *m* temple.
Temperafarbe ['tɛmperafarbə] *f* distemper.
Temperament [tempera'mɛnt] *nt* temperament; (*Schwung*) vivacity, vitality; **sein ~ ist mit ihm durchgegangen** he went over the top; **t~los** *adj* spiritless; **t~voll** *adj* high-spirited, lively.
Temperatur [tempera'tuːr] *f* temperature; **erhöhte ~ haben** to have a temperature.
Tempo¹ ['tɛmpo] (-s, -s) *nt* speed, pace; **~!** get a move on!
Tempo² ['tɛmpo] (-s, Tempi) *nt* (*MUS*) tempo; **das ~ angeben** (*fig*) to set the pace; **~limit** *nt* speed limit.
temporär [tempo'rɛːr] *adj* temporary.
Tempotaschentuch ® *nt* paper handkerchief.
Tendenz [tɛn'dɛnts] *f* tendency; (*Absicht*) intention.
tendenziell [tɛndɛntsi'el] *adj*: **nur ~e Unterschiede** merely differences in emphasis.
tendenziös [tɛndɛntsi'øːs] *adj* bias(s)ed, tendentious.
tendieren [tɛn'diːrən] *vi*: **zu etw ~** to show a tendency to(wards) sth, incline to(wards) sth.
Teneriffa [tene'rɪfa] (-s) *nt* Tenerife.
Tenne ['tɛnə] (-, -n) *f* threshing floor.
Tennis ['tɛnɪs] (-) *nt* tennis; **~platz** *m* tennis court; **~schläger** *m* tennis racket; **~spieler** *m* tennis player.
Tenor [te'noːr] (-s, ̈-e) *m* tenor.
Teppich ['tɛpɪç] (-s, -e) *m* carpet; **~boden** *m* wall-to-wall carpeting; **~kehrmaschine** *f* carpet sweeper; **~klopfer** *m* carpet beater.
Termin [tɛr'miːn] (-s, -e) *m* (*Zeitpunkt*) date; (*Frist*) deadline; (*Arzt~ etc*) appointment; (*JUR: Verhandlung*) hearing; **sich** *dat* **einen ~ geben lassen** to make an appointment; **t~gerecht** *adj* on schedule.

terminieren [tɛrmi'niːrən] *vt* (*befristen*) to limit; (*festsetzen*) to set a date for.
Terminkalender *m* diary, appointments book.
Terminologie [tɛrminolo'giː] *f* terminology.
Termite [tɛr'miːtə] (-, -n) *f* termite.
Terpentin [tɛrpɛn'tiːn] (-s, -e) *nt* turpentine, turps *sing*.
Terrain [tɛ'rɛː] (-s, -s) *nt* land, terrain; (*fig*) territory; **das ~ sondieren** (*MIL*) to reconnoitre the terrain; (*fig*) to see how the land lies.
Terrasse [tɛ'rasə] (-, -n) *f* terrace.
Terrine [tɛ'riːnə] *f* tureen.
territorial [tɛritori'aːl] *adj* territorial.
Territorium [tɛri'toːriʊm] *nt* territory.
Terror ['tɛrɔr] (-s) *m* terror; (*~herrschaft*) reign of terror; **blanker ~** sheer terror; **~anschlag** *m* terrorist attack.
terrorisieren [tɛrori'ziːrən] *vt* to terrorize.
Terrorismus [tɛro'rɪsmʊs] *m* terrorism.
Terrorist(in) *m(f)* terrorist.
terroristisch *adj* terrorist *attr*.
Terrororganisation *f* terrorist organization.
Tertia ['tɛrtsia] (-, Tertien) *f* (*SCH: früher: Unter~/Ober~*) fourth/fifth year of German secondary school.
Terz [tɛrts] (-, -en) *f* (*MUS*) third.
Terzett [tɛr'tsɛt] (-(e)s, -e) *nt* (*MUS*) trio.
Tesafilm ® ['teːzafɪlm] *m* Sellotape ® (*BRIT*), Scotch tape ® (*US*).
Test [tɛst] (-s, -s) *m* test.
Testament [tɛsta'mɛnt] *nt* will, testament; (*REL*) Testament; **Altes/Neues ~** Old/New Testament.
testamentarisch [tɛstamɛn'taːrɪʃ] *adj* testamentary.
Testamentsvollstrecker(in) (-s, -) *m(f)* executor (of a will).
Testat [tɛs'taːt] (-(e)s, -e) *nt* certificate.
Testator [tɛs'taːtɔr] *m* testator.
Test- *zW*: **~bild** *nt* (*TV*) test card; **t~en** *vt* to test; **~fall** *m* test case; **~person** *f* subject (of a test); **~stoppabkommen** *nt* nuclear test ban agreement.
Tetanus ['teːtanʊs] (-) *m* tetanus; **~impfung** *f* (anti-)tetanus injection.
teuer ['tɔyər] *adj* dear, expensive; **teures Geld** good money; **das wird ihn ~ zu stehen kommen** (*fig*) that will cost him dear.
Teuerung *f* increase in prices.
Teuerungszulage *f* cost-of-living bonus.
Teufel ['tɔyfəl] (-s, -) *m* devil; **den ~ an die Wand malen** (*schwarz malen*) to imagine the worst; (*Unheil heraufbeschwören*) to tempt fate *od* providence; **in ~s Küche kommen** to get into a mess; **jdn zum ~ jagen** (*umg*) to send sb packing.
Teufelei [tɔyfə'lai] *f* devilry.
Teufels- *zW*: **~austreibung** *f* exorcism; **~brut**

(umg) f devil's brood; **~kreis** _m_ vicious circle.

teuflisch ['tɔʏflɪʃ] _adj_ fiendish, diabolic.

Text [tɛkst] (-(e)s, -e) _m_ text; _(Lieder~)_ words _pl_; (: _von Schlager)_ lyrics _pl_; **~dichter** _m_ songwriter; **t~en** _vi_ to write the words.

textil [tɛksˈtiːl] _adj_ textile; **T~branche** _f_ textile trade.

Textilien _pl_ textiles _pl._

Textilindustrie _f_ textile industry.

Textilwaren _pl_ textiles _pl._

Text- _zW:_ **~nachrichten** _pl (TEL)_ text messaging; **~stelle** _f_ passage; **~ verarbeitungssystem** _nt_ word processor.

TH (-, -s) _f abk_ (= _technische Hochschule) siehe_ **technisch**.

Thailand ['taɪlant] (-s) _nt_ Thailand.

Thailänder(in) ['taɪlɛndər(ɪn)] (-s, -) _m(f)_ Thai.

Theater [teˈaːtər] (-s, -) _nt_ theatre; _(US);_ _(umg)_ fuss; **(ein)** ~ **machen** to make a (big) fuss; ~ **spielen** to act; _(fig)_ to put on an act; **~besucher** _m_ playgoer; **~kasse** _f_ box office; **~stück** _nt_ (stage) play.

theatralisch [teaˈtraːlɪʃ] _adj_ theatrical.

Theke ['teːkə] (-, -n) _f (Schanktisch)_ bar; _(Ladentisch)_ counter.

Thema ['teːma] (-s, **Themen** _od_ -ta) _nt (MUS, Leitgedanke)_ theme; topic, subject; **beim** ~ **bleiben/vom** ~ **abschweifen** to stick to/ wander off the subject.

thematisch [teˈmaːtɪʃ] _adj_ thematic.

Themenkreis _m_ topic.

Themenpark _m_ theme park.

Themse ['tɛmzə] _f:_ **die** ~ the Thames.

Theologe [teoˈloːgə] (-n, -n) _m_ theologian.

Theologie [teoloˈgiː] _f_ theology.

Theologin _f_ theologian.

theologisch [teoˈloːgɪʃ] _adj_ theological.

Theoretiker(in) [teoˈreːtikər(ɪn)] (-s, -) _m(f)_ theorist.

theoretisch _adj_ theoretical; ~ **gesehen** in theory, theoretically.

Theorie [teoˈriː] _f_ theory.

Therapeut [teraˈpɔʏt] (-en, -en) _m_ therapist.

therapeutisch _adj_ therapeutic.

Therapie [teraˈpiː] _f_ therapy.

Thermalbad [tɛrˈmaːlbaːt] _nt_ thermal bath; _(Badeort)_ thermal spa.

Thermalquelle _f_ thermal spring.

Thermometer [tɛrmoˈmeːtər] (-s, -) _nt_ thermometer.

Thermosflasche ® ['tɛrmɔsflaʃə] _f_ Thermos ® flask.

Thermostat [tɛrmoˈstaːt] (-(e)s _od_ -en, -e(n)) _m_ thermostat.

These ['teːzə] (-, -n) _f_ thesis.

Thrombose [trɔmˈboːsə] (-, -n) _f_ thrombosis.

Thron [troːn] (-(e)s, -e) _m_ throne; **~besteigung** _f_ accession (to the throne).

thronen _vi_ to sit enthroned; _(fig)_ to sit in state.

Thronerbe _m_ heir to the throne.

Thronfolge _f_ succession (to the throne).

Thunfisch ['tuːnfɪʃ] _m_ tuna (fish).

Thüringen ['tyːrɪŋən] (-s) _nt_ Thuringia.

Thymian ['tyːmiaːn] (-s, -e) _m_ thyme.

Tibet ['tiːbɛt] (-s) _nt_ Tibet.

Tick [tɪk] (-(e)s, -s) _m_ tic; _(Eigenart)_ quirk; _(Fimmel)_ craze.

ticken _vi_ to tick; **nicht richtig** ~ _(umg)_ to be off one's rocker.

Ticket ['tɪkət] (-s, -s) _nt_ ticket.

tief [tiːf] _adj_ deep; _(~sinnig)_ profound; _(Ausschnitt, Ton)_ low; **~er Teller** soup plate; ~ **greifend** far-reaching; ~ **schürfend** profound; **bis** ~ **in die Nacht hinein** late into the night; **T~** (-s, -s) _nt (MET)_ depression; _(fig)_ low; **T~bau** _m_ civil engineering _(at or below ground level)_; **T~druck** _m (MET)_ low pressure.

Tiefe (-, -n) _f_ depth.

Tiefebene ['tiːfˌeːbənə] _f_ plain.

Tiefenpsychologie _f_ depth psychology.

Tiefenschärfe _f (PHOT)_ depth of focus.

tief- _zW:_ **~ernst** _adj_ very grave _od_ solemn; **T~flug** _m_ low-level _od_ low-altitude flight; **T~gang** _m (NAUT)_ draught _(BRIT)_, draft _(US)_; _(geistig)_ depth; **T~garage** _f_ underground car park _(BRIT)_ _od_ parking lot _(US)_; **~gekühlt** _adj_ frozen; **T~kühlfach** _nt_ freezer compartment; **T~kühlkost** _f_ frozen food; **T~kühltruhe** _f_ freezer, deep freezer _(US)_; **T~lader** (-s, -) _m_ low-loader; **T~land** _nt_ lowlands _pl_; **T~parterre** _f_ basement; **T~punkt** _m_ low point; _(fig)_ low ebb; **T~schlag** _m (BOXEN, fig)_ blow below the belt; **T~see** _f_ deep parts of the sea; **T~sinn** _m_ profundity; **~sinnig** _adj_ profound; _(umg)_ melancholy; **T~stand** _m_ low level; **~stapeln** _vi_ to be overmodest; **T~start** _m (SPORT)_ crouch start.

Tiefstwert _m_ minimum _od_ lowest value.

Tiegel ['tiːgəl] (-s, -) _m_ saucepan; _(CHEM)_ crucible.

Tier [tiːr] (-(e)s, -e) _nt_ animal; **~arzt** _m_, **~ärztin** _f_ vet(erinary surgeon) _(BRIT)_, veterinarian _(US)_; **~freund** _m_ animal lover; **~garten** _m_ zoo, zoological gardens _pl_; **~handlung** _f_ pet shop _(BRIT)_ _od_ store _(US)_; **t~isch** _adj_ animal _attrib_; _(lit, fig)_ brutish; _(fig: Ernst etc)_ deadly; **~kreis** _m_ zodiac; **~kunde** _f_ zoology; **t~lieb** _adj_, **t~liebend** _adj_ fond of animals; **~quälerei** _f_ cruelty to animals; **~reich** _nt_ animal kingdom; **~schutz** _m_ protection of animals; **~schutzverein** _m_ society for the prevention of cruelty to animals; **~versuch** _m_ animal experiment; **~welt** _f_ animal kingdom.

Tiger ['tiːgər] (-s, -) _m_ tiger; **~in** _f_ tigress.

tilgen ['tɪlgən] _vt_ to erase; _(Sünden)_ to expiate; _(Schulden)_ to pay off.

Tilgung _f_ erasing, blotting out; expiation;

repayment.

Tilgungsfonds m (COMM) sinking fund.

tingeln ['tɪŋgəln] (umg) vi to appear in small night clubs.

Tinktur [tɪŋk'tuːr] f tincture.

Tinte ['tɪntə] (-, -n) f ink.

Tinten- zW: ~**fass▲** nt inkwell; ~**fisch** m cuttlefish; (achtarmig) octopus; ~**fleck** m ink stain od blot; ~**stift** m indelible pencil; ~**strahldrucker** m ink-jet printer.

Tipp▲ [tɪp] (-s, -s) m (SPORT, BÖRSE) tip; (Andeutung) hint; (an Polizei) tip-off.

Tippelbruder (umg) m tramp, gentleman of the road (BRIT), hobo (US).

tippen ['tɪpən] vi to tap, touch; (umg: schreiben) to type; (im Lotto etc) to bet ♦ vt to type; to bet; **auf jdn** ~ (umg: raten) to tip sb, put one's money on sb (fig).

Tippfehler (umg) m typing error.

Tippse (-, -n) (umg) f typist.

tipptopp ['tɪp'tɔp] (umg) adj tiptop.

Tippzettel m (pools) coupon.

Tirade [ti'raːdə] (-, -n) f tirade.

Tirol [ti'roːl] (-s) nt the Tyrol.

Tiroler(in) (-s, -) m(f) Tyrolese, Tyrolean.

tirolerisch adj Tyrolese, Tyrolean.

Tisch [tɪʃ] (-(e)s, -e) m table; **bitte zu** ~! lunch od dinner is served; **bei** ~ at table; **vor/nach** ~ before/after eating; **unter den** ~ **fallen** (fig) to be dropped; ~**decke** f tablecloth.

Tischler (-s, -) m carpenter, joiner.

Tischlerei [tɪʃlə'raɪ] f joiner's workshop; (Arbeit) carpentry, joinery.

Tischlerhandwerk nt cabinetmaking.

tischlern vi to do carpentry etc.

Tisch- zW: ~**nachbar** m neighbour (BRIT) od neighbor (US) (at table); ~**rechner** m desk calculator; ~**rede** f after-dinner speech; ~**tennis** nt table tennis; ~**tuch** nt tablecloth.

Titel ['tiːtəl] (-s, -) m title; ~**anwärter** m (SPORT) challenger; ~**bild** nt cover (picture); (von Buch) frontispiece; ~**geschichte** f headline story; ~**rolle** f title role; ~**seite** f cover; (Buch~) title page; ~**verteidiger** m defending champion, title holder.

Titte ['tɪtə] (-, -n) (umg) f (weibliche Brust) boob, tit (umg).

titulieren [titu'liːrən] vt to entitle; (anreden) to address.

tja [tja] interj well!

Toast [toːst] (-(e)s, -s od -e) m toast.

toasten vi to drink a toast ♦ vt (Brot) to toast; **auf jdn** ~ to toast sb, drink a toast to sb.

Toaster (-s, -) m toaster.

toben ['toːbən] vi to rage; (Kinder) to romp about.

tob- zW: **T~sucht** f raving madness; ~**süchtig** adj maniacal; **T~suchtsanfall** m maniacal fit.

Tochter ['tɔxtər] (-, -̈) f daughter;

~**gesellschaft** f subsidiary (company).

Tod [toːt] (-(e)s, -e) m death; **zu** ~**e betrübt sein** to be in the depths of despair; **eines natürlichen/gewaltsamen** ~**es sterben** to die of natural causes/die a violent death; **t~ernst** (umg) adj deadly serious ♦ adv in dead earnest.

Todes- zW: ~**angst** f mortal fear; ~**ängste ausstehen** (umg) to be scared to death; ~**anzeige** f obituary (notice); ~**fall** m death; ~**kampf** m death throes pl; ~**opfer** nt death, casualty, fatality; ~**qualen** pl: ~**qualen ausstehen** (fig) to suffer agonies; ~**stoß** m deathblow; ~**strafe** f death penalty; ~**tag** m anniversary of death; ~**ursache** f cause of death; ~**urteil** nt death sentence; ~**verachtung** f utter disgust.

Todfeind m deadly od mortal enemy.

todkrank adj dangerously ill.

tödlich ['tøːtlɪç] adj fatal; (Gift) deadly, lethal.

tod- zW: ~**müde** adj dead tired; ~**schick** (umg) adj smart, classy; ~**sicher** (umg) adj absolutely od dead certain; **T~sünde** f deadly sin; ~**traurig** adj extremely sad.

Tofu ['toːfu] (-(s)) m tofu.

Togo ['toːgo] (-s) nt Togo.

Toilette [toa'lɛtə] f toilet, lavatory (BRIT), john (US); (Frisiertisch) dressing table; (Kleidung) outfit; **auf die** ~ **gehen/auf der** ~ **sein** to go to/be in the toilet.

Toiletten- zW: ~**artikel** pl toiletries pl, toilet articles pl; ~**papier** nt toilet paper; ~**tisch** m dressing table.

toi, toi, toi ['tɔy'tɔy'tɔy] (umg) interj good luck; (unberufen) touch wood.

Tokio ['toːkjo] (-s) nt Tokyo.

tolerant [tole'rant] adj tolerant.

Toleranz f tolerance.

tolerieren [tole'riːrən] vt to tolerate.

toll [tɔl] adj mad; (Treiben) wild; (umg) terrific.

tollen vi to romp.

toll- zW: **T~heit** f madness, wildness; **T~kirsche** f deadly nightshade; ~**kühn** adj daring; **T~wut** f rabies.

Tölpel ['tœlpəl] (-s, -) m oaf, clod.

Tomate [to'maːtə] (-, -n) f tomato; **du treulose** ~! (umg) you're a fine friend!

Tomatenmark (-(e)s) nt tomato purée.

Tombola ['tɔmbola] (-, -s od **Tombolen**) f tombola.

Ton¹ [toːn] (-(e)s, -e) m (Erde) clay.

Ton² [toːn] (-(e)s, -̈e) m (Laut) sound; (MUS) note; (Redeweise) tone; (Farb~, Nuance) shade; (Betonung) stress; **keinen** ~ **herausbringen** not to be able to say a word; **den** ~ **angeben** (MUS) to give an A; (fig: Mensch) to set the tone; ~**abnehmer** m pick-up; **t~angebend** adj leading; ~**arm** m pick-up arm; ~**art** f (musical) key; ~**band** nt tape; ~**bandaufnahme** f tape recording;

~**bandgerät** nt tape recorder.

tönen ['tø:nən] vi to sound ♦ vt to shade; (Haare) to tint.

tönern ['tø:nərn] adj clay.

Ton- zW: ~**fall** m intonation; ~**film** m sound film; ~**höhe** f pitch.

Tonika ['to:nika] (-, -iken) f (MUS) tonic.

Tonikum (-s, -ika) nt (MED) tonic.

Ton- zW: ~**ingenieur** m sound engineer; ~**kopf** m recording head; ~**künstler** m musician; ~**leiter** f (MUS) scale; **t~los** adj soundless.

Tonne ['tɔnə] (-, -n) f barrel; (Maß) ton.

Ton- zW: ~**spur** f soundtrack; ~**taube** f clay pigeon; ~**waren** pl pottery sing, earthenware sing.

Topf [tɔpf] (-(e)s, ⁻e) m pot; **alles in einen ~ werfen** (fig) to lump everything together; ~**blume** f pot plant.

Töpfer(in) ['tœpfər(ɪn)] (-s, -) m(f) potter.

Töpferei [tœpfə'raɪ] f (Töpferware) pottery; (Werkstatt) pottery, potter's workshop.

töpfern vi to do pottery.

Töpferscheibe f potter's wheel.

topfit ['tɔp'fɪt] adj in top form.

Topflappen m ovencloth.

topografisch▲ [topo'graːfɪʃ] adj topographic.

topp [tɔp] interj O.K.

Tor¹ [to:r] (-en, -en) m fool.

Tor² (-(e)s, -e) nt gate; (SPORT) goal; ~**bogen** m archway; ~**einfahrt** f entrance gate.

Toresschluss▲ m: **(kurz) vor ~** right at the last minute.

Torf [tɔrf] (-(e)s) m peat; ~**stechen** nt peat-cutting.

Torheit f foolishness; (törichte Handlung) foolish deed.

Torhüter (-s, -) m goalkeeper.

töricht ['tøːrɪçt] adj foolish.

torkeln ['tɔrkəln] vi to stagger, reel.

torpedieren [tɔrpe'diːrən] vt (lit, fig) to torpedo.

Torpedo [tɔr'peːdo] (-s, -s) m torpedo.

Torschlusspanik▲ ['tɔːrʃlʊspaːnik] (umg) f (von Unverheirateten) fear of being left on the shelf.

Torte ['tɔrtə] (-, -n) f cake; (Obst~) flan, tart.

Tortenguss m glaze.

Tortenheber m cake slice.

Tortur [tɔr'tuːr] f ordeal.

Torverhältnis nt goal average.

Torwart (-(e)s, -e) m goalkeeper.

tosen ['toːzən] vi to roar.

Toskana [tɔs'kaːna] f Tuscany.

tot [toːt] adj dead; **er war auf der Stelle ~** he died instantly; **~ geboren** stillborn; **sich ~ stellen** to pretend to be dead; **der ~e Winkel** the blind spot; **einen ~en Punkt haben** to be at one's lowest; **das T~e Meer** the Dead Sea.

total [to'taːl] adj total; **T~ausverkauf** m

clearance sale.

totalitär [totali'tɛːr] adj totalitarian.

Totaloperation f extirpation; (von Gebärmutter) hysterectomy.

Totalschaden m (AUT) complete write-off.

totarbeiten vr to work o.s. to death.

totärgern (umg) vr to get really annoyed.

Tote(r) f(m) dead person.

töten ['tøːtən] vt, vi to kill.

Toten- zW: ~**bett** nt deathbed; **t~blass▲** adj deathly pale, white as a sheet; ~**gräber** (-s, -) m gravedigger; ~**hemd** nt shroud; ~**kopf** m skull; ~**messe** f requiem mass; ~**schein** m death certificate; ~**stille** f deathly silence; ~**tanz** m danse macabre; ~**wache** f wake.

tot- zW: ~**fahren** unreg vt to run over; ~**kriegen** (umg) vt: **nicht ~zukriegen sein** to go on for ever; ~**lachen** (umg) vr to laugh one's head off.

tot- zW: ~**sagen** vt: **jdn ~sagen** to say that sb is dead; **T~schlag** m (JUR) manslaughter, second degree murder (US); ~**schlagen** unreg vt (lit, fig) to kill; **T~schläger** m (Waffe) cosh (BRIT), blackjack (US); ~**schweigen** unreg vt to hush up; ~**treten** unreg vt to trample to death.

Tötung ['tøːtʊŋ] f killing.

Toupet [tu'peː] (-s, -s) nt toupee.

toupieren [tu'piːrən] vt to backcomb.

Tour [tuːr] (-, -en) f tour, trip; (Umdrehung) revolution; (Verhaltensart) way; **auf ~en kommen** (AUT) to reach top speed; (fig) to get into top gear; **auf vollen ~en laufen** (lit) to run at full speed; (fig) to be in full swing; **auf die krumme ~** by dishonest means; **in einer ~** incessantly.

Tourenzahl f number of revolutions.

Tourenzähler m rev counter.

Tourismus [tu'rɪsmʊs] m tourism.

Tourist(in) m(f) tourist.

Touristenklasse f tourist class.

Touristik [tu'rɪstɪk] f tourism.

touristisch adj tourist attr.

Tournee [tur'neː] (-, -s od -n) f (THEAT etc) tour; **auf ~ gehen** to go on tour.

Trab [traːp] (-(e)s) m trot; **auf ~ sein** (umg) to be on the go.

Trabant [tra'bant] m satellite.

Trabantenstadt f satellite town.

traben ['traːbən] vi to trot.

Tracht [traxt] (-, -en) f (Kleidung) costume, dress; **eine ~ Prügel** a sound thrashing.

trachten vi to strive, endeavour (BRIT), endeavor (US); **danach ~, etw zu tun** to strive to do sth; **jdm nach dem Leben ~** to seek to kill sb.

trächtig ['trɛçtɪç] adj (Tier) pregnant.

Tradition [traditsi'oːn] f tradition.

traditionell [traditsio'nɛl] adj traditional.

traf *etc* [traːf] *vb siehe* **treffen**.

Tragbahre *f* stretcher.

tragbar *adj* (*Gerät*) portable; (*Kleidung*) wearable; (*erträglich*) bearable.

träge ['trɛːgə] *adj* sluggish, slow; (*PHYS*) inert.

tragen ['traːgən] *unreg vt* to carry; (*Kleidung, Brille*) to wear; (*Namen, Früchte*) to bear; (*erdulden*) to endure ♦ *vi* (*schwanger sein*) to be pregnant; (*Eis*) to hold; **schwer an etw** *dat* ~ (*lit*) to have a job carrying sth; (*fig*) to find sth hard to bear; **zum T~ kommen** to come to fruition; (*nützlich werden*) to come in useful.

tragend *adj* (*Säule, Bauteil*) load-bearing; (*Idee, Motiv*) fundamental.

Träger ['trɛːgər] (**-s**, **-**) *m* carrier; wearer; bearer; (*Ordens~*) holder; (*an Kleidung*) (shoulder) strap; (*Körperschaft etc*) sponsor; (*Holz~, Beton~*) supporting) beam; (*Stahl~, Eisen~*) girder; (*TECH: Stütze von Brücken etc*) support.

Trägerin *f* (*Person*) *siehe* **Träger**.

Träger- *zW:* ~**kleid** *nt* pinafore dress (*BRIT*), jumper (*US*); ~**rakete** *f* launch vehicle; ~**rock** *m* skirt with shoulder straps.

Tragetasche *f* carrier bag (*BRIT*), carry-all (*US*).

Trag- *zW:* ~**fähigkeit** *f* load-bearing capacity; ~**fläche** *f* (*AVIAT*) wing; ~**flügelboot** *nt* hydrofoil.

Trägheit ['trɛːkhaɪt] *f* laziness; (*PHYS*) inertia.

Tragik ['traːgɪk] *f* tragedy.

tragikomisch [tragi'koːmɪʃ] *adj* tragi-comic.

tragisch *adj* tragic; **etw** ~ **nehmen** (*umg*) to take sth to heart.

Traglast *f* load.

Tragödie [tra'gøːdiə] *f* tragedy.

trägt [trɛːkt] *vb siehe* **tragen**.

Tragweite *f* range; (*fig*) scope; **von großer** ~ **sein** to have far-reaching consequences.

Tragwerk *nt* wing assembly.

Trainer(in) ['trɛːnər(ɪn)] (**-s**, **-**) *m(f)* (*SPORT*) trainer, coach; (*FUSSBALL*) manager.

trainieren [trɛ'niːrən] *vt* to train; (*Übung*) to practise (*BRIT*), practice (*US*) ♦ *vi* to train; **Fußball** ~ to do football practice.

Training (**-s**, **-s**) *nt* training.

Trainingsanzug *m* track suit.

Trakt [trakt] (**-(e)s**, **-e**) *m* (*Gebäudeteil*) section; (*Flügel*) wing.

Traktat [trak'taːt] (**-(e)s**, **-e**) *m od nt* (*Abhandlung*) treatise; (*Flugschrift, religiöse Schrift*) tract.

traktieren (*umg*) *vt* (*schlecht behandeln*) to maltreat; (*quälen*) to torment.

Traktor ['traktɔr] *m* tractor; (*von Drucker*) tractor feed.

trällern ['trɛlərn] *vt, vi* to warble; (*Vogel*) to trill, warble.

trampeln ['trampəln] *vt* to trample;

(*abschütteln*) to stamp ♦ *vi* to stamp.

Trampelpfad *m* track, path.

Trampeltier *nt* (*ZOOL*) (Bactrian) camel; (*fig: umg*) clumsy oaf.

trampen ['trɛmpən] *vi* to hitchhike.

Tramper(in) [trɛmpər(ɪn)] (**-s**, **-**) *m(f)* hitchhiker.

Trampolin [trampo'liːn] (**-s**, **-e**) *nt* trampoline.

Tranchierbesteck *nt* pair of carvers, carvers *pl*.

tranchieren [trã'ʃiːrən] *vt* to carve.

Träne ['trɛːnə] (**-**, **-n**) *f* tear.

tränen *vi* to water.

Tränengas *nt* tear gas.

tranig ['traːnɪç] (*umg*) *adj* slow, sluggish.

trank *etc* [traŋk] *vb siehe* **trinken**.

Tränke ['trɛŋkə] (**-**, **-n**) *f* watering place.

tränken *vt* (*nass machen*) to soak; (*Tiere*) to water.

Transaktion [transˌaktsi'oːn] *f* transaction.

Transchierbesteck *nt* = **Tranchierbesteck**.

transchieren *vt* = **tranchieren**.

Transformator [transfɔr'maːtɔr] *m* transformer.

Transfusion [transfuzi'oːn] *f* transfusion.

Transistor [tran'zistɔr] *m* transistor.

transitiv ['tranzitiːf] *adj* transitive.

Transitverkehr [tran'ziːtfɛrkeːr] *m* transit traffic.

transparent [transpa'rɛnt] *adj* transparent; **T~** (**-(e)s**, **-e**) *nt* (*Bild*) transparency; (*Spruchband*) banner.

transpirieren [transpi'riːrən] *vi* to perspire.

Transplantation [transplantatsi'oːn] *f* transplantation; (*Haut~*) graft(ing).

Transport [trans'pɔrt] (**-(e)s**, **-e**) *m* transport; (*Fracht*) consignment, shipment; **t~fähig** *adj* moveable.

transportieren [transpɔr'tiːrən] *vt* to transport.

Transport- *zW:* ~**kosten** *pl* transport charges *pl*, carriage *sing;* ~**mittel** *nt* means *sing* of transport; ~**unternehmen** *nt* carrier.

transsexuell [transzɛksu'ɛl] *adj* transsexual.

transusig ['traːnzuːzɪç] (*umg*) *adj* sluggish.

Transvestit [transvɛs'tiːt] (**-en**, **-en**) *m* transvestite.

Trapez [tra'peːts] (**-es**, **-e**) *nt* trapeze; (*MATH*) trapezium.

Trara [tra'raː] (**-s**) *nt:* **mit viel** ~ (**um**) (*fig: umg*) with a great hullabaloo (about).

trat *etc* [traːt] *vb siehe* **treten**.

Tratsch [traːtʃ] (**-(e)s**) (*umg*) *m* gossip.

tratschen ['traːtʃən] (*umg*) *vi* to gossip.

Tratte ['tratə] (**-**, **-n**) *f* (*FIN*) draft.

Traube ['traubə] (**-**, **-n**) *f* grape; (*ganze Frucht*) bunch (of grapes).

Traubenlese *f* grape harvest.

Traubenzucker *m* glucose.

trauen ['trauən] *vi* +*dat* to trust ♦ *vr* to dare ♦ *vt* to marry; **jdm/etw** ~ to trust sb/sth.

Trauer ['traʊər] (-) *f* sorrow; (*für Verstorbenen*) mourning; ~**fall** *m* death, bereavement; ~**feier** *f* funeral service; ~**flor** (-**s**, -**e**) *m* black ribbon; ~**gemeinde** *f* mourners *pl*; ~**marsch** *m* funeral march.

trauern *vi* to mourn; **um jdn** ~ to mourn (for) sb.

Trauer- *zW:* ~**rand** *m* black border; ~**spiel** *nt* tragedy; ~**weide** *f* weeping willow.

Traufe ['traʊfə] (-, -**n**) *f* eaves *pl*.

träufeln ['trɔʏfəln] *vt, vi* to drip.

traulich ['traʊlɪç] *adj* cosy, intimate.

Traum [traʊm] (-(**e**)**s**, **Träume**) *m* dream; **aus der** ~! it's all over!

Trauma (-**s**, -**men**) *nt* trauma.

traumatisieren [traʊmati'ziːrən] *vt* to traumatize.

Traumbild *nt* vision.

Traumdeutung *f* interpretation of dreams.

träumen ['trɔʏmən] *vt, vi* to dream; **das hätte ich mir nicht** ~ **lassen** I'd never have thought it possible.

Träumer(in) (-**s**, -) *m(f)* dreamer.

Träumerei [trɔʏmə'raɪ] *f* dreaming.

träumerisch *adj* dreamy.

traumhaft *adj* dreamlike; (*fig*) wonderful.

Traumtänzer *m* dreamer.

traurig ['traʊrɪç] *adj* sad; **T~keit** *f* sadness.

Trauring *m* wedding ring.

Trauschein *m* marriage certificate.

Trauung *f* wedding ceremony.

Trauzeuge *m* witness (to a marriage).

treffen ['trɛfən] *unreg vt* to strike, hit; (*Bemerkung*) to hurt; (*begegnen*) to meet; (*Entscheidung etc*) to make; (*Maßnahmen*) to take ♦ *vi* to hit ♦ *vr* to meet; **er hat es gut getroffen** he did well; **er fühlte sich getroffen** he took it personally; ~ **auf** +*akk* to come across, meet; **es traf sich, dass ...** it so happened that ...; **es trifft sich gut** it's convenient.

Treffen (-**s**, -) *nt* meeting.

treffend *adj* pertinent, apposite.

Treffer (-**s**, -) *m* hit; (*Tor*) goal; (*Los*) winner.

trefflich *adj* excellent.

Treffpunkt *m* meeting place.

Treibeis *nt* drift ice.

treiben ['traɪbən] *unreg vt* to drive; (*Studien etc*) to pursue; (*SPORT*) to do, go in for ♦ *vi* (*Schiff etc*) to drift; (*Pflanzen*) to sprout; (*KOCH: aufgehen*) to rise; (*Medikamente*) to be diuretic; **die ~de Kraft** (*fig*) the driving force; **Handel mit etw/jdm** ~ to trade in sth/with sb; **es zu weit** ~ to go too far; **Unsinn** ~ to fool around; **T~** (-**s**) *nt* activity.

Treib- *zW:* ~**gut** *nt* flotsam and jetsam; ~**haus** *nt* greenhouse; ~**hauseffekt** *m* greenhouse effect; ~**hausgas** *nt* greenhouse gas; ~**jagd** *f* shoot (*in which game is sent up*); (*fig*) witchhunt;

~**sand** *m* quicksand; ~**stoff** *m* fuel.

Trend [trɛnt] (-**s**, -**s**) *m* trend; ~**wende** *f* new trend.

trennbar *adj* separable.

trennen ['trɛnən] *vt* to separate; (*teilen*) to divide ♦ *vr* to separate; **sich** ~ **von** to part with.

Trennschärfe *f* (*RUNDF*) selectivity.

Trennung *f* separation.

Trennungsstrich *m* hyphen.

Trennwand *f* partition (wall).

treppab *adv* downstairs.

treppauf *adv* upstairs.

Treppe ['trɛpə] (-, -**n**) *f* stairs *pl*, staircase; (*im Freien*) steps *pl*; **eine** ~ a staircase, a flight of stairs *od* steps; **sie wohnt zwei** ~**n hoch/höher** she lives two flights up/higher up.

Treppengeländer *nt* banister.

Treppenhaus *nt* staircase.

Tresen ['treːzən] (-**s**, -) *m* (*Theke*) bar; (*Ladentisch*) counter.

Tresor [tre'zoːr] (-**s**, -**e**) *m* safe.

Tretboot *nt* pedal boat, pedalo.

treten ['treːtən] *unreg vi* to step; (*Tränen, Schweiß*) to appear ♦ *vt* (*mit Fußtritt*) to kick; (*nieder*~) to tread, trample; ~ **nach** to kick at; ~ **in** +*akk* to step in(to); **in Verbindung** ~ to get in contact; **in Erscheinung** ~ to appear; **der Fluss trat über die Ufer** the river overflowed its banks; **in Streik** ~ to go on strike.

Treter ['treːtər] (*umg*) *pl* (*Schuhe*) casual shoes *pl*.

Tretmine *f* (*MIL*) (anti-personnel) mine.

Tretmühle *f* (*fig*) daily grind.

treu [trɔʏ] *adj* faithful, true; ~**doof** (*umg*) *adj* naïve.

Treue (-) *f* loyalty, faithfulness.

Treuhand (*umg*) *f*, **Treuhandanstalt** *f* trustee organization (*overseeing the privatization of former GDR state-owned firms*).

TREUHANDANSTALT

The **Treuhandanstalt** *is a now defunct organization set up in 1990 to take over the nationally-owned companies of the former* **DDR**, *to break them down into smaller units and to privatize them. It was based in Berlin and had nine branches. Many companies were closed down by the* **Treuhandanstalt** *because of their outdated equipment and inability to compete with the western firms. This resulted in a rise in unemployment.*

Treuhänder (-**s**, -) *m* trustee.

Treuhandgesellschaft *f* trust company.

treu- *zW:* ~**herzig** *adj* innocent; ~**lich** *adv* faithfully; ~**los** *adj* faithless; ~**los an jdm handeln** to fail sb.

Triathlon ['triːatlɔn] (-**s**, -**s**) *nt* triathlon.

Tribüne [tri'by:nə] (-, -n) *f* grandstand; (*Redner~*) platform.
Tribut [tri'bu:t] (-(e)s, -e) *m* tribute.
Trichter ['trɪçtər] (-s, -) *m* funnel; (*Bomben~*) crater.
Trick [trɪk] (-s, -e *od* -s) *m* trick; ~**film** *m* cartoon.
Trieb (-(e)s, -e) *m* urge, drive; (*Neigung*) inclination; (*BOT*) shoot.
trieb *etc* [tri:p] *vb siehe* **treiben**.
Trieb- *zW:* ~**feder** *f* (*fig*) motivating force; **t**~**haft** *adj* impulsive; ~**kraft** *f* (*fig*) drive; ~**täter** *m* sex offender; ~**wagen** *m* (*EISENB*) railcar; ~**werk** *nt* engine.
triefen ['tri:fən] *vi* to drip.
trifft [trɪft] *vb siehe* **treffen**.
triftig ['trɪftɪç] *adj* convincing; (*Grund etc*) good.
Trigonometrie [trigonome'tri:] *f* trigonometry.
Trikot [tri'ko:] (-s, -s) *nt* vest; (*SPORT*) shirt ♦ *m* (*Gewebe*) tricot.
Triller ['trɪlər] (-s, -) *m* (*MUS*) trill.
trillern *vi* to trill, warble.
Trillerpfeife *f* whistle.
Trilogie [trilo'gi:] *f* trilogy.
Trimester [tri'mɛstər] (-s, -) *nt* term.
Trimm-Aktion *f* keep-fit campaign.
Trimm-dich-Pfad *m* keep-fit trail.
trimmen *vt* (*Hund*) to trim; (*umg: Mensch, Tier*) to teach, train ♦ *vr* to keep fit.
trinkbar *adj* drinkable.
trinken ['trɪŋkən] *unreg vt, vi* to drink.
Trinker(in) (-s, -) *m(f)* drinker.
Trink- *zW:* **t**~**fest** *adj:* **ich bin nicht sehr t~fest** I can't hold my drink very well; ~**geld** *nt* tip; ~**halle** *f* (*Kiosk*) refreshment kiosk; ~**halm** *m* (drinking) straw; ~**milch** *f* milk; ~**spruch** *m* toast; ~**wasser** *nt* drinking water.
Trio ['tri:o] (-s, -s) *nt* trio.
trippeln ['trɪpəln] *vi* to toddle.
Tripper ['trɪpər] (-s, -) *m* gonorrhoea (*BRIT*), gonorrhea (*US*).
trist [trɪst] *adj* dreary, dismal; (*Farbe*) dull.
tritt [trɪt] *vb siehe* **treten**.
Tritt (-(e)s, -e) *m* step; (*Fuß~*) kick.
Trittbrett *nt* (*EISENB*) step; (*AUT*) running board.
Trittleiter *f* stepladder.
Triumph [tri'ʊmf] (-(e)s, -e) *m* triumph; ~**bogen** *m* triumphal arch.
triumphieren [triʊm'fi:rən] *vi* to triumph; (*jubeln*) to exult.
trivial [trivi'a:l] *adj* trivial; **T**~**literatur** *f* light fiction.
trocken ['trɔkən] *adj* dry; **sich ~ rasieren** to use an electric razor; **T**~**automat** *m* tumble dryer; **T**~**dock** *nt* dry dock; **T**~**eis** *nt* dry ice; **T**~**element** *nt* dry cell; **T**~**haube** *f* hairdryer; **T**~**heit** *f* dryness; ~**legen** *vt* (*Sumpf*) to

drain; (*Kind*) to put a clean nappy (*BRIT*) *od* diaper (*US*) on; **T**~**milch** *f* dried milk; **T**~**zeit** *f* (*Jahreszeit*) dry season.
trocknen *vt, vi* to dry.
Trockner (-s, -) *m* dryer.
Troddel ['trɔdəl] (-, -n) *f* tassel.
Trödel ['trø:dəl] (-s) (*umg*) *m* junk; ~**markt** *m* flea market.
trödeln (*umg*) *vi* to dawdle.
Trödler (-s, -) *m* secondhand dealer.
Trog (-(e)s, ̈-e) *m* trough.
trog *etc* [tro:k] *vb siehe* **trügen**.
trollen ['trɔlən] (*umg*) *vr* to push off.
Trommel ['trɔməl] (-, -n) *f* drum; **die ~ rühren** (*fig: umg*) to drum up support; ~**fell** *nt* eardrum; ~**feuer** *nt* drumfire, heavy barrage.
trommeln *vt, vi* to drum.
Trommelrevolver *m* revolver.
Trommelwaschmaschine *f* tumble-action washing machine.
Trommler(in) ['trɔmlər(ɪn)] (-s, -) *m(f)* drummer.
Trompete [trɔm'pe:tə] (-, -n) *f* trumpet.
Trompeter (-s, -) *m* trumpeter.
Tropen ['tro:pən] *pl* tropics *pl*; **t**~**beständig** *adj* suitable for the tropics; ~**helm** *m* topee, sun helmet.
Tropf¹ [trɔpf] (-(e)s, ̈-e) (*umg*) *m* rogue; **armer ~** poor devil.
Tropf² (-(e)s) (*umg*) *m* (*MED: Infusion*) drip (*umg*); **am ~ hängen** to be on a drip.
tröpfeln ['trœpfəln] *vi* to drip, trickle.
Tropfen (-s, -) *m* drop; **ein guter** *od* **edler ~** a good wine; **ein ~ auf den heißen Stein** (*fig: umg*) a drop in the ocean.
tropfen *vt, vi* to drip ♦ *vi unpers:* **es tropft** a few raindrops are falling.
tropfenweise *adv* in drops.
tropfnass▲ *adj* dripping wet.
Tropfsteinhöhle *f* stalactite cave.
Trophäe [tro'fɛ:ə] (-, -n) *f* trophy.
tropisch ['tro:pɪʃ] *adj* tropical.
Trost [tro:st] (-es) *m* consolation, comfort; **t**~**bedürftig** *adj* in need of consolation.
trösten ['trø:stən] *vt* to console, comfort.
Tröster(in) (-s, -) *m(f)* comfort(er).
tröstlich *adj* comforting.
trost- *zW:* ~**los** *adj* bleak; (*Verhältnisse*) wretched; **T**~**pflaster** *nt* (*fig*) consolation; **T**~**preis** *m* consolation prize; ~**reich** *adj* comforting.
Tröstung ['trø:stʊŋ] *f* comfort, consolation.
Trott [trɔt] (-(e)s, -e) *m* trot; (*Routine*) routine.
Trottel (-s, -) (*umg*) *m* fool, dope.
trotten *vi* to trot.
Trottoir [trɔto'a:r] (-s, -s *od* -e) *nt* (*veraltet*) pavement (*BRIT*), sidewalk (*US*).
trotz [trɔts] *präp* (*+gen od dat*) in spite of.
Trotz (-es) *m* pig-headedness; **etw aus ~ tun**

to do sth just to show them; **jdm zum** ~ **in defiance of sb.**
Trotzalter *nt* obstinate phase.
trotzdem *adv* nevertheless ◆ *konj* although.
trotzen *vi +dat* to defy; (*der Kälte, dem Klima etc*) to withstand; (*der Gefahr*) to brave; (*trotzig sein*) to be awkward.
trotzig *adj* defiant; (*Kind*) difficult, awkward.
Trotzkopf *m* obstinate child.
Trotzreaktion *f* fit of pique.
trüb [try:p] *adj* dull; (*Flüssigkeit, Glas*) cloudy; (*fig*) gloomy; ~**e Tasse** (*umg*) drip.
Trubel ['tru:bəl] (-s) *m* hurly-burly.
trüben ['try:bən] *vt* to cloud ◆ *vr* to become clouded.
Trübheit *f* dullness; cloudiness; gloom.
Trübsal (-, -e) *f* distress; ~ **blasen** (*umg*) to mope.
trüb- *zW:* ~**selig** *adj* sad, melancholy; **T**~**sinn** *m* depression; ~**sinnig** *adj* depressed, gloomy.
trudeln ['tru:dəln] *vi* (*AVIAT*) to (go into a) spin.
Trüffel ['tryfəl] (-, -n) *f* truffle.
Trug (-(e)s) *m* (*liter*) deception; (*der Sinne*) illusion.
trug *etc* [tru:k] *vb siehe* **tragen**.
trügen ['try:gən] *unreg vt* to deceive ◆ *vi* to be deceptive; **wenn mich nicht alles trügt** unless I am very much mistaken.
trügerisch *adj* deceptive.
Trugschluss▲ ['tru:gʃlʊs] *m* false conclusion.
Truhe ['tru:ə] (-, -n) *f* chest.
Trümmer ['trymər] *pl* wreckage *sing*; (*Bau~*) ruins *pl*; ~**feld** *nt* expanse of rubble *od* ruins; (*fig*) scene of devastation; ~**frauen** *pl* (*German*) *women who cleared away the rubble after the war*; ~**haufen** *m* heap of rubble.
Trumpf [trʊmpf] (-(e)s, ⁻e) *m* (*lit, fig*) trump; **t**~**en** *vt, vi* to trump.
Trunk [trʊŋk] (-(e)s, ⁻e) *m* drink.
trunken *adj* intoxicated; **T**~**bold** (-(e)s, -e) *m* drunkard; **T**~**heit** *f* intoxication; **T**~**heit am Steuer** drink-driving.
Trunksucht *f* alcoholism.
Trupp [trʊp] (-s, -s) *m* troop.
Truppe (-, -n) *f* troop; (*Waffengattung*) force; (*Schauspiel~*) troupe; **nicht von der schnellen** ~ **sein** (*umg*) to be slow.
Truppen *pl* troops *pl*; ~**abbau** *m* cutback in troop numbers; ~**führer** *m* (*military*) commander; ~**teil** *m* unit; ~**übungsplatz** *m* training area.
Trust [trast] (-(e)s, -e *od* -s) *m* trust.
Truthahn ['tru:tha:n] *m* turkey.
Tschad [tʃat] (-s) *m*: **der** ~ Chad.
Tscheche ['tʃɛçə] (-n, -n) *m*, **Tschechin** *f* Czech.
tschechisch *adj* Czech; **die T**~**e Republik** the

Czech Republic.
Tschechoslowakei [tʃɛçoslovaːˈkai] *f* (*früher*): **die** ~ Czechoslovakia.
tschüss▲ [tʃʏs] (*umg*) *interj* cheerio (*BRIT*), so long (*US*).
T-Shirt ['tiːʃəːt] (-s, -s) *nt* T-shirt.
TU (-) *f abk* (= *technische Universität*) ≈ polytechnic.
Tuba ['tuːba] (-, **Tuben**) *f* (*MUS*) tuba.
Tube ['tuːbə] (-, -n) *f* tube.
Tuberkulose [tubɛrkuˈloːzə] (-, -n) *f* tuberculosis.
Tuch [tuːx] (-(e)s, ⁻er) *nt* cloth; (*Hals~*) scarf; (*Kopf~*) (head)scarf; (*Hand~*) towel; ~**fühlung** *f* physical contact.
tüchtig ['tʏçtɪç] *adj* efficient; (*fähig*) able, capable; (*umg: kräftig*) good, sound; **etwas T**~**es lernen/werden** (*umg*) to get a proper training/job; **T**~**keit** *f* efficiency; ability.
Tücke ['tʏkə] (-, -n) *f* (*Arglist*) malice; (*Trick*) trick; (*Schwierigkeit*) difficulty, problem; **seine** ~**n haben** to be temperamental.
tückisch *adj* treacherous; (*böswillig*) malicious.
tüfteln ['tʏftəln] (*umg*) *vi* to puzzle; (*basteln*) to fiddle about.
Tugend ['tuːgənt] (-, -en) *f* virtue; **t**~**haft** *adj* virtuous.
Tüll [tʏl] (-s, -e) *m* tulle.
Tülle (-, -n) *f* spout.
Tulpe ['tʊlpə] (-, -n) *f* tulip.
tummeln ['tʊməln] *vr* to romp (about); (*sich beeilen*) to hurry.
Tummelplatz *m* play area; (*fig*) hotbed.
Tumor ['tuːmɔr] (-s, -e) *m* tumour (*BRIT*), tumor (*US*).
Tümpel ['tʏmpəl] (-s, -) *m* pond.
Tumult [tuˈmʊlt] (-(e)s, -e) *m* tumult.
tun [tuːn] *unreg vt* to do; (*legen*) to put ◆ *vi* to act ◆ *vr*: **es tut sich etwas/viel** something/a lot is happening; **jdm etw** ~ to do sth to sb; **etw tut es auch** sth will do; **das tut nichts** that doesn't matter; **das tut nichts zur Sache** that's neither here nor there; **du kannst** ~ **und lassen, was du willst** you can do as you please; **so** ~, **als ob** to act as if; **zu** ~ **haben** (*beschäftigt sein*) to be busy, have things *od* something to do.
Tünche ['tʏnçə] (-, -n) *f* whitewash.
tünchen *vt* to whitewash.
Tunesien [tuˈneːziən] (-s) *nt* Tunisia.
Tunesier(in) (-s, -) *m(f)* Tunisian.
tunesisch *adj* Tunisian.
Tunfisch▲ *m* = **Thunfisch**.
Tunke ['tʊŋkə] (-, -n) *f* sauce.
tunken *vt* to dip, dunk.
tunlichst ['tuːnlɪçst] *adv* if at all possible; ~ **bald** as soon as possible.
Tunnel ['tʊnəl] (-s, -s *od* -) *m* tunnel.
Tunte ['tʊntə] (-, -n) (*pej: umg*) *f* fairy (*pej*).

Tüpfel ['tʏpfəl] (**-s**, -) *m* dot; ~**chen** *nt* (small) dot.

tüpfeln ['tʏpfəln] *vt* to dab.

tupfen ['tʊpfən] *vt* to dab; (*mit Farbe*) to dot; **T~** (**-s**, -) *m* dot, spot.

Tupfer (**-s**, -) *m* swab.

Tür [tyːr] (**-**, **-en**) *f* door; **an die ~ gehen** to answer the door; **zwischen ~ und Angel** in passing; **Weihnachten steht vor der ~** (*fig*) Christmas is just around the corner; **mit der ~ ins Haus fallen** (*umg*) to blurt it *od* things out; ~**angel** *f* (door) hinge.

Turbine [tʊr'biːnə] *f* turbine.

turbulent [tʊrbu'lɛnt] *adj* turbulent.

Türke ['tʏrkə] (**-n**, **-n**) *m* Turk.

Türkei [tʏr'kaɪ] *f*: **die ~** Turkey.

Türkin *f* Turk.

Türkis [tʏr'kiːs] (**-es**, **-e**) *m* turquoise; **t~** *adj* turquoise.

türkisch *adj* Turkish.

Türklinke *f* door handle.

Turm [tʊrm] (**-(e)s**, **ᵘe**) *m* tower; (*Kirch~*) steeple; (*Sprung~*) diving platform; (*SCHACH*) castle, rook.

türmen ['tʏrmən] *vr* to tower up ♦ *vt* to heap up ♦ *vi* (*umg*) to scarper, bolt.

Turmuhr *f* clock (on a tower); (*Kirch~*) church clock.

Turnanzug *m* gym costume.

turnen ['tʊrnən] *vi* to do gymnastic exercises; (*herumklettern*) to climb about; (*Kind*) to romp ♦ *vt* to perform; **T~** (**-s**) *nt* gymnastics *sing*; (*SCH*) physical education, P.E.

Turner(in) (**-s**, -) *m(f)* gymnast.

Turnhalle *f* gym(nasium).

Turnhose *f* gym shorts *pl*.

Turnier [tʊr'niːr] (**-s**, **-e**) *nt* tournament.

Turn- *zW*: ~**lehrer(in)** *m(f)* gym *od* PE teacher; ~**schuh** *m* gym shoe; ~**stunde** *f* gym *od* PE lesson.

Turnus ['tʊrnʊs] (**-**, **-se**) *m* rota; **im ~** in rotation.

Turnverein *m* gymnastics club.

Turnzeug *nt* gym kit.

Türöffner *m* buzzer.

turteln ['tʊrtəln] (*umg*) *vi* to bill and coo; (*fig*) to whisper sweet nothings.

Tusch [tʊʃ] (**-(e)s**, **-e**) *m* (*MUS*) flourish.

Tusche ['tʊʃə] (**-**, **-n**) *f* Indian ink.

tuscheln ['tʊʃəln] *vt*, *vi* to whisper.

Tuschkasten *m* paintbox.

Tussi ['tʊsɪ] (**-**, **-s**) (*umg*) *f* (*Frau, Freundin*) bird (*BRIT*), chick (*US*).

tust [tuːst] *vb siehe* **tun**.

tut [tuːt] *vb siehe* **tun**.

Tüte ['tyːtə] (**-**, **-n**) *f* bag; **in die ~ blasen** (*umg*) to be breathalyzed; **das kommt nicht in die ~!** (*umg*) no way!

tuten ['tuːtən] *vi* (*AUT*) to hoot (*BRIT*), honk (*US*); **von T~ und Blasen keine Ahnung**

haben (*umg*) not to have a clue.

TÜV [tʏf] *m abk* (= *Technischer Überwachungs-Verein*) ≈ MOT (*BRIT*); **durch den ~ kommen** (*AUT*) to pass its test *od* MOT (*Brit*).

TÜV

The **TÜV** (*Technischer Überwachungsverein*) is the organization responsible for checking the safety of machinery, particularly vehicles. Cars over three years old have to be examined every two years for their safety and for their exhaust emissions. The **TÜV** is the German equivalent of the MOT.

TV (-) *nt abk* (= *Television*) TV ♦ *m abk* = **Turnverein**.

Twen [tvɛn] (**-(s)**, **-s**) *m person in his/her twenties*.

Typ [tyːp] (**-s**, **-en**) *m* type.

Type (**-**, **-n**) *f* (*TYP*) type.

Typenrad *nt* (*Drucker*) daisywheel; ~**drucker** *m* daisywheel printer.

Typhus ['tyːfʊs] (-) *m* typhoid (fever).

typisch ['tyːpɪʃ] *adj*: ~ (**für**) typical (of).

Tyrann [ty'ran] (**-en**, **-en**) *m(f)* tyrant.

Tyrannei [tyra'naɪ] *f* tyranny.

Tyrannin *f* tyrant.

tyrannisch *adj* tyrannical.

tyrannisieren [tyrani'ziːrən] *vt* to tyrannize.

tyrrhenisch [ty'reːnɪʃ] *adj* Tyrrhenian; **T~es Meer** Tyrrhenian Sea.

U, u

U, u [uː] *nt* U, u; ~ **wie Ulrich** ≈ U for Uncle.

u. *abk* = **und**.

u. a. *abk* (= *und andere(s)*) and others; (= *unter anderem*) amongst other things.

u. Ä. *abk* (= *und Ähnliche(s)*) and similar.

u. A. w. g. *abk* (= *um Antwort wird gebeten*) R.S.V.P.

U-Bahn ['uːbaːn] *f abk* (= *Untergrundbahn*) underground (*BRIT*), subway (*US*).

übel ['yːbəl] *adj* bad; **jdm ist ~** sb feels sick; **~ gelaunt** bad-tempered, sullen; **jdm eine Bemerkung** *etc* ~ **nehmen** to be offended at sb's remark *etc*; ~ **wollend** malevolent; **Ü~** (**-s**, -) *nt* evil; (*Krankheit*) disease; **zu allem Ü~ ...** to make matters worse ...; **Ü~keit** *f* nausea; **Ü~stand** *m* bad state of affairs; **Ü~täter** *m* wrongdoer.

üben ['yːbən] *vt*, *vi*, *vr* to practise (*BRIT*), practice (*US*); (*Gedächtnis, Muskeln*) to exercise; **Kritik an etw** *dat* ~ to criticize sth.

===================== *SCHLÜSSELWORT*

über ['y:bər] *präp +dat* **1** (*räumlich*) over, above; **zwei Grad** ~ **null** two degrees above zero.
2 (*zeitlich*) over; ~ **der Arbeit einschlafen** to fall asleep over one's work.

♦ *präp +akk* **1** (*räumlich*) over; (*hoch* ~) above; (*quer* ~) across; **er lachte** ~ **das ganze Gesicht** he was beaming all over his face; **Macht** ~ **jdn haben** to have power over sb.
2 (*zeitlich*) over; ~ **Weihnachten** over Christmas; ~ **kurz oder lang** sooner or later.
3 (*auf dem Wege*) via; **nach Köln** ~ **Aachen** to Cologne via Aachen; **ich habe es** ~ **die Auskunft erfahren** I found out from information.
4 (*betreffend*) about; **ein Buch** ~ ... a book about *od* on ...; ~ **jdn/etw lachen** to laugh about *od* at sb/sth; **ein Scheck** ~ **100 Euro** a cheque for 100 euros.
5: Fehler ~ **Fehler** mistake after mistake.

♦ *adv* **1** (*mehr als*) over, more than; **Kinder** ~ **12 Jahren** children over *od* above 12 years of age; **sie liebt ihn** ~ **alles** she loves him more than anything.
2: ~ **und** ~ over and over; **den ganzen Tag/ die ganze Zeit** ~ all day long/all the time; **jdm in etw** *dat* ~ **sein** to be superior to sb in sth.

─────────────────────

überall [y:bər'|al] *adv* everywhere; **~hin** *adv* everywhere.
überaltert [y:bər'|altərt] *adj* obsolete.
Überangebot ['y:bər|angəbo:t] *nt:* ~ **(an** +*dat*) surplus (of).
überanstrengen [y:bər'|anʃtrɛŋən] *vt untr* to overexert ♦ *vr untr* to overexert o.s.
überantworten [y:bər'|antvɔrtən] *vt untr* to hand over, deliver (up).
überarbeiten [y:bər'|arbaitən] *vt untr* to revise, rework ♦ *vr untr* to overwork (o.s.).
überaus ['y:bər|aus] *adv* exceedingly.
überbacken [y:bər'bakən] *unreg vt untr* to put in the oven/under the grill.
Überbau ['y:bərbau] *m* (*Gebäude, Philosophie*) superstructure.
überbeanspruchen ['y:bərbə|anʃpruxən] *vt untr* (*Menschen, Körper, Maschine*) to overtax.
überbelichten ['y:bərbəliçtən] *vt untr* (*PHOT*) to overexpose.
Überbesetzung ['y:bərbəzetsuŋ] *f* overmanning.
überbewerten ['y:bərbəve:rtən] *vt untr* (*fig*) to overrate; (*Äußerungen*) to attach too much importance to.
überbieten [y:bər'bi:tən] *unreg vt untr* to outbid; (*übertreffen*) to surpass; (*Rekord*) to break ♦ *vr untr:* **sich in etw** *dat* (*gegenseitig*) ~ to vie with each other in sth.

Überbleibsel ['y:bərblaipsəl] (**-s, -**) *nt* residue, remainder.
Überblick ['y:bərblik] *m* view; (*fig: Darstellung*) survey, overview; (*Fähigkeit*): ~ (**über** +*akk*) overall view (of), grasp (of); **den** ~ **verlieren** to lose track (of things); **sich** *dat* **einen** ~ **verschaffen** to get a general idea.
überblicken [y:bər'blikən] *vt untr* to survey; (*fig*) to see; (: *Lage etc*) to grasp.
überbringen [y:bər'briŋən] *unreg vt untr* to deliver, hand over.
Überbringer (**-s, -**) *m* bearer.
Überbringung *f* delivery.
überbrücken [y:bər'brykən] *vt untr* to bridge.
Überbrückung *f:* **100 Euro zur** ~ 100 euros to tide me/him over.
Überbrückungskredit *m* bridging loan.
überbuchen ['y:bərbu:xən] *vt* to overbook.
überdauern [y:bər'dauərn] *vt untr* to outlast.
überdenken [y:bər'dɛŋkən] *unreg vt untr* to think over.
überdies [y:bər'di:s] *adv* besides.
überdimensional ['y:bərdimɛnziona:l] *adj* oversize.
Überdosis ['y:bərdo:zis] *f* overdose, OD (*umg*); (*zu große Zumessung*) excessive amount.
überdrehen [y:bər'dre:ən] *vt untr* (*Uhr etc*) to overwind.
überdreht *adj:* ~ **sein** (*fig*) to be hyped up, be overexcited.
Überdruck ['y:bərdruk] *m* (*TECH*) excess pressure.
Überdruss▲ ['y:bərdrus] (**-es**) *m* weariness; **bis zum** ~ ad nauseam.
überdrüssig ['y:bərdrysiç] *adj* +*gen* tired of, sick of.
überdurchschnittlich ['y:bərdurçʃnitliç] *adj* above-average ♦ *adv* exceptionally.
übereifrig ['y:bər|aifriç] *adj* overzealous.
übereignen [y:bər'|aignən] *vt untr:* **jdm etw** ~ (*geh*) to make sth over to sb.
übereilen [y:bər'|ailən] *vt untr* to hurry.
übereilt *adj* (over)hasty.
übereinander [y:bər|ai'nandər] *adv* one upon the other; (*sprechen*) about each other; ~ **schlagen** (*Arme*) to fold; (*Beine*) to cross.
übereinkommen [y:bər'|ainkɔmən] *unreg vi* to agree.
Übereinkunft [y:bər'|ainkunft] (**-, -künfte**) *f* agreement.
übereinstimmen [y:bər'|ainʃtimən] *vi* to agree; (*Angaben, Messwerte etc*) to tally; (*mit Tatsachen*) to fit.
Übereinstimmung *f* agreement.
überempfindlich ['y:bər|ɛmpfintliç] *adj* hypersensitive.
überfahren[1] ['y:bərfa:rən] *unreg vt* to take across ♦ *vi* to cross, go across.
überfahren[2] [y:bər'fa:rən] *unreg vt untr* (*AUT*) to run over; (*fig*) to walk all over.

Überfahrt ['y:bərfa:rt] *f* crossing.
Überfall ['y:bərfal] *m* (*Bank~*, *MIL*) raid; (*auf jdn*) assault.
überfallen [y:bər'falən] *unreg vt untr* to attack; (*Bank*) to raid; (*besuchen*) to drop in on, descend (up)on.
überfällig ['y:bərfɛlıç] *adj* overdue.
Überfallkommando *nt* flying squad.
überfliegen [y:bər'fli:gən] *unreg vt untr* to fly over, overfly; (*Buch*) to skim through.
Überflieger *m* (*fig*) high-flier.
überflügeln [y:bər'fly:gəln] *vt untr* to outdo.
Überfluss▲ ['y:bərflʊs] *m*: ~ (an +*dat*) (super)abundance (of), excess (of); **zu allem** *od* **zum** ~ (*unnötigerweise*) superfluously; (*obendrein*) to crown it all (*umg*); ~**gesellschaft** *f* affluent society.
überflüssig ['y:bərflʏsıç] *adj* superfluous.
überfluten [y:bər'flu:tən] *vt untr* (*lit*) to flood; (*fig*) to flood, inundate.
überfordern [y:bər'fordərn] *vt untr* to demand too much of; (*Kräfte etc*) to overtax.
überfragt [y:bər'fra:kt] *adj*: **da bin ich** ~ there you've got me, you've got me there.
überführen¹ ['y:bərfy:rən] *vt* to transfer; (*Leiche etc*) to transport.
überführen² [y:bər'fy:rən] *vt untr* (*Täter*) to have convicted.
Überführung *f* (*siehe vbs*) transfer; transport; conviction; (*Brücke*) bridge, overpass.
überfüllt [y:bər'fʏlt] *adj* overcrowded; (*Kurs*) oversubscribed.
Übergabe ['y:bərga:bə] *f* handing over; (*MIL*) surrender.
Übergang ['y:bərgaŋ] *m* crossing; (*Wandel*, *Überleitung*) transition.
Übergangs- *zW*: ~**erscheinung** *f* transitory phenomenon; ~**finanzierung** *f* (*FIN*) accommodation; **ü~los** *adj* without a transition; ~**lösung** *f* provisional solution, stopgap; ~**stadium** *nt* state of transition; ~**zeit** *f* transitional period.
übergeben [y:bər'ge:bən] *unreg vt untr* to hand over; (*MIL*) to surrender ♦ *vr untr* to be sick; **dem Verkehr** ~ to open to traffic.
übergehen¹ ['y:bərge:ən] *unreg vi* (*Besitz*) to pass; (*zum Feind etc*) to go over, defect; (*überwechseln*): (**zu etw**) ~ to go on (to sth); ~ **in** +*akk* to turn into.
übergehen² [y:bər'ge:ən] *unreg vt untr* to pass over, omit.
übergeordnet ['y:bərgə|ordnət] *adj* (*Behörde*) higher.
Übergepäck ['y:bərgəpɛk] *nt* excess baggage.
übergeschnappt ['y:bərgəʃnapt] (*umg*) *adj* crazy.
Übergewicht ['y:bərgəvıçt] *nt* excess weight; (*fig*) preponderance.
übergießen [y:bər'gi:sən] *unreg vt untr* to pour

over; (*Braten*) to baste.
überglücklich ['y:bərglʏklıç] *adj* overjoyed.
übergreifen ['y:bərgraıfən] *unreg vi*: ~ (**auf** +*akk*) (*auf Rechte etc*) to encroach (on); (*Feuer*, *Streik*, *Krankheit etc*) to spread (to); **ineinander** ~ to overlap.
übergroß ['y:bərgro:s] *adj* outsize, huge.
Übergröße ['y:bərgrø:sə] *f* oversize.
überhaben ['y:bərha:bən] *unreg* (*umg*) *vt* to be fed up with.
überhand [y:bər'hant] *adv*: ~ **nehmen** to gain the ascendancy.
überhängen ['y:bərhɛŋən] *unreg vi* to overhang.
überhäufen [y:bər'hoʏfən] *vt untr*: **jdn mit Geschenken/Vorwürfen** ~ to heap presents/reproaches on sb.
überhaupt [y:bər'haupt] *adv* at all; (*im Allgemeinen*) in general; (*besonders*) especially; ~ **nicht** not at all; **wer sind Sie** ~**?** who do you think you are?
überheblich [y:bər'he:plıç] *adj* arrogant; **Ü~keit** *f* arrogance.
überhöht [y:bər'hø:t] *adj* (*Forderungen*, *Preise*) exorbitant, excessive.
überholen [y:bər'ho:lən] *vt untr* to overtake; (*TECH*) to overhaul.
Überholspur *f* overtaking lane.
überholt *adj* out-of-date, obsolete.
Überholverbot [y:bər'ho:lfɛrbo:t] *nt* overtaking (*BRIT*) *od* passing ban.
überhören [y:bər'hø:rən] *vt untr* to not hear; (*absichtlich*) to ignore; **das möchte ich überhört haben!** (I'll pretend) I didn't hear that!
Überich▲ ['y:bər|ıç] (**-s**) *nt* superego.
überirdisch ['y:bər|ırdıʃ] *adj* supernatural, unearthly.
überkapitalisieren ['y:bərkapitali'zi:rən] *vt untr* to overcapitalize.
überkochen ['y:bərkɔxən] *vi* to boil over.
überkompensieren ['y:bərkɔmpɛnzi:rən] *vt untr* to overcompensate for.
überladen [y:bər'la:dən] *unreg vt untr* to overload ♦ *adj* (*fig*) cluttered.
überlassen [y:bər'lasən] *unreg vt untr*: **jdm etw** ~ to leave sth to sb ♦ *vr untr*: **sich einer Sache** *dat* ~ to give o.s. over to sth; **das bleibt Ihnen** ~ that's up to you; **jdn sich** *dat* **selbst** ~ to leave sb to his/her own devices.
überlasten [y:bər'lastən] *vt untr* to overload; (*jdn*) to overtax.
überlaufen¹ ['y:bərlaufən] *unreg vi* (*Flüssigkeit*) to flow over; (*zum Feind etc*) to go over, defect.
überlaufen² [y:bər'laufən] *unreg vt untr* (*Schauer etc*) to come over ♦ *adj* overcrowded; ~ **sein** to be inundated *od* besieged.
Überläufer ['y:bərloʏfər] *m* deserter.

überleben [y:bər'le:bən] *vt untr* to survive.
Überlebende(r) *f(m)* survivor.
überlebensgroß *adj* larger-than-life.
überlegen [y:bər'le:gən] *vt untr* to consider
♦ *adj* superior; **ich habe es mir anders** *od*
noch einmal überlegt I've changed my
mind; **Ü~heit** *f* superiority.
Überlegung *f* consideration, deliberation.
überleiten ['y:bərlaɪtən] *vt* (*Abschnitt etc*): **~ in**
+*akk* to link up with.
überlesen [y:bər'le:zən] *unreg vt untr*
(*übersehen*) to overlook, miss.
überliefern [y:bər'li:fərn] *vt untr* to hand down,
transmit.
Überlieferung *f* tradition; **schriftliche ~en**
(written) records.
überlisten [y:bər'lɪstən] *vt untr* to outwit.
überm ['y:bərm] = **über dem**.
Übermacht ['y:bərmaxt] *f* superior force,
superiority.
übermächtig ['y:bərmɛçtɪç] *adj* superior (in
strength); (*Gefühl etc*) overwhelming.
übermannen [y:bər'manən] *vt untr* to
overcome.
Übermaß ['y:bərma:s] *nt*: **~ (an** +*dat*) excess
(of).
übermäßig ['y:bərmɛ:sɪç] *adj* excessive.
Übermensch ['y:bərmɛnʃ] *m* superman;
ü~lich *adj* superhuman.
übermitteln [y:bər'mɪtəln] *vt untr* to convey.
übermorgen ['y:bərmɔrgən] *adv* the day after
tomorrow.
Übermüdung [y:bər'my:duŋ] *f* overtiredness.
Übermut ['y:bərmu:t] *m* exuberance.
übermütig ['y:bərmy:tɪç] *adj* exuberant, high-
spirited; **~ werden** to get overconfident.
übernächste(r, s) ['y:bərnɛ:çstə(r, s)] *adj* next
... but one; (*Woche, Jahr etc*) after next.
übernachten [y:bər'naxtən] *vi untr*: **(bei jdm) ~**
to spend the night (at sb's place).
übernächtigt [y:bər'nɛçtɪçt] *adj* sleepy, tired.
Übernachtung *f*: **~ mit Frühstück** bed and
breakfast.
Übernahme ['y:bərna:mə] **(-, -n)** *f* taking over
od on; (*von Verantwortung*) acceptance;
~angebot *nt* takeover bid.
übernatürlich ['y:bərnaty:rlɪç] *adj*
supernatural.
übernehmen [y:bər'ne:mən] *unreg vt untr* to
take on, accept; (*Amt, Geschäft*) to take over
♦ *vr untr* to take on too much; (*sich
überanstrengen*) to overdo it.
überparteilich ['y:bərpartaɪlɪç] *adj* (*Zeitung*)
independent; (*Amt, Präsident etc*) above
party politics.
überprüfen [y:bər'pry:fən] *vt untr* to examine,
check; (*POL: jdn*) to screen.
Überprüfung *f* examination.
überqueren [y:bər'kve:rən] *vt untr* to cross.
überragen [y:bər'ra:gən] *vt untr* to tower

above; (*fig*) to surpass.
überragend *adj* outstanding; (*Bedeutung*)
paramount.
überraschen [y:bər'raʃən] *vt untr* to surprise.
Überraschung *f* surprise.
überreden [y:bər're:dən] *vt untr* to persuade;
jdn zu etw ~ to talk sb into sth.
Überredungskunst *f* powers *pl* of
persuasion.
überregional ['y:bərregiona:l] *adj* national;
(*Zeitung, Sender*) nationwide.
überreichen [y:bər'raɪçən] *vt untr* to hand over;
(*feierlich*) to present.
überreichlich *adj* (more than) ample.
überreizt [y:bər'raɪtst] *adj* overwrought.
Überreste ['y:bərrɛstə] *pl* remains *pl*,
remnants *pl*.
überrumpeln [y:bər'rumpəln] *vt untr* to take by
surprise; (*umg: überwältigen*) to overpower.
überrunden [y:bər'rundən] *vt untr* (*SPORT*) to
lap.
übers ['y:bərs] = **über das**.
übersättigen [y:bər'zɛtɪgən] *vt untr* to satiate.
Überschall- [y:bərʃal] *in zW* supersonic;
~flugzeug *nt* supersonic jet;
~geschwindigkeit *f* supersonic speed.
überschatten [y:bər'ʃatən] *vt untr* to
overshadow.
überschätzen [y:bər'ʃɛtsən] *vt untr, vr untr* to
overestimate.
überschaubar [y:bər'ʃauba:r] *adj* (*Plan*) easily
comprehensible, clear.
überschäumen ['y:bərʃɔymən] *vi* to froth
over; (*fig*) to bubble over.
überschlafen [y:bər'ʃla:fən] *unreg vt untr*
(*Problem*) to sleep on.
Überschlag ['y:bərʃla:k] *m* (*FIN*) estimate;
(*SPORT*) somersault.
überschlagen[1] [y:bər'ʃla:gən] *unreg vt untr*
(*berechnen*) to estimate; (*auslassen: Seite*) to
omit ♦ *vr untr* to somersault; (*Stimme*) to
crack; (*AVIAT*) to loop the loop ♦ *adj*
lukewarm, tepid.
überschlagen[2] ['y:bərʃla:gən] *unreg vt* (*Beine*)
to cross; (*Arme*) to fold ♦ *vi* (*Hilfsverb sein*:
Wellen) to break; (: *Funken*) to flash over; **in
etw** *akk* **~** (*Stimmung etc*) to turn into sth.
überschnappen ['y:bərʃnapən] *vi* (*Stimme*) to
crack; (*umg: Mensch*) to flip one's lid.
überschneiden [y:bər'ʃnaɪdən] *unreg vr untr* (*lit,
fig*) to intersect.
überschreiben [y:bər'ʃraɪbən] *unreg vt untr* to
provide with a heading; (*COMPUT*) to
overwrite; **jdm etw ~** to transfer *od* make
over sth to sb.
überschreiten [y:bər'ʃraɪtən] *unreg vt untr* to
cross over; (*fig*) to exceed; (*verletzen*) to
transgress.
Überschrift ['y:bərʃrɪft] *f* heading, title.
überschuldet [y:bər'ʃuldət] *adj* heavily in

debt; (*Grundstück*) heavily mortgaged.

Überschuss▲ ['y:bərʃʊs] *m*: ~ **(an** +*dat*) surplus (of).

überschüssig ['y:bərʃʏsɪç] *adj* surplus, excess.

überschütten [y:bər'ʃʏtən] *vt untr*: **jdn/etw mit etw** ~ (*lit*) to pour sth over sb/sth; **jdn mit etw** ~ (*fig*) to shower sb with sth.

Überschwang ['y:bərʃvaŋ] *m* exuberance.

überschwänglich▲ ['y:bərʃvɛŋlɪç] *adj* effusive; **Ü~keit** *f* effusion.

überschwappen ['y:bərʃvapən] *vi* to splash over.

überschwemmen [y:bər'ʃvɛmən] *vt untr* to flood.

Überschwemmung *f* flood.

überschwenglich△ ['y:bərʃvɛŋlɪç] *adj siehe* **überschwänglich**; **Ü~keit**△ *f siehe* **Überschwänglichkeit**.

Übersee ['y:bərze:] *f*: **nach/in** ~ overseas.

überseeisch *adj* overseas.

übersehbar [y:bər'ze:ba:r] *adj* (*fig: Folgen, Zusammenhänge etc*) clear; (*Kosten, Dauer etc*) assessable.

übersehen [y:bər'ze:ən] *unreg vt untr* to look (out) over; (*fig: Folgen*) to see, get an overall view of; (: *nicht beachten*) to overlook.

übersenden [y:bər'zɛndən] *unreg vt untr* to send, forward.

übersetzen¹ [y:bər'zɛtsən] *vt untr, vi untr* to translate.

übersetzen² ['y:bərzɛtsən] *vi* (*Hilfsverb sein*) to cross.

Übersetzer(in) [y:bər'zɛtsər(ɪn)] (**-s, -**) *m(f)* translator.

Übersetzung [y:bər'zɛtsʊŋ] *f* translation; (*TECH*) gear ratio.

Übersicht ['y:bərzɪçt] *f* overall view; (*Darstellung*) survey; **die** ~ **verlieren** to lose track; **ü~lich** *adj* clear; (*Gelände*) open; **~lichkeit** *f* clarity, lucidity.

übersiedeln¹ ['y:bərzi:dəln] *vi* to move.

übersiedeln² [y:bər'zi:dəln] *vi untr* to move.

überspannen [y:bər'ʃpanən] *vt untr* (*zu sehr spannen*) to overstretch; (*überdecken*) to cover.

überspannt *adj* eccentric; (*Idee*) wild, crazy; **Ü~heit** *f* eccentricity.

überspielen [y:bər'ʃpi:lən] *vt untr* (*verbergen*) to cover (up); (*übertragen: Aufnahme*) to transfer.

überspitzt [y:bər'ʃpɪtst] *adj* exaggerated.

überspringen [y:bər'ʃprɪŋən] *unreg vt untr* to jump over; (*fig*) to skip.

übersprudeln ['y:bərʃpru:dəln] *vi* to bubble over.

überstehen¹ [y:bər'ʃte:ən] *unreg vt untr* to overcome, get over; (*Winter etc*) to survive, get through.

überstehen² ['y:bərʃte:ən] *unreg vi* to project.

übersteigen [y:bər'ʃtaɪgən] *unreg vt untr* to climb over; (*fig*) to exceed.

übersteigert [y:bər'ʃtaɪgərt] *adj* excessive.

überstimmen [y:bər'ʃtɪmən] *vt untr* to outvote.

überstrapazieren ['y:bərʃtrapatsi:rən] *vt untr* to wear out ♦ *vr* to wear o.s. out.

überstreifen ['y:bərʃtraɪfən] *vt*: **(sich** *dat*) **etw** ~ to slip sth on.

überströmen¹ [y:bər'ʃtrø:mən] *vt untr*: **von Blut überströmt sein** to be streaming with blood.

überströmen² ['y:bərʃtrø:mən] *vi* (*lit, fig*): ~ **(vor** +*dat*) to overflow (with).

Überstunden ['y:bərʃtʊndən] *pl* overtime *sing*.

überstürzen [y:bər'ʃtʏrtsən] *vt untr* to rush ♦ *vr untr* to follow (one another) in rapid succession.

überstürzt *adj* (over)hasty.

übertariflich ['y:bərtarɪflɪç] *adj*, *adv* above the agreed *od* union rate.

übertölpeln [y:bər'tœlpln] *vt untr* to dupe.

übertönen [y:bər'tø:nən] *vt untr* to drown (out).

Übertrag ['y:bərtra:k] (**-(e)s, -träge**) *m* (*COMM*) amount brought forward.

übertragbar [y:bər'tra:kba:r] *adj* transferable; (*MED*) infectious.

übertragen [y:bər'tra:gən] *unreg vt untr* to transfer; (*RUNDF*) to broadcast; (*anwenden: Methode*) to apply; (*übersetzen*) to render; (*Krankheit*) to transmit ♦ *vr untr* to spread ♦ *adj* figurative; ~ **auf** +*akk* to transfer to; to apply to; **sich** ~ **auf** +*akk* to spread to; **jdm etw** ~ to assign sth to sb; (*Verantwortung etc*) to give sb *od* sth to do.

Übertragung *f* (*siehe vb*) transference; broadcast; rendering; transmission.

übertreffen [y:bər'trɛfən] *unreg vt untr* to surpass.

übertreiben [y:bər'traɪbən] *unreg vt untr* to exaggerate; **man kann es auch** ~ you can overdo things.

Übertreibung *f* exaggeration.

übertreten¹ [y:bər'tre:tən] *unreg vt untr* to cross; (*Gebot etc*) to break.

übertreten² ['y:bərtre:tən] *unreg vi* (*über Linie, Gebiet*) to step (over); (*SPORT*) to overstep; (*zu anderem Glauben*) to be converted; ~ **(in** +*akk*) (*POL*) to go over (to).

Übertretung [y:bər'tre:tʊŋ] *f* violation, transgression.

übertrieben [y:bər'tri:bən] *adj* exaggerated, excessive.

Übertritt ['y:bərtrɪt] *m* (*zu anderem Glauben*) conversion; (*bes zu anderer Partei*) defection.

übertrumpfen [y:bər'trʊmpfən] *vt untr* to outdo; (*KARTEN*) to overtrump.

übertünchen [y:bər'tʏnçən] *vt untr* to whitewash; (*fig*) to cover up, whitewash.

übervölkert [y:bər'fœlkərt] *adj* overpopulated.

übervoll ['y:bərfɔl] *adj* overfull.
übervorteilen [y:bər'fɔrtaɪlən] *vt untr* to dupe, cheat.
überwachen [y:bər'vaxən] *vt untr* to supervise; (*Verdächtigen*) to keep under surveillance.
Überwachung *f* supervision; surveillance.
überwältigen [y:bər'vɛltɪgən] *vt untr* to overpower.
überwältigend *adj* overwhelming.
überwechseln ['y:bərvɛksəln] *vi*: ~ (in +*akk*) to move (to); (*zu Partei etc*): ~ (**zu**) to go over (to).
überweisen [y:bər'vaɪzən] *unreg vt untr* to transfer; (*Patienten*) to refer.
Überweisung *f* transfer; (*von Patient*) referral.
überwerfen[1] ['y:bərvɛrfən] *unreg vt* (*Kleidungsstück*) to put on; (*sehr rasch*) to throw on.
überwerfen[2] [y:bər'vɛrfən] *unreg vr untr*: **sich (mit jdm)** ~ to fall out (with sb).
überwiegen [y:bər'vi:gən] *unreg vi untr* to predominate.
überwiegend *adj* predominant.
überwinden [y:bər'vɪndən] *unreg vt untr* to overcome ♦ *vr untr*: **sich** ~, **etw zu tun** to make an effort to do sth, bring o.s. to do sth.
Überwindung *f* overcoming; (*Selbst~*) effort of will.
überwintern [y:bər'vɪntərn] *vi untr* to (spend the) winter; (*umg: Winterschlaf halten*) to hibernate.
Überwurf ['y:bərvurf] *m* wrap.
Überzahl ['y:bərtsa:l] *f* superior numbers *pl*, superiority; **in der** ~ **sein** to be numerically superior.
überzählig ['y:bərtsɛ:lɪç] *adj* surplus.
überzeugen [y:bər'tsɔygən] *vt untr* to convince.
überzeugend *adj* convincing.
überzeugt *adj attrib* (*Anhänger etc*) dedicated; (*Vegetarier*) strict; (*Christ, Moslem*) devout.
Überzeugung *f* conviction; **zu der** ~ **gelangen, dass** ... to become convinced that ...
Überzeugungskraft *f* power of persuasion.
überziehen[1] ['y:bərtsi:ən] *unreg vt* to put on.
überziehen[2] [y:bər'tsi:ən] *unreg vt untr* to cover; (*Konto*) to overdraw; (*Redezeit etc*) to overrun ♦ *vr untr* (*Himmel*) to cloud over; **ein Bett frisch** ~ to change a bed, change the sheets (on a bed).
Überziehungskredit *m* overdraft.
überzüchten [y:bər'tsyçtən] *vt untr* to overbreed.
Überzug ['y:bərtsu:k] *m* cover; (*Belag*) coating.
üblich ['y:plɪç] *adj* usual; **allgemein** ~ **sein** to

be common practice.
U-Boot ['u:bo:t] *nt* U-boat, submarine.
übrig ['y:brɪç] *adj* remaining; **für jdn etwas** ~ **haben** (*umg*) to be fond of sb; **die Ü~en** the others; **das Ü~e** the rest; **im Ü~en** besides; ~ **bleiben** to remain, be left (over); ~ **lassen** to leave (over); **einiges/viel zu wünschen** ~ **lassen** (*umg*) to leave something/a lot to be desired.
übrigens ['y:brɪgəns] *adv* besides; (*nebenbei bemerkt*) by the way.
Übung ['y:bʊŋ] *f* practice; (*Turn~, Aufgabe etc*) exercise; ~ **macht den Meister** (*Sprichwort*) practice makes perfect.
Übungsarbeit *f* (*SCH*) mock test.
Übungsplatz *m* training ground; (*MIL*) drill ground.
u. d. M. *abk* (= *unter dem Meeresspiegel*) below sea level.
ü. d. M. *abk* (= *über dem Meeresspiegel*) above sea level.
u. E. *abk* (= *unseres Erachtens*) in our opinion.
Ufer ['u:fər] (**-s, -**) *nt* bank; (*Meeres~*) shore; ~**befestigung** *f* embankment.
u~los *adj* endless; (*grenzenlos*) boundless; **ins U~lose gehen** (*Kosten*) to go up and up; (*Debatte etc*) to go on forever.
UFO, Ufo ['u:fo] (**-(s), -s**) *nt abk* (= *unbekanntes Flugobjekt*) UFO, ufo.
Uganda [u'ganda] (**-s**) *nt* Uganda.
Ugander(in) (**-s, -**) *m(f)* Ugandan.
ugandisch *adj* Ugandan.
U-Haft ['u:haft] *f abk* = **Untersuchungshaft**.
Uhr [u:r] (**-, -en**) *f* clock; (*Armband~*) watch; **wie viel** ~ **ist es?** what time is it?; **um wie viel** ~**?** at what time?; **1** ~ 1 o'clock; **20** ~ 8 o'clock, 20.00 (twenty hundred) hours; ~**band** *nt* watchstrap; ~**(en)gehäuse** *nt* clock case; watch case; ~**kette** *f* watch chain; ~**macher** *m* watchmaker; ~**werk** *nt* (*auch fig*) clockwork mechanism; ~**zeiger** *m* hand; ~**zeigersinn** *m*: **im** ~**zeigersinn** clockwise; **entgegen dem** ~**zeigersinn** anticlockwise; ~**zeit** *f* time (of day).
Uhu ['u:hu] (**-s, -s**) *m* eagle owl.
Ukraine [ukra'i:nə] *f* Ukraine.
Ukrainer(in) [ukra'i:nər(ɪn)] (**-s, -**) *m(f)* Ukrainian.
ukrainisch *adj* Ukrainian.
UKW *abk* (= *Ultrakurzwelle*) VHF.
Ulk [ʊlk] (**-s, -e**) *m* lark.
ulkig ['ʊlkɪç] *adj* funny.
Ulme ['ʊlmə] (**-, -n**) *f* elm.
Ulster ['ʊlstər] (**-s**) *nt* Ulster.
Ultimatum [ʊlti'ma:tʊm] (**-s, Ultimaten**) *nt* ultimatum; **jdm ein** ~ **stellen** to give sb an ultimatum.
Ultra- *zW*: ~**kurzwelle** *f* very high frequency; ~**leichtflugzeug** *nt* microlight; ~**schall** *m* (*PHYS*) ultrasound; **u~violett** *adj* ultraviolet.

======================= SCHLÜSSELWORT

um [ʊm] *präp* +*akk* **1** (~ *herum*) (a)round;
~ **Weihnachten** around Christmas; **er schlug**
~ **sich** he hit about him.
2 (*mit Zeitangabe*) at; ~ **acht (Uhr)** at eight
(o'clock).
3 (*mit Größenangabe*) by; **etw** ~ **4 cm kürzen**
to shorten sth by 4 cm; ~ **10% teurer** 10%
more expensive; ~ **vieles besser** better by
far; ~ **nichts besser** not in the least bit
better; *siehe auch* **umso.**
4: der Kampf ~ **den Titel** the battle for the
title; ~ **Geld spielen** to play for money; **es
geht** ~ **das Prinzip** it's a question of
principle; **Stunde** ~ **Stunde** hour after hour;
Auge ~ **Auge** an eye for an eye.
♦ *präp* +*gen*: ~ **... willen** for the sake of ...;
~ **Gottes willen** for goodness *od* (*stärker*)
God's sake.
♦ *konj*: ~ **... zu** (in order) to ...; **zu klug,** ~ **zu**
... too clever to ...; *siehe auch* **umso.**
♦ *adv* **1** (*ungefähr*) about; ~ **(die) 30 Leute**
about *od* around 30 people.
2 (*vorbei*): **die zwei Stunden sind** ~ the two
hours are up.

umadressieren [ʊm|adrɛsiːrən] *vt untr* to
readdress.
umändern [ʊm|ɛndərn] *vt* to alter.
Umänderung *f* alteration.
umarbeiten [ʊm|arbaɪtən] *vt* to remodel;
(*Buch etc*) to revise, rework.
umarmen [ʊm|armən] *vt untr* to embrace.
Umbau [ʊmbaʊ] (-(e)s, -e *od* -ten) *m*
reconstruction, alteration(s *pl*).
umbauen [ʊmbaʊən] *vt* to rebuild,
reconstruct.
umbenennen [ʊmbənɛnən] *unreg vt untr* to
rename.
umbesetzen [ʊmbəzɛtsən] *vt untr* (*THEAT*) to
recast; (*Mannschaft*) to change; (*Posten,
Stelle*) to find someone else for.
umbiegen [ʊmbiːgən] *unreg vt* to bend (over).
umbilden [ʊmbɪldən] *vt* to reorganize; (*POL:
Kabinett*) to reshuffle.
umbinden¹ [ʊmbɪndən] *unreg vt* (*Krawatte etc*)
to put on.
umbinden² [ʊmbɪndən] *unreg vt untr*: **etw mit
etw** ~ to tie sth round sth.
umblättern [ʊmblɛtərn] *vt* to turn over.
umblicken [ʊmblɪkən] *vr* to look around.
umbringen [ʊmbrɪŋən] *unreg vt* to kill.
Umbruch [ʊmbrʊx] *m* radical change; (*TYP*)
make-up (into page).
umbuchen [ʊmbuːxən] *vi* to change one's
reservation *od* flight *etc* ♦ *vt* to change.
umdenken [ʊmdɛŋkən] *unreg vi* to adjust one's
views.
umdisponieren [ʊmdɪsponiːrən] *vi untr* to

change one's plans.
umdrängen [ʊmdrɛŋən] *vt untr* to crowd
round.
umdrehen [ʊmdreːən] *vt* to turn (round);
(*Hals*) to wring ♦ *vr* to turn (round); **jdm den
Arm** ~ to twist sb's arm.
Umdrehung *f* turn; (*PHYS*) revolution,
rotation.
umeinander [ʊm|aɪnandər] *adv* round one
another; (*füreinander*) for one another.
umerziehen [ʊm|ɛrtsiːən] *unreg vt* (*POL: euph*):
jdn (zu etw) ~ to re-educate sb (to become
sth).
umfahren¹ [ʊmfaːrən] *unreg vt* to run over.
umfahren² [ʊmfaːrən] *unreg vt untr* to drive
round; (*die Welt*) to sail round.
umfallen [ʊmfalən] *unreg vi* to fall down *od*
over; (*fig: umg: nachgeben*) to give in.
Umfang [ʊmfaŋ] *m* extent; (*von Buch*) size;
(*Reichweite*) range; (*Fläche*) area; (*MATH*)
circumference; **in großem** ~ on a large
scale; **u~reich** *adj* extensive; (*Buch etc*)
voluminous.
umfassen [ʊmfasən] *vt untr* to embrace; (*umgeben*) to surround; (*enthalten*) to include.
umfassend *adj* comprehensive; (*umfangreich*)
extensive.
Umfeld [ʊmfɛlt] *nt*: **zum** ~ **von etw gehören**
to be associated with sth.
umformatieren [ʊmfɔrmatiːrən] *vt untr*
(*COMPUT*) to reformat.
umformen [ʊmfɔrmən] *vi* to transform.
Umformer (-s, -) *m* (*ELEK*) converter.
umformulieren [ʊmfɔrmuliːrən] *vt untr* to
redraft.
Umfrage [ʊmfraːgə] *f* poll; ~ **halten** to ask
around.
umfüllen [ʊmfʏlən] *vt* to transfer; (*Wein*) to
decant.
umfunktionieren [ʊmfʊŋktsioniːrən] *vt untr* to
convert.
Umgang [ʊmgaŋ] *m* company; (*mit jdm*)
dealings *pl*; (*Behandlung*) dealing.
umgänglich [ʊmgɛŋlɪç] *adj* sociable.
Umgangs- *zW*: **~formen** *pl* manners *pl*;
~sprache *f* colloquial language;
u~sprachlich *adj* colloquial.
umgeben [ʊmgeːbən] *unreg vt untr* to surround.
Umgebung *f* surroundings *pl*; (*Milieu*)
environment; (*Personen*) people in one's
circle; **in der näheren/weiteren** ~ **Münchens**
on the outskirts/in the environs of Munich.
umgehen¹ [ʊmgeːən] *unreg vi* to go (a)round;
im Schlosse ~ to haunt the castle; **mit jdm/
etw** ~ **können** to know how to handle sb/sth;
mit jdm grob *etc* ~ to treat sb roughly *etc*;
mit Geld sparsam ~ to be careful with one's
money.
umgehen² [ʊmgeːən] *unreg vt untr* to bypass;
(*MIL*) to outflank; (*Gesetz, Vorschrift etc*) to

circumvent; (*vermeiden*) to avoid.
umgehend *adj* immediate.
Umgehung *f* (*siehe vb*) bypassing;
outflanking; circumvention; avoidance.
Umgehungsstraße *f* bypass.
umgekehrt ['ʊmgəke:rt] *adj* reverse(d);
(*gegenteilig*) opposite ♦ *adv* the other way
around; **und** ~ and vice versa.
umgestalten ['ʊmgəʃtaltən] *vt untr* to alter;
(*reorganisieren*) to reorganize; (*umordnen*) to
rearrange.
umgewöhnen ['ʊmgəvø:nən] *vr* to readapt.
umgraben ['ʊmgra:bən] *unreg vt* to dig up.
umgruppieren ['ʊmgrupi:rən] *vt untr* to
regroup.
Umhang ['ʊmhaŋ] *m* wrap, cape.
umhängen ['ʊmhɛŋən] *vt* (*Bild*) to hang
somewhere else; **jdm etw** ~ to put sth on sb.
Umhängetasche *f* shoulder bag.
umhauen ['ʊmhauən] *vt* to fell; (*fig*) to bowl
over.
umher [ʊm'he:r] *adv* about, around; ~**gehen**
unreg vi to walk about; ~**irren** *vi* to wander
around; (*Blick, Augen*) to roam about;
~**reisen** *vi* to travel about; ~**schweifen** *vi* to
roam about; ~**ziehen** *unreg vi* to wander from
place to place.
umhinkönnen [ʊm'hɪnkœnən] *unreg vi:* **ich
kann nicht umhin, das zu tun** I can't help
doing it.
umhören ['ʊmhø:rən] *vr* to ask around.
umkämpfen [ʊm'kɛmpfən] *vt untr*
(*Entscheidung*) to dispute; (*Wahlkreis, Sieg*) to
contest.
Umkehr ['ʊmke:r] (-) *f* turning back;
(*Änderung*) change.
umkehren *vi* to turn back; (*fig*) to change
one's ways ♦ *vt* to turn round, reverse;
(*Tasche etc*) to turn inside out; (*Gefäß etc*) to
turn upside down.
umkippen ['ʊmkɪpən] *vt* to tip over ♦ *vi* to
overturn; (*umg: ohnmächtig werden*) to keel
over; (*fig: Meinung ändern*) to change one's
mind.
umklammern [ʊm'klamərn] *vt untr* (*mit
Händen*) to clasp; (*festhalten*) to cling to.
umklappen ['ʊmklapən] *vt* to fold down.
Umkleidekabine ['ʊmklaɪdəkabi:nə] *f*
changing cubicle (*BRIT*), dressing room
(*US*).
Umkleideraum ['ʊmklaɪdəraum] *m* changing
room; (*US, THEAT*) dressing room.
umknicken ['ʊmknɪkən] *vt* (*Ast*) to snap;
(*Papier*) to fold (over) ♦ *vi:* **mit dem Fuß** ~ to
twist one's ankle.
umkommen ['ʊmkɔmən] *unreg vi* to die,
perish; (*Lebensmittel*) to go bad.
Umkreis ['ʊmkraɪs] *m* neighbourhood (*BRIT*),
neighborhood (*US*); **im** ~ **von** within a
radius of.

umkreisen [ʊm'kraɪzən] *vt untr* to circle
(round); (*Satellit*) to orbit.
umkrempeln ['ʊmkrɛmpəln] *vt* to turn up;
(*mehrmals*) to roll up; (*umg: Betrieb*) to shake
up.
umladen ['ʊmla:dən] *unreg vt* to transfer,
reload.
Umlage ['ʊmla:gə] *f* share of the costs.
Umlauf *m* (*Geld*~) circulation; (*von Gestirn*)
revolution; (*Schreiben*) circular; **in**
~ **bringen** to circulate; ~**bahn** *f* orbit.
umlaufen ['ʊmlaufən] *unreg vi* to circulate.
Umlaufkapital *nt* working capital.
Umlaufvermögen *nt* current assets *pl*.
Umlaut ['ʊmlaut] *m* umlaut.
umlegen ['ʊmle:gən] *vt* to put on; (*verlegen*) to
move, shift; (*Kosten*) to share out;
(*umkippen*) to tip over; (*umg: töten*) to bump
off.
umleiten ['ʊmlaɪtən] *vt* to divert.
Umleitung *f* diversion.
umlernen ['ʊmlɛrnən] *vi* to learn something
new; (*fig*) to adjust one's views.
umliegend ['ʊmli:gənt] *adj* surrounding.
ummelden ['ʊmmɛldən] *vt, vr:* **jdn/sich** ~ to
notify (the police of) a change in sb's/one's
address.
Umnachtung [ʊm'naxtʊŋ] *f* mental
derangement.
umorganisieren ['ʊm|ɔrganizi:rən] *vt untr* to
reorganize.
umpflanzen ['ʊmpflantsən] *vt* to transplant.
umquartieren ['ʊmkvarti:rən] *vt untr* to move;
(*Truppen*) to requarter.
umrahmen [ʊm'ra:mən] *vt untr* to frame.
umranden [ʊm'randən] *vt untr* to border, edge.
umräumen ['ʊmrɔymən] *vt* (*anders anordnen*)
to rearrange ♦ *vi* to rearrange things, move
things around.
umrechnen ['ʊmrɛçnən] *vt* to convert.
Umrechnung *f* conversion.
Umrechnungskurs *m* rate of exchange.
umreißen [ʊm'raɪsən] *unreg vt untr* to outline.
umrennen ['ʊmrɛnən] *unreg vt* to (run into
and) knock down.
umringen [ʊm'rɪŋən] *vt untr* to surround.
Umriss▲ ['ʊmrɪs] *m* outline.
umrühren ['ʊmry:rən] *vt, vi* to stir.
umrüsten ['ʊmrystən] *vt* (*TECH*) to adapt;
(*MIL*) to re-equip; ~ **auf** +*akk* to adapt to.
ums [ʊms] = **um das.**
umsatteln ['ʊmzatəln] (*umg*) *vi* to change
one's occupation, switch jobs.
Umsatz ['ʊmzats] *m* turnover; ~**beteiligung** *f*
commission; ~**einbuße** *f* loss of profit;
~**steuer** *f* turnover tax.
umschalten ['ʊmʃaltən] *vt* to switch ♦ *vi* to
push/pull a lever; (*auf anderen Sender*):
~ (**auf** +*akk*) to change over (to); (*AUT*): ~ **in**
+*akk* to change (*BRIT*) *od* shift into; **„wir**

schalten jetzt um nach Hamburg" "and now we go over to Hamburg".
Umschalttaste f shift key.
Umschau f look(ing) round; ~ **halten nach** to look around for.
umschauen ['ʊmʃaʊən] vr to look round.
Umschlag ['ʊmʃlaːk] m cover; (Buch~) jacket, cover; (MED) compress; (Brief~) envelope; (Gütermenge) volume of traffic; (Wechsel) change; (von Hose) turn-up (BRIT), cuff (US).
umschlagen ['ʊmʃlaːgən] unreg vi to change; (NAUT) to capsize ♦ vt to knock over; (Ärmel) to turn up; (Seite) to turn over; (Waren) to transfer.
Umschlag- zW: ~**hafen** m port of transshipment; ~**platz** m (COMM) distribution centre (BRIT) od center (US); ~**seite** f cover page.
umschlingen [ʊm'ʃlɪŋən] unreg vt untr (Pflanze) to twine around; (jdn) to embrace.
umschreiben[1] ['ʊmʃraɪbən] unreg vt (neu ~) to rewrite; (übertragen) to transfer; ~ **auf** +akk to transfer to.
umschreiben[2] [ʊm'ʃraɪbən] unreg vt untr to paraphrase; (abgrenzen) to circumscribe, define.
Umschuldung ['ʊmʃʊldʊŋ] f rescheduling (of debts).
umschulen ['ʊmʃuːlən] vt to retrain; (Kind) to send to another school.
umschwärmen [ʊm'ʃvɛrmən] vt untr to swarm round; (fig) to surround, idolize.
Umschweife ['ʊmʃvaɪfə] pl: **ohne** ~ without beating about the bush, straight out.
umschwenken ['ʊmʃvɛnkən] vi (Kran) to swing out; (fig) to do an about-turn (BRIT) od about-face (US); (Wind) to veer.
Umschwung ['ʊmʃvʊŋ] m (GYMNASTIK) circle; (fig: ins Gegenteil) change (around).
umsegeln [ʊm'zeːgəln] vt untr to sail around; (Erde) to circumnavigate.
umsehen ['ʊmzeːən] unreg vr to look around od about; (suchen): **sich** ~ **(nach)** to look out (for); **ich möchte mich nur mal** ~ (in Geschäft) I'm just looking.
umseitig ['ʊmzaɪtɪç] adv overleaf.
umsetzen ['ʊmzɛtsən] vt (Waren) to turn over ♦ vr (Schüler) to change places; **etw in die Tat** ~ to translate sth into action.
Umsicht ['ʊmzɪçt] f prudence, caution.
umsichtig adj prudent, cautious.
umsiedeln ['ʊmziːdəln] vt to resettle.
Umsiedler(in) (-s, -) m(f) resettler.
umso▲ ['ʊmzo] konj: ~ **besser/schlimmer** so much the better/worse; ~ **mehr, als ...** all the more considering ...
umsonst [ʊm'zɔnst] adv in vain; (gratis) for nothing.
umspringen ['ʊmʃprɪŋən] unreg vi to change; **mit jdm** ~ to treat sb badly.

Umstand ['ʊmʃtant] m circumstance; **Umstände** pl (fig: Schwierigkeiten) fuss sing; **in anderen Umständen sein** to be pregnant; **Umstände machen** to go to a lot of trouble; **den Umständen entsprechend** much as one would expect (under the circumstances); **die näheren Umstände** further details; **unter Umständen** possibly; **mildernde Umstände** (JUR) extenuating circumstances.
umständehalber adv owing to circumstances.
umständlich ['ʊmʃtɛntlɪç] adj (Methode) cumbersome, complicated; (Ausdrucksweise, Erklärung) long-winded; (ungeschickt) ponderous; **etw** ~ **machen** to make heavy weather of (doing) sth.
Umstandskleid nt maternity dress.
Umstandswort nt adverb.
umstehend ['ʊmʃteːənt] adj attrib (umseitig) overleaf; **die U~en** pl the bystanders pl.
Umsteigekarte f transfer ticket.
umsteigen ['ʊmʃtaɪgən] unreg vi (EISENB) to change; (fig: umg): ~ **(auf** +akk) to change over (to), switch (over) (to).
umstellen[1] ['ʊmʃtɛlən] vt (an anderen Ort) to change round, rearrange; (TECH) to convert ♦ vr: **sich** ~ **(auf** +akk) to adapt o.s. (to).
umstellen[2] [ʊm'ʃtɛlən] vt untr to surround.
Umstellung f change; (Umgewöhnung) adjustment; (TECH) conversion.
umstimmen ['ʊmʃtɪmən] vt (MUS) to retune; **jdn** ~ to make sb change his mind.
umstoßen ['ʊmʃtoːsən] unreg vt (lit) to overturn; (Plan etc) to change, upset.
umstritten [ʊm'ʃtrɪtən] adj disputed; (fraglich) controversial.
Umsturz ['ʊmʃtʊrts] m overthrow.
umstürzen ['ʊmʃtʏrtsən] vt (umwerfen) to overturn ♦ vi to collapse, fall down; (Wagen) to overturn.
umstürzlerisch adj revolutionary.
Umtausch ['ʊmtaʊʃ] m exchange; **diese Waren sind vom** ~ **ausgeschlossen** these goods cannot be exchanged.
umtauschen vt to exchange.
Umtriebe ['ʊmtriːbə] pl machinations pl, intrigues pl.
umtun ['ʊmtuːn] unreg vr: **sich nach etw** ~ to look for sth.
umverteilen ['ʊmfɛrtaɪlən] vt untr to redistribute.
umwälzend ['ʊmvɛltsənt] adj (fig) radical; (Veränderungen) sweeping; (Ereignisse) revolutionary.
Umwälzung f (fig) radical change.
umwandeln ['ʊmvandəln] vt to change, convert; (ELEK) to transform.
umwechseln ['ʊmvɛksəln] vt to change.
Umweg ['ʊmveːk] m detour; (fig) roundabout way.

Umwelt ['ʊmvɛlt] *f* environment; **~allergie** *f* environmental allergy; **~auto** (*umg*) *nt* environment-friendly vehicle; **~belastung** *f* environmental pollution; **~bewusstsein▲** *nt* environmental awareness; **u~freundlich** *adj* environment-friendly; **~kriminalität** *f* crimes *pl* against the environment; **~ministerium** *nt* Ministry of the Environment; **u~schädlich** *adj* harmful to the environment; **~schutz** *m* environmental protection; **~schützer** (**-s, -**) *m* environmentalist; **~verschmutzung** *f* pollution (of the environment); **u~verträglich** *adj* not harmful to the environment; **~verträglichkeit** *f* ecofriendliness.

umwenden ['ʊmvɛndən] *unreg vt, vr* to turn (round).

umwerben [ʊm'vɛrbən] *unreg vt untr* to court, woo.

umwerfen ['ʊmvɛrfən] *unreg vt* (*lit*) to upset, overturn; (*Mantel*) to throw on; (*fig: erschüttern*) to upset, throw.

umwerfend (*umg*) *adj* fantastic.

umziehen ['ʊmtsiːən] *unreg vt, vr* to change ♦ *vi* to move.

umzingeln [ʊm'tsɪŋəln] *vt untr* to surround, encircle.

Umzug ['ʊmtsuːk] *m* procession; (*Wohnungs~*) move, removal.

UN *pl abk* (= *United Nations*): **die ~** the UN *sing*.

un- -*zW:* **~abänderlich** *adj* irreversible, unalterable; **~abänderlich feststehen** to be absolutely certain; **~abdingbar** *adj* indispensable, essential; (*Recht*) inalienable; **~abhängig** *adj* independent; **U~abhängigkeit** *f* independence; **~abkömmlich** *adj* indispensable; **zur Zeit ~abkömmlich** not free at the moment; **~ablässig** *adj* incessant, constant; **~absehbar** *adj* immeasurable; (*Folgen*) unforeseeable; (*Kosten*) incalculable; **~absichtlich** *adj* unintentional; **~abwendbar** *adj* inevitable.

unachtsam ['ʊn|axtzaːm] *adj* careless; **U~keit** *f* carelessness.

un- -*zW:* **~anfechtbar** *adj* indisputable; **~angebracht** *adj* uncalled-for; **~angefochten** *adj* unchallenged; (*Testament, Wahlkandidat, Urteil*) uncontested; **~angemeldet** *adj* unannounced; (*Besucher*) unexpected; **~angemessen** *adj* inadequate; **~angenehm** *adj* unpleasant; (*peinlich*) embarrassing; **~angepasst▲** *adj* nonconformist; **U~annehmlichkeit** *f* inconvenience; **Unannehmlichkeiten** *pl* trouble *sing*; **~ansehnlich** *adj* unsightly; **~anständig** *adj* indecent, improper; **U~anständigkeit** *f* indecency, impropriety; **~antastbar** *adj* inviolable, sacrosanct.

unappetitlich ['ʊn|apetiːtlɪç] *adj* unsavoury

(*BRIT*), unsavory (*US*).

Unart ['ʊn|aːrt] *f* bad manners *pl*; (*Angewohnheit*) bad habit.

unartig *adj* naughty, badly behaved.

un- -*zW:* **~aufdringlich** *adj* unobtrusive; (*Parfüm*) discreet; (*Mensch*) unassuming; **~auffällig** *adj* unobtrusive; (*Kleidung*) inconspicuous; **~auffindbar** *adj* not to be found; **~aufgefordert** *adj* unsolicited ♦ *adv* unasked, spontaneously; **~aufgefordert zugesandte Manuskripte** unsolicited manuscripts; **~aufhaltsam** *adj* irresistible; **~aufhörlich** *adj* incessant, continuous; **~aufmerksam** *adj* inattentive; **~aufrichtig** *adj* insincere.

un- -*zW:* **~ausbleiblich** *adj* inevitable, unavoidable; **~ausgeglichen** *adj* volatile; **~ausgegoren** *adj* immature; (*Idee, Plan*) half-baked; **~ausgesetzt** *adj* incessant, constant; **~ausgewogen** *adj* unbalanced; **~aussprechlich** *adj* inexpressible; **~ausstehlich** *adj* intolerable; **~ausweichlich** *adj* inescapable, ineluctable.

unbändig ['ʊnbɛndɪç] *adj* extreme, excessive.

unbarmherzig ['ʊnbarmhɛrtsɪç] *adj* pitiless, merciless.

unbeabsichtigt ['ʊnbə|apzɪçtɪçt] *adj* unintentional.

unbeachtet ['ʊnbə|axtət] *adj* unnoticed; (*Warnung*) ignored.

unbedacht ['ʊnbədaxt] *adj* rash.

unbedarft ['ʊnbədarft] (*umg*) *adj* clueless.

unbedenklich ['ʊnbədɛŋklɪç] *adj* unhesitating; (*Plan*) unobjectionable ♦ *adv* without hesitation.

unbedeutend ['ʊnbədɔʏtənt] *adj* insignificant, unimportant; (*Fehler*) slight.

unbedingt ['ʊnbədɪŋt] *adj* unconditional ♦ *adv* absolutely; **musst du ~ gehen?** do you really have to go?; **nicht ~** not necessarily.

unbefangen ['ʊnbəfaŋən] *adj* impartial, unprejudiced; (*ohne Hemmungen*) uninhibited; **U~heit** *f* impartiality; uninhibitedness.

unbefriedigend ['ʊnbəfriːdɪgənd] *adj* unsatisfactory.

unbefriedigt ['ʊnbəfriːdɪçt] *adj* unsatisfied; (*unzufrieden*) dissatisfied; (*unerfüllt*) unfulfilled.

unbefristet ['ʊnbəfrɪstət] *adj* permanent.

unbefugt ['ʊnbəfuːkt] *adj* unauthorized; **U~en ist der Eintritt verboten** no admittance to unauthorized persons.

unbegabt ['ʊnbəgaːpt] *adj* untalented.

unbegreiflich [ʊnbə'graɪflɪç] *adj* inconceivable.

unbegrenzt ['ʊnbəgrɛntst] *adj* unlimited.

unbegründet ['ʊnbəgründət] *adj* unfounded.

Unbehagen ['ʊnbəhaːgən] *nt* discomfort.

unbehaglich ['ʊnbəhaːklɪç] *adj*

unbeherrscht – uneingeschränkt

uncomfortable; (*Gefühl*) uneasy.

unbeherrscht ['ʊnbəhɛrʃt] *adj* uncontrolled; (*Mensch*) lacking self-control.

unbeholfen ['ʊnbəhɔlfən] *adj* awkward, clumsy; **U~heit** *f* awkwardness, clumsiness.

unbeirrt ['ʊnbə|ɪrt] *adj* imperturbable.

unbekannt ['ʊnbəkant] *adj* unknown; **~e** Größe (*MATH, fig*) unknown quantity.

unbekannterweise *adv*: **grüß(e) sie ~ von mir** give her my regards although I don't know her.

unbekümmert ['ʊnbəkymərt] *adj* unconcerned.

unbelehrbar [ʊnbə'leːrbaːr] *adj* fixed in one's views; (*Rassist etc*) dyed-in-the-wool *attrib*.

unbeliebt ['ʊnbəliːpt] *adj* unpopular; **U~heit** *f* unpopularity.

unbemannt ['ʊnbəmant] *adj* (*Raumflug*) unmanned; (*Flugzeug*) pilotless.

unbemerkt ['ʊnbəmɛrkt] *adj* unnoticed.

unbenommen [ʊnbə'nɔmən] *adj* (*form*): **es bleibt** *od* **ist Ihnen ~, zu ...** you are at liberty to ...

unbequem ['ʊnbəkveːm] *adj* (*Stuhl*) uncomfortable; (*Mensch*) bothersome; (*Regelung*) inconvenient.

unberechenbar [ʊnbə'rɛçənbaːr] *adj* incalculable; (*Mensch, Verhalten*) unpredictable.

unberechtigt ['ʊnbərɛçtɪçt] *adj* unjustified; (*nicht erlaubt*) unauthorized.

unberücksichtigt [ʊnbə'rʏkzɪçtɪçt] *adj*: **etw ~ lassen** not to consider sth.

unberufen [ʊnbə'ruːfən] *interj* touch wood!

unberührt ['ʊnbəryːrt] *adj* untouched; (*Natur*) unspoiled; **sie ist noch ~** she is still a virgin.

unbeschadet [ʊnbə'ʃaːdət] *präp +gen* (*form*) regardless of.

unbescheiden ['ʊnbəʃaɪdən] *adj* presumptuous.

unbescholten ['ʊnbəʃɔltən] *adj* respectable; (*Ruf*) spotless.

unbeschrankt ['ʊnbəʃraŋkt] *adj* (*Bahnübergang*) unguarded.

unbeschränkt [ʊnbə'ʃrɛŋkt] *adj* unlimited.

unbeschreiblich [ʊnbə'ʃraɪplɪç] *adj* indescribable.

unbeschwert ['ʊnbəʃveːrt] *adj* (*sorgenfrei*) carefree; (*Melodien*) light.

unbesehen [ʊnbə'zeːən] *adv* indiscriminately; (*ohne es anzusehen*) without looking at it.

unbesonnen ['ʊnbəzɔnən] *adj* unwise, rash, imprudent.

unbesorgt ['ʊnbəzɔrkt] *adj* unconcerned; **Sie können ganz ~ sein** you can set your mind at rest.

unbespielt ['ʊnbəʃpiːlt] *adj* (*Kassette*) blank.

unbest. *abk* = **unbestimmt**.

unbeständig ['ʊnbəʃtɛndɪç] *adj* (*Mensch*) inconstant; (*Wetter*) unsettled; (*Lage*)

unstable.

unbestechlich [ʊnbə'ʃtɛçlɪç] *adj* incorruptible.

unbestimmt ['ʊnbəʃtɪmt] *adj* indefinite; (*Zukunft*) uncertain; **U~heit** *f* vagueness.

unbestritten ['ʊnbəʃtrɪtən] *adj* undisputed.

unbeteiligt [ʊnbə'taɪlɪçt] *adj* unconcerned; (*uninteressiert*) indifferent.

unbeugsam ['ʊnbɔykzaːm] *adj* stubborn, inflexible; (*Wille*) unbending.

unbewacht ['ʊnbəvaxt] *adj* unguarded, unwatched.

unbewaffnet ['ʊnbəvafnət] *adj* unarmed.

unbeweglich ['ʊnbəveːklɪç] *adj* immovable.

unbewegt *adj* motionless; (*fig: unberührt*) unmoved.

unbewohnt ['ʊnbəvoːnt] *adj* (*Gegend*) uninhabited; (*Haus*) unoccupied.

unbewusst▲ ['ʊnbəvʊst] *adj* unconscious.

unbezahlbar [ʊnbə'tsaːlbaːr] *adj* prohibitively expensive; (*fig*) priceless; (*nützlich*) invaluable.

unbezahlt ['ʊnbətsaːlt] *adj* unpaid.

unblutig ['ʊnbluːtɪç] *adj* bloodless.

unbrauchbar ['ʊnbrauxbaːr] *adj* (*nutzlos*) useless; (*Gerät*) unusable; **U~keit** *f* uselessness.

unbürokratisch ['ʊnbyrokratɪʃ] *adj* without any red tape.

und [ʊnt] *konj* and; **~ so weiter** and so on.

Undank ['ʊndaŋk] *m* ingratitude; **u~bar** *adj* ungrateful; **~barkeit** *f* ingratitude.

undefinierbar [ʊndefi'niːrbaːr] *adj* indefinable.

undenkbar [ʊn'dɛŋkbaːr] *adj* inconceivable.

undeutlich ['ʊndɔytlɪç] *adj* indistinct; (*Schrift*) illegible; (*Ausdrucksweise*) unclear.

undicht ['ʊndɪçt] *adj* leaky.

undifferenziert ['ʊndɪfərɛntsiːrt] *adj* simplistic.

Unding ['ʊndɪŋ] *nt* absurdity.

unduldsam ['ʊnduldsaːm] *adj* intolerant.

un- *zW*: **~durchdringlich** *adj* (*Urwald*) impenetrable; (*Gesicht*) inscrutable; **~durchführbar** *adj* impracticable; **~durchlässig** *adj* impervious; (*wasserundurchlässig*) waterproof, impermeable; **~durchschaubar** *adj* inscrutable; **~durchsichtig** *adj* opaque; (*Motive*) obscure; (*fig: pej: Mensch, Methoden*) devious.

uneben ['ʊn|eːbən] *adj* uneven.

unecht ['ʊn|ɛçt] *adj* artificial, fake; (*pej: Freundschaft, Lächeln*) false.

unehelich ['ʊn|eːəlɪç] *adj* illegitimate.

uneigennützig ['ʊn|aɪɡənnʏtsɪç] *adj* unselfish.

uneinbringlich [ʊn|aɪn'brɪŋlɪç] *adj*: **~e Forderungen** (*COMM*) bad debts *pl*.

uneingeschränkt ['ʊn|aɪŋɡəʃrɛŋkt] *adj* absolute, total; (*Rechte, Handel*) unrestricted; (*Zustimmung*) unqualified.

uneinig ['ʊn|aɪnɪç] *adj* divided; ~ **sein** to disagree; **U~keit** *f* discord, dissension.
uneinnehmbar [ʊn|aɪn'neːmbaːr] *adj* impregnable.
uneins ['ʊn|aɪns] *adj* at variance, at odds.
unempfänglich ['ʊn|ɛmpfɛŋlɪç] *adj*: ~ **(für)** not susceptible (to).
unempfindlich ['ʊn|ɛmpfɪntlɪç] *adj* insensitive; **U~keit** *f* insensitivity.
unendlich [ʊn'|ɛntlɪç] *adj* infinite ♦ *adv* endlessly; (*fig: sehr*) terribly; **U~keit** *f* infinity.
un- *zW:* **~entbehrlich** *adj* indispensable; **~entgeltlich** *adj* free (of charge); **~entschieden** *adj* undecided; **~entschieden enden** (*SPORT*) to end in a draw; **~entschlossen** *adj* undecided; (*entschlusslos*) irresolute; **~entwegt** *adj* unswerving; (*unaufhörlich*) incessant.
un- *zW:* **~erbittlich** *adj* unyielding, inexorable; **~erfahren** *adj* inexperienced; **~erfreulich** *adj* unpleasant; **U~erfreuliches** (*schlechte Nachrichten*) bad news *sing*; (*Übles*) bad things *pl*; **~erfüllt** *adj* unfulfilled; **~ergiebig** *adj* (*Quelle, Thema*) unproductive; (*Ernte, Nachschlagewerk*) poor; **~ergründlich** *adj* unfathomable; **~erheblich** *adj* unimportant; **~erhört** *adj* unheard-of; (*unverschämt*) outrageous; (*Bitte*) unanswered; **~erlässlich ▲** *adj* indispensable; **~erlaubt** *adj* unauthorized; **~erledigt** *adj* unfinished; (*Post*) unanswered; (*Rechnung*) outstanding; (*schwebend*) pending; **~ermesslich ▲** *adj* immeasurable, immense; **~ermüdlich** *adj* indefatigable; **~ersättlich** *adj* insatiable; **~erschlossen** *adj* (*Land*) undeveloped; (*Boden*) unexploited; (*Vorkommen, Markt*) untapped; **~erschöpflich** *adj* inexhaustible; **~erschrocken** *adj* intrepid, courageous; **~erschütterlich** *adj* unshakeable; **~erschwinglich** *adj* (*Preis*) prohibitive; **~ersetzlich** *adj* irreplaceable; **~erträglich** *adj* unbearable; (*Frechheit*) insufferable; **~erwartet** *adj* unexpected; **~erwünscht** *adj* undesirable, unwelcome; **~erzogen** *adj* ill-bred, rude.
unfähig ['ʊnfɛːɪç] *adj* incapable (*attrib*) incompetent; **zu etw ~ sein** to be incapable of sth; **U~keit** *f* inability; incompetence.
unfair ['ʊnfɛːr] *adj* unfair.
Unfall ['ʊnfal] *m* accident; **~flucht** *f* hit-and-run (driving); **~opfer** *nt* casualty; **~station** *f* emergency ward; **~stelle** *f* scene of the accident; **~versicherung** *f* accident insurance; **~wagen** *m car involved in an accident*; (*umg: Rettungswagen*) ambulance.
unfassbar ▲ [ʊn'fasbaːr] *adj* inconceivable.
unfehlbar [ʊn'feːlbaːr] *adj* infallible ♦ *adv* without fail; **U~keit** *f* infallibility.
unfertig ['ʊnfɛrtɪç] *adj* unfinished, incomplete;

(*Mensch*) immature.
unflätig ['ʊnflɛːtɪç] *adj* rude.
unfolgsam ['ʊnfɔlkzaːm] *adj* disobedient.
unförmig ['ʊnfœrmɪç] *adj* (*formlos*) shapeless; (*groß*) cumbersome; (*Füße, Nase*) unshapely.
unfrankiert ['ʊnfraŋkiːrt] *adj* unfranked.
unfrei ['ʊnfraɪ] *adj* not free.
unfreiwillig *adj* involuntary.
unfreundlich ['ʊnfrɔʏntlɪç] *adj* unfriendly; **U~keit** *f* unfriendliness.
Unfriede(n) ['ʊnfriːdə(n)] *m* dissension, strife.
unfruchtbar ['ʊnfrʊxtbaːr] *adj* infertile; (*Gespräche*) fruitless; **U~keit** *f* infertility; fruitlessness.
Unfug ['ʊnfuːk] (**-s**) *m* (*Benehmen*) mischief; (*Unsinn*) nonsense; **grober ~** (*JUR*) gross misconduct.
Ungar(in) ['ʊŋɡar(ɪn)] (**-n, -n**) *m(f)* Hungarian; **u~isch** *adj* Hungarian.
Ungarn (**-s**) *nt* Hungary.
ungeachtet ['ʊnɡə|axtət] *präp +gen* notwithstanding.
ungeahndet ['ʊnɡə|aːndət] *adj* (*JUR*) unpunished.
ungeahnt ['ʊnɡə|aːnt] *adj* unsuspected, undreamt-of.
ungebeten ['ʊnɡəbeːtən] *adj* uninvited.
ungebildet ['ʊnɡəbɪldət] *adj* uncultured; (*ohne Bildung*) uneducated.
ungeboren ['ʊnɡəboːrən] *adj* unborn.
ungebräuchlich ['ʊnɡəbrɔʏçlɪç] *adj* unusual, uncommon.
ungebraucht ['ʊnɡəbraʊxt] *adj* unused.
ungebührlich ['ʊnɡəbyːrlɪç] *adj*: **sich ~ aufregen** to get unduly excited.
ungebunden ['ʊnɡəbʊndən] *adj* (*Buch*) unbound; (*Leben*) (fancy-)free; (*ohne festen Partner*) unattached; (*POL*) independent.
ungedeckt ['ʊnɡədɛkt] *adj* (*schutzlos*) unprotected; (*Scheck*) uncovered.
Ungeduld ['ʊnɡədʊlt] *f* impatience.
ungeduldig ['ʊnɡədʊldɪç] *adj* impatient.
ungeeignet ['ʊnɡə|aɪɡnət] *adj* unsuitable.
ungefähr ['ʊnɡəfɛːr] *adj* rough, approximate ♦ *adv* roughly, approximately; **so ~!** more or less!; **das kommt nicht von ~** that's hardly surprising.
ungefährlich ['ʊnɡəfɛːrlɪç] *adj* not dangerous, harmless.
ungehalten ['ʊnɡəhaltən] *adj* indignant.
ungeheuer ['ʊnɡəhɔʏər] *adj* huge ♦ *adv* (*umg*) enormously; **U~** (**-s, -**) *nt* monster; **~lich** [ʊnɡə'hɔʏərlɪç] *adj* monstrous.
ungehindert ['ʊnɡəhɪndərt] *adj* unimpeded.
ungehobelt ['ʊnɡəhoːbəlt] *adj* (*fig*) uncouth.
ungehörig ['ʊnɡəhøːrɪç] *adj* impertinent, improper; **U~keit** *f* impertinence.
ungehorsam ['ʊnɡəhoːrzaːm] *adj* disobedient; **U~** *m* disobedience.
ungeklärt ['ʊnɡəklɛːrt] *adj* not cleared up;

(*Rätsel*) unsolved; (*Abwasser*) untreated.

ungekürzt ['ʊngəkyrtst] *adj* not shortened; (*Film*) uncut.

ungeladen ['ʊngəlaːdən] *adj* not loaded; (*ELEK*) uncharged; (*Gast*) uninvited.

ungelegen ['ʊngəleːgən] *adj* inconvenient; **komme ich (Ihnen)** ~? is this an inconvenient time for you?

ungelernt ['ʊngəlɛrnt] *adj* unskilled.

ungelogen ['ʊngəloːgən] *adv* really, honestly.

ungemein ['ʊngəmaɪn] *adj* immense.

ungemütlich ['ʊngəmyːtlɪç] *adj* uncomfortable; (*Person*) disagreeable; **er kann ~ werden** he can get nasty.

ungenau ['ʊngənaʊ] *adj* inaccurate.

Ungenauigkeit *f* inaccuracy.

ungeniert ['ʊnʒeniːrt] *adj* free and easy; (*bedenkenlos, taktlos*) uninhibited ♦ *adv* without embarrassment, freely.

ungenießbar ['ʊngəniːsbaːr] *adj* inedible; (*nicht zu trinken*) undrinkable; (*umg*) unbearable.

ungenügend ['ʊngənyːgənt] *adj* insufficient, inadequate; (*SCH*) unsatisfactory.

ungenutzt ['ʊngənʊtst] *adj*: **eine Chance ~ lassen** to miss an opportunity.

ungepflegt ['ʊngəpfleːkt] *adj* (*Garten etc*) untended; (*Person*) unkempt; (*Hände*) neglected.

ungerade ['ʊngəraːdə] *adj* odd, uneven (*US*).

ungerecht ['ʊngəreçt] *adj* unjust.

ungerechtfertigt *adj* unjustified.

Ungerechtigkeit *f* unfairness, injustice.

ungeregelt ['ʊngəreːgəlt] *adj* irregular.

ungereimt ['ʊngəraɪmt] *adj* (*Verse*) unrhymed; (*fig*) inconsistent.

ungern ['ʊngɛrn] *adv* unwillingly, reluctantly.

ungerufen ['ʊngəruːfən] *adj* without being called.

ungeschehen ['ʊngəʃeːən] *adj*: **~ machen** to undo.

Ungeschicklichkeit ['ʊngəʃɪklɪçkaɪt] *f* clumsiness.

ungeschickt *adj* awkward, clumsy.

ungeschliffen ['ʊngəʃlɪfən] *adj* (*Edelstein*) uncut; (*Messer etc*) blunt; (*fig: Benehmen*) uncouth.

ungeschmälert ['ʊngəʃmɛːlɐrt] *adj* undiminished.

ungeschminkt ['ʊngəʃmɪŋkt] *adj* without make-up; (*fig*) unvarnished.

ungeschoren ['ʊngəʃoːrən] *adj*: **jdn ~ lassen** (*umg*) to spare sb; (*ungestraft*) to let sb off.

ungesetzlich ['ʊngəzɛtslɪç] *adj* illegal.

ungestempelt ['ʊngəʃtɛmpəlt] *adj* (*Briefmarke*) unfranked, mint.

ungestört ['ʊngəʃtøːrt] *adj* undisturbed.

ungestraft ['ʊngəʃtraːft] *adv* with impunity.

ungestüm ['ʊngəʃtyːm] *adj* impetuous; **U~** (**-(e)s**) *nt* impetuosity.

ungesund ['ʊngəzʊnt] *adj* unhealthy.

ungetrübt ['ʊngətryːpt] *adj* clear; (*fig*) untroubled; (*Freude*) unalloyed.

Ungetüm ['ʊngətyːm] (**-(e)s, -e**) *nt* monster.

ungeübt ['ʊngəˈyːpt] *adj* unpractised (*BRIT*), unpracticed (*US*); (*Mensch*) out of practice.

ungewiss▲ ['ʊngəvɪs] *adj* uncertain; **U~heit** *f* uncertainty.

ungewöhnlich ['ʊngəvøːnlɪç] *adj* unusual.

ungewohnt ['ʊngəvoːnt] *adj* unusual.

ungewollt ['ʊngəvɔlt] *adj* unintentional.

Ungeziefer ['ʊngətsiːfɐr] (**-s**) *nt* vermin *pl*.

ungezogen ['ʊngətsoːgən] *adj* rude, impertinent; **U~heit** *f* rudeness, impertinence.

ungezwungen ['ʊngətsvʊŋən] *adj* natural, unconstrained.

ungläubig ['ʊnglɔybɪç] *adj* unbelieving; **ein ~er Thomas** a doubting Thomas; **die U~en** the infidel(s *pl*).

unglaublich [ʊn'glaʊplɪç] *adj* incredible.

unglaubwürdig ['ʊnglaʊpvyrdɪç] *adj* untrustworthy, unreliable; (*Geschichte*) improbable; **sich ~ machen** to lose credibility.

ungleich ['ʊnglaɪç] *adj* dissimilar; (*Mittel, Waffen*) unequal ♦ *adv* incomparably; **~artig** *adj* different; **U~behandlung** *f* (*von Frauen, Ausländern*) unequal treatment; **U~heit** *f* dissimilarity; inequality; **~mäßig** *adj* uneven; (*Atemzüge, Gesichtszüge, Puls*) irregular.

Unglück ['ʊnglʏk] *nt* misfortune; (*Pech*) bad luck; (*~sfall*) calamity, disaster; (*Verkehrs~*) accident; **zu allem ~** to make matters worse; **u~lich** *adj* unhappy; (*erfolglos*) unlucky; (*unerfreulich*) unfortunate; **u~licherweise** *adv* unfortunately; **u~selig** *adj* calamitous; (*Person*) unfortunate.

Unglücksfall *m* accident, mishap.

Unglücksrabe (*umg*) *m* unlucky thing.

Ungnade ['ʊngnaːdə] *f*: **bei jdm in ~ fallen** to fall out of favour (*BRIT*) *od* favor (*US*) with sb.

ungültig ['ʊngʏltɪç] *adj* invalid; **etw für ~ erklären** to declare sth null and void; **U~keit** *f* invalidity.

ungünstig ['ʊngʏnstɪç] *adj* unfavourable (*BRIT*), unfavorable (*US*); (*Termin*) inconvenient; (*Augenblick, Wetter*) bad; (*nicht preiswert*) expensive.

ungut ['ʊnguːt] *adj* (*Gefühl*) uneasy; **nichts für ~!** no offence!

unhaltbar ['ʊnhaltbaːr] *adj* untenable.

unhandlich ['ʊnhantlɪç] *adj* unwieldy.

Unheil ['ʊnhaɪl] *nt* evil; (*Unglück*) misfortune; **~ anrichten** to cause mischief; **~ bringend** fatal, fateful.

unheilbar [ʊn'haɪlbaːr] *adj* incurable.

unheilvoll *adj* disastrous.

unheimlich ['ʊnhaɪmlɪç] adj weird, uncanny
♦ adv (umg) tremendously; **das/er ist mir** ~
it/he gives me the creeps (umg).
unhöflich ['ʊnhøːflɪç] adj impolite; **U~keit** f
impoliteness.
unhörbar [ʊn'høːrbaːr] adj silent; (Frequenzen)
inaudible.
unhygienisch ['ʊnhygieːnɪʃ] adj unhygienic.
Uni ['ʊni] (-, -s) (umg) f university.
uni ['yniː] adj self-coloured (BRIT), self-colored
(US).
Uniform [uni'fɔrm] (-, -en) f uniform.
uniformiert [unifɔr'miːrt] adj uniformed.
Unikum ['uːnɪkʊm] (-s, -s od Unika) (umg) nt
real character.
uninteressant ['ʊn|ɪntɛrɛsant] adj
uninteresting.
uninteressiert ['ʊn|ɪntərɛ'siːrt] adj: ~ **(an** +dat)
uninterested (in), not interested (in).
Union [uni'oːn] f union.
Unionsparteien pl (BRD POL) CDU and CSU
parties pl.
universal [univer'zaːl] adj universal.
universell [univer'zɛl] adj universal.
Universität [univerzi'tɛːt] f university; **auf die**
~ **gehen, die** ~ **besuchen** to go to
university.
Universum [uni'vɛrzʊm] (-s) nt universe.
unkenntlich ['ʊnkɛntlɪç] adj unrecognizable;
U~keit f: **bis zur U~keit** beyond recognition.
Unkenntnis ['ʊnkɛntnɪs] f ignorance.
unklar ['ʊnklaːr] adj unclear; **im U~en sein**
über +akk to be in the dark about; **U~heit** f
unclarity; (Unentschiedenheit) uncertainty.
unklug ['ʊnkluːk] adj unwise.
unkompliziert ['ʊnkɔmplitsiːrt] adj
straightforward, uncomplicated.
unkontrolliert ['ʊnkɔntrɔliːrt] adj unchecked.
unkonzentriert ['ʊnkɔntsɛntriːrt] adj lacking
in concentration.
Unkosten ['ʊnkɔstən] pl expense(s pl); **sich in**
~ **stürzen** (umg) to go to a lot of expense.
Unkraut ['ʊnkraʊt] nt weed; weeds pl;
~ **vergeht nicht** (Sprichwort) it would take
more than that to finish me/him etc off;
~**vertilgungsmittel** nt weedkiller.
unlängst ['ʊnlɛŋst] adv not long ago.
unlauter ['ʊnlaʊtər] adj unfair.
unleserlich ['ʊnleːzərlɪç] adj illegible.
unleugbar ['ʊnlɔykbaːr] adj undeniable,
indisputable.
unlogisch ['ʊnloːgɪʃ] adj illogical.
unlösbar [ʊn'løːsbar] adj insoluble.
unlöslich [ʊn'løːslɪç] adj insoluble.
Unlust ['ʊnlʊst] f lack of enthusiasm.
unlustig adj unenthusiastic ♦ adv without
enthusiasm.
unmännlich ['ʊnmɛnlɪç] adj unmanly.
Unmasse ['ʊnmasə] (umg) f load.
unmäßig ['ʊnmɛːsɪç] adj immoderate.

Unmenge ['ʊnmɛŋə] f tremendous number,
vast number.
Unmensch ['ʊnmɛnʃ] m ogre, brute; **u~lich**
adj inhuman, brutal; (ungeheuer) awful.
unmerklich [ʊn'mɛrklɪç] adj imperceptible.
unmissverständlich▲ ['ʊnmɪsfɛrʃtɛntlɪç] adj
unmistakable.
unmittelbar ['ʊnmɪtəlbaːr] adj immediate; ~**er**
Kostenaufwand direct expense.
unmöbliert ['ʊnmøbliːrt] adj unfurnished.
unmöglich ['ʊnmøːklɪç] adj impossible; **ich**
kann es ~ **tun** I can't possibly do it;
~ **aussehen** (umg) to look ridiculous; **U~keit**
f impossibility.
unmoralisch ['ʊnmoraːlɪʃ] adj immoral.
unmotiviert ['ʊnmotiviːrt] adj unmotivated.
unmündig ['ʊnmyndɪç] adj (minderjährig)
underage.
Unmut ['ʊnmuːt] m ill humour (BRIT) od
humor (US).
unnachahmlich ['ʊnnaːx|a:mlɪç] adj
inimitable.
unnachgiebig ['ʊnnaːxgiːbɪç] adj unyielding.
unnahbar [ʊn'naːbaːr] adj unapproachable.
unnatürlich ['ʊnnatyːrlɪç] adj unnatural.
unnormal ['ʊnnɔrmaːl] adj abnormal.
unnötig ['ʊnnøːtɪç] adj unnecessary.
unnötigerweise adv unnecessarily.
unnütz ['ʊnnyts] adj useless.
UNO ['uːno] f abk (= United Nations
Organization): **die** ~ the UN.
unordentlich ['ʊn|ɔrdəntlɪç] adj untidy.
Unordnung ['ʊn|ɔrdnʊŋ] f disorder;
(Durcheinander) mess.
unorganisiert ['ʊn|ɔrganiziːrt] adj
disorganized.
unparteiisch ['ʊnpartaiɪʃ] adj impartial.
Unparteiische(r) f(m) umpire; (FUSSBALL)
referee.
unpassend ['ʊnpasənt] adj inappropriate;
(Zeit) inopportune.
unpässlich▲ ['ʊnpɛslɪç] adj unwell.
unpersönlich ['ʊnpɛrzøːnlɪç] adj impersonal.
unpolitisch ['ʊnpoliːtɪʃ] adj apolitical.
unpraktisch ['ʊnpraktɪʃ] adj impractical,
unpractical.
unproduktiv ['ʊnprodʊktiːf] adj unproductive.
unproportioniert ['ʊnprɔpɔrtsioniːrt] adj out
of proportion.
unpünktlich ['ʊnpyŋktlɪç] adj unpunctual.
unqualifiziert ['ʊnkvalifitsiːrt] adj unqualified;
(Äußerung) incompetent.
unrasiert ['ʊnraziːrt] adj unshaven.
Unrat ['ʊnraːt] (-(e)s) m (geh) refuse; (fig) filth.
unrationell ['ʊnratsionɛl] adj inefficient.
unrecht ['ʊnrɛçt] adj wrong; **das ist mir gar**
nicht so ~ I don't really mind; **U~** nt wrong;
zu U~ wrongly; **nicht zu U~** not without
good reason; **U~ haben, im U~ sein** to be
wrong.

unrechtmäßig *adj* unlawful, illegal.
unredlich ['ʊnreːtlɪç] *adj* dishonest; **U~keit** *f* dishonesty.
unreell ['ʊnreɛl] *adj* unfair; (*unredlich*) dishonest; (*Preis*) unreasonable.
unregelmäßig ['ʊnreːɡəlmɛːsɪç] *adj* irregular; **U~keit** *f* irregularity.
unreif ['ʊnraɪf] *adj* (*Obst*) unripe; (*fig*) immature.
Unreife *f* immaturity.
unrein ['ʊnraɪn] *adj* not clean; (*Ton, Gedanken, Taten*) impure; (*Atem, Haut*) bad.
unrentabel ['ʊnrɛntaːbəl] *adj* unprofitable.
unrichtig ['ʊnrɪçtɪç] *adj* incorrect, wrong.
Unruh ['ʊnruː] (-, -en) *f* (*von Uhr*) balance.
Unruhe (-, -n) *f* unrest; **~herd** *m* trouble spot; **~stifter** *m* troublemaker.
unruhig *adj* restless; (*nervös*) fidgety; (*belebt*) noisy; (*Schlaf*) fitful; (*Zeit etc, Meer*) troubled.
unrühmlich ['ʊnryːmlɪç] *adj* inglorious.
uns [ʊns] *pron akk, dat von* **wir** us; (*reflexiv*) ourselves.
unsachgemäß ['ʊnzaxɡəmɛːs] *adj* improper.
unsachlich ['ʊnzaxlɪç] *adj* not to the point, irrelevant; (*persönlich*) personal.
unsagbar [ʊn'zaːkbaːr] *adj* indescribable.
unsäglich [ʊn'zɛːklɪç] *adj* indescribable.
unsanft ['ʊnzanft] *adj* rough.
unsauber ['ʊnzaʊbər] *adj* (*schmutzig*) dirty; (*fig*) crooked; (: *Klang*) impure.
unschädlich ['ʊnʃɛːtlɪç] *adj* harmless; **jdn/etw ~ machen** to render sb/sth harmless.
unscharf ['ʊnʃarf] *adj* indistinct; (*Bild etc*) out of focus, blurred.
unschätzbar [ʊn'ʃɛtsbaːr] *adj* incalculable; (*Hilfe*) invaluable.
unscheinbar ['ʊnʃaɪnbaːr] *adj* insignificant; (*Aussehen, Haus etc*) unprepossessing.
unschlagbar [ʊn'ʃlaːkbaːr] *adj* invincible.
unschlüssig ['ʊnʃlʏsɪç] *adj* undecided.
unschön ['ʊnʃøːn] *adj* unsightly; (*lit, fig: Szene*) ugly; (*Vorfall*) unpleasant.
Unschuld ['ʊnʃʊlt] *f* innocence.
unschuldig ['ʊnʃʊldɪç] *adj* innocent.
Unschuldsmiene *f* innocent expression.
unschwer ['ʊnʃveːr] *adv* easily, without difficulty.
unselbstständig ['ʊnzɛlpstʃtɛndɪç]▲, **unselbständig** ['ʊnzɛlpʃtɛndɪç] *adj* dependent, over-reliant on others.
unselig ['ʊnzeːlɪç] *adj* unfortunate; (*verhängnisvoll*) ill-fated.
unser ['ʊnzər] *poss pron* our ♦ *pron gen von* **wir** of us.
unsere(r, s) *poss pron* ours; **wir tun das ~ od U~** (*geh*) we are doing our bit.
unsereiner *pron* the likes of us.
unsereins *pron* the likes of us.
unser(er)seits ['ʊnzər(ər)'zaɪts] *adv* on our part.

unseresgleichen *pron* the likes of us.
unserige(r, s) *poss pron*: **der/die/das ~** *od* **U~** ours.
unseriös ['ʊnzeriøːs] *adj* (*unehrlich*) not straight, untrustworthy.
unsertwegen ['ʊnzərt've:gən] *adv* (*für uns*) for our sake; (*wegen uns*) on our account.
unsertwillen ['ʊnzərt'vɪlən] *adv*: **um ~ =** **unsertwegen**.
unsicher ['ʊnzɪçər] *adj* uncertain; (*Mensch*) insecure; **die Gegend ~ machen** (*fig: umg*) to knock about the district; **U~heit** *f* uncertainty; insecurity.
unsichtbar ['ʊnzɪçtbaːr] *adj* invisible; **U~keit** *f* invisibility.
Unsinn ['ʊnzɪn] *m* nonsense.
unsinnig *adj* nonsensical.
Unsitte ['ʊnzɪtə] *f* deplorable habit.
unsittlich ['ʊnzɪtlɪç] *adj* indecent; **U~keit** *f* indecency.
unsolide ['ʊnzoliːdə] *adj* (*Mensch, Leben*) loose; (*Firma*) unreliable.
unsozial ['ʊnzotsiaːl] *adj* (*Verhalten*) antisocial; (*Politik*) unsocial.
unsportlich ['ʊnʃpɔrtlɪç] *adj* not sporty; (*Verhalten*) unsporting.
unsre *etc* ['ʊnzrə] *poss pron* = **unsere** *etc siehe auch* **unser**.
unsrige(r, s) ['ʊnzrɪɡə(r, s)] *poss pron* = **unserige**.
unsterblich ['ʊnʃtɛrplɪç] *adj* immortal; **U~keit** *f* immortality.
unstet ['ʊnʃteːt] *adj* (*Mensch*) restless; (*wankelmütig*) changeable; (*Leben*) unsettled.
Unstimmigkeit ['ʊnʃtɪmɪçkaɪt] *f* inconsistency; (*Streit*) disagreement.
Unsumme ['ʊnzʊmə] *f* vast sum.
unsympathisch ['ʊnzympaːtɪʃ] *adj* unpleasant; **er ist mir ~** I don't like him.
untad(e)lig ['ʊntaːd(ə)lɪç] *adj* impeccable; (*Mensch*) beyond reproach.
Untat ['ʊntaːt] *f* atrocity.
untätig ['ʊntɛːtɪç] *adj* idle.
untauglich ['ʊntaʊklɪç] *adj* unsuitable; (*MIL*) unfit; **U~keit** *f* unsuitability; unfitness.
unteilbar [ʊn'taɪlbaːr] *adj* indivisible.
unten ['ʊntən] *adv* below; (*im Haus*) downstairs; (*an der Treppe etc*) at the bottom; **~ genannt** undermentioned; **siehe ~** see below; **nach ~** down; **~ am Berg etc** at the bottom of the mountain *etc*; **er ist bei mir ~ durch** (*umg*) I'm through with him; **~an** *adv* (*am unteren Ende*) at the far end; (*lit, fig*) at the bottom.

══════════════ *SCHLÜSSELWORT*

unter ['ʊntər] *präp +dat* **1** (*räumlich*) under; (*drunter*) underneath.
2 (*zwischen*) among(st); **sie waren ~ sich** they were by themselves; **einer ~ ihnen** one

of them; ~ **anderem** among other things;
~ **der Hand** secretly; (*verkaufen*) privately
♦ **präp** +*akk* under, below.
♦ *adv* (*weniger als*) under; **Mädchen ~ 18
Jahren** girls under *od* less than 18 (years of
age).

Unter- *zW:* ~**abteilung** *f* subdivision; ~**arm** *m*
forearm; **u~belegt** *adj* (*Kurs*) under-
subscribed; (*Hotel etc*) not full.
unterbelichten ['ʊntərbəlɪçtən] *vt untr* (*PHOT*)
to underexpose.
Unterbeschäftigung ['ʊntərbəʃɛftɪɡʊŋ] *f*
underemployment.
unterbesetzt ['ʊntərbəzɛtst] *adj* understaffed.
Unterbewusstsein▲ ['ʊntərbəvʊstzaɪn] *nt*
subconscious.
unterbezahlt ['ʊntərbətsaːlt] *adj* underpaid.
unterbieten [ʊntər'biːtən] *unreg vt untr* (*COMM*)
to undercut; (*fig*) to surpass.
unterbinden [ʊntər'bɪndən] *unreg vt untr* to
stop, call a halt to.
unterbleiben [ʊntər'blaɪbən] *unreg vi untr*
(*aufhören*) to stop; (*versäumt werden*) to be
omitted.
Unterbodenschutz [ʊntər'boːdənʃʊts] *m*
(*AUT*) underseal.
unterbrechen [ʊntər'breçən] *unreg vt untr* to
interrupt.
Unterbrechung *f* interruption.
unterbreiten [ʊntər'braɪtən] *vt untr* (*Plan*) to
present.
unterbringen ['ʊntərbrɪŋən] *unreg vt* (*in Koffer*)
to stow; (*in Zeitung*) to place; (*Person: in Hotel
etc*) to accommodate, put up; (: *beruflich*):
~ **(bei)** to fix up (with).
unterbuttern ['ʊntərbʊtərn] (*umg*) *vt*
(*zuschießen*) to throw in; (*unterdrücken*) to
ride roughshod over.
unterdessen [ʊntər'dɛsən] *adv* meanwhile.
Unterdruck ['ʊntərdrʊk] *m* (*TECH*) below
atmospheric pressure.
unterdrücken [ʊntər'drykən] *vt untr* to
suppress; (*Leute*) to oppress.
untere(r, s) ['ʊntərə(r, s)] *adj* lower.
untereinander [ʊntər|aɪ'nandər] *adv*
(*gegenseitig*) each other; (*miteinander*)
among themselves *etc*.
unterentwickelt ['ʊntər|ɛntvɪkəlt] *adj*
underdeveloped.
unterernährt ['ʊntər|ɛrnɛːrt] *adj*
undernourished.
Unterernährung *f* malnutrition.
Unterfangen [ʊntər'faŋən] *nt* undertaking.
Unterführung [ʊntər|fyːrʊŋ] *f* subway,
underpass.
Untergang ['ʊntərɡaŋ] *m* (down)fall, decline;
(*NAUT*) sinking; (*von Gestirn*) setting; **dem
~ geweiht sein** to be doomed.
untergeben [ʊntər'ɡeːbən] *adj* subordinate.

Untergebene(r) *f(m)* subordinate.
untergehen ['ʊntərɡeːən] *unreg vi* to go down;
(*Sonne*) to set, go down; (*Staat*) to fall; (*Volk*)
to perish; (*Welt*) to come to an end; (*im
Lärm*) to be drowned.
untergeordnet ['ʊntərɡə|ɔrdnət] *adj* (*Dienst-
stelle*) subordinate; (*Bedeutung*) secondary.
Untergeschoss▲ ['ʊntərɡəʃɔs] *nt* basement.
Untergewicht ['ʊntərɡəvɪçt] *nt*: **(10 Kilo)
~ haben** to be (10 kilos) underweight.
untergliedern [ʊntər'ɡliːdərn] *vt untr* to
subdivide.
untergraben [ʊntər'ɡraːbən] *unreg vt untr* to
undermine.
Untergrund ['ʊntərɡrʊnt] *m* foundation; (*POL*)
underground; ~**bahn** *f* underground (*BRIT*),
subway (*US*); ~**bewegung** *f* underground
(movement).
unterhaken ['ʊntərhaːkən] *vr*: **sich bei jdm ~**
to link arms with sb.
unterhalb ['ʊntərhalp] *präp* +*gen* below ♦ *adv*
below; ~ **von** below.
Unterhalt ['ʊntərhalt] *m* maintenance; **seinen
~ verdienen** to earn one's living.
unterhalten [ʊntər'haltən] *unreg vt untr* to
maintain; (*belustigen*) to entertain;
(*versorgen*) to support; (*Geschäft, Kfz*) to run;
(*Konto*) to have ♦ *vr untr* to talk; (*sich
belustigen*) to enjoy o.s.
unterhaltend, unterhaltsam
[ʊntər'haltzaːm] *adj* entertaining.
Unterhaltskosten *pl* maintenance costs *pl*.
Unterhaltszahlung *f* maintenance payment.
Unterhaltung *f* maintenance; (*Belustigung*)
entertainment, amusement; (*Gespräch*) talk.
Unterhaltungskosten *pl* running costs *pl*.
Unterhaltungsmusik *f* light music.
Unterhändler ['ʊntərhɛntlər] *m* negotiator.
Unterhaus ['ʊntərhaʊs] *nt* House of Commons
(*BRIT*), House of Representatives (*US*),
Lower House.
Unterhemd ['ʊntərhɛmt] *nt* vest (*BRIT*),
undershirt (*US*).
unterhöhlen [ʊntər'høːlən] *vt untr* (*lit, fig*) to
undermine.
Unterholz ['ʊntərhɔlts] *nt* undergrowth.
Unterhose ['ʊntərhoːzə] *f* underpants *pl*.
unterirdisch ['ʊntər|ɪrdɪʃ] *adj* underground.
unterjubeln ['ʊntərjuːbəln] (*umg*) *vt*: **jdm etw
~** to palm sth off on sb.
unterkapitalisiert [ʊntərkapitali'ziːrt] *adj*
undercapitalized.
unterkellern [ʊntər'kɛlərn] *vt untr* to build with
a cellar.
Unterkiefer ['ʊntərkiːfər] *m* lower jaw.
unterkommen ['ʊntərkɔmən] *unreg vi* to find
shelter; (*Stelle finden*) to find work; **das ist
mir noch nie untergekommen** I've never
met with that; **bei jdm ~** to stay at sb's
(place).

unterkriegen ['ʊntərkri:gən] (*umg*) *vt*: **sich nicht ~ lassen** not to let things get one down.

unterkühlt [ʊntər'ky:lt] *adj* (*Körper*) affected by hypothermia; (*fig: Mensch, Atmosphäre*) cool.

Unterkunft ['ʊntərkʊnft] (-, -künfte) *f* accommodation (*BRIT*), accommodations *pl* (*US*); ~ **und Verpflegung** board and lodging.

Unterlage ['ʊntərla:gə] *f* foundation; (*Beleg*) document; (*Schreib~ etc*) pad.

unterlassen [ʊntər'lasən] *unreg vt untr* (*versäumen*) to fail to do; (*sich enthalten*) to refrain from.

unterlaufen [ʊntər'laʊfən] *unreg vi untr* to happen ♦ *adj*: **mit Blut ~** suffused with blood; (*Augen*) bloodshot; **mir ist ein Fehler ~** I made a mistake.

unterlegen¹ ['ʊntərle:gən] *vt* to lay *od* put under.

unterlegen² [ʊntər'le:gən] *adj* inferior; (*besiegt*) defeated.

Unterleib ['ʊntərlaɪp] *m* abdomen.

unterliegen [ʊntər'li:gən] *unreg vi untr +dat* to be defeated *od* overcome (by); (*unterworfen sein*) to be subject (to).

Unterlippe ['ʊntərlɪpə] *f* bottom *od* lower lip.

unterm = unter dem.

untermalen [ʊntər'ma:lən] *vt untr* (*mit Musik*) to provide with background music.

Untermalung *f*: **musikalische ~** background music.

untermauern [ʊntər'maʊərn] *vt untr* (*Gebäude, fig*) to underpin.

Untermiete ['ʊntərmi:tə] *f* subtenancy; **bei jdm zur ~ wohnen** to rent a room from sb.

Untermieter(in) *m(f)* lodger.

untern = unter den.

unternehmen [ʊntər'ne:mən] *unreg vt untr* to do; (*durchführen*) to undertake; (*Versuch, Reise*) to make; **U~** (-s, -) *nt* undertaking, enterprise (*auch COMM*); (*Firma*) business.

unternehmend *adj* enterprising, daring.

Unternehmensberater *m* management consultant.

Unternehmensplanung *f* corporate planning, management planning.

Unternehmer(in) [ʊntər'ne:mər(ɪn)] (-s, -) *m(f)* (business) employer; (*alten Stils*) entrepreneur; ~**verband** *m* employers' association.

Unternehmungsgeist *m* spirit of enterprise.

unternehmungslustig *adj* enterprising.

Unteroffizier ['ʊntərɔfɪtsi:r] *m* noncommissioned officer, NCO.

unterordnen ['ʊntər|ɔrdnən] *vt*: **~ (+dat)** to subordinate (to).

Unterordnung *f* subordination.

Unterprima ['ʊntərpri:ma] *f* (*früher*) eighth year of German secondary school.

Unterprogramm ['ʊntərprogram] *nt* (*COMPUT*) subroutine.

Unterredung [ʊntər're:dʊŋ] *f* discussion, talk.

Unterricht ['ʊntərrɪçt] (-(e)s) *m* teaching; (*Stunden*) lessons *pl*; **jdm ~ (in etw** *dat*) **geben** to teach sb (sth).

unterrichten [ʊntər'rɪçtən] *vt untr* to instruct; (*SCH*) to teach ♦ *vr untr*: **sich ~ (über** +*akk*) to inform o.s. (about), obtain information (about).

Unterrichts- *zW*: ~**gegenstand** *m* topic, subject; ~**methode** *f* teaching method; ~**stoff** *m* teaching material; ~**stunde** *f* lesson; ~**zwecke** *pl*: **zu** ~**zwecken** for teaching purposes.

Unterrock ['ʊntərrɔk] *m* petticoat, slip.

unters = unter das.

untersagen [ʊntər'za:gən] *vt untr* to forbid; **jdm etw ~** to forbid sb to do sth.

Untersatz ['ʊntərzats] *m* mat; (*für Blumentöpfe etc*) base.

unterschätzen [ʊntər'ʃɛtsən] *vt untr* to underestimate.

unterscheiden [ʊntər'ʃaɪdən] *unreg vt untr* to distinguish ♦ *vr untr* to differ.

Unterscheidung *f* (*Unterschied*) distinction; (*Unterscheiden*) differentiation.

Unterschenkel ['ʊntərʃɛŋkəl] *m* lower leg.

Unterschicht ['ʊntərʃɪçt] *f* lower class.

unterschieben [ʊntər'ʃi:bən] *unreg vt* (*fig*): **jdm etw ~** to foist sth on sb.

Unterschied ['ʊntərʃi:t] (-(e)s, -e) *m* difference, distinction; **im ~ zu** as distinct from; **u~lich** *adj* varying, differing; (*diskriminierend*) discriminatory.

unterschiedslos *adv* indiscriminately.

unterschlagen [ʊntər'ʃlagən] *unreg vt untr* to embezzle; (*verheimlichen*) to suppress.

Unterschlagung *f* embezzlement; (*von Briefen, Beweis*) withholding.

Unterschlupf ['ʊntərʃlʊpf] (-(e)s, -schlüpfe) *m* refuge.

unterschlüpfen ['ʊntərʃlʏpfən] (*umg*) *vi* to take cover *od* shelter; (*Versteck finden*): (**bei jdm**) **~** to hide out (at sb's) (*umg*).

unterschreiben [ʊntər'ʃraɪbən] *unreg vt untr* to sign.

Unterschrift ['ʊntərʃrɪft] *f* signature; (*Bild~*) caption.

unterschwellig ['ʊntərʃvɛlɪç] *adj* subliminal.

Unterseeboot ['ʊntərze:bo:t] *nt* submarine.

Unterseite ['ʊntərzaɪtə] *f* underside.

Untersekunda ['ʊntərzekunda] *f* (*früher*) sixth year of German secondary school.

Untersetzer ['ʊntərzɛtsər] *m* tablemat; (*für Gläser*) coaster.

untersetzt [ʊntər'zɛtst] *adj* stocky.

unterste(r, s) ['ʊntərstə(r, s)] *adj* lowest, bottom.

unterstehen[1] [ʊntər'ʃteːən] *unreg vi untr +dat* to be under ♦ *vr untr* to dare.

unterstehen[2] ['ʊntərʃteːən] *unreg vi* to shelter.

unterstellen[1] [ʊntər'ʃtɛlən] *vt untr* to subordinate; (*fig*) to impute; **jdm/etw unterstellt sein** to be under sb/sth; (*in Firma*) to report to sb/sth.

unterstellen[2] ['ʊntərʃtɛlən] *vt* (*Auto*) to garage, park ♦ *vr* to take shelter.

Unterstellung *f* (*falsche Behauptung*) misrepresentation; (*Andeutung*) insinuation.

unterstreichen [ʊntər'ʃtraɪçən] *unreg vt untr* (*lit, fig*) to underline.

Unterstufe ['ʊntərʃtuːfə] *f* lower grade.

unterstützen [ʊntər'ʃtʏtsən] *vt untr* to support.

Unterstützung *f* support, assistance.

untersuchen [ʊntər'zuːxən] *vt untr* (*MED*) to examine; (*Polizei*) to investigate; **sich ärztlich ~ lassen** to have a medical (*BRIT*) *od* physical (*US*) (examination), have a check-up.

Untersuchung *f* examination; investigation, inquiry.

Untersuchungs- *zW:* **~ausschuss**▲ *m* committee of inquiry; **~ergebnis** *nt* (*JUR*) findings *pl*; (*MED*) result of an examination; **~haft** *f* custody; **in ~haft sein** to be remanded in custody; **~richter** *m* examining magistrate.

Untertagebau [ʊntər'taːgəbau] *m* underground mining.

Untertan ['ʊntərtaːn] (**-s, -en**) *m* subject.

untertänig ['ʊntərtɛːnɪç] *adj* submissive, humble.

Untertasse ['ʊntərtasə] *f* saucer.

untertauchen ['ʊntərtauxən] *vi* to dive; (*fig*) to disappear, go underground.

Unterteil ['ʊntərtail] *nt od m* lower part, bottom.

unterteilen [ʊntər'tailən] *vt untr* to divide up.

Untertertia ['ʊntərtɛrtia] *f* (*früher*) fourth year of German secondary school.

Untertitel ['ʊntərtiːtəl] *m* subtitle; (*für Bild*) caption.

unterwandern [ʊntər'vandərn] *vt untr* to infiltrate.

Unterwäsche ['ʊntərvɛʃə] *f* underwear.

unterwegs [ʊntər'veːks] *adv* on the way; (*auf Reisen*) away.

unterweisen [ʊntər'vaizən] *unreg vt untr* to instruct.

Unterwelt ['ʊntərvɛlt] *f* (*lit, fig*) underworld.

unterwerfen [ʊntər'vɛrfən] *unreg vt untr* to subject; (*Volk*) to subjugate ♦ *vr untr* to submit.

unterwürfig [ʊntər'vʏrfɪç] *adj* obsequious.

unterzeichnen [ʊntər'tsaiçnən] *vt untr* to sign.

Unterzeichner *m* signatory.

unterziehen [ʊntər'tsiːən] *unreg vt untr +dat* to subject ♦ *vr untr +dat* to undergo; (*einer Prüfung*) to take.

Untiefe ['ʊntiːfə] *f* shallow.

Untier ['ʊntiːr] *nt* monster.

untragbar [ʊn'traːkbaːr] *adj* intolerable, unbearable.

untreu ['ʊntrɔy] *adj* unfaithful; **sich** *dat* **selbst ~ werden** to be untrue to o.s.

Untreue *f* unfaithfulness.

untröstlich [ʊn'trøːstlɪç] *adj* inconsolable.

Untugend ['ʊntuːgənt] *f* vice; (*Angewohnheit*) bad habit.

un- *zW:* **~überbrückbar** *adj* (*fig: Gegensätze etc*) irreconcilable; (*Kluft*) unbridgeable; **~überlegt** *adj* ill-considered ♦ *adv* without thinking; **~übersehbar** *adj* (*Schaden etc*) incalculable; (*Menge*) vast, immense; (*auffällig: Fehler etc*) obvious; **~übersichtlich** *adj* (*Gelände*) broken; (*Kurve*) blind; (*System, Plan*) confused; **~übertroffen** *adj* unsurpassed.

un- *zW:* **~umgänglich** *adj* indispensable, vital; **~umstößlich** *adj* (*Tatsache*) incontrovertible; (*Entschluss*) irrevocable; **~umstritten** *adj* undisputed; **~umwunden** [-ʊm'vʊndən] *adj* candid ♦ *adv* straight out.

ununterbrochen ['ʊn|ʊntərbrɔxən] *adj* uninterrupted.

un- *zW:* **~veränderlich** *adj* unchangeable; **~verantwortlich** *adj* irresponsible; (*~entschuldbar*) inexcusable; **~verarbeitet** *adj* (*lit, fig*) raw; **~veräußerlich** [-fɛr'ɔysərlɪç] *adj* inalienable; (*Besitz*) unmarketable; **~verbesserlich** *adj* incorrigible; **~verbindlich** *adj* not binding; (*Antwort*) curt ♦ *adv* (*COMM*) without obligation; **~verbleit** [-fɛrblait] *adj* (*Benzin*) unleaded; **~verblümt** [-fɛr'blyːmt] *adj* plain, blunt ♦ *adv* plainly, bluntly; **~verdaulich** *adj* indigestible; **~verdorben** *adj* unspoilt; **~verdrossen** *adj* undeterred; (*~ermüdlich*) untiring; **~vereinbar** *adj* incompatible; **~verfälscht** [-fɛrfɛlʃt] *adj* (*auch fig*) unadulterated; (*Dialekt*) pure; (*Natürlichkeit*) unaffected; **~verfänglich** *adj* harmless; **~verfroren** *adj* impudent; **~vergänglich** *adj* immortal; (*Eindruck, Erinnerung*) everlasting; **~vergesslich**▲ *adj* unforgettable; **~vergleichlich** *adj* unique, incomparable; **~verhältnismäßig** *adv* disproportionately; (*übermäßig*) excessively; **~verheiratet** *adj* unmarried; **~verhofft** *adj* unexpected; **~verhohlen** [-fɛrhoːlən] *adj* open, unconcealed; **~verkäuflich** *adj*: "**~verkäuflich**" "not for sale"; **~verkennbar** *adj* unmistakable; **~verletzlich** *adj* (*fig: Rechte*) inviolable; (*lit*) invulnerable; **~verletzt** *adj* uninjured; **~vermeidlich** *adj* unavoidable; **~vermittelt** *adj* (*plötzlich*) sudden, unexpected; **U~vermögen** *nt* inability; **~vermutet** *adj*

unexpected; ~**vernünftig** *adj* foolish;
~**verrichtet** *adj*: ~**verrichteter Dinge** empty-handed; ~**verschämt** *adj* impudent;
U~**verschämtheit** *f* impudence, insolence;
~**verschuldet** *adj* occurring through no fault of one's own; ~**versehens** *adv* all of a sudden; ~**versehrt** [-fɛrzeːrt] *adj* uninjured;
~**versöhnlich** *adj* irreconcilable; **U**~**verstand**
m lack of judgement; (*Torheit*) folly;
~**verständlich** *adj* unintelligible; ~**versucht**
adj: **nichts** ~**versucht lassen** to try everything; ~**verträglich** *adj* quarrelsome;
(*Meinungen, MED*) incompatible;
~**verwechselbar** *adj* unmistakable,
distinctive; ~**verwüstlich** *adj* indestructible;
(*Mensch*) irrepressible; ~**verzeihlich** *adj* unpardonable; ~**verzinslich** *adj* interest-free;
~**verzüglich** [-fɛr'tsyːklɪç] *adj* immediate;
~**vollendet** *adj* unfinished; ~**vollkommen** *adj* imperfect; ~**vollständig** *adj* incomplete;
~**vorbereitet** *adj* unprepared;
~**voreingenommen** *adj* unbiased;
~**vorhergesehen** *adj* unforeseen; ~**vorsichtig**
adj careless, imprudent; ~**vorstellbar** *adj* inconceivable; ~**vorteilhaft** *adj* disadvantageous.
unwahr ['ʊnvaːr] *adj* untrue; ~**haftig** *adj* untruthful; **U**~**heit** *f* untruth; **die U**~**heit sagen** not to tell the truth; ~**scheinlich** *adj* improbable, unlikely ♦ *adv* (*umg*) incredibly;
U~**scheinlichkeit** *f* improbability,
unlikelihood.
unwegsam ['ʊnveːkzaːm] *adj* (*Gelände etc*) rough.
unweigerlich [ʊn'vaɪɡərlɪç] *adj* unquestioning ♦ *adv* without fail.
unweit ['ʊnvaɪt] *präp +gen* not far from ♦ *adv* not far.
Unwesen ['ʊnveːzən] *nt* nuisance; (*Unfug*) mischief; **sein** ~ **treiben** to wreak havoc;
(*Mörder etc*) to be at large.
unwesentlich *adj* inessential, unimportant;
~ **besser** marginally better.
Unwetter ['ʊnvetər] *nt* thunderstorm.
unwichtig ['ʊnvɪçtɪç] *adj* unimportant.
un- *zW*: ~**widerlegbar** *adj* irrefutable;
~**widerruflich** *adj* irrevocable;
~**widerstehlich** [-viːdər'ʃteːlɪç] *adj* irresistible.
unwiederbringlich [ʊnviːdər'brɪŋlɪç] *adj* (*geh*) irretrievable.
Unwille(n) ['ʊnvɪlə(n)] *m* indignation.
unwillig *adj* indignant; (*widerwillig*) reluctant.
unwillkürlich ['ʊnvɪlkyːrlɪç] *adj* involuntary ♦ *adv* instinctively; (*lachen*) involuntarily.
unwirklich ['ʊnvɪrklɪç] *adj* unreal.
unwirksam ['ʊnvɪrkzaːm] *adj* ineffective.
unwirsch ['ʊnvɪrʃ] *adj* cross, surly.
unwirtlich ['ʊnvɪrtlɪç] *adj* inhospitable.
unwirtschaftlich ['ʊnvɪrtʃaftlɪç] *adj*

uneconomical.
unwissend ['ʊnvɪsənt] *adj* ignorant.
Unwissenheit *f* ignorance.
unwissenschaftlich *adj* unscientific.
unwissentlich *adv* unwittingly,
unknowingly.
unwohl ['ʊnvoːl] *adj* unwell, ill; **U**~**sein** (**-s**) *nt* indisposition.
unwürdig ['ʊnvʏrdɪç] *adj* unworthy.
Unzahl ['ʊntsaːl] *f*: **eine** ~ **von** ... a whole host of ...
unzählig [ʊn'tsɛːlɪç] *adj* innumerable,
countless.
unzeitgemäß ['ʊntsaɪtɡəmɛːs] *adj* (*altmodisch*) old-fashioned.
un- *zW*: ~**zerbrechlich** *adj* unbreakable;
~**zerreißbar** *adj* untearable; ~**zerstörbar** *adj* indestructible; ~**zertrennlich** *adj* inseparable.
Unzucht ['ʊntsʊxt] *f* sexual offence.
unzüchtig ['ʊntsʏçtɪç] *adj* immoral.
un- *zW*: ~**zufrieden** *adj* dissatisfied;
U~**zufriedenheit** *f* discontent; ~**zugänglich**
adj (*Gegend*) inaccessible; (*Mensch*) inapproachable; ~**zulänglich** *adj* inadequate;
~**zulässig** *adj* inadmissible; ~**zumutbar** *adj* unreasonable; ~**zurechnungsfähig** *adj* irresponsible; **jdn für** ~**zurechnungsfähig erklären lassen** (*JUR*) to have sb certified (insane); ~**zusammenhängend** *adj* disconnected; (*Äußerung*) incoherent;
~**zustellbar** *adj*: **falls** ~**zustellbar, bitte an Absender zurück** if undelivered, please return to sender; ~**zutreffend** *adj* incorrect;
„**U**~**zutreffendes bitte streichen"** "delete as applicable"; ~**zuverlässig** *adj* unreliable.
unzweckmäßig ['ʊntsvɛkmɛːsɪç] *adj* (*nicht ratsam*) inadvisable; (*unpraktisch*) impractical; (*ungeeignet*) unsuitable.
unzweideutig ['ʊntsvaɪdɔʏtɪç] *adj* unambiguous.
unzweifelhaft ['ʊntsvaɪfəlhaft] *adj* indubitable.
üppig ['ʏpɪç] *adj* (*Frau*) curvaceous; (*Essen*) sumptuous, lavish; (*Vegetation*) luxuriant,
lush; (*Haar*) thick.
Ur- ['uːr] *in zW* original.
Urabstimmung ['uːrʔapʃtɪmʊŋ] *f* ballot.
Ural [u'raːl] (**-s**) *m*: **der** ~ the Ural mountains
pl, **die Urals** *pl*; ~**gebirge** *nt* Ural mountains.
uralt ['uːrʔalt] *adj* ancient, very old.
Uran [u'raːn] (**-s**) *nt* uranium.
Uraufführung *f* first performance.
urbar *adj*: **die Wüste/Land** ~ **machen** to reclaim the desert/cultivate land.
Urdu ['ʊrdu] (**-**) *nt* Urdu.
Ur- *zW*: ~**einwohner** *m* original inhabitant;
~**eltern** *pl* ancestors *pl*; ~**enkel(in)** *m(f)* great-grandchild; ~**fassung** *f* original version; ~**großmutter** *f* great-grandmother;

~**großvater** *m* great-grandfather.
Urheber (-s, -) *m* originator; (*Autor*) author;
~**recht** *nt*: ~**recht** (**an** *+dat*) copyright (on);
u~**rechtlich** *adv*: **u**~**rechtlich geschützt**
copyright.
urig ['u:rɪç] (*umg*) *adj* (*Mensch, Atmosphäre*)
earthy.
Urin [u'ri:n] (-s, -e) *m* urine.
urkomisch *adj* incredibly funny.
Urkunde *f* document; (*Kauf*~) deed.
urkundlich ['u:rkʊntlɪç] *adj* documentary.
urladen ['u:rla:dən] *vt* (*COMPUT*) to boot.
Urlader *m* (*COMPUT*) bootstrap.
Urlaub ['u:rlaʊp] (-(e)s, -e) *m* holiday(s *pl*)
(*BRIT*), vacation (*US*); (*MIL etc*) leave; ~**er** (-s,
-) *m* holiday-maker (*BRIT*), vacationer (*US*).
Urlaubs- *zW*: ~**geld** *nt* holiday (*BRIT*) *od*
vacation (*US*) money; ~**ort** *m* holiday (*BRIT*)
od vacation (*US*) resort; **u**~**reif** *adj* in need of
a holiday (*BRIT*) *od* vacation (*US*).
Urmensch *m* primitive man.
Urne ['ʊrnə] (-, -n) *f* urn; **zur** ~ **gehen** to go to
the polls.
urplötzlich ['u:r'plœtslɪç] (*umg*) *adv* all of a
sudden.
Ursache ['u:rzaxə] *f* cause; **keine** ~! (*auf Dank*)
don't mention it, you're welcome; (*auf
Entschuldigung*) that's all right.
ursächlich ['u:rzɛçlɪç] *adj* causal.
Urschrei ['u:rʃraɪ] *m* (*PSYCH*) primal scream.
Ursprung ['u:rʃprʊŋ] *m* origin, source; (*von
Fluss*) source.
ursprünglich ['u:rʃprʏŋlɪç] *adj* original ♦ *adv*
originally.
Ursprungsland *nt* (*COMM*) country of origin.
Ursprungszeugnis *nt* certificate of origin.
Urteil ['ʊrtaɪl] (-s, -e) *nt* opinion; (*JUR*)
sentence, judgement; **sich** *dat* **ein** ~ **über**
etw *akk* **erlauben** to pass judgement on sth;
ein ~ **über etw** *akk* **fällen** to pass judgement
on sth; **u**~**en** *vi* to judge.
Urteilsbegründung *f* (*JUR*) opinion.
Urteilsspruch *m* sentence; verdict.
Uruguay [uru'gua:i] (-s) *nt* Uruguay.
Uruguayer(in) (-s, -) *m(f)* Uruguayan.
uruguayisch *adj* Uruguayan.
Ur- *zW*: ~**wald** *m* jungle; **u**~**wüchsig** *adj*
natural; (*Landschaft*) unspoilt; (*Humor*)
earthy; ~**zeit** *f* prehistoric times *pl*.
USA [u:'ɛs'a:] *pl abk*: **die** ~ the USA *sing*.
USB *abk* (= *universal serial bus*) USB.
Usbekistan [ʊs'be:kista:n] (-s) *nt* Uzbekistan.
usw. *abk* (= *und so weiter*) etc.
Utensilien [utɛn'zi:liən] *pl* utensils *pl*.
Utopie [uto'pi:] *f* pipe dream.
utopisch [u'to:pɪʃ] *adj* utopian.
u. U. *abk* (= *unter Umständen*) possibly.
UV *abk* (= *ultraviolett*) U.V.
u. v. a. *abk* (= *und viele(s) andere*) and much/
many more.

u. v. a. m. *abk* (= *und viele(s) andere mehr*) and
much/many more.
u. W. *abk* (= *unseres Wissens*) to our
knowledge.
Ü-Wagen *m* (*RUNDF, TV*) outside broadcast
vehicle.
uzen ['u:tsən] (*umg*) *vt, vi* to tease, kid.
u. zw. *abk* = **und zwar**.

V, v

V¹, v [faʊ] *nt* V, v; ~ **wie Viktor** ≈ V for
Victor.
V² [faʊ] *abk* (= *Volt*) v.
VAE *pl abk* (= *Vereinigte Arabische Emirate*)
UAE.
vag(e) *adj* vague.
Vagina [va'gi:na] (-, **Vaginen**) *f* vagina.
Vakuum ['va:kuʊm] (-s, **Vakua** *od* **Vakuen**) *nt*
vacuum; **v**~**verpackt** *adj* vacuum-packed.
Vandalismus [vanda'lɪsmʊs] *m* vandalism.
Vanille [va'nɪljə] (-) *f* vanilla; ~**zucker** *m*
vanilla sugar.
Vanillinzucker *m* vanilla sugar.
variabel [vari'a:bəl] *adj*: **variable Kosten**
variable costs.
Variable [vari'a:blə] (-, -n) *f* variable.
Variante [vari'antə] (-, -n) *f*: ~ (**zu**) variant
(on).
Variation [variatsi'o:n] *f* variation.
variieren [vari'i:rən] *vt, vi* to vary.
Vase ['va:zə] (-, -n) *f* vase.
Vater ['fa:tər] (-s, ⸚) *m* father; ~ **Staat** (*umg*)
the State; ~**land** *nt* native country; (*bes
Deutschland*) Fatherland; ~**landsliebe** *f*
patriotism.
väterlich ['fɛ:tərlɪç] *adj* fatherly.
väterlicherseits *adv* on the father's side.
Vaterschaft *f* paternity.
Vaterschaftsklage *f* paternity suit.
Vaterstelle *f*: ~ **bei jdm vertreten** to take the
place of sb's father.
Vaterunser (-s, -) *nt* Lord's Prayer.
Vati ['fa:ti] (-s, -s) (*umg*) *m* dad(dy).
Vatikan [vati'ka:n] (-s) *m* Vatican.
V-Ausschnitt ['faʊ|aʊsʃnɪt] *m* V-neck.
VB *abk* (= *Verhandlungsbasis*) o.i.r.o.
v. Chr. *abk* (= *vor Christus*) B.C.
Vegetarier(in) [vege'ta:riər(ɪn)] (-s, -) *m(f)*
vegetarian.
vegetarisch *adj* vegetarian.
Vegetation [vegetatsi'o:n] *f* vegetation.
vegetativ [vegeta'ti:f] *adj* (*BIOL*) vegetative;

(*MED*) autonomic.

vegetieren [vege'ti:rən] *vi* to vegetate; (*kärglich leben*) to eke out a bare existence.

Vehikel [ve'hi:kəl] (**-s**, **-**) (*pej: umg*) *nt* boneshaker.

Veilchen ['faɪlçən] *nt* violet; (*umg: blaues Auge*) shiner, black eye.

Velours (**-**, **-**) *nt* suede; ~**leder** *nt* suede.

Vene ['ve:nə] (**-**, **-n**) *f* vein.

Venedig [ve'ne:dɪç] (**-s**) *nt* Venice.

Venezianer(in) [venetsi'a:nər(ɪn)] (**-s**, **-**) *m(f)* Venetian.

venezianisch [venetsi'a:nɪʃ] *adj* Venetian.

Venezolaner(in) [venetso'la:nər(ɪn)] (**-s**, **-**) *m(f)* Venezuelan.

venezolanisch *adj* Venezuelan.

Venezuela [venetsu'e:la] (**-s**) *nt* Venezuela.

Ventil [vɛn'ti:l] (**-s**, **-e**) *nt* valve.

Ventilator [vɛnti'la:tɔr] *m* ventilator.

verabreden [fɛr'|apre:dən] *vt* to arrange; (*Termin*) to agree upon ♦ *vr* to arrange to meet; **sich (mit jdm)** ~ to arrange to meet (*sb*); **schon verabredet sein** to have a prior engagement (*form*), have something else on.

Verabredung *f* arrangement; (*Treffen*) appointment; **ich habe eine** ~ I'm meeting somebody.

verabreichen [fɛr'|apraɪçən] *vt* (*Tracht Prügel etc*) to give; (*Arznei*) to administer (*form*).

verabscheuen [fɛr'|apʃɔyən] *vt* to detest, abhor.

verabschieden [fɛr'|apʃi:dən] *vt* (*Gäste*) to say goodbye to; (*entlassen*) to discharge; (*Gesetz*) to pass ♦ *vr*: **sich** ~ **(von)** to take one's leave (of).

Verabschiedung *f* (*von Beamten etc*) discharge; (*von Gesetz*) passing.

verachten [fɛr'|axtən] *vt* to despise; **nicht zu** ~ (*umg*) not to be scoffed at.

verächtlich [fɛr'|ɛçtlɪç] *adj* contemptuous; (*verachtenswert*) contemptible; **jdn** ~ **machen** to run sb down.

Verachtung *f* contempt; **jdn mit** ~ **strafen** to treat sb with contempt.

veralbern [fɛr'|albərn] (*umg*) *vt* to make fun of.

verallgemeinern [fɛr|algə'maɪnərn] *vt* to generalize.

Verallgemeinerung *f* generalization.

veralten [fɛr'|altən] *vi* to become obsolete *od* out-of-date.

Veranda [ve'randa] (**-**, **Veranden**) *f* veranda.

veränderlich [fɛr'|ɛndərlɪç] *adj* variable; (*Wetter*) changeable; **V~keit** *f* variability; changeability.

verändern *vt*, *vr* to change.

Veränderung *f* change; **eine berufliche** ~ a change of job.

verängstigen [fɛr'|ɛŋstɪgən] *vt* (*erschrecken*) to frighten; (*einschüchtern*) to intimidate.

verankern [fɛr'|aŋkərn] *vt* (*NAUT, TECH*) to anchor; (*fig*): ~ **(in** +*dat*) to embed (in).

veranlagen [fɛr'|anla:gən] *vt*: **etw** ~ **(mit)** to assess sth (at).

veranlagt *adj*: **praktisch** ~ **sein** to be practically-minded; **zu** *od* **für etw** ~ **sein** to be cut out for sth.

Veranlagung *f* disposition, aptitude.

veranlassen [fɛr'|anlasən] *vt* to cause; **Maßnahmen** ~ to take measures; **sich veranlasst sehen** to feel prompted; **etw** ~ to arrange for sth; (*befehlen*) to order sth.

Veranlassung *f* cause; motive; **auf jds** ~ *akk* **(hin)** at sb's instigation.

veranschaulichen [fɛr'|anʃaʊlɪçən] *vt* to illustrate.

veranschlagen [fɛr'|anʃla:gən] *vt* to estimate.

veranstalten [fɛr'|anʃtaltən] *vt* to organize, arrange.

Veranstalter(in) (**-s**, **-**) *m(f)* organizer; (*COMM: von Konzerten etc*) promoter.

Veranstaltung *f* (*Veranstalten*) organizing; (*Veranstaltetes*) event; (*feierlich, öffentlich*) function.

verantworten [fɛr'|antvɔrtən] *vt* to accept responsibility for; (*Folgen etc*) to answer for ♦ *vr* to justify o.s.; **etw vor jdm** ~ to answer to sb for sth.

verantwortlich *adj* responsible.

Verantwortung *f* responsibility; **jdn zur** ~ **ziehen** to call sb to account.

verantwortungs- *zW*: ~**bewusst▲** *adj* responsible; **V**~**gefühl** *nt* sense of responsibility; ~**los** *adj* irresponsible; ~**voll** *adj* responsible.

verarbeiten [fɛr'|arbaɪtən] *vt* to process; (*geistig*) to assimilate; (*Erlebnis etc*) to digest; **etw zu etw** ~ to make sth into sth; ~**de Industrie** processing industries *pl*.

verarbeitet *adj*: **gut** ~ (*Kleid etc*) well finished.

Verarbeitung *f* processing; assimilation.

verärgern [fɛr'|ɛrgərn] *vt* to annoy.

verarmen [fɛr'|armən] *vi* (*lit, fig*) to become impoverished.

verarschen [fɛr'|arʃən] (*umg!*) *vt*: **jdn** ~ to take the mickey out of sb.

verarzten [fɛr'|a:rtstən] *vt* to fix up (*umg*).

verausgaben [fɛr'|aʊsga:bən] *vr* to run out of money; (*fig*) to exhaust o.s.

veräußern [fɛr'|ɔysərn] *vt* (*form: verkaufen*) to dispose of.

Verb [vɛrp] (**-s**, **-en**) *nt* verb.

Verb. *abk* (= *Verband*) assoc.

Verband [fɛr'bant] (**-(e)s**, **ˉe**) *m* (*MED*) bandage, dressing; (*Bund*) association, society; (*MIL*) unit.

verband *etc vb siehe* **verbinden**.

Verband- *zW*: ~**(s)kasten** *m* medicine chest, first-aid box; ~**(s)päckchen** *nt* gauze

bandage; **~stoff** *m* bandage, dressing material; **~zeug** *nt* bandage, dressing material.
verbannen [fɛr'banən] *vt* to banish.
Verbannung *f* exile.
verbarrikadieren [fɛrbarika'diːrən] *vt* to barricade ◆ *vr* to barricade o.s. in.
verbauen [fɛr'bauən] *vt*: **sich** *dat* **alle Chancen** ~ to spoil one's chances.
verbergen [fɛr'bɛrgən] *unreg vt, vr*: **(sich)** ~ **(vor** +*dat*) to hide (from).
verbessern [fɛr'bɛsərn] *vt* to improve; (*berichtigen*) to correct ◆ *vr* to improve; to correct o.s.
verbessert *adj* revised; improved; **eine neue, ~e Auflage** a new revised edition.
Verbesserung *f* improvement; correction.
verbeugen [fɛr'bɔygən] *vr* to bow.
Verbeugung *f* bow.
verbiegen [fɛr'biːgən] *unreg vi* to bend.
verbiestert [fɛr'biːstərt] (*umg*) *adj* crotchety.
verbieten [fɛr'biːtən] *unreg vt* to forbid; (*amtlich*) to prohibit; (*Zeitung, Partei*) to ban; **jdm etw** ~ to forbid sb to do sth.
verbilligen [fɛr'bɪlɪgən] *vt* to reduce (the price of) ◆ *vr* to become cheaper, go down.
verbinden [fɛr'bɪndən] *unreg vt* to connect; (*kombinieren*) to combine; (*MED*) to bandage ◆ *vr* to combine (*auch CHEM*), join (together); **jdm die Augen** ~ to blindfold sb.
verbindlich [fɛr'bɪntlɪç] *adj* binding; (*freundlich*) obliging; ~ **zusagen** to accept definitely; **V~keit** *f* obligation; (*Höflichkeit*) civility; **Verbindlichkeiten** *pl* (*JUR*) obligations *pl*; (*COMM*) liabilities *pl*.
Verbindung *f* connection; (*Zusammensetzung*) combination; (*CHEM*) compound; (*UNIV*) club; (*TEL: Anschluss*) line; **mit jdm in** ~ **stehen** to be in touch *od* contact with sb; ~ **mit jdm aufnehmen** to contact sb.
Verbindungsmann (-(e)s, *pl* **-männer** *od* **-leute**) *m* intermediary; (*Agent*) contact.
verbissen [fɛr'bɪsən] *adj* grim; (*Arbeiter*) dogged; **V~heit** *f* grimness; doggedness.
verbitten [fɛr'bɪtən] *unreg vt*: **sich** *dat* **etw** ~ not to tolerate sth, not to stand for sth.
verbittern [fɛr'bɪtərn] *vt* to embitter ◆ *vi* to get bitter.
verblassen [fɛr'blasən] *vi* to fade.
Verbleib [fɛr'blaip] (-(e)s) *m* whereabouts.
verbleiben [fɛr'blaibən] *unreg vi* to remain; **wir sind so verblieben, dass wir ...** we agreed to ...
verbleit [fɛr'blait] *adj* leaded.
Verblendung [fɛr'blɛnduŋ] *f* (*fig*) delusion.
verblöden [fɛr'bløːdən] *vi* (*Hilfsverb sein*) to get stupid.
verblüffen [fɛr'blʏfən] *vt* to amaze; (*verwirren*) to baffle.
Verblüffung *f* stupefaction.

verblühen [fɛr'blyːən] *vi* to wither, fade.
verbluten [fɛr'bluːtən] *vi* to bleed to death.
verbohren [fɛr'boːrən] (*umg*) *vr*: **sich in etw** *akk* ~ to become obsessed with sth.
verbohrt *adj* (*Haltung*) stubborn, obstinate.
verborgen [fɛr'bɔrgən] *adj* hidden; **~e Mängel** latent defects *pl*.
Verbot [fɛr'boːt] (-(e)s, -e) *nt* prohibition, ban.
verboten *adj* forbidden; **Rauchen** ~**!** no smoking; **er sah** ~ **aus** (*umg*) he looked a real sight.
verbotenerweise *adv* though it is forbidden.
Verbotsschild *nt* prohibitory sign.
verbrämen [fɛr'brɛːmən] *vt* (*fig*) to gloss over; (*Kritik*): ~ **(mit)** to veil (in).
Verbrauch [fɛr'braux] (-(e)s) *m* consumption.
verbrauchen *vt* to use up; **der Wagen verbraucht 10 Liter Benzin auf 100 km** the car does 10 kms to the litre (*BRIT*) *od* liter (*US*).
Verbraucher(in) (-s, -) *m(f)* consumer; **~markt** *m* hypermarket; **v~nah** *adj* consumer-friendly; **~schutz** *m* consumer protection; **~verband** *m* consumer council.
Verbrauchsgüter *pl* consumer goods *pl*.
verbraucht *adj* used up, finished; (*Luft*) stale; (*Mensch*) worn-out.
Verbrechen (-s, -) *nt* crime.
Verbrecher(in) (-s, -) *m(f)* criminal; **v~isch** *adj* criminal; **~kartei** *f* file of offenders, ≈ rogues' gallery; **~tum** (-s) *nt* criminality.
verbreiten [fɛr'braitən] *vt* to spread; (*Licht*) to shed; (*Wärme, Ruhe*) to radiate ◆ *vr* to spread; **eine (weit) verbreitete Ansicht** a widely held opinion; **sich über etw** *akk* ~ to expound on sth.
verbreitern [fɛr'braitərn] *vt* to broaden.
Verbreitung *f* spread(ing); shedding; radiation.
verbrennbar *adj* combustible.
verbrennen [fɛr'brɛnən] *unreg vt* to burn; (*Leiche*) to cremate; (*versengen*) to scorch; (*Haar*) to singe; (*verbrühen*) to scald.
Verbrennung *f* burning; (*in Motor*) combustion; (*von Leiche*) cremation.
Verbrennungsanlage *f* incineration plant.
Verbrennungsmotor *m* internal-combustion engine.
verbriefen [fɛr'briːfən] *vt* to document.
verbringen [fɛr'brɪŋən] *unreg vt* to spend.
Verbrüderung [fɛr'bryːdəruŋ] *f* fraternization.
verbrühen [fɛr'bryːən] *vt* to scald.
verbuchen [fɛr'buːxən] *vt* (*FIN*) to register; (*Erfolg*) to enjoy; (*Misserfolg*) to suffer.
verbummeln [fɛr'buməln] (*umg*) *vt* (*verlieren*) to lose; (*Zeit*) to waste, fritter away; (*Verabredung*) to miss.
verbunden [fɛr'bundən] *adj* connected; **jdm** ~ **sein** to be obliged *od* indebted to sb; **ich/**

er *etc* **war falsch** ~ (*TEL*) it was a wrong number.

verbünden [fɛr'bʏndən] *vr* to form an alliance.

Verbundenheit *f* bond, relationship.

Verbündete(r) *f(m)* ally.

Verbundglas [fɛr'bʊntglaːs] *nt* laminated glass.

verbürgen [fɛr'bʏrgən] *vr*: **sich** ~ **für** to vouch for; **ein verbürgtes Recht** an established right.

verbüßen [fɛr'byːsən] *vt*: **eine Strafe** ~ to serve a sentence.

verchromt [fɛr'kroːmt] *adj* chromium-plated.

Verdacht [fɛr'daxt] (-(e)s) *m* suspicion; ~ **schöpfen (gegen jdn)** to become suspicious (of sb); **jdn in** ~ **haben** to suspect sb; **es besteht** ~ **auf Krebs** *akk* cancer is suspected.

verdächtig *adj* suspicious.

verdächtigen [fɛr'dɛçtɪgən] *vt* to suspect.

Verdächtigung *f* suspicion.

verdammen [fɛr'damən] *vt* to damn, condemn.

Verdammnis (-) *f* perdition, damnation.

verdammt (*umg*) *adj, adv* damned; ~ **noch mal!** bloody hell (!), damn (!).

verdampfen [fɛr'dampfən] *vt, vi* (*vi Hilfsverb sein*) to vaporize; (*KOCH*) to boil away.

verdanken [fɛr'daŋkən] *vt*: **jdm etw** ~ to owe sb sth.

verdarb *etc* [fɛr'darp] *vb siehe* **verderben**.

verdattert [fɛr'datərt] (*umg*) *adj, adv* flabbergasted.

verdauen [fɛr'dauən] *vt* (*lit, fig*) to digest ◆ *vi* (*lit*) to digest.

verdaulich [fɛr'daulɪç] *adj* digestible; **das ist schwer** ~ that is hard to digest.

Verdauung *f* digestion.

Verdauungsspaziergang *m* constitutional.

Verdauungsstörung *f* indigestion.

Verdeck [fɛr'dɛk] (-(e)s, -e) *nt* (*AUT*) soft top; (*NAUT*) deck.

verdecken *vt* to cover (up); (*verbergen*) to hide.

verdenken [fɛr'dɛŋkən] *unreg vt*: **jdm etw** ~ to blame sb for sth, hold sth against sb.

verderben [fɛr'dɛrbən] *unreg vt* to spoil; (*schädigen*) to ruin; (*moralisch*) to corrupt ◆ *vi* (*Essen*) to spoil, rot; (*Mensch*) to go to the bad; **es mit jdm** ~ to get into sb's bad books.

Verderben (-s) *nt* ruin.

verderblich *adj* (*Einfluss*) pernicious; (*Lebensmittel*) perishable.

verderbt *adj* (*veraltet*) depraved; **V~heit** *f* depravity.

verdeutlichen [fɛr'dɔʏtlɪçən] *vt* to make clear.

verdichten [fɛr'dɪçtən] *vt* (*PHYS, fig*) to compress ◆ *vr* to thicken; (*Verdacht, Eindruck*)

to deepen.

verdienen [fɛr'diːnən] *vt* to earn; (*moralisch*) to deserve ◆ *vi* (*Gewinn machen*): ~ **(an** +*dat*) to make (a profit) (on).

Verdienst [fɛr'diːnst] (-(e)s, -e) *m* earnings *pl* ◆ *nt* merit; (*Dank*) credit; (*Leistung*): ~ **(um)** service (to), contribution (to); **v~voll** *adj* commendable.

verdient [fɛr'diːnt] *adj* well-earned; (*Person*) of outstanding merit; (*Lohn, Strafe*) rightful; **sich um etw** ~ **machen** to do a lot for sth.

verdirbst [fɛr'dɪrpst] *vb siehe* **verderben**.

verdirbt [fɛr'dɪrpt] *vb siehe* **verderben**.

verdonnern [fɛr'dɔnərn] (*umg*) *vt* (*zu Haft etc*): ~ **(zu)** to sentence (to); **jdn zu etw** ~ to order sb to do sth.

verdoppeln [fɛr'dɔpəln] *vt* to double.

Verdopp(e)lung *f* doubling.

verdorben [fɛr'dɔrbən] *pp von* **verderben** ◆ *adj* spoilt; (*geschädigt*) ruined; (*moralisch*) corrupt.

verdorren [fɛr'dɔrən] *vi* to wither.

verdrängen [fɛr'drɛŋən] *vt* to oust; (*auch PHYS*) to displace; (*PSYCH*) to repress.

Verdrängung *f* displacement; (*PSYCH*) repression.

verdrehen [fɛr'dreːən] *vt* (*lit, fig*) to twist; (*Augen*) to roll; **jdm den Kopf** ~ (*fig*) to turn sb's head.

verdreht (*umg*) *adj* crazy; (*Bericht*) confused.

verdreifachen [fɛr'draɪfaxən] *vt* to treble.

verdrießen [fɛr'driːsən] *unreg vt* to annoy.

verdrießlich [fɛr'driːslɪç] *adj* peevish, annoyed.

verdross *etc*▲ [fɛr'drɔs] *vb siehe* **verdrießen**.

verdrossen [fɛr'drɔsən] *pp von* **verdrießen** ◆ *adj* cross, sulky.

verdrücken [fɛr'drʏkən] (*umg*) *vt* to put away, eat ◆ *vr* to disappear.

Verdruss▲ [fɛr'drʊs] (-es, -e) *m* frustration; **zu jds** ~ to sb's annoyance.

verduften [fɛr'dʊftən] *vi* to evaporate; (*umg*) to disappear.

verdummen [fɛr'dʊmən] *vt* to make stupid ◆ *vi* to grow stupid.

verdunkeln [fɛr'dʊŋkəln] *vt* to darken; (*fig*) to obscure ◆ *vr* to darken.

Verdunk(e)lung *f* blackout; (*fig*) obscuring.

verdünnen [fɛr'dʏnən] *vt* to dilute.

Verdünner (-s, -) *m* thinner.

verdünnisieren [fɛrdʏni'ziːrən] (*umg*) *vr* to make o.s. scarce.

verdunsten [fɛr'dʊnstən] *vi* to evaporate.

verdursten [fɛr'dʊrstən] *vi* to die of thirst.

verdutzt [fɛr'dʊtst] *adj* nonplussed (*BRIT*), nonplused (*US*), taken aback.

verebben [fɛr'|ɛbən] *vi* to subside.

veredeln [fɛr'|eːdəln] *vt* (*Metalle, Erdöl*) to refine; (*Fasern*) to finish; (*BOT*) to graft.

verehren [fɛr'|eːrən] *vt* to venerate, worship

(*auch REL*); **jdm etw** ~ to present sb with sth.

Verehrer(in) (**-s, -**) *m(f)* admirer, worshipper (*BRIT*), worshiper (*US*).

verehrt *adj* esteemed; (**sehr**) ~**e Anwesende/** ~**es Publikum** Ladies and Gentlemen.

Verehrung *f* respect; (*REL*) worship.

vereidigen [fɛrˈaɪdɪɡən] *vt* to put on oath; **jdn auf etw** *akk* ~ to make sb swear on sth.

Vereidigung *f* swearing in.

Verein [fɛrˈaɪn] (**-(e)s, -e**) *m* club, association; **ein wohltätiger** ~ a charity.

vereinbar *adj* compatible.

vereinbaren [fɛrˈaɪnbaːrən] *vt* to agree upon.

Vereinbarkeit *f* compatibility.

Vereinbarung *f* agreement.

vereinfachen [fɛrˈaɪnfaxən] *vt* to simplify.

Vereinfachung *f* simplification.

vereinheitlichen [fɛrˈaɪnhaɪtlɪçən] *vt* to standardize.

vereinigen [fɛrˈaɪnɪɡən] *vt, vr* to unite.

vereinigt *adj* united; **V~e Arabische Emirate** *pl* United Arab Emirates; **V~es Königreich** *nt* United Kingdom; **V~e Staaten** *pl* United States.

Vereinigung *f* union; (*Verein*) association.

vereinnahmen [fɛrˈaɪnnaːmən] *vt* (*geh*) to take; **jdn** ~ (*fig*) to make demands on sb.

vereinsamen [fɛrˈaɪnzaːmən] *vi* to become lonely.

vereint [fɛrˈaɪnt] *adj* united; **V~e Nationen** *pl* United Nations.

vereinzelt [fɛrˈaɪntsəlt] *adj* isolated.

vereisen [fɛrˈaɪzən] *vi* to freeze, ice over ♦ *vt* (*MED*) to freeze.

vereiteln [fɛrˈaɪtəln] *vt* to frustrate.

vereitern [fɛrˈaɪtərn] *vi* to suppurate, fester.

Verelendung [fɛrˈeːlɛndʊŋ] *f* impoverishment.

verenden [fɛrˈɛndən] *vi* to perish, die.

verengen [fɛrˈɛŋən] *vr* to narrow.

vererben [fɛrˈɛrbən] *vt* to bequeath; (*BIOL*) to transmit ♦ *vr* to be hereditary.

vererblich [fɛrˈɛrplɪç] *adj* hereditary.

Vererbung *f* bequeathing; (*BIOL*) transmission; **das ist** ~ (*umg*) it's hereditary.

verewigen [fɛrˈeːvɪɡən] *vt* to immortalize ♦ *vr* (*umg*) to leave one's name.

Verf. *abk* = **Verfasser**.

verfahren [fɛrˈfaːrən] *unreg vi* to act ♦ *vr* to get lost ♦ *adj* tangled; ~ **mit** to deal with.

Verfahren (**-s, -**) *nt* procedure; (*TECH*) process; (*JUR*) proceedings *pl*.

Verfahrenstechnik *f* (*Methode*) process.

Verfahrensweise *f* procedure.

Verfall [fɛrˈfal] (**-(e)s**) *m* decline; (*von Haus*) dilapidation; (*FIN*) expiry.

verfallen *unreg vi* to decline; (*Haus*) to be falling down; (*FIN*) to lapse ♦ *adj* (*Gebäude*) dilapidated, ruined; (*Karten, Briefmarken*)

invalid; (*Strafe*) lapsed; (*Pass*) expired; ~ **in** *+akk* to lapse into; ~ **auf** *+akk* to hit upon; **einem Laster** ~ **sein** to be addicted to a vice; **jdm völlig** ~ **sein** to be completely under sb's spell.

Verfallsdatum *nt* expiry date; (*der Haltbarkeit*) best-before date.

verfänglich [fɛrˈfɛŋlɪç] *adj* awkward, tricky; (*Aussage, Beweismaterial etc*) incriminating; (*gefährlich*) dangerous.

verfärben [fɛrˈfɛrbən] *vr* to change colour (*BRIT*) *od* color (*US*).

verfassen [fɛrˈfasən] *vt* to write; (*Gesetz, Urkunde*) to draw up.

Verfasser(in) (**-s, -**) *m(f)* author, writer.

Verfassung *f* constitution (*auch POL*); (*körperlich*) state of health; (*seelisch*) state of mind; **sie ist in guter/schlechter** ~ she is in good/bad shape.

Verfassungs- *zW:* **v~feindlich** *adj* anticonstitutional; ~**gericht** *nt* constitutional court; **v~mäßig** *adj* constitutional; ~**schutz** *m* (*Aufgabe*) defence of the constitution; (*Amt*) office responsible for defending the constitution; ~**schützer(in)** *m(f)* defender of the constitution; **v~widrig** *adj* unconstitutional.

verfaulen [fɛrˈfaʊlən] *vi* to rot.

verfechten [fɛrˈfɛçtən] *unreg vt* to defend; (*Lehre*) to advocate.

Verfechter(in) [fɛrˈfɛçtər(ɪn)] (**-s, -**) *m(f)* champion; defender.

verfehlen [fɛrˈfeːlən] *vt* to miss; **das Thema** ~ to be completely off the subject.

verfehlt *adj* unsuccessful; (*unangebracht*) inappropriate; **etw für** ~ **halten** to regard sth as mistaken.

Verfehlung *f* (*Vergehen*) misdemeanour (*BRIT*), misdemeanor (*US*); (*Sünde*) transgression.

verfeinern [fɛrˈfaɪnərn] *vt* to refine.

Verfettung [fɛrˈfɛtʊŋ] *f* (*von Organ, Muskeln*) fatty degeneration.

verfeuern [fɛrˈfɔʏərn] *vt* to burn; (*Munition*) to fire; (*umg*) to use up.

verfilmen [fɛrˈfɪlmən] *vt* to film, make a film of.

Verfilmung *f* film (version).

Verfilzung [fɛrˈfɪltsʊŋ] *f* (*fig: von Firmen, Parteien*) entanglements *pl*.

verflachen [fɛrˈflaxən] *vi* to flatten out; (*fig: Diskussion*) to become superficial.

verfliegen [fɛrˈfliːɡən] *unreg vi* to evaporate; (*Zeit*) to pass, fly ♦ *vr* to stray (past).

verflixt [fɛrˈflɪkst] (*umg*) *adj, adv* darned.

verflossen [fɛrˈflɔsən] *adj* past, former.

verfluchen [fɛrˈfluːxən] *vt* to curse.

verflüchtigen [fɛrˈflʏçtɪɡən] *vr* to evaporate; (*Geruch*) to fade.

verflüssigen [fɛrˈflʏsɪɡən] *vr* to become

liquid.
verfolgen [fɛr'fɔlgən] vt to pursue; (gerichtlich) to prosecute; (grausam, bes POL) to persecute.
Verfolger(in) (-s, -) m(f) pursuer.
Verfolgte(r) f(m) (politisch) victim of persecution.
Verfolgung f pursuit; persecution; **strafrechtliche** ~ prosecution.
Verfolgungswahn m persecution mania.
verfrachten [fɛr'fraxtən] vt to ship.
verfremden [fɛr'frɛmdən] vt to alienate, distance.
verfressen [fɛr'frɛsən] (umg) adj greedy.
verfrüht [fɛr'fry:t] adj premature.
verfügbar adj available.
verfügen [fɛr'fy:gən] vt to direct, order ♦ vr to proceed ♦ vi: ~ **über** +akk to have at one's disposal; **über etw** akk **frei ~ können** to be able to do as one wants with sth.
Verfügung f direction, order; (JUR) writ; **zur ~** at one's disposal; **jdm zur ~ stehen** to be available to sb.
Verfügungsgewalt f (JUR) right of disposal.
verführen [fɛr'fy:rən] vt to tempt; (sexuell) to seduce; (die Jugend, das Volk etc) to lead astray.
Verführer m tempter; seducer.
Verführerin f temptress; seductress.
verführerisch adj seductive.
Verführung f seduction; (Versuchung) temptation.
Vergabe [fɛr'ga:bə] f (von Arbeiten) allocation; (von Stipendium, Auftrag etc) award.
vergällen [fɛr'gɛlən] vt (geh): **jdm die Freude/ das Leben** ~ to spoil sb's fun/sour sb's life.
vergaloppieren [fɛrgalɔ'pi:rən] (umg) vr (sich irren) to be on the wrong track.
vergammeln [fɛr'gaməln] (umg) vi to go to seed; (Nahrung) to go off; (Zeit) to waste.
vergangen [fɛr'gaŋən] adj past; **V~heit** f past; **V~heitsbewältigung** f coming to terms with the past.
vergänglich [fɛr'gɛŋlɪç] adj transitory; **V~keit** f transitoriness, impermanence.
vergasen [fɛr'ga:zən] vt to gasify; (töten) to gas.
Vergaser (-s, -) m (AUT) carburettor (BRIT), carburetor (US).
vergaß etc [fɛr'ga:s] vb siehe **vergessen**.
vergeben [fɛr'ge:bən] unreg vt to forgive; (weggeben) to give away; (fig: Chance) to throw away; (Auftrag, Preis) to award; (Studienplätze, Stellen) to allocate; **jdm (etw)** ~ to forgive sb (sth); ~ **an** +akk to award to; to allocate to; ~ **sein** to be occupied; (umg: Mädchen) to be spoken for.
vergebens adv in vain.
vergeblich [fɛr'ge:plɪç] adv in vain ♦ adj vain, futile.

Vergebung f forgiveness.
vergegenwärtigen [fɛrge:gən'vɛrtɪgən] vr: **sich** dat **etw** ~ to visualize sth; (erinnern) to recall sth.
vergehen [fɛr'ge:ən] unreg vi to pass by od away ♦ vr to commit an offence (BRIT) od offense (US); **vor Angst** ~ to be scared to death; **jdm vergeht etw** sb loses sth; **sich an jdm** ~ to (sexually) assault sb; **V~** (-s, -) nt offence (BRIT), offense (US).
vergeigen [fɛr'gaigən] (umg) vt to cock up.
vergeistigt [fɛr'gaistɪçt] adj spiritual.
vergelten [fɛr'gɛltən] unreg vt: **jdm etw** ~ to pay sb back for sth, repay sb for sth.
Vergeltung f retaliation, reprisal.
Vergeltungsmaßnahme f retaliatory measure.
Vergeltungsschlag m (MIL) reprisal.
vergesellschaften [fɛrgə'zɛlʃaftən] vt (POL) to nationalize.
vergessen [fɛr'gɛsən] unreg vt to forget; **V~heit** f oblivion; **in V~heit geraten** to fall into oblivion.
vergesslich▲ [fɛr'gɛslɪç] adj forgetful; **V~keit** f forgetfulness.
vergeuden [fɛr'gɔydən] vt to squander, waste.
vergewaltigen [fɛrgə'valtɪgən] vt to rape; (fig) to violate.
Vergewaltigung f rape.
vergewissern [fɛrgə'vɪsərn] vr to make sure; **sich einer Sache** gen od **über etw** akk ~ to make sure of sth.
vergießen [fɛr'gi:sən] unreg vt to shed.
vergiften [fɛr'gɪftən] vt to poison.
Vergiftung f poisoning.
vergilbt [fɛr'gɪlpt] adj yellowed.
Vergissmeinnicht▲ [fɛr'gɪsmainnɪçt] (-(e)s, -e) nt forget-me-not.
vergisst▲ [fɛr'gɪst] vb siehe **vergessen**.
vergittert [fɛr'gɪtərt] adj: ~**e Fenster** barred windows.
verglasen [fɛr'gla:zən] vt to glaze.
Vergleich [fɛr'glaiç] (-(e)s, -e) m comparison; (JUR) settlement; **einen** ~ **schließen** (JUR) to reach a settlement; **in keinem** ~ **zu etw stehen** to be out of all proportion to sth; **im** ~ **mit** od **zu** compared with od to; **v~bar** adj comparable.
vergleichen unreg vt to compare ♦ vr (JUR) to reach a settlement.
vergleichsweise adv comparatively.
verglühen [fɛr'gly:ən] vi (Feuer) to die away; (Draht) to burn out; (Raumkapsel, Meteor etc) to burn up.
vergnügen [fɛr'gny:gən] vr to enjoy od amuse o.s.; **V~** (-s, -) nt pleasure; **das war ein teures V~** (umg) that was an expensive bit of fun; **viel V~!** enjoy yourself!
vergnüglich adj enjoyable.
vergnügt [fɛr'gny:kt] adj cheerful.

Vergnügung *f* pleasure, amusement.
Vergnügungs- *zW:* ~**park** *m* amusement park; **v~süchtig** *adj* pleasure-loving; ~**viertel** *nt* entertainments district.
vergolden [fɛr'gɔldən] *vt* to gild.
vergönnen [fɛr'gœnən] *vt* to grant.
vergöttern [fɛr'gœtərn] *vt* to idolize.
vergraben [fɛr'graːbən] *unreg vt* to bury.
vergrämt [fɛr'grɛːmt] *adj* (*Gesicht*) troubled.
vergreifen [fɛr'graɪfən] *unreg vr:* **sich an jdm** ~ to lay hands on sb; **sich an etw** *dat* ~ to misappropriate sth; **sich im Ton** ~ to say the wrong thing.
vergriffen [fɛr'grɪfən] *adj* (*Buch*) out of print; (*Ware*) out of stock.
vergrößern [fɛr'grøːsərn] *vt* to enlarge; (*mengenmäßig*) to increase; (*Lupe*) to magnify.
Vergrößerung *f* enlargement; increase; magnification.
Vergrößerungsglas *nt* magnifying glass.
vergünstigt *adj* (*Lage*) improved; (*Preis*) reduced.
Vergünstigung [fɛr'gynstɪɡʊŋ] *f* concession; (*Vorteil*) privilege.
vergüten [fɛr'gyːtən] *vt:* **jdm etw** ~ to compensate sb for sth; (*Arbeit, Leistung*) to pay sb for sth.
Vergütung *f* compensation; payment.
verh. *abk* = **verheiratet**.
verhaften [fɛr'haftən] *vt* to arrest.
Verhaftete(r) *f(m)* prisoner.
Verhaftung *f* arrest.
verhallen [fɛr'halən] *vi* to die away.
verhalten [fɛr'haltən] *unreg vr* (*Sache*) to be, stand; (*sich benehmen*) to behave; (*MATH*) to be in proportion to ♦ *vr unpers:* **wie verhält es sich damit?** (*wie ist die Lage?*) how do things stand?; (*wie wird das gehandhabt?*) how do you go about it? ♦ *adj* restrained; **sich ruhig** ~ to keep quiet; (*sich nicht bewegen*) to keep still; **wenn sich das so verhält ...** if that is the case ...; **V~** (**-s**) *nt* behaviour (*BRIT*), behavior (*US*).
Verhaltens- *zW:* ~**forschung** *f* behavioural (*BRIT*) *od* behavioral (*US*) science; **v~gestört** *adj* disturbed; ~**maßregel** *f* rule of conduct.
Verhältnis [fɛr'hɛltnɪs] (**-ses, -se**) *nt* relationship; (*Liebes~*) affair; (*MATH*) proportion, ratio; (*Einstellung*): ~ (**zu**) attitude (to); **Verhältnisse** *pl* (*Umstände*) conditions *pl*; **aus was für** ~**sen kommt er?** what sort of background does he come from?; **für klare** ~**se sorgen, klare** ~**se schaffen** to get things straight; **über seine** ~**se leben** to live beyond one's means; **v~mäßig** *adj* relative, comparative ♦ *adv* relatively, comparatively; ~**wahl** *f* proportional representation; ~**wahlrecht** *nt* (system of) proportional representation.

verhandeln [fɛr'handəln] *vi* to negotiate; (*JUR*) to hold proceedings ♦ *vt* to discuss; (*JUR*) to hear; **über etw** *akk* ~ to negotiate sth *od* about sth.
Verhandlung *f* negotiation; (*JUR*) proceedings *pl*; ~**en führen** to negotiate.
Verhandlungspaket *nt* (*COMM*) package deal.
Verhandlungstisch *m* negotiating table.
verhangen [fɛr'haŋən] *adj* overcast.
verhängen [fɛr'hɛŋən] *vt* (*fig*) to impose, inflict.
Verhängnis [fɛr'hɛŋnɪs] (**-ses, -se**) *nt* fate; **jdm zum** ~ **werden** to be sb's undoing; **v~voll** *adj* fatal, disastrous.
verharmlosen [fɛr'harmloːzən] *vt* to make light of, play down.
verharren [fɛr'harən] *vi* to remain; (*hartnäckig*) to persist.
verhärten [fɛr'hɛrtən] *vr* to harden.
verhaspeln [fɛr'haspəln] (*umg*) *vr* to get into a muddle *od* tangle.
verhasst▲ [fɛr'hast] *adj* odious, hateful.
verhätscheln [fɛr'hɛːtʃəln] *vt* to spoil, pamper.
Verhau [fɛr'hau] (**-(e)s, -e**) *m* (*zur Absperrung*) barrier; (*Käfig*) coop.
verhauen *unreg* (*umg*) *vt* (*verprügeln*) to beat up; (*Prüfung etc*) to muff.
verheben [fɛr'heːbən] *unreg vr* to hurt o.s. lifting sth.
verheerend [fɛr'heːrənt] *adj* disastrous, devastating.
verhehlen [fɛr'heːlən] *vt* to conceal.
verheilen [fɛr'haɪlən] *vi* to heal.
verheimlichen [fɛr'haɪmlɪçən] *vt:* (**jdm**) **etw** ~ to keep sth secret (from sb).
verheiratet [fɛr'haɪraːtət] *adj* married.
verheißen [fɛr'haɪsən] *unreg vt:* **jdm etw** ~ to promise sb sth.
verheißungsvoll *adj* promising.
verheizen [fɛr'haɪtsən] *vt* to burn, use as fuel.
verhelfen [fɛr'hɛlfən] *unreg vi:* **jdm zu etw** ~ to help sb to get sth.
verherrlichen [fɛr'hɛrlɪçən] *vt* to glorify.
verheult [fɛr'hɔylt] *adj* (*Augen, Gesicht*) puffy (*from crying*).
verhexen [fɛr'hɛksən] *vt* to bewitch; **es ist wie verhext** it's jinxed.
verhindern [fɛr'hɪndərn] *vt* to prevent; **verhindert sein** to be unable to make it; **das lässt sich leider nicht** ~ it can't be helped, unfortunately; **ein verhinderter Politiker** (*umg*) a would-be politician.
Verhinderung *f* prevention.
verhöhnen [fɛr'høːnən] *vt* to mock, sneer at.
verhohnepipeln [fɛr'hoːnəpiːpəln] (*umg*) *vt* to send up (*BRIT*), ridicule.
verhökern [fɛr'høːkərn] (*umg*) *vt* to turn into cash.

Verhör [fɛrˈhøːr] (-(e)s, -e) nt interrogation; (gerichtlich) (cross-)examination.
verhören vt to interrogate; to (cross-) examine ♦ vr to mishear.
verhüllen [fɛrˈhʏlən] vt to veil; (Haupt, Körperteil) to cover.
verhungern [fɛrˈhʊŋərn] vi to starve, die of hunger.
verhunzen [fɛrˈhʊntsən] (umg) vt to ruin.
verhüten [fɛrˈhyːtən] vt to prevent, avert.
Verhütung f prevention.
Verhütungsmittel nt contraceptive.
verifizieren [verifiˈtsiːrən] vt to verify.
verinnerlichen [fɛrˈ|ɪnərlɪçən] vt to internalize.
verirren [fɛrˈ|ɪrən] vr to get lost, lose one's way; (fig) to go astray; (Tier, Kugel) to stray.
verjagen [fɛrˈjaːɡən] vt to drive away od out.
verjähren [fɛrˈjɛːrən] vi to come under the statute of limitations; (Anspruch) to lapse.
Verjährungsfrist f limitation period.
verjubeln [fɛrˈjuːbəln] (umg) vt (Geld) to blow.
verjüngen [fɛrˈjʏŋən] vt to rejuvenate ♦ vr to taper.
verkabeln [fɛrˈkaːbəln] vt (TV) to link up to the cable network.
Verkabelung f (TV) linking up to the cable network.
verkalken [fɛrˈkalkən] vi to calcify; (umg) to become senile.
verkalkulieren [fɛrkalkuˈliːrən] vr to miscalculate.
verkannt [fɛrˈkant] adj unappreciated.
verkatert [fɛrˈkaːtərt] (umg) adj hung over.
Verkauf [fɛrˈkaʊf] m sale; **zum ~ stehen** to be up for sale.
verkaufen vt, vi to sell; „**zu ~**" "for sale".
Verkäufer(in) [fɛrˈkɔʏfər(ɪn)] (-s, -) m(f) seller; (im Außendienst) salesman, saleswoman; (in Laden) shop assistant (BRIT), sales clerk (US).
verkäuflich [fɛrˈkɔʏflɪç] adj saleable.
Verkaufs- zW: ~**abteilung** f sales department; ~**automat** m slot machine; ~**bedingungen** pl (COMM) terms and conditions of sale; ~**kampagne** f sales drive; ~**leiter** m sales manager; **v~offen** adj: **v~offener Samstag** Saturday on which the shops are open all day; ~**schlager** m big seller; ~**stelle** f outlet; ~**tüchtigkeit** f salesmanship.
Verkehr [fɛrˈkeːr] (-s, -e) m traffic; (Umgang, bes sexuell) intercourse; (Umlauf) circulation; **aus dem ~ ziehen** to withdraw from service; **für den ~ freigeben** (Straße etc) to open to traffic; (Transportmittel) to bring into service.
verkehren vi (Fahrzeug) to ply, run ♦ vt, vr to turn, transform; **~ mit** to associate with; **mit jdm brieflich** od **schriftlich ~** (form) to correspond with sb; **bei jdm ~** to visit sb

regularly.
Verkehrs- zW: ~**ampel** f traffic lights pl; ~**amt** nt tourist (information) office; ~**aufkommen** nt volume of traffic; **v~beruhigt** adj traffic-calmed; ~**beruhigung** f traffic-calming; ~**betriebe** pl transport services pl; ~**delikt** nt traffic offence (BRIT) od violation (US); ~**erziehung** f road safety training; **v~günstig** adj convenient; ~**insel** f traffic island; ~**knotenpunkt** m traffic junction; ~**mittel** nt: **öffentliche/private ~mittel** public/private transport sing; ~**schild** nt road sign; **v~sicher** adj (Fahrzeug) roadworthy; ~**sicherheit** f road safety; ~**stockung** f traffic jam, stoppage; ~**sünder** (umg) m traffic offender; ~**teilnehmer** m road user; **v~tüchtig** adj (Fahrzeug) roadworthy; (Mensch) fit to drive; ~**unfall** m traffic accident; ~**verein** m tourist information office; **v~widrig** adj contrary to traffic regulations; ~**zeichen** nt road sign.
verkehrt adj wrong; (umgekehrt) the wrong way round.
verkennen [fɛrˈkɛnən] unreg vt to misjudge; (unterschätzen) to underestimate.
Verkettung [fɛrˈkɛtʊŋ] f: **eine ~ unglücklicher Umstände** an unfortunate chain of events.
verklagen [fɛrˈklaːɡən] vt to take to court.
verklappen [fɛrˈklapən] vt to dump (at sea).
verklären [fɛrˈklɛːrən] vt to transfigure; **verklärt lächeln** to smile radiantly.
verklausulieren [fɛrklaʊzuˈliːrən] vt (Vertrag) to hedge in with (restrictive) clauses.
verkleben [fɛrˈkleːbən] vt to glue up, stick ♦ vi to stick together.
verkleiden [fɛrˈklaɪdən] vt to disguise; (kostümieren) to dress up; (Schacht, Tunnel) to line; (vertäfeln) to panel; (Heizkörper) to cover in ♦ vr to disguise o.s.; to dress up.
Verkleidung f disguise; (ARCHIT) panelling (BRIT), paneling (US).
verkleinern [fɛrˈklaɪnərn] vt to make smaller, reduce in size.
verklemmt [fɛrˈklɛmt] adj (fig) inhibited.
verklickern [fɛrˈklɪkərn] (umg) vt: **jdm etw ~** to make sth clear to sb.
verklingen [fɛrˈklɪŋən] unreg vi to die away.
verknacksen [fɛrˈknaksən] (umg) vt: **sich** dat **den Fuß ~** to twist one's ankle.
verknallen [fɛrˈknalən] (umg) vr: **sich in jdn ~** to fall for sb.
verkneifen [fɛrˈknaɪfən] (umg) vt: **sich** dat **etw ~** to stop o.s. from doing sth; **ich konnte mir das Lachen nicht ~** I couldn't help laughing.
verknöchert [fɛrˈknœçərt] adj (fig) fossilized.
verknüpfen [fɛrˈknʏpfən] vt to tie (up), knot; (fig) to connect.
Verknüpfung f connection.
verkochen [fɛrˈkɔxən] vt, vi (Flüssigkeit) to boil away.

verkohlen [fɛr'koːlən] *vi* to carbonize ♦ *vt* to carbonize; (*umg*): **jdn ~** to have sb on.

verkommen [fɛr'kɔmən] *unreg vi* to deteriorate, decay; (*Mensch*) to go downhill, come down in the world ♦ *adj* (*moralisch*) dissolute, depraved; **V~heit** *f* depravity.

verkorksen [fɛr'kɔrksən] (*umg*) *vt* to ruin, mess up.

verkörpern [fɛr'kœrpərn] *vt* to embody, personify.

verköstigen [fɛr'kœstɪgən] *vt* to feed.

verkrachen [fɛr'kraxən] (*umg*) *vr*: **sich (mit jdm) ~** to fall out (with sb).

verkracht (*umg*) *adj* (*Leben*) ruined.

verkraften [fɛr'kraftən] *vt* to cope with.

verkrampfen [fɛr'krampfən] *vr* (*Muskeln*) to go tense.

verkrampft [fɛr'krampft] *adj* (*fig*) tense.

verkriechen [fɛr'kriːçən] *unreg vr* to creep away, creep into a corner.

verkrümeln [fɛr'kryːməln] (*umg*) *vr* to disappear.

verkrümmt [fɛr'krymt] *adj* crooked.

Verkrümmung *f* bend, warp; (*ANAT*) curvature.

verkrüppelt [fɛr'krypəlt] *adj* crippled.

verkrustet [fɛr'krʊstət] *adj* encrusted.

verkühlen [fɛr'kyːlən] *vr* to get a chill.

verkümmern [fɛr'kymərn] *vi* to waste away; **emotionell/geistig ~** to become emotionally/intellectually stunted.

verkünden [fɛr'kyndən] *vt* to proclaim; (*Urteil*) to pronounce.

verkündigen [fɛr'kyndɪgən] *vt* to proclaim; (*ironisch*) to announce; (*Evangelium*) to preach.

verkuppeln [fɛr'kʊpəln] *vt*: **jdn an jdn ~** (*Zuhälter*) to procure sb for sb.

verkürzen [fɛr'kyrtsən] *vt* to shorten; (*Wort*) to abbreviate; **sich** *dat* **die Zeit ~** to while away the time; **verkürzte Arbeitszeit** shorter working hours *pl*.

Verkürzung *f* shortening; abbreviation.

Verl. *abk* (= *Verlag*) publ.

verladen [fɛr'laːdən] *unreg vt* to load.

Verlag [fɛr'laːk] (*-(e)s, -e*) *m* publishing firm.

verlagern [fɛr'laːgərn] *vt, vr* (*lit, fig*) to shift.

Verlagsanstalt *f* publishing firm.

Verlagswesen *nt* publishing.

verlangen [fɛr'laŋən] *vt* to demand; (*wollen*) to want ♦ *vi*: **~ nach** to ask for; **Sie werden am Telefon verlangt** you are wanted on the phone; **~ Sie Herrn X** ask for Mr X; **V~** (*-s, -*) *nt*: **V~** (*nach*) desire (for); **auf jds V~** *akk* (**hin**) at sb's request.

verlängern [fɛr'lɛŋərn] *vt* to extend; (*länger machen*) to lengthen; (*zeitlich*) to prolong; (*Pass, Abonnement etc*) to renew; **ein verlängertes Wochenende** a long weekend.

Verlängerung *f* extension; (*SPORT*) extra

time.

Verlängerungsschnur *f* extension cable.

verlangsamen [fɛr'laŋzaːmən] *vt, vr* to decelerate, slow down.

Verlass▲ [fɛr'las] *m*: **auf ihn/das ist kein ~** he/it cannot be relied upon.

verlassen [fɛr'lasən] *unreg vt* to leave ♦ *vr*: **sich ~ auf** *+akk* to depend on ♦ *adj* desolate; (*Mensch*) abandoned; **einsam und ~** so all alone; **V~heit** *f* loneliness (*BRIT*), lonesomeness (*US*).

verlässlich▲ [fɛr'lɛslɪç] *adj* reliable.

Verlauf [fɛr'laʊf] *m* course; **einen guten/ schlechten ~ nehmen** to go well/badly.

verlaufen *unreg vi* (*zeitlich*) to pass; (*Farben*) to run ♦ *vr* to get lost; (*Menschenmenge*) to disperse.

Verlautbarung *f* announcement.

verlauten [fɛr'laʊtən] *vi*: **etw ~ lassen** to disclose sth; **wie verlautet** as reported.

verleben [fɛr'leːbən] *vt* to spend.

verlebt [fɛr'leːpt] *adj* dissipated, worn-out.

verlegen [fɛr'leːgən] *vt* to move; (*verlieren*) to mislay; (*Kabel, Fliesen etc*) to lay; (*Buch*) to publish; (*verschieben*): **~ (auf** *+akk*) to postpone (until) ♦ *vr*: **sich auf etw** *akk* **~** to resort to sth ♦ *adj* embarrassed; **nicht ~ um** never at a loss for; **V~heit** *f* embarrassment; (*Situation*) difficulty, scrape.

Verleger [fɛr'leːgər] (*-s, -*) *m* publisher.

verleiden [fɛr'laɪdən] *vt*: **jdm etw ~** to put sb off sth.

Verleih [fɛr'laɪ] (*-(e)s, -e*) *m* hire service; (*das ~en*) renting (out), hiring (out) (*BRIT*); (*Film~*) distribution.

verleihen *unreg vt*: **etw (an jdn) ~** to lend sth (to sb), lend (sb) sth; (*gegen Gebühr*) to rent sth (out) (to sb), hire sth (out) (to sb) (*BRIT*); (*Kraft, Anschein*) to confer sth (on sb), bestow sth (on sb); (*Preis, Medaille*) to award sth (to sb), award (sb) sth.

Verleiher (*-s, -*) *m* hire (*BRIT*) *od* rental firm; (*von Filmen*) distributor; (*von Büchern*) lender.

Verleihung *f* lending; (*von Kraft etc*) bestowal; (*von Preis*) award.

verleiten [fɛr'laɪtən] *vt* to lead astray; **~ zu** to talk into, tempt into.

verlernen [fɛr'lɛrnən] *vt* to forget, unlearn.

verlesen [fɛr'leːzən] *unreg vt* to read out; (*aussondern*) to sort out ♦ *vr* to make a mistake in reading.

verletzbar *adj* vulnerable.

verletzen [fɛr'lɛtsən] *vt* (*lit, fig*) to injure, hurt; (*Gesetz etc*) to violate.

verletzend *adj* (*fig: Worte*) hurtful.

verletzlich *adj* vulnerable.

Verletzte(r) *f(m)* injured person.

Verletzung *f* injury; (*Verstoß*) violation,

infringement.

verleugnen [fɛrˈlɔygnən] *vt* to deny; (*Menschen*) to disown; **er lässt sich immer (vor ihr) verleugnen** he always pretends not to be there (when she calls).

Verleugnung *f* denial.

verleumden [fɛrˈlɔymdən] *vt* to slander; (*schriftlich*) to libel.

verleumderisch *adj* slanderous; libellous (*BRIT*), libelous (*US*).

Verleumdung *f* slander; libel.

verlieben *vr*: **sich** ~ **(in** +*akk*) to fall in love (with).

verliebt [fɛrˈliːpt] *adj* in love; **V~heit** *f* being in love.

verlieren [fɛrˈliːrən] *unreg vt, vi* to lose ♦ *vr* to get lost; (*verschwinden*) to disappear; **das/er hat hier nichts verloren** (*umg*) that/he has no business to be here.

Verlierer(in) (**-s, -**) *m(f)* loser.

Verlies [fɛrˈliːs] (**-es, -e**) *nt* dungeon.

verloben [fɛrˈloːbən] *vr*: **sich** ~ **(mit)** to get engaged (to); **verlobt sein** to be engaged.

Verlobte(r) [fɛrˈloːptə(r)] *f(m)*: **mein** ~**r** my fiancé; **meine** ~ my fiancée.

Verlobung *f* engagement.

verlocken [fɛrˈlɔkən] *vt* to entice, lure.

verlockend *adj* (*Angebot, Idee*) tempting.

Verlockung *f* temptation, attraction.

verlogen [fɛrˈloːgən] *adj* untruthful; (*Komplimente, Versprechungen*) false; (*Moral, Gesellschaft*) hypocritical; **V~heit** *f* untruthfulness.

verlor *etc* [fɛrˈloːr] *vb siehe* **verlieren**.

verloren *pp von* **verlieren** ♦ *adj* lost; (*Eier*) poached; **der** ~**e Sohn** the prodigal son; **auf** ~**em Posten kämpfen** *od* **stehen** to be fighting a losing battle; **etw** ~ **geben** to give sth up for lost; ~ **gehen** to get lost; **an ihm ist ein Sänger** ~ **gegangen** he would have made a (good) singer.

verlöschen [fɛrˈlœʃən] *vi* (*Hilfsverb sein*) to go out; (*Inschrift, Farbe, Erinnerung*) to fade.

verlosen [fɛrˈloːzən] *vt* to raffle (off), draw lots for.

Verlosung *f* raffle, lottery.

verlottern [fɛrˈlɔtərn] (*umg*) *vi* to go to the dogs.

verludern [fɛrˈluːdərn] (*umg*) *vi* to go to the dogs.

Verlust [fɛrˈlʊst] (**-(e)s, -e**) *m* loss; (*MIL*) casualty; **mit** ~ **verkaufen** to sell at a loss; ~**anzeige** *f* "lost" notice; ~**geschäft** *nt*: **das war ein** ~**geschäft** I/he *etc* made a loss; ~**zeit** *f* (*INDUSTRIE*) waiting time.

vermachen [fɛrˈmaxən] *vt* to bequeath, leave.

Vermächtnis [fɛrˈmɛçtnɪs] (**-ses, -se**) *nt* legacy.

vermählen [fɛrˈmɛːlən] *vr* to marry.

Vermählung *f* wedding, marriage.

vermarkten [fɛrˈmarktən] *vt* to market; (*fig: Persönlichkeit*) to promote.

Vermarktung [fɛrˈmarktʊŋ] *f* marketing.

vermasseln [fɛrˈmasəln] (*umg*) *vt* to mess up.

vermehren [fɛrˈmeːrən] *vt, vr* to multiply; (*Menge*) to increase.

Vermehrung *f* multiplying; increase.

vermeiden [fɛrˈmaɪdən] *unreg vt* to avoid.

vermeidlich *adj* avoidable.

vermeintlich [fɛrˈmaɪntlɪç] *adj* supposed.

vermengen [fɛrˈmɛŋən] *vt* to mix; (*fig*) to mix up, confuse.

Vermenschlichung [fɛrˈmɛnʃlɪçʊŋ] *f* humanization.

Vermerk [fɛrˈmɛrk] (**-(e)s, -e**) *m* note; (*in Ausweis*) endorsement.

vermerken *vt* to note.

vermessen [fɛrˈmɛsən] *unreg vt* to survey ♦ *vr* (*falsch messen*) to measure incorrectly ♦ *adj* presumptuous, bold; **V~heit** *f* presumptuousness.

Vermessung *f* survey(ing).

Vermessungsamt *nt* land survey(ing) office.

Vermessungsingenieur *m* land surveyor.

vermiesen [fɛrˈmiːzən] (*umg*) *vt* to spoil.

vermieten [fɛrˈmiːtən] *vt* to let (*BRIT*), rent (out); (*Auto*) to hire out, rent.

Vermieter(in) (**-s, -**) *m(f)* landlord, landlady.

Vermietung *f* letting, renting (out); (*von Autos*) hiring (out), rental.

vermindern [fɛrˈmɪndərn] *vt, vr* to lessen, decrease.

Verminderung *f* reduction.

verminen [fɛrˈmiːnən] *vt* to mine.

vermischen [fɛrˈmɪʃən] *vt, vr* to mix; (*Teesorten etc*) to blend; **vermischte Schriften** miscellaneous writings.

vermissen [fɛrˈmɪsən] *vt* to miss; **vermisst sein, als vermisst gemeldet sein** to be reported missing; **wir haben dich bei der Party vermisst** we didn't see you at the party.

Vermisste(r)▲ *f(m)* missing person.

Vermisstenanzeige▲ *f* missing persons report.

vermitteln [fɛrˈmɪtəln] *vi* to mediate ♦ *vt* to arrange; (*Gespräch*) to connect; (*Stelle*) to find; (*Gefühl, Bild, Idee etc*) to convey; (*Wissen*) to impart; ~**de Worte** conciliatory words; **jdm etw** ~ to help sb to obtain sth; (*Stelle*) to find sth for sb.

Vermittler(in) [fɛrˈmɪtlər(ɪn)] (**-s, -**) *m(f)* (*COMM*) agent; (*Schlichter*) mediator.

Vermittlung *f* procurement; (*Stellen*~) agency; (*TEL*) exchange; (*Schlichtung*) mediation.

Vermittlungsgebühr *f* commission.

vermögen [fɛrˈmøːgən] *unreg vt* to be capable of; ~ **zu** to be able to; **V~** (**-s, -**) *nt* wealth; (*Fähigkeit*) ability; **mein ganzes V~ besteht**

aus my entire assets consist of ...; **ein V~ kosten** to cost a fortune.

vermögend *adj* wealthy.

Vermögens- *zW:* **~steuer** *f* property tax, wealth tax; **~wert** *m* asset; **v~wirksam** *adj:* **sein Geld v~wirksam anlegen** to invest one's money profitably; **v~wirksame Leistungen** *employers' contributions to tax-deductible savings scheme.*

vermummen [fɛr'mʊmən] *vr* to wrap up (warm); (*sich verkleiden*) to disguise.

Vermummungsverbot (-(e)s) *nt law against disguising o.s. at demonstrations.*

vermurksen [fɛr'mʊrksən] (*umg*) *vt* to make a mess of.

vermuten [fɛr'muːtən] *vt* to suppose; (*argwöhnen*) to suspect.

vermutlich *adj* supposed, presumed ♦ *adv* probably.

Vermutung *f* supposition; suspicion; **die ~ liegt nahe, dass ...** there are grounds for assuming that ...

vernachlässigen [fɛr'naːxlɛsɪgən] *vt* to neglect ♦ *vr* to neglect o.s. *od* one's appearance.

Vernachlässigung *f* neglect.

vernarben [fɛr'narbən] *vi* to heal up.

vernarren [fɛr'narən] (*umg*) *vr:* **in jdn/etw vernarrt sein** to be crazy about sb/sth.

vernaschen [fɛr'naʃən] *vt* (*Geld*) to spend on sweets; (*umg: Mädchen, Mann*) to make it with.

vernehmen [fɛr'neːmən] *unreg vt* to hear, perceive; (*erfahren*) to learn; (*JUR*) to (cross-)examine; (*Polizei*) to question; **V~** *nt:* **dem V~ nach** from what I/we *etc* hear.

vernehmlich *adj* audible.

Vernehmung *f* (cross-)examination.

vernehmungsfähig *adj* in a condition to be (cross-)examined.

verneigen [fɛr'naɪgən] *vr* to bow.

verneinen [fɛr'naɪnən] *vt* (*Frage*) to answer in the negative; (*ablehnen*) to deny; (*GRAM*) to negate.

verneinend *adj* negative.

Verneinung *f* negation.

vernichten [fɛr'nɪçtən] *vt* to destroy, annihilate.

vernichtend *adj* (*fig*) crushing; (*Blick*) withering; (*Kritik*) scathing.

Vernichtung *f* destruction, annihilation.

Vernichtungsschlag *m* devastating blow.

verniedlichen [fɛr'niːtlɪçən] *vt* to play down.

Vernunft [fɛr'nʊnft] (-) *f* reason; **~ annehmen** to see reason; **~ehe** *f*, **~heirat** *f* marriage of convenience.

vernünftig [fɛr'nʏnftɪç] *adj* sensible, reasonable.

Vernunftmensch *m* rational person.

veröden [fɛr'|øːdən] *vi* to become desolate ♦ *vt*

(*MED*) to remove.

veröffentlichen [fɛr'|œfəntlɪçən] *vt* to publish.

Veröffentlichung *f* publication.

verordnen [fɛr'|ɔrdnən] *vt* (*MED*) to prescribe.

Verordnung *f* order, decree; (*MED*) prescription.

verpachten [fɛr'paxtən] *vt* to lease (out).

verpacken [fɛr'pakən] *vt* to pack; (*verbrauchergerecht*) to package; (*einwickeln*) to wrap.

Verpackung *f* packing; packaging; wrapping.

verpassen [fɛr'pasən] *vt* to miss; **jdm eine Ohrfeige ~** (*umg*) to give sb a clip round the ear.

verpatzen [fɛr'patsən] (*umg*) *vt* to spoil, mess up.

verpennen [fɛr'pɛnən] (*umg*) *vi, vr* to oversleep.

verpesten [fɛr'pɛstən] *vt* to pollute.

verpetzen [fɛr'pɛtsən] (*umg*) *vt:* **jdn ~ (bei)** to tell on sb (to).

verpfänden [fɛr'pfɛndən] *vt* to pawn; (*JUR*) to mortgage.

verpfeifen [fɛr'pfaɪfən] *unreg* (*umg*) *vt:* **jdn ~ (bei)** to grass on sb (to).

verpflanzen [fɛr'pflantsən] *vt* to transplant.

Verpflanzung *f* transplanting; (*MED*) transplant.

verpflegen [fɛr'pfleːgən] *vt* to feed, cater for (*BRIT*).

Verpflegung *f* catering; (*Kost*) food; (*in Hotel*) board.

verpflichten [fɛr'pflɪçtən] *vt* to oblige, bind; (*anstellen*) to engage ♦ *vr* to undertake; (*MIL*) to sign on ♦ *vi* to carry obligations; **jdm verpflichtet sein** to be under an obligation to sb; **sich zu etw ~** to commit o.s. to doing sth; **jdm zu Dank verpflichtet sein** to be obliged to sb.

verpflichtend *adj* (*Zusage*) binding.

Verpflichtung *f* obligation; (*Aufgabe*) duty.

verpfuschen [fɛr'pfʊʃən] (*umg*) *vt* to bungle, make a mess of.

verplanen [fɛr'plaːnən] *vt* (*Zeit*) to book up; (*Geld*) to budget.

verplappern [fɛr'plapərn] (*umg*) *vr* to open one's big mouth.

verplempern [fɛr'plɛmpərn] (*umg*) *vt* to waste.

verpönt [fɛr'pøːnt] *adj:* **~ (bei)** frowned upon (by).

verprassen [fɛr'prasən] *vt* to squander.

verprügeln [fɛr'pryːgəln] (*umg*) *vt* to beat up.

verpuffen [fɛr'pʊfən] *vi* to (go) pop; (*fig*) to fall flat.

Verputz [fɛr'pʊts] *m* plaster; (*Rauputz*) roughcast; **v~en** *vt* to plaster; (*umg: Essen*) to put away.

verqualmen [fɛr'kvalmən] *vt* (*Zimmer*) to fill with smoke.

verquollen [fɛr'kvɔlən] *adj* swollen; (*Holz*) warped.

verrammeln [fɛr'raməln] *vt* to barricade.

Verrat [fɛr'raːt] (-(e)s) *m* treachery; (*POL*) treason; ~ **an jdm üben** to betray sb.

verraten *unreg vt* to betray; (*fig: erkennen lassen*) to show; (*Geheimnis*) to divulge ♦ *vr* to give o.s. away.

Verräter(in) [fɛr'rɛːtər(ɪn)] (-s, -) *m(f)* traitor, traitress; **v~isch** *adj* treacherous.

verrauchen [fɛr'rauxən] *vi* (*fig: Zorn*) to blow over.

verrechnen [fɛr'rɛçnən] *vt*: ~ **mit** to set off against ♦ *vr* to miscalculate.

Verrechnung *f*: **nur zur ~** (*auf Scheck*) a/c payee only.

Verrechnungsscheck *m* crossed cheque (*BRIT*).

verregnet [fɛr'reːgnət] *adj* rainy, spoilt by rain.

verreisen [fɛr'raizən] *vi* to go away (on a journey); **er ist geschäftlich verreist** he's away on business.

verreißen [fɛr'raisən] *unreg vt* to pull to pieces.

verrenken [fɛr'rɛŋkən] *vt* to contort; (*MED*) to dislocate; **sich** *dat* **den Knöchel ~** to sprain one's ankle.

Verrenkung *f* contortion; (*MED*) dislocation.

verrennen [fɛr'rɛnən] *unreg vr*: **sich in etw** *akk* ~ to get stuck on sth.

verrichten [fɛr'rɪçtən] *vt* (*Arbeit*) to do, perform.

verriegeln [fɛr'riːgəln] *vt* to bolt.

verringern [fɛr'rɪŋərn] *vt* to reduce ♦ *vr* to decrease.

Verringerung *f* reduction; decrease.

verrinnen [fɛr'rɪnən] *unreg vi* to run out *od* away; (*Zeit*) to elapse.

Verriss▲ [fɛr'rɪs] *m* slating review.

verrohen [fɛr'roːən] *vi* to become brutalized.

verrosten [fɛr'rɔstən] *vi* to rust.

verrotten [fɛr'rɔtən] *vi* to rot.

verrucht [fɛr'ruːxt] *adj* despicable; (*verrufen*) disreputable.

verrücken [fɛr'rʏkən] *vt* to move, shift.

verrückt *adj* crazy, mad; **V~e(r)** *f(m)* lunatic; **V~heit** *f* madness, lunacy.

Verruf [fɛr'ruːf] *m*: **in ~ geraten/bringen** to fall/bring into disrepute.

verrufen *adj* disreputable.

verrutschen [fɛr'rʊtʃən] *vi* to slip.

Vers [fɛrs] (-es, -e) *m* verse.

versacken [fɛr'zakən] *vi* (*lit*) to sink; (*fig: umg: herunterkommen*) to go downhill; (: *lange zechen*) to get involved in a booze-up (*BRIT*) *od* a drinking spree.

versagen [fɛr'zaːgən] *vt*: **jdm/sich etw ~** to deny sb/o.s. sth ♦ *vi* to fail; **V~** (-s) *nt* failure; **menschliches V~** human error.

Versager (-s, -) *m* failure.

versalzen [fɛr'zaltsən] *vt* to put too much salt in; (*fig*) to spoil.

versammeln [fɛr'zaməln] *vt*, *vr* to assemble, gather.

Versammlung *f* meeting, gathering.

Versammlungsfreiheit *f* freedom of assembly.

Versand [fɛr'zant] (-(e)s) *m* dispatch; (~*abteilung*) dispatch department; ~**bahnhof** *m* dispatch station; ~**haus** *nt* mail-order firm; ~**kosten** *pl* transport(ation) costs *pl*; ~**weg** *m*: **auf dem ~weg** by mail order.

versäumen [fɛr'zɔymən] *vt* to miss; (*Pflicht*) to neglect; (*Zeit*) to lose.

Versäumnis (-ses, -se) *nt* neglect; (*Unterlassung*) omission.

verschachern [fɛr'ʃaxərn] (*umg*) *vt* to sell off.

verschachtelt [fɛr'ʃaxtəlt] *adj* (*Satz*) complex.

verschaffen [fɛr'ʃafən] *vt*: **jdm/sich etw ~** to get *od* procure sth for sb/o.s.

verschämt [fɛr'ʃɛːmt] *adj* bashful.

verschandeln [fɛr'ʃandəln] (*umg*) *vt* to spoil.

verschanzen [fɛr'ʃantsən] *vr*: **sich hinter etw** *dat* ~ to dig in behind sth; (*fig*) to take refuge behind sth.

verschärfen [fɛr'ʃɛrfən] *vt* to intensify; (*Lage*) to aggravate; (*strenger machen: Kontrollen, Gesetze*) to tighten up ♦ *vr* to intensify; to become aggravated; to become tighter.

Verschärfung *f* intensification; (*der Lage*) aggravation; (*von Kontrollen etc*) tightening.

verscharren [fɛr'ʃarən] *vt* to bury.

verschätzen [fɛr'ʃɛtsən] *vr* to miscalculate.

verschenken [fɛr'ʃɛŋkən] *vt* to give away.

verscherzen [fɛr'ʃɛrtsən] *vt*: **sich** *dat* **etw ~** to lose sth, throw sth away.

verscheuchen [fɛr'ʃɔyçən] *vt* to frighten away.

verschicken [fɛr'ʃɪkən] *vt* to send off; (*Sträfling*) to transport.

verschieben [fɛr'ʃiːbən] *unreg vt* to shift; (*EISENB*) to shunt; (*Termin*) to postpone; (*umg: Waren, Devisen*) to traffic in.

Verschiebung *f* shift, displacement; shunting; postponement.

verschieden [fɛr'ʃiːdən] *adj* different; **das ist ganz ~** (*wird ~ gehandhabt*) that varies, that just depends; **sie sind ~ groß** they are of different sizes; ~**artig** *adj* various, of different kinds; **zwei so ~artige ...** two such differing ...; **V~e▲** *pron pl* various people; various things *pl*; **V~es▲** *pron* various things *pl*; **etwas V~es** something different; **V~heit** *f* difference.

verschiedentlich *adv* several times.

verschiffen [fɛr'ʃɪfən] *vt* to ship; (*Sträfling*) to transport.

verschimmeln [fɛr'ʃɪməln] *vi* (*Nahrungsmittel*) to go mouldy (*BRIT*) *od* moldy (*US*); (*Leder,*

Papier etc) to become mildewed.

verschlafen [fɛrˈʃlaːfən] *unreg vt* to sleep through; (*fig: versäumen*) to miss ♦ *vi, vr* to oversleep ♦ *adj* sleepy.

Verschlag [fɛrˈʃlaːk] *m* shed.

verschlagen [fɛrˈʃlaːgən] *unreg vt* to board up; (*TENNIS*) to hit out of play; (*Buchseite*) to lose ♦ *adj* cunning; **jdm den Atem ~ to take sb's breath away; an einen Ort ~ werden** to wind up in a place.

verschlampen [fɛrˈʃlampən] *vi* (*Hilfsverb sein: Mensch*) to go to seed (*umg*) ♦ *vt* to lose, mislay.

verschlechtern [fɛrˈʃlɛçtərn] *vt* to make worse ♦ *vr* to deteriorate, get worse; (*gehaltlich*) to take a lower-paid job.

Verschlechterung *f* deterioration.

Verschleierung [fɛrˈʃlaɪərʊŋ] *f* veiling; (*fig*) concealment; (*MIL*) screening.

Verschleierungstaktik *f* smoke-screen tactics *pl*.

Verschleiß [fɛrˈʃlaɪs] (**-es, -e**) *m* wear and tear.

verschleißen *unreg vt, vi, vr* to wear out.

verschleppen [fɛrˈʃlɛpən] *vt* to carry off, abduct; (*zeitlich*) to drag out, delay; (*verbreiten: Seuche*) to spread.

verschleudern [fɛrˈʃlɔydərn] *vt* to squander; (*COMM*) to sell dirt-cheap.

verschließbar *adj* lockable.

verschließen [fɛrˈʃliːsən] *unreg vt* to lock ♦ *vr*: **sich einer Sache** *dat* ~ to close one's mind to sth.

verschlimmern [fɛrˈʃlɪmərn] *vt* to make worse, aggravate ♦ *vr* to get worse, deteriorate.

Verschlimmerung *f* deterioration.

verschlingen [fɛrˈʃlɪŋən] *unreg vt* to devour, swallow up; (*Fäden*) to twist.

verschliss *etc*▲ [fɛrˈʃlɪs] *vb siehe* **verschleißen**.

verschlissen [fɛrˈʃlɪsən] *pp von* **verschleißen** ♦ *adj* worn(-out).

verschlossen [fɛrˈʃlɔsən] *adj* locked; (*fig*) reserved; (*schweigsam*) tight-lipped; **V~heit** *f* reserve.

verschlucken [fɛrˈʃlʊkən] *vt* to swallow ♦ *vr* to choke.

Verschluss▲ [fɛrˈʃlʊs] *m* lock; (*von Kleid etc*) fastener; (*PHOT*) shutter; (*Stöpsel*) plug; **unter ~ halten** to keep under lock and key.

verschlüsseln [fɛrˈʃlʏsəln] *vt* to encode.

verschmachten [fɛrˈʃmaxtən] *vi*: ~ (**vor** +*dat*) to languish (for); **vor Durst ~** to be dying of thirst.

verschmähen [fɛrˈʃmɛːən] *vt* to scorn.

verschmelzen [fɛrˈʃmɛltsən] *unreg vt, vi* to merge, blend.

verschmerzen [fɛrˈʃmɛrtsən] *vt* to get over.

verschmiert [fɛrˈʃmiːrt] *adj* (*Hände*) smeary; (*Schminke*) smudged.

verschmitzt [fɛrˈʃmɪtst] *adj* mischievous.

verschmutzen [fɛrˈʃmʊtsən] *vt* to soil; (*Umwelt*) to pollute.

Verschmutzung *f* pollution.

verschnaufen [fɛrˈʃnaʊfən] (*umg*) *vi, vr* to have a breather.

verschneiden [fɛrˈʃnaɪdən] *vt* (*Whisky etc*) to blend.

verschneit [fɛrˈʃnaɪt] *adj* covered in snow, snowed up.

Verschnitt [fɛrˈʃnɪt] *m* (*von Whisky etc*) blend.

verschnörkelt [fɛrˈʃnœrkəlt] *adj* ornate.

verschnupft [fɛrˈʃnʊpft] (*umg*) *adj*: ~ **sein** to have a cold; (*beleidigt*) to be peeved (*umg*).

verschnüren [fɛrˈʃnyːrən] *vt* to tie up.

verschollen [fɛrˈʃɔlən] *adj* lost, missing.

verschonen [fɛrˈʃoːnən] *vt*: **jdn mit etw ~** to spare sb sth; **von etw verschont bleiben** to escape sth.

verschönern [fɛrˈʃøːnərn] *vt* to decorate; (*verbessern*) to improve.

verschossen [fɛrˈʃɔsən] *adj*: ~ **sein** (*fig: umg*) to be in love.

verschränken [fɛrˈʃrɛŋkən] *vt* to cross; (*Arme*) to fold.

verschreckt [fɛrˈʃrɛkt] *adj* frightened, scared.

verschreiben [fɛrˈʃraɪbən] *unreg vt* (*Papier*) to use up; (*MED*) to prescribe ♦ *vr* to make a mistake (in writing); **sich einer Sache** *dat* ~ to devote o.s. to sth.

verschrie(e)n [fɛrˈʃriː(ə)n] *adj* notorious.

verschroben [fɛrˈʃroːbən] *adj* eccentric, odd.

verschrotten [fɛrˈʃrɔtən] *vt* to scrap.

verschüchtert [fɛrˈʃʏçtərt] *adj* subdued, intimidated.

verschulden [fɛrˈʃʊldən] *vt* to be guilty of ♦ *vi* (*in Schulden geraten*) to get into debt; **V~** (**-s**) *nt* fault.

verschuldet *adj* in debt.

Verschuldung *f* debts *pl*.

verschütten [fɛrˈʃʏtən] *vt* to spill; (*zuschütten*) to fill; (*unter Trümmer*) to bury.

verschwand *etc* [fɛrˈʃvant] *vb siehe* **verschwinden**.

verschweigen [fɛrˈʃvaɪgən] *unreg vt* to keep secret; **jdm etw ~** to keep sth from sb.

verschwenden [fɛrˈʃvɛndən] *vt* to squander.

Verschwender(in) (**-s, -**) *m(f)* spendthrift; **v~isch** *adj* wasteful; (*Leben*) extravagant.

Verschwendung *f* waste.

verschwiegen [fɛrˈʃviːgən] *adj* discreet; (*Ort*) secluded; **V~heit** *f* discretion; seclusion; **zur V~heit verpflichtet** bound to secrecy.

verschwimmen [fɛrˈʃvɪmən] *unreg vi* to grow hazy, become blurred.

verschwinden [fɛrˈʃvɪndən] *unreg vi* to disappear, vanish; **verschwinde!** clear off! (*umg*); **V~** (**-s**) *nt* disappearance.

verschwindend *adj* (*Anzahl, Menge*) insignificant.

verschwitzen [fɛr'ʃvɪtsən] vt to stain with sweat; (umg) to forget.

verschwitzt adj (Kleidung) sweat-stained; (Mensch) sweaty.

verschwommen [fɛr'ʃvɔmən] adj hazy, vague.

verschworen [fɛr'ʃvoːrən] adj (Gesellschaft) sworn.

verschwören [fɛr'ʃvøːrən] unreg vr to conspire, plot.

Verschwörer(in) (-s, -) m(f) conspirator.

Verschwörung f conspiracy, plot.

verschwunden [fɛr'ʃvʊndən] pp von **verschwinden** ♦ adj missing.

versehen [fɛr'zeːən] unreg vt to supply, provide; (Pflicht) to carry out; (Amt) to fill; (Haushalt) to keep ♦ vr (fig) to make a mistake; **ehe er (es) sich ~ hatte ...** before he knew it ...; **V~** (-s, -) nt oversight; **aus V~** by mistake.

versehentlich adv by mistake.

Versehrte(r) [fɛr'zeːrtə(r)] f(m) disabled person.

verselbstständigen▲ [fɛr'zɛlpstʃtɛndɪgən], **verselbständigen** [fɛr'zɛlpʃtɛndɪgən] vr to become independent.

versenden [fɛr'zɛndən] unreg vt to send; (COMM) to forward.

versengen [fɛr'zɛŋən] vt to scorch; (Feuer) to singe; (umg: verprügeln) to wallop.

versenken [fɛr'zɛŋkən] vt to sink ♦ vr: **sich ~ in** +akk to become engrossed in.

versessen [fɛr'zɛsən] adj: **~ auf** +akk mad about, hellbent on.

versetzen [fɛr'zɛtsən] vt to transfer; (verpfänden) to pawn; (umg: vergeblich warten lassen) to stand up; (nicht geradlinig anordnen) to stagger; (SCH: in höhere Klasse) to move up ♦ vr: **sich in jdn od in jds Lage ~** to put o.s. in sb's place; **jdm einen Tritt/ Schlag ~** to kick/hit sb; **etw mit etw ~** to mix sth with sth; **jdm einen Stich ~** (fig) to cut sb to the quick, wound sb (deeply); **jdn in gute Laune ~** to put sb in a good mood.

Versetzung f transfer; **seine ~ ist gefährdet** (SCH) he's in danger of having to repeat a year.

verseuchen [fɛr'zɔʏçən] vt to contaminate.

Versicherer (-s, -) m insurer; (bei Schiffen) underwriter.

versichern [fɛr'zɪçərn] vt to assure; (mit Geld) to insure ♦ vr: **sich ~ +gen** to make sure of.

Versicherte(r) f(m) insured.

Versicherung f assurance; insurance.

Versicherungs- zW: **~beitrag** m insurance premium; (bei staatlicher Versicherung etc) social security contribution; **~gesellschaft** f insurance company; **~nehmer** (-s, -) m (form) insured, policy holder; **~police** f insurance policy; **~schutz** m insurance

cover; **~summe** f sum insured; **~träger** m insurer.

versickern [fɛr'zɪkərn] vi to seep away; (fig: Interesse etc) to peter out.

versiegeln [fɛr'ziːgəln] vt to seal (up).

versiegen [fɛr'ziːgən] vi to dry up.

versiert [vɛr'ziːrt] adj: **in etw** dat **~ sein** to be experienced od well versed in sth.

versilbert [fɛr'zɪlbərt] adj silver-plated.

versinken [fɛr'zɪŋkən] unreg vi to sink; **ich hätte im Boden** od **vor Scham ~ mögen** I wished the ground would swallow me up.

versinnbildlichen [fɛr'zɪnbɪltlɪçən] vt to symbolize.

Version [vɛrzi'oːn] f version.

Versmaß ['fɛrsmaːs] nt metre (BRIT), meter (US).

versohlen [fɛr'zoːlən] (umg) vt to belt.

versöhnen [fɛr'zøːnən] vt to reconcile ♦ vr to become reconciled.

versöhnlich adj (Ton, Worte) conciliatory; (Ende) happy.

Versöhnung f reconciliation.

versonnen [fɛr'zɔnən] adj (Gesichtsausdruck) pensive, thoughtful; (träumerisch: Blick) dreamy.

versorgen [fɛr'zɔrgən] vt to provide, supply; (Familie etc) to look after ♦ vr to look after o.s.

Versorger(in) (-s, -) m(f) (Ernährer) provider, breadwinner; (Belieferer) supplier.

Versorgung f provision; (Unterhalt) maintenance; (Alters~ etc) benefit, assistance.

Versorgungs- zW: **~amt** nt pension office; **~betrieb** m public utility; **~netz** nt (Wasserversorgung etc) (supply) grid; (von Waren) supply network.

verspannen [fɛr'ʃpanən] vr (Muskeln) to tense up.

verspäten [fɛr'ʃpɛːtən] vr to be late.

verspätet adj late.

Verspätung f delay; **~ haben** to be late; **mit zwanzig Minuten ~** twenty minutes late.

versperren [fɛr'ʃpɛrən] vt to bar, obstruct.

verspielen [fɛr'ʃpiːlən] vt, vi to lose; **(bei jdm) verspielt haben** to have had it (as far as sb is concerned).

verspielt [fɛr'ʃpiːlt] adj playful.

versponnen [fɛr'ʃpɔnən] adj crackpot.

verspotten [fɛr'ʃpɔtən] vt to ridicule, scoff at.

versprach etc [fɛr'ʃpraːx] vb siehe **versprechen**.

versprechen [fɛr'ʃprɛçən] unreg vt to promise ♦ vr (etwas Nichtgemeintes sagen) to make a slip of the tongue; **sich** dat **etw von etw ~** to expect sth from sth; **V~** (-s, -) nt promise.

Versprecher (-s, -) (umg) m slip (of the tongue).

verspricht [fɛr'ʃprɪçt] vb siehe **versprechen**.

verspüren [fɛr'ʃpyːrən] vt to feel, be

conscious of.

verstaatlichen [fɛr'ʃtaːtlɪçən] *vt* to nationalize.

verstaatlicht *adj*: ~**er Industriezweig** nationalized industry.

Verstaatlichung *f* nationalization.

Verstand [fɛr'ʃtant] *m* intelligence; (*Intellekt*) mind; (*Fähigkeit zu denken*) reason; **den** ~ **verlieren** to go out of one's mind; **über jds** ~ *akk* **gehen** to be beyond sb.

verstand *etc vb siehe* **verstehen**.

verstanden [fɛr'ʃtandən] *pp von* **verstehen**.

verstandesmäßig *adj* rational.

verständig [fɛr'ʃtɛndɪç] *adj* sensible.

verständigen [fɛr'ʃtɛndɪɡən] *vt* to inform ♦ *vr* to communicate; (*sich einigen*) to come to an understanding.

Verständigkeit *f* good sense.

Verständigung *f* communication; (*Benachrichtigung*) informing; (*Einigung*) agreement.

verständlich [fɛr'ʃtɛntlɪç] *adj* understandable, comprehensible; (*hörbar*) audible; **sich** ~ **machen** to make o.s. understood; (*sich klar ausdrücken*) to make o.s. clear.

verständlicherweise *adv* understandably (enough).

Verständlichkeit *f* clarity, intelligibility.

Verständnis (-ses, -se) *nt* understanding; **für etw kein** ~ **haben** to have no understanding *od* sympathy for sth; (*für Kunst etc*) to have no appreciation of sth; **v~los** *adj* uncomprehending; **v~voll** *adj* understanding, sympathetic.

verstärken [fɛr'ʃtɛrkən] *vt* to strengthen; (*Ton*) to amplify; (*erhöhen*) to intensify ♦ *vr* to intensify.

Verstärker (-s, -) *m* amplifier.

Verstärkung *f* strengthening; (*Hilfe*) reinforcements *pl*; (*von Ton*) amplification.

verstaubt [fɛr'ʃtaʊpt] *adj* dusty; (*fig: Ansichten*) fuddy-duddy (*umg*).

verstauchen [fɛr'ʃtaʊxən] *vt* to sprain.

verstauen [fɛr'ʃtaʊən] *vt* to stow away.

Versteck [fɛr'ʃtɛk] (-(e)s, -e) *nt* hiding (place).

verstecken *vt*, *vr* to hide.

versteckt *adj* hidden; (*Tür*) concealed; (*fig: Lächeln, Blick*) furtive; (*Andeutung*) veiled.

verstehen [fɛr'ʃteːən] *unreg vt, vi* to understand; (*können, beherrschen*) to know ♦ *vr* (*auskommen*) to get on; **das ist nicht wörtlich zu** ~ that isn't to be taken literally; **das versteht sich von selbst** that goes without saying; **die Preise** ~ **sich einschließlich Lieferung** prices are inclusive of delivery; **sich auf etw** *akk* ~ to be an expert at sth.

versteifen [fɛr'ʃtaɪfən] *vt* to stiffen, brace ♦ *vr* (*fig*): **sich** ~ **auf** +*akk* to insist on.

versteigen [fɛr'ʃtaɪɡən] *unreg vr*: **sie hat sich zu**

der Behauptung verstiegen, dass ... she presumed to claim that ...

versteigern [fɛr'ʃtaɪɡərn] *vt* to auction.

Versteigerung *f* auction.

verstellbar *adj* adjustable, variable.

verstellen [fɛr'ʃtɛlən] *vt* to move, shift; (*Uhr*) to adjust; (*versperren*) to block; (*fig*) to disguise ♦ *vr* to pretend, put on an act.

Verstellung *f* pretence (*BRIT*), pretense (*US*).

versteuern [fɛr'ʃtɔʏərn] *vt* to pay tax on; **zu** ~ taxable.

verstiegen [fɛr'ʃtiːɡən] *adj* exaggerated.

verstimmt [fɛr'ʃtɪmt] *adj* out of tune; (*fig*) cross, put out; (: *Magen*) upset.

Verstimmung *f* (*fig*) disgruntled state, peevishness.

verstockt [fɛr'ʃtɔkt] *adj* stubborn; **V~heit** *f* stubbornness.

verstohlen [fɛr'ʃtoːlən] *adj* stealthy.

verstopfen [fɛr'ʃtɔpfən] *vt* to block, stop up; (*MED*) to constipate.

Verstopfung *f* obstruction; (*MED*) constipation.

verstorben [fɛr'ʃtɔrbən] *adj* deceased, late.

Verstorbene(r) *f(m)* deceased.

verstört [fɛr'ʃtøːrt] *adj* (*Mensch*) distraught.

Verstoß [fɛr'ʃtoːs] *m*: ~ **(gegen)** infringement (of), violation (of).

verstoßen *unreg vt* to disown, reject ♦ *vi*: ~ **gegen** to offend against.

Verstrebung [fɛr'ʃtreːbʊŋ] *f* (*Strebebalken*) support(ing beam).

verstreichen [fɛr'ʃtraɪçən] *unreg vt* to spread ♦ *vi* to elapse; (*Zeit*) to pass (by); (*Frist*) to expire.

verstreuen [fɛr'ʃtrɔʏən] *vt* to scatter (about).

verstricken [fɛr'ʃtrɪkən] *vt* (*fig*) to entangle, ensnare ♦ *vr*: **sich** ~ **in** +*akk* to get entangled in.

verströmen [fɛr'ʃtrøːmən] *vt* to exude.

verstümmeln [fɛr'ʃtʏməln] *vt* to maim, mutilate (*auch fig*).

verstummen [fɛr'ʃtʊmən] *vi* to go silent; (*Lärm*) to die away.

Versuch [fɛr'zuːx] (-(e)s, -e) *m* attempt; (*CHEM etc*) experiment; **das käme auf einen** ~ **an** we'll have to have a try.

versuchen *vt* to try; (*verlocken*) to tempt ♦ *vr*: **sich an etw** *dat* ~ to try one's hand at sth.

Versuchs- *zW*: ~**anstalt** *f* research institute; ~**bohrung** *f* experimental drilling; ~**kaninchen** *nt* guinea pig; ~**objekt** *nt* test object; (*fig: Mensch*) guinea pig; ~**reihe** *f* series of experiments; **v~weise** *adv* tentatively.

Versuchung *f* temptation.

versumpfen [fɛr'zʊmpfən] *vi* (*Gebiet*) to become marshy; (*fig: umg*) to go to pot; (*lange zechen*) to get involved in a booze-up (*BRIT*) *od* drinking spree (*US*).

versündigen [fɛr'zʏndɪɡən] *vr* (*geh*): **sich an jdm/etw** ~ to sin against sb/sth.

versunken [fɛr'zʊŋkən] *adj* sunken; ~ **sein in** +*akk* to be absorbed *od* engrossed in; **V~heit** *f* absorption.

versüßen [fɛr'zy:sən] *vt*: **jdm etw** ~ (*fig*) to make sth more pleasant for sb.

vertagen [fɛr'ta:ɡən] *vt, vi* to adjourn. **Vertagung** *f* adjournment.

vertauschen [fɛr'tauʃən] *vt* to exchange; (*versehentlich*) to mix up; **vertauschte Rollen** reversed roles.

verteidigen [fɛr'taɪdɪɡən] *vt* to defend ♦ *vr* to defend o.s.; (*vor Gericht*) to conduct one's own defence (*BRIT*) *od* defense (*US*).

Verteidiger(in) (**-s, -**) *m(f)* defender; (*Anwalt*) defence (*BRIT*) *od* defense (*US*) lawyer.

Verteidigung *f* defence (*BRIT*), defense (*US*).

Verteidigungsfähigkeit *f* ability to defend.

Verteidigungsminister *m* Minister of Defence (*BRIT*), Defense Secretary (*US*).

verteilen [fɛr'taɪlən] *vt* to distribute; (*Rollen*) to assign; (*Salbe*) to spread.

Verteiler (**-s, -**) *m* (*COMM, AUT*) distributor.

Verteilung *f* distribution.

Verteuerung [fɛr'tɔyərʊŋ] *f* increase in price.

verteufeln [fɛr'tɔyfəln] *vt* to condemn.

verteufelt (*umg*) *adj* awful, devilish ♦ *adv* awfully, devilishly.

vertiefen [fɛr'ti:fən] *vt* to deepen; (*SCH*) to consolidate ♦ *vr*: **sich in etw** *akk* ~ to become engrossed *od* absorbed in sth.

Vertiefung *f* depression.

vertikal [vɛrti'ka:l] *adj* vertical.

vertilgen [fɛr'tɪlɡən] *vt* to exterminate; (*umg*) to eat up, consume.

Vertilgungsmittel *nt* weedkiller; (*Insekten~*) pesticide.

vertippen [fɛr'tɪpən] *vr* to make a typing mistake.

vertonen [fɛr'to:nən] *vt* to set to music; (*Film etc*) to add a soundtrack to.

vertrackt [fɛr'trakt] *adj* awkward, tricky, complex.

Vertrag [fɛr'tra:k] (**-(e)s, ⁻e**) *m* contract, agreement; (*POL*) treaty.

vertragen [fɛr'tra:ɡən] *unreg vt* to tolerate, stand ♦ *vr* to get along; (*sich aussöhnen*) to become reconciled; **viel** ~ **können** (*umg*: *Alkohol*) to be able to hold one's drink; **sich mit etw** ~ (*Nahrungsmittel, Farbe*) to go with sth; (*Aussage, Verhalten*) to be consistent with sth.

vertraglich *adj* contractual.

verträglich [fɛr'trɛ:klɪç] *adj* good-natured; (*Speisen*) easily digested; (*MED*) easily tolerated; **V~keit** *f* good nature; digestibility.

Vertrags- *zW*: **~bruch** *m* breach of contract; **v~brüchig** *adj* in breach of contract; **v~fähig** *adj* (*JUR*) competent to contract; **v~mäßig** *adj, adv* (as) stipulated, according to contract; **~partner** *m* party to a contract; **~spieler** *m* (*SPORT*) player under contract; **v~widrig** *adj, adv* contrary to contract.

vertrauen [fɛr'trauən] *vi*: **jdm** ~ to trust sb; ~ **auf** +*akk* to rely on; **V~** (**-s**) *nt* confidence; **jdn ins V~ ziehen** to take sb into one's confidence; **V~ zu jdm fassen** to gain confidence in sb; **V~ erweckend** inspiring trust.

Vertrauens- *zW*: **~mann** (**-(e)s**, *pl* **-männer** *od* **-leute**) *m* intermediary; **~sache** *f* (*vertrauliche Angelegenheit*) confidential matter; (*Frage des Vertrauens*) question of trust; **v~selig** *adj* trusting; **v~voll** *adj* trustful; **~votum** *nt* (*PARL*) vote of confidence; **v~würdig** *adj* trustworthy.

vertraulich [fɛr'trauliç] *adj* familiar; (*geheim*) confidential; **V~keit** *f* familiarity; confidentiality.

verträumt [fɛr'trɔymt] *adj* dreamy; (*Städtchen etc*) sleepy.

vertraut [fɛr'traut] *adj* familiar; **sich mit dem Gedanken** ~ **machen, dass** ... to get used to the idea that ...

Vertraute(r) *f(m)* confidant(e), close friend.

Vertrautheit *f* familiarity.

vertreiben [fɛr'traɪbən] *unreg vt* to drive away; (*aus Land*) to expel; (*COMM*) to sell; (*Zeit*) to pass.

Vertreibung *f* expulsion.

vertretbar *adj* justifiable; (*Theorie, Argument*) tenable.

vertreten [fɛr'tre:tən] *unreg vt* to represent; (*Ansicht*) to hold, advocate; (*ersetzen*) to replace; (*Kollegen*) to cover for; (*COMM*) to be the agent for; **sich** *dat* **die Beine** ~ to stretch one's legs.

Vertreter(in) (**-s, -**) *m(f)* representative; (*Verfechter*) advocate; (*COMM: Firma*) agent; **~provision** *f* agent's commission.

Vertretung *f* representation; advocacy; **die** ~ **übernehmen (für)** to stand in (for).

Vertretungsstunde *f* (*SCH*) cover lesson.

Vertrieb [fɛr'tri:p] (**-(e)s, -e**) *m* marketing; **den** ~ **für eine Firma haben** to have the (selling) agency for a firm.

Vertriebene(r) [fɛr'tri:bənə(r)] *f(m)* exile.

Vertriebskosten *pl* marketing costs *pl*.

vertrocknen [fɛr'trɔknən] *vi* to dry up.

vertrödeln [fɛr'trø:dəln] (*umg*) *vt* to fritter away.

vertrösten [fɛr'trø:stən] *vt* to put off.

vertun [fɛr'tu:n] *unreg vt* to waste ♦ *vr* (*umg*) to make a mistake.

vertuschen [fɛr'tuʃən] *vt* to hush *od* cover up.

verübeln [fɛr'¦y:bəln] *vt*: **jdm etw** ~ to be cross *od* offended with sb on account of sth.

verüben [fɛr'¦y:bən] *vt* to commit.

verulken [fɛr'|ʊlkən] (*umg*) *vt* to make fun of.
verunglimpfen [fɛr'|ʊnglɪmpfən] *vt* to disparage.
verunglücken [fɛr'|ʊnglʏkən] *vi* to have an accident; (*fig: umg: misslingen*) to go wrong; **tödlich** ~ to be killed in an accident.
Verunglückte(r) *f(m)* accident victim.
verunreinigen [fɛr'|ʊnraɪnɪgən] *vt* to soil; (*Umwelt*) to pollute.
verunsichern [fɛr'|ʊnzɪçərn] *vt* to rattle (*fig*).
verunstalten [fɛr'|ʊnʃtaltən] *vt* to disfigure; (*Gebäude etc*) to deface.
veruntreuen [fɛr'|ʊntrɔʏən] *vt* to embezzle.
verursachen [fɛr'|uːrzaxən] *vt* to cause.
verurteilen [fɛr'|uːrtaɪlən] *vt* to condemn; (*zu Strafe*) to sentence; (*für schuldig befinden*): **jdn** ~ **(für)** to convict sb (of).
Verurteilung *f* condemnation; (*JUR*) sentence; conviction.
vervielfachen [fɛr'fiːlfaxən] *vt* to multiply.
vervielfältigen [fɛr'fiːlfɛltɪgən] *vt* to duplicate, copy.
Vervielfältigung *f* duplication, copying.
vervollkommnen [fɛr'fɔlkɔmnən] *vt* to perfect.
vervollständigen [fɛr'fɔlʃtɛndɪgən] *vt* to complete.
verw. *abk* = **verwitwet**.
verwachsen [fɛr'vaksən] *adj* (*Mensch*) deformed; (*verkümmert*) stunted; (*überwuchert*) overgrown.
verwackeln [fɛr'vakəln] *vt* (*Foto*) to blur.
verwählen [fɛr'vɛːlən] *vr* (*TEL*) to dial the wrong number.
verwahren [fɛr'vaːrən] *vt* to keep (safe) ♦ *vr* to protest.
verwahrlosen *vi* to become neglected; (*moralisch*) to go to the bad.
verwahrlost *adj* neglected; (*moralisch*) wayward.
Verwahrung *f* (*von Geld etc*) keeping; (*von Täter*) custody, detention; **jdn in** ~ **nehmen** to take sb into custody.
verwaist [fɛr'vaɪst] *adj* orphaned.
verwalten [fɛr'valtən] *vt* to manage; (*Behörde*) to administer.
Verwalter(in) (**-s, -**) *m(f)* adminstrator; (*Vermögens~*) trustee.
Verwaltung *f* management; administration.
Verwaltungs- *zW:* **~apparat** *m* administrative machinery; **~bezirk** *m* administrative district; **~gericht** *nt* Administrative Court.
verwandeln [fɛr'vandəln] *vt* to change, transform ♦ *vr* to change.
Verwandlung *f* change, transformation.
verwandt [fɛr'vant] *adj:* ~ **(mit)** related (to); **geistig** ~ **sein** (*fig*) to be kindred spirits.
Verwandte(r) *f(m)* relative, relation.
Verwandtschaft *f* relationship; (*Menschen*) relatives *pl*, relations *pl*; (*fig*) affinity.
verwarnen [fɛr'varnən] *vt* to caution.
Verwarnung *f* caution.
verwaschen [fɛr'vaʃən] *adj* faded; (*fig*) vague.
verwässern [fɛr'vɛsərn] *vt* to dilute, water down.
verwechseln [fɛr'vɛksəln] *vt:* ~ **mit** to confuse with; **zum V~ ähnlich** as like as two peas.
Verwechslung *f* confusion, mixing up; **das muss eine** ~ **sein** there must be some mistake.
verwegen [fɛr've:gən] *adj* daring, bold; **V~heit** *f* daring, audacity, boldness.
verwehren [fɛr've:rən] *vt* (*geh*): **jdm etw** ~ to refuse *od* deny sb sth.
Verwehung [fɛr've:ʊŋ] *f* (*Schnee~*) snowdrift; (*Sand~*) sanddrift.
verweichlichen [fɛr'vaɪçlɪçən] *vt* to mollycoddle.
verweichlicht *adj* effeminate, soft.
verweigern [fɛr'vaɪgərn] *vt:* **jdm etw** ~ to refuse sb sth; **den Gehorsam/die Aussage** ~ to refuse to obey/testify.
Verweigerung *f* refusal.
verweilen [fɛr'vaɪlən] *vi* to stay; (*fig*): ~ **bei** to dwell on.
verweint [fɛr'vaɪnt] *adj* (*Augen*) swollen with tears *od* with crying; (*Gesicht*) tear-stained.
Verweis [fɛr'vaɪs] (**-es, -e**) *m* reprimand, rebuke; (*Hinweis*) reference.
verweisen [fɛr'vaɪzən] *unreg vt* to refer; **jdn auf etw** *akk***/an jdn** ~ (*hinweisen*) to refer sb to sth/sb; **jdn vom Platz** *od* **des Spielfeldes** ~ (*SPORT*) to send sb off; **jdn von der Schule** ~ to expel sb (from school); **jdn des Landes** ~ to deport sb.
Verweisung *f* reference; (*Landes~*) deportation.
verwelken [fɛr'vɛlkən] *vi* to fade; (*Blumen*) to wilt.
verweltlichen [fɛr'vɛltlɪçən] *vt* to secularize.
verwendbar [fɛr'vɛndbaːr] *adj* usable.
verwenden [fɛr'vɛndən] *unreg vt* to use; (*Mühe, Zeit, Arbeit*) to spend ♦ *vr* to intercede.
Verwendung *f* use.
Verwendungsmöglichkeit *f* (possible) use.
verwerfen [fɛr'vɛrfən] *unreg vt* to reject; (*Urteil*) to quash; (*kritisieren: Handlungsweise*) to condemn.
verwerflich [fɛr'vɛrflɪç] *adj* reprehensible.
verwertbar *adj* usable.
verwerten [fɛr've:rtən] *vt* to utilize.
Verwertung *f* utilization.
verwesen [fɛr've:zən] *vi* to decay.
Verwesung *f* decomposition.
verwickeln [fɛr'vɪkəln] *vt* to tangle (up); (*fig*) to involve ♦ *vr* to get tangled (up); **jdn** ~ **in** *+akk* to involve sb in, get sb involved in; **sich** ~ **in** *+akk* to get involved in.

verwickelt–viel

verwickelt *adj* involved.
Verwicklung *f* entanglement, complication.
verwildern [fɛr'vɪldərn] *vi* to run wild.
verwildert *adj* wild; (*Garten*) overgrown; (*jds Aussehen*) unkempt.
verwinden [fɛr'vɪndən] *unreg vt* to get over.
verwirken [fɛr'vɪrkən] *vt* (*geh*) to forfeit.
verwirklichen [fɛr'vɪrklɪçən] *vt* to realize, put into effect.
Verwirklichung *f* realization.
verwirren [fɛr'vɪrən] *vt* to tangle (up); (*fig*) to confuse.
Verwirrspiel *nt* confusing tactics *pl*.
Verwirrung *f* confusion.
verwischen [fɛr'vɪʃən] *vt* (*verschmieren*) to smudge; (*lit, fig: Spuren*) to cover over; (*fig: Erinnerungen*) to blur.
verwittern [fɛr'vɪtərn] *vi* to weather.
verwitwet [fɛr'vɪtvət] *adj* widowed.
verwöhnen [fɛr'vøːnən] *vt* to spoil, pamper.
Verwöhnung *f* spoiling, pampering.
verworfen [fɛr'vɔrfən] *adj* depraved; **V~heit** *f* depravity.
verworren [fɛr'vɔrən] *adj* confused.
verwundbar [fɛr'vʊntbaːr] *adj* vulnerable.
verwunden [fɛr'vʊndən] *vt* to wound.
verwunderlich [fɛr'vʊndərlɪç] *adj* surprising; (*stärker*) astonishing.
verwundern *vt* to astonish ♦ *vr*: **sich ~ über** +*akk* to be astonished at.
Verwunderung *f* astonishment.
Verwundete(r) *f(m)* injured person; **die ~n** the injured; (*MIL*) the wounded.
Verwundung *f* wound, injury.
verwünschen [fɛr'vynʃən] *vt* to curse.
verwurzelt [fɛr'vʊrtsəlt] *adj*: **(fest) in etw** *dat* *od* **mit etw ~** (*fig*) deeply rooted in sth.
verwüsten [fɛr'vyːstən] *vt* to devastate.
Verwüstung *f* devastation.
Verz. *abk* = **Verzeichnis**.
verzagen [fɛr'tsaːgən] *vi* to despair.
verzagt [fɛr'tsaːkt] *adj* disheartened.
verzählen [fɛr'tsɛːlən] *vr* to miscount.
verzahnen [fɛr'tsaːnən] *vt* to dovetail; (*Zahnräder*) to cut teeth in.
verzapfen [fɛr'tsapfən] (*umg*) *vt*: **Unsinn ~** to talk nonsense.
verzaubern [fɛr'tsaʊbərn] *vt* (*lit*) to cast a spell on; (*fig: jdn*) to enchant.
verzehren [fɛr'tseːrən] *vt* to consume.
verzeichnen [fɛr'tsaɪçnən] *vt* to list; (*Niederlage, Verlust*) to register.
Verzeichnis (**-ses, -se**) *nt* list, catalogue (*BRIT*), catalog (*US*); (*in Buch*) index; (*COMPUT*) directory.
verzeihen [fɛr'tsaɪən] *unreg vt, vi* to forgive; **jdm etw ~** to forgive sb (for) sth; **~ Sie!** excuse me!
verzeihlich *adj* pardonable.
Verzeihung *f* forgiveness, pardon; **~!** sorry!,

excuse me!; (**jdn**) **um ~ bitten** to apologize (to sb).
verzerren [fɛr'tsɛrən] *vt* to distort; (*Sehne, Muskel*) to strain, pull.
verzetteln [fɛr'tsɛtəln] *vr* to waste a lot of time.
Verzicht [fɛr'tsɪçt] (**-(e)s, -e**) *m*: **~ (auf** +*akk*) renunciation (of); **v~en** *vi*: **v~en auf** +*akk* to forego, give up.
verziehen [fɛr'tsiːən] *unreg vi* (*Hilfsverb sein*) to move ♦ *vt* to put out of shape; (*Kind*) to spoil; (*Pflanzen*) to thin out ♦ *vr* to go out of shape; (*Gesicht*) to contort; (*verschwinden*) to disappear; **verzogen** (*Vermerk*) no longer at this address; **keine Miene ~** not to turn a hair; **das Gesicht ~** to pull a face.
verzieren [fɛr'tsiːrən] *vt* to decorate.
Verzierung *f* decoration.
verzinsen [fɛr'tsɪnzən] *vt* to pay interest on.
verzinslich *adj*: **(fest)~ sein** to yield (a fixed rate of) interest.
verzogen [fɛr'tsoːgən] *adj* (*Kind*) spoilt; *siehe auch* **verziehen**.
verzögern [fɛr'tsøːgərn] *vt* to delay.
Verzögerung *f* delay.
Verzögerungstaktik *f* delaying tactics *pl*.
verzollen [fɛr'tsɔlən] *vt* to pay duty on; **haben Sie etwas zu ~?** have you anything to declare?
verzücken [fɛr'tsʏkən] *vt* to send into ecstasies, enrapture.
Verzug [fɛr'tsuːk] *m* delay; (*FIN*) arrears *pl*; **mit etw in ~ geraten** to fall behind with sth.
verzweifeln [fɛr'tsvaɪfəln] *vi* to despair.
verzweifelt *adj* desperate.
Verzweiflung *f* despair.
verzweigen [fɛr'tsvaɪgən] *vr* to branch out.
verzwickt [fɛr'tsvɪkt] (*umg*) *adj* awkward, complicated.
Vesper ['fɛspər] (**-, -n**) *f* vespers *pl*.
Vesuv [ve'zuːf] (**-(s)**) *m* Vesuvius.
Veto ['veːto] (**-s, -s**) *nt* veto.
Vetter ['fɛtər] (**-s, -n**) *m* cousin.
vgl. *abk* (= *vergleiche*) cf.
v. H. *abk* (= *vom Hundert*) pc.
VHS (**-**) *f abk* = **Volkshochschule**.
Viadukt [via'dʊkt] (**-(e)s, -e**) *m* viaduct.
Vibrator [vi'braːtɔr] *m* vibrator.
vibrieren [vi'briːrən] *vi* to vibrate.
Video ['viːdeo] (**-s, -s**) *nt* video; **~aufnahme** *f* video (recording), **~kamera** *f* video camera; **~rekorder** *m* video recorder; **~spiel** *nt* video game; **~text** *m* teletext.
Vieh [fiː] (**-(e)s**) *nt* cattle *pl*; (*Nutztiere*) livestock; (*umg: Tier*) animal; **v~isch** *adj* bestial; **~zucht** *f* (live)stock *od* cattle breeding.
viel [fiːl] *adj* a lot of, much ♦ *adv* a lot, much; **in ~em** in many respects; **noch (ein)mal so ~** (*Zeit etc*) as much (time *etc*) again; **einer zu**

~ **one too many;** ~ **zu wenig** much too little;
~ **beschäftigt** very busy; ~**e** *pl* a lot of,
many; **gleich** ~**e** (**Angestellte/Anteile** *etc*) the
same number (of employees/shares *etc*);
~ **geprüft** (*hum*) sorely tried; ~ **sagend**
significant; ~ **versprechend** promising.
vielerlei *adj* a great variety of.
vielerorts *adv* in many places.
viel- *zW:* ~**fach** *adj, adv* many times; **auf**
~**fachen Wunsch** at the request of many
people; **V**~**fache(s)** *nt* (*MATH*) multiple; **um**
ein V~**faches** many times over; **V**~**falt** (-) *f*
variety; ~**fältig** *adj* varied, many-sided;
V~**fraß** *m* glutton.
vielleicht [fiˈlaɪçt] *adv* perhaps; (*in Bitten*) by
any chance; **du bist** ~ **ein Idiot!** (*umg*) you
really are an idiot!
viel- *zW:* ~**mal(s)** *adv* many times; **danke**
~**mals** many thanks; **ich bitte** ~**mals um**
Entschuldigung! I do apologize!; ~**mehr** *adv*
rather, on the contrary; ~**schichtig** *adj* (*fig*)
complex; ~**seitig** *adj* many-sided;
(*Ausbildung*) all-round *attr*; (*Interessen*)
varied; (*Mensch, Gerät*) versatile;
V~**völkerstaat** *m* multinational state.
vier [fiːr] *num* four; **alle** ~**e von sich strecken**
(*umg*) to stretch out; **V**~**beiner** *m* (*hum*)
four-legged friend; **V**~**eck** (-(e)s, -e) *nt* four-
sided figure; (*gleichseitig*) square; ~**eckig** *adj*
four-sided; square; ~**hundert** *num* four
hundred; ~**kant** *adj, adv* (*NAUT*) square;
~**köpfig** *adj:* **eine** ~**köpfige Familie** a family
of four; **V**~**mächteabkommen** *nt* four-power
agreement.
viert *adj:* **wir gingen zu** ~ four of us went.
Viertaktmotor *m* four-stroke engine.
vierte(r, s) [ˈfiːrtə(r, s)] *adj* fourth.
vierteln *vt* to quarter.
Viertel [ˈfɪrtəl] (-s, -) *nt* quarter; **ein**
~ **Leberwurst** a quarter of liver sausage;
~**finale** *nt* quarter finals *pl*; ~**jahr** *nt* three
months *pl*, quarter (*COMM, FIN*);
~**jahresschrift** *f* quarterly; **v**~**jährlich** *adj*
quarterly; ~**note** *f* crotchet (*BRIT*), quarter
note (*US*); ~**stunde** *f* quarter of an hour.
vier- *zW:* ~**türig** *adj* four-door *attr;*
V~**waldstättersee** *m* Lake Lucerne; ~**zehn**
[ˈfɪrtseːn] *num* fourteen; **in** ~**zehn Tagen** in a
fortnight (*BRIT*), in two weeks (*US*);
~**zehntägig** *adj* fortnightly; ~**zehnte(r, s)** *adj*
fourteenth.
vierzig [ˈfɪrtsɪç] *num* forty; **V**~**stundenwoche** *f*
forty-hour week.
Vierzimmerwohnung *f* four-room flat (*BRIT*)
od apartment (*US*).
Vietnam [vietˈnam] (-s) *nt* Vietnam.
Vietnamese [vietnaˈmeːzə] (-n, -n) *m*,
Vietnamesin *f* Vietnamese.
vietnamesisch *adj* Vietnamese.
Vikar [viˈkaːr] (-s, -e) *m* curate.

Villa [ˈvɪla] (-, **Villen**) *f* villa.
Villenviertel *nt* (prosperous) residential
area.
violett [vioˈlɛt] *adj* violet.
Violinbogen *m* violin bow.
Violine [vioˈliːnə] (-, -n) *f* violin.
Violinkonzert *nt* violin concerto.
Violinschlüssel *m* treble clef.
virtuell [vɪrtuˈɛl] *adj* (*COMPUT*) virtual; ~**e**
Realität virtual reality.
virtuos [vɪrtuˈoːs] *adj* virtuoso *attrib.*
Virtuose [vɪrtuˈoːzə] (-n, -n) *m* virtuoso.
Virtuosin [vɪrtuˈoːzɪn] *f* virtuoso.
Virtuosität [vɪrtuoziˈtɛt] *f* virtuosity.
Virus [ˈviːrʊs] (-, **Viren**) *m od nt* (*also COMPUT*)
virus.
Virus- *in zW* viral; ~**infektion** *f* virus
infection.
Visage [viˈzaːʒə] (-, -n) (*pej*) *f* face, (ugly) mug
(*umg*).
Visagist(in) [vizaˈʒɪst(ɪn)] *m(f)* make-up artist.
vis-a-vis▲, **vis-à-vis** [vizaˈviː] *adv* (*veraltet*):
~ **(von)** opposite (to) ♦ *präp +dat* opposite
(to).
Visier [viˈziːr] (-s, -e) *nt* gunsight; (*am Helm*)
visor.
Vision [viziˈoːn] *f* vision.
Visite [viˈziːtə] (-, -n) *f* (*MED*) visit.
Visitenkarte *f* visiting card.
visuell [vizuˈɛl] *adj* visual.
Visum [ˈviːzʊm] (-s, **Visa** *od* **Visen**) *nt* visa;
~**zwang** *m* obligation to hold a visa.
vital [viˈtaːl] *adj* lively, full of life;
(*lebenswichtig*) vital.
Vitamin [vitaˈmiːn] (-s, -e) *nt* vitamin;
~**mangel** *m* vitamin deficiency.
Vitrine [viˈtriːnə] (-, -n) *f* (*Schrank*) glass
cabinet; (*Schaukasten*) showcase, display
case.
Vivisektion [vivizɛktsiˈoːn] *f* vivisection.
Vize [ˈfiːtsə] *m* (*umg*) number two; (: ~*meister*)
runner-up ♦ *in zW* vice-.
v. J. *abk* (= *vorigen Jahres*) of the previous *od*
last year.
Vlies [fliːs] (-es, -e) *nt* fleece.
v. M. *abk* (= *vorigen Monats*) ult.
V-Mann *m abk* = **Verbindungsmann**;
Vertrauensmann.
VN *pl abk* (= *Vereinte Nationen*) UN.
VO *abk* = **Verordnung**.
Vogel [ˈfoːgəl] (-s, ⸚) *m* bird; **einen** ~ **haben**
(*umg*) to have bats in the belfry; **den**
~ **abschießen** (*umg*) to surpass everyone
(*ironisch*); ~**bauer** *nt* birdcage; ~**beerbaum** *m*
rowan (tree); ~**dreck** *m* bird droppings *pl;*
~**perspektive** *f* bird's-eye view; ~**schau** *f*
bird's-eye view; ~**scheuche** *f* scarecrow;
~**schutzgebiet** *nt* bird sanctuary; ~**Strauß-**
Politik *f* head-in-the-sand policy.
Vogesen [voˈgeːzən] *pl* Vosges *pl.*

Vokabel [vo'ka:bəl] (-, -n) f word.
Vokabular [vokabu'la:r] (-s, -e) nt vocabulary.
Vokal [vo'ka:l] (-s, -e) m vowel.
Volk [fɔlk] (-(e)s, ⸚er) nt people; (*Nation*) nation; **etw unters ~ bringen** (*Nachricht*) to spread sth.
Völker- zW: **~bund** m League of Nations; **~kunde** f ethnology; **~mord** m genocide; **~recht** nt international law; **v~rechtlich** adj according to international law; **~verständigung** f international understanding; **~wanderung** f migration.
Volks- zW: **~abstimmung** f referendum; **~armee** f People's Army; **~begehren** nt petition for a referendum; **~deutsche(r)** dekl wie adj f(m) ethnic German; **v~eigen** adj (*DDR*) nationally-owned; **~feind** m enemy of the people; **~fest** nt popular festival; (*Jahrmarkt*) fair.
Volkshochschule f adult education classes pl.

VOLKSHOCHSCHULE
The **Volkshochschule** (*VHS*) is an institution which offers *Adult Education* classes. No set qualifications are necessary to attend. For a small fee adults can attend both vocational and non-vocational classes in the daytime or evening.

Volks- zW: **~lauf** m fun run; **~lied** nt folk song; **~mund** m vernacular; **~polizei** f (*DDR*) People's Police; **~republik** f people's republic; **~schule** f ≈ primary school (*BRIT*), elementary school (*US*); **~seuche** f epidemic; **~stamm** m tribe; **~stück** nt folk play in dialect; **~tanz** m folk dance; **~trauertag** m ≈ Remembrance Day (*BRIT*), Memorial Day (*US*); **v~tümlich** adj popular; **~wirtschaft** f national economy; (*Fach*) economics sing, political economy; **~wirtschaftler** m economist; **~zählung** f (national) census.
voll [fɔl] adj full ♦ adv fully; **etw ~ laufen lassen** to fill sth up; **~ machen** to fill (up); **~ schreiben** (*Heft, Seite*) to fill; (*Tafel*) to cover (with writing); **jdn für ~ nehmen** (*umg*) to take sb seriously; **aus dem V~en schöpfen** to draw on unlimited resources; **~ tanken** to fill up; **in ~er Größe** (*Bild*) life-size(d); (*bei plötzlicher Erscheinung etc*) large as life; **~ sein** (*umg: satt*) to be full (up); (: *betrunken*) to be plastered; **~ und ganz** completely.
vollauf [fɔl'|auf] adv amply; **~ zu tun haben** to have quite enough to do.
voll- zW: **V~bad** nt (proper) bath; **V~bart** m full beard; **V~beschäftigung** f full employment; **V~besitz** m: **im V~besitz** +gen in full possession of; **V~blut** nt

thoroughbred; **~blütig** adj full-blooded; **V~bremsung** f emergency stop; **~bringen** unreg vt untr to accomplish; **V~dampf** m (*NAUT*): **mit V~dampf** at full steam; **~enden** vt untr to finish, complete; **~endet** adj (*vollkommen*) perfect; (*Tänzer etc*) accomplished; **~ends** adv completely; **V~endung** f completion.
voller adj fuller; **~ Flecken/Ideen** full of stains/ideas.
Völlerei [fœlə'rai] f gluttony.
Volleyball ['vɔlibal] (-(e)s) m volleyball.
voll- zW: **~fett** adj full-fat; **V~gas** nt: **mit V~gas** at full throttle; **V~gas geben** to step on it.
völlig ['fœlıç] adj complete ♦ adv completely.
voll- zW: **~jährig** adj of age; **V~kaskoversicherung** f fully comprehensive insurance; **~kommen** adj perfect; (*völlig*) complete, absolute; **V~kommenheit** f perfection; **V~kornbrot** nt wholemeal (*BRIT*) od whole-wheat (*US*) bread; **V~macht** f authority, power of attorney; **V~matrose** m able-bodied seaman; **V~milch** f full-cream milk; **V~mond** m full moon; **V~narkose** f general anaesthetic (*BRIT*) od anesthetic (*US*); **V~pension** f full board; **~schlank** adj plump, stout; **~ständig** adj complete; **~strecken** vt untr to execute; **V~treffer** m (*lit, fig*) bull's-eye; **V~versammlung** f general meeting; **V~waise** f orphan; **~wertig** adj full attrib; (*Stellung*) equal; **V~wertkost** f wholefoods pl; **~zählig** adj complete; (*anwesend*) in full number; **~ziehen** unreg vt untr to carry out ♦ vr untr to happen; **V~zug** m execution.
Volontär(in) [volɔn'tɛ:r(ın)] (-s, -e) m(f) trainee.
Volt [vɔlt] (- od -(e)s, -) nt volt.
Volumen [vo'lu:mən] (-s, - od **Volumina**) nt volume.
vom [fɔm] = **von dem**.

von [fɔn] präp +dat **1** (*Ausgangspunkt*) from; **~ ... bis** from ... to; **~ morgens bis abends** from morning till night; **~ ... nach ... from ...** to ...; **~ ... an** from ...; **~ ... aus** from ...; **~ dort aus** from there; **etw ~ sich aus tun** to do sth of one's own accord; **~ mir aus** (*umg*) if you like, I don't mind; **~ wo/wann ...?** where/when ... from?
2 (*Ursache, im Passiv*) by; **ein Gedicht ~ Schiller** a poem by Schiller; **~ etw müde** tired from sth.
3 (*als Genitiv*) of; **ein Freund ~ mir** a friend of mine; **nett ~ dir** nice of you; **jeweils zwei ~ zehn** two out of every ten.
4 (*über*) about; **er erzählte vom Urlaub** he talked about his holiday.
5: ~ wegen! (*umg*) no way!

---

voneinander *adv* from each other.
vonseiten▲, von Seiten▲ [vɔn'zaɪtn] *präp* +*gen* on the part of.
vonstatten [fɔn'ʃtatən] *adv*: ~ **gehen** to proceed, go.

═══════════ *SCHLÜSSELWORT*

vor [foːr] *präp* +*dat* **1** (*räumlich*) in front of.
2 (*zeitlich, Reihenfolge*) before; **ich war** ~ **ihm da** I was there before him; **X kommt** ~ **Y** X comes before Y; ~ **zwei Tagen** two days ago; **5 (Minuten)** ~ **4** 5 (minutes) to 4; ~ **kurzem** a little while ago.
3 (*Ursache*) with; ~ **Wut/Liebe** with rage/love; ~ **Hunger sterben** to die of hunger; ~ **lauter Arbeit** because of work.
4: ~ **allem**, ~ **allen Dingen** above all.
♦ *präp* +*akk* (*räumlich*) in front of; ~ **sich hin summen** to hum to oneself.
♦ *adv*: ~ **und zurück** backwards and forwards.

Vor- *zW*: ~**abdruck** *m* preprint; ~**abend** *m* evening before, eve; ~**ahnung** *f* presentiment, premonition.
voran [fo'ran] *adv* before, ahead; ~**bringen** *unreg vt* to make progress with; ~**gehen** *unreg vi* to go ahead; **einer Sache** *dat* ~**gehen** to precede sth; ~**gehend** *adj* previous; ~**kommen** *unreg vi* to make progress, come along.
Voranschlag ['foːr|anʃlaːk] *m* estimate.
voranstellen [fo'ranʃtɛlən] *vt* +*dat* to put in front (of); (*fig*) to give precedence (over).
Vorarbeiter ['foːr|arbaɪtər] *m* foreman.
voraus [fo'raʊs] *adv* ahead; (*zeitlich*) in advance; **jdm** ~ **sein** to be ahead of sb; **im V**~ in advance; ~**bezahlen** *vt* to pay in advance; ~**gehen** *unreg vi* to go (on) ahead; (*fig*) to precede; ~**haben** *unreg vt*: **jdm etw** ~**haben** to have the edge on sb in sth; **V**~**sage** *f* prediction; ~**sagen** *vt* to predict; ~**sehen** *unreg vt* to foresee; ~**setzen** *vt* to assume; (*sicher annehmen*) to take for granted; (*erfordern: Kenntnisse, Geduld*) to require, demand; ~**gesetzt, dass ...** provided that ...; **V**~**setzung** *f* requirement, prerequisite; **unter der V**~**setzung, dass ...** on condition that ...; **V**~**sicht** *f* foresight; **aller V**~**sicht nach** in all probability; **in der V**~**sicht, dass ...** anticipating that ...; ~**sichtlich** *adv* probably; **V**~**zahlung** *f* advance payment.
Vorbau ['foːrbaʊ] (-**(e)s, -ten**) *m* porch; (*Balkon*) balcony.
vorbauen ['foːrbaʊən] *vt* to build up in front ♦ *vi* +*dat* to take precautions (against).
Vorbedacht ['foːrbədaxt] *m*: **mit/ohne** ~ (*Überlegung*) with/without due

consideration; (*Absicht*) intentionally/unintentionally.
Vorbedingung ['foːrbədɪŋʊŋ] *f* precondition.
Vorbehalt ['foːrbəhalt] *m* reservation, proviso; **unter dem** ~, **dass ...** with the reservation that ...
vorbehalten *unreg vt*: **sich/jdm etw** ~ to reserve sth (for o.s.)/for sb; **alle Rechte** ~ all rights reserved.
vorbehaltlich *präp* +*gen* (*form*) subject to.
vorbehaltlos *adj* unconditional ♦ *adv* unconditionally.
vorbei [fɔr'baɪ] *adv* by, past; **aus und** ~ over and done with; **damit ist es nun** ~ that's all over now; ~**bringen** *unreg* (*umg*) *vt* to drop off; ~**gehen** *unreg vi* to pass by, go past; ~**kommen** *unreg vi*: **bei jdm** ~**kommen** to drop *od* call in on sb; ~**reden** *vi*: **an etw** *dat* ~**reden** to talk around sth.
vorbelastet ['foːrbəlastət] *adj* (*fig*) handicapped (*BRIT*), handicaped (*US*).
Vorbemerkung ['foːrbəmɛrkʊŋ] *f* introductory remark.
vorbereiten ['foːrbəraɪtən] *vt* to prepare.
Vorbereitung *f* preparation.
vorbestellen ['foːrbəʃtɛlən] *vt* to book (in advance), reserve.
Vorbestellung *f* advance booking.
vorbestraft ['foːrbəʃtraft] *adj* previously convicted, with a record.
Vorbeugehaft *f* preventive custody.
vorbeugen ['foːrbɔʏɡən] *vt, vr* to lean forward ♦ *vi* +*dat* to prevent.
vorbeugend *adj* preventive.
Vorbeugung *f* prevention; **zur** ~ **gegen** for the prevention of.
Vorbild ['foːrbɪlt] *nt* model; **sich** *dat* **jdn zum** ~ **nehmen** to model o.s. on sb; **v**~**lich** *adj* model, ideal.
Vorbildung ['foːrbɪldʊŋ] *f* educational background.
Vorbote ['foːrboːtə] *m* (*fig*) herald.
vorbringen ['foːrbrɪŋən] *unreg vt* to voice; (*Meinung etc*) to advance, state; (*umg: nach vorne*) to bring to the front.
vordatieren ['foːrdatiːrən] *vt* (*Schreiben*) to postdate.
Vorder- *zW*: ~**achse** *f* front axle; ~**ansicht** *f* front view; ~**asien** *nt* Near East.
vordere(r, s) *adj* front.
Vorder- *zW*: ~**grund** *m* foreground; **im** ~**grund stehen** (*fig*) to be to the fore; ~**grundprogramm** *nt* (*COMPUT*) foreground program; ~**hand** *adv* for the present; ~**mann** (-**(e)s**, *pl* -**männer**) *m* man in front; **jdn auf** ~**mann bringen** (*umg*) to get sb to shape up; ~**seite** *f* front (side); ~**sitz** *m* front seat.
vorderste(r, s) *adj* front.
vordrängen ['foːrdrɛŋən] *vr* to push to the

front.

vordringen ['foːrdrɪŋən] *unreg vi:* **bis zu jdm/ etw ~** to get as far as sb/sth.

vordringlich *adj* urgent.

Vordruck ['foːrdrʊk] *m* form.

vorehelich ['foːr|eːəlɪç] *adj* premarital.

voreilig ['foːr|aɪlɪç] *adj* hasty, rash; **~e Schlüsse ziehen** to jump to conclusions.

voreinander [foːr|aɪ'nandər] *adv* (*räumlich*) in front of each other; (*einander gegenüber*) face to face.

voreingenommen ['foːr|aɪngənɔmən] *adj* bias(s)ed; **V~heit** *f* bias.

voreingestellt ['foːr|aɪngəftɛlt] *adj:* **~er Parameter** (*COMPUT*) default (parameter).

vorenthalten ['foːr|ɛnthaltən] *unreg vt:* **jdm etw ~** to withhold sth from sb.

Vorentscheidung ['foːr|ɛntʃaɪdʊŋ] *f* preliminary decision.

vorerst ['foːr|eːrst] *adv* for the moment *od* present.

Vorfahr ['foːrfaːr] (**-en, -en**) *m* ancestor.

vorfahren *unreg vi* to drive (on) ahead; (*vors Haus etc*) to drive up.

Vorfahrt *f* (*AUT*) right of way; „**~ (be)achten"** "give way" (*BRIT*), "yield" (*US*).

Vorfahrts- *zW:* **~regel** *f* rule of right of way; **~schild** *nt* "give way" (*BRIT*) *od* "yield" (*US*) sign; **~straße** *f* major road.

Vorfall ['foːrfal] *m* incident.

vorfallen *unreg vi* to occur.

Vorfeld ['foːrfɛlt] *nt* (*fig*): **im ~** (*+gen*) in the run-up (to).

Vorfilm ['foːrfɪlm] *m* short.

vorfinden ['foːrfɪndən] *unreg vt* to find.

Vorfreude ['foːrfrɔʏdə] *f* anticipation.

vorfühlen ['foːrfyːlən] *vi* (*fig*) to put out feelers.

vorführen ['foːrfyːrən] *vt* to show, display; (*Theaterstück, Kunststücke*): **(jdm) etw ~** to perform sth (to *od* in front of sb); **dem Gericht ~** to bring before the court.

Vorgabe ['foːrgaːbə] *f* (*SPORT*) handicap.

Vorgang ['foːrgaŋ] *m* (*Ereignis*) event; (*Ablauf*) course of events; (*CHEM etc*) process.

Vorgänger(in) ['foːrgɛŋər(ɪn)] (**-s, -**) *m(f)* predecessor.

vorgaukeln ['foːrgaʊkəln] *vt:* **jdm etw ~** to lead sb to believe in sth.

vorgeben ['foːrgeːbən] *unreg vt* to pretend, use as a pretext; (*SPORT*) to give an advantage *od* a start of.

Vorgebirge ['foːrgəbɪrgə] *nt* foothills *pl*.

vorgefasst▲ ['foːrgəfast] *adj* preconceived.

vorgefertigt ['foːrgəfɛrtɪçt] *adj* prefabricated.

Vorgefühl ['foːrgəfyːl] *nt* anticipation; (*etwas Böses*) presentiment.

vorgehen ['foːrgeːən] *unreg vi* (*voraus*) to go (on) ahead; (*nach vorn*) to go forward; (*handeln*) to act, proceed; (*Uhr*) to be fast;

(*Vorrang haben*) to take precedence; (*passieren*) to go on.

Vorgehen (**-s**) *nt* action.

Vorgehensweise *f* proceedings *pl*.

vorgerückt ['foːrgərʏkt] *adj* (*Stunde*) late; (*Alter*) advanced.

Vorgeschichte ['foːrgəʃɪçtə] *f* prehistory; (*von Fall, Krankheit*) past history.

Vorgeschmack ['foːrgəʃmak] *m* foretaste.

Vorgesetzte(r) ['foːrgəzɛtstə(r)] *f(m)* superior.

vorgestern ['foːrgɛstərn] *adv* the day before yesterday; **von ~** (*fig*) antiquated.

vorgreifen ['foːrgraɪfən] *unreg vi +dat* to anticipate; **jdm ~** to forestall sb.

vorhaben ['foːrhaːbən] *unreg vt* to intend; **hast du schon was vor?** have you got anything on?

Vorhaben (**-s, -**) *nt* intention.

Vorhalle ['foːrhalə] *f* (*Diele*) entrance hall; (*von Parlament*) lobby.

vorhalten ['foːrhaltən] *unreg vt* to hold *od* put up ♦ *vi* to last; **jdm etw ~** to reproach sb for sth.

Vorhaltung *f* reproach.

Vorhand ['foːrhant] *f* forehand.

vorhanden [foːr'handən] *adj* existing; (*erhältlich*) available; **V~sein** (**-s**) *nt* existence, presence.

Vorhang ['foːrhaŋ] *m* curtain.

Vorhängeschloss▲ ['foːrhɛŋəʃlɔs] *nt* padlock.

Vorhaut ['foːrhaʊt] *f* (*ANAT*) foreskin.

vorher [foːr'heːr] *adv* before(hand); **~bestimmen** *vt* (*Schicksal*) to preordain; **~gehen** *unreg vi* to precede.

vorherig [foːr'heːrɪç] *adj* previous.

Vorherrschaft ['foːrhɛrʃaft] *f* predominance, supremacy.

vorherrschen *vi* to predominate.

vorher- *zW:* **V~sage** *f* forecast; **~sagen** *vt* to forecast, predict; **~sehbar** *adj* predictable; **~sehen** *unreg vt* to foresee.

vorhin [foːr'hɪn] *adv* not long ago, just now.

Vorhinein▲ ['foːrhɪnaɪn] *adv:* **im ~** beforehand.

Vorhof ['foːrhoːf] *m* forecourt.

vorig ['foːrɪç] *adj* previous, last.

Vorjahr ['foːrjaːr] *nt* previous year, year before.

vorjährig ['foːrjɛːrɪç] *adj* of the previous year.

vorjammern ['foːrjamərn] *vt, vi:* **jdm (etwas) ~** to moan to sb (about sth).

Vorkämpfer(in) ['foːrkɛmpfər(ɪn)] *m(f)* pioneer.

Vorkaufsrecht ['foːrkaʊfsrɛçt] *nt* option to buy.

Vorkehrung ['foːrkeːrʊŋ] *f* precaution.

Vorkenntnis ['foːrkɛntnɪs] *f* previous knowledge.

vorknöpfen ['foːrknœpfən] *vt* (*fig: umg*): **sich** *dat* **jdn ~** to take sb to task.

vorkommen ['foːrkɔmən] *unreg vi* to come forward; (*geschehen, sich finden*) to occur; (*scheinen*) to seem (to be); **so was soll ~!** that's life!; **sich** *dat* **dumm** *etc* ~ to feel stupid *etc*.

Vorkommen *nt* occurrence; (*MIN*) deposit.

Vorkommnis ['foːrkɔmnɪs] (**-ses, -se**) *nt* occurrence.

Vorkriegs- ['foːrkriːks] *in zW* pre-war.

vorladen ['foːrlaːdən] *unreg vt* (*bei Gericht*) to summons.

Vorladung *f* summons.

Vorlage ['foːrlaːgə] *f* model, pattern; (*das Vorlegen*) presentation; (*von Beweismaterial*) submission; (*Gesetzes~*) bill; (*SPORT*) pass.

vorlassen ['foːrlasən] *unreg vt* to admit; (*überholen lassen*) to let pass; (*vorgehen lassen*) to allow to go in front.

Vorlauf ['foːrlauf] *m* (preliminary) heat (*of running event*).

Vorläufer *m* forerunner.

vorläufig ['foːrlɔyfɪç] *adj* temporary; (*provisorisch*) provisional.

vorlaut ['foːrlaut] *adj* impertinent, cheeky.

Vorleben ['foːrleːbən] *nt* past (life).

vorlegen ['foːrleːgən] *vt* to put in front, present; (*Beweismaterial etc*) to produce, submit; **jdm etw** ~ to put sth before sb.

Vorleger (**-s, -**) *m* mat.

Vorleistung ['foːrlaɪstʊŋ] *f* (*FIN*: *Vorausbezahlung*) advance (payment); (*Vorarbeit*) preliminary work; (*POL*) prior concession.

vorlesen ['foːrleːzən] *unreg vt* to read (out).

Vorlesung *f* (*UNIV*) lecture.

Vorlesungsverzeichnis *nt* lecture timetable.

vorletzte(r, s) ['foːrlɛtstə(r, s)] *adj* last but one, penultimate.

vorlieb▲ [foːr'liːp] *adv*: ~ **nehmen mit** to make do with.

Vorliebe ['foːrliːbə] *f* preference, special liking; **etw mit** ~ **tun** to particularly like doing sth.

vorliegen ['foːrliːgən] *unreg vi* to be (here); **etw liegt jdm vor** sb has sth; **etw liegt gegen jdn vor** sb is charged with sth.

vorliegend *adj* present, at issue.

vorm. *abk* (= *vormittags*) a.m.; (= *vormals*) formerly.

vormachen ['foːrmaxən] *vt*: **jdm etw** ~ to show sb how to do sth; **jdm etwas** ~ (*fig*) to fool sb; **mach mir doch nichts vor** don't try and fool me.

Vormachtstellung ['foːrmaxtʃtɛlʊŋ] *f* supremacy.

vormals ['foːrmals] *adv* formerly.

Vormarsch ['foːrmarʃ] *m* advance.

vormerken ['foːrmɛrkən] *vt* to book; (*notieren*) to make note of; (*bei Bestellung*) to take an order for.

Vormittag ['foːrmɪtaːk] *m* morning; **am** ~ in the morning.

vormittags *adv* in the morning, before noon.

Vormund ['foːrmʊnt] (**-(e)s, -e** *od* **-münder**) *m* guardian.

vorn [fɔrn] *adv* in front; **von** ~ **anfangen** to start at the beginning; **nach** ~ to the front; **er betrügt sie von** ~ **bis hinten** he deceives her right, left and centre.

Vorname ['foːrnaːmə] *m* first *od* Christian name.

vornan [fɔrn'|an] *adv* at the front.

vorne ['fɔrnə] = **vorn**.

vornehm ['foːrneːm] *adj* distinguished; (*Manieren etc*) refined; (*Kleid*) elegant; **in ~en Kreisen** in polite society.

vornehmen *unreg vt* (*fig*) to carry out; **sich** *dat* **etw** ~ to start on sth; (*beschließen*) to decide to do sth; **sich** *dat* **zu viel** ~ to take on too much; **sich** *dat* **jdn** ~ to tell sb off.

vornehmlich *adv* chiefly, specially.

vorn(e)weg ['fɔrn(ə)vɛk] *adv* in front; (*als Erstes*) first.

vornherein ['fɔrnhɛraɪn] *adv*: **von** ~ from the start.

Vorort ['foːr|ɔrt] *m* suburb; **~zug** *m* commuter train.

vorprogrammiert ['foːrprogramiːrt] *adj* (*Erfolg, Antwort*) automatic.

Vorrang ['foːrraŋ] *m* precedence, priority.

vorrangig *adj* of prime importance, primary.

Vorrat ['foːrraːt] *m* stock, supply; **solange der** ~ **reicht** (*COMM*) while stocks last.

vorrätig ['foːrrɛːtɪç] *adj* in stock.

Vorratskammer *f* store cupboard; (*für Lebensmittel*) larder.

Vorraum *m* anteroom; (*Büro*) outer office.

vorrechnen ['foːrrɛçnən] *vt*: **jdm etw** ~ to calculate sth for sb; (*als Kritik*) to point sth out to sb.

Vorrecht ['foːrrɛçt] *nt* privilege.

Vorrede ['foːrreːdə] *f* introductory speech; (*THEAT*) prologue (*BRIT*), prolog (*US*).

Vorrichtung ['foːrrɪçtʊŋ] *f* device, gadget.

vorrücken ['foːrrykən] *vi* to advance ♦ *vt* to move forward.

Vorruhestand ['foːrruːəʃtant] *m* early retirement.

Vorrunde ['foːrrʊndə] *f* (*SPORT*) preliminary round.

Vors. *abk* = **Vorsitzende(r)**.

vorsagen ['foːrzaːgən] *vt* to recite; (*SCH*: *zuflüstern*) to tell secretly, prompt.

Vorsaison ['foːrzɛzõː] *f* early season, low season.

Vorsatz ['foːrzats] *m* intention; (*JUR*) intent; **einen** ~ **fassen** to make a resolution.

vorsätzlich ['foːrzɛtslɪç] *adj* intentional; (*JUR*) premeditated ♦ *adv* intentionally.

Vorschau ['foːrʃau] *f* (*RUNDF, TV*)

(programme (*BRIT*) *od* program (*US*)) preview; (*Film*) trailer.

Vorschein ['foːrʃaɪn] *m*: **zum ~ kommen** (*lit*: *sichtbar werden*) to appear; (*fig*: *entdeckt werden*) to come to light.

vorschieben ['foːrʃiːbən] *unreg vt* to push forward; (*vor etw*) to push across; (*fig*) to put forward as an excuse; **jdn ~** to use sb as a front.

vorschießen ['foːrʃiːsən] *unreg* (*umg*) *vt*: **jdm Geld ~** to advance sb money.

Vorschlag ['foːrʃlaːk] *m* suggestion, proposal.

vorschlagen ['foːrʃlaːgən] *unreg vt* to suggest, propose.

Vorschlaghammer *m* sledgehammer.

vorschnell ['foːrʃnɛl] *adj* hasty, too quick.

vorschreiben ['foːrʃraɪbən] *unreg vt* (*Dosis*) to prescribe; (*befehlen*) to specify; (**jdm**) **etw ~** (*lit*) to write sth out (for sb); **ich lasse mir nichts ~** I won't be dictated to.

Vorschrift ['foːrʃrɪft] *f* regulation(s *pl*), rule(s *pl*); (*Anweisungen*) instruction(s *pl*); **jdm ~en machen** to give sb orders; **Dienst nach ~** work-to-rule (*BRIT*), slowdown (*US*).

vorschriftsmäßig *adv* as per regulations/ instructions.

Vorschub ['foːrʃuːp] *m*: **jdm/einer Sache ~ leisten** to encourage sb/sth.

Vorschule ['foːrʃuːlə] *f* nursery school.

vorschulisch ['foːrʃuːlɪʃ] *adj* preschool *attr*.

Vorschuss▲ ['foːrʃʊs] *m* advance.

vorschützen ['foːrʃʏtsən] *vt* to put forward as a pretext; (*Unwissenheit*) to plead.

vorschweben ['foːrʃveːbən] *vi*: **jdm schwebt etw vor** sb has sth in mind.

vorsehen ['foːrzeːən] *unreg vt* to provide for; (*planen*) to plan ♦ *vr* to take care, be careful.

Vorsehung *f* providence.

vorsetzen ['foːrzɛtsən] *vt* to move forward; (*davor setzen*): **~ vor +akk** to put in front of; (*anbieten*): **jdm etw ~** to offer sb sth.

Vorsicht ['foːrzɪçt] *f* caution, care; **~! look out!**, **take care!**; (*auf Schildern*) caution!, danger!; **~ Stufe!** mind the step!; **etw mit ~ genießen** (*umg*) to take sth with a pinch of salt.

vorsichtig *adj* cautious, careful.

vorsichtshalber *adv* just in case.

Vorsichtsmaßnahme *f* precaution.

Vorsilbe ['foːrzɪlbə] *f* prefix.

vorsintflutlich ['foːrzɪntfluːtlɪç] (*umg*) *adj* antiquated.

Vorsitz ['foːrzɪts] *m* chair(manship); **den ~ führen** to chair the meeting.

Vorsitzende(r) *f(m)* chairman/-woman, chair(person).

Vorsorge ['foːrzɔrgə] *f* precaution(s *pl*); (*Fürsorge*) provision(s *pl*).

vorsorgen *vi*: **~ für** to make provision(s *pl*) for.

Vorsorgeuntersuchung ['foːrzɔrgə- |ʊntərzuːxʊŋ] *f* medical check-up.

vorsorglich ['foːrzɔrklɪç] *adv* as a precaution.

Vorspann ['foːrʃpan] *m* (*FILM, TV*) opening credits *pl*; (*PRESSE*) opening paragraph.

vorspannen *vt* (*Pferde*) to harness.

Vorspeise ['foːrʃpaɪzə] *f* hors d'œuvre, starter.

Vorspiegelung ['foːrʃpiːgəlʊŋ] *f*: **das ist (eine) ~ falscher Tatsachen** it's all sham.

Vorspiel ['foːrʃpiːl] *nt* prelude; (*bei Geschlechtsverkehr*) foreplay.

vorspielen *vt*: **jdm etw ~** (*MUS*) to play sth to sb; (*THEAT*) to act sth to sb; (*fig*) to act out a sham of sth in front of sb.

vorsprechen ['foːrʃprɛçən] *unreg vt* to say out loud; (*vortragen*) to recite ♦ *vi* (*THEAT*) to audition; **bei jdm ~** to call on sb.

vorspringend ['foːrʃprɪŋənt] *adj* projecting; (*Nase, Kinn*) prominent.

Vorsprung ['foːrʃprʊŋ] *m* projection; (*Fels~*) ledge; (*fig*) advantage, start.

Vorstadt ['foːrʃtat] *f* suburbs *pl*.

Vorstand ['foːrʃtant] *m* executive committee; (*COMM*) board (of directors); (*Person*) director; (*Leiter*) head.

Vorstandssitzung *f* (*von Firma*) board meeting.

Vorstandsvorsitzende(r) *f(m)* chairperson.

vorstehen ['foːrʃteːən] *unreg vi* to project; **einer Sache** *dat* **~** (*fig*) to be the head of sth.

Vorsteher(in) (**-s, -**) *m(f)* (*von Abteilung*) head; (*von Gefängnis*) governor; (*Bahnhofs~*) stationmaster.

vorstellbar *adj* conceivable.

vorstellen ['foːrʃtɛlən] *vt* to put forward; (*vor etw*) to put in front of; (*bekannt machen*) to introduce; (*darstellen*) to represent ♦ *vr* to introduce o.s.; (*bei Bewerbung*) to go for an interview; **sich** *dat* **etw ~** to imagine sth; **stell dir das nicht so einfach vor** don't think it's so easy.

Vorstellung *f* (*Bekanntmachen*) introduction; (*THEAT etc*) performance; (*Gedanke*) idea.

Vorstellungsgespräch *nt* interview.

Vorstellungsvermögen *nt* powers of imagination *pl*.

Vorstoß ['foːrʃtoːs] *m* advance; (*fig*: *Versuch*) attempt.

vorstoßen *unreg vt, vi* to push forward.

Vorstrafe ['foːrʃtraːfə] *f* previous conviction.

vorstrecken ['foːrʃtrɛkən] *vt* to stretch out; (*Geld*) to advance.

Vorstufe ['foːrʃtuːfə] *f* first step(s *pl*).

Vortag ['foːrtaːk] *m*: **am ~ einer Sache** *gen* on the day before sth.

Vortal ['foːrtaːl] *nt* (*COMPUT*) vortal.

vortasten ['foːrtastən] *vr*: **sich langsam zu etw ~** to approach sth carefully.

vortäuschen ['foːrtɔyʃən] *vt* to pretend, feign.

Vortäuschung *f:* unter ~ **falscher Tatsachen** under false pretences (*BRIT*) *od* pretenses (*US*).

Vorteil ['fɔːrtaɪl] **(-s, -e)** *m:* ~ **(gegenüber)** advantage (over); **im** ~ **sein** to have the advantage; **die Vor- und Nachteile** the pros and cons; **v~haft** *adj* advantageous; (*Kleider*) flattering; (*Geschäft*) lucrative.

Vortr. *abk* = **Vortrag.**

Vortrag ['fɔːrtraːk] **(-(e)s, Vorträge)** *m* talk, lecture; (~*sart*) delivery; (*von Gedicht*) rendering; (*COMM*) balance carried forward; **einen** ~ **halten** to give a lecture *od* talk.

vortragen ['fɔːrtraːgən] *unreg vt* to carry forward (*auch COMM*); (*fig*) to recite; (*Rede*) to deliver; (*Lied*) to perform; (*Meinung etc*) to express.

Vortragsabend *m* lecture evening; (*mit Musik*) recital; (*mit Gedichten*) poetry reading.

Vortragsreihe *f* series of lectures.

vortrefflich [fɔːrˈtrɛflɪç] *adj* excellent.

vortreten ['fɔːrtreːtən] *unreg vi* to step forward; (*Augen etc*) to protrude.

Vortritt ['fɔːrtrɪt] *m:* **jdm den** ~ **lassen** (*lit, fig*) to let sb go first.

vorüber [foˈryːbər] *adv* past, over; ~**gehen** *unreg vi* to pass (by); ~**gehen an** +*dat* (*fig*) to pass over; ~**gehend** *adj* temporary, passing.

Voruntersuchung ['fɔːr|ʊntərzuːxʊŋ] *f* (*MED*) preliminary examination; (*JUR*) preliminary investigation.

Vorurteil ['fɔːr|ʊrtaɪl] *nt* prejudice.

vorurteilsfrei *adj* unprejudiced, open-minded.

Vorverkauf ['fɔːrfɛrkaʊf] *m* advance booking.

Vorverkaufsssstelle *f* advance booking office.

vorverlegen ['fɔːrfɛrleːgən] *vt* (*Termin*) to bring forward.

Vorw. *abk* = **Vorwort.**

vorwagen ['fɔːrvaːgən] *vr* to venture forward.

Vorwahl ['fɔːrvaːl] *f* preliminary election; (*TEL*) dialling (*BRIT*) *od* area (*US*) code.

Vorwand ['fɔːrvant] **(-(e)s, Vorwände)** *m* pretext.

Vorwarnung ['fɔːrvarnʊŋ] *f* (advance) warning.

vorwärts ['fɔːrvɛrts] *adv* forward; ~ **gehen** to progress; ~ **kommen** to get on, make progress; ~! (*umg*) let's go!; (*MIL*) forward march!; **V~gang** *m* (*AUT etc*) forward gear.

Vorwäsche *f* prewash.

Vorwaschgang *m* prewash.

vorweg [fɔːrˈvɛk] *adv* in advance; **V~nahme** **(-, -n)** *f* anticipation; ~**nehmen** *unreg vt* to anticipate.

vorweisen ['fɔːrvaɪzən] *unreg vt* to show, produce.

vorwerfen ['fɔːrvɛrfən] *unreg vt:* **jdm etw** ~ to reproach sb for sth, accuse sb of sth; **sich** *dat* **nichts vorzuwerfen haben** to have nothing to reproach o.s. with; **das wirft er mir heute noch vor** he still holds it against me; **Tieren/Gefangenen etw** ~ (*lit*) to throw sth down for the animals/prisoners.

vorwiegend ['fɔːrviːgənt] *adj* predominant ♦ *adv* predominantly.

vorwitzig *adj* saucy, cheeky.

Vorwort ['fɔːrvɔrt] **(-(e)s, -e)** *nt* preface.

Vorwurf ['fɔːrvʊrf] **(-(e)s, ⁻e)** *m* reproach; **jdm/sich Vorwürfe machen** to reproach sb/o.s.

vorwurfsvoll *adj* reproachful.

Vorzeichen ['fɔːrtsaɪçən] *nt* (*Omen*) omen; (*MED*) early symptom; (*MATH*) sign.

vorzeigen ['fɔːrtsaɪgən] *vt* to show, produce.

Vorzeit ['fɔːrtsaɪt] *f* prehistoric times *pl*.

vorzeitig *adj* premature.

vorziehen ['fɔːrtsiːən] *unreg vt* to pull forward; (*Gardinen*) to draw; (*zuerst behandeln, abfertigen*) to give priority to; (*lieber haben*) to prefer.

Vorzimmer ['fɔːrtsɪmər] *nt* anteroom; (*Büro*) outer office.

Vorzug ['fɔːrtsuːk] *m* preference; (*gute Eigenschaft*) merit, good quality; (*Vorteil*) advantage; (*EISENB*) relief train; **einer Sache** *dat* **den** ~ **geben** (*form*) to prefer sth; (*Vorrang geben*) to give sth precedence.

vorzüglich [fɔːrˈtsyːklɪç] *adj* excellent, first-rate.

Vorzugsaktien *pl* preference shares (*BRIT*), preferred stock (*US*).

vorzugsweise *adv* preferably; (*hauptsächlich*) chiefly.

Votum ['voːtʊm] **(-s, Voten)** *nt* vote.

Voyeur [voaˈjøːr] **(-s, -e)** *m* voyeur; **Voyeurismus** [voajøˈrɪsmʊs] *m* voyeurism.

v. T. *abk* (= *vom Tausend*) per thousand.

vulgär [vʊlˈgɛːr] *adj* vulgar.

Vulkan [vʊlˈkaːn] **(-s, -e)** *m* volcano; ~**ausbruch** *m* volcanic eruption.

vulkanisieren [vʊlkaniˈziːrən] *vt* to vulcanize.

v. u. Z. *abk* (= *vor unserer Zeitrechnung*) B.C.

vo company can rely on another outside independent company yes skills + assets that are central to its comp advantage

W, w

W, w [ve:] nt W, w; ~ **wie Wilhelm** ≈ W for William.

W. abk (= West(en)) W.

w. abk = **wenden, werktags, westlich** (= **weiblich**) f.

Waage ['va:gə] (-, -n) f scales pl; (ASTROL) Libra; **sich** dat **die ~ halten** (fig) to balance one another; **w~recht** adj horizontal.

Waagschale f (scale) pan; **(schwer) in die ~ fallen** (fig) to carry weight.

wabb(e)lig ['vab(ə)liç] adj wobbly.

Wabe ['va:bə] (-, -n) f honeycomb.

wach [vax] adj awake; (fig) alert; ~ **werden** to wake up.

Wachablösung f changing of the guard; (Mensch) relief guard; (fig: Regierungswechsel) change of government.

Wache (-, -n) f guard, watch; ~ **halten** to keep watch; ~ **stehen** od **schieben** (umg) to be on guard (duty).

wachen vi to be awake; (Wache halten) to keep watch; **bei jdm** ~ to sit up with sb.

wachhabend adj attrib duty.

Wachhund m watchdog, guard dog; (fig) watchdog.

Wacholder [va'xɔldər] (-s, -) m juniper.

wachrütteln ['vaxrʏtəln] vt (fig) to (a)rouse.

Wachs [vaks] (-es, -e) nt wax.

wachsam ['vaxza:m] adj watchful, vigilant, alert; **W~keit** f vigilance.

wachsen[1] unreg vi to grow.

wachsen[2] vt (Skier) to wax.

Wachsfigurenkabinett nt waxworks (exhibition).

Wachs(mal)stift m wax crayon.

wächst [vɛkst] vb siehe **wachsen**[1].

Wachstuch ['vakstu:x] nt oilcloth.

Wachstum ['vakstu:m] (-s) nt growth.

Wachstums- zW: **~branche** f growth industry; **~grenze** f limits of growth; **w~hemmend** adj growth-inhibiting; **~rate** f growth rate; **~schmerzen** pl growing pains; **~störung** f disturbance of growth.

Wachtel ['vaxtəl] (-, -n) f quail.

Wächter ['vɛçtər] (-s, -) m guard; (Park~) warden, keeper; (Museums~, Parkplatz~) attendant.

Wachtmeister m officer.

Wachtposten m guard, sentry.

Wach(t)turm m watchtower.

Wach- und Schließgesellschaft f security corps.

wack(e)lig adj shaky, wobbly; **auf ~en Beinen stehen** to be wobbly on one's legs; (fig) to be unsteady.

Wackelkontakt m loose connection.

wackeln vi to shake; (fig: Position) to be shaky; **mit den Hüften/dem Schwanz** ~ to wiggle one's hips/wag its tail.

wacker ['vakər] adj valiant, stout; **sich ~ schlagen** (umg) to put up a brave fight.

Wade ['va:də] (-, -n) f (ANAT) calf.

Waffe ['vafə] (-, -n) f weapon; **jdn mit seinen eigenen ~n schlagen** (fig) to beat sb at his own game.

Waffel ['vafəl] (-, -n) f waffle; (Eis~) wafer.

Waffen- zW: **~gewalt** f: **mit ~gewalt** by force of arms; **~lager** nt (von Armee) ordnance depot; (von Terroristen) cache; **~schein** m firearms od gun licence (BRIT), firearms license (US); **~schmuggel** m gunrunning, arms smuggling; **~stillstand** m armistice, truce.

Wagemut ['va:gəmu:t] m daring.

Wagen ['va:gən] (-s, -) m vehicle; (Auto) car, automobile (US); (EISENB) car, carriage (BRIT); (Pferde~) wag(g)on, cart.

wagen vt to venture, dare.

Wagen- zW: **~führer** m driver; **~heber** (-s, -) m jack; **~park** m fleet of cars; **~rückholtaste** f (Schreibmaschine) carriage return (key); **~rücklauf** m carriage return.

Waggon [va'gõ:] (-s, -s) m wag(g)on; (Güter~) goods van (BRIT), freight truck (US).

waghalsig ['va:khalziç] adj foolhardy.

Wagnis ['va:knɪs] (-ses, -se) nt risk.

Wagon▲ (-s, -s) m = **Waggon**.

Wahl [va:l] (-, -en) f choice; (POL) election; **erste** ~ (Qualität) top quality; (Gemüse, Eier) grade one; **zweite** ~ (COMM) seconds pl; **aus freier** ~ of one's own free choice; **wer die ~ hat, hat die Qual** (Sprichwort) he is od you are etc spoilt for choice; **die** ~ **fiel auf ihn** he was chosen; **sich zur** ~ **stellen** (POL etc) to stand (BRIT) od run (for parliament etc).

wählbar adj eligible.

Wahl- zW: **w~berechtigt** adj entitled to vote; **~beteiligung** f poll, turnout; **~bezirk** m (POL) ward.

wählen ['vɛːlən] vt to choose; (POL) to elect, vote for; (TEL) to dial ♦ vi to choose; (POL) to vote; (TEL) to dial.

Wähler(in) (-s, -) m(f) voter; **~abwanderung** f voter drift; **w~isch** adj fastidious, particular; **~schaft** f electorate.

Wahl- zW: **~fach** nt optional subject; **w~frei** adj: **w~freier Zugriff** (COMPUT) random access; **~gang** m ballot; **~geschenk** nt pre-election vote-catching gimmick; **~heimat** f country of adoption; **~helfer** m (im ~kampf)

election assistant; (*bei der* ~) polling officer;
~**kabine** *f* polling booth; ~**kampf** *m* election
campaign; ~**kreis** *m* constituency; ~**leiter** *m*
returning officer; ~**liste** *f* electoral register;
~**lokal** *nt* polling station; **w**~**los** *adv* at
random; (*nicht wählerisch*) indiscriminately;
~**recht** *nt* franchise; **allgemeines** ~**recht**
universal franchise; **das aktive** ~**recht** the
right to vote; **das passive** ~**recht** eligibility
(for political office); ~**spruch** *m* motto;
~**urne** *f* ballot box; **w**~**weise** *adv*
alternatively.
Wählzeichen *nt* (*TEL*) dialling tone (*BRIT*),
dial tone (*US*).
Wahn [vaːn] (**-(e)s**) *m* delusion; ~**sinn** *m*
madness; **w**~**sinnig** *adj* insane, mad ♦ *adv*
(*umg*) incredibly; **w**~**witzig** *adj* crazy *attrib*
♦ *adv* terribly.
wahr [vaːr] *adj* true; **da ist (et)was W**~**es dran**
there's some truth in that.
wahren *vt* to maintain, keep.
während ['vɛːrən] *vi* to last.
während *präp* +*gen* during ♦ *konj* while;
~**dessen** *adv* meanwhile.
wahr- *zW:* ~**haben** *unreg vt:* **etw nicht** ~**haben**
wollen to refuse to admit sth; ~**haft** *adv*
(*tatsächlich*) truly; ~**haftig** *adj* true, real ♦ *adv*
really.
Wahrheit *f* truth; **die** ~ **sagen** to tell the
truth.
wahrheitsgetreu *adj* (*Bericht*) truthful;
(*Darstellung*) faithful.
wahrnehmen *unreg vt* to perceive; (*Frist*) to
observe; (*Veränderungen etc*) to be aware of;
(*Gelegenheit*) to take; (*Interessen, Rechte*) to
look after.
Wahrnehmung *f* perception; observing;
awareness; taking; looking after.
wahrsagen *vi* to predict the future, tell
fortunes.
Wahrsager *m* fortune-teller.
wahrscheinlich [vaːrˈʃaɪnlɪç] *adj* probable
♦ *adv* probably; **W**~**keit** *f* probability; **aller**
W~**keit nach** in all probability.
Währung ['vɛːrʊŋ] *f* currency.
Währungs- *zW:* ~**einheit** *f* monetary unit;
~**politik** *f* monetary policy; ~**raum** *m*
currency area; ~**reserven** *pl* official
reserves *pl*; ~**union** *f* monetary union.
Wahrzeichen *nt* (*Gebäude, Turm etc*) symbol;
(*von Stadt, Verein*) emblem.
Waise ['vaɪzə] (**-, -n**) *f* orphan.
Waisen- *zW:* ~**haus** *nt* orphanage; ~**kind** *nt*
orphan; ~**knabe** *m:* **gegen dich ist er ein**
~**knabe** (*umg*) he's no match for you;
~**rente** *f* orphan's allowance.
Wal [vaːl] (**-(e)s, -e**) *m* whale.
Wald [valt] (**-(e)s, ̈er**) *m* wood(s *pl*); (*groß*)
forest; ~**brand** *m* forest fire.
Wäldchen ['vɛltçən] *nt* copse, grove.

Waldhorn *nt* (*MUS*) French horn.
waldig ['valdɪç] *adj* wooded.
Wald- *zW:* ~**lehrpfad** *m* nature trail; ~**meister**
m (*BOT*) woodruff; ~**sterben** *nt* loss of trees
due to pollution.
Wald- und Wiesen- (*umg*) *in zW* common-or-
garden.
Waldweg *m* woodland *od* forest path.
Wales [weɪlz] *nt* Wales.
Walfang ['vaːlfaŋ] *m* whaling.
Walfisch ['valfɪʃ] *m* whale.
Waliser(in) [vaˈliːzər(ɪn)] (**-s, -**) *m(f)* Welshman,
Welshwoman.
walisisch *adj* Welsh.
Walkman ® ['wɔːkman] (**-s, Walkmen**) *m*
Walkman ®, personal stereo.
Wall [val] (**-(e)s, ̈e**) *m* embankment; (*Bollwerk*)
rampart.
wallfahren *vi untr* to go on a pilgrimage.
Wallfahrer(in) *m(f)* pilgrim.
Wallfahrt *f* pilgrimage.
Wallis ['valɪs] (**-**) *nt:* **das** ~ Valais.
Wallone [vaˈloːnə] (**-n, -n**) *m*, **Wallonin** *f*
Walloon.
Walnuss▲ ['valnʊs] *f* walnut.
Walross▲ ['valrɔs] *nt* walrus.
walten ['valtən] *vi* (*geh*): **Vernunft** ~ **lassen** to
let reason prevail.
Walzblech (**-(e)s**) *nt* sheet metal.
Walze ['valtsə] (**-, -n**) *f* (*Gerät*) cylinder;
(*Fahrzeug*) roller.
walzen *vt* to roll (out).
wälzen ['vɛltsən] *vt* to roll (over); (*Bücher*) to
hunt through; (*Probleme*) to deliberate on
♦ *vr* to wallow; (*vor Schmerzen*) to roll about;
(*im Bett*) to toss and turn.
Walzer ['valtsər] (**-s, -**) *m* waltz.
Wälzer ['vɛltsər] (**-s, -**) (*umg*) *m* tome.
Wampe ['vampə] (**-, -n**) (*umg*) *f* paunch.
Wand (**-, ̈e**) *f* wall; (*Trenn*~) partition;
(*Berg*~) precipice; (*Fels*~) (rock) face; (*fig*)
barrier; **weiß wie die** ~ as white as a sheet;
jdn an die ~ **spielen** to put sb in the shade;
(*SPORT*) to outplay sb.
wand *etc* [vant] *vb siehe* **winden**.
Wandel ['vandəl] (**-s**) *m* change; **w**~**bar** *adj*
changeable, variable.
Wandelhalle *f* foyer.
wandeln *vt, vr* to change ♦ *vi* (*gehen*) to walk.
Wanderausstellung *f* touring exhibition.
Wanderbühne *f* touring theatre (*BRIT*) *od*
theater (*US*).
Wanderer (**-s, -**) *m* hiker, rambler.
Wanderin *f* hiker, rambler.
Wanderkarte *f* hiker's map.
Wanderlied *nt* hiking song.
wandern *vi* to hike; (*Blick*) to wander;
(*Gedanken*) to stray; (*umg: in den Papierkorb*
etc) to land.
Wanderpreis *m* challenge trophy.

Wanderschaft f travelling (BRIT), traveling (US).

Wanderung f walk, hike; (von Tieren, Völkern) migration.

Wanderweg m trail, (foot)path.

Wandgemälde nt mural.

Wandlung f change; (völlige Um~) transformation; (REL) transubstantiation.

Wand- zW: ~**malerei** f mural painting; ~**schirm** m (folding) screen; ~**schrank** m cupboard.

wandte etc ['vantə] vb siehe **wenden**.

Wandteppich m tapestry.

Wandverkleidung f panelling.

Wange ['vaŋə] (-, -n) f cheek.

wankelmütig ['vaŋkəlmy:tıç] adj fickle, inconstant.

wanken ['vankən] vi to stagger; (fig) to waver.

wann [van] adv when; **seit ~ bist/hast du ...?** how long have you been/have you had ...?

Wanne ['vanə] (-, -n) f tub.

Wanze ['vantsə] (-, -n) f (ZOOL, Abhörgerät) bug.

WAP nt abk (COMPUT: = Wireless Application Protocol) WAP; ~**-Handy** nt WAP phone.

Wappen ['vapən] (-s, -) nt coat of arms, crest; ~**kunde** f heraldry.

wappnen vr (fig) to prepare o.s.; **gewappnet sein** to be forearmed.

war etc [va:r] vb siehe **sein**.

warb etc [varp] vb siehe **werben**.

Ware ['va:rə] (-, -n) f ware; **Waren** pl goods pl.

wäre etc ['vɛ:rə] vb siehe **sein**.

Waren- zW: ~**bestand** m stock; ~**haus** nt department store; ~**lager** nt stock, store; ~**muster** nt sample; ~**probe** f sample; ~**rückstände** pl backlog sing; ~**sendung** f trade sample (sent by post); ~**zeichen** nt trademark.

warf etc [varf] vb siehe **werfen**.

warm [varm] adj warm; (Essen) hot; (umg: homosexuell) queer; **mir ist ~** I'm warm; **mit jdm ~ werden** (umg) to get close to sb; **sich** dat **jdn ~ halten** (fig) to keep in with sb; ~ **laufen** (AUT) to warm up.

Wärme ['vɛrmə] (-, -n) f warmth; **10 Grad ~** 10 degrees above zero.

wärmen vt, vr to warm (up), heat (up).

Wärmflasche f hot-water bottle.

warm- zW: **W~front** f (MET) warm front; ~**herzig** adj warm-hearted; **W~wassertank** m hot-water tank.

Warnblinkanlage f (AUT) hazard warning lights pl.

Warndreieck nt warning triangle.

warnen ['varnən] vt to warn.

Warnstreik m token strike.

Warnung f warning.

Warschau ['varʃaʊ] (-s) nt Warsaw; ~**er Pakt** m Warsaw Pact.

Warte (-, -n) f observation point; (fig) viewpoint.

warten ['vartən] vi to wait ♦ vt (Auto, Maschine) to service; ~ **auf** +akk to wait for; **auf sich ~ lassen** to take a long time; **warte mal!** wait a minute!; (überlegend) let me see; **mit dem Essen auf jdn ~** to wait for sb before eating.

Wärter(in) ['vɛrtər(ın)] (-s, -) m(f) attendant.

Wartesaal m (EISENB) waiting room.

Wartezimmer nt waiting room.

Wartung f (von Auto, Maschine) servicing; ~ **und Instandhaltung** maintenance.

warum [va'rʊm] adv why; ~ **nicht gleich so!** that's better.

Warze ['vartsə] (-, -n) f wart.

was [vas] pron what; (umg: etwas) something; **das, ~ ...** that which ...; ~ **für ...?** what sort od kind of ...?

Wasch- zW: ~**anlage** f (für Autos) car wash; **w~bar** adj washable; ~**becken** nt washbasin.

Wäsche ['vɛʃə] (-, -n) f wash(ing); (Bett~) linen; (Unter~) underwear; **dumm aus der ~ gucken** (umg) to look stupid.

waschecht adj (Farbe) fast; (fig) genuine.

Wäsche- zW: ~**klammer** f clothes peg (BRIT), clothespin (US); ~**korb** m dirty clothes basket; ~**leine** f washing line (BRIT), clothes line (US).

waschen ['vaʃən] unreg vt, vi to wash ♦ vr to (have a) wash; **sich** dat **die Hände ~** to wash one's hands; ~ **und legen** (Haare) to shampoo and set.

Wäscherei [vɛʃə'raɪ] f laundry.

Wäscheschleuder f spin-dryer.

Wasch- zW: ~**gang** m stage of the washing programme (BRIT) od program (US); ~**küche** f laundry room; ~**lappen** m face cloth od flannel (BRIT), washcloth (US); (umg) softy; ~**maschine** f washing machine; ~**mittel** nt detergent; ~**pulver** nt washing powder; ~**salon** m Launderette ® (BRIT), Laundromat ® (US).

wäscht [vɛʃt] vb siehe **waschen**.

Waschtisch m washstand.

Washington ['wɔʃɪŋtən] (-s) nt Washington.

Wasser¹ ['vasər] (-s, -) nt water; ~ **abstoßend** water-repellent; **dort wird auch nur mit ~ gekocht** (fig) they're no different from anybody else (them); **ins ~ fallen** (fig) to fall through; **mit allen ~n gewaschen sein** (umg) to be a shrewd customer; ~ **lassen** (euph) to pass water; **jdm das ~ abgraben** (fig) to take the bread from sb's mouth, take away sb's livelihood.

Wasser² (-s, ⁻) nt (Flüssigkeit) water; (MED) lotion; (Parfüm) cologne; (Mineral~) mineral water.

Wässerchen nt: **er sieht aus, als ob er kein ~ trüben könnte** he looks as if butter wouldn't melt in his mouth.

Wasser- *zW:* **w~dicht** *adj* watertight; (*Stoff, Uhr*) waterproof; **~fall** *m* waterfall; **~farbe** *f* watercolour (*BRIT*), watercolor (*US*); **w~gekühlt** *adj* (*AUT*) water-cooled; **~graben** *m* (*SPORT*) water jump; (*um Burg*) moat; **~hahn** *m* tap, faucet (*US*).

wässerig ['vɛsəriç] *adj* watery.

Wasser- *zW:* **~kessel** *m* kettle; (*TECH*) boiler; **~kraftwerk** *nt* hydroelectric power station; **~leitung** *f* water pipe; (*Anlagen*) plumbing; **~mann** *m* (*ASTROL*) Aquarius.

wassern *vi* to land on the water.

wässern ['vɛsərn] *vt, vi* to water.

Wasser- *zW:* **~scheide** *f* watershed; **w~scheu** *adj* afraid of water; **~schutzpolizei** *f* (*auf Flüssen*) river police; (*im Hafen*) harbour (*BRIT*) *od* harbor (*US*) police; (*auf der See*) coastguard service; **~ski** *nt* water-skiing; **~spiegel** *m* (*Oberfläche*) surface of the water; (*~stand*) water level; **~stand** *m* water level; **~stoff** *m* hydrogen; **~stoffbombe** *f* hydrogen bomb; **~verbrauch** *m* water consumption; **~waage** *f* spirit level; **~welle** *f* shampoo and set; **~werfer (-s, -)** *m* water cannon; **~werk** *nt* waterworks; **~zeichen** *nt* watermark.

waten ['va:tən] *vi* to wade.

watscheln ['va:tʃəln] *vi* to waddle.

Watt¹ [vat] **(-(e)s, -en)** *nt* mud flats *pl*.

Watt² **(-s, -)** *nt* (*ELEK*) watt.

Watte (-, -n) *f* cotton wool (*BRIT*), absorbent cotton (*US*).

Wattenmeer (-(e)s) *nt* mud flats *pl*.

Wattestäbchen *nt* cotton(-wool) swab.

wattieren [va'ti:rən] *vt* to pad.

WC [ve:'tse:] **(-s, -s)** *nt abk* (= *Wasserklosett*) WC.

Web [wɛb] *nt* (*COMPUT*): **das ~** the Web; **im ~** on the Web; **~page** *nt* web page; **~seite** *f* Web page, web site.

weben ['ve:bən] *unreg vt* to weave.

Weber(in) **(-s, -)** *m(f)* weaver.

Weberei [ve:bə'raɪ] *f* (*Betrieb*) weaving mill.

Webstuhl ['ve:pʃtu:l] *m* loom.

Wechsel ['vɛksəl] **(-s, -)** *m* change; (*Geld~*) exchange; (*COMM*) bill of exchange; **~bäder** *pl* alternating hot and cold baths *pl*; **~beziehung** *f* correlation; **~forderungen** *pl* (*COMM*) bills receivable *pl*; **~geld** *nt* change; **w~haft** *adj* (*Wetter*) variable; **~inhaber** *m* bearer; **~jahre** *pl* change of life, menopause; **in die ~jahre kommen** to start the change; **~kurs** *m* rate of exchange; **~kursmechanismus** *m* Exchange Rate Mechanism, ERM.

wechseln *vt* to change; (*Blicke*) to exchange ♦ *vi* to change; (*einander ablösen*) to alternate.

wechselnd *adj* changing; (*Stimmungen*)

changeable; (*Winde, Bewölkung*) variable.

Wechsel- *zW:* **w~seitig** *adj* reciprocal; **~sprechanlage** *f* two-way intercom; **~strom** *m* alternating current; **~stube** *f* currency exchange, bureau de change; **~verbindlichkeiten** *pl* bills payable *pl*; **w~weise** *adv* alternately; **~wirkung** *f* interaction.

wecken ['vɛkən] *vt* to wake (up); (*fig*) to arouse; (*Bedarf*) to create; (*Erinnerungen*) to revive.

Wecker (-s, -) *m* alarm clock; **jdm auf den ~ fallen** (*umg*) to get on sb's nerves.

Weckglas ® *nt* preserving jar.

Weckruf *m* (*TEL*) alarm call.

wedeln ['ve:dəln] *vi* (*mit Schwanz*) to wag; (*mit Fächer*) to fan; (*SKI*) to wedel.

weder ['ve:dər] *konj* neither; **~ ... noch ...** neither ... nor ...

Weg [ve:k] **(-(e)s, -e)** *m* way; (*Pfad*) path; (*Route*) route; **sich auf den ~ machen** to be on one's way; **jdm aus dem ~ gehen** to keep out of sb's way; **jdm nicht über den ~ trauen** (*fig*) not to trust sb an inch; **den ~ des geringsten Widerstandes gehen** to follow the line of least resistance; **etw in die ~e leiten** to arrange sth; **jdm Steine in den ~ legen** (*fig*) to put obstacles in sb's way; *siehe auch* **zuwege**.

weg [vɛk] *adv* away, off; **über etw** *akk* **~ sein** to be over sth; **er war schon ~** he had already left; **nichts wie** *od* **nur ~ von hier!** let's get out of here!; **~ damit!** (*mit Schere etc*) put it/them away!; **Finger ~!** hands off!

Wegbereiter (-s, -) *m* pioneer.

wegblasen *unreg vt* to blow away; **wie weggeblasen sein** (*fig*) to have vanished.

wegbleiben *unreg vi* to stay away; **mir bleibt die Spucke weg!** (*umg*) I am absolutely flabbergasted!

wegen ['ve:gən] (*umg*) *präp +gen od* (*umg*) *+dat* because of; **von ~!** you must be joking!

weg- *zW:* **~fahren** *unreg vi* to drive away; (*abfahren*) to leave; **W~fahrsperre** *f* (*AUT*): **(elektronische) W~fahrsperre** (electronic) immobilizer; **~fallen** *unreg vi* to be left out; (*Ferien, Bezahlung*) to be cancelled; (*aufhören*) to cease; **~gehen** *unreg vi* to go away, leave; (*umg: Ware*) to sell; **~hören** *vi* to turn a deaf ear; **~jagen** *vt* to chase away; **~kommen** *unreg vi*: **(bei etw) gut/schlecht ~kommen** (*umg*) to come off well/badly (with sth); **~lassen** *unreg vt* to leave out; **~laufen** *unreg vi* to run away *od* off; **das läuft (dir) nicht ~!** (*fig hum*) that can wait; **~legen** *vt* to put aside; **~machen** (*umg*) *vt* to get rid of; **~müssen** *unreg* (*umg*) *vi* to have to go; **~nehmen** *unreg vt* to take away.

Wegrand ['ve:krant] *m* wayside.

weg- *zW:* **~räumen** *vt* to clear away;

~**schaffen** vt to clear away; ~**schließen** unreg
vt to lock away; ~**schnappen** vt: (**jdm**) **etw**
~**schnappen** to snatch sth away (from sb);
~**stecken** vt to put away; (umg: verkraften) to
cope with; ~**treten** unreg vi (MIL): ~**treten!**
dismiss!; **geistig** ~**getreten sein** (umg:
geistesabwesend) to be away with the
fairies; ~**tun** unreg vt to put away.
wegweisend ['veːgvaɪzənt] adj pioneering
attrib, revolutionary.
Wegweiser ['veːgvaɪzər] (-**s**, -) m road sign,
signpost; (fig: Buch etc) guide.
Wegwerf- ['vɛkvɛrf] in zW disposable.
weg- zW: ~**werfen** unreg vt to throw away;
~**werfend** adj disparaging;
W~werfgesellschaft f throw-away society;
~**wollen** unreg vi (verreisen) to want to go
away; ~**ziehen** unreg vi to move away.
weh [veː] adj sore.
Wehe ['veːə] (-, -**n**) f drift.
wehe interj: ~, **wenn du ...** you'll regret it if
you ...; ~ **dir!** you dare!
Wehen pl (MED) contractions pl; **in den**
~ **liegen** to be in labour (BRIT) od labor (US).
wehen vt, vi to blow; (Fahnen) to flutter.
weh- zW: ~**klagen** vi untr to wail; ~**leidig** adj
oversensitive to pain; (jammernd) whiny,
whining; **W~mut** f melancholy; ~**mütig** adj
melancholy.
Wehr¹ [veːr] (-(**e**)**s**, -**e**) nt weir.
Wehr² [veːr] (-, -**en**) f (Feuer~) fire brigade
(BRIT) od department (US) ♦ in zW defence
(BRIT), defense (US); **sich zur** ~ **setzen** to
defend o.s.
Wehrdienst m military service.

WEHRDIENST

Wehrdienst is military service which is still
compulsory in Germany. All young men receive
their call-up papers at 18 and all who are pronounced
physically fit are required to spend ten months in the
Bundeswehr. Conscientious objectors are
allowed to do **Zivildienst** as an alternative, on
attending a hearing and presenting their case.

Wehrdienstverweigerer m ≈ conscientious
objector.
wehren vr to defend o.s.
Wehr- zW: **w~los** adj defenceless (BRIT),
defenseless (US); **jdm w~los ausgeliefert**
sein to be at sb's mercy; ~**macht** f armed
forces pl; ~**pflicht** f conscription;
w~pflichtig adj liable for military service;
~**übung** f reserve duty training exercise.
wehtun▲ ['veːtuːn] unreg vt: **jdm/sich** ~ to
hurt sb/o.s.
Wehwehchen (umg) nt (minor) complaint.
Weib [vaɪp] (-(**e**)**s**, -**er**) nt woman, female (pej).
Weibchen nt (Ehefrau) little woman; (ZOOL)
female.
weibisch ['vaɪbɪʃ] adj effeminate.
weiblich adj feminine.
weich [vaɪç] adj soft; (Ei) soft-boiled; ~**e**
Währung soft currency.
Weiche (-, -**n**) f (EISENB) points pl; **die** ~**n**
stellen (lit) to switch the points; (fig) to set
the course.
weichen unreg vi to yield, give way; (**nicht**)
von jdm od **von jds Seite** ~ (not) to leave
sb's side.
Weichensteller (-**s**, -) m pointsman.
weich- zW: **W~heit** f softness; **W~käse** m soft
cheese; ~**lich** adj soft, namby-pamby;
W~ling m wimp; **W~spüler** (-**s**, -) m fabric
conditioner; **W~teile** pl soft parts pl; **W~tier**
nt mollusc (BRIT), mollusk (US).
Weide ['vaɪdə] (-, -**n**) f (Baum) willow; (Gras)
pasture.
weiden vi to graze ♦ vr: **sich an etw** dat ~ to
delight in sth.
Weidenkätzchen nt willow catkin.
weidlich ['vaɪtlɪç] adv thoroughly.
weigern ['vaɪgərn] vr to refuse.
Weigerung ['vaɪgərʊŋ] f refusal.
Weihe ['vaɪə] (-, -**n**) f consecration; (Priester~)
ordination.
weihen vt to consecrate; (widmen) to
dedicate; **dem Untergang geweiht** (liter)
doomed.
Weiher (-**s**, -) m pond.
Weihnachten (-) nt Christmas; **fröhliche** ~!
happy od merry Christmas!; **w~** vi unpers: **es**
weihnachtet sehr (poetisch, ironisch)
Christmas is very much in evidence.
weihnachtlich adj Christmas(sy).
Weihnachts- zW: ~**abend** m Christmas Eve;
~**baum** m Christmas tree; ~**geld** nt
Christmas bonus; ~**geschenk** nt Christmas
present; ~**lied** nt Christmas carol; ~**mann** m
Father Christmas (BRIT), Santa Claus.
Weihnachtsmarkt m Christmas fair.

WEIHNACHTSMARKT

The **Weihnachtsmarkt** is a market held in most
large towns in Germany in the weeks prior to
Christmas. People visit it to buy presents, toys and
Christmas decorations, and to enjoy the festive
atmosphere. Food and drink associated with the
Christmas festivities can also be eaten and drunk
there, for example gingerbread and mulled wine.

Weihnachtstag m: (**erster**) ~ Christmas day;
zweiter ~ Boxing Day (BRIT).
Weihrauch m incense.
Weihwasser nt holy water.
weil [vaɪl] konj because.
Weile ['vaɪlə] (-) f while, short time.
Weiler ['vaɪlər] (-**s**, -) m hamlet.

Weimarer Republik ['vaɪmarər repu'bliːk] *f* Weimar Republic.

Wein [vaɪn] (-(e)s, -e) *m* wine; (*Pflanze*) vine; **jdm reinen ~ einschenken** (*fig*) to tell sb the truth; **~bau** *m* cultivation of vines; **~bauer** *m* wine-grower; **~beere** *f* grape; **~berg** *m* vineyard; **~bergschnecke** *f* snail; **~brand** *m* brandy.

weinen *vt, vi* to cry; **das ist zum W~** it's enough to make you cry *od* weep.

weinerlich *adj* tearful.

Wein- *zW:* **~gegend** *f* wine-growing area; **~geist** *m* (ethyl) alcohol; **~glas** *nt* wine glass; **~gut** *nt* wine-growing estate; **~karte** *f* wine list.

Weinkrampf *m* crying fit.

Wein- *zW:* **~lese** *f* vintage; **~probe** *f* wine tasting; **~rebe** *f* vine; **w~rot** *adj* (*Farbe*) claret; **w~selig** *adj* merry with wine; **~stein** *m* tartar; **~stock** *m* vine; **~stube** *f* wine bar; **~traube** *f* grape.

weise ['vaɪzə] *adj* wise.

Weise (-, -n) *f* manner, way; (*Lied*) tune; **auf diese ~** in this way.

Weise(r) *f(m)* wise man, wise woman, sage.

weisen *unreg vt* to show; **etw (weit) von sich ~** (*fig*) to reject sth (emphatically).

Weisheit ['vaɪshaɪt] *f* wisdom.

Weisheitszahn *m* wisdom tooth.

weismachen ['vaɪsmaxən] *vt:* **er wollte uns ~, dass ...** he would have us believe that ...

weiß¹ [vaɪs] *vb siehe* **wissen**.

weiß² *adj* white; **W~blech** *nt* tin plate; **W~brot** *nt* white bread; **~en** *vt* to whitewash; **W~glut** *f* (*TECH*) incandescence; **jdn zur W~glut bringen** (*fig*) to make sb see red; **W~kohl** *m* (white) cabbage.

Weißrussland▲ *nt* B(y)elorussia.

weißt [vaɪst] *vb siehe* **wissen**.

Weiß- *zW:* **~waren** *pl* linen *sing;* **~wein** *m* white wine; **~wurst** *f* veal sausage.

Weisung ['vaɪzʊŋ] *f* instruction.

weit [vaɪt] *adj* wide; (*Begriff*) broad; (*Reise, Wurf*) long ♦ *adv* far; **~ blickend** far-seeing; **~ hergeholt** far-fetched; **~ reichend** (*fig*) far-reaching; **~ verbreitet** widespread; **~ verzweigt** (*Straßensystem*) extensive; **in ~er Ferne** in the far distance; **wie ~ ist es ...?** how far is it ...?; **das geht zu ~** that's going too far; **~ und breit** for miles around; **~ gefehlt!** far from it; **es so ~ bringen, dass ...** to bring it about that ...; **~ zurückliegen** to be far behind; **von ~em** from a long way off; **~ab** *adv:* **~ab von** (away) from; **~aus** *adv* by far; **W~blick** *m* (*fig*) far-sightedness; **~blickend** *adj siehe* **weit**.

Weite (-, -n) *f* width; (*Raum*) space; (*von Entfernung*) distance.

weiten *vt, vr* to widen.

weiter ['vaɪtər] *adj* wider; (*zusätzlich*) further

♦ *adv* further; **wenn es ~ nichts ist ...** well, if that's all (it is), ...; **das hat ~ nichts zu sagen** that doesn't really matter; **immer ~** on and on; (*Anweisung*) keep on (going); **~ nichts/niemand** nothing/nobody else; **~arbeiten** *vi* to go on working; **~bilden** *vr* to continue one's studies; **W~bildung** *f* further education.

Weitere(s) *nt* further details *pl;* **bis auf w~s** for the time being; **ohne w~s** without further ado, just like that.

weiter- *zW:* **~empfehlen** *unreg vt* to recommend (to others); **~erzählen** *vt* (*Geheimnis*) to pass on; **W~fahrt** *f* continuation of the journey; **~führend** *adj* (*Schule*) secondary (*BRIT*), high (*US*); **~gehen** *unreg vi* to go on; **~hin** *adv:* **etw ~hin tun** to go on doing sth; **~kommen** *unreg vi:* **nicht ~kommen** (*fig*) to be bogged down; **~leiten** *vt* to pass on; **~machen** *vt, vi* to continue; **~reisen** *vi* to continue one's journey; **~sagen** *vt:* **nicht ~sagen!** don't tell anyone!; **~sehen** *unreg vi:* **dann sehen wir ~** then we'll see; **~verarbeiten** *vt* to process; **~wissen** *unreg vi:* **nicht (mehr) ~wissen** (*verzweifelt sein*) to be at one's wits' end.

weit- *zW:* **~gehend** *adj* considerable ♦ *adv* largely; **~hin** *adv* widely; (*~gehend*) to a large extent; **~läufig** *adj* (*Gebäude*) spacious; (*Erklärung*) lengthy; (*Verwandter*) distant; **~schweifig** *adj* long-winded; **~sichtig** *adj* (*lit*) long-sighted (*BRIT*), far-sighted (*US*); (*fig*) far-sighted; **W~sprung** *m* long jump; **W~winkelobjektiv** *nt* (*PHOT*) wide-angle lens.

Weizen ['vaɪtsən] (-s, -) *m* wheat; **~bier** *nt* light, fizzy wheat beer; **~keime** *pl* (*KOCH*) wheatgerm *sing*.

welch [vɛlç] *pron:* **~ ein(e) ...** what a ...

welche(r, s) *interrog pron* which; **~r von beiden?** which (one) of the two?; **~n hast du genommen?** which (one) did you take?; **~ Freude!** what joy!

♦ *indef pron* some; (*in Fragen*) any; **ich habe ~** I have some; **haben Sie ~?** do you have any?

♦ *rel pron* (*bei Menschen*) who; (*bei Sachen*) which, that; **~(r, s) auch immer** whoever/whichever/whatever.

welk [vɛlk] *adj* withered; **~en** *vi* to wither.

Wellblech *nt* corrugated iron.

Welle ['vɛlə] (-, -n) *f* wave; (*TECH*) shaft; **(hohe) ~n schlagen** (*fig*) to create (quite) a stir.

Wellen- *zW:* **~bereich** *m* waveband; **~brecher** *m* breakwater; **~gang** *m:* **starker ~gang** heavy sea(s) *od* swell; **~länge** *f* (*lit, fig*) wavelength; **mit jdm auf einer ~länge sein**

(*fig*) to be on the same wavelength as sb;
~**linie** *f* wavy line.
Wellensittich *m* budgerigar.
Wellpappe *f* corrugated cardboard.
Welpe ['vɛlpə] (-**n, -n**) *m* pup, whelp; (*von Wolf etc*) cub.
Welt [vɛlt] (-, -**en**) *f* world; **aus der ~ schaffen** to eliminate; **in aller ~** all over the world; **vor aller ~** in front of everybody; **auf die ~ kommen** to be born; ~**all** *nt* universe; ~**anschauung** *f* philosophy of life; **w~berühmt** *adj* world-famous; **w~bewegend** *adj* world-shattering; ~**bild** *nt* conception of the world; (*jds Ansichten*) philosophy.
Weltenbummler(in) *m(f)* globetrotter.
Weltergewicht ['vɛltərgəvɪçt] *nt* (*SPORT*) welterweight.
weltfremd *adj* unworldly.
Weltgesundheitsorganisation *f* World Health Organization.
Welt- *zW*: **w~gewandt** *adj* sophisticated; ~**kirchenrat** *m* World Council of Churches; ~**krieg** *m* world war; **w~lich** *adj* worldly; (*nicht kirchlich*) secular; ~**literatur** *f* world literature; ~**macht** *f* world power; **w~männisch** *adj* sophisticated; ~**meister** *m* world champion; ~**meisterschaft** *f* world *od* world's (*US*) championship; (*FUSSBALL etc*) World Cup; ~**rang** *m*: **von ~rang** world-famous; ~**raum** *m* space; ~**raumforschung** *f* space research; ~**raumstation** *f* space station; ~**reise** *f* trip round the world; ~**ruf** *m* world-wide reputation; ~**sicherheitsrat** *m* (*POL*) United Nations Security Council; ~**stadt** *f* metropolis; ~**untergang** *m* (*lit, fig*) end of the world; **w~weit** *adj* world-wide; ~**wirtschaft** *f* world economy; ~**wirtschaftskrise** *f* world economic crisis; ~**wunder** *nt* wonder of the world.
wem [ve:m] *dat von* **wer** ♦ *pron* to whom.
wen [ve:n] *akk von* **wer** ♦ *pron* whom.
Wende ['vɛndə] (-, -**n**) *f* turn; (*Veränderung*) change; **die ~** (*POL*) (the) reunification (of Germany); ~**kreis** *m* (*GEOG*) tropic; (*AUT*) turning circle.
Wendeltreppe *f* spiral staircase.
wenden *unreg vt, vi, vr* to turn; **bitte ~!** please turn over; **sich an jdn ~** to go/come to sb.
Wendepunkt *m* turning point.
wendig *adj* (*lit, fig*) agile; (*Auto etc*) manoeuvrable (*BRIT*), maneuverable (*US*).
Wendung *f* turn; (*Rede~*) idiom.
wenig [ve:nɪç] *adj, adv* little; **ein ~ a little; er hat zu ~ Geld** he doesn't have enough money; **ein Exemplar zu ~** one copy too few.
wenige ['ve:nɪgə] *pl* few *pl*; **in ~n Tagen** in (just) a few days.
weniger *adj* less; (*mit pl*) fewer ♦ *adv* less.
Wenigkeit *f* trifle; **meine ~** (*umg*) little me.

wenigste(r, s) *adj* least.
wenigstens *adv* at least.
wenn [vɛn] *konj* if; (*zeitlich*) when; **~ auch** ... even if ...; **~ ich doch** ... if only I ...; **~ wir erst die neue Wohnung haben** once we get the new flat.
Wenn *nt*: **ohne ~ und Aber** unequivocally.
wennschon *adv*: **na ~** so what?; **~, dennschon!** in for a penny, in for a pound!
wer [ve:r] *pron* who.
Werbe- *zW*: ~**agentur** *f* advertising agency; ~**aktion** *f* advertising campaign; ~**antwort** *f* business reply card; ~**banner** *nt* banner; ~**fernsehen** *nt* commercial television; ~**film** *m* promotional film; ~**geschenk** *nt* promotional gift, freebie (*umg*); (*zu Gekauftem*) free gift; ~**grafiker(in)** *m(f)* commercial artist; ~**kampagne** *f* advertising campaign.
werben ['vɛrbən] *unreg vt* to win; (*Mitglied*) to recruit ♦ *vi* to advertise; **um jdn/etw ~** to try to win sb/sth; **für jdn/etw ~** to promote sb/sth.
Werbe- *zW*: ~**spot** *m* commercial; ~**texter** (-**s**, -) *m* copywriter; ~**trommel** *f*: **die ~trommel (für etw) rühren** (*umg*) to beat the big drum (for sth); **w~wirksam** *adj*: **w~wirksam sein** to be good publicity.
Werbung *f* advertising; (*von Mitgliedern*) recruitment; (*TV etc: Werbeblock*) commercial break; **~ um jdn/etw** promotion of sb/sth.
Werbungskosten *pl* professional *od* business expenses *pl*.
Werdegang ['ve:rdəgaŋ] *m* development; (*beruflich*) career.

════════════════ *SCHLÜSSELWORT*

werden ['ve:rdən] *unreg* (*pt* **wurde,** *pp* **geworden** *od* (*bei Passiv*) **worden**) *vi* to become; **was ist aus ihm/aus der Sache geworden?** what became of him/it; **es ist nichts/gut geworden** it came to nothing/turned out well; **es wird Nacht/Tage** it's getting dark/light; **es wird bald ein Jahr, dass** ... it's almost a year since ...; **er wird am 8. Mai 36** he will be 36 on the 8th May; **mir wird kalt** I'm getting cold; **mir wird schlecht** I feel ill; **Erster ~** to come *od* be first; **das muss anders ~** that will have to change; **rot/zu Eis ~** to turn red/to ice; **was willst du (mal) ~?** what do you want to be?; **die Fotos sind gut geworden** the photos turned out well.

♦ *Hilfsverb* **1** (*bei Futur*): **er wird es tun** he will *od* he'll do it; **er wird das nicht tun** he will not *od* he won't do it; **es wird gleich regnen** it's going to rain any moment.
2 (*bei Konjunktiv*): **ich würde** ... I would ...; **er würde gern** ... he would *od* he'd like to ...; **ich würde lieber** I would *od* I'd rather ...

3 (*bei Vermutung*): **sie wird in der Küche sein** she will be in the kitchen.
4 (*bei Passiv*): **gebraucht ~** to be used; **er ist erschossen worden** he has *od* he's been shot; **mir wurde gesagt, dass** I was told that ...

werdend *adj*: **~e Mutter** expectant mother.
werfen ['vɛrfən] *unreg vt* to throw ♦ *vi* (*Tier*) to have its young; „**nicht ~**" "handle with care".
Werft [vɛrft] (-, **-en**) *f* shipyard; (*für Flugzeuge*) hangar.
Werk [vɛrk] (**-(e)s, -e**) *nt* work; (*Tätigkeit*) job; (*Fabrik, Mechanismus*) works *pl*; **ans ~ gehen** to set to work; **das ist sein ~** this is his doing; **ab ~** (*COMM*) ex works.
werkeln ['vɛrkəln] (*umg*) *vi* to potter about (*BRIT*), putter around (*US*).
Werken (**-s**) *nt* (*SCH*) handicrafts *pl*.
Werkschutz *m* works security service.
Werksgelände *nt* factory premises *pl*.
Werk- *zW*: **~statt** (-, **-stätten**) *f* workshop; (*AUT*) garage; **~stoff** *m* material; **~student** *m* self-supporting student; **~tag** *m* working day; **w~tags** *adv* on working days; **w~tätig** *adj* working; **~zeug** *nt* tool; **~zeugkasten** *m* toolbox; **~zeugmaschine** *f* machine tool; **~zeugschrank** *m* tool chest.
Wermut ['veːrmuːt] (**-(e)s, -s**) *m* wormwood; (*Wein*) vermouth.
Wermutstropfen *m* (*fig*) drop of bitterness.
Wert [veːrt] (**-(e)s, -e**) *m* worth; (*FIN*) value; **~ legen auf** +*akk* to attach importance to; **es hat doch keinen ~** it's useless; **im ~e von** to the value of.
wert [veːrt] *adj* worth; (*geschätzt*) dear; (*würdig*) worthy; **das ist nichts/viel ~** it's not worth anything/it's worth a lot; **das ist es/er mir ~** it's/he's worth that to me; **ein Auto ist viel ~** (*nützlich*) a car is very useful.
Wertangabe *f* declaration of value.
wertbeständig *adj* stable in value.
werten *vt* to rate; (*beurteilen*) to judge; (*SPORT*: **als gültig ~**) to allow; **~ als** to rate as; to judge to be.
Wert- *zW*: **~gegenstand** *m* article of value; **w~los** *adj* worthless; **~losigkeit** *f* worthlessness; **~maßstab** *m* standard; **~papier** *nt* security; **~steigerung** *f* appreciation.
Wertung *f* (*SPORT*) score.
Wert- *zW*: **w~voll** *adj* valuable; **~vorstellung** *f* moral concept; **~zuwachs** *m* appreciation.
Wesen ['veːzən] (**-s, -**) *nt* (*Geschöpf*) being; (*Natur, Character*) nature.
wesentlich *adj* significant; (*beträchtlich*) considerable; **im W~en** essentially; (*im Großen*) in the main.
weshalb [vɛs'halp] *adv* why.

Wespe ['vɛspə] (-, **-n**) *f* wasp.
wessen ['vɛsən] *gen von* **wer** ♦ *pron* whose.
Wessi ['vɛsɪ] (**-s, -s**) (*umg*) *m* West German.

WESSI

A **Wessi** *is a colloquial and often derogatory word used to describe a German from the former West Germany. The expression "Besserwessi" is used by East Germans to describe a West German who is considered to be a know-all.*

West- *zW*: **w~deutsch** *adj* West German; **~deutsche(r)** *f(m)* West German; **~deutschland** *nt* (*POL: früher*) West Germany; (*GEOG*) Western Germany.
Weste ['vɛstə] (-, **-n**) *f* waistcoat, vest (*US*); **eine reine ~ haben** (*fig*) to have a clean slate.
Westen (**-s**) *m* west.
Westentasche *f*: **etw wie seine ~ kennen** (*umg*) to know sth like the back of one's hand.
Westerwald ['vɛstərvalt] (**-s**) *m* Westerwald (Mountains *pl*).
Westeuropa *nt* Western Europe.
westeuropäisch ['vɛst|ɔyro'pɛːɪʃ] *adj* West(ern) European; **~e Zeit** Greenwich Mean Time.
Westfale [vɛst'faːlə] (**-n, -n**) *m* Westphalian.
Westfalen (**-s**) *nt* Westphalia.
Westfälin [vɛst'fɛːlɪn] *f* Westphalian.
westfälisch *adj* Westphalian.
Westindien ['vɛst|ɪndɪən] (**-s**) *nt* West Indies *pl*.
westindisch *adj* West Indian; **die W~en Inseln** the West Indies.
west- *zW*: **~lich** *adj* western ♦ *adv* to the west; **W~mächte** *pl* (*POL: früher*): **die W~mächte** the Western powers *pl*; **~wärts** *adv* westwards.
weswegen [vɛs've:gən] *adv* why.
wett [vɛt] *adj* even; **~ sein** to be quits.
Wettbewerb *m* competition.
Wettbewerbsbeschränkung *f* restraint of trade.
wettbewerbsfähig *adj* competitive.
Wette (-, **-n**) *f* bet, wager; **um die ~ laufen** to run a race (with each other).
Wetteifer *m* rivalry.
wetteifern *vi untr*: **mit jdm um etw wetteifern** to compete with sb for sth.
wetten ['vɛtən] *vt, vi* to bet; **so haben wir nicht gewettet!** that's not part of the bargain!
Wetter ['vɛtər] (**-s, -**) *nt* weather; (*MIN*) air; **~amt** *nt* meteorological office; **~aussichten** *pl* weather outlook *sing*; **~bericht** *m* weather report; **~dienst** *m* meteorological service; **w~fest** *adj* weatherproof; **w~fühlig** *adj* sensitive to changes in the weather; **~karte**

f weather chart; **~lage** *f* (weather) situation.
wettern ['vɛtərn] *vi* to curse and swear.
Wetter- *zW:* **~umschlag** *m* sudden change in the weather; **~vorhersage** *f* weather forecast; **~warte** *f* weather station; **w~wendisch** *adj* capricious.
Wett- *zW:* **~kampf** *m* contest; **~lauf** *m* race; **ein ~lauf mit der Zeit** a race against time.
wettmachen *vt* to make good.
Wett- *zW:* **~rüsten** *nt* arms race; **~spiel** *nt* match; **~streit** *m* contest.
wetzen ['vɛtsən] *vt* to sharpen ♦ *vi* (*umg*) to scoot.
WEU *f abk* (= *Westeuropäische Union*) WEU.
WEZ *abk* (= *westeuropäische Zeit*) GMT.
WG *abk* = **Wohngemeinschaft.**
Whisky ['vɪski] (**-s, -s**) *m* whisky (*BRIT*), whiskey (*US, Ireland*).
WHO (-) *f abk* (= *World Health Organization*) WHO.
wich *etc* [vɪç] *vb siehe* **weichen.**
wichsen ['vɪksən] *vt* (*Schuhe*) to polish ♦ *vi* (*umg!: onanieren*) to jerk *od* toss off (!).
Wichser (*umg!*) *m* wanker (!).
Wicht [vɪçt] (**-(e)s, -e**) *m* titch; (*pej*) worthless creature.
wichtig *adj* important; **sich selbst/etw (zu) ~ nehmen** to take o.s./sth (too) seriously; **W~keit** *f* importance; **W~tuer(in)** (*pej*) *m(f)* pompous ass (*umg*).
Wicke ['vɪkə] (**-, -n**) *f* (*BOT*) vetch; (*Garten~*) sweet pea.
Wickelkleid *nt* wrap-around dress.
wickeln ['vɪkəln] *vt* to wind; (*Haare*) to set; (*Kind*) to change; **da bist du schief gewickelt!** (*fig: umg*) you're very much mistaken; **jdn/etw in etw** *akk* **~** to wrap sb/sth in sth.
Wickeltisch *m* baby's changing table.
Widder ['vɪdər] (**-s, -**) *m* ram; (*ASTROL*) Aries.
wider ['viːdər] *präp +akk* against.
widerfahren *unreg vi untr:* **jdm widerfahren** to happen to sb.
Widerhaken ['viːdərhaːkən] *m* barb.
Widerhall ['viːdərhal] *m* echo; **keinen ~ (bei jdm) finden** (*Interesse*) to meet with no response (from sb).
widerlegen *vt untr* to refute.
widerlich ['viːdərlɪç] *adj* disgusting, repulsive; **W~keit** *f* repulsiveness.
widerrechtlich *adj* unlawful.
Widerrede *f* contradiction; **keine ~!** don't argue!
Widerruf ['viːdərruːf] *m* retraction; countermanding; **bis auf ~** until revoked.
widerrufen *unreg vt untr* to retract; (*Anordnung*) to revoke; (*Befehl*) to countermand.
Widersacher(in) ['viːdərzaxər(ɪn)] (**-s, -**) *m(f)* adversary.
widersetzen *vr untr:* **sich jdm widersetzen** to

oppose sb; (*der Polizei*) to resist sb; **sich einer Sache widersetzen** to oppose sth; (*einem Befehl*) to refuse to comply with sth.
widerspenstig ['viːdərʃpɛnstɪç] *adj* wilful (*BRIT*), willful (*US*); **W~keit** *f* wilfulness (*BRIT*), willfulness (*US*).
widerspiegeln ['viːdərʃpiːgəln] *vt* to reflect.
widersprechen *unreg vi untr:* **jdm widersprechen** to contradict sb.
widersprechend *adj* contradictory.
Widerspruch ['viːdərʃprʊx] *m* contradiction; **ein ~ in sich** a contradiction in terms.
widersprüchlich ['viːdərʃprɣçlɪç] *adj* contradictory, inconsistent.
widerspruchslos *adv* without arguing.
Widerstand ['viːdərʃtant] *m* resistance; **der Weg des geringsten ~es** the line of least resistance; **jdm/etw ~ leisten** to resist sb/sth.
Widerstands- *zW:* **~bewegung** *f* resistance (movement); **w~fähig** *adj* resistant, tough; **w~los** *adj* unresisting.
widerstehen *unreg vi untr:* **jdm/etw widerstehen** to withstand sb/sth.
widerstreben *vi untr:* **es widerstrebt mir, so etwas zu tun** I am reluctant to do anything like that.
widerstrebend *adj* reluctant; (*gegensätzlich*) conflicting.
Wider- *zW:* **~streit** *m* conflict; **w~wärtig** *adj* nasty, horrid; **~wille** *m:* **~wille (gegen)** aversion (to); (*Abneigung*) distaste (for); (*~streben*) reluctance; **w~willig** *adj* unwilling, reluctant; **~worte** *pl* answering back *sing*.
widmen ['vɪtmən] *vt* to dedicate ♦ *vr* to devote o.s.
Widmung *f* dedication.
widrig ['viːdrɪç] *adj* (*Umstände*) adverse; (*Mensch*) repulsive.

═══════════════════ *SCHLÜSSELWORT*

wie [viː] *adv* how; **~ groß/schnell?** how big/fast?; **~ viel** how much; **~ viel Menschen** how many people; **~ wärs?** how about it?; **~ wärs mit einem Whisky?** (*umg*) how about a whisky?; **~ nennt man das?** what is that called?; **~ ist er?** what's he like?; **~ gut du das kannst!** you're very good at it; **~ bitte?** pardon? (*BRIT*), pardon me? (*US*); (*entrüstet*) I beg your pardon!; **und ~!** and how!
♦ *konj* **1** (*bei Vergleichen*): **so schön ~ ...** as beautiful as ...; **~ ich schon sagte** as I said; **~ noch nie** as never before; **~ du like you**; **singen ~ ein ...** to sing like a ...; **~ (zum Beispiel)** such as (for example).
2 (*zeitlich*): **~ er das hörte, ging er** when he heard that he left; **er hörte, ~ der Regen fiel** he heard the rain falling.

wieder ['viːdər] *adv* again; ~ **aufbereiten** to recycle; (*Atommüll*) to reprocess; ~ **aufnehmen** to resume; (*Gedanken, Hobby*) to take up again; (*Thema*) to revert to; (*JUR: Verfahren*) to reopen; ~ **beleben** to revive; ~ **erkennen** to recognize; ~ **gutmachen** to make up for; (*Fehler*) to put right; ~ **herstellen** (*Ruhe, Frieden*) to restore; ~ **vereinigen** to reunite; ~ **da sein** to be back (again); **gehst du schon** ~? are you off again?; ~ **ein(e)** ... another ...; **das ist auch** ~ **wahr** that's true enough; **da sieht man mal** ~ ... it just shows ...

wieder- *zW:* **W~aufbau** [-'|aufbau] *m* rebuilding; **W~aufbereitungsanlage** *f* reprocessing plant; **W~aufnahme** [-'|aufnaːmə] *f* resumption; ~**bekommen** *unreg vt* to get back; ~**bringen** *unreg vt* to bring back; **W~erstattung** *f* reimbursement; ~**finden** *unreg vt* (*fig: Selbstachtung etc*) to regain.

Wiedergabe *f* (*von Rede, Ereignis*) account; (*Wiederholung*) repetition; (*Darbietung*) performance; (*Reproduktion*) reproduction; ~**gerät** *nt* playback unit.

wieder- *zW:* ~**geben** *unreg vt* (*zurückgeben*) to return; (*Erzählung etc*) to repeat; (*Gefühle etc*) to convey; **W~geburt** *f* rebirth; **W~gutmachung** *f* reparation; ~**herstellen** *vt* (*Gesundheit, Gebäude*) to restore.

wiederholen *vt untr* to repeat.

wiederholt *adj:* **zum** ~**en Male** once again.

Wiederholung *f* repetition.

Wiederholungstäter(in) *m(f)* (*JUR*) second-time offender; (*mehrmalig*) persistent offender.

wieder- *zW:* **W~hören** *nt:* **auf W~hören** (*TEL*) goodbye; ~**käuen** *vi* to ruminate ♦ *vt* to ruminate; (*fig: umg*) to go over again and again; **W~kehr** (-) *f* return; (*von Vorfall*) repetition, recurrence; ~**kehrend** *adj* recurrent; **W~kunft** (-, ⸚e) *f* return; ~**sehen** *unreg vt* to see again; **auf W~sehen** goodbye; ~**um** *adv* again; (*seinerseits etc*) in turn; (*andererseits*) on the other hand; **W~vereinigung** *f* reunification; **W~verkäufer** *m* distributor; **W~wahl** *f* re-election.

Wiege ['viːgə] (-, -n) *f* cradle.

wiegen[1] *vt* (*schaukeln*) to rock; (*Kopf*) to shake.

wiegen[2] *unreg vt, vi* to weigh; **schwer** ~ (*fig*) to carry a lot of weight; (*Irrtum*) to be serious.

wiehern ['viːərn] *vi* to neigh, whinny.

Wien [viːn] (-s) *nt* Vienna.

Wiener(in) (-s, -) *m(f)* Viennese ♦ *adj attrib* Viennese; ~ **Schnitzel** Wiener schnitzel.

wies *etc* [viːs] *vb siehe* **weisen**.

Wiese ['viːzə] (-, -n) *f* meadow.

Wiesel ['viːzəl] (-s, -) *nt* weasel; **schnell** *od* **flink wie ein** ~ quick as a flash.

wieso [viˈzoː] *adv* why.

wievielmal [viːˈfiːlmaːl] *adv* how often.

wievielte(r, s) *adj:* **zum** ~**n Mal?** how many times?; **den W~n haben wir?** what's the date?; **an** ~**r Stelle?** in what place?; **der** ~ **Besucher war er?** how many visitors were there before him?

wieweit [viːˈvait] *adv* to what extent.

Wikinger ['viːkiŋər] (-s, -) *m* Viking.

wild [vilt] *adj* wild; ~**er Streik** unofficial strike; **in** ~**er Ehe leben** (*veraltet, hum*) to live in sin; ~ **entschlossen** (*umg*) dead set.

Wild (-(e)s) *nt* game.

Wild- *zW:* ~**bahn** *f:* **in freier** ~**bahn** in the wild; ~**bret** *nt* game; (*von Rotwild*) venison; ~**dieb** *m* poacher.

Wilde(r) ['vildə(r)] *f(m)* savage.

wildern ['vildərn] *vi* to poach.

wild- *zW:* **W~fang** *m* little rascal; ~**fremd** ['vilt'frɛmt] (*umg*) *adj* quite strange *od* unknown; **W~heit** *f* wildness; **W~leder** *nt* suede.

Wildnis (-, -se) *f* wilderness.

Wild- *zW:* ~**schwein** *nt* (wild) boar; ~**wechsel** *m:* „~**wechsel**" "wild animals"; ~**westroman** *m* western.

will [vil] *vb siehe* **wollen**.

Wille ['vilə] (-ns, -n) *m* will; **jdm seinen** ~**n lassen** to let sb have his own way; **seinen eigenen** ~**n haben** to be self-willed.

willen *präp +gen:* **um** ... ~ for the sake of ...

willenlos *adj* weak-willed.

willens *adj* (*geh*): ~ **sein** to be willing.

willensstark *adj* strong-willed.

willentlich ['viləntliç] *adj* wilful (*BRIT*), willful (*US*), deliberate.

willig *adj* willing.

willkommen [vilˈkɔmən] *adj* welcome; **jdn** ~ **heißen** to welcome sb; **herzlich** ~ (**in** +*dat*) welcome (to); **W~** (-s, -) *nt* welcome.

willkürlich *adj* arbitrary; (*Bewegung*) voluntary.

willst [vilst] *vb siehe* **wollen**.

Wilna ['vilna] (-s) *nt* Vilnius.

wimmeln ['viməln] *vi:* ~ (**von**) to swarm (with).

wimmern ['vimərn] *vi* to whimper.

Wimper ['vimpər] (-, -n) *f* eyelash; **ohne mit der** ~ **zu zucken** (*fig*) without batting an eyelid.

Wimperntusche *f* mascara.

Wind [vint] (-(e)s, -e) *m* wind; **den Mantel** *od* **das Fähnchen nach dem** ~ **hängen** to trim one's sails to the wind; **etw in den** ~ **schlagen** to turn a deaf ear to sth.

Windbeutel *m* cream puff; (*fig*) windbag.

Winde ['vində] (-, -n) *f* (*TECH*) winch, windlass; (*BOT*) bindweed.

Windel ['vindəl] (-, -n) *f* nappy (*BRIT*), diaper (*US*).

windelweich *adj*: **jdn ~ schlagen** (*umg*) to beat the living daylights out of sb.

winden¹ ['vɪndən] *vi unpers* to be windy.

winden² *unreg vt* to wind; (*Kranz*) to weave; (*ent~*) to twist ♦ *vr* to wind; (*Person*) to writhe; (*fig: ausweichen*) to try to wriggle out.

Windenergie *f* wind power.

Windeseile *f*: **sich in** *od* **mit Windeseile verbreiten** to spread like wildfire.

Windhose *f* whirlwind.

Windhund *m* greyhound; (*Mensch*) fly-by-night.

windig ['vɪndɪç] *adj* windy; (*fig*) dubious.

Wind- *zW*: **~jacke** *f* windcheater, windbreaker (*US*); **~kanal** *m* (*TECH*) wind tunnel; **~kraft** *f* wind power; **~kraftanlage** *f* wind power station; **~mühle** *f* windmill; **gegen ~mühlen (an)kämpfen** (*fig*) to tilt at windmills; **~park** *m* wind farm.

Windpocken *pl* chickenpox *sing*.

Wind- *zW*: **~rose** *f* (*NAUT*) compass card; (*MET*) wind rose; **~schatten** *m* lee; (*von Fahrzeugen*) slipstream; **~schutzscheibe** *f* (*AUT*) windscreen (*BRIT*), windshield (*US*); **~stärke** *f* wind force; **w~still** *adj* (*Tag*) windless; **es ist w~still** there's no wind; **~stille** *f* calm; **~stoß** *m* gust of wind; **~surfen** *nt* windsurfing.

Windung *f* (*von Weg, Fluss etc*) meander; (*von Schlange, Spule*) coil; (*von Schraube*) thread.

Wink [vɪŋk] (**-(e)s, -e**) *m* (*mit Kopf*) nod; (*mit Hand*) wave; (*Tipp, Hinweis*) hint; **ein ~ mit dem Zaunpfahl** a broad hint.

Winkel ['vɪŋkəl] (**-s, -**) *m* (*MATH*) angle; (*Gerät*) set square; (*in Raum*) corner; **~advokat** (*pej*) *m* incompetent lawyer; **~messer** *m* protractor; **~zug** *m*: **mach keine ~züge** stop evading the issue.

winken ['vɪŋkən] *vt, vi* to wave; **dem Sieger winkt eine Reise nach Italien** the (lucky) winner will receive a trip to Italy.

winseln ['vɪnzəln] *vi* to whine.

Winter ['vɪntər] (**-s, -**) *m* winter; **~garten** *m* conservatory; **w~lich** *adj* wintry; **~reifen** *m* winter tyre (*BRIT*) *od* tire (*US*); **~schlaf** *m* (*ZOOL*) hibernation; **~schlussverkauf**▲ *m* winter sale; **~semester** *nt* (*UNIV*) winter semester (*bes US*), ≈ autumn term (*BRIT*); **~spiele** *pl*: (**Olympische**) **~spiele** Winter Olympics *pl*; **~sport** *m* winter sports *pl*.

Winzer(in) ['vɪntsər(ɪn)] (**-s, -**) *m(f)* wine-grower.

winzig ['vɪntsɪç] *adj* tiny.

Wipfel ['vɪpfəl] (**-s, -**) *m* treetop.

Wippe ['vɪpə] (**-, -n**) *f* seesaw.

wir [viːr] *pron* we; **~ alle** all of us, we all.

Wirbel ['vɪrbəl] (**-s, -**) *m* whirl, swirl; (*Trubel*) hurly-burly; (*Aufsehen*) fuss; (*ANAT*) vertebra; **~ um jdn/etw machen** to make a

fuss about sb/sth.

wirbellos *adj* (*ZOOL*) invertebrate.

wirbeln *vi* to whirl, swirl.

Wirbel- *zW*: **~säule** *f* spine; **~tier** *nt* vertebrate; **~wind** *m* whirlwind.

wirbst *vb siehe* **werben**.

wirbt [vɪrpt] *vb siehe* **werben**.

wird [vɪrt] *vb siehe* **werden**.

wirfst *vb siehe* **werfen**.

wirft [vɪrft] *vb siehe* **werfen**.

wirken ['vɪrkən] *vi* to have an effect; (*erfolgreich sein*) to work; (*scheinen*) to seem ♦ *vt* (*Wunder*) to work; **etw auf sich** *akk* **~ lassen** to take sth in.

wirklich ['vɪrklɪç] *adj* real; **W~keit** *f* reality; **~keitsgetreu** *adj* realistic.

wirksam ['vɪrkzaːm] *adj* effective; **W~keit** *f* effectiveness.

Wirkstoff *m* active substance.

Wirkung ['vɪrkʊŋ] *f* effect.

Wirkungs- *zW*: **~bereich** *m* field (of activity *od* interest *etc*); (*Domäne*) domain; **w~los** *adj* ineffective; **w~los bleiben** to have no effect; **w~voll** *adj* effective.

wirr [vɪr] *adj* confused; (*unrealistisch*) wild; (*Haare etc*) tangled.

Wirren *pl* disturbances *pl*.

Wirrwarr ['vɪrvar] (**-s**) *m* disorder, chaos; (*von Stimmen*) hubbub; (*von Fäden, Haaren etc*) tangle.

Wirsing(kohl) ['vɪrzɪŋ(koːl)] (**-s**) *m* savoy cabbage.

wirst [vɪrst] *vb siehe* **werden**.

Wirt(in) [vɪrt(ɪn)] (**-(e)s, -e**) *m(f)* landlord, landlady.

Wirtschaft ['vɪrtʃaft] *f* (*Gaststätte*) pub; (*Haushalt*) housekeeping; (*eines Landes*) economy; (*Geschäftsleben*) industry and commerce; (*umg: Durcheinander*) mess; **w~en** *vi* (*sparsam sein*): **gut w~en können** to be economical; **~er** *m* (*Verwalter*) manager; **~erin** *f* (*im Haushalt, Heim etc*) housekeeper; **w~lich** *adj* economical; (*POL*) economic; **~lichkeit** *f* economy; (*von Betrieb*) viability.

Wirtschafts- *zW*: **~geld** *nt* housekeeping (money); **~geografie**▲ *f* economic geography; **~hilfe** *f* economic aid; **~krise** *f* economic crisis; **~minister** *m* minister of economic affairs; **~ordnung** *f* economic system; **~politik** *f* economic policy; **~prüfer** *m* chartered accountant (*BRIT*), certified public accountant (*US*); **~spionage** *f* industrial espionage; **~wachstum** *nt* economic growth; **~wissenschaft** *f* economics *sing*; **~wunder** *nt* economic miracle; **~zweig** *m* branch of industry.

Wirtshaus *nt* inn.

Wisch [vɪʃ] (**-(e)s, -e**) *m* scrap of paper.

wischen *vt* to wipe.

Wischer (**-s, -**) *m* (*AUT*) wiper.

Wischiwaschi [vɪʃiːˈvaʃiː] (-s) (*pej: umg*) *nt* drivel.

Wisent [ˈviːzɛnt] (-s, -e) *m* bison.

WiSo [ˈvizo] *abk* (= *Wirtschafts- und Sozialwissenschaften*) economics and social sciences.

wispern [ˈvɪspərn] *vt, vi* to whisper.

Wiss. *abk* = **Wissenschaft**.

wiss. *abk* = **wissenschaftlich**.

Wissbegier(de)▲ [ˈvɪsbəgiːr(də)] *f* thirst for knowledge.

wissbegierig▲ *adj* eager for knowledge.

wissen [ˈvɪsən] *unreg vt, vi* to know; **von jdm/ etw nichts ~ wollen** not to be interested in sb/sth; **sie hält sich für wer weiß wie klug** (*umg*) she doesn't half think she's clever; **gewusst wie/wo!** *etc* sheer brilliance!; **ich weiß seine Adresse nicht mehr** (*sich erinnern*) I can't remember his address; **W~** (-s) *nt* knowledge; **etw gegen (sein) besseres W~ tun** to do sth against one's better judgement; **nach bestem W~ und Gewissen** to the best of one's knowledge and belief.

Wissenschaft [ˈvɪsənʃaft] *f* science.

Wissenschaftler(in) (-s, -) *m(f)* scientist; (*Geistes~*) academic.

wissenschaftlich *adj* scientific; **W~er Assistent** assistant lecturer.

wissenswert *adj* worth knowing.

wissentlich *adj* knowing.

wittern [ˈvɪtərn] *vt* to scent; (*fig*) to suspect.

Witterung *f* weather; (*Geruch*) scent.

Witwe [ˈvɪtvə] (-, -n) *f* widow.

Witwer (-s, -) *m* widower.

Witz [vɪts] (-es, -e) *m* joke; **der ~ an der Sache ist, dass ...** the great thing about it is that ...; **~bold** (-(e)s, -e) *m* joker.

witzeln *vi* to joke.

witzig *adj* funny.

witzlos (*umg*) *adj* (*unsinnig*) pointless, futile.

WM (-) *f abk* = **Weltmeisterschaft**.

wo [voː] *adv* where; (*umg: irgend~*) somewhere ♦ *konj* (*wenn*) if; **im Augenblick, ~ ...** the moment (that) ...; **die Zeit, ~ ...** the time when ...

woanders [voːˈʔandərs] *adv* elsewhere.

wob *etc* [voːp] *vb siehe* **weben**.

wobei [voːˈbaɪ] *adv* (*rel*) ... in/by/with which; (*interrog*) how; what ... in/by/with; **~ mir gerade einfällt ...** which reminds me ...

Woche [ˈvɔxə] (-, -n) *f* week.

Wochenbett *nt*: **im ~ sterben** to die in childbirth.

Wochen- *zW*: **~ende** *nt* weekend; **~endhaus** *nt* weekend house; **~karte** *f* weekly ticket; **w~lang** *adj* lasting weeks ♦ *adv* for weeks; **~schau** *f* newsreel; **~tag** *m* weekday.

wöchentlich [ˈvœçəntlɪç] *adj, adv* weekly.

Wochenzeitung *f* weekly (paper).

Wöchnerin [ˈvœçnərɪn] *f* woman who has

recently given birth.

wodurch [voːˈdʊrç] *adv* (*rel*) through which; (*interrog*) what ... through.

wofür [voːˈfyːr] *adv* (*rel*) for which; (*interrog*) what ... for.

Wodka [ˈvɔtka] (-s, -s) *m* vodka.

wog *etc* [voːk] *vb siehe* **wiegen**[2].

Woge [ˈvoːgə] (-, -n) *f* wave.

wogegen [voːˈgeːgən] *adv* (*rel*) against which; (*interrog*) what ... against.

wogen *vi* to heave, surge.

woher [voːˈheːr] *adv* where ... from; **~ kommt es eigentlich, dass ...?** how is it that ...?

wohin [voːˈhɪn] *adv* where ... to; **~ man auch schaut** wherever you look.

wohingegen *konj* whereas, while.

Wohl (-(e)s) *nt* welfare; **zum ~!** cheers!

═══════════════════════ *SCHLÜSSELWORT*

wohl [voːl] *adv* **1** well; (*behaglich*) at ease, comfortable; **sich ~ fühlen** (*zufrieden*) to feel happy; (*gesundheitlich*) to feel well; **~ gemeint** well-intentioned; **jdm ~ tun** to do sb good; **bei dem Gedanken ist mir nicht ~** I'm not very happy at the thought; **~ oder übel** whether one likes it or not; **er weiß das sehr ~** he knows that perfectly well. **2** (*wahrscheinlich*) probably; (*vermutlich*) I suppose; (*gewiss*) certainly; (*vielleicht*) perhaps; **sie ist ~ zu Hause** she's probably at home; **sie wird ~ das Haus verkaufen** I suppose *od* presumably she's going to sell the house; **das ist doch ~ nicht dein Ernst!** surely you're not serious!; **das mag ~ sein** that may well be; **ob das ~ stimmt?** I wonder if that's true.

wohl- *zW*: **~auf** [voːlˈʔaʊf] *adj* well, in good health; **W~befinden** *nt* well-being; **W~behagen** *nt* comfort; **~behalten** *adj* safe and sound; **W~ergehen** *nt* welfare; **W~fahrt** *f* welfare; **W~fahrtsstaat** *m* welfare state; **W~gefallen** *nt*: **sich in W~gefallen auflösen** (*hum: Gegenstände, Probleme*) to vanish into thin air; (*zerfallen*) to fall apart; **~gemerkt** *adv* mark you; **~habend** *adj* wealthy.

wohlig *adj* contented; (*gemütlich*) comfortable.

wohl- *zW*: **W~klang** *m* melodious sound; **~meinend** *adj* well-meaning; **~schmeckend** *adj* delicious; **W~stand** *m* prosperity; **W~standsgesellschaft** *f* affluent society; **W~tat** *f* (*Gefallen*) favour (*BRIT*), favor (*US*); (*gute Tat*) good deed; (*Erleichterung*) relief; **W~täter** *m* benefactor; **~tätig** *adj* charitable; **W~tätigkeit** *f* charity; **~tuend** *adj* pleasant; **~verdient** *adj* (*Ruhe*) well-earned; (*Strafe*) well-deserved; **~weislich** *adv* prudently; **W~wollen** (-s) *nt* good will; **~wollend** *adj* benevolent.

Wohnblock ['voːnblɔk] **(-s, -s)** *m* block of flats (*BRIT*), apartment house (*US*).

wohnen ['voːnən] *vi* to live.

wohn- *zW:* **W~fläche** *f* living space; **W~geld** *nt* housing benefit; **W~gemeinschaft** *f* people sharing a flat (*BRIT*) *od* apartment (*US*); (*von Hippies*) commune; **~haft** *adj* resident; **W~ heim** *nt* (*für Studenten*) hall (of residence), dormitory (*US*); (*für Senioren*) home; (*bes für Arbeiter*) hostel; **W~komfort** *m:* **mit sämtlichem W~komfort** with all mod cons (*BRIT*); **~lich** *adj* comfortable; **W~mobil** *nt* motor caravan (*BRIT*), motor home (*US*); **W~ort** *m* domicile; **W~silo** *nt* concrete block of flats (*BRIT*) *od* apartment block (*US*); **W~sitz** *m* place of residence; **ohne festen W~sitz** of no fixed abode.

Wohnung *f* house; (*Etagen~*) flat (*BRIT*), apartment (*US*).

Wohnungs- *zW:* **~amt** *nt* housing office; **~bau** *m* house-building; **~markt** *m* housing market; **~not** *f* housing shortage.

wohn- *zW:* **W~viertel** *nt* residential area; **W~wagen** *m* caravan (*BRIT*), trailer (*US*); **W~zimmer** *nt* living room.

wölben ['vœlbən] *vt, vr* to curve.

Wölbung *f* curve.

Wolf [vɔlf] **(-(e)s, ⁻e)** *m* wolf; (*TECH*) shredder; (*Fleisch~*) mincer (*BRIT*), grinder (*US*).

Wölfin ['vœlfɪn] *f* she-wolf.

Wolke ['vɔlkə] **(-, -n)** *f* cloud; **aus allen ~n fallen** (*fig*) to be flabbergasted (*umg*).

Wolken- *zW:* **~bruch** *m* cloudburst; **w~bruchartig** *adj* torrential; **~kratzer** *m* skyscraper; **~kuckucksheim** *nt* cloud-cuckoo-land (*BRIT*), cloudland (*US*); **w~los** *adj* cloudless.

wolkig ['vɔlkɪç] *adj* cloudy.

Wolle ['vɔlə] **(-, -n)** *f* wool; **sich mit jdm in die ~ kriegen** (*fig: umg*) to start squabbling with sb.

═══════════════ *SCHLÜSSELWORT*

wollen¹ ['vɔlən] *unreg* (*pt* **wollte**, *pp* **gewollt** *od* (*als Hilfsverb*) **wollen**) *vt, vi* to want; **ich will nach Hause** I want to go home; **er will nicht** he doesn't want to; **sie wollte das nicht** she didn't want it; **wenn du willst** if you like; **ich will, dass du mir zuhörst** I want you to listen to me; **oh, das hab ich nicht gewollt** oh, I didn't mean to do that; **ich weiß nicht, was er will** (*verstehe ihn nicht*) I don't know what he's on about.

♦ *Hilfsverb:* **er will ein Haus kaufen** he wants to buy a house; **ich wollte, ich wäre ...** I wish I were ...; **etw gerade tun ~** to be just about to *od* going to do sth; **und so jemand** *od* **etwas will Lehrer sein!** (*umg*) and he calls himself a teacher!; **das will alles gut überlegt sein** that needs a lot of thought.

wollen² *adj* woollen (*BRIT*), woolen (*US*).

Wollsachen *pl* wool(l)ens *pl*.

wollüstig ['vɔlʏstɪç] *adj* lusty, sensual.

wo- *zW:* **~mit** [vo'mɪt] *adv* (*rel*) with which; (*interrog*) what ... with; **~mit kann ich dienen?** what can I do for you?; **~möglich** [vo'møːklɪç] *adv* probably, I suppose; **~nach** [vo'naːx] *adv* (*rel*) after/for which; (*interrog*) what ... after.

Wonne ['vɔnə] **(-, -n)** *f* joy, bliss.

woran [vo'ran] *adv* (*rel*) on/at which; (*interrog*) what ... on/at; **~ liegt das?** what's the reason for it?

worauf [vo'rauf] *adv* (*rel*) on which; (*interrog*) what ... on; (*zeitlich*) whereupon; **~ du dich verlassen kannst** of that you can be sure.

woraus [vo'raus] *adv* (*rel*) from/out of which; (*interrog*) what ... from/out of.

worin [vo'rɪn] *adv* (*rel*) in which; (*interrog*) what ... in.

Wort [vɔrt] **(-(e)s, ⁻er** *od* **-e)** *nt* word; **jdn beim ~ nehmen** to take sb at his word; **ein ernstes ~ mit jdm reden** to have a serious talk with sb; **man kann sein eigenes ~ nicht (mehr) verstehen** you can't hear yourself speak; **jdm aufs ~ gehorchen** to obey sb's every word; **zu ~ kommen** to get a chance to speak; **jdm das ~ erteilen** to allow sb to speak; **~art** *f* (*GRAM*) part of speech; **w~brüchig** *adj* not true to one's word.

Wörtchen *nt:* **da habe ich wohl ein ~ mitzureden** (*umg*) I think I have some say in that.

Wörterbuch ['vœrtərbuːx] *nt* dictionary.

Wort- *zW:* **~fetzen** *pl* snatches *pl* of conversation; **~führer** *m* spokesman; **w~getreu** *adj* true to one's word; (*Übersetzung*) literal; **w~gewaltig** *adj* eloquent; **w~karg** *adj* taciturn; **~laut** *m* wording; **im ~laut** verbatim.

wörtlich ['vœrtlɪç] *adj* literal.

Wort- *zW:* **w~los** *adj* mute; **~meldung** *f:* **wenn es keine weiteren ~meldungen gibt, ...** if nobody else wishes to speak ...; **w~reich** *adj* wordy, verbose; **~schatz** *m* vocabulary; **~spiel** *nt* play on words, pun; **~wechsel** *m* dispute; **w~wörtlich** *adj* word-for-word ♦ *adv* quite literally.

worüber [vo'ryːbər] *adv* (*rel*) over/about which; (*interrog*) what ... over/about.

worum [vo'rum] *adv* (*rel*) about/round which; (*interrog*) what ... about/round; **~ handelt es sich?** what's it about?

worunter [vo'runtər] *adv* (*rel*) under which; (*interrog*) what ... under.

wo- *zW:* **~von** [vo'fɔn] *adv* (*rel*) from which; (*interrog*) what ... from; **~vor** [vo'fɔr] *adv* (*rel*) in front of/before which; (*interrog*) in front of/before what; **~zu** [vo'tsu] *adv* (*rel*) to/for which; (*interrog*) what ... for/to; (*warum*) why; **~zu soll das gut sein?** what's the point of that?

Wrack [vrak] **(-(e)s, -s)** *nt* wreck.

wrang *etc* [vraŋ] *vb siehe* **wringen.**

wringen ['vrɪŋən] *unreg vt* to wring.

WS *abk* = **Wintersemester.**

WSV *abk* = **Winterschlussverkauf.**

Wucher ['vu:xər] **(-s)** *m* profiteering; **~er (-s, -)** *m*, **~in** *f* profiteer; **w~isch** *adj* profiteering.

wuchern *vi* (*Pflanzen*) to grow wild.

Wucherpreis *m* exorbitant price.

Wucherung *f* (*MED*) growth.

Wuchs [vu:ks] **(-es)** *m* (*Wachstum*) growth; (*Statur*) build.

wuchs *etc vb siehe* **wachsen¹.**

Wucht [vʊxt] **(-)** *f* force.

wuchtig *adj* massive, solid.

wühlen ['vy:lən] *vi* to scrabble; (*Tier*) to root; (*Maulwurf*) to burrow; (*umg: arbeiten*) to slave away ♦ *vt* to dig.

Wühlmaus *f* vole.

Wühltisch *m* (*in Kaufhaus*) bargain counter.

Wulst [vʊlst] **(-es, ⁼e)** *m* bulge; (*an Wunde*) swelling.

wulstig *adj* bulging; (*Rand, Lippen*) thick.

wund [vʊnt] *adj* sore; **sich** *dat* **die Füße ~ laufen** (*lit*) to get sore feet from walking; (*fig*) to walk one's legs off; **ein ~er Punkt** a sore point; **W~brand** *m* gangrene.

Wunde ['vʊndə] **(-, -n)** *f* wound; **alte ~n wieder aufreißen** (*fig*) to open up old wounds.

Wunder (-s, -) *nt* miracle; **es ist kein ~** it's no wonder; **meine Eltern denken ~ was passiert ist** my parents think goodness knows what has happened; **w~bar** *adj* wonderful, marvellous (*BRIT*), marvelous (*US*); **~kerze** *f* sparkler; **~kind** *nt* child prodigy; **w~lich** *adj* odd, peculiar.

wundern *vt* to surprise ♦ *vr*: **sich ~ über** +*akk* to be surprised at.

Wunder- *zW*: **w~schön** *adj* beautiful; **~tüte** *f* lucky bag; **w~voll** *adj* wonderful.

Wundfieber (-s) *nt* traumatic fever.

Wundstarrkrampf ['vʊntʃtarkrampf] *m* tetanus, lockjaw.

Wunsch [vʊnʃ] **(-(e)s, ⁼e)** *m* wish; **haben Sie (sonst) noch einen ~?** (*beim Einkauf etc*) is there anything else you'd like?; **auf jds (besonderen/ausdrücklichen) ~ hin** at sb's (special/express) request; **~denken** *nt* wishful thinking.

Wünschelrute ['vynʃəlru:tə] *f* divining rod.

wünschen ['vynʃən] *vt* to wish ♦ *vi*: **zu ~/viel zu ~ übrig lassen** to leave something/a great deal to be desired; **sich** *dat* **etw ~** to want sth, wish for sth; **was ~ Sie?** (*in Geschäft*) what can I do for you?; (*in Restaurant*) what would you like?

wünschenswert *adj* desirable.

Wunsch- *zW*: **~kind** *nt* planned child; **~konzert** *nt* (*RUNDF*) musical request programme (*BRIT*) *od* program (*US*); **w~los** *adj*: **w~los glücklich** perfectly happy; **~traum** *m* dream; (*unrealistisch*) pipe dream; **~zettel** *m* list of things one would like.

wurde *etc* ['vʊrdə] *vb siehe* **werden.**

Würde ['vyrdə] **(-, -n)** *f* dignity; (*Stellung*) honour (*BRIT*), honor (*US*); **unter aller ~ sein** to be beneath contempt.

Würdenträger *m* dignitary.

würdevoll *adj* dignified.

würdig ['vyrdɪç] *adj* worthy; (*würdevoll*) dignified.

würdigen ['vyrdɪgən] *vt* to appreciate; **etw zu ~ wissen** to appreciate sth; **jdn keines Blickes ~** not to so much as look at sb.

Wurf [vʊrf] **(-(e)s, ⁼e)** *m* throw; (*Junge*) litter.

Würfel ['vyrfəl] **(-s, -)** *m* dice; (*MATH*) cube; **die ~ sind gefallen** the die is cast; **~becher** *m* (dice) cup.

würfeln *vi* to play dice ♦ *vt* to dice.

Würfelspiel *nt* game of dice.

Würfelzucker *m* lump sugar.

Wurf- *zW*: **~geschoss▲** *nt* projectile; **~sendung** *f* circular; **~sendungen** *pl* (*Reklame*) junk mail.

Würgegriff (-(e)s) *m* (*lit, fig*) stranglehold.

würgen ['vyrgən] *vt, vi* to choke; **mit Hängen und W~** by the skin of one's teeth.

Wurm [vʊrm] **(-(e)s, ⁼er)** *m* worm; **da steckt der ~ drin** (*fig: umg*) there's something wrong somewhere; (*verdächtig*) there's something fishy about it (*umg*).

wurmen (*umg*) *vt* to rile, nettle.

Wurmfortsatz *m* (*MED*) appendix.

wurmig *adj* worm-eaten.

wurmstichig *adj* worm-ridden.

Wurst [vʊrst] **(-, ⁼e)** *f* sausage; **das ist mir ~** (*umg*) I don't care, I don't give a damn; **jetzt geht es um die ~** (*fig: umg*) the moment of truth has come.

Würstchen ['vyrstçən] *nt* frankfurter, hot dog sausage; **~bude** *f*, **~stand** *m* hot dog stall.

Württemberg ['vyrtəmberk] *nt* Württemberg.

Würze ['vyrtsə] **(-, -n)** *f* seasoning.

Wurzel ['vʊrtsəl] **(-, -n)** *f* root; **~n schlagen** (*lit*) to root; (*fig*) to put down roots; **die ~ aus 4 ist 2** (*MATH*) the square root of 4 is 2.

würzen *vt* to season; (*würzig machen*) to spice.

würzig *adj* spicy.

wusch *etc* ['vu:ʃ] *vb siehe* **waschen.**

wusste *etc*▲ ['vʊstə] *vb siehe* **wissen.**

Wust [vu:st] **(-(e)s)** (*umg*) *m* (*Durcheinander*) jumble; (*Menge*) pile.

wüst [vy:st] *adj* untidy, messy; (*ausschweifend*) wild; (*öde*) waste; (*umg: heftig*) terrible; **jdn ~ beschimpfen** to use vile language to sb.

Wüste (-, -n) *f* desert; **die ~ Gobi** the Gobi Desert; **jdn in die ~ schicken** (*fig*) to send sb packing.
Wut [vuːt] (-) *f* rage, fury; **eine ~ (auf jdn/ etw) haben** to be furious (with sb/sth); **~anfall** *m* fit of rage.
wüten ['vyːtən] *vi* to rage.
wütend *adj* furious, enraged.
wutentbrannt *adj* furious, enraged.
Wz *abk* (= *Warenzeichen*) ®.

X, x

X, x [ɪks] *nt* X, x; **~ wie Xanthippe** ≈ X for Xmas; **jdm ein ~ für ein U vormachen** to put one over on sb (*umg*).
X-Beine ['ɪksbaɪnə] *pl* knock-knees *pl*.
x-beliebig [ɪksbə'liːbiç] *adj* any (... whatever).
Xerografie▲ [kserogra'fiː] *f* xerography.
xerokopieren [kseroko'piːrən] *vt* to xerox, photocopy.
x-fach ['ɪksfax] *adj*: **die ~e Menge** (*MATH*) n times the amount.
x-mal ['ɪksmaːl] *adv* any number of times, n times.
XML *abk* (*COMPUT*: = *extensible markup language*) XML.
x-te ['ɪkstə] *adj* (*MATH*: *umg*) nth; **zum ~n Male** (*umg*) for the nth *od* umpteenth time.
Xylofon▲, Xylophon [ksylo'foːn] (-s, -e) *nt* xylophone.

Y, y

Y, y ['ʏpsilɔn] *nt* Y, y; **~ wie Ypsilon** ≈ Y for Yellow, Y for Yoke (*US*).
Yen [jɛn] (-(s), -(s)) *m* yen.
Yoga ['joːga] (-(s)) *m od nt* yoga.
Ypsilon ['ʏpsilɔn] (-(s), -s) *nt* the letter Y.

Z, z

Z, z [tsɛt] *nt* Z, z; **~ wie Zacharias** ≈ Z for Zebra.
Zack [tsak] *m*: **auf ~ sein** (*umg*) to be on the ball.
Zacke ['tsakə] (-, -n) *f* point; (*Berg~*) jagged peak; (*Gabel~*) prong; (*Kamm~*) tooth.
zackig ['tsakɪç] *adj* jagged; (*umg*) smart; (: *Tempo*) brisk.
zaghaft ['tsaːkhaft] *adj* timid.
Zaghaftigkeit *f* timidity.
Zagreb ['zaːgrɛp] (-s) *nt* Zagreb.
zäh [tsɛː] *adj* tough; (*Mensch*) tenacious; (*Flüssigkeit*) thick; (*schleppend*) sluggish; **~flüssig** *adj* viscous; (*Verkehr*) slow-moving.
Zähigkeit *f* toughness; tenacity.
Zahl [tsaːl] (-, -en) *f* number.
zahlbar *adj* payable.
zahlen *vt, vi* to pay; **~ bitte!** the bill *od* check (*US*) please!
zählen ['tsɛːlən] *vt* to count ♦ *vi* (*sich verlassen*): **~ auf** *+akk* to count on; **seine Tage sind gezählt** his days are numbered; **~ zu** to be numbered among.
Zahlen- *zW*: **~angabe** *f* figure; **~kombination** *f* combination of figures; **z~mäßig** *adj* numerical; **~schloss▲** *nt* combination lock.
Zahler (-s, -) *m* payer.
Zähler (-s, -) *m* (*TECH*) meter; (*MATH*) numerator; **~stand** *m* meter reading.
Zahl- *zW*: **~grenze** *f* fare stage; **~karte** *f* transfer form; **z~los** *adj* countless; **~meister** *m* (*NAUT*) purser; **z~reich** *adj* numerous; **~tag** *m* payday.
Zahlung *f* payment; **in ~ geben/nehmen** to give/take in part exchange.
Zahlungs- *zW*: **~anweisung** *f* transfer order; **~aufforderung** *f* request for payment; **z~fähig** *adj* solvent; **~mittel** *nt* means *sing* of payment; (*Münzen, Banknoten*) currency; **~rückstände** *pl* arrears *pl*; **z~unfähig** *adj* insolvent; **~verzug** *m* default.
Zahlwort *nt* numeral.
zahm [tsaːm] *adj* tame.
zähmen ['tsɛːmən] *vt* to tame; (*fig*) to curb.
Zahn [tsaːn] (-(e)s, ¨e) *m* tooth; **die dritten Zähne** (*umg*) false teeth *pl*; **einen ~ draufhaben** (*umg*: *Geschwindigkeit*) to be going like the clappers (*BRIT*) *od* like crazy (*US*); **jdm auf den ~ fühlen** (*fig*) to sound sb out; **einen ~ zulegen** (*fig*) to get a move on;

~**arzt** *m*, ~**ärztin** *f* dentist; ~**belag** *m* plaque; ~**bürste** *f* toothbrush; ~**creme** *f* toothpaste; **z**~**en** *vi* to teethe; ~**ersatz** *m* denture; ~**fäule** (-) *f* tooth decay, caries *sing*; ~**fleisch** *nt* gums *pl*; **auf dem** ~**fleisch gehen** (*fig: umg*) to be all in, be at the end of one's tether; **z**~**los** *adj* toothless; ~**medizin** *f* dentistry; ~**pasta** *f*, ~**paste** *f* toothpaste; ~**rad** *nt* cog(wheel); ~**radbahn** *f* rack railway; ~**schmelz** *m* (tooth) enamel; ~**schmerzen** *pl* toothache *sing*; ~**seide** *f* dental floss; ~**spange** *f* brace; ~**stein** *m* tartar; ~**stocher** (-s, -) *m* toothpick; ~**techniker(in)** *m(f)* dental technician; ~**weh** *nt* toothache.

Zaire [za'i:r] (-s) *nt* Zaire.

Zange ['tsaŋə] (-, -n) *f* pliers *pl*; (*Zucker*~ etc) tongs *pl*; (*Beiß*~, *ZOOL*) pincers *pl*; (*MED*) forceps *pl*; **jdn in die** ~ **nehmen** (*fig*) to put the screws on sb (*umg*).

Zangengeburt *f* forceps delivery.

Zankapfel *m* bone of contention.

zanken ['tsaŋkən] *vi*, *vr* to quarrel.

zänkisch ['tsɛŋkɪʃ] *adj* quarrelsome.

Zäpfchen ['tsɛpfçən] *nt* (*ANAT*) uvula; (*MED*) suppository.

Zapfen ['tsapfən] (-s, -) *m* plug; (*BOT*) cone; (*Eis*~) icicle.

zapfen *vt* to tap.

Zapfenstreich *m* (*MIL*) tattoo.

Zapfsäule *f* petrol (*BRIT*) od gas (*US*) pump.

zappelig ['tsapəlɪç] *adj* wriggly; (*unruhig*) fidgety.

zappeln ['tsapəln] *vi* to wriggle; to fidget; **jdn** ~ **lassen** (*fig: umg*) to keep sb in suspense.

Zar [tsa:r] (-en, -en) *m* tzar, czar.

zart [tsart] *adj* (*weich, leise*) soft; (*Braten etc*) tender; (*fein, schwächlich*) delicate; ~ **besaitet** highly sensitive; ~**bitter** *adj* (*Schokolade*) plain (*BRIT*), bittersweet (*US*); **Z**~**gefühl** *nt* tact; **Z**~**heit** *f* softness; tenderness; delicacy.

zärtlich ['tsɛːrtlɪç] *adj* tender, affectionate; **Z**~**keit** *f* tenderness; **Zärtlichkeiten** *pl* caresses *pl*.

Zäsium ['tsɛːziʊm] *nt* caesium (*BRIT*), cesium (*US*).

Zäsur [tsɛ'zuːr] *f* caesura; (*fig*) break.

Zauber ['tsaʊbər] (-s, -) *m* magic; (~*bann*) spell; **fauler** ~ (*umg*) humbug.

Zauberei [tsaʊbə'raɪ] *f* magic.

Zauberer (-s, -) *m* magician; (*Zauberkünstler*) conjurer.

Zauber- *zW*: **z**~**haft** *adj* magical, enchanting; ~**in** *f* magician; conjurer; ~**künstler** *m* conjurer; ~**kunststück** *nt* conjuring trick; ~**mittel** *nt* magical cure; (*Trank*) magic potion.

zaubern *vi* to conjure, do magic.

Zauberspruch *m* (magic) spell.

Zauberstab *m* magic wand.

zaudern ['tsaʊdərn] *vi* to hesitate.

Zaum [tsaʊm] (-(e)s, Zäume) *m* bridle; **etw im** ~ **halten** to keep sth in check.

Zaun [tsaʊn] (-(e)s, Zäune) *m* fence; **vom** ~**(e) brechen** (*fig*) to start; ~**gast** *m* (*Person*) mere onlooker; ~**könig** *m* wren.

z. B. *abk* (= *zum Beispiel*) e.g.

z. d. A. *abk* (= *zu den Akten*) to be filed.

ZDF

*The **ZDF** (Zweites Deutsches Fernsehen) is the second German television channel. It was founded in 1961 and is based in Mainz. It is financed by licence fees and advertising. About 40% of its transmissions are news and educational programmes.*

Zebra ['tseːbra] (-s, -s) *nt* zebra; ~**streifen** *m* pedestrian crossing (*BRIT*), crosswalk (*US*).

Zeche ['tsɛçə] (-, -n) *f* (*Rechnung*) bill, check (*US*); (*Bergbau*) mine.

zechen *vi* to booze (*umg*).

Zechprellerei [tsɛçprɛlə'raɪ] *f* skipping payment in restaurants etc.

Zecke ['tsɛkə] (-, -n) *f* tick.

Zeder ['tseːdər] (-, -n) *f* cedar.

Zeh [tseː] (-s, -en) *m* toe.

Zehe ['tseːə] (-, -n) *f* toe; (*Knoblauch*~) clove.

Zehenspitze *f*: **auf** ~**n** on tiptoe.

zehn [tseːn] *num* ten.

Zehnerpackung *f* packet of ten.

Zehnfingersystem *nt* touch-typing method.

Zehnkampf *m* (*SPORT*) decathlon.

zehnte(r, s) *adj* tenth.

Zehntel (-s, -) *nt* tenth (part).

zehren ['tseːrən] *vi*: **an jdm/etw** ~ (*an Mensch, Kraft*) to wear sb/sth out.

Zeichen ['tsaɪçən] (-s, -) *nt* sign; (*COMPUT*) character; **jdm ein** ~ **geben** to give sb a signal; **unser/Ihr** ~ (*COMM*) our/your reference; ~**block** *m* sketch pad; ~**erklärung** *f* key; (*auf Karten*) legend; ~**folge** *f* (*COMPUT*) string; ~**kette** *f* (*COMPUT*) character string; ~**kode** *m* (*COMPUT*) character code; ~**satz** *m* (*COMPUT*) character set; ~**setzung** *f* punctuation; ~**trickfilm** *m* (animated) cartoon.

zeichnen *vt* to draw; (*kenn*~) to mark; (*unter*~) to sign ♦ *vi* to draw; to sign.

Zeichner(in) (-s, -) *m(f)* artist; **technischer** ~ draughtsman (*BRIT*), draftsman (*US*).

Zeichnung *f* drawing; (*Markierung*) markings *pl*.

zeichnungsberechtigt *adj* authorized to sign.

Zeigefinger *m* index finger.

zeigen ['tsaɪgən] *vt* to show ♦ *vi* to point ♦ *vr* to show o.s.; ~ **auf** +*akk* to point to; **es wird sich** ~ time will tell; **es zeigte sich, dass ...** it turned out that ...

Zeiger (-s, -) *m* pointer; (*Uhr~*) hand.
Zeile ['tsaɪlə] (-, -n) *f* line; (*Häuser~*) row.
Zeilen- *zW:* ~**abstand** *m* line spacing;
~**ausrichtung** *f* justification; ~**drucker** *m* line
printer; ~**umbruch** *m* (*COMPUT*)
wraparound; ~**vorschub** *m* (*COMPUT*) line
feed.
zeit [tsaɪt] *präp +gen:* ~ **meines Lebens** in my
lifetime.
Zeit (-, -en) *f* time; (*GRAM*) tense; **sich** *dat*
~ **lassen** to take one's time; **eine Stunde**
~ **haben** to have an hour (to spare); **sich** *dat*
für jdn/etw ~ **nehmen** to devote time to sb/
sth; **eine** ~ **lang** a while, a time; **von** ~ **zu** ~
from time to time; ~**raubend** time-
consuming; **in letzter** ~ recently; **nach**
~ **bezahlt werden** to be paid by the hour; **zu**
der ~, **als** ... (at the time) when ...; *siehe auch*
zurzeit.
Zeit- *zW:* ~**alter** *nt* age; ~**ansage** *f* (*RUNDF*)
time check; (*TEL*) speaking clock; ~**arbeit** *f*
temporary work; ~**aufwand** *m* time (*needed*
for a task); ~**bombe** *f* time bomb; ~**druck** *m*:
unter ~**druck stehen** to be under pressure;
~**geist** *m* spirit of the times; **z**~**gemäß** *adj* in
keeping with the times; ~**genosse** *m*
contemporary; **z**~**genössisch** ['tsaɪtgənœsɪʃ]
adj contemporary.
zeitig *adj, adv* early.
Zeit- *zW:* ~**karte** *f* season ticket; **z**~**kritisch** *adj*
(*Aufsatz*) commenting on contemporary
issues; **z**~**lebens** *adv* all one's life; **z**~**lich** *adj*
temporal ♦ *adv:* **das kann sie z**~**lich nicht**
einrichten she can't find (the) time for that;
das ~**liche segnen** (*euph*) to depart this life;
z~**los** *adj* timeless; ~**lupe** *f* slow motion;
~**lupentempo** *nt:* **im** ~**lupentempo** at a
snail's pace; ~**not** *f:* **in** ~**not geraten** to run
short of time; ~**plan** *m* schedule; ~**punkt** *m*
moment, point in time; ~**raffer** (-s) *m* time-
lapse photography; ~**raum** *m* period;
~**rechnung** *f* time, era; **nach/vor unserer**
~**rechnung** A.D./B.C.; ~**schrift** *f* periodical;
~**tafel** *f* chronological table.
Zeitung *f* newspaper.
Zeitungs- *zW:* ~**anzeige** *f* newspaper
advertisement; ~**ausschnitt** *m* press cutting;
~**händler** *m* newsagent (*BRIT*), newsdealer
(*US*); ~**papier** *nt* newsprint; ~**stand** *m*
newsstand.
Zeit- *zW:* ~**verschwendung** *f* waste of time;
~**vertreib** *m* pastime, diversion; **z**~**weilig** *adj*
temporary; **z**~**weise** *adv* for a time; ~**wort** *nt*
verb; ~**zeichen** *nt* (*RUNDF*) time signal;
~**zone** *f* time zone; ~**zünder** *m* time fuse.
Zelle ['tsɛlə] (-, -n) *f* cell; (*Telefon~*) callbox
(*BRIT*), booth.
Zellkern *m* cell, nucleus.
Zellophan [tsɛlo'faːn] (-s) *nt* cellophane.
Zellstoff *m* cellulose.

Zelt [tsɛlt] (-(e)s, -e) *nt* tent; **seine** ~**e**
aufschlagen/abbrechen to settle down/pack
one's bags; ~**bahn** *f* groundsheet; **z**~**en** *vi* to
camp; ~**lager** *nt* camp; ~**platz** *m* camp site.
Zement [tse'mɛnt] (-(e)s, -e) *m* cement.
zementieren [tsemɛn'tiːrən] *vt* to cement.
Zementmaschine *f* cement mixer.
Zenit [tse'niːt] (-(e)s) *m* (*lit, fig*) zenith.
zensieren [tsɛn'ziːrən] *vt* to censor; (*SCH*) to
mark.
Zensur [tsɛn'zuːr] *f* censorship; (*SCH*) mark.
Zensus ['tsɛnzʊs] (-, -) *m* census.
Zentimeter [tsɛnti'meːtər] *m od nt* centimetre
(*BRIT*), centimeter (*US*); ~**maß** *nt* (metric)
tape measure.
Zentner ['tsɛntnər] (-s, -) *m* hundredweight.
zentral [tsɛn'traːl] *adj* central.
Zentrale (-, -n) *f* central office; (*TEL*)
exchange.
Zentraleinheit *f* (*COMPUT*) central
processing unit.
Zentralheizung *f* central heating.
zentralisieren [tsɛntrali'ziːrən] *vt* to
centralize.
Zentralverriegelung *f* (*AUT*) central locking.
Zentrifugalkraft [tsɛntrifu'gaːlkraft] *f*
centrifugal force.
Zentrifuge [tsɛntri'fuːgə] (-, -n) *f* centrifuge;
(*für Wäsche*) spin-dryer.
Zentrum ['tsɛntrʊm] (-s, Zentren) *nt* centre
(*BRIT*), center (*US*).
Zepter ['tsɛptər] (-s, -) *nt* sceptre (*BRIT*),
scepter (*US*).
zerbrechen *unreg vt, vi* to break.
zerbrechlich *adj* fragile.
zerbröckeln [tsɛr'brœkəln] *vt, vi* to crumble (to
pieces).
zerdeppern [tsɛr'dɛpərn] *vt* to smash.
zerdrücken *vt* to squash; to crush; (*Kartoffeln*)
to mash.
Zeremonie [tseremo'niː] *f* ceremony.
Zeremoniell [tseremoni'ɛl] (-s, -e) *nt*
ceremonial.
zerfahren *adj* scatterbrained, distracted.
Zerfall *m* decay, disintegration; (*von Kultur,*
Gesundheit) decline; **z**~**en** *unreg vi* to
disintegrate, decay; (*sich gliedern*): **z**~**en in**
+akk to fall into.
zerfetzen [tsɛr'fɛtsən] *vt* to tear to pieces.
zerfleischen [tsɛr'flaɪʃən] *vt* to tear to pieces.
zerfließen *unreg vi* to dissolve, melt away.
zerfressen *unreg vt* to eat away; (*Motten,*
Mäuse etc) to eat.
zergehen *unreg vi* to melt, dissolve.
zerkleinern [tsɛr'klaɪnərn] *vt* to reduce to
small pieces.
zerklüftet [tsɛr'klyftət] *adj:* **tief** ~**es Gestein**
deeply fissured rock.
zerknirscht [tsɛr'knɪrʃt] *adj* overcome with
remorse.

zerknüllen [tsɛr'knʏlən] vt to crumple up.
zerlaufen unreg vi to melt.
zerlegbar [tsɛr'leːkbaːr] adj able to be dismantled.
zerlegen vt to take to pieces; (Fleisch) to carve; (Satz) to analyse.
zerlumpt [tsɛr'lʊmpt] adj ragged.
zermalmen [tsɛr'malmən] vt to crush.
zermürben [tsɛr'mʏrbən] vt to wear down.
zerpflücken vt (lit, fig) to pick to pieces.
zerplatzen vi to burst.
zerquetschen vt to squash.
Zerrbild ['tsɛrbɪlt] nt (fig) caricature, distorted picture.
zerreden vt (Problem) to flog to death.
zerreiben unreg vt to grind down.
zerreißen unreg vt to tear to pieces ♦ vi to tear, rip.
Zerreißprobe f (lit) pull test; (fig) real test.
zerren ['tsɛrən] vt to drag ♦ vi: ~ (an +dat) to tug (at).
zerrinnen unreg vi to melt away; (Geld) to disappear.
zerrissen [tsɛr'rɪsən] pp von **zerreißen** ♦ adj torn, tattered; **Z~heit** f tattered state; (POL) disunion, discord; (innere) disintegration.
Zerrspiegel ['tsɛrʃpiːgəl] m (lit) distorting mirror; (fig) travesty.
Zerrung f: **eine** ~ a pulled ligament/muscle.
zerrütten [tsɛr'rʏtən] vt to wreck, destroy.
zerrüttet adj wrecked, shattered.
Zerrüttungsprinzip nt (bei Ehescheidung) principle of irretrievable breakdown.
zerschellen [tsɛr'ʃɛlən] vi (Schiff, Flugzeug) to be smashed to pieces.
zerschießen unreg vt to shoot to pieces.
zerschlagen unreg vt to shatter, smash; (fig: Opposition) to crush; (: Vereinigung) to break up ♦ vr to fall through.
zerschleißen [tsɛr'ʃlaɪsən] unreg vt, vi to wear out.
zerschmelzen unreg vi to melt.
zerschmettern unreg vt to shatter; (Feind) to crush ♦ vi to shatter.
zerschneiden unreg vt to cut up.
zersetzen vt, vr to decompose, dissolve.
zersetzend adj (fig) subversive.
zersplittern [tsɛr'ʃplɪtərn] vt, vi to split (into pieces); (Glas) to shatter.
zerspringen unreg vi to shatter ♦ vi (fig) to burst.
zerstäuben [tsɛr'ʃtɔʏbən] vt to spray.
Zerstäuber (-s, -) m atomizer.
zerstören vt to destroy.
Zerstörer (-s, -) m (NAUT) destroyer.
Zerstörung f destruction.
Zerstörungswut f destructive mania.
zerstoßen unreg vt to pound, pulverize.
zerstreiten unreg vr to fall out, break up.
zerstreuen vt to disperse, scatter; (Zweifel

etc) to dispel ♦ vr (sich verteilen) to scatter; (fig) to be dispelled; (sich ablenken) to take one's mind off things.
zerstreut adj scattered; (Mensch) absent-minded; **Z~heit** f absent-mindedness.
Zerstreuung f dispersion; (Ablenkung) diversion.
zerstritten adj: **mit jdm zerstritten sein** to be on very bad terms with sb.
zerstückeln [tsɛr'ʃtʏkəln] vt to cut into pieces.
zerteilen vt to divide into parts.
Zertifikat [tsɛrtifi'kaːt] (-(e)s, -e) nt certificate.
zertreten unreg vt to crush underfoot.
zertrümmern [tsɛr'trʏmərn] vt to shatter; (Gebäude etc) to demolish.
zerwühlen vt to ruffle up, tousle; (Bett) to rumple (up).
Zerwürfnis [tsɛr'vʏrfnɪs] (-ses, -se) nt dissension, quarrel.
zerzausen [tsɛr'tsaʊzən] vt (Haare) to ruffle up, tousle.
zetern ['tseːtərn] (pej) vi to clamour (BRIT), clamor (US); (keifen) to scold.
Zettel ['tsɛtəl] (-s, -) m piece od slip of paper; (Notiz~) note; (Formular) form; „~ **ankleben verboten**" "stick no bills"; **~kasten** m card index (box); **~wirtschaft** (pej) f: **eine ~wirtschaft haben** to have bits of paper everywhere.
Zeug [tsɔʏk] (-(e)s, -e) (umg) nt stuff; (Ausrüstung) gear; **dummes ~** (stupid) nonsense; **das ~ haben zu** to have the makings of; **sich ins ~ legen** to put one's shoulder to the wheel; **was das ~ hält** for all one is worth; **jdm am ~ flicken** to find fault with sb.
Zeuge ['tsɔʏgə] (-n, -n) m witness.
zeugen vi to bear witness, testify ♦ vt (Kind) to father; **es zeugt von ...** it testifies to ...
Zeugenaussage f evidence.
Zeugenstand m witness box (BRIT) od stand (US).
Zeugin f witness.
Zeugnis ['tsɔʏgnɪs] (-ses, -se) nt certificate; (SCH) report; (Referenz) reference; (Aussage) evidence, testimony; ~ **geben von** to be evidence of, testify to; ~**konferenz** f (SCH) staff meeting to decide on marks etc.
Zeugung ['tsɔʏgʊŋ] f procreation.
zeugungsunfähig adj sterile.
ZH abk = **Zentralheizung**.
z. H., z. Hd. abk (= zu Händen) att., attn.
Zicken ['tsɪkən] (umg) pl: ~ **machen** to make trouble.
zickig adj (albern) silly; (prüde) prudish.
Zickzack ['tsɪktsak] (-(e)s, -e) m zigzag.
Ziege ['tsiːgə] (-, -n) f goat; (pej: umg: Frau) cow (!).
Ziegel ['tsiːgəl] (-s, -) m brick; (Dach~) tile.
Ziegelei [tsiːgə'laɪ] f brickworks.

Ziegelstein *m* brick.
Ziegenbock *m* billy goat.
Ziegenleder *nt* kid.
Ziegenpeter *m* mumps *sing*.
Ziehbrunnen *m* well.
ziehen ['tsiːən] *unreg vt* to draw; (*zerren*) to pull; (*SCHACH etc*) to move; (*züchten*) to rear ♦ *vi* to draw; (*um~, wandern*) to move; (*Rauch, Wolke etc*) to drift; (*reißen*) to pull ♦ *vb unpers*: **es zieht** there is a draught (*BRIT*) *od* draft (*US*), it's draughty (*BRIT*) *od* drafty (*US*) ♦ *vr* (*Gummi*) to stretch; (*Grenze etc*) to run; (*Gespräche*) to be drawn out; **etw nach sich ~** to lead to sth, entail sth; **etw ins Lächerliche ~** to ridicule sth; **so was zieht bei mir nicht** I don't like that sort of thing; **zu jdm ~** to move in with sb; **mir ziehts im Rücken** my back hurts; **Z~** (**-s, -**) *nt* (*Schmerz*) ache; (*im Unterleib*) dragging pain.
Ziehharmonika ['tsiːharmoːnika] *f* concertina.
Ziehung ['tsiːʊŋ] *f* (*Los~*) drawing.
Ziel [tsiːl] (**-(e)s, -e**) *nt* (*einer Reise*) destination; (*SPORT*) finish; (*MIL*) target; (*Absicht*) goal, aim; **jdm/sich ein ~ stecken** to set sb/o.s. a goal; **am ~ sein** to be at one's destination; (*fig*) to have reached one's goal; **über das ~ hinausschießen** (*fig*) to overshoot the mark; **z~bewusst▲** *adj* purposeful; **z~en** *vi*: **z~en (auf +akk)** to aim (at); **~fernrohr** *nt* telescopic sight; **~foto** *nt* (*SPORT*) photofinish, photograph; **~gruppe** *f* target group; **~linie** *f* (*SPORT*) finishing line; **z~los** *adj* aimless; **~ort** *m* destination; **~scheibe** *f* target; **z~strebig** *adj* purposeful.
ziemen ['tsiːmən] *vr unpers* (*geh*): **das ziemt sich nicht (für dich)** it is not proper for (for you).
ziemlich ['tsiːmlɪç] *adj attrib* (*Anzahl*) fair ♦ *adv* quite, pretty (*umg*); (*beinahe*) almost, nearly; **eine ~e Anstrengung** quite an effort; **~ lange** quite a long time; **~ fertig** almost *od* nearly ready.
Zierde ['tsiːrdə] (**-, -n**) *f* ornament, decoration; (*Schmuckstück*) adornment.
zieren ['tsiːrən] *vr* to act coy.
Zierleiste *f* border; (*an Wand, Möbeln*) moulding (*BRIT*), molding (*US*); (*an Auto*) trim.
zierlich *adj* dainty; **Z~keit** *f* daintiness.
Zierstrauch *m* flowering shrub.
Ziffer ['tsɪfər] (**-, -n**) *f* figure, digit; **römische/ arabische ~n** roman/arabic numerals; **~blatt** *nt* dial, (clock *od* watch) face.
zig [tsɪk] (*umg*) *adj* umpteen.
Zigarette [tsigaˈrɛtə] *f* cigarette.
Zigaretten- *zW*: **~automat** *m* cigarette machine; **~pause** *f* break for a cigarette; **~schachtel** *f* cigarette packet *od* pack (*US*); **~spitze** *f* cigarette holder.
Zigarillo [tsigaˈrɪlo] (**-s, -s**) *nt od m* cigarillo.

Zigarre [tsiˈgarə] (**-, -n**) *f* cigar.
Zigeuner(in) [tsiˈgɔʏnər(ɪn)] (**-s, -**) *m(f)* gipsy; **~schnitzel** *nt* (*KOCH*) cutlet served in a spicy sauce with green and red peppers; **~sprache** *f* Romany (language).
Zimmer ['tsɪmər] (**-s, -**) *nt* room; **~antenne** *f* indoor aerial; **~decke** *f* ceiling; **~lautstärke** *f* reasonable volume; **~mädchen** *nt* chambermaid; **~mann** (**-(e)s,** *pl* **-leute**) *m* carpenter.
zimmern *vt* to make from wood.
Zimmer- *zW*: **~nachweis** *m* accommodation service; **~pflanze** *f* indoor plant; **~vermittlung** *f* accommodation (*BRIT*) *od* accommodations (*US*) service.
zimperlich ['tsɪmpərlɪç] *adj* squeamish; (*pingelig*) fussy, finicky.
Zimt [tsɪmt] (**-(e)s, -e**) *m* cinnamon; **~stange** *f* cinnamon stick.
Zink [tsɪŋk] (**-(e)s**) *nt* zinc.
Zinke (**-, -n**) *f* (*Gabel~*) prong; (*Kamm~*) tooth.
Zinken (**-s, -**) (*umg*) *m* (*Nase*) hooter.
zinken *vt* (*Karten*) to mark.
Zinksalbe *f* zinc ointment.
Zinn [tsɪn] (**-(e)s**) *nt* (*Element*) tin; (*in ~waren*) pewter; **~becher** *m* pewter tankard.
zinnoberrot [tsɪˈnoːbərrot] *adj* vermilion.
Zinnsoldat *m* tin soldier.
Zinnwaren *pl* pewter *sing*.
Zins [tsɪns] (**-es, -en**) *m* interest.
Zinseszins *m* compound interest.
Zins- *zW*: **~fuß** *m* rate of interest; **z~los** *adj* interest-free; **~satz** *m* rate of interest; **~steuer** *f* tax on interest.
Zionismus [tsioˈnɪsmʊs] *m* Zionism.
Zipfel ['tsɪpfəl] (**-s, -**) *m* corner; (*von Land*) tip; (*Hemd~*) tail; (*Wurst~*) end; **~mütze** *f* pointed cap.
zirka ['tsɪrka] *adv* (round) about.
Zirkel ['tsɪrkəl] (**-s, -**) *m* circle; (*MATH*) pair of compasses; **~kasten** *m* geometry set.
zirkulieren [tsɪrkuˈliːrən] *vi* to circulate.
Zirkus ['tsɪrkʊs] (**-, -se**) *m* circus; (*umg: Getue*) fuss, to-do.
zirpen ['tsɪrpən] *vi* to chirp, cheep.
Zirrhose [tsɪˈroːzə] (**-, -n**) *f* cirrhosis.
zischeln ['tsɪʃəln] *vt, vi* to whisper.
zischen ['tsɪʃən] *vi* to hiss; (*Limonade*) to fizz; (*Fett*) to sizzle.
Zitat [tsiˈtaːt] (**-(e)s, -e**) *nt* quotation, quote.
zitieren [tsiˈtiːrən] *vt* to quote; (*vorladen, rufen*): **~ (vor +akk)** to summon (before).
Zitronat [tsitroˈnaːt] (**-(e)s, -e**) *nt* candied lemon peel.
Zitrone [tsiˈtroːnə] (**-, -n**) *f* lemon.
Zitronen- *zW*: **~limonade** *f* lemonade; **~saft** *m* lemon juice; **~säure** *f* citric acid; **~scheibe** *f* lemon slice.
zitt(e)rig ['tsɪt(ə)rɪç] *adj* shaky.
zittern ['tsɪtərn] *vi* to tremble; **vor jdm ~** to be

terrified of sb.

Zitze ['tsɪtsə] (-, -n) *f* teat, dug.

Zivi ['tsivi] (-s, -s) *m abk* = **Zivildienstleistender**.

zivil [tsi'viːl] *adj* civilian; (*anständig*) civil; (*Preis*) moderate; ~**er Ungehorsam** civil disobedience; **Z~** (-s) *nt* plain clothes *pl*; (*MIL*) civilian clothing; **Z~bevölkerung** *f* civilian population; **Z~courage** *f* courage of one's convictions.

Zivildienst *m* alternative service (for conscientious objectors).

ZIVILDIENST

A young German has to complete his 13 months' **Zivildienst** *or community service if he has opted out of military service as a conscientious objector. This service is usually done in a hospital or old people's home. Many young Germans choose to do this as an alternative to the* **Wehrdienst**, *although it lasts three months longer.*

Zivildienstleistender *m conscientious objector doing community service.*

Zivilisation [tsivilizatsi'oːn] *f* civilization.

Zivilisationserscheinung *f* phenomenon of civilization.

Zivilisationskrankheit *f* disease of civilized man.

zivilisieren [tsivili'ziːrən] *vt* to civilize.

zivilisiert *adj* civilized.

Zivilist [tsivi'lɪst] *m* civilian.

Zivilrecht *nt* civil law.

ZK (-s, -s) *nt abk* (= *Zentralkomitee*) central committee.

Zobel ['tsoːbəl] (-s, -) *m* (*auch*: ~**pelz**) sable (fur).

Zofe ['tsoːfə] (-, -n) *f* lady's maid; (*von Königin*) lady-in-waiting.

zog *etc* [tsoːk] *vb siehe* **ziehen**.

zögern ['tsøːgərn] *vi* to hesitate.

Zölibat [tsøli'baːt] (-(e)s) *nt od m* celibacy.

Zoll¹ [tsɔl] (-(e)s, -) *m* (*Maß*) inch.

Zoll² (-(e)s, ⁻e) *m* customs *pl*; (*Abgabe*) duty; ~**abfertigung** *f* customs clearance; ~**amt** *nt* customs office; ~**beamte(r)** *m* customs official; ~**erklärung** *f* customs declaration; **z~frei** *adj* duty-free; ~**gutlager** *nt* bonded warehouse; ~**kontrolle** *f* customs (check); **z~pflichtig** *adj* liable to duty, dutiable.

Zollstock *m* inch rule.

Zone ['tsoːnə] (-, -n) *f* zone; (*von Fahrkarte*) fare stage.

Zoo [tsoː] (-s, -s) *m* zoo; ~**handlung** *f* pet shop.

Zoologe [tsoo'loːgə] (-n, -n) *m* zoologist.

Zoologie *f* zoology.

Zoologin *f* zoologist.

zoologisch *adj* zoological.

Zoom [zuːm] (-s, -s) *nt* zoom shot; (*Objektiv*) zoom lens.

Zopf [tsɔpf] (-(e)s, ⁻e) *m* plait; pigtail; **alter** ~ antiquated custom.

Zorn [tsɔrn] (-(e)s) *m* anger.

zornig *adj* angry.

Zote ['tsoːtə] (-, -n) *f* smutty joke/remark.

zottig ['tsɔtɪç] *adj* shaggy.

ZPO *abk* (= *Zivilprozessordnung*) ≈ General Practice Act (*US*).

z. T. *abk* = **zum Teil**.

=================================== *SCHLÜSSELWORT*

zu [tsuː] *präp +dat* **1** (*örtlich*) to; ~**m Bahnhof/ Arzt gehen** to go to the station/doctor; ~**r Schule/Kirche gehen** to go to school/church; **sollen wir** ~ **Euch gehen?** shall we go to your place?; **sie sah** ~ **ihm hin** she looked towards him; ~**m Fenster herein** through the window; ~ **meiner Linken** to *od* on my left.

2 (*zeitlich*) at; ~ **Ostern** at Easter; **bis** ~**m 1. Mai** until May 1st; (*nicht später als*) by May 1st; ~ **meiner Zeit** in my time.

3 (*Zusatz*) with; **Wein** ~**m Essen trinken** to drink wine with one's meal; **sich** ~ **jdm setzen** to sit down beside sb; **setz dich doch** ~ **uns** (come and) sit with us; **Anmerkungen** ~ **etw** notes on sth.

4 (*Zweck*) for; **Wasser** ~**m Waschen** water for washing; **Papier** ~**m Schreiben** paper to write on; **etw** ~**m Geburtstag bekommen** to get sth for one's birthday; **es ist** ~ **seinem Besten** it's for his own good.

5 (*Veränderung*) into; ~ **etw werden** to turn into sth; **jdn** ~ **etw machen** to make sb (into) sth; ~ **Asche verbrennen** to burn to ashes.

6 (*mit Zahlen*): **3** ~ **2** (*SPORT*) 3-2; **das Stück** ~ **5 Euro** at 5 euros each; ~**m ersten Mal** for the first time.

7: ~ **meiner Freude** *etc* to my joy *etc*; ~**m Glück** luckily; ~ **Fuß** on foot; **es ist** ~**m Weinen** it's enough to make you cry.

♦ *konj* to; **etw** ~ **essen** sth to eat; **um besser sehen** ~ **können** in order to see better; **ohne es** ~ **wissen** without knowing it; **noch** ~ **bezahlende Rechnungen** outstanding bills.

♦ *adv* **1** (*allzu*) too; ~ **sehr** too much; ~ **viel** too much; (*umg: zu viele*) too many; **er kriegt** ~ **viel** (*umg*) he gets annoyed; ~ **wenig** too little; (*umg: zu wenige*) too few.

2 (*örtlich*) toward(s); **er kam auf mich** ~ he came towards *od* up to me.

3 (*geschlossen*) shut; closed; **die Geschäfte haben** ~ the shops are closed; ~ **sein** to be closed; **auf/zu** (*Wasserhahn etc*) on/off.

4 (*umg: los*): **nur** ~! just keep at it!; **mach** ~! hurry up!

zuallererst *adv* first of all.

zuallerletzt adv last of all.

zubauen ['tsu:bauən] vt (Lücke) to fill in; (Platz, Gebäude) to build up.

Zubehör ['tsu:bəhø:r] (-(e)s, -e) nt accessories pl.

Zuber ['tsu:bər] (-s, -) m tub.

zubereiten ['tsu:bəraitən] vt to prepare.

zubilligen ['tsu:bilɪgən] vt to grant.

zubinden ['tsu:bindən] unreg vt to tie up; **jdm die Augen** ~ to blindfold sb.

zubleiben ['tsu:blaibən] unreg vi to stay shut.

zubringen ['tsu:brɪŋən] unreg vt to spend; (herbeibringen) to bring, take; (umg: Tür) to get shut.

Zubringer (-s, -) m (TECH) feeder, conveyor; (Verkehrsmittel) shuttle; (zum Flughafen) airport bus; ~**(bus)** m shuttle (bus); ~**straße** f slip road (BRIT), entrance ramp (US).

Zucchini [tsʊ'ki:ni:] pl courgettes pl (BRIT), zucchini(s) pl (US).

Zucht [tsʊxt] (-, -en) f (von Tieren) breeding; (von Pflanzen) cultivation; (Rasse) breed; (Erziehung) raising; (Disziplin) discipline; ~**bulle** m breeding bull.

züchten ['tsʏçtən] vt (Tiere) to breed; (Pflanzen) to cultivate, grow.

Züchter(in) (-s, -) m(f) breeder; grower.

Zuchthaus nt prison, penitentiary (US).

Zuchthengst m stallion, stud.

züchtig ['tsʏçtɪç] adj modest, demure.

züchtigen ['tsʏçtɪgən] vt to chastise.

Züchtigung f chastisement; **körperliche** ~ corporal punishment.

Zuchtperle f cultured pearl.

Züchtung f (von Tieren) breeding; (von Pflanzen) cultivation; (Zuchtart: von Tier) breed; (: von Pflanze) strain.

zucken ['tsʊkən] vi to jerk, twitch; (Strahl etc) to flicker ♦ vt to shrug; **der Schmerz zuckte (mir) durch den ganzen Körper** the pain shot right through my body.

zücken ['tsʏkən] vt (Schwert) to draw; (Geldbeutel) to pull out.

Zucker ['tsʊkər] (-s, -) m sugar; (MED) diabetes; ~ **haben** (umg) to be a diabetic; ~**dose** f sugar bowl; ~**erbse** f mangetout (BRIT), sugar pea (US); ~**gussA** m icing; ~**hut** m sugar loaf; z~**krank** adj diabetic; ~**krankheit** f diabetes sing; ~**lecken** nt: **das ist kein** ~**lecken** it's no picnic.

zuckern vt to sugar.

Zucker- zW: ~**rohr** nt sugar cane; ~**rübe** f sugar beet; ~**spiegel** m (MED) (blood) sugar level; z~**süß** adj sugary; ~**watte** f candy floss (BRIT), cotton candy (US).

Zuckung f convulsion, spasm; (leicht) twitch.

zudecken ['tsu:dɛkən] vt to cover (up); (im Bett) to tuck up od in.

zudem [tsu'de:m] adv in addition (to this).

zudrehen ['tsu:dre:ən] vt to turn off.

zudringlich ['tsu:drɪŋlɪç] adj forward, pushy; (Nachbar etc) intrusive; ~ **werden** to make advances; **Z~keit** f forwardness; intrusiveness.

zudrücken ['tsu:drʏkən] vt to close; **jdm die Kehle** ~ to throttle sb; **ein Auge** ~ to turn a blind eye.

zueinander [tsu|ai'nandər] adv to one other; (in Verbverbindung) together.

zuerkennen ['tsu:|ɛrkɛnən] unreg vt: **jdm etw** ~ to award sth to sb, award sb sth.

zuerst [tsu'|e:rst] adv first; (zu Anfang) at first; ~ **einmal** first of all.

Zufahrt ['tsu:fa:rt] f approach; „**keine** ~ **zum Krankenhaus**" "no access to hospital".

Zufahrtsstraße f approach road; (von Autobahn etc) slip road (BRIT), entrance ramp (US).

Zufall ['tsu:fal] m chance; (Ereignis) coincidence; **durch** ~ by accident; **so ein** ~! what a coincidence!

zufallen unreg vi to close, shut; (Anteil, Aufgabe): **jdm** ~ to fall to sb.

zufällig ['tsu:fɛlɪç] adj chance ♦ adv by chance; (in Frage) by any chance.

Zufallstreffer m fluke.

zufassen ['tsu:fasən] vi (zugreifen) to take hold (of it od them); (fig: schnell handeln) to seize the opportunity; (helfen) to lend a hand.

zufliegen ['tsu:fli:gən] unreg vi: **ihm fliegt alles nur so zu** (fig) everything comes so easily to him.

Zuflucht ['tsu:flʊxt] f recourse; (Ort) refuge; **zu etw** ~ **nehmen** (fig) to resort to sth.

Zufluchtsort m, **Zufluchtsstätte** f place of refuge.

ZuflussA ['tsu:flʊs] m (Zufließen) inflow, influx; (GEOG) tributary; (COMM) supply.

zufolge [tsu'fɔlgə] präp +dat od +gen (laut) according to; (aufgrund) as a result of.

zufrieden [tsu'fri:dən] adj content(ed); **er ist mit nichts** ~ nothing pleases him; **sich mit etw** ~ **geben** to be satisfied with sth; **lass mich damit** ~! (umg) shut up about it!; ~ **stellen** to satisfy; ~ **stellend** satisfactory; **Z~heit** f contentedness; (Befriedigtsein) satisfaction.

zufrieren ['tsu:fri:rən] unreg vi to freeze up od over.

zufügen ['tsu:fy:gən] vt to add; (Leid etc): **jdm etw** ~ to cause sb sth.

Zufuhr ['tsu:fu:r] (-, -en) f (Herbeibringen) supplying; (MET) influx; (MIL) supplies pl.

zuführen ['tsu:fy:rən] vt (bringen) to bring; (transportieren) to convey; (versorgen) to supply ♦ vi: **auf etw** akk ~ to lead to sth.

Zug [tsu:k] (-(e)s, ″-e) m (Eisenbahn~) train; (Luft~) draught (BRIT), draft (US); (Ziehen) pull(ing); (Gesichts~) feature; (SCHACH etc) move; (Klingel~) pull; (Schrift~, beim

Schwimmen) stroke; *(Atem~)* breath; *(Charakter~)* trait; *(an Zigarette)* puff, pull, drag; *(Schluck)* gulp; *(Menschengruppe)* procession; *(von Vögeln)* migration; *(MIL)* platoon; **etw in vollen Zügen genießen** to enjoy sth to the full; **in den letzten Zügen liegen** *(umg)* to be at one's last gasp; **im ~(e)** *+gen (im Verlauf)* in the course of; **~ um ~** *(fig)* step by step; **zum ~(e) kommen** *(umg)* to get a look-in; **etw in groben Zügen darstellen** *od* **umreißen** to outline sth; **das war kein schöner ~ von dir** that wasn't nice of you.

Zugabe ['tsu:ga:bə] *f* extra; *(in Konzert etc)* encore.

Zugabteil *nt* train compartment.

Zugang ['tsu:gaŋ] *m* entrance; *(Zutritt, fig)* access.

zugänglich ['tsu:gɛŋlɪç] *adj* accessible; *(öffentliche Einrichtungen)* open; *(Mensch)* approachable.

Zugbegleiter *m (EISENB)* guard *(BRIT)*, conductor *(US)*.

Zugbrücke *f* drawbridge.

zugeben ['tsu:ge:bən] *unreg vt (beifügen)* to add, throw in; *(zugestehen)* to admit; *(erlauben)* to permit; **zugegeben ... granted ...**

zugegebenermaßen ['tsu:gegə:bənər'ma:sən] *adv* admittedly.

zugegen [tsu'ge:gən] *adv (geh):* **~ sein** to be present.

zugehen ['tsu:ge:ən] *unreg vi (schließen)* to shut ♦ *vi unpers (sich ereignen)* to go on, happen; **auf jdn/etw ~** to walk towards sb/sth; **dem Ende ~** to be finishing; **er geht schon auf die siebzig zu** he's getting on for seventy; **hier geht es nicht mit rechten Dingen zu** there's something odd going on here; **dort geht es ... zu** things are ... there.

Zugehörigkeit ['tsu:gəhø:rɪçkaɪt] *f:* **~ (zu)** membership (of), belonging (to).

Zugehörigkeitsgefühl *nt* feeling of belonging.

zugeknöpft ['tsu:gəknœpft] *(umg) adj* reserved, stand-offish.

Zügel ['tsy:gəl] *(-s, -) m* rein, reins *pl;* *(fig)* rein, curb; **die ~ locker lassen** to slacken one's hold on the reins; **die ~ locker lassen bei** *(fig)* to give free rein to.

zugelassen ['tsu:gəlasən] *adj* authorized; *(Heilpraktiker)* registered; *(Kfz)* licensed.

zügellos *adj* unrestrained; *(sexuell)* licentious.

Zügellosigkeit *f* lack of restraint; licentiousness.

zügeln *vt* to curb; *(Pferd)* to rein in.

zugesellen *vr:* **sich jdm ~** to join sb, join up with sb.

Zugeständnis ['tsu:gəʃtɛntnɪs] *(-ses, -se) nt*

concession; **~se machen** to make allowances.

zugestehen *unreg vt* to admit; *(Rechte)* to concede.

zugetan ['tsu:gəta:n] *adj:* **jdm/etw ~ sein** to be fond of sb/sth.

Zugewinn *(-(e)s) m (JUR) property acquired during marriage.*

Zugezogene(r) ['tsu:gətso:gənə(r)] *f(m)* newcomer.

Zugführer *m (EISENB)* chief guard *(BRIT) od* conductor *(US)*; *(MIL)* platoon commander.

zugig *adj* draughty *(BRIT)*, drafty *(US)*.

zügig ['tsy:gɪç] *adj* speedy, swift.

zugkräftig *adj (fig: Werbetext, Titel)* eye-catching; *(Schauspieler)* crowd-pulling *attr,* popular.

zugleich [tsu'glaɪç] *adv (zur gleichen Zeit)* at the same time; *(ebenso)* both.

Zugluft *f* draught *(BRIT)*, draft *(US)*.

Zugmaschine *f* traction engine, tractor.

zugreifen ['tsu:graɪfən] *unreg vi* to seize *od* grab it/them; *(helfen)* to help; *(beim Essen)* to help o.s.

Zugriff ['tsu:grɪf] *m (COMPUT)* access; **sich dem ~ der Polizei entziehen** *(fig)* to evade justice.

zugrunde, zu Grunde▲ [tsu'grʊndə] *adv:* **~ gehen** to collapse; *(Mensch)* to perish; **er wird daran nicht ~ gehen** he'll survive; *(finanziell)* it won't ruin him; **einer Sache** *dat* **etw ~ legen** to base sth on sth; **einer Sache** *dat* **~ liegen** to be based on sth; **~ richten** to ruin, destroy.

zugunsten, zu Gunsten▲ [tsu'gʊnstən] *präp* *+gen od +dat* in favour *(BRIT) od* favor *(US)* of.

zugute [tsu'gu:tə] *adv:* **jdm etw ~ halten** to concede sth to sb; **jdm ~ kommen** to be of assistance to sb.

Zug- *zW:* **~verbindung** *f* train connection; **~vogel** *m* migratory bird; **~zwang** *m* *(SCHACH)* zugzwang; **unter ~zwang stehen** *(fig)* to be in a tight spot.

zuhalten ['tsu:haltən] *unreg vt* to hold shut ♦ *vi:* **auf jdn/etw ~** to make for sb/sth; **sich** *dat* **die Nase ~** to hold one's nose.

Zuhälter ['tsu:hɛltər] *(-s, -) m* pimp.

zuhause▲ [tsu'hauzə] *(ÖSTERR, SCHWEIZ) adv* at home.

Zuhause *(-s) nt* home.

Zuhilfenahme [tsu'hɪlfəna:mə] *f:* **unter ~ von** with the help of.

zuhören ['tsu:hø:rən] *vi* to listen.

Zuhörer *(-s, -) m* listener; **~schaft** *f* audience.

zujubeln ['tsu:ju:bəln] *vi:* **jdm ~** to cheer sb.

zukehren ['tsu:ke:rən] *vt (zuwenden)* to turn.

zuklappen ['tsu:klapən] *vt (Buch, Deckel)* to close ♦ *vi (Hilfsverb sein: Tür etc)* to click shut.

zukleben ['tsu:kle:bən] *vt* to paste up.

zukneifen ['tsu:knaɪfən] *vt* (*Augen*) to screw up; (*Mund*) to shut tight(ly).

zuknöpfen ['tsu:knœpfən] *vt* to button (up), fasten (up).

zukommen ['tsu:kɔmən] *unreg vi* to come up; **auf jdn ~** to come up to sb; **jdm ~** (*sich gehören*) to be fitting for sb; **diesem Treffen kommt große Bedeutung zu** this meeting is of the utmost importance; **jdm etw ~ lassen** to give sb sth; **die Dinge auf sich** *akk* **~ lassen** to take things as they come.

Zukunft ['tsu:kʊnft] (*-, no pl*) *f* future.

zukünftig ['tsu:kʏnftɪç] *adj* future ◆ *adv* in future; **mein ~er Mann** my husband-to-be.

Zukunfts- *zW:* **~aussichten** *pl* future prospects *pl;* **~musik** (*umg*) *f* wishful thinking; **~roman** *m* science-fiction novel; **z~trächtig** *adj* promising for the future; **z~weisend** *adj* trend-setting.

Zulage ['tsu:la:gə] *f* bonus.

zulande [tsu'landə] *adv:* **bei uns ~** in our country.

zulangen ['tsu:laŋən] (*umg*) *vi* (*Dieb, beim Essen*) to help o.s.

zulassen ['tsu:lasən] *unreg vt* (*hereinlassen*) to admit; (*erlauben*) to permit; (*Auto*) to license; (*umg: nicht öffnen*) to keep shut.

zulässig ['tsu:lɛsɪç] *adj* permissible, permitted; **~e Höchstgeschwindigkeit** (upper) speed limit.

Zulassung *f* (*amtlich*) authorization; (*von Kfz*) licensing; (*als praktizierender Arzt*) registration.

Zulauf *m:* **großen ~ haben** (*Geschäft*) to be very popular.

zulaufen ['tsu:laʊfən] *unreg vi:* **~ auf** *+akk* to run towards; **jdm ~** (*Tier*) to adopt sb; **spitz ~** to come to a point.

zulegen ['tsu:le:gən] *vt* to add; (*Geld*) to put in; (*Tempo*) to accelerate, quicken; (*schließen*) to cover over; **sich** *dat* **etw ~** (*umg*) to get oneself sth.

zuleide [tsu'laɪdə] *adj:* **jdm etw ~ tun** to harm sb.

zuleiten ['tsu:laɪtən] *vt* (*Wasser*) to supply; (*schicken*) to send.

Zuleitung *f* (*TECH*) supply.

zuletzt [tsu'lɛtst] *adv* finally, at last; **wir blieben bis ~** we stayed to the very end; **nicht ~ wegen** not least because of.

zuliebe [tsu'li:bə] *adv:* **jdm ~** (in order) to please sb.

Zulieferbetrieb ['tsu:li:fərbətri:p] *m* (*COMM*) supplier.

zum [tsʊm] = **zu dem;** **~ dritten Mal** for the third time; **~ Scherz** as a joke; **~ Trinken** for drinking; **bis ~ 15. April** until 15th April; (*nicht später als*) by 15th April; **~ ersten Mal(e)** for the first time; **es ist ~ Weinen** it's enough to make you (want to) weep;

~ Glück luckily.

zumachen ['tsu:maxən] *vt* to shut; (*Kleidung*) to do up, fasten ◆ *vi* to shut; (*umg*) to hurry up.

zumal [tsu'ma:l] *konj* especially (as).

zumeist [tsu'maɪst] *adv* mostly.

zumessen ['tsu:mɛsən] *unreg vt* (*+dat*) (*Zeit*) to allocate (for); (*Bedeutung*) to attach (to).

zumindest [tsu'mɪndəst] *adv* at least.

zumutbar ['tsu:mu:tba:r] *adj* reasonable.

zumute [tsu'mu:tə] *adv:* **wie ist ihm ~?** how does he feel?

zumuten ['tsu:mu:tən] *vt:* **(jdm) etw ~** to expect *od* ask sth (of sb); **sich** *dat* **zuviel ~** to take on too much.

Zumutung *f* unreasonable expectation *od* demand; (*Unverschämtheit*) impertinence; **das ist eine ~!** that's a bit much!

zunächst [tsu'nɛːçst] *adv* first of all; **~ einmal** to start with.

zunageln ['tsu:na:gəln] *vt* (*Fenster etc*) to nail up; (*Kiste etc*) to nail down.

zunähen ['tsu:nɛ:ən] *vt* to sew up.

Zunahme ['tsu:na:mə] (*-, -n*) *f* increase.

Zuname ['tsu:na:mə] *m* surname.

zünden ['tsʏndən] *vi* (*Feuer*) to light, ignite; (*Motor*) to fire; (*fig*) to kindle enthusiasm ◆ *vt* to ignite; (*Rakete*) to fire.

zündend *adj* fiery.

Zünder (*-s, -*) *m* fuse; (*MIL*) detonator.

Zünd- *zW:* **~holz** *nt* match; **~kabel** *nt* (*AUT*) plug lead; **~kerze** *f* (*AUT*) spark(ing) plug; **~plättchen** *nt* cap; **~schlüssel** *m* ignition key; **~schnur** *f* fuse wire; **~stoff** *m* fuel; (*fig*) dynamite.

Zündung *f* ignition.

zunehmen ['tsu:ne:mən] *unreg vi* to increase, grow; (*Mensch*) to put on weight.

zunehmend *adj:* **mit ~em Alter** with advancing age.

zuneigen ['tsu:naɪgən] *vi* to incline, lean; **sich dem Ende ~** to draw to a close; **einer Auffassung ~** to incline towards a view; **jdm zugeneigt sein** to be attracted to sb.

Zuneigung *f* affection.

Zunft [tsʊnft] (*-, ⸚e*) *f* guild.

zünftig ['tsʏnftɪç] *adj* (*Arbeit*) professional; (*umg: ordentlich*) proper, real.

Zunge ['tsʊŋə] *f* tongue; (*Fisch*) sole; **böse ~n behaupten, ...** malicious gossip has it ...

züngeln ['tsʏŋəln] *vi* (*Flammen*) to lick.

Zungenbrecher *m* tongue-twister.

zungenfertig *adj* glib.

Zünglein ['tsʏŋlaɪn] *nt:* **das ~ an der Waage sein** (*fig*) to tip the scales.

zunichte [tsu'nɪçtə] *adv:* **~ machen** to ruin, destroy; **~ werden** to come to nothing.

zunutze [tsu'nʊtsə] *adv:* **sich** *dat* **etw ~ machen** to make use of sth.

zuoberst [tsu'|o:bərst] *adv* at the top.

Spelling Reform: ▲ *new spelling* △ *old spelling (to be phased out)*

zuordnen ['tsu:|ɔrdnən] *vt* to assign.

zupacken ['tsu:pakən] (*umg*) *vi* (*zugreifen*) to make a grab for it; (*bei der Arbeit*) to get down to it; **mit ~** (*helfen*) to give me/them *etc* a hand.

zupfen ['tsʊpfən] *vt* to pull, pick, pluck; (*Gitarre*) to pluck.

zur [tsu:r] = **zu der**.

zurate▲, zu Rate [tsu'ra:tə] *adv*: **jdn ~ ziehen** to consult sb.

zurechnungsfähig ['tsu:rɛçnʊŋsfɛ:ɪç] *adj* (*JUR*) responsible, of sound mind; **Z~keit** *f* responsibility, accountability.

zurecht- *zW*: **~biegen** *unreg vt* to bend into shape; (*fig*) to twist; **~finden** *unreg vr* to find one's way (about); **~kommen** *unreg vi* (*rechtzeitig kommen*) to come in time; (*schaffen*) to cope; (*finanziell*) to manage; **~legen** *vt* to get ready; (*Ausrede etc*) to have ready; **~machen** *vt* to prepare ♦ *vr* to get ready; (*sich schminken*) to put on one's make-up; **~weisen** *unreg vt* to reprimand; **Z~weisung** *f* reprimand, rebuff.

zureden ['tsu:re:dən] *vi*: **jdm ~** to persuade sb, urge sb.

zureiten ['tsuraɪtən] *unreg vt* (*Pferd*) to break in.

Zürich ['tsy:rɪç] (**-s**) *nt* Zurich.

zurichten ['tsu:rɪçtən] *vt* (*Essen*) to prepare; (*beschädigen*) to batter, bash up.

zürnen ['tsʏrnən] *vi*: **jdm ~** to be angry with sb.

zurück [tsu'rʏk] *adv* back; (*mit Zahlungen*) behind; (*fig: ~geblieben: von Kind*) backward; **~!** get back!; **~behalten** *unreg vt* to keep back; **er hat Schäden ~behalten** he suffered lasting damage; **~bekommen** *unreg vt* to get back; **~bezahlen** *vt* to repay, pay back; **~bleiben** *unreg vi* (*Mensch*) to remain behind; (*nicht nachkommen*) to fall behind, lag; (*Schaden*) to remain; **~bringen** *unreg vt* to bring back; **~datieren** *vt* to backdate; **~drängen** *vt* (*Gefühle*) to repress; (*Feind*) to push back; **~drehen** *vt* to turn back; **~erobern** *vt* to reconquer; **~erstatten** *vt* to refund; **~fahren** *unreg vi* to travel back; (*vor Schreck*) to recoil ♦ *vt* to drive back; **~fallen** *unreg vi* to fall back; (*in Laster*) to relapse; (*in Leistungen*) to fall behind; (*an Besitzer*): **~fallen an** +*akk* to revert to; **~finden** *unreg vi* to find one's way back; **~fordern** *vt* to demand back; **~führen** *vt* to lead back; **etw auf etw** *akk* **~führen** to trace sth back to sth; **~geben** *unreg vt* to give back; (*antworten*) to retort with; **~geblieben** *adj* retarded; **~gehen** *unreg vi* to go back; (*fallen*) to go down, fall; (*zeitlich*): **~gehen (auf** +*akk*) to date back (to); **Waren ~gehen lassen** to send back goods; **~gezogen** *adj* retired, withdrawn; **~greifen** *unreg vi*: **~greifen (auf** +*akk*) (*fig*) to fall back (upon); (*zeitlich*) to go back (to); **~halten** *unreg vt* to hold back; (*Mensch*) to restrain; (*hindern*) to prevent ♦ *vr* (*reserviert sein*) to be reserved; (*im Essen*) to hold back; (*im Hintergrund bleiben*) to keep in the background; (*bei Verhandlung*) to keep a low profile; **~haltend** *adj* reserved; **Z~haltung** *f* reserve; **~holen** *vt* (*COMPUT: Daten*) to retrieve; **~kehren** *vi* to return; **~kommen** *unreg vi* to come back; **auf etw** *akk* **~kommen** to return to sth; **~lassen** *unreg vt* to leave behind; **~legen** *vt* to put back; (*Geld*) to put by; (*reservieren*) to keep back; (*Strecke*) to cover ♦ *vr* to lie back; **~liegen** *unreg vi*: **der Unfall liegt etwa eine Woche ~** the accident was about a week ago; **~nehmen** *unreg vt* to take back; **~reichen** *vi* (*Tradition etc*): **~reichen (in** +*akk*) to go back (to); **~rufen** *unreg vt, vi* to call back; **etw ins Gedächtnis ~rufen** to recall sth; **~schrauben** *vt*: **seine Ansprüche ~schrauben** to lower one's sights; **~schrecken** *vi*: **~schrecken vor** +*dat* to shrink from; **vor nichts ~schrecken** to stop at nothing; **~setzen** *vt* to put back; (*im Preis*) to reduce; (*benachteiligen*) to put at a disadvantage ♦ *vi* (*mit Fahrzeug*) to reverse, back; **~stecken** *vt* to put back ♦ *vi* (*fig*) to moderate one's wishes; **~stellen** *vt* to put back, replace; (*aufschieben*) to put off, postpone; (*MIL*) to turn down; (*Interessen*) to defer; (*Ware*) to keep; **persönliche Interessen hinter etw** *dat* **~stellen** to put sth before one's personal interests; **~stoßen** *unreg vt* to repulse; **~stufen** *vt* to downgrade; **~treten** *unreg vi* to step back; (*vom Amt*) to retire; (*von einem Vertrag etc*): **~treten (von)** to withdraw (from); **gegenüber** *od* **hinter etw** *dat* **~treten** to diminish in importance in view of sth; **bitte ~treten!** stand back, please!; **~verfolgen** *vt* (*fig*) to trace back; **~versetzen** *vt* (*in alten Zustand*): **~versetzen (in** +*akk*) to restore (to) ♦ *vr*: **sich ~versetzen (in** +*akk*) to think back (to); **~weichen** *unreg vi*: **~weichen (vor** +*dat*) to shrink back (from); **~weisen** *unreg vt* to turn down; (*Mensch*) to reject; **~werfen** *unreg vt* (*Ball, Kopf*) to throw back; (*Strahlen, Schall*) to reflect; (*fig: Feind*) to repel; (: *wirtschaftlich*): **~werfen (um)** to set back (by); **~zahlen** *vt* to pay back, repay; **Z~zahlung** *f* repayment; **~ziehen** *unreg vt* to pull back; (*Angebot*) to withdraw ♦ *vr* to retire.

Zuruf ['tsu:ru:f] *m* shout, cry.

zurzeit▲ [tsʊr'tsaɪt] *adv* at the moment.

zus. *abk* = **zusammen**; **zusätzlich**.

Zusage ['tsu:za:gə] *f* promise; (*Annahme*) consent.

zusagen *vt* to promise ♦ *vi* to accept; **jdm etw auf den Kopf ~** (*umg*) to tell sb sth outright; **jdm ~** (*gefallen*) to appeal to *od* please sb.

zusammen [tsu'zamən] *adv* together; **Z~arbeit** *f* cooperation; **~arbeiten** *vi* to cooperate; **Z~ballung** *f* accumulation; **~bauen** *vt* to assemble; **~beißen** *unreg vt* (*Zähne*) to clench; **~bleiben** *unreg vi* to stay together; **~brauen** (*umg*) *vt* to concoct ♦ *vr* (*Gewitter, Unheil etc*) to be brewing; **~brechen** *unreg vi* (*Hilfsverb sein*) to collapse; (*Mensch*) to break down, collapse; (*Verkehr etc*) to come to a standstill; **~bringen** *unreg vt* to bring *od* get together; (*Geld*) to get; (*Sätze*) to put together; **Z~bruch** *m* collapse; (*COMPUT*) crash; **~fahren** *unreg vi* to collide; (*erschrecken*) to start; **~fallen** *unreg vi* (*einstürzen*) to collapse; (*Ereignisse*) to coincide; **~fassen** *vt* to summarize; (*vereinigen*) to unite; **~fassend** *adj* summarizing ♦ *adv* to summarize; **Z~fassung** *f* summary, résumé; **~finden** *unreg vi, vr* to meet (together); **~fließen** *unreg vi* to flow together, meet; **Z~fluss**▲ *m* confluence; **~fügen** *vt* to join (together), unite; **~führen** *vt* to bring together; (*Familie*) to reunite; **~gehören** *vi* to belong together; (*Paar*) to match; **Z~gehörigkeitsgefühl** *nt* sense of belonging; **~gesetzt** *adj* compound, composite; **~gewürfelt** *adj* motley; **~halten** *unreg vt* to hold together ♦ *vi* to hold together; (*Freunde, fig*) to stick together; **Z~hang** *m* connection; **im/aus dem Z~hang** in/out of context; **etw aus dem Z~hang reißen** to take sth out of its context; **~hängen** *unreg vi* to be connected *od* linked; **~hängend** *adj* (*Erzählung*) coherent; **~hang(s)los** *adj* incoherent; **~klappbar** *adj* folding, collapsible; **~klappen** *vt* (*Messer etc*) to fold ♦ *vi* (*umg: Mensch*) to flake out; **~knüllen** *vt* to crumple up; **~kommen** *unreg vi* to meet, assemble; (*sich ereignen*) to occur at once *od* together; **~kramen** *vt* to gather (together); **Z~kunft** (-, **-künfte**) *f* meeting; **~laufen** *unreg vi* to run *od* come together; (*Straßen, Flüsse etc*) to converge, meet; (*Farben*) to run into one another; **~legen** *vt* to put together; (*stapeln*) to pile up; (*falten*) to fold; (*verbinden*) to combine, unite; (*Termine, Feste*) to combine; (*Geld*) to collect; **~nehmen** *unreg vt* to summon up ♦ *vr* to pull o.s. together; **alles ~genommen** all in all; **~passen** *vi* to go well together, match; **Z~prall** *m* (*lit*) collision; (*fig*) clash; **~prallen** *vi* (*Hilfsverb sein*) to collide; **~reimen** (*umg*) *vt*: **das kann ich mir nicht ~reimen** I can't make head nor tail of this; **~reißen** *unreg vr* to pull o.s. together; **~rotten** *unreg* (*pej*) *vr* to gang up; **~schlagen** *unreg vt* (*jdn*) to beat up; (*Dinge*) to smash up; (*falten*) to fold; (*Hände*) to clap; (*Hacken*) to click; **~schließen** *unreg vt, vr* to join (together); **Z~schluss**▲ *m* amalgamation; **~schmelzen** *unreg vi*

(*verschmelzen*) to fuse; (*zerschmelzen*) to melt (away); (*Anzahl*) to dwindle; **~schrecken** *unreg vi* to start; **~schreiben** *unreg vt* to write together; (*Bericht*) to put together; **~schrumpfen** *vi* (*Hilfsverb sein*) to shrink, shrivel up; **Z~sein** (-s) *nt* get-together; **~setzen** *vt* to put together ♦ *vr*: **sich ~setzen aus** to consist of; **Z~spiel** *nt* teamwork; (*von Kräften etc*) interaction; **~stellen** *vt* to put together; **Z~stellung** *f* list; (*Vorgang*) compilation; **Z~stoß** *m* collision; **~stoßen** *unreg vi* (*Hilfsverb sein*) to collide; **~strömen** *vi* (*Hilfsverb sein: Menschen*) to flock together; **~tragen** *unreg vt* to collect; **Z~treffen** *nt* meeting; (*Zufall*) coincidence; **~treffen** *unreg vi* (*Hilfsverb sein*) to coincide; (*Menschen*) to meet; **~treten** *unreg vi* (*Verein etc*) to meet; **~wachsen** *unreg vi* to grow together; **~wirken** *vi* to combine; **~zählen** *vt* to add up; **~ziehen** *unreg vt* (*verengern*) to draw together; (*vereinigen*) to bring together; (*addieren*) to add up ♦ *vr* to shrink; (*sich bilden*) to form, develop; **~zucken** *vi* (*Hilfsverb sein*) to start.

Zusatz ['tsu:zats] *m* addition; **~antrag** *m* (*POL*) amendment; **~gerät** *nt* attachment.

zusätzlich ['tsu:zɛtslɪç] *adj* additional.

Zusatzmittel *nt* additive.

zuschauen ['tsu:ʃauən] *vi* to watch, look on.

Zuschauer (-s, -) *m* spectator ♦ *pl* (*THEAT*) audience *sing*.

zuschicken ['tsu:ʃɪkən] *vt*: **jdm etw ~** to send *od* forward sth to sb.

zuschießen ['tsu:ʃi:sən] *unreg vt* to fire; (*Geld*) to put in ♦ *vi*: **~ auf** +*akk* to rush towards.

Zuschlag ['tsu:ʃla:k] *m* extra charge; (*Erhöhung*) surcharge; (*EISENB*) supplement.

zuschlagen ['tsu:ʃla:gən] *unreg vt* (*Tür*) to slam; (*Ball*) to hit; (*bei Auktion*) to knock down; (*Steine etc*) to knock into shape ♦ *vi* (*Fenster, Tür*) to shut; (*Mensch*) to hit, punch.

zuschlagfrei *adj* (*EISENB*) not subject to a supplement.

zuschlagpflichtig *adj* subject to surcharge.

Zuschlagskarte *f* (*EISENB*) supplementary ticket.

zuschließen ['tsu:ʃli:sən] *unreg vt* to lock (up).

zuschmeißen ['tsu:ʃmaɪsən] *unreg* (*umg*) *vt* to slam, bang shut.

zuschmieren ['tsu:ʃmi:rən] *vt* to smear over; (*Löcher*) to fill in.

zuschneiden ['tsu:ʃnaɪdən] *unreg vt* to cut to size; (*NÄHEN*) to cut out; **auf etw** *akk* **zugeschnitten sein** (*fig*) to be geared to sth.

zuschnüren ['tsu:ʃny:rən] *vt* to tie up; **die Angst schnürte ihm die Kehle zu** (*fig*) he was choked with fear.

zuschrauben ['tsu:ʃraubən] *vt* to screw shut.

zuschreiben ['tsu:ʃraɪbən] *unreg vt* (*fig*) to

ascribe, attribute; (*COMM*) to credit; **das hast du dir selbst zuzuschreiben** you've only got yourself to blame.

Zuschrift ['tsu:ʃrɪft] *f* letter, reply.

zuschulden, zu Schulden▲ [tsu'ʃʊldən] *adv*: **sich** *dat* **etw ~ kommen lassen** to make o.s. guilty of sth.

Zuschuss▲ ['tsu:ʃʊs] *m* subsidy.

Zuschussbetrieb▲ *m* loss-making concern.

zuschütten ['tsu:ʃʏtən] *vt* to fill up.

zusehen ['tsu:zeːən] *unreg vi* to watch; (*dafür sorgen*) to take care; (*etw dulden*) to sit back (and watch); **jdm/etw ~** to watch sb/sth.

zusehends *adv* visibly.

zu sein▲ ['tsu:zaɪn] *siehe* **zu.**

zusenden ['tsu:zɛndən] *unreg vt* to forward, send on.

zusetzen ['tsu:zɛtsən] *vt* (*beifügen*) to add; (*Geld*) to lose ♦ *vi*: **jdm ~** to harass sb; (*Krankheit*) to take a lot out of sb; (*unter Druck setzen*) to lean on sb (*umg*); (*schwer treffen*) to hit sb hard.

zusichern ['tsu:zɪçərn] *vt*: **jdm etw ~** to assure sb of sth.

Zusicherung *f* assurance.

zusperren ['tsu:ʃpɛrən] *vt* to bar.

zuspielen ['tsu:ʃpiːlən] *vt, vi* to pass; **jdm etw ~** to pass sth to sb; (*fig*) to pass sth on to sb; **etw der Presse ~** to leak sth to the press.

zuspitzen ['tsu:ʃpɪtsən] *vt* to sharpen ♦ *vr* (*Lage*) to become critical.

zusprechen ['tsu:ʃprɛçən] *unreg vt* (*zuerkennen*): **jdm etw ~** to award sb sth, award sth to sb ♦ *vi*: **jdm ~** to speak to sb; **jdm Trost ~** to comfort sb; **dem Essen/ Alkohol ~** to eat/drink a lot.

Zuspruch ['tsu:ʃprʊx] *m* encouragement; (*Anklang*) popularity.

Zustand ['tsu:ʃtant] *m* state, condition; **in gutem/schlechtem ~** in good/poor condition; (*Haus*) in good/bad repair; **Zustände bekommen** *od* **kriegen** (*umg*) to have a fit.

zustande, zu Stande▲ [tsu'ʃtandə] *adv*: **~ bringen** to bring about; **~ kommen** to come about.

zuständig ['tsu:ʃtɛndɪç] *adj* competent, responsible; **Z~keit** *f* competence, responsibility; **Z~keitsbereich** *m* area of responsibility.

zustatten [tsu'ʃtatən] *adj*: **jdm ~ kommen** (*geh*) to come in useful for sb.

zustehen ['tsu:ʃteːən] *unreg vi*: **jdm ~** to be sb's right.

zusteigen ['tsu:ʃtaɪɡən] *unreg vi*: **noch jemand zugestiegen?** (*in Zug*) any more tickets?

zustellen ['tsu:ʃtɛlən] *vt* (*verstellen*) to block; (*Post etc*) to send.

Zustellung *f* delivery.

zusteuern ['tsu:ʃtɔyərn] *vi*: **auf etw** *akk* **~** to

head for sth; (*beim Gespräch*) to steer towards sth ♦ *vt* (*beitragen*) to contribute.

zustimmen ['tsu:ʃtɪmən] *vi* to agree.

Zustimmung *f* agreement; (*Einwilligung*) consent; **allgemeine ~ finden** to meet with general approval.

zustoßen ['tsu:ʃtoːsən] *unreg vi* (*fig*): **jdm ~** to happen to sb.

Zustrom ['tsu:ʃtroːm] *m* (*fig: Menschenmenge*) stream (of visitors *etc*); (*hineinströmend*) influx; (*MET*) inflow.

zustürzen ['tsu:ʃtʏrtsən] *vi*: **auf jdn/etw ~** to rush up to sb/sth.

zutage, zu Tage▲ [tsu'taːɡə] *adv*: **~ bringen** to bring to light; **~ treten** to come to light.

Zutaten ['tsu:taːtən] *pl* ingredients *pl*; (*fig*) accessories *pl*.

zuteil [tsu'taɪl] *adv* (*geh*): **jdm wird etw ~** sb is granted sth, sth is granted to sb.

zuteilen ['tsu:taɪlən] *vt* to allocate, assign.

zutiefst [tsu'tiːfst] *adv* deeply.

zutragen ['tsu:traːɡən] *unreg vt*: **jdm etw ~** to bring sb sth, bring sth to sb ♦ *vt* (*Klatsch*) to tell sb sth ♦ *vr* to happen.

zuträglich ['tsu:trɛːklɪç] *adj* beneficial.

zutrauen ['tsu:traʊən] *vt*: **jdm etw ~** to credit sb with sth; **sich** *dat* **nichts ~** to have no confidence in o.s.; **jdm viel ~** to think a lot of sb; **jdm wenig ~** not to think much of sb; **Z~ (-s)** *nt*: **Z~ (zu)** trust (in); **zu jdm Z~ fassen** to begin to trust sb.

zutraulich *adj* trusting; (*Tier*) friendly; **Z~keit** *f* trust.

zutreffen ['tsu:trɛfən] *unreg vi* to be correct; (*gelten*) to apply.

zutreffend *adj* (*richtig*) accurate; **Z~es bitte unterstreichen** please underline where applicable.

zutrinken ['tsu:trɪŋkən] *unreg vi*: **jdm ~** to drink to sb.

Zutritt ['tsu:trɪt] *m* access; (*Einlass*) admittance; **kein ~, ~ verboten** no admittance.

zutun ['tsu:tuːn] *unreg vt* to add; (*schließen*) to shut.

Zutun (-s) *nt* assistance.

zuunterst [tsu'ʊntərst] *adv* right at the bottom.

zuverlässig ['tsu:fɛrlɛsɪç] *adj* reliable; **Z~keit** *f* reliability.

Zuversicht ['tsu:fɛrzɪçt] (-) *f* confidence; **z~lich** *adj* confident; **~lichkeit** *f* confidence.

zu viel▲ [tsu'fiːl] *siehe* **zu.**

zuvor [tsu'foːr] *adv* before, previously.

zuvorderst [tsu'fordərst] *adv* right at the front.

zuvorkommen *unreg vi* +*dat* to anticipate; (*Gefahr etc*) to forestall; **jdm ~** to beat sb to it.

zuvorkommend *adj* courteous; (*gefällig*)

obliging.

Zuwachs ['tsu:vaks] (-es) *m* increase, growth; (*umg*) addition.

zuwachsen *unreg vi* to become overgrown; (*Wunde*) to heal (up).

Zuwachsrate *f* rate of increase.

zuwandern ['tsu:vandərn] *vi* to immigrate.

zuwege, zu Wege▲ [tsu've:gə] *adv*: **etw ~ bringen** to accomplish sth; **mit etw ~ kommen** to manage sth; **gut ~ sein** to be (doing) well.

zuweilen [tsu'vaɪlən] *adv* at times, now and then.

zuweisen ['tsu:vaɪzən] *unreg vt* to assign, allocate.

zuwenden ['tsu:vɛndən] *unreg vt +dat* to turn towards ♦ *vr +dat* to turn to; (*sich widmen*) to devote o.s. to; **jdm seine Aufmerksamkeit ~** to give sb one's attention.

Zuwendung *f* (*Geld*) financial contribution; (*Liebe*) love and care.

zu wenig▲ [tsu've:nɪç] *siehe* **zu**.

zuwerfen ['tsu:vɛrfən] *unreg vt*: **jdm etw ~ to** throw sth to sb, throw sb sth.

zuwider [tsu'vi:dər] *adv*: **etw ist jdm ~ sb** loathes sth, sb finds sth repugnant ♦ *präp +dat* contrary to; **~handeln** *vi +dat* to act contrary to; **einem Gesetz ~handeln** to contravene a law; **Z~handlung** *f* contravention; **~laufen** *unreg vi*: **einer Sache** *dat* **~laufen** to run counter to sth.

zuz. *abk* = **zuzüglich**.

zuzahlen ['tsu:tsa:lən] *vt*: **10 Euro ~** to pay another 10 euros.

zuziehen ['tsu:tsi:ən] *unreg vt* (*schließen*: *Vorhang*) to draw, close; (*herbeirufen*: *Experten*) to call in ♦ *vi* to move in, come; **sich** *dat* **etw ~** (*Krankheit*) to catch sth; (*Zorn*) to incur sth; **sich** *dat* **eine Verletzung ~** (*form*) to sustain an injury.

Zuzug ['tsu:tsuk] (-(e)s) *m* (*Zustrom*) influx; (*von Familie etc*): **~ nach** move to.

zuzüglich ['tsu:tsy:klɪç] *präp +gen* plus, with the addition of.

zuzwinkern ['tsu:tsvɪnkərn] *vi*: **jdm ~** to wink at sb.

ZVS *f abk* (= *Zentralstelle für die Vergabe von Studienplätzen*) *central body organizing the granting of places at university.*

Zwang (-(e)s, ⁻e) *m* compulsion; (*Gewalt*) coercion; **gesellschaftliche Zwänge** social constraints; **tu dir keinen ~ an** don't feel you have to be polite.

zwang *etc* [tsvaŋ] *vb siehe* **zwingen**.

zwängen ['tsvɛŋən] *vt, vr* to squeeze.

Zwang- *zW*: **z~haft** *adj* compulsive; **z~los** *adj* informal; **~losigkeit** *f* informality.

Zwangs- *zW*: **~abgabe** *f* (*COMM*) compulsory levy; **~arbeit** *f* forced labour (*BRIT*) *od* labor (*US*); **~ernährung** *f* force-feeding; **~jacke** *f*

straitjacket; **~lage** *f* predicament, tight corner; **z~läufig** *adj* inevitable; **~maßnahme** *f* compulsory measure; (*POL*) sanction; **~vollstreckung** *f* execution; **~vorstellung** *f* (*PSYCH*) obsession; **z~weise** *adv* compulsorily.

zwanzig ['tsvantsɪç] *num* twenty.

zwanzigste(r, s) *adj* twentieth.

zwar [tsva:r] *adv* to be sure, indeed; **das ist ~ ..., aber ...** that may be ... but ...; **und ~ in** fact, actually; **und ~ am Sonntag** on Sunday to be precise; **und ~ so schnell, dass ...** in fact so quickly that ...

Zweck [tsvɛk] (-(e)s, -e) *m* purpose, aim; **es hat keinen ~, darüber zu reden** there is no point (in) talking about it; **z~dienlich** *adj* practical; (*nützlich*) useful; **z~dienliche Hinweise** (any) relevant information.

Zwecke (-, -n) *f* hobnail; (*Heft~*) drawing pin (*BRIT*), thumbtack (*US*).

Zweck- *zW*: **z~entfremden** *vt untr* to use for another purpose; **~entfremdung** *f* misuse; **z~frei** *adj* (*Forschung etc*) pure; **z~los** *adj* pointless; **z~mäßig** *adj* suitable, appropriate; **~mäßigkeit** *f* suitability.

zwecks *präp +gen* (*form*) for (the purpose of).

zweckwidrig *adj* unsuitable.

zwei [tsvaɪ] *num* two; **Z~bettzimmer** *nt* twin-bedded room; **~deutig** *adj* ambiguous; (*unanständig*) suggestive; **Z~drittelmehrheit** *f* (*PARL*) two-thirds majority; **~eiig** *adj* (*Zwillinge*) non-identical.

zweierlei ['tsvaɪər'laɪ] *adj* two kinds *od* sorts of; **~ Stoff** two different kinds of material; **~ zu tun haben** to have two different things to do.

zweifach *adj* double.

Zweifel ['tsvaɪfəl] (-s, -) *m* doubt; **ich bin mir darüber im ~** I'm in two minds about it; **z~haft** *adj* doubtful, dubious; **z~los** *adj* doubtless.

zweifeln *vi*: (**an etw** *dat*) **~** to doubt (sth).

Zweifelsfall *m*: **im ~** in case of doubt.

Zweifrontenkrieg *m* war(fare) on two fronts.

Zweig [tsvaɪk] (-(e)s, -e) *m* branch; **~geschäft** *nt* (*COMM*) branch.

zweigleisig ['tsvaɪglaɪzɪç] *adj*: **~ argumentieren** to argue along two different lines.

Zweigstelle *f* branch (office).

zwei- *zW*: **~händig** *adj* two-handed; (*MUS*) for two hands; **Z~heit** *f* duality; **~hundert** *num* two hundred; **Z~kampf** *m* duel; **~mal** *adv* twice; **das lasse ich mir nicht ~mal sagen** I don't have to be told twice; **~motorig** *adj* twin-engined; **~reihig** *adj* (*Anzug*) double-breasted; **Z~samkeit** *f* togetherness; **~schneidig** *adj* (*fig*) double-edged; **Z~sitzer** (-s, -) *m* two-seater; **~sprachig** *adj* bilingual;

~**spurig** *adj* (*AUT*) two-lane;
Z~**spur(tonband)gerät** *nt* twin-track (tape)
recorder; ~**stellig** *adj* (*Zahl*) two-digit *attrib*,
with two digits; ~**stimmig** *adj* for two
voices.
zweit [tsvait] *adv*: **zu** ~ (*in Paaren*) in twos.
Zweitaktmotor *m* two-stroke engine.
zweitbeste(r, s) *adj* second best.
zweite(r, s) *adj* second; **Bürger ~r Klasse**
second-class citizen(s *pl*).
zweiteilig ['tsvaitailiç] *adj* (*Buch, Film etc*) in
two parts; (*Kleidung*) two-piece.
zweitens *adv* secondly.
zweit- *zW:* ~**größte(r, s)** *adj* second largest;
~**klassig** *adj* second-class; ~**letzte(r, s)** *adj*
last but one, penultimate; ~**rangig** *adj*
second-rate; Z~**schlüssel** *m* duplicate key;
Z~**stimme** *f* second vote; *siehe auch*
Erststimme.
zweitürig ['tsvaityriç] *adj* two-door.
Zweitwagen *m* second car.
Zweitwohnung *f* second home.
zweizeilig *adj* two-lined; (*TYP: Abstand*)
double-spaced.
Zweizimmerwohnung *f* two-room(ed) flat
(*BRIT*) *od* apartment (*US*).
Zwerchfell ['tsverçfel] *nt* diaphragm.
Zwerg(in) [tsverk, 'tsvergin] (-(e)s, -e) *m(f)*
dwarf; (*fig: Knirps*) midget; ~**schule** (*umg*) *f*
village school.
Zwetsch(g)e ['tsvetʃ(g)ə] (-, -n) *f* plum.
Zwickel ['tsvikəl] (-s, -) *m* gusset.
zwicken ['tsvikən] *vt* to pinch, nip.
Zwickmühle ['tsvikmy:lə] *f*: **in der ~ sitzen**
(*fig*) to be in a dilemma.
Zwieback ['tsvi:bak] (-(e)s, -e *od* -bäcke) *m*
rusk.
Zwiebel ['tsvi:bəl] (-, -n) *f* onion; (*Blumen~*)
bulb; z~**artig** *adj* bulbous; ~**turm** *m* (tower
with an) onion dome.
Zwie- *zW:* ~**gespräch** *nt* dialogue (*BRIT*), dialog
(*US*); ~**licht** *nt* twilight; **ins ~licht geraten
sein** (*fig*) to appear in an unfavourable
(*BRIT*) *od* unfavorable (*US*) light; z~**lichtig**
adj shady, dubious; ~**spalt** *m* conflict;
(*zwischen Menschen*) rift, gulf; z~**spältig** *adj*
(*Gefühle*) conflicting; (*Charakter*)
contradictory; ~**tracht** *f* discord, dissension.
Zwilling ['tsviliŋ] (-s, -e) *m* twin; **Zwillinge** *pl*
(*ASTROL*) Gemini.
zwingen ['tsviŋən] *unreg vt* to force.
zwingend *adj* (*Grund etc*) compelling; (*logisch
notwendig*) necessary; (*Schluss, Beweis*)
conclusive.
Zwinger (-s, -) *m* (*Käfig*) cage; (*Hunde~*) run.
zwinkern ['tsviŋkərn] *vi* to blink; (*absichtlich*)

to wink.
Zwirn [tsvirn] (-(e)s, -e) *m* thread.
zwischen ['tsviʃən] *präp* (+*akk od dat*)
between; (*bei mehreren*) among;
Z~**aufenthalt** *m* stopover; Z~**bemerkung** *f*
(incidental) remark; Z~**bilanz** *f* (*COMM*)
interim balance; ~**blenden** *vt* (*FILM, RUNDF,
TV*) to insert; Z~**ding** *nt* cross; Z~**dividende** *f*
interim dividend; ~**durch** *adv* in between;
(*räumlich*) here and there; Z~**ergebnis** *nt*
intermediate result; Z~**fall** *m* incident;
Z~**frage** *f* question; Z~**größe** *f* in-between
size; Z~**handel** *m* wholesaling; Z~**händler** *m*
middleman, agent; Z~**lagerung** *f* temporary
storage; Z~**landung** *f* (*AVIAT*) stopover;
Z~**lösung** *f* temporary solution; ~**mahlzeit** *f*
snack (*between meals*); ~**menschlich** *adj*
interpersonal; Z~**prüfung** *f* intermediate
examination; Z~**raum** *m* gap, space; Z~**ruf** *m*
interjection, interruption; **Zwischenrufe** *pl*
heckling *sing*; Z~**saison** *f* low season; Z~**spiel**
nt (*THEAT, fig*) interlude; (*MUS*) intermezzo;
~**staatlich** *adj* interstate; (*international*)
international; Z~**station** *f* intermediate
station; Z~**stecker** *m* (*ELEK*) adapter;
Z~**stück** *nt* connecting piece; Z~**summe** *f*
subtotal; Z~**wand** *f* partition; Z~**zeit** *f*
interval; **in der Z~zeit** in the interim,
meanwhile; Z~**zeugnis** *nt* (*SCH*) interim
report.
Zwist [tsvist] (-es, -e) *m* dispute.
zwitschern ['tsvitʃərn] *vt, vi* to twitter, chirp;
einen ~ (*umg*) to have a drink.
Zwitter ['tsvitər] (-s, -) *m* hermaphrodite.
zwo [tsvo:] *num* (*TEL, MIL*) two.
zwölf [tsvœlf] *num* twelve; **fünf Minuten vor ~**
(*fig*) at the eleventh hour.
Zwölffingerdarm *m* duodenum.
Zyankali [tsya:n'ka:li] (-s) *nt* (*CHEM*)
potassium cyanide.
Zyklon [tsy'klo:n] (-s, -e) *m* cyclone.
Zyklus ['tsy:klus] (-, **Zyklen**) *m* cycle.
Zylinder [tsi'lindər] (-s, -) *m* cylinder; (*Hut*) top
hat; z~**förmig** *adj* cylindrical.
Zyniker(in) ['tsy:nikər(in)] (-s, -) *m(f)* cynic.
zynisch ['tsy:niʃ] *adj* cynical.
Zynismus [tsy'nismus] *m* cynicism.
Zypern ['tsy:pərn] (-s) *nt* Cyprus.
Zypresse [tsy'presə] (-, -n) *f* (*BOT*) cypress.
Zypriot(in) [tsypri'o:t(in)] (-en, -en) *m(f)*
Cypriot.
zypriotisch *adj* Cypriot, Cyprian.
zyprisch ['tsy:priʃ] *adj* Cypriot, Cyprian.
Zyste ['tsystə] (-, -n) *f* cyst.
zz., zzt. *abk* = **zurzeit.**
z. Z(t). *abk* = **zur Zeit.**

A, a

A¹, a [eɪ] n (letter) A nt, a nt; (SCOL) ≈ Eins f, sehr gut nt; ~ **for Andrew, (US)** ~ **for Able** ≈ A wie Anton; ~ **road** (BRIT: AUT) Hauptverkehrsstraße f; ~ **shares** (BRIT: STOCK EXCHANGE) stimmrechtslose Aktien pl.

A² [eɪ] n (MUS) A nt, a nt.

a [ə] (before vowel or silent h: **an**) indef art **1** ein; (before feminine noun) eine; ~ **book** ein Buch; ~ **lamp** eine Lampe; **she's** ~ **doctor** sie ist Ärztin; **I haven't got** ~ **car** ich habe kein Auto; ~ **hundred/thousand** etc **pounds** einhundert/eintausend etc Pfund.
2 (in expressing ratios, prices etc) pro; **3** ~ **day/week** 3 pro Tag/Woche, 3 am Tag/in der Woche; **10 km an hour** 10 km pro Stunde.

a. abbr = **acre**.
A2 (BRIT) n (SCOL) Mit "A2" wird das zweite Jahr der britischen Sekundarstufe II bezeichnet, in dem die übrigen drei Wahlpflichtfächer unterrichtet und am Ende des Schuljahres geprüft werden. Die Note für den "A level" setzt sich aus den Noten der Jahre "AS" und "A2" zusammen.
AA n abbr (BRIT: = Automobile Association) Autofahrerorganisation, ≈ ADAC m; (US: = Associate in/of Arts) akademischer Grad für Geisteswissenschaftler; (= Alcoholics Anonymous) Anonyme Alkoholiker pl, AA pl.
AAA n abbr (= American Automobile Association) Autofahrerorganisation, ≈ ADAC m; (BRIT: = Amateur Athletics Association) Leichtathletikverband der Amateure.
A & R n abbr (MUS: = artists and repertoire): ~ **person** Talentsucher(in) m(f).
abaci ['æbəsaɪ] npl of **abacus**.
aback [ə'bæk] adv: **to be taken** ~ verblüfft sein.
abacus ['æbəkəs] (pl **abaci**) n Abakus m.
abandon [ə'bændən] vt verlassen; (child) aussetzen; (give up) aufgeben ♦ n (wild behaviour): **with** ~ selbstvergessen; **to** ~ **ship** das Schiff verlassen.

abandoned [ə'bændənd] adj verlassen; (child) ausgesetzt; (unrestrained) selbstvergessen.
abase [ə'beɪs] vt: **to** ~ **o.s.** sich erniedrigen; **to** ~ **o.s. so far as to do sth** sich dazu erniedrigen, etw zu tun.
abashed [ə'bæʃt] adj verlegen.
abate [ə'beɪt] vi nachlassen, sich legen.
abatement [ə'beɪtmənt] n: **noise** ~ **society** Gesellschaft f zur Lärmbekämpfung.
abattoir ['æbətwɑːʳ] (BRIT) n Schlachthof m.
abbey ['æbɪ] n Abtei f.
abbot ['æbət] n Abt m.
abbreviate [ə'briːvɪeɪt] vt abkürzen; (essay etc) kürzen.
abbreviation [əbriːvɪ'eɪʃən] n Abkürzung f.
ABC n abbr (= American Broadcasting Companies) Fernsehsender.
abdicate ['æbdɪkeɪt] vt verzichten auf +acc ♦ vi (monarch) abdanken.
abdication [æbdɪ'keɪʃən] n (see vb) Verzicht m; Abdankung f.
abdomen ['æbdəmən] n Unterleib m.
abdominal [æb'dɔmɪnl] adj (pain etc) Unterleibs-.
abduct [æb'dʌkt] vt entführen.
abduction [æb'dʌkʃən] n Entführung f.
Aberdonian [æbə'dəʊnɪən] adj (GEOG) Aberdeener inv ♦ n Aberdeener(in) m(f).
aberration [æbə'reɪʃən] n Anomalie f; **in a moment of mental** ~ in einem Augenblick geistiger Verwirrung.
abet [ə'bet] vt see **aid**.
abeyance [ə'beɪəns] n: **in** ~ (law) außer Kraft; (matter) ruhend.
abhor [əb'hɔːʳ] vt verabscheuen.
abhorrent [əb'hɔrənt] adj abscheulich.
abide [ə'baɪd] vt: **I can't** ~ **it/him** ich kann es/ ihn nicht ausstehen.
▶ **abide by** vt fus sich halten an +acc.
abiding [ə'baɪdɪŋ] adj (memory, impression) bleibend.
ability [ə'bɪlɪtɪ] n Fähigkeit f; **to the best of my** ~ so gut ich es kann.
abject ['æbdʒekt] adj (poverty) bitter; (apology) demütig; (coward) erbärmlich.
ablaze [ə'bleɪz] adj in Flammen; ~ **with light**

hell erleuchtet.

able ['eɪbl] *adj* fähig; **to be ~ to do sth** etw tun können.

able-bodied ['eɪbl'bɔdɪd] *adj* kräftig; **~ seaman** (*BRIT*) Vollmatrose *m*.

ablutions [ə'bluːʃənz] *npl* Waschungen *pl*.

ably ['eɪblɪ] *adv* gekonnt.

ABM *n abbr* (= *antiballistic missile*) Anti-Raketen-Rakete *f*.

abnormal [æb'nɔːməl] *adj* abnorm; (*child*) anormal.

abnormality [æbnɔː'mælɪtɪ] *n* Abnormität *f*.

aboard [ə'bɔːd] *adv* (*NAUT*, *AVIAT*) an Bord ♦ *prep* an Bord +*gen*; **~ the train/bus** im Zug/Bus.

abode [ə'bəʊd] *n* (*LAW*): **of no fixed ~** ohne festen Wohnsitz.

abolish [ə'bɔlɪʃ] *vt* abschaffen.

abolition [æbə'lɪʃən] *n* Abschaffung *f*.

abominable [ə'bɔmɪnəbl] *adj* scheußlich.

abominably [ə'bɔmɪnəblɪ] *adv* scheußlich.

Aborigine [æbə'rɪdʒɪnɪ] *n* Ureinwohner(in) *m(f)* Australiens.

abort [ə'bɔːt] *vt* abtreiben; (*MED*: *miscarry*) fehlgebären; (*COMPUT*) abbrechen.

abortion [ə'bɔːʃən] *n* Abtreibung *f*; (*miscarriage*) Fehlgeburt *f*; **to have an ~** abtreiben lassen.

abortionist [ə'bɔːʃənɪst] *n* Abtreibungshelfer(in) *m(f)*.

abortive [ə'bɔːtɪv] *adj* misslungen.

abound [ə'baʊnd] *vi* im Überfluss vorhanden sein; **to ~ in** *or* **with** reich sein an +*dat*.

———————————— *KEYWORD*

about [ə'baʊt] *adv* **1** (*approximately*) etwa, ungefähr; **~ a hundred/thousand** *etc* etwa hundert/tausend *etc*; **at ~ 2 o'clock** etwa um 2 Uhr; **I've just ~ finished** ich bin gerade fertig.

2 (*referring to place*) herum; **to run/walk** *etc* **~** herumlaufen/-gehen *etc*; **is Paul ~?** ist Paul da?

3: **to be ~ to do sth** im Begriff sein, etw zu tun; **he was ~ to cry** er fing fast an zu weinen; **she was ~ to leave/wash the dishes** sie wollte gerade gehen/das Geschirr spülen

♦ *prep* **1** (*relating to*) über +*acc*; **what is it ~?** worum geht es?; (*book etc*) wovon handelt es?; **we talked ~ it** wir haben darüber geredet; **what** *or* **how ~ going to the cinema?** wollen wir ins Kino gehen?

2 (*referring to place*) um ... herum; **to walk ~ the town** durch die Stadt gehen; **her clothes were scattered ~ the room** ihre Kleider waren über das ganze Zimmer verstreut.

———————————

about-face [ə'baʊt'feɪs] (*US*) *n* = **about-turn**.

about-turn [ə'baʊt'tɔːn] (*BRIT*) *n* Kehrtwendung *f*.

above [ə'bʌv] *adv* oben; (*greater, more*) darüber ♦ *prep* über +*dat*; **to cost ~ £10** mehr als £10 kosten; **mentioned ~** oben genannt; **he's not ~ a bit of blackmail** er ist sich *dat* nicht zu gut für eine kleine Erpressung; **~ all** vor allem.

above board *adj* korrekt.

abrasion [ə'breɪʒən] *n* Abschürfung *f*.

abrasive [ə'breɪzɪv] *adj* (*substance*) Scheuer-; (*person, manner*) aggressiv.

abreast [ə'brest] *adv* nebeneinander; **three ~** zu dritt nebeneinander; **to keep ~ of** (*fig*) auf dem Laufenden bleiben mit.

abridge [ə'brɪdʒ] *vt* kürzen.

abroad [ə'brɔːd] *adv* (*be*) im Ausland; (*go*) ins Ausland; **there is a rumour ~ that ...** (*fig*) ein Gerücht geht um *or* kursiert, dass ...

abrupt [ə'brʌpt] *adj* abrupt; (*person, behaviour*) schroff.

abruptly [ə'brʌptlɪ] *adv* abrupt.

abscess ['æbsɪs] *n* Abszess *m*.

abscond [əb'skɔnd] *vi*: **to ~ with** sich davonmachen mit; **to ~ (from)** fliehen (aus).

abseil ['æbseɪl] *vi* sich abseilen.

absence ['æbsəns] *n* Abwesenheit *f*; **in the ~ of** (*person*) in Abwesenheit +*gen*; (*thing*) in Ermangelung +*gen*.

absent ['æbsənt] *adj* abwesend, nicht da ♦ *vt*: **to ~ o.s. from** fernbleiben +*dat*; **to be ~** fehlen; **to be ~ without leave** (*MIL*) sich unerlaubt von der Truppe entfernen.

absentee [æbsən'tiː] *n* Abwesende(r) *f(m)*.

absenteeism [æbsən'tiːɪzəm] *n* (*from school*) Schwänzen *nt*; (*from work*) Nichterscheinen *nt* am Arbeitsplatz.

absent-minded ['æbsənt'maɪndɪd] *adj* zerstreut.

absent-mindedly ['æbsənt'maɪndɪdlɪ] *adv* zerstreut; (*look*) abwesend.

absent-mindedness ['æbsənt'maɪndɪdnɪs] *n* Zerstreutheit *f*.

absolute ['æbsəluːt] *adj* absolut; (*power*) uneingeschränkt.

absolutely [æbsə'luːtlɪ] *adv* absolut; (*agree*) vollkommen; **~!** genau!

absolution [æbsə'luːʃən] *n* Lossprechung *f*.

absolve [əb'zɔlv] *vt*: **to ~ sb (from)** jdn lossprechen (von); (*responsibility*) jdn entbinden (von).

absorb [əb'zɔːb] *vt* aufnehmen (*also fig*); (*light, heat*) absorbieren; (*group, business*) übernehmen; **to be ~ed in a book** in ein Buch vertieft sein.

absorbent [əb'zɔːbənt] *adj* saugfähig.

absorbent cotton (*US*) *n* Watte *f*.

absorbing [əb'zɔːbɪŋ] *adj* saugfähig; (*book, film, work etc*) fesselnd.

absorption [əb'sɔːpʃən] *n* (*see vb*) Aufnahme *f*; Absorption *f*; Übernahme *f*; (*interest*) Faszination *f*.

abstain [əb'steɪn] *vi* (*voting*) sich (der Stimme) enthalten; **to ~ (from)** (*eating,* *drinking etc*) sich enthalten (+*gen*).

abstemious [əb'stiːmɪəs] *adj* enthaltsam.

abstention [əb'stɛnʃən] *n* (Stimm)enthaltung *f*.

abstinence ['æbstɪnəns] *n* Enthaltsamkeit *f*.

abstract ['æbstrækt] *adj* abstrakt ♦ *n* (*summary*) Zusammenfassung *f* ♦ *vt*: **to ~ sth (from)** (*summarize*) etw entnehmen (aus); (*remove*) etw entfernen (aus).

abstruse [æb'struːs] *adj* abstrus.

absurd [əb'səːd] *adj* absurd.

absurdity [əb'səːdɪtɪ] *n* Absurdität *f*.

ABTA ['æbtə] *n abbr* (= *Association of British Travel Agents*) *Verband der Reiseveranstalter.*

Abu Dhabi ['æbuː'dɑːbɪ] *n* (*GEOG*) Abu Dhabi *nt*.

abundance [ə'bʌndəns] *n* Reichtum *m*; **an ~ of** eine Fülle von; **in ~** in Hülle und Fülle.

abundant [ə'bʌndənt] *adj* reichlich.

abundantly [ə'bʌndəntlɪ] *adv* reichlich; **~ clear** völlig klar.

abuse [ə'bjuːs] *n* (*insults*) Beschimpfungen *pl*; (*ill-treatment*) Misshandlung *f*, (*misuse*) Missbrauch *m* ♦ *vt* (*see n*) beschimpfen; misshandeln; missbrauchen; **to be open to ~** sich leicht missbrauchen lassen.

abuser [ə'bjuːzə*] *n* (*drug abuser*) jd, der Drogen missbraucht; (*child abuser*) jd, der Kinder missbraucht oder misshandelt.

abusive [ə'bjuːsɪv] *adj* beleidigend.

abysmal [ə'bɪzməl] *adj* entsetzlich; (*ignorance etc*) grenzenlos.

abysmally [ə'bɪzməlɪ] *adv* (*see adj*) entsetzlich; grenzenlos.

abyss [ə'bɪs] *n* Abgrund *m*.

AC *abbr* = **alternating current**; (*US*: = *athletic club*) ≈ SV *m*.

a/c *abbr* (*BANKING etc*) = **account** (= *account current*) Girokonto *nt*.

academic [ækə'dɛmɪk] *adj* akademisch (*also pej*); (*work*) wissenschaftlich; (*person*) intellektuell ♦ *n* Akademiker(in) *m(f)*.

academic year *n* (*university year*) Universitätsjahr *nt*; (*school year*) Schuljahr *nt*.

academy [ə'kædəmɪ] *n* Akademie *f*; (*school*) Hochschule *f*; **~ of music** Musikhochschule *f*; **military/naval ~** Militär-/Marineakademie *f*.

ACAS ['eɪkæs] (*BRIT*) *n abbr* (= *Advisory, Conciliation and Arbitration Service*) *Schlichtungsstelle für Arbeitskonflikte.*

accede [æk'siːd] *vi*: **to ~ to** zustimmen +*dat*.

accelerate [æk'sɛləreɪt] *vt* beschleunigen ♦ *vi* (*AUT*) Gas geben.

acceleration [æksɛlə'reɪʃən] *n* Beschleunigung *f*.

accelerator [æk'sɛləreɪtə*] *n* Gaspedal *nt*.

accent ['æksɛnt] *n* Akzent *m*; (*fig: emphasis, stress*) Betonung *f*; **to speak with an Irish ~** mit einem irischen Akzent sprechen; **to**

have a strong ~ einen starken Akzent haben.

accentuate [æk'sɛntjueɪt] *vt* betonen; (*need, difference etc*) hervorheben.

accept [ək'sɛpt] *vt* annehmen; (*fact, situation*) sich abfinden mit; (*risk*) in Kauf nehmen; (*responsibility*) übernehmen; (*blame*) auf sich *acc* nehmen.

acceptable [ək'sɛptəbl] *adj* annehmbar.

acceptance [ək'sɛptəns] *n* Annahme *f*; **to meet with general ~** allgemeine Anerkennung finden.

access ['æksɛs] *n* Zugang *m* ♦ *vt* (*COMPUT*) zugreifen auf +*dat*; **the burglars gained ~ through a window** die Einbrecher gelangten durch ein Fenster hinein.

accessible [æk'sɛsəbl] *adj* erreichbar; (*knowledge, art etc*) zugänglich.

accession [æk'sɛʃən] *n* Antritt *m*; (*of monarch*) Thronbesteigung *f*; (*to library*) Neuanschaffung *f*.

accessory [æk'sɛsərɪ] *n* Zubehörteil *nt*; (*DRESS*) Accessoire *nt*; (*LAW*): **~ to** Mitschuldige(r) *f(m)* an +*dat*; **accessories** *npl* Zubehör *nt*; **toilet accessories** (*BRIT*) Toilettenartikel *pl*.

access road *n* Zufahrt(sstraße) *f*.

access time *n* (*COMPUT*) Zugriffszeit *f*.

accident ['æksɪdənt] *n* Zufall *m*; (*mishap, disaster*) Unfall *m*; **to meet with** *or* **to have an ~** einen Unfall haben, verunglücken; **~s at work** Arbeitsunfälle *pl*; **by ~** zufällig.

accidental [æksɪ'dɛntl] *adj* zufällig; (*death, damage*) Unfall-.

accidentally [æksɪ'dɛntəlɪ] *adv* zufällig.

accident insurance *n* Unfallversicherung *f*.

accident-prone ['æksɪdənt'prəun] *adj* vom Pech verfolgt.

acclaim [ə'kleɪm] *n* Beifall *m* ♦ *vt*: **to be ~ed for one's achievements** für seine Leistungen gefeiert werden.

acclamation [æklə'meɪʃən] *n* Anerkennung *f*; (*applause*) Beifall *m*.

acclimate [ə'klaɪmət] (*US*) *vt* = **acclimatize**.

acclimatize [ə'klaɪmətaɪz], (*US*) **acclimate** [ə'klaɪmət] *vt*: **to become ~d** sich akklimatisieren; **to become ~d to** sich gewöhnen an +*acc*.

accolade ['ækəleɪd] *n* (*fig*) Auszeichnung *f*.

accommodate [ə'kɔmədeɪt] *vt* unterbringen; (*subj: car, hotel etc*) Platz bieten +*dat*; (*oblige, help*) entgegenkommen +*dat*; **to ~ one's plans to** seine Pläne anpassen an +*acc*.

accommodating [ə'kɔmədeɪtɪŋ] *adj* entgegenkommend.

accommodation [əkɔmə'deɪʃən] *n* Unterkunft *f*; **accommodations** (*US*) *npl* Unterkunft *f*; **have you any ~?** haben Sie eine Unterkunft?; **"~ to let"** „Zimmer zu vermieten"; **they have ~ for 500** sie können 500 Personen unterbringen; **the hall has seating ~ for 600** (*BRIT*) in dem Saal können

600 Personen sitzen.

accompaniment [ə'kʌmpənɪmənt] n Begleitung f.

accompanist [ə'kʌmpənɪst] n Begleiter(in) m(f).

accompany [ə'kʌmpənɪ] vt begleiten.

accomplice [ə'kʌmplɪs] n Komplize m, Komplizin f.

accomplish [ə'kʌmplɪʃ] vt vollenden; (achieve) erreichen.

accomplished [ə'kʌmplɪʃt] adj ausgezeichnet.

accomplishment [ə'kʌmplɪʃmənt] n Vollendung f; (achievement) Leistung f; (skill: gen pl) Fähigkeit f.

accord [ə'kɔːd] n Übereinstimmung f; (treaty) Vertrag m ♦ vt gewähren; **of his own ~** freiwillig; **with one ~** geschlossen; **to be in ~** übereinstimmen.

accordance [ə'kɔːdəns] n: **in ~ with** in Übereinstimmung mit.

according [ə'kɔːdɪŋ] prep: **~ to** zufolge +dat; **~ to plan** wie geplant.

accordingly [ə'kɔːdɪŋlɪ] adv entsprechend; (as a result) folglich.

accordion [ə'kɔːdɪən] n Akkordeon nt.

accost [ə'kɒst] vt ansprechen.

account [ə'kaunt] n (COMM: bill) Rechnung f; (in bank, department store) Konto nt; (report) Bericht m; **accounts** npl (COMM) Buchhaltung f; (BOOKKEEPING) (Geschäfts)bücher pl; **"~ payee only"** (BRIT) „nur zur Verrechnung"; **to keep an ~ of** Buch führen über +acc; **to bring sb to ~ for sth/for having embezzled £50,000** jdn für etw/für die Unterschlagung von £50.000 zur Rechenschaft ziehen; **by all ~s** nach allem, was man hört; **of no ~** ohne Bedeutung; **on ~** auf Kredit; **to pay £5 on ~** eine Anzahlung von £5 leisten; **on no ~** auf keinen Fall; **on ~ of** wegen +gen; **to take into ~, take ~ of** berücksichtigen.

▶ **account for** vt fus erklären; (expenditure) Rechenschaft ablegen für; (represent) ausmachen; **all the children were ~ed for** man wusste, wo alle Kinder waren; **4 people are still not ~ed for** 4 Personen werden immer noch vermisst.

accountability [əkauntə'bɪlɪtɪ] n Verantwortlichkeit f.

accountable [ə'kauntəbl] adj: **~ (to)** verantwortlich (gegenüber +dat); **to be held ~ for sth** für etw verantwortlich gemacht werden.

accountancy [ə'kauntənsɪ] n Buchhaltung f.

accountant [ə'kauntənt] n Buchhalter(in) m(f).

accounting [ə'kauntɪŋ] n Buchhaltung f.

accounting period n Abrechnungszeitraum m.

account number n Kontonummer f.

accounts payable npl Verbindlichkeiten pl.

accounts receivable npl Forderungen pl.

accredited [ə'krɛdɪtɪd] adj anerkannt.

accretion [ə'kriːʃən] n Ablagerung f.

accrue [ə'kruː] vi sich ansammeln; **to ~ to** zufließen +dat.

accrued interest n aufgelaufene Zinsen pl.

accumulate [ə'kjuːmjuleɪt] vt ansammeln ♦ vi sich ansammeln.

accumulation [əkjuːmju'leɪʃən] n Ansammlung f.

accuracy ['ækjʊrəsɪ] n Genauigkeit f.

accurate ['ækjʊrɪt] adj genau.

accurately ['ækjʊrɪtlɪ] adv genau; (answer) richtig.

accusation [ækjuː'zeɪʃən] n Vorwurf m; (instance) Beschuldigung f; (LAW) Anklage f.

accusative [ə'kjuːzətɪv] n Akkusativ m.

accuse [ə'kjuːz] vt: **to ~ sb (of sth)** jdn (einer Sache gen) beschuldigen; (LAW) jdn (wegen etw dat) anklagen.

accused [ə'kjuːzd] n (LAW): **the ~** der/die Angeklagte.

accuser [ə'kjuːzə] n Ankläger(in) m(f).

accusing [ə'kjuːzɪŋ] adj anklagend.

accustom [ə'kʌstəm] vt gewöhnen; **to ~ o.s. to sth** sich an etw acc gewöhnen.

accustomed [ə'kʌstəmd] adj gewohnt; (in the habit): **~ to** gewohnt an +acc.

AC/DC abbr (= alternating current/direct current) WS/GS.

ACE [eɪs] n abbr (= American Council on Education) akademischer Verband für das Erziehungswesen.

ace [eɪs] n As nt.

acerbic [ə'səːbɪk] adj scharf.

acetate ['æsɪteɪt] n Acetat nt.

ache [eɪk] n Schmerz m ♦ vi schmerzen, wehtun; (yearn): **to ~ to do sth** sich danach sehnen, etw zu tun; **I've got (a) stomach ~** ich habe Magenschmerzen; **I'm aching all over** mir tut alles weh; **my head ~s** mir tut der Kopf weh.

achieve [ə'tʃiːv] vt (aim, result) erreichen; (success) erzielen; (victory) erringen.

achievement [ə'tʃiːvmənt] n (act of achieving) Erreichen nt; (success, feat) Leistung f.

Achilles heel [ə'kɪliːz-] n Achillesferse f.

acid ['æsɪd] adj sauer ♦ n (CHEM) Säure f; (inf: LSD) Acid nt.

Acid House n Acid House nt, elektronische Funk-Diskomusik.

acidic [ə'sɪdɪk] adj sauer.

acidity [ə'sɪdɪtɪ] n Säure f.

acid rain n saurer Regen m.

acid test n (fig) Feuerprobe f.

acknowledge [ək'nɒlɪdʒ] vt (also: **~ receipt of**) den Empfang +gen bestätigen; (fact) zugeben; (situation) zur Kenntnis nehmen; (person) grüßen.

acknowledgement [ək'nɒlɪdʒmənt] n Empfangsbestätigung f; **acknowledgements** npl (in book) ≈ Danksagung f.

ACLU n abbr (= American Civil Liberties Union) Bürgerrechtsverband.

acme ['ækmɪ] n Gipfel m, Höhepunkt m.
acne ['æknɪ] n Akne f.
acorn ['eɪkɔːn] n Eichel f.
acoustic [ə'kuːstɪk] adj akustisch.
acoustic coupler n (COMPUT)
Akustikkoppler m.
acoustics [ə'kuːstɪks] n Akustik f.
acoustic screen n Trennwand f zur
Schalldämpfung.
acquaint [ə'kweɪnt] vt: **to ~ sb with sth** jdn
mit etw vertraut machen; **to be ~ed with**
(person) bekannt sein mit; (fact) vertraut
sein mit.
acquaintance [ə'kweɪntəns] n Bekannte(r)
f(m); (with person) Bekanntschaft f; (with
subject) Kenntnis f; **to make sb's ~** jds
Bekanntschaft machen.
acquiesce [ækwɪ'ɛs] vi einwilligen; **to ~ (to)**
(demand, arrangement, request) einwilligen
(in +acc).
acquire [ə'kwaɪə*] vt erwerben; (interest)
entwickeln; (habit) annehmen.
acquired [ə'kwaɪəd] adj erworben; **whisky is
an ~ taste** man muss sich an Whisky erst
gewöhnen.
acquisition [ækwɪ'zɪʃən] n (see vb) Erwerb m,
Entwicklung f, Annahme f; (thing acquired)
Errungenschaft f.
acquisitive [ə'kwɪzɪtɪv] adj habgierig; **the
~ society** die Erwerbsgesellschaft.
acquit [ə'kwɪt] vt freisprechen; **to ~ o.s. well**
seine Sache gut machen.
acquittal [ə'kwɪtl] n Freispruch m.
acre ['eɪkə*] n Morgen m.
acreage ['eɪkərɪdʒ] n Fläche f.
acrid ['ækrɪd] adj bitter; (smoke, fig) beißend.
acrimonious [ækrɪ'məʊnɪəs] adj bitter;
(dispute) erbittert.
acrimony ['ækrɪmənɪ] n Erbitterung f.
acrobat ['ækrəbæt] n Akrobat(in) m(f).
acrobatic [ækrə'bætɪk] adj akrobatisch.
acrobatics [ækrə'bætɪks] npl Akrobatik f.
acronym ['ækrənɪm] n Akronym nt.
Acropolis [ə'krɔpəlɪs] n: **the ~** (GEOG) die
Akropolis.
across [ə'krɔs] prep über +acc; (on the other side
of) auf der anderen Seite +gen ♦ adv
(direction) hinüber, herüber; (measurement)
breit; **to take sb ~ the road** jdn über die
Straße bringen; **a road ~ the wood** eine
Straße durch den Wald; **the lake is 12 km ~**
der See ist 12 km breit; **~ from** gegenüber
+dat; **to get sth ~ (to sb)** (jdm) etw
klarmachen.
acrylic [ə'krɪlɪk] adj (acid, paint, blanket) Acryl-
♦ n Acryl nt; **acrylics** npl: **he paints in ~s** er
malt mit Acrylfarbe.
ACT n abbr (= American College Test)
Eignungstest für Studienbewerber.
act [ækt] n Tat f; (of play) Akt m; (in a show etc)
Nummer f; (LAW) Gesetz nt ♦ vi handeln;
(behave) sich verhalten; (have effect) wirken;

(THEAT) spielen ♦ vt spielen; **it's only an ~**
es ist nur Schau; **~ of God** (LAW) höhere
Gewalt f; **to be in the ~ of doing sth** dabei
sein, etw zu tun; **to catch sb in the ~** jdn auf
frischer Tat ertappen; **to ~ the fool** (BRIT)
herumalbern; **he is only ~ing** er tut (doch)
nur so; **to ~ as** fungieren als; **it ~s as a
deterrent** es dient zur Abschreckung.
► **act on** vt: **to ~ on sth** (take action) auf etw
+acc hin handeln.
► **act out** vt (event) durchspielen; (fantasies)
zum Ausdruck bringen.
acting ['æktɪŋ] adj stellvertretend ♦ n
(profession) Schauspielkunst f; (activity)
Spielen nt; **~ in my capacity as chairman ...**
in meiner Eigenschaft als Vorsitzender ...
action ['ækʃən] n Tat f; (motion) Bewegung f;
(MIL) Kampf m, Gefecht nt; (LAW) Klage f; **to
bring an ~ against sb** (LAW) eine Klage
gegen jdn anstrengen; **killed in ~** (MIL)
gefallen; **out of ~** (person) nicht
einsatzfähig; (thing) außer Betrieb; **to take
~** etwas unternehmen; **to put a plan into ~**
einen Plan in die Tat umsetzen.
action replay n (TV) Wiederholung f.
activate ['æktɪveɪt] vt in Betrieb setzen;
(CHEM, PHYS) aktivieren.
active ['æktɪv] adj aktiv; (volcano) tätig; **to
play an ~ part in sth** sich aktiv an etw dat
beteiligen.
active duty (US) n (MIL) Einsatz m.
actively ['æktɪvlɪ] adv aktiv; (dislike) offen.
active partner n (COMM) aktiver Teilhaber
m.
active service (BRIT) n (MIL) Einsatz m.
active suspension n (AUT) aktives or
computergesteuertes Fahrwerk nt.
activist ['æktɪvɪst] n Aktivist(in) m(f).
activity [æk'tɪvɪtɪ] n Aktivität f; (pastime,
pursuit) Betätigung f.
activity holiday n Aktivurlaub m.
actor ['æktə*] n Schauspieler m.
actress ['æktrɪs] n Schauspielerin f.
actual ['æktjuəl] adj wirklich; (emphatic use)
eigentlich.
actually ['æktjuəlɪ] adv wirklich; (in fact)
tatsächlich; (even) sogar.
actuary ['æktjuərɪ] n Aktuar m.
actuate ['æktjueɪt] vt auslösen.
acuity [ə'kjuːɪtɪ] n Schärfe f.
acumen ['ækjumən] n Scharfsinn m; **business
~** Geschäftssinn m.
acupuncture ['ækjupʌŋktʃə*] n Akupunktur f.
acute [ə'kjuːt] adj akut; (anxiety) heftig; (mind)
scharf; (person) scharfsinnig; (MATH: angle)
spitz; (LING): **~ accent** Akut m.
AD adv abbr (= Anno Domini) n. Chr. ♦ n abbr
(US: MIL) = **active duty**.
ad [æd] (inf) n abbr = **advertisement**.
adage ['ædɪdʒ] n Sprichwort nt.
adamant ['ædəmənt] adj: **to be ~ that ...**
darauf bestehen, dass ...; **to be ~ about sth**

auf etw *dat* bestehen.
Adam's apple ['ædəmz-] *n* Adamsapfel *m*.
adapt [ə'dæpt] *vt* anpassen; (*novel etc*)
bearbeiten ♦ *vi*: **to ~ (to)** sich anpassen (an
+acc).
adaptability [ədæptə'bɪlɪtɪ] *n*
Anpassungsfähigkeit *f*.
adaptable [ə'dæptəbl] *adj* anpassungsfähig;
(*device*) vielseitig.
adaptation [ædæp'teɪʃən] *n* (*of novel etc*)
Bearbeitung *f*; (*of machine etc*) Umstellung *f*.
adapter [ə'dæptə*] *n* (*ELEC*) Adapter *m*; (: *for
several plugs*) Mehrfachsteckdose *f*.
adaptor [ə'dæptə*] *n* = **adapter**.
ADC *n abbr* (*MIL*) = **aide-de-camp**; (*US*: = *Aid to
Dependent Children*) *Beihilfe für
sozialschwache Familien*.
add [æd] *vt* hinzufügen; (*figures: also*: **~ up**)
zusammenzählen ♦ *vi*: **to ~ to** (*increase*)
beitragen zu.
▶ **add on** *vt* (*amount*) dazurechnen; (*room*)
anbauen.
▶ **add up** *vt* (*figures*) zusammenzählen ♦ *vi*
(*fig*): **it doesn't ~ up** es ergibt keinen Sinn; **it
doesn't ~ up to much** (*fig*) das ist nicht
berühmt (*inf*).
addenda [ə'dɛndə] *npl of* **addendum**.
addendum [ə'dɛndəm] (*pl* **addenda**) *n*
Nachtrag *m*.
adder ['ædə*] *n* Kreuzotter *f*, Viper *f*.
addict ['ædɪkt] *n* Süchtige(r) *f(m)*; (*enthusiast*)
Anhänger(in) *m(f)*.
addicted [ə'dɪktɪd] *adj*: **to be ~ to drugs/drink**
drogensüchtig/alkoholsüchtig sein; **to be
~ to football** (*fig*) ohne Fußball nicht mehr
leben können.
addiction [ə'dɪkʃən] *n* Sucht *f*.
addictive [ə'dɪktɪv] *adj*: **to be ~** (*drug*) süchtig
machen; (*activity*) zur Sucht werden können.
adding machine ['ædɪŋ-] *n* Addiermaschine *f*.
Addis Ababa ['ædɪs'æbəbə] *n* (*GEOG*) Addis
Abeba *nt*.
addition [ə'dɪʃən] *n* (*adding up*)
Zusammenzählen *nt*; (*thing added*) Zusatz *m*;
(: *to payment, bill*) Zuschlag *m*; (: *to building*)
Anbau *m*; **in ~ (to)** zusätzlich (zu).
additional [ə'dɪʃənl] *adj* zusätzlich.
additive ['ædɪtɪv] *n* Zusatz *m*.
addled ['ædld] *adj* (*BRIT*: *egg*) faul; (*brain*)
verwirrt.
address [ə'drɛs] *n* Adresse *f*; (*speech*)
Ansprache *f* ♦ *vt* adressieren; (*speak to*:
person) ansprechen; (: *audience*) sprechen
zu; **form of ~** (Form *f* der) Anrede *f*; **what
form of ~ do you use for ...?** wie redet man
... an?; **absolute/relative ~** (*COMPUT*)
absolute/relative Adresse; **to ~ (o.s. to)**
(*problem*) sich befassen mit.
address book *n* Adressbuch *nt*.
addressee [ædrɛ'si:] *n* Empfänger(in) *m(f)*.
Aden ['eɪdən] *n* (*GEOG*): **Gulf of ~** Golf *m* von
Aden.

adenoids ['ædɪnɔɪdz] *npl* Rachenmandeln *pl*.
adept ['ædɛpt] *adj*: **to be ~ at** gut sein in *+dat*.
adequacy ['ædɪkwəsɪ] *n* (*of resources*)
Adäquatheit *f*; (*of performance, proposals etc*)
Angemessenheit *f*.
adequate ['ædɪkwɪt] *adj* ausreichend,
adäquat; (*satisfactory*) angemessen.
adequately ['ædɪkwɪtlɪ] *adv* ausreichend;
(*satisfactorily*) zufrieden stellend.
adhere [əd'hɪə*] *vi*: **to ~ to** haften an *+dat*; (*fig*:
abide by) sich halten an *+acc*; (: *hold to*)
festhalten an *+dat*.
adhesion [əd'hi:ʒən] *n* Haften *nt*, Haftung *f*.
adhesive [əd'hi:zɪv] *adj* klebend, Klebe- ♦ *n*
Klebstoff *m*.
adhesive tape *n* (*BRIT*) Klebstreifen *m*; (*US*:
MED) Heftpflaster *nt*.
ad hoc [æd'hɔk] *adj* (*committee, decision*) Ad-
hoc- ♦ *adv* ad hoc.
ad infinitum ['ædɪnfɪ'naɪtəm] *adv* ad infinitum.
adjacent [ə'dʒeɪsənt] *adj*: **~ to** neben *+dat*.
adjective ['ædʒɛktɪv] *n* Adjektiv *nt*,
Eigenschaftswort *nt*.
adjoin [ə'dʒɔɪn] *vt*: **the hotel ~ing the station**
das Hotel neben dem Bahnhof.
adjoining [ə'dʒɔɪnɪŋ] *adj* benachbart, Neben-.
adjourn [ə'dʒə:n] *vt* vertagen ♦ *vi* sich
vertagen; **to ~ a meeting till the following
week** eine Besprechung auf die nächste
Woche vertagen; **they ~ed to the pub** (*BRIT*:
inf) sie begaben sich in die Kneipe.
adjournment [ə'dʒə:nmənt] *n* Unterbrechung
f.
Adjt. *abbr* (*MIL*) = **adjutant**.
adjudicate [ə'dʒu:dɪkeɪt] *vt* (*contest*)
Preisrichter sein bei; (*claim*) entscheiden
♦ *vi* entscheiden; **to ~ on** urteilen bei *+dat*.
adjudication [ədʒu:dɪ'keɪʃən] *n* Entscheidung
f.
adjudicator [ə'dju:dɪkeɪtə*] *n*
Schiedsrichter(in) *m(f)*; (*in contest*)
Preisrichter(in) *m(f)*.
adjust [ə'dʒʌst] *vt* anpassen; (*change*) ändern;
(*clothing*) zurechtrücken; (*machine etc*)
einstellen; (*INSURANCE*) regulieren ♦ *vi*: **to
~ (to)** sich anpassen (an *+acc*).
adjustable [ə'dʒʌstəbl] *adj* verstellbar.
adjuster [ə'dʒʌstə*] *n see* **loss**.
adjustment [ə'dʒʌstmənt] *n* Anpassung *f*; (*to
machine*) Einstellung *f*.
adjutant ['ædʒətənt] *n* Adjutant *m*.
ad-lib [æd'lɪb] *vi*, *vt* improvisieren ♦ *adv*: **ad lib**
aus dem Stegreif.
adman ['ædmæn] (*inf: irreg: like* **man**) *n*
Werbefachmann *m*.
admin ['ædmɪn] (*inf*) *n abbr* = **administration**.
administer [əd'mɪnɪstə*] *vt* (*country,
department*) verwalten; (*justice*) sprechen;
(*oath*) abnehmen; (*MED*: *drug*) verabreichen.
administration [ədmɪnɪs'treɪʃən] *n*
(*management*) Verwaltung *f*; (*government*)
Regierung *f*; **the A~** (*US*) die Regierung.

administrative [əd'mınıstrətıv] *adj* (*department, reform etc*) Verwaltungs-.
administrator [əd'mınıstreıtə*] *n* Verwaltungsbeamte(r) *f(m)*.
admirable ['ædmərəbl] *adj* bewundernswert.
admiral ['ædmərəl] *n* Admiral *m*.
Admiralty ['ædmərəltı] (*BRIT*) *n*: **the ~** (*also*: **the ~ Board**) das Marineministerium.
admiration [ædmə'reıʃən] *n* Bewunderung *f*; **to have great ~ for sb/sth** jdn/etw sehr bewundern.
admire [əd'maıə*] *vt* bewundern.
admirer [əd'maıərə*] *n* (*suitor*) Verehrer *m*; (*fan*) Bewunderer *m*, Bewunderin *f*.
admiring [əd'maıərıŋ] *adj* bewundernd.
admissible [əd'mısəbl] *adj* (*evidence, as evidence*) zulässig.
admission [əd'mıʃən] *n* (*admittance*) Zutritt *m*; (*to exhibition, night club etc*) Einlass *m*; (*to club, hospital*) Aufnahme *f*; (*entry fee*) Eintritt(spreis) *m*; (*confession*) Geständnis *nt*; **"~ free"**, **"~ free"** „Eintritt frei"; **by his own ~** nach eigenem Eingeständnis.
admit [əd'mıt] *vt* (*confess*) gestehen; (*permit to enter*) einlassen; (*to club, hospital*) aufnehmen; (*responsibility etc*) anerkennen; **"children not ~ted"** „kein Zutritt für Kinder"; **this ticket ~s two** diese Karte ist für zwei Personen; **I must ~ that ...** ich muss zugeben, dass ...; **to ~ defeat** sich geschlagen geben.
▶ **admit of** *vt fus* (*interpretation etc*) erlauben.
▶ **admit to** *vt fus* (*murder etc*) gestehen.
admittance [əd'mıtəns] *n* Zutritt *m*; **"no ~"** „kein Zutritt".
admittedly [əd'mıtıdlı] *adv* zugegebenermaßen.
admonish [əd'mɒnıʃ] *vt* ermahnen.
ad nauseam [æd'nɔːsıæm] *adv* (*talk*) endlos; (*repeat*) bis zum Gehtnichtmehr (*inf*).
ado [ə'duː] *n*: **without (any) more ~** ohne weitere Umstände.
adolescence [ædəu'lɛsns] *n* Jugend *f*.
adolescent [ædəu'lɛsnt] *adj* heranwachsend; (*remark, behaviour*) pubertär ♦ *n* Jugendliche(r) *f(m)*.
adopt [ə'dɒpt] *vt* adoptieren; (*POL: candidate*) aufstellen; (*policy, attitude, accent*) annehmen.
adopted [ə'dɒptıd] *adj* (*child*) adoptiert.
adoption [ə'dɒpʃən] *n* (*see vb*) Adoption *f*; Aufstellung *f*; Annahme *f*.
adoptive [ə'dɒptıv] *adj* (*parents etc*) Adoptiv-; **~ country** Wahlheimat *f*.
adorable [ə'dɔːrəbl] *adj* entzückend.
adoration [ædə'reıʃən] *n* Verehrung *f*.
adore [ə'dɔː*] *vt* (*person*) verehren; (*film, activity etc*) schwärmen für.
adoring [ə'dɔːrıŋ] *adj* (*fans etc*) ihn/sie bewundernd; (*husband/wife*) sie/ihn innig liebend.
adoringly [ə'dɔːrıŋlı] *adv* bewundernd.

adorn [ə'dɔːn] *vt* schmücken.
adornment [ə'dɔːnmənt] *n* Schmuck *m*.
ADP *n abbr* = **automatic data processing**.
adrenalin [ə'drɛnəlın] *n* Adrenalin *nt*; **it gets the ~ going** das bringt einen in Fahrt.
Adriatic [eıdrı'ætık] *n*: **the ~ (Sea)** (*GEOG*) die Adria, das Adriatische Meer.
adrift [ə'drıft] *adv* (*NAUT*) treibend; (*fig*) ziellos; **to be ~** (*NAUT*) treiben; **to come ~** (*boat*) sich losmachen; (*fastening etc*) sich lösen.
adroit [ə'drɔıt] *adj* gewandt.
adroitly [ə'drɔıtlı] *adv* gewandt.
ADT (*US*) *abbr* (= *Atlantic Daylight Time*) atlantische Sommerzeit.
adulation [ædju'leıʃən] *n* Verherrlichung *f*.
adult ['ædʌlt] *n* Erwachsene(r) *f(m)* ♦ *adj* erwachsen; (*animal*) ausgewachsen; (*literature etc*) für Erwachsene.
adult education *n* Erwachsenenbildung *f*.
adulterate [ə'dʌltəreıt] *vt* verunreinigen; (*with water*) panschen.
adulterer [ə'dʌltərə*] *n* Ehebrecher *m*.
adulteress [ə'dʌltərıs] *n* Ehebrecherin *f*.
adultery [ə'dʌltərı] *n* Ehebruch *m*.
adulthood ['ædʌlthud] *n* Erwachsenenalter *nt*.
advance [əd'vɑːns] *n* (*movement*) Vorrücken *nt*; (*progress*) Fortschritt *m*; (*money*) Vorschuss *m* ♦ *vt* (*money*) vorschießen; (*theory, idea*) vorbringen ♦ *vi* (*move forward*) vorrücken; (*make progress*) Fortschritte machen ♦ *adj*: **~ booking** Vorverkauf *m*; **to make ~s (to sb)** Annäherungsversuche (bei jdm) machen; **in ~** im Voraus; **to give sb ~ notice** jdm frühzeitig Bescheid sagen; **to give sb ~ warning** jdn vorwarnen.
advanced [əd'vɑːnst] *adj* (*SCOL: studies*) für Fortgeschrittene; (*country*) fortgeschritten; (*child*) weit entwickelt; (*ideas*) fortschrittlich; **~ in years** in fortgeschrittenem Alter.
Advanced Higher (*SCOT*) *n* (*SCOL*) Mit "*Advanced Higher*" wird das Ausbildungsjahr nach "*Higher*" bezeichnet dessen erfolgreicher Abschluss eine Hochschulzugangsberechtigung darstellt.
advancement [əd'vɑːnsmənt] *n* (*improvement*) Förderung *f*; (*in job, rank*) Aufstieg *m*.
advantage [əd'vɑːntıdʒ] *n* Vorteil *m*; **to take ~ of** ausnutzen; (*opportunity*) nutzen; **it's to our ~ (to)** es ist für uns von Vorteil(, wenn wir).
advantageous [ædvən'teıdʒəs] *adj*: **~ (to)** vorteilhaft (für), von Vorteil (für).
advent ['ædvɛnt] *n* (*of innovation*) Aufkommen *nt*; (*REL*): **A~** Advent *m*.
Advent calendar *n* Adventskalender *m*.
adventure [əd'vɛntʃə*] *n* Abenteuer *nt*.
adventure playground *n* Abenteuerspielplatz *m*.
adventurous [əd'vɛntʃərəs] *adj* abenteuerlustig; (*bold*) mutig.
adverb ['ædvəːb] *n* Adverb *nt*.
adversarial [ædvə'sɛərıəl] *adj* konfliktreich.

adversary ['ædvəsərı] n Widersacher(in) m(f).

adverse ['ædvɔːs] adj ungünstig; **in ~ circumstances** unter widrigen Umständen; **~ to** ablehnend gegenüber +dat.

adversity [əd'vɔːsıtı] n Widrigkeit f.

advert ['ædvɔːt] (BRIT) n abbr = **advertisement**.

advertise ['ædvətaız] vi (COMM) werben; (in newspaper) annoncieren, inserieren ♦ vt (product, event) werben für; (job) ausschreiben; **to ~ for** (staff, accommodation etc) (per Anzeige) suchen.

advertisement [əd'vɔːtısmənt] n (COMM) Werbung f, Reklame f; (in classified ads) Anzeige f, Inserat nt.

advertiser ['ædvətaızəˀ] n (in newspaper) Inserent(in) m(f); (on television etc) Firma, die im Fernsehen etc wirbt.

advertising ['ædvətaızıŋ] n Werbung f.

advertising agency n Werbeagentur f.

advertising campaign n Werbekampagne f.

advice [əd'vaıs] n Rat m; (notification) Benachrichtigung f, Avis m or nt (COMM); **a piece of ~** ein Rat(schlag); **to ask sb for ~** jdn um Rat fragen; **to take legal ~** einen Rechtsanwalt zurate or zu Rate ziehen.

advice note (BRIT) n (COMM) Avis m or nt.

advisable [əd'vaızəbl] adj ratsam.

advise [əd'vaız] vt (person) raten +dat; (company etc) beraten; **to ~ sb of sth** jdn von etw in Kenntnis setzen; **to ~ against sth** von etw abraten; **to ~ against doing sth** davon abraten, etw zu tun; **you would be well-/ill-~d to go** Sie wären gut/schlecht beraten, wenn Sie gingen.

advisedly [əd'vaızıdlı] adv bewusst.

adviser [əd'vaızəˀ] n Berater(in) m(f).

advisor [əd'vaızəˀ] n = **adviser**.

advisory [əd'vaızərı] adj beratend, Beratungs-; **in an ~ capacity** in beratender Funktion.

advocate ['ædvəkıt] vt befürworten ♦ n (LAW) (Rechts)anwalt m, (Rechts)anwältin f; (supporter, upholder): **~ of** Befürworter(in) m(f) +gen; **to be an ~ of sth** etw befürworten.

advt. abbr = **advertisement**.

AEA (BRIT) n abbr (= Atomic Energy Authority) britische Atomenergiebehörde; (BRIT: SCOL: = Advanced Extension Award) eine besondere Qualifikation für leistungsstarke Schüler des "A level".

AEC (US) n abbr (= Atomic Energy Commission) amerikanische Atomenergiebehörde.

AEEU (BRIT) n abbr (= Amalgamated Engineering and Electrical Union) Gewerkschaft der Ingenieure und Elektriker.

Aegean [iː'dʒiːən] n: **the ~ (Sea)** (GEOG) die Ägäis, das Ägäische Meer.

aegis ['iːdʒıs] n: **under the ~ of** unter der Schirmherrschaft +gen.

aeon ['iːən] n Äon m, Ewigkeit f.

aerial ['ɛərıəl] n Antenne f ♦ adj (view,

bombardment etc) Luft-.

aero... ['ɛərə(u)] pref Luft-.

aerobatics ['ɛərəu'bætıks] npl fliegerische Kunststücke pl.

aerobics [ɛə'rəubıks] n Aerobic nt.

aerodrome ['ɛərədrəum] (BRIT) n Flugplatz m.

aerodynamic ['ɛərəudaı'næmık] adj aerodynamisch.

aeronautics [ɛərə'nɔːtıks] n Luftfahrt f, Aeronautik f.

aeroplane ['ɛərəpleın] (BRIT) n Flugzeug nt.

aerosol ['ɛərəsɔl] n Sprühdose f.

aerospace industry ['ɛərəuspeıs-] n Raumfahrtindustrie f.

aesthetic [iːs'θɛtık] adj ästhetisch.

aesthetically [iːs'θɛtıklı] adv ästhetisch.

afar [ə'faːˀ] adv: **from ~** aus der Ferne.

AFB (US) n abbr (= Air Force Base) Luftwaffenstützpunkt m.

affable ['æfəbl] adj umgänglich, freundlich.

affair [ə'fɛəˀ] n Angelegenheit f; (romance: also: **love ~**) Verhältnis nt; **affairs** npl Geschäfte pl.

affect [ə'fɛkt] vt (influence) sich auswirken auf +acc; (subj: disease) befallen; (move deeply) bewegen; (concern) betreffen; (feign) vortäuschen; **to be ~ed by sth** von etw beeinflusst werden.

affectation [æfɛk'teıʃən] n Affektiertheit f.

affected [ə'fɛktıd] adj affektiert.

affection [ə'fɛkʃən] n Zuneigung f.

affectionate [ə'fɛkʃənıt] adj liebevoll, zärtlich; (animal) anhänglich.

affectionately [ə'fɛkʃənıtlı] adv liebevoll, zärtlich.

affidavit [æfı'deıvıt] n (LAW) eidesstattliche Erklärung f.

affiliated [ə'fılıeıtıd] adj angeschlossen.

affinity [ə'fınıtı] n: **to have an ~ with** or **for** sich verbunden fühlen mit; (resemblance): **to have an ~ with** verwandt sein mit.

affirm [ə'fɔːm] vt versichern; (profess) sich bekennen zu.

affirmation [æfə'meıʃən] n (of facts) Bestätigung f; (of beliefs) Bekenntnis nt.

affirmative [ə'fɔːmətıv] adj bejahend ♦ n: **to reply in the ~** mit "Ja" antworten.

affix [ə'fıks] vt aufkleben.

afflict [ə'flıkt] vt quälen; (misfortune) heimsuchen.

affliction [ə'flıkʃən] n Leiden nt.

affluence ['æfluəns] n Wohlstand m.

affluent ['æfluənt] adj wohlhabend; **the ~ society** die Wohlstandsgesellschaft.

afford [ə'fɔːd] vt sich dat leisten; (time) aufbringen; (provide) bieten; **can we ~ a car?** können wir uns ein Auto leisten?; **I can't ~ the time** ich habe einfach nicht die Zeit.

affordable [ə'fɔːdəbl] adj erschwinglich.

affray [ə'freı] (BRIT) n Schlägerei f.

affront [ə'frʌnt] n Beleidigung f.

affronted [ə'frʌntɪd] adj beleidigt.
Afghan ['æfgæn] adj afghanisch ♦ n Afghane m, Afghanin f.
Afghanistan [æf'gænɪstæn] n Afghanistan nt.
afield [ə'fiːld] adv: **far** ~ weit fort; **from far** ~ aus weiter Ferne.
AFL-CIO n abbr (= American Federation of Labor and Congress of Industrial Organizations) amerikanischer Gewerkschafts-Dachverband.
afloat [ə'fləut] adv auf dem Wasser ♦ adj: **to be** ~ schwimmen; **to stay** ~ sich über Wasser halten; **to keep/get a business** ~ ein Geschäft über Wasser halten/auf die Beine stellen.
afoot [ə'fut] adv: **there is something** ~ da ist etwas im Gang.
aforementioned [ə'fɔːmenʃənd] adj oben erwähnt.
aforesaid [ə'fɔːsed] adj = **aforementioned**.
afraid [ə'freɪd] adj ängstlich; **to be** ~ **of** Angst haben vor +dat; **to be** ~ **of doing sth** or **to do sth** Angst davor haben, etw zu tun; **I am** ~ **that** ... leider ...; **I am** ~ **so/not** leider ja/nein.
afresh [ə'freʃ] adv von neuem, neu.
Africa ['æfrɪkə] n Afrika nt.
African ['æfrɪkən] adj afrikanisch ♦ n Afrikaner(in) m(f).
Afrikaans [æfrɪ'kɑːns] n Afrikaans nt.
Afrikaner [æfrɪ'kɑːnə*] n Afrika(a)nder(in) m(f).
Afro-American ['æfrəuə'merɪkən] adj afro-amerikanisch.
AFT (US) n abbr (= American Federation of Teachers) Lehrergewerkschaft.
aft [ɑːft] adv (be) achtern; (go) nach achtern.
after ['ɑːftə*] prep nach +dat; (of place) hinter +dat ♦ adv danach ♦ conj nachdem; ~ **dinner** nach dem Essen; **the day** ~ **tomorrow** übermorgen; **what are you** ~? was willst du; **who are you** ~? wen suchst du?; **the police are** ~ **him** die Polizei ist hinter ihm her; **to name sb** ~ **sb** jdn nach jdm nennen; **it's twenty** ~ **eight** (US) es ist zwanzig nach acht; **to ask** ~ **sb** nach jdm fragen; ~ **all** schließlich; ~ **you!** nach Ihnen!; ~ **he left** nachdem er gegangen war; ~ **having shaved** nachdem er sich rasiert hatte.
afterbirth ['ɑːftəbɜːθ] n Nachgeburt f.
aftercare ['ɑːftəkeə*] (BRIT) n Nachbehandlung f.
aftereffects ['ɑːftərɪfekts] npl Nachwirkungen pl.
afterlife ['ɑːftəlaɪf] n Leben nt nach dem Tod.
aftermath ['ɑːftəmɑːθ] n Auswirkungen pl; **in the** ~ **of** nach +dat.
afternoon ['ɑːftə'nuːn] n Nachmittag m.
afters ['ɑːftəz] (BRIT: inf) n Nachtisch m.
after-sales service [ɑːftə'seɪlz-] (BRIT) n Kundendienst m.
aftershave (lotion) ['ɑːftəʃeɪv-] n Rasierwasser nt.
aftershock ['ɑːftəʃɔk] n Nachbeben nt.
aftersun ['ɑːftəsʌn] n After-Sun-Lotion f.
aftertaste ['ɑːftəteɪst] n Nachgeschmack m.
afterthought ['ɑːftəθɔːt] n: **as an** ~ nachträglich; **I had an** ~ mir ist noch etwas eingefallen.
afterwards, (US) **afterward** ['ɑːftəwəd(z)] adv danach.
again [ə'gen] adv (once more) noch einmal; (repeatedly) wieder; **not him** ~! nicht schon wieder er!; **to do sth** ~ etw noch einmal tun; **to begin** ~ noch einmal anfangen; **to see** ~ wieder sehen; **he's opened it** ~ er hat er schon wieder geöffnet; ~ **and** ~ immer wieder; **now and** ~ ab und zu, hin und wieder.
against [ə'genst] prep gegen +acc; (leaning on) an +acc; (compared to) gegenüber +dat; ~ **a blue background** vor einem blauen Hintergrund; **(as)** ~ gegenüber +dat.
age [eɪdʒ] n Alter nt; (period) Zeitalter nt ♦ vi altern, alt werden ♦ vt alt machen; **what** ~ **is he?** wie alt ist er?; **20 years of** ~ 20 Jahre alt; **under** ~ minderjährig; **to come of** ~ mündig werden; **it's been** ~**s since** ... es ist ewig her, seit ...
aged¹ [eɪdʒd] adj: ~ **ten** zehn Jahre alt, zehnjährig.
aged² [eɪdʒɪd] npl: **the** ~ die Alten pl.
age group n Altersgruppe f; **the 40 to 50** ~ die Gruppe der Vierzig- bis Fünfzigjährigen.
ageing ['eɪdʒɪŋ] adj (person, population) alternd; (thing) älter werdend; (system, technology) veraltend.
ageless ['eɪdʒlɪs] adj zeitlos.
age limit n Altersgrenze f.
agency ['eɪdʒənsɪ] n Agentur f; (government body) Behörde f; **through** or **by the** ~ **of** durch die Vermittlung von.
agenda [ə'dʒendə] n Tagesordnung f.
agent ['eɪdʒənt] n (COMM) Vertreter(in) m(f); (representative, spy) Agent(in) m(f); (CHEM) Mittel nt; (fig) Kraft f.
aggravate ['ægrəveɪt] vt verschlimmern; (inf: annoy) ärgern.
aggravating ['ægrəveɪtɪŋ] (inf) adj ärgerlich.
aggravation [ægrə'veɪʃən] (inf) n Ärger m.
aggregate ['ægrɪgɪt] n Gesamtmenge f ♦ vt zusammenzählen; **on** ~ (SPORT) nach Toren.
aggression [ə'greʃən] n Aggression f.
aggressive [ə'gresɪv] adj aggressiv.
aggressiveness [ə'gresɪvnɪs] n Aggressivität f.
aggressor [ə'gresə*] n Aggressor(in) m(f), Angreifer(in) m(f).
aggrieved [ə'griːvd] adj verärgert.
aggro ['ægrəu] (BRIT: inf) n (hassle) Ärger m, Theater nt; (aggressive behaviour) Aggressivität f.

aghast [ə'gɑːst] adj entsetzt.

agile ['ædʒaɪl] adj beweglich, wendig.

agility [ə'dʒɪlɪtɪ] n Beweglichkeit f, Wendigkeit f; (of mind) (geistige) Beweglichkeit f.

agitate ['ædʒɪteɪt] vt aufregen; (liquid: stir) aufrühren; (: shake) schütteln ♦ vi: to ~ for/against sth für/gegen etw agitieren.

agitated ['ædʒɪteɪtɪd] adj aufgeregt.

agitator ['ædʒɪteɪtəʳ] n Agitator(in) m(f).

AGM n abbr (= annual general meeting) JHV f.

agnostic [æg'nɒstɪk] n Agnostiker(in) m(f).

ago [ə'gəʊ] adv: **2 days** ~ vor 2 Tagen; **not long** ~ vor kurzem; **as long** ~ **as 1960** schon 1960; **how long** ~? wie lange ist das her?

agog [ə'gɒg] adj gespannt.

agonize ['ægənaɪz] vi: **to** ~ **over sth** sich dat den Kopf über etw acc zermartern.

agonizing ['ægənaɪzɪŋ] adj qualvoll; (pain etc) quälend.

agony ['ægənɪ] n (pain) Schmerz m; (torment) Qual f; **to be in** ~ Qualen leiden.

agony aunt (BRIT: inf) n Briefkastentante f.

agony column n Kummerkasten m.

agree [ə'griː] vt (price, date) vereinbaren ♦ vi übereinstimmen; (consent) zustimmen; **to** ~ **with sb** (subj: person) jdm zustimmen; (: food) jdm bekommen; **to** ~ **to sth** einer Sache dat zustimmen; **to** ~ **to do sth** sich bereit erklären, etw zu tun; **to** ~ **on sth** sich auf etw acc einigen; **to** ~ **that** (admit) zugeben, dass; **garlic doesn't** ~ **with me** Knoblauch vertrage ich nicht; **it was** ~d **that ...** es wurde beschlossen, dass ...; **they** ~d **on this** sie haben sich in diesem Punkt geeinigt; **they** ~d **on going** sie einigten sich darauf, zu gehen; **they** ~d **on a price** sie vereinbarten einen Preis.

agreeable [ə'griːəbl] adj angenehm; (willing) einverstanden; **are you** ~ **to this?** sind Sie hiermit einverstanden?

agreed [ə'griːd] adj vereinbart; **to be** ~ sich dat einig sein.

agreement [ə'griːmənt] n (concurrence) Übereinstimmung f; (consent) Zustimmung f; (arrangement) Abmachung f; (contract) Vertrag m; **to be in** ~ **(with sb)** (mit jdm) einer Meinung sein; **by mutual** ~ in gegenseitigem Einverständnis.

agricultural [ægrɪ'kʌltʃərəl] adj landwirtschaftlich; (show) Landwirtschafts-.

agriculture ['ægrɪkʌltʃəʳ] n Landwirtschaft f.

aground [ə'graund] adv: **to run** ~ auf Grund laufen.

ahead [ə'hɛd] adv vor uns/ihnen etc; ~ **of** (in advance of) +dat; **to be** ~ **of sb** (in progress, ranking) vor jdm liegen; **to be** ~ **of schedule** schneller als geplant vorankommen; ~ **of time** zeitlich voraus; **to arrive** ~ **of time** zu früh ankommen; **go right** or **straight** ~ gehen/fahren Sie geradeaus;

go ~! (fig) machen Sie nur!, nur zu!; **they were (right)** ~ **of us** sie waren (genau) vor uns.

AI n abbr (= Amnesty International) AI no art; (COMPUT) = **artificial intelligence**.

AIB (BRIT) n abbr (= Accident Investigation Bureau) Untersuchungsstelle für Unglücksfälle.

AID n abbr (= artificial insemination by donor) künstliche Besamung durch Samenspender; (US: = Agency for International Development) Abteilung zur Koordination von Entwicklungshilfe und Außenpolitik.

aid [eɪd] n Hilfe f; (to less developed country) Entwicklungshilfe f; (device) Hilfsmittel nt ♦ vt (help) helfen, unterstützen; **with the** ~ **of** mit Hilfe von; **in** ~ **of** zugunsten or zu Gunsten +gen; **to** ~ **and abet** Beihilfe leisten; see also **hearing aid**.

aide [eɪd] n Berater(in) m(f); (MIL) Adjutant m.

aide-de-camp ['eɪddə'kɒŋ] n (MIL) Adjutant m.

AIDS [eɪdz] n abbr (= acquired immune deficiency syndrome) AIDS nt.

AIH n abbr (= artificial insemination by husband) künstliche Besamung durch den Ehemann/Partner.

ailing ['eɪlɪŋ] adj kränklich; (economy, industry etc) krank.

ailment ['eɪlmənt] n Leiden nt.

aim [eɪm] vt: **to** ~ **at** (gun, missile, camera) richten auf +acc; (blow) zielen auf +acc; (remark) richten an +acc ♦ vi (also: **take** ~) zielen ♦ n (objective) Ziel nt; (in shooting) Zielsicherheit f; **to** ~ **at** zielen auf +acc; (objective) anstreben +acc; **to** ~ **to do sth** vorhaben, etw zu tun.

aimless ['eɪmlɪs] adj ziellos.

aimlessly ['eɪmlɪslɪ] adv ziellos.

ain't [eɪnt] (inf) = **am not**; = **aren't**; = **isn't**.

air [ɛəʳ] n Luft f; (tune) Melodie f; (appearance) Auftreten nt; (demeanour) Haltung f; (of house etc) Atmosphäre f ♦ vt lüften; (grievances, views) Luft machen +dat; (knowledge) zur Schau stellen; (ideas) darlegen ♦ cpd Luft-; **into the** ~ in die Luft; **by** ~ mit dem Flugzeug; **to be on the** ~ (RADIO, TV: programme) gesendet werden; (: station) senden; (: person) auf Sendung sein.

air base n Luftwaffenstützpunkt m.

air bed (BRIT) n Luftmatratze f.

airborne ['ɛəbɔːn] adj in der Luft; (plane, particles) in der Luft befindlich; (troops) Luftlande-.

air cargo n Luftfracht f.

air-conditioned ['ɛəkən'dɪʃənd] adj klimatisiert.

air conditioning n Klimaanlage f.

air-cooled ['ɛəkuːld] adj (engine) luftgekühlt.

aircraft ['ɛəkrɑːft] n inv Flugzeug nt.

aircraft carrier n Flugzeugträger m.

air cushion n Luftkissen nt.

airfield ['ɛəfiːld] n Flugplatz m.
Air Force n Luftwaffe f.
air freight n Luftfracht f.
air freshener n Raumspray nt.
air gun n Luftgewehr nt.
air hostess (BRIT) n Stewardess f.
airily ['ɛərɪlɪ] adv leichtfertig.
airing ['ɛərɪŋ] n: **to give an ~ to** (fig: ideas) darlegen; (: views) Luft machen +dat.
air letter (BRIT) n Luftpostbrief m.
airlift ['ɛəlɪft] n Luftbrücke f.
airline ['ɛəlaɪn] n Fluggesellschaft f.
airliner ['ɛəlaɪnə*] n Verkehrsflugzeug nt.
airlock ['ɛəlɔk] n (in pipe etc) Luftblase f; (compartment) Luftschleuse f.
air mail n: **by ~** per or mit Luftpost.
air mattress n Luftmatratze f.
airplane ['ɛəpleɪn] (US) n Flugzeug nt.
air pocket n Luftloch nt.
airport ['ɛəpɔːt] n Flughafen m.
air raid n Luftangriff m.
air rifle n Luftgewehr nt.
airsick ['ɛəsɪk] adj luftkrank.
airspace ['ɛəspeɪs] n Luftraum m.
airspeed ['ɛəspiːd] n Fluggeschwindigkeit f.
airstrip ['ɛəstrɪp] n Start-und-Lande-Bahn f.
air terminal n Terminal m or nt.
airtight ['ɛətaɪt] adj luftdicht.
airtime ['ɛətaɪm] n (RADIO, TV) Sendezeit f.
air-traffic control ['ɛətræfɪk-] n Flugsicherung f.
air-traffic controller ['ɛətræfɪk-] n Fluglotse m.
air waybill n Luftfrachtbrief m.
airy ['ɛərɪ] adj luftig; (casual) lässig.
aisle [aɪl] n Gang m; (section of church) Seitenschiff nt.
aisle seat n Sitz m am Gang.
ajar [ə'dʒɑː*] adj angelehnt.
AK (US) abbr (POST: = Alaska).
a.k.a. abbr (= also known as) alias.
akin [ə'kɪn] adj: **~ to** ähnlich +dat.
AL (US) abbr (POST: = Alabama).
ALA n abbr (= American Library Association) akademischer Verband für das Bibliothekswesen.
Ala. (US) abbr (POST: = Alabama).
alabaster ['æləbɑːstə*] n Alabaster m.
à la carte adv à la carte.
alacrity [ə'lækrɪtɪ] n Bereitwilligkeit f; **with ~** ohne zu zögern.
alarm [ə'lɑːm] n (anxiety) Besorgnis f; (in shop, bank) Alarmanlage f ♦ vt (worry) beunruhigen; (frighten) erschrecken.
alarm call n Weckruf m.
alarm clock n Wecker m.
alarmed [ə'lɑːmd] adj beunruhigt; **don't be ~** erschrecken Sie nicht.
alarming [ə'lɑːmɪŋ] adj (worrying) beunruhigend; (frightening) erschreckend.
alarmingly [ə'lɑːmɪŋlɪ] adv erschreckend.
alarmist [ə'lɑːmɪst] n Panikmacher(in) m(f).

alas [ə'læs] excl leider.
Alaska [ə'læskə] n Alaska nt.
Albania [æl'beɪnɪə] n Albanien nt.
Albanian [æl'beɪnɪən] adj albanisch ♦ n (LING) Albanisch nt.
albatross ['ælbətrɔs] n Albatros m.
albeit [ɔːl'biːɪt] conj wenn auch.
album ['ælbəm] n Album nt.
albumen ['ælbjumɪn] n Albumen nt.
alchemy ['ælkɪmɪ] n Alchimie f, Alchemie f.
alcohol ['ælkəhɔl] n Alkohol m.
alcoholic [ælkə'hɔlɪk] adj alkoholisch ♦ n Alkoholiker(in) m(f).
alcoholism ['ælkəhɔlɪzəm] n Alkoholismus m.
alcove ['ælkəuv] n Alkoven m, Nische f.
Ald. abbr = alderman.
alderman ['ɔːldəmən] (irreg: like man) n ≈ Stadtrat m.
ale [eɪl] n Ale nt.
alert [ə'ləːt] adj aufmerksam ♦ n Alarm m ♦ vt alarmieren; **to be ~ to** (danger, opportunity) sich dat bewusst sein +gen; **to be on the ~** wachsam sein; **to ~ sb (to sth)** jdn (vor etw dat) warnen.
Aleutian Islands [ə'luːʃən-] npl Aleuten pl.
A level (BRIT) n ≈ Abschluss m der Sekundarstufe 2, Abitur nt.
Alexandria [ælɪg'zɑːndrɪə] n Alexandria nt.
alfresco [æl'freskəu] adj, adv im Freien.
algebra ['ældʒɪbrə] n Algebra f.
Algeria [æl'dʒɪərɪə] n Algerien nt.
Algerian [æl'dʒɪərɪən] adj algerisch ♦ n Algerier(in) m(f).
Algiers [æl'dʒɪəz] n Algier nt.
algorithm ['ælgərɪðəm] n (MATH) Algorithmus m.
alias ['eɪlɪəs] adv alias ♦ n Deckname m.
alibi ['ælɪbaɪ] n Alibi nt.
alien ['eɪlɪən] n Ausländer(in) m(f); (extraterrestrial) außerirdisches Wesen nt ♦ adj: **~ (to)** fremd (+dat).
alienate ['eɪlɪəneɪt] vt entfremden; (antagonize) befremden.
alienation [eɪlɪə'neɪʃən] n Entfremdung f.
alight [ə'laɪt] adj brennend; (eyes, expression) leuchtend ♦ vi (bird) sich niederlassen; (passenger) aussteigen.
align [ə'laɪn] vt ausrichten.
alignment [ə'laɪnmənt] n Ausrichtung f; **it's out of ~ (with)** es ist nicht richtig ausgerichtet (nach).
alike [ə'laɪk] adj ähnlich ♦ adv (similarly) ähnlich; (equally) gleich; **to look ~** sich dat ähnlich sehen; **winter and summer ~** Sommer wie Winter.
alimony ['ælɪmənɪ] n Unterhalt m.
alive [ə'laɪv] adj (living) lebend; (lively) lebendig; (active) lebhaft; **~ with** erfüllt von; **to be ~ to sth** sich dat einer Sache gen bewusst sein.
alkali ['ælkəlaɪ] n Base f, Lauge f.
alkaline ['ælkəlaɪn] adj basisch, alkalisch.

══════════════ KEYWORD

all [ɔːl] adj alle(r, s); ~ **day/night** den ganzen Tag/die ganze Nacht (über); ~ **men are equal** alle Menschen sind gleich; ~ **five came** alle fünf kamen; ~ **the books** die ganzen Bücher, alle Bücher; ~ **the food** das ganze Essen; ~ **the time** die ganze Zeit (über); ~ **his life** sein ganzes Leben (lang) ♦ pron **1** alles; **I ate it** ~, **I ate** ~ **of it** ich habe alles gegessen; ~ **of us/the boys went** wir alle/alle Jungen gingen; **we** ~ **sat down** wir setzten uns alle; **is that** ~**?** ist das alles?; (in shop) sonst noch etwas?

2 (in phrases): **above** ~ vor allem; **after** ~ schließlich; ~ **in** ~ alles in allem ♦ adv ganz; ~ **alone** ganz allein; **it's not as hard as** ~ **that** so schwer ist es nun auch wieder nicht; ~ **the more/the better** um so mehr/besser; ~ **but** (all except for) alle außer; (almost) fast; **the score is 2** ~ der Spielstand ist 2 zu 2.

──────────────────────────

allay [əˈleɪ] vt (fears) zerstreuen.
all clear n Entwarnung f.
allegation [ælɪˈgeɪʃən] n Behauptung f.
allege [əˈledʒ] vt behaupten; **he is** ~**d to have said that ...** er soll angeblich gesagt haben, dass ...
alleged [əˈledʒd] adj angeblich.
allegedly [əˈledʒɪdlɪ] adv angeblich.
allegiance [əˈliːdʒəns] n Treue f.
allegory [ˈælɪgərɪ] n Allegorie f.
all-embracing [ˈɔːlɪmˈbreɪsɪŋ] adj (all)umfassend.
allergic [əˈlɜːdʒɪk] adj (rash, reaction) allergisch; (person): ~ **to** allergisch gegen.
allergy [ˈælədʒɪ] n Allergie f.
alleviate [əˈliːvɪeɪt] vt lindern.
alley [ˈælɪ] n Gasse f.
alleyway [ˈælɪweɪ] n Durchgang m.
alliance [əˈlaɪəns] n Bündnis nt.
allied [ˈælaɪd] adj verbündet, alliiert; (products, industries) verwandt.
alligator [ˈælɪgeɪtə*] n Alligator m.
all-important [ˈɔːlɪmˈpɔːtənt] adj entscheidend, äußerst wichtig.
all in (BRIT) adv inklusive.
all-in [ˈɔːlɪn] (BRIT) adj (price) Inklusiv-.
all-in wrestling n (esp BRIT) Freistilringen nt.
alliteration [əlɪtəˈreɪʃən] n Alliteration f.
all-night [ˈɔːlˈnaɪt] adj (café, cinema) die ganze Nacht geöffnet; (party) die ganze Nacht dauernd.
allocate [ˈæləkeɪt] vt zuteilen.
allocation [æləʊˈkeɪʃən] n Verteilung f; (of money, resources) Zuteilung f.
allot [əˈlɒt] vt: to ~ (to) zuteilen (+dat); **in the** ~**ed time** in der vorgesehenen Zeit.
allotment [əˈlɒtmənt] n (share) Anteil m; (garden) Schrebergarten m.
all-out [ˈɔːlaut] adj (effort, dedication etc)

äußerste(r, s); (strike) total ♦ adv: **all out** mit aller Kraft; **to go all out for** sein Letztes or Äußerstes geben für.
allow [əˈlau] vt erlauben; (behaviour) zulassen; (sum, time) einplanen; (claim, goal) anerkennen; (concede): **to** ~ **that** annehmen, dass; **to** ~ **sb to do sth** jdm erlauben, etw zu tun; **he is** ~**ed to ...** er darf ...; **smoking is not** ~**ed** Rauchen ist nicht gestattet; **we must** ~ **3 days for the journey** wir müssen für die Reise 3 Tage einplanen.
► **allow for** vt fus einplanen, berücksichtigen.
allowance [əˈlauəns] n finanzielle Unterstützung f; (welfare payment) Beihilfe f; (pocket money) Taschengeld nt; (tax allowance) Freibetrag m; **to make** ~**s for** (person) Zugeständnisse machen für; (thing) berücksichtigen.
alloy [ˈælɔɪ] n Legierung f.
all right adv (well) gut; (correctly) richtig; (as answer) okay, in Ordnung.
all-rounder [ɔːlˈraundə*] n Allrounder m; (athlete etc) Allroundsportler(in) m(f).
allspice [ˈɔːlspaɪs] n Piment m or nt.
all-time [ˈɔːlˈtaɪm] adj aller Zeiten.
allude [əˈluːd] vi: **to** ~ **to** anspielen auf +acc.
alluring [əˈljuərɪŋ] adj verführerisch.
allusion [əˈluːʒən] n Anspielung f.
alluvium [əˈluːvɪəm] n Anschwemmung f.
ally [ˈælaɪ] n Verbündete(r) f(m); (during wars) Alliierte(r) f(m) ♦ vt: **to** ~ **o.s. with** sich verbünden mit.
almighty [ɔːlˈmaɪtɪ] adj allmächtig; (tremendous) mächtig.
almond [ˈɑːmənd] n Mandel f; (tree) Mandelbaum m.
almost [ˈɔːlməust] adv fast, beinahe; **he** ~ **fell** er wäre beinahe gefallen.
alms [ɑːmz] npl Almosen pl.
aloft [əˈlɒft] adv (hold, carry) empor.
alone [əˈləun] adj, adv allein; **to leave sb** ~ jdn in Ruhe lassen; **to leave sth** ~ die Finger von etw lassen; **let** ~ **...** geschweige denn ...
along [əˈlɒŋ] prep entlang +acc ♦ adv: **is he coming** ~ **with us?** kommt er mit?; **he was hopping/limping** ~ er hüpfte/humpelte daher; ~ **with** (together with) zusammen mit; **all** ~ (all the time) die ganze Zeit.
alongside [əˈlɒŋˈsaɪd] prep neben +dat; (ship) längsseits +gen ♦ adv (come) nebendran; (be) daneben; **we brought our boat** ~ wir brachten unser Boot heran; **a car drew up** ~ ein Auto fuhr neben mich/ihn etc heran.
aloof [əˈluːf] adj unnahbar ♦ adv: **to stand** ~ abseits stehen.
aloofness [əˈluːfnɪs] n Unnahbarkeit f.
aloud [əˈlaud] adv laut.
alphabet [ˈælfəbɛt] n Alphabet nt.
alphabetical [ælfəˈbɛtɪkl] adj alphabetisch; **in** ~ **order** in alphabetischer Reihenfolge.
alphanumeric [ˈælfənjuːˈmɛrɪk] adj alphanumerisch.

alpine ['ælpaɪn] adj alpin, Alpen-.

Alps [ælps] npl: **the** ~ die Alpen.

already [ɔːl'rɛdɪ] adv schon.

alright ['ɔːl'raɪt] (BRIT) adv = **all right**.

Alsace ['ælsæs] n Elsass nt.

Alsatian [æl'seɪʃən] (BRIT) n (dog) Schäferhund m.

also ['ɔːlsəʊ] adv (too) auch; (moreover) außerdem.

altar ['ɔltə*] n Altar m.

alter ['ɔltə*] vt ändern; (clothes) umändern ♦ vi sich (ver)ändern.

alteration [ɔltə'reɪʃən] n Änderung f; (to clothes) Umänderung f; (to building) Umbau m; **alterations** npl (SEWING) Änderungen pl; (ARCHIT) Umbau m.

altercation [ɔltə'keɪʃən] n Auseinandersetzung f.

alternate [adj ɔl'tɜːnɪt, vi 'ɔltəneɪt] adj abwechselnd; (US: alternative: plans etc) Alternativ- ♦ vi: **to** ~ **(with)** sich abwechseln (mit); **on** ~ **days** jeden zweiten Tag.

alternately [ɔl'tɜːnɪtlɪ] adv abwechselnd.

alternating current ['ɔltəneɪtɪŋ-] n Wechselstrom m.

alternative [ɔl'tɜːnətɪv] adj alternativ; (solution etc) Alternativ- ♦ n Alternative f.

alternative energy n Alternativenergie f.

alternatively [ɔl'tɜːnətɪvlɪ] adv: ~ **one could** ... oder man könnte ...

alternative medicine n Alternativmedizin f.

alternative society n Alternativgesellschaft f.

alternator ['ɔltəneɪtə*] n (AUT) Lichtmaschine f.

although [ɔːl'ðəʊ] conj obwohl.

altitude ['æltɪtjuːd] n Höhe f.

alto ['æltəʊ] n Alt m.

altogether [ɔːltə'gɛðə*] adv ganz; (on the whole, in all) im Ganzen, insgesamt; **how much is that** ~? was macht das zusammen?

altruism ['æltruɪzəm] n Altruismus m.

altruistic [æltru'ɪstɪk] adj uneigennützig, altruistisch.

aluminium [ælju'mɪnɪəm], (US) **aluminum** [ə'luːmɪnəm] n Aluminium nt.

always ['ɔːlweɪz] adv immer; **we can** ~ ... (if all else fails) wir können ja auch ...

Alzheimer's (disease) n (MED) Alzheimerkrankheit f.

AM abbr (= amplitude modulation) AM, ≈ MW; (BRIT: POL: = Assembly Member) Mitglied nt der walisischen Versammlung.

am [æm] vb see **be**.

a.m. adv abbr (= ante meridiem) morgens; (later) vormittags.

AMA n abbr (= American Medical Association) Medizinerverband.

amalgam [ə'mælgəm] n Amalgam nt; (fig) Mischung f.

amalgamate [ə'mælgəmeɪt] vi, vt fusionieren.

amalgamation [əmælgə'meɪʃən] n Fusion f.

amass [ə'mæs] vt anhäufen; (evidence) zusammentragen.

amateur ['æmətə*] n Amateur m ♦ adj (SPORT) Amateur-; ~ **dramatics** Laientheater nt.

amateurish ['æmətərɪʃ] adj (pej) dilettantisch, stümperhaft.

amaze [ə'meɪz] vt erstaunen; **to be** ~**d (at)** erstaunt sein (über +acc).

amazement [ə'meɪzmənt] n Erstaunen nt.

amazing [ə'meɪzɪŋ] adj erstaunlich; (bargain, offer) sensationell.

amazingly [ə'meɪzɪŋlɪ] adv erstaunlich.

Amazon ['æməzən] n (river) Amazonas m; **the** ~ **basin** das Amazonastiefland; **the** ~ **jungle** der Amazonas-Regenwald.

Amazonian [æmə'zəʊnɪən] adj amazonisch.

ambassador [æm'bæsədə*] n Botschafter(in) m(f).

amber ['æmbə*] n Bernstein m; **at** ~ (BRIT: traffic lights) auf Gelb; (: move off) bei Gelb.

ambidextrous [æmbɪ'dɛkstrəs] adj beidhändig.

ambience ['æmbɪəns] n Atmosphäre f.

ambiguity [æmbɪ'gjuɪtɪ] n Zweideutigkeit f; (lack of clarity) Unklarheit f.

ambiguous [æm'bɪgjuəs] adj zweideutig; (not clear) unklar.

ambition [æm'bɪʃən] n Ehrgeiz m; (desire) Ambition f; **to achieve one's** ~ seine Ambitionen erfüllen.

ambitious [æm'bɪʃəs] adj ehrgeizig.

ambivalence [æm'bɪvələns] n Ambivalenz f.

ambivalent [æm'bɪvələnt] adj ambivalent.

amble ['æmbl] vi schlendern.

ambulance ['æmbjuləns] n Krankenwagen m.

ambulanceman ['æmbjulənsmən] (irreg: like man) n Sanitäter m.

ambush ['æmbuʃ] n Hinterhalt m; (attack) Überfall m aus dem Hinterhalt ♦ vt (aus dem Hinterhalt) überfallen.

ameba [ə'miːbə] (US) n = **amoeba**.

ameliorate [ə'miːlɪəreɪt] vt verbessern.

amen ['ɑː'mɛn] excl amen.

amenable [ə'miːnəbl] adj: ~ **to** zugänglich +dat; (to flattery etc) empfänglich für; ~ **to the law** dem Gesetz verantwortlich.

amend [ə'mɛnd] vt ändern; (habits, behaviour) bessern.

amendment [ə'mɛndmənt] n Änderung f; (to law) Amendement nt.

amends [ə'mɛndz] npl: **to make** ~ es wieder gutmachen; **to make** ~ **for sth** etw wieder gutmachen.

amenities [ə'miːnɪtɪz] npl Einkaufs-, Unterhaltungs- und Transportmöglichkeiten.

amenity [ə'miːnɪtɪ] n (Freizeit)einrichtung f.

America [ə'mɛrɪkə] n Amerika nt.

American [ə'mɛrɪkən] adj amerikanisch ♦ n Amerikaner(in) m(f).

Americanize [ə'mɛrɪkənaɪz] vt amerikanisieren.

amethyst ['æmɪθɪst] n Amethyst m.
Amex ['æmɛks] n abbr (= American Stock Exchange) US-Börse; (= American Express ®) Kreditkarte.
amiable ['eɪmɪəbl] adj liebenswürdig.
amiably ['eɪmɪəblɪ] adv liebenswürdig.
amicable ['æmɪkəbl] adj freundschaftlich; (settlement) gütlich.
amicably ['æmɪkəblɪ] adv (part, discuss) in aller Freundschaft; (settle) gütlich.
amid(st) [ə'mɪd(st)] prep inmitten +gen.
amiss [ə'mɪs] adj, adv: **to take sth** ~ **etw** übel nehmen; **there's something** ~ da stimmt irgend etwas nicht.
ammeter ['æmɪtə*] n Amperemeter nt.
ammo ['æməu] (inf) n abbr = **ammunition**.
ammonia [ə'məunɪə] n Ammoniak nt.
ammunition [æmju'nɪʃən] n Munition f.
ammunition dump n Munitionslager nt.
amnesia [æm'niːzɪə] n Amnesie f, Gedächtnisschwund m.
amnesty ['æmnɪstɪ] n Amnestie f; **to grant an** ~ **to** amnestieren.
Amnesty International n Amnesty International no art.
amoeba, (US) ameba [ə'miːbə] n Amöbe f.
amok [ə'mɔk] adv: **to run** ~ Amok laufen.
among(st) [ə'mʌŋ(st)] prep unter +dat.
amoral [æ'mɔrəl] adj unmoralisch.
amorous ['æmərəs] adj amourös.
amorphous [ə'mɔːfəs] adj formlos, gestaltlos.
amortization [əmɔːtaɪ'zeɪʃən] n Amortisation f.
amount [ə'maunt] n (quantity) Menge f; (sum of money) Betrag m; (total) Summe f; (of bill etc) Höhe f ♦ vi: **to** ~ **to** (total) sich belaufen auf +acc; (be same as) gleichkommen +dat; **the total** ~ (of money) die Gesamtsumme.
amp(ère) ['æmp(ɛə*)] n Ampere nt; **a 3** ~ **fuse** eine Sicherung von 3 Ampere; **a 13** ~ **plug** ein Stecker mit einer Sicherung von 13 Ampere.
ampersand ['æmpəsænd] n Et-Zeichen nt, Und-Zeichen nt.
amphetamine [æm'fɛtəmiːn] n Amphetamin nt.
amphibian [æm'fɪbɪən] n Amphibie f.
amphibious [æm'fɪbɪəs] adj amphibisch; (vehicle) Amphibien-.
amphitheatre, (US) amphitheater ['æmfɪθɪətə*] n Amphitheater nt.
ample ['æmpl] adj (large) üppig; (abundant) reichlich; (enough) genügend; **this is** ~ das ist reichlich; **to have** ~ **time/room** genügend Zeit/Platz haben.
amplifier ['æmplɪfaɪə*] n Verstärker m.
amplify ['æmplɪfaɪ] vt verstärken; (expand: idea etc) genauer ausführen.
amply ['æmplɪ] adv reichlich.
ampoule, (US) ampule ['æmpuːl] n Ampulle f.
amputate ['æmpjuteɪt] vt amputieren.
amputation [æmpju'teɪʃən] n Amputation f.

amputee [æmpju'tiː] n Amputierte(r) f(m).
Amsterdam ['æmstədæm] n Amsterdam nt.
amt abbr = **amount**.
amuck [ə'mʌk] adv = **amok**.
amuse [ə'mjuːz] vt (entertain) unterhalten; (make smile) amüsieren, belustigen; **to** ~ **o.s. with sth/by doing sth** sich die Zeit mit etw vertreiben/damit vertreiben, etw zu tun; **to be** ~**d at** sich amüsieren über +acc; **he was not** ~**d** er fand das gar nicht komisch or zum Lachen.
amusement [ə'mjuːzmənt] n (mirth) Vergnügen nt; (pleasure) Unterhaltung f; (pastime) Zeitvertreib m; **much to my** ~ zu meiner großen Belustigung.
amusement arcade n Spielhalle f.
amusement park n Vergnügungspark m.
amusing [ə'mjuːzɪŋ] adj amüsant, unterhaltsam.
an [æn, ən] indef art see **a.**
ANA n abbr (= American Newspaper Association) amerikanischer Zeitungsverband; (= American Nurses Association) Verband amerikanischer Krankenschwestern und Krankenpfleger.
anachronism [ə'nækrənɪzəm] n Anachronismus m.
anaemia, (US) anemia [ə'niːmɪə] n Anämie f.
anaemic, (US) anemic [ə'niːmɪk] adj blutarm.
anaesthetic, (US) anesthetic [ænɪs'θɛtɪk] n Betäubungsmittel nt; **under (the)** ~ unter Narkose; **local** ~ örtliche Betäubung f; **general** ~ Vollnarkose f.
anaesthetist [æ'niːsθɪtɪst] n Anästhesist(in) m(f).
anagram ['ænəgræm] n Anagramm nt.
anal ['eɪnl] adj anal, Anal-.
analgesic [ænæl'dʒiːsɪk] adj schmerzstillend ♦ n Schmerzmittel nt, schmerzstillendes Mittel nt.
analogous [ə'næləgəs] adj: ~ (**to** or **with**) analog (zu).
analogue, (US) analog ['ænəlɔg] adj (watch, computer) Analog-.
analogy [ə'nælədʒɪ] n Analogie f; **to draw an** ~ **between** eine Analogie herstellen zwischen +dat; **by** ~ durch einen Analogieschluss.
analyse, (US) analyze ['ænəlaɪz] vt analysieren; (CHEM, MED) untersuchen; (person) psychoanalytisch behandeln.
analyses [ə'næləsiːz] npl of **analysis.**
analysis [ə'næləsɪs] (pl **analyses**) n (see vb) Analyse f; Untersuchung f; Psychoanalyse f; **in the last** ~ letzten Endes.
analyst ['ænəlɪst] n Analytiker(in) m(f); (US) Psychoanalytiker(in) m(f).
analytic(al) [ænə'lɪtɪk(l)] adj analytisch.
analyze ['ænəlaɪz] (US) vt = **analyse.**
anarchic [æ'naːkɪk] adj anarchisch.
anarchist ['ænəkɪst] adj anarchistisch ♦ n Anarchist(in) m(f).

anarchy ['ænəkı] n Anarchie f.
anathema [ə'næθımə] n: **that is ~ to him** das ist ihm ein Gräuel.
anatomical [ænə'tɔmıkl] adj anatomisch.
anatomy [ə'nætəmı] n Anatomie f; (body) Körper m.
ANC n abbr (= African National Congress) ANC m.
ancestor ['ænsıstə*] n Vorfahr(in) m(f).
ancestral [æn'sɛstrəl] adj angestammt; **~ home** Stammsitz m.
ancestry ['ænsıstrı] n Abstammung f.
anchor ['æŋkə*] n Anker m ♦ vi (also: **to drop ~**) ankern, vor Anker gehen ♦ vt (fig): **to ~ sth to** etw verankern in +dat; **to weigh ~** den Anker lichten.
anchorage ['æŋkərıdʒ] n Ankerplatz m.
anchorman [æŋkəmæn] (irreg: like **man**) n (TV, RADIO) ≈ Moderator m.
anchorwoman [æŋkəwumən] (irreg: like **woman**) n (TV, RADIO) ≈ Moderatorin f.
anchovy ['æntʃəvı] n Sardelle f, An(s)chovis f.
ancient ['eınʃənt] adj alt; (person, car) uralt.
ancient monument n historisches Denkmal nt.
ancillary [æn'sılərı] adj Hilfs-.
and [ænd] conj und; **~ so on** und so weiter; **try ~ come please** bitte versuche zu kommen; **better ~ better** immer besser.
Andes ['ændi:z] npl: **the ~** die Anden pl.
Andorra [æn'dɔ:rə] n Andorra nt.
anecdote ['ænıkdəut] n Anekdote f.
anemia etc [ə'ni:mıə] (US) = **anaemia** etc.
anemone [ə'nɛmənı] n (BOT) Anemone f, Buschwindröschen nt.
anesthetic etc [ænıs'θetık] (US) = **anaesthetic** etc.
anew [ə'nju:] adv von neuem.
angel ['eındʒəl] n Engel m.
angel dust (inf) n als halluzinogene Droge missbrauchtes Medikament.
angelic [æn'dʒɛlık] adj engelhaft.
anger ['æŋgə*] n Zorn m ♦ vt ärgern; (enrage) erzürnen; **red with ~** rot vor Wut.
angina [æn'dʒaınə] n Angina pectoris f.
angle ['æŋgl] n Winkel m; (viewpoint): **from their ~** von ihrem Standpunkt aus ♦ vi: **to ~ for** (invitation) aus sein auf +acc; (compliments) fischen nach ♦ vt: **to ~ sth towards** or **to** etw ausrichten auf +acc.
angler ['æŋglə*] n Angler(in) m(f).
Anglican ['æŋglıkən] adj anglikanisch ♦ n Anglikaner(in) m(f).
anglicize ['æŋglısaız] vt anglisieren.
angling ['æŋglıŋ] n Angeln nt.
Anglo- ['æŋgləu] pref Anglo-, anglo-.
Anglo-German ['æŋgləu'dʒɔ:mən] adj englisch-deutsch.
Anglo-Saxon ['æŋgləu'sæksən] adj angelsächsisch ♦ n Angelsachse m, Angelsächsin f.
Angola [æŋ'gəulə] n Angola nt.

Angolan [æŋ'gəulən] adj angolanisch ♦ n Angolaner(in) m(f).
angrily ['æŋgrılı] adv verärgert.
angry ['æŋgrı] adj verärgert; (wound) entzündet; **to be ~ with sb** auf jdn böse sein; **to be ~ at sth** über etw acc verärgert sein; **to get ~** wütend werden; **to make sb ~** jdn wütend machen.
anguish ['æŋgwıʃ] n Qual f.
anguished ['æŋgwıʃt] adj gequält.
angular ['æŋgjulə*] adj eckig; (features) kantig.
animal ['ænıməl] n Tier nt; (living creature) Lebewesen nt; (pej: person) Bestie f ♦ adj tierhaft; (attraction etc) animalisch.
animal spirits npl Vitalität f.
animate [vt ænımeıt, adj ænımıt] vt beleben ♦ adj lebend.
animated ['ænımeıtıd] adj lebhaft; (film) Zeichentrick-.
animation [ænı'meıʃən] n (liveliness) Lebhaftigkeit f; (film) Animation f.
animosity [ænı'mɔsıtı] n Feindseligkeit f.
aniseed ['ænısi:d] n Anis m.
Ankara ['æŋkərə] n Ankara nt.
ankle ['æŋkl] n Knöchel m.
ankle sock (BRIT) n Söckchen nt.
annex ['ænɛks] n (also: **~e**: BRIT) Anhang m; (building) Nebengebäude nt; (extension) Anbau m ♦ vt (take over) annektieren.
annexation [ænɛk'seıʃən] n Annexion f.
annihilate [ə'naıəleıt] vt (also fig) vernichten.
annihilation [ənaıə'leıʃən] n Vernichtung f.
anniversary [ænı'və:sərı] n Jahrestag m.
anno Domini adv anno Domini, nach Christus.
annotate ['ænəuteıt] vt kommentieren.
announce [ə'nauns] vt ankündigen; (birth, death etc) anzeigen; **he ~d that he wasn't going** er verkündete, dass er nicht gehen würde.
announcement [ə'naunsmənt] n Ankündigung f; (official) Bekanntmachung f; (of birth, death etc) Anzeige f; **I'd like to make an ~** ich möchte etwas bekannt geben.
announcer [ə'naunsə*] n Ansager(in) m(f).
annoy [ə'nɔı] vt ärgern; **to be ~ed (at sth/with sb)** sich (über etw/jdn) ärgern; **don't get ~ed!** reg dich nicht auf!
annoyance [ə'nɔıəns] n Ärger m.
annoying [ə'nɔııŋ] adj ärgerlich; (person, habit) lästig.
annual ['ænjuəl] adj jährlich; (income) Jahres- ♦ n (BOT) einjährige Pflanze f; (book) Jahresband m.
annual general meeting (BRIT) n Jahreshauptversammlung f.
annually ['ænjuəlı] adv jährlich.
annual report n Geschäftsbericht m.
annuity [ə'nju:ıtı] n Rente f; **life ~** Rente f auf Lebenszeit.
annul [ə'nʌl] vt annullieren; (law) aufheben.
annulment [ə'nʌlmənt] n (see vb)

Annullierung f; Aufhebung f.
annum ['ænəm] n see **per.**
Annunciation [ənʌnsɪ'eɪʃən] n Mariä
Verkündigung f.
anode ['ænəud] n Anode f.
anodyne ['ænədaɪn] (fig) n Wohltat f ♦ adj
schmerzlos.
anoint [ə'nɔɪnt] vt salben.
anomalous [ə'nɒmələs] adj anomal.
anomaly [ə'nɒməlɪ] n Anomalie f.
anon. [ə'nɒn] abbr = **anonymous.**
anonymity [ænə'nɪmɪtɪ] n Anonymität f.
anonymous [ə'nɒnɪməs] adj anonym.
anorak ['ænəræk] n Anorak m.
anorexia [ænə'rɛksɪə] n Magersucht f,
Anorexie f.
anorexic [ænə'rɛksɪk] adj magersüchtig.
another [ə'nʌðə*] pron (additional) noch eine(r,
s); (different) ein(e) andere(r, s) ♦ adj:
~ **book** (one more) noch ein Buch; (a
different one) ein anderes Buch; ~ **drink?**
noch etwas zu trinken?; **in** ~ **5 years** in
weiteren 5 Jahren; see also **one.**
ANSI [eɪɛnɛs'aɪ] n abbr (= American National
Standards Institute) amerikanischer
Normenausschuss.
answer ['ɑːnsə*] n Antwort f; (to problem)
Lösung f ♦ vi antworten; (TEL) sich melden
♦ vt (reply to: person) antworten +dat; (: letter,
question) beantworten; (problem) lösen;
(prayer) erhören; **in** ~ **to your letter** in
Beantwortung Ihres Schreibens; **to** ~ **the
phone** ans Telefon gehen; **to** ~ **the bell** or
the door die Tür aufmachen.
▶ **answer back** vi widersprechen; (child)
frech sein.
▶ **answer for** vt fus (person) verantwortlich
sein für, sich verbürgen für.
▶ **answer to** vt fus (description) entsprechen
+dat.
answerable ['ɑːnsərəbl] adj: **to be** ~ **to sb for
sth** jdm gegenüber für etw verantwortlich
sein; **I am** ~ **to no-one** ich brauche mich vor
niemandem zu verantworten.
answering machine ['ɑːnsərɪŋ-] n
Anrufbeantworter m.
ant [ænt] n Ameise f.
ANTA n abbr (= American National Theater and
Academy) Nationaltheater und
Schauspielerakademie.
antagonism [æn'tægənɪzəm] n Feindseligkeit
f, Antagonismus m.
antagonist [æn'tægənɪst] n Gegner(in) m(f),
Antagonist(in) m(f).
antagonistic [æntægə'nɪstɪk] adj feindselig.
antagonize [æn'tægənaɪz] vt gegen sich
aufbringen.
Antarctic [ænt'ɑːktɪk] n: **the** ~ die Antarktis.
Antarctica [ænt'ɑːktɪkə] n Antarktik f.
Antarctic Circle n: **the** ~ der südliche
Polarkreis.
Antarctic Ocean n: **the** ~ das Südpolarmeer.

ante ['æntɪ] n: **to up the** ~ den Einsatz
erhöhen.
ante... ['æntɪ] pref vor-.
anteater ['æntiːtə*] n Ameisenbär m.
antecedent [æntɪ'siːdənt] n Vorläufer m; (of
living creature) Vorfahr m; **antecedents** npl
Herkunft f.
antechamber ['æntɪtʃeɪmbə*] n Vorzimmer nt.
antelope ['æntɪləup] n Antilope f.
antenatal ['æntɪ'neɪtl] adj vor der Geburt,
Schwangerschafts-.
antenatal clinic n Sprechstunde f für
werdende Mütter.
antenna [æn'tɛnə] (pl ~**e**) n (of insect) Fühler
m; (RADIO, TV) Antenne f.
antennae [æn'tɛniː] npl of **antenna.**
anteroom ['æntɪrum] n Vorzimmer nt.
anthem ['ænθəm] n: **national** ~
Nationalhymne f.
ant hill n Ameisenhaufen m.
anthology [æn'θɒlədʒɪ] n Anthologie f.
anthropologist [ænθrə'pɒlədʒɪst] n
Anthropologe m, Anthropologin f.
anthropology [ænθrə'pɒlədʒɪ] n
Anthropologie f.
anti... ['æntɪ] pref Anti-, anti-.
anti-aircraft ['æntɪ'ɛəkrɑːft] adj (gun, rocket)
Flugabwehr-.
anti-aircraft defence n Luftverteidigung f.
antiballistic ['æntɪbə'lɪstɪk] adj (missile) Anti-
Raketen-.
antibiotic ['æntɪbaɪ'ɔtɪk] n Antibiotikum nt.
antibody ['æntɪbɒdɪ] n Antikörper m.
anticipate [æn'tɪsɪpeɪt] vt erwarten; (foresee)
vorhersehen; (look forward to) sich freuen
auf +acc; (forestall) vorwegnehmen; **this is
worse than I** ~**d** es ist schlimmer, als ich
erwartet hatte; **as** ~**d** wie erwartet.
anticipation [æntɪsɪ'peɪʃən] n Erwartung f;
(eagerness) Vorfreude f; **thanking you in** ~
vielen Dank im Voraus.
anticlimax [æntɪ'klaɪmæks] n Enttäuschung f.
anticlockwise ['æntɪ'klɔkwaɪz] (BRIT) adv
gegen den Uhrzeigersinn.
antics ['æntɪks] npl Mätzchen pl; (of politicians
etc) Gehabe nt.
anticyclone ['æntɪ'saɪkləun] n
Hoch(druckgebiet) nt.
antidote ['æntɪdəut] n Gegenmittel nt.
antifreeze ['æntɪfriːz] n Frostschutzmittel nt.
antihistamine ['æntɪ'hɪstəmɪn] n
Antihistamin nt.
Antilles [æn'tɪliːz] npl: **the** ~ die Antillen pl.
antipathy [æn'tɪpəθɪ] n Antipathie f,
Abneigung f.
antiperspirant ['æntɪ'pəːspɪrənt] n
Antitranspirant nt.
antipodean [æntɪpə'diːən] adj antipodisch.
Antipodes [æn'tɪpədiːz] npl: **the** ~ Australien
und Neuseeland nt.
antiquarian [æntɪ'kwɛərɪən] n (collector)
Antiquitätensammler(in) m(f); (seller)

Antiquitätenhändler(in) *m(f)* ♦ *adj*:
~ **bookshop** Antiquariat *nt*.

antiquated ['æntɪkweɪtɪd] *adj* antiquiert.

antique [æn'tiːk] *n* Antiquität *f* ♦ *adj* antik.

antique dealer *n* Antiquitätenhändler *m*.

antique shop *n* Antiquitätenladen *m*.

antiquity [æn'tɪkwɪtɪ] *n* (*period*) Antike *f*;
antiquities *npl* (*objects*) Altertümer *pl*.

anti-Semitic ['æntɪsɪ'mɪtɪk] *adj* antisemitisch.

anti-Semitism ['æntɪ'semɪtɪzəm] *n*
Antisemitismus *m*.

antiseptic [æntɪ'septɪk] *n* Antiseptikum *nt*
♦ *adj* antiseptisch.

antisocial ['æntɪ'səʊʃəl] *adj* unsozial; (*person*)
ungesellig.

antitank ['æntɪ'tæŋk] *adj* Panzerabwehr-.

antitheses [æn'tɪθɪsiːz] *npl of* antithesis.

antithesis [æn'tɪθɪsɪs] (*pl* **antitheses**) *n*
Gegensatz *m*; **she's the** ~ **of a good cook** sie
ist das genaue Gegenteil einer guten
Köchin.

antitrust ['æntɪ'trʌst] (*US*) *adj*: ~ **legislation**
Kartellgesetzgebung *f*.

antlers ['æntlɒz] *npl* Geweih *nt*.

Antwerp ['æntwɔːp] *n* Antwerpen *nt*.

anus ['eɪnəs] *n* After *m*.

anvil ['ænvɪl] *n* Amboss *m*.

anxiety [æŋ'zaɪətɪ] *n* (*worry*) Sorge *f*; (*MED*)
Angstzustand *m*; (*eagerness*): ~ **to do sth**
Verlangen (danach), etw zu tun.

anxious ['æŋkʃəs] *adj* (*worried*) besorgt;
(*situation*) Angst einflößend; (*question,
moments*) bang(e); (*keen*): **to be** ~ **to do sth**
etw unbedingt tun wollen; **I'm very** ~ **about
you** ich mache mir große Sorgen um dich.

anxiously ['æŋkʃəslɪ] *adv* besorgt.

═══════════════════════ *KEYWORD*

any ['enɪ] *adj* **1** (*in questions etc*): **have you**
~ **butter/children?** haben Sie Butter/
Kinder?; **if there are** ~ **tickets left** falls noch
Karten da sind.
2 (*with negative*) kein(e); **I haven't** ~ **money/
books** ich habe kein Geld/keine Bücher.
3 (*no matter which*) irgendein(e); **choose**
~ **book you like** nehmen Sie irgendein Buch
or ein beliebiges Buch.
4 (*in phrases*): **in** ~ **case** in jedem Fall; ~ **day
now** jeden Tag; **at** ~ **moment** jeden
Moment; **at** ~ **rate** auf jeden Fall; ~ **time** (*at
any moment*) jeden Moment; (*whenever*)
jederzeit
♦ *pron* **1** (*in questions etc*): **have you got** ~**?**
haben Sie welche?; **can** ~ **of you sing?** kann
(irgend)einer von euch singen?
2 (*with negative*) **I haven't** ~ (**of them**) ich
habe keine (davon).
3 (*no matter which one(s)*) egal welche; **take**
~ **of those books** (**you like**) nehmen Sie
irgendwelche von diesen Büchern
♦ *adv* **1** (*in questions etc*): **do you want**
~ **more soup/sandwiches?** möchtest du

noch Suppe/Butterbrote?; **are you feeling**
~ **better?** geht es Ihnen etwas besser?
2 (*with negative*): **I can't hear him** ~ **more** ich
kann ihn nicht mehr hören; **don't wait**
~ **longer** warte nicht noch länger.

anybody ['enɪbɒdɪ] *pron* = **anyone**.

═══════════════════════ *KEYWORD*

anyhow ['enɪhaʊ] *adv* **1** (*at any rate*) sowieso,
ohnehin; **I shall go** ~ ich gehe auf jeden
Fall.
2 (*haphazard*): **do it** ~ **you like** machen Sie
es, wie Sie wollen.

anyone ['enɪwʌn] *pron* **1** (*in questions etc*)
(irgend)jemand; **can you see** ~**?** siehst du
jemanden?
2 (*with negative*) keine(r); **I can't see** ~ ich
kann keinen *or* niemanden sehen.
3 (*no matter who*) jede(r); ~ **could do it** das
kann jeder.

anyplace ['enɪpleɪs] (*US*) *adv* = **anywhere**.

═══════════════════════ *KEYWORD*

anything ['enɪθɪŋ] *pron* **1** (*in questions etc*)
(irgend)etwas; **can you see** ~**?** kannst du
etwas sehen?
2 (*with negative*) nichts; **I can't see** ~ ich
kann nichts sehen.
3 (*no matter what*) irgendetwas; **you can say**
~ **you like** du kannst sagen, was du willst;
~ **between 15 and 20 pounds** (ungefähr)
zwischen 15 und 20 Pfund.

═══════════════════════ *KEYWORD*

anyway ['enɪweɪ] *adv* **1** (*at any rate*) sowieso; **I
shall go** ~ ich gehe auf jeden Fall.
2 (*besides*): ~, **I can't come** jedenfalls kann
ich nicht kommen; **why are you phoning,** ~**?**
warum rufst du überhaupt *or* eigentlich an?

═══════════════════════ *KEYWORD*

anywhere ['enɪwɛə'] *adv* **1** (*in questions etc*)
irgendwo; **can you see him** ~**?** kannst du ihn
irgendwo sehen?
2 (*with negative*) nirgendwo, nirgends; **I can't
see him** ~ ich kann ihn nirgendwo *or*
nirgends sehen.
3 (*no matter where*) irgendwo; **put the books
down** ~ legen Sie die Bücher irgendwohin.

Anzac ['ænzæk] *n abbr* (= *Australia-New Zealand
Army Corps*) (*soldier*) australischer/
neuseeländischer Soldat *m*.

ANZAC DAY

Anzac Day, *der 25 April, ist in Australien und
Neuseeland ein Feiertag zum Gedenken an die
Landung der australischen und neuseeländischen
Truppen in Gallipoli im ersten Weltkrieg (1915).*

apace [ə'peɪs] *adv*: **to continue** ~ (*negotiations, preparations etc*) rasch vorangehen.

apart [ə'pɑːt] *adv* (*be*) entfernt; (*move*) auseinander; (*aside*) beiseite; (*separately*) getrennt; **10 miles** ~ 10 Meilen voneinander entfernt; **a long way** ~ weit auseinander; **they are living** ~ sie leben getrennt; **with one's legs** ~ mit gespreizten Beinen; **to take** ~ auseinander nehmen; ~ **from** (*excepting*) abgesehen von; (*in addition*) außerdem.

apartheid [ə'pɑːteɪt] *n* Apartheid *f*.

apartment [ə'pɑːtmənt] *n* (*US: flat*) Wohnung *f*; (*room*) Raum *m*, Zimmer *nt*.

apartment building (*US*) *n* Wohnblock *m*.

apathetic [æpə'θetɪk] *adj* apathisch, teilnahmslos.

apathy ['æpəθɪ] *n* Apathie *f*, Teilnahmslosigkeit *f*.

APB (*US*) *n abbr* (= *all points bulletin*) *polizeiliche Fahndung.*

ape [eɪp] *n* (Menschen)affe *m* ♦ *vt* nachahmen.

Apennines ['æpənaɪnz] *npl*: **the** ~ die Apenninen *pl*, der Appenin.

apéritif *n* Aperitif *m*.

aperture ['æpətʃjuə*] *n* Öffnung *f*; (*PHOT*) Blende *f*.

APEX ['eɪpɛks] *n abbr* (*AVIAT, RAIL:* = *advance purchase excursion*) APEX.

apex ['eɪpɛks] *n* Spitze *f*.

aphid ['æfɪd] *n* Blattlaus *f*.

aphorism ['æfərɪzəm] *n* Aphorismus *m*.

aphrodisiac [æfrəu'dɪzɪæk] *adj* aphrodisisch ♦ *n* Aphrodisiakum *nt*.

API *n abbr* (= *American Press Institute*) *amerikanischer Presseverband.*

apiece [ə'piːs] *adv* (*each person*) pro Person; (*each thing*) pro Stück.

aplomb [ə'plɔm] *n* Gelassenheit *f*.

APO (*US*) *n abbr* (= *Army Post Office*) *Poststelle der Armee.*

apocalypse [ə'pɔkəlɪps] *n* Apokalypse *f*.

apolitical [eɪpə'lɪtɪkl] *adj* apolitisch.

apologetic [əpɔlə'dʒetɪk] *adj* entschuldigend; **to be very** ~ **(about sth)** sich (wegen etw *gen*) sehr entschuldigen.

apologize [ə'pɔlədʒaɪz] *vi*: **to** ~ **(for sth to sb)** sich (für etw bei jdm) entschuldigen.

apology [ə'pɔlədʒɪ] *n* Entschuldigung *f*; **to send one's apologies** sich entschuldigen lassen; **please accept my apologies** ich bitte um Verzeihung.

apoplectic [æpə'plɛktɪk] *adj* (*MED*) apoplektisch; (*fig*): **to be** ~ **with rage** vor Wut fast platzen.

apoplexy ['æpəplɛksɪ] *n* Schlaganfall *m*.

apostle [ə'pɔsl] *n* Apostel *m*.

apostrophe [ə'pɔstrəfɪ] *n* Apostroph *m*, Auslassungszeichen *nt*.

apotheosis [əpɔθɪ'əusɪs] *n* Apotheose *f*.

appal [ə'pɔːl] *vt* entsetzen; **to be** ~**led by** entsetzt sein über +*acc*.

Appalachian Mountains [æpə'leɪʃən-] *npl*: **the** ~ die Appalachen *pl*.

appalling [ə'pɔːlɪŋ] *adj* entsetzlich; **she's an** ~ **cook** sie kann überhaupt nicht kochen.

apparatus [æpə'reɪtəs] *n* Gerät *nt*; (*in gymnasium*) Geräte *pl*; (*of organization*) Apparat *m*; **a piece of** ~ ein Gerät *nt*.

apparel [ə'pærəl] (*US*) *n* Kleidung *f*.

apparent [ə'pærənt] *adj* (*seeming*) scheinbar; (*obvious*) offensichtlich; **it is** ~ **that** ... es ist klar, dass ...

apparently [ə'pærəntlɪ] *adv* anscheinend.

apparition [æpə'rɪʃən] *n* Erscheinung *f*.

appeal [ə'piːl] *vi* (*LAW*) Berufung einlegen ♦ *n* (*LAW*) Berufung *f*; (*plea*) Aufruf *m*; (*charm*) Reiz *m*; **to** ~ **(to sb) for** (jdn) bitten um; **to** ~ **to** (*be attractive to*) gefallen +*dat*; **it doesn't** ~ **to me** es reizt mich nicht; **right of** ~ (*LAW*) Berufungsrecht *nt*; **on** ~ (*LAW*) in der Berufung.

appealing [ə'piːlɪŋ] *adj* ansprechend; (*touching*) rührend.

appear [ə'pɪə*] *vi* erscheinen; (*seem*) scheinen; **to** ~ **on TV/in "Hamlet"** im Fernsehen/in „Hamlet" auftreten; **it would** ~ **that** ... anscheinend ...

appearance [ə'pɪərəns] *n* Erscheinen *nt*; (*look*) Aussehen *nt*; (*in public, on TV*) Auftritt *m*; **to put in** *or* **make an** ~ sich sehen lassen; **in** *or* **by order of** ~ (*THEAT etc*) in der Reihenfolge ihres Auftritts; **to keep up** ~**s** den (äußeren) Schein wahren; **to all** ~**s** allem Anschein nach.

appease [ə'piːz] *vt* beschwichtigen.

appeasement [ə'piːzmənt] *n* Beschwichtigung *f*.

append [ə'pɛnd] *vt* (*COMPUT*) anhängen.

appendage [ə'pɛndɪdʒ] *n* Anhängsel *nt*.

appendices [ə'pɛndɪsiːz] *npl of* **appendix**.

appendicitis [əpɛndɪ'saɪtɪs] *n* Blinddarmentzündung *f*.

appendix [ə'pɛndɪks] (*pl* **appendices**) *n* (*ANAT*) Blinddarm *m*; (*to publication*) Anhang *m*; **to have one's** ~ **out** sich *dat* den Blinddarm herausnehmen lassen.

appetite ['æpɪtaɪt] *n* Appetit *m*; (*fig*) Lust *f*; **that walk has given me an** ~ von dem Spaziergang habe ich Appetit bekommen.

appetizer ['æpɪtaɪzə*] *n* (*food*) Appetit-happen *m*; (*drink*) appetitanregendes Getränk *nt*.

appetizing ['æpɪtaɪzɪŋ] *adj* appetitanregend.

applaud [ə'plɔːd] *vi* applaudieren, klatschen ♦ *vt* (*actor etc*) applaudieren +*dat*, Beifall spenden *or* klatschen +*dat*; (*action, attitude*) loben; (*decision*) begrüßen.

applause [ə'plɔːz] *n* Applaus *m*, Beifall *m*.

apple ['æpl] *n* Apfel *m*; **he's the** ~ **of her eye** er ist ihr ein und alles.

apple tree *n* Apfelbaum *m*.

apple turnover *n* Apfeltasche *f*.

appliance [ə'plaɪəns] n Gerät nt.

applicable [ə'plɪkəbl] adj: ~ **(to)** anwendbar (auf +acc); (on official forms) zutreffend (auf +acc); **the law is** ~ **from January** das Gesetz gilt ab Januar.

applicant ['æplɪkənt] n Bewerber(in) m(f).

application [æplɪ'keɪʃən] n (for job) Bewerbung f; (for grant etc) Antrag m; (hard work) Fleiß m; (applying: of paint etc) Auftragen nt; **on** ~ auf Antrag.

application form n (for a job) Bewerbungsformular nt; (for a grant etc) Antragsformular nt.

application program n (COMPUT) Anwendungsprogramm nt.

applications package n (COMPUT) Anwendungspaket nt.

applied [ə'plaɪd] adj angewandt.

apply [ə'plaɪ] vt anwenden; (paint etc) auftragen ♦ vi: **to** ~ **(to)** (be applicable) gelten (für); **to** ~ **the brakes** die Bremse betätigen, bremsen; **to** ~ **o.s. to sth** sich bei etw anstrengen; **to** ~ **to** (ask) sich wenden an +acc; **to** ~ **for** (permit, grant) beantragen; (job) sich bewerben um.

appoint [ə'pɔɪnt] vt ernennen; (date, place) festlegen, festsetzen.

appointed [ə'pɔɪntɪd] adj: **at the** ~ **time** zur festgesetzten Zeit.

appointee [əpɔɪn'tiː] n Ernannte(r) f(m).

appointment [ə'pɔɪntmənt] n Ernennung f; (post) Stelle f; (arranged meeting) Termin m; **to make an** ~ **(with sb)** einen Termin (mit jdm) vereinbaren; **by** ~ nach Anmeldung, mit Voranmeldung.

apportion [ə'pɔːʃən] vt aufteilen; (blame) zuweisen; **to** ~ **sth to sb** jdm etw zuteilen.

apposition [æpə'zɪʃən] n Apposition f, Beifügung f; **A is in** ~ **to B** A ist eine Apposition zu B.

appraisal [ə'preɪzl] n Beurteilung f.

appraise [ə'preɪz] vt beurteilen.

appreciable [ə'priːʃəbl] adj merklich, deutlich.

appreciably [ə'priːʃəblɪ] adv merklich.

appreciate [ə'priːʃɪeɪt] vt (like) schätzen; (be grateful for) zu schätzen wissen; (understand) verstehen; (be aware of) sich dat bewusst sein +gen ♦ vi (COMM: currency, shares) im Wert steigen; **I** ~ **your help** ich weiß Ihre Hilfe zu schätzen.

appreciation [əpriːʃɪ'eɪʃən] n (enjoyment) Wertschätzung f; (understanding) Verständnis nt; (gratitude) Dankbarkeit f; (COMM: in value) (Wert)steigerung f.

appreciative [ə'priːʃɪətɪv] adj dankbar; (comment) anerkennend.

apprehend [æprɪ'hɛnd] vt (arrest) festnehmen; (understand) verstehen.

apprehension [æprɪ'hɛnʃən] n (fear) Besorgnis f; (arrest) Festnahme f.

apprehensive [æprɪ'hɛnsɪv] adj ängstlich; **to**

be ~ **about sth** sich dat Gedanken or Sorgen um etw machen.

apprentice [ə'prɛntɪs] n Lehrling m, Auszubildende(r) f(m) ♦ vt: **to be** ~**d to sb** bei jdm in der Lehre sein.

apprenticeship [ə'prɛntɪsʃɪp] n Lehre f, Lehrzeit f; **to serve one's** ~ seine Lehre machen.

appro. ['æprəu] (BRIT: inf) abbr (COMM: = approval): **on** ~ zur Ansicht.

approach [ə'prəutʃ] vi sich nähern; (event) nahen ♦ vt (come to) sich nähern +dat; (ask, apply to: person) herantreten an +acc, ansprechen; (situation, problem) herangehen an +acc, angehen ♦ n (advance) (Heran)nahen nt; (access) Zugang m; (: for vehicles) Zufahrt f; (to problem etc) Ansatz m; **to** ~ **sb about sth** jdn wegen etw ansprechen.

approachable [ə'prəutʃəbl] adj (person) umgänglich; (place) zugänglich.

approach road n Zufahrtsstraße f.

approbation [æprə'beɪʃən] n Zustimmung f.

appropriate [adj ə'prəuprɪɪt, vt ə'prəuprɪeɪt] adj (apt) angebracht; (relevant) entsprechend ♦ vt sich dat aneignen; **it would not be** ~ **for me to comment** es wäre nicht angebracht, wenn ich mich dazu äußern würde.

appropriately [ə'prəuprɪɪtlɪ] adv entsprechend.

appropriation [əprəuprɪ'eɪʃən] n Zuteilung f, Zuweisung f.

approval [ə'pruːvəl] n (approbation) Zustimmung f, Billigung f; (permission) Einverständnis f; **to meet with sb's** ~ jds Zustimmung or Beifall finden; **on** ~ (COMM) zur Probe.

approve [ə'pruːv] vt billigen; (motion, decision) annehmen.

▶ **approve of** vt fus etwas halten von; **I don't** ~ **of it/him** ich halte nichts davon/von ihm.

approved school [ə'pruːvd-] (BRIT) n Erziehungsheim nt.

approvingly [ə'pruːvɪŋlɪ] adv zustimmend.

approx. abbr = **approximately**.

approximate [adj ə'prɒksɪmɪt, vb ə'prɒksɪmeɪt] adj ungefähr ♦ vt, vi: **to** ~ **(to)** nahe kommen +dat.

approximately [ə'prɒksɪmɪtlɪ] adv ungefähr.

approximation [əprɒksɪ'meɪʃən] n Annäherung f.

APR n abbr (= annual(ized) percentage rate) Jahreszinssatz m.

Apr. abbr = **April**.

apricot ['eɪprɪkɒt] n Aprikose f.

April ['eɪprəl] n April m; ~ **fool!** April, April!; see also **July**.

apron ['eɪprən] n Schürze f; (AVIAT) Vorfeld nt.

apse [æps] n Apsis f.

APT (BRIT) n abbr (= Advanced Passenger Train) Hochgeschwindigkeitszug m.

Apt. abbr = **apartment**.

apt [æpt] adj (suitable) passend, treffend;

(*likely*): **to be ~ to do sth** dazu neigen, etw zu tun.
aptitude ['æptɪtjuːd] *n* Begabung *f*.
aptitude test *n* Eignungstest *m*.
aptly ['æptlɪ] *adv* passend, treffend.
aqualung ['ækwəlʌŋ] *n* Tauchgerät *nt*.
aquarium [ə'kwɛərɪəm] *n* Aquarium *nt*.
Aquarius [ə'kwɛərɪəs] *n* Wassermann *m*; **to be ~** (ein) Wassermann sein.
aquatic [ə'kwætɪk] *adj* (*plants etc*) Wasser-; (*life*) im Wasser.
aqueduct ['ækwɪdʌkt] *n* Aquädukt *m or nt*.
AR (*US*) *abbr* (*POST:* = *Arkansas*).
ARA (*BRIT*) *n abbr* (= *Associate of the Royal Academy*) Qualifikationsnachweis im künstlerischen Bereich.
Arab ['ærəb] *adj* arabisch ♦ *n* Araber(in) *m(f)*.
Arabia [ə'reɪbɪə] *n* Arabien *nt*.
Arabian [ə'reɪbɪən] *adj* arabisch.
Arabian Desert *n*: **the ~** die Arabische Wüste.
Arabian Sea *n*: **the ~** das Arabische Meer.
Arabic ['ærəbɪk] *adj* arabisch ♦ *n* (*LING*) Arabisch *nt*.
arable ['ærəbl] *adj* (*land*) bebaubar; **~ farm** Bauernhof, der ausschließlich Ackerbau betreibt.
ARAM (*BRIT*) *n abbr* (= *Associate of the Royal Academy of Music*) Qualifikationsnachweis in Musik.
arbiter ['ɑːbɪtə*] *n* Vermittler *m*.
arbitrary ['ɑːbɪtrərɪ] *adj* willkürlich.
arbitrate ['ɑːbɪtreɪt] *vi* vermitteln.
arbitration [ɑːbɪ'treɪʃən] *n* Schlichtung *f*; **the dispute went to ~** der Streit wurde vor eine Schlichtungskommission gebracht.
arbitrator ['ɑːbɪtreɪtə*] *n* Vermittler(in) *m(f)*; (*INDUSTRY*) Schlichter(in) *m(f)*.
ARC *n abbr* (= *American Red Cross*) ≈ DRK *nt*.
arc [ɑːk] *n* Bogen *m*.
arcade [ɑː'keɪd] *n* Arkade *f*; (*shopping mall*) Passage *f*.
arch [ɑːtʃ] *n* Bogen *m*; (*of foot*) Gewölbe *nt* ♦ *vt* (*back*) krümmen ♦ *adj* schelmisch ♦ *pref* Erz-.
archaeological [ɑːkɪə'lɒdʒɪkl] *adj* archäologisch.
archaeologist [ɑːkɪ'ɒlədʒɪst] *n* Archäologe *m*, Archäologin *f*.
archaeology, (*US*) **archeology** [ɑːkɪ'ɒlədʒɪ] *n* Archäologie *f*.
archaic [ɑː'keɪɪk] *adj* altertümlich; (*language*) veraltet, archaisch.
archangel ['ɑːkeɪndʒəl] *n* Erzengel *m*.
archbishop [ɑːtʃ'bɪʃəp] *n* Erzbischof *m*.
archenemy ['ɑːtʃ'ɛnəmɪ] *n* Erzfeind(in) *m(f)*.
archeology *etc* [ɑːkɪ'ɒlədʒɪ] (*US*) = **archaeology** *etc.*
archery ['ɑːtʃərɪ] *n* Bogenschießen *nt*.
archetypal ['ɑːkɪtaɪpəl] *adj* (arche)typisch.
archetype ['ɑːkɪtaɪp] *n* Urbild *nt*, Urtyp *m*.
archipelago [ɑːkɪ'pɛlɪgəu] *n* Archipel *m*.
architect ['ɑːkɪtɛkt] *n* Architekt(in) *m(f)*.

architectural [ɑːkɪ'tɛktʃərəl] *adj* architektonisch.
architecture ['ɑːkɪtɛktʃə*] *n* Architektur *f*.
archive file *n* (*COMPUT*) Archivdatei *f*.
archives ['ɑːkaɪvz] *npl* Archiv *nt*.
archivist ['ɑːkɪvɪst] *n* Archivar(in) *m(f)*.
archway ['ɑːtʃweɪ] *n* Torbogen *m*.
ARCM (*BRIT*) *n abbr* (= *Associate of the Royal College of Music*) Qualifikationsnachweis in Musik.
Arctic ['ɑːktɪk] *adj* arktisch ♦ *n*: **the ~** die Arktis.
Arctic Circle *n*: **the ~** der nördliche Polarkreis.
Arctic Ocean *n*: **the ~** das Nordpolarmeer.
ARD (*US*) *n abbr* (*MED:* = *acute respiratory disease*) akute Erkrankung der Atemwege.
ardent ['ɑːdənt] *adj* leidenschaftlich; (*admirer*) glühend.
ardour, (*US*) **ardor** ['ɑːdə*] *n* Leidenschaft *f*.
arduous ['ɑːdjuəs] *adj* mühsam.
are [ɑː*] *vb see* **be**.
area ['ɛərɪə] *n* Gebiet *nt*; (*GEOM etc*) Fläche *f*; (*dining area etc*) Bereich *m*; **in the London ~** im Raum London.
area code (*US*) *n* Vorwahl(nummer) *f*.
arena [ə'riːnə] *n* Arena *f*.
aren't [ɑːnt] = **are not**.
Argentina [ɑːdʒən'tiːnə] *n* Argentinien *nt*.
Argentinian [ɑːdʒən'tɪnɪən] *adj* argentinisch ♦ *n* Argentinier(in) *m(f)*.
arguable ['ɑːgjuəbl] *adj*: **it is ~ whether ...** es ist (noch) die Frage, ob ...; **it is ~ that ...** man kann (wohl) sagen, dass ...
arguably ['ɑːgjuəblɪ] *adv* wohl; **it is ~ ...** es dürfte wohl ... sein.
argue ['ɑːgjuː] *vi* (*quarrel*) sich streiten; (*reason*) diskutieren ♦ *vt* (*debate*) diskutieren, erörtern; **to ~ that ...** den Standpunkt vertreten, dass ...; **to ~ about sth** sich über etw *acc* streiten; **to ~ for/against sth** sich für/gegen etw aussprechen.
argument ['ɑːgjumənt] *n* (*reasons*) Argument *nt*; (*quarrel*) Streit *m*, Auseinandersetzung *f*; (*debate*) Diskussion *f*; **~ for/against** Argument für/gegen; **to have an ~** sich streiten.
argumentative [ɑːgju'mɛntətɪv] *adj* streitlustig.
aria ['ɑːrɪə] *n* Arie *f*.
ARIBA [ə'riːbə] (*BRIT*) *n abbr* (= *Associate of the Royal Institute of British Architects*) Qualifikationsnachweis in Architektur.
arid ['ærɪd] *adj* (*land*) dürr; (*subject*) trocken.
aridity [ə'rɪdɪtɪ] *n* Dürre *f*, Trockenheit *f*.
Aries ['ɛərɪz] *n* Widder *m*; **to be ~** (ein) Widder sein.
arise [ə'raɪz] (*pt* **arose**, *pp* **arisen**) *vi* (*difficulty etc*) sich ergeben; (*question*) sich stellen; **to ~ from** sich ergeben aus, herrühren von; **should the need ~** falls es nötig wird.
arisen [ə'rɪzn] *pp* of **arise**.

aristocracy [ærɪs'tɔkrəsɪ] n Aristokratie f, Adel m.

aristocrat ['ærɪstəkræt] n Aristokrat(in) m(f), Ad(e)lige(r) f(m).

aristocratic [ærɪstə'krætɪk] adj aristokratisch, ad(e)lig.

arithmetic [ə'rɪθmətɪk] n Rechnen nt; (calculation) Rechnung f.

arithmetical [ærɪθ'metɪkl] adj rechnerisch, arithmetisch.

Ariz. (US) abbr (POST: = Arizona).

ark [ɑːk] n: **Noah's A**~ die Arche Noah.

arm [ɑːm] n Arm m; (of clothing) Ärmel m; (of chair) Armlehne f; (of organization etc) Zweig m ♦ vt bewaffnen; **arms** npl (weapons) Waffen pl; (HERALDRY) Wappen nt.

armaments ['ɑːməmənts] npl (weapons) (Aus)rüstung f.

armband ['ɑːmbænd] n Armbinde f.

armchair ['ɑːmtʃeə'] n Sessel m, Lehnstuhl m.

armed [ɑːmd] adj bewaffnet; **the ~ forces** die Streitkräfte pl.

armed robbery n bewaffneter Raubüberfall m.

Armenia [ɑː'miːnɪə] n Armenien nt.

Armenian [ɑː'miːnɪən] adj armenisch ♦ n Armenier(in) m(f); (LING) Armenisch nt.

armful ['ɑːmful] n Arm m voll.

armistice ['ɑːmɪstɪs] n Waffenstillstand m.

armour, (US) **armor** ['ɑːmə'] n (HIST) Rüstung f; (also: ~-plating) Panzerplatte f; (MIL: tanks) Panzerfahrzeuge pl.

armoured car ['ɑːməd-] n Panzerwagen m.

armoury ['ɑːmərɪ] n Waffenlager nt.

armpit ['ɑːmpɪt] n Achselhöhle f.

armrest ['ɑːmrest] n Armlehne f.

arms control [ɑːmz-] n Rüstungskontrolle f.

arms race [ɑːmz-] n: **the ~** das Wettrüsten.

army ['ɑːmɪ] n Armee f, Heer nt; (fig: host) Heer.

aroma [ə'rəumə] n Aroma nt, Duft m.

aromatherapy [ərəumə'θerəpɪ] n Aromatherapie f.

aromatic [ærə'mætɪk] adj aromatisch, duftend.

arose [ə'rəuz] pt of **arise**.

around [ə'raund] adv (about) herum; (in the area) in der Nähe ♦ prep (encircling) um ... herum; (near) in der Nähe von; (fig: about: dimensions) etwa; (: time) gegen; (: date) um; **is he ~?** ist er da?; **~ £5** um die £5, etwa £5; **~ 3 o'clock** gegen 3 Uhr.

arousal [ə'rauzəl] n (sexual) Erregung f; (of feelings, interest) Weckung f.

arouse [ə'rauz] vt (feelings, interest) wecken.

arpeggio [ɑː'pedʒɪəu] n Arpeggio nt.

arrange [ə'reɪndʒ] vt (meeting etc) vereinbaren; (tour etc) planen; (books etc) anordnen; (flowers) arrangieren; (MUS) arrangieren, bearbeiten ♦ vi: **we have ~d for a car to pick you up** wir haben veranlasst, dass Sie mit dem Auto abgeholt werden; **it was ~d that ...** es wurde

vereinbart, dass ...; **to ~ to do sth** vereinbaren or ausmachen, etw zu tun.

arrangement [ə'reɪndʒmənt] n (agreement) Vereinbarung f; (layout) Anordnung f; (MUS) Arrangement nt, Bearbeitung f; **arrangements** npl Pläne pl; (preparations) Vorbereitungen pl; **to come to an ~ with sb** eine Regelung mit jdm treffen; **home deliveries by ~** nach Vereinbarung Lieferung ins Haus; **I'll make ~s for you to be met** ich werde veranlassen, dass Sie abgeholt werden.

arrant ['ærənt] adj (coward, fool etc) Erz-; (nonsense) total.

array [ə'reɪ] n: **an ~ of** (things) eine Reihe von; (people) Aufgebot an +dat; (MATH, COMPUT) (Daten)feld nt.

arrears [ə'rɪəz] npl Rückstand m; **to be in ~ with one's rent** mit seiner Miete im Rückstand sein.

arrest [ə'rest] vt (person) verhaften; (sb's attention) erregen ♦ n Verhaftung f; **under ~** verhaftet.

arresting [ə'restɪŋ] adj (fig) atemberaubend.

arrival [ə'raɪvl] n Ankunft f; (COMM: of goods) Sendung f; **new ~** (person) Neuankömmling m; (baby) Neugeborene(s) nt.

arrive [ə'raɪv] vi ankommen.

▶ **arrive at** vt fus (fig: conclusion) kommen zu; (: situation) es bringen zu.

arrogance ['ærəgəns] n Arroganz f, Überheblichkeit f.

arrogant ['ærəgənt] adj arrogant, überheblich.

arrow ['ærəu] n Pfeil m.

arse [ɑːs] (BRIT: inf!) n Arsch m (!).

arsenal ['ɑːsɪnl] n Waffenlager nt; (stockpile) Arsenal nt.

arsenic ['ɑːsnɪk] n Arsen nt.

arson ['ɑːsn] n Brandstiftung f.

art [ɑːt] n Kunst f; **Arts** npl (SCOL) Geisteswissenschaften pl; **work of ~** Kunstwerk nt.

art and design (BRIT) n (SCOL) ≈ Kunst und Design.

artefact ['ɑːtɪfækt] n Artefakt nt.

arterial [ɑː'tɪərɪəl] adj arteriell; **~ road** Fernverkehrsstraße f; **~ line** (RAIL) Hauptstrecke f.

artery ['ɑːtərɪ] n Arterie f, Schlagader f; (fig) Verkehrsader f.

artful ['ɑːtful] adj raffiniert.

art gallery n Kunstgalerie f.

arthritic [ɑː'θrɪtɪk] adj arthritisch.

arthritis [ɑː'θraɪtɪs] n Arthritis f.

artichoke ['ɑːtɪtʃəuk] n (also: **globe ~**) Artischocke f; (also: **Jerusalem ~**) Topinambur m.

article ['ɑːtɪkl] n Artikel m; (object, item) Gegenstand m; **articles** (BRIT) npl (LAW) (Rechts)referendarzeit f; **~ of clothing** Kleidungsstück nt.

articles of association npl (COMM)

Gesellschaftsvertrag *m*.

articulate [*adj* ɔ:'tɪkjulɪt, *vt, vi* ɔ:'tɪkjuleɪt] *adj* (*speech, writing*) klar; (*speaker*) redegewandt ♦ *vt* darlegen ♦ *vi* artikulieren; **to be ~** (*person*) sich gut ausdrücken können.

articulated lorry (*BRIT*) *n* Sattelschlepper *m*.

artifice ['ɑːtɪfɪs] *n* List *f*.

artificial [ɑːtɪ'fɪʃəl] *adj* künstlich; (*manner*) gekünstelt; **to be ~** (*person*) gekünstelt *or* unnatürlich wirken.

artificial insemination [-ɪnsɛmɪ'neɪʃən] *n* künstliche Besamung *f*.

artificial intelligence *n* künstliche Intelligenz *f*.

artificial respiration *n* künstliche Beatmung *f*.

artillery [ɑː'tɪləri] *n* Artillerie *f*.

artisan ['ɑːtɪzæn] *n* Handwerker *m*.

artist ['ɑːtɪst] *n* Künstler(in) *m(f)*.

artistic [ɑː'tɪstɪk] *adj* künstlerisch.

artistry ['ɑːtɪstrɪ] *n* künstlerisches Geschick *nt*.

artless ['ɑːtlɪs] *adj* arglos.

art school *n* Kunstakademie *f*, Kunsthochschule *f*.

artwork ['ɑːtwɜːk] *n* (*for advert etc, material for printing*) Druckvorlage *f*; (*in book*) Bildmaterial *nt*.

ARV *n abbr* (*BIBLE*: = *American Revised Version*) *amerikanische revidierte Bibelübersetzung*.

AS (*US*) *n abbr* (= *Associate in/of Science*) *akademischer Grad in Naturwissenschaften* ♦ *abbr* (*POST*: = *American Samoa*).

========================= *KEYWORD*

as [æz] *conj* **1** (*referring to time*) als; **~ the years went by** mit den Jahren; **he came in ~ I was leaving** als er hereinkam, ging ich gerade; **~ from tomorrow** ab morgen.

2 (*in comparisons*): **~ big ~** so groß wie; **twice ~ big ~** zweimal so groß wie; **~ much/many ~** so viel/so viele wie; **~ soon ~** sobald; **much ~ I admire her ...** sosehr ich sie auch bewundere ...

3 (*since, because*) da, weil; **~ you can't come I'll go without you** da du nicht mitkommen kannst, gehe ich ohne dich.

4 (*referring to manner, way*) wie; **do ~ you wish** mach, was du willst; **~ she said** wie sie sagte; **he gave it to me ~ a present** er gab es mir als Geschenk; **~ it were** sozusagen.

5 (*in the capacity of*) als; **he works ~ a driver** er arbeitet als Fahrer.

6 (*concerning*): **~ for** *or* **to that** was das betrifft *or* angeht.

7: **~ if** *or* **though** als ob; *see also* **long, such, well**.

─────────────────────────────

ASA *n abbr* (= *American Standards Association*) *amerikanischer Normenausschuss*.

a.s.a.p. *adv abbr* (= *as soon as possible*)

baldmöglichst.

asbestos [æz'bɛstɔs] *n* Asbest *m*.

ascend [ə'sɛnd] *vt* hinaufsteigen; (*throne*) besteigen.

ascendancy [ə'sɛndənsɪ] *n* Vormachtstellung *f*; **~ over sb** Vorherrschaft *f* über jdn.

ascendant [ə'sɛndənt] *n*: **to be in the ~** im Aufstieg begriffen sein.

ascension [ə'sɛnʃən] *n*: **the A~** (*REL*) die Himmelfahrt *f* (Christi).

Ascension Island *n* Ascension *nt*.

ascent [ə'sɛnt] *n* Aufstieg *m*.

ascertain [æsə'teɪn] *vt* feststellen.

ascetic [ə'sɛtɪk] *adj* asketisch.

asceticism [ə'sɛtɪsɪzəm] *n* Askese *f*.

ASCII ['æskiː] *n abbr* (*COMPUT*: = *American Standard Code for Information Interchange*) ASCII.

ascribe [ə'skraɪb] *vt*: **to ~ sth to** etw zuschreiben +*dat*; (*cause*) etw zurückführen auf +*acc*.

ASCU (*US*) *n abbr* (= *Association of State Colleges and Universities*) *Verband staatlicher Bildungseinrichtungen*.

ASEAN ['æsɪæn] *n abbr* (= *Association of Southeast Asian Nations*) ASEAN *f* (*Gemeinschaft südostasiatischer Staaten*).

ASH [æʃ] (*BRIT*) *n abbr* (= *Action on Smoking and Health*) *Antiraucherinitiative*.

ash [æʃ] *n* Asche *f*; (*wood, tree*) Esche *f*.

ashamed [ə'feɪmd] *adj* beschämt; **to be ~ of** sich schämen für; **to be ~ of o.s. for having done sth** sich schämen, dass man etw getan hat.

A shares *npl* stimmrechtslose Aktien *pl*.

ashen ['æʃən] *adj* (*face*) aschfahl.

ashore [ə'fɔː'] *adv* an Land.

ashtray ['æftreɪ] *n* Aschenbecher *m*.

Ash Wednesday *n* Aschermittwoch *m*.

Asia ['eɪfə] *n* Asien *nt*.

Asia Minor *n* Kleinasien *nt*.

Asian ['eɪfən] *adj* asiatisch ♦ *n* Asiat(in) *m(f)*.

Asiatic [eɪsɪ'ætɪk] *adj* asiatisch.

aside [ə'saɪd] *adv* zur Seite; (*take*) beiseite ♦ *n* beiseite gesprochene Worte *pl*; **to brush objections ~** Einwände beiseite schieben.

aside from *prep* außer +*dat*.

ask [ɑːsk] *vt* fragen; (*invite*) einladen; **to ~ sb to do sth** jdn bitten, etw zu tun; **to ~ (sb) sth** (jdn) etw fragen; **to ~ sb a question** jdm eine Frage stellen; **to ~ sb the time** jdn nach der Uhrzeit fragen; **to ~ sb about sth** jdn nach etw fragen; **to ~ sb out to dinner** jdn zum Essen einladen.

▶ **ask after** *vt fus* fragen nach.

▶ **ask for** *vt fus* bitten um; (*trouble*) haben wollen; **it's just ~ing for trouble/it** das kann ja nicht gut gehen.

askance [ə'skɑːns] *adv*: **to look ~ at sb** jdn misstrauisch ansehen; **to look ~ at sth** etw mit Misstrauen betrachten.

askew [ə'skjuː] *adv* schief.

asking price ['ɑːskɪŋ-] n: **the ~** der geforderte Preis.

asleep [ə'sliːp] adj schlafend; **to be ~** schlafen; **to fall ~** einschlafen.

AS level n abbr (= Advanced Subsidiary level) Mit "AS level" wird das erste Jahr der Sekundarstufe II bezeichnet, nach dessen Abschluss Prüfungen in drei der ingesamt sechs für den "A level" benötigten Wahlpflichtfächern abgehalten werden.

asp [æsp] n Natter f.

asparagus [əs'pærəgəs] n Spargel m.

asparagus tips npl Spargelspitzen pl.

ASPCA n abbr (= American Society for the Prevention of Cruelty to Animals) Tierschutzverein.

aspect ['æspɛkt] n (of subject) Aspekt m; (of building etc) Lage f; (quality, air) Erscheinung f; **to have a south-westerly ~** nach Südwesten liegen.

aspersions [əs'pɔːʃənz] npl: **to cast ~ on** sich abfällig äußern über +acc.

asphalt ['æsfælt] n Asphalt m.

asphyxiate [æs'fɪksɪeɪt] vt ersticken.

asphyxiation [æsfɪksɪ'eɪʃən] n Erstickung f.

aspirate ['æspəreɪt] vt aspirieren, behauchen.

aspirations [æspə'reɪʃənz] npl Hoffnungen pl; **to have ~ to(wards) sth** etw anstreben.

aspire [əs'paɪə*] vi: **to ~ to** streben nach.

aspirin ['æsprɪn] n Kopfschmerztablette f, Aspirin ® nt.

aspiring [əs'paɪərɪŋ] adj aufstrebend.

ass [æs] n (also fig) Esel m; (US: inf!) Arsch! m.

assail [ə'seɪl] vt angreifen; (fig): **to be ~ed by doubts** von Zweifeln geplagt werden.

assailant [ə'seɪlənt] n Angreifer(in) m(f).

assassin [ə'sæsɪn] n Attentäter(in) m(f).

assassinate [ə'sæsɪneɪt] vt ermorden, ein Attentat verüben auf +acc.

assassination [əsæsɪ'neɪʃən] n Ermordung f, (geglücktes) Attentat nt.

assault [ə'sɔːlt] n Angriff m ♦ vt angreifen; (sexually) vergewaltigen; **~ and battery** (LAW) Körperverletzung f.

assemble [ə'sɛmbl] vt versammeln; (car, machine) montieren; (furniture etc) zusammenbauen ♦ vi sich versammeln.

assembly [ə'sɛmblɪ] n Versammlung f; (of car, machine) Montage f; (of furniture) Zusammenbau m.

assembly language n (COMPUT) Assemblersprache f.

assembly line n Fließband nt.

assent [ə'sɛnt] n Zustimmung f ♦ vi: **to ~ to** zustimmen (+dat).

assert [ə'sɜːt] vt behaupten; (innocence) beteuern; (authority) geltend machen; **to ~ o.s.** sich durchsetzen.

assertion [ə'sɜːʃən] n Behauptung f.

assertive [ə'sɜːtɪv] adj (person) selbstbewusst; (manner) bestimmt.

assess [ə'sɛs] vt (situation) einschätzen; (abilities etc) beurteilen; (tax) festsetzen; (damages, property etc) schätzen.

assessment [ə'sɛsmənt] n (see vt) Einschätzung f; Beurteilung f; Festsetzung f; Schätzung f.

assessor [ə'sɛsə*] n (LAW) Gutachter(in) m(f).

asset ['æsɛt] n Vorteil m; (person) Stütze f; **assets** npl (property, funds) Vermögen nt; (COMM) Aktiva pl.

asset-stripping ['æsɛt'strɪpɪŋ] n (COMM) Aufkauf von finanziell gefährdeten Firmen und anschließender Verkauf ihrer Vermögenswerte.

assiduous [ə'sɪdjuəs] adj gewissenhaft.

assign [ə'saɪn] vt: **to ~ (to)** (date) zuweisen (+dat); (task) übertragen (+dat); (person) einteilen (für); (cause) zuschreiben (+dat); (meaning) zuordnen (+dat); **to ~ sb to do sth** jdn damit beauftragen, etw zu tun.

assignment [ə'saɪnmənt] n Aufgabe f.

assimilate [ə'sɪmɪleɪt] vt aufnehmen; (immigrants) integrieren.

assimilation [əsɪmɪ'leɪʃən] n (see vt) Aufnahme f; Integration f.

assist [ə'sɪst] vt helfen; (with money etc) unterstützen.

assistance [ə'sɪstəns] n Hilfe f; (with money etc) Unterstützung f.

assistant [ə'sɪstənt] n Assistent(in) m(f); (BRIT: also: **shop ~**) Verkäufer(in) m(f).

assistant manager n stellvertretender Geschäftsführer m, stellvertretende Geschäftsführerin f.

associate [adj, n ə'səʊʃɪɪt, vt, vi ə'səʊʃɪeɪt] adj (director) assoziiert; (member, professor) außerordentlich ♦ n (at work) Kollege m, Kollegin f ♦ vt in Verbindung bringen ♦ vi: **to ~ with sb** mit jdm verkehren.

associated company [ə'səʊʃɪeɪtɪd-] n Partnerfirma f.

association [əsəʊsɪ'eɪʃən] n (group) Verband m; (involvement) Verbindung f; (PSYCH) Assoziation f; **in ~ with** in Zusammenarbeit mit.

association football n Fußball m.

assorted [ə'sɔːtɪd] adj gemischt; (various) diverse(r, s); **in ~ sizes** in verschiedenen Größen.

assortment [ə'sɔːtmənt] n Mischung f; (of books, people etc) Ansammlung f.

Asst abbr = **assistant**.

assuage [ə'sweɪdʒ] vt (grief, pain) lindern; (thirst, appetite) stillen, befriedigen.

assume [ə'sjuːm] vt annehmen; (responsibilities etc) übernehmen.

assumed name [ə'sjuːmd-] n Deckname m.

assumption [ə'sʌmpʃən] n Annahme f; (of power etc) Übernahme f; **on the ~ that ...** vorausgesetzt, dass ...

assurance [ə'ʃʊərəns] n Versicherung f; (promise) Zusicherung f; (confidence) Zuversicht f; **I can give you no ~s** ich kann Ihnen nichts versprechen.

assure [əˈʃuəˀ] *vt* versichern; (*guarantee*) sichern.

assured [əˈʃuəd] *n* (*BRIT*) Versicherte(r) *f(m)* ♦ *adj* sicher.

AST (*US*) *abbr* (= *Atlantic Standard Time*) Ortszeit in Ostkanada.

asterisk [ˈæstərɪsk] *n* Sternchen *nt*.

astern [əˈstəːn] *adv* achtern.

asteroid [ˈæstərɔɪd] *n* Asteroid *m*.

asthma [ˈæsmə] *n* Asthma *nt*.

asthmatic [æsˈmætɪk] *adj* asthmatisch ♦ *n* Asthmatiker(in) *m(f)*.

astigmatism [əˈstɪgmətɪzəm] *n* Astigmatismus *m*.

astir [əˈstəːˀ] *adv*: **to be** ~ (*out of bed*) auf sein.

astonish [əˈstɔnɪʃ] *vt* erstaunen.

astonishing [əˈstɔnɪʃɪŋ] *adj* erstaunlich; **I find it** ~ **that** ... es überrascht mich, dass ...

astonishingly [əˈstɔnɪʃɪŋlɪ] *adv* erstaunlich; ~, ... erstaunlicherweise ...

astonishment [əˈstɔnɪʃmənt] *n* Erstaunen *nt*.

astound [əˈstaund] *vt* verblüffen, sehr erstaunen.

astounded [əˈstaundɪd] *adj* (höchst) erstaunt.

astounding [əˈstaundɪŋ] *adj* erstaunlich.

astray [əˈstreɪ] *adv*: **to go** ~ (*letter*) verloren gehen; (*fig*) auf Abwege geraten; **to lead** ~ auf Abwege bringen; **to go** ~ **in one's calculations** sich verrechnen.

astride [əˈstraɪd] *adv* (*sit, ride*) rittlings; (*stand*) breitbeinig ♦ *prep* rittlings auf +*dat*; breitbeinig über +*dat*.

astringent [əsˈtrɪndʒənt] *adj* adstringierend; (*fig: caustic*) ätzend, beißend ♦ *n* Adstringens *nt*.

astrologer [əsˈtrɔlədʒəˀ] *n* Astrologe *m*, Astrologin *f*.

astrology [əsˈtrɔlədʒɪ] *n* Astrologie *f*.

astronaut [ˈæstrənɔːt] *n* Astronaut(in) *m(f)*.

astronomer [əsˈtrɔnəməˀ] *n* Astronom(in) *m(f)*.

astronomical [æstrəˈnɔmɪkl] *adj* (*also fig*) astronomisch.

astronomy [əsˈtrɔnəmɪ] *n* Astronomie *f*.

astrophysics [ˈæstrəuˈfɪzɪks] *n* Astrophysik *f*.

astute [əsˈtjuːt] *adj* scharfsinnig; (*operator, behaviour*) geschickt.

asunder [əˈsʌndəˀ] *adv*: **to tear** ~ auseinander reißen.

ASV *n abbr* (*BIBLE*: = *American Standard Version*) amerikanische Standard-Bibelübersetzung.

asylum [əˈsaɪləm] *n* Asyl *nt*; (*mental hospital*) psychiatrische Klinik *f*; **to seek political** ~ um (politisches) Asyl bitten.

asymmetrical [eɪsɪˈmetrɪkl] *adj* asymmetrisch.

—————————————————— *KEYWORD*

at [æt] *prep* **1** (*referring to position, direction*) an +*dat*, in +*dat*; ~ **the top** an der Spitze; ~ **home** zu Hause, zuhause (*ÖSTERR, SCHWEIZ*); ~ **school** in der Schule; ~ **the**

baker's beim Bäcker; **to look** ~ **sth** auf etw *acc* blicken.

2 (*referring to time*): ~ **4 o'clock** um 4 Uhr; ~ **night/dawn** bei Nacht/Tagesanbruch; ~ **Christmas** zu Weihnachten; ~ **times** zuweilen.

3 (*referring to rates, speed etc*): ~ **£2 a kilo** zu £2 pro Kilo; **two** ~ **a time** zwei auf einmal; ~ **50 km/h** mit 50 km/h.

4 (*referring to activity*): **to be** ~ **work** (*in office etc*) auf der Arbeit sein; **to play** ~ **cowboys** Cowboy spielen; **to be good** ~ **sth** gut in etw *dat* sein.

5 (*referring to cause*): **shocked/surprised/ annoyed** ~ **sth** schockiert/überrascht/ verärgert über etw *acc*; **I went** ~ **his suggestion** ich ging auf seinen Vorschlag hin.

6: **not** ~ **all** (*in answer to question*) überhaupt nicht, ganz und gar nicht; (*in answer to thanks*) nichts zu danken, keine Ursache; **I'm not** ~ **all tired** ich bin überhaupt nicht müde; **anything** ~ **all** irgendetwas.

——————————————————

ate [eɪt] *pt of* **eat**.

atheism [ˈeɪθɪɪzəm] *n* Atheismus *m*.

atheist [ˈeɪθɪɪst] *n* Atheist(in) *m(f)*.

Athenian [əˈθiːnɪən] *adj* Athener ♦ *n* Athener(in) *m(f)*.

Athens [ˈæθɪnz] *n* Athen *nt*.

athlete [ˈæθliːt] *n* Athlet(in) *m(f)*.

athletic [æθˈletɪk] *adj* sportlich; (*muscular*) athletisch.

athletics [æθˈletɪks] *n* Leichtathletik *f*.

Atlantic [ətˈlæntɪk] *adj* atlantisch; (*coast etc*) Atlantik- ♦ *n*: **the** ~ (*Ocean*) der Atlantik.

atlas [ˈætləs] *n* Atlas *m*.

Atlas Mountains *npl*: **the** ~ der Atlas, das Atlasgebirge.

ATM *abbr* (= *automated telling machine*) Geldautomat *m*.

atmosphere [ˈætməsfɪəˀ] *n* Atmosphäre *f*; (*air*) Luft *f*.

atmospheric [ætməsˈferɪk] *adj* atmosphärisch.

atmospherics [ætməsˈferɪks] *npl* atmosphärische Störungen *pl*.

atoll [ˈætɔl] *n* Atoll *nt*.

atom [ˈætəm] *n* Atom *nt*.

atomic [əˈtɔmɪk] *adj* atomar; (*energy, weapons*) Atom-.

atom(ic) bomb *n* Atombombe *f*.

atomizer [ˈætəmaɪzəˀ] *n* Zerstäuber *m*.

atone [əˈtəun] *vi*: **to** ~ **for** büßen für.

atonement [əˈtəunmənt] *n* Buße *f*.

A to Z ® *n* Stadtplan *m*.

ATP *n abbr* (= *Association of Tennis Professionals*) Tennis-Profiverband.

atrocious [əˈtrəuʃəs] *adj* grauenhaft.

atrocity [əˈtrɔsɪtɪ] *n* Gräueltat *f*.

atrophy [ˈætrəfɪ] *n* Schwund *m*, Atrophie *f* ♦ *vt* schwinden lassen ♦ *vi* schwinden, verkümmern.

attach [ə'tætʃ] vt befestigen; (*document, letter*) anheften, beiheften; (*employee, troops*) zuteilen; (*importance etc*) beimessen; **to be ~ed to sb/sth** (*like*) an jdm/etw hängen; (*be connected with*) mit jdm/etw zu tun haben; **the ~ed letter** der beiliegende Brief.

attaché [ə'tæʃeɪ] n Attaché m.

attaché case n Aktenkoffer m.

attachment [ə'tætʃmənt] n (*tool*) Zubehörteil nt; (*love*): **~ (to sb)** Zuneigung f (zu jdm).

attack [ə'tæk] vt angreifen; (*subj: criminal*) überfallen; (*task, problem etc*) in Angriff nehmen ♦ n (*also fig*) Angriff m; (*on sb's life*) Anschlag m; (*of illness*) Anfall m; **heart ~** Herzanfall m, Herzinfarkt m.

attacker [ə'tækə*] n Angreifer(in) m(f).

attain [ə'teɪn] vt (*also:* **~ to**) erreichen; (*knowledge*) erlangen.

attainments [ə'teɪnmənts] npl Fähigkeiten pl.

attempt [ə'tɛmpt] n Versuch m ♦ vt versuchen; **to make an ~ on sb's life** einen Anschlag auf jdn verüben.

attempted [ə'tɛmptɪd] adj versucht; **~ murder/suicide** Mord-/Selbstmordversuch m; **~ theft** versuchter Diebstahl.

attend [ə'tɛnd] vt besuchen; (*patient*) behandeln.

▶ **attend to** vt fus sich kümmern um; (*needs*) nachkommen +dat; (*customer*) bedienen.

attendance [ə'tɛndəns] n Anwesenheit f; (*people present*) Besucherzahl f; (*SPORT*) Zuschauerzahl f.

attendant [ə'tɛndənt] n (*helper*) Begleiter(in) m(f); (*in garage*) Tankwart m; (*in museum*) Aufseher(in) m(f) ♦ adj damit verbunden.

attention [ə'tɛnʃən] n Aufmerksamkeit f; (*care*) Fürsorge f ♦ excl (*MIL*) Achtung!; **attentions** npl (*acts of courtesy*) Aufmerksamkeiten pl; **for the ~ of ...** zu Händen von ...; **it has come to my ~ that ...** ich bin darauf aufmerksam geworden, dass ...; **to stand to** or **at ~** (*MIL*) stillstehen.

attentive [ə'tɛntɪv] adj aufmerksam.

attentively [ə'tɛntɪvlɪ] adv aufmerksam.

attenuate [ə'tɛnjueɪt] vt abschwächen ♦ vi schwächer werden.

attest [ə'tɛst] vt, vi: **to ~ (to)** bezeugen.

attic ['ætɪk] n Dachboden m.

attire [ə'taɪə*] n Kleidung f.

attitude ['ætɪtjuːd] n (*posture, manner*) Haltung f; (*mental*): **~ to** or **towards** Einstellung f zu.

attorney [ə'tɜːnɪ] n (*US: lawyer*) (Rechts)anwalt m, (Rechts)anwältin f; (*having proxy*) Bevollmächtigte(r) f(m); **power of ~** Vollmacht f.

Attorney General n (*BRIT*) ≈ Justizminister(in) m(f); (*US*) ≈ General-bundesanwalt m, Generalbundesanwältin f.

attract [ə'trækt] vt (*draw*) anziehen; (*interest*) auf sich acc lenken; (*attention*) erregen.

attraction [ə'trækʃən] n Anziehungskraft f; (*of house, city*) Reiz m; (*gen pl: amusements*) Attraktion f; (*fig*) **to feel an ~ towards sb/sth** sich von jdm/etw angezogen fühlen.

attractive [ə'træktɪv] adj attraktiv; (*price, idea, offer*) verlockend, reizvoll.

attribute [n ætrɪbjuːt, vt ə'trɪbjuːt] n Eigenschaft f ♦ vt: **to ~ sth to** (*cause*) etw zurückführen auf +acc; (*poem, painting*) etw zuschreiben +dat; (*quality*) etw beimessen +dat.

attribution [ætrɪ'bjuːʃən] n (*see vt*) Zurückführung f; Zuschreibung f; Beimessung f.

attrition [ə'trɪʃən] n: **war of ~** Zermürbungskrieg m.

Atty. Gen. abbr = **Attorney General**.

ATV n abbr (= *all-terrain vehicle*) Geländefahrzeug nt.

atypical [eɪ'tɪpɪkl] adj atypisch.

aubergine ['əubəʒiːn] n Aubergine f; (*colour*) Aubergine nt.

auburn ['ɔːbən] adj rotbraun.

auction ['ɔːkʃən] n (*also:* **sale by ~**) Versteigerung f, Auktion f ♦ vt versteigern.

auctioneer [ɔːkʃə'nɪə*] n Versteigerer m.

auction room n Auktionssaal m.

audacious [ɔː'deɪʃəs] adj wagemutig, kühn.

audacity [ɔː'dæsɪtɪ] n Kühnheit f, Verwegenheit f; (*pej: impudence*) Dreistigkeit f.

audible ['ɔːdɪbl] adj hörbar.

audience ['ɔːdɪəns] n Publikum nt; (*RADIO*) Zuhörer pl; (*TV*) Zuschauer pl; (*with queen etc*) Audienz f.

audiotypist ['ɔːdɪəu'taɪpɪst] n Fonotypist(in) m(f), Phonotypist(in) m(f).

audiovisual ['ɔːdɪəu'vɪzjuəl] adj audiovisuell.

audiovisual aid n audiovisuelles Lehrmittel nt.

audit ['ɔːdɪt] vt (*COMM*) prüfen ♦ n Buchprüfung f, Rechnungsprüfung f.

audition [ɔː'dɪʃən] n Vorsprechprobe f ♦ vi: **to ~ (for)** vorsprechen (für).

auditor ['ɔːdɪtə*] n Buchprüfer(in) m(f), Rechnungsprüfer(in) m(f).

auditorium [ɔːdɪ'tɔːrɪəm] n (*building*) Auditorium nt; (*audience area*) Zuschauerraum m.

Aug. abbr = **August**.

augment [ɔːg'mɛnt] vt vermehren; (*income, diet*) verbessern.

augur ['ɔːgə*] vi: **it ~s well** das ist ein gutes Zeichen or Omen.

August ['ɔːgəst] n August m; *see also* **July**.

august [ɔː'gʌst] adj erhaben.

aunt [ɑːnt] n Tante f.

auntie ['ɑːntɪ] n dimin of **aunt**.

aunty ['ɑːntɪ] n dimin of **aunt**.

au pair ['əu'pɛə*] n (*also:* **~ girl**)

Aupair(mädchen) *nt*, Au-pair(-Mädchen) *nt*.
aura ['ɔːrə] *n* Aura *f*.
auspices ['ɔːspɪsɪz] *npl*: **under the** ~ **of** unter der Schirmherrschaft +*gen*.
auspicious [ɔːs'pɪʃəs] *adj* verheißungsvoll; (*opening, start*) viel versprechend.
austere [ɔs'tɪə˟] *adj* streng; (*room, decoration*) schmucklos; (*person, lifestyle*) asketisch.
austerity [ɔs'tɛrɪtɪ] *n* Strenge *f*; (*of room etc*) Schmucklosigkeit *f*; (*hardship*) Entbehrung *f*.
Australasia [ɔːstrə'leɪzɪə] *n* Australien und Ozeanien *nt*.
Australasian [ɔːstrə'leɪzɪən] *adj* ozeanisch, südwestpazifisch.
Australia [ɒs'treɪlɪə] *n* Australien *nt*.
Australian [ɒs'treɪlɪən] *adj* australisch ♦ *n* Australier(in) *m(f)*.
Austria ['ɒstrɪə] *n* Österreich *nt*.
Austrian ['ɒstrɪən] *adj* österreichisch ♦ *n* Österreicher(in) *m(f)*.
AUT (*BRIT*) *n abbr* (= *Association of University Teachers*) *Gewerkschaft der Universitätsdozenten*.
authentic [ɔː'θɛntɪk] *adj* authentisch.
authenticate [ɔː'θɛntɪkeɪt] *vt* beglaubigen.
authenticity [ɔːθɛn'tɪsɪtɪ] *n* Echtheit *f*.
author ['ɔːθə˟] *n* (*of text*) Verfasser(in) *m(f)*; (*profession*) Autor(in) *m(f)*, Schriftsteller(in) *m(f)*; (*creator*) Urheber(in) *m(f)*; (: *of plan*) Initiator(in) *m(f)*.
authoritarian [ɔːθɔrɪ'tɛərɪən] *adj* autoritär.
authoritative [ɔː'θɔrɪtətɪv] *adj* (*person, manner*) bestimmt, entschieden; (*source, account*) zuverlässig; (*study, treatise*) maßgeblich, maßgebend.
authority [ɔː'θɔrɪtɪ] *n* Autorität *f*; (*government body*) Behörde *f*, Amt *nt*; (*official permission*) Genehmigung *f*; **the authorities** *npl* (*ruling body*) die Behörden *pl*; **to have the** ~ **to do sth** befugt sein, etw zu tun.
authorization [ɔːθəraɪ'zeɪʃən] *n* Genehmigung *f*.
authorize ['ɔːθəraɪz] *vt* genehmigen; **to** ~ **sb to do sth** jdn ermächtigen, etw zu tun.
authorized capital ['ɔːθəraɪzd-] *n* autorisiertes Aktienkapital *nt*.
authorship ['ɔːθəʃɪp] *n* Autorschaft *f*, Verfasserschaft *f*.
autistic [ɔː'tɪstɪk] *adj* autistisch.
auto ['ɔːtəu] (*US*) *n* Auto *nt*, Wagen *m*.
autobiographical ['ɔːtəbaɪə'græfɪkl] *adj* autobiografisch.
autobiography [ɔːtəbaɪ'ɔgrəfɪ] *n* Autobiografie *f*.
autocratic [ɔːtə'krætɪk] *adj* autokratisch.
Autocue ® ['ɔːtəukjuː] *n* Teleprompter *m*.
autograph ['ɔːtəgrɑːf] *n* Autogramm *nt* ♦ *vt* signieren.
autoimmune [ɔːtɔɪ'mjuːn] *adj* (*disease*) Autoimmun-.
automat ['ɔːtəmæt] *n* Automat *m*; (*US*) Automatenrestaurant *nt*.

automata [ɔː'tɔmətə] *npl of* **automaton**.
automate ['ɔːtəmeɪt] *vt* automatisieren.
automatic [ɔːtə'mætɪk] *adj* automatisch ♦ *n* (*gun*) automatische Waffe; (*washing machine*) Waschautomat *m*; (*car*) Automatikwagen *m*.
automatically [ɔːtə'mætɪklɪ] *adv* automatisch.
automatic data processing *n* automatische Datenverarbeitung *f*.
automation [ɔːtə'meɪʃən] *n* Automatisierung *f*.
automaton [ɔː'tɔmətən] (*pl* **automata**) *n* Roboter *m*.
automobile ['ɔːtəməbiːl] (*US*) *n* Auto(mobil) *nt*.
autonomous [ɔː'tɔnəməs] *adj* autonom.
autonomy [ɔː'tɔnəmɪ] *n* Autonomie *f*.
autopsy ['ɔːtɔpsɪ] *n* Autopsie *f*.
autumn ['ɔːtəm] *n* Herbst *m*; **in** ~ im Herbst.
autumnal [ɔː'tʌmnəl] *adj* herbstlich.
auxiliary [ɔːg'zɪlɪərɪ] *adj* (*tool, verb*) Hilfs- ♦ *n* (*assistant*) Hilfskraft *f*.
AV *n abbr* (*BIBLE*: = *Authorized Version*) *englische Bibelübersetzung von 1611* ♦ *abbr* = **audiovisual**.
Av. *abbr* = **avenue**.
avail [ə'veɪl] *vt*: **to** ~ **o.s. of** Gebrauch machen von ♦ *n*: **to no** ~ vergeblich, erfolglos.
availability [əveɪlə'bɪlɪtɪ] *n* Erhältlichkeit *f*; (*of staff*) Vorhandensein *nt*.
available [ə'veɪləbl] *adj* erhältlich; (*person: unoccupied*) frei, abkömmlich; (: *unattached*) zu haben; (*time*) frei, verfügbar; **every** ~ **means** alle verfügbaren Mittel; **is the manager** ~? ist der Geschäftsführer zu sprechen?; **to make sth** ~ **to sb** jdm etw zur Verfügung stellen.
avalanche ['ævəlɑːnʃ] *n* (*also fig*) Lawine *f*.
avant-garde ['ævɑ̃ː'gɑːd] *adj* avantgardistisch.
avarice ['ævərɪs] *n* Habsucht *f*.
avaricious [ævə'rɪʃəs] *adj* habsüchtig.
avdp. *abbr* (= *avoirdupois*) *Handelsgewicht*.
Ave *abbr* = **avenue**.
avenge [ə'vɛndʒ] *vt* rächen.
avenue ['ævənjuː] *n* Straße *f*; (*drive*) Auffahrt *f*; (*means*) Weg *m*.
average ['ævərɪdʒ] *n* Durchschnitt *m* ♦ *adj* durchschnittlich, Durchschnitts- ♦ *vt* (*reach an average of*) einen Durchschnitt erreichen von; **on** ~ im Durchschnitt, durchschnittlich; **above/below (the)** ~ über/unter dem Durchschnitt.
► **average out** *vi*: **to** ~ **out at** durchschnittlich ausmachen.
averse [ə'vɜːs] *adj*: **to be** ~ **to sth/doing sth** eine Abneigung gegen etw haben/dagegen haben, etw zu tun; **I wouldn't be** ~ **to a drink** ich hätte nichts gegen einen Drink.
aversion [ə'vɜːʃən] *n* Abneigung *f*; **to have an** ~ **to sb/sth** eine Abneigung gegen jdn/etw haben.

avert [ə'vɜːt] vt (prevent) verhindern; (ward off) abwehren; (turn away) abwenden.
aviary ['eɪvɪərɪ] n Vogelhaus nt.
aviation [eɪvɪ'eɪʃən] n Luftfahrt f.
avid ['ævɪd] adj begeistert, eifrig.
avidly ['ævɪdlɪ] adv begeistert, eifrig.
avocado [ævə'kɑːdəʊ] (BRIT) n (also: ~ pear) Avocado f.
avoid [ə'vɔɪd] vt (person, obstacle) ausweichen +dat; (trouble) vermeiden; (danger) meiden.
avoidable [ə'vɔɪdəbl] adj vermeidbar.
avoidance [ə'vɔɪdəns] n (of tax) Umgehung f; (of issue) Vermeidung f.
avowed [ə'vaʊd] adj erklärt.
AVP (US) n abbr (= assistant vice president) stellvertretender Vizepräsident.
avuncular [ə'vʌŋkjʊlə°] adj onkelhaft.
AWACS ['eɪwæks] n abbr (= airborne warning and control system) AWACS.
await [ə'weɪt] vt warten auf +acc; ~ing attention/delivery zur Bearbeitung/Lieferung bestimmt; long ~ed lang ersehnt.
awake [ə'weɪk] (pt awoke, pp awoken or awaked) adj wach ♦ vt wecken ♦ vi erwachen, aufwachen; ~ to sich dat bewusst werden +gen.
awakening [ə'weɪknɪŋ] n (also fig) Erwachen nt.
award [ə'wɔːd] n Preis m; (for bravery) Auszeichnung f; (damages) Entschädigung(ssumme) f ♦ vt (prize) verleihen; (damages) zusprechen.
aware [ə'weə°] adj: ~ (of) bewusst (+gen); to become ~ of sich dat bewusst werden +gen; to become ~ that ... sich dat bewusst werden, dass ...; politically/socially ~ politik-/sozialbewusst; I am fully ~ that es ist mir völlig klar or bewusst, dass.
awareness [ə'weənɪs] n Bewusstsein nt; to develop people's ~ of sth den Menschen etw zu Bewusstsein bringen.
awash [ə'wɒʃ] adj (also fig) überflutet.
away [ə'weɪ] adv weg, fort; (position) entfernt; two kilometres ~ zwei Kilometer entfernt; two hours ~ by car zwei Autostunden entfernt; the holiday was two weeks ~ es war noch zwei Wochen bis zum Urlaub; he's ~ for a week er ist eine Woche nicht da; he's ~ in Milan er ist in Mailand; to take ~ (from) (remove) entfernen (von); (subtract) abziehen (von); to work/pedal etc ~ unablässig arbeiten/strampeln etc; to fade ~ (colour, light) verblassen; (sound) verhallen; (enthusiasm) schwinden.
away game n Auswärtsspiel nt.
awe [ɔː] n Ehrfurcht f.
awe-inspiring ['ɔːɪnspaɪərɪŋ] adj Ehrfurcht gebietend.
awesome ['ɔːsəm] adj Ehrfurcht gebietend; (fig: inf) überwältigend.
awe-struck ['ɔːstrʌk] adj von Ehrfurcht ergriffen.

awful ['ɔːfəl] adj furchtbar, schrecklich; an ~ lot (of) furchtbar viel(e).
awfully ['ɔːfəlɪ] adv furchtbar, schrecklich.
awhile [ə'waɪl] adv eine Weile.
awkward ['ɔːkwəd] adj (clumsy) unbeholfen; (inconvenient, difficult) ungünstig; (embarrassing) peinlich.
awkwardness ['ɔːkwədnɪs] n (see adj) Unbeholfenheit f; Ungünstigkeit f; Peinlichkeit f.
awl [ɔːl] n Ahle f, Pfriem m.
awning ['ɔːnɪŋ] n (of tent, caravan) Vordach nt; (of shop etc) Markise f.
awoke [ə'wəʊk] pt of awake.
awoken [ə'wəʊkən] pp of awake.
AWOL ['eɪwɒl] abbr (MIL: = absent without leave) see absent.
awry [ə'raɪ] adv: to be ~ (clothes) schief sitzen; to go ~ schief gehen.
axe, (US) **ax** [æks] n Axt f, Beil nt ♦ vt (employee) entlassen; (project, jobs etc) streichen; to have an ~ to grind (fig) ein persönliches Interesse haben.
axes¹ ['æksɪz] npl of ax(e).
axes² ['æksiːz] npl of axis.
axiom ['æksɪəm] n Axiom nt, Grundsatz m.
axiomatic [æksɪəʊ'mætɪk] adj axiomatisch.
axis ['æksɪs] (pl axes) n Achse f.
axle ['æksl] n (also: ~tree) Achse f.
aye [aɪ] excl (yes) ja ♦ n: the ~s die Jastimmen pl.
AYH n abbr (= American Youth Hostels) Jugendherbergsverband, ≈ DJHV m.
AZ (US) abbr (POST: = Arizona).
azalea [ə'zeɪlɪə] n Azalee f.
Azerbaijan [æzəbaɪ'dʒɑːn] n Aserbaidschan nt.
Azerbaijani [æzəbaɪ'dʒɑːnɪ], **Azeri** [ə'zeərɪ] adj aserbaidschanisch ♦ n Aserbaidschaner(in) m(f).
Azores [ə'zɔːz] npl: the ~ die Azoren pl.
AZT n abbr (= azidothymidine) AZT nt.
Aztec ['æztɛk] adj aztekisch ♦ n Azteke m, Aztekin f.
azure ['eɪʒə°] adj azurblau, tiefblau.

B, b

B¹, b [biː] n (letter) B nt, b nt; (SCOL) ≈ Zwei f, Gut nt; ~ for Benjamin, (US) ~ for Baker ≈ B wie Bertha; ~ road (BRIT) Landstraße f.
B² [biː] n (MUS) H nt, h nt.
b. abbr = born.
BA n abbr (= Bachelor of Arts) see bachelor; (= British Academy) Verband zur Förderung der Künste und Geisteswissenschaften.

babble ['bæbl] *vi* schwatzen; (*baby*) plappern; (*brook*) plätschern ♦ *n*: **a ~ of voices** ein Stimmengewirr *nt*.

babe [beɪb] *n* (*liter*) Kindlein *nt*; (*esp US: address*) Schätzchen *nt*; **~ in arms** Säugling *m*.

baboon [bə'buːn] *n* Pavian *m*.

baby ['beɪbɪ] *n* Baby *nt*; (*US: inf: darling*) Schatz *m*, Schätzchen *nt*.

baby carriage (*US*) *n* Kinderwagen *m*.

baby grand *n* (*also:* ~ **piano**) Stutzflügel *m*.

babyhood ['beɪbɪhud] *n* frühe Kindheit *f*.

babyish ['beɪbɪʃ] *adj* kindlich.

baby-minder ['beɪbɪ'maɪndə*] (*BRIT*) *n* Tagesmutter *f*.

baby-sit ['beɪbɪsɪt] *vi* babysitten.

baby-sitter ['beɪbɪsɪtə*] *n* Babysitter(in) *m(f)*.

baby wipe *n* Ölpflegetuch *nt*.

bachelor ['bætʃələ*] *n* Junggeselle *m*; **B~ of Arts/Science (degree)** ≈ Magister *m* der philosophischen Fakultät/der Naturwissenschaften.

bachelorhood ['bætʃələhud] *n* Junggesellentum *nt*.

bachelor party (*US*) *n* Junggesellenparty *f*.

back [bæk] *n* Rücken *m*; (*of house, page*) Rückseite *f*; (*of chair*) (Rücken)lehne *f*; (*of train*) Ende *nt*; (*FOOTBALL*) Verteidiger *m* ♦ *vt* (*candidate: also:* ~ **up**) unterstützen; (*horse*) setzen *or* wetten auf +*acc*; (*car*) zurücksetzen, zurückfahren ♦ *vi* (*also:* ~ **up**: *person*) rückwärts gehen; (*car etc*) zurücksetzen, zurückfahren ♦ *cpd* (*payment, rent*) ausstehend ♦ *adv* hinten; **in the ~ (of the car)** hinten (im Auto); **at the ~ of the book/crowd/audience** hinten im Buch/in der Menge/im Publikum; **~ to front** verkehrt herum; **to break the ~ of a job** (*BRIT*) mit einer Arbeit über den Berg sein; **to have one's ~ to the wall** (*fig*) in die Enge getrieben sein; **~ room** Hinterzimmer *nt*; **~ garden** Garten *m* (hinter dem Haus); **~ seat** (*AUT*) Rücksitz *m*; **to take a ~ seat** (*fig*) sich zurückhalten; ~ **wheels** Hinterräder *pl*; **he's ~** er ist zurück *or* wieder da; **throw the ball** ~ wirf den Ball zurück; **he called** ~ er rief zurück; **he ran** ~ er rannte zurück; **when will you be** ~**?** wann kommen Sie wieder?; **can I have it** ~**?** kann ich es zurückhaben *or* wiederhaben?

▶ **back down** *vi* nachgeben.

▶ **back on to** *vt fus*: **the house ~s on to the golf course** das Haus grenzt hinten an den Golfplatz an.

▶ **back out** *vi* (*of promise*) einen Rückzieher machen.

▶ **back up** *vt* (*support*) unterstützen; (*COMPUT*) sichern.

backache ['bækeɪk] *n* Rückenschmerzen *pl*.

backbencher ['bæk'bentʃə*] (*BRIT*) *n* Abgeordnete(r) *f(m)* (*in den hinteren Reihen im britischen Parlament*), Hinterbänkler(in) *m(f)* (*pej*); *see also* **back bench**.

backbiting ['bækbaɪtɪŋ] *n* Lästern *nt*.

backbone ['bækbəun] *n* (*also fig*) Rückgrat *nt*.

backchat ['bæktʃæt] (*BRIT: inf*) *n* Widerrede *f*.

backcloth ['bækklɒθ] (*BRIT*) *n* Hintergrund *m*.

backcomb ['bækkəum] (*BRIT*) *vt* toupieren.

backdate [bæk'deɪt] *vt* (zu)rückdatieren; **~d pay rise** rückwirkend geltende Gehaltserhöhung *f*.

backdrop ['bækdrɒp] *n* = **backcloth**.

backer ['bækə*] *n* (*COMM*) Geldgeber *m*.

backfire [bæk'faɪə*] *vi* (*AUT*) Fehlzündungen haben; (*plans*) ins Auge gehen.

backgammon ['bækgæmən] *n* Backgammon *nt*.

background ['bækgraund] *n* Hintergrund *m*; (*basic knowledge*) Grundkenntnisse *pl*; (*experience*) Erfahrung *f* ♦ *cpd* (*music*) Hintergrund-; **family** ~ Herkunft *f*; ~ **noise** Geräuschkulisse *f*; ~ **reading** vertiefende Lektüre *f*.

backhand ['bækhænd] *n* (*TENNIS: also:* ~ **stroke**) Rückhand *f*.

backhanded ['bæk'hændɪd] *adj* (*fig: compliment*) zweifelhaft.

backhander ['bæk'hændə*] (*BRIT*) *n* Schmiergeld *nt*.

backing ['bækɪŋ] *n* (*fig, COMM*) Unterstützung *f*; (*MUS*) Begleitung *f*.

backlash ['bæklæʃ] *n* (*fig*) Gegenreaktion *f*.

backlog ['bæklɒg] *n*: **to have a ~ of work** mit der Arbeit im Rückstand sein.

back number *n* alte Ausgabe *f or* Nummer *f*.

backpack ['bækpæk] *n* Rucksack *m*.

backpacker ['bækpækə*] *n* Rucksacktourist(in) *m(f)*.

back pay n Nachzahlung f.

back-pedal ['bækpɛdl] vi (fig) einen Rückzieher machen.

back-seat driver n Mitfahrer, der dem Fahrer dazwischenredet.

backside ['bæksaɪd] (inf) n Hintern m.

backslash ['bækslæʃ] n Backslash m.

backslide ['bækslaɪd] vi rückfällig werden.

backspace ['bækspeɪs] vi (in typing) die Rücktaste betätigen.

backstage [bæk'steɪdʒ] adv (THEAT) hinter den Kulissen; (: in dressing-room area) in der Garderobe.

backstreet ['bækstriːt] n Seitenstraße f ♦ cpd: ~ **abortionist** Engelmacher(in) m(f).

backstroke ['bækstrəʊk] n Rückenschwimmen nt.

backtrack ['bæktræk] vi (fig) einen Rückzieher machen.

backup ['bækʌp] adj (train, plane) Entlastungs-; (COMPUT: copy etc) Sicherungs- ♦ n (support) Unterstützung f; (COMPUT: also: ~ **disk**, ~ **file**) Sicherungskopie f, Back-up nt, Backup nt.

backward ['bækwəd] adj (movement) Rückwärts-; (person) zurückgeblieben; (country) rückständig; ~ **and forward movement** Vor- und Zurückbewegung f; ~ **step/glance** Blick m/Schritt m zurück.

backwards ['bækwədz] adv rückwärts; (read) von hinten nach vorne; (fall) nach hinten; (in time) zurück; **to know sth** ~ or (US) ~ **and forwards** etw in- und auswendig kennen.

backwater ['bækwɔːtə*] n (fig) Kaff nt.

back yard n Hinterhof m.

bacon ['beɪkən] n (Frühstücks)speck m, (Schinken)speck m.

bacteria [bæk'tɪərɪə] npl Bakterien pl.

bacteriology [bæktɪərɪ'ɔlədʒɪ] n Bakteriologie f.

bad [bæd] adj schlecht; (naughty) unartig, ungezogen; (mistake, accident, injury) schwer; **his** ~ **leg** sein schlimmes Bein; **to go** ~ verderben, schlecht werden; **to have a** ~ **time of it** es schwer haben; **I feel** ~ **about it** es tut mir Leid; **in** ~ **faith** mit böser Absicht.

bad debt n uneinbringliche Forderung f.

baddy ['bædɪ] (inf) n Bösewicht m.

bade [bæd] pt of **bid**.

badge [bædʒ] n Plakette f; (stick-on) Aufkleber m; (fig) Merkmal nt.

badger ['bædʒə*] n Dachs m ♦ vt zusetzen +dat.

badly ['bædlɪ] adv schlecht; ~ **wounded** schwer verletzt; **he needs it** ~ er braucht es dringend; **things are going** ~ es sieht schlecht or nicht gut aus; **to be** ~ **off (for money)** wenig Geld haben.

bad-mannered ['bæd'mænəd] adj ungezogen, unhöflich.

badminton ['bædmɪntən] n Federball m.

bad-tempered ['bæd'tɛmpəd] adj schlecht

gelaunt; (by nature) übellaunig.

baffle ['bæfl] vt verblüffen.

baffling ['bæflɪŋ] adj rätselhaft, verwirrend.

bag [bæg] n Tasche f; (made of paper, plastic) Tüte f; (handbag) (Hand)tasche f; (satchel) Schultasche f; (case) Reisetasche f; (of hunter) Jagdbeute f; (pej: woman) Schachtel f; ~**s of** (inf: lots of) jede Menge; **to pack one's** ~**s** die Koffer packen; ~**s under the eyes** Ringe pl unter den Augen.

bagful ['bægful] n: **a** ~ **of** eine Tasche/Tüte voll.

baggage ['bægɪdʒ] n Gepäck nt.

baggage allowance n Freigepäck nt.

baggage car (US) n Gepäckwagen m.

baggage claim n Gepäckausgabe f.

baggy ['bægɪ] adj weit; (out of shape) ausgebeult.

Baghdad [bæg'dæd] n Bagdad nt.

bag lady (esp US) n Stadtstreicherin f.

bagpipes ['bægpaɪps] npl Dudelsack m.

bag-snatcher ['bægsnætʃə*] (BRIT) n Handtaschendieb(in) m(f).

Bahamas [bə'hɑːməz] npl: **the** ~ die Bahamas pl, die Bahamainseln pl.

Bahrain [bɑː'reɪn] n Bahrain nt.

bail [beɪl] n (LAW: payment) Kaution f; (: release) Freilassung f gegen Kaution ♦ vt (prisoner) gegen Kaution freilassen; (boat: also: ~ **out**) ausschöpfen; **to be on** ~ gegen Kaution freigelassen sein; **to be released on** ~ gegen Kaution freigelassen werden; see also **bale**.

▶ **bail out** vt (prisoner) gegen Kaution freibekommen; (firm, friend) aus der Patsche helfen +dat.

bailiff ['beɪlɪf] n (LAW: BRIT) Gerichtsvollzieher(in) m(f); (: US) Gerichtsdiener(in) m(f); (BRIT: factor) (Guts)verwalter(in) m(f).

bait [beɪt] n Köder m ♦ vt (hook, trap) mit einem Köder versehen; (tease) necken.

baize [beɪz] n Flausch m; **green** ~ Billardtuch nt.

bake [beɪk] vt backen; (clay etc) brennen ♦ vi backen.

baked beans [beɪkt-] npl gebackene Bohnen pl (in Tomatensauce).

baked potato n in der Schale gebackene Kartoffel f.

baker ['beɪkə*] n Bäcker(in) m(f).

baker's dozen n dreizehn (Stück).

bakery ['beɪkərɪ] n Bäckerei f.

baking ['beɪkɪŋ] n Backen nt; (batch) Ofenladung f ♦ adj (inf: hot) wie im Backofen.

baking powder n Backpulver nt.

baking tin n Backform f.

baking tray n Backblech nt.

balaclava [bælə'klɑːvə] n (also: ~ **helmet**) Kapuzenmütze f.

balance ['bæləns] n (equilibrium)

Gleichgewicht nt; (COMM: sum) Saldo m;
(remainder) Restbetrag m; (scales) Waage f
♦ vt ausgleichen; (AUT: wheels) auswuchten;
(pros and cons) (gegeneinander) abwägen;
on ~ alles in allem; ~ of trade/payments
Handels-/Zahlungsbilanz f; ~ carried
forward or brought forward (COMM)
Saldovortrag m, Saldoübertrag m; to ~ the
books (COMM) die Bilanz ziehen or machen.
balanced ['bælənst] adj ausgeglichen; (report)
ausgewogen.
balance sheet n Bilanz f.
balance wheel n Unruh f.
balcony ['bælkənı] n Balkon m; (in theatre)
oberster Rang m.
bald [bɔːld] adj kahl; (tyre) abgefahren;
(statement) knapp.
baldness ['bɔːldnıs] n Kahlheit f.
bale [beıl] n (AGR) Bündel nt; (of papers etc)
Packen m.
▶ **bale out** vi (of a plane) abspringen ♦ vt
(water) schöpfen; (boat) ausschöpfen.
Balearic Islands [bælı'ærık-] npl: the ~ die
Balearen pl.
baleful ['beılful] adj böse.
balk [bɔːk] vi: to ~ (at) (subj: person)
zurückschrecken (vor +dat); (: horse)
scheuen (vor +dat).
Balkan ['bɔːlkən] adj (countries etc) Balkan-
♦ n: the ~s der Balkan, die Balkanländer pl.
ball [bɔːl] n Ball m; (of wool, string) Knäuel m or
nt; to set the ~ rolling (fig) den Stein ins
Rollen bringen; to play ~ (with sb) (fig) (mit
jdm) mitspielen; to be on the ~ (fig:
competent) am Ball sein; (: alert) auf Draht
or Zack sein; the ~ is in their court (fig) sie
sind am Ball.
ballad ['bæləd] n Ballade f.
ballast ['bæləst] n Ballast m.
ball bearing npl Kugellager nt; (individual ball)
Kugellagerkugel f.
ball cock n Schwimmerhahn m.
ballerina [bælə'riːnə] n Ballerina f.
ballet ['bæleı] n Ballett nt.
ballet dancer n Balletttänzer(in) m(f).
ballistic [bə'lıstık] adj ballistisch.
ballistic missile n Raketengeschoss nt.
ballistics [bə'lıstıks] n Ballistik f.
balloon [bə'luːn] n (Luft)ballon m; (hot air
balloon) Heißluftballon m; (in comic strip)
Sprechblase f.
balloonist [bə'luːnıst] n Ballonfahrer(in) m(f).
ballot ['bælət] n (geheime) Abstimmung f.
ballot box n Wahlurne f.
ballot paper n Stimmzettel m.
ballpark ['bɔːlpɑːk] n (US) n (SPORT)
Baseballstadion nt.
ballpark figure (inf) n Richtzahl f.
ballpoint (pen) ['bɔːlpɔınt(-)] n
Kugelschreiber m.
ballroom ['bɔːlrum] n Tanzsaal m.
balls [bɔːlz] (inf!) npl (testicles) Eier pl (!);

(courage) Schneid m, Mumm m ♦ excl red
keinen Scheiß! (!).
balm [bɑːm] n Balsam m.
balmy ['bɑːmı] adj (breeze) sanft; (air) lau,
lind; (BRIT: inf) = **barmy**.
BALPA ['bælpə] n abbr (= British Airline Pilots'
Association) Flugpilotengewerkschaft.
balsam ['bɔːlsəm] n Balsam m.
balsa (wood) ['bɔːlsə-] n Balsaholz nt.
Baltic ['bɔːltık] n: the ~ (Sea) die Ostsee.
balustrade [bæləs'treıd] n Balustrade f.
bamboo [bæm'buː] n Bambus m.
bamboozle [bæm'buːzl] (inf) vt hereinlegen;
to ~ sb into doing sth jdn durch Tricks
dazu bringen, etw zu tun.
ban [bæn] n Verbot nt ♦ vt verbieten; he was
~ned from driving (BRIT) ihm wurde
Fahrverbot erteilt.
banal [bə'nɑːl] adj banal.
banana [bə'nɑːnə] n Banane f.
band [bænd] n (group) Gruppe f, Schar f;
(MUS: jazz, rock etc) Band f; (: military etc)
(Musik)kapelle f; (strip, range) Band nt;
(stripe) Streifen m.
▶ **band together** vi sich
zusammenschließen.
bandage ['bændıdʒ] n Verband m ♦ vt
verbinden.
Band-Aid ® ['bændeıd] (US) n Heftpflaster nt.
B & B n abbr = **bed and breakfast**.
bandit ['bændıt] n Bandit m.
bandstand ['bændstænd] n Musikpavillion m.
bandwagon ['bændwægən] n: to jump on the
~ (fig) auf den fahrenden Zug aufspringen.
bandy ['bændı] vt (jokes) sich erzählen; (ideas)
diskutieren; (insults) sich an den Kopf
werfen.
▶ **bandy about** vt (word, expression) immer
wieder gebrauchen; (name) immer wieder
nennen.
bandy-legged ['bændı'legıd] adj o-beinig, O-
beinig.
bane [beın] n: it/he is the ~ of my life das/er
ist noch mal mein Ende.
bang [bæŋ] n (of door) Knallen nt; (of gun,
exhaust) Knall m; (blow) Schlag m ♦ excl peng
♦ vt (door) zuschlagen, zuknallen; (one's
head etc) sich dat stoßen +acc ♦ vi knallen
♦ adv: to be ~ on time (BRIT: inf) auf die
Sekunde pünktlich sein; to ~ at the door
gegen die Tür hämmern; to ~ into sth sich
an etw dat stoßen.
banger ['bæŋə°] (BRIT: inf) n (car: also: old ~)
Klapperkiste f; (sausage) Würstchen nt;
(firework) Knallkörper m.
Bangkok [bæŋ'kɔk] n Bangkok nt.
Bangladesh [bæŋglə'deʃ] n Bangladesch nt.
bangle ['bæŋgl] n Armreif(en) m.
bangs [bæŋz] (US) npl (fringe) Pony m.
banish ['bænıʃ] vt verbannen.
banister(s) ['bænıstə(z)] n(pl) Geländer nt.
banjo ['bændʒəu] (pl ~es or ~s) n Banjo nt.

bank [bæŋk] *n* Bank *f*; (*of river, lake*) Ufer *nt*; (*of earth*) Wall *m*; (*of switches*) Reihe *f* ♦ *vi* (*AVIAT*) sich in die Kurve legen; (*COMM*): **they ~ with Pitt's** sie haben ihr Konto bei Pitt's.
▶ **bank on** *vt fus* sich verlassen auf +*acc*.
bank account *n* Bankkonto *nt*.
bank balance *n* Kontostand *m*.
bank card *n* Scheckkarte *f*.
bank charges (*BRIT*) *npl* Kontoführungsgebühren *pl*.
bank draft *n* Bankanweisung *f*.
banker ['bæŋkə'] *n* Bankier *m*.
banker's card (*BRIT*) *n* = **bank card**.
banker's order (*BRIT*) *n* Dauerauftrag *m*.
bank giro *n* Banküberweisung *f*.
bank holiday (*BRIT*) *n* (öffentlicher) Feiertag *m*.

BANK HOLIDAY

Als **bank holiday** *wird in Großbritannien ein gesetzlicher Feiertag bezeichnet, an dem die Banken geschlossen sind. Die meisten dieser Feiertage, abgesehen von Weihnachten und Ostern, fallen auf Montage im Mai und August. An diesen langen Wochenenden (*bank holiday weekends*) fahren viele Briten in Urlaub, sodass dann auf den Straßen, Flughäfen und bei der Bahn sehr viel Betrieb ist.*

---

banking ['bæŋkɪŋ] *n* Bankwesen *nt*.
banking hours *npl* Schalterstunden *pl*.
bank loan *n* Bankkredit *m*.
bank manager *n* Filialleiter(in) *m(f)* (einer Bank).
banknote ['bæŋknəut] *n* Geldschein *m*, Banknote *f*.
bank rate *n* Diskontsatz *m*.
bankrupt ['bæŋkrʌpt] *adj* bankrott ♦ *n* Bankrotteur(in) *m(f)*; **to go ~** Bankrott machen.
bankruptcy ['bæŋkrʌptsɪ] *n* (*COMM, fig*) Bankrott *m*.
bank statement *n* Kontoauszug *m*.
banner ['bænə'] *n* Banner *nt*; (*in demonstration*) Spruchband *nt*.
banner headline *n* Schlagzeile *f*.
bannister(s) ['bænɪstə(z)] *n(pl)* = **banister(s)**.
banns [bænz] *npl* Aufgebot *nt*.
banquet ['bæŋkwɪt] *n* Bankett *nt*.
bantamweight ['bæntəmweɪt] *n* Bantamgewicht *nt*.
banter ['bæntə'] *n* Geplänkel *nt*.
BAOR *n abbr* (= *British Army of the Rhine*) *britische Rheinarmee.*
baptism ['bæptɪzəm] *n* Taufe *f*.
Baptist ['bæptɪst] *n* Baptist(in) *m(f)*.
baptize [bæp'taɪz] *vt* taufen.
bar [ba'] *n* (*for drinking*) Lokal *nt*; (*counter*) Theke *f*; (*rod*) Stange *f*; (*on window etc*) (Gitter)stab *m*; (*slab: of chocolate*) Tafel *f*; (*fig: obstacle*) Hindernis *nt*; (*prohibition*) Verbot *nt*; (*MUS*) Takt *m* ♦ *vt* (*road*) blockieren, versperren; (*window*) verriegeln; (*person*) ausschließen; (*activity*) verbieten; **~ of soap** Stück *nt* Seife; **behind ~s** hinter Gittern; **the B~** (*LAW*) die Anwaltschaft; **~ none** ohne Ausnahme.
Barbados [ba:'beɪdɔs] *n* Barbados *nt*.
barbaric [ba:'bærɪk] *adj* barbarisch.
barbarous ['ba:bərəs] *adj* barbarisch.
barbecue ['ba:bɪkju:] *n* Grill *m*; (*meal, party*) Barbecue *nt*.
barbed wire ['ba:bd-] *n* Stacheldraht *m*.
barber ['ba:bə'] *n* (Herren)friseur *m*.
barbiturate [ba:'bɪtjurɪt] *n* Schlafmittel *nt*, Barbiturat *nt*.
Barcelona [ba:sə'ləunə] *n* Barcelona *nt*.
bar chart *n* Balkendiagramm *nt*.
bar code *n* Strichkode *m*.
bare [bɛə'] *adj* nackt; (*trees, countryside*) kahl; (*minimum*) absolut ♦ *vt* entblößen; (*teeth*) blecken; **the ~ essentials, the ~ necessities** das Allernotwendigste; **to ~ one's soul** sein Innerstes entblößen.
bareback ['bɛəbæk] *adv* ohne Sattel.
barefaced ['bɛəfeɪst] *adj* (*fig*) unverfroren, schamlos.
barefoot ['bɛəfut] *adj* barfüßig ♦ *adv* barfuß.
bareheaded [bɛə'hɛdɪd] *adj* barhäuptig ♦ *adv* ohne Kopfbedeckung.
barely ['bɛəlɪ] *adv* kaum.
Barents Sea ['bærənts-] *n*: **the ~** die Barentssee.
bargain ['ba:gɪn] *n* (*deal*) Geschäft *nt*; (*transaction*) Handel *m*; (*good offer*) Sonderangebot *nt*; (*good buy*) guter Kauf *m* ♦ *vi*: **to ~ (with sb)** (mit jdm) verhandeln; (*haggle*) (mit jdm) handeln; **into the ~** obendrein.
▶ **bargain for** *vt fus*: **he got more than he ~ed for** er bekam mehr, als er erwartet hatte.
bargaining ['ba:gənɪŋ] *n* Verhandeln *nt*.
bargaining position *n* Verhandlungsposition *f*.
barge [ba:dʒ] *n* Lastkahn *m*, Frachtkahn *m*.
▶ **barge in** *vi* (*enter*) hereinplatzen; (*interrupt*) unterbrechen.
▶ **barge into** *vt fus* (*place*) hereinplatzen; (*person*) anrempeln.
bargepole ['ba:dʒpəul] *n*: **I wouldn't touch it with a ~** (*fig*) das würde ich nicht mal mit der Kneifzange anfassen.
baritone ['bærɪtəun] *n* Bariton *m*.
barium meal ['bɛərɪəm-] *n* Kontrastbrei *m*.
bark [ba:k] *n* (*of tree*) Rinde *f*; (*of dog*) Bellen *nt* ♦ *vi* bellen; **she's ~ing up the wrong tree** (*fig*) sie ist auf dem Holzweg.
barley ['ba:lɪ] *n* Gerste *f*.
barley sugar *n* Malzbonbon *nt or m*.
barmaid ['ba:meɪd] *n* Bardame *f*.
barman ['ba:mən] (*irreg: like* **man**) *n* Barmann *m*.
barmy ['ba:mɪ] (*BRIT: inf*) *adj* bekloppt.

barn [bɑːn] n Scheune f.
barnacle ['bɑːnəkl] n Rankenfußkrebs m.
barn owl n Schleiereule f.
barometer [bə'rɒmɪtə*] n Barometer nt.
baron ['bærən] n Baron m; **industrial ~** Industriemagnat m; **press ~** Pressezar m.
baroness ['bærənɪs] n (baron's wife) Baronin f; (baron's daughter) Baroness f, Baronesse f.
baronet ['bærənɪt] n Baronet m.
barracking ['bærəkɪŋ] n Buhrufe pl.
barracks ['bærəks] npl Kaserne f.
barrage ['bærɑːʒ] n (MIL) Sperrfeuer nt; (dam) Staustufe f; (fig: of criticism, questions etc) Hagel m.
barrel ['bærəl] n Fass nt; (of oil) Barrel nt; (of gun) Lauf m.
barrel organ n Drehorgel f.
barren ['bærən] adj unfruchtbar.
barricade [bærɪ'keɪd] n Barrikade f ♦ vt (road, entrance) verbarrikadieren; **to ~ o.s. (in)** sich verbarrikadieren.
barrier ['bærɪə*] n (at frontier, entrance) Schranke f; (BRIT: also: **crash ~**) Leitplanke f; (fig) Barriere f; (: to progress etc) Hindernis nt.
barrier cream (BRIT) n Hautschutzcreme f.
barring ['bɑːrɪŋ] prep außer im Falle +gen.
barrister ['bærɪstə*] (BRIT) n Rechtsanwalt m, Rechtsanwältin f.

BARRISTER

Barrister oder barrister-at-law ist in England die Bezeichnung für einen Rechtsanwalt, der seine Klienten vor allem vor Gericht vertritt; im Gegensatz zum solicitor, der nicht vor Gericht auftritt, sondern einen barrister mit dieser Aufgabe beauftragt.

---

barrow ['bærəʊ] n Schubkarre f, Schubkarren m; (cart) Karren m.
bar stool n Barhocker m.
Bart. (BRIT) abbr = **baronet**.
bartender ['bɑːtendə*] (US) n Barmann m.
barter ['bɑːtə*] n Tauschhandel m ♦ vt: **to ~ sth for sth** etw gegen etw tauschen.
base [beɪs] n (of tree etc) Fuß m; (of cup, box etc) Boden m; (foundation) Grundlage f; (centre) Stützpunkt m, Standort m; (for organization) Sitz m ♦ adj gemein, niederträchtig ♦ vt: **to ~ sth on** etw gründen or basieren auf +acc; **to be ~d at** (troops) stationiert sein in +dat; (employee) arbeiten in +dat; **I'm ~d in London** ich wohne in London; **a Paris-~d firm** eine Firma mit Sitz in Paris; **coffee-~d** auf Kaffeebasis.
baseball ['beɪsbɔːl] n Baseball m.
baseboard ['beɪsbɔːd] (US) n Fußleiste f.
base camp n Basislager nt, Versorgungslager nt.
Basel [bɑːl] n = **Basle**.
baseline ['beɪslaɪn] n (TENNIS) Grundlinie f; (fig: standard) Ausgangspunkt m.

basement ['beɪsmənt] n Keller m.
base rate n Eckzins m, Leitzins m.
bases[1] ['beɪsɪz] npl of **base**.
bases[2] ['beɪsiːz] npl of **basis**.
bash [bæʃ] (inf) vt schlagen, hauen ♦ n: **I'll have a ~ (at it)** (BRIT) ich probier's mal.
► **bash up** vt (car) demolieren; (BRIT: person) vermöbeln.
bashful ['bæʃful] adj schüchtern.
bashing ['bæʃɪŋ] (inf) n Prügel pl; **Paki-/queer-~** Überfälle pl auf Pakistaner/Schwule.
BASIC ['beɪsɪk] n (COMPUT) BASIC nt.
basic ['beɪsɪk] adj (method, needs etc) Grund-; (principles) grundlegend; (problem) grundsätzlich; (knowledge) elementar; (facilities) primitiv.
basically ['beɪsɪklɪ] adv im Grunde.
basic rate n Eingangssteuersatz m.
basics ['beɪsɪks] npl: **the ~** das Wesentliche.
basil ['bæzl] n Basilikum nt.
basin ['beɪsn] n Gefäß nt; (BRIT: for food) Schüssel f; (also: **wash ~**) (Wasch)becken nt; (of river, lake) Becken nt.
basis ['beɪsɪs] (pl **bases**) n Basis f, Grundlage f; **on a part-time ~** stundenweise; **on a trial ~** zur Probe; **on the ~ of what you've said** aufgrund or auf Grund dessen, was Sie gesagt haben.
bask [bɑːsk] vi: **to ~ in the sun** sich sonnen.
basket ['bɑːskɪt] n Korb m; (smaller) Körbchen nt.
basketball ['bɑːskɪtbɔːl] n Basketball m.
basketball player n Basketballspieler(in) m(f).
Basle [bɑːl] n Basel nt.
basmati rice [bəz'mætɪ-] n Basmatireis m.
Basque [bæsk] adj baskisch ♦ n Baske m, Baskin f.
bass [beɪs] n Bass m.
bass clef n Bassschlüssel m.
bassoon [bə'suːn] n Fagott nt.
bastard ['bɑːstəd] n uneheliches Kind nt; (inf!) Arschloch nt (!).
baste [beɪst] vt (CULIN) (mit Fett und Bratensaft) begießen; (SEWING) heften, reihen.
bastion ['bæstɪən] n Bastion f.
bat [bæt] n (ZOOL) Fledermaus f; (for cricket, baseball etc) Schlagholz nt; (BRIT: for table tennis) Schläger m ♦ vt: **he didn't ~ an eyelid** er hat nicht mit der Wimper gezuckt; **off one's own ~** auf eigene Faust.
batch [bætʃ] n (of bread) Schub m; (of letters, papers) Stoß m, Stapel m; (of applicants) Gruppe f; (of work) Schwung m; (of goods) Ladung f, Sendung f.
batch processing n (COMPUT) Stapelverarbeitung f.
bated ['beɪtɪd] adj: **with ~ breath** mit angehaltenem Atem.
bath [bɑːθ] n Bad nt; (bathtub) (Bade)wanne f

♦ *vt* baden; **to have a** ~ baden, ein Bad
nehmen; *see also* **baths**.
bathe [beɪð] *vi, vt* (*also fig*) baden.
bather [ˈbeɪðəʳ] *n* Badende(r) *f(m)*.
bathing [ˈbeɪðɪŋ] *n* Baden *nt*.
bathing cap *n* Bademütze *f*, Badekappe *f*.
bathing costume, (*US*) **bathing suit** *n*
Badeanzug *m*.
bath mat *n* Bademattе *f*, Badevorleger *m*.
bathrobe [ˈbɑːθrəʊb] *n* Bademantel *m*.
bathroom [ˈbɑːθrʊm] *n* Bad(ezimmer) *nt*.
baths [bɑːðz] *npl* (*also*: **swimming** ~)
(Schwimm)bad *nt*.
bath towel *n* Badetuch *nt*.
bathtub [ˈbɑːθtʌb] *n* (Bade)wanne *f*.
batman [ˈbætmən] *n* (*irreg: like* **man**) (*BRIT*) *n*
(*MIL*) (Offiziers)bursche *m*.
baton [ˈbætən] *n* (*MUS*) Taktstock *m*;
(*ATHLETICS*) Staffelholz *nt*; (*policeman's*)
Schlagstock *m*.
battalion [bəˈtælɪən] *n* Bataillon *nt*.
batten [ˈbætn] *n* Leiste *f*, Latte *f*; (*NAUT: on
sail*) Segellatte *f*.
► **batten down** *vt* (*NAUT*): **to** ~ **down the
hatches** die Luken dicht machen.
batter [ˈbætəʳ] *vt* schlagen, misshandeln;
(*subj: rain*) schlagen; (*wind*) rütteln ♦ *n*
(*CULIN*) Teig *m*; (*for frying*) (Ausback)teig *m*.
battered [ˈbætəd] *adj* (*hat, pan*) verbeult;
~ **wife** misshandelte Ehefrau; ~ **child**
misshandeltes Kind.
battering ram [ˈbætərɪŋ-] *n* Rammbock *m*.
battery [ˈbætərɪ] *n* Batterie *f*; (*of tests,
reporters*) Reihe *f*.
battery charger *n* (Batterie)ladegerät *nt*.
battery farming *n* Batteriehaltung *f*.
battle [ˈbætl] *n* (*MIL*) Schlacht *f*; (*fig*) Kampf *m*
♦ *vi* kämpfen; **that's half the** ~ damit ist
schon viel gewonnen; **it's a losing** ~, **we're
fighting a losing** ~ (*fig*) es ist ein
aussichtsloser Kampf.
battledress [ˈbætldrɛs] *n* Kampfanzug *m*.
battlefield [ˈbætlfiːld] *n* Schlachtfeld *nt*.
battlements [ˈbætlmənts] *npl* Zinnen *pl*.
battleship [ˈbætlʃɪp] *n* Schlachtschiff *nt*.
batty [ˈbætɪ] (*inf*) *adj* verrückt.
bauble [ˈbɔːbl] *n* Flitter *m*.
baud [bɔːd] *n* (*COMPUT*) Baud *nt*.
baud rate *n* (*COMPUT*) Baudrate *f*.
baulk [bɔːlk] *vi* = **balk**.
bauxite [ˈbɔːksaɪt] *n* Bauxit *m*.
Bavaria [bəˈvɛərɪə] *n* Bayern *nt*.
Bavarian [bəˈvɛərɪən] *adj* bay(e)risch ♦ *n*
Bayer(in) *m(f)*.
bawdy [ˈbɔːdɪ] *adj* derb, obszön.
bawl [bɔːl] *vi* brüllen, schreien.
bay [beɪ] *n* Bucht *f*; (*BRIT: for parking*)
Parkbucht *f*; (: *for loading*) Ladeplatz *m*;
(*horse*) Braune(r) *m*; **to hold sb at** ~ jdn in
Schach halten.
bay leaf *n* Lorbeerblatt *nt*.
bayonet [ˈbeɪənɪt] *n* Bajonett *nt*.

bay tree *n* Lorbeerbaum *m*.
bay window *n* Erkerfenster *nt*.
bazaar [bəˈzɑːʳ] *n* Basar *m*.
bazooka [bəˈzuːkə] *n* Panzerfaust *f*.
BB (*BRIT*) *n abbr* (= *Boys' Brigade*)
Jugendorganisation für Jungen.
BBB (*US*) *n abbr* (= *Better Business Bureau*)
amerikanische Verbraucherbehörde.
BBC *n abbr* BBC *f*.

BBC

BBC (*Abkürzung für British Broadcasting
Corporation*) *ist die staatliche britische Rundfunk-
und Fernsehanstalt. Die Fernsehsender BBC1 und
BBC2 bieten beide ein umfangsreiches
Fernsehprogramm, wobei BBC1 mehr Sendungen
von allgemeinem Interesse wie z.B. leichte
Unterhaltung, Sport, Aktuelles, Kinderprogramme
und Außenübertragungen zeigt. BBC2
berücksichtigt Reisesendungen, Drama, Musik und
internationale Filme. Die 5 landesweiten
Radiosender bieten von Popmusik bis Kricket etwas
für jeden Geschmack; dazu gibt es noch 37 regionale
Radiosender. Der BBC World Service ist auf der
ganzen Welt auf Englisch oder in einer von 35
anderen Sprachen zu empfangen. Finanziert wird
die BBC vor allem durch Fernsehgebühren und ins
Ausland verkaufte Sendungen. Obwohl die BBC
dem Parlament gegenüber verantwortlich ist,
werden die Sendungen nicht vom Staat kontrolliert.*

BC *adv abbr* (= *before Christ*) v. Chr. ♦ *abbr*
(*CANADA*: = *British Columbia*) Britisch-
Kolumbien *nt*.
BCG *n abbr* (= *bacille Calmette-Guérin*) BCG *m*.
BD *n abbr* (= *Bachelor of Divinity*) *akademischer
Grad in Theologie*.
B/D *abbr* = **bank draft**.
BDS *n abbr* (= *Bachelor of Dental Surgery*)
akademischer Grad in Zahnmedizin.
B/E *abbr* = **bill of exchange**.

═══════════════════════════════ *KEYWORD*

be [biː] (*pt* **was, were**, *pp* **been**) *aux vb* **1** (*with
present participle: forming continuous tenses*):
what are you doing? was machst du?; **it is
raining** es regnet; **have you been to Rome?**
waren Sie schon einmal in Rom?
2 (*with pp: forming passives*) werden; **to**
~ **killed** getötet werden; **the box had been
opened** die Kiste war geöffnet worden.
3 (*in tag questions*): **he's good-looking, isn't
he?** er sieht gut aus, nicht (wahr)?; **she's
back again, is she?** sie ist wieder da, oder?
4 (+ **to** + *infinitive*): **the house is to** ~ **sold** das
Haus soll verkauft werden; **he's not to open
it** er darf es nicht öffnen
♦ *vb* + *complement* **1** sein; **I'm tired/English** ich
bin müde/Engländer(in); **I'm hot/cold** mir
ist heiß/kalt; **2 and 2 are 4** 2 und 2 ist *or*
macht 4; **she's tall/pretty** sie ist groß/

hübsch; ~ **careful/quiet** sei vorsichtig/
ruhig.
2 (*of health*): **how are you?** wie geht es
Ihnen?
3 (*of age*): **how old are you?** wie alt bist du?;
I'm sixteen (years old) ich bin sechzehn
(Jahre alt).
4 (*cost*) kosten; **how much was the meal?**
was hat das Essen gekostet?; **that'll ~ 5
pounds please** das macht 5 Pfund, bitte
♦ *vi* **1** (*exist, occur etc*) sein; **there is/are** es
gibt; **is there a God?** gibt es einen Gott?;
~ **that as it may** wie dem auch sei; **so ~ it**
gut (und schön).
2 (*referring to place*) sein, liegen; **Edinburgh
is in Scotland** Edinburgh liegt *or* ist in
Schottland; **I won't ~ here tomorrow**
morgen bin ich nicht da.
3 (*referring to movement*) sein; **where have
you been?** wo warst du?
♦ *impers vb* **1** (*referring to time, distance,
weather*) sein; **it's 5 o'clock** es ist 5 Uhr; **it's
10 km to the village** es sind 10 km bis zum
Dorf; **it's too hot/cold** es ist zu heiß/kalt.
2 (*emphatic*): **it's only me** ich bins nur; **it's
only the postman** es ist nur der Briefträger.

beach [biːtʃ] *n* Strand *m* ♦ *vt* (*boat*) auf (den)
Strand setzen.
beach buggy *n* Strandbuggy *m*.
beachcomber ['biːtʃkəʊmə*] *n*
Strandgutsammler *m*.
beachwear ['biːtʃwɛə*] *n* Strandkleidung *f*.
beacon ['biːkən] *n* Leuchtfeuer *nt*; (*marker*)
Bake *f*; (*also:* **radio ~**) Funkfeuer *nt*.
bead [biːd] *n* Perle *f*; **beads** *npl* (*necklace*)
Perlenkette *f*.
beady ['biːdɪ] *adj*: ~ **eyes** Knopfaugen *pl*.
beagle ['biːgl] *n* Beagle *m*.
beak [biːk] *n* Schnabel *m*.
beaker ['biːkə*] *n* Becher *m*.
beam [biːm] *n* (*ARCHIT*) Balken *m*; (*of light*)
Strahl *m*; (*RADIO*) Leitstrahl *m* ♦ *vi* (*smile*)
strahlen ♦ *vt* ausstrahlen, senden; **to ~ at sb**
jdn anstrahlen; **to drive on full** *or* **main** *or*
high ~ mit Fernlicht fahren.
beaming ['biːmɪŋ] *adj* strahlend.
bean [biːn] *n* Bohne *f*; **runner** ~ Stangenbohne
f; **broad** ~ dicke Bohne; **coffee** ~
Kaffeebohne *f*.
beanpole ['biːnpəʊl] *n* (*lit, fig*) Bohnenstange *f*.
beanshoots ['biːnʃuːts] *npl*
Sojabohnensprossen *pl*.
beansprouts ['biːnsprauts] *npl* = **beanshoots**.
bear [bɛə*] (*pt* **bore**, *pp* **borne**) *n* Bär *m*; (*STOCK
EXCHANGE*) Baissier *m* ♦ *vt* tragen; (*tolerate,
endure*) ertragen; (*examination*) standhalten
+*dat*; (*traces, signs*) aufweisen, zeigen;
(*COMM: interest*) tragen, bringen; (*produce:
children*) gebären; (: *fruit*) tragen ♦ *vi*: **to
~ right/left** (*AUT*) sich rechts/links halten;
to ~ the responsibility of die

Verantwortung tragen für; **to ~ comparison
with** einem Vergleich standhalten mit; **I
can't ~ him** ich kann ihn nicht ausstehen; **to
bring pressure to ~ on sb** Druck auf jdn
ausüben.
▸ **bear out** *vt* (*person, suspicions etc*)
bestätigen.
▸ **bear up** *vi* Haltung bewahren; **he bore up
well** er hat sich gut gehalten.
▸ **bear with** *vt fus* Nachsicht haben mit;
~ **with me a minute** bitte gedulden Sie sich
einen Moment.
bearable ['bɛərəbl] *adj* erträglich.
beard [bɪəd] *n* Bart *m*.
bearded ['bɪədɪd] *adj* bärtig.
bearer ['bɛərə*] *n* (*of letter, news*)
Überbringer(in) *m(f)*; (*of cheque, passport,
title etc*) Inhaber(in) *m(f)*.
bearing ['bɛərɪŋ] *n* (*posture*) Haltung *f*; (*air*)
Auftreten *nt*; (*connection*) Bezug *m*; (*TECH*)
Lager *nt*; **bearings** *npl* (*also:* **ball ~s**)
Kugellager *nt*; **to take a ~ with a compass**
den Kompasskurs feststellen; **to get one's
~s** sich zurechtfinden.
beast [biːst] *n* (*animal*) Tier *nt*; (*inf: person*)
Biest *nt*.
beastly ['biːstlɪ] *adj* scheußlich.
beat [biːt] (*pt* **beat**, *pp* **beaten**) *n* (*of heart*)
Schlag *m*; (*MUS*) Takt *m*; (*of policeman*)
Revier *nt* ♦ *vt* schlagen; (*record*) brechen ♦ *vi*
schlagen; **to ~ time** den Takt schlagen; **to
~ it** (*inf*) abhauen, verschwinden; **that ~s
everything** das ist doch wirklich der Gipfel
or die Höhe; **to ~ about the bush** um den
heißen Brei herumreden; **off the ~en track**
abgelegen.
▸ **beat down** *vt* (*door*) einschlagen; (*price*)
herunterhandeln; (*seller*) einen niedrigeren
Preis aushandeln mit ♦ *vi* (*rain*)
herunterprasseln; (*sun*) herunterbrennen.
▸ **beat off** *vt* (*attack, attacker*) abwehren.
▸ **beat up** *vt* (*person*) zusammenschlagen;
(*mixture, eggs*) schlagen.
beater ['biːtə*] *n* (*for eggs, cream*)
Schneebesen *m*.
beating ['biːtɪŋ] *n* Schläge *pl*, Prügel *pl*; **to
take a ~** (*fig*) eine Schlappe einstecken.
beat-up ['biːtʌp] (*inf*) *adj* zerbeult,
ramponiert.
beautician [bjuːˈtɪʃən] *n* Kosmetiker(in) *m(f)*.
beautiful ['bjuːtɪful] *adj* schön.
beautifully ['bjuːtɪflɪ] *adv* (*play, sing, drive etc*)
hervorragend; (*quiet, empty etc*) schön.
beautify ['bjuːtɪfaɪ] *vt* verschönern.
beauty ['bjuːtɪ] *n* Schönheit *f*; (*fig: attraction*)
Schöne *nt*; **the ~ of it is that** ... das Schöne
daran ist, dass ...
beauty contest *n* Schönheitswettbewerb *m*.
beauty queen *n* Schönheitskönigin *f*.
beauty salon *n* Kosmetiksalon *m*.
beauty sleep *n* (Schönheits)schlaf *m*.
beauty spot (*BRIT*) *n* besonders schöner

Ort *m*.

beaver ['bi:və*] *n* Biber *m*.

becalmed [bɪ'kɑːmd] *adj*: **to be** ~ (*sailing ship*) in eine Flaute geraten.

became [bɪ'keɪm] *pt of* **become**.

because [bɪ'kɔz] *conj* weil; ~ **of** wegen +*gen or* (*inf*) +*dat*.

beck [bɛk] *n*: **to be at sb's** ~ **and call** nach jds Pfeife tanzen.

beckon ['bɛkən] *vt* (*also*: ~ **to**) winken ♦ *vi* locken.

become [bɪ'kʌm] (*irreg: like* **come**) *vi* werden; **it became known that** es wurde bekannt, dass; **what has** ~ **of him?** was ist aus ihm geworden?

becoming [bɪ'kʌmɪŋ] *adj* (*behaviour*) schicklich; (*clothes*) kleidsam.

BECTU ['bɛktu] (*BRIT*) *n abbr* (= *Broadcasting, Entertainment, Cinematographic and Theatre Union*) Gewerkschaft für Beschäftigte in der Unterhaltungsindustrie.

BEd *n abbr* (= *Bachelor of Education*) akademischer Grad im Erziehungswesen.

bed [bɛd] *n* Bett *nt*; (*of coal*) Flöz *nt*; (*of clay*) Schicht *f*; (*of river*) (Fluss)bett *nt*; (*of sea*) (Meeres)boden *m*, (Meeres)grund *m*; (*of flowers*) Beet *nt*; **to go to** ~ ins *or* zu Bett gehen.

▶ **bed down** *vi* sein Lager aufschlagen.

bed and breakfast *n* (*place*) (Frühstücks)pension *f*; (*terms*) Übernachtung *f* mit Frühstück.

BED AND BREAKFAST

Bed and breakfast bedeutet „*Übernachtung mit Frühstück*", wobei sich dies in Großbritannien nicht auf Hotels, sondern auf kleinere Pensionen, Privathäuser und Bauernhöfe bezieht, wo man wesentlich preisgünstiger übernachten kann als in Hotels. Oft wird für Bed and Breakfast, auch **B & B** genannt, durch ein entsprechendes Schild im Garten oder an der Einfahrt geworben.

---

bedbug ['bɛdbʌg] *n* Wanze *f*.

bedclothes ['bɛdkləʊðz] *npl* Bettzeug *nt*.

bedding ['bɛdɪŋ] *n* Bettzeug *nt*.

bedevil [bɪ'dɛvl] *vt* (*person*) heimsuchen; (*plans*) komplizieren; **to be** ~**led by misfortune/bad luck** vom Schicksal/Pech verfolgt sein.

bedfellow ['bɛdfɛləʊ] *n*: **they are strange** ~**s** (*fig*) sie sind ein merkwürdiges Gespann.

bedlam ['bɛdləm] *n* Chaos *nt*.

bedpan ['bɛdpæn] *n* Bettpfanne *f*, Bettschüssel *f*.

bedpost ['bɛdpəʊst] *n* Bettpfosten *m*.

bedraggled [bɪ'dræɡld] *adj* (*wet*) triefnass, tropfnass; (*dirty*) verdreckt.

bedridden ['bɛdrɪdn] *adj* bettlägerig.

bedrock ['bɛdrɔk] *n* (*fig*) Fundament *nt*; (*GEOG*) Grundgebirge *nt*, Grundgestein *nt*.

bedroom ['bɛdrum] *n* Schlafzimmer *nt*.

Beds [bɛdz] (*BRIT*) *abbr* (*POST*: = *Bedfordshire*).

bed settee *n* Sofabett *nt*.

bedside ['bɛdsaɪd] *n*: **at sb's** ~ an jds Bett; ~ **lamp** Nachttischlampe *f*; ~ **book** Bettlektüre *f*.

bedsit(ter) ['bɛdsɪt(ə*)] (*BRIT*) *n* möbliertes Zimmer *nt*.

bedspread ['bɛdsprɛd] *n* Tagesdecke *f*.

bedtime ['bɛdtaɪm] *n* Schlafenszeit *f*; **it's** ~ **es ist Zeit, ins Bett zu gehen.**

bee [biː] *n* Biene *f*; **to have a** ~ **in one's bonnet about cleanliness** einen Sauberkeitsfimmel *or* Sauberkeitstick haben.

beech [biːtʃ] *n* Buche *f*.

beef [biːf] *n* Rind(fleisch) *nt*; **roast** ~ Rinderbraten *m*.

▶ **beef up** (*inf*) *vt* aufmotzen; (*essay*) auswalzen.

beefburger ['biːfbɔːɡə*] *n* Hamburger *m*.

beefeater ['biːfiːtə*] *n* Beefeater *m*.

beehive ['biːhaɪv] *n* Bienenstock *m*.

beekeeping ['biːkiːpɪŋ] *n* Bienenzucht *f*, Imkerei *f*.

beeline ['biːlaɪn] *n*: **to make a** ~ **for** schnurstracks zugehen auf +*acc*.

been [biːn] *pp of* **be**.

beep [biːp] (*inf*) *n* Tut(tut) *nt* ♦ *vi* tuten ♦ *vt*: **to** ~ **one's horn** hupen.

beer [bɪə*] *n* Bier *nt*.

beer belly (*inf*) *n* Bierbauch *m*.

beer can *n* Bierdose *f*.

beet [biːt] *n* Rübe *f*; (*US*: *also*: **red** ~) Rote Bete *f*.

beetle ['biːtl] *n* Käfer *m*.

beetroot ['biːtruːt] (*BRIT*) *n* Rote Bete *f*.

befall [bɪ'fɔːl] (*irreg: like* **fall**) *vi* sich zutragen ♦ *vt* widerfahren +*dat*.

befit [bɪ'fɪt] *vt* sich gehören für.

before [bɪ'fɔː*] *prep* vor +*dat*; (*with movement*) vor +*acc* ♦ *conj* bevor ♦ *adv* (*time*) vorher; (*space*) davor; ~ **going** bevor er/sie *etc* geht/ging; ~ **she goes** bevor sie geht; **the week** ~ die Woche davor; **I've never seen it** ~ ich habe es noch nie gesehen.

beforehand [bɪ'fɔːhænd] *adv* vorher.

befriend [bɪ'frɛnd] *vt* sich annehmen +*gen*.

befuddled [bɪ'fʌdld] *adj*: **to be** ~ verwirrt sein.

beg [bɛg] *vi* betteln ♦ *vt* (*food, money*) betteln um; (*favour, forgiveness etc*) bitten um; **to** ~ **for** (*food etc*) betteln um; (*forgiveness, mercy etc*) bitten um; **to** ~ **sb to do sth** jdn bitten, etw zu tun; **I** ~ **your pardon** (*apologizing*) entschuldigen Sie bitte; (: *not hearing*) (wie) bitte?; **to** ~ **the question** der Frage ausweichen; *see also* **pardon**.

began [bɪ'gæn] *pt of* **begin**.

beggar ['bɛgə*] *n* Bettler(in) *m(f)*.

begin [bɪ'gɪn] (*pt* **began**, *pp* **begun**) *vt, vi* beginnen, anfangen; **to** ~ **doing** *or* **to do sth** anfangen, etw zu tun; ~**ning (from) Monday**

ab Montag; **I can't ~ to thank you** ich kann Ihnen gar nicht genug danken; **we'll have soup to ~ with** als Vorspeise hätten wir gern Suppe; **to ~ with, I'd like to know ...** zunächst einmal möchte ich wissen, ...

beginner [bɪ'gɪnə*] *n* Anfänger(in) *m(f)*.

beginning [bɪ'gɪnɪŋ] *n* Anfang *m*; **right from the ~** von Anfang an.

begrudge [bɪ'grʌdʒ] *vt*: **to ~ sb sth** jdm etw missgönnen *or* nicht gönnen.

beguile [bɪ'gaɪl] *vt* betören.

beguiling [bɪ'gaɪlɪŋ] *adj* (*charming*) verführerisch; (*deluding*) betörend.

begun [bɪ'gʌn] *pp of* **begin**.

behalf [bɪ'hɑːf] *n*: **on ~ of, (*US*) in ~ of** (*as representative of*) im Namen von; (*for benefit of*) zugunsten *or* zu Gunsten von; **on my/his ~** in meinem/seinem Namen; zu meinen/ seinen Gunsten.

behave [bɪ'heɪv] *vi* (*person*) sich verhalten, sich benehmen; (*thing*) funktionieren; (*also:* **~ o.s.**) sich benehmen.

behaviour, (*US*) **behavior** [bɪ'heɪvjə*] *n* Verhalten *nt*; (*manner*) Benehmen *nt*.

behead [bɪ'hed] *vt* enthaupten.

beheld [bɪ'held] *pt, pp of* **behold**.

behind [bɪ'haɪnd] *prep* hinter ♦ *adv* (*at/towards the back*) hinten ♦ *n* (*buttocks*) Hintern *m*, Hinterteil *nt*; **~ the scenes** (*fig*) hinter den Kulissen; **we're ~ them in technology** auf dem Gebiet der Technologie liegen wir hinter ihnen zurück; **to be ~** (*schedule*) im Rückstand *or* Verzug sein; **to leave/stay ~** zurücklassen/-bleiben.

behold [bɪ'həʊld] (*irreg: like* **hold**) *vt* sehen, erblicken.

beige [beɪʒ] *adj* beige.

Beijing ['beɪ'dʒɪŋ] *n* Peking *nt*.

being ['biːɪŋ] *n* (*creature*) (Lebe)wesen *nt*; (*existence*) Leben *nt*, (Da)sein *nt*; **to come into ~** entstehen.

Beirut [beɪ'ruːt] *n* Beirut *nt*.

Belarus [bɛlə'rus] *n* Weißrussland *nt*.

Belarussian *adj* belarussisch, weißrussisch ♦ *n* Weißrusse *m*, Weißrussin *f*; (*LING*) Weißrussisch *nt*.

belated [bɪ'leɪtɪd] *adj* verspätet.

belch [bɛltʃ] *vi* rülpsen ♦ *vt* (*also:* **belch out**: *smoke etc*) ausstoßen.

beleaguered [bɪ'liːgɪd] *adj* (*city*) belagert; (*army*) eingekesselt; (*fig*) geplagt.

Belfast ['bɛlfɑːst] *n* Belfast *nt*.

belfry ['bɛlfrɪ] *n* Glockenstube *f*.

Belgian ['bɛldʒən] *adj* belgisch ♦ *n* Belgier(in) *m(f)*.

Belgium ['bɛldʒəm] *n* Belgien *nt*.

Belgrade [bɛl'greɪd] *n* Belgrad *nt*.

belie [bɪ'laɪ] *vt* (*contradict*) im Widerspruch stehen zu; (*give false impression of*) hinwegtäuschen über +*acc*; (*disprove*) widerlegen, Lügen strafen.

belief [bɪ'liːf] *n* Glaube *m*; (*opinion*)

Überzeugung *f*; **it's beyond ~** es ist unglaublich *or* nicht zu glauben; **in the ~ that** im Glauben, dass.

believable [bɪ'liːvəbl] *adj* glaubhaft.

believe [bɪ'liːv] *vt* glauben ♦ *vi* (an Gott) glauben; **he is ~d to be abroad** es heißt, dass er im Ausland ist; **to ~ in** (*God, ghosts*) glauben an +*acc*; (*method etc*) Vertrauen haben zu; **I don't ~ in corporal punishment** ich halte nicht viel von der Prügelstrafe.

believer [bɪ'liːvə*] *n* (*in idea, activity*) Anhänger(in) *m(f)*; (*REL*) Gläubige(r) *f(m)*; **she's a great ~ in healthy eating** sie ist sehr für eine gesunde Ernährung.

belittle [bɪ'lɪtl] *vt* herabsetzen.

Belize [be'liːz] *n* Belize *nt*.

bell [bɛl] *n* Glocke *f*; (*small*) Glöckchen *nt*, Schelle *f*; (*on door*) Klingel *f*; **that rings a ~** (*fig*) das kommt mir bekannt vor.

bell-bottoms ['bɛlbɒtəmz] *npl* Hose *f* mit Schlag.

bellboy ['bɛlbɔɪ] (*BRIT*) *n* Page *m*, Hoteljunge *m*.

bellhop ['bɛlhɒp] (*US*) *n* = **bellboy**.

belligerence [bɪ'lɪdʒərəns] *n* Angriffslust *f*.

belligerent [bɪ'lɪdʒərənt] *adj* angriffslustig.

bellow ['bɛləʊ] *vi, vt* brüllen.

bellows ['bɛləʊz] *npl* Blasebalg *m*.

bell push (*BRIT*) *n* Klingel *f*.

belly ['bɛlɪ] *n* Bauch *m*.

bellyache ['bɛlɪeɪk] (*inf*) *n* Bauchschmerzen *pl* ♦ *vi* murren.

bellybutton ['bɛlɪbʌtn] *n* Bauchnabel *m*.

bellyful ['bɛlɪfʊl] (*inf*) *n*: **I've had a ~ of that** davon habe ich die Nase voll.

belong [bɪ'lɒŋ] *vi*: **to ~ to** (*person*) gehören +*dat*; (*club etc*) angehören +*dat*; **this book ~s here** dieses Buch gehört hierher.

belongings [bɪ'lɒŋɪŋz] *npl* Sachen *pl*, Habe *f*; **personal ~** persönlicher Besitz *m*, persönliches Eigentum *nt*.

Belorussia [bɛleu'rʌʃə] *n* Weißrussland *nt*.

Belorussian [bɛleu'rʌʃən] *adj, n* = **Belarussian**.

beloved [bɪ'lʌvɪd] *adj* geliebt ♦ *n* Geliebte(r) *f(m)*.

below [bɪ'ləʊ] *prep* (*beneath*) unterhalb +*gen*; (*less than*) unter +*dat* ♦ *adv* (*beneath*) unten; **see ~** siehe unten; **temperatures ~ normal** Temperaturen unter dem Durchschnitt.

belt [bɛlt] *n* Gürtel *m*; (*TECH*) (Treib)riemen *m* ♦ *vt* schlagen ♦ *vi* (*BRIT: inf*): **to ~ along** rasen; **to ~ down/into** hinunter-/ hineinrasen; **industrial ~** Industriegebiet *nt*.

► **belt out** *vt* (*song*) schmettern.

► **belt up** (*BRIT: inf*) *vi* den Mund *or* die Klappe halten.

beltway ['bɛltweɪ] (*US*) *n* Umgehungsstraße *f*, Ringstraße *f*; (*motorway*) Umgehungsautobahn *f*.

bemoan [bɪ'məʊn] *vt* beklagen.

bemused [bɪ'mjuːzd] *adj* verwirrt.

bench [bɛntʃ] *n* Bank *f*; (*work bench*)

Werkbank *f;* **the B~** (*LAW: judges*) die Richter *pl,* der Richterstand.

benchmark ['bɛntʃmɑːk] *n* (*fig*) Maßstab *m.*

bend [bɛnd] (*pt, pp* **bent**) *vt* (*leg, arm*) beugen; (*pipe*) biegen ♦ *vi* (*person*) sich beugen ♦ *n* (*BRIT: in road*) Kurve *f;* (*in pipe, river*) Biegung *f;* **bends** *npl* (*MED*): **the ~s** die Taucherkrankheit.

▶ **bend down** *vi* sich bücken.

▶ **bend over** *vi* sich bücken.

beneath [bɪ'niːθ] *prep* unter +*dat* ♦ *adv* darunter.

benefactor ['bɛnɪfæktə*] *n* Wohltäter *m.*

benefactress ['bɛnɪfæktrɪs] *n* Wohltäterin *f.*

beneficial [bɛnɪ'fɪʃəl] *adj* (*effect*) nützlich; (*influence*) vorteilhaft; **~ (to)** gut (für).

beneficiary [bɛnɪ'fɪʃərɪ] *n* (*LAW*) Nutznießer(in) *m(f).*

benefit ['bɛnɪfɪt] *n* (*advantage*) Vorteil *m;* (*money*) Beihilfe *f;* (*also:* **~ concert, ~ match**) Benefizveranstaltung *f* ♦ *vt* nützen +*dat,* zugute kommen +*dat* ♦ *vi:* **he'll ~ from it** er wird davon profitieren.

Benelux ['bɛnɪlʌks] *n* die Beneluxstaaten *pl.*

benevolent [bɪ'nɛvələnt] *adj* wohlwollend; (*organization*) Wohltätigkeits-.

BEng *n abbr* (= *Bachelor of Engineering*) *akademischer Grad für Ingenieure.*

benign [bɪ'naɪn] *adj* gütig; (*MED*) gutartig.

bent [bɛnt] *pt, pp of* **bend** ♦ *n* Neigung *f* ♦ *adj* (*wire, pipe*) gebogen; (*inf: dishonest*) korrupt; (: *pej: homosexual*) andersrum; **to be ~ on** entschlossen sein zu.

bequeath [bɪ'kwiːð] *vt* vermachen.

bequest [bɪ'kwɛst] *n* Vermächtnis *nt,* Legat *nt.*

bereaved [bɪ'riːvd] *adj* leidtragend ♦ *npl:* **the ~** die Hinterbliebenen *pl.*

bereavement [bɪ'riːvmənt] *n* schmerzlicher Verlust *m.*

bereft [bɪ'rɛft] *adj:* **~ of** beraubt +*gen.*

beret ['bɛreɪ] *n* Baskenmütze *f.*

Bering Sea ['beɪrɪŋ-] *n:* **the ~** das Beringmeer.

berk [bəːk] (*inf*) *n* Dussel *m.*

Berks [baːks] (*BRIT*) *abbr* (*POST:* = *Berkshire*).

Berlin [bəː'lɪn] *n* Berlin *nt;* **East/West ~** (*formerly*) Ost-/Westberlin *nt.*

berm [bəːm] (*US*) *n* Seitenstreifen *m.*

Bermuda [bəː'mjuːdə] *n* Bermuda *nt,* die Bermudinseln *pl.*

Bermuda shorts *npl* Bermudashorts *pl.*

Bern [bəːn] *n* Bern *nt.*

berry ['bɛrɪ] *n* Beere *f.*

berserk [bə'səːk] *adj:* **to go ~** wild werden.

berth [bəːθ] *n* (*bed*) Bett *nt;* (*on ship*) Koje *f;* (*on train*) Schlafwagenbett *nt;* (*for ship*) Liegeplatz *m* ♦ *vi* anlegen; **to give sb a wide ~** (*fig*) einen großen Bogen um jdn machen.

beseech [bɪ'siːtʃ] (*pt, pp* **besought**) *vt* anflehen.

beset [bɪ'sɛt] (*pt, pp* **beset**) *vt* (*subj: difficulties*) bedrängen; (: *fears, doubts*) befallen; **~ with** (*problems, dangers etc*) voller +*dat.*

beside [bɪ'saɪd] *prep* neben +*dat;* (*with movement*) neben +*acc;* **to be ~ o.s.** außer sich sein; **that's ~ the point** das hat damit nichts zu tun.

besides [bɪ'saɪdz] *adv* außerdem ♦ *prep* außer +*dat.*

besiege [bɪ'siːdʒ] *vt* belagern; (*fig*) belagern, bedrängen.

besmirch [bɪ'sməːtʃ] *vt* besudeln.

besotted [bɪ'sɔtɪd] (*BRIT*) *adj:* **~ with** vernarrt in +*acc.*

besought [bɪ'sɔːt] *pt, pp of* **beseech.**

bespectacled [bɪ'spɛktɪkld] *adj* bebrillt.

bespoke [bɪ'spəuk] (*BRIT*) *adj* (*garment*) maßgeschneidert; (*suit*) Maß-; **~ tailor** Maßschneider *m.*

best [bɛst] *adj* beste(r, s) ♦ *adv* am besten ♦ *n:* **at ~** bestenfalls; **the ~ thing to do is ...** das Beste ist ...; **the ~ part of** der größte Teil +*gen;* **to make the ~ of sth** das Beste aus etw machen; **to do one's ~** sein Bestes tun; **to the ~ of my knowledge** meines Wissens; **to the ~ of my ability** so gut ich kann; **he's not exactly patient at the ~ of times** er ist schon normalerweise ziemlich ungeduldig.

best-before date *n* Mindesthaltbarkeitsdatum *nt.*

bestial ['bɛstɪəl] *adj* bestialisch.

best man *n* Trauzeuge *m* (*des Bräutigams*).

bestow [bɪ'stəu] *vt* schenken; **to ~ sth on sb** (*honour, praise*) jdm etw zuteil werden lassen; (*title*) jdm etw verleihen.

best seller *n* Bestseller *m.*

bet [bɛt] (*pt, pp* **bet** *or* **betted**) *n* Wette *f* ♦ *vi* wetten ♦ *vt:* **to ~ sb sth** mit jdm um etw wetten; **it's a safe ~** (*fig*) es ist so gut wie sicher; **to ~ money on sth** Geld auf etw *acc* setzen.

Bethlehem ['bɛθlɪhɛm] *n* Bethlehem *nt.*

betray [bɪ'treɪ] *vt* verraten; (*trust, confidence*) missbrauchen.

betrayal [bɪ'treɪəl] *n* Verrat *m.*

better ['bɛtə*] *adj, adv* besser ♦ *vt* verbessern ♦ *n:* **to get the ~ of sb** jdn unterkriegen; (*curiosity*) über jdn siegen; **I had ~ go** ich gehe jetzt (wohl) besser; **you had ~ do it** tun Sie es lieber; **he thought ~ of it** er überlegte es sich *dat* anders; **to get ~** gesund werden; **that's ~!** so ist es besser!; **a change for the ~** eine Wendung zum Guten.

better off *adj* (*wealthier*) besser gestellt; (*more comfortable etc*) besser dran; (*fig*): **you'd be ~ this way** so wäre es besser für Sie.

betting ['bɛtɪŋ] *n* Wetten *nt.*

betting shop (*BRIT*) *n* Wettbüro *nt.*

between [bɪ'twiːn] *prep* zwischen +*dat;* (*with movement*) zwischen +*acc;* (*amongst*) unter +*acc or dat* ♦ *adv* dazwischen; **the road ~ here and London** die Straße zwischen hier und London; **we only had £5 ~ us** wir hatten zusammen nur £5.

bevel ['bɛvəl] n (also: ~ **edge**) abgeschrägte Kante f.

bevelled ['bɛvəld] adj: **a ~ edge** eine Schrägkante, eine abgeschrägte Kante.

beverage ['bɛvərɪdʒ] n Getränk nt.

bevy ['bɛvɪ] n: **a ~ of** eine Schar +gen.

bewail [bɪ'weɪl] vt beklagen.

beware [bɪ'wɛə'] vi: **to ~ (of)** sich in Acht nehmen (vor +dat); "~ **of the dog**" „Vorsicht, bissiger Hund".

bewildered [bɪ'wɪldəd] adj verwirrt.

bewildering [bɪ'wɪldrɪŋ] adj verwirrend.

bewitching [bɪ'wɪtʃɪŋ] adj bezaubernd, hinreißend.

beyond [bɪ'jɔnd] prep (in space) jenseits +gen; (exceeding) über +acc … hinaus; (after) nach; (above) über +dat ♦ adv (in space) dahinter; (in time) darüber hinaus; **it is ~ doubt** es steht außer Zweifel; **~ repair** nicht mehr zu reparieren; **it is ~ my understanding** es übersteigt mein Begriffsvermögen; **it's ~ me** das geht über meinen Verstand.

b/f abbr (COMM: = brought forward) Übertr.

BFPO n abbr (= British Forces Post Office) Postbehörde der britischen Armee.

bhp n abbr (AUT: = brake horsepower) Bremsleistung f.

bi... [baɪ] pref Bi-, bi-.

biannual [baɪ'ænjuəl] adj zweimal jährlich.

bias ['baɪəs] n (prejudice) Vorurteil nt; (preference) Vorliebe f.

bias(s)ed ['baɪəst] adj voreingenommen; **to be ~ against** voreingenommen sein gegen.

biathlon [baɪ'æθlən] n Biathlon nt.

bib [bɪb] n Latz m.

Bible ['baɪbl] n Bibel f.

biblical ['bɪblɪkl] adj biblisch.

bibliography [bɪblɪ'ɔgrəfɪ] n Bibliografie f.

bicarbonate of soda [baɪ'kɑːbənɪt-] n Natron nt.

bicentenary [baɪsɛn'tiːnərɪ] n Zweihundertjahrfeier f.

bicentennial [baɪsɛn'tɛnɪəl] (US) n = bicentenary.

biceps ['baɪsɛps] n Bizeps m.

bicker ['bɪkə'] vi sich zanken.

bickering ['bɪkərɪŋ] n Zankerei f.

bicycle ['baɪsɪkl] n Fahrrad nt.

bicycle path n (Fahr)radweg m.

bicycle pump n Luftpumpe f.

bicycle track n (Fahr)radweg m.

bid [bɪd] (pt **bade** or **bid**, pp **bidden** or **bid**) n (at auction) Gebot nt; (in tender) Angebot nt; (attempt) Versuch m ♦ vi bieten; (CARDS) bieten, reizen ♦ vt bieten; **to ~ sb good day** jdm einen guten Tag wünschen.

bidder ['bɪdə'] n: **the highest ~** der/die Höchstbietende or Meistbietende.

bidding ['bɪdɪŋ] n Steigern nt, Bieten nt; (order, command): **to do sb's ~** tun, was jd einem sagt.

bide [baɪd] vt: **to ~ one's time** den rechten Augenblick abwarten.

bidet ['biːdeɪ] n Bidet nt.

bidirectional ['baɪdɪ'rɛkʃənl] adj (COMPUT) bidirektional.

biennial [baɪ'ɛnɪəl] adj zweijährlich ♦ n zweijährige Pflanze f.

bifocals [baɪ'fəuklz] npl Bifokalbrille f.

big [bɪg] adj groß; **to do things in a ~ way** alles im großen Stil tun.

bigamist ['bɪgəmɪst] n Bigamist(in) m(f).

bigamous ['bɪgəməs] adj bigamistisch.

bigamy ['bɪgəmɪ] n Bigamie f.

big dipper [-'dɪpə'] n Achterbahn f.

big end n (AUT) Pleuelfuß m, Schubstangenkopf m.

biggish ['bɪgɪʃ] adj ziemlich groß.

bigheaded ['bɪg'hɛdɪd] adj eingebildet.

big-hearted ['bɪg'hɑːtɪd] adj großherzig.

bigot ['bɪgət] n Eiferer m; (about religion) bigotter Mensch m.

bigoted ['bɪgətɪd] adj (see n) eifernd; bigott.

bigotry ['bɪgətrɪ] n (see n) eifernde Borniertheit f; Bigotterie f.

big toe n große Zehe f.

big top n Zirkuszelt nt.

big wheel n Riesenrad nt.

bigwig ['bɪgwɪg] (inf) n hohes Tier nt.

bike [baɪk] n (Fahr)rad nt; (motorcycle) Motorrad nt.

bike lane n Fahrradspur f.

bikini [bɪ'kiːnɪ] n Bikini m.

bilateral [baɪ'lætərəl] adj bilateral.

bile [baɪl] n Galle(nflüssigkeit) f; (fig: invective) Beschimpfungen pl.

bilingual [baɪ'lɪŋwəl] adj zweisprachig.

bilious ['bɪlɪəs] adj unwohl; (fig: colour) widerlich; **he felt ~** ihm war schlecht or übel.

bill [bɪl] n Rechnung f; (POL) (Gesetz)entwurf m, (Gesetzes)vorlage f; (US: banknote) Banknote f, (Geld)schein m; (of bird) Schnabel m ♦ vt (item) in Rechnung stellen, berechnen; (customer) eine Rechnung ausstellen +dat; "**post no ~s**" „Plakate ankleben verboten"; **on the ~** (THEAT) auf dem Programm; **to fit** or **fill the ~** (fig) der/die/das Richtige sein; **~ of exchange** Wechsel m, Tratte f; **~ of fare** Speisekarte f; **~ of lading** Seefrachtbrief m, Konnossement nt; **~ of sale** Verkaufsurkunde f.

billboard ['bɪlbɔːd] n Reklametafel f.

billet ['bɪlɪt] (MIL) n Quartier nt ♦ vt einquartieren.

billfold ['bɪlfəuld] (US) n Brieftasche f.

billiards ['bɪljədz] n Billard nt.

billion ['bɪljən] n (BRIT) Billion f; (US) Milliarde f.

billionaire [bɪljə'nɛə'] n Milliardär(in) m(f).

billow ['bɪləu] n (of smoke) Schwaden m ♦ vi (smoke) in Schwaden aufsteigen; (sail) sich blähen.

billy goat ['bɪlɪ-] n Ziegenbock m.

bimbo ['bɪmbəu] (inf: pej) n (woman) Puppe f, Häschen nt.

bin [bɪn] n (BRIT) Mülleimer m; (container) Behälter m.

binary ['baɪnərɪ] adj binär.

bind [baɪnd] (pt, pp **bound**) vt binden; (tie together: hands and feet) fesseln; (constrain, oblige) verpflichten ♦ n (inf: nuisance) Last f.

► **bind over** vt rechtlich verpflichten.

► **bind up** vt (wound) verbinden; **to be bound up in** sehr beschäftigt sein mit; **to be bound up with** verbunden or verknüpft sein mit.

binder ['baɪndə*] n (file) Hefter m; (for magazines) Mappe f.

binding ['baɪndɪŋ] adj bindend, verbindlich ♦ n (of book) Einband m.

binge [bɪndʒ] (inf) n: **to go on a ~** auf eine Sauftour gehen.

bingo ['bɪŋgəu] n Bingo nt.

bin liner n Müllbeutel m.

binoculars [bɪ'nɔkjuləz] npl Fernglas nt.

biochemistry [baɪə'kemɪstrɪ] n Biochemie f.

biodegradable ['baɪəudɪ'greɪdəbl] adj biologisch abbaubar.

biodiversity ['baɪəudaɪ'vɜːsɪtɪ] n biologische Vielfalt f.

biofuel n Biotreibstoff m.

biographer [baɪ'ɔgrəfə*] n Biograf(in) m(f).

biographic(al) [baɪə'græfɪk(l)] adj biografisch.

biography [baɪ'ɔgrəfɪ] n Biografie f.

biological [baɪə'lɔdʒɪkl] adj biologisch.

biological clock n biologische Uhr f.

biologist [baɪ'ɔlədʒɪst] n Biologe m, Biologin f.

biology [baɪ'ɔlədʒɪ] n Biologie f.

biophysics ['baɪəu'fɪzɪks] n Biophysik f.

biopic ['baɪəupɪk] n Filmbiografie f.

biopsy ['baɪɔpsɪ] n Biopsie f.

biosphere ['baɪəsfɪə*] n Biosphäre f.

biotechnology ['baɪəutek'nɔlədʒɪ] n Biotechnik f.

biped ['baɪped] n Zweifüßer m.

birch [bɜːtʃ] n Birke f.

bird [bɜːd] n Vogel m; (BRIT: inf: girl) Biene f.

bird of prey n Raubvogel m.

bird's-eye view ['bɜːdzaɪ-] n Vogelperspektive f; (overview) Überblick m.

bird-watcher ['bɜːdwɔtʃə*] n Vogelbeobachter(in) m(f).

Biro ® ['baɪərəu] n Kugelschreiber m, Kuli m (inf).

birth [bɜːθ] n Geburt f; **to give ~ to** (subj: woman) gebären, entbunden werden von; (: animal) werfen.

birth certificate n Geburtsurkunde f.

birth control n Geburtenkontrolle f, Geburtenregelung f.

birthday ['bɜːθdeɪ] n Geburtstag m ♦ cpd Geburtstags-; see also **happy**.

birthmark ['bɜːθmɑːk] n Muttermal nt.

birthplace ['bɜːθpleɪs] n Geburtsort m; (house)

Geburtshaus nt; (fig) Entstehungsort m.

birth rate ['bɜːθreɪt] n Geburtenrate f, Geburtenziffer f.

Biscay ['bɪskeɪ] n: **the Bay of ~** der Golf von Biskaya.

biscuit ['bɪskɪt] n (BRIT) Keks m or nt; (US) Brötchen nt.

bisect [baɪ'sekt] vt halbieren.

bisexual ['baɪ'seksjuəl] adj bisexuell ♦ n Bisexuelle(r) f(m).

bishop ['bɪʃəp] n (REL) Bischof m; (CHESS) Läufer m.

bistro ['biːstrəu] n Bistro nt.

bit [bɪt] pt of **bite** ♦ n (piece) Stück nt; (of drill) (Bohr)einsatz m, Bohrer m; (of plane) (Hobel)messer nt; (COMPUT) Bit nt; (of horse) Gebiss nt; (US): **two/four/six ~s** 25/50/75 Cent(s); **a ~ of** ein bisschen; **a ~ mad** ein bisschen verrückt; **a ~ dangerous** etwas gefährlich; **~ by ~** nach und nach; **to come to ~s** kaputtgehen; **bring all your ~s and pieces** bringen Sie Ihre (Sieben)sachen mit; **to do one's ~** sein(en) Teil tun or beitragen.

bitch [bɪtʃ] n (dog) Hündin f; (inf!: woman) Miststück nt.

bite [baɪt] (pt **bit**, pp **bitten**) vt, vi beißen; (subj: insect etc) stechen ♦ n (insect bite) Stich m; (mouthful) Bissen m; **to ~ one's nails** an seinen Nägeln kauen; **let's have a ~ (to eat)** (inf) lasst uns eine Kleinigkeit essen.

biting ['baɪtɪŋ] adj (wind) schneidend; (wit) scharf.

bit part n kleine Nebenrolle f.

bitten ['bɪtn] pp of **bite**.

bitter ['bɪtə*] adj bitter; (person) verbittert; (wind, weather) bitterkalt, eisig; (criticism) scharf ♦ n (BRIT: beer) halbdunkles obergäriges Bier; **to the ~ end** bis zum bitteren Ende.

bitterly ['bɪtəlɪ] adv (complain, weep) bitterlich; (oppose) erbittert; (criticize) scharf; (disappointed) bitter; (jealous) sehr; **it's ~ cold** es ist bitterkalt.

bitterness ['bɪtənɪs] n Bitterkeit f.

bittersweet ['bɪtəswiːt] adj bittersüß.

bitty ['bɪtɪ] (BRIT: inf) adj zusammengestoppelt, zusammengestückelt.

bitumen ['bɪtjumɪn] n Bitumen nt.

bivouac ['bɪvuæk] n Biwak nt.

bizarre [bɪ'zɑː*] adj bizarr.

bk abbr = **bank**, **book**.

BL n abbr (= Bachelor of Law) akademischer Grad für Juristen; (= Bachelor of Letters) akademischer Grad für Literaturwissenschaftler; (US: = Bachelor of Literature) akademischer Grad für Literaturwissenschaftler.

b.l. abbr = **bill of lading**.

blab [blæb] (inf) vi quatschen.

black [blæk] adj schwarz ♦ vt (BRIT: INDUSTRY) boykottieren ♦ n Schwarz nt; (person): **B~** Schwarze(r) f(m); **to give sb a ~ eye** jdm ein

blaues Auge schlagen; ~ **and blue** grün und blau; **there it is in** ~ **and white** (*fig*) da steht es schwarz auf weiß; **to be in the** ~ in den schwarzen Zahlen sein.
▶ **black out** *vi* (*faint*) ohnmächtig werden.
black belt *n* (*US*) Gebiet in den *Südstaaten der USA, das vorwiegend von Schwarzen bewohnt wird*; (*JUDO*) schwarzer Gürtel *m*.
blackberry ['blækbərɪ] *n* Brombeere *f*.
blackbird ['blækbɔːd] *n* Amsel *f*.
blackboard ['blækbɔːd] *n* Tafel *f*.
black box *n* (*AVIAT*) Flugschreiber *m*.
black coffee *n* schwarzer Kaffee *m*.
Black Country (*BRIT*) *n*: **the** ~ *Industriegebiet in den englischen Midlands*.
blackcurrant ['blæk'kʌrənt] *n* Johannisbeere *f*.
black economy *n*: **the** ~ die Schattenwirtschaft.
blacken ['blækn] *vt*: **to** ~ **sb's name/ reputation** (*fig*) jdn verunglimpfen.
Black Forest *n*: **the** ~ der Schwarzwald.
blackhead ['blækhɛd] *n* Mitesser *m*.
black hole *n* schwarzes Loch *nt*.
black ice *n* Glatteis *nt*.
blackjack ['blækdʒæk] *n* (*CARDS*) Siebzehnundvier *nt*; (*US: truncheon*) Schlagstock *m*.
blackleg ['blæklɛg] (*BRIT*) *n* Streikbrecher(in) *m(f)*.
blacklist ['blæklɪst] *n* schwarze Liste *f* ▶ *vt* auf die schwarze Liste setzen.
blackmail ['blækmeɪl] *n* Erpressung *f* ▶ *vt* erpressen.
blackmailer ['blækmeɪlə⁻] *n* Erpresser(in) *m(f)*.
black market *n* Schwarzmarkt *m*.
blackout ['blækaut] *n* (*in wartime*) Verdunkelung *f*; (*power cut*) Stromausfall *m*; (*TV, RADIO*) Ausfall *m*; (*faint*) Ohnmachtsanfall *m*.
black pepper *n* schwarzer Pfeffer *m*.
Black Sea *n*: **the** ~ das Schwarze Meer.
black sheep *n* (*fig*) schwarzes Schaf *nt*.
blacksmith ['blæksmɪθ] *n* Schmied *m*.
black spot *n* (*AUT*) Gefahrenstelle *f*; (*for unemployment etc*) *Gebiet, in dem ein Problem besonders ausgeprägt ist*.
bladder ['blædə⁻] *n* Blase *f*.
blade [bleɪd] *n* (*of knife etc*) Klinge *f*; (*of oar, propeller*) Blatt *nt*; **a** ~ **of grass** ein Grashalm *m*.
Blairite ['blɛəraɪt] (*POL*) *adj* blairistisch ▶ *n* Blair-Anhänger(in) *m(f)*.
blame [bleɪm] *n* Schuld *f* ▶ *vt*: **to** ~ **sb for sth** jdm die Schuld an etw *dat* geben; **to be to** ~ Schuld daran haben, schuld sein; **who's to** ~? wer hat Schuld *or* ist schuld?; **I'm not to** ~ es ist nicht meine Schuld.
blameless ['bleɪmlɪs] *adj* schuldlos.
blanch [blɑːntʃ] *vi* blass werden ▶ *vt* (*CULIN*) blanchieren.
blancmange [blə'mɒnʒ] *n* Pudding *m*.
bland [blænd] *adj* (*taste, food*) fade.

blank [blæŋk] *adj* (*paper*) leer, unbeschrieben; (*look*) ausdruckslos ▶ *n* (*on form*) Lücke *f*; (*cartridge*) Platzpatrone *f*; **my mind was a** ~ ich hatte ein Brett vor dem Kopf; **we drew a** ~ (*fig*) wir hatten kein Glück.
blank cheque *n* Blankoscheck *m*; **to give sb a** ~ **to do sth** (*fig*) jdm freie Hand geben, etw zu tun.
blanket ['blæŋkɪt] *n* Decke *f* ▶ *adj* (*statement*) pauschal; (*agreement*) Pauschal-.
blanket cover *n* umfassende Versicherung *f*.
blare [blɛə⁻] *vi* (*brass band*) schmettern; (*horn*) tuten; (*radio*) plärren.
▶ **blare out** *vi* (*radio, stereo*) plärren.
blasé ['blɑːzeɪ] *adj* blasiert.
blaspheme [blæs'fiːm] *vi* Gott lästern.
blasphemous ['blæsfɪməs] *adj* lästerlich, blasphemisch.
blasphemy ['blæsfɪmɪ] *n* (*Gottes*)lästerung *f*, Blasphemie *f*.
blast [blɑːst] *n* (*of wind*) Windstoß *m*; (*of whistle*) Trillern *nt*; (*shock wave*) Druckwelle *f*; (*of air, steam*) Schwall *m*; (*of explosive*) Explosion *f* ▶ *vt* (*blow up*) sprengen ▶ *excl* (*BRIT: inf*) verdammt!, so ein Mist!; **at full** ~ (*play music*) mit voller Lautstärke; (*move, work*) auf Hochtouren.
▶ **blast off** *vi* (*SPACE*) abheben, starten.
blast furnace *n* Hochofen *m*.
blastoff ['blɑːstɒf] *n* (*SPACE*) Abschuss *m*.
blatant ['bleɪtənt] *adj* offensichtlich.
blatantly ['bleɪtəntlɪ] *adv* (*lie*) unverfroren; **it's** ~ **obvious** es ist überdeutlich.
blaze [bleɪz] *n* (*fire*) Feuer *nt*, Brand *m*; (*fig: of colour*) Farbenpracht *f*; (: *of glory*) Glanz *m* ▶ *vi* (*fire*) lodern; (*guns*) feuern; (*fig: eyes*) glühen ▶ *vt*: **to** ~ **a trail** (*fig*) den Weg bahnen; **in a** ~ **of publicity** mit viel Publicity.
blazer ['bleɪzə⁻] *n* Blazer *m*.
bleach [bliːtʃ] *n* (*also*: **household** ~) ≈ Reinigungsmittel *nt* ▶ *vt* bleichen.
bleached [bliːtʃt] *adj* gebleicht.
bleachers ['bliːtʃəz] (*US*) *npl* unüberdachte Zuschauertribüne *f*.
bleak [bliːk] *adj* (*countryside*) öde; (*weather, situation*) trostlos; (*prospect*) trüb; (*expression, voice*) deprimiert.
bleary-eyed ['blɪərɪ'aɪd] *adj* triefäugig.
bleat [bliːt] *vi* (*goat*) meckern; (*sheep*) blöken ▶ *n* Meckern *nt*; Blöken *nt*.
bled [blɛd] *pt, pp of* **bleed**.
bleed [bliːd] (*pt, pp* **bled**) *vi* bluten; (*colour*) auslaufen ▶ *vt* (*brakes, radiator*) entlüften; **my nose is** ~**ing** ich habe Nasenbluten.
bleep [bliːp] *n* Piepton *m* ▶ *vi* piepen ▶ *vt* (*doctor etc*) rufen, anpiepen (*inf*).
bleeper ['bliːpə⁻] *n* Piepser *m* (*inf*), Funkrufempfänger *m*.
blemish ['blɛmɪʃ] *n* Makel *m*.
blend [blɛnd] *n* Mischung *f* ▶ *vt* (*CULIN*) mischen, mixen; (*colours, styles, flavours etc*)

vermischen ♦ *vi* (*colours etc: also:* ~ **in**) harmonieren.

blender ['blɛndə*] *n* (*CULIN*) Mixer *m*.

bless [blɛs] (*pt, pp* **blessed** *or* **blest**) *vt* segnen; **to be** ~**ed with** gesegnet sein mit; ~ **you!** (*after sneeze*) Gesundheit!

blessed ['blɛsɪd] *adj* heilig; (*happy*) selig; **it rains every** ~ **day** (*inf*) es regnet aber auch jeden Tag.

blessing ['blɛsɪŋ] *n* (*approval*) Zustimmung *f*; (*REL, fig*) Segen *m*; **to count one's** ~**s** von Glück sagen können; **it was a** ~ **in disguise** es war schließlich doch ein Segen.

blew [bluː] *pt of* **blow**.

blight [blaɪt] *vt* zerstören; (*hopes*) vereiteln; (*life*) verderben ♦ *n* (*of plants*) Brand *m*.

blimey ['blaɪmɪ] (*BRIT: inf*) *excl* Mensch!

blind [blaɪnd] *adj* blind ♦ *n* (*for window*) Rollo *nt*, Rouleau *nt*; (*also:* **Venetian** ~) Jalousie *f* ♦ *vt* blind machen; (*dazzle*) blenden; (*deceive: with facts etc*) verblenden; **the blind** *npl* (*blind people*) die Blinden *pl*; **to turn a** ~ **eye (on** *or* **to)** ein Auge zudrücken (bei); **to be** ~ **to sth** (*fig*) blind für etw sein.

blind alley *n* (*fig*) Sackgasse *f*.

blind corner (*BRIT*) *n* unübersichtliche Ecke *f*.

blind date *n* Rendezvous *nt* mit einem/einer Unbekannten.

blinders ['blaɪndəz] (*US*) *npl* = **blinkers**.

blindfold ['blaɪndfəʊld] *n* Augenbinde *f* ♦ *adj, adv* mit verbundenen Augen ♦ *vt* die Augen verbinden +*dat*.

blinding ['blaɪndɪŋ] *adj* (*dazzling*) blendend; (*remarkable*) bemerkenswert.

blindly ['blaɪndlɪ] *adv* (*without seeing*) wie blind; (*without thinking*) blindlings.

blindness ['blaɪndnɪs] *n* Blindheit *f*.

blind spot *n* (*AUT*) toter Winkel *m*; (*fig: weak spot*) schwacher Punkt *m*.

blink [blɪŋk] *vi* blinzeln; (*light*) blinken ♦ *n*: **the TV's on the** ~ (*inf*) der Fernseher ist kaputt.

blinkers ['blɪŋkəz] *npl* Scheuklappen *pl*.

blinking ['blɪŋkɪŋ] (*BRIT: inf*) *adj*: **this** ~ ... diese(r, s) verflixte ...

blip [blɪp] *n* (*on radar screen*) leuchtender Punkt *m*; (*in a straight line*) Ausschlag *m*; (*fig*) (zeitweilige) Abweichung *f*.

bliss [blɪs] *n* Glück *nt*, Seligkeit *f*.

blissful ['blɪsful] *adj* (*event, day*) herrlich; (*smile*) selig; **a** ~ **sigh** ein wohliger Seufzer *m*; **in** ~ **ignorance** in herrlicher Ahnungslosigkeit.

blissfully ['blɪsfəlɪ] *adv* selig; ~ **happy** überglücklich; ~ **unaware of** ... ohne auch nur zu ahnen, dass ...

blister ['blɪstə*] *n* Blase *f* ♦ *vi* (*paint*) Blasen werfen.

blithely ['blaɪðlɪ] *adv* (*unconcernedly*) unbekümmert, munter; (*joyfully*) fröhlich.

blithering ['blɪðərɪŋ] (*inf*) *adj*: **this** ~ **idiot** dieser Trottel.

BLit(t) *n abbr* (= *Bachelor of Literature; Bachelor of Letters*) akademischer Grad *für* Literaturwissenschaftler.

blitz [blɪts] *n* (*MIL*) Luftangriff *m*; **to have a** ~ **on sth** (*fig*) einen Großangriff auf etw *acc* starten.

blizzard ['blɪzəd] *n* Schneesturm *m*.

BLM (*US*) *n abbr* (= *Bureau of Land Management*) Behörde zur Verwaltung von Grund und Boden.

bloated ['bləʊtɪd] *adj* aufgedunsen; (*full*) (über)satt.

blob [blɔb] *n* Tropfen *m*; (*sth indistinct*) verschwommener Fleck *m*.

bloc [blɔk] *n* Block *m*; **the Eastern** ~ (*HIST*) der Ostblock.

block [blɔk] *n* Block *m*; (*toy*) Bauklotz *m*; (*in pipes*) Verstopfung *f* ♦ *vt* blockieren; (*progress*) aufhalten; (*COMPUT*) blocken; ~ **of flats** (*BRIT*) Wohnblock *m*; **3** ~**s from here** 3 Blocks *or* Straßen weiter; **mental** ~ geistige Sperre *f*, Mattscheibe *f* (*inf*); ~ **and tackle** Flaschenzug *m*.

▶ **block up** *vt, vi* verstopfen.

blockade [blɔ'keɪd] *n* Blockade *f* ♦ *vt* blockieren.

blockage ['blɔkɪdʒ] *n* Verstopfung *f*.

block booking *n* Gruppenbuchung *f*.

blockbuster ['blɔkbʌstə*] *n* Knüller *m*.

block capitals *npl* Blockschrift *f*.

blockhead ['blɔkhɛd] (*inf*) *n* Dummkopf *m*.

block letters *npl* Blockschrift *f*.

block release (*BRIT*) *n* blockweise Freistellung von Auszubildenden zur Weiterbildung.

block vote (*BRIT*) *n* Stimmenblock *m*.

bloke [bləʊk] (*BRIT: inf*) *n* Typ *m*.

blond(e) [blɔnd] *adj* blond ♦ *n*: ~ (*woman*) Blondine *f*.

blood [blʌd] *n* Blut *nt*; **new** ~ (*fig*) frisches Blut *nt*.

blood bank *n* Blutbank *f*.

blood bath *n* Blutbad *nt*.

blood count *n* Blutbild *nt*.

bloodcurdling ['blʌdkɜːdlɪŋ] *adj* Grauen erregend.

blood donor *n* Blutspender(in) *m(f)*.

blood group *n* Blutgruppe *f*.

bloodhound ['blʌdhaund] *n* Bluthund *m*.

bloodless ['blʌdlɪs] *adj* (*victory*) unblutig; (*pale*) blutleer.

blood-letting ['blʌdlɛtɪŋ] *n* (*also fig*) Aderlass *m*.

blood poisoning *n* Blutvergiftung *f*.

blood pressure *n* Blutdruck *m*; **to have high/low** ~ hohen/niedrigen Blutdruck haben.

bloodshed ['blʌdʃɛd] *n* Blutvergießen *nt*.

bloodshot ['blʌdʃɔt] *adj* (*eyes*) blutunterlaufen.

blood sport *n* Jagdsport *m* (*und andere Sportarten, bei denen Tiere getötet werden*).

bloodstained ['blʌdsteɪnd] adj blutbefleckt.
bloodstream ['blʌdstriːm] n Blut nt, Blutkreislauf m.
blood test n Blutprobe f.
bloodthirsty ['blʌdθəːstɪ] adj blutrünstig.
blood transfusion n Blutübertragung f, (Blut)transfusion f.
blood type n Blutgruppe f.
blood vessel n Blutgefäß nt.
bloody ['blʌdɪ] adj blutig; (BRIT: inf!): this ~ ... diese(r, s) verdammte ...; ~ strong (inf!) verdammt stark; ~ good (inf!) echt gut.
bloody-minded ['blʌdɪ'maɪndɪd] (BRIT: inf) adj stur.
bloom [bluːm] n Blüte f ♦ vi blühen; to be in ~ in Blüte stehen.
blooming ['bluːmɪŋ] (BRIT: inf) adj: this ~ ... diese(r, s) verflixte ...
blossom ['blɒsəm] n Blüte f ♦ vi blühen; (fig): to ~ into erblühen or aufblühen zu.
blot [blɒt] n Klecks m; (fig: on name etc) Makel m ♦ vt (liquid) aufsaugen; (make blot on) beklecksen; to be a ~ on the landscape ein Schandfleck in der Landschaft sein; to ~ one's copy book (fig) sich unmöglich machen.
▸ **blot out** vt (view) verdecken; (memory) auslöschen.
blotchy ['blɒtʃɪ] adj fleckig.
blotter ['blɒtə*] n (Tinten)löscher m.
blotting paper ['blɒtɪŋ-] n Löschpapier nt.
blotto ['blɒtəʊ] (inf) adj (drunk) sternhagelvoll.
blouse [blaʊz] n Bluse f.
blow [bləʊ] (pt **blew**, pp **blown**) n (also fig) Schlag m ♦ vi (wind) wehen; (person) blasen ♦ vt (subj: wind) wehen; (instrument, whistle) blasen; (fuse) durchbrennen lassen; to come to ~s handgreiflich werden; to ~ off course (ship) vom Kurs abgetrieben werden; to ~ one's nose sich dat die Nase putzen; to ~ a whistle pfeifen.
▸ **blow away** vt wegblasen ♦ vi wegfliegen.
▸ **blow down** vt umwehen.
▸ **blow off** vt wegwehen ♦ vi wegfliegen.
▸ **blow out** vi ausgehen.
▸ **blow over** vi sich legen.
▸ **blow up** vi ausbrechen ♦ vt (bridge) in die Luft jagen; (tyre) aufblasen; (PHOT) vergrößern.
blow-dry ['bləʊdraɪ] vt föhnen ♦ n: to have a ~ sich föhnen lassen.
blowlamp ['bləʊlæmp] (BRIT) n Lötlampe f.
blown [bləʊn] pp of **blow**.
blowout ['bləʊaʊt] n Reifenpanne f; (inf: big meal) Schlemmerei f; (of oil-well) Ölausbruch m.
blowtorch ['bləʊtɔːtʃ] n = **blowlamp**.
blow-up ['bləʊʌp] n Vergrößerung f.
blowzy ['blaʊzɪ] (BRIT) adj schlampig.
BLS (US) n abbr (= Bureau of Labor Statistics) Amt für Arbeitsstatistik.
blubber ['blʌbə*] n Walfischspeck m ♦ vi (pej)

heulen.
bludgeon ['blʌdʒən] vt niederknüppeln; (fig): to ~ sb into doing sth jdm so lange zusetzen, bis er etw tut.
blue [bluː] adj blau; (depressed) deprimiert, niedergeschlagen ♦ n: out of the ~ (fig) aus heiterem Himmel; **blues** n (MUS): the ~s der Blues; ~ **film** Pornofilm m; ~ **joke** schlüpfriger Witz m; (only) once in a ~ **moon** (nur) alle Jubeljahre einmal; to have the ~s deprimiert or niedergeschlagen sein.
blue baby n Baby nt mit angeborenem Herzfehler.
bluebell ['bluːbɛl] n Glockenblume f.
bluebottle ['bluːbɒtl] n Schmeißfliege f.
blue cheese n Blauschimmelkäse m.
blue-chip ['bluːtʃɪp] adj: ~ **investment** sichere Geldanlage f.
blue-collar worker ['bluːkɒlə*-] n Arbeiter(in) m(f).
blue jeans npl (Blue)jeans pl.
blueprint ['bluːprɪnt] n (fig): a ~ (for) ein Plan m or Entwurf m (für).
bluff [blʌf] vi bluffen ♦ n Bluff m; (cliff) Klippe f; (promontory) Felsvorsprung m; to call sb's ~ es darauf ankommen lassen.
blunder ['blʌndə*] n (dummer) Fehler m ♦ vi einen (dummen) Fehler machen; to ~ into sb jdm zusammenstoßen; to ~ into sth in etw acc (hinein)tappen.
blunt [blʌnt] adj stumpf; (person) direkt; (talk) unverblümt ♦ vt stumpf machen; ~ **instrument** (LAW) stumpfer Gegenstand m.
bluntly ['blʌntlɪ] adv (speak) unverblümt.
bluntness ['blʌntnɪs] n (of person) Direktheit f.
blur [bləː*] n (shape) verschwommener Fleck m; (scene etc) verschwommenes Bild nt; (memory) verschwommene Erinnerung f ♦ vt (vision) trüben; (distinction) verwischen.
blurb [bləːb] n Informationsmaterial nt.
blurred [bləːd] adj (photograph, TV picture etc) verschwommen; (distinction) verwischt.
blurt out [bləːt-] vt herausplatzen mit.
blush [blʌʃ] vi erröten ♦ n Röte f.
blusher ['blʌʃə*] n Rouge nt.
bluster ['blʌstə*] n Toben nt, Geschrei nt ♦ vi toben.
blustering ['blʌstərɪŋ] adj polternd.
blustery ['blʌstərɪ] adj stürmisch.
Blvd abbr = boulevard.
BM n abbr (= British Museum) Britisches Museum nt; (= Bachelor of Medicine) akademischer Grad für Mediziner.
BMA n abbr (= British Medical Association) Dachverband der Ärzte.
BMJ n abbr (= British Medical Journal) vom BMA herausgegebene Zeitschrift.
BMus n abbr (= Bachelor of Music) akademischer Grad für

Musikwissenschaftler.
BMX *n abbr* (= *bicycle motocross*): ~ **bike**
BMX-Rad *nt*.
bn *abbr* = **billion**.
BO *n abbr* (*inf*: = *body odour*) Körpergeruch *m*;
(*US*) = **box office**.
boar [bɔː⁺] *n* (*male pig*) Eber *m*; (*wild pig*)
Keiler *m*.
board [bɔːd] *n* Brett *nt*; (*cardboard*) Pappe *f*;
(*committee*) Ausschuss *m*; (*in firm*) Vorstand
m ♦ *vt* (*ship*) an Bord +*gen* gehen; (*train*)
einsteigen in +*acc*; **on** ~ (*NAUT, AVIAT*) an
Bord; **full/half** ~ (*BRIT*) Voll-/Halbpension *f*;
~ **and lodging** Unterkunft und Verpflegung
f; **to go by the** ~ (*fig*) unter den Tisch fallen;
above ~ (*fig*) korrekt; **across the** ~ (*fig*)
allgemein; (: *criticize, reject*) pauschal.
▶ **board up** *vt* mit Brettern vernageln.
boarder [ˈbɔːdə⁺] *n* Internatsschüler(in) *m(f)*.
board game *n* Brettspiel *nt*.
boarding card [ˈbɔːdɪŋ-] *n* (*AVIAT, NAUT*)
= **boarding pass**.
boarding house [ˈbɔːdɪŋ-] *n* Pension *f*.
boarding party [ˈbɔːdɪŋ-] *n* (*NAUT*)
Enterkommando *nt*.
boarding pass [ˈbɔːdɪŋ-] *n* Bordkarte *f*.
boarding school [ˈbɔːdɪŋ-] *n* Internat *nt*.
board meeting *n* Vorstandssitzung *f*.
boardroom [ˈbɔːdruːm] *n* Sitzungssaal *m*.
boardwalk [ˈbɔːdwɔːk] (*US*) *n* Holzsteg *m*.
boast [bəʊst] *vi* prahlen ♦ *vt* (*fig: possess*) sich
rühmen +*gen*, besitzen; **to** ~ **about** *or* **of**
prahlen mit.
boastful [ˈbəʊstful] *adj* prahlerisch.
boastfulness [ˈbəʊstfulnɪs] *n* Prahlerei *f*.
boat [bəʊt] *n* Boot *nt*; (*ship*) Schiff *nt*; **to go by**
~ mit dem Schiff fahren; **to be in the same**
~ (*fig*) in einem Boot *or* im gleichen Boot
sitzen.
boater [ˈbəʊtə⁺] *n* steifer Strohhut *m*,
Kreissäge *f* (*inf*).
boating [ˈbəʊtɪŋ] *n* Bootfahren *nt*.
boat people *npl* Bootsflüchtlinge *pl*.
boatswain [ˈbəʊsn] *n* Bootsmann *m*.
bob [bɒb] *vi* (*also:* ~ **up and down**) sich auf
und ab bewegen ♦ *n* (*BRIT*: *inf*) = **shilling**.
▶ **bob up** *vi* auftauchen.
bobbin [ˈbɒbɪn] *n* Spule *f*.
bobby [ˈbɒbɪ] (*BRIT*: *inf*) *n* Bobby *m*, Polizist *m*.
bobsleigh [ˈbɒbsleɪ] *n* Bob *m*.
bode [bəʊd] *vi*: **to** ~ **well/ill (for)** ein gutes/
schlechtes Zeichen sein (für).
bodice [ˈbɒdɪs] *n* (*of dress*) Oberteil *nt*.
bodily [ˈbɒdɪlɪ] *adj* körperlich; (*needs*) leiblich
♦ *adv* (*lift, carry*) mit aller Kraft.
body [ˈbɒdɪ] *n* Körper *m*; (*corpse*) Leiche *f*;
(*main part*) Hauptteil *m*; (*of car*) Karosserie *f*;
(*of plane*) Rumpf *m*; (*group*) Gruppe *f*;
(*organization*) Organ *nt*; **ruling** ~
amtierendes Organ; **in a** ~ geschlossen; **a**
~ **of facts** Tatsachenmaterial *nt*.
body blow *n* (*fig: setback*) schwerer Schlag *m*.

body building *n* Bodybuilding *nt*.
body double *n* (*FILM, TV*) Double *für Szenen,
in denen Körperpartien in Nahaufnahme
gezeigt werden.*
bodyguard [ˈbɒdɪgɑːd] *n* (*group*) Leibwache *f*;
(*one person*) Leibwächter *m*.
body language *n* Körpersprache *f*.
body repairs *npl* Karosseriearbeiten *pl*.
body search *n* Leibesvisitation *f*.
body stocking *n* Body(stocking) *m*.
bodywork [ˈbɒdɪwɜːk] *n* Karosserie *f*.
boffin [ˈbɒfɪn] (*BRIT*) *n* Fachidiot *m*.
bog [bɒg] *n* Sumpf *m* ♦ *vt*: **to get** ~**ged down**
(*fig*) sich verzetteln.
bogey [ˈbəʊgɪ] *n* Schreckgespenst *nt*; (*also:*
~**man**) Butzemann *m*, schwarzer Mann *m*.
boggle [ˈbɒgl] *vi*: **the mind** ~**s** das ist nicht *or*
kaum auszumalen.
bogie [ˈbəʊgɪ] *n* Drehgestell *nt*; (*trolley*)
Draisine *f*.
Bogotá [bəʊgəˈtɑː] *n* Bogotá *nt*.
bogus [ˈbəʊgəs] *adj* (*workman etc*) falsch;
(*claim*) erfunden.
Bohemia [bəʊˈhiːmɪə] *n* Böhmen *nt*.
Bohemian [bəʊˈhiːmɪən] *adj* böhmisch ♦ *n*
Böhme *m*, Böhmin *f*; (*also:* **b**~) Bohemien *m*.
boil [bɔɪl] *vt, vi* kochen ♦ *n* (*MED*) Furunkel *nt or*
m; **to come to the** (*BRIT*) *or* **a** (*US*) ~ zu
kochen anfangen.
▶ **boil down to** *vt fus* (*fig*) hinauslaufen auf
+*acc*.
▶ **boil over** *vi* überkochen.
boiled egg [bɔɪld-] *n* gekochtes Ei *nt*.
boiled potatoes *npl* Salzkartoffeln *pl*.
boiler [ˈbɔɪlə⁺] *n* Boiler *m*.
boiler suit (*BRIT*) *n* Overall *m*.
boiling [ˈbɔɪlɪŋ] *adj*: **I'm** ~ (**hot**) (*inf*) mir ist
fürchterlich heiß; **it's** ~ es ist eine
Affenhitze (*inf*).
boiling point *n* Siedepunkt *m*.
boil-in-the-bag [bɔɪlɪnðəˈbæg] *adj* (*meals*)
Kochbeutel-.
boisterous [ˈbɔɪstərəs] *adj* ausgelassen.
bold [bəʊld] *adj* (*brave*) mutig; (*pej: cheeky*)
dreist; (*pattern, colours*) kräftig.
boldly [ˈbəʊldlɪ] *adv* (*see adj*) mutig; dreist;
kräftig.
boldness [ˈbəʊldnɪs] *n* Mut *m*; (*cheekiness*)
Dreistigkeit *f*.
bold type *n* Fettdruck *m*.
Bolivia [bəˈlɪvɪə] *n* Bolivien *nt*.
Bolivian [bəˈlɪvɪən] *adj* bolivisch, bolivianisch
♦ *n* Bolivier(in) *m(f)*, Bolivianer(in) *m(f)*.
bollard [ˈbɒləd] (*BRIT*) *n* Poller *m*.
bolshy [ˈbɒlʃɪ] (*BRIT*: *inf*) *adj* (*stroppy*) pampig.
bolster [ˈbəʊlstə⁺] *n* Nackenrolle *f*.
▶ **bolster up** *vt* stützen; (*case*) untermauern.
bolt [bəʊlt] *n* Riegel *m*; (*with nut*) Schraube *f*;
(*of lightning*) Blitz(strahl) *m* ♦ *vt* (*door*)
verriegeln; (*also:* ~ **together**) verschrauben;
(*food*) hinunterschlingen ♦ *vi* (*run away:*
person) weglaufen; (: *horse*) durchgehen

♦ *adv*: ~ **upright** kerzengerade; **a** ~ **from the blue** (*fig*) ein Blitz *m* aus heiterem Himmel.

bomb [bɔm] *n* Bombe *f* ♦ *vt* bombardieren; (*plant bomb in or near*) einen Bombenanschlag verüben auf +*acc*.

bombard [bɔm'bɑːd] *vt* (*also fig*) bombardieren.

bombardment [bɔm'bɑːdmənt] *n* Bombardierung *f*, Bombardement *nt*.

bombastic [bɔm'bæstɪk] *adj* bombastisch.

bomb disposal *n*: ~ **unit** Bombenräumkommando *nt*; ~ **expert** Bombenräumexperte *m*, Bombenräumexpertin *f*.

bomber ['bɔmə*] *n* Bomber *m*; (*terrorist*) Bombenattentäter(in) *m(f)*.

bombing ['bɔmɪŋ] *n* Bombenangriff *m*.

bomb scare *n* Bombenalarm *m*.

bombshell ['bɔmʃel] *n* (*fig: revelation*) Bombe *f*.

bomb site *n* Trümmergrundstück *nt*.

bona fide ['bəʊnə'faɪdɪ] *adj* echt; ~ **offer** Angebot *nt* auf Treu und Glauben.

bonanza [bə'nænzə] *n* (*ECON*) Boom *m*.

bond [bɔnd] *n* Band *nt*, Bindung *f*; (*FIN*) festverzinsliches Wertpapier *nt*, Bond *m*.

bondage ['bɔndɪdʒ] *n* Sklaverei *f*.

bonded warehouse ['bɔndɪd] *n* Zolllager *nt*.

bone [bəʊn] *n* Knochen *m*; (*of fish*) Gräte *f* ♦ *vt* (*meat*) die Knochen herauslösen aus; (*fish*) entgräten; **I've got a** ~ **to pick with you** ich habe mit Ihnen (noch) ein Hühnchen zu rupfen.

bone china *n* ≈ feines Porzellan *nt*.

bone-dry ['bəʊn'draɪ] *adj* knochentrocken.

bone idle *adj* stinkfaul.

bone marrow *n* Knochenmark *nt*.

boner ['bəʊnə*] (*US*) *n* Schnitzer *m*.

bonfire ['bɔnfaɪə*] *n* Feuer *nt*.

bonk [bɔŋk] (*inf*) *vt*, *vi* (*have sex (with)*) bumsen.

bonkers ['bɔŋkəz] (*BRIT: inf*) *adj* (*mad*) verrückt.

Bonn [bɔn] *n* Bonn *nt*.

bonnet ['bɔnɪt] *n* Haube *f*; (*for baby*) Häubchen *nt*; (*BRIT: of car*) Motorhaube *f*.

bonny ['bɔnɪ] (*SCOT, Northern English*) *adj* schön, hübsch.

bonus ['bəʊnəs] *n* Prämie *f*; (*on wages*) Zulage *f*; (*at Christmas*) Gratifikation *f*; (*fig: additional benefit*) Plus *nt*.

bony ['bəʊnɪ] *adj* knochig; (*MED*) knöchern; (*tissue*) knochenartig; (*meat*) mit viel Knochen; (*fish*) mit viel Gräten.

boo [buː] *excl* buh ♦ *vt* auspfeifen, ausbuhen.

boob [buːb] (*inf*) *n* (*breast*) Brust *f*; (*BRIT: mistake*) Schnitzer *m*.

booby prize ['buːbɪ-] *n* Scherzpreis für den schlechtesten Teilnehmer.

booby trap ['buːbɪ-] *n* versteckte Bombe *f*; (*fig: joke etc*) als Schabernack versteckt angebrachte Falle.

booby-trapped ['buːbɪtræpt] *adj*: **a** ~ **car** ein Auto *nt*, in dem eine Bombe versteckt ist.

book [buk] *n* Buch *nt*; (*of stamps, tickets*)

Heftchen *nt* ♦ *vt* bestellen; (*seat, room*) buchen, reservieren lassen; (*subj: traffic warden, policeman*) aufschreiben; (: *referee*) verwarnen; **books** *npl* (*COMM: accounts*) Bücher *pl*; **to keep the** ~**s** die Bücher führen; **by the** ~ nach Vorschrift; **to throw the** ~ **at sb** jdn nach allen Regeln der Kunst fertig machen.

▶ **book in** (*BRIT*) *vi* sich eintragen.

▶ **book up** *vt*: **all seats are** ~**ed up** es ist bis auf den letzten Platz ausverkauft; **the hotel is** ~**ed up** das Hotel ist ausgebucht.

bookable ['bukəbl] *adj*: **all seats are** ~ Karten für alle Plätze können vorbestellt werden.

bookcase ['bukkeɪs] *n* Bücherregal *nt*.

book ends *npl* Bücherstützen *pl*.

booking ['bukɪŋ] (*BRIT*) *n* Bestellung *f*; (*of seat, room*) Buchung *f*, Reservierung *f*.

booking office (*BRIT*) *n* (*RAIL*) Fahrkartenschalter *m*; (*THEAT*) Vorverkaufsstelle *f*, Vorverkaufskasse *f*.

book-keeping ['buk'kiːpɪŋ] *n* Buchhaltung *f*, Buchführung *f*.

booklet ['buklɪt] *n* Broschüre *f*.

bookmaker ['bukmeɪkə*] *n* Buchmacher *m*.

bookmark ['bukmɑːk] *n* Lesezeichen *nt*; (*COMPUT*) Bookmark *nt* ♦ *vt* (*COMPUT*) ein Bookmark einrichten für, bookmarken.

bookseller ['buksɛlə*] *n* Buchhändler(in) *m(f)*.

bookshelf ['bukʃɛlf] *n* Bücherbord *nt*; **bookshelves** *npl* Bücherregal *nt*.

bookshop ['bukʃɔp] *n* Buchhandlung *f*.

bookstall ['bukstɔːl] *n* Bücher- und Zeitungskiosk *m*.

book store *n* = **bookshop**.

book token *n* Buchgutschein *m*.

book value *n* Buchwert *m*, Bilanzwert *m*.

bookworm ['bukwɔːm] *n* (*fig*) Bücherwurm *m*.

boom [buːm] *n* Donnern *nt*, Dröhnen *nt*; (*in prices, population etc*) rapider Anstieg *m*; (*ECON*) Hochkonjunktur *f*; (*busy period*) Boom *m* ♦ *vi* (*guns*) donnern; (*thunder*) hallen; (*voice*) dröhnen; (*business*) florieren.

boomerang ['buːməræŋ] *n* Bumerang *m* ♦ *vi* (*fig*) einen Bumerangeffekt haben.

boom town *n* Goldgräberstadt *f*.

boon [buːn] *n* Segen *m*.

boorish ['buərɪʃ] *adj* rüpelhaft.

boost [buːst] *n* Auftrieb *m* ♦ *vt* (*confidence*) stärken; (*sales, economy etc*) ankurbeln; **to give a** ~ **to sb/sb's spirits** jdm Auftrieb geben.

booster ['buːstə*] *n* (*MED*) Wiederholungsimpfung *f*; (*TV*) Zusatzgleichrichter *m*; (*ELEC*) Puffersatz *m*; (*also:* ~ **rocket**) Booster *m*, Startrakete *f*.

booster seat *n* (*AUT*) Sitzerhöhung *f*.

boot [buːt] *n* Stiefel *m*; (*ankle boot*) hoher Schuh *m*; (*BRIT: of car*) Kofferraum *m* ♦ *vt* (*COMPUT*) laden; **... to** ~ (*in addition*) obendrein ...; **to give sb the** ~ (*inf*) jdn rauswerfen *or* rausschmeißen.

booth – bounce

booth [buːð] n (at fair) Bude f, Stand m; (telephone booth) Zelle f; (voting booth) Kabine f.

bootleg ['buːtlɛg] adj (alcohol) schwarzgebrannt; (fuel) schwarz hergestellt; (tape etc) schwarz mitgeschnitten.

bootlegger ['buːtlɛgə*] n Bootlegger m, Schwarzhändler m.

booty ['buːtɪ] n Beute f.

booze [buːz] (inf) n Alkohol m ♦ vi saufen.

boozer ['buːzə*] (inf) n (person) Säufer(in) m(f); (BRIT: pub) Kneipe f.

border ['bɔːdə*] n Grenze f; (for flowers) Rabatte f; (on cloth etc) Bordüre f ♦ vt (road) säumen; (another country: also: ~ on) grenzen an +acc; **Borders** n: **the B~s** das Grenzgebiet zwischen England und Schottland.

  ▸ **border on** vt fus (fig) grenzen an +acc.

borderline ['bɔːdəlaɪn] n (fig): **on the ~** an der Grenze.

borderline case n Grenzfall m.

bore [bɔː*] pt of **bear** ♦ vt bohren; (person) langweilen ♦ n Langweiler m; (of gun) Kaliber nt; **to be ~d** sich langweilen; **he's ~d to tears** or **~d to death** or **~d stiff** er langweilt sich zu Tode.

boredom ['bɔːdəm] n Langeweile f; (boring quality) Langweiligkeit f.

boring ['bɔːrɪŋ] adj langweilig.

born [bɔːn] adj: **to be ~** geboren werden; **I was ~ in 1960** ich bin or wurde 1960 geboren; **~ blind** blind geboren, von Geburt (an) blind; **a ~ comedian** ein geborener Komiker.

born-again [bɔːnə'gɛn] adj wieder geboren.

borne [bɔːn] pp of **bear**.

Borneo ['bɔːnɪəu] n Borneo nt.

borough ['bʌrə] n Bezirk m, Stadtgemeinde f.

borrow ['bɔrəu] vt: **to ~ sth** etw borgen, sich dat etw leihen; (from library) sich dat etw ausleihen; **may I ~ your car?** kann ich deinen Wagen leihen?

borrower ['bɔrəuə*] n (of loan etc) Kreditnehmer(in) m(f).

borrowing ['bɔrəuɪŋ] n Kreditaufnahme f.

borstal ['bɔːstl] (BRIT) n (formerly) Besserungsanstalt f.

Bosnia ['bɔznɪə] n Bosnien nt.

Bosnia-Herzegovina n Bosnien-Herzegowina nt.

Bosnian ['bɔznɪən] adj bosnisch ♦ n Bosnier(in) m(f).

bosom ['buzəm] n Busen m; (fig: of family) Schoß m.

bosom friend n Busenfreund(in) m(f).

boss [bɔs] n Chef(in) m(f); (leader) Boss m ♦ vt (also: ~ around, ~ about) herumkommandieren; **stop ~ing everyone about!** hör auf mit dem ständigen Herumkommandieren!

bossy ['bɔsɪ] adj herrisch.

bosun ['bəusn] n Bootsmann m.

botanical [bə'tænɪkl] adj botanisch.

botanist ['bɔtənɪst] n Botaniker(in) m(f).

botany ['bɔtənɪ] n Botanik f.

botch [bɔtʃ] vt (also: ~ up) verpfuschen.

both [bəuθ] adj beide ♦ pron beide; (two different things) beides ♦ adv: **~ A and B** sowohl A als auch B; **~ (of them)** (alle) beide; **~ of us went, we ~ went** wir gingen beide; **they sell ~ the fabric and the finished curtains** sie verkaufen sowohl den Stoff als auch die fertigen Vorhänge.

bother ['bɔðə*] vt Sorgen machen +dat; (disturb) stören ♦ vi (also: ~ o.s.) sich dat Sorgen or Gedanken machen ♦ n (trouble) Mühe f; (nuisance) Plage f ♦ excl Mist! (inf); **don't ~ phoning** du brauchst nicht anzurufen; **I'm sorry to ~ you** es tut mir Leid, dass ich Sie belästigen muss; **I can't be ~ed** ich habe keine Lust; **please don't ~** bitte machen Sie sich keine Umstände; **don't ~!** lass es!; **it is a ~ to have to shave every morning** es ist wirklich lästig, sich jeden Morgen rasieren zu müssen; **it's no ~** es ist kein Problem.

Botswana [bɔt'swɑːnə] n Botswana nt.

bottle ['bɔtl] n Flasche f; (BRIT: inf: courage) Mumm m ♦ vt in Flaschen abfüllen; (fruit) einmachen; **a ~ of wine/milk** eine Flasche Wein/Milch; **wine/milk ~** Wein-/Milchflasche f.

  ▸ **bottle up** vt in sich dat aufstauen.

bottle bank n Altglascontainer m.

bottle-fed ['bɔtlfɛd] adj mit der Flasche ernährt.

bottleneck ['bɔtlnɛk] n (also fig) Engpass m.

bottle-opener ['bɔtləupnə*] n Flaschenöffner m.

bottom ['bɔtəm] n Boden m; (buttocks) Hintern m; (of page, list) Ende nt; (of chair) Sitz m; (of mountain, tree) Fuß m ♦ adj (lower) untere(r, s); (last) unterste(r, s); **at the ~ of** unten an/in +dat; **at the ~ of the page/list** unten auf der Seite/Liste; **to be at the ~ of the class** der/die Letzte in der Klasse sein; **to get to the ~ of sth** (fig) einer Sache dat auf den Grund kommen.

bottomless ['bɔtəmlɪs] adj (fig) unerschöpflich.

bottom line n (of accounts) Saldo m; (fig): **that's the ~ (of it)** (what it amounts to) darauf läuft es im Endeffekt hinaus.

botulism ['bɔtjulɪzəm] n Botulismus m, Nahrungsmittelvergiftung f.

bough [bau] n Ast m.

bought [bɔːt] pt, pp of **buy**.

boulder ['bəuldə*] n Felsblock m.

boulevard ['buːləvɑːd] n Boulevard m.

bounce [bauns] vi (auf)springen; (cheque) platzen ♦ vt (ball) (auf)springen lassen; (signal) reflektieren ♦ n Aufprall m; **he's got plenty of ~** (fig) er hat viel Schwung.

bouncer ['baunsə*] (inf) n Rausschmeißer m.

bouncy castle ['baunsi-] n aufblasbare Spielfläche in Form eines Schlosses, auf dem Kinder herumspringen können.

bound [baund] pt, pp of **bind** ♦ n Sprung m; (gen pl: limit) Grenze f ♦ vi springen ♦ vt begrenzen ♦ adj: ~ **by** gebunden durch; **to be** ~ **to do sth** (obliged) verpflichtet sein, etw zu tun; (very likely) etw bestimmt tun; **he's** ~ **to fail** es kann ihm ja gar nicht gelingen; ~ **for** nach; **the area is out of** ~**s** das Betreten des Gebiets ist verboten.

boundary ['baundri] n Grenze f.

boundless ['baundlis] adj grenzenlos.

bountiful ['bauntiful] adj großzügig; (God) gütig; (supply) reichlich.

bounty ['baunti] n Freigebigkeit f; (reward) Kopfgeld nt.

bounty hunter n Kopfgeldjäger m.

bouquet ['bukei] n (Blumen)strauß m; (of wine) Bukett nt, Blume f.

bourbon ['buəbən] (US) n (also: ~ **whiskey**) Bourbon m.

bourgeois ['buəʒwɑː] adj bürgerlich, spießig (pej) ♦ n Bürger(in) m(f), Bourgeois m.

bout [baut] n Anfall m; (BOXING etc) Kampf m.

boutique [buːˈtiːk] n Boutique f.

bow¹ [bəu] n Schleife f; (weapon, MUS) Bogen m.

bow² [bau] n Verbeugung f; (NAUT: also: ~**s**) Bug m ♦ vi sich verbeugen; (yield): **to** ~ **to** or **before** sich beugen +dat; **to** ~ **to the inevitable** sich in das Unvermeidliche fügen.

bowels ['bauəlz] npl Darm m; (of the earth etc) Innere nt.

bowl [bəul] n Schüssel f; (shallower) Schale f; (ball) Kugel f; (of pipe) Kopf m; (US: stadium) Stadion nt ♦ vi werfen.

▶ **bowl over** vt (fig) überwältigen.

bow-legged ['bəuˈlɛgɪd] adj o-beinig, O-beinig.

bowler ['bəulə*] n Werfer(in) m(f); (BRIT: also: ~ **hat**) Melone f.

bowling ['bəulɪŋ] n Kegeln nt; (on grass) Bowling nt.

bowling alley n Kegelbahn f.

bowling green n Bowlingrasen m.

bowls [bəulz] n Bowling nt.

bow tie [bəu-] n Fliege f.

box [bɔks] n Schachtel f; (cardboard box) Karton m; (crate) Kiste f; (THEAT) Loge f; (BRIT: AUT) gelb schraffierter Kreuzungsbereich; (on form) Feld nt ♦ vt (in eine Schachtel etc) verpacken; (fighter) boxen ♦ vi boxen; **to** ~ **sb's ears** jdm eine Ohrfeige geben.

▶ **box in** vt einkeilen.

▶ **box off** vt abtrennen.

boxer ['bɔksə*] n (person, dog) Boxer m.

box file n Sammelordner m.

boxing ['bɔksɪŋ] n Boxen nt.

Boxing Day (BRIT) n zweiter Weihnachts(feier)tag m.

---

boxing gloves npl Boxhandschuhe pl.

boxing ring n Boxring m.

box number n Chiffre f.

box office n Kasse f.

boxroom ['bɔksrum] n Abstellraum m.

boy [bɔi] n Junge m.

boycott ['bɔikɔt] n Boykott m ♦ vt boykottieren.

boyfriend ['bɔifrɛnd] n Freund m.

boyish ['bɔiiʃ] adj jungenhaft; (woman) knabenhaft.

boy scout n Pfadfinder m.

Bp abbr = **bishop**.

BR abbr = **British Rail**.

bra [brɑː] n BH m.

brace [breis] n (on teeth) (Zahn)klammer f, (Zahn)spange f; (tool) (Hand)bohrer m; (also: ~ **bracket**) geschweifte Klammer f ♦ vt spannen; **braces** npl (BRIT) Hosenträger pl; **to** ~ **o.s.** (for weight) sich stützen; (for shock) sich innerlich vorbereiten.

bracelet ['breislit] n Armband nt.

bracing ['breisiŋ] adj belebend.

bracken ['brækən] n Farn m.

bracket ['brækit] n Träger m; (group, range) Gruppe f; (also: **round** ~) (runde) Klammer f; (also: **brace** ~) geschweifte Klammer f; (also: **square** ~) eckige Klammer f ♦ vt (also: ~ **together**) zusammenfassen; (word, phrase) einklammern; **income** ~ Einkommensgruppe f; **in** ~**s** in Klammern.

brackish ['brækiʃ] adj brackig.

brag [bræg] vi prahlen.

braid [breid] n Borte f; (of hair) Zopf m.

Braille [breil] n Blindenschrift f, Brailleschrift f.

brain [brein] n Gehirn nt; **brains** npl (CULIN) Hirn nt; (intelligence) Intelligenz f; **he's got** ~**s** er hat Köpfchen or Grips.

brainchild ['breinʃaild] n Geistesprodukt nt.

braindead ['breindɛd] adj hirntot; (inf) hirnlos.

brain drain n Abwanderung f von Wissenschaftlern, Braindrain m.

brainless ['breinlis] adj dumm.

brainstorm ['breinstɔːm] n (fig) Anfall m geistiger Umnachtung; (US: brain wave) Geistesblitz m.

brainwash ['breinwɔʃ] vt einer Gehirnwäsche dat unterziehen.

brain wave n Geistesblitz m.
brainy ['breɪnɪ] adj intelligent.
braise [breɪz] vt schmoren.
brake [breɪk] n Bremse f ♦ vi bremsen.
brake fluid n Bremsflüssigkeit f.
brake light n Bremslicht nt.
brake pedal n Bremspedal nt.
bramble ['bræmbl] n Brombeerstrauch m; (fruit) Brombeere f.
bran [bræn] n Kleie f.
branch [brɑːntʃ] n Ast m; (of family, organization) Zweig m; (COMM) Filiale f, Zweigstelle f; (: bank, company etc) Geschäftsstelle f ♦ vi sich gabeln.
▶ **branch out** vi (fig): **to ~ out into** seinen (Geschäfts)bereich erweitern auf +acc.
branch line n (RAIL) Zweiglinie f, Nebenlinie f.
branch manager n Zweigstellenleiter(in) m(f), Filialleiter(in) m(f).
brand [brænd] n (also: ~ **name**) Marke f; (fig: type) Art f ♦ vt mit einem Brandzeichen kennzeichnen; (fig: pej): **to ~ sb a communist** jdn als Kommunist brandmarken.
brandish ['brændɪʃ] vt schwingen.
brand name n Markenname m.
brand-new ['brænd'njuː] adj nagelneu, brandneu.
brandy ['brændɪ] n Weinbrand m.
brash [bræʃ] adj dreist.
Brasilia [brə'zɪlɪə] n Brasilia nt.
brass [brɑːs] n Messing nt; **the ~** (MUS) die Blechbläser pl.
brass band n Blaskapelle f.
brassière ['bræsɪə*] n Büstenhalter m.
brass tacks npl: **to get down to ~** zur Sache kommen.
brassy ['brɑːsɪ] adj (colour) messingfarben; (sound) blechern; (appearance, behaviour) auffällig.
brat [bræt] (pej) n Balg m or nt, Gör nt.
bravado [brə'vɑːdəu] n Draufgängertum nt.
brave [breɪv] adj mutig; (attempt, smile) tapfer ♦ n (indianischer) Krieger m ♦ vt trotzen +dat.
bravely ['breɪvlɪ] adv (see adj) mutig; tapfer.
bravery ['breɪvərɪ] n (see adj) Mut m; Tapferkeit f.
bravo [brɑː'vəu] excl bravo.
brawl [brɔːl] n Schlägerei f ♦ vi sich schlagen.
brawn [brɔːn] n Muskeln pl; (meat) Schweinskopfsülze f.
brawny ['brɔːnɪ] adj muskulös, kräftig.
bray [breɪ] vi schreien ♦ n (Esels)schrei m.
brazen ['breɪzn] adj unverschämt, dreist; (lie) schamlos ♦ vt: **to ~ it out** durchhalten.
brazier ['breɪzɪə*] n (container) Kohlenbecken nt.
Brazil [brə'zɪl] n Brasilien nt.
Brazilian [brə'zɪljən] adj brasilianisch ♦ n Brasilianer(in) m(f).

Brazil nut n Paranuss f.
breach [briːtʃ] vt (defence) durchbrechen; (wall) eine Bresche schlagen in +acc ♦ n (gap) Bresche f; (estrangement) Bruch m; (breaking): **~ of contract** Vertragsbruch m; **~ of the peace** öffentliche Ruhestörung f; **~ of trust** Vertrauensbruch m.
bread [bred] n Brot nt; (inf: money) Moos nt, Kies m; **to earn one's daily ~** sein Brot verdienen; **to know which side one's ~ is buttered (on)** wissen, wo etwas zu holen ist.
bread and butter n Butterbrot nt; (fig) Broterwerb m.
bread bin (BRIT) n Brotkasten m.
breadboard ['bredbɔːd] n Brot(schneide)brett nt; (COMPUT) Leiterplatte f.
bread box (US) n Brotkasten m.
breadcrumbs ['bredkrʌmz] npl Brotkrumen pl; (CULIN) Paniermehl nt.
breadline ['bredlaɪn] n: **to be on the ~** nur das Allernotwendigste zum Leben haben.
breadth [bretθ] n (also fig) Breite f.
breadwinner ['bredwɪnə*] n Ernährer(in) m(f).
break [breɪk] (pt **broke**, pp **broken**) vt zerbrechen; (leg, arm) sich dat brechen; (promise, record) brechen; (law) verstoßen gegen ♦ vi zerbrechen, kaputtgehen; (storm) losbrechen; (weather) umschlagen; (dawn) anbrechen; (story, news) bekannt werden ♦ n Pause f; (gap) Lücke f; (fracture) Bruch m; (chance) Chance f, Gelegenheit f; (holiday) Urlaub m; **to ~ the news to sb** es jdm sagen; **to ~ even** seine (Un)kosten decken; **to ~ with sb** mit jdm brechen, sich von jdm trennen; **to ~ free** or **loose** sich losreißen; **to take a ~** (eine) Pause machen; (holiday) Urlaub machen; **without a ~** ohne Unterbrechung or Pause, ununterbrochen; **a lucky ~** ein Durchbruch m.
▶ **break down** vt (figures, data) aufschlüsseln; (door etc) einrennen ♦ vi (car) eine Panne haben; (machine) kaputtgehen; (person, resistance) zusammenbrechen; (talks) scheitern.
▶ **break in** vt (horse) zureiten ♦ vi einbrechen; (interrupt) unterbrechen.
▶ **break into** vt fus einbrechen in +acc.
▶ **break off** vi abbrechen ♦ vt (talks) abbrechen; (engagement) lösen.
▶ **break open** vt, vi aufbrechen.
▶ **break out** vi ausbrechen; **to ~ out in spots/a rash** Pickel/einen Ausschlag bekommen.
▶ **break through** vi: **the sun broke through** die Sonne kam durch ♦ vt fus durchbrechen.
▶ **break up** vi (ship) zerbersten; (crowd, meeting, partnership) sich auflösen; (marriage) scheitern; (friends) sich trennen; (SCOL) in die Ferien gehen ♦ vt zerbrechen; (journey, fight etc) unterbrechen; (meeting) auflösen; (marriage) zerstören.
breakable ['breɪkəbl] adj zerbrechlich ♦ n: **~s**

zerbrechliche Ware *f*.

breakage ['breɪkɪdʒ] *n* Bruch *m*; **to pay for ~s** für zerbrochene Ware *or* für Bruch bezahlen.

breakaway ['breɪkəweɪ] *adj (group etc)* Splitter-.

break dancing *n* Breakdance *m*.

breakdown ['breɪkdaun] *n (AUT)* Panne *f*; *(in communications)* Zusammenbruch *m*; *(of marriage)* Scheitern *nt*; *(also:* **nervous ~**) (Nerven)zusammenbruch *m*; *(of statistics)* Aufschlüsselung *f*.

breakdown service *(BRIT) n* Pannendienst *m*.

breakdown van *(BRIT) n* Abschleppwagen *m*.

breaker ['breɪkə*] *n (wave)* Brecher *m*.

breakeven ['breɪk'iːvn] *cpd*: **~ chart** Gewinnschwellendiagramm *nt*; **~ point** Gewinnschwelle *f*.

breakfast ['brɛkfəst] *n* Frühstück *nt ♦ vi* frühstücken.

breakfast cereal *n* Getreideflocken *pl*.

break-in ['breɪkɪn] *n* Einbruch *m*.

breaking and entering ['breɪkɪŋən'entrɪŋ] *n (LAW)* Einbruch *m*.

breaking point ['breɪkɪŋ-] *(fig)*: **to reach ~** völlig am Ende sein.

breakthrough ['breɪkθruː] *n* Durchbruch *m*.

break-up ['breɪkʌp] *n (of partnership)* Auflösung *f*; *(of marriage)* Scheitern *nt*.

break-up value *n (COMM)* Liquidationswert *m*.

breakwater ['breɪkwɔːtə*] *n* Wellenbrecher *m*.

breast [brɛst] *n* Brust *f*; *(of meat)* Brust *f*, Bruststück *nt*.

breast-feed ['brɛstfiːd] *(irreg: like* **feed***) vt, vi* stillen.

breast pocket *n* Brusttasche *f*.

breaststroke ['brɛststrəuk] *n* Brustschwimmen *nt*.

breath [brɛθ] *n* Atem *m*; *(a breath)* Atemzug *m*; **to go out for a ~ of air** an die frische Luft gehen, frische Luft schnappen gehen; **out of ~** außer Atem, atemlos; **to get one's ~ back** wieder zu Atem kommen.

breathalyse ['brɛθəlaɪz] *vt* blasen lassen *(inf)*.

Breathalyser ® ['brɛθəlaɪzə*] *n* Promillemesser *m*.

breathe [briːð] *vt, vi* atmen; **I won't ~ a word about it** ich werde kein Sterbenswörtchen darüber sagen.

▶ **breathe in** *vt, vi* einatmen.

▶ **breathe out** *vt, vi* ausatmen.

breather ['briːðə*] *n* Atempause *f*, Verschnaufpause *f*.

breathing ['briːðɪŋ] *n* Atmung *f*.

breathing space *n (fig)* Atempause *f*, Ruhepause *f*.

breathless ['brɛθlɪs] *adj* atemlos, außer Atem; *(MED)* an Atemnot leidend; **I was ~ with excitement** die Aufregung verschlug mir den Atem.

breathtaking ['brɛθteɪkɪŋ] *adj* atemberaubend.

breath test *n* Atemalkoholtest *m*.

bred [brɛd] *pt, pp of* **breed**.

-bred *suff*: **well/ill-~** gut/schlecht erzogen.

breed [briːd] *(pt, pp* **bred***) vt* züchten; *(fig: give rise to)* erzeugen; *(: hate, suspicion)* hervorrufen ♦ *vi* Junge *pl* haben ♦ *n* Rasse *f*; *(type, class)* Art *f*.

breeder ['briːdə*] *n* Züchter(in) *m(f)*; *(also: ~* **reactor***)* Brutreaktor *m*, Brüter *m*.

breeding ['briːdɪŋ] *n* Erziehung *f*.

breeding ground *n (also fig)* Brutstätte *f*.

breeze [briːz] *n* Brise *f*.

breeze block *(BRIT) n* Ytong ® *m*.

breezy ['briːzɪ] *adj (manner, tone)* munter; *(weather)* windig.

Breton ['brɛtən] *adj* bretonisch ♦ *n* Bretone *m*, Bretonin *f*.

brevity ['brɛvɪtɪ] *n* Kürze *f*.

brew [bruː] *vt (tea)* aufbrühen, kochen; *(beer)* brauen ♦ *vi (tea)* ziehen; *(beer)* gären; *(storm, fig)* sich zusammenbrauen.

brewer ['bruːə*] *n* Brauer *m*.

brewery ['bruːərɪ] *n* Brauerei *f*.

briar ['braɪə*] *n* Dornbusch *m*; *(wild rose)* wilde Rose *f*.

bribe [braɪb] *n* Bestechungsgeld *nt ♦ vt* bestechen; **to ~ sb to do sth** jdn bestechen, damit er etw tut.

bribery ['braɪbərɪ] *n* Bestechung *f*.

bric-a-brac ['brɪkəbræk] *n* Nippes *pl*, Nippsachen *pl*.

brick [brɪk] *n* Ziegelstein *m*, Backstein *m*; *(of ice cream)* Block *m*.

bricklayer ['brɪkleɪə*] *n* Maurer(in) *m(f)*.

brickwork ['brɪkwɜːk] *n* Mauerwerk *nt*.

bridal ['braɪdl] *adj (gown, veil etc)* Braut-.

bride [braɪd] *n* Braut *f*.

bridegroom ['braɪdgruːm] *n* Bräutigam *m*.

bridesmaid ['braɪdzmeɪd] *n* Brautjungfer *f*.

bridge [brɪdʒ] *n* Brücke *f*; *(NAUT)* (Kommando)brücke *f*; *(of nose)* Sattel *m*; *(CARDS)* Bridge *nt ♦ vt (river)* eine Brücke schlagen *or* bauen über *+acc*; *(fig)* überbrücken.

bridging loan ['brɪdʒɪŋ-] *(BRIT) n* Überbrückungskredit *m*.

bridle ['braɪdl] *n* Zaum *m ♦ vt* aufzäumen ♦ *vi*: **to ~ (at)** sich entrüstet wehren (gegen).

bridle path *n* Reitweg *m*.

brief [briːf] *adj* kurz ♦ *n (LAW)* Auftrag *m*; *(task)* Aufgabe *f ♦ vt* instruieren; *(MIL etc)*: **to ~ sb (about)** jdn instruieren (über *+acc*); **briefs** *npl* Slip *m*; **in ~** ... kurz (gesagt) ...

briefcase ['briːfkeɪs] *n* Aktentasche *f*.

briefing ['briːfɪŋ] *n* Briefing *nt*, Lagebesprechung *f*.

briefly ['briːflɪ] *adv* kurz; **to glimpse sth ~** einen flüchtigen Blick von etw erhaschen.

Brig. *abbr* = **brigadier**.

brigade [brɪ'geɪd] *n* Brigade *f*.

brigadier [brɪgə'dɪə*] n Brigadegeneral m.
bright [braɪt] adj (light, room) hell; (weather) heiter; (clever) intelligent; (lively) heiter, fröhlich; (colour) leuchtend; (outlook, future) glänzend; **to look on the ~ side** die Dinge von der positiven Seite betrachten.
brighten ['braɪtn] (also: ~ **up**) vt aufheitern; (event) beleben ♦ vi (weather, face) sich aufheitern; (person) fröhlicher werden; (prospects) sich verbessern.
brightly ['braɪtlɪ] adv (shine) hell; (smile) fröhlich; (talk) heiter.
brill [brɪl] (BRIT: inf) adj toll.
brilliance ['brɪljəns] n Strahlen nt; (of person) Genialität f, Brillanz f; (of talent, skill) Großartigkeit f.
brilliant ['brɪljənt] adj strahlend; (person, idea) genial, brillant; (career) großartig; (inf: holiday etc) fantastisch.
brilliantly ['brɪljəntlɪ] adv (see adj) strahlend; genial, brillant; großartig; fantastisch.
brim [brɪm] n Rand m; (of hat) Krempe f.
brimful ['brɪm'ful] adj: ~ **(of)** randvoll (mit); (fig) voll (von).
brine [braɪn] n Lake f.
bring [brɪŋ] (pt, pp brought) vt bringen; (with you) mitbringen; **to ~ sth to an end** etw zu Ende bringen; **I can't ~ myself to fire him** ich kann es nicht über mich bringen, ihn zu entlassen.
▶ **bring about** vt herbeiführen.
▶ **bring back** vt (restore) wieder einführen; (return) zurückbringen.
▶ **bring down** vt (government) zu Fall bringen; (plane) herunterholen; (price) senken.
▶ **bring forward** vt (meeting) vorverlegen; (proposal) vorbringen; (BOOKKEEPING) übertragen.
▶ **bring in** vt (money) (ein)bringen; (include) einbeziehen; (person) einschalten; (legislation) einbringen; (verdict) fällen.
▶ **bring off** vt (plan) durchführen; (deal) zustande or zu Stande bringen.
▶ **bring out** vt herausholen; (meaning, book, album) herausbringen.
▶ **bring round** vt (after faint) wieder zu Bewusstsein bringen.
▶ **bring up** vt heraufbringen; (educate) erziehen; (question, subject) zur Sprache bringen; (food) erbrechen.
bring-and-buy sale n Basar m (wo mitgebrachte Sachen verkauft werden).
brink [brɪŋk] n Rand m; **on the ~ of doing sth** nahe daran, etw zu tun; **she was on the ~ of tears** sie war den Tränen nahe.
brisk [brɪsk] adj (abrupt: person, tone) forsch; (pace) flott; (trade) lebhaft, rege; **to go for a ~ walk** einen ordentlichen Spaziergang machen; **business is ~** das Geschäft ist rege.
bristle ['brɪsl] n Borste f; (of beard) Stoppel f

♦ vi zornig werden; **bristling with** strotzend von.
bristly ['brɪslɪ] adj borstig; (chin) stoppelig.
Brit [brɪt] (inf) n abbr (= British person) Brite m, Britin f.
Britain ['brɪtən] n (also: **Great** ~) Großbritannien nt.
British ['brɪtɪʃ] adj britisch ♦ npl: **the** ~ die Briten pl.
British Isles npl: **the** ~ die Britischen Inseln.
British Rail n britische Eisenbahngesellschaft.
British Summer Time n britische Sommerzeit f.
Briton ['brɪtən] n Brite m, Britin f.
Brittany ['brɪtənɪ] n die Bretagne.
brittle ['brɪtl] adj spröde; (glass) zerbrechlich; (bones) schwach.
broach [brəutʃ] vt (subject) anschneiden.
broad [brɔːd] adj breit; (general) allgemein; (accent) stark ♦ n (US: inf) Frau f; **in ~ daylight** am helllichten Tag; ~ **hint** deutlicher Wink m.
broadband ['brɔːdbænd] (COMPUT) adj Breitband- ♦ n Breitband nt.
broad bean n dicke Bohne f, Saubohne f.
broadcast ['brɔːdkɑːst] (pt, pp broadcast) n Sendung f ♦ vt, vi senden.
broadcaster ['brɔːdkɑːstə*] n (RADIO, TV) Rundfunk-/Fernsehpersönlichkeit f.
broadcasting ['brɔːdkɑːstɪŋ] n (RADIO) Rundfunk m; (TV) Fernsehen nt.
broadcasting station n (RADIO) Rundfunkstation f; (TV) Fernsehstation f.
broaden ['brɔːdn] vt erweitern ♦ vi breiter werden, sich verbreitern; **to ~ one's mind** seinen Horizont erweitern.
broadly ['brɔːdlɪ] adv (in general terms) in großen Zügen; ~ **speaking** allgemein or generell gesagt.
broad-minded ['brɔːd'maɪndɪd] adj tolerant.
broadsheet ['brɔːdʃiːt] n (newspaper) großformatige Zeitung f.
broccoli ['brɔkəlɪ] n Brokkoli pl, Spargelkohl m.
brochure ['brəuʃjuə*] n Broschüre f.
brogue [brəug] n Akzent m; (shoe) fester Schuh m.
broil [brɔɪl] (US) vt grillen.
broiler ['brɔɪlə*] n Brathähnchen nt.
broke [brəuk] pt of break ♦ adj (inf) pleite; **to go ~** Pleite gehen.
broken ['brəukn] pp of break ♦ adj zerbrochen; (machine: also: ~ **down**) kaputt; (promise, vow) gebrochen; **a ~ leg** ein gebrochenes Bein; **a ~ marriage** eine gescheiterte Ehe; **a ~ home** zerrüttete Familienverhältnisse pl; **in ~ English/German** in gebrochenem Englisch/Deutsch.
broken-down ['brəukn'daun] adj kaputt; (house) baufällig.
brokenhearted [brəukn'hɑːtɪd] adj untröstlich.

broker ['brəukə'] *n* Makler(in) *m(f)*.
brokerage ['brəukrɪdʒ] *n* (*commission*) Maklergebühr *f*; (*business*) Maklergeschäft *nt*.
brolly ['brɒlɪ] (*BRIT: inf*) *n* (Regen)schirm *m*.
bronchitis [brɒŋ'kaɪtɪs] *n* Bronchitis *f*.
bronze [brɒnz] *n* Bronze *f*.
bronzed [brɒnzd] *adj* braun, (sonnen)gebräunt.
brooch [brəutʃ] *n* Brosche *f*.
brood [bru:d] *n* Brut *f* ♦ *vi* (*hen*) brüten; (*person*) grübeln.
► **brood on** *vt fus* nachgrübeln über +*acc*.
► **brood over** *vt fus* = **brood on**.
broody ['bru:dɪ] *adj* (*person*) grüblerisch; (*hen*) brütig.
brook [bruk] *n* Bach *m*.
broom [brum] *n* Besen *m*; (*BOT*) Ginster *m*.
broomstick ['brumstɪk] *n* Besenstiel *m*.
Bros. *abbr* (*COMM*: = *brothers*) Gebr.
broth [brɒθ] *n* Suppe *f*, Fleischbrühe *f*.
brothel ['brɒθl] *n* Bordell *nt*.
brother ['brʌðə'] *n* Bruder *m*; (*in trade union, society etc*) Kollege *m*.
brotherhood ['brʌðəhud] *n* Brüderlichkeit *f*.
brother-in-law ['brʌðərɪn'lɔ:] *n* Schwager *m*.
brotherly ['brʌðəlɪ] *adj* brüderlich.
brought [brɔ:t] *pt, pp of* **bring**.
brought forward *adj* (*COMM*) vorgetragen.
brow [brau] *n* Stirn *f*; (*eyebrow*) (Augen)braue *f*; (*of hill*) (Berg)kuppe *f*.
browbeat ['braubi:t] *vt*: **to ~ sb (into doing sth)** jdn (so) unter Druck setzen(, dass er etw tut).
brown [braun] *adj* braun ♦ *n* Braun *nt* ♦ *vt* (*CULIN*) (an)bräunen; **to go ~** braun werden.
brown bread *n* Graubrot *nt*, Mischbrot *nt*.
Brownie ['braunɪ] *n* (*also*: **~ Guide**) Wichtel *m*.
brownie ['braunɪ] (*US*) *n kleiner Schokoladenkuchen*.
brown paper *n* Packpapier *nt*.
brown rice *n* Naturreis *m*.
brown sugar *n* brauner Zucker *m*.
browse [brauz] *vi* (*in shop*) sich umsehen; (*animal*) weiden; (: *deer*) äsen ♦ *vti* (*COMPUT*) browsen ♦ *n*: **to have a ~ (around)** sich umsehen; **to ~ through a book** in einem Buch schmökern.
browser ['brauzə'] *n* (*COMPUT*) Browser *m*.
bruise [bru:z] *n* blauer Fleck *m*, Bluterguss *m*; (*on fruit*) Druckstelle *f* ♦ *vt* (*arm, leg etc*) sich *dat* stoßen; (*person*) einen blauen Fleck schlagen; (*fruit*) beschädigen ♦ *vi* (*fruit*) eine Druckstelle bekommen; **to ~ one's arm** sich *dat* den Arm stoßen, sich *dat* einen blauen Fleck am Arm holen.
bruising ['bru:zɪŋ] *adj* (*experience, encounter*) schmerzhaft ♦ *n* Quetschung *f*.
Brum [brʌm] (*BRIT: inf*) *n abbr* (= *Birmingham*).
Brummie ['brʌmɪ] (*inf*) *n aus Birmingham stammende oder dort wohnhafte Person*, Birminghamer(in) *m(f)*.

brunch [brʌntʃ] *n* Brunch *m*.
brunette [bru:'nɛt] *n* Brünette *f*.
brunt [brʌnt] *n*: **to bear the ~ of** die volle Wucht +*gen* tragen.
brush [brʌʃ] *n* Bürste *f*; (*for painting, shaving etc*) Pinsel *m*; (*quarrel*) Auseinandersetzung *f* ♦ *vt* fegen; (*groom*) bürsten; (*teeth*) putzen; (*also*: **~ against**) streifen; **to have a ~ with sb** (*verbally*) sich mit jdm streiten; (*physically*) mit jdm aneinander geraten; **to have a ~ with the police** mit der Polizei aneinander geraten.
► **brush aside** *vt* abtun.
► **brush past** *vt* streifen.
► **brush up** *vt* auffrischen.
brushed [brʌʃt] *adj* (*steel, chrome etc*) gebürstet; (*denim etc*) aufgeraut; **~ nylon** Nylonvelours *m*.
brushoff ['brʌʃɒf] (*inf*) *n*: **to give sb the ~** jdm eine Abfuhr erteilen.
brushwood ['brʌʃwud] *n* Reisig *nt*.
brusque [bru:sk] *adj* brüsk; (*tone*) schroff.
Brussels ['brʌslz] *n* Brüssel *nt*.
Brussels sprouts *npl* Rosenkohl *m*.
brutal ['bru:tl] *adj* brutal.
brutality [bru:'tælɪtɪ] *n* Brutalität *f*.
brutalize ['bru:təlaɪz] *vt* brutalisieren; (*ill-treat*) brutal behandeln.
brute [bru:t] *n* brutaler Kerl *m*; (*animal*) Tier *nt* ♦ *adj*: **by ~ force** mit roher Gewalt.
brutish ['bru:tɪʃ] *adj* tierisch.
BS (*US*) *n abbr* (= *Bachelor of Science*) *akademischer Grad für Naturwissenschaftler*.
BSA *n abbr* (= *Boy Scouts of America*) *amerikanische Pfadfinderorganisation*.
BSc *abbr* (= *Bachelor of Science*) *akademischer Grad für Naturwissenschaftler*.
BSE *n abbr* (= *bovine spongiform encephalopathy*) BSE *f*.
BSI *n abbr* (= *British Standards Institution*) *britischer Normenausschuss*.
BST *abbr* = **British Summer Time**.
Bt (*BRIT*) *abbr* = **baronet**.
btu *n abbr* (= *British thermal unit*) *britische Wärmeeinheit*.
bubble ['bʌbl] *n* Blase *f* ♦ *vi* sprudeln; (*sparkle*) perlen; (*fig: person*) übersprudeln.
bubble bath *n* Schaumbad *nt*.
bubble gum *n* Bubble-Gum *m*.
bubble-jet printer *n* Bubblejetdrucker *m*, Bubble-Jet-Drucker *m*.
bubble pack *n* (Klar)sichtpackung *f*.
bubbly ['bʌblɪ] *adj* (*person*) lebendig; (*liquid*) sprudelnd ♦ *n* (*inf: champagne*) Schampus *m*.
Bucharest [bu:kə'rɛst] *n* Bukarest *nt*.
buck [bʌk] *n* (*rabbit*) Rammler *m*; (*deer*) Bock *m*; (*US: inf*) Dollar *m* ♦ *vi* bocken; **to pass the ~** die Verantwortung abschieben; **to pass the ~ to sb** jdm die Verantwortung zuschieben.
► **buck up** *vi* (*cheer up*) aufleben ♦ *vt*: **to**

~ **one's ideas up** sich zusammenreißen.
bucket ['bʌkɪt] n Eimer m ♦ vi (BRIT: inf): **the
rain is** ~**ing (down)** es gießt or schüttet (wie
aus Kübeln).

BUCKINGHAM PALACE

Buckingham Palace ist die offizielle Londoner
Residenz der britischen Monarchen und liegt am
St James Park. Der Palast wurde 1703 für den
Herzog von Buckingham erbaut, 1762 von Georg
III. gekauft, zwischen 1821 und 1836 von John
Nash umgebaut und Anfang des 20. Jahrhunderts
teilweise neu gestaltet. Teile des **Buckingham
Palace** sind heute der Öffentlichkeit zugänglich.

---

buckle ['bʌkl] n Schnalle f ♦ vt zuschnallen;
(wheel) verbiegen ♦ vi sich verbiegen.
▶ **buckle down** vi sich dahinter klemmen; **to
** ~ **down to sth** sich hinter etw acc klemmen.
Bucks [bʌks] (BRIT) abbr (POST:
= Buckinghamshire).
bud [bʌd] n Knospe f ♦ vi knospen, Knospen
treiben.
Budapest [bju:dəˈpɛst] n Budapest nt.
Buddha ['budə] n Buddha m.
Buddhism ['budɪzəm] n Buddhismus m.
Buddhist ['budɪst] adj buddhistisch ♦ n
Buddhist(in) m(f).
budding ['bʌdɪŋ] adj angehend.
buddy ['bʌdɪ] (US) n Kumpel m.
budge [bʌdʒ] vt (von der Stelle) bewegen; (fig)
zum Nachgeben bewegen ♦ vi sich von der
Stelle rühren; (fig) nachgeben.
budgerigar ['bʌdʒərɪgɑː'] n Wellensittich
m.
budget ['bʌdʒɪt] n Budget nt, Etat m, Haushalt
m ♦ vi Haus halten, haushalten,
wirtschaften; **I'm on a tight** ~ ich habe
nicht viel Geld zur Verfügung; **she works
out her** ~ **every month** sie macht (sich dat)
jeden Monat einen Haushaltsplan; **to** ~ **for
sth** etw kostenmäßig einplanen.
budgie ['bʌdʒɪ] n = budgerigar.
Buenos Aires ['bweinɔsˈaɪrɪz] n Buenos Aires
nt.
buff [bʌf] adj gelbbraun ♦ n (inf) Fan m.
buffalo ['bʌfələu] (pl ~ or ~es) n (BRIT) Büffel
m; (US) Bison m.
buffer ['bʌfə'] n (COMPUT) Puffer m,
Pufferspeicher m; (RAIL) Prellbock m; (fig)
Polster nt.
buffering ['bʌfərɪŋ] n (COMPUT) Pufferung
f.
buffer state n Pufferstaat m.
buffer zone n Pufferzone f.
buffet[1] ['bufeɪ] (BRIT) n Büfett nt,
Bahnhofsrestaurant nt; (food) kaltes Buffet
nt.
buffet[2] ['bʌfɪt] vt (subj: sea) hin und her
werfen; (: wind) schütteln.
buffet car (BRIT) n Speisewagen m.

buffet lunch n Buffet nt.
buffoon [bəˈfuːn] n Clown m.
bug [bʌg] n (esp US) Insekt nt; (COMPUT: of
program) Programmfehler m; (: of
equipment) Fehler m; (fig: germ) Bazillus m;
(hidden microphone) Wanze f ♦ vt (inf)
nerven; (telephone etc) abhören; (room)
verwanzen; **I've got the travel** ~ (fig) mich
hat die Reiselust gepackt.
bugbear ['bʌgbɛə'] n Schreckgespenst nt.
bugger ['bʌgə'] (inf!) n Scheißkerl m,
Arschloch m ♦ vb: ~ **off!** hau ab!; ~ **(it)!**
Scheiße!
buggy ['bʌgɪ] n (for baby) Sportwagen m.
bugle ['bjuːgl] n Bügelhorn nt.
build [bɪld] (pt, pp **built**) n Körperbau m ♦ vt
bauen.
▶ **build on** vt fus (fig) aufbauen auf +dat.
▶ **build up** vt aufbauen; (production) steigern;
(morale) stärken; (stocks) anlegen; **don't**
~ **your hopes up too soon** mach dir nicht zu
früh Hoffnungen.
builder ['bɪldə'] n Bauunternehmer m.
building ['bɪldɪŋ] n (industry) Bauindustrie f;
(construction) Bau m; (structure) Gebäude nt,
Bau.
building contractor n Bauunternehmer m.
building industry n Bauindustrie f.
building site n Baustelle f.
building society (BRIT) n Bausparkasse f.
building trade n = building industry.
build-up ['bɪldʌp] n Ansammlung f; (publicity):
to give sb/sth a good ~ jdn/etw ganz groß
herausbringen.
built [bɪlt] pt, pp of build ♦ adj: ~-**in** eingebaut,
Einbau-; (safeguards) eingebaut; **well-**~ gut
gebaut.
built-up area ['bɪltʌp-] n bebautes Gebiet nt.
bulb [bʌlb] n (Blumen)zwiebel f; (ELEC)
(Glüh)birne f.
bulbous ['bʌlbəs] adj knollig.
Bulgaria [bʌlˈgɛərɪə] n Bulgarien nt.
Bulgarian [bʌlˈgɛərɪən] adj bulgarisch ♦ n
Bulgare m, Bulgarin f; (LING) Bulgarisch
nt.
bulge [bʌldʒ] n Wölbung f; (in birth rate, sales)
Zunahme f ♦ vi (pocket) prall gefüllt sein;
(cheeks) voll sein; (file) (zum Bersten) voll
sein; **to be bulging with** prall gefüllt sein
mit.
bulimia [bəˈlɪmɪə] n Bulimie f.
bulk [bʌlk] n (of thing) massige Form f; (of
person) massige Gestalt f; **in** ~ im Großen,
en gros; **the** ~ **of** der Großteil +gen.
bulk buying [-ˈbaɪɪŋ] n Mengeneinkauf m,
Großeinkauf m.
bulk carrier n Bulkcarrier m.
bulkhead ['bʌlkhɛd] n Schott nt.
bulky ['bʌlkɪ] adj sperrig.
bull [bul] n Stier m; (male elephant or whale)
Bulle m; (STOCK EXCHANGE) Haussier m,
Haussespekulant m; (REL) Bulle f.

bulldog ['buldɔg] *n* Bulldogge *f*.

bulldoze ['buldəuz] *vt* mit Bulldozern wegräumen; (*building*) mit Bulldozern abreißen; **I was ~d into it** (*fig: inf*) ich wurde gezwungen *or* unter Druck gesetzt, es zu tun.

bulldozer ['buldəuzə*] *n* Bulldozer *m*, Planierraupe *f*.

bullet ['bulɪt] *n* Kugel *f*.

bulletin ['bulɪtɪn] *n* (*TV etc*) Kurznachrichten *pl*; (*journal*) Bulletin *nt*.

bulletin board *n* (*COMPUT*) schwarzes Brett *nt*.

bulletproof ['bulɪtpruːf] *adj* kugelsicher.

bullfight ['bulfaɪt] *n* Stierkampf *m*.

bullfighter ['bulfaɪtə*] *n* Stierkämpfer *m*.

bullfighting ['bulfaɪtɪŋ] *n* Stierkampf *m*.

bullion ['buljən] *n*: **gold/silver ~** Barrengold *nt*/-silber *nt*.

bullock ['bulək] *n* Ochse *m*.

bullring ['bulrɪŋ] *n* Stierkampfarena *f*.

bull's-eye ['bulzaɪ] *n* (*on a target*): **the ~** der Scheibenmittelpunkt, das Schwarze.

bullshit ['bulʃɪt] (*inf!*) *n* Scheiß *m*, Quatsch *m* ♦ *vi* Scheiß erzählen; **~!** Quatsch!

bully ['bulɪ] *n* Tyrann *m* ♦ *vt* tyrannisieren; (*frighten*) einschüchtern.

bullying ['bulɪŋ] *n* Tyrannisieren *nt*.

bum [bʌm] (*inf*) *n* Hintern *m*; (*esp US: good-for-nothing*) Rumtreiber *m*; (*tramp*) Penner *m*.

▶ **bum around** (*inf*) *vi* herumgammeln.

bumblebee ['bʌmblbiː] *n* Hummel *f*.

bumf [bʌmf] (*inf*) *n* Papierkram *m*.

bump [bʌmp] *n* Zusammenstoß *m*; (*jolt*) Erschütterung *f*; (*swelling*) Beule *f*; (*on road*) Unebenheit *f* ♦ *vt* stoßen; (*car*) eine Delle fahren in +*acc*.

▶ **bump along** *vi* entlangholpern.

▶ **bump into** *vt fus* (*obstacle*) stoßen gegen; (*inf: person*) treffen.

bumper ['bʌmpə*] *n* Stoßstange *f* ♦ *adj*: **~ crop**, **~ harvest** Rekordernte *f*.

bumper cars *npl* Autoskooter *pl*.

bumper sticker *n* Aufkleber *m*.

bumph [bʌmf] *n* = **bumf**.

bumptious ['bʌmpʃəs] *adj* wichtigtuerisch.

bumpy ['bʌmpɪ] *adj* holperig; **it was a ~ flight/ride** während des Fluges/auf der Fahrt wurden wir tüchtig durchgerüttelt.

bun [bʌn] *n* Brötchen *nt*; (*of hair*) Knoten *m*.

bunch [bʌntʃ] *n* Strauß *m*; (*of keys*) Bund *m*; (*of bananas*) Büschel *nt*; (*of people*) Haufen *m*; **bunches** *npl* (*in hair*) Zöpfe *pl*; **~ of grapes** Weintraube *f*.

bundle ['bʌndl] *n* Bündel *nt* ♦ *vt* (*also: ~ up*) bündeln; (*put*): **to ~ sth into** etw stopfen *or* packen in +*acc*; **to ~ sb into** jdn schaffen in +*acc*.

▶ **bundle off** *vt* schaffen.

▶ **bundle out** *vt* herausschaffen.

bun fight (*BRIT: inf*) *n* Festivitäten *pl*; (*tea party*) Teegesellschaft *f*.

bung [bʌŋ] *n* Spund *m*, Spundzapfen *m* ♦ *vt* (*BRIT: inf: also: ~ in*) schmeißen; (*also: ~ up*) verstopfen; **my nose is ~ed up** meine Nase ist verstopft.

bungalow ['bʌŋgələu] *n* Bungalow *m*.

bungee jumping ['bʌndʒiː'dʒʌmpɪŋ] *n* Bungeespringen *nt*.

bungle ['bʌŋgl] *vt* verpfuschen.

bunion ['bʌnjən] *n* entzündeter Ballen *m*.

bunk [bʌŋk] *n* Bett *nt*, Koje *f*; **to do a ~** (*inf*) abhauen.

▶ **bunk off** (*inf*) *vi* abhauen.

bunk beds *npl* Etagenbett *nt*.

bunker ['bʌŋkə*] *n* Kohlenbunker *m*; (*MIL, GOLF*) Bunker *m*.

bunny ['bʌnɪ] *n* (*also: ~ rabbit*) Hase *m*, Häschen *nt*.

bunny girl (*BRIT*) *n* Häschen *nt*.

bunny hill (*US*) *n* (*SKI*) Anfängerhügel *m*.

bunting ['bʌntɪŋ] *n* (*flags*) Wimpel *pl*, Fähnchen *pl*.

buoy [bɔɪ] *n* Boje *f*.

▶ **buoy up** *vt* (*fig*) Auftrieb geben +*dat*.

buoyancy ['bɔɪənsɪ] *n* (*of ship, object*) Schwimmfähigkeit *f*.

buoyant ['bɔɪənt] *adj* (*ship, object*) schwimmfähig; (*market*) fest; (*economy*) stabil; (*prices, currency*) fest, stabil; (*person, nature*) heiter.

burden ['bəːdn] *n* Belastung *f*; (*load*) Last *f* ♦ *vt*: **to ~ sb with sth** jdn mit etw belasten; **to be a ~ to sb** jdm zur Last fallen.

bureau ['bjuərəu] (*pl* **~x**) *n* (*BRIT: writing desk*) Sekretär *m*; (*US: chest of drawers*) Kommode *f*; (*office*) Büro *nt*.

bureaucracy [bjuə'rɔkrəsɪ] *n* Bürokratie *f*.

bureaucrat ['bjuərəkræt] *n* Bürokrat(in) *m(f)*.

bureaucratic [bjuərə'krætɪk] *adj* bürokratisch.

bureaux ['bjuərəuz] *npl of* **bureau**.

burgeon ['bəːdʒən] *vi* hervorsprießen.

burger ['bəːgə*] (*inf*) *n* Hamburger *m*.

burglar ['bəːglə*] *n* Einbrecher(in) *m(f)*.

burglar alarm *n* Alarmanlage *f*.

burglarize ['bəːgləraɪz] (*US*) *vt* einbrechen in +*acc*.

burglary ['bəːglərɪ] *n* Einbruch *m*.

burgle ['bəːgl] *vt* einbrechen in +*acc*.

Burgundy ['bəːgəndɪ] *n* Burgund *nt*.

burial ['berɪəl] *n* Beerdigung *f*.

burial ground *n* Begräbnisstätte *f*.

burlesque [bəː'lesk] *n* (*parody*) Persiflage *f*; (*US: THEAT*) Burleske *f*.

burly ['bəːlɪ] *adj* kräftig, stämmig.

Burma ['bəːmə] *n* Birma *nt*, Burma *nt*.

Burmese [bəː'miːz] *adj* birmanisch, burmesisch ♦ *n inv* Birmane *m*, Burmese *m*, Birmanin *f*, Burmesin *f* ♦ *n* (*LING*) Birmanisch *nt*, Burmesisch *nt*.

burn [bəːn] (*pt, pp* **burned** *or* **burnt**) *vt* verbrennen; (*fuel*) als Brennstoff verwenden; (*food*) anbrennen lassen; (*house etc*) niederbrennen ♦ *vi* brennen; (*food*) anbrennen ♦ *n* Verbrennung *f*; **the cigarette ~t a hole in her dress** die Zigarette brannte ein Loch in ihr Kleid; **I've ~t myself!** ich habe mich verbrannt!

▶ **burn down** *vt* abbrennen.

▶ **burn out** *vt*: **to ~ o.s. out** (*writer etc*) sich völlig verausgaben; **the fire ~t itself out** das Feuer brannte aus.

burner ['bəːnəʳ] *n* Brenner *m*.

burning ['bəːnɪŋ] *adj* brennend; (*sand, desert*) glühend heiß.

burnish ['bəːnɪʃ] *vt* polieren.

BURNS' NIGHT

Burns' Night *ist der am 25. Januar begangene Gedenktag für den schottischen Dichter Robert Burns (1759 - 1796). Wo Schotten leben, sei es in Schottland oder im Ausland, wird dieser Tag mit einem Abendessen gefeiert, bei dem es als Hauptgericht* **haggis** *gibt, der mit Dudelsackbegleitung aufgetischt wird. Dazu isst man Steckrüben- und Kartoffelpüree und trinkt Whisky. Während des Essens werden Burns' Gedichte vorgelesen, seine Lieder gesungen, bestimmte Reden gehalten und Trinksprüche ausgegeben.*

---

burnt [bəːnt] *pt, pp of* **burn**.

burnt sugar (*BRIT*) *n* Karamell *m*.

burp [bəːp] (*inf*) *n* Rülpser *m* ♦ *vt* (*baby*) aufstoßen lassen ♦ *vi* rülpsen.

burrow ['bʌrəu] *n* Bau *m* ♦ *vi* graben; (*rummage*) wühlen.

bursar ['bəːsəʳ] *n* Schatzmeister *m*, Finanzverwalter *m*.

bursary ['bəːsərɪ] (*BRIT*) *n* Stipendium *nt*.

burst [bəːst] (*pt, pp* burst) *vt* zum Platzen bringen, platzen lassen ♦ *vi* platzen ♦ *n* Salve *f*; (*also:* ~ **pipe**) (Rohr)bruch *m*; **the river has ~ its banks** der Fluss ist über die Ufer getreten; **to ~ into flames** in Flammen aufgehen; **to ~ into tears** in Tränen ausbrechen; **to ~ out laughing** in Lachen ausbrechen; **~ blood vessel** geplatzte Ader *f*; **to be ~ing with** zum Bersten voll sein mit; (*pride*) fast platzen vor +*dat*; **to ~ open** aufspringen; **a ~ of energy** ein Ausbruch *m* von Energie; **a ~ of enthusiasm** ein Begeisterungsausbruch *m*; **a ~ of speed** ein Spurt *m*; **~ of laughter** Lachsalve *f*; **~ of applause** Beifallssturm *m*.

▶ **burst in on** *vt fus*: **to ~ in on sb** bei jdm hereinplatzen.

▶ **burst into** *vt fus* (*into room*) platzen in +*acc*.

▶ **burst out of** *vt fus* (*of room*) stürmen *or* stürzen aus.

bury ['bɛrɪ] *vt* begraben; (*at funeral*) beerdigen; **to ~ one's face in one's hands** das Gesicht in den Händen vergraben; **to ~ one's head in the sand** (*fig*) den Kopf in den Sand stecken; **to ~ the hatchet** (*fig*) das Kriegsbeil begraben.

bus [bʌs] *n* (Auto)bus *m*, (Omni)bus *m*; (*double decker*) Doppeldecker *m* (*inf*).

bus boy (*US*) *n* Bedienungshilfe *f*.

bush [buʃ] *n* Busch *m*, Strauch *m*; (*scrubland*) Busch; **to beat about the ~** um den heißen Brei herumreden.

bushed [buʃt] (*inf*) *adj* (*exhausted*) groggy.

bushel ['buʃl] *n* Scheffel *m*.

bushfire *n* Buschfeuer *nt*.

bushy ['buʃɪ] *adj* buschig.

busily ['bɪzɪlɪ] *adv* eifrig; **to be ~ doing sth** eifrig etw tun.

business ['bɪznɪs] *n* (*matter*) Angelegenheit *f*; (*trading*) Geschäft *nt*; (*firm*) Firma *f*, Betrieb *m*; (*occupation*) Beruf *m*; **to be away on ~** geschäftlich unterwegs sein; **I'm here on ~** ich bin geschäftlich hier; **he's in the insurance/transport ~** er arbeitet in der Versicherungs-/Transportbranche; **to do ~ with sb** Geschäfte *pl* mit jdm machen; **it's my ~ to ...** es ist meine Aufgabe, zu ...; **it's none of my ~** es geht mich nichts an; **he means ~** er meint es ernst.

business address *n* Geschäftsadresse *f*.

business card *n* (Visiten)karte *f*.

businesslike ['bɪznɪslaɪk] *adj* geschäftsmäßig.

businessman ['bɪznɪsmən] (*irreg: like* **man**) *n* Geschäftsmann *m*.

business trip *n* Geschäftsreise *f*.

businesswoman ['bɪznɪswumən] (*irreg: like* **woman**) *n* Geschäftsfrau *f*.

busker ['bʌskəʳ] (*BRIT*) *n* Straßenmusikant(in) *m(f)*.

bus lane (*BRIT*) *n* Busspur *f*.

bus shelter *n* Wartehäuschen *nt*.

bus station *n* Busbahnhof *m*.

bus stop *n* Bushaltestelle *f*.

bust [bʌst] *n* Busen *m*; (*measurement*) Oberweite *f*; (*sculpture*) Büste *f* ♦ *adj* (*inf*) kaputt ♦ *vt* (*inf*) verhaften; **to go ~** Pleite gehen.

bustle ['bʌsl] *n* Betrieb *m* ♦ *vi* eilig herumlaufen.

bustling ['bʌslɪŋ] *adj* belebt.

bust-up ['bʌstʌp] (*BRIT: inf*) *n* Krach *m*.

busty ['bʌstɪ] *adj* (*woman*) vollbusig.

BUSWE (*BRIT*) *n abbr* (= *British Union of Social Work Employees*) Sozialarbeitergewerkschaft.

busy ['bɪzɪ] *adj* (*person*) beschäftigt; (*shop, street*) belebt; (*TEL: esp US*) besetzt ♦ *vt*: **to ~ o.s. with** sich beschäftigen mit; **he's a ~ man** er ist ein viel beschäftigter Mann; **he's ~** er hat (zurzeit) viel zu tun.

busybody ['bɪzɪbɔdɪ] *n*: **to be a ~** sich ständig einmischen.

busy signal (*US*) *n* (*TEL*) Besetztzeichen *nt*.

=============================== *KEYWORD*

but [bʌt] *conj* **1** (*yet*) aber; **not blue ~ red** nicht blau, sondern rot; **he's not very bright, ~ he's hard-working** er ist nicht sehr intelligent, aber er ist fleißig.

2 (*however*): **I'd love to come, ~ I'm busy** ich würde gern kommen, bin aber beschäftigt.

3 (*showing disagreement, surprise etc*): **~ that's far too expensive!** aber das ist viel zu teuer!; **~ that's fantastic!** das ist doch toll!

♦ *prep* (*apart from, except*) außer +*dat*; **nothing ~ trouble** nichts als Ärger; **no-one ~ him can do it** keiner außer ihm kann es machen; **~ for you** wenn Sie nicht gewesen wären; **~ for your help** ohne Ihre Hilfe; **I'll do anything ~ that** ich mache alles, nur nicht das; **the last house ~ one** das vorletzte Haus; **the next street ~ one** die übernächste Straße

♦ *adv* (*just, only*) nur; **she's ~ a child** sie ist doch noch ein Kind; **I can ~ try** ich kann es ja versuchen.

butane ['bjuːteɪn] *n* (*also:* **~ gas**) Butan(gas) *nt*.
butch [butʃ] (*inf*) *adj* maskulin.
butcher ['butʃəʳ] *n* Fleischer *m*, Metzger *m*; (*pej: murderer*) Schlächter *m* ♦ *vt* schlachten; (*prisoners etc*) abschlachten.
butcher's (shop) ['butʃəz-] *n* Fleischerei *f*, Metzgerei *f*.
butler ['bʌtləʳ] *n* Butler *m*.
butt [bʌt] *n* großes Fass *nt*, Tonne *f*; (*thick end*) dickes Ende *nt*; (*of gun*) Kolben *m*; (*of cigarette*) Kippe *f*; (*BRIT, fig: target*) Zielscheibe *f*; (*US: inf!*) Arsch *m* ♦ *vt* (*goat*) mit den Hörnern stoßen; (*person*) mit dem Kopf stoßen.
► **butt in** *vi* sich einmischen, dazwischenfunken (*inf*).
butter ['bʌtəʳ] *n* Butter *f* ♦ *vt* buttern.
buttercup ['bʌtəkʌp] *n* Butterblume *f*.
butter dish *n* Butterdose *f*.
butterfingers ['bʌtəfɪŋgəz] (*inf*) *n* Schussel *m*.
butterfly ['bʌtəflaɪ] *n* Schmetterling *m*; (*SWIMMING: also:* **~ stroke**) Schmetterlingsstil *m*, Butterfly *m*.
buttocks ['bʌtəks] *npl* Gesäß *nt*.
button ['bʌtn] *n* Knopf *m*; (*US: badge*) Plakette *f* ♦ *vt* (*also:* **~ up**) zuknöpfen ♦ *vi* geknöpft werden.
buttonhole ['bʌtnhəʊl] *n* Knopfloch *nt*; (*flower*) Blume *f* im Knopfloch ♦ *vt* zu fassen bekommen, sich *dat* schnappen (*inf*).
buttress ['bʌtrɪs] *n* Strebepfeiler *m*.
buxom ['bʌksəm] *adj* drall.
buy [baɪ] (*pt, pp* **bought**) *vt* kaufen; (*company*) aufkaufen ♦ *n* Kauf *m*; **that was a good/bad ~** das war ein guter/schlechter Kauf; **to ~ sb sth** jdm etw kaufen; **to ~ sth from sb**

etw bei jdm kaufen; (*from individual*) jdm etw abkaufen; **to ~ sb a drink** jdm einen ausgeben (*inf*).
► **buy back** *vt* zurückkaufen.
► **buy in** (*BRIT*) *vt* einkaufen.
► **buy into** (*BRIT*) *vt fus* sich einkaufen in +*acc*.
► **buy off** *vt* kaufen.
► **buy out** *vt* (*partner*) auszahlen; (*business*) aufkaufen.
► **buy up** *vt* aufkaufen.
buyer ['baɪəʳ] *n* Käufer(in) *m(f)*; (*COMM*) Einkäufer(in) *m(f)*.
buyer's market ['baɪəz-] *n* Käufermarkt *m*.
buyout ['baɪaʊt] *n* (*of firm: by workers, management*) Aufkauf *m*.
buzz [bʌz] *vi* summen, brummen; (*saw*) kreischen ♦ *vt* rufen; (*with buzzer*) (mit dem Summer) rufen; (*AVIAT: plane, building*) dicht vorbeifliegen an +*dat* ♦ *n* Summen *nt*, Brummen *nt*; (*inf*): **to give sb a ~** jdn anrufen; **my head is ~ing** mir schwirrt der Kopf.
► **buzz off** (*inf*) *vi* abhauen.
buzzard ['bʌzəd] *n* Bussard *m*.
buzzer ['bʌzəʳ] *n* Summer *m*.
buzz word (*inf*) *n* Modewort *nt*.

=============================== *KEYWORD*

by [baɪ] *prep* **1** (*referring to cause, agent*) von +*dat*, durch +*acc*; **killed ~ lightning** vom Blitz *or* durch einen Blitz getötet; **a painting ~ Picasso** ein Bild von Picasso.

2 (*referring to method, manner, means*): **~ bus/car/train** mit dem Bus/Auto/Zug; **to pay ~ cheque** mit *or* per Scheck bezahlen; **~ saving hard, he was able to ...** indem er eisern sparte, konnte er ...

3 (*via, through*) über +*acc*; **we came ~ Dover** wir sind über Dover gekommen.

4 (*close to*) bei +*dat*, an +*dat*; **the house ~ the river** das Haus am Fluss.

5 (*past*) an ... *dat* vorbei; **she rushed ~ me** sie eilte an mir vorbei.

6 (*not later than*) bis +*acc*; **~ 4 o'clock** bis 4 Uhr; **~ this time tomorrow** morgen um diese Zeit.

7 (*amount*): **~ the kilo/metre** kilo-/meterweise; **to be paid ~ the hour** stundenweise bezahlt werden.

8 (*MATH, measure*): **to divide ~ 3** durch 3 teilen; **to multiply ~ 3** mit 3 malnehmen; **it missed me ~ inches** es hat mich um Zentimeter verfehlt.

9 (*according to*): **to play ~ the rules** sich an die Regeln halten; **it's all right ~ me** von mir aus ist es in Ordnung.

10: (**all**) **~ myself/himself** *etc* (ganz) allein.

11: **~ the way** übrigens

♦ *adv* **1** *see* **go, pass** *etc*.

2: **~ and ~** irgendwann.

3: **~ and large** im Großen und Ganzen.

bye(-bye) ['baɪ('baɪ)] *excl* (auf) Wiedersehen, tschüss (*inf*).

bye-law ['baɪlɔ:] *n* Verordnung *f*.

by-election ['baɪɪlɛkʃən] (*BRIT*) *n* Nachwahl *f*.

Byelorussia [bjɛləʊ'rʌʃə] *n* = **Belorussia**.

Byelorussian [bjɛləʊ'rʌʃən] *adj*, *n* = **Belarussian**.

bygone ['baɪgɔn] *adj* (längst) vergangen ♦ *n*: **let ~s be ~s** wir sollten die Vergangenheit ruhen lassen.

by-law ['baɪlɔ:] *n* = **bye-law**.

bypass ['baɪpɑːs] *n* Umgehungsstraße *f*; (*MED*) Bypassoperation *f* ♦ *vt* (*also fig*) umgehen.

by-product ['baɪprɒdʌkt] *n* Nebenprodukt *nt*.

byre ['baɪə*] (*BRIT*) *n* Kuhstall *m*.

bystander ['baɪstændə*] *n* Zuschauer(in) *m(f)*.

byte [baɪt] *n* (*COMPUT*) Byte *nt*.

byway ['baɪweɪ] *n* Seitenweg *m*.

byword ['baɪwɜːd] *n*: **to be a ~ for** der Inbegriff +*gen* sein, gleichbedeutend sein mit.

by-your-leave ['baɪjɔː'liːv] *n*: **without so much as a ~** ohne auch nur (um Erlaubnis) zu fragen.

C, c

C¹, c¹ [siː] *n* (*letter*) C *nt*, c *nt*; (*SCOL*) ≈ Drei *f*, Befriedigend *nt*; **~ for Charlie** ≈ C wie Cäsar.

C² [siː] *n* (*MUS*) C *nt*, c *nt*.

C³ [siː] *abbr* = **Celsius**; **centigrade**.

c² *abbr* = **century** (= *circa*) ca.; (*US etc*: = *cent(s)*) Cent.

CA *n abbr* (*BRIT*) = **chartered accountant** ♦ *abbr* = **Central America**; (*US: POST*: = *California*).

C/A *abbr* (*COMM*) = **capital account**; **credit account**; **current account**.

ca. *abbr* (= *circa*) ca.

CAA *n abbr* (*BRIT*) = **Civil Aviation Authority**; (*US*: = *Civil Aeronautics Authority*) Zivilluftfahrtbehörde *f*.

CAB (*BRIT*) *n abbr* = **Citizens' Advice Bureau**.

cab [kæb] *n* Taxi *nt*; (*of truck, train etc*) Führerhaus *nt*; (*horse-drawn*) Droschke *f*.

cabaret ['kæbəreɪ] *n* Kabarett *nt*.

cabbage ['kæbɪdʒ] *n* Kohl *m*.

cabbie, cabby ['kæbɪ] *n* Taxifahrer(in) *m(f)*.

cab driver *n* Taxifahrer(in) *m(f)*.

cabin ['kæbɪn] *n* Kabine *f*; (*house*) Hütte *f*.

cabin cruiser *n* Kajütboot *nt*.

cabinet ['kæbɪnɪt] *n* kleiner Schrank *m*; (*also*: **display ~**) Vitrine *f*; (*POL*) Kabinett *nt*.

cabinet-maker ['kæbɪnɪt'meɪkə*] *n* Möbeltischler *m*.

cabinet minister *n* Mitglied *nt* des Kabinetts, Minister(in) *m(f)*.

cable ['keɪbl] *n* Kabel *nt* ♦ *vt* kabeln.

cable car *n* (Draht)seilbahn *f*.

cablegram ['keɪblgræm] *n* (Übersee)telegramm *nt*, Kabel *nt*.

cable railway *n* Seilbahn *f*.

cable television *n* Kabelfernsehen *nt*.

cable TV *n* = **cable television**.

cache [kæʃ] *n* Versteck *nt*, geheimes Lager *nt*; **a ~ of food** ein geheimes Proviantlager.

cackle ['kækl] *vi* (*person: laugh*) meckernd lachen; (*hen*) gackern.

cacti ['kæktaɪ] *npl of* **cactus**.

cactus ['kæktəs] (*pl* **cacti**) *n* Kaktus *m*.

CAD *n abbr* (= *computer-aided design*) CAD *nt*.

caddie ['kædɪ] *n* (*GOLF*) Caddie *m*.

caddy ['kædɪ] *n* = **caddie**.

cadence ['keɪdəns] *n* (*of voice*) Tonfall *m*.

cadet [kə'dɛt] *n* Kadett *m*; **police ~** Polizeianwärter(in) *m(f)*.

cadge [kædʒ] (*inf*) *vt*: **to ~ (from** *or* **off)** schnorren (bei *or* von +*dat*); **to ~ a lift with sb** von jdm mitgenommen werden.

cadger ['kædʒə*] (*BRIT: inf*) *n* Schnorrer(in) *m(f)*.

cadre ['kædrɪ] *n* Kader *m*.

Caesarean [siː'zɛərɪən] *n*: **~ (section)** Kaiserschnitt *m*.

CAF (*BRIT*) *abbr* (= *cost and freight*) cf.

café ['kæfeɪ] *n* Café *nt*.

cafeteria [kæfɪ'tɪərɪə] *n* Cafeteria *f*.

caffein(e) ['kæfiːn] *n* Koffein *nt*.

cage [keɪdʒ] *n* Käfig *m*; (*of lift*) Fahrkorb *m* ♦ *vt* einsperren.

cagey ['keɪdʒɪ] (*inf*) *adj* vorsichtig; (*evasive*) ausweichend.

cagoule [kə'guːl] *n* Regenjacke *f*.

cahoots [kə'huːts] (*inf*) *n*: **to be in ~ with** unter einer Decke stecken mit.

CAI *n abbr* (= *computer-aided instruction*) CAI *nt*.

Cairo ['kaɪərəʊ] *n* Kairo *nt*.

cajole [kə'dʒəʊl] *vt*: **to ~ sb into doing sth** jdn bereden, etw zu tun.

cake [keɪk] *n* Kuchen *m*; (*small*) Gebäckstück *nt*; (*of soap*) Stück *nt*; **it's a piece of ~** (*inf*) das ist ein Kinderspiel *or* ein Klacks; **he wants to have his ~ and eat it (too)** (*fig*) er will das eine, ohne das andere zu lassen.

caked [keɪkt] *adj*: **~ with** (*mud, blood*) verkrustet mit.

cake shop *n* Konditorei *f*.

Cal. (*US*) *abbr* (*POST*: = *California*).

calamine lotion ['kæləmaɪn-] *n* Galmeilotion *f*.

calamitous [kə'læmɪtəs] *adj* katastrophal.

calamity [kə'læmɪtɪ] *n* Katastrophe *f*.

calcium ['kælsɪəm] *n* Kalzium *nt*.

calculate ['kælkjuleɪt] *vt* (*work out*) berechnen; (*estimate*) abschätzen.

▶ **calculate on** *vt fus*: **to ~ on sth** mit etw

rechnen; **to ~ on doing sth** damit rechnen, etw zu tun.

calculated ['kælkjuleɪtɪd] *adj* (*insult*) bewusst; (*action*) vorsätzlich; **a ~ risk** ein kalkuliertes Risiko.

calculating ['kælkjuleɪtɪŋ] *adj* (*scheming*) berechnend.

calculation [kælkju'leɪʃən] *n* (*see vt*) Berechnung *f*; Abschätzung *f*; (*sum*) Rechnung *f*.

calculator ['kælkjuleɪtə*] *n* Rechner *m*.

calculus ['kælkjuləs] *n* Infinitesimalrechnung *f*; **integral/differential ~** Integral-/ Differenzialrechnung *f*.

calendar ['kæləndə*] *n* Kalender *m*; (*timetable, schedule*) (Termin)kalender *m*.

calendar month *n* Kalendermonat *m*.

calendar year *n* Kalenderjahr *nt*.

calf [kɑːf] (*pl* **calves**) *n* Kalb *nt*; (*of elephant, seal etc*) Junge(s) *nt*; (*also:* **~skin**) Kalb(s)leder *nt*; (*ANAT*) Wade *f*.

caliber ['kælɪbə*] (*US*) *n* = **calibre**.

calibrate ['kælɪbreɪt] *vt* (*gun etc*) kalibrieren; (*scale of measuring instrument*) eichen.

calibre, (*US*) **caliber** ['kælɪbə*] *n* Kaliber *nt*; (*of person*) Format *nt*.

calico ['kælɪkəu] *n* (*BRIT*) Kattun *m*, Kaliko *m*; (*US*) bedruckter Kattun.

Calif. (*US*) *abbr* (*POST:* = *California*).

California [kælɪ'fɔːnɪə] *n* Kalifornien *nt*.

calipers ['kælɪpəz] (*US*) *npl* = **callipers**.

call [kɔːl] *vt* (*name, consider*) nennen; (*shout out, summon*) rufen; (*TEL*) anrufen; (*witness, flight*) aufrufen; (*meeting*) einberufen; (*strike*) ausrufen ♦ *vi* rufen; (*TEL*) anrufen; (*visit: also:* **~ in, ~ round**) vorbeigehen, vorbeikommen ♦ *n* Ruf *m*; (*TEL*) Anruf *m*; (*visit*) Besuch *m*; (*for a service etc*) Nachfrage *f*, (*for flight etc*) Aufruf *m*; (*fig: lure*) Ruf *m*, Verlockung *f*; **to be ~ed** (*named*) heißen; **who is ~ing?** (*TEL*) wer spricht da bitte?; **London ~ing** (*RADIO*) hier ist London; **please give me a ~ at 7** rufen Sie mich bitte um 7 an; **to make a ~** ein (Telefon)gespräch führen; **to pay a ~ on sb** jdn besuchen; **to be on ~** einsatzbereit sein; (*doctor etc*) Bereitschaftsdienst haben; **there's not much ~ for these items** es besteht keine große Nachfrage nach diesen Dingen.

▶ **call at** *vt fus* (*subj: ship*) anlaufen; (*: train*) halten in *+dat*.

▶ **call back** *vi* (*return*) wiederkommen; (*TEL*) zurückrufen ♦ *vt* (*TEL*) zurückrufen.

▶ **call for** *vt fus* (*demand*) fordern; (*fetch*) abholen.

▶ **call in** *vt* (*doctor, expert, police*) zurate *or* zu Rate ziehen; (*books, cars, stock etc*) aus dem Verkehr ziehen ♦ *vi* vorbeigehen, vorbeikommen.

▶ **call off** *vt* absagen.

▶ **call on** *vt fus* besuchen; (*appeal to*) appellieren an *+acc*; **to ~ on sb to do sth** jdn

bitten *or* auffordern, etw zu tun.

▶ **call out** *vi* rufen ♦ *vt* rufen; (*police, troops*) alarmieren.

▶ **call up** *vt* (*MIL*) einberufen; (*TEL*) anrufen.

Callanetics ® *n sing* Callanetics *f*.

call box (*BRIT*) *n* Telefonzelle *f*.

call centre *n* Telefoncenter *nt*, Callcenter *nt*.

caller ['kɔːlə*] *n* Besucher(in) *m(f)*; (*TEL*) Anrufer(in) *m(f)*; **hold the line, ~!** (*TEL*) bitte bleiben Sie am Apparat!

call girl *n* Callgirl *nt*.

call-in ['kɔːlɪn] (*US*) *n* (*RADIO, TV*) Phone-in *nt*.

calling ['kɔːlɪŋ] *n* (*trade*) Beruf *m*; (*vocation*) Berufung *f*.

calling card (*US*) *n* Visitenkarte *f*.

callipers, (*US*) **calipers** ['kælɪpəz] *npl* (*MATH*) Tastzirkel *m*; (*MED*) Schiene *f*.

callous ['kæləs] *adj* herzlos.

callousness ['kæləsnɪs] *n* Herzlosigkeit *f*.

callow ['kæləu] *adj* unreif.

calm [kɑːm] *adj* ruhig; (*unworried*) gelassen ♦ *n* Ruhe *f* ♦ *vt* beruhigen; (*fears*) zerstreuen; (*grief*) lindern.

▶ **calm down** *vt* beruhigen ♦ *vi* sich beruhigen.

calmly ['kɑːmlɪ] *adv* (*see adj*) ruhig; gelassen.

calmness ['kɑːmnɪs] *n* (*see adj*) Ruhe *f*; Gelassenheit *f*.

Calor gas ® ['kælə*-] *n* Butangas *nt*.

calorie ['kælərɪ] *n* Kalorie *f*; **low-~ product** kalorienarmes Produkt *nt*.

calve [kɑːv] *vi* kalben.

calves [kɑːvz] *npl of* **calf**.

CAM *n abbr* (= *computer-aided manufacture*) CAM *nt*.

camber ['kæmbə*] *n* Wölbung *f*.

Cambodia [kæm'bəudɪə] *n* Kambodscha *nt*.

Cambodian [kæm'bəudɪən] *adj* kambodschanisch ♦ *n* Kambodschaner(in) *m(f)*.

Cambs (*BRIT*) *abbr* (*POST:* = *Cambridgeshire*).

camcorder ['kæmkɔːdə*] *n* Camcorder *m*, Kamerarekorder *m*.

came [keɪm] *pt of* **come**.

camel ['kæməl] *n* Kamel *nt*.

cameo ['kæmɪəu] *n* Kamee *f*; (*THEAT, LITER*) Miniatur *f*.

camera ['kæmərə] *n* (*CINE, PHOT*) Kamera *f*; (*also:* **cine ~, movie ~**) Filmkamera *f*; **35 mm ~** Kleinbildkamera *f*; **in ~** (*LAW*) unter Ausschluss der Öffentlichkeit.

cameraman ['kæmərəmæn] (*irreg: like* **man**) *n* Kameramann *m*.

Cameroon [kæmə'ruːn] *n* Kamerun *nt*.

Cameroun [kæmə'ruːn] *n* = **Cameroon**.

camomile ['kæməumaɪl] *n* Kamille *f*.

camouflage ['kæməflɑːʒ] *n* Tarnung *f* ♦ *vt* tarnen.

camp [kæmp] *n* Lager *nt*; (*barracks*) Kaserne *f* ♦ *vi* zelten ♦ *adj* (*effeminate*) tuntenhaft (*inf*).

campaign [kæm'peɪn] *n* (*MIL*) Feldzug *m*; (*POL etc*) Kampagne *f* ♦ *vi* kämpfen; **to ~ for/**

against sich einsetzen für/gegen.
campaigner [kæm'peɪnə*] n: ~ **for**
Befürworter(in) m(f) +gen; ~ **against**
Gegner(in) m(f) +gen.
camp bed (BRIT) n Campingliege f.
camper ['kæmpə*] n (person) Camper m;
(vehicle) Wohnmobil nt.
camping ['kæmpɪŋ] n Camping nt; **to go ~**
zelten gehen, campen.
camp(ing) site n Campingplatz m.
campus ['kæmpəs] n (UNIV)
Universitätsgelände nt, Campus m.
camshaft ['kæmʃɑːft] n Nockenwelle f.
can¹ [kæn] n Büchse f, Dose f; (for oil, water)
Kanister m ♦ vt eindosen, in Büchsen or
Dosen einmachen; **a ~ of beer** eine Dose
Bier; **he had to carry the ~** (BRIT: inf) er
musste die Sache ausbaden.

============================= KEYWORD

can² (negative **cannot, can't**, conditional and pt
could) aux vb **1** (be able to, know how to)
können; **you ~ do it if you try** du kannst es,
wenn du es nur versuchst; **I can't see you**
ich kann dich nicht sehen; **I ~ swim/drive**
ich kann schwimmen/Auto fahren; **~ you
speak English?** sprechen Sie Englisch?
2 (may) können, dürfen; **~ I use your phone?**
kann or darf ich Ihr Telefon benutzen?;
could I have a word with you? könnte ich
Sie mal sprechen?
3 (expressing disbelief, puzzlement): **it can't be
true!** das darf doch nicht wahr sein!
4 (expressing possibility, suggestion, etc): **he
could be in the library** er könnte in der
Bibliothek sein.

Canada ['kænədə] n Kanada nt.
Canadian [kə'neɪdɪən] adj kanadisch ♦ n
Kanadier(in) m(f).
canal [kə'næl] n (also ANAT) Kanal m.
Canaries [kə'nɛərɪz] npl = **Canary Islands**.
canary [kə'nɛərɪ] n Kanarienvogel m.
Canary Islands [kə'nɛərɪ 'aɪləndz] npl: **the ~**
die Kanarischen Inseln pl.
Canberra ['kænbərə] n Canberra nt.
cancel ['kænsəl] vt absagen; (reservation)
abbestellen; (train, flight) ausfallen lassen;
(contract) annullieren; (order) stornieren;
(cross out) durchstreichen; (stamp)
entwerten; (cheque) ungültig machen.
▶ **cancel out** vt aufheben; **they ~ each other
out** sie heben sich gegenseitig auf.
cancellation [kænsə'leɪʃən] n Absage f; (of
reservation) Abbestellung f; (of train, flight)
Ausfall m; (TOURISM) Rücktritt m.
cancer ['kænsə*] n (also: **C~**: ASTROL) Krebs m;
to be C~ (ein) Krebs sein.
cancerous ['kænsrəs] adj krebsartig.
cancer patient n Krebskranke(r) f(m).
cancer research n Krebsforschung f.
c and f (BRIT) abbr (COMM: = cost and freight)

cf.
candid ['kændɪd] adj offen, ehrlich.
candidacy ['kændɪdəsɪ] n Kandidatur f.
candidate ['kændɪdeɪt] n Kandidat(in) m(f);
(for job) Bewerber(in) m(f).
candidature ['kændɪdətʃə*] (BRIT) n
= **candidacy**.
candied ['kændɪd] adj kandiert; ~ **apple** (US)
kandierter Apfel m.
candle ['kændl] n Kerze f; (of tallow) Talglicht
nt.
candleholder ['kændlhəuldə*] n see
candlestick.
candlelight ['kændllaɪt] n: **by ~** bei
Kerzenlicht.
candlestick ['kændlstɪk] n (also: **candleholder**)
Kerzenhalter m; (bigger, ornate)
Kerzenleuchter m.
candour, (US) candor ['kændə*] n Offenheit f.
C & W n abbr = **country and western (music)**.
candy ['kændɪ] n (also: **sugar-~**)
Kandis(zucker) m; (US) Bonbon nt or m.
candyfloss ['kændɪflɒs] (BRIT) n Zuckerwatte
f.
candy store (US) n Süßwarenhandlung f.
cane [keɪn] n Rohr nt; (stick) Stock m; (: for
walking) (Spazier)stock m ♦ vt (BRIT: SCOL)
mit dem Stock schlagen.
canine ['keɪnaɪn] adj (species) Hunde-.
canister ['kænɪstə*] n Dose f; (pressurized
container) Sprühdose f; (of gas, chemicals etc)
Kanister m.
cannabis ['kænəbɪs] n Haschisch nt; (also:
~ **plant**) Hanf m, Cannabis m.
canned [kænd] adj Dosen-; (inf: music) aus der
Konserve; (US: inf: worker) entlassen,
rausgeschmissen inf.
cannibal ['kænɪbəl] n Kannibale m, Kannibalin
f.
cannibalism ['kænɪbəlɪzəm] n Kannibalismus
m.
cannon ['kænən] n (pl ~ or ~**s**) n Kanone f.
cannonball ['kænənbɔːl] n Kanonenkugel f.
cannon fodder n Kanonenfutter nt.
cannot ['kænɒt] = **can not**.
canny ['kænɪ] adj schlau.
canoe [kə'nuː] n Kanu nt.
canoeing [kə'nuːɪŋ] n Kanusport m.
canon ['kænən] n Kanon m; (clergyman)
Kanoniker m, Kanonikus m.
canonize ['kænənaɪz] vt kanonisieren, heilig
sprechen.
can-opener ['kænəupnə*] n Dosenöffner m,
Büchsenöffner m.
canopy ['kænəpɪ] n (also fig) Baldachin m.
cant [kænt] n scheinheiliges Gerede nt.
can't [kænt] = **can not**.
Cantab. (BRIT) abbr (in degree titles:
= Cantabrigiensis) der Universität
Cambridge.
cantankerous [kæn'tæŋkərəs] adj mürrisch.
canteen [kæn'tiːn] n (in school, workplace)

Kantine *f*; (: *mobile*) Feldküche *f*; (*BRIT*: *of cutlery*) Besteckkasten *m*.

canter ['kæntə'] *vi* leicht galoppieren, kantern ♦ *n* leichter Galopp *m*, Kanter *m*.

cantilever ['kæntɪliːvə'] *n* Ausleger *m*.

canvas ['kænvəs] *n* Leinwand *f*; (*painting*) Gemälde *nt*; (*NAUT*) Segeltuch *nt*; **under ~** im Zelt.

canvass ['kænvəs] *vt* (*opinions, views*) erforschen; (*person*) für seine Partei zu gewinnen suchen; (*place*) Wahlwerbung machen in +*dat* ♦ *vi*: **to ~ for ...** (*POL*) um Stimmen für ... werben.

canvasser ['kænvəsə'] *n* (*POL*) Wahlhelfer(in) *m(f)*.

canvassing ['kænvəsɪŋ] *n* (*POL*) Wahlwerbung *f*.

canyon ['kænjən] *n* Cañon *m*.

CAP *n abbr* (= *Common Agricultural Policy*) gemeinsame Agrarpolitik *f* der EG.

cap [kæp] *n* Mütze *f*, Kappe *f*; (*of pen*) (Verschluss)kappe *f*; (*of bottle*) Verschluss *m*, Deckel *m*; (*contraceptive*: *also*: ~) Pessar *nt*; (*for toy gun*) Zündplättchen *nt*; (*for swimming*) Bademütze *f*, Badekappe *f*; (*SPORT*) Ehrenkappe, *die Nationalspielern verliehen wird* ♦ *vt* (*outdo*) überbieten; (*SPORT*) für die Nationalmannschaft aufstellen; **~ped with ...** mit ... obendrauf; **and to ~ it all, ...** und obendrein ...

capability [keɪpə'bɪlɪtɪ] *n* Fähigkeit *f*; (*MIL*) Potenzial *nt*.

capable ['keɪpəbl] *adj* fähig; **to be ~ of doing sth** etw tun können, fähig sein, etw zu tun; **to be ~ of sth** (*interpretation etc*) etw zulassen.

capacious [kə'peɪʃəs] *adj* geräumig.

capacity [kə'pæsɪtɪ] *n* Fassungsvermögen *nt*; (*of lift etc*) Höchstlast *f*; (*capability*) Fähigkeit *f*; (*position, role*) Eigenschaft *f*; (*of factory*) Kapazität *f*; **filled to ~** randvoll; (*stadium etc*) bis auf den letzten Platz besetzt; **in his ~ as** ... in seiner Eigenschaft als ...; **this work is beyond my ~** zu dieser Arbeit bin ich nicht fähig; **in an advisory ~** in beratender Funktion; **to work at full ~** voll ausgelastet sein.

cape [keɪp] *n* Kap *nt*; (*cloak*) Cape *nt*, Umhang *m*.

Cape of Good Hope *n*: **the ~** das Kap der guten Hoffnung.

caper ['keɪpə'] *n* (*CULIN*: *usu pl*) Kaper *f*; (*prank*) Eskapade *f*, Kapriole *f*.

Cape Town *n* Kapstadt *nt*.

capita ['kæpɪtə] *see* **per capita**.

capital ['kæpɪtl] *n* (*also*: ~ **city**) Hauptstadt *f*; (*money*) Kapital *nt*; (*also*: ~ **letter**) Großbuchstabe *m*.

capital account *n* Kapitalverkehrsbilanz *f*; (*of country*) Kapitalkonto *nt*.

capital allowance *n* (Anlage)abschreibung *f*.

capital assets *npl* Kapitalvermögen *nt*.

capital expenditure *n* Kapitalaufwendungen *pl*.

capital gains tax *n* Kapitalertragssteuer *f*.

capital goods *npl* Investitionsgüter *pl*.

capital-intensive ['kæpɪtlɪn'tɛnsɪv] *adj* kapitalintensiv.

capitalism ['kæpɪtəlɪzəm] *n* Kapitalismus *m*.

capitalist ['kæpɪtəlɪst] *adj* kapitalistisch ♦ *n* Kapitalist(in) *m(f)*.

capitalize ['kæpɪtəlaɪz] *vt* (*COMM*) kapitalisieren ♦ *vi*: **to ~ on** Kapital schlagen aus.

capital punishment *n* Todesstrafe *f*.

capital transfer tax (*BRIT*) *n* Erbschafts- und Schenkungssteuer *f*.

Capitol ['kæpɪtl] *n*: **the ~** das Kapitol.

CAPITOL

Capitol *ist das Gebäude in Washington auf dem Capitol Hill, in dem der Kongress der USA zusammentritt. Die Bezeichnung wird in vielen amerikanischen Bundesstaaten auch für das Parlamentsgebäude des jeweiligen Staates verwendet.*

---

capitulate [kə'pɪtjuleɪt] *vi* kapitulieren.

capitulation [kəpɪtju'leɪʃən] *n* Kapitulation *f*.

capricious [kə'prɪʃəs] *adj* launisch.

Capricorn ['kæprɪkɔːn] *n* (*ASTROL*) Steinbock *m*; **to be ~** (ein) Steinbock sein.

caps [kæps] *abbr* (= *capital letters*) Großbuchstaben *pl*.

capsize [kæp'saɪz] *vt* zum Kentern bringen ♦ *vi* kentern.

capstan ['kæpstən] *n* Poller *m*.

capsule ['kæpsjuːl] *n* Kapsel *f*.

Capt. *abbr* (*MIL*) = **captain**.

captain ['kæptɪn] *n* Kapitän *m*; (*of plane*) (Flug)kapitän *m*; (*in army*) Hauptmann *m* ♦ *vt* (*ship*) befehligen; (*team*) anführen.

caption ['kæpʃən] *n* Bildunterschrift *f*.

captivate ['kæptɪveɪt] *vt* fesseln.

captive ['kæptɪv] *adj* gefangen ♦ *n* Gefangene(r) *f(m)*.

captivity [kæp'tɪvɪtɪ] *n* Gefangenschaft *f*.

captor ['kæptə'] *n*: **his ~s** diejenigen, die ihn gefangen nahmen.

capture ['kæptʃə'] *vt* (*animal*) (ein)fangen; (*person*) gefangen nehmen; (*town, country, share of market*) erobern; (*attention*) erregen; (*COMPUT*) erfassen ♦ *n* (*of animal*) Einfangen *nt*; (*of person*) Gefangennahme *f*; (*of town etc*) Eroberung *f*; (*data capture*) Erfassung *f*.

car [kɑː'] *n* Auto *nt*, Wagen *m*; (*RAIL*) Wagen *m*; **by ~** mit dem Auto *or* Wagen.

Caracas [kə'rækəs] *n* Caracas *nt*.

carafe [kə'ræf] *n* Karaffe *f*.

caramel ['kærəməl] *n* Karamelle *f*, Karamellbonbon *m or nt*; (*burnt sugar*) Karamell *m*.

carat ['kærət] n Karat nt; **18 ~ gold** achtzehnkarätiges Gold.

caravan ['kærəvæn] n (BRIT) Wohnwagen m; (in desert) Karawane f.

caravan site (BRIT) n Campingplatz m für Wohnwagen.

caraway seed n Kümmel m.

carbohydrate [ka:bəu'haɪdreɪt] n Kohle(n)hydrat nt.

carbolic acid [ka:'bɔlɪk-] n Karbolsäure f.

car bomb n Autobombe f.

carbon ['ka:bən] n Kohlenstoff m.

carbonated ['ka:bəneɪtɪd] adj mit Kohlensäure (versetzt).

carbon copy n Durchschlag m.

carbon dioxide n Kohlendioxid nt.

carbon monoxide [mɔ'nɔksaɪd] n Kohlenmonoxid nt.

carbon paper n Kohlepapier nt.

carbon ribbon n Kohlefarbband nt.

car-boot sale n auf einem Parkplatz stattfindender Flohmarkt mit dem Kofferraum als Auslage.

carburettor, (US) **carburetor** [ka:bju'retə*] n Vergaser m.

carcass ['ka:kəs] n Kadaver m.

carcinogenic [ka:sɪnə'dʒenɪk] adj Krebs erregend, karzinogen.

card [ka:d] n Karte f; (material) (dünne) Pappe f, Karton m; (record card, index card etc) (Kartei)karte f; (membership card) (Mitglieds)ausweis m; (playing card) (Spiel)karte f; (visiting card) (Visiten)karte f; **to play ~s** Karten spielen.

cardamom ['ka:dəməm] n Kardamom m.

cardboard ['ka:dbɔ:d] n Pappe f.

cardboard box n (Papp)karton m.

card-carrying ['ka:d'kærɪɪŋ] adj: **~ member** eingetragenes Mitglied nt.

card game n Kartenspiel nt.

cardiac ['ka:dɪæk] adj (failure, patient) Herz-.

cardigan ['ka:dɪgən] n Strickjacke f.

cardinal ['ka:dɪnl] adj (principle, importance) Haupt- ♦ n Kardinal m; **~ number** Kardinalzahl f; **~ sin** Todsünde f.

card index n Kartei f.

cardphone n Kartentelefon nt.

cardsharp ['ka:dʃa:p] n Falschspieler m.

card vote (BRIT) n Abstimmung f durch Wahlmänner.

CARE [keə*] n abbr (= Cooperative for American Relief Everywhere) karitative Organisation.

care [keə*] n (attention) Versorgung f; (worry) Sorge f; (charge) Obhut f, Fürsorge f ♦ vi: **to ~ about** sich kümmern um; **~ of** bei; "**handle with ~**" „Vorsicht, zerbrechlich"; **in sb's ~** in jds dat Obhut; **to take ~** aufpassen; **to take ~ to do sth** sich bemühen, etw zu tun; **to take ~ of** sich kümmern um; **the child has been taken into ~** das Kind ist in Pflege genommen worden; **would you ~ to/for ...?** möchten Sie gerne

...?; **I wouldn't ~ to do it** ich möchte es nicht gern tun; **I don't ~** es ist mir egal or gleichgültig; **I couldn't ~ less** es ist mir völlig egal or gleichgültig.

▶ **care for** vt fus (look after) sich kümmern um; (like) mögen.

career [kə'rɪə*] n Karriere f; (job, profession) Beruf m; (life) Laufbahn f ♦ vi (also: **~ along**) rasen.

career girl n Karrierefrau f.

careers officer [kə'rɪəz-] n Berufsberater(in) m(f).

career woman n Karrierefrau f.

carefree ['keəfri:] adj sorglos.

careful ['keəful] adj vorsichtig; (thorough) sorgfältig; **(be) ~!** Vorsicht!, pass auf!; **to be ~ with one's money** sein Geld gut zusammenhalten.

carefully ['keəfəlɪ] adv vorsichtig; (methodically) sorgfältig.

careless ['keəlɪs] adj leichtsinnig; (negligent) nachlässig; (remark) gedankenlos.

carelessly ['keəlɪslɪ] adv (see adj) leichtsinnig; nachlässig; gedankenlos.

carelessness ['keəlɪsnɪs] n (see adj) Leichtsinn m; Nachlässigkeit f; Gedankenlosigkeit f.

caress [kə'res] n Streicheln nt ♦ vt streicheln.

caretaker ['keəteɪkə*] n Hausmeister(in) m(f).

caretaker government (BRIT) n geschäftsführende Regierung f.

car ferry n Autofähre f.

cargo ['ka:gəu] (pl **~es**) n Fracht f, Ladung f.

cargo boat n Frachter m, Frachtschiff nt.

cargo plane n Transportflugzeug nt.

car hire (BRIT) n Autovermietung f.

Caribbean [kærɪ'bi:ən] adj karibisch ♦ n: **the ~ (Sea)** die Karibik, das Karibische Meer.

caricature ['kærɪkətjuə*] n Karikatur f.

caring ['keərɪŋ] adj liebevoll; (society, organization) sozial; (behaviour) fürsorglich.

carjacking n Angriff durch Banditen, die gewaltsam in PKWs eindringen und den Wagen samt Insassen entführen.

carnage ['ka:nɪdʒ] n (MIL) Blutbad nt, Gemetzel nt.

carnal ['ka:nl] adj fleischlich, sinnlich.

carnation [ka:'neɪʃən] n Nelke f.

carnival ['ka:nɪvl] n Karneval m; (US: funfair) Kirmes f.

carnivorous [ka:'nɪvərəs] adj Fleisch fressend.

carol ['kærəl] n: **(Christmas) ~** Weihnachtslied nt.

carouse [kə'rauz] vi zechen.

carousel [kærə'sel] (US) n Karussell nt.

carp [ka:p] n Karpfen m.

▶ **carp at** vt fus herumnörgeln an +dat.

car park (BRIT) n Parkplatz m; (building) Parkhaus nt.

carpenter ['ka:pɪntə*] n Zimmermann m.

carpentry ['ka:pɪntrɪ] n Zimmerhandwerk nt;

(*school subject, hobby*) Tischlern *nt*.
carpet ['kɑːpɪt] *n* (*also fig*) Teppich *m* ♦ *vt* (mit
Teppichen/Teppichboden) auslegen; **fitted**
~ (*BRIT*) Teppichboden *m*.
carpet bombing *n* Flächenbombardierung *f*.
carpet slippers *npl* Pantoffeln *pl*.
carpet-sweeper ['kɑːpɪtswiːpəˈ] *n*
Teppichkehrer *m*.
car phone *n* (*TELEC*) Autotelefon *nt*.
carport ['kɑːpɔːt] *n* Einstellplatz *m*.
car rental *n* Autovermietung *f*.
carriage ['kærɪdʒ] *n* (*RAIL, of typewriter*) Wagen
m; (*horse-drawn vehicle*) Kutsche *f*; (*of goods*)
Beförderung *f*; (*transport costs*)
Beförderungskosten *pl*; ~ **forward** Fracht
zahlt Empfänger; ~ **free** frachtfrei; ~ **paid**
frei Haus.
carriage return *n* (*on typewriter*)
Wagenrücklauf *m*; (*COMPUT*) Return *nt*.
carriageway ['kærɪdʒweɪ] (*BRIT*) *n* Fahrbahn *f*.
carrier ['kærɪəˈ] *n* Spediteur *m*,
Transportunternehmer *m*; (*MED*)
Überträger *m*.
carrier bag (*BRIT*) *n* Tragetasche *f*, Tragetüte
f.
carrier pigeon *n* Brieftaube *f*.
carrion ['kærɪən] *n* Aas *nt*.
carrot ['kærət] *n* Möhre *f*, Mohrrübe *f*, Karotte
f; (*fig*) Köder *m*.
carry ['kærɪ] *vt* tragen; (*transport*)
transportieren; (*a motion, bill*) annehmen;
(*reponsibilities etc*) mit sich bringen; (*disease,
virus*) übertragen ♦ *vi* (*sound*) tragen; **to get
carried away** (*fig*) sich hinreißen lassen; **this
loan carries 10% interest** dieses Darlehen
wird mit 10% verzinst.
▶ **carry forward** *vt* übertragen, vortragen.
▶ **carry on** *vi* weitermachen; (*inf: make a fuss*)
(ein) Theater machen ♦ *vt* fortführen; **to
~ on with sth** mit etw weitermachen; **to
~ on singing/eating** weitersingen/-essen.
▶ **carry out** *vt* (*orders*) ausführen;
(*investigation*) durchführen; (*idea*) in die Tat
umsetzen; (*threat*) wahrmachen.
carrycot ['kærɪkɔt] (*BRIT*) *n* Babytragetasche
f.
carry-on ['kærɪˈɔn] (*inf*) *n* Theater *nt*.
cart [kɑːt] *n* Wagen *m*, Karren *m*; (*for
passengers*) Wagen *m*; (*handcart*)
(Hand)wagen *m* ♦ *vt* (*inf*) mit sich
herumschleppen.
carte blanche ['kɑːt'blɒŋʃ] *n*: **to give sb** ~
jdm Carte blanche *or* (eine)
Blankovollmacht geben.
cartel [kɑːˈtɛl] *n* Kartell *nt*.
cartilage ['kɑːtɪlɪdʒ] *n* Knorpel *m*.
cartographer [kɑːˈtɔgrəfəˈ] *n* Kartograf(in)
m(f).
cartography [kɑːˈtɔgrəfɪ] *n* Kartografie *f*.
carton ['kɑːtən] *n* (Papp)karton *m*; (*of yogurt*)
Becher *m*; (*of milk*) Tüte *f*; (*of cigarettes*)
Stange *f*.

cartoon [kɑːˈtuːn] *n* (*drawing*) Karikatur *f*;
(*BRIT*: *comic strip*) Cartoon *m*; (*CINE*)
Zeichentrickfilm *m*.
cartoonist [kɑːˈtuːnɪst] *n* Karikaturist(in) *m(f)*.
cartridge ['kɑːtrɪdʒ] *n* (*for gun, pen*) Patrone *f*;
(*music tape, for camera*) Kassette *f*; (*of
record-player*) Tonabnehmer *m*.
cartwheel ['kɑːtwiːl] *n* Rad *nt*; **to turn a** ~ Rad
schlagen.
carve [kɑːv] *vt* (*meat*) (ab)schneiden; (*wood*)
schnitzen; (*stone*) meißeln; (*initials, design*)
einritzen.
▶ **carve up** *vt* (*land etc*) aufteilen; (*meat*)
aufschneiden.
carving ['kɑːvɪŋ] *n* Skulptur *f*; (*in wood etc*)
Schnitzerei *f*.
carving knife *n* Tran(s)chiermesser *nt*.
car wash *n* Autowaschanlage *f*.
Casablanca [kæsəˈblæŋkə] *n* Casablanca *nt*.
cascade [kæsˈkeɪd] *n* Wasserfall *m*, Kaskade *f*;
(*of money*) Regen *m*; (*of hair*) wallende Fülle
f ♦ *vi* (in Kaskaden) herabfallen; (*hair etc*)
wallen; (*people*) strömen.
case [keɪs] *n* Fall *m*; (*for spectacles etc*) Etui *nt*;
(*BRIT: also*: **suit**~) Koffer *m*; (*of wine, whisky
etc*) Kiste *f*; (*TYP*): **lower/upper** ~ klein-/
großgeschrieben; **to have a good** ~ gute
Chancen haben, durchzukommen; **there's a
strong** ~ **for reform** es spricht viel für eine
Reform; **in** ~ ... **falls** ...; **in** ~ **of fire** bei
Feuer; **in** ~ **of emergency** im Notfall; **in**
~ **he comes** falls er kommt; **in any** ~
sowieso; **just in** ~ für alle Fälle.
case-hardened ['keɪʃɑːdnd] *adj* (*fig*)
abgebrüht (*inf*).
case history *n* (*MED*) Krankengeschichte *f*.
case study *n* Fallstudie *f*.
cash [kæʃ] *n* (Bar)geld *nt* ♦ *vt* (*cheque etc*)
einlösen; **to pay (in)** ~ bar bezahlen; ~ **on
delivery** per Nachnahme; ~ **with order**
zahlbar bei Bestellung.
▶ **cash in** *vt* einlösen.
▶ **cash in on** *vt fus* Kapital schlagen aus.
cash account *n* Kassenbuch *nt*.
cash-and-carry [kæʃənˈkærɪ] *n* Abholmarkt *m*.
cash-book ['kæʃbuk] *n* Kassenkonto *nt*.
cash box *n* (Geld)kassette *f*.
cash card (*BRIT*) *n* (Geld)automatenkarte *f*.
cash crop *n* zum Verkauf bestimmte Ernte *f*.
cash desk (*BRIT*) *n* Kasse *f*.
cash discount *n* Skonto *m or nt*.
cash dispenser (*BRIT*) *n* Geldautomat *m*.
cashew [kæˈʃuː] *n* (*also*: ~ **nut**) Cashewnuss *f*.
cash flow *n* Cashflow *m*.
cashier [kæˈʃɪəˈ] *n* Kassierer(in) *m(f)*.
cashmere ['kæʃmɪəˈ] *n* Kaschmir *m*.
cash point *n* Geldautomat *m*.
cash price *n* Bar(zahlungs)preis *m*.
cash register *n* Registrierkasse *f*.
cash sale *n* Barverkauf *m*.
casing ['keɪsɪŋ] *n* Gehäuse *nt*.
casino [kəˈsiːnəu] *n* Kasino *nt*.

cask [kɑːsk] n Fass nt.

casket ['kɑːskɪt] n Schatulle f; (US: coffin) Sarg m.

Caspian Sea ['kæspɪən-] n: **the** ~ das Kaspische Meer.

casserole ['kæsərəul] n Auflauf m; (pot, container) Kasserolle f.

cassette [kæ'sɛt] n Kassette f.

cassette deck n Kassettendeck nt.

cassette player n Kassettenrekorder m.

cassette recorder n Kassettenrekorder m.

cast [kɑːst] (pt, pp cast) vt werfen; (net, fishing-line) auswerfen; (metal, statue) gießen ♦ vi die Angel auswerfen ♦ n (THEAT) Besetzung f; (mould) (Guss)form f; (also: **plaster** ~) Gipsverband m; **to** ~ **sb as Hamlet** (THEAT) die Rolle des Hamlet auf jdm besetzen; **to** ~ **one's vote** seine Stimme abgeben; **to** ~ **one's eyes over sth** einen Blick auf etw acc werfen; **to** ~ **aspersions on sb/sth** abfällige Bemerkungen über jdn/etw machen; **to** ~ **doubts on sth** etw in Zweifel ziehen; **to** ~ **a spell on sb/sth** jdn/etw verzaubern; **to** ~ **its skin** sich häuten.

▶ **cast aside** vt fallen lassen.

▶ **cast off** vi (NAUT) losmachen; (KNITTING) abketten ♦ vt abketten.

▶ **cast on** vi, vt (KNITTING) anschlagen, aufschlagen.

castaway ['kɑːstəweɪ] n Schiffbrüchige(r) f(m).

caste [kɑːst] n Kaste f; (system) Kastenwesen nt.

caster sugar ['kɑːstə-] (BRIT) n Raffinade f.

casting vote ['kɑːstɪŋ-] (BRIT) n ausschlaggebende Stimme f.

cast iron n Gusseisen nt ♦ adj: **cast-iron** (fig: will) eisern; (: alibi, excuse etc) hieb- und stichfest.

castle ['kɑːsl] n Schloss nt; (manor) Herrenhaus nt; (fortified) Burg f; (CHESS) Turm m.

cast off n abgelegtes Kleidungsstück nt.

castor ['kɑːstə-] n Rolle f.

castor oil n Rizinusöl nt.

castrate [kæs'treɪt] vt kastrieren.

casual ['kæʒjul] adj (by chance) zufällig; (work etc) Gelegenheits-; (unconcerned) lässig, gleichgültig; (clothes) leger; ~ **wear** Freizeitkleidung f.

casual labour n Gelegenheitsarbeit f.

casually ['kæʒjulɪ] adv lässig; (glance) beiläufig; (dress) leger; (by chance) zufällig.

casualty ['kæʒjultɪ] n (of war etc) Opfer nt; (someone injured) Verletzte(r) f(m); (someone killed) Tote(r) f(m); (MED) Unfallstation f; **heavy casualties** (MIL) schwere Verluste pl.

casualty ward (BRIT) n Unfallstation f.

cat [kæt] n Katze f; (lion etc) (Raub)katze f.

catacombs ['kætəkuːmz] npl Katakomben pl.

catalogue, (US) **catalog** ['kætələg] n Katalog m ♦ vt katalogisieren.

catalyst ['kætəlɪst] n Katalysator m.

catalytic converter [kætə'lɪtɪk kən'vɜːtə-] n (AUT) Katalysator m.

catapult ['kætəpʌlt] (BRIT) n Schleuder f; (MIL) Katapult nt or m ♦ vi geschleudert or katapultiert werden ♦ vt schleudern, katapultieren.

cataract ['kætərækt] n (MED) grauer Star m.

catarrh [kə'tɑːʳ] n Katarr(h) m.

catastrophe [kə'tæstrəfɪ] n Katastrophe f.

catastrophic [kætə'strɔfɪk] adj katastrophal.

catcalls ['kætkɔːlz] npl Pfiffe und Buhrufe pl.

catch-22 ['kætʃtwɛntɪ'tuː] n: **it's a** ~ **situation** es ist eine Zwickmühle.

catch [kætʃ] (pt, pp **caught**) vt fangen; (take: bus, train etc) nehmen; (arrest) festnehmen; (surprise) erwischen, ertappen; (breath) holen; (attention) erregen; (hit) treffen; (hear) mitbekommen; (illness) sich dat zuziehen or holen; (person: also: ~ **up**) einholen ♦ vi (fire) (anfangen zu) brennen; (become trapped) hängen bleiben ♦ n Fang m; (trick, hidden problem) Haken m; (of lock) Riegel m; (game) Fangen nt; **to** ~ **sb's attention/eye** jdn auf sich acc aufmerksam machen; **to** ~ **fire** Feuer fangen; **to** ~ **sight of** erblicken.

▶ **catch on** vi (grow popular) sich durchsetzen; **to** ~ **on (to sth)** (etw) kapieren.

▶ **catch out** (BRIT) vt (fig) hereinlegen.

▶ **catch up** vi (fig: with person) mitkommen; (: on work) aufholen ♦ vt: **to** ~ **sb up, to** ~ **up with sb** jdn einholen.

catching ['kætʃɪŋ] adj ansteckend.

catchment area ['kætʃmənt-] (BRIT) n Einzugsgebiet nt.

catch phrase n Schlagwort nt, Slogan m.

catchy ['kætʃɪ] adj (tune) eingängig.

catechism ['kætɪkɪzəm] n Katechismus m.

categoric(al) [kætɪ'gɔrɪk(l)] adj kategorisch.

categorize ['kætɪgəraɪz] vt kategorisieren.

category ['kætɪgərɪ] n Kategorie f.

cater ['keɪtə-] vi: **to** ~ **(for)** die Speisen und Getränke liefern (für).

▶ **cater for** (BRIT) vt fus (needs, tastes) gerecht werden +dat; (readers, consumers) eingestellt or ausgerichtet sein auf +acc.

caterer ['keɪtərə-] n Lieferant(in) m(f) von Speisen und Getränken; (company) Lieferfirma f für Speisen und Getränke.

catering ['keɪtərɪŋ] n Gastronomie f.

caterpillar ['kætəpɪlə-] n Raupe f ♦ cpd (vehicle) Raupen-.

caterpillar track n Raupenkette f, Gleiskette f.

cat flap n Katzentür f.

cathedral [kə'θiːdrəl] n Kathedrale f, Dom m.

cathode ['kæθəud] n Kat(h)ode f.

cathode-ray tube [kæθəud'reɪ-] n Kat(h)odenstrahlröhre f.

Catholic ['kæθəlɪk] adj katholisch ♦ n

Katholik(in) *m(f)*.
catholic ['kæθəlɪk] *adj* vielseitig.
CAT scanner *n abbr (MED*: = *computerized axial tomography scanner)* CAT-Scanner *m*.
Catseye ® ['kæts'aɪ] *(BRIT) n (AUT)* Katzenauge *nt*.
catsup ['kætsəp] *(US) n* Ket(s)chup *m or nt*.
cattle ['kætl] *npl* Vieh *nt*.
catty ['kætɪ] *adj* gehässig.
catwalk ['kætwɔːk] *n* Steg *m*; *(for models)* Laufsteg *m*.
Caucasian [kɔː'keɪzɪən] *adj* kaukasisch ♦ *n* Kaukasier(in) *m(f)*.
Caucasus ['kɔːkəsəs] *n* Kaukasus *m*.
caucus ['kɔːkəs] *n (group)* Gremium *nt*, Ausschuss *m*; *(US)* Parteiversammlung *f*.

CAUCUS

Caucus bedeutet vor allem in den USA ein privates Treffen von Parteifunktionären, bei dem z. B. Kandidaten ausgewählt oder Grundsatzentscheidungen getroffen werden. Meist wird ein solches Treffen vor einer öffentlichen Parteiversammlung abgehalten. Der Begriff bezieht sich im weiteren Sinne auch auf den kleinen, aber mächtigen Kreis von Parteifunktionären, der beim caucus zusammentrifft.

---

caught [kɔːt] *pt, pp of* **catch**.
cauliflower ['kɔlɪflauə°] *n* Blumenkohl *m*.
cause [kɔːz] *n* Ursache *f*; *(reason)* Grund *m*; *(aim)* Sache *f* ♦ *vt* verursachen; **there is no** ~ **for concern** es besteht kein Grund zur Sorge; **to** ~ **sth to be done** veranlassen, dass etw getan wird; **to** ~ **sb to do sth** jdn veranlassen, etw zu tun.
causeway ['kɔːzweɪ] *n* Damm *m*.
caustic ['kɔːstɪk] *adj* ätzend, kaustisch; *(remark)* bissig.
cauterize ['kɔːtəraɪz] *vt* kauterisieren.
caution ['kɔːʃən] *n* Vorsicht *f*; *(warning)* Warnung *f*; (: *LAW)* Verwarnung *f* ♦ *vt* warnen; *(LAW)* verwarnen.
cautious ['kɔːʃəs] *adj* vorsichtig.
cautiously ['kɔːʃəslɪ] *adv* vorsichtig.
cautiousness ['kɔːʃəsnɪs] *n* Vorsicht *f*.
cavalier [kævə'lɪə°] *adj* unbekümmert.
cavalry ['kævəlrɪ] *n* Kavallerie *f*.
cave [keɪv] *n* Höhle *f* ♦ *vi*: **to go caving** auf Höhlenexpedition(en) gehen.
▶ **cave in** *vi* einstürzen; *(to demands)* nachgeben.
caveman ['keɪvmæn] *(irreg: like* **man**) *n* Höhlenmensch *m*.
cavern ['kævən] *n* Höhle *f*.
caviar(e) ['kævɪɑː°] *n* Kaviar *m*.
cavity ['kævɪtɪ] *n* Hohlraum *m*; *(in tooth)* Loch *nt*.
cavity wall insulation *n* Schaumisolierung *f*.
cavort [kə'vɔːt] *vi* tollen, toben.
cayenne [keɪ'ɛn] *n (also:* ~ **pepper)**

Cayennepfeffer *m*.
CB *n abbr* (= *Citizens' Band (Radio)*) CB-Funk *m*.
CBC *n abbr* (= *Canadian Broadcasting Corporation*) *kanadische Rundfunkgesellschaft*.
CBE *(BRIT) n abbr* (= *Commander of (the Order of) the British Empire)* britischer Ordenstitel.
CBI *n abbr* (= *Confederation of British Industry)* britischer Unternehmerverband, ≈ BDI *m*.
CBS *(US) n abbr* (= *Columbia Broadcasting System) Rundfunkgesellschaft*.
CC *(BRIT) abbr* = **county council**.
cc *abbr* (= *cubic centimetre)* ccm; = **carbon copy**.
CCTV *n abbr* = **closed-circuit television**.
CCU *(US) n abbr* (= *cardiac or coronary care unit) Intensivstation für Herzpatienten*.
CD *abbr (BRIT*: = *Corps Diplomatique)* CD ♦ *n abbr (MIL*: *BRIT*: = *Civil Defence (Corps))* Zivilschutz *m*; (: *US*: = *Civil Defense)* Zivilschutz *m*; (= *compact disk)* CD *f*; ~ **player** CD-Spieler *m*.
CDC *(US) n abbr* (= *Center for Disease Control)* Seuchenkontrollbehörde.
CD-I *n abbr* (= *Compact Disk Interactive)* CD-I *f*.
Cdr *abbr (MIL)* = **commander**.
CD-ROM *n abbr* (= *compact disc read-only memory)* CD-ROM *f*.
CDT *(US) abbr* (= *Central Daylight Time) mittelamerikanische Sommerzeit*; *(BRIT*: *SCOL) abbr* (= *Craft, Design and Technology)* Arbeitslehre *f*.
cease [siːs] *vt* beenden ♦ *vi* aufhören.
ceasefire ['siːsfaɪə°] *n* Waffenruhe *f*.
ceaseless ['siːslɪs] *adj* endlos, unaufhörlich.
CED *(US) n abbr* (= *Committee for Economic Development) Komitee für wirtschaftliche Entwicklung*.
cedar ['siːdə°] *n* Zeder *f*; *(wood)* Zedernholz *nt*.
cede [siːd] *vt* abtreten.
cedilla [sɪ'dɪlə] *n* Cedille *f*.
CEEB *(US) n abbr* (= *College Entry Examination Board) akademische Zulassungsstelle*.
ceilidh ['keɪlɪ] *(SCOT) n* Fest mit Volksmusik, Gesang und Tanz.
ceiling ['siːlɪŋ] *n* Decke *f*; *(upper limit)* Obergrenze *f*, Höchstgrenze *f*.
celebrate ['sɛlɪbreɪt] *vt* feiern; *(mass)* zelebrieren ♦ *vi* feiern.
celebrated ['sɛlɪbreɪtɪd] *adj* gefeiert.
celebration [sɛlɪ'breɪʃən] *n* Feier *f*.
celebrity [sɪ'lɛbrɪtɪ] *n* berühmte Persönlichkeit *f*.
celeriac [sə'lɛrɪæk] *n* (Knollen)sellerie *f*.
celery ['sɛlərɪ] *n* (Stangen)sellerie *f*.
celestial [sɪ'lɛstɪəl] *adj* himmlisch.
celibacy ['sɛlɪbəsɪ] *n* Zölibat *nt or m*.
cell [sɛl] *n* Zelle *f*.
cellar ['sɛlə°] *n* Keller *m*; *(for wine)* (Wein)keller *m*.
cellist ['tʃɛlɪst] *n* Cellist(in) *m(f)*.
cello ['tʃɛləu] *n* Cello *nt*.

cellophane ['sɛləfeɪn] n Cellophan nt.
cellphone ['sɛlfəun] n Funktelefon nt.
cellular ['sɛljulə*] adj (BIOL) zellular, Zell-; (fabrics) aus porösem Material.
Celluloid ® ['sɛljulɔɪd] n Zelluloid nt.
cellulose ['sɛljuləus] n Zellulose f, Zellstoff m.
Celsius ['sɛlsɪəs] adj (scale) Celsius-.
Celt [kɛlt] n Kelte m, Keltin f.
Celtic ['kɛltɪk] adj keltisch ♦ n (LING) Keltisch nt.

cement [sə'mɛnt] n Zement m; (concrete) Beton m; (glue) Klebstoff m ♦ vt zementieren; (stick, glue) kleben; (fig) festigen.
cement mixer n Betonmischmaschine f.
cemetery ['sɛmɪtrɪ] n Friedhof m.
cenotaph ['sɛnətɑːf] n Ehrenmal nt.
censor ['sɛnsə*] n Zensor(in) m(f) ♦ vt zensieren.
censorship ['sɛnsəʃɪp] n Zensur f.
censure ['sɛnʃə*] vt tadeln ♦ n Tadel m.
census ['sɛnsəs] n Volkszählung f.
cent [sɛnt] n Cent m; see also **per cent.**
centenary [sɛn'tiːnərɪ] n hundertster Jahrestag m.
centennial [sɛn'tɛnɪəl] (US) n = **centenary.**
center etc ['sɛntə*] (US) = **centre** etc.
centigrade ['sɛntɪɡreɪd] adj (scale) Celsius-.
centilitre, (US) **centiliter** ['sɛntɪliːtə*] n Zentiliter m or nt.
centimetre, (US) **centimeter** ['sɛntɪmiːtə*] n Zentimeter m or nt.
centipede ['sɛntɪpiːd] n Tausendfüßler m.
central ['sɛntrəl] adj zentral; (committee, government) Zentral-; (idea) wesentlich.
Central African Republic n Zentralafrikanische Republik f.
Central America n Mittelamerika nt.
central heating n Zentralheizung f.
centralize ['sɛntrəlaɪz] vt zentralisieren.
central processing unit n (COMPUT) Zentraleinheit f.
central reservation (BRIT) n Mittelstreifen m.
centre, (US) **center** ['sɛntə*] n Mitte f; (health centre etc, town centre) Zentrum nt; (of attention, interest) Mittelpunkt m; (of action, belief etc) Kern m ♦ vt zentrieren; (ball) zur Mitte spielen ♦ vi (concentrate): **to ~ on** sich konzentrieren auf +acc.
centrefold, (US) **centerfold** ['sɛntəfəuld] n doppelseitiges Bild in der Mitte einer Zeitschrift.
centre forward n Mittelstürmer(in) m(f).
centre half n Stopper(in) m(f).
centrepiece, (US) **centerpiece** ['sɛntəpiːs] n Tafelaufsatz m; (fig) Kernstück nt.
centre spread (BRIT) n Doppelseite in der Mitte einer Zeitschrift.
centre-stage [sɛntə'steɪdʒ] (fig) adv: **to be ~** im Mittelpunkt stehen ♦ n **to take centre stage** in den Mittelpunkt rücken.

centrifugal [sɛn'trɪfjugl] adj (force) Zentrifugal-.
centrifuge ['sɛntrɪfjuːʒ] n Zentrifuge f, Schleuder f.
century ['sɛntjurɪ] n Jahrhundert nt; (CRICKET) Hundert f; **in the twentieth ~** im zwanzigsten Jahrhundert.
CEO (US) n abbr = **chief executive officer.**
ceramic [sɪ'ræmɪk] adj keramisch; (tiles) Keramik-.
ceramics [sɪ'ræmɪks] npl Keramiken pl.
cereal ['siːrɪəl] n Getreide nt; (food) Getreideflocken pl (Cornflakes etc).
cerebral ['sɛrɪbrəl] adj (MED) zerebral; (intellectual) geistig.
ceremonial [sɛrɪ'məunɪəl] n Zeremoniell nt ♦ adj zeremoniell.
ceremony ['sɛrɪmənɪ] n Zeremonie f; (behaviour) Förmlichkeit f; **to stand on ~** förmlich sein.
cert [sɜːt] (BRIT: inf) n: **it's a dead ~** es ist todsicher.
certain ['sɜːtən] adj sicher; **a ~ Mr Smith** ein gewisser Herr Smith; **~ days/places** bestimmte Tage/Orte; **a ~ coldness** eine gewisse Kälte; **to make ~ of** sich vergewissern +gen; **for ~** ganz sicher, ganz genau.
certainly ['sɜːtənlɪ] adv bestimmt; (of course) sicherlich; **~!** (aber) sicher!
certainty ['sɜːtəntɪ] n Sicherheit f; (inevitability) Gewissheit f.
certificate [sə'tɪfɪkɪt] n Urkunde f; (diploma) Zeugnis nt.
certified letter ['sɜːtɪfaɪd-] (US) n Einschreibebrief m.
certified mail (US) n Einschreiben nt.
certified public accountant ['sɜːtɪfaɪd-] (US) n geprüfter Buchhalter m, geprüfte Buchhalterin f.
certify ['sɜːtɪfaɪ] vt bescheinigen; (award a diploma to) ein Zeugnis verleihen +dat; (declare insane) für unzurechnungsfähig erklären ♦ vi: **to ~ to** sich verbürgen für.
cervical ['sɜːvɪkl] adj: **~ cancer** Gebärmutterhalskrebs m; **~ smear** Abstrich m.
cervix ['sɜːvɪks] n Gebärmutterhals m.
Cesarean [sɪ'zɛərɪən] (US) n = **Caesarean.**
cessation [sə'seɪʃən] n (of hostilities etc) Einstellung f, Ende nt.
cesspit ['sɛspɪt] n (sewage tank) Senkgrube f.
CET abbr (= Central European Time) MEZ.
Ceylon [sɪ'lɔn] n Ceylon nt.
cf. abbr (= compare) vgl.
c/f abbr (COMM: = carried forward) Übertr.
CFC n abbr (= chlorofluorocarbon) FCKW m.
CG (US) n abbr = **coastguard.**
cg abbr (= centigram) cg.
CH (BRIT) n abbr (= Companion of Honour) britischer Ordenstitel.
ch. abbr (= chapter) Kap.

c.h. (BRIT) abbr (= central heating) ZH.
Chad [tʃæd] n Tschad m.
chafe [tʃeɪf] vt (wund) reiben ♦ vi (fig): **to
~ against** sich ärgern über +acc.
chaffinch [ˈtʃæfɪntʃ] n Buchfink m.
chagrin [ˈʃægrɪn] n Ärger m.
chain [tʃeɪn] n Kette f ♦ vt (also: ~ **up**: prisoner)
anketten; (: dog) an die Kette legen.
chain reaction n Kettenreaktion f.
chain-smoke [ˈtʃeɪnsməʊk] vi eine Zigarette
nach der anderen rauchen.
chain store n Kettenladen m.
chair [tʃɛə*] n Stuhl m; (armchair) Sessel m; (of
university) Lehrstuhl m; (of meeting,
committee) Vorsitz m ♦ vt den Vorsitz führen
bei; **the ~** (US) der elektrische Stuhl.
chair lift n Sessellift m.
chairman [ˈtʃɛəmən] (irreg: like **man**) n
Vorsitzende(r) f(m); (BRIT: of company)
Präsident m.
chairperson [ˈtʃɛəpɜːsn] n Vorsitzende(r) f(m).
chairwoman [ˈtʃɛəwʊmən] (irreg: like **woman**)
n Vorsitzende f.
chalet [ˈʃæleɪ] n Chalet nt.
chalice [ˈtʃælɪs] n Kelch m.
chalk [tʃɔːk] n Kalkstein m, Kreide f; (for
writing) Kreide f.
▸ **chalk up** vt aufschreiben, notieren; (fig:
success etc) verbuchen.
challenge [ˈtʃælɪndʒ] n (of new job)
Anforderungen pl; (of unknown etc) Reiz m;
(to authority etc) Infragestellung f; (dare)
Herausforderung f ♦ vt herausfordern;
(authority, right, idea etc) infrage or in Frage
stellen; **to ~ sb to do sth** jdn dazu
auffordern, etw zu tun; **to ~ sb to a fight/
game** jdn zu einem Kampf/Spiel
herausfordern.
challenger [ˈtʃælɪndʒə*] n Herausforderer m,
Herausforderin f.
challenging [ˈtʃælɪndʒɪŋ] adj (career, task)
anspruchsvoll; (tone, look etc)
herausfordernd.
chamber [ˈtʃeɪmbə*] n Kammer f; (BRIT: LAW:
gen pl: of barristers) Kanzlei f; (: of judge)
Amtszimmer nt; **~ of commerce**
Handelskammer f.
chambermaid [ˈtʃeɪmbəmeɪd] n
Zimmermädchen nt.
chamber music n Kammermusik f.
chamber pot n Nachttopf m.
chameleon [kəˈmiːlɪən] n Chamäleon nt.
chamois [ˈʃæmwɑː] n Gämse f; (cloth)
Ledertuch nt, Fensterleder nt.
chamois leather [ˈʃæmɪ-] n Ledertuch nt,
Fensterleder nt.
champagne [ʃæmˈpeɪn] n Champagner m.
champers [ˈʃæmpəz] (inf) n (champagne)
Schampus m.
champion [ˈtʃæmpɪən] n Meister(in) m(f); (of
cause, principle) Verfechter(in) m(f); (of
person) Fürsprecher(in) m(f) ♦ vt eintreten

für, sich engagieren für.
championship [ˈtʃæmpɪənʃɪp] n
Meisterschaft f; (title) Titel m.
chance [tʃɑːns] n (hope) Aussicht f; (likelihood,
possibility) Möglichkeit f; (opportunity)
Gelegenheit f; (risk) Risiko nt ♦ vt riskieren
♦ adj zufällig; **the ~s are that ...** aller
Wahrscheinlichkeit nach ..., wahrscheinlich
...; **there is little ~ of his coming** es ist
unwahrscheinlich, dass er kommt; **to take a
~** es darauf ankommen lassen; **by ~** durch
Zufall, zufällig; **it's the ~ of a lifetime** es ist
eine einmalige Chance; **to ~ to do sth**
zufällig etw tun; **to ~ it** es riskieren.
▸ **chance (up)on** vt fus (person) zufällig
begegnen +dat, zufällig treffen; (thing)
zufällig stoßen auf +acc.
chancel [ˈtʃɑːnsəl] n Altarraum m.
chancellor [ˈtʃɑːnsələ*] n Kanzler m.
Chancellor of the Exchequer (BRIT) n
Schatzkanzler m, Finanzminister m.
chancy [ˈtʃɑːnsɪ] adj riskant.
chandelier [ʃændəˈlɪə*] n Kronleuchter m.
change [tʃeɪndʒ] vt ändern; (wheel, job, money,
baby's nappy) wechseln; (bulb) auswechseln;
(baby) wickeln ♦ vi sich verändern; (traffic
lights) umspringen ♦ n Veränderung f;
(difference) Abwechslung f; (coins) Kleingeld
nt; (money returned) Wechselgeld nt; **to ~ sb
into** jdn verwandeln in +acc; **to ~ gear** (AUT)
schalten; **to ~ one's mind** seine Meinung
ändern, es sich dat anders überlegen; **to
~ hands** den Besitzer wechseln; **to
~ (trains/buses/planes etc)** umsteigen; **to
~ (one's clothes)** sich umziehen; **to ~ into**
(be transformed) sich verwandeln in +acc; **she
~d into an old skirt** sie zog einen alten Rock
an; **a ~ of clothes** Kleidung f zum Wechseln;
~ of government/climate/job Regierungs-/
Klima-/Berufswechsel m; **small ~** Kleingeld
nt; **to give sb ~ for** or **of £10** jdm £10
wechseln; **keep the ~** das stimmt so, der
Rest ist für Sie; **for a ~** zur Abwechslung.
changeable [ˈtʃeɪndʒəbl] adj (weather)
wechselhaft, veränderlich; (mood)
wechselnd; (person) unbeständig.
change machine n (Geld)wechselautomat m.
changeover [ˈtʃeɪndʒəʊvə*] n Umstellung f.
changing [ˈtʃeɪndʒɪŋ] adj sich verändernd.
changing room (BRIT) n (Umkleide)kabine f;
(SPORT) Umkleideraum m.
channel [ˈtʃænl] n (TV) Kanal m; (of river,
waterway) (Fluss)bett nt; (for boats)
Fahrrinne f; (groove) Rille f; (fig: means) Weg
m ♦ vt leiten; (fig): **to ~ into** lenken auf +acc;
through the usual ~s auf dem üblichen
Wege; **green ~** (CUSTOMS) „nichts zu
verzollen"; **red ~** (CUSTOMS) „Waren zu
verzollen"; **the (English) C~** der
Ärmelkanal; **the C~ Islands** die Kanalinseln
pl.
channel-hopping [ˈtʃænlhɒpɪŋ] n (TV)

ständiges Umschalten.

Channel Tunnel *n*: **the** ~ der Kanaltunnel.

chant [tʃɑ:nt] *n* Sprechchor *m*; (*REL*) Gesang *m* ♦ *vt* im (Sprech)chor rufen; (*REL*) singen ♦ *vi* Sprechchöre anstimmen; (*REL*) singen; **the demonstrators ~ed their disapproval** die Demonstranten machten ihrem Unmut in Sprechchören Luft.

chaos ['keɪɔs] *n* Chaos *nt*, Durcheinander *nt*.

chaos theory *n* Chaostheorie *f*.

chaotic [keɪ'ɔtɪk] *adj* chaotisch.

chap [tʃæp] (*BRIT: inf*) *n* Kerl *m*, Typ *m*; **old** ~ alter Knabe *or* Junge.

chapel ['tʃæpl] *n* Kapelle *f*; (*BRIT: non-conformist chapel*) Sektenkirche *f*; (: *of union*) *Betriebsgruppe innerhalb der Gewerkschaft der Drucker und Journalisten*.

chaperone ['ʃæpərəʊn] *n* Anstandsdame *f* ♦ *vt* begleiten.

chaplain ['tʃæplɪn] *n* Pfarrer(in) *m(f)*; (*Roman Catholic*) Kaplan *m*.

chapped [tʃæpt] *adj* aufgesprungen, rau.

chapter ['tʃæptə*] *n* Kapitel *nt*; **a** ~ **of accidents** eine Serie von Unfällen.

char [tʃɑ:*] *vt* verkohlen ♦ *vi* (*BRIT*) putzen gehen ♦ *n* (*BRIT*) = **charlady**.

character ['kærɪktə*] *n* Charakter *m*; (*personality*) Persönlichkeit *f*; (*in novel, film*) Figur *f*, Gestalt *f*; (*eccentric*) Original *nt*; (*letter: also COMPUT*) Zeichen *nt*; **a person of good** ~ ein guter Mensch.

character code *n* (*COMPUT*) Zeichenkode *m*.

characteristic [kærɪktə'rɪstɪk] *n* Merkmal *nt* ♦ *adj*: ~ (**of**) charakteristisch (für), typisch (für).

characterize ['kærɪktəraɪz] *vt* kennzeichnen, charakterisieren; (*describe the character of*): **to** ~ (**as**) beschreiben (als).

charade [ʃə'rɑ:d] *n* Scharade *f*.

charcoal ['tʃɑ:kəʊl] *n* Holzkohle *f*; (*for drawing*) Kohle *f*, Kohlestift *m*.

charge [tʃɑ:dʒ] *n* (*fee*) Gebühr *f*; (*accusation*) Anklage *f*; (*responsibility*) Verantwortung *f*; (*attack*) Angriff *m* ♦ *vt* (*customer*) berechnen +*dat*; (*sum*) berechnen; (*battery*) (auf)laden; (*gun*) laden; (*enemy*) angreifen; (*sb with task*) beauftragen ♦ *vi* angreifen; (*usu with: up, along etc*) stürmen; **charges** *npl* Gebühren *pl*; **labour** ~**s** Arbeitskosten *pl*; **to reverse the** ~**s** (*BRIT: TEL*) ein R-Gespräch führen; **is there a** ~? kostet das etwas?; **there's no** ~ es ist umsonst, es kostet nichts; **at no extra** ~ ohne Aufpreis; **free of** ~ kostenlos, gratis; **to take** ~ **of** (*child*) sich kümmern um; (*company*) übernehmen; **to be in** ~ **of** die Verantwortung haben für; (*business*) leiten; **they** ~**d us £10 for the meal** das Essen kostete £10; **how much do you** ~? was verlangen Sie?; **to** ~ **an expense (up) to sb's account** eine Ausgabe auf jds Rechnung *acc* setzen; **to** ~ **sb (with)** (*LAW*) jdn anklagen

(wegen).

charge account *n* Kunden(kredit)konto *nt*.

charge card *n* Kundenkreditkarte *f*.

chargé d'affaires *n* Chargé d'affaires *m*.

charge hand (*BRIT*) *n* Vorarbeiter(in) *m(f)*.

charger ['tʃɑ:dʒə*] *n* (*also*: **battery** ~) Ladegerät *nt*; (*warhorse*) (Schlacht)ross *nt*.

chariot ['tʃærɪət] *n* (Streit)wagen *m*.

charisma [kæ'rɪsmə] *n* Charisma *nt*.

charitable ['tʃærɪtəbl] *adj* (*organization*) karitativ, Wohltätigkeits-; (*remark*) freundlich.

charity ['tʃærɪtɪ] *n* (*organization*) karitative Organisation *f*, Wohltätigkeitsverein *m*; (*kindness, generosity*) Menschenfreundlichkeit *f*; (*money, gifts*) Almosen *nt*.

charlady ['tʃɑ:leɪdɪ] (*irreg: like* **lady**) (*BRIT*) *n* Putzfrau *f*, Reinemachefrau *f*.

charlatan ['ʃɑ:lətən] *n* Scharlatan *m*.

charm [tʃɑ:m] *n* Charme *m*; (*to bring good luck*) Talisman *m*; (*on bracelet etc*) Anhänger *m* ♦ *vt* bezaubern.

charm bracelet *n* Armband *nt* mit Anhängern.

charming ['tʃɑ:mɪŋ] *adj* reizend, charmant; (*place*) bezaubernd.

chart [tʃɑ:t] *n* Schaubild *nt*, Diagramm *nt*; (*map*) Karte *f*; (*weather chart*) Wetterkarte *f* ♦ *vt* (*course*) planen; (*progress*) aufzeichnen; **charts** *npl* (*hit parade*) Hitliste *f*.

charter ['tʃɑ:tə*] *vt* chartern ♦ *n* Charta *f*; (*of university, company*) Gründungsurkunde *f*; **on** ~ gechartert.

chartered accountant ['tʃɑ:təd-] (*BRIT*) *n* Wirtschaftsprüfer(in) *m(f)*.

charter flight *n* Charterflug *m*.

charwoman ['tʃɑ:wʊmən] (*irreg: like* **woman**) *n* Putzfrau *f*, Reinemachefrau *f*.

chary ['tʃɛərɪ] *adj*: **to be** ~ **of doing sth** zögern, etw zu tun.

chase [tʃeɪs] *vt* jagen, verfolgen; (*also*: ~ **away**) wegjagen, vertreiben; (*business, job etc*) her sein hinter +*dat* (*inf*) ♦ *n* Verfolgungsjagd *f*.

▶ **chase down** (*US*) *vt* = **chase up**.

▶ **chase up** (*BRIT*) *vt* (*person*) rankriegen (*inf*); (*information*) ranschaffen (*inf*).

chasm ['kæzəm] *n* Kluft *f*.

chassis ['ʃæsɪ] *n* Fahrgestell *nt*.

chaste [tʃeɪst] *adj* keusch.

chastened ['tʃeɪsnd] *adj* zur Einsicht gebracht.

chastening ['tʃeɪsnɪŋ] *adj* ernüchternd.

chastise [tʃæs'taɪz] *vt* (*scold*) schelten.

chastity ['tʃæstɪtɪ] *n* Keuschheit *f*.

chat [tʃæt] *vi* (*also*: **have a** ~) plaudern, sich unterhalten ♦ *n* Plauderei *f*, Unterhaltung *f*.

▶ **chat up** (*BRIT: inf*) *vt* anmachen.

chatline ['tʃætlaɪn] *n* Telefondienst, der *Anrufern die Teilnahme an einer Gesprächsrunde ermöglicht.*

chat show (*BRIT*) *n* Talkshow *f*.
chattel ['tʃætl] *n*: **goods and ~s** *see* **good.**
chatter ['tʃætə*] *vi* schwatzen; (*monkey*)
schnattern; (*teeth*) klappern ♦ *n* (*see vi*)
Schwatzen *nt*; Schnattern *nt*; Klappern *nt*;
my teeth are ~ing mir klappern die Zähne.
chatterbox ['tʃætəbɔks] (*inf*) *n* Quasselstrippe
f.
chattering classes ['tʃætərɪŋ 'klɑːsɪz] *npl*: **the**
~ die intellektuellen Schwätzer *pl*.
chatty ['tʃætɪ] *adj* geschwätzig; (*letter*) im
Plauderton.
chauffeur ['ʃəʊfə*] *n* Chauffeur *m*, Fahrer *m*.
chauvinism ['ʃəʊvɪnɪzəm] *n* (*also*: **male ~**)
Chauvinismus *m*.
chauvinist ['ʃəʊvɪnɪst] *n* Chauvinist *m*.
chauvinistic [ʃəʊvɪ'nɪstɪk] *adj* chauvinistisch.
ChE *abbr* (= *chemical engineer*) *Titel für*
Chemotechniker.
cheap [tʃiːp] *adj* billig; (*reduced*) ermäßigt;
(*poor quality*) billig, minderwertig;
(*behaviour, joke*) ordinär ♦ *adv*: **to buy/sell**
sth ~ etw billig kaufen/verkaufen.
cheap day return *n* Tagesrückfahrkarte *f* (*zu*
einem günstigen Tarif).
cheapen ['tʃiːpn] *vt* entwürdigen.
cheaper ['tʃiːpə*] *adj* billiger.
cheaply ['tʃiːplɪ] *adv* billig.
cheat [tʃiːt] *vi* mogeln (*inf*), schummeln (*inf*)
♦ *n* Betrüger(in) *m(f)* ♦ *vt*: **to ~ sb (out of sth)**
jdn (um etw) betrügen; **to ~ on sb** (*inf*) jdn
betrügen.
cheating ['tʃiːtɪŋ] *n* Mogeln *nt* (*inf*),
Schummeln *nt* (*inf*).
check [tʃɛk] *vt* überprüfen; (*passport, ticket*)
kontrollieren; (*facts*) nachprüfen; (*enemy,*
disease) aufhalten; (*impulse*) unterdrücken;
(*person*) zurückhalten ♦ *vi* nachprüfen ♦ *n*
Kontrolle *f*, (*curb*) Beschränkung *f*; (*US*)
= **cheque**; (: *bill*) Rechnung *f*; (*pattern: gen pl*)
Karo(muster) *nt* ♦ *adj* kariert; **to ~ o.s.** sich
beherrschen; **to ~ with sb** bei jdm
nachfragen; **to keep a ~ on sb/sth** jdn/etw
kontrollieren.
▶ **check in** *vi* (*at hotel*) sich anmelden; (*at*
airport) einchecken ♦ *vt* (*luggage*) abfertigen
lassen.
▶ **check off** *vt* abhaken.
▶ **check out** *vi* (*of hotel*) abreisen ♦ *vt*
(*luggage*) abfertigen; (*investigate*)
überprüfen.
▶ **check up** *vi*: **to ~ up on sth** etw
überprüfen; **to ~ up on sb**
Nachforschungen über jdn anstellen.
checkered ['tʃɛkəd] (*US*) *adj* = **chequered.**
checkers ['tʃɛkəz] (*US*) *npl* Damespiel *nt*.
check guarantee card (*US*) *n* Scheckkarte *f*.
check-in (desk) ['tʃɛkɪn-] *n* (*at airport*)
Abfertigung *f*, Abfertigungsschalter *m*.
checking account ['tʃɛkɪŋ-] (*US*) *n* Girokonto
nt.
check list *n* Prüfliste *f*, Checkliste *f*.

checkmate ['tʃɛkmeɪt] *n* Schachmatt *nt*.
checkout ['tʃɛkaut] *n* Kasse *f*.
checkpoint ['tʃɛkpɔɪnt] *n* Kontrollpunkt *m*.
checkroom ['tʃɛkrum] (*US*) *n* (*left-luggage*
office) Gepäckaufbewahrung *f*.
checkup ['tʃɛkʌp] *n* Untersuchung *f*.
cheek [tʃiːk] *n* Backe *f*; (*impudence*) Frechheit
f; (*nerve*) Unverschämtheit *f*.
cheekbone ['tʃiːkbəun] *n* Backenknochen *m*.
cheeky ['tʃiːkɪ] *adj* frech.
cheep [tʃiːp] *vi* (*bird*) piep(s)en ♦ *n* Piep(s) *m*,
Piepser *m*.
cheer [tʃɪə*] *vt* zujubeln +*dat*; (*gladden*)
aufmuntern, aufheitern ♦ *vi* jubeln, hurra
rufen ♦ *n* (*gen pl*) Hurraruf *m*, Beifallsruf *m*;
cheers *npl* Hurrageschrei *nt*, Jubel *m*; **~s!**
prost!
▶ **cheer on** *vt* anspornen, anfeuern.
▶ **cheer up** *vi* vergnügter *or* fröhlicher
werden ♦ *vt* aufmuntern, aufheitern.
cheerful ['tʃɪəful] *adj* fröhlich.
cheerfulness ['tʃɪəfulnɪs] *n* Fröhlichkeit *f*.
cheerio [tʃɪərɪ'əu] (*BRIT*) *excl* tschüss (*inf*).
cheerleader ['tʃɪəliːdə*] *n jd, der bei*
Sportveranstaltungen etc die Zuschauer zu
Beifallsrufen anfeuert.
cheerless ['tʃɪəlɪs] *adj* freudlos, trüb; (*room*)
trostlos.
cheese [tʃiːz] *n* Käse *m*.
cheeseboard ['tʃiːzbɔːd] *n* Käsebrett *nt*; (*with*
cheese on it) Käseplatte *f*.
cheeseburger ['tʃiːzbəːgə*] *n* Cheeseburger
m.
cheesecake ['tʃiːzkeɪk] *n* Käsekuchen *m*.
cheetah ['tʃiːtə] *n* Gepard *m*.
chef [ʃɛf] *n* Küchenchef(in) *m(f)*.
chemical ['kɛmɪkl] *adj* chemisch ♦ *n*
Chemikalie *f*.
chemical engineering *n* Chemotechnik *f*.
chemist ['kɛmɪst] *n* (*BRIT: pharmacist*)
Apotheker(in) *m(f)*; (*scientist*) Chemiker(in)
m(f).
chemistry ['kɛmɪstrɪ] *n* Chemie *f*.
chemist's (shop) ['kɛmɪsts-] (*BRIT*) *n*
Drogerie *f*; (*also*: **dispensing chemist's**)
Apotheke *f*.
chemotherapy [kiːməu'θɛrəpɪ] *n*
Chemotherapie *f*.
cheque [tʃɛk] (*BRIT*) *n* Scheck *m*; **to pay by ~**
mit (einem) Scheck bezahlen.
chequebook ['tʃɛkbuk] *n* Scheckbuch *nt*.
cheque card (*BRIT*) *n* Scheckkarte *f*.
chequered, (*US*) **checkered** ['tʃɛkəd] *adj* (*fig*)
bewegt.
cherish ['tʃɛrɪʃ] *vt* (*person*) liebevoll sorgen
für; (*memory*) in Ehren halten; (*dream*) sich
hingeben +*dat*; (*hope*) hegen.
cheroot [ʃə'ruːt] *n* Stumpen *m*.
cherry ['tʃɛrɪ] *n* Kirsche *f*; (*also*: **~ tree**)
Kirschbaum *m*.
chervil ['tʃəːvɪl] *n* Kerbel *m*.
Ches. (*BRIT*) *abbr* (*POST*: = *Cheshire*).

chess [tʃɛs] n Schach(spiel) nt.
chessboard ['tʃɛsbɔːd] n Schachbrett nt.
chessman ['tʃɛsmən] (irreg: like **man**) n Schachfigur f.
chess player n Schachspieler(in) m(f).
chest [tʃɛst] n Brust f, Brustkorb m; (box) Kiste f, Truhe f; **to get sth off one's ~** (inf) sich dat etw von der Seele reden.
chest measurement n Brustweite f, Brustumfang m.
chestnut ['tʃɛsnʌt] n Kastanie f ♦ adj kastanienbraun.
chest of drawers n Kommode f.
chesty ['tʃɛstɪ] adj (cough) tief sitzend.
chew [tʃuː] vt kauen.
chewing gum ['tʃuːɪŋ-] n Kaugummi m.
chic [ʃiːk] adj schick, elegant.
chick [tʃɪk] n Küken nt; (inf: girl) Mieze f.
chicken ['tʃɪkɪn] n Huhn nt; (meat) Hähnchen nt; (inf: coward) Feigling m.
► **chicken out** (inf) vi: **to ~ out of doing sth** davor kneifen, etw zu tun.
chicken feed n (inf: money) ein paar Pfennige pl (HIST); (as salary) ein Hungerlohn m.
chickenpox ['tʃɪkɪnpɔks] n Windpocken pl.
chickpea ['tʃɪkpiː] n Kichererbse f.
chicory ['tʃɪkərɪ] n (in coffee) Zichorie f; (salad vegetable) Chicorée f or m, Schikoree f or m.
chide [tʃaɪd] vt: **to ~ sb (for)** jdn schelten (wegen).
chief [tʃiːf] n Häuptling m; (of organization, department) Leiter(in) m(f), Chef(in) m(f) ♦ adj Haupt-, wichtigste(r, s).
chief constable (BRIT) n Polizeipräsident m, Polizeichef m.
chief executive, (US) **chief executive officer** n Generaldirektor(in) m(f).
chiefly ['tʃiːflɪ] adv hauptsächlich.
Chief of Staff n Stabschef m.
chiffon ['ʃɪfɔn] n Chiffon m.
chilblain ['tʃɪlbleɪn] n Frostbeule f.
child [tʃaɪld] (pl **~ren**) n Kind nt; **do you have any ~ren?** haben Sie Kinder?
child benefit (BRIT) n Kindergeld nt.
childbirth ['tʃaɪldbəːθ] n Geburt f, Entbindung f.
childhood ['tʃaɪldhud] n Kindheit f.
childish ['tʃaɪldɪʃ] adj kindisch.
childless ['tʃaɪldlɪs] adj kinderlos.
childlike ['tʃaɪldlaɪk] adj kindlich.
child minder (BRIT) n Tagesmutter f.
child prodigy n Wunderkind nt.
children ['tʃɪldrən] npl of **child**.
children's home ['tʃɪldrənz-] n Kinderheim nt.
child's play ['tʃaɪldz-] n: **it was ~** es war ein Kinderspiel.
Chile ['tʃɪlɪ] n Chile nt.
Chilean ['tʃɪlɪən] adj chilenisch ♦ n Chilene m, Chilenin f.
chill [tʃɪl] n Kühle f; (illness) Erkältung f ♦ adj kühl; (fig: reminder) erschreckend ♦ vt

kühlen; (person) frösteln or frieren lassen; **"serve ~ed"** „gekühlt servieren".
chilli, (US) **chili** ['tʃɪlɪ] n Peperoni pl.
chilling ['tʃɪlɪn] adj (wind, morning) eisig; (fig: effect, prospect etc) beängstigend.
chill out (inf) vi sich entspannen, relaxen.
chilly ['tʃɪlɪ] adj kühl; (person, response, look) kühl, frostig; **to feel ~** frösteln, frieren.
chime [tʃaɪm] n Glockenspiel nt ♦ vi läuten.
chimney ['tʃɪmnɪ] n Schornstein m.
chimney sweep n Schornsteinfeger(in) m(f).
chimpanzee [tʃɪmpæn'ziː] n Schimpanse m.
chin [tʃɪn] n Kinn nt.
China ['tʃaɪnə] n China nt.
china ['tʃaɪnə] n Porzellan nt.
Chinese [tʃaɪ'niːz] adj chinesisch ♦ n inv Chinese m, Chinesin f; (LING) Chinesisch nt.
chink [tʃɪŋk] n (in door, wall etc) Ritze f, Spalt m; (of bottles etc) Klirren nt.
chintz [tʃɪnts] n Chintz m.
chinwag ['tʃɪnwæg] (BRIT: inf) n Schwatz m.
chip [tʃɪp] n (gen pl) Pommes frites pl; (US: also: **potato ~**) Chip m; (of wood) Span m; (of glass, stone) Splitter m; (in glass, cup etc) abgestoßene Stelle f; (in gambling) Chip m, Spielmarke f; (COMPUT: also: **microchip**) Chip m ♦ vt (cup, plate) anschlagen; **when the ~s are down** (fig) wenn es drauf ankommt.
► **chip in** (inf) vi (contribute) etwas beisteuern; (interrupt) sich einschalten.
chipboard ['tʃɪpbɔːd] n Spanplatte f.
chipmunk ['tʃɪpmʌŋk] n Backenhörnchen nt.
chippings ['tʃɪpɪŋz] npl: **loose ~** (on road) Schotter m.

CHIP SHOP

Chip shop, auch „fish-and-chip shop", ist die traditionelle britische Imbissbude, in der vor allem frittierte Fischfilets und Pommes frites, aber auch andere einfache Mahlzeiten angeboten werden. Früher wurde das Essen zum Mitnehmen in Zeitungspapier verpackt. Manche chip shops haben auch einen Essraum.

---

chiropodist [kɪ'rɔpədɪst] (BRIT) n Fußpfleger(in) m(f).
chiropody [kɪ'rɔpədɪ] (BRIT) n Fußpflege f.
chirp [tʃəːp] vi (bird) zwitschern; (crickets) zirpen.
chirpy ['tʃəːpɪ] (inf) adj munter.
chisel ['tʃɪzl] n (for stone) Meißel m; (for wood) Beitel m.
chit [tʃɪt] n Zettel m.
chitchat ['tʃɪttʃæt] n Plauderei f.
chivalrous ['ʃɪvəlrəs] adj ritterlich.
chivalry ['ʃɪvəlrɪ] n Ritterlichkeit f.
chives [tʃaɪvz] npl Schnittlauch m.
chloride ['klɔːraɪd] n Chlorid nt.
chlorinate ['klɔrɪneɪt] vt chloren.
chlorine ['klɔːriːn] n Chlor nt.
chock [tʃɔk] n Bremskeil m, Bremsklotz m.

chock-a-block ['tʃɔkə'blɔk] _adj_ gerammelt voll.

chock-full [tʃɔk'ful] _adj_ = **chock-a-block.**

chocolate ['tʃɔklɪt] _n_ Schokolade _f_; (_drink_) Kakao _m_, Schokolade _f_; (_sweet_) Praline _f_ ♦ _cpd_ Schokoladen-.

choice [tʃɔɪs] _n_ Auswahl _f_; (_option_) Möglichkeit _f_; (_preference_) Wahl _f_ ♦ _adj_ Qualitäts-, erstklassig; **I did it by** _or_ **from** ~ ich habe es mir so ausgesucht; **a wide** ~ eine große Auswahl.

choir ['kwaɪə*] _n_ Chor _m_.

choirboy ['kwaɪə'bɔɪ] _n_ Chorknabe _m_.

choke [tʃəuk] _vi_ ersticken; (_with smoke, dust, anger etc_) keine Luft mehr bekommen ♦ _vt_ erwürgen, erdrosseln ♦ _n_ (_AUT_) Choke _m_, Starterklappe _f_; **to be** ~**d (with)** verstopft sein (mit).

cholera ['kɔlərə] _n_ Cholera _f_.

cholesterol [kə'lestərɔl] _n_ Cholesterin _nt_.

choose [tʃuːz] (_pt_ **chose**, _pp_ **chosen**) _vt_ (aus)wählen; (_profession, friend_) sich _dat_ aussuchen ♦ _vi_: **to** ~ **between** wählen zwischen +_dat_, eine Wahl treffen zwischen +_dat_; **to** ~ **from** wählen aus _or_ unter +_dat_, eine Wahl treffen aus _or_ unter +_dat_; **to** ~ **to do sth** beschließen, etw zu tun.

choosy ['tʃuːzɪ] _adj_ wählerisch.

chop [tʃɔp] _vt_ (_wood_) hacken; (_also:_ ~ **up:** _vegetables, fruit, meat_) klein schneiden ♦ _n_ Kotelett _nt_; **chops** (_inf_) _npl_ (_of animal_) Maul _nt_; (_of person_) Mund _m_; **to get the** ~ (_BRIT: inf_: _project_) dem Rotstift zum Opfer fallen; (: _be sacked_) rausgeschmissen werden.

► **chop down** _vt_ (_tree_) fällen.

chopper ['tʃɔpə*] (_inf_) _n_ Hubschrauber _m_.

choppy ['tʃɔpɪ] _adj_ (_sea_) kabbelig, bewegt.

chopsticks ['tʃɔpstɪks] _npl_ Stäbchen _pl_.

choral ['kɔːrəl] _adj_ (_singing_) Chor-; (_society_) Gesang-.

chord [kɔːd] _n_ Akkord _m_; (_MATH_) Sehne _f_.

chore [tʃɔː*] _n_ Hausarbeit _f_; (_routine task_) lästige Routinearbeit _f_; **household** ~**s** Hausarbeit.

choreographer [kɔrɪ'ɔgrəfə*] _n_ Choreograf(in) _m(f)_.

choreography [kɔrɪ'ɔgrəfɪ] _n_ Choreografie _f_.

chorister ['kɔrɪstə*] _n_ Chorsänger(in) _m(f)_.

chortle ['tʃɔːtl] _vi_ glucksen.

chorus ['kɔːrəs] _n_ Chor _m_; (_refrain_) Refrain _m_; (_of complaints_) Flut _f_.

chose [tʃəuz] _pt of_ **choose.**

chosen ['tʃəuzn] _pp of_ **choose.**

chow [tʃau] _n_ Chow-Chow _m_.

chowder ['tʃaudə*] _n_ (sämige) Fischsuppe _f_.

Christ [kraɪst] _n_ Christus _m_.

christen ['krɪsn] _vt_ taufen.

christening ['krɪsnɪŋ] _n_ Taufe _f_.

Christian ['krɪstɪən] _adj_ christlich ♦ _n_ Christ(in) _m(f)_.

Christianity [krɪstɪ'ænɪtɪ] _n_ Christentum _nt_.

Christian name _n_ Vorname _m_.

Christmas ['krɪsməs] _n_ Weihnachten _nt_; **Happy** _or_ **Merry** ~! frohe _or_ fröhliche Weihnachten!

Christmas card _n_ Weihnachtskarte _f_.

Christmas Day _n_ der erste Weihnachtstag.

Christmas Eve _n_ Heiligabend _m_.

Christmas Island _n_ Weihnachtsinsel _f_.

Christmas tree _n_ Weihnachtsbaum _m_, Christbaum _m_.

chrome [krəum] _n_ = **chromium.**

chromium ['krəumɪəm] _n_ Chrom _nt_; (_also:_ ~ **plating**) Verchromung _f_.

chromosome ['krəuməsəum] _n_ Chromosom _nt_.

chronic ['krɔnɪk] _adj_ (_also fig_) chronisch; (_severe_) schlimm.

chronicle ['krɔnɪkl] _n_ Chronik _f_.

chronological [krɔnə'lɔdʒɪkl] _adj_ chronologisch.

chrysanthemum [krɪ'sænθəməm] _n_ Chrysantheme _f_.

chubby ['tʃʌbɪ] _adj_ pummelig; ~ **cheeks** Pausbacken _pl_.

chuck [tʃʌk] (_inf_) _vt_ werfen, schmeißen; (_BRIT_: _also_: ~ **up,** ~ **in**) (_job_) hinschmeißen; (: _person_) Schluss machen mit.

► **chuck out** _vt_ (_person_) rausschmeißen; (_rubbish etc_) wegschmeißen.

chuckle ['tʃʌkl] _vi_ leise in sich _acc_ hineinlachen.

chuffed [tʃʌft] (_BRIT: inf_) _adj_ vergnügt und zufrieden; (_flattered_) gebauchpinselt.

chug [tʃʌg] _vi_ (_also:_ ~ **along**) tuckern.

chum [tʃʌm] _n_ Kumpel _m_.

chump [tʃʌmp] (_inf_) _n_ Trottel _m_.

chunk [tʃʌŋk] _n_ großes Stück _nt_.

chunky ['tʃʌŋkɪ] _adj_ (_furniture etc_) klobig; (_person_) stämmig, untersetzt; (_knitwear_) dick.

church [tʃəːtʃ] _n_ Kirche _f_; **the C~ of England** die anglikanische Kirche.

churchyard ['tʃəːtʃjɑːd] _n_ Friedhof _m_.

churlish ['tʃəːlɪʃ] _adj_ griesgrämig; (_behaviour_) ungehobelt.

churn [tʃəːn] _n_ Butterfass _nt_; (_also:_ **milk** ~) Milchkanne _f_.

► **churn out** _vt_ am laufenden Band produzieren.

chute [ʃuːt] _n_ (_also:_ **rubbish** ~) Müllschlucker _m_; (_for coal, parcels etc_) Rutsche _f_; (_BRIT: slide_) Rutschbahn _f_, Rutsche _f_.

chutney ['tʃʌtnɪ] _n_ Chutney _nt_.

CIA (_US_) _n abbr_ (= _Central Intelligence Agency_) CIA _f or m_.

cicada [sɪ'kɑːdə] _n_ Zikade _f_.

CID (_BRIT_) _n abbr_ = **Criminal Investigation Department.**

cider ['saɪdə*] _n_ Apfelwein _m_.

c.i.f. _abbr_ (_COMM_: = _cost, insurance and freight_) cif.

cigar [sɪ'gɑː*] _n_ Zigarre _f_.

cigarette [sɪgə'ret] _n_ Zigarette _f_.

cigarette case n Zigarettenetui nt.
cigarette end n Zigarettenstummel m.
cigarette holder n Zigarettenspitze f.
C in C abbr (MIL) = **commander in chief**.
cinch [sɪntʃ] (inf) n: **it's a** ~ das ist ein
Kinderspiel or ein Klacks.
Cinderella [sɪndəˈrɛlə] n Aschenputtel nt,
Aschenbrödel nt.
cinders [ˈsɪndəz] npl Asche f.
cine camera [ˈsɪnɪ-] (BRIT) n
(Schmal)filmkamera f.
cine film (BRIT) n Schmalfilm m.
cinema [ˈsɪnəmə] n Kino nt; (film-making) Film
m.
cine projector (BRIT) n Filmprojektor m.
cinnamon [ˈsɪnəmən] n Zimt m.
cipher [ˈsaɪfəʳ] n (code) Chiffre f; (fig)
Niemand m; **in** ~ chiffriert.
circa [ˈsəːkə] prep zirka, circa.
circle [ˈsəːkl] n Kreis m; (in cinema, theatre)
Rang m ♦ vi kreisen ♦ vt kreisen um;
(surround) umgeben.
circuit [ˈsəːkɪt] n Runde f; (ELEC) Stromkreis
m; (track) Rennbahn f.
circuit board n Platine f, Leiterplatte f.
circuitous [səːˈkjuɪtəs] adj umständlich.
circular [ˈsəːkjuləʳ] adj rund; (route) Rund- ♦ n
(letter) Rundschreiben nt, Rundbrief m; (as
advertisement) Wurfsendung f; ~ **argument**
Zirkelschluss m.
circulate [ˈsəːkjuleɪt] vi (traffic) fließen; (blood,
report) zirkulieren; (news, rumour)
kursieren, in Umlauf sein; (person) die
Runde machen ♦ vt herumgehen or
zirkulieren lassen.
circulating capital [səːkjuˈleɪtɪŋ-] n (COMM)
flüssiges Kapital nt, Umlaufkapital nt.
circulation [səːkjuˈleɪʃən] n (of traffic) Fluss m;
(of air etc) Zirkulation f; (of newspaper)
Auflage f; (MED: of blood) Kreislauf m.
circumcise [ˈsəːkəmsaɪz] vt beschneiden.
circumference [səˈkʌmfərəns] n Umfang m;
(edge) Rand m.
circumflex [ˈsəːkəmflɛks] n (also: ~ **accent**)
Zirkumflex m.
circumscribe [ˈsəːkəmskraɪb] vt (MATH) einen
Kreis umbeschreiben; (fig) eingrenzen.
circumspect [ˈsəːkəmspɛkt] adj umsichtig.
circumstances [ˈsəːkəmstənsɪz] npl Umstände
pl; (financial condition) (finanzielle)
Verhältnisse pl; **in the** ~ unter diesen
Umständen; **under no** ~ unter (gar) keinen
Umständen, auf keinen Fall.
circumstantial [səːkəmˈstænʃl] adj
ausführlich; ~ **evidence** Indizienbeweis m.
circumvent [səːkəmˈvɛnt] vt umgehen.
circus [ˈsəːkəs] n Zirkus m; (also: **C**~: in place
names) Platz m.
cirrhosis [sɪˈrəusɪs] n (also: ~ **of the liver**)
Leberzirrhose f.
CIS n abbr (= Commonwealth of Independent
States) GUS f.

cissy [ˈsɪsɪ] n, adj see **sissy**.
cistern [ˈsɪstən] n Zisterne f; (of toilet)
Spülkasten m.
citation [saɪˈteɪʃən] n Zitat nt; (US)
Belobigung f; (LAW) Vorladung f (vor
Gericht).
cite [saɪt] vt zitieren; (example) anführen;
(LAW) vorladen.
citizen [ˈsɪtɪzn] n Staatsbürger(in) m(f); (of
town) Bürger(in) m(f).
Citizens' Advice Bureau [ˈsɪtɪznz-] n ≈
Bürgerberatungsstelle f.
citizenship [ˈsɪtɪznʃɪp] n Staatsbürgerschaft f;
(BRIT: SCOL) Gesellschaftskunde f.
citric acid [ˈsɪtrɪk-] n Zitronensäure f.
citrus fruit [ˈsɪtrəs-] n Zitrusfrucht f.
city [ˈsɪtɪ] n (Groß)stadt f; **the C**~ (FIN) die
City, das Londoner Banken- und
Börsenviertel.
city centre n Stadtzentrum nt, Innenstadt f.
City Hall n Rathaus nt; (US: municipal
government) Stadtverwaltung f.
civic [ˈsɪvɪk] adj (authorities etc) Stadt-,
städtisch; (duties, pride) Bürger-,
bürgerlich.
civic centre (BRIT) n Stadtverwaltung f.
civil [ˈsɪvɪl] adj (disturbances, rights) Bürger-;
(liberties, law) bürgerlich; (polite) höflich.
Civil Aviation Authority (BRIT) n Behörde f
für Zivilluftfahrt.
civil defence n Zivilschutz m.
civil disobedience n ziviler Ungehorsam m.
civil engineer n Bauingenieur(in) m(f).
civil engineering n Hoch- und Tiefbau m.
civilian [sɪˈvɪlɪən] adj (population) Zivil- ♦ n
Zivilist m; ~ **casualties** Verluste pl unter der
Zivilbevölkerung.
civilization [sɪvɪlaɪˈzeɪʃən] n Zivilisation f; (a
society) Kultur f.
civilized [ˈsɪvɪlaɪzd] adj zivilisiert; (person)
kultiviert; (place, experience) gepflegt.
civil law n Zivilrecht nt, bürgerliches Recht
nt.
civil liberties n (bürgerliche)
Freiheitsrechte pl.
civil rights npl Bürgerrechte pl.
civil servant n (Staats)beamter m,
(Staats)beamtin f.
Civil Service n Beamtenschaft f.
civil war n Bürgerkrieg m.
civvies [ˈsɪvɪz] (inf) npl Zivilklamotten pl.
cl abbr (= centilitre) cl.
clad [klæd] adj: ~ **(in)** gekleidet (in +acc).
claim [kleɪm] vt (assert) behaupten;
(responsibility) übernehmen; (credit) in
Anspruch nehmen; (rights, inheritance)
Anspruch erheben auf +acc; (expenses) sich
dat zurückerstatten lassen; (compensation,
damages) verlangen ♦ vi (for insurance)
Ansprüche geltend machen ♦ n (assertion)
Behauptung f; (for pension, wage rise,
compensation) Forderung f; (right: to

inheritance, land) Anspruch m; (for expenses)
Spesenabrechnung f; **(insurance)** ~
(Versicherungs)anspruch m; **to put in a**
~ **for** beantragen.
claimant ['kleimənt] n Antragsteller(in) m(f).
claim form n Antragsformular nt.
clairvoyant [klɛə'vɔɪənt] n Hellseher(in) m(f).
clam [klæm] n Venusmuschel f.
▶ **clam up** (inf) vi keinen Piep (mehr) sagen.
clamber ['klæmbə*] vi klettern.
clammy ['klæmɪ] adj feucht.
clamour, (US) **clamor** ['klæmə*] n Lärm m;
(protest) Protest m, Aufschrei m ♦ vi: **to** ~ **for**
schreien nach.
clamp [klæmp] n Schraubzwinge f, Klemme f
♦ vt (two things) zusammenklemmen; (one
thing on another) klemmen; (wheel) krallen.
▶ **clamp down on** vt fus rigoros vorgehen
gegen.
clampdown ['klæmpdaun] n: ~ **(on)** hartes
Durchgreifen nt (gegen).
clan [klæn] n Clan m.
clandestine [klæn'dɛstɪn] adj geheim,
Geheim-.
clang [klæŋ] vi klappern; (bell) läuten ♦ n (see
vi) Klappern nt; Läuten nt.
clanger ['klæŋə*] (BRIT: inf) n Fauxpas m; **to
drop a** ~ ins Fettnäpfchen treten.
clansman ['klænzmən] n (irreg: like **man**)
Clanmitglied nt.
clap [klæp] vi (Beifall) klatschen ♦ vt: **to**
~ **(one's hands)** (in die Hände) klatschen
♦ n: **a** ~ **of thunder** ein Donnerschlag m.
clapping ['klæpɪŋ] n Beifall m.
claptrap ['klæptræp] (inf) n Geschwafel nt.
claret ['klærət] n roter Bordeaux(wein) m.
clarification [klærɪfɪ'keɪʃən] n Klärung f.
clarify ['klærɪfaɪ] vt klären.
clarinet [klærɪ'nɛt] n Klarinette f.
clarity ['klærɪtɪ] n Klarheit f.
clash [klæʃ] n (fight) Zusammenstoß m;
(disagreement) Streit m, Auseinandersetzung
f; (of beliefs, ideas, views) Konflikt m; (of
colours, styles, personalities)
Unverträglichkeit f; (of events, dates,
appointments) Überschneidung f; (noise)
Klirren nt ♦ vi (fight) zusammenstoßen;
(disagree) sich streiten, eine
Auseinandersetzung haben; (beliefs, ideas,
views) aufeinander prallen; (colours) sich
beißen; (styles, personalities) nicht
zusammenpassen; (two events, dates,
appointments) sich überschneiden; (make
noise) klirrend aneinander schlagen.
clasp [klɑːsp] n Griff m; (embrace)
Umklammerung f; (of necklace, bag)
Verschluss m ♦ vt (er)greifen; (embrace)
umklammern.
class [klɑːs] n Klasse f; (lesson)
(Unterrichts)stunde f ♦ adj (struggle,
distinction) Klassen- ♦ vt einordnen,
einstufen.

class-conscious ['klɑːs'kɒnʃəs] adj
klassenbewusst, standesbewusst.
class-consciousness ['klɑːs'kɒnʃəsnɪs] n
Klassenbewusstsein nt, Standesbewusstsein
nt.
classic ['klæsɪk] adj klassisch ♦ n Klassiker m;
(race) bedeutendes Pferderennen für
dreijährige Pferde; **classics** npl (SCOL)
Altphilologie f.
classical ['klæsɪkl] adj klassisch.
classification [klæsɪfɪ'keɪʃən] n Klassifikation
f; (category) Klasse f; (system) Einteilung f.
classified ['klæsɪfaɪd] adj geheim.
classified advertisement n Kleinanzeige f.
classify ['klæsɪfaɪ] vt klassifizieren,
(ein)ordnen.
classless ['klɑːslɪs] adj: ~ **society** klassenlose
Gesellschaft f.
classmate ['klɑːsmeɪt] n Klassenkamerad(in)
m(f).
classroom ['klɑːsrum] n Klassenzimmer nt.
classroom assistant n Assistenzlehrkraft f.
classy ['klɑːsɪ] (inf) adj nobel, exklusiv;
(person) todschick.
clatter ['klætə*] n Klappern nt; (of hooves)
Trappeln nt ♦ vi (see n) klappern; trappeln.
clause [klɔːz] n (LAW) Klausel f; (LING) Satz m.
claustrophobia [klɔːstrə'fəubɪə] n
Klaustrophobie f, Platzangst f.
claustrophobic [klɔːstrə'fəubɪk] adj (place,
situation) beengend; (person): **to be/feel** ~
Platzangst haben/bekommen.
claw [klɔː] n Kralle f; (of lobster) Schere f,
Zange f.
▶ **claw at** vt fus sich krallen an +acc.
clay [kleɪ] n Ton m; (soil) Lehm m.
clean [kliːn] adj sauber; (fight) fair; (record,
reputation) einwandfrei; (joke, story)
stubenrein, anständig; (edge, MED: fracture)
glatt ♦ vt sauber machen; (car, hands, face
etc) waschen ♦ adv: **he** ~ **forgot** er hat es
glatt(weg) vergessen; **to have a** ~ **driving
licence** or (US) **record** keine Strafpunkte
haben; **to** ~ **one's teeth** (BRIT) sich dat die
Zähne putzen; **the thief got** ~ **away** der
Dieb konnte entkommen; **to come** ~ (inf)
auspacken.
▶ **clean off** vt abwaschen, abwischen.
▶ **clean out** vt gründlich sauber machen; (inf:
person) ausnehmen.
▶ **clean up** vt aufräumen; (child) sauber
machen; (fig) für Ordnung sorgen in +dat ♦ vi
aufräumen, sauber machen; (inf: make profit)
absahnen.
clean-cut ['kliːn'kʌt] adj gepflegt; (situation)
klar.
cleaner ['kliːnə*] n Raumpfleger(in) m(f);
(woman) Putzfrau f; (substance)
Reinigungsmittel nt, Putzmittel nt.
cleaner's ['kliːnəz] n (also: **dry** ~) Reinigung f.
cleaning ['kliːnɪŋ] n Putzen nt.
cleaning lady n Putzfrau f, Reinemache-

frau f.
cleanliness ['klɛnlɪnɪs] n Sauberkeit f,
Reinlichkeit f.
cleanly ['kliːnlɪ] adv sauber.
cleanse [klɛnz] vt (purify) läutern; (face, cut)
reinigen.
cleanser ['klɛnzə'] n (for face)
Reinigungscreme f, Reinigungsmilch f.
clean-shaven ['kliːn'ʃeɪvn] adj glatt rasiert.
cleansing department ['klɛnzɪŋ-] (BRIT) n ≈
Stadtreinigung f.
clean sweep n: **to make a ~** (SPORT) alle
Preise einstecken.
clean-up ['kliːnʌp] n: **to give sth a ~** etw
gründlich sauber machen.
clear [klɪə'] adj klar; (footprint) deutlich;
(photograph) scharf; (commitment)
eindeutig; (glass, plastic) durchsichtig; (road,
way, floor etc) frei; (conscience, skin) rein ♦ vt
(room) ausräumen; (trees) abholzen; (weeds
etc) entfernen; (slums etc, stock) räumen;
(LAW) freisprechen; (fence, wall)
überspringen; (cheque) verrechnen ♦ vi
(weather, sky) aufklaren; (fog, smoke) sich
auflösen; (room etc) sich leeren ♦ adv: **to be
~ of the ground** den Boden nicht berühren
♦ n: **to be in the ~** (out of debt) schuldenfrei
sein; (free of suspicion) von jedem Verdacht
frei sein; (out of danger) außer Gefahr sein;
~ profit Reingewinn m; **I have a ~ day
tomorrow** (BRIT) ich habe morgen nichts
vor; **to make o.s. ~** sich klar ausdrücken; **to
make it ~ to sb that ...** es jdm
(unmissverständlich) klarmachen, dass ...;
to ~ the table den Tisch abräumen; **to ~ a
space (for sth)** (für etw) Platz schaffen; **to
~ one's throat** sich räuspern; **to ~ a profit**
einen Gewinn machen; **to keep ~ of sb** jdm
aus dem Weg gehen; **to keep ~ of sth** etw
meiden; **to keep ~ of trouble** allem Ärger
aus dem Weg gehen.
▶ **clear off** (inf) vi abhauen, verschwinden.
▶ **clear up** vt aufräumen; (mystery)
aufklären; (problem) lösen ♦ vi (bad weather)
sich aufklären; (illness) sich bessern.
clearance ['klɪərəns] n (of slums) Räumung f;
(of trees) Abholzung f; (permission)
Genehmigung f; (free space) lichte Höhe f.
clearance sale n Räumungsverkauf m.
clear-cut ['klɪə'kʌt] adj klar.
clearing ['klɪərɪŋ] n Lichtung f; (BRIT:
BANKING) Clearing nt.
clearing bank (BRIT) n Clearingbank f.
clearing house n (COMM) Clearingstelle f.
clearly ['klɪəlɪ] adv klar; (obviously) eindeutig.
clearway ['klɪəweɪ] (BRIT) n Straße f mit
Halteverbot.
cleavage ['kliːvɪdʒ] n (of woman's breasts)
Dekolletee nt, Dekolleté nt.
cleaver ['kliːvə'] n Hackbeil nt.
clef [klɛf] n (Noten)schlüssel m.
cleft [klɛft] n Spalte f.

cleft palate n (MED) Gaumenspalte f.
clemency ['klɛmənsɪ] n Milde f.
clement ['klɛmənt] adj mild.
clench [klɛntʃ] vt (fist) ballen; (teeth)
zusammenbeißen.
clergy ['klɜːdʒɪ] n Klerus m, Geistlichkeit f.
clergyman ['klɜːdʒɪmən] (irreg: like **man**) n
Geistliche(r) m.
clerical ['klɛrɪkl] adj (job, worker) Büro-; (error)
Schreib-; (REL) geistlich.
clerk [klɑːk, (US) klɜːrk] n (BRIT)
Büroangestellte(r) f(m); (US: sales person)
Verkäufer(in) m(f).
Clerk of Court n Protokollführer(in) m(f).
clever ['klɛvə'] adj klug; (deft, crafty) schlau,
clever (inf); (device, arrangement) raffiniert.
cleverly ['klɛvəlɪ] adv geschickt.
clew [kluː] (US) n = **clue**.
cliché ['kliːʃeɪ] n Klischee nt.
click [klɪk] vi klicken ♦ vt: **to ~ one's tongue**
mit der Zunge schnalzen; **to ~ one's heels**
die Hacken zusammenschlagen.
client ['klaɪənt] n Kunde m, Kundin f; (of bank,
lawyer) Klient(in) m(f); (of restaurant) Gast m.
clientele [kliː[-ɑ]ːnˈtɛl] n Kundschaft f.
cliff [klɪf] n Kliff nt.
cliffhanger ['klɪfhæŋə'] n spannungsgeladene
Szene am Ende einer Filmepisode,
Cliffhanger m.
climactic [klaɪˈmæktɪk] adj: **~ point**
Höhepunkt m.
climate ['klaɪmɪt] n Klima nt.
climax ['klaɪmæks] n (also: **sexual**) Höhepunkt
m.
climb [klaɪm] vi klettern; (plane, sun, prices,
shares) steigen ♦ vt (stairs, ladder)
hochsteigen, hinaufsteigen; (tree) klettern
auf +acc; (hill) steigen auf +acc ♦ n Aufstieg
m; (of prices etc) Anstieg m; **to ~ over a wall/
into a car** über eine Mauer/in ein Auto
steigen or klettern.
▶ **climb down** (BRIT) vi (fig) nachgeben.
climb-down ['klaɪmdaun] n Nachgeben nt,
Rückzieher m (inf).
climber ['klaɪmə'] n Bergsteiger(in) m(f);
(plant) Kletterpflanze f.
climbing ['klaɪmɪŋ] n Bergsteigen nt.
clinch [klɪntʃ] vt (deal) perfekt machen;
(argument) zum Abschluss bringen.
clincher ['klɪntʃə'] n ausschlaggebender
Faktor m.
cling [klɪŋ] (pt, pp clung) vi: **to ~ to** (mother,
support) sich festklammern an +dat; (idea,
belief) festhalten an +dat; (subj: clothes, dress)
sich anschmiegen +dat.
clingfilm ['klɪŋfɪlm] n Frischhaltefolie f.
clinic ['klɪnɪk] n Klinik f; (session)
Sprechstunde f; (: SPORT) Trainingsstunde f.
clinical ['klɪnɪkl] adj klinisch; (fig) nüchtern,
kühl; (: building, room) steril.
clink [klɪŋk] vi klirren.
clip [klɪp] n (also: **paper ~**) Büroklammer f;

(*BRIT*: *also*: **bulldog** ~) Klammer *f*; (*holding wire, hose etc*) Klemme *f*; (*for hair*) Spange *f*; (*TV, CINE*) Ausschnitt *m* ♦ *vt* festklemmen; (*also*: ~ **together**) zusammenheften; (*cut*) schneiden.

clippers ['klɪpəz] *npl* (*for gardening*) Schere *f*; (*also*: **nail** ~) Nagelzange *f*.

clipping ['klɪpɪŋ] *n* (*from newspaper*) Ausschnitt *m*.

clique [kliːk] *n* Clique *f*, Gruppe *f*.

clitoris ['klɪtərɪs] *n* Klitoris *f*.

cloak [kləuk] *n* Umhang *m* ♦ *vt* (*fig*) hüllen.

cloakroom ['kləukrum] *n* Garderobe *f*; (*BRIT*: *WC*) Toilette *f*.

clobber ['klɔbə*] (*inf*) *n* Klamotten *pl* ♦ *vt* (*hit*) hauen, schlagen; (*defeat*) in die Pfanne hauen.

clock [klɔk] *n* Uhr *f*; **round the** ~ rund um die Uhr; **30,000 on the** ~ (*BRIT*: *AUT*) ein Tachostand von 30.000; **to work against the** ~ gegen die Uhr arbeiten.
► **clock in** (*BRIT*) *vi* (den Arbeitsbeginn) stempeln *or* stechen.
► **clock off** (*BRIT*) *vi* (das Arbeitsende) stempeln *or* stechen.
► **clock on** (*BRIT*) *vi* = **clock in**.
► **clock out** (*BRIT*) *vi* = **clock off**.
► **clock up** *vt* (*miles*) fahren; (*hours*) arbeiten.

clockwise ['klɔkwaɪz] *adv* im Uhrzeigersinn.

clockwork ['klɔkwəːk] *n* Uhrwerk *nt* ♦ *adj* aufziehbar, zum Aufziehen; **like** ~ wie am Schnürchen.

clog [klɔg] *n* Clog *m*; (*wooden*) Holzschuh *m* ♦ *vt* verstopfen ♦ *vi* (*also*: ~ **up**) verstopfen.

cloister ['klɔɪstə*] *n* Kreuzgang *m*.

clone [kləun] *n* Klon *m*.

close[1] [kləus] *adj* (*writing, friend, contact*) eng; (*texture*) dicht, fest; (*relative*) nahe; (*examination*) genau, gründlich; (*watch*) streng, scharf; (*contest*) knapp; (*weather*) schwül; (*room*) stickig ♦ *adv* nahe; ~ **(to)** nahe (+*gen*); ~ **to** in der Nähe +*gen*; ~ **by**, ~ **at hand** in der Nähe; **how** ~ **is Edinburgh to Glasgow?** wie weit ist Edinburgh von Glasgow entfernt?; **a** ~ **friend** ein guter *or* enger Freund; **to have a** ~ **shave** (*fig*) gerade noch davonkommen; **at** ~ **quarters** aus der Nähe.

close[2] [kləuz] *vt* schließen, zumachen; (*sale, deal, case*) abschließen; (*speech*) schließen, beenden ♦ *vi* schließen, zumachen; (*door, lid*) sich schließen, zugehen; (*end*) aufhören ♦ *n* Ende *nt*, Schlus *m*; **to bring sth to a** ~ etw beenden.
► **close down** *vi* (*factory*) stillgelegt werden; (*magazine etc*) eingestellt werden.
► **close in** *vi* (*night*) hereinbrechen; (*fog*) sich verdichten; **to** ~ **in on sb/sth** jdm/etw auf den Leib rücken; **the days are closing in** die Tage werden kürzer.
► **close off** *vt* (*area*) abriegeln; (*road*) sperren.

closed [kləuzd] *adj* geschlossen; (*road*) gesperrt.

closed-circuit television *n* Fernsehüberwachungsanlage *f*.

closed shop *n* Betrieb *m* mit Gewerkschaftszwang.

close-knit ['kləus'nɪt] *adj* eng zusammengewachsen.

closely ['kləuslɪ] *adv* (*examine, watch*) genau; (*connected*) eng; **we are** ~ **related** wir sind nah verwandt; **a** ~ **guarded secret** ein streng gehütetes Geheimnis.

close season ['kləus-] *n* Schonzeit *f*; (*SPORT*) Sommerpause *f*.

closet ['klɔzɪt] *n* Wandschrank *m*.

close-up ['kləusʌp] *n* Nahaufnahme *f*.

closing ['kləuzɪŋ] *adj* (*stages*) Schluss-; (*remarks*) abschließend.

closing price *n* (*STOCK EXCHANGE*) Schlusskurs *m*, Schlussnotierung *f*.

closing time (*BRIT*) *n* (*in pub*) Polizeistunde *f*, Sperrstunde *f*.

closure ['kləuʒə*] *n* (*of factory*) Stilllegung *f*; (*of magazine*) Einstellung *f*; (*of road*) Sperrung *f*; (*of border*) Schließung *f*.

clot [klɔt] *n* (*blood clot*) (Blut)gerinnsel *nt*; (*inf*: *idiot*) Trottel *m* ♦ *vi* gerinnen; (*external bleeding*) zum Stillstand kommen.

cloth [klɔθ] *n* (*material*) Stoff *m*, Tuch *nt*; (*rag*) Lappen *m*; (*BRIT*: *also*: **teacloth**) (Spül)tuch *nt*; (*also*: **tablecloth**) Tischtuch *nt*, Tischdecke *f*.

clothe [kləuð] *vt* anziehen, kleiden.

clothes [kləuðz] *npl* Kleidung *f*, Kleider *pl*; **to put one's** ~ **on** sich anziehen; **to take one's** ~ **off** sich ausziehen.

clothes brush *n* Kleiderbürste *f*.

clothesline ['kləuðzlaɪn] *n* Wäscheleine *f*.

clothes peg, (*US*) **clothes pin** *n* Wäscheklammer *f*.

clothing ['kləuðɪŋ] *n* = **clothes**.

clotted cream ['klɔtɪd-] (*BRIT*) *n* Sahne aus erhitzter Milch.

cloud [klaud] *n* Wolke *f* ♦ *vt* trüben; **every** ~ **has a silver lining** (*proverb*) auf Regen folgt Sonnenschein; **to** ~ **the issue** es unnötig kompliziert machen; (*deliberately*) die Angelegenheit verschleiern.
► **cloud over** *vi* (*sky*) sich bewölken, sich bedecken; (*face, eyes*) sich verfinstern.

cloudburst ['klaudbəːst] *n* Wolkenbruch *m*.

cloud-cuckoo-land [klaud'kuːkuːlænd] (*BRIT*) *n* Wolkenkuckucksheim *nt*.

cloudy ['klaudɪ] *adj* wolkig, bewölkt; (*liquid*) trüb.

clout [klaut] *vt* schlagen, hauen ♦ *n* (*fig*) Schlagkraft *f*.

clove [kləuv] *n* Gewürznelke *f*; ~ **of garlic** Knoblauchzehe *f*.

clover ['kləuvə*] *n* Klee *m*.

cloverleaf ['kləuvəliːf] *n* Kleeblatt *nt*.

clown [klaun] *n* Clown *m* ♦ *vi* (*also*: ~ **about**, ~ **around**) herumblödeln, herumkaspern.

cloying ['klɔɪɪŋ] adj süßlich.

club [klʌb] n Klub m, Verein m; (weapon) Keule f, Knüppel m; (also: **golf** ~: object) Golfschläger m ♦ vt knüppeln ♦ vi: **to** ~ **together** zusammenlegen; **clubs** npl (CARDS) Kreuz nt.

club car (US) n Speisewagen m.

club class n Club-Klasse f, Businessklasse f.

clubhouse ['klʌbhaus] n Klubhaus nt.

club soda (US) n (soda water) Sodawasser nt.

cluck [klʌk] vi glucken.

clue [kluː] n Hinweis m, Anhaltspunkt m; (in crossword) Frage f; **I haven't a** ~ ich habe keine Ahnung.

clued-up ['kluːdʌp], (US: inf) **clued in** adj: **to be** ~ **on sth** über etw acc im Bilde sein.

clueless ['kluːlɪs] adj ahnungslos, unbedarft.

clump [klʌmp] n Gruppe f.

clumsy ['klʌmzɪ] adj ungeschickt; (object) unförmig; (effort, attempt) plump.

clung [klʌŋ] pt, pp of cling.

cluster ['klʌstə*] n Gruppe f ♦ vi (people) sich scharen; (houses) sich drängen.

clutch [klʌtʃ] n Griff m; (AUT) Kupplung f ♦ vt (purse, hand) umklammern; (stick) sich festklammern an +dat ♦ vi: **to** ~ **at** sich klammern an +acc.

clutter ['klʌtə*] vt (also: ~ **up**: room) voll stopfen; (: table) voll stellen ♦ n Kram m (inf).

CM (US) abbr (POST: = North Mariana Islands).

cm abbr (= centimetre) cm.

CNAA (BRIT) n abbr (= Council for National Academic Awards) Zentralstelle zur Vergabe von Qualifikationsnachweisen.

CND n abbr (= Campaign for Nuclear Disarmament) Organisation für atomare Abrüstung.

CO n abbr = **commanding officer**; (BRIT: = Commonwealth Office) Regierungsstelle für Angelegenheiten des Commonwealth ♦ abbr (US: POST: = Colorado).

Co. abbr = **company, county**.

c/o abbr (= care of) bei, c/o.

coach [kəutʃ] n (Reise)bus m; (horse-drawn) Kutsche f; (of train) Wagen m; (SPORT) Trainer m; (SCOL) Nachhilfelehrer(in) m(f) ♦ vt trainieren; (student) Nachhilfeunterricht geben +dat.

coach trip n Busfahrt f.

coagulate [kəu'ægjuleɪt] vi (blood) gerinnen; (paint etc) eindicken ♦ vt (blood) gerinnen lassen; (paint) dick werden lassen.

coal [kəul] n Kohle f.

coalface ['kəulfeɪs] n Streb m.

coalfield ['kəulfiːld] n Kohlenrevier nt.

coalition [kəuə'lɪʃən] n (POL) Koalition f; (of pressure groups etc) Zusammenschluss m.

coalman ['kəulmən] (irreg: like man) n Kohlenhändler m.

coal merchant n = **coalman**.

coal mine n Kohlenbergwerk nt, Zeche f.

coal miner n Bergmann m, Kumpel m (inf).

coal mining n (Kohlen)bergbau m.

coarse [kɔːs] adj (texture) grob; (vulgar) gewöhnlich, derb; (salt, sand etc) grobkörnig.

coast [kəust] n Küste f ♦ vi (im Leerlauf) fahren.

coastal ['kəustl] adj Küsten-.

coaster ['kəustə*] n (NAUT) Küstenfahrzeug nt; (for glass) Untersetzer m.

coastguard ['kəustgɑːd] n (officer) Küstenwächter m; (service) Küstenwacht f.

coastline ['kəustlaɪn] n Küste f.

coat [kəut] n Mantel m; (of animal) Fell nt; (layer) Schicht f; (: of paint) Anstrich m ♦ vt überziehen.

coat hanger n Kleiderbügel m.

coating ['kəutɪŋ] n (of chocolate etc) Überzug m; (of dust etc) Schicht f.

coat of arms n Wappen nt.

coauthor ['kəu'ɔːθə*] n Mitautor(in) m(f), Mitverfasser(in) m(f).

coax [kəuks] vt (person) überreden.

cob [kɔb] n see **corn**.

cobbler ['kɔblə*] n Schuster m.

cobbles ['kɔblz] npl Kopfsteinpflaster nt.

cobblestones ['kɔblstəunz] npl = **cobbles**.

COBOL ['kəubɔl] n COBOL nt.

cobra ['kəubrə] n Kobra f.

cobweb ['kɔbwɛb] n Spinnennetz nt.

cocaine [kə'keɪn] n Kokain nt.

cock [kɔk] n Hahn m; (male bird) Männchen nt ♦ vt (gun) entsichern; **to** ~ **one's ears** (fig) die Ohren spitzen.

cock-a-hoop [kɔkə'huːp] adj ganz aus dem Häuschen.

cockerel ['kɔkərl] n junger Hahn m.

cock-eyed ['kɔkaɪd] adj (fig) verrückt, widersinnig.

cockle ['kɔkl] n Herzmuschel f.

cockney ['kɔknɪ] n Cockney m, echter Londoner m; (LING) Cockney nt.

cockpit ['kɔkpɪt] n Cockpit nt.

cockroach ['kɔkrəutʃ] n Küchenschabe f, Kakerlak m.

cocktail ['kɔkteɪl] n Cocktail m; **fruit** ~ Obstsalat m; **prawn** ~ Krabbencocktail m.

cocktail cabinet n Hausbar f.

cocktail party n Cocktailparty f.

cocktail shaker [-'ʃeɪkə*] n Mixbecher m.

cock-up ['kɔkʌp] (inf!) n Schlamassel m.

cocky ['kɔkɪ] adj großspurig.

cocoa ['kəukəu] n Kakao m.

coconut ['kəukənʌt] n Kokosnuss f.

cocoon [kə'kuːn] n Puppe f, Kokon m; (fig) schützende Umgebung f.

COD abbr (BRIT) = **cash on delivery**; (US) = **collect on delivery**.

cod [kɔd] n Kabeljau m.

code [kəud] n (cipher) Chiffre f; (dialling code) Vorwahl f; (post code) Postleitzahl f; ~ **of behaviour** Sittenkodex m; ~ **of practice**

Verfahrensregeln *pl.*
codeine ['kəʊdiːn] *n* Kodein *nt.*
codger ['kɒdʒə*] (*inf*) *n*: **old ~** komischer Kauz *m.*
codicil ['kɒdɪsɪl] *n* (*LAW*) Kodizill *nt.*
codify ['kəʊdɪfaɪ] *vt* kodifizieren.
cod-liver oil ['kɒdlɪvə-] *n* Lebertran *m.*
co-driver ['kəʊ'draɪvə*] *n* Beifahrer(in) *m(f).*
co-ed ['kəʊ'ɛd] (*SCOL*) *adj abbr* = **coeducational**
♦ *n abbr* (*US: female pupil/student*) Schülerin/ Studentin an einer gemischten Schule/ Universität; (*BRIT: school*) gemischte Schule *f.*
coeducational ['kəʊɛdju'keɪʃənl] *adj* (*school*) Koedukations-, gemischt.
coerce [kəʊ'əːs] *vt* zwingen.
coercion [kəʊ'əːʃən] *n* Zwang *m.*
coexistence ['kəʊɪg'zɪstəns] *n* Koexistenz *f.*
C of C *n abbr* = **chamber of commerce.**
C of E *abbr* = **Church of England.**
coffee ['kɒfɪ] *n* Kaffee *m*; **black ~** schwarzer Kaffee *m*; **white ~** Kaffee mit Milch; **~ with cream** Kaffee mit Sahne.
coffee bar (*BRIT*) *n* Café *nt.*
coffee bean *n* Kaffeebohne *f.*
coffee break *n* Kaffeepause *f.*
coffee cake (*US*) *n* Kuchen *m* zum Kaffee.
coffee cup *n* Kaffeetasse *f.*
coffeepot ['kɒfɪpɒt] *n* Kaffeekanne *f.*
coffee table *n* Couchtisch *m.*
coffin ['kɒfɪn] *n* Sarg *m.*
C of I *abbr* (= *Church of Ireland*) anglikanische Kirche Irlands.
C of S *abbr* (= *Church of Scotland*) presbyterianische Kirche in Schottland.
cog [kɒg] *n* (*wheel*) Zahnrad *nt*; (*tooth*) Zahn *m.*
cogent ['kəʊdʒənt] *adj* stichhaltig, zwingend.
cognac ['kɒnjæk] *n* Kognak *m.*
cogwheel ['kɒgwiːl] *n* Zahnrad *nt.*
cohabit [kəʊ'hæbɪt] *vi* (*formal*) in eheähnlicher Gemeinschaft leben; **to ~ (with sb)** (mit jdm) zusammenleben.
coherent [kəʊ'hɪərənt] *adj* (*speech*) zusammenhängend; (*answer, theory*) schlüssig; (*person*) bei klarem Verstand.
cohesion [kəʊ'hiːʒən] *n* Geschlossenheit *f.*
cohesive [kəʊ'hiːsɪv] *adj* geschlossen.
coil [kɔɪl] *n* Rolle *f*; (*one loop*) Windung *f*; (*of smoke*) Kringel *m*; (*AUT, ELEC*) Spule *f*; (*contraceptive*) Spirale *f* ♦ *vt* aufrollen, aufwickeln.
coin [kɔɪn] *n* Münze *f* ♦ *vt* prägen.
coinage ['kɔɪnɪdʒ] *n* Münzen *pl*; (*LING*) Prägung *f.*
coin box (*BRIT*) *n* Münzfernsprecher *m.*
coincide [kəʊɪn'saɪd] *vi* (*events*) zusammenfallen; (*ideas, views*) übereinstimmen.
coincidence [kəʊ'ɪnsɪdəns] *n* Zufall *m.*
coin-operated ['kɔɪn'ɒpəreɪtɪd] *adj* Münz-.
Coke ® [kəʊk] *n* Coca-Cola ® *nt or f*, Coke ® *nt.*
coke [kəʊk] *n* Koks *m.*

Col. *abbr* = **colonel.**
COLA (*US*) *n abbr* (= *cost-of-living adjustment*) Anpassung der Löhne und Gehälter an steigende Lebenshaltungskosten.
colander ['kɒləndə*] *n* Durchschlag *m.*
cold [kəʊld] *adj* kalt; (*unemotional*) kalt, kühl ♦ *n* Kälte *f*; (*MED*) Erkältung *f*; **it's ~** es ist kalt; **to be/feel ~** (*person*) frieren; (*object*) kalt sein; **in ~ blood** kaltblütig; **to have ~ feet** (*fig*) kalte Füße bekommen; **to give sb the ~ shoulder** jdm die kalte Schulter zeigen; **to catch ~, to catch a ~** sich erkälten.
cold-blooded ['kəʊld'blʌdɪd] *adj* kaltblütig.
cold calling *n* (*COMM: on phone*) unaufgeforderte Telefonwerbung; (: *visit*) unaufgeforderter Vertreterbesuch.
cold cream *n* (halbfette) Feuchtigkeitscreme *f.*
coldly ['kəʊldlɪ] *adv* kalt, kühl.
cold-shoulder [kəʊld'ʃəʊldə*] *vt* die kalte Schulter zeigen +*dat.*
cold sore *n* Bläschenausschlag *m.*
cold sweat *n*: **to come out in a ~ (about sth)** (wegen etw) in kalten Schweiß ausbrechen.
cold turkey *n*: **to do ~** Totalentzug machen.
Cold War *n*: **the ~** der Kalte Krieg.
coleslaw ['kəʊlslɔː] *n* Krautsalat *m.*
colic ['kɒlɪk] *n* Kolik *f.*
colicky ['kɒlɪkɪ] *adj*: **to be ~** Kolik *f or* Leibschmerzen *pl* haben.
collaborate [kə'læbəreɪt] *vi* zusammenarbeiten; (*with enemy*) kollaborieren.
collaboration [kəlæbə'reɪʃən] *n* (*see vb*) Zusammenarbeit *f*; Kollaboration *f.*
collaborator [kə'læbəreɪtə*] *n* (*see vb*) Mitarbeiter(in) *m(f)*; Kollaborateur(in) *m(f).*
collage [kɒ'lɑːʒ] *n* Collage *f.*
collagen ['kɒlədʒən] *n* Kollagen *nt.*
collapse [kə'læps] *vi* zusammenbrechen; (*building*) einstürzen; (*plans*) scheitern; (*government*) stürzen ♦ *n* (*see vb*) Zusammenbruch *m*; Einsturz *m*; Scheitern *nt*; Sturz *m.*
collapsible [kə'læpsəbl] *adj* Klapp-, zusammenklappbar.
collar ['kɒlə*] *n* Kragen *m*; (*of dog, cat*) Halsband *nt*; (*TECH*) Bund *m* ♦ *vt* (*inf*) schnappen.
collarbone ['kɒləbəʊn] *n* Schlüsselbein *nt.*
collate [kə'leɪt] *vt* vergleichen.
collateral [kə'lætərl] *n* (*COMM*) (zusätzliche) Sicherheit *f.*
collateral damage *n* (*MIL*) Schäden *pl* in Wohngebieten; (: *casualties*) Opfer *pl* unter der Zivilbevölkerung.
collation [kə'leɪʃən] *n* Vergleich *m*; (*CULIN*): **a cold ~** ein kalter Imbiss *m.*
colleague ['kɒliːg] *n* Kollege *m*, Kollegin *f.*
collect [kə'lɛkt] *vt* sammeln; (*mail, BRIT: fetch*) abholen; (*debts*) eintreiben; (*taxes*)

einziehen ♦ *vi* sich ansammeln ♦ *adv* (*US: TEL*): **to call** ~ ein R-Gespräch führen; **to ~ one's thoughts** seine Gedanken ordnen, sich sammeln; ~ **on delivery** (*US: COMM*) per Nachnahme.

collected [kə'lɛktɪd] *adj*: ~ **works** gesammelte Werke *pl*.

collection [kə'lɛkʃən] *n* Sammlung *f*, (*from place, person, of mail*) Abholung *f*; (*in church*) Kollekte *f*.

collective [kə'lɛktɪv] *adj* kollektiv, gemeinsam ♦ *n* Kollektiv *nt*; ~ **farm** landwirtschaftliche Produktionsgenossenschaft *f*.

collective bargaining *n* Tarifverhandlungen *pl*.

collector [kə'lɛktə°] *n* Sammler(in) *m(f)*; (*of taxes etc*) Einnehmer(in) *m(f)*; (*of rent, cash*) Kassierer(in) *m(f)*; ~'**s item** *or* **piece** Sammlerstück *nt*, Liebhaberstück *nt*.

college ['kɔlɪdʒ] *n* College *nt*; (*of agriculture, technology*) Fachhochschule *f*; **to go to** ~ studieren; ~ **of education** pädagogische Hochschule *f*.

collide [kə'laɪd] *vi*: **to** ~ **(with)** zusammenstoßen (mit); (*fig: clash*) eine heftige Auseinandersetzung haben (mit).

collie ['kɔlɪ] *n* Collie *m*.

colliery ['kɔlɪərɪ] (*BRIT*) *n* (Kohlen)bergwerk *nt*, Zeche *f*.

collision [kə'lɪʒən] *n* Zusammenstoß *m*; **to be on a** ~ **course** (*also fig*) auf Kollisionskurs sein.

collision damage waiver *n* (*INSURANCE*) Verzicht auf Haftungsbeschränkung bei Unfällen mit Mietwagen.

colloquial [kə'ləukwɪəl] *adj* umgangssprachlich.

collusion [kə'luːʒən] *n* (geheime) Absprache *f*; **to be in** ~ **with** gemeinsame Sache machen mit.

Colo. (*US*) *abbr* (*POST*: = *Colorado*).

Cologne [kə'ləun] *n* Köln *nt*.

cologne [kə'ləun] *n* (*also*: **eau de** ~) Kölnischwasser *nt*, Eau de Cologne *nt*.

Colombia [kə'lɔmbɪə] *n* Kolumbien *nt*.

Colombian [kə'lɔmbɪən] *adj* kolumbianisch ♦ *n* Kolumbianer(in) *m(f)*.

colon ['kəulən] *n* Doppelpunkt *m*; (*ANAT*) Dickdarm *m*.

colonel ['kɔːnl] *n* Oberst *m*.

colonial [kə'ləunɪəl] *adj* Kolonial-.

colonize ['kɔlənaɪz] *vt* kolonisieren.

colony ['kɔlənɪ] *n* Kolonie *f*.

color *etc* ['kʌlə°] (*US*) = **colour** *etc*.

Colorado beetle [kɔlə'rɑːdəu-] *n* Kartoffelkäfer *m*.

colossal [kə'lɔsl] *adj* riesig, kolossal.

colour, (*US*) **color** ['kʌlə°] *n* Farbe *f*; (*skin colour*) Hautfarbe *f*; (*of spectacle etc*) Atmosphäre *f* ♦ *vt* bemalen; (*with crayons*) ausmalen; (*dye*) färben; (*fig*) beeinflussen ♦ *vi* (*blush*) erröten, rot werden ♦ *cpd* Farb-;

colours *npl* (*of party, club etc*) Farben *pl*; **in** ~ (*film*) in Farbe; (*illustrations*) bunt.

▶ **colour in** *vt* ausmalen.

colour bar *n* Rassenschranke *f*.

colour-blind ['kʌləblaɪnd] *adj* farbenblind.

coloured ['kʌləd] *adj* farbig; (*photo*) Farb-; (*illustration etc*) bunt.

colour film *n* Farbfilm *m*.

colourful ['kʌləful] *adj* bunt; (*account, story*) farbig, anschaulich; (*personality*) schillernd.

colouring ['kʌlərɪŋ] *n* Gesichtsfarbe *f*, Teint *m*; (*in food*) Farbstoff *m*.

colour scheme *n* Farbzusammenstellung *f*.

colour supplement (*BRIT*) *n* Farbbeilage *f*, Magazin *nt*.

colour television *n* Farbfernsehen *nt*; (*set*) Farbfernseher *m*.

colt [kəult] *n* Hengstfohlen *nt*.

column ['kɔləm] *n* Säule *f*; (*of people*) Kolonne *f*; (*of print*) Spalte *f*; (*gossip/sports column*) Kolumne *f*; **the editorial** ~ der Leitartikel.

columnist ['kɔləmnɪst] *n* Kolumnist(in) *m(f)*.

coma ['kəumə] *n* Koma *nt*; **to be in a** ~ im Koma liegen.

comb [kəum] *n* Kamm *m* ♦ *vt* kämmen; (*area*) durchkämmen.

combat ['kɔmbæt] *n* Kampf *m* ♦ *vt* bekämpfen.

combination [kɔmbɪ'neɪʃən] *n* Kombination *f*.

combination lock *n* Kombinationsschloss *nt*.

combine [*vti* kəm'baɪn, *n* 'kɔmbaɪn] *vt* verbinden ♦ *vi* sich zusammenschließen; (*CHEM*) sich verbinden ♦ *n* Konzern *m*; (*AGR*) = **combine harvester** ~**d effort** vereintes Unternehmen.

combine harvester *n* Mähdrescher *m*.

combo ['kɔmbəu] *n* Combo *f*.

combustible [kəm'bʌstɪbl] *adj* brennbar.

combustion [kəm'bʌstʃən] *n* Verbrennung *f*.

════════════════════════ *KEYWORD*

come [kʌm] (*pt* **came**, *pp* **come**) *vi* **1** (*movement towards*) kommen; ~ **with me** kommen Sie mit mir; **to** ~ **running** angelaufen kommen; **coming!** ich komme!

2 (*arrive*) kommen; **they came to a river** sie kamen an einen Fluss; **to** ~ **home** nach Hause kommen.

3 (*reach*): **to** ~ **to** kommen an +*acc*; **her hair came to her waist** ihr Haar reichte ihr bis zur Hüfte; **to** ~ **to a decision** zu einer Entscheidung kommen.

4 (*occur*): **an idea came to me** mir kam eine Idee.

5 (*be, become*) werden; **I've** ~ **to like him** mittlerweile mag ich ihn; **if it** ~**s to it** wenn es darauf ankommt.

▶ **come about** *vi* geschehen.

▶ **come across** *vt fus* (*find: person, thing*) stoßen auf +*acc* ♦ *vi*: **to** ~ **across well/badly** (*idea etc*) gut/schlecht ankommen; (*meaning*) gut/schlecht verstanden werden.

▶ **come along** *vi* (*arrive*) daherkommen;

(*make progress*) vorankommen; ~ **along!** komm schon!

▶ **come apart** *vi* (*break in pieces*) auseinander gehen.

▶ **come away** *vi* (*leave*) weggehen; (*become detached*) abgehen.

▶ **come back** *vi* (*return*) zurückkommen;: **to ~ back into fashion** wieder in Mode kommen.

▶ **come by** *vt fus* (*acquire*) kommen zu.

▶ **come down** *vi* (*price*) sinken, fallen; (*building: be demolished*) abgerissen werden; (*tree: during storm*) umstürzen.

▶ **come forward** *vi* (*volunteer*) sich melden.

▶ **come from** *vt fus* kommen von, stammen aus; (*person*) kommen aus.

▶ **come in** *vi* (*enter*) hereinkommen; (*report, news*) eintreffen; (*on deal etc*) sich beteiligen; ~ **in!** herein!

▶ **come in for** *vt fus* (*criticism etc*) einstecken müssen.

▶ **come into** *vt fus* (*inherit: money*) erben; **to ~ into fashion** in Mode kommen; **money doesn't ~ into it** Geld hat nichts damit zu tun.

▶ **come off** *vi* (*become detached: button, handle*) sich lösen; (*succeed: attempt, plan*) klappen ♦ *vt fus* (*inf*): ~ **off it!** mach mal halblang!

▶ **come on** *vi* (*pupil, work, project*) vorankommen; (*lights etc*) angehen; ~ **on!** (*hurry up*) mach schon!; (*giving encouragement*) los!

▶ **come out** *vi* herauskommen; (*stain*) herausgehen; **to ~ out (on strike)** in den Streik treten.

▶ **come over** *vt fus*: **I don't know what's ~ over him!** ich weiß nicht, was in ihn gefahren ist.

▶ **come round** *vi* (*after faint, operation*) wieder zu sich kommen; (*visit*) vorbeikommen; (*agree*) zustimmen.

▶ **come through** *vi* (*survive*) durchkommen; (*telephone call*) (durch)kommen ♦ *vt fus* (*illness etc*) überstehen.

▶ **come to** *vi* (*regain consciousness*) wieder zu sich kommen ♦ *vt fus* (*add up to*): **how much does it ~ to?** was macht das zusammen?

▶ **come under** *vt fus* (*heading*) kommen unter +*acc*; (*criticism, pressure, attack*) geraten unter +*acc*.

▶ **come up** *vi* (*approach*) herankommen; (*sun*) aufgehen; (*problem*) auftauchen; (*event*) bevorstehen; (*in conversation*) genannt werden; **something's come up** etwas ist dazwischengekommen.

▶ **come up against** *vt fus* (*resistance, difficulties*) stoßen auf +*acc*.

▶ **come upon** *vt fus* (*find*) stoßen auf +*acc*.

▶ **come up to** *vt fus*: **the film didn't come up to our expectations** der Film entsprach

nicht unseren Erwartungen; **it's coming up to 10 o'clock** es ist gleich 10 Uhr.

▶ **come up with** *vt fus* (*idea*) aufwarten mit; (*money*) aufbringen.

comeback ['kʌmbæk] *n* (*of film star etc*) Come-back *nt*, Comeback *nt*; (*reaction, response*) Reaktion *f*.

Comecon ['kɔmɪkɔn] *n abbr* (= *Council for Mutual Economic Assistance*) Comecon *m*.

comedian [kə'miːdɪən] *n* Komiker *m*.

comedienne [kəmiːdɪ'ɛn] *n* Komikerin *f*.

comedown ['kʌmdaʊn] (*inf*) *n* Enttäuschung *f*; (*professional*) Abstieg *m*.

comedy ['kɔmɪdɪ] *n* Komödie *f*; (*humour*) Witz *m*.

comet ['kɔmɪt] *n* Komet *m*.

comeuppance [kʌm'ʌpəns] *n*: **to get one's ~** die Quittung bekommen.

comfort ['kʌmfət] *n* (*physical*) Behaglichkeit *f*; (*material*) Komfort *m*; (*solace, relief*) Trost *m* ♦ *vt* trösten; **comforts** *npl* (*of home etc*) Komfort *m*, Annehmlichkeiten *pl*.

comfortable ['kʌmfətəbl] *adj* bequem; (*room*) komfortabel; (*walk, climb etc*) geruhsam; (*income*) ausreichend; (*majority*) sicher; **to be ~** (*physically*) sich wohl fühlen; (*financially*) sehr angenehm leben; **the patient is ~** dem Patienten geht es den Umständen entsprechend gut; **I don't feel very ~ about it** mir ist nicht ganz wohl bei der Sache.

comfortably ['kʌmfətəblɪ] *adv* (*sit*) bequem; (*live*) angenehm.

comforter ['kʌmfətə*] (*US*) *n* Schnuller *m*.

comfort station (*US*) *n* öffentliche Toilette *f*.

comic ['kɔmɪk] *adj* (*also*: ~**al**) komisch ♦ *n* Komiker(in) *m(f)*; (*BRIT: magazine*) Comicheft *nt*.

comical ['kɔmɪkl] *adj* komisch.

comic strip *n* Comicstrip *m*.

coming ['kʌmɪŋ] *n* Ankunft *f*, Kommen *nt* ♦ *adj* kommend; (*next*) nächste(r, s); **in the ~ weeks** in den nächsten Wochen.

coming(s) and going(s) *n(pl)* Kommen und Gehen *nt*.

Comintern ['kɔmɪntəːn] *n* (*POL*) Komintern *f*.

comma ['kɔmə] *n* Komma *nt*.

command [kə'maːnd] *n* (*also COMPUT*) Befehl *m*; (*control, charge*) Führung *f*; (*MIL: authority*) Kommando *nt*, Befehlsgewalt *f*; (*mastery*) Beherrschung *f* ♦ *vt* (*troops*) befehligen, kommandieren; (*be able to get*) verfügen über +*acc*; (*deserve: respect, admiration etc*) verdient haben; **to be in ~ of** das Kommando *or* den (Ober)befehl haben über +*acc*; **to have ~ of** das Kommando haben über +*acc*; **to take ~ of** das Kommando übernehmen +*gen*; **to have at one's ~** verfügen über +*acc*; **to ~ sb to do sth** jdm befehlen, etw zu tun.

commandant ['kɔməndænt] *n* Kommandant

m.

command economy *n* Kommandowirtschaft *f.*

commandeer [kɔmən'dɪə'] *vt* requirieren, beschlagnahmen; (*fig*) sich aneignen.

commander [kə'mɑːndə'] *n* Befehlshaber *m*, Kommandant *m.*

commander in chief *n* Oberbefehlshaber *m.*

commanding [kə'mɑːndɪŋ] *adj* (*appearance*) imposant; (*voice, tone*) gebieterisch; (*lead*) entscheidend; (*position*) vorherrschend.

commanding officer *n* befehlshabender Offizier *m.*

commandment [kə'mɑːndmənt] *n* Gebot *nt.*

command module *n* Kommandokapsel *f.*

commando [kə'mɑːndəu] *n* Kommando *nt*, Kommandotrupp *m*; (*soldier*) Angehörige(r) *m* eines Kommando(trupp)s.

commemorate [kə'mɛməreɪt] *vt* gedenken +*gen.*

commemoration [kəmɛmə'reɪʃən] *n* Gedenken *nt.*

commemorative [kə'mɛmərətɪv] *adj* Gedenk-.

commence [kə'mɛns] *vt, vi* beginnen.

commend [kə'mɛnd] *vt* loben; **to ~ sth to sb** jdm etw empfehlen.

commendable [kə'mɛndəbl] *adj* lobenswert.

commendation [kɔmɛn'deɪʃən] *n* Auszeichnung *f.*

commensurate [kə'mɛnʃərɪt] *adj*: **~ with** *or* **to** entsprechend +*dat.*

comment ['kɔmɛnt] *n* Bemerkung *f*; (*on situation etc*) Kommentar *m* ♦ *vi*: **to ~ (on)** sich äußern (über +*acc or* zu); (*on situation etc*) einen Kommentar abgeben (zu); "**no ~**" „kein Kommentar!"; **to ~ that ...** bemerken, dass ...

commentary ['kɔməntərɪ] *n* Kommentar *m*; (*SPORT*) Reportage *f.*

commentator ['kɔmənteɪtə'] *n* Kommentator(in) *m(f)*; (*SPORT*) Reporter(in) *m(f).*

commerce ['kɔmɜːs] *n* Handel *m.*

commercial [kə'mɜːʃəl] *adj* kommerziell; (*organization*) Wirtschafts- ♦ *n* (*advertisement*) Werbespot *m.*

commercial bank *n* Handelsbank *f.*

commercial break *n* Werbung *f.*

commercial college *n* Fachschule *f* für kaufmännische Berufe.

commercialism [kə'mɜːʃəlɪzəm] *n* Kommerzialisierung *f.*

commercialize [kə'mɜːʃəlaɪz] *vt* kommerzialisieren.

commercialized [kə'mɜːʃəlaɪzd] (*pej*) *adj* kommerzialisiert.

commercial radio *n* kommerzielles Radio *nt.*

commercial television *n* kommerzielles Fernsehen *nt.*

commercial traveller *n* Handelsvertreter(in) *m(f).*

commercial vehicle *n* Lieferwagen *m.*

commiserate [kə'mɪzəreɪt] *vi*: **to ~ with sb** jdm sein Mitgefühl zeigen.

commission [kə'mɪʃən] *n* (*order for work*) Auftrag *m*; (*COMM*) Provision *f*; (*committee*) Kommission *f*; (*MIL*) Offizierspatent *nt* ♦ *vt* (*work of art*) in Auftrag geben; (*MIL*) (zum Offizier) ernennen; **out of ~** außer Betrieb; (*NAUT*) nicht im Dienst; **I get 10% ~** ich bekomme 10% Provision; **~ of inquiry** Untersuchungsausschuss *m*, Untersuchungskommission *f*; **to ~ sb to do sth** jdn damit beauftragen, etw zu tun; **to ~ sth from sb** jdm etw in Auftrag geben.

commissionaire [kəmɪʃə'nɛə'] (*BRIT*) *n* Portier *m.*

commissioner [kə'mɪʃənə'] *n* Polizeipräsident *m.*

commit [kə'mɪt] *vt* (*crime*) begehen; (*money, resources*) einsetzen; (*to sb's care*) anvertrauen; **to ~ o.s.** sich festlegen; **to ~ o.s. to do sth** (dazu) verpflichten, etw zu tun; **to ~ suicide** Selbstmord begehen; **to ~ to writing** zu Papier bringen; **to ~ sb for trial** jdn einem Gericht überstellen.

commitment [kə'mɪtmənt] *n* Verpflichtung *f*; (*to ideology, system*) Engagement *nt.*

committed [kə'mɪtɪd] *adj* engagiert.

committee [kə'mɪtɪ] *n* Ausschuss *m*, Komitee *nt*; **to be on a ~** in einem Ausschuss *or* Komitee sein *or* sitzen.

committee meeting *n* Ausschusssitzung *f.*

commodity [kə'mɔdɪtɪ] *n* Ware *f*; (*food*) Nahrungsmittel *nt.*

common ['kɔmən] *adj* (*shared by all*) gemeinsam; (*good*) Gemein-; (*property*) Gemeinschafts-; (*usual, ordinary*) häufig; (*vulgar*) gewöhnlich ♦ *n* Gemeindeland *nt*; **the Commons** (*BRIT: POL*) *npl* das Unterhaus; **in ~ use** allgemein gebräuchlich; **it's ~ knowledge that** es ist allgemein bekannt, dass; **to the ~ good** für das Gemeinwohl; **to have sth in ~ (with sb)** etw (mit jdm) gemein haben.

common cold *n* Schnupfen *m.*

common denominator *n* (*MATH, fig*) gemeinsamer Nenner *m.*

commoner ['kɔmənə'] *n* Bürgerliche(r) *f(m).*

common ground *n* (*fig*) gemeinsame Basis *f.*

common land *n* Gemeindeland *nt.*

common law *n* Gewohnheitsrecht *nt.*

common-law ['kɔmənlɔː] *adj*: **she is his ~ wife** sie lebt mit ihm in eheähnlicher Gemeinschaft.

commonly ['kɔmənlɪ] *adv* häufig.

Common Market *n*: **the ~** der Gemeinsame Markt.

commonplace ['kɔmənpleɪs] *adj* alltäglich.

common room *n* Aufenthaltsraum *m*, Tagesraum *m.*

common sense *n* gesunder Menschenverstand *m.*

Commonwealth ['kɔmənwɛlθ] (*BRIT*) n: **the ~** das Commonwealth.

COMMONWEALTH

*Das **Commonwealth**, offiziell Commonwealth of Nations, ist ein lockerer Zusammenschluss aus souveränen Staaten, die früher unter britischer Regierung standen, und von Großbritannien abhängigen Gebieten. Die Mitgliedstaaten erkennen den britischen Monarchen als Oberhaupt des Commonwealth an. Bei der Commonwealth Conference, einem Treffen der Staatsoberhäupter der Commonwealthländer, werden Angelegenheiten von gemeinsamem Interesse diskutiert.*

---

commotion [kə'məuʃən] n Tumult m.
communal ['kɔmjuːnl] adj gemeinsam, Gemeinschafts-; (*life*) Gemeinschafts-.
commune [n 'kɔmjuːn, vi kə'mjuːn] n Kommune f; vi: **to ~ with** Zwiesprache halten mit.
communicate [kə'mjuːnɪkeɪt] vt mitteilen; (*idea, feeling*) vermitteln ♦ vi: **to ~ (with**) (*by speech, gesture*) sich verständigen (mit); (*in writing*) in Verbindung or Kontakt stehen (mit).
communication [kəmjuːnɪ'keɪʃən] n Kommunikation f; (*letter, call*) Mitteilung f.
communication cord (*BRIT*) n Notbremse f.
communications network [kəmjuːnɪ'keɪʃənz-] n Kommunikationsnetz nt.
communications satellite n Kommunikationssatellit m, Nachrichtensatellit m.
communicative [kə'mjuːnɪkətɪv] adj gesprächig, mitteilsam.
communion [kə'mjuːnɪən] n (*also:* **Holy C~**: *Catholic*) Kommunion f; (: *Protestant*) Abendmahl nt.
communiqué [kə'mjuːnɪkeɪ] n Kommunikee nt, Kommuniqué nt, (amtliche) Verlautbarung f.
communism ['kɔmjunɪzəm] n Kommunismus m.
communist ['kɔmjunɪst] adj kommunistisch ♦ n Kommunist(in) m(f).
community [kə'mjuːnɪtɪ] n Gemeinschaft f; (*within larger group*) Bevölkerungsgruppe f.
community centre n Gemeindezentrum nt.
community charge (*BRIT*) n (*formerly*) Gemeindesteuer f.
community chest (*US*) n Wohltätigkeitsfonds m, Hilfsfonds m.
community health centre n Gemeinde-Ärztezentrum nt.
community home (*BRIT*) n Erziehungsheim nt.
community service n Sozialdienst m.
community spirit n Gemeinschaftssinn m.
commutation ticket [kɔmju'teɪʃən-] (*US*) n Zeitkarte f.

commute [kə'mjuːt] vi pendeln ♦ vt (*LAW, MATH*) umwandeln.
commuter [kə'mjuːtə*] n Pendler(in) m(f).
compact [adj kəm'pækt, n 'kɔmpækt] adj kompakt ♦ n (*also:* **powder ~**) Puderdose f.
compact disc n Compactdisk f, Compact Disk f, CD f.
compact disc player n CD-Spieler m.
companion [kəm'pænjən] n Begleiter(in) m(f).
companionship [kəm'pænjənʃɪp] n Gesellschaft f.
companionway [kəm'pænjənweɪ] n (*NAUT*) Niedergang m.
company ['kʌmpənɪ] n Firma f; (*THEAT*) (Schauspiel)truppe f; (*MIL*) Kompanie f; (*companionship*) Gesellschaft f; **he's good ~** seine Gesellschaft ist angenehm; **to keep sb ~** jdm Gesellschaft leisten; **to part ~ with** sich trennen von; **Smith and C~** Smith & Co.
company car n Firmenwagen m.
company director n Direktor(in) m(f), Firmenchef(in) m(f).
company secretary (*BRIT*) n ≈ Prokurist(in) m(f).
comparable ['kɔmpərəbl] adj vergleichbar.
comparative [kəm'pærətɪv] adj relativ; (*study, literature*) vergleichend; (*LING*) komparativ.
comparatively [kəm'pærətɪvlɪ] adv relativ.
compare [kəm'pɛə*] vt: **to ~ (with** or **to)** vergleichen (mit) ♦ vi: **to ~ (with**) sich vergleichen lassen (mit); **how do the prices ~?** wie lassen sich die Preise vergleichen?; **~d with** or **to** im Vergleich zu, verglichen mit.
comparison [kəm'pærɪsn] n Vergleich m; **in ~ (with**) im Vergleich (zu).
compartment [kəm'paːtmənt] n (*RAIL*) Abteil nt; (*section*) Fach nt.
compass ['kʌmpəs] n Kompass m; (*fig: scope*) Bereich m; **compasses** npl (*also:* **pair of ~es**) Zirkel m; **within the ~ of** im Rahmen or Bereich +gen; **beyond the ~ of** über den Rahmen or Bereich +gen hinaus.
compassion [kəm'pæʃən] n Mitgefühl nt.
compassionate [kəm'pæʃənɪt] adj mitfühlend; **on ~ grounds** aus familiären Gründen.
compassionate leave n (*esp MIL*) Beurlaubung wegen Krankheit oder Trauerfall in der Familie.
compatibility [kəmpætɪ'bɪlɪtɪ] n (*see adj*) Vereinbarkeit f; Zueinanderpassen nt; Kompatibilität f.
compatible [kəm'pætɪbl] adj (*ideas etc*) vereinbar; (*people*) zueinander passend; (*COMPUT*) kompatibel.
compel [kəm'pɛl] vt zwingen.
compelling [kəm'pɛlɪŋ] adj zwingend.
compendium [kəm'pɛndɪəm] n Kompendium nt.
compensate ['kɔmpənseɪt] vt entschädigen

♦ *vi*: **to** ~ **for** (*loss*) ersetzen; (*disappointment, change etc*) (wieder) ausgleichen.
compensation [kɔmpən'seɪʃən] *n* (*see vb*) Entschädigung *f*; Ersatz *m*; Ausgleich *m*; (*money*) Schaden(s)ersatz *m*.
compère ['kɔmpɛə'] *n* Conférencier *m*.
compete [kəm'piːt] *vi* (*in contest, game*) teilnehmen; (*two theories, statements*) unvereinbar sein; **to** ~ (**with**) (*companies, rivals*) konkurrieren (mit).
competence ['kɔmpɪtəns] *n* Fähigkeit *f*.
competent ['kɔmpɪtənt] *adj* fähig.
competing [kəm'piːtɪŋ] *adj* konkurrierend.
competition [kɔmpɪ'tɪʃən] *n* Konkurrenz *f*; (*contest*) Wettbewerb *m*; **in** ~ **with** im Wettbewerb mit.
competitive [kəm'pɛtɪtɪv] *adj* (*industry, society*) wettbewerbsbetont, wettbewerbsorientiert; (*person*) vom Konkurrenzdenken geprägt; (*price, product*) wettbewerbsfähig, konkurrenzfähig; (*sport*) (Wett)kampf-.
competitive examination *n* (*for places*) Auswahlprüfung *f*; (*for prizes*) Wettbewerb *m*.
competitor [kəm'pɛtɪtə'] *n* Konkurrent(in) *m(f)*; (*participant*) Teilnehmer(in) *m(f)*.
compilation [kɔmpɪ'leɪʃən] *n* Zusammenstellung *f*.
compile [kəm'paɪl] *vt* zusammenstellen; (*book*) verfassen.
complacency [kəm'pleɪsnsɪ] *n* Selbstzufriedenheit *f*, Selbstgefälligkeit *f*.
complacent [kəm'pleɪsnt] *adj* selbstzufrieden, selbstgefällig.
complain [kəm'pleɪn] *vi* (*protest*) sich beschweren; **to** ~ (**about**) sich beklagen (über +*acc*); **to** ~ **of** (*headache etc*) klagen über +*acc*.
complaint [kəm'pleɪnt] *n* Klage *f*; (*in shop etc*) Beschwerde *f*; (*illness*) Beschwerden *pl*.
complement ['kɔmplɪmənt] *n* Ergänzung *f*; (*esp ship's crew*) Besatzung *f* ♦ *vt* ergänzen; **to have a full** ~ **of** … (*people*) die volle Stärke an … *dat* haben; (*items*) die volle Zahl an … *dat* haben.
complementary [kɔmplɪ'mɛntərɪ] *adj* komplementär, einander ergänzend.
complete [kəm'pliːt] *adj* (*total: silence*) vollkommen; (: *change*) völlig; (: *success*) voll; (*whole*) ganz; (: *set*) vollständig; (: *edition*) Gesamt-; (*finished*) fertig ♦ *vt* fertig stellen; (*task*) beenden; (*set, group etc*) vervollständigen; (*fill in*) ausfüllen; **it's a** ~ **disaster** es ist eine totale Katastrophe.
completely [kəm'pliːtlɪ] *adv* völlig, vollkommen.
completion [kəm'pliːʃən] *n* Fertigstellung *f*; (*of contract*) Abschluss *m*; **to be nearing** ~ kurz vor dem Abschluss sein *or* stehen; **on** ~ **of the contract** bei Vertragsabschluss.
complex ['kɔmplɛks] *adj* kompliziert ♦ *n*

Komplex *m*.
complexion [kəm'plɛkʃən] *n* Teint *m*, Gesichtsfarbe *f*; (*of event etc*) Charakter *m*; (*political, religious*) Anschauung *f*; **to put a different** ~ **on sth** etw in einem anderen Licht erscheinen lassen.
complexity [kəm'plɛksɪtɪ] *n* Kompliziertheit *f*.
compliance [kəm'plaɪəns] *n* Fügsamkeit *f*; (*agreement*) Einverständnis *nt*; ~ **with** Einverständnis mit, Zustimmung *f* zu; **in** ~ **with** gemäß +*dat*.
compliant [kəm'plaɪənt] *adj* gefällig, entgegenkommend.
complicate ['kɔmplɪkeɪt] *vt* komplizieren.
complicated ['kɔmplɪkeɪtɪd] *adj* kompliziert.
complication [kɔmplɪ'keɪʃən] *n* Komplikation *f*.
complicity [kəm'plɪsɪtɪ] *n* Mittäterschaft *f*.
compliment [*n* 'kɔmplɪmənt, *vt* 'kɔmplɪmɛnt] *n* Kompliment *nt* ♦ *vt* ein Kompliment/ Komplimente machen; **compliments** *npl* (*regards*) Grüße *pl*; **to pay sb a** ~ jdm ein Kompliment machen; **to** ~ **sb** (**on sth**) jdm Komplimente (wegen etw) machen; **to** ~ **sb on doing sth** jdm Komplimente machen, dass er/sie etw getan hat.
complimentary [kɔmplɪ'mɛntərɪ] *adj* schmeichelhaft; (*ticket, copy of book etc*) Frei-.
compliments slip *n* Empfehlungszettel *m*.
comply [kəm'plaɪ] *vi*: **to** ~ **with** (*law*) einhalten +*acc*; (*ruling*) sich richten nach.
component [kəm'pəunənt] *adj* einzeln ♦ *n* Bestandteil *m*.
compose [kəm'pəuz] *vt* (*music*) komponieren; (*poem*) verfassen; (*letter*) abfassen; **to be** ~**d of** bestehen aus; **to** ~ **o.s.** sich sammeln.
composed [kəm'pəuzd] *adj* ruhig, gelassen.
composer [kəm'pəuzə'] *n* Komponist(in) *m(f)*.
composite ['kɔmpəzɪt] *adj* zusammengesetzt; (*BOT*) Korbblütler-; (*MATH*) teilbar; (*BOT*): ~ **plant** Korbblütler *m*.
composition [kɔmpə'zɪʃən] *n* Zusammensetzung *f*; (*essay*) Aufsatz *m*; (*MUS*) Komposition *f*.
compositor [kəm'pɔzɪtə'] *n* (*Schrift*)setzer(in) *m(f)*.
compos mentis ['kɔmpɔs 'mɛntɪs] *adj* zurechnungsfähig.
compost ['kɔmpɔst] *n* Kompost *m*; (*also*: **potting** ~) Blumenerde *f*.
composure [kəm'pəuʒə'] *n* Fassung *f*, Beherrschung *f*.
compound [*n, adj* 'kɔmpaund, *vt* kəm'paund] *n* (*CHEM*) Verbindung *f*; (*enclosure*) umzäuntes Gebiet *or* Gelände *nt*; (*LING*) Kompositum *nt* ♦ *adj* zusammengesetzt; (*eye*) Facetten-, Fassetten- ♦ *vt* verschlimmern, vergrößern.
compound fracture *n* komplizierter Bruch *m*.
compound interest *n* Zinseszins *m*.
comprehend [kɔmprɪ'hɛnd] *vt* begreifen,

verstehen.

comprehension [kɔmprɪ'hɛnʃən] n Verständnis nt.

comprehensive [kɔmprɪ'hɛnsɪv] adj umfassend; (insurance) Vollkasko- ♦ n = **comprehensive school**.

comprehensive school (BRIT) n Gesamtschule f.

COMPREHENSIVE SCHOOL

Comprehensive school ist in Großbritannien eine nicht selektive, weiterführende Schule, an der alle Kinder aus einem Einzugsgebiet gemeinsam unterrichtet werden. An einer solchen Gesamtschule können alle Schulabschlüsse gemacht werden. Die meisten staatlichen Schulen in Großbritannien sind comprehensive schools.

---

compress [vt kəm'prɛs, n 'kɔmprɛs] vt (information etc) verdichten; (air) komprimieren; (cotton, paper etc) zusammenpressen ♦ n (MED) Kompresse f.

compressed air [kəm'prɛst-] n Druckluft f, Pressluft f.

compression [kəm'prɛʃən] n (see vb) Verdichtung f; Kompression f; Zusammenpressen nt.

comprise [kəm'praɪz] vt (also: be ~d of) bestehen aus; (constitute) bilden, ausmachen.

compromise ['kɔmprəmaɪz] n Kompromiss m ♦ vt (beliefs, principles) verraten; (person) kompromittieren ♦ vi Kompromisse schließen ♦ cpd (solution etc) Kompromiss-.

compulsion [kəm'pʌlʃən] n Zwang m; (force) Druck m, Zwang m; **under** ~ unter Druck or Zwang.

compulsive [kəm'pʌlsɪv] adj zwanghaft; **it makes** ~ **viewing/reading** das muss man einfach sehen/lesen; **he's a** ~ **smoker** das Rauchen ist bei ihm zur Sucht geworden.

compulsory [kəm'pʌlsərɪ] adj obligatorisch; (retirement) Zwangs-.

compulsory purchase n Enteignung f.

compunction [kəm'pʌŋkʃən] n Schuldgefühle pl, Gewissensbisse pl; **to have no** ~ **about doing sth** etw tun, ohne sich schuldig zu fühlen.

computer [kəm'pjuːtə*] n Computer m, Rechner m ♦ cpd Computer-; **the process is done by** ~ das Verfahren wird per Computer durchgeführt.

computer game n Computerspiel nt.

computerization [kəmpjuːtəraɪ'zeɪʃən] n Computerisierung f.

computerize [kəm'pjuːtəraɪz] vt auf Computer umstellen; (information) computerisieren.

computer literate adj: **to be** ~ Computerkenntnisse haben.

computer programmer n

Programmierer(in) m(f).

computer programming n Programmieren nt.

computer science n Informatik f.

computer scientist n Informatiker(in) m(f).

computing [kəm'pjuːtɪŋ] n Informatik f; (activity) Computerarbeit f.

comrade ['kɔmrɪd] n Genosse m, Genossin f; (friend) Kamerad(in) m(f).

comradeship ['kɔmrɪdʃɪp] n Kameradschaft f.

comsat ['kɔmsæt] n abbr = **communications satellite**.

con [kɔn] vt betrügen; (cheat) hereinlegen ♦ n Schwindel m; **to** ~ **sb into doing sth** jdn durch einen Trick dazu bringen, dass er/sie etw tut.

concave ['kɔnkeɪv] adj konkav.

conceal [kən'siːl] vt verbergen; (information) verheimlichen.

concede [kən'siːd] vt zugeben ♦ vi nachgeben; (admit defeat) sich geschlagen geben; **to** ~ **defeat** sich geschlagen geben; **to** ~ **a point to sb** jdm in einem Punkt Recht geben.

conceit [kən'siːt] n Einbildung f.

conceited [kən'siːtɪd] adj eingebildet.

conceivable [kən'siːvəbl] adj denkbar, vorstellbar; **it is** ~ **that** ... es ist denkbar, dass ...

conceivably [kən'siːvəblɪ] adv: **he may** ~ **be right** es ist durchaus denkbar, dass er Recht hat.

conceive [kən'siːv] vt (child) empfangen; (plan) kommen auf +acc; (policy) konzipieren ♦ vi empfangen; **to** ~ **of sth** sich dat etw vorstellen; **to** ~ **of doing sth** sich dat vorstellen, etw zu tun.

concentrate ['kɔnsəntreɪt] vi sich konzentrieren ♦ vt konzentrieren.

concentration [kɔnsən'treɪʃən] n Konzentration f.

concentration camp n Konzentrationslager nt, KZ nt.

concentric [kɔn'sɛntrɪk] adj konzentrisch.

concept ['kɔnsɛpt] n Vorstellung f; (principle) Begriff m.

conception [kən'sɛpʃən] n Vorstellung f; (of child) Empfängnis f.

concern [kən'sɜːn] n Angelegenheit f; (anxiety, worry) Sorge f; (COMM) Konzern m ♦ vt Sorgen machen +dat; (involve) angehen; (relate to) betreffen; **to be** ~**ed (about)** sich dat Sorgen machen (um); **"to whom it may** ~**"** (on certificate) „Bestätigung"; (on reference) „Zeugnis"; **as far as I am** ~**ed** was mich betrifft; **to be** ~**ed with** sich interessieren für; **the department** ~**ed** (under discussion) die betreffende Abteilung; (involved) die zuständige Abteilung.

concerning [kən'sɜːnɪŋ] prep bezüglich +gen, hinsichtlich +gen.

concert ['kɒnsət] n Konzert nt; **in** ~ (MUS) live; (activities, actions etc) gemeinsam.

concerted [kən'sɔːtɪd] adj gemeinsam.

concert hall n Konzerthalle f, Konzertsaal m.

concertina [kɒnsə'tiːnə] n Konzertina f ♦ vi sich wie eine Ziehharmonika zusammenschieben.

concerto [kən'tʃɔːtəʊ] n Konzert nt.

concession [kən'sɛʃən] n Zugeständnis nt, Konzession f; (COMM) Konzession; **tax** ~ Steuervergünstigung f.

concessionaire [kənsɛʃə'nɛə*] n Konzessionär m.

concessionary [kən'sɛʃənrɪ] adj ermäßigt.

conciliation [kənsɪlɪ'eɪʃən] n Schlichtung f.

conciliatory [kən'sɪlɪətrɪ] adj versöhnlich.

concise [kən'saɪs] adj kurz gefasst, prägnant.

conclave ['kɒnkleɪv] n Klausur f; (REL) Konklave f.

conclude [kən'kluːd] vt beenden, schließen; (treaty, deal etc) abschließen; (decide) schließen, folgern ♦ vi schließen; (events): **to** ~ (with) enden (mit); **"That," he** ~**d, "is why we did it."** „Darum", schloss er, „haben wir es getan"; **I** ~ **that ...** ich komme zu dem Schluss, dass ...

concluding [kən'kluːdɪŋ] adj (remarks etc) abschließend, Schluss-.

conclusion [kən'kluːʒən] n (see vb) Ende nt; Schluss m; Abschluss m; Folgerung f; **to come to the** ~ **that ...** zu dem Schluss kommen, dass ...

conclusive [kən'kluːsɪv] adj (evidence) schlüssig; (defeat) endgültig.

concoct [kən'kɒkt] vt (excuse etc) sich dat ausdenken; (meal, sauce) improvisieren.

concoction [kən'kɒkʃən] n Zusammenstellung f; (drink) Gebräu nt.

concord ['kɒnkɔːd] n Eintracht f; (treaty) Vertrag m.

concourse ['kɒnkɔːs] n (Eingangs)halle f; (crowd) Menge f.

concrete ['kɒnkriːt] n Beton m ♦ adj (ceiling, block) Beton-; (proposal, idea) konkret.

concrete mixer n Betonmischmaschine f.

concur [kən'kɔː*] vi übereinstimmen; **to** ~ **with** beipflichten +dat.

concurrently [kən'kʌrntlɪ] adv gleichzeitig.

concussion [kən'kʌʃən] n Gehirnerschütterung f.

condemn [kən'dɛm] vt verurteilen; (building) für abbruchreif erklären.

condemnation [kɒndɛm'neɪʃən] n Verurteilung f.

condensation [kɒndɛn'seɪʃən] n Kondenswasser nt.

condense [kən'dɛns] vi kondensieren, sich niederschlagen ♦ vt zusammenfassen.

condensed milk [kən'dɛnst-] n Kondensmilch f, Büchsenmilch f.

condescend [kɒndɪ'sɛnd] vi herablassend sein; **to** ~ **to do sth** sich dazu herablassen,

etw zu tun.

condescending [kɒndɪ'sɛndɪŋ] adj herablassend.

condition [kən'dɪʃən] n Zustand m; (requirement) Bedingung f; (illness) Leiden nt ♦ vt konditionieren; (hair) in Form bringen; **conditions** npl (circumstances) Verhältnisse pl; **in good/poor** ~ (person) in guter/ schlechter Verfassung; (thing) in gutem/ schlechtem Zustand; **a heart** ~ ein Herzleiden nt; **weather** ~**s** die Wetterlage; **on** ~ **that ...** unter der Bedingung, dass ...

conditional [kən'dɪʃənl] adj bedingt; **to be** ~ **upon** abhängen von.

conditioner [kən'dɪʃənə*] n (for hair) Pflegespülung f; (for fabrics) Weichspüler m.

condo ['kɒndəʊ] (US: inf) n abbr = **condominium**.

condolences [kən'dəʊlənsɪz] npl Beileid nt.

condom ['kɒndəm] n Kondom m or nt.

condominium [kɒndə'mɪnɪəm] (US) n Haus nt mit Eigentumswohnungen; (rooms) Eigentumswohnung f.

condone [kən'dəʊn] vt gutheißen.

conducive [kən'djuːsɪv] adj: ~ **to** förderlich +dat.

conduct [n 'kɒndʌkt, vt kən'dʌkt] n Verhalten nt ♦ vt (investigation etc) durchführen; (manage) führen; (orchestra, choir etc) dirigieren; (heat, electricity) leiten; **to** ~ **o.s.** sich verhalten.

conducted tour [kən'dʌktɪd-] n Führung f.

conductor [kən'dʌktə*] n (of orchestra) Dirigent(in) m(f); (on bus) Schaffner m; (US: on train) Zugführer(in) m(f); (ELEC) Leiter m.

conductress [kən'dʌktrɪs] n (on bus) Schaffnerin f.

conduit ['kɒndjuɪt] n (TECH) Leitungsrohr nt; (ELEC) Isolierrohr nt.

cone [kəʊn] n Kegel m; (on road) Leitkegel m; (BOT) Zapfen m; (ice cream cornet) (Eis)tüte f.

confectioner [kən'fɛkʃənə*] n (maker) Süßwarenhersteller(in) m(f); (seller) Süßwarenhändler(in) m(f); (of cakes) Konditor(in) m(f).

confectioner's (shop) [kən'fɛkʃənəz-] n Süßwarenladen m; (cake shop) Konditorei f.

confectionery [kən'fɛkʃənrɪ] n Süßwaren pl, Süßigkeiten pl; (cakes) Konditorwaren pl.

confederate [kən'fɛdrɪt] adj verbündet ♦ n (pej) Komplize m, Komplizin f; (US: HIST) **the C~s** die Konföderierten pl.

confederation [kənfɛdə'reɪʃən] n Bund m; (POL) Bündnis nt; (COMM) Verband m.

confer [kən'fɔː*] vt: **to** ~ **sth (on sb)** (jdm) etw verleihen ♦ vi sich beraten; **to** ~ **with sb about sth** sich mit jdm über etw acc beraten, etw mit jdm besprechen.

conference ['kɒnfərəns] n Konferenz f; (more informal) Besprechung f; **to be in** ~ in or bei einer Konferenz/Besprechung sein.

conference room n Konferenzraum m; (smaller) Besprechungszimmer nt.

confess [kən'fɛs] *vt* bekennen; (*sin*) beichten; (*crime*) zugeben, gestehen ♦ *vi* (*admit*) gestehen; **to ~ to sth** (*crime*) etw gestehen; (*weakness etc*) sich zu etw bekennen; **I must ~ that I didn't enjoy it at all** ich muss sagen, dass es mir überhaupt keinen Spaß gemacht hat.

confession [kən'fɛʃən] *n* Geständnis *nt*; (*REL*) Beichte *f*; **to make a ~** ein Geständnis ablegen.

confessor [kən'fɛsə*] *n* Beichtvater *m*.

confetti [kən'fɛtɪ] *n* Konfetti *nt*.

confide [kən'faɪd] *vi*: **to ~ in** sich anvertrauen +*dat*.

confidence ['kɒnfɪdns] *n* Vertrauen *nt*; (*self-assurance*) Selbstvertrauen *nt*; (*secret*) vertrauliche Mitteilung *f*, Geheimnis *nt*; **to have ~ in sb/sth** Vertrauen zu jdm/etw haben; **to have (every) ~ that ...** ganz zuversichtlich sein, dass ...; **motion of no ~** Misstrauensantrag *m*; **to tell sb sth in strict ~** jdm etw ganz im Vertrauen sagen; **in ~** vertraulich.

confidence trick *n* Schwindel *m*.

confident ['kɒnfɪdənt] *adj* (selbst)sicher; (*positive*) zuversichtlich.

confidential [kɒnfɪ'dɛnʃəl] *adj* vertraulich; (*secretary*) Privat-.

confidentiality [kɒnfɪdɛnʃɪ'ælɪtɪ] *n* Vertraulichkeit *f*.

configuration [kənfɪɡjʊ'reɪʃən] *n* Anordnung *f*; (*COMPUT*) Konfiguration *f*.

confine [kən'faɪn] *vt* (*shut up*) einsperren; **to ~ (to)** beschränken (auf +*acc*); **to ~ o.s. to sth** sich auf etw *acc* beschränken; **to ~ o.s. to doing sth** sich darauf beschränken, etw zu tun.

confined [kən'faɪnd] *adj* begrenzt.

confinement [kən'faɪnmənt] *n* Haft *f*.

confines ['kɒnfaɪnz] *npl* Grenzen *pl*; (*of situation*) Rahmen *m*.

confirm [kən'fə:m] *vt* bestätigen; **to be ~ed** (*REL*) konfirmiert werden.

confirmation [kɒnfə'meɪʃən] *n* Bestätigung *f*; (*REL*) Konfirmation *f*.

confirmed [kən'fə:md] *adj* (*bachelor*) eingefleischt; (*teetotaller*) überzeugt.

confiscate ['kɒnfɪskeɪt] *vt* beschlagnahmen, konfiszieren.

confiscation [kɒnfɪs'keɪʃən] *n* Beschlagnahme *f*, Konfiszierung *f*.

conflagration [kɒnflə'ɡreɪʃən] *n* Feuersbrunst *f*.

conflict ['kɒnflɪkt] *n* Konflikt *m*; (*fighting*) Zusammenstoß *m*, Kampf *m* ♦ *vi*: **to ~ (with)** im Widerspruch stehen (zu).

conflicting [kən'flɪktɪŋ] *adj* widersprüchlich.

conform [kən'fɔ:m] *vi* sich anpassen; **to ~ to** entsprechen +*dat*.

conformist [kən'fɔ:mɪst] *n* Konformist(in) *m(f)*.

confound [kən'faʊnd] *vt* verwirren; (*amaze*) verblüffen.

confounded [kən'faʊndɪd] *adj* verdammt, verflixt (*inf*).

confront [kən'frʌnt] *vt* (*problems, task*) sich stellen +*dat*; (*enemy, danger*) gegenübertreten +*dat*.

confrontation [kɒnfrən'teɪʃən] *n* Konfrontation *f*.

confuse [kən'fju:z] *vt* verwirren; (*mix up*) verwechseln; (*complicate*) durcheinander bringen.

confused [kən'fju:zd] *adj* (*person*) verwirrt; (*situation*) verworren, konfus; **to get ~** konfus werden.

confusing [kən'fju:zɪŋ] *adj* verwirrend.

confusion [kən'fju:ʒən] *n* (*mix-up*) Verwechslung *f*; (*perplexity*) Verwirrung *f*; (*disorder*) Durcheinander *nt*.

congeal [kən'dʒi:l] *vi* (*blood*) gerinnen; (*sauce, oil*) erstarren.

congenial [kən'dʒi:nɪəl] *adj* ansprechend, sympathisch; (*atmosphere, place, work, company*) angenehm.

congenital [kən'dʒɛnɪtl] *adj* angeboren.

conger eel ['kɒŋɡər-] *n* Seeaal *m*.

congested [kən'dʒɛstɪd] *adj* (*road*) verstopft; (*area*) überfüllt; (*nose*) verstopft; **his lungs are ~** in seiner Lunge hat sich Blut angestaut.

congestion [kən'dʒɛstʃən] *n* (*MED*) Blutstau *m*; (*of road*) Verstopfung *f*; (*of area*) Überfüllung *f*.

congestion charge *n* City-Maut *f*.

conglomerate [kən'ɡlɒmərɪt] *n* (*COMM*) Konglomerat *nt*.

conglomeration [kənɡlɒmə'reɪʃən] *n* Ansammlung *f*.

Congo ['kɒŋɡəʊ] *n* (*state*) Kongo *m*.

congratulate [kən'ɡrætjʊleɪt] *vt* gratulieren; **to ~ sb (on sth)** jdm (zu etw) gratulieren.

congratulations [kənɡrætjʊ'leɪʃənz] *npl* Glückwunsch *m*, Glückwünsche *pl*; **~!** herzlichen Glückwunsch!; **~ on** Glückwünsche zu.

congregate ['kɒŋɡrɪɡeɪt] *vi* sich versammeln.

congregation [kɒŋɡrɪ'ɡeɪʃən] *n* Gemeinde *f*.

congress ['kɒŋɡrɛs] *n* Kongress *m*; (*US*): **C~** der Kongress.

CONGRESS

Der **Congress** *ist die nationale gesetzgebende Versammlung der USA, die in Washington im* **Capitol** *zusammentritt. Der Kongress besteht aus dem Repräsentantenhaus (435 Abgeordnete, entsprechend den Bevölkerungszahlen auf die einzelnen Bundesstaaten verteilt und jeweils für 2 Jahre gewählt) und dem Senat (100 Senatoren, 2 für jeden Bundesstaat, für 6 Jahre gewählt, wobei ein Drittel alle zwei Jahre neu gewählt wird). Sowohl die Abgeordneten als auch die Senatoren werden in direkter Wahl vom Volk gewählt.*

congressman ['kɔŋgrɛsmən] (*US*) *n* (*irreg: like man*) Kongressabgeordnete(r) *m*.

congresswoman ['kɔŋgrɛswumən] (*US: irreg: like* woman*) n* Kongressabgeordnete *f*.

conical ['kɔnɪkl] *adj* kegelförmig, konisch.

conifer ['kɔnɪfəʳ] *n* Nadelbaum *m*.

coniferous [kə'nɪfərəs] *adj* Nadel-.

conjecture [kən'dʒɛktʃəʳ] *n* Vermutung *f*, Mutmaßung *f* ♦ *vi* vermuten, mutmaßen.

conjugal ['kɔndʒugl] *adj* ehelich.

conjugate ['kɔndʒugeɪt] *vt* konjugieren.

conjugation [kɔndʒə'geɪʃən] *n* Konjugation *f*.

conjunction [kən'dʒʌŋkʃən] *n* Konjunktion *f*; **in ~ with** zusammen mit, in Verbindung mit.

conjunctivitis [kəndʒʌŋktɪ'vaɪtɪs] *n* Bindehautentzündung *f*.

conjure ['kʌndʒəʳ] *vi* zaubern ♦ *vt* (*also fig*) hervorzaubern.

▶ **conjure up** *vt* (*ghost, spirit*) beschwören; (*memories*) heraufbeschwören.

conjurer ['kʌndʒərəʳ] *n* Zauberer *m*, Zauberkünstler(in) *m(f)*.

conjuring trick ['kʌndʒərɪŋ-] *n* Zaubertrick *m*, Zauberkunststück *nt*.

conker ['kɔŋkəʳ] (*BRIT*) *n* (Ross)kastanie *f*.

conk out [kɔŋk-] (*inf*) *vi* den Geist aufgeben.

con man *n* Schwindler *m*.

Conn. (*US*) *abbr* (*POST:* = *Connecticut*).

connect [kə'nɛkt] *vt* verbinden; (*ELEC*) anschließen; (*TEL: caller*) verbinden; (*: subscriber*) anschließen; (*fig: associate*) in Zusammenhang bringen ♦ *vi*: **to ~ with** (*train, plane etc*) Anschluss haben an +*acc*; **to ~ sth to sth** etw mit einer Sache verbinden; **to be ~ed with** (*associated*) in einer Beziehung *or* in Verbindung stehen zu; (*have dealings with*) zu tun haben mit; **I am trying to ~ you** (*TEL*) ich versuche, Sie zu verbinden.

connection [kə'nɛkʃən] *n* Verbindung *f*; (*ELEC*) Kontakt *m*; (*train, plane etc, TEL: subscriber*) Anschluss *m*; (*fig: association*) Beziehung *f*, Zusammenhang *m*; **in ~ with** in Zusammenhang mit; **what is the ~ between them?** welche Verbindung besteht zwischen ihnen?; **business ~s** Geschäftsbeziehungen *pl*; **to get/miss one's ~** seinen Anschluss erreichen/verpassen.

connexion [kə'nɛkʃən] (*BRIT*) *n* = **connection**.

conning tower ['kɔnɪŋ-] *n* Kommandoturm *m*.

connive [kə'naɪv] *vi*: **to ~ at** stillschweigend dulden.

connoisseur [kɔnɪ'səːʳ] *n* Kenner(in) *m(f)*.

connotation [kɔnə'teɪʃən] *n* Konnotation *f*.

connubial [kə'njuːbɪəl] *adj* ehelich.

conquer ['kɔŋkəʳ] *vt* erobern; (*enemy, fear, feelings*) besiegen.

conqueror ['kɔŋkərəʳ] *n* Eroberer *m*.

conquest ['kɔŋkwɛst] *n* Eroberung *f*.

cons [kɔnz] *npl see* **convenience**, **pro**.

conscience ['kɔnʃəns] *n* Gewissen *nt*; **to have a guilty/clear ~** ein schlechtes/gutes Gewissen haben; **in all ~** allen Ernstes.

conscientious [kɔnʃɪ'ɛnʃəs] *adj* gewissenhaft.

conscientious objector *n* Wehrdienst- *or* Kriegsdienstverweigerer *m* (*aus Gewissensgründen*).

conscious ['kɔnʃəs] *adj* bewusst; (*awake*) bei Bewusstsein; **to become ~ of sth** sich *dat* einer Sache *gen* bewusst werden; **to become ~ that** ... sich *dat* bewusst werden, dass ...

consciousness ['kɔnʃəsnɪs] *n* Bewusstsein *nt*; **to lose ~** bewusstlos werden; **to regain ~** wieder zu sich kommen.

conscript ['kɔnskrɪpt] *n* Wehrpflichtige(r) *m*.

conscription [kən'skrɪpʃən] *n* Wehrpflicht *f*.

consecrate ['kɔnsɪkreɪt] *vt* weihen.

consecutive [kən'sɛkjutɪv] *adj* aufeinander folgend; **on three ~ occasions** dreimal hintereinander.

consensus [kən'sɛnsəs] *n* Übereinstimmung *f*; **the ~ (of opinion)** die allgemeine Meinung.

consent [kən'sɛnt] *n* Zustimmung *f* ♦ *vi*: **to ~ to** zustimmen +*dat*; **age of ~** Ehemündigkeitsalter *nt*; **by common ~** auf allgemeinen Wunsch.

consenting [kən'sɛntɪŋ] *adj*: **between ~ adults** ≈ zwischen Erwachsenen.

consequence ['kɔnsɪkwəns] *n* Folge *f*; **of ~** bedeutend, wichtig; **it's of little ~** es spielt kaum eine Rolle; **in ~** folglich.

consequently ['kɔnsɪkwəntlɪ] *adv* folglich.

conservation [kɔnsə'veɪʃən] *n* Erhaltung *f*, Schutz *m*; (*of energy*) Sparen *nt*; (*also:* **nature ~**) Umweltschutz *m*; (*of paintings, books*) Erhaltung *f*, Konservierung *f*; **energy ~** Energieeinsparung *f*.

conservationist [kɔnsə'veɪʃnɪst] *n* Umweltschützer(in) *m(f)*.

conservative [kən'səːvətɪv] *adj* konservativ; (*cautious*) vorsichtig; (*BRIT: POL*): **C~** konservativ ♦ *n* (*BRIT: POL*): **C~** Konservative(r) *f(m)*.

Conservative Party *n*: **the ~** die Konservative Partei *f*.

conservatory [kən'səːvətrɪ] *n* Wintergarten *m*; (*MUS*) Konservatorium *nt*.

conserve [kən'səːv] *vt* erhalten; (*supplies, energy*) sparen ♦ *n* Konfitüre *f*.

consider [kən'sɪdəʳ] *vt* (*study*) sich *dat* überlegen; (*take into account*) in Betracht ziehen; **to ~ that** ... der Meinung sein, dass ...; **to ~ sb/sth as** ... jdn/etw für ... halten; **to ~ doing sth** in Erwägung ziehen, etw zu tun; **they ~ themselves to be superior** sie halten sich für etwas Besseres; **she ~ed it a disaster** sie betrachtete es als eine Katastrophe; **~ yourself lucky** Sie können sich glücklich schätzen; **all things ~ed** alles in allem.

considerable [kən'sɪdərəbl] *adj* beträchtlich.

considerably [kən'sɪdərəblɪ] *adv* beträchtlich; (*bigger, smaller etc*) um einiges.

considerate [kən'sɪdərɪt] *adj* rücksichtsvoll.

consideration [kənsɪdə'reɪʃən] *n* Überlegung *f*; (*factor*) Gesichtspunkt *m*, Faktor *m*; (*thoughtfulness*) Rücksicht *f*; (*reward*) Entgelt *nt*; **out of ~ for** aus Rücksicht auf +*acc*; **to be under ~** geprüft werden; **my first ~ is my family** ich denke zuerst an meine Familie.

considered [kən'sɪdəd] *adj*: **~ opinion** ernsthafte Überzeugung *f*.

considering [kən'sɪdərɪŋ] *prep* in Anbetracht +*gen*; **~ (that)** wenn man bedenkt(, dass).

consign [kən'saɪn] *vt*: **to ~ to** (*object: to place*) verbannen in +*acc*; (*person: to sb's care*) anvertrauen +*dat*; (: *to poverty*) verurteilen zu; (*send*) versenden an +*acc*.

consignment [kən'saɪnmənt] *n* Sendung *f*, Lieferung *f*.

consignment note *n* Frachtbrief *m*.

consist [kən'sɪst] *vi*: **to ~ of** bestehen aus.

consistency [kən'sɪstənsɪ] *n* (*of actions etc*) Konsequenz *f*; (*of cream etc*) Konsistenz *f*, Dicke *f*.

consistent [kən'sɪstənt] *adj* konsequent; (*argument, idea*) logisch, folgerichtig; **to be ~ with** entsprechen +*dat*.

consolation [kənsə'leɪʃən] *n* Trost *m*.

console [kən'səul] *vt* trösten ♦ *n* (*panel*) Schalttafel *f*.

consolidate [kən'sɔlɪdeɪt] *vt* festigen.

consols ['kɔnsɔlz] (*BRIT*) *npl* (*STOCK EXCHANGE*) Konsols *pl*, konsolidierte Staatsanleihen *pl*.

consommé [kən'sɔmeɪ] *n* Kraftbrühe *f*, Consommé *f*.

consonant ['kɔnsənənt] *n* Konsonant *m*, Mitlaut *m*.

consort ['kɔnsɔːt] *n* Gemahl(in) *m(f)*, Gatte *m*, Gattin *f* ♦ *vi*: **to ~ with sb** mit jdm verkehren; **prince ~** Prinzgemahl *m*.

consortium [kən'sɔːtɪəm] *n* Konsortium *nt*.

conspicuous [kən'spɪkjuəs] *adj* auffallend; **to make o.s. ~** auffallen.

conspiracy [kən'spɪrəsɪ] *n* Verschwörung *f*, Komplott *nt*.

conspiratorial [kənspɪrə'tɔːrɪəl] *adj* verschwörerisch.

conspire [kən'spaɪə*] *vi* sich verschwören; (*events*) zusammenkommen.

constable ['kʌnstəbl] (*BRIT*) *n* Polizist *m*; **chief ~** Polizeipräsident *m*, Polizeichef *m*.

constabulary [kən'stæbjulərɪ] (*BRIT*) *n* Polizei *f*.

constant ['kɔnstənt] *adj* dauernd, ständig; (*fixed*) konstant, gleich bleibend.

constantly ['kɔnstəntlɪ] *adv* (an)dauernd, ständig.

constellation [kɔnstə'leɪʃən] *n* Sternbild *nt*.

consternation [kɔnstə'neɪʃən] *n* Bestürzung *f*.

constipated ['kɔnstɪpeɪtɪd] *adj*: **to be ~**

Verstopfung haben, verstopft sein.

constipation [kɔnstɪ'peɪʃən] *n* Verstopfung *f*.

constituency [kən'stɪtjuənsɪ] *n* (*POL*) Wahlkreis *m*; (*electors*) Wähler *pl* (*eines Wahlkreises*).

constituency party *n* Parteiorganisation *in einem Wahlkreis*.

constituent [kən'stɪtjuənt] *n* (*POL*) Wähler(in) *m(f)*; (*component*) Bestandteil *m*.

constitute ['kɔnstɪtjuːt] *vt* (*represent*) darstellen; (*make up*) bilden, ausmachen.

constitution [kɔnstɪ'tjuːʃən] *n* (*POL*) Verfassung *f*; (*of club etc*) Satzung *f*; (*health*) Konstitution *f*, Gesundheit *f*; (*make-up*) Zusammensetzung *f*.

constitutional [kɔnstɪ'tjuːʃənl] *adj* (*government*) verfassungsmäßig; (*reform etc*) Verfassungs-.

constitutional monarchy *n* konstitutionelle Monarchie *f*.

constrain [kən'streɪn] *vt* zwingen.

constrained [kən'streɪnd] *adj* gezwungen.

constraint [kən'streɪnt] *n* Beschränkung *f*, Einschränkung *f*; (*compulsion*) Zwang *m*; (*embarrassment*) Befangenheit *f*.

constrict [kən'strɪkt] *vt* einschnüren; (*blood vessel*) verengen; (*limit, restrict*) einschränken.

constriction [kən'strɪkʃən] *n* Einschränkung *f*; (*tightness*) Verengung *f*; (*squeezing*) Einschnürung *f*.

construct [kən'strʌkt] *vt* bauen; (*machine*) konstruieren; (*theory, argument*) entwickeln.

construction [kən'strʌkʃən] *n* Bau *m*; (*structure*) Konstruktion *f*; (*fig: interpretation*) Deutung *f*; **under ~** in *or* im Bau.

construction industry *n* Bauindustrie *f*.

constructive [kən'strʌktɪv] *adj* konstruktiv.

construe [kən'struː] *vt* auslegen, deuten.

consul ['kɔnsl] *n* Konsul(in) *m(f)*.

consulate ['kɔnsjulɪt] *n* Konsulat *nt*.

consult [kən'sʌlt] *vt* (*doctor, lawyer*) konsultieren; (*friend*) sich beraten *or* besprechen mit; (*reference book*) nachschlagen in +*dat*; **to ~ sb (about sth)** jdn (wegen etw) fragen.

consultancy [kən'sʌltənsɪ] *n* Beratungsbüro *nt*; (*MED: job*) Facharztstelle *f*.

consultant [kən'sʌltənt] *n* (*MED*) Facharzt *m*, Fachärztin *f*; (*other specialist*) Berater(in) *m(f)* ♦ *cpd*: **~ engineer** beratender Ingenieur *m*; **~ paediatrician** Facharzt/-ärztin *m/f* für Pädiatrie *or* Kinderheilkunde; **legal/ management ~** Rechts-/ Unternehmensberater(in) *m(f)*.

consultation [kɔnsəl'teɪʃən] *n* (*MED, LAW*) Konsultation *f*; (*discussion*) Beratung *f*, Besprechung *f*; **in ~ with** in gemeinsamer Beratung mit.

consultative [kən'sʌltətɪv] *adj* beratend.

consulting room [kən'sʌltɪŋ-] (*BRIT*) *n* Sprechzimmer *nt*.

consume [kən'sjuːm] *vt* (*food, drink*) zu sich nehmen, konsumieren; (*fuel, energy*) verbrauchen; (*time*) in Anspruch nehmen; (*subj: emotion*) verzehren; (: *fire*) vernichten.

consumer [kən'sjuːmə*] *n* Verbraucher(in) *m(f)*.

consumer credit *n* Verbraucherkredit *m*.

consumer durables *npl* (langlebige) Gebrauchsgüter *pl*.

consumer goods *npl* Konsumgüter *pl*.

consumerism [kən'sjuːmərɪzəm] *n* Verbraucherschutz *m*.

consumer society *n* Konsumgesellschaft *f*.

consumer watchdog *n* Verbraucherschutzorganisation *f*.

consummate ['kɒnsʌmeɪt] *vt* (*marriage*) vollziehen; (*ambition etc*) erfüllen.

consumption [kən'sʌmpʃən] *n* Verbrauch *m*; (*of food*) Verzehr *m*; (*of drinks, buying*) Konsum *m*; (*MED*) Schwindsucht *f*; **not fit for human** ~ zum Verzehr ungeeignet.

cont. *abbr* (= *continued*) Forts.

contact ['kɒntækt] *n* Kontakt *m*; (*touch*) Berührung *f*; (*person*) Kontaktperson *f* ♦ *vt* sich in Verbindung setzen mit; **to be in** ~ **with sb/sth** mit jdm/etw in Verbindung *or* Kontakt stehen; (*touch*) jdn/etw berühren; **business** ~**s** Geschäftsverbindungen *pl*.

contact lenses *npl* Kontaktlinsen *pl*.

contagious [kən'teɪdʒəs] *adj* ansteckend.

contain [kən'teɪn] *vt* enthalten; (*growth, spread*) in Grenzen halten; (*feeling*) beherrschen; **to** ~ **o.s.** an sich *acc* halten.

container [kən'teɪnə*] *n* Behälter *m*; (*for shipping etc*) Container *m* ♦ *cpd* Container-.

containerize [kən'teɪnəraɪz] *vt* in Container verpacken; (*port*) auf Container umstellen.

container ship *n* Containerschiff *nt*.

contaminate [kən'tæmɪneɪt] *vt* (*water, food*) verunreinigen; (*soil etc*) verseuchen.

contamination [kəntæmɪ'neɪʃən] *n* (*see vb*) Verunreinigung *f*; Verseuchung *f*.

cont'd *abbr* (= *continued*) Forts.

contemplate ['kɒntəmpleɪt] *vt* nachdenken über +*acc*; (*course of action*) in Erwägung ziehen; (*person, painting etc*) betrachten.

contemplation [kɒntəm'pleɪʃən] *n* Betrachtung *f*.

contemporary [kən'tɛmpərərɪ] *adj* zeitgenössisch; (*present-day*) modern ♦ *n* Altersgenosse *m*, Altersgenossin *f*; **Samuel Pepys and his contemporaries** Samuel Pepys und seine Zeitgenossen.

contempt [kən'tɛmpt] *n* Verachtung *f*; ~ **of court** (*LAW*) Missachtung *f* (der Würde) des Gerichts, Ungebühr *f* vor Gericht; **to have** ~ **for sb/sth** jdn/etw verachten; **to hold sb in** ~ jdn verachten.

contemptible [kən'tɛmptəbl] *adj* verachtenswert.

contemptuous [kən'tɛmptjuəs] *adj* verächtlich, geringschätzig.

contend [kən'tɛnd] *vt*: **to** ~ **that ... behaupten, dass ...; to** ~ **with** fertig werden mit; **to** ~ **for** kämpfen um; **to have to** ~ **with** es zu tun haben mit; **he has a lot to** ~ **with** er hat viel um die Ohren.

contender [kən'tɛndə*] *n* (*SPORT*) Wettkämpfer(in) *m(f)*; (*for title*) Anwärter(in) *m(f)*; (*POL*) Kandidat(in) *m(f)*.

content [*adj, vt* kən'tɛnt, *n* 'kɒntɛnt] *adj* zufrieden ♦ *vt* zufrieden stellen ♦ *n* Inhalt *m*; (*fat content, moisture content etc*) Gehalt *m*; **contents** *npl* Inhalt; (*table of*) ~**s** Inhaltsverzeichnis *nt*; **to be** ~ **with** zufrieden sein mit; **to** ~ **o.s. with sth** sich mit etw zufrieden geben *or* begnügen; **to** ~ **o.s. with doing sth** sich damit zufrieden geben *or* begnügen, etw zu tun.

contented [kən'tɛntɪd] *adj* zufrieden.

contentedly [kən'tɛntɪdlɪ] *adv* zufrieden.

contention [kən'tɛnʃən] *n* Behauptung *f*; (*disagreement, argument*) Streit *m*; **bone of** ~ Zankapfel *m*.

contentious [kən'tɛnʃəs] *adj* strittig, umstritten.

contentment [kən'tɛntmənt] *n* Zufriedenheit *f*.

contest [*n* 'kɒntɛst, *vt* kən'tɛst] *n* (*competition*) Wettkampf *m*; (*for control, power etc*) Kampf *m* ♦ *vt* (*election, competition*) teilnehmen an +*dat*; (*compete for*) kämpfen um; (*statement*) bestreiten; (*decision*) anfechten; (*LAW*) anfechten.

contestant [kən'tɛstənt] *n* (*in quiz*) Kandidat(in) *m(f)*; (*in competition*) Teilnehmer(in) *m(f)*; (*in fight*) Kämpfer(in) *m(f)*.

context ['kɒntɛkst] *n* Zusammenhang *m*, Kontext *m*; **in** ~ im Zusammenhang; **out of** ~ aus dem Zusammenhang gerissen.

continent ['kɒntɪnənt] *n* Kontinent *m*, Erdteil *m*; **the C**~ (*BRIT*) (Kontinental)europa *nt*; **on the C**~ in (Kontinental)europa, auf dem Kontinent.

continental [kɒntɪ'nɛntl] *adj* kontinental; (*European*) europäisch ♦ *n* (*BRIT*) (Festlands)europäer(in) *m(f)*.

continental breakfast *n* kleines Frühstück *nt*.

continental quilt (*BRIT*) *n* Steppdecke *f*.

contingency [kən'tɪndʒənsɪ] *n* möglicher Fall *m*, Eventualität *f*.

contingency plan *n* Plan *m* für den Eventualfall.

contingent [kən'tɪndʒənt] *n* Kontingent *nt* ♦ *adj*: **to be** ~ **upon** abhängen von.

continual [kən'tɪnjuəl] *adj* ständig; (*process*) ununterbrochen.

continually [kən'tɪnjuəlɪ] *adv* (*see adj*) ständig; ununterbrochen.

continuation [kəntɪnju'eɪʃən] *n* Fortsetzung *f*; (*extension*) Weiterführung *f*.

continue [kən'tɪnjuː] *vi* andauern;

(*performance, road*) weitergehen; (*person: talking*) fortfahren ♦ *vt* fortsetzen; **to ~ to do sth/doing sth** etw weiter tun; **"to be ~d"** „Fortsetzung folgt"; **"~d on page 10"** „Fortsetzung auf Seite 10".

continuing education [kən'tɪnjuɪŋ-] *n* Erwachsenenbildung *f*.

continuity [kɒntɪ'njuːɪtɪ] *n* Kontinuität *f* ♦ *cpd* (*TV*): **~ announcer** Ansager(in) *m(f)*; **~ studio** Ansagestudio *nt*.

continuous [kən'tɪnjuəs] *adj* ununterbrochen; (*growth etc*) kontinuierlich; **~ form** (*LING*) Verlaufsform *f*; **~ performance** (*CINE*) durchgehende Vorstellung *f*.

continuously [kən'tɪnjuəslɪ] *adv* dauernd, ständig; (*uninterruptedly*) ununterbrochen.

continuous stationery *n* (*COMPUT*) Endlospapier *nt*.

contort [kən'tɔːt] *vt* (*body*) verrenken, verdrehen; (*face*) verziehen.

contortion [kən'tɔːʃən] *n* Verrenkung *f*.

contortionist [kən'tɔːʃənɪst] *n* Schlangenmensch *m*.

contour ['kɒntuə*] *n* (*also:* **~ line**) Höhenlinie *f*; (*shape, outline: gen pl*) Kontur *f*, Umriss *m*.

contraband ['kɒntrəbænd] *n* Schmuggelware *f* ♦ *adj* Schmuggel-.

contraception [kɒntrə'sepʃən] *n* Empfängnisverhütung *f*.

contraceptive [kɒntrə'septɪv] *adj* empfängnisverhütend ♦ *n* Verhütungsmittel *nt*.

contract [*n, cpd* 'kɒntrækt, *vb* kən'trækt] *n* Vertrag *m* ♦ *vi* schrumpfen; (*metal, muscle*) sich zusammenziehen ♦ *vt* (*illness*) erkranken an +*dat* ♦ *cpd* vertraglich festgelegt; (*work*) Auftrags-; **~ of employment/service** Arbeitsvertrag *m*; **to ~ to do sth** (*COMM*) sich vertraglich verpflichten, etw zu tun.

▶ **contract in** (*BRIT*) *vi* beitreten.

▶ **contract out** (*BRIT*) *vi* austreten.

contraction [kən'trækʃən] *n* Zusammenziehen *nt*; (*LING*) Kontraktion *f*; (*MED*) Wehe *f*.

contractor [kən'træktə*] *n* Auftragnehmer *m*; (*building contractor*) Bauunternehmer *m*.

contractual [kən'træktʃuəl] *adj* vertraglich.

contradict [kɒntrə'dɪkt] *vt* widersprechen +*dat*.

contradiction [kɒntrə'dɪkʃən] *n* Widerspruch *m*; **to be in ~ with** im Widerspruch stehen zu; **a ~ in terms** ein Widerspruch in sich.

contradictory [kɒntrə'dɪktərɪ] *adj* widersprüchlich.

contralto [kən'træltəu] *n* (*MUS*) Altistin *f*; (: *voice*) Alt *m*.

contraption [kən'træpʃən] (*pej*) *n* (*device*) Vorrichtung *f*; (*machine*) Gerät *nt*, Apparat *m*.

contrary¹ ['kɒntrərɪ] *adj* entgegengesetzt; (*ideas, opinions*) gegensätzlich; (*unfavourable*) widrig ♦ *n* Gegenteil *nt*; **~ to**

what we thought im Gegensatz zu dem, was wir dachten; **on the ~** im Gegenteil; **unless you hear to the ~** sofern Sie nichts Gegenteiliges hören.

contrary² [kən'trɛərɪ] *adj* widerspenstig.

contrast ['kɒntrɑːst] *n* Gegensatz *m*, Kontrast *m* ♦ *vt* vergleichen, gegenüberstellen; **in ~ to** *or* **with** im Gegensatz zu.

contrasting [kən'trɑːstɪŋ] *adj* (*colours*) kontrastierend; (*attitudes*) gegensätzlich.

contravene [kɒntrə'viːn] *vt* verstoßen gegen.

contravention [kɒntrə'venʃən] *n* Verstoß *m*; **to be in ~ of sth** gegen etw verstoßen.

contribute [kən'trɪbjuːt] *vi* beitragen ♦ *vt*: **to ~ £10/an article to** £10/einen Artikel beisteuern zu; **to ~ to** (*charity*) spenden für; (*newspaper*) schreiben für; (*discussion, problem etc*) beitragen zu.

contribution [kɒntrɪ'bjuːʃən] *n* Beitrag *m*; (*donation*) Spende *f*.

contributor [kən'trɪbjutə*] *n* (*to appeal*) Spender(in) *m(f)*; (*to newspaper*) Mitarbeiter(in) *m(f)*.

contributory [kən'trɪbjutərɪ] *adj*: **a ~ cause** ein Faktor, der mit eine Rolle spielt; **it was a ~ factor in ...** es trug zu ... bei.

contributory pension scheme (*BRIT*) *n* beitragspflichtige Rentenversicherung *f*.

contrite ['kɒntraɪt] *adj* zerknirscht.

contrivance [kən'traɪvəns] *n* (*scheme*) List *f*; (*device*) Vorrichtung *f*.

contrive [kən'traɪv] *vt* (*meeting*) arrangieren ♦ *vi*: **to ~ to do sth** es fertig bringen, etw zu tun.

control [kən'trəul] *vt* (*country*) regieren; (*organization*) leiten; (*machinery, process*) steuern; (*wages, prices*) kontrollieren; (*temper*) zügeln; (*disease, fire*) unter Kontrolle bringen ♦ *n* (*of country*) Kontrolle *f*; (*of organization*) Leitung *f*; (*of oneself, emotions*) Beherrschung *f*; (*SCI: also:* **~ group**) Kontrollgruppe *f*; **controls** *npl* (*of vehicle*) Steuerung *f*; (*on radio, television etc*) Bedienungsfeld *nt*; (*governmental*) Kontrolle *f*; **to ~ o.s.** sich beherrschen; **to take ~ of** die Kontrolle über etw +*acc* (*COMM*) übernehmen; **to be in ~ of** unter Kontrolle haben; (*in charge of*) unter sich *dat* haben; **out of/under ~** außer/unter Kontrolle; **everything is under ~** ich habe/ wir haben *etc* die Sache im Griff (*inf*); **the car went out of ~** der Fahrer verlor die Kontrolle über den Wagen; **circumstances beyond our ~** unvorhersehbare Umstände.

control key *n* (*COMPUT*) Controltaste *f*, Steuerungstaste *f*.

controlled substance *n* verschreibungspflichtiges Medikament.

controller [kən'trəulə*] *n* (*RADIO, TV*) Intendant(in) *m(f)*.

controlling interest [kən'trəulɪŋ-] *n* Mehrheitsanteil *m*.

control panel *n* Schalttafel *f*; (*on television*) Bedienungsfeld *nt*.

control point *n* Kontrollpunkt *m*, Kontrollstelle *f*.

control room *n* (*NAUT*) Kommandoraum *m*; (*MIL*) (Operations)zentrale *f*; (*RADIO, TV*) Regieraum *m*.

control tower *n* Kontrollturm *m*.

control unit *n* (*COMPUT*) Steuereinheit *f*.

controversial [kɔntrə'vɜːʃl] *adj* umstritten, kontrovers.

controversy ['kɔntrəvɜːsɪ] *n* Streit *m*, Kontroverse *f*.

conurbation [kɔnə'beɪʃən] *n* Ballungsgebiet *nt*, Ballungsraum *m*.

convalesce [kɔnvə'lɛs] *vi* genesen.

convalescence [kɔnvə'lɛsns] *n* Genesungszeit *f*.

convalescent [kɔnvə'lɛsnt] *adj* (*leave etc*) Genesungs-, Kur- ♦ *n* Genesende(r) *f(m)*.

convector [kən'vɛktə*] *n* Heizlüfter *m*.

convene [kən'viːn] *vt* einberufen ♦ *vi* zusammentreten.

convener [kən'viːnə*] *n* (*organizer*) Organisator(in) *m(f)*; (*chairperson*) Vorsitzende(r) *f(m)*.

convenience [kən'viːnɪəns] *n* Annehmlichkeit *f*; (*suitability*): **the ~ of this arrangement/ location** diese günstige Vereinbarung/Lage; **I like the ~ of having a shower** mir gefällt, wie angenehm es ist, eine Dusche zu haben; **I like the ~ of living in the city** mir gefällt, wie praktisch es ist, in der Stadt zu wohnen; **at your ~** wann es Ihnen passt; **at your earliest ~** möglichst bald, baldmöglichst; **with all modern ~s** *or* (*BRIT*) **all mod cons** mit allem modernen Komfort; *see also* **public convenience.**

convenience foods *npl* Fertiggerichte *pl*.

convenient [kən'viːnɪənt] *adj* günstig; (*handy*) praktisch; (*house etc*) günstig gelegen; **if it is ~ to you** wenn es Ihnen (so) passt, wenn es Ihnen keine Umstände macht.

conveniently [kən'viːnɪəntlɪ] *adv* (*happen*) günstigerweise; (*situated*) günstig.

convenor [kən'viːnə*] *n* = **convener.**

convent ['kɔnvənt] *n* Kloster *nt*.

convention [kən'vɛnʃən] *n* Konvention *f*; (*conference*) Tagung *f*, Konferenz *f*; (*agreement*) Abkommen *nt*.

conventional [kən'vɛnʃənl] *adj* konventionell.

convent school *n* Klosterschule *f*.

converge [kən'vɜːdʒ] *vi* (*roads*) zusammenlaufen ♦ *vi* sich einander annähern; **to ~ on sb/a place** (*people*) von überallher zu jdm/an einen Ort strömen.

conversant [kən'vɜːsnt] *adj*: **to be ~ with** vertraut sein mit.

conversation [kɔnvə'seɪʃən] *n* Gespräch *nt*, Unterhaltung *f*.

conversational [kɔnvə'seɪʃənl] *adj* (*tone, style*) Unterhaltungs-; (*language*) gesprochen;

~ mode (*COMPUT*) Dialogbetrieb *m*.

conversationalist [kɔnvə'seɪʃnəlɪst] *n* Unterhalter(in) *m(f)*, Gesprächspartner(in) *m(f)*.

converse [*n* 'kɔnvɜːs, *vi* kən'vɜːs] *n* Gegenteil *nt* ♦ *vi*: **to ~ (with sb) (about sth)** sich (mit jdm) (über etw) unterhalten.

conversely [kɔn'vɜːslɪ] *adv* umgekehrt.

conversion [kən'vɜːʃən] *n* Umwandlung *f*; (*of weights etc*) Umrechnung *f*; (*REL*) Bekehrung *f*; (*BRIT: of house*) Umbau *m*.

conversion table *n* Umrechnungstabelle *f*.

convert [*vt* kən'vɜːt, *n* 'kɔnvɜːt] *vt* umwandeln; (*person*) bekehren; (*building*) umbauen; (*vehicle*) umrüsten; (*COMM*) konvertieren; (*RUGBY*) verwandeln ♦ *n* Bekehrte(r) *f(m)*.

convertible [kən'vɜːtəbl] *adj* (*currency*) konvertierbar ♦ *n* (*AUT*) Kabriolett *nt*.

convex ['kɔnvɛks] *adj* konvex.

convey [kən'veɪ] *vt* (*information etc*) vermitteln; (*cargo, traveller*) befördern; (*thanks*) übermitteln.

conveyance [kən'veɪəns] *n* Beförderung *f*, Spedition *f*; (*vehicle*) Gefährt *nt*.

conveyancing [kən'veɪənsɪŋ] *n* (Eigentums)übertragung *f*.

conveyor belt *n* Fließband *nt*.

convict [*vt* kən'vɪkt, *n* 'kɔnvɪkt] *vt* verurteilen ♦ *n* Sträfling *m*.

conviction [kən'vɪkʃən] *n* Überzeugung *f*; (*LAW*) Verurteilung *f*.

convince [kən'vɪns] *vt* überzeugen; **to ~ sb (of sth)** jdn (von etw) überzeugen; **to ~ sb that ...** jdn davon überzeugen, dass ...

convinced [kən'vɪnst] *adj*: **~ (of)** überzeugt (von); **~ that ...** überzeugt davon, dass ...

convincing [kən'vɪnsɪŋ] *adj* überzeugend.

convincingly [kən'vɪnsɪŋlɪ] *adv* überzeugend.

convivial [kən'vɪvɪəl] *adj* freundlich; (*event*) gesellig.

convoluted ['kɔnvəluːtɪd] *adj* verwickelt, kompliziert; (*shape*) gewunden.

convoy ['kɔnvɔɪ] *n* Konvoi *m*.

convulse [kən'vʌls] *vt*: **to be ~d with laughter/pain** sich vor Lachen schütteln/ Schmerzen krümmen.

convulsion [kən'vʌlʃən] *n* Schüttelkrampf *m*.

coo [kuː] *vi* gurren.

cook [kuk] *vt* kochen, zubereiten ♦ *vi* (*person, food*) kochen; (*fry, roast*) braten; (*pie*) backen ♦ *n* Koch *m*, Köchin *f*.

► **cook up** (*inf*) *vt* sich *dat* einfallen lassen, zurechtbasteln.

cookbook ['kukbuk] *n* Kochbuch *nt*.

cook-chill ['kuktʃɪl] *adj* durch rasches Kühlen haltbar gemacht.

cooker ['kukə*] *n* Herd *m*.

cookery ['kukərɪ] *n* Kochen *nt*, Kochkunst *f*.

cookery book (*BRIT*) *n* = **cookbook.**

cookie ['kukɪ] (*US*) *n* Keks *m or nt*, Plätzchen *nt*.

cooking ['kukɪŋ] *n* Kochen *nt*; (*food*) Essen *nt*

♦ *cpd* Koch-; (*chocolate*) Block-.

cookout ['kukaut] (*US*) *n* ≈ Grillparty *f*.

cool [kuːl] *adj* kühl; (*dress, clothes*) leicht, luftig; (*person: calm*) besonnen; (: *unfriendly*) kühl ♦ *vt* kühlen ♦ *vi* abkühlen; **it's** ~ es ist kühl; **to keep sth** ~ *or* **in a** ~ **place** etw kühl aufbewahren; **to keep one's** ~ die Ruhe bewahren.

▶ **cool down** *vi* abkühlen; (*fig*) sich beruhigen.

coolant ['kuːlənt] *n* Kühlflüssigkeit *f*.

cool box *n* Kühlbox *f*.

cooler ['kuːlə*] (*US*) *n* = **cool box**.

cooling ['kuːlɪŋ] *adj* (*drink, shower*) kühlend; (*feeling, emotion*) abkühlend.

cooling tower ['kuːlɪŋ-] *n* Kühlturm *m*.

coolly ['kuːlɪ] *adv* (*calmly*) besonnen, ruhig; (*in unfriendly way*) kühl.

coolness ['kuːlnɪs] *n* (*see adj*) Kühle *f*; Leichtigkeit *f*, Luftigkeit *f*; Besonnenheit *f*.

coop [kuːp] *n* (*for rabbits*) Kaninchenstall *m*; (*for poultry*) Hühnerstall *m* ♦ *vt*: **to** ~ **up** (*fig*) einsperren.

co-op ['kəuɔp] *n abbr* (= *cooperative (society)*) Genossenschaft *f*.

cooperate [kəu'ɔpəreɪt] *vi* zusammenarbeiten; (*assist*) mitmachen, kooperieren; **to** ~ **with sb** mit jdm zusammenarbeiten.

cooperation [kəuɔpə'reɪʃən] *n* (*see vb*) Zusammenarbeit *f*; Mitarbeit *f*, Kooperation *f*.

cooperative [kəu'ɔpərətɪv] *adj* (*farm, business*) auf Genossenschaftsbasis; (*person*) kooperativ; (: *helpful*) hilfsbereit ♦ *n* Genossenschaft *f*, Kooperative *f*.

coopt [kəu'ɔpt] *vt*: **to** ~ **sb onto a committee** jdn in ein Komitee hinzuwählen *or* kooptieren.

coordinate [kəu'ɔːdɪneɪt] *vt* koordinieren ♦ *n* (*MATH*) Koordinate *f*; **coordinates** *npl* (*clothes*) Kleidung *f* zum Kombinieren.

coordination [kəuɔːdɪ'neɪʃən] *n* Koordinierung *f*, Koordination *f*.

coownership [kəu'əunəʃɪp] *n* Mitbesitz *m*.

cop [kɔp] (*inf*) *n* Polizist(in) *m(f)*, Bulle *m* (*pej*).

cope [kəup] *vi* zurechtkommen; **to** ~ **with** fertig werden mit.

Copenhagen ['kəupn'heɪgən] *n* Kopenhagen *nt*.

copier ['kɔpɪə*] *n* (*also*: **photocopier**) Kopiergerät *nt*, Kopierer *m*.

copilot ['kəupaɪlət] *n* Kopilot(in) *m(f)*.

copious ['kəupɪəs] *adj* reichlich.

copper ['kɔpə*] *n* Kupfer *nt*; (*BRIT*: *inf*) Polizist(in) *m(f)*, Bulle *m* (*pej*); **coppers** *npl* (*small change, coins*) Kleingeld *nt*.

coppice ['kɔpɪs] *n* Wäldchen *nt*.

copse [kɔps] *n* = **coppice**.

copulate ['kɔpjuleɪt] *vi* kopulieren.

copy ['kɔpɪ] *n* Kopie *f*; (*of book, record, newspaper*) Exemplar *nt*; (*for printing*) Artikel *m* ♦ *vt* (*person*) nachahmen; (*idea etc*) nachmachen; (*something written*) abschreiben; **this murder story will make good** ~ (*PRESS*) aus diesem Mord kann man etwas machen.

▶ **copy out** *vt* abschreiben.

copycat ['kɔpɪkæt] (*pej*) *n* Nachahmer(in) *m(f)*.

copyright ['kɔpɪraɪt] *n* Copyright *nt*, Urheberrecht *nt*; ~ **reserved** urheberrechtlich geschützt.

copy typist *n* Schreibkraft *f* (*die mit Textvorlagen arbeitet*).

copywriter ['kɔpɪraɪtə*] *n* Werbetexter(in) *m(f)*.

coral ['kɔrəl] *n* Koralle *f*.

coral reef *n* Korallenriff *nt*.

Coral Sea *n*: **the** ~ das Korallenmeer.

cord [kɔːd] *n* Schnur *f*; (*string*) Kordel *f*; (*ELEC*) Kabel *nt*, Schnur *f*; (*fabric*) Kord(samt) *m*; **cords** *npl* (*trousers*) Kordhosen *pl*.

cordial ['kɔːdɪəl] *adj* herzlich ♦ *n* (*BRIT*) Fruchtsaftkonzentrat *nt*.

cordless ['kɔːdlɪs] *adj* schnurlos.

cordon ['kɔːdn] *n* Kordon *m*, Absperrkette *f*.

▶ **cordon off** *vt* (*area*) absperren, abriegeln; (*crowd*) mit einer Absperrkette zurückhalten.

corduroy ['kɔːdərɔɪ] *n* Kord(samt) *m*.

CORE [kɔː*] (*US*) *n abbr* (= *Congress of Racial Equality*) Ausschuss für Rassengleichheit.

core [kɔː*] *n* Kern *m*; (*of fruit*) Kerngehäuse *nt* ♦ *vt* das Kerngehäuse ausschneiden aus; **rotten to the** ~ durch und durch schlecht.

Corfu [kɔː'fuː] *n* Korfu *nt*.

coriander [kɔrɪ'ændə*] *n* Koriander *m*.

cork [kɔːk] *n* (*stopper*) Korken *m*; (*substance*) Kork *m*.

corkage ['kɔːkɪdʒ] *n* Korkengeld *nt*.

corked [kɔːkt] *adj*: **the wine is** ~ der Wein schmeckt nach Kork.

corkscrew ['kɔːkskruː] *n* Korkenzieher *m*.

corky ['kɔːkɪ] (*US*) *adj* = **corked**.

corm [kɔːm] *n* Knolle *f*.

cormorant ['kɔːmərnt] *n* Kormoran *m*.

Corn (*BRIT*) *abbr* (*POST*: = *Cornwall*).

corn [kɔːn] *n* (*BRIT*) Getreide *nt*, Korn *nt*; (*US*) Mais *m*; (*on foot*) Hühnerauge *nt*; ~ **on the cob** Maiskolben *m*.

cornea ['kɔːnɪə] *n* Hornhaut *f*.

corned beef ['kɔːnd-] *n* Cornedbeef *nt*, Corned Beef *nt*.

corner ['kɔːnə*] *n* Ecke *f*; (*bend*) Kurve *f* ♦ *vt* in die Enge treiben; (*COMM: market*) monopolisieren ♦ *vi* (*in car*) die Kurve nehmen; **to cut** ~**s** (*fig*) das Verfahren abkürzen.

corner flag *n* Eckfahne *f*.

corner kick *n* Eckball *m*.

cornerstone ['kɔːnəstəun] *n* (*fig*) Grundstein *m*, Eckstein *m*.

cornet ['kɔːnɪt] *n* (*MUS*) Kornett *nt*; (*BRIT*: *for ice cream*) Eistüte *f*.

cornflakes ['kɔːnfleɪks] *npl* Cornflakes *pl*.

cornflour ['kɔːnflauə*] (*BRIT*) n Stärkemehl nt.
cornice ['kɔːnɪs] n (Ge)sims nt.
Cornish ['kɔːnɪʃ] adj kornisch, aus Cornwall.
corn oil n (Mais)keimöl nt.
cornstarch ['kɔːnstɑːtʃ] (*US*) n = cornflour.
cornucopia [kɔːnjuˈkəupɪə] n Fülle f.
Cornwall ['kɔːnwəl] n Cornwall nt.
corny ['kɔːnɪ] (*inf*) adj (*joke*) blöd.
corollary [kəˈrɔlərɪ] n (logische) Folge f.
coronary ['kɔrənərɪ] n (*also:* ~ **thrombosis**) Herzinfarkt m.
coronation [kɔrəˈneɪʃən] n Krönung f.
coroner ['kɔrənə*] n Beamter, der Todesfälle untersucht, die nicht eindeutig eine natürliche Ursache haben.
coronet ['kɔrənɪt] n Krone f.
Corp. abbr = corporation; (*MIL*) = corporal.
corporal ['kɔːpərl] n Stabsunteroffizier m.
corporal punishment n Prügelstrafe f.
corporate ['kɔːpərɪt] adj (*organization*) körperschaftlich; (*action, effort, ownership*) gemeinschaftlich; (*finance*) Unternehmens-; (*image, identity*) Firmen-.
corporate hospitality n Empfänge, Diners etc auf Kosten der ausrichtenden Firma.
corporation [kɔːpəˈreɪʃən] n (*COMM*) Körperschaft f; (*of town*) Gemeinde f, Stadt f.
corporation tax n Körperschaftssteuer f.
corps [kɔː*] (pl ~) n Korps nt; **the press** ~ die Presse.
corpse [kɔːps] n Leiche f.
corpuscle ['kɔːpʌsl] n Blutkörperchen nt.
corral [kəˈrɑːl] n Korral m.
correct [kəˈrɛkt] adj richtig; (*proper*) korrekt ♦ vt korrigieren; (*mistake*) berichtigen, verbessern; **you are** ~ Sie haben Recht.
correction [kəˈrɛkʃən] n (*see vb*) Korrektur f; Berichtigung f, Verbesserung f.
correctly [kəˈrɛktlɪ] adv (*see adj*) richtig; korrekt.
correlate ['kɔrɪleɪt] vt zueinander in Beziehung setzen ♦ vi: **to** ~ **with** in einer Beziehung stehen zu.
correlation [kɔrɪˈleɪʃən] n Beziehung f, Zusammenhang m.
correspond [kɔrɪsˈpɔnd] vi: **to** ~ (**with**) (*write*) korrespondieren (mit); (*be in accordance*) übereinstimmen (mit); **to** ~ **to** (*be equivalent*) entsprechen +dat.
correspondence [kɔrɪsˈpɔndəns] n Korrespondenz f, Briefwechsel m; (*relationship*) Beziehung f.
correspondence column n Leserbriefspalte f.
correspondence course n Fernkurs m.
correspondent [kɔrɪsˈpɔndənt] n Korrespondent(in) m(f).
corresponding [kɔrɪsˈpɔndɪŋ] adj entsprechend.
corridor ['kɔrɪdɔː*] n Korridor m; (*in train*) Gang m.

corroborate [kəˈrɔbəreɪt] vt bestätigen.
corrode [kəˈrəud] vt zerfressen ♦ vi korrodieren.
corrosion [kəˈrəuʒən] n Korrosion f.
corrosive [kəˈrəuzɪv] adj korrosiv.
corrugated ['kɔrəgeɪtɪd] adj (*roof*) gewellt; (*cardboard*) Well-.
corrugated iron n Wellblech nt.
corrupt [kəˈrʌpt] adj korrupt; (*depraved*) verdorben ♦ vt korrumpieren; (*morally*) verderben; ~ **practices** Korruption f.
corruption [kəˈrʌpʃən] n Korruption f.
corset ['kɔːsɪt] n Korsett nt; (*MED*) Stützkorsett nt.
Corsica ['kɔːsɪkə] n Korsika nt.
Corsican ['kɔːsɪkən] adj korsisch ♦ n Korse m, Korsin f.
cortège [kɔːˈteɪʒ] n (*also:* **funeral** ~) Leichenzug m.
cortisone ['kɔːtɪzəun] n Kortison nt.
coruscating ['kɔrəskeɪtɪŋ] adj sprühend.
c.o.s. abbr (= cash on shipment) Barzahlung bei Versand.
cosh [kɔʃ] (*BRIT*) n Totschläger m.
cosignatory ['kəuˈsɪgnətərɪ] n Mitunterzeichner(in) m(f).
cosiness ['kəuzɪnɪs] n Gemütlichkeit f, Behaglichkeit f.
cos lettuce ['kɔs-] n römischer Salat m.
cosmetic [kɔzˈmɛtɪk] n Kosmetikum nt ♦ adj kosmetisch; ~ **surgery** (*MED*) kosmetische Chirurgie f.
cosmic ['kɔzmɪk] adj kosmisch.
cosmonaut ['kɔzmənɔːt] n Kosmonaut(in) m(f).
cosmopolitan [kɔzməˈpɔlɪtn] adj kosmopolitisch.
cosmos ['kɔzmɔs] n: **the** ~ der Kosmos.
cosset ['kɔsɪt] vt verwöhnen.
cost [kɔst] (pt, pp cost) n Kosten pl; (*fig: loss, damage etc*) Preis m ♦ vt kosten; (*find out cost of*) (pt, pp costed) veranschlagen; **costs** npl (*COMM, LAW*) Kosten pl; **the** ~ **of living** die Lebenshaltungskosten pl; **at all** ~s um jeden Preis; **how much does it** ~? wie viel or was kostet es?; **it** ~s **£5/too much** es kostet £5/ ist zu teuer; **what will it** ~ **to have it repaired?** wie viel kostet die Reparatur?; **to** ~ **sb time/effort** jdn Zeit/Mühe kosten; **it** ~ **him his life/job** es kostete ihn das Leben/seine Stelle.
cost accountant n Kostenbuchhalter(in) m(f).
co-star ['kəustɑː*] n einer der Hauptdarsteller m, eine der Hauptdarstellerinnen f; **she was Sean Connery's** ~ **in** ... sie spielte neben Sean Connery in ...
Costa Rica ['kɔstəˈriːkə] n Costa Rica nt.
cost centre n Kostenstelle f.
cost control n Kostenkontrolle f.
cost-effective ['kɔstɪˈfɛktɪv] adj rentabel;

(*COMM*) kostengünstig.
cost-effectiveness ['kɔstɪ'fɛktɪvnɪs] *n*
Rentabilität *f*.
costing ['kɔstɪŋ] *n* Kalkulation *f*.
costly ['kɔstlɪ] *adj* teuer, kostspielig; (*in time,
effort*) aufwändig, aufwendig.
cost-of-living ['kɔstəv'lɪvɪŋ] *adj*
Lebenshaltungskosten-; (*index*)
Lebenshaltungs-.
cost price (*BRIT*) *n* Selbstkostenpreis *m*; **to
sell/buy at** ~ zum Selbstkostenpreis
verkaufen/kaufen.
costume ['kɔstjuːm] *n* Kostüm *nt*; (*BRIT: also:
swimming* ~) Badeanzug *m*.
costume jewellery *n* Modeschmuck *m*.
cosy, (*US*) **cozy** ['kəuzɪ] *adj* gemütlich,
behaglich; (*bed, scarf, gloves*) warm; (*chat,
evening*) gemütlich; **I'm very** ~ **here** ich
fühle mich hier sehr wohl, ich finde es hier
sehr gemütlich.
cot [kɔt] *n* (*BRIT*) Kinderbett *nt*; (*US: campbed*)
Feldbett *nt*.
cot death *n* Krippentod *m*, plötzlicher
Kindstod *m*.
Cotswolds ['kɔtswəuldz] *npl*: **the** ~ die
Cotswolds *pl*.
cottage ['kɔtɪdʒ] *n* Cottage *nt*, Häuschen *nt*.
cottage cheese *n* Hüttenkäse *m*.
cottage industry *n* Heimindustrie *f*.
cottage pie *n* Hackfleisch mit Kartoffelbrei
überbacken.
cotton ['kɔtn] *n* (*fabric*) Baumwollstoff *m*;
(*plant*) Baumwollstrauch *m*; (*thread*)
(Baumwoll)garn *nt* ♦ *cpd* (*dress etc*)
Baumwoll-.
▶ **cotton on** (*inf*) *vi*: **to** ~ **on** es kapieren *or*
schnallen; **to** ~ **on to sth** etw kapieren *or*
schnallen.
cotton candy (*US*) *n* Zuckerwatte *f*.
cotton wool (*BRIT*) *n* Watte *f*.
couch [kautʃ] *n* Couch *f* ♦ *vt* formulieren.
couchette [kuː'ʃɛt] *n* Liegewagen(platz) *m*.
couch potato (*esp US: inf*) *n* Dauerglotzer(in)
m(f).
cough [kɔf] *vi* husten; (*engine*) stottern ♦ *n*
Husten *m*.
cough drop *n* Hustenpastille *f*.
cough mixture *n* Hustensaft *m*.
cough syrup *n* = **cough mixture**.
could [kud] *pt of* **can²**.
couldn't ['kudnt] = **could not**.
council ['kaunsl] *n* Rat *m*; **city/town** ~
Stadtrat *m*; **C**~ **of Europe** Europarat *m*.
council estate (*BRIT*) *n* Siedlung *f* mit
Sozialwohnungen.
council house (*BRIT*) *n* Sozialwohnung *f*.
council housing *n* sozialer Wohnungsbau *m*;
(*accommodation*) Sozialwohnungen *pl*.
councillor ['kaunslə*] *n* Stadtrat *m*, Stadträtin
f.
council tax (*BRIT*) *n* Gemeindesteuer *f*.
counsel ['kaunsl] *n* Rat(schlag) *m*; (*lawyer*)

Rechtsanwalt *m*, Rechtsanwältin *f* ♦ *vt*
beraten; **to** ~ **sth** etw raten *or* empfehlen; **to**
~ **sb to do sth** jdm raten *or* empfehlen, etw
zu tun; ~ **for the defence** Verteidiger(in)
m(f); ~ **for the prosecution** Vertreter(in) *m(f)*
der Anklage.
counsellor ['kaunslə*] *n* Berater(in) *m(f)*; (*US:
lawyer*) Rechtsanwalt *m*, Rechtsanwältin *f*.
count [kaunt] *vt* zählen; (*include*) mitrechnen,
mitzählen ♦ *vi* zählen; (*be considered*)
betrachtet *or* angesehen werden ♦ *n*
Zählung *f*; (*level*) Zahl *f*; (*nobleman*) Graf *m*;
to ~ (**up**) **to 10** bis 10 zählen; **not** ~**ing the
children** die Kinder nicht mitgerechnet; **10**
~**ing him** 10, wenn man ihn mitrechnet; **to**
~ **the cost of sth** die Folgen von etw
abschätzen; **it** ~**s for very little** es zählt nicht
viel; ~ **yourself lucky** Sie können sich
glücklich schätzen; **to keep** ~ **of sth** die
Übersicht über etw *acc* behalten; **blood** ~
Blutbild *nt*; **cholesterol/alcohol** ~
Cholesterin-/Alkoholspiegel *m*.
▶ **count on** *vt fus* rechnen mit; (*depend on*)
sich verlassen auf +*acc*; **to** ~ **on doing sth**
die feste Absicht haben, etw zu tun.
▶ **count up** *vt* zusammenzählen,
zusammenrechnen.
countdown ['kauntdaun] *n* Count-down *m*,
Countdown *m*.
countenance ['kauntɪnəns] *n* Gesicht *nt* ♦ *vt*
gutheißen.
counter ['kauntə*] *n* (*in shop*) Ladentisch *m*; (*in
café*) Theke *f*; (*in bank, post office*) Schalter *m*;
(*in game*) Spielmarke *f*; (*TECH*) Zähler *m* ♦ *vt*
(*oppose: sth said, sth done*) begegnen +*dat*;
(*blow*) kontern ♦ *adv*: ~ **to** gegen +*acc*; **to buy
sth under the** ~ (*fig*) etw unter dem
Ladentisch bekommen; **to** ~ **sth with sth**
auf etw *acc* mit etw antworten; **to** ~ **sth by
doing sth** einer Sache damit begegnen, dass
man etw tut.
counteract ['kauntər'ækt] *vt* entgegenwirken
+*dat*; (*effect*) neutralisieren.
counterattack ['kauntərə'tæk] *n*
Gegenangriff *m* ♦ *vi* einen Gegenangriff
starten.
counterbalance ['kauntə'bæləns] *vt*
Gegengewicht *nt*.
counterclockwise ['kauntə'klɔkwaɪz] *adv*
gegen den Uhrzeigersinn.
counterespionage ['kauntər'ɛspɪənɑːʒ] *n*
Gegenspionage *f*, Spionageabwehr *f*.
counterfeit ['kauntəfɪt] *n* Fälschung *f* ♦ *vt*
fälschen ♦ *adj* (*coin*) Falsch-.
counterfoil ['kauntəfɔɪl] *n* Kontrollabschnitt
m.
counterintelligence ['kauntərɪn'tɛlɪdʒəns] *n*
Gegenspionage *f*, Spionageabwehr *f*.
countermand ['kauntəmɑːnd] *vt* aufheben,
widerrufen.
countermeasure ['kauntəmɛʒə*] *n*
Gegenmaßnahme *f*.

counteroffensive [ˈkauntərəˈfɛnsɪv] n
Gegenoffensive f.

counterpane [ˈkauntəpeɪn] n Tagesdecke f.

counterpart [ˈkauntəpɑːt] n Gegenüber nt; (of
document etc) Gegenstück nt, Pendant nt.

counterproductive [ˈkauntəprəˈdʌktɪv] adj
widersinnig.

counterproposal [ˈkauntəprəˈpəuzl] n
Gegenvorschlag m.

countersign [ˈkauntəsaɪn] vt gegenzeichnen.

countersink [ˈkauntəsɪŋk] vt senken.

countess [ˈkauntɪs] n Gräfin f.

countless [ˈkauntlɪs] adj unzählig, zahllos.

countrified [ˈkʌntrɪfaɪd] adj ländlich.

country [ˈkʌntrɪ] n Land nt; (native land)
Heimatland nt; **in the** ~ auf dem Land;
mountainous ~ gebirgige Landschaft f.

country and western (music) n Country-
und-Western-Musik f.

country dancing (BRIT) n Volkstanz m.

country house n Landhaus nt.

countryman [ˈkʌntrɪmən] (irreg: like **man**) n
(compatriot) Landsmann m; (country dweller)
Landmann m.

countryside [ˈkʌntrɪsaɪd] n Land nt; (scenery)
Landschaft f, Gegend f.

country-wide [ˈkʌntrɪˈwaɪd] adj, adv
landesweit.

county [ˈkauntɪ] n (BRIT) Grafschaft f; (US)
(Verwaltungs)bezirk m.

county council (BRIT) n Gemeinderat m (einer
Grafschaft).

county town (BRIT) n Hauptstadt einer
Grafschaft.

coup [kuː] (pl ~**s**) n (also: ~ **d'état**)
Staatsstreich m, Coup d'Etat m;
(achievement) Coup m.

coupé [kuːˈpeɪ] n Coupé nt, Kupee nt.

couple [ˈkʌpl] n Paar nt; (married couple)
Ehepaar nt ♦ vt verbinden; (vehicles)
koppeln; **a** ~ **of** (two) zwei; (a few) ein paar.

couplet [ˈkʌplɪt] n Verspaar nt.

coupling [ˈkʌplɪŋ] n Kupplung f.

coupon [ˈkuːpɔn] n Gutschein m; (detachable
form) Abschnitt m; (COMM) Kupon m,
Coupon m.

courage [ˈkʌrɪdʒ] n Mut m.

courageous [kəˈreɪdʒəs] adj mutig.

courgette [kuəˈʒɛt] (BRIT) n Zucchino m.

courier [ˈkurɪəʳ] n (messenger) Kurier(in) m(f);
(for tourists) Reiseleiter(in) m(f).

course [kɔːs] n (SCOL) Kurs(us) m; (of ship)
Kurs m; (of life, events, time etc, of river) Lauf
m; (of argument) Richtung f; (part of meal)
Gang m; (for golf) Platz m; **of** ~ natürlich; **of**
~**!** (aber) natürlich!, (aber)
selbstverständlich!; (**no) of** ~ **not!** natürlich
nicht!; **in the** ~ **of the next few days**
während or im Laufe der nächsten paar
Tage; **in due** ~ zu gegebener Zeit; ~ (**of
action**) Vorgehensweise f; **the best** ~ **would
be to** ... das Beste wäre es, zu ...; **we have no**

other ~ **but to** ... es bleibt uns nichts
anderes übrig, als zu ...; ~ **of lectures**
Vorlesungsreihe f; ~ **of treatment** (MED)
Behandlung f; **first/last** ~ erster/letzter
Gang, Vor-/Nachspeise f.

court [kɔːt] n Hof m; (LAW) Gericht nt; (for
tennis, badminton etc) Platz m ♦ vt den Hof
machen +dat; (favour, popularity) werben um;
(death, disaster) herausfordern; **out of** ~
(LAW) außergerichtlich; **to take to** ~ (LAW)
verklagen, vor Gericht bringen.

courteous [ˈkəːtɪəs] adj höflich.

courtesan [kɔːtɪˈzæn] n Kurtisane f.

courtesy [ˈkəːtəsɪ] n Höflichkeit f; **(by)** ~ **of**
freundlicherweise zur Verfügung gestellt
von.

courtesy bus, courtesy coach n
gebührenfreier Bus m.

courtesy light n Innenleuchte f.

courthouse [ˈkɔːthaus] (US) n
Gerichtsgebäude nt.

courtier [ˈkɔːtɪəʳ] n Höfling m.

court martial (pl **courts martial**) n
Militärgericht nt.

court of appeal (pl **courts of appeal**) n
Berufungsgericht nt.

court of inquiry (pl **courts of inquiry**) n
Untersuchungskommission f.

courtroom [ˈkɔːtrum] n Gerichtssaal m.

court shoe n Pumps m.

courtyard [ˈkɔːtjɑːd] n Hof m.

cousin [ˈkʌzn] n (male) Cousin m, Vetter m;
(female) Cousine f, Kusine f; **first** ~
Cousin(e) ersten Grades.

cove [kəuv] n (kleine) Bucht f.

covenant [ˈkʌvənənt] n Schwur m ♦ vt: **to**
~ **£200 per year to a charity** sich vertraglich
verpflichten, £200 im Jahr für wohltätige
Zwecke zu spenden.

Coventry [ˈkɔvəntrɪ] n: **to send sb to** ~ (fig)
jdn schneiden (inf).

cover [ˈkʌvəʳ] vt bedecken; (distance)
zurücklegen; (INSURANCE) versichern;
(topic) behandeln; (include) erfassen;
(PRESS: report on) berichten über +acc ♦ n
(for furniture) Bezug m; (for typewriter, PC etc)
Hülle f; (of book, magazine) Umschlag m;
(shelter) Schutz m; (INSURANCE)
Versicherung f; (fig: for illegal activities)
Tarnung f; **to be** ~**ed in** or **with** bedeckt sein
mit; **£10 will** ~ **my expenses** £10 decken
meine Unkosten; **to take** ~ (from rain) sich
unterstellen; **under** ~ geschützt; **under** ~ **of
darkness** im Schutz(e) der Dunkelheit;
under separate ~ getrennt.

▶ **cover up** vt zudecken; (fig: facts, feelings)
verheimlichen; (: mistakes) vertuschen ♦ vi
(fig): **to** ~ **up for sb** jdn decken.

coverage [ˈkʌvərɪdʒ] n Berichterstattung f;
television ~ **of the conference**
Fernsehberichte pl über die Konferenz; **to
give full** ~ **to** ausführlich berichten über

+*acc.*

coveralls ['kʌvərɔːlz] (*US*) *npl* Overall *m*.

cover charge *n* Kosten *pl* für ein Gedeck.

covering ['kʌvərɪŋ] *n* Schicht *f*; (*of snow, dust etc*) Decke *f*.

covering letter, (*US*) **cover letter** *n* Begleitbrief *m*.

cover note *n* (*INSURANCE*) Deckungszusage *f*.

cover price *n* Einzel(exemplar)preis *m*.

covert ['kʌvət] *adj* versteckt; (*glance*) verstohlen.

cover-up ['kʌvərʌp] *n* Vertuschung *f*, Verschleierung *f*.

covet ['kʌvɪt] *vt* begehren.

cow [kau] *n* (*animal, inf!: woman*) Kuh *f* ♦ *cpd* Kuh- ♦ *vt* einschüchtern.

coward ['kauəd] *n* Feigling *m*.

cowardice ['kauədɪs] *n* Feigheit *f*.

cowardly ['kauədlɪ] *adj* feige.

cowboy ['kaubɔɪ] *n* (*in US*) Cowboy *m*; (*pej: tradesman*) Pfuscher *m*.

cow elephant *n* Elefantenkuh *f*.

cower ['kauə*] *vi* sich ducken; (*squatting*) kauern.

cowshed ['kauʃɛd] *n* Kuhstall *m*.

cowslip ['kauslɪp] *n* Schlüsselblume *f*.

cox [kɔks] *n abbr* = **coxswain**.

coxswain ['kɔksn] *n* Steuermann *m*; (*of ship*) Boot(s)führer *m*.

coy [kɔɪ] *adj* verschämt.

coyote [kɔɪ'əutɪ] *n* Kojote *m*.

cozy ['kəuzɪ] (*US*) *adj* = **cosy**.

CP *n abbr* (= *Communist Party*) KP *f*.

cp. *abbr* (= *compare*) vgl.

c/p (*BRIT*) *abbr* = **carriage paid**.

CPA (*US*) *n abbr* = **certified public accountant**.

CPI *n abbr* (= *Consumer Price Index*) (Verbraucher)preisindex *m*.

Cpl *abbr* (*MIL*) = **corporal**.

CP/M *n abbr* (= *Control Program for Microprocessors*) CP/M *nt*.

cps *abbr* (*COMPUT, TYP*: = *characters per second*) cps, Zeichen *pl* pro Sekunde.

CPSA (*BRIT*) *n abbr* (= *Civil and Public Services Association*) Gewerkschaft im öffentlichen Dienst.

CPU *n abbr* (*COMPUT*) = **central processing unit**.

cr. *abbr* = **credit, creditor**.

crab [kræb] *n* Krabbe *f*, Krebs *m*; (*meat*) Krabbe *f*.

crab apple *n* Holzapfel *m*.

crack [kræk] *n* (*noise*) Knall *m*; (*of wood breaking*) Knacks *m*; (*gap*) Spalte *f*; (*in bone, dish, glass*) Sprung *m*; (*in wall*) Riss *m*; (*joke*) Witz *m*; (*DRUGS*) Crack *nt* ♦ *vt* (*whip*) knallen mit; (*twig*) knacken mit; (*dish, glass*) einen Sprung machen in +*acc*; (*bone*) anbrechen; (*nut, code*) knacken; (*wall*) rissig machen; (*problem*) lösen; (*joke*) reißen ♦ *adj* erstklassig; **to have a ~ at sth** (*inf*) etw mal

probieren; **to ~ jokes** (*inf*) Witze reißen; **to get ~ing** (*inf*) loslegen.

▶ **crack down on** *vt fus* hart durchgreifen gegen.

▶ **crack up** *vi* durchdrehen, zusammenbrechen.

crackdown ['krækdaun] *n*: **~ (on)** scharfes Durchgreifen *nt* (gegen).

cracked [krækt] (*inf*) *adj* übergeschnappt.

cracker ['krækə*] *n* (*biscuit*) Kräcker *m*; (*Christmas cracker*) Knallbonbon *nt*; (*firework*) Knallkörper *m*, Kracher *m*; **a ~ of a ...** (*BRIT: inf*) ein(e) tolle(r, s) ...; **he's ~s** (*BRIT: inf*) er ist übergeschnappt.

crackle ['krækl] *vi* (*fire*) knistern, prasseln; (*twig*) knacken.

crackling ['kræklɪŋ] *n* (*of fire*) Knistern *nt*, Prasseln *nt*; (*of twig, on radio, telephone*) Knacken *nt*; (*of pork*) Kruste *f* (*des Schweinebratens*).

crackpot ['krækpɔt] (*inf*) *n* Spinner(in) *m(f)* ♦ *adj* verrückt.

cradle ['kreɪdl] *n* Wiege *f* ♦ *vt* fest in den Armen halten.

craft [krɑːft] *n* (*skill*) Geschicklichkeit *f*; (*art*) Kunsthandwerk *nt*; (*trade*) Handwerk *nt*; (*pl inv: boat*) Boot *nt*; (*pl inv: plane*) Flugzeug *nt*.

craftsman ['krɑːftsmən] (*irreg: like* **man**) *n* Handwerker *m*.

craftsmanship ['krɑːftsmənʃɪp] *n* handwerkliche Ausführung *f*.

crafty ['krɑːftɪ] *adj* schlau, clever.

crag [kræg] *n* Fels *m*.

craggy ['krægɪ] *adj* (*mountain*) zerklüftet; (*cliff*) felsig; (*face*) kantig.

cram [kræm] *vt* voll stopfen ♦ *vi* pauken (*inf*), büffeln (*inf*); **to ~ with** voll stopfen mit; **to ~ sth into** etw hineinstopfen in +*acc*.

cramming ['kræmɪŋ] *n* (*for exams*) Pauken *nt*, Büffeln *nt*.

cramp [kræmp] *n* Krampf *m* ♦ *vt* hemmen.

cramped [kræmpt] *adj* eng.

crampon ['kræmpən] *n* Steigeisen *nt*.

cranberry ['krænbərɪ] *n* Preiselbeere *f*.

crane [kreɪn] *n* Kran *m*; (*bird*) Kranich *m* ♦ *vt*: **to ~ one's neck** den Hals recken ♦ *vi*: **to ~ forward** den Hals recken.

crania ['kreɪnɪə] *npl of* **cranium**.

cranium ['kreɪnɪəm] (*pl* **crania**) *n* Schädel *m*.

crank [kræŋk] *n* Spinner(in) *m(f)*; (*handle*) Kurbel *f*.

crankshaft ['kræŋkʃɑːft] *n* Kurbelwelle *f*.

cranky ['kræŋkɪ] *adj* verrückt.

cranny ['krænɪ] *n see* **nook**.

crap [kræp] (*inf!*) *n* Scheiße *f* (!) ♦ *vi* scheißen (!); **to have a ~** scheißen (!).

crappy ['kræpɪ] (*inf!*) *adj* beschissen (!).

crash [kræʃ] *n* (*noise*) Krachen *nt*; (*of car*) Unfall *m*; (*of plane etc*) Unglück *nt*; (*collision*) Zusammenstoß *m*; (*of stock market, business etc*) Zusammenbruch *m* ♦ *vt* (*car*) einen Unfall haben mit; (*plane etc*) abstürzen mit

♦ vi (plane) abstürzen; (car) einen Unfall
haben; (two cars) zusammenstoßen; (market)
zusammenbrechen; (firm) Pleite machen; **to**
~ into krachen or knallen gegen; **he ~ed the**
car into a wall er fuhr mit dem Auto gegen
eine Mauer.

crash barrier (BRIT) n Leitplanke f.

crash course n Schnellkurs m, Intensivkurs
m.

crash helmet n Sturzhelm m.

crash-landing ['kræʃlændɪŋ] n Bruchlandung
f.

crass [kræs] adj krass; (behaviour) unfein,
derb.

crate [kreɪt] n (also inf) Kiste f; (for bottles)
Kasten m.

crater ['kreɪtə*] n Krater m.

cravat [krə'væt] n Halstuch nt.

crave [kreɪv] vt, vi: **to ~ (for)** sich sehnen nach.

craven ['kreɪvən] adj feige.

craving ['kreɪvɪŋ] n: **~ (for)** Verlangen nt
(nach).

crawl [krɔːl] vi kriechen; (child) krabbeln ♦ n
(SWIMMING) Kraulstil m, Kraul(en) nt; **to**
~ to sb (inf) vor jdm kriechen; **to drive**
along at a ~ im Schneckentempo or
Kriechtempo vorankommen.

crawler lane (BRIT) n (AUT) Kriechspur f.

crayfish ['kreɪfɪʃ] n inv (freshwater) Flusskrebs
m; (saltwater) Languste f.

crayon ['kreɪən] n Buntstift m.

craze [kreɪz] n Fimmel m; **to be all the ~**
große Mode sein.

crazed [kreɪzd] adj wahnsinnig; (pottery, glaze)
rissig.

crazy ['kreɪzɪ] adj wahnsinnig, verrückt;
~ about sb/sth (inf) verrückt or wild auf
jdn/etw; **to go ~** wahnsinnig or verrückt
werden.

crazy paving (BRIT) n Mosaikpflaster nt.

creak [kriːk] vi knarren.

cream [kriːm] n Sahne f, Rahm m (SÜDD);
(artificial cream, cosmetic) Creme f; (élite)
Creme f, Elite f ♦ adj cremefarben; **whipped**
~ Schlagsahne f.

▶ **cream off** vt absahnen (inf).

cream cake n Sahnetorte f; (small)
Sahnetörtchen nt.

cream cheese n (Doppelrahm)frischkäse m.

creamery ['kriːmərɪ] n (shop) Milchgeschäft
nt; (factory) Molkerei f.

creamy ['kriːmɪ] adj (colour) cremefarben;
(taste) sahnig.

crease [kriːs] n Falte f; (in trousers) Bügelfalte
f ♦ vt zerknittern; (forehead) runzeln ♦ vi
knittern; (forehead) sich runzeln.

crease-resistant ['kriːsrɪzɪstənt] adj
knitterfrei.

create [kriː'eɪt] vt schaffen; (interest)
hervorrufen; (problems) verursachen;
(produce) herstellen; (design) entwerfen,
kreieren; (impression, fuss) machen.

creation [kriː'eɪʃən] n (see vb) Schaffung f;
Hervorrufen nt; Verursachung f;
Herstellung f; Entwurf m, Kreation f; (REL)
Schöpfung f.

creative [kriː'eɪtɪv] adj kreativ, schöpferisch.

creativity [kriːeɪ'tɪvɪtɪ] n Kreativität f.

creator [kriː'eɪtə*] n Schöpfer(in) m(f).

creature ['kriːtʃə*] n Geschöpf nt; (living
animal) Lebewesen nt.

creature comforts [- 'kʌmfəts] npl
Lebensgenüsse pl.

crèche [krɛʃ] n (Kinder)krippe f; (all day)
(Kinder)tagesstätte f.

credence ['kriːdns] n: **to lend** or **give ~ to sth**
etw glaubwürdig erscheinen lassen or
machen.

credentials [krɪ'dɛnʃlz] npl Referenzen pl,
Zeugnisse pl; (papers of identity)
(Ausweis)papiere pl.

credibility [krɛdɪ'bɪlɪtɪ] n Glaubwürdigkeit f.

credible ['krɛdɪbl] adj glaubwürdig.

credit ['krɛdɪt] n (loan) Kredit m; (recognition)
Anerkennung f; (SCOL) Schein m ♦ adj
(COMM: terms etc) Kredit- ♦ vt (COMM)
gutschreiben; (believe: also: **give ~ to**)
glauben; **credits** npl (CINE, TV: at beginning)
Vorspann m; (: at end) Nachspann m; **to be in**
~ (person) Geld auf dem Konto haben; (bank
account) im Haben sein; **on ~** auf Kredit; **it**
is to his ~ that ... es ehrt ihn, dass ...; **to take**
the ~ for das Verdienst in Anspruch
nehmen für; **it does him ~** es spricht für
ihn; **he's a ~ to his family** er macht seiner
Familie Ehre; **to ~ sb with sth** (fig) jdm etw
zuschreiben; **to ~ £5 to sb** jdm £5
gutschreiben.

creditable ['krɛdɪtəbl] adj lobenswert,
anerkennenswert.

credit account n Kreditkonto nt.

credit agency (BRIT) n Kreditauskunftei f.

credit balance n Kontostand m.

credit bureau (US) n = **credit agency**.

credit card n Kreditkarte f.

credit control n Kreditüberwachung f.

credit facilities npl (COMM)
Kreditmöglichkeiten pl.

credit limit n Kreditgrenze f.

credit note (BRIT) n Gutschrift f.

creditor ['krɛdɪtə*] n Gläubiger m.

credit transfer n Banküberweisung f.

creditworthy ['krɛdɪtwɜːðɪ] adj kreditwürdig.

credulity [krɪ'djuːlɪtɪ] n Leichtgläubigkeit f.

creed [kriːd] n Glaubensbekenntnis nt.

creek [kriːk] n (kleine) Bucht f; (US: stream)
Bach m; **to be up the ~** (inf) in der Tinte
sitzen.

creel [kriːl] n (also: **lobster ~**)
Hummer(fang)korb m.

creep [kriːp] n (pt, pp **crept**) vi schleichen; (plant:
horizontally) kriechen; (: vertically) klettern
♦ n (inf) Kriecher m; **to ~ up on sb** sich an
jdn heranschleichen; (time etc) langsam auf

jdn zukommen; **he's a** ~ er ist ein
widerlicher or fieser Typ; **it gives me the** ~**s**
davon kriege ich das kalte Grausen.
creeper ['kriːpə*] n Kletterpflanze f.
creepers ['kriːpəz] (US) npl Schuhe mit
weichen Sohlen.
creepy ['kriːpɪ] adj gruselig; (experience)
unheimlich, gruselig.
creepy-crawly ['kriːpɪ'krɔːlɪ] (inf) n
Krabbeltier nt.
cremate [krɪ'meɪt] vt einäschern.
cremation [krɪ'meɪʃən] n Einäscherung f,
Kremation f.
crematoria [krɛmə'tɔːrɪə] npl of **crematorium**.
crematorium [krɛmə'tɔːrɪəm] (pl **crematoria**)
n Krematorium nt.
creosote ['krɪəsəut] n Kreosot nt.
crepe [kreɪp] n Krepp m; (rubber)
Krepp(gummi) m.
crepe bandage (BRIT) n elastische Binde f.
crepe paper n Krepppapier nt.
crepe sole n Kreppsohle f.
crept [krɛpt] pt, pp of **creep**.
crescendo [krɪ'ʃɛndəu] n Höhepunkt m; (MUS)
Crescendo nt.
crescent ['krɛsnt] n Halbmond m; (street)
halbkreisförmig verlaufende Straße.
cress [krɛs] n Kresse f.
crest [krɛst] n (of hill) Kamm m; (of bird)
Haube f; (coat of arms) Wappen nt.
crestfallen ['krɛstfɔːlən] adj
niedergeschlagen.
Crete [kriːt] n Kreta nt.
crevasse [krɪ'væs] n Gletscherspalte f.
crevice ['krɛvɪs] n Spalte f.
crew [kruː] n Besatzung f; (TV, CINE) Crew f;
(gang) Bande f.
crew cut n Bürstenschnitt m.
crew neck n runder (Hals)ausschnitt m.
crib [krɪb] n Kinderbett nt; (REL) Krippe f ♦ vt
(inf: copy) abschreiben.
cribbage ['krɪbɪdʒ] n Cribbage nt.
crib death (US) n = **cot death**.
crick [krɪk] n Krampf m.
cricket ['krɪkɪt] n Kricket nt; (insect) Grille f.
cricketer ['krɪkɪtə*] n Kricketspieler(in) m(f).
crime [kraɪm] n (no pl: illegal activities)
Verbrechen pl; (illegal action, fig)
Verbrechen nt; **minor** ~ kleinere Vergehen
pl.
crime wave n Verbrechenswelle f.
criminal ['krɪmɪnl] n Kriminelle(r) f(m),
Verbrecher(in) m(f) ♦ adj kriminell;
C~ **Investigation Department**
Kriminalpolizei f.
criminal code n Strafgesetzbuch nt.
crimp [krɪmp] vt kräuseln; (hair) wellen.
crimson ['krɪmzn] adj purpurrot.
cringe [krɪndʒ] vi (in fear) zurückweichen; (in
embarrassment) zusammenzucken.
crinkle ['krɪŋkl] vt (zer)knittern.
cripple ['krɪpl] n Krüppel m ♦ vt zum Krüppel

machen; (ship, plane) aktionsunfähig
machen; (production, exports) lahm legen,
lähmen; ~**d with rheumatism** von Rheuma
praktisch gelähmt.
crippling ['krɪplɪŋ] adj (disease) schwer;
(taxation, debts) erdrückend.
crises ['kraɪsiːz] npl of **crisis**.
crisis ['kraɪsɪs] (pl **crises**) n Krise f.
crisp [krɪsp] adj (vegetables etc) knackig;
(bacon etc) knusprig; (weather) frisch;
(manner, tone, reply) knapp.
crisps [krɪsps] (BRIT) npl Chips pl.
crisscross ['krɪskrɔs] adj (pattern) Kreuz- ♦ vt
kreuz und quer durchziehen.
criteria [kraɪ'tɪərɪə] npl of **criterion**.
criterion [kraɪ'tɪərɪən] (pl **criteria**) n Kriterium
nt.
critic ['krɪtɪk] n Kritiker(in) m(f).
critical ['krɪtɪkl] adj kritisch; **to be** ~ **of sb/sth**
jdn/etw kritisieren; **he is in a** ~ **condition**
sein Zustand ist kritisch.
critically ['krɪtɪklɪ] adv kritisch; (ill) schwer.
criticism ['krɪtɪsɪzəm] n Kritik f.
criticize ['krɪtɪsaɪz] vt kritisieren.
critique [krɪ'tiːk] n Kritik f.
croak [krəuk] vi (frog) quaken; (bird, person)
krächzen.
Croat n Kroate m, Kroatin f; (LING) Kroatisch
nt.
Croatia [krəu'eɪʃə] n Kroatien nt.
Croatian [krəu'eɪʃən] adj kroatisch.
crochet ['krəuʃeɪ] n (activity) Häkeln nt; (result)
Häkelei f.
crock [krɔk] n Topf m; (inf: also: **old** ~) (vehicle)
Kiste f; (: person) Wrack nt.
crockery ['krɔkərɪ] n Geschirr nt.
crocodile ['krɔkədaɪl] n Krokodil nt.
crocus ['krəukəs] n Krokus m.
croft [krɔft] (BRIT) n kleines Pachtgut nt.
crofter ['krɔftə*] (BRIT) n Kleinpächter(in)
m(f).
crone [krəun] n alte Hexe f.
crony ['krəunɪ] (inf: pej) n Kumpan(in) m(f).
crook [kruk] n (criminal) Gauner m; (of
shepherd) Hirtenstab m; (of arm) Beuge f.
crooked ['krukɪd] adj krumm; (dishonest)
unehrlich.
crop [krɔp] n (Feld)frucht f; (amount produced)
Ernte f; (riding crop) Reitpeitsche f; (of bird)
Kropf m ♦ vt (hair) stutzen; (subj: animal:
grass) abfressen.
▶ **crop up** vi aufkommen.
cropper ['krɔpə*] (inf) n: **to come a** ~
hinfallen; (fig: fail) auf die Nase fallen.
crop spraying [-'spreɪɪŋ] n
Schädlingsbekämpfung f (durch Besprühen).
croquet ['krəukeɪ] (BRIT) n Krocket nt.
croquette [krə'kɛt] n Krokette f.
cross [krɔs] n Kreuz nt; (BIOL, BOT) Kreuzung f
♦ vt (street) überqueren; (room etc)
durchqueren; (cheque) zur Verrechnung
ausstellen; (arms) verschränken; (legs)

übereinander schlagen; (*animal, plant*) kreuzen; (*thwart: person*) verärgern; (: *plan*) durchkreuzen ♦ *adj* ärgerlich, böse ♦ *vi:* **the boat ~es from ... to ...** das Schiff fährt von ... nach ...; **to ~ o.s.** sich bekreuzigen; **we have a ~ed line** (*BRIT*) es ist jemand in der Leitung; **they've got their lines** *or* **wires ~ed** (*fig*) sie reden aneinander vorbei; **to be/get ~ with sb (about sth)** mit jdm *or* auf jdn (wegen etw) böse sein/werden.

▶ **cross out** *vt* streichen.
▶ **cross over** *vi* hinübergehen.

crossbar ['krɔsbɑː'] *n* (*SPORT*) Querlatte *f*; (*of bicycle*) Stange *f*.
crossbow *n* Armbrust *f*.
crossbreed ['krɔsbriːd] *n* Kreuzung *f*.
cross-Channel ferry ['krɔs't∫ænl-] *n* Kanalfähre *f*.
crosscheck ['krɔst∫ɛk] *n* Gegenprobe *f* ♦ *vt* überprüfen.
cross-country (race) ['krɔs'kʌntrɪ-] *n* Querfeldeinrennen *nt*.
cross-dressing [krɔs'drɛsɪŋ] *n* (*transvestism*) Transvestismus *m*.
cross-examination ['krɔsɪgzæmɪ'neɪ∫ən] *n* Kreuzverhör *nt*.
cross-examine ['krɔsɪg'zæmɪn] *vt* ins Kreuzverhör nehmen.
cross-eyed ['krɔsaɪd] *adj* schielend; **to be ~** schielen.
crossfire ['krɔsfaɪə'] *n* Kreuzfeuer *nt*; **to get caught in the ~** (*also fig*) ins Kreuzfeuer geraten.
crossing ['krɔsɪŋ] *n* Überfahrt *f*; (*also:* **pedestrian ~**) Fußgängerüberweg *m*.
crossing guard (*US*) *n* ≈ Schülerlotse *m*.
crossing point *n* Übergangsstelle *f*.
cross-purposes ['krɔs'pəːpəsɪz] *npl:* **to be at ~ with sb** jdn missverstehen; **we're (talking) at ~** wir reden aneinander vorbei.
cross-question ['krɔs'kwɛst∫ən] *vt* ins Kreuzverhör nehmen.
cross-reference ['krɔs'rɛfrəns] *n* (Quer)verweis *m*.
crossroads ['krɔsrəudz] *n* Kreuzung *f*.
cross section *n* Querschnitt *m*.
crosswalk ['krɔswɔːk] (*US*) *n* Fußgängerüberweg *m*.
crosswind ['krɔswɪnd] *n* Seitenwind *m*.
crosswise ['krɔswaɪz] *adv* quer.
crossword ['krɔswəːd] *n* (*also:* **~ puzzle**) Kreuzworträtsel *nt*.
crotch [krɔt∫] *n* Unterleib *m*; (*of garment*) Schritt *m*.
crotchet ['krɔt∫ɪt] *n* Viertelnote *f*.
crotchety ['krɔt∫ɪtɪ] *adj* reizbar.
crouch [kraut∫] *vi* kauern.
croup [kruːp] *n* (*MED*) Krupp *m*.
croupier ['kruːpɪə'] *n* Croupier *m*.
crouton ['kruːtɔn] *n* Crouton *m*.
crow [krəu] *n* (*bird*) Krähe *f*; (*of cock*) Krähen *nt* ♦ *vi* krähen; (*fig*) sich brüsten, angeben.

crowbar ['krəubɑː'] *n* Brechstange *f*.
crowd [kraud] *n* (Menschen)menge *f* ♦ *vt* (*room, stadium*) füllen ♦ *vi:* **to ~ round** sich herumdrängen; **~s of people** Menschenmassen *pl;* **the/our ~** (*of friends*) die/unsere Clique *f*; **to ~ sb/sth in** jdn/etw hineinstopfen; **to ~ sb/sth into** jdn pferchen/etw stopfen in +*acc*; **to ~ in** sich hineindrängen.
crowded ['kraudɪd] *adj* überfüllt; (*densely populated*) dicht besiedelt; **~ with** voll von.
crowd scene *n* Massenszene *f*.
crown [kraun] *n* (*also of tooth*) Krone *f*; (*of head*) Wirbel *m*; (*of hill*) Kuppe *f*; (*of hat*) Kopf *m* ♦ *vt* krönen; (*tooth*) überkronen; **the C~** die Krone; **and to ~ it all ...** (*fig*) und zur Krönung des Ganzen ....

CROWN COURT

Crown Court ist ein Strafgericht, das in etwa 90 verschiedenen Städten in England und Wales zusammentritt. Schwere Verbrechen wie Mord, Totschlag, Vergewaltigung und Raub werden nur vor dem crown court unter Vorsitz eines Richters mit Geschworenen verhandelt.

---

crowning ['kraunɪŋ] *adj* krönend.
crown jewels *npl* Kronjuwelen *pl*.
crown prince *n* Kronprinz *m*.
crow's-feet ['krəuzfiːt] *npl* Krähenfüße *pl*.
crow's-nest ['krəuznɛst] *n* Krähennest *nt*, Mastkorb *m*.
crucial ['kruː∫l] *adj* (*decision*) äußerst wichtig; (*vote*) entscheidend; **~ to** äußerst wichtig für.
crucifix ['kruːsɪfɪks] *n* Kruzifix *nt*.
crucifixion [kruːsɪ'fɪk∫ən] *n* Kreuzigung *f*.
crucify ['kruːsɪfaɪ] *vt* kreuzigen; (*fig*) in der Luft zerreißen.
crude [kruːd] *adj* (*oil, fibre*) Roh-; (*fig: basic*) primitiv; (: *vulgar*) ordinär ♦ *n* = **crude oil**.
crude oil *n* Rohöl *nt*.
cruel ['kruəl] *adj* grausam.
cruelty ['kruəltɪ] *n* Grausamkeit *f*.
cruet ['kruːɪt] *n* Gewürzständer *m*.
cruise [kruːz] *n* Kreuzfahrt *f* ♦ *vi* (*ship*) kreuzen; (*car*) (mit Dauergeschwindigkeit) fahren; (*aircraft*) (mit Reisegeschwindigkeit) fliegen; (*taxi*) gemächlich fahren.
cruise missile *n* Marschflugkörper *m*.
cruiser ['kruːzə'] *n* Motorboot *nt*; (*warship*) Kreuzer *m*.
cruising speed *n* Reisegeschwindigkeit *f*.
crumb [krʌm] *n* Krümel *m*; (*fig: of information*) Brocken *m*; **a ~ of comfort** ein winziger Trost.
crumble ['krʌmbl] *vt* (*bread*) zerbröckeln; (*biscuit etc*) zerkrümeln ♦ *vi* (*building, earth etc*) zerbröckeln; (*plaster*) abbröckeln; (*fig: opposition*) sich auflösen; (: *belief*) ins

Wanken geraten.

crumbly ['krʌmblɪ] *adj* krümelig.

crummy ['krʌmɪ] (*inf*) *adj* mies.

crumpet ['krʌmpɪt] *n* Teekuchen *m* (*zum Toasten*).

crumple ['krʌmpl] *vt* zerknittern.

crunch [krʌntʃ] *vt* (*biscuit, apple etc*) knabbern; (*underfoot*) zertreten ♦ *n:* **the ~** der große Krach; **if it comes to the ~** wenn es wirklich dahin kommt; **when the ~ comes** wenn es hart auf hart geht.

crunchy ['krʌntʃɪ] *adj* knusprig; (*apple etc*) knackig; (*gravel, snow etc*) knirschend.

crusade [kru:'seɪd] *n* Feldzug *m* ♦ *vi:* **to ~ for/against sth** für/gegen etw zu Felde ziehen.

crusader [kru:'seɪdə*] *n* Kreuzritter *m*; (*fig*): **~ (for)** Apostel (+*gen*).

crush [krʌʃ] *n* (*crowd*) Gedränge *nt* ♦ *vt* quetschen; (*grapes*) zerquetschen; (*paper, clothes*) zerknittern; (*garlic, ice*) (zer)stoßen; (*defeat*) niederschlagen; (*devastate*) vernichten; **to have a ~ on sb** (*love*) für jdn schwärmen; **lemon ~** Zitronensaftgetränk *nt*.

crush barrier (*BRIT*) *n* Absperrung *f*.

crushing ['krʌʃɪŋ] *adj* vernichtend.

crust [krʌst] *n* Kruste *f*.

crustacean [krʌs'teɪʃən] *n* Schalentier *nt*, Krustazee *f*.

crusty ['krʌstɪ] *adj* knusprig.

crutch [krʌtʃ] *n* Krücke *f*; (*support*) Stütze *f*; *see also* **crotch**.

crux [krʌks] *n* Kern *m*.

cry [kraɪ] *vi* weinen; (*also:* **~ out**) aufschreien ♦ *n* Schrei *m*; (*shout*) Ruf *m*; **what are you ~ing about?** warum weinst du?; **to ~ for help** um Hilfe rufen; **she had a good ~** sie hat sich (mal richtig) ausgeweint; **it's a far ~ from ...** (*fig*) das ist etwas ganz anderes als ...

▶ **cry off** (*inf*) *vi* absagen.

crying ['kraɪɪŋ] *adj* (*fig: need*) dringend; **it's a ~ shame** es ist ein Jammer.

crypt [krɪpt] *n* Krypta *f*.

cryptic ['krɪptɪk] *adj* hintergründig, rätselhaft; (*clue*) verschlüsselt.

crystal ['krɪstl] *n* Kristall *m*; (*glass*) Kristall(glas) *nt*.

crystal clear *adj* glasklar.

crystallize ['krɪstəlaɪz] *vt* (*opinion, thoughts*) (feste) Form geben +*dat* ♦ *vi* (*sugar etc*) kristallisieren; **~d fruits** (*BRIT*) kandierte Früchte *pl*.

CSA *n abbr* (= *Child Support Agency*) Amt zur Regelung von Unterhaltszahlungen für Kinder.

CSC *n abbr* (= *Civil Service Commission*) Einstellungsbehörde für den öffentlichen Dienst.

CSE (*BRIT*) *n abbr* (*formerly:* = *Certificate of Secondary Education*) Schulabschlusszeugnis, ≈ mittlere Reife *f*.

CS gas (*BRIT*) *n* ≈ Tränengas *nt*.

CST (*US*) *abbr* (= *Central Standard Time*) mittelamerikanische Standardzeit.

CT (*US*) *abbr* (*POST:* = *Connecticut*).

ct *abbr* = **carat**.

CTC (*BRIT*) *n abbr* = **city technology college**.

CT scanner *n abbr* (*MED:* = *computerized tomography scanner*) CT-Scanner *m*.

cu. *abbr* = **cubic**.

cub [kʌb] *n* Junge(s) *nt*; (*also:* **~ scout**) Wölfling *m*.

Cuba ['kju:bə] *n* Kuba *nt*.

Cuban ['kju:bən] *adj* kubanisch ♦ *n* Kubaner(in) *m(f)*.

cubbyhole ['kʌbɪhəʊl] *n* (*room*) Kabuff *nt*; (*space*) Eckchen *nt*.

cube [kju:b] *n* Würfel *m*; (*MATH: of number*) dritte Potenz *f* ♦ *vt* (*MATH*) in die dritte Potenz erheben, hoch drei nehmen.

cube root *n* Kubikwurzel *f*.

cubic ['kju:bɪk] *adj* (*volume*) Kubik-; **~ metre** *etc* Kubikmeter *m etc*.

cubic capacity *n* Hubraum *m*.

cubicle ['kju:bɪkl] *n* Kabine *f*; (*in hospital*) Bettnische *f*.

cuckoo ['kuku:] *n* Kuckuck *m*.

cuckoo clock *n* Kuckucksuhr *f*.

cucumber ['kju:kʌmbə*] *n* Gurke *f*.

cud [kʌd] *n:* **to chew the ~** (*animal*) wiederkäuen; (*fig: person*) vor sich *acc* hin grübeln.

cuddle ['kʌdl] *vt* in den Arm nehmen, drücken ♦ *vi* schmusen.

cuddly ['kʌdlɪ] *adj* (*toy*) zum Liebhaben *or* Drücken; (*person*) knuddelig (*inf*).

cudgel ['kʌdʒl] *n* Knüppel *m* ♦ *vt:* **to ~ one's brains** sich *dat* das (Ge)hirn zermartern.

cue [kju:] *n* (*SPORT*) Billardstock *m*, Queue *nt*; (*THEAT: word*) Stichwort *nt*; (: *action*) (Einsatz)zeichen *nt*; (*MUS*) Einsatz *m*.

cuff [kʌf] *n* (*of sleeve*) Manschette *f*; (*US: of trousers*) Aufschlag *m*; (*blow*) Klaps *m* ♦ *vt* einen Klaps geben +*dat*; **off the ~** aus dem Stegreif.

cuff links *npl* Manschettenknöpfe *pl*.

cu. in. *abbr* = *cubic inches*) Kubikzoll.

cuisine [kwɪ'zi:n] *n* Küche *f*.

cul-de-sac ['kʌldəsæk] *n* Sackgasse *f*.

culinary ['kʌlɪnərɪ] *adj* (*skill*) Koch-; (*delight*) kulinarisch.

cull [kʌl] *vt* (zusammen)sammeln; (*animals*) ausmerzen ♦ *n* Erlegen überschüssiger Tierbestände.

culminate ['kʌlmɪneɪt] *vi:* **to ~ in** gipfeln in +*dat*.

culmination [kʌlmɪ'neɪʃən] *n* Höhepunkt *m*.

culottes [kju:'lɒts] *npl* Hosenrock *m*.

culpable ['kʌlpəbl] *adj* schuldig.

culprit ['kʌlprɪt] *n* Täter(in) *m(f)*.

cult [kʌlt] *n* Kult *m*.

cult figure *n* Kultfigur *f*.

cultivate ['kʌltɪveɪt] *vt* (*land*) bebauen,

landwirtschaftlich nutzen; (*crop*) anbauen; (*feeling*) entwickeln; (*person*) sich *dat* warm halten (*inf*), die Beziehung pflegen zu.
cultivation [kʌltɪ'veɪʃən] n (*of land*) Bebauung f, landwirtschaftliche Nutzung f; (*of crop*) Anbau m.
cultural ['kʌltʃərəl] adj kulturell.
culture ['kʌltʃəʳ] n Kultur f.
cultured ['kʌltʃəd] adj kultiviert; (*pearl*) Zucht-.
cumbersome ['kʌmbəsəm] adj (*suitcase etc*) sperrig, unhandlich; (*piece of machinery*) schwer zu handhaben; (*clothing*) hinderlich; (*process*) umständlich.
cumin ['kʌmɪn] n Kreuzkümmel m.
cumulative ['kjuːmjulətɪv] adj (*effect, result*) Gesamt-.
cunning ['kʌnɪŋ] n Gerissenheit f ♦ adj gerissen; (*device, idea*) schlau.
cunt [kʌnt] (*inf!*) n (*vagina*) Fotze f (*!*); (*term of abuse*) Arsch m (*!*).
cup [kʌp] n Tasse f; (*as prize*) Pokal m; (*of bra*) Körbchen nt; **a ~ of tea** eine Tasse Tee.
cupboard ['kʌbəd] n Schrank m.
cup final (*BRIT*) n Pokalendspiel nt.
cupful ['kʌpful] n Tasse f.
Cupid ['kjuːpɪd] n Amor m; (*figurine*) Amorette f.
cupidity [kjuː'pɪdɪtɪ] n Begierde f, Gier f.
cupola ['kjuːpələ] n Kuppel f.
cuppa ['kʌpə] (*BRIT: inf*) n Tasse f Tee.
cup tie (*BRIT*) n Pokalspiel nt.
curable ['kjuərəbl] adj heilbar.
curate ['kjuərɪt] n Vikar m.
curator [kjuə'reɪtəʳ] n Kustos m.
curb [kəːb] vt einschränken; (*person*) an die Kandare nehmen ♦ n Einschränkung f; (*US: kerb*) Bordstein m.
curd cheese n Weißkäse m.
curdle ['kəːdl] vi gerinnen.
curds [kəːdz] npl ≈ Quark m.
cure [kjuəʳ] vt heilen; (*CULIN: salt*) pökeln; (*: smoke*) räuchern; (*: dry*) trocknen; (*problem*) abhelfen +*dat* ♦ n (*remedy*) (Heil)mittel nt; (*treatment*) Heilverfahren nt; (*solution*) Abhilfe f; **to be ~d of sth** von etw geheilt sein.
cure-all ['kjuərɔːl] n (*also fig*) Allheilmittel nt.
curfew ['kəːfjuː] n Ausgangssperre f; (*time*) Sperrstunde f.
curio ['kjuərɪəu] n Kuriosität f.
curiosity [kjuərɪ'ɒsɪtɪ] n (*see adj*) Wissbegier(de) f; Neugier f; Merkwürdigkeit f.
curious ['kjuərɪəs] adj (*interested*) wissbegierig; (*nosy*) neugierig; (*strange, unusual*) sonderbar, merkwürdig; **I'm ~ about him** ich bin gespannt auf ihn.
curiously ['kjuərɪəslɪ] adv neugierig; (*inquisitively*) wissbegierig; **~ enough, ...** merkwürdigerweise ...
curl [kəːl] n Locke f; (*of smoke etc*) Kringel m

♦ vt (*hair: loosely*) locken; (*: tightly*) kräuseln; ♦ vi sich locken; sich kräuseln; (*smoke*) sich kringeln.
► **curl up** vi sich zusammenrollen.
curler ['kəːləʳ] n Lockenwickler m; (*SPORT*) Curlingspieler(in) m(f).
curlew ['kəːluː] n Brachvogel m.
curling ['kəːlɪŋ] n (*SPORT*) Curling nt.
curling tongs, (*US*) **curling irons** npl Lockenschere f, Brennschere f.
curly ['kəːlɪ] adj lockig; (*tightly curled*) kraus.
currant ['kʌrnt] n Korinthe f; (*blackcurrant, redcurrant*) Johannisbeere f.
currency ['kʌrnsɪ] n (*system*) Währung f; (*money*) Geld nt; **foreign ~** Devisen pl; **to gain ~** (*fig*) sich verbreiten, um sich greifen.
current ['kʌrnt] n Strömung f; (*ELEC*) Strom m; (*of opinion*) Tendenz f, Trend m ♦ adj gegenwärtig; (*expression*) gebräuchlich; (*idea, custom*) verbreitet; **direct/alternating ~** (*ELEC*) Gleich-/Wechselstrom m; **the ~ issue of a magazine** die neueste *or* letzte Nummer einer Zeitschrift; **in ~ use** allgemein gebräuchlich.
current account (*BRIT*) n Girokonto nt.
current affairs npl Tagespolitik f.
current assets npl (*COMM*) Umlaufvermögen nt.
current liabilities npl (*COMM*) kurzfristige Verbindlichkeiten pl.
currently ['kʌrntlɪ] adv zurzeit.
curricula [kə'rɪkjulə] npl of **curriculum.**
curriculum [kə'rɪkjuləm] (pl **~s** or **curricula**) n Lehrplan m.
curriculum vitae [-'viːtaɪ] n Lebenslauf m.
curry ['kʌrɪ] n (*dish*) Currygericht nt ♦ vt: **to ~ favour with** sich einschmeicheln bei.
curry powder n Curry m or nt, Currypulver nt.
curse [kəːs] vi fluchen ♦ vt verfluchen ♦ n Fluch m.
cursor ['kəːsəʳ] n (*COMPUT*) Cursor m.
cursory ['kəːsərɪ] adj flüchtig; (*examination*) oberflächlich.
curt [kəːt] adj knapp, kurz angebunden.
curtail [kəː'teɪl] vt einschränken; (*visit etc*) abkürzen.
curtain ['kəːtn] n Vorhang m; (*net*) Gardine f; **to draw the ~s** (*together*) die Vorhänge zuziehen; (*apart*) die Vorhänge aufmachen.
curtain call n (*THEAT*) Vorhang m.
curts(e)y ['kəːtsɪ] vi knicksen ♦ n Knicks m.
curvature ['kəːvətʃəʳ] n Krümmung f.
curve [kəːv] n Bogen m; (*in the road*) Kurve f ♦ vi einen Bogen machen; (*surface, arch*) sich wölben ♦ vt biegen.
curved [kəːvd] adj (*line*) gebogen; (*table legs etc*) geschwungen; (*surface, arch, sides of ship*) gewölbt.
cushion ['kuʃən] n Kissen nt ♦ vt dämpfen; (*seat*) polstern.

cushy ['kuʃɪ] (*inf*) *adj*: **a ~ job** ein gemütlicher *or* ruhiger Job; **to have a ~ time** eine ruhige Kugel schieben.

custard ['kʌstəd] *n* (*for pouring*) Vanillesoße *f*.

custard powder (*BRIT*) *n* Vanillesoßenpulver *nt*.

custodial [kʌs'təudɪəl] *adj*: **~ sentence** Gefängnisstrafe *f*.

custodian [kʌs'təudɪən] *n* Verwalter(in) *m(f)*; (*of museum etc*) Aufseher(in) *m(f)*, Wächter(in) *m(f)*.

custody ['kʌstədɪ] *n* (*of child*) Vormundschaft *f*; (*for offenders*) (polizeilicher) Gewahrsam *m*, Haft *f*; **to take into ~** verhaften; **in the ~ of** unter der Obhut +*gen*; **the mother has ~ of the children** die Kinder sind der Mutter zugesprochen worden.

custom ['kʌstəm] *n* Brauch *m*; (*habit*) (An)gewohnheit *f*; (*LAW*) Gewohnheitsrecht *nt*; (*COMM*) Kundschaft *f*.

customary ['kʌstəmərɪ] *adj* (*conventional*) üblich; (*habitual*) gewohnt; **it is ~ to do it** es ist üblich, es zu tun.

custom-built ['kʌstəm'bɪlt] *adj* speziell angefertigt.

customer ['kʌstəmə*] *n* Kunde *m*, Kundin *f*; **he's an awkward ~** (*inf*) er ist ein schwieriger Typ.

customer profile *n* Kundenprofil *nt*.

customized ['kʌstəmaɪzd] *adj* individuell aufgemacht.

custom-made ['kʌstəm'meɪd] *adj* (*shirt etc*) maßgefertigt, nach Maß; (*car etc*) speziell angefertigt.

customs ['kʌstəmz] *npl* Zoll *m*; **to go through (the) ~** durch den Zoll gehen.

Customs and Excise (*BRIT*) *n* die Zollbehörde *f*.

customs duty *n* Zoll *m*.

customs officer *n* Zollbeamte(r) *m*, Zollbeamtin *f*.

cut [kʌt] (*pt, pp* **cut**) *vt* schneiden; (*text, programme, spending*) kürzen; (*prices*) senken, heruntersetzen, herabsetzen; (*supply*) einschränken; (*cloth*) zuschneiden; (*road*) schlagen, (*inf*: *lecture, appointment*) schwänzen ♦ *vi* schneiden; (*lines*) sich schneiden ♦ *n* Schnitt *m*; (*in skin*) Schnittwunde *f*; (*in salary, spending etc*) Kürzung *f*; (*of meat*) Stück *nt*; (*of jewel*) Schnitt *m*, Schliff *m*; **to ~ a tooth** zahnen, einen Zahn bekommen; **to ~ one's finger/ hand/knee** sich in den Finger/in die Hand/ am Knie schneiden; **to get one's hair ~** sich *dat* die Haare schneiden lassen; **to ~ sth short** etw vorzeitig abbrechen; **to ~ sb dead** jdn wie Luft behandeln; **cold ~s** (*US*) Aufschnitt *m*; **power ~** Stromausfall *m*.

▶ **cut back** *vt* (*plants*) zurückschneiden; (*production*) zurückschrauben; (*expenditure*) einschränken.

▶ **cut down** *vt* (*tree*) fällen; (*consumption*)

einschränken; **to ~ sb down to size** (*fig*) jdn auf seinen Platz verweisen.

▶ **cut down on** *vt fus* einschränken.

▶ **cut in** *vi* (*AUT*) sich direkt vor ein anderes Auto setzen; **to ~ in (on)** (*conversation*) sich einschalten (in +*acc*).

▶ **cut off** *vt* abschneiden; (*supply*) sperren; (*TEL*) unterbrechen; **we've been ~ off** (*TEL*) wir sind unterbrochen worden.

▶ **cut out** *vt* ausschneiden; (*an activity etc*) aufhören mit; (*remove*) herausschneiden.

▶ **cut up** *vt* klein schneiden; **it really ~ me up** (*inf*) es hat mich ziemlich mitgenommen; **to feel ~ up about sth** (*inf*) betroffen über etw *acc* sein.

cut and dried *adj* (*also*: **cut-and-dry**: *answer*) eindeutig; (: *solution*) einfach.

cutaway ['kʌtəweɪ] *n* (*coat*) Cut(away) *m*; (*drawing*) Schnittdiagramm *nt*; (*model*) Schnittmodell *nt*; (*CINE, TV*) Schnitt *m*.

cutback ['kʌtbæk] *n* Kürzung *f*.

cute [kju:t] *adj* süß, niedlich; (*clever*) schlau.

cut glass *n* geschliffenes Glas *nt*.

cuticle ['kju:tɪkl] *n* Nagelhaut *f*; **~ remover** Nagelhautentferner *m*.

cutlery ['kʌtlərɪ] *n* Besteck *nt*.

cutlet ['kʌtlɪt] *n* Schnitzel *nt*; (*vegetable cutlet, nut cutlet*) Bratling *m*.

cutoff ['kʌtɒf] *n* (*also*: **~ point**) Trennlinie *f*.

cutoff switch *n* Ausschaltmechanismus *m*.

cutout ['kʌtaut] *n* (*switch*) Unterbrecher *m*; (*shape*) Ausschneidemodell *nt*; (*paper figure*) Ausschneidepuppe *f*.

cut-price ['kʌt'praɪs] *adj* (*goods*) heruntergesetzt; (*offer*) Billig-.

cut-rate ['kʌt'reɪt] (*US*) *adj* = **cut-price**.

cutthroat ['kʌtθrəut] *n* Mörder(in) *m(f)* ♦ *adj* unbarmherzig, mörderisch.

cutting ['kʌtɪŋ] *adj* (*edge, remark*) scharf ♦ *n* (*BRIT*: *from newspaper*) Ausschnitt *m*; (: *RAIL*) Durchstich *m*; (*from plant*) Ableger *m*.

cutting edge *n* (*fig*) Spitzenstellung *f*; **on the ~ (of)** an der Spitze +*gen*.

cuttlefish ['kʌtlfɪʃ] *n* Tintenfisch *m*.

CV *n abbr* = **curriculum vitae**.

c.w.o. *abbr* (*COMM*) = **cash with order**.

cwt *abbr* = **hundredweight**.

cyanide ['saɪənaɪd] *n* Zyanid *nt*.

cybercafé ['saɪbəkæfeɪ] *n* Internet-Café *nt*.

cybernetics [saɪbə'nɛtɪks] *n* Kybernetik *f*.

cyclamen ['sɪkləmən] *n* Alpenveilchen *nt*.

cycle ['saɪkl] *n* (*bicycle*) (Fahr)rad *nt*; (*series: of seasons, songs etc*) Zyklus *m*; (: *of events*) Gang *m*; (: *TECH*) Periode *f* ♦ *vi* Rad fahren.

cycle lane, cycle path *n* (Fahr)radweg *m*.

cycle race *n* Radrennen *nt*.

cycle rack *n* Fahrradständer *m*.

cycling ['saɪklɪŋ] *n* Radfahren *nt*; **to go on a ~ holiday** (*BRIT*) Urlaub mit dem Fahrrad machen.

cyclist ['saɪklɪst] *n* (Fahr)radfahrer(in) *m(f)*.

cyclone ['saɪkləun] *n* Zyklon *m*.

cygnet ['sɪgnɪt] *n* Schwanjunge(s) *nt*.
cylinder ['sɪlɪndə*] *n* Zylinder *m*; (*of gas*)
Gasflasche *f*.
cylinder block *n* Zylinderblock *m*.
cylinder head *n* Zylinderkopf *m*.
cylinder-head gasket ['sɪlɪndəhed-] *n*
Zylinderkopfdichtung *f*.
cymbals ['sɪmblz] *npl* (*MUS*) Becken *nt*.
cynic ['sɪnɪk] *n* Zyniker(in) *m(f)*.
cynical ['sɪnɪkl] *adj* zynisch.
cynicism ['sɪnɪsɪzəm] *n* Zynismus *m*.
CYO (*US*) *n abbr* (= *Catholic Youth Organization*)
katholische Jugendorganisation.
cypress ['saɪprɪs] *n* Zypresse *f*.
Cypriot ['sɪprɪət] *adj* zypriotisch, zyprisch ♦ *n*
Zypriot(in) *m(f)*.
Cyprus ['saɪprəs] *n* Zypern *nt*.
cyst [sɪst] *n* Zyste *f*.
cystitis [sɪs'taɪtɪs] *n* Blasenentzündung *f*,
Zystitis *f*.
CZ (*US*) *n abbr* (= *Canal Zone*) *Bereich des
Panamakanals*.
czar [zɑ:*] *n* = **tsar**.
Czech [tʃɛk] *adj* tschechisch ♦ *n* Tscheche *m*,
Tschechin *f*; (*language*) Tschechisch *nt*; **the
~ Republic** die Tschechische Republik *f*.
Czechoslovak [tʃɛkə'sləuvæk] *adj*, *n*
= **Czechoslovak(ian)**.
Czechoslovakia [tʃɛkəslə'vækɪə] *n* (*formerly*)
die Tschechoslowakei *f*.
Czechoslovak(ian) [tʃɛkə'sləuvæk,
tʃɛkəslə'vækɪən] (*formerly*) *adj*
tschechoslowakisch ♦ *n* Tschechoslowake
m, Tschechoslowakin *f*.

D, d

D¹, d¹ [di:] *n* (*letter*) D *nt*, d *nt*; **~ for David**,
(*US*) **~ for Dog** ≈ D wie Dora.
D² [di:] *n* (*MUS*) D *nt*, d *nt*.
D³ [di:] (*US*) *abbr* (*POL*) = **democrat;
democratic.**
d² (*BRIT: formerly*) *abbr* = **penny.**
d. *abbr* (= *died*): **Henry Jones, ~ 1754** Henry
Jones, gest. 1754.
DA (*US*) *n abbr* = **district attorney.**
dab [dæb] *vt* betupfen; (*paint, cream*) tupfen
♦ *n* Tupfer *m*; **to be a ~ hand at sth** gut in
etw *dat* sein; **to be a ~ hand at doing sth**
sich darauf verstehen, etw zu tun.
▶ **dab at** *vt* betupfen.
dabble ['dæbl] *vi*: **to ~ in** sich (nebenbei)
beschäftigen mit.
dachshund ['dækshund] *n* Dackel *m*.
dad [dæd] (*inf*) *n* Papa *m*, Vati *m*.

daddy ['dædɪ] (*inf*) *n* = **dad.**
daddy-longlegs [dædɪ'lɔŋlɛgz] (*inf*) *n* Schnake
f.
daffodil ['dæfədɪl] *n* Osterglocke *f*, Narzisse *f*.
daft [dɑ:ft] (*inf*) *adj* doof (*inf*), blöd (*inf*); **to be
~ about sb/sth** verrückt nach jdm/etw sein.
dagger ['dægə*] *n* Dolch *m*; **to be at ~s drawn
with sb** mit jdm auf Kriegsfuß stehen; **to
look ~s at sb** jdn mit Blicken durchbohren.
dahlia ['deɪljə] *n* Dahlie *f*.
daily ['deɪlɪ] *adj* täglich; (*wages*) Tages- ♦ *n*
(*paper*) Tageszeitung *f*; (*BRIT: also:* ~ **help**)
Putzfrau *f* ♦ *adv* täglich; **twice ~** zweimal
täglich *or* am Tag.
dainty ['deɪntɪ] *adj* zierlich.
dairy ['dɛərɪ] *n* (*BRIT: shop*) Milchgeschäft *nt*;
(*company*) Molkerei *f*; (*on farm*)
Milchkammer *f* ♦ *cpd* Milch-; (*herd, industry,
farming*) Milchvieh-.
dairy farm *n auf Milchviehhaltung
spezialisierter Bauernhof*.
dairy products *npl* Milchprodukte *pl*,
Molkereiprodukte *pl*.
dairy store (*US*) *n* Milchgeschäft *nt*.
dais ['deɪɪs] *n* Podium *nt*.
daisy ['deɪzɪ] *n* Gänseblümchen *nt*.
daisywheel ['deɪzɪwi:l] *n* Typenrad *nt*.
daisywheel printer *n* Typenraddrucker *m*.
Dakar ['dækə*] *n* Dakar *nt*.
dale [deɪl] (*BRIT*) *n* Tal *nt*.
dally ['dælɪ] *vi* (herum)trödeln; **to ~ with**
(*plan, idea*) spielen mit.
dalmatian [dæl'meɪʃən] *n* Dalmatiner *m*.
dam [dæm] *n* (Stau)damm *m*; (*reservoir*)
Stausee *m* ♦ *vt* stauen.
damage ['dæmɪdʒ] *n* Schaden *m* ♦ *vt* schaden
+*dat*; (*spoil, break*) beschädigen; **damages** *npl*
(*LAW*) Schaden(s)ersatz *m*; **~ to property**
Sachbeschädigung *f*; **to pay £5,000 in ~s**
5000 Pfund Schaden(s)ersatz (be)zahlen.
damaging ['dæmɪdʒɪŋ] *adj*: **~ (to)** schädlich
(für).
Damascus [də'mɑ:skəs] *n* Damaskus *nt*.
dame [deɪm] *n* Dame *f*; (*US: inf*) Weib *nt*;
(*THEAT*) (komische) Alte *f* (*von einem Mann
gespielt*).
damn [dæm] *vt* verfluchen; (*condemn*)
verurteilen ♦ *adj* (*inf: also:* ~**ed**) verdammt
♦ *n* (*inf*): **I don't give a ~** das ist mir
scheißegal (*!*); **~ (it)!** verdammt (noch mal)!
damnable ['dæmnəbl] *adj* grässlich.
damnation [dæm'neɪʃən] *n* Verdammnis *f*
♦ *excl* (*inf*) verdammt.
damning ['dæmɪŋ] *adj* belastend.
damp [dæmp] *adj* feucht ♦ *n* Feuchtigkeit *f* ♦ *vt*
(*also:* ~**en**) befeuchten, anfeuchten;
(*enthusiasm etc*) dämpfen.
dampcourse ['dæmpkɔ:s] *n* Dämmschicht *f*.
damper ['dæmpə*] *n* (*MUS*) Dämpfer *m*; (*of
fire*) (Luft)klappe *f*; **to put a ~ on** (*fig*) einen
Dämpfer aufsetzen +*dat*.
dampness ['dæmpnɪs] *n* Feuchtigkeit *f*.

damson ['dæmzən] n Damaszenerpflaume f.
dance [dɑ:ns] n Tanz m; (social event)
Tanz(abend) m ♦ vi tanzen; **to ~ about**
(herum)tänzeln.
dance hall n Tanzsaal m.
dancer ['dɑ:nsə*] n Tänzer(in) m(f).
dancing ['dɑ:nsɪŋ] n Tanzen nt ♦ cpd (teacher,
school, class etc) Tanz-.
D and C n abbr (MED: = dilation and curettage)
Ausschabung f.
dandelion ['dændɪlaɪən] n Löwenzahn m.
dandruff ['dændrəf] n Schuppen pl.
D and T (BRIT) n abbr (SCOL) = design and
technology.
dandy ['dændɪ] n Dandy m ♦ adj (US: inf)
prima.
Dane [deɪn] n Däne m, Dänin f.
danger ['deɪndʒə*] n Gefahr f; **there is ~ of**
fire/poisoning es besteht Feuer-/
Vergiftungsgefahr; **there is a ~ of sth**
happening es besteht die Gefahr, dass etw
geschieht; **"~!"** „Achtung!"; **in ~** in
Gefahr; **to be in ~ of doing sth** Gefahr
laufen, etw zu tun; **out of ~** außer Gefahr.
danger list n: **on the ~** in Lebensgefahr.
dangerous ['deɪndʒrəs] adj gefährlich.
dangerously ['deɪndʒrəslɪ] adv gefährlich;
(close) bedenklich; **~ ill** schwer krank.
danger zone n Gefahrenzone f.
dangle ['dæŋgl] vt baumeln lassen ♦ vi
baumeln.
Danish ['deɪnɪʃ] adj dänisch ♦ n (LING)
Dänisch nt.
Danish pastry n Plundergebäck nt.
dank [dæŋk] adj (unangenehm) feucht.
Danube ['dænju:b] n: **the ~** die Donau.
dapper ['dæpə*] adj gepflegt.
Dardanelles [dɑ:də'nelz] npl: **the ~** die
Dardanellen pl.
dare [dɛə*] vt: **to ~ sb to do sth** jdn dazu
herausfordern, etw zu tun ♦ vi: **to ~ (to) do**
sth es wagen, etw zu tun; **I ~n't tell him**
(BRIT) ich wage nicht, es ihm zu sagen; **I**
~ say ich nehme an.
daredevil ['dɛədɛvl] n Draufgänger m.
Dar-es-Salaam ['dɑ:rɛssə'lɑ:m] n Daressalam
nt.
daring ['dɛərɪŋ] adj kühn, verwegen; (bold)
gewagt ♦ n Kühnheit f.
dark [dɑ:k] adj dunkel; (look) finster ♦ n: **in the**
~ im Dunkeln; **to be in the ~ about** (fig)
keine Ahnung haben von; **after ~** nach
Einbruch der Dunkelheit; **it is/is getting ~**
es ist/wird dunkel; **~ chocolate**
Zartbitterschokolade f.
Dark Ages npl: **the ~** das finstere Mittelalter.
darken [dɑ:kn] vt dunkel machen ♦ vi sich
verdunkeln.
dark glasses npl Sonnenbrille f.
dark horse n (in competition) Unbekannte(r)
f(m) (mit Außenseiterchancen); (quiet
person) stilles Wasser nt.

darkly ['dɑ:klɪ] adv finster.
darkness ['dɑ:knɪs] n Dunkelheit f, Finsternis f.
darkroom ['dɑ:krum] n Dunkelkammer f.
darling ['dɑ:lɪŋ] adj lieb ♦ n Liebling m; **to be**
the ~ of der Liebling +gen sein; **she is a ~** sie
ist ein Schatz.
darn [dɑ:n] vt stopfen.
dart [dɑ:t] n (in game) (Wurf)pfeil m; (in
sewing) Abnäher m ♦ vi: **to ~ towards** (also:
make a ~ towards) zustürzen auf +acc; **to**
~ away/along davon-/entlangflitzen.
dartboard ['dɑ:tbɔ:d] n Dartscheibe f.
darts [dɑ:ts] n Darts nt, Pfeilwurfspiel nt.
dash [dæʃ] n (sign) Gedankenstrich m; (rush)
Jagd f ♦ vt (throw) schleudern; (hopes)
zunichte machen ♦ vi: **to ~ towards**
zustürzen auf +acc; **a ~ of ...** (small quantity)
etwas ..., ein Schuss m ...; **to make a ~ for**
sth auf etw acc zustürzen; **we'll have to**
make a ~ for it wir müssen rennen, so
schnell wir können.
▶ **dash away** vi losstürzen.
▶ **dash off** vi = dash away.
dashboard ['dæʃbɔ:d] n Armaturenbrett n.
dashing ['dæʃɪŋ] adj flott.
dastardly ['dæstədlɪ] adj niederträchtig.
DAT n abbr (= digital audio tape) DAT nt.
data ['deɪtə] npl Daten pl.
database ['deɪtəbeɪs] n Datenbank f.
data capture n Datenerfassung f.
data processing n Datenverarbeitung f.
data transmission n Datenübertragung f.
date [deɪt] n Datum nt; (with friend)
Verabredung f; (fruit) Dattel f ♦ vt datieren;
(person) ausgehen mit; **what's the ~ today?**
der Wievielte ist heute?; **~ of birth**
Geburtsdatum nt; **closing ~**
Einsendeschluss m; **to ~** bis heute; **out of ~**
altmodisch; (expired) abgelaufen; **up to ~**
auf dem neuesten Stand; **to bring up to ~**
auf den neuesten Stand bringen; (person)
über den neuesten Stand der Dinge
informieren; **a letter ~d 5th July** or (US) **July**
5th ein vom 5. Juli datierter Brief.
dated ['deɪtɪd] adj altmodisch.
dateline ['deɪtlaɪn] n (GEOG) Datumsgrenze f;
(PRESS) Datumszeile f.
date rape n Vergewaltigung f einer
Bekannten (mit der der Täter eine Verabredung
hatte).
date stamp n Datumsstempel m.
dative ['deɪtɪv] n Dativ m.
daub [dɔ:b] vt schmieren; **to ~ with**
beschmieren mit.
daughter ['dɔ:tə*] n Tochter f.
daughter-in-law ['dɔ:tərɪnlɔ:] n
Schwiegertochter f.
daunt [dɔ:nt] vt entmutigen.
daunting ['dɔ:ntɪŋ] adj entmutigend.
dauntless ['dɔ:ntlɪs] adj unerschrocken,
beherzt.
dawdle ['dɔ:dl] vi trödeln; **to ~ over one's**

work bei der Arbeit bummeln *or* trödeln.
dawn [dɔːn] *n* Tagesanbruch *m*,
Morgengrauen *nt*; (*of period*) Anbruch *m* ♦ *vi*
dämmern; (*fig*): **it ~ed on him that ... es**
dämmerte ihm, dass ...; **from ~ to dusk** von
morgens bis abends.
dawn chorus (*BRIT*) *n* Morgenkonzert *nt* der
Vögel.
day [deɪ] *n* Tag *m*; (*heyday*) Zeit *f*; **the**
~ before/after am Tag zuvor/danach; **the**
~ after tomorrow übermorgen; **the ~ before**
yesterday vorgestern; **(on) the following ~**
am Tag danach; **the ~ that ...** (am Tag,) als
...; **~ by ~** jeden Tag, täglich; **by ~**
tagsüber; **paid by the ~** tageweise bezahlt;
to work an eight hour ~ einen
Achtstundentag haben; **these ~s, in the**
present ~ heute, heutzutage.
daybook ['deɪbuk] (*BRIT*) *n* Journal *nt*.
dayboy ['deɪbɔɪ] *n* Externe(r) *m*.
daybreak ['deɪbreɪk] *n* Tagesanbruch *m*.
day-care centre ['deɪkɛə-] *n* (*for children*)
(Kinder)tagesstätte *f*; (*for old people*)
Altentagesstätte *f*.
daydream ['deɪdriːm] *vi* (mit offenen Augen)
träumen ♦ *n* Tagtraum *m*, Träumerei *f*.
daygirl ['deɪgəːl] *n* Externe *f*.
daylight ['deɪlaɪt] *n* Tageslicht *nt*.
daylight robbery (*inf*) *n* Halsabschneiderei *f*.
daylight-saving time (*US*) *n* Sommerzeit *f*.
day release *n*: **to be on ~** tageweise (zur
Weiterbildung) freigestellt sein.
day return (*BRIT*) *n* Tagesrückfahrkarte *f*.
day shift *n* Tagschicht *f*.
daytime ['deɪtaɪm] *n* Tag *m*; **in the ~**
tagsüber, bei Tage.
day-to-day ['deɪtə'deɪ] *adj* täglich, Alltags-;
on a ~ basis tageweise.
day trader *n* (*STOCK EXCHANGE*)
Daytrader(in) *m(f)*, Tageshändler(in) *m(f)*.
day trip *n* Tagesausflug *m*.
day-tripper ['deɪ'trɪpə*] *n* Tagesausflügler(in)
m(f).
daze [deɪz] *vt* benommen machen ♦ *n*: **in a ~**
ganz benommen.
dazed [deɪzd] *adj* benommen.
dazzle ['dæzl] *vt* blenden.
dazzling ['dæzlɪŋ] *adj* (*light*) blendend; (*smile*)
strahlend; (*career, achievements*) glänzend.
DC *abbr* = **direct current**.
DCC *n abbr* (= *digital compact cassette*) DCC *f*.
DD *n abbr* (= *Doctor of Divinity*) ≈ Dr. theol.
D/D *abbr* = **direct debit**.
dd. *abbr* (*COMM*: = *delivered*) geliefert.
D-day ['diːdeɪ] *n* der Tag X.
DDS (*US*) *n abbr* (= *Doctor of Dental Surgery*) ≈
Dr. med. dent.
DDT *n abbr* (= *dichlorodiphenyltrichloroethane*)
DDT *nt*.
DEA (*US*) *n abbr* (= *Drug Enforcement*
Administration) *amerikanische*
Drogenbehörde.

deacon ['diːkən] *n* Diakon *m*.
dead [dɛd] *adj* tot; (*flowers*) verwelkt; (*numb*)
abgestorben, taub; (*battery*) leer; (*place*) wie
ausgestorben ♦ *adv* total, völlig; (*directly,*
exactly) genau ♦ *npl*: **the ~** die Toten *pl*; **to**
shoot sb ~ jdn erschießen; **~ silence**
Totenstille *f*; **in the ~ centre (of)** genau in
der Mitte +*gen*; **the line has gone ~** (*TEL*) die
Leitung ist tot; **~ on time** auf die Minute
pünktlich; **~ tired** todmüde; **to stop ~**
abrupt stehen bleiben.
dead beat (*inf*) *adj* (*tired*) völlig kaputt.
deaden [dɛdn] *vt* (*blow*) abschwächen; (*pain*)
mildern; (*sound*) dämpfen.
dead end *n* Sackgasse *f*.
dead-end ['dɛdɛnd] *adj*: **a ~ job** ein Job *m*
ohne Aufstiegsmöglichkeiten.
dead heat *n*: **to finish in a ~** unentschieden
ausgehen.
dead letter office *n* Amt *nt* für unzustellbare
Briefe.
deadline ['dɛdlaɪn] *n* (letzter) Termin *m*; **to**
work to a ~ auf einen Termin hinarbeiten.
deadlock ['dɛdlɔk] *n* Stillstand *m*; **the meeting**
ended in ~ die Verhandlung war
festgefahren.
dead loss (*inf*) *n*: **to be a ~** ein
hoffnungsloser Fall sein.
deadly ['dɛdlɪ] *adj* tödlich ♦ *adv*: **~ dull**
todlangweilig.
deadpan ['dɛdpæn] *adj* (*look*) unbewegt; (*tone*)
trocken.
Dead Sea *n*: **the ~** das Tote Meer.
dead season *n* tote Saison *f*.
deaf [dɛf] *adj* taub; (*partially*) schwerhörig; **to**
turn a ~ ear to sth sich einer Sache *dat*
gegenüber taub stellen.
deaf aid (*BRIT*) *n* Hörgerät *nt*.
deaf-and-dumb ['dɛfən'dʌm] *adj* taubstumm;
~ alphabet Taubstummensprache *f*.
deafen ['dɛfn] *vt* taub machen.
deafening ['dɛfnɪŋ] *adj* ohrenbetäubend.
deaf-mute ['dɛfmjuːt] *n* Taubstumme(r) *f(m)*.
deafness ['dɛfnɪs] *n* Taubheit *f*.
deal [diːl] (*pt, pp* **dealt**) *n* Geschäft *nt*, Handel *m*
♦ *vt* (*blow*) versetzen; (*card*) geben,
austeilen; **to strike a ~ with sb** ein Geschäft
mit jdm abschließen; **it's a ~!** (*inf*)
abgemacht!; **he got a fair/bad ~ from them**
er ist von ihnen anständig/schlecht
behandelt worden; **a good ~** (*a lot*) ziemlich
viel; **a great ~ (of)** ziemlich viel.
▶ **deal in** *vt fus* handeln mit.
▶ **deal with** *vt fus* (*person*) sich kümmern um;
(*problem*) sich befassen mit; (*successfully*)
fertig werden mit; (*subject*) behandeln.
dealer ['diːlə*] *n* Händler(in) *m(f)*; (*in drugs*)
Dealer *m*; (*CARDS*) Kartengeber(in) *m(f)*.
dealership ['diːləʃɪp] *n* (Vertrags)händler *m*.
dealings ['diːlɪŋz] *npl* Geschäfte *pl*; (*relations*)
Beziehungen *pl*.
dealt [dɛlt] *pt, pp of* **deal**.

dean [di:n] *n* Dekan *m*; (*US: SCOL: administrator*) Schul- oder Collegeverwalter mit Beratungs- und Disziplinarfunktion.

dear [dɪə*] *adj* lieb; (*expensive*) teuer ♦ *n*: (**my**) ~ (mein) Liebling *m* ♦ *excl*: ~ **me!** (ach) du liebe Zeit!; **D~ Sir/Madam** Sehr geehrte Damen und Herren; **D~ Mr/Mrs X** Sehr geehrter Herr/geehrte Frau X; (*less formal*) Lieber Herr/Liebe Frau X.

dearly ['dɪəlɪ] *adv* (*love*) von ganzem Herzen; (*pay*) teuer.

dear money *n* (*COMM*) teures Geld *nt*.

dearth [də:θ] *n*: **a** ~ **of** ein Mangel *m* an +*dat*.

death [dɛθ] *n* Tod *m*; (*fatality*) Tote(r) *f(m)*, Todesfall *m*.

deathbed ['dɛθbɛd] *n*: **to be on one's** ~ auf dem Sterbebett liegen.

death certificate *n* Sterbeurkunde *f*, Totenschein *m*.

deathly ['dɛθlɪ] *adj* (*silence*) eisig ♦ *adv* (*pale etc*) toten-.

death penalty *n* Todesstrafe *f*.

death rate *n* Sterbeziffer *f*.

death row [-rəu] (*US*) *n* Todestrakt *m*.

death sentence *n* Todesurteil *nt*.

death squad *n* Todeskommando *nt*.

death toll *n* Zahl *f* der Todesopfer *or* Toten.

deathtrap ['dɛθtræp] *n* Todesfalle *f*.

deb [dɛb] (*inf*) *n abbr* = **debutante**.

debacle [deɪ'bɑ:kl] *n* Debakel *nt*.

debar [dɪ'bɑ:*] *vt*: **to** ~ **sb from doing sth** jdn davon ausschließen, etw zu tun; **to** ~ **sb from a club** jdn aus einem Klub ausschließen.

debase [dɪ'beɪs] *vt* (*value, quality*) mindern, herabsetzen; (*person*) erniedrigen, entwürdigen.

debatable [dɪ'beɪtəbl] *adj* fraglich.

debate [dɪ'beɪt] *n* Debatte *f* ♦ *vt* debattieren über +*acc*; (*course of action*) überlegen ♦ *vi*: **to** ~ **whether** hin und her überlegen, ob.

debauchery [dɪ'bɔ:tʃərɪ] *n* Ausschweifungen *pl*.

debenture [dɪ'bɛntʃə*] *n* Schuldschein *m*.

debilitate [dɪ'bɪlɪteɪt] *vt* schwächen.

debilitating [dɪ'bɪlɪteɪtɪŋ] *adj* schwächend.

debit ['dɛbɪt] *n* Schuldposten *m* ♦ *vt*: **to** ~ **a sum to sb/sb's account** jdn/jds Konto mit einer Summe belasten; *see also* **direct**.

debit balance *n* Sollsaldo *nt*, Debetsaldo *nt*.

debit note *n* Lastschriftanzeige *f*.

debonair *adj* flott.

debrief [di:'bri:f] *vt* befragen.

debriefing [di:'bri:fɪŋ] *n* Befragung *f*.

debris ['dɛbri:] *n* Trümmer *pl*, Schutt *m*.

debt [dɛt] *n* Schuld *f*; (*state of owing money*) Schulden *pl*, Verschuldung *f*; **to be in** ~ Schulden haben, verschuldet sein; **bad** ~ uneinbringliche Forderung *f*.

debt collector *n* Inkassobeauftragte(r) *f(m)*, Schuldeneintreiber(in) *m(f)*.

debtor ['dɛtə*] *n* Schuldner(in) *m(f)*.

debug ['di:'bʌg] *vt* (*COMPUT*) Fehler beseitigen in +*dat*.

debunk [di:'bʌŋk] *vt* (*myths, ideas*) bloßstellen; (*claim*) entlarven; (*person, institution*) vom Sockel stoßen.

debut ['deɪbju:] *n* Debüt *nt*.

debutante ['dɛbjutænt] *n* Debütantin *f*.

Dec. *abbr* = **December**.

decade ['dɛkeɪd] *n* Jahrzehnt *nt*.

decadence ['dɛkədəns] *n* Dekadenz *f*.

decadent ['dɛkədənt] *adj* dekadent.

decaff ['di:kæf] *n* koffeinfreier Kaffee *m*.

decaffeinated [dɪ'kæfɪneɪtɪd] *adj* koffeinfrei.

decamp [dɪ'kæmp] (*inf*) *vi* verschwinden, sich aus dem Staub machen.

decant [dɪ'kænt] *vt* umfüllen.

decanter [dɪ'kæntə*] *n* Karaffe *f*.

decarbonize [di:'kɑ:bənaɪz] *vt* entkohlen.

decathlon [dɪ'kæθlən] *n* Zehnkampf *m*.

decay [dɪ'keɪ] *n* Verfall *m*; (*of tooth*) Fäule *f* ♦ *vi* (*body*) verwesen; (*teeth*) faulen; (*leaves*) verrotten; (*fig: society etc*) verfallen.

decease [dɪ'si:s] *n* (*LAW*): **upon your** ~ bei Ihrem Ableben.

deceased [dɪ'si:st] *n*: **the** ~ der/die Tote *or* Verstorbene.

deceit [dɪ'si:t] *n* Betrug *m*.

deceitful [dɪ'si:tful] *adj* betrügerisch.

deceive [dɪ'si:v] *vt* täuschen; (*husband, wife etc*) betrügen; **to** ~ **o.s.** sich *dat* etwas vormachen.

decelerate [di:'sɛləreɪt] *vi* (*car etc*) langsamer werden; (*driver*) die Geschwindigkeit herabsetzen.

December [dɪ'sɛmbə*] *n* Dezember *m*; *see also* **July**.

decency ['di:sənsɪ] *n* (*propriety*) Anstand *m*; (*kindness*) Anständigkeit *f*.

decent ['di:sənt] *adj* anständig; **we expect you to do the** ~ **thing** wir erwarten, dass Sie die Konsequenzen ziehen; **they were very** ~ **about it** sie haben sich sehr anständig verhalten; **that was very** ~ **of him** das war sehr anständig von ihm; **are you** ~? (*dressed*) hast du etwas an?

decently ['di:səntlɪ] *adv* anständig.

decentralization [di:sentrəlaɪ'zeɪʃən] *n* Dezentralisierung *f*.

decentralize [di:'sentrəlaɪz] *vt* dezentralisieren.

deception [dɪ'sɛpʃən] *n* Täuschung *f*, Betrug *m*.

deceptive [dɪ'sɛptɪv] *adj* irreführend, täuschend.

decibel ['dɛsɪbɛl] *n* Dezibel *nt*.

decide [dɪ'saɪd] *vt* entscheiden; (*persuade*) veranlassen ♦ *vi* sich entscheiden; **to** ~ **to do sth/that** beschließen, etw zu tun/dass; **to** ~ **on sth** sich für etw entscheiden; **to** ~ **on/against doing sth** sich dafür/dagegen entscheiden, etw zu tun.

decided [dɪ'saɪdɪd] *adj* entschieden; (*character*)

entschlossen; (*difference*) deutlich.
decidedly [dɪˈsaɪdɪdlɪ] *adv* entschieden;
(*emphatically*) entschlossen.
deciding [dɪˈsaɪdɪŋ] *adj* entscheidend.
deciduous [dɪˈsɪdjuəs] *adj* (*tree, woods*) Laub-.
decimal [ˈdɛsɪməl] *adj* (*system, number*)
Dezimal- ♦ *n* Dezimalzahl *f*; **to three**
~ **places** auf drei Dezimalstellen.
decimalize [ˈdɛsɪməlaɪz] (*BRIT*) *vt* auf das
Dezimalsystem umstellen.
decimal point *n* Komma *nt*.
decimate [ˈdɛsɪmeɪt] *vt* dezimieren.
decipher [dɪˈsaɪfə*] *vt* entziffern.
decision [dɪˈsɪʒən] *n* Entscheidung *f*;
(*decisiveness*) Bestimmtheit *f*,
Entschlossenheit *f*; **to make a** ~ eine
Entscheidung treffen.
decisive [dɪˈsaɪsɪv] *adj* (*action etc*)
entscheidend; (*person*) entschlussfreudig;
(*manner, reply*) bestimmt, entschlossen.
deck [dɛk] *n* Deck *nt*; (*record deck*)
Plattenspieler *m*; (*of cards*) Spiel *nt*; **to go up**
on ~ an Deck gehen; **below** ~ unter Deck;
top ~ (*of bus*) Oberdeck *nt*; **cassette** ~
Tapedeck *nt*.
deck chair *n* Liegestuhl *m*.
deck hand *n* Deckshelfer(in) *m(f)*.
declaration [dɛkləˈreɪʃən] *n* Erklärung *f*.
declare [dɪˈklɛə*] *vt* erklären; (*result*) bekannt
geben, veröffentlichen; (*income etc*)
angeben; (*goods at customs*) verzollen.
declassify [diːˈklæsɪfaɪ] *vt* freigeben.
decline [dɪˈklaɪn] *n* Rückgang *m*; (*decay*)
Verfall *m* ♦ *vt* ablehnen ♦ *vi* (*strength*)
nachlassen; (*business*) zurückgehen; (*old
person*) abbauen; ~ **in/of** Rückgang *m* +*gen*;
~ **in living standards** Sinken *nt* des
Lebensstandards.
declutch [ˈdiːˈklʌtʃ] *vi* auskuppeln.
decode [ˈdiːˈkəʊd] *vt* entschlüsseln.
decoder [diːˈkəʊdə*] *n* Decoder *m*.
decompose [diːkəmˈpəʊz] *vi* (*organic matter*)
sich zersetzen; (*corpse*) verwesen.
decomposition [diːkɒmpəˈzɪʃən] *n*
Zersetzung *f*.
decompression [diːkəmˈprɛʃən] *n*
Dekompression *f*, Druckverminderung *f*.
decompression chamber *n*
Dekompressionskammer *f*.
decongestant [diːkənˈdʒɛstənt] *n* (*MED*)
abschwellendes Mittel *nt*; (: *drops*)
Nasentropfen *pl*.
decontaminate [diːkənˈtæmɪneɪt] *vt* entgiften.
decontrol [diːkənˈtrəʊl] *vt* freigeben.
décor [ˈdeɪkɔː*] *n* Ausstattung *f*; (*THEAT*)
Dekor *m* or *nt*.
decorate [ˈdɛkəreɪt] *vt*: **to** ~ **(with)** verzieren
(mit), (*tree, building*) schmücken (mit) ♦ *vt*
(*room, house: from bare walls*) anstreichen
und tapezieren; (: *redecorate*) renovieren.
decoration [dɛkəˈreɪʃən] *n* Verzierung *f*; (*on
tree, building*) Schmuck *m*; (*act: see verb*)

Verzieren *nt*; Schmücken *nt*; (An)streichen
nt; Tapezieren *nt*; (*medal*) Auszeichnung *f*.
decorative [ˈdɛkərətɪv] *adj* dekorativ.
decorator [ˈdɛkəreɪtə*] *n* Maler(in) *m(f)*,
Anstreicher(in) *m(f)*.
decorum [dɪˈkɔːrəm] *n* Anstand *m*.
decoy [ˈdiːkɔɪ] *n* Lockvogel *m*; (*object*) Köder
m; **they used him as a** ~ **for the enemy** sie
benutzten ihn dazu, den Feind anzulocken.
decrease [ˈdiːkriːs] *vt* verringern, reduzieren
♦ *vi* abnehmen, zurückgehen ♦ *n*: ~ **(in)**
Abnahme (+*gen*); Rückgang (+*gen*); **to be on
the** ~ abnehmen, zurückgehen.
decreasing [diːˈkriːsɪŋ] *adj* abnehmend,
zurückgehend.
decree [dɪˈkriː] *n* (*ADMIN, LAW*) Verfügung *f*;
(*POL*) Erlass *m*; (*REL*) Dekret *nt* ♦ *vt*: **to**
~ **(that)** verfügen(, dass), verordnen(,
dass).
decree absolute *n* endgültiges
Scheidungsurteil *nt*.
decree nisi [-ˈnaɪsaɪ] *n* vorläufiges
Scheidungsurteil *nt*.
decrepit [dɪˈkrɛpɪt] *adj* (*shack*) baufällig;
(*person*) klapprig (*inf*).
decry [dɪˈkraɪ] *vt* schlecht machen.
dedicate [ˈdɛdɪkeɪt] *vt*: **to** ~ **to** widmen +*dat*.
dedicated [ˈdɛdɪkeɪtɪd] *adj* hingebungsvoll,
engagiert; (*COMPUT*) dediziert; ~ **word
processor** dediziertes
Textverarbeitungssystem *nt*.
dedication [dɛdɪˈkeɪʃən] *n* Hingabe *f*; (*in book,
on radio*) Widmung *f*.
deduce [dɪˈdjuːs] *vt*: **to** ~ **(that)** schließen(,
dass), folgern(, dass).
deduct [dɪˈdʌkt] *vt* abziehen; **to** ~ **sth (from)**
etw abziehen (von); (*esp from wage etc*) etw
einbehalten (von).
deduction [dɪˈdʌkʃən] *n* (*act of deducting*)
Abzug *m*; (*act of deducing*) Folgerung *f*.
deed [diːd] *n* Tat *f*; (*LAW*) Urkunde *f*; ~ **of
covenant** Vertragsurkunde *f*.
deem [diːm] *vt* (*formal*) erachten für, halten
für; **to** ~ **it wise/helpful to do sth** es für
klug/hilfreich halten, etw zu tun.
deep [diːp] *adj* tief ♦ *adv*: **the spectators stood
20** ~ die Zuschauer standen in 20 Reihen
hintereinander; **to be 4 metres** ~ 4 Meter
tief sein; **knee-**~ **in water** bis zu den Knien
im Wasser; **he took a** ~ **breath** er holte tief
Luft.
deepen [ˈdiːpn] *vt* vertiefen ♦ *vi* (*crisis*) sich
verschärfen; (*mystery*) größer werden.
deepfreeze [ˈdiːpˈfriːz] *n* Tiefkühltruhe *f*.
deep-fry [ˈdiːpˈfraɪ] *vt* frittieren.
deeply [ˈdiːplɪ] *adv* (*breathe*) tief; (*interested*)
höchst; (*moved, grateful*) zutiefst.
deep-rooted [ˈdiːpˈruːtɪd] *adj* tief verwurzelt;
(*habit*) fest eingefahren.
deep-sea [ˈdiːpˈsiː] *cpd* Tiefsee-; (*fishing*)
Hochsee-.
deep-seated [ˈdiːpˈsiːtɪd] *adj* tief sitzend.

deep-set ['diːpsɛt] *adj* tief liegend.
deer [dɪəʳ] *n inv* Reh *nt*; (*male*) Hirsch *m*; **(red)** ~ Rotwild *nt*; **(roe)** ~ Reh *nt*; **(fallow)** ~ Damwild *nt*.
deerskin ['dɪəskɪn] *n* Hirschleder *nt*, Rehleder *nt*.
deerstalker ['dɪəstɔːkəʳ] *n* ≈ Sherlock-Holmes-Mütze *f*.
deface [dɪ'feɪs] *vt* (*with paint etc*) beschmieren; (*slash, tear*) zerstören.
defamation [dɛfə'meɪʃən] *n* Diffamierung *f*, Verleumdung *f*.
defamatory [dɪ'fæmətrɪ] *adj* diffamierend, verleumderisch.
default [dɪ'fɔːlt] *n* (*also:* ~ **value**) Voreinstellung *f* ♦ *vi:* **to** ~ **on a debt** einer Zahlungsverpflichtung nicht nachkommen; **to win by** ~ kampflos gewinnen.
defaulter [dɪ'fɔːltəʳ] *n* säumiger Zahler *m*, säumige Zahlerin *f*.
default option *n* Voreinstellung *f*.
defeat [dɪ'fiːt] *vt* besiegen, schlagen ♦ *n* (*failure*) Niederlage *f*; (*of enemy*): ~ **(of)** Sieg *m* (über +*acc.*)
defeatism [dɪ'fiːtɪzəm] *n* Defätismus *m*.
defeatist [dɪ'fiːtɪst] *adj* defätistisch ♦ *n* Defätist(in) *m(f)*.
defect [*n* 'diːfɛkt, *vi* dɪ'fɛkt] *n* Fehler *m* ♦ *vi:* **to** ~ **to the enemy** zum Feind überlaufen; **physical/mental** ~ körperlicher/geistiger Schaden *m or* Defekt *m*; **to** ~ **to the West** sich in den Westen absetzen.
defective [dɪ'fɛktɪv] *adj* fehlerhaft.
defector [dɪ'fɛktəʳ] *n* Überläufer(in) *m(f)*.
defence, (*US*) **defense** [dɪ'fɛns] *n* Verteidigung *f*; (*justification*) Rechtfertigung *f*; **in** ~ **of** zur Verteidigung +*gen*; **witness for the** ~ Zeuge *m*/Zeugin *f* der Verteidigung; **the Ministry of D**~, (*US*) **the Department of Defense** das Verteidigungsministerium.
defenceless [dɪ'fɛnslɪs] *adj* schutzlos.
defend [dɪ'fɛnd] *vt* verteidigen.
defendant [dɪ'fɛndənt] *n* Angeklagte(r) *f(m)*; (*in civil case*) Beklagte(r) *f(m)*.
defender [dɪ'fɛndəʳ] *n* Verteidiger(in) *m(f)*.
defending champion [dɪ'fɛndɪŋ-] *n* (*SPORT*) Titelverteidiger(in) *m(f)*.
defending counsel [dɪ'fɛndɪŋ-] *n* Verteidiger(in) *m(f)*.
defense [dɪ'fɛns] (*US*) *n* = **defence**.
defensive [dɪ'fɛnsɪv] *adj* defensiv ♦ *n:* **on the** ~ in der Defensive.
defer [dɪ'fɜːʳ] *vt* verschieben.
deference ['dɛfərəns] *n* Achtung *f*, Respekt *m*; **out of** *or* **in** ~ **to** aus Rücksicht auf +*acc.*
deferential [dɛfə'rɛnʃəl] *adj* ehrerbietig, respektvoll.
defiance [dɪ'faɪəns] *n* Trotz *m*; **in** ~ **of sth** einer Sache *dat* zum Trotz, unter Missachtung einer Sache *gen*.
defiant [dɪ'faɪənt] *adj* trotzig; (*challenging*) herausfordernd.

defiantly [dɪ'faɪəntlɪ] *adv* (*see adj*) trotzig; herausfordernd.
deficiency [dɪ'fɪʃənsɪ] *n* Mangel *m*; (*defect*) Unzulänglichkeit *f*; (*deficit*) Defizit *nt*.
deficiency disease *n* Mangelkrankheit *f*.
deficient [dɪ'fɪʃənt] *adj:* **sb/sth is** ~ **in sth** jdm/etw fehlt es an etw *dat*.
deficit ['dɛfɪsɪt] *n* Defizit *nt*.
defile [dɪ'faɪl] *vt* (*memory*) beschmutzen; (*statue etc*) schänden ♦ *n* Hohlweg *m*.
define [dɪ'faɪn] *vt* (*limits, boundaries*) bestimmen, festlegen; (*word*) definieren.
definite ['dɛfɪnɪt] *adj* definitiv; (*date etc*) fest; (*clear, obvious*) klar, eindeutig; (*certain*) bestimmt; **he was** ~ **about it** er war sich *dat* sehr sicher.
definite article *n* bestimmter Artikel *m*.
definitely ['dɛfɪnɪtlɪ] *adv* bestimmt; (*decide*) fest, definitiv.
definition [dɛfɪ'nɪʃən] *n* (*of word*) Definition *f*; (*of photograph etc*) Schärfe *f*.
definitive [dɪ'fɪnɪtɪv] *adj* (*account*) definitiv; (*version*) maßgeblich.
deflate [diː'fleɪt] *vt* (*tyre, balloon*) die Luft ablassen aus; (*person*) einen Dämpfer versetzen +*dat*; (*ECON*) deflationieren.
deflation [diː'fleɪʃən] *n* Deflation *f*.
deflationary [diː'fleɪʃənrɪ] *adj* deflationistisch.
deflect [dɪ'flɛkt] *vt* (*attention*) ablenken; (*criticism*) abwehren; (*shot*) abfälschen; (*light*) brechen, beugen.
defog ['diː'fɒg] (*US*) *vt* von Beschlag freimachen.
defogger ['diː'fɒgəʳ] (*US*) *n* Gebläse *nt*.
deform [dɪ'fɔːm] *vt* deformieren, verunstalten.
deformed [dɪ'fɔːmd] *adj* deformiert, missgebildet.
deformity [dɪ'fɔːmɪtɪ] *n* Deformität *f*, Missbildung *f*.
defraud [dɪ'frɔːd] *vt:* **to** ~ **sb (of sth)** jdn (um etw) betrügen.
defray [dɪ'freɪ] *vt:* **to** ~ **sb's expenses** jds Unkosten tragen *or* übernehmen.
defrost [diː'frɒst] *vt* (*fridge*) abtauen; (*windscreen*) entfrosten; (*food*) auftauen.
defroster [diː'frɒstəʳ] (*US*) *n* (*AUT*) Gebläse *nt*.
deft [dɛft] *adj* geschickt.
defunct [dɪ'fʌŋkt] *adj* (*industry*) stillgelegt; (*organization*) nicht mehr bestehend.
defuse [diː'fjuːz] *vt* entschärfen.
defy [dɪ'faɪ] *vt* sich widersetzen +*dat*; (*challenge*) auffordern; **it defies description** es spottet jeder Beschreibung.
degenerate [dɪ'dʒɛnəreɪt] *vi* degenerieren ♦ *adj* degeneriert.
degradation [dɛgrə'deɪʃən] *n* Erniedrigung *f*.
degrade [dɪ'greɪd] *vt* erniedrigen; (*reduce the quality of*) degradieren.
degrading [dɪ'greɪdɪŋ] *adj* erniedrigend.
degree [dɪ'griː] *n* Grad *m*; (*SCOL*) akademischer Grad *m*; **10** ~**s below (zero)**

10 Grad unter null; **6 ~s of frost** 6 Grad
Kälte *or* unter null; **a considerable ~ of risk**
ein gewisses Risiko; **a ~ in maths** ein
Hochschulabschluss *m* in Mathematik; **by
~s nach und nach; to some ~, to a certain ~**
einigermaßen, in gewissem Maße.
dehydrated [diːhaɪˈdreɪtɪd] *adj* ausgetrocknet,
dehydriert; (*milk, eggs*) pulverisiert,
Trocken-.
dehydration [diːhaɪˈdreɪʃən] *n* Austrocknung
f, Dehydration *f*.
de-ice [ˈdiːˈaɪs] *vt* enteisen.
de-icer [ˈdiːˈaɪsəˈ] *n* Defroster *m*.
deign [deɪn] *vi*: **to ~ to do sth** sich
herablassen, etw zu tun.
deity [ˈdiːɪtɪ] *n* Gottheit *f*.
dejected [dɪˈdʒɛktɪd] *adj* niedergeschlagen,
deprimiert.
dejection [dɪˈdʒɛkʃən] *n*
Niedergeschlagenheit *f*, Depression *f*.
Del. (*US*) *abbr* (*POST:* = *Delaware*).
del. *abbr* = **delete**.
delay [dɪˈleɪ] *vt* (*decision, ceremony*)
verschieben, aufschieben; (*person, plane,
train*) aufhalten ♦ *vi* zögern ♦ *n* Verzögerung
f; (*postponement*) Aufschub *m*; **to be ~ed**
(*person*) sich verspäten; (*departure etc*)
verspätet sein; (*flight etc*) Verspätung
haben; **without ~** unverzüglich.
delayed-action [dɪˈleɪdˈækʃən] *adj* (*bomb,
mine*) mit Zeitzünder; (*PHOT*): **~ shutter
release** Selbstauslöser *m*.
delectable [dɪˈlɛktəbl] *adj* (*person*) reizend;
(*food*) köstlich.
delegate [ˈdɛlɪgɪt] *n* Delegierte(r) *f(m)* ♦ *vt*
delegieren; **to ~ sth to sb** jdm mit etw
beauftragen; **to ~ sb to do sth** jdn damit
beauftragen, etw zu tun.
delegation [dɛlɪˈgeɪʃən] *n* Delegation *f*;
(*group*) Abordnung *f*, Delegation *f*.
delete [dɪˈliːt] *vt* streichen; (*COMPUT*)
löschen.
Delhi [ˈdɛlɪ] *n* Delhi *nt*.
deli [ˈdɛlɪ] *n* Feinkostgeschäft *nt*.
deliberate [*adj* dɪˈlɪbərɪt, *vi* dɪˈlɪbəreɪt] *adj*
absichtlich; (*action, insult*) bewusst; (*slow*)
bedächtig ♦ *vi* überlegen.
deliberately [dɪˈlɪbərɪtlɪ] *adv* absichtlich,
bewusst; (*slowly*) bedächtig.
deliberation [dɪlɪbəˈreɪʃən] *n* Überlegung *f*;
(*usu pl: discussions*) Beratungen *pl*.
delicacy [ˈdɛlɪkəsɪ] *n* Feinheit *f*, Zartheit *f*; (*of
problem*) Delikatheit *f*; (*choice food*)
Delikatesse *f*.
delicate [ˈdɛlɪkɪt] *adj* fein; (*colour, health*) zart;
(*approach*) feinfühlig; (*problem*) delikat,
heikel.
delicately [ˈdɛlɪkɪtlɪ] *adv* zart, fein; (*act,
express*) feinfühlig.
delicatessen [dɛlɪkəˈtɛsn] *n* Feinkostgeschäft
nt.
delicious [dɪˈlɪʃəs] *adj* köstlich; (*feeling,

person) herrlich.
delight [dɪˈlaɪt] *n* Freude *f* ♦ *vt* erfreuen; **sb
takes (a) ~ in sth** etw bereitet jdm große
Freude; **sb takes (a) ~ in doing sth** es
bereitet jdm große Freude, etw zu tun; **to
be the ~ of** die Freude +*gen* sein; **she was a
~ to interview** es war eine Freude, sie zu
interviewen; **the ~s of country life** die
Freuden des Landlebens.
delighted [dɪˈlaɪtɪd] *adj*: **~ (at *or* with)** erfreut
(über +*acc*), entzückt (über +*acc*); **to be ~ to
do sth** etw gern tun; **I'd be ~** ich würde
mich sehr freuen.
delightful [dɪˈlaɪtful] *adj* reizend, wunderbar.
delimit [diːˈlɪmɪt] *vt* abgrenzen.
delineate [dɪˈlɪnɪeɪt] *vt* (*fig*) beschreiben.
delinquency [dɪˈlɪŋkwənsɪ] *n* Kriminalität *f*.
delinquent [dɪˈlɪŋkwənt] *adj* straffällig ♦ *n*
Delinquent(in) *m(f)*.
delirious [dɪˈlɪrɪəs] *adj*: **to be ~ (with fever)** im
Delirium sein; (*with excitement*) im Taumel
sein.
delirium [dɪˈlɪrɪəm] *n* Delirium *nt*.
deliver [dɪˈlɪvəˈ] *vt* liefern; (*letters, papers*)
zustellen; (*hand over*) übergeben; (*message*)
überbringen; (*speech*) halten; (*blow*)
versetzen; (*MED: baby*) zur Welt bringen;
(*warning*) geben; (*ultimatum*) stellen; (*free*):
to ~ (from) befreien (von); **to ~ the goods**
(*fig*) halten, was man versprochen hat.
deliverance [dɪˈlɪvrəns] *n* Befreiung *f*.
delivery [dɪˈlɪvərɪ] *n* Lieferung *f*; (*of letters,
papers*) Zustellung *f*; (*of speaker*) Vortrag *m*;
(*MED*) Entbindung *f*; **to take ~ of sth** etw in
Empfang nehmen.
delivery note *n* Lieferschein *m*.
delivery van, (*US*) **delivery truck** *n*
Lieferwagen *m*.
delouse [ˈdiːˈlaus] *vt* entlausen.
delta [ˈdɛltə] *n* Delta *nt*.
delude [dɪˈluːd] *vt* täuschen; **to ~ o.s.** sich *dat*
etwas vormachen.
deluge [ˈdɛljuːdʒ] *n* (*of rain*) Guss *m*; (*fig: of
petitions, requests*) Flut *f*.
delusion [dɪˈluːʒən] *n* Irrglaube *m*; **to have ~s
of grandeur** größenwahnsinnig sein.
de luxe [dəˈlʌks] *adj* (*hotel, model*) Luxus-.
delve [dɛlv] *vi*: **to ~ into** (*subject*) sich
eingehend befassen mit; (*cupboard,
handbag*) tief greifen in +*acc*.
Dem. (*US*) *abbr* (*POL*) = **democrat, democratic**.
demagogue [ˈdɛməgɔg] *n* Demagoge *m*,
Demagogin *f*.
demand [dɪˈmaːnd] *vt* verlangen; (*rights*)
fordern; (*need*) erfordern, verlangen ♦ *n*
Verlangen *nt*; (*claim*) Forderung *f*; (*ECON*)
Nachfrage *f*; **to ~ sth (from *or* of sb)** etw
(von jdm) verlangen *or* fordern; **to be in ~**
gefragt sein; **on ~** (*available*) auf Verlangen;
(*payable*) bei Vorlage *or* Sicht.
demand draft *n* Sichtwechsel *m*.
demanding [dɪˈmaːndɪŋ] *adj* anspruchsvoll;

(*work, child*) anstrengend.

demarcation [diːmɑːˈkeɪʃən] n (*of area, tasks*) Abgrenzung f.

demarcation dispute n Streit m um den Zuständigkeitsbereich.

demean [dɪˈmiːn] vt: **to ~ o.s.** sich erniedrigen.

demeanour, (*US*) **demeanor** [dɪˈmiːnəʳ] n Benehmen nt, Auftreten nt.

demented [dɪˈmɛntɪd] adj wahnsinnig.

demilitarized zone [diːˈmɪlɪtəraɪzd-] n entmilitarisierte Zone f.

demise [dɪˈmaɪz] n Ende nt; (*death*) Tod m.

demist [diːˈmɪst] (*BRIT*) vt (*AUT: windscreen*) von Beschlag freimachen.

demister [diːˈmɪstəʳ] (*BRIT*) n (*AUT*) Gebläse nt.

demo [ˈdɛməʊ] (*inf*) n abbr = **demonstration**.

demob [diːˈmɔb] (*inf*) vt = **demobilize**.

demobilize [diːˈməʊbɪlaɪz] vt aus dem Kriegsdienst entlassen, demobilisieren.

democracy [dɪˈmɔkrəsɪ] n Demokratie f.

democrat [ˈdɛməkræt] n Demokrat(in) m(f).

democratic [dɛməˈkrætɪk] adj demokratisch.

Democratic Party (*US*) n: **the ~** die Demokratische Partei.

demography [dɪˈmɔgrəfɪ] n Demografie f.

demolish [dɪˈmɔlɪʃ] vt abreißen, abbrechen; (*fig: argument*) widerlegen.

demolition [dɛməˈlɪʃən] n Abriss m, Abbruch m; (*of argument*) Widerlegung f.

demon [ˈdiːmən] n Dämon m ♦ adj teuflisch gut.

demonstrate [ˈdɛmənstreɪt] vt (*theory*) demonstrieren; (*skill*) zeigen, beweisen; (*appliance*) vorführen ♦ vi: **to ~ (for/against)** demonstrieren (für/gegen).

demonstration [dɛmənˈstreɪʃən] n Demonstration f; (*of gadget, machine etc*) Vorführung f; **to hold a ~** eine Demonstration veranstalten *or* durchführen.

demonstrative [dɪˈmɔnstrətɪv] adj demonstrativ.

demonstrator [ˈdɛmənstreɪtəʳ] n Demonstrant(in) m(f); (*sales person*) Vorführer(in) m(f); (*car*) Vorführwagen m; (*computer etc*) Vorführgerät nt.

demoralize [dɪˈmɔrəlaɪz] vt entmutigen.

demote [dɪˈməʊt] vt zurückstufen; (*MIL*) degradieren.

demotion [dɪˈməʊʃən] n Zurückstufung f; (*MIL*) Degradierung f.

demur [dɪˈmɜːʳ] (*form*) vi Einwände pl erheben ♦ n: **without ~** widerspruchslos; **they ~red at the suggestion** sie erhoben Einwände gegen den Vorschlag.

demure [dɪˈmjʊəʳ] adj zurückhaltend; (*smile*) höflich; (*dress*) schlicht.

demurrage [dɪˈmʌrɪdʒ] n Liegegeld nt.

den [dɛn] n Höhle f; (*of fox*) Bau m; (*room*) Bude f.

denationalization [diːnæʃnəlaɪˈzeɪʃən] n Privatisierung f.

denationalize [diːˈnæʃnəlaɪz] vt privatisieren.

denatured alcohol [diːˈneɪtʃəd-] (*US*) n vergällter Alkohol m.

denial [dɪˈnaɪəl] n Leugnen nt; (*of rights*) Verweigerung f.

denier [ˈdɛnɪəʳ] n Denier nt.

denigrate [ˈdɛnɪgreɪt] vt verunglimpfen.

denim [ˈdɛnɪm] n Jeansstoff m; **denims** npl (Blue) Jeans pl.

denim jacket n Jeansjacke f.

denizen [ˈdɛnɪzn] n Bewohner(in) m(f); (*person in town*) Einwohner(in) m(f); (*foreigner*) eingebürgerter Ausländer m, eingebürgerte Ausländerin f.

Denmark [ˈdɛnmɑːk] n Dänemark nt.

denomination [dɪnɔmɪˈneɪʃən] n (*of money*) Nennwert m; (*REL*) Konfession f.

denominator [dɪˈnɔmɪneɪtəʳ] n Nenner m.

denote [dɪˈnəʊt] vt (*indicate*) hindeuten auf +acc; (*represent*) bezeichnen.

denounce [dɪˈnaʊns] vt (*person*) anprangern; (*action*) verurteilen.

dense [dɛns] adj dicht; (*inf: person*) beschränkt.

densely [ˈdɛnslɪ] adv dicht.

density [ˈdɛnsɪtɪ] n Dichte f; **single/double- ~ disk** (*COMPUT*) Diskette f mit einfacher/doppelter Dichte.

dent [dɛnt] n Beule f; (*in pride, ego*) Knacks m ♦ vt (*also*: **make a ~ in**) einbeulen; (*pride, ego*) anknacksen.

dental [ˈdɛntl] adj (*filling, hygiene etc*) Zahn-; (*treatment*) zahnärztlich.

dental floss [-flɔs] n Zahnseide f.

dental surgeon n Zahnarzt m, Zahnärztin f.

dentifrice [ˈdɛntɪfrɪs] n Zahnpasta f.

dentist [ˈdɛntɪst] n Zahnarzt m, Zahnärztin f; (*also*: **~'s (surgery)**) Zahnarzt m, Zahnarztpraxis f.

dentistry [ˈdɛntɪstrɪ] n Zahnmedizin f.

dentures [ˈdɛntʃəz] npl Zahnprothese f; (*full*) Gebiss nt.

denuded [diːˈnjuːdɪd] adj: **~ of** entblößt von.

denunciation [dɪnʌnsɪˈeɪʃən] n (*of person*) Anprangerung f; (*of action*) Verurteilung f.

deny [dɪˈnaɪ] vt leugnen; (*involvement*) abstreiten; (*permission, chance*) verweigern; (*country, religion etc*) verleugnen; **he denies having said it** er leugnet *or* bestreitet, das gesagt zu haben.

deodorant [diːˈəʊdərənt] n Deodorant nt.

depart [dɪˈpɑːt] vi (*visitor*) abreisen; (: *on foot*) weggehen; (*bus, train*) abfahren; (*plane*) abfliegen; **to ~ from** (*fig*) abweichen von.

departed [dɪˈpɑːtɪd] adj: **the (dear) ~** der/die (liebe) Verstorbene m/f, die (lieben) Verstorbenen pl.

department [dɪˈpɑːtmənt] n Abteilung f; (*SCOL*) Fachbereich m; (*POL*) Ministerium nt; **that's not my ~** (*fig*) dafür bin ich nicht zuständig; **D~ of State** (*US*) Außenministerium *nt*.

departmental [dɪːpɑːt'mentl] *adj* (*budget, costs*) der Abteilung, (*level*) Abteilungs-; **~ manager** Abteilungsleiter(in) *m(f)*.

department store *n* Warenhaus *nt*.

departure [dɪ'pɑːtʃə*] *n* (*of visitor*) Abreise *f*; (*on foot, of employee etc*) Weggang *m*; (*of bus, train*) Abfahrt *f*; (*of plane*) Abflug *m*; (*fig*): **~ from** Abweichen *nt* von; **a new ~** ein neuer Weg *m*.

departure lounge *n* Abflughalle *f*.

depend [dɪ'pend] *vi*: **to ~ on** abhängen von; (*rely on, trust*) sich verlassen auf *+acc*; (*financially*) abhängig sein von, angewiesen sein auf *+acc*; **it ~s** es kommt darauf an; **~ing on the result ...** je nachdem, wie das Ergebnis ausfällt, ...

dependable [dɪ'pendəbl] *adj* zuverlässig.

dependant [dɪ'pendənt] *n* abhängige(r) (Familien)angehörige(r) *f(m)*.

dependence [dɪ'pendəns] *n* Abhängigkeit *f*.

dependent [dɪ'pendənt] *adj*: **to be ~ on** (*person*) abhängig sein von, angewiesen sein auf *+acc*; (*decision*) abhängen von ♦ *n* = **dependant**.

depict [dɪ'pɪkt] *vt* (*in picture*) darstellen; (*describe*) beschreiben.

depilatory [dɪ'pɪlətrɪ] *n* (*also*: **~ cream**) Enthaarungsmittel *nt*.

depleted [dɪ'pliːtɪd] *adj* (*reserves*) aufgebraucht; (*stocks*) erschöpft.

deplorable [dɪ'plɔːrəbl] *adj* bedauerlich.

deplore [dɪ'plɔː*] *vt* verurteilen.

deploy [dɪ'plɔɪ] *vt* einsetzen.

depopulate [diː'pɒpjuleɪt] *vt* entvölkern.

depopulation ['diːpɒpju'leɪʃən] *n* Entvölkerung *f*.

deport [dɪ'pɔːt] *vt* (*criminal*) deportieren; (*illegal immigrant*) abschieben.

deportation [diːpɔː'teɪʃən] *n* (*see vb*) Deportation *f*; Abschiebung *f*.

deportation order *n* Ausweisung *f*.

deportee [diːpɔː'tiː] *n* Deportierte(r) *f(m)*.

deportment [dɪ'pɔːtmənt] *n* Benehmen *nt*.

depose [dɪ'pəuz] *vt* absetzen.

deposit [dɪ'pɒzɪt] *n* (*in account*) Guthaben *nt*; (*down payment*) Anzahlung *f*; (*for hired goods etc*) Sicherheit *f*, Kaution *f*; (*on bottle etc*) Pfand *nt*; (*CHEM*) Ablagerung *f*; (*of ore, oil*) Lagerstätte *f* ♦ *vt* deponieren; (*subj: river, sand etc*) ablagern; **to put down a ~ of £50** eine Anzahlung von £50 machen.

deposit account *n* Sparkonto *nt*.

depositary [dɪ'pɒzɪtərɪ] *n* Treuhänder(in) *m(f)*.

depositor [dɪ'pɒzɪtə*] *n* Deponent(in) *m(f)*, Einzahler(in) *m(f)*.

depository [dɪ'pɒzɪtərɪ] *n* (*person*) Treuhänder(in) *m(f)*; (*place*) Lager(haus) *nt*.

depot ['depəu] *n* Lager(haus) *nt*; (*for vehicles*) Depot *nt*; (*US: station*) Bahnhof *m*; (*: bus station*) Busbahnhof *m*.

depraved [dɪ'preɪvd] *adj* verworfen.

depravity [dɪ'prævɪtɪ] *n* Verworfenheit *f*.

deprecate ['deprɪkeɪt] *vt* missbilligen.

deprecating ['deprɪkeɪtɪŋ] *adj* (*disapproving*) missbilligend; (*apologetic*) entschuldigend.

depreciate [dɪ'priːʃeɪt] *vi* an Wert verlieren; (*currency*) an Kaufkraft verlieren; (*value*) sinken.

depreciation [dɪpriːʃɪ'eɪʃən] *n* (*see vb*) Wertminderung *f*; Kaufkraftverlust *m*; Sinken *nt*.

depress [dɪ'pres] *vt* deprimieren; (*price, wages*) drücken; (*press down*) herunterdrücken.

depressant [dɪ'presnt] *n* Beruhigungsmittel *nt*.

depressed [dɪ'prest] *adj* deprimiert, niedergeschlagen; (*price*) gesunken; (*industry*) geschwächt; (*area*) Notstands-; **to get ~** deprimiert werden.

depressing [dɪ'presɪŋ] *adj* deprimierend.

depression [dɪ'preʃən] *n* (*PSYCH*) Depressionen *pl*; (*ECON*) Wirtschaftskrise *f*; (*MET*) Tief(druckgebiet) *nt*; (*hollow*) Vertiefung *f*.

deprivation [deprɪ'veɪʃən] *n* Entbehrung *f*, Not *f*; (*of freedom, rights etc*) Entzug *m*.

deprive [dɪ'praɪv] *vt*: **to ~ sb of sth** (*liberty*) jdm etw entziehen; (*life*) jdm etw nehmen.

deprived [dɪ'praɪvd] *adj* benachteiligt; (*area*) Not leidend.

dept *abbr* = **department**.

depth [depθ] *n* Tiefe *f*; **in the ~s of** in den Tiefen *+gen*; **in the ~s of despair** in tiefster Verzweiflung; **in the ~s of winter** im tiefsten Winter; **at a ~ of 3 metres** in 3 Meter Tiefe; **to be out of one's ~** (*in water*) nicht mehr stehen können; (*fig*) überfordert sein; **to study sth in ~** etw gründlich *or* eingehend studieren.

depth charge *n* Wasserbombe *f*.

deputation [depju'teɪʃən] *n* Abordnung *f*.

deputize ['depjutaɪz] *vi*: **to ~ for sb** jdn vertreten.

deputy ['depjutɪ] *cpd* stellvertretend ♦ *n* (Stell)vertreter(in) *m(f)*; (*POL*) Abgeordnete(r) *f(m)*; (*US: also*: **~ sheriff**) Hilfssheriff *m*; **~ head** (*BRIT: SCOL*) Konrektor(in) *m(f)*.

derail [dɪ'reɪl] *vt*: **to be ~ed** entgleisen.

derailment [dɪ'reɪlmənt] *n* Entgleisung *f*.

deranged [dɪ'reɪndʒd] *adj*: **to be mentally ~** geistesgestört sein.

derby ['dɜːrbɪ] *n* Derby *nt*; (*US: hat*) Melone *f*.

Derbys (*BRIT*) *abbr* (*POST*: = **Derbyshire**).

deregulate [dɪ'regjuleɪt] *vt* staatliche Kontrollen aufheben bei.

deregulation [dɪ'regju'leɪʃən] *n* Aufhebung *f* staatlicher Kontrollen.

derelict ['derɪlɪkt] *adj* verfallen.

deride [dɪ'raɪd] *vt* sich lustig machen über *+acc*.

derision [dɪ'rɪʒən] n Hohn m, Spott m.
derisive [dɪ'raɪsɪv] adj spöttisch.
derisory [dɪ'raɪsərɪ] adj spöttisch; (sum) lächerlich.
derivation [dɛrɪ'veɪʃən] n Ableitung f.
derivative [dɪ'rɪvətɪv] n (LING) Ableitung f; (CHEM) Derivat nt ♦ adj nachahmend.
derive [dɪ'raɪv] vt: to ~ (from) gewinnen (aus); (benefit) ziehen (aus) ♦ vi: to ~ from (originate in) sich herleiten or ableiten von; to ~ pleasure from Freude haben an +dat.
dermatitis [də:mə'taɪtɪs] n Hautentzündung f, Dermatitis f.
dermatology [də:mə'tɔlədʒɪ] n Dermatologie f.
derogatory [dɪ'rɔgətərɪ] adj abfällig.
derrick ['dɛrɪk] n (on ship) Derrickkran m; (on well) Bohrturm m.
derv [də:v] (BRIT) n (AUT) Diesel(kraftstoff) m.
desalination [di:sælɪ'neɪʃən] n Entsalzung f.
descend [dɪ'sɛnd] vt hinuntergehen, hinuntersteigen; (lift, vehicle) hinunterfahren; (road) hinunterführen ♦ vi hinuntergehen; (lift) nach unten fahren; to ~ from abstammen von; to ~ to sich erniedrigen zu; in ~ing order of importance nach Wichtigkeit geordnet.
▶ **descend on** vt fus überfallen; (subj: misfortune) hereinbrechen über +acc; (: gloom) befallen; (: silence) sich senken auf +acc; **visitors ~ed (up)on us** der Besuch hat uns überfallen.
descendant [dɪ'sɛndənt] n Nachkomme m.
descent [dɪ'sɛnt] n Abstieg m; (origin) Abstammung f.
describe [dɪs'kraɪb] vt beschreiben.
description [dɪs'krɪpʃən] n Beschreibung f; (sort): **of every ~** aller Art.
descriptive [dɪs'krɪptɪv] adj deskriptiv.
desecrate ['dɛsɪkreɪt] vt schänden.
desegregate [di:'sɛgrɪgeɪt] vt die Rassentrennung aufheben in +dat.
desert [n 'dɛzət, vb dɪ'zə:t] n Wüste f ♦ vt verlassen ♦ vi desertieren; see also **deserts**.
deserter [dɪ'zə:tə*] n Deserteur m.
desertion [dɪ'zə:ʃən] n Desertion f, Fahnenflucht f; (LAW) böswilliges Verlassen nt.
desert island n einsame or verlassene Insel f.
deserts [dɪ'zə:ts] npl: **to get one's just ~** bekommen, was man verdient.
deserve [dɪ'zə:v] vt verdienen.
deservedly [dɪ'zə:vɪdlɪ] adv verdientermaßen.
deserving [dɪ'zə:vɪŋ] adj verdienstvoll.
desiccated ['dɛsɪkeɪtɪd] adj vertrocknet; (coconut) getrocknet.
design [dɪ'zaɪn] n Design nt; (process) Entwurf m, Gestaltung f; (sketch) Entwurf m; (layout, shape) Form f; (pattern) Muster nt; (of car) Konstruktion f; (intention) Plan m, Absicht f ♦ vt entwerfen; **to have ~s on** es abgesehen

haben auf +acc; **well-~ed** mit gutem Design.
design and technology (BRIT) n (SCOL) ≈ Design und Technologie.
designate [vt 'dɛzɪgneɪt, adj 'dɛzɪgnɪt] vt bestimmen, ernennen ♦ adj designiert.
designation [dɛzɪg'neɪʃən] n Bezeichnung f.
designer [dɪ'zaɪnə*] n Designer(in) m(f); (TECH) Konstrukteur(in) m(f); (fashion designer) Modeschöpfer(in) m(f) ♦ adj (clothes etc) Designer-.
desirability [dɪzaɪərə'bɪlɪtɪ] n: **they discussed the ~ of the plan** sie besprachen, ob der Plan wünschenswert sei.
desirable [dɪ'zaɪərəbl] adj (proper) wünschenswert; (attractive) reizvoll, attraktiv.
desire [dɪ'zaɪə*] n Wunsch m; (sexual) Verlangen nt, Begehren nt ♦ vt wünschen; (lust after) begehren; **to ~ to do sth/that** wünschen, etw zu tun/dass.
desirous [dɪ'zaɪərəs] adj: **to be ~ of doing sth** den Wunsch haben, etw zu tun.
desist [dɪ'zɪst] vi: **to ~ (from)** absehen (von), Abstand nehmen (von).
desk [dɛsk] n Schreibtisch m; (for pupil) Pult nt; (in hotel) Empfang m; (at airport) Schalter m; (BRIT: in shop, restaurant) Kasse f.
desk job n Bürojob m.
desktop ['dɛsktɔp] n Arbeitsfläche f.
desktop publishing n Desktoppublishing nt, Desktop-Publishing nt.
desolate ['dɛsəlɪt] adj trostlos.
desolation [dɛsə'leɪʃən] n Trostlosigkeit f.
despair [dɪs'pɛə*] n Verzweiflung f ♦ vi: **to ~** alle Hoffnung aufgeben auf +acc; **to be in ~** verzweifelt sein.
despatch [dɪs'pætʃ] n, vt = **dispatch**.
desperate ['dɛspərɪt] adj verzweifelt; (shortage) akut; (criminal) zum Äußersten entschlossen; **to be ~ for sth/to do sth** etw dringend brauchen/unbedingt tun wollen.
desperately ['dɛspərɪtlɪ] adv (shout, struggle etc) verzweifelt; (ill) schwer; (unhappy etc) äußerst.
desperation [dɛspə'reɪʃən] n Verzweiflung f; **in (sheer) ~** aus (reiner) Verzweiflung.
despicable [dɪs'pɪkəbl] adj (action) verabscheuungswürdig; (person) widerwärtig.
despise [dɪs'paɪz] vt verachten.
despite [dɪs'paɪt] prep trotz +gen.
despondent [dɪs'pɔndənt] adj niedergeschlagen, mutlos.
despot ['dɛspɔt] n Despot m.
dessert [dɪ'zə:t] n Nachtisch m, Dessert nt.
dessertspoon [dɪ'zə:tspu:n] n Dessertlöffel m.
destabilize [di:'steɪbɪlaɪz] vt destabilisieren.
destination [dɛstɪ'neɪʃən] n (Reise)ziel nt; (of mail) Bestimmungsort m.
destined ['dɛstɪnd] adj: **to be ~ to do sth** dazu bestimmt or ausersehen sein, etw zu tun; **to**

be ~ **for** bestimmt *or* ausersehen sein für.
destiny ['dɛstɪnɪ] *n* Schicksal *nt*.
destitute ['dɛstɪtjuːt] *adj* mittellos.
destroy [dɪs'trɔɪ] *vt* zerstören; (*animal*) töten.
destroyer [dɪs'trɔɪə·] *n* Zerstörer *m*.
destruction [dɪs'trʌkʃən] *n* Zerstörung *f*.
destructive [dɪs'trʌktɪv] *adj* zerstörerisch; (*child, criticism etc*) destruktiv.
desultory ['dɛsəltərɪ] *adj* flüchtig; (*conversation*) zwanglos.
detach [dɪ'tætʃ] *vt* (*remove*) entfernen; (*unclip*) abnehmen; (*unstick*) ablösen.
detachable [dɪ'tætʃəbl] *adj* abnehmbar.
detached [dɪ'tætʃt] *adj* distanziert; (*house*) frei stehend, Einzel-.
detachment [dɪ'tætʃmənt] *n* Distanz *f*; (*MIL*) Sonderkommando *nt*.
detail ['diːteɪl] *n* Einzelheit *f*; (*no pl: in picture, one's work etc*) Detail *nt*; (*trifle*) unwichtige Einzelheit ♦ *vt* (einzeln) aufführen; **in** ~ in Einzelheiten; **to go into** ~**s** auf Einzelheiten eingehen, ins Detail gehen.
detailed ['diːteɪld] *adj* detailliert, genau.
detain [dɪ'teɪn] *vt* aufhalten; (*in captivity*) in Haft halten; (*in hospital*) festhalten.
detainee [diːteɪ'niː] *n* Häftling *m*.
detect [dɪ'tɛkt] *vt* wahrnehmen; (*MED, TECH*) feststellen; (*MIL*) ausfindig machen.
detection [dɪ'tɛkʃən] *n* Entdeckung *f*, Feststellung *f*; **crime** ~ Ermittlungsarbeit *f*; **to escape** ~ (*criminal*) nicht gefasst werden; (*mistake*) der Aufmerksamkeit *dat* entgehen.
detective [dɪ'tɛktɪv] *n* Kriminalbeamte(r) *m*; **private** ~ Privatdetektiv *m*.
detective story *n* Kriminalgeschichte *f*, Detektivgeschichte *f*.
detector [dɪ'tɛktə·] *n* Detektor *m*.
détente [deɪ'tɑːnt] *n* Entspannung *f*, Détente *f*.
detention [dɪ'tɛnʃən] *n* (*arrest*) Festnahme *f*; (*captivity*) Haft *f*; (*SCOL*) Nachsitzen *nt*.
deter [dɪ'təː·] *vt* (*discourage*) abschrecken; (*dissuade*) abhalten.
detergent [dɪ'təːdʒənt] *n* Reinigungsmittel *nt*; (*for clothes*) Waschmittel *nt*; (*for dishes*) Spülmittel *nt*.
deteriorate [dɪ'tɪərɪəreɪt] *vi* sich verschlechtern.
deterioration [dɪtɪərɪə'reɪʃən] *n* Verschlechterung *f*.
determination [dɪtəːmɪ'neɪʃən] *n* Entschlossenheit *f*; (*establishment*) Festsetzung *f*.
determine [dɪ'təːmɪn] *vt* (*facts*) feststellen; (*limits etc*) festlegen; **to** ~ **that** beschließen, dass; **to** ~ **to do sth** sich entschließen, etw zu tun.
determined [dɪ'təːmɪnd] *adj* entschlossen; (*quantity*) bestimmt; **to be** ~ **to do sth** (fest) entschlossen sein, etw zu tun.
deterrence [dɪ'tɛrəns] *n* Abschreckung *f*.
deterrent [dɪ'tɛrənt] *n* Abschreckungsmittel *nt*; **to act as a** ~ als Abschreckung(smittel)

dienen.
detest [dɪ'tɛst] *vt* verabscheuen.
detestable [dɪ'tɛstəbl] *adj* abscheulich, widerwärtig.
detonate ['dɛtəneɪt] *vi* detonieren ♦ *vt* zur Explosion bringen.
detonator ['dɛtəneɪtə·] *n* Sprengkapsel *f*.
detour ['diːtuə·] *n* Umweg *m*; (*US: AUT*) Umleitung *f*.
detract [dɪ'trækt] *vi*: **to** ~ **from** schmälern; (*effect*) beeinträchtigen.
detractor [dɪ'træktə·] *n* Kritiker(in) *m(f)*.
detriment ['dɛtrɪmənt] *n*: **to the** ~ **of** zum Schaden +*gen*; **without** ~ **to** ohne Schaden für.
detrimental [dɛtrɪ'mɛntl] *adj*: **to be** ~ **to** schaden +*dat*.
deuce [djuːs] *n* (*TENNIS*) Einstand *m*.
devaluation [diːvæljuˈeɪʃən] *n* Abwertung *f*.
devalue ['diːˈvæljuː] *vt* abwerten.
devastate ['dɛvəsteɪt] *vt* verwüsten; (*fig: shock*): **to be** ~**d by** niedergeschmettert sein von.
devastating ['dɛvəsteɪtɪŋ] *adj* verheerend; (*announcement, news*) niederschmetternd.
devastation [dɛvəs'teɪʃən] *n* Verwüstung *f*.
develop [dɪ'vɛləp] *vt* entwickeln; (*business*) erweitern, ausbauen; (*land, resource*) erschließen; (*disease*) bekommen ♦ *vi* sich entwickeln; (*facts*) an den Tag kommen; (*symptoms*) auftreten; **to** ~ **a taste for sth** Geschmack an etw finden; **the machine/car** ~**ed a fault/engine trouble** an dem Gerät/ dem Wagen trat ein Defekt/ein Motorschaden auf; **to** ~ **into** sich entwickeln zu, werden.
developer [dɪ'vɛləpə·] *n* (*also*: **property** ~) *Bauunternehmer und Immobilienmakler*.
developing country [dɪ'vɛləpɪŋ-] *n* Entwicklungsland *nt*.
development [dɪ'vɛləpmənt] *n* Entwicklung *f*; (*of land*) Erschließung *f*.
development area *n* Entwicklungsgebiet *nt*.
deviant ['diːvɪənt] *adj* abweichend.
deviate ['diːvɪeɪt] *vi*: **to** ~ **(from)** abweichen (von).
deviation [diːvɪ'eɪʃən] *n* Abweichung *f*.
device [dɪ'vaɪs] *n* Gerät *nt*; (*ploy, stratagem*) Trick *m*; **explosive** ~ Sprengkörper *m*.
devil ['dɛvl] *n* Teufel *m*; **go on, be a** ~! nur zu, riskier mal was!; **talk of the** ~! wenn man vom Teufel spricht!
devilish ['dɛvlɪʃ] *adj* teuflisch.
devil's advocate ['dɛvlz-] *n* Advocatus Diaboli *m*.
devious ['diːvɪəs] *adj* (*person*) verschlagen; (*route, path*) gewunden.
devise [dɪ'vaɪz] *vt* sich *dat* ausdenken; (*machine*) entwerfen.
devoid [dɪ'vɔɪd] *adj*: ~ **of** bar +*gen*, ohne +*acc*.
devolution [diːvə'luːʃən] *n* Dezentralisierung *f*.

devolve [dɪ'vɔlv] *vt* übertragen ♦ *vi*: to ~ (up)on übergehen auf +*acc*.
devote [dɪ'vəut] *vt*: to ~ sth/o.s. to etw/sich widmen +*dat*.
devoted [dɪ'vəutɪd] *adj* treu; (*admirer*) eifrig; to be ~ to sb jdn innig lieben; the book is ~ to politics das Buch widmet sich ganz der Politik *dat*.
devotee [dɛvəu'tiː] *n* (*fan*) Liebhaber(in) *m(f)*; (*REL*) Anhänger(in) *m(f)*.
devotion [dɪ'vəuʃən] *n* (*affection*) Ergebenheit *f*; (*dedication*) Hingabe *f*; (*REL*) Andacht *f*.
devour [dɪ'vauə*] *vt* verschlingen.
devout [dɪ'vaut] *adj* fromm.
dew [djuː] *n* Tau *m*.
dexterity [dɛks'tɛrɪtɪ] *n* Geschicklichkeit *f*; (*mental*) Gewandtheit *f*.
dext(e)rous ['dɛkstrəs] *adj* geschickt.
DfEE (*BRIT*) *n abbr* (= *Department for Education and Employment*) Ministerium *nt* für Bildung und Arbeit.
dg *abbr* (= *decigram*) dg.
DH (*BRIT*) *n abbr* (= *Department of Health*) ≈ Gesundheitsministerium *nt*.
DHSS (*BRIT*) *n abbr* (*formerly*: = *Department of Health and Social Security*) *Ministerium für Gesundheit und Sozialfürsorge*.
diabetes [daɪə'biːtiːz] *n* Zuckerkrankheit *f*.
diabetic [daɪə'bɛtɪk] *adj* zuckerkrank; (*chocolate, jam*) Diabetiker- ♦ *n* Diabetiker(in) *m(f)*.
diabolical [daɪə'bɔlɪkl] (*inf*) *adj* schrecklich, fürchterlich.
diaeresis [daɪ'ɛrɪsɪs] *n* Diärese *f*.
diagnose [daɪəg'nəuz] *vt* diagnostizieren.
diagnoses [-siːz] *pl of* **diagnosis**.
diagnosis [daɪəg'nəusɪs] (*pl* **diagnoses**) *n* Diagnose *f*.
diagonal [daɪ'ægənl] *adj* diagonal ♦ *n* Diagonale *f*.
diagram ['daɪəgræm] *n* Diagramm *nt*, Schaubild *nt*.
dial ['daɪəl] *n* Zifferblatt *nt*; (*on radio set*) Einstellskala *f*; (*of phone*) Wählscheibe *f* ♦ *vt* wählen; to ~ a wrong number sich verwählen; can I ~ London direct? kann ich nach London durchwählen?
dial. *abbr* = **dialect**.
dial code (*US*) *n* = **dialling code**.
dialect ['daɪəlɛkt] *n* Dialekt *m*.
dialling code ['daɪəlɪŋ-], (*US*) **dial code** *n* Vorwahl *f*.
dialling tone, (*US*) **dial tone** *n* Amtszeichen *nt*.
dialogue, (*US*) **dialog** ['daɪəlɔg] *n* Dialog *m*; (*conversation*) Gespräch *nt*, Dialog *m*.
dial tone (*US*) *n* = **dialling tone**.
dialysis [daɪ'ælɪsɪs] *n* Dialyse *f*.
diameter [daɪ'æmɪtə*] *n* Durchmesser *m*.
diametrically [daɪə'mɛtrɪklɪ] *adv*: ~ opposed (to) diametral entgegengesetzt (+*dat*).
diamond ['daɪəmənd] *n* Diamant *m*; (*shape*)

Raute *f*; **diamonds** *npl* (*CARDS*) Karo *nt*.
diamond ring *n* Diamantring *m*.
diaper ['daɪəpə*] (*US*) *n* Windel *f*.
diaphragm ['daɪəfræm] *n* Zwerchfell *nt*; (*contraceptive*) Pessar *nt*.
diarrhoea, (*US*) **diarrhea** [daɪə'riːə] *n* Durchfall *m*.
diary ['daɪərɪ] *n* (Termin)kalender *m*; (*daily account*) Tagebuch *nt*; to keep a ~ Tagebuch führen.
diatribe ['daɪətraɪb] *n* Schmährede *f*; (*written*) Schmähschrift *f*.
dice [daɪs] *n inv* Würfel *m* ♦ *vt* in Würfel schneiden.
dicey ['daɪsɪ] (*inf*) *adj* riskant.
dichotomy [daɪ'kɔtəmɪ] *n* Dichotomie *f*, Kluft *f*.
dickhead ['dɪkhɛd] (*inf*) *n* Knallkopf *m*.
Dictaphone ® ['dɪktəfəun] *n* Diktafon *nt*, Diktaphon *nt*, Diktiergerät *nt*.
dictate [dɪk'teɪt] *vt* diktieren ♦ *n* Diktat *nt*; (*principle*): the ~s of die Gebote +*gen* ♦ *vi*: to ~ to diktieren +*dat*; I won't be ~d to ich lasse mir keine Vorschriften machen.
dictation [dɪk'teɪʃən] *n* Diktat *nt*; at ~ speed im Diktiertempo.
dictator [dɪk'teɪtə*] *n* Diktator *m*.
dictatorship [dɪk'teɪtəʃɪp] *n* Diktatur *f*.
diction ['dɪkʃən] *n* Diktion *f*.
dictionary ['dɪkʃənrɪ] *n* Wörterbuch *nt*.
did [dɪd] *pt of* **do**.
didactic [daɪ'dæktɪk] *adj* didaktisch.
diddle ['dɪdl] (*inf*) *vt* übers Ohr hauen.
didn't ['dɪdnt] = **did not**.
die [daɪ] *n* (*pl*: **dice**) Würfel *m*; (*: dies*) Gussform *f* ♦ *vi* sterben; (*plant*) eingehen; (*fig*: *noise*) aufhören; (*: smile*) vergehen; (*engine*) stehen bleiben; to ~ of *or* from sterben an +*dat*; to be dying im Sterben liegen; to be dying for sth etw unbedingt brauchen; to be dying to do sth darauf brennen, etw zu tun.
► **die away** *vi* (*sound*) schwächer werden; (*light*) nachlassen.
► **die down** *vi* (*wind*) sich legen; (*fire*) herunterbrennen; (*excitement, noise*) nachlassen.
► **die out** *vi* aussterben.
die-hard ['daɪhɑːd] *n* Ewiggestrige(r) *f(m)*.
diesel ['diːzl] *n* (*vehicle*) Diesel *m*; (*also*: ~ oil) Diesel(kraftstoff) *m*.
diesel engine *n* Dieselmotor *m*.
diet ['daɪət] *n* Ernährung *f*; (*MED*) Diät *f*; (*when slimming*) Schlankheitskur *f* ♦ *vi* (*also*: be on a ~) eine Schlankheitskur machen; to live on a ~ of sich ernähren von, leben von.
dietician [daɪə'tɪʃən] *n* Diätassistent(in) *m(f)*.
differ ['dɪfə*] *vi* (*be different*): to ~ (from) sich unterscheiden (von); (*disagree*): to ~ (about) anderer Meinung sein (über +*acc*); to agree to ~ sich *dat* verschiedene Meinungen zugestehen.
difference ['dɪfrəns] *n* Unterschied *m*;

(*disagreement*) Differenz *f*,
Auseinandersetzung *f*; **it makes no ~ to me**
das ist mir egal *or* einerlei; **to settle one's**
~s die Differenzen *or*
Meinungsverschiedenheiten beilegen.

different ['dɪfrənt] *adj* (*various people, things*)
verschieden, unterschiedlich; **to be**
~ (from) anders sein (als).

differential [dɪfə'renʃəl] *n* (*MATH*)
Differenzial *nt*; (*BRIT: in wages*)
(Einkommens)unterschied *m*.

differentiate [dɪfə'renʃɪeɪt] *vi*: **to ~ (between)**
unterscheiden (zwischen) ♦ *vt*: **to ~ A from**
B A von B unterscheiden.

differently ['dɪfrəntlɪ] *adv* anders; (*shaped,
designed*) verschieden, unterschiedlich.

difficult ['dɪfɪkəlt] *adj* schwierig; (*task,
problem*) schwer, schwierig; **~ to
understand** schwer zu verstehen.

difficulty ['dɪfɪkəltɪ] *n* Schwierigkeit *f*; **to be
in/get into difficulties** in Schwierigkeiten
sein/geraten.

diffidence ['dɪfɪdəns] *n* Bescheidenheit *f*,
Zurückhaltung *f*.

diffident ['dɪfɪdənt] *adj* bescheiden,
zurückhaltend.

diffuse [dɪ'fjuːs] *adj* diffus ♦ *vt* verbreiten.

dig [dɪg] (*pt, pp* **dug**) *vt* graben; (*garden*)
umgraben ♦ *n* (*prod*) Stoß *m*; (*archaeological*)
(Aus)grabung *f*; (*remark*) Seitenhieb *m*,
spitze Bemerkung *f*; **to ~ one's nails into
sth** seine Nägel in etw *acc* krallen.

▶ **dig in** *vi* (*fig: inf: eat*) reinhauen ♦ *vt*
(*compost*) untergraben, eingraben; (*knife*)
hineinstoßen; (*claw*) festkrallen; **to ~ one's
heels in** (*fig*) sich auf die Hinterbeine stellen
(*inf*).

▶ **dig into** *vt fus* (*savings*) angreifen; (*snow,
soil*) ein Loch graben in +*acc*; **to ~ into one's
pockets for sth** in seinen Taschen nach etw
suchen *or* wühlen.

▶ **dig out** *vt* ausgraben.

▶ **dig up** *vt* ausgraben.

digest [daɪ'dʒest] *vt* verdauen ♦ *n* Digest *m or*
nt, Auswahl *f*.

digestible [dɪ'dʒestəbl] *adj* verdaulich.

digestion [dɪ'dʒestʃən] *n* Verdauung *f*.

digestive [dɪ'dʒestɪv] *adj* (*system, upsets*)
Verdauungs- ♦ *n* Keks aus Vollkornmehl.

digit ['dɪdʒɪt] *n* (*number*) Ziffer *f*; (*finger*)
Finger *m*.

digital ['dɪdʒɪtl] *adj* (*watch, display etc*) Digital-.

digital computer *n* Digitalrechner *m*.

digital TV *n* Digitalfernsehen *nt*.

dignified ['dɪgnɪfaɪd] *adj* würdevoll.

dignitary ['dɪgnɪtərɪ] *n* Würdenträger(in) *m(f)*.

dignity ['dɪgnɪtɪ] *n* Würde *f*.

digress [daɪ'gres] *vi*: **to ~ (from)** abschweifen
(von).

digression [daɪ'greʃən] *n* Abschweifung *f*.

digs [dɪgz] (*BRIT: inf*) *npl* Bude *f*.

dike [daɪk] *n* = **dyke**.

dilapidated [dɪ'læpɪdeɪtɪd] *adj* verfallen.

dilate [daɪ'leɪt] *vi* sich weiten ♦ *vt* weiten.

dilatory ['dɪlətərɪ] *adj* langsam.

dilemma [daɪ'lemə] *n* Dilemma *nt*; **to be in a ~**
sich in einem Dilemma befinden, in der
Klemme sitzen (*inf*).

diligence ['dɪlɪdʒəns] *n* Fleiß *m*.

diligent ['dɪlɪdʒənt] *adj* fleißig; (*research*)
sorgfältig, genau.

dill [dɪl] *n* Dill *m*.

dilly-dally ['dɪlɪ'dælɪ] *vi* trödeln.

dilute [daɪ'luːt] *vt* verdünnen; (*belief, principle*)
schwächen ♦ *adj* verdünnt.

dim [dɪm] *adj* schwach; (*outline, figure*)
undeutlich, verschwommen; (*room*)
dämmerig; (*future*) düster; (*prospects*)
schlecht; (*inf: person*) schwer von Begriff
♦ *vt* (*light*) dämpfen; (*US: AUT*) abblenden; **to
take a ~ view of sth** wenig *or* nicht viel von
etw halten.

dime [daɪm] (*US*) *n* Zehncentstück *nt*.

dimension [daɪ'menʃən] *n* (*aspect*) Dimension
f; (*measurement*) Abmessung *f*, Maß *nt*; (*also
pl: scale, size*) Ausmaß *nt*.

-dimensional [dɪ'menʃənl] *adj suff*
-dimensional.

diminish [dɪ'mɪnɪʃ] *vi* sich verringern ♦ *vt*
verringern.

diminished responsibility *n* verminderte
Zurechnungsfähigkeit *f*.

diminutive [dɪ'mɪnjutɪv] *adj* winzig ♦ *n*
Verkleinerungsform *f*.

dimly ['dɪmlɪ] *adv* schwach; (*see*) undeutlich,
verschwommen.

dimmer ['dɪmə*] *n* (*also:* **~ switch**) Dimmer *m*;
(*US: AUT*) Abblendschalter *m*.

dimmers ['dɪməz] (*US*) *npl* (*AUT: dipped
headlights*) Abblendlicht *nt*; (*parking lights*)
Parklicht *nt*.

dimmer (switch) ['dɪmə-] *n* (*ELEC*) Dimmer
m; (*US: AUT*) Abblendschalter *m*.

dimple ['dɪmpl] *n* Grübchen *nt*.

dim-witted ['dɪm'wɪtɪd] (*inf*) *adj* dämlich.

din [dɪn] *n* Lärm *m*, Getöse *nt* ♦ *vt* (*inf*): **to
~ sth into sb** jdm etw einbleuen.

dine [daɪn] *vi* speisen.

diner ['daɪnə*] *n* Gast *m*; (*US: restaurant*)
Esslokal *nt*.

dinghy ['dɪŋgɪ] *n* (*also:* **rubber ~**)
Schlauchboot *nt*; (*also:* **sailing ~**) Dingi *nt*.

dingy ['dɪndʒɪ] *adj* schäbig; (*clothes, curtains
etc*) schmuddelig.

dining car ['daɪnɪŋ-] (*BRIT*) *n* Speisewagen *m*.

dining room *n* Esszimmer *nt*; (*in hotel*)
Speiseraum *m*.

dinner ['dɪnə*] *n* (*evening meal*) Abendessen *nt*;
(*lunch*) Mittagessen *nt*; (*banquet*) (Fest)essen
nt.

dinner jacket *n* Smokingjackett *nt*.

dinner party *n* Abendgesellschaft *f* (mit
Essen).

dinner service *n* Tafelservice *nt*.

dinner time *n* Essenszeit *f.*
dinosaur ['daɪnɔsɔː'] *n* Dinosaurier *m.*
dint [dɪnt] *n*: **by ~ of** durch +*acc.*
diocese ['daɪəsɪs] *n* Diözese *f.*
dioxide [daɪ'ɔksaɪd] *n* Dioxid *nt.*
Dip. (*BRIT*) *abbr* = **diploma.**
dip [dɪp] *n* Senke *f;* (*in sea*) kurzes Bad *nt;* (*CULIN*) Dip *m;* (*for sheep*) Desinfektionslösung *f* ♦ *vt* eintauchen; (*BRIT: AUT*) abblenden ♦ *vi* abfallen.
diphtheria [dɪf'θɪərɪə] *n* Diphtherie *f.*
diphthong ['dɪfθɒŋ] *n* Diphthong *m.*
diploma [dɪ'pləʊmə] *n* Diplom *nt.*
diplomacy [dɪ'pləʊməsɪ] *n* Diplomatie *f.*
diplomat ['dɪpləmæt] *n* Diplomat(in) *m(f).*
diplomatic [dɪplə'mætɪk] *adj* diplomatisch; **to break off ~ relations (with)** die diplomatischen Beziehungen abbrechen (mit).
diplomatic corps *n* diplomatisches Korps *nt.*
diplomatic immunity *n* Immunität *f.*
dip rod ['dɪprɒd] (*US*) *n* Ölmessstab *m.*
dipstick ['dɪpstɪk] (*BRIT*) *n* Ölmessstab *m.*
dip switch (*BRIT*) *n* Abblendschalter *m.*
dire [daɪə'] *adj* schrecklich.
direct [daɪ'rɛkt] *adj, adv* direkt ♦ *vt* richten; (*company, project, programme etc*) leiten; (*play, film*) Regie führen bei; **to ~ sb to do sth** jdn anweisen, etw zu tun; **can you ~ me to ...?** können Sie mir den Weg nach ... sagen?
direct access *n* (*COMPUT*) Direktzugriff *m.*
direct cost *n* direkte Kosten *pl.*
direct current *n* Gleichstrom *m.*
direct debit (*BRIT*) *n* Einzugsauftrag *m;* (*transaction*) automatische Abbuchung *f.*
direct dialling *n* Selbstwahl *f.*
direct hit *n* Volltreffer *m.*
direction [dɪ'rɛkʃən] *n* Richtung *f;* (*TV, RADIO*) Leitung *f;* (*CINE*) Regie *f;* **directions** *npl* (*instructions*) Anweisungen *pl;* **sense of ~** Orientierungssinn *m;* **~s for use** Gebrauchsanweisung *f,* Gebrauchsanleitung *f;* **to ask for ~s** nach dem Weg fragen; **in the ~ of** in Richtung.
directional [dɪ'rɛkʃənl] *adj* (*aerial*) Richt-.
directive [dɪ'rɛktɪv] *n* Direktive *f,* Weisung *f;* **government ~** Regierungserlass *m.*
direct labour *n* (*COMM*) Produktionsarbeit *f;* (*BRIT*) eigene Arbeitskräfte *pl.*
directly [dɪ'rɛktlɪ] *adv* direkt; (*at once*) sofort, gleich.
direct mail *n* Werbebriefe *pl.*
direct mailshot (*BRIT*) *n* Direktwerbung *f* per Post.
directness [daɪ'rɛktnɪs] *n* Direktheit *f.*
director [dɪ'rɛktə'] *n* Direktor(in) *m(f);* (*of project, TV, RADIO*) Leiter(in) *m(f);* (*CINE*) Regisseur(in) *m(f).*
Director of Public Prosecutions (*BRIT*) *n* ≈ Generalstaatsanwalt *m,* Generalstaatsanwältin *f.*

directory [dɪ'rɛktərɪ] *n* (*also:* **telephone ~**) Telefonbuch *nt;* (*also:* **street ~**) Einwohnerverzeichnis *nt;* (*COMPUT*) Verzeichnis *nt;* (*COMM*) Branchenverzeichnis *nt.*
directory enquiries, (*US*) **directory assistance** *n* (Fernsprech)auskunft *f.*
dirt [dɔːt] *n* Schmutz *m;* (*earth*) Erde *f,* **to treat sb like ~** jdn wie (den letzten) Dreck behandeln.
dirt-cheap ['dɔːt'tʃiːp] *adj* spottbillig.
dirt road *n* unbefestigte Straße *f.*
dirty ['dɔːtɪ] *adj* schmutzig; (*story*) unanständig ♦ *vt* beschmutzen.
dirty bomb *n* schmutzige Bombe.
dirty trick *n* gemeiner Trick *m.*
disability [dɪsə'bɪlɪtɪ] *n* Behinderung *f.*
disability allowance *n* Behindertenbeihilfe *f.*
disable [dɪs'eɪbl] *vt* zum Invaliden machen; (*tank, gun*) unbrauchbar machen.
disabled [dɪs'eɪbld] *adj* behindert ♦ *npl:* **the ~** die Behinderten *pl.*
disabuse [dɪsə'bjuːz] *vt:* **to ~ sb (of)** jdn befreien (von).
disadvantage [dɪsəd'vɑːntɪdʒ] *n* Nachteil *m;* (*detriment*) Schaden *m;* **to be at a ~** benachteiligt *or* im Nachteil sein.
disadvantaged [dɪsəd'vɑːntɪdʒd] *adj* benachteiligt.
disadvantageous [dɪsædvɑːn'teɪdʒəs] *adj* ungünstig.
disaffected [dɪsə'fɛktɪd] *adj* entfremdet.
disaffection [dɪsə'fɛkʃən] *n* Entfremdung *f.*
disagree [dɪsə'griː] *vi* nicht übereinstimmen; (*to be against, think differently*): **to ~ (with)** nicht einverstanden sein (mit); **I ~ with you** ich bin anderer Meinung; **garlic ~s with me** ich vertrage keinen Knoblauch, Knoblauch bekommt mir nicht.
disagreeable [dɪsə'griːəbl] *adj* unangenehm; (*person*) unsympathisch.
disagreement [dɪsə'griːmənt] *n* Uneinigkeit *f;* (*argument*) Meinungsverschiedenheit *f;* **to have a ~ with sb** sich mit jdm nicht einig sein.
disallow ['dɪsə'lau] *vt* (*appeal*) abweisen; (*goal*) nicht anerkennen, nicht geben.
disappear [dɪsə'pɪə'] *vi* verschwinden; (*custom etc*) aussterben.
disappearance [dɪsə'pɪərəns] *n* (*see vi*) Verschwinden *nt;* Aussterben *nt.*
disappoint [dɪsə'pɔɪnt] *vt* enttäuschen.
disappointed [dɪsə'pɔɪntɪd] *adj* enttäuscht.
disappointing [dɪsə'pɔɪntɪŋ] *adj* enttäuschend.
disappointment [dɪsə'pɔɪntmənt] *n* Enttäuschung *f.*
disapproval [dɪsə'pruːvəl] *n* Missbilligung *f.*
disapprove [dɪsə'pruːv] *vi* dagegen sein; **to ~ of** missbilligen +*acc.*
disapproving [dɪsə'pruːvɪŋ] *adj* missbilligend.

disarm [dɪs'ɑːm] *vt* entwaffnen; (*criticism*) zum Verstummen bringen ♦ *vi* abrüsten.

disarmament [dɪs'ɑːməmənt] *n* Abrüstung *f*.

disarming [dɪs'ɑːmɪŋ] *adj* entwaffnend.

disarray [dɪsə'reɪ] *n*: **in** ~ (*army, organization*) in Auflösung (begriffen); (*hair, clothes*) unordentlich; (*thoughts*) durcheinander; **to throw into** ~ durcheinander bringen.

disaster [dɪ'zɑːstə*] *n* Katastrophe *f*; (*AVIAT etc*) Unglück *nt*; (*fig: mess*) Fiasko *nt*.

disaster area *n* Katastrophengebiet *nt*; (*fig: person*) Katastrophe *f*; **my office is a** ~ **in** meinem Büro sieht es katastrophal aus.

disastrous [dɪ'zɑːstrəs] *adj* katastrophal.

disband [dɪs'bænd] *vt* auflösen ♦ *vi* sich auflösen.

disbelief ['dɪsbə'liːf] *n* Ungläubigkeit *f*; **in** ~ ungläubig.

disbelieve ['dɪsbə'liːv] *vt* (*person*) nicht glauben +*dat*; (*story*) nicht glauben; **I don't** ~ **you** ich bezweifle nicht, was Sie sagen.

disc [dɪsk] *n* (*ANAT*) Bandscheibe *f*; (*record*) Platte *f*; (*COMPUT*) = **disk**.

disc. *abbr* (*COMM*) = **discount**.

discard [dɪs'kɑːd] *vt* ausrangieren; (*fig: idea, plan*) verwerfen.

disc brake *n* Scheibenbremse *f*.

discern [dɪ'sɜːn] *vt* wahrnehmen; (*identify*) erkennen.

discernible [dɪ'sɜːnəbl] *adj* erkennbar; (*object*) wahrnehmbar.

discerning [dɪ'sɜːnɪŋ] *adj* (*judgement*) scharfsinnig; (*look*) kritisch; (*listeners etc*) anspruchsvoll.

discharge [dɪs'tʃɑːdʒ] *vt* (*duties*) nachkommen +*dat*; (*debt*) begleichen; (*waste*) ablassen; (*ELEC*) entladen; (*MED*) ausscheiden, absondern; (*patient, employee, soldier*) entlassen; (*defendant*) freisprechen ♦ *n* (*of gas*) Ausströmen *nt*; (*of liquid*) Ausfließen *nt*; (*ELEC*) Entladung *f*; (*MED*) Ausfluss *m*; (*of patient, employee, soldier*) Entlassung *f*; (*of defendant*) Freispruch *m*; **to** ~ **a gun** ein Gewehr abfeuern.

discharged bankrupt [dɪs'tʃɑːdʒd-] *n* (*LAW*) entlasteter Konkursschuldner *m*, entlastete Konkursschuldnerin *f*.

disciple [dɪ'saɪpl] *n* Jünger *m*; (*fig: follower*) Schüler(in) *m(f)*.

disciplinary ['dɪsɪplɪnərɪ] *adj* (*powers etc*) Disziplinar-; **to take** ~ **action against sb** ein Disziplinarverfahren gegen jdn einleiten.

discipline ['dɪsɪplɪn] *n* Disziplin *f* ♦ *vt* disziplinieren; (*punish*) bestrafen; **to** ~ **o.s. to do sth** sich dazu anhalten *or* zwingen, etw zu tun.

disc jockey *n* Diskjockey *m*.

disclaim [dɪs'kleɪm] *vt* (*knowledge*) abstreiten; (*responsibility*) von sich weisen.

disclaimer [dɪs'kleɪmə*] *n* Dementi *nt*; **to issue a** ~ eine Gegenerklärung abgeben.

disclose [dɪs'kləuz] *vt* enthüllen, bekannt geben.

disclosure [dɪs'kləuʒə*] *n* Enthüllung *f*.

disco ['dɪskəu] *n abbr* = **discotheque**.

discolor *etc* [dɪs'kʌlə*] (*US*) = **discolour** *etc*.

discolour [dɪs'kʌlə*] *vt* verfärben ♦ *vi* sich verfärben.

discolouration [dɪskʌlə'reɪʃən] *n* Verfärbung *f*.

discoloured [dɪs'kʌləd] *adj* verfärbt.

discomfort [dɪs'kʌmfət] *n* (*unease*) Unbehagen *nt*; (*physical*) Beschwerden *pl*.

disconcert [dɪskən'sɜːt] *vt* beunruhigen, irritieren.

disconcerting [dɪskən'sɜːtɪŋ] *adj* beunruhigend, irritierend.

disconnect [dɪskə'nɛkt] *vt* abtrennen; (*ELEC, RADIO*) abstellen; **I've been** ~**ed** (*TEL*) das Gespräch ist unterbrochen worden; (*supply, connection*) man hat mir das Telefon/den Strom/das Gas *etc* abgestellt.

disconnected [dɪskə'nɛktɪd] *adj* unzusammenhängend.

disconsolate [dɪs'kɔnsəlɪt] *adj* niedergeschlagen.

discontent [dɪskən'tɛnt] *n* Unzufriedenheit *f*.

discontented [dɪskən'tɛntɪd] *adj* unzufrieden.

discontinue [dɪskən'tɪnjuː] *vt* einstellen; **"~d"** (*COMM*) „ausgelaufene Serie".

discord ['dɪskɔːd] *n* Zwietracht *f*; (*MUS*) Dissonanz *f*.

discordant [dɪs'kɔːdənt] *adj* unharmonisch.

discotheque ['dɪskəutɛk] *n* Diskothek *f*.

discount [*n* 'dɪskaunt, *vt* dɪs'kaunt] *n* Rabatt *m* ♦ *vt* nachlassen; (*idea, fact*) unberücksichtigt lassen; **to give sb a** ~ **on sth** jdm auf etw *acc* Rabatt geben; ~ **for cash** Skonto *nt or* *m* (bei Barzahlung); **at a** ~ mit Rabatt.

discount house *n* Diskontbank *f*; (*also*: **discount store**) Diskontgeschäft *nt*.

discount rate *n* Diskontsatz *m*.

discourage [dɪs'kʌrɪdʒ] *vt* entmutigen; **to** ~ **sb from doing sth** jdm davon abraten, etw zu tun.

discouragement [dɪs'kʌrɪdʒmənt] *n* Mutlosigkeit *f*; **to act as a** ~ **to sb** entmutigend für jdn sein.

discouraging [dɪs'kʌrɪdʒɪŋ] *adj* entmutigend.

discourteous [dɪs'kəːtɪəs] *adj* unhöflich.

discover [dɪs'kʌvə*] *vt* entdecken; (*missing person*) finden; **to** ~ **that** ... herausfinden, dass ...

discovery [dɪs'kʌvərɪ] *n* Entdeckung *f*.

discredit [dɪs'krɛdɪt] *vt* in Misskredit bringen ♦ *n*: **to sb's** ~ zu jds Schande.

discreet [dɪs'kriːt] *adj* diskret; (*unremarkable*) dezent.

discreetly [dɪs'kriːtlɪ] *adv* diskret; (*unremarkably*) dezent.

discrepancy [dɪs'krɛpənsɪ] *n* Diskrepanz *f*.

discretion [dɪs'krɛʃən] *n* Diskretion *f*; **at the** ~ **of** im Ermessen +*gen*; **use your own** ~ Sie müssen nach eigenem Ermessen handeln.

discretionary [dɪs'kreʃənrɪ] *adj*: ~ **powers** Ermessensspielraum *m*; ~ **payments** Ermessenszahlungen *pl*.

discriminate [dɪs'krɪmɪneɪt] *vi*: **to** ~ **between** unterscheiden zwischen +*dat*; **to** ~ **against** diskriminieren +*acc*.

discriminating [dɪs'krɪmɪneɪtɪŋ] *adj* anspruchsvoll, kritisch; (*tax, duty*) Differenzial-.

discrimination [dɪskrɪmɪ'neɪʃən] *n* Diskriminierung *f*; (*discernment*) Urteilsvermögen *nt*; **racial** ~ Rassendiskriminierung *f*; **sexual** ~ Diskriminierung aufgrund *or* auf Grund des Geschlechts.

discus ['dɪskəs] *n* Diskus *m*; (*event*) Diskuswerfen *nt*.

discuss [dɪs'kʌs] *vt* besprechen; (*debate*) diskutieren; (*analyse*) erörtern, behandeln.

discussion [dɪs'kʌʃən] *n* Besprechung *f*; (*debate*) Diskussion *f*; **under** ~ in der Diskussion.

disdain [dɪs'deɪn] *n* Verachtung *f* ♦ *vt* verachten ♦ *vi*: **to** ~ **to do sth** es für unter seiner Würde halten, etw zu tun.

disease [dɪ'ziːz] *n* Krankheit *f*.

diseased [dɪ'ziːzd] *adj* krank; (*tree*) befallen.

disembark [dɪsɪm'bɑːk] *vt* ausschiffen ♦ *vi* (*passengers*) von Bord gehen.

disembarkation [dɪsembɑː'keɪʃən] *n* Ausschiffung *f*.

disembodied ['dɪsɪm'bɒdɪd] *adj* (*voice*) geisterhaft; (*hand*) körperlos.

disembowel ['dɪsɪm'bauəl] *vt* die Eingeweide herausnehmen +*dat*.

disenchanted ['dɪsɪn'tʃɑːntɪd] *adj*: ~ **(with)** enttäuscht (von).

disenfranchise ['dɪsɪn'fræntʃaɪz] *vt* (*POL*) das Wahlrecht entziehen +*dat*; (*COMM*) die Konzession entziehen +*dat*.

disengage [dɪsɪn'geɪdʒ] *vt* (*TECH*) ausrasten; **to** ~ **the clutch** auskuppeln.

disengagement [dɪsɪn'geɪdʒmənt] *n* (*POL*) Disengagement *nt*.

disentangle [dɪsɪn'tæŋgl] *vt* befreien; (*wool, wire*) entwirren.

disfavour, (*US*) **disfavor** [dɪs'feɪvəˀ] *n* Missfallen *nt*; **to fall into** ~ **(with sb)** (bei jdm) in Ungnade fallen.

disfigure [dɪs'fɪgəˀ] *vt* entstellen; (*object, place*) verunstalten.

disgorge [dɪs'gɔːdʒ] *vt* (*liquid*) ergießen; (*people*) ausspeien.

disgrace [dɪs'greɪs] *n* Schande *f*; (*scandal*) Skandal *m* ♦ *vt* Schande bringen über +*acc*.

disgraceful [dɪs'greɪsful] *adj* skandalös.

disgruntled [dɪs'grʌntld] *adj* verärgert.

disguise [dɪs'gaɪz] *n* Verkleidung *f* ♦ *vt*: **to** ~ **(as)** (*person*) verkleiden (als); (*object*) tarnen (als); **in** ~ (*person*) verkleidet; **there's no disguising the fact that ...** es kann nicht geleugnet werden, dass ...; **to** ~ **o.s. as** sich verkleiden als.

disgust [dɪs'gʌst] *n* Abscheu *m* ♦ *vt* anwidern; **she walked off in** ~ sie ging voller Empörung weg.

disgusting [dɪs'gʌstɪŋ] *adj* widerlich.

dish [dɪʃ] *n* Schüssel *f*; (*flat*) Schale *f*; (*recipe, food*) Gericht *nt*; (*also*: **satellite** ~) Parabolantenne *f*, Schüssel (*inf*); **to do** *or* **wash the** ~**es** Geschirr spülen, abwaschen.

▶ **dish out** *vt* verteilen; (*food, money*) austeilen; (*advice*) erteilen.

▶ **dish up** *vt* (*food*) auftragen, servieren; (*facts, statistics*) auftischen (*inf*).

dishcloth ['dɪʃklɒθ] *n* Spültuch *nt*, Spüllappen *m*.

dishearten [dɪs'hɑːtn] *vt* entmutigen.

dishevelled, (*US*) **disheveled** [dɪ'ʃevəld] *adj* unordentlich; (*hair*) zerzaust.

dishonest [dɪs'ɒnɪst] *adj* unehrlich; (*means*) unlauter.

dishonesty [dɪs'ɒnɪstɪ] *n* Unehrlichkeit *f*.

dishonor *etc* [dɪs'ɒnəˀ] (*US*) = **dishonour** *etc*.

dishonour [dɪs'ɒnəˀ] *n* Schande *f*.

dishonourable [dɪs'ɒnərəbl] *adj* unehrenhaft.

dish soap (*US*) *n* Spülmittel *nt*.

dishtowel ['dɪʃtauəl] (*US*) *n* Geschirrtuch *nt*.

dishwasher ['dɪʃwɒʃəˀ] *n* (*machine*) (Geschirr)spülmaschine *f*.

dishy ['dɪʃɪ] (*inf*: *BRIT*) *adj* attraktiv.

disillusion [dɪsɪ'luːʒən] *vt* desillusionieren ♦ *n* = **disillusionment**: **to become** ~**ed (with)** seine Illusionen (über +*acc*) verlieren.

disillusionment [dɪsɪ'luːʒənmənt] *n* Desillusionierung *f*.

disincentive [dɪsɪn'sentɪv] *n* Entmutigung *f*; **it's a** ~ es hält die Leute ab; **to be a** ~ **to sb** jdm keinen Anreiz bieten.

disinclined [dɪsɪn'klaɪnd] *adj*: **to be** ~ **to do sth** abgeneigt sein, etw zu tun.

disinfect [dɪsɪn'fekt] *vt* desinfizieren.

disinfectant [dɪsɪn'fektənt] *n* Desinfektionsmittel *nt*.

disinflation [dɪsɪn'fleɪʃən] *n* (*ECON*) Rückgang *m* einer inflationären Entwicklung.

disinformation [dɪsɪnfə'meɪʃən] *n* Desinformation *f*.

disingenuous [dɪsɪn'dʒenjuəs] *adj* unaufrichtig.

disinherit [dɪsɪn'herɪt] *vt* enterben.

disintegrate [dɪs'ɪntɪgreɪt] *vi* zerfallen; (*marriage, partnership*) scheitern; (*organization*) sich auflösen.

disinterested [dɪs'ɪntrəstɪd] *adj* (*advice*) unparteiisch, unvoreingenommen; (*help*) uneigennützig.

disjointed [dɪs'dʒɔɪntɪd] *adj* unzusammenhängend.

disk [dɪsk] *n* Diskette *f*; **single-/double-sided** ~ einseitige/zweiseitige Diskette.

disk drive *n* Diskettenlaufwerk *nt*.

diskette [dɪs'ket] (*US*) *n* = **disk**.

disk operating system *n* Betriebssystem *nt*.

dislike [dɪs'laɪk] n Abneigung f ♦ vt nicht mögen; **to take a ~ to sb/sth** eine Abneigung gegen jdn/etw entwickeln; **I ~ the idea** die Idee gefällt mir nicht; **he ~s it** er kann es nicht leiden, er mag es nicht.

dislocate ['dɪsləkeɪt] vt verrenken, ausrenken; **he has ~d his shoulder** er hat sich dat den Arm ausgekugelt.

dislodge [dɪs'lɔdʒ] vt verschieben.

disloyal [dɪs'lɔɪəl] adj illoyal.

dismal ['dɪzml] adj trübe, trostlos; (song, person, mood) trübsinnig; (failure) kläglich.

dismantle [dɪs'mæntl] vt (machine) demontieren.

dismast [dɪs'mɑːst] vt (NAUT) entmasten.

dismay [dɪs'meɪ] n Bestürzung f ♦ vt bestürzen; **much to my ~** zu meiner Bestürzung; **in ~** bestürzt.

dismiss [dɪs'mɪs] vt entlassen; (case) abweisen; (possibility, idea) abtun.

dismissal [dɪs'mɪsl] n Entlassung f.

dismount [dɪs'maunt] vi absteigen.

disobedience [dɪsə'biːdɪəns] n Ungehorsam m.

disobedient [dɪsə'biːdɪənt] adj ungehorsam.

disobey [dɪsə'beɪ] vt nicht gehorchen +dat; (order) nicht befolgen.

disorder [dɪs'ɔːdə*] n Unordnung f; (rioting) Unruhen pl; (MED) (Funktions)störung f; **civil ~** öffentliche Unruhen pl.

disorderly [dɪs'ɔːdəlɪ] adj unordentlich; (meeting) undiszipliniert; (behaviour) ungehörig.

disorderly conduct n (LAW) ungebührliches Benehmen nt.

disorganize [dɪs'ɔːgənaɪz] vt durcheinander bringen.

disorganized [dɪs'ɔːgənaɪzd] adj chaotisch.

disorientated [dɪs'ɔːrɪenteɪtɪd] adj desorientiert, verwirrt.

disown [dɪs'əun] vt (action) verleugnen; (child) verstoßen.

disparaging [dɪs'pærɪdʒɪŋ] adj (remarks) abschätzig, geringschätzig; **to be ~ about sb/sth** (person) abschätzig or geringschätzig über jdn/etw urteilen.

disparate ['dɪspərɪt] adj völlig verschieden.

disparity [dɪs'pærɪtɪ] n Unterschied m.

dispassionate [dɪs'pæʃənət] adj nüchtern.

dispatch [dɪs'pætʃ] vt senden, schicken; (deal with) erledigen; (kill) töten ♦ n Senden nt, Schicken nt; (PRESS) Bericht m; (MIL) Depesche f.

dispatch department n Versandabteilung f.

dispatch rider n (MIL) Meldefahrer m.

dispel [dɪs'pel] vt (myths) zerstören; (fears) zerstreuen.

dispensary [dɪs'pensərɪ] n Apotheke f; (in chemist's) Raum in einer Apotheke, wo Arzneimittel abgefüllt werden.

dispensation [dɪspən'seɪʃən] n (of treatment) Vergabe f; (special permission) Dispens m;

dispense [dɪs'pens] vt (medicines) abgeben; (charity) austeilen; (advice) erteilen.

▶ **dispense with** vt fus verzichten auf +acc.

dispenser [dɪs'pensə*] n (machine) Automat m.

dispensing chemist [dɪs'pensɪŋ-] (BRIT) n (shop) Apotheke f.

dispersal [dɪs'pəːsl] n (of objects) Verstreuen nt; (of group, crowd) Auflösung f, Zerstreuen nt.

disperse [dɪs'pəːs] vt (objects) verstreuen; (crowd etc) auflösen, zerstreuen; (knowledge, information) verbreiten ♦ vi (crowd) sich auflösen or zerstreuen.

dispirited [dɪs'pɪrɪtɪd] adj entmutigt.

displace [dɪs'pleɪs] vt ablösen.

displaced person [dɪs'pleɪst-] n Verschleppte(r) f(m).

displacement [dɪs'pleɪsmənt] n Ablösung f; (of people) Vertreibung f; (PHYS) Verdrängung f.

display [dɪs'pleɪ] n (in shop) Auslage f; (exhibition) Ausstellung f; (of feeling) Zeigen nt; (pej) Zurschaustellung f; (COMPUT, TECH) Anzeige f ♦ vt zeigen; (ostentatiously) zur Schau stellen; (results, departure times) aushängen; **on ~** ausgestellt.

display advertising n Displaywerbung f.

displease [dɪs'pliːz] vt verstimmen, verärgern.

displeased [dɪs'pliːzd] adj: **I am very ~ with you** ich bin sehr enttäuscht von dir.

displeasure [dɪs'pleʒə*] n Missfallen nt.

disposable [dɪs'pəuzəbl] adj (lighter) Wegwerf-; (bottle) Einweg-; (income) verfügbar.

disposable nappy (BRIT) n Papierwindel f.

disposal [dɪs'pəuzl] n (of goods for sale) Loswerden nt; (of property, belongings: by selling) Verkauf m; (: by giving away) Abgeben nt; (of rubbish) Beseitigung f; **at one's ~** zur Verfügung; **to put sth at sb's ~** jdm etw zur Verfügung stellen.

dispose [dɪs'pəuz]: **~ of** vt fus (body) aus dem Weg schaffen; (unwanted goods) loswerden; (problem, task) erledigen; (stock) verkaufen.

disposed [dɪs'pəuzd] adj: **to be ~ to do sth** (inclined) geneigt sein, etw zu tun; (willing) bereit sein, etw zu tun; **to be well ~ towards sb** jdm wohl wollen.

disposition [dɪspə'zɪʃən] n (nature) Veranlagung f; (inclination) Neigung f.

dispossess [dɪspə'zes] vt enteignen; **to ~ sb of his/her land** jds Land enteignen.

disproportion [dɪsprə'pɔːʃən] n Missverhältnis nt.

disproportionate [dɪsprə'pɔːʃənət] adj unverhältnismäßig; (amount) unverhältnismäßig hoch/niedrig.

disprove [dɪs'pruːv] vt widerlegen.

dispute [dɪs'pjuːt] n Streit m; (also: **industrial ~**) Auseinandersetzung f zwischen

Arbeitgebern und Arbeitnehmern; (POL, MIL) Streitigkeiten pl ♦ vt bestreiten; (ownership etc) anfechten; **to be in** or **under ~** umstritten sein.

disqualification [dɪskwɔlɪfɪ'keɪʃən] n: **~ (from)** Ausschluss m (von); (SPORT) Disqualifizierung f (von); **~ (from driving)** (BRIT) Führerscheinentzug m.

disqualify [dɪs'kwɔlɪfaɪ] vt disqualifizieren; **to ~ sb for sth** jdn für etw ungeeignet machen; **to ~ sb from doing sth** jdn ungeeignet machen, etw zu tun; **to ~ sb from driving** (BRIT) jdm den Führerschein entziehen.

disquiet [dɪs'kwaɪət] n Unruhe f.

disquieting [dɪs'kwaɪətɪŋ] adj beunruhigend.

disregard [dɪsrɪ'gɑːd] vt nicht beachten, ignorieren ♦ n: **~ (for)** Missachtung (+gen); (for danger, money) Geringschätzung (+gen).

disrepair ['dɪsrɪ'pɛə*] n: **to fall into ~** (machine) vernachlässigt werden; (building) verfallen.

disreputable [dɪs'rɛpjutəbl] adj (person) unehrenhaft; (behaviour) unfein.

disrepute ['dɪsrɪ'pjuːt] n schlechter Ruf m; **to bring/fall into ~** in Verruf bringen/kommen.

disrespectful [dɪsrɪ'spɛktful] adj respektlos.

disrupt [dɪs'rʌpt] vt (plans) durcheinander bringen; (conversation, proceedings) unterbrechen.

disruption [dɪs'rʌpʃən] n Unterbrechung f; (disturbance) Störung f.

disruptive [dɪs'rʌptɪv] adj störend; (action) Stör-.

dissatisfaction [dɪssætɪs'fækʃən] n Unzufriedenheit f.

dissatisfied [dɪs'sætɪsfaɪd] adj: **~ (with)** unzufrieden (mit).

dissect [dɪ'sɛkt] vt sezieren.

disseminate [dɪ'sɛmɪneɪt] vt verbreiten.

dissent [dɪ'sɛnt] n abweichende Meinungen pl.

dissenter [dɪ'sɛntə*] n Abweichler(in) m(f).

dissertation [dɪsə'teɪʃən] n (speech) Vortrag m; (piece of writing) Abhandlung f; (for PhD) Dissertation f.

disservice [dɪs'sɔːvɪs] n: **to do sb a ~** jdm einen schlechten Dienst erweisen.

dissident ['dɪsɪdnt] adj anders denkend; (voice) kritisch ♦ n Dissident(in) m(f).

dissimilar [dɪ'sɪmɪlə*] adj: **~ (to)** anders (als).

dissipate ['dɪsɪpeɪt] vt (heat) neutralisieren; (clouds) auflösen; (money, effort) verschwenden.

dissipated ['dɪsɪpeɪtɪd] adj zügellos, ausschweifend.

dissociate [dɪ'səʊʃɪeɪt] vt trennen; **to ~ o.s. from** sich distanzieren von.

dissolute ['dɪsəluːt] adj zügellos, ausschweifend.

dissolution [dɪsə'luːʃən] n Auflösung f.

dissolve [dɪ'zɔlv] vt auflösen ♦ vi sich auflösen; **to ~ in(to) tears** in Tränen zerfließen.

dissuade [dɪ'sweɪd] vt: **to ~ sb (from sth)** jdn (von etw) abbringen.

distaff ['dɪstɑːf] n: **the ~ side** die mütterliche Seite.

distance ['dɪstns] n Entfernung f; (in time) Abstand m; (reserve) Abstand, Distanz f ♦ vt: **to ~ o.s. (from)** sich distanzieren (von); **in the ~** in der Ferne; **what's the ~ to London?** wie weit ist es nach London?; **it's within walking ~** es ist zu Fuß erreichbar; **at a ~ of 2 metres** in 2 Meter(n) Entfernung; **keep your ~!** halten Sie Abstand!

distant ['dɪstnt] adj (place) weit entfernt, fern; (time) weit zurückliegend; (relative) entfernt; (manner) distanziert, kühl.

distaste [dɪs'teɪst] n Widerwille m.

distasteful [dɪs'teɪstful] adj widerlich; **to be ~ to sb** jdm zuwider sein.

Dist. Atty. (US) abbr = district attorney.

distemper [dɪs'tɛmpə*] n (paint) Temperafarbe f; (disease of dogs) Staupe f.

distend [dɪs'tɛnd] vt blähen ♦ vi sich blähen.

distended [dɪs'tɛndɪd] adj aufgebläht.

distil, (US) **distill** [dɪs'tɪl] vt destillieren; (fig) (heraus)destillieren.

distillery [dɪs'tɪlərɪ] n Brennerei f.

distinct [dɪs'tɪŋkt] adj deutlich, klar; (possibility) eindeutig; (different) verschieden; **as ~ from** im Unterschied zu.

distinction [dɪs'tɪŋkʃən] n Unterschied m; (honour) Ehre f; (in exam) Auszeichnung f; **to draw a ~ between** einen Unterschied machen zwischen +dat; **a writer of ~** ein Schriftsteller von Rang.

distinctive [dɪs'tɪŋktɪv] adj unverwechselbar.

distinctly [dɪs'tɪŋktlɪ] adv deutlich, klar; (tell) ausdrücklich; (unhappy) ausgeprochen; (better) entschieden.

distinguish [dɪs'tɪŋgwɪʃ] vt unterscheiden; (details etc) erkennen, ausmachen; **to ~ (between)** unterscheiden (zwischen +dat); **to ~ o.s.** sich hervortun.

distinguished [dɪs'tɪŋgwɪʃt] adj von hohem Rang; (career) hervorragend; (in appearance) distinguiert.

distinguishing [dɪs'tɪŋgwɪʃɪŋ] adj charakteristisch.

distort [dɪs'tɔːt] vt verzerren; (argument) verdrehen.

distortion [dɪs'tɔːʃən] n (see vb) Verzerrung f; Verdrehung f.

distract [dɪs'trækt] vt ablenken.

distracted [dɪs'træktɪd] adj unaufmerksam; (anxious) besorgt, beunruhigt.

distraction [dɪs'trækʃən] n Unaufmerksamkeit f; (confusion) Verstörtheit f; (sth which distracts) Ablenkung f; (amusement) Zerstreuung f; **to drive sb to ~** jdn zur Verzweiflung treiben.

distraught [dɪs'trɔːt] *adj* verzweifelt.

distress [dɪs'trɛs] *n* Verzweiflung *f* ♦ *vt* Kummer machen +*dat*; **in** ~ (*ship*) in Seenot; (*person*) verzweifelt; **~ed area** (*BRIT*) Notstandsgebiet *nt*.

distressing [dɪs'trɛsɪŋ] *adj* beunruhigend.

distress signal *n* Notsignal *nt*.

distribute [dɪs'trɪbjuːt] *vt* verteilen; (*profits*) aufteilen.

distribution [dɪstrɪ'bjuːʃən] *n* Vertrieb *m*; (*of profits*) Aufteilung *f*.

distribution costs *npl* Vertriebskosten *pl*.

distributor [dɪs'trɪbjutə°] *n* (*COMM*) Vertreiber(in) *m(f)*; (*AUT, TECH*) Verteiler *m*.

district ['dɪstrɪkt] *n* Gebiet *nt*; (*of town*) Stadtteil *m*; (*ADMIN*) (Verwaltungs)bezirk *m*.

district attorney (*US*) *n* Bezirksstaatsanwalt *m*, Bezirksstaatsanwältin *f*.

DISTRICT COUNCIL

District Council heißt der in jedem der britischen **districts** (*Bezirke*) alle vier Jahre neu gewählte Bezirksrat, der für bestimmte Bereiche der Kommunalverwaltung (*Gesundheitswesen, Wohnungsbeschaffung, Baugenehmigungen, Müllabfuhr*) zuständig ist. Die **district councils** werden durch Kommunalabgaben und durch einen Zuschuss von der Regierung finanziert. Ihre Ausgaben werden von einer unabhängigen Prüfungskommission kontrolliert, und bei zu hohen Ausgaben wird der Regierungszuschuss gekürzt.

---

district nurse (*BRIT*) *n* Gemeindeschwester *f*.

distrust [dɪs'trʌst] *n* Misstrauen *nt* ♦ *vt* misstrauen +*dat*.

distrustful [dɪs'trʌstful] *adj*: ~ (**of**) misstrauisch (gegenüber +*dat*).

disturb [dɪs'tɜːb] *vt* stören; (*upset*) beunruhigen; (*disorganize*) durcheinander bringen; **sorry to** ~ **you** entschuldigen Sie bitte die Störung.

disturbance [dɪs'tɜːbəns] *n* Störung *f*; (*political etc*) Unruhe *f*; (*violent event*) Unruhen *pl*; (*by drunks etc*) (Ruhe)störung *f*; **to cause a** ~ Unruhe/eine Ruhestörung verursachen; ~ **of the peace** Ruhestörung.

disturbed [dɪs'tɜːbd] *adj* beunruhigt; (*childhood*) unglücklich; **mentally/emotionally** ~ geistig/seelisch gestört.

disturbing [dɪs'tɜːbɪŋ] *adj* beunruhigend.

disuse [dɪs'juːs] *n*: **to fall into** ~ nicht mehr benutzt werden.

disused [dɪs'juːzd] *adj* (*building*) leer stehend; (*airfield*) stillgelegt.

ditch [dɪtʃ] *n* Graben *m* ♦ *vt* (*inf: partner*) sitzen lassen; (: *plan*) sausen lassen; (: *car etc*) loswerden.

dither ['dɪðə°] (*pej*) *vi* zaudern.

ditto ['dɪtəu] *adv* dito, ebenfalls.

divan [dɪ'væn] *n* (*also:* ~ **bed**) Polsterbett *nt*.

dive [daɪv] *n* Sprung *m*; (*underwater*) Tauchen *nt*; (*of submarine*) Untertauchen *nt*; (*pej: place*) Spelunke *f* (*inf*) ♦ *vi* springen; (*under water*) tauchen; (*bird*) einen Sturzflug machen; (*submarine*) untertauchen; **to** ~ **into** (*bag, drawer etc*) greifen in +*acc*; (*shop, car etc*) sich stürzen in +*acc*.

diver ['daɪvə°] *n* Taucher(in) *m(f)*; (*deep-sea diver*) Tiefseetaucher(in) *m(f)*.

diverge [daɪ'vɜːdʒ] *vi* auseinander gehen.

divergent [daɪ'vɜːdʒənt] *adj* unterschiedlich; (*views*) voneinander abweichend; (*interests*) auseinander gehend.

diverse [daɪ'vɜːs] *adj* verschiedenartig.

diversification [daɪvɜːsɪfɪ'keɪʃən] *n* Diversifikation *f*.

diversify [daɪ'vɜːsɪfaɪ] *vi* diversifizieren.

diversion [daɪ'vɜːʃən] *n* (*BRIT: AUT*) Umleitung *f*; (*distraction*) Ablenkung *f*; (*of funds*) Umlenkung *f*.

diversionary [daɪ'vɜːʃənrɪ] *adj*: ~ **tactics** Ablenkungsmanöver *pl*.

diversity [daɪ'vɜːsɪtɪ] *n* Vielfalt *f*.

divert [daɪ'vɔːt] *vt* (*sb's attention*) ablenken; (*funds*) umlenken; (*re-route*) umleiten.

divest [daɪ'vɛst] *vt*: **to** ~ **sb of office/his authority** jdn seines Amtes entkleiden/seiner Macht entheben.

divide [dɪ'vaɪd] *vt* trennen; (*MATH*) dividieren, teilen; (*share out*) verteilen ♦ *vi* sich teilen; (*road*) sich gabeln; (*people, groups*) sich aufteilen ♦ *n* Kluft *f*; (**between** *or* **among**) aufteilen (unter +*dat*); **40** ~**d by 5** 40 geteilt *or* dividiert durch 5.

► **divide out** *vt*: **to** ~ **out** (**between** *or* **among**) aufteilen (unter +*dat*).

divided [dɪ'vaɪdɪd] *adj* geteilt; **to be** ~ **about** *or* **over sth** geteilter Meinung über etw *acc* sein.

divided highway (*US*) *n* ≈ Schnellstraße *f*.

dividend ['dɪvɪdɛnd] *n* Dividende *f*; (*fig*): **to pay** ~**s** sich bezahlt machen.

dividend cover *n* (*COMM*) Dividendendeckung *f*.

dividers [dɪ'vaɪdəz] *npl* (*MATH, TECH*) Stechzirkel *m*; (*between pages*) Register *nt*.

divine [dɪ'vaɪn] *adj* göttlich ♦ *vt* (*future*) weissagen, prophezeien; (*truth*) erahnen; (*water, metal*) aufspüren.

diving ['daɪvɪŋ] *n* Tauchen *nt*; (*SPORT*) Kunstspringen *nt*.

diving board *n* Sprungbrett *nt*.

diving suit *n* Taucheranzug *m*.

divinity [dɪ'vɪnɪtɪ] *n* Göttlichkeit *f*; (*god or goddess*) Gottheit *f*; (*SCOL*) Theologie *f*.

divisible [dɪ'vɪzəbl] *adj*: ~ (**by**) teilbar (durch); **to be** ~ **into** teilbar sein in +*acc*.

division [dɪ'vɪʒən] *n* Teilung *f*; (*MATH*) Teilen *nt*, Division *f*; (*sharing out*) Verteilung *f*; (*disagreement*) Uneinigkeit *f*; (*BRIT: POL*) Abstimmung *f* durch Hammelsprung; (*COMM*) Abteilung *f*; (*MIL*) Division *f*; (*esp FOOTBALL*) Liga *f*; ~ **of labour**

Arbeitsteilung *f*.

divisive [dɪ'vaɪsɪv] *adj*: **to be ~** (*tactics*) auf Spaltung abzielen; (*system*) zu Feindseligkeit führen.

divorce [dɪ'vɔːs] *n* Scheidung *f* ♦ *vt* sich scheiden lassen von; (*dissociate*) trennen.

divorced [dɪ'vɔːst] *adj* geschieden.

divorcee [dɪvɔː'siː] *n* Geschiedene(r) *f(m)*.

divot ['dɪvət] *n vom Golfschläger etc ausgehacktes Rasenstück*.

divulge [daɪ'vʌldʒ] *vt* preisgeben.

DIY (*BRIT*) *n abbr* = **do-it-yourself**.

dizziness ['dɪzɪnɪs] *n* Schwindel *m*.

dizzy ['dɪzɪ] *adj* schwind(e)lig; (*turn, spell*) Schwindel-; (*height*) Schwindel erregend; **I feel ~** mir ist *or* ich bin schwind(e)lig.

DJ *n abbr* = **disc jockey**.

d.j. *n abbr* = **dinner jacket**.

Djakarta [dʒə'kɑːtə] *n* Jakarta *nt*.

DJIA (*US*) *n abbr* (= *Dow-Jones Industrial Average*) Dow-Jones-Index *m*.

dl *abbr* (= *decilitre*) dl.

DLit(t) *n abbr* (= *Doctor of Literature, Doctor of Letters*) *akademischer Grad in Literaturwissenschaft*.

dm *abbr* (= *decimetre*) dm.

DMus *n abbr* (= *Doctor of Music*) *Doktor der Musikwissenschaft*.

DMZ *n abbr* = **demilitarized zone**.

DNA *n abbr* (= *deoxyribonucleic acid*) DNS *f*.

DNA test *n* DNS-Test *m*.

════════════════════════ *KEYWORD*

do [duː] (*pt* **did**, *pp* **done**) *aux vb* **1** (*in negative constructions*): **I don't understand** ich verstehe nicht.

2 (*to form questions*): **didn't you know?** wusstest du das nicht?; **what ~ you think?** was meinst du?

3 (*for emphasis*): **she does seem rather upset** sie scheint wirklich recht aufgeregt zu sein; **~ sit down/help yourself** bitte nehmen Sie Platz/bedienen Sie sich; **oh ~ shut up!** halte endlich den Mund!

4 (*to avoid repeating vb*): **she swims better than I ~** sie schwimmt besser als ich; **she lives in Glasgow - so ~ I** sie wohnt in Glasgow - ich auch; **who made this mess? - I did** wer hat dieses Durcheinander gemacht? - ich.

5 (*in question tags*): **you like him, don't you?** du magst ihn, nicht wahr?; **I don't know him, ~ I?** ich kenne ihn nicht, oder?

♦ *vt* **1** (*carry out, perform*) tun, machen; **what are you ~ing tonight?** was machen Sie heute Abend?; **what ~ you ~ (for a living)?** was machen Sie beruflich?; **to ~ one's teeth/nails** sich *dat* die Zähne putzen/die Nägel schneiden.

2 (*AUT etc*) fahren; **the car was ~ing 100** das Auto fuhr 100

♦ *vi* **1** (*act, behave*): **~ as I ~** mach es wie ich.

2 (*get on, fare*): **he's ~ing well/badly at school** er ist gut/schlecht in der Schule; **the company is ~ing well** der Firma geht es gut; **how ~ you ~?** guten Tag/Morgen/ Abend!

3 (*suit, be sufficient*) reichen; **will that ~?** reicht das?; **will this dress ~ for the party?** ist dieses Kleid gut genug für die Party?; **will £10 ~?** reichen £10?; **that'll ~ das** reicht; (*in annoyance*) jetzt reichts aber!; **to make ~ with** auskommen mit

♦ *n* (*inf*: *party etc*) Party *f*, Fete *f*; **it was quite a ~** es war ganz schön was los.

► **do away with** *vt fus* (*get rid of*) abschaffen.

► **do for** (*inf*) *vt fus*: **to be done for** erledigt sein.

► **do in** (*inf*) *vt* (*kill*) umbringen.

► **do out of** (*inf*) *vt* (*deprive*) bringen um.

► **do up** *vt fus* (*laces, dress, buttons*) zumachen; (*renovate: room, house*) renovieren.

► **do with** *vt fus* **1** (*need*) brauchen; **I could ~ with some help/a drink** ich könnte Hilfe/ einen Drink gebrauchen.
2 **it has to ~ with money** es hat mit Geld zu tun.

► **do without** *vt fus* auskommen ohne.

DOA *abbr* (= *dead on arrival*) bei Einlieferung ins Krankenhaus bereits tot.

d.o.b. *abbr* = **date of birth**.

doc [dɔk] (*inf*) *n* Doktor *m*.

docile ['dəʊsaɪl] *adj* sanft(mütig).

dock [dɔk] *n* Dock *nt*; (*LAW*) Anklagebank *f*; (*BOT*) Ampfer *m* ♦ *vi* anlegen; (*SPACE*) docken ♦ *vt*: **they ~ed a third of his wages** sie kürzten seinen Lohn um ein Drittel; **docks** *npl* (*NAUT*) Hafen *m*.

dock dues [-djuːz] *npl* Hafengebühr *f*.

docker ['dɔkə*] *n* Hafenarbeiter *m*, Docker *m*.

docket ['dɔkɪt] *n* Inhaltserklärung *f*; (*on parcel etc*) Warenbegleitschein *m*, Laufzettel *m*.

dockyard ['dɔkjɑːd] *n* Werft *f*.

doctor ['dɔktə*] *n* Arzt *m*, Ärztin *f*; (*PhD etc*) Doktor *m* ♦ *vt*: **to ~ a drink** *etc* einem Getränk *etc* etwas beimischen; **~'s office** (*US*) Sprechzimmer *nt*.

doctorate ['dɔktərɪt] *n* Doktorwürde *f*.

┌─────────────────────────────────┐
│ **DOCTORATE**   │
│   │
│ **Doctorate** *ist der höchste akademische Grad auf jedem Wissensgebiet und wird nach erfolgreicher Vorlage einer Doktorarbeit verliehen. Die Studienzeit (meist mindestens 3 Jahre) und Länge der Doktorarbeit ist je nach Hochschule verschieden. Am häufigsten wird der Titel* **PhD** *(Doctor of Philosophy) auf dem Gebiet der Geisteswissenschaften, Naturwissenschaften und des Ingenieurwesens verliehen, obwohl es auch andere Doktortitel (in Musik, Jura usw.) gibt. Siehe auch* **bachelor's degree, master's degree.** │
└─────────────────────────────────┘

Doctor of Philosophy *n* Doktor *m* der Philosophie.

doctrine ['dɔktrɪn] *n* Doktrin *f*.

docudrama ['dɔkjudrɑːmə] *n* Dokumentarspiel *nt*.

document ['dɔkjumənt] *n* Dokument *nt* ♦ *vt* dokumentieren.

documentary [dɔkju'mentərɪ] *adj* dokumentarisch ♦ *n* Dokumentarfilm *m*.

documentation [dɔkjumən'teɪʃən] *n* Dokumentation *f*.

DOD (*US*) *n abbr* (= *Department of Defense*) Verteidigungsministerium *nt*.

doddering ['dɔdərɪŋ] *adj* (*shaky, unsteady*) zittrig.

doddery ['dɔdərɪ] *adj* = **doddering**.

doddle ['dɔdl] (*inf*) *n*: **a** ~ ein Kinderspiel *nt*.

Dodecanese (Islands) [dəudɪkə'niːz ('aɪləndz)] *n(pl)*: **the** ~ der Dodekanes.

dodge [dɔdʒ] *n* Trick *m* ♦ *vt* ausweichen +*dat*; (*tax*) umgehen ♦ *vi* ausweichen; **to** ~ **out of the way** zur Seite springen; **to** ~ **through the traffic** sich durch den Verkehr schlängeln.

dodgems ['dɔdʒəmz] (*BRIT*) *npl* Autoskooter *pl*.

dodgy ['dɔdʒɪ] (*inf*) *adj* (*person*) zweifelhaft; (*plan etc*) gewagt.

DOE *n abbr* (*BRIT*: = *Department of the Environment*) Umweltministerium; (*US*: = *Department of Energy*) Energieministerium.

doe [dəu] *n* Reh *nt*, Ricke *f*; (*rabbit*) (Kaninchen)weibchen *nt*.

does [dʌz] *vb see* **do**.

doesn't ['dʌznt] = **does not**.

dog [dɔg] *n* Hund *m* ♦ *vt* (*subj: person*) auf den Fersen bleiben +*dat*; (: *bad luck, memory etc*) verfolgen; **to go to the** ~**s** (*inf*) vor die Hunde gehen.

dog biscuits *npl* Hundekuchen *pl*.

dog collar *n* Hundehalsband *nt*; (*REL*) Kragen *m* des Geistlichen.

dog-eared ['dɔgɪəd] *adj* mit Eselsohren.

dog food *n* Hundefutter *nt*.

dogged ['dɔgɪd] *adj* beharrlich.

doggy ['dɔgɪ] *n* Hündchen *nt*.

doggy bag ['dɔgɪ-] *n* Tüte für Essensreste, die man nach Hause mitnehmen möchte.

dogma ['dɔgmə] *n* Dogma *nt*.

dogmatic [dɔg'mætɪk] *adj* dogmatisch.

do-gooder [duː'gudə*] (*pej*) *n* Weltverbesserer(in) *m(f)*.

dogsbody ['dɔgzbɔdɪ] (*BRIT: inf*) *n* Mädchen *nt* für alles.

doily ['dɔɪlɪ] *n* Deckchen *nt*.

doing ['duːɪŋ] *n*: **this is your** ~ das ist dein Werk.

doings ['duːɪŋz] *npl* Treiben *nt*.

do-it-yourself ['duːɪtjɔː'self] *n* Heimwerken *nt*, Do-it-yourself *nt*.

doldrums ['dɔldrəmz] *npl*: **to be in the** ~ (*person*) niedergeschlagen sein; (*business*) in einer Flaute stecken.

dole [dəul] (*BRIT*) *n* Arbeitslosenunterstützung *f*; **on the** ~ arbeitslos.

▶ **dole out** *vt* austeilen, verteilen.

doleful ['dəulful] *adj* traurig.

doll [dɔl] *n* (*toy, also US*: *inf*: *woman*) Puppe *f*.

dollar ['dɔlə*] (*US etc*) *n* Dollar *m*.

dollar area *n* Dollarblock *m*.

dolled up (*inf*) *adj* aufgedonnert.

dollop ['dɔləp] (*inf*) *n* Schlag *m*.

dolly ['dɔlɪ] (*inf*) *n* (*doll, woman*) Puppe *f*.

Dolomites ['dɔləmaɪts] *npl*: **the** ~ die Dolomiten *pl*.

dolphin ['dɔlfɪn] *n* Delfin *m*, Delphin *m*.

domain [də'meɪn] *n* Bereich *m*; (*empire*) Reich *nt*.

dome [dəum] *n* Kuppel *f*.

domestic [də'mestɪk] *adj* (*trade*) Innen-; (*situation*) innenpolitisch; (*news*) Inland-, aus dem Inland; (*tasks, appliances*) Haushalts-; (*animal*) Haus-; (*duty, happiness*) häuslich.

domesticated [də'mestɪkeɪtɪd] *adj* (*animal*) zahm; (*person*) häuslich.

domesticity [dəumes'tɪsɪtɪ] *n* häusliches Leben *nt*.

domestic servant *n* Hausangestellte(r) *f(m)*.

domicile ['dɔmɪsaɪl] *n* Wohnsitz *m*.

dominant ['dɔmɪnənt] *adj* dominierend; (*share*) größte(r, s).

dominate ['dɔmɪneɪt] *vt* dominieren, beherrschen.

domination [dɔmɪ'neɪʃən] *n* (Vor)herrschaft *f*.

domineering [dɔmɪ'nɪərɪŋ] *adj* herrschsüchtig.

Dominican Republic [də'mɪnɪkən-] *n*: **the** ~ die Dominikanische Republik.

dominion [də'mɪnɪən] *n* (*territory*) Herrschaftsgebiet *nt*; (*authority*): **to have** ~ **over** Macht haben über +*acc*.

domino ['dɔmɪnəu] (*pl* ~**es**) *n* (*block*) Domino(stein) *m*.

domino effect *n* Dominoeffekt *m*.

dominoes ['dɔmɪnəuz] *n* (*game*) Domino(spiel) *nt*.

don [dɔn] *n* (*BRIT*) (Universitäts)dozent *m* (*besonders in Oxford und Cambridge*) ♦ *vt* anziehen.

donate [də'neɪt] *vt*: **to** ~ (**to**) (*organization, cause*) spenden (für).

donation [də'neɪʃən] *n* (*act of donating*) Spenden *nt*; (*contribution*) Spende *f*.

done [dʌn] *pp of* **do**.

donkey ['dɔŋkɪ] *n* Esel *m*.

donkey-work ['dɔŋkɪwɔːk] (*BRIT: inf*) *n* Dreckarbeit *f*.

donor ['dəunə*] *n* Spender(in) *m(f)*.

donor card *n* Organspenderausweis *m*.

don't [dəunt] = **do not**.

donut ['dəunʌt] (*US*) *n* = **doughnut**.

doodle ['du:dl] _vi_ Männchen malen ♦ _n_
Kritzelei _f_.

doom [du:m] _n_ Unheil _nt_ ♦ _vt_: **to be ~ed to
failure** zum Scheitern verurteilt sein.

doomsday ['du:mzdeɪ] _n_ der Jüngste Tag.

door [dɔ:ˡ] _n_ Tür _f_; **to go from ~ to ~** von Tür
zu Tür gehen.

door bell _n_ Türklingel _f_.

door handle _n_ Türklinke _f_; (_of car_) Türgriff
_m_.

doorman ['dɔ:mən] (_irreg: like_ **man**) _n_ Portier
_m_.

doormat ['dɔ:mæt] _n_ Fußmatte _f_; (_fig_)
Fußabtreter _m_.

doorpost ['dɔ:pəʊst] _n_ Türpfosten _m_.

doorstep ['dɔ:stɛp] _n_ Eingangsstufe _f_,
Türstufe _f_; **on the ~** vor der Haustür.

door-to-door ['dɔ:tə'dɔ:ˡ] _adj_ (_selling_) von
Haus zu Haus; **~ salesman** Vertreter _m_.

doorway ['dɔ:weɪ] _n_ Eingang _m_.

dope [dəʊp] _n_ (_inf_) Stoff _m_, Drogen _pl_;
(: _person_) Esel _m_, Trottel _m_; (: _information_)
Informationen _pl_ ♦ _vt_ dopen.

dopey ['dəʊpɪ] (_inf_) _adj_ (_groggy_) benebelt;
(_stupid_) blöd, bekloppt.

dormant ['dɔ:mənt] _adj_ (_plant_) ruhend;
(_volcano_) untätig; (_idea, report etc_): **to lie ~**
schlummern.

dormer ['dɔ:məˡ] _n_ (_also: ~_ **window**)
Mansardenfenster _nt_.

dormice ['dɔ:maɪs] _npl of_ **dormouse**.

dormitory ['dɔ:mɪtrɪ] _n_ Schlafsaal _m_; (_US:
building_) Wohnheim _nt_.

dormouse ['dɔ:maʊs] (_pl_ **dormice**) _n_
Haselmaus _f_.

Dors (_BRIT_) _abbr_ (_POST: = Dorset_).

DOS [dɒs] _n abbr_ (_COMPUT: = disk operating
system_) DOS.

dosage ['dəʊsɪdʒ] _n_ Dosis _f_; (_on label_)
Dosierung _f_.

dose [dəʊs] _n_ Dosis _f_; (_BRIT: bout_) Ration _f_ ♦ _vt_:
to ~ o.s. Medikamente nehmen; **a ~ of flu**
eine Grippe.

dosser ['dɒsəˡ] (_BRIT: inf_) _n_ Penner(in) _m(f)_.

dosshouse ['dɒshaʊs] (_BRIT: inf_) _n_
Obdachlosenheim _nt_.

dossier ['dɒsɪeɪ] _n_ Dossier _nt_.

DOT (_US_) _n abbr_ (_= Department of
Transportation_) ≈ Verkehrsministerium _nt_.

dot [dɒt] _n_ Punkt _m_ ♦ _vt_: **~ted with** übersät
mit; **on the ~** (auf die Minute) pünktlich.

dote [dəʊt]: **~ on** _vt fus_ abgöttisch lieben.

dot-matrix printer [dɒt'meɪtrɪks-] _n_
Nadeldrucker _m_.

dotted line ['dɒtɪd-] _n_ punktierte Linie _f_; **to
sign on the ~** (_fig_) seine formelle
Zustimmung geben.

dotty ['dɒtɪ] (_inf_) _adj_ schrullig.

double ['dʌbl] _adj_ doppelt; (_chin_) Doppel- ♦ _adv_
(_cost_) doppelt so viel ♦ _n_ Doppelgänger(in)
_m(f)_ ♦ _vt_ verdoppeln; (_paper, blanket_) (einmal)
falten ♦ _vi_ sich verdoppeln; **~ five two six**

(5526) (_BRIT: TEL_) fünfundfünfzig
sechsundzwanzig; **it's spelt with a ~ "l"** es
wird mit zwei l geschrieben; **an egg with a
~ yolk** ein Ei mit zwei Dottern; **on the ~**,
(_BRIT_) **at the ~** (_quickly_) schnell;
(_immediately_) unverzüglich; **to ~ as ...**
(_person_) auch als ... fungieren; (_thing_) auch
als ... dienen.

▶ **double back** _vi_ kehrtmachen,
zurückgehen/-fahren.

▶ **double up** _vi_ sich krümmen; (_share room_)
sich ein Zimmer teilen.

double bass _n_ Kontrabass _m_.

double bed _n_ Doppelbett _nt_.

double bend (_BRIT_) _n_ S-Kurve _f_.

double-blind _adj_: **~ experiment**
Doppelblindversuch _m_.

double-breasted ['dʌbl'brɛstɪd] _adj_ (_jacket,
coat_) zweireihig.

double-check ['dʌbl'tʃɛk] _vt_ noch einmal
(über)prüfen ♦ _vi_ es noch einmal
(über)prüfen.

double-clutch ['dʌbl'klʌtʃ] (_US_) _vi_ mit
Zwischengas schalten.

double cream (_BRIT_) _n_ Sahne _f_ mit hohem
Fettgehalt, ≈ Schlagsahne _f_.

double-cross [dʌbl'krɔs] _vt_ ein Doppelspiel
treiben mit.

double-decker [dʌbl'dɛkəˡ] _n_ Doppeldecker
_m_.

double-declutch ['dʌbldi:'klʌtʃ] (_BRIT_) _vi_ mit
Zwischengas schalten.

double exposure _n_ doppelt belichtetes Foto
_nt_.

double glazing [-'gleɪzɪŋ] (_BRIT_) _n_
Doppelverglasung _f_.

double-page spread ['dʌblpeɪdʒ-] _n_
Doppelseite _f_.

double-parking [dʌbl'pɑ:kɪŋ] _n_ Parken _nt_ in
der zweiten Reihe.

double room _n_ Doppelzimmer _nt_.

doubles ['dʌblz] _n_ (_TENNIS_) Doppel _nt_.

double time _n_ doppelter Lohn _m_.

double whammy [-'wæmɪ] (_inf_) _n_
Doppelschlag _m_.

doubly ['dʌblɪ] _adv_ (ganz) besonders.

doubt [daʊt] _n_ Zweifel _m_ ♦ _vt_ bezweifeln;
without (a) ~ ohne Zweifel; **to ~ sb** jdm
nicht glauben; **I ~ it (very much)** das
bezweifle ich (sehr), das möchte ich (stark)
bezweifeln; **to ~ if** _or_ **whether ...** bezweifeln,
dass ...; **I don't ~ that ...** ich bezweifle nicht,
dass ...

doubtful ['daʊtful] _adj_ zweifelhaft; **to be
~ about sth** an etw _dat_ zweifeln; **to be
~ about doing sth** Bedenken haben, ob man
etw tun soll; **I'm a bit ~** ich bin nicht ganz
sicher.

doubtless ['daʊtlɪs] _adv_ ohne Zweifel,
sicherlich.

dough [dəʊ] _n_ Teig _m_; (_inf: money_) Kohle _f_,
Knete _f_.

doughnut, (US) **donut** ['dəʊnʌt] n ≈ Berliner (Pfannkuchen) m.

dour [dʊə*] adj mürrisch, verdrießlich.

douse [daʊz] vt Wasser schütten über +acc; (extinguish) löschen; **to ~ with** übergießen mit.

dove [dʌv] n Taube f.

Dover ['dəʊvə*] n Dover nt.

dovetail ['dʌvteɪl] vi übereinstimmen ♦ n (also: ~ **joint**) Schwalbenschwanzverbindung f.

dowager ['daʊədʒə*] n (adlige) Witwe f.

dowdy ['daʊdɪ] adj ohne jeden Schick; (clothes) unmodern.

Dow-Jones average ['dau'dʒəunz-] (US) n Dow-Jones-Index m.

down [daʊn] n Daunen pl ♦ adv hinunter, herunter; (on the ground) unten ♦ prep hinunter, herunter; (movement along) entlang ♦ vt (inf: drink) runterkippen; **~ there/here** da/hier unten; **the price of meat is ~** die Fleischpreise sind gefallen; **I've got it ~ in my diary** ich habe es in meinem Kalender notiert; **to pay £2 ~** £2 anzahlen; **England is two goals ~** England liegt mit zwei Toren zurück; **to ~ tools** (BRIT) die Arbeit niederlegen; **~ with ...!** nieder mit ...!

down-and-out ['daʊnəndaut] n Penner(in) m(f) (inf).

down-at-heel ['daʊnət'hiːl] adj (appearance, person) schäbig, heruntergekommen; (shoes) abgetreten.

downbeat ['daʊnbiːt] n (MUS) erster betonter Taktteil m ♦ adj zurückhaltend.

downcast ['daʊnkɑːst] adj niedergeschlagen.

downer ['daʊnə*] (inf) n (drug) Beruhigungsmittel nt; **to be on a ~** deprimiert sein.

downfall ['daʊnfɔːl] n Ruin m; (of dictator etc) Sturz m, Fall m.

downgrade ['daʊngreɪd] vt herunterstufen.

downhearted ['daʊn'hɑːtɪd] adj niedergeschlagen, entmutigt.

downhill ['daʊn'hɪl] adv bergab ♦ n (SKI: also: ~ **race**) Abfahrtslauf m; **to go ~** (road) bergab führen; (person) hinuntergehen, heruntergehen; (car) hinunterfahren, herunterfahren; (fig) auf dem absteigenden Ast sein.

DOWNING STREET

Downing Street ist die Straße in London, die von Whitehall zum St James Park führt und in der sich der offizielle Wohnsitz des Premierministers (Nr.10) und des Finanzministers (Nr. 11) befindet. Im weiteren Sinne bezieht sich der Begriff **Downing Street** auf die britische Regierung.

---

download ['daʊnləʊd] vt laden.

down-market ['daʊn'mɑːkɪt] adj (product) für den Massenmarkt.

down payment n Anzahlung f.

downplay ['daʊnpleɪ] (US) vt herunterspielen.

downpour ['daʊnpɔː*] n Wolkenbruch m.

downright ['daʊnraɪt] adj (liar etc) ausgesprochen; (refusal, lie) glatt.

Downs [daʊnz] (BRIT) npl: **the ~** die Downs pl, Hügellandschaft in Südengland.

downsize ['daʊnsaɪz] vi (ECON: company) sich verkleinern.

Down's syndrome n (MED) Down-Syndrom nt.

downstairs ['daʊn'stɛəz] adv unten; (downwards) nach unten.

downstream ['daʊnstriːm] adv flussabwärts, stromabwärts.

downtime ['daʊntaɪm] n Ausfallzeit f.

down-to-earth ['daʊntuːˈɜːθ] adj (person) nüchtern; (solution) praktisch.

downtown ['daʊn'taʊn] (esp US) adv im Zentrum, in der (Innen)stadt; (go) ins Zentrum, in die (Innen)stadt ♦ adj: **~ Chicago** das Zentrum von Chicago.

downtrodden ['daʊntrɒdn] adj unterdrückt, geknechtet.

down under adv (be) in Australien/ Neuseeland; (go) nach Australien/ Neuseeland.

downward ['daʊnwəd] adj, adv nach unten; **a ~ trend** ein Abwärtstrend m.

downwards ['daʊnwədz] adv = **downward**.

dowry ['daʊrɪ] n Mitgift f.

doz. abbr = **dozen**.

doze [dəʊz] vi ein Nickerchen nt machen.

▶ **doze off** vi einschlafen, einnicken.

dozen ['dʌzn] n Dutzend nt; **a ~ books** ein Dutzend Bücher; **80p a ~** 80 Pence das Dutzend; **~s of** dutzende or Dutzende von.

DPh n abbr (= Doctor of Philosophy) ≈ Dr. phil.

DPhil n abbr (= Doctor of Philosophy) ≈ Dr. phil.

DPP (BRIT) n abbr = **Director of Public Prosecutions**.

DPT n abbr (= diphtheria, pertussis, tetanus) Diphtherie, Keuchhusten und Tetanus.

DPW (US) n abbr (= Department of Public Works) Ministerium für öffentliche Bauprojekte.

Dr abbr = **doctor**; (in street names: = Drive) ≈ Str.

dr abbr (COMM) = **debtor**.

drab [dræb] adj trist.

draft [drɑːft] n Entwurf m; (bank draft) Tratte f; (US: call-up) Einberufung f ♦ vt entwerfen; see also **draught**.

draftsman etc ['drɑːftsmən] (US) n = **draughtsman** etc.

drag [dræg] vt schleifen, schleppen; (river) absuchen ♦ vi sich hinziehen ♦ n (AVIAT) Luftwiderstand m; (NAUT) Wasserwiderstand m; (inf): **to be a ~** (boring) langweilig sein; (a nuisance) lästig sein; (women's clothing): **in ~** in Frauenkleidung.

▶ **drag away** vt: **to ~ away (from)**

wegschleppen *or* wegziehen (von).

▶ **drag on** *vi* sich hinziehen.

dragnet ['drægnɛt] *n* Schleppnetz *nt*; (*fig*) groß angelegte Polizeiaktion *f*.

dragon ['drægn] *n* Drache *m*.

dragonfly ['drægənflaɪ] *n* Libelle *f*.

dragoon [drə'guːn] *n* Dragoner *m* ♦ *vt*: **to ~ sb into doing sth** (*BRIT*) jdn zwingen, etw zu tun.

drain [dreɪn] *n* Belastung *f*; (*in street*) Gully *m* ♦ *vt* entwässern; (*pond*) trockenlegen; (*vegetables*) abgießen; (*glass, cup*) leeren ♦ *vi* ablaufen; **to feel ~ed** (*of energy/emotion*) sich ausgelaugt fühlen.

drainage ['dreɪnɪdʒ] *n* Entwässerungssystem *nt*; (*process*) Entwässerung *f*.

draining board ['dreɪnɪŋ-], (*US*) **drainboard** ['dreɪnbɔːd] *n* Ablaufbrett *nt*.

drainpipe ['dreɪnpaɪp] *n* Abflussrohr *nt*.

drake [dreɪk] *n* Erpel *m*, Enterich *m*.

dram [dræm] (*SCOTT*) *n* (*drink*) Schluck *m*.

drama ['drɑːmə] *n* Drama *nt*.

dramatic [drə'mætɪk] *adj* dramatisch; (*theatrical*) theatralisch.

dramatically [drə'mætɪklɪ] *adv* dramatisch; (*say, announce, pause*) theatralisch.

dramatist ['dræmətɪst] *n* Dramatiker(in) *m(f)*.

dramatize ['dræmətaɪz] *vt* dramatisieren; (*for TV/cinema*) für das Fernsehen/den Film bearbeiten.

drank [dræŋk] *pt of* **drink**.

drape [dreɪp] *vt* drapieren.

drapes [dreɪps] (*US*) *npl* Vorhänge *pl*.

drastic ['dræstɪk] *adj* drastisch.

drastically ['dræstɪklɪ] *adv* drastisch.

draught, (*US*) **draft** [drɑːft] *n* (Luft)zug *m*; (*NAUT*) Tiefgang *m*; (*of chimney*) Zug *m*; **on ~** vom Fass.

draught beer *n* Bier *nt* vom Fass.

draughtboard ['drɑːftbɔːd] (*BRIT*) *n* Damebrett *nt*.

draughts [drɑːfts] (*BRIT*) *n* Damespiel *nt*.

draughtsman, (*US*) **draftsman** ['drɑːftsmən] (*irreg: like* **man**) *n* Zeichner(in) *m(f)*; (*as job*) technischer Zeichner *m*, technische Zeichnerin *f*.

draughtsmanship, (*US*) **draftsmanship** ['drɑːftsmənʃɪp] *n* zeichnerisches Können *nt*; (*art*) Zeichenkunst *f*.

draw [drɔː] (*pt* **drew**, *pp* **drawn**) *vt* zeichnen; (*cart, gun, tooth, conclusion*) ziehen; (*curtain: open*) aufziehen; (: *close*) zuziehen; (*admiration, attention*) erregen; (*money*) abheben; (*wages*) bekommen ♦ *vi* (*SPORT*) unentschieden spielen ♦ *n* (*SPORT*) Unentschieden *nt*; (*lottery*) Lotterie *f*; (: *picking of ticket*) Ziehung *f*; **to ~ a comparison/distinction (between)** einen Vergleich ziehen/Unterschied machen (zwischen +*dat*); **to ~ near** näher kommen; (*event*) nahen; **to ~ to a close** zu Ende gehen.

▶ **draw back** *vi*: **to ~ back (from)** zurückweichen (von).

▶ **draw in** *vi* (*BRIT: car*) anhalten; (: *train*) einfahren; (*nights*) länger werden.

▶ **draw on** *vt* (*resources*) zurückgreifen auf +*acc*; (*imagination*) zu Hilfe nehmen; (*person*) einsetzen.

▶ **draw out** *vi* länger werden ♦ *vt* (*money*) abheben.

▶ **draw up** *vi* (an)halten ♦ *vt* (*chair etc*) heranziehen; (*document*) aufsetzen.

drawback ['drɔːbæk] *n* Nachteil *m*.

drawbridge ['drɔːbrɪdʒ] *n* Zugbrücke *f*.

drawee [drɔː'iː] *n* Bezogene(r) *f(m)*.

drawer [drɔːʳ] *n* Schublade *f*.

drawing ['drɔːɪŋ] *n* Zeichnung *f*; (*skill, discipline*) Zeichnen *nt*.

drawing board *n* Reißbrett *nt*; **back to the ~** (*fig*) das muss noch einmal neu überdacht werden.

drawing pin (*BRIT*) *n* Reißzwecke *f*.

drawing room *n* Salon *m*.

drawl [drɔːl] *n* schleppende Sprechweise *f* ♦ *vi* schleppend sprechen.

drawn [drɔːn] *pp of* **draw** ♦ *adj* abgespannt.

drawstring ['drɔːstrɪŋ] *n* Kordel *f* zum Zuziehen.

dread [drɛd] *n* Angst *f*, Furcht *f* ♦ *vt* große Angst haben vor +*dat*.

dreadful ['drɛdful] *adj* schrecklich, furchtbar; **I feel ~!** (*ill*) ich fühle mich schrecklich; (*ashamed*) es ist mir schrecklich peinlich.

dream [driːm] (*pt*, *pp* **dreamed** *or* **dreamt**) *n* Traum *m* ♦ *vt*, *vi* träumen; **to have a ~ about sb/sth** von jdm/etw träumen; **sweet ~s!** träume süß!

▶ **dream up** *vt* sich *dat* einfallen lassen, sich *dat* ausdenken.

dreamer ['driːməʳ] *n* Träumer(in) *m(f)*.

dreamt [drɛmt] *pt*, *pp of* **dream**.

dream world *n* Traumwelt *f*.

dreamy ['driːmɪ] *adj* verträumt; (*music*) zum Träumen.

dreary ['drɪərɪ] *adj* langweilig; (*weather*) trüb.

dredge [drɛdʒ] *vt* ausbaggern.

▶ **dredge up** *vt* ausbaggern; (*fig: unpleasant facts*) ausgraben.

dredger ['drɛdʒəʳ] *n* (*ship*) Schwimmbagger *m*; (*machine*) Bagger *m*; (*BRIT: also:* **sugar ~**) Zuckerstreuer *m*.

dregs [drɛgz] *npl* Bodensatz *m*; (*of humanity*) Abschaum *m*.

drench [drɛntʃ] *vt* durchnässen; **~ed to the skin** nass bis auf die Haut.

dress [drɛs] *n* Kleid *nt*; (*no pl: clothing*) Kleidung *f* ♦ *vt* anziehen; (*wound*) verbinden ♦ *vi* sich anziehen; **she ~es very well** sie kleidet sich sehr gut; **to ~ a shop window** ein Schaufenster dekorieren; **to get ~ed** sich anziehen.

▶ **dress up** *vi* sich fein machen; (*in fancy dress*) sich verkleiden.

dress circle (*BRIT*) n (*THEAT*) erster Rang m.
dress designer n Modezeichner(in) m(f).
dresser ['drɛsə*] n (*BRIT*) Anrichte f; (*US*) Kommode f; (*also:* **window ~**) Dekorateur(in) m(f).
dressing ['drɛsɪŋ] n Verband m; (*CULIN*) (Salat)soße f.
dressing gown (*BRIT*) n Morgenrock m.
dressing room n Umkleidekabine f; (*THEAT*) (Künstler)garderobe f.
dressing table n Frisierkommode f.
dressmaker ['drɛsmeɪkə*] n (Damen)schneider(in) m(f).
dressmaking ['drɛsmeɪkɪŋ] n Schneidern nt.
dress rehearsal n Generalprobe f.
dressy ['drɛsɪ] (*inf*) adj elegant.
drew [dru:] pt of **draw**.
dribble ['drɪbl] vi tropfen; (*baby*) sabbern; (*FOOTBALL*) dribbeln ♦ vt (*ball*) dribbeln mit.
dried [draɪd] adj (*fruit*) getrocknet, Dörr-; **~ egg** Trockenei nt, Eipulver nt; **~ milk** Trockenmilch f, Milchpulver nt.
drier ['draɪə*] n = **dryer**.
drift [drɪft] n Strömung f; (*of snow*) Schneewehe f; (*of questions*) Richtung f ♦ vi treiben; (*sand*) wehen; **to let things ~** die Dinge treiben lassen; **to ~ apart** sich auseinander leben; **I get** *or* **catch your ~** ich verstehe, worauf Sie hinauswollen.
drifter ['drɪftə*] n: **to be a ~** sich treiben lassen.
driftwood ['drɪftwud] n Treibholz nt.
drill [drɪl] n Bohrer m; (*machine*) Bohrmaschine f; (*MIL*) Drill m ♦ vt bohren; (*troops*) drillen ♦ vi: **to ~ (for)** bohren (nach); **to ~ pupils in grammar** mit den Schülern Grammatik pauken.
drilling ['drɪlɪŋ] n Bohrung f.
drilling rig n Bohrturm m; (*at sea*) Bohrinsel f.
drily ['draɪlɪ] adv = **dryly**.
drink [drɪŋk] (*pt* **drank**, *pp* **drunk**) n Getränk nt; (*alcoholic*) Glas nt, Drink m; (*sip*) Schluck m ♦ vt, vi trinken; **to have a ~** etwas trinken; **a ~ of water** etwas Wasser; **we had ~s before lunch** vor dem Mittagessen gab es einen Drink; **would you like something to ~?** möchten Sie etwas trinken?
▶ **drink in** vt (*fresh air*) einatmen, einsaugen; (*story, sight*) (begierig) in sich aufnehmen.
drinkable ['drɪŋkəbl] adj trinkbar.
drink-driving ['drɪŋk'draɪvɪŋ] n Trunkenheit f am Steuer.
drinker ['drɪŋkə*] n Trinker(in) m(f).
drinking ['drɪŋkɪŋ] n Trinken nt.
drinking fountain n Trinkwasserbrunnen m.
drinking water n Trinkwasser nt.
drip [drɪp] n Tropfen nt; (*one drip*) Tropfen m; (*MED*) Tropf m ♦ vi tropfen; (*wall*) triefnass sein.
drip-dry ['drɪp'draɪ] adj bügelfrei.
drip-feed ['drɪpfi:d] vt künstlich ernähren ♦ n: **to be on a ~** künstlich ernährt werden.

dripping ['drɪpɪŋ] n Bratenfett nt ♦ adj triefend; **I'm ~** ich bin klatschnass (*inf*); **~ wet** triefnass.
drive [draɪv] (*pt* **drove**, *pp* **driven**) n Fahrt f; (*also:* **~way**) Einfahrt f; (: *longer*) Auffahrt f; (*energy*) Schwung m, Elan m; (*campaign*) Aktion f; (*SPORT*) Treibschlag m; (*COMPUT: also:* **disk ~**) Laufwerk nt ♦ vt fahren; (*TECH*) antreiben ♦ vi fahren; **to go for a ~** ein bisschen (raus)fahren; **it's 3 hours' ~ from London** es ist drei Stunden Fahrt von London (entfernt); **left-/right-hand ~** Links-/Rechtssteuerung f; **front-/rear-wheel ~** Vorderrad-/Hinterradantrieb m; **he ~s a taxi** er ist Taxifahrer; **to ~ sth into sth** (*nail, stake etc*) etw in etw schlagen *acc*; (*animal*) treiben; (*ball*) weit schlagen; (*incite, encourage: also:* **~ on**) antreiben; **to ~ sb home/to the airport** jdn nach Hause/zum Flughafen fahren; **to ~ sb mad** jdn verrückt machen; **to ~ sb to (do) sth** jdn dazu treiben, etw zu tun; **to ~ at 50 km an hour** mit (einer Geschwindigkeit von) 50 Stundenkilometern fahren; **what are you driving at?** worauf wollen Sie hinaus?
▶ **drive off** vt vertreiben.
▶ **drive out** vt (*evil spirit*) austreiben; (*person*) verdrängen.
drive-by shooting ['draɪvbaɪ-] n *Schusswaffenangriff aus einem vorbeifahrenden Wagen.*
drive-in ['draɪvɪn] (*esp US*) adj, n: **~ (cinema)** Autokino nt; **~ (restaurant)** Autorestaurant nt.
drive-in window (*US*) n Autoschalter m.
drivel ['drɪvl] (*inf*) n Blödsinn m.
driven ['drɪvn] pp of **drive**.
driver ['draɪvə*] n Fahrer(in) m(f); (*RAIL*) Führer(in) m(f).
driver's license ['draɪvəz-] (*US*) n Führerschein m.
driveway ['draɪvweɪ] n Einfahrt f; (*longer*) Auffahrt f.
driving ['draɪvɪŋ] n Fahren nt ♦ adj: **~ rain** strömender Regen m; **~ snow** Schneetreiben nt.
driving belt n Treibriemen m.
driving force n treibende Kraft f.
driving instructor n Fahrlehrer(in) m(f).
driving lesson n Fahrstunde f.
driving licence (*BRIT*) n Führerschein m.
driving mirror n Rückspiegel m.
driving school n Fahrschule f.
driving test n Fahrprüfung f.
drizzle ['drɪzl] n Nieselregen m ♦ vi nieseln.
droll [drəul] adj drollig.
dromedary ['drɒmədərɪ] n Dromedar nt.
drone [drəun] n Brummen nt; (*male bee*) Drohne f ♦ vi brummen; (*bee*) summen; (*also:* **~ on**) eintönig sprechen.
drool [dru:l] vi sabbern; **to ~ over sth/sb** etw/jdn sehnsüchtig anstarren.

droop [druːp] *vi* (*flower*) den Kopf hängen lassen; **his shoulders/head** ~**ed** er ließ die Schultern/den Kopf herabhängen.

drop [drɔp] *n* Tropfen *m*; (*lessening*) Rückgang *m*; (*distance*) Höhenunterschied *m*; (*in salary*) Verschlechterung *f*; (*also:* **parachute** ~) (Ab)sprung *m* ♦ *vt* fallen lassen; (*voice, eyes, price*) senken; (*set down from car*) absetzen; (*omit*) weglassen ♦ *vi* (herunter)fallen; (*wind*) sich legen; **drops** *npl* Tropfen *pl*; **a 300 ft** ~ ein Höhenunterschied von 300 Fuß; **a** ~ **of 10%** ein Rückgang um 10%; **cough** ~**s** Hustentropfen *pl*; **to** ~ **anchor** ankern, vor Anker gehen; **to** ~ **sb a line** jdm ein paar Zeilen schreiben.

▶ **drop in** (*inf*) *vi*: **to** ~ **in** (**on sb**) (bei jdm) vorbeikommen.

▶ **drop off** *vi* einschlafen ♦ *vt* (*passenger*) absetzen.

▶ **drop out** *vi* (*withdraw*) ausscheiden; (*student*) sein Studium abbrechen.

droplet ['drɔplɪt] *n* Tröpfchen *nt*.

dropout ['drɔpaut] *n* Aussteiger(in) *m(f)*; (*SCOL*) Studienabbrecher(in) *m(f)*.

dropper ['drɔpə*] *n* Pipette *f*.

droppings ['drɔpɪŋz] *npl* Kot *m*.

dross [drɔs] *n* Schlacke *f*; (*fig*) Schund *m*.

drought [draut] *n* Dürre *f*.

drove [drəuv] *pt of* **drive** ♦ *n*: ~**s of people** Scharen *pl* von Menschen.

drown [draun] *vt* ertränken; (*fig: also:* ~ **out**) übertönen ♦ *vi* ertrinken.

drowse [drauz] *vi* (vor sich *acc* hin) dösen *or* dämmern.

drowsy ['drauzɪ] *adj* schläfrig.

drudge [drʌdʒ] *n* Arbeitstier *nt*.

drudgery ['drʌdʒərɪ] *n* (stumpfsinnige) Plackerei *f* (*inf*); **housework is sheer** ~ Hausarbeit ist eine einzige Plackerei.

drug [drʌg] *n* Medikament *nt*, Arzneimittel *nt*; (*narcotic*) Droge *f*, Rauschgift *nt* ♦ *vt* betäuben; **to be on** ~**s** drogensüchtig sein; **hard/soft** ~**s** harte/weiche Drogen *pl*.

drug addict *n* Drogensüchtige(r) *f(m)*, Rauschgiftsüchtige(r) *f(m)*.

druggist ['drʌgɪst] (*US*) *n* Drogist(in) *m(f)*.

drug peddler *n* Drogenhändler(in) *m(f)*, Dealer *m* (*inf*).

drugstore ['drʌgstɔː*] (*US*) *n* Drogerie *f*.

drum [drʌm] *n* Trommel *f*; (*for oil, petrol*) Fass *nt* ♦ *vi* trommeln; **drums** *npl* (*kit*) Schlagzeug *nt*.

▶ **drum up** *vt* (*enthusiasm*) erwecken; (*support*) auftreiben.

drummer ['drʌmə*] *n* Trommler(in) *m(f)*; (*in band, pop group*) Schlagzeuger(in) *m(f)*.

drum roll *n* Trommelwirbel *m*.

drumstick ['drʌmstɪk] *n* Trommelstock *m*; (*of chicken*) Keule *f*.

drunk [drʌŋk] *pp of* **drink** ♦ *adj* betrunken ♦ *n* (*also:* ~**ard**) Trinker(in) *m(f)*; **to get** ~ sich betrinken; **a** ~ **driving offence** Trunkenheit *f*

am Steuer.

drunken ['drʌŋkən] *adj* betrunken; (*party*) feucht-fröhlich; ~ **driving** Trunkenheit *f* am Steuer.

drunkenness ['drʌŋkənnɪs] *n* (*state*) Betrunkenheit *f*; (*habit*) Trunksucht *f*.

dry [draɪ] *adj* trocken ♦ *vt, vi* trocknen; **on** ~ **land** auf festem Boden; **to** ~ **one's hands/hair/eyes** sich *dat* die Hände (ab)trocknen/die Haare trocknen/die Tränen abwischen; **to** ~ **the dishes** (das Geschirr) abtrocknen.

▶ **dry up** *vi* austrocknen; (*in speech*) den Faden verlieren.

dry-clean ['draɪ'kliːn] *vt* chemisch reinigen.

dry-cleaner ['draɪ'kliːnə*] *n* (*job*) Inhaber(in) *m(f)* einer chemischen Reinigung; (*shop: also:* ~'**s**) chemische Reinigung *f*.

dry-cleaning ['draɪ'kliːnɪŋ] *n* (*process*) chemische Reinigung *f*.

dry dock *n* Trockendock *nt*.

dryer ['draɪə*] *n* Wäschetrockner *m*; (*US: spin-dryer*) Wäscheschleuder *f*.

dry goods *npl* Kurzwaren *pl*.

dry ice *n* Trockeneis *nt*.

dryly ['draɪlɪ] *adv* (*say, remark*) trocken.

dryness ['draɪnɪs] *n* Trockenheit *f*.

dry rot *n* (Haus)schwamm *m*, (Holz)schwamm *m*.

dry run *n* (*fig*) Probe *f*.

dry ski slope *n* Trockenskipiste *f*.

DSc *n abbr* (= *Doctor of Science*) ≈ Dr. rer. nat.

DSS (*BRIT*) *n abbr* (= *Department of Social Security*) Ministerium *für* Sozialfürsorge.

DST (*US*) *abbr* = **daylight-saving time**.

DT *n abbr* (*COMPUT*) = **data transmission**.

DTI (*BRIT*) *n abbr* (= *Department of Trade and Industry*) ≈ Wirtschaftsministerium *nt*.

DTP *n abbr* (= *desktop publishing*) DTP *nt*; *see also* **desktop publishing**.

DT's (*inf*) *npl abbr* (= *delirium tremens*) Delirium tremens *nt*; **to have the** ~ vom Trinken den Tatterich haben (*inf*).

dual ['djuəl] *adj* doppelt; (*personality*) gespalten.

dual carriageway (*BRIT*) *n* ≈ Schnellstraße *f*.

dual nationality *n* doppelte Staatsangehörigkeit *f*.

dual-purpose ['djuəl'pəːpəs] *adj* zweifach verwendbar.

dubbed [dʌbd] *adj* synchronisiert; (*nicknamed*) getauft.

dubious ['djuːbɪəs] *adj* zweifelhaft; **I'm very** ~ **about it** ich habe da (doch) starke Zweifel.

Dublin ['dʌblɪn] *n* Dublin *nt*.

Dubliner ['dʌblɪnə*] *n* Dubliner(in) *m(f)*.

duchess ['dʌtʃɪs] *n* Herzogin *f*.

duck [dʌk] *n* Ente *f* ♦ *vi* (*also:* ~ **down**) sich ducken ♦ *vt* (*blow*) ausweichen +*dat*; (*duty, responsibility*) aus dem Weg gehen +*dat*.

duckling ['dʌklɪŋ] *n* Entenküken *nt*; (*CULIN*)

(junge) Ente *f*.

duct [dʌkt] *n* Rohr *nt*; (*ANAT*) Röhre *f*; **tear** ~ Tränenkanal *m*.

dud [dʌd] *n* Niete *f* (*inf*); (*note*) Blüte *f* (*inf*)
♦ *adj*: ~ **cheque** (*BRIT*) ungedeckter Scheck *m*.

due [dju:] *adj* fällig; (*attention etc*) gebührend; (*consideration*) reiflich ♦ *n*: **to give sb his/her** ~ jdn gerecht behandeln ♦ *adv*: ~ **north** direkt nach Norden; **dues** *npl* Beitrag *m*; (*in harbour*) Gebühren *pl*; **in** ~ **course** zu gegebener Zeit; (*eventually*) im Laufe der Zeit; ~ **to** (*owing to*) wegen +*gen*, aufgrund *or* auf Grund +*gen*; **to be** ~ **to do sth** etw tun sollen; **the rent is** ~ **on the 30th** die Miete ist am 30. fällig; **the train is** ~ **at 8** der Zug soll (laut Fahrplan) um 8 ankommen; **she is** ~ **back tomorrow** sie müsste morgen zurück sein; **I am** ~ **6 days' leave** mir stehen 6 Tage Urlaub zu.

due date *n* Fälligkeitsdatum *nt*.

duel ['djuəl] *n* Duell *nt*.

duet [dju:'et] *n* Duett *nt*.

duff [dʌf] (*BRIT*: *inf*) *adj* kaputt.

▶ **duff up** *vt* vermöbeln.

duffel bag ['dʌfl-] *n* Matchbeutel *m*.

duffel coat *n* Dufflecoat *m*.

duffer ['dʌfə'] (*inf*) *n* Versager *m*, Flasche *f*.

dug [dʌg] *pt*, *pp of* **dig**.

dugout ['dʌgaut] *n* (*canoe*) Einbaum *m*; (*shelter*) Unterstand *m*.

duke [dju:k] *n* Herzog *m*.

dull [dʌl] *adj* trüb; (*intelligence*, *wit*) schwerfällig, langsam; (*event*) langweilig; (*sound*, *pain*) dumpf ♦ *vt* (*pain*, *grief*) betäuben; (*mind*, *senses*) abstumpfen.

duly ['dju:lɪ] *adv* (*properly*) gebührend; (*on time*) pünktlich.

dumb [dʌm] *adj* stumm; (*pej*: *stupid*) dumm, doof (*inf*); **he was struck** ~ es verschlug ihm die Sprache.

dumbbell ['dʌmbel] *n* Hantel *f*.

dumbfounded [dʌm'faundɪd] *adj* verblüfft.

dummy ['dʌmɪ] *n* (Schneider)puppe *f*; (*mockup*) Attrappe *f*; (*SPORT*) Finte *f*; (*BRIT*: *for baby*) Schnuller *m* ♦ *adj* (*firm*) fiktiv; ~ **bullets** Übungsmunition *f*.

dummy run *n* Probe *f*.

dump [dʌmp] *n* (*also*: **rubbish** ~) Abfallhaufen *m*; (*inf*: *place*) Müllkippe *f*; (*MIL*) Depot *nt* ♦ *vt* fallen lassen; (*get rid of*) abladen; (*car*) abstellen; (*COMPUT*: *data*) ausgeben; **to be down in the** ~**s** (*inf*) deprimiert *or* down sein; **"no** ~**ing"** „Schuttabladen verboten".

dumpling ['dʌmplɪŋ] *n* Kloß *m*, Knödel *m*.

dumpy ['dʌmpɪ] *adj* pummelig.

dunce [dʌns] *n* Niete *f*.

dune [dju:n] *n* Düne *f*.

dung [dʌŋ] *n* (*AGR*) Dünger *m*, Mist *m*; (*ZOOL*) Dung *m*.

dungarees [dʌŋgə'ri:z] *npl* Latzhose *f*.

dungeon ['dʌndʒən] *n* Kerker *m*, Verlies *nt*.

dunk [dʌŋk] *vt* (ein)tunken.

Dunkirk [dʌn'kə:k] *n* Dünkirchen *nt*.

duo ['dju:əu] *n* Duo *nt*.

duodenal [dju:əu'di:nl] *adj* Duodenal-; ~ **ulcer** Zwölffingerdarmgeschwür *nt*.

duodenum [dju:əu'di:nəm] *n* Zwölffingerdarm *m*.

dupe [dju:p] *n* Betrogene(r) *f*(*m*) ♦ *vt* betrügen.

duplex ['dju:pleks] (*US*) *n* Zweifamilienhaus *nt*; (*apartment*) zweistöckige Wohnung *f*.

duplicate [*n*, *adj* 'dju:plɪkət, *vt* 'dju:plɪkeɪt] *n* (*also*: ~ **copy**) Duplikat *nt*, Kopie *f*; (*also*: ~ **key**) Zweitschlüssel *m* ♦ *adj* doppelt ♦ *vt* kopieren; (*repeat*) wiederholen; **in** ~ in doppelter Ausfertigung.

duplicating machine ['dju:plɪkeɪtɪŋ-] *n* Vervielfältigungsapparat *m*.

duplicator ['dju:plɪkeɪtə'] *n* Vervielfältigungsapparat *m*.

duplicity [dju:'plɪsɪtɪ] *n* Doppelspiel *nt*.

Dur. (*BRIT*) *abbr* (*POST*: = *Durham*).

durability [djuərə'bɪlɪtɪ] *n* Haltbarkeit *f*.

durable ['djuərəbl] *adj* haltbar.

duration [djuə'reɪʃən] *n* Dauer *f*.

duress [djuə'res] *n*: **under** ~ unter Zwang.

Durex ® ['djuəreks] (*BRIT*) *n* Gummi *m* (*inf*).

during ['djuərɪŋ] *prep* während +*gen*.

dusk [dʌsk] *n* (Abend)dämmerung *f*.

dusky ['dʌskɪ] *adj* (*room*) dunkel; (*light*) Dämmer-.

dust [dʌst] *n* Staub *m* ♦ *vt* abstauben; (*cake etc*): **to** ~ **with** bestäuben mit.

▶ **dust off** *vt* abwischen, wegwischen; (*fig*) hervorkramen.

dustbin ['dʌstbɪn] (*BRIT*) *n* Mülltonne *f*.

dustbin liner (*BRIT*) *n* Müllsack *m*.

duster ['dʌstə'] *n* Staubtuch *nt*.

dust jacket *n* (Schutz)umschlag *m*.

dustman ['dʌstmən] (*BRIT*: *irreg*: *like* **man**) *n* Müllmann *m*.

dustpan ['dʌstpæn] *n* Kehrschaufel *f*, Müllschaufel *f*.

dusty ['dʌstɪ] *adj* staubig.

Dutch [dʌtʃ] *adj* holländisch, niederländisch ♦ *n* Holländisch *nt*, Niederländisch *nt* ♦ *adv*: **to go** ~ (*inf*) getrennte Kasse machen; **the Dutch** *npl* die Holländer *pl*, die Niederländer *pl*.

Dutch auction *n* *Versteigerung mit stufenweise erniedrigtem Ausbietungspreis.*

Dutchman ['dʌtʃmən] (*irreg*: *like* **man**) *n* Holländer *m*, Niederländer *m*.

Dutchwoman ['dʌtʃwumən] (*irreg*: *like* **woman**) *n* Holländerin *f*, Niederländerin *f*.

dutiable ['dju:tɪəbl] *adj* zollpflichtig.

dutiful ['dju:tɪful] *adj* pflichtbewusst; (*son*, *daughter*) gehorsam.

duty ['dju:tɪ] *n* Pflicht *f*; (*tax*) Zoll *m*; **duties** *npl* (*functions*) Aufgaben *pl*; **to make it one's** ~ **to do sth** es sich *dat* zur Pflicht machen, etw zu tun; **to pay** ~ **on sth** Zoll auf etw *acc* zahlen; **on/off** ~ im/nicht im Dienst.

duty-free ['djuːtɪ'friː] *adj* zollfrei; ~ **shop** Dutyfreeshop *m*, Duty-free-Shop *m*.
duty officer *n* Offizier *m* vom Dienst.
duvet ['duːveɪ] (*BRIT*) *n* Federbett *nt*.
DV *abbr* (= *Deo volente*) so Gott will.
DVD *n abbr* (= *digital versatile or video disc*) DVD *f*.
DVLA *n abbr* (= *Driver and Vehicle Licensing Authority*) Zulassungsbehörde für Kraftfahrzeuge.
DVLC (*BRIT*) *n abbr* (= *Driver and Vehicle Licensing Centre*) Zulassungsstelle für Kraftfahrzeuge.
DVM (*US*) *n abbr* (= *Doctor of Veterinary Medicine*) ≈ Dr. med. vet.
dwarf [dwɔːf] (*pl* **dwarves**) *n* Zwerg(in) *m(f)* ♦ *vt*: **to be** ~**ed by sth** neben etw *dat* klein erscheinen.
dwarves [dwɔːvz] *npl of* **dwarf**.
dwell [dwɛl] (*pt, pp* **dwelt**) *vi* wohnen, leben.
► **dwell on** *vt fus* (in Gedanken) verweilen bei.
dweller ['dwɛləʳ] *n* Bewohner(in) *m(f)*; **city ~** Stadtbewohner(in) *m(f)*.
dwelling ['dwɛlɪŋ] *n* Wohnhaus *nt*.
dwelt [dwɛlt] *pt, pp of* **dwell**.
dwindle ['dwɪndl] *vi* abnehmen; (*interest*) schwinden; (*attendance*) zurückgehen.
dwindling ['dwɪndlɪŋ] *adj* (*strength, interest*) schwindend; (*resources, supplies*) versiegend.
dye [daɪ] *n* Farbstoff *m*; (*for hair*) Färbemittel *nt* ♦ *vt* färben.
dyestuffs ['daɪstʌfs] *npl* Farbstoffe *pl*.
dying ['daɪɪŋ] *adj* sterbend; (*moments, words*) letzte(r, s).
dyke [daɪk] *n* (*BRIT: wall*) Deich *m*, Damm *m*; (*channel*) (Entwässerungs)graben *m*; (*causeway*) Fahrdamm *m*.
dynamic [daɪ'næmɪk] *adj* dynamisch.
dynamics [daɪ'næmɪks] *n or npl* Dynamik *f*.
dynamite ['daɪnəmaɪt] *n* Dynamit *nt* ♦ *vt* sprengen.
dynamo ['daɪnəməu] *n* Dynamo *m*; (*AUT*) Lichtmaschine *f*.
dynasty ['dɪnəstɪ] *n* Dynastie *f*.
dysentery ['dɪsntrɪ] *n* (*MED*) Ruhr *f*.
dyslexia [dɪs'lɛksɪə] *n* Legasthenie *f*.
dyslexic [dɪs'lɛksɪk] *adj* legasthenisch ♦ *n* Legastheniker(in) *m(f)*.
dyspepsia [dɪs'pɛpsɪə] *n* Dyspepsie *f*, Verdauungsstörung *f*.
dystrophy ['dɪstrəfɪ] *n* Dystrophie *f*, Ernährungsstörung *f*; **muscular ~** Muskelschwund *m*.

E, e

E¹, e [iː] *n* (*letter*) E *nt*, e *nt*; ~ **for Edward,** (*US*) ~ **for Easy** E wie Emil.
E² [iː] *n* (*MUS*) E *nt*, e *nt*.
E³ [iː] *abbr* (= *east*) O ♦ *n abbr* (*drug*: = *Ecstasy*) Ecstasy *nt*.
e- [iː] *pref* E-, elektronisch.
E111 *n abbr* (*also*: **form ~**) E111-Formular *nt*.
E.A. (*US*) *n abbr* (= *educational age*) Bildungsstand *m*.
ea. *abbr* = **each**.
each [iːtʃ] *adj, pron* jede(r, s); ~ **other** sich, einander; **they hate ~ other** sie hassen sich *or* einander; **you are jealous of ~ other** ihr seid eifersüchtig aufeinander; ~ **day** jeden Tag; **they have 2 books** ~ sie haben je 2 Bücher; **they cost £5** ~ sie kosten 5 Pfund das Stück; ~ **of us** jede(r, s) von uns.
eager ['iːgəʳ] *adj* eifrig; **to be** ~ **to do sth** etw unbedingt tun wollen; **to be** ~ **for sth** auf etw *acc* erpicht *or* aus (*inf*) sein.
eagerly ['iːgəlɪ] *adv* eifrig; (*awaited*) gespannt, ungeduldig.
eagle ['iːgl] *n* Adler *m*.
ear [ɪəʳ] *n* Ohr *nt*; (*of corn*) Ähre *f*; **to be up to one's ~s in debt/work** bis über beide Ohren in Schulden/Arbeit stecken; **to be up to one's ~s in paint/baking** mitten im Anstreichen/Backen stecken; **to give sb a thick ~** jdm ein paar hinter die Ohren geben; **we'll play it by ~** (*fig*) wir werden es auf uns zukommen lassen.
earache ['ɪəreɪk] *n* Ohrenschmerzen *pl*.
eardrum ['ɪədrʌm] *n* Trommelfell *nt*.
earful ['ɪəful] (*inf*) *n*: **to give sb an ~** jdm was erzählen; **to get an ~** was zu hören bekommen.
earl [əːl] (*BRIT*) *n* Graf *m*.
earlier ['əːlɪəʳ] *adj, adv* früher; **I can't come any ~** ich kann nicht früher *or* eher kommen.
early ['əːlɪ] *adv* früh; (*ahead of time*) zu früh ♦ *adj* früh; (*Christians*) Ur-; (*death, departure*) vorzeitig; (*reply*) baldig; ~ **in the morning** früh am Morgen; **to have an ~ night** früh ins Bett gehen; **in the ~ hours** in den frühen Morgenstunden; **in the ~ or ~ in the spring/19th century** Anfang des Frühjahrs/ des 19. Jahrhunderts; **take the ~ train** nimm den früheren Zug; **you're ~!** Sie sind früh dran!; **she's in her ~ forties** sie ist Anfang Vierzig; **at your earliest convenience** so bald wie möglich.
early retirement *n*: **to take ~** vorzeitig in den Ruhestand gehen.

early warning system *n* Frühwarnsystem *nt*.

earmark ['ɪəmɑːk] *vt*: **to ~ (for)** bestimmen (für), vorsehen (für).

earn [ɜːn] *vt* verdienen; (*interest*) bringen; **to ~ one's living** seinen Lebensunterhalt verdienen; **this ~ed him much praise, he ~ed much praise for this** das trug ihm viel Lob ein; **he's ~ed his rest/reward** er hat sich seine Pause/Belohnung verdient.

earned income [ɜːnd-] *n* Arbeitseinkommen *nt*.

earnest ['ɜːnɪst] *adj* ernsthaft; (*wish, desire*) innig ♦ *n* (*also*: **~ money**) Angeld *nt*; **in ~** (*adv*) richtig; (*adj*): **to be in ~** es ernst meinen; **work on the tunnel soon began in ~** die Tunnelarbeiten begannen bald richtig; **is the Minister in ~ about these proposals?** meint der Minister diese Vorschläge ernst?

earnings ['ɜːnɪŋz] *npl* Verdienst *m*; (*of company etc*) Ertrag *m*.

ear, nose and throat specialist *n* Hals-Nasen-Ohren-Arzt *m*, Hals-Nasen-Ohren-Ärztin *f*.

earphones ['ɪəfəʊnz] *npl* Kopfhörer *pl*.

earplugs ['ɪəplʌgz] *npl* Ohropax ® *nt*.

earring ['ɪərɪŋ] *n* Ohrring *m*.

earshot ['ɪəʃɒt] *n*: **within/out of ~** in/außer Hörweite.

earth [ɜːθ] *n* Erde *f*; (*of fox*) Bau *m* ♦ *vt* (*BRIT*: *ELEC*) erden.

earthenware ['ɜːθnwɛə'] *n* Tongeschirr *nt* ♦ *adj* Ton-.

earthly ['ɜːθlɪ] *adj* irdisch; **~ paradise** Paradies *nt* auf Erden; **there is no ~ reason to think ...** es besteht nicht der geringste Grund für die Annahme ...

earthquake ['ɜːθkweɪk] *n* Erdbeben *nt*.

earthshattering ['ɜːθʃætərɪŋ] *adj* (*fig*) weltbewegend.

earth tremor *n* Erdstoß *m*.

earthworks ['ɜːθwɜːks] *npl* Erdarbeiten *pl*.

earthworm ['ɜːθwɜːm] *n* Regenwurm *m*.

earthy ['ɜːθɪ] *adj* (*humour*) derb.

earwig ['ɪəwɪg] *n* Ohrwurm *m*.

ease [iːz] *n* Leichtigkeit *f*; (*comfort*) Behagen *nt* ♦ *vt* (*problem*) vereinfachen; (*pain*) lindern; (*tension*) verringern; (*loosen*) lockern ♦ *vi* nachlassen; (*situation*) sich entspannen; **to ~ sth in/out** (*push/pull*) etw behutsam hineinschieben/herausziehen; **at ~!** (*MIL*) rührt euch!; **with ~** mit Leichtigkeit; **life of ~** Leben *nt* der Muße; **to ~ in the clutch** die Kupplung behutsam kommen lassen.

► **ease off** *vi* nachlassen; (*slow down*) langsamer werden.

► **ease up** *vi* = ease off.

easel ['iːzl] *n* Staffelei *f*.

easily ['iːzɪlɪ] *adv* (*see adj*) leicht; ungezwungen; bequem.

easiness ['iːzɪnɪs] *n* Leichtigkeit *f*; (*of manner*) Ungezwungenheit *f*.

east [iːst] *n* Osten *m* ♦ *adj* (*coast, Asia etc*) Ost- ♦ *adv* ostwärts, nach Osten; **the E~** der Osten.

Easter ['iːstə'] *n* Ostern *nt* ♦ *adj* (*holidays etc*) Oster-.

Easter egg *n* Osterei *nt*.

Easter Island *n* Osterinsel *f*.

easterly ['iːstəlɪ] *adj* östlich; (*wind*) Ost-.

Easter Monday *n* Ostermontag *m*.

eastern ['iːstən] *adj* östlich; **E~ Europe** Osteuropa *nt*; **the E~ bloc** (*formerly*) der Ostblock.

Easter Sunday *n* Ostersonntag *m*.

East Germany *n* (*formerly*) die DDR *f*.

eastward(s) ['iːstwəd(z)] *adv* ostwärts, nach Osten.

easy ['iːzɪ] *adj* leicht; (*relaxed*) ungezwungen; (*comfortable*) bequem ♦ *adv*: **to take it/things ~** (*go slowly*) sich *dat* Zeit lassen; (*not worry*) es nicht so schwer nehmen; (*rest*) sich schonen; **payment on ~ terms** Zahlung zu günstigen Bedingungen; **that's easier said than done** das ist leichter gesagt als getan; **I'm ~** (*inf*) mir ist alles recht.

easy chair *n* Sessel *m*.

easy-going ['iːzɪ'gəʊɪŋ] *adj* gelassen.

easy touch (*inf*) *n*: **to be an ~** (*for money etc*) leicht anzuzapfen sein.

eat [iːt] (*pt* **ate**, *pp* **eaten**) *vt*, *vi* essen; (*animal*) fressen.

► **eat away** *vt* (*subj*: *sea*) auswaschen; (: *acid*) zerfressen.

► **eat away at** *vt fus* (*metal*) anfressen; (*savings*) angreifen.

► **eat into** *vt fus* = eat away at.

► **eat out** *vi* essen gehen.

► **eat up** *vt* aufessen; **it ~s up electricity** es verbraucht viel Strom.

eatable ['iːtəbl] *adj* genießbar.

eau de Cologne ['əʊdəkə'ləʊn] *n* Kölnischwasser *nt*, Eau de Cologne *nt*.

eaves [iːvz] *npl* Dachvorsprung *m*.

eavesdrop ['iːvzdrɒp] *vi* lauschen; **to ~ on** belauschen *+acc*.

ebb [ɛb] *n* Ebbe *f* ♦ *vi* ebben; (*fig*: *also*: **~ away**) dahinschwinden; (: *feeling*) abebben; **the ~ and flow** (*fig*) das Auf und Ab; **to be at a low ~** (*fig*) auf einem Tiefpunkt angelangt sein.

ebb tide *n* Ebbe *f*.

ebony ['ɛbənɪ] *n* Ebenholz *nt*.

ebullient [ɪ'bʌlɪənt] *adj* überschäumend, übersprudelnd.

EC *n abbr* (= *European Community*) EG *f*.

ECB *n abbr* (= *European Central Bank*) EZB *f*.

eccentric [ɪk'sɛntrɪk] *adj* exzentrisch ♦ *n* Exzentriker(in) *m(f)*.

ecclesiastic(al) [ɪkliːzɪ'æstɪk(l)] *adj* kirchlich.

ECG *n abbr* (= *electrocardiogram*) EKG *nt*.

echo ['ɛkəʊ] (*pl* **~es**) *n* Echo *nt* ♦ *vt* wiederholen ♦ *vi* widerhallen; (*place*) hallen.

éclair – effectiveness

éclair [eɪ'klɛə*] n Eclair nt.
eclipse [ɪ'klɪps] n Finsternis f ♦ vt in den Schatten stellen.
ECM (US) n abbr (= European Common Market) EG f.
eco- ['iːkəʊ] pref Öko-, öko-.
ecofriendly adj umweltfreundlich.
ecological [iːkə'lɔdʒɪkəl] adj ökologisch; (damage, disaster) Umwelt-.
ecologist [ɪ'kɔlədʒɪst] n Ökologe m, Ökologin f.
ecology [ɪ'kɔlədʒɪ] n Ökologie f.
e-commerce [iː'kɒmɜːs] n E-Commerce nt, elektronischer Handel.
economic [iːkə'nɔmɪk] adj (system, policy etc) Wirtschafts-; (profitable) wirtschaftlich.
economical [iːkə'nɔmɪkl] adj wirtschaftlich; (person) sparsam.
economically [iːkə'nɔmɪklɪ] adv wirtschaftlich; (thriftily) sparsam.
economics [iːkə'nɔmɪks] n Wirtschaftswissenschaften pl ♦ npl Wirtschaftlichkeit f; (of situation) wirtschaftliche Seite f.
economist [ɪ'kɔnəmɪst] n Wirtschaftswissenschaftler(in) m(f).
economize [ɪ'kɔnəmaɪz] vi sparen.
economy [ɪ'kɔnəmɪ] n Wirtschaft f; (financial prudence) Sparsamkeit f; **economies of scale** (COMM) Einsparungen pl durch erhöhte Produktion.
economy class n Touristenklasse f.
economy size n Sparpackung f.
ecosystem ['iːkəʊsɪstəm] n Ökosystem nt.
ecotourism ['iːkəʊ'tʊərɪzm] n Ökotourismus m.
ECSC n abbr (= European Coal and Steel Community) Europäische Gemeinschaft für Kohle und Stahl.
ecstasy ['ɛkstəsɪ] n Ekstase f; (drug) Ecstasy nt; **to go into ecstasies over** in Verzückung geraten über +acc; **in ~** verzückt.
ecstatic [ɛks'tætɪk] adj ekstatisch.
ECT n abbr = electroconvulsive therapy.
Ecuador ['ɛkwədɔː*] n Ecuador nt, Ekuador nt.
ecumenical [iːkjuː'mɛnɪkl] adj ökumenisch.
eczema ['ɛksɪmə] n Ekzem nt.
eddy ['ɛdɪ] n Strudel m.
edge [ɛdʒ] n Rand m; (of table, chair) Kante f; (of lake) Ufer nt; (of knife etc) Schneide f ♦ vt einfassen ♦ vi: **to ~ forward** sich nach vorne schieben; **on ~** (fig) = edgy **to have the ~ on** überlegen sein +dat; **to ~ away from** sich allmählich entfernen von; **to ~ past** sich vorbeischieben, sich vorbeidrücken.
edgeways ['ɛdʒweɪz] adv: **he couldn't get a word in ~** er kam überhaupt nicht zu Wort.
edging ['ɛdʒɪŋ] n Einfassung f.
edgy ['ɛdʒɪ] adj nervös.
edible ['ɛdɪbl] adj essbar, genießbar.
edict ['iːdɪkt] n Erlass m.
edifice ['ɛdɪfɪs] n Gebäude nt.

edifying ['ɛdɪfaɪɪŋ] adj erbaulich.
Edinburgh ['ɛdɪnbərə] n Edinburg(h) nt.
edit ['ɛdɪt] vt (text) redigieren; (book) lektorieren; (film, broadcast) schneiden, cutten; (newspaper, magazine) herausgeben; (COMPUT) editieren.
edition [ɪ'dɪʃən] n Ausgabe f.
editor ['ɛdɪtə*] n Redakteur(in) m(f); (of newspaper, magazine) Herausgeber(in) m(f); (of book) Lektor(in) m(f); (CINE, RADIO, TV) Cutter(in) m(f).
editorial [ɛdɪ'tɔːrɪəl] adj redaktionell; (staff) Redaktions- ♦ n Leitartikel m.
EDP n abbr (COMPUT: = electronic data processing) EDV f.
EDT (US) abbr (= Eastern Daylight Time) ostamerikanische Sommerzeit.
educate ['ɛdjʊkeɪt] vt erziehen; **~d at ...** zur Schule/Universität gegangen in ...
educated ['ɛdjʊkeɪtɪd] adj gebildet.
educated guess ['ɛdjʊkeɪtɪd-] n wohl begründete Vermutung f.
education [ɛdjʊ'keɪʃən] n Erziehung f; (schooling) Ausbildung f; (knowledge, culture) Bildung f; **primary** or (US) **elementary ~** Grundschul(aus)bildung f; **secondary ~** höhere Schul(aus)bildung f.
educational [ɛdjʊ'keɪʃənl] adj pädagogisch; (experience) lehrreich; (toy) pädagogisch wertvoll; **~ technology** Unterrichtstechnologie f.
Edwardian [ɛd'wɔːdɪən] adj aus der Zeit Edwards VII.
EE abbr = electrical engineer.
EEC n abbr (formerly: = European Economic Community) EWG f.
EEG n abbr (= electroencephalogram) EEG nt.
eel [iːl] n Aal m.
EENT (US) n abbr (MED: = eye, ear, nose and throat) Augen und Hals-Nasen-Ohren.
EEOC (US) n abbr (= Equal Employment Opportunity Commission) Kommission für Gleichberechtigung am Arbeitsplatz.
eerie ['ɪərɪ] adj unheimlich.
EET abbr (= Eastern European Time) OEZ f.
efface [ɪ'feɪs] vt auslöschen; **to ~ o.s.** sich im Hintergrund halten.
effect [ɪ'fɛkt] n Wirkung f, Effekt m ♦ vt bewirken; (repairs) durchführen; **effects** npl Effekten pl; (THEAT, CINE etc) Effekte pl; **to take ~** (law) in Kraft treten; (drug) wirken; **to put into ~** in Kraft setzen; **to have an ~ on sb/sth** eine Wirkung auf jdn/etw haben; **in ~** eigentlich, praktisch; **his letter is to the ~ that ...** sein Brief hat zum Inhalt, dass ...
effective [ɪ'fɛktɪv] adj effektiv, wirksam; (actual) eigentlich, wirklich; **to become ~** in Kraft treten; **~ date** Zeitpunkt m des In-Kraft-Tretens.
effectively [ɪ'fɛktɪvlɪ] adv effektiv.
effectiveness [ɪ'fɛktɪvnɪs] n Wirksamkeit f,

Effektivität f.

effeminate [ɪˈfɛmɪnɪt] adj feminin, effeminiert.

effervescent [ɛfəˈvɛsnt] adj sprudelnd.

efficacy [ˈɛfɪkəsɪ] n Wirksamkeit f.

efficiency [ɪˈfɪʃənsɪ] n (see adj) Fähigkeit f, Tüchtigkeit f; Rationalität f; Leistungsfähigkeit f.

efficiency apartment (US) n Einzimmerwohnung f.

efficient [ɪˈfɪʃənt] adj fähig, tüchtig; (organization) rationell; (machine) leistungsfähig.

efficiently [ɪˈfɪʃəntlɪ] adv gut, effizient.

effigy [ˈɛfɪdʒɪ] n Bildnis nt.

effluent [ˈɛfluənt] n Abwasser nt.

effort [ˈɛfət] n Anstrengung f; (attempt) Versuch m; **to make an ~ to do sth** sich bemühen, etw zu tun.

effortless [ˈɛfətlɪs] adj mühelos; (style) flüssig.

effrontery [ɪˈfrʌntərɪ] n Unverschämtheit f; **to have the ~ to do sth** die Frechheit besitzen, etw zu tun.

effusive [ɪˈfjuːsɪv] adj überschwänglich.

EFL n abbr (SCOL: = English as a Foreign Language) Englisch nt als Fremdsprache.

EFTA [ˈɛftə] n abbr (= European Free Trade Association) EFTA f.

e.g. adv abbr (= exempli gratia) z. B.

egalitarian [ɪgælɪˈtɛərɪən] adj egalitär; (principles) Gleichheits- ♦ n Verfechter(in) m(f) des Egalitarismus.

egg [ɛg] n Ei nt; **hard-boiled/soft-boiled ~** hart/weich gekochtes Ei nt.
► **egg on** vt anstacheln.

egg cup n Eierbecher m.

eggplant [ˈɛgplɑːnt] n (esp US) Aubergine f.

eggshell [ˈɛgʃɛl] n Eierschale f ♦ adj eierschalenfarben.

egg timer n Eieruhr f.

egg white n Eiweiß nt.

egg yolk n Eigelb nt.

ego [ˈiːgəu] n (self-esteem) Selbstbewusstsein nt.

egoism [ˈɛgəuɪzəm] n Egoismus m.

egoist [ˈɛgəuɪst] n Egoist(in) m(f).

egotism [ˈɛgəutɪzəm] n Ichbezogenheit f, Egotismus m.

egotist [ˈɛgəutɪst] n ichbezogener Mensch m, Egotist(in) m(f).

ego trip (inf) n Egotrip m.

Egypt [ˈiːdʒɪpt] n Ägypten nt.

Egyptian [ɪˈdʒɪpʃən] adj ägyptisch ♦ n Ägypter(in) m(f).

eiderdown [ˈaɪdədaun] n Federbett nt, Daunendecke f.

eight [eɪt] num acht.

eighteen [eɪˈtiːn] num achtzehn.

eighteenth [eɪˈtiːnθ] num achtzehnte(r, s).

eighth [eɪtθ] num achte(r, s) ♦ n Achtel nt.

eighty [ˈeɪtɪ] num achtzig.

Eire [ˈɛərə] n (Republik f) Irland nt.

EIS n abbr (= Educational Institute of Scotland) schottische Lehrergewerkschaft.

either [ˈaɪðəˈ] adj (one or other) eine(r, s) (von beiden); (both, each) beide pl, jede(r, s) ♦ pron: **~ (of them)** eine(r, s) (davon) ♦ adv auch nicht ♦ conj: **~ yes or no** entweder ja oder nein; **on ~ side** (on both sides) auf beiden Seiten; (on one or other side) auf einer der beiden Seiten; **I don't like ~** ich mag beide nicht or keinen von beiden; **no, I don't ~** nein, ich auch nicht; **I haven't seen ~ one or the other** ich habe weder den einen noch den anderen gesehen.

ejaculation [ɪdʒækjuˈleɪʃən] n Ejakulation f, Samenerguss m.

eject [ɪˈdʒɛkt] vt ausstoßen; (tenant, gatecrasher) hinauswerfen ♦ vi den Schleudersitz betätigen.

ejector seat [ɪˈdʒɛktəˈ] n Schleudersitz m.

eke out vt (make last) strecken.

EKG (US) n abbr = **electrocardiogram**.

el [ɛl] (US: inf) n abbr = **elevated railroad**.

elaborate [adj ɪˈlæbərɪt, vb ɪˈlæbəreɪt] adj kompliziert; (plan) ausgefeilt ♦ vt näher ausführen; (refine) ausarbeiten ♦ vi mehr ins Detail gehen; **to ~ on** näher ausführen.

elapse [ɪˈlæps] vi vergehen, verstreichen.

elastic [ɪˈlæstɪk] n Gummi nt ♦ adj elastisch.

elastic band (BRIT) n Gummiband nt.

elasticity [ɪlæsˈtɪsɪtɪ] n Elastizität f.

elated [ɪˈleɪtɪd] adj: **to be ~** hocherfreut or in Hochstimmung sein.

elation [ɪˈleɪʃən] n große Freude f, Hochstimmung f.

elbow [ˈɛlbəu] n Ell(en)bogen m ♦ vt: **to ~ one's way through the crowd** sich durch die Menge boxen.

elbow grease (inf) n Muskelkraft f.

elbowroom [ˈɛlbəurum] n Ellbogenfreiheit f.

elder [ˈɛldəˈ] adj älter ♦ n (BOT) Holunder m; (older person: gen pl) Ältere(r) f(m).

elderly [ˈɛldəlɪ] adj ältere(r, s) ♦ npl: **the ~** ältere Leute pl.

elder statesman n erfahrener Staatsmann m.

eldest [ˈɛldɪst] adj älteste(r, s) ♦ n Älteste(r) f(m).

elect [ɪˈlɛkt] vt wählen ♦ adj: **the president ~** der designierte or künftige Präsident; **to ~ to do sth** sich dafür entscheiden, etw zu tun.

election [ɪˈlɛkʃən] n Wahl f; **to hold an ~** eine Wahl abhalten.

election campaign n Wahlkampf m.

electioneering [ɪlɛkʃəˈnɪərɪŋ] n Wahlkampf m.

elector [ɪˈlɛktəˈ] n Wähler(in) m(f).

electoral [ɪˈlɛktərəl] adj Wähler-.

electoral college n Wahlmännergremium nt.

electorate [ɪˈlɛktərɪt] n Wähler pl, Wählerschaft f.

electric [ɪˈlɛktrɪk] adj elektrisch.

electrical [ɪˈlɛktrɪkl] adj elektrisch; (appliance)

Elektro-; (*failure*) Strom-.
electrical engineer *n* Elektrotechniker *m*.
electric blanket *n* Heizdecke *f*.
electric chair (*US*) *n* elektrischer Stuhl *m*.
electric cooker *n* Elektroherd *m*.
electric current *n* elektrischer Strom *m*.
electric fire (*BRIT*) *n* elektrisches Heizgerät *nt*.
electrician [ɪlɛkˈtrɪʃən] *n* Elektriker(in) *m(f)*.
electricity [ɪlɛkˈtrɪsɪtɪ] *n* Elektrizität *f*; (*supply*) (elektrischer) Strom *m* ♦ *cpd* Strom-; **to switch on/off the** ~ den Strom an-/abschalten.
electric light *n* elektrisches Licht *nt*.
electric shock *n* elektrischer Schlag *m*, Stromschlag *m*.
electrify [ɪˈlɛktrɪfaɪ] *vt* (*fence*) unter Strom setzen; (*rail network*) elektrifizieren; (*audience*) elektrisieren.
electro... [ɪˈlɛktrəʊ] *pref* Elektro-.
electrocardiogram [ɪˈlɛktrəˈkɑːdɪəgræm] *n* Elektrokardiogramm *nt*.
electroconvulsive therapy [ɪˈlɛktrəkən'vʌlsɪv-] *n* Elektroschocktherapie *f*.
electrocute [ɪˈlɛktrəkjuːt] *vt* durch einen Stromschlag töten; (*US: criminal*) auf dem elektrischen Stuhl hinrichten.
electrode [ɪˈlɛktrəʊd] *n* Elektrode *f*.
electroencephalogram [ɪˈlɛktrəʊenˈsɛfələgræm] *n* Elektroenzephalogramm *nt*.
electrolysis [ɪlɛkˈtrɒlɪsɪs] *n* Elektrolyse *f*.
electromagnetic [ɪˈlɛktrəmæg'nɛtɪk] *adj* elektromagnetisch.
electron [ɪˈlɛktrɒn] *n* Elektron *nt*.
electronic [ɪlɛkˈtrɒnɪk] *adj* elektronisch.
electronic data processing *n* elektronische Datenverarbeitung *f*.
electronic mail *n* elektronische Post *f*.
electronics [ɪlɛkˈtrɒnɪks] *n* Elektronik *f*.
electron microscope *n* Elektronenmikroskop *nt*.
electroplated [ɪˈlɛktrəˈpleɪtɪd] *adj* galvanisiert.
electrotherapy [ɪˈlɛktrəˈθɛrəpɪ] *n* Elektrotherapie *f*.
elegance [ˈɛlɪgəns] *n* Eleganz *f*.
elegant [ˈɛlɪgənt] *adj* elegant.
element [ˈɛlɪmənt] *n* Element *nt*; (*of heater, kettle etc*) Heizelement *nt*.
elementary [ɛlɪˈmɛntərɪ] *adj* grundlegend; ~ **school** Grundschule *f*; ~ **education** Elementarunterricht *m*; ~ **maths** Grundbegriffe *pl* der Mathematik.

ELEMENTARY SCHOOL

Elementary school *ist in den USA und Kanada eine Grundschule, in der ein Kind die ersten sechs bis acht Schuljahre verbringt. In den USA heißt diese Schule auch grade school oder grammar school. Siehe auch* **high school**.

---

elephant [ˈɛlɪfənt] *n* Elefant *m*.
elevate [ˈɛlɪveɪt] *vt* erheben; (*physically*) heben.
elevated [ˈɛlɪveɪtɪd] *adj* erhöht; (*language*) gehoben.
elevated railroad [ˈɛlɪveɪtɪd-] (*US*) *n* Hochbahn *f*.
elevation [ɛlɪˈveɪʃən] *n* Erhebung *f*; (*height*) Höhe *f* über dem Meeresspiegel; (*ARCHIT*) Aufriss *m*.
elevator [ˈɛlɪveɪtə*] *n* (*US*) Aufzug *m*, Fahrstuhl *m*; (*in warehouse etc*) Lastenaufzug *m*.
eleven [ɪˈlɛvn] *num* elf.
elevenses [ɪˈlɛvnzɪz] (*BRIT*) *npl* zweites Frühstück *nt*.
eleventh [ɪˈlɛvnθ] *num* elfte(r, s); **at the** ~ **hour** (*fig*) in letzter Minute.
elf [ɛlf] (*pl* **elves**) *n* Elf *m*, Elfe *f*; (*mischievous*) Kobold *m*.
elicit [ɪˈlɪsɪt] *vt*: **to** ~ **(from sb)** (*information*) (aus jdm) herausbekommen; (*reaction, response*) (von jdm) bekommen.
eligible [ˈɛlɪdʒəbl] *adj* (*marriage partner*) begehrt; **to be** ~ **for sth** für etw infrage *or* in Frage kommen; **to be** ~ **for a pension** pensionsberechtigt sein.
eliminate [ɪˈlɪmɪneɪt] *vt* beseitigen; (*candidate etc*) ausschließen; (*team, contestant*) aus dem Wettbewerb werfen.
elimination [ɪlɪmɪˈneɪʃən] *n* (*see vb*) Beseitigung *f*; Ausschluss *m*; Ausscheiden *nt*; **by process of** ~ durch negative Auslese.
élite [eɪˈliːt] *n* Elite *f*.
élitist [eɪˈliːtɪst] (*pej*) *adj* elitär.
elixir [ɪˈlɪksə*] *n* Elixier *nt*; ~ **of life** Lebenselixier *nt*.
Elizabethan [ɪlɪzəˈbiːθən] *adj* elisabethanisch.
elk [ɛlk] *n* Elch *m*; **Canadian** ~ Wapiti(hirsch) *m*.
ellipse [ɪˈlɪps] *n* Ellipse *f*.
elliptical [ɪˈlɪptɪkl] *adj* elliptisch.
elm [ɛlm] *n* Ulme *f*.
elocution [ɛləˈkjuːʃən] *n* Sprechtechnik *f*.
elongated [ˈiːlɒŋgeɪtɪd] *adj* lang gestreckt; (*shadow*) verlängert.
elope [ɪˈləʊp] *vi* weglaufen.
elopement [ɪˈləʊpmənt] *n* Weglaufen *nt*.
eloquence [ˈɛləkwəns] *n* (*see adj*) Beredtheit *f*, Wortgewandtheit *f*; Ausdrucksfülle *f*.
eloquent [ˈɛləkwənt] *adj* beredt, wortgewandt; (*speech, description*) ausdrucksvoll.
else [ɛls] *adv* andere(r, s); **something** ~ etwas anderes; **somewhere** ~ woanders, anderswo; **everywhere** ~ sonst überall; **where** ~? wo sonst?; **is there anything** ~ **I can do?** kann ich sonst noch etwas tun?; **there was little** ~ **to do** es gab nicht viel anderes zu tun; **everyone** ~ alle anderen; **nobody** ~ **spoke** niemand anders sagte etwas, sonst sagte niemand etwas.

elsewhere [ɛls'wɛə*] *adv* woanders, anderswo; (*go*) woandershin, anderswohin.

ELT *n abbr* (*SCOL:* = *English Language Teaching*) Englisch als Unterrichtsfach.

elucidate [ɪ'lu:sɪdeɪt] *vt* erläutern.

elude [ɪ'lu:d] *vt* (*captor*) entkommen +*dat*; (*capture*) sich entziehen +*dat*; **this fact/idea** ~**d him** diese Tatsache/Idee entging ihm.

elusive [ɪ'lu:sɪv] *adj* schwer zu fangen; (*quality*) unerreichbar; **he's very** ~ er ist sehr schwer zu erreichen.

elves [ɛlvz] *npl of* **elf.**

emaciated [ɪ'meɪsɪeɪtɪd] *adj* abgezehrt, ausgezehrt.

E-mail *n abbr* (= *electronic mail*) E-Mail *f*.

emanate [ˈɛmaneɪt] *vi*: **to** ~ **from** stammen von; (*sound, light etc*) ausgehen von.

emancipate [ɪ'mænsɪpeɪt] *vt* (*women*) emanzipieren; (*poor*) befreien; (*slave*) freilassen.

emancipation [ɪmænsɪ'peɪʃən] *n* (*see vb*) Emanzipation *f*; Befreiung *f*; Freilassung *f*.

emasculate [ɪ'mæskjuleɪt] *vt* schwächen.

embalm [ɪm'bɑ:m] *vt* einbalsamieren.

embankment [ɪm'bæŋkmənt] *n* Böschung *f*; (*of railway*) Bahndamm *m*; (*of river*) Damm *m*.

embargo [ɪm'bɑ:gəʊ] (*pl* ~**es**) *n* Embargo *nt* ♦ *vt* mit einem Embargo belegen; **to put** *or* **impose** *or* **place an** ~ **on sth** ein Embargo über etw *acc* verhängen; **to lift an** ~ ein Embargo aufheben.

embark [ɪm'bɑ:k] *vt* einschiffen ♦ *vi*: **to** ~ **(on)** sich einschiffen (auf); **to** ~ **on** (*journey*) beginnen; (*task*) in Angriff nehmen; (*course of action*) einschlagen.

embarkation [ɛmbɑː'keɪʃən] *n* Einschiffung *f*.

embarkation card *n* Bordkarte *f*.

embarrass [ɪm'bærəs] *vt* in Verlegenheit bringen.

embarrassed [ɪm'bærəst] *adj* verlegen.

embarrassing [ɪm'bærəsɪŋ] *adj* peinlich.

embarrassment [ɪm'bærəsmənt] *n* Verlegenheit *f*; (*embarrassing problem*) Peinlichkeit *f*.

embassy [ˈɛmbəsɪ] *n* Botschaft *f*; **the Swiss E**~ die Schweizer Botschaft.

embedded [ɪm'bɛdɪd] *adj* eingebettet; (*attitude, belief, feeling*) verwurzelt.

embellish [ɪm'bɛlɪʃ] *vt* (*account*) ausschmücken; **to be** ~**ed with** geschmückt sein mit.

embers [ˈɛmbəz] *npl* Glut *f*.

embezzle [ɪm'bɛzl] *vt* unterschlagen.

embezzlement [ɪm'bɛzlmənt] *n* Unterschlagung *f*.

embezzler [ɪm'bɛzlə*] *n jd, der eine Unterschlagung begangen hat.*

embitter [ɪm'bɪtə*] *vt* verbittern.

embittered [ɪm'bɪtəd] *adj* verbittert.

emblem [ˈɛmbləm] *n* Emblem *nt*; (*symbol*) Wahrzeichen *nt*.

embodiment [ɪm'bɒdɪmənt] *n* Verkörperung *f*; **to be the** ~ **of** ... (*subj: thing*) ... verkörpern; (: *person*) ... in Person sein.

embody [ɪm'bɒdɪ] *vt* verkörpern; (*include, contain*) enthalten.

embolden [ɪm'bəʊldn] *vt* ermutigen.

embolism [ˈɛmbəlɪzəm] *n* Embolie *f*.

embossed [ɪm'bɒst] *adj* geprägt; ~ **with a logo** mit geprägtem Logo.

embrace [ɪm'breɪs] *vt* umarmen; (*include*) umfassen ♦ *vi* sich umarmen ♦ *n* Umarmung *f*.

embroider [ɪm'brɔɪdə*] *vt* (*cloth*) besticken; (*fig: story*) ausschmücken.

embroidery [ɪm'brɔɪdərɪ] *n* Stickerei *f*; (*activity*) Sticken *nt*.

embroil [ɪm'brɔɪl] *vt*: **to become** ~**ed (in sth)** (in etw *acc*) verwickelt *or* hineingezogen werden.

embryo [ˈɛmbrɪəʊ] *n* Embryo *m*; (*fig*) Keim *m*.

emcee [ɛm'siː] *n* Conférencier *m*.

emend [ɪ'mɛnd] *vt* verbessern, korrigieren.

emerald [ˈɛmərəld] *n* Smaragd *m*.

emerge [ɪ'mɜːdʒ] *vi*: **to** ~ **(from)** auftauchen (aus); (*from sleep*) erwachen (aus); (*from imprisonment*) entlassen werden (aus); (*from discussion etc*) sich herausstellen (bei); (*new idea, industry, society*) entstehen (aus); **it** ~**s that** (*BRIT*) es stellt sich heraus, dass.

emergence [ɪ'mɜːdʒəns] *n* Entstehung *f*.

emergency [ɪ'mɜːdʒənsɪ] *n* Notfall *m* ♦ *cpd* Not-; (*repair*) notdürftig; **in an** ~ im Notfall; **state of** ~ Notstand *m*.

emergency cord (*US*) *n* Notbremse *f*.

emergency exit *n* Notausgang *m*.

emergency landing *n* Notlandung *f*.

emergency lane (*US*) *n* Seitenstreifen *m*.

emergency road service (*US*) *n* Pannendienst *m*.

emergency services *npl*: **the** ~ der Notdienst.

emergency stop (*BRIT*) *n* Vollbremsung *f*.

emergent [ɪ'mɜːdʒənt] *adj* jung, aufstrebend.

emeritus [ɪ'mɛrɪtəs] *adj* emeritiert.

emery board [ˈɛmərɪ-] *n* Papiernagelfeile *f*.

emery paper [ˈɛmərɪ-] *n* Schmirgelpapier *nt*.

emetic [ɪ'mɛtɪk] *n* Brechmittel *nt*.

emigrant [ˈɛmɪgrənt] *n* Auswanderer *m*, Auswanderin *f*, Emigrant(in) *m(f)*.

emigrate [ˈɛmɪgreɪt] *vi* auswandern, emigrieren.

emigration [ɛmɪ'greɪʃən] *n* Auswanderung *f*, Emigration *f*.

émigré [ˈɛmɪgreɪ] *n* Emigrant(in) *m(f)*.

eminence [ˈɛmɪnəns] *n* Bedeutung *f*.

eminent [ˈɛmɪnənt] *adj* bedeutend.

eminently [ˈɛmɪnəntlɪ] *adv* ausgesprochen.

emirate [ˈɛmɪrɪt] *n* Emirat *nt*.

emission [ɪ'mɪʃən] *n* Emission *f*.

emissions [ɪ'mɪʃənz] *npl* Emissionen *pl*.

emit [ɪ'mɪt] *vt* abgeben; (*smell*) ausströmen; (*light, heat*) ausstrahlen.

emolument [ɪ'mɒljumənt] *n* (*often pl*)

Vergütung f; (fee) Honorar nt; (salary)
Bezüge pl.
emotion [ɪ'məuʃən] n Gefühl nt.
emotional [ɪ'məuʃənl] adj emotional;
(exhaustion) seelisch; (scene) ergreifend;
(speech) gefühlsbetont.
emotionally [ɪ'məuʃnəlɪ] adv emotional; (be
involved) gefühlsmäßig; (speak) gefühlvoll;
~ **disturbed** seelisch gestört.
emotive [ɪ'məutɪv] adj emotional.
empathy ['empəθɪ] n Einfühlungsvermögen
nt; **to feel ~ with sb** sich in jdn einfühlen.
emperor ['empərə'] n Kaiser m.
emphases ['emfəsi:z] npl of **emphasis**.
emphasis ['emfəsɪs] (pl **emphases**) n
Betonung f; (importance) (Schwer)gewicht
nt; **to lay** or **place ~ on sth** etw betonen; **the
~ is on reading** das Schwergewicht liegt
auf dem Lesen.
emphasize ['emfəsaɪz] vt betonen; (feature)
hervorheben; **I must ~ that** ... ich möchte
betonen, dass ...
emphatic [em'fætɪk] adj nachdrücklich;
(denial) energisch; (person, manner)
bestimmt, entschieden.
emphatically [em'fætɪklɪ] adv nachdrücklich;
(certainly) eindeutig.
emphysema [emfɪ'si:mə] n Emphysem nt.
empire ['empaɪə'] n Reich nt.
empirical [em'pɪrɪkl] adj empirisch.
employ [ɪm'plɔɪ] vt beschäftigen; (tool,
weapon) verwenden; **he's ~ed in a bank** er
ist bei einer Bank angestellt.
employee [ɪmplɔɪ'i:] n Angestellte(r) f(m).
employer [ɪm'plɔɪə'] n Arbeitgeber(in) f(m).
employment [ɪm'plɔɪmənt] n Arbeit f; **to find
~** Arbeit or eine (An)stellung finden;
without ~ stellungslos; **your place of ~** Ihre
Arbeitsstätte f.
employment agency n Stellenvermittlung f.
employment exchange (BRIT) n Arbeitsamt
nt.
empower [ɪm'pauə'] vt: **to ~ sb to do sth** jdn
ermächtigen, etw zu tun.
empress ['emprɪs] n Kaiserin f.
empties ['emptɪz] npl Leergut nt.
emptiness ['emptɪnɪs] n Leere f.
empty ['emptɪ] adj leer; (house, room) leer
stehend; (space) frei ♦ vt leeren; (place,
house etc) räumen ♦ vi sich leeren; (liquid)
abfließen; (river) münden; **on an ~ stomach**
auf nüchternen Magen; **to ~ into** (river)
münden or sich ergießen in +acc.
empty-handed ['emptɪ'hændɪd] adj mit leeren
Händen; **he returned ~** er kehrte
unverrichteter Dinge zurück.
empty-headed ['emptɪ'hedɪd] adj strohdumm.
EMS n abbr (= European Monetary System) EWS
nt.
EMT (US) n abbr (= emergency medical
technician) ≈ Sanitäter(in) m(f).
EMU n abbr (= economic and monetary union)

EWU f.
emu ['i:mju:] n Emu m.
emulate ['emjuleɪt] vt nacheifern +dat.
emulsion [ɪ'mʌlʃən] n Emulsion f; (also:
~ **paint**) Emulsionsfarbe f.
enable [ɪ'neɪbl] vt: **to ~ sb to do sth** (permit)
es jdm erlauben, etw zu tun; (make possible)
es jdm ermöglichen, etw zu tun.
enact [ɪ'nækt] vt (law) erlassen; (play)
aufführen; (role) darstellen, spielen.
enamel [ɪ'næməl] n Email nt, Emaille f; (also:
~ **paint**) Email(le)lack m; (of tooth)
Zahnschmelz m.
enamoured [ɪ'næməd] adj: **to be ~ of** (person)
verliebt sein in +acc; (pastime, idea, belief)
angetan sein von.
encampment [ɪn'kæmpmənt] n Lager nt.
encased [ɪn'keɪst] adj: ~ **in** (shell) umgeben
von; **to be ~ in** (limb) in Gips liegen or sein.
encash [ɪn'kæʃ] (BRIT) vt einlösen.
enchant [ɪn'tʃɑ:nt] vt bezaubern.
enchanted [ɪn'tʃɑ:ntɪd] adj verzaubert.
enchanting [ɪn'tʃɑ:ntɪŋ] adj bezaubernd.
encircle [ɪn'sɜ:kl] vt umgeben; (person)
umringen; (building: police etc) umstellen.
encl. abbr (on letters etc: = enclosed, enclosure)
Anl.
enclave ['enkleɪv] n: **an ~ (of)** eine Enklave
(+gen).
enclose [ɪn'kləuz] vt umgeben; (land, space)
begrenzen; (with fence) einzäunen; (letter
etc): **to ~ (with)** beilegen (+dat); **please find
~d** als Anlage übersenden wir Ihnen.
enclosure [ɪn'kləuʒə'] n eingefriedeter
Bereich m; (in letter etc) Anlage f.
encoder [ɪn'kəudə'] n Kodierer m.
encompass [ɪn'kʌmpəs] vt umfassen.
encore [ɔŋ'kɔ:'] excl Zugabe! ♦ n Zugabe f.
encounter [ɪn'kauntə'] n Begegnung f ♦ vt
begegnen +dat; (problem) stoßen auf +acc.
encourage [ɪn'kʌrɪdʒ] vt (activity, attitude)
unterstützen; (growth, industry) fördern; **to
~ sb (to do sth)** jdn ermutigen(, etw zu tun).
encouragement [ɪn'kʌrɪdʒmənt] n (see vb)
Unterstützung f; Förderung f; Ermutigung f.
encouraging [ɪn'kʌrɪdʒɪŋ] adj ermutigend.
encroach [ɪn'krəutʃ] vi: **to ~ (up)on** (rights)
eingreifen in +acc; (property) eindringen in
+acc; (time) in Anspruch nehmen.
encrusted [ɪn'krʌstɪd] adj: ~ **with** (gems)
besetzt mit; (snow, dirt) verkrustet mit.
encumber [ɪn'kʌmbə'] vt: **to be ~ed with**
beladen sein mit; (debts) belastet sein mit.
encyclop(a)edia [ensaɪkləu'pi:dɪə] n Lexikon
nt, Enzyklopädie f.
end [end] n Ende nt; (of film, book) Schluss m,
Ende nt; (of table) Schmalseite f; (of pointed
object) Spitze f; (aim) Zweck m, Ziel nt ♦ vt
(also: **bring to an ~**, **put an ~ to**) beenden
♦ vi enden; **from ~ to ~** von einem Ende
zum anderen; **to come to an ~** zu Ende
gehen; **to be at an ~** zu Ende sein; **in the ~**

schließlich; **on** ~ hochkant; **to stand on** ~ (*hair*) zu Berge stehen; **for hours on** ~ stundenlang ununterbrochen; **for 5 hours on** ~ 5 Stunden ununterbrochen; **at the** ~ **of the street** am Ende der Straße; **at the** ~ **of the day** (*BRIT, fig*) letztlich; **to this** ~, **with this** ~ in view mit diesem Ziel vor Augen.

▶ **end up** *vi*: **to** ~ **up in** (*place*) landen in +*dat*; **to** ~ **up in trouble** Ärger bekommen; **to** ~ **up doing sth** etw schließlich tun.

endanger [ɪn'deɪndʒəʳ] *vt* gefährden; **an** ~**ed species** eine vom Aussterben bedrohte Art.

endear [ɪn'dɪəʳ] *vt*: **to** ~ **o.s. to sb** sich bei jdm beliebt machen.

endearing [ɪn'dɪərɪŋ] *adj* gewinnend.

endearment [ɪn'dɪəmənt] *n*: **to whisper** ~**s** zärtliche Worte flüstern; **term of** ~ Kosewort *nt*, Kosename *m*.

endeavour, (*US*) **endeavor** [ɪn'dɛvəʳ] *n* Anstrengung *f*, Bemühung *f*; (*effort*) Bestrebung *f* ♦ *vi*: **to** ~ **to do sth** (*attempt*) sich anstrengen *or* bemühen, etw zu tun; (*strive*) bestrebt sein, etw zu tun.

endemic [ɛn'dɛmɪk] *adj* endemisch, verbreitet.

ending ['ɛndɪŋ] *n* Ende *nt*, Schluss *m*; (*LING*) Endung *f*.

endive ['ɛndaɪv] *n* Endivie *f*; (*chicory*) Chicorée *f or m*, Schikoree *f or m*.

endless ['ɛndlɪs] *adj* endlos; (*patience, resources, possibilities*) unbegrenzt.

endorse [ɪn'dɔːs] *vt* (*cheque*) indossieren, auf der Rückseite unterzeichnen; (*proposal, plan*) billigen; (*candidate*) unterstützen.

endorsee [ɪndɔː'siː] *n* Indossat *m*.

endorsement [ɪn'dɔːsmənt] *n* Billigung *f*; (*of candidate*) Unterstützung *f*; (*BRIT: on driving licence*) Strafvermerk *m*.

endow [ɪn'dau] *vt* (*institution*) eine Stiftung machen an +*acc*; **to be** ~**ed with** besitzen.

endowment [ɪn'daumənt] *n* Stiftung *f*; (*quality*) Begabung *f*.

endowment assurance *n* Versicherung *f* auf den Erlebensfall, Erlebens-versicherung *f*.

endowment mortgage *n* Hypothek *f* mit Lebensversicherung.

end product *n* Endprodukt *nt*; (*fig*) Produkt *nt*.

end result *n* Endergebnis *nt*.

endurable [ɪn'djuərəbl] *adj* erträglich.

endurance [ɪn'djuərəns] *n* Durchhaltevermögen *nt*; (*patience*) Geduld *f*.

endurance test *n* Belastungsprobe *f*.

endure [ɪn'djuəʳ] *vt* ertragen ♦ *vi* Bestand haben.

enduring [ɪn'djuərɪŋ] *adj* dauerhaft.

end user *n* (*COMPUT*) Endbenutzer *m*.

enema ['ɛnɪmə] *n* Klistier *nt*, Einlauf *m*.

enemy ['ɛnəmɪ] *adj* feindlich; (*strategy*) des Feindes ♦ *n* Feind(in) *m(f)*; **to make an** ~ **of sb** sich *dat* jdn zum Feind machen.

energetic [ɛnə'dʒɛtɪk] *adj* aktiv.

energy ['ɛnədʒɪ] *n* Energie *f*; **Department of E**~ Energieministerium *nt*.

energy crisis *n* Energiekrise *f*.

energy-saving ['ɛnədʒɪ'seɪvɪŋ] *adj* energiesparend; (*policy*) energiebewusst.

enervating ['ɛnəveɪtɪŋ] *adj* strapazierend.

enforce [ɪn'fɔːs] *vt* (*law, rule, decision*) Geltung verschaffen +*dat*.

enforced [ɪn'fɔːst] *adj* erzwungen.

enfranchise [ɪn'fræntʃaɪz] *vt* das Wahlrecht geben *or* erteilen +*dat*.

engage [ɪn'geɪdʒ] *vt* in Anspruch nehmen; (*employ*) einstellen; (*lawyer*) sich *dat* nehmen; (*MIL*) angreifen ♦ *vi* (*TECH*) einrasten; **to** ~ **the clutch** einkuppeln; **to** ~ **sb in conversation** jdn in ein Gespräch verwickeln; **to** ~ **in** sich beteiligen an +*dat*; **to** ~ **in commerce** kaufmännisch tätig sein; **to** ~ **in study** studieren.

engaged [ɪn'geɪdʒd] *adj* verlobt; (*BRIT: busy, in use*) besetzt; **to get** ~ sich verloben; **he is** ~ **in research/a survey** er ist mit Forschungsarbeit/einer Umfrage beschäftigt.

engaged tone *n* (*BRIT*) *n* Besetztzeichen *nt*.

engagement [ɪn'geɪdʒmənt] *n* Verabredung *f*; (*booking*) Engagement *nt*; (*to marry*) Verlobung *f*; (*MIL*) Gefecht *nt*, Kampf *m*; **I have a previous** ~ ich habe schon eine Verabredung.

engagement ring *n* Verlobungsring *m*.

engaging [ɪn'geɪdʒɪŋ] *adj* einnehmend.

engender [ɪn'dʒɛndəʳ] *vt* erzeugen.

engine ['ɛndʒɪn] *n* Motor *m*; (*RAIL*) Lok(omotive) *f*.

engine driver *n* (*RAIL*) Lok(omotiv)führer(in) *m(f)*.

engineer [ɛndʒɪ'nɪəʳ] *n* Ingenieur(in) *m(f)*; (*BRIT: for repairs*) Techniker(in) *m(f)*; (*US: RAIL*) Lok(omotiv)führer(in) *m(f)*; (*on ship*) Maschinist(in) *m(f)*; **civil/mechanical** ~ Bau-/Maschinenbauingenieur(in) *m(f)*.

engineering [ɛndʒɪ'nɪərɪŋ] *n* Technik *f*; (*design, construction*) Konstruktion *f* ♦ *cpd*: ~ **works** *or* **factory** Maschinenfabrik *f*.

engine failure *n* Maschinenschaden *m*; (*AUT*) Motorschaden *m*.

engine trouble *n* Maschinenschaden *m*; (*AUT*) Motorschaden *m*.

England ['ɪŋglənd] *n* England *nt*.

English ['ɪŋglɪʃ] *adj* englisch ♦ *n* Englisch *nt*; **the English** *npl* die Engländer *pl*; **an** ~ **speaker** *jd, der Englisch spricht*.

English Channel *n*: **the** ~ der Ärmelkanal.

Englishman ['ɪŋglɪʃmən] (*irreg: like* **man**) *n* Engländer *m*.

English-speaking ['ɪŋglɪʃ'spiːkɪŋ] *adj* (*country*) englischsprachig.

Englishwoman ['ɪŋglɪʃwumən] (*irreg: like* **woman**) *n* Engländerin *f*.

engrave [ɪn'greɪv] *vt* gravieren; (*name etc*)

eingravieren; (*fig*) einprägen.
engraving [ɪn'greɪvɪŋ] *n* Stich *m*.
engrossed [ɪn'grəʊst] *adj*: ~ **in** vertieft in *+acc*.
engulf [ɪn'gʌlf] *vt* verschlingen; (*subj: panic, fear*) überkommen.
enhance [ɪn'hɑːns] *vt* verbessern; (*enjoyment, beauty*) erhöhen.
enigma [ɪ'nɪgmə] *n* Rätsel *nt*.
enigmatic [ɛnɪg'mætɪk] *adj* rätselhaft.
enjoy [ɪn'dʒɔɪ] *vt* genießen; (*health, fortune*) sich erfreuen *+gen*; (*success*) haben; **to ~ o.s.** sich amüsieren; **I ~ dancing** ich tanze gerne.
enjoyable [ɪn'dʒɔɪəbl] *adj* nett, angenehm.
enjoyment [ɪn'dʒɔɪmənt] *n* Vergnügen *nt*; (*activity*) Freude *f*.
enlarge [ɪn'lɑːdʒ] *vt* vergrößern; (*scope*) erweitern ♦ *vi*: **to ~ on** weiter ausführen.
enlarged [ɪn'lɑːdʒd] *adj* erweitert; (*MED*) vergrößert.
enlargement [ɪn'lɑːdʒmənt] *n* Vergrößerung *f*.
enlighten [ɪn'laɪtn] *vt* aufklären.
enlightened [ɪn'laɪtnd] *adj* aufgeklärt.
enlightening [ɪn'laɪtnɪŋ] *adj* aufschlussreich.
enlightenment [ɪn'laɪtnmənt] *n* (*also HIST: Enlightenment*) Aufklärung *f*.
enlist [ɪn'lɪst] *vt* anwerben; (*support, help*) gewinnen ♦ *vi*: **to ~ in** eintreten in *+acc*; **~ed man** (*US: MIL*) gemeiner Soldat *m*; (*US: in navy*) Matrose *m*.
enliven [ɪn'laɪvn] *vt* beleben.
enmity ['ɛnmɪtɪ] *n* Feindschaft *f*.
ennoble [ɪ'nəʊbl] *vt* adeln; (*fig: dignify*) erheben.
enormity [ɪ'nɔːmɪtɪ] *n* ungeheure Größe *f*.
enormous [ɪ'nɔːməs] *adj* gewaltig, ungeheuer; (*pleasure, success etc*) riesig.
enormously [ɪ'nɔːməslɪ] *adv* enorm; (*rich*) ungeheuer.
enough [ɪ'nʌf] *adj* genug, genügend ♦ *pron* genug ♦ *adv*: **big ~** groß genug; **he has not worked ~** er hat nicht genug *or* genügend gearbeitet; **have you got ~?** haben Sie genug?; **~ to eat** genug zu essen; **will 5 be ~?** reichen 5?; **I've had ~!** jetzt reichts mir aber!; **it's hot ~ (as it is)** es ist heiß genug; **he was kind ~ to lend me the money** er war so gut und hat mir das Geld geliehen; **~! es** reicht!; **that's ~, thanks** danke, das reicht *or* ist genug; **I've had ~ of him** ich habe genug von ihm; **funnily/oddly ~** ... komischerweise ...
enquire [ɪn'kwaɪə*] *vt, vi* = **inquire**.
enrage [ɪn'reɪdʒ] *vt* wütend machen.
enrich [ɪn'rɪtʃ] *vt* bereichern.
enrol, (*US*) **enroll** [ɪn'rəʊl] *vt* anmelden; (*at university*) einschreiben, immatrikulieren ♦ *vi* (*see vt*) sich anmelden; sich einschreiben, sich immatrikulieren.
enrolment, (*US*) **enrollment** [ɪn'rəʊlmənt] *n*

(*v vb*) Anmeldung *f*; Einschreibung *f*, Immatrikulation *f*.
en route [ɔn'ruːt] *adv* unterwegs; ~ **for** auf dem Weg nach; ~ **from London to Berlin** auf dem Weg von London nach Berlin.
ensconced [ɪn'skɒnst] *adj*: **she is ~ in** ... sie hat es sich *dat* in ... *dat* gemütlich gemacht.
ensemble [ɔn'sɒmbl] *n* Ensemble *nt*.
enshrine [ɪn'ʃraɪn] *vt* bewahren; **to be ~d in** verankert sein in *+dat*.
ensue [ɪn'sjuː] *vi* folgen.
ensuing [ɪn'sjuːɪŋ] *adj* folgend.
ensure [ɪn'ʃuə*] *vt* garantieren; **to ~ that** sicherstellen, dass.
ENT *n abbr* (*MED: = ear, nose and throat*) HNO.
entail [ɪn'teɪl] *vt* mit sich bringen.
entangled [ɪn'tæŋgld] *adj*: **to become ~ (in)** sich verfangen (in *+dat*).
enter ['ɛntə*] *vt* betreten; (*club*) beitreten *+dat*; (*army*) gehen zu; (*profession*) ergreifen; (*race, contest*) sich beteiligen an *+dat*; (*sb for a competition*) anmelden; (*write down*) eintragen; (*COMPUT: data*) eingeben ♦ *vi* (*come in*) hereinkommen; (*go in*) hineingehen.
▸ **enter for** *vt fus* anmelden für.
▸ **enter into** *vt fus* (*discussion, negotiations*) aufnehmen; (*correspondence*) treten in *+acc*; (*agreement*) schließen.
▸ **enter up** *vt* eintragen.
▸ **enter (up)on** *vt fus* (*career, policy*) einschlagen.
enteritis [ɛntə'raɪtɪs] *n* Dünndarmentzündung *f*.
enterprise ['ɛntəpraɪz] *n* Unternehmen *nt*; (*initiative*) Initiative *f*; **free ~** freies Unternehmertum *nt*; **private ~** Privatunternehmertum *nt*.
enterprising ['ɛntəpraɪzɪŋ] *adj* einfallsreich.
entertain [ɛntə'teɪn] *vt* unterhalten; (*invite*) einladen; (*idea, plan*) erwägen.
entertainer [ɛntə'teɪnə*] *n* Unterhalter(in) *m(f)*, Entertainer(in) *m(f)*.
entertaining [ɛntə'teɪnɪŋ] *adj* amüsant ♦ *n*: **to do a lot of ~** sehr oft Gäste haben.
entertainment [ɛntə'teɪnmənt] *n* Unterhaltung *f*; (*show*) Darbietung *f*.
entertainment allowance *n* Aufwandspauschale *f*.
enthral [ɪn'θrɔːl] *vt* begeistern; (*story*) fesseln.
enthralled [ɪn'θrɔːld] *adj* gefesselt; **he was ~ by** *or* **with the book** das Buch fesselte ihn.
enthralling [ɪn'θrɔːlɪŋ] *adj* fesselnd; (*details*) spannend.
enthuse [ɪn'θuːz] *vi*: **to ~ about** *or* **over** schwärmen von.
enthusiasm [ɪn'θuːzɪæzəm] *n* Begeisterung *f*.
enthusiast [ɪn'θuːzɪæst] *n* Enthusiast(in) *m(f)*; **he's a jazz/sports ~** er begeistert sich für Jazz/Sport.
enthusiastic [ɪnθuːzɪ'æstɪk] *adj* begeistert; (*response, reception*) enthusiastisch; **to be**

~ **about** begeistert sein von.

entice [ɪn'taɪs] *vt* locken; (*tempt*) verleiten.

enticing [ɪn'taɪsɪŋ] *adj* verlockend.

entire [ɪn'taɪə*] *adj* ganz.

entirely [ɪn'taɪəlɪ] *adv* völlig.

entirety [ɪn'taɪərətɪ] *n*: **in its** ~ in seiner Gesamtheit.

entitle [ɪn'taɪtl] *vt*: **to** ~ **sb to sth** jdn zu etw berechtigen; **to** ~ **sb to do sth** jdn dazu berechtigen, etw zu tun.

entitled [ɪn'taɪtld] *adj*: **a book/film** *etc* ~ ... ein Buch/Film *etc* mit dem Titel ...; **to be** ~ **to do sth** das Recht haben, etw zu tun.

entity ['ɛntɪtɪ] *n* Wesen *nt*.

entourage [ɔntu'rɑːʒ] *n* Gefolge *nt*.

entrails ['ɛntreɪlz] *npl* Eingeweide *pl*.

entrance [*n* 'ɛntrns, *vt* ɪn'trɑːns] *n* Eingang *m*; (*arrival*) Ankunft *f*; (*on stage*) Auftritt *m* ♦ *vt* bezaubern; **to gain** ~ **to** (*building etc*) sich *dat* Zutritt verschaffen zu; (*university*) die Zulassung erhalten zu; (*profession etc*) Zugang erhalten zu.

entrance examination *n* Aufnahmeprüfung *f*.

entrance fee *n* Eintrittsgeld *nt*.

entrance ramp (*US*) *n* Auffahrt *f*.

entrancing [ɪn'trɑːnsɪŋ] *adj* bezaubernd.

entrant ['ɛntrnt] *n* Teilnehmer(in) *m(f)*; (*BRIT*: *in exam*) Prüfling *m*.

entreat [ɛn'triːt] *vt*: **to** ~ **sb to do sth** jdn anflehen, etw zu tun.

entreaty [ɛn'triːtɪ] *n* (flehentliche) Bitte *f*.

entrée ['ɔntreɪ] *n* Hauptgericht *nt*.

entrenched [ɛn'trɛntʃt] *adj* verankert; (*ideas*) festgesetzt.

entrepreneur ['ɔntrəprə'nɜː*] *n* Unternehmer(in) *m(f)*.

entrepreneurial ['ɔntrəprə'nɜːrɪəl] *adj* unternehmerisch.

entrust [ɪn'trʌst] *vt*: **to** ~ **sth to sb** jdm etw anvertrauen; **to** ~ **sb with sth** (*task*) jdn mit etw betrauen; (*secret, valuables*) jdm etw anvertrauen.

entry ['ɛntrɪ] *n* Eingang *m*; (*in competition*) Meldung *f*; (*in register, account book, reference book*) Eintrag *m*; (*arrival*) Eintritt *m*; (*to country*) Einreise *f*; **"no** ~**"** „Zutritt verboten"; (*AUT*) „Einfahrt verboten"; **single/double** ~ **book-keeping** einfache/doppelte Buchführung *f*.

entry form *n* Anmeldeformular *nt*.

entry phone (*BRIT*) *n* Türsprechanlage *f*.

entwine [ɪn'twaɪn] *vt* verflechten.

enumerate [ɪ'njuːməreɪt] *vt* aufzählen.

enunciate [ɪ'nʌnsɪeɪt] *vt* artikulieren; (*principle, plan etc*) formulieren.

envelop [ɪn'vɛləp] *vt* einhüllen.

envelope ['ɛnvələup] *n* Umschlag *m*.

enviable ['ɛnvɪəbl] *adj* beneidenswert.

envious ['ɛnvɪəs] *adj* neidisch; **to be** ~ **of sth/sb** auf etw/jdn neidisch sein.

environment [ɪn'vaɪərnmənt] *n* Umwelt *f*;

Department of the E~ (*BRIT*) Umweltministerium *nt*.

environmental [ɪnvaɪərn'mɛntl] *adj* (*problems, pollution etc*) Umwelt-; ~ **studies** Umweltkunde *f*.

environmentalist [ɪnvaɪərn'mɛntlɪst] *n* Umweltschützer(in) *m(f)*.

Environmental Protection Agency (*US*) *n* staatliche Umweltbehörde der USA.

environment-friendly *adj* umweltfreundlich.

envisage [ɪn'vɪzɪdʒ] *vt* sich *dat* vorstellen; **I** ~ **that** ... ich stelle mir vor, dass ...

envision [ɪn'vɪʒən] (*US*) *vt* = **envisage**.

envoy ['ɛnvɔɪ] *n* Gesandte(r) *f(m)*.

envy ['ɛnvɪ] *n* Neid *m* ♦ *vt* beneiden; **to** ~ **sb sth** jdn um etw beneiden.

enzyme ['ɛnzaɪm] *n* Enzym *nt*.

eon ['iːən] *n* Äon *m*, Ewigkeit *f*.

EPA (*US*) *n abbr* = **Environmental Protection Agency**.

ephemeral [ɪ'fɛmərl] *adj* kurzlebig.

epic ['ɛpɪk] *n* Epos *nt* ♦ *adj* (*journey*) lang und abenteuerlich.

epicentre, (*US*) **epicenter** ['ɛpɪsentə*] *n* Epizentrum *nt*.

epidemic [ɛpɪ'dɛmɪk] *n* Epidemie *f*.

epigram ['ɛpɪgræm] *n* Epigramm *nt*.

epilepsy ['ɛpɪlɛpsɪ] *n* Epilepsie *f*.

epileptic [ɛpɪ'lɛptɪk] *adj* epileptisch ♦ *n* Epileptiker(in) *m(f)*.

epilogue ['ɛpɪlɔg] *n* Epilog *m*, Nachwort *nt*.

Epiphany [ɪ'pɪfənɪ] *n* Dreikönigsfest *nt*.

episcopal [ɪ'pɪskəpl] *adj* bischöflich; **the E**~ **Church** die Episkopalkirche.

episode ['ɛpɪsəud] *n* Episode *f*; (*TV, RADIO*) Folge *f*.

epistle [ɪ'pɪsl] *n* Epistel *f*; (*REL*) Brief *m*.

epitaph ['ɛpɪtɑːf] *n* Epitaph *nt*; (*on gravestone etc*) Grab(in)schrift *f*.

epithet ['ɛpɪθɛt] *n* Beiname *m*.

epitome [ɪ'pɪtəmɪ] *n* Inbegriff *m*.

epitomize [ɪ'pɪtəmaɪz] *vt* verkörpern.

epoch ['iːpɔk] *n* Epoche *f*.

epoch-making ['iːpɔkmeɪkɪŋ] *adj* epochal; (*discovery*) Epoche machend.

eponymous [ɪ'pɔnɪməs] *adj* namengebend.

equable ['ɛkwəbl] *adj* ausgeglichen; (*reply*) sachlich.

equal ['iːkwl] *adj* gleich ♦ *n* Gleichgestellte(r) *f(m)* ♦ *vt* gleichkommen +*dat*; (*number*) gleich sein +*dat*; **they are roughly** ~ **in size** sie sind ungefähr gleich groß; **the number of exports should be** ~ **to imports** Export- und Importzahlen sollten gleich sein; ~ **opportunities** Chancengleichheit *f*; **to be** ~ **to** (*task*) gewachsen sein +*dat*; **two times two** ~**s four** zwei mal zwei ist (gleich) vier.

equality [iː'kwɔlɪtɪ] *n* Gleichheit *f*; ~ **of opportunity** Chancengleichheit *f*.

equalize ['iːkwəlaɪz] *vt* angleichen ♦ *vi* (*SPORT*) ausgleichen.

equally ['i:kwəlɪ] *adv* gleichmäßig; (*good, bad etc*) gleich; **they are ~ clever** sie sind beide gleich klug.

Equal Opportunities Commission, (*US*) **Equal Employment Opportunity Commission** *n* Ausschuss *m* für Chancengleichheit am Arbeitsplatz.

equal(s) sign *n* Gleichheitszeichen *nt*.

equanimity [ɛkwə'nɪmɪtɪ] *n* Gleichmut *m*, Gelassenheit *f*.

equate [ɪ'kweɪt] *vt*: **to ~ sth with** etw gleichsetzen mit ♦ *vt* (*compare*) auf die gleiche Stufe stellen; **to ~ A to B** A und B auf die gleiche Stufe stellen.

equation [ɪ'kweɪʃən] *n* Gleichung *f*.

equator [ɪ'kweɪtə*] *n* Äquator *m*.

equatorial [ɛkwə'tɔːrɪəl] *adj* äquatorial.

Equatorial Guinea *n* Äquatorial-Guinea *nt*.

equestrian [ɪ'kwɛstrɪən] *adj* (*sport, dress etc*) Reit-; (*statue*) Reiter- ♦ *n* Reiter(in) *m(f)*.

equilibrium [i:kwɪ'lɪbrɪəm] *n* Gleichgewicht *nt*.

equinox ['i:kwɪnɔks] *n* Tagundnachtgleiche *f*; **the spring/autumn ~** die Frühjahrs-/die Herbst-Tagundnachtgleiche *f*.

equip [ɪ'kwɪp] *vt*: **to ~ (with)** (*person, army*) ausrüsten (mit); (*room, car etc*) ausstatten (mit); **to ~ sb for** jdn vorbereiten auf +*acc*; **to be well ~ped** gut ausgerüstet sein.

equipment [ɪ'kwɪpmənt] *n* Ausrüstung *f*.

equitable ['ɛkwɪtəbl] *adj* gerecht.

equities ['ɛkwɪtɪz] (*BRIT*) *npl* Stammaktien *pl*.

equity ['ɛkwɪtɪ] *n* Gerechtigkeit *f*.

equity capital *n* Eigenkapital *nt*.

equivalent [ɪ'kwɪvələnt] *adj* gleich, gleichwertig ♦ *n* Gegenstück *nt*; **to be ~ to** *or* **the ~ of** entsprechen +*dat*.

equivocal [ɪ'kwɪvəkl] *adj* vieldeutig; (*open to suspicion*) zweifelhaft.

equivocate [ɪ'kwɪvəkeɪt] *vi* ausweichen, ausweichend antworten.

equivocation [ɪkwɪvə'keɪʃən] *n* Ausflucht *f*, ausweichende Antwort *f*.

ER (*BRIT*) *abbr* (= *Elizabeth Regina*) *offizieller Namenszug der Königin*.

ERA (*US*) *n abbr* (*POL*: = *Equal Rights Amendment*) *Artikel der amerikanischen Verfassung zur Gleichberechtigung*; (*BASEBALL*: = *earned run average*) *durch Eigenleistung erzielte Läufe*.

era ['ɪərə] *n* Ära *f*, Epoche *f*.

eradicate [ɪ'rædɪkeɪt] *vt* ausrotten.

erase [ɪ'reɪz] *vt* (*tape, COMPUT*) löschen; (*writing*) ausradieren; (*thought, feeling*) auslöschen.

eraser [ɪ'reɪzə*] *n* Radiergummi *m*.

erect [ɪ'rɛkt] *adj* aufrecht; (*tail*) hoch erhoben; (*ears*) gespitzt ♦ *vt* bauen; (*assemble*) aufstellen.

erection [ɪ'rɛkʃən] *n* Bauen *nt*; (*of statue*) Errichten *nt*; (*of tent, machinery etc*) Aufstellen *nt*; (*PHYSIOL*) Erektion *f*.

ergonomics [ə:gə'nɔmɪks] *n sing* Ergonomie *f*, Ergonomik *f*.

ERISA (*US*) *n abbr* (= *Employee Retirement Income Security Act*) *Gesetz zur Regelung der Rentenversicherung*.

Eritrea *n* Eritrea *nt*.

ERM *n abbr* (= *Exchange Rate Mechanism*) Wechselkursmechanismus *m*.

ermine ['ə:mɪn] *n* (*fur*) Hermelin *m*.

ERNIE, Ernie ['ə:nɪ] (*BRIT*) *n abbr* (= *Electronic Random Number Indicator Equipment*) *Gerät zur Ermittlung von Gewinnnummern für Prämiensparer*.

erode [ɪ'rəud] *vt* erodieren, auswaschen; (*metal*) zerfressen; (*confidence, power*) untergraben.

erogenous [ɪ'rɔdʒənəs] *adj* erogen.

erosion [ɪ'rəuʒən] *n* (*see vb*) Erosion *f*, Auswaschen *nt*; Zerfressen *nt*; Untergraben *nt*.

erotic [ɪ'rɔtɪk] *adj* erotisch.

eroticism [ɪ'rɔtɪsɪzəm] *n* Erotik *f*.

err [ə:*] *vi* sich irren; **to ~ on the side of caution/simplicity** (im Zweifelsfall) zur Vorsicht/Vereinfachung neigen.

errand ['ɛrənd] *n* Besorgung *f*; (*to give a message etc*) Botengang *m*; **to run ~s** Besorgungen/Botengänge machen; **~ of mercy** Rettungsaktion *f*.

erratic [ɪ'rætɪk] *adj* unberechenbar; (*attempts*) unkoordiniert; (*noise*) unregelmäßig.

erroneous [ɪ'rəunɪəs] *adj* irrig.

error ['ɛrə*] *n* Fehler *m*; **typing/spelling ~** Tipp-/Rechtschreibfehler *m*; **in ~** irrtümlicherweise; **~s and omissions excepted** Irrtum vorbehalten.

error message *n* Fehlermeldung *f*.

erstwhile ['ə:stwaɪl] *adj* einstig, vormalig.

erudite ['ɛrjudaɪt] *adj* gelehrt.

erupt [ɪ'rʌpt] *vi* ausbrechen.

eruption [ɪ'rʌpʃən] *n* Ausbruch *m*.

ESA *n abbr* (= *European Space Agency*) Europäische Weltraumbehörde *f*.

escalate ['ɛskəleɪt] *vi* eskalieren, sich ausweiten.

escalation [ɛskə'leɪʃən] *n* Eskalation *f*.

escalator ['ɛskəleɪtə*] *n* Rolltreppe *f*.

escalator clause *n* Gleitklausel *f*.

escapade [ɛskə'peɪd] *n* Eskapade *f*.

escape [ɪs'keɪp] *n* Flucht *f*; (*TECH: of liquid*) Ausfließen *nt*; (*of gas*) Ausströmen *nt*; (*of air, heat*) Entweichen *nt* ♦ *vi* entkommen; (*from prison*) ausbrechen; (*liquid*) ausfließen; (*gas*) ausströmen; (*air, heat*) entweichen ♦ *vt* (*pursuers etc*) entkommen +*dat*; (*punishment etc*) entgehen +*dat*; **his name ~s me** sein Name ist mir entfallen; **to ~ from** flüchten aus; (*prison*) ausbrechen aus; (*person*) entkommen +*dat*; **to ~ to Peru** nach Peru fliehen; **to ~ to safety** sich in Sicherheit bringen; **to ~ notice** unbemerkt bleiben.

escape artist *n* Entfesselungskünstler(in)

m(f).

escape clause *n (in contract)*
Befreiungsklausel *f*.

escapee [ɪskeɪ'piː] *n* entwichener Häftling *m*.

escape hatch *n* Notluke *f*.

escape key *n (COMPUT)* Escape-Taste *f*.

escape route *n* Fluchtweg *m*.

escapism [ɪs'keɪpɪzəm] *n* Wirklichkeitsflucht *f*, Eskapismus *m*.

escapist [ɪs'keɪpɪst] *adj* eskapistisch.

escapologist [ɛskə'pɔlədʒɪst] *(BRIT)* *n* = **escape artist**.

escarpment [ɪs'kɑːpmənt] *n* Steilhang *m*.

eschew [ɪs'tʃuː] *vt* meiden.

escort [*n* 'ɛskɔːt, *vt* ɪs'kɔːt] *n* Eskorte *f*; *(companion)* Begleiter(in) *m(f)* ♦ *vt* begleiten; **his** ~ seine Begleiterin; **her** ~ ihr Begleiter.

escort agency *n* Agentur *f* für Begleiter(innen).

Eskimo ['ɛskɪməu] *n* Eskimo(frau) *m(f)*.

ESL *n abbr (SCOL:* = *English as a Second Language)* Englisch *nt* als Zweitsprache.

esophagus [iː'sɔfəgəs] *(US)* *n* = **oesophagus**.

esoteric [ɛsə'tɛrɪk] *adj* esoterisch.

ESP *n abbr* = **extrasensory perception**; *(SCOL:* = *English for Special Purposes)* Englischunterricht *für spezielle Fachbereiche*.

esp. *abbr* = **especially**.

especially [ɪs'pɛʃlɪ] *adv* besonders.

espionage ['ɛspɪənɑːʒ] *n* Spionage *f*.

esplanade [ɛsplə'neɪd] *n* Promenade *f*.

espouse [ɪs'pauz] *vt* eintreten für.

Esquire [ɪs'kwaɪə*] *n (abbr Esq.):* **J. Brown, ~** Herrn J. Brown.

essay ['ɛseɪ] *n* Aufsatz *m*; *(LITER)* Essay *m or nt*.

essence ['ɛsns] *n* Wesen *nt*; *(CULIN)* Essenz *f*; **in ~** im Wesentlichen; **speed is of the ~** Geschwindigkeit ist von entscheidender Bedeutung.

essential [ɪ'sɛnʃl] *adj* notwendig; *(basic)* wesentlich ♦ *n (see adj)* Notwendigste(s) *nt*; Wesentliche(s) *nt*; **it is ~ that** es ist unbedingt *or* absolut erforderlich, dass.

essentially [ɪ'sɛnʃəlɪ] *adv* im Grunde genommen.

EST *(US)* *abbr* (= *Eastern Standard Time)* ostamerikanische Standardzeit.

est. *abbr* = **established, estimate(d)**.

establish [ɪs'tæblɪʃ] *vt* gründen; *(facts)* feststellen; *(proof)* erstellen; *(relations, contact)* aufnehmen; *(reputation)* sich *dat* verschaffen.

established [ɪs'tæblɪʃt] *adj* üblich; *(business)* eingeführt.

establishment [ɪs'tæblɪʃmənt] *n (see vb)* Gründung *f*; Feststellung *f*; Erstellung *f*; Aufnahme *f*; *(of reputation)* Begründung *f*; *(shop etc)* Unternehmen *nt*; **the E~** das Establishment.

estate [ɪs'teɪt] *n* Gut *nt*; *(BRIT: also:* **housing ~**) Siedlung *f*; *(LAW)* Nachlass *m*.

estate agency *(BRIT)* *n* Maklerbüro *nt*.

estate agent *(BRIT)* *n* Immobilienmakler(in) *m(f)*.

estate car *(BRIT)* *n* Kombiwagen *m*.

esteem [ɪs'tiːm] *n:* **to hold sb in high ~** eine hohe Meinung von jdm haben.

esthetic [ɪs'θɛtɪk] *(US)* *adj* = **aesthetic**.

estimate ['ɛstɪmət] *n* Schätzung *f*; *(assessment)* Einschätzung *f*; *(COMM)* (Kosten)voranschlag *m* ♦ *vt* schätzen ♦ *vi* *(BRIT: COMM):* **to ~** für einen Kostenvoranschlag machen für; **to give sb an ~ of sth** jdm eine Schätzung von etw geben; **to ~ for** einen Kostenvoranschlag machen für; **at a rough ~** grob geschätzt, über den Daumen gepeilt *(inf)*; **I ~ that** ich schätze, dass.

estimation [ɛstɪ'meɪʃən] *n* Schätzung *f*; *(opinion)* Einschätzung *f*; **in my ~** meiner Einschätzung nach.

estimator ['ɛstɪmeɪtə*] *n* Schätzer(in) *m(f)*.

Estonia [ɛs'təunɪə] *n* Estland *nt*.

Estonian [ɛs'təunɪən] *adj* estnisch ♦ *n* Este *m*, Estin *f*; *(LING)* Estnisch *nt*.

estranged [ɪs'treɪndʒd] *adj* entfremdet; *(from spouse)* getrennt; *(couple)* getrennt lebend.

estrangement [ɪs'treɪndʒmənt] *n* Entfremdung *f*; *(from spouse)* Trennung *f*.

estrogen ['iːstrəudʒən] *(US)* *n* = **oestrogen**.

estuary ['ɛstjuərɪ] *n* Mündung *f*.

ET *(BRIT)* *n abbr* (= *Employment Training)* Ausbildungsmaßnahmen *für Arbeitslose*.

ETA *n abbr* (= *estimated time of arrival)* voraussichtliche Ankunftszeit *f*.

et al. *abbr* (= *et alii)* u. a.

etc. *abbr* (= *et cetera)* etc.

etch [ɛtʃ] *vt (design, surface:* **with needle)** radieren; *(: with acid)* ätzen; *(: with chisel)* meißeln; **it will be ~ed on my memory** es wird sich tief in mein Gedächtnis eingraben.

etching ['ɛtʃɪŋ] *n* Radierung *f*.

ETD *n abbr* (= *estimated time of departure)* voraussichtliche Abflugzeit *f*.

eternal [ɪ'təːnl] *adj* ewig.

eternity [ɪ'təːnɪtɪ] *n* Ewigkeit *f*.

ether ['iːθə*] *n* Äther *m*.

ethereal [ɪ'θɪərɪəl] *adj* ätherisch.

ethical ['ɛθɪkl] *adj* ethisch.

ethics ['ɛθɪks] *n* Ethik *f* ♦ *npl (morality)* Moral *f*.

Ethiopia [iːθɪ'əupɪə] *n* Äthiopien *nt*.

Ethiopian [iːθɪ'əupɪən] *adj* äthiopisch ♦ *n* Äthiopier(in) *m(f)*.

ethnic ['ɛθnɪk] *adj* ethnisch; *(music)* folkloristisch; *(culture etc)* urwüchsig.

ethnic cleansing [-'klɛnzɪŋ] *n* ethnische Säuberung *f*.

ethnic minority *n* ethnische Minderheit *f*.

ethnology [ɛθ'nɔlədʒɪ] *n* Ethnologie *f*, Völkerkunde *f*.

ethos ['iːθɔs] *n* Ethos *nt*.

etiquette ['ɛtɪkɛt] *n* Etikette *f*.

ETV (*US*) *n abbr* (= *educational television*) Fernsehsender, der Bildungs- und Kulturprogramme ausstrahlt.

etymology [etɪ'mɔlədʒɪ] *n* Etymologie *f*; (*of word*) Herkunft *f*.

EU *n abbr* (= *European Union*) EU *f*.

eucalyptus [juːkə'lɪptəs] *n* Eukalyptus *m*.

Eucharist ['juːkərɪst] *n*: **the** ~ die Eucharistie, das (heilige) Abendmahl.

eulogy ['juːlədʒɪ] *n* Lobrede *f*.

euphemism ['juːfəmɪzəm] *n* Euphemismus *m*.

euphemistic [juːfə'mɪstɪk] *adj* euphemistisch, verhüllend.

euphoria [juː'fɔːrɪə] *n* Euphorie *f*.

Eurasia [juə'reɪʒə] *n* Eurasien *nt*.

Eurasian [juə'reɪʃən] *adj* eurasisch ♦ *n* Eurasier(in) *m(f)*.

Euratom [juə'rætəm] *n abbr* (= *European Atomic Energy Community*) Euratom *f*.

euro ['juərəu] *n* (*FIN*) Euro *m*.

Euro- ['juərəu] *pref* Euro-.

Eurocheque ['juərəutʃɛk] *n* Euroscheck *m*.

Eurocrat ['juərəukræt] *n* Eurokrat(in) *m(f)*.

Eurodollar ['juərəudɔlə*] *n* Eurodollar *m*.

Euroland ['juərəulænd] *n* (*FIN*) Eurozone *f*.

Europe ['juərəp] *n* Europa *nt*.

European [juərə'piːən] *adj* europäisch ♦ *n* Europäer(in) *m(f)*.

European Central Bank *n*: **the** ~ die Europäische Zentralbank.

European Community *n*: **the** ~ die Europäische Gemeinschaft.

European Court of Justice *n*: **the** ~ der Europäische Gerichtshof.

European Economic Community *n* (*formerly*): **the** ~ die Europäische Wirtschaftsgemeinschaft.

Euro-sceptic ['juərəuskeptɪk] *n* Euroskeptiker(in) *m(f)*.

euthanasia [juːθə'neɪzɪə] *n* Euthanasie *f*.

evacuate [ɪ'vækjueɪt] *vt* evakuieren; (*place*) räumen.

evacuation [ɪvækju'eɪʃən] *n* (*see verb*) Evakuierung *f*; Räumung *f*.

evacuee [ɪvækju'iː] *n* Evakuierte(r) *f(m)*.

evade [ɪ'veɪd] *vt* (*person, question*) ausweichen +*dat*; (*tax*) hinterziehen; (*duty, responsibility*) sich entziehen +*dat*.

evaluate [ɪ'væljueɪt] *vt* bewerten; (*situation*) einschätzen.

evangelical [iːvæn'dʒelɪkl] *adj* evangelisch.

evangelist [ɪ'vændʒəlɪst] *n* Evangelist(in) *m(f)*.

evangelize [ɪ'vændʒəlaɪz] *vi* evangelisieren.

evaporate [ɪ'væpəreɪt] *vi* verdampfen; (*feeling, attitude*) dahinschwinden.

evaporated milk [ɪ'væpəreɪtɪd-] *n* Kondensmilch *f*, Büchsenmilch *f*.

evaporation [ɪvæpə'reɪʃən] *n* Verdampfung *f*.

evasion [ɪ'veɪʒən] *n* Ausweichen *nt*; (*of tax*) Hinterziehung *f*.

evasive [ɪ'veɪsɪv] *adj* ausweichend; **to take** ~ **action** ein Ausweichmanöver machen.

eve [iːv] *n*: **on the** ~ **of** am Tag vor +*dat*; **Christmas E**~ Heiligabend *m*; **New Year's E**~ Silvester *m or nt*.

even ['iːvn] *adj* (*level*) eben; (*smooth*) glatt; (*equal*) gleich; (*number*) gerade ♦ *adv* sogar, selbst; (*introducing a comparison*) sogar noch; ~ **if**, ~ **though** selbst wenn; ~ **more** sogar noch mehr; **he loves her** ~ **more** er liebt sie umso mehr; **it's going** ~ **faster now** es fährt jetzt sogar noch schneller; ~ **so** (aber) trotzdem; **not** ~ nicht einmal; ~ **he was there** sogar er war da; **to break** ~ die Kosten decken; **to get** ~ **with sb** es jdm heimzahlen.
  ► **even out** *vi* sich ausgleichen ♦ *vt* ausgleichen.

even-handed ['iːvnhændɪd] *adj* gerecht.

evening ['iːvnɪŋ] *n* Abend *m*; **in the** ~ abends, am Abend; **this** ~ heute Abend; **tomorrow/yesterday** ~ morgen/gestern Abend.

evening class *n* Abendkurs *m*.

evening dress *n* (*no pl*) Abendkleidung *f*; (*woman's*) Abendkleid *nt*.

evenly ['iːvnlɪ] *adv* gleichmäßig.

evensong ['iːvnsɔŋ] *n* Abendandacht *f*.

event [ɪ'vent] *n* Ereignis *nt*; (*SPORT*) Wettkampf *m*; **in the normal course of** ~**s** normalerweise; **in the** ~ **of** im Falle +*gen*; **in the** ~ schließlich; **at all** ~**s** (*BRIT*), **in any** ~ auf jeden Fall.

eventful [ɪ'ventful] *adj* ereignisreich.

eventing [ɪ'ventɪŋ] *n* (*HORSERIDING*) Military *f*.

eventual [ɪ'ventʃuəl] *adj* schließlich; (*goal*) letztlich.

eventuality [ɪventʃu'ælɪtɪ] *n* Eventualität *f*.

eventually [ɪ'ventʃuəlɪ] *adv* endlich; (*in time*) schließlich.

ever ['ɛvə*] *adv* immer; (*at any time*) je(mals); **why** ~ **not?** warum denn bloß nicht?; **the best** ~ der/die/das Allerbeste; **have you** ~ **seen it?** haben Sie es schon einmal gesehen?; **for** ~ für immer; **hardly** ~ kaum je(mals); **better than** ~ besser als je zuvor; ~ **since** adv seitdem ♦ *conj* seit, seitdem; ~ **so pretty** unheimlich hübsch (*inf*); **thank you** ~ **so much** ganz herzlichen Dank; **yours** ~ (*BRIT: in letters*) alles Liebe.

Everest ['ɛvərɪst] *n* (*also:* **Mount** ~) Mount Everest *m*.

evergreen ['ɛvəgriːn] *n* (*tree/bush*) immergrüner Baum/Strauch *m*.

everlasting [ɛvə'lɑːstɪŋ] *adj* ewig.

════════════════════ *KEYWORD*

every ['ɛvrɪ] *adj* **1** jede(r, s); ~ **one of them** (*persons*) jede(r) (Einzelne) von ihnen; (*objects*) jedes einzelne Stück; ~ **day** jeden Tag; ~ **week** jede Woche; ~ **other car** jedes zweite Auto; ~ **other/third day** alle zwei/drei Tage; ~ **shop in the town was closed** alle Geschäfte der Stadt waren

geschlossen; ~ **now and then** ab und zu, hin und wieder.
2 (*all possible*): **I have** ~ **confidence in him** ich habe volles Vertrauen in ihn; **we wish you** ~ **success** wir wünschen Ihnen alles Gute.

everybody ['ɛvrɪbɔdɪ] *pron* jeder, alle *pl*; ~ **knows about it** alle wissen es; ~ **else** alle anderen *pl*.
everyday ['ɛvrɪdeɪ] *adj* täglich; (*usual, common*) alltäglich; (*life, language*) Alltags-.
everyone ['ɛvrɪwʌn] *pron* = **everybody**.
everything ['ɛvrɪθɪŋ] *pron* alles; **he did** ~ **possible** er hat sein Möglichstes getan.
everywhere ['ɛvrɪwɛə*] *adv* überall; (*wherever*) wo auch *or* immer; ~ **you go you meet** ... wo man auch *or* wo immer man hingeht, trifft man ...
evict [ɪ'vɪkt] *vt* zur Räumung zwingen.
eviction [ɪ'vɪkʃən] *n* Ausweisung *f*.
eviction notice *n* Räumungskündigung *f*.
eviction order *n* Räumungsbefehl *m*.
evidence ['ɛvɪdns] *n* Beweis *m*; (*of witness*) Aussage *f*; (*sign, indication*) Zeichen *nt*, Spur *f*; **to give** ~ (als Zeuge) aussagen; **to show** ~ **of** zeigen; **in** ~ sichtbar.
evident ['ɛvɪdnt] *adj* offensichtlich.
evidently ['ɛvɪdntlɪ] *adv* offensichtlich.
evil ['iːvl] *adj* böse; (*influence*) schlecht ♦ *n* Böse(s) *nt*; (*unpleasant situation or activity*) Übel *nt*.
evocative [ɪ'vɔkətɪv] *adj* evokativ.
evoke [ɪ'vəuk] *vt* hervorrufen; (*memory*) wecken.
evolution [iːvə'luːʃən] *n* Evolution *f*; (*development*) Entwicklung *f*.
evolve [ɪ'vɔlv] *vt* entwickeln ♦ *vi* sich entwickeln.
ewe [juː] *n* Mutterschaf *nt*.
ewer ['juːə*] *n* (Wasser)krug *m*.
ex- [ɛks] *pref* Ex-, frühere(r, s); **the price** ~ **works** der Preis ab Werk.
exacerbate [ɛks'æsəbeɪt] *vt* verschärfen; (*pain*) verschlimmern.
exact [ɪg'zækt] *adj* genau; (*word*) richtig ♦ *vt*: **to** ~ **sth (from)** etw verlangen (von); (*payment*) etw eintreiben (von).
exacting [ɪg'zæktɪŋ] *adj* anspruchsvoll.
exactly [ɪg'zæktlɪ] *adv* genau; ~! (ganz) genau!; **not** ~ (*hardly*) nicht gerade.
exaggerate [ɪg'zædʒəreɪt] *vt, vi* übertreiben.
exaggerated [ɪg'zædʒəreɪtɪd] *adj* übertrieben.
exaggeration [ɪgzædʒə'reɪʃən] *n* Übertreibung *f*.
exalt [ɪg'zɔːlt] *vt* preisen.
exalted [ɪg'zɔːltɪd] *adj* hoch; (*elated*) exaltiert.
exam [ɪg'zæm] *n abbr* = **examination**.
examination [ɪgzæmɪ'neɪʃən] *n* (*see vb*) Untersuchung *f*; Prüfung *f*; Verhör *nt*; **to take** *or* (*BRIT*) **sit an** ~ eine Prüfung machen; **the matter is under** ~ die Angelegenheit

wird geprüft *or* untersucht.
examine [ɪg'zæmɪn] *vt* untersuchen; (*accounts, candidate*) prüfen; (*witness*) verhören.
examiner [ɪg'zæmɪnə*] *n* Prüfer(in) *m(f)*.
example [ɪg'zɑːmpl] *n* Beispiel *nt*; **for** ~ zum Beispiel; **to set a good/bad** ~ ein gutes/ schlechtes Beispiel geben.
exasperate [ɪg'zɑːspəreɪt] *vt* (*annoy*) verärgern; (*frustrate*) zur Verzweiflung bringen; ~**d by** *or* **with** verärgert/ verzweifelt über +*acc*.
exasperating [ɪg'zɑːspəreɪtɪŋ] *adj* ärgerlich; (*job*) leidig.
exasperation [ɪgzɑːspə'reɪʃən] *n* Verzweiflung *f*; **in** ~ verzweifelt.
excavate ['ɛkskəveɪt] *vt* ausgraben; (*hole*) graben ♦ *vi* Ausgrabungen machen.
excavation [ɛkskə'veɪʃən] *n* Ausgrabung *f*.
excavator ['ɛkskəveɪtə*] *n* Bagger *m*.
exceed [ɪk'siːd] *vt* übersteigen; (*hopes*) übertreffen; (*limit, budget, powers*) überschreiten.
exceedingly [ɪkˈsiːdɪŋlɪ] *adv* äußerst.
excel [ɪk'sɛl] *vt* übertreffen ♦ *vi*: **to** ~ (**in** *or* **at**) sich auszeichnen (in +*dat*); **to** ~ **o.s.** (*BRIT*) sich selbst übertreffen.
excellence ['ɛksələns] *n* hervorragende Leistung *f*.
Excellency ['ɛksələnsɪ] *n*: **His** ~ Seine Exzellenz.
excellent ['ɛksələnt] *adj* ausgezeichnet, hervorragend.
except [ɪk'sɛpt] *prep* (*also*: ~ **for**) außer +*dat* ♦ *vt*: **to** ~ **sb (from)** jdn ausnehmen (bei); ~ **if**, ~ **when** außer wenn; ~ **that** nur dass.
excepting [ɪk'sɛptɪŋ] *prep* außer +*dat*, mit Ausnahme +*gen*.
exception [ɪk'sɛpʃən] *n* Ausnahme *f*; **to take** ~ **to** Anstoß nehmen an +*dat*; **with the** ~ **of** mit Ausnahme von.
exceptional [ɪk'sɛpʃənl] *adj* außergewöhnlich.
excerpt ['ɛksəːpt] *n* Auszug *m*.
excess [ɪk'sɛs] *n* Übermaß *nt*; (*INSURANCE*) Selbstbeteiligung *f*; **excesses** *npl* Exzesse *pl*; **an** ~ **of £15, a £15** ~ eine Selbstbeteiligung von £15; **in** ~ **of** über +*dat*.
excess baggage *n* Übergepäck *nt*.
excess fare (*BRIT*) *n* Nachlösegebühr *f*.
excessive [ɪk'sɛsɪv] *adj* übermäßig.
excess supply *n* Überangebot *nt*.
exchange [ɪks'tʃeɪndʒ] *n* Austausch *m*; (*conversation*) Wortwechsel *m*; (*also*: **telephone** ~) Fernsprechamt *nt* ♦ *vt*: **to** ~ (**for**) tauschen (gegen); (*in shop*) umtauschen (gegen); **in** ~ **for** für; **foreign** ~ Devisenhandel *m*; (*money*) Devisen *pl*.
exchange control *n* Devisenkontrolle *f*.
exchange market *n* Devisenmarkt *m*.
exchange rate *n* Wechselkurs *m*.
Exchequer [ɪks'tʃɛkə*] (*BRIT*) *n*: **the** ~ das Finanzministerium.
excisable [ɪk'saɪzəbl] *adj* steuerpflichtig.

excise ['ɛksaɪz] _n_ Verbrauchssteuer _f_ ♦ _vt_
entfernen.
excise duties _npl_ Verbrauchssteuern _pl_.
excitable [ɪk'saɪtəbl] _adj_ (leicht) erregbar.
excite [ɪk'saɪt] _vt_ aufregen; (_arouse_) erregen;
to get ~**d** sich aufregen.
excitement [ɪk'saɪtmənt] _n_ Aufregung _f_;
(_exhilaration_) Hochgefühl _nt_.
exciting [ɪk'saɪtɪŋ] _adj_ aufregend.
excl. _abbr_ = **excluding; exclusive (of)**.
exclaim [ɪks'kleɪm] _vi_ aufschreien.
exclamation [ɛksklə'meɪʃən] _n_ Ausruf _m_; ~ **of
joy** Freudenschrei _m_.
exclamation mark _n_ Ausrufezeichen _nt_.
exclude [ɪks'kluːd] _vt_ ausschließen.
excluding [ɪks'kluːdɪŋ] _prep_: ~ **VAT** ohne
Mehrwertsteuer.
exclusion [ɪks'kluːʒən] _n_ Ausschluss _m_; **to
concentrate on sth to the** ~ **of everything
else** sich ausschließlich auf etw _dat_
konzentrieren.
exclusion clause _n_ Freizeichnungsklausel _f_.
exclusion zone _n_ Sperrzone _f_.
exclusive [ɪks'kluːsɪv] _adj_ exklusiv; (_story,
interview_) Exklusiv-; (_use_) ausschließlich ♦ _n_
Exklusivbericht _m_ ♦ _adv_: **from 1st to 15th
March** ~ vom 1. bis zum 15. März
ausschließlich; ~ **of postage** ohne _or_
exklusive Porto; ~ **of tax** ausschließlich _or_
exklusive Steuern; **to be mutually** ~ sich _or_
einander ausschließen.
exclusively [ɪks'kluːsɪvlɪ] _adv_ ausschließlich.
exclusive rights _npl_ Exklusivrechte _pl_.
excommunicate [ɛkskə'mjuːnɪkeɪt] _vt_
exkommunizieren.
excrement ['ɛkskrəmənt] _n_ Kot _m_,
Exkremente _pl_.
excruciating [ɪks'kruːʃɪeɪtɪŋ] _adj_ grässlich,
fürchterlich; (_noise, embarrassment_)
unerträglich.
excursion [ɪks'kəːʃən] _n_ Ausflug _m_.
excursion ticket _n_ verbilligte Fahrkarte _f_.
excusable [ɪks'kjuːzəbl] _adj_ verzeihlich,
entschuldbar.
excuse [ɪks'kjuːs] _n_ Entschuldigung _f_ ♦ _vt_
entschuldigen; (_forgive_) verzeihen; **to** ~ **sb
from sth** jdm etw erlassen; **to** ~ **sb from
doing sth** jdn davon befreien, etw zu tum;
~ **me!** entschuldigen Sie!, Entschuldigung!;
if you will ~ **me** ... entschuldigen Sie mich
bitte ...; **to** ~ **o.s. for sth** sich für _or_ wegen
etw entschuldigen; **to** ~ **o.s. for doing sth**
sich entschuldigen, dass man etw tut; **to
make** ~**s for sb** jdn entschuldigen; **that's no
**~! das ist keine Ausrede!
ex-directory ['ɛksdɪ'rɛktərɪ] (_BRIT_) _adj_
(_number_) geheim; **she's** ~ sie steht nicht im
Telefonbuch.
execrable ['ɛksɪkrəbl] _adj_ scheußlich;
(_manners_) abscheulich.
execute ['ɛksɪkjuːt] _vt_ ausführen; (_person_)
hinrichten.

execution [ɛksɪ'kjuːʃən] _n_ (_see vb_)
Ausführung _f_; Hinrichtung _f_.
executioner [ɛksɪ'kjuːʃnə*] _n_ Scharfrichter _m_.
executive [ɪg'zɛkjutɪv] _n_ leitende(r)
Angestellte(r) _f(m)_; (_committee_) Vorstand _m_
♦ _adj_ geschäftsführend; (_role_) führend;
(_secretary_) Chef-; (_car, chair_) für gehobene
Ansprüche; (_toys_) Manager-; (_plane_) ≈
Privat-.
executive director _n_ leitender Direktor _m_,
leitende Direktorin _f_.
executor [ɪg'zɛkjutə*] _n_
Testamentsvollstrecker(in) _m(f)_.
exemplary [ɪg'zɛmplərɪ] _adj_ vorbildlich,
beispielhaft; (_punishment_) exemplarisch.
exemplify [ɪg'zɛmplɪfaɪ] _vt_ verkörpern;
(_illustrate_) veranschaulichen.
exempt [ɪg'zɛmpt] _adj_: ~ **from** befreit von
♦ _vt_: **to** ~ **sb from** jdn befreien von.
exemption [ɪg'zɛmpʃən] _n_ Befreiung _f_.
exercise ['ɛksəsaɪz] _n_ Übung _f_; (_no pl: keep-fit_)
Gymnastik _f_; (: _energetic movement_)
Bewegung _f_; (: _of authority etc_) Ausübung _f_
♦ _vt_ (_patience_) üben; (_right_) ausüben; (_dog_)
ausführen; (_mind_) beschäftigen ♦ _vi_ (_also:_ **to
take** ~) Sport treiben.
exercise book _n_ (Schul)heft _nt_.
exert [ɪg'zəːt] _vt_ (_influence_) ausüben;
(_authority_) einsetzen; **to** ~ **o.s.** sich
anstrengen.
exertion [ɪg'zəːʃən] _n_ Anstrengung _f_.
ex gratia ['ɛks'greɪʃə] _adj_: ~ **payment**
freiwillige Zahlung _f_.
exhale [ɛks'heɪl] _vt, vi_ ausatmen.
exhaust [ɪg'zɔːst] _n_ (_also:_ ~ **pipe**) Auspuff _m_;
(_fumes_) Auspuffgase _pl_ ♦ _vt_ erschöpfen;
(_money_) aufbrauchen; (_topic_) erschöpfend
behandeln; **to** ~ **o.s.** sich verausgaben.
exhausted [ɪg'zɔːstɪd] _adj_ erschöpft.
exhausting [ɪg'zɔːstɪŋ] _adj_ anstrengend.
exhaustion [ɪg'zɔːstʃən] _n_ Erschöpfung _f_;
nervous ~ nervöse Erschöpfung.
exhaustive [ɪg'zɔːstɪv] _adj_ erschöpfend.
exhibit [ɪg'zɪbɪt] _n_ Ausstellungsstück _nt_;
(_LAW_) Beweisstück _nt_ ♦ _vt_ zeigen, an den
Tag legen; (_paintings_) ausstellen.
exhibition [ɛksɪ'bɪʃən] _n_ Ausstellung _f_; **to
make an** ~ **of o.s.** sich unmöglich
aufführen; **an** ~ **of bad manners** schlechte
Manieren _pl_; **an** ~ **of draughtsmanship**
zeichnerisches Können _nt_.
exhibitionist [ɛksɪ'bɪʃənɪst] _n_
Exhibitionist(in) _m(f)_.
exhibitor [ɪg'zɪbɪtə*] _n_ Aussteller(in) _m(f)_.
exhilarating [ɪg'zɪləreɪtɪŋ] _adj_ erregend,
berauschend; (_news_) aufregend.
exhilaration [ɪgzɪlə'reɪʃən] _n_ Hochgefühl _nt_.
exhort [ɪg'zɔːt] _vt_: **to** ~ **sb to do sth** jdn
ermahnen, etw zu tun.
exile ['ɛksaɪl] _n_ Exil _nt_; (_person_) Verbannte(r)
_f(m)_ ♦ _vt_ verbannen; **in** ~ im Exil.
exist [ɪg'zɪst] _vi_ existieren.

existence [ɪg'zɪstəns] n Existenz f; **to be in ~** existieren.

existentialism [ɛgzɪs'tɛnʃlɪzəm] n Existentialismus m.

existing [ɪg'zɪstɪŋ] adj bestehend.

exit ['ɛksɪt] n Ausgang m; (from motorway) Ausfahrt f; (departure) Abgang m ♦ vi (THEAT) abgehen; (COMPUT: from program/ file etc) das Programm/die Datei etc verlassen; **to ~** from hinausgehen aus; (motorway etc) abfahren von.

exit poll n bei Wählern unmittelbar nach Verlassen der Wahllokale durchgeführte Umfrage.

exit ramp (US) n Ausfahrt f.

exit visa n Ausreisevisum nt.

exodus ['ɛksədəs] n Auszug m; **the ~ to the cities** die Abwanderung in die Städte.

ex officio ['ɛksə'fɪʃɪəu] adj von Amts wegen ♦ adv kraft seines Amtes.

exonerate [ɪg'zɔnəreɪt] vt: **to ~ from** entlasten von.

exorbitant [ɪg'zɔːbɪtnt] adj (prices, rents) astronomisch, unverschämt; (demands) maßlos, übertrieben.

exorcize ['ɛksɔːsaɪz] vt exorzieren; (spirit) austreiben.

exotic [ɪg'zɔtɪk] adj exotisch.

expand [ɪks'pænd] vt erweitern; (staff, numbers etc) vergrößern; (influence) ausdehnen ♦ vi expandieren; (population) wachsen; (gas, metal) sich ausdehnen; **to ~ on** weiter ausführen.

expanse [ɪks'pæns] n Weite f.

expansion [ɪks'pænʃən] n Expansion f; (of population) Wachstum nt; (of gas, metal) Ausdehnung f.

expansionism [ɪks'pænʃənɪzəm] n Expansionspolitik f.

expansionist [ɪks'pænʃənɪst] adj Expansions-, expansionistisch.

expatriate [ɛks'pætrɪət] n im Ausland Lebende(r) f(m).

expect [ɪks'pɛkt] vt erwarten; (suppose) denken, glauben; (count on) rechnen mit ♦ vi: **to be ~ing** ein Kind erwarten; **to ~ sb to do sth** erwarten, dass jd etw tut; **to ~ to do sth** vorhaben, etw zu tun; **as ~ed** wie erwartet; **I ~ so** ich glaube schon.

expectancy [ɪks'pɛktənsɪ] n Erwartung f; **life ~** Lebenserwartung f.

expectant [ɪks'pɛktənt] adj erwartungsvoll.

expectantly [ɪks'pɛktəntlɪ] adv erwartungsvoll.

expectant mother n werdende Mutter f.

expectation [ɛkspɛk'teɪʃən] n Erwartung f; (hope) Hoffnung f; **in ~ of** in Erwartung +gen; **against** or **contrary to all ~(s)** wider Erwarten; **to come** or **live up to sb's ~s** jds Erwartungen dat entsprechen.

expedience [ɪks'piːdɪəns] n = expediency.

expediency [ɪks'piːdɪənsɪ] n Zweckmäßigkeit

f; **for the sake of ~** aus Gründen der Zweckmäßigkeit.

expedient [ɪks'piːdɪənt] adj zweckmäßig ♦ n Hilfsmittel nt.

expedite ['ɛkspədaɪt] vt beschleunigen.

expedition [ɛkspə'dɪʃən] n Expedition f; (for shopping etc) Tour f.

expeditionary force [ɛkspə'dɪʃənrɪ-] n Expeditionskorps nt.

expeditious [ɛkspə'dɪʃəs] adj schnell.

expel [ɪks'pɛl] vt (from school) verweisen; (from organization) ausschließen; (from place) vertreiben; (gas, liquid) ausstoßen.

expend [ɪks'pɛnd] vt ausgeben; (time, energy) aufwenden.

expendable [ɪks'pɛndəbl] adj entbehrlich.

expenditure [ɪks'pɛndɪtʃə*] n Ausgaben pl; (of energy, time) Aufwand m.

expense [ɪks'pɛns] n Kosten pl; (expenditure) Ausgabe f; **expenses** npl Spesen pl; **at the ~ of** auf Kosten +gen; **to go to the ~ of buying a new car** (viel) Geld für ein neues Auto anlegen; **at great/little ~** mit hohen/ geringen Kosten.

expense account n Spesenkonto nt.

expensive [ɪks'pɛnsɪv] adj teuer; **to have ~ tastes** einen teuren Geschmack haben.

experience [ɪks'pɪərɪəns] n Erfahrung f; (event, activity) Erlebnis nt ♦ vt erleben; **by** or **from ~** aus Erfahrung; **to learn by ~** durch eigene Erfahrung lernen.

experienced [ɪks'pɪərɪənst] adj erfahren.

experiment [ɪks'pɛrɪmənt] n Experiment nt, Versuch m ♦ vi: **to ~ (with/on)** experimentieren (mit/an +dat); **to perform** or **carry out an ~** einen Versuch or ein Experiment durchführen; **as an ~** versuchsweise.

experimental [ɪkspɛrɪ'mɛntl] adj experimentell; **at the ~ stage** im Versuchsstadium.

expert ['ɛkspəːt] adj ausgezeichnet, geschickt; (opinion, help etc) eines Fachmanns ♦ n Fachmann m, Fachfrau f, Experte m, Expertin f; **to be ~ in** or **at doing sth** etw ausgezeichnet können; **an ~ on sth/on the subject of sth** ein Experte für etw/auf dem Gebiet einer Sache gen; **~ witness** (LAW) sachverständiger Zeuge m.

expertise [ɛkspəː'tiːz] n Sachkenntnis f.

expire [ɪks'paɪə*] vi ablaufen.

expiry [ɪks'paɪərɪ] n Ablauf m.

expiry date n Ablauftermin m; (of voucher, special offer etc) Verfallsdatum nt.

explain [ɪks'pleɪn] vt erklären.

▸ **explain away** vt eine Erklärung finden für.

explanation [ɛksplə'neɪʃən] n Erklärung f; **to find an ~ for sth** eine Erklärung für etw finden.

explanatory [ɪks'plænətrɪ] adj erklärend.

expletive [ɪks'pliːtɪv] n Kraftausdruck m.

explicable [ɪks'plɪkəbl] *adj* erklärbar; **for no ~ reason** aus unerfindlichen Gründen.

explicit [ɪks'plɪsɪt] *adj* ausdrücklich; (*sex, violence*) deutlich, unverhüllt; **to be ~** (*frank*) sich deutlich ausdrücken.

explode [ɪks'pləʊd] *vi* explodieren; (*population*) sprunghaft ansteigen ♦ *vt* zur Explosion bringen; (*myth, theory*) zu Fall bringen.

exploit ['ɛksplɔɪt] *n* Heldentat *f* ♦ *vt* ausnutzen; (*workers etc*) ausbeuten; (*resources*) nutzen.

exploitation [ɛksplɔɪ'teɪʃən] *n* (*see vb*) Ausnutzung *f*; Ausbeutung *f*; Nutzung *f*.

exploration [ɛksplə'reɪʃən] *n* (*see vb*) Erforschung *f*; Erkundung *f*; Untersuchung *f*.

exploratory [ɪks'plɔrətrɪ] *adj* exploratorisch; (*expedition*) Forschungs-; **~ operation** (*MED*) Explorationsoperation *f*; **~ talks** Sondierungsgespräche *pl*.

explore [ɪks'plɔ:*] *vt* erforschen; (*with hands etc, idea*) untersuchen.

explorer [ɪks'plɔ:rə*] *n* Forschungsreisende(r) *f(m)*; (*of place*) Erforscher(in) *m(f)*.

explosion [ɪks'pləʊʒən] *n* Explosion *f*; (*outburst*) Ausbruch *m*.

explosive [ɪks'pləʊsɪv] *adj* explosiv; (*device*) Spreng-; (*temper*) aufbrausend ♦ *n* Sprengstoff *m*; (*device*) Sprengkörper *m*.

exponent [ɪks'pəʊnənt] *n* Vertreter(in) *m(f)*, Exponent(in) *m(f)*; (*MATH*) Exponent *m*.

exponential [ɛkspəʊ'nɛnʃl] *adj* exponentiell; (*MATH: function etc*) Exponential-.

export [ɛks'pɔ:t] *vt* exportieren, ausführen; (*ideas, values*) verbreiten ♦ *n* Export *m*, Ausfuhr *f*; (*product*) Exportgut *nt* ♦ *cpd* Export-, Ausfuhr-.

exportation [ɛkspɔ:'teɪʃən] *n* Export *m*, Ausfuhr *f*.

exporter [ɛks'pɔ:tə*] *n* Exporteur *m*.

expose [ɪks'pəʊz] *vt* freilegen; (*to heat, radiation*) aussetzen; (*unmask*) entlarven; **to ~ o.s.** sich entblößen.

exposé [ɪk'spəʊzeɪ] *n* Enthüllung *f*.

exposed [ɪks'pəʊzd] *adj* ungeschützt; (*wire*) bloßliegend; **to be ~ to** (*radiation, heat etc*) ausgesetzt sein *+dat*.

exposition [ɛkspə'zɪʃən] *n* Erläuterung *f*; (*exhibition*) Ausstellung *f*.

exposure [ɪks'pəʊʒə*] *n* (*to heat, radiation*) Aussetzung *f*; (*publicity*) Publicity *f*; (*of person*) Entlarvung *f*; (*PHOT*) Belichtung *f*; (: *MED*) Aufnahme *f*; **to be suffering from ~** an Unterkühlung leiden; **to die from ~** erfrieren.

exposure meter *n* Belichtungsmesser *m*.

expound [ɪks'paʊnd] *vt* darlegen, erläutern.

express [ɪks'prɛs] *adj* ausdrücklich; (*intention*) bestimmt; (*BRIT: letter etc*) Express-, Eil- ♦ *n* (*train*) Schnellzug *m*; (*bus*) Schnellbus *m* ♦ *adv* (*send*) per Express ♦ *vt* ausdrücken; (*view, emotion*) zum Ausdruck bringen; **to**

~ o.s. sich ausdrücken.

expression [ɪks'prɛʃən] *n* Ausdruck *m*; (*on face*) (Gesichts)ausdruck *m*.

expressionism [ɪks'prɛʃənɪzəm] *n* Expressionismus *m*.

expressive [ɪks'prɛsɪv] *adj* ausdrucksvoll; **~ ability** Ausdrucksfähigkeit *f*.

expressly [ɪks'prɛslɪ] *adv* ausdrücklich; (*intentionally*) absichtlich.

expressway [ɪks'prɛsweɪ] (*US*) *n* Schnellstraße *f*.

expropriate [ɛks'prəʊprɪeɪt] *vt* enteignen.

expulsion [ɪks'pʌlʃən] *n* (*SCOL*) Verweisung *f*; (*POL*) Ausweisung *f*; (*of gas, liquid etc*) Ausstoßen *nt*.

expurgate ['ɛkspə:geɪt] *vt* zensieren; **the ~d version** die zensierte *or* bereinigte Fassung.

exquisite [ɛks'kwɪzɪt] *adj* exquisit, erlesen; (*keenly felt*) köstlich.

exquisitely [ɛks'kwɪzɪtlɪ] *adv* exquisit; (*carved*) kunstvoll; (*polite, sensitive*) äußerst.

ex-serviceman ['ɛks'sə:vɪsmən] (*irreg: like* **man**) *n* ehemaliger Soldat *m*.

ext. *abbr* (*TEL*) = **extension**.

extemporize [ɪks'tɛmpəraɪz] *vi* improvisieren.

extend [ɪks'tɛnd] *vt* verlängern; (*building*) anbauen an *+acc*; (*offer, invitation*) aussprechen; (*arm, hand*) ausstrecken; (*deadline*) verschieben ♦ *vi* sich erstrecken; (*period*) dauern.

extension [ɪks'tɛnʃən] *n* Verlängerung *f*; (*of building*) Anbau *m*; (*of time*) Aufschub *m*; (*of campaign, rights*) Erweiterung *f*; (*TEL*) (Neben)anschluss *m*; **~ 3718** (*TEL*) Apparat 3718.

extension cable *n* Verlängerungskabel *nt*.

extension lead *n* Verlängerungsschnur *f*.

extensive [ɪks'tɛnsɪv] *adj* ausgedehnt; (*effect*) weitreichend; (*damage*) beträchtlich; (*coverage, discussion*) ausführlich; (*inquiries*) umfangreich; (*use*) häufig.

extensively [ɪks'tɛnsɪvlɪ] *adv*: **he's travelled ~** er ist viel gereist.

extent [ɪks'tɛnt] *n* Ausdehnung *f*; (*of problem, damage, loss etc*) Ausmaß *nt*; **to some ~** bis zu einem gewissen Grade; **to a certain ~** in gewissem Maße; **to a large ~** in hohem Maße; **to the ~ of ...** (*debts*) in Höhe von ...; **to go to the ~ of doing sth** so weit gehen, etw zu tun; **to such an ~ that ...** dermaßen, dass ...; **to what ~?** inwieweit?

extenuating [ɪks'tɛnjueɪtɪŋ] *adj*: **~ circumstances** mildernde Umstände *pl*.

exterior [ɛks'tɪərɪə*] *adj* (*surface, angle, world*) Außen- ♦ *n* Außenseite *f*; (*appearance*) Äußere(s) *nt*.

exterminate [ɪks'tə:mɪneɪt] *vt* ausrotten.

extermination [ɪkstə:mɪ'neɪʃən] *n* Ausrottung *f*.

external [ɛks'tə:nl] *adj* (*wall etc*) Außen-; (*use*) äußerlich; (*evidence*) unabhängig; (*examiner, auditor*) extern ♦ *n*: **the ~s** die

Äußerlichkeiten *pl*; **for** ~ **use only** nur äußerlich (anzuwenden); ~ **affairs** (*POL*) auswärtige Angelegenheiten *pl*.

externally [ɛksˈtɜːnəlɪ] *adv* äußerlich.

extinct [ɪksˈtɪŋkt] *adj* ausgestorben; (*volcano*) erloschen.

extinction [ɪksˈtɪŋkʃən] *n* Aussterben *nt*.

extinguish [ɪksˈtɪŋgwɪʃ] *vt* löschen; (*hope*) zerstören.

extinguisher [ɪksˈtɪŋgwɪʃəˈ] *n* (*also*: **fire** ~) Feuerlöscher *m*.

extol, (*US*) **extoll** [ɪksˈtəul] *vt* preisen, rühmen.

extort [ɪksˈtɔːt] *vt* erpressen; (*confession*) erzwingen.

extortion [ɪksˈtɔːʃən] *n* (*see vb*) Erpressung *f*; Erzwingung *f*.

extortionate [ɪksˈtɔːʃnɪt] *adj* überhöht; (*price*) Wucher-.

extra [ˈɛkstrə] *adj* zusätzlich ♦ *adv* extra ♦ *n* Extra *nt*; (*surcharge*) zusätzliche Kosten *pl*; (*CINE, THEAT*) Statist(in) *m(f)*; **wine will cost** ~ Wein wird extra berechnet.

extra... [ˈɛkstrə] *pref* außer-, extra-.

extract [*vt* ɪksˈtrækt, *n* ˈɛkstrækt] *vt* (*tooth*) ziehen; (*mineral*) gewinnen ♦ *n* Auszug *m*; (*malt extract, vanilla extract etc*) Extrakt *m*; **to** ~ **(from)** (*object*) herausziehen (aus); (*money*) herausholen (aus); (*promise*) abringen +*dat*.

extraction [ɪksˈtrækʃən] *n* (*see vb*) Ziehen *nt*; Gewinnung *f*; Herausziehen *nt*; Herausholen *nt*; Abringen *nt*; (*DENTISTRY*) Extraktion *f*; (*descent*) Herkunft *f*, Abstammung *f*; **to be of Scottish** ~, **to be Scottish by** ~ schottischer Herkunft *or* Abstammung sein.

extractor fan [ɪksˈtræktə-] *n* Sauglüfter *m*.

extracurricular [ˈɛkstrəkəˈrɪkjuləˈ] *adj* außerhalb des Lehrplans.

extradite [ˈɛkstrədaɪt] *vt* ausliefern.

extradition [ɛkstrəˈdɪʃən] *n* Auslieferung *f* ♦ *cpd* Auslieferungs-.

extramarital [ˈɛkstrəˈmærɪtl] *adj* außerehelich.

extramural [ˈɛkstrəˈmjuərl] *adj* außerhalb der Universität; ~ **classes** von der Universität veranstaltete Teilzeitkurse *pl*.

extraneous [ɛksˈtreɪnɪəs] *adj* unwesentlich.

extraordinary [ɪksˈtrɔːdnrɪ] *adj* ungewöhnlich; (*special*) außerordentlich; **the** ~ **thing is that** ... das Merkwürdige ist; dass ...

extraordinary general meeting *n* außerordentliche Hauptversammlung *f*.

extrapolation [ɛkstræpəˈleɪʃən] *n* Extrapolation *f*.

extrasensory perception [ˈɛkstrəˈsɛnsərɪ-] *n* außersinnliche Wahrnehmung *f*.

extra time *n* (*FOOTBALL*) Verlängerung *f*.

extravagance [ɪksˈtrævəgəns] *n* (*no pl*) Verschwendungssucht *f*; (*example of spending*) Luxus *m*.

extravagant [ɪksˈtrævəgənt] *adj* extravagant; (*tastes, gift*) teuer; (*wasteful*) verschwenderisch; (*praise*) übertrieben; (*ideas*) ausgefallen.

extreme [ɪksˈtriːm] *adj* extrem; (*point, edge, poverty*) äußerste(r, s) ♦ *n* Extrem *nt*; **the** ~ **right/left** (*POL*) die äußerste *or* extreme Rechte/Linke; ~**s of temperature** extreme Temperaturen *pl*.

extremely [ɪksˈtriːmlɪ] *adv* äußerst, extrem.

extremist [ɪksˈtriːmɪst] *n* Extremist(in) *m(f)* ♦ *adj* extremistisch.

extremities [ɪksˈtrɛmɪtɪz] *npl* Extremitäten *pl*.

extremity [ɪksˈtrɛmɪtɪ] *n* Rand *m*; (*end*) äußerstes Ende *nt*; (*of situation*) Ausmaß *nt*.

extricate [ˈɛkstrɪkeɪt] *vt*: **to** ~ **sb/sth (from)** jdn/etw befreien (aus).

extrovert [ˈɛkstrəvɜːt] *n* extravertierter Mensch *m*.

exuberance [ɪgˈzjuːbərns] *n* Überschwänglichkeit *f*.

exuberant [ɪgˈzjuːbərnt] *adj* überschwänglich; (*imagination etc*) lebhaft.

exude [ɪgˈzjuːd] *vt* ausstrahlen; (*liquid*) absondern; (*smell*) ausströmen.

exult [ɪgˈzʌlt] *vi*: **to** ~ **(in)** jubeln (über +*acc*).

exultant [ɪgˈzʌltənt] *adj* jubelnd; (*shout*) Jubel-; **to be** ~ jubeln.

exultation [ɛgzʌlˈteɪʃən] *n* Jubel *m*.

eye [aɪ] *n* Auge *nt*; (*of needle*) Öhr *nt* ♦ *vt* betrachten; **to keep an** ~ **on** aufpassen auf +*acc*; **as far as the** ~ **can see** so weit das Auge reicht; **in the public** ~ im Blickpunkt der Öffentlichkeit; **to have an** ~ **for sth** einen Blick für etw haben; **with an** ~ **to doing sth** (*BRIT*) mit der Absicht, etw zu tun; **there's more to this than meets the** ~ da steckt mehr dahinter(, als man auf den ersten Blick meint).

eyeball [ˈaɪbɔːl] *n* Augapfel *m*.

eyebath [ˈaɪbɑːθ] (*BRIT*) *n* Augenbadewanne *f*.

eyebrow [ˈaɪbrau] *n* Augenbraue *f*.

eyebrow pencil *n* Augenbrauenstift *m*.

eye-catching [ˈaɪkætʃɪŋ] *adj* auffallend.

eyecup [ˈaɪkʌp] (*US*) *n* = **eyebath**.

eye drops *npl* Augentropfen *pl*.

eyeful [ˈaɪful] *n*: **to get an** ~ **of sth** (*lit*) etw ins Auge bekommen; (*fig: have a good look*) einiges von etw zu sehen bekommen; **she's quite an** ~ sie hat allerhand zu bieten.

eyeglass [ˈaɪglɑːs] *n* Augenglas *nt*.

eyelash [ˈaɪlæʃ] *n* Augenwimper *f*.

eyelet [ˈaɪlɪt] *n* Öse *f*.

eye level *n*: **at** ~ in Augenhöhe.

eyelevel [ˈaɪlɛvl] *adj* in Augenhöhe.

eyelid [ˈaɪlɪd] *n* Augenlid *nt*.

eyeliner [ˈaɪlaɪnəˈ] *n* Eyeliner *m*.

eye-opener [ˈaɪəupnəˈ] *n* Überraschung *f*; **to be an** ~ **to sb** jdm die Augen öffnen.

eye shadow *n* Lidschatten *m*.

eyesight [ˈaɪsaɪt] *n* Sehvermögen *nt*.

eyesore [ˈaɪsɔːˈ] *n* Schandfleck *m*.

eyestrain ['aɪstreɪn] *n*: **to get ~** seine Augen überanstrengen.

eyetooth ['aɪtuːθ] (*pl* **eyeteeth**) *n* Eckzahn *m*, Augenzahn *m*; **to give one's eyeteeth for sth** alles für etw geben; **to give one's eyeteeth to do sth** alles darum geben, etw zu tun.

eyewash ['aɪwɔʃ] *n* Augenwasser *nt*; (*fig*) Gewäsch *nt*.

eyewitness ['aɪwɪtnɪs] *n* Augenzeuge *m*, Augenzeugin *f*.

eyrie ['ɪərɪ] *n* Horst *m*.

$$F, f$$

F¹, f [ɛf] *n* (*letter*) F *nt*, f *nt*; **~ for Frederick**, *(US)* **~ for Fox** ≈ F wie Friedrich.

F² [ɛf] *n* (*MUS*) F *nt*, f *nt*.

F³ [ɛf] *abbr* (= *Fahrenheit*) F.

FA (*BRIT*) *n abbr* (= *Football Association*) *englischer Fußball-Dachverband*, ≈ DFB *m*.

FAA (*US*) *n abbr* (= *Federal Aviation Administration*) *amerikanische Luftfahrtbehörde*.

fable ['feɪbl] *n* Fabel *f*.

fabric ['fæbrɪk] *n* Stoff *m*; (*of society*) Gefüge *nt*; (*of building*) Bausubstanz *f*.

fabricate ['fæbrɪkeɪt] *vt* herstellen; (*story*) erfinden; (*evidence*) fälschen.

fabrication [fæbrɪ'keɪʃən] *n* Herstellung *f*; (*lie*) Erfindung *f*.

fabric ribbon *n* (*for typewriter*) Gewebefarbband *nt*.

fabulous ['fæbjuləs] *adj* fabelhaft, toll (*inf*); (*extraordinary*) sagenhaft; (*mythical*) legendär.

façade [fə'sɑːd] *n* Fassade *f*.

face [feɪs] *n* Gesicht *nt*; (*expression*) Gesichtsausdruck *m*; (*grimace*) Grimasse *f*; (*of clock*) Zifferblatt *nt*; (*of mountain, cliff*) (Steil)wand *f*; (*of building*) Fassade *f*; (*side, surface*) Seite *f* ♦ *vt* (*subj: person*) gegenübersitzen/-stehen +*dat etc*; (: *building, street etc*) liegen zu; (: *north, south etc*) liegen nach; (*unpleasant situation*) sich gegenübersehen +*dat*; (*facts*) ins Auge sehen +*dat*; **~ down** mit dem Gesicht nach unten; (*card*) mit der Bildseite nach unten; (*object*) mit der Vorderseite nach unten; **to lose/save ~** das Gesicht verlieren/wahren; **to make** *or* **pull a ~** das Gesicht verziehen; **in the ~ of** trotz +*gen*; **on the ~ of it** so, wie es aussieht; **to come ~ to ~ with sb** jdn treffen; **to come ~ to ~ with a problem** einem Problem gegenüberstehen; **to ~ each other** einander gegenüberstehen/-liegen/-

sitzen *etc*; **to ~ the fact that** ... der Tatsache ins Auge sehen, dass ...; **the man facing me** der Mann mir gegenüber.

▶ **face up to** *vt fus* (*obligations, difficulty*) auf sich *acc* nehmen; (*situation, possibility*) sich abfinden mit; (*danger, fact*) ins Auge sehen +*dat*.

face cloth (*BRIT*) *n* Waschlappen *m*.

face cream *n* Gesichtscreme *f*.

faceless ['feɪslɪs] *adj* (*fig*) anonym.

face-lift ['feɪslɪft] *n* Facelifting *nt*; (*of building etc*) Verschönerung *f*.

face powder *n* Gesichtspuder *m*.

face-saving ['feɪs'seɪvɪŋ] *adj*: **a ~ excuse/tactic** eine Entschuldigung/Taktik, um das Gesicht zu wahren.

facet ['fæsɪt] *n* Seite *f*, Aspekt *m*; (*of gem*) Facette *f*, Fassette *f*.

facetious [fə'siːʃəs] *adj* witzelnd.

face-to-face [feɪstə'feɪs] *adj* persönlich; (*confrontation*) direkt.

face value *n* Nennwert *m*; **to take sth at ~** (*fig*) etw für bare Münze nehmen.

facia ['feɪʃə] *n* = **fascia**.

facial ['feɪʃl] *adj* (*expression, massage etc*) Gesichts- ♦ *n* kosmetische Gesichtsbehandlung *f*.

facile ['fæsaɪl] *adj* oberflächlich; (*comment*) nichts sagend.

facilitate [fə'sɪlɪteɪt] *vt* erleichtern.

facilities [fə'sɪlɪtɪz] *npl* Einrichtungen *pl*; **cooking ~** Kochgelegenheit *f*; **credit ~** Kreditmöglichkeiten *pl*.

facility [fə'sɪlɪtɪ] *n* Einrichtung *f*; **to have a ~ for** (*skill, aptitude*) eine Begabung haben für.

facing ['feɪsɪŋ] *prep* gegenüber +*dat* ♦ *n* (*SEWING*) Besatz *m*.

facsimile [fæk'sɪmɪlɪ] *n* Faksimile *nt*; (*also:* **~ machine**) Fernkopierer *m*, (Tele)faxgerät *nt*; (*transmitted document*) Fernkopie *f*, (Tele)fax *nt*.

fact [fækt] *n* Tatsache *f*; (*truth*) Wirklichkeit *f*; **in ~** eigentlich; (*in reality*) tatsächlich, in Wirklichkeit; **to know for a ~ that** ... ganz genau wissen, dass ...; **the ~ (of the matter) is that** ... die Sache ist die, dass ...; **it's a ~ of life that** ... es ist eine Tatsache, dass ...; **to tell sb the ~s of life** (*sex*) jdn aufklären.

fact-finding ['fæktfaɪndɪŋ] *adj*: **a ~ tour** *or* **mission** eine Informationstour *f*.

faction ['fækʃən] *n* Fraktion *f*.

factional ['fækʃənl] *adj* (*dispute, system*) Fraktions-.

factor ['fæktə*] *n* Faktor *m*; (*COMM*) Kommissionär *m*; (: *agent*) Makler *m*; **safety ~** Sicherheitsfaktor *m*; **human ~** menschlicher Faktor.

factory ['fæktərɪ] *n* Fabrik *f*.

factory farming (*BRIT*) *n* industriell betriebene Viehzucht *f*.

factory floor *n*: **the ~** (*workers*) die

Fabrikarbeiter *pl*; **on the** ~ bei *or* unter den Fabrikarbeitern.

factory ship *n* Fabrikschiff *nt*.

factual ['fæktjuəl] *adj* sachlich; (*information*) Sach-.

faculty ['fækəltɪ] *n* Vermögen *nt*, Kraft *f*; (*ability*) Talent *nt*; (*of university*) Fakultät *f*; (*US: teaching staff*) Lehrkörper *m*.

fad [fæd] *n* Fimmel *m*, Tick *m*.

fade [feɪd] *vi* verblassen; (*light*) nachlassen; (*sound*) schwächer werden; (*flower*) verblühen; (*hope*) zerrinnen; (*smile*) verschwinden.

▶ **fade in** *vt sep* allmählich einblenden.

▶ **fade out** *vt sep* ausblenden.

faeces, (*US*) **feces** ['fiːsiːz] *npl* Kot *m*.

fag [fæg] *n* (*BRIT: inf: cigarette*) Glimmstängel *m*; (: *chore*) Schinderei *f* (*inf*), Plackerei *f* (*inf*); (*US: inf: homosexual*) Schwule(r) *m*.

fail [feɪl] *vt* (*exam*) nicht bestehen; (*candidate*) durchfallen lassen; (*subj: courage*) verlassen; (: *leader, memory*) im Stich lassen ♦ *vi* (*candidate*) durchfallen; (*attempt*) fehlschlagen; (*brakes*) versagen; (*also:* **be** ~**ing**: *health*) sich verschlechtern; (: *eyesight, light*) nachlassen; **to** ~ **to do sth** etw nicht tun; (*neglect*) (es) versäumen, etw zu tun; **without** ~ ganz bestimmt.

failing ['feɪlɪŋ] *n* Schwäche *f*, Fehler *m* ♦ *prep* in Ermangelung +*gen*; ~ **that** (oder) sonst, und wenn das nicht möglich ist.

fail-safe ['feɪlseɪf] *adj* (ab)gesichert.

failure ['feɪljə*] *n* Misserfolg *m*; (*person*) Versager(in) *m(f)*; (*of brakes, heart*) Versagen *nt*; (*of engine, power*) Ausfall *m*; (*of crops*) Missernte *f*; (*in exam*) Durchfall *m*; **his** ~ **to turn up meant that we had to ...** weil er nicht auftauchte, mussten wir ...; **it was a complete** ~ es war ein totaler Fehlschlag.

faint [feɪnt] *adj* schwach; (*breeze, trace*) leicht ♦ *n* Ohnmacht *f* ♦ *vi* ohnmächtig werden, in Ohnmacht fallen; **she felt** ~ ihr wurde schwach.

faintest ['feɪntɪst] *adj, n*: **I haven't the** ~ (**idea**) ich habe keinen blassen Schimmer.

faint-hearted ['feɪnt'hɑːtɪd] *adj* zaghaft.

faintly ['feɪntlɪ] *adv* schwach.

fair [fɛə*] *adj* gerecht, fair; (*size, number*) ansehnlich; (*chance, guess*) recht gut; (*hair*) blond; (*skin, complexion*) hell; (*weather*) schön ♦ *adv*: **to play** ~ fair spielen ♦ *n* (*also:* **trade** ~) Messe *f*; (*BRIT: funfair*) Jahrmarkt *m*, Rummel *m*; **it's not** ~! das ist nicht fair!; **a** ~ **amount of** ziemlich viel.

fair copy *n* Reinschrift *f*.

fair game *n*: **to be** ~ (**for**) (*for attack, criticism*) Freiwild *nt* sein (für).

fairground ['fɛəɡraund] *n* Rummelplatz *m*.

fair-haired [fɛə'hɛəd] *adj* blond.

fairly ['fɛəlɪ] *adv* gerecht; (*quite*) ziemlich; **I'm** ~ **sure** ich bin (mir) ziemlich sicher.

fairness ['fɛənɪs] *n* Gerechtigkeit *f*; **in all** ~

gerechterweise, fairerweise.

fair play *n* faires Verhalten *nt*, Fairplay *nt*, Fair Play *nt*.

fairway ['fɛəweɪ] *n* (*GOLF*): **the** ~ das Fairway.

fairy ['fɛərɪ] *n* Fee *f*.

fairy godmother *n* gute Fee *f*.

fairy lights (*BRIT*) *npl* bunte Lichter *pl*.

fairy tale *n* Märchen *nt*.

faith [feɪθ] *n* Glaube *m*; (*trust*) Vertrauen *nt*; **to have** ~ **in sb** jdm vertrauen; **to have** ~ **in sth** Vertrauen in etw *acc* haben.

faithful ['feɪθful] *adj* (*account*) genau; ~ (**to**) (*person*) treu +*dat*.

faithfully ['feɪθfəlɪ] *adv* (*see adj*) genau; treu.

faith healer *n* Gesundbeter(in) *m(f)*.

fake [feɪk] *n* Fälschung *f*; (*person*) Schwindler(in) *m(f)* ♦ *adj* gefälscht ♦ *vt* fälschen; (*illness, emotion*) vortäuschen; **his illness is a** ~ er simuliert seine Krankheit nur.

falcon ['fɔːlkən] *n* Falke *m*.

Falkland Islands ['fɔːlklənd-] *npl*: **the** ~ die Falklandinseln *pl*.

fall [fɔːl] (*pt* **fell**, *pp* **fallen**) *n* Fall *m*; (*of price, temperature*) Sinken *nt*; (: *sudden*) Sturz *m*; (*US: autumn*) Herbst *m* ♦ *vi* fallen; (*night, darkness*) hereinbrechen; (*silence*) eintreten; **falls** *npl* (*waterfall*) Wasserfall *m*; **a** ~ **of snow** ein Schneefall *m*; **a** ~ **of earth** ein Erdrutsch *m*; **to** ~ **flat** auf die Nase fallen; (*plan*) ins Wasser fallen; (*joke*) nicht ankommen; **to** ~ **in love (with sb/sth)** sich (in jdn/etw) verlieben; **to** ~ **short of sb's expectations** jds Erwartungen nicht erfüllen.

▶ **fall apart** *vi* auseinander fallen, kaputtgehen; (*inf: emotionally*) durchdrehen.

▶ **fall back** *vi* zurückweichen.

▶ **fall back on** *vi* zurückgreifen auf +*acc*; **to have sth to** ~ **back on** auf etw *acc* zurückgreifen können.

▶ **fall behind** *vi* zurückbleiben; (*fig: with payment*) in Rückstand geraten.

▶ **fall down** *vi* hinfallen; (*building*) einstürzen.

▶ **fall for** *vt fus* (*trick, story*) hereinfallen auf +*acc*; (*person*) sich verlieben in +*acc*.

▶ **fall in** *vi* einstürzen; (*MIL*) antreten.

▶ **fall in with** *vt fus* eingehen auf +*acc*.

▶ **fall off** *vi* herunterfallen; (*takings, attendance*) zurückgehen.

▶ **fall out** *vi* (*hair, teeth*) ausfallen; **to** ~ **out with sb** sich mit jdm zerstreiten.

▶ **fall over** *vi* hinfallen; (*object*) umfallen ♦ *vt*: **to** ~ **over o.s. to do sth** sich *dat* die größte Mühe geben, etw zu tun.

▶ **fall through** *vi* (*plan, project*) ins Wasser fallen.

fallacy ['fæləsɪ] *n* Irrtum *m*.

fall-back ['fɔːlbæk] *adj*: ~ **position** Rückzugsbasis *f*.

fallen ['fɔːlən] *pp of* **fall**.

fallible ['fæləbl] *adj* fehlbar.
falling ['fɔːlɪŋ] *adj*: ~ **market** (*COMM*) Baissemarkt *m*.
falling off *n* Rückgang *m*.
falling-out ['fɔːlɪŋ'aut] *n* (*break-up*) Bruch *m*.
Fallopian tube [fə'ləupɪən-] *n* Eileiter *m*.
fallout ['fɔːlaut] *n* radioaktiver Niederschlag *m*.
fallout shelter *n* Atombunker *m*.
fallow ['fæləu] *adj* brach(liegend).
false [fɔːls] *adj* falsch; (*imprisonment*) widerrechtlich.
false alarm *n* falscher *or* blinder Alarm *m*.
falsehood ['fɔːlshud] *n* Unwahrheit *f*.
falsely ['fɔːlslɪ] *adv* (*accuse*) zu Unrecht.
false pretences *npl*: **under** ~ unter Vorspiegelung falscher Tatsachen.
false teeth (*BRIT*) *npl* Gebiss *nt*.
falsify ['fɔːlsɪfaɪ] *vt* fälschen.
falter ['fɔːltə'] *vi* stocken; (*hesitate*) zögern.
fame [feɪm] *n* Ruhm *m*.
familiar [fə'mɪlɪə'] *adj* vertraut; (*intimate*) vertraulich; **to be ~ with** vertraut sein mit; **to make o.s. ~ with sth** sich mit etw vertraut machen; **to be on ~ terms with sb** mit jdm auf vertrautem Fuß stehen.
familiarity [fəmɪlɪ'ærɪtɪ] *n* (*see adj*) Vertrautheit *f*; Vertraulichkeit *f*.
familiarize [fə'mɪlɪəraɪz] *vt*: **to ~ o.s. with sth** sich mit etw vertraut machen.
family ['fæmɪlɪ] *n* Familie *f*; (*relations*) Verwandtschaft *f*.
family business *n* Familienbetrieb *m*.
family credit *n* Beihilfe für einkommensschwache Familien.
family doctor *n* Hausarzt *m*, Hausärztin *f*.
family life *n* Familienleben *nt*.
family man *n* (*home-loving*) häuslich veranlagter Mann *m*; (*with a family*) Familienvater *m*.
family planning *n* Familienplanung *f*; ~ **clinic** ≈ Familienberatungsstelle *f*.
family tree *n* Stammbaum *m*.
famine ['fæmɪn] *n* Hungersnot *f*.
famished ['fæmɪʃt] (*inf*) *adj* ausgehungert; **I'm ~** ich sterbe vor Hunger.
famous ['feɪməs] *adj* berühmt.
famously ['feɪməslɪ] *adv* (*get on*) prächtig.
fan [fæn] *n* (*person*) Fan *m*; (*object: folding*) Fächer *m*; (: *ELEC*) Ventilator *m* ♦ *vt* fächeln; (*fire*) anfachen; (*quarrel*) schüren.
▶ **fan out** *vi* ausschwärmen; (*unfurl*) sich fächerförmig ausbreiten.
fanatic [fə'nætɪk] *n* Fanatiker(in) *m(f)*; (*enthusiast*) Fan *m*.
fanatical [fə'nætɪkl] *adj* fanatisch.
fan belt *n* (*AUT*) Keilriemen *m*.
fanciful ['fænsɪful] *adj* (*idea*) abstrus, seltsam; (*design, name*) fantasievoll; (*object*) reich verziert.
fan club *n* Fanklub *m*.
fancy ['fænsɪ] *n* Laune *f*; (*imagination*) Fantasie *f*; (*fantasy*) Fantasievorstellung *f* ♦ *adj* (*clothes, hat*) toll, schick; (*hotel*) fein, vornehm; (*food*) ausgefallen ♦ *vt* mögen; (*imagine*) sich *dat* einbilden; (*think*) glauben; **to take a ~ to sth** Lust auf etw *acc* bekommen; **when the ~ takes him** wenn ihm gerade danach ist; **it took *or* caught my ~** es gefiel mir; **to ~ that ...** meinen, dass ...; **~ that!** (nein) so was!; **he fancies her** (*inf*) sie gefällt ihm.
fancy dress *n* Verkleidung *f*, (Masken)kostüm *nt*.
fancy-dress ball ['fænsɪdrɛs-] *n* Maskenball *m*.
fancy goods *npl* Geschenkartikel *pl*.
fanfare ['fænfɛə'] *n* Fanfare *f*.
fanfold paper ['fænfəuld-] *n* Endlospapier *nt*.
fang [fæŋ] *n* (*tooth*) Fang *m*; (: *of snake*) Giftzahn *m*.
fan heater (*BRIT*) *n* Heizlüfter *m*.
fanlight ['fænlaɪt] *n* Oberlicht *nt*.
fanny ['fænɪ] *n* (*US: inf: bottom*) Po *m*; (*BRIT: infl: genitals*) Möse *f* (!).
fantasize ['fæntəsaɪz] *vi* fantasieren.
fantastic [fæn'tæstɪk] *adj* fantastisch.
fantasy ['fæntəsɪ] *n* Fantasie *f*; (*dream*) Traum *m*.
fanzine ['fænziːn] *n* Fanmagazin *nt*.
FAO *n abbr* (= *Food and Agriculture Organization*) FAO *f*.
f.a.q. *abbr* (= *free alongside quay*) frei Kai.
far [fɑː'] *adj*: **at the ~ side** auf der anderen Seite ♦ *adv* weit; **at the ~ end** am anderen Ende; **the ~ left/right** die extreme Linke/ Rechte; ~ **away,** ~ **off** weit entfernt *or* weg; **her thoughts were ~ away** sie war mit ihren Gedanken weit weg; ~ **from** (*fig*) alles andere als; **by ~** bei weitem; **is it ~ to London?** ist es weit bis nach London?; **it's not ~ from here** es ist nicht weit von hier; **go as ~ as the church** gehen/fahren Sie bis zur Kirche; **as ~ back as the 13th century** schon im 13. Jahrhundert; **as ~ as I know** soweit ich weiß; **as ~ as possible** so weit wie möglich; **how ~?** wie weit?; **how ~ have you got with your work?** wie weit sind Sie mit Ihrer Arbeit (gekommen)?
faraway ['fɑːrəweɪ] *adj* weit entfernt; (*look, voice*) abwesend.
farce [fɑːs] *n* Farce *f*.
farcical ['fɑːsɪkl] *adj* absurd, grotesk.
fare [fɛə'] *n* Fahrpreis *m*; (*money*) Fahrgeld *nt*; (*passenger*) Fahrgast *m*; (*food*) Kost *f* ♦ *vi*: **he ~d well/badly** es ging ihm gut/schlecht; **half/full ~** halber/voller Fahrpreis; **how did you ~?** wie ist es Ihnen ergangen?; **they ~d badly in the recent elections** sie haben bei den letzten Wahlen schlecht abgeschnitten.
Far East *n*: **the ~** der Ferne Osten.
farewell [fɛə'wɛl] *excl* lebe/lebt *etc* wohl! ♦ *n* Abschied *m* ♦ *cpd* Abschieds-.
far-fetched ['fɑː'fɛtʃt] *adj* weit hergeholt.

farm [fɑːm] n Bauernhof m ♦ vt bebauen.
▶ **farm out** vt (work etc) vergeben.
farmer ['fɑːmə˟] n Bauer m, Bäu(e)rin f,
Landwirt(in) m(f).
farm hand n Landarbeiter(in) m(f).
farmhouse ['fɑːmhaus] n Bauernhaus nt.
farming ['fɑːmɪŋ] n Landwirtschaft f; (of
crops) Ackerbau m; (of animals) Viehzucht f;
sheep ~ Schafzucht f; **intensive** ~ (of crops)
Intensivanbau m; (of animals)
Intensivhaltung f.
farm labourer n = **farm hand**.
farmland ['fɑːmlænd] n Ackerland nt.
farm produce n landwirtschaftliche
Produkte pl.
farm worker n = **farm hand**.
farmyard ['fɑːmjɑːd] n Hof m.
Faroe Islands ['fɛərəu-] npl: **the** ~ die Färöer
pl.
Faroes ['fɛərəuz] npl = **Faroe Islands**.
far-reaching ['fɑːˈriːtʃɪŋ] adj weitreichend,
weit reichend.
far-sighted ['fɑːˈsaɪtɪd] adj weitsichtig; (fig)
weitblickend, weit blickend.
fart [fɑːt] vi furzen (inf!) ♦ n Furz m (inf!).
farther ['fɑːðə˟] adv weiter ♦ adj weiter
entfernt.
farthest ['fɑːðɪst] superl of **far**.
FAS, f.a.s. (BRIT) abbr (= free alongside ship)
frei Kai.
fascia ['feɪʃə] n (AUT) Armaturenbrett nt.
fascinate ['fæsɪneɪt] vt faszinieren.
fascinating ['fæsɪneɪtɪŋ] adj faszinierend.
fascination [fæsɪˈneɪʃən] n Faszination f.
fascism ['fæʃɪzəm] n Faschismus m.
fascist ['fæʃɪst] adj faschistisch ♦ n
Faschist(in) m(f).
fashion ['fæʃən] n Mode f; (manner) Art f ♦ vt
formen; **in** ~ modern; **out of** ~ unmodern;
after a ~ recht und schlecht; **in the Greek** ~
im griechischen Stil.
fashionable ['fæʃnəbl] adj modisch, modern;
(subject) Mode-; (club, writer) in Mode.
fashion designer n Modezeichner(in) m(f).
fashion show n Modenschau f.
fast [fɑːst] adj schnell; (dye, colour) farbecht
♦ adv schnell; (stuck, held) fest ♦ n Fasten nt;
(period of fasting) Fastenzeit f ♦ vi fasten; **my
watch is (5 minutes)** ~ meine Uhr geht (5
Minuten) vor; **to be** ~ **asleep** tief or fest
schlafen; **as** ~ **as I can** so schnell ich kann;
to make a boat ~ (BRIT) ein Boot
festmachen.
fasten ['fɑːsn] vt festmachen; (coat, belt etc)
zumachen ♦ vi (see vt) festgemacht werden;
zugemacht werden.
▶ **fasten (up)on** vt fus sich dat in den Kopf
setzen.
fastener ['fɑːsnə˟] n Verschluss m.
fastening ['fɑːsnɪŋ] n = **fastener**.
fast food n Fastfood nt, Fast Food nt,
Schnellgerichte pl.

fast-food ['fɑːstfuːd] cpd (industry, chain)
Fastfood-, Fast-Food-; ~ **restaurant**
Schnellimbiss m.
fastidious [fæsˈtɪdɪəs] adj penibel.
fast lane n (AUT): **the** ~ die Überholspur.
fat [fæt] adj dick; (person) dick, fett (pej);
(animal) fett; (profit) üppig ♦ n Fett nt; **that's
a** ~ **lot of use** (inf) das hilft herzlich wenig;
to live off the ~ **of the land** wie Gott in
Frankreich or wie die Made im Speck
leben.
fatal ['feɪtl] adj tödlich; (mistake)
verhängnisvoll.
fatalistic [feɪtəˈlɪstɪk] adj fatalistisch.
fatality [fəˈtælɪtɪ] n Todesopfer nt.
fatally ['feɪtəlɪ] adv (see adj) tödlich;
verhängnisvoll.
fate [feɪt] n Schicksal nt; **to meet one's** ~ vom
Schicksal ereilt werden.
fated ['feɪtɪd] adj (person) unglückselig;
(project) zum Scheitern verurteilt; (governed
by fate) vorherbestimmt.
fateful ['feɪtful] adj schicksalhaft.
fat-free ['fætfriː] adj fettfrei.
father ['fɑːðə˟] n Vater m.
Father Christmas n der Weihnachtsmann.
fatherhood ['fɑːðəhud] n Vaterschaft f.
father-in-law ['fɑːðərənlɔː] n Schwiegervater
m.
fatherland ['fɑːðəlænd] n Vaterland nt.
fatherly ['fɑːðəlɪ] adj väterlich.
fathom ['fæðəm] n (NAUT) Faden m ♦ vt (also:
~ **out**) verstehen.
fatigue [fəˈtiːg] n Erschöpfung f; **fatigues** npl
(MIL) Arbeitsanzug m; **metal** ~
Metallermüdung f.
fatness ['fætnɪs] n Dicke f.
fatten ['fætn] vt mästen ♦ vi (person) dick
werden; (animal) fett werden; **chocolate is**
~**ing** Schokolade macht dick.
fatty ['fætɪ] adj fett ♦ n (inf) Dickerchen nt.
fatuous ['fætjuəs] adj albern, töricht.
faucet ['fɔːsɪt] (US) n (Wasser)hahn m.
fault [fɔːlt] n Fehler m; (blame) Schuld f; (in
machine) Defekt m; (GEOG) Verwerfung f
♦ vt (also: **find** ~ **with**) etwas auszusetzen
haben an +dat; **it's my** ~ es ist meine Schuld;
at ~ im Unrecht; **generous to a** ~
übermäßig großzügig.
faultless ['fɔːltlɪs] adj fehlerlos.
faulty ['fɔːltɪ] adj defekt.
fauna ['fɔːnə] n Fauna f.
faux pas ['fəuˈpɑː] n inv Fauxpas m.
favor etc (US) = **favour** etc.
favour, (US) **favor** ['feɪvə˟] n (approval)
Wohlwollen nt; (help) Gefallen m ♦ vt
bevorzugen; (be favourable for) begünstigen;
to ask a ~ **of sb** jdn um einen Gefallen
bitten; **to do sb a** ~ jdm einen Gefallen tun;
to find ~ **with sb** bei jdm Anklang finden; **in**
~ **of** (biased) zugunsten or zu Gunsten von;
(rejected) zugunsten or zu Gunsten +gen; **to**

be in ~ **of sth** für etw sein; **to be in** ~ **of doing sth** dafür sein, etw zu tun.
favourable ['feɪvrəbl] *adj* günstig; (*reaction*) positiv; (*comparison*) vorteilhaft.
favourably ['feɪvrəblɪ] *adv* (*react*) positiv; (*compare*) vorteilhaft.
favourite ['feɪvrɪt] *adj* Lieblings- ♦ *n* Liebling *m*; (*in race*) Favorit(in) *m(f)*.
favouritism ['feɪvrɪtɪzəm] *n* Günstlingswirtschaft *f*.
fawn [fɔːn] *n* Rehkitz *nt* ♦ *adj* (*also:* ~-**coloured**) hellbraun ♦ *vi:* **to** ~ (**up)on** sich einschmeicheln bei.
fax [fæks] *n* Fax *nt*; (*machine*) Fax(gerät) *nt* ♦ *vt* faxen.
FBI (*US*) *n abbr* (= *Federal Bureau of Investigation*) FBI *nt*.
FCC (*US*) *n abbr* (= *Federal Communications Commission*) Aufsichtsbehörde im Medienbereich.
FCO (*BRIT*) *n abbr* (= *Foreign and Commonwealth Office*) ≈ Auswärtiges Amt *nt*.
FD (*US*) *n abbr* = **fire department**.
FDA (*US*) *n abbr* (= *Food and Drug Administration*) Nahrungs- und Arzneimittelbehörde.
FE *n abbr* (= *further education*) Fortbildung *f*.
fear [fɪəʳ] *n* Furcht *f*, Angst *f* ♦ *vt* fürchten, Angst haben vor +*dat*; (*be worried about*) befürchten ♦ *vi* sich fürchten; ~ **of heights** Höhenangst *f*; **for** ~ **of doing sth** aus Angst, etw zu tun; **to** ~ **for** fürchten um; **to** ~ **that** ... befürchten, dass ...
fearful ['fɪəful] *adj* (*frightening*) furchtbar, schrecklich; (*apprehensive*) ängstlich; **to be** ~ **of** Angst haben vor +*dat*.
fearfully ['fɪəfəlɪ] *adv* ängstlich; (*inf: very*) furchtbar, schrecklich.
fearless ['fɪəlɪs] *adj* furchtlos.
fearsome ['fɪəsəm] *adj* Furcht erregend.
feasibility [fiːzə'bɪlɪtɪ] *n* Durchführbarkeit *f*.
feasibility study *n* Durchführbarkeitsstudie *f*.
feasible ['fiːzəbl] *adj* machbar; (*proposal, plan*) durchführbar.
feast [fiːst] *n* Festmahl *nt*; (*REL: also:* ~ **day**) Festtag *m*, Feiertag *m* ♦ *vi* schlemmen; **to** ~ **on** sich gütlich tun an +*dat*.
feat [fiːt] *n* Leistung *f*.
feather ['feðəʳ] *n* Feder *f* ♦ *cpd* Feder-; (*mattress*) Federkern- ♦ *vt:* **to** ~ **one's nest** (*fig*) sein Schäfchen ins Trockene bringen.
featherweight ['feðəweɪt] *n* Leichtgewicht *nt*; (*BOXING*) Federgewicht *nt*.
feature ['fiːtʃəʳ] *n* Merkmal *nt*; (*PRESS, TV*) Feature *nt* ♦ *vt:* **the film** ~**s Marlon Brando** Marlon Brando spielt in dem Film mit ♦ *vi:* **to** ~ **in** vorkommen in +*dat*; (*film*) mitspielen in +*dat*; **features** *npl* (*of face*) (Gesichts)züge *pl*; **it** ~**d prominently in** es spielte eine große Rolle in +*dat*; **a special** ~ **on sth/sb** ein Sonderbeitrag *m* über etw/jdn.

feature film *n* Spielfilm *m*.
featureless ['fiːtʃəlɪs] *adj* (*landscape*) eintönig.
Feb. *abbr* (= *February*) Feb.
February ['fɛbruərɪ] *n* Februar *m*; *see also* **July**.
feces ['fiːsiːz] (*US*) *npl* = **faeces**.
feckless ['fɛklɪs] *adj* nutzlos.
Fed (*US*) *abbr* = **federal, federation**.
Fed. [fɛd] (*US: inf*) *n abbr* = **Federal Reserve Board**.
fed [fɛd] *pt, pp of* **feed**.
federal ['fɛdərəl] *adj* föderalistisch.
Federal Republic of Germany *n* Bundesrepublik *f* Deutschland.
Federal Reserve Board (*US*) *n* Kontrollorgan der US-Zentralbank.
Federal Trade Commission (*US*) *n* Handelskontrollbehörde.
federation [fɛdə'reɪʃən] *n* Föderation *f*, Bund *m*.
fed up *adj:* **to be** ~ **with** die Nase voll haben von.
fee [fiː] *n* Gebühr *f*; (*of doctor, lawyer*) Honorar *nt*; **school** ~**s** Schulgeld *nt*; **entrance** ~ Eintrittsgebühr *f*; **membership** ~ Mitgliedsbeitrag *m*; **for a small** ~ gegen eine geringe Gebühr.
feeble ['fiːbl] *adj* schwach; (*joke*) lahm.
feeble-minded ['fiːbl'maɪndɪd] *adj* dümmlich.
feed [fiːd] (*pt, pp* **fed**) *n* Mahlzeit *f*; (*of animal*) Fütterung *f*; (*on printer*) Papiervorschub *m* ♦ *vt* füttern; (*family etc*) ernähren; (*machine*) versorgen; **to** ~ **sth into sth** etw in etw *acc* einfüllen *or* eingeben; (*data, information*) etw in etw *acc* eingeben; **to** ~ **material into sth** Material in etw *acc* eingeben.
▶ **feed back** *vt* zurückleiten.
▶ **feed on** *vt fus* sich nähren von.
feedback ['fiːdbæk] *n* Feed-back *nt*, Feedback *nt*, Rückmeldung *f*; (*from person*) Reaktion *f*.
feeder ['fiːdəʳ] *n* (*road*) Zubringer *m*; (*railway line, air route*) Zubringerlinie *f*; (*baby's bottle*) Flasche *f*.
feeding bottle ['fiːdɪŋ-] (*BRIT*) *n* Flasche *f*.
feel [fiːl] (*pt, pp* **felt**) *n* (*sensation, touch*) Gefühl *nt*; (*impression*) Atmosphäre *f* ♦ *vt* (*object*) fühlen; (*desire, anger, grief*) empfinden; (*pain*) spüren; (*cold*) leiden unter +*dat*; (*think, believe*): **I** ~ **that you ought to do it** ich meine *or* ich bin der Meinung, dass Sie es tun sollten; **it has a soft** ~ es fühlt sich weich an; **I** ~ **hungry** ich habe Hunger; **I** ~ **cold** mir ist kalt; **to** ~ **lonely/better** sich einsam/besser fühlen; **I don't** ~ **well** mir geht es nicht gut; **I** ~ **sorry for him** er tut mir Leid; **it** ~**s soft** es fühlt sich weich an; **it** ~**s colder here** es kommt mir hier kälter vor; **it** ~**s like velvet** es fühlt sich wie Samt an; **to** ~ **like** (*desire*) Lust haben auf +*acc*; **to** ~ **like doing sth** Lust haben, etw zu tun; **to get the** ~ **of sth** ein Gefühl für etw bekommen; **I'm still** ~**ing my way** ich versuche noch, mich zu orientieren.

▶ **feel about** vi umhertasten; **to ~ about** or **around in one's pocket for** in seiner Tasche herumsuchen nach.

▶ **feel around** vi = feel about.

feeler ['fiːlə*] n Fühler m; **to put out a ~** or **~s** (fig) seine Fühler ausstrecken.

feelgood ['fiːlgʊd] adj (film, song) Feelgood-.

feeling ['fiːlɪŋ] n Gefühl nt; (impression) Eindruck m; **~s ran high about it** man ereiferte sich sehr darüber; **what are your ~s about the matter?** was meinen Sie dazu?; **I have a ~ that** ... ich habe das Gefühl, dass ...; **my ~ is that** ... meine Meinung ist, dass ...; **to hurt sb's ~s** jdn verletzen.

fee-paying ['fiːpeɪɪŋ] adj (school) Privat-; **~ pupils** Schüler, deren Eltern Schulgeld zahlen.

feet [fiːt] npl of **foot**.

feign [feɪn] vt vortäuschen.

feigned [feɪnd] adj vorgetäuscht.

feint [feɪnt] n fein liniertes Papier nt.

felicitous [fɪ'lɪsɪtəs] adj glücklich.

feline ['fiːlaɪn] adj (eyes etc) Katzen-; (features, grace) katzenartig.

fell [fɛl] pt of **fall** ♦ vt fällen; (opponent) niederstrecken ♦ n (BRIT: mountain) Berg m; (: moorland): **the ~s** das Moor(land) ♦ adj: **in one ~ swoop** auf einen Schlag.

fellow ['fɛləʊ] n Mann m, Typ m (inf); (comrade) Kamerad m; (of learned society) Mitglied nt; (of university) Fellow m; **their ~ prisoners/students** ihre Mitgefangenen/ Kommilitonen (und Kommilitoninnen); **his ~ workers** seine Kollegen (und Kolleginnen).

fellow citizen n Mitbürger(in) m(f).

fellow countryman (irreg: like **man**) n Landsmann m, Landsmännin f.

fellow men npl Mitmenschen pl.

fellowship ['fɛləʊʃɪp] n Kameradschaft f; (society) Gemeinschaft f; (SCOL) Forschungsstipendium nt.

fell-walking ['fɛlwɔːkɪŋ] (BRIT) n Bergwandern nt.

felon ['fɛlən] n (LAW) (Schwer)verbrecher m.

felony ['fɛlənɪ] n (LAW) (schweres) Verbrechen nt.

felt [fɛlt] pt, pp of **feel** ♦ n Filz m.

felt-tip pen ['fɛlttɪp-] n Filzstift m.

female ['fiːmeɪl] n Weibchen nt; (pej: woman) Frau f, Weib nt (pej) ♦ adj weiblich; (vote etc) Frauen-; (ELEC: connector, plug) Mutter-, Innen-; **male and ~ students** Studenten und Studentinnen.

Femidom ® ['fɛmɪdəm] n Kondom nt für die Frau, Femidom ® nt.

feminine ['fɛmɪnɪn] adj weiblich, feminin ♦ n Femininum nt.

femininity [fɛmɪ'nɪnɪtɪ] n Weiblichkeit f.

feminism ['fɛmɪnɪzəm] n Feminismus m.

feminist ['fɛmɪnɪst] n Feminist(in) m(f).

fen [fɛn] (BRIT) n: **the F~s** die Niederungen in East Anglia.

fence [fɛns] n Zaun m; (SPORT) Hindernis nt ♦ vt (also: **~ in**) einzäunen ♦ vi (SPORT) fechten; **to sit on the ~** (fig) neutral bleiben, nicht Partei ergreifen.

fencing ['fɛnsɪŋ] n (SPORT) Fechten nt.

fend [fɛnd] vi: **to ~ for o.s.** für sich (selbst) sorgen, sich allein durchbringen.

▶ **fend off** vt abwehren.

fender ['fɛndə*] n Kamingitter nt; (on boat) Fender m; (US: of car) Kotflügel m.

fennel ['fɛnl] n Fenchel m.

ferment [vi fə'mɛnt, n 'fɜːmɛnt] vi gären ♦ n (fig: unrest) Unruhe f.

fermentation [fɜːmɛn'teɪʃən] n Gärung f.

fern [fɜːn] n Farn m.

ferocious [fə'rəʊʃəs] adj wild; (behaviour) heftig; (competition) scharf.

ferocity [fə'rɒsɪtɪ] n (see adj) Wildheit f; Heftigkeit f; Schärfe f.

ferret ['fɛrɪt] n Frettchen nt.

▶ **ferret about** vi herumstöbern.

▶ **ferret around** vi = ferret about.

▶ **ferret out** vt aufspüren.

ferry ['fɛrɪ] n (also: **~boat**) Fähre f ♦ vt transportieren; **to ~ sth/sb across** or **over** jdn/etw übersetzen.

ferryman ['fɛrɪmən] (irreg: like **man**) n Fährmann m.

fertile ['fɜːtaɪl] adj fruchtbar; **~ period** fruchtbare Tage pl.

fertility [fə'tɪlɪtɪ] n Fruchtbarkeit f.

fertility drug n Fruchtbarkeitsmedikament nt.

fertilization [fɜːtɪlaɪ'zeɪʃən] n (BIOL) Befruchtung f.

fertilize ['fɜːtɪlaɪz] vt düngen; (BIOL) befruchten.

fertilizer ['fɜːtɪlaɪzə*] n Dünger m.

fervent ['fɜːvənt] adj leidenschaftlich; (admirer) glühend.

fervour, (US) **fervor** ['fɜːvə*] n Leidenschaft f.

fester ['fɛstə*] vi (wound) eitern; (insult) nagen; (row) sich verschlimmern.

festival ['fɛstɪvəl] n Fest nt; (ART, MUS) Festival nt, Festspiele pl.

festive ['fɛstɪv] adj festlich; **the ~ season** (BRIT: Christmas and New Year) die Festzeit f.

festivities [fɛs'tɪvɪtɪz] npl Feierlichkeiten pl.

festoon [fɛs'tuːn] vt: **to ~ with** schmücken mit.

fetch [fɛtʃ] vt holen; (sell for) (ein)bringen; **would you ~ me a glass of water please?** kannst du mir bitte ein Glas Wasser bringen?; **how much did it ~?** wie viel hat es eingebracht?

▶ **fetch up** (inf) vi landen (inf).

fetching ['fɛtʃɪŋ] adj bezaubernd, reizend.

fête [feɪt] n Fest nt.

fetid ['fɛtɪd] adj übel riechend.

fetish ['fɛtɪʃ] n Fetisch m.

fetter ['fɛtə*] vt fesseln; (horse) anpflocken;

(fig) in Fesseln legen.
fetters ['fɛtəz] *npl* Fesseln *pl.*
fettle ['fɛtl] *(BRIT)* *n:* **in fine** ~ **in bester Form.**
fetus ['fiːtəs] *(US)* *n* = **foetus.**
feud [fjuːd] *n* Streit *m* ♦ *vi* im Streit liegen; **a family** ~ ein Familienstreit *m.*
feudal ['fjuːdl] *adj (society etc)* Feudal-.
feudalism ['fjuːdlɪzəm] *n* Feudalismus *m.*
fever ['fiːvə*] *n* Fieber *nt;* **he has a** ~ er hat Fieber.
feverish ['fiːvərɪʃ] *adj* fiebrig; *(activity, emotion)* fieberhaft.
few [fjuː] *adj* wenige; **a** ~ *(adj)* ein paar, einige; *(pron)* ein paar; **a** ~ **more (days)** noch ein paar (Tage); **they were** ~ sie waren nur wenige; ~ **succeed** nur wenigen gelingt es; **very** ~ **survive** nur sehr wenige überleben; **I know a** ~ ich kenne einige; **a good** ~, **quite a** ~ ziemlich viele; **in the next/past** ~ **days** in den nächsten/letzten paar Tagen; **every** ~ **days/months** alle paar Tage/Monate.
fewer ['fjuːə*] *adj* weniger; **there are** ~ **buses on Sundays** Sonntags fahren weniger Busse.
fewest ['fjuːɪst] *adj* die wenigsten.
FFA *n abbr (= Future Farmers of America)* Verband von Landwirtschaftsstudenten.
FH *(BRIT)* *n abbr* = **fire hydrant.**
FHA *(US)* *n abbr (= Federal Housing Administration):* ~ **loan** Baudarlehen *nt.*
fiancé [fɪ'ãːŋseɪ] *n* Verlobte(r) *m.*
fiancée [fɪ'ãːŋseɪ] *n* Verlobte *f.*
fiasco [fɪ'æskəu] *n* Fiasko *nt.*
fib [fɪb] *n* Flunkerei *f (inf).*
fibre, *(US)* **fiber** ['faɪbə*] *n* Faser *f;* *(cloth)* (Faser)stoff *m;* *(roughage)* Ballaststoffe *pl;* *(ANAT: tissue)* Gewebe *nt.*
fibreboard, *(US)* **fiberboard** ['faɪbəbɔːd] *n* Faserplatte *f.*
fibreglass, *(US)* **fiberglass** ['faɪbəglɑːs] *n* Fiberglas *nt.*
fibrositis [faɪbrə'saɪtɪs] *n* Bindegewebsentzündung *f.*
FICA *(US)* *n abbr (= Federal Insurance Contributions Act)* Abgabe zur Sozialversicherung.
fickle ['fɪkl] *adj* unbeständig; *(weather)* wechselhaft.
fiction ['fɪkʃən] *n* Erfindung *f;* *(LITER)* Erzählliteratur *f,* Prosaliteratur *f.*
fictional ['fɪkʃənl] *adj* erfunden.
fictionalize ['fɪkʃnəlaɪz] *vt* fiktionalisieren.
fictitious [fɪk'tɪʃəs] *adj (false)* falsch; *(invented)* fiktiv, frei erfunden.
fiddle ['fɪdl] *n* Fiedel *f (inf),* Geige *f;* *(fraud, swindle)* Schwindelei *f* ♦ *vt (BRIT: accounts)* frisieren *(inf);* **tax** ~ Steuermanipulation *f;* **to work a** ~ ein krummes Ding drehen *(inf).*
▶ **fiddle with** *vt fus* herumspielen mit.
fiddler ['fɪdlə*] *n* Geiger(in) *m(f).*
fiddly ['fɪdlɪ] *adj* knifflig *(inf);* *(object)*

fummelig.
fidelity [fɪ'dɛlɪtɪ] *n* Treue *f;* *(accuracy)* Genauigkeit *f.*
fidget ['fɪdʒɪt] *vi* zappeln.
fidgety ['fɪdʒɪtɪ] *adj* zappelig.
fiduciary [fɪ'djuːʃɪərɪ] *n (LAW)* Treuhänder *m.*
field [fiːld] *n* Feld *nt;* *(SPORT: ground)* Platz *m;* *(subject, area of interest)* Gebiet *nt;* *(COMPUT)* Datenfeld *nt* ♦ *cpd* Feld-; **to lead the** ~ das Feld anführen; ~ **trip** Exkursion *f.*
field day *n:* **to have a** ~ einen herrlichen Tag haben.
field glasses *npl* Feldstecher *m.*
field hospital *n* Feldlazarett *nt.*
field marshal *n* Feldmarschall *m.*
field work *n* Feldforschung *f;* *(ARCHAEOLOGY, GEOG)* Arbeit *f* im Gelände.
fiend [fiːnd] *n* Teufel *m.*
fiendish ['fiːndɪʃ] *adj* teuflisch; *(problem)* verzwickt.
fierce [fɪəs] *adj* wild; *(look)* böse; *(fighting, wind)* heftig; *(loyalty)* leidenschaftlich; *(enemy)* erbittert; *(heat)* glühend.
fiery ['faɪərɪ] *adj* glühend; *(temperament)* feurig, hitzig.
FIFA ['fiːfə] *n abbr (= Fédération Internationale de Football Association)* FIFA *f.*
fifteen [fɪf'tiːn] *num* fünfzehn.
fifteenth [fɪf'tiːnθ] *num* fünfzehnte(r, s).
fifth [fɪfθ] *num* fünfte(r, s) ♦ *n* Fünftel *nt.*
fiftieth ['fɪftɪɪθ] *num* fünfzigste(r, s).
fifty ['fɪftɪ] *num* fünfzig.
fifty-fifty ['fɪftɪ'fɪftɪ] *adj, adv* halbe-halbe, fifty-fifty; **to go/share** ~ **with sb** mit jdm halbe-halbe *or* fifty-fifty machen; **we have a** ~ **chance (of success)** unsere Chancen stehen fifty-fifty.
fig [fɪg] *n* Feige *f.*
fight [faɪt] *(pt, pp fought)* *n* Kampf *m;* *(quarrel)* Streit *m;* *(punch-up)* Schlägerei *f* ♦ *vt* kämpfen mit *or* gegen; *(prejudice etc)* bekämpfen; *(election)* kandidieren bei; *(emotion)* ankämpfen gegen; *(LAW: case)* durchkämpfen, durchfechten ♦ *vi* kämpfen; *(quarrel)* sich streiten; *(punch-up)* sich schlagen; **to put up a** ~ sich zur Wehr setzen; **to** ~ **one's way through a crowd/the undergrowth** sich *dat* einen Weg durch die Menge/das Unterholz bahnen; **to** ~ **against** bekämpfen; **to** ~ **for one's rights** für seine Rechte kämpfen.
▶ **fight back** *vi* zurückschlagen; *(SPORT)* zurückkämpfen; *(after illness)* zu Kräften kommen ♦ *vt fus* unterdrücken.
▶ **fight down** *vt* unterdrücken.
▶ **fight off** *vt* abwehren; *(sleep, urge)* ankämpfen gegen.
▶ **fight out** *vt:* **to** ~ **it out** es untereinander ausfechten.
fighter ['faɪtə*] *n* Kämpfer(in) *m(f);* *(plane)* Jagdflugzeug *nt;* *(fig)* Kämpfernatur *f.*
fighter pilot *n* Jagdflieger *m.*

fighting ['faɪtɪŋ] n Kämpfe pl; (brawl) Schlägereien pl.

figment ['fɪgmənt] n: **a ~ of the imagination** ein Hirngespinst nt, pure Einbildung f.

figurative ['fɪgjurətɪv] adj bildlich, übertragen; (style) gegenständlich.

figure ['fɪgə'] n Figur f; (illustration) Abbildung f; (number, statistic, cipher) Zahl f; (person) Gestalt f; (personality) Persönlichkeit f ♦ vt (esp US) glauben, schätzen ♦ vi eine Rolle spielen; **to put a ~ on sth** eine Zahl für etw angeben; **public ~** Persönlichkeit f des öffentlichen Lebens.

▸ **figure out** vt ausrechnen.

figurehead ['fɪgəhɛd] n Galionsfigur f.

figure of speech n Redensart f, Redewendung f.

figure skating n Eiskunstlaufen nt.

Fiji (Islands) ['fiːdʒiː-] n(pl) Fidschiinseln pl.

filament ['fɪləmənt] n Glühfaden m; (BOT) Staubfaden m.

filch [fɪltʃ] (inf) vt filzen.

file [faɪl] n Akte f, (folder) (Akten)ordner m; (for loose leaf) (Akten)mappe f; (COMPUT) Datei f; (row) Reihe f; (tool) Feile f ♦ vt ablegen, abheften; (claim) einreichen; (wood, metal, fingernails) feilen ♦ vi: **to ~ in/ out** nacheinander hereinkommen/ hinausgehen; **to ~ a suit against sb** eine Klage gegen jdn erheben; **to ~ past** in einer Reihe vorbeigehen; **to ~ for divorce** die Scheidung einreichen.

filename ['faɪlneɪm] n (COMPUT) Dateiname m.

filibuster ['fɪlɪbʌstə'] (esp US: POL) n (also: ~**er**) Dauerredner(in) m(f) ♦ vi filibustern, Obstruktion betreiben.

filing ['faɪlɪŋ] n Ablegen nt, Abheften nt.

filing cabinet n Aktenschrank m.

filing clerk n Angestellte(r) f(m) in der Registratur.

Filipino [fɪlɪ'piːnəu] n Filipino m, Filipina f; (LING) Philippinisch nt.

fill [fɪl] vt füllen; (space, area) ausfüllen; (tooth) plombieren; (need) erfüllen ♦ vi sich füllen ♦ n: **to eat one's ~** sich satt essen; **we've already ~ed that vacancy** wir haben diese Stelle schon besetzt.

▸ **fill in** vt füllen; (time) überbrücken; (form) ausfüllen ♦ vi: **to ~ in for sb** für jdn einspringen; **to ~ sb in on sth** (inf) jdn über etw acc ins Bild setzen.

▸ **fill out** vt ausfüllen.

▸ **fill up** vt füllen ♦ vi (AUT) tanken; **~ it up, please** (AUT) bitte voll tanken.

fillet ['fɪlɪt] n Filet nt ♦ vt filetieren.

fillet steak n Filetsteak nt.

filling ['fɪlɪŋ] n Füllung f; (for tooth) Plombe f.

filling station n Tankstelle f.

fillip ['fɪlɪp] n (stimulus) Ansporn m.

filly ['fɪlɪ] n Stutfohlen nt.

film [fɪlm] n Film m; (of powder etc) Schicht f;

(for wrapping) Plastikfolie f ♦ vt, vi filmen.

film star n Filmstar m.

film strip n Filmstreifen m.

film studio n Filmstudio nt.

Filofax ® ['faɪləufæks] n Filofax ® nt, Terminplaner m.

filter ['fɪltə'] n Filter m ♦ vt filtern.

▸ **filter in** vi durchsickern.

▸ **filter through** vi = filter in.

filter coffee n Filterkaffee m.

filter lane (BRIT) n Abbiegespur f.

filter tip n Filter m.

filter-tipped ['fɪltə'tɪpt] adj (cigarette) Filter-.

filth [fɪlθ] n Dreck m, Schmutz m.

filthy ['fɪlθɪ] adj dreckig, schmutzig; (language) unflätig.

fin [fɪn] n Flosse f; (TECH) Seitenflosse f.

final ['faɪnl] adj letzte(r, s); (ultimate) letztendlich; (definitive) endgültig ♦ n Finale nt, Endspiel nt; **finals** npl (UNIV) Abschlussprüfung f.

final demand n letzte Zahlungsaufforderung f.

finale [fɪ'nɑːlɪ] n Finale nt; (THEAT) Schlussszene f.

finalist ['faɪnəlɪst] n Endrundenteilnehmer(in) m(f), Finalist(in) m(f).

finality [faɪ'nælɪtɪ] n Endgültigkeit f; **with an air of ~** mit Bestimmtheit.

finalize ['faɪnəlaɪz] vt endgültig festlegen.

finally ['faɪnəlɪ] adv endlich, schließlich; (lastly) schließlich, zum Schluss; (irrevocably) endgültig.

finance [faɪ'næns] n Geldmittel pl; (money management) Finanzwesen nt ♦ vt finanzieren; **finances** npl (personal) Finanzen pl, Finanzlage f.

financial [faɪ'nænʃəl] adj finanziell; **~ statement** Bilanz f.

financially [faɪ'nænʃəlɪ] adv finanziell.

financial year n Geschäftsjahr nt.

financier [faɪ'nænsɪə'] n Finanzier m.

find [faɪnd] (pt, pp found) vt finden; (discover) entdecken ♦ n Fund m; **to ~ sb guilty** jdn für schuldig befinden; **to ~ (some) difficulty in doing sth** (einige) Schwierigkeiten haben, etw zu tun.

▸ **find out** vt herausfinden; (person) erwischen ♦ vi: **to ~ out about** etwas herausfinden über +acc; (by chance) etwas erfahren über +acc.

findings ['faɪndɪŋz] npl (LAW) Urteil nt; (of report) Ergebnis nt.

fine [faɪn] adj fein; (excellent) gut; (thin) dünn ♦ adv gut; (small) fein ♦ n Geldstrafe f ♦ vt mit einer Geldstrafe belegen; **he's ~** es geht ihm gut; **the weather is ~** das Wetter ist schön; **that's cutting it (a bit) ~** das ist aber (ein bisschen) knapp; **you're doing ~** das machen Sie gut.

fine arts npl schöne Künste pl.

finely ['faɪnlɪ] adv schön; (chop) klein; (slice)

dünn; (*adjust*) fein.

fine print *n*: **the** ~ das Kleingedruckte *or* klein Gedruckte.

finery ['faɪnərɪ] *n* (*of dress*) Staat *m*.

finesse [fɪ'nɛs] *n* Geschick *nt*.

fine-tooth comb ['faɪntu:θ-] *n*: **to go through sth with a** ~ (*fig*) etw genau unter die Lupe nehmen.

finger ['fɪŋgə*] *n* Finger *m* ♦ *vt* befühlen; **little** ~ kleiner Finger; **index** ~ Zeigefinger *m*.

fingernail ['fɪŋgəneɪl] *n* Fingernagel *m*.

fingerprint ['fɪŋgəprɪnt] *n* Fingerabdruck *m* ♦ *vt* Fingerabdrücke abnehmen +*dat*.

fingerstall ['fɪŋgəstɔ:l] *n* Fingerling *m*.

fingertip ['fɪŋgətɪp] *n* Fingerspitze *f*; **to have sth at one's** ~**s** (*to hand*) etw parat haben; (*know well*) etw aus dem Effeff kennen (*inf*).

finicky ['fɪnɪkɪ] *adj* pingelig.

finish ['fɪnɪʃ] *n* Schluss *m*, Ende *nt*; (*SPORT*) Finish *nt*; (*polish etc*) Verarbeitung *f* ♦ *vt* fertig sein mit; (*work*) erledigen; (*book*) auslesen; (*use up*) aufbrauchen ♦ *vi* enden; (*person*) fertig sein; **to** ~ **doing sth** mit etw fertig werden; **to** ~ **third** als dritter durchs Ziel gehen; **to have** ~**ed with sth** mit etw fertig sein; **she's** ~**ed with him** sie hat mit ihm Schluss gemacht.

▶ **finish off** *vt* fertig machen; (*kill*) den Gnadenstoß geben.

▶ **finish up** *vt* (*food*) aufessen; (*drink*) austrinken ♦ *vi* (*end up*) landen.

finished ['fɪnɪʃt] *adj* fertig; (*performance*) ausgereift; (*inf: tired*) erledigt.

finishing line ['fɪnɪʃɪŋ-] *n* Ziellinie *f*.

finishing school *n* höhere Mädchenschule *f* (*in der auch Etikette und gesellschaftliches Verhalten gelehrt wird*).

finishing touches *npl*: **the** ~ der letzte Schliff.

finite ['faɪnaɪt] *adj* begrenzt; (*verb*) finit.

Finland ['fɪnlənd] *n* Finnland *nt*.

Finn [fɪn] *n* Finne *m*, Finnin *f*.

Finnish ['fɪnɪʃ] *adj* finnisch ♦ *n* (*LING*) Finnisch *nt*.

fjord [fjɔ:d] *n* = **fjord**.

fir [fə:*] *n* Tanne *f*.

fire ['faɪə*] *n* Feuer *nt*; (*in hearth*) (Kamin)feuer *nt*; (*accidental fire*) Brand *m* ♦ *vt* abschießen; (*imagination*) beflügeln; (*enthusiasm*) befeuern; (*inf: dismiss*) feuern ♦ *vi* feuern, schießen; **to** ~ **a gun** ein Gewehr abschießen; **to be on** ~ brennen; **to set** ~ **to sth, set sth on** ~ etw anzünden; **insured against** ~ feuerversichert; **electric/gas** ~ Elektro-/Gasofen *m*; **to come/be under** ~ **(from)** unter Beschuss (von) geraten/ stehen.

fire alarm *n* Feuermelder *m*.

firearm ['faɪərɑ:m] *n* Feuerwaffe *f*, Schusswaffe *f*.

fire brigade *n* Feuerwehr *f*.

fire chief *n* Branddirektor *m*.

fire department (*US*) *n* Feuerwehr *f*.

fire door *n* Feuertür *f*.

fire drill *n* Probealarm *m*.

fire engine *n* Feuerwehrauto *nt*.

fire escape *n* Feuertreppe *f*.

fire-extinguisher ['faɪərɪk'stɪŋgwɪʃə*] *n* Feuerlöscher *m*.

fireguard ['faɪəgɑ:d] (*BRIT*) *n* (Schutz)gitter *nt* (*vor dem Kamin*).

fire hazard *n*: **that's a** ~ das ist feuergefährlich.

fire hydrant *n* Hydrant *m*.

fire insurance *n* Feuerversicherung *f*.

fireman ['faɪəmən] (*irreg: like* **man**) *n* Feuerwehrmann *m*.

fireplace ['faɪəpleɪs] *n* Kamin *m*.

fireplug ['faɪəplʌg] (*US*) *n* = **fire hydrant**.

fire practice *n* = **fire drill**.

fireproof ['faɪəpru:f] *adj* feuerfest.

fire regulations *npl* Brandschutzbestimmungen *pl*.

fire screen *n* Ofenschirm *m*.

fireside ['faɪəsaɪd] *n*: **by the** ~ am Kamin.

fire station *n* Feuerwache *f*.

firewood ['faɪəwud] *n* Brennholz *nt*.

fireworks ['faɪəwə:ks] *npl* Feuerwerkskörper *pl*; (*display*) Feuerwerk *nt*.

firing line ['faɪərɪŋ-] *n* Feuerlinie *f*, Schusslinie *f*; **to be in the** ~ (*fig*) in der Schusslinie sein.

firing squad *n* Exekutionskommando *nt*.

firm [fə:m] *adj* fest; (*mattress*) hart; (*measures*) durchgreifend ♦ *n* Firma *f*; **to be a** ~ **believer in sth** fest von etw überzeugt sein.

firmly ['fə:mlɪ] *adv* (*see adj*) fest; hart; (*definitely*) entschlossen.

firmness ['fə:mnɪs] *n* (*see adj*) Festigkeit *f*; Härte *f*; (*definiteness*) Entschlossenheit *f*.

first [fə:st] *adj* erste(r, s) ♦ *adv* als Erste(r, s); (*before other things*) zuerst; (*when listing reasons etc*) erstens; (*for the first time*) zum ersten Mal ♦ *n* Erste(r, s); (*AUT: also:* ~ **gear**) der erste Gang; (*BRIT: SCOL*) ≈ Eins *f*; **the** ~ **of January** der erste Januar; **at** ~ zuerst, zunächst; ~ **of all** vor allem; **in the** ~ **instance** zuerst *or* zunächst einmal; **I'll do it** ~ **thing (tomorrow)** ich werde es (morgen) als Erstes tun; **from the very** ~ gleich von Anfang an.

first aid *n* erste Hilfe *f*.

first-aid kit [fə:st'eɪd-] *n* Erste-Hilfe-Ausrüstung *f*.

first-class ['fə:st'klɑ:s] *adj* erstklassig; (*carriage, ticket*) Erste(r)-Klasse-; (*post*) bevorzugt befördert ♦ *adv* (*travel, send*) erster Klasse.

first-hand ['fə:st'hænd] *adj* aus erster Hand.

first lady (*US*) *n* First Lady *f*; **the** ~ **of jazz** die Königin des Jazz.

firstly ['fə:stlɪ] *adv* erstens, zunächst einmal.

first name *n* Vorname *m*.

first night n Premiere f.

first-rate ['fəːst'reɪt] adj erstklassig.

first-time buyer ['fəːsttaɪm-] n jd, der zum ersten Mal ein Haus/eine Wohnung kauft.

fir tree n Tannenbaum m.

FIS (BRIT) n abbr (= Family Income Supplement) Beihilfe für einkommensschwache Familien.

fiscal ['fɪskl] adj (year) Steuer-; (policies) Finanz-.

fish [fɪʃ] n inv Fisch m ♦ vt (area) fischen in +dat; (river) angeln in +dat ♦ vi fischen; (as sport, hobby) angeln; **to go ~ing** fischen/angeln gehen.

► **fish out** vt herausfischen.

fish bone n (Fisch)gräte f.

fish cake n Fischfrikadelle f.

fisherman ['fɪʃəmən] (irreg: like man) n Fischer m.

fishery ['fɪʃərɪ] n Fischereigebiet nt.

fish factory (BRIT) n Fischfabrik f.

fish farm n Fischzucht(anlage) f.

fishfingers [fɪʃ'fɪŋɡəz] (BRIT) npl Fischstäbchen pl.

fish-hook ['fɪʃhuk] n Angelhaken m.

fishing boat ['fɪʃɪŋ-] n Fischerboot nt.

fishing line n Angelschnur f.

fishing net n Fischnetz nt.

fishing rod n Angelrute f.

fishing tackle n Angelgeräte pl.

fish market n Fischmarkt m.

fishmonger ['fɪʃmʌŋɡə'] (esp BRIT) n Fischhändler(in) m(f).

fishmonger's (shop) ['fɪʃmʌŋɡəz-] (esp BRIT) n Fischgeschäft nt.

fish slice (BRIT) n Fischvorlegemesser nt.

fish sticks (US) npl = **fishfingers**.

fishy ['fɪʃɪ] (inf) adj verdächtig, faul.

fission ['fɪʃən] n Spaltung f; **atomic** or **nuclear ~** Atomspaltung f, Kernspaltung f.

fissure ['fɪʃə'] n Riss m, Spalte f.

fist [fɪst] n Faust f.

fist fight n Faustkampf m.

fit [fɪt] adj geeignet; (healthy) gesund; (SPORT) fit ♦ vt passen +dat; (adjust) anpassen; (match) entsprechen +dat; (be suitable for) passen auf +acc; (put in) einbauen; (attach) anbringen; (equip) ausstatten ♦ vi passen; (parts) zusammenpassen; (in space, gap) hineinpassen ♦ n (MED) Anfall m; **to ~ the description** der Beschreibung entsprechen; **~ to bereit zu**; **~ to eat** essbar; **~ to drink** trinkbar; **to be ~ to keep** es wert sein, aufbewahrt zu werden; **~ for** geeignet für; **~ for work** arbeitsfähig; **to keep ~** sich fit halten; **do as you think** or **see ~** tun Sie, was Sie für richtig halten; **a ~ of anger** ein Wutanfall m; **a ~ of pride** eine Anwandlung von Stolz; **to have a ~** einen Anfall haben; (inf, fig) einen Anfall kriegen; **this dress is a good ~** dieses Kleid sitzt or passt gut; **by ~s and starts** unregelmäßig.

► **fit in** vi (person) sich einfügen; (object) hineinpassen ♦ vt (fig: appointment) unterbringen, einschieben; (visitor) Zeit finden für; **to ~ in with sb's plans** sich mit jds Plänen vereinbaren lassen.

fitful ['fɪtful] adj unruhig.

fitment ['fɪtmənt] n Einrichtungsgegenstand m.

fitness ['fɪtnɪs] n Gesundheit f; (SPORT) Fitness f.

fitted carpet ['fɪtɪd-] n Teppichboden m.

fitted cupboards npl Einbauschränke pl.

fitted kitchen (BRIT) n Einbauküche f.

fitter ['fɪtə'] n Monteur m; (for machines) (Maschinen)schlosser m.

fitting ['fɪtɪŋ] adj passend; (thanks) gebührend ♦ n (of dress) Anprobe f; (of piece of equipment) Installation f; **fittings** npl Ausstattung f.

fitting room n Anprobe(kabine) f.

five [faɪv] num fünf.

five-day week ['faɪvdeɪ-] n Fünftagewoche f.

fiver ['faɪvə'] (inf) n (BRIT) Fünfpfundschein m; (US) Fünfdollarschein m.

fix [fɪks] vt (attach) befestigen; (arrange) festsetzen, festlegen; (mend) reparieren; (meal, drink) machen; (inf) manipulieren ♦ n: **to be in a ~** in der Patsche or Klemme sitzen; **to ~ sth to/on sth** etw an/auf etw dat befestigen; **to ~ one's eyes/attention on** seinen Blick/seine Aufmerksamkeit richten auf +acc; **the fight was a ~** (inf) der Kampf war eine abgekartete Sache.

► **fix up** vt arrangieren; **to ~ sb up with sth** jdm etw besorgen.

fixation [fɪk'seɪʃən] n Fixierung f.

fixative ['fɪksətɪv] n Fixativ nt.

fixed [fɪkst] adj fest; (ideas) fix; (smile) starr; **~ charge** Pauschale f; **how are you ~ for money?** wie sieht es bei dir mit dem Geld aus?

fixed assets npl Anlagevermögen nt.

fixture ['fɪkstʃə'] n Ausstattungsgegenstand m; (FOOTBALL etc) Spiel nt; (ATHLETICS etc) Veranstaltung f.

fizz [fɪz] vi sprudeln; (firework) zischen.

fizzle out ['fɪzl-] vi (plan) im Sande verlaufen; (interest) sich verlieren.

fizzy ['fɪzɪ] adj sprudelnd.

fjord [fjɔːd] n Fjord m.

FL, Fla. (US) abbr (POST: = Florida).

flabbergasted ['flæbəɡɑːstɪd] adj verblüfft.

flabby ['flæbɪ] adj schwammig, wabbelig (inf).

flag [flæg] n Fahne f; (of country) Flagge f; (for signalling) Signalflagge f; (also: **~stone**) (Stein)platte f ♦ vi erlahmen; **~ of convenience** Billigflagge f; **to ~ down** anhalten.

flagon ['flæɡən] n Flasche f; (jug) Krug m.

flagpole ['flæɡpəʊl] n Fahnenstange f.

flagrant ['fleɪɡrənt] adj flagrant; (injustice) himmelschreiend.

flagship ['flægʃɪp] n Flaggschiff nt.
flagstone ['flægstəun] n (Stein)platte f.
flag stop (US) n Bedarfshaltestelle f.
flair [fleə*] n Talent nt; (style) Flair nt.
flak [flæk] n Flakfeuer nt; **to get a lot of** ~ **(for sth)** (inf: criticism) (wegen etw) unter Beschuss geraten.
flake [fleɪk] n Splitter m; (of snow, soap powder) Flocke f ♦ vi (also: ~ **off**) abblättern, absplittern.
► **flake out** (inf) vi aus den Latschen kippen; (go to sleep) einschlafen.
flaky ['fleɪkɪ] adj brüchig; (skin) schuppig.
flaky pastry n Blätterteig m.
flamboyant [flæm'bɔɪənt] adj extravagant.
flame [fleɪm] n Flamme f; **to burst into** ~s in Flammen aufgehen; **an old** ~ (inf) eine alte Flamme.
flaming ['fleɪmɪŋ] (inf!) adj verdammt.
flamingo [flə'mɪŋgəu] n Flamingo m.
flammable ['flæməbl] adj leicht entzündbar.
flan [flæn] n Kuchen m; ~ **case** Tortenboden m.
Flanders ['flɑːndəz] n Flandern nt.
flange [flændʒ] n Flansch m.
flank [flæŋk] n Flanke f ♦ vt flankieren.
flannel ['flænl] n Flanell m; (BRIT: also: **face** ~) Waschlappen m; (: inf) Geschwafel nt; **flannels** npl (trousers) Flanellhose f.
flannelette [flænə'let] n Baumwollflanell m, Biber m or nt.
flap [flæp] n Klappe f; (of envelope) Lasche f ♦ vt schlagen mit ♦ vi flattern; (inf: also: **be in a** ~) in heller Aufregung sein.
flapjack ['flæpdʒæk] n (US: pancake) Pfannkuchen m; (BRIT: biscuit) Haferkeks m.
flare [fleə*] n Leuchtsignal nt; (in skirt etc) Weite f.
► **flare up** vi auflodern; (person) aufbrausen; (fighting, violence, trouble) ausbrechen; see also **flared**.
flared ['fleəd] adj (trousers) mit Schlag; (skirt) ausgestellt.
flash [flæʃ] n Aufblinken nt; (also: **news**~) Eilmeldung f; (PHOT) Blitz m, Blitzlicht nt; (US: torch) Taschenlampe f ♦ vt aufleuchten lassen; (news, message) durchgeben; (look, smile) zuwerfen ♦ vi aufblinken; (light on ambulance) blinken; (eyes) blitzen; **in a** ~ im Nu; **quick as a** ~ blitzschnell; ~ **of inspiration** Geistesblitz m; **to** ~ **one's headlights** die Lichthupe betätigen; **the thought** ~**ed through his mind** der Gedanke schoss ihm durch den Kopf; **to** ~ **by** or **past** vorbeiflitzen (inf).
flashback ['flæʃbæk] n Rückblende f.
flashbulb ['flæʃbʌlb] n Blitzbirne f.
flash card n Leselernkarte f.
flashcube ['flæʃkjuːb] n Blitzwürfel m.
flasher ['flæʃə*] n (AUT) Lichthupe f; (inf: man) Exhibitionist m.
flashlight ['flæʃlaɪt] n Blitzlicht nt.

flash point n (fig): **to be at** ~ auf dem Siedepunkt sein.
flashy ['flæʃɪ] (pej) adj auffällig, protzig.
flask [flɑːsk] n Flakon m; (CHEM) Glaskolben m; (also: **vacuum** ~) Thermosflasche ® f.
flat [flæt] adj flach; (surface) eben; (tyre) platt; (battery) leer; (beer) schal; (refusal, denial) glatt; (note, voice) zu tief; (rate, fee) Pauschal- ♦ n (BRIT: apartment) Wohnung f; (AUT) (Reifen)panne f; (MUS) Erniedrigungszeichen nt; **to work** ~ **out** auf Hochtouren arbeiten; ~ **rate of pay** Pauschallohn m.
flat-footed ['flæt'futɪd] adj: **to be** ~ Plattfüße pl haben.
flatly ['flætlɪ] adv (refuse, deny) glatt, kategorisch.
flatmate ['flætmeɪt] (BRIT) n Mitbewohner(in) m(f).
flatness ['flætnɪs] n Flachheit f.
flat screen n Flachbildschirm m.
flatten ['flætn] vt (also: ~ **out**) (ein)ebnen; (paper, fabric etc) glätten; (building, city) dem Erdboden gleichmachen; (crop) zu Boden drücken; (inf: person) umhauen; **to** ~ **o.s. against a wall/door** etc sich platt gegen or an eine Wand/Tür etc drücken.
flatter ['flætə*] vt schmeicheln +dat.
flatterer ['flætərə*] n Schmeichler(in) m(f).
flattering ['flætərɪŋ] adj schmeichelhaft; (dress etc) vorteilhaft.
flattery ['flætərɪ] n Schmeichelei f.
flatulence ['flætjuləns] n Blähungen pl.
flaunt [flɔːnt] vt zur Schau stellen, protzen mit.
flavour, (US) **flavor** ['fleɪvə*] n Geschmack m; (of ice-cream etc) Geschmacksrichtung f ♦ vt Geschmack verleihen +dat; **to give** or **add** ~ **to** Geschmack verleihen +dat; **music with an African** ~ (fig) Musik mit einer afrikanischen Note; **strawberry-**~**ed** mit Erdbeergeschmack.
flavouring ['fleɪvərɪŋ] n Aroma nt.
flaw [flɔː] n Fehler m.
flawless ['flɔːlɪs] adj (performance) fehlerlos; (complexion) makellos.
flax [flæks] n Flachs m.
flaxen ['flæksən] adj (hair) flachsblond.
flea [fliː] n Floh m.
flea market n Flohmarkt m.
fleck [flek] n Tupfen m, Punkt m; (of dust) Flöckchen nt; (of mud, paint, colour) Fleck(en) m ♦ vt bespritzen; **brown** ~**ed with white** braun mit weißen Punkten.
fled [fled] pt, pp of **flee**.
fledg(e)ling ['fledʒlɪŋ] n Jungvogel m ♦ adj (inexperienced: actor etc) Nachwuchs-; (newly started: business etc) jung.
flee [fliː] (pt, pp **fled**) vt fliehen or flüchten vor +dat; (country) fliehen or flüchten aus ♦ vi fliehen, flüchten.
fleece [fliːs] n Schafwolle f; (sheep's coat)

Schaffell *nt*, Vlies *nt* ♦ *vt* (*inf: cheat*) schröpfen.
fleecy ['fli:sɪ] *adj* flauschig; (*cloud*) Schäfchen-.
fleet [fli:t] *n* Flotte *f*; (*of lorries, cars*) Fuhrpark *m*.
fleeting ['fli:tɪŋ] *adj* flüchtig.
Flemish ['flemɪʃ] *adj* flämisch ♦ *n* (*LING*) Flämisch *nt*; **the Flemish** *npl* die Flamen.
flesh [fleʃ] *n* Fleisch *nt*; (*of fruit*) Fruchtfleisch *nt*.
► **flesh out** *vt* ausgestalten.
flesh wound [-wu:nd] *n* Fleischwunde *f*.
flew [flu:] *pt of* **fly**.
flex [fleks] *n* Kabel *nt* ♦ *vt* beugen; (*muscles*) spielen lassen.
flexibility [fleksɪ'bɪlɪtɪ] *n* (*see adj*) Flexibilität *f*; Biegsamkeit *f*.
flexible ['fleksəbl] *adj* flexibel; (*material*) biegsam.
flexitime ['fleksɪtaɪm] *n* gleitende Arbeitszeit *f*, Gleitzeit *f*.
flick [flɪk] *n* (*of finger*) Schnipsen *nt*; (*of hand*) Wischen *nt*; (*of whip*) Schnalzen *nt*; (*of towel etc*) Schlagen *nt*; (*of switch*) Knipsen *nt* ♦ *vt* schnipsen; (*with hand*) wischen; (*whip*) knallen mit; (*switch*) knipsen; **flicks** (*inf*) *npl* Kino *nt*; **to ~ a towel at sb** mit einem Handtuch nach jdm schlagen.
► **flick through** *vt fus* durchblättern.
flicker ['flɪkə*] *vi* flackern; (*eyelids*) zucken ♦ *n* Flackern *nt*; (*of pain, fear*) Aufflackern *nt*; (*of smile*) Anflug *m*; (*of eyelid*) Zucken *nt*.
flick knife (*BRIT*) *n* Klappmesser *nt*.
flier ['flaɪə*] *n* Flieger(in) *m(f)*.
flight [flaɪt] *n* Flug *m*; (*escape*) Flucht *f*; (*also:* ~ **of steps**) Treppe *f*; **to take** ~ die Flucht ergreifen; **to put to** ~ in die Flucht schlagen.
flight attendant (*US*) *n* Flugbegleiter(in) *m(f)*.
flight crew *n* Flugbesatzung *f*.
flight deck *n* (*AVIAT*) Cockpit *nt*; (*NAUT*) Flugdeck *nt*.
flight path *n* Flugbahn *f*.
flight recorder *n* Flugschreiber *m*.
flimsy ['flɪmzɪ] *adj* leicht, dünn; (*building*) leicht gebaut; (*excuse*) fadenscheinig; (*evidence*) nicht stichhaltig.
flinch [flɪntʃ] *vi* zusammenzucken; **to ~ from** zurückschrecken vor +*dat*.
fling [flɪŋ] (*pt, pp* **flung**) *vt* schleudern; (*arms*) werfen; (*oneself*) stürzen ♦ *n* (flüchtige) Affäre *f*.
flint [flɪnt] *n* Feuerstein *m*.
flip [flɪp] *vt* (*switch*) knipsen; (*coin*) werfen; (*US: pancake*) umdrehen ♦ *vi*: **to ~ for sth** (*US*) um etw mit einer Münze knobeln.
► **flip through** *vt fus* durchblättern; (*records etc*) durchgehen.
flippant ['flɪpənt] *adj* leichtfertig.
flipper ['flɪpə*] *n* Flosse *f*; (*for swimming*) (Schwimm)flosse *f*.
flip side *n* (*of record*) B-Seite *f*.
flirt [flɜ:t] *vi* flirten; (*with idea*) liebäugeln ♦ *n*: **he/she is a** ~ er/sie flirtet gern.
flirtation [flɜ:'teɪʃən] *n* Flirt *m*.
flit [flɪt] *vi* flitzen; (*expression, smile*) huschen.
float [fləʊt] *n* Schwimmkork *m*; (*for fishing*) Schwimmer *m*; (*lorry*) Festwagen *m*; (*money*) Wechselgeld *nt* ♦ *vi* schwimmen; (*swimmer*) treiben; (*through air*) schweben; (*currency*) floaten ♦ *vt* (*currency*) freigeben, floaten lassen; (*company*) gründen; (*idea, plan*) in den Raum stellen.
► **float around** *vi* im Umlauf sein; (*person*) herumschweben (*inf*); (*object*) herumfliegen (*inf*).
flock [flɒk] *n* Herde *f*; (*of birds*) Schwarm *m* ♦ *vi*: **to ~ to** (*place*) strömen nach; (*event*) in Scharen kommen zu.
floe [fləʊ] *n* (*also:* **ice ~**) Eisscholle *f*.
flog [flɒg] *vt* auspeitschen; (*inf: sell*) verscherbeln.
flood [flʌd] *n* Überschwemmung *f*; (*of letters, imports etc*) Flut *f* ♦ *vt* überschwemmen; (*AUT*) absaufen lassen (*inf*) ♦ *vi* überschwemmt werden; **to be in** ~ Hochwasser führen; **to ~ the market** den Markt überschwemmen; **to ~ into Hungary/the square/the palace** nach Ungarn/auf den Platz/in den Palast strömen.
flooding ['flʌdɪŋ] *n* Überschwemmung *f*.
floodlight ['flʌdlaɪt] *n* Flutlicht *nt* ♦ *vt* (mit Flutlicht) beleuchten; (*building*) anstrahlen.
floodlit ['flʌdlɪt] *pt, pp of* **floodlight** ♦ *adj* (mit Flutlicht) beleuchtet; (*building*) angestrahlt.
flood tide *n* Flut *f*.
floodwater ['flʌdwɔ:tə*] *n* Hochwasser *nt*.
floor [flɔ:*] *n* (Fuß)boden *m*; (*storey*) Stock *m*; (*of sea, valley*) Boden *m* ♦ *vt* (*subj: blow*) zu Boden werfen; (: *question, remark*) die Sprache verschlagen +*dat*; **on the** ~ auf dem Boden; **ground** (*BRIT*) **or first** (*US*) ~ Erdgeschoss *nt*, Erdgeschoß *nt* (*ÖSTERR*); **first** (*BRIT*) **or second** (*US*) ~ erster Stock *m*; **top** ~ oberstes Stockwerk *nt*; **to have the** ~ (*speaker: at meeting*) das Wort haben.
floorboard ['flɔ:bɔ:d] *n* Diele *f*.
flooring ['flɔ:rɪŋ] *n* (Fuß)boden *m*; (*covering*) Fußbodenbelag *m*.
floor lamp (*US*) *n* Stehlampe *f*.
floor show *n* Show *f*, Vorstellung *f*.
floorwalker ['flɔ:wɔ:kə*] (*esp US*) *n* Ladenaufsicht *f*.
floozy ['flu:zɪ] (*inf*) *n* Flittchen *nt*.
flop [flɒp] *n* Reinfall *m* ♦ *vi* (*play, book*) durchfallen; (*fall*) sich fallen lassen; (*scheme*) ein Reinfall sein.
floppy ['flɒpɪ] *adj* schlaff, schlapp ♦ *n* (*also:* ~ **disk**) Diskette *f*, Floppydisk *f*, Floppy Disk *f*; ~ **hat** Schlapphut *m*.
floppy disk *n* Diskette *f*, Floppydisk *f*, Floppy

Disk *f*.

flora ['flɔːrə] *n* Flora *f*.

floral ['flɔːrl] *adj* geblümt.

Florence ['flɔrəns] *n* Florenz *nt*.

Florentine ['flɔrəntaɪn] *adj* florentinisch.

florid ['flɔrɪd] *adj* (*style*) blumig; (*complexion*) kräftig.

florist ['flɔrɪst] *n* Blumenhändler(in) *m(f)*.

florist's (shop) ['flɔrɪsts-] *n* Blumengeschäft *nt*.

flotation [fləʊ'teɪʃən] *n* (*of shares*) Auflegung *f*; (*of company*) Umwandlung *f* in eine Aktiengesellschaft.

flotsam ['flɔtsəm] *n* (*also:* ~ **and jetsam**) Strandgut *nt*; (*floating*) Treibgut *nt*.

flounce [flaʊns] *n* Volant *m*.

▶ **flounce out** *vi* hinausstolzieren.

flounder ['flaʊndəʳ] *vi* sich abstrampeln; (*fig: speaker*) ins Schwimmen kommen; (*economy*) in Schwierigkeiten geraten ♦ *n* Flunder *f*.

flour ['flaʊəʳ] *n* Mehl *nt*.

flourish ['flʌrɪʃ] *vi* gedeihen; (*business*) blühen, florieren ♦ *vt* schwenken ♦ *n* (*in writing*) Schnörkel *m*; (*bold gesture*): **with a** ~ mit einer schwungvollen Bewegung.

flourishing ['flʌrɪʃɪŋ] *adj* gut gehend, florierend.

flout [flaʊt] *vt* sich hinwegsetzen über *+acc*.

flow [fləʊ] *n* Fluss *m*; (*of sea*) Flut *f* ♦ *vi* fließen; (*clothes, hair*) wallen.

flow chart *n* Flussdiagramm *nt*.

flow diagram *n* = **flow chart**.

flower ['flaʊəʳ] *n* Blume *f*; (*blossom*) Blüte *f* ♦ *vi* blühen; **to be in** ~ blühen.

flowerbed ['flaʊəbed] *n* Blumenbeet *nt*.

flowerpot ['flaʊəpɔt] *n* Blumentopf *m*.

flowery ['flaʊərɪ] *adj* blumig; (*pattern*) Blumen-.

flown [fləʊn] *pp of* **fly**.

flu [fluː] *n* Grippe *f*.

fluctuate ['flʌktjʊeɪt] *vi* schwanken; (*opinions, attitudes*) sich ändern.

fluctuation [flʌktjʊ'eɪʃən] *n*: ~ **(in)** Schwankung (*+gen*).

flue [fluː] *n* Rauchfang *m*, Rauchabzug *m*.

fluency ['fluːənsɪ] *n* Flüssigkeit *f*; **his** ~ **in German** sein flüssiges Deutsch.

fluent ['fluːənt] *adj* flüssig; **he speaks** ~ **German, he's** ~ **in German** er spricht fließend Deutsch.

fluently ['fluːəntlɪ] *adv* flüssig; (*speak a language*) fließend.

fluff [flʌf] *n* Fussel *m*; (*fur*) Flaum *m* ♦ *vt* (*inf: do badly*) verpatzen; (*also:* ~ **out**) aufplustern.

fluffy ['flʌfɪ] *adj* flaumig; (*jacket etc*) weich, kuschelig; ~ **toy** Kuscheltier *nt*.

fluid ['fluːɪd] *adj* fließend; (*situation, arrangement*) unklar ♦ *n* Flüssigkeit *f*.

fluid ounce (*BRIT*) *n* flüssige Unze *f* (= 28 *ml*).

fluke [fluːk] (*inf*) *n* Glücksfall *m*; **by a** ~ durch einen glücklichen Zufall.

flummox ['flʌməks] *vt* verwirren, durcheinander bringen.

flung [flʌŋ] *pt, pp of* **fling**.

flunky ['flʌŋkɪ] *n* Lakai *m*.

fluorescent [fluə'rɛsnt] *adj* fluoreszierend; (*paint*) Leucht-; (*light*) Neon-.

fluoride ['fluəraɪd] *n* Fluorid *nt*.

fluorine ['fluəriːn] *n* Fluor *nt*.

flurry ['flʌrɪ] *n* (*of snow*) Gestöber *nt*; **a** ~ **of activity/excitement** hektische Aktivität/Aufregung.

flush [flʌʃ] *n* Röte *f*; (*fig: of beauty etc*) Blüte *f* ♦ *vt* (durch)spülen, (aus)spülen ♦ *vi* erröten ♦ *adj*: ~ **with** auf gleicher Ebene mit; ~ **against** direkt an *+dat*; **in the first** ~ **of youth** in der ersten Jugendblüte; **in the first** ~ **of freedom** im ersten Freiheitstaumel; **hot** ~**es** (*BRIT*) Hitzewallungen *pl*; **to** ~ **the toilet** spülen, die Wasserspülung betätigen.

▶ **flush out** *vt* aufstöbern.

flushed [flʌʃt] *adj* rot.

fluster ['flʌstəʳ] *n*: **in a** ~ nervös; (*confused*) durcheinander ♦ *vt* nervös machen; (*confuse*) durcheinander bringen.

flustered ['flʌstəd] *adj* nervös; (*confused*) durcheinander.

flute [fluːt] *n* Querflöte *f*.

fluted ['fluːtɪd] *adj* gerillt; (*column*) kanneliert.

flutter ['flʌtəʳ] *n* Flattern *nt*; (*of panic, nerves*) kurzer Anfall *m*; (*of excitement*) Beben *nt* ♦ *vi* flattern; (*person*) tänzeln; **to have a** ~ (*BRIT: inf: gamble*) sein Glück (beim Wetten) versuchen.

flux [flʌks] *n*: **in a state of** ~ im Fluss.

fly [flaɪ] (*pt* **flew**, *pp* **flown**) *n* Fliege *f*; (*on trousers: also:* **flies**) (Hosen)schlitz *m* ♦ *vt* fliegen; (*kite*) steigen lassen ♦ *vi* fliegen; (*escape*) fliehen; (*flag*) wehen; **to** ~ **open** auffliegen; **to** ~ **off the handle** an die Decke gehen (*inf*); **pieces of metal went** ~**ing everywhere** überall flogen Metallteile herum; **she came** ~**ing into the room** sie kam ins Zimmer gesaust; **her glasses flew off** die Brille flog ihr aus dem Gesicht.

▶ **fly away** *vi* wegfliegen.

▶ **fly in** *vi* einfliegen; **he flew in yesterday** er ist gestern mit dem Flugzeug gekommen.

▶ **fly off** *vi* = **fly away**.

▶ **fly out** *vi* ausfliegen; **he flew out yesterday** er ist gestern hingeflogen.

fly-fishing ['flaɪfɪʃɪŋ] *n* Fliegenfischen *nt*.

flying ['flaɪɪŋ] *n* Fliegen *nt* ♦ *adj*: **a** ~ **visit** ein Blitzbesuch *m*; **he doesn't like** ~ er fliegt nicht gerne; **with** ~ **colours** mit fliegenden Fahnen.

flying buttress *n* Strebebogen *m*.

flying picket *n* mobiler Streikposten *m*.

flying saucer *n* fliegende Untertasse *f*.

flying squad *n* mobiles Einsatzkommando *nt*.

flying start *n*: **to get off to a** ~ (*SPORT*) hervorragend wegkommen; (*fig*) einen glänzenden Start haben.

flyleaf ['flaɪliːf] n Vorsatzblatt nt.

flyover ['flaɪəʊvə*] n (BRIT) Überführung f; (US) Luftparade f.

fly-past ['flaɪpɑːst] n Luftparade f.

flysheet ['flaɪʃiːt] n (for tent) Überzelt nt.

flyweight ['flaɪweɪt] n Fliegengewicht nt.

flywheel ['flaɪwiːl] n Schwungrad nt.

FM abbr (BRIT: MIL) = **field marshal**; (RADIO: = frequency modulation) FM, ≈ UKW.

FMB (US) n abbr (= Federal Maritime Board) Dachausschuss der Handelsmarine.

FMCS (US) n abbr (= Federal Mediation and Conciliation Service) Schlichtungsstelle für Arbeitskonflikte.

FO (BRIT) n abbr = **Foreign Office**.

foal [fəʊl] n Fohlen nt.

foam [fəʊm] n Schaum m; (also: ~ **rubber**) Schaumgummi m ♦ vi schäumen.

fob [fɔb] vt: **to ~ sb off** jdn abspeisen ♦ n (also: **watch ~**) Uhrkette f.

f.o.b. abbr (COMM: = free on board) frei Schiff.

foc (BRIT) abbr (COMM: = free of charge) gratis.

focal point n Mittelpunkt m; (of camera, telescope etc) Brennpunkt m.

focus ['fəʊkəs] (pl ~**es**) n Brennpunkt m; (of storm) Zentrum nt ♦ vt einstellen; (light rays) bündeln ♦ vi: **to ~ (on)** (with camera) klar or scharf einstellen +acc; (person) sich konzentrieren (auf +acc); **in/out of ~** (camera etc) scharf/unscharf eingestellt; (photograph) scharf/unscharf.

focus group n (POL) Fokusgruppe f.

fodder ['fɔdə*] n Futter nt.

FoE n abbr (= Friends of the Earth) Umweltschutzorganisation.

foe [fəʊ] n Feind(in) m(f).

foetus, (US) **fetus** ['fiːtəs] n Fötus m, Fetus m.

fog [fɔg] n Nebel m.

fogbound ['fɔgbaʊnd] adj (airport) wegen Nebel geschlossen.

foggy ['fɔgɪ] adj neb(e)lig.

fog lamp, (US) **fog light** n (AUT) Nebelscheinwerfer m.

foible ['fɔɪbl] n Eigenheit f.

foil [fɔɪl] vt vereiteln ♦ n Folie f; (complement) Kontrast m; (FENCING) Florett nt; **to act as a ~ to** einen Kontrast darstellen zu.

foist [fɔɪst] vt: **to ~ sth on sb** (goods) jdm etw andrehen; (task) etw an jdn abschieben; (ideas, views) jdm etw aufzwingen.

fold [fəʊld] n Falte f; (AGR) Pferch m; (fig) Schoß m ♦ vt (zusammen)falten; (arms) verschränken ♦ vi (business) eingehen (inf).
► **fold up** vi sich zusammenfalten lassen; (bed, table) sich zusammenklappen lassen; (business) eingehen (inf) ♦ vt zusammenfalten.

folder ['fəʊldə*] n Aktenmappe f; (binder) Hefter m; (brochure) Informationsblatt nt.

folding ['fəʊldɪŋ] adj (chair, bed) Klapp-.

foliage ['fəʊlɪɪdʒ] n Laubwerk nt.

folk [fəʊk] npl Leute pl ♦ cpd Volks-; **my ~s** (parents) meine alten Herrschaften.

folklore ['fəʊklɔː*] n Folklore f.

folk music n Volksmusik f; (contemporary) Folk m.

folk song n Volkslied nt; (contemporary) Folksong m.

follow ['fɔləʊ] vt folgen +dat; (with eyes) verfolgen; (advice, instructions) befolgen ♦ vi folgen; **to ~ in sb's footsteps** in jds Fußstapfen acc treten; **I don't quite ~ you** ich kann Ihnen nicht ganz folgen; **it ~s that** daraus folgt, dass; **to ~ suit** (fig) jds Beispiel dat folgen.
► **follow on** vi (continue): **to ~ on from** aufbauen auf +dat.
► **follow out** vt (idea, plan) zu Ende verfolgen.
► **follow through** vt = **follow out**.
► **follow up** vt nachgehen +dat; (offer) aufgreifen; (case) weiterverfolgen.

follower ['fɔləʊə*] n Anhänger(in) m(f).

following ['fɔləʊɪŋ] adj folgend ♦ n Anhängerschaft f.

follow-up ['fɔləʊʌp] n Weiterführung f ♦ adj: **~ treatment** Nachbehandlung f.

folly ['fɔlɪ] n Torheit f; (building) exzentrisches Bauwerk nt.

fond [fɔnd] adj liebevoll; (memory) lieb; (hopes, dreams) töricht; **to be ~ of** mögen; **she's ~ of swimming** sie schwimmt gerne.

fondle ['fɔndl] vt streicheln.

fondly ['fɔndlɪ] adv liebevoll; (naïvely) törichterweise; **he ~ believed that ...** er war so naiv zu glauben, dass ...

fondness ['fɔndnɪs] n (for things) Vorliebe f; (for people) Zuneigung f; **a special ~ for** eine besondere Vorliebe für/Zuneigung zu.

font [fɔnt] n Taufbecken nt; (TYP) Schrift f.

food [fuːd] n Essen nt; (for animals) Futter nt; (nourishment) Nahrung f; (groceries) Lebensmittel pl.

food chain n Nahrungskette f.

food mixer n Küchenmixer m.

food poisoning n Lebensmittelvergiftung f.

food processor n Küchenmaschine f.

food stamp n Lebensmittelmarke f.

foodstuffs ['fuːdstʌfs] npl Lebensmittel pl.

fool [fuːl] n Dummkopf m; (CULIN) Sahnespeise aus Obstpüree ♦ vt hereinlegen, täuschen ♦ vi herumalbern; **to make a ~ of sb** jdn lächerlich machen; (trick) jdn hereinlegen; **to make a ~ of o.s.** sich blamieren; **you can't ~ me** du kannst mich nicht zum Narren halten.
► **fool about** (pej) vi herumtrödeln; (behave foolishly) herumalbern.
► **fool around** vi = **fool about**.

foolhardy ['fuːlhɑːdɪ] adj tollkühn.

foolish ['fuːlɪʃ] adj dumm.

foolishly ['fuːlɪʃlɪ] adv dumm; **~, I forgot ...** dummerweise habe ich ... vergessen.

foolishness ['fuːlɪʃnɪs] n Dummheit f.

foolproof ['fuːlpruːf] *adj* idiotensicher.
foolscap ['fuːlskæp] *n* ≈ Kanzleipapier *nt*.
foot [fut] (*pl* **feet**) *n* Fuß *m*; (*of animal*) Pfote *f*
  ♦ *vt* (*bill*) bezahlen; **on ~** zu Fuß; **to find
  one's feet** sich eingewöhnen; **to put one's
  ~ down** (*AUT*) Gas geben; (*say no*) ein
  Machtwort sprechen.
footage ['futɪdʒ] *n* Filmmaterial *nt*.
foot-and-mouth (disease) [futən'mauθ-] *n*
  Maul- und Klauenseuche *f*.
football ['futbɔːl] *n* Fußball *m*; (*US*) Football
  m, amerikanischer Fußball *m*.
footballer ['futbɔːlə*] (*BRIT*) *n*
  Fußballspieler(in) *m(f)*.
football ground *n* Fußballplatz *m*.
football match (*BRIT*) *n* Fußballspiel *nt*.
football player (*BRIT*) *n* Fußballspieler(in)
  m(f); (*US*) Footballspieler(in) *m(f)*.

FOOTBALL POOLS

Football Pools, *umgangssprachlich auch* **the
pools** *genannt, ist das in Großbritannien sehr
beliebte Fußballtoto, bei dem auf die Ergebnisse
der samstäglichen Fußballspiele gewettet wird.
Die Gewinne können sehr hoch sein und
gelegentlich Millionen von Pfund betragen.*

---

foot brake *n* Fußbremse *f*.
footbridge ['futbrɪdʒ] *n* Fußgängerbrücke *f*.
foothills ['futhɪlz] *npl* (Gebirgs)ausläufer *pl*.
foothold ['futhəuld] *n* Halt *m*; **to get a ~** Fuß
  fassen.
footing ['futɪŋ] *n* Stellung *f*; (*relationship*)
  Verhältnis *nt*; **to lose one's ~** den Halt
  verlieren; **on an equal ~** auf gleicher Basis.
footlights ['futlaɪts] *npl* Rampenlicht *nt*.
footman ['futmən] (*irreg: like* **man**) *n* Lakai *m*.
footnote ['futnəut] *n* Fußnote *f*.
footpath ['futpɑːθ] *n* Fußweg *m*; (*in street*)
  Bürgersteig *m*.
footprint ['futprɪnt] *n* Fußabdruck *m*; (*of
  animal*) Spur *f*.
footrest ['futrest] *n* Fußstütze *f*.
Footsie ['futsɪ] (*inf*) *n* = FTSE 100 Index.
footsie ['futsɪ] (*inf*) *n*: **to play ~ with sb** mit
  jdm füßeln.
footsore ['futsɔː*] *adj*: **to be ~** wunde Füße
  haben.
footstep ['futstep] *n* Schritt *m*; (*footprint*)
  Fußabdruck *m*; **to follow in sb's ~s** in jds
  Fußstapfen *acc* treten.
footwear ['futwɛə*] *n* Schuhe *pl*, Schuhwerk
  nt.

═══════════════════════ *KEYWORD*

for [fɔː*] *prep* **1** für +*acc*; **is this ~ me?** ist das
  für mich?; **the train ~ London** der Zug nach
  London; **it's time ~ lunch** es ist Zeit zum
  Mittagessen; **what's it ~?** wofür ist das?; **he
  works ~ the government/a local firm** er
  arbeitet für die Regierung/eine Firma am

Ort; **he's mature ~ his age** er ist reif für
sein Alter; **I sold it ~ £20** ich habe es für
£20 verkauft; **I'm all ~ it** ich bin ganz dafür;
G ~ George ≈ G wie Gustav.
2 (*because of*): **~ this reason** aus diesem
Grund; **~ fear of being criticised** aus Angst,
kritisiert zu werden.
3 (*referring to distance*): **there are roadworks
~ 5 km** die Straßenbauarbeiten erstrecken
sich über 5 km; **we walked ~ miles** wir sind
meilenweit gelaufen.
4 (*referring to time*): **he was away ~ 2 years**
er war 2 Jahre lang weg; **I have known her
~ years** ich kenne sie bereits seit Jahren.
5 (*with infinitive clause*): **it is not ~ me to
decide** es liegt nicht an mir, das zu
entscheiden; **~ this to be possible** ... um
dies möglich zu machen, ...
6 (*in spite of*) trotz +*gen or dat*; **~ all his
complaints, he is very fond of her** trotz
seiner vielen Klagen mag er sie sehr
  ♦ *conj* (*form: since, as*) denn; **she was very
angry, ~ he was late again** sie war sehr
böse, denn er kam wieder zu spät.

---

f.o.r. *abbr* (*COMM:* = *free on rail*) frei Bahn.
forage ['fɔrɪdʒ] *n* Futter *nt* ♦ *vi* herumstöbern;
  to ~ (*for food*) nach Futter suchen.
forage cap *n* Schiffchen *nt*.
foray ['fɔreɪ] *n* (Raub)überfall *m*.
forbad(e) [fə'bæd] *pt of* **forbid**.
forbearing [fɔː'bɛərɪŋ] *adj* geduldig.
forbid [fə'bɪd] (*pt* **forbade**, *pp* **forbidden**) *vt*
  verbieten; **to ~ sb to do sth** jdm verbieten,
  etw zu tun.
forbidden [fə'bɪdn] *pp of* **forbid** ♦ *adj* verboten.
forbidding [fə'bɪdɪŋ] *adj* (*look*) streng;
  (*prospect*) grauenhaft.
force [fɔːs] *n* Kraft *f*; (*violence*) Gewalt *f*; (*of
  blow, impact*) Wucht *f*; (*influence*) Macht *f* ♦ *vt*
  zwingen; (*push*) drücken; (*: person*)
  drängen; (*lock, door*) aufbrechen; **the Forces**
  (*BRIT*) *npl* die Streitkräfte *pl*; **in ~** (*law etc*)
  geltend; (*people: arrive etc*) zahlreich; **to
  come into ~** in Kraft treten; **to join ~s** sich
  zusammentun; **a ~ 5 wind** Windstärke 5; **to
  the sales ~** das Verkaufspersonal; **to
  ~ o.s./sb to do sth** sich/jdn zwingen, etw zu
  tun.
▶ **force back** *vt* zurückdrängen; (*tears*)
  unterdrücken.
▶ **force down** *vt* (*food*) hinunterwürgen (*inf*).
forced [fɔːst] *adj* gezwungen; **~ labour**
  Zwangsarbeit *f*; **~ landing** Notlandung *f*.
force-feed ['fɔːsfiːd] *vt* zwangsernähren;
  (*animal*) stopfen.
forceful ['fɔːsful] *adj* energisch; (*attack*)
  wirkungsvoll; (*point*) überzeugend.
forceps ['fɔːseps] *npl* Zange *f*.
forcible ['fɔːsəbl] *adj* gewaltsam; (*reminder,
  lesson*) eindringlich.
forcibly ['fɔːsəblɪ] *adv* mit Gewalt; (*express*)

eindringlich.

ford [fɔːd] n Furt f ♦ vt durchqueren; (on foot) durchwaten.

fore [fɔː*] n: **to come to the ~** ins Blickfeld geraten.

forearm ['fɔːrɑːm] n Unterarm m.

forebear ['fɔːbɛə*] n Vorfahr(in) m(f), Ahn(e) m(f).

foreboding [fɔː'bəudɪŋ] n Vorahnung f.

forecast ['fɔːkɑːst] (irreg: like **cast**) n Prognose f; (of weather) (Wetter)vorhersage f ♦ vt voraussagen.

foreclose [fɔː'kləuz] vt (LAW: also: ~ **on**) kündigen; **to ~ sb** (on loan/mortgage) jds Darlehen/Hypothek kündigen.

foreclosure [fɔː'kləuʒə*] n Zwangsvollstreckung f.

forecourt ['fɔːkɔːt] n Vorplatz m.

forefathers ['fɔːfɑːðəz] npl Vorfahren pl.

forefinger ['fɔːfɪŋgə*] n Zeigefinger m.

forefront ['fɔːfrʌnt] n: **in the ~ of** an der Spitze +gen.

forego [fɔː'gəu] (irreg: like **go**) vt verzichten auf +acc.

foregoing ['fɔːgəuɪŋ] adj vorhergehend ♦ n: **the ~** das Vorhergehende.

foregone ['fɔːgɔn] pp of **forego** ♦ adj: **it's a ~ conclusion** es steht von vornherein fest.

foreground ['fɔːgraund] n Vordergrund m.

forehand ['fɔːhænd] n (TENNIS) Vorhand f.

forehead ['fɔrɪd] n Stirn f.

foreign ['fɔrɪn] adj ausländisch; (holiday) im Ausland; (customs, appearance) fremdartig; (trade, policy) Außen-; (correspondent) Auslands-; (object, matter) fremd; **goods from ~ countries/a ~ country** Waren aus dem Ausland.

foreign body n Fremdkörper m.

foreign currency n Devisen pl.

foreigner ['fɔrɪnə*] n Ausländer(in) m(f).

foreign exchange n Devisenhandel m; (money) Devisen pl.

foreign exchange market n Devisenmarkt m.

foreign exchange rate n Devisenkurs m.

foreign investment n Auslandsinvestition f.

foreign minister n Außenminister(in) m(f).

Foreign Office (BRIT) n Außenministerium nt.

Foreign Secretary (BRIT) n Außenminister(in) m(f).

foreleg ['fɔːlɛg] n Vorderbein nt.

foreman ['fɔːmən] (irreg: like **man**) n Vorarbeiter m; (of jury) Obmann m.

foremost ['fɔːməust] adj führend ♦ adv: **first and ~** zunächst, vor allem.

forename ['fɔːneɪm] n Vorname m.

forensic [fə'rɛnsɪk] adj (test) forensisch; (medicine) Gerichts-; (expert) Spurensicherungs-.

foreplay ['fɔːpleɪ] n Vorspiel nt.

forerunner ['fɔːrʌnə*] n Vorläufer m.

foresee [fɔː'siː] (irreg: like **see**) vt vorhersehen.

foreseeable [fɔː'siːəbl] adj vorhersehbar; **in the ~ future** in absehbarer Zeit.

foreseen [fɔː'siːn] pp of **foresee**.

foreshadow [fɔː'ʃædəu] vt andeuten.

foreshore ['fɔːʃɔː*] n Strand m.

foreshorten [fɔː'ʃɔːtn] vt perspektivisch verkürzen.

foresight ['fɔːsaɪt] n Voraussicht f, Weitblick m.

foreskin ['fɔːskɪn] n (ANAT) Vorhaut f.

forest ['fɔrɪst] n Wald m.

forestall [fɔː'stɔːl] vt zuvorkommen +dat; (discussion) im Keim ersticken.

forestry ['fɔrɪstrɪ] n Forstwirtschaft f.

foretaste ['fɔːteɪst] n: **a ~ of** ein Vorgeschmack von.

foretell [fɔː'tɛl] (irreg: like **tell**) vt vorhersagen.

forethought ['fɔːθɔːt] n Vorbedacht m.

foretold [fɔː'təuld] pt, pp of **foretell**.

forever [fə'rɛvə*] adv für immer; (endlessly) ewig; (consistently) dauernd, ständig; **you're ~ finding difficulties** du findest ständig or dauernd neue Schwierigkeiten.

forewarn [fɔː'wɔːn] vt vorwarnen.

forewent [fɔː'wɛnt] pt of **forego**.

forewoman ['fɔːwumən] (irreg: like **woman**) n Vorarbeiterin f; (of jury) Obmännin f.

foreword ['fɔːwəːd] n Vorwort nt.

forfeit ['fɔːfɪt] n Strafe f, Buße f ♦ vt (right) verwirken; (friendship etc) verlieren; (one's happiness, health) einbüßen.

forgave [fə'geɪv] pt of **forgive**.

forge [fɔːdʒ] n Schmiede f ♦ vt fälschen; (wrought iron) schmieden.

▶ **forge ahead** vi große or schnelle Fortschritte machen.

forger ['fɔːdʒə*] n Fälscher(in) m(f).

forgery ['fɔːdʒərɪ] n Fälschung f.

forget [fə'gɛt] (pt **forgot**, pp **forgotten**) vt vergessen ♦ vi es vergessen; **to ~ o.s.** sich vergessen.

forgetful [fə'gɛtful] adj vergesslich; **~ of sth** (of duties etc) nachlässig gegenüber etw.

forgetfulness [fə'gɛtfulnɪs] n Vergesslichkeit f; (oblivion) Vergessenheit f.

forget-me-not [fə'gɛtmɪnɔt] n Vergissmeinnicht nt.

forgive [fə'gɪv] (pt **forgave**, pp **forgiven**) vt verzeihen +dat, vergeben +dat; **to ~ sb for sth** jdm etw verzeihen or vergeben; **to ~ sb for doing sth** jdm verzeihen or vergeben, dass er etw getan hat; **~ me, but ...** entschuldigen Sie, aber ...; **they could be ~n for thinking that ...** es ist verständlich, wenn sie denken, dass ...

forgiveness [fə'gɪvnɪs] n Verzeihung f.

forgiving [fə'gɪvɪŋ] adj versöhnlich.

forgo [fɔː'gəu] (pt **forwent**, pp **forgone**) vt = **forego**.

forgot [fə'gɔt] pt of **forget**.

forgotten [fə'gɔtn] pp of **forget**.

fork [fɔːk] *n* Gabel *f*; (*in road, river, railway*) Gabelung *f* ♦ *vi* (*road*) sich gabeln.
► **fork out** (*inf*) *vt, vi* (*pay*) blechen.
forked [fɔːkt] *adj* (*lightning*) zickzackförmig.
fork-lift truck ['fɔːklɪft-] *n* Gabelstapler *m*.
forlorn [fə'lɔːn] *adj* verlassen; (*person*) einsam und verlassen; (*attempt*) verzweifelt; (*hope*) schwach.
form [fɔːm] *n* Form *f*; (*SCOL*) Klasse *f*; (*questionnaire*) Formular *nt* ♦ *vt* formen, gestalten; (*queue, organization, group*) bilden; (*idea, habit*) entwickeln; **in the ~ of** in Form von *or +gen*; **in the ~ of Peter** in Gestalt von Peter; **to be in good ~** gut in Form sein; **in top ~** in Hochform; **on ~** in Form; **to ~ part of sth** Teil von etw sein.
formal ['fɔːməl] *adj* offiziell; (*person, behaviour*) förmlich, formell; (*occasion, dinner*) feierlich; (*clothes*) Gesellschafts-; (*garden*) formell angelegt; (*ART, PHILOSOPHY*) formal; ~ **dress** Gesellschaftskleidung *f*.
formalities [fɔː'mælɪtɪz] *npl* Formalitäten *pl*.
formality [fɔː'mælɪtɪ] *n* Förmlichkeit *f*; (*procedure*) Formalität *f*.
formalize ['fɔːməlaɪz] *vt* formell machen.
formally ['fɔːmlɪ] *adv* (*see adj*) offiziell; förmlich, formell; feierlich; **to be ~ invited** ausdrücklich eingeladen sein.
format ['fɔːmæt] *n* Format *nt*; (*form, style*) Aufmachung *f* ♦ *vt* (*COMPUT*) formatieren.
formation [fɔː'meɪʃən] *n* Bildung *f*; (*of theory*) Entstehung *f*; (*of business*) Gründung *f*; (*pattern: of rocks, clouds*) Formation *f*.
formative ['fɔːmətɪv] *adj* (*influence*) prägend; (*years*) entscheidend.
former ['fɔːmə*] *adj* früher; **the ~ ... the latter ...** Erstere(r, s) ... Letztere(r, s); **the ~ president** der ehemalige Präsident; **the ~ East Germany** die ehemalige DDR.
formerly ['fɔːməlɪ] *adv* früher.
form feed *n* (*on printer*) Papiervorschub *m*.
Formica ® [fɔː'maɪkə] *n* Resopal ® *nt*.
formidable ['fɔːmɪdəbl] *adj* (*task*) gewaltig, enorm; (*opponent*) Furcht erregend.
formula ['fɔːmjulə] (*pl* ~**e** *or* ~**s**) *n* Formel *f*; **F~ One** (*AUT*) Formel Eins.
formulate ['fɔːmjuleɪt] *vt* formulieren.
fornicate ['fɔːnɪkeɪt] *vi* Unzucht treiben.
forsake [fə'seɪk] (*pt* **forsook**, *pp* **forsaken**) *vt* im Stich lassen; (*belief*) aufgeben.
forsook [fə'suk] *pt of* **forsake**.
fort [fɔːt] *n* Fort *nt*; **to hold the ~** die Stellung halten.
forte ['fɔːtɪ] *n* Stärke *f*, starke Seite *f*.
forth [fɔːθ] *adv* aus; **back and ~** hin und her; **to go back and ~** auf und ab gehen; **to bring ~** hervorbringen; **and so ~** und so weiter.
forthcoming [fɔːθ'kʌmɪŋ] *adj* (*event*) bevorstehend; (*person*) mitteilsam; **to be ~** (*help*) erfolgen; (*evidence*) geliefert werden.
forthright ['fɔːθraɪt] *adj* offen.

forthwith ['fɔːθ'wɪθ] *adv* umgehend.
fortieth ['fɔːtɪɪθ] *num* vierzigste(r, s).
fortification [fɔːtɪfɪ'keɪʃən] *n* Befestigung *f*, Festungsanlage *f*.
fortified wine ['fɔːtɪfaɪd-] *n* weinhaltiges Getränk *nt* (*Sherry, Portwein etc*).
fortify ['fɔːtɪfaɪ] *vt* (*city*) befestigen; (*person*) bestärken; (*: subj: food, drink*) stärken.
fortitude ['fɔːtɪtjuːd] *n* innere Kraft *or* Stärke *f*.
fortnight ['fɔːtnaɪt] (*BRIT*) *n* vierzehn Tage *pl*, zwei Wochen *pl*; **it's a ~ since ...** es ist vierzehn Tage *or* zwei Wochen her, dass ...
fortnightly ['fɔːtnaɪtlɪ] *adj* vierzehntägig, zweiwöchentlich ♦ *adv* alle vierzehn Tage, alle zwei Wochen.
FORTRAN ['fɔːtræn] *n* FORTRAN *nt*.
fortress ['fɔːtrɪs] *n* Festung *f*.
fortuitous [fɔː'tjuːɪtəs] *adj* zufällig.
fortunate ['fɔːtʃənɪt] *adj* glücklich; **to be ~** Glück haben; **he is ~ to have ...** er kann sich glücklich schätzen, ... zu haben; **it is ~ that ...** es ist ein Glück, dass ...
fortunately ['fɔːtʃənɪtlɪ] *adv* glücklicherweise, zum Glück.
fortune ['fɔːtʃən] *n* Glück *nt*; (*wealth*) Vermögen *nt*; **to make a ~** ein Vermögen machen; **to tell sb's ~** jdm wahrsagen.
fortune-teller ['fɔːtʃəntelə*] *n* Wahrsager(in) *m(f)*.
forty ['fɔːtɪ] *num* vierzig.
forum ['fɔːrəm] *n* Forum *nt*.
forward ['fɔːwəd] *adj* vordere(r, s); (*movement*) Vorwärts-; (*not shy*) dreist; (*COMM: buying, price*) Termin- ♦ *adv* nach vorn; (*movement*) vorwärts; (*in time*) voraus ♦ *n* (*SPORT*) Stürmer *m* ♦ *vt* (*letter etc*) nachsenden; (*career, plans*) voranbringen; ~ **planning** Vorausplanung *f*; **to move ~** vorwärts kommen; **"please ~"** „bitte nachsenden".
forwards ['fɔːwədz] *adv* nach vorn; (*movement*) vorwärts; (*in time*) voraus.
fossil ['fɒsl] *n* Fossil *nt*.
fossil fuel *n* fossiler Brennstoff *m*.
foster ['fɒstə*] *vt* (*child*) in Pflege nehmen; (*idea, activity*) fördern.
foster child *n* Pflegekind *nt*.
foster mother *n* Pflegemutter *f*.
fought [fɔːt] *pt, pp of* **fight**.
foul [faul] *adj* abscheulich; (*taste, smell, temper*) übel; (*water*) faulig; (*air*) schlecht; (*language*) unflätig ♦ *n* (*SPORT*) Foul *nt* ♦ *vt* beschmutzen; (*SPORT*) foulen; (*entangle*) sich verheddern in *+dat*.
foul play *n* unnatürlicher *or* gewaltsamer Tod *m*; ~ **is not suspected** es besteht kein Verdacht auf ein Verbrechen.
found [faund] *pt, pp of* **find** ♦ *vt* gründen.
foundation [faun'deɪʃən] *n* Gründung *f*; (*base: also fig*) Grundlage *f*; (*organization*) Stiftung *f*; (*also:* ~ **cream**) Grundierungscreme *f*;

foundations *npl* (*of building*) Fundament *nt*; **the rumours are without** ~ die Gerüchte entbehren jeder Grundlage; **to lay the ~s** (*fig*) die Grundlagen schaffen.

foundation stone *n* Grundstein *m*.

founder ['faundə*] *n* Gründer(in) *m(f)* ♦ *vi* (*ship*) sinken.

founder member *n* Gründungsmitglied *nt*.

founding ['faundɪŋ] *adj*: ~ **fathers** (*esp US*) Väter *pl*.

foundry ['faundrɪ] *n* Gießerei *f*.

fount [faunt] *n* Quelle *f*; (*TYP*) Schrift *f*.

fountain ['fauntɪn] *n* Brunnen *m*.

fountain pen *n* Füllfederhalter *m*, Füller *m*.

four [fɔ:*] *num* vier; **on all ~s** auf allen vieren.

four-letter word ['fɔ:lɛtə-] *n* Vulgärausdruck *m*.

four-poster ['fɔ:'pəustə*] *n* (*also:* ~ **bed**) Himmelbett *nt*.

foursome ['fɔ:səm] *n* Quartett *nt*; **in** *or* **as a** ~ zu viert.

fourteen ['fɔ:'ti:n] *num* vierzehn.

fourteenth ['fɔ:'ti:nθ] *num* vierzehnte(r, s).

fourth [fɔ:θ] *num* vierte(r, s) ♦ *n* (*AUT: also:* ~ **gear**) der vierte (Gang).

four-wheel drive ['fɔ:wi:l-] *n* (*AUT*): **with** ~ mit Vierradantrieb *m*.

fowl [faul] *n* Vogel *m* (*besonders Huhn, Gans, Ente etc*).

fox [fɔks] *n* Fuchs *m* ♦ *vt* verblüffen.

foxglove ['fɔksglʌv] *n* (*BOT*) Fingerhut *m*.

fox-hunting ['fɔkshʌntɪŋ] *n* Fuchsjagd *f*.

foxtrot ['fɔkstrɔt] *n* Foxtrott *m*.

foyer ['fɔɪeɪ] *n* Foyer *nt*.

FPA (*BRIT*) *n abbr* (= *Family Planning Association*) Organisation *für* Familienplanung.

Fr. *abbr* (*REL*) = **father; friar.**

fr. *abbr* (= *franc*) Fr.

fracas ['fræka:] *n* Aufruhr *m*, Tumult *m*.

fraction ['frækʃən] *n* Bruchteil *m*; (*MATH*) Bruch *m*.

fractionally ['frækʃnəlɪ] *adv* geringfügig.

fractious ['frækʃəs] *adj* verdrießlich.

fracture ['fræktʃə*] *n* Bruch *m* ♦ *vt* brechen.

fragile ['frædʒaɪl] *adj* zerbrechlich; (*economy*) schwach; (*health*) zart; (*person*) angeschlagen.

fragment [*n* 'frægmənt, *vb* fræg'mɛnt] *n* Stück *nt* ♦ *vt* aufsplittern ♦ *vi* sich aufsplittern.

fragmentary ['frægməntərɪ] *adj* fragmentarisch, bruchstückhaft.

fragrance ['freɪgrəns] *n* Duft *m*.

fragrant ['freɪgrənt] *adj* duftend.

frail [freɪl] *adj* schwach, gebrechlich; (*structure*) zerbrechlich.

frame [freɪm] *n* Rahmen *m*; (*of building*) (Grund)gerippe *nt*; (*of human, animal*) Gestalt *f*; (*of spectacles: also:* ~**s**) Gestell *nt* ♦ *vt* (*picture*) rahmen; (*reply*) formulieren; (*law, theory*) entwerfen; ~ **of mind** Stimmung *f*, Laune *f*; **to** ~ **sb** (*inf*) jdm etwas anhängen.

framework ['freɪmwə:k] *n* Rahmen *m*.

France [frɑ:ns] *n* Frankreich *nt*.

franchise ['fræntʃaɪz] *n* Wahlrecht *nt*; (*COMM*) Konzession *f*, Franchise *f*.

franchisee [fræntʃaɪ'zi:] *n* Franchisenehmer(in) *m(f)*.

franchiser ['fræntʃaɪzə*] *n* Franchisegeber(in) *m(f)*.

frank [fræŋk] *adj* offen ♦ *vt* (*letter*) frankieren.

Frankfurt ['fræŋkfə:t] *n* Frankfurt *nt*.

frankfurter ['fræŋkfə:tə*] *n* (Frankfurter) Würstchen *nt*.

franking machine ['fræŋkɪŋ-] *n* Frankiermaschine *f*.

frankly ['fræŋklɪ] *adv* ehrlich gesagt; (*candidly*) offen.

frankness ['fræŋknɪs] *n* Offenheit *f*.

frantic ['fræntɪk] *adj* verzweifelt; (*hectic*) hektisch; (*desperate*) übersteigert.

frantically ['fræntɪklɪ] *adv* verzweifelt; (*hectically*) hektisch.

fraternal [frə'tə:nl] *adj* brüderlich.

fraternity [frə'tə:nɪtɪ] *n* Brüderlichkeit *f*; (*US: UNIV*) Verbindung *f*; **the legal/medical/golfing** ~ die Juristen/Mediziner/Golfer *pl*.

fraternize ['frætənaɪz] *vi* Umgang haben.

fraud [frɔ:d] *n* Betrug *m*; (*person*) Betrüger(in) *m(f)*.

fraudulent ['frɔ:djulənt] *adj* betrügerisch.

fraught [frɔ:t] *adj* (*person*) nervös; **to be** ~ **with danger/problems** voller Gefahren/ Probleme sein.

fray [freɪ] *n*: **the** ~ der Kampf ♦ *vi* (*cloth*) ausfransen; (*rope*) sich durchscheuern; **to return to the** ~ sich wieder ins Getümmel stürzen; **tempers were** ~**ed** die Gemüter erhitzten sich; **her nerves were** ~**ed** sie war mit den Nerven am Ende.

FRB (*US*) *n abbr* = **Federal Reserve Board.**

FRCM (*BRIT*) *n abbr* (= *Fellow of the Royal College of Music*) Qualifikationsnachweis in Musik.

FRCO (*BRIT*) *n abbr* (= *Fellow of the Royal College of Organists*) Qualifikationsnachweis für Organisten.

FRCP (*BRIT*) *n abbr* (= *Fellow of the Royal College of Physicians*) Qualifikationsnachweis für Ärzte.

FRCS (*BRIT*) *n abbr* (= *Fellow of the Royal College of Surgeons*) Qualifikationsnachweis für Chirurgen.

freak [fri:k] *n* Irre(r) *f(m)*; (*in appearance*) Missgeburt *f*; (*event, accident*) außergewöhnlicher Zufall *m*; (*pej: fanatic*): **health** ~ Gesundheitsapostel *m*.

▶ **freak out** (*inf*) *vi* aussteigen; (*on drugs*) ausflippen.

freakish ['fri:kɪʃ] *adj* verrückt.

freckle ['frɛkl] *n* Sommersprosse *f*.

freckled ['frɛkld] *adj* sommersprossig.

free [fri:] *adj* frei; *(costing nothing)* kostenlos, gratis ♦ *vt* freilassen, frei lassen; *(jammed object)* lösen; **to give sb a ~ hand** jdm freie Hand lassen; **~ and easy** ungezwungen; **admission ~** Eintritt frei; **~ (of charge), for ~** umsonst, gratis.

free agent *n*: **to be a ~** sein eigener Herr sein.

freebie ['fri:bɪ] *(inf)* *n* *(promotional gift)* Werbegeschenk *nt*.

freedom ['fri:dəm] *n* Freiheit *f*.

freedom fighter *n* Freiheitskämpfer(in) *m(f)*.

free enterprise *n* freies Unternehmertum *nt*.

Freefone ® ['fri:fəun] *n*: **call ~ 0800** rufen Sie gebührenfrei 0800 an.

free-for-all ['fri:fərɔ:l] *n* Gerangel *nt*; **the fight turned into a ~** schließlich beteiligten sich alle an der Schlägerei.

free gift *n* Werbegeschenk *nt*.

freehold ['fri:həuld] *n* *(of property)* Besitzrecht *nt*.

free kick *n* Freistoß *m*.

freelance ['fri:lɑ:ns] *adj* *(journalist etc)* frei(schaffend), freiberuflich tätig.

freelance work *n* freiberufliche Arbeit *f*.

freeloader ['fri:ləudə*] *(pej)* *n* Schmarotzer(in) *m(f)*.

freely ['fri:lɪ] *adv* frei; *(spend)* mit vollen Händen; *(liberally)* großzügig; **drugs are ~ available in the city** Drogen sind in der Stadt frei erhältlich.

free-market economy ['fri:'mɑ:kɪt-] *n* freie Marktwirtschaft *f*.

Freemason ['fri:meɪsn] *n* Freimaurer *m*.

Freemasonry ['fri:meɪsnrɪ] *n* Freimaurerei *f*.

Freepost ® ['fri:pəust] *n* ≈ „Gebühr zahlt Empfänger".

free-range ['fri:'reɪndʒ] *adj* *(eggs)* von frei laufenden Hühnern.

free sample *n* Gratisprobe *f*.

freesia ['fri:zɪə] *n* Freesie *f*.

free speech *n* Redefreiheit *f*.

freestyle ['fri:staɪl] *n* Freistil *m*.

free trade *n* Freihandel *m*.

freeway ['fri:weɪ] *(US)* *n* Autobahn *f*.

freewheel [fri:'wi:l] *vi* im Freilauf fahren.

free will *n* freier Wille *m*; **of one's own ~** aus freien Stücken.

freeze [fri:z] *(pt* **froze***, pp* **frozen***) vi* frieren; *(liquid)* gefrieren; *(pipe)* einfrieren; *(person: stop moving)* erstarren ♦ *vt* einfrieren; *(water, lake)* gefrieren ♦ *n* Frost *m*; *(on arms, wages)* Stopp *m*.

▶ **freeze over** *vi* *(river)* überfrieren; *(windscreen, windows)* vereisen.

▶ **freeze up** *vi* zufrieren.

freeze-dried ['fri:zdraɪd] *adj* gefriergetrocknet.

freezer ['fri:zə*] *n* Tiefkühltruhe *f*; *(upright)* Gefrierschrank *m*; *(in fridge: also:* **~ compartment***)* Gefrierfach *nt*.

freezing ['fri:zɪŋ] *adj*: **~ (cold)** eiskalt ♦ *n*: **3 degrees below ~** 3 Grad unter null; **I'm ~** mir ist eiskalt.

freezing point *n* Gefrierpunkt *m*.

freight [freɪt] *n* Fracht *f*; *(money charged)* Frachtkosten *pl*; **~ forward** Fracht gegen Nachnahme; **~ inward** Eingangsfracht *f*.

freight car *(US)* *n* Güterwagen *m*.

freighter ['freɪtə*] *n* *(NAUT)* Frachter *m*, Frachtschiff *nt*; *(AVIAT)* Frachtflugzeug *nt*.

freight forwarder [-'fɔ:wədə*] *n* Spediteur *m*.

freight train *(US)* *n* Güterzug *m*.

French [frentʃ] *adj* französisch ♦ *n* *(LING)* Französisch *nt*; **the French** *npl* die Franzosen *pl*.

French bean *(BRIT)* *n* grüne Bohne *f*.

French Canadian *adj* frankokanadisch ♦ *n* Frankokanadier(in) *m(f)*.

French dressing *n* Vinaigrette *f*.

French fried potatoes *npl* Pommes frites *pl*.

French fries [-fraɪz] *(US)* *npl* = **French fried potatoes**.

French Guiana [-gaɪ'ænə] *n* Französisch-Guyana *nt*.

Frenchman ['frentʃmən] *(irreg: like* **man***) n* Franzose *m*.

French Riviera *n*: **the ~** die französische Riviera.

French stick *n* Stangenbrot *nt*.

French window *n* Verandatür *f*.

Frenchwoman ['frentʃwumən] *(irreg: like* **woman***) n* Französin *f*.

frenetic [frə'netɪk] *adj* frenetisch, rasend.

frenzied ['frenzɪd] *adj* rasend.

frenzy ['frenzɪ] *n* Raserei *f*; *(of joy, excitement)* Taumel *m*; **to drive sb into a ~** jdn zum Rasen bringen; **to be in a ~** in wilder Aufregung sein.

frequency ['fri:kwənsɪ] *n* Häufigkeit *f*; *(RADIO)* Frequenz *f*.

frequency modulation *n* Frequenzmodulation *f*.

frequent [*adj* 'fri:kwənt, *vt* frɪ'kwent] *adj* häufig ♦ *vt* *(pub, restaurant)* oft *or* häufig besuchen.

frequently ['fri:kwəntlɪ] *adv* oft, häufig.

fresco ['freskəu] *n* Fresko *nt*.

fresh [freʃ] *adj* frisch; *(instructions, approach, start)* neu; *(cheeky)* frech; **to make a ~ start** einen neuen Anfang machen.

freshen ['freʃən] *vi* *(wind)* auffrischen; *(air)* frisch werden.

▶ **freshen up** *vi* sich frisch machen.

freshener ['freʃnə*] *n*: **skin ~** Gesichtswasser *nt*; **air ~** Raumspray *m or nt*.

fresher ['freʃə*] *(BRIT: inf)* *n* Erstsemester(in) *m(f)*.

freshly ['freʃlɪ] *adv* frisch.

freshman ['freʃmən] *(US: irreg: like* **man***) n* = **fresher**.

freshness ['freʃnɪs] *n* Frische *f*.

freshwater ['freʃwɔ:tə*] *adj* *(fish etc)* Süßwasser-.

fret [fret] *vi* sich *dat* Sorgen machen.

fretful ['frɛtful] adj (child) quengelig.
Freudian ['frɔɪdɪən] adj freudianisch,
freudsch; ~ **slip** freudscher Versprecher
m.
FRG n abbr (= Federal Republic of Germany)
BRD f.
Fri. abbr (= Friday) Fr.
friar ['fraɪə*] n Mönch m, (Ordens)bruder m.
friction ['frɪkʃən] n Reibung f; (between people)
Reibereien pl.
friction feed n (on printer) Friktionsvorschub
m.
Friday ['fraɪdɪ] n Freitag m; see also **Tuesday**.
fridge [frɪdʒ] (BRIT) n Kühlschrank m.
fridge-freezer ['frɪdʒ'friːzə*] n Kühl- und
Gefrierkombination f.
fried [fraɪd] pt, pp of fry ♦ adj gebraten; ~ **egg**
Spiegelei nt; ~ **fish** Bratfisch m.
friend [frɛnd] n Freund(in) m(f); (less intimate)
Bekannte(r) f(m); **to make ~s with** sich
anfreunden mit.
friendliness ['frɛndlɪnɪs] n Freundlichkeit f.
friendly ['frɛndlɪ] adj freundlich; (government)
befreundet; (game, match) Freundschafts-
♦ n (also: ~ **match**) Freundschaftsspiel nt; **to
be ~ with** befreundet sein mit; **to be ~ to**
freundlich or nett sein zu.
friendly fire n Beschuss m durch die eigene
Seite.
friendly society n Versicherungsverein m
auf Gegenseitigkeit.
friendship ['frɛndʃɪp] n Freundschaft f.
frieze [friːz] n Fries m.
frigate ['frɪgɪt] n Fregatte f.
fright [fraɪt] n Schreck(en) m; **to take** ~ es mit
der Angst zu tun bekommen; **she looks a** ~
sie sieht verboten or zum Fürchten aus (inf).
frighten ['fraɪtn] vt erschrecken.
► **frighten away** or **off** vt verscheuchen.
frightened ['fraɪtnd] adj ängstlich; **to be ~ (of)**
Angst haben (vor +dat).
frightening ['fraɪtnɪŋ] adj Furcht erregend.
frightful ['fraɪtful] adj schrecklich, furchtbar.
frightfully ['fraɪtfəlɪ] adv schrecklich,
furchtbar; **I'm ~ sorry** es tut mir
schrecklich Leid.
frigid ['frɪdʒɪd] adj frigide.
frigidity [frɪ'dʒɪdɪtɪ] n Frigidität f.
frill [frɪl] n Rüsche f; **without ~s** (fig) schlicht.
fringe [frɪndʒ] n (BRIT: of hair) Pony m;
(decoration) Fransen pl; (edge: also fig) Rand
m.
fringe benefits npl zusätzliche Leistungen
pl.
fringe theatre n avantgardistisches Theater
nt.
Frisbee ® ['frɪzbɪ] n Frisbee ® nt.
frisk [frɪsk] vt durchsuchen, filzen (inf) ♦ vi
umhertollen.
frisky ['frɪskɪ] adj lebendig, ausgelassen.
fritter ['frɪtə*] n Schmalzgebackenes nt no pl
mit Füllung.

► **fritter away** vt vergeuden.
frivolity [frɪ'vɔlɪtɪ] n Frivolität f.
frivolous ['frɪvələs] adj frivol; (activity)
leichtfertig.
frizzy ['frɪzɪ] adj kraus.
fro [frəu] adv: **to and** ~ hin und her; (walk) auf
und ab.
frock [frɔk] n Kleid nt.
frog [frɔg] n Frosch m; **to have a ~ in one's
throat** einen Frosch im Hals haben.
frogman ['frɔgmən] (irreg: like man) n
Froschmann m.
frogmarch ['frɔgmɑːtʃ] (BRIT) vt: **to ~ sb in/
out** jdn herein-/herausschleppen.
frolic ['frɔlɪk] vi umhertollen ♦ n
Ausgelassenheit f; (fun) Spaß m.

═══════════════════════════════ KEYWORD

from [frɔm] prep **1** (indicating starting place,
origin) von +dat; **where do you come ~?**
woher kommen Sie?; ~ **London to Glasgow**
von London nach Glasgow; **a letter/
telephone call ~ my sister** ein Brief/Anruf
von meiner Schwester; **to drink ~ the bottle**
aus der Flasche trinken.
2 (indicating time) von (... an); ~ **one o'clock
to** or **until** or **till now** von ein Uhr bis jetzt;
~ **January (on)** von Januar an, ab Januar.
3 (indicating distance) von ... entfernt; **the
hotel is 1 km ~ the beach** das Hotel ist 1 km
vom Strand entfernt.
4 (indicating price, number etc): **trousers**
~ **£20** Hosen ab £20; **prices range ~ £10 to
£50** die Preise liegen zwischen £ 10 und
£ 50.
5 (indicating difference): **he can't tell red**
~ **green** er kann Rot und Grün nicht
unterscheiden; **to be different ~ sb/sth**
anders sein als jd/etw.
6 (because of, on the basis of): ~ **what he says**
nach dem, was er sagt; **to act ~ conviction**
aus Überzeugung handeln; **weak ~ hunger**
schwach vor Hunger.

frond [frɔnd] n Wedel m.
front [frʌnt] n Vorderseite f; (of dress)
Vorderteil nt; (promenade: also: sea ~)
Strandpromenade f; (MIL, MET) Front f; (fig:
appearances) Fassade f ♦ adj vorderste(r, s);
(wheel, tooth, view) Vorder- ♦ vi: **to ~ onto
sth** (house) auf etw acc hinausliegen;
(window) auf etw acc hinausgehen; **in ~**
vorne; **in ~ of** vor; **at the ~ of the coach/
train/car** vorne im Bus/Zug/Auto; **on the
political ~, little progress has been made** an
der politischen Front sind kaum
Fortschritte gemacht worden.
frontage ['frʌntɪdʒ] n Vorderseite f, Front f;
(of shop) Front.
frontal ['frʌntl] adj (attack etc) Frontal-.
front bench (BRIT) n (POL) vorderste or erste
Reihe f.

front desk (*US*) *n* Rezeption *f*.
front door *n* Haustür *f*.
frontier ['frʌntɪə°] *n* Grenze *f*.
frontispiece ['frʌntɪspiːs] *n* zweite Titelseite *f*, Frontispiz *nt*.
front page *n* erste Seite *f*, Titelseite *f*.
front room (*BRIT*) *n* Wohnzimmer *nt*.
frontrunner ['frʌntrʌnə°] *n* Spitzenreiter *m*.
front-wheel drive ['frʌntwiːl-] *n* (*AUT*) Vorderradantrieb *m*.
frost [frɔst] *n* Frost *m*; (*also:* **hoar~**) Raureif *m*.
frostbite ['frɔstbaɪt] *n* Erfrierungen *pl*.
frosted ['frɔstɪd] *adj* (*glass*) Milch-; (*esp US*) glasiert, mit Zuckerguss überzogen.
frosting ['frɔstɪŋ] (*esp US*) *n* Zuckerguss *m*.
frosty ['frɔstɪ] *adj* frostig; (*look*) eisig; (*window*) bereift.
froth [frɔθ] *n* Schaum *m*.
frothy ['frɔθɪ] *adj* schäumend.
frown [fraun] *n* Stirnrunzeln *nt* ♦ *vi* die Stirn runzeln.
▶ **frown on** *vt fus* missbilligen.
froze [frəuz] *pt of* **freeze**.
frozen ['frəuzn] *pp of* **freeze** ♦ *adj* tiefgekühlt; (*food*) Tiefkühl-; (*COMM*) eingefroren.
FRS *n abbr* (*BRIT:* = *Fellow of the Royal Society*) *Auszeichnung für Naturwissenschaftler*; (*US:* = *Federal Reserve System*) *amerikanische Zentralbank*.
frugal ['fruːgl] *adj* genügsam; (*meal*) einfach.
fruit [fruːt] *n inv* Frucht *f*; (*collectively*) Obst *nt*; (*fig: results*) Früchte *pl*.
fruiterer ['fruːtərə°] (*esp BRIT*) *n* Obsthändler(in) *m(f)*.
fruitful ['fruːtful] *adj* fruchtbar.
fruition [fruːˈɪʃən] *n*: **to come to ~** (*plan*) Wirklichkeit werden; (*efforts*) Früchte tragen; (*hope*) in Erfüllung gehen.
fruit juice *n* Fruchtsaft *m*.
fruitless ['fruːtlɪs] *adj* fruchtlos, ergebnislos.
fruit machine (*BRIT*) *n* Spielautomat *m*.
fruit salad *n* Obstsalat *m*.
fruity ['fruːtɪ] *adj* (*taste, smell etc*) Frucht-, Obst-; (*wine*) fruchtig; (*voice, laugh*) volltönend.
frump [frʌmp] *n*: **to feel a ~** sich *dat* wie eine Vogelscheuche vorkommen.
frustrate [frʌsˈtreɪt] *vt* frustrieren; (*attempt*) vereiteln; (*plan*) durchkreuzen.

frustrated [frʌsˈtreɪtɪd] *adj* frustriert.
frustrating [frʌsˈtreɪtɪŋ] *adj* frustrierend.
frustration [frʌsˈtreɪʃən] *n* Frustration *f*; (*of attempt*) Vereitelung *f*; (*of plan*) Zerschlagung *f*.
fry [fraɪ] (*pt, pp* **fried**) *vt* braten; *see also* **small**.
frying pan ['fraɪɪŋ-] *n* Bratpfanne *f*.
FT (*BRIT*) *n abbr* (= *Financial Times*) *Wirtschaftszeitung*; **the ~ index** der Aktienindex der „Financial Times".
ft. *abbr* = **foot**; **feet**.
FTC (*US*) *n abbr* = **Federal Trade Commission**.
FTSE 100 Index *n Aktienindex der „Financial Times"*.
fuchsia ['fjuːʃə] *n* Fuchsie *f*.
fuck [fʌk] (*inf!*) *vt, vi* ficken (*!*); **~ off!** (*inf!*) verpiss dich! (*!*).
fuddled ['fʌdld] *adj* verwirrt.
fuddy-duddy ['fʌdɪdʌdɪ] (*pej*) *n* Langweiler *m*.
fudge [fʌdʒ] *n* Fondant *m* ♦ *vt* (*issue, problem*) ausweichen +*dat*, aus dem Weg gehen +*dat*.
fuel ['fjuəl] *n* Brennstoff *m*; (*for vehicle*) Kraftstoff *m*; (: *petrol*) Benzin *nt*; (*for aircraft, rocket*) Treibstoff *m* ♦ *vt* (*furnace etc*) betreiben; (*aircraft, ship etc*) antreiben.
fuel oil *n* Gasöl *nt*.
fuel pump *n* (*AUT*) Benzinpumpe *f*.
fuel tank *n* Öltank *m*; (*in vehicle*) (Benzin)tank *m*.
fug [fʌg] (*BRIT: inf*) *n* Mief *m* (*inf*).
fugitive ['fjuːdʒɪtɪv] *n* Flüchtling *m*.
fulfil, (*US*) **fulfill** [ful'fɪl] *vt* erfüllen; (*order*) ausführen.
fulfilled [ful'fɪld] *adj* ausgefüllt.
fulfilment, (*US*) **fulfillment** [ful'fɪlmənt] *n* Erfüllung *f*.
full [ful] *adj* voll; (*complete*) vollständig; (*skirt*) weit; (*life*) ausgefüllt ♦ *adv*: **to know ~ well that ...** sehr wohl wissen, dass ...; **~ up** (*hotel etc*) ausgebucht; **I'm ~ (up)** ich bin satt; **a ~ two hours** volle zwei Stunden; **~ marks** die beste Note, ≈ eine Eins; (*fig*) höchstes Lob *nt*; **at ~ speed** in voller Fahrt; **in ~** ganz, vollständig; **to pay in ~** den vollen Betrag bezahlen; **to write one's name** *etc* **in ~** seinen Namen *etc* ausschreiben.
fullback ['fulbæk] *n* (*SPORT*) Verteidiger *m*.
full-blooded ['ful'blʌdɪd] *adj* (*vigorous*) kräftig; (*virile*) vollblütig.
full board *n* Vollpension *f*.
full-cream ['ful'kriːm] *adj*: **~ milk** (*BRIT*) Vollmilch *f*.
full employment *n* Vollbeschäftigung *f*.
full grown *adj* ausgewachsen.
full-length ['ful'lɛŋθ] *adj* (*film*) abendfüllend; (*coat*) lang; (*portrait*) lebensgroß; (*mirror*) groß; **~ novel** Roman *m*.
full moon *n* Vollmond *m*.
fullness ['fulnɪs] *n*: **in the ~ of time** zu gegebener Zeit.
full-page ['fulpeɪdʒ] *adj* ganzseitig.
full-scale ['fulskeɪl] *adj* (*war*) richtig; (*attack*)

Groß-; (*model*) in Originalgröße; (*search*) groß angelegt.

full-sized ['ful'saɪzd] *adj* lebensgroß.

full stop *n* Punkt *m*.

full-time ['ful'taɪm] *adj* (*work*) Ganztags-; (*study*) Voll- ♦ *adv* ganztags.

fully ['fulɪ] *adv* völlig; ~ **as big as** mindestens so groß wie.

fully fledged [-'flɛdʒd] *adj* richtiggehend; (*doctor etc*) voll qualifiziert; (*member*) Voll-; (*bird*) flügge.

fulsome ['fulsəm] (*pej*) *adj* übertrieben.

fumble ['fʌmbl] *vi*: **to ~ with** herumfummeln an +*dat* ♦ *vt* (*ball*) nicht sicher fangen.

fume [fju:m] *vi* wütend sein, kochen (*inf*).

fumes [fju:mz] *npl* (*of fire*) Rauch *m*; (*of fuel*) Dämpfe *pl*; (*of car*) Abgase *pl*.

fumigate ['fju:mɪgeɪt] *vt* ausräuchern.

fun [fʌn] *n* Spaß *m*; **he's good ~ (to be with)** es macht viel Spaß, mit ihm zusammen zu sein; **for ~** aus *or* zum Spaß; **it's not much ~** es macht keinen Spaß; **to make ~ of, to poke ~ at** sich lustig machen über +*acc*.

function ['fʌŋkʃən] *n* Funktion *f*; (*social occasion*) Veranstaltung *f*, Feier *f* ♦ *vi* funktionieren; **to ~ as** (*thing*) dienen als; (*person*) fungieren als.

functional ['fʌŋkʃənl] *adj* (*operational*) funktionsfähig; (*practical*) funktionell, zweckmäßig.

function key *n* (*COMPUT*) Funktionstaste *f*.

fund [fʌnd] *n* (*of money*) Fonds *m*; (*source, store*) Schatz *m*, Vorrat *m*; **funds** *npl* (*money*) Mittel *pl*, Gelder *pl*.

fundamental [fʌndə'mɛntl] *adj* fundamental, grundlegend.

fundamentalism [fʌndə'mɛntəlɪzəm] *n* Fundamentalismus *m*.

fundamentalist [fʌndə'mɛntəlɪst] *n* Fundamentalist(in) *m(f)*.

fundamentally [fʌndə'mɛntəlɪ] *adv* im Grunde; (*radically*) von Grund auf.

fundamentals [fʌndə'mɛntlz] *npl* Grundbegriffe *pl*.

funding ['fʌndɪŋ] *n* Finanzierung *f*.

fund-raising ['fʌndreɪzɪŋ] *n* Geldbeschaffung *f*.

funeral ['fju:nərəl] *n* Beerdigung *f*.

funeral director *n* Beerdigungsunternehmer(in) *m(f)*.

funeral parlour *n* Leichenhalle *f*.

funeral service *n* Trauergottesdienst *m*.

funereal [fju:'nɪərɪəl] *adj* traurig, trübselig.

funfair ['fʌnfɛə*] (*BRIT*) *n* Jahrmarkt *m*.

fungi ['fʌŋgaɪ] *npl of* **fungus**.

fungus ['fʌŋgəs] (*pl* **fungi**) *n* Pilz *m*; (*mould*) Schimmel(pilz) *m*.

funicular [fju:'nɪkjulə*] *n* (*also*: ~ **railway**) Seilbahn *f*.

funky ['fʌŋkɪ] *adj* (*music*) Funk-.

funnel ['fʌnl] *n* Trichter *m*; (*of ship*) Schornstein *m*.

funnily ['fʌnɪlɪ] *adv* komisch; ~ **enough** komischerweise.

funny ['fʌnɪ] *adj* komisch; (*strange*) seltsam, komisch.

funny bone *n* Musikantenknochen *m*.

fun run *n* ≈ Volkslauf *m*.

fur [fə:*] *n* Fell *nt*, Pelz *m*; (*BRIT: in kettle etc*) Kesselstein *m*.

fur coat *n* Pelzmantel *m*.

furious ['fjuərɪəs] *adj* wütend; (*argument*) heftig; (*effort*) riesig; (*speed*) rasend; **to be ~ with sb** wütend auf jdn sein.

furiously ['fjuərɪəslɪ] *adv* (*see adj*) wütend; (*struggle etc*) heftig; (*run*) schnell.

furl [fə:l] *vt* (*NAUT*) einrollen.

furlong ['fə:lɔŋ] *n* Achtelmeile *f* (= 201,17 m).

furlough ['fə:ləu] *n* (*MIL*) Urlaub *m*.

furnace ['fə:nɪs] *n* (*in foundry*) Schmelzofen *m*; (*in power plant*) Hochofen *m*.

furnish ['fə:nɪʃ] *vt* einrichten; (*room*) möblieren; **to ~ sb with sth** jdm etw liefern; **~ed flat** *or* (*US*) **apartment** möblierte Wohnung *f*.

furnishings ['fə:nɪʃɪŋz] *npl* Einrichtung *f*.

furniture ['fə:nɪtʃə*] *n* Möbel *pl*; **piece of ~** Möbelstück *nt*.

furniture polish *n* Möbelpolitur *f*.

furore [fjuə'rɔ:rɪ] *n* (*protests*) Proteste *pl*; (*enthusiasm*) Furore *f or nt*.

furrier ['fʌrɪə*] *n* Kürschner(in) *m(f)*.

furrow ['fʌrəu] *n* Furche *f*; (*in skin*) Runzel *f* ♦ *vt* (*brow*) runzeln.

furry ['fə:rɪ] *adj* (*coat, tail*) flauschig; (*animal*) Pelz-; (*toy*) Plüsch-.

further ['fə:ðə*] *adj* weitere(r, s) ♦ *adv* weiter; (*moreover*) darüber hinaus ♦ *vt* fördern; **until ~ notice** bis auf weiteres; **how much ~ is it?** wie weit ist es noch?; ~ **to your letter of ...** (*COMM*) Bezug nehmend auf Ihr Schreiben vom ...

further education (*BRIT*) *n* Weiterbildung *f*, Fortbildung *f*.

furthermore [fə:ðə'mɔ:*] *adv* außerdem.

furthermost ['fə:ðəməust] *adj* äußerste(r, s).

furthest ['fə:ðɪst] *superl of* **far**.

furtive ['fə:tɪv] *adj* verstohlen.

furtively ['fə:tɪvlɪ] *adv* verstohlen.

fury ['fjuərɪ] *n* Wut *f*; **to be in a ~** in Rage sein.

fuse, (*US*) **fuze** [fju:z] *n* (*ELEC*) Sicherung *f*; (*for bomb etc*) Zündschnur *f* ♦ *vt* (*pieces of metal*) verschmelzen; (*fig*) vereinigen ♦ *vi* (*pieces of metal*) sich verbinden; (*fig*) sich vereinigen; **to ~ the lights** (*BRIT*) die Sicherung durchbrennen lassen; **a ~ has blown** eine Sicherung ist durchgebrannt.

fuse box *n* Sicherungskasten *m*.

fuselage ['fju:zəlɑ:ʒ] *n* Rumpf *m*.

fuse wire *n* Schmelzdraht *m*.

fusillade [fju:zɪ'leɪd] *n* Salve *f*.

fusion ['fju:ʒən] *n* Verschmelzung *f*; (*also*: **nuclear ~**) Kernfusion *f*.

fuss [fʌs] *n* Theater *nt* (*inf*) ♦ *vi* sich (unnötig) aufregen ♦ *vt* keine Ruhe lassen +*dat*; **to make a** ~ Krach schlagen (*inf*); **to make a** ~ **of sb** viel Getue um jdn machen (*inf*).

▶ **fuss over** *vt fus* bemuttern.

fusspot ['fʌspɒt] *n* Nörgler(in) *m(f)*.

fussy ['fʌsɪ] *adj* kleinlich, pingelig (*inf*); (*clothes, room etc*) verspielt; **I'm not** ~ es ist mir egal.

fusty ['fʌstɪ] *adj* muffig.

futile ['fjuːtaɪl] *adj* vergeblich; (*existence*) sinnlos; (*comment*) zwecklos.

futility [fjuː'tɪlɪtɪ] *n* (*see adj*) Vergeblichkeit *f*; Sinnlosigkeit *f*; Zwecklosigkeit *f*.

futon ['fuːtɒn] *n* Futon *m*.

future ['fjuːtʃə*] *adj* zukünftig ♦ *n* Zukunft *f*; (*LING*) Futur *nt*; **futures** *npl* (*COMM*) Termingeschäfte *pl*; **in (the)** ~ in Zukunft; **in the near** ~ in der nahen Zukunft; **in the immediate** ~ sehr bald.

futuristic [fjuːtʃə'rɪstɪk] *adj* futuristisch.

fuze [fjuːz] (*US*) *n, vt, vi* = **fuse**.

fuzz [fʌz] (*inf*) *n* (*police*): **the** ~ die Bullen *pl*.

fuzzy ['fʌzɪ] *adj* verschwommen; (*hair*) kraus; (*thoughts*) verworren.

fwd. *abbr* = **forward**.

fwy (*US*) *abbr* = **freeway**.

FY *abbr* (= *fiscal year*) Steuerjahr *nt*.

FYI *abbr* (= *for your information*) zu Ihrer Information.

G, g

G¹, g¹ [dʒiː] *n* (*letter*) G *nt*, g *nt*; ~ **for George** ≈ G wie Gustav.

G² [dʒiː] *n* (*MUS*) G *nt*, g *nt*.

G³ [dʒiː] *n abbr* (*BRIT: SCOL*) = **good**; (*US: CINE*: = *general (audience)*) Klassifikation für jugendfreie Filme; (*PHYS*): ~**-force** g-Druck *m*.

G7 *n abbr* (*POL*: = *Group of Seven*) G7 *f*.

g² *abbr* (= *gram(me)*) g; (*PHYS*) = **gravity**.

GA (*US*) *n abbr* (*POST*: = *Georgia*).

gab [gæb] (*inf*) *n*: **to have the gift of the** ~ reden können, nicht auf den Mund gefallen sein.

gabble ['gæbl] *vi* brabbeln (*inf*).

gaberdine [gæbə'diːn] *n* Gabardine *m*.

gable ['geɪbl] *n* Giebel *m*.

Gabon [gə'bɒn] *n* Gabun *nt*.

gad about [gæd-] (*inf*) *vi* herumziehen.

gadget ['gædʒɪt] *n* Gerät *nt*.

gadgetry ['gædʒɪtrɪ] *n* Geräte *pl*.

Gaelic ['geɪlɪk] *adj* gälisch ♦ *n* (*LING*) Gälisch *nt*.

gaffe [gæf] *n* Fauxpas *m*.

gaffer ['gæfə*] (*BRIT: inf*) *n* (*boss*) Chef *m*; (*foreman*) Vorarbeiter *m*; (*old man*) Alte(r) *m*.

gag [gæg] *n* Knebel *m*; (*joke*) Gag *m* ♦ *vt* knebeln ♦ *vi* würgen.

gaga ['gɑːgɑː] (*inf*) *adj*: **to go** ~ verkalken.

gage [geɪdʒ] (*US*) *n, vt* = **gauge**.

gaiety ['geɪɪtɪ] *n* Fröhlichkeit *f*.

gaily ['geɪlɪ] *adv* fröhlich; ~ **coloured** farbenfroh, farbenprächtig.

gain [geɪn] *n* Gewinn *m* ♦ *vt* gewinnen ♦ *vi* (*clock, watch*) vorgehen; **to do sth for** ~ etw aus Berechnung tun; (*for money*) etw des Geldes wegen tun; ~ **(in)** (*increase*) Zunahme *f* (an +*dat*); (*in rights, conditions*) Verbesserung *f* +*gen*; **to** ~ **ground** (an) Boden gewinnen; **to** ~ **speed** schneller werden; **to** ~ **weight** zunehmen; **to** ~ **3lbs (in weight)** 3 Pfund zunehmen; **to** ~ **(in) confidence** sicherer werden; **to** ~ **from sth** von etw profitieren; **to** ~ **in strength** stärker werden; **to** ~ **by doing sth** davon profitieren, etw zu tun; **to** ~ **on sb** jdn einholen.

gainful ['geɪnful] *adj*: ~ **employment** Erwerbstätigkeit *f*.

gainfully ['geɪnfəlɪ] *adv*: ~ **employed** erwerbstätig.

gainsay [geɪn'seɪ] (*irreg: like* **say**) *vt* widersprechen +*dat*; (*fact*) leugnen.

gait [geɪt] *n* Gang *m*; **to walk with a slow/ confident** ~ mit langsamen Schritten/ selbstbewusst gehen.

gal. *abbr* = **gallon**.

gala ['gɑːlə] *n* Galaveranstaltung *f*; **swimming** ~ großes Schwimmfest *nt*.

Galapagos (Islands) [gə'læpəgəs-] *npl*: **(the)** ~ die Galapagosinseln *pl*.

galaxy ['gæləksɪ] *n* Galaxis *f*, Sternsystem *nt*.

gale [geɪl] *n* Sturm *m*; ~ **force 10** Sturmstärke 10.

gall [gɔːl] *n* Galle *f*; (*fig: impudence*) Frechheit *f* ♦ *vt* maßlos ärgern.

gall. *abbr* = **gallon**.

gallant ['gælənt] *adj* tapfer; (*polite*) galant.

gallantry ['gæləntrɪ] *n* (*see adj*) Tapferkeit *f*; Galanterie *f*.

gall bladder *n* Gallenblase *f*.

galleon ['gælɪən] *n* Galeone *f*.

gallery ['gælərɪ] *n* (*also*: **art** ~) Galerie *f*, Museum *nt*; (*private*) (Privat)galerie *f*; (*in hall, church*) Galerie *f*; (*in theatre*) oberster Rang *m*, Balkon *m*.

galley ['gælɪ] *n* Kombüse *f*; (*ship*) Galeere *f*; (*also*: ~ **proof**) Fahne *f*, Fahnenabzug *m*.

Gallic ['gælɪk] *adj* gallisch; (*French*) französisch.

galling ['gɔːlɪŋ] *adj* äußerst ärgerlich.

gallon ['gælən] *n* Gallone *f* (*BRIT* = 4,5 *l*, *US* = 3,8 *l*).

gallop ['gæləp] *n* Galopp *m* ♦ *vi* galoppieren; ~**ing inflation** galoppierende Inflation *f*.

gallows ['gæləuz] *n* Galgen *m*.

gallstone ['gɔːlstəun] *n* Gallenstein *m*.
Gallup poll ['gæləp-] *n* Meinungsumfrage *f*.
galore [gə'lɔːˈ] *adv* in Hülle und Fülle.
galvanize ['gælvənaɪz] *vt* (*fig*) mobilisieren; **to** ~ **sb into action** jdn plötzlich aktiv werden lassen.
galvanized ['gælvənaɪzd] *adj* (*metal*) galvanisiert.
Gambia ['gæmbɪə] *n* Gambia *nt*.
gambit ['gæmbɪt] *n*: (*opening*) ~ (einleitender) Schachzug *m*; (*in conversation*) (einleitende) Bemerkung *f*.
gamble ['gæmbl] *n* Risiko *nt* ♦ *vt* einsetzen ♦ *vi* ein Risiko eingehen; (*bet*) spielen; (*on horses etc*) wetten; **to** ~ **on the Stock Exchange** an der Börse spekulieren; **to** ~ **on sth** (*horses, race*) auf etw *acc* wetten; (*success, outcome etc*) sich auf etw *acc* verlassen.
gambler ['gæmblə'] *n* Spieler(in) *m(f)*.
gambling ['gæmblɪŋ] *n* Spielen *nt*; (*on horses etc*) Wetten *nt*.
gambol ['gæmbl] *vi* herumtollen.
game [geɪm] *n* Spiel *nt*; (*sport*) Sport *m*; (*strategy, scheme*) Vorhaben *nt*; (*CULIN, HUNTING*) Wild *nt* ♦ *adj*: **to be** ~ (**for**) mitmachen (bei); **games** *npl* (*SCOL*) Sport *m*; **to play a** ~ **of football/tennis** Fußball/(eine Partie) Tennis spielen; **big** ~ Großwild *nt*.
game bird *n* Federwild *nt no pl*.
gamekeeper ['geɪmkiːpə'] *n* Wildhüter(in) *m(f)*.
gamely ['geɪmlɪ] *adv* mutig.
game reserve *n* Wildschutzreservat *nt*.
games console ['geɪmz-] *n* (*COMPUT*) Gameboy ® *m*, Konsole *f*.
game show *n* (*TV*) Spielshow *f*.
gamesmanship ['geɪmzmənʃɪp] *n* Gerissenheit *f* beim Spiel.
gaming ['geɪmɪŋ] *n* (*gambling*) Spielen *nt*.
gammon ['gæmən] *n* Schinken *m*.
gamut ['gæmət] *n* Skala *f*; **to run the** ~ **of** die ganze Skala +*gen* durchlaufen.
gander ['gændə'] *n* Gänserich *m*.
gang [gæŋ] *n* Bande *f*; (*of friends*) Haufen *m*; (*of workmen*) Kolonne *f*.
▶ **gang up** *vi*: **to** ~ **up on sb** sich gegen jdn zusammentun.
Ganges ['gændʒiːz] *n*: **the** ~ der Ganges.
gangland ['gæŋlænd] *adj* (*killer, boss*) Unterwelt-.
gangling ['gæŋglɪŋ] *adj* schlaksig, hoch aufgeschossen.
gangly ['gæŋglɪ] *adj* schlaksig.
gangplank ['gæŋplæŋk] *n* Laufplanke *f*.
gangrene ['gæŋgriːn] *n* (*MED*) Brand *m*.
gangster ['gæŋstə'] *n* Gangster *m*.
gangway ['gæŋweɪ] *n* Laufplanke *f*, Gangway *f*; (*in cinema, bus, plane etc*) Gang *m*.
gantry ['gæntrɪ] *n* (*for crane*) Portal *nt*; (*for railway signal*) Signalbrücke *f*; (*for rocket*) Abschussrampe *f*.
GAO (*US*) *n abbr* (= *General Accounting Office*)

Rechnungshof der USA.
gaol [dʒeɪl] (*BRIT*) *n*, *vt* = **jail**.
gap [gæp] *n* Lücke *f*; (*in time*) Pause *f*; (*difference*): ~ (**between**) Kluft *f* (zwischen +*dat*).
gape [geɪp] *vi* starren, gaffen; (*hole*) gähnen; (*shirt*) offen stehen.
gaping ['geɪpɪŋ] *adj* (*hole*) gähnend; (*shirt*) offen.
garage ['gærɑːʒ] *n* Garage *f*; (*for car repairs*) (Reparatur)werkstatt *f*; (*petrol station*) Tankstelle *f*.
garb [gɑːb] *n* Gewand *nt*, Kluft *f*.
garbage ['gɑːbɪdʒ] *n* (*US: rubbish*) Abfall *m*, Müll *m*; (*inf: nonsense*) Blödsinn *m*, Quatsch *m*; (*fig: film, book*) Schund *m*.
garbage can (*US*) *n* Mülleimer *m*, Abfalleimer *m*.
garbage collector (*US*) *n* Müllmann *m*.
garbage disposal (unit) *n* Müllschlucker *m*.
garbage truck (*US*) *n* Müllwagen *m*.
garbled ['gɑːbld] *adj* (*account*) wirr; (*message*) unverständlich.
garden ['gɑːdn] *n* Garten *m* ♦ *vi* gärtnern; **gardens** *npl* (*public park*) Park *m*; (*private*) Gartenanlagen *pl*; **she was** ~**ing** sie arbeitete im Garten.
garden centre *n* Gartencenter *nt*.
garden city *n* Gartenstadt *f*.
gardener ['gɑːdnə'] *n* Gärtner(in) *m(f)*.
gardening ['gɑːdnɪŋ] *n* Gartenarbeit *f*.
gargle ['gɑːgl] *vi* gurgeln ♦ *n* Gurgelwasser *nt*.
gargoyle ['gɑːgɔɪl] *n* Wasserspeier *m*.
garish ['gɛərɪʃ] *adj* grell.
garland ['gɑːlənd] *n* Kranz *m*.
garlic ['gɑːlɪk] *n* Knoblauch *m*.
garment ['gɑːmənt] *n* Kleidungsstück *nt*.
garner ['gɑːnə'] *vt* sammeln.
garnish ['gɑːnɪʃ] *vt* garnieren.
garret ['gærɪt] *n* Dachkammer *f*, Mansarde *f*.
garrison ['gærɪsn] *n* Garnison *f*.
garrulous ['gæruləs] *adj* geschwätzig.
garter ['gɑːtə'] *n* Strumpfband *nt*; (*US: suspender*) Strumpfhalter *m*.
garter belt (*US*) *n* Strumpfgürtel *m*, Hüftgürtel *m*.
gas [gæs] *n* Gas *nt*; (*US: gasoline*) Benzin *nt* ♦ *vt* mit Gas vergiften; (*MIL*) vergasen; **to be given** ~ (*as anaesthetic*) Lachgas bekommen.
gas cooker (*BRIT*) *n* Gasherd *m*.
gas cylinder *n* Gasflasche *f*.
gaseous ['gæsɪəs] *adj* gasförmig.
gas fire (*BRIT*) *n* Gasofen *m*.
gas-fired ['gæsfaɪəd] *adj* (*heater etc*) Gas-.
gash [gæʃ] *n* klaffende Wunde *f*; (*tear*) tiefer Schlitz *m* ♦ *vt* aufschlitzen.
gasket ['gæskɪt] *n* Dichtung *f*.
gas mask *n* Gasmaske *f*.
gas meter *n* Gaszähler *m*.
gasoline ['gæsəliːn] (*US*) *n* Benzin *nt*.
gasp [gɑːsp] *n* tiefer Atemzug *m* ♦ *vi* keuchen; (*in surprise*) nach Luft schnappen; **to give a**

~ **(of shock/horror)** (vor Schreck/Entsetzen) die Luft anhalten; **to be ~ing for** sich sehnen nach +dat.

▶ **gasp out** vt hervorstoßen.

gas permeable adj (lenses) luftdurchlässig.

gas ring n Gasbrenner m.

gas station (US) n Tankstelle f.

gas stove n (cooker) Gasherd m; (for camping) Gaskocher m.

gassy ['gæsɪ] adj (drink) kohlensäurehaltig.

gas tank n Benzintank m.

gastric ['gæstrɪk] adj (upset, ulcer etc) Magen-.

gastric flu n Darmgrippe f.

gastroenteritis ['gæstrəuentə'raɪtɪs] n Magen-Darm-Katar(h) m.

gastronomy [gæs'trɒnəmɪ] n Gastronomie f.

gasworks ['gæswɔːks] n Gaswerk nt.

gate [geɪt] n (of garden) Pforte f; (of field) Gatter nt; (of building) Tor nt; (at airport) Flugsteig m; (of level crossing) Schranke f; (of lock) Tor nt.

gateau ['gætəu] (pl ~x) n Torte f.

gate-crash ['geɪtkræʃ] (BRIT) vt (party) ohne Einladung besuchen; (concert) eindringen in +acc ♦ vi ohne Einladung hingehen; eindringen.

gate-crasher ['geɪtkræʃə*] n ungeladener Gast m.

gatehouse ['geɪthaus] n Pförtnerhaus nt.

gateway ['geɪtweɪ] n (also fig) Tor nt.

gather ['gæðə*] vt sammeln; (flowers, fruit) pflücken; (understand) schließen; (SEWING) kräuseln ♦ vi (assemble) sich versammeln; (dust) sich ansammeln; (clouds) sich zusammenziehen; **to ~ (from)** schließen (aus); **to ~ (that)** annehmen(, dass); **as far as I can ~** so wie ich es sehe; **to ~ speed** schneller werden.

gathering ['gæðərɪŋ] n Versammlung f.

GATT [gæt] n abbr (= General Agreement on Tariffs and Trade) GATT nt.

gauche [gəuʃ] adj linkisch.

gaudy ['gɔːdɪ] adj knallig.

gauge, (US) **gage** [geɪdʒ] n Messgerät nt, Messinstrument nt; (RAIL) Spurweite f ♦ vt messen; (fig) beurteilen; **petrol ~, fuel ~**, (US) **gas gage** Benzinuhr f; **to ~ the right moment** den richtigen Moment abwägen.

Gaul [gɔːl] n Gallien nt; (person) Gallier(in) m(f).

gaunt [gɔːnt] adj (haggard) hager; (bare, stark) öde.

gauntlet ['gɔːntlɪt] n (Stulpen)handschuh m; (fig): **to run the ~** Spießruten laufen; **to throw down the ~** den Fehdehandschuh hinwerfen.

gauze [gɔːz] n Gaze f.

gave [geɪv] pt of **give**.

gavel ['gævl] n Hammer m.

gawk [gɔːk] (inf) vi gaffen, glotzen.

gawky ['gɔːkɪ] adj schlaksig.

gawp [gɔːp] vi: **to ~ at** angaffen, anglotzen

(inf).

gay [geɪ] adj (homosexual) schwul; (cheerful) fröhlich; (dress) bunt.

gaze [geɪz] n Blick m ♦ vi: **to ~ at sth** etw anstarren.

gazelle [gə'zɛl] n Gazelle f.

gazette [gə'zɛt] n Zeitung f; (official) Amtsblatt nt.

gazetteer [gæzə'tɪə*] n alphabetisches Ortsverzeichnis nt.

gazump [gə'zʌmp] (BRIT) vt: **to be ~ed** ein mündlich zugesagtes Haus an einen Höherbietenden verlieren.

GB abbr (= Great Britain) GB.

GBH (BRIT) n abbr (LAW) = **grievous bodily harm**.

GC (BRIT) n abbr (= George Cross) britische Tapferkeitsmedaille.

GCE (BRIT) n abbr (= General Certificate of Education) Schulabschlusszeugnis, ≈ Abitur nt.

GCHQ (BRIT) n abbr (= Government Communications Headquarters) Zentralstelle des britischen Nachrichtendienstes.

GCSE (BRIT) n abbr (= General Certificate of Secondary Education) Schulabschlusszeugnis, ≈ mittlere Reife f.

Gdns abbr (in street names: = Gardens) ≈ Str.

GDP n abbr = **gross domestic product**.

GDR n abbr (formerly: = German Democratic Republic) DDR f.

gear [gɪə*] n (equipment) Ausrüstung f; (belongings) Sachen pl; (TECH) Getriebe nt; (AUT) Gang m; (on bicycle) Gangschaltung f ♦ vt (fig: adapt): **to ~ sth to** etw ausrichten auf +acc; **top or** (US) **high/low/bottom ~** hoher/niedriger/erster Gang; **to put a car into ~** einen Gang einlegen; **to leave the car in ~** den Gang eingelegt lassen; **to leave out of ~** im Leerlauf lassen; **our service is ~ed to meet the needs of the disabled** unser Betrieb ist auf die Bedürfnisse von Behinderten eingerichtet.

▶ **gear up** vt, vi: **to ~ (o.s.) up (to)** sich vorbereiten (auf +acc) ♦ vt: **to ~ o.s. up to do sth** sich darauf vorbereiten, etw zu tun.

gearbox ['gɪəbɒks] n Getriebe nt.

gear lever, (US) **gear shift** n Schalthebel m.

GED (US) n abbr (SCOL: = general educational development) allgemeine Lernentwicklung.

geese [giːs] npl of **goose**.

geezer ['giːzə*] (inf) n Kerl m, Typ m.

Geiger counter ['gaɪgə-] n Geigerzähler m.

gel [dʒɛl] n Gel nt.

gelatin(e) ['dʒɛlətiːn] n Gelatine f.

gelignite ['dʒɛlɪgnaɪt] n Plastiksprengstoff m.

gem [dʒɛm] n Edelstein m; **she/the house is a ~** (fig) sie/das Haus ist ein Juwel; **a ~ of an idea** eine ausgezeichnete Idee.

Gemini ['dʒɛmɪnaɪ] n (ASTROL) Zwillinge pl; **to be ~** (ein) Zwilling sein.

gen [dʒɛn] (BRIT: inf) n: **to give sb the ~ on sth**

jdn über etw *acc* informieren.

Gen. *abbr* (*MIL:* = *General*) Gen.

gen. *abbr* = **general; generally**.

gender ['dʒɛndə*] *n* Geschlecht *nt*.

gene [dʒiːn] *n* Gen *nt*.

genealogy [dʒiːnɪ'ælədʒɪ] *n* Genealogie *f*, Stammbaumforschung *f*; (*family history*) Stammbaum *m*.

general ['dʒɛnərl] *n* General *m* ♦ *adj* allgemein; (*widespread*) weitverbreitet, weit verbreitet; (*non-specific*) generell; **in ~** im Allgemeinen; **the ~ public** die Öffentlichkeit, die Allgemeinheit; **~ audit** (*COMM*) Jahresabschlussprüfung *f*.

general anaesthetic *n* Vollnarkose *f*.

general delivery (*US*) *n*: **to send sth ~** etw postlagernd schicken.

general election *n* Parlamentswahlen *pl*.

generalization ['dʒɛnrəlaɪ'zeɪʃən] *n* Verallgemeinerung *f*.

generalize ['dʒɛnrəlaɪz] *vi* verallgemeinern.

generally ['dʒɛnrəlɪ] *adv* im Allgemeinen.

general manager *n* Hauptgeschäftsführer(in) *m(f)*.

general practitioner *n* praktischer Arzt *m*, praktische Ärztin *f*.

general strike *n* Generalstreik *m*.

generate ['dʒɛnəreɪt] *vt* erzeugen; (*jobs*) schaffen; (*profits*) einbringen.

generation [dʒɛnə'reɪʃən] *n* Generation *f*; (*of electricity etc*) Erzeugung *f*.

generator ['dʒɛnəreɪtə*] *n* Generator *m*.

generic [dʒɪ'nɛrɪk] *adj* allgemein; **~ term** Oberbegriff *m*.

generosity [dʒɛnə'rɔsɪtɪ] *n* Großzügigkeit *f*.

generous ['dʒɛnərəs] *adj* großzügig; (*measure, remuneration*) reichlich.

genesis ['dʒɛnɪsɪs] *n* Entstehung *f*.

genetic [dʒɪ'nɛtɪk] *adj* genetisch.

genetically *adv* genetisch; **genetically modified** genmanipuliert.

genetic engineering *n* Gentechnologie *f*.

genetic fingerprinting [-'fɪŋɡəprɪntɪŋ] *n* genetische Fingerabdrücke *pl*.

genetics [dʒɪ'nɛtɪks] *n* Genetik *f*.

Geneva [dʒɪ'niːvə] *n* Genf *nt*.

genial ['dʒiːnɪəl] *adj* freundlich; (*climate*) angenehm.

genitals ['dʒɛnɪtlz] *npl* Genitalien *pl*, Geschlechtsteile *pl*.

genitive ['dʒɛnɪtɪv] *n* Genitiv *m*.

genius ['dʒiːnɪəs] *n* Talent *nt*; (*person*) Genie *nt*.

Genoa ['dʒɛnəuə] *n* Genua *nt*.

genocide ['dʒɛnəusaɪd] *n* Völkermord *m*.

Genoese [dʒɛnəu'iːz] *adj* genuesisch ♦ *n inv* Genuese *m*, Genuesin *f*.

gent [dʒɛnt] (*BRIT: inf*) *n abbr* = **gentleman**.

genteel [dʒɛn'tiːl] *adj* vornehm, fein.

gentle ['dʒɛntl] *adj* sanft; (*movement, breeze*) leicht; **a ~ hint** ein zarter Hinweis.

gentleman ['dʒɛntlmən] (*irreg: like* **man**) *n*

Herr *m*; (*referring to social position or good manners*) Gentleman *m*; **~'s agreement** Vereinbarung *f* auf Treu und Glauben.

gentlemanly ['dʒɛntlmənlɪ] *adj* zuvorkommend.

gentleness ['dʒɛntlnɪs] *n* (*see adj*) Sanftheit *f*; Leichtheit *f*; Zartheit *f*.

gently ['dʒɛntlɪ] *adv* (*see adj*) sanft; leicht; zart.

gentry ['dʒɛntrɪ] *n inv*: **the ~** die Gentry, der niedere Adel.

gents [dʒɛnts] *n*: **the ~** die Herrentoilette.

genuine ['dʒɛnjuɪn] *adj* echt; (*person*) natürlich, aufrichtig.

genuinely ['dʒɛnjuɪnlɪ] *adv* wirklich.

geographer [dʒɪ'ɔɡrəfə*] *n* Geograf(in) *m(f)*.

geographic(al) [dʒɪə'ɡræfɪk(l)] *adj* geografisch.

geography [dʒɪ'ɔɡrəfɪ] *n* Geografie *f*; (*SCOL*) Erdkunde *f*.

geological [dʒɪə'lɔdʒɪkl] *adj* geologisch.

geologist [dʒɪ'ɔlədʒɪst] *n* Geologe *m*, Geologin *f*.

geology [dʒɪ'ɔlədʒɪ] *n* Geologie *f*.

geometric(al) [dʒɪə'mɛtrɪk(l)] *adj* geometrisch.

geometry [dʒɪ'ɔmətrɪ] *n* Geometrie *f*.

Geordie ['dʒɔːdɪ] (*inf*) *n* aus dem Gebiet von Newcastle stammende oder dort wohnhafte Person.

Georgia ['dʒɔːdʒə] *n* (*in Eastern Europe*) Georgien *nt*.

Georgian ['dʒɔːdʒən] *adj* georgisch ♦ *n* Georgier(in) *m(f)*; (*LING*) Georgisch *nt*.

geranium [dʒɪ'reɪnɪəm] *n* Geranie *f*.

geriatric [dʒɛrɪ'ætrɪk] *adj* geriatrisch ♦ *n* Greis(in) *m(f)*.

germ [dʒəːm] *n* Bazillus *m*; (*BIOL, fig*) Keim *m*.

German ['dʒəːmən] *adj* deutsch ♦ *n* Deutsche(r) *f(m)*; (*LING*) Deutsch *nt*.

German Democratic Republic *n* (*formerly*) Deutsche Demokratische Republik *f*.

germane [dʒəː'meɪn] *adj*: **~ (to)** von Belang (für).

German measles (*BRIT*) *n* Röteln *pl*.

German Shepherd (dog) (*esp US*) *n* Schäferhund *m*.

Germany ['dʒəːmənɪ] *n* Deutschland *nt*.

germinate ['dʒəːmɪneɪt] *vi* keimen; (*fig*) aufkeimen.

germination [dʒəːmɪ'neɪʃən] *n* Keimung *f*.

germ warfare *n* biologische Kriegsführung *f*, Bakterienkrieg *m*.

gerrymandering ['dʒɛrɪmændərɪŋ] *n* Wahlkreisschiebungen *pl*.

gestation [dʒɛs'teɪʃən] *n* (*of animals*) Trächtigkeit *f*; (*of humans*) Schwangerschaft *f*.

gesticulate [dʒɛs'tɪkjuleɪt] *vi* gestikulieren.

gesture ['dʒɛstjə*] *n* Geste *f*; **as a ~ of friendship** als Zeichen der Freundschaft.

===================== *KEYWORD*

get [gɛt] (*pt, pp* **got**) (*US*) (*pp* **gotten**) *vi* **1**
(*become, be*) werden; **to ~ old/tired/cold**
alt/müde/kalt werden; **to ~ dirty** sich
schmutzig machen; **to ~ killed** getötet
werden; **to ~ married** heiraten.
2 (*go*): **to ~ (from ...) to ...** (von ...) nach ...
kommen; **how did you ~ here?** wie sind Sie
hierhin gekommen?
3 (*begin*): **to ~ to know sb** jdn kennen
lernen; **let's ~ going** *or* **started** fangen wir
an!
♦ *modal aux vb*: **you've got to do it** du musst
es tun
♦ *vt* **1**: **to ~ sth done** (*do oneself*) etw
gemacht bekommen; (*have done*) etw
machen lassen; **to ~ one's hair cut** sich *dat*
die Haare schneiden lassen; **to ~ the car
going** *or* **to go** das Auto in Gang bringen; **to
~ sb to do sth** etw von jdm machen lassen;
(*persuade*) jdn dazu bringen, etw zu tun.
2 (*obtain: money, permission, results*)
erhalten; (*find: job, flat*) finden; (*fetch: person,
doctor, object*) holen; **to ~ sth for sb** jdm etw
besorgen; **can I ~ you a drink?** kann ich
Ihnen etwas zu trinken anbieten?
3 (*receive, acquire: present, prize*) bekommen;
how much did you ~ for the painting? wie
viel haben Sie für das Bild bekommen?
4 (*catch*) bekommen, kriegen (*inf*); (*hit: target
etc*) treffen; **to ~ sb by the arm/throat** jdn
am Arm/Hals packen; **the bullet got him in
the leg** die Kugel traf ihn ins Bein.
5 (*take, move*) bringen; **to ~ sth to sb** jdm
etw zukommen lassen.
6 (*plane, bus etc: take*) nehmen; (*: catch*)
bekommen.
7 (*understand: joke etc*) verstehen; **I ~ it** ich
verstehe.
8 (*have, possess*): **to have got** haben; **how
many have you got?** wie viele hast du?
▶ **get about** *vi* (*person*) herumkommen;
(*news, rumour*) sich verbreiten.
▶ **get across** *vt* (*message, meaning*)
klarmachen.
▶ **get along** *vi* (*be friends*) (miteinander)
auskommen ♦ (*depart*) sich auf den Weg
machen.
▶ **get around** *vt fus* = **get round**.
▶ **get at** *vt fus* (*attack, criticize*) angreifen;
(*reach*) herankommen an +*acc*; **what are you
~ting at?** worauf willst du hinaus?
▶ **get away** *vi* (*leave*) wegkommen; (*on
holiday*) verreisen; (*escape*) entkommen.
▶ **get away with** *vt fus* (*stolen goods*)
entkommen mit; **he'll never ~ away with it!**
damit kommt er nicht durch.
▶ **get back** *vi* (*return*) zurückkommen
♦ *vt* (*regain*) zurückbekommen; **~ back!**
zurück!
▶ **get back at** (*inf*) *vt fus*: **to ~ back at sb for**

sth jdm etw heimzahlen.
▶ **get back to** *vt fus* (*return to*) zurückkehren
zu; (*contact again*) zurückkommen auf +*acc*;
to ~ back to sleep wieder einschlafen.
▶ **get by** *vi* (*pass*) vorbeikommen; (*manage*)
zurechtkommen; **I can ~ by in German** ich
kann mich auf Deutsch verständlich
machen.
▶ **get down** *vi* (*from tree, ladder etc*)
heruntersteigen; (*from horse*) absteigen;
(*leave table*) aufstehen; (*bend down*) sich
bücken; (*duck*) sich ducken ♦ *vt* (*depress:
person*) fertig machen; (*write*)
aufschreiben.
▶ **get down to** *vt fus*: **to ~ down to sth** (*work*)
etw in Angriff nehmen; (*find time*) zu etw
kommen; **to ~ down to business** (*fig*) zur
Sache kommen.
▶ **get in** *vi* (*be elected: candidate, party*)
gewählt werden; (*arrive*) ankommen
♦ *vt* (*bring in: harvest*) einbringen; (*: shopping,
supplies*) (herein)holen.
▶ **get into** *vt fus* (*conversation, argument, fight*)
geraten in +*acc*; (*vehicle*) einsteigen in +*acc*;
(*clothes*) hineinkommen in +*acc*; **to ~ into
bed** ins Bett gehen; **to ~ into the habit of
doing sth** sich *dat* angewöhnen, etw zu tun.
▶ **get off** *vi* (*from train etc*) aussteigen; (*escape
punishment*) davonkommen ♦ *vt* (*remove:
clothes*) ausziehen; (*: stain*)
herausbekommen
♦ *vt fus* (*leave: train, bus*) aussteigen aus; **we
~ 3 days off at Christmas** zu Weihnachten
bekommen wir 3 Tage frei; **to ~ off to a
good start** (*fig*) einen guten Anfang machen.
▶ **get on** *vi* (*be friends*) (miteinander)
auskommen ♦ *vt fus* (*bus, train*) einsteigen in
+*acc*; **how are you ~ting on?** wie kommst du
zurecht?; **time is ~ting on** es wird langsam
spät.
▶ **get on to** (*BRIT*) *vt fus* (*subject, topic*)
übergehen zu; (*contact: person*) sich in
Verbindung setzen mit.
▶ **get on with** *vt fus* (*person*) auskommen mit;
(*meeting, work etc*) weitermachen mit.
▶ **get out** *vi* (*leave: on foot*) hinausgehen; (*of
vehicle*) aussteigen; (*news etc*)
herauskommen ♦ *vt* (*take out: book etc*)
herausholen; (*remove: stain*)
herausbekommen.
▶ **get out of** *vt fus* (*money: bank etc*) abheben
von; (*avoid: duty etc*) herumkommen um
♦ *vt* (*extract: confession etc*)
herausbekommen aus; (*derive: pleasure*)
haben an +*dat*; (*: benefit*) haben von.
▶ **get over** *vt fus* (*overcome*) überwinden;
(*: illness*) sich erholen von; (*communicate:
idea etc*) verständlich machen
♦ *vt*: **to ~ it over with** (*finish*) es hinter sich
acc bringen.
▶ **get round** *vt fus* (*law, rule*) umgehen;
(*person*) herumkriegen.

▶ **get round to** vt fus: **to ~ round to doing sth** dazu kommen, etw zu tun.

▶ **get through** vi (TEL) durchkommen
♦ vt fus (finish: work) schaffen; (: book) lesen.

▶ **get through to** vt fus (TEL) durchkommen zu; (make o.s. understood) durchdringen zu.

▶ **get together** vi (people) zusammenkommen ♦ vt (people) zusammenbringen; (project, plan etc) zusammenstellen.

▶ **get up** vi (rise) aufstehen ♦ vt: **to ~ up enthusiasm for sth** Begeisterung für etw aufbringen.

▶ **get up to** vt fus (prank etc) anstellen.

getaway ['gɛtəweɪ] n: **to make a/one's ~** sich davonmachen.

getaway car n Fluchtauto nt.

get-together ['gɛttəgɛðə*] n Treffen nt; (party) Party f.

get-up ['gɛtʌp] (inf) n Aufmachung f.

get-well card [gɛt'wɛl-] n Karte f mit Genesungswünschen.

geyser ['giːzə*] n Geiser m; (BRIT: water heater) Durchlauferhitzer m.

Ghana ['gɑːnə] n Ghana nt.

Ghanaian [gɑːˈneɪən] adj ghanaisch ♦ n Ghanaer(in) m(f).

ghastly ['gɑːstlɪ] adj grässlich; (complexion) totenblass; **you look ~!** (ill) du siehst grässlich aus!

gherkin ['gəːkɪn] n Gewürzgurke f.

ghetto ['gɛtəʊ] n G(h)etto nt.

ghetto blaster [-'blɑːstə*] (inf) n Ghettoblaster m.

ghost [gəʊst] n Geist m, Gespenst nt ♦ vt für jdn (als Ghostwriter) schreiben; **to give up the ~** den Geist aufgeben.

ghost town n Geisterstadt f.

ghostwriter ['gəʊstraɪtə*] n Ghostwriter(in) m(f).

ghoul [guːl] n böser Geist m.

ghoulish ['guːlɪʃ] adj makaber.

GHQ n abbr (MIL: = general headquarters) Hauptquartier nt.

GHz abbr (= gigahertz) GHz.

GI (US: inf) n abbr (= government issue) GI m.

giant ['dʒaɪənt] n (also fig) Riese m ♦ adj riesig, riesenhaft; **~ (size) packet** Riesenpackung f.

giant killer n (fig) Goliathbezwinger(in) m(f).

gibber ['dʒɪbə*] vi brabbeln.

gibberish ['dʒɪbərɪʃ] n Quatsch m.

gibe [dʒaɪb] n spöttische Bemerkung f ♦ vi: **to ~ at** spöttische Bemerkungen machen über +acc.

giblets ['dʒɪblɪts] npl Geflügelinnereien pl.

Gibraltar [dʒɪˈbrɔːltə*] n Gibraltar nt.

giddiness ['gɪdɪnɪs] n Schwindelgefühl nt.

giddy ['gɪdɪ] adj: **I am/feel ~** mir ist schwind(e)lig; (height) Schwindel erregend; **~ with excitement** vor Aufregung ganz ausgelassen.

gift [gɪft] n Geschenk nt; (donation) Spende f; (COMM: also: **free ~**) (Werbe)geschenk nt; (ability) Gabe f; **to have a ~ for sth** ein Talent für etw haben.

gifted ['gɪftɪd] adj begabt.

gift token n Geschenkgutschein m.

gift voucher n = gift token.

gig [gɪg] (inf) n Konzert nt.

gigabyte ['dʒɪgəbaɪt] n Gigabyte nt.

gigantic [dʒaɪˈgæntɪk] adj riesig, riesengroß.

giggle ['gɪgl] vi kichern ♦ n Spaß m; **to do sth for a ~** etw aus Spaß tun.

GIGO ['gaɪgəʊ] (inf) abbr (COMPUT: = garbage in, garbage out) GIGO.

gild [gɪld] vt vergolden.

gill [dʒɪl] n Gill nt (BRIT: = 15 cl, US = 12 cl).

gills [gɪlz] npl Kiemen pl.

gilt [gɪlt] adj vergoldet ♦ n Vergoldung f; **gilts** npl (COMM) mündelsichere Wertpapiere pl.

gilt-edged ['gɪltɛdʒd] adj (stocks, securities) mündelsicher.

gimlet ['gɪmlɪt] n Handbohrer m.

gimmick ['gɪmɪk] n Gag m; **sales ~** Verkaufsmasche f, Verkaufstrick m.

gin [dʒɪn] n Gin m.

ginger ['dʒɪndʒə*] n Ingwer m ♦ adj (hair) rötlich; (cat) rötlich gelb.

ginger ale n Ginger Ale nt.

ginger beer n Ingwerbier nt.

gingerbread ['dʒɪndʒəbrɛd] n (cake) Ingwerkuchen m; (biscuit) ≈ Pfefferkuchen m.

ginger group (BRIT) n Aktionsgruppe f.

gingerly ['dʒɪndʒəlɪ] adv vorsichtig.

gingham ['gɪŋəm] n (TEXTILE) Gingan m, Gingham m.

ginseng ['dʒɪnsɛŋ] n Ginseng m.

gipsy ['dʒɪpsɪ] n Zigeuner(in) m(f).

gipsy caravan n Zigeunerwagen m.

giraffe [dʒɪˈrɑːf] n Giraffe f.

girder ['gəːdə*] n Träger m.

girdle ['gəːdl] n Hüftgürtel m, Hüfthalter m ♦ vt (fig) umgeben.

girl [gəːl] n Mädchen nt; (young unmarried woman) (junges) Mädchen nt; (daughter) Tochter f; **this is my little ~** das ist mein Töchterchen; **an English ~** eine Engländerin.

girlfriend ['gəːlfrɛnd] n Freundin f.

Girl Guide n Pfadfinderin f.

girlish ['gəːlɪʃ] adj mädchenhaft.

Girl Scout (US) n Pfadfinderin f.

Giro ['dʒaɪrəʊ] n: **the National ~** (BRIT) der Postscheckdienst.

giro ['dʒaɪrəʊ] n Giro nt, Giroverkehr m; (post office giro) Postscheckverkehr m; (BRIT: welfare cheque) Sozialhilfescheck m.

girth [gəːθ] n Umfang m; (of horse) Sattelgurt m.

gist [dʒɪst] n Wesentliche(s) nt.

====================== KEYWORD

give [gɪv] (pt **gave**, pp **given**) vt **1** (hand over): **to ~ sb sth, ~ sth to sb** jdm etw geben; **I'll ~ you £5 for it** ich gebe dir £5 dafür.
2 (used with noun to replace a verb): **to ~ a sigh/cry/laugh** etc seufzen/schreien/lachen etc; **to ~ a speech/a lecture** eine Rede/einen Vortrag halten; **to ~ three cheers** ein dreifaches Hoch ausbringen.
3 (tell, deliver: news, message etc) mitteilen; (: advice, answer) geben.
4 (supply, provide: opportunity, job etc) geben; (: surprise) bereiten; (bestow: title, honour, right) geben, verleihen; **that's given me an idea** dabei kommt mir eine Idee.
5 (devote: time, one's life) geben; (: attention) schenken.
6 (organize: party, dinner etc) geben
♦ vi **1** (also: **~ way**: break, collapse) nachgeben.
2 (stretch: fabric) sich dehnen.
▶ **give away** vt (money, opportunity) verschenken; (secret, information) verraten; (bride) zum Altar führen; **that immediately gave him away** dadurch verriet er sich sofort.
▶ **give back** vt (money, book etc) zurückgeben.
▶ **give in** vi (yield) nachgeben
♦ vt (essay etc) abgeben.
▶ **give off** vt (heat, smoke) abgeben.
▶ **give out** vt (prizes, books, drinks etc) austeilen ♦ vi (be exhausted: supplies) zu Ende gehen; (fail) versagen.
▶ **give up** vt, vi aufgeben; **to ~ up smoking** das Rauchen aufgeben; **to ~ o.s. up** sich stellen; (after siege etc) sich ergeben.
▶ **give way** vi (yield, collapse) nachgeben; (BRIT: AUT) die Vorfahrt achten.

give-and-take ['gɪvənd'teɪk] n (gegenseitiges) Geben und Nehmen nt.
giveaway ['gɪvəweɪ] (inf) n: **her expression was a ~** ihr Gesichtsausdruck verriet alles; **the exam was a ~!** die Prüfung war geschenkt!; **~ prices** Schleuderpreise pl.
given ['gɪvn] pp of **give** ♦ adj (time, amount) bestimmt ♦ conj: **~ the circumstances ...** unter den Umständen ...; **~ that ...** angesichts der Tatsache, dass ...
glacial ['gleɪsɪəl] adj (landscape etc) Gletscher-; (fig) eisig.
glacier ['glæsɪə*] n Gletscher m.
glad [glæd] adj froh; **to be ~ about sth** sich über etw acc freuen; **to be ~ that** sich freuen, dass; **I was ~ of his help** ich war froh über seine Hilfe.
gladden ['glædn] vt erfreuen.
glade [gleɪd] n Lichtung f.
gladioli [glædɪ'əʊlaɪ] npl Gladiolen pl.
gladly ['glædlɪ] adv gern(e).

glamorous ['glæmərəs] adj reizvoll; (model etc) glamourös.
glamour ['glæmə*] n Glanz m, Reiz m.
glance [glɑːns] n Blick m ♦ vi: **to ~ at** einen Blick werfen auf +acc.
▶ **glance off** vt fus abprallen von.
glancing ['glɑːnsɪŋ] adj: **to strike sth a ~ blow** etw streifen.
gland [glænd] n Drüse f.
glandular fever ['glændjʊlə-] (BRIT) n Drüsenfieber nt.
glare [gleə*] n wütender Blick m; (of light) greller Schein m; (of publicity) grelles Licht nt ♦ vi (light) grell scheinen; **to ~ at** (wütend) anstarren.
glaring ['gleərɪŋ] adj eklatant.
glasnost ['glæznɒst] n Glasnost f.
glass [glɑːs] n Glas nt; **glasses** npl (spectacles) Brille f.
glass-blowing ['glɑːsbləʊɪŋ] n Glasbläserei f.
glass ceiling n (fig) gläserne Decke f.
glass fibre n Glasfaser f.
glasshouse ['glɑːshaʊs] n Gewächshaus nt.
glassware ['glɑːsweə*] n Glaswaren pl.
glassy ['glɑːsɪ] adj glasig.
Glaswegian [glæs'wiːdʒən] adj Glasgower ♦ n Glasgower(in) m(f).
glaze [gleɪz] vt (door, window) verglasen; (pottery) glasieren ♦ n Glasur f.
glazed [gleɪzd] adj (eyes) glasig; (pottery, tiles) glasiert.
glazier ['gleɪzɪə*] n Glaser(in) m(f).
gleam [gliːm] vi (light) schimmern; (polished surface, eyes) glänzen ♦ n: **a ~ of hope** ein Hoffnungsschimmer m.
gleaming ['gliːmɪŋ] adj schimmernd, glänzend.
glean [gliːn] vt (information) herausbekommen, ausfindig machen.
glee [gliː] n Freude f.
gleeful ['gliːfʊl] adj fröhlich.
glen [glɛn] n Tal nt.
glib [glɪb] adj (person) glatt; (promise, response) leichthin gemacht.
glibly ['glɪblɪ] adv (talk) gewandt; (answer) leichthin.
glide [glaɪd] vi gleiten ♦ n Gleiten nt.
glider ['glaɪdə*] n Segelflugzeug nt.
gliding ['glaɪdɪŋ] n Segelfliegen nt.
glimmer ['glɪmə*] n Schimmer m; (of interest, hope) Funke m ♦ vi schimmern.
glimpse [glɪmps] n Blick m ♦ vt einen Blick werfen auf +acc; **to catch a ~ (of)** einen flüchtigen Blick erhaschen (von +dat).
glint [glɪnt] vi glitzern; (eyes) funkeln ♦ n (see vb) Glitzern nt; Funkeln nt.
glisten ['glɪsn] vi glänzen.
glitter ['glɪtə*] vi glitzern; (eyes) funkeln ♦ n (see vb) Glitzern nt; Funkeln nt.
glittering ['glɪtərɪŋ] adj glitzernd; (eyes) funkelnd; (career) glänzend.

glitz [glɪts] (*inf*) *n* Glanz *m*.

gloat [gləʊt] *vi*: **to ~ (over)** (*own success*) sich brüsten (mit); (*sb's failure*) sich hämisch freuen (über +*acc*).

global ['gləʊbl] *adj* global.

global warming [-'wɔːmɪŋ] *n* Erwärmung *f* der Erdatmosphäre.

globe [gləʊb] *n* Erdball *m*; (*model*) Globus *m*; (*shape*) Kugel *f*.

globetrotter ['gləʊbtrɒtə*] *n* Globetrotter(in) *m(f)*, Weltenbummler(in) *m(f)*.

globule ['glɒbjuːl] *n* Tröpfchen *nt*.

gloom [gluːm] *n* Düsterkeit *f*; (*sadness*) düstere *or* gedrückte Stimmung *f*.

gloomily ['gluːmɪlɪ] *adv* düster.

gloomy ['gluːmɪ] *adj* düster; (*person*) bedrückt; (*situation*) bedrückend.

glorification [glɔːrɪfɪ'keɪʃən] *n* Verherrlichung *f*.

glorify ['glɔːrɪfaɪ] *vt* verherrlichen.

glorious ['glɔːrɪəs] *adj* herrlich; (*victory*) ruhmreich; (*future*) glanzvoll.

glory ['glɔːrɪ] *n* Ruhm *m*; (*splendour*) Herrlichkeit *f* ♦ *vi*: **to ~ in** sich sonnen in +*dat*.

glory hole (*inf*) *n* Rumpelkammer *f*.

Glos (*BRIT*) *abbr* (*POST*: = *Gloucestershire*).

gloss [glɒs] *n* Glanz *m*; (*also*: **~ paint**) Lack *m*, Lackfarbe *f*.

▶ **gloss over** *vt fus* vom Tisch wischen.

glossary ['glɒsərɪ] *n* Glossar *nt*.

glossy ['glɒsɪ] *adj* glänzend; (*photograph, magazine*) Hochglanz- ♦ *n* (*also*: **~ magazine**) (Hochglanz)magazin *nt*.

glove [glʌv] *n* Handschuh *m*.

glove compartment *n* Handschuhfach *nt*.

glow [gləʊ] *vi* glühen; (*stars, eyes*) leuchten ♦ *n* (*see vb*) Glühen *nt*; Leuchten *nt*.

glower ['glaʊə*] *vi*: **to ~ at sb** jdn finster ansehen.

glowing ['gləʊɪŋ] *adj* glühend; (*complexion*) blühend; (*fig: report, description etc*) begeistert.

glow-worm ['gləʊwəːm] *n* Glühwürmchen *nt*.

glucose ['gluːkəʊs] *n* Traubenzucker *m*.

glue [gluː] *n* Klebstoff *m* ♦ *vt*: **to ~ sth onto sth** etw an etw *acc* kleben; **to ~ sth into place** etw festkleben.

glue-sniffing ['gluːsnɪfɪŋ] *n* (Klebstoff)-Schnüffeln *nt*.

glum [glʌm] *adj* bedrückt, niedergeschlagen.

glut [glʌt] *n*: **~ (of)** Überangebot *nt* (an +*dat*) ♦ *vt*: **to be ~ted (with)** überschwemmt sein (mit); **a ~ of pears** eine Birnenschwemme.

glutinous ['gluːtɪnəs] *adj* klebrig.

glutton ['glʌtn] *n* Vielfraß *m*; **a ~ for work** ein Arbeitstier *nt*; **a ~ for punishment** ein Masochist *m*.

gluttonous ['glʌtənəs] *adj* gefräßig.

gluttony ['glʌtənɪ] *n* Völlerei *f*.

glycerin(e) ['glɪsəriːn] *n* Glyzerin *nt*.

GM *abbr* = **genetically modified**.

gm *abbr* (= *gram(me)*) g.

GMAT (*US*) *n abbr* (= *Graduate Management Admissions Test*) Zulassungsprüfung *für Handelsschulen*.

GMT *abbr* (= *Greenwich Mean Time*) WEZ *f*.

gnarled [nɑːld] *adj* (*tree*) knorrig; (*hand*) knotig.

gnash [næʃ] *vt*: **to ~ one's teeth** mit den Zähnen knirschen.

gnat [næt] *n* (Stech)mücke *f*.

gnaw [nɔː] *vt* nagen an +*dat* ♦ *vi* (*fig*): **to ~ at** quälen.

gnome [nəʊm] *n* Gnom *m*; (*in garden*) Gartenzwerg *m*.

GNP *n abbr* (= *gross national product*) BSP *nt*.

GNVQ (*BRIT*) *n abbr* (= *General National Vocational Qualification*) allgemeine, auf die Arbeitswelt bezogene Qualifikation.

=================================== *KEYWORD*

go [gəʊ] (*pt* **went**, *pp* **gone**) *vi* **1** gehen; (*travel*) fahren; **a car went by** ein Auto fuhr vorbei.
2 (*depart*) gehen; **"I must ~,"** she said „ich muss gehen", sagte sie; **she has gone to Sheffield/Australia** (*permanently*) sie ist nach Sheffield/Australien gegangen.
3 (*attend, take part in activity*) gehen; **she went to university in Oxford** sie ist in Oxford zur Universität gegangen; **to ~ for a walk** spazieren gehen; **to ~ dancing** tanzen gehen.
4 (*work*) funktionieren; **the tape recorder was still ~ing** das Tonband lief noch.
5 (*become*): **to ~ pale/mouldy** blass/schimmelig werden.
6 (*be sold*): **to ~ for £100** für £100 weggehen *or* verkauft werden.
7 (*be about to, intend to*): **we're ~ing to stop in an hour** wir hören in einer Stunde auf; **are you ~ing to come?** kommst du?, wirst du kommen?
8 (*time*) vergehen.
9 (*event, activity*) ablaufen; **how did it ~?** wie wars?
10 (*be given*): **the job is to ~ to someone else** die Stelle geht an jemand anders.
11 (*break etc*) kaputtgehen; **the fuse went** die Sicherung ist durchgebrannt.
12 (*be placed*) hingehören; **the milk goes in the fridge** die Milch kommt in den Kühlschrank

♦ *n* **1** (*try*): **to have a ~ at sth** etw versuchen; **I'll have a ~ at mending it** ich will versuchen, es zu reparieren; **to have a ~** es versuchen.
2 (*turn*): **whose ~ is it?** wer ist dran *or* an der Reihe?
3 (*move*): **to be on the ~** auf Trab sein.

▶ **go about** *vi* (*also*: **~ around:** *rumour*) herumgehen
♦ *vt fus*: **how do I ~ about this?** wie soll ich vorgehen?; **to ~ about one's business**

seinen eigenen Geschäften nachgehen.
► **go after** *vt fus* (*pursue: person*) nachgehen +*dat*; (: *job etc*) sich bemühen um; (: *record*) erreichen wollen.
► **go against** *vt fus* (*be unfavourable to*) ungünstig verlaufen für; (*disregard: advice, wishes etc*) handeln gegen.
► **go ahead** *vi* (*proceed*) weitergehen; **to ~ ahead with** weitermachen mit.
► **go along** *vi* gehen.
► **go along with** *vt fus* (*agree with*) zustimmen +*dat*; (*accompany*) mitgehen mit.
► **go away** *vi* (*leave*) weggehen.
► **go back** *vi* zurückgehen.
► **go back on** *vt fus* (*promise*) zurücknehmen.
► **go by** *vi* (*years, time*) vergehen
  ♦ *vt fus* (*rule etc*) sich richten nach.
► **go down** *vi* (*descend*) hinuntergehen; (*ship, sun*) untergehen; (*price, level*) sinken
  ♦ *vt fus* (*stairs, ladder*) hinuntergehen; **his speech went down well** seine Rede kam gut an.
► **go for** *vt fus* (*fetch*) holen (gehen); (*like*) mögen; (*attack*) losgehen auf +*acc*; (*apply to*) gelten für.
► **go in** *vi* (*enter*) hineingehen.
► **go in for** *vt fus* (*competition*) teilnehmen an +*dat*; (*favour*) stehen auf +*acc*.
► **go into** *vt fus* (*enter*) hineingehen in +*acc*; (*investigate*) sich befassen mit; (*career*) gehen in +*acc*.
► **go off** *vi* (*leave*) weggehen; (*food*) schlecht werden; (*bomb, gun*) losgehen; (*event*) verlaufen; (*lights etc*) ausgehen
  ♦ *vt fus* (*inf*): **I've gone off it/him** ich mache mir nichts mehr daraus/aus ihm; **the gun went off** das Gewehr ging los; **to ~ off to sleep** einschlafen; **the party went off well** die Party verlief gut.
► **go on** *vi* (*continue*) weitergehen; (*happen*) vor sich gehen; (*lights*) angehen
  ♦ *vt fus* (*be guided by*) sich stützen auf +*acc*; **to ~ on doing sth** mit etw weitermachen; **what's ~ing on here?** was geht hier vor?, was ist hier los?
► **go on at** (*inf*) *vt fus* (*nag*) herumnörgeln an +*dat*.
► **go on with** *vt fus* weitermachen mit.
► **go out** *vt fus* (*leave*) hinausgehen
  ♦ *vi* (*for entertainment*) ausgehen; (*fire, light*) ausgehen; (*couple*): **they went out for 3 years** sie gingen 3 Jahre lang miteinander.
► **go over** *vi* hinübergehen ♦ *vt* (*check*) durchgehen; **to ~ over sth in one's mind** etw überdenken.
► **go round** *vi* (*circulate: news, rumour*) umgehen; (*revolve*) sich drehen; (*suffice*) ausreichen; (*visit*): **to ~ round (to sb's)** (bei jdm) vorbeigehen; **there's not enough to ~ round** es reicht nicht (für alle).
► **go through** *vt fus* (*place*) gehen durch; (*by car*) fahren durch; (*undergo*) durchmachen;

(*search through: files, papers*) durchsuchen; (*describe: list, book, story*) durchgehen; (*perform*) durchgehen.
► **go through with** *vt fus* (*plan, crime*) durchziehen; **I couldn't ~ through with it** ich brachte es nicht fertig.
► **go under** *vi* (*sink: person*) untergehen; (*fig: business, project*) scheitern.
► **go up** *vi* (*ascend*) hinaufgehen; (*price, level*) steigen; **to ~ up in flames** in Flammen aufgehen.
► **go with** *vt fus* (*suit*) passen zu.
► **go without** *vt fus* (*food, treats*) verzichten auf +*acc*.

goad [gəud] *vt* aufreizen.
► **goad on** *vt* anstacheln.
go-ahead ['gəuəhɛd] *adj* zielstrebig; (*firm*) fortschrittlich ♦ *n* grünes Licht *nt*; **to give sb the ~** jdm grünes Licht geben.
goal [gəul] *n* Tor *nt*; (*aim*) Ziel *nt*; **to score a ~** ein Tor schießen *or* erzielen.
goal difference *n* Tordifferenz *f*.
goalie ['gəulɪ] (*inf*) *n* Tormann *m*.
goalkeeper ['gəulkiːpə*] *n* Torwart *m*.
goal post *n* Torpfosten *m*.
goat [gəut] *n* Ziege *f*.
gobble ['gɔbl] *vt* (*also: ~ down, ~ up*) verschlingen.
go-between ['gəubɪtwiːn] *n* Vermittler(in) *m(f)*.
Gobi Desert ['gəubɪ-] *n*: **the ~** die Wüste Gobi.
goblet ['gɔblɪt] *n* Pokal *m*.
goblin ['gɔblɪn] *n* Kobold *m*.
go-cart ['gəukɑːt] *n* Gokart *m*.
God [gɔd] *n* Gott *m* ♦ *excl* o Gott!
god [gɔd] *n* Gott *m*.
god-awful [gɔd'ɔːfəl] (*inf*) *adj* beschissen (!).
godchild ['gɔdtʃaɪld] *n* Patenkind *nt*.
goddamn(ed) ['gɔdæm(d)] (*US: inf*) *adj* gottverdammt.
goddaughter ['gɔdɔːtə*] *n* Patentochter *f*.
goddess ['gɔdɪs] *n* Göttin *f*.
godfather ['gɔdfɑːðə*] *n* Pate *m*.
God-fearing ['gɔdfɪərɪŋ] *adj* gottesfürchtig.
godforsaken ['gɔdfəseɪkən] *adj* gottverlassen.
godmother ['gɔdmʌðə*] *n* Patin *f*.
godparent ['gɔdpɛərənt] *n* Pate *m*, Patin *f*.
godsend ['gɔdsɛnd] *n* Geschenk *nt* des Himmels.
godson ['gɔdsʌn] *n* Patensohn *m*.
goes [gəuz] *vb see* **go**.
gofer ['gəufə*] (*inf*) *n* Mädchen *nt* für alles.
go-getter ['gəugɛtə*] (*inf*) *n* Ellbogentyp (*pej, inf*) *m*.
goggle ['gɔgl] (*inf*) *vi*: **to ~ at** anstarren, anglotzen.
goggles ['gɔglz] *npl* Schutzbrille *f*.
going ['gəuɪŋ] *n*: **it was slow/hard ~** (*fig*) es ging nur langsam/schwer voran ♦ *adj*: **the ~ rate** der gängige Preis; **when the ~ gets**

tough wenn es schwierig wird; **a ~ concern** ein gut gehendes Unternehmen.

going-over [gəuɪŋ'əuvə*] (*inf*) *n* (*check*) Untersuchung *f*; (*beating-up*) Abreibung *f*; **to give sb a good ~** jdm eine tüchtige Abreibung verpassen.

goings-on ['gəuɪŋz'ɔn] (*inf*) *npl* Vorgänge *pl*, Dinge *pl*.

go-kart ['gəukɑːt] *n* = **go-cart**.

gold [gəuld] *n* Gold *nt*; (*also*: ~ **medal**) Goldmedaille *f* ♦ *adj* golden; (*reserves, jewellery, tooth*) Gold-.

golden ['gəuldən] *adj* (*also fig*) golden.

golden age *n* Blütezeit *f*.

golden handshake (*BRIT*) *n* Abstandssumme *f*.

golden rule *n* goldene Regel *f*.

goldfish ['gəuldfɪʃ] *n* Goldfisch *m*.

gold leaf *n* Blattgold *nt*.

gold medal *n* Goldmedaille *f*.

gold mine *n* (*also fig*) Goldgrube *f*.

gold-plated ['gəuld'pleɪtɪd] *adj* vergoldet.

goldsmith ['gəuldsmɪθ] *n* Goldschmied(in) *m(f)*.

gold standard *n* Goldstandard *m*.

golf [gɔlf] *n* Golf *nt*.

golf ball *n* (*for game*) Golfball *m*; (*on typewriter*) Kugelkopf *m*.

golf club *n* Golfklub *m*; (*stick*) Golfschläger *m*.

golf course *n* Golfplatz *m*.

golfer ['gɔlfə*] *n* Golfspieler(in) *m(f)*, Golfer(in) *m(f)*.

golfing ['gɔlfɪŋ] *n* Golf(spielen) *nt*; **he does a lot of ~** er spielt viel Golf ♦ *cpd* Golf-.

gondola ['gɔndələ] *n* Gondel *f*.

gondolier [gɔndə'lɪə*] *n* Gondoliere *m*.

gone [gɔn] *pp of* **go** ♦ *adj* weg; (*days*) vorbei.

goner ['gɔnə*] (*inf*) *n*: **to be a ~** hinüber sein.

gong [gɔŋ] *n* Gong *m*.

good [gud] *adj* gut; (*well-behaved*) brav, lieb ♦ *n* (*virtue, morality*) Gute(s) *nt*; (*benefit*) Wohl *nt*; **goods** *npl* (*COMM*) Güter *pl*; **to have a ~ time** sich (gut) amüsieren; **to be ~ at sth** (*swimming, talking etc*) etw gut können; (*science, sports etc*) gut in etw *dat* sein; **to be ~ for sb/sth** gut für jdn/zu etw *dat* sein; **it's ~ for you** das tut dir gut; **it's a ~ thing you were there** gut, dass Sie da waren; **she is ~ with children** sie kann gut mit Kindern umgehen; **she is ~ with her hands** sie ist geschickt; **to feel ~** sich wohl fühlen; **it's ~ to see you** (es ist) schön, Sie zu sehen; **would you be ~ enough to ...?** könnten Sie bitte ...?; **that's very ~ of you** das ist wirklich nett von Ihnen; **a ~ deal (of)** ziemlich viel; **a ~ many** ziemlich viele; **take a ~ look** sieh dir das genau *or* gut an; **a ~ while ago** vor einiger Zeit; **to make ~** (*damage*) wieder gutmachen; (*loss*) ersetzen; **it's no ~ complaining** es ist sinnlos *or* es nützt nichts, sich zu beklagen;

~ morning/afternoon/evening! guten Morgen/Tag/Abend!; **~ night!** gute Nacht!; **he's up to no ~** er führt nichts Gutes im Schilde; **for the common ~** zum Wohle aller; **is this any ~?** (*will it help you?*) können Sie das gebrauchen?; (*is it good enough?*) reicht das?; **is the book/film any ~?** was halten Sie von dem Buch/Film?; **for ~** für immer; **~s and chattels** Hab und Gut *nt*.

goodbye [gud'baɪ] *excl* auf Wiedersehen!; **to say ~** sich verabschieden.

good-for-nothing ['gudfənʌθɪŋ] *adj* nichtsnutzig.

Good Friday *n* Karfreitag *m*.

good-humoured ['gud'hjuːməd] *adj* gut gelaunt; (*good-natured*) gutmütig; (*remark, joke*) harmlos.

good-looking ['gud'lukɪŋ] *adj* gut aussehend.

good-natured ['gud'neɪtʃəd] *adj* gutmütig; (*discussion*) freundlich.

goodness ['gudnɪs] *n* Güte *f*; **for ~ sake!** um Himmels willen!; **~ gracious!** ach du liebe *or* meine Güte!

goods train (*BRIT*) *n* Güterzug *m*.

goodwill [gud'wɪl] *n* Wohlwollen *nt*; (*COMM*) Goodwill *m*.

goody ['gudɪ] (*inf*) *n* Gute(r) *m*, Held *m*.

goody-goody ['gudɪgudɪ] (*pej*) *n* Tugendlamm *nt*, Musterkind (*inf*) *nt*.

gooey ['guːɪ] (*inf*) *adj* (*sticky*) klebrig; (*cake*) üppig; (*fig: sentimental*) rührselig.

goose [guːs] (*pl* **geese**) *n* Gans *f*.

gooseberry ['guzbərɪ] *n* Stachelbeere *f*; **to play ~** (*BRIT*) das fünfte Rad am Wagen sein.

goose flesh *n* = **goose pimples**.

goose pimples *npl* Gänsehaut *f*.

goose step *n* Stechschritt *m*.

GOP (*US: inf*) *n abbr* (*POL*: = *Grand Old Party*) Republikanische Partei.

gopher ['gəufə*] *n* (*ZOOL*) Taschenratte *f*.

gore [gɔː*] *vt* aufspießen ♦ *n* Blut *nt*.

gorge [gɔːdʒ] *n* Schlucht *f* ♦ *vt*: **to ~ o.s. (on)** sich voll stopfen (mit).

gorgeous ['gɔːdʒəs] *adj* herrlich; (*person*) hinreißend.

gorilla [gə'rɪlə] *n* Gorilla *m*.

gormless ['gɔːmlɪs] (*BRIT: inf*) *adj* doof.

gorse [gɔːs] *n* Stechginster *m*.

gory ['gɔːrɪ] *adj* blutig.

go-slow ['gəu'sləu] (*BRIT*) *n* Bummelstreik *m*.

gospel ['gɔspl] *n* Evangelium *nt*; (*doctrine*) Lehre *f*.

gossamer ['gɔsəmə*] *n* Spinnfäden *pl*; (*light fabric*) hauchdünne Gaze *f*.

gossip ['gɔsɪp] *n* (*rumours*) Klatsch *m*, Tratsch *m*; (*chat*) Schwatz *m*; (*person*) Klatschbase *f* ♦ *vi* schwatzen; **a piece of ~** eine Neuigkeit.

gossip column *n* Klatschkolumne *f*, Klatschspalte *f*.

got [gɔt] *pt, pp of* **get**.

Gothic ['gɔθɪk] *adj* gotisch.

gotten ['gɔtn] (US) pp of **get**.

gouge [gaudʒ] vt (also: ~ **out:** hole etc) bohren; (: initials) eingravieren; **to ~ sb's eyes out** jdm die Augen ausstechen.

gourd [guəd] n (container) Kürbisflasche f.

gourmet ['guəmeɪ] n Feinschmecker(in) m(f), Gourmet m.

gout [gaut] n Gicht f.

govern ['gʌvən] vt (also LING) regieren; (event, conduct) bestimmen.

governess ['gʌvənɪs] n Gouvernante f.

governing ['gʌvənɪŋ] adj (POL) regierend.

governing body n Vorstand m.

government ['gʌvnmənt] n Regierung f ♦ cpd Regierungs-; **local ~** Kommunalverwaltung f, Gemeindeverwaltung f.

governmental [gʌvn'mentl] adj Regierungs-.

government stocks npl Staatspapiere pl, Staatsanleihen pl.

governor ['gʌvənə'] n Gouverneur(in) m(f); (of bank, hospital, BRIT: of prison) Direktor(in) m(f); (of school) ≈ Mitglied nt des Schulbeirats.

Govt abbr = **government**.

gown [gaun] n (Abend)kleid nt; (of teacher, BRIT: of judge) Robe f.

GP n abbr = **general practitioner**.

GPMU (BRIT) n abbr (= Graphical Paper and Media Union) Mediengewerkschaft.

GPO n abbr (BRIT: formerly: = general post office) Postbehörde f; (US: = Government Printing Office) regierungsamtliche Druckanstalt.

gr. abbr (COMM) = **gross** (= gram(me)) g.

grab [græb] vt packen; (chance, opportunity) (beim Schopf) ergreifen ♦ vi: **to ~ at** greifen or grapschen nach +dat; **to ~ some food** schnell etwas essen; **to ~ a few hours sleep** ein paar Stunden schlafen.

grace [greɪs] n Gnade f; (gracefulness) Anmut f ♦ vt (honour) beehren; (adorn) zieren; **5 days' ~** 5 Tage Aufschub; **with (a) good ~** anstandslos; **with (a) bad ~** widerwillig; **his sense of humour is his saving ~** was einen mit ihm versöhnt, ist sein Sinn für Humor; **to say ~** das Tischgebet sprechen.

graceful ['greɪsful] adj anmutig; (style, shape) gefällig; (refusal, behaviour) charmant.

gracious ['greɪʃəs] adj (kind, courteous) liebenswürdig; (compassionate) gnädig; (smile) freundlich; (house, mansion etc) stilvoll; (living etc) kultiviert ♦ excl: **(good) ~!** (ach) du meine Güte!, (ach du) lieber Himmel!

gradation [grə'deɪʃən] n Abstufung f.

grade [greɪd] n (COMM) (Güte)klasse f; (in hierarchy) Rang m; (SCOL: mark) Note f; (US: school class) Klasse f; (: gradient: upward) Neigung f, Steigung f; (: downward) Neigung f, Gefälle nt ♦ vt klassifizieren; (work, student) einstufen; **to make the ~** (fig) es schaffen.

grade crossing (US) n Bahnübergang m.

grade school (US) n Grundschule f.

gradient ['greɪdɪənt] n (upward) Neigung f, Steigung f; (downward) Neigung f, Gefälle nt; (GEOM) Gradient m.

gradual ['grædjuəl] adj allmählich.

gradually ['grædjuəlɪ] adv allmählich.

graduate [n 'grædjuɪt, vi 'grædjueɪt] n (of university) Hochschulabsolvent(in) m(f); (US: of high school) Schulabgänger(in) m(f) ♦ vi (from university) graduieren; (US) die (Schul)abschlussprüfung bestehen.

graduated pension ['grædjueɪtɪd-] n gestaffelte Rente f.

graduation [grædju'eɪʃən] n (Ab)schlussfeier f.

graffiti [grə'fiːtɪ] n, npl Graffiti pl.

graft [graːft] n (AGR) (Pfropf)reis nt; (MED) Transplantat nt; (BRIT: inf: hard work) Schufterei f; (bribery) Schiebung f ♦ vt: **to ~ (onto)** (AGR) (auf)pfropfen (auf +acc); (MED) übertragen (auf +acc), einpflanzen (in +acc); (fig) aufpfropfen +dat.

grain [greɪn] n Korn nt; (no pl: cereals) Getreide nt; (US: corn) Getreide nt, Korn nt; (of wood) Maserung f; **it goes against the ~** (fig) es geht einem gegen den Strich.

gram [græm] n Gramm nt.

grammar ['græmə'] n Grammatik f, Sprachlehre f.

grammar school (BRIT) n ≈ Gymnasium nt.

grammatical [grə'mætɪkl] adj grammat(ikal)isch.

gramme [græm] n = **gram**.

gramophone ['græməfəun] (BRIT) n Grammofon nt, Grammophon nt.

granary ['grænərɪ] n Kornspeicher m; ® (Granary): **G~ bread/loaf** Körnerbrot nt.

grand [grænd] adj großartig; (inf: wonderful) fantastisch ♦ n (inf) ≈ Riese m (1000 Pfund/ Dollar).

grandchild ['græntʃaɪld] (irreg: like **child**) n Enkelkind nt, Enkel(in) m(f).

granddad ['grændæd] (inf) n Opa m.

granddaughter ['grændɔːtə'] n Enkelin f.

grandeur ['grændjə'] n (of scenery etc) Erhabenheit f; (of building) Vornehmheit f.

grandfather ['grændfɑːðə'] n Großvater m.

grandiose ['grændɪəus] (also pej) adj grandios.

grand jury (US) n Großes Geschworenengericht nt.

grandma ['grænmaː] (inf) n Oma f.

grandmother ['grænmʌðə'] n Großmutter f.

grandpa ['grænpaː] (inf) n Opa m.

grandparents ['grændpɛərənts] npl Großeltern pl.

grand piano n Flügel m.

Grand Prix ['grãː'priː] n (AUT) Grand Prix m.

grandson ['grænsʌn] n Enkel m.

grandstand ['grændstænd] n Haupttribüne f.

grand total n Gesamtsumme f, Endsumme f.

granite ['grænɪt] n Granit m.

granny ['grænɪ] (inf) n Oma f.

grant [graːnt] vt (money) bewilligen; (request

etc) gewähren; (*visa*) erteilen; (*admit*)
zugeben ♦ *n* Stipendium *nt*; (*subsidy*)
Subvention *f*; **to take sth for** ~**ed** etw für
selbstverständlich halten; **to take sb for**
~**ed** jdn als selbstverständlich hinnehmen;
to ~ **that** zugeben, dass.

granulated sugar ['grænjuleɪtɪd-] *n*
(Zucker)raffinade *f*.

granule ['grænjuːl] *n* Körnchen *nt*.

grape [greɪp] *n* (Wein)traube *f*; **a bunch of** ~**s**
eine (ganze) Weintraube.

grapefruit ['greɪpfruːt] (*pl* ~ *or* ~**s**) *n*
Pampelmuse *f*, Grapefruit *f*.

grapevine ['greɪpvaɪn] *n* Weinstock *m*; **I heard
it on the** ~ (*fig*) es ist mir zu Ohren
gekommen.

graph [grɑːf] *n* (*diagram*) grafische
Darstellung *f*, Schaubild *nt*.

graphic ['græfɪk] *adj* plastisch, anschaulich;
(*art, design*) grafisch; *see also* **graphics**.

graphic designer *n* Grafiker(in) *m(f)*.

graphic equalizer [-iːkwəlaɪzə*] *n* (Graphic)
Equalizer *m*.

graphics ['græfɪks] *n* Grafik *f* ♦ *npl* (*drawings*)
Zeichnungen *pl*, grafische Darstellungen *pl*.

graphite ['græfaɪt] *n* Graphit *m*.

graph paper *n* Millimeterpapier *nt*.

grapple ['græpl] *vi*: **to** ~ **with sb/sth** mit jdm/
etw kämpfen; **to** ~ **with a problem** sich mit
einem Problem herumschlagen.

grasp [grɑːsp] *vt* (*seize*) ergreifen; (*hold*)
festhalten; (*understand*) begreifen ♦ *n* Griff
m; (*understanding*) Verständnis *nt*; **it slipped
from my** ~ es entglitt mir; **to have sth
within one's** ~ etw in greifbarer Nähe
haben; **to have a good** ~ **of sth** (*fig*) etw gut
beherrschen.

▶ **grasp at** *vt fus* greifen nach; (*fig:
opportunity*) ergreifen.

grasping ['grɑːspɪŋ] *adj* habgierig.

grass [grɑːs] *n* Gras *nt*; (*lawn*) Rasen *m*; (*BRIT:
inf: informer*) (Polizei)spitzel *m*.

grasshopper ['grɑːshɔpə*] *n* Grashüpfer *m*,
Heuschrecke *f*.

grass-roots ['grɑːsruːts] *npl* (*of party etc*) Basis
f ♦ *adj* (*opinion*) des kleinen Mannes; **at**
~ **level** an der Basis.

grass snake *n* Ringelnatter *f*.

grassy ['grɑːsɪ] *adj* Gras-, grasig.

grate [greɪt] *n* (Feuer)rost *m* ♦ *vt* reiben;
(*carrots etc*) raspeln ♦ *vi*: **to** ~ (**on**) kratzen
(auf +*dat*).

grateful ['greɪtful] *adj* dankbar; (*thanks*)
aufrichtig.

gratefully ['greɪtfəlɪ] *adv* dankbar.

grater ['greɪtə*] *n* Reibe *f*.

gratification [grætɪfɪ'keɪʃən] *n* (*pleasure*)
Genugtuung *f*; (*satisfaction*) Befriedigung *f*.

gratify ['grætɪfaɪ] *vt* (*please*) erfreuen; (*satisfy*)
befriedigen.

gratifying ['grætɪfaɪɪŋ] *adj* (*see vt*) erfreulich;
befriedigend.

grating ['greɪtɪŋ] *n* Gitter *nt* ♦ *adj* (*noise*)
knirschend; (*voice*) schrill.

gratitude ['grætɪtjuːd] *n* Dankbarkeit *f*.

gratuitous [grə'tjuːɪtəs] *adj* unnötig.

gratuity [grə'tjuːɪtɪ] *n* Trinkgeld *nt*.

grave [greɪv] *n* Grab *nt* ♦ *adj* (*decision, mistake*)
schwer (wiegend), schwerwiegend;
(*expression, person*) ernst.

grave digger *n* Totengräber *m*.

gravel ['grævl] *n* Kies *m*.

gravely ['greɪvlɪ] *adv* (*see adj*) schwer, ernst;
~ **ill** schwer krank.

gravestone ['greɪvstəun] *n* Grabstein *m*.

graveyard ['greɪvjɑːd] *n* Friedhof *m*.

gravitas ['grævɪtæs] *n* Seriosität *f*.

gravitate ['grævɪteɪt] *vi*: **to** ~ **towards**
angezogen werden von.

gravity ['grævɪtɪ] *n* Schwerkraft *f*;
(*seriousness*) Ernst *m*, Schwere *f*.

gravy ['greɪvɪ] *n* (*juice*) (Braten)saft *m*; (*sauce*)
(Braten)soße *f*.

gravy boat *n* Sauciere *f*, Soßenschüssel *f*.

gravy train (*inf*) *n*: **to ride the** ~ leichtes Geld
machen.

gray [greɪ] (*US*) *adj* = **grey**.

graze [greɪz] *vi* grasen, weiden ♦ *vt* streifen;
(*scrape*) aufschürfen ♦ *n* (*MED*)
Abschürfung *f*.

grazing ['greɪzɪŋ] *n* Weideland *nt*.

grease [griːs] *n* (*lubricant*) Schmiere *f*; (*fat*)
Fett *nt* ♦ *vt* (*see n*) schmieren; fetten; **to**
~ **the skids** (*US, fig*) die Maschinerie in
Gang halten.

grease gun *n* Fettspritze *f*, Fettpresse *f*.

greasepaint ['griːspeɪnt] *n* (Fett)schminke *f*.

greaseproof paper ['griːspruːf-] (*BRIT*) *n*
Pergamentpapier *nt*.

greasy ['griːsɪ] *adj* fettig; (*food: containing
grease*) fett; (*tools*) schmierig, ölig; (*clothes*)
speckig; (*BRIT: road, surface*) glitschig,
schlüpfrig.

great [greɪt] *adj* groß; (*city*) bedeutend; (*inf:
terrific*) prima, toll; **they're** ~ **friends** sie sind
gute Freunde; **we had a** ~ **time** wir haben
uns glänzend amüsiert; **it was** ~! es war
toll!; **the** ~ **thing is that ...** das Wichtigste
ist, dass ...

Great Barrier Reef *n*: **the** ~ das Große
Barriereriff.

Great Britain *n* Großbritannien *nt*.

greater ['greɪtə*] *adj see* **great** größer;
bedeutender; **people in G**~ **Calcutta** die
Leute in Kalkutta und Umgebung;
G~ **Manchester** Groß-Manchester *nt*.

great-grandchild [greɪt'grænt∫aɪld] (*irreg: like
child*) *n* Urenkel(in) *m(f)*.

great-grandfather [greɪt'grænfɑːðə*] *n*
Urgroßvater *m*.

great-grandmother [greɪt'grænmʌðə*] *n*
Urgroßmutter *f*.

Great Lakes *npl*: **the** ~ die Großen Seen *pl*.

greatly ['greɪtlɪ] *adv* sehr; (*influenced*) stark.

greatness ['greɪtnɪs] n Bedeutung f.

Grecian ['gri:ʃən] adj griechisch.

Greece [gri:s] n Griechenland nt.

greed [gri:d] n (also: ~iness): ~ **for** Gier f nach; ~ **for power** Machtgier f; ~ **for money** Geldgier f.

greedily ['gri:dɪlɪ] adv gierig.

greedy ['gri:dɪ] adj gierig.

Greek [gri:k] adj griechisch ♦ n Grieche m, Griechin f; (LING) Griechisch nt; **ancient/ modern** ~ Alt-/Neugriechisch nt.

green [gri:n] adj (also ecological) grün ♦ n (also GOLF) Grün nt; (stretch of grass) Rasen m, Grünfläche f; (also: village ~) Dorfwiese f, Anger m; **greens** npl (vegetables) Grüngemüse nt; (POL): **the G~s** die Grünen pl; **to have** ~ **fingers** or (US) **a** ~ **thumb** (fig) eine Hand für Pflanzen haben; **to give sb the** ~ **light** jdm grünes Licht geben.

green belt n Grüngürtel m.

green card n (AUT) grüne (Versicherungs)karte f; (US) ≈ Aufenthaltserlaubnis f.

greenery ['gri:nərɪ] n Grün nt.

greenfly ['gri:nflaɪ] (BRIT) n Blattlaus f.

greengage ['gri:ngeɪdʒ] n Reineclaude f, Reneklode f.

greengrocer ['gri:ngrəʊsə*] (BRIT) n Obst- und Gemüsehändler(in) m(f).

greenhouse ['gri:nhaʊs] n Gewächshaus nt, Treibhaus nt; ~ **effect** Treibhauseffekt m; ~ **gas** Treibhausgas nt.

greenish ['gri:nɪʃ] adj grünlich.

Greenland ['gri:nlənd] n Grönland nt.

Greenlander ['gri:nləndə*] n Grönländer(in) m(f).

green light n grünes Licht nt; **to give sb the** ~ jdm grünes Licht or freie Fahrt geben.

Green Party n (POL): **the** ~ die Grünen pl.

green pepper n grüne Paprikaschote f.

green pound n grünes Pfund nt.

greet [gri:t] vt begrüßen; (news) aufnehmen.

greeting ['gri:tɪŋ] n Gruß m; (welcome) Begrüßung f; **Christmas** ~**s** Weihnachtsgrüße pl; **birthday** ~**s** Geburtstagsglückwünsche pl; **Season's** ~**s** frohe Weihnachten und ein glückliches neues Jahr.

greeting(s) card n Grußkarte f; (congratulating) Glückwunschkarte f.

gregarious [grə'gɛərɪəs] adj gesellig.

grenade [grə'neɪd] n (also: **hand** ~) (Hand)granate f.

grew [gru:] pt of **grow**.

grey, (US) **gray** [greɪ] adj grau; (dismal) trüb, grau; **to go** ~ grau werden.

grey-haired [greɪ'hɛəd] adj grauhaarig.

greyhound ['greɪhaʊnd] n Windhund m.

grid [grɪd] n Gitter nt; (ELEC) (Verteiler)netz nt; (US: AUT: intersection) Kreuzung f.

griddle ['grɪdl] n gusseiserne Pfanne zum Braten und Pfannkuchenbacken.

gridiron ['grɪdaɪən] n Bratrost m.

gridlock ['grɪdlɔk] n (esp US: on road) totaler Stau m; (stalemate) Patt nt ♦ vt: **to be** ~**ed** (roads) total verstopft sein; (talks etc) festgefahren sein.

grief [gri:f] n Kummer m, Trauer f; **to come to** ~ (plan) scheitern; (person) zu Schaden kommen; **good** ~! ach du liebe Gute!

grievance ['gri:vəns] n Beschwerde f; (feeling of resentment) Groll m.

grieve [gri:v] vi trauern ♦ vt Kummer bereiten +dat, betrüben; **to** ~ **for** trauern um.

grievous ['gri:vəs] adj (mistake) schwer; (situation) beträchtlich; ~ **bodily harm** (LAW) schwere Körperverletzung f.

grill [grɪl] n (grilled food: also: **mixed** ~) Grillgericht nt; (restaurant) = **grillroom** ♦ vt (BRIT) grillen; (inf: question) in die Zange nehmen, ausquetschen.

grille [grɪl] n (screen) Gitter nt; (AUT) Kühlergrill m.

grillroom ['grɪlrum] n Grillrestaurant nt.

grim [grɪm] adj trostlos; (serious, stern) grimmig.

grimace [grɪ'meɪs] n Grimasse f ♦ vi Grimassen schneiden.

grime [graɪm] n Dreck m, Schmutz m.

grimy ['graɪmɪ] adj dreckig, schmutzig.

grin [grɪn] n Grinsen nt ♦ vi grinsen; **to** ~ **at sb** jdn angrinsen.

grind [graɪnd] (pt, pp **ground**) vt zerkleinern; (coffee, pepper etc) mahlen; (US: meat) hacken, durch den Fleischwolf drehen; (knife) schleifen, wetzen; (gem, lens) schleifen ♦ vi (car gears) knirschen ♦ n (work) Schufterei f; **to** ~ **one's teeth** mit den Zähnen knirschen; **to** ~ **to a halt** (vehicle) quietschend zum Stehen kommen; (fig: talks, scheme) sich festfahren; (work) stocken; (production) zum Erliegen kommen; **the daily** ~ (inf) der tägliche Trott.

grinder ['graɪndə*] n (for coffee) Kaffeemühle f; (for waste disposal etc) Müllzerkleinerungsanlage f.

grindstone ['graɪndstəʊn] n: **to keep one's nose to the** ~ hart arbeiten.

grip [grɪp] n Griff m; (of tyre, shoe) Halt m; (holdall) Reisetasche f ♦ vt packen; (audience, attention) fesseln; **to come to** ~**s with sth** etw in den Griff bekommen; **to lose one's** ~ den Halt verlieren; (fig) nachlassen; **to** ~ **the road** (car) gut auf der Straße liegen.

gripe [graɪp] (inf) n (complaint) Meckerei f ♦ vi meckern; **the** ~**s** (MED) Kolik f, Bauchschmerzen pl.

gripping ['grɪpɪŋ] adj fesselnd, packend.

grisly ['grɪzlɪ] adj grässlich, grausig.

grist [grɪst] n (fig): **it's all** ~ **to the mill** das kann man alles verwerten.

gristle ['grɪsl] n Knorpel m.

grit [grɪt] n (for icy roads: sand) Sand m;

(*crushed stone*) Splitt *m*; (*determination, courage*) Mut *m* ♦ *vt* (*road*) streuen; **grits** *npl* (*US*) Grütze *f*; **I've got a piece of ~ in my eye** ich habe ein Staubkorn im Auge; **to ~ one's teeth** die Zähne zusammenbeißen.

grizzle ['grɪzl] (*BRIT*) *vi* quengeln.

grizzly ['grɪzlɪ] *n* (*also:* ~ **bear**) Grislibär *m*, Grizzlybär *m*.

groan [grəʊn] *n* Stöhnen *nt* ♦ *vi* stöhnen; (*tree, floorboard etc*) ächzen, knarren.

grocer ['grəʊsə*] *n* Lebensmittelhändler(in) *m(f)*.

groceries ['grəʊsərɪz] *npl* Lebensmittel *pl*.

grocer's (shop) *n* Lebensmittelgeschäft *nt*.

grog [grɒg] *n* Grog *m*.

groggy ['grɒgɪ] *adj* angeschlagen.

groin [grɔɪn] *n* Leistengegend *f*.

groom [gruːm] *n* Stallbursche *m*; (*also:* **bride~**) Bräutigam *m* ♦ *vt* (*horse*) striegeln; (*fig*): **to ~ sb for** (*job*) jdn aufbauen für; **well-~ed** gepflegt.

groove [gruːv] *n* Rille *f*.

grope [grəʊp] *vi*: **to ~ for** tasten nach; (*fig*: *try to think of*) suchen nach.

grosgrain ['grəʊgreɪn] *n* grob gerippter Stoff *m*.

gross [grəʊs] *adj* (*neglect*) grob; (*injustice*) krass; (*behaviour, speech*) grob, derb; (*COMM: income, weight*) Brutto- ♦ *n inv* Gros *nt* ♦ *vt*: **to ~ £500,000** £500 000 brutto einnehmen.

gross domestic product *n* Bruttoinlandsprodukt *nt*.

grossly ['grəʊslɪ] *adv* äußerst; (*exaggerated*) grob.

gross national product *n* Bruttosozialprodukt *nt*.

grotesque [grə'tɛsk] *adj* grotesk.

grotto ['grɒtəʊ] *n* Grotte *f*.

grotty ['grɒtɪ] (*inf*) *adj* mies.

grouch [graʊtʃ] (*inf*) *vi* schimpfen ♦ *n* (*person*) Miesepeter *m*, Muffel *m*.

ground [graʊnd] *pt, pp of* **grind** ♦ *n* Boden *m*, Erde *f*; (*land*) Land *nt*; (*SPORT*) Platz *m*, Feld *nt*; (*US: ELEC: also:* ~ **wire**) Erde *f*; (*reason: gen pl*) Grund *m* ♦ *vt* (*plane*) aus dem Verkehr ziehen; (*US: ELEC*) erden ♦ *adj* (*coffee etc*) gemahlen ♦ *vi* (*ship*) auflaufen; **grounds** *npl* (*of coffee etc*) Satz *m*; (*gardens etc*) Anlagen *pl*; **below** ~ unter der Erde; **to gain/lose** ~ Boden gewinnen/verlieren; **common** ~ Gemeinsame(s) *nt*; **on the ~s that** mit der Begründung, dass.

ground cloth (*US*) *n* = **groundsheet**.

ground control *n* (*AVIAT, SPACE*) Bodenkontrolle *f*.

ground floor *n* Erdgeschoss *nt*, Erdgeschoß *nt* (*ÖSTERR*).

grounding ['graʊndɪŋ] *n* (*in education*) Grundwissen *nt*.

groundless ['graʊndlɪs] *adj* grundlos, unbegründet.

groundnut ['graʊndnʌt] *n* Erdnuss *f*.

ground rent (*BRIT*) *n* Erbbauzins *m*.

ground rule *n* Grundregel *f*.

groundsheet ['graʊndʃiːt] (*BRIT*) *n* Zeltboden *m*.

groundskeeper ['graʊndzkiːpə*] (*US*) *n* = **groundsman**.

groundsman ['graʊndzmən] (*irreg: like* **man**) *n* (*SPORT*) Platzwart *m*.

ground staff *n* (*AVIAT*) Bodenpersonal *nt*.

ground swell *n*: **there was a ~ of public opinion against him** die Öffentlichkeit wandte sich gegen ihn.

ground-to-air missile ['graʊndtə'ɛə*-] *n* Boden-Luft-Rakete *f*.

ground-to-ground missile ['graʊndtə'graʊnd-] *n* Boden-Boden-Rakete *f*.

groundwork ['graʊndwɜːk] *n* Vorarbeit *f*.

group [gruːp] *n* Gruppe *f*; (*COMM*) Konzern *m* ♦ *vt* (*also:* ~ **together**: *in one group*) zusammentun; (: *in several groups*) in Gruppen einteilen ♦ *vi* (*also:* ~ **together**) sich zusammentun.

groupie ['gruːpɪ] (*inf*) *n* Groupie *nt*.

group therapy *n* Gruppentherapie *f*.

grouse [graʊs] *n inv* schottisches Moorhuhn *nt* ♦ *vi* (*complain*) schimpfen.

grove [grəʊv] *n* Hain *m*, Wäldchen *nt*.

grovel ['grɒvl] *vi* (*crawl*) kriechen; (*fig*): **to ~ (before)** kriechen (vor +*dat*).

grow [grəʊ] (*pt* **grew**, *pp* **grown**) *vi* wachsen; (*increase*) zunehmen; (*become*) werden ♦ *vt* (*roses*) züchten; (*vegetables*) anbauen, ziehen; (*beard*) sich *dat* wachsen lassen; **to ~ tired of waiting** das Warten leid sein; **to ~ (out of or from)** (*develop*) entstehen (aus).
► **grow apart** *vi* (*fig*) sich auseinander entwickeln.
► **grow away from** *vt fus* (*fig*) sich entfremden +*dat*.
► **grow on** *vt fus*: **that painting is ~ing on me** allmählich finde ich Gefallen an dem Bild.
► **grow out of** *vt fus* (*clothes*) herauswachsen aus; (*habit*) ablegen; **he'll ~ out of it** diese Phase geht auch vorbei.
► **grow up** *vi* aufwachsen; (*mature*) erwachsen werden; (*idea, friendship*) entstehen.

grower ['grəʊə*] *n* (*BOT*) Züchter(in) *m(f)*; (*AGR*) Pflanzer(in) *m(f)*.

growing ['grəʊɪŋ] *adj* wachsend; (*number*) zunehmend; ~ **pains** Wachstumsschmerzen *pl*; (*fig*) Kinderkrankheiten *pl*, Anfangsschwierigkeiten *pl*.

growl [graʊl] *vi* knurren.

grown [grəʊn] *pp of* **grow**.

grown-up [grəʊn'ʌp] *n* Erwachsene(r) *f(m)*.

growth [grəʊθ] *n* Wachstum *nt*; (*what has grown: of weeds, beard etc*) Wuchs *m*; (*of person, character*) Entwicklung *f*; (*MED*) Gewächs *nt*, Wucherung *f*.

growth rate *n* Wachstumsrate *f*,

Zuwachsrate *f*.

grub [grʌb] *n* (*larva*) Larve *f*; (*inf: food*)
Fressalien *pl*, Futter *nt* ♦ *vi*: **to ~ about** *or*
around (for) (herum)wühlen (nach).

grubby ['grʌbɪ] *adj* (*dirty*) schmuddelig; (*fig*)
schmutzig.

grudge [grʌdʒ] *n* Groll *m* ♦ *vt*: **to ~ sb sth** jdm
etw nicht gönnen; **to bear sb a ~** jdm böse
sein, einen Groll gegen jdn hegen.

grudging ['grʌdʒɪŋ] *adj* widerwillig.

grudgingly ['grʌdʒɪŋlɪ] *adv* widerwillig.

gruelling, (*US*) **grueling** ['gruəlɪŋ] *adj*
(*encounter*) aufreibend; (*trip, journey*)
äußerst strapaziös.

gruesome ['gruːsəm] *adj* grauenhaft.

gruff [grʌf] *adj* barsch, schroff.

grumble ['grʌmbl] *vi* murren, schimpfen.

grumpy ['grʌmpɪ] *adj* mürrisch, brummig.

grunge [grʌndʒ] (*inf*) *n* Grunge *nt*.

grunt [grʌnt] *vi* grunzen ♦ *n* Grunzen *nt*.

G-string ['dʒiːstrɪŋ] *n* Minislip *m*, Tangaslip
m.

GSUSA *n abbr* (= *Girl Scouts of the United States
of America*) *amerikanische Pfadfinderinnen.*

GT *abbr* (*AUT*: = *gran turismo*) GT.

GU (*US*) *abbr* (*POST*: = *Guam*).

guarantee [gærən'tiː] *n* Garantie *f* ♦ *vt*
garantieren; **he can't ~ (that) he'll come** er
kann nicht dafür garantieren, dass er
kommt.

guarantor [gærən'tɔːʳ] *n* (*COMM*) Bürge *m*.

guard [gɑːd] *n* Wache *f*; (*BOXING, FENCING*)
Deckung *f*; (*BRIT: RAIL*) Schaffner(in) *m(f)*;
(*on machine*) Schutz *m*, Schutzvorrichtung *f*;
(*also:* **fire~**) (Schutz)gitter *nt* ♦ *vt* (*prisoner*)
bewachen; (*protect*): **to ~ (against)**
(be)schützen (vor +*dat*); (*secret*) hüten (vor
+*dat*); **to be on one's ~** auf der Hut sein.
  ▶ **guard against** *vt fus* (*disease*) vorbeugen
+*dat*; (*damage, accident*) verhüten.

guard dog *n* Wachhund *m*.

guarded ['gɑːdɪd] *adj* vorsichtig,
zurückhaltend.

guardian ['gɑːdɪən] *n* Vormund *m*; (*defender*)
Hüter *m*.

guardrail ['gɑːdreɪl] *n* (Schutz)geländer *nt*.

guard's van (*BRIT*) *n* (*RAIL*) Schaffnerabteil
nt, Dienstwagen *m*.

Guatemala [gwɑːtɪ'mɑːlə] *n* (*GEOG*)
Guatemala *nt*.

Guatemalan [gwɑːtɪ'mɑːlən] *adj*
guatemaltekisch, aus Guatemala.

Guernsey ['gɜːnzɪ] *n* Guernsey *nt*.

guerrilla [gə'rɪlə] *n* Guerilla *m*,
Guerillakämpfer(in) *m(f)*.

guerrilla warfare *n* Guerillakrieg *m*.

guess [gɛs] *vt* schätzen; (*answer*) (er)raten;
(*US: think*) schätzen (*inf*) ♦ *vi* (*see vt*)
schätzen; raten ♦ *n* Vermutung *f*; **I ~ you're
right** da haben Sie wohl Recht; **to keep sb
~ing** jdn im Ungewissen lassen; **to take** *or*
have a ~ raten; (*estimate*) schätzen; **my ~ is**

that ich schätze *or* vermute, dass ...

guesstimate ['gɛstɪmɪt] (*inf*) *n* grobe
Schätzung *f*.

guesswork ['gɛswɜːk] *n* Vermutungen *pl*; **I
got the answer by ~** ich habe die Antwort
nur geraten.

guest [gɛst] *n* Gast *m*; **be my ~** (*inf*) nur zu!

guesthouse ['gɛsthaus] *n* Pension *f*.

guest room *n* Gästezimmer *nt*.

guff [gʌf] (*inf*) *n* Quatsch *m*, Käse *m*.

guffaw [gʌ'fɔː] *vi* schallend lachen ♦ *n*
schallendes Lachen *nt*.

guidance ['gaɪdəns] *n* Rat *m*, Beratung *f*;
under the ~ of unter der Leitung von;
vocational ~ Berufsberatung *f*; **marriage ~**
Eheberatung *f*.

guide [gaɪd] *n* (*person*) Führer(in) *m(f)*; (*book*)
Führer *m*; (*BRIT: also:* **girl ~**) Pfadfinderin *f*
♦ *vt* führen; (*direct*) lenken; **to be ~d by sb/
sth** sich von jdm/etw leiten lassen.

guidebook ['gaɪdbuk] *n* Führer *m*.

guided missile *n* Lenkwaffe *f*.

guide dog *n* Blindenhund *m*.

guidelines ['gaɪdlaɪnz] *npl* Richtlinien *pl*.

guild [gɪld] *n* Verein *m*.

guildhall ['gɪldhɔːl] (*BRIT*) *n* Gildehaus *nt*.

guile [gaɪl] *n* Arglist *f*.

guileless ['gaɪllɪs] *adj* arglos.

guillotine ['gɪlətiːn] *n* Guillotine *f*, Fallbeil *nt*;
(*for paper*) (Papier)schneidemaschine *f*.

guilt [gɪlt] *n* Schuld *f*; (*remorse*) Schuldgefühl
nt.

guilty ['gɪltɪ] *adj* schuldig; (*expression*)
schuldbewusst; (*secret*) dunkel; **to plead ~/
not ~** sich schuldig/nicht schuldig
bekennen; **to feel ~ about doing sth** ein
schlechtes Gewissen haben, etw zu tun.

Guinea ['gɪnɪ] *n*: **Republic of ~** Guinea *nt*.

guinea ['gɪnɪ] (*BRIT*) *n* (*old*) Guinee *f*.

guinea pig *n* Meerschweinchen *nt*; (*fig:
person*) Versuchskaninchen *nt*.

guise [gaɪz] *n*: **in** *or* **under the ~ of** in der
Form +*gen*, in Gestalt +*gen*.

guitar [gɪ'tɑːʳ] *n* Gitarre *f*.

guitarist [gɪ'tɑːrɪst] *n* Gitarrist(in) *m(f)*.

gulch [gʌltʃ] (*US*) *n* Schlucht *f*.

gulf [gʌlf] *n* Golf *m*; (*abyss*) Abgrund *m*; (*fig:
difference*) Kluft *f*; **the (Persian) G~** der
(Persische) Golf.

Gulf States *npl*: **the ~** die Golfstaaten *pl*.

Gulf Stream *n*: **the ~** der Golfstrom.

Gulf War *n*: **the ~** der Golfkrieg.

gull [gʌl] *n* Möwe *f*.

gullet ['gʌlɪt] *n* Speiseröhre *f*.

gullibility [gʌlɪ'bɪlɪtɪ] *n* Leichtgläubigkeit *f*.

gullible ['gʌlɪbl] *adj* leichtgläubig.

gully ['gʌlɪ] *n* Schlucht *f*.

gulp [gʌlp] *vi* schlucken ♦ *vt* (*also:* **~ down**)
hinunterschlucken ♦ *n*: **at one ~** mit einem
Schluck.

gum [gʌm] *n* (*ANAT*) Zahnfleisch *nt*; (*glue*)
Klebstoff *m*; (*also:* **~drop**) Weingummi *nt*;

(*also:* **chewing-~**) Kaugummi *m* ♦ *vt:* **to ~ (together)** (zusammen)kleben.

▶ **gum up** *vt:* **to ~ up the works** (*inf*) alles vermasseln.

gumboots ['gʌmbuːts] (*BRIT*) *npl* Gummistiefel *pl.*

gumption ['gʌmpʃən] *n* Grips *m* (*inf*).

gumtree ['gʌmtriː] *n:* **to be up a ~** (*fig: inf*) aufgeschmissen sein.

gun [gʌn] *n* (*small*) Pistole *f*; (*medium-sized*) Gewehr *nt*; (*large*) Kanone *f* ♦ *vt* (*also:* **~ down**) erschießen; **to stick to one's ~s** (*fig*) nicht nachgeben, festbleiben.

gunboat ['gʌnbəʊt] *n* Kanonenboot *nt.*

gun dog *n* Jagdhund *m.*

gunfire ['gʌnfaɪə*] *n* Geschützfeuer *nt.*

gunge [gʌndʒ] (*inf*) *n* Schmiere *f.*

gung ho ['gʌŋ'həʊ] (*inf*) *adj* übereifrig.

gunman ['gʌnmən] (*irreg: like* **man**) *n* bewaffneter Verbrecher *m.*

gunner ['gʌnə*] *n* (*MIL*) Kanonier *m*, Artillerist *m.*

gunpoint ['gʌnpɔɪnt] *n:* **at ~** mit vorgehaltener Pistole; mit vorgehaltenem Gewehr.

gunpowder ['gʌnpaʊdə*] *n* Schießpulver *nt.*

gunrunner ['gʌnrʌnə*] *n* Waffenschmuggler(in) *m(f)*, Waffenschieber(in) *m(f).*

gunrunning ['gʌnrʌnɪŋ] *n* Waffenschmuggel *m*, Waffenschieberei *f.*

gunshot ['gʌnʃɔt] *n* Schuss *m.*

gunsmith ['gʌnsmɪθ] *n* Büchsenmacher *m.*

gurgle ['gɜːgl] *vi* (*baby*) glucksen; (*water*) gluckern.

guru ['guruː] *n* Guru *m.*

gush [gʌʃ] *vi* hervorquellen, hervorströmen; (*person*) schwärmen ♦ *n* Strahl *m.*

gushing ['gʌʃɪŋ] *adj* (*fig*) überschwänglich.

gusset ['gʌsɪt] *n* Keil *m*, Zwickel *m.*

gust [gʌst] *n* Windstoß *m*, Bö(e) *f*; (*of smoke*) Wolke *f.*

gusto ['gʌstəʊ] *n:* **with ~** mit Genuss, mit Schwung.

gusty ['gʌstɪ] *adj* (*wind*) böig; (*day*) stürmisch.

gut [gʌt] *n* (*ANAT*) Darm *m*; (*for violin, racket*) Darmsaiten *pl* ♦ *vt* (*poultry, fish*) ausnehmen; (*building*) ausräumen; (*by fire*) ausbrennen; **guts** *npl* (*ANAT*) Eingeweide *pl*; (*inf: courage*) Mumm *m*; **to hate sb's ~s** jdn auf den Tod nicht ausstehen können.

gut reaction *n* rein gefühlsmäßige Reaktion *f.*

gutsy ['gʌtsɪ] (*inf*) *adj* (*vivid*) rasant; (*courageous*) mutig.

gutter ['gʌtə*] *n* (*in street*) Gosse *f*, Rinnstein *m*; (*of roof*) Dachrinne *f.*

gutter press *n* Boulevardpresse *f.*

guttural ['gʌtərl] *adj* guttural.

guy [gaɪ] *n* (*inf: man*) Typ *m*, Kerl *m*; (*also:* **~rope**) Haltetau *nt*, Halteseil *nt*; (*for Guy Fawkes' night*) (Guy-Fawkes-)Puppe *f.*

GUY FAWKES' NIGHT

Guy Fawkes' Night, *auch "bonfire night" genannt, erinnert an den "Gunpowder Plot", einen Attentatsversuch auf James I. und sein Parlament am 5. November 1605. Einer der Verschwörer, Guy Fawkes, wurde auf frischer Tat ertappt, als er das Parlamentsgebäude in die Luft sprengen wollte. Vor der Guy Fawkes' Night basteln Kinder in Großbritannien eine Puppe des Guy Fawkes, mit der sie Geld für Feuerwerkskörper von Passanten erbetteln, und die dann am 5. November auf einem Lagerfeuer mit Feuerwerk verbrannt wird.*

---

guzzle ['gʌzl] *vt* (*food*) futtern; (*drink*) saufen (*inf*).

gym [dʒɪm] *n* (*also:* **gymnasium**) Turnhalle *f*; (*also:* **gymnastics**) Gymnastik *f*, Turnen *nt.*

gymkhana [dʒɪm'kɑːnə] *n* Reiterfest *nt.*

gymnasium [dʒɪm'neɪzɪəm] *n* Turnhalle *f.*

gymnast ['dʒɪmnæst] *n* Turner(in) *m(f).*

gymnastics [dʒɪm'næstɪks] *n* Gymnastik *f*, Turnen *nt.*

gym shoes *npl* Turnschuhe *pl.*

gymslip ['dʒɪmslɪp] (*BRIT*) *n* (Schul)trägerrock *m.*

gynaecologist, (*US*) **gynecologist** [gaɪnɪ'kɔlədʒɪst] *n* Gynäkologe *m*, Gynäkologin *f*, Frauenarzt *m*, Frauenärztin *f.*

gynaecology, (*US*) **gynecology** [gaɪnɪ'kɔlədʒɪ] *n* Gynäkologie *f*, Frauenheilkunde *f.*

gypsy ['dʒɪpsɪ] *n* = **gipsy**.

gyrate [dʒaɪ'reɪt] *vi* kreisen, sich drehen.

gyroscope ['dʒaɪərəskəʊp] *n* Gyroskop *nt.*

H, h

H, h [eɪtʃ] *n* (*letter*) H, h *nt*; **~ for Harry**, (*US*) **~ for How** ≈ H wie Heinrich.

habeas corpus ['heɪbɪəs'kɔːpəs] *n* Habeaskorpusakte *f.*

haberdashery [hæbə'dæʃərɪ] (*BRIT*) *n* Kurzwaren *pl.*

habit ['hæbɪt] *n* Gewohnheit *f*; (*esp undesirable*) Angewohnheit *f*; (*addiction*) Sucht *f*; (*REL*) Habit *m or nt*; **to get out of/into the ~ of doing sth** sich abgewöhnen/ angewöhnen, etw zu tun; **to be in the ~ of doing sth** die (An)gewohnheit haben, etw zu tun.

habitable ['hæbɪtəbl] *adj* bewohnbar.

habitat ['hæbɪtæt] *n* Heimat *f*; (*of animals*) Lebensraum *m*, Heimat *f.*

habitation [hæbɪ'teɪʃən] *n* Wohnstätte *f*; **fit for**

human ~ für Wohnzwecke geeignet, bewohnbar.
habitual [hə'bɪtjuəl] adj (action) gewohnt; (drinker) Gewohnheits-; (liar) gewohnheitsmäßig.
habitually [hə'bɪtjuəlɪ] adv ständig.
hack [hæk] vt, vi (also COMPUT) hacken ♦ n (pej: writer) Schreiberling m; (horse) Mietpferd nt.
hacker ['hækə*] n (COMPUT) Hacker m.
hackles ['hæklz] npl: **to make sb's** ~ **rise** (fig) jdn auf die Palme bringen (inf).
hackney cab ['hæknɪ-] n Taxi nt.
hackneyed ['hæknɪd] adj abgedroschen.
hacksaw ['hæksɔː] n Metallsäge f.
had [hæd] pt, pp of **have**.
haddock ['hædək] (pl ~ or ~s) n Schellfisch m.
hadn't ['hædnt] = **had not**.
haematology, (US) **hematology** ['hiːmə'tɒlədʒɪ] n Hämatologie f.
haemoglobin, (US) **hemoglobin** ['hiːmə'gləubɪn] n Hämoglobin nt.
haemophilia, (US) **hemophilia** ['hiːmə'fɪlɪə] n Bluterkrankheit f.
haemorrhage, (US) **hemorrhage** ['hɛmərɪdʒ] n Blutung f.
haemorrhoids, (US) **hemorrhoids** ['hɛmərɔɪdz] npl Hämorr(ho)iden pl.
hag [hæg] n alte Hexe f; (witch) Hexe f.
haggard ['hægəd] adj ausgezehrt; (from worry) abgehärmt; (from tiredness) abgespannt.
haggis ['hægɪs] (SCOT) n Gericht aus gehackten Schafsinnereien und Haferschrot, im Schafsmagen gekocht.
haggle ['hægl] vi: **to** ~ **(over)** feilschen (um).
haggling ['hæglɪŋ] n Feilschen nt.
Hague [heɪg] n: **The** ~ Den Haag m.
hail [heɪl] n Hagel m ♦ vt (person) zurufen +dat; (taxi) herbeiwinken, anhalten; (acclaim: person) zujubeln +dat; (: event etc) bejubeln ♦ vi hageln; **he** ~s **from Scotland** er kommt or stammt aus Schottland.
hailstone ['heɪlstəun] n Hagelkorn nt.
hailstorm ['heɪlstɔːm] n Hagelschauer m.
hair [hɛə*] n (collectively: of person) Haar nt, Haare pl; (: of animal) Fell nt; (single hair) Haar nt; **to do one's** ~ sich frisieren; **by a** ~**'s breadth** um Haaresbreite.
hairbrush ['hɛəbrʌʃ] n Haarbürste f.
haircut ['hɛəkʌt] n Haarschnitt m; (style) Frisur f.
hairdo ['hɛəduː] n Frisur f.
hairdresser ['hɛədrɛsə*] n Friseur m, Friseuse f.
hairdresser's ['hɛədrɛsəz] n Friseursalon m.
hair dryer n Haartrockner m, Föhn m, Fön ® m.
-haired [hɛəd] suff: **fair-**~ blond; **long-**~ langhaarig.
hairgrip ['hɛəgrɪp] n Haarklemme f.
hairline ['hɛəlaɪn] n Haaransatz m.
hairline fracture n Haarriss m.

hairnet ['hɛənɛt] n Haarnetz nt.
hair oil n Haaröl nt.
hairpiece ['hɛəpiːs] n Haarteil nt; (for men) Toupet nt.
hairpin ['hɛəpɪn] n Haarnadel f.
hairpin bend, (US) **hairpin curve** n Haarnadelkurve f.
hair-raising ['hɛəreɪzɪŋ] adj haarsträubend.
hair remover n Enthaarungscreme f.
hair slide n Haarspange f.
hair spray n Haarspray nt.
hairstyle ['hɛəstaɪl] n Frisur f.
hairy ['hɛərɪ] adj behaart; (inf: situation) brenzlig, haarig.
Haiti ['heɪtɪ] n Haiti nt.
hake [heɪk] (pl ~ or ~s) n Seehecht m.
halcyon ['hælsɪən] adj glücklich.
hale [heɪl] adj: ~ **and hearty** gesund und munter.
half [hɑːf] (pl halves) n Hälfte f; (of beer etc) kleines Bier nt etc; (RAIL, bus) Fahrkarte f zum halben Preis ♦ adj, adv halb; **first/second** ~ (SPORT) erste/zweite Halbzeit f; **two and a** ~ zweieinhalb; ~-**an-hour** eine halbe Stunde; ~ **a dozen/pound** ein halbes Dutzend/Pfund; **a week and a** ~ eineinhalb or anderthalb Wochen; ~ (**of it**) die Hälfte; ~ (**of**) die Hälfte (von or +gen); ~ **the amount of** die halbe Menge an +dat; **to cut sth in** ~ etw halbieren; ~ **past three** halb vier; **to go halves (with sb)** (mit jdm) halbe-halbe machen; **she never does things by halves** sie macht keine halben Sachen; **he's too clever by** ~ er ist ein richtiger Schlaumeier; ~ **empty** halb leer; ~ **closed** halb geschlossen.
half-baked ['hɑːf'beɪkt] adj blödsinnig (inf).
half board n Halbpension f.
half-breed ['hɑːfbriːd] n = **half-caste**.
half-brother ['hɑːfbrʌðə*] n Halbbruder m.
half-caste ['hɑːfkɑːst] n Mischling m.
half-day [hɑːf'deɪ] n halber freier Tag m.
half-hearted ['hɑːf'hɑːtɪd] adj halbherzig, lustlos.
half-hour [hɑːf'auə*] n halbe Stunde f.
half-life ['hɑːflaɪf] n (TECH) Halbwertszeit f.
half-mast ['hɑːf'mɑːst]: **at** ~ adv (auf) halbmast.
halfpenny ['heɪpnɪ] (BRIT) n halber Penny m.
half-price ['hɑːf'praɪs] adj, adv zum halben Preis.
half-sister ['hɑːfsɪstə*] n Halbschwester f.
half term (BRIT) n kleine Ferien pl (in der Mitte des Trimesters).
half-timbered [hɑːf'tɪmbəd] adj (house) Fachwerk-.
half-time [hɑːf'taɪm] n (SPORT) Halbzeit f.
halfway ['hɑːf'weɪ] adv: ~ **to** auf halbem Wege nach; ~ **through** mitten in +dat; **to meet sb** ~ (fig) jdm auf halbem Wege entgegenkommen.
halfway house n (hostel) offene Anstalt f;

(*fig*) Zwischending *nt*; (: *compromise*) Kompromiss *m*.

halfwit ['hɑːfwɪt] *n* Schwachsinnige(r) *f(m)*; (*fig: inf*) Schwachkopf *m*.

half-yearly [hɑːf'jɪəlɪ] *adv* halbjährlich, jedes halbe Jahr ♦ *adj* halbjährlich.

halibut ['hælɪbət] *n inv* Heilbutt *m*.

halitosis [hælɪ'təʊsɪs] *n* schlechter Atem *m*, Mundgeruch *m*.

hall [hɔːl] *n* Diele *f*, (Haus)flur *m*; (*corridor*) Korridor *m*, Flur *m*; (*mansion*) Herrensitz *m*, Herrenhaus *nt*; (*for concerts etc*) Halle *f*; **to live in ~** (*BRIT*) im Wohnheim wohnen.

hallmark ['hɔːlmɑːk] *n* (*on gold, silver*) (Feingehalts)stempel *m*; (*of writer, artist etc*) Kennzeichen *nt*.

hallo [hə'ləʊ] *excl* = **hello**.

hall of residence (*pl* **halls of residence**) (*BRIT*) *n* Studentenwohnheim *nt*.

hallowed ['hæləʊd] *adj* (*ground*) heilig; (*fig: respected, revered*) geheiligt.

Hallowe'en ['hæləʊ'iːn] *n* der Tag vor Allerheiligen.

hallucination [həluːsɪ'neɪʃən] *n* Halluzination *f*.

hallucinogenic [həluːsɪnəʊ'dʒɛnɪk] *adj* (*drug*) halluzinogen ♦ *n* Halluzinogen *nt*.

hallway ['hɔːlweɪ] *n* Diele *f*, (Haus)flur *m*.

halo ['heɪləʊ] *n* Heiligenschein *m*; (*circle of light*) Hof *m*.

halt [hɔːlt] *vt* anhalten; (*progress etc*) zum Stillstand bringen ♦ *vi* anhalten, zum Stillstand kommen ♦ *n*: **to come to a ~** zum Stillstand kommen; **to call a ~ to sth** (*fig*) einer Sache *dat* ein Ende machen.

halter ['hɔːltə*] *n* Halfter *nt*.

halter-neck ['hɔːltənɛk] *adj* (*dress*) rückenfrei mit Nackenverschluss.

halve [hɑːv] *vt* halbieren.

halves [hɑːvz] *pl of* **half**.

ham [hæm] *n* Schinken *m*; (*inf: also:* **radio ~**) Funkamateur *m*; (: *actor*) Schmierenkomödiant(in) *m(f)*.

Hamburg ['hæmbəːg] *n* Hamburg *nt*.

hamburger ['hæmbəːgə*] *n* Hamburger *m*.

ham-fisted ['hæm'fɪstɪd], (*US*) **ham-handed** ['hæm'hændɪd] *adj* ungeschickt.

hamlet ['hæmlɪt] *n* Weiler *m*, kleines Dorf *nt*.

hammer ['hæmə*] *n* Hammer *m* ♦ *vt* hämmern; (*fig: criticize*) vernichtend kritisieren; (: *defeat*) vernichtend schlagen ♦ *vi*

hämmern; **to ~ sth into sb, to ~ sth across to sb** jdm etw einhämmern *or* einbläuen.

▶ **hammer out** *vt* hämmern; (*solution, agreement*) ausarbeiten.

hammock ['hæmək] *n* Hängematte *f*.

hamper ['hæmpə*] *vt* behindern ♦ *n* Korb *m*.

hamster ['hæmstə*] *n* Hamster *m*.

hamstring ['hæmstrɪŋ] *n* Kniesehne *f* ♦ *vt* einengen.

hand [hænd] *n* Hand *f*; (*of clock*) Zeiger *m*; (*handwriting*) Hand(schrift) *f*; (*worker*) Arbeiter(in) *m(f)*; (*of cards*) Blatt *nt*; (*measurement: of horse*) ≈ 10 cm ♦ *vt* geben, reichen; **to give** *or* **lend sb a ~** jdm helfen; **at ~** (*place*) in der Nähe; (*time*) unmittelbar bevorstehend; **by ~** von Hand; **in ~** (*time*) zur Verfügung; (*job*) anstehend; (*situation*) unter Kontrolle; **we have the matter in ~** wir haben die Sache im Griff; **on ~** zur Verfügung; **out of ~** *adj* außer Kontrolle ♦ *adv* (*reject etc*) rundweg; **to ~** zur Hand; **on the one ~ ..., on the other ~ ...** einerseits ... andererseits ...; **to force sb's ~** jdn zwingen; **to have a free ~** freie Hand haben; **to change ~s** den Besitzer wechseln; **to have in one's ~** (*also fig*) in der Hand halten; **"~s off!"** „Hände weg!"

▶ **hand down** *vt* (*knowledge*) weitergeben; (*possessions*) vererben; (*LAW: judgement, sentence*) fällen.

▶ **hand in** *vt* abgeben, einreichen.

▶ **hand out** *vt* verteilen; (*information*) austeilen; (*punishment*) verhängen.

▶ **hand over** *vt* übergeben.

▶ **hand round** *vt* (*BRIT*) verteilen; (*chocolates etc*) herumreichen.

handbag ['hændbæg] *n* Handtasche *f*.

hand baggage *n* Handgepäck *nt*.

handball ['hændbɔːl] *n* Handball *m*.

hand basin *n* Handwaschbecken *nt*.

handbook ['hændbuk] *n* Handbuch *nt*.

handbrake ['hændbreɪk] *n* Handbremse *f*.

h & c (*BRIT*) *abbr* (= *hot and cold (water)*) h. u. k.

hand cream *n* Handcreme *f*.

handcuff ['hændkʌf] *vt* Handschellen anlegen +*dat*.

handcuffs ['hændkʌfs] *npl* Handschellen *pl*.

handful ['hændful] *n* Hand *f* voll.

hand-held ['hænd'hɛld] *adj* (*camera*) Hand-.

handicap ['hændɪkæp] *n* Behinderung *f*; (*disadvantage*) Nachteil *m*; (*SPORT*) Handicap *nt* ♦ *vt* benachteiligen; **mentally/physically ~ped** geistig/körperlich behindert.

handicraft ['hændɪkrɑːft] *n* Kunsthandwerk *nt*; (*object*) Kunsthandwerksarbeit *f*.

handiwork ['hændɪwɔːk] *n* Arbeit *f*; **this looks like his ~** (*pej*) das sieht nach seiner Arbeit aus.

handkerchief ['hæŋkətʃɪf] *n* Taschentuch *nt*.

handle ['hændl] *n* Griff *m*; (*of door*) Klinke *f*; (*of cup*) Henkel *m*; (*of broom, brush etc*) Stiel *m*; (*for winding*) Kurbel *f*; (*CB RADIO*: *name*) Sendezeichen *nt* ♦ *vt* anfassen, berühren; (*problem etc*) sich befassen mit; (: *successfully*) fertig werden mit; (*people*) umgehen mit; "~ with care" „Vorsicht - zerbrechlich"; **to fly off the** ~ an die Decke gehen; **to get a** ~ **on a problem** (*inf*) ein Problem in den Griff bekommen.

handlebar(s) ['hændlbɑ:(z)] *n(pl)* Lenkstange *f*.

handling ['hændlɪŋ] *n*: ~ (**of**) (*of plant, animal, issue etc*) Behandlung *f* +*gen*; (*of person, tool, machine etc*) Umgang *m* (mit); (*ADMIN*) Bearbeitung *f* +*gen*.

handling charges *npl* Bearbeitungsgebühr *f*; (*BANKING*) Kontoführungsgebühr *f*.

hand luggage *n* Handgepäck *nt*.

handmade ['hænd'meɪd] *adj* handgearbeitet.

hand-out ['hændaut] *n* (*money, food etc*) Unterstützung *f*; (*publicity leaflet*) Flugblatt *nt*; (*summary*) Informationsblatt *nt*.

hand-picked ['hænd'pɪkt] *adj* von Hand geerntet; (*staff etc*) handverlesen.

handrail ['hændreɪl] *n* Geländer *nt*.

handset ['hændsɛt] *n* (*TEL*) Hörer *m*.

hands-free ['hændzfri:] *adj* (*telephone, microphone*) Freisprech-.

handshake ['hændʃeɪk] *n* Händedruck *m*.

handsome ['hænsəm] *adj* gut aussehend; (*building*) schön; (*gift*) großzügig; (*profit, return*) ansehnlich.

hands-on ['hændz'ɔn] *adj* (*training*) praktisch; (*approach etc*) aktiv; ~ **experience** praktische Erfahrung.

handstand ['hændstænd] *n*: **to do a** ~ einen Handstand machen.

hand-to-mouth ['hændtə'mauθ] *adj*: **to lead a** ~ **existence** von der Hand in den Mund leben.

handwriting ['hændraɪtɪŋ] *n* Handschrift *f*.

handwritten ['hændrɪtn] *adj* handgeschrieben.

handy ['hændɪ] *adj* praktisch; (*skilful*) geschickt; (*close at hand*) in der Nähe; **to come in** ~ sich als nützlich erweisen.

handyman ['hændɪmæn] (*irreg: like* **man**) *n* (*at home*) Heimwerker *m*; (*in hotel etc*) Faktotum *nt*.

hang [hæŋ] (*pt, pp* **hung**) *vt* aufhängen; (*criminal*) (*pt, pp* **hanged**) hängen; (*head*) hängen lassen ♦ *vi* hängen; (*hair, drapery*) fallen ♦ *n*: **to get the** ~ **of sth** (*inf*) den richtigen Dreh (bei etw) herauskriegen.

▶ **hang about** *vi* herumlungern.

▶ **hang around** *vi* = **hang about**.

▶ **hang back** *vi*: **to** ~ **back (from doing sth)** zögern(, etw zu tun).

▶ **hang on** *vi* warten ♦ *vt fus* (*depend on*) abhängen von; **to** ~ **on to** festhalten; (*for protection, support*) sich festhalten an +*dat*; (*hope, position*) sich klammern an +*acc*; (*ideas*) festhalten an +*dat*; (*keep*) behalten.

▶ **hang out** *vt* draußen aufhängen ♦ *vi*

heraushängen; (*inf: live*) wohnen.

▶ **hang together** *vi* (*argument*) folgerichtig *or* zusammenhängend sein; (*story, explanation*) zusammenhängend sein; (*statements*) zusammenpassen.

▶ **hang up** *vt* aufhängen ♦ *vi* (*TEL*): **to** ~ **up (on sb)** einfach auflegen.

hangar ['hæŋə'] *n* Hangar *m*, Flugzeughalle *f*.

hangdog ['hæŋdɔg] *adj* zerknirscht.

hanger ['hæŋə'] *n* Bügel *m*.

hanger-on [hæŋər'ɔn] *n* (*parasite*) Trabant *m* (*inf*); **the** ~**s-** ~ der Anhang.

hang-glide ['hæŋglaɪd] *vi* drachenfliegen.

hang-glider ['hæŋglaɪdə'] *n* (Flug)drachen *m*.

hang-gliding ['hæŋglaɪdɪŋ] *n* Drachenfliegen *nt*.

hanging ['hæŋɪŋ] *n* (*execution*) Hinrichtung *f* durch den Strang; (*for wall*) Wandbehang *m*.

hangman ['hæŋmən] (*irreg: like* **man**) *n* Henker *m*.

hangover ['hæŋəuvə'] *n* Kater *m*; (*from past*) Überbleibsel *nt*.

hang-up ['hæŋʌp] *n* Komplex *m*.

hank [hæŋk] *n* Strang *m*.

hanker ['hæŋkə'] *vi*: **to** ~ **after** sich sehnen nach.

hankering ['hæŋkərɪŋ] *n*: ~ (**for**) Verlangen *nt* (nach).

hankie, hanky ['hæŋkɪ] *n abbr* = **handkerchief**.

haphazard [hæp'hæzəd] *adj* planlos, wahllos.

hapless ['hæplɪs] *adj* glücklos.

happen ['hæpən] *vi* geschehen; **to** ~ **to do sth** zufällig(erweise) etw tun; **as it** ~**s** zufälligerweise; **what's** ~**ing?** was ist los?; **she** ~**ed to be free** sie hatte zufällig(erweise) gerade Zeit; **if anything** ~**ed to him** wenn ihm etwas zustoßen *or* passieren sollte.

▶ **happen (up)on** *vt fus* zufällig stoßen auf +*acc*; (*person*) zufällig treffen.

happening ['hæpnɪŋ] *n* Ereignis *nt*, Vorfall *m*.

happily ['hæpɪlɪ] *adv* (*luckily*) glücklicherweise; (*cheerfully*) fröhlich.

happiness ['hæpɪnɪs] *n* Glück *nt*.

happy ['hæpɪ] *adj* glücklich; (*cheerful*) fröhlich; **to be** ~ (**with**) zufrieden sein (mit); **to be** ~ **to do sth** etw gerne tun; ~ **birthday!** herzlichen Glückwunsch zum Geburtstag!

happy-go-lucky ['hæpɪgəu'lʌkɪ] *adj* unbekümmert.

happy hour *n* Zeit, in der Bars, Pubs usw Getränke zu ermäßigten Preisen anbieten.

harangue [hə'ræŋ] *vt* predigen +*dat* (*inf*).

harass ['hærəs] *vt* schikanieren.

harassed ['hærəst] *adj* geplagt.

harassment ['hærəsmənt] *n* Schikanierung *f*; **sexual** ~ sexuelle Belästigung *f*.

harbour, (*US*) **harbor** ['hɑ:bə'] *n* Hafen *m* ♦ *vt* (*hope, fear, grudge etc*) hegen; (*criminal, fugitive*) Unterschlupf gewähren +*dat*.

harbour dues *npl* Hafengebühren *pl*.

harbour master n Hafenmeister m.
hard [hɑːd] adj hart; (question, problem)
  schwierig; (evidence) gesichert ♦ adv (work)
  hart, schwer; (think) scharf; (try) sehr;
  ~ **luck!** Pech!; **no** ~ **feelings!** ich nehme es
  dir nicht übel; **to be** ~ **of hearing**
  schwerhörig sein; **to be** ~ **done by**
  ungerecht behandelt werden; **I find it** ~ **to**
  believe that ... ich kann es kaum glauben,
  dass ...; **to look** ~ **at sth** (object) sich +dat etw
  genau ansehen; (idea) etw gründlich prüfen.
hard-and-fast ['hɑːdən'fɑːst] adj fest.
hardback ['hɑːdbæk] n gebundene Ausgabe f.
hardboard ['hɑːdbɔːd] n Hartfaserplatte f.
hard-boiled egg ['hɑːd'bɔɪld-] n hart
  gekochtes Ei nt.
hard cash n Bargeld nt.
hard copy n (COMPUT) Ausdruck m.
hard core n harter Kern m.
hard-core ['hɑːd'kɔː'] adj (pornography) hart;
  (supporters) zum harten Kern gehörend.
hard court n (TENNIS) Hartplatz m.
hard disk n (COMPUT) Festplatte f.
harden ['hɑːdn] vt härten; (attitude, person)
  verhärten ♦ vi hart werden, sich verhärten.
hardened ['hɑːdnd] adj (criminal)
  Gewohnheits-; **to be** ~ **to sth** gegen etw
  abgehärtet sein.
hardening ['hɑːdnɪŋ] n Verhärtung f.
hard graft n: **by sheer** ~ durch harte Arbeit.
hard-headed ['hɑːd'hɛdɪd] adj nüchtern.
hardhearted ['hɑːd'hɑːtɪd] adj hartherzig.
hard-hitting ['hɑːd'hɪtɪŋ] adj (fig: speech,
  journalist etc) knallhart.
hard labour n Zwangsarbeit f.
hardliner [hɑːd'laɪnə'] n Vertreter(in) m(f) der
  harten Linie.
hard-luck story ['hɑːd'lʌk-] n
  Leidensgeschichte f.
hardly ['hɑːdlɪ] adv kaum; (harshly) hart,
  streng; **it's** ~ **the case** (ironic) das ist wohl
  kaum der Fall; **I can** ~ **believe it** ich kann es
  kaum glauben.
hard-nosed [hɑːd'nəuzd] adj abgebrüht.
hard-pressed [hɑːd'prɛst] adj: **to be** ~ unter
  Druck sein; ~ **for money** in Geldnot.
hard sell n aggressive Verkaufstaktik f.
hardship ['hɑːdʃɪp] n Not f.
hard shoulder (BRIT) n (AUT) Seitenstreifen
  m.
hard up (inf) adj knapp bei Kasse.
hardware ['hɑːdwɛə'] n Eisenwaren pl;
  (household goods) Haushaltswaren pl;
  (COMPUT) Hardware f; (MIL) Waffen pl.
hardware shop n Eisenwarenhandlung f.
hard-wearing [hɑːd'wɛərɪŋ] adj
  strapazierfähig.
hard-won [hɑːd'wʌn] adj schwer erkämpft.
hard-working [hɑːd'wɜːkɪŋ] adj fleißig.
hardy ['hɑːdɪ] adj (animals) zäh; (people)
  abgehärtet; (plant) winterhart.
hare [hɛə'] n Hase m.

harebrained ['hɛəbreɪnd] adj verrückt.
harelip ['hɛəlɪp] n Hasenscharte f.
harem [hɑː'riːm] n Harem m.
hark back [hɑːk-] vi: **to** ~ **to** zurückkommen
  auf +acc.
harm [hɑːm] n Schaden m; (injury) Verletzung
  f ♦ vt schaden +dat; (person: physically)
  verletzen; **to mean no** ~ es nicht böse
  meinen; **out of** ~'**s way** in Sicherheit;
  there's no ~ **in trying** es kann nicht
  schaden, es zu versuchen.
harmful ['hɑːmful] adj schädlich.
harmless ['hɑːmlɪs] adj harmlos.
harmonic [hɑː'mɔnɪk] adj harmonisch.
harmonica [hɑː'mɔnɪkə] n Harmonika f.
harmonics [hɑː'mɔnɪks] npl Harmonik f.
harmonious [hɑː'məunɪəs] adj harmonisch.
harmonium [hɑː'məunɪəm] n Harmonium nt.
harmonize ['hɑːmənaɪz] vi (MUS)
  mehrstimmig singen/spielen; (: one person)
  die zweite Stimme singen/spielen; (colours,
  ideas) harmonieren.
harmony ['hɑːmənɪ] n Einklang m; (MUS)
  Harmonie f.
harness ['hɑːnɪs] n (for horse) Geschirr nt; (for
  child) Laufgurt m; (safety harness)
  Sicherheitsgurt m ♦ vt (resources, energy etc)
  nutzbar machen; (horse, dog) anschirren.
harp [hɑːp] n Harfe f ♦ vi: **to** ~ **on about** (pej)
  herumreiten auf +dat.
harpist ['hɑːpɪst] n Harfenspieler(in) m(f).
harpoon [hɑː'puːn] n Harpune f.
harpsichord ['hɑːpsɪkɔːd] n Cembalo nt.
harried ['hærɪd] adj bedrängt.
harrow ['hærəu] n Egge f.
harrowing ['hærəuɪŋ] adj (film) erschütternd;
  (experience) grauenhaft.
harry ['hærɪ] vt bedrängen, zusetzen +dat.
harsh [hɑːʃ] adj (sound, light) grell; (judge,
  winter) streng; (criticism, life) hart.
harshly ['hɑːʃlɪ] adv (judge) streng; (say)
  barsch; (criticize) hart.
harshness ['hɑːʃnɪs] n (see adj) Grelle f;
  Strenge f; Härte f.
harvest ['hɑːvɪst] n Ernte f ♦ vt ernten.
harvester ['hɑːvɪstə'] n (also: **combine** ~)
  Mähdrescher m.
has [hæz] vb see **have**.
has-been ['hæzbiːn] (inf) n: **he's/she's a** ~ er/
  sie ist eine vergangene or vergessene
  Größe.
hash [hæʃ] n (CULIN) Haschee nt; (fig) **to make**
  a ~ **of sth** etw verpfuschen (inf); (inf) ♦ n abbr
  (= hashish) Hasch nt.
hashish ['hæʃɪʃ] n Haschisch nt.
hasn't ['hæznt] = **has not**.
hassle ['hæsl] (inf) n (bother) Theater nt ♦ vt
  schikanieren.
haste [heɪst] n Hast f; (speed) Eile f; **in** ~ in
  Eile; **to make** ~ **(to do sth)** sich beeilen(,
  etw zu tun).
hasten ['heɪsn] vt beschleunigen ♦ vi: **to** ~ **to**

do sth sich beeilen, etw zu tun; **I ~ to add ...** ich muss allerdings hinzufügen, ...; **she ~ed back to the house** sie eilte zum Haus zurück.

hastily ['heɪstɪlɪ] *adv (see adj)* hastig, eilig; vorschnell.

hasty ['heɪstɪ] *adj* hastig, eilig; *(rash)* vorschnell.

hat [hæt] *n* Hut *m*; **to keep sth under one's ~** etw für sich behalten.

hatbox ['hætbɔks] *n* Hutschachtel *f*.

hatch [hætʃ] *n (NAUT: also: ~way)* Luke *f*; *(also:* **service ~)** Durchreiche *f* ♦ *vi (bird)* ausschlüpfen ♦ *vt* ausbrüten; **the eggs ~ed after 10 days** nach 10 Tagen schlüpften die Jungen aus.

hatchback ['hætʃbæk] *n (AUT: car)* Heckklappenmodell *nt*.

hatchet ['hætʃɪt] *n* Beil *nt*; **to bury the ~** das Kriegsbeil begraben.

hatchet job *(inf) adj:* **to do a ~ on sb** jdn fertig machen.

hatchet man *(inf) n (fig)* Vollstrecker *m*.

hate [heɪt] *vt* hassen ♦ *n* Hass *m*; **I ~ him/milk** ich kann ihn/Milch nicht ausstehen; **to ~ to do/doing sth** es hassen, etw zu tun; *(weaker)* etw ungern tun; **I ~ to trouble you, but ...** es ist mir sehr unangenehm, dass ich Sie belästigen muss, aber ...

hateful ['heɪtful] *adj* abscheulich.

hatred ['heɪtrɪd] *n* Hass *m*; *(dislike)* Abneigung *f*.

hat trick *n* Hattrick *m*.

haughty ['hɔːtɪ] *adj* überheblich.

haul [hɔːl] *vt* ziehen; *(by lorry)* transportieren; *(NAUT)* den Kurs ändern *+gen* ♦ *n (booty)* Beute *f*, *(catch: of fish)* Fang *m*; **he ~ed himself out of the pool** er stemmte sich aus dem Schwimmbecken.

haulage ['hɔːlɪdʒ] *n (cost)* Transportkosten *pl*; *(business)* Transport *m*.

haulage contractor *(BRIT) n* Transportunternehmen *nt*, Spedition *f*; *(person)* Transportunternehmer(in) *m(f)*, Spediteur *m*.

hauler ['hɔːlə*] *(US) n* Transportunternehmer(in) *m(f)*, Spediteur *m*.

haulier ['hɔːlɪə*] *(BRIT) n* Transportunternehmer(in) *m(f)*, Spediteur *m*.

haunch [hɔːntʃ] *n* Hüftpartie *f*; *(of meat)* Keule *f*.

haunt [hɔːnt] *vt (place)* spuken in *+dat*, umgehen in *+dat*; *(person, also fig)* verfolgen ♦ *n* Lieblingsplatz *m*; *(of crooks etc)* Treffpunkt *m*.

haunted ['hɔːntɪd] *adj (expression)* gehetzt, gequält; **this building/room is ~** in diesem Gebäude/Zimmer spukt es.

haunting ['hɔːntɪŋ] *adj (music)* eindringlich; **a ~ sight** ein Anblick, der einen nicht loslässt.

Havana [hə'vænə] *n* Havanna *nt*.

have [hæv] *(pt, pp* **had***) aux vb* **1** haben; *(with verbs of motion)* sein; **to ~ arrived/gone** angekommen/gegangen sein; **to ~ eaten/slept** gegessen/geschlafen haben; **he has been promoted** er ist befördert worden; **having eaten** *or* **when he had eaten, he left** nachdem er gegessen hatte, ging er

2 *(in tag questions):* **you've done it, ~n't you?** du hast es gemacht, nicht wahr?; **he hasn't done it, has he?** er hat es nicht gemacht, oder?

3 *(in short answers and questions):* **you've made a mistake - no I ~n't/so I ~** du hast einen Fehler gemacht - nein(, das habe ich nicht)/ja, stimmt; **we ~n't paid - yes we ~!** wir haben nicht bezahlt - doch!; **I've been there before - ~ you?** ich war schon einmal da - wirklich *or* tatsächlich?

♦ *modal aux vb (be obliged):* **to ~ (got) to do sth** etw tun müssen; **this has (got) to be a mistake** das muss ein Fehler sein

♦ *vt* **1** *(possess)* haben; **she has (got) blue eyes/dark hair** sie hat blaue Augen/dunkle Haare; **I ~ (got) an idea** ich habe eine Idee.

2 *(referring to meals etc):* **to ~ breakfast** frühstücken; **to ~ lunch/dinner** zu Mittag/Abend essen; **to ~ a drink** etwas trinken; **to ~ a cigarette** eine Zigarette rauchen.

3 *(receive, obtain etc)* haben; **may I ~ your address?** kann ich Ihre Adresse haben *or* bekommen?; **to ~ a baby** ein Kind bekommen.

4 *(allow):* **I won't ~ this nonsense** dieser Unsinn kommt nicht infrage *or* in Frage!; **we can't ~ that** das kommt nicht infrage *or* in Frage.

5: to ~ sth done etw machen lassen; **to ~ one's hair cut** sich *dat* die Haare schneiden lassen; **to ~ sb do sth** *(order)* jdn etw tun lassen; **he soon had them all laughing/working** bald hatte er alle zum Lachen/Arbeiten gebracht.

6 *(experience, suffer):* **to ~ a cold/flu** eine Erkältung/die Grippe haben; **she had her bag stolen** ihr *dat* wurde die Tasche gestohlen.

7 *(+ noun: take, hold etc):* **to ~ a swim** schwimmen gehen; **to ~ a walk** spazieren gehen; **to ~ a rest** sich ausruhen; **to ~ a meeting** eine Besprechung haben; **to ~ a party** eine Party geben.

8 *(inf: dupe):* **you've been had** man hat dich hereingelegt.

▶ **have in** *(inf) vt:* **to ~ it in for sb** jdn auf dem Kieker haben.

▶ **have on** *vt (wear)* anhaben; *(BRIT: inf: tease)* auf den Arm nehmen; **I don't ~ any money on me** ich habe kein Geld bei mir; **do you ~** *or* **~ you anything on tomorrow?** haben Sie

morgen etwas vor?
▶ **have out** vt: to ~ it out with sb (settle a problem etc) ein Wort mit jdm reden.

haven ['heɪvn] n Hafen m; (safe place) Zufluchtsort m.
haven't ['hævnt] = have not.
haversack ['hævəsæk] n Rucksack m.
haves [hævz] (inf) npl: the ~ and the have-nots die Betuchten und die Habenichtse.
havoc ['hævək] n Verwüstung f; (confusion) Chaos nt; to play ~ with sth (disrupt) etw völlig durcheinander bringen.
Hawaii [hə'waɪiː] n Hawaii nt.
Hawaiian [hə'waɪjən] adj hawaiisch ♦ n Hawaiianer(in) m(f); (LING) Hawaiisch nt.
hawk [hɔːk] n Habicht m.
hawker ['hɔːkə*] n Hausierer(in) m(f).
hawkish ['hɔːkɪʃ] adj (person, approach) knallhart.
hawthorn ['hɔːθɔːn] n Weißdorn m, Rotdorn m.
hay [heɪ] n Heu nt.
hay fever n Heuschnupfen m.
haystack ['heɪstæk] n Heuhaufen m; like looking for a needle in a ~ als ob man eine Stecknadel im Heuhaufen suchte.
haywire ['heɪwaɪə*] (inf) adj: to go ~ (machine) verrückt spielen; (plans etc) über den Haufen geworfen werden.
hazard ['hæzəd] n Gefahr f ♦ vt riskieren; to be a health/fire ~ eine Gefahr für die Gesundheit/feuergefährlich sein; to ~ a guess (es) wagen, eine Vermutung anzustellen.
hazardous ['hæzədəs] adj gefährlich.
hazard pay (US) n Gefahrenzulage f.
hazard (warning) lights npl (AUT) Warnblinkanlage f.
haze [heɪz] n Dunst m.
hazel ['heɪzl] n Hasel(nuss)strauch m, Haselbusch m ♦ adj haselnussbraun.
hazelnut ['heɪzlnʌt] n Haselnuss f.
hazy ['heɪzɪ] adj dunstig, diesig; (idea, memory) unklar, verschwommen; I'm rather ~ about the details an die Einzelheiten kann ich mich nur vage or verschwommen erinnern; (ignorant) die genauen Einzelheiten sind mir nicht bekannt.
H-bomb ['eɪtʃbɔm] n H-Bombe f.
HE abbr (REL, DIPLOMACY: = His/Her Excellency) Seine/Ihre Exzellenz; (= high explosive) hochexplosiver Sprengstoff m.
he [hiː] pron er ♦ pref männlich; ~ who ... wer ...

head [hɛd] n Kopf m; (of table) Kopfende nt; (of queue) Spitze f; (of company, organization) Leiter(in) m(f); (of school) Schulleiter(in) m(f); (on coin) Kopfseite f; (on tape recorder) Tonkopf m ♦ vt anführen, an der Spitze stehen von; (group, company) leiten; (FOOTBALL: ball) köpfen; ~s (or tails) Kopf

(oder Zahl); ~ over heels Hals über Kopf; (in love) bis über beide Ohren; £10 a or per ~ 10 Pfund pro Kopf; at the ~ of the list oben auf der Liste; to have a ~ for business einen guten Geschäftssinn haben; to have no ~ for heights nicht schwindelfrei sein; to come to a ~ sich zuspitzen; they put their ~s together sie haben sich zusammengesetzt; off the top of my etc ~ ohne lange zu überlegen; on your own ~ be it! auf Ihre eigene Verantwortung or Kappe (inf)!; to bite or snap sb's ~ off jdn grob anfahren; he won't bite your ~ off er wird dir schon nicht den Kopf abreißen; it went to my ~ es ist mir in den Kopf or zu Kopf gestiegen; to lose/keep one's ~ den Kopf verlieren/nicht verlieren; I can't make ~ nor tail of this hieraus werde ich nicht schlau; he's off his ~! (inf) er ist nicht (ganz) bei Trost!
▶ **head for** vt fus (on foot) zusteuern auf +acc; (by car) in Richtung ... fahren; (plane, ship) Kurs nehmen auf +acc; you are ~ing for trouble du wirst Ärger bekommen.
▶ **head off** vt abwenden.
headache ['hɛdeɪk] n Kopfschmerzen pl, Kopfweh nt; (fig) Problem nt; to have a ~ Kopfschmerzen or Kopfweh haben.
headband ['hɛdbænd] n Stirnband nt.
headboard ['hɛdbɔːd] n Kopfteil nt.
head cold n Kopfgrippe f.
headdress ['hɛddrɛs] (BRIT) n Kopfschmuck m.
headed notepaper ['hɛdɪd-] n Schreibpapier nt mit Briefkopf.
header ['hɛdə*] (BRIT: inf) n (FOOTBALL) Kopfball m.
headfirst ['hɛd'fɜːst] adv (lit) kopfüber; (fig) Hals über Kopf.
headgear ['hɛdgɪə*] n Kopfbedeckung f.
head-hunt ['hɛdhʌnt] vt abwerben.
head-hunter ['hɛdhʌntə*] n (COMM) Kopfjäger(in) m(f).
heading ['hɛdɪŋ] n Überschrift f.
headlamp ['hɛdlæmp] (BRIT) n = headlight.
headland ['hɛdlənd] n Landspitze f.
headlight ['hɛdlaɪt] n Scheinwerfer m.
headline ['hɛdlaɪn] n Schlagzeile f; (RADIO, TV): (news) ~s Nachrichtenüberblick m.
headlong ['hɛdlɔŋ] adv kopfüber; (rush) Hals über Kopf.
headmaster ['hɛd'mɑːstə*] n Schulleiter m.
headmistress ['hɛd'mɪstrɪs] n Schulleiterin f.
head office n Zentrale f.
head of state (pl heads of state) n Staatsoberhaupt nt.
head-on ['hɛd'ɔn] adj (collision) frontal; (confrontation) direkt.
headphones ['hɛdfəunz] npl Kopfhörer pl.
headquarters ['hɛdkwɔːtəz] npl Zentrale f; (MIL) Hauptquartier nt.
headrest ['hɛdrɛst] n (AUT) Kopfstütze f.

headroom ['hɛdrʊm] n (in car) Kopfraum m; (under bridge) lichte Höhe f.
headscarf ['hɛdskɑːf] n Kopftuch nt.
headset ['hɛdsɛt] n = **headphones**.
head start n Vorsprung m.
headstone ['hɛdstəʊn] n Grabstein m.
headstrong ['hɛdstrɒŋ] adj eigensinnig.
head waiter n Oberkellner m.
headway ['hɛdweɪ] n: **to make ~** vorankommen.
headwind ['hɛdwɪnd] n Gegenwind m.
heady ['hɛdɪ] adj (experience etc) aufregend; (drink, atmosphere) berauschend.
heal [hiːl] vt, vi heilen.
health [hɛlθ] n Gesundheit f.
health care n Gesundheitsfürsorge f.
health centre (BRIT) n Ärztezentrum nt.
health food n Reformkost f, Naturkost f.
health food shop n Reformhaus nt, Naturkostladen m.
health hazard n Gefahr f für die Gesundheit.
health service (BRIT) n: **the Health Service** das Gesundheitswesen.
healthy ['hɛlθɪ] adj gesund; (profit) ansehnlich.
heap [hiːp] n Haufen m ♦ vt: **to ~ (up)** (auf)häufen; **~s of** (inf) jede Menge; **to ~ sth with** etw beladen mit; **to ~ sth on** etw häufen auf +acc; **to ~ favours/gifts** etc **on sb** jdn mit Gefälligkeiten/Geschenken etc überhäufen; **to ~ praises on sb** jdn mit Lob überschütten.
hear [hɪə*] (pt, pp **heard**) vt hören; (LAW: case) verhandeln; (: witness) vernehmen; **to ~ about** hören von; **to ~ from sb** von jdm hören; **I've never heard of that book** von dem Buch habe ich noch nie etwas gehört; **I wouldn't ~ of it!** davon will ich nichts hören.
▶ **hear out** vt ausreden lassen.
heard [hɜːd] pt, pp of **hear**.
hearing ['hɪərɪŋ] n Gehör nt; (of facts, by committee) Anhörung f; (of witnesses) Vernehmung f; (of a case) Verhandlung f; **to give sb a ~** (BRIT) jdn anhören.
hearing aid n Hörgerät nt.
hearsay ['hɪəseɪ] n Gerüchte pl; **by ~** vom Hörensagen.
hearse [hɜːs] n Leichenwagen m.
heart [hɑːt] n Herz nt; (of problem) Kern m; **hearts** npl (CARDS) Herz nt; **to lose ~** den Mut verlieren; **to take ~** Mut fassen; **at ~** im Grunde; **by ~** auswendig; **to set one's ~ on sth** sein Herz an etw acc hängen; **to set one's ~ on doing sth** alles daransetzen, etw zu tun; **the ~ of the matter** der Kern der Sache.
heartache ['hɑːteɪk] n Kummer m.
heart attack n Herzanfall m.
heartbeat ['hɑːtbiːt] n Herzschlag m.
heartbreak ['hɑːtbreɪk] n großer Kummer m, Leid nt.
heartbreaking ['hɑːtbreɪkɪŋ] adj

herzzerreißend.
heartbroken ['hɑːtbrəʊkən] adj: **to be ~** todunglücklich sein.
heartburn ['hɑːtbɜːn] n Sodbrennen nt.
-hearted ['hɑːtɪd] suff: **kind-~** gutherzig.
heartening ['hɑːtnɪŋ] adj ermutigend.
heart failure n Herzversagen nt.
heartfelt ['hɑːtfɛlt] adj tief empfunden.
hearth [hɑːθ] n ≈ Kamin m.
heartily ['hɑːtɪlɪ] adv (see adj) (laut und) herzlich; herzhaft; tief; ungeteilt.
heartland ['hɑːtlænd] n Herz nt; **Britain's industrial ~** Großbritanniens Industriezentrum nt.
heartless ['hɑːtlɪs] adj herzlos.
heartstrings ['hɑːtstrɪŋz] npl: **to tug at sb's ~** bei jdm auf die Tränendrüsen drücken.
heart-throb ['hɑːtθrɒb] (inf) n Schwarm m.
heart-to-heart ['hɑːt'tə'hɑːt] adj, adv ganz im Vertrauen.
heart transplant n Herztransplantation f, Herzverpflanzung f.
heart-warming ['hɑːtwɔːmɪŋ] adj herzerfreuend.
hearty ['hɑːtɪ] adj (person) laut und herzlich; (laugh, appetite) herzhaft; (welcome) herzlich; (dislike) tief; (support) ungeteilt.
heat [hiːt] n Hitze f; (warmth) Wärme f; (temperature) Temperatur f; (SPORT: also: **qualifying ~**) Vorrunde f ♦ vt erhitzen, heiß machen; (room, house) heizen; **in** or (BRIT) **on ~** (ZOOL) brünstig, läufig.
▶ **heat up** vi sich erwärmen, warm werden ♦ vt aufwärmen; (water, room) erwärmen.
heated ['hiːtɪd] adj geheizt; (pool) beheizt; (argument) hitzig.
heater ['hiːtə*] n (Heiz)ofen m; (in car) Heizung f.
heath [hiːθ] (BRIT) n Heide f.
heathen ['hiːðn] n Heide m, Heidin f.
heather ['hɛðə*] n Heidekraut nt, Erika f.
heating ['hiːtɪŋ] n Heizung f.
heat-resistant ['hiːtrɪzɪstənt] adj hitzebeständig.
heat-seeking ['hiːtsiːkɪŋ] adj Wärme suchend.
heatstroke ['hiːtstrəʊk] n Hitzschlag m.
heat wave n Hitzewelle f.
heave [hiːv] vt (pull) ziehen; (push) schieben; (lift) (hoch)heben ♦ vi sich heben und senken; (retch) sich übergeben ♦ n (see vt) Zug m; Stoß m; Heben nt; **to ~ a sigh** einen Seufzer ausstoßen.
▶ **heave to** (pt, pp **hove**) vi (NAUT) beidrehen.
heaven ['hɛvn] n Himmel m; **thank ~!** Gott sei Dank!; **~ forbid!** bloß nicht!; **for ~'s sake!** um Himmels or Gottes willen!
heavenly ['hɛvnlɪ] adj himmlisch.
heaven-sent [hɛvn'sɛnt] adj ideal.
heavily ['hɛvɪlɪ] adv schwer; (drink, smoke, depend, rely) stark; (sleep, sigh) tief; (say) mit schwerer Stimme.
heavy ['hɛvɪ] adj schwer; (clothes) dick; (rain,

snow, drinker, smoker) stark; (*build, frame*) kräftig; (*breathing, sleep*) tief; (*schedule, week*) anstrengend; (*weather*) drückend, schwül; **the conversation was ~ going** die Unterhaltung war mühsam; **the book was ~ going** das Buch las sich schwer.

heavy cream (*US*) *n Sahne mit hohem Fettgehalt*, ≈ Schlagsahne *f*.

heavy-duty ['hɛvɪ'djuːtɪ] *adj* strapazierfähig.

heavy goods vehicle *n* Lastkraftwagen *m*.

heavy-handed ['hɛvɪ'hændɪd] *adj* schwerfällig, ungeschickt.

heavy industry *n* Schwerindustrie *f*.

heavy metal *n* (*MUS*) Heavymetal *nt*.

heavyset ['hɛvɪ'sɛt] (*esp US*) *adj* kräftig gebaut.

heavyweight ['hɛvɪweɪt] *n* (*SPORT*) Schwergewicht *nt*.

Hebrew ['hiːbruː] *adj* hebräisch ♦ *n* (*LING*) Hebräisch *nt*.

Hebrides ['hɛbrɪdiːz] *npl*: **the ~** die Hebriden *pl*.

heck [hɛk] (*inf*) *interj*: **oh ~**! zum Kuckuck! ♦ *n*: **a ~ of a lot** irrsinnig viel.

heckle ['hɛkl] *vt* durch Zwischenrufe stören.

heckler ['hɛklə*] *n* Zwischenrufer(in) *m(f)*, Störer(in) *m(f)*.

hectare ['hɛktɑː*] (*BRIT*) *n* Hektar *nt or m*.

hectic ['hɛktɪk] *adj* hektisch.

hector ['hɛktə*] *vt* tyrannisieren.

he'd [hiːd] = **he would; he had**.

hedge [hɛdʒ] *n* Hecke *f* ♦ *vi* ausweichen, sich nicht festlegen ♦ *vt*: **to ~ one's bets** (*fig*) sich absichern; **as a ~ against inflation** als Absicherung *or* Schutz gegen die Inflation.

▶ **hedge in** *vt* (*person*) (in seiner Freiheit) einschränken; (*proposals etc*) behindern.

hedgehog ['hɛdʒhɒg] *n* Igel *m*.

hedgerow ['hɛdʒrəʊ] *n* Hecke *f*.

hedonism ['hiːdənɪzəm] *n* Hedonismus *m*.

heed [hiːd] *vt* (*also*: **take ~ of**) beachten ♦ *n*: **to pay (no) ~ to, take (no) ~ of** (nicht) beachten.

heedless ['hiːdlɪs] *adj* achtlos; **~ of sb/sth** ohne auf jdn/etw zu achten.

heel [hiːl] *n* Ferse *f*; (*of shoe*) Absatz *m* ♦ *vt* (*shoe*) mit einem neuen Absatz versehen; **to bring to ~** (*dog*) bei Fuß gehen lassen; (*fig: person*) an die Kandare nehmen; **to take to one's ~s** (*inf*) sich aus dem Staub machen.

hefty ['hɛftɪ] *adj* kräftig; (*parcel etc*) schwer; (*profit*) ansehnlich.

heifer ['hɛfə*] *n* Färse *f*.

height [haɪt] *n* Höhe *f*; (*of person*) Größe *f*; (*fig: of luxury, good taste etc*) Gipfel *m*; **what ~ are you?** wie groß bist du?; **of average ~** durchschnittlich groß; **to be afraid of ~s** nicht schwindelfrei sein; **it's the ~ of fashion** das ist die neueste Mode; **at the ~ of the tourist season** in der Hauptsaison.

heighten ['haɪtn] *vt* erhöhen.

heinous ['heɪnəs] *adj* abscheulich,

verabscheuungswürdig.

heir [ɛə*] *n* Erbe *m*; **the ~ to the throne** der Thronfolger.

heir apparent *n* gesetzlicher Erbe *m*.

heiress ['ɛərɛs] *n* Erbin *f*.

heirloom ['ɛəluːm] *n* Erbstück *nt*.

heist [haɪst] (*US: inf*) *n* Raubüberfall *m*.

held [hɛld] *pt, pp of* **hold**.

helicopter ['hɛlɪkɒptə*] *n* Hubschrauber *m*.

heliport ['hɛlɪpɔːt] *n* Hubschrauberflugplatz *m*, Heliport *m*.

helium ['hiːlɪəm] *n* Helium *nt*.

hell [hɛl] *n* Hölle *f*; **~!** (*inf!*) verdammt! (*inf!*); **a ~ of a lot** (*inf*) verdammt viel (*inf*); **a ~ of a mess** (*inf*) ein wahnsinniges Chaos (*inf*); **a ~ of a noise** (*inf*) ein Höllenlärm *m*; **a ~ of a nice guy** ein wahnsinnig netter Typ.

he'll [hiːl] = **he will; he shall**.

hellbent [hɛl'bɛnt] *adj*: **~ (on)** versessen (auf +*acc*)

hellish ['hɛlɪʃ] (*inf*) *adj* höllisch.

hello [hə'ləʊ] *excl* hallo; (*expressing surprise*) nanu, he.

Hell's Angels *npl* Hell's Angels *pl*.

helm [hɛlm] *n* Ruder *nt*, Steuer *nt*; **at the ~** am Ruder.

helmet ['hɛlmɪt] *n* Helm *m*.

helmsman ['hɛlmzmən] (*irreg: like* **man**) *n* Steuermann *m*.

help [hɛlp] *n* Hilfe *f*; (*charwoman*) (Haushalts)hilfe *f* ♦ *vt* helfen +*dat*; **with the ~ of** (*person*) mit (der) Hilfe +*gen*; (*tool etc*) mithilfe *or* mit Hilfe +*gen*; **to be of ~ to sb** jdm behilflich sein, jdm helfen; **can I ~ you?** (*in shop*) womit kann ich Ihnen dienen?; **~ yourself** bedienen Sie sich; **he can't ~ it** er kann nichts dafür; **I can't ~ thinking that** ... ich kann mir nicht helfen, ich glaube, dass ...

helper ['hɛlpə*] *n* Helfer(in) *m(f)*.

helpful ['hɛlpful] *adj* hilfsbereit; (*advice, suggestion*) nützlich, hilfreich.

helping ['hɛlpɪŋ] *n* Portion *f*.

helping hand *n*: **to give** *or* **lend sb a ~** jdm behilflich sein.

helpless ['hɛlplɪs] *adj* hilflos.

helplessly ['hɛlplɪslɪ] *adv* hilflos.

helpline ['hɛlplaɪn] *n* (*for emergencies*) Notruf *m*; (*for information*) Informationsdienst *m*.

Helsinki ['hɛlsɪŋkɪ] *n* Helsinki *nt*.

helter-skelter ['hɛltə'skɛltə*] (*BRIT*) *n* Rutschbahn *f*.

hem [hɛm] *n* Saum *m* ♦ *vt* säumen.

▶ **hem in** *vt* einschließen, umgeben; **to feel ~med in** (*fig*) sich eingeengt fühlen.

hematology ['hiːmə'tɒlədʒɪ] (*US*) *n* = **haematology**.

hemisphere ['hɛmɪsfɪə*] *n* Hemisphäre *f*; (*of sphere*) Halbkugel *f*.

hemlock ['hɛmlɒk] *n* Schierling *m*.

hemoglobin ['hiːmə'gləʊbɪn] (*US*) *n* = **haemoglobin**.

hemophilia ['hiːməˈfɪlɪə] (*US*) *n*
= **haemophilia**.
hemorrhage ['hɛmərɪdʒ] (*US*) *n*
= **haemorrhage**.
hemorrhoids ['hɛmərɔɪdz] (*US*) *npl*
= **haemorrhoids**.
hemp [hɛmp] *n* Hanf *m*.
hen [hɛn] *n* Henne *f*, Huhn *nt*; (*female bird*)
Weibchen *nt*.
hence [hɛns] *adv* daher; **2 years** ~ **in** zwei
Jahren.
henceforth [hɛnsˈfɔːθ] *adv* von nun an; (*from
that time on*) von da an.
henchman ['hɛntʃmən] (*irreg: like* **man**) (*pej*) *n*
Spießgeselle *m*.
hen night, **hen party** (*inf*) *n*
Damenkränzchen *nt*.

HEN NIGHT

Als **hen night** *bezeichnet man eine feuchtfröhliche
Frauenparty, die kurz vor einer Hochzeit von der
Braut und ihren Freundinnen meist in einem
Gasthaus oder Nachtklub abgehalten wird und bei
der die Freundinnen dafür sorgen, dass vor allem
die Braut große Mengen an Alkohol konsumiert.
Siehe auch* **stag night**.

---

henpecked ['hɛnpɛkt] *adj*: **to be** ~ unter dem
Pantoffel stehen; ~ **husband** Pantoffelheld
m.
hepatitis [hɛpəˈtaɪtɪs] *n* Hepatitis *f*.
her [hɜː*] *pron* sie; (*indirect*) ihr ♦ *adj* ihr; **I see**
~ ich sehe sie; **give** ~ **a book** gib ihr ein
Buch; **after** ~ nach ihr; *see also* **me**, **my**.
herald ['hɛrəld] *n* (Vor)bote *m* ♦ *vt* ankündigen.
heraldic [hɛˈrældɪk] *adj* heraldisch, Wappen-.
heraldry ['hɛrəldrɪ] *n* Wappenkunde *f*,
Heraldik *f*; (*coats of arms*) Wappen *pl*.
herb [hɜːb] *n* Kraut *nt*.
herbaceous [hɜːˈbeɪʃəs] *adj*: ~ **border**
Staudenrabatte *f*; ~ **plant** Staude *f*.
herbal ['hɜːbl] *adj* (*tea, medicine*) Kräuter-.
herbicide ['hɜːbɪsaɪd] *n* Herbizid *nt*.
herd [hɜːd] *n* Herde *f*; (*of wild animals*) Rudel *nt*
♦ *vt* treiben; (*gather*) zusammentreiben; ~**ed
together** zusammengetrieben.
here [hɪə*] *adv* hier; **she left** ~ **yesterday** sie
ist gestern von hier abgereist; ~ **is/are...**
hier ist/sind...; ~ **you are** (*giving*) (hier,)
bitte; ~ **we are!** (*finding sth*) da ist es ja!;
~ **she is!** da ist sie ja!; ~ **she comes** da
kommt sie ja; **come** ~! komm hierher *or*
hierhin!; ~ **and there** hier und da; "~'s **to**
..." "auf ... *acc*".
hereabouts ['hɪərəˈbaʊts] *adv* hier.
hereafter [hɪərˈɑːftə*] *adv* künftig.
hereby [hɪəˈbaɪ] *adv* hiermit.
hereditary [hɪˈrɛdɪtrɪ] *adj* erblich, Erb-.
heredity [hɪˈrɛdɪtɪ] *n* Vererbung *f*.
heresy ['hɛrəsɪ] *n* Ketzerei *f*.
heretic ['hɛrətɪk] *n* Ketzer(in) *m(f)*.

heretical [hɪˈrɛtɪkl] *adj* ketzerisch.
herewith [hɪəˈwɪð] *adv* hiermit.
heritage ['hɛrɪtɪdʒ] *n* Erbe *nt*.
hermetically [hɜːˈmɛtɪklɪ] *adv*: ~ **sealed**
hermetisch verschlossen.
hermit ['hɜːmɪt] *n* Einsiedler(in) *m(f)*.
hernia ['hɜːnɪə] *n* Bruch *m*.
hero ['hɪərəʊ] (*pl* ~**es**) *n* Held *m*; (*idol*) Idol *nt*.
heroic [hɪˈrəʊɪk] *adj* heldenhaft.
heroin ['hɛrəʊɪn] *n* Heroin *nt*.
heroin addict *n* Heroinsüchtige(r) *f(m)*.
heroine ['hɛrəʊɪn] *n* Heldin *f*; (*idol*) Idol *nt*.
heroism ['hɛrəʊɪzəm] *n* Heldentum *nt*.
heron ['hɛrən] *n* Reiher *m*.
hero worship *n* Heldenverehrung *f*.
herring ['hɛrɪŋ] *n* Hering *m*.
hers [hɜːz] *pron* ihre(r, s); **a friend of** ~ ein
Freund von ihr; **this is** ~ das gehört ihr; *see
also* **mine**.
herself [hɜːˈsɛlf] *pron* sich; (*emphatic*) (sie)
selbst; *see also* **oneself**.
Herts [hɑːts] (*BRIT*) *abbr* (= *Hertfordshire*).
he's [hiːz] = **he is**; = **he has**.
hesitant ['hɛzɪtənt] *adj* zögernd; **to be** ~ **about
doing sth** zögern, etw zu tun.
hesitate ['hɛzɪteɪt] *vi* zögern; (*be unwilling*)
Bedenken haben; **to** ~ **about** Bedenken
haben wegen; **don't** ~ **to see a doctor if you
are worried** gehen Sie ruhig zum Arzt, wenn
Sie sich Sorgen machen.
hesitation [hɛzɪˈteɪʃən] *n* Zögern *nt*;
Bedenken *pl*; **to have no** ~ **in saying sth** etw
ohne weiteres sagen können.
hessian ['hɛsɪən] *n* Sackleinwand *f*, Rupfen *m*.
heterogenous [hɛtəˈrɒdʒɪnəs] *adj* heterogen.
heterosexual ['hɛtərəʊˈsɛksjʊəl] *adj*
heterosexuell ♦ *n* Heterosexuelle(r) *f(m)*.
het up [hɛt-] (*inf*) *adj*: **to get** ~ (**about**) sich
aufregen (über +*acc*).
HEW (*US*) *n abbr* (= *Department of Health,
Education and Welfare*) *Ministerium für
Gesundheit, Erziehung und Sozialfürsorge*.
hew [hjuː] (*pt, pp* **hewed** *or* **hewn**) *vt* (*stone*)
behauen; (*wood*) hacken.
hex [hɛks] (*US*) *n* Fluch *m* ♦ *vt* verhexen.
hexagon ['hɛksəgən] *n* Sechseck *nt*.
hexagonal [hɛkˈsægənl] *adj* sechseckig.
hey [heɪ] *excl* he; (*to attract attention*) he du/Sie.
heyday ['heɪdeɪ] *n*: **the** ~ **of** (*person*) die
Glanzzeit +*gen*; (*nation, group etc*) die
Blütezeit +*gen*.
HF *n abbr* (= *high frequency*) HF.
HGV (*BRIT*) *n abbr* (= *heavy goods vehicle*) LKW
m.
HI (*US*) *abbr* (= *Hawaii*).
hi [haɪ] *excl* hallo.
hiatus [haɪˈeɪtəs] *n* Unterbrechung *f*.
hibernate ['haɪbəneɪt] *vi* Winterschlaf halten.
hibernation [haɪbəˈneɪʃən] *n* Winterschlaf *m*.
hiccough, **hiccup** ['hɪkʌp] *vi* hicksen.
hiccoughs, **hiccups** ['hɪkʌps] *npl* Schluckauf
m; **to have (the)** ~ den Schluckauf haben.

hick [hɪk] (*US: inf*) *n* Hinterwäldler *m*.
hid [hɪd] *pt of* **hide**.
hidden ['hɪdn] *pp of* **hide** ♦ *adj* (*advantage, danger*) unsichtbar; (*place*) versteckt; **there are no ~ extras** es gibt keine versteckten Extrakosten.
hide [haɪd] (*pt* **hid**, *pp* **hidden**) *n* Haut *f*, Fell *nt*; (*of birdwatcher etc*) Versteck *nt* ♦ *vt* verstecken; (*feeling, information*) verbergen; (*obscure*) verdecken ♦ *vi*: **to ~ (from sb)** sich (vor jdm) verstecken; **to ~ sth (from sb)** etw (vor jdm) verstecken.
hide-and-seek ['haɪdən'si:k] *n* Versteckspiel *nt*; **to play ~** Verstecken spielen.
hideaway ['haɪdəweɪ] *n* Zufluchtsort *m*.
hideous ['hɪdɪəs] *adj* scheußlich; (*conditions*) furchtbar.
hideously ['hɪdɪəslɪ] *adv* furchtbar.
hide-out ['haɪdaut] *n* Versteck *nt*.
hiding ['haɪdɪŋ] *n* Tracht *f* Prügel; **to be in ~** (*concealed*) sich versteckt halten.
hiding place *n* Versteck *nt*.
hierarchy ['haɪərɑːkɪ] *n* Hierarchie *f*.
hieroglyphics [haɪərə'glɪfɪks] *npl* Hieroglyphen *pl*.
hi-fi ['haɪfaɪ] *n abbr* (= **high fidelity**) Hi-Fi *nt* ♦ *adj* (*equipment etc*) Hi-Fi-.
higgledy-piggledy ['hɪgldɪ'pɪgldɪ] *adj* durcheinander.
high [haɪ] *adj* hoch; (*wind*) stark; (*risk*) groß; (*quality*) gut; (*inf: on drugs*) high; (: *on drink*) blau; (*BRIT: food*) schlecht; (: *game*) anbrüchig ♦ *adv* hoch ♦ *n*: **exports have reached a new ~** der Export hat einen neuen Höchststand erreicht; **to pay a ~ price for sth** etw teuer bezahlen; **it's ~ time you did it** es ist höchste Zeit, dass du es machst; **~ in the air** hoch oben in der Luft.
highboy ['haɪbɔɪ] (*US*) *n* hohe Kommode *f*.
highbrow ['haɪbrau] *adj* intellektuell; (*book, discussion etc*) anspruchsvoll.
highchair ['haɪtʃɛə*] *n* Hochstuhl *m*.
high-class ['haɪ'klɑːs] *adj* erstklassig; (*neighbourhood*) vornehm.

HIGH COURT

High Court *ist in England und Wales die Kurzform für „High Court of Justice" und bildet zusammen mit dem Berufungsgericht den Obersten Gerichtshof. In Schottland ist es die Kurzform für „High Court of Justiciary", das höchste Strafgericht in Schottland, das in Edinburgh und anderen Großstädten (immer mit Richter und Geschworenen) zusammentritt und für Verbrechen wie Mord, Vergewaltigung und Hochverrat zuständig ist. Weniger schwere Verbrechen werden vor dem „sheriff court" verhandelt und leichtere Vergehen vor dem „district court".*

---

high-energy ['haɪ'ɛnədʒɪ] *adj* (*particle, food*) energiereich.

higher ['haɪə*] *adj* (*form of study, life etc*) höher (entwickelt) ♦ *adv* höher ♦ *n* (*SCOT: SCOL*): **H~** *mit "Higher" wird die Fortgeschrittenenstufe des "Scottish certificate of education" und auch der Abschluss dieses Ausbildungsjahrs bezeichnet.*
higher education *n* Hochschulbildung *f*.
highfalutin [haɪfə'luːtɪn] (*inf*) *adj* hochtrabend.
high-flier, high-flyer [haɪ'flaɪə*] *n* Senkrechtstarter(in) *m(f)*.
high-flying [haɪ'flaɪɪŋ] *adj* (*person*) erfolgreich; (*lifestyle*) exklusiv.
high-handed [haɪ'hændɪd] *adj* eigenmächtig.
high-heeled [haɪ'hiːld] *adj* hochhackig.
high heels *npl* hochhackige Schuhe *pl*.
high jump *n* Hochsprung *m*.
Highlands ['haɪləndz] *npl*: **the ~** das Hochland.
high-level ['haɪlɛvl] *adj* (*talks etc*) auf höchster Ebene; **~ language** (*COMPUT*) höhere Programmiersprache *f*; **~ official** Spitzenfunktionär(in).
highlight ['haɪlaɪt] *n* (*of event*) Höhepunkt *m*; (*in hair*) Strähnchen *nt* ♦ *vt* (*problem, need*) ein Schlaglicht werfen auf +*acc*; **this ~s the fact that ...** das verdeutlicht die Tatsache, dass ...
highlighter ['haɪlaɪtə*] *n* Textmarker *m*.
highly ['haɪlɪ] *adv* hoch-; **to speak ~ of** sich sehr positiv äußern über +*acc*; **to think ~ of** eine hohe Meinung haben von; **~ recommended** sehr empfehlenswert; **~ unlikely** äußerst *or* höchst unwahrscheinlich.
highly strung *adj* nervös.
High Mass ['haɪ'mæs] *n* Hochamt *nt*.
highness ['haɪnɪs] *n*: **Her/His/Your H~** Ihre/ Seine/Eure Hoheit *f*.
high-pitched [haɪ'pɪtʃt] *adj* hoch.
high point *n* Höhepunkt *m*.
high-powered ['haɪ'pauəd] *adj* (*engine*) Hochleistungs-; (*job*) Spitzen-; (*businessman*) dynamisch; (*person*) äußerst fähig; (*course*) anspruchsvoll.
high-pressure ['haɪprɛʃə*] *adj* (*area, system*) Hochdruck-; (*inf: sales technique*) aggressiv.
high-rise ['haɪraɪz] *adj* (*apartment, block*) Hochhaus-; **~ building/flats** Hochhaus *nt*.
high school *n* ≈ Oberschule *f*.

HIGH SCHOOL

High school *ist eine weiterführende Schule in den USA. Man unterscheidet zwischen „junior high school" (im Anschluss an die Grundschule, umfasst das 7., 8. und 9. Schuljahr) und „senior high school" (10., 11. und 12. Schuljahr, mit akademischen und berufsbezogenen Fächern). Weiterführende Schulen in Großbritannien werden manchmal auch als* **high school** *bezeichnet. Siehe auch* **elementary school.**

high season (*BRIT*) n Hochsaison f.
high spirits npl Hochstimmung f.
high street (*BRIT*) n Hauptstraße f.
high strung (*US*) adj = **highly strung**.
high tide n Flut f.
highway ['haɪweɪ] (*US*) n Straße f; (*between towns, states*) Landstraße f; **information ~** Datenautobahn f.
Highway Code (*BRIT*) n Straßenverkehrsordnung f.
highwayman ['haɪweɪmən] (*irreg: like* **man**) n Räuber m, Wegelagerer m.
hijack ['haɪdʒæk] vt entführen ♦ n (*also:* ~**ing**) Entführung f.
hijacker ['haɪdʒækə*] n Entführer(in) m(f).
hike [haɪk] vi wandern ♦ n Wanderung f; (*inf: in prices etc*) Erhöhung f ♦ vt (*inf*) erhöhen.
hiker ['haɪkə*] n Wanderer m, Wanderin f.
hiking ['haɪkɪŋ] n Wandern nt.
hilarious [hɪ'lɛərɪəs] adj urkomisch.
hilarity [hɪ'lærɪtɪ] n übermütige Ausgelassenheit f.
hill [hɪl] n Hügel m; (*fairly high*) Berg m; (*slope*) Hang m; (*on road*) Steigung f.
hillbilly ['hɪlbɪlɪ] (*US*) n Hillbilly m; (*pej*) Hinterwäldler(in) m(f), Landpomeranze f.
hillock ['hɪlək] n Hügel m, Anhöhe f.
hillside ['hɪlsaɪd] n Hang m.
hill start n (*AUT*) Anfahren nt am Berg.
hilltop ['hɪltɒp] n Gipfel m.
hill walking n Bergwandern nt.
hilly ['hɪlɪ] adj hügelig.
hilt [hɪlt] n (*of sword, knife*) Heft nt; **to the ~** voll und ganz.
him [hɪm] pron ihn; (*indirect*) ihm; *see also* **me**.
Himalayas [hɪmə'leɪəz] npl: **the ~** der Himalaja.
himself [hɪm'sɛlf] pron sich; (*emphatic*) (er) selbst; *see also* **oneself**.
hind [haɪnd] adj (*legs*) Hinter- ♦ n (*female deer*) Hirschkuh f.
hinder ['hɪndə*] vt behindern; **to ~ sb from doing sth** jdn daran hindern, etw zu tun.
hindquarters ['haɪnd'kwɔːtəz] npl Hinterteil nt.
hindrance ['hɪndrəns] n Behinderung f.
hindsight ['haɪndsaɪt] n: **with ~** im nachhinein.
Hindu ['hɪnduː] adj hinduistisch, Hindu-.
hinge [hɪndʒ] n (*on door*) Angel f ♦ vi: **to ~ on** anhängen von.
hint [hɪnt] n Andeutung f; (*advice*) Tipp m; (*sign, glimmer*) Spur f ♦ vt: **to ~ that** andeuten, dass ♦ vi: **to ~ at** andeuten; **to drop a ~** eine Andeutung machen; **give me a ~** geben Sie mir einen Hinweis; **white with a ~ of pink** weiß mit einem Hauch von Rosa.
hip [hɪp] n Hüfte f.
hip flask n Taschenflasche f, Flachmann m (*inf*).

hip-hop ['hɪphɒp] n Hip-Hop nt.
hippie ['hɪpɪ] n Hippie m.
hippo ['hɪpəʊ] n Nilpferd nt.
hip pocket n Gesäßtasche f.
hippopotamus [hɪpə'pɒtəməs] (*pl* ~**es** *or* **hippopotami**) n Nilpferd nt.
hippy ['hɪpɪ] n = **hippie**.
hire ['haɪə*] vt (*BRIT*) mieten; (*worker*) einstellen ♦ n (*BRIT*) Mieten nt; **for ~** (*taxi*) frei; (*boat*) zu vermieten; **on ~** gemietet.
▶ **hire out** vt vermieten.
hire(d) car (*BRIT*) n Mietwagen m, Leihwagen m.
hire-purchase [haɪə'pɜːtʃɪs] (*BRIT*) n Ratenkauf m; **to buy sth on ~** etw auf Raten kaufen.
his [hɪz] pron seine(r, s) ♦ adj sein; *see also* **my**, **mine**[2].
hiss [hɪs] vi zischen; (*cat*) fauchen ♦ n Zischen nt; (*of cat*) Fauchen nt.
histogram ['hɪstəgræm] n Histogramm nt.
historian [hɪ'stɔːrɪən] n Historiker(in) m(f).
historic [hɪ'stɒrɪk] adj historisch.
historical [hɪ'stɒrɪkl] adj historisch.
history ['hɪstərɪ] n Geschichte f; **there's a ~ of heart disease in his family** Herzleiden liegen bei ihm in der Familie; **medical ~** Krankengeschichte f.
hit [hɪt] (*pt, pp* **hit**) vt schlagen; (*reach, affect*) treffen; (*vehicle: another vehicle*) zusammenstoßen mit; (: *wall, tree*) fahren gegen; (: *more violently*) prallen gegen; (: *person*) anfahren ♦ n Schlag m; (*success*) Erfolg m; (*song*) Hit m; **to ~ it off with sb** sich gut mit jdm verstehen; **to ~ the headlines** Schlagzeilen machen; **to ~ the road** (*inf*) sich auf den Weg *or* die Socken (*inf*) machen; **to ~ the roof** (*inf*) an die Decke *or* in die Luft gehen.
▶ **hit back** vi: **to ~ back at sb** jdn zurückschlagen; (*fig*) jdm Kontra geben.
▶ **hit out at** vt fus auf jdn losschlagen; (*fig*) jdn scharf angreifen.
▶ **hit (up)on** vt fus stoßen auf +acc, finden.
hit-and-miss ['hɪtən'mɪs] adj = **hit-or-miss**.
hit-and-run driver ['hɪtən'rʌn-] n unfallflüchtiger Fahrer m, unfallflüchtige Fahrerin f.
hitch [hɪtʃ] vt festmachen, anbinden; (*also:* ~ **up:** *trousers, skirt*) hochziehen ♦ n Schwierigkeit f, Problem nt; **to ~ a lift** trampen, per Anhalter fahren; **technical ~** technische Panne f.
▶ **hitch up** vt anspannen; *see also* **hitch**.
hitchhike ['hɪtʃhaɪk] vi trampen, per Anhalter fahren.
hitchhiker ['hɪtʃhaɪkə*] n Tramper(in) m(f), Anhalter(in) m(f).
hi-tech ['haɪ'tɛk] adj Hightech-, hoch technisiert ♦ n Hightech nt, Hochtechnologie f.

hitherto [hɪðə'tuː] *adv* bisher, bis jetzt.

hit list *n* Abschussliste *f*.

hit man (*inf*) *n* Killer *m*.

hit-or-miss ['hɪtə'mɪs] *adj* ungeplant; **to be a ~ affair** eine unsichere Sache sein; **it's ~ whether ...** es ist nicht zu sagen, ob ...

hit parade *n* Hitparade *f*.

HIV *n abbr* (= *human immunodeficiency virus*) HIV; **~-negative** HIV-negativ; **~-positive** HIV-positiv.

hive [haɪv] *n* Bienenkorb *m*; **to be a ~ of activity** einem Bienenhaus gleichen.
▶ **hive off** (*inf*) *vt* ausgliedern, abspalten.

hl *abbr* (= *hectolitre*) hl.

HM *abbr* (= *His/Her Majesty*) S./I.M.

HMG (*BRIT*) *abbr* (= *His/Her Majesty's Government*) die Regierung Seiner/Ihrer Majestät.

HMI (*BRIT*) *n abbr* (*SCOL*: = *His/Her Majesty's Inspector*) *regierungsamtlicher Schulaufsichtsbeauftragter*.

HMO (*US*) *n abbr* (= *health maintenance organization*) *Organisation zur Gesundheitsfürsorge*.

HMS (*BRIT*) *abbr* (= *His (or Her) Majesty's Ship*) *Namensteil von Schiffen der Kriegsmarine*.

HMSO (*BRIT*) *n abbr* (= *His (or Her) Majesty's Stationery Office*) *regierungsamtliche Druckerei*.

HNC (*BRIT*) *n abbr* (= *Higher National Certificate*) *Berufsschulabschluss*.

HND (*BRIT*) *n abbr* (= *Higher National Diploma*) *Qualifikationsnachweis in technischen Fächern*.

hoard [hɔːd] *n* (*of food*) Vorrat *m*; (*of money, treasure*) Schatz *m* ♦ *vt* (*food*) hamstern; (*money*) horten.

hoarding ['hɔːdɪŋ] (*BRIT*) *n* Plakatwand *f*.

hoarfrost ['hɔːfrɒst] *n* (Rau)reif *m*.

hoarse [hɔːs] *adj* heiser.

hoax [həʊks] *n* (*false alarm*) blinder Alarm *m*.

hob [hɒb] *n* Kochmulde *f*.

hobble ['hɒbl] *vi* humpeln.

hobby ['hɒbɪ] *n* Hobby *nt*, Steckenpferd *nt*.

hobbyhorse ['hɒbɪhɔːs] *n* (*fig*) Lieblingsthema *nt*.

hobnail boot ['hɒbneɪl-] *n* Nagelschuh *m*.

hobnob ['hɒbnɒb] *vi*: **to ~ with** auf Du und Du stehen mit.

hobo ['həʊbəʊ] (*US*) *n* Penner *m* (*inf*).

hock [hɒk] *n* (*BRIT*) weißer Rheinwein *m*; (*of animal*) Sprunggelenk *nt*; (*US*: *CULIN*) Gelenkstück *nt*; (*inf*): **to be in ~** (*person: in debt*) in Schulden stecken; (*object*) verpfändet *or* im Leihhaus sein.

hockey ['hɒkɪ] *n* Hockey *nt*.

hocus-pocus ['həʊkəs'pəʊkəs] *n* Hokuspokus *m*; (*trickery*) faule Tricks *pl*; (*jargon*) Jargon *m*.

hod [hɒd] *n* (*for bricks etc*) Tragemulde *f*.

hodgepodge ['hɒdʒpɒdʒ] (*US*) *n* = **hotchpotch**.

hoe [həʊ] *n* Hacke *f* ♦ *vt* hacken.

hog [hɒg] *n* (Mast)schwein *nt* ♦ *vt* (*road*) für sich beanspruchen; (*telephone etc*) in Beschlag nehmen; **to go the whole ~** Nägel mit Köpfen machen.

Hogmanay [hɒgmə'neɪ] (*SCOT*) *n* Silvester *nt*.

hogwash ['hɒgwɒʃ] (*inf*) *n* (*nonsense*) Quatsch *m*.

ho hum ['həʊ'hʌm] *interj* na gut.

hoist [hɔɪst] *n* Hebevorrichtung *f* ♦ *vt* hochheben; (*flag, sail*) hissen.

hoity-toity [hɔɪtɪ'tɔɪtɪ] (*inf*: *pej*) *adj* hochnäsig.

hold [həʊld] (*pt, pp* **held**) *vt* halten; (*contain*) enthalten; (*power, qualification*) haben; (*opinion*) vertreten; (*meeting*) abhalten; (*conversation*) führen; (*prisoner, hostage*) festhalten ♦ *vi* halten; (*be valid*) gelten; (*weather*) sich halten ♦ *n* (*grasp*) Griff *m*; (*of ship, plane*) Laderaum *m*; **to ~ one's head up** den Kopf hochhalten; **to ~ sb responsible/ liable** *etc* jdn verantwortlich/haftbar *etc* machen; **~ the line!** (*TEL*) bleiben Sie am Apparat!; **~ it!** Moment mal!; **to ~ one's own** sich behaupten; **he ~s the view that ...** er ist der Meinung *or* er vertritt die Ansicht, dass ...; **to ~ firm** *or* **fast** halten; **~ still!**, **~ steady!** stillhalten!; **his luck held** das Glück blieb ihm treu; **I don't ~ with ...** ich bin gegen ...; **to catch** *or* **get (a) ~ of** sich festhalten an +*dat*; **to get ~ of** (*fig*) finden, auftreiben; **to get ~ of o.s.** sich in den Griff bekommen; **to have a ~ over** in der Hand haben.
▶ **hold back** *vt* zurückhalten; (*tears, laughter*) unterdrücken; (*secret*) verbergen; (*information*) geheim halten.
▶ **hold down** *vt* niederhalten; (*job*) sich halten in +*dat*.
▶ **hold forth** *vi*: **to ~ forth (about)** sich ergehen *or* sich auslassen (über +*acc*).
▶ **hold off** *vt* abwehren ♦ *vi*: **if the rain ~s off** wenn es nicht regnet.
▶ **hold on** *vi* sich festhalten; (*wait*) warten; **~ on!** (*TEL*) einen Moment bitte!
▶ **hold on to** *vt fus* sich festhalten an; (*keep*) behalten.
▶ **hold out** *vt* (*hand*) ausstrecken; (*hope*) haben; (*prospect*) bieten ♦ *vi* nicht nachgeben.
▶ **hold over** *vt* vertagen.
▶ **hold up** *vt* hochheben; (*support*) stützen; (*delay*) aufhalten; (*rob*) überfallen.

holdall ['həʊldɔːl] (*BRIT*) *n* Tasche *f*; (*for clothes*) Reisetasche *f*.

holder ['həʊldə*] *n* Halter *m*; (*of ticket, record, office, title etc*) Inhaber(in) *m(f)*.

holding ['həʊldɪŋ] *n* (*share*) Anteil *m*; (*small farm*) Gut *nt* ♦ *adj* (*operation, tactic*) zur Schadensbegrenzung.

holding company *n* Dachgesellschaft *f*, Holdinggesellschaft *f*.

hold-up ['həʊldʌp] *n* bewaffneter

Raubüberfall *m*; (*delay*) Verzögerung *f*; (*BRIT: in traffic*) Stockung *f*.

hole [həul] *n* Loch *nt*; (*unpleasant town*) Kaff *nt* (*inf*) ♦ *vt* (*ship*) leck schlagen; (*building etc*) durchlöchern; ~ **in the heart** Loch im Herz(en); **to pick** ~**s** (*fig*) (über)kritisch sein; **to pick** ~**s in sth** (*fig*) an etw *dat* herumkritisieren.

▶ **hole up** *vi* sich verkriechen.

holiday ['hɒlɪdeɪ] *n* (*BRIT*) Urlaub *m*; (*SCOL*) Ferien *pl*; (*day off*) freier Tag *m*; (*public* ~) Feiertag *m*; **on** ~ im Urlaub, in den Ferien.

holiday camp (*BRIT*) *n* (*also:* **holiday centre**) Feriendorf *nt*.

holiday-maker ['hɒlɪdɪmeɪkə*] (*BRIT*) *n* Urlauber(in) *m(f)*.

holiday pay *n* Lohn-/Gehaltsfortzahlung *während des Urlaubs.*

holiday resort *n* Ferienort *m*.

holiday season *n* Urlaubszeit *f*.

holiness ['həulɪnɪs] *n* Heiligkeit *f*.

holistic [həu'lɪstɪk] *adj* holistisch.

Holland ['hɒlənd] *n* Holland *nt*.

holler ['hɒlə*] (*inf*) *vi* brüllen ♦ *n* Schrei *m*.

hollow ['hɒləu] *adj* hohl; (*eyes*) tief liegend; (*laugh*) unecht; (*sound*) dumpf; (*fig*) leer; (: *victory, opinion*) wertlos ♦ *n* Vertiefung *f* ♦ *vt*: **to** ~ **out** aushöhlen.

holly ['hɒlɪ] *n* Stechpalme *f*, Ilex *m*; (*leaves*) Stechpalmenzweige *pl*.

hollyhock ['hɒlɪhɒk] *n* Malve *f*.

holocaust ['hɒləkɔːst] *n* Inferno *nt*; (*in Third Reich*) Holocaust *m*.

hologram ['hɒləgræm] *n* Hologramm *nt*.

hols [hɒlz] (*inf*) *npl* Ferien *pl*.

holster ['həulstə*] *n* Pistolenhalfter *m or nt*.

holy ['həulɪ] *adj* heilig.

Holy Communion *n* heilige Kommunion *f*.

Holy Father *n* Heiliger Vater *m*.

Holy Ghost *n* Heiliger Geist *m*.

Holy Land *n*: **the** ~ das Heilige Land.

holy orders *npl* Priesterweihe *f*.

Holy Spirit *n* Heiliger Geist *m*.

homage ['hɒmɪdʒ] *n* Huldigung *f*; **to pay** ~ **to** huldigen +*dat*.

home [həum] *n* Heim *nt*; (*house, flat*) Zuhause *nt*; (*area, country*) Heimat *f*; (*institution*) Anstalt *f* ♦ *cpd* Heim-; (*ECON, POL*) Innen- ♦ *adv* (*go etc*) nach Hause, nachhause (*ÖSTERR, SCHWEIZ*), heim; **at** ~ zu Hause, zuhause (*ÖSTERR, SCHWEIZ*); (*in country*) im Inland; **to be** *or* **feel at** ~ (*fig*) sich wohl fühlen; **make yourself at** ~ machen Sie es sich *dat* gemütlich *or* bequem; **to make one's** ~ **somewhere** sich irgendwo niederlassen; **the** ~ **of free enterprise/jazz** *etc* die Heimat des freien Unternehmertums/Jazz *etc*; **when will you be** ~? wann bist du wieder zu Hause?; **a** ~ **from** ~ ein zweites Zuhause *nt*; ~ **and dry** aus dem Schneider; **to drive a nail** ~ einen Nagel einschlagen; **to bring sth** ~ **to sb** jdm etw klarmachen.

▶ **home in on** *vt fus* (*missiles*) sich ausrichten auf +*acc*.

home address *n* Heimatanschrift *f*.

home-brew [həum'bruː] *n* selbst gebrautes Bier *nt*.

homecoming ['həumkʌmɪŋ] *n* Heimkehr *f*.

home computer *n* Heimcomputer *m*.

Home Counties (*BRIT*) *npl*: **the** ~ die Grafschaften, die an London angrenzen.

home economics *n* Hauswirtschaft *f*.

home ground *n* (*SPORT*) eigener Platz *m*; **to be on** ~ (*fig*) sich auf vertrautem Terrain bewegen.

home-grown ['həumgrəun] *adj* (*not foreign*) einheimisch; (*from garden*) selbst gezogen.

home help *n* Haushaltshilfe *f*.

homeland ['həumlænd] *n* Heimat(land *nt*) *f*.

homeless ['həumlɪs] *adj* obdachlos; (*refugee*) heimatlos.

home loan *n* Hypothek *f*.

homely ['həumlɪ] *adj* einfach; (*US: plain*) unscheinbar.

home-made [həum'meɪd] *adj* selbst gemacht.

Home Office (*BRIT*) *n* Innenministerium *nt*.

homeopath ['həumɪəupæθ] (*US*) *n* = **homoeopath**.

homeopathy [həumɪ'ɒpəθɪ] (*US*) *n* = **homoeopathy**.

home page *n* (*COMPUT*) Homepage *f*.

home rule *n* Selbstbestimmung *f*, Selbstverwaltung *f*.

Home Secretary (*BRIT*) *n* Innenminister *m*.

homesick ['həumsɪk] *adj* heimwehkrank; **to be** ~ Heimweh haben.

homestead ['həumstɛd] *n* Heimstätte *f*; (*farm*) Gehöft *nt*.

home town *n* Heimatstadt *f*.

home truth *n* bittere Wahrheit *f*; **to tell sb some** ~**s** jdm deutlich der Meinung sagen.

homeward ['həumwəd] *adj* (*journey*) Heim- ♦ *adv* = **homewards**.

homewards ['həumwədz] *adv* nach Hause, nachhause (*ÖSTERR, SCHWEIZ*), heim.

homework ['həumwɔːk] *n* Hausaufgaben *pl*.

homicidal [hɒmɪ'saɪdl] *adj* gemeingefährlich.

homicide ['hɒmɪsaɪd] (*US*) *n* Mord *m*.

homily ['hɒmɪlɪ] *n* Predigt *f*.

homing ['həumɪŋ] *adj* (*device, missile*) mit Zielsucheinrichtung; ~ **pigeon** Brieftaube *f*.

homoeopath, (*US*) **homeopath** ['həumɪəupæθ] *n* Homöopath(in) *m(f)*.

homoeopathy, (*US*) **homeopathy** [həumɪ'ɒpəθɪ] *n* Homöopathie *f*.

homogeneous [hɒmə'dʒiːnɪəs] *adj* homogen.

homogenize [hə'mɒdʒənaɪz] *vt* homogenisieren.

homosexual [hɒməu'sɛksjuəl] *adj* homosexuell ♦ *n* Homosexuelle(r) *f(m)*.

Hon. *abbr* = **honourable**; **honorary**.

Honduras [hɒn'djuərəs] *n* Honduras *nt*.

hone [həun] *n* Schleifstein *m* ♦ *vt* schleifen; (*fig: groom*) erziehen.

honest ['ɔnɪst] *adj* ehrlich; (*trustworthy*) redlich; (*sincere*) aufrichtig; **to be quite ~ with you** ... um ehrlich zu sein, ...
honestly ['ɔnɪstlɪ] *adv* (*see adj*) ehrlich; redlich; aufrichtig.
honesty ['ɔnɪstɪ] *n* (*see adj*) Ehrlichkeit *f*; Redlichkeit *f*; Aufrichtigkeit *f*.
honey ['hʌnɪ] *n* Honig *m*; (*US: inf*) Schätzchen *nt*.
honeycomb ['hʌnɪkəum] *n* Bienenwabe *f*; (*pattern*) Wabe *f* ♦ *vt*: **to ~ with** durchlöchern mit.
honeymoon ['hʌnɪmuːn] *n* Flitterwochen *pl*; (*trip*) Hochzeitsreise *f*.
honeysuckle ['hʌnɪsʌkl] *n* Geißblatt *nt*.
Hong Kong ['hɔŋ'kɔŋ] *n* Hongkong *nt*.
honk [hɔŋk] *vi* (*AUT*) hupen.
Honolulu [hɔnə'luːluː] *n* Honolulu *nt*.
honor *etc* ['ɔnə*] (*US*) = **honour** *etc*.
honorary ['ɔnərərɪ] *adj* ehrenamtlich; (*title, degree*) Ehren-.
honour, (*US*) **honor** ['ɔnə*] *vt* ehren; (*commitment, promise*) stehen zu ♦ *n* Ehre *f*; (*tribute*) Auszeichnung *f*; **in ~ of** zu Ehren von *or +gen*.
honourable ['ɔnərəbl] *adj* (*person*) ehrenwert; (*action, defeat*) ehrenvoll.
honour-bound ['ɔnə'baund] *adj*: **to be ~ to do sth** moralisch verpflichtet sein, etw zu tun.
honours degree ['ɔnəz-] *n akademischer Grad mit Prüfung im Spezialfach.*

HONOURS DEGREE

Honours Degree *ist ein Universitätsabschluss mit einer guten Note, also der Note I (first class), II:1 (upper second class), II:2 (lower second class), oder III (third class). Wer ein **honours degree** erhalten hat, darf die Abkürzung **Hons** nach seinem Namen und Titel führen, z. B. Mary Smith MA Hons. Heute sind fast alle Universitätsabschlüsse in Großbritannien **honours degrees**. Siehe auch **ordinary degree**.*

---

honours list *n Liste verliehener/zu verleihender Ehrentitel.*

HONOURS LIST

Honours list *ist eine Liste von Adelstiteln und Orden, die der britische Monarch zweimal jährlich (zu Neujahr und am offiziellen Geburtstag des Monarchen) an Bürger in Großbritannien und im Commonwealth verleiht. Die Liste wird vom Premierminister zusammengestellt, aber drei Orden (der Hosenbandorden, der Verdienstorden und der Victoria-Orden) werden vom Monarchen persönlich vergeben. Erfolgreiche Geschäftsleute, Militärangehörige, Sportler und andere Prominente, aber auch im sozialen Bereich besonders aktive Bürger werden auf diese Weise geehrt.*

Hons. *abbr* (*UNIV*) = **honours degree**.
hood [hud] *n* (*of coat etc*) Kapuze *f*; (*of cooker*) Abzugshaube *f*; (*AUT: BRIT: folding roof*) Verdeck *nt*; (*: US: bonnet*) (Motor)haube *f*.
hooded ['hudɪd] *adj* maskiert; (*jacket etc*) mit Kapuze.
hoodlum ['huːdləm] *n* Gangster *m*.
hoodwink ['hudwɪŋk] *vt* (he)reinlegen.
hoof [huːf] (*pl* **hooves**) *n* Huf *m*.
hook [huk] *n* Haken *m* ♦ *vt* festhaken; (*fish*) an die Angel bekommen; **by ~ or by crook** auf Biegen und Brechen; **to be ~ed on** (*inf: film, exhibition, etc*) fasziniert sein von; (*: drugs*) abhängig sein von; (*: person*) stehen auf *+acc*.
▶ **hook up** *vt* (*RADIO, TV etc*) anschließen; **to ~ with sb** sich jdm anschließen.
hook and eye (*pl* **hooks and eyes**) *n* Haken und Öse *pl*.
hooligan ['huːlɪgən] *n* Rowdy *m*.
hooliganism ['huːlɪgənɪzəm] *n* Rowdytum *nt*.
hoop [huːp] *n* Reifen *m*; (*for croquet: arch*) Tor *nt*.
hooray [huː'reɪ] *excl* = **hurrah**.
hoot [huːt] *vi* hupen; (*siren*) heulen; (*owl*) schreien, rufen; (*person*) johlen ♦ *vt* (*horn*) drücken auf *+acc* ♦ *n* (*see vi*) Hupen *nt*; Heulen *nt*; Schreien *nt*, Rufen *nt*; Johlen *nt*; **to ~ with laughter** in johlendes Gelächter ausbrechen.
hooter ['huːtə*] *n* (*BRIT: AUT*) Hupe *f*; (*NAUT, factory*) Sirene *f*.
Hoover ® ['huːvə*] (*BRIT*) *n* Staubsauger *m* ♦ *vt* **hoover** (*carpet*) saugen.
hooves [huːvz] *npl of* **hoof**.
hop [hɔp] *vi* hüpfen ♦ *n* Hüpfer *m*; *see also* **hops**.
hope [həup] *vi* hoffen ♦ *n* Hoffnung *f* ♦ *vt*: **to ~ that** hoffen, dass; **I ~ so** ich hoffe es, hoffentlich; **I ~ not** ich hoffe nicht, hoffentlich nicht; **to ~ for the best** das Beste hoffen; **to have no ~ of sth/doing sth** keine Hoffnung auf etw *+acc* haben/darauf haben, etw zu tun; **in the ~ of/that** in der Hoffnung auf/, dass; **to ~ to do sth** hoffen, etw zu tun.
hopeful ['həupful] *adj* hoffnungsvoll; (*situation*) viel versprechend; **I'm ~ that she'll manage** ich hoffe, dass sie es schafft.
hopefully ['həupfulɪ] *adv* hoffnungsvoll; (*one hopes*) hoffentlich; **~, he'll come back** hoffentlich kommt er wieder.
hopeless ['həuplɪs] *adj* hoffnungslos; (*situation*) aussichtslos; (*useless*): **to be ~ at sth** etw überhaupt nicht können.
hopper ['hɔpə*] *n* Einfülltrichter *m*.
hops [hɔps] *npl* Hopfen *m*.
horde [hɔːd] *n* Horde *f*.
horizon [hə'raɪzn] *n* Horizont *m*.
horizontal [hɔrɪ'zɔntl] *adj* horizontal.
hormone ['hɔːməun] *n* Hormon *nt*.

hormone replacement therapy *n* Hormonersatztherapie *f*.

horn [hɔːn] *n* Horn *nt*; (*AUT*) Hupe *f*.

horned [hɔːnd] *adj* (*animal*) mit Hörnern.

hornet [ˈhɔːnɪt] *n* Hornisse *f*.

horn-rimmed [ˈhɔːnˈrɪmd] *adj* (*spectacles*) Horn-.

horny [ˈhɔːnɪ] (*inf*) *adj* (*aroused*) scharf, geil.

horoscope [ˈhɔrəskəup] *n* Horoskop *nt*.

horrendous [həˈrendəs] *adj* abscheulich, entsetzlich.

horrible [ˈhɔrɪbl] *adj* fürchterlich, schrecklich; (*scream, dream*) furchtbar.

horrid [ˈhɔrɪd] *adj* entsetzlich, schrecklich.

horrific [həˈrɪfɪk] *adj* entsetzlich, schrecklich.

horrify [ˈhɔrɪfaɪ] *vt* entsetzen.

horrifying [ˈhɔrɪfaɪɪŋ] *adj* schrecklich, fürchterlich, entsetzlich.

horror [ˈhɔrəˑ] *n* Entsetzen *nt*, Grauen *nt*; ~ (**of** sth) (*abhorrence*) Abscheu *m* (vor etw *dat*); **the ~s of war** die Schrecken *pl* des Krieges.

horror film *n* Horrorfilm *m*.

horror-stricken [ˈhɔrəstrɪkn] *adj* = **horror-struck**.

horror-struck [ˈhɔrəstrʌk] *adj* von Entsetzen *or* Grauen gepackt.

hors d'oeuvre [ɔːˈdɜːvrə] *n* Hors d'oeuvre *nt*, Vorspeise *f*.

horse [hɔːs] *n* Pferd *nt*.

horseback [ˈhɔːsbæk]: **on ~** *adj, adv* zu Pferd.

horsebox [ˈhɔːsbɔks] *n* Pferdetransporter *m*.

horse chestnut *n* Rosskastanie *f*.

horse-drawn [ˈhɔːsdrɔːn] *adj* von Pferden gezogen.

horsefly [ˈhɔːsflaɪ] *n* (Pferde)bremse *f*.

horseman [ˈhɔːsmən] (*irreg: like* **man**) *n* Reiter *m*.

horsemanship [ˈhɔːsmənʃɪp] *n* Reitkunst *f*.

horseplay [ˈhɔːspleɪ] *n* Alberei *f*, Balgerei *f*.

horsepower [ˈhɔːspauəˑ] *n* Pferdestärke *f*.

horse racing *n* Pferderennen *nt*.

horseradish [ˈhɔːsrædɪʃ] *n* Meerrettich *m*.

horseshoe [ˈhɔːsʃuː] *n* Hufeisen *nt*.

horse show *n* Reitturnier *nt*.

horse trading *n* Kuhhandel *m*.

horse trials *npl* = **horse show**.

horsewhip [ˈhɔːswɪp] *n* Reitpeitsche *f* ♦ *vt* auspeitschen.

horsewoman [ˈhɔːswumən] (*irreg: like* **woman**) *n* Reiterin *f*.

horsey [ˈhɔːsɪ] *adj* pferdenärrisch; (*appearance*) pferdeähnlich.

horticulture [ˈhɔːtɪkʌltʃəˑ] *n* Gartenbau *m*.

hose [həuz] *n* (*also*: ~ **pipe**) Schlauch *m*.

► **hose down** *vt* abspritzen.

hosiery [ˈhəuzɪərɪ] *n* Strumpfwaren *pl*.

hospice [ˈhɔspɪs] *n* Pflegeheim *nt* (*für unheilbar Kranke*).

hospitable [ˈhɔspɪtəbl] *adj* gastfreundlich; (*climate*) freundlich.

hospital [ˈhɔspɪtl] *n* Krankenhaus *nt*; **in ~**, (*US*) **in the ~** im Krankenhaus.

hospitality [hɔspɪˈtælɪtɪ] *n* Gastfreundschaft *f*.

hospitalize [ˈhɔspɪtəlaɪz] *vt* ins Krankenhaus einweisen.

host [həust] *n* Gastgeber *m*; (*REL*) Hostie *f* ♦ *adj* Gast- ♦ *vt* Gastgeber sein bei; **a ~ of** eine Menge.

hostage [ˈhɔstɪdʒ] *n* Geisel *f*; **to be taken/held ~** als Geisel genommen/festgehalten werden.

hostel [ˈhɔstl] *n* (Wohn)heim *nt*; (*also*: **youth ~**) Jugendherberge *f*.

hostelling [ˈhɔstlɪŋ] *n*: **to go (youth) ~** in Jugendherbergen übernachten.

hostess [ˈhəustɪs] *n* Gastgeberin *f*; (*BRIT*: **air hostess**) Stewardess *f*; (*in night-club*) Hostess *f*.

hostile [ˈhɔstaɪl] *adj* (*conditions*) ungünstig; (*environment*) unwirtlich; (*person*): ~ (**to** *or* **towards**) feindselig (gegenüber *+dat*).

hostility [hɔˈstɪlɪtɪ] *n* Feindseligkeit *f*; **hostilities** *npl* (*fighting*) Feindseligkeiten *pl*.

hot [hɔt] *adj* heiß; (*moderately hot*) warm; (*spicy*) scharf; (*temper*) hitzig; **I am** *or* **feel ~** mir ist heiß; **to be ~ on sth** (*knowledgeable etc*) sich gut mit etw auskennen; (*strict*) sehr auf etw *acc* achten.

► **hot up** (*BRIT*: *inf*) *vi* (*situation*) sich verschärfen *or* zuspitzen; (*party*) in Schwung kommen ♦ *vt* (*pace*) steigern; (*engine*) frisieren.

hot air *n* leeres Gerede *nt*.

hot-air balloon [hɔtˈɛəˑ-] *n* Heißluftballon *m*.

hotbed [ˈhɔtbed] *n* (*fig*) Brutstätte *f*.

hot-blooded [hɔtˈblʌdɪd] *adj* heißblütig.

hotchpotch [ˈhɔtʃpɔtʃ] (*BRIT*) *n* Durcheinander *nt*, Mischmasch *m*.

hot dog *n* Hotdog *m or nt*, Hot Dog *m or nt*.

hotel [həuˈtɛl] *n* Hotel *nt*.

hotelier [həuˈtɛlɪəˑ] *n* Hotelier(in) *m(f)*.

hotel industry *n* Hotelgewerbe *nt*.

hotel room *n* Hotelzimmer *nt*.

hot flash (*US*) *n* = **hot flush**.

hot flush *n* (*MED*) Hitzewallung *f*.

hotfoot [ˈhɔtfut] *adv* eilends.

hothead [ˈhɔthed] *n* Hitzkopf *m*.

hot-headed [hɔtˈhedɪd] *adj* hitzköpfig.

hothouse [ˈhɔthaus] *n* Treibhaus *nt*.

hot line *n* (*POL*) heißer Draht *m*.

hotly [ˈhɔtlɪ] *adv* (*contest*) heiß; (*speak, deny*) heftig.

hotplate [ˈhɔtpleɪt] *n* Kochplatte *f*.

hotpot [ˈhɔtpɔt] (*BRIT*) *n* Fleischeintopf *m*.

hot potato (*fig*: *inf*) *n* heißes Eisen *nt*; **to drop sb like a ~** jdn wie eine heiße Kartoffel fallen lassen.

hot seat *n*: **to be in the ~** auf dem Schleudersitz sitzen.

hot spot *n* (*fig*) Krisenherd *m*.

hot spring *n* heiße Quelle *f*, Thermalquelle *f*.

hot stuff *n* große Klasse *f*.

hot-tempered [hɔtˈtempəd] *adj* leicht

aufbrausend, jähzornig.

hot-water bottle [hɔt'wɔːtəˣ-] n Wärmflasche f.

hot-wire (inf) vt (car) kurzschließen.

hound [haund] vt hetzen, jagen ♦ n Jagdhund m; **the** ~**s** die Meute.

hour ['auəˣ] n Stunde f; (time) Zeit f; **at 60 miles an** ~ mit 60 Meilen in der Stunde; **lunch** ~ Mittagspause f; **to pay sb by the** ~ jdn stundenweise bezahlen.

hourly ['auəlɪ] adj stündlich; (rate) Stunden- ♦ adv stündlich; (soon) jederzeit.

house [haus] n Haus nt; (household) Haushalt m; (dynasty) Geschlecht nt, Haus nt; (THEAT: performance) Vorstellung f ♦ vt unterbringen; **at my** ~ bei mir (zu Hause); **to my** ~ zu mir (nach Hause); **on the** ~ (fig) auf Kosten des Hauses; **the H**~ (**of Commons**) (BRIT) das Unterhaus; **the H**~ (**of Lords**) (BRIT) das Oberhaus; **the H**~ (**of Representatives**) (US) das Repräsentantenhaus.

house arrest n Hausarrest m.

houseboat ['hausbəut] n Hausboot nt.

housebound ['hausbaund] adj ans Haus gefesselt.

housebreaking ['hausbreɪkɪŋ] n Einbruch m.

house-broken ['hausbrəukn] (US) adj = house-trained.

housecoat ['hauskəut] n Morgenrock m.

household ['haushəuld] n Haushalt m; **to be a** ~ **name** ein Begriff sein.

householder ['haushəuldəˣ] n Hausinhaber(in) m(f); (of flat) Wohnungsinhaber(in) m(f).

house-hunting ['haushʌntɪŋ] n: **to go** ~ nach einem Haus suchen.

housekeeper ['hauskiːpəˣ] n Haushälterin f.

housekeeping ['hauskiːpɪŋ] n Hauswirtschaft f; (money) Haushaltsgeld nt.

houseman ['hausmən] (BRIT: irreg like man) n (MED) Assistenzarzt m, Assistenzärztin f.

house owner n Hausbesitzer(in) m(f).

house party n mehrtägige Einladung f; (people) Gesellschaft f.

house plant n Zimmerpflanze f.

house-proud ['hauspraud] adj auf Ordnung und Sauberkeit im Haushalt bedacht.

house-to-house ['haustə'haus] adj von Haus zu Haus.

house-trained ['haustreɪnd] (BRIT) adj (animal) stubenrein.

house-warming (party) ['hauswɔːmɪŋ-] n Einzugsparty f.

housewife ['hauswaɪf] n Hausfrau f.

housework ['hauswɜːk] n Hausarbeit f.

housing ['hauzɪŋ] n Wohnungen pl; (provision) Wohnungsbeschaffung f ♦ cpd Wohnungs-.

housing association n Wohnungsbaugesellschaft f.

housing benefit n ≈ Wohngeld nt.

housing conditions npl Wohnbedingungen pl, Wohnverhältnisse pl.

housing development n (Wohn)siedlung f.

housing estate n (Wohn)siedlung f.

hovel ['hɔvl] n (armselige) Hütte f.

hover ['hɔvəˣ] vi schweben; (person) herumstehen; **to** ~ **round sb** jdm nicht von der Seite weichen.

hovercraft ['hɔvəkrɑːft] n Hovercraft nt, Luftkissenfahrzeug nt.

hoverport ['hɔvəpɔːt] n Anlegestelle f für Hovercrafts.

=========== KEYWORD

how [hau] adv **1** (in what way) wie; ~ **was the film?** wie war der Film?; ~ **is school?** was macht die Schule?; ~ **are you?** wie geht es Ihnen?; ~**'s life?** wie gehts?; ~ **come?** (inf) wieso (denn das)?

2 (to what degree): ~ **much milk?** wie viel Milch?; ~ **many people?** wie viele Leute?; ~ **long have you been here?** wie lange sind Sie schon hier?; ~ **old are you?** wie alt bist du?; ~ **lovely/awful!** wie schön/furchtbar!; ~ **nice!** wie nett!

however [hau'ɛvəˣ] conj jedoch, aber ♦ adv wie ... auch; (in questions) wie ... bloß or nur.

howl [haul] vi heulen; (animal) jaulen; (baby, person) schreien ♦ n (see vb) Heulen nt;

Jaulen *nt*; Schreien *nt*.
howler ['haulǝ'] (*inf*) *n* (*mistake*) Schnitzer *m*.
howling ['haulɪŋ] *adj* (*wind, gale*) heulend.
HP (*BRIT*) *n abbr* = **hire-purchase**.
h.p. *abbr* (*AUT*: = *horsepower*) PS.
HQ *abbr* = **headquarters**.
HR (*US*) *n abbr* (*POL*: = *House of Representatives*) Repräsentantenhaus *nt*.
hr *abbr* (= *hour*) Std.
HRH (*BRIT*) *abbr* (= *His/Her Royal Highness*) Seine/Ihre Königliche Hoheit.
hrs *abbr* (= *hours*) Std.
HST (*US*) *abbr* (= *Hawaiian Standard Time*) *Normalzeit in Hawaii*.
HTML (*COMPUT*) *abbr* (= *hypertext markup language*) HTML *f*.
hub [hʌb] *n* (Rad)nabe *f*; (*fig: centre*) Mittelpunkt *m*, Zentrum *nt*.
hubbub ['hʌbʌb] *n* Lärm *m*; (*commotion*) Tumult *m*.
hubcap ['hʌbkæp] *n* Radkappe *f*.
HUD (*US*) *n abbr* (= *Department of Housing and Urban Development*) *Ministerium für Wohnungsbau und Stadtentwicklung*.
huddle ['hʌdl] *vi*: **to ~ together** sich zusammendrängen ♦ *n*: **in a ~** dicht zusammengedrängt.
hue [hju:] *n* Farbton *m*.
hue and cry *n* großes Geschrei *nt*.
huff [hʌf] *n*: **in a ~** beleidigt, eingeschnappt ♦ *vi*: **to ~ and puff** sich aufregen.
huffy ['hʌfɪ] (*inf*) *adj* beleidigt.
hug [hʌg] *vt* umarmen; (*thing*) umklammern ♦ *n* Umarmung *f*; **to give sb a ~** jdn umarmen.
huge [hju:dʒ] *adj* riesig.
hugely ['hju:dʒlɪ] *adv* ungeheuer.
hulk [hʌlk] *n* (*wrecked ship*) Wrack *nt*; (*person, building etc*) Klotz *m*.
hulking ['hʌlkɪŋ] *adj*: **~ great** massig.
hull [hʌl] *n* Schiffsrumpf *m*; (*of nuts*) Schale *f*; (*of fruit*) Blättchen *nt* ♦ *vt* (*fruit*) entstielen.
hullaballoo [hʌləbə'lu:] (*inf*) *n* Spektakel *m*.
hullo [hə'ləu] *excl* = **hello**.
hum [hʌm] *vt* summen ♦ *vi* summen; (*machine*) brummen ♦ *n* Summen *nt*; (*of traffic*) Brausen *nt*; (*of machines*) Brummen *nt*; (*of voices*) Gemurmel *nt*.
human ['hju:mən] *adj* menschlich ♦ *n* (*also*: ~ **being**) Mensch *m*.
humane [hju:'meɪn] *adj* human.
humanism ['hju:mənɪzəm] *n* Humanismus *m*.
humanitarian [hju:mænɪ'tɛərɪən] *adj* humanitär.
humanity [hju:'mænɪtɪ] *n* Menschlichkeit *f*; (*mankind*) Menschheit *f*; (*humaneness*) Humanität *f*; **humanities** *npl* (*SCOL*): **the humanities** die Geisteswissenschaften *pl*.
humanly ['hju:mənlɪ] *adv* menschlich; **if (at all) ~ possible** wenn es irgend möglich ist.
humanoid ['hju:mənɔɪd] *adj* menschenähnlich ♦ *n* menschenähnliches Wesen *nt*.

human rights *npl* Menschenrechte *pl*.
humble ['hʌmbl] *adj* bescheiden ♦ *vt* demütigen.
humbly ['hʌmblɪ] *adv* bescheiden.
humbug ['hʌmbʌg] *n* Humbug *m*, Mumpitz *m*; (*BRIT: sweet*) Pfefferminzbonbon *m or nt*.
humdrum ['hʌmdrʌm] *adj* eintönig, langweilig.
humid ['hju:mɪd] *adj* feucht.
humidifier [hju:'mɪdɪfaɪə'] *n* Luftbefeuchter *m*.
humidity [hju:'mɪdɪtɪ] *n* Feuchtigkeit *f*.
humiliate [hju:'mɪlɪeɪt] *vt* demütigen.
humiliating [hju:'mɪlɪeɪtɪŋ] *adj* demütigend.
humiliation [hju:mɪlɪ'eɪʃən] *n* Demütigung *f*.
humility [hju:'mɪlɪtɪ] *n* Bescheidenheit *f*.
humor *etc* (*US*) = **humour** *etc*.
humorist ['hju:mərɪst] *n* Humorist(in) *m(f)*.
humorous ['hju:mərəs] *adj* (*remark*) witzig; (*book*) lustig; (*person*) humorvoll.
humour, (*US*) **humor** ['hju:mə'] *n* Humor *m*; (*mood*) Stimmung *f* ♦ *vt* seinen Willen lassen +*dat*; **sense of ~** (Sinn *m* für) Humor; **to be in good/bad ~** gute/schlechte Laune haben.
humourless ['hju:mələs] *adj* humorlos.
hump [hʌmp] *n* Hügel *m*; (*of camel*) Höcker *m*; (*deformity*) Buckel *m*.
humpbacked ['hʌmpbækt] *adj*: **~ bridge** gewölbte Brücke *f*.
humus ['hju:məs] *n* Humus *m*.
hunch [hʌntʃ] *n* Gefühl *nt*, Ahnung *f*; **I have a ~ that ...** ich habe den (leisen) Verdacht, dass ...
hunchback ['hʌntʃbæk] *n* Bucklige(r) *f(m)*.
hunched [hʌntʃt] *adj* gebeugt; (*shoulders*) hochgezogen; (*back*) krumm.
hundred ['hʌndrəd] *num* hundert; **a or one ~ books/people/dollars** (ein)hundert Bücher/Personen/Dollar; **~s of** hunderte *or* Hunderte von; **I'm a ~ per cent sure** ich bin absolut sicher.
hundredth ['hʌndrədθ] *num* hundertste(r, s).
hundredweight ['hʌndrɪdweɪt] *n Gewichtseinheit* (*BRIT* = 50,8 *kg*; *US* = 45,3 *kg*), ≈ Zentner *m*.
hung [hʌŋ] *pt, pp of* **hang**.
Hungarian [hʌŋ'gɛərɪən] *adj* ungarisch ♦ *n* Ungar(in) *m(f)*; (*LING*) Ungarisch *nt*.
Hungary ['hʌŋgərɪ] *n* Ungarn *nt*.
hunger ['hʌŋgə'] *n* Hunger *m* ♦ *vi*: **to ~ for** hungern nach.
hunger strike *n* Hungerstreik *m*.
hung over (*inf*) *adj* verkatert.
hungrily ['hʌŋgrəlɪ] *adv* hungrig.
hungry ['hʌŋgrɪ] *adj* hungrig; **to be ~** Hunger haben; **to be ~ for** hungern nach; (*news*) sehnsüchtig warten auf; **to go ~** hungern.
hung up (*inf*) *adj*: **to be ~ on** (*person*) ein gestörtes Verhältnis haben zu; **to be ~ about** nervös sein wegen.
hunk [hʌŋk] *n* großes Stück *nt*; (*inf: man*) (großer, gut aussehender) Mann *m*.

hunt [hʌnt] vt jagen; (criminal, fugitive)
fahnden nach ♦ vi (SPORT) jagen ♦ n (see vb)
Jagd f; Fahndung f; (search) Suche f; **to ~ for**
(search) suchen (nach).
▶ **hunt down** vt Jagd machen auf +acc.
hunter ['hʌntə'] n Jäger(in) m(f).
hunting ['hʌntɪŋ] n Jagd f, Jagen nt.
hurdle ['hə:dl] n Hürde f.
hurl [hə:l] vt schleudern; **to ~ sth at sb** (also
fig) jdm etw entgegenschleudern.
hurling ['hə:lɪŋ] n (SPORT) Hurling nt, irische
Hockeyart.
hurly-burly ['hə:lɪ'bə:lɪ] n Rummel m.
hurrah [huˈrɑ:] n Hurra nt ♦ excl hurra.
hurray [huˈreɪ] n = hurrah.
hurricane ['hʌrɪkən] n Orkan m.
hurried ['hʌrɪd] adj eilig; (departure)
überstürzt.
hurriedly ['hʌrɪdlɪ] adv eilig.
hurry ['hʌrɪ] n Eile f ♦ vi eilen; (to do sth) sich
beeilen ♦ vt (zur Eile) antreiben; (work)
beschleunigen; **to be in a ~** es eilig haben;
to do sth in a ~ etw schnell tun; **there's no**
~ es eilt nicht; **what's the ~?** warum so
eilig?; **they hurried to help him** sie eilten
ihm zu Hilfe; **to ~ home** nach Hause eilen.
▶ **hurry along** vi sich beeilen.
▶ **hurry away** vi schnell weggehen,
forteilen.
▶ **hurry off** vi = hurry away.
▶ **hurry up** vt (zur Eile) antreiben ♦ vi sich
beeilen.
hurt [hə:t] (pt, pp **hurt**) vt wehtun +dat; (injure,
fig) verletzen ♦ vi weh tun ♦ adj verletzt; **I've**
~ my arm ich habe mir am Arm wehgetan;
(injured) ich habe mir den Arm verletzt;
where does it ~? wo tut es weh?
hurtful ['hə:tful] adj verletzend.
hurtle ['hə:tl] vi: **to ~ past** vorbeisausen; **to**
~ down (fall) hinunterfallen.
husband ['hʌzbənd] n (Ehe)mann m.
hush [hʌʃ] n Stille f ♦ vt zum Schweigen
bringen; **~!** pst!
▶ **hush up** vt vertuschen.
hushed [hʌʃt] adj still; (voice) gedämpft.
hush-hush [hʌʃ'hʌʃ] (inf) adj streng geheim.
husk [hʌsk] n Schale f; (of wheat) Spelze f; (of
maize) Hüllblatt nt.
husky ['hʌskɪ] adj (voice) rau ♦ n
Schlittenhund m.
hustings ['hʌstɪŋz] (BRIT) npl (POL)
Wahlkampf m.
hustle ['hʌsl] vt drängen ♦ n: **~ and bustle**
Geschäftigkeit f.
hut [hʌt] n Hütte f.
hutch [hʌtʃ] n (Kaninchen)stall m.
hyacinth ['haɪəsɪnθ] n Hyazinthe f.
hybrid ['haɪbrɪd] n (plant, animal) Kreuzung f;
(mixture) Mischung f ♦ adj Misch-.
hydrant ['haɪdrənt] n (also: **fire ~**) Hydrant m.
hydraulic [haɪ'drɔ:lɪk] adj hydraulisch.
hydraulics [haɪ'drɔ:lɪks] n Hydraulik f.

hydrochloric acid ['haɪdrəu'klɔrɪk-] n
Salzsäure f.
hydroelectric ['haɪdrəuɪ'lektrɪk] adj
hydroelektrisch.
hydrofoil ['haɪdrəfɔɪl] n Tragflächenboot nt,
Tragflügelboot nt.
hydrogen ['haɪdrədʒən] n Wasserstoff m.
hydrogen bomb n Wasserstoffbombe f.
hydrophobia ['haɪdrə'fəubɪə] n Hydrophobie
f, Wasserscheu f.
hydroplane ['haɪdrəpleɪn] n Gleitboot nt;
(plane) Wasserflugzeug nt ♦ vi (boat)
abheben.
hyena [haɪ'i:nə] n Hyäne f.
hygiene ['haɪdʒi:n] n Hygiene f.
hygienic [haɪ'dʒi:nɪk] adj hygienisch.
hymn [hɪm] n Kirchenlied nt.
hype [haɪp] (inf) n Rummel m.
hyperactive ['haɪpər'æktɪv] adj überaktiv.
hyperinflation ['haɪpərɪn'fleɪʃən] n
galoppierende Inflation f.
hypermarket ['haɪpəmɑ:kɪt] (BRIT) n
Verbrauchermarkt m.
hypertension ['haɪpə'tɛnʃən] n Hypertonie f,
Bluthochdruck m.
hypertext ['haɪpətɛkst] n (COMPUT)
Hypertext m.
hyphen ['haɪfn] n Bindestrich m; (at end of
line) Trennungsstrich m.
hyphenated ['haɪfəneɪtɪd] adj mit Bindestrich
(geschrieben).
hypnosis [hɪp'nəusɪs] n Hypnose f.
hypnotic [hɪp'nɔtɪk] adj hypnotisierend;
(trance) hypnotisch.
hypnotism ['hɪpnətɪzəm] n Hypnotismus m.
hypnotist ['hɪpnətɪst] n Hypnotiseur m,
Hypnotiseuse f.
hypnotize ['hɪpnətaɪz] vt hypnotisieren.
hypoallergenic ['haɪpəuælə'dʒɛnɪk] adj für
äußerst empfindliche Haut.
hypochondriac [haɪpə'kɔndrɪæk] n
Hypochonder m.
hypocrisy [hɪ'pɔkrɪsɪ] n Heuchelei f.
hypocrite ['hɪpəkrɪt] n Heuchler(in) m(f).
hypocritical [hɪpə'krɪtɪkl] adj heuchlerisch.
hypodermic [haɪpə'də:mɪk] adj (injection)
subkutan ♦ n (Injektions)spritze f.
hypotenuse [haɪ'pɔtɪnju:z] n Hypotenuse f.
hypothermia [haɪpə'θə:mɪə] n Unterkühlung
f.
hypothesis [haɪ'pɔθɪsɪs] (pl **hypotheses**) n
Hypothese f.
hypothesize [haɪ'pɔθɪsaɪz] vi Hypothesen
aufstellen ♦ vt annehmen.
hypothetic(al) [haɪpəu'θɛtɪk(l)] adj
hypothetisch.
hysterectomy [hɪstə'rɛktəmɪ] n
Hysterektomie f.
hysteria [hɪ'stɪərɪə] n Hysterie f.
hysterical [hɪ'stɛrɪkl] adj hysterisch;
(situation) wahnsinnig komisch; **to become**
~ hysterisch werden.

hysterically [hɪˈstɛrɪklɪ] *adv* hysterisch;
~ **funny** wahnsinnig komisch.
hysterics [hɪˈstɛrɪks] *npl*: **to be in** *or* **to have** ~
einen hysterischen Anfall haben; (*laughter*)
einen Lachanfall haben.
Hz *abbr* (= *hertz*) Hz.

I, i

I¹, i [aɪ] *n* (*letter*) I *nt*, i *nt*; ~ **for Isaac,** *(US)* ~ **for**
Item ≈ I wie Ida.
I² [aɪ] *pron* ich.
I. *abbr* = **island; isle.**
IA (*US*) *abbr* (*POST*: = *Iowa*).
IAEA *n abbr* = **International Atomic Energy**
Agency.
ib *abbr* (= *ibidem*) ib(id).
Iberian [aɪˈbɪərɪən] *adj*: **the** ~ **Peninsula** die
Iberische Halbinsel.
ibid *abbr* (= *ibidem*) ib(id).
i/c (*BRIT*) *abbr* (= *in charge (of)*) *see* **charge.**
ICBM *n abbr* (= *intercontinental ballistic missile*)
Interkontinentalrakete *f*.
ICC *n abbr* = **International Chamber of**
Commerce; (*US*: = *Interstate Commerce*
Commission) *Kommission zur Regelung des*
Warenverkehrs zwischen den US-
Bundesstaaten.
ice [aɪs] *n* Eis *nt*; (*on road*) Glatteis *nt* ♦ *vt* (*cake*)
mit Zuckerguss überziehen, glasieren ♦ *vi*
(*also*: ~ **over,** ~ **up**) vereisen; (*puddle etc*)
zufrieren; **to put sth on** ~ (*fig*) etw auf Eis
legen.
Ice Age *n* Eiszeit *f*.
ice axe *n* Eispickel *m*.
iceberg [ˈaɪsbəːg] *n* Eisberg *m*; **the tip of the** ~
(*fig*) die Spitze des Eisbergs.
icebox [ˈaɪsbɔks] *n* (*US: fridge*) Kühlschrank *m*;
(*BRIT: compartment*) Eisfach *nt*; (*insulated*
box) Kühltasche *f*.
icebreaker [ˈaɪsbreɪkə*] *n* Eisbrecher *m*.
ice bucket *n* Eiskühler *m*.
icecap [ˈaɪskæp] *n* Eisdecke *f*; (*polar*) Eiskappe
f.
ice-cold [ˈaɪsˈkəʊld] *adj* eiskalt.
ice cream *n* Eis *nt*.
ice-cream soda [ˈaɪskriːm-] *n* Eisbecher mit
Sirup und Sodawasser.
ice cube *n* Eiswürfel *m*.
iced [aɪst] *adj* (*cake*) mit Zuckerguss
überzogen, glasiert; (*beer etc*) eisgekühlt;
(*tea, coffee*) Eis-.
ice hockey *n* Eishockey *nt*.
Iceland [ˈaɪslənd] *n* Island *nt*.
Icelander [ˈaɪsləndə*] *n* Isländer(in) *m(f)*.

Icelandic [aɪsˈlændɪk] *adj* isländisch ♦ *n* (*LING*)
Isländisch *nt*.
ice lolly (*BRIT*) *n* Eis *nt* am Stiel.
ice pick *n* Eispickel *m*.
ice rink *n* (Kunst)eisbahn *f*, Schlittschuhbahn
f.
ice skate *n* Schlittschuh *m*.
ice-skate [ˈaɪsskeɪt] *vi* Schlittschuh laufen.
ice-skating [ˈaɪsskeɪtɪŋ] *n* Eislauf *m*,
Schlittschuhlaufen *nt*.
icicle [ˈaɪsɪkl] *n* Eiszapfen *m*.
icing [ˈaɪsɪŋ] *n* (*CULIN*) Zuckerguss *m*; (*AVIAT*
etc) Vereisung *f*.
icing sugar (*BRIT*) *n* Puderzucker *m*.
ICJ *n abbr* = **International Court of Justice.**
icon [ˈaɪkɔn] *n* Ikone *f*; (*COMPUT*) Ikon *nt*.
ICR (*US*) *n abbr* (= *Institute for Cancer Research*)
Krebsforschungsinstitut.
ICRC *n abbr* (= *International Committee of the*
Red Cross) IKRK *nt*.
ICT (*BRIT*) *n abbr* (*SCOL*) = *information and*
communication(s) technology.
ICU *n abbr* (*MED*) = **intensive care unit.**
icy [ˈaɪsɪ] *adj* eisig; (*road*) vereist.
ID, Ida. (*US*) *abbr* (*POST*: = *Idaho*).
I'd [aɪd] = **I would;** = **I had.**
ID card *n* = **identity card.**
IDD (*BRIT*) *n abbr* (*TEL*: = *international direct*
dialling) *Selbstwählferndienst ins Ausland.*
idea [aɪˈdɪə] *n* Idee *f*; (*opinion*) Ansicht *f*;
(*notion*) Vorstellung *f*; (*objective*) Ziel *nt*;
good ~! gute Idee!; **to have a good** ~ **that**
sich *dat* ziemlich sicher sein, dass; **I haven't**
the least ~ ich habe nicht die leiseste
Ahnung.
ideal [aɪˈdɪəl] *n* Ideal *nt* ♦ *adj* ideal.
idealist [aɪˈdɪəlɪst] *n* Idealist(in) *m(f)*.
ideally [aɪˈdɪəlɪ] *adv* ideal; ~ **the book should**
... idealerweise *or* im Idealfall sollte das
Buch ...; **she's** ~ **suited for** ... sie eignet sich
hervorragend für ...
identical [aɪˈdɛntɪkl] *adj* identisch; (*twins*)
eineiig.
identification [aɪdɛntɪfɪˈkeɪʃən] *n*
Identifizierung *f*; (*means of*) ~
Ausweispapiere *pl*.
identify [aɪˈdɛntɪfaɪ] *vt* (*recognize*) erkennen;
(*distinguish*) identifizieren; **to** ~ **sb/sth with**
jdn/etw identifizieren mit.
Identikit ® [aɪˈdɛntɪkɪt] *n*: ~ (**picture**)
Phantombild *nt*.
identity [aɪˈdɛntɪtɪ] *n* Identität *f*.
identity card *n* (Personal)ausweis *m*.
identity papers *npl* Ausweispapiere *pl*.
identity parade (*BRIT*) *n* Gegenüberstellung
f.
ideological [aɪdɪəˈlɔdʒɪkl] *adj* ideologisch,
weltanschaulich.
ideology [aɪdɪˈɔlədʒɪ] *n* Ideologie *f*,
Weltanschauung *f*.
idiocy [ˈɪdɪəsɪ] *n* Idiotie *f*, Dummheit *f*.
idiom [ˈɪdɪəm] *n* (*style*) Ausdrucksweise *f*;

(*phrase*) Redewendung *f*.
idiomatic [ɪdɪə'mætɪk] *adj* idiomatisch.
idiosyncrasy [ɪdɪəu'sɪŋkrəsɪ] *n* Eigenheit *f*, Eigenart *f*.
idiosyncratic [ɪdɪəusɪŋ'krætɪk] *adj* eigenartig; (*way, method, style*) eigen.
idiot ['ɪdɪət] *n* Idiot(in) *m(f)*, Dummkopf *m*.
idiotic [ɪdɪ'ɔtɪk] *adj* idiotisch, blöd(sinnig).
idle ['aɪdl] *adj* untätig; (*lazy*) faul; (*unemployed*) unbeschäftigt; (*machinery, factory*) stillstehend; (*question*) müßig; (*conversation, pleasure*) leer ♦ *vi* leer laufen, im Leerlauf sein; **to lie ~** (*machinery*) außer Betrieb sein; (*factory*) die Arbeit eingestellt haben.
▶ **idle away** *vt* (*time*) vertrödeln, verbummeln.
idleness ['aɪdlnɪs] *n* Untätigkeit *f*, (*laziness*) Faulheit *f*.
idler ['aɪdlə*] *n* Faulenzer(in) *m(f)*.
idle time *n* (*COMM*) Leerlaufzeit *f*.
idly ['aɪdlɪ] *adv* untätig; (*glance*) abwesend.
idol ['aɪdl] *n* Idol *nt*; (*REL*) Götzenbild *nt*.
idolize ['aɪdəlaɪz] *vt* vergöttern.
idyllic [ɪ'dɪlɪk] *adj* idyllisch.
i.e. *abbr* (= *id est*) d. h.

================= *KEYWORD* =================

if [ɪf] *conj* **1** (*given that, providing that etc*) wenn, falls; **~ anyone comes in** wenn *or* falls jemand hereinkommt; **~ necessary** wenn *or* falls nötig; **~ I were you** wenn ich Sie wäre, an Ihrer Stelle.
2 (*whenever*) wenn.
3 (*although*): **(even) ~** auch *or* selbst wenn; **I like it, (even) ~ you don't** mir gefällt es, auch wenn du es nicht magst.
4 (*whether*) ob; **ask him ~ he can come** frag ihn, ob er kommen kann.
5: **~ so/not** falls ja/nein; **~ only** wenn nur; *see also* **as**.

iffy ['ɪfɪ] (*inf*) *adj* (*uncertain*) unsicher; (*plan, proposal*) fragwürdig; **he was a bit ~ about it** er hat sich sehr vage ausgedrückt.
igloo ['ɪglu:] *n* Iglu *m or nt*.
ignite [ɪg'naɪt] *vt* entzünden ♦ *vi* sich entzünden.
ignition [ɪg'nɪʃən] *n* (*AUT*) Zündung *f*.
ignition key *n* (*AUT*) Zündschlüssel *m*.
ignoble [ɪg'nəubl] *adj* schändlich, unehrenhaft.
ignominious [ɪgnə'mɪnɪəs] *adj* schmachvoll.
ignoramus [ɪgnə'reɪməs] *n* Ignorant(in) *m(f)*.
ignorance ['ɪgnərəns] *n* Unwissenheit *f*, Ignoranz *f*; **to keep sb in ~ of sth** jdn in Unkenntnis über etw *acc* lassen.
ignorant ['ɪgnərənt] *adj* unwissend, ignorant; **to be ~ of** (*subject*) sich nicht auskennen in *+dat*; (*events*) nicht informiert sein über *+acc*.
ignore [ɪg'nɔ:*] *vt* ignorieren; (*fact*) außer Acht lassen.
ikon ['aɪkɔn] *n* = **icon**.

IL (*US*) *abbr* (*POST*: = *Illinois*).
ILA (*US*) *n abbr* (= *International Longshoremen's Association*) Hafenarbeitergewerkschaft.
I'll [aɪl] = **I will**; = **I shall**.
ill [ɪl] *adj* krank; (*effects*) schädlich ♦ *n* Übel *nt*; (*trouble*) Schlechte(s) *nt* ♦ *adv*: **to speak ~ of sb** Schlechtes über jdn sagen; **to be taken ~** krank werden; **to think ~ of sb** schlecht von jdm denken.
ill-advised [ɪləd'vaɪzd] *adj* unklug; (*person*) schlecht beraten.
ill at ease *adj* unbehaglich.
ill-considered [ɪlkən'sɪdəd] *adj* unüberlegt.
ill-disposed [ɪldɪs'pəuzd] *adj*: **to be ~ toward sb/sth** jdm/etw nicht wohlgesinnt sein.
illegal [ɪ'li:gl] *adj* illegal.
illegally [ɪ'li:gəlɪ] *adv* illegal.
illegible [ɪ'ledʒɪbl] *adj* unleserlich.
illegitimate [ɪlɪ'dʒɪtɪmət] *adj* (*child*) unehelich; (*activity, treaty*) unzulässig.
ill-fated [ɪl'feɪtɪd] *adj* unglückselig.
ill-favoured, (*US*) **ill-favored** [ɪl'feɪvəd] *adj* ungestalt (*liter*), hässlich.
ill feeling *n* Verstimmung *f*.
ill-gotten [ɪl'gɔtn] *adj*: **~ gains** unrechtmäßig erworbener Gewinn *m*.
ill health *n* schlechter Gesundheitszustand *m*.
illicit [ɪ'lɪsɪt] *adj* verboten.
ill-informed [ɪlɪn'fɔ:md] *adj* (*judgement*) wenig sachkundig; (*person*) schlecht informiert *or* unterrichtet.
illiterate [ɪ'lɪtərət] *adj* (*person*) des Lesens und Schreibens unkundig; (*letter*) voller Fehler.
ill-mannered [ɪl'mænəd] *adj* unhöflich.
illness ['ɪlnɪs] *n* Krankheit *f*.
illogical [ɪ'lɔdʒɪkl] *adj* unlogisch.
ill-suited [ɪl'su:tɪd] *adj* nicht zusammenpassend; **he is ~ to the job** er ist für die Stelle ungeeignet.
ill-timed [ɪl'taɪmd] *adj* ungelegen, unpassend.
ill-treat [ɪl'tri:t] *vt* misshandeln.
ill-treatment [ɪl'tri:tmənt] *n* Misshandlung *f*.
illuminate [ɪ'lu:mɪneɪt] *vt* beleuchten.
illuminated sign [ɪ'lu:mɪneɪtɪd-] *n* Leuchtzeichen *nt*.
illuminating [ɪ'lu:mɪneɪtɪŋ] *adj* aufschlussreich.
illumination [ɪlu:mɪ'neɪʃən] *n* Beleuchtung *f*; **illuminations** *npl* (*decorative lights*) festliche Beleuchtung *f*, Illumination *f*.
illusion [ɪ'lu:ʒən] *n* Illusion *f*; (*trick*) (Zauber)trick *m*; **to be under the ~ that ...** sich *dat* einbilden, dass ...
illusive [ɪ'lu:sɪv] *adj* = **illusory**.
illusory [ɪ'lu:sərɪ] *adj* illusorisch, trügerisch.
illustrate ['ɪləstreɪt] *vt* veranschaulichen; (*book*) illustrieren.
illustration [ɪlə'streɪʃən] *n* Illustration *f*; (*example*) Veranschaulichung *f*.
illustrator ['ɪləstreɪtə*] *n* Illustrator(in) *m(f)*.
illustrious [ɪ'lʌstrɪəs] *adj* (*career*) glanzvoll;

(*predecessor*) berühmt.

ill will n böses Blut nt.

ILO n abbr = **International Labour Organization**.

I'm [aɪm] = **I am**.

image ['ɪmɪdʒ] n Bild nt; (*public face*) Image nt; (*reflection*) Abbild nt.

imagery ['ɪmɪdʒərɪ] n (*in writing*) Metaphorik f; (*in painting etc*) Symbolik f.

imaginable [ɪ'mædʒɪnəbl] adj vorstellbar, denkbar; **we've tried every ~ solution** wir haben jede denkbare Lösung ausprobiert; **she had the prettiest hair ~** sie hatte das schönste Haar, das man sich vorstellen kann.

imaginary [ɪ'mædʒɪnərɪ] adj erfunden; (*being*) Fantasie-; (*danger*) eingebildet.

imagination [ɪmædʒɪ'neɪʃən] n Fantasie f; (*illusion*) Einbildung f; **it's just your ~** das bildest du dir nur ein.

imaginative [ɪ'mædʒɪnətɪv] adj fantasievoll; (*solution*) einfallsreich.

imagine [ɪ'mædʒɪn] vt sich dat vorstellen; (*dream*) sich dat träumen lassen; (*suppose*) vermuten.

imbalance [ɪm'bæləns] n Unausgeglichenheit f.

imbecile ['ɪmbəsiːl] n Schwachkopf m, Idiot m.

imbue [ɪm'bjuː] vt: **to ~ sb/sth with** jdn/etw durchdringen mit.

IMF n abbr (= **International Monetary Fund**) IWF m.

imitate ['ɪmɪteɪt] vt imitieren; (*mimic*) nachahmen.

imitation [ɪmɪ'teɪʃən] n Imitation f, Nachahmung f.

imitator ['ɪmɪteɪtə*] n Imitator(in) m(f), Nachahmer(in) m(f).

immaculate [ɪ'mækjulət] adj makellos; (*appearance, piece of work*) tadellos; (*REL*) unbefleckt.

immaterial [ɪmə'tɪərɪəl] adj unwichtig, unwesentlich.

immature [ɪmə'tjuə*] adj unreif; (*organism*) noch nicht voll entwickelt.

immaturity [ɪmə'tjuərɪtɪ] n Unreife f.

immeasurable [ɪ'mɛʒrəbl] adj unermesslich groß.

immediacy [ɪ'miːdɪəsɪ] n Unmittelbarkeit f, Direktheit f; (*of needs*) Dringlichkeit f.

immediate [ɪ'miːdɪət] adj sofortig; (*need*) dringend; (*neighbourhood, family*) nächste(r, s).

immediately [ɪ'miːdɪətlɪ] adv sofort; (*directly*) unmittelbar; **~ next to** direkt neben.

immense [ɪ'mɛns] adj riesig, enorm.

immensely [ɪ'mɛnslɪ] adv unheimlich; (*grateful, complex etc*) äußerst.

immensity [ɪ'mɛnsɪtɪ] n ungeheure Größe f, Unermesslichkeit f; (*of problems etc*) gewaltiges Ausmaß nt.

immerse [ɪ'mɜːs] vt eintauchen; **to ~ sth in** etw tauchen in +acc; **to be ~d in** (*fig*) vertieft sein in +acc.

immersion heater [ɪ'mɜːʃən-] (*BRIT*) n elektrischer Heißwasserboiler m.

immigrant ['ɪmɪgrənt] n Einwanderer m, Einwanderin f.

immigration [ɪmɪ'greɪʃən] n Einwanderung f; (*at airport etc*) Einwanderungsstelle f ♦ cpd Einwanderungs-.

imminent ['ɪmɪnənt] adj bevorstehend.

immobile [ɪ'məubaɪl] adj unbeweglich.

immobilize [ɪ'məubɪlaɪz] vt (*person*) handlungsunfähig machen; (*machine*) zum Stillstand bringen.

immobilizer [ɪməubɪlaɪzə*] n (*AUT*) Wegfahrsperre f.

immoderate [ɪ'mɒdərət] adj unmäßig; (*opinion, reaction*) extrem; (*demand*) maßlos.

immodest [ɪ'mɒdɪst] adj unanständig; (*boasting*) unbescheiden.

immoral [ɪ'mɒrl] adj unmoralisch; (*behaviour*) unsittlich.

immorality [ɪmə'rælɪtɪ] n (*see adj*) Unmoral f; Unsittlichkeit f.

immortal [ɪ'mɔːtl] adj unsterblich.

immortality [ɪmɔː'tælɪtɪ] n Unsterblichkeit f.

immortalize [ɪ'mɔːtlaɪz] vt unsterblich machen.

immovable [ɪ'muːvəbl] adj unbeweglich; (*person, opinion*) fest.

immune [ɪ'mjuːn] adj: **~ (to)** (*disease*) immun (gegen); (*flattery*) unempfänglich (für); (*criticism*) unempfindlich (gegen); (*attack*) sicher (vor +dat).

immune system n Immunsystem nt.

immunity [ɪ'mjuːnɪtɪ] n (*see adj*) Immunität f; Unempfänglichkeit f; Unempfindlichkeit f; Sicherheit f; (*of diplomat, from prosecution*) Immunität f.

immunization [ɪmjunaɪ'zeɪʃən] n Immunisierung f.

immunize ['ɪmjunaɪz] vt: **to ~ (against)** immunisieren (gegen).

imp [ɪmp] n Kobold m; (*child*) Racker m (*inf*).

impact ['ɪmpækt] n Aufprall m; (*of crash*) Wucht f; (*of law, measure*) (Aus)wirkung f.

impair [ɪm'pɛə*] vt beeinträchtigen.

impaired [ɪm'pɛəd] adj beeinträchtigt; (*hearing*) schlecht; **~ vision** schlechte Augen pl.

impale [ɪm'peɪl] vt: **to ~ sth (on)** etw aufspießen (auf +dat).

impart [ɪm'pɑːt] vt: **to ~ (to)** (*information*) mitteilen +dat; (*flavour*) verleihen +dat.

impartial [ɪm'pɑːʃl] adj unparteiisch.

impartiality [ɪmpɑːʃɪ'ælɪtɪ] n Unparteilichkeit f.

impassable [ɪm'pɑːsəbl] adj unpassierbar.

impasse [æm'pɑːs] n Sackgasse f.

impassive [ɪm'pæsɪv] adj gelassen.

impatience [ɪm'peɪʃəns] n Ungeduld f.

impatient [ɪm'peɪʃənt] adj ungeduldig; **to get**

or **grow** ~ ungeduldig werden; **to be** ~ **to do sth** es nicht erwarten können, etw zu tun.

impatiently [ɪm'peɪʃəntlɪ] *adv* ungeduldig.

impeach [ɪm'piːtʃ] *vt* anklagen; (*public official*) eines Amtsvergehens anklagen.

impeachment [ɪm'piːtʃmənt] *n* Anklage *f* wegen eines Amtsvergehens, Impeachment *nt*.

impeccable [ɪm'pɛkəbl] *adj* (*dress*) untadelig; (*manners*) tadellos.

impecunious [ɪmpɪ'kjuːnɪəs] *adj* mittellos.

impede [ɪm'piːd] *vt* behindern.

impediment [ɪm'pɛdɪmənt] *n* Hindernis *nt*; (*also*: **speech** ~) Sprachfehler *m*.

impel [ɪm'pɛl] *vt*: **to** ~ **sb to do sth** jdn (dazu) nötigen, etw zu tun.

impending [ɪm'pɛndɪŋ] *adj* bevorstehend; (*catastrophe*) drohend.

impenetrable [ɪm'pɛnɪtrəbl] *adj* undurchdringlich; (*fig*) unergründlich.

imperative [ɪm'pɛrətɪv] *adj* dringend; (*tone*) Befehls- ♦ *n* (*LING*) Imperativ *m*, Befehlsform *f*.

imperceptible [ɪmpə'sɛptɪbl] *adj* nicht wahrnehmbar, unmerklich.

imperfect [ɪm'pəːfɪkt] *adj* mangelhaft; (*goods*) fehlerhaft ♦ *n* (*LING*: *also*: ~ **tense**) Imperfekt *nt*, Vergangenheit *f*.

imperfection [ɪmpə'fɛkʃən] *n* Fehler *m*.

imperial [ɪm'pɪərɪəl] *adj* kaiserlich; (*BRIT*: *measure*) britisch.

imperialism [ɪm'pɪərɪəlɪzəm] *n* Imperialismus *m*.

imperil [ɪm'pɛrɪl] *vt* gefährden.

imperious [ɪm'pɪərɪəs] *adj* herrisch, gebieterisch.

impersonal [ɪm'pəːsənl] *adj* unpersönlich.

impersonate [ɪm'pəːsəneɪt] *vt* sich ausgeben als; (*THEAT*) imitieren.

impersonation [ɪmpəːsə'neɪʃən] *n* (*THEAT*) Imitation *f*; ~ **of** (*LAW*) Auftreten *nt* als.

impertinent [ɪm'pəːtɪnənt] *adj* unverschämt.

imperturbable [ɪmpə'təːbəbl] *adj* unerschütterlich.

impervious [ɪm'pəːvɪəs] *adj*: ~ **to** (*criticism, pressure*) unberührt von; (*charm, influence*) unempfänglich für.

impetuous [ɪm'pɛtjuəs] *adj* ungestüm, stürmisch; (*act*) impulsiv.

impetus ['ɪmpɪtəs] *n* Schwung *m*; (*fig: driving force*) treibende Kraft *f*.

impinge [ɪm'pɪndʒ]: **to** ~ **on** *vt fus* sich auswirken auf +*acc*; (*rights*) einschränken.

impish ['ɪmpɪʃ] *adj* schelmisch.

implacable [ɪm'plækəbl] *adj* unerbittlich, erbittert.

implant [ɪm'plɑːnt] *vt* (*MED*) einpflanzen; (*fig: idea, principle*) einimpfen.

implausible [ɪm'plɔːzɪbl] *adj* unglaubwürdig.

implement [*n* 'ɪmplɪmənt, *vt* 'ɪmplɪmɛnt] *n* Gerät *nt*, Werkzeug *nt* ♦ *vt* durchführen.

implicate ['ɪmplɪkeɪt] *vt* verwickeln.

implication [ɪmplɪ'keɪʃən] *n* Auswirkung *f*; (*involvement*) Verwicklung *f*; **by** ~ implizit.

implicit [ɪm'plɪsɪt] *adj* (*inferred*) implizit, unausgesprochen; (*unquestioning*) absolut.

implicitly [ɪm'plɪsɪtlɪ] *adv* (*see adj*) implizit; absolut.

implore [ɪm'plɔː*] *vt* anflehen.

imply [ɪm'plaɪ] *vt* andeuten; (*mean*) bedeuten.

impolite [ɪmpə'laɪt] *adj* unhöflich.

imponderable [ɪm'pɒndərəbl] *adj* unberechenbar ♦ *n* unberechenbare Größe *f*.

import [*vt* ɪm'pɔːt, *n* 'ɪmpɔːt] *vt* importieren, einführen ♦ *n* Import *m*, Einfuhr *f*; (*article*) Importgut *nt* ♦ *cpd* Import-, Einfuhr-.

importance [ɪm'pɔːtns] *n* (*see adj*) Wichtigkeit *f*; Bedeutung *f*; **to be of little/great** ~ nicht besonders wichtig/sehr wichtig sein.

important [ɪm'pɔːtənt] *adj* wichtig; (*influential*) bedeutend; **it's not** ~ es ist unwichtig.

importantly [ɪm'pɔːtəntlɪ] *adv* wichtigtuerisch; **but more** ~ ... aber was noch wichtiger ist, ...

importation [ɪmpɔː'teɪʃən] *n* Import *m*, Einfuhr *f*.

imported [ɪm'pɔːtɪd] *adj* importiert, eingeführt.

importer [ɪm'pɔːtə*] *n* Importeur *m*.

impose [ɪm'pəuz] *vt* auferlegen; (*sanctions*) verhängen ♦ *vi*: **to** ~ **on sb** jdm zur Last fallen.

imposing [ɪm'pəuzɪŋ] *adj* eindrucksvoll.

imposition [ɪmpə'zɪʃən] *n* (*of tax etc*) Auferlegung *f*; **to be an** ~ **on** eine Zumutung sein für.

impossibility [ɪmpɒsə'bɪlɪtɪ] *n* Unmöglichkeit *f*.

impossible [ɪm'pɒsɪbl] *adj* unmöglich; **it's** ~ **for me to leave now** ich kann jetzt unmöglich gehen.

impossibly [ɪm'pɒsɪblɪ] *adv* unmöglich.

imposter [ɪm'pɒstə*] *n* = **impostor**.

impostor [ɪm'pɒstə*] *n* Hochstapler(in) *m(f)*.

impotence ['ɪmpətns] *n* (*see adj*) Machtlosigkeit *f*; Impotenz *f*.

impotent ['ɪmpətnt] *adj* machtlos; (*MED*) impotent.

impound [ɪm'paund] *vt* beschlagnahmen.

impoverished [ɪm'pɒvərɪʃt] *adj* verarmt.

impracticable [ɪm'præktɪkəbl] *adj* (*idea*) undurchführbar; (*solution*) unbrauchbar.

impractical [ɪm'præktɪkl] *adj* (*plan*) undurchführbar; (*person*) unpraktisch.

imprecise [ɪmprɪ'saɪs] *adj* ungenau.

impregnable [ɪm'prɛgnəbl] *adj* uneinnehmbar; (*fig*) unerschütterlich.

impregnate ['ɪmprɛgneɪt] *vt* tränken.

impresario [ɪmprɪ'sɑːrɪəu] *n* (*THEAT*) Impresario *m*.

impress [ɪm'prɛs] *vt* beeindrucken; (*mark*) aufdrücken; **to** ~ **sth on sb** jdm etw einschärfen.

impression [ɪmˈprɛʃən] *n* Eindruck *m*; (*of stamp, seal*) Abdruck *m*; (*imitation*) Nachahmung *f*, Imitation *f*; **to make a good/bad ~ on sb** einen guten/schlechten Eindruck auf jdn machen; **to be under the ~ that** ... den Eindruck haben, dass ...

impressionable [ɪmˈprɛʃnəbl] *adj* leicht zu beeindrucken.

impressionist [ɪmˈprɛʃənɪst] *n* Impressionist(in) *m(f)*; (*entertainer*) Imitator(in) *m(f)*.

impressive [ɪmˈprɛsɪv] *adj* beeindruckend.

imprint [ˈɪmprɪnt] *n* (*of hand etc*) Abdruck *m*; (*PUBLISHING*) Impressum *nt*.

imprinted [ɪmˈprɪntɪd] *adj*: **it is ~ on my memory/mind** es hat sich mir eingeprägt.

imprison [ɪmˈprɪzn] *vt* inhaftieren, einsperren.

imprisonment [ɪmˈprɪznmənt] *n* Gefangenschaft *f*; **three years' ~** drei Jahre Gefängnis *or* Freiheitsstrafe.

improbable [ɪmˈprɒbəbl] *adj* unwahrscheinlich.

impromptu [ɪmˈprɒmptjuː] *adj* improvisiert.

improper [ɪmˈprɒpə] *adj* ungehörig; (*procedure*) unrichtig; (*dishonest*) unlauter.

impropriety [ɪmprəˈpraɪətɪ] *n* (*see adj*) Ungehörigkeit *f*; Unrichtigkeit *f*; Unlauterkeit *f*.

improve [ɪmˈpruːv] *vt* verbessern ♦ *vi* sich bessern; **the patient is improving** dem Patienten geht es besser.

▶ **improve (up)on** *vt fus* verbessern.

improvement [ɪmˈpruːvmənt] *n*: **~ (in)** Verbesserung (+*gen*); **to make ~s to** Verbesserungen durchführen an +*dat*.

improvisation [ɪmprəvaɪˈzeɪʃən] *n* Improvisation *f*.

improvise [ˈɪmprəvaɪz] *vt, vi* improvisieren.

imprudence [ɪmˈpruːdns] *n* Unklugheit *f*.

imprudent [ɪmˈpruːdnt] *adj* unklug.

impudent [ˈɪmpjudnt] *adj* unverschämt.

impugn [ɪmˈpjuːn] *vt* angreifen; (*sincerity, motives, reputation*) in Zweifel ziehen.

impulse [ˈɪmpʌls] *n* Impuls *m*; (*urge*) Drang *m*; **to act on ~** aus einem Impuls heraus handeln.

impulse buy *n* Impulsivkauf *m*.

impulsive [ɪmˈpʌlsɪv] *adj* impulsiv, spontan; (*purchase*) Impulsiv-.

impunity [ɪmˈpjuːnɪtɪ] *n*: **with ~** ungestraft.

impure [ɪmˈpjuə] *adj* unrein; (*adulterated*) verunreinigt.

impurity [ɪmˈpjuərɪtɪ] *n* Verunreinigung *f*.

IN (*US*) *abbr* (*POST*: = *Indiana*).

===================== *KEYWORD*

in [ɪn] *prep* **1** (*indicating place, position*) in +*dat*; (*with motion*) in +*acc*; **~ the house/garden** im Haus/Garten; **~ town** in der Stadt; **~ the country** auf dem Land; **~ here** hierin; **~ there** darin.

2 (*with place names: of town, region, country*) in +*dat*; **~ London/Bavaria** in London/Bayern.

3 (*indicating time*) in +*dat*; **~ spring/summer/May** im Frühling/Sommer/Mai; **~ 1994** 1994; **~ the afternoon** am Nachmittag; **at 4 o'clock ~ the afternoon** um 4 Uhr nachmittags; **I did it ~ 3 hours/days** ich habe es in 3 Stunden/Tagen gemacht; **~ 2 weeks** *or* **2 weeks' time** in 2 Wochen.

4 (*indicating manner, circumstances, state*) in +*dat*; **~ a loud/soft voice** mit lauter/weicher Stimme; **~ English/German** auf Englisch/Deutsch; **~ the sun** in der Sonne; **~ the rain** im Regen; **~ good condition** in guter Verfassung.

5 (*with ratios, numbers*): **1 ~ 10** eine(r, s) von 10; **20 pence ~ the pound** 20 Pence pro Pfund; **they lined up ~ twos** sie stellten sich in Zweierreihen auf.

6 (*referring to people, works*): **the disease is common ~ children** die Krankheit ist bei Kindern verbreitet; **~ (the works of) Dickens** bei Dickens; **they have a good leader ~ him** in ihm haben sie einen guten Führer.

7 (*indicating profession etc*) **to be ~ teaching/the army** Lehrer(in)/beim Militär sein.

8 (*with present participle*): **~ saying this, I ...** wenn ich das sage, ...

♦ *adv*: **to be ~** (*person: at home, work*) da sein; (*train, ship, plane*) angekommen sein; (*in fashion*) in sein; **to ask sb ~** jdn hereinbitten; **to run/limp etc ~** hereinlaufen/-humpeln *etc*

♦ *n*: **the ~s and outs** (*of proposal, situation etc*) die Einzelheiten *pl*.

in. *abbr* = **inch.**

inability [ɪnəˈbɪlɪtɪ] *n* Unfähigkeit *f*.

inaccessible [ɪnəkˈsɛsɪbl] *adj* unzugänglich.

inaccuracy [ɪnˈækjurəsɪ] *n* (*see adj*) Ungenauigkeit *f*; Unrichtigkeit *f*; (*mistake*) Fehler *m*.

inaccurate [ɪnˈækjurət] *adj* ungenau; (*not correct*) unrichtig.

inaction [ɪnˈækʃən] *n* Untätigkeit *f*.

inactive [ɪnˈæktɪv] *adj* untätig.

inactivity [ɪnækˈtɪvɪtɪ] *n* Untätigkeit *f*.

inadequacy [ɪnˈædɪkwəsɪ] *n* Unzulänglichkeit *f*.

inadequate [ɪnˈædɪkwət] *adj* unzulänglich.

inadmissible [ɪnədˈmɪsəbl] *adj* unzulässig.

inadvertently [ɪnədˈvɜːtntlɪ] *adv* ungewollt.

inadvisable [ɪnədˈvaɪzəbl] *adj* unratsam; **it is ~ to** ... es ist nicht ratsam, zu ...

inane [ɪˈneɪn] *adj* dumm.

inanimate [ɪnˈænɪmət] *adj* unbelebt.

inapplicable [ɪnˈæplɪkəbl] *adj* unzutreffend.

inappropriate [ɪnəˈprəuprɪət] *adj* unpassend; (*word, expression*) unangebracht.

inapt [ɪn'æpt] adj unpassend.

inarticulate [ɪnɑː'tɪkjulət] adj (speech) unverständlich; **he is** ~ er kann sich nur schlecht ausdrücken.

inasmuch as [ɪnəz'mʌtʃ-] adv da, weil; (in so far as) insofern als.

inattention [ɪnə'tɛnʃən] n Unaufmerksamkeit f.

inattentive [ɪnə'tɛntɪv] adj unaufmerksam.

inaudible [ɪn'ɔːdɪbl] adj unhörbar.

inaugural [ɪ'nɔːgjurəl] adj (speech, meeting) Eröffnungs-.

inaugurate [ɪ'nɔːgjureɪt] vt einführen; (president, official) (feierlich) in sein/ihr Amt einführen.

inauguration [ɪnɔːgju'reɪʃən] n (see vb) Einführung f; (feierliche) Amtseinführung f.

inauspicious [ɪnɔːs'pɪʃəs] adj Unheil verheißend.

in-between [ɪnbɪ'twiːn] adj Mittel-, Zwischen-.

inborn [ɪn'bɔːn] adj angeboren.

inbred [ɪn'brɛd] adj angeboren; **an** ~ **family** eine Familie, in der Inzucht herrscht.

inbreeding [ɪn'briːdɪŋ] n Inzucht f.

in-built ['ɪnbɪlt] adj (quality) ihm/ihr etc eigen; (feeling etc) angeboren.

Inc. abbr = **incorporated company**.

Inca ['ɪŋkə] adj (also: ~n) Inka-, inkaisch ♦ n Inka mf.

incalculable [ɪn'kælkjuləbl] adj (effect) unabsehbar; (loss) unermesslich.

incapable [ɪn'keɪpəbl] adj hilflos; **to be** ~ **of sth** unfähig zu etw sein; **to be** ~ **of doing sth** unfähig sein, etw zu tun.

incapacitate [ɪnkə'pæsɪteɪt] vt: **to** ~ **sb** jdn unfähig machen.

incapacitated [ɪnkə'pæsɪteɪtɪd] adj (LAW) entmündigt.

incapacity [ɪnkə'pæsɪtɪ] n Hilflosigkeit f; (inability) Unfähigkeit f.

incarcerate [ɪn'kɑːsəreɪt] vt einkerkern.

incarnate [ɪn'kɑːnɪt] adj leibhaftig, in Person; **evil** ~ das leibhaftige Böse.

incarnation [ɪnkɑː'neɪʃən] n Inbegriff m; (REL) Menschwerdung f.

incendiary [ɪn'sɛndɪərɪ] adj (bomb) Brand-; ~ **device** Brandsatz m.

incense [n 'ɪnsɛns, vt ɪn'sɛns] n Weihrauch m; (perfume) Duft m ♦ vt wütend machen.

incense burner n Weihrauchschwenker m.

incentive [ɪn'sɛntɪv] n Anreiz m.

inception [ɪn'sɛpʃən] n Beginn m, Anfang m.

incessant [ɪn'sɛsnt] adj unablässig.

incessantly [ɪn'sɛsntlɪ] adv unablässig.

incest ['ɪnsɛst] n Inzest m.

inch [ɪntʃ] n Zoll m; **to be within an** ~ **of sth** kurz vor etw dat stehen; **he didn't give an** ~ (fig) er gab keinen Fingerbreit nach.

▶ **inch forward** vi sich millimeterweise vorwärts schieben.

incidence ['ɪnsɪdns] n Häufigkeit f.

incident ['ɪnsɪdnt] n Vorfall m; (diplomatic etc) Zwischenfall m.

incidental [ɪnsɪ'dɛntl] adj zusätzlich; (unimportant) nebensächlich; ~ **to** verbunden mit; ~ **expenses** Nebenkosten pl.

incidentally [ɪnsɪ'dɛntəlɪ] adv übrigens.

incidental music n Begleitmusik f.

incident room n Einsatzzentrale f.

incinerate [ɪn'sɪnəreɪt] vt verbrennen.

incinerator [ɪn'sɪnəreɪtə*] n (for waste, refuse) (Müll)verbrennungsanlage f.

incipient [ɪn'sɪpɪənt] adj einsetzend.

incision [ɪn'sɪʒən] n Einschnitt m.

incisive [ɪn'saɪsɪv] adj treffend.

incisor [ɪn'saɪzə*] n Schneidezahn m.

incite [ɪn'saɪt] vt (rioters) aufhetzen; (violence, hatred) schüren.

incl. abbr = **including; inclusive (of)**.

inclement [ɪn'klɛmənt] adj (weather) rauh, unfreundlich.

inclination [ɪnklɪ'neɪʃən] n Neigung f.

incline [n 'ɪnklaɪn, vb ɪn'klaɪn] n Abhang m ♦ vt neigen ♦ vi sich neigen; **to be** ~d **to** neigen zu; **to be well** ~d **towards sb** jdm geneigt or gewogen sein.

include [ɪn'kluːd] vt einbeziehen; (in price) einschließen; **the tip is not** ~d **in the price** Trinkgeld ist im Preis nicht inbegriffen.

including [ɪn'kluːdɪŋ] prep einschließlich; ~ **service charge** inklusive Bedienung.

inclusion [ɪn'kluːʒən] n (see vb) Einbeziehung f; Einschluss m.

inclusive [ɪn'kluːsɪv] adj (terms) inklusive; (price) Inklusiv-, Pauschal-; ~ **of** einschließlich +gen.

incognito [ɪnkɔg'niːtəu] adv inkognito.

incoherent [ɪnkəu'hɪərənt] adj zusammenhanglos; (speech) wirr; (person) sich unklar or undeutlich ausdrückend.

income ['ɪnkʌm] n Einkommen nt; (from property, investment, pension) Einkünfte pl; **gross/net** ~ Brutto-/Nettoeinkommen nt; ~ **and expenditure account** Gewinn- und Verlustrechnung f; ~ **bracket** Einkommensklasse f.

income support n ≈ Sozialhilfe f.

income tax n Einkommensteuer f ♦ cpd Steuer-.

incoming ['ɪnkʌmɪŋ] adj (passenger) ankommend; (flight) landend; (call, mail) eingehend; (government, official) neu; (wave) hereinbrechend; ~ **tide** Flut f.

incommunicado ['ɪnkəmjunɪ'kɑːdəu] adj: **to hold sb** ~ jdn ohne jede Verbindung zur Außenwelt halten.

incomparable [ɪn'kɔmpərəbl] adj unvergleichlich.

incompatible [ɪnkəm'pætɪbl] adj unvereinbar.

incompetence [ɪn'kɔmpɪtns] n Unfähigkeit f.

incompetent [ɪn'kɔmpɪtnt] adj unfähig; (job) unzulänglich.

incomplete [ɪnkəm'pliːt] *adj* unfertig; (*partial*) unvollständig.

incomprehensible [ɪnkɔmprɪ'hensɪbl] *adj* unverständlich.

inconceivable [ɪnkən'siːvəbl] *adj*: **it is ~ (that ...)** es ist unvorstellbar *or* undenkbar(, dass ...).

inconclusive [ɪnkən'kluːsɪv] *adj* (*experiment, discussion*) ergebnislos; (*evidence, argument*) nicht überzeugend; (*result*) unbestimmt.

incongruous [ɪn'kɔŋgruəs] *adj* (*strange*) absurd; (*inappropriate*) unpassend.

inconsequential [ɪnkɔnsɪ'kwɛnʃl] *adj* unbedeutend, unwichtig.

inconsiderable [ɪnkən'sɪdərəbl] *adj*: **not ~** beachtlich; (*sum*) nicht unerheblich.

inconsiderate [ɪnkən'sɪdərət] *adj* rücksichtslos.

inconsistency [ɪnkən'sɪstənsɪ] *n* (*see adj*) Widersprüchlichkeit *f*, Inkonsequenz *f*, Unbeständigkeit *f*.

inconsistent [ɪnkən'sɪstnt] *adj* widersprüchlich; (*person*) inkonsequent; (*work*) unbeständig; **to be ~ with** im Widerspruch stehen zu.

inconsolable [ɪnkən'səuləbl] *adj* untröstlich.

inconspicuous [ɪnkən'spɪkjuəs] *adj* unauffällig; **to make o.s. ~** sich unauffällig benehmen.

incontinence [ɪn'kɔntɪnəns] *n* (*MED*) Unfähigkeit *f*, Stuhl und/oder Harn zurückzuhalten; Inkontinenz *f*.

incontinent [ɪn'kɔntɪnənt] *adj* (*MED*) unfähig, Stuhl und/oder Harn zurückzuhalten, inkontinent.

inconvenience [ɪnkən'viːnjəns] *n* Unannehmlichkeit *f*; (*trouble*) Umstände *pl* ♦ *vt* Umstände bereiten +*dat*; **don't ~ yourself** machen Sie sich keine Umstände.

inconvenient [ɪnkən'viːnjənt] *adj* (*time, place*) ungünstig; (*house*) unbequem, unpraktisch; (*visitor*) ungelegen.

incorporate [ɪn'kɔːpəreɪt] *vt* aufnehmen; (*contain*) enthalten; **safety features have been ~d in the design** in der Konstruktion sind auch Sicherheitsvorkehrungen enthalten.

incorporated company [ɪn'kɔːpəreɪtɪd-] (*US*) *n* eingetragene Gesellschaft *f*.

incorrect [ɪnkə'rɛkt] *adj* falsch.

incorrigible [ɪn'kɔrɪdʒɪbl] *adj* unverbesserlich.

incorruptible [ɪnkə'rʌptɪbl] *adj* unbestechlich.

increase [*vb* ɪn'kriːs, *n* 'ɪnkriːs] *vi* (*level etc*) zunehmen; (*price*) steigen; (*in size*) sich vergrößern; (*in number, quantity*) sich vermehren ♦ *vt* vergrößern; (*price*) erhöhen ♦ *n*: **~ (in)** Zunahme *f* (+*gen*); (*in wages, spending etc*) Erhöhung *f* (+*gen*); **an ~ of 5%** eine Erhöhung von 5%, eine Zunahme um 5%; **to be on the ~** zunehmen.

increasing [ɪn'kriːsɪŋ] *adj* zunehmend.

increasingly [ɪn'kriːsɪŋlɪ] *adv* zunehmend.

incredible [ɪn'krɛdɪbl] *adj* unglaublich; (*amazing, wonderful*) unwahrscheinlich (*inf*), sagenhaft (*inf*).

incredulity [ɪnkrɪ'djuːlɪtɪ] *n* Ungläubigkeit *f*.

incredulous [ɪn'krɛdjuləs] *adj* ungläubig.

increment ['ɪnkrɪmənt] *n* (*in salary*) Erhöhung *f*, Zulage *f*.

incriminate [ɪn'krɪmɪneɪt] *vt* belasten.

incriminating [ɪn'krɪmɪneɪtɪŋ] *adj* belastend.

incrusted [ɪn'krʌstɪd] *adj* = **encrusted**.

incubate ['ɪnkjubeɪt] *vt* ausbrüten ♦ *vi* ausgebrütet werden; (*disease*) zum Ausbruch kommen.

incubation [ɪnkju'beɪʃən] *n* Ausbrüten *nt*; (*of illness*) Inkubation *f*.

incubation period *n* Inkubationszeit *f*.

incubator ['ɪnkjubeɪtə'] *n* (*for babies*) Brutkasten *m*, Inkubator *m*.

inculcate ['ɪnkʌlkeɪt] *vt*: **to ~ sth in(to) sb** jdm etw einprägen.

incumbent [ɪn'kʌmbənt] *n* Amtsinhaber(in) *m(f)* ♦ *adj*: **it is ~ on him to ...** es obliegt ihm *or* es ist seine Pflicht, zu ...

incur [ɪn'kɔː'] *vt* (*expenses, debt*) machen; (*loss*) erleiden; (*disapproval, anger*) sich *dat* zuziehen.

incurable [ɪn'kjuərəbl] *adj* unheilbar.

incursion [ɪn'kɔːʃən] *n* (*MIL*) Einfall *m*.

Ind. (*US*) *abbr* (*POST*: = Indiana).

indebted [ɪn'dɛtɪd] *adj*: **to be ~ to sb** jdm (zu Dank) verpflichtet sein.

indecency [ɪn'diːsnsɪ] *n* Unanständigkeit *f*, Anstößigkeit *f*.

indecent [ɪn'diːsnt] *adj* unanständig, anstößig; (*haste*) ungebührlich.

indecent assault (*BRIT*) *n* Sexualverbrechen *nt*.

indecent exposure *n* Erregung *f* öffentlichen Ärgernisses.

indecipherable [ɪndɪ'saɪfərəbl] *adj* unleserlich; (*expression, glance etc*) unergründlich.

indecision [ɪndɪ'sɪʒən] *n* Unentschlossenheit *f*.

indecisive [ɪndɪ'saɪsɪv] *adj* unentschlossen.

indeed [ɪn'diːd] *adv* aber sicher; (*in fact*) tatsächlich, in der Tat; (*furthermore*) sogar; **yes ~!** oh ja!, das kann man wohl sagen!

indefatigable [ɪndɪ'fætɪgəbl] *adj* unermüdlich.

indefensible [ɪndɪ'fɛnsɪbl] *adj* (*conduct*) unentschuldbar.

indefinable [ɪndɪ'faɪnəbl] *adj* undefinierbar.

indefinite [ɪn'dɛfɪnɪt] *adj* unklar, vage; (*period, number*) unbestimmt.

indefinite article *n* (*LING*) unbestimmter Artikel *m*.

indefinitely [ɪn'dɛfɪnɪtlɪ] *adv* (*continue*) endlos; (*wait*) unbegrenzt (lange); (*postpone*) auf unbestimmte Zeit.

indelible [ɪn'dɛlɪbl] *adj* (*mark, stain*) nicht zu entfernen; **~ pen** Tintenstift *m*; **~ ink** Wäschetinte *f*.

indelicate [ɪn'dɛlɪkɪt] adj taktlos; (not polite) ungehörig.

indemnify [ɪn'dɛmnɪfaɪ] vt entschädigen.

indemnity [ɪn'dɛmnɪtɪ] n (insurance) Versicherung f; (compensation) Entschädigung f.

indent [ɪn'dɛnt] vt (text) einrücken, einziehen.

indentation [ɪndɛn'teɪʃən] n Einkerbung f; (TYP) Einrückung f, Einzug m; (on metal) Delle f.

indenture [ɪn'dɛntʃə*] n Ausbildungsvertrag m, Lehrvertrag m.

independence [ɪndɪ'pɛndns] n Unabhängigkeit f.

INDEPENDENCE DAY

Independence Day (der 4. Juli) ist in den USA ein gesetzlicher Feiertag zum Gedenken an die Unabhängigkeitserklärung vom 4. Juli 1776, mit der die 13 amerikanischen Kolonien ihre Freiheit und Unabhängigkeit von Großbritannien erklärten.

---

independent [ɪndɪ'pɛndnt] adj unabhängig.

independently [ɪndɪ'pɛndntlɪ] adv unabhängig.

in-depth ['ɪndɛpθ] adj eingehend.

indescribable [ɪndɪs'kraɪbəbl] adj unbeschreiblich.

indestructible [ɪndɪs'trʌktəbl] adj unzerstörbar.

indeterminate [ɪndɪ'tə:mɪnɪt] adj unbestimmt.

index ['ɪndɛks] (pl ~es) n (in book) Register nt; (in library etc) Katalog m; (card index) Kartei f; (pl **indices**) (ratio) Index m; (: sign) (An)zeichen nt.

index card n Karteikarte f.

indexed ['ɪndɛkst] (US) adj = **index-linked**.

index finger n Zeigefinger m.

index-linked ['ɪndɛks'lɪŋkt] adj der Inflationsrate dat angeglichen.

India ['ɪndɪə] n Indien nt.

Indian ['ɪndɪən] adj indisch; (American Indian) indianisch ♦ n Inder(in) m(f); **American ~** Indianer(in) m(f).

Indian Ocean n: the **~** der Indische Ozean.

Indian summer n Altweibersommer m.

India paper n Dünndruckpapier nt.

India rubber n Gummi m, Kautschuk m.

indicate ['ɪndɪkeɪt] vt (an)zeigen; (point to) deuten auf +acc; (mention) andeuten ♦ vi (BRIT: AUT): **to ~ left/right** links/rechts blinken.

indication [ɪndɪ'keɪʃən] n (An)zeichen nt.

indicative [ɪn'dɪkətɪv] n (LING) Indikativ m, Wirklichkeitsform f ♦ adj: **to be ~ of sth** auf etw acc schließen lassen.

indicator ['ɪndɪkeɪtə*] n (instrument, gauge) Anzeiger m; (fig) (An)zeichen nt; (AUT) Richtungsanzeiger m, Blinker m.

indices ['ɪndɪsi:z] npl of **index**.

indict [ɪn'daɪt] vt anklagen.

indictable [ɪn'daɪtəbl] adj (person) strafrechtlich verfolgbar; **~ offence** strafbare Handlung f.

indictment [ɪn'daɪtmənt] n Anklage f; **to be an ~ of sth** (fig) ein Armutszeugnis nt für etw sein.

indifference [ɪn'dɪfrəns] n Gleichgültigkeit f.

indifferent [ɪn'dɪfrənt] adj gleichgültig; (mediocre) mittelmäßig.

indigenous [ɪn'dɪdʒɪnəs] adj einheimisch.

indigestible [ɪndɪ'dʒɛstɪbl] adj unverdaulich.

indigestion [ɪndɪ'dʒɛstʃən] n Magenverstimmung f.

indignant [ɪn'dɪgnənt] adj: **to be ~ at sth/with sb** entrüstet über etw/jdn sein.

indignation [ɪndɪg'neɪʃən] n Entrüstung f.

indignity [ɪn'dɪgnɪtɪ] n Demütigung f.

indigo ['ɪndɪgəʊ] n Indigo nt or m.

indirect [ɪndɪ'rɛkt] adj indirekt; **~ way** or **route** Umweg m.

indirectly [ɪndɪ'rɛktlɪ] adv indirekt.

indiscreet [ɪndɪs'kri:t] adj indiskret.

indiscretion [ɪndɪs'krɛʃən] n Indiskretion f.

indiscriminate [ɪndɪs'krɪmɪnət] adj wahllos; (taste) unkritisch.

indispensable [ɪndɪs'pɛnsəbl] adj unentbehrlich.

indisposed [ɪndɪs'pəʊzd] adj unpässlich.

indisputable [ɪndɪs'pju:təbl] adj unbestreitbar.

indistinct [ɪndɪs'tɪŋkt] adj undeutlich; (image) verschwommen; (noise) schwach.

indistinguishable [ɪndɪs'tɪŋgwɪʃəbl] adj: **~ from** nicht zu unterscheiden von.

individual [ɪndɪ'vɪdjuəl] n Individuum nt, Einzelne(r) f(m) ♦ adj eigen; (single) einzeln; (case, portion) Einzel-; (particular) individuell.

individualist [ɪndɪ'vɪdjuəlɪst] n Individualist(in) m(f).

individuality [ɪndɪvɪdju'ælɪtɪ] n Individualität f.

individually [ɪndɪ'vɪdjuəlɪ] adv einzeln, individuell.

indivisible [ɪndɪ'vɪzɪbl] adj unteilbar.

Indochina [ɪndəʊ'tʃaɪnə] n Indochina nt.

indoctrinate [ɪn'dɒktrɪneɪt] vt indoktrinieren.

indoctrination [ɪndɒktrɪ'neɪʃən] n Indoktrination f.

indolence ['ɪndələns] n Trägheit f.

indolent ['ɪndələnt] adj träge.

Indonesia [ɪndə'ni:zɪə] n Indonesien nt.

Indonesian [ɪndə'ni:zɪən] adj indonesisch ♦ n Indonesier(in) m(f); (LING) Indonesisch nt.

indoor ['ɪndɔ:*] adj (plant, aerial) Zimmer-; (clothes, shoes) Haus-; (swimming pool, sport) Hallen-; (games) im Haus.

indoors [ɪn'dɔ:z] adv drinnen; **to go ~** hineingehen.

indubitable [ɪn'dju:bɪtəbl] adj unzweifelhaft.

indubitably [ɪn'dju:bɪtəblɪ] adv zweifellos.

induce [ɪn'dju:s] vt herbeiführen; (persuade)

dazu bringen; (*MED*: *birth*) einleiten; **to ~ sb to do sth** jdn dazu bewegen *or* bringen, etw zu tun.

inducement [ɪn'djuːsmənt] *n* Anreiz *m*; (*pej*: *bribe*) Bestechung *f*.

induct [ɪn'dʌkt] *vt* (in sein/ihr *etc* Amt) einführen.

induction [ɪn'dʌkʃən] *n* (*MED*: *of birth*) Einleitung *f*.

induction course (*BRIT*) *n* Einführungskurs *m*.

indulge [ɪn'dʌldʒ] *vt* nachgeben +*dat*; (*person, child*) verwöhnen ♦ *vi*: **to ~ in** sich hingeben +*dat*.

indulgence [ɪn'dʌldʒəns] *n* (*pleasure*) Luxus *m*; (*leniency*) Nachgiebigkeit *f*.

indulgent [ɪn'dʌldʒənt] *adj* nachsichtig.

industrial [ɪn'dʌstrɪəl] *adj* industriell; (*accident*) Arbeits-; (*city*) Industrie-.

industrial action *n* Arbeitskampfmaßnahmen *pl*.

industrial design *n* Industriedesign *nt*.

industrial estate (*BRIT*) *n* Industriegebiet *nt*.

industrialist [ɪn'dʌstrɪəlɪst] *n* Industrielle(r) *f(m)*.

industrialize [ɪn'dʌstrɪəlaɪz] *vt* industrialisieren.

industrial park (*US*) *n* = **industrial estate**.

industrial relations *npl* Beziehungen *zwischen Arbeitgebern, Arbeitnehmern und Gewerkschaften*.

industrial tribunal (*BRIT*) *n* Arbeitsgericht *nt*.

industrial unrest (*BRIT*) *n* Arbeitsunruhen *pl*.

industrious [ɪn'dʌstrɪəs] *adj* fleißig.

industry ['ɪndəstrɪ] *n* Industrie *f*; (*diligence*) Fleiß *m*.

inebriated [ɪ'niːbrɪeɪtɪd] *adj* betrunken.

inedible [ɪn'edɪbl] *adj* ungenießbar.

ineffective [ɪnɪ'fektɪv] *adj* wirkungslos; (*government*) unfähig.

ineffectual [ɪnɪ'fektʃuəl] *adj* = **ineffective**.

inefficiency [ɪnɪ'fɪʃənsɪ] *n* (*see adj*) Ineffizienz *f*; Leistungsunfähigkeit *f*.

inefficient [ɪnɪ'fɪʃənt] *adj* ineffizient; (*machine*) leistungsunfähig.

inelegant [ɪn'elɪgənt] *adj* unelegant.

ineligible [ɪn'elɪdʒɪbl] *adj* (*candidate*) nicht wählbar; **to be ~ for sth** zu etw nicht berechtigt sein.

inept [ɪ'nept] *adj* (*politician*) unfähig; (*management*) stümperhaft.

ineptitude [ɪ'neptɪtjuːd] *n* (*see adj*) Unfähigkeit *f*; Stümperhaftigkeit *f*.

inequality [ɪnɪ'kwɒlɪtɪ] *n* Ungleichheit *f*.

inequitable [ɪn'ekwɪtəbl] *adj* ungerecht.

inert [ɪ'nɜːt] *adj* unbeweglich; **~ gas** Edelgas *nt*.

inertia [ɪ'nɜːʃə] *n* Trägheit *f*.

inertia-reel seat belt [ɪ'nɜːʃə'riːl-] *n* Automatikgurt *m*.

inescapable [ɪnɪ'skeɪpəbl] *adj* unvermeidlich;

(*conclusion*) zwangsläufig.

inessential [ɪnɪ'senʃl] *adj* unwesentlich; (*furniture etc*) entbehrlich.

inessentials [ɪnɪ'senʃlz] *npl* Nebensächlichkeiten *pl*.

inestimable [ɪn'estɪməbl] *adj* unschätzbar.

inevitability [ɪnevɪtə'bɪlɪtɪ] *n* Unvermeidlichkeit *f*; **it is an ~** es ist nicht zu vermeiden.

inevitable [ɪn'evɪtəbl] *adj* unvermeidlich; (*result*) zwangsläufig.

inevitably [ɪn'evɪtəblɪ] *adv* zwangsläufig; **~, he was late** es konnte ja nicht ausbleiben, dass er zu spät kam; **as ~ happens ...** wie es immer so ist ...

inexact [ɪnɪg'zækt] *adj* ungenau.

inexcusable [ɪnɪks'kjuːzəbl] *adj* unentschuldbar, unverzeihlich.

inexhaustible [ɪnɪg'zɔːstɪbl] *adj* unerschöpflich.

inexorable [ɪn'eksərəbl] *adj* unaufhaltsam.

inexpensive [ɪnɪk'spensɪv] *adj* preisgünstig.

inexperience [ɪnɪk'spɪərɪəns] *n* Unerfahrenheit *f*.

inexperienced [ɪnɪk'spɪərɪənst] *adj* unerfahren; (*swimmer etc*) ungeübt; **to be ~ in sth** wenig Erfahrung mit etw haben.

inexplicable [ɪnɪk'splɪkəbl] *adj* unerklärlich.

inexpressible [ɪnɪk'spresɪbl] *adj* unbeschreiblich.

inextricable [ɪnɪk'strɪkəbl] *adj* unentwirrbar; (*dilemma*) unlösbar.

inextricably [ɪnɪk'strɪkəblɪ] *adv* unentwirrbar; (*linked*) untrennbar.

infallibility [ɪnfælə'bɪlɪtɪ] *n* Unfehlbarkeit *f*.

infallible [ɪn'fælɪbl] *adj* unfehlbar.

infamous ['ɪnfəməs] *adj* niederträchtig.

infamy ['ɪnfəmɪ] *n* Verrufenheit *f*.

infancy ['ɪnfənsɪ] *n* frühe Kindheit *f*; (*of movement, firm*) Anfangsstadium *nt*.

infant ['ɪnfənt] *n* Säugling *m*; (*young child*) Kleinkind *nt* ♦ *cpd* Säuglings-.

infantile ['ɪnfəntaɪl] *adj* kindisch, infantil; (*disease*) Kinder-.

infantry ['ɪnfəntrɪ] *n* Infanterie *f*.

infantryman ['ɪnfəntrɪmən] (*irreg*: *like* **man**) *n* Infanterist *m*.

infant school (*BRIT*) *n* Grundschule *f* (*für die ersten beiden Jahrgänge*).

infatuated [ɪn'fætjueɪtɪd] *adj*: **~ with** vernarrt in +*acc*; **to become ~ with** sich vernarren in +*acc*.

infatuation [ɪnfætju'eɪʃən] *n* Vernarrtheit *f*.

infect [ɪn'fekt] *vt* anstecken (*also fig*), infizieren; (*food*) verseuchen; **to become ~ed** (*wound*) sich entzünden.

infection [ɪn'fekʃən] *n* Infektion *f*, Entzündung *f*; (*contagion*) Ansteckung *f*.

infectious [ɪn'fekʃəs] *adj* ansteckend.

infer [ɪn'fɜː*] *vt* schließen; (*imply*) andeuten.

inference ['ɪnfərəns] *n* (*see vb*) Schluss *m*; Andeutung *f*.

inferior [ɪn'fɪərɪə*] adj (in rank) untergeordnet, niedriger; (in quality) minderwertig; (in quantity, number) geringer ♦ n Untergebene(r) f(m); **to feel** ~ **(to sb)** sich (jdm) unterlegen fühlen.

inferiority [ɪnfɪərɪ'ɔrətɪ] n (see adj) untergeordnete Stellung f, niedriger Rang m; Minderwertigkeit f; geringere Zahl f.

inferiority complex n Minderwertigkeitskomplex m.

infernal [ɪn'fɜːnl] adj höllisch; (temper) schrecklich.

inferno [ɪn'fɜːnəu] n (blaze) Flammenmeer nt.

infertile [ɪn'fɜːtaɪl] adj unfruchtbar.

infertility [ɪnfə:'tɪlɪtɪ] n Unfruchtbarkeit f.

infested [ɪn'fɛstɪd] adj: ~ **(with)** verseucht (mit).

infidelity [ɪnfɪ'dɛlɪtɪ] n Untreue f.

infighting ['ɪnfaɪtɪŋ] n interne Machtkämpfe pl.

infiltrate ['ɪnfɪltreɪt] vt (organization etc) infiltrieren, unterwandern; (: to spy) einschleusen.

infinite ['ɪnfɪnɪt] adj unendlich; (time, money) unendlich viel.

infinitely ['ɪnfɪnɪtlɪ] adv unendlich viel.

infinitesimal [ɪnfɪnɪ'tɛsɪməl] adj unendlich klein, winzig.

infinitive [ɪn'fɪnɪtɪv] n (LING) Infinitiv m, Grundform f.

infinity [ɪn'fɪnɪtɪ] n Unendlichkeit f; (MATH, PHOT) Unendliche nt; **an** ~ **of** ... unendlich viel(e) ...

infirm [ɪn'fɜːm] adj schwach, gebrechlich.

infirmary [ɪn'fɜːmərɪ] n Krankenhaus nt.

infirmity [ɪn'fɜːmɪtɪ] n Schwäche f, Gebrechlichkeit f.

inflame [ɪn'fleɪm] vt aufbringen.

inflamed [ɪn'fleɪmd] adj entzündet.

inflammable [ɪn'flæməbl] adj feuergefährlich.

inflammation [ɪnflə'meɪʃən] n Entzündung f.

inflammatory [ɪn'flæmətərɪ] adj (speech) aufrührerisch, Hetz-.

inflatable [ɪn'fleɪtəbl] adj aufblasbar; (dinghy) Schlauch-.

inflate [ɪn'fleɪt] vt aufpumpen; (balloon) aufblasen; (price) hochtreiben; (expectation) steigern; (position, ideas etc) hochspielen.

inflated [ɪn'fleɪtɪd] adj (value, price) überhöht.

inflation [ɪn'fleɪʃən] n Inflation f.

inflationary [ɪn'fleɪʃənərɪ] adj inflationär; (spiral) Inflations-.

inflexible [ɪn'flɛksɪbl] adj inflexibel; (rule) starr.

inflict [ɪn'flɪkt] vt: **to** ~ **sth on sb** (damage, suffering, wound) jdm etw zufügen; (punishment) jdm etw auferlegen; (fig: problems) jdn mit etw belasten.

infliction [ɪn'flɪkʃən] n (see vb) Zufügen nt; Auferlegung f, Belastung f.

in-flight ['ɪnflaɪt] adj während des Fluges.

inflow ['ɪnfləu] n Zustrom m.

influence ['ɪnfluəns] n Einfluss m ♦ vt beeinflussen; **under the** ~ **of alcohol** unter Alkoholeinfluss.

influential [ɪnflu'ɛnʃl] adj einflussreich.

influenza [ɪnflu'ɛnzə] n (MED) Grippe f.

influx ['ɪnflʌks] n (of refugees) Zustrom m; (of funds) Zufuhr f.

inform [ɪn'fɔːm] vt: **to** ~ **sb of sth** jdn von etw unterrichten, jdn über etw acc informieren ♦ vi: **to** ~ **on sb** jdn denunzieren.

informal [ɪn'fɔːml] adj ungezwungen; (manner, clothes) leger; (unofficial) inoffiziell; (announcement, invitation) informell.

informality [ɪnfɔː'mælɪtɪ] n (see adj) Ungezwungenheit f; legere Art f; inoffizieller Charakter m; informeller Charakter m.

informally [ɪn'fɔːməlɪ] adv (see adj) ungezwungen; leger; inoffiziell; informell.

informant [ɪn'fɔːmənt] n Informant(in) m(f).

information [ɪnfə'meɪʃən] n Informationen pl, Auskunft f; (knowledge) Wissen nt; **to get** ~ **on** sich informieren über +acc; **a piece of** ~ eine Auskunft or Information; **for your** ~ zu Ihrer Information.

information and communication technology (BRIT) n (SCOL) ≈ Informations- und Kommunikationstechnologie.

information bureau n Auskunftsbüro nt.

information desk n Auskunftsschalter m.

information office n Auskunftsbüro nt.

information processing n Informationsverarbeitung f.

information retrieval n Informationsabruf m, Datenabruf m.

information science n Informatik f.

information superhighway n (COMPUT) Datenautobahn f.

information technology n Informationstechnik f.

informative [ɪn'fɔːmətɪv] adj aufschlussreich.

informed [ɪn'fɔːmd] adj informiert; (guess, opinion) wohl begründet; **to be well/better** ~ gut/besser informiert sein.

informer [ɪn'fɔːmə*] n Informant(in) m(f); (also: **police** ~) Polizeispitzel m.

infra dig ['ɪnfrə'dɪg] (inf) adj abbr (= infra dignitatem) unter meiner/seiner etc Würde.

infrared [ɪnfrə'rɛd] adj infrarot.

infrastructure ['ɪnfrəstrʌktʃə*] n Infrastruktur f.

infrequent [ɪn'friːkwənt] adj selten.

infringe [ɪn'frɪndʒ] vt (law) verstoßen gegen, übertreten ♦ vi: **to** ~ **on** (rights) verletzen.

infringement [ɪn'frɪndʒmənt] n (see vb) Verstoß m, Übertretung f; Verletzung f.

infuriate [ɪn'fjuərɪeɪt] vt wütend machen.

infuriating [ɪn'fjuərɪeɪtɪŋ] adj äußerst ärgerlich.

infuse [ɪn'fjuːz] vt (tea etc) aufgießen; **to** ~ **sb with sth** (fig) jdm etw einflößen.

infusion [ɪn'fjuːʒən] n (tea etc) Aufguss m.

ingenious [ɪn'dʒiːnjəs] adj genial.

ingenuity [ɪndʒɪ'njuːɪtɪ] *n* Einfallsreichtum *m*; (*skill*) Geschicklichkeit *f*.

ingenuous [ɪn'dʒɛnjuəs] *adj* offen, aufrichtig; (*innocent*) naiv.

ingot ['ɪŋgət] *n* Barren *m*.

ingrained [ɪn'greɪnd] *adj* (*habit*) fest; (*belief*) unerschütterlich.

ingratiate [ɪn'greɪʃɪeɪt] *vt*: **to ~ o.s. with sb** sich bei jdm einschmeicheln.

ingratiating [ɪn'greɪʃɪeɪtɪŋ] *adj* schmeichlerisch.

ingratitude [ɪn'grætɪtjuːd] *n* Undank *m*.

ingredient [ɪn'griːdɪənt] *n* (*of cake etc*) Zutat *f*; (*of situation*) Bestandteil *m*.

ingrowing ['ɪngrəʊɪŋ] *adj*: **~ toenail** eingewachsener Zehennagel *m*.

inhabit [ɪn'hæbɪt] *vt* bewohnen, wohnen in +*dat*.

inhabitant [ɪn'hæbɪtnt] *n* Einwohner(in) *m(f)*; (*of street, house*) Bewohner(in) *m(f)*.

inhale [ɪn'heɪl] *vt* einatmen ♦ *vi* einatmen; (*when smoking*) inhalieren.

inhaler [ɪn'heɪlə'] *n* Inhalationsapparat *m*.

inherent [ɪn'hɪərənt] *adj*: **~ in** *or* **to** eigen +*dat*.

inherently [ɪn'hɪərəntlɪ] *adv* von Natur aus.

inherit [ɪn'herɪt] *vt* erben.

inheritance [ɪn'herɪtəns] *n* Erbe *nt*.

inhibit [ɪn'hɪbɪt] *vt* hemmen.

inhibited [ɪn'hɪbɪtɪd] *adj* gehemmt.

inhibiting [ɪn'hɪbɪtɪŋ] *adj* hemmend; **~ factor** Hemmnis *nt*.

inhibition [ɪnhɪ'bɪʃən] *n* Hemmung *f*.

inhospitable [ɪnhɒs'pɪtəbl] *adj* ungastlich; (*place, climate*) unwirtlich.

in-house ['ɪn'haus] *adj*, *adv* hausintern.

inhuman [ɪn'hjuːmən] *adj* (*behaviour*) unmenschlich; (*appearance*) nicht menschlich.

inhumane [ɪnhju:'meɪn] *adj* inhuman; (*treatment*) menschenunwürdig.

inimitable [ɪ'nɪmɪtəbl] *adj* unnachahmlich.

iniquitous [ɪ'nɪkwɪtəs] *adj* (*unfair*) ungerecht.

iniquity [ɪ'nɪkwɪtɪ] *n* Ungerechtigkeit *f*; (*wickedness*) Ungeheuerlichkeit *f*.

initial [ɪ'nɪʃl] *adj* anfänglich; (*stage*) Anfangs- ♦ *n* Initiale *f*, Anfangsbuchstabe *m* ♦ *vt* (*document*) abzeichnen; **initials** *npl* Initialen *pl*; (*as signature*) Namenszeichen *nt*.

initialize [ɪ'nɪʃəlaɪz] *vt* initialisieren.

initially [ɪ'nɪʃəlɪ] *adv* zu Anfang; (*first*) zuerst.

initiate [ɪ'nɪʃɪeɪt] *vt* (*talks*) eröffnen; (*process*) einleiten; (*new member*) feierlich aufnehmen; **to ~ sb into a secret** jdn in ein Geheimnis einweihen; **to ~ proceedings against sb** (*LAW*) einen Prozess gegen jdn anstrengen.

initiation [ɪnɪʃɪ'eɪʃən] *n* (*beginning*) Einführung *f*; (*into secret etc*) Einweihung *f*.

initiative [ɪ'nɪʃətɪv] *n* Initiative *f*; **to take the ~** die Initiative ergreifen.

inject [ɪn'dʒɛkt] *vt* (ein)spritzen; (*fig: funds*) hineinpumpen; **to ~ sb with sth** jdm etw

spritzen *or* injizieren; **to ~ money into sth** (*fig*) Geld in etw *acc* pumpen.

injection [ɪn'dʒɛkʃən] *n* Spritze *f*, Injektion *f*; **to give/have an ~** eine Spritze *or* Injektion geben/bekommen; **an ~ of money/funds** (*fig*) eine Finanzspritze.

injudicious [ɪndʒu'dɪʃəs] *adj* unklug.

injunction [ɪn'dʒʌŋkʃən] *n* (*LAW*) gerichtliche Verfügung *f*.

injure ['ɪndʒə'] *vt* verletzen; (*reputation*) schaden +*dat*; **to ~ o.s.** sich verletzen.

injured ['ɪndʒəd] *adj* verletzt; (*tone*) gekränkt; **~ party** (*LAW*) Geschädigte(r) *f(m)*.

injurious [ɪn'dʒuərɪəs] *adj*: **to be ~ to** schaden +*dat*, schädlich sein +*dat*.

injury ['ɪndʒərɪ] *n* Verletzung *f*; **to escape without ~** unverletzt davonkommen.

injury time *n* (*SPORT*) Nachspielzeit *f*; **to play ~** nachspielen.

injustice [ɪn'dʒʌstɪs] *n* Ungerechtigkeit *f*; **you do me an ~** Sie tun mir unrecht.

ink [ɪŋk] *n* Tinte *f*; (*in printing*) Druckfarbe *f*.

ink-jet printer ['ɪŋkdʒɛt-] *n* Tintenstrahldrucker *m*.

inkling ['ɪŋklɪŋ] *n* (dunkle) Ahnung *f*; **to have an ~ of** ahnen.

ink pad *n* Stempelkissen *nt*.

inky ['ɪŋkɪ] *adj* tintenschwarz; (*fingers*) tintenbeschmiert.

inlaid ['ɪnleɪd] *adj* eingelegt.

inland ['ɪnlənd] *adj* (*port, sea, waterway*) Binnen- ♦ *adv* (*travel*) landeinwärts.

Inland Revenue (*BRIT*) *n* ≈ Finanzamt *nt*.

in-laws ['ɪnlɔːz] *npl* (*parents-in-law*) Schwiegereltern *pl*; (*other relatives*) angeheiratete Verwandte *pl*.

inlet ['ɪnlet] *n* (schmale) Bucht *f*.

inlet pipe *n* Zuleitung *f*, Zuleitungsrohr *nt*.

inmate ['ɪnmeɪt] *n* Insasse *m*, Insassin *f*.

inmost ['ɪnməust] *adj* innerst.

inn [ɪn] *n* Gasthaus *nt*.

innards ['ɪnədz] (*inf*) *npl* Innereien *pl*.

innate [ɪ'neɪt] *adj* angeboren.

inner ['ɪnə'] *adj* innere(r, s); (*courtyard*) Innen-.

inner city *n* Innenstadt *f*.

innermost ['ɪnəməust] *adj* = **inmost**.

inner tube *n* (*of tyre*) Schlauch *m*.

innings ['ɪnɪŋz] *n* (*CRICKET*) Innenrunde *f*; **he's had a good ~** (*fig*) er kann auf ein langes, ausgefülltes Leben zurückblicken.

innocence ['ɪnəsns] *n* Unschuld *f*.

innocent ['ɪnəsnt] *adj* unschuldig.

innocuous [ɪ'nɒkjuəs] *adj* harmlos.

innovation [ɪnəu'veɪʃən] *n* Neuerung *f*.

innuendo [ɪnju'ɛndəu] (*pl* ~**es**) *n* versteckte Andeutung *f*.

innumerable [ɪ'njuːmrəbl] *adj* unzählig.

inoculate [ɪ'nɒkjuleɪt] *vt*: **to ~ sb against sth** jdn gegen etw impfen; **to ~ sb with sth** jdm etw einimpfen.

inoculation [ɪnɒkju'leɪʃən] *n* Impfung *f*.

inoffensive [ɪnə'fɛnsɪv] *adj* harmlos.

inopportune [ɪn'ɔpətjuːn] *adj* unangebracht; (*moment*) ungelegen.

inordinate [ɪ'nɔːdɪnət] *adj* (*thirst etc*) unmäßig; (*amount, pleasure*) ungeheuer.

inordinately [ɪ'nɔːdɪnətlɪ] *adv* (*proud*) unmäßig; (*long, large etc*) ungeheuer.

inorganic [ɪnɔː'gænɪk] *adj* anorganisch.

inpatient ['ɪnpeɪʃənt] *n* stationär behandelter Patient *m*, stationär behandelte Patientin *f*.

input ['ɪnput] *n* (*of capital, manpower*) Investition *f*; (*of energy*) Zufuhr *f*; (*COMPUT*) Eingabe *f*, Input *m or nt* ♦ *vt* (*COMPUT*) eingeben.

inquest ['ɪnkwɛst] *n* gerichtliche Untersuchung *f* der Todesursache.

inquire [ɪn'kwaɪə°] *vi*: **to ~ about** sich erkundigen nach, fragen nach ♦ *vt* sich erkundigen nach, fragen nach; **to ~ when/ where/whether** fragen *or* sich erkundigen, wann/wo/ob.

► **inquire after** *vt fus* sich erkundigen nach.

► **inquire into** *vt fus* untersuchen.

inquiring [ɪn'kwaɪərɪŋ] *adj* wissensdurstig.

inquiry [ɪn'kwaɪərɪ] *n* Untersuchung *f*; (*question*) Anfrage *f*; **to hold an ~ into sth** eine Untersuchung +*gen* durchführen.

inquiry desk (*BRIT*) *n* Auskunft *f*, Auskunftsschalter *m*.

inquiry office (*BRIT*) *n* Auskunft *f*, Auskunftsbüro *nt*.

inquisition [ɪnkwɪ'zɪʃən] *n* Untersuchung *f*; (*REL*) **the I~** die Inquisition.

inquisitive [ɪn'kwɪzɪtɪv] *adj* neugierig.

inroads ['ɪnrəudz] *npl*: **to make ~ into** (*savings, supplies*) angreifen.

ins *abbr* (= *inches*) see **inch**.

insane [ɪn'seɪn] *adj* wahnsinnig; (*MED*) geisteskrank.

insanitary [ɪn'sænɪtərɪ] *adj* unhygienisch.

insanity [ɪn'sænɪtɪ] *n* Wahnsinn *m*; (*MED*) Geisteskrankheit *f*.

insatiable [ɪn'seɪʃəbl] *adj* unersättlich.

inscribe [ɪn'skraɪb] *vt* (*on ring*) eingravieren; (*on stone*) einmeißeln; (*on banner*) schreiben; **to ~ a ring/stone/banner with sth** etw in einen Ring eingravieren/in einen Stein einmeißeln/auf ein Spruchband schreiben; **to ~ a book** eine Widmung in ein Buch schreiben.

inscription [ɪn'skrɪpʃən] *n* Inschrift *f*; (*in book*) Widmung *f*.

inscrutable [ɪn'skruːtəbl] *adj* (*comment*) unergründlich; (*expression*) undurchdringlich.

inseam measurement ['ɪnsiːm-] (*US*) *n* innere Beinlänge *f*.

insect ['ɪnsɛkt] *n* Insekt *nt*.

insect bite *n* Insektenstich *m*.

insecticide [ɪn'sɛktɪsaɪd] *n* Insektizid *nt*, Insektengift *nt*.

insect repellent *n* Insektenbekämpfungsmittel *nt*.

insecure [ɪnsɪ'kjuə°] *adj* unsicher.

insecurity [ɪnsɪ'kjuərɪtɪ] *n* Unsicherheit *f*.

insemination [ɪnsɛmɪ'neɪʃən] *n*: **artificial ~** künstliche Besamung *f*.

insensible [ɪn'sɛnsɪbl] *adj* bewusstlos; **~ to** unempfindlich gegen; **~ of** nicht bewusst +*gen*.

insensitive [ɪn'sɛnsɪtɪv] *adj* gefühllos.

insensitivity [ɪnsɛnsɪ'tɪvɪtɪ] *n* Gefühllosigkeit *f*.

inseparable [ɪn'sɛprəbl] *adj* untrennbar; (*friends*) unzertrennlich.

insert [*vt* ɪn'sɔːt, *n* 'ɪnsɔːt] *vt* einfügen; (*into sth*) hineinstecken ♦ *n* (*in newspaper etc*) Beilage *f*; (*in shoe*) Einlage *f*.

insertion [ɪn'sɔːʃən] *n* Hineinstecken *nt*; (*of needle*) Einstechen *nt*; (*of comment*) Einfügen *nt*.

in-service ['ɪn'sɔːvɪs] *adj*: **~ training** (berufsbegleitende) Fortbildung *f*; **~ course** Fortbildungslehrgang *m*.

inshore ['ɪn'ʃɔː°] *adj* (*fishing, waters*) Küsten- ♦ *adv* in Küstennähe; (*move*) auf die Küste zu.

inside ['ɪn'saɪd] *n* Innere(s) *nt*, Innenseite *f*; (*of road*: *BRIT*) linke Spur *f*; (: *US, Europe etc*) rechte Spur *f* ♦ *adj* innere(r, s); (*pocket, cabin, light*) Innen- ♦ *adv* (*go*) nach innen, hinein; (*be*) drinnen ♦ *prep* (*location*) in +*dat*; (*motion*) in +*acc*; **~ 10 minutes** innerhalb von 10 Minuten; **insides** *npl* (*inf*) Bauch *m*; (*innards*) Eingeweide *pl*.

inside forward *n* (*SPORT*) Halbstürmer *m*.

inside information *n* interne Informationen *pl*.

inside lane *n* (*BRIT*) linke Spur *f*; (*US, Europe etc*) rechte Spur *f*.

inside leg measurement (*BRIT*) *n* innere Beinlänge *f*.

inside out *adv* (*know*) in- und auswendig; (*piece of clothing*: *be*) links *or* verkehrt herum; (: *turn*) nach links.

insider [ɪn'saɪdə°] *n* Insider *m*, Eingeweihte(r) *f(m)*.

insider dealing *n* (*STOCK EXCHANGE*) Insiderhandel *m*.

insider trading *n* = **insider dealing**.

inside story *n* Insidestory *f*, Inside Story *f*.

insidious [ɪn'sɪdɪəs] *adj* heimtückisch.

insight ['ɪnsaɪt] *n* Verständnis *nt*; **to gain (an) ~ into** einen Einblick gewinnen in +*acc*.

insignia [ɪn'sɪgnɪə] *npl* Insignien *pl*.

insignificant [ɪnsɪg'nɪfɪknt] *adj* belanglos.

insincere [ɪnsɪn'sɪə°] *adj* unaufrichtig, falsch.

insincerity [ɪnsɪn'sɛrɪtɪ] *n* Unaufrichtigkeit *f*, Falschheit *f*.

insinuate [ɪn'sɪnjueɪt] *vt* anspielen auf +*acc*.

insinuation [ɪnsɪnju'eɪʃən] *n* Anspielung *f*.

insipid [ɪn'sɪpɪd] *adj* fad(e); (*person*) geistlos; (*colour*) langweilig.

insist [ɪn'sɪst] *vi* bestehen; **to ~ on** bestehen auf +*dat*; **to ~ that** darauf bestehen, dass;

(*claim*) behaupten, dass.

insistence [ɪn'sɪstəns] n (*determination*) Bestehen nt.

insistent [ɪn'sɪstənt] adj (*determined*) hartnäckig; (*continual*) andauernd, penetrant (*pej*).

in so far as adv insofern als.

insole ['ɪnsəʊl] n Einlegesohle f.

insolence ['ɪnsələns] n Frechheit f, Unverschämtheit f.

insolent ['ɪnsələnt] adj frech, unverschämt.

insoluble [ɪn'sɒljʊbl] adj unlösbar.

insolvency [ɪn'sɒlvənsɪ] n Zahlungsunfähigkeit f.

insolvent [ɪn'sɒlvənt] adj zahlungsunfähig.

insomnia [ɪn'sɒmnɪə] n Schlaflosigkeit f.

insomniac [ɪn'sɒmnɪæk] n: **to be an ~** an Schlaflosigkeit leiden.

inspect [ɪn'spɛkt] vt kontrollieren; (*examine*) prüfen; (*troops*) inspizieren.

inspection [ɪn'spɛkʃən] n (*see vb*) Kontrolle f; Prüfung f; Inspektion f.

inspector [ɪn'spɛktə*] n Inspektor(in) m(f); (BRIT: *on buses, trains*) Kontrolleur(in) m(f); (: POLICE) Kommissar(in) m(f).

inspiration [ɪnspə'reɪʃən] n Inspiration f; (*idea*) Eingebung f.

inspire [ɪn'spaɪə*] vt inspirieren; (*confidence, hope etc*) (er)wecken.

inspired [ɪn'spaɪəd] adj genial; **in an ~ moment** in einem Augenblick der Inspiration.

inspiring [ɪn'spaɪərɪŋ] adj inspirierend.

inst. (BRIT) abbr (COMM: = *instant*): **of the 16th ~** vom 16. d. M.

instability [ɪnstə'bɪlɪtɪ] n Instabilität f; (*of person*) Labilität f.

install [ɪn'stɔːl] vt installieren; (*telephone*) anschließen; (*official*) einsetzen; **to ~ o.s.** sich niederlassen.

installation [ɪnstə'leɪʃən] n Installation f; (*of telephone*) Anschluss m; (INDUSTRY, MIL: *plant*) Anlage f.

installment plan (US) n Ratenzahlung f.

instalment, (US) **installment** [ɪn'stɔːlmənt] n Rate f; (*of story*) Fortsetzung f; (*of TV serial etc*) (Sende)folge f; **in ~s** in Raten.

instance ['ɪnstəns] n Beispiel nt; **for ~** zum Beispiel; **in that ~** in diesem Fall; **in many ~s** in vielen Fällen; **in the first ~** zuerst or zunächst (einmal).

instant ['ɪnstənt] n Augenblick m ♦ adj (*reaction*) unmittelbar; (*success*) sofortig; **~ food** Schnellgerichte pl; **~ coffee** Instantkaffee m; **the 10th ~** (COMM, ADMIN) der 10. dieses Monats.

instantaneous [ɪnstən'teɪnɪəs] adj unmittelbar.

instantly ['ɪnstəntlɪ] adv sofort.

instant replay n (TV) Wiederholung f.

instead [ɪn'stɛd] adv stattdessen; **~ of** statt +gen; **~ of sb** an jds Stelle dat; **~ of doing sth** anstatt or anstelle or an Stelle etw zu tun.

instep ['ɪnstɛp] n (*of foot*) Spann m; (*of shoe*) Blatt nt.

instigate ['ɪnstɪgeɪt] vt anstiften, anzetteln; (*talks etc*) initiieren.

instigation [ɪnstɪ'geɪʃən] n (*see vb*) Anstiftung f, Anzettelung f; Initiierung f; **at sb's ~** auf jds Betreiben acc.

instil [ɪn'stɪl] vt: **to ~ sth into sb** (*confidence, fear etc*) jdm etw einflößen.

instinct ['ɪnstɪŋkt] n Instinkt m; (*reaction, inclination*) instinktive Reaktion f.

instinctive [ɪn'stɪŋktɪv] adj instinktiv.

instinctively [ɪn'stɪŋktɪvlɪ] adv instinktiv.

institute ['ɪnstɪtjuːt] n Institut nt; (*for teaching*) Hochschule f; (*professional body*) Bund m, Verband m ♦ vt einführen; (*inquiry, course of action*) einleiten; (*proceedings*) anstrengen.

institution [ɪnstɪ'tjuːʃən] n Einführung f; (*organization*) Institution f, Einrichtung f; (*hospital, mental home*) Anstalt f, Heim nt.

institutional [ɪnstɪ'tjuːʃənl] adj (*education*) institutionell; (*value, quality etc*) institutionalisiert; **~ care** Unterbringung f in einem Heim or einer Anstalt; **to be in ~ care** in einem Heim or einer Anstalt sein.

instruct [ɪn'strʌkt] vt: **to ~ sb in sth** jdn in etw dat unterrichten; **to ~ sb to do sth** jdn anweisen, etw zu tun.

instruction [ɪn'strʌkʃən] n Unterricht m; **instructions** npl (*orders*) Anweisungen pl; **~s (for use)** Gebrauchsanweisung f, Gebrauchsanleitung f; **~ book/manual/ leaflet** etc Bedienungsanleitung f.

instructive [ɪn'strʌktɪv] adj lehrreich; (*response*) aufschlussreich.

instructor [ɪn'strʌktə*] n Lehrer(in) m(f).

instrument ['ɪnstrʊmənt] n Instrument nt; (MUS) (Musik)instrument nt.

instrumental [ɪnstrʊ'mɛntl] adj (MUS: *music, accompaniment*) Instrumental-; **to be ~ in** eine bedeutende Rolle spielen bei.

instrumentalist [ɪnstrʊ'mɛntəlɪst] n Instrumentalist(in) m(f).

instrument panel n Armaturenbrett nt.

insubordination [ɪnsəbɔːdɪ'neɪʃən] n Gehorsamsverweigerung f.

insufferable [ɪn'sʌfrəbl] adj unerträglich.

insufficient [ɪnsə'fɪʃənt] adj unzureichend.

insufficiently [ɪnsə'fɪʃəntlɪ] adv unzureichend.

insular ['ɪnsjʊlə*] adj engstirnig.

insulate ['ɪnsjʊleɪt] vt isolieren; (*person, group*) abschirmen.

insulating tape ['ɪnsjʊleɪtɪŋ-] n Isolierband nt.

insulation [ɪnsjʊ'leɪʃən] n (*see vb*) Isolierung f; Abschirmung f.

insulator ['ɪnsjʊleɪtə*] n Isolierstoff m.

insulin ['ɪnsjʊlɪn] n Insulin nt.

insult [n 'ɪnsʌlt, vt ɪn'sʌlt] n Beleidigung f ♦ vt beleidigen.

insulting [ɪn'sʌltɪŋ] adj beleidigend.

insuperable [ɪn'sjuːprəbl] adj unüberwindlich.
insurance [ɪn'ʃuərəns] n Versicherung f; **fire/
life** ~ Brand-/Lebensversicherung f; **to take
out** ~ **(against)** eine Versicherung
abschließen (gegen).
insurance agent n
Versicherungsvertreter(in) m(f).
insurance broker n
Versicherungsmakler(in) m(f).
insurance policy n Versicherungspolice f.
insurance premium n Versicherungsprämie
f.
insure [ɪn'ʃuə*] vt versichern; **to** ~ **o.s./sth
against sth** sich/etw gegen etw versichern;
to ~ **o.s.** or **one's life** eine
Lebensversicherung abschließen; **to**
~ **(o.s.) against sth** (fig) sich gegen etw
absichern; **to be** ~d **for £5,000** für £5000
versichert sein.
insured [ɪn'ʃuəd] n: **the** ~ der/die
Versicherte.
insurer [ɪn'ʃuərə*] n Versicherer m.
insurgent [ɪn'sɔːdʒənt] adj aufständisch ♦ n
Aufständische(r) f(m).
insurmountable [ɪnsə'mauntəbl] adj
unüberwindlich.
insurrection [ɪnsə'rɛkʃən] n Aufstand m.
intact [ɪn'tækt] adj intakt; (whole) ganz;
(unharmed) unversehrt.
intake ['ɪnteɪk] n (of food) Aufnahme f; (of air)
Zufuhr f; (BRIT: SCOL): **an** ~ **of 200 a year**
200 neue Schüler pro Jahr.
intangible [ɪn'tændʒɪbl] adj unbestimmbar;
(idea) vage; (benefit) immateriell.
integer ['ɪntɪdʒə*] n (MATH) ganze Zahl f.
integral ['ɪntɪgrəl] adj wesentlich.
integrate ['ɪntɪgreɪt] vt integrieren ♦ vi sich
integrieren.
integrated circuit ['ɪntɪgreɪtɪd-] n (COMPUT)
integrierter Schaltkreis m.
integration [ɪntɪ'greɪʃən] n Integration f;
racial ~ Rassenintegration f.
integrity [ɪn'tɛgrɪtɪ] n Integrität f; (of group)
Einheit f; (of culture, text) Unversehrtheit f.
intellect ['ɪntəlɛkt] n Intellekt m.
intellectual [ɪntə'lɛktjuəl] adj intellektuell,
geistig ♦ n Intellektuelle(r) f(m).
intelligence [ɪn'tɛlɪdʒəns] n Intelligenz f;
(information) Informationen pl.
intelligence quotient n Intelligenzquotient
m.
intelligence service n Nachrichtendienst m,
Geheimdienst m.
intelligence test n Intelligenztest m.
intelligent [ɪn'tɛlɪdʒənt] adj intelligent;
(decision) klug.
intelligently [ɪn'tɛlɪdʒəntlɪ] adv intelligent.
intelligentsia [ɪntɛlɪ'dʒɛntsɪə] n: **the** ~ die
Intelligenz.
intelligible [ɪn'tɛlɪdʒɪbl] adj verständlich.
intemperate [ɪn'tɛmpərət] adj unmäßig;
(remark) überzogen.

intend [ɪn'tɛnd] vt: **to be** ~**ed for sb** für jdn
gedacht sein; **to** ~ **to do sth** beabsichtigen,
etw zu tun.
intended [ɪn'tɛndɪd] adj (effect, victim)
beabsichtigt; (journey) geplant; (insult)
absichtlich.
intense [ɪn'tɛns] adj intensiv; (anger, joy)
äußerst groß; (person) ernsthaft.
intensely [ɪn'tɛnslɪ] adv äußerst; **I dislike him**
~ ich verabscheue ihn.
intensify [ɪn'tɛnsɪfaɪ] vt intensivieren,
verstärken.
intensity [ɪn'tɛnsɪtɪ] n Intensität f; (of anger)
Heftigkeit f.
intensive [ɪn'tɛnsɪv] adj intensiv.
intensive care n: **to be in** ~ auf der
Intensivstation sein.
intensive care unit n Intensivstation f.
intent [ɪn'tɛnt] n Absicht f ♦ adj (attentive)
aufmerksam; (absorbed): ~ **(on)** versunken
(in +acc); **to all** ~**s and purposes** im Grunde;
to be ~ **on doing sth** entschlossen sein, etw
zu tun.
intention [ɪn'tɛnʃən] n Absicht f.
intentional [ɪn'tɛnʃənl] adj absichtlich.
intentionally [ɪn'tɛnʃnəlɪ] adv absichtlich.
intently [ɪn'tɛntlɪ] adv konzentriert.
inter [ɪn'tɜː*] vt bestatten.
interact [ɪntər'ækt] vi (people) interagieren;
(things) aufeinander einwirken; (ideas) sich
gegenseitig beeinflussen; **to** ~ **with**
interagieren mit; einwirken auf +acc;
beeinflussen.
interaction [ɪntər'ækʃən] n (see vb)
Interaktion f; gegenseitige Einwirkung f;
gegenseitige Beeinflussung f.
interactive [ɪntər'æktɪv] adj (also COMPUT)
interaktiv.
intercede [ɪntə'siːd] vi: **to** ~ **(with sb/on
behalf of sb)** sich (bei jdm/für jdn)
einsetzen.
intercept [ɪntə'sɛpt] vt abfangen.
interception [ɪntə'sɛpʃən] n Abfangen nt.
interchange ['ɪntətʃeɪndʒ] n Austausch m; (on
motorway) (Autobahn)kreuz nt.
interchangeable [ɪntə'tʃeɪndʒəbl] adj
austauschbar.
intercity [ɪntə'sɪtɪ] adj: ~ **train** Intercityzug m.
intercom ['ɪntəkɔm] n (Gegen)sprechanlage f.
interconnect [ɪntəkə'nɛkt] vi (rooms)
miteinander verbunden sein.
intercontinental ['ɪntəkɔntɪ'nɛntl] adj (flight,
missile) Interkontinental-.
intercourse ['ɪntəkɔːs] n (sexual)
(Geschlechts)verkehr m; (social, verbal)
Verkehr m.
interdependence [ɪntədɪ'pɛndəns] n
gegenseitige Abhängigkeit f.
interdependent [ɪntədɪ'pɛndənt] adj
voneinander abhängig.
interest ['ɪntrɪst] n Interesse nt; (COMM: in
company) Anteil m; (: sum of money) Zinsen

pl ♦ *vt* interessieren; **compound** ~ Zinseszins *m*; **simple** ~ einfache Zinsen; **British** ~**s in the Middle East** britische Interessen im Nahen Osten; **his main** ~ **is ...** er interessiert sich hauptsächlich für ...

interested ['ɪntrɪstɪd] *adj* interessiert; (*party, body etc*) beteiligt; **to be** ~ **in sth** für etw interessieren; **to be** ~ **in doing sth** daran interessiert sein, etw zu tun.

interest-free ['ɪntrɪst'friː] *adj, adv* zinslos.

interesting ['ɪntrɪstɪŋ] *adj* interessant.

interest rate *n* Zinssatz *m*.

interface ['ɪntəfeɪs] *n* Verbindung *f*; (*COMPUT*) Schnittstelle *f*.

interfere [ɪntə'fɪə'] *vi*: **to** ~ **in** sich einmischen in +*acc*; **to** ~ **with** (*object*) sich zu schaffen machen an +*dat*; (*plans*) durchkreuzen; (*career, duty, decision*) beeinträchtigen; **don't** ~ misch dich nicht ein.

interference [ɪntə'fɪərəns] *n* Einmischung *f*; (*RADIO, TV*) Störung *f*.

interfering [ɪntə'fɪərɪŋ] *adj* (*person*) sich ständig einmischend.

interim ['ɪntərɪm] *adj* (*agreement, government etc*) Übergangs- ♦ *n*: **in the** ~ in der Zwischenzeit.

interim dividend *n* (*COMM*) Abschlagsdividende *f*.

interior [ɪn'tɪərɪə'] *n* Innere(s) *nt*; (*decor etc*) Innenausstattung *f* ♦ *adj* Innen-.

interior decorator *n* Innenausstatter(in) *m(f)*.

interior designer *n* Innenarchitekt(in) *m(f)*.

interjection [ɪntə'dʒɛkʃən] *n* Einwurf *m*; (*LING*) Interjektion *f*.

interlock [ɪntə'lɔk] *vi* ineinander greifen.

interloper ['ɪntələupə'] *n* Eindringling *m*.

interlude ['ɪntəluːd] *n* Unterbrechung *f*, Pause *f*; (*THEAT*) Zwischenspiel *nt*.

intermarry [ɪntə'mærɪ] *vi* untereinander heiraten.

intermediary [ɪntə'miːdɪərɪ] *n* Vermittler(in) *m(f)*.

intermediate [ɪntə'miːdɪət] *adj* (*stage*) Zwischen-; **an** ~ **student** ein fortgeschrittener Anfänger.

interment [ɪn'təːmənt] *n* Bestattung *f*.

interminable [ɪn'təːmɪnəbl] *adj* endlos.

intermission [ɪntə'mɪʃən] *n* Pause *f*.

intermittent [ɪntə'mɪtnt] *adj* (*noise*) periodisch auftretend; (*publication*) in unregelmäßigen Abständen veröffentlicht.

intermittently [ɪntə'mɪtntlɪ] *adv* (*see adj*) periodisch; in unregelmäßigen Abständen.

intern [*vt* ɪn'təːn, *n* 'ɪntəːn] *vt* internieren ♦ *n* (*US*) Assistenzarzt *m*, Assistenzärztin *f*.

internal [ɪn'təːnl] *adj* innere(r, s); (*pipes*) im Haus; (*politics*) Innen-; (*dispute, reform, memo, structure etc*) intern.

internally [ɪn'təːnəlɪ] *adv*: "**not to be taken** ~" "nicht zum Einnehmen".

Internal Revenue Service (*US*) *n* ≈ Finanzamt *nt*.

international [ɪntə'næʃənl] *adj* international ♦ *n* (*BRIT: SPORT*) Länderspiel *nt*.

International Atomic Energy Agency *n* *Internationale Atomenergiebehörde.*

International Chamber of Commerce *n* Internationale Handelskammer *f*.

International Court of Justice *n* Internationaler Gerichtshof *m*.

international date line *n* Datumsgrenze *f*.

International Labour Organization *n* Internationale Arbeitsorganisation *f*.

internationally [ɪntə'næʃnəlɪ] *adv* international.

International Monetary Fund *n* Internationaler Währungsfonds *m*.

international relations *npl* zwischenstaatliche Beziehungen *pl*.

internecine [ɪntə'niːsaɪn] *adj* mörderisch; (*war*) Vernichtungs-.

internee [ɪntə'niː] *n* Internierte(r) *f(m)*.

Internet ['ɪntənɛt] *n* Internet *nt*.

Internet café *n* Internet-Café *nt*.

internment [ɪn'təːnmənt] *n* Internierung *f*.

interplay ['ɪntəpleɪ] *n*: ~ (**of** *or* **between**) Zusammenspiel *nt* (von).

Interpol ['ɪntəpɔl] *n* Interpol *f*.

interpret [ɪn'təːprɪt] *vt* auslegen, interpretieren; (*translate*) dolmetschen ♦ *vi* dolmetschen.

interpretation [ɪntəːprɪ'teɪʃən] *n* (*see vb*) Auslegung *f*, Interpretation *f*; Dolmetschen *nt*.

interpreter [ɪn'təːprɪtə'] *n* Dolmetscher(in) *m(f)*.

interpreting [ɪn'təːprɪtɪŋ] *n* Dolmetschen *nt*.

interrelated [ɪntərɪ'leɪtɪd] *adj* zusammenhängend.

interrogate [ɪn'tɛrəugeɪt] *vt* verhören; (*witness*) vernehmen.

interrogation [ɪntɛrəu'geɪʃən] *n* (*see vb*) Verhör *nt*; Vernehmung *f*.

interrogative [ɪntə'rɔgətɪv] *adj* (*LING: pronoun*) Interrogativ-, Frage-.

interrogator [ɪn'tɛrəgeɪtə'] *n* (*POLICE*) Vernehmungsbeamte(r) *m*; **the hostage's** ~ derjenige, der die Geisel verhörte.

interrupt [ɪntə'rʌpt] *vt, vi* unterbrechen.

interruption [ɪntə'rʌpʃən] *n* Unterbrechung *f*.

intersect [ɪntə'sɛkt] *vi* sich kreuzen ♦ *vt* durchziehen; (*MATH*) schneiden.

intersection [ɪntə'sɛkʃən] *n* Kreuzung *f*; (*MATH*) Schnittpunkt *m*.

intersperse [ɪntə'spəːs] *vt*: **to be** ~**d with** durchsetzt sein mit; **he** ~**d his lecture with** ... er spickte seine Rede mit ...

intertwine [ɪntə'twaɪn] *vi* sich ineinander verschlingen.

interval ['ɪntəvl] *n* Pause *f*; (*MUS*) Intervall *nt*; **bright** ~**s** (*in weather*) Aufheiterungen *pl*; **at** ~**s** in Abständen.

intervene [ɪntə'viːn] *vi* eingreifen; (*event*) dazwischenkommen; (*time*) dazwischenliegen.

intervening [ıntə'viːnıŋ] *adj (period, years)* dazwischenliegend.

intervention [ıntə'venʃən] *n* Eingreifen *nt*.

interview ['ıntəvjuː] *n (for job)* Vorstellungsgespräch *nt*; *(for place at college etc)* Auswahlgespräch *nt*; *(RADIO, TV etc)* Interview *nt* ♦ *vt (see n)* ein Vorstellungsgespräch/Auswahlgespräch führen mit; interviewen.

interviewee [ıntəvjuˈiː] *n (for job)* Stellenbewerber(in) *m(f)*; *(TV etc)* Interviewgast *m*.

interviewer ['ıntəvjuəˈ] *n* Leiter(in) *m(f)* des Vorstellungsgesprächs/Auswahlgesprächs; *(RADIO, TV etc)* Interviewer(in) *m(f)*.

intestate [ın'testeıt] *adv*: **to die** ~ ohne Testament sterben.

intestinal [ın'testınl] *adj (infection etc)* Darm-.

intestine [ın'testın] *n* Darm *m*.

intimacy ['ıntıməsı] *n* Vertrautheit *f*.

intimate [*adj* 'ıntımət, *vt* 'ıntımeıt] *adj* eng; *(sexual, also restaurant, dinner, atmosphere)* intim; *(conversation, matter, detail)* vertraulich; *(knowledge)* gründlich ♦ *vt* andeuten; *(make known)* zu verstehen geben.

intimately ['ıntımətlı] *adv (see adj)* eng; intim; vertraulich; gründlich.

intimation [ıntıˈmeıʃən] *n* Andeutung *f*.

intimidate [ın'tımıdeıt] *vt* einschüchtern.

intimidation [ıntımıˈdeıʃən] *n* Einschüchterung *f*.

━━━━━━━━ *KEYWORD*

into ['ıntu] *prep* **1** *(indicating motion or direction)* in *+acc*; **to go** ~ **town** in die Stadt gehen; **he worked late** ~ **the night** er arbeitete bis spät in die Nacht; **the car bumped** ~ **the wall** der Wagen fuhr gegen die Mauer. **2** *(indicating change of condition, result)*: **it broke** ~ **pieces** es zerbrach in Stücke; **she translated** ~ **English** sie übersetzte ins Englische; **to change pounds** ~ **dollars** Pfund in Dollar wechseln; **5** ~ **25** 25 durch 5.

intolerable [ın'tɔlərəbl] *adj* unerträglich.

intolerance [ın'tɔlərns] *n* Intoleranz *f*.

intolerant [ın'tɔlərnt] *adj*: ~ **(of)** intolerant (gegenüber).

intonation [ıntəu'neıʃən] *n* Intonation *f*.

intoxicated [ın'tɔksıkeıtıd] *adj* betrunken; *(fig)* berauscht.

intoxication [ıntɔksıˈkeıʃən] *n* (Be)trunkenheit *f*; *(fig)* Rausch *m*.

intractable [ın'træktəbl] *adj* hartnäckig; *(child)* widerspenstig; *(temper)* unbeugsam.

intranet ['ıntrənet] *n (COMPUT)* Intranet *nt*.

intransigence [ın'trænsıdʒəns] *n* Unnachgiebigkeit *f*.

intransigent [ın'trænsıdʒənt] *adj* unnachgiebig.

intransitive [ın'trænsıtıv] *adj (LING)* intransitiv.

intrauterine device ['ıntrəˈjuːtəraın-] *n (MED)* Intrauterinpessar *nt*, Spirale *f (inf)*.

intravenous [ıntrəˈviːnəs] *adj* intravenös.

in-tray ['ıntreı] *n* Ablage *f* für Eingänge.

intrepid [ın'trepıd] *adj* unerschrocken.

intricacy ['ıntrıkəsı] *n* Kompliziertheit *f*.

intricate ['ıntrıkət] *adj* kompliziert.

intrigue [ın'triːg] *n* Intrigen *pl* ♦ *vt* faszinieren.

intriguing [ın'triːgıŋ] *adj* faszinierend.

intrinsic [ın'trınsık] *adj* wesentlich.

introduce [ıntrəˈdjuːs] *vt (sth new)* einführen; *(speaker, TV show etc)* ankündigen; **to** ~ **sb (to sb)** jdn (jdm) vorstellen; **to** ~ **sb to** *(pastime, technique)* jdn einführen in *+acc*; **may I** ~ ...? darf ich ... vorstellen?

introduction [ıntrəˈdʌkʃən] *n* Einführung *f*; *(of person)* Vorstellung *f*; *(to book)* Einleitung *f*; **a letter of** ~ ein Einführungsschreiben *nt*.

introductory [ıntrəˈdʌktərı] *adj* Einführungs-; ~ **remarks** einführende Bemerkungen *pl*; ~ **offer** Einführungsangebot *nt*.

introspection [ıntrəuˈspekʃən] *n* Selbstbeobachtung *f*, Introspektion *f*.

introspective [ıntrəuˈspektıv] *adj* in sich gekehrt.

introvert ['ıntrəuvəːt] *n* Introvertierte(r) *f(m)* ♦ *adj (also:* ~**ed)** introvertiert.

intrude [ın'truːd] *vi* eindringen; **to** ~ **on** stören; *(conversation)* sich einmischen in *+acc*; **am I intruding?** störe ich?

intruder [ın'truːdəˈ] *n* Eindringling *m*.

intrusion [ın'truːʒən] *n* Eindringen *nt*.

intrusive [ın'truːsıv] *adj* aufdringlich.

intuition [ıntjuːˈıʃən] *n* Intuition *f*.

intuitive [ın'tjuːıtıv] *adj* intuitiv; *(feeling)* instinktiv.

inundate ['ınʌndeıt] *vt*: **to** ~ **with** überschwemmen mit.

inure [ın'juəˈ] *vt*: **to** ~ **o.s. to** sich gewöhnen an *+acc*.

invade [ın'veıd] *vt* einfallen in *+acc*; *(fig)* heimsuchen.

invader [ın'veıdəˈ] *n* Invasor *m*.

invalid [*n* 'ınvəlıd, *adj* ın'vælıd] *n* Kranke(r) *f(m)*; *(disabled)* Invalide *m* ♦ *adj* ungültig.

invalidate [ın'vælıdeıt] *vt* entkräften; *(law, marriage, election)* ungültig machen.

invaluable [ın'væljuəbl] *adj* unschätzbar.

invariable [ın'vɛərıəbl] *adj* unveränderlich.

invariably [ın'vɛərıəblı] *adv* ständig, unweigerlich; **she is** ~ **late** sie kommt immer zu spät.

invasion [ın'veıʒən] *n* Invasion *f*; **an** ~ **of privacy** ein Eingriff *m* in die Privatsphäre.

invective [ın'vektıv] *n* Beschimpfungen *pl*.

inveigle [ın'viːgl] *vt*: **to** ~ **sb into sth/doing sth** jdn zu etw verleiten/dazu verleiten, etw zu tun.

invent [ɪn'vɛnt] *vt* erfinden.
invention [ɪn'vɛnʃən] *n* Erfindung *f*.
inventive [ɪn'vɛntɪv] *adj* erfinderisch.
inventiveness [ɪn'vɛntɪvnɪs] *n*
Einfallsreichtum *m*.
inventor [ɪn'vɛntə'] *n* Erfinder(in) *m(f)*.
inventory [ɪn'vəntrɪ] *n* Inventar *nt*.
inventory control *n* (*COMM*)
Bestandskontrolle *f*.
inverse [ɪn'vɜːs] *adj* umgekehrt; **in**
~ **proportion (to)** im umgekehrten
Verhältnis (zu).
invert [ɪn'vɜːt] *vt* umdrehen.
invertebrate [ɪn'vɜːtɪbrət] *n* wirbelloses Tier
nt.
inverted commas [ɪn'vɜːtɪd-] (*BRIT*) *npl*
Anführungszeichen *pl*.
invest [ɪn'vɛst] *vt* investieren ♦ *vi*: ~ **in**
investieren in +*acc*; (*fig*) sich *dat* anschaffen;
to ~ **sb with sth** jdm etw verleihen.
investigate [ɪn'vɛstɪgeɪt] *vt* untersuchen.
investigation [ɪnvɛstɪ'geɪʃən] *n*
Untersuchung *f*.
investigative [ɪn'vɛstɪgeɪtɪv] *adj*: ~ **journalism**
Enthüllungsjournalismus *m*.
investigator [ɪn'vɛstɪgeɪtə'] *n* Ermittler(in)
m(f); **private** ~ Privatdetektiv(in) *m(f)*.
investiture [ɪn'vɛstɪtʃə'] *n* (*of chancellor*)
Amtseinführung *f*; (*of prince*) Investitur *f*.
investment [ɪn'vɛstmənt] *n* Investition *f*.
investment income *n* Kapitalerträge *pl*.
investment trust *n* Investmenttrust *m*.
investor [ɪn'vɛstə'] *n* (Kapital)anleger(in) *m(f)*.
inveterate [ɪn'vɛtərət] *adj* unverbesserlich.
invidious [ɪn'vɪdɪəs] *adj* (*task, job*)
unangenehm; (*comparison, decision*)
ungerecht.
invigilator [ɪn'vɪdʒɪleɪtə'] *n* Aufsicht *f*.
invigorating [ɪn'vɪgəreɪtɪŋ] *adj* belebend;
(*experience etc*) anregend.
invincible [ɪn'vɪnsɪbl] *adj* unbesiegbar; (*belief,
conviction*) unerschütterlich.
inviolate [ɪn'vaɪələt] *adj* sicher; (*truth*)
unantastbar.
invisible [ɪn'vɪzɪbl] *adj* unsichtbar.
invisible mending *n* Kunststopfen *nt*.
invitation [ɪnvɪ'teɪʃən] *n* Einladung *f*; **by**
~ **only** nur auf Einladung; **at sb's** ~ auf jds
Aufforderung *acc* (hin).
invite [ɪn'vaɪt] *vt* einladen; (*discussion*)
auffordern zu; (*criticism*) herausfordern; **to**
~ **sb to do sth** jdn auffordern, etw zu tun;
to ~ **sb to dinner** jdn zum Abendessen
einladen.
▶ **invite out** *vt* einladen.
inviting [ɪn'vaɪtɪŋ] *adj* einladend; (*desirable*)
verlockend.
invoice ['ɪnvɔɪs] *n* Rechnung *f* ♦ *vt* in
Rechnung stellen; **to** ~ **sb for goods** jdm
für Waren eine Rechnung ausstellen.
invoke [ɪn'vəuk] *vt* anrufen; (*feelings,
memories etc*) heraufbeschwören.

involuntary [ɪn'vɔləntrɪ] *adj* unbeabsichtigt;
(*reflex*) unwillkürlich.
involve [ɪn'vɔlv] *vt* (*person*) beteiligen; (*thing*)
verbunden sein mit; (*concern, affect*)
betreffen; **to** ~ **sb in sth** jdn in etw *acc*
verwickeln.
involved [ɪn'vɔlvd] *adj* kompliziert; **the work/
problems** ~ die damit verbundene Arbeit/
verbundenen Schwierigkeiten; **to be** ~ **in**
beteiligt sein an +*dat*; (*be engrossed*)
engagiert sein in +*dat*; **to become** ~ **with sb**
Umgang mit jdm haben; (*emotionally*) mit
jdm eine Beziehung anfangen.
involvement [ɪn'vɔlvmənt] *n* Engagement *nt*;
(*participation*) Beteiligung *f*.
invulnerable [ɪn'vʌlnərəbl] *adj* unverwundbar;
(*ship, building etc*) uneinnehmbar.
inward ['ɪnwəd] *adj* innerste(r, s); (*movement*)
nach innen ♦ *adv* nach innen.
inwardly ['ɪnwədlɪ] *adv* innerlich.
inwards ['ɪnwədz] *adv* nach innen.
I/O *abbr* (*COMPUT*: = *input/output*) E/A.
IOC *n abbr* (= *International Olympic Committee*)
IOC *nt*, IOK *nt*.
iodine ['aɪəudiːn] *n* Jod *nt*.
IOM (*BRIT*) *abbr* (*POST*: = *Isle of Man*).
ion ['aɪən] *n* Ion *nt*.
Ionian Sea [aɪ'əunɪən-] *n*: **the** ~ das Ionische
Meer.
ionizer ['aɪənaɪzə'] *n* Ionisator *m*.
iota [aɪ'əutə] *n* Jota *nt*.
IOU *n abbr* (= *I owe you*) Schuldschein *m*.
IOW (*BRIT*) *abbr* (*POST*: = *Isle of Wight*).
IP *abbr* (*COMPUT*: = *Internet Protocol*) IP.
IPA *n abbr* (= *International Phonetic Alphabet*)
internationale Lautschrift *f*.
IQ *n abbr* (= *intelligence quotient*) IQ *m*.
IRA *n abbr* (= *Irish Republican Army*) IRA *f*; (*US*:
= *individual retirement account*) *privates
Rentensparkonto*.
Iran [ɪ'rɑːn] *n* (der) Iran.
Iranian [ɪ'reɪnɪən] *adj* iranisch ♦ *n* Iraner(in)
m(f); (*LING*) Iranisch *nt*.
Iraq [ɪ'rɑːk] *n* (der) Irak.
Iraqi [ɪ'rɑːkɪ] *adj* irakisch ♦ *n* Iraker(in) *m(f)*.
irascible [ɪ'ræsɪbl] *adj* jähzornig.
irate [aɪ'reɪt] *adj* zornig.
Ireland ['aɪələnd] *n* Irland *nt*; **the Republic of** ~
die Republik Irland.
iris ['aɪrɪs] (*pl* ~**es**) *n* (*ANAT*) Iris *f*,
Regenbogenhaut *f*; (*BOT*) Iris, Schwertlilie *f*.
Irish ['aɪrɪʃ] *adj* irisch ♦ *npl*: **the** ~ die Iren *pl*,
die Irländer *pl*.
Irishman ['aɪrɪʃmən] (*irreg: like* **man**) *n* Ire *m*,
Irländer *m*.
Irish Sea *n*: **the** ~ die Irische See.
Irishwoman ['aɪrɪʃwumən] (*irreg: like* **woman**)
n Irin *f*, Irländerin *f*.
irk [ɜːk] *vt* ärgern.
irksome ['ɜːksəm] *adj* lästig.
IRN *n abbr* (= *Independent Radio News*)
Nachrichtendienst des kommerziellen

Rundfunks.
iron ['aɪən] *n* Eisen *nt*; (*for clothes*) Bügeleisen *nt* ♦ *cpd* Eisen-; (*will, discipline etc*) eisern ♦ *vt* bügeln.
► **iron out** *vt* (*fig*) aus dem Weg räumen.
Iron Curtain *n* **the** ~ der Eiserne Vorhang.
ironic(al) [aɪ'rɒnɪk(l)] *adj* ironisch; (*situation*) paradox, witzig.
ironically [aɪ'rɒnɪklɪ] *adv* ironisch; ~, **the intelligence chief was the last to find out** witzigerweise war der Geheimdienstchef der Letzte, der es erfuhr.
ironing ['aɪənɪŋ] *n* Bügeln *nt*; (*clothes*) Bügelwäsche *f*.
ironing board *n* Bügelbrett *nt*.
iron lung *n* (*MED*) eiserne Lunge *f*.
ironmonger ['aɪənmʌŋgə*] (*BRIT*) *n* Eisen- und Haushaltswarenhändler(in) *m(f)*.
ironmonger's (shop) ['aɪənmʌŋgəz-] (*BRIT*) *n* Eisen- und Haushaltswarenhandlung *f*.
iron ore *n* Eisenerz *nt*.
irons ['aɪənz] *npl* Hand- und Fußschellen *pl*; **to clap sb in** ~ jdn in Eisen legen.
irony ['aɪrənɪ] *n* Ironie *f*; **the** ~ **of it is that ...** das Ironische daran ist, dass ...
irrational [ɪ'ræʃənl] *adj* irrational.
irreconcilable [ɪrɛkən'saɪləbl] *adj* unvereinbar.
irredeemable [ɪrɪ'diːməbl] *adj* (*COMM*) nicht einlösbar; (*loan*) unkündbar; (*fault, character*) unverbesserlich.
irrefutable [ɪrɪ'fjuːtəbl] *adj* unwiderlegbar.
irregular [ɪ'rɛgjulə*] *adj* unregelmäßig; (*surface*) uneben; (*behaviour*) ungehörig.
irregularity [ɪrɛgju'lærɪtɪ] *n* (*see adj*) Unregelmäßigkeit *f*; Unebenheit *f*; Ungehörigkeit *f*.
irrelevance [ɪ'rɛləvəns] *n* Irrelevanz *f*.
irrelevant [ɪ'rɛləvənt] *adj* unwesentlich, irrelevant.
irreligious [ɪrɪ'lɪdʒəs] *adj* unreligiös.
irreparable [ɪ'rɛprəbl] *adj* nicht wieder gutzumachen.
irreplaceable [ɪrɪ'pleɪsəbl] *adj* unersetzlich.
irrepressible [ɪrɪ'prɛsəbl] *adj* (*good humour*) unerschütterlich; (*enthusiasm etc*) unbändig; (*person*) nicht unterzukriegen.
irreproachable [ɪrɪ'prəutʃəbl] *adj* untadelig.
irresistible [ɪrɪ'zɪstɪbl] *adj* unwiderstehlich.
irresolute [ɪ'rɛzəluːt] *adj* unentschlossen.
irrespective [ɪrɪ'spɛktɪv]: ~ **of** *prep* ungeachtet +*gen*.
irresponsible [ɪrɪ'spɒnsɪbl] *adj* verantwortungslos; (*action*) unverantwortlich.
irretrievable [ɪrɪ'triːvəbl] *adj* (*object*) nicht mehr wiederzubekommen; (*loss*) unersetzlich; (*damage*) nicht wieder gutzumachen.
irreverent [ɪ'rɛvərnt] *adj* respektlos.
irrevocable [ɪ'rɛvəkəbl] *adj* unwiderruflich.
irrigate ['ɪrɪgeɪt] *vt* bewässern.
irrigation [ɪrɪ'geɪʃən] *n* Bewässerung *f*.

irritable ['ɪrɪtəbl] *adj* reizbar.
irritant ['ɪrɪtənt] *n* Reizerreger *m*; (*situation etc*) Ärgernis *nt*.
irritate ['ɪrɪteɪt] *vt* ärgern, irritieren; (*MED*) reizen.
irritating ['ɪrɪteɪtɪŋ] *adj* ärgerlich, irritierend; **he is** ~ er kann einem auf die Nerven gehen.
irritation [ɪrɪ'teɪʃən] *n* Ärger *m*; (*MED*) Reizung *f*; (*annoying thing*) Ärgernis *nt*.
IRS (*US*) *n abbr* (= *Internal Revenue Service*) Steuereinzugsbehörde.
is [ɪz] *vb see* **be**.
ISA ['aɪsə] *n abbr* (= *individual savings account*) steuerfreies Sparsystem mit begrenzter Einlagenhöhe.
ISBN *n abbr* (= *International Standard Book Number*) ISBN *f*.
ISDN *n abbr* (= *Integrated Services Digital Network*) ISDN *nt*.
Islam ['ɪzlɑːm] *n* der Islam; (*Islamic countries*) die islamischen Länder *pl*.
Islamic [ɪz'læmɪk] *adj* islamisch.
island ['aɪlənd] *n* Insel *f*; (*also:* **traffic** ~) Verkehrsinsel *f*.
islander ['aɪləndə*] *n* Inselbewohner(in) *m(f)*.
isle [aɪl] *n* Insel *f*.
isn't ['ɪznt] = **is not**.
isobar ['aɪsəubɑː*] *n* Isobare *f*.
isolate ['aɪsəleɪt] *vt* isolieren.
isolated ['aɪsəleɪtɪd] *adj* isoliert; (*place*) abgelegen; ~ **incident** Einzelfall *m*.
isolation [aɪsə'leɪʃən] *n* Isolierung *f*.
isolationism [aɪsə'leɪʃənɪzəm] *n* Isolationismus *m*.
isotope ['aɪsəutəup] *n* Isotop *nt*.
ISP (*COMPUT*) *n abbr* (= *Internet Service Provider*) Provider *m*.
Israel ['ɪzreɪl] *n* Israel *nt*.
Israeli [ɪz'reɪlɪ] *adj* israelisch ♦ *n* Israeli *mf*.
issue ['ɪʃjuː] *n* Frage *f*; (*subject*) Thema *nt*; (*problem*) Problem *nt*; (*of book, stamps etc*) Ausgabe *f*; (*offspring*) Nachkommenschaft *f* ♦ *vt* ausgeben; (*statement*) herausgeben; (*documents*) ausstellen ♦ *vi*: **to** ~ **(from)** dringen (aus); (*liquid*) austreten (aus); **the point at** ~ der Punkt, um den es geht; **to avoid the** ~ ausweichen; **to confuse** *or* **obscure the** ~ es unnötig kompliziert machen; **to** ~ **sth to sb** *or* ~ **sb with sth** jdm etw geben; (*documents*) jdm etw ausstellen; (*gun etc*) jdn mit etw ausstatten; **to take** ~ **with sb (over)** jdm widersprechen (in +*dat*); **to make an** ~ **of sth** etw aufbauschen.
Istanbul [ɪstæn'buːl] *n* Istanbul *nt*.
isthmus ['ɪsməs] *n* Landenge *f*, Isthmus *m*.
IT *n abbr* = **information technology**.

───────── *KEYWORD*

it [ɪt] *pron* **1** (*specific: subject*) er/sie/es; (: *direct object*) ihn/sie/es; (: *indirect object*) ihm/ihr/ihm; **it's on the table** es ist auf dem Tisch; **I**

can't find ~ ich kann es nicht finden; **give ~ to me** gib es mir; **about ~** darüber; **from ~** davon; **in ~** darin; **of ~** davon; **what did you learn from ~?** was hast du daraus gelernt?; **I'm proud of ~** ich bin stolz darauf.

2 (*impersonal*) es; **it's raining** es regnet; **it's Friday tomorrow** morgen ist Freitag; **who is ~? - it's me** wer ist da? - ich bins.

ITA, (*BRIT*) **i.t.a.** *n abbr* (= *initial teaching alphabet*) Alphabet zum Lesenlernen.

Italian [ɪ'tæljən] *adj* italienisch ♦ *n* Italiener(in) *m(f)*; (*LING*) Italienisch *nt*; **the ~s** die Italiener *pl*.

italics [ɪ'tælɪks] *npl* Kursivschrift *f*.

Italy ['ɪtəlɪ] *n* Italien *nt*.

ITC (*BRIT*) *n abbr* (= *Independent Television Commission*) Fernseh-Aufsichtsgremium.

itch [ɪtʃ] *n* Juckreiz *m* ♦ *vi* jucken; **I am ~ing all over** mich juckt es überall; **to ~ to do sth** darauf brennen, etw zu tun.

itchy ['ɪtʃɪ] *adj* juckend; **my back is ~** mein Rücken juckt.

it'd ['ɪtd] = **it would**; **it had**.

item ['aɪtəm] *n* Punkt *m*; (*of collection*) Stück *nt*; (*also:* **news ~**) Meldung *f*; (: *in newspaper*) Zeitungsnotiz *f*; **~s of clothing** Kleidungsstücke *pl*.

itemize ['aɪtəmaɪz] *vt* einzeln aufführen.

itemized bill ['aɪtəmaɪzd-] *n* Rechnung, auf der die Posten einzeln aufgeführt sind.

itinerant [ɪ'tɪnərənt] *adj* (*labourer, priest etc*) Wander-; (*salesman*) reisend.

itinerary [aɪ'tɪnərərɪ] *n* Reiseroute *f*.

it'll ['ɪtl] = **it will**; **it shall**.

ITN (*BRIT*) *n abbr* (*TV:* = *Independent Television News*) Nachrichtendienst des kommerziellen Fernsehens.

its [ɪts] *adj* sein(e), ihr(e) ♦ *pron* seine(r, s), ihre(r, s).

it's [ɪts] = **it is**; **it has**.

itself [ɪt'sɛlf] *pron* sich; (*emphatic*) selbst.

ITV (*BRIT*) *n abbr* (*TV:* = *Independent Television*) kommerzieller Fernsehsender.

ITV

ITV steht für „Independent Television" und ist ein landesweiter privater Fernsehsender in Großbritannien. Unter der Oberaufsicht einer unabhängigen Rundfunkbehörde produzieren Privatfirmen die Programme für die verschiedenen Sendegebiete. **ITV***, das seit 1955 Programme ausstrahlt, wird ganz durch Werbung finanziert und bietet etwa ein Drittel Informationssendungen (Nachrichten, Dokumentarfilme, Aktuelles) und ansonsten Unterhaltung (Sport, Komödien, Drama, Spielshows, Filme).*

IUD *n abbr* = **intrauterine device**.

I've [aɪv] = **I have**.

ivory ['aɪvərɪ] *n* Elfenbein *nt*.

Ivory Coast *n* Elfenbeinküste *f*.

ivory tower *n* (*fig*) Elfenbeinturm *m*.

ivy ['aɪvɪ] *n* Efeu *m*.

Ivy League (*US*) *n* Eliteuniversitäten der USA.

IVY LEAGUE

Als **Ivy League** *bezeichnet man die acht renommiertesten Universitäten im Nordosten der Vereinigten Staaten (Brown, Columbia, Cornell, Dartmouth College, Harvard, Princeton, University of Pennsylvania, Yale), die untereinander Sportwettkämpfe austragen. Der Name bezieht sich auf die efeubewachsenen Mauern der Universitätsgebäude.*

J, j

J, j [dʒeɪ] *n* (*letter*) J *nt*, j *nt*; **~ for Jack**, (*US*) **~ for Jig** ≈ J wie Julius.

JA *n abbr* = **judge advocate**, **joint account**.

J/A *abbr* = **joint account**.

jab [dʒæb] *vt* stoßen; (*with finger, needle*) stechen ♦ *n* (*inf*) Spritze *f* ♦ *vi*: **to ~ at** einstechen auf +*acc*; **to ~ sth into sth** etw in etw *acc* stoßen/stechen.

jack [dʒæk] *n* (*AUT*) Wagenheber *m*; (*BOWLS*) Zielkugel *f*; (*CARDS*) Bube *m*.

▶ **jack in** (*inf*) *vt* aufgeben.

▶ **jack up** *vt* (*AUT*) aufbocken.

jackal ['dʒækl] *n* Schakal *m*.

jackass ['dʒækæs] (*inf*) *n* (*person*) Esel *m*.

jackdaw ['dʒækdɔː] *n* Dohle *f*.

jacket ['dʒækɪt] *n* Jackett *nt*; (*of book*) Schutzumschlag *m*; **potatoes in their ~s, ~ potatoes** in der Schale gebackene Kartoffeln *pl*.

jack-in-the-box ['dʒækɪnðəbɔks] *n* Schachtelteufel *m*, Kastenteufel *m*.

jack-knife ['dʒæknaɪf] *n* Klappmesser *nt* ♦ *vi*: **the lorry ~d** der Anhänger *(des Lastwagens)* hat sich quer gestellt.

jack-of-all-trades ['dʒækəv'ɔːltreɪdz] *n* Alleskönner *m*.

jack plug *n* Bananenstecker *m*.

jackpot ['dʒækpɔt] *n* Hauptgewinn *m*; **to hit the ~** (*fig*) das große Los ziehen.

jacuzzi [dʒə'kuːzɪ] *n* Whirlpool *m*.

jade [dʒeɪd] *n* Jade *m or f*.

jaded ['dʒeɪdɪd] *adj* abgespannt; **to get ~** die Nase voll haben.

JAG *n abbr* = **Judge Advocate General**.

jagged ['dʒægɪd] adj gezackt.
jaguar ['dʒægjuə*] n Jaguar m.
jail [dʒeɪl] n Gefängnis nt ♦ vt einsperren.
jailbird ['dʒeɪlbɜːd] n Knastbruder m (inf).
jailbreak ['dʒeɪlbreɪk] n (Gefängnis)ausbruch m.
jalopy [dʒə'lɒpɪ] (inf) n alte (Klapper)kiste f or Mühle f.
jam [dʒæm] n Marmelade f, Konfitüre f; (also: **traffic** ~) Stau m; (inf: difficulty) Klemme f ♦ vt blockieren; (mechanism, drawer etc) verklemmen; (RADIO) stören ♦ vi klemmen; (gun) Ladehemmung haben; **I'm in a real** ~ (inf) ich stecke wirklich in der Klemme; **to get sb out of a** ~ (inf) jdm aus der Klemme helfen; **to** ~ **sth into sth** etw in etw acc stopfen; **the telephone lines are** ~**med** die Leitungen sind belegt.
Jamaica [dʒə'meɪkə] n Jamaika nt.
Jamaican [dʒə'meɪkən] adj jamaikanisch ♦ n Jamaikaner(in) m(f).
jamb [dʒæm] n (of door) (Tür)pfosten m; (of window) (Fenster)pfosten m.
jamboree [dʒæmbə'riː] n Fest nt.
jam-packed [dʒæm'pækt] adj: ~ **(with)** voll gestopft (mit).
jam session n (MUS) Jamsession f.
Jan. abbr (= January) Jan.
jangle ['dʒæŋgl] vi klimpern.
janitor ['dʒænɪtə*] n Hausmeister(in) m(f).
January ['dʒænjuərɪ] n Januar m; see also **July**.
Japan [dʒə'pæn] n Japan nt.
Japanese [dʒæpə'niːz] adj japanisch ♦ n inv Japaner(in) m(f); (LING) Japanisch nt.
jar [dʒɑː*] n Topf m, Gefäß nt; (glass) Glas nt ♦ vi (sound) gellen; (colours) nicht harmonieren, sich beißen ♦ vt erschüttern; **to** ~ **on sb** jdm auf die Nerven gehen.
jargon ['dʒɑːgən] n Jargon m.
jarring ['dʒɑːrɪŋ] adj (sound) gellend, schrill; (colour) schreiend.
Jas. abbr (= James).
jasmine ['dʒæzmɪn] n Jasmin m.
jaundice ['dʒɔːndɪs] n Gelbsucht f.
jaundiced ['dʒɔːndɪst] adj (view, attitude) zynisch.
jaunt [dʒɔːnt] n Spritztour f.
jaunty ['dʒɔːntɪ] adj munter; (step) schwungvoll.
Java ['dʒɑːvə] n Java nt.
javelin ['dʒævlɪn] n Speer m.
jaw [dʒɔː] n Kiefer m.
jawbone ['dʒɔːbəun] n Kieferknochen m.
jay [dʒeɪ] n Eichelhäher m.
jaywalker ['dʒeɪwɔːkə*] n unachtsamer Fußgänger m, unachtsame Fußgängerin f.
jazz [dʒæz] n Jazz m.
► **jazz up** vt aufpeppen (inf).
jazz band n Jazzband f.
JCB ® n Erdräummaschine f.
JCS (US) n abbr (= Joint Chiefs of Staff) Stabschefs pl.

JD (US) n abbr (= Doctor of Laws) ≈ Dr. jur.; (= Justice Department) ≈ Justizministerium nt.
jealous ['dʒeləs] adj eifersüchtig; (envious) neidisch.
jealously ['dʒeləslɪ] adv eifersüchtig; (enviously) neidisch; (watchfully) sorgsam.
jealousy ['dʒeləsɪ] n Eifersucht f; (envy) Neid m.
jeans [dʒiːnz] npl Jeans pl.
Jeep ® [dʒiːp] n Jeep ® m.
jeer [dʒɪə*] vi höhnische Bemerkungen machen; **to** ~ **at** verhöhnen.
jeering ['dʒɪərɪŋ] adj höhnisch; (crowd) johlend ♦ n Johlen nt.
jeers ['dʒɪəz] npl Buhrufe pl.
jelly ['dʒelɪ] n Götterspeise f; (jam) Gelee m or nt.
jelly baby (BRIT) n Gummibärchen nt.
jellyfish ['dʒelɪfɪʃ] n Qualle f.
jeopardize ['dʒepədaɪz] vt gefährden.
jeopardy ['dʒepədɪ] n: **to be in** ~ gefährdet sein.
jerk [dʒɜːk] n Ruck m; (inf: idiot) Trottel m ♦ vt reißen ♦ vi (vehicle) ruckeln.
jerkin ['dʒɜːkɪn] n Wams nt.
jerky ['dʒɜːkɪ] adj ruckartig.
jerry-built ['dʒerɪbɪlt] adj schlampig gebaut.
jerry can ['dʒerɪ-] n großer Blechkanister m.
Jersey ['dʒɜːzɪ] n Jersey nt.
jersey ['dʒɜːzɪ] n Pullover m; (fabric) Jersey m.
Jerusalem [dʒə'ruːsləm] n Jerusalem nt.
jest [dʒest] n Scherz m.
jester ['dʒestə*] n Narr m.
Jesus ['dʒiːzəs] n Jesus m; ~ **Christ** Jesus Christus m.
jet [dʒet] n Strahl m; (AVIAT) Düsenflugzeug nt; (MINERALOGY, JEWELLERY) Jett m or nt, Gagat m.
jet-black ['dʒet'blæk] adj pechschwarz.
jet engine n Düsentriebwerk nt.
jet lag n Jetlag nt.
jet-propelled ['dʒetprə'peld] adj Düsen-, mit Düsenantrieb.
jetsam ['dʒetsəm] n Strandgut nt; (floating) Treibgut nt.
jet-setter ['dʒetsetə*] n: **to be a** ~ zum Jetset gehören.
jettison ['dʒetɪsn] vt abwerfen; (from ship) über Bord werfen.
jetty ['dʒetɪ] n Landesteg m, Pier m.
Jew [dʒuː] n Jude m, Jüdin f.
jewel ['dʒuːəl] n Edelstein m, Juwel nt (also fig); (in watch) Stein m.
jeweller, (US) **jeweler** ['dʒuːələ*] n Juwelier m.
jeweller's (shop) n Juwelier m, Juweliergeschäft nt.
jewellery, (US) **jewelry** ['dʒuːəlrɪ] n Schmuck m.
Jewess ['dʒuːɪs] n Jüdin f.
Jewish ['dʒuːɪʃ] adj jüdisch.

JFK (*US*) *n abbr* (= *John Fitzgerald Kennedy International Airport*) John-F.-Kennedy-Flughafen *m*.

jib [dʒɪb] *n* (*NAUT*) Klüver *m*; (*of crane*) Ausleger *m* ♦ *vi* (*horse*) scheuen, bocken; **to ~ at doing sth** sich dagegen sträuben, etw zu tun.

jibe [dʒaɪb] *n* = **gibe**.

jiffy ['dʒɪfɪ] (*inf*) *n*: **in a ~** sofort.

jig [dʒɪg] *n lebhafter Volkstanz*.

jigsaw ['dʒɪgsɔ:] *n* (*also:* **~ puzzle**) Puzzle(spiel) *nt*; (*tool*) Stichsäge *f*.

jilt [dʒɪlt] *vt* sitzen lassen.

jingle ['dʒɪŋgl] *n* (*tune*) Jingle *m* ♦ *vi* (*bracelets*) klimpern; (*bells*) bimmeln.

jingoism ['dʒɪŋgəʊɪzəm] *n* Hurrapatriotismus *m*.

jinx [dʒɪŋks] (*inf*) *n* Fluch *m*; **there's a ~ on it** es ist verhext.

jitters ['dʒɪtəz] (*inf*) *npl*: **to get the ~** das große Zittern bekommen.

jittery ['dʒɪtərɪ] (*inf*) *adj* nervös, rappelig.

jiujitsu [dʒu:'dʒɪtsu:] *n* Jiu-Jitsu *nt*.

job [dʒɒb] *n* Arbeit *f*; (*post, employment*) Stelle *f*, Job *m*; **it's not my ~** es ist nicht meine Aufgabe; **a part-time ~** eine Teilzeitbeschäftigung; **a full-time ~** eine Ganztagsstelle; **he's only doing his ~** er tut nur seine Pflicht; **it's a good ~ that ...** nur gut, dass ...; **just the ~!** genau das Richtige!

jobber ['dʒɒbə*] (*BRIT*) *n* Börsenhändler *m*.

jobbing ['dʒɒbɪŋ] (*BRIT*) *adj* Gelegenheits-.

job centre (*BRIT*) *n* Arbeitsamt *nt*.

job creation scheme *n* Arbeitsbeschaffungsmaßnahmen *pl*.

job description *n* Tätigkeitsbeschreibung *f*.

jobless ['dʒɒblɪs] *adj* arbeitslos ♦ *npl*: **the ~** die Arbeitslosen *pl*.

job lot *n* (Waren)posten *m*.

job satisfaction *n* Zufriedenheit *f* am Arbeitsplatz.

job security *n* Sicherheit *f* des Arbeitsplatzes.

job sharing *n* Jobsharing *nt*, Arbeitsplatzteilung *f*.

job specification *n* Tätigkeitsbeschreibung *f*.

Jock [dʒɒk] (*inf*) *n* Schotte *m*.

jockey ['dʒɒkɪ] *n* Jockei *m* ♦ *vi*: **to ~ for position** um eine gute Position rangeln.

jockey box (*US*) *n* (*AUT*) Handschuhfach *nt*.

jocular ['dʒɒkjʊlə*] *adj* spaßig, witzig.

jog [dʒɒg] *vt* (an)stoßen ♦ *vi* joggen, Dauerlauf machen; **to ~ sb's memory** jds Gedächtnis *dat* nachhelfen.

▶ **jog along** *vi* entlangzuckeln (*inf*).

jogger ['dʒɒgə*] *n* Jogger(in) *m(f)*.

jogging ['dʒɒgɪŋ] *n* Jogging *nt*, Joggen *nt*.

john [dʒɒn] (*US: inf*) *n* (*toilet*) Klo *nt*.

join [dʒɔɪn] *vt* (*club, party*) beitreten +*dat*; (*queue*) sich stellen in +*acc*; (*things, places*) verbinden; (*group of people*) sich anschließen +*dat* ♦ *vi* (*roads*) sich treffen; (*rivers*) zusammenfließen ♦ *n* Verbindungsstelle *f*; **to ~ forces (with)** (*fig*) sich zusammentun (mit); **will you ~ us for dinner?** wollen Sie mit uns zu Abend essen?; **I'll ~ you later** ich komme später.

▶ **join in** *vi* mitmachen ♦ *vt fus* sich beteiligen an +*dat*.

▶ **join up** *vi* sich treffen; (*MIL*) zum Militär gehen.

joiner ['dʒɔɪnə*] (*BRIT*) *n* Schreiner(in) *m(f)*.

joinery ['dʒɔɪnərɪ] (*BRIT*) *n* Schreinerei *f*.

joint [dʒɔɪnt] *n* (*in woodwork*) Fuge *f*; (*in pipe etc*) Verbindungsstelle *f*; (*ANAT*) Gelenk *nt*; (*BRIT: CULIN*) Braten *m*; (*inf: place*) Laden *m*; (*: of cannabis*) Joint *m* ♦ *adj* gemeinsam; (*combined*) vereint.

joint account *n* gemeinsames Konto *nt*.

jointly ['dʒɔɪntlɪ] *adv* gemeinsam.

joint ownership *n* Miteigentum *nt*.

joint-stock company ['dʒɔɪnt'stɔk-] *n* Aktiengesellschaft *f*.

joint venture *n* Gemeinschaftsunternehmen *nt*, Jointventure *nt*, Joint Venture *nt*.

joist [dʒɔɪst] *n* Balken *m*, Träger *m*.

joke [dʒəʊk] *n* Witz *m*; (*also:* **practical ~**) Streich *m* ♦ *vi* Witze machen; **to play a ~ on sb** jdm einen Streich spielen.

joker ['dʒəʊkə*] *n* (*CARDS*) Joker *m*.

joking ['dʒəʊkɪŋ] *adj* scherzhaft.

jokingly ['dʒəʊkɪŋlɪ] *adv* scherzhaft, im Spaß.

jollity ['dʒɒlɪtɪ] *n* Fröhlichkeit *f*.

jolly ['dʒɒlɪ] *adj* fröhlich; (*enjoyable*) lustig ♦ *adv* (*BRIT: inf: very*) ganz (schön) ♦ *vt* (*BRIT*): **to ~ sb along** jdm aufmunternd zureden; **~ good!** prima!

jolt [dʒəʊlt] *n* Ruck *m*; (*shock*) Schock *m* ♦ *vt* schütteln; (*subj: bus etc*) durchschütteln; (*emotionally*) aufrütteln.

Jordan ['dʒɔ:dən] *n* Jordanien *nt*; (*river*) Jordan *m*.

Jordanian [dʒɔ:'deɪnɪən] *adj* jordanisch ♦ *n* Jordanier(in) *m(f)*.

joss stick [dʒɒs-] *n* Räucherstäbchen *nt*.

jostle ['dʒɒsl] *vt* anrempeln ♦ *vi* drängeln.

jot [dʒɒt] *n*: **not one ~** kein bisschen.

▶ **jot down** *vt* notieren.

jotter ['dʒɒtə*] (*BRIT*) *n* Notizbuch *nt*; (*pad*) Notizblock *m*.

journal ['dʒə:nl] *n* Zeitschrift *f*; (*diary*) Tagebuch *nt*.

journalese [dʒə:nə'li:z] (*pej*) *n* Pressejargon *m*.

journalism ['dʒə:nəlɪzəm] *n* Journalismus *m*.

journalist ['dʒə:nəlɪst] *n* Journalist(in) *m(f)*.

journey ['dʒə:nɪ] *n* Reise *f* ♦ *vi* reisen; **a 5-hour ~** eine Fahrt von 5 Stunden; **return ~** Rückreise *f*; (*both ways*) Hin- und Rückreise *f*.

jovial ['dʒəʊvɪəl] *adj* fröhlich; (*atmosphere*) freundlich, herzlich.

jowl [dʒaʊl] *n* Backe *f*.

joy [dʒɔɪ] n Freude f.

joyful ['dʒɔɪful] adj freudig.

joyride ['dʒɔɪraɪd] n Spritztour in einem gestohlenen Auto.

joyrider ['dʒɔɪraɪdə*] n Autodieb, der den Wagen nur für eine Spritztour benutzt.

joystick ['dʒɔɪstɪk] n (AVIAT) Steuerknüppel m; (COMPUT) Joystick m.

JP n abbr = **Justice of the Peace.**

Jr abbr (in names: = junior) jun.

JTPA (US) n abbr (= Job Training Partnership Act) Arbeitsbeschaffungsprogramm für benachteiligte Bevölkerungsteile und Minderheiten.

jubilant ['dʒuːbɪlnt] adj überglücklich.

jubilation [dʒuːbɪˈleɪʃən] n Jubel m.

jubilee ['dʒuːbɪliː] n Jubiläum nt; **silver** ~ 25-jähriges Jubiläum; **golden** ~ 50-jähriges Jubiläum.

judge [dʒʌdʒ] n Richter(in) m(f); (in competition) Preisrichter(in) m(f); (fig: expert) Kenner(in) m(f) ♦ vt (LAW: person) die Verhandlung führen über +acc; (: case) verhandeln; (competition) Preisrichter(in) sein bei; (person etc) beurteilen; (consider) halten für; (estimate) einschätzen ♦ vi: **judging by** or **to** ~ **by his expression** seinem Gesichtsausdruck nach zu urteilen; **she's a good** ~ **of character** sie ist ein guter Menschenkenner; **I'll be the** ~ **of that** das müssen Sie mich schon selbst beurteilen lassen; **as far as I can** ~ soweit ich es beurteilen kann; **I** ~**d it necessary to inform him** ich hielt es für nötig, ihn zu informieren.

judge advocate n (MIL) Beisitzer(in) m(f) bei einem Kriegsgericht.

Judge Advocate General n (MIL) Vorsitzender des obersten Militärgerichts.

judg(e)ment ['dʒʌdʒmənt] n Urteil nt; (REL) Gericht nt; (view, opinion) Meinung f; (discernment) Urteilsvermögen nt; **in my** ~ meiner Meinung nach; **to pass** ~ **(on)** (LAW) das Urteil sprechen (über +acc); (fig) ein Urteil fällen (über +acc).

judicial [dʒuːˈdɪʃl] adj gerichtlich, Justiz-; (fig) kritisch; ~ **review** gerichtliche Überprüfung f.

judiciary [dʒuːˈdɪʃɪərɪ] n: **the** ~ die Gerichtsbehörden pl.

judicious [dʒuːˈdɪʃəs] adj klug.

judo ['dʒuːdəu] n Judo nt.

jug [dʒʌg] n Krug m.

jugged hare ['dʒʌgd-] (BRIT) n ≈ Hasenpfeffer m.

juggernaut ['dʒʌgənɔːt] (BRIT) n Fernlastwagen m.

juggle ['dʒʌgl] vi jonglieren.

juggler ['dʒʌglə*] n Jongleur m.

Jugoslav etc ['juːgəuˈslɑːv] = **Yugoslav** etc.

jugular ['dʒʌgjulə*] adj: ~ **(vein)** Drosselvene f.

juice [dʒuːs] n Saft m; (inf: petrol): **we've run out of** ~ wir haben keinen Sprit mehr.

juicy ['dʒuːsɪ] adj saftig.

jukebox ['dʒuːkbɔks] n Musikbox f.

Jul. abbr = **July.**

July [dʒuːˈlaɪ] n Juli m; **the first of** ~ der erste Juli; **on the eleventh of** ~ am elften Juli; **in the month of** ~ im (Monat) Juli; **at the beginning/end of** ~ Anfang/Ende Juli; **in the middle of** ~ Mitte Juli; **during** ~ im Juli; **in** ~ **of next year** im Juli nächsten Jahres; **each** or **every** ~ jedes Jahr im Juli; ~ **was wet this year** der Juli war dieses Jahr ein nasser Monat.

jumble ['dʒʌmbl] n Durcheinander nt; (items for sale) gebrauchte Sachen pl ♦ vt (also: ~ **up**) durcheinander bringen.

JUMBLE SALE

Jumble sale ist ein Wohltätigkeitsbasar, meist in einer Aula oder einem Gemeindehaus abgehalten, bei dem alle möglichen Gebrauchtwaren (vor allem Kleidung, Spielzeug, Bücher, Geschirr und Möbel) verkauft werden. Der Erlös fließt entweder einer Wohltätigkeitsorganisation zu oder wird für örtliche Zwecke verwendet, z. B. die Pfadfinder, die Grundschule, Reparatur der Kirche usw.

---

jumbo (jet) ['dʒʌmbəu-] n Jumbo(jet) m.

jumbo-size ['dʒʌmbəusaɪz] adj (packet etc) Riesen-.

jump [dʒʌmp] vi springen; (with fear, surprise) zusammenzucken; (increase) sprunghaft ansteigen ♦ vt springen über +acc ♦ n (see vb) Sprung m; Zusammenzucken nt; sprunghafter Anstieg m; **to** ~ **the queue** (BRIT) sich vordrängeln.

► **jump about** vi herumspringen.

► **jump at** vt fus (idea) sofort aufgreifen; (chance) sofort ergreifen; **he** ~**ed at the offer** er griff bei dem Angebot sofort zu.

► **jump down** vi herunterspringen.

► **jump up** vi hochspringen; (from seat) aufspringen.

jumped-up ['dʒʌmptʌp] (BRIT: pej) adj eingebildet.

jumper ['dʒʌmpə*] n (BRIT) Pullover m; (US: dress) Trägerkleid nt; (SPORT) Springer(in) m(f).

jumper cables (US) npl = **jump leads.**

jumping jack n Knallfrosch m.

jump jet n Senkrechtstarter m.

jump leads (BRIT) npl Starthilfekabel nt.

jump-start ['dʒʌmpstɑːt] vt (AUT: engine) durch Anschieben des Wagens in Gang bringen.

jump suit n Overall m.

jumpy ['dʒʌmpɪ] adj nervös.

Jun. abbr = **June.**

junction ['dʒʌŋkʃən] (BRIT) n Kreuzung f; (RAIL) Gleisanschluss m.

juncture ['dʒʌŋktʃə*] n: **at this** ~ zu diesem Zeitpunkt.
June [dʒuːn] n Juni m; see also **July**.
jungle ['dʒʌŋgl] n Urwald m, Dschungel m (also fig).
junior ['dʒuːnɪə*] adj jünger; (subordinate) untergeordnet ♦ n Jüngere(r) f(m); (young person) Junior m; **he's ~ to me (by 2 years)**, **he's my ~ (by 2 years)** (younger) er ist (2 Jahre) jünger als ich; **he's ~ to me** (subordinate) er steht unter mir.
junior executive n zweiter Geschäftsführer m, zweite Geschäftsführerin f.
junior high school (US) n ≈ Mittelschule f.
junior minister (BRIT) n Staatssekretär(in) m(f).
junior partner n Juniorpartner(in) m(f).
junior school (BRIT) n ≈ Grundschule f.
junior sizes npl (COMM) Kindergrößen pl.
juniper ['dʒuːnɪpə*] n: ~ **berry** Wacholderbeere f.
junk [dʒʌŋk] n (rubbish) Gerümpel nt; (cheap goods) Ramsch m; (ship) Dschunke f ♦ vt (inf) ausrangieren.
junk bond n (FIN) niedrig eingestuftes Wertpapier mit hohen Ertragschancen bei erhöhtem Risiko.
junket ['dʒʌŋkɪt] n Dickmilch f; (inf. pej: free trip): **to go on a** ~ eine Reise auf Kosten des Steuerzahlers machen.
junk food n ungesundes Essen nt.
junkie ['dʒʌŋkɪ] n (inf) n Fixer(in) m(f).
junk mail n (Post)wurfsendungen pl.
junk room n Rumpelkammer f.
junk shop n Trödelladen m.
Junr abbr (in names: = junior) jun.
junta ['dʒʌntə] n Junta f.
Jupiter ['dʒuːpɪtə*] n Jupiter m.
jurisdiction [dʒuərɪs'dɪkʃən] n Gerichtsbarkeit f; (ADMIN) Zuständigkeit f, Zuständigkeitsbereich m; **it falls** or **comes within/outside my** ~ dafür bin ich zuständig/nicht zuständig.
jurisprudence [dʒuərɪs'pruːdəns] n Jura no art, Rechtswissenschaft f.
juror ['dʒuərə*] n Schöffe m, Schöffin f; (for capital crimes) Geschworene(r) f(m); (in competition) Preisrichter(in) m(f).
jury ['dʒuərɪ] n: **the** ~ die Schöffen pl; (for capital crimes) die Geschworenen pl; (for competition) die Jury, das Preisgericht.
jury box n Schöffenbank f; Geschworenenbank f.
juryman ['dʒuərɪmən] (irreg: like **man**) n = **juror**.
just [dʒʌst] adj gerecht ♦ adv (exactly) genau; (only) nur; **he's** ~ **done it/left** er hat es gerade getan/ist gerade gegangen; ~ **as I expected** genau wie ich erwartet habe; ~ **right** genau richtig; ~ **two o'clock** erst zwei Uhr; **we were** ~ **going** wir wollten gerade gehen; **I was** ~ **about to phone** ich wollte gerade anrufen; **she's** ~ **as clever as**

you sie ist genauso klug wie du; **it's** ~ **as well (that ...)** nur gut, dass ...; ~ **as he was leaving** gerade als er gehen wollte; ~ **before** gerade noch; ~ **enough** gerade genug; ~ **here** genau hier, genau an dieser Stelle; **he** ~ **missed** er hat genau danebengetroffen; **it's** ~ **me** ich bins nur; **it's** ~ **a mistake** es ist nur ein Fehler; ~ **listen** hör mal; ~ **ask someone the way** frage doch einfach jemanden nach dem Weg; **not** ~ **now** nicht gerade jetzt; ~ **a minute!**, ~ **one moment!** einen Moment, bitte!
justice ['dʒʌstɪs] n Justiz f; (of cause, complaint) Berechtigung f; (fairness) Gerechtigkeit f; (US: judge) Richter(in) m(f); **Lord Chief J~** (BRIT) oberster Richter in Großbritannien; **to do** ~ **to** (fig) gerecht werden +dat.
Justice of the Peace n Friedensrichter(in) m(f).
justifiable [dʒʌstɪ'faɪəbl] adj gerechtfertigt, berechtigt.
justifiably [dʒʌstɪ'faɪəblɪ] adv zu Recht, berechtigterweise.
justification [dʒʌstɪfɪ'keɪʃən] n Rechtfertigung f; (TYP) Justierung f.
justify ['dʒʌstɪfaɪ] vt rechtfertigen; (text) justieren; **to be justified in doing sth** etw zu or mit Recht tun.
justly ['dʒʌstlɪ] adv zu or mit Recht; (deservedly) gerecht.
jut [dʒʌt] vi (also: ~ **out**) vorstehen.
jute [dʒuːt] n Jute f.
juvenile ['dʒuːvənaɪl] adj (crime, offenders) Jugend-; (humour, mentality) kindisch, unreif ♦ n Jugendliche(r) f(m).
juvenile delinquency n Jugendkriminalität f.
juvenile delinquent n jugendlicher Straftäter m, jugendliche Straftäterin f.
juxtapose ['dʒʌkstəpəuz] vt nebeneinander stellen.
juxtaposition ['dʒʌkstəpə'zɪʃən] n Nebeneinanderstellung f.

K, k

K¹, k [keɪ] n (letter) K nt, k nt; ~ **for King** ≈ K wie Kaufmann.
K² [keɪ] abbr (= one thousand) K; (COMPUT: = kilobyte) KB; (BRIT: in titles) = **knight**.
kaftan ['kæftæn] n Kaftan m.
Kalahari Desert [kælə'hɑːrɪ-] n: **the** ~ die Kalahari.

kale [keɪl] n Grünkohl m.
kaleidoscope [kə'laɪdəskəup] n Kaleidoskop nt.
kamikaze ['kæmɪ'kɑːzɪ] adj (mission etc) Kamikaze-, Selbstmord-.
Kampala [kæm'pɑːlə] n Kampala nt.
Kampuchea [kæmpu't ʃɪə] n Kampuchea nt.
Kampuchean [kæmpu't ʃɪən] adj kampucheanisch.
kangaroo [kæŋgə'ruː] n Känguru nt.
Kans. (US) abbr (POST: = Kansas).
kaput [kə'put] (inf) adj: **to be ~** kaputt sein.
karaoke [kɑːrə'əukɪ] n Karaoke nt.
karate [kə'rɑːtɪ] n Karate nt.
Kashmir [kæʃ'mɪə] n Kaschmir nt.
kayak ['kaɪæk] n Kajak m or nt.
Kazakhstan [kæzæk'stɑːn] n Kasachstan nt.
KC (BRIT) n abbr (LAW: = King's Counsel) Kronanwalt m.
kd (US) abbr (COMM: = knocked down) (in Einzelteile) zerlegt.
kebab [kə'bæb] n Kebab m.
keel [kiːl] n Kiel m; **on an even ~** (fig) stabil.
▶ **keel over** vi kentern; (person) umkippen.
keen [kiːn] adj begeistert, eifrig; (interest) groß; (desire) heftig; (eye, intelligence, competition, edge) scharf; **to be ~ to do** or **on doing sth** scharf darauf sein, etw zu tun (inf); **to be ~ on sth** an etw dat sehr interessiert sein; **to be ~ on sb** von jdm sehr angetan sein; **I'm not ~ on going** ich brenne nicht gerade darauf, zu gehen.
keenly ['kiːnlɪ] adv (enthusiastically) begeistert; (feel) leidenschaftlich; (look) aufmerksam.
keenness ['kiːnnɪs] n Begeisterung f, Eifer m; **his ~ to go is suspicious** dass er so unbedingt gehen will, ist verdächtig.
keep [kiːp] (pt, pp **kept**) vt behalten; (preserve, store) aufbewahren; (house, shop, accounts, diary) führen; (garden etc) pflegen; (chickens, bees, fig: promise) halten; (family etc) versorgen, unterhalten; (detain) aufhalten; (prevent) abhalten ♦ vi (remain) bleiben; (food) sich halten ♦ n (food etc) Unterhalt m; (of castle) Bergfried m; **to ~ doing sth** etw immer wieder tun; **to ~ sb happy** jdn zufrieden stellen; **to ~ a room tidy** ein Zimmer in Ordnung halten; **to ~ sb waiting** jdn warten lassen; **to ~ an appointment** eine Verabredung einhalten; **to ~ a record of sth** über etw acc Buch führen; **to ~ sth to o.s.** etw für sich behalten; **to ~ sth (back) from sb** etw vor jdm geheim halten; **to ~ sb from doing sth** jdn davon abhalten, etw zu tun; **to ~ sth from happening** etw verhindern; **to ~ time** (clock) genau gehen; **enough for his ~** genug für seinen Unterhalt.
▶ **keep away** vt fern halten ♦ vi: **to ~ away (from)** wegbleiben (von).
▶ **keep back** vt zurückhalten; (tears) unterdrücken; (money) einbehalten ♦ vi zurückbleiben.
▶ **keep down** vt (prices) niedrig halten; (spending) einschränken; (food) bei sich behalten ♦ vi unten bleiben.
▶ **keep in** vt im Haus behalten; (at school) nachsitzen lassen ♦ vi (inf): **to ~ in with sb** sich mit jdm gut stellen.
▶ **keep off** vt fernhalten ♦ vi wegbleiben; "**~ off the grass**" „Betreten des Rasens verboten"; **~ your hands off** Hände weg.
▶ **keep on** vi: **to ~ on doing sth** (continue) etw weiter tun; **to ~ on (about sth)** unaufhörlich (von etw) reden.
▶ **keep out** vt fern halten; "**~ out**" „Zutritt verboten".
▶ **keep up** vt (payments) weiterbezahlen; (standards etc) aufrechterhalten ♦ vi: **to ~ up (with)** mithalten können (mit).
keeper ['kiːpə'] n Wärter(in) m(f).
keep fit n Fitnesstraining nt.
keeping ['kiːpɪŋ] n (care) Obhut f; **in ~ with** in Übereinstimmung mit; **out of ~ with** nicht im Einklang mit; **I'll leave this in your ~** ich vertraue dies deiner Obhut an.
keeps [kiːps] n: **for ~** (inf) für immer.
keepsake ['kiːpseɪk] n Andenken nt.
keg [kɛg] n Fässchen nt; **~ beer** Bier nt vom Fass.
Ken. (US) abbr (POST: = Kentucky).
kennel ['kɛnl] n Hundehütte f.
kennels ['kɛnlz] n Hundeheim nt; **we had to leave our dog in ~ over Christmas** wir mussten unseren Hund über Weihnachten in ein Heim geben.
Kenya ['kɛnjə] n Kenia nt.
Kenyan ['kɛnjən] adj kenianisch ♦ n Kenianer(in) m(f).
kept [kɛpt] pt, pp of **keep**.
kerb [kəːb] (BRIT) n Bordstein m.
kerb crawler [-'krɔːlə'] (inf) n Freier m im Autostrich.
kernel ['kəːnl] n Kern m.
kerosene ['kɛrəsiːn] n Kerosin nt.
kestrel ['kɛstrəl] n Turmfalke m.
ketchup ['kɛtʃəp] n Ket(s)chup m or nt.
kettle ['kɛtl] n Kessel m.
kettledrum ['kɛtldrʌm] n (Kessel)pauke f.
key [kiː] n Schlüssel m; (MUS) Tonart f; (of piano, computer, typewriter) Taste f ♦ cpd (issue etc) Schlüssel- ♦ vt (also: **~ in**) eingeben.
keyboard ['kiːbɔːd] n Tastatur f.
keyboarder ['kiːbɔːdə'] n Datentypist(in) m(f).
keyed up [kiːd-] adj: **to be (all) ~** (ganz) aufgedreht sein (inf).
keyhole ['kiːhəul] n Schlüsselloch nt.
keyhole surgery n Schlüssellochchirurgie f, minimal invasive Chirurgie f.
keynote ['kiːnəut] n Grundton m; (of speech) Leitgedanke m.
keypad ['kiːpæd] n Tastenfeld nt.
key ring n Schlüsselring m.

keystroke ['ki:strəuk] *n* Anschlag *m*.
kg *abbr* (= *kilogram*) kg.
KGB *n abbr* (*POL: formerly*) KGB *m*.
khaki ['kɑːkɪ] *n* K(h)aki *nt*.
kHz *abbr* (= *kilohertz*) kHz.
kibbutz [kɪ'buts] *n* Kibbuz *m*.
kick [kɪk] *vt* treten; (*table, ball*) treten gegen
+*acc*; (*inf: habit*) ablegen; (: *addiction*)
wegkommen von ♦ *vi* (*horse*) ausschlagen
♦ *n* Tritt *m*; (*to ball*) Schuss *m*; (*of rifle*)
Rückstoß *m*; (*thrill*): **he does it for ~s** er
macht es zum Spaß.
► **kick around** (*inf*) *vi* (*person*) rumhängen;
(*thing*) rumliegen.
► **kick off** *vi* (*SPORT*) anstoßen.
kickoff ['kɪkɔf] *n* (*SPORT*) Anstoß *m*.
kick start *n* (*AUT: also:* **~er**) Kickstarter *m*.
kid [kɪd] *n* (*inf: child*) Kind *nt*; (*animal*) Kitz *nt*;
(*leather*) Ziegenleder *nt*, Glacéleder *nt*,
Glaceeleder *nt* ♦ *vi* (*inf*) Witze machen;
~ brother kleiner Bruder *m*; **~ sister** kleine
Schwester *f*.
kid gloves *npl*: **to treat sb with ~** (*fig*) jdn mit
Samthandschuhen anfassen.
kidnap ['kɪdnæp] *vt* entführen, kidnappen.
kidnapper ['kɪdnæpə*] *n* Entführer(in) *m(f)*,
Kidnapper(in) *m(f)*.
kidnapping ['kɪdnæpɪŋ] *n* Entführung *f*,
Kidnapping *nt*.
kidney ['kɪdnɪ] *n* Niere *f*.
kidney bean *n* Gartenbohne *f*.
kidney machine *n* (*MED*) künstliche Niere *f*.
Kilimanjaro [kɪlɪmən'dʒɑːrəu] *n*: **Mount ~** der
Kilimandscharo.
kill [kɪl] *vt* töten; (*murder*) ermorden,
umbringen; (*plant*) eingehen lassen;
(*proposal*) zu Fall bringen; (*rumour*) ein
Ende machen +*dat* ♦ *n* Abschuss *m*; **to ~ time**
die Zeit totschlagen; **to ~ o.s. to do sth** (*fig*)
sich fast umbringen, um etw zu tun; **to
~ o.s. (laughing)** (*fig*) sich totlachen.
► **kill off** *vt* abtöten; (*fig: romance*) beenden.
killer ['kɪlə*] *n* Mörder(in) *m(f)*.
killer instinct *n* (*fig*) Tötungsinstinkt *m*.
killing ['kɪlɪŋ] *n* Töten *nt*; (*instance*) Mord *m*; **to
make a ~** (*inf*) einen Riesengewinn machen.
killjoy ['kɪldʒɔɪ] *n* Spielverderber(in) *m(f)*.
kiln [kɪln] *n* Brennofen *m*.
kilo ['kiːləu] *n* Kilo *nt*.
kilobyte ['kiːləubaɪt] *n* Kilobyte *nt*.
kilogram(me) ['kɪləugræm] *n* Kilogramm *nt*.
kilohertz ['kɪləuhɜːts] *n inv* Kilohertz *nt*.
kilometre, (*US*) **kilometer** ['kɪləmiːtə*] *n*
Kilometer *m*.
kilowatt ['kɪləuwɔt] *n* Kilowatt *nt*.
kilt [kɪlt] *n* Kilt *m*, Schottenrock *m*.
kilter ['kɪltə*] *n*: **out of ~** nicht in Ordnung.
kimono [kɪ'məunəu] *n* Kimono *m*.
kin [kɪn] *n see* **kith, next**.
kind [kaɪnd] *adj* freundlich ♦ *n* Art *f*; (*sort*)
Sorte *f*; **would you be ~ enough to ...?,
would you be so ~ as to ...?** wären Sie

(vielleicht) so nett und ...?; **it's very ~ of you
(to do ...)** es ist wirklich nett von Ihnen(, ...
zu tun); **in ~** (*COMM*) in Naturalien; **a ~ of
... eine Art ...; they are two of a ~** sie sind
beide von der gleichen Art; (*people*) sie sind
vom gleichen Schlag.
kindergarten ['kɪndəgɑːtn] *n* Kindergarten *m*.
kind-hearted [kaɪnd'hɑːtɪd] *adj* gutherzig.
kindle ['kɪndl] *vt* anzünden; (*emotion*) wecken.
kindling ['kɪndlɪŋ] *n* Anzündholz *nt*.
kindly ['kaɪndlɪ] *adj, adv* freundlich, nett; **will
you ~ ...** würden Sie bitte ...; **he didn't take
it ~** er konnte sich damit nicht anfreunden.
kindness ['kaɪndnɪs] *n* Freundlichkeit *f*.
kindred ['kɪndrɪd] *adj*: **~ spirit**
Gleichgesinnte(r) *f(m)*.
kinetic [kɪ'netɪk] *adj* kinetisch.
king [kɪŋ] *n* (*also fig*) König *m*.
kingdom ['kɪndəm] *n* Königreich *nt*.
kingfisher ['kɪŋfɪʃə*] *n* Eisvogel *m*.
kingpin ['kɪŋpɪn] *n* (*TECH*) Bolzen *m*; (*AUT*)
Achsschenkelbolzen *m*; (*fig*) wichtigste
Stütze *f*.
king-size(d) ['kɪŋsaɪz(d)] *adj* extragroß;
(*cigarette*) Kingsize-.
kink [kɪŋk] *n* Knick *m*; (*in hair*) Welle *f*; (*fig*)
Schrulle *f*.
kinky ['kɪŋkɪ] (*pej*) *adj* schrullig; (*sexually*)
abartig.
kinship ['kɪnʃɪp] *n* Verwandtschaft *f*.
kinsman ['kɪnzmən] (*irreg: like* **man**) *n*
Verwandte(r) *m*.
kinswoman ['kɪnzwumən] (*irreg: like* **woman**) *n*
Verwandte *f*.
kiosk ['kiːɔsk] *n* Kiosk *m*; (*BRIT*) (Telefon)zelle
f; (*also:* **newspaper ~**) (Zeitungs)kiosk *m*.
kipper ['kɪpə*] *n* Räucherhering *m*.
Kirghizia [kɜː'gɪzɪə] *n* Kirgistan *nt*.
kiss [kɪs] *n* Kuß *m* ♦ *vt* küssen ♦ *vi* sich küssen;
to ~ (each other) sich küssen; **to ~ sb
goodbye** jdm einen Abschiedskuss geben.
kissagram ['kɪsəgræm] *n durch eine(n)
Angestellte(n) einer Agentur persönlich
übermittelter Kuss.*
kiss of life (*BRIT*) *n*: **the ~** Mund-zu-Mund-
Beatmung *f*.
kit [kɪt] *n* Zeug *nt*, Sachen *pl*; (*equipment: also
MIL*) Ausrüstung *f*; (*set of tools*) Werkzeug *nt*;
(*for assembly*) Bausatz *m*.
► **kit out** (*BRIT*) *vt* ausrüsten, ausstatten.
kitbag ['kɪtbæg] *n* Seesack *m*.
kitchen ['kɪtʃɪn] *n* Küche *f*.
kitchen garden *n* Küchengarten *m*.
kitchen sink *n* Spüle *f*.
kitchen unit (*BRIT*) *n* Küchenschrank *m*.
kitchenware ['kɪtʃɪnwɛə*] *n* Küchengeräte *pl*.
kite [kaɪt] *n* Drachen *m*; (*ZOOL*) Milan *m*.
kith [kɪθ] *n*: **~ and kin** Freunde und
Verwandte *pl*.
kitten ['kɪtn] *n* Kätzchen *nt*.
kitty ['kɪtɪ] *n* (gemeinsame) Kasse *f*.
kiwi (fruit) ['kiːwiː-] *n* Kiwi(frucht) *f*.

KKK (*US*) *n abbr* (= *Ku Klux Klan*) Ku-Klux-Klan *m*.

Kleenex ® ['kli:nɛks] *n* Tempo(taschentuch) ® *nt*.

kleptomaniac [klɛptəʊ'meɪnɪæk] *n* Kleptomane *m*, Kleptomanin *f*.

km *abbr* (= *kilometre*) km.

km/h *abbr* (= *kilometres per hour*) km/h.

knack [næk] *n*: **to have the ~ of doing sth** es heraushaben, wie man etw macht; **there's a ~ to doing this** da ist ein Trick *or* Kniff dabei.

knackered ['nækəd] (*BRIT*: *inf*) *adj* kaputt.

knapsack ['næpsæk] *n* Rucksack *m*.

knead [ni:d] *vt* kneten.

knee [ni:] *n* Knie *nt*.

kneecap ['ni:kæp] *n* Kniescheibe *f*.

kneecapping ['ni:kæpɪŋ] *n* Durchschießen *nt* der Kniescheibe.

knee-deep ['ni:'di:p] *adj, adv*: **the water was ~** das Wasser ging mir *etc* bis zum Knie; **~ in mud** knietief *or* bis zu den Knien im Schlamm.

kneejerk reaction ['ni:dʒə:k-] *n* (*fig*) instinktive Reaktion *f*.

kneel [ni:l] (*pt, pp* **knelt**) *vi* knien; (*also*: **~ down**) niederknien.

kneepad ['ni:pæd] *n* Knieschützer *m*.

knell [nɛl] *n* Totengeläut(e) *nt*; (*fig*) Ende *nt*.

knelt [nɛlt] *pt, pp of* **kneel**.

knew [nju:] *pt of* **know**.

knickers ['nɪkəz] (*BRIT*) *npl* Schlüpfer *m*.

knick-knacks ['nɪknæks] *npl* Nippsachen *pl*.

knife [naɪf] (*pl* **knives**) *n* Messer *nt* ♦ *vt* (*injure, attack*) einstechen auf +*acc*; **~, fork and spoon** Messer, Gabel und Löffel.

knife edge *n*: **to be balanced on a ~** (*fig*) auf Messers Schneide stehen.

knight [naɪt] *n* (*BRIT*) Ritter *m*; (*CHESS*) Springer *m*, Pferd *nt*.

knighthood ['naɪthud] (*BRIT*) *n*: **to get a ~** in den Adelsstand erhoben werden.

knit [nɪt] *vt* stricken ♦ *vi* stricken; (*bones*) zusammenwachsen; **to ~ one's brows** die Stirn runzeln.

knitted ['nɪtɪd] *adj* gestrickt, Strick-.

knitting ['nɪtɪŋ] *n* Stricken *nt*; (*garment being made*) Strickzeug *nt*.

knitting machine *n* Strickmaschine *f*.

knitting needle *n* Stricknadel *f*.

knitting pattern *n* Strickmuster *nt*.

knitwear ['nɪtwɛə*] *n* Strickwaren *pl*.

knives [naɪvz] *npl of* **knife**.

knob [nɔb] *n* Griff *m*; (*of stick*) Knauf *m*; (*on radio, TV etc*) Knopf *m*; **a ~ of butter** (*BRIT*) ein Stückchen *nt* Butter.

knobbly ['nɔblɪ], **knobby** ['nɔbɪ] (*US*) *adj* (*wood*) knorrig; (*surface*) uneben; **~ knees** Knubbelknie *pl* (*inf*).

knock [nɔk] *vt* schlagen; (*bump into*) stoßen gegen +*acc*; (*inf: criticize*) runtermachen ♦ *vi* klopfen ♦ *n* Schlag *m*; (*bump*) Stoß *m*; (*on door*) Klopfen *nt*; **to ~ a nail into sth** einen Nagel in etw *acc* schlagen; **to ~ some sense into sb** jdn zur Vernunft bringen; **to ~ at/ on** klopfen an/auf +*acc*; **he ~ed at the door** er klopfte an, er klopfte an die Tür.

► **knock about** (*inf*) *vt* schlagen, verprügeln ♦ *vi* rumziehen; **~ about with** sich rumtreiben mit.

► **knock around** *vt, vi* = **knock about**.

► **knock back** (*inf*) *vt* (*drink*) sich *dat* hinter die Binde kippen.

► **knock down** *vt* anfahren; (*fatally*) überfahren; (*building etc*) abreißen; (*price: buyer*) herunterhandeln; (: *seller*) heruntergehen mit.

► **knock off** *vi* (*inf*) Feierabend machen ♦ *vt* (*from price*) nachlassen; (*inf: steal*) klauen; **to ~ off £10** £10 nachlassen.

► **knock out** *vt* bewusstlos schlagen; (*subj: drug*) bewusstlos werden lassen; (*BOXING*) k. o. schlagen; (*in game, competition*) besiegen.

► **knock over** *vt* umstoßen; (*with car*) anfahren.

knockdown ['nɔkdaun] *adj*: **~ price** Schleuderpreis *m*.

knocker ['nɔkə*] *n* Türklopfer *m*.

knock-for-knock ['nɔkfə'nɔk] (*BRIT*) *adj*: **~ agreement** Vereinbarung, bei der jede Versicherungsgesellschaft den Schaden am von ihr versicherten Fahrzeug übernimmt.

knocking ['nɔkɪŋ] *n* Klopfen *nt*.

knock-kneed [nɔk'ni:d] *adj* x-beinig, X-beinig; **to be ~** X-Beine haben.

knockout ['nɔkaut] *n* (*BOXING*) K.-o.-Schlag *m*, Ko.-Schlag *m* ♦ *cpd* (*competition etc*) Ausscheidungs-.

knock-up ['nɔkʌp] *n* (*TENNIS*): **to have a ~** ein paar Bälle schlagen.

knot [nɔt] *n* Knoten *m*; (*in wood*) Ast *m* ♦ *vt* einen Knoten machen in +*acc*; (*knot together*) verknoten; **to tie a ~** einen Knoten machen.

knotty ['nɔtɪ] *adj* (*fig*: *problem*) verwickelt.

know [nəʊ] (*pt* **knew**, *pp* **known**) *vt* kennen; (*facts*) wissen; (*language*) können ♦ *vi*: **to ~ about** *or* **of sth/sb** von etw/jdm gehört haben; **to ~ how to swim** schwimmen können; **to get to ~ sth** etw erfahren; (*place*) etw kennen lernen; **I don't ~ him** ich kenne ihn nicht; **to ~ right from wrong** Gut und Böse unterscheiden können; **as far as I ~** soviel ich weiß; **yes, I ~** ja, ich weiß; **I don't ~** ich weiß (es) nicht.

know-all ['nəʊɔ:l] (*BRIT*: *pej*) *n* Alleswisser *m*.

know-how ['nəʊhau] *n* Know-how *nt*, Sachkenntnis *f*.

knowing ['nəʊɪŋ] *adj* wissend.

knowingly ['nəʊɪŋlɪ] *adv* (*purposely*) bewusst; (*smile, look*) wissend.

know-it-all ['nəʊɪtɔ:l] (*US*) *n* = **know-all**.

knowledge ['nɔlɪdʒ] *n* Wissen *nt*, Kenntnis *f*; (*learning, things learnt*) Kenntnisse *pl*; **to have**

no ~ of nichts wissen von; **not to my** ~
nicht, dass ich wüsste; **without my** ~ ohne
mein Wissen; **it is common** ~ **that** ... es ist
allgemein bekannt, dass ...; **it has come to
my** ~ **that** ... ich habe erfahren, dass ...; **to
have a working** ~ **of French**
Grundkenntnisse in Französisch haben.
knowledgeable ['nɔlɪdʒəbl] *adj* informiert.
known [nəun] *pp of* **know ♦** *adj* bekannt;
(*expert*) anerkannt.
knuckle ['nʌkl] *n* (Finger)knöchel *m*.
▶ **knuckle down** (*inf*) *vi* sich dahinter
klemmen; **to** ~ **down to work** sich an die
Arbeit machen.
▶ **knuckle under** (*inf*) *vi* sich fügen, spuren.
knuckle-duster ['nʌkl'dʌstə*] *n* Schlagring *m*.
KO *n abbr* (= *knockout*) K. o. *m* **♦** *vt* k. o.
schlagen.
koala [kəu'ɑ:lə] *n* (*also:* ~ **bear**) Koala(bär) *m*.
kook [ku:k] (*US: inf*) *n* Spinner *m*.
Koran [kɔ'rɑ:n] *n:* **the** ~ der Koran.
Korea [kə'rɪə] *n* Korea *nt;* **North** ~ Nordkorea
nt; **South** ~ Südkorea *nt.*
Korean [kə'rɪən] *adj* koreanisch **♦** *n*
Koreaner(in) *m(f).*
kosher ['kəuʃə*] *adj* koscher.
kowtow ['kau'tau] *vi:* **to** ~ **to sb** vor jdm
dienern *or* einen Kotau machen.
Kremlin ['krɛmlɪn] *n:* **the** ~ der Kreml.
KS (*US*) *abbr* (*POST:* = *Kansas*).
Kt (*BRIT*) *abbr* (*in titles*) = **knight**.
Kuala Lumpur ['kwɑ:lə'lumpuə*] *n* Kuala
Lumpur *nt.*
kudos ['kju:dɔs] *n* Ansehen *nt*, Ehre *f.*
Kurd [kə:d] *n* Kurde *m*, Kurdin *f.*
Kuwait [ku'weɪt] *n* Kuwait *nt.*
Kuwaiti [ku'weɪtɪ] *adj* kuwaitisch **♦** *n*
Kuwaiter(in) *m(f).*
kW *abbr* (= *kilowatt*) kW.
KY (= *US*) *abbr* (*POST:* = *Kentucky*).

L, l

L¹, l¹ [ɛl] *n* (*letter*) L *nt*, l *nt;* ~ **for Lucy,** (*US*)
~ **for Love** ≈ L wie Ludwig.
L² [ɛl] *abbr* (*BRIT: AUT:* = *learner*) am Auto
angebrachtes Kennzeichen für Fahrschüler;
= **lake** (= *large*) gr.; (= *left*) l.
l² *abbr* (= *litre*) l.
LA (*US*) *n abbr* (= *Los Angeles*) **♦** *abbr* (*POST:*
= *Louisiana*).
La. (*US*) *abbr* (*POST:* = *Louisiana*).
lab [læb] *n abbr* = **laboratory**.
label ['leɪbl] *n* Etikett *nt;* (*brand: of record*)
Label *nt* **♦** *vt* etikettieren; (*fig: person*)
abstempeln.

labor *etc* ['leɪbə*] (*US*) *n* = **labour** *etc.*
laboratory [lə'bɔrətərɪ] *n* Labor *nt.*

laborious [lə'bɔ:rɪəs] *adj* mühsam.
labor union (*US*) *n* Gewerkschaft *f.*
labour, (*US*) **labor** ['leɪbə*] *n* Arbeit *f;* (*work
force*) Arbeitskräfte *pl;* (*MED*): **to be in** ~ in
den Wehen liegen **♦** *vi:* **to** ~ **(at sth)** sich
(mit etw) abmühen **♦** *vt:* **to** ~ **a point** auf
einem Thema herumreiten; **L~, the
L~ Party** (*BRIT*) die Labour Party; **hard** ~
Zwangsarbeit *f.*
labour camp *n* Arbeitslager *nt.*
labour cost *n* Lohnkosten *pl.*
labour dispute *n* Arbeitskampf *m.*
laboured ['leɪbəd] *adj* (*breathing*) schwer;
(*movement, style*) schwerfällig.
labourer ['leɪbərə*] *n* Arbeiter(in) *m(f);* **farm** ~
Landarbeiter(in) *m(f).*
labour force *n* Arbeiterschaft *f.*
labour intensive *adj* arbeitsintensiv.
labour market *n* Arbeitsmarkt *m.*
labour pains *npl* Wehen *pl.*
labour relations *npl* Beziehungen *pl*
zwischen Arbeitnehmern, Arbeitgebern
und Gewerkschaften.
labour-saving ['leɪbəseɪvɪŋ] *adj*
arbeitssparend.
laburnum [lə'bə:nəm] *n* (*BOT*) Goldregen *m.*
labyrinth ['læbɪrɪnθ] *n* Labyrinth *nt.*
lace [leɪs] *n* (*fabric*) Spitze *f;* (*of shoe etc*)
(Schuh)band *nt*, Schnürsenkel *m* **♦** *vt* (*also:*
~ **up**) (zu)schnüren; **to** ~ **a drink** einen
Schuss Alkohol in ein Getränk geben.
lacemaking ['leɪsmeɪkɪŋ] *n* Klöppelei *f.*
lacerate ['læsəreɪt] *vt* zerschneiden.
laceration [læsə'reɪʃən] *n* Schnittwunde *f.*
lace-up ['leɪsʌp] *adj* (*shoes etc*) Schnür-.
lack [læk] *n* Mangel *m* **♦** *vt, vi:* **sb** ~**s sth, sb is**
~**ing in sth** jdm fehlt es an etw *dat;* **through**
or **for** ~ **of** aus Mangel an +*dat;* **to be** ~**ing**
fehlen.
lackadaisical [lækə'deɪzɪkl] *adj* lustlos.
lackey ['lækɪ] (*pej*) *n* Lakai *m.*
lacklustre, (*US*) **lackluster** ['læklʌstə*] *adj*
farblos, langweilig.
laconic [lə'kɔnɪk] *adj* lakonisch.
lacquer ['lækə*] *n* Lack *m;* (*also:* **hair** ~)
Haarspray *nt.*
lacrosse [lə'krɔs] *n* Lacrosse *nt.*
lacy ['leɪsɪ] *adj* Spitzen-; (*like lace*) spitzenartig.
lad [læd] *n* Junge *m.*
ladder ['lædə*] *n* (*also fig*) Leiter *f;* (*BRIT: in
tights*) Laufmasche *f* **♦** *vt* (*BRIT*)
Laufmaschen bekommen in +*dat* **♦** *vi* (*BRIT*)

Laufmaschen bekommen.
laden ['leɪdn] *adj:* ~ **(with)** beladen (mit); **fully**
~ voll beladen.
ladle ['leɪdl] *n* Schöpflöffel *m*, (Schöpf)kelle *f*
♦ *vt* schöpfen.
▶ **ladle out** *vt (fig)* austeilen.
lady ['leɪdɪ] *n (woman)* Frau *f*; (: *dignified,
graceful etc)* Dame *f*; *(BRIT: title)* Lady *f*; **ladies
and gentlemen** ... meine Damen und Herren
...; **young** ~ junge Dame; **the ladies' (room)**
die Damentoilette.
ladybird ['leɪdɪbəːd], **ladybug** ['leɪdɪbʌg] *(US)*
n Marienkäfer *m*.
lady-in-waiting ['leɪdɪɪn'weɪtɪŋ] *n* Hofdame *f*.
lady-killer ['leɪdɪkɪlə*] *n* Herzensbrecher *m*.
ladylike ['leɪdɪlaɪk] *adj* damenhaft.
ladyship ['leɪdɪʃɪp] *n:* **your L**~ Ihre
Ladyschaft.
lag [læg] *n (period of time)* Zeitabstand *m* ♦ *vi*
(also: ~ **behind)** zurückbleiben; *(trade,
investment etc)* zurückgehen ♦ *vt (pipes etc)*
isolieren; **old** ~ *(inf: prisoner)* (ehemaliger)
Knacki *m*.
lager ['lɑːgə*] *n* helles Bier *nt*.
lager lout *(BRIT: inf) n* betrunkener Rowdy *m*.
lagging ['lægɪŋ] *n* Isoliermaterial *nt*.
lagoon [lə'guːn] *n* Lagune *f*.
Lagos ['leɪgɔs] *n* Lagos *nt*.
laid [leɪd] *pt, pp of* **lay**.
laid-back [leɪd'bæk] *(inf) adj* locker.
laid up *adj:* **to be** ~ **(with)** im Bett liegen
(mit).
lain [leɪn] *pp of* **lie**.
lair [lɛə*] *n* Lager *nt*; *(cave)* Höhle *f*; (den) Bau
m.
laissez faire [lɛseɪ'fɛə*] *n* Laisser-faire *nt*.
laity ['leɪətɪ] *n or npl* Laien *pl*.
lake [leɪk] *n* See *m*.
Lake District *(BRIT) n:* **the** ~ der Lake
Distrikt, *Seengebiet im NW Englands.*
lamb [læm] *n* Lamm *nt*; *(meat)* Lammfleisch *nt*.
lamb chop *n* Lammkotelett *nt*.
lambskin ['læmskɪn] *n* Lammfell *nt*.
lamb's wool *n* Lammwolle *f*.
lame [leɪm] *adj* lahm; *(argument, answer)*
schwach.
lame duck *n (person)* Niete *f*; *(business)*
unwirtschaftliche Firma *f*.
lamely ['leɪmlɪ] *adv* lahm.
lament [lə'ment] *n* Klage *f* ♦ *vt* beklagen.
lamentable ['læməntəbl] *adj* beklagenswert.
laminated ['læmɪneɪtɪd] *adj* laminiert; *(metal)*
geschichtet; ~ **glass** Verbundglas *nt*;
~ **wood** Sperrholz *nt*.
lamp [læmp] *n* Lampe *f*.
lamplight ['læmplaɪt] *n:* **by** ~ bei
Lampenlicht.
lampoon [læm'puːn] *n* Schmähschrift *f* ♦ *vt*
verspotten.
lamppost ['læmppəust] *(BRIT) n*
Laternenpfahl *m*.
lampshade ['læmpʃeɪd] *n* Lampenschirm *m*.

lance [lɑːns] *n* Lanze *f* ♦ *vt (MED)*
aufschneiden.
lance corporal *(BRIT) n* Obergefreite(r) *m*.
lancet ['lɑːnsɪt] *n (MED)* Lanzette *f*.
Lancs [læŋks] *(BRIT) abbr (POST: = Lancashire).*
land [lænd] *n* Land *nt*; *(as property)* Grund und
Boden *m* ♦ *vi (AVIAT, fig)* landen; *(from ship)*
an Land gehen ♦ *vt (passengers)* absetzen;
(goods) an Land bringen; **to own** ~ Land
besitzen; **to go** *or* **travel by** ~ auf dem
Landweg reisen; **to** ~ **on one's feet** *(fig)* auf
die Füße fallen; **to** ~ **sb with sth** *(inf)* jdm
etw aufhalsen.
▶ **land up** *vi:* **to** ~ **up in/at** landen in *+dat.*
landed gentry ['lændɪd-] *n* Landadel *m*.
landfill site ['lændfɪl-] *n* ≈ Mülldeponie *f*.
landing ['lændɪŋ] *n (of house)* Flur *m*; *(outside
flat door)* Treppenabsatz *m*; *(AVIAT)* Landung
f.
landing card *n* Einreisekarte *f*.
landing craft *n inv* Landungsboot *nt*.
landing gear *n (AVIAT)* Fahrgestell *nt*.
landing stage *n* Landesteg *m*.
landing strip *n* Landebahn *f*.
landlady ['lændleɪdɪ] *n* Vermieterin *f*; *(of pub)*
Wirtin *f*.
landlocked ['lændlɔkt] *adj* von Land
eingeschlossen; ~ **country** Binnenstaat *m*.
landlord ['lændlɔːd] *n* Vermieter *m*; *(of pub)*
Wirt *m*.
landlubber ['lændlʌbə*] *(old) n* Landratte *f*.
landmark ['lændmɑːk] *n* Orientierungspunkt
m; *(famous building)* Wahrzeichen *nt*; *(fig)*
Meilenstein *m*.
landowner ['lændəunə*] *n* Grundbesitzer(in)
m(f).
landscape ['lændskeɪp] *n* Landschaft *f* ♦ *vt*
landschaftlich *or* gärtnerisch gestalten.
landscape architect *n*
Landschaftsarchitekt(in) *m(f)*.
landscape gardener *n*
Landschaftsgärtner(in) *m(f)*.
landscape painting *n* Landschaftsmalerei *f*.
landslide ['lændslaɪd] *n* Erdrutsch *m*; *(fig:
electoral)* Erdrutschsieg *m*.
lane [leɪn] *n (in country)* Weg *m*; *(in town)*
Gasse *f*; *(of carriageway)* Spur *f*; *(of race
course, swimming pool)* Bahn *f*; **shipping** ~
Schifffahrtsweg *m*.
language ['læŋgwɪdʒ] *n* Sprache *f*; **bad** ~
Kraftausdrücke *pl*.
language laboratory *n* Sprachlabor *nt*.
languid ['læŋgwɪd] *adj* träge, matt.
languish ['læŋgwɪʃ] *vi* schmachten; *(project,
case)* erfolglos bleiben.
lank [læŋk] *adj (hair)* strähnig.
lanky ['læŋkɪ] *adj* schlaksig.
lanolin(e) ['lænəlɪn] *n* Lanolin *nt*.
lantern ['læntən] *n* Laterne *f*.
Laos [laus] *n* Laos *nt*.
lap [læp] *n* Schoß *m*; *(in race)* Runde *f* ♦ *vt (also:*
~ **up)** aufschlecken ♦ *vi (water)* plätschern.

lapdog – latter

▶ **lap up** vt (fig) genießen.
lapdog ['læpdɒg] (pej) n (fig) Schoßhund m.
lapel [lə'pɛl] n Aufschlag m, Revers nt or m.
Lapland ['læplænd] n Lappland nt.
Lapp [læp] adj lappländisch ♦ n Lappe m,
Lappin f; (LING) Lappländisch nt.
lapse [læps] n (bad behaviour) Fehltritt m; (of
memory etc) Schwäche f; (of time) Zeitspanne
f ♦ vi ablaufen; (law) ungültig werden; **to
~ into bad habits** in schlechte
Gewohnheiten verfallen.
laptop ['læptɒp] (COMPUT) n Laptop m ♦ cpd
Laptop-.
larceny ['lɑːsənɪ] n Diebstahl m.
larch [lɑːtʃ] n Lärche f.
lard [lɑːd] n Schweineschmalz nt.
larder ['lɑːdə*] n Speisekammer f; (cupboard)
Speiseschrank m.
large [lɑːdʒ] adj groß; (person) korpulent; **to
make ~r** vergrößern; **a ~ number of people**
eine große Anzahl von Menschen; **on a
~ scale** im großen Rahmen; (extensive)
weitreichend, weit reichend; **at ~** (as a
whole) im Allgemeinen; (at liberty) auf
freiem Fuß; **by and ~** im Großen und
Ganzen.
large goods vehicle n Lastkraftwagen m.
largely ['lɑːdʒlɪ] adv (mostly) zum größten
Teil; (mainly) hauptsächlich.
large-scale ['lɑːdʒ'skeɪl] adj im großen
Rahmen; (extensive) weitreichend, weit
reichend; (map, diagram) in einem großen
Maßstab.
largesse [lɑː'ʒɛs] n Großzügigkeit f.
lark [lɑːk] n (bird) Lerche f; (joke) Spaß m, Jux
m.
▶ **lark about** vi herumalbern.
larva ['lɑːvə] (pl ~e) n Larve f.
larvae ['lɑːviː] npl of **larva**.
laryngitis [lærɪn'dʒaɪtɪs] n
Kehlkopfentzündung f.
larynx ['lærɪŋks] n Kehlkopf m.
lasagne [lə'zænjə] n Lasagne pl.
lascivious [lə'sɪvɪəs] adj lüstern.
laser ['leɪzə*] n Laser m.
laser beam n Laserstrahl m.
laser printer n Laserdrucker m.
lash [læʃ] n (also: **eyelash**) Wimper f; (blow with
whip) Peitschenhieb m ♦ vt peitschen; (rain,
wind) peitschen gegen; (tie): **to ~ to**
festbinden an +dat; **to ~ together**
zusammenbinden.
▶ **lash down** vt festbinden ♦ vi (rain)
niederprasseln.
▶ **lash out** vi um sich schlagen; **to ~ out at
sb** auf jdn losschlagen; **to ~ out at** or
against sb (criticize) gegen jdn wettern.
lashing ['læʃɪŋ] n: **~s of** (BRIT: inf)
massenhaft.
lass [læs] (BRIT) n Mädchen nt.
lasso [læ'suː] n Lasso nt ♦ vt mit dem Lasso
einfangen.

last [lɑːst] adj letzte(r, s) ♦ adv (most recently)
zuletzt, das letzte Mal; (finally) als Letztes
♦ vi (continue) dauern; (: in good condition)
sich halten; (money, commodity) reichen;
~ week letzte Woche; **~ night** gestern
Abend; **~ but one** vorletzte(r, s); **the ~ time**
das letzte Mal; **at ~** endlich; **it ~s (for) 2
hours** es dauert 2 Stunden.
last-ditch ['lɑːst'dɪtʃ] adj (attempt)
allerletzte(r, s).
lasting ['lɑːstɪŋ] adj dauerhaft.
lastly ['lɑːstlɪ] adv (finally) schließlich; (last of
all) zum Schluss.
last-minute ['lɑːstmɪnɪt] adj in letzter Minute.
latch [lætʃ] n Riegel m; **to be on the ~** nur
eingeklinkt sein.
▶ **latch on to** vt fus (person) sich anschließen
+dat; (idea) abfahren auf +acc (inf).
latchkey ['lætʃkiː] n Hausschlüssel m.
latchkey child n Schlüsselkind nt.
late [leɪt] adj spät; (not on time) verspätet ♦ adv
spät; (behind time) zu spät; (recently): **~ of
Dechmont** bis vor kurzem in Dechmont
wohnhaft; **the ~ Mr X** (deceased) der
verstorbene Herr X; **in ~ May** Ende Mai; **to
be (10 minutes) ~** (10 Minuten) zu spät
kommen; (train etc) (10 Minuten)
Verspätung haben; **to work ~** länger
arbeiten; **~ in life** relativ spät (im Leben); **of
~** in letzter Zeit.
latecomer ['leɪtkʌmə*] n Nachzügler(in) m(f).
lately ['leɪtlɪ] adv in letzter Zeit.
lateness ['leɪtnɪs] n (of person)
Zuspätkommen nt; (of train, event)
Verspätung f.
latent ['leɪtnt] adj (energy) ungenutzt; (skill,
ability) verborgen.
later ['leɪtə*] adj, adv später; **~ on** nachher.
lateral ['lætərəl] adj seitlich; **~ thinking**
kreatives Denken nt.
latest ['leɪtɪst] adj neueste(r, s) ♦ n: **at the ~**
spätestens.
latex ['leɪtɛks] n Latex m.
lathe [leɪð] n Drehbank f.
lather ['lɑːðə*] n (Seifen)schaum m ♦ vt
einschäumen.
Latin ['lætɪn] n Latein nt; (person)
Südländer(in) m(f) ♦ adj lateinisch;
(temperament etc) südländisch.
Latin America n Lateinamerika nt.
Latin American adj lateinamerikanisch ♦ n
Lateinamerikaner(in) m(f).
Latino [læ'tiːnəʊ] (US) adj aus Lateinamerika
stammend ♦ n Latino mf, in den USA
lebende(r) Lateinamerikaner(in).
latitude ['lætɪtjuːd] n (GEOG) Breite f; (fig:
freedom) Freiheit f.
latrine [lə'triːn] n Latrine f.
latter ['lætə*] adj (of two) letztere(r, s); (later)
spätere(r, s); (second part of period) zweite(r,
s); (recent) letzte(r, s) ♦ n: **the ~** der/die/das
Letztere, die Letzteren.

latter-day ['lætədeɪ] adj modern.
latterly ['lætəlɪ] adv in letzter Zeit.
lattice ['lætɪs] n Gitter nt.
lattice window n Gitterfenster nt.
Latvia ['lætvɪə] n Lettland nt.
Latvian ['lætvɪən] adj lettisch ♦ n Lette m, Lettin f; (LING) Lettisch nt.
laudable ['lɔːdəbl] adj lobenswert.
laudatory ['lɔːdətrɪ] adj (comments) lobend; (speech) Lob-.
laugh [lɑːf] n Lachen nt ♦ vi lachen; (to do sth) for a ~ (etw) aus Spaß (tun).
► **laugh at** vt fus lachen über +acc.
► **laugh off** vt mit einem Lachen abtun.
laughable ['lɑːfəbl] adj lächerlich, lachhaft.
laughing gas ['lɑːfɪŋ-] n Lachgas nt.
laughing matter n: this is no ~ das ist nicht zum Lachen.
laughing stock n: to be the ~ of zum Gespött +gen werden.
laughter ['lɑːftə*] n Lachen nt, Gelächter nt.
launch [lɔːntʃ] n (of rocket, missile) Abschuss m; (of satellite) Start m; (COMM: of product) Einführung f; (: with publicity) Lancierung f; (motorboat) Barkasse f ♦ vt (ship) vom Stapel lassen; (rocket, missile) abschießen; (satellite) starten; (fig: start) beginnen mit; (COMM) auf den Markt bringen; (: with publicity) lancieren.
► **launch into** vt fus (speech) vom Stapel lassen; (activity) in Angriff nehmen.
► **launch out** vi: to ~ out (into) beginnen (mit).
launching ['lɔːntʃɪŋ] n (of ship) Stapellauf m; (of rocket, missile) Abschuss m; (of satellite) Start m; (fig: start) Beginn m; (COMM: of product) Einführung f; (: with publicity) Lancierung f.
launch(ing) pad n Startrampe f, Abschussrampe f.
launder ['lɔːndə*] vt waschen und bügeln; (pej: money) waschen.
Laundrette [lɔːn'drɛt] (BRIT) n Waschsalon m.
Laundromat ® ['lɔːndrəmæt] (US) n Waschsalon m.
laundry ['lɔːndrɪ] n Wäsche f; (dirty) (schmutzige) Wäsche; (business) Wäscherei f; (room) Waschküche f; to do the ~ (Wäsche) waschen.
laureate ['lɔːrɪət] adj see poet laureate.
laurel ['lɔrl] n (tree) Lorbeer(baum) m; to rest on one's ~s sich auf seinen Lorbeeren ausruhen.
Lausanne [ləu'zæn] n Lausanne nt.
lava ['lɑːvə] n Lava f.
lavatory ['lævətərɪ] n Toilette f.
lavatory paper n Toilettenpapier nt.
lavender ['lævəndə*] n Lavendel m.
lavish ['lævɪʃ] adj großzügig; (meal) üppig; (surroundings) feudal; (wasteful) verschwenderisch ♦ vt: to ~ sth on sb jdn mit etw überhäufen.

lavishly ['lævɪʃlɪ] adv (generously) großzügig; (sumptuously) aufwändig, aufwendig.
law [lɔː] n Recht nt; (a rule: also of nature, science) Gesetz nt; (professions connected with law) Rechtswesen nt; (SCOL) Jura no art; against the ~ rechtswidrig; to study ~ Jura or Recht(swissenschaft) studieren; to go to ~ vor Gericht gehen; to break the ~ gegen das Gesetz verstoßen.
law-abiding ['lɔːəbaɪdɪŋ] adj gesetzestreu.
law and order n Ruhe und Ordnung f.
lawbreaker ['lɔːbreɪkə*] n Rechtsbrecher(in) m(f).
law court n Gerichtshof m, Gericht nt.
lawful ['lɔːful] adj rechtmäßig.
lawfully ['lɔːfəlɪ] adv rechtmäßig.
lawless ['lɔːlɪs] adj gesetzwidrig.
Law Lord (BRIT) n Mitglied des Oberhauses mit besonderem Verantwortungsbereich in Rechtsfragen.
lawn [lɔːn] n Rasen m.
lawn mower n Rasenmäher m.
lawn tennis n Rasentennis nt.
law school (US) n juristische Hochschule f.
law student n Jurastudent(in) m(f).
lawsuit ['lɔːsuːt] n Prozess m.
lawyer ['lɔːjə*] n (Rechts)anwalt m, (Rechts)anwältin f.
lax [læks] adj lax.
laxative ['læksətɪv] n Abführmittel nt.
laxity ['læksɪtɪ] n Laxheit f; moral ~ lockere or laxe Moral f.
lay [leɪ] (pt, pp laid) pt of lie ♦ adj (REL: preacher etc) Laien- ♦ vt legen; (table) decken; (carpet, cable etc) verlegen; (plans) schmieden; (trap) stellen; the ~ person (not expert) der Laie; to ~ facts/proposals before sb jdm Tatsachen vorlegen/Vorschläge unterbreiten; to ~ one's hands on sth (fig) etw in die Finger bekommen; to get laid (inf!) bumsen (!).
► **lay aside** vt weglegen, zur Seite legen.
► **lay by** vt beiseite or auf die Seite legen.
► **lay down** vt hinlegen; (rules, laws etc) festlegen; to ~ down the law Vorschriften machen; to ~ down one's life sein Leben geben.
► **lay in** vt (supply) anlegen.
► **lay into** vt fus losgehen auf +acc; (criticize) herunterputzen.
► **lay off** vt (workers) entlassen.
► **lay on** vt (meal) auftischen; (entertainment etc) sorgen für; (water, gas) anschließen; (paint) auftragen.
► **lay out** vt ausbreiten; (inf: spend) ausgeben.
► **lay up** vt (illness) außer Gefecht setzen; see also lay by.
layabout ['leɪəbaut] (inf: pej) n Faulenzer m.
lay-by ['leɪbaɪ] (BRIT) n Parkbucht f.
lay days npl Liegezeit f.
layer ['leɪə*] n Schicht f.
layette [leɪ'ɛt] n Babyausstattung f.

layman ['leɪmən] (*irreg: like* **man**) *n* Laie *m*.
lay-off ['leɪɔf] *n* Entlassung *f*.
layout ['leɪaut] *n* (*of garden*) Anlage *f*; (*of building*) Aufteilung *f*; (*TYP*) Lay-out *nt*, Layout *nt*.
laze [leɪz] *vi* (*also:* ~ **about**) (herum)faulenzen.
laziness ['leɪzɪnɪs] *n* Faulheit *f*.
lazy ['leɪzɪ] *adj* faul; (*movement, action*) langsam, träge.
LB (*CANADA*) *abbr* (= *Labrador*).
lb *abbr* (= *pound (weight)*) *britisches Pfund (0,45 kg),* ≈ Pfd.
lbw *abbr* (*CRICKET*: = *leg before wicket*) *Regelverletzung beim Kricket*.
LC (*US*) *n abbr* (= *Library of Congress*) *Bibliothek des US-Parlaments*.
L/C *abbr* = **letter of credit**.
lc *abbr* (*TYP*: = *lower case*) *see* **case**.
LCD *n abbr* (= *liquid-crystal display*) LCD *nt*.
Ld (*BRIT*) *abbr* (*in titles*) = **lord**.
LDS *n abbr* (*BRIT*: = *Licentiate in Dental Surgery*) ≈ Dr. med. dent. ♦ *n abbr* (= *Latter-day Saints*) Heilige *pl* der Letzten Tage.
LEA (*BRIT*) *n abbr* (= *Local Education Authority*) *örtliche Schulbehörde*.
lead¹ [liːd] (*pt, pp* **led**) *n* (*SPORT, fig*) Führung *f*; (*clue*) Spur *f*; (*in play, film*) Hauptrolle *f*; (*for dog*) Leine *f*; (*ELEC*) Kabel *nt* ♦ *vt* anführen; (*guide*) führen; (*organization, BRIT: orchestra*) leiten ♦ *vi* führen; **to be in the** ~ (*SPORT, fig*) in Führung liegen; **to take the** ~ (*SPORT*) in Führung gehen; **to** ~ **the way** vorangehen; **to** ~ **sb astray** jdn vom rechten Weg abführen; (*mislead*) jdn irreführen; **to** ~ **sb to believe that ...** jdm den Eindruck vermitteln, dass ...; **to** ~ **sb to do sth** jdn dazu bringen, etw zu tun.
▸ **lead away** *vt* wegführen; (*prisoner etc*) abführen.
▸ **lead back** *vt* zurückführen.
▸ **lead off** *vi* (*in conversation etc*) den Anfang machen; (*room, road*) abgehen ♦ *vt fus* abgehen von.
▸ **lead on** *vt* (*tease*) aufziehen.
▸ **lead to** *vt fus* führen zu.
▸ **lead up to** *vt fus* (*events*) vorangehen +*dat*; (*in conversation*) hinauswollen auf +*acc*.
lead² [lɛd] *n* Blei *nt*; (*in pencil*) Mine *f*.
leaded ['lɛdɪd] *adj* (*window*) bleiverglast; (*petrol*) verbleit.
leaden ['lɛdn] *adj* (*sky, sea*) bleiern; (*movements*) bleischwer.
leader ['liːdə*] *n* Führer(in) *m(f)*; (*SPORT*) Erste(r) *f(m)*; (*in newspaper*) Leitartikel *m*; **the L**~ **of the House (of Commons/of Lords)** (*BRIT*) der Führer des Unterhauses/des Oberhauses.
leadership ['liːdəʃɪp] *n* Führung *f*; (*position*) Vorsitz *m*; (*quality*) Führungsqualitäten *pl*.
lead-free ['lɛdfriː] (*old*) *adj* bleifrei.
leading ['liːdɪŋ] *adj* führend; (*role*) Haupt-; (*first, front*) vorderste(r, s).

leading lady *n* (*THEAT*) Hauptdarstellerin *f*.
leading light *n* führende Persönlichkeit *f*.
leading man *n* (*THEAT*) Hauptdarsteller *m*.
leading question *n* Suggestivfrage *f*.
lead pencil [lɛd-] *n* Bleistift *m*.
lead poisoning [lɛd-] *n* Bleivergiftung *f*.
lead singer [liːd-] *n* Leadsänger(in) *m(f)*.
lead time [liːd-] *n* (*COMM*: *for production*) Produktionszeit *f*; (: *for delivery*) Lieferzeit *f*.
lead-up ['liːdʌp] *n*: **the** ~ **to sth** die Zeit vor etw *dat*.
leaf [liːf] (*pl* **leaves**) *n* Blatt *nt*; (*of table*) Ausziehplatte *f*; **to turn over a new** ~ einen neuen Anfang machen; **to take a** ~ **out of sb's book** sich *dat* von jdm eine Scheibe abschneiden.
▸ **leaf through** *vt fus* durchblättern.
leaflet ['liːflɪt] *n* Informationsblatt *nt*.
leafy ['liːfɪ] *adj* (*tree, branch*) belaubt; (*lane, suburb*) grün.
league [liːg] *n* (*of people, clubs*) Verband *m*; (*of countries*) Bund *m*; (*FOOTBALL*) Liga *f*; **to be in** ~ **with sb** mit jdm gemeinsame Sache machen.
league table *n* Tabelle *f*.
leak [liːk] *n* Leck *nt*; (*in roof, pipe etc*) undichte Stelle *f*; (*piece of information*) zugespielte Information *f* ♦ *vi* (*shoes, roof, pipe*) undicht sein; (*ship*) lecken; (*liquid*) auslaufen; (*gas*) ausströmen ♦ *vt* (*information*) durchsickern lassen; **to** ~ **sth to sb** jdm etw zuspielen.
▸ **leak out** *vi* (*liquid*) auslaufen; (*news, information*) durchsickern.
leakage ['liːkɪdʒ] *n* (*of liquid*) Auslaufen *nt*; (*of gas*) Ausströmen *nt*.
leaky ['liːkɪ] *adj* (*roof, container*) undicht.
lean [liːn] (*pt, pp* **leaned** *or* **leant**) *adj* (*person*) schlank; (*meat, fig: time*) mager ♦ *vt*: **to** ~ **sth on sth** etw an etw *acc* lehnen; (*rest*) etw auf etw *acc* stützen ♦ *vi* (*slope*) sich neigen; **to** ~ **against** sich lehnen gegen; **to** ~ **on** sich stützen auf +*acc*; **to** ~ **forward/back** sich vorbeugen/zurücklehnen; **to** ~ **towards** tendieren zu.
▸ **lean out** *vi* sich hinauslehnen.
▸ **lean over** *vi* sich vorbeugen.
leaning ['liːnɪŋ] *n* Hang *m*, Neigung *f*.
leant [lɛnt] *pt, pp of* **lean**.
lean-to ['liːntuː] *n* Anbau *m*.
leap [liːp] (*pt, pp* **leaped** *or* **leapt**) *n* Sprung *m*; (*in price, number etc*) sprunghafter Anstieg *m* ♦ *vi* springen; (*price, number etc*) sprunghaft (an)steigen.
▸ **leap at** *vt fus* (*offer*) sich stürzen auf +*acc*; (*opportunity*) beim Schopf ergreifen.
▸ **leap up** *vi* aufspringen.
leapfrog ['liːpfrɔg] *n* Bockspringen *nt*.
leapt [lɛpt] *pt, pp of* **leap**.
leap year *n* Schaltjahr *nt*.
learn [lɜːn] (*pt, pp* **learned** *or* **learnt**) *vt* lernen; (*facts*) erfahren ♦ *vi* lernen; **to** ~ **about** *or* **of sth** von etw erfahren; **to** ~ **about sth** (*study*)

etw lernen; **to ~ that** ... (*hear, read*)
erfahren, dass ...; **to ~ to do sth** etw lernen.
learned ['lɔːnɪd] *adj* gelehrt; (*book, paper*)
wissenschaftlich.
learner ['lɔːnəʳ] (*BRIT*) *n* (*also:* ~ **driver**)
Fahrschüler(in) *m(f)*.
learning ['lɔːnɪŋ] *n* Gelehrsamkeit *f*.
learnt [lɔːnt] *pt, pp of* **learn**.
lease [liːs] *n* Pachtvertrag *m* ♦ *vt:* **to ~ sth (to
sb)** etw (an jdn) verpachten; **on ~ (to)**
verpachtet (an +*acc*); **to ~ sth (from sb)** etw
(von jdm) pachten.
▶ **lease back** *vt* rückmieten.
leaseback ['liːsbæk] *n* Verkauf und
Rückmiete *pl*.
leasehold ['liːshəuld] *n* Pachtbesitz *m* ♦ *adj*
gepachtet.
leash [liːʃ] *n* Leine *f*.
least [liːst] *adv* am wenigsten ♦ *adj:* **the ~** (+
noun) der/die/das wenigste; (: *slightest*) der/
die/das geringste; **the ~ expensive car** das
billigste Auto; **at ~** mindestens; (*still, rather*)
wenigstens; **you could at ~ have written** du
hättest wenigstens schreiben können; **not in
the ~** nicht im Geringsten; **it was the ~ I
could do** das war das wenigste, was ich tun
konnte.
leather ['lɛðəʳ] *n* Leder *nt*.
leave [liːv] (*pt, pp* **left**) *vt* verlassen; (*leave
behind*) zurücklassen; (*mark, stain*)
hinterlassen; (*object: accidentally*) liegen
lassen, stehen lassen; (*food*) übrig lassen;
(*space, time etc*) lassen ♦ *vi* (*go away*)
(weg)gehen; (*bus, train*) abfahren ♦ *n* Urlaub
m; **to ~ sth to sb** (*money etc*) jdm etw
hinterlassen; **to ~ sb with sth** (*impose*) jdm
etw aufhalsen; (*possession*) jdm etw lassen;
they were left with nothing ihnen blieb
nichts; **to be left** übrig sein; **to be left over**
(*remain*) übrig (geblieben) sein; **to ~ for**
gehen/fahren nach; **to take one's ~ of sb**
sich von jdm verabschieden; **on ~** auf
Urlaub.
▶ **leave behind** *vt* zurücklassen; (*object:
accidentally*) liegen lassen, stehen lassen.
▶ **leave off** *vt* (*cover, lid*) ablassen; (*heating,
light*) auslassen ♦ *vi* (*inf: stop*) aufhören.
▶ **leave on** *vt* (*light, heating*) anlassen.
▶ **leave out** *vt* auslassen.
leave of absence *n* Beurlaubung *f*.
leaves [liːvz] *npl of* **leaf**.
Lebanese [lɛbə'niːz] *adj* libanesisch ♦ *n inv*
Libanese *m*, Libanesin *f*.
Lebanon ['lɛbənən] *n* Libanon *m*.
lecherous ['lɛtʃərəs] (*pej*) *adj* lüstern.
lectern ['lɛktɔːn] *n* Rednerpult *nt*.
lecture ['lɛktʃəʳ] *n* Vortrag *m*; (*UNIV*)
Vorlesung *f* ♦ *vi* Vorträge/Vorlesungen
halten ♦ *vt* (*scold*): **to ~ sb on** or **about sth**
jdm wegen etw eine Strafpredigt halten; **to
give a ~ on** einen Vortrag/eine Vorlesung
halten über +*acc*.

lecture hall *n* Hörsaal *m*.
lecturer ['lɛktʃərəʳ] (*BRIT*) *n* Dozent(in) *m(f)*;
(*speaker*) Redner(in) *m(f)*.
LED *n abbr* (*ELEC*: = *light-emitting diode*) LED *f*.
led [lɛd] *pt, pp of* **lead**[1].
ledge [lɛdʒ] *n* (*of mountain*) (Fels)vorsprung
m; (*of window*) Fensterbrett *nt*; (*on wall*)
Leiste *f*.
ledger ['lɛdʒəʳ] *n* (*COMM*) Hauptbuch *nt*.
lee [liː] *n* Windschatten *m*; (*NAUT*) Lee *f*.
leech [liːtʃ] *n* Blutegel *m*; (*fig*) Blutsauger *m*.
leek [liːk] *n* Porree *m*, Lauch *m*.
leer [lɪəʳ] *vi:* **to ~ at sb** jdm lüsterne Blicke
zuwerfen.
leeward ['liːwəd] (*NAUT*) *adj* (*side etc*) Lee-
♦ *adv* leewärts ♦ *n:* **to ~** an der Leeseite;
(*direction*) nach der Leeseite.
leeway ['liːweɪ] *n* (*fig*): **to have some ~** etwas
Spielraum haben; **there's a lot of ~ to make
up** ein großer Rückstand muss aufgeholt
werden.
left [lɛft] *pt, pp of* **leave** ♦ *adj* (*remaining*) übrig;
(*of position*) links; (*of direction*) nach links ♦ *n*
linke Seite *f* ♦ *adv* links; nach links; **on the ~**,
to the ~ links; **the L~** (*POL*) die Linke.
left-click ['lɛftklɪk] (*COMPUT*) *vi* links klicken
♦ *vt* links klicken auf (+*acc*).
left-hand drive ['lɛfthænd-] *adj* mit
Linkssteuerung.
left-handed [lɛft'hændɪd] *adj* linkshändig.
left-hand side ['lɛfthænd-] *n* linke Seite *f*.
leftie ['lɛftɪ] (*inf*) *n* Linke(r) *f(m)*.
leftist ['lɛftɪst] (*POL*) *n* Linke(r) *f(m)* ♦ *adj*
linke(r, s).
left-luggage (office) [lɛft'lʌgɪdʒ(-)] (*BRIT*) *n*
Gepäckaufbewahrung *f*.
leftovers ['lɛftəuvəz] *npl* Reste *pl*.
left-wing ['lɛft'wɪŋ] *adj* (*POL*) linke(r, s).
left-winger ['lɛft'wɪŋgəʳ] *n* (*POL*) Linke(r) *f(m)*.
lefty ['lɛftɪ] *n* = **leftie**.
leg [lɛg] *n* Bein *nt*; (*CULIN*) Keule *f*; (*SPORT*)
Runde *f*; (: *of relay race*) Teilstrecke *f*; (*of
journey etc*) Etappe *f*; **to stretch one's ~s** sich
dat die Beine vertreten; **to get one's ~ over**
(*inf*) bumsen.
legacy ['lɛgəsɪ] *n* Erbschaft *f*; (*fig*) Erbe *nt*.
legal ['liːgl] *adj* (*requirement*) rechtlich,
gesetzlich; (*system*) Rechts-; (*allowed by law*)
legal, rechtlich zulässig; **to take ~ action** or
proceedings against sb jdn verklagen.
legal adviser *n* juristischer Berater *m*.
legal holiday (*US*) *n* gesetzlicher Feiertag *m*.
legality [lɪ'gælɪtɪ] *n* Legalität *f*.
legalize ['liːgəlaɪz] *vt* legalisieren.
legally ['liːgəlɪ] *adv* rechtlich, gesetzlich; (*in
accordance with the law*) rechtmäßig; **~
binding** rechtsverbindlich.
legal tender *n* gesetzliches Zahlungsmittel
nt.
legation [lɪ'geɪʃən] *n* Gesandtschaft *f*.
legend ['lɛdʒənd] *n* Legende *f*, Sage *f*; (*fig:
person*) Legende *f*.

legendary ['lɛdʒəndərɪ] *adj* legendär; (*very famous*) berühmt.

-legged ['lɛgɪd] *suff* -beinig.

leggings ['lɛgɪŋz] *npl* Leggings *pl*, Leggins *pl*.

leggy ['lɛgɪ] *adj* langbeinig.

legibility [lɛdʒɪ'bɪlɪtɪ] *n* Lesbarkeit *f*.

legible ['lɛdʒəbl] *adj* leserlich.

legibly ['lɛdʒəblɪ] *adv* leserlich.

legion ['liːdʒən] *n* Legion *f* ♦ *adj* zahlreich.

legionnaire [liːdʒə'nɛə*] *n* Legionär *m*.

legionnaire's disease *n* Legionärskrankheit *f*.

legislate ['lɛdʒɪsleɪt] *vi* Gesetze/ein Gesetz erlassen.

legislation [lɛdʒɪs'leɪʃən] *n* Gesetzgebung *f*; (*laws*) Gesetze *pl*.

legislative ['lɛdʒɪslətɪv] *adj* gesetzgebend; ~ **reforms** Gesetzesreformen *pl*.

legislator ['lɛdʒɪsleɪtə*] *n* Gesetzgeber *m*.

legislature ['lɛdʒɪslətʃə*] *n* Legislative *f*.

legitimacy [lɪ'dʒɪtɪməsɪ] *n* (*validity*) Berechtigung *f*; (*legality*) Rechtmäßigkeit *f*.

legitimate [lɪ'dʒɪtɪmət] *adj* (*reasonable*) berechtigt; (*excuse*) begründet; (*legal*) rechtmäßig.

legitimize [lɪ'dʒɪtɪmaɪz] *vt* legitimieren.

legless ['lɛglɪs] (*inf*) *adj* (*drunk*) sternhagelvoll.

legroom ['lɛgruːm] *n* Beinfreiheit *f*.

Leics (*BRIT*) *abbr* (*POST*: = Leicestershire).

leisure ['lɛʒə*] *n* Freizeit *f*; **at** ~ in Ruhe.

leisure centre *n* Freizeitzentrum *nt*.

leisurely ['lɛʒəlɪ] *adj* geruhsam.

leisure suit *n* Freizeitanzug *m*.

lemon ['lɛmən] *n* Zitrone *f*; (*colour*) Zitronengelb *nt*.

lemonade [lɛmə'neɪd] *n* Limonade *f*.

lemon cheese *n* = **lemon curd**.

lemon curd *n* zähflüssiger Brotaufstrich mit Zitronengeschmack.

lemon juice *n* Zitronensaft *m*.

lemon squeezer *n* Zitronenpresse *f*.

lemon tea *n* Zitronentee *m*.

lend [lɛnd] (*pt*, *pp* **lent**) *vt*: **to** ~ **sth to sb** jdm etw leihen; **to** ~ **sb a hand (with sth)** jdm (bei etw) helfen; **it** ~**s itself to ...** es eignet sich für ...

lender ['lɛndə*] *n* Verleiher(in) *m(f)*.

lending library ['lɛndɪŋ-] *n* Leihbücherei *f*.

length [lɛŋθ] *n* Länge *f*; (*piece*) Stück *nt*; (*amount of time*) Dauer *f*; **the** ~ **of the island** (*all along*) die ganze Insel entlang; **2 metres in** ~ 2 Meter lang; **at** ~ (*at last*) schließlich; (*for a long time*) lange; **to go to great** ~**s to do sth** sich *dat* sehr viel Mühe geben, etw zu tun; **to fall full-**~ lang hinfallen; **to lie full-**~ in voller Länge daliegen.

lengthen ['lɛŋθən] *vt* verlängern ♦ *vi* länger werden.

lengthways ['lɛŋθweɪz] *adv* der Länge nach.

lengthy ['lɛŋθɪ] *adj* lang.

leniency ['liːnɪənsɪ] *n* Nachsicht *f*.

lenient ['liːnɪənt] *adj* nachsichtig.

leniently ['liːnɪəntlɪ] *adv* nachsichtig.

lens [lɛnz] *n* (*of spectacles*) Glas *nt*; (*of camera*) Objektiv *nt*; (*of telescope*) Linse *f*.

Lent [lɛnt] *n* Fastenzeit *f*.

lent [lɛnt] *pt*, *pp of* **lend**.

lentil ['lɛntɪl] *n* Linse *f*.

Leo ['liːəu] *n* Löwe *m*; **to be** ~ Löwe sein.

leopard ['lɛpəd] *n* Leopard *m*.

leotard ['liːətɑːd] *n* Gymnastikanzug *m*.

leper ['lɛpə*] *n* Leprakranke(r) *f(m)*.

leper colony *n* Leprasiedlung *f*.

leprosy ['lɛprəsɪ] *n* Lepra *f*.

lesbian ['lɛzbɪən] *adj* lesbisch ♦ *n* Lesbierin *f*.

lesion ['liːʒən] *n* Verletzung *f*.

Lesotho [lɪ'suːtuː] *n* Lesotho *nt*.

less [lɛs] *adj*, *pron*, *adv* weniger ♦ *prep*: ~ **tax/ 10% discount** abzüglich Steuer/10% Rabatt; ~ **than half** weniger als die Hälfte; ~ **than ever** weniger denn je; ~ **and** ~ immer weniger; **the** ~ **he works ...** je weniger er arbeitet ...; **the Prime Minister, no** ~ kein Geringerer als der Premierminister.

lessee [lɛ'siː] *n* Pächter(in) *m(f)*.

lessen ['lɛsn] *vi* nachlassen, abnehmen ♦ *vt* verringern.

lesser ['lɛsə*] *adj* geringer; **to a** ~ **extent** in geringerem Maße.

lesson ['lɛsn] *n* (*class*) Stunde *f*; (*example, warning*) Lehre *f*, **to teach sb a** ~ (*fig*) jdm eine Lektion erteilen.

lessor ['lɛsɔː*] *n* Verpächter(in) *m(f)*.

lest [lɛst] *conj* damit ... nicht.

let [lɛt] (*pt*, *pp* **let**) *vt* (*allow*) lassen; (*BRIT: lease*) vermieten; **to** ~ **sb do sth** jdn etw tun lassen, jdm erlauben, etw zu tun; **to** ~ **sb know sth** jdn etw wissen lassen; ~**'s go** gehen wir!; ~ **him come** lassen Sie ihn kommen; **"to** ~**"** „zu vermieten".

▶ **let down** *vt* (*tyre etc*) die Luft herauslassen aus; (*person*) im Stich lassen; (*dress etc*) länger machen; (*hem*) auslassen; **to** ~ **one's hair down** (*fig*) aus sich herausgehen.

▶ **let go** *vi* loslassen ♦ *vt* (*release*) freilassen; **to** ~ **go of** loslassen; **to** ~ **o.s. go** aus sich herausgehen; (*neglect o.s.*) sich gehen lassen.

▶ **let in** *vt* hereinlassen; (*water*) durchlassen.

▶ **let off** *vt* (*culprit*) laufen lassen; (*firework, bomb*) hochgehen lassen; (*gun*) abfeuern; **to** ~ **sb off sth** (*excuse*) jdm etw erlassen; **to** ~ **off steam** (*inf*, *fig*) sich abreagieren.

▶ **let on** *vi* verraten.

▶ **let out** *vt* herauslassen; (*sound*) ausstoßen; (*house, room*) vermieten.

▶ **let up** *vi* (*cease*) aufhören; (*diminish*) nachlassen.

letdown ['lɛtdaun] *n* Enttäuschung *f*.

lethal ['liːθl] *adj* tödlich.

lethargic [lɛ'θɑːdʒɪk] *adj* träge, lethargisch.

lethargy ['lɛθədʒɪ] *n* Trägheit *f*, Lethargie *f*.

letter ['lɛtə*] *n* Brief *m*; (*of alphabet*) Buchstabe *m*; **small/capital** ~ Klein-/

Großbuchstabe m.
letter bomb n Briefbombe f.
letter box (BRIT) n Briefkasten m.
letterhead ['lɛtəhɛd] n Briefkopf m.
lettering ['lɛtərɪŋ] n Beschriftung f.
letter of credit n Akkreditiv nt.
letter opener n Brieföffner m.
letterpress ['lɛtəprɛs] n Hochdruck m.
letter-quality printer ['lɛtəkwɔlɪtɪ-] n Schönschreibdrucker m.
letters patent npl Patent nt, Patenturkunde f.
lettuce ['lɛtɪs] n Kopfsalat m.
let-up ['lɛtʌp] n Nachlassen nt; **there was no ~** es ließ nicht nach.
leukaemia, (US) **leukemia** [luːˈkiːmɪə] n Leukämie f.
level ['lɛvl] adj eben ♦ n (on scale, of liquid) Stand m; (of lake, river) Wasserstand m; (height) Höhe f; (fig: standard) Niveau nt; (also: **spirit ~**) Wasserwaage f ♦ vt (building) abreißen; (forest etc) einebnen ♦ vi: **to ~ with sb** (inf) ehrlich mit jdm sein ♦ adv: **to draw ~ with** einholen; **to be ~ with** auf gleicher Höhe sein mit; **to do one's ~ best** sein Möglichstes tun; **"A" ~s** (BRIT) ≈ Abitur nt; **"O" ~s** (BRIT) ≈ mittlere Reife f; **on the ~** (fig: honest) ehrlich, reell; **to ~ a gun at sb** ein Gewehr auf jdn richten; **to ~ an accusation at** or **against sb** eine Anschuldigung gegen jdn erheben; **to ~ a criticism at** or **against sb** Kritik an jdm üben.
▶ **level off** vi (prices etc) sich beruhigen.
▶ **level out** vi = **level off**.
level crossing (BRIT) n (beschrankter) Bahnübergang m.
level-headed [lɛvlˈhɛdɪd] adj (calm) ausgeglichen.
levelling ['lɛvlɪŋ] n Nivellierung f.
level playing field n Chancengleichheit f; **to compete on a ~** unter gleichen Bedingungen antreten.
lever ['liːvəʳ] n Hebel m; (bar) Brechstange f; (fig) Druckmittel nt ♦ vt: **to ~ up** hochhieven; **to ~ out** heraushieven.
leverage ['liːvərɪdʒ] n Hebelkraft f; (fig: influence) Einfluss m.
levity ['lɛvɪtɪ] n Leichtfertigkeit f.
levy ['lɛvɪ] n (tax) Steuer f; (charge) Gebühr f ♦ vt erheben.
lewd [luːd] adj (look etc) lüstern; (remark) anzüglich.
lexicographer [lɛksɪˈkɔɡrəfəʳ] n Lexikograf(in) m(f).
lexicography [lɛksɪˈkɔɡrəfɪ] n Lexikografie f.
LGV (BRIT) n abbr (= large goods vehicle) LKW m.
LI (US) abbr (= Long Island).
liability [laɪəˈbɪlɪtɪ] n Belastung f; (LAW) Haftung f; **liabilities** npl (COMM) Verbindlichkeiten pl.
liable ['laɪəbl] adj: **to be ~ to** (subject to)

unterliegen +dat; (prone to) anfällig sein für; **~ for** (responsible) haftbar für; **to be ~ to do sth** dazu neigen, etw zu tun.
liaise [liːˈeɪz] vi: **to ~ (with)** sich in Verbindung setzen (mit).
liaison [liːˈeɪzɔn] n Zusammenarbeit f; (sexual relationship) Liaison f.
liar ['laɪəʳ] n Lügner(in) m(f).
libel ['laɪbl] n Verleumdung f ♦ vt verleumden.
libellous, (US) **libelous** ['laɪbləs] adj verleumderisch.
liberal ['lɪbərl] adj (POL) liberal; (tolerant) aufgeschlossen; (generous: offer) großzügig; (: amount etc) reichlich ♦ n (tolerant person) liberal eingestellter Mensch m; (POL): **L~** Liberale(r) f(m); **~ with** großzügig mit.
Liberal Democrat n Liberaldemokrat(in) m(f).
liberalize ['lɪbərəlaɪz] vt liberalisieren.
liberally ['lɪbrəlɪ] adv großzügig.
liberal-minded ['lɪbərlˈmaɪndɪd] adj liberal (eingestellt).
liberate ['lɪbəreɪt] vt befreien.
liberation [lɪbəˈreɪʃən] n Befreiung f.
liberation theology n Befreiungstheologie f.
Liberia [laɪˈbɪərɪə] n Liberia nt.
Liberian [laɪˈbɪərɪən] adj liberianisch ♦ n Liberianer(in) m(f).
liberty ['lɪbətɪ] n Freiheit f; **to be at ~** (criminal) auf freiem Fuß sein; **to be at ~ to do sth** etw tun dürfen; **to take the ~ of doing sth** sich dat erlauben, etw zu tun.
libido [lɪˈbiːdəu] n Libido f.
Libra ['liːbrə] n Waage f; **to be ~** Waage sein.
librarian [laɪˈbrɛərɪən] n Bibliothekar(in) m(f).
library ['laɪbrərɪ] n Bibliothek f; (institution) Bücherei f.
library book n Buch nt aus der Bücherei.
libretto [lɪˈbrɛtəu] n Libretto nt.
Libya ['lɪbɪə] n Libyen nt.
Libyan ['lɪbɪən] adj libysch ♦ n Libyer(in) m(f).
lice [laɪs] npl of **louse**.
licence, (US) **license** ['laɪsns] n (document) Genehmigung f; (also: **driving ~**) Führerschein m; (COMM) Lizenz f; (excessive freedom) Zügellosigkeit f; **to get a TV ~** ≈ Fernsehgebühren bezahlen; **under ~** (COMM) in Lizenz.
license ['laɪsns] n (US) = **licence** ♦ vt (person, organization) eine Lizenz vergeben an +acc; (activity) eine Genehmigung erteilen für.
licensed ['laɪsnst] adj: **the car is ~** die Kfz-Steuer für das Auto ist bezahlt; **~ hotel/ restaurant** Hotel/Restaurant mit Schankerlaubnis.
licensee [laɪsənˈsiː] n (of bar) Inhaber(in) m(f) einer Schankerlaubnis.
license plate (US) n Nummernschild nt.
licensing hours ['laɪsnsɪŋ-] (BRIT) npl Ausschankzeiten pl.
licentious [laɪˈsɛnʃəs] adj ausschweifend, zügellos.

lichen ['laɪkən] *n* Flechte *f*.

lick [lɪk] *vt* lecken; (*stamp etc*) lecken an +*dat*; (*inf: defeat*) in die Pfanne hauen ♦ *n* Lecken *nt*; **to ~ one's lips** sich *dat* die Lippen lecken; (*fig*) sich *dat* die Finger lecken; **a ~ of paint** ein Anstrich *m*.

licorice ['lɪkərɪs] (*US*) *n* = **liquorice**.

lid [lɪd] *n* Deckel *m*; (*eyelid*) Lid *nt*; **to take the ~ off sth** (*fig*) etw enthüllen *or* aufdecken.

lido ['laɪdəu] (*BRIT*) *n* Freibad *nt*.

lie[1] [laɪ] (*pt, pp* **lied**) *vi* lügen ♦ *n* Lüge *f*; **to tell ~s** lügen.

lie[2] [laɪ] (*pt* **lay**, *pp* **lain**) *vi* (*lit, fig*) liegen; **to ~ low** (*fig*) untertauchen.

▶ **lie about** *vi* herumliegen.

▶ **lie around** *vi* = **lie about**.

▶ **lie back** *vi* sich zurücklehnen; (*fig: accept the inevitable*) sich fügen.

▶ **lie down** *vi* sich hinlegen.

▶ **lie up** *vi* (*hide*) untertauchen; (*rest*) im Bett bleiben.

Liechtenstein ['lɪktənstaɪn] *n* Liechtenstein *nt*.

lie detector *n* Lügendetektor *m*.

lie-down ['laɪdaun] (*BRIT*) *n*: **to have a ~** ein Schläfchen machen.

lie-in ['laɪɪn] (*BRIT*) *n*: **to have a ~** (sich) ausschlafen.

lieu [luː]: **in ~ of** *prep* anstelle *or* an Stelle von, anstatt +*gen*.

Lieut. *abbr* (*MIL*: = *lieutenant*) Lt.

lieutenant [lɛf'tɛnəntɡ, ɡ(USG) luː'tɛnənt] *n* Leutnant *m*.

lieutenant colonel *n* Oberstleutnant *m*.

life [laɪf] (*pl* **lives**) *n* Leben *nt*; (*of machine etc*) Lebensdauer *f*; **true to ~** lebensecht; **painted from ~** aus dem Leben gegriffen; **to be sent to prison for ~** zu einer lebenslänglichen Freiheitsstrafe verurteilt werden; **such is ~** so ist das Leben; **to come to ~** (*fig: person*) munter werden; (: *party etc*) in Schwung kommen.

life annuity *n* Leibrente *f*.

life assurance (*BRIT*) *n* = **life insurance**.

life belt (*BRIT*) *n* Rettungsgürtel *m*.

lifeblood ['laɪfblʌd] *n* (*fig*) Lebensnerv *m*.

lifeboat ['laɪfbəut] *n* Rettungsboot *nt*.

life buoy *n* Rettungsring *m*.

life expectancy *n* Lebenserwartung *f*.

lifeguard ['laɪfɡɑːd] *n* (*at beach*) Rettungsschwimmer(in) *m(f)*; (*at swimming pool*) Bademeister(in) *m(f)*.

life imprisonment *n* lebenslängliche Freiheitsstrafe *f*.

life insurance *n* Lebensversicherung *f*.

life jacket *n* Schwimmweste *f*.

lifeless ['laɪflɪs] *adj* leblos; (*fig: person, party etc*) langweilig.

lifelike ['laɪflaɪk] *adj* lebensecht; (*painting*) naturgetreu.

lifeline ['laɪflaɪn] *n* (*fig*) Rettungsanker *m*; (*rope*) Rettungsleine *f*.

lifelong ['laɪflɔŋ] *adj* lebenslang.

life preserver (*US*) *n* = **life belt**, **life jacket**.

lifer ['laɪfə'] (*inf*) *n* Lebenslängliche(r) *f(m)*.

life raft *n* Rettungsfloß *nt*.

life-saver ['laɪfseɪvə'] *n* Lebensretter(in) *m(f)*.

life sciences *npl* Biowissenschaften *pl*.

life sentence *n* lebenslängliche Freiheitsstrafe *f*.

life-size(d) ['laɪfsaɪz(d)] *adj* in Lebensgröße.

life span *n* Lebensdauer *f*; (*of person*) Lebenszeit *f*.

life style ['laɪfstaɪl] *n* Lebensstil *m*.

life-support system ['laɪfsəpɔːt-] *n* (*MED*) Lebenserhaltungssystem *nt*.

lifetime ['laɪftaɪm] *n* Lebenszeit *f*; (*of thing*) Lebensdauer *f*; (*of parliament*) Legislaturperiode *f*; **in my ~** während meines Lebens; **the chance of a ~** eine einmalige Chance.

lift [lɪft] *vt* (*raise*) heben; (*end: ban etc*) aufheben; (*plagiarize*) abschreiben; (*inf: steal*) mitgehen lassen, klauen ♦ *vi* (*fog*) sich auflösen ♦ *n* (*BRIT*) Aufzug *m*, Fahrstuhl *m*; **to take the ~** mit dem Aufzug *or* Fahrstuhl fahren; **to give sb a ~** (*BRIT*) jdn (im Auto) mitnehmen.

▶ **lift off** *vi* abheben.

▶ **lift up** *vt* hochheben.

liftoff ['lɪftɔf] *n* Abheben *nt*.

ligament ['lɪɡəmənt] *n* (*ANAT*) Band *nt*.

light [laɪt] (*pt, pp* **lit**) *n* Licht *nt* ♦ *vt* (*candle, cigarette, fire*) anzünden; (*room*) beleuchten ♦ *adj* leicht; (*pale, bright*) hell; (*traffic etc*) gering; (*music*) Unterhaltungs- ♦ *adv*: **to travel ~** mit leichtem Gepäck reisen; **lights** *npl* (*AUT: also*: **traffic ~s**) Ampel *f*; **the ~s** (*of car*) die Beleuchtung; **have you got a ~?** haben Sie Feuer?; **to turn the ~ on/off** das Licht an-/ausmachen; **to come to ~** ans Tageslicht kommen; **to cast** *or* **shed** *or* **throw ~ on** (*fig*) Licht bringen in +*acc*; **in the ~ of** angesichts +*gen*; **to make ~ of sth** (*fig*) etw auf die leichte Schulter nehmen; **~ green/blue** *etc* hellblau/-grün *etc*.

▶ **light up** *vi* (*face*) sich erhellen ♦ *vt* (*illuminate*) beleuchten, erhellen.

light bulb *n* Glühbirne *f*.

lighten ['laɪtn] *vt* (*make less heavy*) leichter machen ♦ *vi* (*become less dark*) sich aufhellen.

lighter ['laɪtə'] *n* (*also*: **cigarette ~**) Feuerzeug *nt*.

light-fingered [laɪt'fɪŋɡəd] (*inf*) *adj* langfingerig.

light-headed [laɪt'hɛdɪd] *adj* (*dizzy*) benommen; (*excited*) ausgelassen.

light-hearted [laɪt'hɑːtɪd] *adj* unbeschwert; (*question, remark etc*) scherzhaft.

lighthouse ['laɪthaus] *n* Leuchtturm *m*.

lighting ['laɪtɪŋ] *n* Beleuchtung *f*.

lighting-up time [laɪtɪŋ'ʌp-] *n* *Zeitpunkt, zu dem die Fahrzeugbeleuchtung* *eingeschaltet werden muss.*

lightly ['laɪtlɪ] *adv* leicht; (*not seriously*) leichthin; **to get off** ~ glimpflich davonkommen.

light meter *n* Belichtungsmesser *m*.

lightness ['laɪtnɪs] *n* (*in weight*) Leichtigkeit *f*.

lightning ['laɪtnɪŋ] *n* Blitz *m* ♦ *adj* (*attack etc*) Blitz-; **with** ~ **speed** blitzschnell.

lightning conductor *n* Blitzableiter *m*.

lightning rod (*US*) *n* = **lightning conductor**.

light pen *n* Lichtstift *m*, Lichtgriffel *m*.

lightship ['laɪtʃɪp] *n* Feuerschiff *nt*.

lightweight ['laɪtweɪt] *adj* leicht ♦ *n* (*BOXING*) Leichtgewichtler *m*.

light year *n* Lichtjahr *nt*.

like [laɪk] *vt* mögen ♦ *prep* wie; (*such as*) wie (zum Beispiel) ♦ *n*: **and the** ~ und dergleichen; **I would** ~, **I'd** ~ ich hätte *or* möchte gern; **would you** ~ **a coffee?** möchten Sie einen Kaffee?; **if you** ~ wenn Sie wollen; **to** ~ **sb/sth** jdm/etw ähnlich sein/sehen; **something** ~ **that** so etwas Ähnliches; **what does it look/taste/ sound** ~? wie sieht es aus/schmeckt es/hört es sich an?; **what's he/the weather** ~? wie ist er/das Wetter?; **I feel** ~ **a drink** ich möchte gerne etwas trinken; **there's nothing** ~ ... es geht nichts über +*acc*; **that's just** ~ **him** das sieht ihm ähnlich; **do it** ~ **this** mach es so; **it is nothing** ~ (+*noun*) es ist ganz anders als; (+*adj*) es ist alles andere als; **it is nothing** ~ **as** ... es ist bei weitem nicht so ...; **his** ~**s and dislikes** seine Vorlieben und Abneigungen.

likeable ['laɪkəbl] *adj* sympathisch.

likelihood ['laɪklɪhud] *n* Wahrscheinlichkeit *f*; **there is every** ~ **that** ... es ist sehr wahrscheinlich, dass ...; **in all** ~ aller Wahrscheinlichkeit nach.

likely ['laɪklɪ] *adj* wahrscheinlich; **to be** ~ **to do sth** wahrscheinlich etw tun; **not** ~! (*inf*) wohl kaum!

like-minded ['laɪk'maɪndɪd] *adj* gleich gesinnt.

liken ['laɪkən] *vt*: **to** ~ **sth to sth** etw mit etw vergleichen.

likeness ['laɪknɪs] *n* Ähnlichkeit *f*; **that's a good** ~ (*photo, portrait*) das ist ein gutes Bild von ihm/ihr *etc*.

likewise ['laɪkwaɪz] *adv* ebenso; **to do** ~ das Gleiche tun.

liking ['laɪkɪŋ] *n*: ~ (**for**) (*person*) Zuneigung *f* (zu); (*thing*) Vorliebe *f* (für); **to be to sb's** ~ nach jds Geschmack sein; **to take a** ~ **to sb** an jdm Gefallen finden.

lilac ['laɪlək] *n* (*BOT*) Flieder *m* ♦ *adj* fliederfarben, (zart)lila.

Lilo ® ['laɪləu] *n* Luftmatratze *f*.

lilt [lɪlt] *n* singender Tonfall *m*.

lilting ['lɪltɪŋ] *adj* singend.

lily ['lɪlɪ] *n* Lilie *f*.

lily of the valley *n* Maiglöckchen *nt*.

Lima ['liːmə] *n* Lima *nt*.

limb [lɪm] *n* Glied *nt*; (*of tree*) Ast *m*; **to be out on a** ~ (*fig*) (ganz) allein (da)stehen.

limber up ['lɪmbə*-*] *vi* Lockerungsübungen machen.

limbo ['lɪmbəu] *n*: **to be in** ~ (*fig: plans etc*) in der Schwebe sein; (: *person*) in der Luft hängen (*inf*).

lime [laɪm] *n* (*fruit*) Limone *f*; (*tree*) Linde *f*; (*also*: ~ **juice**) Limonensaft *m*; (*for soil*) Kalk *m*; (*rock*) Kalkstein *m*.

limelight ['laɪmlaɪt] *n*: **to be in the** ~ im Rampenlicht stehen.

limerick ['lɪmərɪk] *n* Limerick *m*.

limestone ['laɪmstəun] *n* Kalkstein *m*.

limit ['lɪmɪt] *n* Grenze *f*; (*restriction*) Beschränkung *f* ♦ *vt* begrenzen, einschränken; **within** ~**s** innerhalb gewisser Grenzen.

limitation [lɪmɪ'teɪʃən] *n* Einschränkung *f*; **limitations** *npl* (*shortcomings*) Grenzen *pl*.

limited ['lɪmɪtɪd] *adj* begrenzt, beschränkt; **to be** ~ **to** beschränkt sein auf +*acc*.

limited edition *n* beschränkte Ausgabe *f*.

limited (liability) company (*BRIT*) *n* ≈ Gesellschaft *f* mit beschränkter Haftung.

limitless ['lɪmɪtlɪs] *adj* grenzenlos.

limousine ['lɪməziːn] *n* Limousine *f*.

limp [lɪmp] *adj* schlaff; (*material etc*) weich ♦ *vi* hinken ♦ *n*: **to have a** ~ hinken.

limpet ['lɪmpɪt] *n* Napfschnecke *f*.

limpid ['lɪmpɪd] *adj* klar.

limply ['lɪmplɪ] *adv* schlaff.

linchpin ['lɪntʃpɪn] *n* (*fig*) wichtigste Stütze *f*.

Lincs [lɪŋks] (*BRIT*) *abbr* (*POST*: = *Lincolnshire*).

line [laɪn] *n* Linie *f*; (*written, printed*) Zeile *f*; (*wrinkle*) Falte *f*; (*row: of people*) Schlange *f*; (: *of things*) Reihe *f*; (*for fishing, washing*) Leine *f*; (*wire, TEL*) Leitung *f*; (*railway track*) Gleise *pl*; (*fig: attitude*) Standpunkt *m*; (: *business*) Branche *f*; (*COMM*: *of product(s)*) Art *f* ♦ *vt* (*road*) säumen; (*container*) auskleiden; (*clothing*) füttern; **hold the** ~ **please!** (*TEL*) bleiben Sie am Apparat!; **to cut in** ~ (*US*) sich vordrängeln; **in** ~ in einer Reihe; **in** ~ **with** im Einklang mit, in Übereinstimmung mit; **to be in** ~ **for sth** mit etw an der Reihe sein; **to bring sth into** ~ **with** etw auf die gleiche Linie wie etw *acc* bringen; **on the right** ~**s** auf dem richtigen Weg; **I draw the** ~ **at that** da mache ich nicht mehr mit; **to** ~ **sth with sth** etw mit etw auskleiden; (*drawers etc*) etw mit etw auslegen; **to** ~ **the streets** die Straßen säumen.

▶ **line up** *vi* sich aufstellen ♦ *vt* (*in a row*) aufstellen; (*engage*) verpflichten; (*prepare*) arrangieren; **to have sb** ~**d up** jdn verpflichtet haben; **to have sth** ~**d up** etw geplant haben.

linear ['lɪnɪə*-*] *adj* linear; (*shape, form*) gerade.

lined [laɪnd] *adj* (*face*) faltig; (*paper*) liniert; (*skirt, jacket*) gefüttert.

line editing n (COMPUT) zeilenweise Aufbereitung f.
line feed n (COMPUT) Zeilenvorschub m.
lineman ['laɪnmən] (US: irreg: like man) n (FOOTBALL) Stürmer m.
linen ['lɪnɪn] n (cloth) Leinen nt; (tablecloths, sheets etc) Wäsche f.
line printer n (COMPUT) Zeilendrucker m.
liner ['laɪnə*] n (ship) Passagierschiff nt; (also: **bin** ~) Müllbeutel m.
linesman ['laɪnzmən] (irreg: like man) n (SPORT) Linienrichter m.
line-up ['laɪnʌp] n (US: queue) Schlange f; (SPORT) Aufstellung f; (at concert etc) Künstleraufgebot nt; (identity parade) Gegenüberstellung f.
linger ['lɪŋgə*] vi (smell) sich halten; (tradition etc) fortbestehen; (person) sich aufhalten.
lingerie ['lænʒəriː] n (Damen)unterwäsche f.
lingering ['lɪŋgərɪŋ] adj bleibend.
lingo ['lɪŋgəu] (pl ~es) (inf) n Sprache f.
linguist ['lɪŋgwɪst] n (person who speaks several languages) Sprachkundige(r) f(m).
linguistic [lɪŋ'gwɪstɪk] adj sprachlich.
linguistics [lɪŋ'gwɪstɪks] n Sprachwissenschaft f.
liniment ['lɪnɪmənt] n Einreibemittel nt.
lining ['laɪnɪŋ] n (cloth) Futter nt; (ANAT: of stomach) Magenschleimhaut f; (TECH) Auskleidung f; (of brakes) (Brems)belag m.
link [lɪŋk] n Verbindung f, Beziehung f; (communications link) Verbindung; (of a chain) Glied nt; (COMPUT) Link m ♦ vi (COMPUT): to ~ **to a site** einen Link zu einer Website haben ♦ vt (join) verbinden; (COMPUT) per Link verbinden; **links** npl (GOLF) Golfplatz m; **rail** ~ Bahnverbindung f.
► **link up** vt verbinden ♦ vi verbunden werden.
linkup ['lɪŋkʌp] n Verbindung f; (of spaceships) Koppelung f.
lino ['laɪnəu] n = **linoleum**.
linoleum [lɪ'nəulɪəm] n Linoleum nt.
linseed oil ['lɪnsiːd-] n Leinöl nt.
lint [lɪnt] n Mull m.
lintel ['lɪntl] n (ARCHIT) Sturz m.
lion ['laɪən] n Löwe m.
lion cub n Löwenjunge(s) nt.
lioness ['laɪənɪs] n Löwin f.
lip [lɪp] n (ANAT) Lippe f; (of cup etc) Rand m; (inf: insolence) Frechheiten pl.
liposuction ['lɪpəusʌkʃən] n Liposuktion f.
lip-read ['lɪpriːd] vi von den Lippen ablesen.
lip salve n Fettstift m.
lip service (pej) n: **to pay** ~ **to sth** ein Lippenbekenntnis nt zu etw ablegen.
lipstick ['lɪpstɪk] n Lippenstift m.
liquefy ['lɪkwɪfaɪ] vt verflüssigen ♦ vi sich verflüssigen.
liqueur [lɪ'kjuə*] n Likör m.
liquid ['lɪkwɪd] adj flüssig ♦ n Flüssigkeit f.
liquid assets npl flüssige Vermögenswerte pl.

liquidate ['lɪkwɪdeɪt] vt liquidieren.
liquidation [lɪkwɪ'deɪʃən] n Liquidation f.
liquidation sale (US) n Verkauf m wegen Geschäftsaufgabe.
liquidator ['lɪkwɪdeɪtə*] n Liquidator m.
liquid-crystal display ['lɪkwɪd'krɪstl-] n Flüssigkristallanzeige f.
liquidity [lɪ'kwɪdɪtɪ] n Liquidität f.
liquidize ['lɪkwɪdaɪz] vt (im Mixer) pürieren.
liquidizer ['lɪkwɪdaɪzə*] n Mixer m.
liquor ['lɪkə*] n Spirituosen pl, Alkohol m; **hard** ~ harte Drinks pl.
liquorice ['lɪkərɪs] (BRIT) n Lakritze f.
liquor store (US) n Spirituosengeschäft nt.
Lisbon ['lɪzbən] n Lissabon nt.
lisp [lɪsp] n Lispeln nt ♦ vi lispeln.
list [lɪst] n Liste f ♦ vt aufführen; (COMPUT) auflisten; (write down) aufschreiben ♦ vi (ship) Schlagseite haben.
listed building ['lɪstɪd-] (BRIT) n unter Denkmalschutz stehendes Gebäude nt.
listed company n börsennotierte Firma f.
listen ['lɪsn] vi hören; **to** ~ **(out) for** horchen auf +acc; **to** ~ **to sb** jdm zuhören; **to** ~ **to sth** etw hören; ~! hör zu!
listener ['lɪsnə*] n Zuhörer(in) m(f); (RADIO) Hörer(in) m(f).
listeria [lɪs'tɪərɪə] n Listeriose f.
listing ['lɪstɪŋ] n Auflistung f; (entry) Eintrag m.
listless ['lɪstlɪs] adj lustlos.
listlessly ['lɪstlɪslɪ] adv lustlos.
list price n Listenpreis m.
lit [lɪt] pt, pp of **light**.
litany ['lɪtənɪ] n Litanei f.
liter ['liːtə*] (US) n = **litre**.
literacy ['lɪtərəsɪ] n die Fähigkeit, lesen und schreiben zu können.
literacy campaign n Kampagne f gegen das Analphabetentum.
literal ['lɪtərəl] adj wörtlich, eigentlich; (translation) (wort)wörtlich.
literally ['lɪtrəlɪ] adv buchstäblich.
literary ['lɪtərərɪ] adj literarisch.
literate ['lɪtərət] adj (educated) gebildet; **to be** ~ lesen und schreiben können.
literature ['lɪtrɪtʃə*] n Literatur f; (printed information) Informationsmaterial nt.
lithe [laɪð] adj gelenkig; (animal) geschmeidig.
lithography [lɪ'θɔgrəfɪ] n Lithografie f.
Lithuania [lɪθju'eɪnɪə] n Litauen nt.
Lithuanian [lɪθju'eɪnɪən] adj litauisch ♦ n Litauer(in) m(f); (LING) Litauisch nt.
litigation [lɪtɪ'geɪʃən] n Prozess m.
litmus paper ['lɪtməs-] n Lackmuspapier nt.
litre, (US) **liter** ['liːtə*] n Liter m or nt.
litter ['lɪtə*] n (rubbish) Abfall m; (young animals) Wurf m.
litter bin (BRIT) n Abfalleimer m.
litterbug ['lɪtəbʌg] n Dreckspatz m.
littered ['lɪtəd] adj: ~ **with** (scattered) übersät mit.

litter lout n Dreckspatz m.
little ['lɪtl] adj klein; (short) kurz ♦ adv wenig; **a** ~ ein wenig, ein bisschen; **a** ~ **bit** ein kleines bisschen; **to have** ~ **time/money** wenig Zeit/Geld haben; ~ **by** ~ nach und nach.
little finger n kleiner Finger m.
little-known ['lɪtl'nəun] adj wenig bekannt.
liturgy ['lɪtədʒɪ] n Liturgie f.
live [vi lɪv, adj laɪv] vi leben; (in house, town) wohnen ♦ adj lebend; (TV, RADIO) live; (performance, pictures etc) Live-; (ELEC) Strom führend; (bullet, bomb etc) scharf; **to** ~ **with sb** mit jdm zusammenleben.
▶ **live down** vt hinwegkommen über +acc.
▶ **live for** vt leben für.
▶ **live in** vi (student/servant) im Wohnheim/ Haus wohnen.
▶ **live off** vt fus leben von; (parents etc) auf Kosten +gen leben.
▶ **live on** vt fus leben von.
▶ **live out** vi (BRIT: student/servant) außerhalb (des Wohnheims/Hauses) wohnen ♦ vt: **to** ~ **out one's days** or **life** sein Leben verbringen.
▶ **live together** vi zusammenleben.
▶ **live up** vt: **to** ~ **it up** einen draufmachen (inf).
▶ **live up to** vt fus erfüllen, entsprechen +dat.
live-in ['lɪvɪn] adj (cook, maid) im Haus wohnend; **her** ~ **lover** ihr Freund, der bei ihr wohnt.
livelihood ['laɪvlɪhud] n Lebensunterhalt m.
liveliness ['laɪvlɪnɪs] n (see adj) Lebhaftigkeit f; Lebendigkeit f.
lively ['laɪvlɪ] adj lebhaft; (place, event, book etc) lebendig.
liven up ['laɪvn-] vt beleben, Leben bringen in +acc; (person) aufmuntern ♦ vi (person) aufleben; (discussion, evening etc) in Schwung kommen.
liver ['lɪvə*] n (ANAT, CULIN) Leber f.
liverish ['lɪvərɪʃ] adj: **to be** ~ sich unwohl fühlen.
Liverpudlian [lɪvə'pʌdlɪən] adj Liverpooler ♦ n Liverpooler(in) m(f).
livery ['lɪvərɪ] n Livree f.
lives [laɪvz] npl of **life**.
livestock ['laɪvstɔk] n Vieh nt.
live wire (inf) n (person) Energiebündel nt.
livid ['lɪvɪd] adj (colour) bleifarben; (inf: furious) fuchsteufelswild.
living ['lɪvɪŋ] adj lebend ♦ n: **to earn** or **make a** ~ sich dat seinen Lebensunterhalt verdienen; **within** ~ **memory** seit Menschengedenken; **the cost of** ~ die Lebenshaltungskosten pl.
living conditions npl Wohnverhältnisse pl.
living expenses npl Lebenshaltungskosten pl.
living room n Wohnzimmer nt.
living standards npl Lebensstandard m.

living wage n ausreichender Lohn m.
lizard ['lɪzəd] n Eidechse f.
llama ['lɑːmə] n Lama nt.
LLB n abbr (= Bachelor of Laws) akademischer Grad für Juristen.
LLD n abbr (= Doctor of Laws) ≈ Dr. jur.
LMT (US) abbr (= Local Mean Time) Ortszeit.
load [ləud] n Last f; (of vehicle) Ladung f; (weight, ELEC) Belastung f ♦ vt (also: ~ **up**) beladen; (gun, COMPUT: program, data) laden; **that's a** ~ **of rubbish** (inf) das ist alles Blödsinn; ~**s of**, **a** ~ **of** (fig) jede Menge; **to** ~ **a camera** einen Film einlegen.
loaded ['ləudɪd] adj (inf: rich) steinreich; (dice) präpariert; (vehicle): **to be** ~ **with** beladen sein mit; **a** ~ **question** eine Fangfrage.
loading bay ['ləudɪŋ-] n Ladeplatz m.
loaf [ləuf] (pl **loaves**) n Brot nt, Laib m ♦ vi (also: ~ **about**, ~ **around**) faulenzen; **use your** ~! (inf) streng deinen Grips an!
loam [ləum] n Lehmerde f.
loan [ləun] n Darlehen nt ♦ vt: **to** ~ **sth to sb** jdm etw leihen; **on** ~ geliehen.
loan account n Darlehenskonto nt.
loan capital n Anleihekapital nt.
loan shark (inf) n Kredithai m.
loath [ləuθ] adj: **to be** ~ **to do sth** etw ungern tun.
loathe [ləuð] vt verabscheuen.
loathing ['ləuðɪŋ] n Abscheu m.
loathsome ['ləuðsəm] adj abscheulich.
loaves [ləuvz] npl of **loaf**.
lob [lɔb] vt (ball) lobben.
lobby ['lɔbɪ] n (of building) Eingangshalle f; (POL: pressure group) Interessenverband m ♦ vt Einfluss nehmen auf +acc.
lobbyist ['lɔbɪɪst] n Lobbyist(in) m(f).
lobe [ləub] n Ohrläppchen nt.
lobster ['lɔbstə*] n Hummer m.
lobster pot n Hummer(fang)korb m.
local ['ləukl] adj örtlich; (council) Stadt-, Gemeinde-; (paper) Lokal- ♦ n (pub) Stammkneipe f; **the locals** npl (local inhabitants) die Einheimischen pl.
local anaesthetic n örtliche Betäubung f.
local authority n Gemeindeverwaltung f, Stadtverwaltung f.
local call n Ortsgespräch nt.
locale [ləu'kɑːl] n Umgebung f.
local government n Kommunalverwaltung f.
locality [ləu'kælɪtɪ] n Gegend f.
localize ['ləukəlaɪz] vt lokalisieren.
locally ['ləukəlɪ] adv am Ort.
locate [ləu'keɪt] vt (find) ausfindig machen; **to be** ~**d** in sich befinden in +dat.
location [ləu'keɪʃən] n Ort m; (position) Lage f; (CINE) Drehort m; **he's on** ~ **in Mexico** er ist bei Außenaufnahmen in Mexiko; **to be filmed on** ~ als Außenaufnahme gedreht werden.
loch [lɔx] (SCOT) n See m.

lock [lɔk] *n* (*of door etc*) Schloss *nt*; (*on canal*) Schleuse *f*; (*also*: ~ **of hair**) Locke *f* ♦ *vt* (*door etc*) abschließen; (*steering wheel*) sperren; (*COMPUT*: *keyboard*) verriegeln ♦ *vi* (*door etc*) sich abschließen lassen; (*wheels, mechanism etc*) blockieren; **on full** ~ (*AUT*) voll eingeschlagen; ~, **stock and barrel** mit allem Drum und Dran; **his jaw** ~**ed** er hatte Mundsperre.

▶ **lock away** *vt* wegschließen; (*criminal*) einsperren.

▶ **lock in** *vt* einschließen.

▶ **lock out** *vt* aussperren.

▶ **lock up** *vt* (*criminal etc*) einsperren; (*house*) abschließen ♦ *vi* abschließen.

locker ['lɔkə*] *n* Schließfach *nt*.

locker room *n* Umkleideraum *m*.

locket ['lɔkɪt] *n* Medaillon *nt*.

lockjaw ['lɔkdʒɔː] *n* Wundstarrkrampf *m*.

lockout ['lɔkaut] *n* Aussperrung *f*.

locksmith ['lɔksmɪθ] *n* Schlosser *m*.

lockup ['lɔkʌp] *n* (*US: inf: jail*) Gefängnis *nt*; (*also*: **lock-up garage**) Garage *f*.

locomotive [ləukə'məutɪv] *n* Lokomotive *f*.

locum ['ləukəm] *n* (*MED*) Vertreter(in) *m(f)*.

locust ['ləukəst] *n* Heuschrecke *f*.

lodge [lɔdʒ] *n* Pförtnerhaus *nt*; (*hunting lodge*) Hütte *f*; (*FREEMASONRY*) Loge *f* ♦ *vt* (*complaint, protest etc*) einlegen ♦ *vi* (*bullet*) stecken bleiben; (*person*): **to** ~ (**with**) zur Untermiete wohnen (bei).

lodger ['lɔdʒə*] *n* Untermieter(in) *m(f)*.

lodging ['lɔdʒɪŋ] *n* Unterkunft *f*.

lodging house *n* Pension *f*.

lodgings ['lɔdʒɪŋz] *npl* möbliertes Zimmer *nt*; (*several rooms*) Wohnung *f*.

loft [lɔft] *n* Boden *m*, Speicher *m*.

lofty ['lɔftɪ] *adj* (*noble*) hoch(fliegend); (*self-important*) hochmütig; (*high*) hoch.

log [lɔg] *n* (*of wood*) Holzblock *m*, Holzklotz *m*; (*written account*) Log *nt* ♦ *n abbr* (*MATH*: = *logarithm*) log ♦ *vt* (ins Logbuch) eintragen.

▶ **log in** *vi* (*COMPUT*) sich anmelden.

▶ **log into** *vt fus* (*COMPUT*) sich anmelden bei.

▶ **log off** *vi* (*COMPUT*) sich abmelden.

▶ **log on** *vi* (*COMPUT*) = **log in**.

▶ **log out** *vi* (*COMPUT*) = **log off**.

logarithm ['lɔgərɪðm] *n* Logarithmus *m*.

logbook ['lɔgbuk] *n* (*NAUT*) Logbuch *nt*; (*AVIAT*) Bordbuch *nt*; (*of car*) Kraftfahrzeugbrief *m*; (*of lorry driver*) Fahrtenbuch *nt*; (*of events*) Tagebuch *nt*; (*of movement of goods etc*) Dienstbuch *nt*.

log fire *n* Holzfeuer *nt*.

logger ['lɔgə*] *n* (*lumberjack*) Holzfäller *m*.

loggerheads ['lɔgəhedz] *npl*: **to be at** ~ Streit haben.

logic ['lɔdʒɪk] *n* Logik *f*.

logical ['lɔdʒɪkl] *adj* logisch.

logically ['lɔdʒɪkəlɪ] *adv* logisch; (*reasonably*) logischerweise.

logistics [lɔ'dʒɪstɪks] *n* Logistik *f*.

log jam *n* (*fig*) Blockierung *f*; **to break the** ~ freie Bahn schaffen.

logo ['ləugəu] *n* Logo *nt*.

loin [lɔɪn] *n* Lende *f*.

loincloth ['lɔɪnklɔθ] *n* Lendenschurz *m*.

loiter ['lɔɪtə*] *vi* sich aufhalten.

loll [lɔl] *vi* (*also*: ~ **about**: *person*) herumhängen; (*head*) herunterhängen; (*tongue*) heraushängen.

lollipop ['lɔlɪpɔp] *n* Lutscher *m*.

lollipop lady (*BRIT*) *n* ≈ Schülerlotsin *f*.

lollipop man (*BRIT*) *n* ≈ Schülerlotse *m*.

LOLLIPOP MAN/LADY

Lollipop man/lady *heißen in Großbritannien die Männer bzw. Frauen, die mithilfe eines runden Stoppschildes den Verkehr anhalten, damit Schulkinder die Straße gefahrlos überqueren können. Der Name bezieht sich auf die Form des Schildes, die an einen Lutscher erinnert.*

---

lollop ['lɔləp] *vi* zockeln.

lolly ['lɔlɪ] (*inf*) *n* (*lollipop*) Lutscher *m*; (*money*) Mäuse *pl*.

London ['lʌndən] *n* London *nt*.

Londoner ['lʌndənə*] *n* Londoner(in) *m(f)*.

lone [ləun] *adj* einzeln, einsam; (*only*) einzig.

loneliness ['ləunlɪnɪs] *n* Einsamkeit *f*.

lonely ['ləunlɪ] *adj* einsam.

lonely hearts *adj*: ~ **ad** Kontaktanzeige *f*; **the** ~ **column** die Kontaktanzeigen *pl*.

lone parent *n* Alleinerziehende(r) *f(m)*, allein Erziehende(r) *f(m)*.

loner ['ləunə*] *n* Einzelgänger(in) *m(f)*.

long [lɔŋ] *adj* lang ♦ *adv* lang(e) ♦ *vi*: **to** ~ **for sth** sich nach etw sehnen; **in the** ~ **run** auf die Dauer; **how** ~ **is the lesson?** wie lange dauert die Stunde?; ~ 6 **metres/months** ~ 6 Meter/Monate lang; **so** *or* **as** ~ **as** (*on condition that*) solange; (*while*) während; **don't be** ~! bleib nicht so lange!; **all night** ~ die ganze Nacht; **he no** ~**er comes** er kommt nicht mehr; ~ **ago** vor langer Zeit; ~ **before/after** lange vorher/danach; **before** ~ bald; **at** ~ **last** schließlich und endlich; **the** ~ **and the short of it is that** ... kurz gesagt, ...

long-distance [lɔŋ'dɪstəns] *adj* (*travel, phone call*) Fern-; (*race*) Langstrecken-.

longevity [lɔn'dʒevɪtɪ] *n* Langlebigkeit *f*.

long-haired ['lɔŋ'heəd] *adj* langhaarig; (*animal*) Langhaar-.

longhand ['lɔŋhænd] *n* Langschrift *f*.

longing ['lɔŋɪŋ] *n* Sehnsucht *f*.

longingly ['lɔŋɪŋlɪ] *adv* sehnsüchtig.

longitude ['lɔŋgɪtjuːd] *n* Länge *f*.

long johns [-dʒɔnz] *npl* lange Unterhose *f*.

long jump *n* Weitsprung *m*.

long-life ['lɔŋlaɪf] *adj* (*batteries etc*) mit langer Lebensdauer; ~ **milk** H-Milch *f*.

long-lost ['lɒŋlɒst] *adj* verloren geglaubt.
long-playing record ['lɒŋpleɪɪŋ-] *n* Langspielplatte *f*.
long-range ['lɒŋ'reɪndʒ] *adj* (*plan, forecast*) langfristig; (*missile, plane etc*) Langstrecken-.
longshoreman ['lɒŋʃɔːmən] (*US: irreg: like* **man**) *n* Hafenarbeiter *m*.
long-sighted ['lɒŋ'saɪtɪd] *adj* weitsichtig.
long-standing ['lɒŋ'stændɪŋ] *adj* langjährig.
long-suffering [lɒŋ'sʌfərɪŋ] *adj* schwer geprüft.
long-term ['lɒŋtəːm] *adj* langfristig.
long wave *n* Langwelle *f*.
long-winded [lɒŋ'wɪndɪd] *adj* umständlich, langatmig.
loo [luː] (*BRIT: inf*) *n* Klo *nt*.
loofah ['luːfə] *n* Luffa(schwamm) *m*.
look [luk] *vi* sehen, schauen, gucken (*inf*); (*seem, appear*) aussehen ♦ *n* (*glance*) Blick *m*; (*appearance*) Aussehen *nt*; (*expression*) Miene *f*; (*FASHION*) Look *m*; **looks** *npl* (*good looks*) (gutes) Aussehen; **to ~ (out) onto the sea/ south** (*building etc*) Blick aufs Meer/nach Süden haben; **~ (here)!** (*expressing annoyance*) hör (mal) zu!; **~!** (*expressing surprise*) sieh mal!; **to ~ like sb/sth** wie jd/ etw aussehen; **it ~s like him** es sieht ihm ähnlich; **it ~s about 4 metres long** es scheint etwa 4 Meter lang zu sein; **it ~s all right to me** es scheint mir in Ordnung zu sein; **to ~ ahead** vorausschauen; **to have a ~ at sth** sich *dat* etw ansehen; **let me have a ~** lass mich mal sehen; **to have a ~ for sth** nach etw suchen.
▶ **look after** *vt fus* sich kümmern um.
▶ **look at** *vt fus* ansehen; (*read quickly*) durchsehen; (*study, consider*) betrachten.
▶ **look back** *vi*: **to ~ back (on)** zurückblicken (auf +*acc*); **to ~ back at sth/sb** sich nach jdm/etw umsehen.
▶ **look down on** *vt fus* (*fig*) herabsehen auf +*acc*.
▶ **look for** *vt fus* suchen.
▶ **look forward to** *vt fus* sich freuen auf +*acc*; **we ~ forward to hearing from you** (*in letters*) wir hoffen, bald von Ihnen zu hören.
▶ **look in** *vi*: **to ~ in on sb** bei jdm vorbeikommen.
▶ **look into** *vt fus* (*investigate*) untersuchen.
▶ **look on** *vi* (*watch*) zusehen.
▶ **look out** *vi* (*beware*) aufpassen.
▶ **look out for** *vt fus* Ausschau halten nach.
▶ **look over** *vt* (*essay etc*) durchsehen; (*house, town etc*) sich *dat* ansehen; (*person*) mustern.
▶ **look round** *vi* sich umsehen.
▶ **look through** *vt fus* durchsehen.
▶ **look to** *vt fus* (*rely on*) sich verlassen auf +*acc*.
▶ **look up** *vi* aufsehen; (*situation*) sich bessern ♦ *vt* (*word etc*) nachschlagen; **things are ~ing up** es geht bergauf.

▶ **look up to** *vt fus* aufsehen zu.
lookalike ['lukəlaɪk] *n* Doppelgänger(in) *m(f)*.
look-in ['lukɪn] *n*: **to get a ~** (*inf*) eine Chance haben.
lookout ['lukaut] *n* (*tower etc*) Ausguck *m*; (*person*) Wachtposten *m*; **to be on the ~ for sth** nach etw Ausschau halten.
loom [luːm] *vi* (*also:* **~ up**: *object, shape*) sich abzeichnen; (*event*) näher rücken ♦ *n* Webstuhl *m*.
loony ['luːnɪ] (*inf*) *adj* verrückt ♦ *n* Verrückte(r) *f(m)*.
loop [luːp] *n* Schlaufe *f*; (*COMPUT*) Schleife *f* ♦ *vt*: **to ~ sth around sth** etw um etw schlingen.
loophole ['luːphəul] *n* Hintertürchen *nt*; **a ~ in the law** eine Lücke im Gesetz.
loose [luːs] *adj* lose, locker; (*clothes etc*) weit; (*long hair*) offen; (*not strictly controlled, promiscuous*) locker; (*definition*) ungenau; (*translation*) frei ♦ *vt* (*animal*) loslassen; (*prisoner*) freilassen; (*set off, unleash*) entfesseln ♦ *n*: **to be on the ~** frei herumlaufen.
loose change *n* Kleingeld *nt*.
loose chippings *npl* Schotter *m*.
loose end *n*: **to be at a ~** *or* (*US*) **at ~s** nichts mit sich *dat* anzufangen wissen; **to tie up ~s** die offen stehenden Probleme lösen.
loose-fitting ['luːsfɪtɪŋ] *adj* weit.
loose-leaf ['luːsliːf] *adj* Loseblatt-; **~ binder** Ringbuch *nt*.
loose-limbed [luːs'lɪmd] *adj* gelenkig, beweglich.
loosely ['luːslɪ] *adv* lose, locker.
loosely-knit ['luːslɪ'nɪt] *adj* (*fig*) locker.
loosen ['luːsn] *vt* lösen, losmachen; (*clothing, belt etc*) lockern.
loosen up *vi* (*before game*) sich auflockern; (*relax*) auftauen.
loot [luːt] *n* (*inf*) Beute *f* ♦ *vt* plündern.
looter ['luːtə] *n* Plünderer *m*.
looting ['luːtɪŋ] *n* Plünderung *f*.
lop off [lɒp-] *vt* abhacken.
lopsided ['lɒp'saɪdɪd] *adj* schief.
lord [lɔːd] *n* (*BRIT*) Lord *m*; **L~ Smith** Lord Smith; **the L~** (*REL*) der Herr; **my ~** (*to bishop*) Exzellenz; (*to noble*) Mylord; (*to judge*) Euer Ehren; **good L~!** ach, du lieber Himmel!; **the (House of) L~s** (*BRIT*) das Oberhaus.
lordly ['lɔːdlɪ] *adj* hochmütig.
lordship ['lɔːdʃɪp] *n*: **your L~** Eure Lordschaft.
lore [lɔː] *n* Überlieferung *pl*.
lorry ['lɒrɪ] (*BRIT*) *n* Lastwagen *m*, Lkw *m*.
lorry driver (*BRIT*) *n* Lastwagenfahrer *m*.
lose [luːz] (*pt, pp* **lost**) *vt* verlieren; (*opportunity*) verpassen; (*pursuers*) abschütteln ♦ *vi* verlieren; **to ~ (time)** (*clock*) nachgehen; **to ~ weight** abnehmen; **to ~ 5 pounds** 5 Pfund abnehmen; **to**

~ **sight of sth** (*also fig*) etw aus den Augen verlieren.

loser ['luːzə*] *n* Verlierer(in) *m(f)*; (*inf: failure*) Versager *m*; **to be a good/bad ~** ein guter/ schlechter Verlierer sein.

loss [lɔs] *n* Verlust *m*; **to make a ~ (of £1,000)** (1000 Pfund) Verlust machen; **to sell sth at a ~** etw mit Verlust verkaufen; **heavy ~es** schwere Verluste *pl*; **to cut one's ~es** aufgeben, bevor es noch schlimmer wird; **to be at a ~** nicht mehr weiterwissen.

loss adjuster *n* Schadenssachverständige(r) *f(m)*.

loss leader *n* (*COMM*) Lockvogelangebot *nt*.

lost [lɔst] *pt, pp of* **lose** ♦ *adj* (*person, animal*) vermisst; (*object*) verloren; **to be ~** sich verlaufen/verfahren haben; **to get ~** sich verlaufen/verfahren; **get ~!** (*inf*) verschwinde!; **~ in thought** in Gedanken verloren.

lost and found (*US*) *n* = **lost property**.

lost cause *n* aussichtslose Sache *f*.

lost property (*BRIT*) *n* Fundsachen *pl*; (*also:* ~ **office**) Fundbüro *nt*.

lot [lɔt] *n* (*kind*) Art *f*; (*group*) Gruppe *f*; (*at auctions, destiny*) Los *nt*; **to draw ~s** losen, Lose ziehen; **the ~** alles; **a ~ (of)** (*a large number (of)*) viele; (*a great deal (of)*) viel; **~s of** viele; **I read a ~** ich lese viel; **this happens a ~** das kommt oft vor.

loth [ləʊθ] *adj* = **loath**.

lotion ['ləʊʃən] *n* Lotion *f*.

lottery ['lɔtərɪ] *n* Lotterie *f*.

loud [laʊd] *adj* laut; (*clothes*) schreiend ♦ *adv* laut; **to be ~ in one's support of sb/sth** jdn/ etw lautstark unterstützen; **out ~** (*read, laugh etc*) laut.

loud-hailer [laʊd'heɪlə*] (*BRIT*) *n* Megafon *nt*, Megaphon *nt*.

loudly ['laʊdlɪ] *adv* laut.

loudmouthed ['laʊdmaʊθt] *adj* großmäulig.

loudspeaker [laʊd'spiːkə*] *n* Lautsprecher *m*.

lounge [laʊndʒ] *n* (*in house*) Wohnzimmer *nt*; (*in hotel*) Lounge *f*; (*at airport, station*) Wartehalle *f*; (*BRIT: also:* ~ **bar**) Salon *m* ♦ *vi* faulenzen.

► **lounge about** *vi* herumliegen, herumsitzen, herumstehen.

► **lounge around** *vi* = **lounge about**.

lounge suit (*BRIT*) *n* Straßenanzug *m*.

louse [laʊs] (*pl* **lice**) *n* Laus *f*.

► **louse up** (*inf*) *vt* vermasseln.

lousy ['laʊzɪ] (*inf*) *adj* (*bad-quality*) lausig, mies; (*despicable*) fies, gemein; (*ill*): **to feel ~** sich miserabel *or* elend fühlen.

lout [laʊt] *n* Lümmel *m*, Flegel *m*.

louvre, (*US*) **louver** ['luːvə*] *adj* (*door, window*) Lamellen-.

lovable ['lʌvəbl] *adj* liebenswert.

love [lʌv] *n* Liebe *f* ♦ *vt* lieben; (*thing, activity etc*) gern mögen; "**~ (from) Anne**" (*on letter*) „mit herzlichen Grüßen, Anne"; **to be in**

~ **with** verliebt sein in +*acc*; **to fall in ~ with** sich verlieben in +*acc*; **to make ~** sich lieben; **~ at first sight** Liebe auf den ersten Blick; **to send one's ~ to sb** jdn grüßen lassen; "**fifteen ~**" (*TENNIS*) „fünfzehn null"; **to ~ doing sth** etw gern tun; **I'd ~ to come** ich würde sehr gerne kommen; **I ~ chocolate** ich esse Schokolade liebend gern.

love affair *n* Verhältnis *nt*, Liebschaft *f*.

love child *n* uneheliches Kind *nt*, Kind *nt* der Liebe.

loved ones ['lʌvdwʌnz] *npl* enge Freunde und Verwandte *pl*.

love-hate relationship ['lʌvheɪt-] *n* Hassliebe *f*.

love letter *n* Liebesbrief *m*.

love life *n* Liebesleben *nt*.

lovely ['lʌvlɪ] *adj* (*beautiful*) schön; (*delightful*) herrlich; (*person*) sehr nett.

lover ['lʌvə*] *n* Geliebte(r) *f(m)*; (*person in love*) Liebende(r) *f(m)*; **~ of art/music** Kunst-/ Musikliebhaber(in) *m(f)*; **to be ~s** ein Liebespaar sein.

lovesick ['lʌvsɪk] *adj* liebeskrank.

love song *n* Liebeslied *nt*.

loving ['lʌvɪŋ] *adj* liebend; (*actions*) liebevoll.

low [ləʊ] *adj* niedrig; (*bow, curtsey*) tief; (*quality*) schlecht; (*sound: deep*) tief; (*: quiet*) leise; (*depressed*) niedergeschlagen, bedrückt ♦ *adv* (*sing*) leise; (*fly*) tief ♦ *n* (*MET*) Tief *nt*; **to be/run ~** knapp sein/ werden; **sb is running ~ on sth** jdm wird etw knapp; **to reach a new** *or* **an all-time ~** einen neuen Tiefstand erreichen.

low-alcohol ['ləʊ'ælkəhɔl] *adj* alkoholarm.

lowbrow ['ləʊbraʊ] *adj* (*geistig*) anspruchslos.

low-calorie ['ləʊ'kælərɪ] *adj* kalorienarm.

low-cut ['ləʊkʌt] *adj* (*dress*) tief ausgeschnitten.

lowdown ['ləʊdaʊn] (*inf*) *n*: **he gave me the ~ on it** er hat mich darüber informiert.

lower ['ləʊə*] *adj* untere(r, s); (*lip, jaw, arm*) Unter- ♦ *vt* senken.

low-fat ['ləʊ'fæt] *adj* fettarm.

low-key ['ləʊ'kiː] *adj* zurückhaltend; (*not obvious*) unaufdringlich.

lowlands ['ləʊləndz] *npl* Flachland *nt*.

low-level language ['ləʊlevl-] *n* (*COMPUT*) niedere Programmiersprache *f*.

low-loader ['ləʊ'ləʊdə*] *n* Tieflader *m*.

lowly ['ləʊlɪ] *adj* (*position*) niedrig; (*origin*) bescheiden.

low-lying ['ləʊ'laɪɪŋ] *adj* tief gelegen.

low-paid [ləʊ'peɪd] *adj* schlecht bezahlt.

low-rise ['ləʊraɪz] *adj* niedrig (gebaut).

low-tech ['ləʊtɛk] *adj* nicht mit Hightech ausgestattet.

loyal ['lɔɪəl] *adj* treu; (*support*) loyal.

loyalist ['lɔɪəlɪst] *n* Loyalist(in) *m(f)*.

loyalty ['lɔɪəltɪ] *n* (*see adj*) Treue *f*; Loyalität *f*.

loyalty card (*BRIT*) *n* (*COMM*) Kundenkarte *f*.
lozenge ['lɔzɪndʒ] *n* Pastille *f*; (*shape*) Raute *f*.
LP *n abbr* (= *long player*) LP *f*; *see also* **long-playing record**.
LPG *abbr* (= *liquefied petroleum gas*) Flüssiggas *nt*.

L-PLATES

Als **L-plates** *werden in Großbritannien die weißen Schilder mit einem roten „L" bezeichnet, die vorne und hinten an jedem von einem Fahrschüler geführten Fahrzeug befestigt werden müssen. Fahrschüler müssen einen vorläufigen Führerschein beantragen und dürfen damit unter der Aufsicht eines erfahrenen Autofahrers auf allen Straßen außer Autobahnen fahren.*

LPN (*US*) *n abbr* (= *Licensed Practical Nurse*) staatlich anerkannte Krankenschwester *f*, staatlich anerkannter Krankenpfleger *m*.
LRAM (*BRIT*) *n abbr* (= *Licentiate of the Royal Academy of Music*) Qualifikationsnachweis *in Musik*.
LSAT (*US*) *n abbr* (= *Law School Admission Test*) Zulassungsprüfung für juristische Hochschulen.
LSD *n abbr* (= *lysergic acid diethylamide*) LSD *nt*; (*BRIT: also*: **L.S.D.**) (= *pounds, shillings and pence*) früheres britisches Währungssystem.
LSE (*BRIT*) *n abbr* (= *London School of Economics*) Londoner Wirtschaftshochschule.
Lt *abbr* (*MIL*: = *lieutenant*) Lt.
Ltd *abbr* (*COMM*: = *limited (liability)*) ≈ GmbH *f*.
lubricant ['luːbrɪkənt] *n* Schmiermittel *nt*.
lubricate ['luːbrɪkeɪt] *vt* schmieren, ölen.
lucid ['luːsɪd] *adj* klar; (*person*) bei klarem Verstand.
lucidity [luːˈsɪdɪtɪ] *n* Klarheit *f*.
luck [lʌk] *n* (*esp good luck*) Glück *nt*; **bad** ~ Unglück *nt*; **good** ~! viel Glück!; **bad** *or* **hard** *or* **tough** ~! so ein Pech!; **hard** *or* **tough** ~! (*showing no sympathy*) Pech gehabt!; **to be in** ~ Glück haben; **to be out of** ~ kein Glück haben.
luckily ['lʌkɪlɪ] *adv* glücklicherweise.
luckless ['lʌklɪs] *adj* glücklos.
lucky ['lʌkɪ] *adj* (*situation, event*) glücklich; (*object*) Glück bringend; (*person*): **to be** ~ Glück haben; **to have a** ~ **escape** noch einmal davonkommen; ~ **charm** Glücksbringer *m*.
lucrative ['luːkrətɪv] *adj* einträglich.
ludicrous ['luːdɪkrəs] *adj* grotesk.
ludo ['luːdəu] *n* Mensch, ärgere dich nicht *nt*.
lug [lʌg] (*inf*) *vt* schleppen.
luggage ['lʌgɪdʒ] *n* Gepäck *nt*.
luggage car (*US*) *n* = **luggage van**.
luggage rack *n* Gepäckträger *m*; (*in train*) Gepäckablage *f*.
luggage van (*BRIT*) *n* (*RAIL*) Gepäckwagen *m*.

lugubrious [luˈguːbrɪəs] *adj* schwermütig.
lukewarm ['luːkwɔːm] *adj* lauwarm; (*fig*: *person, reaction etc*) lau.
lull [lʌl] *n* Pause *f* ♦ *vt*: **to** ~ **sb to sleep** jdn einlullen *or* einschläfern; **to be** ~**ed into a false sense of security** in trügerische Sicherheit gewiegt werden.
lullaby ['lʌləbaɪ] *n* Schlaflied *nt*.
lumbago [lʌmˈbeɪgəu] *n* Hexenschuss *m*.
lumber ['lʌmbəʳ] *n* (*wood*) Holz *nt*; (*junk*) Gerümpel *nt* ♦ *vi*: **to** ~ **about/along** herum-/entlangtapsen.
► **lumber with** *vt*: **to be/get** ~**ed with sth** etw am Hals haben/aufgehalst bekommen.
lumberjack ['lʌmbədʒæk] *n* Holzfäller *m*.
lumber room (*BRIT*) *n* Rumpelkammer *f*.
lumberyard ['lʌmbəjɑːd] (*US*) *n* Holzlager *nt*.
luminous ['luːmɪnəs] *adj* leuchtend, Leucht-.
lump [lʌmp] *n* Klumpen *m*; (*on body*) Beule *f*; (*in breast*) Knoten *m*; (*also*: **sugar** ~) Stück *nt* (Zucker) ♦ *vt*: **to** ~ **together** in einen Topf werfen; **a** ~ **sum** eine Pauschalsumme.
lumpy ['lʌmpɪ] *adj* klumpig.
lunacy ['luːnəsɪ] *n* Wahnsinn *m*.
lunar ['luːnəʳ] *adj* Mond-.
lunatic ['luːnətɪk] *adj* wahnsinnig ♦ *n* Wahnsinnige(r) *f(m)*, Irre(r) *f(m)*.
lunatic asylum *n* Irrenanstalt *f*.
lunatic fringe *n*: **the** ~ die Extremisten *pl*.
lunch [lʌntʃ] *n* Mittagessen *nt*; (*time*) Mittagszeit *f* ♦ *vi* zu Mittag essen.
lunch break *n* Mittagspause *f*.
luncheon ['lʌntʃən] *n* Mittagessen *nt*.
luncheon meat *n* Frühstücksfleisch *nt*.
luncheon voucher (*BRIT*) *n* Essensmarke *f*.
lunch hour *n* Mittagspause *f*.
lunch time *n* Mittagszeit *f*.
lung [lʌŋ] *n* Lunge *f*.
lunge [lʌndʒ] *vi* (*also*: ~ **forward**) sich nach vorne stürzen; **to** ~ **at** sich stürzen auf +*acc*.
lupin ['luːpɪn] *n* Lupine *f*.
lurch [ləːtʃ] *vi* ruckeln; (*person*) taumeln ♦ *n* Ruck *m*; (*of person*) Taumeln *nt*; **to leave sb in the** ~ jdn im Stich lassen.
lure [luəʳ] *n* Verlockung *f* ♦ *vt* locken.
lurid ['luərɪd] *adj* (*story etc*) reißerisch; (*pej*: *brightly coloured*) grell, in grellen Farben.
lurk [ləːk] *vi* (*also fig*) lauern.
luscious ['lʌʃəs] *adj* (*attractive*) fantastisch; (*food*) köstlich, lecker.
lush [lʌʃ] *adj* (*fields*) saftig; (*gardens*) üppig; (*luxurious*) luxuriös.
lust [lʌst] (*pej*) *n* (*sexual*) (sinnliche) Begierde *f*; (*for money, power etc*) Gier *f*.
► **lust after** *vt fus* (*sexually*) begehren; (*crave*) gieren nach.
► **lust for** *vt fus* = **lust after**.
lustful ['lʌstful] *adj* lüstern.
lustre, (*US*) **luster** ['lʌstəʳ] *n* Schimmer *m*, Glanz *m*.
lusty ['lʌstɪ] *adj* gesund und munter.
lute [luːt] *n* Laute *f*.

luvvie, luvvy ['lʌvɪ] (*inf*) *n* Schätzchen *nt*.
Luxembourg ['lʌksəmbɔːg] *n* Luxemburg *nt*.
luxuriant [lʌg'zjuərɪənt] *adj* üppig.
luxuriate [lʌg'zjuərɪeɪt] *vi*: **to ~ in sth** sich in etw *dat* aalen.
luxurious [lʌg'zjuərɪəs] *adj* luxuriös.
luxury ['lʌkʃərɪ] *n* Luxus *m* (*no pl*) ♦ *cpd* (*hotel, car etc*) Luxus-; **little luxuries** kleine Genüsse.
LV *n abbr* = **luncheon voucher**.
LW *abbr* (*RADIO*: = *long wave*) LW.
Lycra ® ['laɪkrə] *n* Lycra *nt*.
lying ['laɪɪŋ] *n* Lügen *nt* ♦ *adj* verlogen.
lynch [lɪntʃ] *vt* lynchen.
lynx [lɪŋks] *n* Luchs *m*.
lyric ['lɪrɪk] *adj* lyrisch.
lyrical ['lɪrɪkl] *adj* lyrisch; (*fig: praise etc*) schwärmerisch.
lyricism ['lɪrɪsɪzəm] *n* Lyrik *f*.
lyrics ['lɪrɪks] *npl* (*of song*) Text *m*.

M, m

M¹, m¹ [ɛm] *n* (*letter*) M *nt*, m *nt*; **~ for Mary**, (*US*) **~ for Mike** ≈ M wie Martha.
M² [ɛm] *n abbr* (*BRIT*: = *motorway*): **the M8** ≈ **die A8** ♦ *abbr* = **medium**.
m² *abbr* (= *metre*) m; = **mile** (= *million*) Mio.
MA *n abbr* (= *Master of Arts*) *akademischer Grad für Geisteswissenschaftler*; (= *military academy*) Militärakademie *f* ♦ *abbr* (*US*: *POST*: = *Massachusetts*).
mac [mæk] (*BRIT*) *n* Regenmantel *m*.
macabre [mə'kɑːbrə] *adj* makaber.
macaroni [mækə'rəʊnɪ] *n* Makkaroni *pl*.
macaroon [mækə'ruːn] *n* Makrone *f*.
mace [meɪs] *n* (*weapon*) Keule *f*; (*ceremonial*) Amtsstab *m*; (*spice*) Muskatblüte *f*.
Macedonia [mæsɪ'dəʊnɪə] *n* Makedonien *nt*.
Macedonian [mæsɪ'dəʊnɪən] *adj* makedonisch ♦ *n* Makedonier(in) *m(f)*; (*LING*) Makedonisch *nt*.
machinations [mækɪ'neɪʃənz] *npl* Machenschaften *pl*.
machine [mə'ʃiːn] *n* Maschine *f*; (*fig: party machine etc*) Apparat *m* ♦ *vt* (*TECH*) maschinell herstellen *or* bearbeiten; (*dress etc*) mit der Maschine nähen.
machine code *n* Maschinenkode *m*.
machine gun *n* Maschinengewehr *nt*.
machine language *n* Maschinensprache *f*.
machine-readable [mə'ʃiːnriːdəbl] *adj* maschinenlesbar.
machinery [mə'ʃiːnərɪ] *n* Maschinen *pl*; (*fig: of government*) Apparat *m*.

machine shop *n* Maschinensaal *m*.
machine tool *n* Werkzeugmaschine *f*.
machine washable *adj* waschmaschinenfest.
machinist [mə'ʃiːnɪst] *n* Maschinist(in) *m(f)*.
macho ['mætʃəʊ] *adj* Macho-; **a ~ man** ein Macho *m*.
mackerel ['mækrl] *n inv* Makrele *f*.
mackintosh ['mækɪntɔʃ] (*BRIT*) *n* Regenmantel *m*.
macro... ['mækrəʊ] *pref* Makro-, makro-.
macroeconomics ['mækrəʊiːkə'nɔmɪks] *npl* Makroökonomie *f*.
mad [mæd] *adj* wahnsinnig, verrückt; (*angry*) böse, sauer (*inf*); **to be ~ about** verrückt sein auf +*acc*; **to be ~ at sb** böse *or* sauer auf jdn sein; **to go ~** (*insane*) verrückt *or* wahnsinnig werden; (*angry*) böse *or* sauer werden.
madam ['mædəm] *n* gnädige Frau *f*; **yes, ~** ja(wohl); **M~ Chairman** Frau Vorsitzende.
madcap ['mædkæp] *adj* (*idea*) versponnen; (*tricks*) toll.
mad cow disease *n* Rinderwahn *m*.
madden ['mædn] *vt* ärgern, fuchsen (*inf*).
maddening ['mædnɪŋ] *adj* unerträglich.
made [meɪd] *pt, pp of* **make**.
Madeira [mə'dɪərə] *n* Madeira *nt*; (*wine*) Madeira *m*.
made-to-measure ['meɪdtə'meʒə*] (*BRIT*) *adj* maßgeschneidert.
madhouse ['mædhaus] *n* (*also fig*) Irrenhaus *nt*.
madly ['mædlɪ] *adv* wie verrückt; **~ in love** bis über beide Ohren verliebt.
madman ['mædmən] (*irreg: like* **man**) *n* Verrückte(r) *m*, Irre(r) *m*.
madness ['mædnɪs] *n* Wahnsinn *m*.
Madrid [mə'drɪd] *n* Madrid *nt*.
Mafia ['mæfɪə] *n* Mafia *f*.
mag [mæg] (*BRIT*: *inf*) *n abbr* = **magazine**.
magazine [mægə'ziːn] *n* Zeitschrift *f*; (*RADIO, TV, of firearm*) Magazin *nt*; (*MIL: store*) Depot *nt*.
maggot ['mægət] *n* Made *f*.
magic ['mædʒɪk] *n* Magie *f*; (*conjuring*) Zauberei *f* ♦ *adj* magisch; (*formula*) Zauber-; (*fig: place, moment etc*) zauberhaft.
magical ['mædʒɪkl] *adj* magisch; (*experience, evening*) zauberhaft.
magician [mə'dʒɪʃən] *n* (*wizard*) Magier *m*; (*conjurer*) Zauberer *m*.
magistrate ['mædʒɪstreɪt] *n* Friedensrichter(in) *m(f)*.
magnanimous [mæg'nænɪməs] *adj* großmütig.
magnate ['mægneɪt] *n* Magnat *m*.
magnesium [mæg'niːzɪəm] *n* Magnesium *nt*.
magnet ['mægnɪt] *n* Magnet *m*.
magnetic [mæg'netɪk] *adj* magnetisch; (*field, compass, pole etc*) Magnet-; (*personality*) anziehend.
magnetic disk *n* (*COMPUT*) Magnetplatte *f*.
magnetic tape *n* Magnetband *nt*.

magnetism ['mægnɪtɪzəm] n Magnetismus m; (of person) Anziehungskraft f.
magnetize ['mægnɪtaɪz] vt magnetisieren.
magnification [mægnɪfɪ'keɪʃən] n Vergrößerung f.
magnificence [mæg'nɪfɪsns] n Großartigkeit f; (of robes) Pracht f.
magnificent [mæg'nɪfɪsnt] adj großartig; (robes) prachtvoll.
magnify ['mægnɪfaɪ] vt vergrößern; (sound) verstärken; (fig: exaggerate) aufbauschen.
magnifying glass ['mægnɪfaɪɪŋ-] n Vergrößerungsglas nt, Lupe f.
magnitude ['mægnɪtjuːd] n (size) Ausmaß nt, Größe f; (importance) Bedeutung f.
magnolia [mæg'nəʊlɪə] n Magnolie f.
magpie ['mægpaɪ] n Elster f.
mahogany [mə'hɒgənɪ] n Mahagoni nt ♦ cpd Mahagoni-.
maid [meɪd] n Dienstmädchen nt; old ~ (pej) alte Jungfer.
maiden ['meɪdn] n (liter) Mädchen nt ♦ adj unverheiratet; (speech, voyage) Jungfern-.
maiden name n Mädchenname m.
mail [meɪl] n Post f ♦ vt aufgeben; by ~ mit der Post.
mailbox ['meɪlbɒks] n (US) Briefkasten m; (COMPUT) Mailbox f, elektronischer Briefkasten m.
mailing list ['meɪlɪŋ-] n Anschriftenliste f.
mailman ['meɪlmæn] (US: irreg: like man) n Briefträger m, Postbote m.
mail order n (system) Versand m ♦ cpd: **mail-order firm** or **business** Versandhaus nt; **mail-order catalogue** Versandhauskatalog m; **by** ~ durch Bestellung per Post.
mailshot ['meɪlʃɒt] (BRIT) n Werbebrief m.
mail train n Postzug m.
mail truck (US) n Postauto nt.
mail van (BRIT) n (AUT) Postauto nt; (RAIL) Postwagen m.
maim [meɪm] vt verstümmeln.
main [meɪn] adj Haupt-, wichtigste(r, s); (door, entrance, meal) Haupt- ♦ n Hauptleitung f; **the mains** npl (ELEC) das Stromnetz; (gas, water) die Hauptleitung; **in the** ~ im Großen und Ganzen.
main course n (CULIN) Hauptgericht nt.
mainframe ['meɪnfreɪm] n (COMPUT) Großrechner m.
mainland ['meɪnlənd] n Festland nt.
mainline ['meɪnlaɪn] adj: ~ **station** Fernbahnhof m ♦ vt (drugs slang) spritzen ♦ vi (drugs slang) fixen.
main line n Hauptstrecke f.
mainly ['meɪnlɪ] adv hauptsächlich.
main road n Hauptstraße f.
mainstay ['meɪnsteɪ] n (foundation) (wichtigste) Stütze f; (chief constituent) Hauptbestandteil m.
mainstream ['meɪnstriːm] n Hauptrichtung f ♦ adj (cinema etc) populär; (politics) der

Mitte.
maintain [meɪn'teɪn] vt (preserve) aufrechterhalten; (keep up) beibehalten; (provide for) unterhalten; (look after: building) instand or in Stand halten; (: equipment) warten; (affirm: opinion) vertreten; (: innocence) beteuern; **to** ~ **that** ... behaupten, dass ...
maintenance ['meɪntənəns] n (of building) Instandhaltung f; (of equipment) Wartung f; (preservation) Aufrechterhaltung f; (LAW: alimony) Unterhalt m.
maintenance contract n Wartungsvertrag m.
maintenance order n (LAW) Unterhaltsurteil nt.
maisonette [meɪzə'nɛt] (BRIT) n Maisonettewohnung f.
maize [meɪz] n Mais m.
Maj. abbr (MIL) = **major**.
majestic [mə'dʒɛstɪk] adj erhaben.
majesty ['mædʒɪstɪ] n (title): **Your M**~ Eure Majestät; (splendour) Erhabenheit f.
major ['meɪdʒə'] n Major m ♦ adj bedeutend; (MUS) Dur ♦ vi (US): **to** ~ **in French** Französisch als Hauptfach belegen; **a** ~ **operation** eine größere Operation.
Majorca [mə'jɔːkə] n Mallorca nt.
major general n Generalmajor m.
majority [mə'dʒɒrɪtɪ] n Mehrheit f ♦ cpd (verdict, holding) Mehrheits-.
make [meɪk] (pt, pp **made**) vt machen; (clothes) nähen; (cake) backen; (speech) halten; (manufacture) herstellen; (earn) verdienen; (cause to be): **to** ~ **sb sad** jdn traurig machen; (force): **to** ~ **sb do sth** jdn zwingen, etw zu tun; (cause) jdn dazu bringen, etw zu tun; (equal): **2 and 2** ~ **4** 2 und 2 ist or macht 4 ♦ n Marke f, Fabrikat nt; **to** ~ **a fool of sb** jdn lächerlich machen; **to** ~ **a profit/loss** Gewinn/Verlust machen; **to** ~ **it** (arrive) es schaffen; (succeed) Erfolg haben; **what time do you** ~ **it?** wie spät hast du?; **to** ~ **good** erfolgreich sein; (threat) wahr machen; (promise) einlösen; (damage) wieder gutmachen; (loss) ersetzen; **to** ~ **do with** auskommen mit.
▶ **make for** vt fus (place) zuhalten auf +acc.
▶ **make off** vi sich davonmachen.
▶ **make out** vt (decipher) entziffern; (understand) verstehen; (see) ausmachen; (write: cheque) ausstellen; (claim, imply) behaupten; (pretend) so tun, als ob; **to** ~ **out a case for sth** für etw argumentieren.
▶ **make over** vt: **to** ~ **over (to)** überschreiben (+dat).
▶ **make up** vt (constitute) bilden; (invent) erfinden; (prepare: bed) zurechtmachen; (: parcel) zusammenpacken ♦ vi (after quarrel) sich versöhnen; (with cosmetics) sich schminken; **to** ~ **up one's mind** sich entscheiden; **to be made up of** bestehen aus.

▶ **make up for** *vt fus* (*loss*) ersetzen; (*disappointment etc*) ausgleichen.

make-believe ['meɪkbɪliːv] *n* Fantasie *f*; **a world of** ~ eine Fantasiewelt; **it's just** ~ es ist nicht wirklich.

maker ['meɪkə'] *n* Hersteller *m*; **film** ~ Filmemacher(in) *m(f)*.

makeshift ['meɪkʃɪft] *adj* behelfsmäßig.

make-up ['meɪkʌp] *n* Make-up *nt*, Schminke *f*.

make-up bag *n* Kosmetiktasche *f*.

make-up remover *n* Make-up-Entferner *m*.

making ['meɪkɪŋ] *n* (*fig*): **in the** ~ im Entstehen; **to have the** ~**s of** das Zeug haben zu.

maladjusted [mælə'dʒʌstɪd] *adj* verhaltensgestört.

maladroit [mælə'drɔɪt] *adj* ungeschickt.

malaise [mæ'leɪz] *n* Unbehagen *f*.

malaria [mə'lɛərɪə] *n* Malaria *f*.

Malawi [mə'lɑːwɪ] *n* Malawi *nt*.

Malay [mə'leɪ] *adj* malaiisch ♦ *n* Malaie *m*, Malaiin *f*; (*LING*) Malaiisch *nt*.

Malaya [mə'leɪə] *n* Malaya *nt*.

Malayan [mə'leɪən] *adj, n* = **Malay**.

Malaysia [mə'leɪzɪə] *n* Malaysia *nt*.

Malaysian [mə'leɪzɪən] *adj* malaysisch ♦ *n* Malaysier(in) *m(f)*.

Maldives ['mɔːldaɪvz] *npl* Malediven *pl*.

male [meɪl] *n* (*animal*) Männchen *nt*; (*man*) Mann *m* ♦ *adj* männlich; (*ELEC*): ~ **plug** Stecker *m*; **because he is** ~ weil er ein Mann/Junge ist; ~ **and female students** Studenten und Studentinnen; **a** ~ **child** ein Junge.

male chauvinist *n* Chauvinist *m*.

male nurse *n* Krankenpfleger *m*.

malevolence [mə'lɛvələns] *n* Boshaftigkeit *f*; (*of action*) Böswilligkeit *f*.

malevolent [mə'lɛvələnt] *adj* boshaft; (*intention*) böswillig.

malfunction [mæl'fʌŋkʃən] *n* (*of computer*) Funktionsstörung *f*; (*of machine*) Defekt *m* ♦ *vi* (*computer*) eine Funktionsstörung haben; (*machine*) defekt sein.

malice ['mælɪs] *n* Bosheit *f*.

malicious [mə'lɪʃəs] *adj* boshaft; (*LAW*) böswillig.

malign [mə'laɪn] *vt* verleumden ♦ *adj* (*influence*) schlecht; (*interpretation*) böswillig.

malignant [mə'lɪgnənt] *adj* bösartig; (*intention*) böswillig.

malingerer [mə'lɪŋgərə'] *n* Simulant(in) *m(f)*.

mall [mɔːl] *n* (*also*: **shopping** ~) Einkaufszentrum *nt*.

malleable ['mælɪəbl] *adj* (*lit, fig*) formbar.

mallet ['mælɪt] *n* Holzhammer *m*.

malnutrition [mælnjuː'trɪʃən] *n* Unterernährung *f*.

malpractice [mæl'præktɪs] *n* Berufsvergehen *nt*.

malt [mɔːlt] *n* Malz *nt*; (*also*: ~ **whisky**) Malt

Whisky *m*.

Malta ['mɔːltə] *n* Malta *nt*.

Maltese [mɔːl'tiːz] *adj* maltesisch ♦ *n inv* Malteser(in) *m(f)*; (*LING*) Maltesisch *nt*.

maltreat [mæl'triːt] *vt* schlecht behandeln; (*violently*) misshandeln.

mammal ['mæml] *n* Säugetier *nt*.

mammoth ['mæməθ] *n* Mammut *nt* ♦ *adj* (*task*) Mammut-.

man [mæn] (*pl* **men**) *n* Mann *m*; (*mankind*) der Mensch, die Menschen *pl*; (*CHESS*) Figur *f* ♦ *vt* (*ship*) bemannen; (*gun, machine*) bedienen; (*post*) besetzen; ~ **and wife** Mann und Frau.

manage ['mænɪdʒ] *vi*: **to** ~ **to do sth** es schaffen, etw zu tun; (*get by financially*) zurechtkommen ♦ *vt* (*business, organization*) leiten; (*control*) zurechtkommen mit; **to** ~ **without sb/sth** ohne jdn/etw auskommen; **well** ~**d** (*business, shop etc*) gut geführt.

manageable ['mænɪdʒəbl] *adj* (*task*) zu bewältigen; (*number*) überschaubar.

management ['mænɪdʒmənt] *n* Leitung *f*, Führung *f*; (*persons*) Unternehmensleitung *f*; **"under new** ~**"** „unter neuer Leitung".

management accounting *n* Kosten- und Leistungsrechnung *f*.

management consultant *n* Unternehmensberater(in) *m(f)*.

manager ['mænɪdʒə'] *n* (*of business*) Geschäftsführer(in) *m(f)*; (*of institution etc*) Direktor(in) *m(f)*; (*of department*) Leiter(in) *m(f)*; (*of pop star*) Manager(in) *m(f)*; (*SPORT*) Trainer(in) *m(f)*; **sales** ~ Verkaufsleiter(in) *m(f)*.

manageress [mænɪdʒə'rɛs] *n* (*of shop, business*) Geschäftsführerin *f*; (*of office, department etc*) Leiterin *f*.

managerial [mænɪ'dʒɪərɪəl] *adj* (*role, post*) leitend; (*decisions*) geschäftlich; ~ **staff/ skills** Führungskräfte *pl*/-qualitäten *pl*.

managing director ['mænɪdʒɪŋ-] *n* Geschäftsführer(in) *m(f)*.

Mancunian [mæŋ'kjuːnɪən] *n* Bewohner(in) *m(f)* Manchesters.

mandarin ['mændərɪn] *n* (*also*: ~ **orange**) Mandarine *f*; (*official: Chinese*) Mandarin *m*; (: *gen*) Funktionär *m*.

mandate ['mændeɪt] *n* Mandat *nt*; (*task*) Auftrag *m*.

mandatory ['mændətərɪ] *adj* obligatorisch.

mandolin(e) ['mændəlɪn] *n* Mandoline *f*.

mane [meɪn] *n* Mähne *f*.

maneuver *etc* [mə'nuːvə'] (*US*) = **manoeuvre** *etc*.

manfully ['mænfəlɪ] *adv* mannhaft, beherzt.

manganese [mæŋgə'niːz] *n* Mangan *nt*.

mangetout ['mɔnʒ'tuː] (*BRIT*) *n* Zuckererbse *f*.

mangle ['mæŋgl] *vt* (übel) zurichten ♦ *n* Mangel *f*.

mango ['mæŋgəu] (*pl* ~**es**) *n* Mango *f*.

mangrove ['mæŋgrəuv] n Mangrove(n)baum m.

mangy ['meɪndʒɪ] adj (animal) räudig.

manhandle ['mænhændl] vt (mistreat) grob behandeln; (move by hand) (von Hand) befördern.

manhole ['mænhəul] n Kanalschacht m.

manhood ['mænhud] n Mannesalter nt.

man-hour ['mænauə'] n Arbeitsstunde f.

manhunt ['mænhʌnt] n Fahndung f.

mania ['meɪnɪə] n Manie f; (craze) Sucht f; persecution ~ Verfolgungswahn m.

maniac ['meɪnɪæk] n Wahnsinnige(r) f(m), Verrückte(r) f(m); (fig) Fanatiker(in) m(f).

manic ['mænɪk] adj (behaviour) manisch; (activity) rasend.

manic-depressive ['mænɪkdɪ'prɛsɪv] n Manisch-Depressive(r) f)m ♦ adj manisch-depressiv.

manicure ['mænɪkjuə'] n Maniküre f ♦ vt maniküren.

manicure set n Nageletui nt, Maniküreetui nt.

manifest ['mænɪfɛst] vt zeigen, bekunden ♦ adj offenkundig ♦ n Manifest nt.

manifestation [mænɪfɛs'teɪʃən] n Anzeichen nt.

manifesto [mænɪ'fɛstəu] n Manifest nt.

manifold ['mænɪfəuld] adj vielfältig ♦ n: exhaust ~ Auspuffkrümmer m.

Manila [mə'nɪlə] n Manila nt.

manila [mə'nɪlə] adj: ~ envelope brauner Briefumschlag m.

manipulate [mə'nɪpjuleɪt] vt manipulieren.

manipulation [mənɪpju'leɪʃən] n Manipulation f.

mankind [mæn'kaɪnd] n Menschheit f.

manliness ['mænlɪnɪs] n Männlichkeit f.

manly ['mænlɪ] adj männlich.

man-made ['mæn'meɪd] adj künstlich; (fibre) synthetisch.

manna ['mænə] n Manna nt.

mannequin ['mænɪkɪn] n (dummy) Schaufensterpuppe f; (fashion model) Mannequin nt.

manner ['mænə'] n (way) Art f, Weise f; (behaviour) Art f; (type, sort): **all ~ of things** die verschiedensten Dinge; **manners** npl (conduct) Manieren pl, Umgangsformen pl; **bad ~s** schlechte Manieren; **that's bad ~s** das gehört sich nicht.

mannerism ['mænərɪzəm] n Eigenheit f.

mannerly ['mænəlɪ] adj wohlerzogen.

manning ['mænɪŋ] n Besatzung f.

manoeuvrable, (US) **maneuverable** [mə'nu:vrəbl] adj manövrierfähig.

manoeuvre, (US) **maneuver** [mə'nu:və'] vt manövrieren; (situation) manipulieren ♦ vi manövrieren ♦ n (skilful move) Manöver nt; **manoeuvres** npl (MIL) Manöver nt, Truppenübungen pl; **to ~ sb into doing sth** jdn dazu bringen, etw zu tun.

manor ['mænə'] n (also: ~ **house**) Herrenhaus nt.

manpower ['mænpauə'] n Personal nt, Arbeitskräfte pl.

Manpower Services Commission (BRIT) n Behörde für Arbeitsbeschaffung, Arbeitsvermittlung und Berufsausbildung.

manservant ['mænsə:vənt] (pl **menservants**) n Diener m.

mansion ['mænʃən] n Villa f.

manslaughter ['mænslɔːtə'] n Totschlag m.

mantelpiece ['mæntlpiːs] n Kaminsims nt or m.

mantle ['mæntl] n Decke f; (fig) Deckmantel m.

man-to-man ['mæntə'mæn] adj, adv von Mann zu Mann.

manual ['mænjuəl] adj manuell, Hand-; (controls) von Hand ♦ n Handbuch nt.

manufacture [mænju'fæktʃə'] vt herstellen ♦ n Herstellung f.

manufactured goods npl Fertigerzeugnisse pl.

manufacturer [mænju'fæktʃərə'] n Hersteller m.

manufacturing [mænju'fæktʃərɪŋ] n Herstellung f.

manure [mə'njuə'] n Dung m.

manuscript ['mænjuskrɪpt] n Manuskript nt; (old document) Handschrift f.

many ['mɛnɪ] adj, pron viele; **a great ~** eine ganze Reihe; **how ~?** wie viele?; **too ~ difficulties** zu viele Schwierigkeiten; **twice as ~** doppelt so viele; **~ a time** so manches Mal.

Maori ['mauri] adj maorisch ♦ n Maori mf.

map [mæp] n (Land)karte f; (of town) Stadtplan m ♦ vt eine Karte anfertigen von.

▶ **map out** vt planen; (plan) entwerfen; (essay) anlegen.

maple ['meɪpl] n (tree, wood) Ahorn m.

Mar. abbr = **March**.

mar [mɑː'] vt (appearance) verunstalten; (day) verderben; (event) stören.

marathon ['mærəθən] n Marathon m ♦ adj: **a ~ session** eine Marathonsitzung.

marathon runner n Marathonläufer(in) m(f).

marauder [mə'rɔːdə'] n (robber) Plünderer m; (killer) Mörder m.

marble ['mɑːbl] n Marmor m; (toy) Murmel f.

marbles ['mɑːblz] n (game) Murmeln pl.

March [mɑːtʃ] n März m; see also **July**.

march [mɑːtʃ] vi marschieren; (protesters) ziehen ♦ n Marsch m; (demonstration) Demonstration f; **to ~ out of/into** (heraus)marschieren aus +dat/ (herein)marschieren in +acc.

marcher ['mɑːtʃə'] n Demonstrant(in) m(f).

marching orders ['mɑːtʃɪŋ-] npl: **to give sb his/her ~** (employee) jdn entlassen; (lover) jdm den Laufpass geben.

march past n Vorbeimarsch m.

mare [mɛə'] n Stute f.

margarine [mɑːdʒə'riːn] n Margarine f.

marge [mɑːdʒ] (*BRIT: inf*) *n abbr* = **margarine**.
margin ['mɑːdʒɪn] *n* Rand *m*; (*of votes*)
Mehrheit *f*; (*for safety, error etc*) Spielraum *m*;
(*COMM*) Gewinnspanne *f*.
marginal ['mɑːdʒɪnl] *adj* geringfügig; (*note*)
Rand-.
marginally ['mɑːdʒɪnəlɪ] *adv* nur wenig,
geringfügig.
marginal (seat) *n* (*POL*) mit knapper
Mehrheit gewonnener Wahlkreis.
marigold ['mærɪɡəʊld] *n* Ringelblume *f*.
marijuana [mærɪ'wɑːnə] *n* Marihuana *nt*.
marina [mə'riːnə] *n* Jachthafen *m*.
marinade [mærɪ'neɪd] *n* Marinade *f* ♦ *vt*
= **marinate**.
marinate ['mærɪneɪt] *vt* marinieren.
marine [mə'riːn] *adj* (*plant, biology*) Meeres-
♦ *n* (*BRIT: soldier*) Marineinfanterist *m*; (*US:
sailor*) Marinesoldat *m*; ~ **engineer**
Schiff(s)bauingenieur *m*; ~ **engineering**
Schiff(s)bau *m*.
marine insurance *n* Seeversicherung *f*.
marital ['mærɪtl] *adj* ehelich; (*problem*) Ehe-;
~ **status** Familienstand *m*.
maritime ['mærɪtaɪm] *adj* (*nation*) Seefahrer-;
(*museum*) Seefahrts-; (*law*) See-.
marjoram ['mɑːdʒərəm] *n* Majoran *m*.
mark [mɑːk] *n* Zeichen *nt*; (*stain*) Fleck *m*; (*in
snow, mud etc*) Spur *f*; (*BRIT: SCOL*) Note *f*;
(*level, point*): **the halfway** ~ die Hälfte *f*;
(*currency*) Mark *f*; (*BRIT: TECH*): **M~ 2/3**
Version *f* 2/3 ♦ *vt* (*with pen*) beschriften;
(*with shoes etc*) schmutzig machen; (*with
tyres etc*) Spuren hinterlassen auf +*dat*;
(*damage*) beschädigen; (*stain*) Flecken
machen auf +*dat*; (*indicate*) markieren;
(: *price*) auszeichnen; (*commemorate*)
begehen; (*characterize*) kennzeichnen; (*BRIT:
SCOL*) korrigieren (und benoten); (*SPORT:
player*) decken; **punctuation ~s** Satzzeichen
pl; **to be quick off the ~ (in doing sth)** (*fig*)
blitzschnell reagieren (und etw tun); **to be
up to the ~** den Anforderungen
entsprechen; **to ~ time** auf der Stelle
treten.
▶ **mark down** *vt* (*prices, goods*) herabsetzen,
heruntersetzen.
▶ **mark off** *vt* (*tick off*) abhaken.
▶ **mark out** *vt* markieren; (*person*)
auszeichnen.
▶ **mark up** *vt* (*price*) heraufsetzen.
marked [mɑːkt] *adj* deutlich.
markedly ['mɑːkɪdlɪ] *adv* deutlich.
marker ['mɑːkə*] *n* Markierung *f*; (*bookmark*)
Lesezeichen *nt*.
market ['mɑːkɪt] *n* Markt *m* ♦ *vt* (*sell*)
vertreiben; (*new product*) auf den Markt
bringen; **to be on the** ~ auf dem Markt sein;
on the open ~ auf dem freien Markt; **to
play the** ~ (*STOCK EXCHANGE*) an der Börse
spekulieren.
marketable ['mɑːkɪtəbl] *adj* marktfähig.

market analysis *n* Marktanalyse *f*.
market day *n* Markttag *m*.
market demand *n* Marktbedarf *m*.
market economy *n* Marktwirtschaft *f*.
market forces *npl* Marktkräfte *pl*.
market garden (*BRIT*) *n*
Gemüseanbaubetrieb *m*.
marketing ['mɑːkɪtɪŋ] *n* Marketing *nt*.
marketing manager *n*
Marketingmanager(in) *m(f)*.
marketplace ['mɑːkɪtpleɪs] *n* Marktplatz *m*;
(*COMM*) Markt *m*.
market price *n* Marktpreis *m*.
market research *n* Marktforschung *f*.
market value *n* Marktwert *m*.
marking ['mɑːkɪŋ] *n* (*on animal*) Zeichnung *f*;
(*on road*) Markierung *f*.
marksman ['mɑːksmən] (*irreg: like* **man**) *n*
Scharfschütze *m*.
marksmanship ['mɑːksmənʃɪp] *n*
Treffsicherheit *f*.
mark-up ['mɑːkʌp] *n* (*COMM: margin*)
Handelsspanne *f*; (: *increase*)
(Preis)aufschlag *m*.
marmalade ['mɑːməleɪd] *n*
Orangenmarmelade *f*.
maroon [mə'ruːn] *vt*: **to be ~ed** festsitzen
♦ *adj* kastanienbraun.
marquee [mɑː'kiː] *n* Festzelt *nt*.
marquess, marquis ['mɑːkwɪs] *n* Marquis *m*.
Marrakech, Marrakesh [mærə'keʃ] *n*
Marrakesch *nt*.
marriage ['mærɪdʒ] *n* Ehe *f*; (*institution*) die
Ehe; (*wedding*) Hochzeit *f*; ~ **of convenience**
Vernunftehe *f*.
marriage bureau *n* Ehevermittlung *f*.
marriage certificate *n* Heiratsurkunde *f*.
marriage guidance, (*US*) **marriage
counseling** *n* Eheberatung *f*.
married ['mærɪd] *adj* verheiratet; (*life*) Ehe-;
(*love*) ehelich; **to get** ~ heiraten.
marrow ['mærəʊ] *n* (*vegetable*) Kürbis *m*;
(*bone marrow*) (Knochen)mark *nt*.
marry ['mærɪ] *vt* heiraten; (*father*)
verheiraten; (*priest*) trauen ♦ *vi* heiraten.
Mars [mɑːz] *n* Mars *m*.
Marseilles [mɑː'seɪlz] *n* Marseilles *nt*.
marsh [mɑːʃ] *n* Sumpf *m*; (*salt marsh*)
Salzsumpf *m*.
marshal ['mɑːʃl] *n* (*MIL: also: field* ~)
(Feld)marschall *m*; (*official*) Ordner *m*; (*US:
of police*) Bezirkspolizeichef *m* ♦ *vt* (*thoughts*)
ordnen; (*support*) auftreiben; (*soldiers*)
aufstellen.
marshalling yard ['mɑːʃlɪŋ-] *n* (*RAIL*)
Rangierbahnhof *m*.
marshmallow [mɑːʃ'mæləʊ] *n* (*BOT*) Eibisch
m; (*sweet*) Marshmallow *nt*.
marshy ['mɑːʃɪ] *adj* sumpfig.
marsupial [mɑː'suːpɪəl] *n* Beuteltier *nt*.
martial ['mɑːʃl] *adj* kriegerisch.
martial arts *npl* Kampfsport *m*; **the** ~ die

Kampfkunst *sing*.

martial law *n* Kriegsrecht *nt*.

Martian ['mɑːʃən] *n* Marsmensch *m*.

martin ['mɑːtɪn] *n* (*also*: **house** ~) Schwalbe *f*.

martyr ['mɑːtə*] *n* Märtyrer(in) *m(f)* ♦ *vt* martern.

martyrdom ['mɑːtədəm] *n* Martyrium *nt*.

marvel ['mɑːvl] *n* Wunder *nt* ♦ *vi*: **to ~ (at)** staunen (über *+acc*).

marvellous, (*US*) **marvelous** ['mɑːvləs] *adj* wunderbar.

Marxism ['mɑːksɪzəm] *n* Marxismus *m*.

Marxist ['mɑːksɪst] *adj* marxistisch ♦ *n* Marxist(in) *m(f)*.

marzipan ['mɑːzɪpæn] *n* Marzipan *nt*.

mascara [mæs'kɑːrə] *n* Wimperntusche *f*.

mascot ['mæskət] *n* Maskottchen *nt*.

masculine ['mæskjulɪn] *adj* männlich; (*atmosphere, woman*) maskulin; (*LING*) männlich, maskulin.

masculinity [mæskju'lɪnɪtɪ] *n* Männlichkeit *f*.

MASH [mæʃ] (*US*) *n abbr* (= *mobile army surgical hospital*) mobiles Lazarett *nt*.

mash [mæʃ] *vt* zerstampfen.

mashed potatoes [mæʃt-] *npl* Kartoffelpüree *nt*, Kartoffelbrei *m*.

mask [mɑːsk] *n* Maske *f* ♦ *vt* (*cover*) verdecken; (*hide*) verbergen; **surgical ~** Mundschutz *m*.

masking tape ['mɑːskɪŋ-] *n* Abdeckband *nt*.

masochism ['mæsəukɪzəm] *n* Masochismus *m*.

masochist ['mæsəukɪst] *n* Masochist(in) *m(f)*.

mason ['meɪsn] *n* (*also*: **stone** ~) Steinmetz *m*; (*also*: **freemason**) Freimaurer *m*.

masonic [mə'sɔnɪk] *adj* (*lodge etc*) Freimaurer-.

masonry ['meɪsnrɪ] *n* Mauerwerk *nt*.

masquerade [mæskə'reɪd] *vi*: **to ~ as** sich ausgeben als ♦ *n* Maskerade *f*.

Mass. (*US*) *abbr* (*POST*: = *Massachusetts*).

mass [mæs] *n* Masse *f*; (*of people*) Menge *f*; (*large amount*) Fülle *f*; (*REL*): **M~** Messe *f* ♦ *cpd* Massen- ♦ *vi* (*troops*) sich massieren; (*protesters*) sich versammeln; **the masses** *npl* (*ordinary people*) die Masse, die Massen *pl*; **to go to M~** zur Messe gehen; **~es of** (*inf*) massenhaft, jede Menge.

massacre ['mæsəkə*] *n* Massaker *nt* ♦ *vt* massakrieren.

massage ['mæsɑːʒ] *n* Massage *f* ♦ *vt* massieren.

masseur [mæ'sɜː*] *n* Masseur *m*.

masseuse [mæ'sɜːz] *n* Masseurin *f*.

massive ['mæsɪv] *adj* (*furniture, person*) wuchtig; (*support*) massiv; (*changes, increase*) enorm.

mass market *n* Massenmarkt *m*.

mass media *npl* Massenmedien *pl*.

mass meeting *n* Massenveranstaltung *f*; (*of everyone concerned*) Vollversammlung *f*; (*POL*) Massenkundgebung *f*.

mass-produce ['mæsprə'djuːs] *vt* in

Massenproduktion herstellen.

mass-production ['mæsprə'dʌkʃən] *n* Massenproduktion *f*.

mast [mɑːst] *n* (*NAUT*) Mast *m*; (*RADIO etc*) Sendeturm *m*.

mastectomy [mæs'tɛktəmɪ] *n* Brustamputation *f*.

master ['mɑːstə*] *n* Herr *m*; (*teacher*) Lehrer *m*; (*title*): **M~ X** (*der junge*) Herr X; (*ART, MUS, of craft etc*) Meister *m* ♦ *cpd*: ~ **baker/ plumber** *etc* Bäcker-/Klempnermeister *etc m* ♦ *vt* meistern; (*feeling*) unter Kontrolle bringen; (*skill, language*) beherrschen.

master disk *n* (*COMPUT*) Stammdiskette *f*.

masterful ['mɑːstəful] *adj* gebieterisch; (*skilful*) meisterhaft.

master key *n* Hauptschlüssel *m*.

masterly ['mɑːstəlɪ] *adj* meisterhaft.

mastermind ['mɑːstəmaɪnd] *n* (*führender*) Kopf *m* ♦ *vt* planen und ausführen.

Master of Arts *n* Magister *m* der philosophischen Fakultät.

Master of Ceremonies *n* Zeremonienmeister *m*; (*for variety show etc*) Conférencier *m*.

Master of Science *n* Magister *m* der naturwissenschaftlichen Fakultät.

masterpiece ['mɑːstəpiːs] *n* Meisterwerk *nt*.

master plan *n* kluger Plan *m*.

MASTER'S DEGREE
Master's Degree *ist ein höherer akademischer Grad, den man in der Regel nach dem* **bachelor's degree** *erwerben kann. Je nach Universität erhält man ein* **master's degree** *nach einem entsprechenden Studium und/oder einer Dissertation. Die am häufigsten verliehenen Grade sind* **MA** (= *Master of Arts*) *und* **MSc** (= *Master of Science*), *die beide Studium und Dissertation erfordern, während für* **MLitt** (= *Master of Letters*) *und* **MPhil** (= *Master of Philosophy*) *meist nur eine Dissertation nötig ist. Siehe auch* **bachelor's degree, doctorate**.

---

masterstroke ['mɑːstəstrəuk] *n* Meisterstück *nt*.

mastery ['mɑːstərɪ] *n* (*of language etc*) Beherrschung *f*; (*skill*) (meisterhaftes) Können *nt*.

mastiff ['mæstɪf] *n* Dogge *f*.

masturbate ['mæstəbeɪt] *vi* masturbieren, onanieren.

masturbation [mæstə'beɪʃən] *n* Masturbation *f*, Onanie *f*.

mat [mæt] *n* Matte *f*; (*also*: **doormat**) Fußmatte *f*; (*also*: **table** ~) Untersetzer *m*; (: *of cloth*) Deckchen *nt* ♦ *adj* = **matt**.

match [mætʃ] *n* Wettkampf *m*; (*team game*) Spiel *nt*; (*TENNIS*) Match *nt*; (*for lighting fire etc*) Streichholz *nt*; (*equivalent*): **to be a good/perfect** ~ gut/perfekt zusammenpassen ♦ *vt* (*go well with*) passen zu; (*equal*) gleichkommen +*dat*; (*correspond to*) entsprechen +*dat*; (*suit*) sich anpassen +*dat*; (*also*: ~ **up**: *pair*) passend zusammenbringen ♦ *vi* zusammenpassen; **to be a good** ~ gut zusammenpassen; **to be no** ~ **for** sich nicht messen können mit; **with shoes to** ~ mit (dazu) passenden Schuhen.

▶ **match up** *vi* zusammenpassen.

matchbox ['mætʃbɔks] *n* Streichholzschachtel *f*.

matching ['mætʃɪŋ] *adj* (dazu) passend.

matchless ['mætʃlɪs] *adj* unvergleichlich.

mate [meɪt] *n* (*inf: friend*) Freund(in) *m(f)*, Kumpel *m*; (*animal*) Männchen *nt*, Weibchen *nt*; (*assistant*) Gehilfe *m*, Gehilfin *f*; (*in merchant navy*) Maat *m* ♦ *vi* (*animals*) sich paaren.

material [mə'tɪərɪəl] *n* Material *nt*; (*cloth*) Stoff *m* ♦ *adj* (*possessions, existence*) materiell; (*relevant*) wesentlich; **materials** *npl* (*equipment*) Material *nt*.

materialistic [mətɪərɪə'lɪstɪk] *adj* materialistisch.

materialize [mə'tɪərɪəlaɪz] *vi* (*event*) zustande kommen; (*plan*) verwirklicht werden; (*hope*) sich verwirklichen; (*problem*) auftreten; (*crisis, difficulty*) eintreten.

maternal [mə'tɜːnl] *adj* mütterlich, Mutter-.

maternity [mə'tɜːnɪtɪ] *n* Mutterschaft *f* ♦ *cpd* (*ward etc*) Entbindungs-; (*care*) für werdende und junge Mütter.

maternity benefit *n* Mutterschaftsgeld *nt*.

maternity dress *n* Umstandskleid *nt*.

maternity hospital *n* Entbindungsheim *nt*.

maternity leave *n* Mutterschaftsurlaub *m*.

matey ['meɪtɪ] (*BRIT: inf*) *adj* kumpelhaft.

math [mæθ] (*US*) *n abbr* = **maths**.

mathematical [mæθə'mætɪkl] *adj* mathematisch.

mathematician [mæθəmə'tɪʃən] *n* Mathematiker(in) *m(f)*.

mathematics [mæθə'mætɪks] *n* Mathematik *f*.

maths [mæθs], (*US*) **math** [mæθ] *n abbr* Mathe *f*.

matinée ['mætɪneɪ] *n* Nachmittagsvorstellung *f*.

mating ['meɪtɪŋ] *n* Paarung *f*.

mating call *n* Lockruf *m*.

mating season *n* Paarungszeit *f*.

matriarchal [meɪtrɪ'ɑːkl] *adj* matriarchalisch.

matrices ['meɪtrɪsiːz] *npl of* **matrix**.

matriculation [mətrɪkju'leɪʃən] *n* Immatrikulation *f*.

matrimonial [mætrɪ'məunɪəl] *adj* Ehe-.

matrimony ['mætrɪmənɪ] *n* Ehe *f*.

matrix ['meɪtrɪks] (*pl* **matrices**) *n* (*MATH*) Matrix *f*; (*framework*) Gefüge *nt*.

matron ['meɪtrən] *n* (*in hospital*) Oberschwester *f*; (*in school*) Schwester *f*.

matronly ['meɪtrənlɪ] *adj* matronenhaft.

matt [mæt] *adj* matt; (*paint*) Matt-.

matted ['mætɪd] *adj* verfilzt.

matter ['mætə*] *n* (*event, situation*) Sache *f*,

Angelegenheit *f*; (*PHYS*) Materie *f*; (*substance, material*) Stoff *m*; (*MED: pus*) Eiter *m* ♦ *vi* (*be important*) wichtig sein; **matters** *npl* (*affairs*) Angelegenheiten *pl*, Dinge *pl*; (*situation*) Lage *f*; **what's the** ~? was ist los?; **no** ~ **what** egal was (passiert); **that's another** ~ das ist etwas anderes; **as a** ~ **of course** selbstverständlich; **as a** ~ **of fact** eigentlich; **it's a** ~ **of habit** es ist eine Gewohnheitssache; **vegetable** ~ pflanzliche Stoffe *pl*; **printed** ~ Drucksachen *pl*; **reading** ~ (*BRIT*) Lesestoff *m*; **it doesn't** ~ es macht nichts.

matter-of-fact ['mætərəv'fækt] *adj* sachlich.

matting ['mætɪŋ] *n* Matten *pl*; **rush** ~ Binsenmatten *pl*.

mattress ['mætrɪs] *n* Matratze *f*.

mature [mə'tjuə*] *adj* reif; (*wine*) ausgereift ♦ *vi* reifen; (*COMM*) fällig werden.

mature student *n* älterer Student *m*, ältere Studentin *f*.

maturity [mə'tjuərɪtɪ] *n* Reife *f*; **to have reached** ~ (*person*) erwachsen sein; (*animal*) ausgewachsen sein.

maudlin ['mɔːdlɪn] *adj* gefühlsselig.

maul [mɔːl] *vt* (anfallen und) übel zurichten.

Mauritania [mɔːrɪ'teɪnɪə] *n* Mauretanien *nt*.

Mauritius [mə'rɪʃəs] *n* Mauritius *nt*.

mausoleum [mɔːsə'lɪəm] *n* Mausoleum *nt*.

mauve [məuv] *adj* mauve.

maverick ['mævrɪk] *n* (*dissenter*) Abtrünnige(r) *m*; (*independent thinker*) Querdenker *m*.

mawkish ['mɔːkɪʃ] *adj* rührselig.

max. *abbr* = **maximum**.

maxim ['mæksɪm] *n* Maxime *f*.

maxima ['mæksɪmə] *npl of* **maximum**.

maximize ['mæksɪmaɪz] *vt* maximieren.

maximum ['mæksɪməm] (*pl* **maxima** *or* ~**s**) *adj* (*amount, speed etc*) Höchst-; (*efficiency*) maximal ♦ *n* Maximum *nt*.

May [meɪ] *n* Mai *m*; *see also* **July**.

may [meɪ] (*conditional* **might**) *vi* (*be possible*) können; (*have permission*) dürfen; **he** ~ **come** vielleicht kommt er; ~ **I smoke?** darf ich rauchen?; ~ **God bless you!** (*wish*) Gott segne dich!; ~ **I sit here?** kann ich mich hier hinsetzen?; **he might be there** er könnte da sein; **you might like to try** vielleicht möchten Sie es mal versuchen; **you** ~ **as well go** Sie können ruhig gehen.

maybe ['meɪbiː] *adv* vielleicht; ~ **he'll** ... es kann sein, dass er ...; ~ **not** vielleicht nicht.

Mayday ['meɪdeɪ] *n* Maydaysignal *nt*, ≈ SOS-Ruf *m*.

May Day *n* der 1. Mai.

mayhem ['meɪhɛm] *n* Chaos *nt*.

mayonnaise [meɪə'neɪz] *n* Majonäse *f*, Mayonnaise *f*.

mayor [mɛə*] *n* Bürgermeister *m*.

mayoress ['mɛərɛs] *n* Bürgermeisterin *f*; (*partner*) Frau *f* des Bürgermeisters.

maypole ['meɪpəul] n Maibaum m.

maze [meɪz] n Irrgarten m; (fig) Wirrwarr m.

MB abbr (COMPUT: = megabyte) MB; (CANADA: = Manitoba).

MBA n abbr (= Master of Business Administration) akademischer Grad in Betriebswirtschaft.

MBE (BRIT) n abbr (= Member of (the Order of) the British Empire) britischer Ordenstitel.

MC n abbr = **Master of Ceremonies**.

MCAT (US) n abbr (= Medical College Admissions Test) Zulassungsprüfung für medizinische Fachschulen.

MCP (BRIT: inf) n abbr (= male chauvinist pig) Chauvinistenschwein nt.

MD n abbr (= Doctor of Medicine) ≈ Dr. med.; (COMM) = **managing director** ♦ abbr (US: POST: = Maryland).

MDT (US) abbr (= Mountain Daylight Time) amerikanische Sommerzeitzone.

ME n abbr (US) = **medical examiner**; (MED: = myalgic encephalomyelitis) krankhafter Energiemangel (oft nach Viruserkrankungen) ♦ abbr (US: POST: = Maine).

═══════════════════ KEYWORD

me [miː] pron **1** (direct) mich; **can you hear ~?** können Sie mich hören?; **it's ~** ich bins.
2 (indirect) mir; **he gave ~ the money, he gave the money to ~** er gab mir das Geld.
3 (after prep): **it's for ~** es ist für mich; **with ~** mit mir; **give them to ~** gib sie mir; **without ~** ohne mich.

meadow ['mɛdəu] n Wiese f.

meagre, (US) **meager** ['miːgə*] adj (amount) kläglich; (meal) dürftig.

meal [miːl] n Mahlzeit f; (food) Essen nt; (flour) Schrotmehl nt; **to go out for a ~** essen gehen; **to make a ~ of sth** (fig) etw auf sehr umständliche Art machen.

meals on wheels n sing Essen nt auf Rädern.

mealtime ['miːltaɪm] n Essenszeit f.

mealy-mouthed ['miːlɪmauðd] adj unaufrichtig; (politician) schönfärberisch.

mean [miːn] (pt, pp **meant**) adj (with money) geizig; (unkind) gemein; (US: inf: animal) bösartig; (shabby) schäbig; (average) Durchschnitts-, mittlere(r, s) ♦ vt (signify) bedeuten; (refer to) meinen; (intend) beabsichtigen ♦ n (average) Durchschnitt m; **means** npl (way) Möglichkeit f; (money) Mittel pl; **by ~s of** durch; **by all ~s!** aber natürlich or selbstverständlich!; **do you ~ it?** meinst du das ernst?; **what do you ~?** was willst du damit sagen?; **to be meant for sb/sth** für jdn/etw bestimmt sein; **to ~ to do sth** etw tun wollen.

meander [mɪ'ændə*] vi (river) sich schlängeln; (person: walking) schlendern; (: talking) abschweifen.

meaning ['miːnɪŋ] n Sinn m; (of word, gesture) Bedeutung f.

meaningful ['miːnɪŋful] adj sinnvoll; (glance, remark) viel sagend, bedeutsam; (relationship) tiefer gehend.

meaningless ['miːnɪŋlɪs] adj sinnlos; (word, song) bedeutungslos.

meanness ['miːnnɪs] n (with money) Geiz m; (unkindness) Gemeinheit f; (shabbiness) Schäbigkeit f.

means test [miːnz-] n Überprüfung f der Einkommens- und Vermögensverhältnisse.

means-tested ['miːnztɛstɪd] adj von den Einkommens- und Vermögensverhältnissen abhängig.

meant [mɛnt] pt, pp of **mean**.

meantime ['miːntaɪm] adv (also: **in the ~**) inzwischen.

meanwhile ['miːnwaɪl] adv = **meantime**.

measles ['miːzlz] n Masern pl.

measly ['miːzlɪ] (inf) adj mick(e)rig.

measurable ['mɛʒərəbl] adj messbar.

measure ['mɛʒə*] vt, vi messen ♦ n (amount) Menge f; (ruler) Messstab m; (of achievement) Maßstab m; (action) Maßnahme f; **a litre ~** ein Messbecher m, der einen Liter fasst; **a/ some ~ of** ein gewisses Maß an +dat; **to take ~s to do sth** Maßnahmen ergreifen, um etw zu tun.

▶ **measure up** vi: **to ~ up to** herankommen an +acc.

measured ['mɛʒəd] adj (tone) bedächtig; (step) gemessen.

measurement ['mɛʒəmənt] n (measure) Maß nt; (act) Messung f; **chest/hip ~** Brust-/Hüftumfang m.

measurements ['mɛʒəmənts] npl Maße pl; **to take sb's ~** bei jdm Maß nehmen.

meat [miːt] n Fleisch nt; **cold ~s** (BRIT) Aufschnitt m; **crab ~** Krabbenfleisch nt.

meatball ['miːtbɔːl] n Fleischkloß m.

meat pie n Fleischpastete f.

meaty ['miːtɪ] adj (meal, dish) mit viel Fleisch; (fig: satisfying: book etc) gehaltvoll; (: brawny: person) kräftig (gebaut).

Mecca ['mɛkə] n (GEOG, fig) Mekka nt.

mechanic [mɪ'kænɪk] n Mechaniker(in) m(f).

mechanical [mɪ'kænɪkl] adj mechanisch.

mechanical engineering n Maschinenbau m.

mechanics [mɪ'kænɪks] n (PHYS) Mechanik f ♦ npl (of reading etc) Technik f; (of government etc) Mechanismus m.

mechanism ['mɛkənɪzəm] n Mechanismus m.

mechanization [mɛkənaɪ'zeɪʃən] n Mechanisierung f.

mechanize ['mɛkənaɪz] vt, vi mechanisieren.

MEd n abbr (= Master of Education) akademischer Grad für Lehrer.

medal ['mɛdl] n Medaille f; (decoration) Orden m.

medallion [mɪ'dælɪən] n Medaillon nt.

medallist, (*US***) medalist** ['mɛdlɪst] *n*
Medaillengewinner(in) *m(f)*.
meddle ['mɛdl] *vi*: **to ~ (in)** sich einmischen
(**in** +*acc*); **to ~ with sb** sich mit jdm
einlassen; **to ~ with sth** (*tamper*) sich *dat* an
etw *dat* zu schaffen machen.
meddlesome ['mɛdlsəm], **meddling** ['mɛdlɪŋ]
adj sich ständig einmischend.
media ['mi:dɪə] *npl* Medien *pl*.
media circus *n* Medienrummel *m*.
mediaeval [mɛdɪ'i:vl] *adj* = **medieval**.
median ['mi:dɪən] (*US*) *n* (*also*: **~ strip**)
Mittelstreifen *m*.
mediate ['mi:dɪeɪt] *vi* vermitteln.
mediation [mi:dɪ'eɪʃən] *n* Vermittlung *f*.
mediator ['mi:dɪeɪtə*] *n* Vermittler(in) *m(f)*.
Medicaid ['mɛdɪkeɪd] (*US*) *n* staatliche
*Krankenversicherung und
Gesundheitsfürsorge für
Einkommensschwache.*
medical ['mɛdɪkl] *adj* (*care*) medizinisch;
(*treatment*) ärztlich ♦ *n* (ärztliche)
Untersuchung *f*.
medical certificate *n* (*confirming health*)
ärztliches Gesundheitszeugnis *nt*;
(*confirming illness*) ärztliches Attest *nt*.
medical examiner (*US*) *n* ≈
Gerichtsmediziner(in) *m(f)*; (*performing
autopsy*) Leichenbeschauer *m*.
medical student *n* Medizinstudent(in) *m(f)*.
Medicare ['mɛdɪkɛə*] (*US*) *n* staatliche
*Krankenversicherung und
Gesundheitsfürsorge für ältere Bürger.*
medicated ['mɛdɪkeɪtɪd] *adj* medizinisch.
medication [mɛdɪ'keɪʃən] *n* Medikamente *pl*.
medicinal [mɛ'dɪsɪnl] *adj* (*substance*) Heil-;
(*qualities*) heilend; (*purposes*) medizinisch.
medicine ['mɛdsɪn] *n* Medizin *f*; (*drug*) Arznei
f.
medicine ball *n* Medizinball *m*.
medicine chest *n* Hausapotheke *f*.
medicine man *n* Medizinmann *m*.
medieval [mɛdɪ'i:vl] *adj* mittelalterlich.
mediocre [mi:dɪ'əukə*] *adj* mittelmäßig.
mediocrity [mi:dɪ'ɔkrɪtɪ] *n* Mittelmäßigkeit *f*.
meditate ['mɛdɪteɪt] *vi* nachdenken; (*REL*)
meditieren.
meditation [mɛdɪ'teɪʃən] *n* Nachdenken *nt*;
(*REL*) Meditation *f*.
Mediterranean [mɛdɪtə'reɪnɪən] *adj* (*country,
climate etc*) Mittelmeer-; **the ~ (Sea)** das
Mittelmeer.
medium ['mi:dɪəm] (*pl* **media** *or* **~s**) *adj*
mittlere(r, s) ♦ *n* (*means*) Mittel *nt*;
(*substance, material*) Medium *nt*; (*pl* **~s**)
(*person*) Medium *nt*; **of ~ height** mittelgroß;
to strike a happy ~ den goldenen Mittelweg
finden.
medium-dry ['mi:dɪəm'draɪ] *adj* (*wine, sherry*)
halbtrocken.
medium-sized ['mi:dɪəm'saɪzd] *adj*
mittelgroß.

medium wave *n* (*RADIO*) Mittelwelle *f*.
medley ['mɛdlɪ] *n* Gemisch *nt*; (*MUS*) Medley
nt.
meek [mi:k] *adj* sanft(mütig), duldsam.
meet [mi:t] (*pt, pp* **met**) *vt* (*encounter*) treffen;
(*by arrangement*) sich treffen mit; (*for the
first time*) kennen lernen; (*go and fetch*)
abholen; (*opponent*) treffen auf +*acc*;
(*condition, standard*) erfüllen; (*need,
expenses*) decken; (*problem*) stoßen auf +*acc*;
(*challenge*) begegnen +*dat*; (*bill*) begleichen;
(*join: line*) sich schneiden mit; (: *road etc*)
treffen auf +*acc* ♦ *vi* (*encounter*) sich
begegnen; (*by arrangement*) sich treffen; (*for
the first time*) sich kennen lernen; (*for talks
etc*) zusammenkommen; (*committee*) tagen;
(*join: lines*) sich schneiden; (: *roads etc*)
aufeinander treffen ♦ *n* (*BRIT: HUNTING*)
Jagd *f*; (*US: SPORT*) Sportfest *nt*; **pleased to
~ you!** (sehr) angenehm!
▶ **meet up** *vi*: **to ~ up with sb** sich mit jdm
treffen.
▶ **meet with** *vt fus* (*difficulty, success*) haben.
meeting ['mi:tɪŋ] *n* (*assembly, people
assembling*) Versammlung *f*; (*COMM, of
committee etc*) Sitzung *f*; (*also*: **business ~**)
Besprechung *f*; (*encounter*) Begegnung *f*;
(: *arranged*) Treffen *nt*; (*POL*) Gespräch *nt*;
(*SPORT*) Veranstaltung *f*; **she's at** *or* **in a ~**
(*COMM*) sie ist bei einer Besprechung; **to
call a ~** eine Sitzung/Versammlung
einberufen.
meeting-place ['mi:tɪŋpleɪs] *n* Treffpunkt *m*.
megabyte ['mɛgəbaɪt] *n* Megabyte *nt*.
megalomaniac [mɛgələ'meɪnɪæk] *n*
Größenwahnsinnige(r) *f(m)*.
megaphone ['mɛgəfəun] *n* Megafon *nt*,
Megaphon *nt*.
megawatt ['mɛgəwɔt] *n* Megawatt *nt*.
melancholy ['mɛlənkəlɪ] *n* Melancholie *f*,
Schwermut *f* ♦ *adj* melancholisch,
schwermütig.
mellow ['mɛləu] *adj* (*sound*) voll, weich; (*light,
colour, stone*) warm; (*weathered*) verwittert;
(*person*) gesetzt; (*wine*) ausgereift ♦ *vi*
(*person*) gesetzter werden.
melodious [mɪ'ləudɪəs] *adj* melodisch.
melodrama ['mɛləudrɑ:mə] *n* Melodrama *nt*.
melodramatic [mɛlədrə'mætɪk] *adj*
melodramatisch.
melody ['mɛlədɪ] *n* Melodie *f*.
melon ['mɛlən] *n* Melone *f*.
melt [mɛlt] *vi* (*lit, fig*) schmelzen ♦ *vt*
schmelzen; (*butter*) zerlassen.
▶ **melt down** *vt* einschmelzen.
meltdown ['mɛltdaun] *n* (*in nuclear reactor*)
Kernschmelze *f*.
melting point ['mɛltɪŋ-] *n* Schmelzpunkt *m*.
melting pot *n* (*lit, fig*) Schmelztiegel *m*; **to be
in the ~** in der Schwebe sein.
member ['mɛmbə*] *n* Mitglied *nt*; (*ANAT*)
Glied *nt* ♦ *cpd*: **~ country** Mitgliedsland *nt*;

~ **state** Mitgliedsstaat *m*; **M~ of Parliament**
(*BRIT*) Abgeordnete(r) *f(m)* (des
Unterhauses); **M~ of the European
Parliament** (*BRIT*) Abgeordnete(r) *f(m)* des
Europaparlaments.
membership ['mɛmbəʃɪp] *n* Mitgliedschaft *f*;
(*members*) Mitglieder *pl*; (*number of
members*) Mitgliederzahl *f*.
membership card *n* Mitgliedsausweis *m*.
membrane ['mɛmbreɪn] *n* Membran(e) *f*.
memento [mə'mɛntəu] *n* Andenken *nt*.
memo ['mɛməu] *n* Memo *nt*, Mitteilung *f*.
memoir ['mɛmwɑː*] *n* Kurzbiografie *f*.
memoirs ['mɛmwɑːz] *npl* Memoiren *pl*.
memo pad *n* Notizblock *m*.
memorable ['mɛmərəbl] *adj* denkwürdig;
(*unforgettable*) unvergesslich.
memorandum [mɛmə'rændəm] (*pl
memoranda) *n* Mitteilung *f*.
memorial [mɪ'mɔːrɪəl] *n* Denkmal *nt* ♦ *adj*
(*service, prize*) Gedenk-.
Memorial Day (*US*) *n* ≈ Volkstrauertag
m.

MEMORIAL DAY

Memorial Day *ist in den USA ein gesetzlicher
Feiertag am letzten Montag im Mai zum Gedenken
an die in allen Kriegen gefallenen amerikanischen
Soldaten. Siehe auch* **Remembrance Sunday**

---

memorize ['mɛməraɪz] *vt* sich *dat* einprägen.
memory ['mɛmərɪ] *n* Gedächtnis *nt*; (*sth
remembered*) Erinnerung *f*; (*COMPUT*)
Speicher *m*; **in ~ of** zur Erinnerung an *+acc*;
to have a good/bad ~ ein gutes/schlechtes
Gedächtnis haben; **loss of ~**
Gedächtnisschwund *m*.
men [mɛn] *npl of* **man**.
menace ['mɛnɪs] *n* Bedrohung *f*; (*nuisance*)
(Land)plage *f* ♦ *vt* bedrohen; **a public ~** eine
Gefahr für die Öffentlichkeit.
menacing ['mɛnɪsɪŋ] *adj* drohend.
menagerie [mɪ'nædʒərɪ] *n* Menagerie *f*.
mend [mɛnd] *vt* reparieren; (*darn*) flicken ♦ *n*:
to be on the ~ auf dem Wege der
Besserung sein; **to ~ one's ways** sich
bessern.
mending ['mɛndɪŋ] *n* Reparaturen *pl*; (*clothes*)
Flickarbeiten *pl*.
menial ['miːnɪəl] (*often pej*) *adj* niedrig,
untergeordnet.
meningitis [mɛnɪn'dʒaɪtɪs] *n*
Hirnhautentzündung *f*.
menopause ['mɛnəupɔːz] *n*: **the ~** die
Wechseljahre *pl*.
menservants ['mɛnsəːvənts] *npl of*
manservant.
men's room (*US*) *n* Herrentoilette *f*.
menstrual ['mɛnstruəl] *adj* (*BIOL: cycle etc*)
Menstruations-; ~ **period** Monatsblutung *f*.
menstruate ['mɛnstrueɪt] *vi* die Menstruation

haben.
menstruation [mɛnstru'eɪʃən] *n* Menstruation
f.
menswear ['mɛnzwɛə*] *n* Herren(be)kleidung
f.
mental ['mɛntl] *adj* geistig; (*illness*) Geistes-;
~ **arithmetic** Kopfrechnen *nt*.
mental hospital *n* psychiatrische Klinik *f*.
mentality [mɛn'tælɪtɪ] *n* Mentalität *f*.
mentally ['mɛntlɪ] *adv*: **to be ~ handicapped**
geistig behindert sein.
menthol ['mɛnθɔl] *n* Menthol *nt*.
mention ['mɛnʃən] *n* Erwähnung *f* ♦ *vt*
erwähnen; **don't ~ it!** (bitte,) gern
geschehen!; **not to ~ ...** von ... ganz zu
schweigen.
mentor ['mɛntɔː*] *n* Mentor *m*.
menu ['mɛnjuː] *n* Menü *nt*; (*printed*)
Speisekarte *f*.
menu-driven ['mɛnjuːdrɪvn] *adj* (*COMPUT*)
menügesteuert.
MEP (*BRIT*) *n abbr* (= *Member of the European
Parliament*) Abgeordnete(r) *f(m)* des
Europaparlaments.
mercantile ['məːkəntaɪl] *adj* (*class, society*)
Handel treibend; (*law*) Handels-.
mercenary ['məːsɪnərɪ] *adj* (*person*) geldgierig
♦ *n* Söldner *m*.
merchandise ['məːtʃəndaɪz] *n* Ware *f*.
merchandiser ['məːtʃəndaɪzə*] *n*
Verkaufsförderungsexperte *m*.
merchant ['məːtʃənt] *n* Kaufmann *m*; **timber/
wine ~** Holz-/Weinhändler *m*.
merchant bank (*BRIT*) *n* Handelsbank *f*.
merchantman ['məːtʃəntmən] (*irreg: like* **man**)
n Handelsschiff *nt*.
merchant navy, (*US*) **merchant marine** *n*
Handelsmarine *f*.
merciful ['məːsɪful] *adj* gnädig; **a ~ release**
eine Erlösung.
mercifully ['məːsɪflɪ] *adv* glücklicherweise.
merciless ['məːsɪlɪs] *adj* erbarmungslos.
mercurial [məː'kjuərɪəl] *adj* (*unpredictable*)
sprunghaft, wechselhaft; (*lively*)
quecksilbrig.
mercury ['məːkjurɪ] *n* Quecksilber *nt*.
mercy ['məːsɪ] *n* Gnade *f*; **to have ~ on sb**
Erbarmen mit jdm haben; **at the ~ of**
ausgeliefert *+dat*.
mercy killing *n* Euthanasie *f*.
mere [mɪə*] *adj* bloß; **his ~ presence irritates
her** schon *or* allein seine Anwesenheit
ärgert sie; **she is a ~ child** sie ist noch ein
Kind; **it's a ~ trifle** es ist eine Lappalie; **by
~ chance** rein durch Zufall.
merely ['mɪəlɪ] *adv* lediglich, bloß.
merge [məːdʒ] *vt* (*combine*) vereinen;
(*COMPUT: files*) mischen ♦ *vi* (*COMM*)
fusionieren; (*colours, sounds, shapes*)
ineinander übergehen; (*roads*)
zusammenlaufen.
merger ['məːdʒə*] *n* (*COMM*) Fusion *f*.

meridian [mə'rɪdɪən] n Meridian m.

meringue [mə'ræŋ] n Baiser nt.

merit ['mɛrɪt] n (worth, value) Wert m;
(advantage) Vorzug m; (achievement)
Verdienst nt ♦ vt verdienen.

meritocracy [mɛrɪ'tɔkrəsɪ] n
Leistungsgesellschaft f.

mermaid ['mɜːmeɪd] n Seejungfrau f,
Meerjungfrau f.

merrily ['mɛrɪlɪ] adv vergnügt.

merriment ['mɛrɪmənt] n Heiterkeit f.

merry ['mɛrɪ] adj vergnügt; (music) fröhlich;
M~ **Christmas!** fröhliche or frohe
Weihnachten!

merry-go-round ['mɛrɪgəʊraund] n Karussell
nt.

mesh [mɛʃ] n Geflecht nt; **wire** ~
Maschendraht m.

mesmerize ['mɛzməraɪz] vt (fig) faszinieren.

mess [mɛs] n Durcheinander nt; (dirt) Dreck
m; (MIL) Kasino nt; **to be in a** ~ (untidy)
unordentlich sein; (in difficulty) in
Schwierigkeiten stecken; **to be a** ~ (fig: life)
verkorkst sein; **to get o.s. in a** ~ **in**
Schwierigkeiten geraten.

► **mess about** (inf) vi (fool around)
herumalbern.

► **mess about with** (inf) vt fus (play around
with) herumfummeln an +dat.

► **mess around** (inf) vi = **mess about.**

► **mess around with** (inf) vt fus = **mess about
with.**

► **mess up** vt durcheinander bringen; (dirty)
verdrecken.

message ['mɛsɪdʒ] n Mitteilung f, Nachricht f;
(meaning) Aussage f; **to get the** ~ (inf, fig)
kapieren.

message switching [-'swɪtʃɪŋ] n (COMPUT)
Speichervermittlung f.

messenger ['mɛsɪndʒəʳ] n Bote m.

Messiah [mɪ'saɪə] n Messias m.

Messrs ['mɛsəz] abbr (on letters: = messieurs)
An (die Herren).

messy ['mɛsɪ] adj (dirty) dreckig; (untidy)
unordentlich.

Met [mɛt] (US) n abbr (= Metropolitan Opera)
Met f.

met [mɛt] pt, pp of **meet.**

met. adj abbr (= meteorological): **the M~ Office**
das Wetteramt.

metabolism [mɛ'tæbəlɪzəm] n Stoffwechsel
m.

metal ['mɛtl] n Metall nt.

metal fatigue n Metallermüdung f.

metalled ['mɛtld] adj (road) asphaltiert.

metallic [mɪ'tælɪk] adj metallisch; (made of
metal) aus Metall.

metallurgy [mɛ'tælədʒɪ] n Metallurgie f.

metalwork ['mɛtlwɜːk] n Metallarbeit f.

metamorphosis [mɛtə'mɔːfəsɪs] (pl
metamorphoses) n Verwandlung f.

metaphor ['mɛtəfəʳ] n Metapher f.

metaphorical [mɛtə'fɔrɪkl] adj metaphorisch.

metaphysics [mɛtə'fɪzɪks] n Metaphysik f.

meteor ['miːtɪəʳ] n Meteor m.

meteoric [miːtɪ'ɔrɪk] adj (fig) kometenhaft.

meteorite ['miːtɪəraɪt] n Meteorit m.

meteorological [miːtɪərə'lɔdʒɪkl] adj
(conditions, office etc) Wetter-.

meteorology [miːtɪə'rɔlədʒɪ] n Wetterkunde f,
Meteorologie f.

mete out [miːt-] vt austeilen; **to** ~ **justice**
Recht sprechen.

meter ['miːtəʳ] n Zähler m; (water meter)
Wasseruhr f; (parking meter) Parkuhr f; (US:
unit) = metre.

methane ['miːθeɪn] n Methan nt.

method ['mɛθəd] n Methode f; ~ **of payment**
Zahlungsweise f.

methodical [mɪ'θɔdɪkl] adj methodisch.

Methodist ['mɛθədɪst] n Methodist(in) m(f).

methodology [mɛθə'dɔlədʒɪ] n Methodik f.

meths [mɛθs] (BRIT) n = **methylated spirit.**

methylated spirit ['mɛθɪleɪtɪd-] (BRIT) n
(Brenn)spiritus m.

meticulous [mɪ'tɪkjuləs] adj sorgfältig; (detail)
genau.

metre, (US) **meter** ['miːtəʳ] n Meter m or nt.

metric ['mɛtrɪk] adj metrisch; **to go** ~ auf das
metrische Maßsystem umstellen.

metrical ['mɛtrɪkl] adj metrisch.

metrication [mɛtrɪ'keɪʃən] n Umstellung f auf
das metrische Maßsystem.

metric system n metrisches Maßsystem nt.

metric ton n Metertonne f.

metronome ['mɛtrənəʊm] n Metronom nt.

metropolis [mɪ'trɔpəlɪs] n Metropole f.

metropolitan [mɛtrə'pɔlɪtn] adj
großstädtisch.

Metropolitan Police (BRIT) n: **the** ~ die
Londoner Polizei.

mettle ['mɛtl] n: **to be on one's** ~ auf dem
Posten sein.

mew [mjuː] vi miauen.

mews [mjuːz] (BRIT) n Gasse f mit ehemaligen
Kutscherhäuschen.

Mexican ['mɛksɪkən] adj mexikanisch ♦ n
Mexikaner(in) m(f).

Mexico ['mɛksɪkəʊ] n Mexiko nt.

Mexico City n Mexico City f.

mezzanine ['mɛtsəniːn] n Mezzanin nt.

MFA (US) n abbr (= Master of Fine Arts)
akademischer Grad in Kunst.

mfr abbr = **manufacture; manufacturer.**

mg abbr (= milligram(me)) mg.

Mgr abbr (= Monseigneur, Monsignor) Mgr.;
(COMM) = **manager.**

MHR (US, AUSTRALIA) n abbr (= Member of the
House of Representatives) Abgeordnete(r) f(m)
des Repräsentantenhauses.

MHz abbr (= megahertz) MHz.

MI (US) abbr (POST: = Michigan).

MI5 (BRIT) n abbr (= Military Intelligence 5)
britischer Spionageabwehrdienst.

MI6 (*BRIT*) *n abbr* (= *Military Intelligence 6*) britischer Geheimdienst.

MIA *abbr* (*MIL*: = *missing in action*) vermisst.

miaow [mi:'au] *vi* miauen.

mice [maɪs] *npl of* **mouse**.

Mich. (*US*) *abbr* (*POST*: = *Michigan*).

micro... ['maɪkrəu] *pref* mikro-, Mikro-.

microbe ['maɪkrəub] *n* Mikrobe *f*.

microbiology [maɪkrəubaɪ'ɔlədʒɪ] *n* Mikrobiologie *f*.

microchip ['maɪkrəutʃɪp] *n* Mikrochip *m*.

micro(computer) ['maɪkrəu(kəm'pju:tə*)] *n* Mikrocomputer *m*.

microcosm ['maɪkrəukɔzəm] *n* Mikrokosmos *m*.

microeconomics ['maɪkrəui:kə'nɔmɪks] *n* Mikroökonomie *f*.

microelectronics ['maɪkrəuɪlek'trɔnɪks] *n* Mikroelektronik *f*.

microfiche ['maɪkrəufi:ʃ] *n* Mikrofiche *m or nt*.

microfilm ['maɪkrəufɪlm] *n* Mikrofilm *m*.

microlight ['maɪkrəulaɪt] *n* Ultraleichtflugzeug *nt*.

micrometer [maɪ'krɔmɪtə*] *n* Messschraube *f*.

microphone ['maɪkrəfəun] *n* Mikrofon *nt*, Mikrophon *nt*.

microprocessor ['maɪkrəu'prəusesə*] *n* Mikroprozessor *m*.

microscope ['maɪkrəskəup] *n* Mikroskop *nt*; **under the** ~ unter dem Mikroskop.

microscopic [maɪkrə'skɔpɪk] *adj* mikroskopisch; (*creature*) mikroskopisch klein.

microwave ['maɪkrəuweɪv] *n* Mikrowelle *f*; (*also:* ~ **oven**) Mikrowellenherd *m*.

mid- [mɪd] *adj*: **in** ~**-May** Mitte Mai; **in** ~**-afternoon** (mitten) am Nachmittag; **in** ~**-air** (mitten) in der Luft; **he's in his** ~**-thirties** er ist Mitte dreißig.

midday [mɪd'deɪ] *n* Mittag *m*.

middle ['mɪdl] *n* Mitte *f* ♦ *adj* mittlere(r, s); **in the** ~ **of the night** mitten in der Nacht; **I'm in the** ~ **of reading it** ich bin mittendrin; **a** ~ **course** ein Mittelweg *m*.

middle age *n* mittleres Lebensalter *nt*.

middle-aged [mɪdl'eɪdʒd] *adj* mittleren Alters.

Middle Ages *npl* Mittelalter *nt*.

middle-class [mɪdl'klɑːs] *adj* mittelständisch.

middle class(es) *n(pl)* Mittelstand *m*.

Middle East *n* Naher Osten *m*.

middleman ['mɪdlmæn] (*irreg: like* **man**) *n* Zwischenhändler *m*.

middle management *n* mittleres Management *nt*.

middle name *n* zweiter Vorname *m*.

middle-of-the-road ['mɪdləvðə'rəud] *adj* gemäßigt; (*politician*) der Mitte; (*MUS*) leicht.

middleweight ['mɪdlweɪt] *n* (*BOXING*) Mittelgewicht *nt*.

middling ['mɪdlɪŋ] *adj* mittelmäßig.

Middx (*BRIT*) *abbr* (*POST*: = *Middlesex*).

midge [mɪdʒ] *n* Mücke *f*.

midget ['mɪdʒɪt] *n* Liliputaner(in) *m(f)*.

midi system ['mɪdɪ-] *n* Midi-System *nt*.

Midlands ['mɪdləndz] (*BRIT*) *npl*: **the** ~ Mittelengland *nt*.

midnight ['mɪdnaɪt] *n* Mitternacht *f* ♦ *cpd* Mitternachts-; **at** ~ um Mitternacht.

midriff ['mɪdrɪf] *n* Taille *f*.

midst [mɪdst] *n*: **in the** ~ **of** mitten in +*dat*; **to be in the** ~ **of doing sth** mitten dabei sein, etw zu tun.

midsummer [mɪd'sʌmə*] *n* Hochsommer *m*; **M**~**('s) Day** Sommersonnenwende *f*.

midway [mɪd'weɪ] *adj*: **we have reached the** ~ **point** wir haben die Hälfte hinter uns *dat* ♦ *adv* auf halbem Weg; ~ **between** (*in space*) auf halbem Weg zwischen; ~ **through** (*in time*) mitten in +*dat*.

midweek [mɪd'wiːk] *adv* mitten in der Woche ♦ *adj* Mitte der Woche.

midwife ['mɪdwaɪf] (*pl* **midwives**) *n* Hebamme *f*.

midwifery ['mɪdwɪfərɪ] *n* Geburtshilfe *f*.

midwinter [mɪd'wɪntə*] *n*: **in** ~ im tiefsten Winter.

miffed [mɪft] (*inf*) *adj*: **to be** ~ eingeschnappt sein.

might [maɪt] *vb see* **may** ♦ *n* Macht *f*; **with all one's** ~ mit aller Kraft.

mighty ['maɪtɪ] *adj* mächtig.

migraine ['miːɡreɪn] *n* Migräne *f*.

migrant ['maɪɡrənt] *adj* (*bird*) Zug-; (*worker*) Wander- ♦ *n* (*bird*) Zugvogel *m*; (*worker*) Wanderarbeiter(in) *m(f)*.

migrate [maɪ'ɡreɪt] *vi* (*bird*) ziehen; (*person*) abwandern.

migration [maɪ'ɡreɪʃən] *n* Wanderung *f*; (*to cities*) Abwanderung *f*; (*of birds*) (Vogel)zug *m*.

mike [maɪk] *n abbr* = **microphone**.

Milan [mɪ'læn] *n* Mailand *nt*.

mild [maɪld] *adj* mild; (*gentle*) sanft; (*slight: infection etc*) leicht; (: *interest*) gering.

mildew ['mɪldjuː] *n* Schimmel *m*.

mildly ['maɪldlɪ] *adv* (*say*) sanft; (*slight*) leicht; **to put it** ~ gelinde gesagt.

mildness ['maɪldnɪs] *n* Milde *f*; (*gentleness*) Sanftheit *f*; (*of infection etc*) Leichtigkeit *f*.

mile [maɪl] *n* Meile *f*; **to do 30** ~**s per gallon** ≈ 9 Liter auf 100 km verbrauchen.

mileage ['maɪlɪdʒ] *n* Meilenzahl *f*; (*fig*) Nutzen *m*; **to get a lot of** ~ **out of sth** etw gründlich ausnutzen; **there is a lot of** ~ **in the idea** aus der Idee lässt sich viel machen.

mileage allowance *n* ≈ Kilometergeld *nt*.

mileometer [maɪ'lɔmɪtə*] *n* ≈ Kilometerzähler *m*.

milestone ['maɪlstəun] *n* (*lit, fig*) Meilenstein *m*.

milieu ['miːljəː] *n* Milieu *nt*.

militant ['mɪlɪtnt] *adj* militant ♦ *n* Militante(r)

f(m).

militarism ['mɪlɪtərɪzəm] *n* Militarismus *m*.

militaristic [mɪlɪtə'rɪstɪk] *adj* militaristisch.

military ['mɪlɪtərɪ] *adj* (*history, leader etc*) Militär- ♦ *n*: **the** ~ das Militär.

military police *n* Militärpolizei *f*.

military service *n* Militärdienst *m*.

militate ['mɪlɪteɪt] *vi*: **to** ~ **against** negative Auswirkungen haben auf +*acc*.

militia [mɪ'lɪʃə] *n* Miliz *f*.

milk [mɪlk] *n* Milch *f* ♦ *vt* (*lit, fig*) melken.

milk chocolate *n* Vollmilchschokolade *f*.

milk float (*BRIT*) *n* Milchwagen *m*.

milking ['mɪlkɪŋ] *n* Melken *nt*.

milkman ['mɪlkmən] (*irreg: like* **man**) *n* Milchmann *m*.

milk shake *n* Milchmixgetränk *nt*.

milk tooth *n* Milchzahn *m*.

milk truck (*US*) *n* = **milk float**.

milky ['mɪlkɪ] *adj* milchig; (*drink*) mit viel Milch; ~ **coffee** Milchkaffee *m*.

Milky Way *n* Milchstraße *f*.

mill [mɪl] *n* Mühle *f*; (*factory*) Fabrik *f*; (*woollen mill*) Spinnerei *f* ♦ *vt* mahlen ♦ *vi* (*also*: ~ **about**) umherlaufen.

millennium [mɪ'lɛnɪəm] (*pl* ~**s** *or* **millennia**) *n* Jahrtausend *nt*.

millennium bug *n* (*COMPUT*) Jahrtausendfehler *m*.

miller ['mɪlə*] *n* Müller *m*.

millet ['mɪlɪt] *n* Hirse *f*.

milli... ['mɪlɪ] *pref* Milli-.

milligram(me) ['mɪlɪgræm] *n* Milligramm *nt*.

millilitre, (*US*) **milliliter** ['mɪlɪliːtə*] *n* Milliliter *m or nt*.

millimetre, (*US*) **millimeter** ['mɪlɪmiːtə*] *n* Millimeter *m or nt*.

millinery ['mɪlɪnərɪ] *n* Hüte *pl*.

million ['mɪljən] *n* Million *f*; **a** ~ **times** (*fig*) tausendmal, x-mal.

millionaire [mɪljə'nɛə*] *n* Millionär *m*.

millipede ['mɪlɪpiːd] *n* Tausendfüßler *m*.

millstone ['mɪlstəʊn] *n* (*fig*): **it's a** ~ **round his neck** es ist für ihn ein Klotz am Bein.

millwheel ['mɪlwiːl] *n* Mühlrad *nt*.

milometer [maɪ'lɒmɪtə*] *n* = **mileometer**.

mime [maɪm] *n* Pantomime *f*; (*actor*) Pantomime *m* ♦ *vt* pantomimisch darstellen.

mimic ['mɪmɪk] *n* Imitator *m* ♦ *vt* (*for amusement*) parodieren; (*animal, person*) imitieren, nachahmen.

mimicry ['mɪmɪkrɪ] *n* Nachahmung *f*.

Min. (*BRIT*) *abbr* (*POL*) = **ministry**.

min. *abbr* (= *minute*) Min.; = **minimum**.

minaret [mɪnə'rɛt] *n* Minarett *nt*.

mince [mɪns] *vt* (*meat*) durch den Fleischwolf drehen ♦ *vi* (*in walking*) trippeln ♦ *n* (*BRIT*: *meat*) Hackfleisch *nt*; **he does not** ~ (**his**) **words** er nimmt kein Blatt vor den Mund.

mincemeat ['mɪnsmiːt] *n* süße Gebäckfüllung aus Dörrobst und Sirup; (*US: meat*) Hackfleisch *nt*; **to make** ~ **of sb** (*inf*)

Hackfleisch aus jdm machen.

mince pie *n* mit Mincemeat gefülltes Gebäck.

mincer ['mɪnsə*] *n* Fleischwolf *m*.

mincing ['mɪnsɪŋ] *adj* (*walk*) trippelnd; (*voice*) geziert.

mind [maɪnd] *n* Geist *m*, Verstand *m*; (*thoughts*) Gedanken *pl*; (*memory*) Gedächtnis *nt* ♦ *vt* aufpassen auf +*acc*; (*office etc*) nach dem Rechten sehen in +*dat*; (*object to*) etwas haben gegen; **to my** ~ meiner Meinung nach; **to be out of one's** ~ verrückt sein; **it is on my** ~ es beschäftigt mich; **to keep** *or* **bear sth in** ~ etw nicht vergessen, an etw denken; **to make up one's** ~ sich entscheiden; **to change one's** ~ es sich *dat* anders überlegen; **to be in two** ~**s about sth** sich *dat* über etw *acc* nicht im Klaren sein; **to have it in** ~ **to do sth** die Absicht haben, etw zu tun; **to have sb/sth in** ~ an jdn/etw denken; **it slipped my** ~ ich habe es vergessen; **to bring** *or* **call sth to** ~ etw in Erinnerung rufen; **I can't get it out of my** ~ es geht mir nicht aus dem Kopf; **his** ~ **was on other things** er war mit den Gedanken woanders; "~ **the step**" „Vorsicht Stufe"; **do you** ~ **if ...?** macht es Ihnen etwas aus, wenn ...?; **I don't** ~ es ist mir egal; ~ **you,** ... allerdings ...; **never** ~! (*it makes no odds*) ist doch egal!; (*don't worry*) macht nichts!

mind-boggling ['maɪndbɒglɪŋ] (*inf*) *adj* atemberaubend.

-minded ['maɪndɪd] *adj*: **fair-**~ gerecht; **an industrially-**~ **nation** ein auf Industrie ausgerichtetes Land.

minder ['maɪndə*] *n* Betreuer(in) *m(f)*; (*inf: bodyguard*) Aufpasser(in) *m(f)*.

mindful ['maɪndful] *adj*: ~ **of** unter Berücksichtigung +*gen*.

mindless ['maɪndlɪs] *adj* (*violence*) sinnlos; (*work*) geistlos.

mine[1] [maɪn] *n* (*coal mine, gold mine*) Bergwerk *nt*; (*bomb*) Mine *f* ♦ *vt* (*coal*) abbauen; (*beach etc*) verminen; (*ship*) eine Mine befestigen an +*dat*.

mine[2] [maɪn] *pron* meine(r, s); **that book is** ~ das Buch ist mein(e)s, das Buch gehört mir; **this is** ~ das ist meins; **a friend of** ~ ein Freund/eine Freundin von mir.

mine detector *n* Minensuchgerät *nt*.

minefield ['maɪnfiːld] *n* Minenfeld *nt*; (*fig*) brisante Situation *f*.

miner ['maɪnə*] *n* Bergmann *m*, Bergarbeiter *m*.

mineral ['mɪnərəl] *adj* (*deposit, resources*) Mineral- ♦ *n* Mineral *nt*; **minerals** *npl* (*BRIT*: *soft drinks*) Erfrischungsgetränke *pl*.

mineralogy [mɪnə'rælədʒɪ] *n* Mineralogie *f*.

mineral water *n* Mineralwasser *nt*.

minesweeper ['maɪnswiːpə*] *n* Minensuchboot *nt*.

mingle ['mɪŋgl] *vi:* **to ~ (with)** sich vermischen (mit); **to ~ with** (*people*) Umgang haben mit; (*at party etc*) sich unterhalten mit; **you should ~ a bit** du solltest dich unter die Leute mischen.

mingy ['mɪndʒɪ] (*inf*) *adj* knick(e)rig; (*amount*) mick(e)rig.

mini... ['mɪnɪ] *pref* Mini-.

miniature ['mɪnətʃə*] *adj* winzig; (*version etc*) Miniatur- ♦ *n* Miniatur *f;* **in ~** im Kleinen, im Kleinformat.

minibus ['mɪnɪbʌs] *n* Kleinbus *m.*

minicab ['mɪnɪkæb] *n* Kleintaxi *nt.*

minicomputer ['mɪnɪkəm'pjuːtə*] *n* Minicomputer *m.*

minim ['mɪnɪm] *n* (*MUS*) halbe Note *f.*

minima ['mɪnɪmə] *npl of* **minimum.**

minimal ['mɪnɪml] *adj* minimal.

minimalist ['mɪnɪməlɪst] *adj* minimalistisch.

minimize ['mɪnɪmaɪz] *vt* auf ein Minimum reduzieren; (*play down*) herunterspielen.

minimum ['mɪnɪməm] (*pl* **minima**) *n* Minimum *nt* ♦ *adj* (*income, speed*) Mindest-; **to reduce to a ~** auf ein Mindestmaß reduzieren; **~ wage** Mindestlohn *m.*

minimum lending rate *n* Diskontsatz *m.*

mining ['maɪnɪŋ] *n* Bergbau *m* ♦ *cpd* Bergbau-.

minion ['mɪnjən] (*pej*) *n* Untergebene(r) *f(m).*

miniseries ['mɪnɪsɪəriːz] *n* Miniserie *f.*

miniskirt ['mɪnɪskəːt] *n* Minirock *m.*

minister ['mɪnɪstə*] *n* (*BRIT: POL*) Minister(in) *m(f);* (*REL*) Pfarrer *m* ♦ *vi:* **to ~ to** sich kümmern um; (*needs*) befriedigen.

ministerial [mɪnɪs'tɪərɪəl] (*BRIT*) *adj* (*POL*) ministeriell.

ministry ['mɪnɪstrɪ] *n* (*BRIT: POL*) Ministerium *nt;* **to join the ~** (*REL*) Geistliche(r) werden.

Ministry of Defence (*BRIT*) *n* Verteidigungsministerium *nt.*

mink [mɪŋk] (*pl* **~s** *or* **~**) *n* Nerz *m.*

mink coat *n* Nerzmantel *m.*

Minn. (*US*) *abbr* (*POST:* = *Minnesota*).

minnow ['mɪnəu] *n* Elritze *f.*

minor ['maɪnə*] *adj* kleinere(r, s); (*poet*) unbedeutend; (*planet*) klein; (*MUS*) Moll ♦ *n* Minderjährige(r) *f(m).*

Minorca [mɪ'nɔːkə] *n* Menorca *nt.*

minority [maɪ'nɔrɪtɪ] *n* Minderheit *f;* **to be in a ~** in der Minderheit sein.

minster ['mɪnstə*] *n* Münster *nt.*

minstrel ['mɪnstrəl] *n* Spielmann *m.*

mint [mɪnt] *n* Minze *f;* (*sweet*) Pfefferminz(bonbon) *nt;* (*place*): **the M~** die Münzanstalt ♦ *vt* (*coins*) prägen; **in ~ condition** neuwertig.

mint sauce *n* Minzsoße *f.*

minuet [mɪnju'et] *n* Menuett *nt.*

minus ['maɪnəs] *n* (*also:* **~ sign**) Minuszeichen *nt* ♦ *prep* minus, weniger; **~ 24°C** 24 Grad unter null.

minuscule ['mɪnəskjuːl] *adj* winzig.

minute¹ [maɪ'njuːt] *adj* winzig; (*search*)

peinlich genau; (*detail*) kleinste(r, s); **in ~ detail** in allen Einzelheiten.

minute² ['mɪnɪt] *n* Minute *f;* (*fig*) Augenblick *m,* Moment *m;* **minutes** *npl* (*of meeting*) Protokoll *nt;* **it is 5 ~s past 3** es ist 5 Minuten nach 3; **wait a ~!** einen Augenblick *or* Moment!; **up-to-the-~** (*news*) hochaktuell; (*technology*) allerneueste(r, s); **at the last ~** in letzter Minute.

minute book *n* Protokollbuch *nt.*

minute hand *n* Minutenzeiger *m.*

minutely [maɪ'njuːtlɪ] *adv* (*in detail*) genauestens; (*by a small amount*) ganz geringfügig.

minutiae [mɪ'njuːʃiː] *npl* Einzelheiten *pl.*

miracle ['mɪrəkl] *n* (*REL, fig*) Wunder *nt.*

miraculous [mɪ'rækjuləs] *adj* wunderbar; (*powers, effect, cure*) Wunder-; (*success, change*) unglaublich; **to have a ~ escape** wie durch ein Wunder entkommen.

mirage ['mɪrɑːʒ] *n* Fata Morgana *f;* (*fig*) Trugbild *nt.*

mire ['maɪə*] *n* Morast *m.*

mirror ['mɪrə*] *n* Spiegel *m* ♦ *vt* (*lit, fig*) widerspiegeln.

mirror image *n* Spiegelbild *nt.*

mirth [məːθ] *n* Heiterkeit *f.*

misadventure [mɪsəd'ventʃə*] *n* Missgeschick *nt;* **death by ~** (*BRIT*) Tod *m* durch Unfall.

misanthropist [mɪ'zænθrəpɪst] *n* Misanthrop *m,* Menschenfeind *m.*

misapply [mɪsə'plaɪ] *vt* (*term*) falsch verwenden; (*rule*) falsch anwenden.

misapprehension ['mɪsæprɪ'henʃən] *n* Missverständnis *nt;* **you are under a ~** Sie befinden sich im Irrtum.

misappropriate [mɪsə'prəuprɪeɪt] *vt* veruntreuen.

misappropriation ['mɪsəprəuprɪ'eɪʃən] *n* Veruntreuung *f.*

misbehave [mɪsbɪ'heɪv] *vi* sich schlecht benehmen.

misbehaviour, (*US*) **misbehavior** [mɪsbɪ'heɪvjə*] *n* schlechtes Benehmen *nt.*

misc. *abbr* = **miscellaneous.**

miscalculate [mɪs'kælkjuleɪt] *vt* falsch berechnen; (*misjudge*) falsch einschätzen.

miscalculation [mɪskælkju'leɪʃən] *n* Rechenfehler *m;* (*misjudgement*) Fehleinschätzung *f.*

miscarriage ['mɪskærɪdʒ] *n* (*MED*) Fehlgeburt *f;* **~ of justice** (*LAW*) Justizirrtum *m.*

miscarry [mɪs'kærɪ] *vi* (*MED*) eine Fehlgeburt haben; (*fail: plans*) fehlschlagen.

miscellaneous [mɪsɪ'leɪnɪəs] *adj* verschieden; (*subjects, items*) divers; **~ expenses** sonstige Unkosten *pl.*

mischance [mɪs'tʃɑːns] *n* unglücklicher Zufall *m.*

mischief ['mɪstʃɪf] *n* (*bad behaviour*) Unfug *m;* (*playfulness*) Verschmitztheit *f;* (*harm*)

Schaden *m*; (*pranks*) Streiche *pl*; **to get into** ~ etwas anstellen; **to do sb a** ~ jdm etwas antun.

mischievous ['mɪstʃɪvəs] *adj* (*naughty*) ungezogen; (*playful*) verschmitzt.

misconception ['mɪskən'sɛpʃən] *n* fälschliche Annahme *f*.

misconduct [mɪs'kɒndʌkt] *n* Fehlverhalten *nt*; **professional** ~ Berufsvergehen *nt*.

misconstrue [mɪskən'struː] *vt* missverstehen.

miscount [mɪs'kaunt] *vt* falsch zählen ♦ *vi* sich verzählen.

misdemeanour, (*US*) **misdemeanor** [mɪsdɪ'miːnə*] *n* Vergehen *nt*.

misdirect [mɪsdɪ'rɛkt] *vt* (*person*) in die falsche Richtung schicken; (*talent*) vergeuden.

miser ['maɪzə*] *n* Geizhals *m*.

miserable ['mɪzərəbl] *adj* (*unhappy*) unglücklich; (*wretched*) erbärmlich, elend; (*unpleasant: weather*) trostlos; (*: person*) gemein; (*contemptible: offer, donation*) armselig; (*: failure*) kläglich; **to feel** ~ sich elend fühlen.

miserably ['mɪzərəblɪ] *adv* (*fail*) kläglich; (*live*) elend; (*smile, speak*) unglücklich; (*small*) jämmerlich.

miserly ['maɪzəlɪ] *adj* geizig; (*amount*) armselig.

misery ['mɪzərɪ] *n* (*unhappiness*) Kummer *m*; (*wretchedness*) Elend *nt*; (*inf: person*) Miesepeter *m*.

misfire [mɪs'faɪə*] *vi* (*plan*) fehlschlagen; (*car engine*) fehlzünden.

misfit ['mɪsfɪt] *n* Außenseiter(in) *m(f)*.

misfortune [mɪs'fɔːtʃən] *n* Pech *nt*, Unglück *nt*.

misgiving [mɪs'gɪvɪŋ] *n* Bedenken *pl*; **to have** ~**s about sth** sich bei etw nicht wohl fühlen.

misguided [mɪs'gaɪdɪd] *adj* töricht; (*opinion, view*) irrig; (*misplaced*) unangebracht.

mishandle [mɪs'hændl] *vt* falsch handhaben.

mishap ['mɪshæp] *n* Missgeschick *nt*.

mishear [mɪs'hɪə*] (*irreg: like* **hear**) *vt* falsch hören ♦ *vi* sich verhören.

misheard [mɪs'hɜːd] *pt, pp of* **mishear**.

mishmash ['mɪʃmæʃ] (*inf*) *n* Mischmasch *m*.

misinform [mɪsɪn'fɔːm] *vt* falsch informieren.

misinterpret [mɪsɪn'tɜːprɪt] *vt* (*gesture, situation*) falsch auslegen; (*comment*) falsch auffassen.

misinterpretation ['mɪsɪntəːprɪ'teɪʃən] *n* falsche Auslegung *f*.

misjudge [mɪs'dʒʌdʒ] *vt* falsch einschätzen.

mislay [mɪs'leɪ] (*irreg: like* **lay**) *vt* verlegen.

mislead [mɪs'liːd] (*irreg: like* **lead**) *vt* irreführen.

misleading [mɪs'liːdɪŋ] *adj* irreführend.

misled [mɪs'lɛd] *pt, pp of* **mislead**.

mismanage [mɪs'mænɪdʒ] *vt* (*business*) herunterwirtschaften; (*institution*) schlecht führen.

mismanagement [mɪs'mænɪdʒmənt] *n* Misswirtschaft *f*.

misnomer [mɪs'nəumə*] *n* unzutreffende Bezeichnung *f*.

misogynist [mɪ'sɒdʒɪnɪst] *n* Frauenfeind *m*.

misplaced [mɪs'pleɪst] *adj* (*misguided*) unangebracht; (*wrongly positioned*) an der falschen Stelle.

misprint ['mɪsprɪnt] *n* Druckfehler *m*.

mispronounce [mɪsprə'nauns] *vt* falsch aussprechen.

misquote ['mɪs'kwəut] *vt* falsch zitieren.

misread [mɪs'riːd] (*irreg: like* **read**) *vt* falsch lesen; (*misinterpret*) falsch verstehen.

misrepresent [mɪsrɛprɪ'zɛnt] *vt* falsch darstellen; **he was** ~**ed** seine Worte wurden verfälscht wiedergegeben.

Miss [mɪs] *n* Fräulein *nt*; **Dear** ~ **Smith** Liebe Frau Smith.

miss [mɪs] *vt* (*train etc, chance, opportunity*) verpassen; (*target*) verfehlen; (*notice loss of, regret absence of*) vermissen; (*class, meeting*) fehlen bei ♦ *vi* danebentreffen; (*missile, object*) danebengehen ♦ *n* Fehltreffer *m*; **you can't** ~ **it** du kannst es nicht verfehlen; **the bus just** ~**ed the wall** der Bus wäre um ein Haar gegen die Mauer gefahren; **you're** ~**ing the point** das geht an der Sache vorbei.

▶ **miss out** (*BRIT*) *vt* auslassen.

▶ **miss out on** *vt fus* (*party*) verpassen; (*fun*) zu kurz kommen bei.

missal ['mɪsl] *n* Messbuch *nt*.

misshapen [mɪs'ʃeɪpən] *adj* missgebildet.

missile ['mɪsaɪl] *n* (*MIL*) Rakete *f*; (*object thrown*) (Wurf)geschoss *nt*, (Wurf)geschoß *nt* (*ÖSTERR*).

missile base *n* Raketenbasis *f*.

missile launcher [-'lɔːntʃə*] *n* Startrampe *f*.

missing ['mɪsɪŋ] *adj* (*lost: person*) vermisst; (*: object*) verschwunden; (*absent, removed*) fehlend; **to be** ~ fehlen; **to go** ~ verschwinden; ~ **person** Vermisste(r) *f(m)*.

mission ['mɪʃən] *n* (*task*) Mission *f*, Auftrag *m*; (*representatives*) Gesandtschaft *f*; (*MIL*) Einsatz *m*; (*REL*) Mission *f*; **on a** ~ **to ...** (*to place/people*) im Einsatz in +*dat*/bei ...

missionary ['mɪʃənrɪ] *n* Missionar(in) *m(f)*.

missive ['mɪsɪv] (*form*) *n* Schreiben *nt*.

misspell ['mɪs'spɛl] (*irreg: like* **spell**) *vt* falsch schreiben.

misspent ['mɪs'spɛnt] *adj* (*youth*) vergeudet.

mist [mɪst] *n* Nebel *m*; (*light*) Dunst *m* ♦ *vi* (*also:* ~ **over**: *eyes*) sich verschleiern; (*BRIT: also:* ~ **over**, ~ **up**) (*windows*) beschlagen.

mistake [mɪs'teɪk] (*irreg: like* **take**) *n* Fehler *m* ♦ *vt* sich irren in +*dat*; (*intentions*) falsch verstehen; **by** ~ aus Versehen; **to make a** ~ (*in writing, calculation*) sich vertun; **to make a** ~ (**about sb/sth**) sich (in jdm/etw) irren; **to** ~ **A for B** A mit B verwechseln.

mistaken [mɪs'teɪkən] *pp of* **mistake** ♦ *adj*

falsch; **to be** ~ sich irren.
mistaken identity n Verwechslung f.
mistakenly [mɪs'teɪkənlɪ] adv
irrtümlicherweise.
mister ['mɪstə*] (inf) n (sir) not translated; see
Mr.
mistletoe ['mɪsltəu] n Mistel f.
mistook [mɪs'tuk] pt of **mistake**.
mistranslation [mɪstræns'leɪʃən] n falsche
Übersetzung f.
mistreat [mɪs'triːt] vt schlecht behandeln.
mistress ['mɪstrɪs] n (lover) Geliebte f; (of
house, servant, situation) Herrin f; (BRIT:
teacher) Lehrerin f.
mistrust [mɪs'trʌst] vt misstrauen +dat ♦ n:
~ (of) Misstrauen nt (gegenüber).
mistrustful [mɪs'trʌstful] adj: ~ (of)
misstrauisch (gegenüber).
misty ['mɪstɪ] adj (day etc) neblig; (glasses,
windows) beschlagen.
misty-eyed ['mɪstɪ'aɪd] adj mit
verschleiertem Blick.
misunderstand [mɪsʌndə'stænd] (irreg: like
understand) vt missverstehen, falsch
verstehen ♦ vi es falsch verstehen.
misunderstanding ['mɪsʌndə'stændɪŋ] n
Missverständnis nt; (disagreement)
Meinungsverschiedenheit f.
misunderstood [mɪsʌndə'stud] pt, pp of
misunderstand.
misuse [n mɪs'juːs, vt mɪs'juːz] n Missbrauch m
♦ vt missbrauchen; (word) falsch
gebrauchen.
MIT (US) n abbr (= Massachusetts Institute of
Technology) private technische
Fachhochschule.
mite [maɪt] n (small quantity) bisschen nt;
(BRIT: small child) Würmchen nt.
miter ['maɪtə*] (US) n = **mitre**.
mitigate ['mɪtɪgeɪt] vt mildern; **mitigating
circumstances** mildernde Umstände pl.
mitigation [mɪtɪ'geɪʃən] n Milderung f.
mitre, (US) **miter** ['maɪtə*] n (of bishop) Mitra
f; (CARPENTRY) Gehrung f.
mitt(en) ['mɪt(n)] n Fausthandschuh m.
mix [mɪks] vt mischen; (drink) mixen; (sauce,
cake) zubereiten; (ingredients) verrühren
♦ vi: to ~ (with) verkehren (mit) ♦ n
Mischung f; to ~ sth with sth etw mit etw
vermischen; to ~ business with pleasure
das Angenehme mit dem Nützlichen
verbinden; cake ~ Backmischung f.
► **mix in** vt (eggs etc) unterrühren.
► **mix up** vt (people) verwechseln; (things)
durcheinander bringen; **to be** ~**ed up in sth**
in etw acc verwickelt sein.
mixed [mɪkst] adj gemischt; ~ **marriage**
Mischehe f.
mixed-ability ['mɪkstə'bɪlɪtɪ] adj (group etc)
mit unterschiedlichen Fähigkeiten.
mixed bag n (of things, problems)
Sammelsurium nt; (of people) gemischter

Haufen m.
mixed blessing n: **it's a** ~ das ist ein
zweischneidiges Schwert.
mixed doubles npl gemischtes Doppel nt.
mixed economy n gemischte
Wirtschaftsform f.
mixed grill (BRIT) n Grillteller m.
mixed-up [mɪkst'ʌp] adj durcheinander.
mixer ['mɪksə*] n (for food) Mixer m; (drink)
Tonic etc zum Auffüllen von alkoholischen
Mixgetränken; **to be a good** ~ (sociable
person) kontaktfreudig sein.
mixer tap n Mischbatterie f.
mixture ['mɪkstʃə*] n Mischung f; (CULIN)
Gemisch nt; (: for cake) Teig m; (MED)
Mixtur f.
mix-up ['mɪksʌp] n Durcheinander nt.
MK (BRIT) abbr (TECH) = **mark**.
mkt abbr = **market**.
MLA (BRIT) n abbr (POL: = Member of the
Legislative Assembly) Abgeordnete(r) f(m)
der gesetzgebenden Versammlung.
MLitt n abbr (= Master of Literature, Master of
Letters) akademischer Grad in
Literaturwissenschaft.
MLR (BRIT) n abbr = **minimum lending rate**.
mm abbr (= millimetre) mm.
MN abbr (BRIT) = **merchant navy**; (US: POST:
= Minnesota).
MO n abbr (= medical officer) Sanitätsoffizier m;
(US: inf) = **modus operandi**.
moan [məun] n Stöhnen nt ♦ vi stöhnen; (inf:
complain): **to** ~ (**about**) meckern (über +acc).
moaner ['məunə*] (inf) n Miesmacher(in) m(f).
moat [məut] n Wassergraben m.
mob [mɔb] n Mob m; (organized) Bande f ♦ vt
herfallen über +acc.
mobile ['məubaɪl] adj beweglich; (workforce,
society) mobil ♦ n (decoration) Mobile nt;
applicants must be ~ Bewerber müssen
motorisiert sein.
mobile home n Wohnwagen m.
mobile phone n Funktelefon nt.
mobility [məu'bɪlɪtɪ] n Beweglichkeit f; (of
workforce etc) Mobilität f.
mobility allowance n Beihilfe für
Gehbehinderte.
mobilize ['məubɪlaɪz] vt mobilisieren; (MIL)
mobil machen ♦ vi (MIL) mobil machen.
moccasin ['mɔkəsɪn] n Mokassin m.
mock [mɔk] vt sich lustig machen über +acc
♦ adj (fake: Elizabethan etc) Pseudo-; (exam)
Probe-; (battle) Schein-.
mockery ['mɔkərɪ] n Spott m; **to make a** ~ **of**
sb jdn zum Gespött machen; **to make a** ~ **of**
sth etw zur Farce machen.
mocking ['mɔkɪŋ] adj spöttisch.
mockingbird ['mɔkɪŋbəːd] n Spottdrossel f.
mock-up ['mɔkʌp] n Modell nt.
MOD (BRIT) n abbr = **Ministry of Defence**.
mod cons ['mɔd'kɔnz] (BRIT) npl abbr
(= modern conveniences) Komfort m.

mode [məud] n Form f; (COMPUT, TECH)
Betriebsart f; ~ **of life** Lebensweise f; ~ **of
transport** Transportmittel nt.

model ['mɔdl] n Modell nt; (fashion model)
Mannequin nt; (example) Muster nt ♦ adj
(excellent) vorbildlich; (small scale: railway
etc) Modell- ♦ vt (clothes) vorführen; (with
clay etc) modellieren, formen ♦ vi (for
designer, photographer etc) als Modell
arbeiten; **to ~ o.s. on sb** sich dat jdn zum
Vorbild nehmen.

modeller, (US) **modeler** ['mɔdlə*] n
Modellbauer m.

model railway n Modelleisenbahn f.

modem ['məudɛm] n Modem nt.

moderate [adj 'mɔdərət, vb 'mɔdəreit] adj
gemäßigt; (amount) nicht allzu groß;
(change) leicht ♦ n Gemäßigte(r) f(m) ♦ vi
(storm, wind etc) nachlassen ♦ vt (tone,
demands) mäßigen.

moderately ['mɔdərətlɪ] adv mäßig;
(expensive, difficult) nicht allzu; (pleased,
happy) einigermaßen; ~ **priced** nicht allzu
teuer.

moderation [mɔdə'reɪʃən] n Mäßigung f; **in ~**
in or mit Maßen.

moderator ['mɔdəreitə*] n (ECCL)
Synodalpräsident m.

modern ['mɔdən] adj modern; ~ **languages**
moderne Fremdsprachen pl.

modernization [mɔdənaɪ'zeɪʃən] n
Modernisierung f.

modernize ['mɔdənaɪz] vt modernisieren.

modest ['mɔdɪst] adj bescheiden; (chaste)
schamhaft.

modestly ['mɔdɪstlɪ] adv bescheiden; (behave)
schamhaft; (to a moderate extent) mäßig.

modesty ['mɔdɪstɪ] n Bescheidenheit f;
(chastity) Schamgefühl nt.

modicum ['mɔdɪkəm] n: **a ~ of** ein wenig or
bisschen.

modification [mɔdɪfɪ'keɪʃən] n Änderung f; (to
policy etc) Modifizierung f; **to make ~s to**
(Ver)änderungen vornehmen an +dat,
modifizieren.

modify ['mɔdɪfaɪ] vt (ver)ändern; (policy etc)
modifizieren.

modish ['məudɪʃ] adj (fashionable) modisch.

Mods [mɔdz] (BRIT) n abbr (SCOL: = Honour)
Moderations) akademische Prüfung an der
Universität Oxford.

modular ['mɔdjulə*] adj (unit, furniture) aus
Bauelementen (zusammengesetzt);
(COMPUT) modular.

modulate ['mɔdjuleit] vt modulieren; (process,
activity) umwandeln.

modulation [mɔdju'leɪʃən] n Modulation f;
(modification) Veränderung f.

module ['mɔdju:l] n (Bau)element nt; (SPACE)
Raumkapsel f; (SCOL) Kurs m.

modus operandi ['məudəsɔpə'rændi:] n
Modus Operandi m.

Mogadishu [mɔgə'dɪʃu:] n Mogadischu nt.

mogul ['məugl] n (fig) Mogul m.

MOH (BRIT) n abbr (= Medical Officer of Health)
Amtsarzt m, Amtsärztin f.

mohair ['məuhɛə*] n Mohair m, Mohär m.

Mohammed [mə'hæmɛd] n Mohammed m.

moist [mɔɪst] adj feucht.

moisten ['mɔɪsn] vt anfeuchten.

moisture ['mɔɪstʃə*] n Feuchtigkeit f.

moisturize ['mɔɪstʃəraɪz] vt (skin) mit einer
Feuchtigkeitscreme behandeln.

moisturizer ['mɔɪstʃəraɪzə*] n
Feuchtigkeitscreme f.

molar ['məulə*] n Backenzahn m.

molasses [mə'læsɪz] n Melasse f.

mold etc [məuld] (US) n, vt = **mould** etc.

Moldavia [mɔl'deɪvɪə] n Moldawien nt.

Moldavian [mɔl'deɪvɪən] adj moldawisch.

Moldova [mɔl'dəuvə] n Moldawien nt.

Moldovan adj moldawisch.

mole [məul] n (on skin) Leberfleck m; (ZOOL)
Maulwurf m; (fig: spy) Spion(in) m(f).

molecular [məu'lɛkjulə*] adj molekular;
(biology) Molekular-.

molecule ['mɔlɪkju:l] n Molekül nt.

molehill ['məulhɪl] n Maulwurfshaufen m.

molest [mə'lɛst] vt (assault sexually) sich
vergehen an +dat; (harass) belästigen.

mollusc ['mɔləsk] n Weichtier m.

mollycoddle ['mɔlɪkɔdl] vt verhätscheln.

Molotov cocktail ['mɔlətɔf-] n
Molotowcocktail m.

molt [məult] (US) vi = **moult**.

molten ['məultən] adj geschmolzen, flüssig.

mom [mɔm] (US) n = **mum**.

moment ['məumənt] n Moment m, Augenblick
m; (importance) Bedeutung f; **for a ~** (für)
einen Moment or Augenblick; **at that ~** in
diesem Moment or Augenblick; **at the ~**
momentan; **for the ~** vorläufig; **in a ~**
gleich; **"one ~ please"** (TEL) „bleiben Sie
am Apparat".

momentarily ['məuməntrɪlɪ] adv für einen
Augenblick or Moment; (US: very soon)
jeden Augenblick or Moment.

momentary ['məuməntərɪ] adj (brief) kurz.

momentous [məu'mɛntəs] adj (occasion)
bedeutsam; (decision) von großer
Tragweite.

momentum [məu'mɛntəm] n (PHYS) Impuls
m; (fig: of movement) Schwung m; (: of events,
change) Dynamik f; **to gather ~** schneller
werden; (fig) richtig in Gang kommen.

mommy ['mɔmɪ] (US) n = **mummy**.

Mon. abbr (= Monday) Mo.

Monaco ['mɔnəkəu] n Monaco nt.

monarch ['mɔnək] n Monarch(in) m(f).

monarchist ['mɔnəkɪst] n Monarchist(in) m(f).

monarchy ['mɔnəkɪ] n Monarchie f; **the M~**
(royal family) die königliche Familie.

monastery ['mɔnəstərɪ] n Kloster nt.

monastic [mə'næstɪk] adj Kloster-,

klösterlich; *(fig)* mönchisch, klösterlich einfach.

Monday ['mʌndɪ] *n* Montag *m*; *see also* Tuesday.

Monegasque [mɔnə'gæsk] *adj* monegassisch ♦ *n* Monegasse *m*, Monegassin *f*.

monetarist ['mʌnɪtərɪst] *n* Monetarist(in) *m(f)* ♦ *adj* monetaristisch.

monetary ['mʌnɪtərɪ] *adj* (*system, union*) Währungs-.

money ['mʌnɪ] *n* Geld *nt*; **to make** ~ (*person*) Geld verdienen; (*business*) etwas einbringen; **danger** ~ (*BRIT*) Gefahrenzulage *f*; **I've got no** ~ **left** ich habe kein Geld mehr.

moneyed ['mʌnɪd] (*form*) *adj* begütert.

moneylender ['mʌnɪlendə*] *n* Geldverleiher(in) *m(f)*.

moneymaker ['mʌnɪmeɪkə*] *n* (*person*) Finanzgenie *nt*; (*idea*) einträgliche Sache *f*; (*product*) Verkaufserfolg *m*.

moneymaking ['mʌnɪmeɪkɪŋ] *adj* einträglich.

money market *n* Geldmarkt *m*.

money order *n* Zahlungsanweisung *f*.

money-spinner ['mʌnɪspɪnə*] (*inf*) *n* Verkaufsschlager *m*; (*person, business*) Goldgrube *f*.

money supply *n* Geldvolumen *nt*.

Mongol ['mɔŋgəl] *n* Mongole *m*, Mongolin *f*; (*LING*) Mongolisch *nt*.

mongol ['mɔŋgəl] (*offensive*) *n* Mongoloide(r) *f(m)*.

Mongolia [mɔŋ'gəulɪə] *n* die Mongolei.

Mongolian [mɔŋ'gəulɪən] *adj* mongolisch ♦ *n* Mongole *m*, Mongolin *f*; (*LING*) Mongolisch *nt*.

mongoose ['mɔŋguːs] *n* Mungo *m*.

mongrel ['mʌŋgrəl] *n* Promenadenmischung *f*.

monitor ['mɔnɪtə*] *n* Monitor *m* ♦ *vt* überwachen; (*broadcasts*) mithören.

monk [mʌŋk] *n* Mönch *m*.

monkey ['mʌŋkɪ] *n* Affe *m*.

monkey business (*inf*) *n* faule Sachen *pl*.

monkey nut (*BRIT*) *n* Erdnuss *f*.

monkey tricks *npl* = **monkey business.**

monkey wrench *n* verstellbarer Schraubenschlüssel *m*.

mono ['mɔnəu] *adj* (*recording etc*) Mono-.

monochrome ['mɔnəkrəum] *adj* (*photograph, television*) Schwarzweiß-; (*COMPUT: screen*) Monochrom-.

monogamous [mə'nɔgəməs] *adj* monogam.

monogamy [mə'nɔgəmɪ] *n* Monogamie *f*.

monogram ['mɔnəgræm] *n* Monogramm *nt*.

monolith ['mɔnəlɪθ] *n* Monolith *m*.

monolithic [mɔnə'lɪθɪk] *adj* monolithisch.

monologue ['mɔnəlɔg] *n* Monolog *m*.

monoplane ['mɔnəpleɪn] *n* Eindecker *m*.

monopolize [mə'nɔpəlaɪz] *vt* beherrschen; (*person*) mit Beschlag belegen; (*conversation*) an sich *acc* reißen.

monopoly [mə'nɔpəlɪ] *n* Monopol *nt*; **to have a** ~ **on** *or* **of sth** (*fig: domination*) etw für sich gepachtet haben; **Monopolies and Mergers Commission** (*BRIT*) ≈ Kartellamt *nt*.

monorail ['mɔnəureɪl] *n* Einschienenbahn *f*.

monosodium glutamate [mɔnə'səudɪəm'gluːtəmeɪt] *n* Glutamat *nt*.

monosyllabic [mɔnəsɪ'læbɪk] *adj* einsilbig.

monosyllable ['mɔnəsɪləbl] *n* einsilbiges Wort *nt*.

monotone ['mɔnətəun] *n*: **in a** ~ monoton.

monotonous [mə'nɔtənəs] *adj* monoton, eintönig.

monotony [mə'nɔtənɪ] *n* Monotonie *f*, Eintönigkeit *f*.

monsoon [mɔn'suːn] *n* Monsun *m*.

monster ['mɔnstə*] *n* Ungetüm *nt*, Monstrum *nt*; (*imaginary creature*) Ungeheuer *nt*, Monster *nt*; (*person*) Unmensch *m*.

monstrosity [mɔn'strɔsɪtɪ] *n* Ungetüm *nt*, Monstrum *nt*.

monstrous ['mɔnstrəs] *adj* (*huge*) riesig; (*ugly*) abscheulich; (*atrocious*) ungeheuerlich.

Mont. (*US*) *abbr* (*POST: = Montana*).

montage [mɔn'taːʒ] *n* Montage *f*.

Mont Blanc [mɔ̃ blɑ̃] *n* Montblanc *m*.

month [mʌnθ] *n* Monat *m*; **every** ~ jeden Monat; **300 dollars a** ~ 300 Dollar im Monat.

monthly ['mʌnθlɪ] *adj* monatlich; (*ticket, magazine*) Monats- ♦ *adv* monatlich; **twice** ~ zweimal im Monat.

Montreal [mɔntrɪ'ɔːl] *n* Montreal *nt*.

monument ['mɔnjumənt] *n* Denkmal *nt*.

monumental [mɔnju'mentl] *adj* (*building, statue*) gewaltig, monumental; (*book, piece of work*) unsterblich; (*storm, row*) ungeheuer.

moo [muː] *vi* muhen.

mood [muːd] *n* Stimmung *f*; (*of person*) Laune *f*, Stimmung *f*; **to be in a good/bad** ~ gut/ schlecht gelaunt sein; **to be in the** ~ **for** aufgelegt sein zu.

moodily ['muːdɪlɪ] *adv* launisch; (*sullenly*) schlecht gelaunt.

moody ['muːdɪ] *adj* launisch; (*sullen*) schlecht gelaunt.

moon [muːn] *n* Mond *m*.

moonlight ['muːnlaɪt] *n* Mondschein *m* ♦ *vi* (*inf*) schwarzarbeiten.

moonlighting ['muːnlaɪtɪŋ] (*inf*) *n* Schwarzarbeit *f*.

moonlit ['muːnlɪt] *adj* (*night*) mondhell.

moonshot ['muːnʃɔt] *n* Mondflug *m*.

moor [muə*] *n* (Hoch)moor *nt*, Heide *f* ♦ *vt* vertäuen ♦ *vi* anlegen.

mooring ['muərɪŋ] *n* Anlegeplatz *m*; **moorings** *npl* (*chains*) Verankerung *f*.

Moorish ['muərɪʃ] *adj* maurisch.

moorland ['muələnd] *n* Moorlandschaft *f*, Heidelandschaft *f*.

moose [muːs] *n inv* Elch *m*.

moot [muːt] *vt*: **to be** ~**ed** vorgeschlagen werden ♦ *adj*: **it's a** ~ **point** das ist fraglich.

mop [mɔp] *n* (*for floor*) Mop *m*; (*for dishes*)

Spülbürste *f*; (*of hair*) Mähne *f* ♦ *vt* (*floor*) wischen; (*face*) abwischen; (*eyes*) sich *dat* wischen; **to ~ the sweat from one's brow** sich *dat* den Schweiß von der Stirn wischen.
▶ **mop up** *vt* aufwischen.
mope [məup] *vi* Trübsal blasen.
▶ **mope about** *vi* mit einer Jammermiene herumlaufen.
▶ **mope around** *vi* = mope about.
moped ['məupɛd] *n* Moped *nt*.
moquette [mɔ'ket] *n* Mokett *m*.
MOR *adj abbr* (*MUS*) = **middle-of-the-road**.
moral ['mɔrl] *adj* moralisch; (*welfare, values*) sittlich; (*behaviour*) moralisch einwandfrei ♦ *n* Moral *f*; **morals** *npl* (*principles, values*) Moralvorstellungen *pl*; **~ support** moralische Unterstützung *f*.
morale [mɔ'rɑːl] *n* Moral *f*.
morality [mɔ'rælɪtɪ] *n* Sittlichkeit *f*; (*system of morals*) Moral *f*, Ethik *f*; (*correctness*) moralische Richtigkeit *f*.
moralize ['mɔrəlaɪz] *vi* moralisieren; **to ~ about** sich moralisch entrüsten über +*acc*.
morally ['mɔrəlɪ] *adv* moralisch; (*live, behave*) moralisch einwandfrei.
moral victory *n* moralischer Sieg *m*.
morass [mə'ræs] *n* Morast *m*, Sumpf *m* (*also fig*).
moratorium [mɔrə'tɔːrɪəm] *n* Stopp *m*; Moratorium *nt*.
morbid ['mɔːbɪd] *adj* (*imagination*) krankhaft; (*interest*) unnatürlich; (*comments, behaviour*) makaber.

========================= *KEYWORD*

more [mɔː*] *adj* **1** (*greater in number etc*) mehr; **~ people/work/letters than we expected** mehr Leute/Arbeit/Briefe, als wir erwarteten; **I have ~ wine/money than you** ich habe mehr Wein/Geld als du.
2 (*additional*): **do you want (some) ~ tea?** möchten Sie noch mehr Tee?; **is there any ~ wine?** ist noch Wein da?; **I have no ~ money, I don't have any ~ money** ich habe kein Geld mehr
♦ *pron* **1** (*greater amount*) mehr; **~ than 10** mehr als 10; **it cost ~ than we expected** es kostete mehr, als wir erwarteten.
2 (*further or additional amount*): **is there any ~?** gibt es noch mehr?; **there's no ~** es ist nichts mehr da; **many/much ~** viel mehr
♦ *adv* mehr; **~ dangerous/difficult/easily** *etc* **(than)** gefährlicher/schwerer/leichter *etc* (als); **~ and ~** mehr und mehr, immer mehr; **~ and ~ excited/expensive** immer aufgeregter/teurer; **~ or less** mehr oder weniger; **~ than ever** mehr denn je, mehr als jemals zuvor; **~ beautiful than ever** schöner denn je; **no ~, not any ~** nicht mehr.

moreover [mɔː'rəuvə*] *adv* außerdem, zudem.

morgue [mɔːg] *n* Leichenschauhaus *nt*.
MORI ['mɔːrɪ] (*BRIT*) *n abbr* (= *Market and Opinion Research Institute*) *Markt- und Meinungsforschungsinstitut.*
moribund ['mɔrɪbʌnd] *adj* dem Untergang geweiht.
Mormon ['mɔːmən] *n* Mormone *m*, Mormonin *f*.
morning ['mɔːnɪŋ] *n* Morgen *m*; (*as opposed to afternoon*) Vormittag *m* ♦ *cpd* Morgen-; **in the ~** morgens; vormittags; (*tomorrow*) morgen früh; **7 o'clock in the ~** 7 Uhr morgens; **this ~** heute Morgen.
morning-after pill ['mɔːnɪŋ'ɑːftə-] *n* Pille *f* danach.
morning sickness *n* (Schwangerschafts)-übelkeit *f*.
Moroccan [mə'rɔkən] *adj* marokkanisch ♦ *n* Marokkaner(in) *m(f)*.
Morocco [mə'rɔkəu] *n* Marokko *nt*.
moron ['mɔːrɔn] (*inf*) *n* Schwachkopf *m*.
moronic [mə'rɔnɪk] (*inf*) *adj* schwachsinnig.
morose [mə'rəus] *adj* missmutig.
morphine ['mɔːfiːn] *n* Morphium *nt*.
morris dancing ['mɔrɪs-] *n* Moriskentanz *m*, *alter englischer Volkstanz.*
Morse [mɔːs] *n* (*also:* **~ code**) Morsealphabet *nt*.
morsel ['mɔːsl] *n* Stückchen *nt*.
mortal ['mɔːtl] *adj* sterblich; (*wound, combat*) tödlich; (*danger*) Todes-; (*sin, enemy*) Tod- ♦ *n* (*human being*) Sterbliche(r) *f(m)*.
mortality [mɔː'tælɪtɪ] *n* Sterblichkeit *f*; (*number of deaths*) Todesfälle *pl*.
mortality rate *n* Sterblichkeitsziffer *f*.
mortar ['mɔːtə*] *n* (*MIL*) Minenwerfer *m*; (*CONSTR*) Mörtel *m*; (*CULIN*) Mörser *m*.
mortgage ['mɔːgɪdʒ] *n* Hypothek *f* ♦ *vt* mit einer Hypothek belasten; **to take out a ~** eine Hypothek aufnehmen.
mortgage company (*US*) *n* Hypotheken-bank *f*.
mortgagee [mɔːgə'dʒiː] *n* Hypotheken-gläubiger *m*.
mortgagor ['mɔːgədʒə*] *n* Hypotheken-schuldner *m*.
mortician [mɔː'tɪʃən] (*US*) *n* Bestattungs-unternehmer *m*.
mortified ['mɔːtɪfaɪd] *adj*: **he was ~** er empfand das als beschämend; (*embarrassed*) es war ihm schrecklich peinlich.
mortify ['mɔːtɪfaɪ] *vt* beschämen.
mortise lock ['mɔːtɪs-] *n* Einsteckschloss *nt*.
mortuary ['mɔːtjuərɪ] *n* Leichenhalle *f*.
mosaic [məu'zeɪɪk] *n* Mosaik *nt*.
Moscow ['mɔskəu] *n* Moskau *nt*.
Moslem ['mɔzləm] *adj*, *n* = **Muslim**.
mosque [mɔsk] *n* Moschee *f*.
mosquito [mɔs'kiːtəu] (*pl* **~es**) *n* Stechmücke *f*; (*in tropics*) Moskito *m*.
mosquito net *n* Moskitonetz *nt*.
moss [mɔs] *n* Moos *nt*.

mossy ['mɒsɪ] *adj* bemoost.

most [məust] *adj* **1** (*almost all: people, things etc*) meiste(r, s); ~ **people** die meisten Leute.

2 (*largest, greatest: interest, money etc*) meiste(r, s); **who has (the)** ~ **money?** wer hat das meiste Geld?

♦ *pron* (*greatest quantity, number*) der/die/das meiste; ~ **of it** das meiste (davon); ~ **of them** die meisten von ihnen; ~ **of the time/ work** die meiste Zeit/Arbeit; ~ **of the time he's very helpful** er ist meistens sehr hilfsbereit; **to make the** ~ **of sth** das Beste aus etw machen; **at the (very)** ~ (aller)höchstens

♦ *adv* (+ *vb: spend, eat, work etc*) am meisten; (+ *adj*): **the** ~ **intelligent/expensive** *etc* der/ die/das intelligenteste/teuerste ... *etc*; (+ *adv: carefully, easily etc*) äußerst; (*very: polite, interesting etc*) höchst; **a** ~ **interesting book** ein höchst interessantes Buch.

mostly ['məustlɪ] *adv* (*chiefly*) hauptsächlich; (*usually*) meistens.

MOT (*BRIT*) *n abbr* (= *Ministry of Transport*): ~ **(test)** ≈ TÜV *m*; **the car failed its** ~ das Auto ist nicht durch den TÜV gekommen.

motel [məu'tɛl] *n* Motel *nt*.

moth [mɒθ] *n* Nachtfalter *m*; (*clothes moth*) Motte *f*.

mothball ['mɒθbɔːl] *n* Mottenkugel *f*.

moth-eaten ['mɒθiːtn] (*pej*) *adj* mottenzerfressen.

mother ['mʌðə*] *n* Mutter *f* ♦ *adj* (*country*) Heimat-; (*company*) Mutter- ♦ *vt* großziehen; (*pamper, protect*) bemuttern.

motherboard ['mʌðəbɔːd] *n* (*COMPUT*) Hauptplatine *f*.

motherhood ['mʌðəhud] *n* Mutterschaft *f*.

mother-in-law ['mʌðərɪnlɔː] *n* Schwiegermutter *f*.

motherly ['mʌðəlɪ] *adj* mütterlich.

mother-of-pearl ['mʌðərəv'pɜːl] *n* Perlmutt *nt*.

mother's help *n* Haushaltshilfe *f*.

mother-to-be ['mʌðətə'biː] *n* werdende Mutter *f*.

mother tongue *n* Muttersprache *f*.

mothproof ['mɒθpruːf] *adj* mottenfest.

motif [məu'tiːf] *n* Motiv *nt*.

motion ['məuʃən] *n* Bewegung *f*; (*proposal*) Antrag *m*; (*BRIT: also: bowel* ~) Stuhlgang *m* ♦ *vt, vi*: **to** ~ **(to) sb to do sth** jdm ein Zeichen geben, dass er/sie etw tun solle; **to be in** ~ (*vehicle*) fahren; **to set in** ~ in Gang bringen; **to go through the** ~**s (of doing sth)** (*fig*) etw der Form halber tun; (*pretend*) so tun, als ob (man etw täte).

motionless ['məuʃənlɪs] *adj* reg(ungs)los.

motion picture *n* Film *m*.

motivate ['məutɪveɪt] *vt* motivieren.

motivated ['məutɪveɪtɪd] *adj* motiviert; ~ **by** getrieben von.

motivation [məutɪ'veɪʃən] *n* Motivation *f*.

motive ['məutɪv] *n* Motiv *nt*, Beweggrund *m* ♦ *adj* (*power, force*) Antriebs-; **from the best (of)** ~**s** mit den besten Absichten.

motley ['mɒtlɪ] *adj* bunt (gemischt).

motor ['məutə*] *n* Motor *m*; (*BRIT: inf: car*) Auto *nt* ♦ *cpd* (*industry, trade*) Auto(mobil)-.

motorbike ['məutəbaɪk] *n* Motorrad *nt*.

motorboat ['məutəbəut] *n* Motorboot *nt*.

motorcade ['məutəkeɪd] *n* Fahrzeugkolonne *f*.

motorcar ['məutəkɑː] (*BRIT*) *n* (Personenkraft)wagen *m*.

motorcoach ['məutəkəutʃ] (*BRIT*) *n* Reisebus *m*.

motorcycle ['məutəsaɪkl] *n* Motorrad *nt*.

motorcycle racing *n* Motorradrennen *nt*.

motorcyclist ['məutəsaɪklɪst] *n* Motorradfahrer(in) *m(f)*.

motoring ['məutərɪŋ] (*BRIT*) *n* Autofahren *nt* ♦ *cpd* Auto-; (*offence, accident*) Verkehrs-.

motorist ['məutərɪst] *n* Autofahrer(in) *m(f)*.

motorized ['məutəraɪzd] *adj* motorisiert.

motor oil *n* Motorenöl *nt*.

motor racing (*BRIT*) *n* Autorennen *nt*.

motor scooter *n* Motorroller *m*.

motor vehicle *n* Kraftfahrzeug *nt*.

motorway ['məutəweɪ] (*BRIT*) *n* Autobahn *f*.

mottled ['mɒtld] *adj* gesprenkelt.

motto ['mɒtəu] (*pl* ~**es**) *n* Motto *nt*.

mould, (*US*) **mold** [məuld] *n* (*cast*) Form *f*; (: *for metal*) Gussform *f*; (*mildew*) Schimmel *m* ♦ *vt* (*lit, fig*) formen.

moulder ['məuldə*] *vi* (*decay*) vermodern.

moulding ['məuldɪŋ] *n* (*ARCHIT*) Zierleiste *f*.

mouldy ['məuldɪ] *adj* schimmelig; (*smell*) moderig.

moult, (*US*) **molt** [məult] *vi* (*animal*) sich haaren; (*bird*) sich mausern.

mound [maund] *n* (*of earth*) Hügel *m*; (*heap*) Haufen *m*.

mount [maunt] *n* (*in proper names*): **M~ Carmel** der Berg Karmel; (*horse*) Pferd *nt*; (*for picture*) Passepartout *nt* ♦ *vt* (*horse*) besteigen; (*exhibition etc*) vorbereiten; (*jewel*) (ein)fassen; (*picture*) mit einem Passepartout versehen; (*staircase*) hochgehen; (*stamp*) aufkleben; (*attack, campaign*) organisieren ♦ *vi* (*increase*) steigen; (: *problems*) sich häufen; (*on horse*) aufsitzen.

► **mount up** *vi* (*costs, savings*) sich summieren, sich zusammenläppern (*inf*).

mountain ['mauntɪn] *n* Berg *m* ♦ *cpd* (*road, stream*) Gebirgs-; **to make a** ~ **out of a molehill** aus einer Mücke einen Elefanten machen.

mountain bike *n* Mountainbike *nt*.

mountaineer [mauntɪ'nɪə*] *n* Bergsteiger(in) *m(f)*.

mountaineering [maʊntɪ'nɪərɪŋ] *n*
Bergsteigen *nt*; **to go ~** bergsteigen gehen.
mountainous ['maʊntɪnəs] *adj* gebirgig.
mountain range *n* Gebirgskette *f*.
mountain rescue team *n* Bergwacht *f*.
mountainside ['maʊntɪnsaɪd] *n* (Berg)hang *m*.
mounted ['maʊntɪd] *adj* (*police etc*) beritten.
Mount Everest *n* Mount Everest *m*.
mourn [mɔːn] *vt* betrauern ♦ *vi*: **to ~ (for)**
trauern (um).
mourner ['mɔːnə*] *n* Trauernde(r) *f(m)*.
mournful ['mɔːnfʊl] *adj* traurig.
mourning ['mɔːnɪŋ] *n* Trauer *f*; **to be in ~**
trauern; (*wear special clothes*) Trauer tragen.
mouse [maʊs] (*pl* **mice**) *n* (*ZOOL, COMPUT*)
Maus *f*; (*fig: person*) schüchternes Mäuschen
nt.
mousetrap ['maʊstræp] *n* Mausefalle *f*.
moussaka [mu'saːkə] *n* Moussaka *f*.
mousse [muːs] *n* (*CULIN*) Mousse *f*; (*cosmetic*)
Schaumstiger *m*.
moustache, (*US*) **mustache** [məs'taːʃ] *n*
Schnurrbart *m*.
mousy ['maʊsɪ] *adj* (*hair*) mausgrau.
mouth [maʊθ] (*pl* **~s**) *n* Mund *m*; (*of cave, hole,
bottle*) Öffnung *f*; (*of river*) Mündung *f*.
mouthful ['maʊθfʊl] *n* (*of food*) Bissen *m*; (*of
drink*) Schluck *m*.
mouth organ *n* Mundharmonika *f*.
mouthpiece ['maʊθpiːs] *n* Mundstück *nt*;
(*spokesman*) Sprachrohr *nt*.
mouth-to-mouth ['maʊθtə'maʊθ] *adj*:
~ resuscitation Mund-zu-Mund-Beatmung *f*.
mouthwash ['maʊθwɒʃ] *n* Mundwasser *nt*.
mouth-watering ['maʊθwɔːtərɪŋ] *adj*
appetitlich.
movable ['muːvəbl] *adj* beweglich; **~ feast**
beweglicher Feiertag *m*.
move [muːv] *n* (*movement*) Bewegung *f*; (*in
game*) Zug *m*; (*change: of house*) Umzug *m*;
(*: of job*) Stellenwechsel *m* ♦ *vt* bewegen;
(*furniture*) (ver)rücken; (*car*) umstellen; (*in
game*) ziehen mit; (*emotionally*) bewegen,
ergreifen; (*POL: resolution etc*) beantragen
♦ *vi* sich bewegen; (*traffic*) vorankommen; (*in
game*) ziehen; (*also: ~ house*) umziehen;
(*develop*) sich entwickeln; **it's my ~** ich bin
am Zug; **to get a ~ on** sich beeilen; **to ~ sb
to do sth** jdn (dazu) veranlassen, etw zu
tun; **to ~ towards** sich nähern +*dat*.
▶ **move about** *vi* sich (hin- und
her)bewegen; (*travel*) unterwegs sein; (*from
place to place*) umherziehen; (*change
residence*) umziehen; (*change job*) die Stelle
wechseln; **I can hear him moving about** ich
höre ihn herumlaufen.
▶ **move along** *vi* weitergehen.
▶ **move around** *vi* = **move about**.
▶ **move away** *vi* (*from town, area*) wegziehen.
▶ **move back** *vi* (*return*) zurückkommen.
▶ **move forward** *vi* (*advance*) vorrücken.
▶ **move in** *vi* (*to house*) einziehen; (*police,
soldiers*) anrücken.
▶ **move off** *vi* (*car*) abfahren.
▶ **move on** *vi* (*leave*) weitergehen; (*travel*)
weiterfahren ♦ *vt* (*onlookers*) zum
Weitergehen auffordern.
▶ **move out** *vi* (*of house*) ausziehen.
▶ **move over** *vi* (*to make room*) (zur Seite)
rücken.
▶ **move up** *vi* (*employee*) befördert werden;
(*pupil*) versetzt werden; (*deputy*) aufrücken.
moveable ['muːvəbl] *adj* = **movable**.
movement ['muːvmənt] *n* (*action, group*)
Bewegung *f*; (*freedom to move*)
Bewegungsfreiheit *f*; (*transportation*)
Beförderung *f*; (*shift*) Trend *m*; (*MUS*) Satz
m; (*MED: also:* **bowel ~**) Stuhlgang *m*.
mover ['muːvə*] *n* (*of proposal*)
Antragsteller(in) *m(f)*.
movie ['muːvɪ] *n* Film *m*; **to go to the ~s** ins
Kino gehen.
movie camera *n* Filmkamera *f*.
moviegoer ['muːvɪɡəʊə*] (*US*) *n*
Kinogänger(in) *m(f)*.
moving ['muːvɪŋ] *adj* beweglich; (*emotional*)
ergreifend; (*instigating*): **the ~ spirit/force**
die treibende Kraft.
mow [məʊ] (*pt* **mowed**, *pp* **mowed** *or* **mown**) *vt*
mähen.
▶ **mow down** *vt* (*kill*) niedermähen.
mower ['məʊə*] *n* (*also:* **lawnmower**)
Rasenmäher *m*.
Mozambique [məʊzəm'biːk] *n* Mosambik *nt*.
MP *n abbr* (= *Member of Parliament*) ≈ MdB;
= **military police**; (*CANADA:* = *Mounted Police*)
berittene Polizei *f*.
MP3 *abbr* (*COMPUT*) MP3.
mpg *n abbr* (= *miles per gallon*) *see* **mile**.
mph *abbr* (= *miles per hour*) Meilen pro
Stunde.
MPhil *n abbr* (= *Master of Philosophy*) ≈ M.A.
MPS (*BRIT*) *n abbr* (= *Member of the
Pharmaceutical Society*)
Qualifikationsnachweis für Pharmazeuten.
Mr, (*US*) **Mr.** ['mɪstə*] *n*: **~ Smith** Herr Smith.
MRC (*BRIT*) *n abbr* (= *Medical Research Council*)
medizinischer Forschungsausschuss.
MRCP (*BRIT*) *n abbr* (= *Member of the Royal
College of Physicians*) *höchster akademischer
Grad in Medizin*.
MRCS (*BRIT*) *n abbr* (= *Member of the Royal
College of Surgeons*) *höchster akademischer
Grad für Chirurgen*.
MRCVS (*BRIT*) *n abbr* (= *Member of the Royal
College of Veterinary Surgeons*) *höchster
akademischer Grad für Tiermediziner*.
Mrs, (*US*) **Mrs.** ['mɪsɪz] *n*: **~ Smith** Frau
Smith.
MS *n abbr* (= *multiple sclerosis*) MS *f*; (*US:
= Master of Science*) *akademischer Grad in
Naturwissenschaften* ♦ *abbr* (*US: POST:
= Mississippi*).
MS. (*pl* **MSS.**) *n abbr* (= *manuscript*) Ms.

Ms, (*US*) **Ms.** [mɪz] *n* (= *Miss or Mrs*): ~ **Smith** Frau Smith.

MSA (*US*) *n abbr* (= *Master of Science in Agriculture*) akademischer Grad in Agronomie.

MSc *n abbr* (= *Master of Science*) akademischer Grad in Naturwissenschaften.

MSG *n abbr* = **monosodium glutamate**.

MSP (*BRIT*) *n abbr* (*POL*: = *Member of the Scottish Parliament*) Abgeordnete(r) *f(m)* des schottischen Parlaments.

MST (*US*) *abbr* (= *Mountain Standard Time*) amerikanische Standardzeitzone.

MSW (*US*) *n abbr* (= *Master of Social Work*) akademischer Grad in Sozialwissenschaft.

MT *n abbr* (*COMPUT*, *LING*: = *machine translation*) maschinelle Übersetzung *f*.

Mt *abbr* (*GEOG*) = **mount**.

MTV (*esp US*) *n abbr* (= *music television*) MTV *nt*.

═══════════════════════ *KEYWORD*

much [mʌtʃ] *adj* (*time, money, effort*) viel; **how ~ money/time do you need?** wie viel Geld/ Zeit brauchen Sie?; **he's done so ~ work for us** er hat so viel für uns gearbeitet; **as ~ as** so viel wie; **I have as ~ money/intelligence as you** ich besitze genauso viel Geld/ Intelligenz wie du

♦ *pron* viel; **how ~ is it?** was kostet es?

♦ *adv* **1** (*greatly, a great deal*) sehr; **thank you very ~** vielen Dank, danke sehr; **I read as ~ as I can** ich lese so viel wie ich kann.

2 (*by far*) viel; **I'm ~ better now** mir geht es jetzt viel besser.

3 (*almost*) fast; **how are you feeling? - ~ the same** wie fühlst du dich? - fast genauso; **the two books are ~ the same** die zwei Bücher sind sich sehr ähnlich.

┕ ─ ─ ─ ─ ─ ─ ─ ─ ─ ─ ─ ─ ─ ─ ─ ─ ┙

muck [mʌk] *n* (*dirt*) Dreck *m*.

▶ **muck about** (*inf*) *vi* (*fool about*) herumalbern ♦ *vt*: **to ~ sb about** mit jdm beliebig umspringen.

▶ **muck around** *vi* = **muck about**.

▶ **muck in** (*BRIT: inf*) *vi* mit anpacken.

▶ **muck out** *vt* (*stable*) ausmisten.

▶ **muck up** (*inf*) *vt* (*exam etc*) verpfuschen.

muckraking ['mʌkreɪkɪŋ] (*fig: inf*) *n* Sensationsmache *f* ♦ *adj* sensationslüstern.

mucky ['mʌkɪ] *adj* (*dirty*) dreckig; (*field*) matschig.

mucus ['mju:kəs] *n* Schleim *m*.

mud [mʌd] *n* Schlamm *m*.

muddle ['mʌdl] *n* (*mess*) Durcheinander *nt*; (*confusion*) Verwirrung *f* ♦ *vt* (*person*) verwirren; (*also*: ~ **up**) durcheinander bringen; **to be in a ~** völlig durcheinander sein; **to get in a ~** (*person*) konfus werden; (*things*) durcheinander geraten.

▶ **muddle along** *vi* vor sich *acc* hin wursteln.

▶ **muddle through** *vi* (*get by*) sich durchschlagen.

muddle-headed [mʌdl'hedɪd] *adj* zerstreut.

muddy ['mʌdɪ] *adj* (*floor*) schmutzig; (*field*) schlammig.

mud flats *npl* Watt(enmeer) *nt*.

mudguard ['mʌdɡɑ:d] (*BRIT*) *n* Schutzblech *nt*.

mudpack ['mʌdpæk] *n* Schlammpackung *f*.

mud-slinging ['mʌdslɪŋɪŋ] *n* (*fig*) Schlechtmacherei *f*.

muesli ['mju:zlɪ] *n* Müsli *nt*.

muffin ['mʌfɪn] *n* (*BRIT*) *weiches, flaches Milchbrötchen, meist warm gegessen*; (*US*) *kleiner runder Rührkuchen*.

muffle ['mʌfl] *vt* (*sound*) dämpfen; (*against cold*) einmummeln.

muffled ['mʌfld] *adj* (*see vt*) gedämpft; eingemummelt.

muffler ['mʌflə*] *n* (*US: AUT*) Auspufftopf *m*; (*scarf*) dicker Schal *m*.

mufti ['mʌftɪ] *n*: **in ~** in Zivil.

mug [mʌɡ] *n* (*cup*) Becher *m*; (*for beer*) Krug *m*; (*inf: face*) Visage *f*; (: *fool*) Trottel *m* ♦ *vt* (*auf der Straße*) überfallen; **it's a ~'s game** (*BRIT*) das ist doch Schwachsinn.

▶ **mug up** (*BRIT: inf*) *vt* (*also*: ~ **up on**) pauken.

mugger ['mʌɡə*] *n* Straßenräuber *m*.

mugging ['mʌɡɪŋ] *n* Straßenraub *m*.

muggins ['mʌɡɪnz] (*BRIT: inf*) *n* Dummkopf *m*; **... and ~ does all the work** ... und ich bin mal wieder der/die Dumme und mache die ganze Arbeit.

muggy ['mʌɡɪ] *adj* (*weather, day*) schwül.

mug shot (*inf*) *n* (*of criminal*) Verbrecherfoto *nt*; (*for passport*) Passbild *nt*.

mulatto [mju:'lætəu] (*pl* ~**es**) *n* Mulatte *m*, Mulattin *f*.

mulberry ['mʌlbrɪ] *n* (*fruit*) Maulbeere *f*; (*tree*) Maulbeerbaum *m*.

mule [mju:l] *n* Maultier *nt*.

mulled [mʌld] *adj*: ~ **wine** Glühwein *m*.

mullioned ['mʌliənd] *adj* (*windows*) längs unterteilt.

mull over [mʌl-] *vt* sich *dat* durch den Kopf gehen lassen.

multi... ['mʌltɪ] *pref* multi-, Multi-.

multi-access ['mʌltɪ'æksɛs] *adj* (*COMPUT: system etc*) Mehrplatz-.

multicoloured, (*US*) **multicolored** ['mʌltɪkʌləd] *adj* mehrfarbig.

multifarious [mʌltɪ'fɛərɪəs] *adj* vielfältig.

multilateral [mʌltɪ'lætərl] *adj* multilateral.

multi-level ['mʌltɪlevl] (*US*) *adj* = **multistorey**.

multimillionaire [mʌltɪmɪljə'nɛə*] *n* Multimillionär *m*.

multinational [mʌltɪ'næʃənl] *adj* multinational ♦ *n* multinationaler Konzern *m*, Multi *m* (*inf*).

multiple ['mʌltɪpl] *adj* (*injuries*) mehrfach; (*interests, causes*) vielfältig ♦ *n* Vielfache(s) *nt*; ~ **collision** Massenkarambolage *f*.

multiple-choice ['mʌltɪpltʃɔɪs] *adj* (*question etc*) Multiplechoice-, Multiple-Choice-.

multiple sclerosis *n* multiple Sklerose *f*.

multiplex ['mʌltɪplɛks] n: ~ **transmitter** Multiplex-Sender m; ~ **cinema** Kinocenter nt.

multiplication [mʌltɪplɪ'keɪʃən] n Multiplikation f; (increase) Vervielfachung f.

multiplication table n Multiplikationstabelle f.

multiplicity [mʌltɪ'plɪsɪtɪ] n: **a** ~ **of** eine Vielzahl von.

multiply ['mʌltɪplaɪ] vt multiplizieren ♦ vi (increase: problems) stark zunehmen; (: number) sich vervielfachen; (breed) sich vermehren.

multiracial [mʌltɪ'reɪʃl] adj gemischtrassig; (school) ohne Rassentrennung; ~ **policy** Politik f der Rassenintegration.

multistorey [mʌltɪ'stɔːrɪ] (BRIT) adj (building, car park) mehrstöckig.

multitude ['mʌltɪtjuːd] n Menge f; **a** ~ **of** eine Vielzahl von, eine Menge.

mum [mʌm] (BRIT: inf) n Mutti f, Mama f ♦ adj: **to keep** ~ den Mund halten; ~**'s the word** nichts verraten!

mumble ['mʌmbl] vt, vi (indistinctly) nuscheln; (quietly) murmeln.

mumbo jumbo ['mʌmbəʊ-] n (nonsense) Geschwafel nt.

mummify ['mʌmɪfaɪ] vt mumifizieren.

mummy ['mʌmɪ] n (BRIT: mother) Mami f; (embalmed body) Mumie f.

mumps [mʌmps] n Mumps m or f.

munch [mʌntʃ] vt, vi mampfen.

mundane [mʌn'deɪn] adj (life) banal; (task) stumpfsinnig.

Munich ['mjuːnɪk] n München nt.

municipal [mjuː'nɪsɪpl] adj städtisch, Stadt-; (elections, administration) Kommunal-.

municipality [mjuːnɪsɪ'pælɪtɪ] n Gemeinde f, Stadt f.

munitions [mjuː'nɪʃənz] npl Munition f.

mural ['mjʊərl] n Wandgemälde nt.

murder ['mɜːdə*] n Mord m ♦ vt ermorden; (spoil: piece of music, language) verhunzen; **to commit** ~ einen Mord begehen.

murderer ['mɜːdərə*] n Mörder m.

murderess ['mɜːdərɪs] n Mörderin f.

murderous ['mɜːdərəs] adj blutrünstig; (attack) Mord-; (fig: look, attack) vernichtend; (: pace, heat) mörderisch.

murk [mɜːk] n Düsternis f.

murky ['mɜːkɪ] adj düster; (water) trübe.

murmur ['mɜːmə*] n (of voices) Murmeln nt; (of wind, waves) Rauschen nt ♦ vt, vi murmeln; **heart** ~ Herzgeräusche pl.

MusB(ac) n abbr (= Bachelor of Music) akademischer Grad in Musikwissenschaft.

muscle ['mʌsl] n Muskel m; (fig: strength) Macht f.

▶ **muscle in** vi: **to** ~ **in (on sth)** (bei etw) mitmischen.

muscular ['mʌskjʊlə*] adj (pain, dystrophy) Muskel-; (person, build) muskulös.

muscular dystrophy n Muskeldystrophie f.

MusD(oc) n abbr (= Doctor of Music) Doktorat in Musikwissenschaft.

muse [mjuːz] vi nachgrübeln ♦ n Muse f.

museum [mjuː'zɪəm] n Museum nt.

mush [mʌʃ] n Brei m; (pej) Schmalz m.

mushroom ['mʌʃrum] n (edible) (essbarer) Pilz m; (poisonous) Giftpilz m; (button mushroom) Champignon m ♦ vi (fig: buildings etc) aus dem Boden schießen; (: town, organization) explosionsartig wachsen.

mushroom cloud n Atompilz m.

mushy ['mʌʃɪ] adj matschig; (consistency) breiig; (inf: sentimental) rührselig; ~ **peas** Erbsenbrei m.

music ['mjuːzɪk] n Musik f; (written music, score) Noten pl.

musical ['mjuːzɪkl] adj musikalisch; (sound, tune) melodisch ♦ n Musical nt.

music(al) box n Spieldose f.

musical chairs n die Reise f nach Jerusalem.

musical instrument n Musikinstrument nt.

music centre n Musik-Center nt.

music hall n Varietee nt.

musician [mjuː'zɪʃən] n Musiker(in) m(f).

music stand n Notenständer m.

musk [mʌsk] n Moschus m.

musket ['mʌskɪt] n Muskete f.

muskrat ['mʌskræt] n Bisamratte f.

musk rose n Moschusrose f.

Muslim ['mʌzlɪm] adj moslemisch ♦ n Moslem m, Moslime f.

muslin ['mʌzlɪn] n Musselin m.

musquash ['mʌskwɒʃ] n Bisamratte f; (fur) Bisam m.

mussel ['mʌsl] n (Mies)muschel f.

must [mʌst] aux vb müssen; (in negative) dürfen ♦ n Muss nt; **I** ~ **do it** ich muss es tun; **you** ~ **not do that** das darfst du nicht tun; **he** ~ **be there by now** jetzt müsste er schon dort sein; **you** ~ **come and see me soon** Sie müssen mich bald besuchen; **why** ~ **he behave so badly?** warum muss er sich so schlecht benehmen?; **I** ~ **have made a mistake** ich muss mich geirrt haben; **the film is a** ~ den Film muss man unbedingt gesehen haben.

mustache ['mʌstæʃ] (US) n = **moustache**.

mustard ['mʌstəd] n Senf m.

mustard gas n (MIL) Senfgas nt.

muster ['mʌstə*] vt (support) zusammenbekommen; (also: ~ **up**: energy, strength, courage) aufbringen; (troops, members) antreten lassen ♦ n: **to pass** ~ den Anforderungen genügen.

mustiness ['mʌstɪnɪs] n Muffigkeit f.

mustn't ['mʌsnt] = **must not**.

musty ['mʌstɪ] adj muffig; (building) moderig.

mutant ['mjuːtənt] n Mutante f.

mutate [mjuː'teɪt] vi (BIOL) mutieren.

mutation [mjuː'teɪʃən] n (BIOL) Mutation f; (alteration) Veränderung f.

mute [mju:t] *adj* stumm.
muted ['mju:tɪd] *adj* (*colour*) gedeckt;
(*reaction, criticism*) verhalten; (*sound,
trumpet, MUS*) gedämpft.
mutilate ['mju:tɪleɪt] *vt* verstümmeln.
mutilation [mju:tɪ'leɪʃən] *n* Verstümmelung *f*.
mutinous ['mju:tɪnəs] *adj* meuterisch;
(*attitude*) rebellisch.
mutiny ['mju:tɪnɪ] *n* Meuterei *f* ♦ *vi* meutern.
mutter ['mʌtə*] *vt, vi* murmeln.
mutton ['mʌtn] *n* Hammelfleisch *nt*.
mutual ['mju:tʃuəl] *adj* (*feeling, attraction*)
gegenseitig; (*benefit*) beiderseitig; (*interest,
friend*) gemeinsam; **the feeling was** ~ das
beruhte auf Gegenseitigkeit.
mutually ['mju:tʃuəlɪ] *adv* (*beneficial,
satisfactory*) für beide Seiten; (*accepted*) von
beiden Seiten; **to be** ~ **exclusive** einander
ausschließen; ~ **incompatible** nicht
miteinander vereinbar.
Muzak ® ['mju:zæk] *n* Berieselungsmusik *f*
(*inf*).
muzzle ['mʌzl] *n* (*of dog*) Maul *nt*; (*of gun*)
Mündung *f*; (*guard: for dog*) Maulkorb *m* ♦ *vt*
(*dog*) einen Maulkorb anlegen +*dat*; (*fig:
press, person*) mundtot machen.
MV *abbr* (= *motor vessel*) MS.
MVP (*US*) *n abbr* (*SPORT*: = *most valuable
player*) wertvollster Spieler *m*, wertvollste
Spielerin *f*.
MW *abbr* (*RADIO*: = *medium wave*) MW.

═══════════════ *KEYWORD*

my [maɪ] *adj* mein(e); **this is** ~ **brother/sister/
house** das ist mein Bruder/meine
Schwester/mein Haus; **I've washed** ~ **hair/
cut** ~ **finger** ich habe mir die Haare
gewaschen/mir *or* mich in den Finger
geschnitten; **is this** ~ **pen or yours?** ist das
mein Stift oder deiner?

Myanmar ['maɪænmɑ:] *n* Myanmar *nt*.
myopic [maɪ'ɒpɪk] *adj* (*MED, fig*) kurzsichtig.
myriad ['mɪrɪəd] *n* Unzahl *f*.
myrrh [mə:*] *n* Myrr(h)e *f*.
myself [maɪ'sɛlf] *pron* (*acc*) mich; (*dat*) mir;
(*emphatic*) selbst; *see also* **oneself**.
mysterious [mɪs'tɪərɪəs] *adj* geheimnisvoll,
mysteriös.
mysteriously [mɪs'tɪərɪəslɪ] *adv* auf
mysteriöse Weise; (*smile*) geheimnisvoll.
mystery ['mɪstərɪ] *n* (*puzzle*) Rätsel *nt*;
(*strangeness*) Rätselhaftigkeit *f* ♦ *cpd* (*guest,
voice*) mysteriös; ~ **tour** Fahrt *f* ins Blaue.
mystery story *n* Kriminalgeschichte *f*.
mystic ['mɪstɪk] *n* Mystiker(in) *m(f)*.
mystic(al) ['mɪstɪk(l)] *adj* mystisch.
mystify ['mɪstɪfaɪ] *vt* vor ein Rätsel stellen.
mystique [mɪs'ti:k] *n* geheimnisvoller
Nimbus *m*.
myth [mɪθ] *n* Mythos *m*; (*fallacy*) Märchen *nt*.
mythical ['mɪθɪkl] *adj* mythisch; (*jobs,

opportunities etc) fiktiv.
mythological [mɪθə'lɒdʒɪkl] *adj* mythologisch.
mythology [mɪ'θɒlədʒɪ] *n* Mythologie *f*.

═══════════ *N, n*

N¹, n [ɛn] *n* (*letter*) N *nt*, n *nt*; ~ **for Nellie**, (*US*)
~ **for Nan** ≈ N wie Nordpol.
N² [ɛn] *abbr* (= *north*) N.
NA (*US*) *n abbr* (= *Narcotics Anonymous*)
Hilfsorganisation für Drogensüchtige;
(= *National Academy*) *Dachverband
verschiedener Forschungsunternehmen*.
n/a *abbr* (= *not applicable*) entf.; (*COMM etc*:
= *no account*) kein Konto.
NAACP (*US*) *n abbr* (= *National Association for
the Advancement of Colored People*)
Vereinigung zur Förderung Farbiger.
NAAFI ['næfɪ] (*BRIT*) *n abbr* (= *Navy, Army and
Air Force Institutes*) *Laden für britische
Armeeangehörige*.
NACU (*US*) *n abbr* (= *National Association of
Colleges and Universities*) *Fachhochschul-
und Universitätsverband*.
nadir ['neɪdɪə*] *n* (*fig*) Tiefstpunkt *m*; (*ASTRON*)
Nadir *m*.
NAFTA *n abbr* (= *North Atlantic Free Trade
Agreement*) *amerikanische
Freihandelszone*.
nag [næg] *vt* herumnörgeln an +*dat* ♦ *vi*
nörgeln ♦ *n* (*pej: horse*) Gaul *m*; (: *person*)
Nörgler(in) *m(f)*; **to** ~ **at sb** jdn plagen, jdm
keine Ruhe lassen.
nagging ['nægɪŋ] *adj* (*doubt, suspicion*)
quälend; (*pain*) dumpf.
nail [neɪl] *n* Nagel *m* ♦ *vt* (*inf: thief etc*)
drankriegen; (: *fraud*) aufdecken; **to** ~ **sth to
sth** etw an etw *acc* nageln; **to** ~ **sb down (to
sth)** jdn (auf etw *acc*) festnageln.
nailbrush ['neɪlbrʌʃ] *n* Nagelbürste *f*.
nailfile ['neɪlfaɪl] *n* Nagelfeile *f*.
nail polish *n* Nagellack *m*.
nail polish remover *n* Nagellackentferner
m.
nail scissors *npl* Nagelschere *f*.
nail varnish (*BRIT*) *n* = **nail polish**.
Nairobi [naɪ'rəubɪ] *n* Nairobi *nt*.
naive [nɑ:'i:v] *adj* naiv.
naïveté [nɑ:i:v'teɪ] *n* = **naivety**.
naivety [naɪ'i:vtɪ] *n* Naivität *f*.
naked ['neɪkɪd] *adj* nackt; (*flame, light*) offen;
with the ~ **eye** mit bloßem Auge; **to the**
~ **eye** für das bloße Auge.
nakedness ['neɪkɪdnɪs] *n* Nacktheit *f*.
NAM (*US*) *n abbr* (= *National Association of

*Manufacturers) nationaler Verband der
verarbeitenden Industrie.*
name [neɪm] *n* Name *m* ♦ *vt* nennen; *(ship)*
taufen; *(identify)* (beim Namen) nennen;
(date etc) bestimmen, festlegen; **what's your
~?** wie heißen Sie?; **my ~ is Peter** ich heiße
Peter; **by ~** mit Namen; **in the ~ of** im
Namen +*gen*; **to give one's ~ and address**
Namen und Adresse angeben; **to make a
~ for o.s.** sich *dat* einen Namen machen; **to
give sb a bad ~** jdn in Verruf bringen; **to
call sb ~s** jdn beschimpfen; **to be ~d after
sb/sth** nach jdm/etw benannt werden.
name-dropping ['neɪmdrɔpɪŋ] *n* Angeberei *f*
mit berühmten Namen.
nameless ['neɪmlɪs] *adj* namenlos; **who/which
shall remain ~** der/die/das ungenannt
bleiben soll.
namely ['neɪmlɪ] *adv* nämlich.
nameplate ['neɪmpleɪt] *n* Namensschild *nt*.
namesake ['neɪmseɪk] *n* Namensvetter(in)
m(f).
nan bread [nɑːn-] *n* Nan-Brot *nt*,
*fladenförmiges Weißbrot als Beilage zu
indischen Gerichten.*
nanny ['nænɪ] *n* Kindermädchen *nt*.
nanny-goat ['nænɪɡəʊt] *n* Geiß *f*.
nap [næp] *n* Schläfchen *nt*; *(of fabric)* Strich *m*
♦ *vi:* **to be caught ~ping** *(fig)* überrumpelt
werden; **to have a ~** ein Schläfchen *or* ein
Nickerchen *(inf)* machen.
NAPA *(US) n abbr* (= *National Association of
Performing Artists) Künstlergewerkschaft.*
napalm ['neɪpɑːm] *n* Napalm *nt*.
nape [neɪp] *n:* **the ~ of the neck** der Nacken.
napkin ['næpkɪn] *n* *(also:* **table ~)** Serviette *f*.
Naples ['neɪplz] *n* Neapel *nt*.
Napoleonic [nəpəʊlɪ'ɔnɪk] *adj* napoleonisch.
nappy ['næpɪ] *(BRIT) n* Windel *f*.
nappy liner *(BRIT) n* Windeleinlage *f*.
nappy rash *n* Wundsein *nt*.
narcissistic [nɑːsɪ'sɪstɪk] *adj* narzisstisch.
narcissus [nɑː'sɪsəs] *(pl* **narcissi***) n* Narzisse *f*.
narcotic [nɑː'kɔtɪk] *adj* narkotisch ♦ *n*
Narkotikum *nt*; **narcotics** *npl (drugs)* Drogen
pl; **~ drug** Rauschgift *nt*.
nark [nɑːk] *(BRIT: inf) vt:* **to be ~ed at sth**
sauer über etw *acc* sein.
narrate [nə'reɪt] *vt* erzählen; *(film, programme)*
kommentieren.
narration [nə'reɪʃən] *n* Kommentar *m*.
narrative ['nærətɪv] *n* Erzählung *f*; *(of journey
etc)* Schilderung *f*.
narrator [nə'reɪtə*] *n* Erzähler(in) *m(f)*; *(in film
etc)* Kommentator(in) *m(f)*.
narrow ['nærəʊ] *adj* eng; *(ledge etc)* schmal;
(majority, advantage, victory, defeat) knapp;
(ideas, view) engstirnig ♦ *vi* sich verengen;
(gap, difference) sich verringern ♦ *vt (gap,
difference)* verringern; *(eyes)*
zusammenkneifen; **to have a ~ escape** mit
knapper Not davonkommen; **to ~ sth down**

(to sth) etw (auf etw *acc*) beschränken.
narrow gauge ['nærəʊɡeɪdʒ] *adj (RAIL)*
Schmalspur-.
narrowly ['nærəʊlɪ] *adv* knapp; *(escape)* mit
knapper Not.
narrow-minded [nærəʊ'maɪndɪd] *adj*
engstirnig.
NAS *(US) n abbr* (= *National Academy of
Sciences) Akademie der Wissenschaften.*
NASA ['næsə] *(US) n abbr* (= *National
Aeronautics and Space Administration)* NASA *f*.
nasal ['neɪzl] *adj* Nasen-; *(voice)* näselnd.
Nassau ['næsɔː] *n* Nassau *nt*.
nastily ['nɑːstɪlɪ] *adv* gemein; *(say)* gehässig.
nastiness ['nɑːstɪnɪs] *n* Gemeinheit *f*; *(of
remark)* Gehässigkeit *f*; *(of smell, taste etc)*
Ekelhaftigkeit *f*.
nasturtium [nəs'tɔːʃəm] *n* Kapuzinerkresse *f*.
nasty ['nɑːstɪ] *adj (remark)* gehässig; *(person)*
gemein; *(taste, smell)* ekelhaft; *(wound,
disease, accident, shock)* schlimm; *(problem,
question)* schwierig; *(weather, temper)*
abscheulich; **to turn ~** unangenehm
werden; **it's a ~ business** es ist schrecklich;
he's got a ~ temper mit ihm ist nicht gut
Kirschen essen.
NAS/UWT *(BRIT) n abbr* (= *National Association
of Schoolmasters/Union of Women Teachers)
Lehrergewerkschaft.*
nation ['neɪʃən] *n* Nation *f*; *(people)* Volk *nt*.
national ['næʃənl] *adj (character, flag)*
National-; *(interests)* Staats-; *(newspaper)*
überregional ♦ *n* Staatsbürger(in) *m(f)*;
foreign ~ Ausländer(in) *m(f)*.
national anthem *n* Nationalhymne *f*.
National Curriculum *n* zentraler Lehrplan
für Schulen in England und Wales.
national debt *n* Staatsverschuldung *f*.
national dress *n* Nationaltracht *f*.
National Guard *(US) n* Nationalgarde *f*.
National Health Service *(BRIT) n*
Staatlicher Gesundheitsdienst *m*.
National Insurance *(BRIT) n*
Sozialversicherung *f*.
nationalism ['næʃnəlɪzəm] *n* Nationalismus *m*.
nationalist ['næʃnəlɪst] *adj* nationalistisch ♦ *n*
Nationalist(in) *m(f)*.
nationality [næʃə'nælɪtɪ] *n*
Staatsangehörigkeit *f*, Nationalität *f*.
nationalization [næʃnəlaɪ'zeɪʃən] *n*
Verstaatlichung *f*.
nationalize ['næʃnəlaɪz] *vt* verstaatlichen.
National Lottery *n ≈* Lotto *nt*.
nationally ['næʃnəlɪ] *adv* landesweit.
national park *n* Nationalpark *m*.
national press *n* überregionale Presse *f*.
National Security Council *(US) n*
Nationaler Sicherheitsrat *m*.
national service *n* Wehrdienst *m*.
National Trust *(BRIT) n Organisation zum
Schutz historischer Bauten und Denkmäler
sowie zum Landschaftsschutz.*

Freikörperkultur.

naught [nɔːt] n = **nought**.

naughtiness ['nɔːtɪnɪs] n (see adj) Unartigkeit f, Ungezogenheit f; Unanständigkeit f.

naughty ['nɔːtɪ] adj (child) unartig, ungezogen; (story, film, words) unanständig.

nausea ['nɔːsɪə] n Übelkeit f.

nauseate ['nɔːsɪeɪt] vt Übelkeit verursachen +dat; (fig) anwidern.

nauseating ['nɔːsɪeɪtɪŋ] adj Ekel erregend; (fig) widerlich.

nauseous ['nɔːsɪəs] adj ekelhaft; **I feel** ~ **mir** ist übel.

nautical ['nɔːtɪkl] adj (chart) See-; (uniform) Seemanns-.

nautical mile n Seemeile f.

naval ['neɪvl] adj Marine-; (battle, forces) See-.

naval officer n Marineoffizier m.

nave [neɪv] n Hauptschiff nt, Mittelschiff nt.

navel ['neɪvl] n Nabel m.

navigable ['nævɪgəbl] adj schiffbar.

navigate ['nævɪgeɪt] vt (river) befahren; (path) begehen ♦ vi navigieren; (AUT) den Fahrer dirigieren.

navigation [nævɪ'geɪʃən] n Navigation f.

navigator ['nævɪgeɪtə*] n (NAUT) Steuermann m; (AVIAT) Navigator(in) m(f); (AUT) Beifahrer(in) m(f).

navvy ['nævɪ] (BRIT) n Straßenarbeiter m.

navy ['neɪvɪ] n (Kriegs)marine f; (ships) (Kriegs)flotte f; **Department of the N~** (US) Marineministerium nt.

navy(-blue) ['neɪvɪ('bluː)] adj marineblau.

Nazareth ['næzərɪθ] n Nazareth nt.

Nazi ['nɑːtsɪ] n Nazi m.

NB abbr (= nota bene) NB; (CANADA: = New Brunswick).

NBA (US) n abbr (= National Basketball Association) Basketball-Dachverband; (= National Boxing Association) Boxsport-Dachverband.

NBC (US) n abbr (= National Broadcasting Company) Fernsehsender.

NBS (US) n abbr (= National Bureau of Standards) amerikanischer Normenausschuss.

NC abbr (COMM etc: = no charge) frei; (US: POST: = North Carolina).

NCC n abbr (BRIT: = Nature Conservancy Council) Naturschutzverband; (US: = National Council of Churches) Zusammenschluss protestantischer und orthodoxer Kirchen.

NCCL (BRIT) n abbr (= National Council for Civil Liberties) Organisation zum Schutz von Freiheitsrechten.

NCO n abbr (MIL: = noncommissioned officer) Uffz.

ND (US) abbr (POST: = North Dakota).

N.Dak. (US) abbr (POST: = North Dakota).

NE abbr = **north-east**; (US: POST: = New England; Nebraska).

NEA (US) n abbr (= National Education

nationwide ['neɪʃənwaɪd] adj, adv landesweit.

native ['neɪtɪv] n Einheimische(r) f(m) ♦ adj einheimisch; (country) Heimat-; (language) Mutter-; (innate) angeboren; **a** ~ **of Germany, a** ~ **German** ein gebürtiger Deutscher, eine gebürtige Deutsche; ~ **to** beheimatet in +dat.

Native American adj indianisch, der Ureinwohner Amerikas ♦ n Ureinwohner(in) m(f) Amerikas.

native speaker n Muttersprachler(in) m(f).

Nativity [nə'tɪvɪtɪ] n: **the** ~ Christi Geburt f.

nativity play n Krippenspiel nt.

NATO ['neɪtəu] n abbr (= North Atlantic Treaty Organization) NATO f.

natter ['nætə*] (BRIT) vi quatschen (inf) ♦ n: **to have a** ~ einen Schwatz halten.

natural ['nætʃrəl] adj natürlich; (disaster) Natur-; (innate) angeboren; (born) geboren; (MUS) ohne Vorzeichen; **to die of** ~ **causes** eines natürlichen Todes sterben; ~ **foods** Naturkost f; **she played F** ~ **not F sharp** sie spielte f statt fis.

natural childbirth n natürliche Geburt f.

natural gas n Erdgas nt.

natural history n Naturkunde f; **the** ~ **of England** die Naturgeschichte Englands.

naturalist ['nætʃrəlɪst] n Naturforscher(in) m(f).

naturalize ['nætʃrəlaɪz] vt: **to become** ~**d** eingebürgert werden.

naturally ['nætʃrəlɪ] adv natürlich; (happen) auf natürlichem Wege; (die) eines natürlichen Todes; (occur: cheerful, talented, blonde) von Natur aus.

naturalness ['nætʃrəlnɪs] n Natürlichkeit f.

natural resources npl Naturschätze pl.

natural selection n natürliche Auslese f.

natural wastage n natürliche Personalreduzierung f.

nature ['neɪtʃə*] n (also: **Nature**) Natur f; (kind, sort) Art f; (character) Wesen nt; **by** ~ von Natur aus; **by its (very)** ~ naturgemäß; **documents of a confidential** ~ Unterlagen vertraulicher Art.

-natured ['neɪtʃəd] suff: **good-**~ gutmütig; **ill-**~ bösartig.

nature reserve (BRIT) n Naturschutzgebiet nt.

nature trail n Naturlehrpfad m.

naturist ['neɪtʃərɪst] n Anhänger(in) m(f) der

Association) Verband für das Erziehungswesen.

neap [ni:p] *n* (*also:* ~ **tide**) Nippflut *f*.

Neapolitan [nɪə'pɔlɪtən] *adj* neapolitanisch ♦ *n* Neapolitaner(in) *m(f)*.

near [nɪə*] *adj* nahe ♦ *adv* nahe; (*almost*) fast, beinahe ♦ *prep* (*also:* ~ **to:** *in space*) nahe an +*dat*; (: *in time*) um *acc* ... herum; (: *in situation, in intimacy*) nahe +*dat* ♦ *vt* sich nähern +*dat*; (*state, situation*) kurz vor +*dat* stehen; **Christmas is** ~ bald ist Weihnachten; **£25,000 or** ~**est offer** (*BRIT*) £25.000 oder das nächstbeste Angebot; **in the** ~ **future** in naher Zukunft, bald; **in** ~ **darkness** fast im Dunkeln; **a** ~ **tragedy** beinahe eine Tragödie; ~ **here/there** hier/dort in der Nähe; **to be** ~ (**to**) **doing sth** nahe daran sein, etw zu tun; **the building is** ~**ing completion** der Bau steht kurz vor dem Abschluss.

nearby [nɪə'baɪ] *adj* nahe gelegen ♦ *adv* in der Nähe.

Near East *n*: **the** ~ der Nahe Osten.

nearer ['nɪərə*] *adj, adv comp of* **near**.

nearest ['nɪərəst] *adj, adv superl of* **near**.

nearly ['nɪəlɪ] *adv* fast; **I** ~ **fell** ich wäre beinahe gefallen; **it's not** ~ **big enough** es ist bei weitem nicht groß genug; **she was** ~ **crying** sie war den Tränen nahe.

near miss *n* Beinahezusammenstoß *m*; **that was a** ~ (*shot*) das war knapp daneben.

nearness ['nɪənɪs] *n* Nähe *f*.

nearside ['nɪəsaɪd] (*AUT*) *adj* (*when driving on left*) linksseitig; (*when driving on right*) rechtsseitig ♦ *n*: **the** ~ (*when driving on left*) die linke Seite; (*when driving on right*) die rechte Seite.

near-sighted [nɪə'saɪtɪd] *adj* kurzsichtig.

neat [ni:t] *adj* ordentlich; (*handwriting*) sauber; (*plan, solution*) elegant; (*description*) prägnant; (*spirits*) pur; **I drink it** ~ ich trinke es pur.

neatly ['ni:tlɪ] *adv* ordentlich; (*conveniently*) sauber.

neatness ['ni:tnɪs] *n* Ordentlichkeit *f*; (*of solution, plan*) Sauberkeit *f*.

Nebr. (*US*) *abbr* (*POST:* = *Nebraska*).

nebulous ['nɛbjuləs] *adj* vage, unklar.

necessarily ['nɛsɪsrɪlɪ] *adv* notwendigerweise; **not** ~ nicht unbedingt.

necessary ['nɛsɪsrɪ] *adj* notwendig, nötig; (*inevitable*) unausweichlich; **if** ~ wenn nötig, nötigenfalls; **it is** ~ **to** ... man muss ...

necessitate [nɪ'sɛsɪteɪt] *vt* erforderlich machen.

necessity [nɪ'sɛsɪtɪ] *n* Notwendigkeit *f*; **of** ~ notgedrungen; **out of** ~ aus Not; **the necessities (of life)** das Notwendigste (zum Leben).

neck [nɛk] *n* Hals *m*; (*of shirt, dress, jumper*) Ausschnitt *m* ♦ *vi* (*inf*) knutschen; ~ **and** ~ Kopf an Kopf; **to stick one's** ~ **out** (*inf*)

necklace ['nɛklɪs] *n* (Hals)kette *f*.

neckline ['nɛklaɪn] *n* Ausschnitt *m*.

necktie ['nɛktaɪ] (*esp US*) *n* Krawatte *f*.

nectar ['nɛktə*] *n* Nektar *m*.

nectarine ['nɛktərɪn] *n* Nektarine *f*.

NEDC (*BRIT*) *n abbr* (= *National Economic Development Council*) *Rat für Wirtschaftsentwicklung.*

Neddy ['nɛdɪ] (*BRIT: inf*) *n abbr* = **NEDC**.

née [neɪ] *prep:* ~ **Scott** geborene Scott.

need [ni:d] *n* Bedarf *m*; (*necessity*) Notwendigkeit *f*; (*requirement*) Bedürfnis *nt*; (*poverty*) Not *f* ♦ *vt* brauchen; (*could do with*) nötig haben; **in** ~ bedürftig; **to be in** ~ **of sth** etw nötig haben; **£10 will meet my immediate** ~**s** mit £ 10 komme ich erst einmal aus; (**there's**) **no** ~ (das ist) nicht nötig; **there's no** ~ **to get so worked up about it** du brauchst dich darüber nicht so aufzuregen; **he had no** ~ **to work** er hatte es nicht nötig zu arbeiten; **I** ~ **to do it** ich muss es tun; **you don't** ~ **to go, you** ~**n't go** du brauchst nicht zu gehen; **a signature is** ~**ed** das bedarf einer Unterschrift *gen*.

needle ['ni:dl] *n* Nadel *f* ♦ *vt* (*fig: inf: goad*) ärgern, piesacken.

needless ['ni:dlɪs] *adj* unnötig; ~ **to say** natürlich.

needlessly ['ni:dlɪslɪ] *adv* unnötig.

needlework ['ni:dlwə:k] *n* Handarbeit *f*.

needn't ['ni:dnt] = **need not**.

needy ['ni:dɪ] *adj* bedürftig ♦ *npl*: **the** ~ die Bedürftigen *pl*.

negation [nɪ'geɪʃən] *n* Verweigerung *f*.

negative ['nɛgətɪv] *adj* negativ; (*answer*) abschlägig ♦ *n* (*PHOT*) Negativ *nt*; (*LING*) Verneinungswort *nt*, Negation *f*; **to answer in the** ~ eine verneinende Antwort geben.

negative equity *n* Differenz zwischen gefallenem Wert und hypothekarischer Belastung eines Wohnungseigentums.

neglect [nɪ'glɛkt] *vt* vernachlässigen; (*writer, artist*) unterschätzen ♦ *n* Vernachlässigung *f*.

neglected [nɪ'glɛktɪd] *adj* vernachlässigt; (*writer, artist*) unterschätzt.

neglectful [nɪ'glɛktful] *adj* nachlässig; (*father*) pflichtvergessen; **to be** ~ **of sth** etw vernachlässigen.

negligee ['nɛglɪʒeɪ] *n* Negligee *nt*, Negligé *nt*.

negligence ['nɛglɪdʒəns] *n* Nachlässigkeit *f*; (*LAW*) Fahrlässigkeit *f*.

negligent ['nɛglɪdʒənt] *adj* nachlässig; (*LAW*) fahrlässig; (*casual*) lässig.

negligently ['nɛglɪdʒəntlɪ] *adv* (*see adj*) nachlässig; fahrlässig; lässig.

negligible ['nɛglɪdʒɪbl] *adj* geringfügig.

negotiable [nɪ'gəʊʃəbl] *adj* verhandlungsfähig; (*path, river*) passierbar; **not** ~ (*on cheque etc*) nicht übertragbar.

negotiate [nɪ'gəʊʃɪeɪt] *vi* verhandeln ♦ *vt* aushandeln; (*obstacle, hill*) überwinden;

(*bend*) nehmen; **to ~ with sb (for sth)** mit jdm (über etw *acc*) verhandeln.

negotiating table [nɪˈgəʊʃɪeɪtɪŋ-] *n* Verhandlungstisch *m*.

negotiation [nɪgəʊʃɪˈeɪʃən] *n* Verhandlung *f*; **the matter is still under ~** über die Sache wird noch verhandelt.

negotiator [nɪˈgəʊʃɪeɪtə*] *n* Unterhändler(in) *m(f)*.

Negress [ˈniːgrɪs] *n* Negerin *f*.

Negro [ˈniːgrəʊ] (*pl* ~**es**) *adj* (*boy, slave*) Neger- ♦ *n* Neger *m*.

neigh [neɪ] *vi* wiehern.

neighbour, (*US*) **neighbor** [ˈneɪbə*] *n* Nachbar(in) *m(f)*.

neighbourhood [ˈneɪbəhud] *n* (*place*) Gegend *f*; (*people*) Nachbarschaft *f*; **in the ~ of** ... in der Nähe von ...; (*sum of money*) so um die ...

neighbourhood watch *n* Vereinigung von Bürgern, die Straßenwachen etc zur Unterstützung der Polizei bei der Verbrechensbekämpfung organisiert.

neighbouring [ˈneɪbərɪŋ] *adj* benachbart, Nachbar-.

neighbourly [ˈneɪbəlɪ] *adj* nachbarlich.

neither [ˈnaɪðə*] *conj*: **I didn't move and ~ did John** ich bewegte mich nicht und John auch nicht ♦ *pron* keine(r, s) (von beiden) ♦ *adv*: **~ ... nor ...** weder ... noch ...; **~ story is true** keine der beiden Geschichten stimmt; **~ is true** beides stimmt nicht; **~ do I/have I** ich auch nicht.

neo... [ˈniːəʊ] *pref* neo-, Neo-.

neolithic [nɪəˈlɪθɪk] *adv* jungsteinzeitlich, neolithisch.

neologism [nɪˈɒlədʒɪzəm] *n* (Wort)neubildung *f*, Neologismus *m*.

neon [ˈniːɒn] *n* Neon *nt*.

neon light *n* Neonlampe *f*.

neon sign *n* Neonreklame *f*.

Nepal [nɪˈpɔːl] *n* Nepal *nt*.

nephew [ˈnɛvjuː] *n* Neffe *m*.

nepotism [ˈnɛpətɪzəm] *n* Vetternwirtschaft *f*.

nerd [nɜːd] (*inf*) *n* Schwachkopf *m*.

nerve [nɜːv] *n* (*ANAT*) Nerv *m*; (*courage*) Mut *m*; (*impudence*) Frechheit *f*; **nerves** *npl* (*anxiety*) Nervosität *f*; (*emotional strength*) Nerven *pl*; **he gets on my ~s** er geht mir auf die Nerven; **to lose one's ~** die Nerven verlieren.

nerve-centre, (*US*) **nerve-center** [ˈnɜːvsɛntə*] *n* (*fig*) Schaltzentrale *f*.

nerve gas *n* Nervengas *nt*.

nerve-racking [ˈnɜːvrækɪŋ] *adj* nervenaufreibend.

nervous [ˈnɜːvəs] *adj* Nerven-, nervlich; (*anxious*) nervös; **to be ~ of/about** Angst haben vor +*dat*.

nervous breakdown *n* Nervenzusammenbruch *m*.

nervously [ˈnɜːvəslɪ] *adv* nervös.

nervousness [ˈnɜːvəsnɪs] *n* Nervosität *f*.

nervous system *n* Nervensystem *nt*.

nervous wreck (*inf*) *n* Nervenbündel *nt*; **to be a ~** mit den Nerven völlig am Ende sein.

nervy [ˈnɜːvɪ] (*inf*) *adj* (*BRIT: tense*) nervös; (*US: cheeky*) dreist.

nest [nɛst] *n* Nest *nt* ♦ *vi* nisten; **a ~ of tables** ein Satz Tische *or* von Tischen.

nest egg *n* Notgroschen *m*.

nestle [ˈnɛsl] *vi* sich kuscheln; (*house*) eingebettet sein.

nestling [ˈnɛstlɪŋ] *n* Nestling *m*.

Net [nɛt] *n*: **the ~** (*COMPUT*) das Internet.

net [nɛt] *n* Netz *nt*; (*fabric*) Tüll *m* ♦ *adj* (*COMM*) Netto-; (*final: result, effect*) End- ♦ *vt* (mit einem Netz) fangen; (*profit*) einbringen; (*deal, sale, fortune*) an Land ziehen; **~ of tax** steuerfrei; **he earns £10,000 ~ per year** er verdient £ 10.000 netto im Jahr; **it weighs 250g ~** es wiegt 250 g netto.

netball [ˈnɛtbɔːl] *n* Netzball *m*.

net curtains *npl* Gardinen *pl*, Stores *pl*.

Netherlands [ˈnɛðələndz] *npl*: **the ~** die Niederlande *pl*.

nett [nɛt] *adj* = **net**.

netting [ˈnɛtɪŋ] *n* (*for fence etc*) Maschendraht *m*; (*fabric*) Netzgewebe *nt*, Tüll *m*.

nettle [ˈnɛtl] *n* Nessel *f*; **to grasp the ~** (*fig*) in den sauren Apfel beißen.

network [ˈnɛtwɜːk] *n* Netz *nt*; (*TV, RADIO*) Sendenetz *nt* ♦ *vt* (*RADIO, TV*) im ganzen Netzbereich ausstrahlen; (*computers*) in einem Netzwerk zusammenschließen.

neuralgia [njʊəˈrældʒə] *n* Neuralgie *f*, Nervenschmerzen *pl*.

neurological [njʊərəˈlɒdʒɪkl] *adj* neurologisch.

neurotic [njʊəˈrɒtɪk] *adj* neurotisch ♦ *n* Neurotiker(in) *m(f)*.

neuter [ˈnjuːtə*] *adj* (*LING*) sächlich ♦ *vt* kastrieren; (*female*) sterilisieren.

neutral [ˈnjuːtrəl] *adj* neutral ♦ *n* (*AUT*) Leerlauf *m*.

neutrality [njuːˈtrælɪtɪ] *n* Neutralität *f*.

neutralize [ˈnjuːtrəlaɪz] *vt* neutralisieren, aufheben.

neutron [ˈnjuːtrɒn] *n* Neutron *nt*.

neutron bomb *n* Neutronenbombe *f*.

Nev. (*US*) *abbr* (*POST:* = *Nevada*).

never [ˈnɛvə*] *adv* nie; (*not*) nicht; **~ in my life** noch nie; **~ again** nie wieder; **well I ~!** nein, so was!; *see also* **mind**.

never-ending [nɛvərˈɛndɪŋ] *adj* endlos.

nevertheless [nɛvəðəˈlɛs] *adv* trotzdem, dennoch.

new [njuː] *adj* neu; (*mother*) jung; **as good as ~** so gut wie neu; **to be ~ to sb** jdm neu sein.

New Age *n* Newage *nt*, New Age *nt*.

newborn [ˈnjuːbɔːn] *adj* neugeboren.

newcomer [ˈnjuːkʌmə*] *n* Neuankömmling *m*; (*in job*) Neuling *m*.

new-fangled [ˈnjuːˈfæŋgld] (*pej*) *adj* neumodisch.

new-found ['nju:faund] *adj* neu entdeckt; (*confidence*) neu geschöpft.

Newfoundland ['nju:fənlənd] *n* Neufundland *nt*.

New Guinea *n* Neuguinea *nt*.

newly ['nju:lɪ] *adv* neu.

newly-weds ['nju:lɪwɛdz] *npl* Neuvermählte *pl*, Frischvermählte *pl*.

new moon *n* Neumond *m*.

newness ['nju:nɪs] *n* Neuheit *f*; (*of cheese, bread etc*) Frische *f*.

New Orleans [-'ɔ:li:ənz] *n* New Orleans *nt*.

news [nju:z] *n* Nachricht *f*; **a piece of** ~ eine Neuigkeit; **the** ~ (*RADIO, TV*) die Nachrichten *pl*; **good/bad** ~ gute/schlechte Nachrichten.

news agency *n* Nachrichtenagentur *f*.

newsagent ['nju:zeɪdʒənt] (*BRIT*) *n* Zeitungshändler(in) *m(f)*.

news bulletin *n* Bulletin *nt*.

newscaster ['nju:zka:stə'] *n* Nachrichtensprecher(in) *m(f)*.

newsdealer ['nju:zdi:lə'] (*US*) *n* = **newsagent**.

newsflash ['nju:zflæʃ] *n* Kurzmeldung *f*.

newsletter ['nju:zlɛtə'] *n* Rundschreiben *nt*, Mitteilungsblatt *nt*.

newspaper ['nju:zpeɪpə'] *n* Zeitung *f*; **daily/weekly** ~ Tages-/Wochenzeitung *f*.

newsprint ['nju:zprɪnt] *n* Zeitungspapier *nt*.

newsreader ['nju:zri:də'] *n* = **newscaster**.

newsreel ['nju:zri:l] *n* Wochenschau *f*.

newsroom ['nju:zru:m] *n* Nachrichtenredaktion *f*; (*RADIO, TV*) Nachrichtenstudio *nt*.

newsstand ['nju:zstænd] *n* Zeitungsstand *m*.

newsworthy ['nju:zwɔ:ðɪ] *adj*: **to be** ~ Neuigkeitswert haben.

newt [nju:t] *n* Wassermolch *m*.

new town (*BRIT*) *n* neue, teilweise mit Regierungsgeldern errichtete städtische Siedlung.

New Year *n* neues Jahr *nt*; (*New Year's Day*) Neujahr *nt*; **Happy** ~! (ein) glückliches *or* frohes neues Jahr!

New Year's Day *n* Neujahr *nt*, Neujahrstag *m*.

New Year's Eve *n* Silvester *nt*.

New York [-'jɔ:k] *n* New York *nt*; (*also*: ~ **State**) der Staat New York.

New Zealand [-'zi:lənd] *n* Neuseeland *nt* ♦ *adj* neuseeländisch.

New Zealander [-'zi:ləndə'] *n* Neuseeländer(in) *m(f)*.

next [nɛkst] *adj* nächste(r, s); (*room*) Neben- ♦ *adv* dann; (*do, happen*) als Nächstes; (*afterwards*) danach; **the** ~ **day** am nächsten *or* folgenden Tag; ~ **time** das nächste Mal; ~ **year** nächstes Jahr; ~ **please!** der Nächste bitte!; **who's** ~? wer ist der Nächste?; **"turn to the** ~ **page"** „bitte umblättern"; **the week after** ~ übernächste Woche; **the** ~ **on the right/left** der/die/das

Nächste rechts/links; **the** ~ **thing I knew** das Nächste, woran ich mich erinnern konnte; ~ **to** neben +*dat*; ~ **to nothing** so gut wie nichts; **when do we meet** ~? wann treffen wir uns wieder *or* das nächste Mal?; **the** ~ **best** der/die/das Nächstbeste.

next door *adv* nebenan ♦ *adj*: **next-door** nebenan; **the house** ~ das Nebenhaus; **to go** ~ nach nebenan gehen; **my next-door neighbour** mein direkter Nachbar.

next-of-kin ['nɛkstəv'kɪn] *n* nächster Verwandter *m*, nächste Verwandte *f*.

NF *n abbr* (*BRIT: POL:* = *National Front*) *rechtsradikale Partei* ♦ *abbr* (*CANADA:* = *Newfoundland*).

NFL (*US*) *n abbr* (= *National Football League*) *Fußball-Nationalliga*.

NG (*US*) *abbr* = **National Guard**.

NGO *n abbr* (= *nongovernmental organization*) *nichtstaatliche Organisation*.

NH (*US*) *abbr* (*POST:* = *New Hampshire*).

NHL (*US*) *n abbr* (= *National Hockey League*) *Hockey-Nationalliga*.

NHS (*BRIT*) *n abbr* = **National Health Service**.

NI *abbr* = **Northern Ireland**; (*BRIT*) = **National Insurance**.

Niagara Falls [naɪ'ægərə-] *npl* Niagarafälle *pl*.

nib [nɪb] *n* Feder *f*.

nibble ['nɪbl] *vt* knabbern; (*bite*) knabbern an +*dat* ♦ *vi*: **to** ~ **at** knabbern an +*dat*.

Nicaragua [nɪkə'rægjuə] *n* Nicaragua *nt*.

Nicaraguan [nɪkə'rægjuən] *adj* nicaraguanisch ♦ *n* Nicaraguaner(in) *m(f)*.

Nice [ni:s] *n* Nizza *nt*.

nice [naɪs] *adj* nett; (*holiday, weather, picture etc*) schön; (*taste*) gut; (*person, clothes etc*) hübsch.

nicely ['naɪslɪ] *adv* (*attractively*) hübsch; (*politely*) nett; (*satisfactorily*) gut; **that will do** ~ das reicht (vollauf).

niceties ['naɪsɪtɪz] *npl*: **the** ~ die Feinheiten *pl*.

niche [ni:ʃ] *n* Nische *f*; (*job, position*) Plätzchen *nt*.

nick [nɪk] *n* Kratzer *m*; (*in metal, wood etc*) Kerbe *f* ♦ *vt* (*BRIT: inf: steal*) klauen; (*: arrest*) einsperren, einlochen; (*cut*): **to** ~ **o.s.** sich schneiden; **in good** ~ (*BRIT: inf*) gut in Schuss; **in the** ~ (*BRIT: inf: in prison*) im Knast; **in the** ~ **of time** gerade noch rechtzeitig.

nickel ['nɪkl] *n* Nickel *nt*; (*US*) Fünfcentstück *nt*.

nickname ['nɪkneɪm] *n* Spitzname *m* ♦ *vt* betiteln, taufen (*inf*).

Nicosia [nɪkə'si:ə] *n* Nikosia *nt*.

nicotine ['nɪkəti:n] *n* Nikotin *nt*.

nicotine patch *n* Nikotinpflaster *nt*.

niece [ni:s] *n* Nichte *f*.

nifty ['nɪftɪ] (*inf*) *adj* flott; (*gadget, tool*) schlau.

Niger ['naɪdʒə'] *n* Niger *m*.

Nigeria [naɪ'dʒɪərɪə] *n* Nigeria *nt*.

Nigerian [naɪ'dʒɪərɪən] *adj* nigerianisch ♦ *n*

Nigerianer(in) m(f).

niggardly ['nɪgədlɪ] adj knauserig; (allowance, amount) armselig.

nigger [nɪgə*] (inf) n Nigger m (inf!).

niggle ['nɪgl] vt plagen, zu schaffen machen +dat ♦ vi herumkritisieren.

niggling ['nɪglɪŋ] adj quälend; (pain, ache) bohrend.

night [naɪt] n Nacht f; (evening) Abend m; **the ~ before last** vorletzte Nacht, vorgestern Abend; **at ~, by ~** nachts, abends; **nine o'clock at ~** um neun Uhr abends; **in the ~, during the ~** in der Nacht; **~ and day** Tag und Nacht.

nightcap ['naɪtkæp] n Schlaftrunk m.

nightclub ['naɪtklʌb] n Nachtlokal nt.

nightdress ['naɪtdrɛs] n Nachthemd nt.

nightfall ['naɪtfɔ:l] n Einbruch m der Dunkelheit.

nightgown ['naɪtgaun] n = **nightdress**.

nightie ['naɪtɪ] n = **nightdress**.

nightingale ['naɪtɪŋgeɪl] n Nachtigall f.

nightlife ['naɪtlaɪf] n Nachtleben nt.

nightly ['naɪtlɪ] adj (all)nächtlich, Nacht-; (every evening) (all)abendlich, Abend- ♦ adv jede Nacht; (every evening) jeden Abend.

nightmare ['naɪtmɛə*] n Albtraum m, Alptraum m.

night porter n Nachtportier m.

night safe n Nachtsafe m.

night school n Abendschule f.

nightshade ['naɪtʃeɪd] n: **deadly ~** Tollkirsche f.

night shift n Nachtschicht f.

night-time ['naɪttaɪm] n Nacht f.

night watchman n Nachtwächter m.

nihilism ['naɪɪlɪzəm] n Nihilismus m.

nil [nɪl] n Nichts nt; (BRIT: SPORT) Null f.

Nile [naɪl] n: **the ~** der Nil.

nimble ['nɪmbl] adj flink; (mind) beweglich.

nine [naɪn] num neun.

nineteen ['naɪn'ti:n] num neunzehn.

nineteenth [naɪn'ti:nθ] num neunzehnte(r, s).

ninety ['naɪntɪ] num neunzig.

ninth [naɪnθ] num neunte(r, s) ♦ n Neuntel nt.

nip [nɪp] vt zwicken ♦ n Biss m; (drink) Schlückchen nt ♦ vi (BRIT: inf): **to ~ out/ down/up** kurz raus-/runter-/raufgehen; **to ~ into a shop** (BRIT: inf) kurz in einen Laden gehen.

nipple ['nɪpl] n (ANAT) Brustwarze f.

nippy ['nɪpɪ] (BRIT) adj (quick: person) flott; (: car) spritzig; (cold) frisch.

nit [nɪt] n Nisse f; (inf: idiot) Dummkopf m.

nitpicking ['nɪtpɪkɪŋ] (inf) n Kleinigkeitskrämerei f.

nitrogen ['naɪtrədʒən] n Stickstoff m.

nitroglycerin(e) ['naɪtrəu'glɪsəri:n] n Nitroglyzerin m.

nitty-gritty ['nɪtɪ'grɪtɪ] (inf) n: **to get down to the ~** zur Sache kommen.

nitwit ['nɪtwɪt] (inf) n Dummkopf m.

NJ (US) abbr (POST: = New Jersey).

NLF n abbr (= National Liberation Front) vietnamesische Befreiungsbewegung während des Vietnamkrieges.

NLQ abbr (COMPUT, TYP: = near letter quality) NLQ.

NLRB (US) n abbr (= National Labor Relations Board) Ausschuss zur Regelung der Beziehungen zwischen Arbeitgebern und Arbeitnehmern.

NM, N.Mex. (US) abbr (POST: = New Mexico).

—————————————————— KEYWORD

no [nəu] (pl **noes**) adv (opposite of "yes") nein; **~ thank you** nein danke
♦ adj (not any) kein(e); **I have ~ money/ time/books** ich habe kein Geld/keine Zeit/ keine Bücher; **"~ entry"** „kein Zutritt"; **"~ smoking"** „Rauchen verboten"
♦ n Nein nt; **there were 20 noes and one abstention** es gab 20 Neinstimmen und eine Enthaltung; **I won't take ~ for an answer** ich bestehe darauf.

no. abbr (= number) Nr.

nobble [nɔbl] (BRIT: inf) vt (bribe) (sich dat) kaufen; (grab) sich dat schnappen; (RACING: horse, dog) lahmlegen.

Nobel Prize [nəu'bɛl-] n Nobelpreis m.

nobility [nəu'bɪlɪtɪ] n Adel m; (quality) Edelmut m.

noble ['nəubl] adj edel, nobel; (aristocratic) ad(e)lig; (impressive) prächtig.

nobleman ['nəublmən] (irreg: like **man**) n Ad(e)lige(r) f(m).

nobly ['nəublɪ] adv edel.

nobody ['nəubədɪ] pron niemand, keiner ♦ n: **he's a ~** er ist ein Niemand m.

no-claims bonus [nəu'kleɪmz-] n Schadenfreiheitsrabatt m.

nocturnal [nɔk'tɜ:nl] adj nächtlich; (animal) Nacht-.

nod [nɔd] vi nicken; (fig: flowers etc) wippen
♦ vt: **to ~ one's head** mit dem Kopf nicken
♦ n Nicken nt; **they ~ded their agreement** sie nickten zustimmend.
▶ **nod off** vi einnicken.

no-fly zone [nəu'flaɪ-] n Sperrzone f für den Flugverkehr.

noise [nɔɪz] n Geräusch nt; (din) Lärm m.

noiseless ['nɔɪzlɪs] adj geräuschlos.

noisily ['nɔɪzɪlɪ] adv laut.

noisy ['nɔɪzɪ] adj laut.

nomad ['nəumæd] n Nomade m, Nomadin f.

nomadic [nəu'mædɪk] adj Nomaden-, nomadisch.

no-man's-land ['nəumænzlænd] n Niemandsland nt.

nominal ['nɔmɪnl] adj nominell.

nominate ['nɔmɪneɪt] vt nominieren; (appoint) ernennen.

nomination [nɔmɪ'neɪʃən] n Nominierung f;

(*appointment*) Ernennung *f*.
nominee [nɔmɪ'niː] *n* Kandidat(in) *m(f)*.
non- [nɔn] *pref* nicht-, Nicht-.
non-alcoholic [nɔnælkə'hɔlɪk] *adj* alkoholfrei.
non-aligned [nɔnə'laɪnd] *adj* blockfrei.
non-breakable [nɔn'breɪkəbl] *adj* unzerbrechlich.
nonce word ['nɔns-] *n* Ad-hoc-Bildung *f*.
nonchalant ['nɔnʃələnt] *adj* lässig, nonchalant.
noncommissioned officer [nɔnkə'mɪʃənd-] *n* Unteroffizier *m*.
non-committal [nɔnkə'mɪtl] *adj* zurückhaltend; (*answer*) unverbindlich.
nonconformist [nɔnkən'fɔːmɪst] *n* Nonkonformist(in) *m(f)* ♦ *adj* nonkonformistisch.
non-cooperation ['nɔnkəuɔpə'reɪʃən] *n* unkooperative Haltung *f*.
nondescript ['nɔndɪskrɪpt] *adj* unauffällig; (*colour*) unbestimmbar.
none [nʌn] *pron* (*not one*) kein(e, er, es); (*not any*) nichts; ~ **of us** keiner von uns; **I've** ~ **left** ('nəut any') ich habe nichts übrig; (*not one*) ich habe kein(e, en, es) übrig; ~ **at all** (*not any*) überhaupt nicht; (*not one*) überhaupt kein(e, er, es); **I was** ~ **the wiser** ich war auch nicht klüger; **she would have** ~ **of it** sie wollte nichts davon hören; **it was** ~ **other than X** es war kein anderer als X.
nonentity [nɔ'nɛntɪtɪ] *n* (*person*) Nichts *nt*, unbedeutende Figur *f*.
non-essential [nɔnɪ'sɛnʃl] *adj* unnötig ♦ *n*: ~**s** nicht (lebens)notwendige Dinge *pl*.
nonetheless ['nʌnðə'lɛs] *adv* nichtsdestoweniger, trotzdem.
nonevent [nɔnɪ'vɛnt] *n* Reinfall *m*.
non-existent [nɔnɪg'zɪstənt] *adj* nicht vorhanden.
non-fiction [nɔn'fɪkʃən] *n* Sachbücher *pl* ♦ *adj* (*book*) Sach-; (*prize*) Sachbuch-.
non-flammable [nɔn'flæməbl] *adj* nicht entzündbar.
non-intervention ['nɔnɪntə'venʃən] *n* Nichteinmischung *f*, Nichteingreifen *nt*.
no-no ['nəunəu] *n*: **it's a** ~ (*inf*) das kommt nicht infrage *or* in Frage.
non obst. *abbr* (= *non obstante*) dennoch.
no-nonsense [nəu'nɔnsəns] *adj* (*approach, look*) nüchtern.
non-payment [nɔn'peɪmənt] *n* Nichtzahlung *f*, Zahlungsverweigerung *f*.
nonplussed [nɔn'plʌst] *adj* verdutzt, verblüfft.
non-profit making ['nɔn'prɔfɪt-] *adj* (*organization*) gemeinnützig.
nonreturnable [nɔnrə'təːnəbl] *adj*: ~ **bottle** Einwegflasche *f*.
nonsense ['nɔnsəns] *n* Unsinn *m*; ~! Unsinn!, Quatsch!; **it is** ~ **to say that** ... es ist dummes Gerede zu sagen, dass ...; **to make (a)** ~ **of sth** etw ad absurdum führen.

nonsensical [nɔn'sɛnsɪkl] *adj* (*idea, action etc*) unsinnig.
non-shrink [nɔn'ʃrɪŋk] (*BRIT*) *adj* nicht einlaufend.
non-smoker ['nɔn'sməukə*] *n* Nichtraucher(in) *m(f)*.
nonstarter [nɔn'stɑːtə*] *n* (*fig*): **it's a** ~ (*idea etc*) es hat keine Erfolgschance.
non-stick ['nɔn'stɪk] *adj* kunststoffbeschichtet, Teflon- ®.
non-stop ['nɔn'stɔp] *adj* ununterbrochen; (*flight*) Nonstop-, Non-Stop- ♦ *adv* ununterbrochen; (*fly*) nonstop.
non-taxable [nɔn'tæksəbl] *adj* nichtsteuerpflichtig.
non-U [nɔn'juː] (*BRIT*: *inf*) *adj abbr* (= *non-upper class*) nicht vornehm.
non-white ['nɔn'waɪt] *adj* farbig ♦ *n* Farbige(r) *f(m)*.
noodles ['nuːdlz] *npl* Nudeln *pl*.
nook [nuk] *n*: **every** ~ **and cranny** jeder Winkel.
noon [nuːn] *n* Mittag *m*.
no-one ['nəuwʌn] *pron* = **nobody**.
noose [nuːs] *n* Schlinge *f*.
nor [nɔː*] *conj, adv* = **neither**.
Norf (*BRIT*) *abbr* (*POST*: = *Norfolk*).
norm [nɔːm] *n* Norm *f*.
normal ['nɔːməl] *adj* normal ♦ *n*: **to return to** ~ sich wieder normalisieren.
normality [nɔː'mælɪtɪ] *n* Normalität *f*.
normally ['nɔːməlɪ] *adv* normalerweise; (*act, behave*) normal.
Normandy ['nɔːməndɪ] *n* Normandie *f*.
north [nɔːθ] *n* Norden *m* ♦ *adj* nördlich, Nord- ♦ *adv* nach Norden; ~ *of* nördlich von.
North Africa *n* Nordafrika *nt*.
North African *adj* nordafrikanisch ♦ *n* Nordafrikaner(in) *m(f)*.
North America *n* Nordamerika *nt*.
North American *adj* nordamerikanisch ♦ *n* Nordamerikaner(in) *m(f)*.
Northants [nɔː'θænts] (*BRIT*) *abbr* (*POST*: = *Northamptonshire*).
northbound ['nɔːθbaund] *adj* in Richtung Norden; (*carriageway*) nach Norden (führend).
Northd (*BRIT*) *abbr* (*POST*: = *Northumberland*).
north-east [nɔːθ'iːst] *n* Nordosten *m* ♦ *adj* nordöstlich, Nordost- ♦ *adv* nach Nordosten; ~ *of* nordöstlich von.
northerly ['nɔːðəlɪ] *adj* nördlich.
northern ['nɔːðən] *adj* nördlich, Nord-.
Northern Ireland *n* Nordirland *nt*.
North Korea *n* Nordkorea *nt*.
North Pole *n*: **the** ~ der Nordpol.
North Sea *n*: **the** ~ die Nordsee *f*.
North Sea oil *n* Nordseeöl *nt*.
northward(s) ['nɔːθwəd(z)] *adv* nach Norden, nordwärts.
north-west [nɔːθ'wɛst] *n* Nordwesten *m* ♦ *adj* nordwestlich, Nordwest- ♦ *adv* nach

Nordwesten; ~ **of** nordwestlich von.
Norway ['nɔːweɪ] n Norwegen nt.
Norwegian [nɔː'wiːdʒən] adj norwegisch ♦ n Norweger(in) m(f); (LING) Norwegisch nt.
nos. abbr (= numbers) Nrn.
nose [nəuz] n Nase f; (of car) Schnauze f ♦ vi (also: ~ **one's way**) sich schieben; **to follow one's** ~ immer der Nase nach gehen; **to get up one's** ~ (inf) auf die Nerven gehen +dat; **to have a (good)** ~ **for sth** eine (gute) Nase für etw haben; **to keep one's** ~ **clean** (inf) eine saubere Weste behalten; **to look down one's** ~ **at sb/sth** (inf) auf jdn/etw herabsehen; **to pay through the** ~ **(for sth)** (inf) (für etw) viel blechen; **to rub sb's** ~ **in sth** (inf) jdm etw unter die Nase reiben; **to turn one's** ~ **up at sth** (inf) die Nase über etw acc rümpfen; **under sb's** ~ vor jds Augen.
► **nose about** vi herumschnüffeln.
► **nose around** vi = **nose about**.
nosebleed ['nəuzbliːd] n Nasenbluten nt.
nose-dive ['nəuzdaɪv] n (of plane) Sturzflug m ♦ vi (plane) im Sturzflug herabgehen.
nose drops npl Nasentropfen pl.
nosey ['nəuzɪ] (inf) adj = **nosy**.
nostalgia [nɔs'tældʒə] n Nostalgie f.
nostalgic [nɔs'tældʒɪk] adj nostalgisch.
nostril ['nɔstrɪl] n Nasenloch nt; (of animal) Nüster f.
nosy ['nəuzɪ] (inf) adj neugierig.

=================== KEYWORD

not [nɔt] adv nicht; **he is** ~ or **isn't here** er ist nicht hier; **you must** ~ or **you mustn't do that** das darfst du nicht tun; **it's too late, isn't it?** es ist zu spät, nicht wahr?; ~ **that I don't like him** nicht, dass ich ihn nicht mag; ~ **yet** noch nicht; ~ **now** nicht jetzt; see also **all, only**.

notable ['nəutəbl] adj bemerkenswert.
notably ['nəutəblɪ] adv hauptsächlich; (markedly) bemerkenswert.
notary ['nəutərɪ] n (also: ~ **public**) Notar(in) m(f).
notation [nəu'teɪʃən] n Notation f; (MUS) Notenschrift f.
notch [nɔtʃ] n Kerbe f; (in blade, saw) Scharte f; (fig) Klasse f.
► **notch up** vt erzielen; (victory) erringen.
note [nəut] n Notiz f; (of lecturer) Manuskript nt; (of student etc) Aufzeichnung f; (in book etc) Anmerkung f; (letter) paar Zeilen pl; (banknote) Note f, Schein m; (MUS: sound) Ton m; (: symbol) Note f; (tone) Ton m, Klang m ♦ vt beachten; (point out) anmerken; (also: ~ **down**) notieren; **of** ~ bedeutend; **to make a** ~ **of sth** sich dat etw notieren; **to take** ~**s** Notizen machen, mitschreiben; **to take** ~ **of sth** etw zur Kenntnis nehmen.
notebook ['nəutbuk] n Notizbuch nt; (for

shorthand) Stenoblock m.
notecase ['nəutkeɪs] (BRIT) n Brieftasche f.
noted ['nəutɪd] adj bekannt.
notepad ['nəutpæd] n Notizblock m.
notepaper ['nəutpeɪpə'] n Briefpapier nt.
noteworthy ['nəutwɜːðɪ] adj beachtenswert.
nothing ['nʌθɪŋ] n nichts; ~ **new/worse** etc nichts Neues/Schlimmeres etc; ~ **much** nicht viel; ~ **else** sonst nichts; **for** ~ umsonst; ~ **at all** überhaupt nichts.
notice ['nəutɪs] n Bekanntmachung f; (sign) Schild nt; (warning) Ankündigung f; (dismissal) Kündigung f; (BRIT: review) Kritik f, Rezension f ♦ vt bemerken; **to bring sth to sb's** ~ jdn auf etw acc aufmerksam machen; **to take no** ~ **of** ignorieren, nicht beachten; **to escape sb's** ~ jdm entgehen; **it has come to my** ~ **that** ... es ist mir zu Ohren gekommen, dass ...; **to give sb** ~ **of sth** jdm von etw Bescheid geben; **without** ~ ohne Ankündigung; **advance** ~ Vorankündigung f; **at short/a moment's** ~ kurzfristig/ innerhalb kürzester Zeit; **until further** ~ bis auf weiteres; **to hand in one's** ~ kündigen; **to be given one's** ~ gekündigt werden +dat.
noticeable ['nəutɪsəbl] adj deutlich.
noticeboard ['nəutɪsbɔːd] (BRIT) n Anschlagbrett nt.
notification [nəutɪfɪ'keɪʃən] n Benachrichtigung f.
notify ['nəutɪfaɪ] vt: **to** ~ **sb (of sth)** jdn (von etw) benachrichtigen.
notion ['nəuʃən] n Vorstellung f; **notions** (US) npl (haberdashery) Kurzwaren pl.
notoriety [nəutə'raɪətɪ] n traurige Berühmtheit f.
notorious [nəu'tɔːrɪəs] adj berüchtigt.
notoriously [nəu'tɔːrɪəslɪ] adv notorisch.
Notts [nɔts] (BRIT) abbr (POST: = Nottinghamshire').
notwithstanding [nɔtwɪθ'stændɪŋ] adv trotzdem ♦ prep trotz +dat.
nougat ['nuːgɑː] n Nugat m, Nougat m.
nought [nɔːt] n Null f.
noun [naun] n Hauptwort nt, Substantiv nt.
nourish ['nʌrɪʃ] vt nähren.
nourishing ['nʌrɪʃɪŋ] adj nahrhaft.
nourishment ['nʌrɪʃmənt] n Nahrung f.
Nov. abbr (= November) Nov.
Nova Scotia ['nəuvə'skəuʃə] n Neuschottland nt.
novel ['nɔvl] n Roman m ♦ adj neu(artig).
novelist ['nɔvəlɪst] n Romanschriftsteller(in) m(f).
novelty ['nɔvəltɪ] n Neuheit f; (object) Kleinigkeit f.
November [nəu'vɛmbə'] n November m; see also **July**.
novice ['nɔvɪs] n Neuling m, Anfänger(in) m(f); (REL) Novize m, Novizin f.
NOW [nau] (US) n abbr (= National Organization for Women) Frauenvereinigung.

now [nau] *adv* jetzt; (*these days*) heute ♦ *conj*:
~ **(that)** jetzt, wo; **right** ~ gleich, sofort; **by**
~ inzwischen, mittlerweile; **that's the
fashion just** ~ das ist gerade modern; **I saw
her just** ~ ich habe sie gerade gesehen;
(every) ~ **and then, (every)** ~ **and again** ab
und zu, gelegentlich; **from** ~ **on** von nun an;
in 3 days from ~ (heute) in 3 Tagen;
between ~ **and Monday** bis Montag; **that's
all for** ~ das ist erst einmal alles; **any day** ~
jederzeit; ~ **then** also.

nowadays ['nauədeɪz] *adv* heute.

nowhere ['nəuwɛə°] *adv* (*be*) nirgends,
nirgendwo; (*go*) nirgendwohin; ~ **else**
nirgendwo anders.

no-win situation [nəu'wɪn-] *n* aussichtslose
Lage *f*.

noxious ['nɔkʃəs] *adj* (*gas, fumes*) schädlich;
(*smell*) übel.

nozzle ['nɔzl] *n* Düse *f*.

NP *n abbr* (*LAW*) = **notary public.**

NS (*CANADA*) *abbr* (= *Nova Scotia*).

NSC (*US*) *n abbr* = **National Security Council.**

NSF (*US*) *n abbr* (= *National Science Foundation*)
Organisation zur Förderung der
Wissenschaft.

NSPCC (*BRIT*) *n abbr* (= *National Society for the
Prevention of Cruelty to Children*)
Kinderschutzbund *m*.

NSW (*AUSTRALIA*) *abbr* (*POST*: = *New South
Wales*).

NT *n abbr* (*BIBLE*: = *New Testament*) NT.

nth [ɛnθ] (*inf*) *adj*: **to the** ~ **degree** in der n-ten
Potenz.

nuance ['njuːɑ̃ːns] *n* Nuance *f*.

nubile ['njuːbaɪl] *adj* gut entwickelt.

nuclear ['njuːklɪə°] *adj* (*bomb, industry etc*)
Atom-; ~ **physics** Kernphysik *f*; ~ **war**
Atomkrieg *m*.

nuclear disarmament *n* nukleare *or*
atomare Abrüstung *f*.

nuclear family *n* Kleinfamilie *f*, Kernfamilie
f.

nuclear-free zone ['njuːklɪə'friː-] *n*
atomwaffenfreie Zone *f*.

nuclei ['njuːklɪaɪ] *npl of* **nucleus.**

nucleus ['njuːklɪəs] (*pl* **nuclei**) *n* Kern *m*.

NUCPS (*BRIT*) *n abbr* (= *National Union of Civil
and Public Servants*) Gewerkschaft für
Beschäftigte im öffentlichen Dienst.

nude [njuːd] *adj* nackt ♦ *n* (*ART*) Akt *m*; **in the**
~ nackt.

nudge [nʌdʒ] *vt* anstoßen.

nudist ['njuːdɪst] *n* Nudist(in) *m(f)*.

nudist colony *n* FKK-Kolonie *f*.

nudity ['njuːdɪtɪ] *n* Nacktheit *f*.

nugget ['nʌgɪt] *n* (*of gold*) Klumpen *m*; (*fig: of
information*) Brocken *m*.

nuisance ['njuːsns] *n*: **to be a** ~ lästig sein;
(*situation*) ärgerlich sein; **he's a** ~ er geht
einem auf die Nerven; **what a** ~! wie
ärgerlich/lästig!

NUJ (*BRIT*) *n abbr* (= *National Union of
Journalists*) Journalistengewerkschaft.

null [nʌl] *adj*: ~ **and void** null und nichtig.

nullify ['nʌlɪfaɪ] *vt* zunichte machen; (*claim,
law*) für null und nichtig erklären.

NUM (*BRIT*) *n abbr* (= *National Union of
Mineworkers*) Bergarbeitergewerkschaft.

numb [nʌm] *adj* taub, gefühllos; (*fig: with fear
etc*) wie betäubt ♦ *vt* taub *or* gefühllos
machen; (*pain, fig: mind*) betäuben.

number ['nʌmbə°] *n* Zahl *f*; (*quantity*) (An)zahl
f; (*of house, bank account, bus etc*) Nummer *f*
♦ *vt* (*pages etc*) nummerieren; (*amount to*)
zählen; **a** ~ **of** einige; **any** ~ **of** beliebig
viele; (*reasons*) alle möglichen; **wrong** ~
(*TEL*) falsch verbunden; **to be** ~ed **among**
zählen zu.

number plate (*BRIT*) *n* (*AUT*)
Nummernschild *nt*.

Number Ten (*BRIT*) *n* (*POL*: = *10 Downing
Street*) Nummer zehn *f* (Downing Street).

numbness ['nʌmnɪs] *n* Taubheit *f*, Starre *f*;
(*fig*) Benommenheit *f*, Betäubung *f*.

numbskull ['nʌmskʌl] *n* = **numskull.**

numeral ['njuːmərəl] *n* Ziffer *f*.

numerate ['njuːmərɪt] (*BRIT*) *adj*: **to be** ~
rechnen können.

numerical [njuː'mɛrɪkl] *adj* numerisch.

numerous ['njuːmərəs] *adj* zahlreich.

numskull ['nʌmskʌl] (*inf*) *n* Holzkopf *m*.

nun [nʌn] *n* Nonne *f*.

nunnery ['nʌnərɪ] *n* (Nonnen)kloster *nt*.

nuptial ['nʌpʃəl] *adj* (*feast, celebration*)
Hochzeits-; ~ **bliss** Eheglück *nt*.

nurse [nɜːs] *n* Krankenschwester *f*; (*also:*
~**maid**) Kindermädchen *nt* ♦ *vt* pflegen;
(*cold, toothache etc*) auskurieren; (*baby*)
stillen; (*fig: desire, grudge*) hegen.

nursery ['nɜːsərɪ] *n* Kindergarten *m*; (*room*)
Kinderzimmer *nt*; (*for plants*) Gärtnerei *f*.

nursery rhyme *n* Kinderreim *m*.

nursery school *n* Kindergarten *m*.

nursery slope (*BRIT*) *n* (*SKI*) Anfängerhügel
m.

nursing ['nɜːsɪŋ] *n* Krankenpflege *f*; (*care*)
Pflege *f*.

nursing home *n* Pflegeheim *nt*.

nursing mother *n* stillende Mutter *f*.

nurture ['nɜːtʃə°] *vt* hegen und pflegen; (*fig:
ideas, creativity*) fördern.

NUS (*BRIT*) *n abbr* (= *National Union of
Students*) Studentengewerkschaft.

NUT (*BRIT*) *n abbr* (= *National Union of
Teachers*) Lehrergewerkschaft.

nut [nʌt] *n* (*TECH*) (Schrauben)mutter *f*; (*BOT*)
Nuss *f*; (*inf: lunatic*) Spinner(in) *m(f)*.

nutcase ['nʌtkeɪs] (*inf*) *n* Spinner(in) *m(f)*.

nutcrackers ['nʌtkrækəz] *npl* Nussknacker *m*.

nutmeg ['nʌtmeg] *n* Muskat *m*, Muskatnuss *f*.

nutrient ['njuːtrɪənt] *n* Nährstoff *m*.

nutrition [njuː'trɪʃən] *n* Ernährung *f*;
(*nourishment*) Nahrung *f*.

nutritionist [nju:'trɪʃənɪst] n
Ernährungswissenschaftler(in) m(f).
nutritious [nju:'trɪʃəs] adj nahrhaft.
nuts [nʌts] (inf) adj verrückt; **he's ~** er spinnt.
nutshell ['nʌtʃɛl] n Nussschale f; **in a ~** (fig)
kurz gesagt.
nutty ['nʌtɪ] adj (flavour) Nuss-; (inf: idea etc)
bekloppt.
nuzzle ['nʌzl] vi: **to ~ up to** sich drücken or
schmiegen an +acc.
NV (US) abbr (POST: = Nevada).
NVQ n abbr (= National Vocational Qualification)
Qualifikation für berufsbegleitende
Ausbildungsinhalte.
NW abbr = **north-west.**
NY (US) abbr (POST: = New York).
nylon ['naɪlɒn] n Nylon nt ♦ adj Nylon-; **nylons**
npl (stockings) Nylonstrümpfe pl.
nymph [nɪmf] n Nymphe f.
nymphomaniac ['nɪmfəu'meɪnɪæk] n
Nymphomanin f.
NYSE (US) n abbr (= New York Stock Exchange)
New Yorker Börse.
NZ abbr = **New Zealand.**

O, o

O, o [əu] n (letter) O nt, o nt; (US: SCOL:
outstanding) ≈ Eins f; (TEL etc) Null f; **~ for
Olive,** (US) **~ for Oboe** ≈ O wie Otto.
oaf [əuf] n Trottel m.
oak [əuk] n (tree, wood) Eiche f ♦ adj (furniture,
door) Eichen-.
O & M n abbr (= organization and method)
Organisation und Arbeitsweise pl.
OAP (BRIT) n abbr = **old age pensioner.**
oar [ɔ:ʳ] n Ruder nt; **to put** or **shove one's ~ in**
(inf, fig) mitmischen, sich einmischen.
oarsman ['ɔ:zmən] (irreg: like **man**) n Ruderer
m.
oarswoman ['ɔ:zwumən] (irreg: like **woman**) n
Ruderin f.
OAS n abbr (= Organization of American States)
OAS f.
oasis [əu'eɪsɪs] (pl **oases**) n (lit, fig) Oase f.
oath [əuθ] n (promise) Eid m, Schwur m; (swear
word) Fluch m; **on** (BRIT) or **under ~** unter
Eid; **to take the ~** (LAW) vereidigt werden.
oatmeal ['əutmi:l] n Haferschrot m; (colour)
Hellbeige nt.
oats [əuts] npl Hafer m; **he's getting his ~**
(BRIT: inf, fig) er kommt im Bett auf seine
Kosten.
OAU n abbr (= Organization of African Unity)
OAU f.

obdurate ['ɒbdjurɪt] adj unnachgiebig.
OBE (BRIT) n abbr (= Officer of (the order of) the
British Empire) britischer Ordenstitel.
obedience [ə'bi:dɪəns] n Gehorsam m; **in ~ to**
gemäß +dat.
obedient [ə'bi:dɪənt] adj gehorsam; **to be ~ to
sb** jdm gehorchen.
obelisk ['ɒbɪlɪsk] n Obelisk m.
obese [əu'bi:s] adj fettleibig.
obesity [əu'bi:sɪtɪ] n Fettleibigkeit f.
obey [ə'beɪ] vt (person) gehorchen +dat, folgen
+dat; (orders, law) befolgen ♦ vi gehorchen.
obituary [ə'bɪtjuərɪ] n Nachruf m.
object [n 'ɒbdʒɪkt, vi əb'dʒɛkt] n (also LING)
Objekt nt; (aim, purpose) Ziel nt, Zweck m ♦ vi
dagegen sein; **to be an ~ of ridicule** (person)
sich lächerlich machen; (thing) lächerlich
wirken; **money is no ~** Geld spielt keine
Rolle; **he ~ed that ...** er wandte ein, dass ...;
I ~! ich protestiere!; **do you ~ to my
smoking?** haben Sie etwas dagegen, wenn
ich rauche?
objection [əb'dʒɛkʃən] n (argument) Einwand
m; **I have no ~ to ...** ich habe nichts
dagegen, dass ...; **if you have no ~** wenn Sie
nichts dagegen haben; **to raise** or **voice an ~**
einen Einwand erheben or vorbringen.
objectionable [əb'dʒɛkʃənəbl] adj (language,
conduct) anstößig; (person) unausstehlich.
objective [əb'dʒɛktɪv] adj objektiv ♦ n Ziel nt.
objectively [əb'dʒɛktɪvlɪ] adv objektiv.
objectivity [ɒbdʒɪk'tɪvɪtɪ] n Objektivität f.
object lesson n: **an ~ in** ein Paradebeispiel
nt für.
objector [əb'dʒɛktəʳ] n Gegner(in) m(f).
obligation [ɒblɪ'geɪʃən] n Pflicht f; **to be under
an ~ to do sth** verpflichtet sein, etw zu tun;
to be under an ~ to sb jdm verpflichtet
sein; **"no ~ to buy"** (COMM) „kein
Kaufzwang".
obligatory [ə'blɪgətərɪ] adj obligatorisch.
oblige [ə'blaɪdʒ] vt (compel) zwingen; (do a
favour for) einen Gefallen tun +dat; **I felt ~d
to invite him in** ich fühlte mich verpflichtet,
ihn hereinzubitten; **to be ~d to sb for sth**
(grateful) jdm für etw dankbar sein;
anything to ~! (inf) stets zu Diensten!
obliging [ə'blaɪdʒɪŋ] adj entgegenkommend.
oblique [ə'bli:k] adj (line, angle) schief;
(reference, compliment) indirekt, versteckt
♦ n (BRIT: also: ~ **stroke**) Schrägstrich m.
obliterate [ə'blɪtəreɪt] vt (village etc)
vernichten; (fig: memory, error) auslöschen.
oblivion [ə'blɪvɪən] n (unconsciousness)
Bewusstlosigkeit f; (being forgotten)
Vergessenheit f; **to sink into ~** (event etc) in
Vergessenheit geraten.
oblivious [ə'blɪvɪəs] adj: **he was ~ of** or **to it** er
war sich dessen nicht bewusst.
oblong ['ɒblɒŋ] adj rechteckig ♦ n Rechteck nt.
obnoxious [əb'nɒkʃəs] adj widerwärtig,
widerlich.

o.b.o. (*US*) *abbr* (*in classified ads*: = *or best offer*) bzw. Höchstgebot.

oboe ['əubəu] *n* Oboe *f*.

obscene [əb'si:n] *adj* obszön; (*fig*: *wealth*) unanständig; (*income etc*) unverschämt.

obscenity [əb'sɛnɪtɪ] *n* Obszönität *f*.

obscure [əb'skjuə*] *adj* (*little known*) unbekannt, obskur; (*difficult to understand*) unklar ♦ *vt* (*obstruct, conceal*) verdecken.

obscurity [əb'skjuərɪtɪ] *n* (*of person, book*) Unbekanntheit *f*; (*of remark etc*) Unklarheit *f*.

obsequious [əb'si:kwɪəs] *adj* unterwürfig.

observable [əb'zə:vəbl] *adj* wahrnehmbar; (*noticeable*) erkennbar.

observance [əb'zə:vəns] *n* (*of law etc*) Befolgung *f*; **religious** ~s religiöse Feste *pl*.

observant [əb'zə:vənt] *adj* aufmerksam.

observation [ɔbzə'veɪʃən] *n* (*remark*) Bemerkung *f*; (*act of observing, MED*) Beobachtung *f*; **she's in hospital under** ~ sie ist zur Beobachtung im Krankenhaus.

observation post *n* Beobachtungsposten *m*.

observatory [əb'zə:vətrɪ] *n* Observatorium *nt*.

observe [əb'zə:v] *vt* (*watch*) beobachten; (*notice, comment*) bemerken; (*abide by: rule etc*) einhalten.

observer [əb'zə:və*] *n* Beobachter(in) *m(f)*.

obsess [əb'sɛs] *vt* verfolgen; **to be ~ed by** *or* **with sb/sth** von jdm/etw besessen sein.

obsession [əb'sɛʃən] *n* Besessenheit *f*.

obsessive [əb'sɛsɪv] *adj* (*person*) zwanghaft; (*interest, hatred, tidiness*) krankhaft; **to be** ~ **about cleaning/tidying up** einen Putz-/ Ordnungsfimmel haben (*inf*).

obsolescence [ɔbsə'lɛsns] *n* Veralten *nt*; **built-in** *or* **planned** ~ (*COMM*) geplanter Verschleiß *m*.

obsolete ['ɔbsəli:t] *adj* veraltet.

obstacle ['ɔbstəkl] *n* (*lit, fig*) Hindernis *nt*.

obstacle race *n* Hindernisrennen *nt*.

obstetrician [ɔbstə'trɪʃən] *n* Geburtshelfer(in) *m(f)*.

obstetrics [əb'stetrɪks] *n* Geburtshilfe *f*.

obstinacy ['ɔbstɪnəsɪ] *n* (*of person*) Starrsinn *m*.

obstinate ['ɔbstɪnɪt] *adj* (*person*) starrsinnig, stur; (*refusal, cough etc*) hartnäckig.

obstruct [əb'strʌkt] *vt* (*road, path*) blockieren; (*traffic, fig*) behindern.

obstruction [əb'strʌkʃən] *n* (*object*) Hindernis *nt*; (*of plan, law*) Behinderung *f*.

obstructive [əb'strʌktɪv] *adj* hinderlich, obstruktiv (*esp POL*); **she's being** ~ sie macht Schwierigkeiten.

obtain [əb'teɪn] *vt* erhalten, bekommen ♦ *vi* (*form*: *exist, be the case*) gelten.

obtainable [əb'teɪnəbl] *adj* erhältlich.

obtrusive [əb'tru:sɪv] *adj* aufdringlich; (*conspicuous*) auffällig.

obtuse [əb'tju:s] *adj* (*person, remark*) einfältig; (*MATH*) stumpf.

obverse ['ɔbvə:s] *n* (*of situation, argument*)

Kehrseite *f*.

obviate ['ɔbvɪeɪt] *vt* (*need, problem etc*) vorbeugen +*dat*.

obvious ['ɔbvɪəs] *adj* offensichtlich; (*lie*) klar; (*predictable*) nahe liegend.

obviously ['ɔbvɪəslɪ] *adv* (*clearly*) offensichtlich; (*of course*) natürlich; ~! selbstverständlich!; ~ **not** offensichtlich nicht; **he was** ~ **not drunk** er war natürlich nicht betrunken; **he was not** ~ **drunk** offenbar war er nicht betrunken.

OCAS *n abbr* (= *Organization of Central American States*) mittelamerikanischer Staatenbund.

occasion [ə'keɪʒən] *n* Gelegenheit *f*; (*celebration etc*) Ereignis *nt* ♦ *vt* (*form*: *cause*) verursachen; **on** ~ (*sometimes*) gelegentlich; **on that** ~ bei der Gelegenheit; **to rise to the** ~ sich der Lage gewachsen zeigen.

occasional [ə'keɪʒənl] *adj* gelegentlich; **he likes the** ~ **cigar** er raucht gelegentlich gern eine Zigarre.

occasionally [ə'keɪʒənəlɪ] *adv* gelegentlich; **very** ~ sehr selten.

occasional table *n* Beistelltisch *m*.

occult [ɔ'kʌlt] *n*: **the** ~ der Okkultismus ♦ *adj* okkult.

occupancy ['ɔkjupənsɪ] *n* (*of room etc*) Bewohnen *nt*.

occupant ['ɔkjupənt] *n* (*of house etc*) Bewohner(in) *m(f)*; (*temporary*: *of car*) Insasse *m*, Insassin *f*; **the** ~ **of this table/ office** derjenige, der an diesem Tisch sitzt/ in diesem Büro arbeitet.

occupation [ɔkju'peɪʃən] *n* (*job*) Beruf *m*; (*pastime*) Beschäftigung *f*; (*of building, country etc*) Besetzung *f*.

occupational guidance [ɔkju'peɪʃənl-] (*BRIT*) *n* Berufsberatung *f*.

occupational hazard *n* Berufsrisiko *nt*.

occupational pension scheme *n* betriebliche Altersversorgung *f*.

occupational therapy *n* Beschäftigungstherapie *f*.

occupier ['ɔkjupaɪə*] *n* Bewohner(in) *m(f)*.

occupy ['ɔkjupaɪ] *vt* (*house, office*) bewohnen; (*place etc*) belegen; (*building, country etc*) besetzen; (*time, attention*) beanspruchen; (*position, space*) einnehmen; **to** ~ **o.s.** (**in** *or* **with sth**) sich (mit etw) beschäftigen; **to** ~ **o.s. in** *or* **with doing sth** sich damit beschäftigen, etw zu tun; **to be occupied in** *or* **with sth** mit etw beschäftigt sein; **to be occupied in** *or* **with doing sth** damit beschäftigt sein, etw zu tun.

occur [ə'kə:*] *vi* (*take place*) geschehen, sich ereignen; (*exist*) vorkommen; **to** ~ **to sb** jdm einfallen.

occurrence [ə'kʌrəns] *n* (*event*) Ereignis *nt*; (*incidence*) Auftreten *nt*.

ocean ['əuʃən] *n* Ozean *m*, Meer *nt*; ~s of (*inf*) jede Menge.

ocean bed *n* Meeresgrund *m*.

ocean-going ['əuʃəngəuiŋ] *adj* (*ship, vessel*) Hochsee-.

Oceania [əuʃɪ'eɪnɪə] *n* Ozeanien *nt*.

ocean liner *n* Ozeandampfer *m*.

ochre, (*US*) **ocher** ['əukə*] *adj* ockerfarben.

o'clock [ə'klɔk] *adv*: **it is 5** ~ es ist 5 Uhr.

OCR *n abbr* (*COMPUT*) = **optical character reader; optical character recogniton**.

Oct. *abbr* (= *October*) Okt.

octagonal [ɔk'tægənl] *adj* achteckig.

octane ['ɔkteɪn] *n* Oktan *nt*; **high-** ~ **petrol** *or* (*US*) **gas** Benzin *nt* mit hoher Oktanzahl.

octave ['ɔktɪv] *n* Oktave *f*.

October [ɔk'təubə*] *n* Oktober *m*; *see also* **July**.

octogenarian ['ɔktəudʒɪ'nɛərɪən] *n* Achtzigjährige(r) *f(m)*.

octopus ['ɔktəpəs] *n* Tintenfisch *m*.

odd [ɔd] *adj* (*person*) sonderbar, komisch; (*behaviour, shape*) seltsam; (*number*) ungerade; (*sock, shoe etc*) einzeln; (*occasional*) gelegentlich; **60-**~ etwa 60; **at** ~ **times** ab und zu; **to be the** ~ **one out** der Außenseiter/die Außenseiterin sein; **add meat or the** ~ **vegetable to the soup** fügen Sie der Suppe Fleisch oder auch etwas Gemüse bei.

oddball ['ɔdbɔːl] (*inf*) *n* komischer Kauz *m*.

oddity ['ɔdɪtɪ] *n* (*person*) Sonderling *m*; (*thing*) Merkwürdigkeit *f*.

odd-job man [ɔd'dʒɔb-] *n* Mädchen *nt* für alles.

odd jobs *npl* Gelegenheitsarbeiten *pl*.

oddly ['ɔdlɪ] *adv* (*behave, dress*) seltsam; *see also* **enough**.

oddments ['ɔdmənts] *npl* (*COMM*) Restposten *m*.

odds [ɔdz] *npl* (*in betting*) Gewinnquote *f*; (*fig*) Chancen *pl*; **the** ~ **are in favour of/against his coming** es sieht so aus, als ob er kommt/nicht kommt; **to succeed against all the** ~ allen Erwartungen zum Trotz erfolgreich sein; **it makes no** ~ es spielt keine Rolle; **to be at** ~ **(with)** (*in disagreement*) uneinig sein (mit); (*at variance*) sich nicht vertragen (mit).

odds and ends *npl* Kleinigkeiten *pl*.

odds-on [ɔdz'ɔn] *adj*: **the** ~ **favourite** der klare Favorit ♦ *adv*: **it's** ~ **that she'll win** es ist so gut wie sicher, dass sie gewinnt.

ode [əud] *n* Ode *f*.

odious ['əudɪəs] *adj* widerwärtig.

odometer [ɔ'dɔmɪtə*] (*US*) *n* Tacho(meter) *m*.

odor *etc* (*US*) = **odour** *etc*.

odour, (*US*) **odor** ['əudə*] *n* Geruch *m*.

odourless ['əudəlɪs] *adj* geruchlos.

OECD *n abbr* (= *Organization for Economic Cooperation and Development*) OECD *f*.

oesophagus, (*US*) **esophagus** [iː'sɔfəgəs] *n* Speiseröhre *f*.

oestrogen, (*US*) **estrogen** ['iːstrəudʒən] *n* Östrogen *nt*.

——————— KEYWORD

of [ɔv] *prep* **1** von; **the history** ~ **Germany** die Geschichte Deutschlands; **a friend** ~ **ours** ein Freund von uns; **a boy** ~ **ten** ein Junge von zehn Jahren, ein zehnjähriger Junge; **that was kind** ~ **you** das war nett von Ihnen; **the city** ~ **New York** die Stadt New York.

2 (*expressing quantity, amount, dates etc*): **a kilo** ~ **flour** ein Kilo Mehl; **how much** ~ **this do you need?** wie viel brauchen Sie davon?; **3** ~ **them** (*people*) 3 von ihnen; (*objects*) 3 davon; **a cup** ~ **tea** eine Tasse Tee; **a vase** ~ **flowers** eine Vase mit Blumen; **the 5th** ~ **July** der 5. Juli.

3 (*from, out of*) aus; **a bracelet** ~ **solid gold** ein Armband aus massivem Gold; **made** ~ **wood** aus Holz (gemacht).

Ofcom ['ɔfkɔm] (*BRIT*) *n abbr* (= *Office of Communications Regulation*) *Regulierungsbehörde für die Kommunikationsindustrie.*

——————— KEYWORD

off [ɔf] *adv* **1** (*referring to distance, time*): **it's a long way** ~ es ist sehr weit weg; **the game is 3 days** ~ es sind noch 3 Tage bis zum Spiel.

2 (*departure*): **to go** ~ **to Paris/Italy** nach Paris/Italien fahren; **I must be** ~ ich muss gehen.

3 (*removal*): **to take** ~ **one's coat/clothes** seinen Mantel/sich ausziehen; **the button came** ~ der Knopf ging ab; **10 %** ~ (*COMM*) 10% Nachlass.

4: **to be** ~ (*on holiday*) im Urlaub sein; (*due to sickness*) krank sein; **I'm** ~ **on Fridays** freitags habe ich frei; **he was** ~ **on Friday** Freitag war er nicht da; **to have a day** ~ (*from work*) einen Tag freihaben; **to be** ~ **sick** wegen Krankheit fehlen

♦ *adj* **1** (*not turned on: machine, light, engine etc*) aus; (: *water, gas*) abgedreht; (: *tap*) zu.

2: **to be** ~ (*meeting, match*) ausfallen; (*agreement*) nicht mehr gelten.

3 (*BRIT: not fresh*) verdorben, schlecht.

4: **on the** ~ **chance that** ... für den Fall, dass ...; **to have an** ~ **day** (*not as good as usual*) nicht in Form sein; **to be badly** ~ sich schlecht stehen

♦ *prep* **1** (*indicating motion, removal etc*) von +*dat*; **to fall** ~ **a cliff** von einer Klippe fallen; **to take a picture** ~ **the wall** ein Bild von der Wand nehmen.

2 (*distant from*): **5 km** ~ **the main road** 5 km von der Hauptstraße entfernt; **an island** ~ **the coast** eine Insel vor der Küste.

3: **I'm** ~ **meat/beer** (*no longer eat/drink it*) ich esse kein Fleisch/trinke kein Bier mehr; (*no longer like it*) ich kann kein Fleisch/Bier *etc* mehr sehen.

offal ['ɔfl] *n* (*CULIN*) Innereien *pl*.

off-beat ['ɔfbiːt] *adj* ausgefallen.
off-centre, *(US)* **off-center** [ɔf'sɛntə*] *adj*
nicht genau in der Mitte, links/rechts von
der Mitte ♦ *adv* asymmetrisch.
off-colour ['ɔf'kʌlə*] *(BRIT) adj (ill)* unpässlich;
to feel ~ sich unwohl fühlen.
offence, *(US)* **offense** [ə'fɛns] *n (crime)*
Vergehen *nt*; *(insult)* Beleidigung *f*,
Kränkung *f*; **to commit an** ~ eine Straftat
begehen; **to take** ~ **(at)** Anstoß nehmen (an
+*dat*); **to give** ~ **(to)** Anstoß erregen (bei);
"no ~**"** „nichts für ungut".
offend [ə'fɛnd] *vt (upset)* kränken; **to**
~ **against** *(law, rule)* verstoßen gegen.
offender [ə'fɛndə*] *n* Straftäter(in) *m(f)*.
offending [ə'fɛndɪŋ] *adj (item etc)* Anstoß
erregend.
offense [ə'fɛns] *(US) n* = **offence**.
offensive [ə'fɛnsɪv] *adj (remark, behaviour)*
verletzend; *(smell etc)* übel; *(weapon)*
Angriffs- ♦ *n (MIL)* Offensive *f*.
offer ['ɔfə*] *n* Angebot *nt* ♦ *vt* anbieten; *(money,
opportunity, service)* bieten; *(reward)*
aussetzen; **to make an** ~ **for sth** ein Angebot
für etw machen; **on** ~ *(COMM: available)*
erhältlich; (: *cheaper*) im Angebot; **to** ~ **sth
to sb** jdm etw anbieten; **to** ~ **to do sth**
anbieten, etw zu tun.
offering ['ɔfərɪŋ] *n* Darbietung *f*; *(REL)*
Opfergabe *f*.
off-hand [ɔf'hænd] *adj (casual)* lässig;
(impolite) kurz angebunden ♦ *adv* auf
Anhieb; **I can't tell you** ~ das kann ich Ihnen
auf Anhieb nicht sagen.
office ['ɔfɪs] *n* Büro *nt*; *(position)* Amt *nt*;
doctor's ~ *(US)* Praxis *f*; **to take** ~ das Amt
antreten; **in** ~ *(minister etc)* im Amt; **through
his good** ~**s** durch seine guten Dienste;
O~ **of Fair Trading** *(BRIT)* Behörde *f* gegen
unlauteren Wettbewerb.
office block, *(US)* **office building** *n*
Bürogebäude *nt*.
office boy *n* Bürogehilfe *m*.
office holder *n* Amtsinhaber(in) *m(f)*.
office hours *npl (COMM)* Bürostunden *pl*; *(US:
MED)* Sprechstunde *f*.
office manager *n* Büroleiter(in) *m(f)*.
officer ['ɔfɪsə*] *n (MIL etc)* Offizier *m*; *(also:
police* ~) Polizeibeamte(r) *m*, Polizeibeamtin *f*; *(of organization)* Funktionär *m*.
office work *n* Büroarbeit *f*.
office worker *n* Büroangestellte(r) *f(m)*.
official [ə'fɪʃl] *adj* offiziell ♦ *n (in government)*
Beamte(r) *m*, Beamtin *f*; *(in trade union etc)*
Funktionär *m*.
officialdom [ə'fɪʃldəm] *(pej) n* Bürokratie *f*.
officially [ə'fɪʃəlɪ] *adv* offiziell.
official receiver *n* Konkursverwalter *m*.
officiate [ə'fɪʃɪeɪt] *vi* amtieren; **to** ~ **at a
marriage** eine Trauung vornehmen.
officious [ə'fɪʃəs] *adj* übereifrig.
offing ['ɔfɪŋ] *n*: **in the** ~ in Sicht.

off-key [ɔf'kiː] *adj (MUS: sing, play)* falsch;
(instrument) verstimmt.
off-licence ['ɔflaɪsns] *(BRIT) n* ≈ Wein- und
Spirituosenhandlung *f*.

OFF-LICENCE

Off-licence *ist ein Geschäft (oder eine Theke in
einer Gaststätte), wo man alkoholische Getränke
kaufen kann, die aber anderswo konsumiert
werden müssen. In solchen Geschäften, die oft
von landesweiten Ketten betrieben werden, kann
man auch andere Getränke, Süßigkeiten,
Zigaretten und Knabbereien kaufen.*

---

off-limits [ɔf'lɪmɪts] *adj* verboten.
off-line [ɔf'laɪn] *(COMPUT) adj* Offline- ♦ *adv*
offline; *(switched off)* abgetrennt.
off-load ['ɔfləud] *vt* abladen.
off-peak ['ɔf'piːk] *adj (heating)*
Nachtspeicher-; *(electricity)* Nacht-; *(train)*
außerhalb der Stoßzeit; ~ **ticket** Fahrkarte *f*
zur Fahrt außerhalb der Stoßzeit.
off-putting ['ɔfputɪŋ] *(BRIT) adj (remark,
behaviour)* abstoßend.
off-season ['ɔf'siːzn] *adj, adv* außerhalb der
Saison.
offset ['ɔfsɛt] *(irreg: like* **set**) *vt (counteract)*
ausgleichen.
offshoot ['ɔfʃuːt] *n (BOT, fig)* Ableger *m*.
offshore [ɔf'ʃɔː*] *adj (breeze)* ablandig; *(oil rig,
fishing)* küstennah.
offside ['ɔf'saɪd] *adj (SPORT)* im Abseits; *(AUT:
when driving on left)* rechtsseitig; (: *when
driving on right)* linksseitig ♦ *n*: **the** ~ *(AUT:
when driving on left)* die rechte Seite; (: *when
driving on right)* die linke Seite.
offspring ['ɔfsprɪŋ] *n inv* Nachwuchs *m*.
offstage [ɔf'steɪdʒ] *adv* hinter den Kulissen.
off-the-cuff [ɔfðə'kʌf] *adj (remark)* aus dem
Stegreif.
off-the-job ['ɔfðə'dʒɔb] *adj*: ~ **training**
außerbetriebliche Weiterbildung *f*.
off-the-peg ['ɔfðə'pɛg], *(US)* **off-the-rack**
['ɔfðə'ræk] *adv* von der Stange.
off-the-record ['ɔfðə'rɛkɔːd] *adj (conversation,
briefing)* inoffiziell; **that's strictly** ~ das ist
ganz im Vertrauen.
off-white ['ɔfwaɪt] *adj* gebrochen weiß.
Ofgas ['ɔfgæs] *n Überwachungsgremium zum
Verbraucherschutz nach Privatisierung der
Gasindustrie.*
Oftel ['ɔftɛl] *n Überwachungsgremium zum
Verbraucherschutz nach Privatisierung der
Telekommunikationsindustrie.*
often ['ɔfn] *adv* oft; **how** ~**?** wie oft?; **more**
~ **than not** meistens; **as** ~ **as not** ziemlich
oft; **every so** ~ ab und zu.
Ofwat ['ɔfwɔt] *n Überwachungsgremium zum
Verbraucherschutz nach Privatisierung der
Wasserindustrie.*
ogle ['əugl] *vt* schielen nach, begaffen *(pej)*.

ogre ['əugə*] n (monster) Menschenfresser m.
OH (US) abbr (POST: = Ohio).
oh [əu] excl oh.
ohm [əum] n Ohm nt.
OHMS (BRIT) abbr (= On His/Her Majesty's
 Service) Aufdruck auf amtlichen
 Postsendungen.
oil [ɔɪl] n Öl nt; (petroleum) (Erd)öl nt ♦ vt ölen.
oilcan ['ɔɪlkæn] n Ölkanne f.
oil change n Ölwechsel m.
oilcloth ['ɔɪlklɔθ] n Wachstuch nt.
oilfield ['ɔɪlfiːld] n Ölfeld nt.
oil filter n Ölfilter m.
oil-fired ['ɔɪlfaɪəd] adj (boiler, central heating)
 Öl-.
oil gauge n Ölstandsmesser m.
oil painting n Ölgemälde nt.
oil refinery n Ölraffinerie f.
oil rig n Ölförderturm m; (at sea) Bohrinsel f.
oilskins ['ɔɪlskɪnz] npl Ölzeug nt.
oil slick n Ölteppich m.
oil tanker n (ship) (Öl)tanker m; (truck)
 Tankwagen m.
oil well n Ölquelle f.
oily ['ɔɪlɪ] adj (substance) ölig; (rag)
 öldurchtränkt; (food) fettig.
ointment ['ɔɪntmənt] n Salbe f.
OK (US) abbr (POST: = Oklahoma).
O.K. ['əu'keɪ] (inf) excl okay; (granted) gut ♦ adj
 (average) einigermaßen; (acceptable) in
 Ordnung ♦ vt genehmigen ♦ n: to give sb/sth
 the ~ jdm/etw seine Zustimmung geben; is
 it ~? ist es in Ordnung?; are you ~? bist du
 in Ordnung?; are you ~ for money? hast du
 (noch) genug Geld?; it's ~ with or by me
 mir ist es recht.
okay ['əu'keɪ] excl = O.K.
Okla. (US) abbr (POST: = Oklahoma).
old [əuld] adj alt; how ~ are you? wie alt bist
 du?; he's 10 years ~ er ist 10 Jahre alt; ~er
 brother ältere(r) Bruder; any ~ thing will
 do for him ihm ist alles recht.
old age n Alter nt.
old age pension n Rente f.
old age pensioner (BRIT) n Rentner(in) m(f).
old-fashioned ['əuld'fæʃnd] adj altmodisch.
old hand n alter Hase m.
old hat adj: to be ~ ein alter Hut sein.
old maid n alte Jungfer f.
old people's home n Altersheim nt.
old-style ['əuldstaɪl] adj im alten Stil.
old-time dancing ['əuldtaɪm-] n Tänze pl im
 alten Stil.
old-timer ['əuld'taɪmə*] (esp US) n Veteran m.
old wives' tale n Ammenmärchen nt.
oleander [əulɪ'ændə*] n Oleander m.
O level (BRIT) n (formerly) ≈ Abschluss m der
 Sekundarstufe 1, mittlere Reife f.
olive ['ɔlɪv] n Olive f; (tree) Olivenbaum m ♦ adj
 (also: ~-green) olivgrün; to offer an ~ branch
 to sb (fig) jdm ein Friedensangebot machen.
olive oil n Olivenöl nt.

Olympic [əu'lɪmpɪk] adj olympisch.
Olympic Games npl: the ~ (also: the
 Olympics) die Olympischen Spiele pl.
OM (BRIT) n abbr (= Order of Merit) britischer
 Verdienstorden.
Oman [əu'maːn] n Oman nt.
OMB (US) n abbr (= Office of Management and
 Budget) Regierungsbehörde für Verwaltung
 und Etat.
ombudsman ['ɔmbudzmən] n Ombudsmann
 m.
omelette, (US) **omelet** ['ɔmlɪt] n Omelett nt;
 ham/cheese omelet(te) Schinken-/
 Käseomelett nt.
omen ['əumən] n Omen nt.
ominous ['ɔmɪnəs] adj (silence, warning)
 ominös; (clouds, smoke) bedrohlich.
omission [əu'mɪʃən] n (thing omitted)
 Auslassung f; (act of omitting) Auslassen nt.
omit [əu'mɪt] vt (deliberately) unterlassen; (by
 mistake) auslassen ♦ vi: to ~ to do sth es
 unterlassen, etw zu tun.
omnivorous [ɔm'nɪvrəs] adj: to be ~
 Allesfresser sein.
ON (CANADA) abbr (= Ontario).

═══════════════════════════════ KEYWORD

on [ɔn] prep 1 (indicating position) auf +dat; (with
 vb of motion) auf +acc; it's ~ the table es ist
 auf dem Tisch; she put the book ~ the table
 sie legte das Buch auf den Tisch; ~ the left
 links; ~ the right rechts; the house is ~ the
 main road das Haus liegt an der
 Hauptstraße.
 2 (indicating means, method, condition etc)
 ~ foot (go, be) zu Fuß; to be ~ the train/
 plane im Zug/Flugzeug sein; to go ~ the
 train/plane mit dem Zug/Flugzeug reisen;
 (to be wanted) ~ the telephone am Telefon
 (verlangt werden) / ~ the radio/television
 im Radio/Fernsehen; to be ~ drugs Drogen
 nehmen; to be ~ holiday im Urlaub sein; I'm
 here ~ business ich bin geschäftlich hier.
 3 (referring to time): ~ Friday am Freitag;
 ~ Fridays freitags; ~ June 20th am 20. Juni;
 ~ Friday, June 20th am Freitag, dem 20.
 Juni; a week ~ Friday Freitag in einer
 Woche; ~ (his) arrival he went straight to his
 hotel bei seiner Ankunft ging er direkt in
 sein Hotel; ~ seeing this he ... als er das
 sah, ... er ...
 4 (about, concerning) über +acc; a book
 ~ physics ein Buch über Physik
 ♦ adv 1 (referring to dress): to have one's coat
 ~ seinen Mantel anhaben; what's she got
 ~? was hat sie an?
 2 (referring to covering) screw the lid
 ~ tightly dreh den Deckel fest zu.
 3 (further, continuously): to walk/drive/read
 ~ weitergehen/-fahren/-lesen
 ♦ adj 1 (functioning, in operation: machine,
 radio, TV, light) an; (: tap) auf; (: handbrake)

angezogen; **there's a good film ~ at the cinema** im Kino läuft ein guter Film. **2: that's not ~!** (*inf: of behaviour*) das ist nicht drin!

ONC (*BRIT*) *n abbr* (= *Ordinary National Certificate*) *höherer Schulabschluss.*

once [wʌns] *adv* (*on one occasion*) einmal; (*formerly*) früher; (*a long time ago*) früher einmal ♦ *conj* (*as soon as*) sobald; **at ~** (*immediately*) sofort; (*simultaneously*) gleichzeitig; **~ a week** einmal pro Woche; **~ more** *or* **again** noch einmal; **~ and for all** ein für alle Mal; **~ upon a time** es war einmal; **~ in a while** ab und zu; **all at ~** (*suddenly*) plötzlich; **for ~** ausnahmsweise (einmal); **~ or twice** ein paar Mal; **~ he had left** sobald er gegangen war; **~ it was done** nachdem es getan war.

oncoming [ˈɔnkʌmɪŋ] *adj* (*traffic etc*) entgegenkommend; (*danger*) nahend, drohend.

OND (*BRIT*) *n abbr* (= *Ordinary National Diploma*) *technisches Diplom.*

═══════════════ *KEYWORD*

one [wʌn] *num* ein(e); (*counting*) eins; **~ hundred and fifty** (ein)hundert(und)fünfzig; **~ day there was a sudden knock at the door** eines Tages klopfte es plötzlich an der Tür; **~ by ~** einzeln
♦ *adj* **1** (*sole*) einzige(r, s); **the ~ book which** ... das einzige Buch, das ...
2 (*same*): **they came in the ~ car** sie kamen in demselben Wagen; **they all belong to the ~ family** sie alle gehören zu ein und derselben Familie
♦ *pron* **1**: **this ~** diese(r, s); **that ~** der/die/das (da); **which ~?** welcher/welche/welches?; **he is ~ of us** er ist einer von uns; **I've already got ~/a red ~** ich habe schon eins/ein rotes.
2: **~ another** einander; **do you two ever see ~ another?** seht ihr zwei euch jemals?
3 (*impersonal*) man; **~ never knows** man weiß nie; **to cut ~'s finger** sich *dat* in den Finger schneiden.

one-day excursion [ˈwʌndeɪ-] (*US*) *n* (*day return*) Tagesrückfahrkarte *f.*
one-man [ˈwʌnˈmæn] *adj* (*business, show*) Einmann-.
one-man band *n* Einmannkapelle *f.*
one-off [ˈwʌnˈɔf] (*BRIT: inf*) *n* einmaliges Ereignis *nt.*
one-parent family [ˈwʌnpɛərənt-] *n* Familie *f* mit nur einem Elternteil, Einelternteilfamilie *nt.*
one-piece [ˈwʌnpiːs] *adj:* **~ swimsuit** einteiliger Badeanzug *m.*
onerous [ˈɔnərəs] *adj* (*duty etc*) schwer.

═══════════════ *KEYWORD*

oneself [wʌnˈself] *pron* (*reflexive: after prep*) sich; (*emphatic*) selbst; **to hurt ~** sich *dat* wehtun; **to keep sth for ~** etw für sich behalten; **to talk to ~** Selbstgespräche führen.

one-shot [ˈwʌnʃɔt] (*US*) *n* = **one-off.**
one-sided [wʌnˈsaɪdɪd] *adj* einseitig.
one-time [ˈwʌntaɪm] *adj* ehemalig.
one-to-one [ˈwʌntəwʌn] *adj* (*relationship, tuition*) Einzel-.
one-upmanship [wʌnˈʌpmənʃɪp] *n:* **the art of ~** die Kunst, anderen um einen Schritt voraus zu sein.
one-way [ˈwʌnweɪ] *adj* (*street, traffic*) Einbahn-; (*ticket*) Einzel-.
ongoing [ˈɔngəʊɪŋ] *adj* (*project*) laufend; (*situation etc*) andauernd.
onion [ˈʌnjən] *n* Zwiebel *f.*
on-line [ˈɔnlaɪn] (*COMPUT*) *adj* (*printer, database*) Online-; (*switched on*) gekoppelt
♦ *adv* online.
onlooker [ˈɔnlʊkə*] *n* Zuschauer(in) *m(f).*
only [ˈəʊnlɪ] *adv* nur ♦ *adj* einzige(r, s) ♦ *conj* nur, bloß; **I ~ took one** ich nahm nur eins; **I saw her ~ yesterday** ich habe sie erst gestern gesehen; **I'd be ~ too pleased to help** ich würde allzu gern helfen; **not ~ ... but (also) ...** nicht nur ..., sondern auch ...; **an ~ child** ein Einzelkind *nt;* **I would come, ~ I'm too busy** ich würde kommen, wenn ich nicht so viel zu tun hätte.
ono (*BRIT*) *abbr* (*in classified ads:* = *or near(est) offer*) *see* **near.**
onset [ˈɔnset] *n* Beginn *m.*
onshore [ˈɔnʃɔː*] *adj* (*wind*) auflandig, See-.
onslaught [ˈɔnslɔːt] *n* Attacke *f.*
on-the-job [ˈɔnðəˈdʒɔb] *adj:* **~ training** Ausbildung *f* am Arbeitsplatz.
onto [ˈɔntu] *prep* = **on to.**
onus [ˈəʊnəs] *n* Last *f,* Pflicht *f;* **the ~ is on him to prove it** er trägt die Beweislast.
onward(s) [ˈɔnwəd(z)] *adv* weiter; **from that time ~** von der Zeit an ♦ *adj* fortschreitend.
onyx [ˈɔnɪks] *n* Onyx *m.*
ooze [uːz] *vi* (*mud, water etc*) triefen.
opacity [əʊˈpæsɪtɪ] *n* (*of substance*) Undurchsichtigkeit *f.*
opal [ˈəʊpl] *n* Opal *m.*
opaque [əʊˈpeɪk] *adj* (*substance*) undurchsichtig, trüb.
OPEC [ˈəʊpɛk] *n abbr* (= *Organization of Petroleum-Exporting Countries*) OPEC *f.*
open [ˈəʊpn] *adj* offen; (*packet, shop, museum*) geöffnet; (*view*) frei; (*meeting, debate*) öffentlich; (*ticket, return*) unbeschränkt; (*vacancy*) verfügbar ♦ *vt* öffnen, aufmachen; (*book, paper etc*) aufschlagen; (*account*) eröffnen; (*blocked road*) frei machen ♦ *vi* (*door, eyes, mouth*) sich öffnen; (*shop, bank*)

etc) aufmachen; (*commence*) beginnen; (*film, play*) Premiere haben; (*flower*) aufgehen; **in the ~ (air)** im Freien; **the ~ sea** das offene Meer; **to have an ~ mind on sth** etw *dat* aufgeschlossen gegenüberstehen; **to be ~ to** (*ideas etc*) offen sein für; **to be ~ to criticism** der Kritik *dat* ausgesetzt sein; **to be ~ to the public** für die Öffentlichkeit zugänglich sein; **to ~ one's mouth** (*speak*) den Mund aufmachen.

▶ **open on to** *vt fus* (*room, door*) führen auf *+acc.*

▶ **open up** *vi* (*unlock*) aufmachen; (*confide*) sich äußern.

open-air [əupn'ɛə°] *adj* im Freien; **~ concert** Openairkonzert *nt*, Open-Air-Konzert *nt*; **~ swimming pool** Freibad *nt*.

open-and-shut ['əupnən'ʃʌt] *adj*: **~ case** klarer Fall *m*.

open day *n* Tag *m* der offenen Tür.

open-ended [əupn'ɛndɪd] *adj* (*question etc*) mit offenem Ausgang; (*contract*) unbefristet.

opener ['əupnə°] *n* (*also*: **tin ~, can ~**) Dosenöffner *m*.

open-heart [əupn'hɑːt] *adj*: **~ surgery** Eingriff *m* am offenen Herzen.

opening ['əupnɪŋ] *adj* (*commencing: stages, scene*) erste(r, s); (*remarks, ceremony etc*) Eröffnungs- ♦ *n* (*gap, hole*) Öffnung *f*; (*of play etc*) Anfang *m*; (*of new building etc*) Eröffnung *f*; (*opportunity*) Gelegenheit *f*.

opening hours *npl* Öffnungszeiten *pl*.

opening night *n* Eröffnungsabend *m*.

open learning *n* Weiterbildungssystem auf Teilzeitbasis.

openly ['əupnlɪ] *adv* offen.

open-minded [əupn'maɪndɪd] *adj* aufgeschlossen.

open-necked ['əupnnɛkt] *adj* (*shirt*) mit offenem Kragen.

openness ['əupnnɪs] *n* (*frankness*) Offenheit *f*.

open-plan ['əupn'plæn] *adj* (*office*) Großraum-.

open prison *n* offenes Gefängnis *nt*.

open sandwich *n* belegtes Brot *nt*.

open shop *n* Unternehmen ohne Gewerkschaftszwang.

Open University (*BRIT*) *n* ≈ Fernuniversität *f*.

OPEN UNIVERSITY

Open University *ist eine 1969 in Großbritannien gegründete Fernuniversität für Spätstudierende. Der Unterricht findet durch Fernseh- und Radiosendungen statt, schriftliche Arbeiten werden mit der Post verschickt, und der Besuch von Sommerkursen ist Pflicht. Die Studenten müssen eine bestimmte Anzahl von Unterrichtseinheiten in einem bestimmten Zeitraum absolvieren und für die Verleihung eines akademischen Grades eine Mindestzahl von Scheinen machen.*

---

open verdict *n* (*LAW*) Todesfeststellung ohne Angabe der Todesursache.

opera ['ɔpərə] *n* Oper *f*.

opera glasses *npl* Opernglas *nt*.

opera house *n* Opernhaus *nt*.

opera singer *n* Opernsänger(in) *m(f)*.

operate ['ɔpəreɪt] *vt* (*machine etc*) bedienen ♦ *vi* (*machine etc*) funktionieren; (*company*) arbeiten; (*laws, forces*) wirken; (*MED*) operieren; **to ~ on sb** jdn operieren.

operatic [ɔpə'rætɪk] *adj* (*singer etc*) Opern-.

operating room ['ɔpəreɪtɪŋ-] (*US*) *n* Operationssaal *m*.

operating system *n* (*COMPUT*) Betriebssystem *nt*.

operating table *n* (*MED*) Operationstisch *m*.

operating theatre *n* (*MED*) Operationssaal *m*.

operation [ɔpə'reɪʃən] *n* (*activity*) Unternehmung *f*; (*of machine etc*) Betrieb *m*; (*MIL, MED*) Operation *f*; (*COMM*) Geschäft *nt*; **to be in ~** (*law, scheme*) in Kraft sein; **to have an ~** (*MED*) operiert werden; **to perform an ~** (*MED*) eine Operation vornehmen.

operational [ɔpə'reɪʃənl] *adj* (*machine etc*) einsatzfähig.

operative ['ɔpərətɪv] *adj* (*measure, system*) wirksam; (*law*) gültig ♦ *n* (*in factory*) Maschinenarbeiter(in) *m(f)*; **the ~ word** das entscheidende Wort.

operator ['ɔpəreɪtə°] *n* (*TEL*) Vermittlung *f*; (*of machine*) Bediener(in) *m(f)*.

operetta [ɔpə'rɛtə] *n* Operette *f*.

ophthalmic [ɔf'θælmɪk] *adj* (*department*) Augen-.

ophthalmic optician *n* Augenoptiker(in) *m(f)*.

ophthalmologist [ɔfθæl'mɔlədʒɪst] *n* Augenarzt *m*, Augenärztin *f*.

opinion [ə'pɪnjən] *n* Meinung *f*; **in my ~** meiner Meinung nach; **to have a good/high ~ of sb/o.s.** eine gute/hohe Meinung von jdm/sich haben; **to be of the ~ that ...** der Ansicht *or* Meinung sein, dass ...; **to get a second ~** (*MED etc*) ein zweites Gutachten einholen.

opinionated [ə'pɪnjəneɪtɪd] (*pej*) *adj* rechthaberisch.

opinion poll *n* Meinungsumfrage *f*.

opium ['əupɪəm] *n* Opium *nt*.

opponent [ə'pəunənt] *n* Gegner(in) *m(f)*.

opportune ['ɔpətjuːn] *adj* (*moment*) günstig.

opportunism [ɔpə'tjuːnɪsəm] (*pej*) *n* Opportunismus *m*.

opportunist [ɔpə'tjuːnɪst] (*pej*) *n* Opportunist(in) *m(f)*.

opportunity [ɔpə'tjuːnɪtɪ] *n* Gelegenheit *f*, Möglichkeit *f*; (*prospects*) Chance *f*; **to take the ~ of doing sth** die Gelegenheit ergreifen, etw zu tun.

oppose [ə'pəuz] *vt* (*opinion, plan*) ablehnen; **to**

be ~d to sth gegen etw sein; **as** ~**d to** im
Gegensatz zu.
opposing [ə'pəuzɪŋ] *adj* (*side, team*)
gegnerisch; (*ideas, tendencies*)
entgegengesetzt.
opposite ['ɔpəzɪt] *adj* (*house, door*)
gegenüberliegend; (*end, direction*)
entgegengesetzt; (*point of view, effect*)
gegenteilig ♦ *adv* gegenüber ♦ *prep* (*in front
of*) gegenüber ♦ (*next to: on list, form etc*)
neben ♦ *n*: **the** ~ das Gegenteil; **the** ~ **sex**
das andere Geschlecht; **"see** ~ **page"**
„siehe gegenüber".
opposite number *n* Gegenspieler(in) *m(f)*.
opposition [ɔpə'zɪʃən] *n* (*resistance*)
Widerstand *m*; (*SPORT*) Gegner *pl*; **the O**~
(*POL*) die Opposition.
oppress [ə'prɛs] *vt* unterdrücken.
oppressed [ə'prɛst] *adj* unterdrückt.
oppression [ə'prɛʃən] *n* Unterdrückung *f*.
oppressive [ə'prɛsɪv] *adj* (*weather, heat*)
bedrückend; (*political regime*) repressiv.
opprobrium [ə'prəubrɪəm] *n* (*form*) Schande *f*,
Schmach *f*.
opt [ɔpt] *vi*: **to** ~ **for** sich entscheiden für;
to ~ **to do sth** sich entscheiden, etw zu
tun.
▶ **opt out (of)** *vi* (*not participate*) sich nicht
beteiligen (an +*dat*); (*of insurance scheme etc*)
kündigen; **to** ~ **out (of local authority
control)** (*POL: hospital, school*) aus der
Kontrolle der Gemeindeverwaltung
austreten.
optical ['ɔptɪkl] *adj* optisch.
optical character reader *n* optischer
Klarschriftleser *m*.
optical character recognition *n* optische
Zeichenerkennung *f*.
optical illusion *n* optische Täuschung *f*.
optician [ɔp'tɪʃən] *n* Optiker(in) *m(f)*.
optics ['ɔptɪks] *n* Optik *f*.
optimism ['ɔptɪmɪzəm] *n* Optimismus *m*.
optimist ['ɔptɪmɪst] *n* Optimist(in) *m(f)*.
optimistic [ɔptɪ'mɪstɪk] *adj* optimistisch.
optimum ['ɔptɪməm] *adj* optimal.
option ['ɔpʃən] *n* (*choice*) Möglichkeit *f*;
(*SCOL*) Wahlfach *nt*; (*COMM*) Option *f*; **to
keep one's** ~**s open** sich *dat* alle
Möglichkeiten offen halten; **to have no** ~
keine (andere) Wahl haben.
optional ['ɔpʃənl] *adj* freiwillig; ~ **extras**
(*COMM*) Extras *pl*.
opulence ['ɔpjuləns] *n* Reichtum *m*.
opulent ['ɔpjulənt] *adj* (*very wealthy*) reich,
wohlhabend.
OR (*US*) *abbr* (*POST*: = Oregon).
or [ɔ:ʳ] *conj* oder; **he hasn't seen** ~ **heard
anything** er hat weder etwas gesehen noch
gehört; ~ **else** (*otherwise*) sonst; **fifty** ~ **sixty
people** fünfzig bis sechzig Leute.
oracle ['ɔrəkl] *n* Orakel *nt*.
oral ['ɔːrəl] *adj* (*test, report*) mündlich; (*MED:

vaccine, contraceptive) zum Einnehmen ♦ *n*
(*exam*) mündliche Prüfung *f*.
orange ['ɔrɪndʒ] *n* Orange *f*, Apfelsine *f* ♦ *adj*
(*colour*) orange.
orangeade [ɔrɪndʒ'eɪd] *n* Orangenlimonade
f.
oration [ɔ:'reɪʃən] *n* Ansprache *f*.
orator ['ɔrətəʳ] *n* Redner(in) *m(f)*.
oratorio [ɔrə'tɔːrɪəu] *n* (*MUS*) Oratorium *nt*.
orb [ɔ:b] *n* Kugel *f*.
orbit ['ɔ:bɪt] *n* (*of planet etc*) Umlaufbahn *f* ♦ *vt*
umkreisen.
orbital motorway ['ɔ:bɪtəl-] *n* Ringautobahn
f.
orchard ['ɔ:tʃəd] *n* Obstgarten *m*; **apple** ~
Obstgarten mit Apfelbäumen.
orchestra ['ɔ:kɪstrə] *n* Orchester *nt*; (*US:
stalls*) Parkett *nt*.
orchestral [ɔ:'kɛstrəl] *adj* (*piece, musicians*)
Orchester-.
orchestrate ['ɔ:kɪstreɪt] *vt* orchestrieren.
orchid ['ɔ:kɪd] *n* Orchidee *f*.
ordain [ɔ:'deɪn] *vt* (*REL*) ordinieren; (*decree*)
verfügen.
ordeal [ɔ:'di:l] *n* Qual *f*.
order ['ɔ:dəʳ] *n* (*command*) Befehl *m*; (*COMM,
in restaurant*) Bestellung *f*; (*sequence*)
Reihenfolge *f*; (*discipline, organization*)
Ordnung *f*; (*REL*) Orden *m* ♦ *vt* (*command*)
befehlen; (*COMM, in restaurant*) bestellen;
(*also:* **put in** ~) ordnen; **in** ~ (*permitted*) in
Ordnung; **in (working)** ~ betriebsfähig; **in**
~ **to do sth** um etw zu tun; **in** ~ **of size** nach
Größe (geordnet); **on** ~ (*COMM*) bestellt;
out of ~ (*not working*) außer Betrieb; (*in the
wrong sequence*) durcheinander; (*motion,
proposal*) nicht zulässig; **to place an** ~ **for
sth with sb** eine Bestellung für etw bei jdm
aufgeben; **made to** ~ (*COMM*) auf
Bestellung (gemacht); **to be under** ~**s to do
sth** die Anweisung haben, etw zu tun; **to
take** ~**s** Befehle entgegennehmen; **a point
of** ~ (*in debate etc*) eine Verfahrensfrage;
"pay to the ~ **of ..."** „zahlbar an +*dat* ...";
of *or* **in the** ~ **of** in der Größenordnung von;
to ~ **sb to do sth** jdn anweisen, etw zu
tun.
▶ **order around** *vt* (*also:* **order about**)
herumkommandieren.
order book *n* (*COMM*) Auftragsbuch *nt*.
order form *n* Bestellschein
m.
orderly ['ɔ:dəlɪ] *n* (*MIL*) Offiziersbursche
m; (*MED*) Pfleger(in) *m(f)* ♦ *adj* (*manner*)
ordentlich; (*sequence, system*)
geordnet.
order number *n* (*COMM*) Bestellnummer *f*.
ordinal ['ɔ:dɪnl] *adj*: ~ **number** Ordinalzahl *f*.
ordinarily ['ɔ:dnrɪlɪ] *adv* normalerweise.
ordinary ['ɔ:dnrɪ] *adj* (*everyday*) gewöhnlich,
normal; (*pej: mediocre*) mittelmäßig; **out of
the** ~ außergewöhnlich.

ordinary seaman (*BRIT*) *n* Leichtmatrose *m*.
ordinary shares *npl* Stammaktien *pl*.
ordination [ɔːdɪˈneɪʃən] *n* (*REL*) Ordination *f*.
ordnance [ˈɔːdnəns] *n* (*unit*) Technische Truppe *f* ♦ *adj* (*factory, supplies*) Munitions-.
Ordnance Survey (*BRIT*) *n* Landesvermessung *f*.
ore [ɔː*] *n* Erz *nt*.
Ore. (*US*) *abbr* (*POST*: = Oregon).
organ [ˈɔːgən] *n* (*ANAT*) Organ *nt*; (*MUS*) Orgel *f*.
organic [ɔːˈgænɪk] *adj* organisch.
organism [ˈɔːgənɪzəm] *n* Organismus *m*.
organist [ˈɔːgənɪst] *n* Organist(in) *m(f)*.
organization [ɔːgənaɪˈzeɪʃən] *n* Organisation *f*.
organization chart *n* Organisationsplan *m*.
organize [ˈɔːgənaɪz] *vt* organisieren; **to get ~d** sich fertig machen.
organized crime *n* organisiertes Verbrechen *nt*.
organized labour *n* organisierte Arbeiterschaft *f*.
organizer [ˈɔːgənaɪzə*] *n* (*of conference etc*) Organisator *m*, Veranstalter *m*.
orgasm [ˈɔːgæzəm] *n* Orgasmus *m*.
orgy [ˈɔːdʒɪ] *n* Orgie *f*; **an ~ of destruction** eine Zerstörungsorgie.
Orient [ˈɔːrɪənt] *n*: **the ~** der Orient.
orient [ˈɔːrɪənt] *vt*: **to ~ o.s. (to)** sich orientieren (in +*dat*); **to be ~ed towards** ausgerichtet sein auf +*acc*.
oriental [ɔːrɪˈɛntl] *adj* orientalisch.
orientate [ˈɔːrɪənteɪt] *vt*: **to ~ o.s.** sich orientieren; (*fig*) sich zurechtfinden; **to be ~d towards** ausgerichtet sein auf +*acc*.
orifice [ˈɔrɪfɪs] *n* (*ANAT*) Öffnung *f*.
origin [ˈɔrɪdʒɪn] *n* Ursprung *m*; (*of person*) Herkunft *f*; **country of ~** Herkunftsland *nt*.
original [əˈrɪdʒɪnl] *adj* (*first*) ursprünglich; (*genuine*) original; (*imaginative*) originell ♦ *n* Original *nt*.
originality [ərɪdʒɪˈnælɪtɪ] *n* Originalität *f*.
originally [əˈrɪdʒɪnəlɪ] *adv* (*at first*) ursprünglich.
originate [əˈrɪdʒɪneɪt] *vi*: **to ~ in** (*idea, custom etc*) entstanden sein in +*dat*; **to ~ with** *or* **from** stammen von.
originator [əˈrɪdʒɪneɪtə*] *n* (*of idea, custom*) Urheber(in) *m(f)*.
Orkneys [ˈɔːknɪz] *npl*: **the ~** (*also*: **the Orkney**

Islands) die Orkneyinseln *pl*.
ornament [ˈɔːnəmənt] *n* (*object*) Ziergegenstand *m*; (*decoration*) Verzierungen *pl*.
ornamental [ɔːnəˈmɛntl] *adj* (*garden, pond*) Zier-.
ornamentation [ɔːnəmɛnˈteɪʃən] *n* Verzierungen *pl*.
ornate [ɔːˈneɪt] *adj* (*necklace, design*) kunstvoll.
ornithologist [ɔːnɪˈθɔlədʒɪst] *n* Ornithologe *m*, Ornithologin *f*.
ornithology [ɔːnɪˈθɔlədʒɪ] *n* Ornithologie *f*.
orphan [ˈɔːfn] *n* Waise *f*, Waisenkind *nt* ♦ *vt*: **to be ~ed** zur Waise werden.
orphanage [ˈɔːfənɪdʒ] *n* Waisenhaus *nt*.
orthodox [ˈɔːθədɔks] *adj* orthodox; **~ medicine** die konventionelle Medizin.
orthodoxy [ˈɔːθədɔksɪ] *n* Orthodoxie *f*.
orthopaedic, (*US*) **orthopedic** [ɔːθəˈpiːdɪk] *adj* orthopädisch.
OS *abbr* (*BRIT*) = **Ordnance Survey**; (*NAUT*) = **ordinary seaman**; (*DRESS*) = **outsize**.
O/S *abbr* (*COMM*: = out of stock) nicht auf Lager.
Oscar [ˈɒskə*] *n* Oscar *m*.
oscillate [ˈɒsɪleɪt] *vi* (*ELEC, PHYS*) schwingen, oszillieren; (*fig*) schwanken.
OSHA (*US*) *n abbr* (= Occupational Safety and Health Administration) Regierungsstelle für Arbeitsschutzvorschriften.
OST *n abbr* (= Office of Science and Technology) Ministerium für Wissenschaft und Technologie.
ostensible [ɒsˈtɛnsɪbl] *adj* angeblich.
ostensibly [ɒsˈtɛnsɪblɪ] *adv* angeblich.
ostentation [ɒstɛnˈteɪʃən] *n* Pomp *m*, Protz *m*.
ostentatious [ɒstɛnˈteɪʃəs] *adj* (*building, car etc*) pompös; (*person*) protzig.
osteopath [ˈɒstɪəpæθ] *n* Osteopath(in) *m(f)*.
ostracize [ˈɒstrəsaɪz] *vt* ächten.
ostrich [ˈɒstrɪtʃ] *n* Strauß *m*.
OT *abbr* (*BIBLE*: = Old Testament) AT.
OTB (*US*) *n abbr* (= offtrack betting) Wetten außerhalb des Rennbahngeländes.
OTE *abbr* (*COMM*: = on-target earnings) Einkommensziel *nt*.
other [ˈʌðə*] *adj* andere(r, s) ♦ *pron*: **the ~ (one)** der/die/das andere; **~s** andere *pl*; **the ~s** die anderen *pl*; **~ than** (*apart from*) außer; **the ~ day** (*recently*) neulich; **some actor or ~** irgendein Schauspieler; **somebody or ~** irgendjemand; **the car was none ~ than Robert's** das Auto gehörte keinem anderen als Robert.
otherwise [ˈʌðəwaɪz] *adv* (*differently*) anders; (*apart from that, if not*) ansonsten; **an ~ good piece of work** eine im Übrigen gute Arbeit.
OTT (*inf*) *abbr* (= over the top) *see* **top**.
otter [ˈɔtə*] *n* Otter *m*.
OU (*BRIT*) *n abbr* = **Open University**.
ouch [autʃ] *excl* autsch.
ought [ɔːt] (*pt* **ought**) *aux vb*: **I ~ to do it** ich

sollte es tun; **this** ~ **to have been corrected**
das hätte korrigiert werden müssen; **he**
~ **to win** (*he probably will win*) er dürfte
wohl gewinnen; **you** ~ **to go and see it** das
solltest du dir ansehen.

ounce [auns] *n* Unze *f*; (*fig: small amount*)
bisschen *nt*.

our ['auə*] *adj* unsere(r, s); *see also* **my**.

ours [auəz] *pron* unsere(r, s); *see also* **mine**[1].

ourselves [auə'sɛlvz] *pron pl* uns (selbst);
(*emphatic*) selbst; **we did it (all) by** ~ wir
haben alles selbst gemacht; *see also* **oneself**.

oust [aust] *vt* (*forcibly remove*) verdrängen.

==================================== *KEYWORD*

out[1] [aut] *adv* **1** (*not in*) draußen; ~ **in the
rain/snow** draußen im Regen/Schnee;
~ **here** hier; ~ **there** dort; **to go/come** *etc* ~
hinausgehen/-kommen *etc*; **to speak** ~ **loud**
laut sprechen.
2 (*not at home, absent*) nicht da.
3 (*indicating distance*): **the boat was 10 km** ~
das Schiff war 10 km weit draußen; **3 days**
~ **from Plymouth** 3 Tage nach dem
Auslaufen von Plymouth.
4 (*SPORT*) aus; **the ball is** ~/**has gone** ~ der
Ball ist aus
♦ *adj* **1**: **to be** ~ (*person: unconscious*)
bewusstlos sein; (: *out of game*)
ausgeschieden sein; (*out of fashion: style,
singer*) out sein.
2 (*have appeared: flowers*) da; (: *news, secret*)
heraus.
3 (*extinguished, finished: fire, light, gas*) aus;
before the week was ~ ehe die Woche zu
Ende war.
4: **to be** ~ **to do sth** (*intend*) etw tun wollen.
5 (*wrong*): **to be** ~ **in one's calculations** sich
in seinen Berechnungen irren.

out[2] [aut] *vt* (*inf: expose as homosexual*) outen.

outage ['autɪdʒ] (*esp US*) *n* (*power failure*)
Stromausfall *m*.

out-and-out ['autəndaut] *adj* (*liar, thief etc*)
ausgemacht.

outback ['autbæk] *n* (*in Australia*): **the** ~ das
Hinterland.

outbid [aut'bɪd] *vt* überbieten.

outboard ['autbɔːd] *n* (*also*: ~ **motor**)
Außenbordmotor *m*.

outbound ['autbaund] *adj* (*ship*) auslaufend.

outbreak ['autbreɪk] *n* (*of war, disease etc*)
Ausbruch *m*.

outbuilding ['autbɪldɪŋ] *n* Nebengebäude *nt*.

outburst ['autbəːst] *n* (*of anger etc*)
Gefühlsausbruch *m*.

outcast ['autkɑːst] *n* Ausgestoßene(r) *f(m)*.

outclass [aut'klɑːs] *vt* deklassieren.

outcome ['autkʌm] *n* Ergebnis *nt*, Resultat *nt*.

outcrop ['autkrɔp] *n* (*of rock*) Block *m*.

outcry ['autkraɪ] *n* Aufschrei *m*.

outdated [aut'deɪtɪd] *adj* (*custom, idea*)

veraltet.

outdo [aut'duː] (*irreg: like* **do**) *vt* übertreffen.

outdoor [aut'dɔː*] *adj* (*activities*) im Freien;
(*clothes*) für draußen; ~ **swimming pool**
Freibad *nt*; **she's an** ~ **person** sie liebt die
freie Natur.

outdoors [aut'dɔːz] *adv* (*play, sleep*) draußen,
im Freien.

outer ['autə*] *adj* äußere(r, s); ~ **suburbs**
(äußere) Vorstädte *pl*; **the** ~ **office** das
Vorzimmer.

outer space *n* der Weltraum.

outfit ['autfɪt] *n* (*clothes*) Kleidung *f*; (*inf: team*)
Verein *m*.

outfitter's ['autfɪtəz] (*BRIT*) *n* (*shop*)
Herrenausstatter *m*.

outgoing ['autgəuɪŋ] *adj* (*extrovert*)
kontaktfreudig; (*retiring: president etc*)
scheidend; (*mail etc*) ausgehend.

outgoings ['autgəuɪŋz] (*BRIT*) *npl* Ausgaben *pl*.

outgrow [aut'grəu] (*irreg: like* **grow**) *vt* (*clothes*)
herauswachsen aus; (*habits etc*) ablegen.

outhouse ['authaus] *n* Nebengebäude *nt*.

outing ['autɪŋ] *n* Ausflug *m*.

outlandish [aut'lændɪʃ] *adj* eigenartig,
seltsam.

outlast [aut'lɑːst] *vt* überleben.

outlaw ['autlɔː] *n* Geächtete(r) *f(m)* ♦ *vt*
verbieten.

outlay ['autleɪ] *n* Auslagen *pl*.

outlet ['autlɛt] *n* (*hole, pipe*) Abfluss *m*; (*US:
ELEC*) Steckdose *f*; (*COMM: also*: **retail** ~)
Verkaufsstelle *f*; (*fig: for grief, anger etc*)
Ventil *nt*.

outline ['autlaɪn] *n* (*shape*) Umriss *m*; (*brief
explanation*) Abriss *m*; (*rough sketch*) Skizze *f*
♦ *vt* (*fig: theory, plan etc*) umreißen,
skizzieren.

outlive [aut'lɪv] *vt* (*survive*) überleben.

outlook ['autluk] *n* (*attitude*) Einstellung *f*;
(*prospects*) Aussichten *pl*; (*for weather*)
Vorhersage *f*.

outlying ['autlaɪɪŋ] *adj* (*area, town etc*)
entlegen.

outmanoeuvre, (*US*) **outmaneuver**
[autmə'nuːvə*] *vt* ausmanövrieren.

outmoded [aut'məudɪd] *adj* veraltet.

outnumber [aut'nʌmbə*] *vt* zahlenmäßig
überlegen sein +*dat*; **to be** ~**ed (by) 5 to 1** im
Verhältnis 5 zu 1 in der Minderheit sein.

==================================== *KEYWORD*

out of *prep* **1** (*outside, beyond: position*) nicht in
+*dat*; (: *motion*) aus +*dat*; **to look** ~ **the
window** aus dem Fenster blicken; **to be**
~ **danger** außer Gefahr sein.
2 (*cause, origin*) aus +*dat*; ~ **curiosity/fear/
greed** aus Neugier/Angst/Habgier; **to drink
sth** ~ **a cup** etw aus einer Tasse trinken.
3 (*from among*) von +*dat*; **one** ~ **every three
smokers** einer von drei Rauchern.
4 (*without*): **to be** ~ **sugar/milk/petrol** *etc*

keinen Zucker/keine Milch/kein Benzin *etc*
mehr haben.

out of bounds *adj*: **to be** ~ verboten sein.
out-of-court [autəv'kɔːt] *adj* (*settlement*)
außergerichtlich; *see also* **court**.
out-of-date [autəv'deɪt] *adj* (*passport, ticket etc*) abgelaufen; (*clothes, idea*) veraltet.
out-of-doors [autəv'dɔːz] *adv* (*play, stay etc*)
im Freien.
out-of-the-way ['autəvðə'weɪ] *adj* (*place*)
entlegen; (*pub, restaurant etc*) kaum bekannt.
out-of-work ['autəvwəːk] *adj* arbeitslos.
outpatient ['autpeɪʃənt] *n* ambulanter Patient *m*, ambulante Patientin *f*.
outpost ['autpəust] *n* (*MIL, COMM*) Vorposten *m*.
outpouring ['autpɔːrɪŋ] *n* (*of emotion etc*)
Erguss *m*.
output ['autput] *n* (*production: of factory, writer etc*) Produktion *f*; (*COMPUT*) Output *m*, Ausgabe *f* ♦ *vt* (*COMPUT*) ausgeben.
outrage ['autreɪdʒ] *n* (*scandal*) Skandal *m*; (*atrocity*) Verbrechen *nt*, Ausschreitung *f*; (*anger*) Empörung *f* ♦ *vt* (*shock, anger*)
empören.
outrageous [aut'reɪdʒəs] *adj* (*remark etc*)
empörend; (*clothes*) unmöglich; (*scandalous*)
skandalös.
outrider ['autraɪdə*] *n* (*on motorcycle*)
Kradbegleiter *m*.
outright [aut'raɪt] *adv* (*kill*) auf der Stelle; (*win*) überlegen; (*buy*) auf einen Schlag; (*ask, refuse*) ohne Umschweife ♦ *adj* (*winner, victory*) unbestritten; (*refusal, hostility*) total.
outrun [aut'rʌn] (*irreg: like* **run**) *vt* schneller laufen als.
outset ['autsɛt] *n* Anfang *m*, Beginn *m*; **from the** ~ von Anfang an; **at the** ~ am Anfang.
outshine [aut'ʃaɪn] (*irreg: like* **shine**) *vt* (*fig*) in den Schatten stellen.
outside [aut'saɪd] *n* (*of building etc*)
Außenseite *f* ♦ *adj* (*wall, lavatory*) Außen-
♦ *adv* (*be, wait*) draußen; (*go*) nach draußen
♦ *prep* außerhalb +*gen*; (*door etc*) vor +*dat*; **at the** ~ (*at the most*) höchstens; (*at the latest*)
spätestens; **an** ~ **chance** eine geringe
Chance.
outside broadcast *n* außerhalb des Studios
produzierte Sendung *f*.
outside lane *n* Überholspur *f*.
outside line *n* (*TEL*) Amtsanschluss *m*.
outsider [aut'saɪdə*] *n* (*stranger*)
Außenstehende(r) *f(m)*; (*odd one out, in race etc*) Außenseiter(in) *m(f)*.
outsize ['autsaɪz] *adj* (*clothes*) übergroß.
outskirts ['autskəːts] *npl* (*of town*) Stadtrand *m*.
outsmart [aut'smaːt] *vt* austricksen (*inf*).
outspoken [aut'spəukən] *adj* offen.
outspread [aut'sprɛd] *adj* (*wings, arms etc*)
ausgebreitet.

outstanding [aut'stændɪŋ] *adj* (*exceptional*)
hervorragend; (*remaining*) ausstehend; **your account is still** ~ Ihr Konto weist noch
Außenstände auf.
outstay [aut'steɪ] *vt*: **to** ~ **one's welcome**
länger bleiben als erwünscht.
outstretched [aut'strɛtʃt] *adj* ausgestreckt.
outstrip [aut'strɪp] *vt* (*competitors, supply*): **to** ~ (**in**) übertreffen (an +*dat*).
out tray *n* Ablage *f* für Ausgänge.
outvote [aut'vəut] *vt* überstimmen.
outward ['autwəd] *adj* (*sign, appearances*)
äußere(r, s); ~ **journey** Hinreise *f*.
outwardly ['autwədlɪ] *adv* (*on the surface*)
äußerlich.
outward(s) ['autwəd(z)] *adv* (*move, face*) nach
außen.
outweigh [aut'weɪ] *vt* schwerer wiegen als.
outwit [aut'wɪt] *vt* überlisten.
ova ['əuvə] *npl of* **ovum**.
oval ['əuvl] *adj* oval ♦ *n* Oval *nt*.

OVAL OFFICE

Oval Office, *ein großer ovaler Raum im Weißen Haus, ist das private Büro des amerikanischen Präsidenten. Im weiteren Sinne bezieht sich dieser Begriff oft auf die Präsidentschaft selbst.*

---

ovarian [əu'vɛərɪən] *adj* (*ANAT*) des
Eierstocks/der Eierstöcke; ~ **cyst** Zyste *f* im
Eierstock.
ovary ['əuvərɪ] *n* (*ANAT, MED*) Eierstock *m*.
ovation [əu'veɪʃən] *n* Ovation *f*.
oven ['ʌvn] *n* (*CULIN*) Backofen *m*.
ovenproof ['ʌvnpruːf] *adj* (*dish etc*) feuerfest.
oven-ready ['ʌvnrɛdɪ] *adj* backfertig.
ovenware ['ʌvnwɛə*] *n* feuerfestes Geschirr
nt.

============== KEYWORD

over ['əuvə*] *adv* **1** (*across: walk, jump, fly etc*)
hinüber; ~ **here** hier; ~ **there** dort (drüben);
to ask sb ~ (*to one's house*) jdn zu sich
einladen.
2 (*indicating movement*): **to fall** ~ (*person*)
hinfallen; (*object*) umfallen; **to knock sth** ~
etw umstoßen; **to turn** ~ (*in bed*) sich
umdrehen; **to bend** ~ sich bücken.
3 (*finished*): **to be** ~ (*game, life, relationship etc*) vorbei sein, zu Ende sein.
4 (*excessively: clever, rich, fat etc*) übermäßig.
5 (*remaining: money, food etc*) übrig; **is there any cake (left)** ~? ist noch Kuchen übrig?
6: all ~ (*everywhere*) überall.
7 (*repeatedly*): ~ **and** ~ (**again**) immer (und
immer) wieder; **five times** ~ fünfmal
♦ *prep* **1** (*on top of, above*) über +*dat*; (*with vb of motion*) über +*acc*; **to spread a sheet** ~ **sth**
ein Laken über etw *acc* breiten.
2 (*on the other side of*): **the pub** ~ **the road**
die Kneipe gegenüber; **he jumped** ~ **the**

wall er sprang über die Mauer.
3 (*more than*) über +*acc*; ~ **200 people** über 200 Leute; ~ **and above my normal duties** über meine normalen Pflichten hinaus; ~ **and above that** darüber hinaus.
4 (*during*) während; **let's discuss it** ~ **dinner** wir sollten es beim Abendessen besprechen.

over... ['əuvəˈ] *pref* über-.
overact [əuvərˈækt] *vi* übertreiben.
overall ['əuvərɔːl] *adj* (*length, cost etc*) Gesamt-; (*impression, view*) allgemein ♦ *adv* (*measure, cost*) insgesamt; (*generally*) im Allgemeinen ♦ *n* (*BRIT*) Kittel *m*; **overalls** *npl* Overall *m*.
overall majority *n* absolute Mehrheit *f*.
overanxious [əuvərˈæŋkʃəs] *adj* überängstlich.
overawe [əuvərˈɔː] *vt*: **to be** ~**d (by)** überwältigt sein (von).
overbalance [əuvəˈbæləns] *vi* das Gleichgewicht verlieren.
overbearing [əuvəˈbɛərɪŋ] *adj* (*person, manner*) aufdringlich.
overboard ['əuvəbɔːd] *adv* (*NAUT*) über Bord; **to go** ~ (*fig*) es übertreiben, zu weit gehen.
overbook [əuvəˈbuk] *vt* überbuchen.
overcame [əuvəˈkeɪm] *pt of* **overcome**.
overcapitalize [əuvəˈkæpɪtəlaɪz] *vt* überkapitalisieren.
overcast ['əuvəkɑːst] *adj* (*day, sky*) bedeckt.
overcharge [əuvəˈtʃɑːdʒ] *vt* zu viel berechnen +*dat*.
overcoat ['əuvəkəut] *n* Mantel *m*.
overcome [əuvəˈkʌm] (*irreg: like* **come**) *vt* (*problem, fear*) überwinden ♦ *adj* überwältigt; **she was** ~ **with grief** der Schmerz übermannte sie.
overconfident [əuvəˈkɒnfɪdənt] *adj* zu selbstsicher.
overcrowded [əuvəˈkraudɪd] *adj* überfüllt.
overcrowding [əuvəˈkraudɪŋ] *n* Überfüllung *f*.
overdo [əuvəˈduː] (*irreg: like* **do**) *vt* übertreiben; **to** ~ **it** es übertreiben.
overdose ['əuvədəus] *n* Überdosis *f*.
overdraft ['əuvədrɑːft] *n* Kontoüberziehung *f*; **to have an** ~ sein Konto überziehen.
overdrawn [əuvəˈdrɔːn] *adj* (*account*) überzogen; **I am** ~ ich habe mein Konto überzogen.
overdrive ['əuvədraɪv] *n* (*AUT*) Schongang *m*.
overdue [əuvəˈdjuː] *adj* überfällig; **that change was long** ~ diese Änderung war schon lange fällig.
overemphasis [əuvərˈɛmfəsɪs] *n*: ~ **on** Überbetonung +*gen*.
overestimate [əuvərˈɛstɪmeɪt] *vt* überschätzen.
overexcited [əuvərɪkˈsaɪtɪd] *adj* ganz aufgeregt.
overexertion [əuvərɪgˈzɔːʃən] *n* Überanstrengung *f*.
overexpose [əuvərɪkˈspəuz] *vt* (*PHOT*) überbelichten.
overflow [əuvəˈfləu] *vi* (*river*) über die Ufer treten; (*bath, jar etc*) überlaufen ♦ *n* (*also*: ~ **pipe**) Überlaufrohr *nt*.
overgenerous [əuvəˈdʒɛnərəs] *adj* allzu großzügig.
overgrown [əuvəˈgrəun] *adj* (*garden*) verwildert; **he's just an** ~ **schoolboy** er ist nur ein großes Kind.
overhang ['əuvəˈhæŋ] (*irreg: like* **hang**) *vt* herausragen über +*acc* ♦ *vi* überhängen ♦ *n* Überhang *m*.
overhaul ['əuvəˈhɔːl] *vt* (*equipment, car etc*) überholen ♦ *n* Überholung *f*.
overhead [əuvəˈhɛd] *adv* (*above*) oben; (*in the sky*) in der Luft ♦ *adj* (*lighting*) Decken-; (*cables, wires*) Überland- ♦ *n* (*US*) = **overheads**; **overheads** *npl* allgemeine Unkosten *pl*.
overhear [əuvəˈhɪə] (*irreg: like* **hear**) *vt* (*zufällig*) mit anhören.
overheat [əuvəˈhiːt] *vi* (*engine*) heißlaufen.
overjoyed [əuvəˈdʒɔɪd] *adj* überglücklich; **to be** ~ **(at)** überglücklich sein (über +*acc*).
overkill ['əuvəkɪl] *n* (*fig*): **it would be** ~ das wäre zu viel des Guten.
overland ['əuvəlænd] *adj* (*journey*) Überland- ♦ *adv* (*travel*) über Land.
overlap [əuvəˈlæp] *vi* (*figures, ideas etc*) sich überschneiden.
overleaf [əuvəˈliːf] *adv* umseitig, auf der Rückseite.
overload [əuvəˈləud] *vt* (*vehicle*) überladen; (*ELEC*) überbelasten; (*fig: with work etc*) überlasten.
overlook [əuvəˈluk] *vt* (*have view over*) überblicken; (*fail to notice*) übersehen; (*excuse, forgive*) hinwegsehen über +*acc*.
overlord ['əuvəlɔːd] *n* oberster Herr *m*.
overmanning [əuvəˈmænɪŋ] *n* Überbesetzung *f*.
overnight [əuvəˈnaɪt] *adv* über Nacht ♦ *adj* (*bag, clothes*) Reise-; (*accommodation, stop*) für die Nacht; **to travel** ~ nachts reisen; **he'll be away** ~ (*tonight*) er kommt erst morgen zurück; **to stay** ~ über Nacht bleiben; ~ **stay** Übernachtung *f*.
overpass ['əuvəpɑːs] (*esp US*) *n* Überführung *f*.
overpay [əuvəˈpeɪ] *vt*: **to** ~ **sb by £50** jdm £ 50 zu viel bezahlen.
overplay [əuvəˈpleɪ] *vt* (*overact*) übertrieben darstellen; **to** ~ **one's hand** den Bogen überspannen.
overpower [əuvəˈpauə] *vt* überwältigen.
overpowering [əuvəˈpauərɪŋ] *adj* (*heat*) unerträglich; (*stench*) durchdringend; (*feeling, desire*) überwältigend.
overproduction ['əuvəprəˈdʌkʃən] *n* Überproduktion *f*.

be ~ **for the course** (*fig*) zu erwarten sein.
parable ['pærəbl] *n* Gleichnis *nt*.
parabola [pə'ræbələ] *n* (*MATH*) Parabel *f*.
parachute ['pærəʃuːt] *n* Fallschirm *m*.
parachute jump *n* Fallschirmabsprung *m*.
parachutist ['pærəʃuːtɪst] *n*
    Fallschirmspringer(in) *m(f)*.
parade [pə'reɪd] *n* (*procession*) Parade *f*;
    (*ceremony*) Zeremonie *f* ♦ *vt* (*people*)
    aufmarschieren lassen; (*wealth, knowledge
    etc*) zur Schau stellen ♦ *vi* (*MIL*)
    aufmarschieren; **fashion** ~ Modenschau *f*.
parade ground *n* Truppenübungsplatz *m*,
    Exerzierplatz *m*.
paradise ['pærədaɪs] *n* (*also fig*) Paradies *nt*.
paradox ['pærədɔks] *n* Paradox *nt*.
paradoxical [pærə'dɔksɪkl] *adj* (*situation*)
    paradox.
paradoxically [pærə'dɔksɪklɪ] *adv*
    paradoxerweise.
paraffin ['pærəfɪn] (*BRIT*) *n* (*also*: ~ **oil**)
    Petroleum *nt*; **liquid** ~ Paraffinöl *nt*.
paraffin heater (*BRIT*) *n* Petroleumofen *m*.
paraffin lamp (*BRIT*) *n* Petroleumlampe *f*.
paragon ['pærəgən] *n*: **a** ~ **of** (*honesty, virtue
    etc*) ein Muster *nt* an +*dat*.
paragraph ['pærəgrɑːf] *n* Absatz *m*, Paragraf
    m; **to begin a new** ~ einen neuen Absatz
    beginnen.
parallel ['pærəlɛl] *adj* (*also COMPUT*) parallel;
    (*fig: similar*) vergleichbar ♦ *n* Parallele *f*;
    (*GEOG*) Breitenkreis *m*; **to run** ~ (**with** *or* **to**)
    (*lit, fig*) parallel verlaufen (zu); **to draw** ~**s
    between/with** Parallelen ziehen zwischen/
    mit; **in** ~ (*ELEC*) parallel.
paralyse ['pærəlaɪz] (*BRIT*) *vt* (*also fig*) lähmen.
paralysis [pə'rælɪsɪs] (*pl* **paralyses**) *n* Lähmung
    f.
paralytic [pærə'lɪtɪk] *adj* paralytisch,
    Lähmungs-; (*BRIT: inf: drunk*) sternhagel-
    voll.
paralyze ['pærəlaɪz] (*US*) *vt* = **paralyse**.
paramedic [pærə'mɛdɪk] *n* Sanitäter(in) *m(f)*;
    (*in hospital*) medizinisch-technischer
    Assistent *m*, medizinisch-technische
    Assistentin *f*.
parameter [pə'ræmɪtə*] *n* (*MATH*) Parameter
    m; (*fig: factor*) Faktor *m*; (: *limit*) Rahmen *m*.
paramilitary [pærə'mɪlɪtərɪ] *adj*
    paramilitärisch.
paramount ['pærəmaʊnt] *adj* vorherrschend;
    of ~ **importance** von höchster *or* größter
    Wichtigkeit.
paranoia [pærə'nɔɪə] *n* Paranoia *f*.
paranoid ['pærənɔɪd] *adj* paranoid.
paranormal [pærə'nɔːml] *adj* übersinnlich,
    paranormal ♦ *n*: **the** ~ das Übersinnliche.
parapet ['pærəpɪt] *n* Brüstung *f*.
paraphernalia [pærəfə'neɪlɪə] *n* Utensilien
    pl.
paraphrase ['pærəfreɪz] *vt* umschreiben.
paraplegic [pærə'pliːdʒɪk] *n* Paraplegiker(in)

m(f), doppelseitig Gelähmte(r) *f(m)*.
parapsychology [pærəsaɪ'kɔlədʒɪ] *n*
    Parapsychologie *f*.
parasite ['pærəsaɪt] *n* (*also fig*) Parasit *m*.
parasol ['pærəsɔl] *n* Sonnenschirm *m*.
paratrooper ['pærətruːpə*] *n* Fallschirmjäger
    m.
parcel ['pɑːsl] *n* Paket *nt* ♦ *vt* (*also*: ~ **up**)
    verpacken.
▶ **parcel out** *vt* aufteilen.
parcel bomb (*BRIT*) *n* Paketbombe *f*.
parcel post *n* Paketpost *f*.
parch [pɑːtʃ] *vt* ausdörren, austrocknen.
parched [pɑːtʃt] *adj* ausgetrocknet; **I'm** ~ (*inf:
    thirsty*) ich bin am Verdursten.
parchment ['pɑːtʃmənt] *n* Pergament *nt*.
pardon ['pɑːdn] *n* (*LAW*) Begnadigung *f*
    ♦ *vt* (*forgive*) verzeihen +*dat*, vergeben
    +*dat*; (*LAW*) begnadigen; ~ **me!, I beg your**
    ~**!** (*I'm sorry!*) verzeihen Sie bitte!; (**I beg
    your**) ~**?**, (*US*) ~ **me?** (*what did you say?*)
    bitte?
pare [pɛə*] *vt* (*BRIT: nails*) schneiden; (*fruit etc*)
    schälen; (*fig: costs etc*) reduzieren.
parent ['pɛərənt] *n* (*mother*) Mutter *f*; (*father*)
    Vater *m*; ~**s** *npl* (*mother and father*) Eltern *pl*.
parentage ['pɛərəntɪdʒ] *n* Herkunft *f*; **of
    unknown** ~ unbekannter Herkunft.
parental [pə'rɛntl] *adj* (*love, control etc*)
    elterlich.
parent company *n* Mutterunternehmen *nt*.
parentheses [pə'rɛnθɪsiːz] *npl of* **parenthesis**.
parenthesis [pə'rɛnθɪsɪs] (*pl* **parentheses**) *n*
    Klammer *f*; **in** ~ in Klammern.
parenthood ['pɛərənthʊd] *n* Elternschaft *f*.
parenting ['pɛərəntɪŋ] *n* elterliche Pflege *f*.
parish ['pærɪʃ] *n* Gemeinde *f*.
parish council (*BRIT*) *n* Gemeinderat *m*.
parishioner [pə'rɪʃənə*] *n* Gemeindemitglied
    nt.
Parisian [pə'rɪzɪən] *adj* Pariser *inv*,
    paris(er)isch ♦ *n* Pariser(in) *m(f)*.
parity ['pærɪtɪ] *n* (*equality*) Gleichstellung *f*.
park [pɑːk] *n* Park *m* ♦ *vt, vi* (*AUT*) parken.
parka ['pɑːkə] *n* Parka *m*.
parking ['pɑːkɪŋ] *n* Parken *nt*; **"no** ~**"**
    „Parken verboten".
parking lights *npl* Parklicht *nt*.
parking lot (*US*) *n* Parkplatz *m*.
parking meter *n* Parkuhr *f*.
parking offence (*BRIT*) *n* Parkvergehen
    nt.
parking place *n* Parkplatz *m*.
parking ticket *n* Strafzettel *m*.
parking violation (*US*) *n* = **parking offence**.
Parkinson's (disease) ['pɑːkɪnsənz-] *n*
    parkinsonsche Krankheit *f*.
parkway ['pɑːkweɪ] (*US*) *n* Allee *f*.
parlance ['pɑːləns] *n*: **in common/modern** ~
    im allgemeinen/modernen Sprach-
    gebrauch.
parliament ['pɑːləmənt] *n* Parlament *nt*.

PARLIAMENT

Parliament *ist die höchste gesetzgebende Versammlung in Großbritannien und tritt im Parlamentsgebäude in London zusammen. Die Legislaturperiode beträgt normalerweise 5 Jahre von einer Wahl zur nächsten. Das Parlament besteht aus zwei Kammern, dem Oberhaus (siehe* **House of Lords** *und dem Unterhaus (siehe* **House of Commons***).*

---

parliamentary [pɑːlə'mɛntərɪ] *adj* parlamentarisch.

parlour, (*US*) **parlor** ['pɑːləˠ] *n* Salon *m*.

parlous ['pɑːləs] *adj* (*state*) prekär.

Parmesan [pɑːmɪ'zæn] *n* (*also:* ~ **cheese**) Parmesan(käse) *m*.

parochial [pə'rəʊkɪəl] (*pej*) *adj* (*person, attitude*) engstirnig.

parody ['pærədɪ] *n* Parodie *f* ♦ *vt* parodieren.

parole [pə'rəʊl] *n* (*LAW*) Bewährung *f*; **on** ~ auf Bewährung.

paroxysm ['pærəksɪzəm] *n* (*also MED*) Anfall *m*.

parquet ['pɑːkeɪ] *n* (*also:* ~ **floor(ing)**) Parkettboden *m*.

parrot ['pærət] *n* Papagei *m*.

parrot-fashion ['pærətfæʃən] *adv* (*say, learn*) mechanisch; (*repeat*) wie ein Papagei.

parry ['pærɪ] *vt* (*blow, argument*) parieren.

parsimonious [pɑːsɪ'məʊnɪəs] *adj* geizig.

parsley ['pɑːslɪ] *n* Petersilie *f*.

parsnip ['pɑːsnɪp] *n* Pastinake *f*.

parson [pɑːsn] *n* Pfarrer *m*.

part [pɑːt] *n* Teil *m*; (*TECH*) Teil *nt*; (*THEAT, CINE etc: role*) Rolle *f*; (*US: in hair*) Scheitel *m*; (*MUS*) Stimme *f* ♦ *adv* = **partly** ♦ *vt* (*separate*) trennen; (*hair*) scheiteln ♦ *vi* (*roads, fig: people*) sich trennen; (*crowd*) sich teilen; **to take** ~ **in** teilnehmen an +*dat*; **to take sth in good** ~ etw nicht übel nehmen; **to take sb's** ~ (*support*) sich auf jds Seite *acc* stellen; **on his** ~ seinerseits; **for my** ~ für meinen Teil; **for the most** ~ (*generally*) zumeist; **for the better** *or* **best** ~ **of the day** die meiste Zeit des Tages; **to be** ~ **and parcel of** dazugehören zu; ~ **of speech** (*LING*) Wortart *f*.
► **part with** *vt fus* sich trennen von.

partake [pɑː'teɪk] (*irreg: like* **take**) *vi* (*form*): **to** ~ **of sth** etw zu sich nehmen.

part exchange (*BRIT*) *n*: **to give/take sth in** ~ etw in Zahlung geben/nehmen.

partial ['pɑːʃl] *adj* (*victory, solution*) Teil-; (*support*) teilweise; (*biassed*) parteiisch; **to be** ~ **to** (*person, drink etc*) eine Vorliebe haben für.

partially ['pɑːʃəlɪ] *adv* (*to some extent*) teilweise, zum Teil.

participant [pɑː'tɪsɪpənt] *n* Teilnehmer(in) *m(f)*.

participate [pɑː'tɪsɪpeɪt] *vi* sich beteiligen; **to** ~ **in** teilnehmen an +*dat*.

participation [pɑːtɪsɪ'peɪʃən] *n* Teilnahme *f*.

participle ['pɑːtɪsɪpl] *n* Partizip *nt*.

particle ['pɑːtɪkl] *n* Teilchen *nt*, Partikel *f*.

particular [pə'tɪkjʊləˠ] *adj* (*distinct: person, time, place etc*) bestimmt, speziell; (*special*) speziell, besondere(r, s) ♦ *n*: **in** ~ im Besonderen, besonders; **particulars** *npl* Einzelheiten *pl*; (*name, address etc*) Personalien *pl*; **to be very** ~ **about sth** (*fussy*) in Bezug auf etw *acc* sehr eigen sein.

particularly [pə'tɪkjʊləlɪ] *adv* besonders.

parting ['pɑːtɪŋ] *n* (*action*) Teilung *f*; (*farewell*) Abschied *m*; (*BRIT: in hair*) Scheitel *m* ♦ *adj* (*words, gift etc*) Abschieds-; **his** ~ **shot was …** (*fig*) seine Bemerkung zum Abschied war …

partisan [pɑːtɪ'zæn] *adj* (*politics, views*) voreingenommen ♦ *n* (*supporter*) Anhänger(in) *m(f)*; (*fighter*) Partisan *m*.

partition [pɑː'tɪʃən] *n* (*wall, screen*) Trennwand *f*; (*of country*) Teilung *f* ♦ *vt* (*room, office*) aufteilen; (*country*) teilen.

partly ['pɑːtlɪ] *adv* teilweise, zum Teil.

partner ['pɑːtnəˠ] *n* Partner(in) *m(f)*; (*COMM*) Partner(in), Teilhaber(in) *m(f)* ♦ *vt* (*at dance, cards etc*) als Partner(in) haben.

partnership ['pɑːtnəʃɪp] *n* (*POL etc*) Partnerschaft *f*; (*COMM*) Teilhaberschaft *f*; **to go into** ~ (**with sb**), **form a** ~ (**with sb**) (mit jdm) eine Partnerschaft eingehen.

part payment *n* Anzahlung *f*.

partridge ['pɑːtrɪdʒ] *n* Rebhuhn *nt*.

part-time ['pɑːt'taɪm] *adj* (*work, staff*) Teilzeit-, Halbtags- ♦ *adv*: **to work** ~ Teilzeit arbeiten; **to study** ~ Teilzeitstudent(in) *m(f)* sein.

part-timer [pɑːt'taɪməˠ] *n* (*also:* **part-time worker**) Teilzeitbeschäftigte(r) *f(m)*.

party ['pɑːtɪ] *n* (*POL, LAW*) Partei *f*; (*celebration, social event*) Party *f*, Fete *f*; (*group of people*) Gruppe *f*, Gesellschaft *f* ♦ *cpd* (*POL*) Partei-; **dinner** ~ Abendgesellschaft *f*; **to give** *or* **throw a** ~ eine Party geben, eine Fete machen; **we're having a** ~ **next Saturday** bei uns ist nächsten Samstag eine Party; **our son's birthday** ~ die Geburtstagsfeier unseres Sohnes; **to be a** ~ **to a crime** an einem Verbrechen beteiligt sein.

party dress *n* Partykleid *nt*.

party line *n* (*TEL*) Gemeinschaftsanschluss *m*; (*POL*) Parteilinie *f*.

party piece (*inf*) *n*: **to do one's** ~ auf einer Party etwas zum Besten geben.

party political *adj* parteipolitisch.

party political broadcast *n* parteipolitische Sendung *f*.

par value *n* (*COMM: of share etc*) Nennwert *m*.

pass [pɑːs] *vt* (*spend: time*) verbringen; (*hand over*) reichen, geben; (*go past*) vorbeikommen an +*dat*; (: *in car*) vorbeifahren an +*dat*; (*overtake*) überholen;

(fig: exceed) übersteigen; (exam) bestehen; (law, proposal) genehmigen ♦ vi (go past) vorbeigehen; (: in car) vorbeifahren; (in exam) bestehen ♦ n (permit) Ausweis m; (in mountains, SPORT) Pass m; to ~ sth through sth etw durch etw führen; to ~ the ball to den Ball zuspielen +dat; could you ~ the vegetables round? könnten Sie das Gemüse herumreichen?; to get a ~ in ... (SCOL) die Prüfung in ... bestehen; things have come to a pretty ~ when ... (BRIT: inf) so weit ist es schon gekommen, dass ...; to make a ~ at sb (inf) jdn anmachen.

► **pass away** vi (die) dahinscheiden.

► **pass by** vi (go past) vorbeigehen; (: in car) vorbeifahren ♦ vt (ignore) vorbeigehen an +dat.

► **pass down** vt (customs, inheritance) weitergeben.

► **pass for** vt: she could ~ for 25 sie könnte für 25 durchgehen.

► **pass on** vi (die) verscheiden ♦ vt: to ~ on (to) weitergeben (an +acc).

► **pass out** vi (faint) ohnmächtig werden; (BRIT: MIL) die Ausbildung beenden.

► **pass over** vt (ignore) übergehen ♦ vi (die) entschlafen.

► **pass up** vt (opportunity) sich dat entgehen lassen.

passable ['pɑːsəbl] adj (road) passierbar; (acceptable) passabel.

passage ['pæsɪdʒ] n Gang m; (in book) Passage f; (way through crowd etc, ANAT) Weg m; (act of passing: of train etc) Durchfahrt f; (journey: on boat) Überfahrt f.

passageway ['pæsɪdʒweɪ] n Gang m.

passenger ['pæsɪndʒəʳ] n (in boat, plane) Passagier m; (in car) Fahrgast m.

passer-by [pɑːsə'baɪ] (pl ~s-~) n Passant(in) m(f).

passing ['pɑːsɪŋ] adj (moment, thought etc) flüchtig; in ~ (incidentally) beiläufig, nebenbei; to mention sth in ~ etw beiläufig or nebenbei erwähnen.

passing place n (AUT) Ausweichstelle f.

passion ['pæʃən] n Leidenschaft f; to have a ~ for sth eine Leidenschaft für etw haben.

passionate ['pæʃənɪt] adj leidenschaftlich.

passion fruit n Passionsfrucht f, Maracuja f.

Passion play n Passionsspiel nt.

passive ['pæsɪv] adj passiv; (LING) Passiv- ♦ n (LING) Passiv nt.

passive smoking n passives Rauchen, Passivrauchen nt.

passkey ['pɑːskiː] n Hauptschlüssel m.

Passover ['pɑːsəʊvəʳ] n Passah(fest) nt.

passport ['pɑːspɔːt] n Pass m; (fig: to success etc) Schlüssel m.

passport control n Passkontrolle f.

passport office n Passamt nt.

password ['pɑːswɜːd] n Kennwort nt; (COMPUT) Passwort nt.

past [pɑːst] prep (in front of) vorbei an +dat; (beyond) hinter +dat; (later than) nach ♦ adj (government etc) früher, ehemalig; (week, month etc) vergangen ♦ n Vergangenheit f ♦ adv: to run ~ vorbeilaufen; he's ~ 40 er ist über 40; it's ~ midnight es ist nach Mitternacht; ten/quarter ~ eight zehn/ Viertel nach acht; he ran ~ me er lief an mir vorbei; I'm ~ caring es kümmert mich nicht mehr; to be ~ it (BRIT: inf: person) es nicht mehr bringen; for the ~ few/3 days während der letzten Tage/3 Tage; in the ~ (also LING) in der Vergangenheit.

pasta ['pæstə] n Nudeln pl.

paste [peɪst] n (wet mixture) Teig m; (glue) Kleister m; (jewellery) Strass m; (fish, tomato etc paste) Paste f ♦ vt (stick) kleben.

pastel ['pæstl] adj (colour) Pastell-.

pasteurized ['pæstʃəraɪzd] adj pasteurisiert.

pastille ['pæstl] n Pastille f.

pastime ['pɑːstaɪm] n Zeitvertreib m, Hobby nt.

past master (BRIT) n: to be a ~ at sth ein Experte m in etw dat sein.

pastor ['pɑːstəʳ] n Pastor(in) m(f).

pastoral ['pɑːstərl] adj (REL: duties etc) als Pastor.

pastry ['peɪstrɪ] n (dough) Teig m; (cake) Gebäckstück nt.

pasture ['pɑːstʃəʳ] n Weide f.

pasty [n 'pæstɪ, adj 'peɪstɪ] n (pie) Pastete f ♦ adj (complexion) blässlich.

pat [pæt] vt (with hand) tätscheln ♦ adj (answer, remark) glatt ♦ n: to give sb/o.s. a ~ on the back (fig) jdm/sich auf die Schulter klopfen; he knows it off ~, (US) he has it down ~ er kennt das in- und auswendig.

patch [pætʃ] n (piece of material) Flicken m; (also: eye ~) Augenklappe f; (damp, bald etc) Fleck m; (of land) Stück nt; (: for growing vegetables etc) Beet nt ♦ vt (clothes) flicken; (to go through) a bad ~ eine schwierige Zeit (durchmachen).

► **patch up** vt (clothes etc) flicken; (quarrel) beilegen.

patchwork ['pætʃwɜːk] n (SEWING) Patchwork nt.

patchy ['pætʃɪ] adj (colour) ungleichmäßig; (information, knowledge etc) lückenhaft.

pate [peɪt] n: a bald ~ eine Glatze.

pâté ['pæteɪ] n Pastete f.

patent ['peɪtnt] n Patent nt ♦ vt patentieren lassen ♦ adj (obvious) offensichtlich.

patent leather n Lackleder nt.

patently ['peɪtntlɪ] adv (obvious, wrong) vollkommen.

patent medicine n patentrechtlich geschütztes Arzneimittel nt.

Patent Office n Patentamt nt.

paternal [pə'tɜːnl] adj väterlich; my ~ grandmother meine Großmutter väterlicherseits.

paternalistic [pətə:nə'lıstık] *adj*
patriarchalisch.
paternity [pə'tə:nıtı] *n* Vaterschaft *f*.
paternity leave *n* Vaterschaftsurlaub *m*.
paternity suit *n* Vaterschaftsprozess *m*.
path [pɑ:θ] *n* (*also fig*) Weg *m*; (*trail, track*) Pfad
m; (*trajectory: of bullet, aircraft, planet*) Bahn *f*.
pathetic [pə'θɛtık] *adj* (*pitiful*)
mitleiderregend; (*very bad*) erbärmlich.
pathological [pæθə'lɔdʒıkl] *adj* (*liar, hatred*)
krankhaft; (*MED*) pathologisch.
pathologist [pə'θɔlədʒıst] *n* Pathologe *m*,
Pathologin *f*.
pathology [pə'θɔlədʒı] *n* Pathologie *f*.
pathos ['peıθɔs] *n* Pathos *nt*.
pathway ['pɑ:θweı] *n* Pfad *m*, Weg *m*; (*fig*)
Weg.
patience ['peıʃns] *n* Geduld *f*; (*BRIT: CARDS*)
Patience *f*; **to lose (one's)** ~ die Geduld
verlieren.
patient ['peıʃnt] *n* Patient(in) *m(f)* ♦ *adj*
geduldig; **to be** ~ **with sb** Geduld mit jdm
haben.
patiently ['peıʃntlı] *adv* geduldig.
patio ['pætıəu] *n* Terrasse *f*.
patriot ['peıtrıət] *n* Patriot(in) *m(f)*.
patriotic [pætrı'ɔtık] *adj* patriotisch.
patriotism ['pætrıətızəm] *n* Patriotismus *m*.
patrol [pə'trəul] *n* (*MIL*) Patrouille *f*; (*POLICE*)
Streife *f* ♦ *vt* (*MIL, POLICE: city, streets etc*)
patrouillieren; **to be on** ~ (*MIL*) auf
Patrouille sein; (*POLICE*) auf Streife sein.
patrol boat *n* Patrouillenboot *nt*.
patrol car *n* Streifenwagen *m*.
patrolman [pə'trəulmən] (*US: irreg: like* **man**) *n*
(*POLICE*) (Streifen)polizist *m*.
patron ['peıtrən] *n* (*customer*) Kunde *m*,
Kundin *f*; (*benefactor*) Förderer *m*; ~ **of the
arts** Kunstmäzen *m*.
patronage ['pætrənıdʒ] *n* (*of artist, charity etc*)
Förderung *f*.
patronize ['pætrənaız] *vt* (*pej: look down on*)
von oben herab behandeln; (*artist etc*)
fördern; (*shop, club*) besuchen.
patronizing ['pætrənaızıŋ] *adj* herablassend.
patron saint *n* Schutzheilige(r) *f(m)*.
patter ['pætə*] *n* (*of feet*) Trappeln *nt*; (*of rain*)
Prasseln *nt*; (*sales talk etc*) Sprüche *pl* ♦ *vi*
(*footsteps*) trappeln; (*rain*) prasseln.
pattern ['pætən] *n* Muster *nt*; (*SEWING*)
Schnittmuster *nt*; **behaviour** ~**s**
Verhaltensmuster *pl*.
patterned ['pætənd] *adj* gemustert; ~ **with
flowers** mit Blumenmuster.
paucity ['pɔ:sıtı] *n*: **a** ~ **of** ein Mangel *m* an
+*dat*.
paunch [pɔ:ntʃ] *n* Bauch *m*, Wanst *m*.
pauper ['pɔ:pə*] *n* Arme(r) *f(m)*; ~**'s grave**
Armengrab *nt*.
pause [pɔ:z] *n* Pause *f* ♦ *vi* eine Pause machen;
(*hesitate*) innehalten; **to** ~ **for breath** eine
Verschnaufpause einlegen.

pave [peıv] *vt* (*street, yard etc*) pflastern; **to**
~ **the way for** (*fig*) den Weg bereiten *or*
bahnen für.
pavement ['peıvmənt] *n* (*BRIT*) Bürgersteig *m*;
(*US: roadway*) Straße *f*.
pavilion [pə'vılıən] *n* (*SPORT*) Klubhaus *nt*.
paving ['peıvıŋ] *n* (*material*) Straßenbelag *m*.
paving stone *n* Pflasterstein *m*.
paw [pɔ:] *n* (*of cat, dog etc*) Pfote *f*; (*of lion, bear
etc*) Tatze *f*, Pranke *f* ♦ *vt* (*pej: touch*)
betatschen; **to** ~ **the ground** (*animal*)
scharren.
pawn [pɔ:n] *n* (*CHESS*) Bauer *m*; (*fig*)
Schachfigur *f* ♦ *vt* versetzen.
pawnbroker ['pɔ:nbrəukə*] *n* Pfandleiher *m*.
pawnshop ['pɔ:nʃɔp] *n* Pfandhaus *nt*.
pay [peı] (*pt, pp* **paid**) *n* (*wage*) Lohn *m*; (*salary*)
Gehalt *nt* ♦ *vt* (*sum of money, wage*) zahlen;
(*bill, person*) bezahlen ♦ *vi* (*be profitable*) sich
bezahlt machen; (*fig*) sich lohnen; **how much
did you** ~ **for it?** wie viel hast du dafür
bezahlt?; **I paid 10 pounds for that book** ich
habe 10 Pfund für das Buch bezahlt, das
Buch hat mich 10 Pfund gekostet; **to**
~ **one's way** seinen Beitrag leisten; **to**
~ **dividends** (*fig*) sich bezahlt machen; **to**
~ **the price/penalty for sth** (*fig*) den Preis/die
Strafe für etw zahlen; **to** ~ **sb a compliment**
jdm ein Kompliment machen; **to**
~ **attention (to)** Acht geben (auf +*acc*); **to**
~ **sb a visit** jdn besuchen; **to** ~ **one's
respects to sb** jdm seine Aufwartung
machen.
► **pay back** *vt* zurückzahlen; **I'll** ~ **you back**
next week ich gebe dir das Geld nächste
Woche zurück.
► **pay for** *vt fus* (*also fig*) (be)zahlen für.
► **pay in** *vt* einzahlen.
► **pay off** *vt* (*debt*) abbezahlen; (*person*)
auszahlen; (*creditor*) befriedigen; (*mortgage*)
tilgen ♦ *vi* sich auszahlen; **to** ~ **sth off in
instalments** etw in Raten (ab)zahlen.
► **pay out** *vt* (*money*) ausgeben; (*rope*)
ablaufen lassen.
► **pay up** *vi* zahlen.
payable ['peıəbl] *adj* zahlbar; **to make a
cheque** ~ **to sb** einen Scheck auf jdn
ausstellen.
pay award *n* Lohn-/Gehaltserhöhung *f*.
payday ['peıdeı] *n* Zahltag *m*.
PAYE (*BRIT*) *n abbr* (= *pay as you earn*)
Lohnsteuerabzugsverfahren *nt*.
payee [peı'i:] *n* Zahlungsempfänger *m*.
pay envelope (*US*) *n* = **pay packet**.
paying guest ['peııŋ-] *n* zahlender Gast *m*.
payload ['peıləud] *n* Nutzlast *f*.
payment ['peımənt] *n* (*act*) Zahlung *f*,
Bezahlung *f*; (*of bill*) Begleichung *f*; (*sum of
money*) Zahlung *f*; **advance** ~ (*part sum*)
Anzahlung *f*; (*total sum*) Vorauszahlung *f*;
deferred ~, ~ **by instalments** Ratenzahlung
f; **monthly** ~ (*sum of money*) Monatsrate *f*;

on ~ of gegen Zahlung von.
pay packet (*BRIT*) *n* Lohntüte *f*.
pay-per-click ['peɪpə'klɪk] *n* (*COMPUT*) Pay-per-Click *nt*.
payphone ['peɪfəʊn] *n* Münztelefon *nt*; (*card phone*) Kartentelefon *nt*.
payroll ['peɪrəʊl] *n* Lohnliste *f*; **to be on a firm's** ~ bei einer Firma beschäftigt sein.
pay slip (*BRIT*) *n see* **pay** Lohnstreifen *m*; Gehaltsstreifen *m*.
pay station (*US*) *n* = **payphone**.
PBS (*US*) *n abbr* (= *Public Broadcasting Service*) öffentliche Rundfunkanstalt.
PC *n abbr* (= *personal computer*) PC *m*; (*BRIT*) = **police constable** ♦ *adj abbr* = **politically correct** ♦ *abbr* (*BRIT*) = **Privy Councillor**.
pc *abbr* = **per cent**; **postcard**.
p/c *abbr* = **petty cash**.
PCB *n abbr* (*ELEC, COMPUT*) = **printed circuit board**; (= *polychlorinated biphenyl*) PCB *nt*.
pcm *abbr* (= *per calendar month*) pro Monat.
PD (*US*) *n abbr* = **police department**.
pd *abbr* (= *paid*) bez.
PDA *abbr* (*COMPUT*: = *personal digital assistant*) PDA *m*.
pdq (*inf*) *adv abbr* (= *pretty damn quick*) verdammt schnell.
PDSA (*BRIT*) *n abbr* (= *People's Dispensary for Sick Animals*) kostenloses Behandlungszentrum für Haustiere.
PDT (*US*) *abbr* (= *Pacific Daylight Time*) pazifische Sommerzeit.
PE *n abbr* (*SCOL*) = **physical education**.
pea [piː] *n* Erbse *f*.
peace [piːs] *n* Frieden *m*; **to be at** ~ **with sb/sth** mit jdm/etw in Frieden leben; **to keep the** ~ (*policeman*) die öffentliche Ordnung aufrechterhalten; (*citizen*) den Frieden wahren.
peaceable ['piːsəbl] *adj* friedlich.
peaceful ['piːsful] *adj* friedlich.
peacekeeper ['piːskiːpə'] *n* Friedenswächter(in) *m(f)*.
peacekeeping force ['piːskiːpɪŋ-] *n* Friedenstruppen *pl*.
peace offering *n* Friedensangebot *nt*.
peach [piːtʃ] *n* Pfirsich *m*.
peacock ['piːkɔk] *n* Pfau *m*.
peak [piːk] *n* (*of mountain*) Spitze *f*, Gipfel *m*; (*of cap*) Schirm *m*; (*fig*) Höhepunkt *m*.
peak hours *npl* Stoßzeit *f*.
peak period *n* Spitzenzeit *f*, Stoßzeit *f*.
peak rate *n* Höchstrate *f*.
peaky ['piːkɪ] (*BRIT: inf*) *adj* blass.
peal [piːl] *n* (*of bells*) Läuten *nt*; ~**s of laughter** schallendes Gelächter *nt*.
peanut ['piːnʌt] *n* Erdnuss *f*.
peanut butter *n* Erdnussbutter *f*.
pear [pɛə'] *n* Birne *f*.
pearl [pɜːl] *n* Perle *f*.
peasant ['pɛznt] *n* Bauer *m*.
peat [piːt] *n* Torf *m*.

pebble ['pɛbl] *n* Kieselstein *m*.
peck [pɛk] *vt* (*bird*) picken; (*also*: ~ **at**) picken an +*dat* ♦ *n* (*of bird*) Schnabelhieb *m*; (*kiss*) Küsschen *nt*.
pecking order ['pɛkɪŋ-] *n* (*fig*) Hackordnung *f*.
peckish ['pɛkɪʃ] (*BRIT: inf*) *adj* (*hungry*) leicht hungrig; **I'm feeling** ~ ich könnte was zu essen gebrauchen.
peculiar [pɪ'kjuːlɪə'] *adj* (*strange*) seltsam; ~ **to** (*exclusive to*) charakteristisch für.
peculiarity [pɪkjuːlɪ'ærɪtɪ] *n* (*strange habit*) Eigenart *f*; (*distinctive feature*) Besonderheit *f*, Eigentümlichkeit *f*.
peculiarly [pɪ'kjuːlɪəlɪ] *adv* (*oddly*) seltsam; (*distinctively*) unverkennbar.
pecuniary [pɪ'kjuːnɪərɪ] *adj* finanziell.
pedal ['pɛdl] *n* Pedal *nt* ♦ *vi* in die Pedale treten.
pedal bin (*BRIT*) *n* Treteimer *m*.
pedant ['pɛdənt] *n* Pedant(in) *m(f)*.
pedantic [pɪ'dæntɪk] *adj* pedantisch.
peddle ['pɛdl] *vt* (*goods*) feilbieten, verkaufen; (*drugs*) handeln mit; (*gossip*) verbreiten.
peddler ['pɛdlə'] *n* (*also*: **drug** ~) Pusher *m*.
pedestal ['pɛdəstl] *n* Sockel *m*.
pedestrian [pɪ'dɛstrɪən] *n* Fußgänger(in) *m(f)* ♦ *adj* Fußgänger-; (*fig*) langweilig.
pedestrian crossing (*BRIT*) *n* Fußgängerüberweg *m*.
pedestrian mall (*US*) *n* Fußgängerzone *f*.
pedestrian precinct (*BRIT*) *n* Fußgängerzone *f*.
pediatrics [piːdɪ'ætrɪks] (*US*) *n* = **paediatrics**.
pedigree ['pɛdɪgriː] *n* (*of animal*) Stammbaum *m*; (*fig*: *background*) Vorgeschichte *f* ♦ *cpd* (*dog*) Rasse-, reinrassig.
pee [piː] (*inf*) *vi* pinkeln.
peek [piːk] *vi*: **to** ~ **at/over/into** *etc* gucken nach/über +*acc*/in +*acc* *etc* ♦ *n*: **to have** *or* **take a** ~ (**at**) einen (kurzen) Blick werfen (auf +*acc*).
peel [piːl] *n* Schale *f* ♦ *vt* schälen ♦ *vi* (*paint*) abblättern; (*wallpaper*) sich lösen; (*skin, back etc*) sich schälen.
▶ **peel back** *vt* abziehen.
peeler ['piːlə'] *n* (*potato peeler etc*) Schälmesser *nt*.
peelings ['piːlɪŋz] *npl* Schalen *pl*.
peep [piːp] *n* (*look*) kurzer Blick *m*; (*sound*) Pieps *m* ♦ *vi* (*look*) gucken; **to have** *or* **take a** ~ (**at**) einen kurzen Blick werfen (auf +*acc*).
▶ **peep out** *vi* (*be visible*) hervorgucken.
peephole ['piːphəʊl] *n* Guckloch *nt*.
peer [pɪə'] *n* (*noble*) Peer *m*; (*equal*) Gleichrangige(r) *f(m)*; (*contemporary*) Gleichaltrige(r) *f(m)* ♦ *vi*: **to** ~ **at** starren auf +*acc*.
peerage ['pɪərɪdʒ] *n* (*title*) Adelswürde *f*; (*position*) Adelsstand *m*; **the** ~ (*all the peers*) der Adel.
peerless ['pɪəlɪs] *adj* unvergleichlich.
peeved [piːvd] *adj* verärgert, sauer (*inf*).

peevish ['piːvɪʃ] *adj* (*bad-tempered*) mürrisch.
peg [pɛg] *n* (*hook, knob*) Haken *m*; (*BRIT*: *also*:
clothes ~) Wäscheklammer *f*; (*also*: **tent** ~)
Hering *m* ♦ *vt* (*washing*) festklammern;
(*prices*) festsetzen; **off the** ~ von der Stange.
pejorative [pɪ'dʒɔrətɪv] *adj* abwertend.
Pekin [piː'kɪn] *n* = **Peking**.
Pekinese [piːkɪ'niːz] *n* = **Pekingese**.
Peking [piː'kɪŋ] *n* Peking *nt*.
Pekingese [piːkɪ'niːz] *n* (*dog*) Pekinese *m*.
pelican ['pɛlɪkən] *n* Pelikan *m*.
pelican crossing (*BRIT*) *n* (*AUT*)
Fußgängerüberweg *m* mit Ampel.
pellet ['pɛlɪt] *n* (*of paper etc*) Kügelchen *nt*; (*of
mud etc*) Klümpchen *nt*; (*for shotgun*)
Schrotkugel *f*.
pell-mell ['pɛl'mɛl] *adv* in heillosem
Durcheinander.
pelmet ['pɛlmɪt] *n* (*wooden*) Blende *f*; (*fabric*)
Querbehang *m*.
pelt [pɛlt] *vi* (*rain*: *also*: ~ **down**)
niederprasseln; (*inf*: *run*) rasen ♦ *n* (*animal
skin*) Pelz *m*, Fell *nt* ♦ *vt*: **to** ~ **sb with sth** jdn
mit etw bewerfen.
pelvis ['pɛlvɪs] *n* Becken *nt*.
pen [pɛn] *n* (*also*: **fountain** ~) Füller *m*; (*also*:
ballpoint ~) Kugelschreiber *m*; (*also*: **felt-tip**
~) Filzstift *m*; (*enclosure: for sheep, pigs etc*)
Pferch *m*; (*US*: *inf*: *prison*) Knast *m*; **to put**
~ **to paper** zur Feder greifen.
penal ['piːnl] *adj* (*LAW: colony, institution*)
Straf-; (: *system, reform*) Strafrechts-;
~ **code** Strafgesetzbuch *nt*.
penalize ['piːnəlaɪz] *vt* (*punish*) bestrafen; (*fig*)
benachteiligen.
penal servitude [-'səːvɪtjuːd] *n* Zwangsarbeit
f.
penalty ['pɛnltɪ] *n* Strafe *f*; (*SPORT*) Strafstoß
m; (: *FOOTBALL*) Elfmeter *m*.
penalty area (*BRIT*) *n* (*SPORT*) Strafraum *m*.
penalty clause *n* Strafklausel *f*.
penalty kick *n* (*RUGBY*) Strafstoß *m*;
(*FOOTBALL*) Elfmeter *m*.
penalty shoot-out [-'ʃuːtaut] *n* (*FOOTBALL*)
Elfmeterschießen *nt*.
penance ['pɛnəns] *n* (*REL*): **to do** ~ **for one's
sins** für seine Sünden Buße tun.
pence [pɛns] *npl of* **penny**.
penchant ['pãːʃãːŋ] *n* Vorliebe *f*, Schwäche *f*,
to have a ~ **for** eine Schwäche haben für.
pencil ['pɛnsl] *n* Bleistift *m* ♦ *vt*: **to** ~ **sb/sth in**
jdn/etw vormerken.
pencil case *n* Federmäppchen *nt*.
pencil sharpener *n* Bleistiftspitzer *m*.
pendant ['pɛndnt] *n* Anhänger *m*.
pending ['pɛndɪŋ] *adj* anstehend ♦ *prep*: ~ **his
return** bis zu seiner Rückkehr; ~ **a decision**
bis eine Entscheidung getroffen ist.
pendulum ['pɛndjuləm] *n* Pendel *nt*.
penetrate ['pɛnɪtreɪt] *vt* (*person: territory etc*)
durchdringen; (*light, water, sound*)
eindringen in +*acc*.

penetrating ['pɛnɪtreɪtɪŋ] *adj* (*sound, gaze*)
durchdringend; (*mind, observation*) scharf.
penetration [pɛnɪ'treɪʃən] *n* Durchdringen *nt*.
pen friend (*BRIT*) *n* Brieffreund(in) *m(f)*.
penguin ['pɛŋgwɪn] *n* Pinguin *m*.
penicillin [pɛnɪ'sɪlɪn] *n* Penizillin *nt*.
peninsula [pə'nɪnsjulə] *n* Halbinsel *f*.
penis ['piːnɪs] *n* Penis *m*.
penitence ['pɛnɪtns] *n* Reue *f*.
penitent ['pɛnɪtnt] *adj* reuig.
penitentiary [pɛnɪ'tɛnʃərɪ] (*US*) *n* Gefängnis
nt.
penknife ['pɛnnaɪf] *n* Taschenmesser *nt*.
Penn. (*US*) *abbr* (*POST*: = *Pennsylvania*).
pen name *n* Pseudonym *nt*.
penniless ['pɛnɪlɪs] *adj* mittellos.
Pennines ['pɛnaɪnz] *npl*: **the** ~ die Pennines *pl*.
penny ['pɛnɪ] (*pl* **pennies** *or* (*BRIT*) **pence**) *n*
Penny *m*; (*US*) Cent *m*; **it was worth every** ~
es war jeden Pfennig wert; **it won't cost
you a** ~ es kostet dich keinen Pfennig.
pen pal *n* Brieffreund(in) *m(f)*.
penpusher ['pɛnpuʃəˀ] *n* Schreiberling *m*.
pension ['pɛnʃən] *n* Rente *f*.
▶ **pension off** *vt* (*vorzeitig*) pensionieren.
pensionable ['pɛnʃnəbl] *adj* (*age*) Pensions-;
(*job*) mit Pensionsberechtigung.
pensioner ['pɛnʃənəˀ] (*BRIT*) *n* Rentner(in)
m(f).
pension scheme *n* Rentenversicherung *f*.
pensive ['pɛnsɪv] *adj* nachdenklich.
pentagon ['pɛntəgən] (*US*) *n*: **the P~** das
Pentagon.

PENTAGON

Pentagon *heißt das fünfeckige Gebäude in
Arlington, Virginia, in dem das amerikanische
Verteidigungsministerium untergebracht ist. Im
weiteren Sinne bezieht sich dieses Wort auf die
amerikanische Militärführung.*

Pentecost ['pɛntɪkɔst] *n* (*in Judaism*)
Erntefest *nt*; (*in Christianity*) Pfingsten *nt*.
penthouse ['pɛnthaus] *n* Penthouse *nt*.
pent-up ['pɛntʌp] *adj* (*feelings*) aufgestaut.
penultimate [pɛ'nʌltɪmət] *adj* vorletzte(r, s).
penury ['pɛnjurɪ] *n* Armut *f*, Not *f*.
people ['piːpl] *npl* (*persons*) Leute *pl*;
(*inhabitants*) Bevölkerung *f* ♦ *n* (*nation, race*)
Volk *nt*; **old** ~ alte Menschen *or* Leute;
young ~ junge Leute; **the room was full of**
~ das Zimmer war voller Leute *or*
Menschen; **several** ~ **came** mehrere (Leute)
kamen; ~ **say that ...** man sagt, dass ...; **the**
~ (*POL*) das Volk; **a man of the** ~ ein Mann
des Volkes.
PEP *n abbr* (= *personal equity plan*)
steuerbegünstigte Kapitalinvestition.
pep [pɛp] (*inf*) *n* Schwung *m*, Pep *m*.
▶ **pep up** *vt* (*person*) aufmöbeln; (*food*)
pikanter machen.

pepper ['pepə*] n (spice) Pfeffer m; (vegetable) Paprika m ♦ vt: **to ~ with** (fig) übersäen mit; **two ~s** zwei Paprikaschoten.
peppercorn ['pepəkɔːn] n Pfefferkorn nt.
pepper mill n Pfeffermühle f.
peppermint ['pepəmɪnt] n (sweet) Pfefferminz nt; (plant) Pfefferminze f.
pepperoni [pepə'rəʊnɪ] n ≈ Pfeffersalami f.
pepper pot n Pfefferstreuer m.
pep talk (inf) n aufmunternde Worte pl.
per [pɜː*] prep (for each) pro; **~ day/person/kilo** pro Tag/Person/Kilo; **~ annum** pro Jahr; **as ~ your instructions** gemäß Ihren Anweisungen.
per capita [-'kæpɪtə] adj (income) Pro-Kopf- ♦ adv pro Kopf.
perceive [pə'siːv] vt (see) wahrnehmen; (view, understand) verstehen.
per cent n Prozent nt; **a 20 ~ discount** 20 Prozent Rabatt.
percentage [pə'sentɪdʒ] n Prozentsatz m; **on a ~ basis** auf Prozentbasis.
percentage point n Prozent nt.
perceptible [pə'septɪbl] adj (difference, change) wahrnehmbar, merklich.
perception [pə'sepʃən] n (insight) Einsicht f; (opinion, understanding) Erkenntnis f; (faculty) Wahrnehmung f.
perceptive [pə'septɪv] adj (person) aufmerksam; (analysis etc) erkenntnisreich.
perch [pɜːtʃ] n (for bird) Stange f; (fish) Flussbarsch m ♦ vi: **to ~ (on)** (bird) sitzen (auf +dat); (person) hocken (auf +dat).
percolate ['pɜːkəleɪt] vt (coffee) (mit einer Kaffeemaschine) zubereiten ♦ vi (coffee) durchlaufen; **to ~ through/into** (idea, light etc) durchsickern durch/in +acc.
percolator ['pɜːkəleɪtə*] n (also: **coffee ~**) Kaffeemaschine f.
percussion [pə'kʌʃən] n (MUS) Schlagzeug nt.
peremptory [pə'remptərɪ] (pej) adj (person) herrisch; (order) kategorisch.
perennial [pə'renɪəl] adj (plant) mehrjährig; (fig: problem, feature etc) immer wiederkehrend ♦ n (BOT) mehrjährige Pflanze f.
perfect [adj, n 'pɜːfɪkt, vt pə'fekt] adj perfekt; (nonsense, idiot etc) ausgemacht ♦ vt (technique) perfektionieren ♦ n: **the ~** (also: **the ~ tense**) das Perfekt; **he's a ~ stranger to me** er ist mir vollkommen fremd.
perfection [pə'fekʃən] n Perfektion f, Vollkommenheit f.
perfectionist [pə'fekʃənɪst] n Perfektionist(in) m(f).
perfectly ['pɜːfɪktlɪ] adv vollkommen; (faultlessly) perfekt; **I'm ~ happy with the situation** ich bin mit der Lage vollkommen zufrieden; **you know ~ well that ...** Sie wissen ganz genau, dass ...
perforate ['pɜːfəreɪt] vt perforieren.
perforated ulcer ['pɜːfəreɪtəd-] n durchgebrochenes Geschwür nt.
perforation [pɜːfə'reɪʃən] n (small hole) Loch nt; (line of holes) Perforation f.
perform [pə'fɔːm] vt (operation, ceremony etc) durchführen; (task) erfüllen; (piece of music, play etc) aufführen ♦ vi auftreten; **to ~ well/badly** eine gute/schlechte Leistung zeigen.
performance [pə'fɔːməns] n Leistung f; (of play, show) Vorstellung f; **the team put up a good ~** die Mannschaft zeigte eine gute Leistung.
performer [pə'fɔːmə*] n Künstler(in) m(f).
performing [pə'fɔːmɪŋ] adj (animal) dressiert.
performing arts npl: **the ~** die darstellenden Künste pl.
perfume ['pɜːfjuːm] n Parfüm nt; (fragrance) Duft m ♦ vt parfümieren.
perfunctory [pə'fʌŋktərɪ] adj flüchtig.
perhaps [pə'hæps] adv vielleicht; **~ he'll come** er kommt vielleicht; **~ not** vielleicht nicht.
peril ['perɪl] n Gefahr f.
perilous ['perɪləs] adj gefährlich.
perilously ['perɪləslɪ] adv: **they came ~ close to being caught** sie wären um ein Haar gefangen worden.
perimeter [pə'rɪmɪtə*] n Umfang m.
perimeter fence n Umzäunung f.
period ['pɪərɪəd] n (length of time) Zeitraum m, Periode f; (era) Zeitalter nt; (SCOL) Stunde f; (esp US: full stop) Punkt m; (MED: also: **menstrual ~**) Periode ♦ adj (costume etc) zeitgenössisch; **for a ~ of 3 weeks** für eine Dauer or einen Zeitraum von 3 Wochen; **the holiday ~** (BRIT) die Urlaubszeit; **I won't do it. P~.** ich mache das nicht, und damit basta!
periodic [pɪərɪ'ɒdɪk] adj periodisch.
periodical [pɪərɪ'ɒdɪkl] n Zeitschrift f ♦ adj periodisch.
periodically [pɪərɪ'ɒdɪklɪ] adv periodisch.
period pains (BRIT) npl Menstruationsschmerzen pl.
peripatetic [perɪpə'tetɪk] adj (BRIT: teacher) an mehreren Schulen tätig; **~ life** Wanderleben nt.
peripheral [pə'rɪfərəl] adj (feature, issue) Rand-, nebensächlich; (vision) peripher ♦ n (COMPUT) Peripheriegerät nt.
periphery [pə'rɪfərɪ] n Peripherie f.
periscope ['perɪskəʊp] n Periskop nt.
perish ['perɪʃ] vi (die) umkommen; (rubber, leather etc) verschleißen.
perishable ['perɪʃəbl] adj (food) leicht verderblich.
perishables ['perɪʃəblz] npl leicht verderbliche Waren pl.
perishing ['perɪʃɪŋ] (BRIT: inf) adj: **it's ~ (cold)** es ist eisig kalt.
peritonitis [perɪtə'naɪtɪs] n Bauchfellentzündung f.
perjure ['pɜːdʒə*] vt: **to ~ o.s.** einen Meineid

leisten.

perjury ['pɜːdʒərɪ] *n* (*in court*) Meineid *m*; (*breach of oath*) Eidesverletzung *f*.

perks [pɜːks] (*inf*) *npl* (*extras*) Vergünstigungen *pl*.

perk up *vi* (*cheer up*) munter werden.

perky ['pɜːkɪ] *adj* (*cheerful*) munter.

perm [pɜːm] *n* Dauerwelle *f* ♦ *vt*: **to have one's hair** ~**ed** sich *dat* eine Dauerwelle machen lassen.

permanence ['pɜːmənəns] *n* Dauerhaftigkeit *f*.

permanent ['pɜːmənənt] *adj* dauerhaft; (*job, position*) fest; ~ **address** ständiger Wohnsitz *m*; **I'm not** ~ **here** ich bin hier nicht fest angestellt.

permanently ['pɜːmənəntlɪ] *adv* (*damage*) dauerhaft; (*stay, live*) ständig; (*locked, open, frozen etc*) dauernd.

permeable ['pɜːmɪəbl] *adj* durchlässig.

permeate ['pɜːmɪeɪt] *vt* durchdringen ♦ *vi*: **to** ~ **through** dringen durch.

permissible [pə'mɪsɪbl] *adj* zulässig.

permission [pə'mɪʃən] *n* Erlaubnis *f*, Genehmigung *f*; **to give sb** ~ **to do sth** jdm die Erlaubnis geben, etw zu tun.

permissive [pə'mɪsɪv] *adj* permissiv.

permit [*n* 'pɜːmɪt, *vt* pə'mɪt] *n* Genehmigung *f* ♦ *vt* (*allow*) erlauben; (*make possible*) gestatten; **fishing** ~ Angelschein *m*; **to** ~ **sb to do sth** jdm erlauben, etw zu tun; **weather** ~**ting** wenn das Wetter es zulässt.

permutation [pɜːmju'teɪʃən] *n* Permutation *f*; (*fig*) Variation *f*.

pernicious [pɜː'nɪʃəs] *adj* (*lie, nonsense*) bösartig; (*effect*) schädlich.

pernickety [pə'nɪkɪtɪ] (*inf*) *adj* pingelig.

perpendicular [pɜːpən'dɪkjulə*] *adj* senkrecht ♦ *n*: **the** ~ die Senkrechte; ~ **to** senkrecht zu.

perpetrate ['pɜːpɪtreɪt] *vt* (*crime*) begehen.

perpetual [pə'pɛtjuəl] *adj* ständig, dauernd.

perpetuate [pə'pɛtjueɪt] *vt* (*custom, belief etc*) bewahren; (*situation*) aufrechterhalten.

perpetuity [pɜːpɪ'tjuːɪtɪ] *n*: **in** ~ auf ewig.

perplex [pə'plɛks] *vt* verblüffen.

perplexing [pə'plɛksɪŋ] *adj* verblüffend.

perquisites ['pɜːkwɪzɪts] (*form*) *npl* Vergünstigungen *pl*.

per se [-seɪ] *adv* an sich.

persecute ['pɜːsɪkjuːt] *vt* verfolgen.

persecution [pɜːsɪ'kjuːʃən] *n* Verfolgung *f*.

perseverance [pɜːsɪ'vɪərns] *n* Beharrlichkeit *f*, Ausdauer *f*.

persevere [pɜːsɪ'vɪə*] *vi* durchhalten, beharren.

Persia ['pɜːʃə] *n* Persien *nt*.

Persian ['pɜːʃən] *adj* persisch ♦ *n* (*LING*) Persisch *nt*; **the** (~) **Gulf** der (Persische) Golf.

Persian cat *n* Perserkatze *f*.

persist [pə'sɪst] *vi*: **to** ~ (**with** *or* **in**) beharren (auf +*dat*), festhalten (an +*dat*); **to** ~ **in doing**

sth darauf beharren, etw zu tun.

persistence [pə'sɪstəns] *n* Beharrlichkeit *f*.

persistent [pə'sɪstənt] *adj* (*person, noise*) beharrlich; (*smell, cough etc*) hartnäckig; (*lateness, rain*) andauernd; ~ **offender** Wiederholungstäter(in) *m(f)*.

persnickety [pə'snɪkɪtɪ] (*US: inf*) *adj* = **pernickety**.

person ['pɜːsn] *n* Person *f*, Mensch *m*; **in** ~ persönlich; **on** *or* **about one's** ~ bei sich; ~ **to** ~ **call** (*TEL*) Gespräch *nt* mit Voranmeldung.

personable ['pɜːsnəbl] *adj* von angenehmer Erscheinung.

personal ['pɜːsnl] *adj* persönlich; (*life*) Privat-; **nothing** ~! nehmen Sie es nicht persönlich!

personal allowance *n* (*TAX*) persönlicher Steuerfreibetrag *m*.

personal assistant *n* persönlicher Referent *m*, persönliche Referentin *f*.

personal column *n* private Kleinanzeigen *pl*.

personal computer *n* Personalcomputer *m*.

personal details *npl* Personalien *pl*.

personal hygiene *n* Körperhygiene *f*.

personal identification number *n* Geheimnummer *f*, PIN-Nummer *f*.

personality [pɜːsə'nælɪtɪ] *n* (*character, person*) Persönlichkeit *f*.

personal loan *n* Personaldarlehen *nt*.

personally ['pɜːsnəlɪ] *adv* persönlich; **to take sth** ~ etw persönlich nehmen.

personal organizer *n* Terminplaner *m*.

personal, social and health education (*BRIT*) *n* (*SCOL*) ≈ Persönlichkeits-, gesellschafts- und gesundheitsbezogene Erziehung.

personal stereo *n* Walkman ® *m*.

personify [pɜː'sɒnɪfaɪ] *vt* personifizieren; (*embody*) verkörpern.

personnel [pɜːsə'nɛl] *n* Personal *nt*.

personnel department *n* Personalabteilung *f*.

personnel manager *n* Personalleiter(in) *m(f)*.

perspective [pə'spɛktɪv] *n* (*also fig*) Perspektive *f*; **to get sth into** ~ (*fig*) etw in Relation zu anderen Dingen sehen.

Perspex ® ['pɜːspɛks] *n* Acrylglas *nt*.

perspicacity [pɜːspɪ'kæsɪtɪ] *n* Scharfsinn *m*.

perspiration [pɜːspɪ'reɪʃən] *n* Transpiration *f*.

perspire [pə'spaɪə*] *vi* transpirieren.

persuade [pə'sweɪd] *vt*: **to** ~ **sb to do sth** jdn dazu überreden, etw zu tun; **to** ~ **sb that** jdn davon überzeugen, dass; **to be** ~**d of sth** von etw überzeugt sein.

persuasion [pə'sweɪʒən] *n* (*act*) Überredung *f*; (*creed*) Überzeugung *f*.

persuasive [pə'sweɪsɪv] *adj* (*person, argument*) überzeugend.

pert [pɜːt] *adj* (*person*) frech; (*nose, buttocks*) keck; (*hat*) kess.

pertaining [pɜː'teɪnɪŋ]: ~ **to** *prep* betreffend

+acc.

pertinent ['pɜːtɪnənt] adj relevant.
perturb [pə'tɜːb] vt beunruhigen.
Peru [pə'ruː] n Peru nt.
perusal [pə'ruːzl] n Durchsicht f.
peruse [pə'ruːz] vt durchsehen.
Peruvian [pə'ruːvjən] adj peruanisch ♦ n Peruaner(in) m(f).
pervade [pə'veɪd] vt (smell, feeling) erfüllen.
pervasive [pə'veɪzɪv] adj (smell) durchdringend; (influence) weitreichend; (mood, atmosphere) allumfassend.
perverse [pə'vɜːs] adj (person) borniert; (behaviour) widernatürlich, pervers.
perversion [pə'vɜːʃən] n (sexual) Perversion f; (of truth, justice) Verzerrung f, Pervertierung f.
perversity [pə'vɜːsɪtɪ] n Widernatürlichkeit f.
pervert [n 'pɜːvɜːt, vt pə'vɜːt] n (sexual deviant) perverser Mensch m ♦ vt (person, mind) verderben; (distort: truth, custom) verfälschen.
pessimism ['pɛsɪmɪzəm] n Pessimismus m.
pessimist ['pɛsɪmɪst] n Pessimist(in) m(f).
pessimistic [pɛsɪ'mɪstɪk] adj pessimistisch.
pest [pɛst] n (insect) Schädling m; (fig: nuisance) Plage f.
pest control n Schädlingsbekämpfung f.
pester ['pɛstə*] vt belästigen.
pesticide ['pɛstɪsaɪd] n Schädlingsbekämpfungsmittel nt, Pestizid nt.
pestilence ['pɛstɪləns] n Pest f.
pestle ['pɛsl] n Stößel m.
pet [pɛt] n (animal) Haustier nt ♦ adj (theory etc) Lieblings- ♦ vt (stroke) streicheln ♦ vi (inf: sexually) herumknutschen; **teacher's** ~ (favourite) Lehrers Liebling m; **a** ~ **rabbit/snake** etc ein Kaninchen/eine Schlange etc (als Haustier); **that's my** ~ **hate** das hasse ich besonders.
petal ['pɛtl] n Blütenblatt nt.
peter out ['piːtə-] vi (road etc) allmählich aufhören, zu Ende gehen; (conversation, meeting) sich totlaufen.
petite [pə'tiːt] adj (woman) zierlich.
petition [pə'tɪʃən] n (signed document) Petition f; (LAW) Klage f ♦ vt ersuchen ♦ vi: **to** ~ **for divorce** die Scheidung einreichen.
pet name (BRIT) n Kosename m.
petrified ['pɛtrɪfaɪd] adj (fig: terrified) starr vor Angst.
petrify ['pɛtrɪfaɪ] vt (fig: terrify) vor Angst erstarren lassen.
petrochemical [pɛtrə'kɛmɪkl] adj petrochemisch.
petrodollars ['pɛtrəudɔləz] npl Petrodollar pl.
petrol ['pɛtrəl] (BRIT) n Benzin nt; **two-star** ~ Normalbenzin nt; **four-star** ~ Super(benzin) nt; **unleaded** ~ bleifreies or unverbleites Benzin.
petrol bomb n Benzinbombe f.

petrol can (BRIT) n Benzinkanister m.
petrol engine (BRIT) n Benzinmotor m.
petroleum [pə'trəuliəm] n Petroleum nt.
petroleum jelly n Vaseline f.
petrol pump (BRIT) n (in garage) Zapfsäule f; (in engine) Benzinpumpe f.
petrol station (BRIT) n Tankstelle f.
petrol tank (BRIT) n Benzintank m.
petticoat ['pɛtɪkəut] n (underskirt: full-length) Unterkleid nt; (: waist) Unterrock m.
pettifogging ['pɛtɪfɔgɪŋ] adj kleinlich.
pettiness ['pɛtɪnɪs] n Kleinlichkeit f.
petty ['pɛtɪ] adj (trivial) unbedeutend; (small-minded) kleinlich; (crime) geringfügig; (official) untergeordnet; (excuse) billig; (remark) spitz.
petty cash n (in office) Portokasse f.
petty officer n Maat m.
petulant ['pɛtjulənt] adj (person, expression) gereizt.
pew [pjuː] n (in church) Kirchenbank f.
pewter ['pjuːtə*] n Zinn nt.
PG n abbr (CINE: = parental guidance) Klassifikation für Filme, die Kinder nur in Begleitung Erwachsener sehen dürfen.
PG 13 (US) abbr (CINE: = Parental Guidance 13) n Klassifikation für Kinofilme, welche Kinder unter 13 Jahren nur in Begleitung Erwachsener sehen dürfen.
PGA n abbr (= Professional Golfers' Association) Golf-Profiverband.
pH n abbr (= potential of hydrogen) pH.
PHA (US) n abbr (= Public Housing Administration) Regierungsbehörde für sozialen Wohnungsbau.
phallic ['fælɪk] adj phallisch; (symbol) Phallus-.
phantom ['fæntəm] n Phantom nt ♦ adj (fig) Phantom-.
Pharaoh ['fɛərəu] n Pharao m.
pharmaceutical [fɑːmə'sjuːtɪkl] adj pharmazeutisch.
pharmaceuticals [fɑːmə'sjuːtɪklz] npl Arzneimittel pl, Pharmaka pl.
pharmacist ['fɑːməsɪst] n Apotheker(in) m(f).
pharmacy ['fɑːməsɪ] n (shop) Apotheke f; (science) Pharmazie f.
phase [feɪz] n Phase f ♦ vt: **to** ~ **sth in/out** etw stufenweise einführen/abschaffen.
PhD n abbr (= Doctor of Philosophy) ≈ Dr. phil.
pheasant ['fɛznt] n Fasan m.
phenomena [fə'nɔmɪnə] npl of **phenomenon**.
phenomenal [fə'nɔmɪnl] adj phänomenal.
phenomenon [fə'nɔmɪnən] (pl **phenomena**) n Phänomen nt.
phew [fjuː] excl puh!
phial ['faɪəl] n Fläschchen nt.
philanderer [fɪ'lændərə*] n Schwerenöter m.
philanthropic [fɪlən'θrɔpɪk] adj philanthropisch.
philanthropist [fɪ'lænθrəpɪst] n Philanthrop(in) m(f).

philatelist [fɪˈlætəlɪst] n Philatelist(in) m(f).
philately [fɪˈlætəlɪ] n Philatelie f.
Philippines [ˈfɪlɪpiːnz] npl: **the ~** die
   Philippinen pl.
Philistine [ˈfɪlɪstaɪn] n (boor) Banause m.
philosopher [fɪˈlɔsəfə*] n Philosoph(in) m(f).
philosophical [fɪləˈsɔfɪkl] adj philosophisch;
   (fig: calm, resigned) gelassen.
philosophize [fɪˈlɔsəfaɪz] vi philosophieren.
philosophy [fɪˈlɔsəfɪ] n Philosophie f.
phlegm [flɛm] n (MED) Schleim m.
phlegmatic [flɛgˈmætɪk] adj phlegmatisch.
phobia [ˈfəubjə] n Phobie f.
phone [fəun] n Telefon nt ♦ vt anrufen ♦ vi
   anrufen, telefonieren; **to be on the ~**
   (possess a phone) Telefon haben; (be calling)
   telefonieren.
▶ **phone back** vt, vi zurückrufen.
▶ **phone up** vt, vi anrufen.
phone book n Telefonbuch nt.
phone booth n Telefonzelle f.
phone box (BRIT) n Telefonzelle f.
phone call n Anruf m.
phonecard [ˈfəunkɑːd] n Telefonkarte f.
phone-in [ˈfəunɪn] (BRIT) n (RADIO, TV)
   Radio-/Fernsehsendung mit Hörer-/
   Zuschauerbeteiligung per Telefon, Phone-in
   nt ♦ adj mit Hörer-/Zuschaueranrufen.
phone tapping [-tæpɪŋ] n Abhören nt von
   Telefonleitungen.
phonetics [fəˈnɛtɪks] n Phonetik f.
phoney [ˈfəunɪ] adj (address) falsch; (accent)
   unecht; (person) unaufrichtig.
phonograph [ˈfəunəgrɑːf] (US) n Grammofon
   nt, Grammophon nt.
phony [ˈfəunɪ] adj = **phoney**.
phosphate [ˈfɔsfeɪt] n Phosphat nt.
phosphorus [ˈfɔsfərəs] n Phosphor m.
photo [ˈfəutəu] n Foto nt.
photo... [ˈfəutəu] pref Foto-.
photocopier [ˈfəutəukɔpɪə*] n Fotokopierer m.
photocopy [ˈfəutəukɔpɪ] n Fotokopie f ♦ vt
   fotokopieren.
photoelectric [fəutəuɪˈlɛktrɪk] adj (effect)
   photoelektrisch; (cell) Photo-.
photo finish n Fotofinish nt.
Photofit ® [ˈfəutəufɪt] n (also: ~ **picture**)
   Phantombild nt.
photogenic [fəutəuˈdʒɛnɪk] adj fotogen.
photograph [ˈfəutəgræf] n Fotografie f ♦ vt
   fotografieren; **to take a ~ of sb** jdn
   fotografieren.
photographer [fəˈtɔgrəfə*] n Fotograf(in)
   m(f).
photographic [fəutəˈgræfɪk] adj (equipment
   etc) fotografisch, Foto-.
photography [fəˈtɔgrəfɪ] n Fotografie f.
photo opportunity n Fototermin m;
   (accidental) Fotogelegenheit f.
photostat [ˈfəutəustæt] n Fotokopie f.
photosynthesis [fəutəuˈsɪnθəsɪs] n
   Photosynthese f.

phrase [freɪz] n Satz m; (LING) Redewendung
   f; (MUS) Phrase f ♦ vt ausdrücken; (letter)
   formulieren.
phrase book n Sprachführer m.
physical [ˈfɪzɪkl] adj (bodily) körperlich;
   (geography, properties) physikalisch; (law,
   explanation) natürlich; **~ examination**
   ärztliche Untersuchung f; **the ~ sciences**
   die Naturwissenschaften.
physical education n Sportunterricht m.
physically [ˈfɪzɪklɪ] adv (fit, attractive)
   körperlich.
physician [fɪˈzɪʃən] n Arzt m, Ärztin f.
physicist [ˈfɪzɪsɪst] n Physiker(in) m(f).
physics [ˈfɪzɪks] n Physik f.
physiological [ˈfɪzɪəˈlɔdʒɪkl] adj
   physiologisch.
physiology [fɪzɪˈɔlədʒɪ] n Physiologie f.
physiotherapist [fɪzɪəuˈθɛrəpɪst] n
   Physiotherapeut(in) m(f).
physiotherapy [fɪzɪəuˈθɛrəpɪ] n
   Physiotherapie f.
physique [fɪˈziːk] n Körperbau m.
pianist [ˈpiːənɪst] n Pianist(in) m(f).
piano [pɪˈænəu] n Klavier nt, Piano nt.
piano accordion (BRIT) n Akkordeon nt.
piccolo [ˈpɪkələu] n Pikkoloflöte f.
pick [pɪk] n (also: ~**axe**) Spitzhacke f ♦ vt
   (select) aussuchen; (gather: fruit, mushrooms)
   sammeln; (: flowers) pflücken; (remove, take
   out) herausnehmen; (lock) knacken; (scab,
   spot) kratzen an +dat; **take your ~** (choose)
   Sie haben die Wahl; **the ~ of** (best) das
   Beste +gen; **to ~ one's nose** in der Nase
   bohren; **to ~ one's teeth** in den Zähnen
   stochern; **to ~ sb's brains** jdn als
   Informationsquelle nutzen; **to ~ sb's pocket**
   jdn bestehlen; **to ~ a quarrel (with sb)** einen
   Streit (mit jdm) anfangen.
▶ **pick at** vt fus (food) herumstochern in +dat.
▶ **pick off** vt (shoot) abschießen.
▶ **pick on** vt fus (criticize) herumhacken auf
   +dat.
▶ **pick out** vt (distinguish) ausmachen; (select)
   aussuchen.
▶ **pick up** vi (health) sich verbessern;
   (economy) sich erholen ♦ vt (from floor etc)
   aufheben; (arrest) festnehmen; (collect:
   person, parcel etc) abholen; (hitchhiker)
   mitnehmen; (for sexual encounter) aufreißen;
   (learn: skill etc) mitbekommen; (RADIO)
   empfangen; **to ~ up where one left off** da
   weitermachen, wo man aufgehört hat; **to**
   ~ up speed schneller werden; **to ~ o.s. up**
   (after falling etc) sich aufrappeln.
pickaxe, (US) **pickax** [ˈpɪkæks] n Spitzhacke f.
picket [ˈpɪkɪt] n (in strike) Streikposten m ♦ vt
   (factory etc) Streikposten aufstellen vor +dat.
picketing [ˈpɪkɪtɪŋ] n Aufstellen nt von
   Streikposten.
picket line n Streikpostenkette f.
pickings [ˈpɪkɪŋz] npl: **there are rich ~ to be**

had **here** hier ist die Ausbeute gut.

pickle ['pɪkl] n (also: ~s: as condiment) Pickles pl ♦ vt einlegen; **to be in a** ~ in der Klemme sitzen; **to get in a** ~ in eine Klemme geraten.

pick-me-up ['pɪkmiːʌp] n Muntermacher m.

pickpocket ['pɪkpɔkɪt] n Taschendieb(in) m(f).

pick-up ['pɪkʌp] n (also: ~ truck) offener Kleintransporter m; (BRIT: on record player) Tonabnehmer m.

picnic ['pɪknɪk] n Picknick nt ♦ vi picknicken.

picnicker ['pɪknɪkə*] n Picknicker(in) m(f).

pictorial [pɪk'tɔːrɪəl] adj (record, coverage etc) bildlich.

picture ['pɪktʃə*] n (also TV, fig) Bild nt; (film) Film m ♦ vt (imagine) sich dat vorstellen; **the ~s** (BRIT: inf: the cinema) das Kino; **to take a** ~ **of sb** ein Bild von jdm machen; **to put sb in the** ~ jdn ins Bild setzen.

picture book n Bilderbuch nt.

picture messaging n (TEL) Picture Messaging nt.

picturesque [pɪktʃə'rɛsk] adj malerisch.

picture window n Aussichtsfenster nt.

piddling ['pɪdlɪŋ] (inf) adj lächerlich.

pidgin ['pɪdʒɪn] adj: ~ **English** Pidgin-Englisch nt.

pie [paɪ] n (vegetable, meat) Pastete f; (fruit) Torte f.

piebald ['paɪbɔːld] adj (horse) scheckig.

piece [piːs] n Stück nt; (DRAUGHTS etc) Stein m; (CHESS) Figur f; **in ~s** (broken) kaputt; (taken apart) auseinander genommen, in Einzelteilen; **a** ~ **of clothing/furniture/music** ein Kleidungs-/Möbel-/Musikstück nt; **a** ~ **of machinery** eine Maschine; **a** ~ **of research** eine Forschungsarbeit; **a** ~ **of advice** ein Rat m; **to take sth to ~s** etw auseinander nehmen; **in one** ~ (object) unbeschädigt; (person) wohlbehalten; **a 10p** ~ (BRIT) ein 10-Pence-Stück nt; ~ **by** ~ Stück für Stück; **a six-~ band** eine sechsköpfige Band; **let her say her** ~ lass sie ausreden.

► **piece together** vt zusammenfügen.

piecemeal ['piːsmiːl] adv stückweise, Stück für Stück.

piecework ['piːswəːk] n Akkordarbeit f.

pie chart n Tortendiagramm nt.

pier [pɪə*] n Pier m.

pierce [pɪəs] vt durchstechen; **to have one's ears ~d** sich dat die Ohrläppchen durchstechen lassen.

piercing ['pɪəsɪŋ] adj (fig: cry, eyes, stare) durchdringend; (wind) schneidend.

piety ['paɪətɪ] n Frömmigkeit f.

piffling ['pɪflɪŋ] (inf) adj lächerlich.

pig [pɪg] n (also pej) Schwein nt; (greedy person) Vielfraß m.

pigeon ['pɪdʒən] n Taube f.

pigeonhole ['pɪdʒənhəul] n (for letters etc) Fach nt; (fig) Schublade f ♦ vt (fig: person) in eine Schublade stecken.

pigeon-toed ['pɪdʒəntəud] adj mit einwärts gerichteten Zehen.

piggy bank ['pɪgɪ-] n Sparschwein nt.

pig-headed ['pɪg'hɛdɪd] (pej) adj dickköpfig.

piglet ['pɪglɪt] n Schweinchen nt, Ferkel nt.

pigment ['pɪgmənt] n Pigment nt.

pigmentation [pɪgmən'teɪʃən] n Pigmentierung f, Färbung f.

pigmy ['pɪgmɪ] n = **pygmy**.

pigskin ['pɪgskɪn] n Schweinsleder nt.

pigsty ['pɪgstaɪ] n (also fig) Schweinestall m.

pigtail ['pɪgteɪl] n Zopf m.

pike [paɪk] n (fish) Hecht m; (spear) Spieß m.

pilchard ['pɪltʃəd] n Sardine f.

pile [paɪl] n (heap) Haufen m; (stack) Stapel m; (of carpet, velvet) Flor m; (pillar) Pfahl m ♦ vt (also: ~ **up**) (auf)stapeln; **in a** ~ in einem Haufen; **to** ~ **into/out of** (vehicle) sich drängen in +acc/aus.

► **pile on** vt: **to** ~ **it on** (inf) zu dick auftragen.

► **pile up** vi sich stapeln.

piles [paɪlz] npl (MED) Hämorr(ho)iden pl.

pile-up ['paɪlʌp] n (AUT) Massenkarambolage f.

pilfer ['pɪlfə*] vt, vi stehlen.

pilfering ['pɪlfərɪŋ] n Diebstahl m.

pilgrim ['pɪlgrɪm] n Pilger(in) m(f).

pilgrimage ['pɪlgrɪmɪdʒ] n Pilgerfahrt f, Wallfahrt f.

pill [pɪl] n Tablette f, Pille f; **the** ~ (contraceptive) die Pille; **to be on the** ~ die Pille nehmen.

pillage ['pɪlɪdʒ] n Plünderung f ♦ vt plündern.

pillar ['pɪlə*] n Säule f; **a** ~ **of society** (fig) eine Säule or Stütze der Gesellschaft.

pillar box (BRIT) n Briefkasten m.

pillion ['pɪljən] n: **to ride** ~ (on motorcycle) auf dem Soziussitz mitfahren; (on horse) hinten auf dem Pferd mitreiten.

pillory ['pɪlərɪ] vt (criticize) anprangern ♦ n Pranger m.

pillow ['pɪləu] n (Kopf)kissen nt.

pillowcase ['pɪləukeɪs] n (Kopf)kissenbezug m.

pillowslip ['pɪləuslɪp] n = **pillowcase**.

pilot ['paɪlət] n (AVIAT) Pilot(in) m(f); (NAUT) Lotse m ♦ adj (scheme, study etc) Pilot- ♦ vt (aircraft) steuern; (fig: new law, scheme) sich zum Fürsprecher machen +gen.

pilot boat n Lotsenboot nt.

pilot light n (on cooker, boiler) Zündflamme f.

pimento [pɪ'mɛntəu] n (spice) Piment nt.

pimp [pɪmp] n Zuhälter m.

pimple ['pɪmpl] n Pickel m.

pimply ['pɪmplɪ] adj pick(e)lig.

PIN n abbr (= personal identification number) PIN; ~ **number** PIN-Nummer f.

pin [pɪn] n (metal: for clothes, papers) Stecknadel f; (TECH) Stift m; (BRIT: also: **drawing** ~) Heftzwecke f; (in grenade) Sicherungsstift m; (BRIT: ELEC) Pol m ♦ vt (fasten with pin) feststecken; ~**s and needles**

(*in arms, legs etc*) Kribbeln *nt*; **to ~ sb against/to sth** jdn gegen/an etw *acc* pressen; **to ~ sth on sb** (*fig*) jdm etw anhängen.

▶ **pin down** *vt* (*fig: person*) festnageln; **there's something strange here but I can't quite ~ it down** hier stimmt etwas nicht, aber ich weiß nicht genau was.

pinafore ['pɪnəfɔː'] (*BRIT*) *n* (*also:* **~ dress**) Trägerkleid *nt*.

pinball ['pɪnbɔːl] *n* (*game*) Flippern *nt*; (*machine*) Flipper *m*.

pincers ['pɪnsəz] *npl* (*tool*) Kneifzange *f*; (*of crab, lobster etc*) Schere *f*.

pinch [pɪntʃ] *n* (*of salt etc*) Prise *f* ♦ *vt* (*with finger and thumb*) zwicken, kneifen; (*inf: steal*) klauen ♦ *vi* (*shoe*) drücken; **at a ~** zur Not; **to feel the ~** (*fig*) die schlechte Lage zu spüren bekommen.

pinched [pɪntʃt] *adj* (*face*) erschöpft; **~ with cold** verfroren.

pincushion ['pɪnkuʃən] *n* Nadelkissen *nt*.

pine [paɪn] *n* (*also:* **~ tree**) Kiefer *f*; (*wood*) Kiefernholz *nt* ♦ *vi:* **to ~ for** sich sehnen nach.

▶ **pine away** *vi* sich (vor Kummer) verzehren.

pineapple ['paɪnæpl] *n* Ananas *f*.

pine cone *n* Kiefernzapfen *m*.

pine needles *npl* Kiefernnadeln *pl*.

ping [pɪŋ] *n* (*noise*) Klingeln *nt*.

Ping-Pong ® ['pɪŋpɔŋ] *n* Pingpong *nt*.

pink [pɪŋk] *adj* rosa *inv* ♦ *n* (*colour*) Rosa *nt*; (*BOT*) Gartennelke *f*.

pinking shears *npl* Zickzackschere *f*.

pin money (*BRIT: inf*) *n* Nadelgeld *nt*.

pinnacle ['pɪnəkl] *n* (*of building, mountain*) Spitze *f*; (*fig*) Gipfel *m*.

pinpoint ['pɪnpɔɪnt] *vt* (*identify*) genau festlegen, identifizieren; (*position of sth*) genau aufzeigen.

pinstripe ['pɪnstraɪp] *adj:* **~ suit** Nadelstreifenanzug *m*.

pint [paɪnt] *n* (*BRIT: = 568 cc*) (britisches) Pint *nt*; (*US: = 473 cc*) (amerikanisches) Pint; **a ~** (*BRIT: inf: of beer*) ≈ eine Halbe.

pin-up ['pɪnʌp] *n* (*picture*) Pin-up-Foto *nt*.

pioneer [paɪə'nɪə'] *n* (*lit, fig*) Pionier *m* ♦ *vt* (*invention etc*) Pionierarbeit leisten für.

pious ['paɪəs] *adj* fromm.

pip [pɪp] *n* (*of apple, orange*) Kern *m* ♦ *vt:* **to be ~ped at the post** (*BRIT, fig*) um Haaresbreite geschlagen werden; **the pips** *npl* (*BRIT: RADIO*) das Zeitzeichen.

pipe [paɪp] *n* (*for water, gas*) Rohr *nt*; (*for smoking*) Pfeife *f*; (*MUS*) Flöte *f* ♦ *vt* (*water, gas, oil*) (durch Rohre) leiten; **pipes** *npl* (*also:* **bagpipes**) Dudelsack *m*.

▶ **pipe down** (*inf*) *vi* (*be quiet*) ruhig sein.

pipe cleaner *n* Pfeifenreiniger *m*.

piped music [paɪpt-] *n* Berieselungsmusik *f*.

pipe dream *n* Hirngespinst *nt*.

pipeline ['paɪplaɪn] *n* Pipeline *f*; **it's in the ~**

(*fig*) es ist in Vorbereitung.

piper ['paɪpə'] *n* (*bagpipe player*) Dudelsackspieler(in) *m(f)*.

pipe tobacco *n* Pfeifentabak *m*.

piping ['paɪpɪŋ] *adv:* **~ hot** kochend heiß.

piquant ['piːkənt] *adj* (*also fig*) pikant.

pique ['piːk] *n:* **in a fit of ~** eingeschnappt, pikiert.

piracy ['paɪərəsi] *n* Piraterie *f*, Seeräuberei *f*; (*COMM*): **to commit ~** ein Plagiat *nt* begehen.

pirate ['paɪərət] *n* Pirat *m*, Seeräuber *m* ♦ *vt* (*COMM: video tape, cassette etc*) illegal herstellen.

pirate radio station (*BRIT*) *n* Piratensender *m*.

pirouette [pɪru'ɛt] *n* Pirouette *f* ♦ *vi* Pirouetten drehen.

Pisces ['paɪsiːz] *n* Fische *pl*; **to be ~** Fische *or* (ein) Fisch sein.

piss [pɪs] (*infl*) *vi* pissen ♦ *n* Pisse *f*; **~ off!** verpiss dich!; **to be ~ed off (with sb/sth)** (von jdm/etw) die Schnauze voll haben; **it's ~ing down** (*BRIT: raining*) es schifft; **to take the ~ out of sb** (*BRIT*) jdn verarschen.

pissed [pɪst] (*infl*) *adj* (*drunk*) besoffen.

pistol ['pɪstl] *n* Pistole *f*.

piston ['pɪstən] *n* Kolben *m*.

pit [pɪt] *n* Grube *f*; (*in surface of road*) Schlagloch *nt*; (*coal mine*) Zeche *f*; (*also:* **orchestra ~**) Orchestergraben *m* ♦ *vt:* **to ~ one's wits against sb** seinen Verstand mit jdm messen; **the pits** *npl* (*AUT*) die Box; **to ~ o.s. against sth** den Kampf gegen etw aufnehmen; **to ~ sb against sb** jdn gegen jdn antreten lassen; **the ~ of one's stomach** die Magengrube.

pitapat ['pɪtə'pæt] (*BRIT*) *adv:* **to go ~** (*heart*) pochen, klopfen; (*rain*) prasseln.

pitch [pɪtʃ] *n* (*BRIT: SPORT: field*) Spielfeld *nt*; (*MUS*) Tonhöhe *f*; (*fig: level, degree*) Grad *m*; (*tar*) Pech *nt*; (*also:* **sales ~**) Verkaufsmasche *f*; (*NAUT*) Stampfen *nt* ♦ *vt* (*throw*) werfen, schleudern; (*set: price, message*) ansetzen ♦ *vi* (*fall forwards*) hinschlagen; (*NAUT*) stampfen; **to ~ a tent** ein Zelt aufschlagen; **to be ~ed forward** vornüber geworfen werden.

pitch-black ['pɪtʃ'blæk] *adj* pechschwarz.

pitched battle [pɪtʃt-] *n* offene Schlacht *f*.

pitcher ['pɪtʃə'] *n* (*jug*) Krug *m*; (*US: BASEBALL*) Werfer *m*.

pitchfork ['pɪtʃfɔːk] *n* Heugabel *f*.

piteous ['pɪtɪəs] *adj* kläglich, erbärmlich.

pitfall ['pɪtfɔːl] *n* Falle *f*.

pith [pɪθ] *n* (*of orange etc*) weiße Haut *f*; (*of plant*) Mark *nt*; (*fig*) Kern *m*.

pithead ['pɪthɛd] *n* Schachtanlagen *pl* über Tage.

pithy ['pɪθɪ] *adj* (*comment etc*) prägnant.

pitiable ['pɪtɪəbl] *adj* Mitleid erregend.

pitiful ['pɪtɪful] *adj* (*sight etc*) Mitleid

erregend; (*excuse, attempt*) jämmerlich, kläglich.

pitifully ['pɪtɪfəlɪ] *adv* (*thin, frail*) jämmerlich; (*inadequate, ill-equipped*) fürchterlich.

pitiless ['pɪtɪlɪs] *adj* mitleidlos.

pittance ['pɪtns] *n* Hungerlohn *m*.

pitted ['pɪtɪd] *adj*: ~ **with** übersät mit; ~ **with rust** voller Rost.

pity ['pɪtɪ] *n* Mitleid *nt* ♦ *vt* bemitleiden, bedauern; **what a** ~! wie schade!; **it is a** ~ **that you can't come** schade, dass du nicht kommen kannst; **to take** ~ **on sb** Mitleid mit jdm haben.

pitying ['pɪtɪɪŋ] *adj* mitleidig.

pivot ['pɪvət] *n* (*TECH*) Drehpunkt *m*; (*fig*) Dreh- und Angelpunkt *m* ♦ *vi* sich drehen.

▶ **pivot on** (*depend on*) abhängen von.

pixel ['pɪksl] *n* (*COMPUT*) Pixel *nt*.

pixie ['pɪksɪ] *n* Elf *m*, Elfe *f*.

pizza ['piːtsə] *n* Pizza *f*.

placard ['plækɑːd] *n* Plakat *nt*, Aushang *m*; (*in march etc*) Transparent *nt*.

placate [plə'keɪt] *vt* beschwichtigen, besänftigen.

placatory [plə'keɪtərɪ] *adj* beschwichtigend, besänftigend.

place [pleɪs] *n* Platz *m*; (*position*) Stelle *f*, Ort *m*; (*seat: on committee etc*) Sitz *m*; (*home*) Wohnung *f*; (*in street names*) ≈ Straße *f* ♦ *vt* (*put: object*) stellen, legen; (*identify: person*) unterbringen; ~ **of birth** Geburtsort *m*; **to take** ~ (*happen*) geschehen, passieren; **at/to his** ~ (*home*) bei/zu ihm; **from** ~ **to** ~ von Ort zu Ort; **all over the** ~ überall; **in** ~**s** stellenweise; **in sb's/sth's** ~ anstelle *or* an Stelle von jdm/etw; **to take sb's/sth's** ~ an die Stelle von jdm/etw treten, jdn/etw ersetzen; **out of** ~ (*inappropriate*) unangebracht; **I feel out of** ~ **here** ich fühle mich hier fehl am Platze; **in the first** ~ (*first of all*) erstens; **to change** ~**s with sb** mit jdm den Platz tauschen; **to put sb in his** ~ (*fig*) jdn in seine Schranken weisen; **he's going** ~**s** er bringt es noch mal weit; **it's not my** ~ **to do it** es ist nicht an mir, das zu tun; **to be** ~**d** (*in race, exam*) platziert sein; **to be** ~**d third** den dritten Platz belegen; **to** ~ **an order with sb (for sth)** eine Bestellung bei jdm (für etw) aufgeben; **how are you** ~**d next week?** wie sieht es bei Ihnen nächste Woche aus?

placebo [plə'siːbəu] *n* Placebo *nt*; (*fig*) Beruhigungsmittel *nt*.

place mat *n* Set *nt or m*.

placement ['pleɪsmənt] *n* Platzierung *f*.

place name *n* Ortsname *m*.

placenta [plə'sɛntə] *n* Plazenta *f*.

place setting *n* Gedeck *nt*.

placid ['plæsɪd] *adj* (*person*) ruhig, gelassen; (*place, river etc*) friedvoll.

plagiarism ['pleɪdʒjərɪzəm] *n* Plagiat *nt*.

plagiarist ['pleɪdʒjərɪst] *n* Plagiator(in) *m(f)*.

plagiarize ['pleɪdʒjəraɪz] *vt* (*idea, work*) kopieren, plagiieren.

plague [pleɪg] *n* (*MED*) Seuche *f*; (*fig: of locusts etc*) Plage *f* ♦ *vt* (*fig: problems etc*) plagen; **to** ~ **sb with questions** jdn mit Fragen quälen.

plaice [pleɪs] *n inv* Scholle *f*.

plaid [plæd] *n* Plaid *nt*.

plain [pleɪn] *adj* (*unpatterned*) einfarbig; (*simple*) einfach, schlicht; (*clear, easily understood*) klar; (*not beautiful*) unattraktiv; (*frank*) offen ♦ *adv* (*wrong, stupid etc*) einfach ♦ *n* (*area of land*) Ebene *f*; (*KNITTING*) rechte Masche *f*; **to make sth** ~ **to sb** jdm etw klarmachen.

plain chocolate *n* Bitterschokolade *f*.

plain-clothes ['pleɪnkləuðz] *adj* (*police officer*) in Zivil.

plainly ['pleɪnlɪ] *adv* (*obviously*) eindeutig; (*clearly*) deutlich, klar.

plainness ['pleɪnnɪs] *n* (*of person*) Reizlosigkeit *f*.

plain speaking *n* Offenheit *f*; **a bit of** ~ ein paar offene Worte.

plain-spoken ['pleɪn'spəukn] *adj* offen.

plaintiff ['pleɪntɪf] *n* Kläger(in) *m(f)*.

plaintive ['pleɪntɪv] *adj* (*cry, voice*) klagend; (*song*) schwermütig; (*look*) traurig.

plait [plæt] *n* (*of hair*) Zopf *m*; (*of rope, leather*) Geflecht *nt* ♦ *vt* flechten.

plan [plæn] *n* Plan *m* ♦ *vt* planen; (*building, schedule*) entwerfen ♦ *vi* planen; **to** ~ **to do sth** planen *or* vorhaben, etw zu tun; **how long do you** ~ **to stay?** wie lange haben Sie vor, zu bleiben?; **to** ~ **for** *or* **on** (*expect*) sich einstellen auf +*acc*; **to** ~ **on doing sth** vorhaben, etw zu tun.

plane [pleɪn] *n* (*AVIAT*) Flugzeug *nt*; (*MATH*) Ebene *f*; (*fig: level*) Niveau *nt*; (*tool*) Hobel *m*; (*also*: ~ **tree**) Platane *f* ♦ *vt* (*wood*) hobeln ♦ *vi* (*NAUT, AUT*) gleiten.

planet ['plænɪt] *n* Planet *m*.

planetarium [plænɪ'tɛərɪəm] *n* Planetarium *nt*.

plank [plæŋk] *n* (*of wood*) Brett *nt*; (*fig: of policy etc*) Schwerpunkt *m*.

plankton ['plæŋktən] *n* Plankton *nt*.

planned economy ['plænd-] *n* Planwirtschaft *f*.

planner ['plænə*] *n* Planer(in) *m(f)*.

planning ['plænɪŋ] *n* Planung *f*.

planning permission (*BRIT*) *n* Baugenehmigung *f*.

plant [plɑːnt] *n* (*BOT*) Pflanze *f*; (*machinery*) Maschinen *pl*; (*factory*) Anlage *f* ♦ *vt* (*seed, plant, crops*) pflanzen; (*field, garden*) bepflanzen; (*microphone, bomb etc*) anbringen; (*incriminating evidence*) schleusen; (*fig: object*) stellen; (: *kiss*) drücken.

plantation [plæn'teɪʃən] *n* Plantage *f*; (*wood*) Anpflanzung *f*.

plant pot (*BRIT*) *n* Blumentopf *m*.

plaque [plæk] *n* (*on building etc*) Tafel *f*,

Plakette f; (on teeth) Zahnbelag m.

plasma ['plæzmə] n Plasma nt.

plaster ['plɑːstə*] n (for walls) Putz m; (also: ~ of Paris) Gips m; (BRIT: also: sticking ~) Pflaster nt ♦ vt (wall, ceiling) verputzen; in ~ (BRIT) in Gips; to ~ with (cover) bepflastern mit.

plasterboard ['plɑːstəbɔːd] n Gipskarton m.

plaster cast n (MED) Gipsverband m; (model, statue) Gipsform f.

plastered ['plɑːstəd] (inf) adj (drunk) sturzbesoffen.

plasterer ['plɑːstərə*] n Gipser m.

plastic ['plæstɪk] n Plastik nt ♦ adj (bucket, cup etc) Plastik-; (flexible) formbar; **the ~ arts** die bildende Kunst.

plastic bag n Plastiktüte f.

plastic bullet n Plastikgeschoss nt.

plastic explosive n Plastiksprengstoff m.

Plasticine ® ['plæstɪsiːn] n Plastilin nt.

plastic surgery n plastische Chirurgie f.

plate [pleɪt] n Teller m; (metal cover) Platte f; (TYP) Druckplatte f; (AUT) Nummernschild nt; (in book: picture) Tafel f; (dental plate) Gaumenplatte f; (on door) Schild nt; (gold/ silver plate) vergoldeter/versilberter Artikel m; **that necklace is just ~** die Halskette ist nur vergoldet/versilbert.

plateau ['plætəu] (pl ~s or ~x) n (GEOG) Plateau nt, Hochebene f; (fig) stabiler Zustand m.

plateful ['pleɪtful] n Teller m.

plate glass n Tafelglas nt.

platen ['plætən] n (on typewriter, printer) (Schreib)walze f.

plate rack n Geschirrständer m.

platform ['plætfɔːm] n (stage) Podium nt; (for landing, loading on etc, BRIT: of bus) Plattform f; (RAIL) Bahnsteig m; (POL) Programm nt; **the train leaves from ~ 7** der Zug fährt von Gleis 7 ab.

platform ticket (BRIT) n (RAIL) Bahnsteigkarte f.

platinum ['plætɪnəm] n Platin nt.

platitude ['plætɪtjuːd] n Plattitüde f, Gemeinplatz m.

platonic [plə'tɒnɪk] adj (relationship) platonisch.

platoon [plə'tuːn] n Zug m.

platter ['plætə*] n Platte f.

plaudits ['plɔːdɪts] npl Ovationen pl.

plausible ['plɔːzɪbl] adj (theory, excuse) plausibel; (liar etc) glaubwürdig.

play [pleɪ] n (THEAT) (Theater)stück nt; (TV) Fernsehspiel nt; (RADIO) Hörspiel nt; (activity) Spiel nt ♦ vt spielen; (team, opponent) spielen gegen ♦ vi spielen; **to bring into ~** ins Spiel bringen; **a ~ on words** ein Wortspiel nt; **to ~ a trick on sb** jdn hereinlegen; **to ~ a part** or **role in sth** (fig) eine Rolle bei etw spielen; **to ~ for time** (fig) auf Zeit spielen, Zeit gewinnen wollen; **to ~ safe** auf Nummer sicher or Sicher gehen; **to ~ into sb's hands** jdm in die Hände spielen.

► **play about with** vt fus = **play around with**.

► **play along with** vt fus (person) sich richten nach; (plan, idea) eingehen auf +acc.

► **play around with** vt fus (fiddle with) herumspielen mit.

► **play at** vt fus (do casually) spielen mit; **to ~ at being sb/sth** jdn/etw spielen.

► **play back** vt (recording) abspielen.

► **play down** vt herunterspielen.

► **play on** vt fus (sb's feelings etc) ausnutzen; **to ~ on sb's mind** jdm im Kopf herumgehen.

► **play up** vi (machine, knee etc) Schwierigkeiten machen; (children) frech werden.

play-act ['pleɪækt] vi Theater spielen.

playboy ['pleɪbɔɪ] n Playboy m.

player ['pleɪə*] n (SPORT, MUS) Spieler(in) m(f); (THEAT) Schauspieler(in) m(f).

playful ['pleɪful] adj (person, gesture) spielerisch; (animal) verspielt.

playgoer ['pleɪgəuə*] n Theaterbesucher(in) m(f).

playground ['pleɪgraund] n (in park) Spielplatz m; (in school) Schulhof m.

playgroup ['pleɪgruːp] n Spielgruppe f.

playing card ['pleɪɪŋ-] n Spielkarte f.

playing field n Sportplatz m.

playmaker ['pleɪmeɪkə*] n (SPORT) Spielmacher(in) m(f).

playmate ['pleɪmeɪt] n Spielkamerad(in) m(f).

play-off ['pleɪɔf] n Entscheidungsspiel nt.

playpen ['pleɪpɛn] n Laufstall m.

playroom ['pleɪruːm] n Spielzimmer nt.

playschool ['pleɪskuːl] n = **playgroup**.

plaything ['pleɪθɪŋ] n (also fig) Spielzeug nt.

playtime ['pleɪtaɪm] n (kleine) Pause f.

playwright ['pleɪraɪt] n Dramatiker(in) m(f).

plc (BRIT) n abbr (= public limited company) ≈ AG f.

plea [pliː] n (request) Bitte f; (LAW): **to enter a ~ of guilty/not guilty** sich schuldig/ unschuldig erklären; (excuse) Vorwand m.

plea bargaining n Verhandlungen zwischen Anklage und Verteidigung mit dem Ziel, bestimmte Anklagepunkte fallen zu lassen, wenn der Angeklagte sich in anderen Punkten schuldig bekennt.

plead [pliːd] vi (LAW) vor Gericht eine Schuld-/Unschuldserklärung abgeben ♦ vt (LAW): **to ~ sb's case** jdn vertreten; (give as excuse: ignorance, ill health etc) vorgeben, sich berufen auf +acc; **to ~ with sb** (beg) jdn inständig bitten; **to ~ for sth** um etw nachsuchen; **to ~ guilty/not guilty** sich schuldig/nicht schuldig bekennen.

pleasant ['plɛznt] adj angenehm; (smile) freundlich.

pleasantly ['plɛzntlɪ] adv (surprised) angenehm; (say, behave) freundlich.

pleasantries ['plɛzntrɪz] *npl* Höflichkeiten *pl*, Nettigkeiten *pl*.

please [pliːz] *excl* bitte ♦ *vt* (*satisfy*) zufrieden stellen ♦ *vi* (*give pleasure*) gefällig sein; ~ **Miss/Sir!** (*to attract teacher's attention*) ≈ Frau/Herr X!; **yes**, ~ ja, bitte; **my bill**, ~ die Rechnung, bitte; ~ **don't cry!** bitte wein doch nicht!; ~ **yourself!** (*inf*) wie du willst!; **do as you** ~ machen Sie, was Sie für richtig halten.

pleased [pliːzd] *adj* (*happy*) erfreut; (*satisfied*) zufrieden; ~ **to meet you** freut mich(, Sie kennen zu lernen); ~ **with** zufrieden mit; **we are** ~ **to inform you that** ... wir freuen uns, Ihnen mitzuteilen, dass ...

pleasing ['pliːzɪŋ] *adj* (*remark, picture etc*) erfreulich; (*person*) sympathisch.

pleasurable ['plɛʒərəbl] *adj* angenehm.

pleasure ['plɛʒə*] *n* (*happiness, satisfaction*) Freude *f*; (*fun, enjoyable experience*) Vergnügen *nt*; **it's a** ~, **my** ~ gern geschehen; **with** ~ gern, mit Vergnügen; **is this trip for business or** ~**?** ist diese Reise geschäftlich oder zum Vergnügen?

pleasure boat *n* Vergnügungsschiff *nt*.

pleasure cruise *n* Vergnügungsfahrt *f*.

pleat [pliːt] *n* Falte *f*.

pleb [plɛb] (*inf: pej*) *n* Prolet *m*.

plebiscite ['plɛbɪsɪt] *n* Volksentscheid *m*, Plebiszit *nt*.

plectrum ['plɛktrəm] *n* Plektron *nt*, Plektrum *nt*.

pledge [plɛdʒ] *n* (*promise*) Versprechen *nt* ♦ *vt* (*promise*) versprechen; **to** ~ **sb to secrecy** jdn zum Schweigen verpflichten.

plenary ['pliːnərɪ] *adj* (*powers*) unbeschränkt; ~ **session** Plenarsitzung *f*; ~ **meeting** Vollversammlung *f*.

plentiful ['plɛntɪful] *adj* reichlich.

plenty ['plɛntɪ] *n* (*lots*) eine Menge; (*sufficient*) reichlich; ~ **of** eine Menge; **we've got** ~ **of time to get there** wir haben jede Menge Zeit, dorthin zu kommen.

plethora ['plɛθərə] *n*: **a** ~ **of** eine Fülle von, eine Unmenge an +*dat*.

pleurisy ['pluərɪsɪ] *n* Rippenfellentzündung *f*.

Plexiglas ® ['plɛksɪglɑːs] (*US*) *n* Plexiglas ® *nt*.

pliable ['plaɪəbl] *adj* (*material*) biegsam; (*fig: person*) leicht beeinflussbar.

pliant ['plaɪənt] *adj* = **pliable**.

pliers ['plaɪəz] *npl* Zange *f*.

plight [plaɪt] *n* (*of person, country*) Not *f*.

plimsolls ['plɪmsəlz] (*BRIT*) *npl* Turnschuhe *pl*.

plinth [plɪnθ] *n* Sockel *m*.

PLO *n abbr* (= *Palestine Liberation Organization*) PLO *f*.

plod [plɒd] *vi* (*walk*) trotten; (*fig*) sich abplagen.

plodder ['plɒdə*] (*pej*) *n* (*slow worker*) zäher Arbeiter *m*, zähe Arbeiterin *f*.

plonk [plɒŋk] (*inf*) *n* (*BRIT: wine*) (billiger)

Wein *m* ♦ *vt*: **to** ~ **sth down** etw hinknallen.

plot [plɒt] *n* (*secret plan*) Komplott *nt*, Verschwörung *f*; (*of story, play, film*) Handlung *f* ♦ *vt* (*sb's downfall etc*) planen; (*on chart, graph*) markieren ♦ *vi* (*conspire*) sich verschwören; **a** ~ **of land** ein Grundstück *nt*; **a vegetable** ~ (*BRIT*) ein Gemüsebeet *nt*.

plotter ['plɒtə*] *n* (*instrument, also COMPUT*) Plotter *m*.

plough, (*US*) **plow** [plau] *n* Pflug *m* ♦ *vt* pflügen; **to** ~ **money into sth** (*project etc*) Geld in etw *acc* stecken.

▶ **plough back** *vt* (*COMM*) reinvestieren.

▶ **plough into** *vt fus* (*crowd*) rasen in +*acc*.

ploughman, (*US*) **plowman** ['plaumən] (*irreg: like* **man**) *n* Pflüger *m*.

ploughman's lunch ['plaumənz-] (*BRIT*) *n* Imbiss aus Brot, Käse und Pickles.

plow *etc* (*US*) = **plough** *etc*.

ploy [plɔɪ] *n* Trick *m*.

pls *abbr* (= *please*) b.

pluck [plʌk] *vt* (*fruit, flower, leaf*) pflücken; (*musical instrument, eyebrows*) zupfen; (*bird*) rupfen ♦ *n* (*courage*) Mut *m*; **to** ~ **up courage** allen Mut zusammennehmen.

plucky ['plʌkɪ] (*inf*) *adj* (*person*) tapfer.

plug [plʌg] *n* (*ELEC*) Stecker *m*; (*stopper*) Stöpsel *m*; (*AUT: also:* **spark(ing)** ~) Zündkerze *f* ♦ *vt* (*hole*) zustopfen; (*inf: advertise*) Reklame machen für; **to give sb/ sth a** ~ für jdn/etw Reklame machen.

▶ **plug in** *vt* (*ELEC*) einstöpseln, anschließen ♦ *vi* angeschlossen werden.

plughole ['plʌghəul] (*BRIT*) *n* Abfluss *m*.

plum [plʌm] *n* (*fruit*) Pflaume *f* ♦ *adj* (*inf*): **a** ~ **job** ein Traumjob *m*.

plumage ['pluːmɪdʒ] *n* Gefieder *nt*.

plumb [plʌm] *vt*: **to** ~ **the depths of despair/ humiliation** die tiefste Verzweiflung/ Erniedrigung erleben.

▶ **plumb in** *vt* anschließen, installieren.

plumber ['plʌmə*] *n* Installateur *m*, Klempner *m*.

plumbing ['plʌmɪŋ] *n* (*piping*) Installationen *pl*, Rohrleitungen *pl*; (*trade*) Klempnerei *f*; (*work*) Installationsarbeiten *pl*.

plumb line *n* Lot *nt*, Senkblei *nt*.

plume [pluːm] *n* (*of bird*) Feder *f*; (*on helmet, horse's head*) Federbusch *m*; ~ **of smoke** Rauchfahne *f*.

plummet ['plʌmɪt] *vi* (*bird, aircraft*) (hinunter)stürzen; (*price, rate*) rapide absacken.

plump [plʌmp] *adj* (*person*) füllig, mollig.

▶ **plump for** (*inf*) *vt fus* sich entscheiden für.

▶ **plump up** *vt* (*cushion*) aufschütteln.

plunder ['plʌndə*] *n* (*activity*) Plünderung *f*; (*stolen things*) Beute *f* ♦ *vt* (*city, tomb*) plündern.

plunge [plʌndʒ] *n* (*of bird, person*) Sprung *m*; (*fig: of prices, rates etc*) Sturz *m* ♦ *vt* (*hand, knife*) stoßen ♦ *vi* (*thing*) stürzen; (*bird,* *person*) sich stürzen; (*fig: prices, rates etc*) abfallen, stürzen; **to take the ~** (*fig*) den Sprung wagen; **the room was ~d into darkness** das Zimmer war in Dunkelheit getaucht.

plunger ['plʌndʒə*] *n* (*for sink*) Sauger *m*.

plunging ['plʌndʒɪŋ] *adj*: **~ neckline** tiefer Ausschnitt *m*.

pluperfect [plu:'pə:fɪkt] *n*: **the ~** das Plusquamperfekt.

plural ['pluərl] *adj* Plural- ♦ *n* Plural *m*, Mehrzahl *f*.

plus [plʌs] *n* (*also:* **~ sign**) Pluszeichen *nt* ♦ *prep, adj* plus; **it's a ~** (*fig*) es ist ein Vorteil *or* ein Pluspunkt; **ten/twenty ~** (*more than*) über zehn/zwanzig; **B ~** (*SCOL*) ≈ Zwei plus.

plus fours *npl* Überfallhose *f*.

plush [plʌʃ] *adj* (*car, hotel etc*) feudal ♦ *n* (*fabric*) Plüsch *m*.

plutonium [plu:'təunɪəm] *n* Plutonium *nt*.

ply [plaɪ] *vt* (*a trade*) ausüben, nachgehen +*dat*; (*tool*) gebrauchen, anwenden ♦ *vi* (*ship*) verkehren ♦ *n* (*of wool, rope*) Stärke *f*; (*also:* **~wood**) Sperrholz *nt*; **to ~ sb with drink** jdn ausgiebig bewirten; **to ~ sb with questions** jdm viele Fragen stellen; **two-/three-~ wool** zwei-/dreifädige Wolle.

plywood ['plaɪwud] *n* Sperrholz *nt*.

PM (*BRIT*) *abbr* = **Prime Minister.**

p.m. *adv abbr* (= *post meridiem*) nachmittags; (*later*) abends.

PMT *abbr* = **premenstrual tension.**

pneumatic [nju:'mætɪk] *adj* pneumatisch.

pneumatic drill *n* Pressluftbohrer *m*.

pneumonia [nju:'məunɪə] *n* Lungenentzündung *f*.

PO *n abbr* = **Post Office**; (*MIL*) = **petty officer.**

p.o. *abbr* = **postal order.**

POA (*BRIT*) *n abbr* (= *Prison Officers' Association*) Gewerkschaft der Gefängnisbeamten.

poach [pəutʃ] *vt* (*steal: fish, animals, birds*) illegal erbeuten, wildern; (*CULIN: egg*) pochieren; (*: fish*) dünsten ♦ *vi* (*steal*) wildern.

poached [pəutʃt] *adj*: **~ eggs** verlorene Eier.

poacher ['pəutʃə*] *n* Wilderer *m*.

PO Box *n abbr* (= *Post Office Box*) Postf.

pocket ['pɔkɪt] *n* Tasche *f*; (*fig: small area*) vereinzelter Bereich *m* ♦ *vt* (*put in one's pocket, steal*) einstecken; **to be out of ~** (*BRIT*) Verlust machen; **~ of resistance** Widerstandsnest *nt*.

pocketbook ['pɔkɪtbuk] *n* (*notebook*) Notizbuch *nt*; (*US: wallet*) Brieftasche *f*; (*: handbag*) Handtasche *f*.

pocket calculator *n* Taschenrechner *m*.

pocketknife ['pɔkɪtnaɪf] *n* Taschenmesser *nt*.

pocket money *n* Taschengeld *nt*.

pocket-sized ['pɔkɪtsaɪzd] *adj* im Taschenformat.

pockmarked ['pɔkmɑːkt] *adj* (*face*) pockennarbig.

pod [pɔd] *n* Hülse *f*.

podgy ['pɔdʒɪ] (*inf*) *adj* rundlich, pummelig.

podiatrist [pɔ'diːətrɪst] (*US*) *n* Fußspezialist(in) *m(f)*.

podiatry [pɔ'diːətrɪ] (*US*) *n* Fußpflege *f*.

podium ['pəudɪəm] *n* Podium *nt*.

POE *n abbr* (= *port of embarkation*) Ausgangshafen *m*; (= *port of entry*) Eingangshafen *m*.

poem ['pəuɪm] *n* Gedicht *nt*.

poet ['pəuɪt] *n* Dichter(in) *m(f)*.

poetic [pəu'ɛtɪk] *adj* poetisch, dichterisch; (*fig*) malerisch.

poetic justice *n* ausgleichende Gerechtigkeit *f*.

poetic licence *n* dichterische Freiheit *f*.

poet laureate *n* Hofdichter *m*.

POET LAUREATE

Poet laureate *ist in Großbritannien ein Dichter, der ein Gehalt als Hofdichter bezieht und kraft seines Amtes ein lebenslanges Mitglied des britischen Königshofes ist. Der* **poet laureate** *schrieb traditionellerweise ausführliche Gedichte zu Staatsanlässen; ein Brauch, der heute kaum noch befolgt wird. Der Erste* **poet laureate** *1616 war Ben Jonson.*

---

poetry ['pəuɪtrɪ] *n* (*poems*) Gedichte *pl*; (*writing*) Poesie *f*.

poignant ['pɔɪnjənt] *adj* ergreifend; (*situation*) herzzerreißend.

point [pɔɪnt] *n* Punkt *m*; (*of needle, knife etc*) Spitze *f*; (*purpose*) Sinn *m*, Zweck *m*; (*significant part*) Entscheidende(s) *nt*; (*moment*) Zeitpunkt *m*; (*ELEC: also:* **power ~**) Steckdose *f*; (*also:* **decimal ~**) ≈ Komma *nt* ♦ *vt* (*show, mark*) deuten auf +*acc* ♦ *vi* (*with finger, stick etc*) zeigen, deuten; **points** *npl* (*AUT*) (Unterbrecher)kontakte *pl*; (*RAIL*) Weichen *pl*; **two ~ five** (= *2.5*) zwei Komma fünf; **good/bad ~s** (*of person*) gute/ schlechte Seiten *or* Eigenschaften; **the train stops at Carlisle and all ~s south** der Zug hält in Carlisle und allen Orten weiter südlich; **to be on the ~ of doing sth** im Begriff sein, etw zu tun; **to make a ~ of doing sth** besonders darauf achten, etw zu tun; (*make a habit of*) Wert darauf legen, etw zu tun; **to get/miss the ~** verstehen/nicht verstehen, worum es geht; **to come** *or* **get to the ~** zur Sache kommen; **to make one's ~** seinen Standpunkt klarmachen; **that's the whole ~!** darum geht es ja gerade!; **what's the ~?** was solls?; **to be beside the ~** unwichtig *or* irrelevant sein; **there's no ~ talking to you** es ist sinnlos, mit dir zu reden; **you've got a ~ there!** da könnten Sie Recht haben!; **in ~ of fact** in Wirklichkeit; **~ of sale** (*COMM*) Verkaufsstelle *f*; **to ~ sth**

at sb (*gun etc*) etw auf jdn richten; (*finger*) mit etw auf jdn *acc* zeigen; **to ~ at** zeigen auf +*acc*; **to ~ to** zeigen auf +*acc*; (*fig*) hinweisen auf +*acc*.

▶ **point out** *vt* hinweisen auf +*acc*.

▶ **point to** *vt fus* hindeuten auf +*acc*.

point-blank ['pɔɪnt'blæŋk] *adv* (*say, ask*) direkt; (*refuse*) glatt; (*also:* **at ~ range**) aus unmittelbarer Entfernung.

point duty (*BRIT*) *n:* **to be on ~** Verkehrsdienst haben.

pointed ['pɔɪntɪd] *adj* spitz; (*fig: remark*) spitz, scharf.

pointedly ['pɔɪntɪdlɪ] *adv* (*ask, reply etc*) spitz, scharf.

pointer ['pɔɪntə*] *n* (*on chart, machine*) Zeiger *m*; (*fig: piece of information or advice*) Hinweis *m*; (*stick*) Zeigestock *m*; (*dog*) Pointer *m*.

pointing ['pɔɪntɪŋ] *n* (*CONSTR*) Ausfugung *f*.

pointless ['pɔɪntlɪs] *adj* sinnlos, zwecklos.

point of view *n* Ansicht *f*, Standpunkt *m*; **from a practical ~** von einem praktischen Standpunkt aus.

poise [pɔɪz] *n* (*composure*) Selbstsicherheit *f*; (*balance*) Haltung *f* ♦ *vt:* **to be ~d for sth** (*fig*) bereit zu etw sein.

poison ['pɔɪzn] *n* Gift *nt* ♦ *vt* vergiften.

poisoning ['pɔɪznɪŋ] *n* Vergiftung *f*.

poisonous ['pɔɪznəs] *adj* (*animal, plant*) Gift-; (*fumes, chemicals etc*) giftig; (*fig: rumours etc*) zersetzend.

poison-pen letter [pɔɪzn'pɛn] *n* anonymer Brief *m* (*mit Indiskretionen*).

poke [pəʊk] *vt* (*with finger, stick etc*) stoßen; (*fire*) schüren ♦ *n* (*jab*) Stoß *m*, Schubs *m* (*inf*); **to ~ sth in(to)** (*put*) etw stecken in +*acc*; **to ~ one's head out of the window** seinen Kopf aus dem Fenster strecken; **to ~ fun at sb** sich über jdn lustig machen.

▶ **poke about** *vi* (*search*) herumstochern.

▶ **poke out** *vi* (*stick out*) vorstehen.

poker ['pəʊkə*] *n* (*metal bar*) Schürhaken *m*; (*CARDS*) Poker *nt*.

poker-faced ['pəʊkə'feɪst] *adj* mit unbewegter Miene, mit Pokergesicht.

poky ['pəʊkɪ] (*pej*) *adj* (*room, house*) winzig.

Poland ['pəʊlənd] *n* Polen *nt*.

polar ['pəʊlə*] *adj* (*icecap*) polar; (*region*) Polar-.

polar bear *n* Eisbär *m*.

polarize ['pəʊləraɪz] *vt* polarisieren.

Pole [pəʊl] *n* Pole *m*, Polin *f*.

pole [pəʊl] *n* (*post, stick*) Stange *f*; (*flag pole, telegraph pole etc*) Mast *m*; (*GEOG, ELEC*) Pol *m*; **to be ~s apart** (*fig*) durch Welten (voneinander) getrennt sein.

poleaxe, (*US*) **poleax** ['pəʊlæks] *vt* (*fig*) umhauen.

pole bean (*US*) *n* (*runner bean*) Stangenbohne *f*.

polecat ['pəʊlkæt] *n* Iltis *m*.

Pol. Econ. ['pɔlɪkɔn] *n abbr* (= *political*

economy) Volkswirtschaft *f*.

polemic [pɔ'lɛmɪk] *n* Polemik *f*.

Pole Star *n* Polarstern *m*.

pole vault ['pəʊlvɔːlt] *n* Stabhochsprung *m*.

police [pə'liːs] *npl* (*organization*) Polizei *f*; (*members*) Polizisten *pl*, Polizeikräfte *pl* ♦ *vt* (*street, area, town*) kontrollieren; **a large number of ~ were hurt** viele Polizeikräfte wurden verletzt.

police car *n* Polizeiauto *nt*.

police constable (*BRIT*) *n* Polizist(in) *m(f)*, Polizeibeamte(r) *m*, Polizeibeamtin *f*.

police department (*US*) *n* Polizei *f*.

police force *n* Polizei *f*.

policeman [pə'liːsmən] (*irreg: like* **man**) *n* Polizist *m*.

police officer *n* = **police constable**.

police record *n:* **to have a ~** vorbestraft sein.

police state *n* (*POL*) Polizeistaat *m*.

police station *n* Polizeiwache *f*.

policewoman [pə'liːswʊmən] (*irreg: like* **woman**) *n* Polizistin *f*.

policy ['pɔlɪsɪ] *n* (*POL, ECON*) Politik *f*; (*also:* **insurance ~**) (Versicherungs)police *f*; (*of newspaper*) Grundsatz *m*; **to take out a ~** (*INSURANCE*) eine Versicherung abschließen.

policyholder ['pɔlɪsɪ'həʊldə*] *n* (*INSURANCE*) Versicherungsnehmer(in) *m(f)*.

policy making *n* Strategieplanung *f*.

polio ['pəʊlɪəʊ] *n* Kinderlähmung *f*, Polio *f*.

Polish ['pəʊlɪʃ] *adj* polnisch ♦ *n* (*LING*) Polnisch *nt*.

polish ['pɔlɪʃ] *n* (*for shoes*) Creme *f*; (*for furniture*) Politur *f*; (*for floors*) Bohnerwachs *nt*; (*shine: on shoes, floor etc*) Glanz *m*; (*fig: refinement*) Schliff *m* ♦ *vt* (*shoes*) putzen; (*floor, furniture etc*) polieren.

▶ **polish off** *vt* (*work*) erledigen; (*food*) verputzen.

polished ['pɔlɪʃt] *adj* (*fig: person*) mit Schliff; (: *style*) geschliffen.

polite [pə'laɪt] *adj* höflich; (*company, society*) fein; **it's not ~ to do that** es gehört sich nicht, das zu tun.

politely [pə'laɪtlɪ] *adv* höflich.

politeness [pə'laɪtnɪs] *n* Höflichkeit *f*.

politic ['pɔlɪtɪk] *adj* klug, vernünftig.

political [pə'lɪtɪkl] *adj* politisch.

political asylum *n* politisches Asyl *nt*.

politically [pə'lɪtɪklɪ] *adv* politisch; **~ correct** politisch korrekt.

politician [pɔlɪ'tɪʃən] *n* Politiker(in) *m(f)*.

politics ['pɔlɪtɪks] *n* Politik *f* ♦ *npl* (*beliefs, opinions*) politische Ansichten *pl*.

polka ['pɔlkə] *n* Polka *f*.

poll [pəʊl] *n* (*also:* **opinion ~**) (Meinungs)umfrage *f*; (*election*) Wahl *f* ♦ *vt* (*in opinion poll*) befragen; (*number of votes*) erhalten; **to go to the ~s** (*voters*) zur Wahl gehen; (*government*) sich den Wählern

stellen.
pollen ['pɔlən] *n* Pollen *m*, Blütenstaub *m*.
pollen count *n* Pollenkonzentration *f*.
pollinate ['pɔlɪneɪt] *vt* bestäuben.
polling booth ['pɔulɪŋ-] (*BRIT*) *n* Wahlkabine
f.
polling day (*BRIT*) *n* Wahltag *m*.
polling station (*BRIT*) *n* Wahllokal *nt*.
pollster ['pɔulstə*] *n* Meinungsforscher(in)
m(f).
poll tax *n* Kopfsteuer *f*.
pollutant [pə'luːtənt] *n* Schadstoff *m*.
pollute [pə'luːt] *vt* verschmutzen.
pollution [pə'luːʃən] *n* (*process*)
Verschmutzung *f*; (*substances*) Schmutz *m*.
polo ['pɔuləu] *n* Polo *nt*.
polo neck *n* (*jumper*) Rollkragenpullover *m*.
polo-necked ['pɔuləunɛkt] *adj* (*jumper,
sweater*) Rollkragen-.
poltergeist ['pɔːltəgaɪst] *n* Poltergeist *m*.
poly ['pɔlɪ] (*BRIT*) *n abbr* = **polytechnic**.
poly bag (*inf*) *n* Plastiktüte *f*.
polyester [pɔlɪ'estə*] *n* Polyester *m*.
polygamy [pə'lɪgəmɪ] *n* Polygamie *f*.
polygraph ['pɔlɪgrɑːf] (*US*) *n* (*lie detector*)
Lügendetektor *m*.
Polynesia [pɔlɪ'niːzɪə] *n* Polynesien *nt*.
Polynesian [pɔlɪ'niːzɪən] *adj* polynesisch ♦ *n*
Polynesier(in) *m(f)*.
polyp ['pɔlɪp] *n* Polyp *m*.
polystyrene [pɔlɪ'staɪriːn] *n* ≈ Styropor ® *nt*.
polytechnic [pɔlɪ'tɛknɪk] *n* technische
Hochschule *f*.
polythene ['pɔlɪθiːn] *n* Polyäthylen *nt*.
polythene bag *n* Plastiktüte *f*.
polyurethane [pɔlɪ'juərɪθeɪn] *n* Polyurethan
nt.
pomegranate ['pɔmɪgrænɪt] *n* Granatapfel *m*.
pommel ['pɔml] *n* (*on saddle*) Sattelknopf *m*
♦ *vt* (*US*) = **pummel**.
pomp [pɔmp] *n* Pomp *m*, Prunk *m*.
pompom ['pɔmpɔm] *n* Troddel *f*.
pompous ['pɔmpəs] (*pej*) *adj* (*person*)
aufgeblasen; (*piece of writing*) geschwollen.
pond [pɔnd] *n* Teich *m*.
ponder ['pɔndə*] *vt* nachdenken über +*acc* ♦ *vi*
nachdenken.
ponderous ['pɔndərəs] *adj* (*style, language*)
schwerfällig.
pong [pɔŋ] (*BRIT: inf*) *n* Gestank *m* ♦ *vi* stinken.
pontiff ['pɔntɪf] *n* Papst *m*.
pontificate [pɔn'tɪfɪkeɪt] *vi* dozieren.
pontoon [pɔn'tuːn] *n* (*floating platform*) Ponton
m; (*CARDS*) Siebzehnundvier *nt*.
pony ['pəunɪ] *n* Pony *nt*.
ponytail ['pəunɪteɪl] *n* Pferdeschwanz *m*; **to
have one's hair in a ~** einen Pferdeschwanz
tragen.
pony trekking (*BRIT*) *n* Ponytrecken *nt*.
poodle ['puːdl] *n* Pudel *m*.
pooh-pooh ['puː'puː] *vt* verächtlich abtun.
pool [puːl] *n* (*pond*) Teich *m*; (*also:* **swimming

~**) Schwimmbad *nt*; (*of blood*) Lache *f*;
(*SPORT*) Poolbillard *nt*; (*of cash, workers*)
Bestand *m*; (*CARDS: kitty*) Kasse *f*; (*COMM:
consortium*) Interessengemeinschaft *f* ♦ *vt*
(*money*) zusammenlegen; (*knowledge,
resources*) vereinigen; **pools** *npl* (*football
pools*) ≈ Fußballtoto *nt*; **a ~ of sunlight/
shade** eine sonnige/schattige Stelle; **car ~**
Fahrgemeinschaft *f*; **typing ~**, (*US*) **secretary
~** Schreibzentrale *f*; **to do the (football) ~s**
≈ im Fußballtoto spielen.
poor [puə*] *adj* arm; (*bad*) schlecht ♦ *npl*: **the ~**
die Armen *pl*; **~ in** (*resources etc*) arm an
+*dat*; **~ Bob** der arme Bob.
poorly ['puəlɪ] *adj* (*ill*) elend, krank ♦ *adv*
(*badly: designed, paid, furnished*) schlecht.
pop [pɔp] *n* (*MUS*) Pop *m*; (*fizzy drink*)
Limonade *f*; (*US: inf: father*) Papa *m*; (*sound*)
Knall *m* ♦ *vi* (*balloon*) platzen; (*cork*) knallen
♦ *vt*: **to ~ sth into/onto sth** etw schnell in
etw *acc* stecken/auf etw *acc* legen; **his eyes
~ped out of his head** (*inf*) ihm fielen fast die
Augen aus dem Kopf; **she ~ped her head
out of the window** sie streckte den Kopf
aus dem Fenster.
▶ **pop in** *vi* vorbeikommen.
▶ **pop out** *vi* kurz weggehen.
▶ **pop up** *vi* auftauchen.
popcorn ['pɔpkɔːn] *n* Popcorn *nt*.
pope [pəup] *n* Papst *m*.
poplar ['pɔplə*] *n* Pappel *f*.
poplin ['pɔplɪn] *n* Popeline *f*.
popper ['pɔpə*] (*BRIT: inf*) *n* (*for fastening*)
Druckknopf *m*.
poppy ['pɔpɪ] *n* Mohn *m*.
poppycock ['pɔpɪkɔk] (*inf*) *n* Humbug *m*,
dummes Zeug *nt*.
Popsicle ® ['pɔpsɪkl] (*US*) *n* Eis *nt* am Stiel.
pop star *n* Popstar *m*.
populace ['pɔpjuləs] *n*: **the ~** die
Bevölkerung, das Volk.
popular ['pɔpjulə*] *adj* (*well-liked, fashionable*)
beliebt, populär; (*general, non-specialist*)
allgemein; (*idea*) weitverbreitet, weit
verbreitet; (*POL: movement*) Volks-; (: *cause*)
des Volkes; **to be ~ with** beliebt sein bei;
the ~ press die Boulevardpresse.
popularity [pɔpju'lærɪtɪ] *n* Beliebtheit *f*,
Popularität *f*.
popularize ['pɔpjuləraɪz] *vt* (*sport, music,
fashion*) populär machen; (*science, ideas*)
popularisieren.
popularly ['pɔpjuləlɪ] *adv* (*commonly*)
allgemein.
population [pɔpju'leɪʃən] *n* Bevölkerung *f*; (*of
a species*) Zahl *f*, Population *f*; **a prison ~ of
44,000** (eine Zahl von) 44.000
Gefängnisinsassen; **the civilian ~** die
Zivilbevölkerung.
population explosion *n*
Bevölkerungsexplosion *f*.
populous ['pɔpjuləs] *adj* dicht besiedelt.

porcelain ['pɔːslɪn] n Porzellan nt.

porch [pɔːtʃ] n (entrance) Vorbau m; (US) Veranda f.

porcupine ['pɔːkjupaɪn] n Stachelschwein nt.

pore [pɔː*] n Pore f ♦ vi: **to ~ over** (book etc) gründlich studieren.

pork [pɔːk] n Schweinefleisch nt.

pork chop n Schweinekotelett nt.

porn [pɔːn] (inf) n Porno m; **~ channel/ magazine/shop** Pornokanal m/-magazin nt/- laden m.

pornographic [pɔːnə'græfɪk] adj pornografisch.

pornography [pɔː'nɔgrəfɪ] n Pornografie f.

porous ['pɔːrəs] adj porös.

porpoise ['pɔːpəs] n Tümmler m.

porridge ['pɔrɪdʒ] n Haferbrei m, Porridge nt.

port [pɔːt] n (harbour) Hafen m; (NAUT: left side) Backbord nt; (wine) Portwein m; (COMPUT) Port m ♦ adj (NAUT) Backbord-; **to ~** (NAUT) an Backbord; **~ of call** (NAUT) Anlaufhafen nt.

portable ['pɔːtəbl] adj (television, typewriter etc) tragbar, portabel.

portal ['pɔːtl] n Portal nt.

portcullis [pɔːt'kʌlɪs] n Fallgitter nt.

portend [pɔː'tend] vt hindeuten auf +acc.

portent ['pɔːtent] n Vorzeichen nt.

porter ['pɔːtə*] n (for luggage) Gepäckträger m; (doorkeeper) Pförtner m; (US: RAIL) Schlafwagenschaffner(in) m(f).

portfolio [pɔːt'fəulɪəu] n (case) Aktenmappe f; (POL) Geschäftsbereich m; (FIN) Portefeuille nt; (of artist) Kollektion f.

porthole ['pɔːthəul] n Bullauge nt.

portico ['pɔːtɪkəu] n Säulenhalle f.

portion ['pɔːʃən] n (part) Teil m; (helping of food) Portion f.

portly ['pɔːtlɪ] adj beleibt, korpulent.

portrait ['pɔːtreɪt] n Porträt nt.

portray [pɔː'treɪ] vt darstellen.

portrayal [pɔː'treɪəl] n Darstellung f.

Portugal ['pɔːtjugl] n Portugal nt.

Portuguese [pɔːtju'giːz] adj portugiesisch ♦ n inv (person) Portugiese m, Portugiesin f; (LING) Portugiesisch nt.

Portuguese man-of-war [-mænəv'wɔː*] n (ZOOL) Röhrenqualle f, Portugiesische Galeere f.

pose [pəuz] n Pose f ♦ vt (question, problem) aufwerfen; (danger) mit sich bringen ♦ vi: **to ~ as** (pretend) sich ausgeben als; **to strike a ~** sich in Positur werfen; **to ~ for** (painting etc) Modell sitzen für, posieren für.

poser ['pəuzə*] n (problem, puzzle) harte Nuss f (inf); (person) = **poseur.**

poseur [pəu'zə:*] n (pej) Angeber(in) m(f).

posh [pɔʃ] (inf) adj vornehm; **to talk ~** vornehm daherreden.

position [pə'zɪʃən] n (place: of thing, person) Position f, Lage f; (of person's body) Stellung f; (job) Stelle f; (in race etc) Platz m; (attitude) Haltung f, Standpunkt m; (situation) Lage ♦ vt (person, thing) stellen; **to be in a ~ to do sth** in der Lage sein, etw zu tun.

positive ['pɔzɪtɪv] adj positiv; (certain) sicher; (decisive: action, policy) konstruktiv.

positively ['pɔzɪtɪvlɪ] adv (emphatic: rude, stupid etc) eindeutig; (encouragingly, also ELEC) positiv; **the body has been ~ identified** die Leiche ist eindeutig identifiziert worden.

posse ['pɔsɪ] (US) n (Polizei)truppe f.

possess [pə'zɛs] vt besitzen; (subj: feeling, belief) Besitz ergreifen von; **like a man ~ed** wie besessen; **whatever ~ed you to do it?** was ist in dich gefahren, das zu tun?

possession [pə'zɛʃən] n Besitz m; **possessions** npl (belongings) Besitz m; **to take ~ of** Besitz ergreifen von.

possessive [pə'zɛsɪv] adj (nature etc) besitzergreifend; (LING: pronoun) Possessiv-; (: adjective) besitzanzeigend; **to be ~ about sb/sth** Besitzansprüche an jdn/ etw acc stellen.

possessiveness [pə'zɛsɪvnɪs] n besitzergreifende Art f.

possessor [pə'zɛsə*] n Besitzer(in) m(f).

possibility [pɔsɪ'bɪlɪtɪ] n Möglichkeit f.

possible ['pɔsɪbl] adj möglich; **it's ~** (may be true) es ist möglich, es kann sein; **it's ~ to do it** es ist machbar or zu machen; **as far as ~** so weit wie möglich; **if ~** falls or wenn möglich; **as soon as ~** so bald wie möglich.

possibly ['pɔsɪblɪ] adv (perhaps) möglicherweise, vielleicht; (conceivably) überhaupt; **if you ~ can** falls überhaupt möglich; **what could they ~ want?** was um alles in der Welt wollen sie?; **I cannot ~ come** ich kann auf keinen Fall kommen.

post [pəust] n (BRIT) Post f; (pole, goal post) Pfosten m; (job) Stelle f; (MIL) Posten m; (also: **trading ~**) Handelsniederlassung f ♦ vt (BRIT: letter) aufgeben; (MIL) aufstellen; **by ~** (BRIT) per Post; **by return of ~** (BRIT) postwendend, umgehend; **to keep sb ~ed** (informed) jdn auf dem Laufenden halten; **to ~ sb to** (town, country) jdn versetzen nach; (embassy, office) jdn versetzen zu; (MIL) jdn abkommandieren nach.
► **post up** vt anschlagen.

post... [pəust] pref Post-, post-; **~-1990** nach 1990.

postage ['pəustɪdʒ] n Porto nt.

postage stamp n Briefmarke f.

postal ['pəustl] adj (charges, service) Post-.

postal order (BRIT) n Postanweisung f.

postbag ['pəustbæg] (BRIT) n Postsack m; (letters) Posteingang m.

postbox ['pəustbɔks] n Briefkasten m.

postcard ['pəustkɑːd] n Postkarte f.

postcode ['pəustkəud] (BRIT) n Postleitzahl f.

postdate ['pəust'deɪt] vt (cheque) vordatieren.

poster ['pəustə*] n Poster nt, Plakat nt.

poste restante [pəust'rɛstã:nt] (*BRIT*) *n* Stelle *f* für postlagernde Sendungen ♦ *adv* postlagernd.

posterior [pɔs'tɪərɪə*] (*hum*) *n* Allerwerteste(r) *m*.

posterity [pɔs'tɛrɪtɪ] *n* die Nachwelt.

poster paint *n* Plakatfarbe *f*.

post exchange (*US*) *n* (*MIL*) Laden für US-Militärpersonal.

post-free [pəust'fri:] (*BRIT*) *adj, adv* portofrei.

postgraduate ['pəust'grædjuət] *n* Graduierte(r) *f(m)* (*im Weiterstudium*).

posthumous ['pɔstjuməs] *adj* posthum.

posthumously ['pɔstjuməslɪ] *adv* posthum.

posting ['pəustɪŋ] *n* (*job*) Stelle *f*.

postman ['pəustmən] (*irreg: like* **man**) *n* Briefträger *m*, Postbote *m*.

postmark ['pəustmɑ:k] *n* Poststempel *m*.

postmaster ['pəustmɑ:stə*] *n* Postmeister *m*.

Postmaster General *n* ≈ Postminister(in) *m(f)*.

postmistress ['pəustmɪstrɪs] *n* Postmeisterin *f*.

postmortem [pəust'mɔ:təm] *n* (*MED*) Obduktion *f*; (*fig*) nachträgliche Erörterung *f*.

postnatal ['pəust'neɪtl] *adj* nach der Geburt, postnatal.

post office *n* (*building*) Post *f*, Postamt *nt*; **the Post Office** (*organization*) die Post.

Post Office Box *n* Postfach *nt*.

post-paid ['pəust'peɪd] *adj, adv* = **post-free**.

postpone [pəus'pəun] *vt* verschieben.

postponement [pəus'pəunmənt] *n* Aufschub *m*.

postscript ['pəustskrɪpt] *n* (*to letter*) Nachschrift *f*, PS *nt*.

postulate ['pɔstjuleɪt] *vt* ausgehen von, postulieren.

posture ['pɔstʃə*] *n* (*also fig*) Haltung *f* ♦ *vi* (*pej*) posieren.

postwar ['pəust'wɔ:*] *adj* Nachkriegs-.

posy ['pəuzɪ] *n* Blumensträußchen *nt*.

pot [pɔt] *n* Topf *m*; (*teapot, coffee pot, potful*) Kanne *f*; (*inf: marijuana*) Pot *nt* ♦ *vt* (*plant*) eintopfen; **to go to** ~ (*inf*) auf den Hund kommen; **~s of** (*BRIT: inf*) jede Menge.

potash ['pɔtæʃ] *n* Pottasche *f*.

potassium [pə'tæsɪəm] *n* Kalium *nt*.

potato [pə'teɪtəu] (*pl* ~**es**) *n* Kartoffel *f*.

potato chips (*US*) *npl* = **potato crisps**.

potato crisps *npl* Kartoffelchips *pl*.

potato flour *n* Kartoffelmehl *nt*.

potato peeler *n* Kartoffelschäler *m*.

potbellied ['pɔtbɛlɪd] *adj* (*from overeating*) dickbäuchig; (*from malnutrition*) blähbäuchig.

potency ['pəutnsɪ] *n* (*sexual*) Potenz *f*; (*of drink, drug*) Stärke *f*.

potent ['pəutnt] *adj* (*powerful*) stark; (*sexually*) potent.

potentate ['pəutnteɪt] *n* Machthaber *m*,

Potentat *m*.

potential [pə'tɛnʃl] *adj* potenziell ♦ *n* Potenzial *nt*; **to have** ~ (*person, machine*) Fähigkeiten *or* Potenzial haben; (*idea, plan*) ausbaufähig sein.

potentially [pə'tɛnʃəlɪ] *adv* potentziell; **it's** ~ **dangerous** es könnte gefährlich sein.

pothole ['pɔthəul] *n* (*in road*) Schlagloch *nt*; (*cave*) Höhle *f*.

potholing ['pɔthəulɪŋ] (*BRIT*) *n*: **to go** ~ Höhlenforschung betreiben.

potion ['pəuʃən] *n* Elixier *nt*.

potluck [pɔt'lʌk] *n*: **to take** ~ sich überraschen lassen.

potpourri [pəu'pʊri:] *n* (*dried petals*) Duftsträußchen *nt*; (*fig*) Sammelsurium *nt*.

pot roast *n* Schmorbraten *m*.

pot shot *n*: **to take a** ~ **at** aufs Geratewohl schießen auf +*acc*.

potted ['pɔtɪd] *adj* (*food*) eingemacht; (*plant*) Topf-; (*abbreviated: history etc*) Kurz-, kurz gefasst.

potter ['pɔtə*] *n* Töpfer(in) *m(f)* ♦ *vi*: **to** ~ **around, ~ about** (*BRIT*) herumhantieren; **to** ~ **around the house** im Haus herumwerkeln.

potter's wheel *n* Töpferscheibe *f*.

pottery ['pɔtərɪ] *n* (*pots, dishes etc*) Keramik *f*, Töpferwaren *pl*; (*work, hobby*) Töpfern *nt*; (*factory, workshop*) Töpferei *f*; **a piece of** ~ ein Töpferstück *nt*.

potty ['pɔtɪ] *adj* (*inf: mad*) verrückt ♦ *n* (*for child*) Töpfchen *nt*.

potty-training ['pɔtɪtreɪnɪŋ] *n* Entwöhnung *f* vom Windeltragen.

pouch [pautʃ] *n* Beutel *m* (*also ZOOL*).

pouf(fe) [pu:f] *n* (*stool*) gepolsterter Hocker *m*.

poultice ['pəultɪs] *n* Umschlag *m*.

poultry ['pəultrɪ] *n* Geflügel *nt*.

poultry farm *n* Geflügelfarm *f*.

poultry farmer *n* Geflügelzüchter(in) *m(f)*.

pounce [pauns] *vi*: **to** ~ **on** (*also fig*) sich stürzen auf +*acc*.

pound [paund] *n* (*unit of money*) Pfund *nt*; (*unit of weight*) (*britisches*) Pfund (= *453,6g*); (*for dogs*) Zwinger *m*; (*for cars*) Abholstelle *f* (*für abgeschleppte Fahrzeuge*) ♦ *vt* (*beat: table, wall etc*) herumhämmern auf +*dat*; (*crush: grain, spice etc*) zerstoßen; (*bombard*) beschießen ♦ *vi* (*heart*) klopfen, pochen; (*head*) dröhnen; **half a** ~ **of butter** ein halbes Pfund Butter; **a five-**~ **note** ein Fünfpfundschein *m*.

pounding ['paundɪŋ] *n*: **to take a** ~ (*fig*) schwer angegriffen werden; (*team*) eine Schlappe einstecken müssen.

pound sterling *n* Pfund *nt* Sterling.

pour [pɔ:*] *vt* (*tea, wine etc*) gießen; (*cereal etc*) schütten ♦ *vi* strömen; **to** ~ **sb a glass of wine/a cup of tea** jdm ein Glas Wein/eine Tasse Tee einschenken; **to** ~ **with rain** in Strömen gießen.

▶ **pour away** vt wegschütten.
▶ **pour in** vi (*people*) hereinströmen; (*letters etc*) massenweise eintreffen.
▶ **pour out** vi (*people*) herausströmen ♦ vt (*tea, wine etc*) eingießen; (*fig: thoughts, feelings, etc*) freien Lauf lassen +*dat*.
pouring ['pɔːrɪŋ] *adj*: ~ **rain** strömender Regen *m*.
pout [paut] *vi* einen Schmollmund ziehen.
poverty ['pɒvətɪ] *n* Armut *f*.
poverty line *n* Armutsgrenze *f*.
poverty-stricken ['pɒvətɪstrɪkn] *adj* verarmt, Not leidend.
poverty trap (*BRIT*) *n* gleich bleibend schlechte wirtschaftliche Situation aufgrund des Wegfalls von Sozialleistungen bei verbessertem Einkommen, Armutsfalle *f*.
POW *n abbr* = **prisoner of war**.
powder ['paudə*] *n* Pulver *nt* ♦ *vt*: **to ~ one's face** sich *dat* das Gesicht pudern; **to ~ one's nose** (*euph*) kurz mal verschwinden.
powder compact *n* Puderdose *f*.
powdered milk ['paudəd-] *n* Milchpulver *nt*.
powder keg *n* (*also fig*) Pulverfass *nt*.
powder puff *n* Puderquaste *f*.
powder room (*euph*) *n* Damentoilette *f*.
power ['pauə*] *n* (*control, legal right*) Macht *f*; (*ability*) Fähigkeit *f*; (*of muscles, ideas, words*) Kraft *f*; (*of explosion, engine*) Gewalt *f*; (*electricity*) Strom *m*; **2 to the ~ (of) 3** (*MATH*) 2 hoch 3; **to do everything in one's ~ to help** alles in seiner Macht Stehende tun, um zu helfen; **a world ~** eine Weltmacht; **the ~s that be** (*authority*) diejenigen, die das Sagen haben; **~ of attorney** Vollmacht *f*; **to be in ~** (*POL etc*) an der Macht sein.
powerboat ['pauəbəut] *n* schnelles Motorboot *nt*, Rennboot *nt*.
power cut *n* Stromausfall *m*.
powered ['pauəd] *adj*: ~ **by** angetrieben von; **nuclear-~ submarine** atomgetriebenes U-Boot.
power failure *n* Stromausfall *m*.
powerful ['pauəful] *adj* (*person, organization*) mächtig; (*body, voice, blow etc*) kräftig; (*engine*) stark; (*unpleasant: smell*) streng; (*emotion*) überwältigend; (*argument, evidence*) massiv.
powerhouse ['pauəhaus] *n*: **he is a ~ of ideas** er hat ständig neue Ideen.
powerless ['pauəlɪs] *adj* machtlos; **to be ~ to do sth** nicht die Macht haben, etw zu tun.
power line *n* Stromkabel *nt*.
power point (*BRIT*) *n* Steckdose *f*.
power station *n* Kraftwerk *nt*.
power steering *n* (*AUT*) Servolenkung *f*.
powwow ['pauwau] *n* Besprechung *f*.
pp *abbr* (= *per procurationem*) ppa.
pp. *abbr* (= *pages*) S.
PPE (*BRIT*) *n abbr* (*UNIV*: = *philosophy, politics and economics*) Studiengang bestehend aus

Philosophie, Politologie und Volkswirtschaft.
PPS *n abbr* (= *post postscriptum*) PPS; (*BRIT*: = *parliamentary private secretary*) Privatsekretär eines Ministers.
PQ (*CANADA*) *abbr* (= *Province of Quebec*).
PR *n abbr* = **public relations**; (*POL*) = **proportional representation** ♦ *abbr* (*US*: *POST*: = *Puerto Rico*).
Pr. *abbr* = **prince**.
practicability [præktɪkə'bɪlɪtɪ] *n* Durchführbarkeit *f*.
practicable ['præktɪkəbl] *adj* (*scheme, idea*) durchführbar.
practical ['præktɪkl] *adj* praktisch; (*person: good with hands*) praktisch veranlagt; (*ideas, methods*) praktikabel.
practicality [præktɪ'kælɪtɪ] *n* (*of person*) praktische Veranlagung *f*; **practicalities** *npl* (*of situation etc*) praktische Einzelheiten *pl*.
practical joke *n* Streich *m*.
practically ['præktɪklɪ] *adv* praktisch.
practice ['præktɪs] *n* (*also MED, LAW*) Praxis *f*; (*custom*) Brauch *m*; (*exercise*) Übung *f* ♦ *vt, vi* (*US*) = **practise** **in ~** in der Praxis; **out of ~** aus der Übung; **2 hours' piano ~** 2 Stunden Klavierübungen; **it's common or standard ~** es ist allgemein üblich; **to put sth into ~** etw in die Praxis umsetzen; **target ~** Zielschießen *nt*.
practice match *n* Übungsspiel *nt*.
practise, (*US*) **practice** ['præktɪs] *vt* (*train at*) üben; (*carry out: custom*) pflegen; (: *activity etc*) ausüben; (*profession*) praktizieren ♦ *vi* (*train*) üben; (*lawyer, doctor etc*) praktizieren.
practised ['præktɪst] (*BRIT*) *adj* (*person, liar*) geübt; (*performance*) gekonnt; **with a ~ eye** mit geschultem Auge.
practising ['præktɪsɪŋ] *adj* praktizierend.
practitioner [præk'tɪʃənə*] *n*: **medical ~** praktischer Arzt *m*, praktische Ärztin *f*; **legal ~** Rechtsanwalt *m*, Rechtsanwältin *f*.
pragmatic [præg'mætɪk] *adj* pragmatisch.
pragmatism ['prægmətɪzəm] *n* Pragmatismus *m*.
Prague [prɑːg] *n* Prag *nt*.
prairie ['prɛərɪ] *n* (*Gras*)steppe *f*; **the ~s** (*US*) die Prärien.
praise [preɪz] *n* Lob *nt* ♦ *vt* loben; (*REL*) loben, preisen.
praiseworthy ['preɪzwɜːðɪ] *adj* lobenswert.
pram [præm] (*BRIT*) *n* Kinderwagen *m*.
prance [prɑːns] *vi* (*horse*) tänzeln; **to ~ about/in/out** (*person*) herum-/hinein-/hinausstolzieren.
prank [præŋk] *n* Streich *m*.
prat [præt] (*BRIT*: *inf*) *n* (*idiot*) Trottel *m*.
prattle ['prætl] *vi*: **to ~ on (about)** pausenlos plappern (über +*acc*).
prawn [prɔːn] *n* (*CULIN, ZOOL*) Garnele *f*, Krabbe *f*; **~ cocktail** Krabbencocktail *m*.
pray [preɪ] *vi* beten; **to ~ for sb/sth** (*REL, fig*)

für jdn/um etw beten.

prayer [prɛəʳ] n Gebet nt; **to say one's ~s** beten.

prayer book n Gebetbuch nt.

pre... [priː] pref Prä-, prä-; **~-1970** vor 1970.

preach [priːtʃ] vi (REL) predigen; (pej: moralize) Predigten halten ♦ vt (sermon) direkt halten; (fig: advocate) predigen, verkünden; **to ~ at sb** (fig) jdm Moralpredigten halten; **to ~ to the converted** (fig) offene Türen einrennen.

preacher ['priːtʃəʳ] n Prediger(in) m(f).

preamble [prɪ'æmbl] n Vorbemerkung f.

prearranged [priːə'reɪndʒd] adj (vorher) vereinbart.

precarious [prɪ'kɛərɪəs] adj prekär.

precaution [prɪ'kɔːʃən] n Vorsichtsmaßnahme f; **to take ~s** Vorsichtsmaßnahmen treffen.

precautionary [prɪ'kɔːʃənrɪ] adj (measure) vorbeugend, Vorsichts-.

precede [prɪ'siːd] vt (event) vorausgehen +dat; (person) vorangehen +dat; (words, sentences) vorangestellt sein +dat.

precedence ['prɛsɪdəns] n (priority) Vorrang m; **to take ~ over** Vorrang haben vor +dat.

precedent ['prɛsɪdənt] n (LAW) Präzedenzfall m; **without ~** noch nie da gewesen; **to establish** or **set a ~** einen Präzedenzfall schaffen.

preceding [prɪ'siːdɪŋ] adj vorhergehend.

precept ['priːsɛpt] n Grundsatz m, Regel f.

precinct ['priːsɪŋkt] n (US: part of city) Bezirk m; **precincts** npl (of cathedral, palace) Gelände nt; **shopping ~** (BRIT) Einkaufsviertel nt; (under cover) Einkaufscenter nt.

precious ['prɛʃəs] adj wertvoll, kostbar; (pej: person, writing) geziert; (ironic: damned) heiß geliebt, wundervoll ♦ adv (inf): **~ little/few** herzlich wenig/wenige.

precious stone n Edelstein m.

precipice ['prɛsɪpɪs] n (also fig) Abgrund m.

precipitate [vt prɪ'sɪpɪteɪt, adj prɪ'sɪpɪtɪt] vt (event) heraufbeschwören ♦ adj (hasty) überstürzt, übereilt.

precipitation [prɪsɪpɪ'teɪʃən] n (rain) Niederschlag m.

precipitous [prɪ'sɪpɪtəs] adj (steep) steil; (hasty) übereilt.

précis ['preɪsiː] n inv Zusammenfassung f.

precise [prɪ'saɪs] adj genau, präzise; **at 4 o'clock to be ~** um 4 Uhr, um genau zu sein.

precisely [prɪ'saɪslɪ] adv genau, exakt; (emphatic) ganz genau; **~!** genau!

precision [prɪ'sɪʒən] n Genauigkeit f, Präzision f.

preclude [prɪ'kluːd] vt ausschließen; **to ~ sb from doing sth** jdn daran hindern, etw zu tun.

precocious [prɪ'kəʊʃəs] adj (child, behaviour) frühreif.

preconceived [priːkən'siːvd] adj (idea)

vorgefasst.

preconception ['priːkən'sɛpʃən] n vorgefasste Meinung f.

precondition ['priːkən'dɪʃən] n Vorbedingung f.

precursor [priː'kəːsəʳ] n Vorläufer m.

predate ['priː'deɪt] vt (precede) vorausgehen +dat.

predator ['prɛdətəʳ] n (ZOOL) Raubtier nt; (fig) Eindringling m.

predatory ['prɛdətərɪ] adj (animal) Raub-; (person, organization) auf Beute lauernd.

predecessor ['priːdɪsɛsəʳ] n Vorgänger(in) m(f).

predestination [priːdɛstɪ'neɪʃən] n Vorherbestimmung f.

predetermine [priːdɪ'təːmɪn] vt vorherbestimmen.

predicament [prɪ'dɪkəmənt] n Notlage f, Dilemma nt; **to be in a ~** in einer Notlage or einem Dilemma stecken.

predicate ['prɛdɪkɪt] n (LING) Prädikat nt.

predict [prɪ'dɪkt] vt vorhersagen.

predictable [prɪ'dɪktəbl] adj vorhersagbar.

predictably [prɪ'dɪktəblɪ] adv (behave, react) wie vorherzusehen; **~ she didn't come** wie vorherzusehen war, kam sie nicht.

prediction [prɪ'dɪkʃən] n Voraussage f.

predispose ['priːdɪs'pəʊz] vt: **to ~ sb to sth** jdn zu etw veranlassen; **to be ~d to do sth** geneigt sein, etw zu tun.

predominance [prɪ'dɔmɪnəns] n Vorherrschaft f.

predominant [prɪ'dɔmɪnənt] adj vorherrschend; **to become ~** vorherrschend werden.

predominantly [prɪ'dɔmɪnəntlɪ] adv überwiegend.

predominate [prɪ'dɔmɪneɪt] vi (in number, size) vorherrschen; (in strength, influence) überwiegen.

pre-eminent [priː'ɛmɪnənt] adj herausragend.

pre-empt [priː'ɛmt] vt zuvorkommen +dat.

pre-emptive [priː'ɛmtɪv] adj: **~ strike** Präventivschlag m.

preen [priːn] vt: **to ~ itself** (bird) sich putzen; **to ~ o.s.** sich herausputzen.

prefab ['priːfæb] n Fertighaus nt.

prefabricated [priː'fæbrɪkeɪtɪd] adj vorgefertigt.

preface ['prɛfəs] n Vorwort nt ♦ vt: **to ~ with/by** (speech, action) einleiten mit/durch.

prefect ['priːfɛkt] (BRIT) n (in school) Aufsichtsschüler(in) m(f).

prefer [prɪ'fəːʳ] vt (like better) vorziehen; **to ~ charges** (LAW) Anklage erheben; **to ~ doing** or **to do sth** (es) vorziehen, etw zu tun; **I ~ tea to coffee** ich mag lieber Tee als Kaffee.

preferable ['prɛfrəbl] adj: **to be ~ (to)** vorzuziehen sein (+dat).

preferably ['prɛfrəblɪ] adv vorzugsweise, am

besten.

preference ['prɛfrəns] n: **to have a ~ for**
(*liking*) eine Vorliebe haben für; **I drink beer
in ~ to wine** ich trinke lieber Bier als Wein;
to give ~ to (*priority*) vorziehen, Vorrang
einräumen +*dat*.

preference shares (*BRIT*) npl (*COMM*)
Vorzugsaktien pl.

preferential [prɛfə'rɛnʃəl] adj: **~ treatment**
bevorzugte Behandlung f; **to give sb
~ treatment** jdn bevorzugt behandeln.

preferred stock [prɪ'fəd-] (*US*) npl
= preference shares.

prefix ['priːfɪks] n (*LING*) Präfix nt.

pregnancy ['prɛgnənsɪ] n (*of woman*)
Schwangerschaft f; (*of female animal*)
Trächtigkeit f.

pregnancy test n Schwangerschaftstest m.

pregnant ['prɛgnənt] adj (*woman*) schwanger;
(*female animal*) trächtig; (*fig: pause, remark*)
bedeutungsschwer; **3 months ~** im vierten
Monat (schwanger).

prehistoric ['priːhɪs'tɔrɪk] adj prähistorisch,
vorgeschichtlich.

prehistory [priː'hɪstərɪ] n Vorgeschichte f.

prejudge [priː'dʒʌdʒ] vt vorschnell
beurteilen.

prejudice ['prɛdʒudɪs] n (*bias against*)
Vorurteil nt; (*bias in favour*)
Voreingenommenheit f ♦ vt beeinträchtigen;
without ~ to (*form*) unbeschadet +*gen*,
Beeinträchtigung +*gen*; **to ~ sb in favour of/
against sth** jdn für/gegen etw einnehmen.

prejudiced ['prɛdʒudɪst] adj (*person, view*)
voreingenommen.

prelate ['prɛlət] n Prälat m.

preliminaries [prɪ'lɪmɪnərɪz] npl
Vorbereitungen pl; (*of competition*)
Vorrunde f.

preliminary [prɪ'lɪmɪnərɪ] adj (*step,
arrangements*) vorbereitend; (*remarks*)
einleitend.

prelude ['prɛljuːd] n (*MUS*) Präludium nt; (:
*as
introduction*) Vorspiel nt; **a ~ to** (*fig*) ein
Vorspiel *or* ein Auftakt zu.

premarital ['priː'mærɪtl] adj vorehelich.

premature ['prɛmətʃuə*] adj (*earlier than
expected*) vorzeitig; (*too early*) verfrüht; **you
are being a little ~** Sie sind etwas voreilig;
~ baby Frühgeburt f.

premeditated [priː'mɛdɪteɪtɪd] adj
vorsätzlich.

premeditation [priː'mɛdɪ'teɪʃən] n Vorsatz m.

premenstrual tension [priː'mɛnstruəl-] n
prämenstruelles Syndrom nt.

premier ['prɛmɪə*] adj (*best*) beste(r, s),
bedeutendste(r, s) ♦ n (*POL*)
Premierminister(in) m(f).

premiere ['prɛmɪɛə*] n Premiere f.

premise ['prɛmɪs] n (*of argument*)
Voraussetzung f; **premises** npl (*of business
etc*) Räumlichkeiten pl; **on the ~s** im Hause.

premium ['priːmɪəm] n (*COMM, INSURANCE*)
Prämie f; **to be at a ~** (*expensive*) zum
Höchstpreis gehandelt werden; (*hard to get*)
Mangelware sein.

premium bond (*BRIT*) n Prämienanleihe f.

PREMIUM BONDS

Premium bonds, *eigentlich* **premium savings
bonds,** *sind Lotterieaktien, die seit 1956 vom
britischen Finanzministerium ausgegeben werden
und keine Zinsen bringen, sondern stattdessen an
einer monatlichen Auslosung teilnehmen. Die
Gewinnnummern für die verschiedenen
Geldpreise werden in Blackpool von einem
Computer namens „ERNIE" (Electronic Random
Number Indicator Equipment) ermittelt.*

---

premium gasoline (*US*) n Super(benzin) nt.

premonition [prɛmə'nɪʃən] n Vorahnung f.

preoccupation [priːɔkju'peɪʃən] n: **~ with**
(*vorrangige*) Beschäftigung mit.

preoccupied [priː'ɔkjupaɪd] adj (*thoughtful*)
gedankenverloren; (*with work, family*)
beschäftigt.

prep [prɛp] (*SCOL*) adj abbr (= preparatory) *see*
preparatory school ♦ n abbr (= preparation)
Hausaufgaben pl.

prepaid [priː'peɪd] adj (*paid in advance*) im
Voraus bezahlt; (*envelope*) frankiert.

preparation [prɛpə'reɪʃən] n Vorbereitung f;
(*food, medicine, cosmetic*) Zubereitung f;
preparations npl Vorbereitungen pl; **in ~ for
sth** als Vorbereitung für etw.

preparatory [prɪ'pærətərɪ] adj vorbereitend;
~ to sth/to doing sth als Vorbereitung für
etw/, um etw zu tun.

PREP(ATORY) SCHOOL

Prep(aratory) school *ist in Großbritannien eine
meist private Schule für Kinder im Alter von 7 bis
13 Jahren, die auf eine weiterführende
Privatschule vorbereiten soll.*

---

prepare [prɪ'pɛə*] vt vorbereiten; (*food, meal*)
zubereiten ♦ vi: **to ~ for** sich vorbereiten
auf +*acc*.

prepared [prɪ'pɛəd] adj: **to be ~ to do sth**
(*willing*) bereit sein, etw zu tun; **to be ~ for
sth** (*ready*) auf etw acc vorbereitet sein.

preponderance [prɪ'pɔndərns] n Übergewicht
nt.

preposition [prɛpə'zɪʃən] n Präposition f.

prepossessing [priːpə'zɛsɪŋ] adj von
angenehmer Erscheinung.

preposterous [prɪ'pɔstərəs] adj grotesk,
widersinnig.

prep school n = preparatory school

prerecorded ['priːrɪ'kɔːdɪd] adj (*broadcast*)
aufgezeichnet; (*cassette, video*) bespielt.

prerequisite [priː'rɛkwɪzɪt] n Vorbedingung f,

Grundvoraussetzung *f*.

prerogative [prɪ'rɔgətɪv] *n* Vorrecht *nt*, Privileg *nt*.

Presbyterian [prɛzbɪ'tɪərɪən] *adj* presbyterianisch ♦ *n* Presbyterianer(in) *m(f)*.

presbytery ['prɛzbɪtərɪ] *n* Pfarrhaus *nt*.

preschool ['priː'skuːl] *adj* (*age, child, education*) Vorschul-.

prescribe [prɪ'skraɪb] *vt* (*MED*) verschreiben; (*demand*) anordnen, vorschreiben.

prescribed *adj* (*duties, period*) vorgeschrieben.

prescription [prɪ'skrɪpʃən] *n* (*MED: slip of paper*) Rezept *nt*; (: *medicine*) Medikament *nt*; **to make up** *or* (*US*) **fill a** ~ ein Medikament zubereiten; "**only available on** ~" „rezeptpflichtig".

prescription charges (*BRIT*) *npl* Rezeptgebühr *f*.

prescriptive [prɪ'skrɪptɪv] *adj* normativ.

presence ['prɛzns] *n* Gegenwart *f*, Anwesenheit *f*; (*fig: personality*) Ausstrahlung *f*; (*spirit, invisible influence*) Erscheinung *f*; **in sb's** ~ in jds *dat* Gegenwart *or* Beisein; ~ **of mind** Geistesgegenwart *f*.

present [*adj, n* 'prɛznt, *vt* prɪ'zɛnt] *adj* (*current*) gegenwärtig, derzeitig; (*in attendance*) anwesend ♦ *n* (*gift*) Geschenk *nt*; (*LING: also:* ~ **tense**) Präsens *nt*, Gegenwart *f* ♦ *vt* (*give: prize etc*) überreichen; (*plan, report*) vorlegen; (*cause, provide, portray*) darstellen; (*information, view*) darlegen; (*RADIO, TV*) leiten; **to be** ~ **at** anwesend *or* zugegen sein bei; **those** ~ die Anwesenden; **to give sb a** ~ jdm ein Geschenk geben; **the** ~ (*actuality*) die Gegenwart; **at** ~ gegenwärtig, im Augenblick; **to** ~ **sth to sb,** ~ **sb with sth** jdm etw übergeben *or* überreichen; **to** ~ **sb** (**to**) (*formally: introduce*) jdn vorstellen +*dat*; **to** ~ **itself** (*opportunity*) sich bieten.

presentable [prɪ'zɛntəbl] *adj* (*person*) präsentabel, ansehnlich.

presentation [prɛzn'teɪʃən] *n* (*of prize*) Überreichung *f*; (*of plan, report etc*) Vorlage *f*; (*appearance*) Erscheinungsbild *nt*; (*talk*) Vortrag *m*; **on** ~ **of** (*voucher etc*) gegen Vorlage +*gen*.

present-day ['prɛzntdeɪ] *adj* heutig, gegenwärtig.

presenter [prɪ'zɛntə*] *n* (*on radio, TV*) Moderator(in) *m(f)*.

presently ['prɛzntlɪ] *adv* (*soon after*) gleich darauf; (*soon*) bald, in Kürze; (*currently*) derzeit, gegenwärtig.

present participle *n* Partizip *nt* Präsens.

preservation [prɛzə'veɪʃən] *n* (*of peace, standards etc*) Erhaltung *f*; (*of furniture, building*) Konservierung *f*.

preservative [prɪ'zəːvətɪv] *n* Konservierungsmittel *nt*.

preserve [prɪ'zəːv] *vt* erhalten; (*peace*) wahren; (*wood*) schützen; (*food*) konservieren ♦ *n* (*often pl: jam, chutney etc*) Eingemachte(s) *nt*; (*for game, fish*) Revier *nt*; **a male** ~ (*fig*) eine männliche Domäne; **a working class** ~ (*fig*) eine Domäne der Arbeiterklasse.

preshrunk ['priː'ʃrʌŋk] *adj* (*jeans etc*) vorgewaschen.

preside [prɪ'zaɪd] *vi:* **to** ~ **over** (*meeting etc*) vorsitzen +*dat*, den Vorsitz haben bei.

presidency ['prɛzɪdənsɪ] *n* (*POL*) Präsidentschaft *f*; (*US: of company*) Vorsitz *m*.

president ['prɛzɪdənt] *n* (*POL*) Präsident(in) *m(f)*; (*of organization*) Vorsitzende(r) *f(m)*.

presidential [prɛzɪ'dɛnʃl] *adj* (*election, campaign etc*) Präsidentschafts-; (*adviser, representative etc*) des Präsidenten.

press [prɛs] *n* (*printing press*) Presse *f*; (*of switch, bell*) Druck *m*; (*for wine*) Kelter *f* ♦ *vt* drücken, pressen; (*button, sb's hand etc*) drücken; (*iron: clothes*) bügeln; (*put pressure on: person*) drängen; (*pursue: idea, claim*) vertreten ♦ *vi* (*squeeze*) drücken, pressen; **the P**~ (*newspapers, journalists*) die Presse; **to go to** ~ (*newspaper*) in Druck gehen; **to be in** ~ (*at the printer's*) im Druck sein; **to be in the** ~ (*in the newspapers*) in der Zeitung stehen; **at the** ~ **of a button** auf Knopfdruck; **to** ~ **sth** (**up)on sb** (*force*) jdm etw aufdrängen; **we are** ~**ed for time/ money** wir sind in Geldnot/Zeitnot; **to** ~ **sb for an answer** auf jds *acc* Antwort drängen; **to** ~ **sb to do** *or* **into doing sth** jdn drängen, etw zu tun; **to** ~ **charges (against sb)** (*LAW*) Klage (gegen jdn) erheben; **to** ~ **for** (*changes etc*) drängen auf +*acc*.

▶ **press ahead** *vi* weitermachen; **to** ~ **ahead with sth** etw durchziehen.

▶ **press on** *vi* weitermachen.

press agency *n* Presseagentur *f*.

press clipping *n* Zeitungsausschnitt *m*.

press conference *n* Pressekonferenz *f*.

press cutting *n* = **press clipping**.

press-gang ['prɛsgæŋ] *vt:* **to** ~ **sb into doing sth** jdn bedrängen, etw zu tun.

pressing ['prɛsɪŋ] *adj* (*urgent*) dringend.

press officer *n* Pressesprecher(in) *m(f)*.

press release *n* Pressemitteilung *f*.

press stud (*BRIT*) *n* Druckknopf *m*.

press-up ['prɛsʌp] (*BRIT*) *n* Liegestütz *m*.

pressure ['prɛʃə*] *n* (*also fig*) Druck *m* ♦ *vt:* **to** ~ **sb to do sth** jdn dazu drängen, etw zu tun; **to put** ~ **on sb (to do sth)** Druck auf jdn ausüben(, etw zu tun); **high/low** ~ (*TECH, MET*) Hoch-/Tiefdruck *m*.

pressure cooker *n* Schnellkochtopf *m*.

pressure gauge *n* Druckmesser *m*, Manometer *nt*.

pressure group *n* Interessenverband *m*, Pressuregroup *f*.

pressurize ['preʃəraız] vt: **to ~ sb (to do sth** or **into doing sth)** jdn unter Druck setzen(, etw zu tun).

pressurized ['preʃəraızd] adj (cabin, container etc) Druck-.

Prestel ® ['prestel] n ≈ Bildschirmtext m, Btx nt.

prestige [pres'tiːʒ] n Prestige nt.

prestigious [pres'tıdʒəs] adj (institution, appointment) mit hohem Prestigewert.

presumably [prı'zjuːməblı] adv vermutlich; ~ **he did it** vermutlich or wahrscheinlich hat er es getan.

presume [prı'zjuːm] vt: **to ~ (that)** (assume) annehmen(, dass); **to ~ to do sth** (dare) sich anmaßen, etw zu tun; **I ~ so** das nehme ich an.

presumption [prı'zʌmpʃən] n (supposition) Annahme f; (audacity) Anmaßung f.

presumptuous [prı'zʌmpʃəs] adj anmaßend.

presuppose [priːsə'pəuz] vt voraussetzen.

presupposition [priːsʌpə'zıʃən] n Voraussetzung f.

pretax [priː'tæks] adj (profit) vor (Abzug der) Steuern.

pretence, (US) **pretense** [prı'tens] n (false appearance) Vortäuschung f; **under false ~s** unter Vorspiegelung falscher Tatsachen; **she is devoid of all ~** sie ist völlig natürlich; **to make a ~ of doing sth** vortäuschen, etw zu tun.

pretend [prı'tend] vt (feign) vorgeben ♦ vi (feign) sich verstellen, so tun, als ob; **I don't ~ to understand it** (claim) ich erhebe nicht den Anspruch, es zu verstehen.

pretense [prı'tens] (US) n = **pretence**.

pretentious [prı'tenʃəs] adj anmaßend.

preterite ['pretərıt] n Imperfekt nt, Präteritum nt.

pretext ['priːtekst] n Vorwand m; **on** or **under the ~ of doing sth** unter dem Vorwand, etw zu tun.

pretty ['prıtı] adj hübsch, nett ♦ adv: ~ **clever** ganz schön schlau; ~ **good** ganz gut.

prevail [prı'veıl] vi (be current) vorherrschen; (triumph) siegen; **to ~ (up)on sb to do sth** (persuade) jdn dazu bewegen or überreden, etw zu tun.

prevailing [prı'veılıŋ] adj (wind, fashion etc) vorherrschend.

prevalent ['prevələnt] adj (belief, custom) vorherrschend.

prevaricate [prı'værıkeıt] vi (by saying sth) Ausflüchte machen; (by doing sth) Ausweichmanöver machen.

prevarication [prıværı'keıʃən] n (see vi) Ausflucht f; Ausweichmanöver nt.

prevent [prı'vent] vt verhindern; **to ~ sb from doing sth** jdn daran hindern, etw zu tun; **to ~ sth from happening** verhindern, dass etw geschieht.

preventable [prı'ventəbl] adj verhütbar,

vermeidbar.

preventative [prı'ventətıv] adj = **preventive**.

prevention [prı'venʃən] n Verhütung f.

preventive [prı'ventıv] adj (measures, medicine) vorbeugend.

preview ['priːvjuː] n (of film) Vorpremiere f; (of exhibition) Vernissage f.

previous ['priːvıəs] adj (earlier) früher; (preceding) vorhergehend; ~ **to** vor +dat.

previously ['priːvıəslı] adv (before) zuvor; (formerly) früher.

prewar [priː'wɔː] adj (period) Vorkriegs-.

prey [preı] n Beute f; **to fall ~ to** (fig) zum Opfer fallen +dat.

▶ **prey on** vt fus (animal) Jagd machen auf +acc; **it was ~ing on his mind** es ließ ihn nicht los.

price [praıs] n (also fig) Preis m ♦ vt (goods) auszeichnen; **what is the ~ of ...?** was kostet ...?; **to go up** or **rise in ~** im Preis steigen, teurer werden; **to put a ~ on sth** (also fig) einen Preis für etw festsetzen; **what ~ his promises now?** wie steht es jetzt mit seinen Versprechungen?; **he regained his freedom, but at a ~** er hat seine Freiheit wieder, aber zu welchem Preis!; **to be ~d at £30** £30 kosten; **to ~ o.s. out of the market** durch zu hohe Preise konkurrenzunfähig werden.

price control n Preiskontrolle f.

price-cutting ['praıskʌtıŋ] n Preissenkungen pl.

priceless ['praıslıs] adj (diamond, painting) von unschätzbarem Wert; (inf: amusing) unbezahlbar, köstlich.

price list n Preisliste f.

price range n Preisklasse f; **it's within my ~** ich kann es mir leisten.

price tag n Preisschild nt; (fig) Preis m.

price war n Preiskrieg m.

pricey ['praısı] (inf) adj kostspielig.

prick [prık] n (sting) Stich m; (inf!: penis) Schwanz m; (: idiot) Arsch m ♦ vt stechen; (sausage, balloon) einstechen; **to ~ up one's ears** die Ohren spitzen.

prickle ['prıkl] n (of plant) Dorn m, Stachel m; (sensation) Prickeln nt.

prickly ['prıklı] adj (plant) stachelig; (fabric) kratzig.

prickly heat n Hitzebläschen pl.

prickly pear n Feigenkaktus m.

pride [praıd] n Stolz m; (pej: arrogance) Hochmut m ♦ vt: **to ~ o.s. on** sich rühmen +gen; **to take (a) ~ in** stolz sein auf +acc; **to take a ~ in doing sth** mit Stolz tun; **to have** or **take ~ of place** (BRIT) die Krönung sein.

priest [priːst] n Priester m.

priestess ['priːstıs] n Priesterin f.

priesthood ['priːsthud] n Priestertum nt.

prig [prıg] n: **he's a ~** er hält sich für ein Tugendlamm.

prim [prım] (pej) adj (person) etepetete.

primacy ['praɪməsɪ] n (supremacy) Vorrang m; (position) Vorrangstellung f.

prima-facie ['praɪmə'feɪʃɪ] adj: **to have a ~ case** (LAW) eine gute Beweisgrundlage haben.

primal ['praɪml] adj ursprünglich; **~ scream** Urschrei m.

primarily ['praɪmərɪlɪ] adv in erster Linie, hauptsächlich.

primary ['praɪmərɪ] adj (principal) Haupt-, hauptsächlich; (education, teacher) Grundschul- ♦ n (US: election) Vorwahl f.

PRIMARY

Als **primary** wird im amerikanischen Präsidentschaftswahlkampf eine Vorwahl bezeichnet, die mitentscheidet, welche Präsidentschaftskandidaten die beiden großen Parteien aufstellen. Vorwahlen werden nach komplizierten Regeln von Februar (New Hampshire) bis Juni in etwa 35 Staaten abgehalten. Der von den Kandidaten in den **primaries** erzielte Stimmenanteil bestimmt, wie viele Abgeordnete bei der endgültigen Auswahl der demokratischen bzw. republikanischen Kandidaten auf den nationalen Parteitagen im Juli/August für sie stimmen.

---

primary colour n Primärfarbe f.
primary school (BRIT) n Grundschule f.

PRIMARY SCHOOL

Primary school ist in Großbritannien eine Grundschule für Kinder im Alter von 5 bis 11 Jahren. Oft wird sie aufgeteilt in „infant school" (5 bis 7 Jahre) und „junior school" (7 bis 11 Jahre). Siehe auch **secondary school**.

---

primate ['praɪmɪt] n (ZOOL) Primat m; (REL) Primas m.

prime [praɪm] adj (most important) oberste(r, s); (best quality) erstklassig ♦ n (of person's life) die besten Jahre pl ♦ vt (wood) grundieren; (fig: person) informieren; (gun) schussbereit machen; (pump) auffüllen; **~ example** erstklassiges Beispiel; **in the ~ of life** im besten Alter.

Prime Minister n Premierminister(in) m(f).
primer ['praɪmə*] n (paint) Grundierung f; (book) Einführung f.
prime time n (RADIO, TV) Hauptsendezeit f.
primeval [praɪ'miːvl] adj (beast) urzeitlich; (fig: feelings) instinktiv; **~ forest** Urwald m.
primitive ['prɪmɪtɪv] adj (tribe, tool, conditions etc) primitiv; (life form, machine etc) frühzeitlich; (man) der Urzeit.
primrose ['prɪmrəʊz] n Primel f, gelbe Schlüsselblume f.
primula ['prɪmjʊlə] n Primel f.
Primus (stove) ® (BRIT) n Primuskocher m.
prince [prɪns] n Prinz m.

Prince Charming (hum) n Märchenprinz m.
princess [prɪn'sɛs] n Prinzessin f.
principal ['prɪnsɪpl] adj (most important) Haupt-, wichtigste(r, s) ♦ n (of school, college) Rektor(in) m(f); (THEAT) Hauptdarsteller(in) m(f); (FIN) Kapitalsumme f.
principality [prɪnsɪ'pælɪtɪ] n Fürstentum nt.
principally ['prɪnsɪplɪ] adv vornehmlich.
principle ['prɪnsɪpl] n Prinzip nt; **in ~** im Prinzip, prinzipiell; **on ~** aus Prinzip.
print [prɪnt] n (type, ART) Druck m; (PHOT) Abzug m; (fabric) bedruckter Stoff m ♦ vt (produce) drucken; (publish) veröffentlichen; (cloth, pattern) bedrucken; (write in capitals) in Druckschrift schreiben; **prints** npl (fingerprints etc) Abdrücke pl; **out of ~** vergriffen; **in ~** erhältlich; **the fine** or **small ~** das Kleingedruckte or klein Gedruckte.
▶ **print out** vt (COMPUT) ausdrucken.
printed circuit ['prɪntɪd-] n gedruckte Schaltung f.
printed circuit board n Leiterplatte f.
printed matter n Drucksache f.
printer ['prɪntə*] n (person) Drucker(in) m(f); (firm) Druckerei f; (machine) Drucker m.
printhead ['prɪnthɛd] n Druckkopf m.
printing ['prɪntɪŋ] n (activity) Drucken nt.
printing press n Druckerpresse f.
print-out ['prɪntaʊt] n (COMPUT) Ausdruck m.
print run n Auflage f.
printwheel ['prɪntwiːl] n (COMPUT) Typenrad nt.
prior ['praɪə*] adj (previous: knowledge, warning) vorherig; (: engagement) früher; (more important: claim, duty) vorrangig ♦ n (REL) Prior m; **without ~ notice** ohne vorherige Ankündigung; **to have a ~ claim on sth** ein Vorrecht auf etw acc haben; **~ to** vor +dat.
priority [praɪ'ɔrɪtɪ] n vorrangige Angelegenheit f; **priorities** npl Prioritäten pl; **to take** or **have ~ (over sth)** Vorrang (vor etw dat) haben; **to give ~ to sb/sth** jdm/etw Vorrang einräumen.
priory ['praɪərɪ] n Kloster nt.
prise [praɪz] (BRIT) vt: **to ~ open** aufbrechen.
prism ['prɪzəm] n Prisma nt.
prison ['prɪzn] n Gefängnis nt ♦ cpd (officer, food, cell etc) Gefängnis-.
prison camp n Gefangenenlager nt.
prisoner ['prɪznə*] n Gefangene(r) f(m); **the ~ at the bar** (LAW) der/die Angeklagte; **to take sb ~** jdn gefangen nehmen.
prisoner of war n Kriegsgefangene(r) f(m).
prissy ['prɪsɪ] (pej) adj zimperlich.
pristine ['prɪstiːn] adj makellos; **in ~ condition** in makellosem Zustand.
privacy ['prɪvəsɪ] n Privatsphäre f.
private ['praɪvɪt] adj privat; (life) Privat-; (thoughts, plans etc) persönlich; (place) abgelegen; (secretive: person) verschlossen

◆ n (MIL) Gefreite(r) m; "~" (on envelope) „vertraulich"; (on door) „privat"; in ~ privat; in (his) ~ life in seinem Privatleben; to be in ~ practice (MED) Privatpatienten haben; ~ hearing (LAW) nichtöffentliche or nicht öffentliche Verhandlung f.

private enterprise n Privatunternehmen nt.

private eye n Privatdetektiv m.

private limited company (BRIT) n (COMM) ≈ Aktiengesellschaft f.

privately ['praɪvɪtlɪ] adv privat; (secretly) insgeheim; a ~ owned company eine Firma im Privatbesitz.

private parts npl (ANAT) Geschlechtsteile pl.

private property n Privatbesitz m.

private school n (fee-paying) Privatschule f.

privation [praɪ'veɪʃən] n Not f.

privatize ['praɪvɪtaɪz] vt privatisieren.

privet ['prɪvɪt] n Liguster m.

privilege ['prɪvɪlɪdʒ] n (advantage) Privileg nt; (honour) Ehre f.

privileged ['prɪvɪlɪdʒd] adj privilegiert; to be ~ to do sth das Privileg or die Ehre haben, etw zu tun.

privy ['prɪvɪ] adj: to be ~ to eingeweiht sein in +acc.

> **PRIVY COUNCIL**
>
> **Privy Council** ist eine Gruppe von königlichen Beratern, die ihren Ursprung im normannischen England hat. Heute hat dieser Rat eine rein formale Funktion. Kabinettsmitglieder und andere bedeutende politische, kirchliche oder juristische Persönlichkeiten sind automatisch Mitglieder.

Privy Councillor (BRIT) n Geheimer Rat m.

prize [praɪz] n Preis m ◆ adj (prize-winning) preisgekrönt; (classic: example) erstklassig ◆ vt schätzen; ~ idiot (inf) Vollidiot m.

prizefighter ['praɪzfaɪtə*] n Preisboxer m.

prizegiving ['praɪzgɪvɪŋ] n Preisverleihung f.

prize money n Geldpreis m.

prizewinner ['praɪzwɪnə*] n Preisträger(in) m(f).

prizewinning ['praɪzwɪnɪŋ] adj preisgekrönt.

PRO n abbr = **public relations officer**.

pro [prəu] n (SPORT) Profi m ◆ prep (in favour of) pro +acc, für +acc; the ~s and cons das Für und Wider.

pro- [prəu] pref (in favour of) Pro-, pro-; ~-disarmament campaign Kampagne f für Abrüstung.

proactive [prəu'æktɪv] adj proaktiv.

probability [prɔbə'bɪlɪtɪ] n Wahrscheinlichkeit f; in all ~ aller Wahrscheinlichkeit nach.

probable ['prɔbəbl] adj wahrscheinlich; it seems ~ that ... es ist wahrscheinlich, dass ...

probably ['prɔbəblɪ] adv wahrscheinlich.

probate ['prəubɪt] n gerichtliche Testamentsbestätigung f.

probation [prə'beɪʃən] n: on ~ (lawbreaker) auf Bewährung; (employee) auf Probe.

probationary [prə'beɪʃnrɪ] adj (period) Probe-.

probationer [prə'beɪʃənə*] n (nurse: female) Lernschwester f; (: male) Lernpfleger m.

probation officer n Bewährungshelfer(in) m(f).

probe [prəub] n (MED, SPACE) Sonde f; (enquiry) Untersuchung f ◆ vt (investigate) untersuchen; (poke) bohren in +dat.

probity ['prəubɪtɪ] n Rechtschaffenheit f.

problem ['prɔbləm] n Problem nt; to have ~s with the car Probleme or Schwierigkeiten mit dem Auto haben; what's the ~? wo fehlts?; I had no ~ finding her ich habe sie ohne Schwierigkeiten gefunden; no ~! kein Problem!

problematic(al) [prɔblə'mætɪk(l)] adj problematisch.

problem-solving ['prɔbləmsɔlvɪŋ] adj (skills, ability) zur Problemlösung ◆ n Problemlösung f.

procedural [prə'siːdjurəl] adj (agreement, problem) verfahrensmäßig.

procedure [prə'siːdʒə*] n Verfahren nt.

proceed [prə'siːd] vi (carry on) fortfahren; (person: go) sich bewegen; to ~ to do sth etw tun; to ~ with fortfahren mit; I am not sure how to ~ ich bin nicht sicher über die weitere Vorgehensweise; to ~ against sb (LAW) gegen jdn gerichtlich vorgehen.

proceedings [prə'siːdɪŋz] npl (organized events) Vorgänge pl; (LAW) Verfahren nt; (records) Protokoll nt.

proceeds ['prəusiːdz] npl Erlös m.

process ['prəusɛs] n (series of actions) Verfahren nt; (BIOL, CHEM) Prozess m ◆ vt (raw materials, food, COMPUT: data) verarbeiten; (application) bearbeiten; (PHOT) entwickeln; in the ~ dabei; to be in the ~ of doing sth (gerade) dabei sein, etw zu tun.

processed cheese ['prəusɛst-], (US) **process cheese** n Schmelzkäse m.

processing ['prəusɛsɪŋ] n (PHOT) Entwickeln nt.

procession [prə'sɛʃən] n Umzug m, Prozession f; wedding/funeral ~ Hochzeits-/Trauerzug m.

proclaim [prə'kleɪm] vt verkünden, proklamieren.

proclamation [prɔklə'meɪʃən] n Proklamation f.

proclivity [prə'klɪvɪtɪ] (form) n Vorliebe f.

procrastinate [prəu'kræstɪneɪt] vi zögern, zaudern.

procrastination [prəukræstɪ'neɪʃən] n Zögern nt, Zaudern nt.

procreation [prəukrɪ'eɪʃən] n Fortpflanzung f.

procurator fiscal ['prɔkjureɪtə-] n (pl **procurators fiscal**) (SCOT) ≈ Staatsanwalt m,

Staatsanwältin *f*.
procure [prə'kjuəˢ] *vt* (*obtain*) beschaffen.
procurement [prə'kjuəmənt] *n* (*COMM*)
Beschaffung *f*.
prod [prɔd] *vt* (*push: with finger, stick etc*)
stoßen, stupsen (*inf*); (*fig: urge*) anspornen
♦ *n* (*with finger, stick etc*) Stoß *m*, Stups *m* (*inf*);
(*fig: reminder*) mahnender Hinweis *m*.
prodigal ['prɔdɪgl] *adj*: ~ **son** verlorener Sohn
m.
prodigious [prə'dɪdʒəs] *adj* (*cost, memory*)
ungeheuer.
prodigy ['prɔdɪdʒɪ] *n* (*person*) Naturtalent *nt*;
child ~ Wunderkind *nt*.
produce [*n* 'prɔdjuːs, *vt* prə'djuːs] *n* (*AGR*)
(Boden)produkte *pl* ♦ *vt* (*result etc*)
hervorbringen; (*goods, commodity*)
produzieren, herstellen; (*BIOL, CHEM*)
erzeugen; (*fig: evidence etc*) liefern;
(: *passport etc*) vorlegen; (*play, film,
programme*) produzieren.
producer [prə'djuːsəˢ] *n* (*person*)
Produzent(in) *m(f)*; (*country, company*)
Produzent *m*, Hersteller *m*.
product ['prɔdʌkt] *n* Produkt *nt*.
production [prə'dʌkʃən] *n* Produktion *f*;
(*THEAT*) Inszenierung *f*; **to go into** ~ (*goods*)
in Produktion gehen; **on** ~ **of** gegen Vorlage
+*gen*.
production agreement (*US*) *n*
Produktivitätsabkommen *nt*.
production line *n* Fließband *nt*,
Fertigungsstraße *f*.
production manager *n*
Produktionsleiter(in) *m(f)*.
productive [prə'dʌktɪv] *adj* produktiv.
productivity [prɔdʌk'tɪvɪtɪ] *n* Produktivität *f*.
productivity agreement (*BRIT*) *n*
Produktivitätsabkommen *nt*.
productivity bonus *n* Leistungszulage *f*.
Prof. *n abbr* (= *professor*) Prof.
profane [prə'feɪn] *adj* (*language etc*) profan;
(*secular*) weltlich.
profess [prə'fɛs] *vt* (*claim*) vorgeben; (*express:
feeling, opinion*) zeigen, bekunden; **I do not**
~ **to be an expert** ich behaupte nicht, ein
Experte zu sein.
professed [prə'fɛst] *adj* (*self-declared*) erklärt.
profession [prə'fɛʃən] *n* Beruf *m*; (*people*)
Berufsstand *m*; **the** ~**s** die gehobenen
Berufe.
professional [prə'fɛʃənl] *adj* (*organization,
musician etc*) Berufs-; (*misconduct, advice*)
beruflich; (*skilful*) professionell ♦ *n* (*doctor,
lawyer, teacher etc*) Fachmann *m*, Fachfrau *f*;
(*SPORT*) Profi *m*; (*skilled person*) Experte *m*,
Expertin *f*; **to seek** ~ **advice**
fachmännischen Rat einholen.
professionalism [prə'fɛʃnəlɪzəm] *n* fachliches
Können *nt*.
professionally [prə'fɛʃnəlɪ] *adv* beruflich; (*for
a living*) berufsmäßig; **I only know him** ~ ich

kenne ihn nur beruflich.
professor [prə'fɛsəˢ] *n* (*BRIT*) Professor(in)
m(f); (*US, CANADA*) Dozent(in) *m(f)*.
professorship [prə'fɛsəʃɪp] *n* Professur *f*.
proffer ['prɔfəˢ] *vt* (*advice, drink, one's hand*)
anbieten; (*apologies*) aussprechen; (*plate etc*)
hinhalten.
proficiency [prə'fɪʃənsɪ] *n* Können *nt*,
Fertigkeiten *pl*.
proficient [prə'fɪʃənt] *adj* fähig; **to be** ~ **at** *or*
in gut sein in +*dat*.
profile ['prəufaɪl] *n* (*of person's face*) Profil *nt*;
(*fig: biography*) Porträt *nt*; **to keep a low** ~
(*fig*) sich zurückhalten; **to have a high** ~ (*fig*)
eine große Rolle spielen.
profit ['prɔfɪt] *n* (*COMM*) Gewinn *m*, Profit *m*
♦ *vi*: **to** ~ **by** *or* **from** (*fig*) profitieren von;
~ **and loss account** Gewinn-und-Verlust-
Rechnung; **to make a** ~ einen Gewinn
machen; **to sell (sth) at a** ~ (etw) mit
Gewinn verkaufen.
profitability [prɔfɪtə'bɪlɪtɪ] *n* Rentabilität *f*.
profitable ['prɔfɪtəbl] *adj* (*business, deal*)
rentabel, einträglich; (*fig: useful*) nützlich.
profit centre *n* Bilanzabteilung *f*.
profiteering [prɔfɪ'tɪərɪŋ] *n* (*pej*) *n*
Profitmacherei *f*.
profit-making ['prɔfɪtmeɪkɪŋ] *adj*
(*organization*) gewinnorientiert.
profit margin *n* Gewinnspanne *f*.
profit-sharing ['prɔfɪtʃɛərɪŋ] *n*
Gewinnbeteiligung *f*.
profits tax (*BRIT*) *n* Ertragssteuer *f*.
profligate ['prɔflɪgɪt] *adj* (*person, spending*)
verschwenderisch; (*waste*) sinnlos; ~ **with**
(*extravagant*) verschwenderisch mit.
pro forma ['prəu'fɔːmə] *adj*: ~ **invoice** Pro-
forma-Rechnung *f*.
profound [prə'faund] *adj* (*shock*) schwer, tief;
(*effect, differences*) weitreichend, weit
reichend; (*idea, book*) tief schürfend.
profuse [prə'fjuːs] *adj* (*apologies*)
überschwänglich.
profusely [prə'fjuːslɪ] *adv* (*apologise, thank*)
vielmals; (*sweat, bleed*) stark.
profusion [prə'fjuːʒən] *n* Überfülle *f*.
progeny ['prɔdʒɪnɪ] *n* Nachkommenschaft *f*.
prognoses [prɔg'nəusiːz] *npl of* **prognosis**.
prognosis [prɔg'nəusɪs] (*pl* **prognoses**) *n* (*MED,
fig*) Prognose *f*.
program [prəu'græm] (*COMPUT*) *n* Programm
nt ♦ *vt* programmieren.
programme, (*US*) **program** ['prəugræm] *n*
Programm *nt* ♦ *vt* (*machine, system*)
programmieren.
programmer ['prəugræməˢ] *n*
Programmierer(in) *m(f)*.
programming, (*US*) **programing**
['prəugræmɪŋ] *n* Programmierung *f*.
programming language *n*
Programmiersprache *f*.
progress [*n* 'prəugrɛs, *vi* prə'grɛs] *n* Fortschritt

m; (*improvement*) Fortschritte *pl* ♦ *vi*
(*advance*) vorankommen; (*become higher in
rank*) aufsteigen; (*continue*) sich fortsetzen;
in ~ (*meeting, battle, match*) im Gange; **to
make** ~ Fortschritte machen.
progression [prə'grɛʃən] *n* (*development*)
Fortschritt *m*; (*series*) Folge *f*.
progressive [prə'grɛsɪv] *adj* (*enlightened*)
fortschrittlich; (*gradual*) fortschreitend.
progressively [prə'grɛsɪvlɪ] *adv* (*gradually*)
zunehmend.
progress report *n* (*MED*) Fortschrittsbericht
m; (*ADMIN*) Tätigkeitsbericht *m*.
prohibit [prə'hɪbɪt] *vt* (*ban*) verbieten; **to** ~ **sb
from doing sth** jdm verbieten *or*
untersagen, etw zu tun; **"smoking ~ed"**
„Rauchen verboten".
prohibition [prəuɪ'bɪʃən] *n* Verbot *nt*; **P~** (*US*)
Prohibition *f*.
prohibitive [prə'hɪbɪtɪv] *adj* (*cost etc*)
untragbar.
project [*n* 'prɔdʒɛkt, *vt, vi* prə'dʒɛkt] *n* (*plan,
scheme*) Projekt *nt*; (*SCOL*) Referat *nt* ♦ *vt*
(*plan*) planen; (*estimate*) schätzen,
voraussagen; (*light, film, picture*) projizieren
♦ *vi* (*stick out*) hervorragen.
projectile [prə'dʒɛktaɪl] *n* Projektil *nt*,
Geschoss *nt*, Geschoß *nt* (*ÖSTERR*).
projection [prə'dʒɛkʃən] *n* (*estimate*)
Schätzung *f*, Voraussage *f*; (*overhang*)
Vorsprung *m*; (*CINE*) Projektion *f*.
projectionist [prə'dʒɛkʃənɪst] *n*
Filmvorführer(in) *m(f)*.
projection room *n* Vorführraum *m*.
projector [prə'dʒɛktə*] *n* Projektor *m*.
proletarian [prəulɪ'tɛərɪən] *adj* proletarisch.
proletariat [prəulɪ'tɛərɪət] *n*: **the** ~ das
Proletariat.
proliferate [prə'lɪfəreɪt] *vi* sich vermehren.
proliferation [prəlɪfə'reɪʃən] *n* Verbreitung *f*.
prolific [prə'lɪfɪk] *adj* (*artist, writer*) produktiv.
prologue, (*US*) **prolog** ['prəulɔg] *n* (*of play,
book*) Prolog *m*.
prolong [prə'lɔŋ] *vt* verlängern.
prom [prɔm] *n abbr* = **promenade**; (*MUS*)
= **promenade concert**; (*US: college ball*)
Studentenball *m*.

PROM

Prom (*promenade concert*) ist in Großbritannien
ein Konzert, bei dem ein Teil der Zuhörer steht
(*ursprünglich spazieren ging*). Die seit 1895
alljährlich stattfindenden **proms** (*seit 1941 immer
in der Londoner Royal Albert Hall*) zählen zu den
bedeutendsten Musikereignissen in England. Der
letzte Abend der **proms** steht ganz um Zeichen
des Patriotismus und gipfelt im Singen des Lieds
„Land of Hope and Glory". In den USA und
Kanada steht das Wort für **promenade**, ein Ball
an einer **high school** oder einem **college**.

---

promenade [prɔmə'nɑːd] *n* Promenade *f*.
promenade concert (*BRIT*) *n*
Promenadenkonzert *nt*.
promenade deck *n* Promenadendeck *nt*.
prominence ['prɔmɪnəns] *n* (*importance*)
Bedeutung *f*; **to rise to** ~ bekannt
werden.
prominent ['prɔmɪnənt] *adj* (*person*)
prominent; (*thing*) bedeutend; (*very
noticeable*) herausragend; **he is** ~ **in the field
of science** er ist eine führende
Persönlichkeit im naturwissenschaftlichen
Bereich.
prominently ['prɔmɪnəntlɪ] *adv* (*display, set*)
deutlich sichtbar; **he figured** ~ **in the case**
er spielte in dem Fall eine bedeutende
Rolle.
promiscuity [prɔmɪs'kjuːɪtɪ] *n* Promiskuität *f*.
promiscuous [prə'mɪskjuəs] *adj* promisk.
promise ['prɔmɪs] *n* (*vow*) Versprechen *nt*;
(*potential, hope*) Hoffnung *f* ♦ *vi* versprechen
♦ *vt*: **to** ~ **sb sth**, ~ **sth to sb** jdm etw
versprechen; **to make/break/keep a** ~ ein
Versprechen geben/brechen/halten; **a
young man of** ~ ein viel versprechender
junger Mann; **she shows** ~ sie gibt zu
Hoffnungen Anlass; **it** ~**s to be lively**
es verspricht lebhaft zu werden; **to** ~
(**sb**) **to do sth** (jdm) versprechen, etw zu
tun.
promising ['prɔmɪsɪŋ] *adj* viel versprechend.
promissory note ['prɔmɪsərɪ-] *n* Schuldschein
m.
promontory ['prɔməntrɪ] *n* Felsvorsprung
m.
promote [prə'məut] *vt* (*employee*) befördern;
(*advertise*) werben für; (*encourage: peace etc*)
fördern; **the team was** ~**d to the first
division** (*BRIT: FOOTBALL*) die Mannschaft
stieg in die erste Division auf.
promoter [prə'məutə*] *n* (*of concert, event*)
Veranstalter(in) *m(f)*; (*of cause, idea*)
Förderer *m*, Förderin *f*.
promotion [prə'məuʃən] *n* (*at work*)
Beförderung *f*; (*of product, event*) Werbung *f*;
(*of idea*) Förderung *f*; (*publicity campaign*)
Werbekampagne *f*.
prompt [prɔmpt] *adj* prompt, sofortig ♦ *adv*
(*exactly*) pünktlich ♦ *n* (*COMPUT*) Prompt *m*
♦ *vt* (*cause*) veranlassen; (*when talking*) auf
die Sprünge helfen *+dat*; (*THEAT*) soufflieren
+dat; **they're very** ~ (*punctual*) sie sind sehr
pünktlich; **he was** ~ **to accept** er nahm
unverzüglich an; **at 8 o'clock** ~ (um) Punkt
8 Uhr; **to** ~ **sb to do sth** jdn dazu
veranlassen, etw zu tun.
prompter ['prɔmptə*] *n* (*THEAT*) Souffleur *m*,
Souffleuse *f*.
promptly ['prɔmptlɪ] *adv* (*immediately*) sofort;
(*exactly*) pünktlich.
promptness ['prɔmptnɪs] *n* Promptheit *f*.
promulgate ['prɔmǝlgeɪt] *vt* (*policy*) bekannt

machen, verkünden; (*idea*) verbreiten.

prone [prəun] *adj* (*face down*) in Bauchlage; **to be ~ to sth** zu etw neigen; **she is ~ to burst into tears if** ... sie neigt dazu, in Tränen auszubrechen, wenn ...

prong [prɔŋ] *n* (*of fork*) Zinke *f*.

pronoun ['prəunaun] *n* Pronomen *nt*, Fürwort *nt*.

pronounce [prə'nauns] *vt* (*word*) aussprechen; (*give verdict, opinion*) erklären ♦ *vi*: **to ~ (up)on** sich äußern zu; **they ~d him dead/unfit to drive** sie erklärten ihn für tot/ fahruntüchtig.

pronounced [prə'naunst] *adj* (*noticeable*) ausgeprägt, deutlich.

pronouncement [prə'naunsmənt] *n* Erklärung *f*.

pronto ['prɔntəu] (*inf*) *adv* fix.

pronunciation [prənʌnsɪ'eɪʃən] *n* Aussprache *f*.

proof [pru:f] *n* (*evidence*) Beweis *m*; (*TYP*) (Korrektur)fahne *f* ♦ *adj*: **~ against** sicher vor +*dat*; **to be 70 % ~** (*alcohol*) ≈ einen Alkoholgehalt von 40% haben.

proofreader ['pru:fri:də*] *n* Korrektor(in) *m(f)*.

Prop. *abbr* (*COMM*: = *proprietor*) Inh.

prop [prɔp] *n* (*support, also fig*) Stütze *f* ♦ *vt* (*lean*): **to ~ sth against sth** etw an etw *acc* lehnen.

▶ **prop up** *vt sep* (*thing*) (ab)stützen; (*fig: government, industry*) unterstützen.

propaganda [prɔpə'gændə] *n* Propaganda *f*.

propagate ['prɔpəgeɪt] *vt* (*plants*) züchten; (*ideas etc*) propagieren ♦ *vi* (*plants, animals*) sich fortpflanzen.

propagation [prɔpə'geɪʃən] *n* (*of ideas etc*) Propagierung *f*; (*of plants, animals*) Fortpflanzung *f*.

propel [prə'pɛl] *vt* (*vehicle, machine*) antreiben; (*person*) schubsen; (*fig: person*) treiben.

propeller [prə'pɛlə*] *n* Propeller *m*.

propelling pencil [prə'pɛlɪŋ-] (*BRIT*) *n* Drehbleistift *m*.

propensity [prə'pɛnsɪtɪ] *n*: **a ~ for** *or* **to sth** ein Hang *m or* eine Neigung zu etw; **to have a ~ to do sth** dazu neigen, etw zu tun.

proper ['prɔpə*] *adj* (*genuine, correct*) richtig; (*socially acceptable*) schicklich; (*inf: real*) echt; **the town/city ~** die Stadt selbst; **to go through the ~ channels** den Dienstweg einhalten.

properly ['prɔpəlɪ] *adv* (*eat, work*) richtig; (*behave*) anständig.

proper noun *n* Eigenname *m*.

property ['prɔpətɪ] *n* (*possessions*) Eigentum *nt*; (*building and its land*) Grundstück *nt*; (*quality*) Eigenschaft *f*; **it's their ~** es gehört ihnen.

property developer *n* ≈ Grundstücksmakler(in) *m(f)*.

property market *n* Immobilienmarkt *m*.

property owner *n* Grundbesitzer(in) *m(f)*.

property tax *n* Vermögenssteuer *f*.

prophecy ['prɔfɪsɪ] *n* Prophezeiung *f*.

prophesy ['prɔfɪsaɪ] *vt* prophezeien ♦ *vi* Prophezeiungen machen.

prophet ['prɔfɪt] *n* Prophet *m*; **~ of doom** Unheilsprophet(in) *m(f)*.

prophetic [prə'fɛtɪk] *adj* prophetisch.

proportion [prə'pɔːʃən] *n* (*part*) Teil *m*; (*number: of people, things*) Anteil *m*; (*ratio*) Verhältnis *nt*; **in ~ to** im Verhältnis zu; **to be out of all ~ to sth** in keinem Verhältnis zu etw stehen; **to get sth in/out of ~** etw im richtigen/falschen Verhältnis sehen; **a sense of ~** (*fig*) ein Sinn für das Wesentliche.

proportional [prə'pɔːʃənl] *adj*: **~ to** proportional zu.

proportional representation *n* Verhältniswahlrecht *nt*.

proportionate [prə'pɔːʃənɪt] *adj* = **proportional**.

proposal [prə'pəuzl] *n* (*plan*) Vorschlag *m*; **~ (of marriage)** Heiratsantrag *m*.

propose [prə'pəuz] *vt* (*plan, idea*) vorschlagen; (*motion*) einbringen; (*toast*) ausbringen ♦ *vi* (*offer marriage*) einen Heiratsantrag machen; **to ~ to do sth** *or* **doing sth** (*intend*) die Absicht haben, etw zu tun.

proposer [prə'pəuzə*] *n* (*of motion etc*) Antragsteller(in) *m(f)*.

proposition [prɔpə'zɪʃən] *n* (*statement*) These *f*; (*offer*) Angebot *nt*; **to make sb a ~** jdm ein Angebot machen.

propound [prə'paund] *vt* (*idea etc*) darlegen.

proprietary [prə'praɪətərɪ] *adj* (*brand, medicine*) Marken-; (*tone, manner*) besitzergreifend.

proprietor [prə'praɪətə*] *n* (*of hotel, shop etc*) Inhaber(in) *m(f)*; (*of newspaper*) Besitzer(in) *m(f)*.

propriety [prə'praɪətɪ] *n* (*seemliness*) Schicklichkeit *f*.

props [prɔps] *npl* (*THEAT*) Requisiten *pl*.

propulsion [prə'pʌlʃən] *n* Antrieb *m*.

pro rata [prəu'rɑːtə] *adj, adv* anteilmäßig; **on a ~ basis** anteilmäßig.

prosaic [prəu'zeɪɪk] *adj* prosaisch, nüchtern.

Pros. Atty. (*US*) *abbr* = **prosecuting attorney**.

proscribe [prə'skraɪb] (*form*) *vt* verbieten, untersagen.

prose [prəuz] *n* (*not poetry*) Prosa *f*; (*BRIT: SCOL: translation*) Übersetzung *f* in die Fremdsprache.

prosecute ['prɔsɪkjuːt] *vt* (*LAW: person*) strafrechtlich verfolgen; (: *case*) die Anklage vertreten in +*dat*.

prosecuting attorney ['prɔsɪkjuːtɪŋ-] (*US*) *n* Staatsanwalt *m*, Staatsanwältin *f*.

prosecution [prɔsɪ'kjuːʃən] *n* (*LAW: action*) strafrechtliche Verfolgung *f*; (: *accusing side*) Anklage(vertretung) *f*.

prosecutor ['prɔsɪkjuːtə*] *n* Anklagevertreter(in) *m(f)*; (*also:* **public ~**)

Staatsanwalt *m*, Staatsanwältin *f*.

prospect [*n* 'prɒspɛkt, *vi* prə'spɛkt] *n* Aussicht *f* ♦ *vi*: **to ~ (for)** suchen (nach); **prospects** *npl* (*for work etc*) Aussichten *pl*, Chancen *pl*; **we are faced with the ~ of higher unemployment** wir müssen mit der Möglichkeit rechnen, dass die Arbeitslosigkeit steigt.

prospecting ['prɒspɛktɪŋ] *n* (*for gold, oil etc*) Suche *f*.

prospective [prə'spɛktɪv] *adj* (*son-in-law*) zukünftig; (*customer, candidate*) voraussichtlich.

prospectus [prə'spɛktəs] *n* (*of college, company*) Prospekt *m*.

prosper ['prɒspə*] *vi* (*person*) Erfolg haben; (*business, city etc*) gedeihen, florieren.

prosperity [prɒ'spɛrɪtɪ] *n* Wohlstand *m*.

prosperous ['prɒspərəs] *adj* (*person*) wohlhabend; (*business, city etc*) blühend.

prostate ['prɒsteɪt] *n* (*also: ~* **gland**) Prostata *f*.

prostitute ['prɒstɪtjuːt] *n* (*female*) Prostituierte *f*; (*male*) männliche(r) Prostituierte(r) *m*, Strichjunge *m* (*inf*) ♦ *vt*: **to ~ o.s.** (*fig*) sich prostituieren, sich unter Wert verkaufen.

prostitution [prɒstɪ'tjuːʃən] *n* Prostitution *f*.

prostrate ['prɒstreɪt] *adj* (*face down*) ausgestreckt (liegend); (*fig*) niedergeschmettert ♦ *vt*: **to ~ o.s. before** sich zu Boden werfen vor *+dat*.

protagonist [prə'tægənɪst] *n* (*of idea, movement*) Verfechter(in) *m(f)*; (*THEAT, LITER*) Protagonist(in) *m(f)*.

protect [prə'tɛkt] *vt* schützen.

protection [prə'tɛkʃən] *n* Schutz *m*; **police ~** Polizeischutz *m*.

protectionism [prə'tɛkʃənɪzəm] *n* Protektionismus *m*.

protection racket *n* Organisation *f* zur Erpressung von Schutzgeld.

protective [prə'tɛktɪv] *adj* (*clothing, layer etc*) Schutz-; (*person*) fürsorglich; **~ custody** Schutzhaft *f*.

protector [prə'tɛktə*] *n* (*person*) Beschützer(in) *m(f)*; (*device*) Schutz *m*.

protégé(e) ['prəʊtɪʒeɪ] *n* Schützling *m*.

protein ['prəʊtiːn] *n* Protein *nt*, Eiweiß *nt*.

pro tem [prəʊ'tɛm] *adv abbr* (= *pro tempore*) vorläufig.

protest [*n* 'prəʊtɛst, *vi, vt* prə'tɛst] *n* Protest *m* ♦ *vi*: **to ~ about** *or* **against** *or* **at sth** gegen etw protestieren ♦ *vt*: **to ~ (that)** (*insist*) beteuern(, dass).

Protestant ['prɒtɪstənt] *adj* protestantisch ♦ *n* Protestant(in) *m(f)*.

protester [prə'tɛstə*] *n* (*in demonstration*) Demonstrant(in) *m(f)*.

protest march *n* Protestmarsch *m*.

protestor [prə'tɛstə*] *n* = **protester**.

protocol ['prəʊtəkɒl] *n* Protokoll *nt*.

prototype ['prəʊtətaɪp] *n* Prototyp *m*.

protracted [prə'træktɪd] *adj* (*meeting etc*) langwierig, sich hinziehend; (*absence*) länger.

protractor [prə'træktə*] *n* (*GEOM*) Winkelmesser *m*.

protrude [prə'truːd] *vi* (*rock, ledge, teeth*) vorstehen.

protuberance [prə'tjuːbərəns] *n* Auswuchs *m*.

proud [praʊd] *adj* stolz; (*arrogant*) hochmütig; **~ of sb/sth** stolz auf jdn/etw; **to be ~ to do sth** stolz (darauf) sein, etw zu tun; **to do sb/o.s. ~** (*inf*) jdn/sich verwöhnen.

proudly ['praʊdlɪ] *adv* stolz.

prove [pruːv] *vt* beweisen ♦ *vi*: **to ~ (to be) correct** sich als richtig herausstellen *or* erweisen; **to ~ (o.s./itself) useful** sich als nützlich erweisen; **he was ~d right in the end** er hat schließlich Recht behalten.

proverb ['prɒvəːb] *n* Sprichwort *nt*.

proverbial [prə'vəːbɪəl] *adj* sprichwörtlich.

provide [prə'vaɪd] *vt* (*food, money, shelter etc*) zur Verfügung stellen; (*answer, example etc*) liefern; **to ~ sb with sth** jdm etw zur Verfügung stellen.

▶ **provide for** *vt fus* (*person*) sorgen für; (*future event*) vorsorgen für.

provided [prə'vaɪdɪd] *conj*: **~ (that)** vorausgesetzt(, dass).

Providence ['prɒvɪdəns] *n* die Vorsehung.

providing [prə'vaɪdɪŋ] *conj*: **~ (that)** vorausgesetzt(, dass).

province ['prɒvɪns] *n* (*of country*) Provinz *f*; (*responsibility etc*) Bereich *m*, Gebiet *nt*; **provinces** *npl*: **the ~s** außerhalb der Hauptstadt liegende Landesteile, Provinz *f*.

provincial [prə'vɪnʃəl] *adj* (*town, newspaper etc*) Provinz-; (*pej: parochial*) provinziell.

provision [prə'vɪʒən] *n* (*supplying*) Bereitstellung *f*; (*preparation*) Vorsorge *f*, Vorkehrungen *pl*; (*stipulation, clause*) Bestimmung *f*; **provisions** *npl* (*food*) Proviant *m*; **to make ~ for** vorsorgen für; (*for people*) sorgen für; **there's no ~ for this in the contract** dies ist im Vertrag nicht vorgesehen.

provisional [prə'vɪʒənl] *adj* vorläufig, provisorisch ♦ *n*: **P~** (*IRISH: POL*) Mitglied *der provisorischen Irisch-Republikanischen Armee*.

provisional licence (*BRIT*) *n* (*AUT*) vorläufige Fahrerlaubnis *f*.

provisionally [prə'vɪʒnəlɪ] *adv* vorläufig.

proviso [prə'vaɪzəʊ] *n* Vorbehalt *m*; **with the ~ that ...** unter dem Vorbehalt, dass ...

Provo ['prɒvəʊ] (*IRISH: inf*) *n abbr* (*POL*) = **Provisional**.

provocation [prɒvə'keɪʃən] *n* Provokation *f*, Herausforderung *f*; **to be under ~** provoziert werden.

provocative [prə'vɒkətɪv] *adj* provozierend, herausfordernd; (*sexually stimulating*) aufreizend.

provoke [prə'vəuk] *vt* (*person*) provozieren, herausfordern; (*fight*) herbeiführen; (*reaction etc*) hervorrufen; **to ~ sb to do** *or* **into doing sth** jdn dazu provozieren, etw zu tun.

provost ['prɔvəst] *n* (*BRIT: of university*) Dekan *m*; (*SCOT*) Bürgermeister(in) *m(f)*.

prow [prau] *n* (*of boat*) Bug *m*.

prowess ['prauɪs] *n* Können *nt*, Fähigkeiten *pl*; **his ~ as a footballer** sein fußballerisches Können.

prowl [praul] *vi* (*also:* **~ about, ~ around**) schleichen ♦ *n*: **on the ~** auf Streifzug.

prowler ['praulə*] *n* Herumtreiber *m*.

proximity [prɔk'sɪmɪtɪ] *n* Nähe *f*.

proxy ['prɔksɪ] *n*: **by ~** durch einen Stellvertreter.

prude [pru:d] *n*: **to be a ~** prüde sein.

prudence ['pru:dns] *n* Klugheit *f*, Umsicht *f*.

prudent ['pru:dnt] *adj* (*sensible*) klug.

prudish ['pru:dɪʃ] *adj* prüde.

prune [pru:n] *n* Backpflaume *f* ♦ *vt* (*plant*) stutzen, beschneiden.

pry [praɪ] *vi*: **to ~ (into)** seine Nase hineinstecken (in +*acc*), herumschnüffeln (in +*dat*).

PS *abbr* (= *postscript*) PS.

psalm [sɑ:m] *n* Psalm *m*.

PSAT (*US*) *n abbr* (= *Preliminary Scholastic Aptitude Test*) Schuleignungstest.

PSBR (*BRIT*) *n abbr* (*ECON:* = *public sector borrowing requirement*) staatlicher Kreditbedarf *m*.

pseud [sju:d] (*BRIT: inf: pej*) *n* Angeber(in) *m(f)*.

pseudo- ['sju:dəu] *pref* Pseudo-.

pseudonym ['sju:dənɪm] *n* Pseudonym *nt*.

PSHE (*BRIT*) *n abbr* (*SCOL*) = *personal, social and health education*.

PST (*US*) *abbr* (= *Pacific Standard Time*) *pazifische Standardzeit*.

psyche ['saɪkɪ] *n* Psyche *f*.

psychedelic [saɪkə'delɪk] *adj* (*drug*) psychedelisch; (*clothes, colours*) in psychedelischen Farben.

psychiatric [saɪkɪ'ætrɪk] *adj* psychiatrisch.

psychiatrist [saɪ'kaɪətrɪst] *n* Psychiater(in) *m(f)*.

psychiatry [saɪ'kaɪətrɪ] *n* Psychiatrie *f*.

psychic ['saɪkɪk] *adj* (*person*) übersinnlich begabt; (*damage, disorder*) psychisch ♦ *n* Mensch *m* mit übersinnlichen Fähigkeiten.

psycho ['saɪkəu] (*US: inf*) *n* Verrückte(r) *f(m)*.

psychoanalyse [saɪkəu'ænəlaɪz] *vt* psychoanalytisch behandeln, psychoanalysieren.

psychoanalysis [saɪkəuə'nælɪsɪs] *n* Psychoanalyse *f*.

psychoanalyst [saɪkəu'ænəlɪst] *n* Psychoanalytiker(in) *m(f)*.

psychological [saɪkə'lɔdʒɪkl] *adj* psychologisch.

psychologist [saɪ'kɔlədʒɪst] *n* Psychologe *m*, Psychologin *f*.

psychology [saɪ'kɔlədʒɪ] *n* (*science*) Psychologie *f*; (*character*) Psyche *f*.

psychopath ['saɪkəupæθ] *n* Psychopath(in) *m(f)*.

psychoses [saɪ'kəusi:z] *npl of* **psychosis**.

psychosis [saɪ'kəusɪs] (*pl* **psychoses**) *n* Psychose *f*.

psychosomatic ['saɪkəusə'mætɪk] *adj* psychosomatisch.

psychotherapy [saɪkəu'θεrəpɪ] *n* Psychotherapie *f*.

psychotic [saɪ'kɔtɪk] *adj* psychotisch.

PT (*BRIT*) *n abbr* (*SCOL:* = *physical training*) Turnen *nt*.

Pt *abbr* (*in place names:* = *Point*) Pt.

pt *abbr* = **pint; point**.

PTA *n abbr* (= *Parent-Teacher Association*) Lehrer- und Elternverband.

Pte (*BRIT*) *abbr* (*MIL*) = *private*.

PTO *abbr* (= *please turn over*) b. w.

PTV (*US*) *n abbr* (= *pay television*) Pay-TV *nt*; (= *public television*) öffentliches Fernsehen *nt*.

pub [pʌb] *n* = **public house**

PUB

Pub *ist ein Gasthaus mit einer Lizenz zum Ausschank von alkoholischen Getränken. Ein* **pub** *besteht meist aus verschiedenen gemütlichen (lounge, snug) oder einfacheren Räumen (public bar), in der oft auch Spiele wie Darts, Domino und Poolbilliard zur Verfügung stehen. In* **pubs** *werden vor allem mittags oft auch Mahlzeiten angeboten.* **Pubs** *sind normalerweise von 11 bis 23 Uhr geöffnet, aber manchmal nachmittags geschlossen.*

---

pub-crawl ['pʌbkrɔ:l] (*inf*) *n*: **to go on a ~** eine Kneipentour machen.

pub lunch *n* in Pubs servierter Imbiss.

puberty ['pju:bətɪ] *n* Pubertät *f*.

pubic ['pju:bɪk] *adj* (*hair*) Scham-; **~ bone** Schambein *nt*.

public ['pʌblɪk] *adj* öffentlich ♦ *n*: **the ~** (*in general*) die Öffentlichkeit; (*particular set of people*) das Publikum; **to be ~ knowledge** allgemein bekannt sein; **to make sth ~** etw bekannt machen; **to go ~** (*COMM*) in eine Aktiengesellschaft umgewandelt werden; **in ~** in aller Öffentlichkeit; **the general ~** die Allgemeinheit.

public-address system [pʌblɪkə'dres-] *n* Lautsprecheranlage *f*.

publican ['pʌblɪkən] *n* Gastwirt(in) *m(f)*.

publication [pʌblɪ'keɪʃən] *n* Veröffentlichung *f*.

public company *n* Aktiengesellschaft *f*.

public convenience (*BRIT*) *n* öffentliche Toilette *f*.

public holiday *n* gesetzlicher Feiertag *m*.

public house (*BRIT*) *n* Gaststätte *f*.
publicity [pʌb'lɪsɪtɪ] *n* (*information*) Werbung *f*;
(*attention*) Publicity *f*.
publicize ['pʌblɪsaɪz] *vt* (*fact*) bekannt
machen; (*event*) Publicity machen für.
public limited company *n* ≈
Aktiengesellschaft *f*.
publicly ['pʌblɪklɪ] *adv* öffentlich; **to be**
~ owned (*COMM*) in Staatsbesitz sein.
public opinion *n* die öffentliche Meinung.
public ownership *n*: **to be taken into ~**
verstaatlicht werden.
Public Prosecutor *n* Staatsanwalt *m*,
Staatsanwältin *f*.
public relations *n* Publicrelations *pl*, Public
Relations *pl*, Öffentlichkeitsarbeit *f*.
public relations officer *n* Beauftragte(r) *f(m)*
für Öffentlichkeitsarbeit.
public school *n* (*BRIT*) Privatschule *f*; (*US*)
staatliche Schule *f*.

PUBLIC SCHOOL

Public school *bezeichnet vor allem in England
eine weiterführende Privatschule, meist eine
Internatsschule mit hohem Prestige, an die oft
auch eine* **preparatory school** *angeschlossen
ist.* **Public schools** *werden von einem
Schulbeirat verwaltet und durch Stiftungen und
Schulgelder, die an den bekanntesten Schulen wie
Eton, Harrow und Westminster sehr hoch sein
können, finanziert. Die meisten Schüler einer*
public school *gehen zur Universität, oft nach
Oxford oder Cambridge. Viele Industrielle,
Abgeordnete und hohe Beamte haben eine* **public
school** *besucht. In Schottland und den USA
bedeutet* **public school** *eine öffentliche, vom
Steuerzahler finanzierte Schule.*

---

public sector *n*: **the ~** der öffentliche Sektor.
public-service vehicle [pʌblɪk'sɜːvɪs-] (*BRIT*)
n öffentliches Verkehrsmittel *nt*.
public-spirited [pʌblɪk'spɪrɪtɪd] *adj*
gemeinsinnig.
public transport *n* öffentliche
Verkehrsmittel *pl*.
public utility *n* öffentlicher
Versorgungsbetrieb *m*.
public works *npl* öffentliche Bauprojekte *pl*.
publish ['pʌblɪʃ] *vt* veröffentlichen.
publisher ['pʌblɪʃə*] *n* (*person*) Verleger(in)
m(f); (*company*) Verlag *m*.
publishing ['pʌblɪʃɪŋ] *n* (*profession*) das
Verlagswesen.
publishing company *n* Verlag *m*,
Verlagshaus *nt*.
puce [pjuːs] *adj* (*face*) hochrot.
puck [pʌk] *n* (*ICE HOCKEY*) Puck *m*.
pucker ['pʌkə*] *vi* (*lips, face*) sich verziehen;
(*fabric etc*) Falten werfen ♦ *vt* (*lips, face*)
verziehen; (*fabric etc*) Falten machen in +*acc*.
pudding ['pudɪŋ] *n* (*cooked sweet food*)

Süßspeise *f*; (*BRIT: dessert*) Nachtisch *m*; **rice**
~ Milchreis *m*; **black ~**, (*US*) **blood ~** ≈
Blutwurst *f*.
puddle ['pʌdl] *n* (*of rain*) Pfütze *f*; (*of blood*)
Lache *f*.
puerile ['pjuəraɪl] *adj* kindisch.
Puerto Rico ['pwɜːtəu'riːkəu] *n* Puerto Rico *nt*.
puff [pʌf] *n* (*of cigarette, pipe*) Zug *m*; (*gasp*)
Schnaufer *m*; (*of air*) Stoß *m*; (*of smoke*)
Wolke *f* ♦ *vt* (*also:* **~ on**, **~ at**: *cigarette, pipe*)
ziehen an +*dat* ♦ *vi* (*gasp*) keuchen,
schnaufen.
▶ **puff out** *vt* (*one's chest*) herausdrücken;
(*one's cheeks*) aufblasen.
puffed [pʌft] (*inf*) *adj* außer Puste.
puffin ['pʌfɪn] *n* Papageientaucher *m*.
puff pastry, (*US*) **puff paste** *n* Blätterteig *m*.
puffy ['pʌfɪ] *adj* (*eye*) geschwollen; (*face*)
aufgedunsen.
pugnacious [pʌg'neɪʃəs] *adj* (*person*)
streitsüchtig.
pull [pul] *vt* (*rope, handle etc*) ziehen an +*dat*;
(*cart etc*) ziehen; (*close: curtain*) zuziehen;
(: *blind*) herunterlassen; (*inf: attract: people*)
anlocken; (: *sexual partner*) aufreißen; (*pint of
beer*) zapfen ♦ *vi* ziehen ♦ *n* (*also fig: attraction*)
Anziehungskraft *f*; **to ~ the trigger**
abdrücken; **to ~ a face** ein Gesicht
schneiden; **to ~ a muscle** sich *dat* einen
Muskel zerren; **not to ~ one's** *or* **any**
punches (*fig*) sich *dat* keine Zurückhaltung
auferlegen; **to ~ to pieces** (*fig*) zerreißen; **to**
~ one's weight (*fig*) sich ins Zeug legen; **to**
~ o.s. together sich zusammenreißen; **to**
~ sb's leg (*fig*) jdn auf den Arm nehmen; **to**
~ strings (for sb) seine Beziehungen (für
jdn) spielen lassen; **to give sth a ~** an etw
dat ziehen.
▶ **pull apart** *vt* (*separate*) trennen.
▶ **pull away** *vi* (*AUT*) losfahren.
▶ **pull back** *vi* (*retreat*) sich zurückziehen; (*fig*)
einen Rückzieher machen (*inf*).
▶ **pull down** *vt* (*building*) abreißen.
▶ **pull in** *vi* (*AUT: at kerb*) anhalten; (*RAIL*)
einfahren ♦ *vt* (*inf: money*) einsacken;
(*crowds, people*) anlocken; (*police: suspect*)
sich *dat* schnappen (*inf*).
▶ **pull off** *vt* (*clothes etc*) ausziehen; (*fig:
difficult thing*) schaffen, bringen (*inf*).
▶ **pull out** *vi* (*AUT: from kerb*) losfahren;
(: *when overtaking*) ausscheren; (*RAIL*)
ausfahren; (*withdraw*) sich zurückziehen
♦ *vt* (*extract*) herausziehen.
▶ **pull over** *vi* (*AUT*) an den Straßenrand
fahren.
▶ **pull through** *vi* (*MED*) durchkommen.
▶ **pull up** *vi* (*AUT, RAIL: stop*) anhalten ♦ *vt*
(*raise*) hochziehen; (*uproot*) herausreißen;
(*chair*) heranrücken.
pullback ['pulbæk] *n* (*retreat*) Rückzug *m*.
pulley ['pulɪ] *n* Flaschenzug *m*.
pull-out ['pulaut] *n* (*in magazine*) Beilage *f* (*zum*

Heraustrennen).

pullover ['puləʊvə'] *n* Pullover *m*.

pulp [pʌlp] *n* (*of fruit*) Fruchtfleisch *nt*; (*for paper*) (Papier)brei *m*; (*LITER: pej*) Schund *m* ♦ *adj* (*pej: magazine, novel*) Schund-; **to reduce sth to a** ~ etw zu Brei machen.

pulpit ['pʊlpɪt] *n* Kanzel *f*.

pulsate [pʌl'seɪt] *vi* (*heart*) klopfen; (*music*) pulsieren.

pulse [pʌls] *n* (*ANAT*) Puls *m*; (*rhythm*) Rhythmus *m*; **pulses** *npl* (*BOT*) Hülsenfrüchte *pl*; (*TECH*) Impuls *m* ♦ *vi* pulsieren; **to take** *or* **feel sb's** ~ jdm den Puls fühlen; **to have one's finger on the** ~ (**of sth**) (*fig*) den Finger am Puls (einer Sache *gen*) haben.

pulverize ['pʌlvəraɪz] *vt* pulverisieren; (*fig: destroy*) vernichten.

puma ['pjuːmə] *n* Puma *m*.

pumice ['pʌmɪs] *n* (*also:* ~ **stone**) Bimsstein *m*.

pummel ['pʌml] *vt* mit Faustschlägen bearbeiten.

pump [pʌmp] *n* Pumpe *f*; (*petrol pump*) Zapfsäule *f*; (*shoe*) Turnschuh *m* ♦ *vt* pumpen; **to** ~ **sb for information** jdn aushorchen; **she had her stomach** ~**ed** ihr wurde der Magen ausgepumpt.

▶ **pump up** *vt* (*inflate*) aufpumpen.

pumpkin ['pʌmpkɪn] *n* Kürbis *m*.

pun [pʌn] *n* Wortspiel *nt*.

punch [pʌntʃ] *n* (*blow*) Schlag *m*; (*fig: force*) Schlagkraft *f*; (*tool*) Locher *m*; (*drink*) Bowle *f*, Punsch *m* ♦ *vt* (*hit*) schlagen; (*make a hole in*) lochen; **to** ~ **a hole in sth** ein Loch in etw *acc* stanzen.

▶ **punch in** (*US*) *vi* (bei Arbeitsbeginn) stempeln.

▶ **punch out** (*US*) *vi* (bei Arbeitsende) stempeln.

Punch and Judy show *n* ≈ Kasper(le)theater *nt*.

punch card, (*US*) **punched card** [pʌntʃt-] *n* Lochkarte *f*.

punch-drunk ['pʌntʃdrʌŋk] (*BRIT*) *adj* (*boxer*) angeschlagen.

punch line *n* Pointe *f*.

punch-up ['pʌntʃʌp] (*BRIT: inf*) *n* Schlägerei *f*.

punctual ['pʌŋktjʊəl] *adj* pünktlich.

punctuality [pʌŋktjuˈælɪtɪ] *n* Pünktlichkeit *f*.

punctually ['pʌŋktjʊəlɪ] *adv* pünktlich; **it will start** ~ **at 6** es beginnt um Punkt 6 *or* pünktlich um 6.

punctuation [pʌŋktjuˈeɪʃən] *n* Zeichensetzung *f*.

punctuation mark *n* Satzzeichen *nt*.

puncture ['pʌŋktʃə'] *n* (*AUT*) Reifenpanne *f* ♦ *vt* durchbohren; **I have a** ~ ich habe eine Reifenpanne.

pundit ['pʌndɪt] *n* Experte *m*, Expertin *f*.

pungent ['pʌndʒənt] *adj* (*smell, taste*) scharf; (*fig: speech, article etc*) spitz, scharf.

punish ['pʌnɪʃ] *vt* bestrafen; **to** ~ **sb for sth**

jdn für etw bestrafen; **to** ~ **sb for doing sth** jdn dafür bestrafen, dass er etw getan hat.

punishable ['pʌnɪʃəbl] *adj* strafbar.

punishing ['pʌnɪʃɪŋ] *adj* (*fig: exercise, ordeal*) hart.

punishment ['pʌnɪʃmənt] *n* (*act*) Bestrafung *f*; (*way of punishing*) Strafe *f*; **to take a lot of** ~ (*fig: car, person etc*) viel abbekommen.

punitive ['pjuːnɪtɪv] *adj* (*action*) Straf-, zur Strafe; (*measure*) (extrem) hart.

punk [pʌŋk] *n* (*also:* ~ **rocker**) Punker(in) *m(f)*; (*also:* ~ **rock**) Punk *m*; (*US: inf: hoodlum*) Gangster *m*.

punnet ['pʌnɪt] *n* (*of raspberries etc*) Körbchen *nt*.

punt[1] [pʌnt] *n* (*boat*) Stechkahn *m* ♦ *vi* mit dem Stechkahn fahren.

punt[2] [pʌnt] (*IRISH*) *n* (*currency*) irisches Pfund *nt*.

punter ['pʌntə'] (*BRIT*) *n* (*gambler*) Wetter(in) *m(f)*; **the** ~**s** (*inf: customers*) die Leute; **the average** ~ (*inf*) Otto Normalverbraucher.

puny ['pjuːnɪ] *adj* (*person, arms etc*) schwächlich; (*efforts*) kläglich, kümmerlich.

pup [pʌp] *n* (*young dog*) Welpe *m*, junger Hund *m*; **seal** ~ Welpenjunge(s) *nt*.

pupil ['pjuːpl] *n* (*SCOL*) Schüler(in) *m(f)*; (*of eye*) Pupille *f*.

puppet ['pʌpɪt] *n* Handpuppe *f*; (*with strings, fig: person*) Marionette *f*.

puppet government *n* Marionettenregierung *f*.

puppy ['pʌpɪ] *n* (*young dog*) Welpe *m*, junger Hund *m*.

purchase ['pɜːtʃɪs] *n* Kauf *m*; (*grip*) Halt *m* ♦ *vt* kaufen; **to get** *or* **gain (a)** ~ **on** (*grip*) Halt finden an +*dat*.

purchase order *n* Bestellung *f*.

purchase price *n* Kaufpreis *m*.

purchaser ['pɜːtʃɪsə'] *n* Käufer(in) *m(f)*.

purchase tax *n* Kaufsteuer *f*.

purchasing power ['pɜːtʃɪsɪŋ-] *n* Kaufkraft *f*.

pure [pjʊə'] *adj* rein; **a** ~ **wool jumper** ein Pullover aus reiner Wolle; **it's laziness** ~ **and simple** es ist nichts als reine Faulheit.

purebred ['pjʊəbrɛd] *adj* reinrassig.

puree ['pjʊəreɪ] *n* Püree *nt*.

purely ['pjʊəlɪ] *adv* rein.

purgatory ['pɜːgətərɪ] *n* (*REL*) das Fegefeuer; (*fig*) die Hölle.

purge [pɜːdʒ] *n* (*POL*) Säuberung *f* ♦ *vt* (*POL: organization*) säubern; (: *extremists etc*) entfernen; (*fig: thoughts, mind etc*) befreien.

purification [pjʊərɪfɪˈkeɪʃən] *n* Reinigung *f*.

purify ['pjʊərɪfaɪ] *vt* reinigen.

purist ['pjʊərɪst] *n* Purist(in) *m(f)*.

puritan ['pjʊərɪtən] *n* Puritaner(in) *m(f)*.

puritanical [pjʊərɪˈtænɪkl] *adj* puritanisch.

purity ['pjʊərɪtɪ] *n* Reinheit *f*.

purl [pɜːl] (*KNITTING*) *n* linke Masche *f* ♦ *vt* links stricken.

purloin [pə:'lɔɪn] (*form*) vt entwenden.

purple ['pə:pl] adj violett.

purport [pə:'pɔ:t] vi: **to ~ to be/do sth** vorgeben, etw zu sein/tun.

purpose ['pə:pəs] n (*reason*) Zweck m; (*aim*) Ziel nt, Absicht f; **on ~** absichtlich; **for illustrative ~s** zu Illustrationszwecken; **for all practical ~s** praktisch (gesehen); **for the ~s of this meeting** zum Zweck dieses Treffens; **to little ~** mit wenig Erfolg; **to no ~** ohne Erfolg; **a sense of ~** ein Zielbewusstsein nt.

purpose-built ['pə:pəs'bɪlt] (*BRIT*) adj speziell angefertigt, Spezial-.

purposeful ['pə:pəsful] adj entschlossen.

purposely ['pə:pəslɪ] adv absichtlich, bewusst.

purr [pə:ʳ] vi (*cat*) schnurren.

purse [pə:s] n (*BRIT: for money*) Geldbörse f, Portemonnaie nt, Portemonee nt; (*US: handbag*) Handtasche f ♦ vt (*lips*) kräuseln.

purser ['pə:səʳ] n (*NAUT*) Zahlmeister m.

purse-snatcher ['pə:ssnætʃəʳ] (*US*) n Handtaschendieb m.

pursue [pə'sju:] vt (*person, vehicle, plan, aim*) verfolgen; (*fig: interest etc*) nachgehen +dat.

pursuer [pə'sju:əʳ] n Verfolger(in) m(f).

pursuit [pə'sju:t] n (*chase*) Verfolgung f; (*pastime*) Beschäftigung f; (*fig*): **~ of** (*of happiness etc*) Streben nt nach; **in ~ of** (*person, car etc*) auf der Jagd nach; (*fig: happiness etc*) im Streben nach.

purveyor [pə'veɪəʳ] (*form*) n (*of goods etc*) Lieferant m.

pus [pʌs] n Eiter m.

push [puʃ] n Stoß m, Schub m ♦ vt (*press*) drücken; (*shove*) schieben; (*fig: put pressure on: person*) bedrängen; (*: promote: product*) werben für; (*inf: sell: drugs*) pushen ♦ vi (*press*) drücken; (*shove*) schieben; **at the ~ of a button** auf Knopfdruck; **at a ~** (*BRIT: inf*) notfalls; **to ~ a door open/shut** eine Tür auf-/zudrücken; **"~"** (*on door*) „drücken"; (*on bell*) „klingeln"; **to be ~ed for time/money** (*inf*) in Zeitnot/Geldnot sein; **she is ~ing fifty** (*inf*) sie geht auf die fünfzig zu; **to ~ for** (*demand*) drängen auf +acc.

▶ **push around** vt (*bully*) herumschubsen.

▶ **push aside** vt beiseite schieben.

▶ **push in** vi sich dazwischendrängeln.

▶ **push off** (*inf*) vi abhauen.

▶ **push on** vi (*continue*) weitermachen.

▶ **push over** vt umstoßen.

▶ **push through** vt (*measure etc*) durchdrücken.

▶ **push up** vt (*total, prices*) hochtreiben.

push-bike ['puʃbaɪk] (*BRIT*) n Fahrrad nt.

push-button ['puʃbʌtn] adj (*machine, calculator*) Drucktasten-.

pushchair ['puʃtʃeəʳ] (*BRIT*) n Sportwagen m.

pusher ['puʃəʳ] n (*drug dealer*) Pusher m.

pushover ['puʃəuvəʳ] (*inf*) n: **it's a ~** das ist ein Kinderspiel.

push-up ['puʃʌp] (*US*) n Liegestütz m.

pushy ['puʃɪ] (*pej*) adj aufdringlich.

puss [pus] (*inf*) n Mieze f.

pussy(cat) ['pusɪ(kæt)] (*inf*) n Mieze(katze) f.

put [put] (*pt, pp* **put**) vt (*thing*) tun; (*: upright*) stellen; (*: flat*) legen; (*person: in room, institution etc*) stecken; (*: in state, situation*) versetzen; (*express: idea etc*) ausdrücken; (*present: case, view*) vorbringen; (*ask: question*) stellen; (*classify*) einschätzen; (*write, type*) schreiben; **to ~ sb in a good/bad mood** jdn gut/schlecht stimmen; **to ~ sb to bed** jdn ins Bett bringen; **to ~ sb to a lot of trouble** jdm viele Umstände machen; **how shall I ~ it?** wie soll ich es sagen or ausdrücken?; **to ~ a lot of time into sth** viel Zeit auf etw acc verwenden; **to ~ money on a horse** Geld auf ein Pferd setzen; **the cost is now ~ at 2 million pounds** die Kosten werden jetzt auf 2 Millionen Pfund geschätzt; **I ~ it to you that ...** (*BRIT*) ich behaupte, dass ...; **to stay ~** (an Ort und Stelle) bleiben.

▶ **put about** vi (*NAUT*) den Kurs ändern ♦ vt (*rumour*) verbreiten.

▶ **put across** vt (*ideas etc*) verständlich machen.

▶ **put around** vt = **put about**.

▶ **put aside** vt (*work*) zur Seite legen; (*idea, problem*) unbeachtet lassen; (*sum of money*) zurücklegen.

▶ **put away** vt (*store*) wegräumen; (*inf: consume*) verdrücken; (*save: money*) zurücklegen; (*imprison*) einsperren.

▶ **put back** vt (*replace*) zurücktun; (*: upright*) zurückstellen; (*: flat*) zurücklegen; (*postpone*) verschieben; (*delay*) zurückwerfen.

▶ **put by** vt (*money, supplies etc*) zurücklegen.

▶ **put down** vt (*upright*) hinstellen; (*flat*) hinlegen; (*cup, glass*) absetzen; (*in writing*) aufschreiben; (*riot, rebellion*) niederschlagen; (*humiliate*) demütigen; (*kill*) töten.

▶ **put down to** vt (*attribute*) zurückführen auf +acc.

▶ **put forward** vt (*ideas etc*) vorbringen; (*watch, clock*) vorstellen; (*date, meeting*) vorverlegen.

▶ **put in** vt (*application, complaint*) einreichen; (*time, effort*) investieren; (*gas, electricity etc*) installieren ♦ vi (*NAUT*) einlaufen.

▶ **put in for** vt fus (*promotion*) sich bewerben um; (*leave*) beantragen.

▶ **put off** vt (*delay*) verschieben; (*distract*) ablenken; **to ~ sb off sth** (*discourage*) jdn von etw abbringen.

▶ **put on** vt (*clothes, brake*) anziehen; (*glasses, kettle*) aufsetzen; (*make-up, ointment etc*) auftragen; (*light, TV*) anmachen; (*play etc*) aufführen; (*record, tape, video*) auflegen; (*dinner etc*) aufsetzen; (*assume: look,* behaviour etc) annehmen; (inf: tease) auf den Arm nehmen; (extra bus, train etc) einsetzen; **to ~ on airs** sich zieren; **to ~ on weight** zunehmen.

▶ **put on to** vt (tell about) vermitteln.

▶ **put out** vt (fire, light) ausmachen; (take out: rubbish) herausbringen; (: cat etc) vor die Tür setzen; (one's hand) ausstrecken; (story, announcement) verbreiten; (BRIT: dislocate: shoulder etc) verrenken; (inf: inconvenience) Umstände machen +dat ♦ vi (NAUT): **to ~ out to sea** in See stechen; **to ~ out from Plymouth** von Plymouth auslaufen.

▶ **put through** vt (TEL: person) verbinden; (: call) durchstellen; (plan, agreement) durchbringen; **~ me through to Ms Blair** verbinden Sie mich mit Frau Blair.

▶ **put together** vt (furniture etc) zusammenbauen; (plan, campaign) ausarbeiten; **more than the rest of them ~ together** mehr als alle anderen zusammen.

▶ **put up** vt (fence, building) errichten; (tent) aufstellen; (umbrella) aufspannen; (hood) hochschlagen; (poster, sign etc) anbringen; (price, cost) erhöhen; (accommodate) unterbringen; **to ~ up resistance** Widerstand leisten; **to ~ up a fight** sich zur Wehr setzen; **to ~ sb up to sth** jdn zu etw anstiften; **to ~ sb up to doing sth** jdn dazu anstiften, etw zu tun; **to ~ sth up for sale** etw zum Verkauf anbieten.

▶ **put upon** vt fus: **to be ~ upon** (imposed on) ausgenutzt werden.

▶ **put up with** vt fus sich abfinden mit.

putative ['pjuːtətɪv] adj mutmaßlich.

putrid ['pjuːtrɪd] adj (mess, meat) faul.

putt [pʌt] n Putt m.

putter ['pʌtə*] n (GOLF) Putter m ♦ vi (US) = **potter**.

putting green ['pʌtɪŋ-] n kleiner Golfplatz m zum Putten.

putty ['pʌtɪ] n Kitt m.

put-up ['pʊtʌp] adj: **a ~ job** ein abgekartetes Spiel nt.

puzzle ['pʌzl] n (game, toy) Geschicklichkeitsspiel nt; (mystery) Rätsel nt ♦ vt verwirren ♦ vi: **to ~ over sth** sich dat über etw acc den Kopf zerbrechen; **to be ~d as to why ...** vor einem Rätsel stehen, warum ...

puzzling ['pʌzlɪŋ] adj verwirrend; (mysterious) rätselhaft.

PVC n abbr (= polyvinyl chloride) PVC nt.

Pvt. (US) abbr (MIL) = **private**.

p.w. abbr (= per week) pro Woche.

pygmy ['pɪgmɪ] n Pygmäe m.

pyjamas, (US) **pajamas** [pə'dʒɑːməz] npl Pyjama m, Schlafanzug m; **a pair of ~** ein Schlafanzug.

pylon ['paɪlən] n Mast m.

pyramid ['pɪrəmɪd] n Pyramide f.

Pyrenean [pɪrə'niːən] adj pyrenäisch.

Pyrenees [pɪrə'niːz] npl: **the ~** die Pyrenäen pl.

Pyrex ® ['paɪrɛks] n ≈ Jenaer Glas ® nt ♦ adj (dish, bowl) aus Jenaer Glas ®.

python ['paɪθən] n Pythonschlange f.

Q, q

Q, q [kjuː] n (letter) Q nt, q nt; **~ for Queen** ≈ Q wie Quelle.

Qatar [kæ'tɑː*] n Katar nt.

QC (BRIT) n abbr (LAW: = Queen's Counsel) Kronanwalt m.

QC

QC (kurz für Queen's Counsel, bzw. **KC** für King's Counsel) ist in Großbritannien ein hoch gestellter **barrister**, der auf Empfehlung des Lordkanzlers ernannt wird und zum Zeichen seines Amtes einen seidenen Umhang trägt und daher auch als **silk** bezeichnet wird. Ein **QC** muss vor Gericht in Begleitung eines rangniedrigeren Anwaltes erscheinen.

QCA (BRIT) n abbr (= Qualifications and Curriculum Authority) Behörde, die in England für die Entwicklung von Lehrplänen und deren Beachtung zuständig ist.

QED abbr (= quod erat demonstrandum) q. e. d.

QM n abbr (MIL) = **quartermaster**.

q.t. (inf) n abbr (= quiet): **on the ~** heimlich.

quack [kwæk] n (of duck) Schnattern nt, Quaken nt; (inf: pej: doctor) Quacksalber m ♦ vi schnattern, quaken.

quad [kwɒd] abbr = **quadrangle**; (= quadruplet) Vierling m.

quadrangle ['kwɒdræŋgl] n (courtyard) Innenhof m.

quadrilateral [kwɒdrɪ'lætərəl] n Viereck nt.

quadruped ['kwɒdrupɛd] n Vierfüßer m.

quadruple [kwɔ'druːpl] vt vervierfachen ♦ vi sich vervierfachen.

quadruplets [kwɔ'druːplɪts] npl Vierlinge pl.

quagmire ['kwægmaɪə*] n (also fig) Sumpf m.

quail [kweɪl] n Wachtel f ♦ vi: **he ~ed at the thought/before her anger** ihm schauderte bei dem Gedanken/vor ihrem Zorn.

quaint [kweɪnt] adj (house, village) malerisch; (ideas, customs) urig, kurios.

quake [kweɪk] vi beben, zittern ♦ n = **earthquake**.

Quaker ['kweɪkə*] n Quäker(in) m(f).

qualification [kwɒlɪfɪ'keɪʃən] n (often pl: degree etc) Qualifikation f; (attribute)

Voraussetzung *f*; (*reservation*) Vorbehalt *m*; **what are your ~s?** welche Qualifikationen haben Sie?

qualified ['kwɔlɪfaɪd] *adj* (*trained: doctor etc*) qualifiziert, ausgebildet; (*limited: agreement, praise*) bedingt; **to be/feel ~ to do sth** (*fit, competent*) qualifiziert sein/sich qualifiziert fühlen, etw zu tun; **it was a ~ success** es war kein voller Erfolg; **he's not ~ for the job** ihm fehlen die Qualifikationen für die Stelle.

qualify ['kwɔlɪfaɪ] *vt* (*entitle*) qualifizieren; (*modify: statement*) einschränken ♦ *vi* (*pass examination*) sich qualifizieren; **to ~ for** (*be eligible*) die Berechtigung erlangen für; (*in competition*) sich qualifizieren für; **to ~ as an engineer** die Ausbildung zum Ingenieur abschließen.

qualifying ['kwɔlɪfaɪɪŋ] *adj*: **~ exam** Auswahlprüfung *f*; **~ round** Qualifikationsrunde *f*.

qualitative ['kwɔlɪtətɪv] *adj* qualitativ.

quality ['kwɔlɪtɪ] *n* Qualität *f*; (*characteristic*) Eigenschaft *f* ♦ *cpd* Qualitäts-; **of good/poor ~** von guter/schlechter Qualität; **~ of life** Lebensqualität *f*.

quality control *n* Qualitätskontrolle *f*.

quality papers (*BRIT*) *npl*: **the ~** die seriösen Zeitungen *pl*.

QUALITY PRESS

Quality press *bezeichnet die seriösen Tages- und Wochenzeitungen im Gegensatz zu den Massenblättern. Diese Zeitungen sind fast alle großformatig und wenden sich an den anspruchsvolleren Leser, der voll informiert sein möchte und bereit ist, für die Zeitungslektüre viel Zeit aufzuwenden. Siehe auch* **tabloid press***.*

---

qualm [kwɑ:m] *n* Bedenken *pl*; **to have ~s about sth** Bedenken wegen etw haben.

quandary ['kwɔndrɪ] *n*: **to be in a ~** in einem Dilemma sein.

quango ['kwæŋgəu] (*BRIT*) *n abbr* (= *quasi-autonomous nongovernmental organization*) ≈ (regierungsunabhängige) Kommission *f*.

quantifiable ['kwɔntɪfaɪəbl] *adj* quantifizierbar.

quantitative ['kwɔntɪtətɪv] *adj* quantitativ.

quantity ['kwɔntɪtɪ] *n* (*amount*) Menge *f*; **in large/small quantities** in großen/kleinen Mengen; **in ~** (*in bulk*) in großen Mengen; **an unknown ~** (*fig*) eine unbekannte Größe.

quantity surveyor *n* Baukostenkalkulator(in) *m(f)*.

quantum leap ['kwɔntəm-] *n* (*PHYS*) Quantensprung *m*; (*fig*) Riesenschritt *m*.

quarantine ['kwɔrnti:n] *n* Quarantäne *f*; **in ~** in Quarantäne.

quark [kwɑ:k] *n* (*cheese*) Quark *m*; (*PHYS*) Quark *nt*.

quarrel ['kwɔrl] *n* (*argument*) Streit *m* ♦ *vi* sich streiten; **to have a ~ with sb** sich mit jdm streiten; **I've no ~ with him** ich habe nichts gegen ihn; **I can't ~ with that** dagegen kann ich nichts einwenden.

quarrelsome ['kwɔrəlsəm] *adj* streitsüchtig.

quarry ['kwɔrɪ] *n* (*for stone*) Steinbruch *m*; (*prey*) Beute *f* ♦ *vt* (*marble etc*) brechen.

quart [kwɔ:t] *n* Quart *nt*.

quarter ['kwɔ:tə*] *n* Viertel *nt*; (*US: coin*) 25-Cent-Stück *nt*; (*of year*) Quartal *nt*; (*district*) Viertel *nt* ♦ *vt* (*divide*) vierteln; (*MIL: lodge*) einquartieren; **quarters** *npl* (*MIL*) Quartier *nt*; (*also:* **living ~s**) Unterkünfte *pl*; **a ~ of an hour** eine Viertelstunde; **it's a ~ to three,** (*US*) **it's a ~ of three** es ist Viertel vor drei; **it's a ~ past three,** (*US*) **it's a ~ after three** es ist Viertel nach drei; **from all ~s** aus allen Richtungen; **at close ~s** aus unmittelbarer Nähe.

quarterback ['kwɔ:təbæk] *n* (*AMERICAN FOOTBALL*) Quarterback *m*.

quarterdeck ['kwɔ:tədɛk] *n* (*NAUT*) Quarterdeck *nt*.

quarterfinal ['kwɔ:tə'faɪnl] *n* Viertelfinale *nt*.

quarterly ['kwɔ:təlɪ] *adj, adv* vierteljährlich ♦ *n* Vierteljahresschrift *f*.

quartermaster ['kwɔ:təmɑ:stə*] *n* (*MIL*) Quartiermeister *m*.

quartet [kwɔ:'tɛt] *n* (*MUS*) Quartett *nt*.

quarto ['kwɔ:təu] *n* (*size of paper*) Quartformat *nt*; (*book*) im Quartformat.

quartz [kwɔ:ts] *n* Quarz *m* ♦ *cpd* (*watch, clock*) Quarz-.

quash [kwɔʃ] *vt* (*verdict*) aufheben.

quasi- ['kweɪzaɪ] *pref* quasi-.

quaver ['kweɪvə*] *n* (*BRIT: MUS*) Achtelnote *f* ♦ *vi* (*voice*) beben, zittern.

quay [ki:] *n* Kai *m*.

quayside ['ki:saɪd] *n* Kai *m*.

queasiness ['kwi:zɪnɪs] *n* Übelkeit *f*.

queasy ['kwi:zɪ] *adj* (*nauseous*) übel; **I feel ~** mir ist übel *or* schlecht.

Quebec [kwɪ'bɛk] *n* Quebec *nt*.

queen [kwi:n] *n* (*also ZOOL*) Königin *f*; (*CARDS, CHESS*) Dame *f*.

queen mother *n* Königinmutter *f*.

Queen's speech (*BRIT*) *n* ≈ Regierungserklärung *f*.

QUEEN'S SPEECH

Queen's Speech *(bzw.* **King's Speech***) ist eine vom britischen Monarchen bei der alljährlichen feierlichen Parlamentseröffnung im Oberhaus vor dem versammelten Ober- und Unterhaus verlesene Rede. Sie wird vom Premierminister in Zusammenarbeit mit dem Kabinett verfasst und enthält die Regierungserklärung.*

---

queer [kwɪə*] *adj* (*odd*) sonderbar, seltsam ♦ *n* (*inf!: pej: male homosexual*) Schwule(r) *m*; **I**

feel ~ (_BRIT: unwell_) mir ist ganz komisch.

quell [kwɛl] _vt_ (_riot_) niederschlagen; (_fears_) überwinden.

quench [kwɛntʃ] _vt:_ **to** ~ **one's thirst** seinen Durst stillen.

querulous ['kwɛrʊləs] _adj_ nörglerisch.

query ['kwɪərɪ] _n_ Anfrage _f_ ♦ _vt_ (_check_) nachfragen bezüglich +_gen_; (_express doubt about_) bezweifeln.

quest [kwɛst] _n_ Suche _f_.

question ['kwɛstʃən] _n_ Frage _f_ ♦ _vt_ (_interrogate_) befragen; (_doubt_) bezweifeln; **to ask sb a** ~, **put a** ~ **to sb** jdm eine Frage stellen; **to bring** _or_ **call sth into** ~ etw infrage _or_ in Frage stellen; **the** ~ **is** ... die Frage ist ...; **there's no** ~ **of him playing for England** es ist ausgeschlossen, dass er für England spielt; **the person/night in** ~ die fragliche Person/Nacht; **to be beyond** ~ außer Frage stehen; **to be out of the** ~ nicht infrage _or_ in Frage kommen.

questionable ['kwɛstʃənəbl] _adj_ fraglich.

questioner ['kwɛstʃənə*] _n_ Fragesteller(in) _m(f)_.

questioning ['kwɛstʃənɪŋ] _adj_ (_look_) fragend; (_mind_) forschend ♦ _n_ (_POLICE_) Vernehmung _f_.

question mark _n_ Fragezeichen _nt_.

questionnaire [kwɛstʃə'nɛə*] _n_ Fragebogen _m_.

queue [kjuː] (_BRIT_) _n_ Schlange _f_ ♦ _vi_ (_also:_ ~ **up**) Schlange stehen.

quibble ['kwɪbl] _vi:_ **to** ~ **about** _or_ **over** sich streiten über +_acc_; **to** ~ **with** herumnörgeln an +_dat_ ♦ _n_ Krittelei _f_.

quiche [kiːʃ] _n_ Quiche _f_.

quick [kwɪk] _adj_ schnell; (_mind, wit_) wach; (_look, visit_) flüchtig ♦ _adv_ schnell ♦ _n:_ **to cut sb to the** ~ (_fig_) jdn tief verletzen; **be** ~! mach schnell!; **to be** ~ **to act** schnell handeln; **she was** ~ **to see that** ... sie begriff schnell, dass ...; **she has a** ~ **temper** sie wird leicht hitzig.

quicken ['kwɪkən] _vt_ beschleunigen ♦ _vi_ schneller werden, sich beschleunigen.

quick-fire ['kwɪkfaɪə*] _adj_ (_questions_) wie aus der Pistole.

quick fix _n_ Sofortlösung _f_.

quicklime ['kwɪklaɪm] _n_ ungelöschter Kalk _m_.

quickly ['kwɪklɪ] _adv_ schnell.

quickness ['kwɪknɪs] _n_ Schnelligkeit _f_; ~ **of mind** Scharfsinn _m_.

quicksand ['kwɪksænd] _n_ Treibsand _m_.

quickstep ['kwɪkstɛp] _n_ Quickstepp _m_.

quick-tempered [kwɪk'tɛmpəd] _adj_ hitzig, leicht erregbar.

quick-witted [kwɪk'wɪtɪd] _adj_ schlagfertig.

quid [kwɪd] (_BRIT: inf_) _n inv_ Pfund _nt_.

quid pro quo [kwɪdprəʊ'kwəʊ] _n_ Gegenleistung _f_.

quiet ['kwaɪət] _adj_ leise; (_place_) ruhig, still; (_silent, reserved_) still; (_business, day_) ruhig; (_without fuss etc: wedding_) in kleinem Rahmen ♦ _n_ (_peacefulness_) Stille _f_, Ruhe _f_; (_silence_) Ruhe _f_ ♦ _vt, vi_ (_US_) = **quieten keep** _or_ **be** ~! sei still!; **I'll have a** ~ **word with him** ich werde mal unter vier Augen mit ihm reden; **on the** ~ (_in secret_) heimlich.

quieten ['kwaɪətn] (_BRIT: also:_ ~ **down**) _vi_ ruhiger werden ♦ _vt_ (_person, animal_) beruhigen.

quietly ['kwaɪətlɪ] _adv_ leise; (_silently_) still; (_calmly_) ruhig; ~ **confident** insgeheim sicher.

quietness ['kwaɪətnɪs] _n_ (_peacefulness_) Ruhe _f_; (_silence_) Stille _f_.

quill [kwɪl] _n_ (_pen_) Feder _f_; (_of porcupine_) Stachel _m_.

quilt [kwɪlt] _n_ Decke _f_; (_also:_ **continental** ~) Federbett _nt_.

quin [kwɪn] (_BRIT_) _n abbr_ (= **quintuplet**) Fünfling _m_.

quince [kwɪns] _n_ Quitte _f_.

quinine [kwɪ'niːn] _n_ Chinin _nt_.

quintet [kwɪn'tɛt] _n_ (_MUS_) Quintett _nt_.

quintuplets [kwɪn'tjuːplɪts] _npl_ Fünflinge _pl_.

quip [kwɪp] _n_ witzige _or_ geistreiche Bemerkung _f_ ♦ _vt_ witzeln.

quire ['kwaɪə*] _n_ (_of paper_) 24 Bogen Papier.

quirk [kwɜːk] _n_ Marotte _f_; **a** ~ **of fate** eine Laune des Schicksals.

quit [kwɪt] (_pt, pp_ **quit** _or_ **quitted**) _vt_ (_smoking_) aufgeben; (_job_) kündigen; (_premises_) verlassen ♦ _vi_ (_give up_) aufgeben; (_resign_) kündigen; **to** ~ **doing sth** aufhören, etw zu tun; ~ **stalling!** (_US: inf_) weichen Sie nicht ständig aus!; **notice to** ~ (_BRIT_) Kündigung _f_.

quite [kwaɪt] _adv_ (_rather_) ziemlich; (_entirely_) ganz; **not** ~ nicht ganz; **I** ~ **like it** ich mag es ganz gern; **I** ~ **understand** ich verstehe; **I don't** ~ **remember** ich erinnere mich nicht genau; **not** ~ **as many as the last time** nicht ganz so viele wie das letzte Mal; **that meal was** ~ **something!** das Essen konnte sich sehen lassen!; **it was** ~ **a sight** das war vielleicht ein Anblick; ~ **a few of them** eine ganze Reihe von Ihnen; ~ **(so)!** ganz recht!

quits [kwɪts] _adj:_ **we're** ~ wir sind quitt; **let's call it** ~ lassen wirs dabei.

quiver ['kwɪvə*] _vi_ zittern.

quiz [kwɪz] _n_ (_game_) Quiz _nt_ ♦ _vt_ (_question_) befragen.

quizzical ['kwɪzɪkl] _adj_ (_look, smile_) wissend.

quoits [kwɔɪts] _npl_ (_game_) Wurfspiel mit Ringen.

quorum ['kwɔːrəm] _n_ Quorum _nt_.

quota ['kwəʊtə] _n_ (_allowance_) Quote _f_.

quotation [kwəʊ'teɪʃən] _n_ (_from book etc_) Zitat _nt_; (_estimate_) Preisangabe _f_; (_COMM_) Kostenvoranschlag _m_.

quotation marks _npl_ Anführungszeichen _pl_.

quote [kwəʊt] _n_ (_from book etc_) Zitat _nt_; (_estimate_) Kostenvoranschlag _m_ ♦ _vt_

zitieren; (*fact, example*) anführen; (*price*) nennen; **quotes** *npl* (*quotation marks*) Anführungszeichen *pl*; **in ~s** in Anführungszeichen; **the figure ~d for the repairs** die für die Reparatur genannte Summe; **~ ...** **unquote** Zitat Anfang ... Zitat Ende.
quotient ['kwəʊʃənt] *n* Quotient *m*.
qv *abbr* (= *quod vide*) s.d.
qwerty keyboard ['kwɜːtɪ-] *n* Qwerty-Tastatur *f*.

R, r

R[1], r [ɑː*] *n* (*letter*) R *nt*, r *nt*; **~ for Robert**, *(US)* **~ for Roger** ≈ R wie Richard.
R[2] [ɑː*] *abbr* (= *Réaumur (scale)*) R; (*US: CINE:* = *restricted*) *Klassifikation für nicht jugendfreie Filme.*
R. *abbr* (= *right*) r.; = *river*; (*US: POL*) = **republican**; (*BRIT: = Rex*) König; (= *Regina*) Königin.
RA *abbr* (*MIL*) = **rear admiral** ♦ *n abbr* (*BRIT:* = *Royal Academy*) *Gesellschaft zur Förderung der Künste*; (= *Royal Academician*) *Mitglied der Royal Academy.*
RAAF *n abbr* (*MIL:* = *Royal Australian Air Force*) *australische Luftwaffe f.*
Rabat [rə'bɑːt] *n* Rabat *nt*.
rabbi ['ræbaɪ] *n* Rabbi *m*.
rabbit ['ræbɪt] *n* Kaninchen *nt* ♦ *vi* (*BRIT: inf: also:* **to ~ on**) quatschen, schwafeln.
rabbit hole *n* Kaninchenbau *m*.
rabbit hutch *n* Kaninchenstall *m*.
rabble ['ræbl] (*pej*) *n* Pöbel *m*.
rabid ['ræbɪd] *adj* (*animal*) tollwütig; (*fig: fanatical*) fanatisch.
rabies ['reɪbiːz] *n* Tollwut *f*.
RAC (*BRIT*) *n abbr* (= *Royal Automobile Club*) *Autofahrerorganisation*, ≈ ADAC *m*.
raccoon [rə'kuːn] *n* Waschbär *m*.
race [reɪs] *n* (*species*) Rasse *f*; (*competition*) Rennen *nt*; (*for power, control*) Wettlauf *m* ♦ *vt* (*horse, pigeon*) an Wettbewerben teilnehmen lassen; (*car etc*) ins Rennen schicken; (*person*) um die Wette laufen mit ♦ *vi* (*compete*) antreten; (*hurry*) rennen; (*pulse, heart*) rasen; (*engine*) durchdrehen; **the human ~** die Menschheit; **a ~ against time** ein Wettlauf mit der Zeit; **he ~d across the road** er raste über die Straße; **to ~ in/out** hinein-/hinausstürzen.
race car (*US*) *n* = **racing car**.
race car driver (*US*) *n* = **racing driver**.
racecourse ['reɪskɔːs] *n* Rennbahn *f*.
racehorse ['reɪshɔːs] *n* Rennpferd *nt*.
race meeting *n* Rennveranstaltung *f*.

race relations *npl* Beziehungen *pl* zwischen den Rassen.
racetrack ['reɪstræk] *n* Rennbahn *f*; (*US*) = **racecourse**.
racial ['reɪʃl] *adj* Rassen-.
racialism ['reɪʃlɪzəm] *n* Rassismus *m*.
racialist ['reɪʃlɪst] *adj* rassistisch ♦ *n* (*pej*) Rassist(in) *m(f)*.
racing ['reɪsɪŋ] *n* (*horse racing*) Pferderennen *nt*; (*motor racing*) Rennsport *m*.
racing car (*BRIT*) *n* Rennwagen *m*.
racing driver (*BRIT*) *n* Rennfahrer *m*.
racism ['reɪsɪzəm] *n* Rassismus *m*.
racist ['reɪsɪst] *adj* rassistisch ♦ *n* (*pej*) Rassist(in) *m(f)*.
rack [ræk] *n* (*also:* **luggage ~**) Gepäckablage *f*; (*also:* **roof ~**) Dachgepäckträger *m*; (*for dresses etc*) Ständer *m*; (*for dishes*) Gestell *nt* ♦ *vt*: **~ed by** (*pain etc*) gemartert von; **magazine/toast ~** Zeitungs-/Toastständer *m*; **to ~ one's brains** sich *dat* den Kopf zerbrechen; **to go to ~ and ruin** (*building*) zerfallen; (*business, country*) herunterkommen.
racket ['rækɪt] *n* (*for tennis etc*) Schläger *m*; (*noise*) Radau *m*; (*swindle*) Schwindel *m*.
racketeer [rækɪ'tɪə*] (*esp US*) *n* Gangster *m*.
racoon [rə'kuːn] *n* = **raccoon**.
racquet ['rækɪt] *n* (*for tennis etc*) Schläger *m*.
racy ['reɪsɪ] *adj* (*book, story*) rasant.
RADA [rɑːdə] *n abbr* (= *Royal Academy of Dramatic Art*) *Schauspielschule.*
radar ['reɪdɑː*] *n* Radar *m or nt* ♦ *cpd* Radar-.
radar trap *n* Radarfalle *f*.
radial ['reɪdɪəl] *adj* (*roads*) strahlenförmig verlaufend; (*pattern*) strahlenförmig ♦ *n* (*also:* **~ tyre**) Gürtelreifen *m*.
radiance ['reɪdɪəns] *n* Glanz *m*.
radiant ['reɪdɪənt] *adj* strahlend; (*PHYS: heat*) Strahlungs-.
radiate ['reɪdɪeɪt] *vt* (*lit, fig*) ausstrahlen ♦ *vi* (*lines, roads*) strahlenförmig verlaufen.
radiation [reɪdɪ'eɪʃən] *n* (*radioactivity*) radioaktive Strahlung *f*; (*from sun etc*) Strahlung *f*.
radiation sickness *n* Strahlenkrankheit *f*.
radiator ['reɪdɪeɪtə*] *n* (*heater*) Heizkörper *m*; (*AUT*) Kühler *m*.
radiator cap *n* (*AUT*) Kühlerdeckel *m*.
radiator grill *n* (*AUT*) Kühlergrill *m*.
radical ['rædɪkl] *adj* radikal ♦ *n* (*person*) Radikale(r) *f(m)*.
radii ['reɪdɪaɪ] *npl of* **radius**.
radio ['reɪdɪəʊ] *n* (*broadcasting*) Radio *nt*, Rundfunk *m*; (*device: for receiving broadcasts*) Radio *nt*; (: *for transmitting and receiving*) Funkgerät *nt* ♦ *vi*: **to ~ to sb** mit jdm per Funk sprechen ♦ *vt* (*person*) per Funk verständigen; (*message, position*) per Funk durchgeben; **on the ~** im Radio.
radio... ['reɪdɪəʊ] *pref* Radio..., radio...
radioactive ['reɪdɪəʊ'æktɪv] *adj* radioaktiv.
radioactivity ['reɪdɪəʊæk'tɪvɪtɪ] *n*

Radioaktivität *f.*

radio announcer *n* Rundfunksprecher(in) *m(f).*

radio-controlled ['reɪdɪəukən'trəuld] *adj* ferngesteuert.

radiographer [reɪdɪ'ɔgrəfə*] *n* Röntgenologe *m,* Röntgenologin *f.*

radiography [reɪdɪ'ɔgrəfɪ] *n* Röntgenografie *f.*

radiologist [reɪdɪ'ɔlədʒɪst] *n* Radiologe *m,* Radiologin *f.*

radiology [reɪdɪ'ɔlədʒɪ] *n* Radiologie *f.*

radio station *n* Radiosender *m.*

radio taxi *n* Funktaxi *nt.*

radiotelephone ['reɪdɪəu'tɛlɪfəun] *n* Funksprechgerät *nt.*

radio telescope *n* Radioteleskop *nt.*

radiotherapist ['reɪdɪəu'θɛrəpɪst] *n* Strahlentherapeut(in) *m(f).*

radiotherapy ['reɪdɪəu'θɛrəpɪ] *n* Strahlentherapie *f.*

radish ['rædɪʃ] *n* Radieschen *nt;* (*long white variety*) Rettich *m.*

radium ['reɪdɪəm] *n* Radium *nt.*

radius ['reɪdɪəs] (*pl* **radii**) *n* Radius *m;* (*area*) Umkreis *m;* **within a ~ of 50 miles** in einem Umkreis von 50 Meilen.

RAF (*BRIT*) *n abbr* = **Royal Air Force.**

raffia ['ræfɪə] *n* Bast *m.*

raffish ['ræfɪʃ] *adj* (*person*) verwegen; (*place*) verkommen.

raffle ['ræfl] *n* Verlosung *f,* Tombola *f* ♦ *vt* (*prize*) verlosen; **~ ticket** Los *nt.*

raft [rɑːft] *n* Floß *nt;* (*also:* **life ~**) Rettungsfloß *nt.*

rafter ['rɑːftə*] *n* Dachsparren *m.*

rag [ræg] *n* (*piece of cloth*) Lappen *m;* (*torn cloth*) Fetzen *m;* (*pej: newspaper*) Käseblatt *nt;* (*BRIT: UNIV*) *studentische Wohltätigkeitsveranstaltung* ♦ *vt* (*BRIT: tease*) aufziehen; **rags** *npl* (*torn clothes*) Lumpen *pl;* **in ~s** (*person*) zerlumpt; **his was a ~s-to-riches story** er brachte es vom Tellerwäscher zum Millionär.

rag-and-bone man [rægən'bəun-] (*BRIT*) *n* Lumpensammler *m.*

ragbag ['rægbæg] *n* (*assortment*) Sammelsurium *nt.*

RAG DAY/WEEK

Rag Day/Week *heißt der Tag bzw. die Woche, wenn Studenten Geld für wohltätige Zwecke sammeln. Diverse gesponserte Aktionen wie Volksläufe, Straßentheater und Kneipentouren werden zur Unterhaltung der Studenten und der Bevölkerung organisiert. Studentenzeitschriften mit schlüpfrigen Witzen werden auf der Straße verkauft, und fast alle Universitäten und Colleges halten einen Ball ab. Der Erlös aller Veranstaltungen fließt Wohltätigkeitsorganisationen zu.*

---

rag doll *n* Stoffpuppe *f.*

rage [reɪdʒ] *n* (*fury*) Wut *f,* Zorn *m* ♦ *vi* toben, wüten; **it's all the ~** (*fashionable*) es ist der letzte Schrei; **to fly into a ~** einen Wutanfall bekommen.

ragged ['rægɪd] *adj* (*jagged*) zackig; (*clothes, person*) zerlumpt; (*beard*) ausgefranst.

raging ['reɪdʒɪŋ] *adj* (*sea, storm, torrent*) tobend, tosend; (*fever*) heftig; (*thirst*) brennend; (*toothache*) rasend.

rag trade (*inf*) *n:* **the ~** die Modebranche *f.*

raid [reɪd] *n* (*MIL*) Angriff *m,* Überfall *m;* (*by police*) Razzia *f;* (*by criminal: forcefully*) Überfall *m;* (: *secretly*) Einbruch *m* ♦ *vt* (*MIL*) angreifen, überfallen; (*police*) stürmen; (*criminal: forcefully*) überfallen; (: *secretly*) einbrechen in +*acc.*

rail [reɪl] *n* Geländer *nt;* (*on deck of ship*) Reling *f;* **rails** *npl* (*for train*) Schienen *pl;* **by ~** mit der Bahn.

railcard ['reɪlkɑːd] (*BRIT*) *n* (*for young people*) ≈ Juniorenpass *m;* (*for pensioners*) ≈ Seniorenpass *m.*

railing(s) ['reɪlɪŋ(z)] *n(pl)* (*fence*) Zaun *m.*

railroad ['reɪlrəud] (*US*) *n* = **railway.**

railway ['reɪlweɪ] (*BRIT*) *n* Eisenbahn *f;* (*track*) Gleis *nt;* (*company*) Bahn *f.*

railway engine (*BRIT*) *n* Lokomotive *f.*

railway line (*BRIT*) *n* Bahnlinie *f;* (*track*) Gleis *nt.*

railwayman ['reɪlweɪmən] (*irreg: like* **man**) (*BRIT*) *n* Eisenbahner *m.*

railway station (*BRIT*) *n* Bahnhof *m.*

rain [reɪn] *n* Regen *m* ♦ *vi* regnen; **in the ~** im Regen; **as right as ~** voll auf der Höhe; **it's ~ing** es regnet; **it's ~ing cats and dogs** es regnet in Strömen.

rainbow ['reɪnbəu] *n* Regenbogen *m.*

rain check (*US*) *n:* **to take a ~ on sth** sich *dat* etw noch einmal überlegen.

raincoat ['reɪnkəut] *n* Regenmantel *m.*

raindrop ['reɪndrɔp] *n* Regentropfen *m.*

rainfall ['reɪnfɔːl] *n* Niederschlag *m.*

rainforest ['reɪnfɔrɪst] *n* Regenwald *m.*

rainproof ['reɪnpruːf] *adj* wasserfest.

rainstorm ['reɪnstɔːm] *n* schwere Regenfälle *pl.*

rainwater ['reɪnwɔːtə*] *n* Regenwasser *nt.*

rainy ['reɪnɪ] *adj* (*day*) regnerisch, verregnet; (*area*) regenreich; **~ season** Regenzeit *f;* **to save sth for a ~ day** etw für schlechte Zeiten aufheben.

raise [reɪz] *n* (*pay rise*) Gehaltserhöhung *f* ♦ *vt* (*lift: hand*) hochheben; (: *window*) hochziehen; (*siege*) beenden; (*embargo*) aufheben; (*increase*) erhöhen; (*improve*) verbessern; (*question etc*) zur Sprache bringen; (*doubts etc*) vorbringen; (*child, cattle*) aufziehen; (*crop*) anbauen; (*army*) aufstellen; (*funds*) aufbringen; (*loan*) aufnehmen; **to ~ a glass to sb/sth** das Glas auf jdn/etw erheben; **to ~ one's voice** die

Stimme erheben; **to ~ sb's hopes** jdm
Hoffnungen machen; **to ~ a laugh/smile**
Gelächter/ein Lächeln hervorrufen;
this ~s the question... das wirft die Frage
auf...

raisin ['reɪzn] *n* Rosine *f.*

Raj [rɑːdʒ] *n*: **the ~** *britische Regierung in
Indien vor 1947.*

rajah ['rɑːdʒə] *n* Radscha *m.*

rake [reɪk] *n* Harke *f*; (*old: person*)
Schwerenöter *m* ♦ *vt* harken; (*light, gun: area*)
bestreichen; **he's raking it in** (*inf*) er
scheffelt das Geld nur so.

rake-off ['reɪkɔf] (*inf*) *n* Anteil *m.*

rally ['rælɪ] *n* (*POL etc*) Kundgebung *f*; (*AUT*)
Rallye *f*; (*TENNIS etc*) Ballwechsel *m* ♦ *vt*
(*support*) sammeln ♦ *vi* (*sick person, Stock
Exchange*) sich erholen; **to ~ one's strength**
seine Kräfte sammeln *or* zusammentun.

▶ **rally round** *vi* sich zusammentun ♦ *vt fus* zu
Hilfe kommen *+dat.*

rallying point ['rælɪŋ-] *n* Sammelstelle *f.*

RAM [ræm] *n abbr* (*COMPUT: = random access
memory*) RAM.

ram [ræm] *n* Widder *m* ♦ *vt* rammen.

ramble ['ræmbl] *n* Wanderung *f* ♦ *vi* wandern;
(*also: ~ on: talk*) schwafeln.

rambler ['ræmblə*] *n* Wanderer *m*, Wanderin *f*;
(*BOT*) Kletterrose *f.*

rambling ['ræmblɪŋ] *adj* (*speech, letter*)
weitschweifig; (*house*) weitläufig; (*BOT*)
rankend, Kletter-.

rambunctious [ræm'bʌŋkʃəs] (*US*) *adj*
= **rumbustious.**

RAMC (*BRIT*) *n abbr* (= *Royal Army Medical
Corps*) *Verband zur Versorgung der
Armee mit Stabsärzten und
Sanitätern.*

ramifications [ræmɪfɪ'keɪʃənz] *npl*
Auswirkungen *pl.*

ramp [ræmp] *n* Rampe *f*; (*in garage*)
Hebebühne *f*; **on ~** (*US: AUT*) Auffahrt *f*; **off
~** (*US: AUT*) Ausfahrt *f.*

rampage [ræm'peɪdʒ] *n*: **to be/go on the ~**
randalieren ♦ *vi*: **they went rampaging
through the town** sie zogen randalierend
durch die Stadt.

rampant ['ræmpənt] *adj*: **to be ~** (*crime,
disease etc*) wild wuchern.

rampart ['ræmpɑːt] *n* Schutzwall *m.*

ram raiding [-reɪdɪŋ] *n Einbruchdiebstahl,
wobei die Diebe mit einem Wagen in die
Schaufensterfront eines Ladens
eindringen.*

ramshackle ['ræmʃækl] *adj* (*house*) baufällig;
(*cart*) klapprig; (*table*) altersschwach.

RAN *n abbr* (= *Royal Australian Navy*)
australische Marine *f.*

ran [ræn] *pt of* **run.**

ranch [rɑːntʃ] *n* Ranch *f.*

rancher ['rɑːntʃə*] *n* Rancher(in) *m(f)*; (*worker*)
Farmhelfer(in) *m(f).*

rancid ['rænsɪd] *adj* ranzig.

rancidity [ræn'sɪdɪtɪ] *n* Ranzigkeit *f.*

rancour, (*US*) **rancor** ['ræŋkə*] *n*
Verbitterung *f.*

R & B *n abbr* (= *rhythm and blues*) R & B.

R & D *n abbr* = **research and development.**

random ['rændəm] *adj* (*arrangement*)
willkürlich; (*selection*) zufällig; (*COMPUT*)
wahlfrei; (*MATH*) Zufalls- ♦ *n*: **at ~** aufs
Geratewohl.

random access *n* (*COMPUT*) wahlfreier
Zugriff *m.*

random access memory *n* (*COMPUT*)
Schreib-Lese-Speicher *m.*

R & R (*US*) *n abbr* (*MIL: = rest and recreation*)
Urlaub *m.*

randy ['rændɪ] (*BRIT: inf*) *adj* geil, scharf.

rang [ræŋ] *pt of* **ring.**

range [reɪndʒ] *n* (*of mountains*) Kette *f*; (*of
missile*) Reichweite *f*; (*of voice*) Umfang *m*;
(*series*) Reihe *f*; (*of products*) Auswahl *f*; (*MIL:
also: rifle ~*) Schießstand *m*; (*also: kitchen ~*)
Herd *m* ♦ *vt* (*place in a line*) anordnen ♦ *vi*: **to
~ over** (*extend*) sich erstrecken über *+acc*;
price ~ Preisspanne *f*; **do you have
anything else in this price ~?** haben Sie noch
etwas anderes in dieser Preisklasse?;
within (**firing**) **~** in Schussweite; **at
close ~** aus unmittelbarer Entfernung;
~d left/right (*text*) links-/rechtsbündig;
to ~ from ... to ... sich zwischen ... und ...
bewegen.

ranger ['reɪndʒə*] *n* Förster(in) *m(f).*

Rangoon [ræŋ'guːn] *n* Rangun *nt.*

rank [ræŋk] *n* (*row*) Reihe *f*; (*MIL*) Rang *m*;
(*social class*) Schicht *f*; (*BRIT: also: taxi ~*)
Taxistand *m* ♦ *vi*: **to ~ as/among** zählen zu
♦ *vt*: **he is ~ed third in the world** er steht
weltweit an dritter Stelle ♦ *adj* (*stinking*)
stinkend; (*sheer: hypocrisy etc*) rein; **the
ranks** *npl* (*MIL*) die Mannschaften *pl*; **the
~ and file** (*ordinary members*) die Basis
f; **to close ~s** (*fig, MIL*) die Reihen
schließen.

rankle ['ræŋkl] *vi* (*insult*) nachwirken; **to
~ with sb** jdn wurmen.

rank outsider *n* totaler Außenseiter *m*, totale
Außenseiterin *f.*

ransack ['rænsæk] *vt* (*search*) durchwühlen;
(*plunder*) plündern.

ransom ['rænsəm] *n* (*money*) Lösegeld *nt*; **to
hold sb to ~** (*hostage*) jdn als Geisel halten;
(*fig*) jdn erpressen.

rant [rænt] *vi* schimpfen, wettern; **to ~ and
rave** herumwettern.

ranting ['ræntɪŋ] *n* Geschimpfe *nt.*

rap [ræp] *vi* klopfen ♦ *vt*: **to ~ sb's knuckles**
jdm auf die Finger klopfen ♦ *n* (*at door*)
Klopfen *nt*; (*also: ~ music*) Rap *m.*

rape [reɪp] *n* Vergewaltigung *f*; (*BOT*) Raps *m*
♦ *vt* vergewaltigen.

rape(seed) oil ['reɪp(siːd)-] *n* Rapsöl *nt.*

rapid ['ræpɪd] *adj* schnell; (*growth, change*) schnell, rapide.
rapidity [rə'pɪdɪtɪ] *n* Schnelligkeit *f*.
rapidly ['ræpɪdlɪ] *adv* schnell; (*grow, change*) schnell, rapide.
rapids ['ræpɪdz] *npl* Stromschnellen *pl*.
rapist ['reɪpɪst] *n* Vergewaltiger *m*.
rapport [ræ'pɔː'] *n* enges Verhältnis *nt*.
rapprochement [ræ'prɔʃmɑ̃ːŋ] *n* Annäherung *f*.
rapt [ræpt] *adj* (*attention*) gespannt; **to be ~ in thought** in Gedanken versunken sein.
rapture ['ræptʃə'] *n* Entzücken *nt*; **to go into ~s over** ins Schwärmen geraten über +*acc*.
rapturous ['ræptʃərəs] *adj* (*applause, welcome*) stürmisch.
rare [rɛə'] *adj* selten; (*steak*) nur angebraten, englisch (gebraten); **it is ~ to find that ...** es kommt nur selten vor, dass ...
rarebit ['rɛəbɪt] *n see* **Welsh rarebit**.
rarefied ['rɛərɪfaɪd] *adj* (*air, atmosphere*) dünn; (*fig*) exklusiv.
rarely ['rɛəlɪ] *adv* selten.
raring ['rɛərɪŋ] *adj:* **~ to go** (*inf*) in den Startlöchern.
rarity ['rɛərɪtɪ] *n* Seltenheit *f*.
rascal ['rɑːskl] *n* (*child*) Frechdachs *m*; (*rogue*) Schurke *m*.
rash [ræʃ] *adj* (*person*) unbesonnen; (*promise, act*) übereilt ♦ *n* (*MED*) Ausschlag *m*; (*of events etc*) Flut *f*; **to come out in a ~** einen Ausschlag bekommen.
rasher ['ræʃə'] *n* (*of bacon*) Scheibe *f*.
rashly ['ræʃlɪ] *adv* (*promise etc*) voreilig.
rasp [rɑːsp] *n* (*tool*) Raspel *f*; (*sound*) Kratzen *nt* ♦ *vt, vi* krächzen.
raspberry ['rɑːzbərɪ] *n* Himbeere *f*; **~ bush** Himbeerstrauch *m*; **to blow a ~** (*inf*) verächtlich schnauben.
rasping ['rɑːspɪŋ] *adj:* **a ~ noise** ein kratzendes Geräusch.
Rastafarian *n* Rastafarier *m*.
rat [ræt] *n* Ratte *f*.
ratable ['reɪtəbl] *adj* = **rateable**.
ratchet ['rætʃɪt] *n* Sperrklinke *f*; **~ wheel** Sperrrad *nt*.
rate [reɪt] *n* (*speed: of change etc*) Tempo *nt*; (*of inflation, unemployment etc*) Rate *f*; (*of interest, taxation*) Satz *m*; (*price*) Preis *m* ♦ *vt* einschätzen; **rates** *npl* (*BRIT: property tax*) Kommunalabgaben *pl*; **at a ~ of 60 kph** mit einem Tempo von 60 km/h; **~ of growth** (*ECON*) Wachstumsrate *f*; **~ of return** (*FIN*) Rendite *f*; **pulse ~** Pulszahl *f*; **at this/that ~** wenn es so weitergeht; **at any ~** auf jeden Fall; **to ~ sb/sth as** jdn/etw einschätzen als; **to ~ sb/sth among** jdn/etw zählen zu; **to ~ sb/sth highly** jdn/etw hoch einschätzen.
rateable ['reɪtəbl] *adj:* **~ value** (*BRIT*) ♦ *n* steuerbarer Wert *m*.
ratepayer ['reɪtpeɪə'] (*BRIT*) *n* Steuerzahler(in) *m(f)*.

rather ['rɑːðə'] *adv* (*somewhat*) etwas; (*very*) ziemlich; **~ a lot** ziemlich *or* recht viel; **I would ~ go** ich würde lieber gehen; **~ than** (*instead of*) anstelle *or* an Stelle von; **or ~** (*more accurately*) oder vielmehr; **I'd ~ not say** das möchte ich lieber nicht sagen; **I ~ think he won't come** ich glaube eher, dass er nicht kommt.
ratification [rætɪfɪ'keɪʃən] *n* Ratifikation *f*.
ratify ['rætɪfaɪ] *vt* (*treaty etc*) ratifizieren.
rating ['reɪtɪŋ] *n* (*score*) Rate *f*; (*assessment*) Beurteilung *f*; (*NAUT: BRIT: sailor*) Matrose *m*; **ratings** *npl* (*RADIO, TV*) Einschaltquote *f*.
ratio ['reɪʃɪəu] *n* Verhältnis *nt*; **a ~ of 5 to 1** ein Verhältnis von 5 zu 1.
ration ['ræʃən] *n* Ration *f* ♦ *vt* rationieren; **rations** *npl* (*MIL*) Rationen *pl*.
rational ['ræʃənl] *adj* rational, vernünftig.
rationale [ræʃə'nɑːl] *n* Grundlage *f*.
rationalization [ræʃnəlaɪ'zeɪʃən] *n* (*justification*) Rechtfertigung *f*; (*of company, system*) Rationalisierung *f*.
rationalize ['ræʃnəlaɪz] *vt* (*see n*) rechtfertigen, rationalisieren.
rationally ['ræʃnəlɪ] *adv* vernünftig, rational.
rationing ['ræʃnɪŋ] *n* Rationierung *f*.
ratpack (*BRIT: inf*) *n* (*reporters*) Pressemeute *f*.
rat poison *n* Rattengift *nt*.
rat race *n:* **the ~** der ständige *or* tägliche Konkurrenzkampf *m*.
rattan [ræ'tæn] *n* Rattan *nt*, Peddigrohr *nt*.
rattle ['rætl] *n* (*of door, window, snake*) Klappern *nt*; (*of train, car etc*) Rattern *nt*; (*of chain*) Rasseln *nt*; (*toy*) Rassel *f* ♦ *vi* (*chains*) rasseln; (*windows*) klappern; (*bottles*) klirren ♦ *vt* (*shake noisily*) rütteln an +*dat*; (*fig: unsettle*) nervös machen; **to ~ along** (*car, bus*) dahinrattern.
rattlesnake ['rætlsneɪk] *n* Klapperschlange *f*.
ratty ['rætɪ] (*inf*) *adj* gereizt.
raucous ['rɔːkəs] *adj* (*voice etc*) rau.
raucously ['rɔːkəslɪ] *adv* rau.
raunchy ['rɔːntʃɪ] *adj* (*voice, song*) lüstern, geil.
ravage ['rævɪdʒ] *vt* verwüsten.
ravages ['rævɪdʒɪz] *npl* (*of war*) Verwüstungen *pl*; (*of weather*) zerstörende Auswirkungen *pl*; (*of time*) Spuren *pl*.
rave [reɪv] *vi* (*in anger*) toben ♦ *adj* (*inf: review*) glänzend; (*scene, culture*) Rave- ♦ *n* (*BRIT: inf: party*) Rave *m*, Fete *f*.
  ► **rave about** schwärmen von.
raven ['reɪvən] *n* Rabe *m*.
ravenous ['rævənəs] *adj* (*person*) ausgehungert; (*appetite*) unersättlich.
ravine [rə'viːn] *n* Schlucht *f*.
raving ['reɪvɪŋ] *adj:* **a ~ lunatic** ein total verrückter Typ.
ravings ['reɪvɪŋz] *npl* Fantastereien *pl*.
ravioli [rævɪ'əulɪ] *n* Ravioli *pl*.
ravishing ['rævɪʃɪŋ] *adj* hinreißend.
raw [rɔː] *adj* roh; (*sore*) wund; (*inexperienced*)

unerfahren; (*weather, day*) rau; **to get a ~ deal** ungerecht behandelt werden.

Rawalpindi [rɔːl'pɪndɪ] n Rawalpindi nt.

raw material n Rohmaterial nt.

ray [reɪ] n Strahl m; **~ of hope** Hoffnungsschimmer m.

rayon ['reɪɔn] n Reyon nt.

raze [reɪz] vt (*also*: **to ~ to the ground**) dem Erdboden gleichmachen.

razor ['reɪzə*] n Rasierapparat m; (*open ~*) Rasiermesser nt.

razor blade n Rasierklinge f.

razzle ['ræzl] (*BRIT*: inf) n: **to be/go on the ~** einen draufmachen.

razzmatazz ['ræzmə'tæz] (inf) n Trubel m.

RC abbr (= *Roman Catholic*) r.-k.

RCAF n abbr (= *Royal Canadian Air Force*) kanadische Luftwaffe f.

RCMP n abbr (= *Royal Canadian Mounted Police*) kanadische berittene Polizei.

RCN n abbr (= *Royal Canadian Navy*) kanadische Marine.

RD (*US*) abbr (*POST*: = *rural delivery*) Landpostzustellung f.

Rd abbr (= *road*) Str.

RDC (*BRIT*) n abbr = **rural district council**.

RE (*BRIT*) n abbr (*SCOL*) = **religious education**; (*MIL*: = *Royal Engineers*) *Königliches Pionierkorps*.

re [riː] prep (*with regard to*) bezüglich +*gen*.

reach [riːtʃ] n (*range*) Reichweite f ♦ vt erreichen; (*conclusion, decision*) kommen zu; (*be able to touch*) kommen an +*acc* ♦ vi (*stretch out one's arm*) langen; **reaches** npl (*of river*) Gebiete pl; **within/out of ~** in/außer Reichweite; **within easy ~ of the supermarket/station** ganz in der Nähe des Supermarkts/Bahnhofs; **beyond the ~ of sb/sth** außerhalb der Reichweite von jdm/ etw; "**keep out of the ~ of children**" „von Kindern fern halten"; **can I ~ you at your hotel?** kann ich Sie in Ihrem Hotel erreichen?

▶ **reach out** vt (*hand*) ausstrecken ♦ vi die Hand ausstrecken; **to ~ out for sth** nach etw greifen.

react [riː'ækt] vi: **to ~ (to)** (*also MED*) reagieren (auf +*acc*); (*CHEM*): **to ~ (with)** reagieren (mit); **to ~ (against)** (*rebel*) sich wehren (gegen).

reaction [riː'ækʃən] n Reaktion f; **reactions** npl (*reflexes*) Reaktionen pl; **a ~ against sth** Widerstand gegen etw.

reactionary [riː'ækʃənrɪ] adj reaktionär ♦ n Reaktionär(in) m(f).

reactor [riː'æktə*] n (*also*: **nuclear ~**) Kernreaktor m.

read [riːd] (*pt, pp* **read**) [rɛd] vi lesen; (*piece of writing etc*) sich lesen ♦ vt lesen; (*meter, thermometer etc*) ablesen; (*understand: mood, thoughts*) sich versetzen in +*acc*; (*meter, thermometer etc: measurement*) anzeigen;

(*study*) studieren; **to ~ sb's lips** jdm von den Lippen ablesen; **to ~ sb's mind** jds Gedanken lesen; **to ~ between the lines** zwischen den Zeilen lesen; **to take sth as ~** (*self-evident*) etw für selbstverständlich halten; **you can take it as ~ that ...** Sie können davon ausgehen, dass ...; **do you ~ me?** (*TEL*) verstehen Sie mich?; **to ~ sth into sb's remarks** etw in jds Bemerkungen hineininterpretieren.

▶ **read out** vt vorlesen.

▶ **read over** vt durchlesen.

▶ **read through** vt durchlesen.

▶ **read up on** vt fus sich informieren über +*acc*.

readable ['riːdəbl] adj (*legible*) lesbar; (*book, author etc*) lesenswert.

reader ['riːdə*] n (*person*) Leser(in) m(f); (*book*) Lesebuch nt; (*BRIT: at university*) ≈ Dozent(in) m(f); **to be an avid/slow ~** eifrig/ langsam lesen.

readership ['riːdəʃɪp] n (*of newspaper etc*) Leserschaft f.

readily ['rɛdɪlɪ] adv (*without hesitation*) bereitwillig; (*easily*) ohne weiteres.

readiness ['rɛdɪnɪs] n Bereitschaft f; **in ~ for** bereit für.

reading ['riːdɪŋ] n Lesen nt; (*understanding*) Verständnis nt; (*from bible, of poetry etc*) Lesung f; (*on meter, thermometer etc*) Anzeige f.

reading lamp n Leselampe f.

reading matter n Lesestoff m.

reading room n Lesesaal m.

readjust [riːə'dʒʌst] vt (*position, knob, instrument etc*) neu einstellen ♦ vi: **to ~ (to)** sich anpassen (an +*acc*).

readjustment [riːə'dʒʌstmənt] n (*fig*) Neuorientierung f.

ready ['rɛdɪ] adj (*prepared*) bereit, fertig; (*willing*) bereit; (*easy*) leicht; (*available*) fertig ♦ n: **at the ~** (*MIL*) einsatzbereit; (*fig*) griffbereit; **~ for use** gebrauchsfertig; **to be ~ to do sth** bereit sein, etw zu tun; **to get ~** sich fertig machen; **to get sth ~** etw bereitmachen.

ready cash n Bargeld nt.

ready-cooked ['rɛdɪkukt] adj vorgekocht.

ready-made ['rɛdɪmeɪd] adj (*clothes*) von der Stange, Konfektions-; **~ meal** Fertiggericht nt.

ready-mix ['rɛdɪmɪks] n (*for cakes etc*) Backmischung f; (*concrete*) Fertigbeton m.

ready money n = **ready cash**.

ready reckoner [-'rɛkənə*] (*BRIT*) n Rechentabelle f.

ready-to-wear ['rɛdɪtə'wɛə*] adj (*clothes*) von der Stange, Konfektions-.

reaffirm [riːə'fəːm] vt bestätigen.

reagent [riː'eɪdʒənt] n: **chemical ~** Reagens nt, Reagenz nt.

real [rɪəl] adj (*reason, result etc*) wirklich;

(leather, gold etc) echt; *(life, feeling)* wahr; *(for emphasis)* echt ♦ *adv (US: inf: very)* echt; **in ~ life** im wahren *or* wirklichen Leben; **in ~ terms** effektiv.

real ale *n* Real Ale *nt*.

real estate *n* Immobilien *pl* ♦ *cpd (US: agent, business etc)* Immobilien-.

realign *vt* neu ausrichten.

realism ['rɪəlɪzəm] *n (also ART)* Realismus *m*.

realist ['rɪəlɪst] *n* Realist(in) *m(f)*.

realistic [rɪə'lɪstɪk] *adj* realistisch.

reality [riː'ælɪtɪ] *n* Wirklichkeit *f*, Realität *f*; **in ~** in Wirklichkeit.

Reality TV *n* Reality-TV *nt*.

realization [rɪəlaɪ'zeɪʃən] *n (understanding)* Erkenntnis *f*; *(fulfilment)* Verwirklichung *f*, Realisierung *f*; *(FIN: of asset)* Realisation *f*.

realize ['rɪəlaɪz] *vt (understand)* verstehen; *(fulfil)* verwirklichen, realisieren; *(FIN: amount, profit)* realisieren; **I ~ that ...** es ist mir klar, dass ...

really ['rɪəlɪ] *adv* wirklich; **what ~ happened** was wirklich geschah; **~?** wirklich?; **~!** *(indicating annoyance)* also wirklich!

realm [rɛlm] *n (fig: field)* Bereich *m*; *(kingdom)* Reich *nt*.

real-time ['riːltaɪm] *adj (COMPUT: processing etc)* Echtzeit-.

Realtor ® ['rɪəltɔːʳ] *(US) n* Immobilienmakler(in) *m(f)*.

ream [riːm] *n (of paper)* Ries *nt*; **reams** *(inf, fig)* Bände *pl*.

reap [riːp] *vt (crop)* einbringen, ernten; *(fig: benefits)* ernten; *(: rewards)* bekommen.

reaper ['riːpəʳ] *n (machine)* Mähdrescher *m*.

reappear [riːə'pɪəʳ] *vi* wieder auftauchen.

reappearance [riːə'pɪərəns] *n* Wiederauftauchen *nt*.

reapply [riːə'plaɪ] *vi*: **to ~ for** sich erneut bewerben um.

reappoint [riːə'pɔɪnt] *vt (to job)* wieder einstellen.

reappraisal [riːə'preɪzl] *n (of idea etc)* Neubeurteilung *f*.

rear [rɪəʳ] *adj* hintere(r, s); *(wheel etc)* Hinter- ♦ *n* Rückseite *f*; *(buttocks)* Hinterteil *nt* ♦ *vt (family, animals)* aufziehen ♦ *vi (also: ~ up: horse)* sich aufbäumen.

rear admiral *n* Konteradmiral *m*.

rear-engined ['rɪər'ɛndʒɪnd] *adj* mit Heckmotor.

rearguard ['rɪəgaːd] *n (MIL)* Nachhut *f*; **to fight a ~ action** *(fig)* sich erbittert wehren.

rearm [riː'aːm] *vi (country)* wieder aufrüsten ♦ *vt* wieder bewaffnen.

rearmament [riː'aːməmənt] *n* Wiederaufrüstung *f*.

rearrange [riːə'reɪndʒ] *vt (furniture)* umstellen; *(meeting)* den Termin ändern +gen.

rear-view mirror ['rɪəvjuː-] *n* Rückspiegel *m*.

reason ['riːzn] *n (cause)* Grund *m*; *(rationality)* Verstand *m*; *(common sense)* Vernunft *f* ♦ *vi*:

to ~ with sb vernünftig mit jdm reden; **the ~ for/why** der Grund für/, warum; **we have ~ to believe that ...** wir haben Grund zu der Annahme, dass ...; **it stands to ~ that ...** es ist zu erwarten, dass ...; **she claims with good ~ that ...** sie behauptet mit gutem Grund *or* mit Recht, dass ...; **all the more ~ why ...** ein Grund mehr, warum ...; **yes, but within ~** ja, solange es sich im Rahmen hält.

reasonable ['riːznəbl] *adj* vernünftig; *(number, amount)* angemessen; *(not bad)* ganz ordentlich; **be ~!** sei doch vernünftig!

reasonably ['riːznəblɪ] *adv (fairly)* ziemlich; *(sensibly)* vernünftig; **one could ~ assume that ...** man könnte durchaus annehmen, dass ...

reasoned ['riːznd] *adj (argument)* durchdacht.

reasoning ['riːznɪŋ] *n* Argumentation *f*.

reassemble [riːə'sɛmbl] *vt (machine)* wieder zusammensetzen ♦ *vi* sich wieder versammeln.

reassert [riːə'səːt] *vt*: **to ~ one's authority** seine Autorität wieder geltend machen.

reassurance [riːə'ʃuərəns] *n (comfort)* Beruhigung *f*; *(guarantee)* Bestätigung *f*.

reassure [riːə'ʃuəʳ] *vt* beruhigen.

reassuring [riːə'ʃuərɪŋ] *adj* beruhigend.

reawakening [riːə'weɪknɪŋ] *n* Wiedererwachen *nt*.

rebate ['riːbeɪt] *n (on tax etc)* Rückerstattung *f*; *(discount)* Ermäßigung *f*.

rebel ['rɛbl] *n* Rebell(in) *m(f)* ♦ *vi* rebellieren.

rebellion [rɪ'bɛljən] *n* Rebellion *f*.

rebellious [rɪ'bɛljəs] *adj* rebellisch.

rebirth [riː'bəːθ] *n* Wiedergeburt *f*.

rebound [rɪ'baund] *vi (ball)* zurückprallen ♦ *n*: **on the ~** *(fig)* als Tröstung.

rebuff [rɪ'bʌf] *n* Abfuhr *f* ♦ *vt* zurückweisen.

rebuild [riː'bɪld] *(irreg: like* **build**) *vt* wieder aufbauen; *(confidence)* wieder herstellen.

rebuke [rɪ'bjuːk] *vt* zurechtweisen, tadeln ♦ *n* Zurechtweisung *f*, Tadel *m*.

rebut [rɪ'bʌt] *(form) vt* widerlegen.

rebuttal [rɪ'bʌtl] *(form) n* Widerlegung *f*.

recalcitrant [rɪ'kælsɪtrənt] *adj* aufsässig.

recall [rɪ'kɔːl] *vt (remember)* sich erinnern an +acc; *(ambassador)* abberufen; *(product)* zurückrufen ♦ *n (of memories)* Erinnerung *f*; *(of ambassador)* Abberufung *f*; *(of product)* Rückruf *m*; **beyond ~** unwiederbringlich.

recant [rɪ'kænt] *vi* widerrufen.

recap ['riːkæp] *vt, vi* zusammenfassen ♦ *n* Zusammenfassung *f*.

recapitulate [riːkə'pɪtjuleɪt] *vt, vi* = **recap**.

recapture [riː'kæptʃəʳ] *vt (town)* wieder einnehmen; *(prisoner)* wieder ergreifen; *(atmosphere etc)* heraufbeschwören.

rec'd *abbr (COMM:* = **received**) erh.

recede [rɪ'siːd] *vi (tide)* zurückgehen; *(lights etc)* verschwinden; *(memory, hope)* schwinden; **his hair is beginning to ~** er

bekommt eine Stirnglatze.
receding [rɪ'siːdɪŋ] adj (hairline)
zurückweichend; (chin) fliehend.
receipt [rɪ'siːt] n (document) Quittung f; (act of
receiving) Erhalt m; **receipts** npl (COMM)
Einnahmen pl; **on ~ of** bei Erhalt +gen; **to be
in ~ of sth** etw erhalten.
receivable [rɪ'siːvəbl] adj (COMM) zulässig;
(owing) ausstehend.
receive [rɪ'siːv] vt erhalten, bekommen;
(injury) erleiden; (treatment) erhalten;
(visitor, guest) empfangen; **to be on the
receiving end of sth** der Leidtragende
von etw sein; **"~d with thanks"** (COMM)
„dankend erhalten".

RECEIVED PRONUNCIATION

Received Pronunciation oder **RP** ist die
hochsprachliche Standardaussprache des
britischen Englisch, die bis vor kurzem in der Ober-
und Mittelschicht vorherrschte und auch noch
großes Ansehen unter höheren Beamten genießt.

---

receiver [rɪ'siːvə*] n (TEL) Hörer m; (RADIO,
TV) Empfänger m; (of stolen goods)
Hehler(in) m(f); (COMM) Empfänger(in) m(f).
receivership [rɪ'siːvəʃɪp] n: **to go into ~** in
Konkurs gehen.
recent ['riːsnt] adj (event) kürzlich; (times)
letzte(r, s); **in ~ years** in den letzten Jahren.
recently ['riːsntlɪ] adv (not long ago) kürzlich;
(lately) in letzter Zeit; **as ~ as** erst; **until ~**
bis vor kurzem.
receptacle [rɪ'sɛptɪkl] n Behälter m.
reception [rɪ'sɛpʃən] n (in hotel, office etc)
Rezeption f; (party, RADIO, TV) Empfang m;
(welcome) Aufnahme f.
reception centre (BRIT) n Aufnahmelager nt.
reception desk n Rezeption f.
receptionist [rɪ'sɛpʃənɪst] n (in hotel)
Empfangschef m, Empfangsdame f; (in
doctor's surgery) Sprechstundenhilfe f.
receptive [rɪ'sɛptɪv] adj aufnahmebereit.
recess [rɪ'sɛs] n (in room) Nische f; (secret
place) Winkel m; (POL etc: holiday) Ferien pl;
(US: LAW: short break) Pause f; (esp US:
SCOL) Pause f.
recession [rɪ'sɛʃən] n (ECON) Rezession f.
recharge [riː'tʃɑːdʒ] vt (battery) aufladen.
rechargeable [riː'tʃɑːdʒəbl] adj (battery)
aufladbar.
recipe ['rɛsɪpɪ] n Rezept nt; **a ~ for success** ein
Erfolgsrezept nt; **to be a ~ for disaster** in
die Katastrophe führen.
recipient [rɪ'sɪpɪənt] n Empfänger(in) m(f).
reciprocal [rɪ'sɪprəkl] adj gegenseitig.
reciprocate [rɪ'sɪprəkeɪt] vt (invitation, feeling)
erwidern ♦ vi sich revanchieren.
recital [rɪ'saɪtl] n (concert) Konzert nt.
recitation [rɛsɪ'teɪʃən] n (of poem etc) Vortrag
m.

recite [rɪ'saɪt] vt (poem) vortragen; (complaints
etc) aufzählen.
reckless ['rɛkləs] adj (driving, driver)
rücksichtslos; (spending) leichtsinnig.
recklessly ['rɛkləslɪ] adv (drive) rücksichtslos;
(spend, gamble) leichtsinnig.
reckon ['rɛkən] vt (consider) halten für;
(calculate) berechnen ♦ vi: **he is somebody to
be ~ed with** mit ihm muss man rechnen; **I
~ that ...** (think) ich schätze, dass ...; **to
~ without sb/sth** nicht mit jdm/etw
rechnen.
► **reckon on** vt fus rechnen mit.
reckoning ['rɛknɪŋ] n (calculation)
Berechnung f; **the day of ~** der Tag der
Abrechnung.
reclaim [rɪ'kleɪm] vt (luggage) abholen; (tax
etc) zurückfordern; (land) gewinnen; (waste
materials) zur Wiederverwertung sammeln.
reclamation [rɛklə'meɪʃən] n (of land)
Gewinnung f.
recline [rɪ'klaɪn] vi (sit or lie back)
zurückgelehnt sitzen.
reclining [rɪ'klaɪnɪŋ] adj (seat) Liege-.
recluse [rɪ'kluːs] n Einsiedler(in) m(f).
recognition [rɛkəg'nɪʃən] n (of person, place)
Erkennen nt; (of problem, fact) Erkenntnis f;
(of achievement) Anerkennung f; **in ~ of** in
Anerkennung +gen; **to gain ~** Anerkennung
finden; **she had changed beyond ~** sie war
nicht wieder zu erkennen.
recognizable ['rɛkəgnaɪzəbl] adj erkennbar.
recognize ['rɛkəgnaɪz] vt (person, place, voice)
wieder erkennen; (sign, problem) erkennen;
(qualifications, government, achievement)
anerkennen; **to ~ sb by/as** jdn erkennen an
+dat/als.
recoil [rɪ'kɔɪl] vi (person): **to ~ from**
zurückweichen vor +dat; (fig)
zurückschrecken vor +dat ♦ n (of gun)
Rückstoß m.
recollect [rɛkə'lɛkt] vt (remember) sich
erinnern an +acc.
recollection [rɛkə'lɛkʃən] n Erinnerung f; **to
the best of my ~** soweit ich mich erinnern
or entsinnen kann.
recommend [rɛkə'mɛnd] vt empfehlen; **she
has a lot to ~ her** es spricht sehr viel für
sie.
recommendation [rɛkəmən'deɪʃən] n
Empfehlung f; **on the ~ of** auf Empfehlung
+gen.
recommended retail price (BRIT) n (COMM)
unverbindlicher Richtpreis m.
recompense ['rɛkəmpɛns] n (reward)
Belohnung f; (compensation) Entschädigung
f.
reconcilable ['rɛkənsaɪləbl] adj (ideas)
(miteinander) vereinbar.
reconcile ['rɛkənsaɪl] vt (people) versöhnen;
(facts, beliefs) (miteinander) vereinbaren, in
Einklang bringen; **to ~ o.s. to sth** sich mit

etw abfinden.

reconciliation [rɛkənsɪlɪ'eɪʃən] *n* (*of people*) Versöhnung *f*; (*of facts, beliefs*) Vereinbarung *f*.

recondite [rɪ'kɒndaɪt] *adj* obskur.

recondition [riːkən'dɪʃən] *vt* (*machine*) überholen.

reconditioned [riːkən'dɪʃənd] *adj* (*engine, TV*) generalüberholt.

reconnaissance [rɪ'kɒnɪsns] *n* (*MIL*) Aufklärung *f*.

reconnoitre, (*US*) **reconnoiter** [rɛkə'nɔɪtə'] *vt* (*MIL*) erkunden.

reconsider [riːkən'sɪdə'] *vt* (noch einmal) überdenken ♦ *vi* es sich *dat* noch einmal überlegen.

reconstitute [riː'kɒnstɪtjuːt] *vt* (*organization*) neu bilden; (*food*) wiederherstellen.

reconstruct [riːkən'strʌkt] *vt* (*building*) wieder aufbauen; (*policy, system*) neu organisieren; (*event, crime*) rekonstruieren.

reconstruction [riːkən'strʌkʃən] *n* Wiederaufbau *m*; (*of crime*) Rekonstruktion *f*.

reconvene [riːkən'viːn] *vi* (*meet again*) wieder zusammenkommen ♦ *vt* (*meeting etc*) wieder einberufen.

record ['rɛkɔːd] *n* (*written account*) Aufzeichnung *f*; (*of meeting*) Protokoll *nt*; (*of decision*) Beleg *m*; (*COMPUT*) Datensatz *m*; (*file*) Akte *f*; (*MUS: disc*) Schallplatte *f*; (*history*) Vorgeschichte *f*; (*also:* **criminal** ~) Vorstrafen *pl*; (*SPORT*) Rekord *m* ♦ *vt* aufzeichnen; (*song etc*) aufnehmen; (*temperature, speed etc*) registrieren ♦ *adj* (*sales, profits*) Rekord-; ~ **of attendance** Anwesenheitsliste *f*; **public** ~**s** Urkunden *pl* des Nationalarchivs; **to keep a** ~ **of sth** etw schriftlich festhalten; **to have a good/poor** ~ gute/schlechte Leistungen vorzuweisen haben; **to have a (criminal)** ~ vorbestraft sein; **to set** *or* **put the** ~ **straight** (*fig*) Klarheit schaffen; **he is on** ~ **as saying that ...** er hat nachweislich gesagt, dass ...; **off the** ~ (*remark*) inoffiziell ♦ *adv* (*speak*) im Vertrauen; **in** ~ **time** in Rekordzeit.

recorded delivery [rɪ'kɔːdɪd-] (*BRIT*) *n* (*POST*) Einschreiben *nt*; **to send sth (by)** ~ etw per Einschreiben senden.

recorder [rɪ'kɔːdə'] *n* (*MUS*) Blockflöte *f*; (*LAW*) *nebenamtlich als Richter tätiger Rechtsanwalt.*

record holder *n* (*SPORT*) Rekordinhaber(in) *m(f)*.

recording [rɪ'kɔːdɪŋ] *n* Aufnahme *f*.

recording studio *n* Aufnahmestudio *nt*.

record library *n* Schallplattenverleih *m*.

record player *n* Plattenspieler *m*.

recount [rɪ'kaʊnt] *vt* (*story etc*) erzählen, wiedergeben.

re-count ['riːkaʊnt] *n* (*of votes*) Nachzählung *f*

♦ *vt* (*votes*) nachzählen.

recoup [rɪ'kuːp] *vt*: **to** ~ **one's losses** seine Verluste ausgleichen.

recourse [rɪ'kɔːs] *n*: **to have** ~ **to sth** Zuflucht zu etw nehmen.

recover [rɪ'kʌvə'] *vt* (*get back*) zurückbekommen; (*stolen goods*) sicherstellen; (*wreck, body*) bergen; (*financial loss*) ausgleichen ♦ *vi* sich erholen; (*regain consciousness*) wieder zu sich kommen.

re-cover [riː'kʌvə'] *vt* (*chair etc*) neu beziehen.

recovery [rɪ'kʌvərɪ] *n* (*from illness etc*) Erholung *f*; (*in economy*) Aufschwung *m*; (*of lost items*) Wiederfinden *nt*; (*of stolen goods*) Sicherstellung *f*; (*of wreck, body*) Bergung *f*; (*of financial loss*) Ausgleich *m*.

re-create [riːkrɪ'eɪt] *vt* (*atmosphere, situation*) wieder herstellen.

recreation [rɛkrɪ'eɪʃən] *n* (*leisure*) Erholung *f*, Entspannung *f*.

recreational [rɛkrɪ'eɪʃənl] *adj* (*facilities etc*) Freizeit-.

recreational drug *n* Freizeitdroge *f*.

recreational sport *n* Freizeitsport *m*.

recreational vehicle (*US*) *n* Caravan *m*.

recrimination [rɪkrɪmɪ'neɪʃən] *n* gegenseitige Anschuldigungen *pl*.

recruit [rɪ'kruːt] *n* (*MIL*) Rekrut *m*; (*in company*) neuer Mitarbeiter *m*, neue Mitarbeiterin *f* ♦ *vt* (*MIL*) rekrutieren; (*staff, new members*) anwerben.

recruiting office [rɪ'kruːtɪŋ-] *n* (*MIL*) Rekrutierungsbüro *nt*.

recruitment [rɪ'kruːtmənt] *n* (*of staff*) Anwerbung *f*.

rectangle ['rɛktæŋgl] *n* Rechteck *nt*.

rectangular [rɛk'tæŋgjulə'] *adj* (*shape*) rechteckig.

rectify ['rɛktɪfaɪ] *vt* (*mistake etc*) korrigieren.

rector ['rɛktə'] *n* (*REL*) Pfarrer(in) *m(f)*.

rectory ['rɛktərɪ] *n* Pfarrhaus *nt*.

rectum ['rɛktəm] *n* Rektum *nt*, Mastdarm *m*.

recuperate [rɪ'kjuːpəreɪt] *vi* (*recover*) sich erholen.

recur [rɪ'kəː'] *vi* (*error, event*) sich wiederholen; (*pain etc*) wiederholt auftreten.

recurrence [rɪ'kəːrns] *n* (*see vi*) Wiederholung *f*; wiederholtes Auftreten *nt*.

recurrent [rɪ'kəːrnt] *adj* (*see vi*) sich wiederholend; wiederholt auftretend.

recurring [rɪ'kəːrɪŋ] *adj* (*problem, dream*) sich wiederholend; (*MATH*): **six point five four** ~ sechs Komma fünf Periode vier.

recycle [riː'saɪkl] *vt* (*waste, paper etc*) recyceln, wieder verwerten.

red [rɛd] *n* Rot *nt*; (*pej: POL*) Rote(r) *f(m)* ♦ *adj* rot; **to be in the** ~ (*business etc*) in den roten Zahlen sein.

red alert *n*: **to be on** ~ in höchster Alarmbereitschaft sein.

red-blooded ['rɛd'blʌdɪd] *adj* heißblütig.

REDBRICK UNIVERSITY

Als **redbrick university** werden die jüngeren britischen Universitäten bezeichnet, die im späten 19. und Anfang des 20. Jh. in Städten wie Manchester, Liverpool und Bristol gegründet wurden. Der Name steht im Gegensatz zu Oxford und Cambridge und bezieht sich auf die roten Backsteinmauern der Universitätsgebäude.

---

red carpet treatment n: **to give sb the** ~ den roten Teppich für jdn ausrollen.
Red Cross n Rotes Kreuz nt.
redcurrant ['rɛdkʌrənt] n rote Johannisbeere f.
redden ['rɛdn] vt röten ♦ vi (blush) erröten.
reddish ['rɛdɪʃ] adj rötlich.
redecorate [riːˈdɛkəreɪt] vt, vi renovieren.
redecoration [riːdɛkəˈreɪʃən] n Renovierung f.
redeem [rɪˈdiːm] vt (situation etc) retten; (voucher, sth in pawn) einlösen; (loan) abzahlen; (REL) erlösen; **to** ~ **oneself for sth** etw wieder gutmachen.
redeemable [rɪˈdiːməbl] adj (voucher etc) einlösbar.
redeeming [rɪˈdiːmɪŋ] adj (feature, quality) versöhnend.
redefine [riːdɪˈfaɪn] vt neu definieren.
redemption [rɪˈdɛmʃən] n (REL) Erlösung f; **past** or **beyond** ~ nicht mehr zu retten.
redeploy [riːdɪˈplɔɪ] vt (resources, staff) umverteilen; (MIL) verlegen.
redeployment [riːdɪˈplɔɪmənt] n (see vt) Umverteilung f; Verlegung f.
redevelop [riːdɪˈvɛləp] vt (area) sanieren.
redevelopment [riːdɪˈvɛləpmənt] n Sanierung f.
red-handed [rɛdˈhændɪd] adj: **to be caught** ~ auf frischer Tat ertappt werden.
redhead ['rɛdhɛd] n Rotschopf m.
red herring n (fig) falsche Spur f.
red-hot [rɛdˈhɒt] adj (metal) rot glühend.
redirect [riːdaɪˈrɛkt] vt (mail) nachsenden; (traffic) umleiten.
rediscover [riːdɪsˈkʌvə*] vt wieder entdecken.
redistribute [riːdɪsˈtrɪbjuːt] vt umverteilen.
red-letter day ['rɛdlɛtə-] n besonderer Tag m.
red light n (AUT): **to go through a** ~ eine Ampel bei Rot überfahren.
red-light district ['rɛdlaɪt-] n Rotlichtviertel nt.
red meat n Rind- und Lammfleisch.
redness ['rɛdnɪs] n Röte f.
redo [riːˈduː] (irreg: like **do**) vt noch einmal machen.
redolent ['rɛdələnt] adj: **to be** ~ **of sth** nach etw riechen; (fig) an etw erinnern.
redouble [riːˈdʌbl] vt: **to** ~ **one's efforts** seine Anstrengungen verdoppeln.
redraft [riːˈdrɑːft] vt (agreement) neu abfassen.

redraw [riːˈdrɔː] vt neu zeichnen.
redress [rɪˈdrɛs] n (compensation) Wiedergutmachung f ♦ vt (error etc) wieder gutmachen; **to** ~ **the balance** das Gleichgewicht wieder herstellen.
Red Sea n: **the** ~ das Rote Meer.
redskin ['rɛdskɪn] (old: offensive) n Rothaut f.
red tape n (fig) Bürokratie f.
reduce [rɪˈdjuːs] vt (spending, numbers, risk etc) vermindern, reduzieren; **to** ~ **sth by/to 5%** etw um/auf 5% acc reduzieren; **to** ~ **sb to tears/silence** jdn zum Weinen/Schweigen bringen; **to** ~ **sb to begging/stealing** jdn zur Bettelei/zum Diebstahl zwingen; "~ **speed now**" (AUT) „langsam fahren".
reduced [rɪˈdjuːst] adj (goods, ticket etc) ermäßigt; "**greatly** ~ **prices**" „Preise stark reduziert".
reduction [rɪˈdʌkʃən] n (in price etc) Ermäßigung f; (in numbers) Verminderung f.
redundancy [rɪˈdʌndənsɪ] (BRIT) n (dismissal) Entlassung f; (unemployment) Arbeitslosigkeit f; **compulsory** ~ Entlassung f; **voluntary** ~ freiwilliger Verzicht m auf den Arbeitsplatz.
redundancy payment (BRIT) n Abfindung f.
redundant [rɪˈdʌndnt] adj (BRIT: worker) arbeitslos; (word, object) überflüssig; **to be made** ~ (worker) den Arbeitsplatz verlieren.
reed [riːd] n (BOT) Schilf nt; (MUS: of clarinet etc) Rohrblatt nt.
re-educate [riːˈɛdjukeɪt] vt umerziehen.
reedy ['riːdɪ] adj (voice) Fistel-.
reef [riːf] n (at sea) Riff nt.
reek [riːk] vi: **to** ~ (**of**) (lit, fig) stinken (nach).
reel [riːl] n (of thread etc, on fishing-rod) Rolle f; (CINE: scene) Szene f; (of film, tape) Spule f; (dance) Reel m ♦ vi (sway) taumeln; **my head is** ~**ing** mir dreht sich der Kopf.
▶ **reel in** vt (fish, line) einholen.
▶ **reel off** vt (say) herunterrasseln.
re-election [riːɪˈlɛkʃən] n Wiederwahl f.
re-enter [riːˈɛntə*] vt (country) wieder einreisen in +acc; (SPACE) wieder eintreten in +acc.
re-entry [riːˈɛntrɪ] n Wiedereinreise f; (SPACE) Wiedereintritt m.
re-examine [riːɪgˈzæmɪn] vt (proposal etc) nochmals prüfen; (witness) nochmals vernehmen.
re-export ['riːɛksˈpɔːt] vt wieder ausführen ♦ n Wiederausfuhr f; (commodity) wieder ausgeführte Ware f.
ref [rɛf] (inf) n abbr (SPORT) = **referee**.
ref. abbr (COMM: = with reference to) betr.; **your** ~ Ihr Zeichen:.
refectory [rɪˈfɛktərɪ] n (in university) Mensa f.
refer [rɪˈfəː*] vt: **to** ~ **sb to** (book etc) jdn verweisen auf +acc; (doctor, hospital) jdn überweisen zu; **to** ~ **sth to** (task, problem) etw übergeben an +acc; **he** ~**red me to the manager** er verwies mich an den Geschäftsführer.
▶ **refer to** vt fus (mention) erwähnen; (relate to)

sich beziehen auf +*acc*; (*consult*)
hinzuziehen.

referee [refə'riː] *n* (*SPORT*) Schiedsrichter(in)
m(f); (*BRIT: for job application*) Referenz *f* ♦ *vt*
als Schiedsrichter(in) leiten.

reference ['rɛfrəns] *n* (*mention*) Hinweis *m*; (*in
book, article*) Quellenangabe *f*; (*for job
application, person*) Referenz *f*; **with ~ to** mit
Bezug auf +*acc*; **"please quote this ~"**
(*COMM*) „bitte dieses Zeichen angeben".

reference book *n* Nachschlagewerk *nt*.

reference library *n* Präsenzbibliothek *f*.

reference number *n* Aktenzeichen *nt*.

referenda [refə'rɛndə] *npl of* **referendum**.

referendum [refə'rɛndəm] (*pl* **referenda**) *n*
Referendum *nt*, Volksentscheid *m*.

referral [rɪ'fəːrəl] *n* (*of matter, problem*)
Weiterleitung *f*; (*to doctor, specialist*)
Überweisung *f*.

refill [riː'fɪl] *vt* nachfüllen ♦ *n* (*for pen etc*)
Nachfüllmine *f*; (*drink*) Nachfüllung *f*.

refine [rɪ'faɪn] *vt* (*sugar, oil*) raffinieren;
(*theory, idea*) verfeinern.

refined [rɪ'faɪnd] *adj* (*person*) kultiviert; (*taste*)
fein, vornehm; (*sugar, oil*) raffiniert.

refinement [rɪ'faɪnmənt] *n* (*of person*)
Kultiviertheit *f*; (*of system, ideas*)
Verfeinerung *f*.

refinery [rɪ'faɪnərɪ] *n* (*for oil etc*) Raffinerie *f*.

refit [riː'fɪt] (*NAUT*) *n* Überholung *f* ♦ *vt* (*ship*)
überholen.

reflate [riː'fleɪt] *vt* (*economy*) ankurbeln.

reflation [riː'fleɪʃən] *n* (*ECON*) Reflation *f*.

reflationary [riː'fleɪʃənrɪ] *adj* (*ECON*)
reflationär.

reflect [rɪ'flɛkt] *vt* reflektieren; (*fig*)
widerspiegeln ♦ *vi* (*think*) nachdenken.
▶ **reflect on** *vt fus* (*discredit*) ein schlechtes
Licht werfen auf +*acc*.

reflection [rɪ'flɛkʃən] *n* (*image*) Spiegelbild *nt*;
(*of light, heat*) Reflexion *f*; (*fig*)
Widerspiegelung *f*; (: *thought*) Gedanke *m*;
on ~ nach genauerer Überlegung; **this is a
~ on** ... (*criticism*) das sagt einiges über ...

reflector [rɪ'flɛktə*] *n* (*AUT etc*) Rückstrahler
m; (*for light, heat*) Reflektor *m*.

reflex ['riːflɛks] *adj* Reflex-; **reflexes** *npl*
(*PHYSIOL, PSYCH*) Reflexe *pl*.

reflexive [rɪ'flɛksɪv] *adj* (*LING*) reflexiv.

reform [rɪ'fɔːm] *n* Reform *f* ♦ *vt* reformieren
♦ *vi* (*criminal etc*) sich bessern.

reformat [riː'fɔːmæt] *vt* (*COMPUT*) neu
formatieren.

Reformation [refə'meɪʃən] *n*: **the** ~ die
Reformation.

reformatory [rɪ'fɔːmətərɪ] (*US*) *n*
Besserungsanstalt *f*.

reformed [rɪ'fɔːmd] *adj* (*character, alcoholic*)
gewandelt.

refrain [rɪ'freɪn] *vi*: **to** ~ **from doing sth** etw
unterlassen ♦ *n* (*of song*) Refrain *m*.

refresh [rɪ'frɛʃ] *vt* erfrischen; **to** ~ **one's**

memory sein Gedächtnis auffrischen.

refresher course [rɪ'frɛʃə-] *n*
Auffrischungskurs *m*.

refreshing [rɪ'frɛʃɪŋ] *adj* erfrischend; (*sleep*)
wohltuend; (*idea etc*) angenehm.

refreshment [rɪ'frɛʃmənt] *n* Erfrischung *f*.

refreshments [rɪ'frɛʃmənts] *npl* (*food and
drink*) Erfrischungen *pl*.

refrigeration [rɪfrɪdʒə'reɪʃən] *n* Kühlung *f*.

refrigerator [rɪ'frɪdʒəreɪtə*] *n* Kühlschrank *m*.

refuel [riː'fjuəl] *vt, vi* auftanken.

refuelling [riː'fjuəlɪŋ] *n* Auftanken *nt*.

refuge ['rɛfjuːdʒ] *n* Zuflucht *f*; **to seek/take
~ in** Zuflucht suchen/nehmen in +*dat*.

refugee [refju'dʒiː] *n* Flüchtling *m*; **a political
~** ein politischer Flüchtling.

refugee camp *n* Flüchtlingslager *nt*.

refund ['riːfʌnd] *n* Rückerstattung *f* ♦ *vt*
(*money*) zurückerstatten.

refurbish [riː'fəːbɪʃ] *vt* (*shop etc*) renovieren.

refurbishment [riː'fəːbɪʃmənt] *n* (*of shop etc*)
Renovierung *f*.

refurnish [riː'fəːnɪʃ] *vt* neu möblieren.

refusal [rɪ'fjuːzəl] *n* Ablehnung *f*; **a ~ to do sth**
eine Weigerung, etw zu tun; **to give sb first
~ on sth** jdm etw zuerst anbieten.

refuse[1] [rɪ'fjuːz] *vt* (*request, offer etc*)
ablehnen; (*gift*) zurückweisen; (*permission*)
verweigern ♦ *vi* ablehnen; (*horse*) verweigern; **to ~ to do sth** sich weigern, etw zu tun.

refuse[2] ['rɛfjuːs] *n* (*rubbish*) Abfall *m*, Müll *m*.

refuse collection *n* Müllabfuhr *f*.

refuse disposal *n* Müllbeseitigung *f*.

refusenik [rɪ'fjuːznɪk] *n* (*inf*) Verweigerer(in)
m(f); (*in former USSR*) *sowjetischer Jude,
dem die Emigration nach Israel verweigert
wurde*.

refute [rɪ'fjuːt] *vt* (*argument*) widerlegen.

regain [rɪ'geɪn] *vt* wiedererlangen.

regal ['riːgl] *adj* königlich.

regale [rɪ'geɪl] *vt*: **to ~ sb with sth** jdn mit etw
verwöhnen.

regard [rɪ'gɑːd] *n* (*esteem*) Achtung *f* ♦ *vt*
(*consider*) ansehen, betrachten; (*view*)
betrachten; **to give one's ~s to sb** jdm
Grüße bestellen; **"with kindest ~s"** „mit
freundlichen Grüßen"; **as ~s, with ~ to**
bezüglich +*gen*.

regarding [rɪ'gɑːdɪŋ] *prep* bezüglich +*gen*.

regardless [rɪ'gɑːdlɪs] *adv* trotzdem ♦ *adj*: ~ **of**
ohne Rücksicht auf +*acc*.

regatta [rɪ'gætə] *n* Regatta *f*.

regency ['riːdʒənsɪ] *n* Regentschaft *f* ♦ *adj*: **R~**
(*furniture etc*) Regency-.

regenerate [rɪ'dʒenəreɪt] *vt* (*inner cities, arts*)
erneuern; (*person, feelings*) beleben ♦ *vi*
(*BIOL*) sich regenerieren.

regent ['riːdʒənt] *n* Regent(in) *m(f)*.

reggae ['rɛgeɪ] *n* Reggae *m*.

regime [reɪ'ʒiːm] *n* (*government*) Regime *nt*;
(*diet etc*) Kur *f*.

regiment ['rɛdʒɪmənt] *n* (*MIL*) Regiment *nt* ♦ *vt*

reglementieren.

regimental [rɛdʒɪ'mɛntl] adj Regiments-.

regimentation [rɛdʒɪmɛn'teɪʃən] n
Reglementierung f.

region ['riːdʒən] n (of land) Gebiet nt; (of body)
Bereich m; (administrative division of country)
Region f; **in the ~ of** (approximately) im
Bereich von.

regional ['riːdʒənl] adj regional.

regional development n regionale
Entwicklung f.

register ['rɛdʒɪstəʳ] n (list, MUS) Register nt;
(also: **electoral ~**) Wählerverzeichnis nt;
(SCOL) Klassenbuch nt ♦ vt registrieren;
(car) anmelden; (letter) als Einschreiben
senden; (amount, measurement) verzeichnen
♦ vi (person) sich anmelden; (: at doctor's)
sich (als Patient) eintragen; (amount etc)
registriert werden; (make impression)
(einen) Eindruck machen; **to ~ a protest**
Protest anmelden.

registered ['rɛdʒɪstəd] adj (letter, parcel)
eingeschrieben; (drug addict, childminder etc)
(offiziell) eingetragen.

registered company n eingetragene
Gesellschaft f.

registered nurse (US) n staatlich geprüfte
Krankenschwester f, staatlich geprüfter
Krankenpfleger m.

registered trademark n eingetragenes
Warenzeichen nt.

register office n = registry office.

registrar ['rɛdʒɪstrɑːʳ] n (in registry office)
Standesbeamte(r) m, Standesbeamtin f; (in
college etc) Kanzler m; (BRIT: in hospital)
Krankenhausarzt m, Krankenhausärztin f.

registration [rɛdʒɪs'treɪʃən] n Registrierung f;
(of students, unemployed etc) Anmeldung f.

registration number (BRIT) n (AUT)
polizeiliches Kennzeichen nt.

registry ['rɛdʒɪstrɪ] n Registratur f.

registry office (BRIT) n Standesamt nt; **to get
married in a ~** standesamtlich heiraten.

regret [rɪ'grɛt] n Bedauern nt ♦ vt bedauern;
with ~ mit Bedauern; **to have no ~s** nichts
bereuen; **we ~ to inform you that ...** wir
müssen Ihnen leider mitteilen, dass ...

regretfully [rɪ'grɛtfəlɪ] adv mit Bedauern.

regrettable [rɪ'grɛtəbl] adj bedauerlich.

regrettably [rɪ'grɛtəblɪ] adv
bedauerlicherweise; **~, he said ...**
bedauerlicherweise sagte er ...

Regt abbr (MIL: = regiment) Rgt.

regular ['rɛgjuləʳ] adj (also LING) regelmäßig;
(usual: time, doctor) üblich; (: customer)
Stamm-; (soldier) Berufs-; (COMM: size)
normal ♦ n (client) Stammkunde m,
Stammkundin f.

regularity [rɛgju'lærɪtɪ] n Regelmäßigkeit f.

regularly ['rɛgjuləlɪ] adv regelmäßig; (breathe,
beat: evenly) gleichmäßig.

regulate ['rɛgjuleɪt] vt regulieren.

regulation [rɛgju'leɪʃən] n Regulierung f;
(rule) Vorschrift f.

regulatory [rɛgju'leɪtrɪ] adj (system)
Regulierungs-; (body, agency)
Überwachungs-.

rehabilitate [riːə'bɪlɪteɪt] vt (criminal, drug
addict) (in die Gesellschaft) wieder
eingliedern; (invalid) rehabilitieren.

rehabilitation ['riːəbɪlɪ'teɪʃən] n (see vt)
Wiedereingliederung f (in die Gesellschaft);
Rehabilitation f.

rehash [riː'hæʃ] (inf) vt (idea etc) aufwärmen.

rehearsal [rɪ'həːsəl] n (THEAT) Probe f; **dress
~** Generalprobe f.

rehearse [rɪ'həːs] vt (play, speech etc) proben.

rehouse [riː'hauz] vt neu unterbringen.

reign [reɪn] n (lit, fig) Herrschaft f ♦ vi (lit, fig)
herrschen.

reigning ['reɪnɪŋ] adj regierend; (champion)
amtierend.

reimburse [riːɪm'bəːs] vt die Kosten erstatten
+dat.

rein [reɪn] n Zügel m; **to give sb free ~** (fig) jdm
freie Hand lassen; **to keep a tight ~ on sth**
(fig) bei etw die Zügel kurz halten.

reincarnation [riːɪnkɑː'neɪʃən] n (belief) die
Wiedergeburt f; (person) Reinkarnation f.

reindeer ['reɪndɪəʳ] n inv Ren(tier) nt.

reinforce [riːɪn'fɔːs] vt (strengthen)
verstärken; (support: idea etc) stützen;
(: prejudice) stärken.

reinforced concrete n Stahlbeton m.

reinforcement [riːɪn'fɔːsmənt] n
(strengthening) Verstärkung f; (of attitude etc)
Stärkung f; **reinforcements** npl (MIL)
Verstärkung f.

reinstate [riːɪn'steɪt] vt (employee) wieder
einstellen; (tax, law) wieder einführen; (text)
wieder einfügen.

reinstatement [riːɪn'steɪtmənt] n (of
employee) Wiedereinstellung f.

reissue [riː'ɪʃjuː] vt neu herausgeben.

reiterate [riː'ɪtəreɪt] vt wiederholen.

reject ['riːdʒɛkt] n (COMM) Ausschuss m no pl
♦ vt ablehnen; (admirer) abweisen; (goods)
zurückweisen; (machine: coin) nicht
annehmen; (MED: heart, kidney) abstoßen.

rejection [rɪ'dʒɛkʃən] n Ablehnung f; (of
admirer) Abweisung f; (MED) Abstoßung f.

rejoice [rɪ'dʒɔɪs] vi: **to ~ at** or **over** jubeln
über +acc.

rejoinder [rɪ'dʒɔɪndəʳ] n Erwiderung f.

rejuvenate [rɪ'dʒuːvəneɪt] vt (person)
verjüngen; (organization etc) beleben.

rekindle [riː'kɪndl] vt (interest, emotion etc)
wieder erwecken.

relapse [rɪ'læps] n (MED) Rückfall m ♦ vi: **to
~ into** zurückfallen in +acc.

relate [rɪ'leɪt] vt (tell) berichten; (connect) in
Verbindung bringen ♦ vi: **to ~ to** (empathize
with: person, subject) eine Beziehung finden
zu; (connect with) zusammenhängen mit.

related [rɪ'leɪtɪd] *adj*: to be ~ (miteinander) verwandt sein; (*issues etc*) zusammenhängen.

relating to [rɪ'leɪtɪŋ-] *prep* bezüglich +*gen*, mit Bezug auf +*acc*.

relation [rɪ'leɪʃən] *n* (*member of family*) Verwandte(r) *f(m)*; (*connection*) Beziehung *f*; **relations** *npl* (*contact*) Beziehungen *pl*; **diplomatic/international** ~s diplomatische/ internationale Beziehungen; **in** ~ **to** im Verhältnis zu; **to bear no** ~ **to** in keinem Verhältnis stehen zu.

relationship [rɪ'leɪʃənʃɪp] *n* Beziehung *f*; (*between countries*) Beziehung *pl*; (*affair*) Verhältnis *nt*; **they have a good** ~ sie haben ein gutes Verhältnis zueinander.

relative ['relətɪv] *n* Verwandte(r) *f(m)* ♦ *adj* relativ; **all her** ~s ihre ganze Verwandtschaft; ~ **to** im Vergleich zu; **it's all** ~ es ist alles relativ.

relatively ['relətɪvlɪ] *adv* relativ.

relative pronoun *n* Relativpronomen *nt*.

relax [rɪ'læks] *vi* (*person, muscle*) sich entspannen; (*calm down*) sich beruhigen ♦ *vt* (*one's grip*) lockern; (*mind, person*) entspannen; (*control etc*) lockern.

relaxation [riːlæk'seɪʃən] *n* Entspannung *f*; (*of control etc*) Lockern *nt*.

relaxed [rɪ'lækst] *adj* (*person, atmosphere*) entspannt; (*discussion*) locker.

relaxing [rɪ'læksɪŋ] *adj* entspannend.

relay ['riːleɪ] *n* (*race*) Staffel *f*, Staffellauf *m* ♦ *vt* (*message etc*) übermitteln; (*broadcast*) übertragen.

release [rɪ'liːs] *n* (*from prison*) Entlassung *f*; (*from obligation, situation*) Befreiung *f*; (*of documents, funds etc*) Freigabe *f*; (*of gas etc*) Freisetzung *f*; (*of film, book, record*) Herausgabe *f*; (*record, film*) Veröffentlichung *f*; (*TECH: device*) Auslöser *m* ♦ *vt* (*from prison*) entlassen; (*person: from obligation, from wreckage*) befreien; (*gas etc*) freisetzen; (*TECH, AUT: catch, brake etc*) lösen; (*record, film*) herausbringen; (*news, figures*) bekannt geben; **on general** ~ (*film*) überall in den Kinos; *see also* **press release**.

relegate ['reləɡeɪt] *vt* (*downgrade*) herunterstufen; (*BRIT: SPORT*): **to be** ~d absteigen.

relent [rɪ'lent] *vi* (*give in*) nachgeben.

relentless [rɪ'lentlɪs] *adj* (*heat, noise*) erbarmungslos; (*enemy etc*) unerbittlich.

relevance ['reləvəns] *n* Relevanz *f*, Bedeutung *f*; **the** ~ **of religion to society** die Relevanz *or* Bedeutung der Religion für die Gesellschaft.

relevant ['reləvənt] *adj* relevant; (*chapter, area*) entsprechend; ~ **to** relevant für.

reliability [rɪlaɪə'bɪlɪtɪ] *n* Zuverlässigkeit *f*.

reliable [rɪ'laɪəbl] *adj* zuverlässig.

reliably [rɪ'laɪəblɪ] *adv*: **to be** ~ **informed that** ... zuverlässige Informationen darüber

haben, dass ...

reliance [rɪ'laɪəns] *n*: ~ (**on**) (*person*) Angewiesenheit *f* (auf +*acc*); (*drugs, financial support*) Abhängigkeit *f* (von).

reliant [rɪ'laɪənt] *adj*: **to be** ~ **on sth/sb** auf etw/jdn angewiesen sein.

relic ['relɪk] *n* (*REL*) Reliquie *f*; (*of the past*) Relikt *nt*.

relief [rɪ'liːf] *n* (*from pain etc*) Erleichterung *f*; (*aid*) Hilfe *f*; (*ART, GEOG*) Relief *nt* ♦ *cpd* (*bus*) Entlastungs-; (*driver*) zur Ablösung; **light** ~ leichte Abwechslung *f*.

relief map *n* Reliefkarte *f*.

relief road (*BRIT*) *n* Entlastungsstraße *f*.

relieve [rɪ'liːv] *vt* (*pain*) lindern; (*fear, worry*) mildern; (*take over from*) ablösen; **to** ~ **sb of sth** (*load*) jdm etw abnehmen; (*duties, post*) jdn einer Sache *gen* entheben; **to** ~ **o.s.** (*euphemism*) sich erleichtern.

relieved [rɪ'liːvd] *adj* erleichtert; **I'm** ~ **to hear it** es erleichtert mich, das zu hören.

religion [rɪ'lɪdʒən] *n* Religion *f*.

religious [rɪ'lɪdʒəs] *adj* religiös.

religious education *n* Religionsunterricht *m*.

religiously [rɪ'lɪdʒəslɪ] *adv* (*regularly, thoroughly*) gewissenhaft.

relinquish [rɪ'lɪŋkwɪʃ] *vt* (*control etc*) aufgeben; (*claim*) verzichten auf +*acc*.

relish ['relɪʃ] *n* (*CULIN*) würzige Soße *f*, Relish *nt*; (*enjoyment*) Genuss *m* ♦ *vt* (*enjoy*) genießen; **to** ~ **doing sth** etw mit Genuss tun.

relive [riː'lɪv] *vt* noch einmal durchleben.

reload [riː'ləud] *vt* (*gun*) neu laden.

relocate [riːləu'keɪt] *vt* verlegen ♦ *vi* den Standort wechseln; **to** ~ **in** seinen Standort verlegen nach.

reluctance [rɪ'lʌktəns] *n* Widerwille *m*.

reluctant [rɪ'lʌktənt] *adj* unwillig, widerwillig; **I'm** ~ **to do that** es widerstrebt mir, das zu tun.

reluctantly [rɪ'lʌktəntlɪ] *adv* widerwillig, nur ungern.

rely on [rɪ'laɪ-] *vt fus* (*be dependent on*) abhängen von; (*trust*) sich verlassen auf +*acc*.

remain [rɪ'meɪn] *vi* bleiben; (*survive*) übrig bleiben; **to** ~ **silent** weiterhin schweigen; **to** ~ **in control** die Kontrolle behalten; **much** ~s **to be done** es ist noch viel zu tun; **the fact** ~s **that** ... Tatsache ist und bleibt, dass ...; **it** ~s **to be seen whether** ... es bleibt abzuwarten, ob ...

remainder [rɪ'meɪndə*] *n* Rest *m* ♦ *vt* (*COMM*) zu ermäßigtem Preis anbieten.

remaining [rɪ'meɪnɪŋ] *adj* übrig.

remains [rɪ'meɪnz] *npl* (*of meal*) Überreste *pl*; (*of building etc*) Ruinen *pl*; (*of body*) sterbliche Überreste *pl*.

remand [rɪ'mɑːnd] *n*: **to be on** ~ in Untersuchungshaft sein ♦ *vt*: **to be** ~ed **in**

custody in Untersuchungshaft bleiben müssen.

remand home (*formerly*: BRIT) *n* Untersuchungsgefängnis *nt* für Jugendliche.

remark [rɪˈmɑːk] *n* Bemerkung *f* ♦ *vt* bemerken ♦ *vi*: **to ~ on sth** Bemerkungen über etw *acc* machen; **to ~ that** die Bemerkung machen, dass.

remarkable [rɪˈmɑːkəbl] *adj* bemerkenswert.

remarry [riːˈmærɪ] *vi* wieder heiraten.

remedial [rɪˈmiːdɪəl] *adj* (*tuition, classes*) Förder-; **~ exercise** Heilgymnastik *f*.

remedy [ˈrɛmədɪ] *n* (*lit, fig*) (Heil)mittel *nt* ♦ *vt* (*mistake, situation*) abhelfen +*dat*.

remember [rɪˈmɛmbə*] *vt* (*call back to mind*) sich erinnern an +*acc*; (*bear in mind*) denken an +*acc*; **~ me to him** (*send greetings*) grüße ihn von mir; **I ~ seeing it, I ~ having seen it** ich erinnere mich (daran), es gesehen zu haben; **she ~ed to do it** sie hat daran gedacht, es zu tun.

remembrance [rɪˈmɛmbrəns] *n* Erinnerung *f*; **in ~ of sb/sth** im Gedenken an +*acc*.

Remembrance Sunday (BRIT) *n* ≈ Volkstrauertag *m*.

REMEMBRANCE SUNDAY

Remembrance Sunday *oder* **Remembrance Day** *ist der britische Gedenktag für die Gefallenen der beiden Weltkriege und anderer Konflikte. Er fällt auf einen Sonntag vor oder nach dem 11. November (am 11. November 1918 endete der erste Weltkrieg) und wird mit einer Schweigeminute, Kranzniederlegungen an Kriegerdenkmälern und dem Tragen von Anstecknadeln in Form einer Mohnblume begangen.*

---

remind [rɪˈmaɪnd] *vt*: **to ~ sb to do sth** jdn daran erinnern, etw zu tun; **to ~ sb of sth** jdn an etw *acc* erinnern; **to ~ sb that ...** jdn daran erinnern, dass ...; **she ~s me of her mother** sie erinnert mich an ihre Mutter; **that ~s me!** dabei fällt mir etwas ein!

reminder [rɪˈmaɪndə*] *n* (*of person, place etc*) Erinnerung *f*; (*letter*) Mahnung *f*.

reminisce [rɛmɪˈnɪs] *vi*: **to ~ (about)** sich in Erinnerungen ergehen (über +*acc*).

reminiscences [rɛmɪˈnɪsnsɪz] *npl* Erinnerungen *pl*.

reminiscent [rɛmɪˈnɪsnt] *adj*: **to be ~ of sth** an etw *acc* erinnern.

remiss [rɪˈmɪs] *adj* nachlässig; **it was ~ of him** es war nachlässig von ihm.

remission [rɪˈmɪʃən] *n* (*of sentence*) Straferlass *m*; (*MED*) Remission *f*; (*REL*) Erlass *m*.

remit [rɪˈmɪt] *vt* (*money*) überweisen ♦ *n* (*of official etc*) Aufgabenbereich *m*.

remittance [rɪˈmɪtns] *n* Überweisung *f*.

remnant [ˈrɛmnənt] *n* Überrest *m*; (*COMM: of cloth*) Rest *m*.

remonstrate [ˈrɛmənstreɪt] *vi*: **to ~ (with sb about sth)** sich beschweren (bei jdm wegen etw).

remorse [rɪˈmɔːs] *n* Reue *f*.

remorseful [rɪˈmɔːsful] *adj* reumütig.

remorseless [rɪˈmɔːslɪs] *adj* (*noise, pain*) unbarmherzig.

remote [rɪˈməut] *adj* (*distant: place, time*) weit entfernt; (*aloof*) distanziert; (*slight: chance etc*) entfernt; **there is a ~ possibility that ...** es besteht eventuell die Möglichkeit, dass ...

remote control *n* Fernsteuerung *f*; (*TV etc*) Fernbedienung *f*.

remote-controlled [rɪˈməutkən'trəuld] *adj* ferngesteuert.

remotely [rɪˈməutlɪ] *adv* (*slightly*) entfernt.

remoteness [rɪˈməutnɪs] *n* (*of place*) Entlegenheit *f*; (*of person*) Distanziertheit *f*.

remould [ˈriːməuld] (BRIT) *n* (AUT) runderneuerter Reifen *m*.

removable [rɪˈmuːvəbl] *adj* (*detachable*) abnehmbar.

removal [rɪˈmuːvəl] *n* (*of object etc*) Entfernung *f*; (*of threat etc*) Beseitigung *f*; (BRIT: *from house*) Umzug *m*; (*dismissal*) Entlassung *f*; (MED: *of kidney etc*) Entfernung *f*.

removal man (BRIT) *n* Möbelpacker *m*.

removal van (BRIT) *n* Möbelwagen *m*.

remove [rɪˈmuːv] *vt* entfernen; (*clothing*) ausziehen; (*bandage etc*) abnehmen; (*employee*) entlassen; (*name: from list*) streichen; (*doubt, threat, obstacle*) beseitigen; **my first cousin once ~d** mein Vetter ersten Grades.

remover [rɪˈmuːvə*] *n* (*for paint, varnish*) Entferner *m*; **stain ~** Fleckentferner *m*; **make-up ~** Make-up-Entferner *m*.

remunerate [rɪˈmjuːnəreɪt] *vt* vergüten.

remuneration [rɪmjuːnəˈreɪʃən] *n* Vergütung *f*.

Renaissance [rɪˈneɪsɑ̃ːs] *n*: **the ~** die Renaissance.

renal [ˈriːnl] *adj* (MED) Nieren-.

renal failure *n* Nierenversagen *nt*.

rename [riːˈneɪm] *vt* umbenennen.

rend [rɛnd] (*pt, pp* **rent**) *vt* (*air, silence*) zerreißen.

render [ˈrɛndə*] *vt* (*give: assistance, aid*) leisten; (*cause to become: unconscious, harmless, useless*) machen; (*submit*) vorlegen.

rendering [ˈrɛndərɪŋ] (BRIT) *n* = **rendition**.

rendezvous [ˈrɒndɪvuː] *n* (*meeting*) Rendezvous *nt*; (*place*) Treffpunkt *m* ♦ *vi* (*people*) sich treffen; (*spacecraft*) ein Rendezvousmanöver durchführen; **to ~ with sb** sich mit jdm treffen.

rendition [rɛnˈdɪʃən] *n* (*of song etc*) Vortrag *m*.

renegade [ˈrɛnɪgeɪd] *n* Renegat(in) *m(f)*, Überläufer(in) *m(f)*.

renew [rɪ'njuː] *vt* erneuern; (*attack, negotiations*) wieder aufnehmen; (*loan, contract etc*) verlängern; (*relationship etc*) wieder aufleben lassen.

renewables *npl* erneuerbare Energien *pl*.

renewal [rɪ'njuːəl] *n* Erneuerung *f*; (*of conflict*) Wiederaufnahme *f*; (*of contract etc*) Verlängerung *f*.

renounce [rɪ'nauns] *vt* verzichten auf +*acc*; (*belief*) aufgeben.

renovate ['rɛnəveɪt] *vt* (*building*) restaurieren; (*machine*) überholen.

renovation [rɛnə'veɪʃən] *n* (*see vb*) Restaurierung *f*; Überholung *f*.

renown [rɪ'naun] *n* Ruf *m*.

renowned [rɪ'naund] *adj* berühmt.

rent [rɛnt] *pt, pp of* **rend** ♦ *n* (*for house*) Miete *f* ♦ *vt* mieten; (*also:* ~ **out**) vermieten.

rental ['rɛntl] *n* (*for television, car*) Mietgebühr *f*.

rent boy (*inf*) *n* Strichjunge *m*.

rent strike *n* Mietstreik *m*.

renunciation [rɪnʌnsɪ'eɪʃən] *n* Verzicht *m*; (*of belief*) Aufgabe *f*; (*self-denial*) Selbstverleugnung *f*.

reopen [riː'əupən] *vt* (*shop etc*) wieder eröffnen; (*negotiations, legal case etc*) wieder aufnehmen.

reopening [riː'əupnɪŋ] *n* (*see vt*) Wiedereröffnung *f*; Wiederaufnahme *f*.

reorder [riː'ɔːdə*] *vt* (*rearrange*) umordnen.

reorganization ['riːɔːɡənaɪ'zeɪʃən] *n* Umorganisation *f*.

reorganize [riː'ɔːɡənaɪz] *vt* umorganisieren.

Rep. (*US*) *abbr* (*POL*) = **representative; republican**.

rep [rɛp] *n abbr* (*COMM*) = **representative**; (*THEAT*) = **repertory**.

repair [rɪ'pɛə*] *n* Reparatur *f* ♦ *vt* reparieren; (*clothes, road*) ausbessern; **in good/bad** ~ in gutem/schlechtem Zustand; **beyond** ~ nicht mehr zu reparieren; **to be under** ~ (*road*) ausgebessert werden.

repair kit *n* (*for bicycle*) Flickzeug *nt*.

repair man *n* Handwerker *m*.

repair shop *n* Reparaturwerkstatt *f*.

repartee [rɛpɑː'tiː] *n* (*exchange*) Schlagabtausch *m*; (*reply*) schlagfertige Bemerkung *f*.

repast [rɪ'pɑːst] (*form*) *n* Mahl *nt*.

repatriate [riː'pætrɪeɪt] *vt* repatriieren.

repay [riː'peɪ] (*irreg: like* **pay**) *vt* zurückzahlen; (*sb's efforts, attention*) belohnen; (*favour*) erwidern; **I'll** ~ **you next week** ich zahle es dir nächste Woche zurück.

repayment [riː'peɪmənt] *n* Rückzahlung *f*.

repeal [rɪ'piːl] *n* (*of law*) Aufhebung *f* ♦ *vt* (*law*) aufheben.

repeat [rɪ'piːt] *n* (*RADIO, TV*) Wiederholung *f* ♦ *vt, vi* wiederholen ♦ *cpd* (*performance*) Wiederholungs-; (*order*) Nach-; **to** ~ **o.s./ itself** sich wiederholen; **to** ~ **an order for sth**

etw nachbestellen.

repeatedly [rɪ'piːtɪdlɪ] *adv* wiederholt.

repel [rɪ'pɛl] *vt* (*drive away*) zurückschlagen; (*disgust*) abstoßen.

repellent [rɪ'pɛlənt] *adj* abstoßend ♦ *n*: **insect** ~ Insekten(schutz)mittel *nt*.

repent [rɪ'pɛnt] *vi*: **to** ~ **of sth** etw bereuen.

repentance [rɪ'pɛntəns] *n* Reue *f*.

repercussions [riːpə'kʌʃənz] *npl* Auswirkungen *pl*.

repertoire ['rɛpətwɑː*] *n* (*MUS, THEAT*) Repertoire *nt*; (*fig*) Spektrum *nt*.

repertory ['rɛpətərɪ] *n* (*also:* ~ **theatre**) Repertoiretheater *nt*.

repertory company *n* Repertoire-Ensemble *nt*.

repetition [rɛpɪ'tɪʃən] *n* (*repeat*) Wiederholung *f*.

repetitious [rɛpɪ'tɪʃəs] *adj* (*speech etc*) voller Wiederholungen.

repetitive [rɪ'pɛtɪtɪv] *adj* eintönig, monoton.

replace [rɪ'pleɪs] *vt* (*put back: upright*) zurückstellen; (: *flat*) zurücklegen; (*take the place of*) ersetzen; **to** ~ **X with Y** X durch Y ersetzen; "~ **the receiver**" (*TEL*) „Hörer auflegen".

replacement [rɪ'pleɪsmənt] *n* Ersatz *m*.

replacement part *n* Ersatzteil *nt*.

replay ['riːpleɪ] *n* (*of match*) Wiederholungsspiel *nt* ♦ *vt* (*match*) wiederholen; (*track, song: on tape*) nochmals abspielen.

replenish [rɪ'plɛnɪʃ] *vt* (*glass, stock etc*) auffüllen.

replete [rɪ'pliːt] *adj* (*after meal*) gesättigt; ~ **with** reichlich ausgestattet mit.

replica ['rɛplɪkə] *n* (*of object*) Nachbildung *f*.

reply [rɪ'plaɪ] *n* Antwort *f* ♦ *vi*: **to** ~ (**to sb/sth**) (jdm/auf etw *acc*) antworten; **in** ~ **to** als Antwort auf +*acc*; **there's no** ~ (*TEL*) es meldet sich niemand.

reply coupon *n* Antwortschein *m*.

report [rɪ'pɔːt] *n* Bericht *m*; (*BRIT: also:* **school** ~) Zeugnis *nt*; (*of gun*) Knall *m* ♦ *vt* berichten; (*casualties, damage, theft etc*) melden; (*person: to police*) anzeigen ♦ *vi* (*make a report*) Bericht erstatten; **to** ~ **to sb** (*present o.s. to*) sich bei jdm melden; (*be responsible to*) jdm unterstellt sein; **to** ~ **on sth** über etw *acc* Bericht erstatten; **to** ~ **sick** sich krankmelden; **it is** ~**ed that** es wird berichtet *or* gemeldet, dass ...

report card (*US, SCOT*) *n* Zeugnis *nt*.

reportedly [rɪ'pɔːtɪdlɪ] *adv*: **she is** ~ **living in Spain** sie lebt angeblich in Spanien.

reported speech *n* (*LING*) indirekte Rede *f*.

reporter [rɪ'pɔːtə*] *n* Reporter(in) *m(f)*.

repose [rɪ'pəuz] *n*: **in** ~ in Ruhestellung.

repository [rɪ'pɔzɪtərɪ] *n* (*person: of knowledge*) Quelle *f*; (*place: of collection etc*) Lager *nt*.

repossess ['riːpə'zɛs] *vt* (wieder) in Besitz

nehmen.

repossession order [ri:pə'zɛʃən-] n Beschlagnahmungsverfügung f.

reprehensible [rɛprɪ'hɛnsɪbl] adj verwerflich.

represent [rɛprɪ'zɛnt] vt (person, nation) vertreten; (show: view, opinion) darstellen; (symbolize: idea) symbolisieren, verkörpern; **to ~ sth as** (describe) etw darstellen als.

representation [rɛprɪzɛn'teɪʃən] n (state of being represented) Vertretung f; (picture etc) Darstellung f; **representations** npl (protest) Proteste pl.

representative [rɛprɪ'zɛntətɪv] n (also COMM) Vertreter(in) m(f); (US: POL) Abgeordnete(r) f(m) des Repräsentantenhauses ♦ adj repräsentativ; **~ of** repräsentativ für.

repress [rɪ'prɛs] vt unterdrücken.

repression [rɪ'prɛʃən] n Unterdrückung f.

repressive [rɪ'prɛsɪv] adj repressiv.

reprieve [rɪ'pri:v] n (cancellation) Begnadigung f; (postponement) Strafaufschub m; (fig) Gnadenfrist f ♦ vt: **he was ~d** (see n) er wurde begnadigt; ihm wurde Strafaufschub gewährt.

reprimand ['rɛprɪmɑːnd] n Tadel m ♦ vt tadeln.

reprint ['riːprɪnt] n Nachdruck m ♦ vt nachdrucken.

reprisal [rɪ'praɪzl] n Vergeltung f; **reprisals** npl Repressalien pl; (in war) Vergeltungsaktionen pl; **to take ~s** zu Repressalien greifen; (in war) Vergeltungsaktionen durchführen.

reproach [rɪ'prəutʃ] n (rebuke) Vorwurf m ♦ vt: **to ~ sb for sth** jdm etw zum Vorwurf machen; **beyond ~** über jeden Vorwurf erhaben; **to ~ sb with sth** jdm etw vorwerfen.

reproachful [rɪ'prəutʃful] adj vorwurfsvoll.

reproduce [riːprə'djuːs] vt reproduzieren ♦ vi (BIOL) sich vermehren.

reproduction [riːprə'dʌkʃən] n Reproduktion f; (BIOL) Fortpflanzung f.

reproductive [riːprə'dʌktɪv] adj (system, organs) Fortpflanzungs-.

reproof [rɪ'pruːf] n (rebuke) Tadel m; **with ~** tadelnd.

reprove [rɪ'pruːv] vt tadeln; **to ~ sb for sth** jdn wegen etw tadeln.

reproving [rɪ'pruːvɪŋ] adj tadelnd.

reptile ['rɛptaɪl] n Reptil nt.

Repub. (US) abbr (POL) = **republican**.

republic [rɪ'pʌblɪk] n Republik f.

republican [rɪ'pʌblɪkən] adj republikanisch ♦ n Republikaner(in) m(f); **the R~s** (US: POL) die Republikaner.

repudiate [rɪ'pjuːdɪeɪt] vt (accusation) zurückweisen; (violence) ablehnen; (old: friend, wife etc) verstoßen.

repugnance [rɪ'pʌgnəns] n Abscheu m.

repugnant [rɪ'pʌgnənt] adj abstoßend.

repulse [rɪ'pʌls] vt (attack etc) zurückschlagen; (sight, picture etc) abstoßen.

repulsion [rɪ'pʌlʃən] n Abscheu m.

repulsive [rɪ'pʌlsɪv] adj widerwärtig, abstoßend.

reputable ['rɛpjutəbl] adj (make, company etc) angesehen.

reputation [rɛpju'teɪʃən] n Ruf m; **to have a ~ for** einen Ruf haben für; **he has a ~ for being awkward** er gilt als schwierig.

repute [rɪ'pjuːt] n: **of ~** angesehen; **to be held in high ~** in hohem Ansehen stehen.

reputed [rɪ'pjuːtɪd] adj angeblich; **he is ~ to be rich** er ist angeblich reich.

reputedly [rɪ'pjuːtɪdlɪ] adv angeblich.

request [rɪ'kwɛst] n (polite) Bitte f; (formal) Ersuchen nt; (RADIO) Musikwunsch m ♦ vt (politely) bitten um; (formally) ersuchen; **at the ~ of** auf Wunsch von; **"you are ~ed not to smoke"** „bitte nicht rauchen".

request stop (BRIT) n Bedarfshaltestelle f.

requiem ['rɛkwɪəm] n (REL: also: ~ **mass**) Totenmesse f; (MUS) Requiem nt.

require [rɪ'kwaɪə*] vt (need) benötigen; (: situation) erfordern; (demand) verlangen; **to ~ sb to do sth** von jdm verlangen, etw zu tun; **if ~d** falls nötig; **what qualifications are ~d?** welche Qualifikationen werden verlangt?; **~d by law** gesetzlich vorgeschrieben.

required [rɪ'kwaɪəd] adj erforderlich.

requirement [rɪ'kwaɪəmənt] n (need) Bedarf m; (condition) Anforderung f; **to meet sb's ~s** jds Anforderungen erfüllen.

requisite ['rɛkwɪzɪt] adj erforderlich; **requisites** npl: **toilet/travel ~s** Toiletten-/Reiseartikel pl.

requisition [rɛkwɪ'zɪʃən] n: ~ **(for)** (demand) Anforderung f (von) ♦ vt (MIL) beschlagnahmen.

reroute [riː'ruːt] vt (train etc) umleiten.

resale [riː'seɪl] n Weiterverkauf m; **"not for ~"** „nicht zum Weiterverkauf bestimmt".

resale price maintenance n Preisbindung f.

rescind [rɪ'sɪnd] vt (law, order) aufheben; (decision) rückgängig machen; (agreement) widerrufen.

rescue ['rɛskjuː] n Rettung f ♦ vt retten; **to come to sb's ~** jdm zu Hilfe kommen.

rescue party n Rettungsmannschaft f.

rescuer ['rɛskjuə*] n Retter(in) m(f).

research [rɪ'səːtʃ] n Forschung f ♦ vt erforschen ♦ vi: **to ~ into sth** etw erforschen; **to do ~** Forschung betreiben; **a piece of ~** eine Forschungsarbeit; ~ **and development** Forschung und Entwicklung.

researcher [rɪ'səːtʃə*] n Forscher(in) m(f).

research work n Forschungsarbeit f.

research worker n = **researcher**.

resell [riː'sɛl] (irreg: like **sell**) vt weiterverkaufen.

resemblance [rɪ'zɛmbləns] n Ähnlichkeit f; **bear a strong ~ to** starke Ähnlichkeit haben mit; **it bears no ~ to ...** es hat keine

Ähnlichkeit mit ...
resemble [rɪ'zɛmbl] *vt* ähneln +*dat*, gleichen +*dat*.
resent [rɪ'zɛnt] *vt* (*attitude, treatment*) missbilligen; (*person*) ablehnen.
resentful [rɪ'zɛntful] *adj* (*person*) gekränkt; (*attitude*) missbilligend.
resentment [rɪ'zɛntmənt] *n* Verbitterung *f*.
reservation [rɛzə'veɪʃən] *n* (*booking*) Reservierung *f*; (*doubt*) Vorbehalt *m*; (*land*) Reservat *nt*; **to make a ~** (*in hotel etc*) eine Reservierung vornehmen; **with ~(s)** (*doubts*) unter Vorbehalt.
reservation desk *n* Reservierungsschalter *m*.
reserve [rɪ'zə:v] *n* Reserve *f*, Vorrat *m*; (*fig: of talent etc*) Reserve *f*; (*SPORT*) Reservespieler(in) *m(f)*; (*also:* **nature ~**) Naturschutzgebiet *nt*; (*restraint*) Zurückhaltung *f* ♦ *vt* reservieren; (*table, ticket*) reservieren lassen; **reserves** *npl* (*MIL*) Reserve *f*; **in ~** in Reserve.
reserve currency *n* Reservewährung *f*.
reserved [rɪ'zə:vd] *adj* (*restrained*) zurückhaltend; (*seat*) reserviert.
reserve price (*BRIT*) *n* Mindestpreis *m*.
reserve team (*BRIT*) *n* Reservemannschaft *f*.
reservist [rɪ'zə:vɪst] *n* (*MIL*) Reservist *m*.
reservoir [ˈrɛzəvwɑː*] *n* (*lit, fig*) Reservoir *nt*.
reset [riː'sɛt] (*irreg: like* **set**) *vt* (*watch*) neu stellen; (*broken bone*) wieder einrichten; (*COMPUT*) zurückstellen.
reshape [riː'ʃeɪp] *vt* (*policy, view*) umgestalten.
reshuffle [riː'ʃʌfl] *n*: **cabinet ~** Kabinettsumbildung *f*.
reside [rɪ'zaɪd] *vi* (*live: person*) seinen/ihren Wohnsitz haben.
▶ **reside in** *vt fus* (*exist*) liegen in +*dat*.
residence [ˈrɛzɪdəns] *n* (*form: home*) Wohnsitz *m*; (*length of stay*) Aufenthalt *m*; **to take up ~** sich niederlassen; **in ~** (*queen etc*) anwesend; **writer/artist in ~** *Schriftsteller/ Künstler, der in einer Ausbildungsstätte bei freier Unterkunft lehrt und arbeitet.*
residence permit (*BRIT*) *n* Aufenthaltserlaubnis *f*.
resident [ˈrɛzɪdənt] *n* (*of country, town*) Einwohner(in) *m(f)*; (*in hotel*) Gast *m* ♦ *adj* (*in country, town*) wohnhaft; (*population*) ansässig; (*doctor*) hauseigen; (*landlord*) im Hause wohnend.
residential [rɛzɪ'dɛnʃəl] *adj* (*area*) Wohn-; (*course*) mit Wohnung am Ort; (*staff*) im Hause wohnend.
residue [ˈrɛzɪdjuː] *n* (*CHEM*) Rückstand *m*; (*fig*) Überrest *m*.
resign [rɪ'zaɪn] *vt* (*one's post*) zurücktreten von ♦ *vi* (*from post*) zurücktreten; **to ~ o.s. to** (*situation etc*) sich abfinden mit.
resignation [rɛzɪg'neɪʃən] *n* (*from post*) Rücktritt *m*; (*state of mind*) Resignation *f*; **to tender one's ~** seine Kündigung einreichen.

resigned [rɪ'zaɪnd] *adj*: **to be ~ to sth** sich mit etw abgefunden haben.
resilience [rɪ'zɪlɪəns] *n* (*of material*) Widerstandsfähigkeit *f*; (*of person*) Unverwüstlichkeit *f*.
resilient [rɪ'zɪlɪənt] *adj* (*see n*) widerstandsfähig; unverwüstlich.
resin [ˈrɛzɪn] *n* Harz *nt*.
resist [rɪ'zɪst] *vt* (*change, demand*) sich widersetzen +*dat*; (*attack etc*) Widerstand leisten +*dat*; (*urge etc*) widerstehen +*dat*; **I couldn't ~ (doing) it** ich konnte nicht widerstehen(, es zu tun).
resistance [rɪ'zɪstəns] *n* (*also ELEC*) Widerstand *m*; (*to illness*) Widerstandsfähigkeit *f*.
resistant [rɪ'zɪstənt] *adj*: **~ (to)** (*to change etc*) widerstandsfähig (gegenüber); (*to antibiotics etc*) resistent (gegen).
resolute [ˈrɛzəluːt] *adj* (*person*) entschlossen, resolut; (*refusal*) entschieden.
resolution [rɛzə'luːʃən] *n* (*decision*) Beschluss *m*; (*determination*) Entschlossenheit *f*; (*of problem*) Lösung *f*; **to make a ~** einen Entschluss fassen.
resolve [rɪ'zɔlv] *n* (*determination*) Entschlossenheit *f* ♦ *vt* (*problem*) lösen; (*difficulty*) beseitigen ♦ *vi*: **to ~ to do sth** beschließen, etw zu tun.
resolved [rɪ'zɔlvd] *adj* (*determined*) entschlossen.
resonance [ˈrɛzənəns] *n* Resonanz *f*.
resonant [ˈrɛzənənt] *adj* (*sound, voice*) volltönend; (*place*) widerhallend.
resort [rɪ'zɔːt] *n* (*town*) Urlaubsort *m*; (*recourse*) Zuflucht *f* ♦ *vi*: **to ~ to** Zuflucht nehmen zu; **seaside ~** Seebad *nt*; **winter sports ~** Wintersportort *m*; **as a last ~** als letzter Ausweg; **in the last ~** schlimmstenfalls.
resound [rɪ'zaʊnd] *vi*: **to ~ (with)** widerhallen (von).
resounding [rɪ'zaʊndɪŋ] *adj* (*noise*) widerhallend; (*voice*) schallend; (*fig: success*) durchschlagend; (: *victory*) überlegen.
resource [rɪ'sɔːs] *n* (*raw material*) Bodenschatz *m*; **resources** *npl* (*coal, oil etc*) Energiequellen *pl*; (*money*) Mittel *pl*, Ressourcen *pl*; **natural ~s** Naturschätze *pl*.
resourceful [rɪ'sɔːsful] *adj* einfallsreich.
resourcefulness [rɪ'sɔːsfulnɪs] *n* Einfallsreichtum *m*.
respect [rɪs'pɛkt] *n* (*consideration, esteem*) Respekt *m* ♦ *vt* respektieren; **respects** *npl* (*greetings*) Grüße *pl*; **to have ~ for sb/sth** Respekt vor jdm/etw haben; **to show sb/sth ~** Respekt vor jdm/etw zeigen; **out of ~ for** aus Rücksicht auf +*acc*; **with ~ to in ~ of** in Bezug auf +*acc*; **in this ~** in dieser Hinsicht; **in some/many ~s** in gewisser/vielfacher Hinsicht; **with (all due) ~** bei allem Respekt.

respectability [rɪspɛktə'bɪlɪtɪ] n Anständigkeit f.

respectable [rɪs'pɛktəbl] adj anständig; (amount, income) ansehnlich; (standard, mark etc) ordentlich.

respected [rɪs'pɛktɪd] adj angesehen.

respectful [rɪs'pɛktful] adj respektvoll.

respectfully [rɪs'pɛktfəlɪ] adv (behave) respektvoll.

respective [rɪs'pɛktɪv] adj jeweilig.

respectively [rɪs'pɛktɪvlɪ] adv beziehungsweise; **Germany and Britain were 3rd and 4th** ~ Deutschland und Großbritannien belegten den 3. beziehungsweise 4. Platz.

respiration [rɛspɪ'reɪʃən] n see **artificial**.

respirator ['rɛspɪreɪtə'] n Respirator m, Beatmungsgerät nt.

respiratory ['rɛspərətərɪ] adj (system, failure) Atmungs-.

respite ['rɛspaɪt] n (rest) Ruhepause f.

resplendent [rɪs'plɛndənt] adj (clothes) prächtig.

respond [rɪs'pɔnd] vi (answer) antworten; (react) reagieren.

respondent [rɪs'pɔndənt] n (LAW) Beklagte(r) f(m).

response [rɪs'pɔns] n (to question) Antwort f; (to event etc) Reaktion f; **in** ~ **to** als Antwort/Reaktion auf +acc.

responsibility [rɪspɔnsɪ'bɪlɪtɪ] n Verantwortung f; **to take** ~ **for sth/sb** die Verantwortung für etw/jdn übernehmen.

responsible [rɪs'pɔnsɪbl] adj verantwortlich; (reliable, important) verantwortungsvoll; **to be** ~ **for sth** für etw verantwortlich sein; **to be** ~ **for doing sth** dafür verantwortlich sein, etw zu tun; **to be** ~ **to sb** jdm gegenüber verantwortlich sein.

responsibly [rɪs'pɔnsɪblɪ] adv verantwortungsvoll.

responsive [rɪs'pɔnsɪv] adj (person) ansprechbar.

rest [rɛst] n (relaxation) Ruhe f; (pause) Ruhepause f; (remainder) Rest m; (support) Stütze f; (MUS) Pause f ♦ vi (relax) sich ausruhen ♦ vt (eyes, legs etc) ausruhen; **the** ~ **of them** die Übrigen; **to put** or **set sb's mind at** ~ jdn beruhigen; **to come to** ~ (object) zum Stillstand kommen; **to lay sb to** ~ jdn zur letzten Ruhe betten; **to** ~ **on sth** (lit, fig) sich auf etw acc stützen; **to let the matter** ~ die Sache auf sich beruhen lassen; ~ **assured that** ... seien Sie versichert, dass ...; **I won't** ~ **until** ... ich werde nicht ruhen, bis ...; **may he/she** ~ **in peace** möge er/sie in Frieden ruhen; **to** ~ **sth on/against sth** (lean) etw an acc/gegen etw lehnen; **to** ~ **one's eyes** or **gaze on sth** den Blick auf etw heften; **I** ~ **my case** mehr brauche ich dazu wohl nicht zu sagen.

restart [riː'stɑːt] vt (engine) wieder anlassen; (work) wieder aufnehmen.

restaurant ['rɛstərɔŋ] n Restaurant nt.

restaurant car (BRIT) n (RAIL) Speisewagen m.

rest cure n Erholung f.

restful ['rɛstful] adj (music) ruhig; (lighting) beruhigend; (atmosphere) friedlich.

rest home n Pflegeheim nt.

restitution [rɛstɪ'tjuːʃən] n: **to make** ~ **to sb of sth** jdm etw zurückerstatten; (as compensation) jdn für etw entschädigen.

restive ['rɛstɪv] adj (person, crew) unruhig; (horse) störrisch.

restless ['rɛstlɪs] adj rastlos; (audience) unruhig; **to get** ~ unruhig werden.

restlessly ['rɛstlɪslɪ] adv (walk around) rastlos; (turn over) unruhig.

restock [riː'stɔk] vt (shop, freezer) wieder auffüllen; (lake, river: with fish) wieder besetzen.

restoration [rɛstə'reɪʃən] n (of painting etc) Restauration f; (of law and order, health, sight etc) Wiederherstellung f; (of land, rights) Rückgabe f; (HIST): **the R**~ die Restauration.

restorative [rɪ'stɔrətɪv] adj (power, treatment) stärkend ♦ n (old: drink) Stärkungsmittel nt.

restore [rɪ'stɔː'] vt (painting etc) restaurieren; (law and order, faith etc) wieder herstellen; (health) wiederherstellen; (property) zurückgeben; **to** ~ **sth to** (to former state) etw zurückverwandeln in +acc; **to** ~ **sb to power** jdn wieder an die Macht bringen.

restorer [rɪ'stɔːrə'] n (ART etc) Restaurator(in) m(f).

restrain [rɪs'treɪn] vt (person) zurückhalten; (feeling) unterdrücken; (growth, inflation) dämpfen; **to** ~ **sb from doing sth** jdn davon abhalten, etw zu tun; **to** ~ **o.s. from doing sth** sich beherrschen, etw nicht zu tun.

restrained [rɪs'treɪnd] adj (person) beherrscht; (style etc) zurückhaltend.

restraint [rɪs'treɪnt] n (restriction) Einschränkung f; (moderation) Zurückhaltung f; **wage** ~ Zurückhaltung f bei Lohnforderungen.

restrict [rɪs'trɪkt] vt beschränken.

restricted area (BRIT) n (AUT) Bereich m mit Geschwindigkeitsbeschränkung.

restriction [rɪs'trɪkʃən] n Beschränkung f.

restrictive [rɪs'trɪktɪv] adj (law, measure) restriktiv; (clothing) beengend.

restrictive practices (BRIT) npl (INDUSTRY) wettbewerbshemmende Geschäftspraktiken pl.

rest room (US) n Toilette f.

restructure [riː'strʌktʃə'] vt umstrukturieren.

result [rɪ'zʌlt] n Resultat nt; (of match, election, exam etc) Ergebnis nt ♦ vi: **to** ~ **in** führen zu; **as a** ~ **of the accident** als Folge des Unfalls; **he missed the train as a** ~ **of sleeping in** er verpasste den Zug, weil er verschlafen hatte; **to** ~ **from** resultieren or sich ergeben

aus; **as a ~ it is too expensive** folglich ist es zu teuer.
resultant [rɪ'zʌltənt] *adj* resultierend, sich ergebend.
resume [rɪ'zjuːm] *vt* (*work, journey*) wieder aufnehmen; (*seat*) wieder einnehmen ♦ *vi* (*start again*) von neuem beginnen.
résumé ['reɪzjuːmeɪ] *n* Zusammenfassung *f*; (*US: curriculum vitae*) Lebenslauf *m*.
resumption [rɪ'zʌmpʃən] *n* (*of work etc*) Wiederaufnahme *f*.
resurgence [rɪ'səːdʒəns] *n* Wiederaufleben *nt*.
resurrection [rɛzə'rɛkʃən] *n* (*of hopes, fears*) Wiederaufleben *nt*; (*of custom etc*) Wiederbelebung *f*; (*REL*): **the R~** die Auferstehung *f*.
resuscitate [rɪ'sʌsɪteɪt] *vt* (*MED, fig*) wieder beleben.
resuscitation [rɪsʌsɪ'teɪʃən] *n* Wiederbelebung *f*.
retail ['riːteɪl] *adj* (*trade, department*) Verkaufs-; (*shop, goods*) Einzelhandels- ♦ *adv* im Einzelhandel ♦ *vt* (*sell*) (im Einzelhandel) verkaufen ♦ *vi*: **to ~ at** (im Einzelhandel) kosten; **this product ~s at £25** dieses Produkt kostet im Laden £25.
retailer ['riːteɪlə*] *n* Einzelhändler(in) *m(f)*.
retail outlet *n* Einzelhandelsverkaufsstelle *f*.
retail price *n* Einzelhandelspreis *m*.
retail price index *n* Einzelhandelspreisindex *m*.
retain [rɪ'teɪn] *vt* (*keep*) behalten; (*: heat, moisture*) zurückhalten.
retainer [rɪ'teɪnə*] *n* (*fee*) Vorauszahlung *f*.
retaliate [rɪ'tælɪeɪt] *vi* Vergeltung üben.
retaliation [rɪtælɪ'eɪʃən] *n* Vergeltung *f*; **in ~ for** als Vergeltung für.
retaliatory [rɪ'tælɪətərɪ] *adj* (*move, attack*) Vergeltungs-.
retarded [rɪ'tɑːdɪd] *adj* zurückgeblieben; **mentally ~** geistig zurückgeblieben.
retch [rɛtʃ] *vi* würgen.
retention [rɪ'tɛnʃən] *n* (*of tradition etc*) Beibehaltung *f*; (*of land, memories*) Behalten *nt*; (*of heat, fluid etc*) Zurückhalten *nt*.
retentive [rɪ'tɛntɪv] *adj* (*memory*) merkfähig.
rethink ['riː'θɪŋk] *vt* noch einmal überdenken.
reticence ['rɛtɪsns] *n* Zurückhaltung *f*.
reticent ['rɛtɪsnt] *adj* zurückhaltend.
retina ['rɛtɪnə] *n* Netzhaut *f*.
retinue ['rɛtɪnjuː] *n* Gefolge *nt*.
retire [rɪ'taɪə*] *vi* (*give up work*) in den Ruhestand treten; (*withdraw, go to bed*) sich zurückziehen.
retired [rɪ'taɪəd] *adj* (*person*) im Ruhestand.
retirement [rɪ'taɪəmənt] *n* (*state*) Ruhestand *m*; (*act*) Pensionierung *f*.
retirement age *n* Rentenalter *nt*.
retiring [rɪ'taɪərɪŋ] *adj* (*leaving*) ausscheidend; (*shy*) zurückhaltend.
retort [rɪ'tɔːt] *vi* erwidern ♦ *n* (*reply*) Erwiderung *f*.

retrace [riː'treɪs] *vt*: **to ~ one's steps** (*lit, fig*) seine Schritte zurückverfolgen.
retract [rɪ'trækt] *vt* (*promise*) zurücknehmen; (*confession*) zurückziehen; (*claws, undercarriage*) einziehen.
retractable [rɪ'træktəbl] *adj* (*undercarriage, aerial*) einziehbar.
retrain [riː'treɪn] *vt* umschulen ♦ *vi* umgeschult werden.
retraining [riː'treɪnɪŋ] *n* Umschulung *f*.
retread ['riːtrɛd] *n* (*tyre*) runderneuerter Reifen *m*.
retreat [rɪ'triːt] *n* (*place*) Zufluchtsort *m*; (*withdrawal: also MIL*) Rückzug *m* ♦ *vi* sich zurückziehen; **to beat a hasty ~** schleunigst den Rückzug antreten.
retrial [rɪ'traɪəl] *n* erneute Verhandlung *f*.
retribution [rɛtrɪ'bjuːʃən] *n* Strafe *f*.
retrieval [rɪ'triːvəl] *n* (*of object*) Zurückholen *nt*; (*COMPUT*) Abruf *m*.
retrieve [rɪ'triːv] *vt* (*object*) zurückholen; (*situation*) retten; (*error*) wieder gutmachen; (*dog*) apportieren; (*COMPUT*) abrufen.
retriever [rɪ'triːvə*] *n* (*dog*) Apportierhund *m*.
retroactive [rɛtrəu'æktɪv] *adj* rückwirkend.
retrograde ['rɛtrəgreɪd] *adj* (*step*) Rück-.
retrospect ['rɛtrəspɛkt] *n*: **in ~** rückblickend, im Rückblick.
retrospective [rɛtrə'spɛktɪv] *adj* (*opinion etc*) im Nachhinein; (*law, tax*) rückwirkend ♦ *n* (*ART*) Retrospektive *f*.
return [rɪ'təːn] *n* (*going or coming back*) Rückkehr *f*; (*of sth stolen etc*) Rückgabe *f*; (*also: ~ ticket: BRIT*) Rückfahrkarte *f*; (*FIN: from investment etc*) Ertrag *m*; (*of merchandise*) Rücksendung *f*; (*official report*) Erklärung *f* ♦ *cpd* (*journey*) Rück- ♦ *vi* (*person etc: come or go back*) zurückkehren; (*feelings, symptoms etc*) wiederkehren ♦ *vt* (*favour, greetings etc*) erwidern; (*sth stolen etc*) zurückgeben; (*LAW: verdict*) fällen; (*POL: candidate*) wählen; (*ball*) zurückspielen; **returns** *npl* (*COMM*) Gewinne *pl*; **in ~ (for)** als Gegenleistung (für); **by ~ of post** postwendend; **many happy ~s (of the day)!** herzlichen Glückwunsch zum Geburtstag!; **~ match** Rückspiel *nt*.
▸ **return to** *vt fus* (*regain: consciousness, power*) wiedererlangen.
returnable [rɪ'təːnəbl] *adj* (*bottle etc*) Mehrweg-.
returner *n* jd, der nach längerer Abwesenheit wieder in die Arbeitswelt zurückkehrt.
returning officer [rɪ'təːnɪŋ-] (*BRIT*) *n* Wahlleiter(in) *m(f)*.
return key *n* (*COMPUT*) Return-Taste *f*.
reunion [riː'juːnɪən] *n* Treffen *nt*; (*after long separation*) Wiedervereinigung *f*.
reunite [riːjuː'naɪt] *vt* wieder vereinigen.
Rev. *abbr* (*REL*) = **Reverend.**
rev [rɛv] *n abbr* (*AUT*: = *revolution per minute*) Umdrehung *f* pro Minute, U/min. ♦ *vt* (*also*:

~ **up:** *engine)* aufheulen lassen.

revaluation [riːˈvæljuˈeɪʃən] *n (of property)*
Neuschätzung *f*; *(of currency)* Aufwertung *f*;
(of attitudes) Neubewertung *f*.

revamp [riːˈvæmp] *vt (company, system)* auf
Vordermann bringen.

rev counter *(BRIT) n (AUT)* Drehzahlmesser
m.

Revd. *abbr (REL)* = **Reverend.**

reveal [rɪˈviːl] *vt (make known)* enthüllen;
(make visible) zum Vorschein bringen.

revealing [rɪˈviːlɪŋ] *adj (comment, action)*
aufschlussreich; *(dress)* tief ausgeschnitten.

reveille [rɪˈvælɪ] *n (MIL)* Wecksignal *nt*.

revel [ˈrɛvl] *vi:* **to ~ in sth** in etw schwelgen;
to ~ in doing sth es genießen, etw zu tun.

revelation [rɛvəˈleɪʃən] *n (disclosure)*
Enthüllung *f*.

reveller [ˈrɛvlə*] *n* Zecher(in) *m(f)*.

revelry [ˈrɛvlrɪ] *n* Gelage *nt*.

revenge [rɪˈvɛndʒ] *n (for insult etc)* Rache *f* ♦ *vt*
rächen; **to get one's ~ (for sth)** seine Rache
(für etw) bekommen; **to ~ o.s.** *or* **take one's
~ (on sb)** sich (an jdm) rächen.

revengeful [rɪˈvɛndʒful] *adj* rachsüchtig.

revenue [ˈrɛvənjuː] *n (of person, company)*
Einnahmen *pl*; *(of government)*
Staatseinkünfte *pl*.

reverberate [rɪˈvɜːbəreɪt] *vi (sound etc)*
widerhallen; *(fig: shock etc)* Nachwirkungen
haben.

reverberation [rɪvɜːbəˈreɪʃən] *n (of sound)*
Widerhall *m*; *(fig: of event etc)*
Nachwirkungen *pl*.

revere [rɪˈvɪə*] *vt* verehren.

reverence [ˈrɛvərəns] *n* Ehrfurcht *f*.

Reverend [ˈrɛvərənd] *adj (in titles)* Pfarrer; **the
~ John Smith** Pfarrer John Smith.

reverent [ˈrɛvərənt] *adj* ehrfürchtig.

reverie [ˈrɛvərɪ] *n* Träumerei *f*.

reversal [rɪˈvɜːsl] *n (of policy, trend)* Umkehr *f*;
a ~ of roles ein Rollentausch *m*.

reverse [rɪˈvɜːs] *n (opposite)* Gegenteil *nt*;
(back: of cloth) linke Seite *f*; *(: of coin, paper)*
Rückseite *f*; *(AUT: also: ~ gear)*
Rückwärtsgang *m*; *(setback)* Rückschlag *m*
♦ *adj (side)* Rück-; *(process)* umgekehrt ♦ *vt*
(position, trend etc) umkehren; *(LAW: verdict)*
revidieren; *(roles)* vertauschen; *(car)*
zurücksetzen ♦ *vi (BRIT: AUT)* zurücksetzen;
in ~ umgekehrt; **to go into ~** den
Rückwärtsgang einlegen; **in ~ order** in
umgekehrter Reihenfolge; **to ~ direction**
sich um 180 Grad drehen.

reverse-charge call [rɪˈvɜːstʃɑːdʒ-] *(BRIT) n*
R-Gespräch *nt*.

reverse video *n (COMPUT)* invertierte
Darstellung *f*.

reversible [rɪˈvɜːsəbl] *adj (garment)* auf beiden
Seiten tragbar; *(decision, operation)*
umkehrbar.

reversing lights [rɪˈvɜːsɪŋ-] *(BRIT) npl*

Rückfahrscheinwerfer *m*.

reversion [rɪˈvɜːʃən] *n:* **~ to** Rückfall in +*acc*;
(ZOOL) Rückentwicklung *f*.

revert [rɪˈvɜːt] *vi:* **to ~ to** *(former state)*
zurückkehren zu, zurückfallen in +*acc*;
(LAW: money, property) zurückfallen an +*acc*.

review [rɪˈvjuː] *n (magazine)* Zeitschrift *f*;
(MIL) Inspektion *f*; *(of book, film etc)* Kritik *f*,
Besprechung *f*, Rezension *f*; *(of policy etc)*
Überprüfung *f* ♦ *vt (MIL: troops)* inspizieren;
(book, film etc) besprechen, rezensieren;
(policy etc) überprüfen; **to be/come under ~**
überprüft werden.

reviewer [rɪˈvjuːə*] *n* Kritiker(in) *m(f)*,
Rezensent(in) *m(f)*.

revile [rɪˈvaɪl] *vt* schmähen.

revise [rɪˈvaɪz] *vt (manuscript)* überarbeiten,
revidieren; *(opinion etc)* ändern; *(price,
procedure)* revidieren ♦ *vi (study)*
wiederholen; **~d edition** überarbeitete
Ausgabe.

revision [rɪˈvɪʒən] *n (of manuscript, law etc)*
Überarbeitung *f*, Revision *f*; *(for exam)*
Wiederholung *f*.

revitalize [riːˈvaɪtəlaɪz] *vt* neu beleben.

revival [rɪˈvaɪvl] *n (recovery)* Aufschwung *m*;
(of interest, faith) Wiederaufleben *nt*; *(THEAT)*
Wiederaufnahme *f*.

revive [rɪˈvaɪv] *vt (person)* wieder beleben;
(economy etc) Auftrieb geben +*dat*; *(custom)*
wieder aufleben lassen; *(hope, interest etc)*
neu beleben; *(play)* wieder aufnehmen ♦ *vi*
(person) wieder zu sich kommen; *(activity,
economy etc)* wieder aufblühen; *(hope,
interest etc)* wieder erweckt werden.

revoke [rɪˈvəuk] *vt (law etc)* aufheben; *(title,
licence)* entziehen +*dat*; *(promise, decision)*
widerrufen.

revolt [rɪˈvəult] *n* Revolte *f*, Aufstand *m* ♦ *vi*
rebellieren ♦ *vt* abstoßen; **to ~ against sb/
sth** gegen jdn/etw rebellieren.

revolting [rɪˈvəultɪŋ] *adj (disgusting)*
abscheulich, ekelhaft.

revolution [rɛvəˈluːʃən] *n (POL etc)* Revolution
f; *(rotation)* Umdrehung *f*.

revolutionary [rɛvəˈluːʃənrɪ] *adj* revolutionär;
(leader, army) Revolutions- ♦ *n*
Revolutionär(in) *m(f)*.

revolutionize [rɛvəˈluːʃənaɪz] *vt*
revolutionieren.

revolve [rɪˈvɔlv] *vi* sich drehen; **to ~ (a)round**
sich drehen um.

revolver [rɪˈvɔlvə*] *n* Revolver *m*.

revolving [rɪˈvɔlvɪŋ] *adj (chair)* Dreh-;
(sprinkler etc) drehbar.

revolving door *n* Drehtür *f*.

revue [rɪˈvjuː] *n (THEAT)* Revue *f*.

revulsion [rɪˈvʌlʃən] *n (disgust)* Abscheu *m*,
Ekel *m*.

reward [rɪˈwɔːd] *n* Belohnung *f*; *(satisfaction)*
Befriedigung *f* ♦ *vt* belohnen.

rewarding [rɪˈwɔːdɪŋ] *adj* lohnend; **financially**

~ einträglich.

rewind [riːˈwaɪnd] (*irreg: like* **wind**) *vt* (*tape etc*) zurückspulen.

rewire [riːˈwaɪə*] *vt* neu verkabeln.

reword [riːˈwɜːd] *vt* (*message, note*) umformulieren.

rework [riːˈwɜːk] *vt* (*use again: theme etc*) wieder verarbeiten; (*revise*) neu fassen.

rewrite [riːˈraɪt] (*irreg: like* **write**) *vt* neu schreiben.

Reykjavik [ˈreɪkjəviːk] *n* Reykjavik *nt*.

RFD (*US*) *abbr* (*POST: = rural free delivery*) *freie Landpostzustellung.*

RGN (*BRIT*) *n abbr* (= *Registered General Nurse*) staatlich geprüfte Krankenschwester *f*, staatlich geprüfter Krankenpfleger *m*.

Rh *abbr* (*MED: = rhesus*) Rh.

rhapsody [ˈræpsədɪ] *n* (*MUS*) Rhapsodie *f*.

rhesus negative *adj* Rhesus negativ.

rhesus positive *adj* Rhesus positiv.

rhetoric [ˈretərɪk] *n* Rhetorik *f*.

rhetorical [rɪˈtɒrɪkl] *adj* rhetorisch.

rheumatic [ruːˈmætɪk] *adj* rheumatisch.

rheumatism [ˈruːmətɪzəm] *n* Rheuma *nt*, Rheumatismus *m*.

rheumatoid arthritis [ˈruːmətɔɪd-] *n* Gelenkrheumatismus *m*.

Rhine [raɪn] *n*: **the** ~ der Rhein.

rhinestone [ˈraɪnstəun] *n* Rheinkiesel *m*.

rhinoceros [raɪˈnɒsərəs] *n* Rhinozeros *nt*.

Rhodes [rəudz] *n* Rhodos *nt*.

Rhodesia [rəuˈdiːʒə] (*formerly*) *n* (*GEOG*) Rhodesien *nt*.

rhododendron [rəudəˈdɛndrən] *n* Rhododendron *m or nt*.

Rhone [rəun] *n*: **the** ~ die Rhone.

rhubarb [ˈruːbɑːb] *n* Rhabarber *m*.

rhyme [raɪm] *n* Reim *m*; (*verse*) Verse *pl* ♦ *vi*: **to** ~ **(with)** sich reimen (mit); **without** ~ **or reason** ohne Sinn und Verstand.

rhythm [ˈrɪðm] *n* Rhythmus *m*.

rhythmic(al) [ˈrɪðmɪk(l)] *adj* rhythmisch.

rhythmically [ˈrɪðmɪklɪ] *adv* (*move, beat*) rhythmisch, im Rhythmus.

rhythm method *n* Knaus-Ogino-Methode *f*.

RI *n abbr* (*BRIT: SCOL: = religious instruction*) Religionsunterricht *m* ♦ *abbr* (*US: POST: = Rhode Island*).

rib [rɪb] *n* Rippe *f* ♦ *vt* (*mock*) aufziehen.

ribald [ˈrɪbəld] *adj* (*laughter, joke*) rüde; (*person*) anzüglich.

ribbed [rɪbd] *adj* (*socks, sweater*) gerippt.

ribbon [ˈrɪbən] *n* (*for hair, decoration*) Band *nt*; (*of typewriter*) Farbband *nt*; **in ~s** (*torn*) in Fetzen.

rice [raɪs] *n* Reis *m*.

ricefield [ˈraɪsfiːld] *n* Reisfeld *nt*.

rice pudding *n* Milchreis *m*.

rich [rɪtʃ] *adj* reich; (*soil*) fruchtbar; (*food*) schwer; (*diet*) reichhaltig; (*colour*) satt; (*voice*) volltönend; (*tapestries, silks*) prächtig ♦ *npl*: **the** ~ die Reichen; ~ **in** reich an +*dat*.

riches [ˈrɪtʃɪz] *npl* Reichtum *m*.

richly [ˈrɪtʃlɪ] *adv* (*decorated, carved*) reich; (*reward, benefit*) reichlich; ~ **deserved/earned** wohlverdient.

richness [ˈrɪtʃnɪs] *n* (*wealth*) Reichtum *m*; (*of life, culture, food*) Reichhaltigkeit *f*; (*of soil*) Fruchtbarkeit *f*; (*of costumes, furnishings*) Pracht *f*.

rickets [ˈrɪkɪts] *n* Rachitis *f*.

rickety [ˈrɪkɪtɪ] *adj* (*chair etc*) wackelig.

rickshaw [ˈrɪkʃɔː] *n* Rikscha *f*.

ricochet [ˈrɪkəʃeɪ] *vi* abprallen ♦ *n* Abpraller *m*.

rid [rɪd] (*pt, pp* **rid**) *vt*: **to** ~ **sb/sth of** jdn/etw befreien von; **to get** ~ **of** loswerden; (*inhibitions, illusions etc*) sich befreien von.

riddance [ˈrɪdns] *n*: **good** ~! gut, dass wir den/die/das los sind!

ridden [ˈrɪdn] *pp of* **ride**.

riddle [ˈrɪdl] *n* Rätsel *nt* ♦ *vt*: **to be** ~**d with** (*guilt, doubts*) geplagt sein von; (*holes, corruption*) durchsetzt sein von.

ride [raɪd] (*pt* **rode**, *pp* **ridden**) *n* (*in car, on bicycle*) Fahrt *f*; (*on horse*) Ritt *m*; (*path*) Reitweg *m* ♦ *vi* (*on horse*) reiten; (*on bicycle, bus etc*) fahren ♦ *vt* (*see vi*) reiten; fahren; **car** ~ Autofahrt *f*; **to go for a** ~ eine Fahrt/einen Ausritt machen; **to take sb for a** ~ (*fig*) jdn hereinlegen; **we rode all day/all the way** wir sind den ganzen Tag/den ganzen Weg geritten/gefahren; **to** ~ **at anchor** (*NAUT*) vor Anker liegen; **can you** ~ **a bike?** kannst du Fahrrad fahren?

▶ **ride out** *vt*: **to** ~ **out the storm** (*fig*) den Sturm überstehen.

rider [ˈraɪdə*] *n* (*on horse*) Reiter(in) *m(f)*; (*on bicycle etc*) Fahrer(in) *m(f)*; (*in document etc*) Zusatz *m*.

ridge [rɪdʒ] *n* (*of hill*) Grat *m*; (*of roof*) First *m*; (*in sand etc*) Rippelmarke *f*.

ridicule [ˈrɪdɪkjuːl] *n* Spott *m* ♦ *vt* (*person*) verspotten; (*proposal, system etc*) lächerlich machen; **she was the object of** ~ alle machten sich über sie lustig.

ridiculous [rɪˈdɪkjuləs] *adj* lächerlich.

riding [ˈraɪdɪŋ] *n* Reiten *nt*.

riding school *n* Reitschule *f*.

rife [raɪf] *adj*: **to be** ~ (*corruption, disease etc*) grassieren; **to be** ~ **with** (*rumours etc*) durchsetzt sein von.

riffraff [ˈrɪfræf] *n* Gesindel *nt*.

rifle [ˈraɪfl] *n* (*gun*) Gewehr *nt* ♦ *vt* (*wallet etc*) plündern.

▶ **rifle through** *vt fus* (*papers etc*) durchwühlen.

rifle range *n* Schießstand *m*.

rift [rɪft] *n* Spalt *m*; (*fig*) Kluft *f*.

rig [rɪg] *n* (*also*: **oil** ~: *at sea*) Bohrinsel *f*; (: *on land*) Bohrturm *m* ♦ *vt* (*election, game etc*) manipulieren.

▶ **rig out** (*BRIT*) *vt*: **to** ~ **sb out as/in** jdn ausstaffieren als/in +*dat*.

▶ **rig up** *vt* (*device*) montieren.
rigging ['rɪgɪŋ] *n* (*NAUT*) Takelage *f*.
right [raɪt] *adj* (*correct*) richtig; (*not left*) rechte(r, s) ♦ *n* Recht *nt* ♦ *adv* (*correctly, properly*) richtig; (*directly, exactly*) genau; (*not on the left*) rechts ♦ *vt* (*ship, car etc*) aufrichten; (*fault, situation*) korrigieren, berichtigen ♦ *excl* okay; **the ~ time** (*exact*) die genaue Zeit; (*most suitable*) die richtige Zeit; **to be ~** (*person*) Recht haben; (*answer, fact*) richtig sein; (*clock*) genau gehen; (*reading etc*) korrekt sein; **to get sth ~** etw richtig machen; **let's get it ~ this time!** diesmal machen wir es richtig!; **you did the ~ thing** du hast das Richtige getan; **to put sth ~** (*mistake etc*) etw berichtigen; **on/to the ~** rechts; **the R~** (*POL*) die Rechte; **by ~s** richtig genommen; **to be in the ~** im Recht sein; **you're within your ~s (to do that)** es ist dein gutes Recht(, das zu tun); **he is a well-known author in his own ~** er ist selbst auch ein bekannter Autor; **film ~s** Filmrechte *pl*; **~ now** im Moment; **~ before/after the party** gleich vor/nach der Party; **~ against the wall** unmittelbar an der Wand; **~ ahead** geradeaus; **~ away** (*immediately*) sofort; **~ in the middle** genau in der Mitte; **he went ~ to the end of the road** er ging bis ganz ans Ende der Straße.
right angle *n* rechter Winkel *m*.
right-click ['raɪtklɪk] (*COMPUT*) *vi* rechts klicken ♦ *vt* rechts klicken auf (*+acc*).
righteous ['raɪtʃəs] *adj* (*person*) rechtschaffen; (*indignation*) gerecht.
righteousness ['raɪtʃəsnɪs] *n* Rechtschaffenheit *f*.
rightful ['raɪtful] *adj* rechtmäßig.
rightfully ['raɪtfəlɪ] *adv* von Rechts wegen.
right-hand drive *adj* (*vehicle*) mit Rechtssteuerung.
right-handed [raɪt'hændɪd] *adj* rechtshändig.
right-hand man *n* rechte Hand *f*.
right-hand side *n* rechte Seite *f*.
rightly ['raɪtlɪ] *adv* (*with reason*) zu Recht; **if I remember ~** (*BRIT*) wenn ich mich recht entsinne.
right-minded [raɪt'maɪndɪd] *adj* vernünftig.
right of way *n* (*on path etc*) Durchgangsrecht *f*; (*AUT*) Vorfahrt *f*.
rights issue *n* (*STOCK EXCHANGE*) Bezugsrechtsemission *f*.
right wing *n* (*POL, SPORT*) rechter Flügel *m*.
right-wing [raɪt'wɪŋ] *adj* (*POL*) rechtsgerichtet.
right-winger [raɪt'wɪŋə*] *n* (*POL*) Rechte(r) *f(m)*; (*SPORT*) Rechtsaußen *m*.
rigid ['rɪdʒɪd] *adj* (*structure, views*) starr; (*principle, control etc*) streng.
rigidity [rɪ'dʒɪdɪtɪ] *n* (*of structure etc*) Starrheit *f*; (*of attitude, views etc*) Strenge *f*.
rigidly ['rɪdʒɪdlɪ] *adv* (*hold, fix etc*) starr; (*control, interpret*) streng.

rigmarole ['rɪgmərəul] *n* Gedöns *nt* (*inf*).
rigor ['rɪgə*] (*US*) *n* = **rigour**.
rigor mortis ['rɪgə'mɔːtɪs] *n* Totenstarre *f*.
rigorous ['rɪgərəs] *adj* (*control etc*) streng; (*training*) gründlich.
rigorously ['rɪgərəslɪ] *adv* (*test, assess etc*) streng.
rigour, (*US*) **rigor** ['rɪgə*] *n* (*of argument, law*) Strenge *f*; (*of research*) Gründlichkeit; **the ~s of life/winter** die Härten des Lebens/des Winters.
rig-out ['rɪgaut] (*BRIT*: *inf*) *n* Aufzug *m*.
rile [raɪl] *vt* ärgern.
rim [rɪm] *n* (*of glass, spectacles*) Rand *m*; (*of wheel*) Felge *f*, Radkranz *m*.
rimless ['rɪmlɪs] *adj* (*spectacles*) randlos.
rimmed [rɪmd] *adj*: **~ with** umrandet von; **gold-~ spectacles** Brille *f* mit Goldfassung *or* Goldrand.
rind [raɪnd] *n* (*of bacon*) Schwarte *f*; (*of lemon, melon*) Schale *f*; (*of cheese*) Rinde *f*.
ring [rɪŋ] (*pt* **rang**, *pp* **rung**) *n* Ring *m*; (*of people, objects*) Kreis *m*; (*of circus*) Manege *f*; (*bullring*) Arena *f*; (*sound of telephone*) Klingeln *nt*; (*sound of bell*) Läuten *nt*; (*on cooker*) Kochstelle *m* ♦ *vi* (*TEL*: *person*) anrufen; (*telephone, doorbell*) klingeln; (*bell*) läuten; (*also*: **~ out**) ertönen ♦ *vt* (*BRIT*: *TEL*) anrufen; (*bell etc*) läuten; (*encircle*) einen Kreis machen um; **to give sb a ~** (*BRIT*: *TEL*) jdn anrufen; **that has a ~ of truth about it** das könnte stimmen; **to run ~s round sb** (*inf, fig*) jdn in die Tasche stecken; **to ~ true/false** wahr/falsch klingen; **my ears are ~ing** mir klingen die Ohren; **to ~ the doorbell** klingeln; **the name doesn't ~ a bell (with me)** der Name sagt mir nichts.
▶ **ring back** (*BRIT*) *vt, vi* (*TEL*) zurückrufen.
▶ **ring off** (*BRIT*) *vi* (*TEL*) (den Hörer) auflegen.
▶ **ring up** (*BRIT*) *vt* (*TEL*) anrufen.
ring binder *n* Ringbuch *nt*.
ring finger *n* Ringfinger *m*.
ringing ['rɪŋɪŋ] *n* (*of telephone*) Klingeln *nt*; (*of bell*) Läuten *nt*; (*in ears*) Klingen *nt*.
ringing tone (*BRIT*) *n* (*TEL*) Rufzeichen *nt*.
ringleader ['rɪŋliːdə*] *n* Rädelsführer(in) *m(f)*.
ringlets ['rɪŋlɪts] *npl* Ringellocken *pl*; **in ~** in Ringellocken.
ring road (*BRIT*) *n* Ringstraße *f*.
rink [rɪŋk] *n* (*also*: **ice ~**) Eisbahn *f*; (*also*: **roller skating ~**) Rollschuhbahn *f*.
rinse [rɪns] *n* Spülen *nt*; (*of hands*) Abspülen *nt*; (*hair dye*) Tönung *f* ♦ *vt* spülen; (*hands*) abspülen; (*also*: **~ out**: *clothes*) auswaschen; (: *mouth*) ausspülen; **to give sth a ~** etw spülen; (*dishes*) etw abspülen.
Rio (de Janeiro) ['riːəu(dədʒə'nɪərəu)] *n* Rio (de Janeiro) *nt*.
riot ['raɪət] *n* (*disturbance*) Aufruhr *m* ♦ *vi* randalieren; **a ~ of colours** ein Farbenmeer *nt*; **to run ~** randalieren.

rioter ['raɪətə*] n Randalierer m.

riot gear n Schutzausrüstung f.

riotous ['raɪətəs] adj (crowd) randalierend; (nights, party) ausschweifend; (welcome etc) tumultartig.

riotously ['raɪətəslɪ] adv: ~ **funny** or **comic** urkomisch.

riot police n Bereitschaftspolizei f; **hundreds of** ~ hunderte or Hunderte von Bereitschaftspolizisten.

RIP abbr (= rest in peace) R.I.P.

rip [rɪp] n (tear) Riss m ♦ vt zerreißen ♦ vi reißen.

▶ **rip off** vt (clothes) herunterreißen; (inf: swindle) übers Ohr hauen.

▶ **rip up** vt zerreißen.

ripcord ['rɪpkɔːd] n Reißleine f.

ripe [raɪp] adj reif; **to be** ~ **for sth** (fig) reif für etw sein; **he lived to a** ~ **old age** er erreichte ein stolzes Alter.

ripen ['raɪpn] vt reifen lassen ♦ vi reifen.

ripeness ['raɪpnɪs] n Reife f.

rip-off ['rɪpɔf] (inf) n: **it's a** ~! das ist Wucher!

riposte [rɪ'pɔst] n scharfe Entgegnung f.

ripple ['rɪpl] n (wave) kleine Welle f; (of laughter, applause) Welle f ♦ vi (water) sich kräuseln; (muscles) spielen ♦ vt (surface) kräuseln.

rise [raɪz] (pt **rose**, pp **risen**) n (incline) Steigung f; (BRIT: salary increase) Gehaltserhöhung f; (in prices, temperature etc) Anstieg m; (fig: to fame etc) Aufstieg m ♦ vi (prices, water) steigen; (sun, moon) aufgehen; (wind) aufkommen; (from bed, chair) aufstehen; (sound, voice) ansteigen; (also: ~ **up**: tower, rebel) sich erheben; (in rank) aufsteigen; **to give** ~ **to** Anlass geben zu; **to** ~ **to power** an die Macht kommen.

risen [rɪzn] pp of **rise**.

rising ['raɪzɪŋ] adj (increasing) steigend; (up-and-coming) aufstrebend.

rising damp n aufsteigende Feuchtigkeit f.

rising star n (fig: person) Aufsteiger(in) m(f).

risk [rɪsk] n (danger, chance) Gefahr f; (deliberate) Risiko nt ♦ vt riskieren; **to take a** ~ ein Risiko eingehen; **to run the** ~ **of sth** etw zu fürchten haben; **to run the** ~ **of doing sth** Gefahr laufen, etw zu tun; **at** ~ in Gefahr; **at one's own** ~ auf eigene Gefahr; **at the** ~ **of sounding rude** ... auf die Gefahr hin, unhöflich zu klingen, ...; **it's a fire/health** ~ es ist ein Feuer-/Gesundheitsrisiko; **I'll** ~ **it** ich riskiere es.

risk capital n Risikokapital nt.

risky ['rɪskɪ] adj riskant.

risqué ['riːskeɪ] adj (joke) gewagt.

rissole ['rɪsəul] n (of meat, fish etc) Frikadelle f.

rite [raɪt] n Ritus m; **last** ~**s** (REL) Letzte Ölung f.

ritual ['rɪtjuəl] adj (law, murder) Ritual-; (dance) rituell ♦ n Ritual nt.

rival ['raɪvl] n Rivale m, Rivalin f ♦ adj (firm, newspaper etc) Konkurrenz-; (teams, groups etc) rivalisierend ♦ vt (match) sich messen können mit; **to** ~ **sth/sb in sth** sich mit etw/ jdm in Bezug auf etw messen können.

rivalry ['raɪvlrɪ] n Rivalität f.

river ['rɪvə*] n Fluss m; (fig: of blood etc) Strom m ♦ cpd (port, traffic) Fluss-; **up/down** ~ flussaufwärts/-abwärts.

river bank n Flussufer nt.

river bed n Flussbett nt.

riverside ['rɪvəsaɪd] n = **river bank**.

rivet ['rɪvɪt] n Niete f ♦ vt (fig: attention) fesseln; (: eyes) heften.

riveting ['rɪvɪtɪŋ] adj (fig) fesselnd.

Riviera [rɪvɪ'ɛərə] n: **the (French)** ~ die (französische) Riviera; **the Italian** ~ die italienische Riviera.

Riyadh [rɪ'jɑːd] n Riad nt.

RMT n abbr (= National Union of Rail, Maritime and Transport Workers) Gewerkschaft der Eisenbahner, Seeleute und Transportarbeiter.

RN n abbr (BRIT) = **Royal Navy**; (US) = **registered nurse**.

RNA n abbr (= ribonucleic acid) RNS f.

RNLI (BRIT) n abbr (= Royal National Lifeboat Institution) durch Spenden finanzierter Seenot-Rettungsdienst, ≈ DLRG f.

RNZAF n abbr (= Royal New Zealand Air Force) neuseeländische Luftwaffe f.

RNZN n abbr (= Royal New Zealand Navy) neuseeländische Marine f.

road [rəud] n Straße f; (fig) Weg m ♦ cpd (accident, sense) Verkehrs-; **main** ~ Hauptstraße f; **it takes four hours by** ~ man braucht vier Stunden mit dem Auto; **let's hit the** ~ machen wir uns auf den Weg!; **to be on the** ~ (salesman etc) unterwegs sein; (pop group etc) auf Tournee sein; **on the** ~ **to success** auf dem Weg zum Erfolg; **major/ minor** ~ Haupt-/Nebenstraße f.

road accident n Verkehrsunfall m.

roadblock ['rəudblɔk] n Straßensperre f.

road haulage n Spedition f.

roadhog ['rəudhɔg] n Verkehrsrowdy m.

road map n Straßenkarte f.

road rage n Aggressivität f im Straßenverkehr.

road safety n Verkehrssicherheit f.

roadside ['rəudsaɪd] n Straßenrand m ♦ cpd (building, sign etc) am Straßenrand; **by the** ~ am Straßenrand.

road sign n Verkehrszeichen nt.

roadsweeper ['rəudswiːpə*] (BRIT) n (person) Straßenkehrer(in) m(f); (vehicle) Straßenkehrmaschine f.

road user n Verkehrsteilnehmer(in) m(f).

roadway ['rəudweɪ] n Fahrbahn f.

road works npl Straßenbauarbeiten pl.

roadworthy ['rəudwɔːðɪ] adj verkehrstüchtig.

roam [rəum] vi wandern, streifen ♦ vt (streets, countryside) durchstreifen.

roar [rɔː] n (of animal, crowd) Brüllen nt; (of vehicle) Getöse nt; (of storm) Heulen nt ♦ vi (animal, person) brüllen; (engine, wind etc) heulen; ~s of laughter brüllendes Gelächter; to ~ with laughter vor Lachen brüllen.

roaring ['rɔːrɪŋ] adj: a ~ fire ein prasselndes Feuer; a ~ success ein Bombenerfolg m; to do a ~ trade (in sth) ein Riesengeschäft (mit etw) machen.

roast [rəust] n Braten m ♦ vt (meat, potatoes) braten; (coffee) rösten.

roast beef n Roastbeef nt.

roasting ['rəustɪŋ] (inf) adj (hot) knallheiß ♦ n (criticism) Verriss m; (telling-off) Standpauke f; to give sb a ~ (criticize) jdn verreißen; (scold) jdm eine Standpauke halten.

rob [rɔb] vt (person) bestehlen; (house, bank) ausrauben; to ~ sb of sth jdm etw rauben; (fig: deprive) jdm etw vorenthalten.

robber ['rɔbə] n Räuber(in) m(f).

robbery ['rɔbərɪ] n Raub m.

robe [rəub] n (for ceremony etc) Gewand nt; (also: bath ~) Bademantel m; (US) Morgenrock m ♦ vt: to be ~d in (form) (festlich) in etw acc gekleidet sein.

robin ['rɔbɪn] n Rotkehlchen nt.

robot ['rəubɔt] n Roboter m.

robotics [rə'bɔtɪks] n Robotik f.

robust [rəu'bʌst] adj robust; (appetite) gesund.

rock [rɔk] n (substance) Stein m; (boulder) Felsen m; (US: small stone) Stein m; (BRIT: sweet) ≈ Zuckerstange f; (MUS: also: ~ music) Rock m, Rockmusik f ♦ vt (swing gently: cradle) schaukeln; (: child) wiegen; (shake: also fig) erschüttern ♦ vi (object) schwanken; (person) schaukeln; on the ~s (drink) mit Eis; (ship) (auf Felsen) aufgelaufen; (marriage etc) gescheitert; to ~ the boat (fig) Unruhe stiften.

rock and roll n Rock and Roll m.

rock bottom ['rɔk'bɔtəm] adj (prices) Tiefst- ♦ n: to reach or touch or hit rock bottom (person, prices) den Tiefpunkt erreichen.

rock cake n ≈ Rosinenbrötchen nt.

rock climber n Felsenkletterer(in) m(f).

rock climbing n Felsenklettern nt.

rockery ['rɔkərɪ] n Steingarten m.

rocket ['rɔkɪt] n Rakete f ♦ vi (prices) in die Höhe schießen.

rocket launcher n Raketenwerfer m.

rock face n Felswand f.

rock fall n Steinschlag m.

rocking chair ['rɔkɪŋ-] n Schaukelstuhl m.

rocking horse n Schaukelpferd nt.

rocky ['rɔkɪ] adj (path, ground) felsig; (fig: business, marriage) wackelig.

Rocky Mountains npl: the ~ die Rocky Mountains pl.

rod [rɔd] n (also TECH) Stange f; (also: fishing ~) Angelrute f.

rode [rəud] pt of ride.

rodent ['rəudnt] n Nagetier nt.

rodeo ['rəudɪəu] (US) n Rodeo nt.

roe [rəu] n (CULIN): hard ~ Rogen m; soft ~ Milch f.

roe deer n inv Reh nt.

rogue [rəug] n Gauner m.

roguish ['rəugɪʃ] adj schelmisch.

role [rəul] n Rolle f.

role model n Rollenmodell nt.

role play n Rollenspiel nt.

roll [rəul] n (of paper) Rolle f; (of cloth) Ballen m; (of banknotes) Bündel nt; (also: bread ~) Brötchen nt; (register, list) Verzeichnis nt; (of drums etc) Wirbel m ♦ vt rollen; (also: ~ up: string) aufrollen; (: sleeves) aufkrempeln; (cigarette) drehen; (also: ~ out: pastry) ausrollen; (flatten: lawn, road) walzen ♦ vi rollen; (drum) wirbeln; (thunder) grollen; (ship) schlingern; (tears, sweat) fließen; (camera, printing press) laufen; cheese/ham ~ Käse-/Schinkenbrötchen nt; he's ~ing in it (inf: rich) er schwimmt im Geld.
► **roll about** vi sich wälzen.
► **roll around** vi = roll about.
► **roll in** vi (money, invitations) hereinströmen.
► **roll over** vi sich umdrehen.
► **roll up** vi (inf: arrive) aufkreuzen ♦ vt (carpet, umbrella etc) aufrollen; to ~ o.s. up into a ball sich zusammenrollen.

roll call n namentlicher Aufruf m.

rolled gold [rəuld-] n Dubleegold nt, Doublégold nt.

roller ['rəulə] n Rolle f; (for lawn, road) Walze f; (for hair) Lockenwickler m.

rollerblades npl Rollerblades pl.

roller blind n Rollo nt.

roller coaster n Achterbahn f.

roller skates npl Rollschuhe pl.

rollicking ['rɔlɪkɪŋ] adj toll, Mords-; to have a ~ time sich ganz toll amüsieren.

rolling ['rəulɪŋ] adj (hills) wellig.

rolling mill n Walzwerk nt.

rolling pin n Nudelholz nt.

rolling stock n (RAIL) Fahrzeuge pl.

roll-on-roll-off ['rəulɔn'rəulɔf] (BRIT) adj (ferry) Roll-on-roll-off-.

roly-poly ['rəulɪ'pəulɪ] (BRIT) n ≈ Strudel m.

ROM [rɔm] n abbr (COMPUT: = read only memory) ROM.

Roman ['rəumən] adj römisch ♦ n (person) Römer(in) m(f).

Roman Catholic adj römisch-katholisch ♦ n Katholik(in) m(f).

romance [rə'mæns] n (love affair) Romanze f; (romanticism) Romantik f; (novel) fantastische Erzählung f.

Romanesque [rəumə'nesk] adj romanisch.

Romania [rəu'meɪnɪə] n Rumänien nt.

Romanian [rəu'meɪnɪən] adj rumänisch ♦ n (person) Rumäne m, Rumänin f; (LING) Rumänisch nt.

Roman numeral n römische Ziffer f.

romantic [rə'mæntɪk] *adj* romantisch.

romanticism [rə'mæntɪsɪzəm] *n* (*also ART, LITER*) Romantik *f*.

Romany ['rɔmənɪ] *adj* Roma- ♦ *n* (*person*) Roma *mf*; (*LING*) Romani *nt*.

Rome [rəum] *n* Rom *nt*.

romp [rɔmp] *n* Klamauk *m* ♦ *vi* (*also:* ~ *about*) herumtollen; **to** ~ **home** (*horse*) spielend gewinnen.

rompers ['rɔmpəz] *npl* (*clothing*) einteiliger Spielanzug *für Babys*.

rondo ['rɔndəu] *n* (*MUS*) Rondo *nt*.

roof [ru:f] (*pl* ~**s**) *n* Dach *nt* ♦ *vt* (*house etc*) überdachen; **the** ~ **of the mouth** der Gaumen.

roof garden *n* Dachgarten *m*.

roofing ['ru:fɪŋ] *n* Deckung *f*; ~ **felt** Dachpappe *f*.

roof rack *n* Dachgepäckträger *m*.

rook [ruk] *n* (*bird*) Saatkrähe *f*; (*CHESS*) Turm *m*.

rookie ['rukɪ] (*inf*) *n* (*esp MIL*) Grünschnabel *m*.

room [ru:m] *n* (*in house, hotel*) Zimmer *nt*; (*space*) Raum *m*, Platz *m*; (*scope: for change etc*) Raum *m* ♦ *vi*: **to** ~ **with sb** (*esp US*) ein Zimmer mit jdm teilen; **rooms** *npl* (*lodging*) Zimmer *pl*; "~**s to let**", (*US*) "~**s for rent**" „Zimmer zu vermieten"; **single/double** ~ Einzel-/Doppelzimmer *nt*; **is there** ~ **for this?** ist dafür Platz vorhanden?; **to make** ~ **for sb** für jdn Platz machen; **there is** ~ **for improvement** es gibt Möglichkeiten zur Verbesserung.

rooming house ['ru:mɪŋ-] (*US*) *n* Mietshaus *nt*.

roommate ['ru:mmeɪt] *n* Zimmergenosse *m*, Zimmergenossin *f*.

room service *n* Zimmerservice *m*.

room temperature *n* Zimmertemperatur *f*.

roomy ['ru:mɪ] *adj* (*building, car*) geräumig.

roost [ru:st] *vi* (*birds*) sich niederlassen.

rooster ['ru:stə*] (*esp US*) *n* Hahn *m*.

root [ru:t] *n* (*also MATH*) Wurzel *f* ♦ *vi* (*plant*) Wurzeln schlagen ♦ *vt*: **to be** ~**ed in** verwurzelt sein in +*dat*; **roots** *npl* (*family origins*) Wurzeln *pl*; **to take** ~ (*plant, idea*) Wurzeln schlagen; **the** ~ **cause of the problem** die Wurzel des Problems.

▶ **root about** *vi* (*search*) herumwühlen.

▶ **root for** *vt fus* (*support*) anfeuern.

▶ **root out** *vt* ausrotten.

root beer (*US*) *n* kohlensäurehaltiges Getränk aus Wurzel- und Kräuterextrakten.

rope [rəup] *n* Seil *nt*; (*NAUT*) Tau *nt* ♦ *vt* (*tie*) festbinden; (*also:* ~ *together*) zusammenbinden; **to know the** ~**s** (*fig*) sich auskennen.

▶ **rope in** *vt* (*fig: person*) einspannen.

▶ **rope off** *vt* (*area*) mit einem Seil absperren.

rope ladder *n* Strickleiter *f*.

rop(e)y (*inf*) *adj* (*ill, poor quality*) miserabel.

rosary ['rəuzərɪ] *n* Rosenkranz *m*.

rose [rəuz] *pt of* **rise** ♦ *n* (*flower*) Rose *f*; (*also:* ~**bush**) Rosenstrauch *m*; (*on watering can*) Brause *f* ♦ *adj* rosarot.

rosé ['rəuzeɪ] *n* (*wine*) Rosé *m*.

rosebed ['rəuzbɛd] *n* Rosenbeet *nt*.

rosebud ['rəuzbʌd] *n* Rosenknospe *f*.

rosebush ['rəuzbuʃ] *n* Rosenstrauch *m*.

rosemary ['rəuzmərɪ] *n* Rosmarin *m*.

rosette ['rəu'zɛt] *n* Rosette *f*.

ROSPA ['rɔspə] (*BRIT*) *n abbr* (= *Royal Society for the Prevention of Accidents*) *Verband, der Maßnahmen zur Unfallverhütung propagiert*.

roster ['rɔstə*] *n*: **duty** ~ Dienstplan *m*.

rostrum ['rɔstrəm] *n* Rednerpult *nt*.

rosy ['rəuzɪ] *adj* (*colour*) rosarot; (*face, situation*) rosig; **a** ~ **future** eine rosige Zukunft.

rot [rɔt] *n* (*decay*) Fäulnis *f*; (*fig: rubbish*) Quatsch *m* ♦ *vt* verfaulen lassen ♦ *vi* (*teeth, wood, fruit etc*) verfaulen; **to stop the** ~ (*BRIT, fig*) den Verfall stoppen; **dry** ~ Holzschwamm *m*; **wet** ~ Nassfäule *f*.

rota ['rəutə] *n* Dienstplan *m*; **on a** ~ **basis** reihum nach Plan.

rotary ['rəutərɪ] *adj* (*cutter*) rotierend; (*motion*) Dreh-.

rotate [rəu'teɪt] *vt* (*spin*) drehen, rotieren lassen; (*crops*) im Wechsel anbauen; (*jobs*) turnusmäßig wechseln ♦ *vi* (*revolve*) rotieren, sich drehen.

rotating [rəu'teɪtɪŋ] *adj* (*revolving*) rotierend; (*drum, mirror*) Dreh-.

rotation [rəu'teɪʃən] *n* (*of planet, drum etc*) Rotation *f*, Drehung *f*; (*of crops*) Wechsel *m*; (*of jobs*) turnusmäßiger Wechsel *m*; **in** ~ der Reihe nach.

rote [rəut] *n*: **by** ~ auswendig.

rotor ['rəutə*] *n* (*also:* ~ **blade**) Rotor *m*.

rotten ['rɔtn] *adj* (*decayed*) faul, verfault; (*inf: person, situation*) gemein; (: *film, weather, driver etc*) mies; **to feel** ~ sich elend fühlen.

rotund [rəu'tʌnd] *adj* (*person*) rundlich.

rouble, (*US*) **ruble** ['ru:bl] *n* Rubel *m*.

rouge [ru:ʒ] *n* Rouge *nt*.

rough [rʌf] *adj* rau; (*terrain, road*) uneben; (*person, plan, drawing, guess*) grob; (*life, conditions, journey*) hart; (*sea, crossing*) stürmisch ♦ *n* (*GOLF*): **in the** ~ im Rough ♦ *vt*: **to** ~ **it** primitiv *or* ohne Komfort leben; **the sea is** ~ **today** die See ist heute stürmisch; **to have a** ~ **time** eine harte Zeit durchmachen; **can you give me a** ~ **idea of the cost?** können Sie mir eine ungefähre Vorstellung von den Kosten geben?; **to feel** ~ (*BRIT*) sich elend fühlen; **to sleep** ~ (*BRIT*) im Freien übernachten; **to play** ~ (*fig*) auf die grobe Tour kommen.

▶ **rough out** *vt* (*drawing, idea etc*) skizzieren.

roughage ['rʌfɪdʒ] *n* Ballaststoffe *pl*.

rough-and-ready ['rʌfən'rɛdɪ] *adj*

provisorisch.
rough-and-tumble [ˈrʌfənˈtʌmbl] n (*fighting*)
Balgerei f; (*fig*) Schlachtfeld nt.
roughcast [ˈrʌfkɑːst] n Rauputz m.
rough copy n Entwurf m.
rough draft n = **rough copy**.
rough justice n Justizwillkür f.
roughly [ˈrʌflɪ] adv grob; (*approximately*)
ungefähr; ~ **speaking** grob gesagt.
roughness [ˈrʌfnɪs] n Rauheit f; (*of manner*)
Grobheit f.
roughshod [ˈrʌfʃɔd] adv: **to ride** ~ **over** sich
rücksichtslos hinwegsetzen über +acc.
roulette [ruːˈlɛt] n Roulette nt.
Roumania etc [ruːˈmeɪnɪə] n = **Romania** etc.
round [raund] adj rund ♦ n Runde f; (*of
ammunition*) Ladung f ♦ vt (*corner*) biegen
um; (*cape*) umrunden ♦ prep um ♦ adv: **all** ~
rundherum; **in** ~ **figures** rund gerechnet;
the daily ~ (*fig*) der tägliche Trott; **a** ~ **of
applause** Beifall m; **a** ~ **of** (*drinks*) eine
Runde; **a** ~ **of sandwiches** ein Butterbrot; **a**
~ **of toast** (*BRIT*) eine Scheibe Toast; **it's just**
~ **the corner** (*fig*) es steht vor der Tür; **to go**
~ **the back** hinten herum gehen; **to go** ~ (**an
obstacle**) (um ein Hindernis) herumgehen;
~ **the clock** rund um die Uhr; ~ **his neck/
the table** um seinen Hals/den Tisch; **to sail**
~ **the world** die Welt umsegeln; **to walk**
~ **the room/park** im Zimmer/Park
herumgehen; ~ **about 300** (*approximately*)
ungefähr 300; **the long way** ~ auf
Umwegen; **all (the) year** ~ das ganze Jahr
über; **the wrong way** ~ falsch herum; **to ask
sb** ~ jdn zu sich einladen; **I'll be** ~ **at 6
o'clock** ich komme um 6 Uhr; **to go** ~
(*rotate*) sich drehen; **to go** ~ **to sb's (house)**
jdn (zu Hause) besuchen; **enough to go** ~
genug für alle.
► **round off** vt abrunden.
► **round up** vt (*cattle etc*) zusammentreiben;
(*people*) versammeln; (*figure*) aufrunden.
roundabout [ˈraundəbaut] (*BRIT*) n (*AUT*)
Kreisverkehr m; (*at fair*) Karussell nt ♦ adj:
by a ~ **route** auf Umwegen; **in a** ~ **way** auf
Umwegen.
rounded [ˈraundɪd] adj (*hill, figure etc*)
rundlich.
rounders [ˈraundəz] n ≈ Schlagball m.
roundly [ˈraundlɪ] adv (*fig: criticize etc*)
nachdrücklich.
round robin n (*esp US*) n (*SPORT*) Wettkampf,
bei dem jeder gegen jeden spielt.
round-shouldered [ˈraundˈʃəuldəd] adj mit
runden Schultern.
round trip n Rundreise f.
roundup [ˈraundʌp] n (*of news etc*)
Zusammenfassung f; (*of animals*)
Zusammentreiben nt; (*of criminals*)
Aufgreifen nt; **a** ~ **of the latest news** ein
Nachrichtenüberblick m.
rouse [rauz] vt (*wake up*) aufwecken; (*stir up*)

reizen.
rousing [ˈrauzɪŋ] adj (*speech*) mitreißend;
(*welcome*) stürmisch.
rout [raut] (*MIL*) n totale Niederlage f ♦ vt
(*defeat*) vernichtend schlagen.
route [ruːt] n Strecke f; (*of bus, train, shipping*)
Linie f; (*of procession, fig*) Weg m; **"all ~s"**
(*AUT*) „alle Richtungen"; **the best** ~ **to
London** der beste Weg nach London.
route map n (*BRIT*) n Streckenkarte f.
routine [ruːˈtiːn] adj (*work, check etc*) Routine-
♦ n (*habits*) Routine f; (*drudgery*) Stumpfsinn
m; (*THEAT*) Nummer f; ~ **procedure**
Routinesache f.
rove [rəuv] vt (*area, streets*) ziehen durch.
roving reporter [ˈrəuvɪŋ-] n Reporter(in) m(f)
im Außendienst.
row¹ [rəu] n (*line*) Reihe f ♦ vi (*in boat*) rudern
♦ vt (*boat*) rudern; **three times in a** ~
dreimal hintereinander.
row² [rau] n (*din*) Krach m, Lärm m; (*dispute*)
Streit m ♦ vi (*argue*) sich streiten; **to have a**
~ sich streiten.
rowboat [ˈrəubəut] (*US*) n = **rowing boat**.
rowdiness [ˈraudɪnɪs] n Rowdytum nt.
rowdy [ˈraudɪ] adj (*person*) rüpelhaft; (*party
etc*) lärmend.
rowdyism [ˈraudɪɪzəm] n = **rowdiness**.
rowing [ˈrəuɪŋ] n (*sport*) Rudern nt.
rowing boat (*BRIT*) n Ruderboot nt.
rowlock [ˈrɔlək] (*BRIT*) n Dolle f.
royal [ˈrɔɪəl] adj königlich; **the** ~ **family** die
königliche Familie.

ROYAL ACADEMY

Die **Royal Academy** *oder* **Royal Academy of
Arts**, *eine Akademie zur Förderung der Malerei,
Bildhauerei und Architektur, wurde 1768 unter der
Schirmherrschaft von George II. gegründet und
befindet sich seit 1869 in Burlington House,
Piccadilly, London. Jeden Sommer findet dort eine
Ausstellung mit Werken zeitgenössischer Künstler
statt. Die* **Royal Academy** *unterhält auch
Schulen, an denen Malerei, Bildhauerei und
Architektur unterrichtet wird.*

Royal Air Force (*BRIT*) n: **the** ~ die
Königliche Luftwaffe.
royal blue adj königsblau.
royalist [ˈrɔɪəlɪst] n Royalist(in) m(f) ♦ adj
royalistisch.
Royal Navy (*BRIT*) n: **the** ~ die Königliche
Marine.
royalty [ˈrɔɪəltɪ] n (*royal persons*) die
königliche Familie; **royalties** npl (*to author*)
Tantiemen pl; (*to inventor*) Honorar nt.
RP (*BRIT*) n abbr (= received pronunciation)
Standardaussprache des Englischen; see also
receive.
rpm abbr (= revolutions per minute) U/min.
RR (*US*) abbr = **railroad.**

RRP (*BRIT*) *n abbr* = **recommended retail price**.

RSA (*BRIT*) *n abbr* (= *Royal Society of Arts*) *akademischer Verband zur Vergabe von Diplomen*; (= *Royal Scottish Academy*) *Kunstakademie*.

RSI *n abbr* (*MED*: = *repetitive strain injury*) RSI *nt, Schmerzempfindung durch ständige Wiederholung bestimmter Bewegungen.*

RSPB (*BRIT*) *n abbr* (= *Royal Society for the Protection of Birds*) *Vogelschutzorganisation.*

RSPCA (*BRIT*) *n abbr* (= *Royal Society for the Prevention of Cruelty to Animals*) Tierschutzverein *m*.

RSVP *abbr* (= *répondez s'il vous plaît*) u. A. w. g.

RTA *n abbr* (= *road traffic accident*) Verkehrsunfall *m*.

Rt Hon. (*BRIT*) *abbr* (= *Right Honourable*) Titel *für Abgeordnete des Unterhauses.*

Rt Rev. *abbr* (*REL*: = *Right Reverend*) *Titel für Bischöfe.*

rub [rʌb] *vt* reiben ♦ *n*: **to give sth a ~** (*polish*) etw polieren; **he ~bed his hands together** er rieb sich *dat* die Hände; **to ~ sb up** *or* (*US*) **~ sb the wrong way** bei jdm anecken.
▶ **rub down** *vt* (*body, horse*) abreiben.
▶ **rub in** *vt* (*ointment*) einreiben; **don't ~ it in!** (*fig*) reite nicht so darauf herum!
▶ **rub off** *vi* (*paint*) abfärben.
▶ **rub off on** *vt fus* abfärben auf +*acc*.
▶ **rub out** *vt* (*with eraser*) ausradieren.

rubber ['rʌbə*] *n* (*also inf*: *condom*) Gummi *nt or m*; (*BRIT*: *eraser*) Radiergummi *m*.

rubber band *n* Gummiband *nt*.

rubber bullet *n* Gummigeschoss *nt*.

rubber plant *n* Gummibaum *m*.

rubber ring *n* (*for swimming*) Schwimmreifen *m*.

rubber stamp *n* Stempel *m*.

rubber-stamp [rʌbə'stæmp] *vt* (*fig: decision*) genehmigen.

rubbery ['rʌbərɪ] *adj* (*material*) gummiartig; (*meat, food*) wie Gummi.

rubbish ['rʌbɪʃ] (*BRIT*) *n* (*waste*) Abfall *m*; (*fig: junk*) Schrott *m*; (: *pej: nonsense*) Quatsch *m* ♦ *vt* (*inf*) heruntermachen; ~! Quatsch!

rubbish bin (*BRIT*) *n* Abfalleimer *m*.

rubbish dump (*BRIT*) *n* Müllabladeplatz *m*.

rubbishy ['rʌbɪʃɪ] (*BRIT*: *inf*) *adj* miserabel, mies.

rubble ['rʌbl] *n* (*debris*) Trümmer *pl*; (*CONSTR*) Schutt *m*.

ruble ['ru:bl] (*US*) *n* = **rouble**.

ruby ['ru:bɪ] *n* (*gem*) Rubin *m* ♦ *adj* (*red*) rubinrot.

RUC (*BRIT*) *n abbr* (= *Royal Ulster Constabulary*) *nordirische Polizeibehörde.*

rucksack ['rʌksæk] *n* Rucksack *m*.

ructions ['rʌkʃənz] (*inf*) *npl* Krach *m*, Ärger *m*.

rudder ['rʌdə*] *n* (*of ship, plane*) Ruder *nt*.

ruddy ['rʌdɪ] *adj* (*complexion etc*) rötlich; (*inf*: *damned*) verdammt.

rude [ru:d] *adj* (*impolite*) unhöflich; (*naughty*)

unanständig; (*unexpected: shock etc*) böse; (*crude: table, shelter etc*) primitiv; **to be ~ to sb** unhöflich zu jdm sein; **a ~ awakening** ein böses Erwachen.

rudely ['ru:dlɪ] *adv* (*interrupt*) unhöflich; (*say, push*) grob.

rudeness ['ru:dnɪs] *n* (*impoliteness*) Unhöflichkeit *f*.

rudimentary [ru:dɪ'mentərɪ] *adj* (*equipment*) primitiv; (*knowledge*) Grund-.

rudiments ['ru:dɪmənts] *npl* Grundlagen *pl*.

rue [ru:] *vt* bereuen.

rueful ['ru:ful] *adj* (*expression, person*) reuevoll.

ruff [rʌf] *n* (*collar*) Halskrause *f*.

ruffian ['rʌfɪən] *n* Rüpel *m*.

ruffle ['rʌfl] *vt* (*hair, feathers*) zerzausen; (*water*) kräuseln; (*fig: person*) aus der Fassung bringen.

rug [rʌg] *n* (*on floor*) Läufer *m*; (*BRIT*: *blanket*) Decke *f*.

rugby ['rʌgbɪ] *n* (*also*: ~ **football**) Rugby *nt*.

rugged ['rʌgɪd] *adj* (*landscape*) rauh; (*man*) robust; (*features, face*) markig; (*determination, independence*) wild.

rugger ['rʌgə*] (*BRIT*: *inf*) *n* Rugby *nt*.

ruin ['ru:ɪn] *n* (*destruction, downfall*) Ruin *m*; (*remains*) Ruine *f* ♦ *vt* ruinieren; (*building*) zerstören; (*clothes, carpet etc*) verderben; **ruins** *npl* (*of castle*) Ruinen *pl*; (*of building*) Trümmer *pl*; **in ~s** (*lit, fig*) in Trümmern.

ruination [ru:ɪ'neɪʃən] *n* (*of building etc*) Zerstörung *f*; (*of person, life*) Ruinierung *f*.

ruinous ['ru:ɪnəs] *adj* (*expense, interest*) ruinös.

rule [ru:l] *n* (*norm*) Regel *f*; (*regulation*) Vorschrift *f*; (*government*) Herrschaft *f*; (*also*: **ruler**) Lineal *nt* ♦ *vt* (*country, people*) herrschen über +*acc* ♦ *vi* (*monarch etc*) herrschen; **it's against the ~s** das ist nicht gestattet; **as a ~ of thumb** als Faustregel; **under British ~** unter britischer Herrschaft; **as a ~** in der Regel; **to ~ in favour of/against/on sth** (*LAW*) für/gegen/über etw *acc* entscheiden; **to ~ that ...** (*umpire, judge etc*) entscheiden, dass ...
▶ **rule out** *vt* (*possibility etc*) ausschließen; **murder cannot be ~d out** Mord ist nicht auszuschließen.

ruled [ru:ld] *adj* (*paper*) liniert.

ruler ['ru:lə*] *n* (*sovereign*) Herrscher(in) *m(f)*; (*for measuring*) Lineal *nt*.

ruling ['ru:lɪŋ] *adj* (*party*) Regierungs-; (*body*) maßgebend ♦ *n* (*LAW*) Entscheidung *f*; **the ~ class** die herrschende Klasse.

rum [rʌm] *n* Rum *m* ♦ *adj* (*BRIT*: *inf*: *peculiar*) komisch.

Rumania *etc n* = **Romania** *etc*.

rumble ['rʌmbl] *n* (*of thunder*) Grollen *nt*; (*of traffic*) Rumpeln *nt*; (*of guns*) Donnern *nt*; (*of voices*) Gemurmel *nt* ♦ *vi* (*stomach*) knurren; (*thunder*) grollen; (*traffic*) rumpeln; (*guns*) donnern.

rumbustious [rʌmˈbʌstʃəs] *adj* (*person*) ungebärdig.

ruminate [ˈruːmɪneɪt] *vi* (*person*) grübeln; (*cow, sheep etc*) wiederkäuen.

rummage [ˈrʌmɪdʒ] *vi* herumstöbern.

rummage sale (*US*) *n* Trödelmarkt *m*.

rumour, (*US*) **rumor** [ˈruːmə*] *n* Gerücht *nt* ♦ *vt*: **it is ~ed that ...** man sagt, dass ...

rump [rʌmp] *n* (*of animal*) Hinterteil *nt*; (*of group etc*) Rumpf *m*.

rumple [ˈrʌmpl] *vt* (*clothes etc*) zerknittern; (*hair*) zerzausen.

rump steak *n* Rumpsteak *nt*.

rumpus [ˈrʌmpəs] *n* Krach *m*; **to kick up a ~** Krach schlagen.

run [rʌn] (*pt* **ran,** *pp* **run**) *n* (*as exercise, sport*) Lauf *m*; (*in car, train etc*) Fahrt *f*; (*series*) Serie *f*; (*SKI*) Abfahrt *f*; (*CRICKET, BASEBALL*) Run *m*; (*THEAT*) Spielzeit *f*; (*in tights etc*) Laufmasche *f* ♦ *vt* (*race, distance*) laufen, rennen; (*operate: business*) leiten; (: *hotel, shop*) führen; (: *competition, course*) durchführen; (*COMPUT: program*) laufen lassen; (*hand, fingers*) streichen mit; (*water, bath*) einlaufen lassen; (*PRESS: feature, article*) bringen ♦ *vi* laufen, rennen; (*flee*) weglaufen; (*bus, train*) fahren; (*river, tears*) fließen; (*colours*) auslaufen; (*jumper*) färben; (*in election*) antreten; (*road, railway etc*) verlaufen; **to go for a ~** (*as exercise*) einen Dauerlauf machen; **to break into a ~** zu laufen *or* rennen beginnen; **a ~ of good/bad luck** eine Glücks-/Pechsträhne; **to have the ~ of sb's house** jds Haus zur freien Verfügung haben; **there was a ~ on ...** (*meat, tickets*) es gab einen Ansturm auf +*acc*; **in the long ~** langfristig; **in the short ~** kurzfristig; **to make a ~ for it** die Beine in die Hand nehmen; **on the ~** (*fugitive*) auf der Flucht; **I'll ~ you to the station** ich fahre dich zum Bahnhof; **to ~ the risk of doing sth** Gefahr laufen, etw zu tun; **she ran her finger down the list** sie fuhr mit dem Finger durch; **it's very cheap to ~** (*car, machine*) es ist sehr billig im Verbrauch; **to ~ a bath** das Badewasser einlaufen lassen; **to be ~ off one's feet** (*BRIT*) in Trab sein; **the baby's nose was ~ning** dem Baby lief die Nase; **the train ~s between Gatwick and Victoria** der Zug verkehrt zwischen Gatwick und Victoria; **the bus ~s every 20 minutes** der Bus fährt alle 20 Minuten; **to ~ on petrol/off batteries** mit Benzin/auf Batterie laufen; **to ~ for president** für das Amt des Präsidenten kandidieren; **to ~ dry** (*well etc*) austrocknen; **tempers were ~ning high** alle waren sehr erregt; **unemployment is ~ning at 20 per cent** die Arbeitslosigkeit beträgt 20 Prozent; **blonde hair ~s in the family** blonde Haare liegen in der Familie.

▶ **run across** *vt fus* (*find*) stoßen auf +*acc*.

▶ **run after** *vt fus* nachlaufen +*dat*.

▶ **run away** *vi* weglaufen.

▶ **run down** *vt* (*production*) verringern; (*factory*) allmählich stilllegen; (*AUT: person*) überfahren; (*criticize*) schlecht machen ♦ *vi* (*battery*) leer werden.

▶ **run in** (*BRIT*) *vt* (*car*) einfahren.

▶ **run into** *vt fus* (*meet: person*) begegnen +*dat*; (: *trouble etc*) bekommen; (*collide with*) laufen/fahren gegen; **to ~ into debt** in Schulden geraten; **their losses ran into millions** ihre Schulden gingen in die Millionen.

▶ **run off** *vt* (*liquid*) ablassen; (*copies*) machen ♦ *vi* weglaufen.

▶ **run out** *vi* (*time, passport*) ablaufen; (*money*) ausgehen; (*luck*) zu Ende gehen.

▶ **run out of** *vt fus*: **we're ~ning out of money/petrol** uns geht das Geld/das Benzin aus; **we're ~ning out of time** wir haben keine Zeit mehr.

▶ **run over** *vt* (*AUT*) überfahren ♦ *vt fus* (*repeat*) durchgehen ♦ *vi* (*bath, water*) überlaufen.

▶ **run through** *vt fus* (*instructions, lines*) durchgehen.

▶ **run up** *vt* (*debt*) anhäufen.

▶ **run up against** *vt fus* (*difficulties*) stoßen auf +*acc*.

runabout [ˈrʌnəbaut] *n* (*AUT*) Flitzer *m*.

run-around [ˈrʌnəraund] (*inf*) *n*: **to give sb the ~** jdn an der Nase herumführen.

runaway [ˈrʌnəweɪ] *adj* (*horse*) ausgerissen; (*truck, train*) außer Kontrolle geraten; (*child, slave*) entlaufen; (*fig: inflation*) unkontrollierbar; (: *success*) überwältigend.

rundown [ˈrʌndaun] *n* (*of industry etc*) allmähliche Stillegung *f* ♦ *adj*: **to be run-down** (*person*) total erschöpft sein; (*building, area*) heruntergekommen.

rung [rʌŋ] *pp of* **ring** ♦ *n* (*also fig*) Sprosse *f*.

run-in [ˈrʌnɪn] (*inf*) *n* Auseinandersetzung *f*.

runner [ˈrʌnə*] *n* Läufer(in) *m(f)*; (*horse*) Rennpferd *nt*; (*on sledge, drawer etc*) Kufe *f*.

runner bean (*BRIT*) *n* Stangenbohne *f*.

runner-up [rʌnərˈʌp] *n* Zweitplatzierte(r) *f(m)*.

running [ˈrʌnɪŋ] *n* (*sport*) Laufen *nt*; (*of business etc*) Leitung *f*; (*of machine etc*) Betrieb *m* ♦ *adj* (*water, stream*) laufend; **to be in/out of the ~ for sth** bei etw im Rennen liegen/aus dem Rennen sein; **to make the ~** (*in race, fig*) das Rennen machen; **6 days ~** 6 Tage hintereinander; **to have a ~ battle with sb** ständig im Streit mit jdm liegen; **to give a ~ commentary on sth** etw fortlaufend kommentieren; **a ~ sore** eine nässende Wunde.

running costs *npl* (*of car, machine*) Unterhaltskosten *pl*.

running head *n* (*TYP, COMPUT*) Kolumnentitel *m*.

running mate (*US*) *n* (*POL*)

Vizepräsidentschaftskandidat m.

runny ['rʌnɪ] adj (egg, butter) dünnflüssig; (nose, eyes) triefend.

run-off ['rʌnɔf] n (in contest, election) Entscheidungsrunde f; (extra race) Entscheidungsrennen nt.

run-of-the-mill ['rʌnəvðə'mɪl] adj gewöhnlich.

runt [rʌnt] n (animal) kleinstes und schwächstes Tier eines Wurfs; (pej: person) Zwerg m.

run-through ['rʌnθru:] n (rehearsal) Probe f.

run-up ['rʌnʌp] n: the ~ to (election etc) die Zeit vor +dat.

runway ['rʌnweɪ] n (AVIAT) Start- und Landebahn f.

rupee [ru:'pi:] n Rupie f.

rupture ['rʌptʃə*] n (MED) Bruch m; (conflict) Spaltung f ♦ vt: to ~ o.s. (MED) sich dat einen Bruch zuziehen.

rural ['ruərl] adj ländlich; (crime) auf dem Lande.

rural district council (BRIT) n Landbezirksverwaltung f.

ruse [ru:z] n List f.

rush [rʌʃ] n (hurry) Eile f, Hetze f; (COMM: sudden demand) starke Nachfrage f; (of water, air) Stoß m; (of feeling) Woge f ♦ vt (lunch, job etc) sich beeilen bei; (person, supplies etc) schnellstens bringen ♦ vi (person) sich beeilen; (air, water) strömen; **rushes** npl (BOT) Schilf nt; (for chair, basket etc) Binsen pl; **is there any ~ for this?** eilt das?; **we've had a ~ of orders** wir hatten einen Zustrom von Bestellungen; **I'm in a ~ (to do sth)** ich habe es eilig (, etw zu tun); **gold ~** Goldrausch m; **don't ~ me!** drängen Sie mich nicht!; **to ~ sth off** (send) etw schnellstens abschicken; **to ~ sb into doing sth** jdn dazu drängen, etw zu tun.
▶ **rush through** vt (order, application) schnellstens erledigen.

rush hour n Hauptverkehrszeit f, Rushhour f.

rush job n Eilauftrag m.

rush matting n Binsenmatte f.

rusk [rʌsk] n Zwieback m.

Russia ['rʌʃə] n Russland nt.

Russian ['rʌʃən] adj russisch ♦ n (person) Russe m, Russin f; (LING) Russisch nt.

rust [rʌst] n Rost m ♦ vi rosten.

rustic ['rʌstɪk] adj (style, furniture) rustikal ♦ n (pej: person) Bauer m.

rustle ['rʌsl] vi (paper, leaves) rascheln ♦ vt (paper) rascheln mit; (US: cattle) stehlen.

rustproof ['rʌstpru:f] adj nichtrostend.

rustproofing ['rʌstpru:fɪŋ] n Rostschutz m.

rusty ['rʌstɪ] adj (car) rostig; (fig: skill etc) eingerostet.

rut [rʌt] n (in path etc) Furche f; (ZOOL: season) Brunft f, Brunst f; **to be in a ~** (fig) im Trott stecken.

rutabaga [ru:tə'beɪgə] (US) n Steckrübe f.

ruthless ['ru:θlɪs] adj rücksichtslos.

ruthlessness ['ru:θlɪsnɪs] n Rücksichtslosigkeit f.

RV abbr (BIBLE: = revised version) englische Bibelübersetzung von 1885 ♦ n abbr (US) = recreational vehicle.

Rwanda [ru'ændə] n Ruanda nt.

Rwandan [ru'ændən] adj ruandisch.

rye [raɪ] n (cereal) Roggen m.

rye bread n Roggenbrot nt.

S, s

S¹, s [ɛs] n (letter) S nt, s nt; (US: SCOL: satisfactory) ≈ 3; ~ **for sugar** ≈ S wie Samuel.

S² [ɛs] abbr (= saint) St.; (= small) kl.; (= south) S.

SA abbr = **South Africa**; **South America**; (= South Australia) Südaustralien nt.

Sabbath ['sæbəθ] n (Jewish) Sabbat m; (Christian) Sonntag m.

sabbatical [sə'bætɪkl] n (also: ~ **year**) Forschungsjahr nt.

sabotage ['sæbətɑ:ʒ] n Sabotage f ♦ vt einen Sabotageakt verüben auf +acc; (plan, meeting) sabotieren.

sabre ['seɪbə*] n Säbel m.

sabre-rattling ['seɪbərætlɪŋ] n Säbelrasseln nt.

saccharin(e) ['sækərɪn] n Sa(c)charin nt ♦ adj (fig) zuckersüß.

sachet ['sæʃeɪ] n (of shampoo) Beutel m; (of sugar etc) Tütchen nt.

sack [sæk] n Sack m ♦ vt (dismiss) entlassen; (plunder) plündern; **to get the ~** rausfliegen (inf); **to give sb the ~** jdn rausschmeißen (inf).

sackful ['sækful] n: **a ~ of** ein Sack.

sacking ['sækɪŋ] n (dismissal) Entlassung f; (material) Sackleinen nt.

sacrament ['sækrəmənt] n Sakrament nt.

sacred ['seɪkrɪd] adj heilig; (music, history) geistlich; (memory) geheiligt; (building) sakral.

sacred cow n (lit, fig) heilige Kuh f.

sacrifice ['sækrɪfaɪs] n Opfer nt ♦ vt opfern; **to make ~s (for sb)** (für jdn) Opfer bringen.

sacrilege ['sækrɪlɪdʒ] n Sakrileg nt; **that would be ~** das wäre ein Sakrileg.

sacrosanct ['sækrəusæŋkt] adj (lit, fig) sakrosankt.

sad [sæd] adj traurig; **he was ~ to see her go** er war traurig (darüber), dass sie wegging.

sadden ['sædn] vt betrüben.

saddle ['sædl] n Sattel m ♦ vt (horse) satteln; **to be ~d with sb/sth** (inf) jdn/etw am Hals haben.

saddlebag ['sædlbæg] n Satteltasche f.

sadism ['seɪdɪzəm] n Sadismus m.

sadist ['seɪdɪst] n Sadist(in) m(f).

sadistic [sə'dɪstɪk] adj sadistisch.

sadly ['sædlɪ] adv traurig, betrübt; (unfortunately) leider, bedauerlicherweise; (seriously) schwer; **he is ~ lacking in humour** ihm fehlt leider jeglicher Humor.

sadness ['sædnɪs] n Traurigkeit f.

sadomasochism [seɪdəʊ'mæsəkɪzəm] n Sadomasochismus m.

s.a.e. (BRIT) abbr (= stamped addressed envelope) see **stamp**.

safari [sə'fɑːrɪ] n Safari f; **to go on ~** auf Safari gehen.

safari park n Safaripark m.

safe [seɪf] adj sicher; (out of danger) in Sicherheit ♦ n Safe m or nt, Tresor m; **~ from** sicher vor +dat; **~ and sound** gesund und wohlbehalten; **(just) to be on the ~ side** (nur) um sicherzugehen; **to play ~** auf Nummer sicher or Sicher gehen (inf); **it is ~ to say that ...** man kann wohl sagen, dass ...; **~ journey!** gute Fahrt or Reise!

safe bet n: **it's a ~ that ...** es ist sicher, dass ...

safe-breaker ['seɪfbreɪkə*] (BRIT) n Safeknacker m (inf).

safe-conduct [seɪf'kɒndʌkt] n freies or sicheres Geleit nt.

safe-cracker ['seɪfkrækə*] n = **safe-breaker**.

safe-deposit ['seɪfdɪpɒzɪt] n (vault) Tresorraum m; (also: ~ **box**) Banksafe m.

safeguard ['seɪfgɑːd] n Schutz m ♦ vt schützen; (interests) wahren; (future) sichern; **as a ~ against** zum Schutz gegen.

safe haven n Zufluchtsort m.

safe house n geheimer Unterschlupf m.

safekeeping ['seɪf'kiːpɪŋ] n sichere Aufbewahrung f.

safely ['seɪflɪ] adv sicher; (assume, say) wohl, ruhig; (arrive) wohlbehalten; **I can ~ say ...** ich kann wohl sagen ...

safe passage n sichere Durchreise f.

safe sex n Safer Sex m, Safersex m.

safety ['seɪftɪ] n Sicherheit f; **~ first!** Sicherheit geht vor!

safety belt n Sicherheitsgurt m.

safety catch n (on gun) Sicherung f; (on window, door) Sperre f.

safety net n Sprungnetz nt, Sicherheitsnetz nt; (fig) Sicherheitsvorkehrung f.

safety pin n Sicherheitsnadel f.

safety valve n Sicherheitsventil nt.

saffron ['sæfrən] n Safran m.

sag [sæg] vi durchhängen; (breasts) hängen; (fig: spirits, demand) sinken.

saga ['sɑːgə] n Saga f; (fig) Geschichte f.

sage [seɪdʒ] n (herb) Salbei m; (wise man) Weise(r) m.

Sagittarius [sædʒɪ'tɛərɪəs] n Schütze m; **to be**

~ Schütze sein.

sago ['seɪgəʊ] n Sago m.

Sahara [sə'hɑːrə] n: **the ~ (Desert)** die (Wüste) Sahara.

Sahel [sæ'hɛl] n Sahel m, Sahelzone f.

said [sɛd] pt, pp of **say**.

Saigon [saɪ'gɒn] n Saigon nt.

sail [seɪl] n Segel nt ♦ vt segeln ♦ vi fahren; (SPORT) segeln; (begin voyage: ship) auslaufen; (: passenger) abfahren; (fig: ball etc) fliegen, segeln; **to go for a ~** segeln gehen; **to set ~** losfahren, abfahren.

▶ **sail through** vt fus (fig: exam etc) spielend schaffen.

sailboat ['seɪlbəʊt] (US) n = **sailing boat**.

sailing ['seɪlɪŋ] n (SPORT) Segeln nt; (voyage) Überfahrt f; **to go ~** segeln gehen.

sailing boat n Segelboot nt.

sailing ship n Segelschiff nt.

sailor ['seɪlə*] n Seemann m, Matrose m.

saint [seɪnt] n (lit, fig) Heilige(r) f(m).

saintly ['seɪntlɪ] adj heiligmäßig; (expression) fromm.

sake [seɪk] n: **for the ~ of sb/sth, for sb's/sth's ~** um jds/einer Sache gen willen; (out of consideration for) jdm/etw zuliebe; **he enjoys talking for talking's ~** er redet gerne, nur damit etwas gesagt wird; **for the ~ of argument** rein theoretisch; **art for art's ~** Kunst um der Kunst willen; **for heaven's ~!** um Gottes willen!

salad ['sæləd] n Salat m; **tomato ~** Tomatensalat m; **green ~** grüner Salat m.

salad bowl n Salatschüssel f.

salad cream (BRIT) n ≈ Majonäse f, Mayonnaise f.

salad dressing n Salatsoße f.

salami [sə'lɑːmɪ] n Salami f.

salaried ['sælərɪd] adj: **~ staff** Gehaltsempfänger pl.

salary ['sælərɪ] n Gehalt nt.

salary scale n Gehaltsskala f.

sale [seɪl] n Verkauf m; (at reduced prices) Ausverkauf m; (auction) Auktion f; **sales** npl (total amount sold) Absatz m ♦ cpd (campaign) Verkaufs-; (conference) Vertreter-; (figures) Absatz-; **"for ~"** „zu verkaufen"; **on ~** im Handel; **on ~ or return** auf Kommissionsbasis; **closing-down** or (US) **liquidation ~** Räumungsverkauf m.

sale and lease back n (COMM) Verkauf m mit Rückmiete.

saleroom ['seɪlruːm] n Auktionsraum m.

sales assistant, (US) **sales clerk** [seɪlz-] n Verkäufer(in) m(f).

sales force n Vertreterstab m.

salesman ['seɪlzmən] (irreg: like **man**) n Verkäufer m; (representative) Vertreter m.

sales manager n Verkaufsleiter m.

salesmanship ['seɪlzmənʃɪp] n Verkaufstechnik f.

sales tax (US) n Verkaufssteuer f.

saleswoman ['seɪlzwumən] (*irreg: like* **woman**) *n* Verkäuferin *f*; (*representative*) Vertreterin *f*.

salient ['seɪlɪənt] *adj* (*features*) hervorstechend; (*points*) Haupt-.

saline ['seɪlaɪn] *adj* (*solution etc*) Salz-.

saliva [sə'laɪvə] *n* Speichel *m*.

sallow ['sæləʊ] *adj* (*complexion*) fahl.

sally forth ['sælɪ-] (*old*) *vi* sich aufmachen.

sally out *vi* = **sally forth**.

salmon ['sæmən] *n inv* Lachs *m*.

salmon trout *n* Lachsforelle *f*.

salon ['sælɒn] *n* Salon *m*.

saloon [sə'luːn] *n* (*US: bar*) Saloon *m*; (*BRIT: AUT*) Limousine *f*; (*ship's lounge*) Salon *m*.

SALT [sɔːlt] *n abbr* (= *Strategic Arms Limitation Talks/Treaty*) SALT.

salt [sɔːlt] *n* Salz *nt* ♦ *vt* (*preserve*) einsalzen; (*put salt on*) salzen; (*road*) mit Salz streuen ♦ *cpd* Salz-; (*pork, beef*) gepökelt; **the ~ of the earth** (*fig*) das Salz der Erde; **to take sth with a pinch** *or* **grain of ~** (*fig*) etw nicht ganz so ernst nehmen.

salt cellar *n* Salzstreuer *m*.

salt-free ['sɔːlt'friː] *adj* salzlos.

salt mine *n* Salzbergwerk *nt*.

saltwater ['sɔːlt'wɔːtə'] *adj* (*fish, plant*) Meeres-.

salty ['sɔːltɪ] *adj* salzig.

salubrious [sə'luːbrɪəs] *adj* (*district etc*) fein; (*air, living conditions*) gesund.

salutary ['sæljutərɪ] *adj* heilsam.

salute [sə'luːt] *n* (*MIL, greeting*) Gruß *m*; (*MIL: with guns*) Salut *m* ♦ *vt* (*MIL*) grüßen, salutieren vor +*dat*; (*fig*) begrüßen.

salvage ['sælvɪdʒ] *n* Bergung *f*; (*things saved*) Bergungsgut *nt* ♦ *vt* bergen; (*fig*) retten.

salvage vessel *n* Bergungsschiff *nt*.

salvation [sæl'veɪʃən] *n* (*REL*) Heil *nt*; (*economic etc*) Rettung *f*.

Salvation Army *n* Heilsarmee *f*.

salver ['sælvə'] *n* Tablett *nt*.

salvo ['sælvəʊ] (*pl* ~**es**) *n* Salve *f*.

Samaritan [sə'mærɪtən] *n*: **the ~s** ≈ die Telefonseelsorge.

same [seɪm] *adj* (*similar*) gleiche(r, s); (*identical*) selbe(r, s) ♦ *pron*: **the ~** (*similar*) der/die/das Gleiche; (*identical*) derselbe/ dieselbe/dasselbe; **the ~ book as** das gleiche Buch wie; **they are the ~ age** sie sind gleichaltrig; **they are exactly the ~** sie sind genau gleich; **on the ~ day** am gleichen *or* selben Tag; **at the ~ time** (*simultaneously*) gleichzeitig, zur gleichen Zeit; (*yet*) doch; **they're one and the ~** (*person*) das ist doch ein und derselbe/ dieselbe; (*thing*) das ist doch dasselbe; **~ again** (*in bar etc*) das Gleiche noch mal; **all** *or* **just the ~** trotzdem; **to do the ~** (**as sb**) das Gleiche (wie jd) tun; **the ~ to you!** (*danke*) gleichfalls!; **~ here!** ich/wir *etc* auch!; **thanks all the ~** trotzdem vielen

Dank; **it's all the ~ to me** es ist mir egal.

sample ['saːmpl] *n* Probe *f*; (*of merchandise*) Probe *f*, Muster *nt* ♦ *vt* probieren; **to take a ~** eine Stichprobe machen; **free ~** kostenlose Probe.

sanatorium [sænə'tɔːrɪəm] (*pl* **sanatoria**) *n* Sanatorium *nt*.

sanctify ['sæŋktɪfaɪ] *vt* heiligen.

sanctimonious [sæŋktɪ'məʊnɪəs] *adj* scheinheilig.

sanction ['sæŋkʃən] *n* Zustimmung *f* ♦ *vt* sanktionieren; **sanctions** *npl* (*POL*) Sanktionen *pl*; **to impose economic ~s on** *or* **against** Wirtschaftssanktionen verhängen gegen.

sanctity ['sæŋktɪtɪ] *n* (*holiness*) Heiligkeit *f*; (*inviolability*) Unantastbarkeit *f*.

sanctuary ['sæŋktjuərɪ] *n* (*for birds/animals*) Schutzgebiet *nt*; (*place of refuge*) Zuflucht *f*; (*REL: in church*) Altarraum *m*.

sand [sænd] *n* Sand *m* ♦ *vt* (*also:* ~ **down**) abschmirgeln; *see also* **sands**.

sandal ['sændl] *n* Sandale *f*.

sandbag ['sændbæg] *n* Sandsack *m*.

sandblast ['sændblɑːst] *vt* sandstrahlen.

sandbox ['sændbɒks] (*US*) *n* Sandkasten *m*.

sandcastle ['sændkɑːsl] *n* Sandburg *f*.

sand dune *n* Sanddüne *f*.

sander ['sændə'] *n* (*tool*) Schleifmaschine *f*.

S & M (*US*) *n abbr* (= *sadomasochism*) S/M.

sandpaper ['sændpeɪpə'] *n* Schmirgelpapier *nt*.

sandpit ['sændpɪt] *n* Sandkasten *m*.

sands [sændz] *npl* (*beach*) Sandstrand *m*.

sandstone ['sændstəʊn] *n* Sandstein *m*.

sandstorm ['sændstɔːm] *n* Sandsturm *m*.

sandwich ['sændwɪtʃ] *n* Sandwich *nt* ♦ *vt*: ~**ed between** eingequetscht zwischen; **cheese/ ham ~** Käse-/Schinkenbrot *nt*.

sandwich board *n* Reklametafel *f*.

sandwich course (*BRIT*) *n* Ausbildungsgang, bei dem sich Theorie und Praxis abwechseln.

sandwich man *n* Sandwichmann *m*, Plakatträger *m*.

sandy ['sændɪ] *adj* sandig; (*beach*) Sand-; (*hair*) rotblond.

sane [seɪn] *adj* geistig gesund; (*sensible*) vernünftig.

sang [sæŋ] *pt of* **sing**.

sanguine ['sæŋgwɪn] *adj* zuversichtlich.

sanitarium [sænɪ'tɛərɪəm] (*US*) (*pl* **sanitaria**) *n* = **sanatorium**.

sanitary ['sænɪtərɪ] *adj* hygienisch; (*facilities*) sanitär; (*inspector*) Gesundheits-.

sanitary towel, (*US*) **sanitary napkin** *n* Damenbinde *f*.

sanitation [sænɪ'teɪʃən] *n* Hygiene *f*; (*toilets etc*) sanitäre Anlagen *pl*; (*drainage*) Kanalisation *f*.

sanitation department (*US*) *n* Stadtreinigung *f*.

sanity ['sænɪtɪ] *n* geistige Gesundheit *f*;
(*common sense*) Vernunft *f*.
sank [sæŋk] *pt of* **sink**.
Santa Claus [sæntə'klɔ:z] *n* ≈ der
Weihnachtsmann.
Santiago [sæntɪ'ɑ:gəʊ] *n* (*also*: ~ **de Chile**)
Santiago (de Chile) *nt*.
sap [sæp] *n* Saft *m* ♦ *vt* (*strength*) zehren an
+*dat*; (*confidence*) untergraben.
sapling ['sæplɪŋ] *n* junger Baum *m*.
sapphire ['sæfaɪə*] *n* Saphir *m*.
sarcasm ['sɑ:kæzm] *n* Sarkasmus *m*.
sarcastic [sɑ:'kæstɪk] *adj* sarkastisch.
sarcophagus [sɑ:'kɔfəgəs] (*pl* **sarcophagi**) *n*
Sarkophag *m*.
sardine [sɑ:'di:n] *n* Sardine *f*.
Sardinia [sɑ:'dɪnɪə] *n* Sardinien *nt*.
Sardinian [sɑ:'dɪnɪən] *adj* sardinisch, sardisch
♦ *n* (*person*) Sardinier(in) *m(f)*; (*LING*)
Sardinisch *nt*.
sardonic [sɑ:'dɔnɪk] *adj* (*smile*) süffisant.
sari ['sɑ:rɪ] *n* Sari *m*.
SARS [sɑ:z] *n abbr* (= *severe acute respiratory
syndrome*) SARS *nt*, Sars *nt*.
sartorial [sɑ:'tɔ:rɪəl] *adj*: **his** ~ **elegance** seine
elegante Art, sich zu kleiden.
SAS (*BRIT*) *n abbr* (*MIL*: = *Special Air Service*)
Spezialeinheit der britischen Armee.
SASE (*US*) *n abbr* (= *self-addressed stamped
envelope*) frankierter Rückumschlag *m*.
sash [sæʃ] *n* Schärpe *f*; (*of window*)
Fensterrahmen *m*.
sash window *n* Schiebefenster *nt*.
SAT (*US*) *n abbr* (= *Scholastic Aptitude Test*)
Hochschulaufnahmeprüfung.
sat [sæt] *pt, pp of* **sit**.
Sat. *abbr* (= *Saturday*) Sa.
Satan ['seɪtn] *n* Satan *m*.
satanic [sə'tænɪk] *adj* satanisch.
satanism ['seɪtnɪzəm] *n* Satanismus *m*.
satchel ['sætʃl] *n* (*child's*) Schultasche *f*.
sated ['seɪtɪd] *adj* gesättigt; **to be** ~ **with sth**
(*fig*) von etw übersättigt sein.
satellite ['sætəlaɪt] *n* Satellit *m*; (*also*: ~ **state**)
Satellitenstaat *m*.
satellite dish *n* Satellitenantenne *f*,
Parabolantenne *f*.
satellite television *n* Satellitenfernsehen *nt*.
satiate ['seɪʃɪeɪt] *vt* (*food*) sättigen; (*fig*:
pleasure etc) übersättigen.
satin ['sætɪn] *n* Satin *m* ♦ *adj* (*dress etc*) Satin-;
with a ~ **finish** mit Seidenglanz.
satire ['sætaɪə*] *n* Satire *f*.
satirical [sə'tɪrɪkl] *adj* satirisch.
satirist ['sætɪrɪst] *n* Satiriker(in) *m(f)*.
satirize ['sætɪraɪz] *vt* satirisch darstellen.
satisfaction [sætɪs'fækʃən] *n* Befriedigung *f*;
to get ~ **from sb** (*refund, apology etc*)
Genugtuung von jdm erhalten; **has it been
done to your** ~? sind Sie damit zufrieden?
satisfactorily [sætɪs'fæktərɪlɪ] *adv* zufrieden
stellend.

satisfactory [sætɪs'fæktərɪ] *adj* zufrieden
stellend.
satisfied ['sætɪsfaɪd] *adj* zufrieden.
satisfy ['sætɪsfaɪ] *vt* zufrieden stellen; (*needs,
demand*) befriedigen; (*requirements,
conditions*) erfüllen; **to** ~ **sb/o.s. that ...** jdn/
sich davon überzeugen, dass ...
satisfying ['sætɪsfaɪɪŋ] *adj* befriedigend;
(*meal*) sättigend.
satsuma [sæt'su:mə] *n* Satsuma *f*.
saturate ['sætʃəreɪt] *vt*: **to** ~ (**with**)
durchnässen (mit); (*CHEM, fig: market*)
sättigen; (*fig: area etc*) überschwemmen.
saturated fat ['sætʃəreɪtɪd-] *n* gesättigtes Fett
nt.
saturation [sætʃə'reɪʃən] *n* (*CHEM, fig*)
Sättigung *f*; ~ **advertising** flächendeckende
Werbung *f*; ~ **bombing**
Flächenbombardierung *f*.
Saturday ['sætədɪ] *n* Samstag *m*; *see also*
Tuesday.
sauce [sɔ:s] *n* Soße *f*, Sauce *f*.
saucepan ['sɔ:spən] *n* Kochtopf *m*.
saucer ['sɔ:sə*] *n* Untertasse *f*.
saucy ['sɔ:sɪ] *adj* frech.
Saudi ['saudi-] *adj* (*also*: ~ **Arabian**) saudisch,
saudi-arabisch.
Saudi Arabia ['saudi-] *n* Saudi-Arabien *nt*.
sauna ['sɔ:nə] *n* Sauna *f*.
saunter ['sɔ:ntə*] *vi* schlendern.
sausage ['sɔsɪdʒ] *n* Wurst *f*.
sausage roll *n* Wurst *f* im Schlafrock.
sauté ['səʊteɪ] *vt* kurz anbraten ♦ *adj*: ~**ed
potatoes** Bratkartoffeln *pl*.
savage ['sævɪdʒ] *adj* (*attack etc*) brutal; (*dog*)
gefährlich; (*criticism*) schonungslos ♦ *n* (*old:
pej*) Wilde(r) *f(m)* ♦ *vt* (*maul*) zerfleischen; (*fig:
criticize*) verreißen.
savagely ['sævɪdʒlɪ] *adv* (*attack etc*) brutal;
(*criticize*) schonungslos.
savagery ['sævɪdʒrɪ] *n* (*of attack*) Brutalität *f*.
save [seɪv] *vt* (*rescue*) retten; (*money, time*)
sparen; (*food etc*) aufheben; (*work, trouble*)
(er)sparen; (*keep: receipts etc*) aufbewahren;
(: *seat etc*) freihalten; (*COMPUT: file*)
abspeichern; (*SPORT: shot, ball*) halten ♦ *vi*
(*also*: ~ **up**) sparen ♦ *n* (*SPORT*) (Ball)abwehr
f ♦ *prep* (*form*) außer +*dat*; **it will** ~ **me an
hour** dadurch spare ich eine Stunde; **to**
~ **face** das Gesicht wahren; **God** ~ **the
Queen!** Gott schütze die Königin!
saving ['seɪvɪŋ] *n* (*on price etc*) Ersparnis *f*
♦ *adj*: **the** ~ **grace of sth** das einzig Gute an
etw *dat*; **savings** *npl* (*money*) Ersparnisse *pl*;
to make ~**s** sparen.
savings account *n* Sparkonto *nt*.
savings bank *n* Sparkasse *f*.
saviour, (*US*) **savior** ['seɪvjə*] *n* Retter(in)
m(f); (*REL*) Erlöser *m*.
savoir-faire ['sævwɑ:fɛə*] *n* Gewandtheit *f*.
savour, (*US*) **savor** ['seɪvə*] *vt* genießen ♦ *n*
(*of food*) Geschmack *m*.

savoury, (US) **savory** ['seɪvərɪ] adj pikant.
savvy ['sævɪ] (inf) n Grips m; **he hasn't got much** ~ er hat keine Ahnung.
saw [sɔ:] (pt **sawed,** pp **sawed** or **sawn**) vt sägen ♦ n Säge f ♦ pt of **see to** ~ **sth up** etw zersägen.
sawdust ['sɔ:dʌst] n Sägemehl nt.
sawmill ['sɔ:mɪl] n Sägewerk nt.
sawn [sɔ:n] pp of **saw.**
sawn-off ['sɔ:nɔf], (US) **sawed-off** ['sɔ:dɔf] adj: ~ **shotgun** Gewehr nt mit abgesägtem Lauf.
saxophone ['sæksəfəun] n Saxofon nt, Saxophon nt.
say [seɪ] (pt, pp **said**) vt sagen ♦ n: **to have one's** ~ seine Meinung äußern; **could you** ~ **that again?** können Sie das wiederholen?; **my watch** ~**s 3 o'clock** auf meiner Uhr ist es 3 Uhr; **it** ~**s on the sign "No Smoking"** auf dem Schild steht „Rauchen verboten"; **shall we** ~ **Tuesday?** sagen wir Dienstag?; **come for dinner at,** ~, **8 o'clock** kommt um, sagen wir mal 8 Uhr, zum Essen; **that doesn't** ~ **much for him** das spricht nicht gerade für ihn; **when all is said and done** letzten Endes; **there is something/a lot to be said for it** es spricht einiges/vieles dafür; **you can** ~ **that again!** das kann man wohl sagen!; **that is to** ~ das heißt; **that goes without** ~**ing** das versteht sich von selbst; **to** ~ **nothing of** ... von ... ganz zu schweigen; ~ **(that)** ... angenommen, (dass) ...; **to have a** or **some** ~ **in sth** ein Mitspracherecht bei etw haben.
saying ['seɪɪŋ] n Redensart f.
say-so ['seɪsəu] n Zustimmung f; **to do sth on sb's** ~ etw auf jds Anweisung acc hin tun.
SBA (US) n abbr (= Small Business Administration) Regierungsstelle zur Unterstützung kleiner und mittelständischer Betriebe.
SC (US) n abbr = **Supreme Court** ♦ abbr (POST: = South Carolina).
s/c abbr = **self-contained.**
scab [skæb] n (on wound) Schorf m; (pej) Streikbrecher(in) m(f).
scabby ['skæbɪ] (pej) adj (hands, skin) schorfig.
scaffold ['skæfəld] n (for execution) Schafott nt.
scaffolding ['skæfəldɪŋ] n Gerüst nt.
scald [skɔ:ld] n Verbrühung f ♦ vt (burn) verbrühen.
scalding ['skɔ:ldɪŋ] adj (also: ~ **hot**) siedend heiß.
scale [skeɪl] n Skala f; (of fish) Schuppe f; (MUS) Tonleiter f; (size, extent) Ausmaß nt, Umfang m; (of map, model) Maßstab m ♦ vt (cliff, tree) erklettern; **(pair of) scales** npl (for weighing) Waage f; **pay** ~ Lohnskala f; **to draw sth to** ~ etw maßstabgetreu zeichnen; **a small-**~ **model** ein Modell in verkleinertem Maßstab; **on a large** ~ im großen Rahmen; ~ **of charges**

Gebührenordnung f.
▶ **scale down** vt verkleinern; (fig) verringern.
scaled-down [skeɪld'daun] adj verkleinert; (project, forecast) eingeschränkt.
scale drawing n maßstabgetreue Zeichnung f.
scallion ['skæljən] n Frühlingszwiebel f; (US: shallot) Schalotte f; (: leek) Lauch m.
scallop ['skɔləp] n (ZOOL) Kammmuschel f; (SEWING) Bogenkante f.
scalp [skælp] n Kopfhaut f ♦ vt skalpieren.
scalpel ['skælpl] n Skalpell nt.
scalper ['skælpə*] (US: inf) n (ticket tout) (Karten)schwarzhändler(in) m(f).
scam [skæm] (inf) n Betrug m.
scamp [skæmp] (inf) n Frechdachs m.
scamper ['skæmpə*] vi: **to** ~ **away** or **off** verschwinden.
scampi ['skæmpɪ] (BRIT) npl Scampi pl.
scan [skæn] vt (horizon) absuchen; (newspaper etc) überfliegen; (TV, RADAR) abtasten ♦ vi (poetry) das richtige Versmaß haben ♦ n (MED) Scan m.
scandal ['skændl] n Skandal m; (gossip) Skandalgeschichten pl.
scandalize ['skændəlaɪz] vt schockieren.
scandalous ['skændələs] adj skandalös.
Scandinavia [skændɪ'neɪvɪə] n Skandinavien nt.
Scandinavian [skændɪ'neɪvɪən] adj skandinavisch ♦ n Skandinavier(in) m(f).
scanner ['skænə*] n (MED) Scanner m; (RADAR) Richtantenne f.
scant [skænt] adj wenig.
scantily ['skæntɪlɪ] adv: ~ **clad** or **dressed** spärlich bekleidet.
scanty ['skæntɪ] adj (information) dürftig; (meal) kärglich; (bikini) knapp.
scapegoat ['skeɪpgəut] n Sündenbock m.
scar [skɑ:] n Narbe f; (fig) Wunde f ♦ vt eine Narbe hinterlassen auf +dat; (fig) zeichnen.
scarce [skɛəs] adj knapp; **to make o.s.** ~ (inf) verschwinden.
scarcely ['skɛəslɪ] adv kaum; (certainly not) wohl kaum; ~ **anybody** kaum jemand; **I can** ~ **believe it** ich kann es kaum glauben.
scarcity ['skɛəsɪtɪ] n Knappheit f; ~ **value** Seltenheitswert m.
scare [skɛə*] n (fright) Schreck(en) m; (public fear) Panik f ♦ vt (frighten) erschrecken; (worry) Angst machen +dat; **to give sb a** ~ jdm einen Schrecken einjagen; **bomb** ~ Bombendrohung f.
▶ **scare away** vt (animal) verscheuchen; (investor, buyer) abschrecken.
▶ **scare off** vt = **scare away.**
scarecrow ['skɛəkrəu] n Vogelscheuche f.
scared [skɛəd] adj: **to be** ~ Angst haben; **to be** ~ **stiff** fürchterliche Angst haben.
scaremonger ['skɛəmʌŋgə*] n Panikmacher m.

scarf [skɑːf] (*pl* ~**s** *or* **scarves**) *n* Schal *m*; (*headscarf*) Kopftuch *nt*.

scarlet ['skɑːlɪt] *adj* (scharlach)rot.

scarlet fever *n* Scharlach *m*.

scarper ['skɑːpə*] (*BRIT: inf*) *vi* abhauen.

scarred [skɑːd] *adj* narbig; (*fig*) gezeichnet.

SCART socket ['skɑːtsɔkɪt] *n* (*COMPUT*) SCART-Büchse *f*.

scarves [skɑːvz] *npl of* **scarf**.

scary ['skɛərɪ] (*inf*) *adj* unheimlich; (*film*) gruselig.

scathing ['skeɪðɪŋ] *adj* (*comments*) bissig; (*attack*) scharf; **to be ~ about sth** bissige Bemerkungen über etw *acc* machen.

scatter ['skætə*] *vt* verstreuen; (*flock of birds*) aufscheuchen; (*crowd*) zerstreuen ♦ *vi* (*crowd*) sich zerstreuen.

scatterbrained ['skætəbreɪnd] (*inf*) *adj* schusselig.

scattered ['skætəd] *adj* verstreut; **~ showers** vereinzelte Regenschauer *pl*.

scatty ['skætɪ] (*BRIT: inf*) *adj* schusselig.

scavenge ['skævəndʒ] *vi*: **to ~ for sth** nach etw suchen.

scavenger ['skævəndʒə*] *n* (*person*) Aasgeier *m* (*inf*); (*animal, bird*) Aasfresser *m*.

SCE *n abbr* (= *Scottish Certificate of Education*) *Schulabschlusszeugnis in Schottland*.

scenario [sɪ'nɑːrɪəu] *n* (*THEAT, CINE*) Szenarium *nt*; (*fig*) Szenario *nt*.

scene [siːn] *n* (*lit, fig*) Szene *f*; (*of crime*) Schauplatz *m*; (*of accident*) Ort *m*; (*sight*) Anblick *m*; **behind the ~s** (*fig*) hinter den Kulissen; **to make a ~** (*inf: fuss*) eine Szene machen; **to appear on the ~** (*fig*) auftauchen, auf der Bildfläche erscheinen; **the political ~** die politische Landschaft.

scenery ['siːnərɪ] *n* (*THEAT*) Bühnenbild *nt*; (*landscape*) Landschaft *f*.

scenic ['siːnɪk] *adj* malerisch, landschaftlich schön.

scent [sɛnt] *n* (*fragrance*) Duft *m*; (*track*) Fährte *f*; (*fig*) Spur *f*; (*liquid perfume*) Parfüm *nt*; **to put** *or* **throw sb off the ~** (*fig*) jdn von der Spur abbringen.

sceptic, (*US*) **skeptic** ['skɛptɪk] *n* Skeptiker(in) *m(f)*.

sceptical, (*US*) **skeptical** ['skɛptɪkl] *adj* skeptisch.

scepticism, (*US*) **skepticism** ['skɛptɪsɪzəm] *n* Skepsis *f*.

sceptre, (*US*) **scepter** ['sɛptə*] *n* Zepter *nt*.

schedule ['ʃɛdjuːl, (*US*) 'skɛdjuːl] *n* (*of trains, buses*) Fahrplan *m*; (*of events*) Programm *nt*; (*of prices, details etc*) Liste *f* ♦ *vt* planen; (*visit, meeting etc*) ansetzen; **on ~** wie geplant, pünktlich; **we are working to a very tight ~** wir arbeiten nach einem sehr knappen Zeitplan; **everything went according to ~** alles ist planmäßig verlaufen; **to be ahead of/behind ~** dem Zeitplan voraus sein/im Rückstand sein; **he was ~d to leave**

yesterday laut Zeitplan hätte er gestern abfahren sollen.

scheduled ['ʃɛdjuːld, (*US*) 'skɛdjuːld] *adj* (*date, time*) vorgesehen; (*visit, event*) geplant; (*train, bus, stop*) planmäßig.

scheduled flight *n* Linienflug *m*.

schematic [skɪ'mætɪk] *adj* schematisch.

scheme [skiːm] *n* (*personal plan*) Plan *m*; (*plot*) raffinierter Plan *m*, Komplott *nt*; (*formal plan*) Programm *nt* ♦ *vi* Pläne schmieden, intrigieren; **colour ~** Farbzusammenstellung *f*; **pension ~** Rentenversicherung *f*.

scheming ['skiːmɪŋ] *adj* intrigierend ♦ *n* Machenschaften *pl*.

schism ['skɪzəm] *n* Spaltung *f*.

schizophrenia [skɪtsə'friːnɪə] *n* Schizophrenie *f*.

schizophrenic [skɪtsə'frɛnɪk] *adj* schizophren ♦ *n* Schizophrene(r) *f(m)*.

scholar ['skɔlə*] *n* Gelehrte(r) *f(m)*; (*pupil*) Student(in) *m(f)*, Schüler(in) *m(f)*; (*scholarship holder*) Stipendiat(in) *m(f)*.

scholarly ['skɔləlɪ] *adj* gelehrt; (*text, approach*) wissenschaftlich.

scholarship ['skɔləʃɪp] *n* Gelehrsamkeit *f*; (*grant*) Stipendium *nt*.

school [skuːl] *n* Schule *f*; (*US: inf: university*) Universität *f*; (*of whales, porpoises etc*) Schule *f*, Schwarm *m* ♦ *cpd* Schul-.

school age *n* Schulalter *nt*.

schoolbook ['skuːlbuk] *n* Schulbuch *nt*.

schoolboy ['skuːlbɔɪ] *n* Schuljunge *m*, Schüler *m*.

schoolchildren ['skuːltʃɪldrən] *npl* Schulkinder *pl*, Schüler *pl*.

schooldays ['skuːldeɪz] *npl* Schulzeit *f*.

schooled [skuːld] *adj* geschult; **to be ~ in sth** über etw *acc* gut Bescheid wissen.

schoolgirl ['skuːlɡɜːl] *n* Schulmädchen *nt*, Schülerin *f*.

schooling ['skuːlɪŋ] *n* Schulbildung *f*.

school-leaver [skuːl'liːvə*] (*BRIT*) *n* Schulabgänger(in) *m(f)*.

schoolmaster ['skuːlmɑːstə*] *n* Lehrer *m*.

schoolmistress ['skuːlmɪstrɪs] *n* Lehrerin *f*.

school report (*BRIT*) *n* Zeugnis *nt*.

schoolroom ['skuːlruːm] *n* Klassenzimmer *nt*.

schoolteacher ['skuːltiːtʃə*] *n* Lehrer(in) *m(f)*.

schoolyard ['skuːljɑːd] *n* Schulhof *m*.

schooner ['skuːnə*] *n* (*ship*) Schoner *m*; (*BRIT: for sherry*) großes Sherryglas *nt*; (*US etc: for beer*) großes Bierglas *nt*.

sciatica [saɪ'ætɪkə] *n* Ischias *m or nt*.

science ['saɪəns] *n* Naturwissenschaft *f*; (*branch of knowledge*) Wissenschaft *f*; **the ~s** Naturwissenschaften *pl*.

science fiction *n* Sciencefiction *f*.

scientific [saɪən'tɪfɪk] *adj* wissenschaftlich.

scientist ['saɪəntɪst] *n* Wissenschaftler(in) *m(f)*.

sci-fi ['saɪfaɪ] (*inf*) *n abbr* (= *science fiction*) SF.

Scillies ['sɪlɪz] *npl* = **Scilly Isles**.
Scilly Isles ['sɪlɪ'aɪlz] *npl*: **the** ~ **die**
Scillyinseln *pl*.
scintillating ['sɪntɪleɪtɪŋ] *adj* (*fig: conversation*)
faszinierend; (*wit*) sprühend.
scissors ['sɪzəz] *npl* Schere *f*; **a pair of** ~ **eine**
Schere.
sclerosis [sklɪ'rəʊsɪs] *n* Sklerose *f*.
scoff [skɒf] *vt* (*BRIT: inf: eat*) futtern,
verputzen ♦ *vi*: **to** ~ (**at**) (*mock*) spotten
(über +*acc*), sich lustig machen (über +*acc*).
scold [skəʊld] *vt* ausschimpfen.
scolding ['skəʊldɪŋ] *n* Schelte *f*; **to get a** ~
ausgeschimpft werden.
scone [skɒn] *n* brötchenartiges Teegebäck.
scoop [skuːp] *n* (*for flour etc*) Schaufel *f*; (*for ice
cream etc*) Portionierer *m*; (*amount*) Kugel *f*;
(*PRESS*) Knüller *m*.
▶ **scoop out** *vt* aushöhlen.
▶ **scoop up** *vt* aufschaufeln; (*liquid*)
aufschöpfen.
scooter ['skuːtə*] *n* (*also*: **motor** ~)
Motorroller *m*; (*toy*) (Tret)roller *m*.
scope [skəʊp] *n* (*opportunity*) Möglichkeiten
pl; (*range*) Ausmaß *nt*, Umfang *m*; (*freedom*)
Freiheit *f*; **within the** ~ **of** im Rahmen +*gen*;
there is plenty of ~ **for improvement** (*BRIT*)
es könnte noch viel verbessert werden.
scorch [skɔːtʃ] *vt* versengen; (*earth, grass*)
verbrennen.
scorched earth policy *n* (*MIL*) Politik *f* der
verbrannten Erde.
scorcher ['skɔːtʃə*] (*inf*) *n* heißer Tag *m*.
scorching ['skɔːtʃɪŋ] *adj* (*day, weather*)
brütend heiß.
score [skɔː*] *n* (*number of points*)
(Punkte)stand *m*; (*of game*) Spielstand *m*;
(*MUS*) Partitur *f*; (*twenty*) zwanzig ♦ *vt* (*goal*)
schießen; (*point, success*) erzielen; (*mark*)
einkerben; (*cut*) einritzen ♦ *vi* (*in game*)
einen Punkt/Punkte erzielen; (*FOOTBALL
etc*) ein Tor schießen; (*keep score*) (Punkte)
zählen; **to settle an old** ~ **with sb** (*fig*) eine
alte Rechnung mit jdm begleichen; **what's
the** ~? (*SPORT*) wie stehts?; ~**s of** hunderte
or Hunderte von; **on that** ~ in dieser
Hinsicht; **to** ~ **well** gut abschneiden; **to** ~ **6
out of 10** 6 von 10 Punkten erzielen; **to** ~ (**a
point**) **over sb** (*fig*) jdn ausstechen.
▶ **score out** *vt* ausstreichen.
scoreboard ['skɔːbɔːd] *n* Anzeigetafel *f*.
scorecard ['skɔːkɑːd] *n* (*SPORT*)
Spielprotokoll *nt*.
score line *n* (*SPORT*) Spielstand *m*; (: *final
score*) Endergebnis *nt*.
scorer ['skɔːrə*] *n* (*FOOTBALL etc*) Torschütze
m, Torschützin *f*; (*person keeping score*)
Anschreiber(in) *m(f)*.
scorn [skɔːn] *n* Verachtung *f* ♦ *vt* verachten;
(*reject*) verschmähen.
scornful ['skɔːnful] *adj* verächtlich, höhnisch.
Scorpio ['skɔːpɪəʊ] *n* Skorpion *m*; **to be** ~

Skorpion sein.
scorpion ['skɔːpɪən] *n* Skorpion *m*.
Scot [skɒt] *n* Schotte *m*, Schottin *f*.
Scotch [skɒtʃ] *n* Scotch *m*.
scotch [skɒtʃ] *vt* (*rumour*) aus der Welt
schaffen; (*plan, idea*) unterbinden.
Scotch tape ® *n* ≈ Tesafilm ® *m*.
scot-free ['skɒt'friː] *adv*: **to get off** ~
ungeschoren davonkommen.
Scotland ['skɒtlənd] *n* Schottland *nt*.
Scots [skɒts] *adj* schottisch.
Scotsman ['skɒtsmən] (*irreg: like* **man**) *n*
Schotte *m*.
Scotswoman ['skɒtswumən] (*irreg: like*
woman) *n* Schottin *f*.
Scottish ['skɒtɪʃ] *adj* schottisch.
Scottish National Party *n* Partei, die für die
Unabhängigkeit Schottlands eintritt.
scoundrel ['skaundrl] *n* Schurke *m*.
scour ['skauə*] *vt* (*search*) absuchen; (*clean*)
scheuern.
scourer ['skauərə*] *n* Topfkratzer *m*.
scourge [skɔːdʒ] *n* (*lit, fig*) Geißel *f*.
scout [skaut] *n* (*MIL*) Kundschafter *m*, Späher
m; (*also*: **boy** ~) Pfadfinder *m*; **girl** ~ (*US*)
Pfadfinderin *f*.
▶ **scout around** *vi* sich umsehen.
scowl [skaul] *vi* ein böses Gesicht machen ♦ *n*
böses Gesicht *nt*; **to** ~ **at sb** jdn böse
ansehen.
scrabble ['skræbl] *vi* (*also*: ~ **around**)
herumtasten ♦ *n*: **S**~ ® Scrabble ® *nt*; **to**
~ **at sth** nach etw krallen; **to** ~ **about** *or*
around for sth nach etw herumsuchen.
scraggy ['skrægɪ] *adj* (*animal*) mager; (*body,
neck etc*) dürr.
scram [skræm] (*inf*) *vi* abhauen,
verschwinden.
scramble ['skræmbl] *n* (*climb*) Kletterpartie *f*;
(*rush*) Hetze *f*; (*struggle*) Gerangel *nt* ♦ *vi*: **to**
~ **up/over** klettern auf/über +*acc*; **to** ~ **for**
sich drängeln um; **to go scrambling** (*SPORT*)
Querfeldeinrennen fahren.
scrambled eggs ['skræmbld-] *n* Rührei *nt*.
scrap [skræp] *n* (*bit*) Stückchen *nt*; (*fig: of truth,
evidence*) Spur *f*; (*fight*) Balgerei *f*; (*also*:
~ **metal**) Altmetall *nt*, Schrott *m* ♦ *vt*
(*machines etc*) verschrotten; (*fig: plans etc*)
fallen lassen ♦ *vi* (*fight*) sich balgen; **scraps**
npl (*leftovers*) Reste *pl*; **to sell sth for** ~ etw
als Schrott *or* zum Verschrotten verkaufen.
scrapbook ['skræpbuk] *n* Sammelalbum *nt*.
scrap dealer *n* Schrotthändler(in) *m(f)*.
scrape [skreɪp] *vt* abkratzen; (*hand etc*)
abschürfen; (*car*) verschrammen ♦ *n*: **to get
into a** ~ (*difficult situation*) in Schwulitäten *pl*
kommen (*inf*).
▶ **scrape through** *vt* (*exam etc*)
durchrutschen durch (*inf*).
▶ **scrape together** *vt* (*money*)
zusammenkratzen.
scraper ['skreɪpə*] *n* Kratzer *m*.

scrap heap n: **to be on the ~** (fig) zum alten Eisen gehören.

scrap merchant (BRIT) n Schrotthändler(in) m(f).

scrap metal n Altmetall nt, Schrott m.

scrap paper n Schmierpapier nt.

scrappy ['skræpɪ] adj zusammengestoppelt (inf).

scrap yard n Schrottplatz m.

scratch [skrætʃ] n Kratzer m ♦ vt kratzen; (one's nose etc) sich kratzen an +dat; (paint, car, record) verkratzen; (COMPUT) löschen ♦ vi sich kratzen ♦ cpd (team, side) zusammengewürfelt; **to start from ~** ganz von vorne anfangen; **to be up to ~** den Anforderungen entsprechen; **to ~ the surface** (fig) an der Oberfläche bleiben.

scratch pad (US) n Notizblock m.

scrawl [skrɔːl] n Gekritzel nt; (handwriting) Klaue f (inf) ♦ vt hinkritzeln.

scrawny ['skrɔːnɪ] adj dürr.

scream [skriːm] n Schrei m ♦ vi schreien; **to be a ~** (inf) zum Schreien sein; **to ~ at sb (to do sth)** jdn anschreien(, etw zu tun).

scree [skriː] n Geröll nt.

screech [skriːtʃ] vi kreischen; (tyres, brakes) quietschen ♦ n Kreischen nt; (of tyres, brakes) Quietschen nt.

screen [skriːn] n (CINE) Leinwand f; (TV, COMPUT) Bildschirm m; (movable barrier) Wandschirm m; (fig: cover) Tarnung f; (also: **windscreen**) Windschutzscheibe f ♦ vt (protect) abschirmen; (from the wind etc) schützen; (conceal) verdecken; (film) zeigen, vorführen; (programme) senden; (candidates etc) überprüfen; (for illness): **to ~ sb for sth** jdn auf etw acc (hin) untersuchen.

screen editing n (COMPUT) Bildschirmaufbereitung f.

screening ['skriːnɪŋ] n (MED) Untersuchung f; (of film) Vorführung f; (TV) Sendung f; (for security) Überprüfung f.

screen memory n (COMPUT) Bildschirmspeicher m.

screenplay ['skriːnpleɪ] n Drehbuch nt.

screen saver n (COMPUT) Bildschirmschoner m.

screen test n Probeaufnahmen pl.

screw [skruː] n Schraube f ♦ vt schrauben; (inf!) bumsen (!); **to ~ sth in** etw einschrauben; **to ~ sth to the wall** etw an der Wand festschrauben; **to have one's head ~ed on** (fig) ein vernünftiger Mensch sein.

▶ **screw up** vt (paper etc) zusammenknüllen; (inf: ruin) vermasseln; **to ~ up one's eyes** die Augen zusammenkneifen.

screwdriver ['skruːdraɪvə*] n Schraubenzieher m.

screwed-up ['skruːd'ʌp] (inf) adj: **to be/get ~ about sth** sich wegen etw ganz verrückt machen.

screwy ['skruːɪ] (inf) adj verrückt.

scribble ['skrɪbl] n Gekritzel nt ♦ vt, vi kritzeln; **to ~ sth down** etw hinkritzeln.

scribe [skraɪb] n Schreiber m.

script [skrɪpt] n (CINE) Drehbuch nt; (of speech, play etc) Text m; (alphabet) Schrift f; (in exam) schriftliche Arbeit f.

scripted ['skrɪptɪd] adj vorbereitet.

scripture(s) ['skrɪptʃə(z)] n(pl) (heilige) Schrift f; **the S~(s)** (the Bible) die Heilige Schrift f.

scriptwriter ['skrɪptraɪtə*] n (RADIO, TV) Autor(in) m(f); (CINE) Drehbuchautor(in) m(f).

scroll [skrəul] n Schriftrolle f ♦ vi (COMPUT) scrollen.

scroll bar n (COMPUT) Bildlaufleiste f.

scrotum ['skrəutəm] n Hodensack m.

scrounge [skraundʒ] (inf) vt: **to ~ sth off sb** etw bei jdm schnorren ♦ vi schnorren ♦ n: **on the ~** am Schnorren.

scrounger ['skraundʒə*] (inf) n Schnorrer(in) m(f).

scrub [skrʌb] n Gestrüpp nt ♦ vt (floor etc) schrubben; (inf: idea, plan) fallen lassen.

scrubbing brush ['skrʌbɪŋ-] n Scheuerbürste f.

scruff [skrʌf] n: **by the ~ of the neck** am Genick.

scruffy ['skrʌfɪ] adj gammelig, verwahrlost.

scrum(mage) ['skrʌm(ɪdʒ)] n (RUGBY) Gedränge nt.

scruple ['skruːpl] n (gen pl) Skrupel m, Bedenken nt; **to have no ~s about doing sth** keine Skrupel or Bedenken haben, etw zu tun.

scrupulous ['skruːpjuləs] adj gewissenhaft; (honesty) unbedingt.

scrupulously ['skruːpjuləslɪ] adv gewissenhaft; (honest, fair) äußerst; (clean) peinlich.

scrutinize ['skruːtɪnaɪz] vt prüfend ansehen; (data, records etc) genau prüfen or untersuchen.

scrutiny ['skruːtɪnɪ] n genaue Untersuchung f; **under the ~ of sb** unter jds prüfendem Blick.

scuba ['skuːbə] n (Schwimm)tauchgerät nt.

scuba diving n Sporttauchen nt.

scuff [skʌf] vt (shoes, floor) abwetzen.

scuffle ['skʌfl] n Handgemenge nt.

scull [skʌl] n Skull nt.

scullery ['skʌlərɪ] n (old) Spülküche f.

sculptor ['skʌlptə*] n Bildhauer(in) m(f).

sculpture ['skʌlptʃə*] n (art) Bildhauerei f; (object) Skulptur f.

scum [skʌm] n (on liquid) Schmutzschicht f; (pej) Abschaum m.

scupper ['skʌpə*] (BRIT: inf) vt (plan, idea) zerschlagen.

scurrilous ['skʌrɪləs] adj verleumderisch.

scurry ['skʌrɪ] vi huschen.

▸ **scurry off** vi forthasten.
scurvy ['skə:vɪ] n Skorbut m.
scuttle ['skʌtl] n (also: **coal** ~) Kohleneimer m
♦ vt (ship) versenken ♦ vi: **to** ~ **away** or **off**
verschwinden.
scythe [saɪð] n Sense f.
SD, S.Dak. (US) abbr (POST: = South Dakota).
SDI (US) n abbr (MIL: = Strategic Defense
Initiative) SDI f.
SDLP (BRIT) n abbr (POL: = Social Democratic
and Labour Party) sozialdemokratische
Partei in Nordirland.
SDP (BRIT) n abbr (POL: formerly: = Social
Democratic Party) sozialdemokratische
Partei.
SE abbr (= south-east) SO.
sea [si:] n Meer nt, See f; (fig) Meer nt ♦ cpd
See-; **by** ~ (travel) mit dem Schiff; **beside** or
by the ~ (holiday) am Meer, an der See;
(village) am Meer; **on the** ~ (boat) auf See;
at ~ auf See; **to be all at** ~ (fig) nicht
durchblicken (inf); **out to** ~ aufs Meer
(hinaus); **to look out to** ~ aufs Meer
hinausblicken; **heavy/rough** ~(s) schwere/
raue See f.
sea anemone n Seeanemone f.
sea bed n Meeresboden m.
seaboard ['si:bɔ:d] n Küste f.
seafarer ['si:fɛərə*] n Seefahrer m.
seafaring ['si:fɛərɪŋ] adj (life, nation)
Seefahrer-.
seafood ['si:fu:d] n Meeresfrüchte pl.
seafront ['si:frʌnt] n Strandpromenade f.
seagoing ['si:gəʊɪŋ] adj hochseetüchtig.
seagull ['si:gʌl] n Möwe f.
seal [si:l] n (animal) Seehund m; (official stamp)
Siegel nt; (in machine etc) Dichtung f; (on
bottle etc) Verschluss m ♦ vt (envelope)
zukleben; (crack, opening) abdichten; (with
seal) versiegeln; (agreement, sb's fate)
besiegeln; **to give sth one's** ~ **of approval**
einer Sache dat seine offizielle Zustimmung
geben.
▸ **seal off** vt (place) abriegeln.
sea level n Meeresspiegel m; **2,000 ft above/**
below ~ 2000 Fuß über/unter dem
Meeresspiegel.
sealing wax ['si:lɪŋ-] n Siegelwachs nt.
sea lion n Seelöwe m.
sealskin ['si:lskɪn] n Seehundfell nt.
seam [si:m] n Naht f; (of coal etc) Flöz nt; **the hall**
was bursting at the ~**s** der Saal platzte aus
allen Nähten.
seaman ['si:mən] (irreg: like **man**) n Seemann
m.
seamanship ['si:mənʃɪp] n Seemannschaft f.
seamless ['si:mlɪs] adj (lit, fig) nahtlos.
seamy ['si:mɪ] adj zwielichtig; **the** ~ **side of**
life die Schattenseite des Lebens.
séance ['seɪɒns] n spiritistische Sitzung f.
seaplane ['si:pleɪn] n Wasserflugzeug nt.

seaport ['si:pɔ:t] n Seehafen m.
search [sə:tʃ] n Suche f; (inspection)
Durchsuchung f; (COMPUT) Suchlauf m ♦ vt
durchsuchen; (mind, memory)
durchforschen ♦ vi: **to** ~ **for** suchen nach;
"~ **and replace**" (COMPUT) „suchen und
ersetzen"; **in** ~ **of** auf der Suche nach.
▸ **search through** vt fus durchsuchen.
searcher ['sə:tʃə*] n Suchende(r) f(m).
searching ['sə:tʃɪŋ] adj (question) bohrend;
(look) prüfend; (examination) eingehend.
searchlight ['sə:tʃlaɪt] n Suchscheinwerfer m.
search party n Suchtrupp m; **to send out a** ~
einen Suchtrupp ausschicken.
search warrant n Durchsuchungsbefehl m.
searing ['sɪərɪŋ] adj (heat) glühend; (pain)
scharf.
seashore ['si:ʃɔ:*] n Strand m; **on the** ~ am
Strand.
seasick ['si:sɪk] adj seekrank.
seasickness ['si:sɪknɪs] n Seekrankheit f.
seaside ['si:saɪd] n Meer nt, See f; **to go to the**
~ ans Meer or an die See fahren; **at the** ~
am Meer, an der See.
seaside resort n Badeort m.
season ['si:zn] n Jahreszeit f; (AGR) Zeit f;
(SPORT, of films etc) Saison f; (THEAT)
Spielzeit f ♦ vt (food) würzen; **strawberries**
are in ~/**out of** ~ für Erdbeeren ist jetzt die
richtige Zeit/nicht die richtige Zeit; **the**
busy ~ die Hochsaison f; **the open** ~
(HUNTING) die Jagdzeit f.
seasonal ['si:znl] adj (work) Saison-.
seasoned ['si:znd] adj (fig: traveller) erfahren;
(wood) abgelagert; **she's a** ~ **campaigner** sie
ist eine alte Kämpferin.
seasoning ['si:znɪŋ] n Gewürz nt.
season ticket n (RAIL) Zeitkarte f; (SPORT)
Dauerkarte f; (THEAT) Abonnement nt.
seat [si:t] n (chair, of government, POL) Sitz m;
(place) Platz m; (buttocks) Gesäß nt; (of
trousers) Hosenboden m; (of learning) Stätte f
♦ vt setzen; (have room for) Sitzplätze bieten
für; **are there any** ~**s left?** sind noch Plätze
frei?; **to take one's** ~ sich setzen; **please be**
~**ed** bitte nehmen Sie Platz; **to be** ~**ed**
sitzen.
seat belt n Sicherheitsgurt m.
seating arrangements ['si:tɪŋ-] npl
Sitzordnung f.
seating capacity n Sitzplätze pl.
SEATO ['si:təʊ] n abbr (= Southeast Asia Treaty
Organization) SEATO f.
sea urchin n Seeigel m.
sea water n Meerwasser nt.
seaweed ['si:wi:d] n Seetang m.
seaworthy ['si:wə:ðɪ] adj seetüchtig.
SEC (US) n abbr (= Securities and Exchange
Commission) amerikanische
Börsenaufsichtsbehörde.
sec. abbr (= second) Sek.
secateurs [sɛkə'tə:z] npl Gartenschere f.

secede [sɪ'siːd] vi (POL): **to ~ (from)** sich abspalten (von).

secluded [sɪ'kluːdɪd] adj (place) abgelegen; (life) zurückgezogen.

seclusion [sɪ'kluːʒən] n Abgeschiedenheit f; **in ~** zurückgezogen.

second¹ [sɪ'kɔnd] (BRIT) vt (employee) abordnen.

second² ['sɛkənd] adj zweite(r, s) ♦ adv (come, be placed) Zweite(r, s); (when listing) zweitens ♦ n (time) Sekunde f; (AUT: also: **~ gear**) der zweite Gang; (person) Zweite(r) f(m); (COMM: imperfect) zweite Wahl f ♦ vt (motion) unterstützen; **upper/lower ~** (BRIT: UNIV) ≈ Zwei plus/minus; **Charles the S~** Karl der Zweite; **just a ~**! einen Augenblick!; **~ floor** (BRIT) zweiter Stock m; (US) erster Stock m; **to ask for a ~ opinion** ein zweites Gutachten einholen.

secondary ['sɛkəndərɪ] adj weniger wichtig.

secondary education n höhere Schulbildung f.

secondary picketing n Aufstellung von Streikposten bei nur indirekt beteiligten Firmen.

secondary school n höhere Schule f.

SECONDARY SCHOOL

Secondary school ist in Großbritannien eine weiterführende Schule für Kinder von 11 bis 18 Jahren. Manche Schüler gehen schon mit 16 Jahren, wenn die allgemeine Schulpflicht endet, von der Schule ab. Die meisten **secondary schools** sind heute Gesamtschulen, obwohl es auch noch selektive Schulen gibt. Siehe auch **comprehensive school, primary school**.

---

second-best [sɛkənd'bɛst] adj zweitbeste(r, s) ♦ n: **as a ~** als Ausweichlösung; **don't settle for ~** gib dich nur mit dem Besten zufrieden.

second-class ['sɛkənd'klɑːs] adj zweitklassig; (citizen) zweiter Klasse; (RAIL, POST) Zweite-Klasse- ♦ adv (RAIL, POST) zweiter Klasse; **to send sth ~** etw zweiter Klasse schicken; **to travel ~** zweiter Klasse reisen.

second cousin n Cousin m/Cousine f or Kusine f zweiten Grades.

seconder ['sɛkəndə*] n Befürworter(in) m(f).

second-guess ['sɛkənd'gɛs] vt vorhersagen; **to ~ sb** vorhersagen, was jd machen wird.

secondhand ['sɛkənd'hænd] adj gebraucht; (clothing) getragen ♦ adv (buy) gebraucht; **to hear sth ~** etw aus zweiter Hand haben; **~ car** Gebrauchtwagen m.

second hand n (on clock) Sekundenzeiger m.

second-in-command ['sɛkəndɪnkə'mɑːnd] n (MIL) stellvertretender Kommandeur m; (ADMIN) stellvertretender Leiter m.

secondly ['sɛkəndlɪ] adv zweitens.

secondment [sɪ'kɔndmənt] (BRIT) n Abordnung f; **to be on ~** abgeordnet sein.

second-rate ['sɛkənd'reɪt] adj zweitklassig.

second thoughts npl: **on ~** or (US) **thought** wenn ich es mir (recht) überlege; **to have ~ (about doing sth)** es sich dat anders überlegen (und etw doch nicht tun).

Second World War n: **the ~** der Zweite Weltkrieg.

secrecy ['siːkrəsɪ] n Geheimhaltung f; (of person) Verschwiegenheit f; **in ~** heimlich.

secret ['siːkrɪt] adj geheim; (admirer) heimlich ♦ n Geheimnis nt; **in ~** heimlich; **~ passage** Geheimgang m; **to keep sth ~ from sb** etw vor jdm geheim halten; **can you keep a ~?** kannst du schweigen?; **to make no ~ of sth** kein Geheimnis or keinen Hehl aus etw machen.

secret agent n Geheimagent(in) m(f).

secretarial [sɛkrɪ'tɛərɪəl] adj (work) Büro-; (course) Sekretärinnen-; (staff) Sekretariats-.

secretariat [sɛkrɪ'tɛərɪət] n (POL, ADMIN) Sekretariat nt.

secretary ['sɛkrətərɪ] n (COMM) Sekretär(in) m(f); (of club) Schriftführer(in) m(f); **S~ of State (for)** (BRIT: POL) Minister(in) m(f) (für); **S~ of State** (US: POL) Außenminister(in) m(f).

secretary-general ['sɛkrətərɪ'dʒɛnərl] (pl **secretaries-general**) n Generalsekretär(in) m(f).

secrete [sɪ'kriːt] vt (ANAT, BIOL, MED) absondern; (hide) verbergen.

secretion [sɪ'kriːʃən] n (substance) Sekret nt.

secretive ['siːkrətɪv] adj verschlossen; (pej) geheimnistuerisch.

secretly ['siːkrɪtlɪ] adv heimlich; (hope) insgeheim.

secret police n Geheimpolizei f.

secret service n Geheimdienst m.

sect [sɛkt] n Sekte f.

sectarian [sɛk'tɛərɪən] adj (killing etc) konfessionell motiviert; **~ violence** gewalttätige Konfessionsstreitigkeiten pl.

section ['sɛkʃən] n (part) Teil m; (department) Abteilung f; (of document) Absatz m; (cross-section) Schnitt m ♦ vt (divide) teilen; **the business/sport ~** (PRESS) der Wirtschafts-/ Sportteil.

sectional ['sɛkʃənl] adj: **~ drawing** Darstellung f im Schnitt.

sector ['sɛktə*] n Sektor m.

secular ['sɛkjulə*] adj weltlich.

secure [sɪ'kjuə*] adj sicher; (firmly fixed) fest ♦ vt (fix) festmachen; (votes etc) erhalten; (contract etc) (sich dat) sichern; (COMM: loan) (ab)sichern; **to make sth ~** etw sichern; **to ~ sth for sb** jdm etw sichern.

secured creditor [sɪ'kjuəd-] n (COMM) abgesicherter Gläubiger m.

securely [sɪ'kjuəlɪ] adv (firmly) fest; (safely) sicher.

security [sɪ'kjuərɪtɪ] n Sicherheit f; (*freedom from anxiety*) Geborgenheit f; **securities** npl (*STOCK EXCHANGE*) Effekten pl, Wertpapiere pl; **to increase/tighten** ~ die Sicherheitsvorkehrungen verschärfen; ~ **of tenure** Kündigungsschutz m.

Security Council n Sicherheitsrat m.

security forces npl Sicherheitskräfte pl.

security guard n Sicherheitsbeamte(r) m; (*transporting money*) Wachmann m.

security risk n Sicherheitsrisiko nt.

secy. abbr = **secretary.**

sedan [sə'dæn] (*US*) n (*AUT*) Limousine f.

sedate [sɪ'deɪt] adj (*person*) ruhig, gesetzt; (*life*) geruhsam; (*pace*) gemächlich ♦ vt (*MED*) Beruhigungsmittel geben +dat.

sedation [sɪ'deɪʃən] n (*MED*) Beruhigungsmittel pl; **to be under** ~ unter dem Einfluss von Beruhigungsmitteln stehen.

sedative ['sɛdɪtɪv] n (*MED*) Beruhigungsmittel nt.

sedentary ['sɛdntrɪ] adj (*occupation, work*) sitzend.

sediment ['sɛdɪmənt] n (*in bottle*) (Boden)satz m; (*in lake etc*) Ablagerung f.

sedimentary [sɛdɪ'mɛntərɪ] adj (*GEOG*) sedimentär; ~ **rock** Sedimentgestein nt.

sedition [sɪ'dɪʃən] n Aufwiegelung f.

seduce [sɪ'djuːs] vt verführen; **to** ~ **sb into doing sth** jdn dazu verleiten, etw zu tun.

seduction [sɪ'dʌkʃən] n (*attraction*) Verlockung f; (*act of seducing*) Verführung f.

seductive [sɪ'dʌktɪv] adj verführerisch; (*fig: offer*) verlockend.

see [siː] (*pt* **saw**, *pp* **seen**) vt sehen; (*look at*) sich dat ansehen; (*understand*) verstehen, (ein)sehen; (*doctor etc*) aufsuchen ♦ vi sehen ♦ n (*REL*) Bistum nt; **to** ~ **that** (*ensure*) dafür sorgen, dass; **to** ~ **sb to the door** jdn zur Tür bringen; **there was nobody to be** ~**n** es war niemand zu sehen; **to go and** ~ **sb** jdn besuchen (gehen); **to** ~ **a doctor** zum Arzt gehen; ~ **you!** tschüss! (*inf*); ~ **you soon!** bis bald!; **let me** ~ (*show me*) lass mich mal sehen; (*let me think*) lass mich mal überlegen; **I** ~ ich verstehe, aha; (*annoyed*) ach so; **you** ~ weißt du, siehst du; ~ **for yourself** überzeug dich doch selbst; **I don't know what she** ~**s in him** ich weiß nicht, was sie an ihm findet; **as far as I can** ~ so wie ich das sehe.

▶ **see about** vt fus sich kümmern um +acc.

▶ **see off** vt verabschieden.

▶ **see through** vt fus durchschauen ♦ vt: **to** ~ **sb through sth** jdm in etw dat beistehen; **to** ~ **sth through to the end** etw zu Ende bringen; **this should** ~ **you through** das müsste dir reichen.

▶ **see to** vt fus sich kümmern um +acc.

seed [siːd] n Samen m; (*of fruit*) Kern m; (*fig: usu pl*) Keim m; (*TENNIS*) gesetzter Spieler

m, gesetzte Spielerin f; **to go to** ~ (*plant*) Samen bilden; (*lettuce etc*) schießen; (*fig: person*) herunterkommen.

seedless ['siːdlɪs] adj kernlos.

seedling ['siːdlɪŋ] n (*BOT*) Sämling m.

seedy ['siːdɪ] adj (*person, place*) zwielichtig, zweifelhaft.

seeing ['siːɪŋ] conj: ~ **as** or **that** da.

seek [siːk] (*pt, pp* **sought**) vt suchen; **to** ~ **advice from sb** jdn um Rat fragen; **to** ~ **help from sb** jdn um Hilfe bitten.

▶ **seek out** vt ausfindig machen.

seem [siːm] vi scheinen; **there** ~**s to be a mistake** da scheint ein Fehler zu sein; **it** ~**s (that)** es scheint(, dass); **it** ~**s to me that ...** mir scheint, dass ...; **what** ~**s to be the trouble?** worum geht es denn?; (*doctor*) was fehlt Ihnen denn?

seemingly ['siːmɪŋlɪ] adv anscheinend.

seemly ['siːmlɪ] adj schicklich.

seen [siːn] pp of **see.**

seep [siːp] vi sickern.

seersucker ['sɪəsʌkə°] n Krepp m, Seersucker m.

seesaw ['siːsɔː] n Wippe f.

seethe [siːð] vi: **to** ~ **with** (*place*) wimmeln von; **to** ~ **with anger** vor Wut kochen.

see-through ['siːθruː] adj durchsichtig.

segment ['sɛgmənt] n Teil m; (*of orange*) Stück nt.

segregate ['sɛgrɪgeɪt] vt trennen, absondern.

segregation [sɛgrɪ'geɪʃən] n Trennung f.

Seine [seɪn] n: **the** ~ die Seine f.

seismic shock n Erdstoß m.

seize [siːz] vt packen, ergreifen; (*fig: opportunity*) ergreifen; (*power, control*) an sich acc reißen; (*territory, airfield*) besetzen; (*hostage*) nehmen; (*LAW*) beschlagnahmen.

▶ **seize up** vi (*engine*) sich festfressen.

▶ **seize (up)on** vt fus sich stürzen auf +acc.

seizure ['siːʒə°] n (*MED*) Anfall m; (*of power*) Ergreifung f; (*LAW*) Beschlagnahmung f.

seldom ['sɛldəm] adv selten.

select [sɪ'lɛkt] adj exklusiv ♦ vt (aus)wählen; (*SPORT*) aufstellen; **a** ~ **few** wenige Auserwählte pl.

selection [sɪ'lɛkʃən] n (*being chosen*) Wahl f; (*range*) Auswahl f.

selection committee n Auswahlkomitee nt.

selective [sɪ'lɛktɪv] adj wählerisch; (*not general*) selektiv.

selector [sɪ'lɛktə°] n (*SPORT*) Mannschaftsaufsteller(in) m(f); (*TECH*) Wählschalter m; (: *button*) Taste f.

self [sɛlf] (*pl* **selves**) n Selbst nt, Ich nt; **she was her normal** ~ **again** sie war wieder ganz die Alte.

self... [sɛlf] pref selbst-, Selbst-.

self-addressed ['sɛlfə'drɛst] adj: ~ **envelope** addressierter Rückumschlag m.

self-adhesive [sɛlfəd'hiːzɪv] adj selbstklebend.

self-appointed [sɛlfə'pɔɪntɪd] *adj* selbst ernannt.

self-assertive [sɛlfə'sɔ:tɪv] *adj* selbstbewusst.

self-assurance [sɛlfə'ʃuərəns] *n* Selbstsicherheit *f*.

self-assured [sɛlfə'ʃuəd] *adj* selbstsicher.

self-catering [sɛlf'keɪtərɪŋ] (*BRIT*) *adj* (*holiday, flat*) für Selbstversorger.

self-centred, (*US*) **self-centered** [sɛlf'sɛntəd] *adj* egozentrisch, ichbezogen.

self-cleaning [sɛlf'kli:nɪŋ] *adj* selbstreinigend.

self-confessed [sɛlfkən'fɛst] *adj* erklärt.

self-confidence [sɛlf'kɒnfɪdns] *n* Selbstbewusstsein *nt*, Selbstvertrauen *nt*.

self-confident [sɛlf'kɒnfɪdənt] *adj* selbstbewusst, selbstsicher.

self-conscious [sɛlf'kɒnʃəs] *adj* befangen, gehemmt.

self-contained [sɛlfkən'teɪnd] (*BRIT*) *adj* (*flat*) abgeschlossen; (*person*) selb(st)ständig.

self-control [sɛlfkən'trəʊl] *n* Selbstbeherrschung *f*.

self-defeating [sɛlfdɪ'fi:tɪŋ] *adj* unsinnig.

self-defence, (*US*) **self-defense** [sɛlfdɪ'fɛns] *n* Selbstverteidigung *f*; (*LAW*) Notwehr *f*; **in ~** zu seiner/ihrer *etc* Verteidigung; (*LAW*) in Notwehr.

self-discipline [sɛlf'dɪsɪplɪn] *n* Selbstdisziplin *f*.

self-employed [sɛlfɪm'plɔɪd] *adj* selbstständig.

self-esteem [sɛlfɪs'ti:m] *n* Selbstachtung *f*.

self-evident [sɛlf'ɛvɪdnt] *adj* offensichtlich.

self-explanatory [sɛlfɪks'plænətrɪ] *adj* unmittelbar verständlich.

self-financing [sɛlffaɪ'nænsɪŋ] *adj* selbstfinanzierend.

self-governing [sɛlf'gʌvənɪŋ] *adj* selbst verwaltet.

self-help [sɛlf'hɛlp] *n* Selbsthilfe *f*.

self-importance [sɛlfɪm'pɔ:tns] *n* Aufgeblasenheit *f*.

self-indulgent [sɛlfɪn'dʌldʒənt] *adj* genießerisch; **to be ~** sich verwöhnen.

self-inflicted [sɛlfɪn'flɪktɪd] *adj* selbst zugefügt.

self-interest [sɛlf'ɪntrɪst] *n* Eigennutz *m*.

selfish [sɛlfɪʃ] *adj* egoistisch, selbstsüchtig.

selfishly [sɛlfɪʃlɪ] *adv* egoistisch, selbstsüchtig.

selfishness [sɛlfɪʃnɪs] *n* Egoismus *m*, Selbstsucht *f*.

selfless [sɛlflɪs] *adj* selbstlos.

selflessly [sɛlflɪslɪ] *adv* selbstlos.

selflessness [sɛlflɪsnɪs] *n* Selbstlosigkeit *f*.

self-made [sɛlfmeɪd] *adj*: **~ man** Selfmademan *m*.

self-pity [sɛlf'pɪtɪ] *n* Selbstmitleid *nt*.

self-portrait [sɛlf'pɔ:treɪt] *n* Selbstporträt *nt*, Selbstbildnis *nt*.

self-possessed [sɛlfpə'zɛst] *adj* selbstbeherrscht.

self-preservation [sɛlfprɛzə'veɪʃən] *n* Selbsterhaltung *f*.

self-raising [sɛlf'reɪzɪŋ], (*US*) **self-rising** [sɛlf'raɪzɪŋ] *adj*: **~ flour** Mehl *mit bereits beigemischtem Backpulver*.

self-reliant [sɛlfrɪ'laɪənt] *adj* selb(st)ständig.

self-respect [sɛlfrɪs'pɛkt] *n* Selbstachtung *f*.

self-respecting [sɛlfrɪs'pɛktɪŋ] *adj* mit Selbstachtung; (*genuine*) der/die/das etwas auf sich hält.

self-righteous [sɛlf'raɪtʃəs] *adj* selbstgerecht.

self-rising [sɛlf'raɪzɪŋ] (*US*) *adj* = **self-raising**.

self-sacrifice [sɛlf'sækrɪfaɪs] *n* Selbstaufopferung *f*.

self-same [sɛlfseɪm] *adj*: **the ~** genau derselbe/dieselbe/dasselbe.

self-satisfied [sɛlf'sætɪsfaɪd] *adj* selbstzufrieden.

self-sealing [sɛlf'si:lɪŋ] *adj* selbstklebend.

self-service [sɛlf'sɜ:vɪs] *adj* (*shop, restaurant etc*) Selbstbedienungs-.

self-styled [sɛlfstaɪld] *adj* selbst ernannt.

self-sufficient [sɛlfsə'fɪʃənt] *adj* (*country*) autark; (*person*) selb(st)ständig, unabhängig; **to be ~ in coal** seinen Kohlebedarf selbst decken können.

self-supporting [sɛlfsə'pɔ:tɪŋ] *adj* (*business*) sich selbst tragend.

self-taught [sɛlf'tɔ:t] *adj*: **to be ~** Autodidakt sein; **he is a ~ pianist** er hat sich das Klavierspielen selbst beigebracht.

self-test [sɛlftɛst] *n* (*COMPUT*) Selbsttest *m*.

sell [sɛl] (*pt, pp* **sold**) *vt* verkaufen; (*shop: goods*) führen, haben (*inf*); (*fig: idea*) schmackhaft machen +*dat*, verkaufen (*inf*) ♦ *vi* sich verkaufen (lassen); **to ~ at or for 10 pounds** für 10 Pfund verkauft werden; **to ~ sb sth** jdm etw verkaufen; **to ~ o.s.** sich verkaufen.

▶ **sell off** *vt* verkaufen.

▶ **sell out** *vi*: **we/the tickets are sold out** wir/die Karten sind ausverkauft; **we have sold out of …** wir haben kein … mehr, … ist ausverkauft.

▶ **sell up** *vi* sein Haus/seine Firma *etc* verkaufen.

sell-by date [sɛlbaɪ-] *n* ≈ Haltbarkeitsdatum *nt*.

seller [sɛlə*] *n* Verkäufer(in) *m(f)*; **~'s market** Verkäufermarkt *m*.

selling price [sɛlɪŋ-] *n* Verkaufspreis *m*.

sellotape ® [sɛləteɪp] (*BRIT*) *n* Klebeband *nt*, ≈ Tesafilm ® *m*.

sellout [sɛlaʊt] *n* (*inf: betrayal*) Verrat *m*; **the match was a ~** das Spiel war ausverkauft.

selves [sɛlvz] *pl of* **self**.

semantic [sɪ'mæntɪk] *adj* semantisch.

semantics [sɪ'mæntɪks] *n* (*LING*) Semantik *f*.

semaphore [sɛməfɔ:*] *n* Flaggenalphabet *nt*.

semblance [sɛmblns] *n* Anschein *m*.

semen [si:mən] *n* Samenflüssigkeit *f*, Sperma *nt*.

semester [sɪ'mɛstə*] (*esp US*) *n* Semester *nt*.

semi ['sɛmɪ] *n* = **semidetached (house)**.
semi... ['sɛmɪ] *pref* halb-, Halb-.
semibreve ['sɛmɪbriːv] (*BRIT*) *n* (*MUS*) ganze
Note *f*.
semicircle ['sɛmɪsəːkl] *n* Halbkreis *m*.
semicircular ['sɛmɪ'səːkjuləʳ] *adj*
halbkreisförmig.
semicolon [sɛmɪ'kəʊlən] *n* Strichpunkt *m*,
Semikolon *nt*.
semiconductor [sɛmɪkən'dʌktəʳ] *n* Halbleiter
m.
semiconscious [sɛmɪ'kɒnʃəs] *adj* halb
bewusstlos.
semidetached (house) (*BRIT*) *n*
Doppelhaushälfte *f*.
semifinal [sɛmɪ'faɪnl] *n* Halbfinale *nt*.
seminar ['sɛmɪnaː] *n* Seminar *nt*.
seminary ['sɛmɪnərɪ] *n* (*REL*) Priesterseminar
nt.
semi-precious stone *n* Halbedelstein *m*.
semiquaver ['sɛmɪkweɪvəʳ] (*BRIT*) *n* (*MUS*)
Sechzehntelnote *f*.
semiskilled [sɛmɪ'skɪld] *adj* (*work*) Anlern-;
(*worker*) angelernt.
semi-skimmed [sɛmɪ'skɪmd] *adj* (*milk*)
teilentrahmt, Halbfett-.
semitone ['sɛmɪtəʊn] *n* (*MUS*) Halbton *m*.
semolina [sɛmə'liːnə] *n* Grieß *m*.
SEN (*BRIT*) *n abbr* (*formerly: = State Enrolled
Nurse*) staatlich anerkannte
Krankenschwester *f*, staatlich anerkannter
Krankenpfleger *m*.
Sen., sen. *abbr* (*US*) = **senator**; (*in names*:
= *senior*) sen.
senate ['sɛnɪt] *n* Senat *m*.

SENATE

Senate *ist das Oberhaus des amerikanischen
Kongresses (das Unterhaus ist das* **House of
Representatives***). Der Senat besteht aus 100
Senatoren, zwei für jeden Bundesstaat, die für
sechs Jahre gewählt werden, wobei ein Drittel alle
zwei Jahre neu gewählt wird. Die Senatoren
werden in direkter Wahl vom Volk gewählt. Siehe
auch* **congress***.

---

senator ['sɛnɪtəʳ] *n* Senator(in) *m(f)*.
send [sɛnd] (*pt, pp* **sent**) *vt* schicken; (*transmit*)
senden; **to ~ sth by post** *or* (*US*) **mail** etw
mit der Post schicken; **to ~ sb for sth** (*for
check-up etc*) jdn zu etw schicken; **to ~ word
that** ... Nachricht geben, dass ...; **she ~s
(you) her love** sie lässt dich grüßen; **to ~ sb
to Coventry** (*BRIT*) jdn schneiden (*inf*); **to
~ sb to sleep** jdn einschläfern; **to ~ sth
flying** etw umwerfen.
▶ **send away** *vt* wegschicken.
▶ **send away for** *vt fus* (per Post) anfordern.
▶ **send back** *vt* zurückschicken.
▶ **send for** *vt fus* (per Post) anfordern; (*doctor,
police*) rufen.

▶ **send in** *vt* einsenden, einschicken.
▶ **send off** *vt* abschicken; (*BRIT: player*) vom
Platz weisen.
▶ **send on** *vt* (*BRIT: letter*) nachsenden;
(*luggage etc*) vorausschicken.
▶ **send out** *vt* verschicken; (*light, heat*)
abgeben; (*signal*) aussenden.
▶ **send round** *vt* schicken; (*circulate*)
zirkulieren lassen.
▶ **send up** *vt* (*astronaut*) hochschießen; (*price,
blood pressure*) hochtreiben; (*BRIT: parody*)
verulken (*inf*).
sender ['sɛndəʳ] *n* Absender(in) *m(f)*.
sending-off ['sɛndɪŋɒf] *n* (*SPORT*)
Platzverweis *m*.
send-off ['sɛndɒf] *n*: **a good ~** eine große
Verabschiedung.
send-up ['sɛndʌp] *n* Verulkung *f* (*inf*).
Senegal [sɛnɪ'gɔːl] *n* Senegal *nt*.
Senegalese [sɛnɪgə'liːz] *adj* senegalesisch ♦ *n
inv* Senegalese *m*, Senegalesin *f*.
senile ['siːnaɪl] *adj* senil.
senility [sɪ'nɪlɪtɪ] *n* Senilität *f*.
senior ['siːnɪəʳ] *adj* (*staff, manager*) leitend;
(*officer*) höher; (*post, position*) leitend ♦ *n*
(*SCOL*): **the ~s** die Oberstufenschüler *pl*; **to
be ~ to sb** jdm übergeordnet sein; **she is 15
years his ~** sie ist 15 Jahre älter als er; **P.
Jones ~** P. Jones senior.
senior citizen *n* Senior(in) *m(f)*.
senior high school (*US*) *n* Oberstufe *f*.
seniority [siːnɪ'ɒrɪtɪ] *n* (*in service*) (längere)
Betriebszugehörigkeit *f*; (*in rank*) (höhere)
Position *f*.
sensation [sɛn'seɪʃən] *n* (*feeling*) Gefühl *nt*;
(*great success*) Sensation *f*; **to cause a ~**
großes Aufsehen erregen.
sensational [sɛn'seɪʃənl] *adj* (*wonderful*)
wunderbar; (*result*) sensationell; (*headlines
etc*) reißerisch.
sense [sɛns] *n* Sinn *m*; (*feeling*) Gefühl *nt*;
(*good sense*) Verstand *m*, gesunder
Menschenverstand *m*; (*meaning*) Bedeutung
f, Sinn *m* ♦ *vt* spüren; **~ of smell**
Geruchssinn *m*; **it makes ~** (*can be
understood*) es ergibt einen Sinn; (*is sensible*)
es ist vernünftig *or* sinnvoll; **there's no ~ in
that** das hat keinen Sinn; **there is no ~ in
doing that** es hat keinen Sinn, das zu tun; **to
come to one's ~s** Vernunft annehmen; **to
take leave of one's ~s** den Verstand
verlieren.
senseless ['sɛnslɪs] *adj* (*pointless*) sinnlos;
(*unconscious*) besinnungslos, bewusstlos.
sense of humour *n* Sinn *m* für Humor.
sensibility [sɛnsɪ'bɪlɪtɪ] *n* Empfindsamkeit *f*;
(*sensitivity*) Empfindlichkeit *f*; **to offend sb's
sensibilities** jds Zartgefühl verletzen.
sensible ['sɛnsɪbl] *adj* vernünftig; (*shoes,
clothes*) praktisch.
sensitive ['sɛnsɪtɪv] *adj* empfindlich;
(*understanding*) einfühlsam; (*touchy: person*)

sensibel; (: *issue*) heikel; **to be ~ to sth** in Bezug auf etw *acc* empfindlich sein; **he is very ~ about it/to criticism** er reagiert sehr empfindlich darauf/auf Kritik.

sensitivity [sɛnsɪ'tɪvɪtɪ] *n* Empfindlichkeit *f*; (*understanding*) Einfühlungsvermögen *nt*; (*of issue etc*) heikle Natur *f*; **an issue of great ~** ein sehr heikles Thema.

sensual ['sɛnsjuəl] *adj* sinnlich; (*person, life*) sinnenfroh.

sensuous ['sɛnsjuəs] *adj* sinnlich.

sent [sɛnt] *pt, pp of* **send**.

sentence ['sɛntns] *n* (*LING*) Satz *m*; (*LAW: judgement*) Urteil *nt*; (: *punishment*) Strafe *f* ♦ *vt*: **to ~ sb to death/to 5 years in prison** jdn zum Tode/zu 5 Jahren Haft verurteilen; **to pass ~ on sb** das Urteil über jdn verkünden; (*fig*) jdn verurteilen; **to serve a life ~** eine lebenslängliche Freiheitsstrafe verbüßen.

sentiment ['sɛntɪmənt] *n* Sentimentalität *f*; (*also pl: opinion*) Ansicht *f*.

sentimental [sɛntɪ'mɛntl] *adj* sentimental.

sentimentality [sɛntɪmɛn'tælɪtɪ] *n* Sentimentalität *f*.

sentry ['sɛntrɪ] *n* Wachtposten *m*.

sentry duty *n*: **to be on ~** auf Wache sein.

Seoul [səul] *n* Seoul *nt*.

separable ['sɛprəbl] *adj*: **to be ~ from** trennbar sein von.

separate ['sɛprɪt] *adj* getrennt; (*occasions*) verschieden; (*rooms*) separat ♦ *vt* trennen ♦ *vi* sich trennen; **~ from** getrennt von; **to go ~ ways** getrennte Wege gehen; **under ~ cover** (*COMM*) mit getrennter Post; **to ~ into** aufteilen in *+acc*; *see also* **separates**.

separately ['sɛprɪtlɪ] *adv* getrennt.

separates ['sɛprɪts] *npl* (*clothes*) kombinierbare Einzelteile *pl*.

separation [sɛpə'reɪʃən] *n* Trennung *f*.

sepia ['siːpjə] *adj* sepiafarben.

Sept. *abbr* (= *September*) Sept.

September [sɛp'tɛmbə*] *n* September *m*; *see also* **July**.

septic ['sɛptɪk] *adj* vereitert, septisch; **to go ~** eitern.

septicaemia, (*US*) **septicemia** [sɛptɪ'siːmɪə] *n* Blutvergiftung *f*.

septic tank *n* Faulbehälter *m*.

sequel ['siːkwl] *n* (*follow-up*) Nachspiel *nt*; (*of film, story*) Fortsetzung *f*.

sequence ['siːkwəns] *n* Folge *f*; (*dance/film sequence*) Sequenz *f*; **in ~** der Reihe nach.

sequential [sɪ'kwɛnʃəl] *adj* aufeinander folgend; **~ access** (*COMPUT*) sequenzieller Zugriff *m*.

sequestrate [sɪ'kwɛstreɪt] *vt* (*LAW, COMM*) sequestrieren, beschlagnahmen.

sequin ['siːkwɪn] *n* Paillette *f*.

Serbia ['səːbɪə] *n* Serbien *nt*.

Serbian ['səːbɪən] *adj* serbisch ♦ *n* Serbier(in) *m(f)*; (*LING*) Serbisch *nt*.

Serbo-Croat ['səːbəu'krəuæt] *n* (*LING*) Serbokroatisch *nt*.

serenade [sɛrə'neɪd] *n* Serenade *f* ♦ *vt* ein Ständchen *nt* bringen *+dat*.

serene [sɪ'riːn] *adj* (*landscape etc*) friedlich; (*expression*) heiter; (*person*) gelassen.

serenity [sə'rɛnɪtɪ] *n* (*of landscape*) Friedlichkeit *f*; (*of expression*) Gelassenheit *f*.

sergeant ['sɑːdʒənt] *n* (*MIL etc*) Feldwebel *m*; (*POLICE*) Polizeimeister *m*.

sergeant-major ['sɑːdʒənt'meɪdʒə*] *n* Oberfeldwebel *m*.

serial ['sɪərɪəl] *n* (*TV*) Serie *f*; (*RADIO*) Sendereihe *f*; (*in magazine*) Fortsetzungsroman *m* ♦ *adj* (*COMPUT*) seriell.

serialize ['sɪərɪəlaɪz] *vt* in Fortsetzungen veröffentlichen; (*TV, RADIO*) in Fortsetzungen senden.

serial killer *n* Serienmörder(in) *m(f)*.

serial number *n* Seriennummer *f*.

series ['sɪərɪz] *n inv* (*group*) Serie *f*, Reihe *f*; (*of books*) Reihe *f*; (*TV*) Serie *f*.

serious ['sɪərɪəs] *adj* ernst; (*important*) wichtig; (: *illness*) schwer; (: *condition*) bedenklich; **are you ~ (about it)?** meinst du das ernst?

seriously ['sɪərɪəslɪ] *adv* ernst; (*talk, interested*) ernsthaft; (*ill, hurt, damaged*) schwer; (*not jokingly*) im Ernst; **to take sb/sth ~** jdn/etw ernst nehmen; **do you ~ believe that ...** glauben Sie ernsthaft *or* im Ernst, dass ...

seriousness ['sɪərɪəsnɪs] *n* Ernst *m*, Ernsthaftigkeit *f*; (*of problem*) Bedenklichkeit *f*.

sermon ['səːmən] *n* Predigt *f*; (*fig*) Moralpredigt *f*.

serrated [sɪ'reɪtɪd] *adj* gezackt; **~ knife** Sägemesser *m*.

serum ['sɪərəm] *n* Serum *nt*.

servant ['səːvənt] *n* (*lit, fig*) Diener(in) *m(f)*; (*domestic*) Hausangestellte(r) *f(m)*.

serve [səːv] *vt* dienen *+dat*; (*in shop, with food/ drink*) bedienen; (*food, meal*) servieren; (*purpose*) haben; (*apprenticeship*) durchmachen; (*prison term*) verbüßen ♦ *vi* (*at table*) auftragen, servieren; (*TENNIS*) aufschlagen; (*soldier*) dienen; (*be useful*): **to ~ as/for** dienen als ♦ *n* (*TENNIS*) Aufschlag *m*; **are you being ~d?** werden Sie schon bedient?; **to ~ its purpose** seinen Zweck erfüllen; **to ~ sb's purpose** jds Zwecken dienen; **it ~s him right** das geschieht ihm recht; **to ~ on a committee** einem Ausschuss angehören; **to ~ on a jury** Geschworene(r) *f(m)* sein; **it's my turn to ~** (*TENNIS*) ich habe Aufschlag; **it ~s to show/explain ...** das zeigt/erklärt ...

▶ **serve out** *vt* (*food*) auftragen, servieren.

▶ **serve up** *vt* = **serve out**.

service ['səːvɪs] *n* Dienst *m*; (*commercial*) Dienstleistung *f*; (*in hotel, restaurant*)

Bedienung f, Service m; (also: **train** ~)
Bahnverbindung f; (: generally) Zugverkehr
m; (REL) Gottesdienst m; (AUT) Inspektion f;
(TENNIS) Aufschlag m; (plates etc) Service nt
♦ vt (car, machine) warten; **the Services** npl
(army, navy etc) die Streitkräfte pl; **military/
national** ~ Militärdienst m; **to be of** ~ **to sb**
jdm nützen; **to do sb a** ~ jdm einen Dienst
erweisen; **to put one's car in for a** ~ sein
Auto zur Inspektion geben; **dinner** ~
Essservice nt, Ess-Service nt.
serviceable ['sə:vɪsəbl] adj zweckmäßig.
service area n (on motorway) Raststätte f.
service charge (BRIT) n Bedienungsgeld nt.
service industry n Dienstleistungsbranche f.
serviceman ['sə:vɪsmən] (irreg: like **man**) n
Militärangehörige(r) m.
service station n Tankstelle f.
serviette [sə:vɪ'ɛt] (BRIT) n Serviette f.
servile ['sə:vaɪl] adj unterwürfig.
session ['sɛʃən] n Sitzung f; (US, SCOT: SCOL)
Studienjahr nt; (: term) Semester nt;
recording ~ Aufnahme f; **to be in** ~ tagen.
session musician n Session-Musiker(in) m(f).
set [sɛt] (pt, pp **set**) n (of saucepans, books, keys
etc) Satz m; (group) Reihe f; (of cutlery)
Garnitur f; (also: **radio** ~) Radio(gerät) nt;
(also: **TV** ~) Fernsehgerät nt; (TENNIS) Satz
m; (group of people) Kreis m; (MATH) Menge
f; (THEAT: stage) Bühne f; (: scenery)
Bühnenbild nt; (CINE) Drehort m;
(HAIRDRESSING) (Ein)legen nt ♦ adj (fixed)
fest; (ready) fertig, bereit ♦ vt (table)
decken; (place) auflegen; (time, price, rules
etc) festsetzen; (record) aufstellen; (alarm,
watch, task) stellen; (exam)
zusammenstellen; (TYP) setzen ♦ vi (sun)
untergehen; (jam, jelly, concrete) fest
werden; (bone) zusammenwachsen; **a** ~ **of
false teeth** ein Gebiss nt; **a** ~ **of dining-room
furniture** eine Esszimmergarnitur; **a chess**
~ ein Schachspiel nt; **to be** ~ **on doing sth**
etw unbedingt tun wollen; **to be all** ~ **to do
sth** bereit sein, etw zu tun; **he's** ~ **in his
ways** er ist in seinen Gewohnheiten
festgefahren; **a** ~ **phrase** eine feste
Redewendung; **a novel** ~ **in Rome** ein
Roman, der in Rom spielt; **to** ~ **to music**
vertonen; **to** ~ **on fire** anstecken; **to** ~ **free**
freilassen; **to** ~ **sail** losfahren.
▶ **set about** vt fus (task) anpacken; **to** ~ **about
doing sth** sich daranmachen, etw zu tun.
▶ **set aside** vt (money etc) beiseite legen;
(time) einplanen.
▶ **set back** vt: **to** ~ **sb back 5 pounds** jdn 5
Pfund kosten; **to** ~ **sb back (by)** (in time) jdn
zurückwerfen (um); **a house** ~ **back from
the road** ein Haus, das etwas von der Straße
abliegt.
▶ **set in** vi (bad weather) einsetzen; (infection)
sich einstellen; **the rain has** ~ **in for the day**
es hat sich für heute eingeregnet.

▶ **set off** vi (depart) aufbrechen ♦ vt (bomb)
losgehen lassen; (alarm, chain of events)
auslösen; (show up well) hervorheben.
▶ **set out** vi (depart) aufbrechen ♦ vt (goods
etc) ausbreiten; (chairs etc) aufstellen;
(arguments) darlegen; **to** ~ **out to do sth**
sich dat vornehmen, etw zu tun; **to** ~ **out
from home** zu Hause aufbrechen.
▶ **set up** vt (organization) gründen;
(monument) errichten; **to** ~ **up shop** ein
Geschäft eröffnen; (fig) sich selb(st)ständig
machen.
setback ['sɛtbæk] n Rückschlag m.
set menu n Menü nt.
set square n Zeichendreieck nt.
settee [sɛ'ti:] n Sofa nt.
setting ['sɛtɪŋ] n (background) Rahmen m;
(position) Einstellung f; (of jewel) Fassung f.
setting lotion n (Haar)festiger m.
settle ['sɛtl] vt (matter) regeln; (argument)
beilegen; (accounts) begleichen; (affairs,
business) in Ordnung bringen; (colonize: land)
besiedeln ♦ vi (also: ~ **down**) sich
niederlassen; (sand, dust etc) sich legen;
(sediment) sich setzen; (calm down) sich
beruhigen; **to** ~ **one's stomach** den Magen
beruhigen; **that's** ~**d then!** das ist also
abgemacht!; **to** ~ **down to work** sich an die
Arbeit setzen; **to** ~ **down to watch TV** es sich
dat vor dem Fernseher gemütlich machen.
▶ **settle for** vt fus sich zufrieden geben mit.
▶ **settle in** vi sich einleben; (in job etc) sich
eingewöhnen.
▶ **settle on** vt fus sich entscheiden für.
▶ **settle up** vi: **to** ~ **up with sb** mit jdm
abrechnen.
settlement ['sɛtlmənt] n (payment)
Begleichung f; (LAW) Vergleich m;
(agreement) Übereinkunft f; (of conflict)
Beilegung f; (village etc) Siedlung f,
Niederlassung f; (colonization) Besiedelung f;
in ~ **of our account** (COMM) zum Ausgleich
unseres Kontos.
settler ['sɛtlə'] n Siedler(in) m(f).
setup, set-up ['sɛtʌp] n (organization)
Organisation f; (system) System nt;
(COMPUT) Setup nt.
seven ['sɛvn] num sieben.
seventeen [sɛvn'ti:n] num siebzehn.
seventh ['sɛvnθ] num siebte(r, s).
seventy ['sɛvntɪ] num siebzig.
sever ['sɛvə'] vt durchtrennen; (fig: relations)
abbrechen; (: ties) lösen.
several ['sɛvərl] adj einige, mehrere ♦ pron
einige; ~ **of us** einige von uns; ~ **times**
einige Male, mehrmals.
severance ['sɛvərəns] n (of relations) Abbruch
m.
severance pay n Abfindung f.
severe [sɪ'vɪə'] adj (damage, shortage) schwer;
(pain) stark; (person, expression, dress, winter)
streng; (punishment) hart; (climate) rauh.

severely [sɪ'vɪəlɪ] adv (damage) stark; (punish) hart; (wounded, ill) schwer.

severity [sɪ'vɛrɪtɪ] n (gravity: of punishment) Härte f; (: of manner, voice, winter) Strenge f; (: of austerity) Rauheit f; (austerity) Strenge f.

sew [səu] (pt **sewed**, pp **sewn**) vt, vi nähen.

▶ **sew up** vt (zusammen)nähen; **it is all ~n up** (fig) es ist unter Dach und Fach.

sewage ['suːɪdʒ] n Abwasser nt.

sewage works n Kläranlage f.

sewer ['suːə'] n Abwasserkanal m.

sewing ['səuɪŋ] n Nähen nt; (items) Näharbeit f.

sewing machine n Nähmaschine f.

sewn [səun] pp of **sew**.

sex [sɛks] n (gender) Geschlecht nt; (lovemaking) Sex m; **to have ~ with sb** (Geschlechts)verkehr mit jdm haben.

sex act n Geschlechtsakt m.

sex appeal n Sexappeal m.

sex education n Sexualerziehung f.

sexism ['sɛksɪzəm] n Sexismus m.

sexist ['sɛksɪst] adj sexistisch.

sex life n Sexualleben nt.

sex object n Sexualobjekt nt.

sextet [sɛks'tɛt] n Sextett nt.

sexual ['sɛksjuəl] adj sexuell; (reproduction) geschlechtlich; (equality) der Geschlechter.

sexual assault n Vergewaltigung f.

sexual harassment n sexuelle Belästigung f.

sexual intercourse n Geschlechtsverkehr m.

sexually ['sɛksjuəlɪ] adv sexuell; (segregate) nach Geschlechtern; (discriminate) aufgrund or auf Grund des Geschlechts; (reproduce) geschlechtlich.

sexual orientation n sexuelle Orientierung f.

sexy ['sɛksɪ] adj sexy; (pictures, underwear) sexy, aufreizend.

Seychelles [seɪ'ʃɛl(z)] npl: **the ~** die Seychellen pl.

SF n abbr (= science fiction) SF.

SG (US) n abbr (MIL, MED) = **Surgeon General**.

Sgt abbr (POLICE, MIL) = **sergeant**.

shabbiness ['ʃæbɪnɪs] n Schäbigkeit f.

shabby ['ʃæbɪ] adj schäbig.

shack [ʃæk] n Hütte f. _Shooming + Cavosgil_

▶ **shack up** (inf) vi: **to ~ up (with sb)** (mit jdm) zusammenziehen.

shackles ['ʃæklz] npl Ketten pl; (fig) Fesseln pl.

shade [ʃeɪd] n Schatten m; (for lamp) (Lampen)schirm m; (of colour) (Farb)ton m; (US: also: **window ~**) Jalousie f, Rollo nt ♦ vt beschatten; (eyes) abschirmen; **shades** npl (inf: sunglasses) Sonnenbrille f; **in the ~** im Schatten; **a ~ of blue** ein Blauton; **a ~ (more/too large)** (small quantity) etwas or eine Spur (mehr/zu groß).

shadow ['ʃædəu] n Schatten m ♦ vt (follow) beschatten; **without** or **beyond a ~ of a doubt** ohne den geringsten Zweifel.

shadow cabinet (BRIT) n Schattenkabinett nt.

shadowy ['ʃædəuɪ] adj schattig; (figure, shape) schattenhaft.

shady ['ʃeɪdɪ] adj schattig; (fig: dishonest) zwielichtig; **~ deals** dunkle Geschäfte.

shaft [ʃɑːft] n (of arrow, spear) Schaft m; (AUT, TECH) Welle f; (of mine, lift) Schacht m; (of light) Strahl m; **ventilation ~** Luftschacht m.

shaggy ['ʃægɪ] adj zottelig; (dog, sheep) struppig.

shake [ʃeɪk] (pt **shook**, pp **shaken**) vt schütteln; (weaken, upset, surprise) erschüttern; (weaken: resolve) ins Wanken bringen ♦ vi zittern, beben; (building, table) wackeln; (earth) beben ♦ n Schütteln nt; **to ~ one's head** den Kopf schütteln; **to ~ hands with sb** jdm die Hand schütteln; **to ~ one's fist (at sb)** (jdm) mit der Faust drohen; **give it a good ~** schütteln Sie es gut durch; **a ~ of the head** ein Kopfschütteln.

▶ **shake off** vt (lit, fig) abschütteln.

▶ **shake up** vt schütteln; (fig: upset) erschüttern.

shake-out ['ʃeɪkaut] n Freisetzung f von Arbeitskräften.

shake-up ['ʃeɪkʌp] n (radikale) Veränderung f.

shakily ['ʃeɪkɪlɪ] adv (reply) mit zittriger Stimme; (walk, stand) unsicher, wackelig.

shaky ['ʃeɪkɪ] adj (hand, voice) zittrig; (memory) schwach; (knowledge, prospects, future, start) unsicher.

shale [ʃeɪl] n Schiefer m.

shall [ʃæl] aux vb: **I ~ go** ich werde gehen; **~ I open the door?** soll ich die Tür öffnen?; **I'll go, ~ I?** soll ich gehen?

shallot [ʃə'lɔt] (BRIT) n Schalotte f.

shallow ['ʃæləu] adj flach; (fig) oberflächlich; **the shallows** npl die Untiefen pl.

sham [ʃæm] n Heuchelei f; (person) Heuchler(in) m(f); (object) Attrappe f ♦ adj unecht; (fight) Schein- ♦ vt vortäuschen.

shambles ['ʃæmblz] n heilloses Durcheinander nt; **the economy is (in) a complete ~** die Wirtschaft befindet sich in einem totalen Chaos.

shambolic [ʃæm'bɔlɪk] (inf) adj chaotisch.

shame [ʃeɪm] n Scham f; (disgrace) Schande f ♦ vt beschämen; **it is a ~ that ...** es ist eine Schande, dass ...; **what a ~!** wie schade!; **to bring ~ on** Schande bringen über +acc; **to put sb/sth to ~** jdn/etw in den Schatten stellen.

shamefaced ['ʃeɪmfeɪst] adj betreten.

shameful ['ʃeɪmful] adj schändlich.

shameless ['ʃeɪmlɪs] adj schamlos.

shampoo [ʃæm'puː] n Shampoo(n) nt ♦ vt waschen.

shampoo and set n Waschen und Legen nt.

shamrock ['ʃæmrɔk] n (plant) Klee m; (leaf) Kleeblatt nt.

shandy ['ʃændɪ] n Bier nt mit Limonade,

Radler m.

shan't [ʃɑːnt] = shall not.

shantytown ['ʃæntɪtaun] n Elendsviertel nt.

SHAPE [ʃeɪp] n abbr (MIL: = Supreme Headquarters Allied Powers, Europe) Hauptquartier der alliierten Streitkräfte in Europa während des 2. Weltkriegs.

shape [ʃeɪp] n Form f ♦ vt gestalten; (form) formen; (sb's ideas) prägen; (sb's life) bestimmen; **to take** ~ Gestalt annehmen; **in the** ~ **of a heart** in Herzform; **I can't bear gardening in any** ~ **or form** ich kann Gartenarbeit absolut nicht ausstehen; **to get (o.s.) into** ~ in Form kommen.
▶ **shape up** vi sich entwickeln.

-shaped [ʃeɪpt] suff: **heart-**~ herzförmig.

shapeless ['ʃeɪplɪs] adj formlos.

shapely ['ʃeɪplɪ] adj (woman) wohlproportioniert; (legs) wohlgeformt, wohl geformt.

share [ʃɛəˀ] n (part) Anteil m; (contribution) Teil m; (COMM) Aktie f ♦ vt teilen; (room, bed, taxi) sich dat teilen; (have in common) gemeinsam haben; **to** ~ **in** (joy, sorrow) teilen; (profits) beteiligt sein an +dat; (work) sich beteiligen an +dat.
▶ **share out** vt aufteilen.

share capital n Aktienkapital nt.

share certificate n Aktienurkunde f.

shareholder ['ʃɛəhəuldəˀ] n Aktionär(in) m(f).

share index n Aktienindex m; **the 100 Share Index** Aktienindex der Financial Times.

share issue n Aktienemission f.

shark [ʃɑːk] n Hai(fisch) m.

sharp [ʃɑːp] adj scharf; (point, nose, chin) spitz; (pain) heftig; (cold) schneidend; (MUS) zu hoch; (increase) stark; (person: quick-witted) clever; (: dishonest) gerissen ♦ n (MUS) Kreuz nt ♦ adv: **at 2 o'clock** ~ um Punkt 2 Uhr; **turn** ~ **left** biegen Sie scharf nach links ab; **to be** ~ **with sb** schroff mit jdm sein; ~ **practices** (COMM) unsaubere Geschäfte pl; **C** ~ (MUS) Cis nt; **look** ~! (ein bisschen) dalli! (inf).

sharpen ['ʃɑːpn] vt schleifen, schärfen; (pencil, stick etc) (an)spitzen; (fig: appetite) anregen.

sharpener ['ʃɑːpnəˀ] n (also: **pencil** ~) (Bleistift)spitzer m; (also: **knife** ~) Schleifgerät nt.

sharp-eyed [ʃɑːpˈaɪd] adj scharfsichtig.

sharpish ['ʃɑːpɪʃ] (inf) adj (instantly) auf der Stelle.

sharply ['ʃɑːplɪ] adv scharf; (stop) plötzlich; (retort) schroff.

sharp-tempered [ʃɑːpˈtɛmpəd] adj jähzornig.

sharp-witted [ʃɑːpˈwɪtɪd] adj scharfsinnig.

shatter ['ʃætəˀ] vt zertrümmern; (fig: hopes, dreams) zunichte machen; (: confidence) zerstören ♦ vi zerbrechen, zerspringen.

shattered ['ʃætəd] adj erschüttert; (inf: exhausted) fertig, kaputt.

shattering ['ʃætərɪŋ] adj erschütternd, niederschmetternd; (exhausting) äußerst anstrengend.

shatterproof ['ʃætəpruːf] adj splitterfest, splitterfrei.

shave [ʃeɪv] vt rasieren ♦ vi sich rasieren ♦ n: **to have a** ~ sich rasieren.

shaven ['ʃeɪvn] adj (head) kahl geschoren.

shaver ['ʃeɪvəˀ] n (also: **electric** ~) Rasierapparat m.

shaving ['ʃeɪvɪŋ] n Rasieren nt; **shavings** npl (of wood etc) Späne pl.

shaving brush n Rasierpinsel m.

shaving cream n Rasiercreme f.

shaving foam n Rasierschaum m.

shaving point n Steckdose f für Rasierapparate.

shaving soap n Rasierseife f.

shawl [ʃɔːl] n (Woll)tuch nt.

she [ʃiː] pron sie ♦ pref weiblich; ~-**bear** Bärin f; **there** ~ **is** da ist sie.

sheaf [ʃiːf] (pl **sheaves**) n (of corn) Garbe f; (of papers) Bündel nt.

shear [ʃɪəˀ] (pt **sheared**, pp **shorn**) vt scheren.
▶ **shear off** vi abbrechen.

shears ['ʃɪəz] npl (for hedge) Heckenschere f.

sheath [ʃiːθ] n (of knife) Scheide f; (contraceptive) Kondom nt.

sheathe [ʃiːð] vt ummanteln; (sword) in die Scheide stecken.

sheath knife n Fahrtenmesser nt.

sheaves [ʃiːvz] npl of **sheaf**.

shed [ʃɛd] (pt, pp **shed**) n Schuppen m; (INDUSTRY, RAIL) Halle f ♦ vt (tears, blood) vergießen; (load) verlieren; (workers) entlassen; **to** ~ **its skin** sich häuten; **to** ~ **light on** (problem) erhellen.

she'd [ʃiːd] = she had, she would.

sheen [ʃiːn] n Glanz m.

sheep [ʃiːp] n inv Schaf nt.

sheepdog ['ʃiːpdɔg] n Hütehund m.

sheep farmer n Schaffarmer m.

sheepish ['ʃiːpɪʃ] adj verlegen.

sheepskin ['ʃiːpskɪn] n Schaffell nt ♦ cpd Schaffell-.

sheer [ʃɪəˀ] adj (utter) rein; (steep) steil; (almost transparent) (hauch)dünn ♦ adv (straight up) senkrecht; **by** ~ **chance** rein zufällig.

sheet [ʃiːt] n (on bed) (Bett)laken nt; (of paper) Blatt nt; (of glass, metal) Platte f; (of ice) Fläche f.

sheet feed n (on printer) Papiereinzug m.

sheet lightning n Wetterleuchten nt.

sheet metal n Walzblech nt.

sheet music n Notenblätter pl.

sheik(h) [ʃeɪk] n Scheich m.

shelf [ʃɛlf] (pl **shelves**) n Brett nt, Bord nt; **set of shelves** Regal nt.

shelf life n Lagerfähigkeit f.

shell [ʃɛl] n (on beach) Muschel f; (of egg, nut etc) Schale f; (explosive) Granate f; (of building) Mauern pl ♦ vt (peas) enthülsen; (MIL: fire on) (mit Granaten) beschießen.

▶ **shell out** (inf) vt: **to ~ out (for)** blechen (für).

she'll [ʃiːl] = **she will; she shall**.

shellfish ['ʃɛlfɪʃ] n inv Schalentier nt; (scallop etc) Muschel f; (as food) Meeresfrüchte pl.

shelter ['ʃɛltə*] n (building) Unterstand m; (refuge) Schutz m; (also: **bus ~**) Wartehäuschen nt; (also: **night ~**) Obdachlosenasyl nt ♦ vt (protect) schützen; (homeless, refugees) aufnehmen; (wanted man) Unterschlupf gewähren +dat ♦ vi sich unterstellen; (from storm) Schutz suchen; **to take ~ (from)** (from danger) sich in Sicherheit bringen (vor +dat); (from storm etc) Schutz suchen (vor +dat).

sheltered ['ʃɛltəd] adj (life) behütet; (spot) geschützt; **~ housing** (for old people) Altenwohnungen pl; (for handicapped people) Behindertenwohnungen pl.

shelve [ʃɛlv] vt (fig: plan) ad acta legen.

shelves [ʃɛlvz] npl of **shelf**.

shelving ['ʃɛlvɪŋ] n Regale pl.

shepherd ['ʃɛpəd] n Schäfer m ♦ vt (guide) führen.

shepherdess ['ʃɛpədɪs] n Schäferin f.

shepherd's pie (BRIT) n Auflauf aus Hackfleisch und Kartoffelbrei.

sherbet ['ʃəːbət] n (BRIT: powder) Brausepulver nt; (US: water ice) Fruchteis nt.

sheriff ['ʃɛrɪf] (US) n Sheriff m.

sherry ['ʃɛrɪ] n Sherry m.

she's [ʃiːz] = **she is; she has**.

Shetland ['ʃɛtlənd] n (also: **the ~ Islands**) die Shetlandinseln pl.

Shetland pony n Shetlandpony nt.

shield [ʃiːld] n (MIL) Schild m; (trophy) Trophäe f; (fig: protection) Schutz m ♦ vt: **to ~ (from)** schützen (vor +dat).

shift [ʃɪft] n (change) Änderung f; (work-period, workers) Schicht f ♦ vt (move) bewegen; (furniture) (ver)rücken; (stain) herausbekommen ♦ vi (move) sich bewegen; (wind) drehen; **a ~ in demand** (COMM) eine Nachfrageverschiebung.

shift key n Umschalttaste f.

shiftless ['ʃɪftlɪs] adj träge.

shift work n Schichtarbeit f; **to do ~** Schicht arbeiten.

shifty ['ʃɪftɪ] adj verschlagen.

Shiite ['ʃiːaɪt] adj schiitisch ♦ n Schiit(in) m(f).

shilling ['ʃɪlɪŋ] (BRIT: old) n Shilling m.

shilly-shally ['ʃɪlɪʃælɪ] vi unschlüssig sein.

shimmer ['ʃɪmə*] vi schimmern.

shimmering ['ʃɪmərɪŋ] adj schimmernd.

shin [ʃɪn] n Schienbein nt ♦ vi: **to ~ up a tree** einen Baum hinaufklettern.

shindig ['ʃɪndɪg] (inf) n Remmidemmi nt.

shine [ʃaɪn] (pt, pp **shone**) n Glanz m ♦ vi (sun, light) scheinen; (eyes) leuchten; (hair, fig: person) glänzen ♦ vt (polish: pt, pp **shined**)

polieren; **to ~ a torch on sth** etw mit einer Taschenlampe anleuchten.

shingle ['ʃɪŋgl] n (on beach) Kiesel(steine) pl; (on roof) Schindel f.

shingles ['ʃɪŋglz] npl (MED) Gürtelrose f.

shining ['ʃaɪnɪŋ] adj glänzend; (example) leuchtend.

shiny ['ʃaɪnɪ] adj glänzend.

ship [ʃɪp] n Schiff nt ♦ vt verschiffen; (send) versenden; (water) übernehmen; **on board ~** an Bord.

shipbuilder ['ʃɪpbɪldə*] n Schiffbauer m.

shipbuilding ['ʃɪpbɪldɪŋ] n Schiffbau m.

ship canal n Seekanal m.

ship chandler [-'tʃɑːndlə*] n Schiffsausrüster m.

shipment ['ʃɪpmənt] n (of goods) Versand m; (amount) Sendung f.

shipowner ['ʃɪpəunə*] n Schiffseigner m; (of many ships) Reeder m.

shipper ['ʃɪpə*] n (person) Spediteur m; (company) Spedition f.

shipping ['ʃɪpɪŋ] n (transport) Versand m; (ships) Schiffe pl.

shipping agent n Reeder m.

shipping company n Schifffahrtslinie f, Reederei f.

shipping lane n Schifffahrtsstraße f.

shipping line n = **shipping company**.

shipshape ['ʃɪpʃeɪp] adj tipptopp (inf).

shipwreck ['ʃɪprɛk] n Schiffbruch m; (ship) Wrack n ♦ vt: **to be ~ed** schiffbrüchig sein.

shipyard ['ʃɪpjɑːd] n Werft f.

shire ['ʃaɪə*] (BRIT) n Grafschaft f.

shirk [ʃəːk] vt sich drücken vor +dat.

shirt [ʃəːt] n (Ober)hemd nt; (woman's) (Hemd)bluse f; **in (one's) ~ sleeves** in Hemdsärmeln.

shirty ['ʃəːtɪ] (BRIT: inf) adj sauer (inf).

shit [ʃɪt] (inf!) excl Scheiße (!).

shiver ['ʃɪvə*] n Schauer m ♦ vi zittern; **to ~ with cold** vor Kälte zittern.

shoal [ʃəul] n (of fish) Schwarm m; (also: **~s**, fig) Scharen pl.

shock [ʃɔk] n Schock m; (impact) Erschütterung f; (also: **electric ~**) Schlag m ♦ vt (upset) erschüttern; (offend) schockieren; **to be suffering from ~** (MED) einen Schock haben; **to be in ~** unter Schock stehen; **it gave us a ~** es hat uns erschreckt; **it came as a ~ to hear that ...** wir hörten mit Bestürzung, dass ...

shock absorber n (AUT) Stoßdämpfer m.

shocker ['ʃɔkə*] (inf) n (film etc) Schocker m, Reißer m; **that's a real ~** (event etc) das haut einen echt um.

shocking ['ʃɔkɪŋ] adj schrecklich, fürchterlich; (outrageous) schockierend.

shockproof ['ʃɔkpruːf] adj stoßfest.

shock therapy n Schocktherapie f.

shock treatment n = **shock therapy**.

shock wave n (lit) Druckwelle f; (fig)

Schockwelle f.
shod [ʃɔd] pt, pp of **shoe**.
shoddy ['ʃɔdɪ] adj minderwertig.
shoe [ʃuː] (pt, pp **shod**) n Schuh m; (for horse) Hufeisen nt; (also: **brake ~**) Bremsbacke f ♦ vt (horse) beschlagen.
shoebrush ['ʃuːbrʌʃ] n Schuhbürste f.
shoehorn ['ʃuːhɔːn] n Schuhanzieher m.
shoelace ['ʃuːleɪs] n Schnürsenkel m.
shoemaker ['ʃuːmeɪkə*] n Schuhmacher m, Schuster m.
shoe polish n Schuhcreme f.
shoe shop n Schuhgeschäft nt.
shoestring ['ʃuːstrɪŋ] n (fig): **on a ~** mit ganz wenig Geld.
shoetree ['ʃuːtriː] n Schuhspanner m.
shone [ʃɔn] pt, pp of **shine**.
shoo [ʃuː] excl (to dog etc) pfui ♦ vt (also: **~ away**, **~ off**, etc) verscheuchen; (somewhere) scheuchen.
shook [ʃuk] pt of **shake**.
shoot [ʃuːt] (pt, pp **shot**) n (on branch) Trieb m; (seedling) Sämling m; (SPORT) Jagd f ♦ vt (gun) abfeuern; (arrow, goal) schießen; (kill, execute) erschießen; (wound) anschießen; (BRIT: game birds) schießen; (film) drehen ♦ vi: **to ~ (at)** schießen (auf +acc); **to ~ past (sb/sth)** (an jdm/etw) vorbeischießen.
► **shoot down** vt abschießen.
► **shoot in** vi hereingeschossen kommen.
► **shoot out (of)** vi herausgeschossen kommen (aus +dat).
► **shoot up** vi (fig: increase) in die Höhe schnellen.
shooting ['ʃuːtɪŋ] n Schießen nt, Schüsse pl; (attack) Schießerei f; (murder) Erschießung f; (CINE) Drehen nt; (HUNTING) Jagen nt.
shooting range n Schießplatz m.
shooting star n Sternschnuppe f.
shop [ʃɔp] n Geschäft nt, Laden m; (workshop) Werkstatt f ♦ vi (also: **go ~ping**) einkaufen (gehen); **repair ~** Reparaturwerkstatt f; **to talk ~** (fig) über die Arbeit reden.
► **shop around** vi Preise vergleichen; (fig) sich umsehen.
shopaholic ['ʃɔpə'hɔlɪk] (inf) n: **to be a ~** einen Einkaufsfimmel haben.
shop assistant (BRIT) n Verkäufer(in) m(f).
shop floor (BRIT) n (workers) Arbeiter pl; **on the ~** bei or unter den Arbeitern.
shopkeeper ['ʃɔpkiːpə*] n Geschäftsinhaber(in) m(f), Ladenbesitzer(in) m(f).
shoplifter ['ʃɔplɪftə*] n Ladendieb(in) m(f).
shoplifting ['ʃɔplɪftɪŋ] n Ladendiebstahl m.
shopper ['ʃɔpə*] n Käufer(in) m(f).
shopping ['ʃɔpɪŋ] n (goods) Einkäufe pl.
shopping bag n Einkaufstasche f.
shopping centre, (US) **shopping center** n Einkaufszentrum nt.
shopping mall n Shoppingcenter nt.
shop-soiled ['ʃɔpsɔɪld] adj angeschmutzt.

shop steward (BRIT) n gewerkschaftlicher Vertrauensmann m.
shop window n Schaufenster nt.
shore [ʃɔː*] n Ufer nt; (beach) Strand m ♦ vt: **to ~ (up)** abstützen; **on ~** an Land.
shore leave n (NAUT) Landurlaub m.
shorn [ʃɔːn] pp of **shear to be ~ of** (power etc) entkleidet sein +gen.
short [ʃɔːt] adj kurz; (person) klein; (curt) schroff, kurz angebunden (inf); (scarce) knapp ♦ n (also: **~ film**) Kurzfilm m; **to be ~ of ...** zu wenig ... haben; **I'm 3 ~** ich habe 3 zu wenig, mir fehlen 3; **in ~** kurz gesagt; **to be in ~ supply** knapp sein; **it is ~ for ...** es ist die Kurzform von ...; **a ~ time ago** vor kurzem; **in the ~ term** auf kurze Sicht; **~ of doing sth** außer etw zu tun; **to cut ~** abbrechen; **everything ~ of ...** alles außer ... +dat; **to fall ~ of sth** etw nicht erreichen; (expectations) etw nicht erfüllen; **to run ~ of ...** nicht mehr viel ... haben; **to stop ~** plötzlich innehalten; **to stop ~ of** Halt machen vor +dat; see also **shorts**.
shortage ['ʃɔːtɪdʒ] n: **a ~ of** ein Mangel m an +dat.
shortbread ['ʃɔːtbrɛd] n Mürbegebäck nt.
short-change [ʃɔːtʃeɪndʒ] vt: **to ~ sb** jdm zu wenig Wechselgeld geben.
short circuit n Kurzschluss m.
shortcoming ['ʃɔːtkʌmɪŋ] n Fehler m, Mangel m.
shortcrust pastry (BRIT) n Mürbeteig m.
short cut n Abkürzung f; (fig) Schnellverfahren nt.
shorten ['ʃɔːtn] vt verkürzen.
shortening ['ʃɔːtnɪŋ] n (Back)fett nt.
shortfall ['ʃɔːtfɔːl] n Defizit nt.
shorthand ['ʃɔːthænd] n Kurzschrift f, Stenografie f; (fig) Kurzform f; **to take sth down in ~** etw stenografieren.
shorthand notebook (BRIT) n Stenoblock m.
shorthand typist (BRIT) n Stenotypist(in) m(f).
short list (BRIT) n Auswahlliste f; **to be on the ~** in der engeren Wahl sein.
short-list ['ʃɔːtlɪst] (BRIT) vt in die engere Wahl ziehen; **to be ~ed** in die engere Wahl kommen.
short-lived ['ʃɔːt'lɪvd] adj kurzlebig; **to be ~** nicht von Dauer sein.
shortly ['ʃɔːtlɪ] adv bald.
shorts [ʃɔːts] npl: **(a pair of) ~** Shorts pl.
short-sighted [ʃɔːt'saɪtɪd] (BRIT) adj (lit, fig) kurzsichtig.
short-sightedness [ʃɔːt'saɪtɪdnɪs] n Kurzsichtigkeit f.
short-staffed [ʃɔːt'stɑːft] adj: **to be ~** zu wenig Personal haben.
short story n Kurzgeschichte f.
short-tempered [ʃɔːt'tɛmpəd] adj gereizt.
short-term ['ʃɔːtɜːm] adj kurzfristig.
short time n: **to work ~**, **to be on ~**

kurzarbeiten, Kurzarbeit haben.
short-wave ['ʃɔːtweɪv] (*RADIO*) *adj* auf
Kurzwelle ♦ *n* Kurzwelle *f*.
shot [ʃɔt] *pt, pp of* shoot ♦ *n* Schuss *m*; (*shotgun
pellets*) Schrot *m*; (*injection*) Spritze *f*; (*PHOT*)
Aufnahme *f*; **to fire a ~ at sb/sth** einen
Schuss auf jdn/etw abgeben; **to have a ~ at
(doing) sth** etw mal versuchen; **to get ~ of
sb/sth** (*inf*) jdn/etw loswerden; **a big ~** (*inf*)
ein hohes Tier; **a good/poor ~** (*person*) ein
guter/schlechter Schütze; **like a ~** sofort.
shotgun ['ʃɔtɡʌn] *n* Schrotflinte *f*.
should [ʃud] *aux vb*: **I ~ go now** ich sollte jetzt
gehen; **he ~ be there now** er müsste
eigentlich schon da sein; **I ~ go if I were you**
an deiner Stelle würde ich gehen; **I ~ like to**
ich möchte gerne, ich würde gerne; **~ he
phone** ... falls er anruft ...
shoulder ['ʃəuldə*] *n* Schulter *f* ♦ *vt* (*fig*) auf
sich *acc* nehmen; **to rub ~s with sb** (*fig*) mit
jdm in Berührung kommen; **to give sb the
cold ~** (*fig*) jdm die kalte Schulter zeigen.
shoulder bag *n* Umhängetasche *f*.
shoulder blade *n* Schulterblatt *nt*.
shoulder strap *n* (*on clothing*) Träger *m*; (*on
bag*) Schulterriemen *m*.
shouldn't ['ʃudnt] = **should not**.
shout [ʃaut] *n* Schrei *m*, Ruf *m* ♦ *vt* schreien,
rufen ♦ *vi* (*also*: **~ out**) aufschreien; **to give
sb a ~** jdn rufen.
► **shout down** *vt* niederbrüllen.
shouting ['ʃautɪŋ] *n* Geschrei *nt*.
shouting match (*inf*) *n*: **to have a ~** sich
gegenseitig anschreien.
shove [ʃʌv] *vt* schieben; (*with one push*)
stoßen, schubsen (*inf*) ♦ *n*: **to give sb a ~** jdn
stoßen *or* schubsen (*inf*); **to give sth a ~** etw
verrücken; (*door*) gegen etw stoßen; **to
~ sth in sth** (*inf*: *put*) etw in etw *acc* stecken;
he ~d me out of the way er stieß mich zur
Seite.
► **shove off** (*inf*) *vi* abschieben.
shovel ['ʃʌvl] *n* Schaufel *f*; (*mechanical*)
Bagger *m* ♦ *vt* schaufeln.
show [ʃəu] (*pt* showed, *pp* shown) *n*
(*exhibition*) Ausstellung *f*, Schau *f*; (*THEAT*)
Aufführung *f*; (*TV*) Show *f*; (*CINE*)
Vorstellung *f* ♦ *vt* zeigen; (*exhibit*) ausstellen
♦ *vi*: **it ~s** man sieht es; (*is evident*) man
merkt es; **to ask for a ~ of hands** um
Handzeichen bitten; **without any ~ of
emotion** ohne jede Gefühlsregung; **it's just
for ~** es ist nur zur Schau; **on ~** ausgestellt,
zu sehen; **who's running the ~ here?** (*inf*)
wer ist hier verantwortlich?; **to ~ sb to his
seat/to the door** jdn an seinen Platz/zur Tür
bringen; **to ~ a profit/loss** Gewinn/Verlust
aufweisen; **it just goes to ~ that** ... da sieht
mans mal wieder, dass.
► **show in** *vt* hereinführen.
► **show off** (*pej*) *vi* angeben ♦ *vt* vorführen.
► **show out** *vt* hinausbegleiten.

► **show up** *vi* (*stand out*) sich abheben; (*inf*:
turn up) auftauchen ♦ *vt* (*uncover*) deutlich
erkennen lassen; (*shame*) blamieren.
showbiz *n* = **show business**.
show business *n* Showgeschäft *nt*.
showcase ['ʃəukeɪs] *n* Schaukasten *m*; (*fig*)
Werbung *f*.
showdown ['ʃəudaun] *n* Kraftprobe *f*.
shower ['ʃauə*] *n* (*of rain*) Schauer *m*; (*of
stones etc*) Hagel *m*; (*for bathing in*) Dusche *f*;
(*US: party*) *Party, bei der jeder ein
Geschenk für den Ehrengast mitbringt* ♦ *vi*
duschen ♦ *vt*: **to ~ sb with** (*gifts etc*) jdn
überschütten mit; (*missiles, abuse etc*) auf
jdn niederhageln lassen; **to have** *or* **take a ~**
duschen; **a ~ of sparks** ein Funkenregen *m*.
showercap ['ʃauəkæp] *n* Duschhaube *f*.
showerproof ['ʃauəpruːf] *adj* regenfest.
showery ['ʃauərɪ] *adj* regnerisch.
showground ['ʃəuɡraund] *n*
Ausstellungsgelände *nt*.
showing ['ʃəuɪŋ] *n* (*of film*) Vorführung *f*.
show jumping *n* Springreiten *nt*.
showman ['ʃəumən] (*irreg: like* man) *n* (*at fair*)
Schausteller *m*; (*at circus*) Artist *m*; (*fig*)
Schauspieler *m*.
showmanship ['ʃəumənʃɪp] *n* Talent *nt* für
effektvolle Darbietung.
shown [ʃəun] *pp of* show.
show-off ['ʃəuɔf] (*inf*) *n* Angeber(in) *m(f)*.
showpiece ['ʃəupiːs] *n* (*of exhibition etc*)
Schaustück *nt*; (*best example*) Paradestück
nt; (*prime example*) Musterbeispiel *nt*.
showroom ['ʃəurum] *n* Ausstellungsraum *m*.
show trial *n* Schauprozess *m*.
showy ['ʃəuɪ] *adj* auffallend.
shrank [ʃræŋk] *pt of* shrink.
shrapnel ['ʃræpnl] *n* Schrapnell *nt*.
shred [ʃred] *n* (*gen pl*) Fetzen *m*; (*fig*): **not a
~ of truth** kein Fünkchen Wahrheit; **not a
~ of evidence** keine Spur eines Beweises
♦ *vt* zerfetzen; (*CULIN*) raspeln.
shredder ['ʃredə*] *n* (*vegetable shredder*)
Raspel *f*; (*document shredder*) Reißwolf *m*;
(*garden shredder*) Häcksler *m*.
shrew [ʃruː] *n* (*ZOOL*) Spitzmaus *f*; (*pej:
woman*) Xanthippe *f*.
shrewd [ʃruːd] *adj* klug.
shrewdness ['ʃruːdnɪs] *n* Klugheit *f*.
shriek [ʃriːk] *n* schriller Schrei *m* ♦ *vi*
schreien; **to ~ with laughter** vor Lachen
quietschen.
shrift [ʃrɪft] *n*: **to give sb short ~** jdn kurz
abfertigen.
shrill [ʃrɪl] *adj* schrill.
shrimp [ʃrɪmp] *n* Garnele *f*.
shrine [ʃraɪn] *n* Schrein *m*; (*fig*) Gedenkstätte *f*.
shrink [ʃrɪŋk] (*pt* shrank, *pp* shrunk) *vi* (*cloth*)
einlaufen; (*profits, audiences*) schrumpfen;
(*forests*) schwinden; (*also*: **~ away**)
zurückweichen ♦ *vt* (*cloth*) einlaufen lassen
♦ *n* (*inf. pej*) Klapsdoktor *m*; **to ~ from sth**

vor etw *dat* zurückschrecken; **to ~ from doing sth** davor zurückschrecken, etw zu tun.

shrinkage ['ʃrɪŋkɪdʒ] *n* (*of clothes*) Einlaufen *nt*.

shrink-wrap ['ʃrɪŋkræp] *vt* einschweißen.

shrivel ['ʃrɪvl] (*also*: ~ **up**) *vt* austrocknen ♦ *vi* austrocknen, verschrumpeln.

shroud [ʃraud] *n* Leichentuch *nt* ♦ *vt*: ~**ed in mystery** von einem Geheimnis umgeben.

Shrove Tuesday ['ʃrəuv-] *n* Fastnachtsdienstag *m*.

shrub [ʃrʌb] *n* Strauch *m*, Busch *m*.

shrubbery ['ʃrʌbərɪ] *n* Gebüsch *nt*.

shrug [ʃrʌg] *n*: ~ (**of the shoulders**) Achselzucken *nt* ♦ *vi, vt*: **to ~ (one's shoulders)** mit den Achseln zucken.

▶ **shrug off** *vt* (*criticism*) auf die leichte Schulter nehmen; (*illness*) abschütteln.

shrunk [ʃrʌŋk] *pp of* **shrink**.

shrunken ['ʃrʌŋkn] *adj* (ein)geschrumpft.

shudder ['ʃʌdə*] *n* Schauder *m* ♦ *vi* schaudern; **I ~ to think of it** (*fig*) mir graut, wenn ich nur daran denke.

shuffle ['ʃʌfl] *vt* (*cards*) mischen ♦ *vi* schlurfen; **to ~ (one's feet)** mit den Füßen scharren.

shun [ʃʌn] *vt* meiden; (*publicity*) scheuen.

shunt [ʃʌnt] *vt* rangieren.

shunting yard ['ʃʌntɪŋ-] *n* Rangierbahnhof *m*.

shush [ʃuʃ] *excl* pst!, sch!

shut [ʃʌt] (*pt, pp* **shut**) *vt* schließen, zumachen (*inf*) ♦ *vi* sich schließen, zugehen; (*shop*) schließen, zumachen (*inf*).

▶ **shut down** *vt* (*factory etc*) schließen; (*machine*) abschalten ♦ *vi* schließen, zumachen (*inf*).

▶ **shut off** *vt* (*gas, electricity*) abstellen; (*oil supplies etc*) abschneiden.

▶ **shut out** *vt* (*person*) aussperren; (*cold, noise*) nicht hereinlassen; (*view*) versperren; (*memory, thought*) verdrängen.

▶ **shut up** *vi* (*inf: keep quiet*) den Mund halten ♦ *vt* (*silence*) zum Schweigen bringen.

shutdown ['ʃʌtdaun] *n* Schließung *f*.

shutter ['ʃʌtə*] *n* Fensterladen *m*; (*PHOT*) Verschluss *m*.

shuttle ['ʃʌtl] *n* (*plane*) Pendelflugzeug *nt*; (*train*) Pendelzug *m*; (*space shuttle*) Raumtransporter *m*; (*also*: ~ **service**) Pendelverkehr *m*; (*for weaving*) Schiffchen *nt* ♦ *vi*: **to ~ to and fro** pendeln; **to ~ between** pendeln zwischen ♦ *vt* (*passengers*) transportieren.

shuttlecock ['ʃʌtlkɔk] *n* Federball *m*.

shuttle diplomacy *n* Reisediplomatie *f*.

shy [ʃaɪ] *adj* schüchtern; (*animal*) scheu ♦ *vi*: **to ~ away from doing sth** (*fig*) davor zurückschrecken, etw zu tun; **to fight ~ of** aus dem Weg gehen +*dat*; **to be ~ of doing sth** Hemmungen haben, etw zu tun.

shyly ['ʃaɪlɪ] *adv* schüchtern, scheu.

shyness ['ʃaɪnɪs] *n* Schüchternheit *f*, Scheu *f*.

Siam [saɪ'æm] *n* Siam *nt*.

Siamese [saɪə'miːz] *adj*: ~ **cat** Siamkatze *f*; ~ **twins** siamesische Zwillinge *pl*.

Siberia [saɪ'bɪərɪə] *n* Sibirien *nt*.

sibling ['sɪblɪŋ] *n* Geschwister *nt*.

Sicilian [sɪ'sɪljən] *adj* sizilianisch ♦ *n* Sizilianer(in) *m(f)*.

Sicily ['sɪsɪlɪ] *n* Sizilien *nt*.

sick [sɪk] *adj* krank; (*humour, joke*) makaber; **to be ~** (*vomit*) brechen, sich übergeben; **I feel ~** mir ist schlecht; **to fall ~** krank werden; **to be (off)** ~ wegen Krankheit fehlen; **a ~ person** ein Kranker, eine Kranke; **to be ~ of** (*fig*) satt haben +*acc*.

sickbag ['sɪkbæg] *n* Spucktüte *f*.

sickbay ['sɪkbeɪ] *n* Krankenrevier *nt*.

sickbed ['sɪkbed] *n* Krankenbett *nt*.

sick building syndrome *n* Kopfschmerzen, Allergien etc, die in modernen, vollklimatisierten Bürogebäuden entstehen.

sicken ['sɪkn] *vt* (*disgust*) anwidern ♦ *vi*: **to be ~ing for a cold/flu** eine Erkältung/Grippe bekommen.

sickening ['sɪknɪŋ] *adj* (*fig*) widerlich, ekelhaft.

sickle ['sɪkl] *n* Sichel *f*.

sick leave *n*: **to be on ~** krankgeschrieben sein.

sickle-cell anaemia *n* Sichelzellenanämie *f*.

sick list *n*: **to be on the ~** auf der Krankenliste stehen.

sickly ['sɪklɪ] *adj* kränklich; (*causing nausea*) widerlich, ekelhaft.

sickness ['sɪknɪs] *n* Krankheit *f*; (*vomiting*) Erbrechen *nt*.

sickness benefit *n* Krankengeld *nt*.

sick note *n* Krankmeldung *f*.

sick pay *n* Lohnfortzahlung *f* im Krankheitsfall; (*paid by insurance*) Krankengeld *nt*.

sickroom ['sɪkruːm] *n* Krankenzimmer *nt*.

side [saɪd] *n* Seite *f*; (*team*) Mannschaft *f*; (*in conflict etc*) Partei *f*, Seite *f*; (*of hill*) Hang *m* ♦ *adj* (*door, entrance*) Seiten-, Neben- ♦ *vi*: **to ~ with sb** jds Partei ergreifen; **by the ~ of** neben +*dat*; ~ **by ~** Seite an Seite; **the right/wrong ~** (*of cloth*) die rechte/linke Seite; **they are on our ~** sie stehen auf unserer Seite; **she never left my ~** sie wich mir nicht von der Seite; **to put sth to one ~** etw beiseite legen; **from ~ to ~** von einer Seite zur anderen; **to take ~s (with)** Partei ergreifen (für); **a ~ of beef** ein halbes Rind; **a ~ of bacon** eine ganze Speckseite.

sideboard ['saɪdbɔːd] *n* Sideboard *nt*; **sideboards** (*BRIT*) *npl* = **sideburns**.

sideburns ['saɪdbəːnz] *npl* Koteletten *pl*.

sidecar ['saɪdkɑː*] *n* Beiwagen *m*.

side dish *n* Beilage *f*.

side drum *n* kleine Trommel *f*.

side effect *n* (*MED, fig*) Nebenwirkung *f*.

sidekick ['saɪdkɪk] (inf) n Handlanger m.

sidelight ['saɪdlaɪt] n (AUT) Begrenzungsleuchte f.

sideline ['saɪdlaɪn] n (SPORT) Seitenlinie f; (fig: job) Nebenerwerb m; **to stand on the ~s** (fig) unbeteiligter Zuschauer sein; **to wait on the ~s** (fig) in den Kulissen warten.

sidelong ['saɪdlɒŋ] adj (glance) Seiten-; (: surreptitious) verstohlen; **to give sb a ~ glance** jdn kurz aus den Augenwinkeln ansehen.

side plate n kleiner Teller m.

side road n Nebenstraße f.

side-saddle ['saɪdsædl] adv (ride) im Damensitz.

sideshow ['saɪdʃəu] n Nebenattraktion f.

sidestep ['saɪdstɛp] vt (problem) umgehen; (question) ausweichen +dat ♦ vi (BOXING etc) seitwärts ausweichen.

side street n Seitenstraße f.

sidetrack ['saɪdtræk] vt (fig) ablenken.

sidewalk ['saɪdwɔːk] (US) n Bürgersteig m.

sideways ['saɪdweɪz] adv seitwärts; (lean, look) zur Seite.

siding ['saɪdɪŋ] n Abstellgleis nt.

sidle ['saɪdl] vi: **to ~ up (to)** sich heranschleichen (an +acc).

SIDS n abbr (MED: = sudden infant death syndrome) plötzlicher Kindstod m.

siege [siːdʒ] n Belagerung f; **to be under ~** belagert sein; **to lay ~ to** belagern.

siege economy n Belagerungswirtschaft f.

siege mentality n Belagerungsmentalität f.

Sierra Leone [sɪˈɛrəlɪˈəun] n Sierra Leone f.

siesta [sɪˈɛstə] n Siesta f.

sieve [sɪv] n Sieb nt ♦ vt sieben.

sift [sɪft] vt sieben; (also: ~ **through**) durchgehen.

sigh [saɪ] n Seufzer m ♦ vi seufzen; **to breathe a ~ of relief** erleichtert aufseufzen.

sight [saɪt] n (faculty) Sehvermögen nt, Augenlicht nt; (spectacle) Anblick m; (on gun) Visier nt ♦ vt sichten; **in ~** in Sicht; **on ~** (shoot) sofort; **out of ~** außer Sicht; **at ~** (COMM) bei Sicht; **at first ~** auf den ersten Blick; **I know her by ~** ich kenne sie vom Sehen; **to catch ~ of sb/sth** jdn/etw sehen; **to lose ~ of sth** (fig) etw aus den Augen verlieren; **to set one's ~s on sth** ein Auge auf etw werfen.

sighted ['saɪtɪd] adj sehend; **partially ~** sehbehindert.

sightseeing ['saɪtsiːɪŋ] n Besichtigungen pl; **to go ~** auf Besichtigungstour gehen.

sightseer ['saɪtsiːə*] n Tourist(in) m(f).

sign [saɪn] n Zeichen nt; (notice) Schild nt; (evidence) Anzeichen nt; (also: **road ~**) Verkehrsschild nt ♦ vt unterschreiben; (player) verpflichten; **a ~ of the times** ein Zeichen unserer Zeit; **it's a good/bad ~** es ist ein gutes/schlechtes Zeichen; **plus/minus ~** Plus-/Minuszeichen nt; **there's no**

~ of her changing her mind nichts deutet darauf hin, dass sie es sich anders überlegen wird; **he was showing ~s of improvement** er ließ Anzeichen einer Verbesserung erkennen; **to ~ one's name** unterschreiben; **to ~ sth over to sb** jdm etw überschreiben.

▶ **sign away** vt (rights etc) verzichten auf +acc.

▶ **sign in** vi sich eintragen.

▶ **sign off** vi (RADIO, TV) sich verabschieden; (in letter) Schluss machen.

▶ **sign on** vi (MIL) sich verpflichten; (BRIT: as unemployed) sich arbeitslos melden; (for course) sich einschreiben ♦ vt (MIL) verpflichten; (employee) anstellen.

▶ **sign out** vi (from hotel etc) sich (aus dem Hotelgästebuch etc) austragen.

▶ **sign up** vi (MIL) sich verpflichten; (for course) sich einschreiben ♦ vt (player, recruit) verpflichten.

signal ['sɪgnl] n Zeichen nt; (RAIL) Signal nt ♦ vi (AUT) Zeichen/ein Zeichen geben ♦ vt ein Zeichen geben +dat; **to ~ a right/left turn** (AUT) rechts/links blinken.

signal box n Stellwerk nt.

signalman ['sɪgnlmən] (irreg: like man) n Stellwerkswärter m.

signatory ['sɪgnətərɪ] n Unterzeichner m; (state) Signatarstaat m.

signature ['sɪgnətʃə*] n Unterschrift f; (ZOOL, BIOL) Kennzeichen nt.

signature tune n Erkennungsmelodie f.

signet ring ['sɪgnət-] n Siegelring m.

significance [sɪgˈnɪfɪkəns] n Bedeutung f; **that is of no ~** das ist belanglos or bedeutungslos.

significant [sɪgˈnɪfɪkənt] adj bedeutend, wichtig; (look, smile) viel sagend, bedeutsam; **it is ~ that ...** es ist bezeichnend, dass ...

significantly [sɪgˈnɪfɪkəntlɪ] adv bedeutend; (smile) viel sagend, bedeutsam.

signify ['sɪgnɪfaɪ] vt bedeuten; (person) zu erkennen geben.

sign language n Zeichensprache f.

signpost ['saɪnpəust] n (lit, fig) Wegweiser m.

Sikh [siːk] n Sikh mf ♦ adj (province etc) Sikh-.

silage ['saɪlɪdʒ] n Silage f, Silofutter nt.

silence ['saɪləns] n Stille f; (of person) Schweigen nt ♦ vt zum Schweigen bringen; **in ~** still; (not talking) schweigend.

silencer ['saɪlənsə*] n (on gun) Schalldämpfer m; (BRIT: AUT) Auspufftopf m.

silent ['saɪlənt] adj still; (machine) ruhig; **~ film** Stummfilm m; **to remain ~** still bleiben; (about sth) sich nicht äußern.

silently ['saɪləntlɪ] adv lautlos; (not talking) schweigend.

silent partner n stiller Teilhaber m.

silhouette [sɪluːˈɛt] n Silhouette f, Umriss m ♦ vt: **to be ~d against sth** sich als Silhouette

gegen etw abheben.
silicon ['sılıkən] *n* Silizium *nt*.
silicon chip *n* Silikonchip *m*.
silicone ['sılıkəun] *n* Silikon *nt*.
silk [sılk] *n* Seide *f* ♦ *adj* (*dress etc*) Seiden-.
silky ['sılkı] *adj* seidig.
sill [sıl] *n* (*also*: **window** ~) (Fenster)sims *m or nt*; (*of door*) Schwelle *f*; (*AUT*) Türleiste *f*.
silly ['sılı] *adj* (*person*) dumm; **to do something** ~ etwas Dummes tun.
silo ['saıləu] *n* Silo *nt*; (*for missile*) Raketensilo *nt*.
silt [sılt] *n* Schlamm *m*, Schlick *m*.
► **silt up** *vi* verschlammen ♦ *vt* verschlämmen.
silver ['sılvə*] *n* Silber *nt*; (*coins*) Silbergeld *nt* ♦ *adj* silbern.
silver foil (*BRIT*) *n* Alufolie *f*.
silver paper (*BRIT*) *n* Silberpapier *nt*.
silver-plated [sılvə'pleıtıd] *adj* versilbert.
silversmith ['sılvəsmıθ] *n* Silberschmied(in) *m(f)*.
silverware ['sılvəwεə*] *n* Silber *nt*.
silver wedding (anniversary) *n* Silberhochzeit *f*.
silvery ['sılvrı] *adj* silbern; (*sound*) silberhell.
SIM card ['sımka:d] *n* (*TEL*: = *Subscriber Identity Module card*) SIM-Karte *f*.
similar ['sımılə*] *adj*: ~ **(to)** ähnlich (*wie or* +*dat*).
similarity [sımı'lærıtı] *n* Ähnlichkeit *f*.
similarly ['sımıləlı] *adv* ähnlich; (*likewise*) genauso.
simile ['sımılı] *n* (*LING*) Vergleich *m*.
simmer ['sımə*] *vi* auf kleiner Flamme kochen.
► **simmer down** (*inf*) *vi* (*fig*) sich abregen.
simper ['sımpə*] *vi* geziert lächeln.
simpering ['sımprıŋ] *adj* geziert.
simple ['sımpl] *adj* einfach; (*dress*) einfach, schlicht; (*foolish*) einfältig; **the** ~ **truth is that ...** es ist einfach so, dass ...
simple interest *n* Kapitalzinsen *pl*.
simple-minded [sımpl'maındıd] (*pej*) *adj* einfältig.
simpleton ['sımpltən] (*pej*) *n* Einfaltspinsel *m*.
simplicity [sım'plısıtı] *n* Einfachheit *f*; (*of dress*) Schlichtheit *f*.
simplification [sımplıfı'keıʃən] *n* Vereinfachung *f*.
simplify ['sımplıfaı] *vt* vereinfachen.
simply ['sımplı] *adv* (*just, merely*) nur, bloß; (*in a simple way*) einfach.
simulate ['sımjuleıt] *vt* vortäuschen, spielen; (*illness*) simulieren.
simulated ['sımjuleıtıd] *adj* (*hair, fur*) imitiert; (*TECH*) simuliert.
simulation [sımju'leıʃən] *n* Vortäuschung *f*; (*simulated object*) Imitation *f*; (*TECH*) Simulation *f*.
simultaneous [sıməl'teınıəs] *adj* gleichzeitig; (*translation, interpreting*) Simultan-.

simultaneously [sıməl'teınıəslı] *adv* gleichzeitig.
sin [sın] *n* Sünde *f* ♦ *vi* sündigen.
since [sıns] *adv* inzwischen, seitdem ♦ *prep* seit ♦ *conj* (*time*) seit(dem); (*because*) da; ~ **then**, **ever** ~ seitdem.
sincere [sın'sıə*] *adj* aufrichtig, offen; (*apology, belief*) aufrichtig.
sincerely [sın'sıəlı] *adv* aufrichtig, offen; **yours** ~ (*in letter*) mit freundlichen Grüßen.
sincerity [sın'sεrıtı] *n* Aufrichtigkeit *f*.
sine [saın] *n* Sinus *m*.
sine qua non [sınıkwa:'nɔn] *n* unerlässliche Voraussetzung *f*.
sinew ['sınju:] *n* Sehne *f*.
sinful ['sınful] *adj* sündig, sündhaft.
sing [sıŋ] (*pt* **sang**, *pp* **sung**) *vt, vi* singen.
Singapore [sıŋgə'pɔ:*] *n* Singapur *nt*.
singe [sındʒ] *vt* versengen; (*lightly*) ansengen.
singer ['sıŋə*] *n* Sänger(in) *m(f)*.
Singhalese [sıŋə'li:z] *adj* = **Sinhalese**.
singing ['sıŋıŋ] *n* Singen *nt*, Gesang *m*; **a** ~ **in the ears** ein Dröhnen in den Ohren.
single ['sıŋgl] *adj* (*solitary*) einzige(r, s); (*individual*) einzeln; (*unmarried*) ledig, unverheiratet; (*not double*) einfach ♦ *n* (*BRIT*: *also*: ~ **ticket**) Einzelfahrschein *m*; (*record*) Single *f*; **not a** ~ **one was left** es war kein Einziges mehr übrig; **every** ~ **day** jeden Tag; ~ **spacing** einfacher Zeilenabstand *m*.
► **single out** *vt* auswählen; **to** ~ **out for praise** lobend erwähnen.
single bed *n* Einzelbett *nt*.
single-breasted ['sıŋglbrestıd] *adj* einreihig.
Single European Market *n*: **the** ~ der Europäische Binnenmarkt.
single file *n*: **in** ~ im Gänsemarsch.
single-handed [sıŋgl'hændıd] *adv* ganz allein.
single-minded [sıŋgl'maındıd] *adj* zielstrebig.
single parent *n* Alleinerziehende(r) *f(m)*, allein Erziehende(r) *f(m)*.
single parent family *n* Einelternfamilie *f*.
single room *n* Einzelzimmer *nt*.
singles ['sıŋglz] *npl* (*TENNIS*) Einzel *nt*.
singles bar *n* Singles-Bar *f*.
single-sex school *n* reine Jungen-/Mädchenschule *f*; **education in** ~**s** nach Geschlechtern getrennte Schulerziehung.
singly ['sıŋglı] *adv* einzeln.
singsong ['sıŋsɔŋ] *adj* (*tone*) singend ♦ *n*: **to have a** ~ zusammen singen.
singular ['sıŋgjulə*] *adj* (*odd*) eigenartig; (*outstanding*) einzigartig; (*LING*: *form etc*) Singular- ♦ *n* (*LING*) Singular *m*, Einzahl *f*; **in the** ~ im Singular.
singularly ['sıŋgjuləlı] *adv* außerordentlich.
Sinhalese [sınhə'li:z] *adj* singhalesisch.
sinister ['sınıstə*] *adj* unheimlich.
sink [sıŋk] (*pt* **sank**, *pp* **sunk**) *n* Spülbecken *nt* ♦ *vt* (*ship*) versenken; (*well*) bohren; (*foundations*) absenken ♦ *vi* (*ship*) sinken, untergehen; (*ground*) sich senken; (*person*)

sinken; **to ~ one's teeth/claws into sth** die Zähne/seine Klauen in etw *acc* schlagen; **his heart/spirits sank at the thought** bei dem Gedanken verließ ihn der Mut; **he sank into the mud/a chair** er sank in den Schlamm ein/in einen Sessel.
► **sink back** *vi* (zurück)sinken.
► **sink down** *vi* (nieder)sinken.
► **sink in** *vi* (*fig*) verstanden werden; **it's only just sunk in** ich begreife es erst jetzt.
sinking ['sɪŋkɪŋ] *n* (*of ship*) Untergang *m*; (: *deliberate*) Versenkung *f* ♦ *adj*: ~ **feeling** flaues Gefühl *nt* (im Magen).
sinking fund *n* Tilgungsfonds *m*.
sink unit *n* Spüle *f*.
sinner ['sɪnə*] *n* Sünder(in) *m(f)*.
Sinn Féin [ʃɪn'feɪn] *n* republikanisch-nationalistische irische Partei.
Sino- ['saɪnəʊ] *pref* chinesisch-.
sinuous ['sɪnjuəs] *adj* (*snake*) gewunden; (*dance*) geschmeidig.
sinus ['saɪnəs] *n* (Nasen)nebenhöhle *f*.
sip [sɪp] *n* Schlückchen *nt* ♦ *vt* nippen an *+dat*.
siphon ['saɪfən] *n* Heber *m*; (*also*: **soda ~**) Siphon *m*.
► **siphon off** *vt* absaugen; (*petrol*) abzapfen.
SIPS *n abbr* (= *side impact protection system*) Seitenaufprallschutz *m*.
sir [sə*] *n* mein Herr, Herr X; **S~ John Smith** Sir John Smith; **yes, ~** ja(, Herr X); **Dear S~ (or Madam)** (*in letter*) Sehr geehrte (Damen und) Herren!
siren ['saɪərn] *n* Sirene *f*.
sirloin ['sɜːlɔɪn] *n* (*also*: ~ **steak**) Filetsteak *nt*.
sirocco [sɪ'rɒkəʊ] *n* Schirokko *m*.
sisal ['saɪsəl] *n* Sisal *m*.
sissy ['sɪsɪ] (*inf*: *pej*) *n* Waschlappen *m* ♦ *adj* weichlich.
sister ['sɪstə*] *n* Schwester *f*; (*nun*) (Ordens)schwester *f*; (*BRIT*: *nurse*) Oberschwester *f* ♦ *cpd*: ~ **organization** Schwesterorganisation *f*; ~ **ship** Schwesterschiff *nt*.
sister-in-law ['sɪstərɪnlɔː] *n* Schwägerin *f*.
sit [sɪt] (*pt, pp* **sat**) *vi* (*sit down*) sich setzen; (*be sitting*) sitzen; (*assembly*) tagen; (*for painter*) Modell sitzen ♦ *vt* (*exam*) machen; **to ~ on a committee** in einem Ausschuss sitzen; **to ~ tight** abwarten.
► **sit about** *vi* herumsitzen.
► **sit around** *vi* = **sit about**.
► **sit back** *vi* sich zurücklehnen.
► **sit down** *vi* sich (hin)setzen; **to be ~ting down** sitzen.
► **sit in on** *vt fus* dabei sein bei.
► **sit up** *vi* sich aufsetzen; (*straight*) sich gerade hinsetzen; (*not go to bed*) aufbleiben.
sitcom ['sɪtkɒm] *n abbr* (*TV*) = **situation comedy**.
sit-down ['sɪtdaʊn] *adj*: **a ~ strike** ein Sitzstreik *m*; **a ~ meal** eine richtige Mahlzeit.

site [saɪt] *n* (*place*) Platz *m*; (*of crime*) Ort *m*; (*also*: **building ~**) Baustelle *f*; (*COMPUT*) Site *f* ♦ *vt* (*factory*) legen; (*missiles*) stationieren.
sit-in ['sɪtɪn] *n* Sit-in *nt*.
siting ['saɪtɪŋ] *n* (*location*) Lage *f*.
sitter ['sɪtə*] *n* (*for painter*) Modell *nt*; (*also*: **baby-~**) Babysitter *m*.
sitting ['sɪtɪŋ] *n* Sitzung *f*; **we have two ~s for lunch** bei uns wird das Mittagessen in zwei Schüben serviert; **at a single ~** auf einmal.
sitting member *n* (*POL*) (derzeitiger) Abgeordnete(r) *m*, (derzeitige) Abgeordnete *f*.
sitting room *n* Wohnzimmer *nt*.
sitting tenant (*BRIT*) *n* (derzeitiger) Mieter *m*.
situate ['sɪtjueɪt] *vt* legen.
situated ['sɪtjueɪtɪd] *adj* gelegen; **to be ~** liegen.
situation [sɪtju'eɪʃən] *n* Situation *f*, Lage *f*; (*job*) Stelle *f*; (*location*) Lage *f*; **"~s vacant"** (*BRIT*) „Stellenangebote".
situation comedy *n* (*TV*) Situationskomödie *f*.
six [sɪks] *num* sechs.
six-pack ['sɪkspæk] *n* Sechserpack *m*.
sixteen [sɪks'tiːn] *num* sechzehn.
sixth [sɪksθ] *num* sechste(r, s); **the upper/lower ~** (*BRIT*: *SCOL*) ≈ die Ober-/Unterprima.
sixty ['sɪkstɪ] *num* sechzig.
size [saɪz] *n* Größe *f*; (*extent*) Ausmaß *nt*; **I take ~ 14** ich habe Größe 14; **the small/large ~** (*of soap powder etc*) die kleine/große Packung; **it's the ~ of ...** es ist so groß wie ...; **cut to ~** auf die richtige Größe zurechtschneiden.
► **size up** *vt* einschätzen.
sizeable ['saɪzəbl] *adj* ziemlich groß; (*income etc*) ansehnlich.
sizzle ['sɪzl] *vi* brutzeln.
SK (*CANADA*) *abbr* (= *Saskatchewan*).
skate [skeɪt] *n* (*ice skate*) Schlittschuh *m*; (*roller skate*) Rollschuh *m*; (*fish*: *pl inv*) Rochen *m* ♦ *vi* Schlittschuh laufen.
► **skate around** *vt fus* (*problem, issue*) einfach übergehen.
► **skate over** *vt fus* = **skate around**.
skateboard ['skeɪtbɔːd] *n* Skateboard *nt*.
skater ['skeɪtə*] *n* Schlittschuhläufer(in) *m(f)*.
skating ['skeɪtɪŋ] *n* Eislauf *m*.
skating rink *n* Eisbahn *f*.
skeleton ['skelɪtn] *n* Skelett *nt* ♦ *attrib* (*plan, outline*) skizzenhaft.
skeleton key *n* Dietrich *m*; Nachschlüssel *m*.
skeleton staff *n* Minimalbesetzung *f*.
skeptic *etc* ['skeptɪk] (*US*) = **sceptic** *etc*.
sketch [sketʃ] *n* Skizze *f*; (*THEAT, TV*) Sketch *m* ♦ *vt* skizzieren; (*also*: ~ **out**: *ideas*) umreißen.
sketchbook ['sketʃbʊk] *n* Skizzenbuch *nt*.
sketchpad ['sketʃpæd] *n* Skizzenblock *m*.
sketchy ['sketʃɪ] *adj* (*coverage*) oberflächlich;

(*notes etc*) bruchstückhaft.
skew [skjuː] *adj* schief.
skewed [skjuːd] *adj* (*distorted*) verzerrt.
skewer ['skjuːəʳ] *n* Spieß *m*.
ski [skiː] *n* Ski *m*, Schi *m* ♦ *vi* Ski laufen *or* fahren.
ski boot *n* Skistiefel *m*.
skid [skɪd] *n* (*AUT*) Schleudern *nt* ♦ *vi* rutschen; (*AUT*) schleudern; **to go into a** ~ ins Schleudern geraten *or* kommen.
skid marks *npl* Reifenspuren *pl*; (*from braking*) Bremsspuren *pl*.
skier ['skiːəʳ] *n* Skiläufer(in) *m(f)*, Skifahrer(in) *m(f)*.
skiing ['skiːɪŋ] *n* Skilaufen *nt*, Skifahren *nt*; **to go** ~ Ski laufen *or* Ski fahren gehen.
ski instructor *n* Skilehrer(in) *m(f)*.
ski jump *n* (*event*) Skispringen *nt*; (*ramp*) Sprungschanze *f*.
skilful, (*US*) **skillful** ['skɪlful] *adj* geschickt.
skilfully *adv* geschickt.
ski lift *n* Skilift *m*.
skill [skɪl] *n* (*ability*) Können *nt*; (*dexterity*) Geschicklichkeit *f*; **skills** (*acquired abilities*) Fähigkeiten *pl*; **computer/language** ~**s** Computer-/Sprachkenntnisse *pl*; **to learn a new** ~ etwas Neues lernen.
skilled [skɪld] *adj* (*skilful*) geschickt; (*trained*) ausgebildet; (*work*) qualifiziert.
skillet ['skɪlɪt] *n* Bratpfanne *f*.
skillful *etc* ['skɪlful] (*US*) = **skilful** *etc*.
skim [skɪm] *vt* (*also:* ~ **off:** *cream, fat*) abschöpfen; (*glide over*) gleiten über +*acc* ♦ *vi*: **to** ~ **through** (*book etc*) überfliegen.
skimmed milk [skɪmd-] *n* Magermilch *f*.
skimp [skɪmp] (*also:* ~ **on**) *vt* (*work etc*) nachlässig machen; (*cloth etc*) sparen an +*dat*.
skimpy ['skɪmpɪ] *adj* (*meagre*) dürftig; (*too small*) knapp.
skin [skɪn] *n* Haut *f*; (*fur*) Fell *nt*; (*of fruit*) Schale *f* ♦ *vt* (*animal*) häuten; **wet** *or* **soaked to the** ~ nass bis auf die Haut.
skin cancer *n* Hautkrebs *m*.
skin-deep ['skɪn'diːp] *adj* oberflächlich.
skin diver *n* Sporttaucher(in) *m(f)*.
skin diving *n* Sporttauchen *nt*.
skinflint ['skɪnflɪnt] *n* Geizkragen *m*.
skin graft *n* Hautverpflanzung *f*.
skinhead ['skɪnhɛd] *n* Skinhead *m*.
skinny ['skɪnɪ] *adj* dünn.
skin test *n* Hauttest *m*.
skintight ['skɪntaɪt] *adj* hauteng.
skip [skɪp] *n* Sprung *m*, Hüpfer *m*; (*BRIT: container*) (Müll)container *m* ♦ *vi* springen, hüpfen; (*with rope*) seilspringen ♦ *vt* überspringen; (*miss: lunch, lecture*) ausfallen lassen; **to** ~ **school** (*esp US*) die Schule schwänzen.
ski pants *npl* Skihose *f*.
ski pass *n* Skipass *nt*.
ski pole *n* Skistock *m*.

skipper ['skɪpəʳ] *n* (*NAUT*) Kapitän *m*; (*inf: SPORT*) Mannschaftskapitän *m* ♦ *vt*: **to** ~ **a boat/team** Kapitän eines Schiffes/einer Mannschaft sein.
skipping rope ['skɪpɪŋ-] (*BRIT*) *n* Sprungseil *nt*.
ski resort *n* Wintersportort *m*.
skirmish ['skəːmɪʃ] *n* (*MIL*) Geplänkel *nt*; (*political etc*) Zusammenstoß *m*.
skirt [skəːt] *n* Rock *m* ♦ *vt* (*fig*) umgehen.
skirting board ['skəːtɪŋ-] (*BRIT*) *n* Fußleiste *f*.
ski run *n* Skipiste *f*.
ski slope *n* Skipiste *f*.
ski suit *n* Skianzug *m*.
skit [skɪt] *n* Parodie *f*.
ski tow *n* Schlepplift *m*.
skittle ['skɪtl] *n* Kegel *m*.
skittles ['skɪtlz] *n* (*game*) Kegeln *nt*.
skive [skaɪv] (*BRIT: inf*) *vi* blaumachen; (*from school*) schwänzen.
skulk [skʌlk] *vi* sich herumdrücken.
skull [skʌl] *n* Schädel *m*.
skullcap ['skʌlkæp] *n* Scheitelkäppchen *nt*.
skunk [skʌŋk] *n* Skunk *m*, Stinktier *nt*; (*fur*) Skunk *m*.
sky [skaɪ] *n* Himmel *m*; **to praise sb to the skies** jdn in den Himmel heben.
sky-blue [skaɪ'bluː] *adj* himmelblau.
skydiving ['skaɪdaɪvɪŋ] *n* Fallschirmspringen *nt*.
sky-high ['skaɪ'haɪ] *adj* (*prices, confidence*) himmelhoch ♦ *adv*: **to blow a bridge** ~ eine Brücke in die Luft sprengen.
skylark ['skaɪlɑːk] *n* Feldlerche *f*.
skylight ['skaɪlaɪt] *n* Dachfenster *nt*.
skyline ['skaɪlaɪn] *n* (*horizon*) Horizont *m*; (*of city*) Skyline *f*, Silhouette *f*.
skyscraper ['skaɪskreɪpəʳ] *n* Wolkenkratzer *m*.
slab [slæb] *n* (*stone*) Platte *f*; (*of wood*) Tafel *f*; (*of cake, cheese*) großes Stück *nt*.
slack [slæk] *adj* (*loose*) locker; (*rope*) durchhängend; (*skin*) schlaff; (*careless*) nachlässig; (*COMM: market*) flau; (: *demand*) schwach; (*period*) ruhig ♦ *n* (*in rope etc*) durchhängendes Teil *nt*; **slacks** *npl* (*trousers*) Hose *f*; **business is** ~ das Geschäft geht schlecht.
slacken ['slækn] *vi* (*also:* ~ **off:** *speed, rain*) nachlassen; (: *pace*) langsamer werden; (: *demand*) zurückgehen ♦ *vt* (*grip*) lockern; (*speed*) verringern; (*pace*) verlangsamen.
slag heap [slæg-] *n* Schlackenhalde *f*.
slag off (*BRIT: inf*) *vt* (*criticize*) (he)runtermachen.
slain [sleɪn] *pp of* **slay**.
slake [sleɪk] *vt* (*thirst*) stillen.
slalom ['slɑːləm] *n* Slalom *m*.
slam [slæm] *vt* (*door*) zuschlagen, zuknallen (*inf*); (*throw*) knallen (*inf*); (*criticize*) verreißen ♦ *vi* (*door*) zuschlagen, zuknallen (*inf*); **to** ~ **on the brakes** (*AUT*) auf die Bremse steigen (*inf*).

slammer ['slæmə*] (*inf*) n (*prison*) Knast m.

slander ['slɑːndə*] n (*LAW*) Verleumdung f; (*insult*) Beleidigung f ♦ vt verleumden.

slanderous ['slɑːndrəs] *adj* verleumderisch.

slang [slæŋ] n Slang m; (*jargon*) Jargon m.

slanging match ['slæŋɪŋ-] n gegenseitige Beschimpfungen pl.

slant [slɑːnt] n Neigung f, Schräge f, (*fig: approach*) Perspektive f ♦ vi (*floor*) sich neigen; (*ceiling*) schräg sein.

slanted ['slɑːntɪd] *adj* (*roof*) schräg; (*eyes*) schräg gestellt.

slanting ['slɑːntɪŋ] *adj* = **slanted**.

slap [slæp] n Schlag m, Klaps m ♦ vt schlagen ♦ *adv* (*inf: directly*) direkt; **to ~ sth on sth** etw auf etw *acc* klatschen; **it fell ~(-bang) in the middle** es fiel genau in die Mitte.

slapdash ['slæpdæʃ] *adj* nachlässig, schludrig (*inf*).

slapstick ['slæpstɪk] n Klamauk m.

slap-up ['slæpʌp] *adj*: **a ~ meal** (*BRIT*) ein Essen mit allem Drum und Dran.

slash [slæʃ] vt aufschlitzen; (*fig: prices*) radikal senken; **to ~ one's wrists** sich *dat* die Pulsadern aufschneiden.

slat [slæt] n Leiste f, Latte f.

slate [sleɪt] n Schiefer m; (*piece*) Schieferplatte f ♦ vt (*criticize*) verreißen.

slaughter ['slɔːtə*] n (*of animals*) Schlachten nt; (*of people*) Gemetzel nt ♦ vt (*animals*) schlachten; (*people*) abschlachten.

slaughterhouse ['slɔːtəhaus] n Schlachthof m.

Slav [slɑːv] *adj* slawisch ♦ n Slawe m, Slawin f.

slave [sleɪv] n Sklave m, Sklavin f ♦ vi (*also*: **~ away**) sich abplagen, schuften (*inf*); **to ~ (away) at sth** sich mit etw herumschlagen.

slave-driver ['sleɪvdraɪvə*] n Sklaventreiber(in) m(f).

slave labour n Sklavenarbeit f; **it's just ~** (*fig*) es ist die reinste Sklavenarbeit.

slaver ['slævə*] vi (*dribble*) geifern.

slavery ['sleɪvərɪ] n Sklaverei f.

Slavic ['slævɪk] *adj* slawisch.

slavish ['sleɪvɪʃ] *adj* slawisch.

slavishly ['sleɪvɪʃlɪ] *adv* sklavisch.

Slavonic [slə'vɒnɪk] *adj* slawisch.

slay [sleɪ] (*pt* **slew**, *pp* **slain**) vt (*liter*) erschlagen.

SLD (*BRIT*) n abbr (*POL*: = *Social and Liberal Democratic Party*) sozialliberale Partei.

sleazy ['sliːzɪ] *adj* schäbig.

sledge [sledʒ] n Schlitten m.

sledgehammer ['sledʒhæmə*] n Vorschlaghammer m.

sleek [sliːk] *adj* glatt, glänzend; (*car, boat etc*) schnittig.

sleep [sliːp] (*pt, pp* **slept**) n Schlaf m ♦ vi schlafen ♦ vt: **we can ~ 4** bei uns können 4 Leute schlafen; **to go to ~** einschlafen; **to have a good night's ~** sich richtig ausschlafen; **to put to ~** (*euph: kill*) einschläfern; **to ~ lightly** einen leichten Schlaf haben; **to ~ with sb** (*euph: have sex*) mit jdm schlafen.

▶ **sleep around** vi mit jedem/jeder schlafen.

▶ **sleep in** vi (*oversleep*) verschlafen; (*rise late*) lange schlafen.

sleeper ['sliːpə*] n (*train*) Schlafwagenzug m; (*berth*) Platz m im Schlafwagen; (*BRIT: on track*) Schwelle f; (*person*) Schläfer(in) m(f).

sleepily ['sliːpɪlɪ] *adv* müde, schläfrig.

sleeping accommodation n (*beds etc*) Schlafgelegenheiten pl.

sleeping arrangements npl Bettenverteilung f.

sleeping bag n Schlafsack m.

sleeping car n Schlafwagen m.

sleeping partner (*BRIT*) = **silent partner**.

sleeping pill n Schlaftablette f.

sleeping sickness n Schlafkrankheit f.

sleepless ['sliːplɪs] *adj* (*night*) schlaflos.

sleeplessness ['sliːplɪsnɪs] n Schlaflosigkeit f.

sleepwalk ['sliːpwɔːk] vi schlafwandeln.

sleepwalker ['sliːpwɔːkə*] n Schlafwandler(in) m(f).

sleepy ['sliːpɪ] *adj* müde, schläfrig; (*fig: village etc*) verschlafen; **to be** or **feel ~** müde sein.

sleet [sliːt] n Schneeregen m.

sleeve [sliːv] n Ärmel m; (*of record*) Hülle f; **to have sth up one's ~** (*fig*) etw in petto haben.

sleeveless ['sliːvlɪs] *adj* (*garment*) ärmellos.

sleigh [sleɪ] n (Pferde)schlitten m.

sleight [slaɪt] n: **~ of hand** Fingerfertigkeit f.

slender ['slendə*] *adj* schlank, schmal; (*small*) knapp.

slept [slept] *pt, pp of* **sleep**.

sleuth [sluːθ] n Detektiv m.

slew [sluː] vi (*BRIT: also*: **~ round**) herumschwenken; **the bus ~ed across the road** der Bus rutschte über die Straße ♦ *pt of* **slay**.

slice [slaɪs] n Scheibe f; (*utensil*) Wender m ♦ vt (in Scheiben) schneiden; **~d bread** aufgeschnittenes Brot nt; **the best thing since ~d bread** der/die/das Allerbeste.

slick [slɪk] *adj* professionell; (*pej*) glatt ♦ n (*also*: **oil ~**) Ölteppich m.

slid [slɪd] *pt, pp of* **slide**.

slide [slaɪd] (*pt, pp* **slid**) n (*on ice etc*) Rutschen nt; (*fig: to ruin etc*) Abgleiten nt; (*in playground*) Rutschbahn f; (*PHOT*) Dia nt; (*BRIT: also*: **hair ~**) Spange f; (*microscope slide*) Objektträger m; (*in prices*) Preisrutsch m ♦ vt schieben ♦ vi (*slip*) rutschen; (*glide*) gleiten; **to let things ~** (*fig*) die Dinge schleifen lassen.

slide projector n Diaprojektor m.

slide rule n Rechenschieber m.

sliding ['slaɪdɪŋ] *adj* (*door, window etc*) Schiebe-.

sliding roof n (*AUT*) Schiebedach nt.

sliding scale n gleitende Skala f.

slight [slaɪt] *adj* zierlich; (*small*) gering; (*error, accent, pain etc*) leicht; (*trivial*) leicht ♦ *n*: **a ~ (on sb/sth)** ein Affront *m* (gegen jdn/etw); **the ~est noise** der geringste Lärm; **the ~est problem** das kleinste Problem; **I haven't the ~est idea** ich habe nicht die geringste Ahnung; **not in the ~est** nicht im Geringsten.

slightly ['slaɪtlɪ] *adv* etwas, ein bisschen; **~ built** zierlich.

slim [slɪm] *adj* schlank; (*chance*) gering ♦ *vi* eine Schlankheitskur machen, abnehmen.

slime [slaɪm] *n* Schleim *m*.

slimming ['slɪmɪŋ] *n* Abnehmen *nt*.

slimy ['slaɪmɪ] *adj* (*lit, fig*) schleimig.

sling [slɪŋ] (*pt, pp* **slung**) *n* Schlinge *f*; (*for baby*) Tragetuch *nt*; (*weapon*) Schleuder *f* ♦ *vt* schleudern; **to have one's arm in a ~** den Arm in der Schlinge tragen.

slingshot ['slɪŋʃɔt] *n* Steinschleuder *f*.

slink [slɪŋk] (*pt, pp* **slunk**) *vi*: **to ~ away** *or* **off** sich davonschleichen.

slinky ['slɪŋkɪ] *adj* (*dress*) eng anliegend.

slip [slɪp] *n* (*fall*) Ausrutschen *nt*; (*mistake*) Fehler *m*, Schnitzer *m*; (*underskirt*) Unterrock *m*; (*also:* **~ of paper**) Zettel *m* ♦ *vt* (*slide*) stecken ♦ *vi* ausrutschen; (*decline*) fallen; **he had a nasty ~** er ist ausgerutscht und böse gefallen; **to give sb the ~** jdm entwischen; **a ~ of the tongue** ein Versprecher *m*; **to ~ into/out of sth, to ~ sth on/off** in etw *acc*/aus etw schlüpfen; **to let a chance ~ by** eine Gelegenheit ungenutzt lassen; **it ~ped from her hand** es rutschte ihr aus der Hand.

► **slip away** *vi* sich davonschleichen.

► **slip in** *vt* stecken in *+acc*.

► **slip out** *vi* kurz weggehen.

► **slip up** *vi* sich vertun (*inf*).

slip-on ['slɪpɔn] *adj* zum Überziehen; **~ shoes** Slipper *pl*.

slipped disc [slɪpt-] *n* Bandscheibenschaden *m*.

slipper ['slɪpə*] *n* Pantoffel *m*, Hausschuh *m*.

slippery ['slɪpərɪ] *adj* (*lit, fig*) glatt; (*fish etc*) schlüpfrig.

slippy ['slɪpɪ] *adj* (*slippery*) glatt.

slip road (*BRIT*) *n* (*to motorway etc*) Auffahrt *f*; (*from motorway etc*) Ausfahrt *f*.

slipshod ['slɪpʃɔd] *adj* schludrig (*inf*).

slipstream ['slɪpstriːm] *n* (*TECH*) Sog *m*; (*AUT*) Windschatten *m*.

slip-up ['slɪpʌp] *n* Fehler *m*, Schnitzer *m*.

slipway ['slɪpweɪ] *n* (*NAUT*) Ablaufbahn *f*.

slit [slɪt] (*pt, pp* **slit**) *n* Schlitz *m*; (*tear*) Riss *m* ♦ *vt* aufschlitzen; **to ~ sb's throat** jdm die Kehle aufschlitzen.

slither ['slɪðə*] *vi* rutschen; (*snake etc*) gleiten.

sliver ['slɪvə*] *n* (*of glass, wood*) Splitter *m*; (*of cheese etc*) Scheibchen *nt*.

slob [slɔb] (*inf*) *n* Drecksau *f* (!).

slog [slɔg] (*BRIT*) *vi* (*work hard*) schuften ♦ *n*: **it**

was a hard ~ es war eine ganz schöne Schufterei; **to ~ away at sth** sich mit etw abrackern.

slogan ['sləugən] *n* Slogan *m*.

slop [slɔp] *vi* schwappen ♦ *vt* verschütten.

► **slop out** *vi* (*in prison etc*) den Toiletteneimer ausleeren.

slope [sləup] *n* Hügel *m*; (*side of mountain*) Hang *m*; (*ski slope*) Piste *f*; (*slant*) Neigung *f* ♦ *vi*: **to ~ down** abfallen; **to ~ up** ansteigen.

sloping ['sləupɪŋ] *adj* (*upwards*) ansteigend; (*downwards*) abfallend; (*roof, handwriting*) schräg.

sloppy ['slɔpɪ] *adj* (*work*) nachlässig; (*appearance*) schlampig; (*sentimental*) rührselig.

slops [slɔps] *npl* Abfallbrühe *f*.

slosh [slɔʃ] (*inf*) *vi*: **to ~ around** *or* **about** (*person*) herumplan(t)schen; (*liquid*) herumschwappen.

sloshed [slɔʃt] (*inf*) *adj* (*drunk*) blau.

slot [slɔt] *n* Schlitz *m*; (*fig: in timetable*) Termin *m*; (*: RADIO, TV*) Sendezeit *f* ♦ *vt*: **to ~ sth in** etw hineinstecken ♦ *vi*: **to ~ into** sich einfügen lassen in *+acc*.

sloth [sləuθ] *n* (*laziness*) Trägheit *f*, Faulheit *f*; (*ZOOL*) Faultier *nt*.

slot machine *n* (*BRIT*) Münzautomat *m*; (*for gambling*) Spielautomat *m*.

slot meter (*BRIT*) *n* Münzzähler *m*.

slouch [slautʃ] *vi* eine krumme Haltung haben; (*when walking*) krumm gehen ♦ *n*: **he's no ~** er hat etwas los (*inf*); **she was ~ed in a chair** sie hing auf einem Stuhl.

Slovak ['sləuvæk] *adj* slowakisch ♦ *n* Slowake *m*, Slowakin *f*; (*LING*) Slowakisch *nt*; **the ~ Republic** die Slowakische Republik.

Slovakia [sləu'vækɪə] *n* die Slowakei.

Slovakian [sləu'vækɪən] *adj, n* = **Slovak**.

Slovene ['sləuviːn] *n* Slowene *m*, Slowenin *f*; (*LING*) Slowenisch *nt* ♦ *adj* slowenisch.

Slovenia [sləu'viːnɪə] *n* Slowenien *nt*.

Slovenian [sləu'viːnɪən] *adj, n* = **Slovene**.

slovenly ['slʌvənlɪ] *adj* schlampig; (*careless*) nachlässig, schludrig (*inf*).

slow [sləu] *adj* langsam; (*not clever*) langsam, begriffsstutzig ♦ *adv* langsam ♦ *vt* (*also:* **~ down, ~ up**) verlangsamen; (*business*) verschlechtern ♦ *vi* (*also:* **~ down, ~ up**) sich verlangsamen; (*business*) schlechter gehen; **to be ~** (*watch, clock*) nachgehen; **"~"** „langsam fahren"; **at a ~ speed** langsam; **to be ~ to act** sich *dat* Zeit lassen; **to be ~ to decide** lange brauchen, um sich zu entscheiden; **my watch is 20 minutes ~** meine Uhr geht 20 Minuten nach; **business is ~** das Geschäft geht schlecht; **to go ~** (*driver*) langsam fahren; (*BRIT: in industrial dispute*) einen Bummelstreik machen.

slow-acting [sləu'æktɪŋ] *adj* mit Langzeitwirkung.

slowly ['sləulɪ] *adv* langsam.

slow motion *n*: **in ~** in Zeitlupe.
slow-moving [sləu'muːvɪŋ] *adj* langsam;
(*traffic*) kriechend.
slowness ['sləunɪs] *n* Langsamkeit *f*.
sludge [slʌdʒ] *n* Schlamm *m*.
slue [sluː] (*US*) *vi* = **slew**.
slug [slʌg] *n* Nacktschnecke *f*; (*US: inf: bullet*)
Kugel *f*.
sluggish ['slʌgɪʃ] *adj* träge; (*engine*) lahm;
(*COMM*) flau.
sluice [sluːs] *n* Schleuse *f*; (*channel*)
(Wasch)rinne *f* ♦ *vt*: **to ~ down** *or* **out**
abspritzen.
slum [slʌm] *n* Slum *m*, Elendsviertel *nt*.
slumber ['slʌmbə*] *n* Schlaf *m*.
slump [slʌmp] *n* Rezession *f* ♦ *vi* fallen; **~ in
sales** Absatzflaute *f*; **~ in prices** Preissturz
m; **he was ~ed over the wheel** er war über
dem Steuer zusammengesackt.
slung [slʌŋ] *pt, pp of* **sling**.
slunk [slʌŋk] *pt, pp of* **slink**.
slur [sləː*] *n* (*fig*): **~ (on)** Beleidigung *f* (für)
♦ *vt* (*words*) undeutlich aussprechen; **to cast
a ~ on** verunglimpfen.
slurp [sləːp] (*inf*) *vt, vi* schlürfen.
slurred [sləːd] *adj* (*speech, voice*) undeutlich.
slush [slʌʃ] *n* (*melted snow*) Schneematsch *m*.
slush fund *n* Schmiergelder *pl*,
Schmiergeldfonds *m*.
slushy ['slʌʃɪ] *adj* matschig; (*BRIT, fig*)
schmalzig.
slut [slʌt] (*pej*) *n* Schlampe *f*.
sly [slaɪ] *adj* (*smile, expression*) wissend;
(*remark*) viel sagend; (*person*) schlau,
gerissen; **on the ~** heimlich.
S/M *n abbr* (= *sadomasochism*) S/M.
smack [smæk] *n* Klaps *m*; (*on face*) Ohrfeige *f*
♦ *vt* (*hit*) schlagen; (: *child*) einen Klaps
geben +*dat*; (: *on face*) ohrfeigen ♦ *vi*: **to ~ of**
riechen nach ♦ *adv*: **it fell ~ in the middle**
(*inf*) es fiel genau in die Mitte; **to ~ one's
lips** schmatzen.
smacker ['smækə*] (*inf*) *n* (*kiss*) Schmatzer *m*.
small [smɔːl] *adj* klein ♦ *n*: **the ~ of the back**
das Kreuz; **to get** *or* **grow ~er** (*thing*)
kleiner werden; (*numbers*) zurückgehen; **to
make ~er** (*amount, income*) kürzen; (*object,
garment*) kleiner machen; **a ~ shopkeeper**
der Inhaber eines kleinen Geschäfts; **a
~ business** ein Kleinunternehmen *nt*.
small ads (*BRIT*) *npl* Kleinanzeigen *pl*.
small arms *n* Handfeuerwaffen *pl*.
small business *n* Kleinunternehmen *nt*.
small change *n* Kleingeld *nt*.
small fry *npl* (*unimportant people*) kleine
Fische *pl*.
smallholder ['smɔːlhəuldə*] (*BRIT*) *n*
Kleinbauer *m*.
smallholding ['smɔːlhəuldɪŋ] (*BRIT*) *n* kleiner
Landbesitz *m*.
small hours *npl*: **in the ~** in den frühen
Morgenstunden.

smallish ['smɔːlɪʃ] *adj* ziemlich klein.
small-minded [smɔːl'maɪndɪd] *adj* engstirnig.
smallpox ['smɔːlpɒks] *n* Pocken *pl*.
small print *n*: **the ~** das Kleingedruckte *or*
klein Gedruckte.
small-scale ['smɔːlskeɪl] *adj* (*map, model*) in
verkleinertem Maßstab; (*business, farming*)
klein angelegt.
small talk *n* (oberflächliche) Konversation *f*.
small-time ['smɔːltaɪm] *adj* (*farmer etc*) klein; **a
~ thief** ein kleiner Ganove.
small-town ['smɔːltaun] *adj* kleinstädtisch.
smarmy ['smɑːmɪ] (*BRIT: pej*) *adj* schmierig.
smart [smɑːt] *adj* (*neat*) ordentlich, gepflegt;
(*fashionable*) schick, elegant; (*clever*)
intelligent, clever (*inf*); (*quick*) schnell ♦ *vi*
(*sting*) brennen; (*suffer*) leiden; **the ~ set** die
Schickeria (*inf*); **and look ~ (about it)!** und
zwar ein bisschen plötzlich! (*inf*).
smart card *n* Chipkarte *f*.
smarten up ['smɑːtn-] *vi* sich fein machen
♦ *vt* verschönern.
smash [smæʃ] *n* (*also: ~-up*) Unfall *m*; (*sound*)
Krachen *nt*; (*song, play, film*) Superhit *m*;
(*TENNIS*) Schmetterball *m* ♦ *vt* (*break*)
zerbrechen; (*car etc*) kaputtfahren; (*hopes*)
zerschlagen; (*SPORT: record*) haushoch
schlagen ♦ *vi* (*break*) zerbrechen; (*against
wall, into sth etc*) krachen.
▶ **smash up** *vt* (*car*) kaputtfahren; (*room*)
kurz und klein schlagen (*inf*).
smash hit *n* Superhit *m*.
smashing ['smæʃɪŋ] (*inf*) *adj* super, toll.
smattering ['smætərɪŋ] *n*: **a ~ of Greek** *etc* ein
paar Brocken Griechisch *etc*.
smear [smɪə*] *n* (*trace*) verschmierter Fleck
m; (*insult*) Verleumdung *f*; (*MED*) Abstrich *m*
♦ *vt* (*spread*) verschmieren; (*make dirty*)
beschmieren; **his hands were ~ed with oil/
ink** seine Hände waren mit Öl/Tinte
beschmiert.
smear campaign *n* Verleumdungskampagne
f.
smear test *n* Abstrich *m*.
smell [smɛl] (*pt, pp* **smelt** *or* **smelled**) *n* Geruch
m; (*sense*) Geruchssinn *m* ♦ *vt* riechen ♦ *vi*
riechen; (*pej*) stinken; (*pleasantly*) duften; **to
~ of** riechen nach.
smelly ['smɛlɪ] (*pej*) *adj* stinkend.
smelt [smɛlt] *pt, pp of* **smell** ♦ *vt* schmelzen.
smile [smaɪl] *n* Lächeln *nt* ♦ *vi* lächeln.
smiling ['smaɪlɪŋ] *adj* lächelnd.
smirk [sməːk] (*pej*) *n* Grinsen *nt*.
smithy ['smɪðɪ] *n* Schmiede *f*.
smitten ['smɪtn] *adj*: **~ with** vernarrt in +*acc*.
smock [smɒk] *n* Kittel *m*; (*US: overall*) Overall
m.
smog [smɒg] *n* Smog *m*.
smoke [sməuk] *n* Rauch *m* ♦ *vi, vt* rauchen; **to
have a ~** eine rauchen; **to go up in ~** in
Rauch (und Flammen) aufgehen; (*fig*) sich
in Rauch auflösen; **do you ~?** rauchen Sie?

smoked [sməukt] *adj* geräuchert, Räucher-;
~ **glass** Rauchglas *nt*.
smokeless fuel ['sməuklıs-] *n* rauchlose
Kohle *f*.
smokeless zone (*BRIT*) *n* rauchfreie Zone *f*.
smoker ['sməukə*] *n* Raucher(in) *m(f)*; (*RAIL*)
Raucherabteil *nt*.
smoke screen *n* Rauchvorhang *m*; (*fig*)
Deckmantel *m*.
smoke shop (*US*) *n* Tabakladen *m*.
smoking ['sməukıŋ] *n* Rauchen *nt*; "**no** ~"
„Rauchen verboten".
smoking compartment, (*US*) **smoking car**
n Raucherabteil *nt*.
smoking room *n* Raucherzimmer *nt*.
smoky ['sməukı] *adj* verraucht; (*taste*)
rauchig.
smolder ['sməuldə*] (*US*) *vi* = **smoulder**.
smoochy ['smu:tʃı] *adj* (*music, tape*) zum
Schmusen.
smooth [smu:ð] *adj* (*lit, fig: pej*) glatt; (*flavour,
whisky*) weich; (*movement*) geschmeidig;
(*flight*) ruhig.
▶ **smooth out** *vt* glätten; (*fig: difficulties*) aus
dem Weg räumen.
▶ **smooth over** *vt*: **to** ~ **things over** (*fig*) die
Sache bereinigen.
smoothly ['smu:ðlı] *adv* reibungslos, glatt;
everything went ~ alles ging glatt über die
Bühne.
smoothness ['smu:ðnıs] *n* Glätte *f*; (*of flight*)
Ruhe *f*.
smother ['smʌðə*] *vt* (*fire, person*) ersticken;
(*repress*) unterdrücken.
smoulder, (*US*) **smolder** ['sməuldə*] *vi* (*lit, fig*)
glimmen, schwelen.
smudge [smʌdʒ] *n* Schmutzfleck *m* ♦ *vt*
verwischen.
smug [smʌg] (*pej*) *adj* selbstgefällig.
smuggle ['smʌgl] *vt* schmuggeln; **to** ~ **in/out**
einschmuggeln/herausschmuggeln.
smuggler ['smʌglə*] *n* Schmuggler(in) *m(f)*.
smuggling ['smʌglıŋ] *n* Schmuggel *m*.
smut [smʌt] *n* (*grain of soot*) Rußflocke *f*; (*in
conversation etc*) Schmutz *m*.
smutty ['smʌtı] *adj* (*fig: joke, book*) schmutzig.
snack [snæk] *n* Kleinigkeit *f* (zu essen); **to
have a** ~ eine Kleinigkeit essen.
snack bar *n* Imbissstube *f*.
snag [snæg] *n* Haken *m*, Schwierigkeit *f*.
snail [sneıl] *n* Schnecke *f*.
snake [sneık] *n* Schlange *f*.
snap [snæp] *n* Knacken *nt*; (*photograph*)
Schnappschuss *m*; (*card game*) ≈
Schnippschnapp *nt* ♦ *adj* (*decision*) plötzlich,
spontan ♦ *vt* (*break*) (zer)brechen ♦ *vi* (*break*)
(zer)brechen; (*rope, thread etc*) reißen; **a cold**
~ ein Kälteeinbruch *m*; **his patience** ~**ped**
ihm riss der Geduldsfaden; **his temper**
~**ped** er verlor die Beherrschung; **to**
~ **one's fingers** mit den Fingern schnipsen
or schnalzen; **to** ~ **open/shut** auf-/

zuschnappen.
▶ **snap at** *vt fus* (*dog*) schnappen nach; (*fig:
person*) anschnauzen (*inf*).
▶ **snap off** *vt* (*break*) abbrechen.
▶ **snap up** *vt* (*bargains*) wegschnappen.
snap fastener *n* Druckknopf *m*.
snappy ['snæpı] (*inf*) *adj* (*answer*) kurz und
treffend; (*slogan*) zündend; **make it** ~ ein
bisschen dalli!; **he is a** ~ **dresser** er zieht
sich flott an.
snapshot ['snæpʃɔt] *n* Schnappschuss *m*.
snare [snɛə*] *n* Falle *f* ♦ *vt* (*lit, fig*) fangen.
snarl [snɑ:l] *vi* knurren ♦ *vt*: **to get** ~**ed up**
(*plans*) durcheinander kommen; (*traffic*)
stocken.
snarl-up ['snɑ:lʌp] *n* Verkehrschaos *nt*.
snatch [snætʃ] *n* (*of conversation*) Fetzen *m*; (*of
song*) paar Takte *pl* ♦ *vt* (*grab*) greifen; (*steal*)
stehlen, klauen (*inf*); (*child*) entführen; (*fig:
opportunity*) ergreifen; (: *look*) werfen ♦ *vi*:
don't ~! nicht grapschen!; **to** ~ **a sandwich**
schnell ein Butterbrot essen; **to** ~ **some
sleep** etwas Schlaf ergattern.
▶ **snatch up** *vt* schnappen.
snazzy ['snæzı] (*inf*) *adj* flott.
sneak [sni:k] (*pt* (*US*) *also* **snuck**) *vi*: **to** ~ **in/out**
sich einschleichen/sich hinausschleichen
♦ *vt*: **to** ~ **a look at sth** heimlich auf etw *acc*
schielen ♦ *n* (*inf: pej*) Petze *f*.
▶ **sneak up** *vi*: **to** ~ **up on sb** sich an jdn
heranschleichen.
sneakers ['sni:kəz] *npl* Freizeitschuhe *pl*.
sneaking ['sni:kıŋ] *adj*: **to have a** ~ **feeling/
suspicion that ...** das ungute Gefühl/den
leisen Verdacht haben, dass ...
sneaky ['sni:kı] (*pej*) *adj* raffiniert.
sneer [snıə*] *vi* (*smile nastily*) spöttisch
lächeln; (*mock*): **to** ~ **at** verspotten ♦ *n*
(*smile*) spöttisches Lächeln *nt*; (*remark*)
spöttische Bemerkung *f*.
sneeze [sni:z] *n* Niesen *nt* ♦ *vi* niesen.
▶ **sneeze at** *vt fus*: **it's not to be** ~**d at** es ist
nicht zu verachten.
snicker ['snıkə*] *vi see* **snigger**.
snide [snaıd] (*pej*) *adj* abfällig.
sniff [snıf] *n* Schniefen *nt*; (*smell*) Schnüffeln
nt ♦ *vi* schniefen ♦ *vt* riechen, schnuppern an
+*dat*; (*glue*) schnüffeln.
sniffer dog ['snıfə-] *n* Spürhund *m*.
snigger ['snıgə*] *vi* kichern.
snip [snıp] *n* Schnitt *m*; (*BRIT: inf: bargain*)
Schnäppchen *nt* ♦ *vt* schnippeln; **to** ~ **sth
off/through sth** etw abschnippeln/
durchschnippeln.
sniper ['snaıpə*] *n* Heckenschütze *m*.
snippet ['snıpıt] *n* (*of information*) Bruchstück
nt; (*of conversation*) Fetzen *m*.
snivelling, (*US*) **sniveling** ['snıvlıŋ] *adj*
heulend.
snob [snɔb] *n* Snob *m*.
snobbery ['snɔbərı] *n* Snobismus *m*.
snobbish ['snɔbıʃ] *adj* snobistisch, versnobt

(*inf*).

snog [snɔg] (*BRIT: inf*) *n* Knutscherei *f*; **to have a ~ with sb** mit jdm (rum)knutschen ♦ *vi* (rum)knutschen.

snooker ['snuːkə°] *n* Snooker *nt* ♦ *vt* (*BRIT: inf*): **to be ~ed** festsitzen.

snoop [snuːp] *vi*: **to ~ about** herumschnüffeln; **to ~ on sb** jdm nachschnüffeln.

snooper ['snuːpə°] *n* Schnüffler(in) *m(f)*.

snooty ['snuːtɪ] *adj* hochnäsig.

snooze [snuːz] *n* Schläfchen *nt* ♦ *vi* ein Schläfchen machen.

snore [snɔː°] *n* Schnarchen *nt* ♦ *vi* schnarchen.

snoring ['snɔːrɪŋ] *n* Schnarchen *nt*.

snorkel ['snɔːkl] *n* Schnorchel *m*.

snort [snɔːt] *n* Schnauben *nt* ♦ *vi* (*animal*) schnauben; (*person*) prusten ♦ *vt* (*inf: cocaine*) schnüffeln.

snotty ['snɔtɪ] (*inf*) *adj* (*handkerchief, nose*) Rotz-; (*pej: snobbish*) hochnäsig.

snout [snaut] *n* Schnauze *f*.

snow [snəu] *n* Schnee *m* ♦ *vi* schneien ♦ *vt*: **to be ~ed under with work** mit Arbeit reichlich eingedeckt sein; **it's ~ing** es schneit.

snowball ['snəubɔːl] *n* Schneeball *m* ♦ *vi* (*fig: problem*) eskalieren; (: *campaign*) ins Rollen kommen.

snowbound ['snəubaund] *adj* eingeschneit.

snow-capped ['snəukæpt] *adj* schneebedeckt.

snowdrift ['snəudrɪft] *n* Schneewehe *f*.

snowdrop ['snəudrɔp] *n* Schneeglöckchen *nt*.

snowfall ['snəufɔːl] *n* Schneefall *m*.

snowflake ['snəufleɪk] *n* Schneeflocke *f*.

snowline ['snəulaɪn] *n* Schneegrenze *f*.

snowman ['snəumæn] (*irreg: like* **man**) *n* Schneemann *m*.

snowplough, (*US*) **snowplow** ['snəuplau] *n* Schneepflug *m*.

snowshoe ['snəuʃuː] *n* Schneeschuh *m*.

snowstorm ['snəustɔːm] *n* Schneesturm *m*.

snowy ['snəuɪ] *adj* schneeweiß; (*covered with snow*) verschneit.

SNP (*BRIT*) *n abbr* (*POL*) = **Scottish National Party**.

snub [snʌb] *vt* (*person*) vor den Kopf stoßen ♦ *n* Abfuhr *f*.

snub-nosed [snʌb'nəuzd] *adj* stupsnasig.

snuff [snʌf] *n* Schnupftabak *m* ♦ *vt* (*also: ~ out: candle*) auslöschen.

snuff movie *n* Pornofilm, in dem jemand tatsächlich stirbt.

snug [snʌg] *adj* behaglich, gemütlich; (*well-fitting*) gut sitzend; **it's a ~ fit** es passt genau.

snuggle ['snʌgl] *vi*: **to ~ up to sb** sich an jdn kuscheln; **to ~ down in bed** sich ins Bett kuscheln.

snugly ['snʌglɪ] *adv* behaglich; **it fits ~** (*object in pocket etc*) es passt genau hinein; (*garment*) es passt wie angegossen.

SO *n abbr* (*BANKING*) = **standing order**.

═══════════════════ *KEYWORD*

so [səu] *adv* **1** (*thus, likewise*) so; **~ saying he walked away** mit diesen Worten ging er weg; **if ~** falls ja; **I didn't do it - you did ~!** ich hab es nicht getan - hast du wohl!; **~ do I, ~ am I** *etc* ich auch; **it's 5 o'clock - ~ it is!** es ist 5 Uhr - tatsächlich!; **I hope/think ~** ich hoffe/glaube ja; **~ far** bis jetzt.

2 (*in comparisons etc: to such a degree*) so; **~ big/quickly (that)** so groß/schnell(, dass); **I'm ~ glad to see you** ich bin ja so froh, dich zu sehen.

3: **~ much** so viel; **I've got ~ much work** ich habe so viel Arbeit; **I love you ~ much** ich liebe dich so sehr; **~ many** so viele.

4 (*phrases*): **10 or ~** 10 oder so; **~ long!** (*inf: goodbye*) tschüss!

♦ *conj* **1** (*expressing purpose*): **~ as to do sth** um etw zu tun; **~ (that)** damit.

2 (*expressing result*) also; **~ I was right after all** ich hatte also doch Recht; **~ you see, I could have gone** wie Sie sehen, hätte ich gehen können; **~ (what)?** na und?

─────────────────────────

soak [səuk] *vt* (*drench*) durchnässen; (*steep*) einweichen ♦ *vi* einweichen; **to be ~ed through** völlig durchnässt sein.

▶ **soak in** *vi* einziehen.

▶ **soak up** *vt* aufsaugen.

soaking ['səukɪŋ] *adj* (*also: ~ wet*) patschnass.

so-and-so ['səuənsəu] *n* (*somebody*) Soundso *no art*; **Mr/Mrs ~** Herr/Frau Soundso; **the little ~!** (*pej*) das Biest!

soap [səup] *n* Seife *f*; (*TV: also: ~ opera*) Fernsehserie *f*, Seifenoper *f* (*inf*).

soapbox ['səupbɔks] *n* (*lit*) Seifenkiste *f*; (*fig: platform*) Apfelsinenkiste *f*.

soapflakes ['səupfleɪks] *npl* Seifenflocken *pl*.

soap opera *n* (*TV*) Fernsehserie *f*, Seifenoper *f* (*inf*).

soap powder *n* Seifenpulver *nt*.

soapsuds ['səupsʌds] *npl* Seifenschaum *m*.

soapy ['səupɪ] *adj* seifig; **~ water** Seifenwasser *nt*.

soar [sɔː°] *vi* aufsteigen; (*price, temperature*) hochschnellen; (*building etc*) aufragen.

soaring ['sɔːrɪŋ] *adj* (*prices*) in die Höhe schnellend; (*inflation*) unaufhaltsam.

sob [sɔb] *n* Schluchzer *m* ♦ *vi* schluchzen.

s.o.b. (*US: inf!*) *n abbr* (= *son of a bitch*) Scheißkerl *m*.

sober ['səubə°] *adj* nüchtern; (*serious*) ernst; (*colour*) gedeckt; (*style*) schlicht.

▶ **sober up** *vt* nüchtern machen ♦ *vi* nüchtern werden.

sobriety [sə'braɪətɪ] *n* Nüchternheit *f*; (*seriousness*) Ernst *m*.

sobriquet ['səubrɪkeɪ] *n* Spitzname *m*.

sob story *n* rührselige Geschichte *f*.

Soc. *abbr* (= *society*) Ges.

so-called ['səu'kɔːld] *adj* so genannt.
soccer ['sɔkə*] *n* Fußball *m*.
soccer pitch *n* Fußballplatz *m*.
soccer player *n* Fußballspieler(in) *m(f)*.
sociable ['səuʃəbl] *adj* gesellig.
social ['səuʃl] *adj* sozial; (*history*) Sozial-;
(*structure*) Gesellschafts-; (*event, contact*)
gesellschaftlich; (*person*) gesellig; (*animal*)
gesellig lebend ♦ *n* (*party*) geselliger Abend
m; ~ **life** gesellschaftliches Leben *nt*; **to
have no** ~ **life** nicht mit anderen Leuten
zusammenkommen.
social class *n* Gesellschaftsklasse *f*.
social climber (*pej*) *n* Emporkömmling *m*,
sozialer Aufsteiger *m*.
social club *n* Klub *m* für geselliges
Beisammensein.
Social Democrat *n* Sozialdemokrat(in) *m(f)*.
social insurance (*US*) *n* Sozialversicherung
f.
socialism ['səuʃəlɪzəm] *n* Sozialismus *m*.
socialist ['səuʃəlɪst] *adj* sozialistisch ♦ *n*
Sozialist(in) *m(f)*.
socialite ['səuʃəlaɪt] *n* Angehörige(r) *f(m)* der
Schickeria.
socialize ['səuʃəlaɪz] *vi* unter die Leute
kommen; **to** ~ **with** (*meet socially*)
gesellschaftlich verkehren mit; (*chat to*)
sich unterhalten mit.
socially ['səuʃəlɪ] *adv* (*visit*) privat; (*acceptable*)
in Gesellschaft.
social science *n* Sozialwissenschaft *f*.
social security (*BRIT*) *n* Sozialhilfe *f*;
Department of Social Security Ministerium
nt für Soziales.
social services *npl* soziale Einrichtungen *pl*.
social welfare *n* soziales Wohl *nt*.
social work *n* Sozialarbeit *f*.
social worker *n* Sozialarbeiter(in) *m(f)*.
society [sə'saɪətɪ] *n* Gesellschaft *f*; (*people,
their lifestyle*) die Gesellschaft; (*club*) Verein
m; (*also:* **high** ~) Highsociety *f* ♦ *cpd* (*party,
lady*) Gesellschafts-.
socioeconomic ['səusɪəui:kə'nɔmɪk] *adj*
sozioökonomisch.
sociological [səusɪə'lɔdʒɪkl] *adj* soziologisch.
sociologist [səusɪ'ɔlədʒɪst] *n* Soziologe *m*,
Soziologin *f*.
sociology [səusɪ'ɔlədʒɪ] *n* Soziologie *f*.
sock [sɔk] *n* Socke *f* ♦ *vt* (*inf: hit*) hauen; **to pull
one's** ~**s up** (*fig*) sich am Riemen reißen.
socket ['sɔkɪt] *n* (*of eye*) Augenhöhle *f*; (*of
joint*) Gelenkpfanne *f*; (*BRIT: ELEC: wall
socket*) Steckdose *f*; (: *for light bulb*) Fassung
f.
sod [sɔd] *n* (*earth*) Sode *f*; (*BRIT: inf!*) Sau *f* (!);
the poor ~ das arme Schwein.
▶ **sod off** (*BRIT: inf!*) *vi*: **sod off!** verpiss dich!
soda ['səudə] *n* Soda *nt*; (*also:* ~ **water**)
Soda(wasser) *nt*; (*US: also:* ~ **pop**) Brause *f*.
sodden ['sɔdn] *adj* durchnässt.
sodium ['səudɪəm] *n* Natrium *nt*.

sodium chloride *n* Natriumchlorid *nt*,
Kochsalz *nt*.
sofa ['səufə] *n* Sofa *nt*.
Sofia ['səufɪə] *n* Sofia *nt*.
soft [sɔft] *adj* weich; (*not rough*) zart; (*voice,
music, light, colour*) gedämpft; (*lenient*)
nachsichtig; ~ **in the head** (*inf*) nicht ganz
richtig im Kopf.
soft-boiled ['sɔftbɔild] *adj* (*egg*) weich
(gekocht).
soft drink *n* alkoholfreies Getränk *nt*.
soft drugs *npl* weiche Drogen *pl*.
soften ['sɔfn] *vt* weich machen; (*effect, blow*)
mildern ♦ *vi* weich werden; (*voice,
expression*) sanfter werden.
softener ['sɔfnə*] *n* (*water softener*)
Enthärtungsmittel *nt*; (*fabric softener*)
Weichspüler *m*.
soft fruit (*BRIT*) *n* Beerenobst *nt*.
soft furnishings *npl* Raumtextilien *pl*.
soft-hearted [sɔft'hɑːtɪd] *adj* weichherzig.
softly ['sɔftlɪ] *adv* (*gently*) sanft; (*quietly*) leise.
softness ['sɔftnɪs] *n* Weichheit *f*; (*gentleness*)
Sanftheit *f*.
soft option *n* Weg *m* des geringsten
Widerstandes.
soft sell *n* weiche Verkaufstaktik *f*.
soft spot *n*: **to have a** ~ **for sb** eine Schwäche
für jdn haben.
soft target *n* leicht verwundbares Ziel *nt*.
soft toy *n* Stofftier *nt*.
software ['sɔftwɛə*] *n* (*COMPUT*) Software *f*.
software package *n* (*COMPUT*)
Softwarepaket *nt*.
soft water *n* weiches Wasser *nt*.
soggy ['sɔgɪ] *adj* (*ground*) durchweicht;
(*sandwiches etc*) matschig.
soil [sɔil] *n* Erde *f*, Boden *m* ♦ *vt* beschmutzen.
soiled [sɔild] *adj* schmutzig.
sojourn ['sɔdʒəːn] *n* (*form*) Aufenthalt *m*.
solace ['sɔlɪs] *n* Trost *m*.
solar ['səulə*] *adj* (*eclipse, power station etc*)
Sonnen-.
solarium [sə'lɛərɪəm] *n* (*pl* **solaria**) *n* Solarium *nt*.
solar panel *n* Sonnenkollektor *m*.
solar plexus [-'plɛksəs] *n* (*ANAT*) Solarplexus
m, Magengrube *f*.
solar power *n* Sonnenenergie *f*.
solar system *n* Sonnensystem *nt*.
solar wind *n* Sonnenwind *m*.
sold [səuld] *pt, pp of* **sell**.
solder ['səuldə*] *vt* löten ♦ *n* Lötmittel *nt*.
soldier ['səuldʒə*] *n* Soldat *m* ♦ *vi*: **to** ~ **on**
unermüdlich weitermachen; **toy** ~
Spielzeugsoldat *m*.
sold out *adj* ausverkauft.
sole [səul] *n* Sohle *f*; (*fish: pl inv*) Seezunge *f*
♦ *adj* einzig, Allein-; (*exclusive*) alleinig; **the**
~ **reason** der einzige Grund.
solely ['səullɪ] *adv* nur, ausschließlich; **I will
hold you** ~ **responsible** ich mache Sie allein
dafür verantwortlich.

solemn ['sɔləm] *adj* feierlich; (*person*) ernst.

sole trader *n* (*COMM*) Einzelunternehmer *m*.

solicit [sə'lɪsɪt] *vt* (*request*) erbitten, bitten um ♦ *vi* (*prostitute*) Kunden anwerben.

solicitor [sə'lɪsɪtə*] (*BRIT*) *n* Rechtsanwalt *m*, Rechtsanwältin *f*.

solid ['sɔlɪd] *adj* (*not hollow, pure*) massiv; (*not liquid*) fest; (*reliable*) zuverlässig; (*strong*: *structure*) stabil; (: *foundations*) solide; (*substantial*: *advice*) gut; (: *experience*) solide; (*unbroken*) ununterbrochen ♦ *n* (*solid object*) Festkörper *m*; **solids** *npl* (*food*) feste Nahrung *f*; **to be on ~ ground** (*fig*) sich auf festem Boden befinden; **I read for 2 hours ~** ich habe 2 Stunden ununterbrochen gelesen.

solidarity [sɔlɪ'dærɪtɪ] *n* Solidarität *f*.

solid fuel *n* fester Brennstoff *m*.

solidify [sə'lɪdɪfaɪ] *vi* fest werden ♦ *vt* fest werden lassen.

solidity [sə'lɪdɪtɪ] *n* (*of structure*) Stabilität *f*; (*of foundations*) Solidität *f*; (*of support*) Geschlossenheit *f*.

solidly ['sɔlɪdlɪ] *adv* (*built*) solide; (*in favour*) geschlossen, einmütig; **a ~ respectable family** eine durch und durch respektable Familie.

solid-state ['sɔlɪdsteɪt] *adj* (*ELEC*: *equipment*) Halbleiter-.

soliloquy [sə'lɪləkwɪ] *n* Monolog *m*.

solitaire [sɔlɪ'tɛə*] *n* (*gem*) Solitär *m*; (*game*) Patience *f*.

solitary ['sɔlɪtərɪ] *adj* einsam; (*single*) einzeln.

solitary confinement *n* Einzelhaft *f*.

solitude ['sɔlɪtjuːd] *n* Einsamkeit *f*; **to live in ~** einsam leben.

solo ['səʊləʊ] *n* Solo *nt* ♦ *adv* (*fly*) allein; (*play, perform*) solo; **~ flight** Alleinflug *m*.

soloist ['səʊləʊɪst] *n* Solist(in) *m(f)*.

Solomon ['sɔləmən] *n* Salomo(n) *m*.

Solomon Islands ['sɔləmən-] *npl*: **the ~** die Salomoninseln *pl*.

solstice ['sɔlstɪs] *n* Sonnenwende *f*.

soluble ['sɔljubl] *adj* löslich.

solution [sə'luːʃən] *n* (*answer, liquid*) Lösung *f*; (*to crossword*) Auflösung *f*; (*of crime*) Aufklärung *f*.

solve [sɔlv] *vt* lösen; (*mystery*) enträtseln.

solvency ['sɔlvənsɪ] *n* (*COMM*) Zahlungsfähigkeit *f*.

solvent ['sɔlvənt] *adj* (*COMM*) zahlungsfähig ♦ *n* (*CHEM*) Lösungsmittel *nt*.

solvent abuse *n* Lösungsmittelmissbrauch *m*.

Som. (*BRIT*) *abbr* (*POST*: = *Somerset*).

Somali [sə'mɑːlɪ] *adj* somalisch ♦ *n* Somalier(in) *m(f)*.

Somalia [sə'mɑːlɪə] *n* Somalia *nt*.

Somaliland *n* (*formerly*) Somaliland *nt*.

sombre, (*US*) **somber** ['sɔmbə*] *adj* (*dark*) dunkel, düster; (*serious*) finster.

some [sʌm] *adj* **1** (*a certain amount or number of*) einige; **~ tea/water/money** etwas Tee/Wasser/Geld; **~ biscuits** ein paar Plätzchen; **~ children came** einige Kinder kamen; **he asked me ~ questions** er stellte mir ein paar Fragen.

2 (*certain*: *in contrasts*) manche(r, s); **~ people say that …** manche Leute sagen, dass …; **~ films were excellent** einige *or* manche Filme waren ausgezeichnet.

3 (*unspecified*) irgendein(e); **~ woman was asking for you** eine Frau hat nach Ihnen gefragt; **~ day** eines Tages; **~ day next week** irgendwann nächste Woche; **that's ~ house!** das ist vielleicht ein Haus!

♦ *pron* **1** (*a certain number*) einige; **I've got ~** (*books etc*) ich habe welche.

2 (*a certain amount*) etwas; **I've got ~** (*money, milk*) ich habe welche(s); **I've read ~ of the book** ich habe das Buch teilweise gelesen

♦ *adv*: **~ 10 people** etwa 10 Leute.

somebody ['sʌmbədɪ] *pron* = **someone.**

someday ['sʌmdeɪ] *adv* irgendwann.

somehow ['sʌmhaʊ] *adv* irgendwie.

someone ['sʌmwʌn] *pron* (*in irgend*)jemand; **there's ~ coming** es kommt jemand; **I saw ~ in the garden** ich habe jemanden im Garten gesehen.

someplace ['sʌmpleɪs] (*US*) *adv* = **somewhere.**

somersault ['sʌməsɔːlt] *n* Salto *m* ♦ *vi* einen Salto machen; (*vehicle*) sich überschlagen.

something ['sʌmθɪŋ] *pron* etwas; **~ nice** etwas Schönes; **there's ~ wrong** da stimmt etwas nicht; **would you like ~ to eat/drink?** möchten Sie etwas zu essen/trinken?

sometime ['sʌmtaɪm] *adv* irgendwann; **~ last month** irgendwann letzten Monat; **I'll finish it ~** ich werde es irgendwann fertig machen.

sometimes ['sʌmtaɪmz] *adv* manchmal.

somewhat ['sʌmwɔt] *adv* etwas, ein wenig; **~ to my surprise** ziemlich zu meiner Überraschung.

somewhere ['sʌmwɛə*] *adv* (*be*) irgendwo; (*go*) irgendwohin; **~ (or other) in Scotland** irgendwo in Schottland; **~ else** (*be*) woanders; (*go*) woandershin.

son [sʌn] *n* Sohn *m*.

sonar ['səʊnɑː*] *n* Sonar(gerät) *nt*, Echolot *nt*.

sonata [sə'nɑːtə] *n* Sonate *f*.

song [sɔŋ] *n* Lied *nt*; (*of bird*) Gesang *m*.

songbook ['sɔŋbʊk] *n* Liederbuch *nt*.

songwriter ['sɔŋraɪtə*] *n* Liedermacher *m*.

sonic ['sɔnɪk] *adj* (*speed*) Schall-; **~ boom** Überschallknall *m*.

son-in-law ['sʌnɪnlɔː] *n* Schwiegersohn *m*.

sonnet ['sɔnɪt] *n* Sonett *nt*.

sonny ['sʌnɪ] (*inf*) *n* Junge *m*.

soon [suːn] *adv* bald; (*a short time after*) bald,

schnell; (*early*) früh; ~ **afterwards** kurz or
bald danach; **quite** ~ ziemlich bald; **how
~ can you finish it?** bis wann haben Sie es
fertig?; **how ~ can you come back?** wann
können Sie frühestens wiederkommen?; **see
you ~!** bis bald!; *see also* **as**.

sooner ['suːnəʳ] *adv* (*time*) früher, eher;
(*preference*) lieber; **I would ~ do that** das
würde ich lieber tun; ~ **or later** früher oder
später; **the ~ the better** je eher, desto
besser; **no ~ said than done** gesagt, getan;
no ~ had we left than ... wir waren gerade
gegangen, da ...

soot [sut] *n* Ruß *m*.

soothe [suːð] *vt* beruhigen; (*pain*) lindern.

soothing ['suːðɪŋ] *adj* beruhigend; (*ointment
etc*) schmerzlindernd; (*drink*) wohltuend;
(*bath*) entspannend.

SOP *n abbr* (= *standard operating procedure*)
normale Vorgehensweise *f*.

sop [sɔp] *n*: **that's only a ~** das soll nur zur
Beschwichtigung dienen.

sophisticated [sə'fɪstɪkeɪtɪd] *adj* (*woman,
lifestyle*) kultiviert; (*audience*)
anspruchsvoll; (*machinery*) hoch entwickelt;
(*arguments*) differenziert.

sophistication [səfɪstɪ'keɪʃən] *n* (*of person*)
Kultiviertheit *f*; (*of machine*) hoher
Entwicklungsstand *m*; (*of argument etc*)
Differenziertheit *f*.

sophomore ['sɔfəmɔːʳ] (*US*) *n* Student(in) im
2. Studienjahr.

soporific [sɔpə'rɪfɪk] *adj* einschläfernd ♦ *n*
Schlafmittel *nt*.

sopping ['sɔpɪŋ] *adj*: ~ **(wet)** völlig
durchnässt.

soppy ['sɔpɪ] (*pej*) *adj* (*person*) sentimental;
(*film*) schmalzig.

soprano [sə'prɑːnəu] *n* Sopranist(in) *m(f)*.

sorbet ['sɔːbeɪ] *n* Sorbet *nt or m*, Fruchteis *nt*.

sorcerer ['sɔːsərəʳ] *n* Hexenmeister *m*.

sordid ['sɔːdɪd] *adj* (*dirty*) verkommen;
(*wretched*) elend.

sore [sɔːʳ] *adj* wund; (*esp US: offended*)
verärgert, sauer (*inf*) ♦ *n* wunde Stelle *f*; **to
have a ~ throat** Halsschmerzen haben; **it's a
~ point** (*fig*) es ist ein wunder Punkt.

sorely ['sɔːlɪ] *adv*: **I am ~ tempted (to)** ich bin
sehr in Versuchung, zu).

soreness ['sɔːnɪs] *n* (*pain*) Schmerz *m*.

sorrel ['sɔrəl] *n* (*BOT*) (großer) Sauerampfer
m.

sorrow ['sɔrəu] *n* Trauer *f*; **sorrows** *npl*
(*troubles*) Sorgen und Nöte *pl*.

sorrowful ['sɔrəuful] *adj* traurig.

sorry ['sɔrɪ] *adj* traurig; (*excuse*) faul; (*sight*)
jämmerlich; ~**!** Entschuldigung!,
Verzeihung!; ~**?** wie bitte?; **I feel ~ for him**
er tut mir Leid; **I'm ~ to hear that ...** es tut
mir Leid, dass ...; **I'm ~ about ...** es tut mir
Leid wegen ...

sort [sɔːt] *n* Sorte *f*; (*make: of car etc*) Marke *f*

♦ *vt* (*also*: ~ **out**) sortieren; (: *problems*) ins
Reine bringen; (*COMPUT*) sortieren; **all ~s
of reasons** alle möglichen Gründe; **what
~ do you want?** welche Sorte möchten Sie?;
what ~ of car? was für ein Auto?; **I'll do
nothing of the ~!** das kommt überhaupt
nicht infrage or in Frage!; **it's ~ of awkward**
(*inf*) es ist irgendwie schwierig; **to ~ sth out**
etw in Ordnung bringen.

sort code *n* Bankleitzahl *f*.

sortie ['sɔːtɪ] *n* (*MIL*) Ausfall *m*; (*fig*) Ausflug *m*.

sorting office ['sɔːtɪŋ-] *n* Postverteilstelle *f*.

SOS *n abbr* (= *save our souls*) SOS *nt*.

so-so ['səusəu] *adv, adj* so lala.

soufflé ['suːfleɪ] *n* Soufflé *nt*, Soufflee *nt*.

sought [sɔːt] *pt, pp of* **seek**.

sought-after ['sɔːtɑːftəʳ] *adj* begehrt,
gesucht; **a much ~ item** ein viel begehrtes
Stück.

soul [səul] *n* Seele *f*; (*MUS*) Soul *m*; **the poor
~ had nowhere to sleep** der Ärmste hatte
keine Unterkunft; **I didn't see a ~** ich habe
keine Menschenseele gesehen.

soul-destroying ['səuldɪstrɔɪɪŋ] *adj*
geisttötend.

soulful ['səulful] *adj* (*eyes*) seelenvoll; (*music*)
gefühlvoll.

soulless ['səullɪs] *adj* (*place*) seelenlos; (*job*)
eintönig.

soul mate *n* Seelenfreund(in) *m(f)*.

soul-searching ['səulsɔːtʃɪŋ] *n*: **after much ~**
nach reiflicher Überlegung.

sound [saund] *adj* (*healthy*) gesund; (*safe,
secure*) sicher; (*not damaged*) einwandfrei;
(*reliable*) solide; (*thorough*) gründlich;
(*sensible, valid*) vernünftig ♦ *adv*: **to be
~ asleep** tief und fest schlafen ♦ *n*
Geräusch *nt*; (*MUS*) Klang *m*; (*on TV etc*) Ton
m; (*GEOG*) Meerenge *f*, Sund *m* ♦ *vt*: **to ~ the
alarm** Alarm schlagen ♦ *vi* (*alarm, horn*)
ertönen; (*fig: seem*) sich anhören, klingen; **to
be of ~ mind** bei klarem Verstand sein; **I
don't like the ~ of it** das klingt gar nicht
gut; **to ~ one's horn** (*AUT*) hupen; **to ~ like**
sich anhören wie; **that ~s like them arriving**
das hört sich so an, als ob sie ankommen; **it
~s as if ...** es klingt or es hört sich so an, als
ob ...

▶ **sound off** (*inf*) *vi*: **to ~ off (about)** sich
auslassen (über +*acc*).

▶ **sound out** *vt* (*person*) aushorchen;
(*opinion*) herausbekommen.

sound barrier *n* Schallmauer *f*.

sound bite *n* prägnantes Zitat *nt*.

sound effects *npl* Toneffekte *pl*.

sound engineer *n* Toningenieur(in) *m(f)*.

sounding ['saundɪŋ] *n* (*NAUT*) Loten *nt*,
Peilung *f*.

sounding board *n* (*MUS*) Resonanzboden *m*;
(*fig*): **to use sb as a ~ for one's ideas** seine
Ideen an jdm testen.

soundly ['saundlɪ] *adv* (*sleep*) tief und fest;

(*beat*) tüchtig.

soundproof ['saundpru:f] *adj* schalldicht ♦ *vt* schalldicht machen.

sound system *n* Verstärkersystem *nt*.

soundtrack ['saundtræk] *n* Filmmusik *f*.

sound wave *n* Schallwelle *f*.

soup [su:p] *n* Suppe *f*; **to be in the ~** (*fig*) in der Tinte sitzen.

soup kitchen *n* Suppenküche *f*.

soup plate *n* Suppenteller *m*.

soupspoon ['su:pspu:n] *n* Suppenlöffel *m*.

sour [sauɔ*] *adj* sauer; (*fig: bad-tempered*) säuerlich; **to go** *or* **turn ~** (*milk, wine*) sauer werden; (*fig: relationship*) sich trüben; **it's ~ grapes** (*fig*) die Trauben hängen zu hoch.

source [sɔːs] *n* Quelle *f*; (*fig: of problem, anxiety*) Ursache *f*; **I have it from a reliable ~ that** ... ich habe es aus sicherer Quelle, dass ...

south [sauθ] *n* Süden *m* ♦ *adj* südlich, Süd- ♦ *adv* nach Süden; (**to the**) **~ of** im Süden *or* südlich von; **to travel ~** nach Süden fahren; **the S~ of France** Südfrankreich *nt*.

South Africa *n* Südafrika *nt*.

South African *adj* südafrikanisch ♦ *n* Südafrikaner(in) *m(f)*.

South America *n* Südamerika *nt*.

South American *adj* südamerikanisch ♦ *n* Südamerikaner(in) *m(f)*.

southbound ['sauθbaund] *adj* in Richtung Süden; (*carriageway*) Richtung Süden.

south-east [sauθ'iːst] *n* Südosten *m*.

South-East Asia *n* Südostasien *nt*.

southerly ['sʌðəlɪ] *adj* südlich; (*wind*) aus südlicher Richtung.

southern ['sʌðən] *adj* südlich, Süd-; **the ~ hemisphere** die südliche Halbkugel *or* Hemisphäre.

South Korea *n* Südkorea *nt*.

South Pole *n* Südpol *m*.

South Sea Islands *npl* Südseeinseln *pl*.

South Seas *npl* Südsee *f*.

southward(s) ['sauθwəd(z)] *adv* nach Süden, in Richtung Süden.

south-west [sauθ'wɛst] *n* Südwesten *m*.

souvenir [su:və'nɪə*] *n* Andenken *nt*, Souvenir *nt*.

sovereign ['sɔvrɪn] *n* Herrscher(in) *m(f)*.

sovereignty ['sɔvrɪntɪ] *n* Oberhoheit *f*, Souveränität *f*.

soviet ['səuvɪət] (*formerly*) *adj* sowjetisch ♦ *n* Sowjetbürger(in) *m(f)*; **the S~ Union** die Sowjetunion *f*.

sow¹ [sau] *n* Sau *f*.

sow² [səu] (*pt* **sowed**, *pp* **sown**) *vt* (*lit, fig*) säen.

soya ['sɔɪə], **soy** [sɔɪ] (*US*) *n*: **~ bean** Sojabohne *f*; **~ sauce** Sojasoße *f*.

sozzled ['sɔzld] (*BRIT: inf*) *adj* besoffen.

spa [spɑː] *n* (*town*) Heilbad *nt*; (*US: also:* **health ~**) Fitnesszentrum *nt*.

space [speɪs] *n* Platz *m*, Raum *m*; (*gap*) Lücke

f; (*beyond Earth*) der Weltraum; (*interval, period*) Zeitraum *m* ♦ *cpd* Raum- ♦ *vt* (*also:* **~ out**) verteilen; **to clear a ~ for sth** für etw Platz schaffen; **in a confined ~** auf engem Raum; **in a short ~ of time** in kurzer Zeit; **(with)in the ~ of an hour** innerhalb einer Stunde.

space bar *n* (*on keyboard*) Leertaste *f*.

spacecraft ['speɪskrɑːft] *n* Raumfahrzeug *nt*.

spaceman ['speɪsmæn] (*irreg: like* **man**) *n* Raumfahrer *m*.

spaceship ['speɪsʃɪp] *n* Raumschiff *nt*.

space shuttle *n* Raumtransporter *m*.

spacesuit ['speɪssuːt] *n* Raumanzug *m*.

spacewoman ['speɪswumən] (*irreg: like* **woman**) *n* Raumfahrerin *f*.

spacing ['speɪsɪŋ] *n* Abstand *m*; **single/double ~** einfacher/doppelter Zeilenabstand.

spacious ['speɪʃəs] *adj* geräumig.

spade [speɪd] *n* Spaten *m*; (*child's*) Schaufel *f*; **spades** *npl* (*CARDS*) Pik *nt*.

spadework ['speɪdwəːk] *n* (*fig*) Vorarbeit *f*.

spaghetti [spə'gɛtɪ] *n* Spag(h)etti *pl*.

Spain [speɪn] *n* Spanien *nt*.

spam [spæm] (*COMPUT*) *n* Spam *m* ♦ *vt* mit Werbung bombardieren.

span [spæn] *n* (*of bird, plane, arch*) Spannweite *f*; (*in time*) Zeitspanne *f* ♦ *vt* überspannen; (*fig: time*) sich erstrecken über +*acc*.

Spaniard ['spænjəd] *n* Spanier(in) *m(f)*.

spaniel ['spænjəl] *n* Spaniel *m*.

Spanish ['spænɪʃ] *adj* spanisch ♦ *n* (*LING*) Spanisch *nt*; **the Spanish** *npl* die Spanier *pl*; **~ omelette** Omelett mit Paprikaschoten, Zwiebeln, Tomaten *etc*.

spank [spæŋk] *vt*: **to ~ sb's bottom** jdm den Hintern versohlen (*inf*).

spanner ['spænə*] (*BRIT*) *n* Schraubenschlüssel *m*.

spar [spɑː*] *n* (*NAUT*) Sparren *m* ♦ *vi* (*BOXING*) ein Sparring *nt* machen.

spare [spɛə*] *adj* (*free*) frei; (*extra: part, fuse etc*) Ersatz- ♦ *n* = **spare part** ♦ *vt* (*save: trouble etc*) (er)sparen; (*make available*) erübrigen; (*afford to give*) (übrig) haben; (*refrain from hurting*) verschonen; **these 2 are going ~** diese beiden sind noch übrig; **to ~** (*surplus*) übrig; **to ~ no expense** keine Kosten scheuen, an nichts sparen; **can you ~ the time?** haben Sie Zeit?; **I've a few minutes to ~** ich habe ein paar Minuten Zeit; **there is no time to ~** es ist keine Zeit; **~ me the details** verschone mich mit den Einzelheiten.

spare part *n* Ersatzteil *nt*.

spare room *n* Gästezimmer *nt*.

spare time *n* Freizeit *f*.

spare tyre *n* Reservereifen *m*.

spare wheel *n* Reserverad *nt*.

sparing ['spɛərɪŋ] *adj*: **to be ~ with** sparsam umgehen mit.

sparingly ['spɛərɪŋlɪ] *adv* sparsam.

spark [spɑːk] *n* (*lit, fig*) Funke *m*.

spark(ing) plug ['spɑːk(ɪŋ)-] *n* Zündkerze *f*.
sparkle ['spɑːkl] *n* Funkeln *nt*, Glitzern *nt* ♦ *vi* funkeln, glitzern.
sparkler ['spɑːklə*] *n* (*firework*) Wunderkerze *f*.
sparkling ['spɑːklɪŋ] *adj* (*water*) mit Kohlensäure; (*conversation*) vor Geist sprühend; (*performance*) glänzend; ~ **wine** Schaumwein *m*.
sparring partner ['spɑːrɪŋ-] *n* (*also fig*) Sparringspartner *m*.
sparrow ['spærəu] *n* Spatz *m*.
sparse [spɑːs] *adj* spärlich; (*population*) dünn.
spartan ['spɑːtən] *adj* (*fig*) spartanisch.
spasm ['spæzəm] *n* (*MED*) Krampf *m*; (*fig: of anger etc*) Anfall *m*.
spasmodic [spæz'mɔdɪk] *adj* (*fig*) sporadisch.
spastic ['spæstɪk] (*old*) *n* Spastiker(in) *m(f)* ♦ *adj* spastisch.
spat [spæt] *pt, pp of* **spit** ♦ *n* (*US: quarrel*) Krach *m*.
spate [speɪt] *n* (*fig*): **a** ~ **of** eine Flut von; **to be in full** ~ (*river*) Hochwasser führen.
spatial ['speɪʃl] *adj* räumlich.
spatter ['spætə*] *vt* (*liquid*) verspritzen; (*surface*) bespritzen ♦ *vi* spritzen.
spatula ['spætjulə] *n* (*CULIN*) Spachtel *m*; (*MED*) Spatel *m*.
spawn [spɔːn] *vi* laichen ♦ *vt* hervorbringen, erzeugen ♦ *n* Laich *m*.
SPCA (*US*) *n abbr* (= *Society for the Prevention of Cruelty to Animals*) Tierschutzverein *m*.
SPCC (*US*) *n abbr* (= *Society for the Prevention of Cruelty to Children*) Kinderschutzbund *m*.
speak [spiːk] (*pt* **spoke**, *pp* **spoken**) *vt* (*say*) sagen; (*language*) sprechen ♦ *vi* sprechen, reden; (*make a speech*) sprechen; **to** ~ **one's mind** seine Meinung sagen; **to** ~ **to sb/of** *or* **about sth** mit jdm/über etw *acc* sprechen *or* reden; ~ **up!** sprich lauter!; **to** ~ **at a conference** bei einer Tagung einen Vortrag halten; **to** ~ **in a debate** in einer Debatte sprechen; **he has no money to** ~ **of** er hat so gut wie kein Geld; **so to** ~ sozusagen.
▶ **speak for** *vt fus*: **to** ~ **for sb** (*on behalf of*) in jds Namen *dat or* für jdn sprechen; **that picture is already spoken for** (*in shop*) das Bild ist schon verkauft *or* vergeben; ~ **for yourself!** das meinst auch nur du!
speaker ['spiːkə*] *n* (*in public*) Redner(in) *m(f)*; (*also*: **loudspeaker**) Lautsprecher *m*; (*POL*): **the S**~ (*BRIT, US*) der Sprecher, die Sprecherin; **are you a Welsh** ~? sprechen Sie Walisisch?
speaking ['spiːkɪŋ] *adj* sprechend; **Italian-** ~ **people** Italienisch Sprechende *pl*; **to be on** ~ **terms** miteinander reden *or* sprechen; ~ **clock** telefonische Zeitansage.
spear [spɪə*] *n* Speer *m* ♦ *vt* aufspießen.
spearhead ['spɪəhed] *vt* (*MIL, fig*) anführen.
spearmint ['spɪəmɪnt] *n* Grüne Minze *f*.
spec [spek] (*inf*) *n*: **on** ~ auf Verdacht, auf gut Glück; **to buy/go on** ~ auf gut Glück

kaufen/hingehen.
spec. *n abbr* (*TECH*) = **specification**.
special ['speʃl] *adj* besondere(r, s); (*service, performance, adviser, permission, school*) Sonder- ♦ *n* (*train*) Sonderzug *m*; **take** ~ **care** pass besonders gut auf; **nothing** ~ nichts Besonderes; **today's** ~ (*at restaurant*) Tagesgericht *nt*.
special agent *n* Agent(in) *m(f)*.
special correspondent *n* Sonderberichterstatter(in) *m(f)*.
special delivery *n* (*POST*): **by** ~ durch Eilzustellung.
special effects *npl* Spezialeffekte *pl*.
specialist ['speʃəlɪst] *n* Spezialist(in) *m(f)*; (*MED*) Facharzt *m*, Fachärztin *f*; **heart** ~ Facharzt *m*/Fachärztin *f* für Herzkrankheiten.
speciality [speʃɪ'ælɪtɪ] *n* Spezialität *f*; (*study*) Spezialgebiet *nt*.
specialize ['speʃəlaɪz] *vi*: **to** ~ **(in)** sich spezialisieren (auf +*acc*).
specially ['speʃlɪ] *adv* besonders, extra.
special offer *n* Sonderangebot *nt*.
specialty ['speʃəltɪ] (*esp US*) = **speciality**.
species ['spiːʃiːz] *n inv* Art *f*.
specific [spə'sɪfɪk] *adj* (*fixed*) bestimmt; (*exact*) genau; **to be** ~ **to** es eigentümlich sein für.
specifically [spə'sɪfɪklɪ] *adv* (*specially*) speziell; (*exactly*) genau; **more** ~ und zwar.
specification [spesɪfɪ'keɪʃən] *n* genaue Angabe *f*; (*requirement*) Bedingung *f*; **specifications** *npl* (*TECH*) technische Daten *pl*.
specify ['spesɪfaɪ] *vt* angeben; **unless otherwise specified** wenn nicht anders angegeben.
specimen ['spesɪmən] *n* Exemplar *nt*; (*MED*) Probe *f*.
specimen copy *n* Belegexemplar *nt*, Probeexemplar *nt*.
specimen signature *n* Unterschriftsprobe *f*.
speck [spek] *n* Fleckchen *nt*; (*of dust*) Körnchen *nt*.
speckled ['spekld] *adj* gesprenkelt.
specs [speks] (*inf*) *npl* Brille *f*.
spectacle ['spektəkl] *n* (*scene*) Schauspiel *nt*; (*sight*) Anblick *m*; (*grand event*) Spektakel *nt*; **spectacles** *npl* (*glasses*) Brille *f*.
spectacle case (*BRIT*) *n* Brillenetui *nt*.
spectacular [spek'tækjulə*] *adj* sensationell; (*success*) spektakulär ♦ *n* (*THEAT etc*) Show *f*.
spectator [spek'teɪtə*] *n* Zuschauer(in) *m(f)*; ~ **sport** Publikumssport *m*.
spectra ['spektrə] *npl of* **spectrum**.
spectre, (*US*) **specter** ['spektə*] *n* Gespenst *nt*; (*fig*) (Schreck)gespenst *nt*.
spectrum ['spektrəm] (*pl* **spectra**) *n* (*lit, fig*) Spektrum *nt*.
speculate ['spekjuleɪt] *vi* (*FIN*) spekulieren; **to** ~ **about** spekulieren *or* Vermutungen anstellen über +*acc*.

speculation [spɛkju'leɪʃən] n Spekulation f.
speculative ['spɛkjulətɪv] adj spekulativ.
speculator ['spɛkjuleɪtə*] n Spekulant(in) m(f).
sped [spɛd] pt, pp of **speed**.
speech [spiːtʃ] n Sprache f; (manner of speaking) Sprechweise f; (enunciation) (Aus)sprache f; (formal talk: THEAT) Rede f.
speech day (BRIT) n (SCOL) ≈ Schulfeier f.
speech impediment n Sprachfehler m.
speechless ['spiːtʃlɪs] adj sprachlos.
speech therapist n Logopäde m, Logopädin f, Sprachtherapeut(in) m(f).
speech therapy n Logopädie f, Sprachtherapie f.
speed [spiːd] (pt, pp **sped**) n Geschwindigkeit f, Schnelligkeit f ♦ vi (exceed speed limit) zu schnell fahren; **to ~ along** dahinsausen; **to ~ by** (car etc) vorbeischießen; (years) verfliegen; **at ~** (BRIT) mit hoher Geschwindigkeit; **at full** or **top ~** mit Höchstgeschwindigkeit; **at a ~ of 70km/h** mit (einer Geschwindigkeit or einem Tempo von) 70 km/h; **shorthand/typing ~s** Silben/Anschläge pro Minute; **a five-~ gearbox** ein Fünfganggetriebe nt.
▶ **speed up** (pt, pp **speeded up**) vi beschleunigen; (fig) sich beschleunigen ♦ vt beschleunigen.
speedboat ['spiːdbəʊt] n Rennboot nt.
speedily ['spiːdɪlɪ] adv schnell.
speeding ['spiːdɪŋ] n Geschwindigkeitsüberschreitung f.
speed limit n Tempolimit nt, Geschwindigkeitsbegrenzung f.
speedometer [spɪ'dɒmɪtə*] n Tachometer m.
speed trap n Radarfalle f.
speedway ['spiːdweɪ] n (also: ~ **racing**) Speedwayrennen nt.
speedy ['spiːdɪ] adj schnell; (reply, settlement) prompt.
speleologist [spɛlɪ'ɒlədʒɪst] n Höhlenkundler(in) m(f).
spell [spɛl] (pt, pp **spelt** (BRIT) or **spelled**) n (also: **magic ~**) Zauber m; (incantation) Zauberspruch m; (period of time) Zeit f, Weile f ♦ vt schreiben; (also: ~ **out**: aloud) buchstabieren; (signify) bedeuten; **to cast a ~ on sb** jdn verzaubern; **cold ~** Kältewelle f; **how do you ~ your name?** wie schreibt sich Ihr Name?; **can you ~ it for me?** können Sie das bitte buchstabieren?; **he can't ~** er kann keine Rechtschreibung.
spellbound ['spɛlbaʊnd] adj gebannt.
spelling ['spɛlɪŋ] n Schreibweise f; (ability) Rechtschreibung f; **~ mistake** Rechtschreibfehler m.
spelt [spɛlt] pt, pp of **spell**.
spend [spɛnd] (pt, pp **spent**) vt (money) ausgeben; (time, life) verbringen; **to ~ time/money/effort on sth** Zeit/Geld/Mühe für etw aufbringen.
spending ['spɛndɪŋ] n Ausgaben pl;

government ~ öffentliche Ausgaben pl.
spending money n Taschengeld nt.
spending power n Kaufkraft f.
spendthrift ['spɛndθrɪft] n Verschwender(in) m(f).
spent [spɛnt] pt, pp of **spend** ♦ adj (patience) erschöpft; (cartridge, bullets) verbraucht; (match) abgebrannt.
sperm [spɜːm] n Samenzelle f, Spermium nt.
sperm bank n Samenbank f.
sperm whale n Pottwal m.
spew [spjuː] vt (also: ~ **up**) erbrechen; (fig) ausspucken.
sphere [sfɪə*] n Kugel f; (area) Gebiet nt, Bereich m.
spherical ['sfɛrɪkl] adj kugelförmig.
sphinx [sfɪŋks] n Sphinx f.
spice [spaɪs] n Gewürz nt ♦ vt würzen.
spick-and-span ['spɪkən'spæn] adj blitzsauber.
spicy ['spaɪsɪ] adj stark gewürzt.
spider ['spaɪdə*] n Spinne f; **~'s web** Spinnengewebe nt, Spinnennetz nt.
spidery ['spaɪdərɪ] adj (handwriting) krakelig.
spiel [spiːl] (inf) n Sermon m.
spike [spaɪk] n (point) Spitze f; (BOT) Ähre f; (ELEC) Spannungsspitze f; **spikes** npl (SPORT) Spikes pl.
spike heel (US) n Pfennigabsatz m.
spiky ['spaɪkɪ] adj stachelig; (branch) dornig.
spill [spɪl] (pt, pp **spilt** or **spilled**) vt verschütten ♦ vi verschüttet werden; **to ~ the beans** (inf, fig) alles ausplaudern.
▶ **spill out** vi (people) herausströmen.
▶ **spill over** vi überlaufen; (fig: spread) sich ausbreiten; **to ~ over into** sich auswirken auf +acc.
spillage ['spɪlɪdʒ] n (act) Verschütten nt; (quantity) verschüttete Menge f.
spin [spɪn] (pt **spun**, **span**, pp **spun**) n (trip) Spritztour f; (revolution) Drehung f; (AVIAT) Trudeln nt; (on ball) Drall m ♦ vt (wool etc) spinnen; (ball, coin) (hoch)werfen; (wheel) drehen; (BRIT: also: ~-**dry**) schleudern ♦ vi (make thread) spinnen; (person) sich drehen; (car etc) schleudern; **to ~ a yarn** Seemannsgarn spinnen; **to ~ a coin** (BRIT) eine Münze werfen; **my head is ~ning** mir dreht sich alles.
▶ **spin out** vt (talk) ausspinnen; (job, holiday) in die Länge ziehen; (money) strecken.
spina bifida ['spaɪnə'bɪfɪdə] n offene Wirbelsäule f, Spina bifida f.
spinach ['spɪnɪtʃ] n Spinat m.
spinal ['spaɪnl] adj (injury etc) Rückgrat-.
spinal column n Wirbelsäule f.
spinal cord n Rückenmark nt.
spindly ['spɪndlɪ] adj spindeldürr.
spin doctor n PR-Fachmann m, PR-Fachfrau f.
spin-dry ['spɪn'draɪ] vt schleudern.
spin-dryer [spɪn'draɪə*] (BRIT) n

(Wäsche)schleuder *f*.

spine [spaɪn] *n* (*ANAT*) Rückgrat *nt*; (*thorn*) Stachel *m*.

spine-chilling ['spaɪntʃɪlɪŋ] *adj* schaurig, gruselig.

spineless ['spaɪnlɪs] *adj* (*fig*) rückgratlos.

spinner ['spɪnə*] *n* (*of thread*) Spinner(in) *m(f)*.

spinning ['spɪnɪŋ] *n* (*art*) Spinnen *nt*.

spinning top *n* Kreisel *m*.

spinning wheel *n* Spinnrad *nt*.

spin-off ['spɪnɔf] *n* (*fig*) Nebenprodukt *nt*.

spinster ['spɪnstə*] *n* unverheiratete Frau; (*pej*) alte Jungfer.

spiral ['spaɪərl] *n* Spirale *f* ♦ *vi* (*fig: prices etc*) in die Höhe klettern; **the inflationary** ~ die Inflationsspirale.

spiral staircase *n* Wendeltreppe *f*.

spire ['spaɪə*] *n* Turmspitze *f*.

spirit ['spɪrɪt] *n* Geist *m*; (*soul*) Seele *f*; (*energy*) Elan *m*, Schwung *m*; (*courage*) Mut *m*; (*sense*) Geist *m*, Sinn *m*; (*frame of mind*) Stimmung *f*; **spirits** *npl* (*drink*) Spirituosen *pl*; **in good** ~**s** guter Laune; **community** ~ Gemeinschaftssinn *m*.

spirited ['spɪrɪtɪd] *adj* (*resistance, defence*) mutig; (*performance*) lebendig.

spirit level *n* Wasserwaage *f*.

spiritual ['spɪrɪtjʊəl] *adj* geistig, seelisch; (*religious*) geistlich ♦ *n* (*also:* **Negro** ~) Spiritual *nt*.

spiritualism ['spɪrɪtjʊəlɪzəm] *n* Spiritismus *m*.

spit [spɪt] (*pt, pp* **spat**) *n* (*for roasting*) Spieß *m*; (*saliva*) Spucke *f* ♦ *vi* spucken; (*fire*) Funken sprühen; (*cooking*) spritzen; (*inf: rain*) tröpfeln.

spite [spaɪt] *n* Boshaftigkeit *f* ♦ *vt* ärgern; **in** ~ **of** trotz *+gen*.

spiteful ['spaɪtful] *adj* boshaft, gemein.

spitroast ['spɪtrəust] *n* Spießbraten *m*.

spitting ['spɪtɪŋ] *n*: "~ **prohibited**" „Spucken verboten" ♦ *adj*: **to be the** ~ **image of sb** jdm wie aus dem Gesicht geschnitten sein.

spittle ['spɪtl] *n* Speichel *m*, Spucke *f*.

spiv [spɪv] (*BRIT: inf: pej*) *n* schmieriger Typ *m*.

splash [splæʃ] *n* (*sound*) Platschen *nt*; (*of colour*) Tupfer *m* ♦ *excl* platsch! ♦ *vt* bespritzen ♦ *vi* (*also:* ~ **about**) herumplan(t)schen; (*water, rain*) spritzen; **to** ~ **paint on the floor** den Fußboden mit Farbe bespritzen.

splashdown ['splæʃdaun] *n* (*SPACE*) Wasserung *f*.

splayfooted ['spleɪfutɪd] *adj* mit nach außen gestellten Füßen.

spleen [spliːn] *n* Milz *f*.

splendid ['splendɪd] *adj* hervorragend, ausgezeichnet; (*impressive*) prächtig.

splendour, (*US*) **splendor** ['splendə*] *n* Pracht *f*; **splendours** *npl* Pracht *f*.

splice [splaɪs] *vt* spleißen, kleben.

splint [splɪnt] *n* Schiene *f*.

splinter ['splɪntə*] *n* Splitter *m* ♦ *vi* (zer)splittern.

splinter group *n* Splittergruppe *f*.

split [splɪt] (*pt, pp* **split**) *n* (*tear*) Riss *m*; (*fig: division*) Aufteilung *f*; (: *difference*) Kluft *f*; (*POL*) Spaltung *f* ♦ *vt* (*divide*) aufteilen; (*party*) spalten; (*share equally*) teilen ♦ *vi* (*divide*) sich aufteilen; (*tear*) reißen; **to do the** ~**s** (einen) Spagat machen; **let's** ~ **the difference** teilen wir uns die Differenz.

► **split up** *vi* sich trennen; (*meeting*) sich auflösen.

split-level ['splɪtlevl] *adj* mit versetzten Geschossen.

split peas *npl* getrocknete (halbe) Erbsen *pl*.

split personality *n* gespaltene Persönlichkeit *f*.

split second *n* Bruchteil *m* einer Sekunde.

splitting ['splɪtɪŋ] *adj*: **a** ~ **headache** rasende Kopfschmerzen *pl*.

splutter ['splʌtə*] *vi* (*engine etc*) stottern; (*person*) prusten.

spoil [spɔɪl] (*pt, pp* **spoilt** *or* **spoiled**) *vt* verderben; (*child*) verwöhnen; (*ballot paper, vote*) ungültig machen ♦ *vi*: **to be** ~**ing for a fight** Streit suchen.

spoils [spɔɪlz] *npl* Beute *f*; (*fig*) Gewinn *m*.

spoilsport ['spɔɪlspɔːt] (*pej*) *n* Spielverderber *m*.

spoilt [spɔɪlt] *pt, pp of* **spoil** ♦ *adj* (*child*) verwöhnt; (*ballot paper*) ungültig.

spoke [spəuk] *pt of* **speak** ♦ *n* Speiche *f*.

spoken ['spəukn] *pp of* **speak**.

spokesman ['spəuksmən] (*irreg: like* **man**) *n* Sprecher *m*.

spokesperson ['spəukspɜːsn] *n* Sprecher(in) *m(f)*.

spokeswoman ['spəukswumən] (*irreg: like* **woman**) *n* Sprecherin *f*.

sponge [spʌndʒ] *n* Schwamm *m*; (*also:* ~ **cake**) Biskuit(kuchen) *m* ♦ *vt* mit einem Schwamm waschen ♦ *vi*: **to** ~ **off** *or* **on sb** jdm auf der Tasche liegen.

sponge bag (*BRIT*) *n* Waschbeutel *m*, Kulturbeutel *m*.

sponger ['spʌndʒə*] (*pej*) *n* Schmarotzer *m*.

spongy ['spʌndʒɪ] *adj* schwammig.

sponsor ['spɒnsə*] *n* Sponsor(in) *m(f)*, Geldgeber(in) *m(f)*; (*BRIT: for charitable event*) Sponsor(in) *m(f)*; (*for application, bill etc*) Befürworter(in) *m(f)* ♦ *vt* sponsern, finanziell unterstützen; (*fund-raiser*) unterstützen; (*applicant*) unterstützen; (*proposal, bill etc*) befürworten; **I** ~**ed him at 3p a mile** (*in fund-raising race*) ich habe mich verpflichtet, ihm 3 Pence pro Meile zu geben.

sponsorship ['spɒnsəʃɪp] *n* finanzielle Unterstützung *f*.

spontaneity [spɒntə'neɪɪtɪ] *n* Spontaneität *f*.

spontaneous [spɒn'teɪnɪəs] *adj* spontan; ~ **combustion** Selbstentzündung *f*.

spoof [spuːf] *n* (*parody*) Parodie *f*; (*hoax*) Ulk *m*.

spooky ['spu:kɪ] (*inf*) *adj* gruselig.
spool [spu:l] *n* Spule *f*.
spoon [spu:n] *n* Löffel *m*.
spoon-feed ['spu:nfi:d] *vt* (mit dem Löffel) füttern; (*fig*) gängeln.
spoonful ['spu:nful] *n* Löffel *m*.
sporadic [spə'rædɪk] *adj* sporadisch, vereinzelt.
sport [spɔːt] *n* Sport *m*; (*type*) Sportart *f*; (*also*: **good ~**: *person*) feiner Kerl *m* ♦ *vt* (*wear*) tragen; **indoor ~s** Hallensport *m*; **outdoor ~s** Sport *m* im Freien.
sporting ['spɔːtɪŋ] *adj* (*event etc*) Sport-; (*generous*) großzügig; **to give sb a ~ chance** jdm eine faire Chance geben.
sport jacket (*US*) *n* = **sports jacket**.
sports car *n* Sportwagen *m*.
sports centre *n* Sportzentrum *nt*.
sports ground *n* Sportplatz *m*.
sports jacket (*BRIT*) *n* Sakko *m*.
sportsman ['spɔːtsmən] (*irreg: like* **man**) *n* Sportler *m*.
sportsmanship ['spɔːtsmənʃɪp] *n* Sportlichkeit *f*.
sports page *n* Sportseite *f*.
sportswear ['spɔːtswɛəˢ] *n* Sportkleidung *f*.
sportswoman ['spɔːtswumən] (*irreg: like* **woman**) *n* Sportlerin *f*.
sporty ['spɔːtɪ] *adj* sportlich.
spot [spɔt] *n* (*mark*) Fleck *m*; (*dot*) Punkt *m*; (*on skin*) Pickel *m*; (*place*) Stelle *f*, Platz *m*; (*RADIO, TV*) Nummer *f*, Auftritt *m*; (*also*: **~ advertisement**) Werbespot *m*; (*small amount*): **a ~ of** ein bisschen ♦ *vt* entdecken; **on the ~** (*in that place*) an Ort und Stelle; (*immediately*) auf der Stelle; **to be in a ~** in der Klemme sitzen; **to put sb on the ~** jdn in Verlegenheit bringen; **to come out in ~s** Pickel bekommen.
spot check *n* Stichprobe *f*.
spotless ['spɔtlɪs] *adj* makellos sauber.
spotlight ['spɔtlaɪt] *n* Scheinwerfer *m*; (*in room*) Strahler *m*.
spot-on [spɔt'ɔn] (*BRIT*: *inf*) *adj* genau richtig.
spot price *n* Kassapreis *m*.
spotted ['spɔtɪd] *adj* gepunktet.
spotty ['spɔtɪ] *adj* pickelig.
spouse [spaus] *n* (*male*) Gatte *m*; (*female*) Gattin *f*.
spout [spaut] *n* (*of jug, teapot*) Tülle *f*; (*of pipe*) Ausfluss *m*; (*of liquid*) Strahl *m* ♦ *vi* spritzen; (*flames*) sprühen.
sprain [spreɪn] *n* Verstauchung *f* ♦ *vt*: **to ~ one's ankle/wrist** sich *dat* den Knöchel/ das Handgelenk verstauchen.
sprang [spræŋ] *pt of* **spring**.
sprawl [sprɔːl] *vi* (*person*) sich ausstrecken; (*place*) wild wuchern ♦ *n*: **urban ~** wild wuchernde Ausbreitung des Stadtgebietes; **to send sb ~ing** jdn zu Boden werfen.
spray [spreɪ] *n* (*small drops*) Sprühnebel *m*; (*sea spray*) Gischt *m or f*; (*container*)

Sprühdose *f*; (*garden spray*) Sprühgerät *nt*; (*of flowers*) Strauß *m* ♦ *vt* sprühen, spritzen; (*crops*) spritzen ♦ *cpd* (*deodorant*) Sprüh-; **~ can** Sprühdose *f*.
spread [sprɛd] (*pt, pp* **spread**) *n* (*range*) Spektrum *nt*; (*selection*) Auswahl *f*; (*distribution*) Verteilung *f*; (*for bread*) (Brot)aufstrich *m*; (*inf*: *food*) Festessen *nt*; (*PRESS, TYP*: *two pages*) Doppelseite *f* ♦ *vt* ausbreiten; (*butter*) streichen; (*workload, wealth, repayments etc*) verteilen; (*scatter*) verstreuen; (*rumour, disease*) verbreiten ♦ *vi* (*disease, news*) sich verbreiten; (*also*: **~ out**: *stain*) sich ausbreiten; **to get a middle-age ~** in den mittleren Jahren Speck ansetzen.
▶ **spread out** *vi* (*move apart*) sich verteilen.
spread-eagled ['sprɛdiːgld] *adj* mit ausgestreckten Armen und Beinen; **to be** *or* **lie ~** mit ausgestreckten Armen und Beinen daliegen.
spreadsheet ['sprɛdʃiːt] *n* (*COMPUT*) Tabellenkalkulation *f*.
spree [spriː] *n*: **to go on a ~** (*drinking*) eine Zechtour machen; (*spending*) groß einkaufen gehen.
sprig [sprɪg] *n* Zweig *m*.
sprightly ['spraɪtlɪ] *adj* rüstig.
spring [sprɪŋ] (*pt* **sprang**, *pp* **sprung**) *n* (*coiled metal*) Sprungfeder *f*; (*season*) Frühling *m*, Frühjahr *nt*; (*of water*) Quelle *f* ♦ *vi* (*leap*) springen ♦ *vt*: **to ~ a leak** (*pipe etc*) undicht werden; **in ~** im Frühling *or* Frühjahr; **to walk with a ~ in one's step** mit federnden Schritten gehen; **to ~ from** (*result*) herrühren von; **to ~ into action** aktiv werden; **he sprang the news on me** er hat mich mit der Nachricht überrascht.
▶ **spring up** *vi* (*building, plant*) aus dem Boden schießen.
springboard ['sprɪŋbɔːd] *n* (*SPORT, fig*) Sprungbrett *nt*.
spring-clean(ing) [sprɪŋ'kliːn(ɪŋ)] *n* Frühjahrsputz *m*.
spring onion (*BRIT*) *n* Frühlingszwiebel *f*.
spring roll *n* Frühlingsrolle *f*.
springtime ['sprɪŋtaɪm] *n* Frühling *m*.
springy ['sprɪŋɪ] *adj* federnd; (*mattress*) weich gefedert.
sprinkle ['sprɪŋkl] *vt* (*liquid*) sprenkeln; (*salt, sugar*) streuen; **to ~ water on, ~ with water** mit Wasser besprengen; **to ~ sugar etc on, ~ with sugar** *etc* mit Zucker *etc* bestreuen.
sprinkler ['sprɪŋkləˢ] *n* (*for lawn*) Rasensprenger *m*; (*to put out fire*) Sprinkler *m*.
sprinkling ['sprɪŋklɪŋ] *n*: **a ~ of** (*water*) ein paar Tropfen; (*salt, sugar*) eine Prise; (*fig*) ein paar ...
sprint [sprɪnt] *n* Sprint *m* ♦ *vi* rennen; (*SPORT*) sprinten; **the 200 metres ~** der 200-Meter-Lauf.
sprinter ['sprɪntəˢ] *n* Sprinter(in) *m(f)*.

sprite [spraɪt] *n* Kobold *m*.
spritzer ['sprɪtsə*] *n* Schorle *f*.
sprocket ['sprɔkɪt] *n* Kettenzahnrad *nt*.
sprout [spraut] *vi* sprießen; (*vegetable*) keimen.
sprouts [sprauts] *npl* (*also*: **Brussels ~**) Rosenkohl *m*.
spruce [spru:s] *n inv* Fichte *f* ♦ *adj* gepflegt, adrett.
▶ **spruce up** *vt* auf Vordermann bringen (*inf*); **to ~ o.s. up** sein Äußeres pflegen.
sprung [sprʌŋ] *pp of* **spring**.
spry [spraɪ] *adj* rüstig.
SPUC *n abbr* (= *Society for the Protection of the Unborn Child*) *Gesellschaft zum Schutz des ungeborenen Lebens.*
spud [spʌd] (*inf*) *n* Kartoffel *f*.
spun [spʌn] *pt*, *pp of* **spin**.
spur [spə:*] *n* Sporn *m*; (*fig*) Ansporn *m* ♦ *vt* (*also*: **~ on**, *fig*) anspornen; **on the ~ of the moment** ganz spontan.
spurious ['spjuərɪəs] *adj* falsch.
spurn [spə:n] *vt* verschmähen.
spurt [spə:t] *n* (*of blood etc*) Strahl *m*; (*of energy*) Anwandlung *f* ♦ *vi* (*blood*) (heraus)spritzen; **to put on a ~** (*lit, fig*) einen Spurt einlegen.
sputter ['spʌtə*] *vi* = **splutter**.
spy [spaɪ] *n* Spion(in) *m(f)* ♦ *vi*: **to ~ on** nachspionieren +*dat* ♦ *vt* sehen ♦ *cpd* (*film, story*) Spionage-.
spying ['spaɪɪŋ] *n* Spionage *f*.
Sq. *abbr* (*in address*: = *square*) ≈ Pl.
sq. *abbr* = **square**.
squabble ['skwɔbl] *vi* (sich) zanken ♦ *n* Streit *m*.
squad [skwɔd] *n* (*MIL*) Trupp *m*; (*POLICE*) Kommando *nt*; (: *drug/fraud squad*) Dezernat *nt*; (*SPORT*) Mannschaft *f*; **flying ~** (*POLICE*) Überfallkommando *nt*.
squad car (*BRIT*) *n* (*POLICE*) Streifenwagen *m*.
squaddie ['skwɔdɪ] (*BRIT*) *n* (*private soldier*) Gefreite(r) *m*.
squadron ['skwɔdrn] *n* (*MIL*) Schwadron *f*; (*AVIAT*) Staffel *f*; (*NAUT*) Geschwader *nt*.
squalid ['skwɔlɪd] *adj* verkommen; (*conditions*) elend; (*sordid*) erbärmlich.
squall [skwɔ:l] *n* Bö(e) *f*.
squalor ['skwɔlə*] *n* Elend *nt*.
squander ['skwɔndə*] *vt* verschwenden; (*chances*) vertun.
square [skwɛə*] *n* Quadrat *nt*; (*in town*) Platz *m*; (*US: block of houses*) Block *m*; (*also*: **set ~**) Zeichendreieck *nt*; (*inf: person*) Spießer *m* ♦ *adj* quadratisch; (*inf: ideas, person*) spießig ♦ *vt* (*arrange*) ausrichten; (*MATH*) quadrieren; (*reconcile*) in Einklang bringen ♦ *vi* (*accord*) übereinstimmen; **we're back to ~ one** jetzt sind wir wieder da, wo wir angefangen haben; **all ~** (*SPORT*) unentschieden; (*fig*) quitt; **a ~ meal** eine ordentliche Mahlzeit; **2 metres ~** 2 Meter

im Quadrat; **2 ~ metres** 2 Quadratmeter; **I'll ~ it with him** (*inf*) ich mache das mit ihm ab; **can you ~ it with your conscience?** können Sie das mit Ihrem Gewissen vereinbaren?
▶ **square up** (*BRIT*) *vi* abrechnen.
square bracket *n* eckige Klammer *f*.
squarely ['skwɛəlɪ] *adv* (*directly*) direkt, genau; (*firmly*) fest; (*honestly*) ehrlich; (*fairly*) gerecht, fair.
square root *n* Quadratwurzel *f*.
squash [skwɔʃ] *n* (*BRIT*): **lemon/orange ~** Zitronen-/Orangensaftgetränk *nt*; (*US: marrow etc*) Kürbis *m*; (*SPORT*) Squash *nt* ♦ *vt* zerquetschen.
squat [skwɔt] *adj* gedrungen ♦ *vi* (*also*: **~ down**) sich (hin)hocken; (*on property*): **to ~ (in a house)** ein Haus besetzen.
squatter ['skwɔtə*] *n* Hausbesetzer(in) *m(f)*.
squawk [skwɔ:k] *vi* kreischen.
squeak [skwi:k] *vi* quietschen; (*mouse etc*) piepsen ♦ *n* Quietschen *nt*; (*of mouse etc*) Piepsen *nt*.
squeaky-clean [skwi:kɪ'kli:n] (*inf*) *adj* blitzsauber.
squeal [skwi:l] *vi* quietschen.
squeamish ['skwi:mɪʃ] *adj* empfindlich.
squeeze [skwi:z] *n* Drücken *nt*; (*ECON*) Beschränkung *f*; (*also*: **credit ~**) Kreditbeschränkung *f* ♦ *vt* drücken; (*lemon etc*) auspressen ♦ *vi*: **to ~ past sth** sich an etw *dat* vorbeidrücken; **to ~ under sth** sich unter etw *dat* durchzwängen; **to give sth a ~** etw drücken; **a ~ of lemon** ein Spritzer *m* Zitronensaft.
▶ **squeeze out** *vt* (*juice etc*) (her)auspressen; (*fig: exclude*) hinausdrängen.
squelch [skweltʃ] *vi* (*mud etc*) quatschen.
squib [skwɪb] *n* Knallfrosch *m*.
squid [skwɪd] *n* Tintenfisch *m*.
squiggle ['skwɪgl] *n* Schnörkel *m*.
squint [skwɪnt] *vi* (*in the sunlight*) blinzeln ♦ *n* (*MED*) Schielen *nt*; **he has a ~** er schielt.
squire ['skwaɪə*] (*BRIT*) *n* Gutsherr *m*; (*inf*) Chef *m*.
squirm [skwə:m] *vi* (*lit, fig*) sich winden.
squirrel ['skwɪrəl] *n* Eichhörnchen *nt*.
squirt [skwə:t] *vi, vi* spritzen.
Sr *abbr* (*in names*: = *senior*) sen.; (*REL*) = **sister**.
SRC (*BRIT*) *n abbr* (= *Students' Representative Council*) *studentische Vertretung.*
Sri Lanka [srɪ'læŋkə] *n* Sri Lanka *nt*.
SRN (*BRIT*) *n abbr* (*formerly*: = *State Registered Nurse*) staatlich geprüfte Krankenschwester *f*, staatlich geprüfter Krankenpfleger *m*.
SRO (*US*) *abbr* (= *standing room only*) nur Stehplätze.
SS *abbr* = **steamship**.
SSA (*US*) *n abbr* (= *Social Security Administration*) *Sozialversicherungsbehörde.*
SST (*US*) *n abbr* (= *supersonic transport*)

Überschallverkehr *m*.
ST (*US*) *abbr* = **standard time**.
St *abbr* (= *saint*) St.; (= *street*) Str.
stab [stæb] *n* Stich *m*, Stoß *m*; (*inf*: *try*): **to have
a** ~ **at sth** etw probieren ♦ *vt* (*person*)
niederstechen; (*body*) einstechen auf +*acc*; **a**
~ **of pain** ein stechender Schmerz; **to** ~ **sb
to death** jdn erstechen.
stabbing ['stæbɪŋ] *n* Messerstecherei *f* ♦ *adj*
(*pain*) stechend.
stability [stə'bɪlɪtɪ] *n* Stabilität *f*.
stabilization [steɪbəlaɪ'zeɪʃən] *n*
Stabilisierung *f*.
stabilize ['steɪbəlaɪz] *vt* stabilisieren ♦ *vi* sich
stabilisieren.
stabilizer ['steɪbəlaɪzə*] *n* (*AVIAT*)
Stabilisierungsfläche *f*; (*NAUT, food additive*)
Stabilisator *m*.
stable ['steɪbl] *adj* stabil; (*marriage*) dauerhaft
♦ *n* Stall *m*; **riding** ~**s** Reitstall *m*.
staccato [stə'kɑːtəu] *adv* (*MUS*) stakkato ♦ *adj*
abgehackt.
stack [stæk] *n* Stapel *m*; (*of books etc*) Stoß *m*
♦ *vt* (*also*: ~ **up**) aufstapeln; ~**s of time** (*BRIT*:
inf) jede Menge Zeit; **to** ~ **with** voll stapeln
mit.
stadia ['steɪdɪə] *npl of* **stadium**.
stadium ['steɪdɪəm] (*pl* **stadia** *or* ~**s**) *n* Stadion
nt.
staff [stɑːf] *n* (*workforce, servants*) Personal *nt*;
(*BRIT*: *also*: **teaching** ~) (Lehrer)kollegium *nt*;
(*stick*: *MIL*) Stab *m* ♦ *vt* (mit Personal)
besetzen; **one of his** ~ einer seiner
Mitarbeiter; **a member of** ~ ein(e)
Mitarbeiter(in) *m(f)*; (*SCOL*) ein(e)
Lehrer(in) *m(f)*.
staffroom ['stɑːfruːm] *n* (*SCOL*)
Lehrerzimmer *nt*.
Staffs (*BRIT*) *abbr* (*POST*: = *Staffordshire*).
stag [stæg] *n* Hirsch *m*; (*BRIT*: *STOCK
EXCHANGE*) Spekulant *m* (*der junge Aktien
aufkauft*); ~ **market** (*BRIT*: *STOCK EXCHANGE*)
Spekulantenmarkt *m*.
stage [steɪdʒ] *n* Bühne *f*; (*platform*) Podium *nt*;
(*point, period*) Stadium *nt* ♦ *vt* (*play*)
aufführen; (*demonstration*) organisieren;
(*perform: recovery etc*) schaffen; **the** ~ das
Theater, die Bühne; **in** ~**s** etappenweise; **to
go through a difficult** ~ eine schwierige
Phase durchmachen; **in the early/final** ~**s** im
Anfangs-/Endstadium.
stagecoach ['steɪdʒkəutʃ] *n* Postkutsche *f*.
stage door *n* Bühneneingang *m*.
stage fright *n* Lampenfieber *nt*.
stagehand ['steɪdʒhænd] *n*
Bühnenarbeiter(in) *m(f)*.
stage-manage ['steɪdʒmænɪdʒ] *vt* (*fig*)
inszenieren.
stage manager *n* Inspizient(in) *m(f)*.
stagger ['stægə*] *vi* schwanken, taumeln ♦ *vt*
(*amaze*) die Sprache verschlagen +*dat*;
(*hours, holidays*) staffeln.

staggering ['stægərɪŋ] *adj* (*amazing*)
atemberaubend.
staging post ['steɪdʒɪŋ-] *n* Zwischenstation *f*.
stagnant ['stægnənt] *adj* (*water*) stehend;
(*economy etc*) stagnierend.
stagnate [stæg'neɪt] *vi* (*economy etc*)
stagnieren; (*person*) verdummen.
stagnation [stæg'neɪʃən] *n* Stagnation *f*.
stag night, **stag party** *n* Herrenabend *m*.

STAG NIGHT

Als **stag night** bezeichnet man eine
feuchtfröhliche Männerparty, die kurz vor einer
Hochzeit vom Bräutigam und seinen Freunden
meist in einem Gasthaus oder Nachtklub
abgehalten wird. Diese Feiern sind oft sehr
ausgelassen und können manchmal auch zu weit
gehen (wenn dem betrunkenen Bräutigam ein
Streich gespielt wird). Siehe auch **hen night**.

---

staid [steɪd] *adj* gesetzt.
stain [steɪn] *n* Fleck *m*; (*colouring*) Beize *f* ♦ *vt*
beflecken; (*wood*) beizen.
stained glass window [steɪnd-] *n* buntes
Glasfenster *nt*.
stainless steel ['steɪnlɪs-] *n* (rostfreier)
Edelstahl *m*.
stain remover *n* Fleckentferner *m*.
stair [stɛə*] *n* (*step*) Stufe *f*; **stairs** *npl* (*flight of
steps*) Treppe *f*; **on the** ~**s** auf der Treppe.
staircase ['stɛəkeɪs] *n* Treppe *f*.
stairway ['stɛəweɪ] *n* = **staircase**.
stairwell ['stɛəwɛl] *n* Treppenhaus *nt*.
stake [steɪk] *n* (*post*) Pfahl *m*, Pfosten *m*;
(*COMM*) Anteil *m*; (*BETTING*: *gen pl*) Einsatz
m ♦ *vt* (*money*) setzen; (*also*: ~ **out**: *area*)
abstecken; **to be at** ~ auf dem Spiel stehen;
to have a ~ **in sth** einen Anteil an etw *dat*
haben; **to** ~ **a claim (to sth)** sich *dat* ein
Anrecht (auf etw *acc*) sichern; **to** ~ **one's
life on sth** seinen Kopf auf etw *acc* wetten;
to ~ **one's reputation on sth** sich für etw
verbürgen.
stakeout ['steɪkaut] *n* (*surveillance*)
Überwachung *f*.
stalactite ['stæləktaɪt] *n* Stalaktit *m*.
stalagmite ['stæləgmaɪt] *n* Stalagmit *m*.
stale [steɪl] *adj* (*bread*) altbacken; (*food*) alt;
(*smell*) muffig; (*air*) verbraucht; (*beer*) schal.
stalemate ['steɪlmeɪt] *n* (*CHESS*) Patt *nt*; (*fig*)
Sackgasse *f*.
stalk [stɔːk] *n* Stiel *m* ♦ *vt* sich heranpirschen
an +*acc* ♦ *vi*: **to** ~ **out/off** hinaus-/
davonstolzieren.
stall [stɔːl] *n* (*BRIT*: *in market etc*) Stand *m*; (*in
stable*) Box *f* ♦ *vt* (*engine, car*) abwürgen; (*fig*:
person) hinhalten; (: *decision etc*)
hinauszögern ♦ *vi* (*engine*) absterben; (*car*)
stehen bleiben; (*fig*: *person*) ausweichen;
stalls *npl* (*BRIT*: *in cinema, theatre*) Parkett *nt*;
a seat in the ~**s** ein Platz im Parkett; **a**

clothes/flower ~ ein Kleidungs-/
Blumenstand; **to** ~ **for time** versuchen, Zeit
zu gewinnen.
stallholder ['stɔːlhəʊldəˀ] (*BRIT*) *n*
Standbesitzer(in) *m(f)*.
stallion ['stæljən] *n* Hengst *m*.
stalwart ['stɔːlwət] *adj* treu.
stamen ['steimɛn] *n* Staubgefäß *nt*.
stamina ['stæmɪnə] *n* Ausdauer *f*.
stammer ['stæməˀ] *n* Stottern *nt* ♦ *vi* stottern;
to have a ~ stottern.
stamp [stæmp] *n* (*lit, fig*) Stempel *m*; (*postage
stamp*) Briefmarke *f* ♦ *vi* stampfen; (*also:*
~ **one's foot**) (mit dem Fuß) aufstampfen
♦ *vt* stempeln; (*with postage stamp*)
frankieren; ~**ed addressed envelope**
frankierter Rückumschlag.
▶ **stamp out** *vt* (*fire*) austreten; (*fig: crime*)
ausrotten; (: *opposition*) unterdrücken.
stamp album *n* Briefmarkenalbum *nt*.
stamp collecting *n* Briefmarkensammeln *nt*.
stamp duty (*BRIT*) *n* (Stempel)gebühr *f*.
stampede [stæm'piːd] *n* (*of animals*) wilde
Flucht *f*; (*fig*) Massenandrang *m*.
stamp machine *n* Briefmarkenautomat *m*.
stance [stæns] *n* Haltung *f*; (*fig*) Einstellung *f*.
stand [stænd] (*pt, pp* **stood**) *n* (*COMM*) Stand *m*;
(*SPORT*) Tribüne *f*; (*piece of furniture*)
Ständer *m* ♦ *vi* stehen; (*rise*) aufstehen;
(*remain*) bestehen bleiben; (*in election etc*)
kandidieren ♦ *vt* stellen; (*tolerate, withstand*)
ertragen; **to make a** ~ **against sth**
Widerstand gegen etw leisten; **to take a**
~ **on sth** einen Standpunkt zu etw
vertreten; **to take the** ~ (*US: LAW*) in den
Zeugenstand treten; **to** ~ **at** (*value, score etc*)
betragen; (*level*) liegen bei; **to** ~ **for
parliament** (*BRIT*) in den Parlamentswahlen
kandidieren; **to** ~ **to gain/lose sth** etw
gewinnen/verlieren können; **it** ~**s to reason**
es ist einleuchtend; **as things** ~ nach Lage
der Dinge; **to** ~ **sb a drink/meal** jdm einen
Drink/ein Essen spendieren; **I can't** ~ **him**
ich kann ihn nicht leiden *or* ausstehen; **we
don't** ~ **a chance** wir haben keine Chance;
to ~ **trial** vor Gericht stehen.
▶ **stand by** *vi* (*be ready*) sich bereithalten;
(*fail to help*) (unbeteiligt) danebenstehen ♦ *vt
fus* (*opinion, decision*) stehen zu; (*person*)
halten zu.
▶ **stand down** *vi* zurücktreten.
▶ **stand for** *vt fus* (*signify*) bedeuten;
(*represent*) stehen für; (*tolerate*) sich *dat*
gefallen lassen.
▶ **stand in for** *vt fus* vertreten.
▶ **stand out** *vi* hervorstechen.
▶ **stand up** *vi* aufstehen.
▶ **stand up for** *vt fus* eintreten für.
▶ **stand up to** *vt fus* standhalten +*dat*; (*person*)
sich behaupten gegenüber +*dat*.
stand-alone ['stændəlaʊn] *adj* (*COMPUT*)
selb(st)ständig.

standard ['stændəd] *n* (*level*) Niveau *nt*; (*norm*)
Norm *f*; (*criterion*) Maßstab *m*; (*flag*)
Standarte *f* ♦ *adj* (*size, model, value etc*)
Standard-; (*normal*) normal; **standards** *npl*
(*morals*) (sittliche) Maßstäbe *pl*; **to be** *or* **to
come up to** ~ den Anforderungen genügen;
to apply a double ~ mit zweierlei Maß
messen.
Standard Grade *n* (*SCOT SCOL*)
Schulabschlusszeugnis, ≈ mittlere Reife *f*.
standardization [stændədaɪ'zeɪʃən] *n*
Vereinheitlichung *f*.
standardize ['stændədaɪz] *vt* vereinheitlichen.
standard lamp (*BRIT*) *n* Stehlampe *f*.
standard of living *n* Lebensstandard *m*.
standard time *n* Normalzeit *f*.
stand-by, standby ['stændbaɪ] *n* Reserve *f*;
(*also:* **standby ticket**) Stand-by-Ticket *nt* ♦ *adj*
(*generator*) Reserve-, Ersatz-; **to be on** ~
(*doctor*) Bereitschaftsdienst haben; (*crew,
firemen etc*) in Bereitschaft sein,
einsatzbereit sein.
stand-by ticket *n* Stand-by-Ticket *nt*.
stand-in ['stændɪn] *n* Ersatz *m*.
standing ['stændɪŋ] *adj* (*permanent*) ständig;
(*army*) stehend ♦ *n* (*status*) Rang *m*, Stellung
f; **a** ~ **ovation** stürmischer Beifall; **of many
years'** ~ von langjähriger Dauer; **a
relationship of 6 months'** ~ eine seit 6
Monaten bestehende Beziehung; **a man of
some** ~ ein angesehener Mann.
standing joke *n* Standardwitz *m*.
standing order (*BRIT*) *n* (*at bank*)
Dauerauftrag *m*.
standing room *n* Stehplätze *pl*.
standoff *n* (*situation*) ausweglose *or*
verfahrene Situation *f*.
stand-offish [stænd'ɔfɪʃ] *adj* distanziert.
standpat ['stændpæt] (*US*) *adj* konservativ.
standpipe ['stændpaɪp] *n* Steigrohr *nt*.
standpoint ['stændpɔɪnt] *n* Standpunkt *m*.
standstill ['stændstɪl] *n*: **to be at a** ~
stillstehen; (*fig: negotiations*) in eine
Sackgasse geraten sein; **to come to a** ~
(*traffic*) zum Stillstand kommen.
stank [stæŋk] *pt of* **stink**.
stanza ['stænzə] *n* Strophe *f*.
staple ['steɪpl] *n* (*for papers*) Heftklammer *f*;
(*chief product*) Hauptartikel *m* ♦ *adj* (*food,
diet*) Grund-, Haupt- ♦ *vt* heften.
stapler ['steɪpləˀ] *n* Hefter *m*.
star [stɑːˀ] *n* Stern *m*; (*celebrity*) Star *m* ♦ *vt*
(*THEAT, CINE*) in der Hauptrolle zeigen ♦ *vi*:
to ~ **in** die Hauptrolle haben in; **the stars** *npl*
(*horoscope*) das Horoskop; **4-**~ **hotel** 4-
Sterne-Hotel *nt*; **2-**~ **petrol** (*BRIT*)
Normal(benzin) *nt*; **4-**~ **petrol** (*BRIT*)
Super(benzin) *nt*.
star attraction *n* Hauptattraktion *f*.
starboard ['stɑːbɔːd] *adj* (*side*) Steuerbord-; **to**
~ (nach) Steuerbord.
starch [stɑːtʃ] *n* Stärke *f*.

starched [stɑːtʃt] *adj* gestärkt.

starchy ['stɑːtʃɪ] *adj (food)* stärkehaltig; *(pej: person)* steif.

stardom ['stɑːdəm] *n* Berühmtheit *f*.

stare [stɛə*] *n* starrer Blick *m* ♦ *vi*: **to ~ at** anstarren.

starfish ['stɑːfɪʃ] *n* Seestern *m*.

stark [stɑːk] *adj (bleak)* kahl; *(simplicity)* schlicht; *(colour)* eintönig; *(reality, poverty)* nackt ♦ *adv*: **~ naked** splitternackt.

starkers ['stɑːkəz] *(inf) adj* splitter(faser)nackt.

starlet ['stɑːlɪt] *n* (Film)sternchen *nt*, Starlet *nt*.

starlight ['stɑːlaɪt] *n* Sternenlicht *nt*.

starling ['stɑːlɪŋ] *n* Star *m*.

starlit ['stɑːlɪt] *adj* sternklar.

starry ['stɑːrɪ] *adj* sternklar; **~ sky** Sternenhimmel *m*.

starry-eyed [stɑːrɪˈaɪd] *adj (innocent)* arglos, blauäugig; *(from wonder)* verzückt.

Stars and Stripes *n sing* Sternenbanner *nt*.

star sign *n* Sternzeichen *nt*.

star-studded ['stɑːstʌdɪd] *adj*: **a ~ cast** eine Starbesetzung *f*.

START *n abbr (MIL: = Strategic Arms Reduction Talks)* START.

start [stɑːt] *n* Beginn *m*, Anfang *m*; *(departure)* Aufbruch *m*; *(advantage)* Vorsprung *m* ♦ *vt* anfangen mit; *(panic)* auslösen; *(fire)* anzünden; *(found)* gründen; *(: restaurant etc)* eröffnen; *(engine)* anlassen; *(car)* starten ♦ *vi* anfangen; *(with fright)* zusammenfahren; *(engine etc)* anspringen; **at the ~** am Anfang, zu Beginn; **for a ~** erstens; **to make an early ~** frühzeitig aufbrechen; **to give a ~** zusammenfahren; **to wake up with a ~** aus dem Schlaf hochschrecken; **to ~ doing** *or* **to do sth** anfangen, etw zu tun; **to ~ (off) with ...** *(firstly)* erstens; *(at the beginning)* zunächst.

▶ **start off** *vi (begin)* anfangen; *(begin moving)* losgehen/-fahren.

▶ **start out** *vi (leave)* sich aufmachen.

▶ **start over** *(US) vi* noch einmal von vorn anfangen.

▶ **start up** *vt (business)* gründen; *(restaurant etc)* eröffnen; *(car)* starten; *(engine)* anlassen.

starter ['stɑːtə*] *n (AUT)* Anlasser *m*; *(SPORT: official, runner, horse)* Starter *m*; *(BRIT: CULIN)* Vorspeise *f*; **for ~s** *(inf)* für den Anfang.

starting point ['stɑːtɪŋ-] *n (lit, fig)* Ausgangspunkt *m*.

starting price *n (at auction)* Ausgangsangebot *nt*.

startle ['stɑːtl] *vt* erschrecken.

startling ['stɑːtlɪŋ] *adj (news etc)* überraschend.

star turn *(BRIT) n* Sensation *f*, Hauptattraktion *f*.

starvation [stɑːˈveɪʃən] *n* Hunger *m*; **to die**

of/from ~ verhungern.

starve [stɑːv] *vi* hungern; *(to death)* verhungern ♦ *vt* hungern lassen; *(fig: deprive)*: **to ~ sb of sth** jdm etw vorenthalten; **I'm starving** ich sterbe vor Hunger.

Star Wars *n* Krieg *m* der Sterne.

stash [stæʃ] *vi (also:* **~ away***)* beiseite schaffen ♦ *n (secret store)* geheimes Lager *nt*.

state [steɪt] *n (condition)* Zustand *m*; *(POL)* Staat *m* ♦ *vt (say)* feststellen; *(declare)* erklären; **the States** *npl (GEOG)* die (Vereinigten) Staaten *pl*; **to be in a ~** aufgeregt sein; *(on edge)* nervös sein; *(in a mess)* in einem schrecklichen Zustand sein; **to get into a ~** durchdrehen *(inf)*; **in ~** feierlich; **to lie in ~** (feierlich) aufgebahrt sein; **~ of emergency** Notstand *m*; **~ of mind** Verfassung *f*.

state control *n* staatliche Kontrolle *f*.

stated ['steɪtɪd] *adj* erklärt.

State Department *(US) n* Außenministerium *nt*.

state education *(BRIT) n* staatliche Erziehung *f*; *(system)* staatliches Bildungswesen *nt*.

stateless ['steɪtlɪs] *adj* staatenlos.

stately ['steɪtlɪ] *adj* würdevoll; *(walk)* gemessen; **~ home** Schloss *nt*.

statement ['steɪtmənt] *n (thing said)* Feststellung *f*; *(declaration)* Erklärung *f*; *(FIN)* (Konto)auszug *m*; **official ~** (amtliche) Erklärung *f*; **bank ~** Kontoauszug *m*.

state of the art *n*: **the ~** der neueste Stand der Technik ♦ *adj*: **state-of-the-art** auf dem neuesten Stand der Technik; *(technology)* Spitzen-.

state-owned ['steɪtəund] *adj* staatseigen.

state school *n* öffentliche Schule *f*.

state secret *n* Staatsgeheimnis *nt*.

statesman ['steɪtsmən] *(irreg: like* **man***) n* Staatsmann *m*.

statesmanship ['steɪtsmənʃɪp] *n* Staatskunst *f*.

static ['stætɪk] *n (RADIO, TV)* atmosphärische Störungen *pl* ♦ *adj (not moving)* konstant.

static electricity *n* Reibungselektrizität *f*.

station ['steɪʃən] *n (RAIL)* Bahnhof *m*; *(also:* **bus ~***)* Busbahnhof *m*; *(also:* **police ~***)* (Polizei)wache *f*; *(RADIO)* Sender *m* ♦ *vt (guards etc)* postieren; *(soldiers etc)* stationieren; **action ~s** *(MIL)* Stellung *f*; **above one's ~** über seinem Stand.

stationary ['steɪʃnərɪ] *adj (vehicle)* haltend; **to be ~** stehen.

stationer ['steɪʃənə*] *n* Schreibwarenhändler(in) *m(f)*.

stationer's (shop) *n* Schreibwarenhandlung *f*.

stationery ['steɪʃnərɪ] *n* Schreibwaren *pl*; *(writing paper)* Briefpapier *nt*.

stationmaster ['steɪʃənmɑːstə*] *n* Bahnhofsvorsteher *m*.

station wagon (*US*) *n* Kombi(wagen) *m*.

statistic [stə'tɪstɪk] *n* Statistik *f*.

statistical [stə'tɪstɪkl] *adj* statistisch.

statistics [stə'tɪstɪks] *n* (*science*) Statistik *f*.

statue ['stætjuː] *n* Statue *f*.

statuesque [stætju'ɛsk] *adj* stattlich.

statuette [stætju'ɛt] *n* Statuette *f*.

stature ['stætʃə*] *n* Wuchs *m*, Statur *f*; (*fig: reputation*) Format *nt*.

status ['steɪtəs] *n* Status *m*; (*position*) Stellung *f*; **the ~ quo** der Status quo.

status line *n* (*COMPUT*) Statuszeile *f*.

status symbol *n* Statussymbol *nt*.

statute ['stætjuːt] *n* Gesetz *nt*; **statutes** *npl* (*of club etc*) Satzung *f*.

statute book *n*: **to be on the ~** geltendes Recht sein.

statutory ['stætjutrɪ] *adj* gesetzlich; **~ declaration** eidesstattliche Erklärung *f*.

staunch [stɔːntʃ] *adj* treu ♦ *vt* (*flow*) stauen; (*blood*) stillen.

stave [steɪv] *n* (*MUS*) Notensystem *nt*.
▶ **stave off** *vt* (*attack*) abwehren; (*threat*) abwenden.

stay [steɪ] *n* Aufenthalt *m* ♦ *vi* bleiben; (*with sb, as guest*) wohnen; (*in hotel*) übernachten; **~ of execution** (*LAW*) Aussetzung *f*; **to ~ put** bleiben; **to ~ with friends** bei Freunden untergebracht sein; **to ~ the night** übernachten.
▶ **stay behind** *vi* zurückbleiben.
▶ **stay in** *vi* (*at home*) zu Hause bleiben.
▶ **stay on** *vi* bleiben.
▶ **stay out** *vi* (*of house*) wegbleiben; (*remain on strike*) weiterstreiken.
▶ **stay up** *vi* (*at night*) aufbleiben.

staying power ['steɪɪŋ-] *n* Stehvermögen *nt*, Durchhaltevermögen *nt*.

STD *n abbr* (*BRIT: TEL*: = *subscriber trunk dialling*) Selbstwählferndienst *m*; (*MED*: = *sexually transmitted disease*) durch Geschlechtsverkehr übertragene Krankheit *f*.

stead [stɛd] *n*: **in sb's ~** an jds Stelle; **to stand sb in good ~** jdm zugute *or* zustatten kommen.

steadfast ['stɛdfɑːst] *adj* standhaft.

steadily ['stɛdɪlɪ] *adv* (*regularly*) regelmäßig; (*constantly*) stetig; (*fixedly*) fest, unverwandt.

steady ['stɛdɪ] *adj* (*job, boyfriend, girlfriend, look*) fest; (*income*) regelmäßig; (*speed*) gleichmäßig; (*rise*) stetig; (*person, character*) zuverlässig, solide; (*voice, hand etc*) ruhig ♦ *vt* (*stabilize*) ruhig halten; (*nerves*) beruhigen; **to ~ o.s. on sth** sich auf etw *acc* stützen; **to ~ o.s. against sth** sich an etw *dat* abstützen.

steak [steɪk] *n* Steak *nt*; (*fish*) Filet *nt*.

steakhouse ['steɪkhaus] *n* Steakrestaurant *nt*.

steal [stiːl] (*pt* **stole**, *pp* **stolen**) *vt* stehlen ♦ *vi* stehlen; (*move secretly*) sich stehlen, schleichen.
▶ **steal away** *vi* sich davonschleichen.

stealth [stɛlθ] *n*: **by ~** heimlich.

stealthy ['stɛlθɪ] *adj* heimlich, verstohlen.

steam [stiːm] *n* Dampf *m* ♦ *vt* (*CULIN*) dämpfen, dünsten ♦ *vi* dampfen; **covered with ~** (*window etc*) beschlagen; **under one's own ~** (*fig*) allein, ohne Hilfe; **to run out of ~** (*fig*) den Schwung verlieren; **to let off ~** (*inf, fig*) Dampf ablassen.
▶ **steam up** *vi* (*window*) beschlagen; **to get ~ed up about sth** (*inf, fig*) sich über etw *acc* aufregen.

steam engine *n* (*RAIL*) Dampflok(omotive) *f*.

steamer ['stiːmə*] *n* Dampfer *m*; (*CULIN*) Dämpfer *m*.

steam iron *n* Dampfbügeleisen *nt*.

steamroller ['stiːmrəulə*] *n* Dampfwalze *f*.

steamship ['stiːmʃɪp] *n* = **steamer**.

steamy ['stiːmɪ] *adj* (*room*) dampfig; (*window*) beschlagen; (*book, film*) heiß.

steed [stiːd] (*liter*) *n* Ross *nt*.

steel [stiːl] *n* Stahl *m* ♦ *adj* (*girder, wool etc*) Stahl-.

steel band *n* (*MUS*) Steelband *f*.

steel industry *n* Stahlindustrie *f*.

steel mill *n* Stahlwalzwerk *nt*.

steelworks ['stiːlwɜːks] *n* Stahlwerk *nt*.

steely ['stiːlɪ] *adj* (*determination*) eisern; (*eyes, gaze*) hart, stählern.

steep [stiːp] *adj* steil; (*increase, rise*) stark; (*price, fees*) gepfeffert ♦ *vt* einweichen; **to be ~ed in history** geschichtsträchtig sein.

steeple ['stiːpl] *n* Kirchturm *m*.

steeplechase ['stiːpltʃeɪs] *n* (*for horses*) Hindernisrennen *nt*; (*for runners*) Hindernislauf *m*.

steeplejack ['stiːpldʒæk] *n* Turmarbeiter *m*.

steeply ['stiːplɪ] *adv* steil.

steer [stɪə*] *vt* steuern; (*car etc*) lenken; (*person*) lotsen ♦ *vi* steuern; (*in car etc*) lenken; **to ~ for** zusteuern auf +*acc*; **to ~ clear of sb** (*fig*) jdm aus dem Weg gehen; **to ~ clear of sth** (*fig*) etw meiden.

steering ['stɪərɪŋ] *n* (*AUT*) Lenkung *f*.

steering column *n* (*AUT*) Lenksäule *f*.

steering committee *n* Lenkungsausschuss *m*.

steering wheel *n* (*AUT*) Lenkrad *nt*, Steuer *nt*.

stellar ['stɛlə*] *adj* stellar.

stem [stɛm] *n* Stiel *m*; (*of pipe*) Hals *m* ♦ *vt* aufhalten; (*flow*) eindämmen; (*bleeding*) zum Stillstand bringen.
▶ **stem from** *vt fus* zurückgehen auf +*acc*.

stench [stɛntʃ] (*pej*) *n* Gestank *m*.

stencil ['stɛnsl] *n* Schablone *f* ♦ *vt* mit Schablone zeichnen.

stenographer [stɛ'nɔgrəfə*] (*US*) *n* Stenograf(in) *m(f)*.

stenography [stɛ'nɔgrəfɪ] (*US*) *n* Stenografie *f*.

step [stɛp] *n* (*lit, fig*) Schritt *m*; (*of stairs*) Stufe *f* ♦ *vi*: **to ~ forward/back** vor-/zurücktreten; **steps** *npl* (*BRIT*) = **stepladder**; **~ by ~** (*fig*) Schritt für Schritt; **in/out of ~** (**with**) im/ nicht im Tritt (mit); (*fig*) im/nicht im Gleichklang (mit).
▶ **step down** *vi* (*fig: resign*) zurücktreten.
▶ **step in** *vi* (*fig*) eingreifen.
▶ **step off** *vt fus* aussteigen aus +*dat*.
▶ **step on** *vt fus* treten auf +*acc*.
▶ **step over** *vt fus* steigen über +*acc*.
▶ **step up** *vt* (*efforts*) steigern; (*pace etc*) beschleunigen.

stepbrother ['stɛpbrʌðə*] *n* Stiefbruder *m*.
stepchild ['stɛptʃaɪld] *n* Stiefkind *nt*.
stepdaughter ['stɛpdɔːtə*] *n* Stieftochter *f*.
stepfather ['stɛpfɑːðə*] *n* Stiefvater *m*.
stepladder ['stɛplædə*] (*BRIT*) *n* Trittleiter *f*.
stepmother ['stɛpmʌðə*] *n* Stiefmutter *f*.
stepping stone ['stɛpɪŋ-] *n* Trittstein *m*; (*fig*) Sprungbrett *nt*.
stepsister ['stɛpsɪstə*] *n* Stiefschwester *f*.
stepson ['stɛpsʌn] *n* Stiefsohn *m*.

stereo ['stɛrɪəu] *n* (*system*) Stereoanlage *f* ♦ *adj* (*sound etc*) Stereo-; **in ~** in Stereo.
stereotype ['stɪərɪətaɪp] *n* Klischee *nt*, Klischeevorstellung *f* ♦ *vt* in ein Klischee zwängen; **~d** stereotyp.

sterile ['stɛraɪl] *adj* steril, keimfrei; (*barren*) unfruchtbar; (*fig: debate*) fruchtlos.
sterility [stɛ'rɪlɪtɪ] *n* Unfruchtbarkeit *f*.
sterilization [stɛrɪlaɪ'zeɪʃən] *n* Sterilisation *f*, Sterilisierung *f*.
sterilize ['stɛrɪlaɪz] *vt* sterilisieren.
sterling ['stɜːlɪŋ] *adj* (*silver*) Sterling-; (*fig*) gediegen ♦ *n* (*ECON*) das Pfund Sterling, das englische Pfund; **one pound ~** ein Pfund Sterling.
sterling area *n* (*ECON*) Sterlingländer *pl*.
stern [stɜːn] *adj* streng ♦ *n* Heck *nt*.
sternum ['stɜːnəm] *n* Brustbein *nt*.
steroid ['stɪərɔɪd] *n* Steroid *nt*.
stethoscope ['stɛθəskəup] *n* Stethoskop *nt*.
stevedore ['stiːvədɔː*] *n* Stauer *m*, Schauermann *m*.
stew [stjuː] *n* Eintopf *m* ♦ *vt* schmoren; (*fruit, vegetables*) dünsten ♦ *vi* schmoren; **~ed tea** bitterer Tee *m*; **~ed fruit** (Obst)kompott *nt*.
steward ['stjuːəd] *n* Steward *m*; (*at public event*) Ordner(in) *m(f)*; (*also:* **shop ~**) gewerkschaftliche Vertrauensperson *f*.
stewardess ['stjuːədɛs] *n* Stewardess *f*.
stewardship ['stjuːədʃɪp] *n* Verwaltung *f*.
stewing steak, (*US*) **stew meat** ['stjuːɪŋ-] *n* (Rinder)schmorfleisch *nt*.
St. Ex. *abbr* = **stock exchange**.
stg *abbr* = **sterling**.
stick [stɪk] (*pt, pp* **stuck**) *n* Zweig *m*; (*of dynamite*) Stange *f*; (*of chalk etc*) Stück *nt*; (*as weapon*) Stock *m*; (*also:* **walking ~**)

(Spazier)stock *m* ♦ *vt* (*with glue etc*) kleben; (*inf: put*) tun, stecken; (*thrust*) stoßen ♦ *vi*: **to ~** (**to**) kleben (an +*dat*); (*remain*) (hängen) bleiben; (*door etc*) klemmen; (*lift*) stecken bleiben; **to get hold of the wrong end of the ~** (*BRIT, fig*) es falsch verstehen; **to ~ in sb's mind** jdm im Gedächtnis (haften) bleiben.
▶ **stick around** (*inf*) *vi* hier-/dableiben.
▶ **stick out** *vi* (*ears etc*) abstehen ♦ *vt*: **to ~ it out** (*inf*) durchhalten.
▶ **stick to** *vt fus* (*one's word, promise*) halten; (*agreement, rules*) sich halten an +*acc*; (*the truth, facts*) bleiben bei.
▶ **stick up** *vi* hochstehen.
▶ **stick up for** *vt fus* eintreten für.
sticker ['stɪkə*] *n* Aufkleber *m*.
sticking plaster ['stɪkɪŋ-] *n* Heftpflaster *nt*.
sticking point *n* Hindernis *nt*; (*in discussion etc*) strittiger Punkt *m*.
stickleback ['stɪklbæk] *n* Stichling *m*.
stickler ['stɪklə*] *n*: **to be a ~ for sth** es mit etw peinlich genau nehmen.
stick shift (*US*) *n* Schaltknüppel *m*; (*car*) Wagen *m* mit Handschaltung.
stick-up ['stɪkʌp] (*inf*) *n* Überfall *m*.
sticky ['stɪkɪ] *adj* klebrig; (*label, tape*) Klebe-; (*weather, day*) schwül.
stiff [stɪf] *adj* steif; (*hard, firm*) hart; (*paste, egg-white*) fest; (*door, zip etc*) schwer gehend; (*competition*) hart; (*sentence*) schwer; (*drink*) stark ♦ *adv* (*bored, worried, scared*) zu Tode; **to be** *or* **feel ~** steif sein; **to have a ~ neck** einen steifen Hals haben; **to keep a ~ upper lip** (*BRIT, fig*) die Haltung bewahren.
stiffen ['stɪfn] *vi* steif werden; (*body*) erstarren.
stiffness ['stɪfnɪs] *n* Steifheit *f*.
stifle ['staɪfl] *vt* unterdrücken; (*heat*) erdrücken.
stifling ['staɪflɪŋ] *adj* (*heat*) drückend.
stigma ['stɪgmə] *n* Stigma *nt*; (*BOT*) Narbe *f*, Stigma *nt*; **stigmata** *npl* (*MED*) Wundmal *nt*.
stile [staɪl] *n* Zaunübertritt *m*.
stiletto [stɪ'lɛtəu] (*BRIT*) *n* (*also:* **~ heel**) Bleistiftabsatz *m*.
still [stɪl] *adj* (*motionless*) bewegungslos; (*tranquil*) ruhig; (*air, water*) still; (*BRIT: drink*) ohne Kohlensäure ♦ *adv* (immer) noch; (*yet, even*) noch; (*nonetheless*) trotzdem ♦ *n* (*CINE*) Standfoto *nt*; **to stand ~** (*machine, motor*) stillstehen; (*motionless*) still stehen; **keep ~!** halte still!; **he ~ hasn't arrived** er ist immer noch nicht angekommen.
stillborn ['stɪlbɔːn] *adj* tot geboren.
still life *n* Stillleben *nt*.
stilt [stɪlt] *n* (*pile*) Pfahl *m*; (*for walking on*) Stelze *f*.
stilted ['stɪltɪd] *adj* gestelzt.
stimulant ['stɪmjulənt] *n* Anregungsmittel *nt*.
stimulate ['stɪmjuleɪt] *vt* anregen,

stimulieren; (*demand*) ankurbeln.

stimulating ['stɪmjuleɪtɪŋ] *adj* anregend, stimulierend.

stimulation [stɪmju'leɪʃən] *n* Anregung *f*, Stimulation *f*.

stimuli ['stɪmjulaɪ] *npl of* **stimulus**.

stimulus ['stɪmjuləs] (*pl* **stimuli**) *n* (*incentive*) Anreiz *m*; (*BIOL*) Reiz *m*; (*PSYCH*) Stimulus *m*.

sting [stɪŋ] (*pt, pp* **stung**) *n* Stich *m*; (*pain*) Stechen *nt*; (*organ: of insect*) Stachel *m*; (*inf: confidence trick*) Ding *nt* ♦ *vt* stechen; (*fig*) treffen, verletzen ♦ *vi* stechen; (*eyes, ointment, plant etc*) brennen; **my eyes are ~ing** mir brennen die Augen.

stingy ['stɪndʒɪ] (*pej*) *adj* geizig, knauserig.

stink [stɪŋk] (*pt* **stank**, *pp* **stunk**) *n* Gestank *m* ♦ *vi* stinken.

stinker ['stɪŋkə°] (*inf*) *n* (*problem*) harter Brocken *m*; (*person*) Ekel *nt*.

stinking ['stɪŋkɪŋ] (*inf*) *adj* (*fig*) beschissen (*!*); **a ~ cold** eine scheußliche Erkältung; **~ rich** stinkreich.

stint [stɪnt] *n* (*period*) Zeit *f*; (*batch of work*) Pensum *nt*; (*share*) Teil *m* ♦ *vi*: **to ~ on** sparen mit.

stipend ['staɪpɛnd] *n* Gehalt *nt*.

stipendiary [staɪ'pɛndɪərɪ] *adj*: **~ magistrate** bezahlter Friedensrichter *m*.

stipulate ['stɪpjuleɪt] *vt* festsetzen; (*condition*) stellen.

stipulation [stɪpju'leɪʃən] *n* Bedingung *f*, Auflage *f*.

stir [stə:°] *n* (*fig*) Aufsehen *nt* ♦ *vt* umrühren; (*fig: emotions*) aufwühlen; (: *person*) bewegen ♦ *vi* sich bewegen; **to give sth a ~** etw umrühren; **to cause a ~** Aufsehen erregen.

▶ **stir up** *vt*: **to ~ up trouble** Unruhe stiften; **to ~ things up** stänkern.

stir-fry ['stə:'fraɪ] *vt* unter Rühren kurz anbraten ♦ *n* Pfannengericht *nt* (*das unter Rühren kurz angebraten wurde*).

stirring ['stə:rɪŋ] *adj* bewegend.

stirrup ['stɪrəp] *n* Steigbügel *m*.

stitch [stɪtʃ] *n* (*SEWING*) Stich *m*; (*KNITTING*) Masche *f*; (*MED*) Faden *m*; (*pain*) Seitenstiche *pl* ♦ *vt* nähen; **he had to have ~es** er musste genäht werden.

stoat [stəut] *n* Wiesel *nt*.

stock [stɔk] *n* Vorrat *m*; (*COMM*) Bestand *m*; (*AGR*) Vieh *nt*; (*CULIN*) Brühe *f*; (*descent, origin*) Abstammung *f*, Herkunft *f*; (*FIN*) Wertpapiere *pl*; (*RAIL: also:* **rolling ~**) rollendes Material *nt* ♦ *adj* (*reply, excuse etc*) Standard- ♦ *vt* (*in shop*) führen; **in/out of ~** vorrätig/nicht vorrätig; **~s and shares** (Aktien und) Wertpapiere *pl*; **government ~** Staatsanleihe *f*; **to take ~ of** (*fig*) Bilanz ziehen über +*acc*; **well-~ed** (*shop*) mit gutem Sortiment.

▶ **stock up** *vi*: **to ~ up (with)** sich eindecken (mit).

stockade [stɔ'keɪd] *n* Palisade *f*.

stockbroker ['stɔkbrəukə°] *n* Börsenmakler *m*.

stock control *n* Bestandsüberwachung *f*.

stock cube (*BRIT*) *n* Brühwürfel *m*.

stock exchange *n* Börse *f*.

stockholder ['stɔkhəuldə°] (*esp US*) *n* Aktionär(in) *m(f)*.

Stockholm ['stɔkhəum] *n* Stockholm *nt*.

stocking ['stɔkɪŋ] *n* Strumpf *m*.

stock-in-trade ['stɔkɪn'treɪd] *n* (*fig*): **it's his ~** es gehört zu seinem festen Repertoire.

stockist ['stɔkɪst] (*BRIT*) *n* Händler *m*.

stock market (*BRIT*) *n* Börse *f*.

stock phrase *n* Standardsatz *m*.

stockpile ['stɔkpaɪl] *n* Vorrat *m*; (*of weapons*) Lager *nt* ♦ *vt* horten.

stockroom ['stɔkru:m] *n* Lager *nt*, Lagerraum *m*.

stocktaking ['stɔkteɪkɪŋ] (*BRIT*) *n* Inventur *f*.

stocky ['stɔkɪ] *adj* stämmig.

stodgy ['stɔdʒɪ] *adj* (*food*) pappig (*inf*), schwer.

stoic ['stəuɪk] *n* Stoiker(in) *m(f)*.

stoic(al) ['stəuɪk(l)] *adj* stoisch.

stoke [stəuk] *vt* (*fire*) schüren; (*furnace, boiler*) heizen.

stoker ['stəukə°] *n* Heizer *m*.

stole [stəul] *pt of* **steal** ♦ *n* Stola *f*.

stolen ['stəuln] *pp of* **steal**.

stolid ['stɔlɪd] *adj* phlegmatisch, stur (*inf*).

stomach ['stʌmək] *n* Magen *m*; (*belly*) Bauch *m* ♦ *vt* (*fig*) vertragen.

stomach ache *n* Magenschmerzen *pl*.

stomach pump *n* Magenpumpe *f*.

stomach ulcer *n* Magengeschwür *nt*.

stomp [stɔmp] *vi* stapfen.

stone [stəun] *n* Stein *m*; (*BRIT: weight*) Gewichtseinheit (= *6,35 kg*) ♦ *adj* (*wall, jar etc*) Stein-, steinern ♦ *vt* (*person*) mit Steinen bewerfen; (*fruit*) entkernen, entsteinen; **within a ~'s throw of the station** nur einen Katzensprung vom Bahnhof entfernt.

Stone Age *n* Steinzeit *f*.

stone-cold ['stəun'kəuld] *adj* eiskalt.

stoned [stəund] (*inf*) *adj* (*on drugs*) stoned; (*drunk*) total zu.

stone-deaf ['stəun'dɛf] *adj* stocktaub.

stonemason ['stəunmeɪsn] *n* Steinmetz *m*.

stonewall ['stəun'wɔ:l] *vi* mauern; (*in answering questions*) ausweichen.

stonework ['stəunwə:k] *n* Mauerwerk *nt*.

stony ['stəunɪ] *adj* steinig; (*fig: silence etc*) steinern.

stood [stud] *pt, pp of* **stand**.

stooge [stu:dʒ] *n* (*inf*) Handlanger(in) *m(f)*; (*THEAT*) Stichwortgeber(in) *m(f)*.

stool [stu:l] *n* Hocker *m*.

stoop [stu:p] *vi* (*also:* **~ down**) sich bücken; (*walk*) gebeugt gehen; **to ~ to sth** (*fig*) sich zu etw herablassen; **to ~ to doing sth** sich dazu herablassen, etw zu tun.

stop [stɔp] *n* Halt *m*; (*short stay*) Aufenthalt *m*;

(*in punctuation: also:* **full** ~) Punkt *m*; (*bus stop etc*) Haltestelle *f* ♦ *vt* stoppen; (*car etc*) anhalten; (*block*) sperren; (*prevent*) verhindern ♦ *vi* (*car etc*) anhalten; (*train*) halten; (*pedestrian, watch, clock*) stehen bleiben; (*end*) aufhören; **to come to a** ~ anhalten; **to put a** ~ **to** einen Riegel vorschieben +*dat*; **to** ~ **doing sth** aufhören, etw zu tun; **to** ~ **sb (from) doing sth** jdn davon abhalten, etw zu tun; ~ **it!** lass das!, hör auf!

► **stop by** *vi* kurz vorbeikommen.

► **stop off** *vi* kurz Halt machen, Zwischenstation machen.

► **stop up** *vt* (*hole*) zustopfen.

stopcock ['stɔpkɔk] *n* Absperrhahn *m*.

stopgap ['stɔpgæp] *n* (*person*) Lückenbüßer *m*; (*thing*) Notbehelf *m*; ~ **measure** Überbrückungsmaßnahme *f*.

stop-go [stɔp'gəu] *adj* (*economic cycle etc*) mit ständigem Auf und Ab.

stoplights ['stɔplaɪts] *npl* (*AUT*) Bremslichter *pl*.

stopover ['stɔpəuvə*] *n* Zwischenaufenthalt *m*; (*AVIAT*) Zwischenlandung *f*.

stoppage ['stɔpɪdʒ] *n* (*strike*) Streik *m*; (*blockage*) Unterbrechung *f*; (*of pay, cheque*) Sperrung *f*; (*deduction*) Abzug *m*.

stopper ['stɔpə*] *n* Stöpsel *m*.

stop press *n* letzte Meldungen *pl*.

stopwatch ['stɔpwɔtʃ] *n* Stoppuhr *f*.

storage ['stɔːrɪdʒ] *n* Lagerung *f*; (*also:* ~ **space**) Stauraum *m*; (*COMPUT*) Speicherung *f*.

storage capacity *n* (*COMPUT*) Speicherkapazität *f*.

storage heater (*BRIT*) *n* (Nacht)speicherofen *m*.

store [stɔː*] *n* Vorrat *m*; (*depot*) Lager *nt*; (*BRIT: large shop*) Geschäft *nt*, Kaufhaus *nt*; (*US: shop*) Laden *m*; (*fig*): **a** ~ **of** eine Fülle an +*dat* ♦ *vt* lagern; (*information etc, COMPUT*) speichern; (*food, medicines etc*) aufbewahren; (*in filing system*) ablegen; **stores** *npl* (*provisions*) Vorräte *pl*; **in** ~ eingelagert; **who knows what's in** ~ **for us?** wer weiß, was uns bevorsteht?; **to set great/little** ~ **by sth** viel/wenig von etw halten.

► **store up** *vt* einen Vorrat anlegen von; (*memories*) im Gedächtnis bewahren.

storehouse ['stɔːhaus] *n* (*US: COMM*) Lager(haus) *nt*; (*fig*) Fundgrube *f*.

storekeeper ['stɔːkiːpə*] (*US*) *n* Ladenbesitzer(in) *m(f)*.

storeroom ['stɔːruːm] *n* Lagerraum *m*.

storey, (*US*) **story** ['stɔːrɪ] *n* Stock *m*, Stockwerk *nt*.

stork [stɔːk] *n* Storch *m*.

storm [stɔːm] *n* (*lit, fig*) Sturm *m*; (*bad weather*) Unwetter *nt*; (*also:* **electrical** ~) Gewitter *nt* ♦ *vi* (*fig*) toben ♦ *vt* (*attack*) stürmen.

storm cloud *n* Gewitterwolke *f*.

storm door *n* äußere Windfangtür *f*.

stormy ['stɔːmɪ] *adj* (*lit, fig*) stürmisch.

story ['stɔːrɪ] *n* Geschichte *f*; (*PRESS*) Artikel *m*; (*lie*) Märchen *nt*; (*US*) = **storey**.

storybook ['stɔːrɪbuk] *n* Geschichtenbuch *nt*.

storyteller ['stɔːrɪtɛlə*] *n* Geschichtenerzähler(in) *m(f)*.

stout [staut] *adj* (*strong*) stark; (*fat*) untersetzt; (*resolute*) energisch ♦ *n* Starkbier *nt*.

stove [stəuv] *n* Herd *m*; (*small*) Kocher *m*; (*for heating*) (Heiz)ofen *m*; **gas** ~ Gasherd *m*.

stow [stəu] *vt* (*also:* ~ **away**) verstauen.

stowaway ['stəuəweɪ] *n* blinder Passagier *m*.

straddle ['strædl] *vt* (*sitting*) rittlings sitzen auf +*dat*; (*standing*) breitbeinig stehen über +*dat*; (*jumping*) grätschen über +*acc*; (*fig*) überspannen.

strafe [strɑːf] *vt* beschießen.

straggle ['strægl] *vi* (*houses etc*) verstreut liegen; (*people etc*) zurückbleiben.

straggler ['stræglə*] *n* Nachzügler *m*.

straggly ['strælgɪ] *adj* (*hair*) unordentlich.

straight [streɪt] *adj* gerade; (*hair*) glatt; (*honest*) offen, direkt; (*simple*) einfach; (*: fight*) direkt; (*THEAT*) ernst; (*inf: heterosexual*) hetero; (*whisky etc*) pur ♦ *adv* (*in time*) sofort; (*in direction*) direkt; (*drink*) pur ♦ *n* (*SPORT*) Gerade *f*; **to put** *or* **get sth** ~ (*make clear*) etw klären; (*make tidy*) etw in Ordnung bringen; **let's get this** ~ das wollen wir mal klarstellen; **10** ~ **wins** 10 Siege hintereinander; **to win in** ~ **sets** (*TENNIS*) ohne Satzverlust gewinnen; **to go** ~ **home** direkt nach Hause gehen; ~ **out** rundheraus; ~ **away**, ~ **off** sofort, gleich.

straighten ['streɪtn] *vt* (*skirt, sheet etc*) geradeziehen.

► **straighten out** *vt* (*fig*) klären.

straight-faced [streɪt'feɪst] *adj*: **to be/remain** ~ ernst bleiben ♦ *adv* ohne zu lachen.

straightforward [streɪt'fɔːwəd] *adj* (*simple*) einfach; (*honest*) offen.

straight sets *npl* (*TENNIS*): **to win in** ~ ohne Satzverlust gewinnen.

strain [streɪn] *n* Belastung *f*; (*MED: also:* **back** ~) überanstrengter Rücken *m*; (*: tension*) Überlastung *f*; (*of virus*) Art *f*; (*breed*) Sorte *f* ♦ *vt* (*back etc*) überanstrengen; (*resources*) belasten; (*CULIN*) abgießen ♦ *vi*: **to** ~ **to do sth** sich anstrengen, etw zu tun; **strains** *npl* (*MUS*) Klänge *pl*; **he's been under a lot of** ~ er hat unter großem Stress gestanden.

strained [streɪnd] *adj* (*back*) überanstrengt; (*muscle*) gezerrt; (*forced*) gezwungen; (*relations*) gespannt.

strainer ['streɪnə*] *n* Sieb *nt*.

strait [streɪt] *n* Meerenge *f*, Straße *f*; **straits** *npl* (*fig*): **to be in dire** ~**s** in großen Nöten sein.

straitjacket ['streɪtdʒækɪt] *n* Zwangsjacke *f*.

strait-laced [streɪt'leɪst] *adj* prüde,

puritanisch.
strand [strænd] *n* (*lit, fig*) Faden *m*; (*of wire*)
Litze *f*; (*of hair*) Strähne *f*.
stranded ['strændɪd] *adj*: **to be** ~ (*traveller*)
festsitzen; (*ship, sea creature*) gestrandet.
strange [streɪndʒ] *adj* fremd; (*odd*) seltsam,
merkwürdig.
strangely ['streɪndʒlɪ] *adv* seltsam,
merkwürdig; *see also* **enough**.
stranger ['streɪndʒə*] *n* Fremde(r) *f(m)*; **I'm a**
~ **here** ich bin hier fremd.
strangle ['stræŋgl] *vt* erwürgen, erdrosseln;
(*fig: economy etc*) ersticken.
stranglehold ['stræŋglhəʊld] *n* (*fig*) absolute
Machtposition *f*.
strangulation [stræŋgjʊ'leɪʃən] *n* Erwürgen
nt, Erdrosseln *nt*.
strap [stræp] *n* Riemen *m*; (*of dress etc*) Träger
m ♦ *vt* (*also*: ~ **in**) anschnallen; (*also*: ~ **on**)
umschnallen.
straphanging ['stræphæŋɪŋ] *n* Pendeln *nt* (als
stehender Fahrgast).
strapless ['stræplɪs] *adj* trägerlos,
schulterfrei.
strapped [stræpt] (*inf*) *adj*: ~ **(for cash)** pleite.
strapping ['stræpɪŋ] *adj* stramm.
Strasbourg ['stræzbɔːg] *n* Straßburg *nt*.
strata ['strɑːtə] *npl of* **stratum**.
stratagem ['strætɪdʒəm] *n* List *f*.
strategic [strə'tiːdʒɪk] *adj* strategisch; (*error*)
taktisch.
strategist ['strætɪdʒɪst] *n* Stratege *m*,
Strategin *f*.
strategy ['strætɪdʒɪ] *n* Strategie *f*.
stratosphere ['strætəsfɪə*] *n* Stratosphäre *f*.
stratum ['strɑːtəm] (*pl* **strata**) *n* Schicht *f*.
straw [strɔː] *n* Stroh *nt*; (*drinking straw*)
Strohhalm *m*; **that's the last** ~! das ist der
Gipfel!
strawberry ['strɔːbərɪ] *n* Erdbeere *f*.
stray [streɪ] *adj* (*animal*) streunend; (*bullet*)
verirrt; (*scattered*) einzeln, vereinzelt ♦ *vi*
(*children*) sich verirren; (*animals*) streunen;
(*thoughts*) abschweifen.
streak [striːk] *n* Streifen *m*; (*in hair*) Strähne *f*;
(*fig: of madness etc*) Zug *m* ♦ *vt* streifen ♦ *vi*:
to ~ **past** vorbeiflitzen; **a winning/losing** ~
eine Glücks-/Pechsträhne.
streaker ['striːkə*] (*inf*) *n* Blitzer(in) *m(f)*.
streaky ['striːkɪ] *adj* (*bacon*) durchwachsen.
stream [striːm] *n* (*small river*) Bach *m*; (*current*)
Strömung *f*; (*of people, vehicles*) Strom *m*; (*of
questions, insults etc*) Flut *f*, Schwall *m*; (*of
smoke*) Schwaden *m*; (*SCOL*)
Leistungsgruppe *f* ♦ *vt* (*SCOL*) in
Leistungsgruppen einteilen ♦ *vi* strömen;
against the ~ gegen den Strom; **to come on**
~ (*new power plant etc*) in Betrieb
genommen werden.
streamer ['striːmə*] *n* Luftschlange *f*.
stream feed *n* automatischer Papiereinzug
m.

streamline ['striːmlaɪn] *vt* Stromlinienform
geben +*dat*; (*fig*) rationalisieren.
streamlined ['striːmlaɪnd] *adj*
stromlinienförmig; (*AVIAT, AUT*)
windschlüpfrig; (*fig*) rationalisiert.
street [striːt] *n* Straße *f*; **the back** ~**s** die
Seitensträßchen *pl*; **to be on the** ~**s**
(*homeless*) obdachlos sein; (*as prostitute*) auf
den Strich gehen.
streetcar ['striːtkɑː*] (*US*) *n* Straßenbahn *f*.
street cred [-kred] (*inf*) *n* Glaubwürdigkeit *f*.
street lamp *n* Straßenlaterne *f*.
street lighting *n* Straßenbeleuchtung *f*.
street map *n* Stadtplan *m*.
street market *n* Straßenmarkt *m*.
street plan *n* Stadtplan *m*.
streetwise ['striːtwaɪz] (*inf*) *adj*: **to be** ~
wissen, wos langgeht.
strength [streŋθ] *n* (*lit, fig*) Stärke *f*; (*physical*)
Kraft *f*, Stärke *f*; (*of girder etc*) Stabilität *f*; (*of
knot etc*) Festigkeit *f*; (*of chemical solution*)
Konzentration *f*; (*of wine*) Schwere *f*; **on the**
~ **of** aufgrund *or* auf Grund +*gen*; **at full** ~
vollzählig; **to be below** ~ nicht die volle
Stärke haben.
strengthen ['streŋθən] *vt* (*lit, fig*) verstärken;
(*muscle*) kräftigen; (*economy, currency,
relationship*) festigen.
strenuous ['strenjʊəs] *adj* anstrengend;
(*determined*) unermüdlich.
strenuously ['strenjʊəslɪ] *adv* energisch; **she**
~ **denied the rumour** sie leugnete das
Gerücht hartnäckig.
stress [stres] *n* Druck *m*; (*mental*) Belastung *f*,
Stress *m*; (*LING*) Betonung *f*; (*emphasis*)
Akzent *m*, Gewicht *nt* ♦ *vt* betonen; **to lay
great** ~ **on sth** großen Wert auf etw *acc*
legen; **to be under** ~ großen Belastungen
ausgesetzt sein, unter Stress stehen.
stressful ['stresful] *adj* anstrengend, stressig;
(*situation*) angespannt.
stretch [stretʃ] *n* (*of sand, water etc*) Stück *nt*;
(*of time*) Zeit *f* ♦ *vi* (*person, animal*) sich
strecken; (*land, area*) sich erstrecken ♦ *vt*
(*pull*) spannen; (*fig: job, task*) fordern; **at a** ~
an einem Stück, ohne Unterbrechung; **by no**
~ **of the imagination** beim besten Willen
nicht; **to** ~ **to** *or* **as far as the frontier**
(*extend*) sich bis zur Grenze erstrecken; **to**
~ **one's legs** sich *dat* die Beine vertreten.
▶ **stretch out** *vi* sich ausstrecken ♦ *vt*
ausstrecken.
▶ **stretch to** *vt fus* (*be enough*) reichen für.
stretcher ['stretʃə*] *n* (Trag)bahre *f*.
stretcher-bearer ['stretʃəbeərə*] *n*
Krankenträger *m*.
stretch marks *npl* Dehnungsstreifen *pl*;
(*through pregnancy*)
Schwangerschaftsstreifen *pl*.
strewn [struːn] *adj*: ~ **with** übersät mit.
stricken ['strɪkən] *adj* (*person*) leidend; (*city,
industry etc*) Not leidend; ~ **with** (*disease*)

geschlagen mit; (*fear etc*) erfüllt von.

strict [strɪkt] *adj* streng; (*precise*) genau; **in the ~est confidence** streng vertraulich; **in the ~ sense of the word** streng genommen.

strictly ['strɪktlɪ] *adv* streng; (*exactly*) genau; (*solely*) ausschließlich; **~ confidential** streng vertraulich; **~ speaking** genau genommen; **not ~ true** nicht ganz richtig; **~ between ourselves** ganz unter uns.

strictness ['strɪktnɪs] *n* Strenge *f*.

stridden ['strɪdn] *pp of* stride.

stride [straɪd] (*pt* strode, *pp* stridden) *n* Schritt *m* ♦ *vi* schreiten; **to take sth in one's ~** (*fig*) mit etw spielend fertig werden.

strident ['straɪdnt] *adj* schrill, durchdringend; (*demands*) lautstark.

strife [straɪf] *n* Streit *m*, Zwietracht *f*.

strike [straɪk] (*pt*, *pp* struck) *n* Streik *m*, Ausstand *m*; (*MIL*) Angriff *m* ♦ *vt* (*hit*) schlagen; (*fig: idea, thought*) in den Sinn kommmen +*dat*; (*oil etc*) finden, stoßen auf +*acc*; (*bargain, deal*) aushandeln; (*coin, medal*) prägen ♦ *vi* streiken; (*illness, killer*) zuschlagen; (*disaster*) hereinbrechen; (*clock*) schlagen; **on ~** streikend; **to be on ~** streiken; **to ~ a balance** einen Mittelweg finden; **to be struck by lightning** vom Blitz getroffen werden; **to ~ a match** ein Streichholz anzünden.

► **strike back** *vi* (*MIL*) zurückschlagen; (*fig*) sich wehren.

► **strike down** *vt* niederschlagen.

► **strike off** *vt* (*from list*) (aus)streichen; (*doctor etc*) die Zulassung entziehen +*dat*.

► **strike out** *vi* losziehen, sich aufmachen ♦ *vt* (*word, sentence*) (aus)streichen.

► **strike up** *vt* (*MUS*) anstimmen; (*conversation*) anknüpfen; (*friendship*) schließen.

strikebreaker ['straɪkbreɪkə*] *n* Streikbrecher *m*.

strike pay *n* Streikgeld *nt*.

striker ['straɪkə*] *n* Streikende(r) *f(m)*; (*SPORT*) Stürmer *m*.

striking ['straɪkɪŋ] *adj* auffallend; (*attractive*) attraktiv.

strimmer ['strɪmə*] *n* Rasentrimmer *m*.

string [strɪŋ] (*pt*, *pp* strung) *n* Schnur *f*; (*of islands*) Kette *f*; (*of people, cars*) Schlange *f*; (*series*) Serie *f*; (*COMPUT*) Zeichenfolge *f*; (*MUS*) Saite *f* ♦ *vt*: **to ~ together** aneinander reihen; **the strings** *npl* (*MUS*) die Streichinstrumente *pl*; **to pull ~s** (*fig*) Beziehungen spielen lassen; **with no ~s attached** (*fig*) ohne Bedingungen; **to ~ sth out** etw verteilen.

string bean *n* grüne Bohne *f*.

stringed instrument *n* Saiteninstrument *nt*.

stringent ['strɪndʒənt] *adj* streng; (*measures*) drastisch.

string quartet *n* Streichquartett *nt*.

strip [strɪp] *n* Streifen *m*; (*of metal*) Band *nt*;

(*SPORT*) Trikot *nt*, Dress *m* ♦ *vt* (*undress*) ausziehen; (*paint*) abbeizen; (*also: ~ down: machine etc*) auseinander nehmen ♦ *vi* (*undress*) sich ausziehen.

strip cartoon *n* Comic(strip) *m*.

stripe [straɪp] *n* Streifen *m*; **stripes** *npl* (*MIL, POLICE*) (Ärmel)streifen *pl*.

striped [straɪpt] *adj* gestreift.

strip lighting (*BRIT*) *n* Neonlicht *nt*.

stripper ['strɪpə*] *n* Stripper(in) *m(f)*, Stripteasetänzer(in) *m(f)*.

strip-search ['strɪpsɜːtʃ] *n* Leibesvisitation *f* (*bei der man sich ausziehen muss*) ♦ *vt*: **to be ~ed** sich ausziehen müssen und durchsucht werden.

striptease ['strɪptiːz] *n* Striptease *m or nt*.

strive [straɪv] (*pt* strove, *pp* striven) *vi*: **to ~ for sth** nach etw streben; **to ~ to do sth** danach streben, etw zu tun.

striven ['strɪvn] *pp of* strive.

strobe [strəub] *n* (*also: ~ lights*) Stroboskoplicht *nt*.

strode [strəud] *pt of* stride.

stroke [strəuk] *n* Schlag *m*, Hieb *m*; (*SWIMMING: style*) Stil *m*; (*MED*) Schlaganfall *m*; (*of clock*) Schlag *m*; (*of paintbrush*) Strich *m* ♦ *vt* (*caress*) streicheln; **at a ~** mit einem Schlag; **on the ~ of 5** Punkt 5 (Uhr); **a ~ of luck** ein Glücksfall *m*; **a 2-~ engine** ein Zweitaktmotor *m*.

stroll [strəul] *n* Spaziergang *m* ♦ *vi* spazieren; **to go for a ~, have** *or* **take a ~** einen Spaziergang machen.

stroller ['strəulə*] (*US*) *n* (*pushchair*) Sportwagen *m*.

strong [strɔŋ] *adj* stark; (*person, arms, grip*) stark, kräftig; (*healthy*) kräftig; (*object, material*) solide, stabil; (*letter*) geharnischt; (*measure*) drastisch; (*language*) derb; (*nerves*) gut; (*taste, smell*) stark ♦ *adv*: **to be going ~** (*company*) sehr erfolgreich sein; (*person*) gut in Schuss sein; **I have no ~ feelings about it** es ist mir ziemlich egal; **they are 50 ~** sie sind insgesamt 50.

strong-arm ['strɔŋɑːm] *adj* brutal.

strongbox ['strɔŋbɔks] *n* (Geld)kassette *f*.

stronghold ['strɔŋhəuld] *n* Festung *f*; (*fig*) Hochburg *f*.

strongly ['strɔŋlɪ] *adv* (*solidly*) stabil; (*forcefully*) entschieden; (*deeply*) fest; **to feel ~ that ...** fest davon überzeugt sein, dass ...; **I feel ~ about it** mir liegt sehr viel daran; (*negatively*) ich bin sehr dagegen.

strongman ['strɔŋmæn] (*irreg: like* man) *n* (*lit, fig*) starker Mann *m*.

strongroom ['strɔŋruːm] *n* Tresorraum *m*.

stroppy ['strɔpɪ] (*BRIT: inf*) *adj* pampig; (*obstinate*) stur.

strove [strəuv] *pt of* strive.

struck [strʌk] *pt*, *pp of* strike.

structural ['strʌktʃrəl] *adj* strukturell; (*damage*) baulich; (*defect*) Konstruktions-.

structurally ['strʌktʃrəlɪ] *adv*: ~ **sound** mit guter Bausubstanz.

structure ['strʌktʃəʳ] *n* Struktur *f*, Aufbau *m*; (*building*) Gebäude *nt*.

struggle ['strʌgl] *n* Kampf *m*; (*difficulty*) Anstrengung *f* ♦ *vi* (*try hard*) sich abmühen; (*fight*) kämpfen; (*in self-defence*) sich wehren; **to have a ~ to do sth** Mühe haben, etw zu tun; **to be a ~ for sb** jdm große Schwierigkeiten bereiten.

strum [strʌm] *vt* (*guitar*) klimpern auf +*dat*.

strung [strʌŋ] *pt, pp of* **string**.

strut [strʌt] *n* Strebe *f*, Stütze *f* ♦ *vi* stolzieren.

strychnine ['strɪkniːn] *n* Strychnin *nt*.

stub [stʌb] *n* (*of cheque, ticket etc*) Abschnitt *m*; (*of cigarette*) Kippe *f* ♦ *vt*: **to ~ one's toe** sich *dat* den Zeh stoßen.

▸ **stub out** *vt* (*cigarette*) ausdrücken.

stubble ['stʌbl] *n* Stoppeln *pl*.

stubborn ['stʌbən] *adj* hartnäckig; (*child*) störrisch.

stubby ['stʌbɪ] *adj* kurz und dick.

stucco ['stʌkəu] *n* Stuck *m*.

stuck [stʌk] *pt, pp of* **stick** ♦ *adj*: **to be ~** (*jammed*) klemmen; (*unable to answer*) nicht klarkommen; **to get ~** stecken bleiben; (*fig*) nicht weiterkommen.

stuck-up [stʌk'ʌp] (*inf*) *adj* hochnäsig.

stud [stʌd] *n* (*on clothing etc*) Niete *f*; (*on collar*) Kragenknopf *m*; (*earring*) Ohrstecker *m*; (*on boot*) Stollen *m*; (*also*: ~ **farm**) Gestüt *nt*; (*also*: ~ **horse**) Zuchthengst *m* ♦ *vt* (*fig*): ~**ded with** übersät mit; (*with jewels*) dicht besetzt mit.

student ['stjuːdənt] *n* Student(in) *m(f)*; (*at school*) Schüler(in) *m(f)* ♦ *cpd* Studenten-; **law/medical** ~ Jura-/Medizinstudent(in) *m(f)*; ~ **nurse** Krankenpflegeschüler(in) *m(f)*; ~ **teacher** Referendar(in) *m(f)*.

student driver (*US*) *n* Fahrschüler(in) *m(f)*.

students' union ['stjuːdənts-] (*BRIT*) *n* Studentenvereinigung *f*, ≈ AStA *m*; (*building*) Gebäude *nt* der Studentenvereinigung.

studied ['stʌdɪd] *adj* (*expression*) einstudiert; (*attitude*) berechnet.

studio ['stjuːdɪəu] *n* Studio *nt*; (*sculptor's etc*) Atelier *nt*.

studio flat, (*US*) **studio apartment** *n* Einzimmerwohnung *f*.

studious ['stjuːdɪəs] *adj* lernbegierig.

studiously ['stjuːdɪəslɪ] *adv* (*carefully*) sorgsam.

study ['stʌdɪ] *n* Studium *nt*, Lernen *nt*; (*room*) Arbeitszimmer *nt* ♦ *vt* studieren; (*face*) prüfend ansehen; (*evidence*) prüfen ♦ *vi* studieren, lernen; **studies** *npl* (*studying*) Studien *pl*; **to make a ~ of sth** etw untersuchen; (*academic*) etw studieren; **to ~ for an exam** sich auf eine Prüfung vorbereiten.

stuff [stʌf] *n* Zeug *nt* ♦ *vt* ausstopfen; (*CULIN*) füllen; (*inf: push*) stopfen; **my nose is ~ed**

up ich habe eine verstopfte Nase; **get ~ed!** (*inf!*) du kannst mich mal!

stuffed toy [stʌft-] *n* Stofftier *nt*.

stuffing ['stʌfɪŋ] *n* Füllung *f*; (*in sofa etc*) Polstermaterial *nt*.

stuffy ['stʌfɪ] *adj* (*room*) stickig; (*person, ideas*) spießig.

stumble ['stʌmbl] *vi* stolpern; **to ~ across** *or* **on** (*fig*) (zufällig) stoßen auf +*acc*.

stumbling block ['stʌmblɪŋ-] *n* Hürde *f*, Hindernis *nt*.

stump [stʌmp] *n* Stumpf *m* ♦ *vt*: **to be ~ed** überfragt sein.

stun [stʌn] *vt* betäuben; (*news*) fassungslos machen.

stung [stʌŋ] *pt, pp of* **sting**.

stunk [stʌŋk] *pp of* **stink**.

stunning ['stʌnɪŋ] *adj* (*news, event*) sensationell; (*girl, dress*) hinreißend.

stunt [stʌnt] *n* (*in film*) Stunt *m*; (*publicity stunt*) (Werbe)gag *m*.

stunted ['stʌntɪd] *adj* verkümmert.

stuntman ['stʌntmæn] (*irreg: like* **man**) *n* Stuntman *m*.

stupefaction [stjuːpɪ'fækʃən] *n* Verblüffung *f*.

stupefy ['stjuːpɪfaɪ] *vt* benommen machen; (*fig*) verblüffen.

stupendous [stjuː'pɛndəs] *adj* enorm.

stupid ['stjuːpɪd] *adj* dumm.

stupidity [stjuː'pɪdɪtɪ] *n* Dummheit *f*.

stupidly ['stjuːpɪdlɪ] *adv* dumm.

stupor ['stjuːpəʳ] *n* Benommenheit *f*; **in a ~** benommen.

sturdily ['stəːdɪlɪ] *adv*: ~ **built** (*person*) kräftig gebaut; (*thing*) stabil gebaut.

sturdy ['stəːdɪ] *adj* (*person*) kräftig; (*thing*) stabil.

sturgeon ['stəːdʒən] *n* Stör *m*.

stutter ['stʌtəʳ] *n* Stottern *nt* ♦ *vi* stottern; **to have a ~** stottern.

Stuttgart ['stutgɑːt] *n* Stuttgart *nt*.

sty [staɪ] *n* Schweinestall *m*.

stye [staɪ] *n* Gerstenkorn *nt*.

style [staɪl] *n* Stil *m*; (*design*) Modell *nt*; **in the latest** ~ nach der neuesten Mode; **hair** ~ Frisur *f*.

styli ['staɪlaɪ] *npl of* **stylus**.

stylish ['staɪlɪʃ] *adj* elegant.

stylist ['staɪlɪst] *n* (*hair stylist*) Friseur *m*, Friseuse *f*; (*literary stylist*) Stilist(in) *m(f)*.

stylized ['staɪlaɪzd] *adj* stilisiert.

stylus ['staɪləs] (*pl* **styli** *or* ~**es**) *n* Nadel *f*.

Styrofoam ® ['staɪrəfəum] *n* ≈ Styropor *nt* ®.

suave [swɑːv] *adj* zuvorkommend.

sub [sʌb] *n abbr* (*NAUT*) = **submarine**; (*ADMIN*) = **subscription**; (*BRIT: PRESS*) = **subeditor**.

sub... [sʌb] *pref* Unter-, unter-.

subcommittee ['sʌbkəmɪtɪ] *n* Unterausschuss *m*.

subconscious [sʌb'kɔnʃəs] *adj* unterbewusst.

subcontinent [sʌb'kɔntɪnənt] *n*: **the (Indian)** ~ der (indische) Subkontinent.

subcontract [vt 'sʌbkən'trækt, n 'sʌb'kɔntrækt] vt (vertraglich) weitervergeben ♦ n Nebenvertrag m.

subcontractor ['sʌbkən'træktə'] n Subunternehmer m.

subdivide [sʌbdɪ'vaɪd] vt unterteilen.

subdivision ['sʌbdɪvɪʒən] n Unterteilung f.

subdue [səb'djuː] vt unterwerfen; (emotions) dämpfen.

subdued [səb'djuːd] adj (light) gedämpft; (person) bedrückt.

subeditor [sʌb'ɛdɪtə'] (BRIT) n Redakteur(in) m(f).

subject [n 'sʌbdʒɪkt, vt sʌb'dʒɛkt] n (matter) Thema nt; (SCOL) Fach nt; (of country) Staatsbürger(in) m(f); (GRAM) Subjekt nt ♦ vt: to ~ sb to sth jdn einer Sache dat unterziehen; (expose) jdn einer Sache dat aussetzen; to change the ~ das Thema wechseln; to be ~ to (law, tax) unterworfen sein +dat; (heart attacks etc) anfällig sein für; ~ to confirmation in writing vorausgesetzt, es wird schriftlich bestätigt.

subjection [səb'dʒɛkʃən] n Unterwerfung f.

subjective [səb'dʒɛktɪv] adj subjektiv.

subject matter n Stoff m; (content) Inhalt m.

sub judice [sʌb'djuːdɪsɪ] adj (LAW): to be ~ verhandelt werden.

subjugate ['sʌbdʒugeɪt] vt unterwerfen.

subjunctive [səb'dʒʌŋktɪv] n Konjunktiv m; in the ~ im Konjunktiv.

sublet [sʌb'lɛt] vt untervermieten.

sublime [sə'blaɪm] adj erhaben, vollendet; that's going from the ~ to the ridiculous das ist ein Abstieg ins Profane.

subliminal [sʌb'lɪmɪnl] adj unterschwellig.

submachine gun ['sʌbmə'ʃiːn-] n Maschinenpistole f.

submarine [sʌbmə'riːn] n Unterseeboot nt, U-Boot nt.

submerge [səb'mɜːdʒ] vt untertauchen; (flood) überschwemmen ♦ vi tauchen; ~d unter Wasser.

submersion [səb'mɜːʃən] n Untertauchen nt; (of submarine) Tauchen nt; (by flood) Überschwemmung f.

submission [səb'mɪʃən] n (subjection) Unterwerfung f; (of plan, application etc) Einreichung f; (proposal) Vorlage f.

submissive [səb'mɪsɪv] adj gehorsam; (gesture) demütig.

submit [səb'mɪt] vt (proposal) vorlegen; (application etc) einreichen ♦ vi: to ~ to sth sich einer Sache dat unterwerfen.

subnormal [sʌb'nɔːml] adj (below average) unterdurchschnittlich; (old: child etc) minderbegabt; **educationally** ~ lernbehindert.

subordinate [sə'bɔːdɪnət] n Untergebene(r) f(m); (LING): ~ **clause** Nebensatz m ♦ adj untergeordnet; **to be** ~ **to sb** jdm untergeordnet sein.

subpoena [səb'piːnə] n (LAW) Vorladung f ♦ vt vorladen.

subroutine [sʌbru:'ti:n] n (COMPUT) Unterprogramm nt.

subscribe [səb'skraɪb] vi spenden; **to** ~ **to** (opinion, theory) sich anschließen +dat; (fund, charity) regelmäßig spenden an +acc; (magazine etc) abonnieren.

subscriber [səb'skraɪbə'] n (to magazine) Abonnent(in) m(f); (TEL) Teilnehmer(in) m(f).

subscript ['sʌbskrɪpt] n tiefgestelltes Zeichen nt.

subscription [səb'skrɪpʃən] n (to magazine etc) Abonnement nt; (membership dues) (Mitglieds)beitrag m; **to take out a** ~ **to** (magazine etc) abonnieren.

subsequent ['sʌbsɪkwənt] adj später, nachfolgend; (further) weiter; ~ **to** im Anschluss an +acc.

subsequently ['sʌbsɪkwəntlɪ] adv später.

subservient [səb'sə:vɪənt] adj unterwürfig; (less important) untergeordnet; **to be** ~ **to** untergeordnet sein +dat.

subside [səb'saɪd] vi (feeling, pain) nachlassen; (flood) sinken; (earth) sich senken.

subsidence [səb'saɪdns] n Senkung f.

subsidiarity [səbsɪdɪ'ærɪtɪ] n Subsidiarität f.

subsidiary [səb'sɪdɪərɪ] adj (question, role, BRIT: SCOL: subject) Neben- ♦ n (also: ~ **company**) Tochtergesellschaft f.

subsidize ['sʌbsɪdaɪz] vt subventionieren.

subsidy ['sʌbsɪdɪ] n Subvention f.

subsist [səb'sɪst] vi: **to** ~ **on sth** sich von etw ernähren.

subsistence [səb'sɪstəns] n Existenz f; **enough for** ~ genug zum (Über)leben.

subsistence allowance n Unterhaltszuschuss m.

subsistence level n Existenzminimum nt.

substance ['sʌbstəns] n Substanz f, Stoff m; (fig: essence) Kern m; **a man of** ~ ein vermögender Mann; **to lack** ~ (book) keine Substanz haben; (argument) keine Durchschlagskraft haben.

substance abuse n Missbrauch von Alkohol, Drogen, Arzneimitteln etc.

substandard [sʌb'stændəd] adj minderwertig; (housing) unzulänglich.

substantial [səb'stænʃl] adj (solid) solide; (considerable) beträchtlich, größere(r, s); (meal) kräftig.

substantially [səb'stænʃəlɪ] adv erheblich; (in essence) im Wesentlichen.

substantiate [səb'stænʃɪeɪt] vt erhärten, untermauern.

substitute ['sʌbstɪtjuːt] n Ersatz m ♦ vt: **to** ~ **A for B** B durch A ersetzen.

substitute teacher (US) n Vertretung f.

substitution [sʌbstɪ'tjuːʃən] n Ersetzen nt; (FOOTBALL) Auswechseln nt.

subterfuge ['sʌbtəfjuːdʒ] n Tricks pl; (trickery) Täuschung f.

subterranean [sʌbtə'reɪnɪən] *adj* unterirdisch.
subtitle ['sʌbtaɪtl] *n* Untertitel *m*.
subtle ['sʌtl] *adj* fein; *(indirect)* raffiniert.
subtlety ['sʌtltɪ] *n* Feinheit *f*; *(art of being subtle)* Finesse *f*.
subtly ['sʌtlɪ] *adv (change, vary)* leicht; *(different)* auf subtile Weise; *(persuade)* raffiniert.
subtotal [sʌb'təʊtl] *n* Zwischensumme *f*.
subtract [səb'trækt] *vt* abziehen, subtrahieren.
subtraction [səb'trækʃən] *n* Abziehen *nt*, Subtraktion *f*.
subtropical [sʌb'trɒpɪkl] *adj* subtropisch.
suburb ['sʌbɜːb] *n* Vorort *m*.
suburban [sə'bɜːbən] *adj (train etc)* Vorort-; *(lifestyle etc)* spießig, kleinbürgerlich.
suburbia [sə'bɜːbɪə] *n* die Vororte *pl*.
subvention [səb'vɛnʃən] *n* Subvention *f*.
subversion [səb'vɜːʃən] *n* Subversion *f*.
subversive [səb'vɜːsɪv] *adj* subversiv.
subway ['sʌbweɪ] *n (US)* Untergrundbahn *f*, U-Bahn *f*; *(BRIT: underpass)* Unterführung *f*.
sub-zero [sʌb'zɪərəʊ] *adj*: ~ **temperatures** Temperaturen unter null.
succeed [sək'siːd] *vi (plan etc)* gelingen, erfolgreich sein; *(person)* erfolgreich sein, Erfolg haben ♦ *vt (in job)* Nachfolger werden +*gen*; *(in order)* folgen +*dat*; **sb ~s in doing sth** es gelingt jdm, etw zu tun.
succeeding [sək'siːdɪŋ] *adj* folgend; ~ **generations** spätere *or* nachfolgende Generationen *pl*.
success [sək'sɛs] *n* Erfolg *m*; **without** ~ ohne Erfolg, erfolglos.
successful [sək'sɛsful] *adj* erfolgreich; **to be** ~ erfolgreich sein, Erfolg haben; **sb is** ~ **in doing sth** es gelingt jdm, etw zu tun.
successfully [sək'sɛsfəlɪ] *adv* erfolgreich, mit Erfolg.
succession [sək'sɛʃən] *n* Folge *f*, Serie *f*; *(to throne etc)* Nachfolge *f*; **3 years in** ~ 3 Jahre nacheinander *or* hintereinander.
successive [sək'sɛsɪv] *adj* aufeinander folgend; **on 3** ~ **days** 3 Tage nacheinander *or* hintereinander.
successor [sək'sɛsə*] *n* Nachfolger(in) *m(f)*.
succinct [sək'sɪŋkt] *adj* knapp, prägnant.
succulent ['sʌkjulənt] *adj* saftig ♦ *n* Fettpflanze *f*, Sukkulente *f*.
succumb [sə'kʌm] *vi*: **to** ~ **to** *(temptation)* erliegen +*dat*; *(illness: become affected by)* bekommen; (: *die of*) erliegen +*dat*.
such [sʌtʃ] *adj (of that kind)*: ~ **a book** so ein Buch; *(so much)*: ~ **courage** so viel Mut; *(emphasizing similarity)*: **or some** ~ **place/name** *etc* oder so ähnlich ♦ *adv* so; ~ **books** solche Bücher; ~ **a lot of** so viel; **she made** ~ **a noise that ...** sie machte so einen Lärm, dass ...; ~ **books as I have** was ich an Büchern habe; **I said no** ~ **thing** das habe ich nie gesagt; ~ **a long trip** so eine lange Reise; ~ **as** wie (zum Beispiel); **as** ~ an sich.
such-and-such ['sʌtʃənsʌtʃ] *adj* die und die, der und der, das und das.
suchlike ['sʌtʃlaɪk] *(inf)* *pron*: **and** ~ und dergleichen.
suck [sʌk] *vt (sweet etc)* lutschen; *(ice-lolly)* lutschen an +*dat*; *(baby)* saugen an +*dat*; *(pump, machine)* saugen.
sucker ['sʌkə*] *n (ZOOL)* Saugnapf *m*; *(TECH)* Saugfuß *m*; *(BOT)* unterirdischer Ausläufer *m*; *(inf)* Dummkopf *m*.
suckle ['sʌkl] *vt (baby)* stillen; *(animal)* säugen.
sucrose ['suːkrəʊz] *n* (pflanzlicher) Zucker *m*.
suction ['sʌkʃən] *n* Saugwirkung *f*.
suction pump *n* Saugpumpe *f*.
Sudan [su'dɑːn] *n* der Sudan.
Sudanese [suːdə'niːz] *adj* sudanesisch ♦ *n* Sudanese *m*, Sudanesin *f*.
sudden ['sʌdn] *adj* plötzlich; **all of a** ~ ganz plötzlich.
sudden death *n (also:* **sudden-death play-off)** Stichkampf *m*.
suddenly ['sʌdnlɪ] *adv* plötzlich.
suds [sʌdz] *npl* Seifenschaum *m*.
sue [suː] *vt* verklagen ♦ *vi* klagen, vor Gericht gehen; **to** ~ **sb for damages** jdn auf Schadenersatz verklagen; **to** ~ **for divorce** die Scheidung einreichen.
suede [sweɪd] *n* Wildleder *nt* ♦ *cpd* Wildleder-.
suet ['suɪt] *n* Nierenfett *nt*.
Suez ['suːɪz] *n*: **the** ~ **Canal** der Suezkanal.
Suff. *(BRIT) abbr (POST:* = **Suffolk)**.
suffer ['sʌfə*] *vt* erleiden; *(rudeness etc)* ertragen ♦ *vi* leiden; **to** ~ **from** leiden an +*dat*; **to** ~ **the effects of sth** an den Folgen von etw leiden.
sufferance ['sʌfərns] *n*: **he was only there on** ~ er wurde dort nur geduldet.
sufferer ['sʌfərə*] *n* Leidende(r) *f(m)*.
suffering ['sʌfərɪŋ] *n* Leid *nt*.
suffice [sə'faɪs] *vi* genügen.
sufficient [sə'fɪʃənt] *adj* ausreichend; ~ **money** genug Geld.
sufficiently [sə'fɪʃəntlɪ] *adv* genug, ausreichend; ~ **powerful/enthusiastic** mächtig/begeistert genug.
suffix ['sʌfɪks] *n* Suffix *nt*, Nachsilbe *f*.
suffocate ['sʌfəkeɪt] *vi (lit, fig)* ersticken.
suffocation [sʌfə'keɪʃən] *n* Ersticken *nt*.
suffrage ['sʌfrɪdʒ] *n* Wahlrecht *nt*.
suffragette [sʌfrə'dʒɛt] *n* Suffragette *f*.
suffused [sə'fjuːzd] *adj*: ~ **with** erfüllt von; ~ **with light** lichtdurchflutet.
sugar ['ʃugə*] *n* Zucker *m* ♦ *vt* zuckern.
sugar beet *n* Zuckerrübe *f*.
sugar bowl *n* Zuckerdose *f*.
sugar cane *n* Zuckerrohr *nt*.
sugar-coated ['ʃugə'kəutɪd] *adj* mit Zucker überzogen.
sugar lump *n* Zuckerstück *nt*.

sugar refinery n Zuckerraffinerie f.
sugary ['ʃugərɪ] adj süß; (fig: smile, phrase)
süßlich.
suggest [sə'dʒɛst] vt vorschlagen; (indicate)
andeuten, hindeuten auf +acc; **what do you
~ I do?** was schlagen Sie vor?
suggestion [sə'dʒɛstʃən] n Vorschlag m;
(indication) Anflug m; (trace) Spur f.
suggestive [sə'dʒɛstɪv] (pej) adj anzüglich.
suicidal [sʊɪ'saɪdl] adj selbstmörderisch;
(person) selbstmordgefährdet; **to be** or **feel
~** Selbstmordgedanken haben.
suicide ['sʊɪsaɪd] n (lit, fig) Selbstmord m;
(person) Selbstmörder(in) m(f); see also
commit.
suicide attempt, suicide bid n
Selbstmordversuch m.
suit [suːt] n (man's) Anzug m; (woman's)
Kostüm nt; (LAW) Prozess m, Verfahren nt;
(CARDS) Farbe f ♦ vt passen +dat; (colour,
clothes) stehen +dat; **to bring a ~ against sb**
(LAW) gegen jdn Klage erheben or einen
Prozess anstrengen; **to follow ~** (fig) das
Gleiche tun; **to ~ sth to** etw anpassen an
+acc; **to be ~ed to do sth** sich dafür eignen,
etw zu tun; **~ yourself!** wie du willst!; **well
~ed** (couple) gut zusammenpassend.
suitability [suːtə'bɪlɪtɪ] n Eignung f.
suitable ['suːtəbl] adj (convenient) passend;
(appropriate) geeignet; **would tomorrow be
~?** würde Ihnen morgen passen?; **Monday
isn't ~** Montag passt nicht; **we found
somebody ~** wir haben jemand Passenden
gefunden.
suitably ['suːtəblɪ] adv passend; (impressed)
gebührend.
suitcase ['suːtkeɪs] n Koffer m.
suite [swiːt] n (of rooms) Suite f, Zimmerflucht
f; (MUS) Suite f; **bedroom/dining room ~**
Schlafzimmer-/Esszimmereinrichtung f; **a
three-piece ~** eine dreiteilige
Polstergarnitur.
suitor ['suːtə*] n Kläger(in) m(f).
sulfate ['sʌlfeɪt] (US) n = **sulphate**.
sulfur ['sʌlfə*] (US) n = **sulphur**.
sulfuric [sʌl'fjuərɪk] (US) adj = **sulphuric**.
sulk [sʌlk] vi schmollen.
sulky ['sʌlkɪ] adj schmollend.
sullen ['sʌlən] adj mürrisch, verdrossen.
sulphate, (US) **sulfate** ['sʌlfeɪt] n Sulfat nt,
schwefelsaures Salz nt.
sulphur, (US) **sulfur** ['sʌlfə*] n Schwefel m.
sulphur dioxide n Schwefeldioxid nt.
sulphuric, (US) **sulfuric** [sʌl'fjuərɪk] adj:
~ acid Schwefelsäure f.
sultan ['sʌltən] n Sultan m.
sultana [sʌl'tɑːnə] n Sultanine f.
sultry ['sʌltrɪ] adj schwül.
sum [sʌm] n (calculation) Rechenaufgabe f;
(amount) Summe f, Betrag m.
▶ **sum up** vt zusammenfassen; (evaluate
rapidly) einschätzen ♦ vi zusammenfassen.

Sumatra [su'mɑːtrə] n Sumatra nt.
summarize ['sʌməraɪz] vt zusammenfassen.
summary ['sʌmərɪ] n Zusammenfassung f
♦ adj (justice, executions) im
Schnellverfahren.
summer ['sʌmə*] n Sommer m ♦ cpd Sommer-;
in ~ im Sommer.
summer camp (US) n Ferienlager nt.
summer holidays npl Sommerferien pl.
summerhouse ['sʌməhaus] n (in garden)
Gartenhaus nt, Gartenlaube f.
summertime ['sʌmətaɪm] n Sommer m,
Sommerszeit f.
summer time n Sommerzeit f.
summery ['sʌmərɪ] adj sommerlich.
summing-up [sʌmɪŋ'ʌp] n (LAW) Resümee nt.
summit ['sʌmɪt] n Gipfel m; (also:
~ conference/meeting) Gipfelkonferenz f/-
treffen nt.
summon ['sʌmən] vt rufen, kommen lassen;
(help) holen; (meeting) einberufen; (LAW:
witness) vorladen.
▶ **summon up** vt aufbringen.
summons ['sʌmənz] n (LAW) Vorladung f; (fig)
Aufruf m ♦ vt (LAW) vorladen; **to serve a
~ on sb** jdn vor Gericht laden.
sumo (wrestling) ['suːməu] n Sumo(-Ringen)
nt.
sump [sʌmp] (BRIT) n Ölwanne f.
sumptuous ['sʌmptjuəs] adj (meal) üppig;
(costume) aufwändig, aufwendig.
Sun. abbr (= Sunday) So.
sun [sʌn] n Sonne f; **to catch the ~** einen
Sonnenbrand bekommen; **everything under
the ~** alles Mögliche.
sunbathe ['sʌnbeɪð] vi sich sonnen.
sunbeam ['sʌnbiːm] n Sonnenstrahl m.
sunbed ['sʌnbɛd] n (with sun lamp)
Sonnenbank f.
sunblock n Sonnenschutzcreme f.
sunburn ['sʌnbəːn] n Sonnenbrand m.
sunburned ['sʌnbəːnd] adj = **sunburnt**.
sunburnt ['sʌnbəːnt] adj sonnenverbrannt,
sonnengebräunt; **to be ~** (painfully) einen
Sonnenbrand haben.
sun-cream ['sʌnkriːm] n Sonnencreme f.
sundae ['sʌndeɪ] n Eisbecher m.
Sunday ['sʌndɪ] n Sonntag m; see also **Tuesday**.
Sunday paper n Sonntagszeitung f.

SUNDAY PAPERS

Die **Sunday papers** umfassen sowohl
Massenblätter als auch seriöse Zeitungen. „The
Observer" ist die älteste überregionale
Sonntagszeitung der Welt. Die Sonntagszeitungen
sind alle sehr umfangreich mit vielen Farb- und
Sonderbeilagen. Zu den meisten Tageszeitungen
gibt es parallele Sonntagsblätter, die aber
separate Redaktionen haben.

Sunday school n Sonntagsschule f.

sundial ['sʌndaɪəl] *n* Sonnenuhr *f*.
sundown ['sʌndaun] (*esp US*) *n* Sonnenuntergang *m*.
sundries ['sʌndrɪz] *npl* Verschiedenes *nt*.
sundry ['sʌndrɪ] *adj* verschiedene; **all and ~** jedermann.
sunflower ['sʌnflauə*] *n* Sonnenblume *f*.
sunflower oil *n* Sonnenblumenöl *nt*.
sung [sʌŋ] *pp of* **sing**.
sunglasses ['sʌnglɑːsɪz] *npl* Sonnenbrille *f*.
sunk [sʌŋk] *pp of* **sink**.
sunken ['sʌŋkn] *adj* versunken; (*eyes*) tief liegend; (*cheeks*) eingefallen; (*bath*) eingelassen.
sunlamp ['sʌnlæmp] *n* Höhensonne *f*.
sunlight ['sʌnlaɪt] *n* Sonnenlicht *nt*.
sunlit ['sʌnlɪt] *adj* sonnig, sonnenbeschienen.
sunny ['sʌnɪ] *adj* sonnig; (*fig*) heiter.
sunrise ['sʌnraɪz] *n* Sonnenaufgang *m*.
sun roof *n* (*AUT*) Schiebedach *nt*; (*on building*) Sonnenterrasse *f*.
sun screen *n* Sonnenschutzmittel *nt*.
sunset ['sʌnsɛt] *n* Sonnenuntergang *m*.
sunshade ['sʌnʃeɪd] *n* Sonnenschirm *m*.
sunshine ['sʌnʃaɪn] *n* Sonnenschein *m*.
sunspot ['sʌnspɒt] *n* Sonnenfleck *m*.
sunstroke ['sʌnstrəuk] *n* Sonnenstich *m*.
suntan ['sʌntæn] *n* (Sonnen)bräune *f*; **to get a ~** braun werden.
suntan lotion *n* Sonnenmilch *f*.
suntanned ['sʌntænd] *adj* braun (gebrannt).
suntan oil *n* Sonnenöl *nt*.
suntrap ['sʌntræp] *n* sonniges Eckchen *nt*.
super ['su:pə*] (*inf*) *adj* fantastisch, toll.
superannuation [su:pərænju'eɪʃən] *n* Beitrag *m* zur Rentenversicherung.
superb [su:'pɜːb] *adj* ausgezeichnet, großartig; (*meal*) vorzüglich.
Super Bowl *n* Superbowl *m*, Super Bowl *m*, *American-Football-Turnier zwischen den Spitzenreitern der Nationalligen*.
supercilious [su:pə'sɪlɪəs] *adj* herablassend.
superconductor [su:pəkən'dʌktə*] *n* (*PHYS*) Superleiter *m*.
superficial [su:pə'fɪʃəl] *adj* oberflächlich.
superficially [su:pə'fɪʃəlɪ] *adv* oberflächlich; (*from a superficial point of view*) oberflächlich gesehen.
superfluous [su'pɜːfluəs] *adj* überflüssig.
superglue ['su:pəglu:] *n* Sekundenkleber *m*.
superhighway (*US*) *n* ≈ Autobahn *f*; **information ~** Datenautobahn *f*.
superhuman [su:pə'hju:mən] *adj* übermenschlich.
superimpose ['su:pərɪm'pəuz] *vt* (*two things*) übereinander legen; **to ~ on** legen auf *+acc*; **to ~ with** überlagern mit.
superintend [su:pərɪn'tɛnd] *vt* beaufsichtigen, überwachen.
superintendent [su:pərɪn'tɛndənt] *n* Aufseher(in) *m(f)*; (*POLICE*) Kommissar(in) *m(f)*.

superior [su'pɪərɪə*] *adj* besser, überlegen *+dat*; (*more senior*) höher gestellt; (*smug*) überheblich; (: *smile*) überlegen ♦ *n* Vorgesetzte(r) *f(m)*; **Mother S~** (*REL*) Mutter Oberin.
superiority [supɪərɪ'ɒrɪtɪ] *n* Überlegenheit *f*.
superlative [su'pɜːlətɪv] *n* Superlativ *m* ♦ *adj* überragend.
superman ['su:pəmæn] (*irreg: like* **man**) *n* Übermensch *m*.
supermarket ['su:pəmɑːkɪt] *n* Supermarkt *m*.
supermodel ['su:pəmɒdl] *n* Supermodell *nt*.
supernatural [su:pə'nætʃərəl] *adj* übernatürlich ♦ *n*: **the ~** das Übernatürliche.
supernova [su:pə'nəuvə] *n* Supernova *f*.
superpower ['su:pəpauə*] *n* Supermacht *f*.
superscript ['su:pəskrɪpt] *n* hochgestelltes Zeichen *nt*.
supersede [su:pə'si:d] *vt* ablösen, ersetzen.
supersonic ['su:pə'sɒnɪk] *adj* (*aircraft etc*) Überschall-.
superstar ['su:pəstɑː*] *n* Superstar *m*.
superstition [su:pə'stɪʃən] *n* Aberglaube *m*.
superstitious [su:pə'stɪʃəs] *adj* abergläubisch.
superstore ['su:pəstɔː*] (*BRIT*) *n* Großmarkt *m*.
supertanker ['su:pətæŋkə*] *n* Supertanker *m*.
supertax ['su:pətæks] *n* Höchststeuer *f*.
supervise ['su:pəvaɪz] *vt* beaufsichtigen.
supervision [su:pə'vɪʒən] *n* Beaufsichtigung *f*; **under medical ~** unter ärztlicher Aufsicht.
supervisor ['su:pəvaɪzə*] *n* Aufseher(in) *m(f)*; (*of students*) Tutor(in) *m(f)*.
supervisory ['su:pəvaɪzərɪ] *adj* beaufsichtigend, Aufsichts-.
supine ['su:paɪn] *adj*: **to be ~** auf dem Rücken liegen ♦ *adv* auf dem Rücken.
supper ['sʌpə*] *n* Abendessen *nt*; **to have ~** zu Abend essen.
supplant [sə'plɑːnt] *vt* ablösen, ersetzen.
supple ['sʌpl] *adj* geschmeidig; (*person*) gelenkig.
supplement ['sʌplɪmənt] *n* Zusatz *m*; (*of book*) Ergänzungsband *m*; (*of newspaper etc*) Beilage *f* ♦ *vt* ergänzen.
supplementary [sʌplɪ'mɛntərɪ] *adj* zusätzlich, ergänzend.
supplementary benefit (*BRIT: old*) *n* ≈ Sozialhilfe *f*.
supplier [sə'plaɪə*] *n* Lieferant(in) *m(f)*.
supply [sə'plaɪ] *vt* liefern; (*provide*) sorgen für; (*a need*) befriedigen ♦ *n* Vorrat *m*; (*supplying*) Lieferung *f*; **supplies** *npl* (*food*) Vorräte *pl*; (*MIL*) Nachschub *m*; **to ~ sth to sb** jdm etw liefern; **to ~ sth with sth** etw mit etw versorgen; **it comes supplied with an adaptor** es wird mit einem Adapter geliefert; **office supplies** Bürobedarf *m*; **to be in short ~** knapp sein; **the electricity/water/gas ~** die Strom-/Wasser-/Gasversorgung *f*; **~ and demand** Angebot *nt*

und Nachfrage.
supply teacher (*BRIT*) *n* Vertretung *f*.
support [səˈpɔːt] *n* Unterstützung *f*; (*TECH*)
Stütze *f* ♦ *vt* unterstützen, eintreten für;
(*financially*: *family etc*) unterhalten; (: *party
etc*) finanziell unterstützen; (*TECH*)
(ab)stützen; (*theory etc*) untermauern; **they
stopped work in ~ of** ... sie sind in den
Streik getreten, um für ... einzutreten; **to
~ o.s.** (*financially*) finanziell unabhängig
sein; **to ~ Arsenal** Arsenal-Fan sein.
supporter [səˈpɔːtə*] *n* (*POL etc*) Anhänger(in)
m(f); (*SPORT*) Fan *m*.
supporting [səˈpɔːtɪŋ] *adj*: **~ role** Nebenrolle
f; **~ actor** Schauspieler *m* in einer
Nebenrolle; **~ film** Vorfilm *m*.
supportive [səˈpɔːtɪv] *adj* hilfreich; **to be ~ of
sb/sth** jdn/etw unterstützen.
suppose [səˈpəʊz] *vt* annehmen, glauben;
(*imagine*) sich *dat* vorstellen; **to be ~d to do
sth** etw tun sollen; **it was worse than she'd
~d** es war schlimmer, als sie es sich
vorgestellt hatte; **I don't ~ she'll come** ich
glaube kaum, dass sie kommt; **he's about
sixty, I ~** er muss wohl so um die Sechzig
sein; **he's ~d to be an expert** er ist
angeblich ein Experte; **I ~ so/not** ich
glaube schon/nicht.
supposedly [səˈpəʊzɪdlɪ] *adv* angeblich.
supposing [səˈpəʊzɪŋ] *conj* angenommen.
supposition [sʌpəˈzɪʃən] *n* Annahme *f*.
suppository [səˈpɒzɪtrɪ] *n* Zäpfchen *nt*.
suppress [səˈpres] *vt* unterdrücken;
(*publication*) verbieten.
suppression [səˈpreʃən] *n* Unterdrückung *f*.
suppressor [səˈpresə*] *n* (*ELEC etc*)
Entstörungselement *nt*.
supremacy [suˈpreməsɪ] *n* Vormachtstellung
f.
supreme [suˈpriːm] *adj* Ober-, oberste(r, s);
(*effort*) äußerste(r, s); (*achievement*)
höchste(r, s).
Supreme Court (*US*) *n* Oberster Gerichtshof
m.
supremo [suˈpriːməʊ] (*BRIT*: *inf*) *n* Boss *m*.
Supt *abbr* (*POLICE*) = **superintendent**.
surcharge [ˈsɜːtʃɑːdʒ] *n* Zuschlag *m*.
sure [ʃʊə*] *adj* sicher; (*reliable*) zuverlässig,
sicher ♦ *adv* (*inf*: *esp US*): **that ~ is pretty,
that's ~ pretty** das ist aber schön; **to make
~ of sth** sich einer Sache *gen* vergewissern;
to make ~ that sich vergewissern, dass; **I'm
~ of it** ich bin mir da sicher; **I'm not
~ how/why/when** ich bin mir nicht sicher
or ich weiß nicht genau, wie/warum/wann;
to be ~ of o.s. selbstsicher sein; **~! klar!;
~ enough** tatsächlich.
sure-fire [ˈʃʊəfaɪə*] (*inf*) *adj* todsicher.
sure-footed [ʃʊəˈfʊtɪd] *adj* trittsicher.
surely [ˈʃʊəlɪ] *adv* sicherlich, bestimmt; **~ you
don't mean that!** das meinen Sie doch
bestimmt *or* sicher nicht (so)!

surety [ˈʃʊərətɪ] *n* Bürgschaft *f*, Sicherheit *f*;
to go *or* **stand ~ for sb** für jdn bürgen.
surf [sɜːf] *n* Brandung *f*.
surface [ˈsɜːfɪs] *n* Oberfläche *f* ♦ *vt* (*road*) mit
einem Belag versehen ♦ *vi* (*lit, fig*)
auftauchen; (*feeling*) hochkommen; (*rise
from bed*) hochkommen; **on the ~** (*fig*)
oberflächlich betrachtet.
surface area *n* Fläche *f*.
surface mail *n* Post *f* auf dem Land-/Seeweg.
surface-to-surface [ˈsɜːfɪstəˈsɜːfɪs] *adj*
(*missile*) Boden-Boden-.
surfboard [ˈsɜːfbɔːd] *n* Surfbrett *nt*.
surfeit [ˈsɜːfɪt] *n*: **a ~ of** ein Übermaß an *+dat*.
surfer [ˈsɜːfə*] *n* Surfer(in) *m(f)*.
surfing [ˈsɜːfɪŋ] *n* Surfen *nt*; **to go ~** surfen
gehen.
surge [sɜːdʒ] *n* Anstieg *m*; (*fig*: *of emotion*)
Woge *f*; (*ELEC*) Spannungsstoß *m* ♦ *vi* (*water*)
branden; (*people*) sich drängen; (*vehicles*)
sich wälzen; (*emotion*) aufwallen; (*ELEC*:
power) ansteigen; **to ~ forward** nach vorne
drängen.
surgeon [ˈsɜːdʒən] *n* Chirurg(in) *m(f)*.
Surgeon General (*US*) *n* (*MED*) ≈
Gesundheitsminister(in) *m(f)*; (*MIL*)
Sanitätsinspekteur(in) *m(f)*.
surgery [ˈsɜːdʒərɪ] *n* Chirurgie *f*; (*BRIT*: *room*)
Sprechzimmer *nt*; (: *building*) Praxis *f*; (*also*:
~ hours: *of doctor, MP etc*) Sprechstunde *f*; **to
have ~** operiert werden; **to need ~** operiert
werden müssen.
surgical [ˈsɜːdʒɪkl] *adj* chirurgisch; (*treatment*)
operativ.
surgical spirit (*BRIT*) *n* Wundbenzin *nt*.
surly [ˈsɜːlɪ] *adj* verdrießlich, mürrisch.
surmise [sɜːˈmaɪz] *vt* vermuten, mutmaßen.
surmount [sɜːˈmaʊnt] *vt* (*fig*) überwinden.
surname [ˈsɜːneɪm] *n* Nachname *m*.
surpass [sɜːˈpɑːs] *vt* übertreffen.
surplus [ˈsɜːpləs] *n* Überschuss *m* ♦ *adj*
überschüssig; **it is ~ to our requirements**
das benötigen wir nicht.
surprise [səˈpraɪz] *n* Überraschung *f* ♦ *vt*
überraschen; (*astonish*) erstaunen; (*army*)
überrumpeln; (*thief*) ertappen; **to take sb by
~** jdn überraschen.
surprising [səˈpraɪzɪŋ] *adj* überraschend;
(*situation*) erstaunlich; **it is ~ how/that** es
ist erstaunlich, wie/dass.
surprisingly [səˈpraɪzɪŋlɪ] *adv* überraschend,
erstaunlich; (**somewhat**) **~, he agreed**
erstaunlicherweise war er damit
einverstanden.
surrealism [səˈrɪəlɪzəm] *n* Surrealismus *m*.
surrealist [səˈrɪəlɪst] *adj* surrealistisch.
surrender [səˈrendə*] *n* Kapitulation *f* ♦ *vi* sich
ergeben ♦ *vt* aufgeben.
surrender value *n* Rückkaufswert *m*.
surreptitious [sʌrəpˈtɪʃəs] *adj* heimlich,
verstohlen.
surrogate [ˈsʌrəgɪt] *n* Ersatz *m* ♦ *adj* (*parents*)

Ersatz-.

surrogate mother *n* Leihmutter *f*.

surround [sə'raund] *vt* umgeben; (*MIL, POLICE etc*) umstellen.

surrounding [sə'raundɪŋ] *adj* umliegend; **the ~ area** die Umgebung.

surroundings [sə'raundɪŋz] *npl* Umgebung *f*.

surtax ['sɔːtæks] *n* Steuerzuschlag *m*.

surveillance [sɔː'veɪləns] *n* Überwachung *f*; **to be under ~** überwacht werden.

survey ['sɔːveɪ] *n* (*of land*) Vermessung *f*; (*of house*) Begutachtung *f*; (*investigation*) Untersuchung *f*; (*report*) Gutachten *nt*; (*comprehensive view*) Überblick *m* ♦ *vt* (*land*) vermessen; (*house*) inspizieren; (*look at*) betrachten.

surveying [sə'veɪɪŋ] *n* (*of land*) Vermessung *f*.

surveyor [sə'veɪəˀ] *n* (*of land*) Landvermesser(in) *m(f)*; (*of house*) Baugutachter(in) *m(f)*.

survival [sə'vaɪvl] *n* Überleben *nt*; (*relic*) Überbleibsel *nt*; **~ course/kit** Überlebenstraining *nt*/-ausrüstung *f*; **~ bag** Expeditionsschlafsack *m*.

survive [sə'vaɪv] *vi* überleben; (*custom etc*) weiterbestehen ♦ *vt* überleben.

survivor [sə'vaɪvəˀ] *n* Überlebende(r) *f(m)*.

susceptible [sə'sɛptəbl] *adj*: **~ (to)** anfällig (für); (*influenced by*) empfänglich (für).

suspect ['sʌspɛkt] *adj* verdächtig ♦ *n* Verdächtige(r) *f(m)* ♦ *vt*: **to ~ sb of** jdn verdächtigen +*gen*; (*think*) vermuten; (*doubt*) bezweifeln.

suspected [sə'pɛktɪd] *adj* (*terrorist etc*) mutmaßlich; **he is a ~ member of this organization** er steht im Verdacht, Mitglied dieser Organisation zu sein.

suspend [sə'spɛnd] *vt* (*hang*) (auf)hängen; (*delay, stop*) einstellen; (*from employment*) suspendieren; **to be ~ed (from)** (*hang*) hängen (an +*dat*).

suspended animation [sə'spɛndɪd-] *n* vorübergehender Stillstand aller Körperfunktionen.

suspended sentence *n* (*LAW*) zur Bewährung ausgesetzte Strafe *f*.

suspender belt [sə'spɛndəˀ-] *n* Strumpfhaltergürtel *m*.

suspenders [sə'spɛndəz] *npl* (*BRIT*) Strumpfhalter *pl*; (*US*) Hosenträger *pl*.

suspense [sə'spɛns] *n* Spannung *f*; (*uncertainty*) Ungewissheit *f*; **to keep sb in ~** jdn auf die Folter spannen.

suspension [sə'spɛnʃən] *n* (*from job*) Suspendierung *f*; (*from team*) Sperrung *f*; (*AUT*) Federung *f*; (*of driving licence*) zeitweiliger Entzug *m*; (*of payment*) zeitweilige Einstellung *f*.

suspension bridge *n* Hängebrücke *f*.

suspicion [sə'spɪʃən] *n* Verdacht *m*; (*distrust*) Misstrauen *nt*; (*trace*) Spur *f*; **to be under ~** unter Verdacht stehen; **arrested on ~ of**

murder wegen Mordverdacht(s) festgenommen.

suspicious [sə'spɪʃəs] *adj* (*suspecting*) misstrauisch; (*causing suspicion*) verdächtig; **to be ~ of** *or* **about sb/sth** jdn/etw mit Misstrauen betrachten.

suss out [sʌs-] (*BRIT: inf*) *vt* (*discover*) rauskriegen; (*understand*) durchschauen.

sustain [sə'steɪn] *vt* (*continue*) aufrechterhalten; (*food, drink*) bei Kräften halten; (*suffer: injury*) erleiden.

sustainable [sə'steɪnəbl] *adj*: **to be ~** aufrechtzuerhalten sein; **~ growth** stetiges Wachstum *nt*.

sustained [sə'steɪnd] *adj* (*effort*) ausdauernd; (*attack*) anhaltend.

sustenance ['sʌstɪnəns] *n* Nahrung *f*.

suture ['suːtʃəˀ] *n* Naht *f*.

SVQ *n abbr* (= *Scottish Vocational Qualification*) Qualifikation für berufsbegleitende Ausbildungsinhalte in Schottland.

SW *abbr* (= *south-west*) SW; (*RADIO*: = *short-wave*) KW.

swab [swɔb] *n* (*MED*) Tupfer *m* ♦ *vt* (*NAUT: also*: **~ down**) wischen.

swagger ['swægəˀ] *vi* stolzieren.

swallow ['swɔləu] *n* (*bird*) Schwalbe *f*; (*of food, drink etc*) Schluck *m* ♦ *vt* (herunter)schlucken; (*fig: story, insult, one's pride*) schlucken; **to ~ one's words** (*speak indistinctly*) seine Worte verschlucken; (*retract*) alles zurücknehmen.

▶ **swallow up** *vt* verschlingen.

swam [swæm] *pt of* **swim**.

swamp [swɔmp] *n* Sumpf *m* ♦ *vt* (*lit, fig*) überschwemmen.

swampy ['swɔmpɪ] *adj* sumpfig.

swan [swɔn] *n* Schwan *m*.

swank [swæŋk] (*inf*) *vi* angeben.

swan song *n* (*fig*) Schwanengesang *m*.

swap [swɔp] *n* Tausch *m* ♦ *vt*: **to ~ (for)** (ein)tauschen (gegen).

SWAPO ['swɑːpəu] *n abbr* (= *South-West Africa People's Organization*) SWAPO *f*.

swarm [swɔːm] *n* Schwarm *m*; (*of people*) Schar *f* ♦ *vi* (*bees, people*) schwärmen; **to be ~ing with** wimmeln von.

swarthy ['swɔːðɪ] *adj* (*person, face*) dunkelhäutig; (*complexion*) dunkel.

swastika ['swɔstɪkə] *n* Hakenkreuz *nt*.

SWAT (*US*) *n abbr* (= *Special Weapons and Tactics*): **~ team** ≈ schnelle Eingreiftruppe *f*.

swat [swɔt] *vt* totschlagen ♦ *n* (*BRIT: also*: **fly ~**) Fliegenklatsche *f*.

swathe [sweɪð] *vt*: **to ~ in** wickeln in +*acc*.

swatter ['swɔtəˀ] *n* (*also*: **fly ~**) Fliegenklatsche *f*.

sway [sweɪ] *vi* schwanken ♦ *vt* (*influence*) beeinflussen ♦ *n*: **to hold ~** herrschen; **to hold ~ over sb** jdn beherrschen *or* in seiner Macht haben.

swear [swɛəʳ] (*pt* **swore**, *pp* **sworn**) *vi* (*curse*)
fluchen ♦ *vt* (*promise*) schwören; **to ~ an
oath** einen Eid ablegen.
▶ **swear in** *vt* vereidigen.
swearword ['swɛəwɜːd] *n* Fluch *m*,
Kraftausdruck *m*.
sweat [swɛt] *n* Schweiß *m* ♦ *vi* schwitzen; **to
be in a ~** schwitzen.
sweatband ['swɛtbænd] *n* Schweißband *nt*.
sweater ['swɛtəʳ] *n* Pullover *m*.
sweatshirt ['swɛtʃɜːt] *n* Sweatshirt *nt*.
sweatshop ['swɛtʃɔp] (*pej*) *n*
Ausbeuterbetrieb *m*.
sweaty ['swɛtɪ] *adj* verschwitzt; (*hands*)
schweißig.
Swede [swiːd] *n* Schwede *m*, Schwedin *f*.
swede [swiːd] (*BRIT*) *n* Steckrübe *f*.
Sweden ['swiːdn] *n* Schweden *nt*.
Swedish ['swiːdɪʃ] *adj* schwedisch ♦ *n*
Schwedisch *nt*.
sweep [swiːp] (*pt*, *pp* **swept**) *n*: **to give sth a ~**
etw fegen *or* kehren; (*curve*) Bogen *m*;
(*range*) Bereich *m*; (*also*: **chimney ~**)
Kaminkehrer *m*, Schornsteinfeger *m* ♦ *vt*
fegen, kehren; (*current*) reißen ♦ *vi* (*through
air*) gleiten; (*wind*) fegen.
▶ **sweep away** *vt* hinwegfegen.
▶ **sweep past** *vi* vorbeirauschen.
▶ **sweep up** *vi* zusammenfegen,
zusammenkehren.
sweeper ['swiːpəʳ] *n* (*FOOTBALL*) Ausputzer *m*.
sweeping ['swiːpɪŋ] *adj* (*gesture*) weit
ausholend; (*changes, reforms*) weitreichend,
weit reichend; (*statement*)
verallgemeinernd.
sweepstake ['swiːpsteɪk] *n* Pferdewette, bei
der der Preis aus der Summe der Einsätze
besteht.
sweet [swiːt] *n* (*candy*) Bonbon *nt* or *m*; (*BRIT*:
CULIN) Nachtisch *m* ♦ *adj* süß; (*air, water*)
frisch; (*kind*) lieb ♦ *adv*: **to smell/taste ~** süß
duften/schmecken; **~ and sour** süß-sauer.
sweetbread ['swiːtbrɛd] *n* Bries *nt*.
sweetcorn ['swiːtkɔːn] *n* Mais *m*.
sweeten ['swiːtn] *vt* süßen; (*temper*) bessern;
(*person*) gnädig stimmen.
sweetener ['swiːtnəʳ] *n* Süßstoff *m*; (*fig*)
Anreiz *m*.
sweetheart ['swiːthɑːt] *n* Freund(in) *m(f)*; (*in
speech, writing*) Schatz *m*, Liebling *m*.
sweetness ['swiːtnɪs] *n* Süße *f*; (*kindness*)
Liebenswürdigkeit *f*.
sweet pea *n* (Garten)wicke *f*.
sweet potato *n* Süßkartoffel *f*, Batate *f*.
sweet shop (*BRIT*) *n* Süßwarengeschäft *nt*.
sweet tooth *n*: **to have a ~** gern Süßes
essen.
swell [swɛl] (*pt* **swelled**, *pp* **swollen** *or* **swelled**)
n Seegang *m* ♦ *adj* (*US*: *inf*) toll, prima ♦ *vi*
(*increase*) anwachsen; (*sound*) anschwellen;
(*feeling*) stärker werden; (*also*: **~ up**)
anschwellen.

swelling ['swɛlɪŋ] *n* Schwellung *f*.
sweltering ['swɛltərɪŋ] *adj* (*heat*) glühend;
(*weather, day*) glühend heiß.
swept [swɛpt] *pt*, *pp of* **sweep**.
swerve [swɜːv] *vi* (*animal*) ausbrechen; (*driver,
vehicle*) ausschwenken; **to ~ off the road**
ausschwenken und von der Straße
abkommen.
swift [swɪft] *n* Mauersegler *m* ♦ *adj* schnell.
swiftly ['swɪftlɪ] *adv* schnell.
swiftness ['swɪftnɪs] *n* Schnelligkeit *f*.
swig [swɪg] (*inf*) *n* Schluck *m* ♦ *vt*
herunterkippen.
swill [swɪl] *vt* (*also*: **~ out**) ausspülen; (*also*:
~ down) abspülen ♦ *n* (*for pigs*)
Schweinefutter *nt*.
swim [swɪm] (*pt* **swam**, *pp* **swum**) *vi*
schwimmen; (*before one's eyes*)
verschwimmen ♦ *vt* (*the Channel etc*)
durchschwimmen; (*a length*) schwimmen
♦ *n*: **to go for a ~** schwimmen gehen; **to go
~ming** schwimmen gehen; **my head is
~ming** mir dreht sich der Kopf.
swimmer ['swɪməʳ] *n* Schwimmer(in) *m(f)*.
swimming ['swɪmɪŋ] *n* Schwimmen *nt*.
swimming baths (*BRIT*) *npl* Schwimmbad *nt*.
swimming cap *n* Badekappe *f*, Bademütze *f*.
swimming costume (*BRIT*) *n* Badeanzug *m*.
swimmingly ['swɪmɪŋlɪ] (*inf*) *adv* glänzend.
swimming pool *n* Schwimmbad *nt*.
swimming trunks *npl* Badehose *f*.
swimsuit ['swɪmsuːt] *n* Badeanzug *m*.
swindle ['swɪndl] *n* Schwindel *m*, Betrug *m*
♦ *vt*: **to ~ sb (out of sth)** jdn (um etw)
betrügen *or* beschwindeln.
swindler ['swɪndləʳ] *n* Schwindler(in) *m(f)*.
swine [swaɪn] (*inf!*) *n* Schwein *nt*.
swing [swɪŋ] (*pt*, *pp* **swung**) *n* (*in playground*)
Schaukel *f*; (*movement*) Schwung *m*; (*change*)
Umschwung *m*; (*MUS*) Swing *m* ♦ *vt* (*arms,
legs*) schwingen (mit); (*also*: **~ round**)
herumschwenken ♦ *vi* schwingen; (*also*:
~ round) sich umdrehen; (*vehicle*)
herumschwenken; **a ~ to the left** (*POL*) ein
Linksruck *m*; **to get into the ~ of things**
richtig reinkommen; **to be in full ~** (*party
etc*) in vollem Gang sein.
swing bridge *n* Drehbrücke *f*.
swing door, (*US*) **swinging door** *n*
Pendeltür *f*.
swingeing ['swɪndʒɪŋ] (*BRIT*) *adj* (*blow*) hart;
(*attack*) scharf; (*cuts, increases*) extrem.
swinging ['swɪŋɪŋ] *adj* (*music*) schwungvoll;
(*movement*) schaukelnd.
swipe [swaɪp] *vt* (*also*: **~ at**) schlagen nach;
(*inf*: *steal*) klauen ♦ *n* Schlag *m*.
swirl [swɜːl] *vi* wirbeln ♦ *n* Wirbeln *nt*.
swish [swɪʃ] *vi* rauschen; (*tail*) schlagen ♦ *n*
Rauschen *nt*; (*of tail*) Schlagen *nt* ♦ *adj* (*inf*)
schick.
Swiss [swɪs] *adj* schweizerisch, Schweizer ♦ *n*
inv Schweizer(in) *m(f)*.

Swiss French *adj* französischschweizerisch.
Swiss German *adj* deutschschweizerisch.
Swiss roll *n* Biskuitrolle *f*.
switch [swɪtʃ] *n* Schalter *m*; (*change*)
Änderung *f* ♦ *vt* (*change*) ändern; (*exchange*)
tauschen, wechseln; **to ~ (round** *or* **over**)
vertauschen.
► **switch off** *vt* abschalten; (*light*)
ausschalten ♦ *vi* abschalten.
► **switch on** *vt* einschalten; (*radio*) anstellen;
(*engine*) anlassen.
switchback ['swɪtʃbæk] (*BRIT*) *n* (*road*) auf
und ab führende Straße *f*; (*roller-coaster*)
Achterbahn *f*.
switchblade ['swɪtʃbleɪd] *n* Schnappmesser
nt.
switchboard ['swɪtʃbɔːd] *n* Vermittlung *f*,
Zentrale *f*.
switchboard operator *n* Telefonist(in) *m(f)*.
Switzerland ['swɪtsələnd] *n* die Schweiz *f*.
swivel ['swɪvl] *vi* (*also*: ~ **round**) sich
(herum)drehen.
swollen ['swəulən] *pp of* **swell** ♦ *adj*
geschwollen; (*lake etc*) angeschwollen.
swoon [swuːn] *vi* beinahe ohnmächtig
werden ♦ *n* Ohnmacht *f*.
swoop [swuːp] *n* (*by police etc*) Razzia *f*; (*of
bird etc*) Sturzflug *m* ♦ *vi* (*also*: ~ **down**: *bird*)
herabstoßen; (*plane*) einen Sturzflug
machen.
swop [swɔp] = **swap**.
sword [sɔːd] *n* Schwert *nt*.
swordfish ['sɔːdfɪʃ] *n* Schwertfisch *m*.
swore [swɔːʳ] *pt of* **swear**.
sworn [swɔːn] *pp of* **swear** ♦ *adj* (*statement*)
eidlich; (*evidence*) unter Eid; (*enemy*)
geschworen.
swot [swɔt] *vi* pauken ♦ *n* (*pej*) Streber(in)
m(f).
► **swot up** *vt*: **to ~ up (on)** pauken (+*acc*).
swum [swʌm] *pp of* **swim**.
swung [swʌŋ] *pt, pp of* **swing**.
sycamore ['sɪkəmɔːʳ] *n* Bergahorn *m*.
sycophant ['sɪkəfænt] *n* Kriecher *m*,
Speichellecker *m*.
sycophantic [sɪkə'fæntɪk] *adj* kriecherisch.
Sydney ['sɪdnɪ] *n* Sydney *nt*.
syllable ['sɪləbl] *n* Silbe *f*.
syllabus ['sɪləbəs] *n* Lehrplan *m*; **on the ~** im
Lehrplan.
symbol ['sɪmbl] *n* Symbol *nt*.
symbolic(al) [sɪm'bɔlɪk(l)] *adj* symbolisch; **to
be ~ of sth** etw symbolisieren, ein Symbol
für etw sein.
symbolism ['sɪmbəlɪzəm] *n* Symbolismus
m.
symbolize ['sɪmbəlaɪz] *vt* symbolisieren.
symmetrical [sɪ'mɛtrɪkl] *adj* symmetrisch.
symmetry ['sɪmɪtrɪ] *n* Symmetrie *f*.
sympathetic [sɪmpə'θɛtɪk] *adj* (*understanding*)
verständnisvoll; (*showing pity*) mitfühlend;
(*likeable*) sympathisch; (*supportive*)

wohlwollend; **to be ~ to a cause** (*well-
disposed*) einer Sache wohlwollend
gegenüberstehen.
sympathetically [sɪmpə'θɛtɪklɪ] *adv* (*showing
understanding*) verständnisvoll; (*showing
support*) wohlwollend.
sympathize ['sɪmpəθaɪz] *vi*: **to ~ with** (*person*)
Mitleid haben mit; (*feelings*) Verständnis
haben für; (*cause*) sympathisieren mit.
sympathizer ['sɪmpəθaɪzəʳ] *n* (*POL*)
Sympathisant(in) *m(f)*.
sympathy ['sɪmpəθɪ] *n* Mitgefühl *nt*;
sympathies *npl* (*support, tendencies*)
Sympathien *pl*; **with our deepest ~** mit
aufrichtigem *or* herzlichem Beileid; **to
come out in ~** (*workers*) in einen
Sympathiestreik treten.
symphonic [sɪm'fɔnɪk] *adj* sinfonisch.
symphony ['sɪmfənɪ] *n* Sinfonie *f*.
symphony orchestra *n* Sinfonieorchester
nt.
symposia [sɪm'pəuzɪə] *npl of* **symposium**.
symposium [sɪm'pəuzɪəm] (*pl* ~**s** *or*
symposia) *n* Symposium *nt*.
symptom ['sɪmptəm] *n* (*MED, fig*) Symptom *nt*,
Anzeichen *nt*.
symptomatic [sɪmptə'mætɪk] *adj*: ~ **of**
symptomatisch für.
synagogue ['sɪnəgɔg] *n* Synagoge *f*.
sync [sɪŋk] *n abbr* (= *synchronization*): **in ~**
synchron; **out of ~** nicht synchron.
synchromesh [sɪŋkrəu'mɛʃ] *n*
Synchrongetriebe *nt*.
synchronize ['sɪŋkrənaɪz] *vt* (*watches*)
gleichstellen; (*movements*) aufeinander
abstimmen; (*sound*) synchronisieren
♦ *vi*: **to ~ with** (*sound*) synchron sein
mit.
synchronized swimming ['sɪŋkrənaɪzd-] *n*
Synchronschwimmen *nt*.
syncopated ['sɪŋkəpeɪtɪd] *adj* synkopiert.
syndicate ['sɪndɪkɪt] *n*
Interessengemeinschaft *f*; (*of businesses*)
Verband *m*; (*of newspapers*) Pressezentrale
f.
syndrome ['sɪndrəum] *n* Syndrom *nt*; (*fig*)
Phänomen *nt*.
synonym ['sɪnənɪm] *n* Synonym *nt*.
synonymous [sɪ'nɔnɪməs] *adj* (*fig*): ~ **(with)**
gleichbedeutend (mit).
synopses [sɪ'nɔpsiːz] *npl of* **synopsis**.
synopsis [sɪ'nɔpsɪs] (*pl* **synopses**) *n* Abriss *m*,
Zusammenfassung *f*.
syntactic [sɪn'tæktɪk] *adj* syntaktisch.
syntax ['sɪntæks] *n* Syntax *f*.
syntax error *n* (*COMPUT*) Syntaxfehler *m*.
syntheses ['sɪnθəsiːz] *npl of* **synthesis**.
synthesis ['sɪnθəsɪs] (*pl* **syntheses**) *n* Synthese
f.
synthesizer ['sɪnθəsaɪzəʳ] *n* Synthesizer *m*.
synthetic [sɪn'θɛtɪk] *adj* synthetisch; (*speech*)
künstlich; **synthetics** *npl* (*man-made fabrics*)

Synthetik *f*.
syphilis ['sɪfɪlɪs] *n* Syphilis *f*.
syphon ['saɪfən] = **siphon**.
Syria ['sɪrɪə] *n* Syrien *nt*.
Syrian ['sɪrɪən] *adj* syrisch ♦ *n* Syrer(in) *m(f)*.
syringe [sɪ'rɪndʒ] *n* Spritze *f*.
syrup ['sɪrəp] *n* Sirup *m*; (*also*: **golden ~**) (gelber) Sirup *m*.
syrupy ['sɪrəpɪ] *adj* sirupartig; (*pej, fig*: *sentimental*) schmalzig.
system ['sɪstəm] *n* System *nt*; (*body*) Körper *m*; (*ANAT*) Apparat *m*, System *nt*; **it was a shock to his ~** er hatte schwer damit zu schaffen.
systematic [sɪstə'mætɪk] *adj* systematisch.
system disk *n* (*COMPUT*) Systemdiskette *f*.
systems analyst ['sɪstəmz-] *n* Systemanalytiker(in) *m(f)*.

T, t

T, t [tiː] *n* (*letter*) T *nt*, t *nt*; **~ for Tommy** ≈ T wie Theodor.
TA (*BRIT*) *n abbr* = **Territorial Army**.
ta [tɑː] (*BRIT*: *inf*) *interj* danke.
tab [tæb] *n abbr* = **tabulator** ♦ *n* (*on drinks can*) Ring *m*; (*on garment*) Etikett *nt*; **to keep ~s on sb/sth** (*fig*) jdn/etw im Auge behalten.
tabby ['tæbɪ] *n* (*also*: **~ cat**) getigerte Katze *f*.
tabernacle ['tæbənækl] *n* Tabernakel *nt*.
table ['teɪbl] *n* Tisch *m*; (*MATH, CHEM etc*) Tabelle *f* ♦ *vt* (*BRIT*: *PARL*: *motion etc*) einbringen; **to lay** *or* **set the ~** den Tisch decken; **to clear the ~** den Tisch abräumen; **league ~** (*BRIT*: *SPORT*) Tabelle *f*.
tablecloth ['teɪblklɒθ] *n* Tischdecke *f*.
table d'hôte [tɑːbl'dəut] *adj* (*menu, meal*) Tagesmenü *nt*.
table lamp *n* Tischlampe *f*.
tablemat ['teɪblmæt] *n* (*of cloth*) Set *nt or m*; (*for hot dish*) Untersatz *m*.
table of contents *n* Inhaltsverzeichnis *nt*.
table salt *n* Tafelsalz *nt*.
tablespoon ['teɪblspuːn] *n* Esslöffel *m*; (*also*: **~ful**) Esslöffel *m* (voll).
tablet ['tæblɪt] *n* (*MED*) Tablette *f*; (*HIST*: *for writing*) Tafel *f*; (*plaque*) Plakette *f*; **~ of soap** (*BRIT*) Stück *nt* Seife.
table tennis *n* Tischtennis *nt*.
table wine *n* Tafelwein *m*.
tabloid ['tæblɔɪd] *n* (*newspaper*) Boulevardzeitung *f*; **the ~s** die Boulevardpresse.

TABLOID PRESS

*Des Ausdruck **tabloid press** bezieht sich auf kleinformatige Zeitungen (ca 30 x 40cm); diese sind in Großbritannien fast ausschließlich Massenblätter. Im Gegensatz zur **quality press** verwenden sie viele Fotos und einen knappern, oft reißerischen Stil. Sie kommen denjenigen Lesern entgegen, die mehr Wert auf Unterhaltung legen.*

---

taboo [tə'buː] *n* Tabu *nt* ♦ *adj* tabu; **a ~ subject/word** ein Tabuthema/Tabuwort.
tabulate ['tæbjuleɪt] *vt* tabellarisieren.
tabulator ['tæbjuleɪtə*] *n* Tabulator *m*.
tachograph ['tækəgrɑːf] *n* Fahrtenschreiber *m*.
tachometer [tæ'kɒmɪtə*] *n* Tachometer *m*.
tacit ['tæsɪt] *adj* stillschweigend.
taciturn ['tæsɪtɜːn] *adj* schweigsam.
tack [tæk] *n* (*nail*) Stift *m* ♦ *vt* (*nail*) anheften; (*stitch*) heften ♦ *vi* (*NAUT*) kreuzen; **to change ~** (*fig*) den Kurs ändern; **to ~ sth on to (the end of) sth** etw (hinten) an etw *acc* anheften.
tackle ['tækl] *n* (*for fishing*) Ausrüstung *f*; (*for lifting*) Flaschenzug *m*; (*FOOTBALL, RUGBY*) Angriff *m* ♦ *vt* (*deal with*: *difficulty*) in Angriff nehmen; (*challenge*: *person*) zur Rede stellen; (*physically, also SPORT*) angreifen.
tacky ['tækɪ] *adj* (*sticky*) klebrig; (*pej*: *cheap-looking*) schäbig.
tact [tækt] *n* Takt *m*.
tactful ['tæktful] *adj* taktvoll; **to be ~** taktvoll sein.
tactfully ['tæktfəlɪ] *adv* taktvoll.
tactical ['tæktɪkl] *adj* taktisch; **~ error** taktischer Fehler; **~ voting** taktische Stimmabgabe.
tactician [tæk'tɪʃən] *n* Taktiker(in) *m(f)*.
tactics ['tæktɪks] *npl* Taktik *f*.
tactless ['tæktlɪs] *adj* taktlos.
tactlessly ['tæktlɪslɪ] *adv* taktlos.
tadpole ['tædpəul] *n* Kaulquappe *f*.
taffy ['tæfɪ] (*US*) *n* (*toffee*) Toffee *nt*.
tag [tæg] *n* (*label*) Anhänger *m*; **price-/name ~** Preis-/Namensschild *nt*.
▶ **tag along** *vi* sich anschließen.
Tahiti [tɑː'hiːtɪ] *n* Tahiti *nt*.
tail [teɪl] *n* (*of animal*) Schwanz *m*; (*of plane*) Heck *nt*; (*of shirt, coat*) Schoß *m* ♦ *vt* (*follow*) folgen +*dat*; **tails** *npl* (*formal suit*) Frack *m*; **to turn ~** die Flucht ergreifen; *see also* **head**.
▶ **tail off** *vi* (*in size etc*) abnehmen; (*voice*) schwächer werden.
tailback ['teɪlbæk] (*BRIT*) *n* (*AUT*) Stau *m*.
tail coat *n* = **tails**.
tail end *n* Ende *nt*.
tailgate ['teɪlgeɪt] *n* (*AUT*) Heckklappe *f*.
taillight ['teɪllaɪt] *n* (*AUT*) Rücklicht *nt*.
tailor ['teɪlə*] *n* Schneider(in) *m(f)* ♦ *vt*: **to ~ sth (to)** etw abstimmen (auf +*acc*); **~'s**

shop Schneiderei *f*.
tailoring ['teɪlərɪŋ] *n* (*craft*) Schneiderei *f*; (*cut*) Verarbeitung *f*.
tailor-made ['teɪlə'meɪd] *adj* (*also fig*) maßgeschneidert.
tailwind ['teɪlwɪnd] *n* Rückenwind *m*.
taint [teɪnt] *vt* (*meat, food*) verderben; (*fig: reputation etc*) beschmutzen.
tainted ['teɪntɪd] *adj* (*food, water, air*) verdorben; (*fig: profits, reputation etc*): ~ **with** behaftet mit.
Taiwan ['taɪ'wɑːn] *n* Taiwan *nt*.
Tajikistan [tɑːdʒɪkɪ'stɑːn] *n* Tadschikistan *nt*.
take [teɪk] (*pt* **took**, *pp* **taken**) *vt* nehmen; (*photo, notes*) machen; (*decision*) fällen; (*require: courage, time*) erfordern; (*tolerate: pain etc*) ertragen; (*hold: passengers etc*) fassen; (*accompany: person*) begleiten; (*carry, bring*) mitnehmen; (*exam, test*) machen; (*conduct: meeting*) leiten; (*: class*) unterrichten ♦ *vi* (*have effect: drug*) wirken; (*: dye*) angenommen werden ♦ *n* (*CINE*) Aufnahme *f*; **to ~ sth from** (*drawer etc*) etw nehmen aus +*dat*; **I ~ it (that)** ich nehme an(, dass); **I took him for a doctor** (*mistake*) ich hielt ihn für einen Arzt; **to ~ sb's hand** jds Hand nehmen; **to ~ sb for a walk** mit jdm spazieren gehen; **to be ~n ill** krank werden; **to ~ it upon o.s. to do sth** es auf sich nehmen, etw zu tun; **~ the first (street) on the left** nehmen Sie die erste Straße links; **to ~ Russian at university** Russisch studieren; **it won't ~ long** es dauert nicht lange; **I was quite ~n with her/it** (*attracted to*) ich war von ihr/davon recht angetan.
▶ **take after** *vt fus* (*resemble*) ähneln +*dat*.
▶ **take apart** *vt* auseinander nehmen.
▶ **take away** *vt* wegnehmen; (*carry off*) wegbringen; (*MATH*) abziehen ♦ *vi*: **to ~ away from** (*detract from*) schmälern, beeinträchtigen.
▶ **take back** *vt* (*return*) zurückbringen; (*one's words*) zurücknehmen.
▶ **take down** *vt* (*write down*) aufschreiben; (*dismantle*) abreißen.
▶ **take in** *vt* (*deceive: person*) hereinlegen, täuschen; (*understand*) begreifen; (*include*) einschließen; (*lodger*) aufnehmen; (*orphan, stray dog*) zu sich nehmen; (*dress, waistband*) enger machen.
▶ **take off** *vi* (*AVIAT*) starten; (*go away*) sich absetzen ♦ *vt* (*clothes*) ausziehen; (*glasses*) abnehmen; (*make-up*) entfernen; (*time*) frei nehmen; (*imitate: person*) nachmachen.
▶ **take on** *vt* (*work, responsibility*) übernehmen; (*employee*) einstellen; (*compete against*) antreten gegen.
▶ **take out** *vt* (*invite*) ausgehen mit; (*remove: tooth*) herausnehmen; (*licence*) erwerben; **to ~ sth out of sth** (*drawer, pocket etc*) etw aus etw nehmen; **don't ~ it out on me!** lass es nicht an mir aus!

▶ **take over** *vt* (*business*) übernehmen; (*country*) Besitz ergreifen von ♦ *vi* (*replace*): **to ~ over from sb** jdn ablösen.
▶ **take to** *vt fus* (*person, thing*) mögen; (*activity*) Gefallen finden an +*dat*; (*form habit of*): **to ~ to doing sth** sich *dat* angewöhnen, etw zu tun.
▶ **take up** *vt* (*hobby, sport*) anfangen mit; (*job*) antreten; (*idea etc*) annehmen; (*time, space*) beanspruchen; (*continue: task, story*) fortfahren mit; (*shorten: hem, garment*) kürzer machen ♦ *vi* (*befriend*): **to ~ up with sb** sich mit jdm anfreunden; **to ~ sb up on an offer/a suggestion** auf jds Angebot/Vorschlag eingehen.
takeaway ['teɪkəweɪ] (*BRIT*) *n* (*shop, restaurant*) ≈ Schnellimbiss *m*; (*food*) Imbiss *m* (*zum Mitnehmen*).
take-home pay ['teɪkhəum-] *n* Nettolohn *m*.
taken ['teɪkən] *pp of* **take**.
takeoff ['teɪkɔf] *n* (*AVIAT*) Start *m*.
takeout ['teɪkaut] (*US*) *n* = **takeaway**.
takeover ['teɪkəuvə*] *n* (*COMM*) Übernahme *f*; (*of country*) Inbesitznahme *f*.
takeover bid *n* Übernahmeangebot *nt*.
takings ['teɪkɪŋz] *npl* Einnahmen *pl*.
talc [tælk] *n* (*also:* **talcum powder**) Talkumpuder *nt*.
tale [teɪl] *n* Geschichte *f*; **to tell ~s (to sb)** (*child*) (jdm) Geschichten erzählen.
talent ['tælnt] *n* Talent *nt*.
talented ['tæləntɪd] *adj* talentiert, begabt.
talent scout *n* Talentsucher(in) *m(f)*.
talisman ['tælɪzmən] *n* Talisman *m*.
talk [tɔːk] *n* (*speech*) Vortrag *m*; (*conversation, discussion*) Gespräch *nt*; (*gossip*) Gerede *nt* ♦ *vi* (*speak*) sprechen; (*chat*) reden; (*gossip*) klatschen; **talks** *npl* (*POL etc*) Gespräche *pl*; **to give a ~** einen Vortrag halten; **to ~ about** (*discuss*) sprechen *or* reden über; **~ing of films, have you seen ...?** da wir gerade von Filmen sprechen: hast du ... gesehen?; **to ~ sb into doing sth** jdn zu etw überreden; **to ~ sb out of doing sth** jdm etw ausreden.
▶ **talk over** *vt* (*problem etc*) besprechen.
talkative ['tɔːkətɪv] *adj* gesprächig.
talker ['tɔːkə*] *n*: **to be a good/fast** *etc* ~ gut/amüsant/schnell *etc* reden können.
talking point ['tɔːkɪŋ-] *n* Gesprächsthema *nt*.
talking-to ['tɔːkɪŋtu] *n*: **to give sb a (good) ~** jdm eine (ordentliche) Standpauke halten (*inf*).
talk show *n* Talkshow *f*.
tall [tɔːl] *adj* (*person*) groß; (*glass, bookcase, tree, building*) hoch; (*ladder*) lang; **to be 6 feet ~** (*person*) ≈ 1,80m groß sein; **how ~ are you?** wie groß bist du?
tallboy ['tɔːlbɔɪ] (*BRIT*) *n* Kommode *f*.
tallness ['tɔːlnɪs] *n* (*of person*) Größe *f*; (*of tree, building etc*) Höhe *f*.
tall story *n* unglaubliche Geschichte *f*.
tally ['tælɪ] *n* (*of marks, amounts etc*) aktueller

Stand *m* ♦ *vi*: **to** ~ **(with)** (*figures, stories etc*) übereinstimmen mit; **to keep a** ~ **of sth** über etw *acc* Buch führen.

talon ['tælən] *n* Kralle *f*.

tambourine [tæmbə'riːn] *n* Tamburin *nt*.

tame [teɪm] *adj* (*animal, bird*) zahm; (*fig: story, party, performance*) lustlos, lahm (*inf*).

Tamil ['tæmɪl] *adj* tamilisch ♦ *n* Tamile *m*, Tamilin *f*; (*LING*) Tamil *nt*.

tamper ['tæmpə'] *vi*: **to** ~ **with sth** an etw *dat* herumpfuschen (*inf*).

tampon ['tæmpɔn] *n* Tampon *m*.

tan [tæn] *n* (*also*: **suntan**) (Sonnen)bräune *f* ♦ *vi* (*person, skin*) braun werden ♦ *vt* (*hide*) gerben; (*skin*) bräunen ♦ *adj* (*colour*) hellbraun; **to get a** ~ braun werden.

tandem ['tændəm] *n* Tandem *nt*; (*together*): **in** ~ (*fig*) zusammen.

tandoori [tæn'duərɪ] *n*: ~ **oven** Tandoori-Ofen *m*; ~ **chicken** *im Tandoori-Ofen gebratenes Huhn*.

tang [tæŋ] *n* (*smell*) Geruch *m*; (*taste*) Geschmack *m*.

tangent ['tændʒənt] *n* (*MATH*) Tangente *f*; **to go off at a** ~ (*fig*) vom Thema abschweifen.

tangerine [tændʒə'riːn] *n* (*fruit*) Mandarine *f*; (*colour*) Orangerot *nt*.

tangible ['tændʒəbl] *adj* greifbar; ~ **assets** (*COMM*) Sachanlagevermögen *nt*.

Tangier [tæn'dʒɪə'] *n* Tanger *nt*.

tangle ['tæŋgl] *n* (*of branches, wire etc*) Gewirr *nt*; **to be in a** ~ verheddert sein; (*fig*) durcheinander sein; **to get in a** ~ sich verheddern; (*fig*) durcheinander geraten.

tango ['tæŋgəu] *n* Tango *m*.

tank [tæŋk] *n* Tank *m*; (*for photographic processing*) Wanne *f*; (*also*: **fish** ~) Aquarium *nt*; (*MIL*) Panzer *m*.

tankard ['tæŋkəd] *n* Bierkrug *m*.

tanker ['tæŋkə'] *n* (*ship*) Tanker *m*; (*truck*) Tankwagen *m*.

tanned [tænd] *adj* (*person*) braun gebrannt; (*hide*) gegerbt.

tannin ['tænɪn] *n* Tannin *nt*.

tanning ['tænɪŋ] *n* (*of leather*) Gerben *nt*.

Tannoy ® ['tænɔɪ] (*BRIT*) *n* Lautsprechersystem *nt*; **over the** ~ über Lautsprecher.

tantalizing ['tæntəlaɪzɪŋ] *adj* (*smell*) verführerisch; (*possibility*) verlockend.

tantamount ['tæntəmaunt] *adj*: ~ **to** gleichbedeutend mit.

tantrum ['tæntrəm] *n* Wutanfall *m*; **to throw a** ~ einen Wutanfall bekommen.

Tanzania [tænzə'nɪə] *n* Tansania *nt*.

Tanzanian [tænzə'nɪən] *adj* tansanisch ♦ *n* (*person*) Tansanier(in) *m(f)*.

tap [tæp] *n* (*on sink, gas tap*) Hahn *m*; (*gentle blow*) leichter Schlag *m*, Klaps *m* ♦ *vt* (*hit gently*) klopfen; (*exploit: resources, energy*) nutzen; (*telephone*) abhören, anzapfen; **on** ~ (*fig: resources, information*) zur Verfügung;

(*beer*) vom Fass.

tap-dancing ['tæpdɑːnsɪŋ] *n* Stepptanz *m*.

tape [teɪp] *n* (*also*: **magnetic** ~) Tonband *nt*; (*cassette*) Kassette *f*; (*also*: **sticky** ~) Klebeband *nt*; (*for tying*) Band *nt* ♦ *vt* (*record, conversation*) aufnehmen, aufzeichnen; (*stick with tape*) mit Klebeband befestigen; **on** ~ (*song etc*) auf Band.

tape deck *n* Tapedeck *nt*.

tape measure *n* Bandmaß *nt*.

taper ['teɪpə'] *n* (*candle*) lange, dünne Kerze ♦ *vi* sich verjüngen.

tape recorder *n* Tonband(gerät) *nt*.

tape recording *n* Tonbandaufnahme *f*.

tapered ['teɪpəd] *adj* (*skirt, jacket*) nach unten enger werdend.

tapering ['teɪpərɪŋ] *adj* spitz zulaufend.

tapestry ['tæpɪstrɪ] *n* (*on wall*) Wandteppich *m*; (*fig*) Kaleidoskop *nt*.

tapeworm ['teɪpwɔːm] *n* Bandwurm *m*.

tapioca [tæpɪ'əukə] *n* Tapioka *f*.

tappet ['tæpɪt] *n* (*AUT*) Stößel *m*.

tar [tɑː] *n* Teer *m*; **low/middle** ~ **cigarettes** Zigaretten mit niedrigem/mittlerem Teergehalt.

tarantula [tə'ræntjulə] *n* Tarantel *f*.

tardy ['tɑːdɪ] *adj* (*reply, letter*) verspätet; (*progress*) langsam.

target ['tɑːgɪt] *n* Ziel *nt*; (*fig: of joke, criticism etc*) Zielscheibe *f*; **to be on** ~ (*project, work*) nach Plan verlaufen.

target practice *n* Zielschießen *nt*.

tariff ['tærɪf] *n* (*tax on goods*) Zoll *m*; (*BRIT: in hotels etc*) Preisliste *f*.

tariff barrier *n* Zollschranke *f*.

tarmac ® ['tɑːmæk] *n* (*BRIT: on road*) Asphalt *m*; (*AVIAT*): **on the** ~ auf dem Rollfeld ♦ *vt* (*BRIT: road etc*) asphaltieren.

tarn [tɑːn] *n* Bergsee *m*.

tarnish ['tɑːnɪʃ] *vt* (*silver, brass etc*) stumpf werden lassen; (*fig: reputation etc*) beflecken, in Mitleidenschaft ziehen.

tarot ['tærəu] *n* Tarot *nt* or *m*.

tarpaulin [tɑː'pɔːlɪn] *n* Plane *f*.

tarragon ['tærəgən] *n* Estragon *m*.

tart [tɑːt] *n* (*CULIN*) Torte *f*; (: *small*) Törtchen *nt*; (*BRIT: inf. prostitute*) Nutte *f* ♦ *adj* (*apple, grapefruit etc*) säuerlich.

▶ **tart up** (*BRIT: inf*) *vt* (*room, building*) aufmotzen; **to** ~ **o.s. up** sich fein machen; (*pej*) sich auftakeln.

tartan ['tɑːtn] *n* Tartan *m*, Schottenstoff *m* ♦ *adj* (*scarf etc*) mit Schottenmuster.

tartar ['tɑːtə'] *n* (*on teeth*) Zahnstein *m*; (*pej: person*) Tyrann(in) *m(f)*.

tartar(e) sauce ['tɑːtə-] *n* Remouladensoße *f*.

task [tɑːsk] *n* Aufgabe *f*; **to take sb to** ~ jdn ins Gebet nehmen.

task force *n* (*MIL*) Sonderkommando *nt*; (*POLICE*) Spezialeinheit *f*.

taskmaster ['tɑːskmɑːstə'] *n*: **a hard** ~ ein strenger Lehrmeister.

Tasmania [tæz'meɪnɪə] n Tasmanien nt.
tassel ['tæsl] n Quaste f.
taste [teɪst] n Geschmack m; (sample)
Kostprobe f; (fig: of suffering, freedom etc)
Vorgeschmack m ♦ vt (get flavour of)
schmecken; (test) probieren, versuchen ♦ vi:
to ~ of/like sth nach/wie etw schmecken;
sense of ~ Geschmackssinn m; **to have a
~ of sth** (sample) etw probieren; **to acquire
a ~ for sth** (liking) Geschmack an etw dat
finden; **to be in good/bad ~** (joke etc)
geschmackvoll/geschmacklos sein; **you can
~ the garlic (in it)** (detect) man schmeckt
den Knoblauch durch; **what does it ~ like?**
wie schmeckt es?
taste buds npl Geschmacksknospen pl.
tasteful ['teɪstful] adj geschmackvoll.
tastefully ['teɪstfəlɪ] adv geschmackvoll.
tasteless ['teɪstlɪs] adj geschmacklos.
tasty ['teɪstɪ] adj schmackhaft.
tattered ['tætəd] adj (clothes, paper etc)
zerrissen; (fig: hopes etc) angeschlagen.
tatters ['tætəz] npl: **to be in ~** (clothes) in
Fetzen sein.
tattoo [tə'tu:] n (on skin) Tätowierung f;
(spectacle) Zapfenstreich m ♦ vt: **to ~ sth on
sth** etw auf etw acc tätowieren.
tatty ['tætɪ] adj (BRIT: inf) adj schäbig.
taught [tɔ:t] pt, pp of **teach**.
taunt [tɔ:nt] n höhnische Bemerkung f ♦ vt
(person) verhöhnen.
Taurus ['tɔ:rəs] n Stier m; **to be ~** (ein) Stier
sein.
taut [tɔ:t] adj (skin, thread etc) straff.
tavern ['tævən] n Taverne f.
tawdry ['tɔ:drɪ] adj billig.
tawny ['tɔ:nɪ] adj gelbbraun.
tawny owl n Waldkauz m.
tax [tæks] n Steuer f ♦ vt (earnings, goods etc)
besteuern; (fig: memory, knowledge)
strapazieren; (: patience etc) auf die Probe
stellen; **before/after ~** vor/nach Abzug der
Steuern; **free of ~** steuerfrei.
taxable ['tæksəbl] adj steuerpflichtig; (income)
steuerbar.
tax allowance n Steuerfreibetrag m.
taxation [tæk'seɪʃən] n (system) Besteuerung
f; (money paid) Steuern pl.
tax avoidance n Steuerumgehung f.
tax collector n Steuerbeamte(r) m,
Steuerbeamtin f.
tax disc (BRIT) n (AUT) Steuerplakette f.
tax evasion n Steuerhinterziehung f.
tax exemption n Steuerbefreiung f.
tax exile (person) n Steuerflüchtling m.
tax-free ['tæksfri:] adj steuerfrei.
tax haven n Steuerparadies nt.
taxi ['tæksɪ] n Taxi nt ♦ vi (AVIAT: plane) rollen.
taxidermist ['tæksɪdəmɪst] n Taxidermist(in)
m(f), Tierpräparator(in) m(f).
taxi driver n Taxifahrer(in) m(f).
tax inspector (BRIT) n Steuerinspektor(in)

m(f).
taxi rank (BRIT) n Taxistand m.
taxi stand n = **taxi rank**.
taxpayer ['tækspeɪə*] n Steuerzahler(in) m(f).
tax rebate n Steuerrückvergütung f.
tax relief n Steuernachlass m.
tax return n Steuererklärung f.
tax shelter n (COMM) System zur
Verhinderung von Steuerbelastung.
tax year n Steuerjahr nt.
TB n abbr (= tuberculosis) Tb f, Tbc f.
tbc abbr (= to be confirmed) noch zu
bestätigen.
TD (US) n abbr = **Treasury Department**;
(FOOTBALL) = **touchdown**.
tea [ti:] n (drink) Tee m; (BRIT: evening meal)
Abendessen nt; **afternoon ~** (BRIT)
Nachmittagstee m.
tea bag n Teebeutel m.
tea break (BRIT) n Teepause f.
teacake ['ti:keɪk] (BRIT) n Rosinenbrötchen nt.
teach [ti:tʃ] (pt, pp taught) vt: **to ~ sb sth,
~ sth to sb** (instruct) jdm etw beibringen; (in
school) jdn in etw dat unterrichten ♦ vi
unterrichten; **it taught him a lesson** (fig) er
hat seine Lektion gelernt.
teacher ['ti:tʃə*] n Lehrer(in) m(f); **German ~**
Deutschlehrer(in) m(f).
teacher training college n (for primary
schools) ≈ pädagogische Hochschule f; (for
secondary schools) ≈ Studienseminar nt.
teaching ['ti:tʃɪŋ] n (work of teacher)
Unterricht m.
teaching aids npl Lehrmittel pl.
teaching hospital (BRIT) n
Ausbildungskrankenhaus nt.
teaching staff (BRIT) n Lehrerkollegium nt.
tea cosy n Teewärmer m.
teacup ['ti:kʌp] n Teetasse f.
teak [ti:k] n Teak nt.
tea leaves npl Teeblätter pl.
team [ti:m] n (of experts etc) Team nt; (SPORT)
Mannschaft f, Team nt; (of horses, oxen)
Gespann nt.
▶ **team up** vi: **to ~ up (with)** sich
zusammentun (mit).
team game n Mannschaftsspiel nt.
team spirit n Teamgeist m.
teamwork ['ti:mwɜ:k] n Teamwork nt,
Teamarbeit f.
tea party n Teegesellschaft f.
teapot ['ti:pɔt] n Teekanne f.
tear[1] [tɛə*] (pt **tore**, pp **torn**) n (hole) Riss m
♦ vt (rip) zerreißen ♦ vi (become torn) reißen;
to ~ sth to pieces or **bits** or **shreds** (lit, fig)
etw in Stücke reißen; **to ~ sb to pieces** jdn
fertig machen.
▶ **tear along** vi (rush) entlangrasen.
▶ **tear apart** vt (book, clothes, people)
auseinander reißen; (upset: person) hin- und
herreißen.
▶ **tear away** vt: **to ~ o.s. away (from sth)** (fig)

sich (von etw) losreißen.
▶ **tear out** vt (*sheet of paper etc*)
herausreißen.
▶ **tear up** vt (*sheet of paper etc*) zerreißen.
tear² [tɪə*] n (*in eye*) Träne f; **in ~s** in Tränen;
to burst into ~s in Tränen ausbrechen.
tearaway ['tɛərəweɪ] (*BRIT: inf*) n Rabauke m.
teardrop ['tɪədrɔp] n Träne f.
tearful ['tɪəful] adj (*person*) weinend; (*face*)
tränenüberströmt.
tear gas n Tränengas nt.
tearing ['tɛərɪŋ] adj: **to be in a ~ hurry** es
unheimlich eilig haben.
tearoom ['tiːruːm] n = **teashop**.
tease [tiːz] vt necken; (*unkindly*) aufziehen ♦ n:
she's a real ~ sie zieht einen ständig auf.
tea set n Teeservice nt.
teashop ['tiːʃɔp] (*BRIT*) n Teestube f.
Teasmade ® ['tiːzmeɪd] n Teemaschine f (*mit
Zeiteinstellung*).
teaspoon ['tiːspuːn] n Teelöffel m; (*also: ~ful:
measure*) Teelöffel m (voll).
tea strainer n Teesieb nt.
teat [tiːt] n (*on bottle*) Sauger m.
teatime ['tiːtaɪm] n Teestunde f.
tea towel (*BRIT*) n Geschirrtuch nt.
tea urn n Teespender m.
tech [tɛk] (*inf*) n abbr = **technical college,
technology**.
technical ['tɛknɪkl] adj technisch; (*terms,
language*) Fach-.
technical college (*BRIT*) n technische
Fachschule f.
technicality [tɛknɪ'kælɪtɪ] n (*point of law*)
Formalität f; (*detail*) technische Einzelheit f;
on a (legal) ~ aufgrund or auf Grund einer
(juristischen) Formalität.
technically ['tɛknɪklɪ] adv (*strictly speaking*)
genau genommen; (*regarding technique*)
technisch (gesehen).
technician [tɛk'nɪʃən] n Techniker(in) m(f).
technique [tɛk'niːk] n Technik f.
techno ['tɛknəu] n (*MUS*) Techno nt.
technocrat ['tɛknəkræt] n Technokrat(in) m(f).
technological [tɛknə'lɔdʒɪkl] adj
technologisch.
technologist [tɛk'nɔlədʒɪst] n Technologe m,
Technologin f.
technology [tɛk'nɔlədʒɪ] n Technologie f.
technology college n Oberstufenkolleg mit
technischem Schwerpunkt.
teddy (bear) ['tɛdɪ(-)] n Teddy(bär) m.
tedious ['tiːdɪəs] adj langweilig.
tedium ['tiːdɪəm] n Langeweile f.
tee [tiː] n (*GOLF*) Tee nt.
▶ **tee off** vi (vom Tee) abschlagen.
teem [tiːm] vi: **to ~ with** (*tourists etc*)
wimmeln von; **it is ~ing down** es gießt in
Strömen.
teenage ['tiːneɪdʒ] adj (*fashions etc*) Jugend-;
(*children*) im Teenageralter.
teenager ['tiːneɪdʒə*] n Teenager m,

Jugendliche(r) f(m).
teens [tiːnz] npl: **to be in one's ~** im
Teenageralter sein.
tee shirt n = **T-shirt**.
teeter ['tiːtə*] vi (*also fig*) schwanken, taumeln.
teeth [tiːθ] npl of **tooth**.
teethe [tiːð] vi Zähne bekommen, zahnen.
teething ring ['tiːðɪŋ-] n Beißring m.
teething troubles npl (*fig*)
Kinderkrankheiten pl.
teetotal ['tiː'təutl] adj (*person*) abstinent.
teetotaller, (*US*) **teetotaler** ['tiː'təutlə*] n
Abstinenzler(in) m(f), Antialkoholiker(in)
m(f).
TEFL ['tɛfl] n abbr (= *Teaching of English as a
Foreign Language*) Unterricht in Englisch als
Fremdsprache.
Teflon ® ['tɛflɔn] n Teflon ® nt.
Teheran [tɛə'rɑːn] n Teheran nt.
tel. abbr (= *telephone*) Tel.
Tel Aviv ['tɛlə'viːv] n Tel Aviv nt.
telecast ['tɛlɪkɑːst] n Fernsehsendung f.
telecommunications ['tɛlɪkəmjuːnɪ'keɪʃənz]
n Nachrichtentechnik f.
teleconferencing [tɛlɪ'kɔnfərənsɪŋ] n
Telekonferenzen pl.
telegram ['tɛlɪgræm] n Telegramm nt.
telegraph ['tɛlɪgrɑːf] n (*system*) Telegraf m.
telegraphic [tɛlɪ'græfɪk] adj (*equipment*)
telegrafisch.
telegraph pole n Telegrafenmast m.
telegraph wire n Telegrafenleitung f.
telepathic [tɛlɪ'pæθɪk] adj telepathisch.
telepathy [tə'lɛpəθɪ] n Telepathie f.
telephone ['tɛlɪfəun] n Telefon nt ♦ vt (*person*)
anrufen ♦ vi anrufen, telefonieren; **to be on
the ~** (*talking*) telefonieren; (*possessing
phone*) ein Telefon haben.
telephone box, (*US*) **telephone booth** n
Telefonzelle f.
telephone call n Anruf m.
telephone directory n Telefonbuch nt.
telephone exchange n Telefonzentrale f.
telephone number n Telefonnummer f.
telephone operator n Telefonist(in) m(f).
telephone tapping n Abhören nt von
Telefonleitungen.
telephonist [tə'lɛfənɪst] (*BRIT*) n
Telefonist(in) m(f).
telephoto ['tɛlɪ'fəutəu] adj: **~ lens**
Teleobjektiv nt.
teleprinter ['tɛlɪprɪntə*] n Fernschreiber m.
Teleprompter ® ['tɛlɪprɔmptə*] (*US*) n
Teleprompter m.
telesales ['tɛlɪseɪlz] n Verkauf m per Telefon.
telescope ['tɛlɪskəup] n Teleskop nt ♦ vi (*fig:
bus, lorry*) sich ineinander schieben ♦ vt
(*make shorter*) zusammenschieben.
telescopic [tɛlɪ'skɔpɪk] adj (*legs, aerial*)
ausziehbar; **~ lens** Fernrohrlinse f.
Teletext ® ['tɛlɪtɛkst] n Videotext m.
telethon ['tɛlɪθɔn] n Spendenaktion für

wohltätige Zwecke in Form einer vielstündigen Fernsehsendung.

televise ['tɛlɪvaɪz] *vt* (im Fernsehen) übertragen.

television ['tɛlɪvɪʒən] *n* Fernsehen *nt*; (*set*) Fernseher *m*, Fernsehapparat *m*; **to be on ~** im Fernsehen sein.

television licence (*BRIT*) *n* Fernsehgenehmigung *f*.

television programme *n* Fernsehprogramm *nt*.

television set *n* Fernseher *m*, Fernsehapparat *m*.

teleworking ['tɛlɪwə:kɪŋ] *n* Telearbeit *f*.

telex ['tɛlɛks] *n* (*system, machine, message*) Telex *nt* ♦ *vt* (*message*) telexen; (*person*) ein Telex schicken +*dat* ♦ *vi* telexen.

tell [tɛl] (*pt, pp* **told**) *vt* (*say*) sagen; (*relate: story*) erzählen; (*distinguish*): **to ~ sth from** etw unterscheiden von; (*be sure*) wissen ♦ *vi* (*have an effect*) sich auswirken; **to ~ sb to do sth** jdm sagen, etw zu tun; **to ~ sb of** *or* **about sth** jdm von etw erzählen; **to be able to ~ the time** (*know how to*) die Uhr kennen; **can you ~ me the time?** können Sie mir sagen, wie spät es ist?; **(I) ~ you what, let's go to the cinema** weißt du was? Lass uns ins Kino gehen!; **I can't ~ them apart** ich kann sie nicht unterscheiden.

▶ **tell off** *vt*: **to ~ sb off** jdn ausschimpfen.

▶ **tell on** *vt fus* (*inform against*) verpetzen.

teller ['tɛlə*] *n* (*in bank*) Kassierer(in) *m(f)*.

telling ['tɛlɪŋ] *adj* (*remark etc*) verräterisch.

telltale ['tɛlteɪl] *adj* verräterisch ♦ *n* (*pej*) Petzer *m*, Petze *f*.

telly ['tɛlɪ] (*BRIT: inf*) *n abbr* = **television**.

temerity [tə'mɛrɪtɪ] *n* Unverschämtheit *f*.

temp [tɛmp] (*BRIT: inf*) *n abbr* (= *temporary office worker*) Zeitarbeitskraft *f* ♦ *vi* als Zeitarbeitskraft arbeiten.

temper ['tɛmpə*] *n* (*nature*) Naturell *nt*; (*mood*) Laune *f* ♦ *vt* (*moderate*) mildern; **a (fit of) ~** ein Wutanfall *m*; **to be in a ~** gereizt sein; **to lose one's ~** die Beherrschung verlieren.

temperament ['tɛmprəmənt] *n* Temperament *nt*.

temperamental [tɛmprə'mɛntl] *adj* (*person, car*) launisch.

temperate ['tɛmprət] *adj* gemäßigt.

temperature ['tɛmprətʃə*] *n* Temperatur *f*; **to have** *or* **run a ~** Fieber haben; **to take sb's ~** bei jdm Fieber messen.

temperature chart *n* (*MED*) Fiebertabelle *f*.

tempered ['tɛmpəd] *adj* (*steel*) gehärtet.

tempest ['tɛmpɪst] *n* Sturm *m*.

tempestuous [tɛm'pɛstjuəs] *adj* (*also fig*) stürmisch; (*person*) leidenschaftlich.

tempi ['tɛmpiː] *npl of* **tempo**.

template ['tɛmplɪt] *n* Schablone *f*.

temple ['tɛmpl] *n* (*building*) Tempel *m*; (*ANAT*) Schläfe *f*.

tempo ['tɛmpəu] (*pl ~s or* **tempi**) *n* (*MUS, fig*)

Tempo *nt*.

temporal ['tɛmpərl] *adj* (*non-religious*) weltlich; (*relating to time*) zeitlich.

temporarily ['tɛmpərərɪlɪ] *adv* vorübergehend; (*unavailable, alone etc*) zeitweilig.

temporary ['tɛmpərərɪ] *adj* (*arrangement*) provisorisch; (*worker, job*) Aushilfs-; **~ secretary** Sekretärin zur Aushilfe; **~ teacher** Aushilfslehrer(in) *m(f)*.

temporize ['tɛmpəraɪz] *vi* ausweichen.

tempt [tɛmpt] *vt* in Versuchung führen; **to ~ sb into doing sth** jdn dazu verleiten, etw zu tun; **to be ~ed to do sth** versucht sein, etw zu tun.

temptation [tɛmp'teɪʃən] *n* Versuchung *f*.

tempting ['tɛmptɪŋ] *adj* (*offer*) verlockend; (*food*) verführerisch.

ten [tɛn] *num* zehn ♦ *n*: **~s of thousands** zehntausende *pl*, Zehntausende *pl*.

tenable ['tɛnəbl] *adj* (*argument, position*) haltbar.

tenacious [tə'neɪʃəs] *adj* zäh, hartnäckig.

tenacity [tə'næsɪtɪ] *n* Zähigkeit *f*, Hartnäckigkeit *f*.

tenancy ['tɛnənsɪ] *n* (*of room*) Mietverhältnis *nt*; (*of land*) Pachtverhältnis *nt*.

tenant ['tɛnənt] *n* (*of room*) Mieter(in) *m(f)*; (*of land*) Pächter(in) *m(f)*.

tend [tɛnd] *vt* (*crops, sick person*) sich kümmern um ♦ *vi*: **to ~ to do sth** dazu neigen *or* tendieren, etw zu tun.

tendency ['tɛndənsɪ] *n* (*of person*) Neigung *f*; (*of thing*) Tendenz *f*.

tender ['tɛndə*] *adj* (*person, care*) zärtlich; (*heart*) gut; (*sore*) empfindlich; (*meat, age*) zart ♦ *n* (*COMM*) Angebot *nt*; (*money*): **legal ~** gesetzliches Zahlungsmittel *nt* ♦ *vt* (*offer*) vorlegen; (*resignation*) einreichen; (*apology*) anbieten; **to put in a ~ (for)** ein Angebot vorlegen (für); **to put work out to ~** (*BRIT*) Arbeiten ausschreiben.

tenderize ['tɛndəraɪz] *vt* (*meat*) zart machen.

tenderly ['tɛndəlɪ] *adv* zärtlich, liebevoll.

tenderness ['tɛndənɪs] *n* (*affection*) Zärtlichkeit *f*; (*of meat*) Zartheit *f*.

tendon ['tɛndən] *n* Sehne *f*.

tendril ['tɛndrɪl] *n* (*BOT*) Ranke *f*; (*of hair etc*) Strähne *f*.

tenement ['tɛnəmənt] *n* Mietshaus *nt*.

Tenerife [tɛnə'riːf] *n* Teneriffa *nt*.

tenet ['tɛnət] *n* Prinzip *nt*.

Tenn. (*US*) *abbr* (*POST*: = *Tennessee*).

tenner ['tɛnə*] (*BRIT: inf*) *n* Zehner *m*.

tennis ['tɛnɪs] *n* Tennis *nt*.

tennis ball *n* Tennisball *m*.

tennis club *n* Tennisklub *m*.

tennis court *n* Tennisplatz *m*.

tennis elbow *n* (*MED*) Tennisell(en)bogen *m*.

tennis match *n* Tennismatch *nt*.

tennis player *n* Tennisspieler(in) *m(f)*.

tennis racket *n* Tennisschläger *m*.

tennis shoes *npl* Tennisschuhe *pl*.

tenor ['tɛnə*] n (MUS) Tenor m; (of speech etc) wesentlicher Gehalt m.
tenpin bowling ['tɛnpɪn-] (BRIT) n Bowling nt.
tense [tɛns] adj (person, muscle) angespannt; (smile) verkrampft; (period, situation) gespannt ♦ n (LING) Zeit f, Tempus nt ♦ vt (muscles) anspannen.
tenseness ['tɛnsnɪs] n Gespanntheit f.
tension ['tɛnʃən] n (nervousness) Angespanntheit f; (between ropes etc) Spannung f.
tent [tɛnt] n Zelt nt.
tentacle ['tɛntəkl] n (ZOOL) Fangarm m; (fig) Klaue f.
tentative ['tɛntətɪv] adj (person, smile) zögernd; (step) unsicher; (conclusion, plans) vorläufig.
tentatively ['tɛntətɪvlɪ] adv (suggest) versuchsweise; (wave etc) zögernd.
tenterhooks ['tɛntəhuks] npl: **to be on** ~ wie auf glühenden Kohlen sitzen.
tenth [tɛnθ] num zehnte(r, s) ♦ n Zehntel nt.
tent peg n Hering m.
tent pole n Zeltstange f.
tenuous ['tɛnjuəs] adj (hold, links etc) schwach.
tenure ['tɛnjuə*] n (of land etc) Nutzungsrecht nt; (of office) Amtszeit f; (UNIV): **to have** ~ eine Dauerstellung haben.
tepid ['tɛpɪd] adj (also fig) lauwarm.
Ter. abbr (in street names: = terrace) ≈ Str.
term [tə:m] n (word) Ausdruck m; (period in power etc) Amtszeit f; (SCOL: three per year) Trimester nt ♦ vt (call) nennen; **terms** npl (also COMM) Bedingungen pl; **in economic** ~**s** wirtschaftlich gesehen; **in** ~**s of business** was das Geschäft angeht or betrifft; ~ **of imprisonment** Gefängnisstrafe f; "**easy** ~**s**" (COMM) „günstige Bedingungen"; **in the short/long** ~ auf kurze/lange Sicht; **to be on good** ~**s with sb** sich mit jdm gut verstehen; **to come to** ~**s with** (problem) sich abfinden mit.
terminal ['tə:mɪnl] adj (disease, patient) unheilbar ♦ n (AVIAT, COMM, COMPUT) Terminal nt; (ELEC) Anschluss m; (BRIT: also: **bus** ~) Endstation f.
terminate ['tə:mɪneɪt] vt beenden ♦ vi: **to** ~ **in** enden in +dat.
termination [tə:mɪ'neɪʃən] n Beendigung f; (expiry: of contract) Ablauf m; (MED: of pregnancy) Abbruch m.
termini ['tə:mɪnaɪ] npl of **terminus**.
terminology [tə:mɪ'nɔlədʒɪ] n Terminologie f.
terminus ['tə:mɪnəs] (pl **termini**) n (for buses, trains) Endstation f.
termite ['tə:maɪt] n Termite f.
term paper (US) n (UNIV) ≈ Semesterarbeit f.
Terr. abbr (in street names: = terrace) ≈ Str.
terrace ['tɛrəs] n (BRIT: row of houses) Häuserreihe f; (AGR, patio) Terrasse f; **the terraces** npl (BRIT: SPORT) die Ränge pl.

terraced ['tɛrəst] adj (house) Reihen-; (garden) terrassenförmig angelegt.
terracotta ['tɛrə'kɔtə] n (clay) Terrakotta f; (colour) Braunrot nt ♦ adj (pot, roof etc) Terrakotta-.
terrain [tɛ'reɪn] n Gelände nt, Terrain nt.
terrible ['tɛrɪbl] adj schrecklich, furchtbar.
terribly ['tɛrɪblɪ] adv (very) furchtbar; (very badly) entsetzlich.
terrier ['tɛrɪə*] n Terrier m.
terrific [tə'rɪfɪk] adj (very great: thunderstorm, speed) unheimlich; (time, party) sagenhaft.
terrify ['tɛrɪfaɪ] vt erschrecken; **to be terrified** schreckliche Angst haben.
terrifying ['tɛrɪfaɪɪŋ] adj entsetzlich, grauenvoll.
territorial [tɛrɪ'tɔ:rɪəl] adj (boundaries, dispute) territorial, Gebiets-; (waters) Hoheits- ♦ n (MIL) Soldat m der Territorialarmee.
Territorial Army (BRIT) n (MIL): **the** ~ die Territorialarmee.
territorial waters npl Hoheitsgewässer pl.
territory ['tɛrɪtərɪ] n (also fig) Gebiet nt.
terror ['tɛrə*] n (great fear) panische Angst f.
terror attack n Terrorangriff m.
terrorism ['tɛrərɪzəm] n Terrorismus m.
terrorist ['tɛrərɪst] n Terrorist(in) m(f).
terrorize ['tɛrəraɪz] vt terrorisieren.
terse [tə:s] adj knapp.
tertiary ['tə:ʃərɪ] adj tertiär; ~ **education** (BRIT) Universitätsausbildung f.
Terylene® ['tɛrɪli:n] n Terylen® nt ♦ adj Terylen-.
TESL ['tɛsl] n abbr (= Teaching of English as a Second Language) Unterricht in Englisch als Zweitsprache.
TESSA ['tɛsə] (BRIT) n abbr (= Tax Exempt Special Savings Account) steuerfreies Sparsystem mit begrenzter Einlagehöhe.
test [tɛst] n Test m; (of courage etc) Probe f; (SCOL) Prüfung f; (also: **driving** ~) Fahrprüfung f ♦ vt testen; (check, SCOL) prüfen; **to put sth to the** ~ etw auf die Probe stellen; **to** ~ **sth for sth** etw auf etw acc prüfen.
testament ['tɛstəmənt] n Zeugnis nt; **the Old/ New T**~ das Alte/Neue Testament; **last will and** ~ Testament nt.
test ban n (also: **nuclear** ~) Teststopp m.
test card n (TV) Testbild nt.
test case n (LAW) Musterfall m; (fig) Musterbeispiel nt.
testes ['tɛsti:z] npl Testikel pl, Hoden pl.
test flight n Testflug m.
testicle ['tɛstɪkl] n Hoden m.
testify ['tɛstɪfaɪ] vi (LAW) aussagen; **to** ~ **to sth** (LAW, fig) etw bezeugen.
testimonial [tɛstɪ'məunɪəl] n (BRIT: reference) Referenz f; (SPORT: also: ~ **match**) Benefizspiel, dessen Erlös einem verdienten Spieler zugute kommt.
testimony ['tɛstɪmənɪ] n (statement) Aussage

f; (*clear proof*): **to be (a)** ~ **to** ein Zeugnis *nt* sein für.

testing ['tɛstɪŋ] *adj* schwierig.

test match *n* (*CRICKET, RUGBY*) Testmatch *nt*, Test Match *nt*, Länderspiel *nt*.

testosterone [tɛs'tɔstərəun] *n* Testosteron *nt*.

test paper *n* (*SCOL*) Klassenarbeit *f.*

test pilot *n* Testpilot(in) *m(f)*.

test tube *n* Reagenzglas *nt*.

test-tube baby ['tɛsttjuːb-] *n* Retortenbaby *nt*.

testy ['tɛstɪ] *adj* gereizt.

tetanus ['tɛtənəs] *n* Tetanus *m.*

tetchy ['tɛtʃɪ] *adj* gereizt.

tether ['tɛðə*] *vt* (*animal*) festbinden ♦ *n*: **to be at the end of one's** ~ völlig am Ende sein.

text [tɛkst] *n* Text *m* ♦ *vt* (*on mobile phone*) eine SMS schreiben (+*dat*).

textbook ['tɛkstbuk] *n* Lehrbuch *nt.*

textiles ['tɛkstaɪlz] *npl* Textilien *pl.*

text message *n* (*TEL*) SMS *f.*

text messaging ['tɛkst,mɛsədʒɪŋ] *n* (*TEL*) Textnachrichten *pl.*

textual ['tɛkstjuəl] *adj* (*analysis etc*) Text-.

texture ['tɛkstʃə*] *n* Beschaffenheit *f,* Struktur *f.*

TGWU (*BRIT*) *n abbr* (= *Transport and General Workers' Union*) *Transportarbeitergewerkschaft.*

Thai [taɪ] *adj* thailändisch ♦ *n* Thailänder(in) *m(f).*

Thailand ['taɪlænd] *n* Thailand *nt.*

thalidomide® [θə'lɪdəmaɪd] *n* Contergan® *nt.*

Thames [tɛmz] *n*: **the** ~ die Themse.

than [ðæn] *conj* (*in comparisons*) als; **more** ~ **10** mehr als 10; **she is older** ~ **you think** sie ist älter, als Sie denken; **more** ~ **once** mehr als einmal.

thank [θæŋk] *vt* danken +*dat*; ~ **you** danke; ~ **you very much** vielen Dank; ~ **God!** Gott sei Dank!

thankful ['θæŋkful] *adj*: ~ (**for/that**) dankbar (für/, dass).

thankfully ['θæŋkfəlɪ] *adv* dankbar; ~ **there were few victims** zum Glück gab es nur wenige Opfer.

thankless ['θæŋklɪs] *adj* undankbar.

thanks [θæŋks] *npl* Dank *m* ♦ *excl* (*also*: **many** ~, ~ **a lot**) danke, vielen Dank; ~ **to** dank +*gen*.

Thanksgiving (Day) ['θæŋksgɪvɪŋ(-)] (*US*) *n* Thanksgiving Day *m.*

THANKSGIVING (DAY)

Thanksgiving (Day) *ist ein Feiertag in den USA, der auf den vierten Donnerstag im November fällt. Er soll daran erinnern, wie die Pilgerväter die gute Ernte im Jahre 1621 feierten. In Kanada gibt es einen ähnlichen Erntedanktag (der aber nichts mit den Pilgervätern zu tun hat) am zweiten Montag im Oktober.*

=== *KEYWORD*

that [ðæt, ðət] (*pl* **those**) *adj* (*demonstrative*) der/die/das; ~ **man** der Mann; ~ **woman** die Frau; ~ **book** das Buch; ~ **one** der/die/das da; **I want this one, not** ~ **one** ich will dieses (hier), nicht das (da)

♦ *pron* **1** (*demonstrative*) das; **who's/what's** ~**?** wer/was ist das?; **is** ~ **you?** bist du das?; **will you eat all** ~**?** isst du das alles?; **that's what he said** das hat er gesagt; **what happened after** ~**?** was geschah danach?; ~ **is (to say)** das heißt; **and that's that!** und damit Schluss!

2 (*relative: subject*) der/die/das; (: *pl*) die; (: *direct object*) den/die/das; (: *pl*) die; (: *indirect object*) dem/der/dem; (: *pl*) denen; **the man** ~ **I saw** der Mann, den ich gesehen habe; **all** ~ **I have** alles was ich habe; **the people** ~ **I spoke to** die Leute, mit denen ich geredet habe.

3 (*relative: of time*) **the day** ~ **he came** der Tag, an dem er kam; **the winter** ~ **he came to see us** der Winter, in dem er uns besuchte

♦ *conj* dass; **he thought** ~ **I was ill** er dachte, dass ich krank sei, er dachte, ich sei krank

♦ *adv* (*demonstrative*) so; **I can't work** ~ **much** ich kann nicht so viel arbeiten; ~ **high** so hoch.

---

thatched [θætʃt] *adj* (*roof, cottage*) strohgedeckt.

Thatcherism ['θætʃərɪzəm] *n* Thatcherismus *m.*

Thatcherite ['θætʃəraɪt] *adj* thatcheristisch ♦ *n* Thatcher Anhänger(in) *m(f).*

thaw [θɔː] *n* Tauwetter *nt* ♦ *vi* (*ice*) tauen; (*food*) auftauen ♦ *vt* (*also*: ~ **out**) auftauen; **it's** ~**ing** es taut.

=== *KEYWORD*

the [ðiː, ðə] *def art* **1** (*before masculine noun*) der; (*before feminine noun*) die; (*before neuter noun*) das; (*before plural noun*) die; **to play** ~ **piano/violin** Klavier/Geige spielen; **I'm going to** ~ **butcher's/the cinema** ich gehe zum Metzger/ins Kino.

2 (+ *adj to form noun*): ~ **rich and** ~ **poor** die Reichen und die Armen; **to attempt** ~ **impossible** das Unmögliche versuchen.

3 (*in titles*): **Elizabeth** ~ **First** Elisabeth die Erste; **Peter** ~ **Great** Peter der Große.

4 (*in comparisons*): ~ **more he works** ~ **more he earns** je mehr er arbeitet, desto mehr verdient er; ~ **sooner** ~ **better** je eher, desto besser.

---

theatre, (*US*) **theater** ['θɪətə*] *n* Theater *nt*; (*also*: **lecture** ~) Hörsaal *m*; (*also*: **operating** ~) Operationssaal *m.*

theatre-goer ['θɪətəɡəuə*] *n*

theatrical – thing

Theaterbesucher(in) *m(f)*.

theatrical [θɪ'ætrɪkl] *adj* (*event, production*) Theater-; (*gestures etc*) theatralisch.

theft [θɛft] *n* Diebstahl *m*.

their [ðɛə°] *adj* ihr.

theirs [ðɛəz] *pron* ihre(r, s); **it is** ~ es gehört ihnen; **a friend of** ~ ein Freund/eine Freundin von ihnen; *see also* **my, mine**[1].

them [ðɛm] *pron* (*direct*) sie; (*indirect*) ihnen; **I see** ~ ich sehe sie; **give** ~ **the** book gib ihnen das Buch; **give me a few of** ~ geben Sie mir ein paar davon; **with** ~ mit ihnen; **without** ~ ohne sie; *see also* **me**.

theme [θiːm] *n* (*also MUS*) Thema *nt*.

theme park *n* Themenpark *m*.

theme song *n* Titelmusik *f*.

theme tune *n* Titelmelodie *f*.

themselves [ðəm'sɛlvz] *pl pron* (*reflexive, after prep*) sich; (*emphatic, alone*) selbst; **between** ~ unter sich.

then [ðɛn] *adv* (*at that time*) damals; (*next, later*) dann ♦ *conj* (*therefore*) also ♦ *adj*: **the** ~ **president** der damalige Präsident; **by** ~ (*past*) bis dahin; (*future*) bis dann; **from** ~ **on** von da an; **before** ~ davor; **until** ~ bis dann; **and** ~ **what?** und was dann?; **what do you want me to do** ~? was soll ich dann machen?; **... but** ~ **(again) he's the boss ...** aber er ist ja der Chef.

theologian [θɪə'ləudʒən] *n* Theologe *m*, Theologin *f*.

theological [θɪə'lɒdʒɪkl] *adj* theologisch.

theology [θɪ'ɒlədʒɪ] *n* Theologie *f*.

theorem ['θɪərəm] *n* Lehrsatz *m*.

theoretical [θɪə'rɛtɪkl] *adj* theoretisch.

theorize ['θɪəraɪz] *vi* theoretisieren.

theory ['θɪərɪ] *n* Theorie *f*; **in** ~ theoretisch.

therapeutic [θɛrə'pjuːtɪk] *adj* therapeutisch.

therapist ['θɛrəpɪst] *n* Therapeut(in) *m(f)*.

therapy ['θɛrəpɪ] *n* Therapie *f*.

========================== *KEYWORD*

there [ðɛə°] *adv* **1**: ~ **is/are** da ist/sind; (*there exist(s)*) es gibt; ~ **are 3 of them** es gibt 3 davon; ~ **has been an accident** da war ein Unfall; ~ **will be a meeting tomorrow** morgen findet ein Treffen statt.
2 (*referring to place*) da, dort; **down/over** ~ da unten/drüben; **put it in/on** ~ leg es dorthinein/-hinauf; **I want that book** ~ ich möchte das Buch da; ~ **he is!** da ist er ja!
3: ~, ~ (*esp to child*) ist ja gut.

thereabouts ['ðɛərə'bauts] *adv*: **or** ~ (*place*) oder dortherum; (*amount, time*) oder so.

thereafter [ðɛər'ɑːftə°] *adv* danach.

thereby ['ðɛəbaɪ] *adv* dadurch.

therefore ['ðɛəfɔː°] *adv* daher, deshalb.

there's ['ðɛəz] = **there is; there has**.

thereupon [ðɛərə'pɒn] *adv* (*at that point*) darauf(hin).

thermal ['θəːml] *adj* (*springs*) Thermal-;

(*underwear, paper, printer*) Thermo-.

thermodynamics ['θəːmədaɪ'næmɪks] *n* Thermodynamik *f*.

thermometer [θə'mɒmɪtə°] *n* Thermometer *nt*.

thermonuclear ['θəːməu'njuːklɪə°] *adj* thermonuklear.

Thermos ® ['θəːməs] *n* (*also*: ~ **flask**) Thermosflasche ® *f*.

thermostat ['θəːməustæt] *n* Thermostat *m*.

thesaurus [θɪ'sɔːrəs] *n* Synonymwörterbuch *nt*.

these [ðiːz] *pl adj, pl pron* diese.

theses ['θiːsiːz] *npl of* **thesis**.

thesis ['θiːsɪs] (*pl* **theses**) *n* These *f*; (*for doctorate etc*) Dissertation *f*, Doktorarbeit *f*.

they [[ðeɪ]] *pl pron* sie; ~ **say that ...** (*it is said that*) man sagt, dass ...

they'd [ðeɪd] = **they had; they would**.

they'll [ðeɪl] = **they shall; they will**.

they're [ðɛə°] = **they are**.

they've [ðeɪv] = **they have**.

thick [θɪk] *adj* dick; (*sauce etc*) dickflüssig; (*fog, forest, hair etc*) dicht; (*inf: stupid*) blöd ♦ *n*: **in the** ~ **of the battle** mitten im Gefecht; **it's 20 cm** ~ es ist 20 cm dick.

thicken ['θɪkn] *vi* (*fog etc*) sich verdichten ♦ *vt* (*sauce etc*) eindicken; **the plot** ~s die Sache wird immer verwickelter.

thicket ['θɪkɪt] *n* Dickicht *nt*.

thickly ['θɪklɪ] *adv* (*spread, cut*) dick; ~ **populated** dicht bevölkert.

thickness ['θɪknɪs] *n* (*of rope, wire*) Dicke *f*; (*layer*) Lage *f*.

thickset [θɪk'sɛt] *adj* (*person, body*) gedrungen.

thick-skinned [θɪk'skɪnd] *adj* (*also fig*) dickhäutig.

thief [θiːf] (*pl* **thieves**) *n* Dieb(in) *m(f)*.

thieves [θiːvz] *npl of* **thief**.

thieving ['θiːvɪŋ] *n* Stehlen *nt*.

thigh [θaɪ] *n* Oberschenkel *m*.

thighbone ['θaɪbəun] *n* Oberschenkelknochen *m*.

thimble ['θɪmbl] *n* Fingerhut *m*.

thin [θɪn] *adj* dünn; (*fog*) leicht; (*hair, crowd*) spärlich ♦ *vt*: **to** ~ **(down)** (*sauce, paint*) verdünnen ♦ *vi* (*fog, crowd*) sich lichten; **his hair is** ~**ning** sein Haar lichtet sich.

thing [θɪŋ] *n* Ding *nt*; (*matter*) Sache *f*; (*inf*): **to have a** ~ **about sth** (*be fascinated by*) wie besessen sein von etw; (*hate*) etw nicht ausstehen können; **things** *npl* (*belongings*) Sachen *pl*; **to do sth first** ~ (*every morning/tomorrow morning*) etw (morgens/morgen früh) als Erstes tun; **I look awful first** ~ **in the morning** ich sehe frühmorgens immer furchtbar aus; **to do sth last** ~ (*at night*) etw als Letztes (am Abend) tun; **the** ~ **is ...** die Sache ist die: ...; **for one** ~ zunächst mal; **don't worry about a** ~ du brauchst dir überhaupt keine Sorgen zu machen; **you'll do no such ~!** das lässt du schön bleiben!; **poor ~** armes Ding; **the best ~ would be to** ... das Beste wäre, zu ...; **how are ~s?** wie gehts?

think [θɪŋk] (*pt, pp* **thought**) *vi* (*reflect*) nachdenken; (*reason*) denken ♦ *vt* (*be of the opinion*) denken; (*believe*) glauben; **to ~ of** denken an +*acc*; (*recall*) sich erinnern an +*acc*; **what did you ~ of them?** was hielten Sie von ihnen?; **to ~ about sth/sb** (*ponder*) über etw/jdn nachdenken; **I'll ~ about it** ich werde es mir überlegen; **to ~ of doing sth** daran denken, etw zu tun; **to ~ highly of sb** viel von jdm halten; **to ~ aloud** laut nachdenken; **~ again!** denk noch mal nach!; **I ~ so/not** ich glaube ja/nein.
► **think over** *vt* (*offer, suggestion*) überdenken; **I'd like to ~ things over** ich möchte mir die Sache noch einmal überlegen.
► **think through** *vt* durchdenken.
► **think up** *vt* sich *dat* ausdenken.

thinking ['θɪŋkɪŋ] *n* Denken *nt*; **to my (way of) ~** meiner Meinung *or* Ansicht nach.

think-tank ['θɪŋktæŋk] *n* Expertengremium *nt*.

thinly ['θɪnlɪ] *adv* dünn; (*disguised, veiled*) kaum.

thinness ['θɪnnɪs] *n* Dünne *f*.

third [θəːd] *num* dritte(r, s) ♦ *n* (*fraction*) Drittel *nt*; (*AUT: also: ~* **gear**) dritter Gang *m*; (*BRIT: SCOL: degree*) ≈ Ausreichend *nt*; **a ~ of** ein Drittel +*gen*.

third-degree burns ['θəːdɪgriː-] *npl* Verbrennungen *pl* dritten Grades.

thirdly ['θəːdlɪ] *adv* drittens.

third party insurance (*BRIT*) *n* ≈ Haftpflichtversicherung *f*.

third-rate ['θəːd'reɪt] (*pej*) *adj* drittklassig.

Third World *n*: **the ~** die Dritte Welt ♦ *adj* der Dritten Welt.

thirst [θəːst] *n* Durst *m*.

thirsty ['θəːstɪ] *adj* durstig; **to be ~** Durst haben; **gardening is ~ work** Gartenarbeit macht durstig.

thirteen [θəː'tiːn] *num* dreizehn.

thirteenth [θəː'tiːnθ] *num* dreizehnte(r, s).

thirtieth ['θəːtɪɪθ] *num* dreißigste(r, s).

thirty ['θəːtɪ] *num* dreißig.

━━━━━━━━━━━ *KEYWORD*

this [ðɪs] (*pl* **these**) *adj* (*demonstrative*) diese(r, s); **~ man** dieser Mann; **~ woman** diese Frau; **~ book** dieses Buch; **~ one** diese(r, s) (hier)
♦ *pron* (*demonstrative*) dies, das; **who/what is ~?** wer/was ist das?; **~ is where I live** hier wohne ich; **~ is what he said** das hat er gesagt; **~ is Mr Brown** (*in introductions, photo*) das ist Herr Brown; (*on telephone*) hier ist Herr Brown

♦ *adv* (*demonstrative*): **~ high/long** *etc* so hoch/lang *etc*.

thistle ['θɪsl] *n* Distel *f*.

thong [θɒŋ] *n* Riemen *m*.

thorn [θɔːn] *n* Dorn *m*.

thorny ['θɔːnɪ] *adj* dornig; (*fig: problem*) heikel.

thorough ['θʌrə] *adj* gründlich.

thoroughbred ['θʌrəbred] *n* Vollblüter *m*.

thoroughfare ['θʌrəfɛə*] *n* (*road*) Durchgangsstraße *f*; **"no ~"** (*BRIT*) „Durchfahrt verboten".

thoroughgoing ['θʌrəgəʊɪŋ] *adj* (*changes, reform*) grundlegend; (*investigation*) gründlich.

thoroughly ['θʌrəlɪ] *adv* gründlich; (*very*) äußerst; **I ~ agree** ich stimme vollkommen zu.

thoroughness ['θʌrənɪs] *n* Gründlichkeit *f*.

those [ðəʊz] *pl adj, pl pron* die (da); **~ (of you) who ...** diejenigen (von Ihnen), die ...

though [ðəʊ] *conj* obwohl ♦ *adv* aber; **even ~** obwohl; **it's not easy, ~** es ist aber nicht einfach.

thought [θɔːt] *pt, pp of* **think** ♦ *n* Gedanke *m*; **thoughts** *npl* (*opinion*) Gedanken *pl*; **after much ~** nach langer Überlegung; **I've just had a ~** mir ist gerade etwas eingefallen; **to give sth some ~** sich *dat* Gedanken über etw *acc* machen.

thoughtful ['θɔːtful] *adj* (*deep in thought*) nachdenklich; (*considerate*) aufmerksam.

thoughtfully ['θɔːtfəlɪ] *adv* (*look etc*) nachdenklich; (*behave etc*) rücksichtsvoll; (*provide*) rücksichtsvollerweise.

thoughtless ['θɔːtlɪs] *adj* gedankenlos.

thoughtlessly ['θɔːtlɪslɪ] *adv* gedankenlos.

thoughtlessness ['θɔːtlɪsnɪs] *n* Gedankenlosigkeit *f*.

thought-out [θɔːt'aut] *adj* durchdacht.

thought-provoking ['θɔːtprəvəʊkɪŋ] *adj*: **to be ~** Denkanstöße geben.

thousand ['θaʊzənd] *num* (ein)tausend; **two ~** zweitausend; **~s of** tausende *or* Tausende von.

thousandth ['θaʊzəntθ] *num* tausendste(r, s).

thrash [θræʃ] *vt* (*beat*) verprügeln; (*defeat*) (vernichtend) schlagen.
► **thrash about** *vi* um sich schlagen.
► **thrash around** *vi* = thrash about.
► **thrash out** *vt* (*problem*) ausdiskutieren.

thrashing ['θræʃɪŋ] *n*: **to give sb a ~** jdn verprügeln.

thread [θrɛd] *n* (*yarn*) Faden *m*; (*of screw*) Gewinde *nt* ♦ *vt* (*needle*) einfädeln; **to ~ one's way between** sich hindurchschlängeln zwischen.

threadbare ['θrɛdbɛə*] *adj* (*clothes*) abgetragen; (*carpet*) abgelaufen.

threat [θrɛt] *n* Drohung *f*; (*fig*): **~ (to)** Gefahr *f* (für); **to be under ~ of** (*closure etc*) bedroht sein von.

threaten ['θrɛtn] vi bedrohen ♦ vt: **to ~ sb
with sth** jdm mit etw drohen; **to ~ to do sth**
(damit) drohen, etw zu tun.
threatening ['θrɛtnɪŋ] adj drohend,
bedrohlich.
three [θriː] num drei.
three-dimensional [θriːdɪ'mɛnʃənl] adj
dreidimensional.
threefold ['θriːfəuld] adv: **to increase ~**
dreifach or um das Dreifache ansteigen.
three-piece suit ['θriːpiːs-] n dreiteiliger
Anzug m.
three-piece suite n dreiteilige
Polstergarnitur f.
three-ply [θriː'plaɪ] adj (wool) dreifädig;
(wood) dreilagig.
three-quarters [θriː'kwɔːtəz] npl drei Viertel
pl; **~ full** drei viertel voll.
three-wheeler ['θriː'wiːlə*] n (car)
Dreiradwagen m.
thresh [θrɛʃ] vt dreschen.
threshing machine ['θrɛʃɪŋ-] n
Dreschmaschine f.
threshold ['θrɛʃhəuld] n Schwelle f; **to be on
the ~ of sth** (fig) an der Schwelle zu etw
sein or stehen.
threshold agreement n (ECON)
Tarifvereinbarung über der Inflationsrate
angeglichene Lohnerhöhungen.
threw [θruː] pt of **throw**.
thrift [θrɪft] n Sparsamkeit f.
thrifty ['θrɪftɪ] adj sparsam.
thrill [θrɪl] n (excitement) Aufregung f;
(shudder) Erregung f ♦ vi zittern ♦ vt (person,
audience) erregen; **to be ~ed** (with gift etc)
sich riesig freuen.
thriller ['θrɪlə*] n Thriller m.
thrilling ['θrɪlɪŋ] adj (ride, performance etc)
erregend; (news) aufregend.
thrive [θraɪv] (pt thrived or throve, pp thrived)
vi gedeihen; **to ~ on sth** von etw leben.
thriving ['θraɪvɪŋ] adj (business, community)
blühend, florierend.
throat [θrəut] n Kehle f; **to have a sore ~**
Halsschmerzen haben.
throb [θrɔb] n (of heart) Klopfen nt; (pain)
Pochen nt; (of engine) Dröhnen nt ♦ vi (heart)
klopfen; (pain) pochen; (machine) dröhnen;
my head is ~bing ich habe rasende
Kopfschmerzen.
throes [θrəuz] npl: **in the ~ of** (war, moving
house etc) mitten in +dat; **death ~**
Todeskampf m.
thrombosis [θrɔm'bəusɪs] n Thrombose f.
throne [θrəun] n Thron m; **on the ~** auf dem
Thron.
throng ['θrɔŋ] n Masse f ♦ vi (streets etc) sich
drängen in +dat ♦ vt: **to ~ to** strömen zu; **a
~ of people** eine Menschenmenge; **to be
~ed with** wimmeln von.
throttle ['θrɔtl] n (in car) Gaspedal nt; (on
motorcycle) Gashebel m ♦ vt (strangle)

erdrosseln.
through [θruː] prep durch; (time) während;
(owing to) infolge +gen ♦ adj (ticket, train)
durchgehend ♦ adv durch; **(from) Monday
~ Friday** (US) von Montag bis Freitag; **to be
~** (TEL) verbunden sein; **to be ~ with sb/sth**
mit jdm/etw fertig sein; **we're ~!** es ist aus
zwischen uns!; **"no ~ road** or (US) **traffic"**
„keine Durchfahrt"; **to let sb ~** jdn
durchlassen; **to put sb ~ to sb** (TEL) jdn mit
jdm verbinden.
throughout [θruː'aut] adv (everywhere)
überall; (the whole time) die ganze Zeit über
♦ prep (place) überall in +dat; (time): **~ the
morning/afternoon** während des ganzen
Morgens/Nachmittags; **~ her life** ihr ganzes
Leben lang.
throughput ['θruːput] n (also COMPUT)
Durchsatz m.
throve [θrəuv] pt of **thrive**.
throw [θrəu] (pt threw, pp thrown) n Wurf m
♦ vt werfen; (rider) abwerfen; (fig: confuse)
aus der Fassung bringen; (pottery) töpfern;
to ~ a party eine Party geben; **to ~ open**
(doors, windows) aufreißen; (debate) öffnen.
▶ **throw about** vt (money) herumwerfen mit.
▶ **throw around** vt = **throw about**.
▶ **throw away** vt wegwerfen; (waste)
verschwenden.
▶ **throw off** vt (get rid of: burden) abwerfen.
▶ **throw out** vt (rubbish) wegwerfen; (idea)
verwerfen; (person) hinauswerfen.
▶ **throw together** vt (meal) hinhauen;
(clothes) zusammenpacken.
▶ **throw up** vi (vomit) sich übergeben.
throwaway ['θrəuəweɪ] adj (cutlery etc)
Einweg-; (line, remark) beiläufig.
throwback ['θrəubæk] n: **it's a ~ to** (reminder)
es erinnert an +acc.
throw-in ['θrəuɪn] n (FOOTBALL) Einwurf m.
thrown [θrəun] pp of **throw**.
thru [θruː] (US) prep, adj, adv = **through**.
thrush [θrʌʃ] n (bird) Drossel f; (MED: esp in
children) Soor m; (: BRIT: in women) vaginale
Pilzerkrankung f.
thrust [θrʌst] (pt, pp thrust) n (TECH)
Schubkraft f; (push) Stoß m; (fig: impetus)
Stoßkraft f ♦ vt stoßen.
thud [θʌd] n dumpfes Geräusch nt.
thug [θʌg] n Schlägertyp m.
thumb [θʌm] n Daumen m ♦ vt: **to ~ a lift** per
Anhalter fahren; **to give sb/sth the ~s up**
(approve) jdm/etw dat grünes Licht geben; **to
give sb/sth the ~s down** (disapprove) jdn/
etw ablehnen.
▶ **thumb through** vt fus (book)
durchblättern.
thumb index n Daumenregister nt.
thumbnail ['θʌmneɪl] n Daumennagel m.
thumbnail sketch n kurze Darstellung f.
thumbtack ['θʌmtæk] (US) n Heftzwecke f.
thump [θʌmp] n (blow) Schlag m; (sound)

dumpfer Schlag m ♦ vt schlagen auf +acc ♦ vi (heart etc) heftig pochen.

thumping ['θʌmpɪŋ] adj (majority, victory etc) Riesen-; (headache, cold) fürchterlich.

thunder ['θʌndə*] n Donner m ♦ vi donnern; (shout angrily) brüllen; **to** ~ **past** (train etc) vorbeidonnern.

thunderbolt ['θʌndəbəult] n Blitzschlag m.

thunderclap ['θʌndəklæp] n Donnerschlag m.

thunderous ['θʌndrəs] adj donnernd.

thunderstorm ['θʌndəstɔːm] n Gewitter nt.

thunderstruck ['θʌndəstrʌk] adj: **to be** ~ (shocked) wie vom Donner gerührt sein.

thundery ['θʌndərɪ] adj (weather) gewitterig.

Thur(s). abbr (= Thursday) Do.

Thursday ['θəːzdɪ] n Donnerstag m; see also **Tuesday.**

thus [ðʌs] adv (in this way) so; (consequently) somit.

thwart [θwɔːt] vt (person) einen Strich durch die Rechnung machen +dat; (plans) vereiteln.

thyme [taɪm] n Thymian m.

thyroid ['θaɪrɔɪd] n (also: ~ **gland**) Schilddrüse f.

tiara [tɪ'ɑːrə] n Diadem nt.

Tiber ['taɪbə*] n: **the** ~ der Tiber.

Tibet [tɪ'bɛt] n Tibet nt.

Tibetan [tɪ'bɛtən] adj tibetanisch ♦ n (person) Tibetaner(in) m(f); (LING) Tibetisch nt.

tibia ['tɪbɪə] n Schienbein n.

tic [tɪk] n nervöse Zuckung f, Tic m, Tick m.

tick [tɪk] n (sound) Ticken nt; (mark) Häkchen nt; (ZOOL) Zecke f; (BRIT: inf: moment) Augenblick m; (: credit): **to buy sth on** ~ etw auf Pump kaufen ♦ vi (clock, watch) ticken ♦ vt (item on list) abhaken; **to put a** ~ **against sth** etw abhaken; **what makes him** ~? was ist er für ein Mensch?

► **tick off** vt (item on list) abhaken; (person) rüffeln.

► **tick over** vi (engine) im Leerlauf sein; (fig: business etc) sich über Wasser halten.

ticker tape ['tɪkəteɪp] n Lochstreifen m; (US: in celebrations) ≈ Luftschlangen pl.

ticket ['tɪkɪt] n (for public transport) Fahrkarte f; (for theatre etc) Eintrittskarte f; (in shop: on goods) Preisschild nt; (: from cash register) Kassenbon m; (for raffle) Los nt; (for library) Ausweis m; (also: **parking** ~: fine) Strafzettel m; (US: POL) Wahlliste f; **to get a (parking)** ~ (AUT) einen Strafzettel bekommen.

ticket agency n (THEAT) Vorverkaufsstelle f.

ticket collector n (RAIL: at station) Fahrkartenkontrolleur(in) m(f); (on train) Schaffner(in) m(f).

ticket holder n Karteninhaber(in) m(f).

ticket inspector n Fahrkartenkontrolleur(in) m(f).

ticket office n (RAIL) Fahrkartenschalter m; (THEAT) Theaterkasse f.

tickle ['tɪkl] vt kitzeln; (fig: amuse) amüsieren

♦ vi kitzeln; **it** ~**s!** das kitzelt!

ticklish ['tɪklɪʃ] adj (person, situation) kitzlig.

tidal ['taɪdl] adj (force) Gezeiten-, der Gezeiten; (river) Tide-.

tidal wave n Flutwelle f.

tidbit ['tɪdbɪt] (US) n = **titbit.**

tiddlywinks ['tɪdlɪwɪŋks] n Flohhüpfen nt.

tide [taɪd] n (in sea) Gezeiten pl; (fig: of events, opinion etc) Trend m; **high** ~ Flut f; **low** ~ Ebbe f; **the** ~ **is in/out** es ist Flut/Ebbe; **the** ~ **is coming in** die Flut kommt.

► **tide over** vt über die Runden helfen +dat.

tidily ['taɪdɪlɪ] adv ordentlich.

tidiness ['taɪdɪnɪs] n Ordentlichkeit f.

tidy ['taɪdɪ] adj (room, desk) ordentlich, aufgeräumt; (person) ordnungsliebend; (sum, income) ordentlich ♦ vt (also: ~ **up**) aufräumen.

tie [taɪ] n (BRIT: also: **necktie**) Krawatte f; (string etc) Band n; (fig: link) Verbindung f; (SPORT: match) Spiel nt; (in competition: draw) Unentschieden nt ♦ vt (parcel) verschnüren; (shoelaces) zubinden; (ribbon) binden ♦ vi (SPORT etc): **to** ~ **with sb for first place** sich mit jdm den ersten Platz teilen; **"black** ~**"** „Abendanzug"; **"white** ~**"** „Frackzwang"; **family** ~**s** familiäre Bindungen; **to** ~ **sth in a bow** etw zu einer Schleife binden; **to** ~ **a knot in sth** einen Knoten in etw acc machen.

► **tie down** vt (fig: restrict) binden; (: to date, price etc) festlegen.

► **tie in** vi: **to** ~ **in with** zusammenpassen mit.

► **tie on** vt (BRIT) anbinden.

► **tie up** vt (parcel) verschnüren; (dog) anbinden; (boat) festmachen; (person) fesseln; (arrangements) unter Dach und Fach bringen; **to be** ~**d up** (busy) zu tun haben, beschäftigt sein.

tie-break(er) ['taɪbreɪk(ə*)] n (TENNIS) Tiebreak m, Tie-Break m; (in quiz) Entscheidungsfrage f.

tie-on ['taɪɔn] (BRIT) adj (label) Anhänge-.

tiepin ['taɪpɪn] (BRIT) n Krawattennadel f.

tier [tɪə*] n (of stadium etc) Rang m; (of cake) Lage f.

tie-tack ['taɪtæk] (US) n = **tiepin.**

tiff [tɪf] n Krach m.

tiger ['taɪgə*] n Tiger m.

tight [taɪt] adj (screw, knot, grip) fest; (shoes, clothes, bend) eng; (security) streng; (budget, money) knapp; (schedule) gedrängt; (inf: drunk) voll; (: stingy) knickerig ♦ adv fest; **to be packed** ~ (suitcase) prallvoll sein; (room) gerammelt voll sein; **everybody hold** ~**!** alle festhalten!

tighten ['taɪtn] vt (rope, strap) straffen; (screw, bolt) anziehen; (grip) festigen; (security) verschärfen ♦ vi (grip) sich festigen; (rope etc) sich spannen.

tightfisted [taɪt'fɪstɪd] adj knickerig (inf).

tight-lipped ['taɪt'lɪpt] adj (fig: silence) eisern; **to be** ~ **about sth** über etw acc schweigen.

tightly ['taɪtlɪ] adv fest.

tightrope ['taɪtrəʊp] n Seil nt; **to be on** or **walking a** ~ (fig) einen Balanceakt vollführen.

tightrope walker n Seiltänzer(in) m(f).

tights [taɪts] (BRIT) npl Strumpfhose f.

tigress ['taɪgrɪs] n Tigerin f.

tilde ['tɪldə] n Tilde f.

tile [taɪl] n (on roof) Ziegel m; (on floor) Fliese f; (on wall) Kachel f ♦ vt (floor) mit Fliesen auslegen; (bathroom) kacheln.

tiled [taɪld] adj (floor) mit Fliesen ausgelegt; (wall) gekachelt.

till [tɪl] n (in shop etc) Kasse f ♦ vt (land) bestellen ♦ prep, conj = **until**.

tiller ['tɪlə*] n (NAUT) Ruderpinne f.

tilt [tɪlt] vt neigen ♦ vi sich neigen ♦ n (slope) Neigung f; **to wear one's hat at a** ~ den Hut schief aufhaben; **(at) full** ~ mit Volldampf.

timber ['tɪmbə*] n (material) Holz nt; (trees) Nutzholz nt.

time [taɪm] n Zeit f; (occasion) Gelegenheit f, Mal nt; (MUS) Takt m ♦ vt (measure time of) die Zeit messen bei; (runner) stoppen; (fix moment for: visit etc) den Zeitpunkt festlegen für; **a long** ~ eine lange Zeit; **for the** ~ **being** vorläufig; **4 at a** ~ 4 auf einmal; **from** ~ **to** ~ von Zeit zu Zeit; ~ **after** ~, ~ **and again** immer (und immer) wieder; **at** ~**s** manchmal, zuweilen; **in** ~ (soon enough) rechtzeitig; (eventually) mit der Zeit; (MUS) im Takt; **in a week's** ~ in einer Woche; **in no** ~ im Handumdrehen; **any** ~ jederzeit; **on** ~ rechtzeitig; **to be 30 minutes behind/ahead of** ~ 30 Minuten zurück/voraus sein; **by the** ~ **he arrived** als er ankam; **5** ~**s 5** 5 mal 5; **what** ~ **is it?** wie spät ist es?; **to have a good** ~ sich amüsieren; **we/they** etc **had a hard** ~ wir/sie etc hatten es schwer; ~**'s up!** die Zeit ist um!; **I've no** ~ **for it** (fig) dafür habe ich nichts übrig; **he'll do it in his own (good)** ~ (without being hurried) er macht es, ohne sich hetzen zu lassen; **he'll do it in** or (US) **on his own** ~ (out of working hours) er macht es in seiner Freizeit; **to be behind the** ~**s** rückständig sein; **to** ~ **sth well/badly** den richtigen/falschen Zeitpunkt für etw wählen; **the bomb was** ~**d to go off 5 minutes later** die Bombe war so eingestellt, dass sie 5 Minuten später explodieren sollte.

time-and-motion study ['taɪmənd'məʊʃən-] n Arbeitsstudie f.

time bomb n (also fig) Zeitbombe f.

time card n Stechkarte f.

time clock n (in factory etc) Stechuhr f.

time-consuming ['taɪmkənsjuːmɪŋ] adj Zeit raubend.

time difference n Zeitunterschied m.

time frame n zeitlicher Rahmen m.

time-honoured, (US) **time-honored** ['taɪmɒnəd] adj althergebracht.

timekeeper ['taɪmkiːpə*] n: **she's a good** ~ sie erfüllt ihr Zeitsoll.

time-lag ['taɪmlæg] n Verzögerung f.

timeless ['taɪmlɪs] adj zeitlos.

time limit n zeitliche Grenze f.

timely ['taɪmlɪ] adj (arrival) rechtzeitig; (reminder) zur rechten Zeit.

time off n: **to take** ~ sich dat freinehmen.

timer ['taɪmə*] n (time switch) Schaltuhr f; (on cooker) Zeitmesser m; (on video) Timer m.

time-saving ['taɪmseɪvɪŋ] adj Zeit sparend.

timescale ['taɪmskeɪl] (BRIT) n Zeitspanne f.

time-share ['taɪmʃeə*] n Ferienwohnung f auf Timesharingbasis.

time-sharing ['taɪmʃeərɪŋ] n (of property, COMPUT) Timesharing nt.

time sheet n = **time card**.

time signal n (RADIO) Zeitzeichen nt.

time switch n Zeitschalter m.

timetable ['taɪmteɪbl] n (RAIL etc) Fahrplan m; (SCOL) Stundenplan m; (programme of events) Programm nt.

time zone n Zeitzone f.

timid ['tɪmɪd] adj (person) schüchtern; (animal) scheu.

timidity [tɪ'mɪdɪtɪ] n (shyness) Schüchternheit f.

timing ['taɪmɪŋ] n (SPORT) Timing nt; **the** ~ **of his resignation** der Zeitpunkt seines Rücktritts.

timing device n (on bomb) Zeitzünder m.

timpani ['tɪmpənɪ] npl Kesselpauken pl.

tin [tɪn] n (metal) Blech nt; (container) Dose f; (: for baking) Form f; (: BRIT: can) Büchse f, Dose f; **two** ~**s of paint** zwei Dosen Farbe.

tinfoil ['tɪnfɔɪl] n Alufolie f.

tinge [tɪndʒ] n (of colour) Färbung f; (fig: of emotion etc) Anflug m, Anstrich m ♦ vt: ~**d with blue/red** leicht blau/rot gefärbt; **to be** ~**d with sth** (fig: emotion etc) einen Anstrich von etw haben.

tingle ['tɪŋgl] vi prickeln; (from cold) kribbeln; **I was tingling with excitement** ich zitterte vor Aufregung.

tinker ['tɪŋkə*] n (gipsy) Kesselflicker m.
► **tinker with** vt fus herumbasteln an +dat.

tinkle ['tɪŋkl] vi klingeln ♦ n (inf): **to give sb a** ~ (TEL) bei jdm anklingeln.

tin mine n Zinnbergwerk nt.

tinned [tɪnd] (BRIT) adj (food, peas) Dosen-, in Dosen.

tinnitus ['tɪnɪtəs] n Tinnitus m, Ohrensummen nt.

tinny ['tɪnɪ] (pej) adj (sound) blechern; (car etc) Schrott-.

tin-opener ['tɪnəʊpnə*] (BRIT) n Dosenöffner m.

tinsel ['tɪnsl] n Rauschgoldgirlanden pl.

tint [tɪnt] n (colour) Ton m; (for hair) Tönung f ♦ vt (hair) tönen.

tinted ['tɪntɪd] adj getönt.

tiny ['taɪnɪ] adj winzig.

tip [tɪp] *n* (*end*) Spitze *f*; (*gratuity*) Trinkgeld *nt*; (*BRIT: for rubbish*) Müllkippe *f*; (: *for coal*) Halde *f*; (*advice*) Tipp *m*, Hinweis *m* ♦ *vt* (*waiter*) ein Trinkgeld geben +*dat*; (*tilt*) kippen; (*also:* ~ **over:** *overturn*) umkippen; (*also:* ~ **out:** *empty*) leeren; (*predict: winner etc*) tippen *or* setzen auf +*acc*; **he ~ped out the contents of the box** er kippte den Inhalt der Kiste aus.
▶ **tip off** *vt* einen Tipp *or* Hinweis geben +*dat*.
tip-off ['tɪpɔf] *n* Hinweis *m*.
tipped ['tɪpt] *adj* (*BRIT: cigarette*) Filter-; **steel-** ~ mit Stahlspitze.
Tipp-Ex ® ['tɪpɛks] *n* Tipp-Ex ® *nt*.
tipple ['tɪpl] (*BRIT*) *vi* picheln ♦ *n:* **to have a** ~ einen trinken.
tipster ['tɪpstə*] *n* jd, der bei Pferderennen, Börsengeschäften *etc* Tipps gegen Bezahlung weitergibt.
tipsy ['tɪpsɪ] (*inf*) *adj* beschwipst.
tiptoe ['tɪptəu] *n:* **on** ~ auf Zehenspitzen.
tip-top ['tɪp'tɔp] *adj:* **in** ~ **condition** tipptopp.
tirade [taɪ'reɪd] *n* Tirade *f*.
tire ['taɪə*] *n* (*US*) = **tyre** ♦ *vt* müde machen, ermüden ♦ *vi* (*become tired*) müde werden; **to** ~ **of sth** genug von etw haben.
▶ **tire out** *vt* erschöpfen.
tired ['taɪəd] *adj* müde; **to be/look** ~ müde sein/aussehen; **to feel** ~ sich müde fühlen; **to be** ~ **of sth** etw satt haben; **to be** ~ **of doing sth** es satt haben, etw zu tun.
tiredness ['taɪədnɪs] *n* Müdigkeit *f*.
tireless ['taɪəlɪs] *adj* unermüdlich.
tiresome ['taɪəsəm] *adj* lästig.
tiring ['taɪərɪŋ] *adj* ermüdend, anstrengend.
tissue ['tɪʃuː] *n* (*ANAT, BIOL*) Gewebe *nt*; (*paper handkerchief*) Papiertaschentuch *nt*.
tissue paper *n* Seidenpapier *nt*.
tit [tɪt] *n* (*bird*) Meise *f*; (*inf: breast*) Titte *f*; ~ **for tat** wie du mir, so ich dir.
titanium [tɪ'teɪnɪəm] *n* Titan *nt*.
titbit, (*US*) **tidbit** ['tɪtbɪt] *n* (*food, news*) Leckerbissen *m*.
titillate ['tɪtɪleɪt] *vt* erregen, reizen.
titivate ['tɪtɪveɪt] *vt* fein machen.
title ['taɪtl] *n* Titel *m*; (*LAW*): ~ **to** Anspruch auf +*acc*.
title deed *n* Eigentumsurkunde *f*.
title page *n* Titelseite *f*.
title role *n* Titelrolle *f*.
title track *n* Titelstück *nt*.
titter ['tɪtə*] *vi* kichern.
tittle-tattle ['tɪtltætl] (*inf*) *n* Klatsch *m*, Gerede *nt*.
tizzy ['tɪzɪ] *n:* **to be in a** ~ aufgeregt sein; **to get in a** ~ sich aufregen.
T-junction ['tiː'dʒʌŋkʃən] *n* T-Kreuzung *f*.
TM *abbr* (= *trademark*) Wz; = **transcendental meditation.**
TN (*US*) *abbr* (*POST:* = *Tennessee*).
TNT *n abbr* (= *trinitrotoluene*) TNT *nt*.

=================== *KEYWORD*

to [tuː] *prep* **1** (*direction*) nach +*dat*, zu +*dat*; **to go** ~ **France/London/school/the station** nach Frankreich/nach London/zur Schule/ zum Bahnhof gehen; ~ **the left/right** nach links/rechts; **I have never been** ~ **Germany** ich war noch nie in Deutschland.
2 (*as far as*) bis; **to count** ~ **10** bis 10 zählen.
3 (*with expressions of time*) vor +*dat*; **a quarter** ~ **5** (*BRIT*) Viertel vor 5.
4 (*for, of*): **the key** ~ **the front door** der Schlüssel für die Haustür; **a letter** ~ **his wife** ein Brief an seine Frau.
5 (*expressing indirect object*): **to give sth** ~ **sb** jdm etw geben; **to talk** ~ **sb** mit jdm sprechen; **I sold it** ~ **a friend** ich habe es an einen Freund verkauft; **you've done something** ~ **your hair** du hast etwas mit deinem Haar gemacht.
6 (*in relation to*) zu; **A is** ~ **B as C is** ~ **D** A verhält sich zu B wie C zu D; **3 goals** ~ **2** 3 zu 2 Tore; **40 miles** ~ **the gallon** 40 Meilen pro Gallone.
7 (*purpose, result*) zu; **to sentence sb** ~ **death** jdn zum Tode verurteilen; ~ **my surprise** zu meiner Überraschung
♦ *with vb* **1** (*simple infinitive*): ~ **go** gehen; ~ **eat** essen.
2 (*following another vb*): **to want** ~ **do sth** etw tun wollen; **to try/start** ~ **do sth** versuchen/anfangen, etw zu tun.
3 (*with vb omitted*): **I don't want** ~ ich will nicht; **you ought** ~ du solltest es tun.
4 (*purpose, result*) (um ...) zu; **I did it** ~ **help** you ich habe es getan, um dir zu helfen.
5 (*equivalent to relative clause*) zu; **he has a lot** ~ **lose** er hat viel zu verlieren; **the main thing is** ~ **try** die Hauptsache ist, es zu versuchen.
6 (*after adjective etc*): **ready** ~ **use** gebrauchsfertig; **too old/young** ~ **...** zu alt/ jung, um zu ...; **it's too heavy** ~ **lift** es ist zu schwer zu heben
♦ *adv:* **to push/pull the door** ~ die Tür zudrücken/zuziehen; ~ **and fro** hin und her.

toad [təud] *n* Kröte *f*.
toadstool ['təudstuːl] *n* Giftpilz *m*.
toady ['təudɪ] (*pej*) *vi:* **to** ~ **to sb** vor jdm kriechen.
toast [təust] *n* (*CULIN, drink*) Toast *m* ♦ *vt* (*bread etc*) toasten; (*drink to*) einen Toast *or* Trinkspruch ausbringen auf +*acc*; **a piece** *or* **slice of** ~ eine Scheibe Toast.
toaster ['təustə*] *n* Toaster *m*.
toastmaster ['təustmɑːstə*] *n* Zeremonienmeister *m*.
toast rack *n* Toastständer *m*.
tobacco [tə'bækəu] *n* Tabak *m*; **pipe** ~ Pfeifentabak *m*.
tobacconist [tə'bækənɪst] *n* Tabakhändler(in)

m(f).

tobacconist's (shop) [tə'bækənɪsts-] n Tabakwarenladen m.

Tobago [tə'beɪgəu] n see **Trinidad**.

toboggan [tə'bɔgən] n Schlitten m.

today [tə'deɪ] adv, n heute; **what day is it ~?** welcher Tag ist heute?; **what date is it ~?** der Wievielte ist heute?; **~ is the 4th of March** heute ist der 4. März; **a week ago ~** heute vor einer Woche; **~'s paper** die Zeitung von heute.

toddle ['tɔdl] (inf) vi: **to ~ in/off/along** herein-/davon-/entlangwatscheln.

toddler ['tɔdlə*] n Kleinkind nt.

to-do [tə'du:] n Aufregung f, Theater nt.

toe [təu] n Zehe f, Zeh m; (of shoe, sock) Spitze f; **to ~ the line** (fig) auf Linie bleiben; **big/ little ~** großer/kleiner Zeh.

toehold ['təuhəuld] n (in climbing) Halt m für die Fußspitzen; (fig): **to get/gain a ~ (in)** einen Einstieg bekommen/sich dat einen Einstieg verschaffen (in +dat).

toenail ['təuneɪl] n Zehennagel m.

toffee ['tɔfɪ] n Toffee m.

toffee apple (BRIT) n ≈ kandierter Apfel m.

tofu ['təufu:] n Tofu m.

toga ['təugə] n Toga f.

together [tə'gɛðə*] adv zusammen; (at the same time) gleichzeitig; **~ with** gemeinsam mit.

togetherness [tə'gɛðənɪs] n Beisammensein nt.

toggle switch ['tɔgl-] n (COMPUT) Toggle-Schalter m.

Togo ['təugəu] n Togo nt.

togs [tɔgz] (inf) npl Klamotten pl.

toil [tɔɪl] n Mühe f ♦ vi sich abmühen.

toilet ['tɔɪlət] n Toilette f ♦ cpd (kit, accessories etc) Toiletten-; **to go to the ~** auf die Toilette gehen.

toilet bag (BRIT) n Kulturbeutel m.

toilet bowl n Toilettenbecken nt.

toilet paper n Toilettenpapier nt.

toiletries ['tɔɪlətrɪz] npl Toilettenartikel pl.

toilet roll n Rolle f Toilettenpapier.

toilet soap n Toilettenseife f.

toilet water n Toilettenwasser nt.

to-ing and fro-ing ['tu:ɪŋən'frəuɪŋ] (BRIT) n Hin und Her nt.

token ['təukən] n (sign, souvenir) Zeichen nt; (substitute coin) Wertmarke f ♦ adj (strike, payment etc) symbolisch; **by the same ~** (fig) in gleicher Weise; **book/record/gift ~** (BRIT) Bücher-/Platten-/Geschenkgutschein m.

tokenism ['təukənɪzəm] n: **to be (pure) ~** (nur) eine Alibifunktion haben.

Tokyo ['təukjəu] n Tokio nt.

told [təuld] pt, pp of **tell**.

tolerable ['tɔlərəbl] adj (bearable) erträglich; (fairly good) passabel.

tolerably ['tɔlərəblɪ] adv: **~ good** ganz annehmbar or passabel.

tolerance ['tɔlərns] n Toleranz f.

tolerant ['tɔlərnt] adj tolerant; **to be ~ of sth** tolerant gegenüber etw sein.

tolerate ['tɔləreɪt] vt (pain, noise) erdulden, ertragen; (injustice) tolerieren.

toleration [tɔlə'reɪʃən] n (of person, pain etc) Duldung f; (REL, POL) Toleranz f.

toll [təul] n (of casualties, deaths) (Gesamt)zahl f; (tax, charge) Gebühr f ♦ vi (bell) läuten; **the work took its ~ on us** die Arbeit blieb nicht ohne Auswirkungen auf uns.

tollbridge ['təulbrɪdʒ] n gebührenpflichtige Brücke f, Mautbrücke f.

toll call (US) n Ferngespräch nt.

toll-free ['təulfri:] (US) adj gebührenfrei.

toll road n gebührenpflichtige Straße f, Mautstraße f.

tomato [tə'mɑːtəu] (pl ~es) n Tomate f.

tomato purée n Tomatenmark nt.

tomb [tu:m] n Grab nt.

tombola [tɔm'bəulə] n Tombola f.

tomboy ['tɔmbɔɪ] n Wildfang m.

tombstone ['tu:mstəun] n Grabstein m.

tomcat ['tɔmkæt] n Kater m.

tome [təum] (form) n Band m.

tomorrow [tə'mɔrəu] adv morgen ♦ n morgen; (future) Zukunft f; **the day after ~** übermorgen; **a week ~** morgen in einer Woche; **~ morning** morgen früh.

ton [tʌn] n (BRIT) (britische) Tonne f; (US: also: **short ~**) (US-)Tonne f (ca. 907 kg); (metric ton) (metrische) Tonne f; **~s of** (inf) Unmengen von.

tonal ['təunl] adj (MUS) klanglich, tonal.

tone [təun] n Ton m ♦ vi (also: **~ in**: colours) (farblich) passen.

► **tone down** vt (also fig) abschwächen.

► **tone up** vt (muscles) kräftigen.

tone-deaf [təun'dɛf] adj ohne Gefühl für Tonhöhen.

toner ['təunə*] n (for photocopier) Toner m.

Tonga ['tɔŋə] n Tonga nt.

tongs [tɔŋz] npl Zange f; (also: **curling ~**) Lockenstab m.

tongue [tʌŋ] n Zunge f; (form: language) Sprache f; **~-in-cheek** (speak, say) ironisch.

tongue-tied ['tʌŋtaɪd] adj (fig) sprachlos.

tongue-twister ['tʌŋtwɪstə*] n Zungenbrecher m.

tonic ['tɔnɪk] n (MED) Tonikum nt; (fig) Wohltat f; (also: **~ water**) Tonic nt; (MUS) Tonika f, Grundton m.

tonight [tə'naɪt] adv (this evening) heute Abend; (this night) heute Nacht ♦ n (this evening) der heutige Abend; (this night) die kommende Nacht; **(I'll) see you ~!** bis heute Abend!

tonnage ['tʌnɪdʒ] n Tonnage f.

tonne [tʌn] (BRIT) n (metric ton) Tonne f.

tonsil ['tɔnsl] n Mandel f; **to have one's ~s out** sich dat die Mandeln herausnehmen lassen.

tonsillitis [tɔnsɪ'laɪtɪs] n Mandelentzündung f.

too [tu:] adv (excessively) zu; (also) auch; **it's ~ sweet** es ist zu süß; **I went ~** ich bin auch mitgegangen; **~ much** (adj) zu viel; (adv) zu sehr; **~ many** zu viele; **~ bad!** das ist eben Pech!

took [tuk] pt of **take**.

tool [tu:l] n (also fig) Werkzeug nt.

tool box n Werkzeugkasten m.

tool kit n Werkzeugsatz m.

toot [tu:t] n (of horn) Hupton m; (of whistle) Pfeifton m ♦ vi (with car-horn) hupen.

tooth [tu:θ] (pl **teeth**) n (also TECH) Zahn m; **to have a ~ out** or (US) **pulled** sich dat einen Zahn ziehen lassen; **to brush one's teeth** sich dat die Zähne putzen; **by the skin of one's teeth** (fig) mit knapper Not.

toothache ['tu:θeɪk] n Zahnschmerzen pl; **to have ~** Zahnschmerzen haben.

toothbrush ['tu:θbrʌʃ] n Zahnbürste f.

toothpaste ['tu:θpeɪst] n Zahnpasta f.

toothpick ['tu:θpɪk] n Zahnstocher m.

tooth powder n Zahnpulver nt.

top [tɒp] n (of mountain, tree, ladder) Spitze f; (of cupboard, table, box) Oberseite f; (of street) Ende nt; (lid) Verschluss m; (AUT: also: ~ **gear**) höchster Gang m; (also: **spinning ~**: toy) Kreisel m; (of blouse etc) Oberteil nt; (of pyjamas) Jacke f ♦ adj höchste(r, s); (highest in rank) oberste(r, s); (: golfer etc) Top- ♦ vt (poll, vote, list) anführen; (estimate etc) übersteigen; **at the ~ of the stairs/page** oben auf der Treppe/Seite; **at the ~ of the street** am Ende der Straße; **on ~ of** (above) auf +dat; (in addition to) zusätzlich zu; **from ~ to bottom** von oben bis unten; **from ~ to toe** (BRIT) von Kopf bis Fuß; **at the ~ of the list** oben auf der Liste; **at the ~ of his voice** so laut er konnte; **over the ~** (inf: behaviour etc) übertrieben; **to go over the ~** (inf) übertreiben; **at ~ speed** bei Höchstgeschwindigkeit.

▶ **top up**, (US) **top off** vt (drink) nachfüllen; (salary) aufbessern.

topaz ['təʊpæz] n Topas m.

top-class ['tɒp'klɑːs] adj erstklassig; (hotel, player etc) Spitzen-.

topcoat ['tɒpkəʊt] n (overcoat) Mantel m; (of paint) Deckanstrich m.

top floor n oberster Stock m.

top hat n Zylinder m.

top-heavy [tɒp'hevɪ] adj (also fig) kopflastig.

topic ['tɒpɪk] n Thema nt.

topical ['tɒpɪkl] adj (issue etc) aktuell.

topless ['tɒplɪs] adj (waitress) Oben-ohne-; (bather) barbusig ♦ adv oben ohne.

top-level ['tɒplevl] adj auf höchster Ebene.

topmost ['tɒpməʊst] adj oberste(r, s).

top-notch ['tɒp'nɒtʃ] adj erstklassig.

topography [tə'pɒgrəfɪ] n Topografie f.

topping ['tɒpɪŋ] n (CULIN) Überzug m.

topple ['tɒpl] vt (government etc) stürzen ♦ vi (person) stürzen; (object) fallen.

top-ranking ['tɒpræŋkɪŋ] adj (official) hoch gestellt.

top-secret ['tɒp'siːkrɪt] adj streng geheim.

top-security ['tɒpsə'kjuərɪtɪ] (BRIT) adj (prison, wing) Hochsicherheits-.

topsy-turvy ['tɒpsɪ'tɜːvɪ] adj auf den Kopf gestellt ♦ adv durcheinander; (fall, land) verkehrt herum.

top-up ['tɒpʌp] n: **would you like a ~?** darf ich Ihnen nachschenken?

top-up loan n Ergänzungsdarlehen nt.

torch [tɔːtʃ] n Fackel f; (BRIT: electric) Taschenlampe f.

tore [tɔː'] pt of **tear**.

torment [n 'tɔːment, vt tɔː'ment] n Qual f ♦ vt quälen; (annoy) ärgern.

torn [tɔːn] pp of **tear¹** ♦ adj: **~ between** (fig) hin- und hergerissen zwischen.

tornado [tɔː'neɪdəʊ] (pl **~es**) n (storm) Tornado m.

torpedo [tɔː'piːdəʊ] (pl **~es**) n Torpedo m.

torpedo boat n Torpedoboot nt.

torpor ['tɔːpə'] n Trägheit f.

torrent ['tɔrnt] n (flood) Strom m; (fig) Flut f.

torrential [tɔ'renʃl] adj (rain) wolkenbruchartig.

torrid ['tɔrɪd] adj (weather, love affair) heiß.

torso ['tɔːsəʊ] n Torso m.

tortoise ['tɔːtəs] n Schildkröte f.

tortoiseshell ['tɔːtəʃel] adj (jewellery, ornaments) aus Schildpatt; (cat) braungelbschwarz, braun-gelb-schwarz.

tortuous ['tɔːtjuəs] adj (path) gewunden; (argument, mind) umständlich.

torture ['tɔːtʃə'] n Folter f; (fig) Qual f ♦ vt foltern; (fig: torment) quälen; **it was ~** (fig) es war eine Qual.

torturer ['tɔːtʃərə'] n Folterer m.

Tory ['tɔːrɪ] (BRIT: POL) adj konservativ ♦ n Tory m, Konservative(r) f(m).

toss [tɒs] vt (throw) werfen; (one's head) zurückwerfen; (salad) anmachen; (pancake) wenden ♦ n: **with a ~ of her head** mit einer Kopfbewegung; **to ~ a coin** eine Münze werfen; **to win/lose the ~** die Entscheidung per Münzwurf gewinnen/verlieren; **to ~ up for sth** etw per Münzwurf entscheiden; **to ~ and turn** (in bed) sich hin und her wälzen.

tot [tɒt] n (BRIT: drink) Schluck m; (child) Knirps m.

▶ **tot up** (BRIT) vt (figures) zusammenzählen.

total ['təʊtl] adj (number etc) gesamt; (failure, wreck etc) völlig, total ♦ n Gesamtzahl f ♦ vt (add up) zusammenzählen; (add up to) sich belaufen auf +dat; **in ~** insgesamt.

totalitarian [təʊtælɪ'teərɪən] adj totalitär.

totality [təʊ'tælɪtɪ] n Gesamtheit f.

totally ['təʊtəlɪ] adv völlig.

totem pole n ['təʊtəm-] n Totempfahl m.

totter ['tɒtə'] vi (person) wanken, taumeln; (fig: government) im Wanken sein.

touch [tʌtʃ] n (sense of touch) Gefühl nt;

(*contact*) Berührung *f*; (*skill: of pianist etc*) Hand *f* ♦ *vt* berühren; (*tamper with*) anrühren; (*emotionally*) rühren ♦ *vi* (*make contact*) sich berühren; **the personal** ~ **die** persönliche Note; **to put the finishing** ~**es to sth** letzte Hand an etw *acc* legen; **a** ~ **of** (*fig: frost etc*) etwas, ein Hauch von; **in** ~ **with** (*person, group*) in Verbindung mit; **to get in** ~ **with sb** mit jdm in Verbindung treten; **I'll be in** ~ ich melde mich; **to lose** ~ (*friends*) den Kontakt verlieren; **to be out of** ~ **with sb** keine Verbindung mehr zu jdm haben; **to be out of** ~ **with events** nicht auf dem Laufenden sein; ~ **wood!** hoffen wir das Beste!

▶ **touch on** *vt fus* (*topic*) berühren.

▶ **touch up** *vt* (*car etc*) ausbessern.

touch-and-go ['tʌt∫ən'gəu] *adj* (*situation*) auf der Kippe; **it was** ~ **whether we'd succeed** es war völlig offen, ob wir Erfolg haben würden.

touchdown ['tʌt∫daun] *n* (*of rocket, plane*) Landung *f*; (*US: FOOTBALL*) Touch-down *m*, Touchdown *m*.

touched [tʌt∫t] *adj* (*moved*) gerührt; (*inf: mad*) plemplem.

touching ['tʌt∫ɪŋ] *adj* rührend.

touchline ['tʌt∫laɪn] *n* (*SPORT*) Seitenlinie *f*.

touch-sensitive ['tʌt∫'sɛnsɪtɪv] *adj* berührungsempfindlich; (*switch*) Kontakt-.

touch-type ['tʌt∫taɪp] *vi* blind schreiben.

touchy ['tʌt∫ɪ] *adj* (*person, subject*) empfindlich.

tough [tʌf] *adj* (*strong, firm, difficult*) hart; (*resistant*) widerstandsfähig; (*meat, animal, person*) zäh; (*rough*) rauh; ~ **luck!** Pech!

toughen ['tʌfn] *vt* (*sb's character*) hart machen; (*glass etc*) härten.

toughness ['tʌfnɪs] *n* Härte *f*.

toupee ['tu:peɪ] *n* Toupet *nt*.

tour ['tuə*] *n* (*journey*) Reise *f*, Tour *f*; (*of factory, museum etc*) Rundgang *m*; () (*also:* **guided** ~) Führung *f*; (*by pop group etc*) Tournee *f* ♦ *vt* (*country, factory etc: on foot*) ziehen durch; (: *in car*) fahren durch; **to go on a** ~ **of a museum/castle** an einer Museums-/Schlossführung teilnehmen; **to go on a** ~ **of the Highlands** die Highlands bereisen; **to go/be on** ~ (*pop group, theatre company etc*) auf Tournee gehen/sein.

tour guide *n* Reiseleiter(in) *m(f)*.

touring ['tuərɪŋ] *n* Umherreisen *nt*.

tourism ['tuərɪzm] *n* Tourismus *m*.

tourist ['tuərɪst] *n* Tourist(in) *m(f)* ♦ *cpd* (*attractions, season*) Touristen-; **the** ~ **trade** die Tourismusbranche.

tourist class *n* Touristenklasse *f*.

tourist information centre (*BRIT*) *n* Touristen-Informationszentrum *nt*.

tourist office *n* Verkehrsamt *nt*.

tournament ['tuənəmənt] *n* Turnier *nt*.

tourniquet ['tuənɪkeɪ] *n* Aderpresse *f*.

tour operator (*BRIT*) *n* Reiseveranstalter *m*.

tousled ['tauzld] *adj* (*hair*) zerzaust.

tout [taut] *vi*: **to** ~ **for business** die Reklametrommel schlagen; **to** ~ **for custom** auf Kundenfang gehen ♦ *n* (*also:* **ticket** ~) *Schwarzhändler, der Eintrittskarten zu überhöhten Preisen verkauft.*

tow [təu] *vt* (*vehicle*) abschleppen; (*caravan, trailer*) ziehen ♦ *n*: **to give sb a** ~ (*AUT*) jdn abschleppen; **"on** *or (US)* **in** ~**"** „Fahrzeug wird abgeschleppt".

▶ **tow away** *vt* (*vehicle*) abschleppen.

toward(s) [tə'wɔːd(z)] *prep* (*direction*) zu; (*attitude*) gegenüber +*dat*; (*purpose*) für; (*in time*) gegen; ~ **noon/the end of the year** gegen Mittag/Ende des Jahres; **to feel friendly** ~ **sb** jdm freundlich gesinnt sein.

towel ['tauəl] *n* Handtuch *nt*; **to throw in the** ~ (*fig*) das Handtuch werfen.

towelling ['tauəlɪŋ] *n* Frottee *nt or m*.

towel rail, (*US*) **towel rack** *n* Handtuchstange *f*.

tower ['tauə*] *n* Turm *m* ♦ *vi* aufragen; **to** ~ **above** *or* **over sb/sth** über jdm/etw aufragen.

tower block (*BRIT*) *n* Hochhaus *nt*.

towering ['tauərɪŋ] *adj* hoch aufragend.

towline ['təulaɪn] *n* Abschleppseil *nt*.

town [taun] *n* Stadt *f*; **to go (in)to** ~ in die Stadt gehen; **to go to** ~ **on sth** (*fig*) sich bei etw ins Zeug legen; **in** ~ in der Stadt; **to be out of** ~ (*person*) nicht in der Stadt sein.

town centre *n* Stadtzentrum *nt*.

town clerk *n* Stadtdirektor(in) *m(f)*.

town council *n* Stadtrat *m*.

town crier [-'kraɪə*] *n* Ausrufer *m*.

town hall *n* Rathaus *nt*.

town house *n* (städtisches) Wohnhaus *nt*; (*US: in a complex*) Reihenhaus *nt*.

townie ['taunɪ] (*inf*) *n* (*town-dweller*) Städter(in) *m(f)*.

town plan *n* Stadtplan *m*.

town planner *n* Stadtplaner(in) *m(f)*.

town planning *n* Stadtplanung *f*.

township ['taun∫ɪp] *n* Stadt(gemeinde) *f*; (*formerly: in South Africa*) Township *f*.

townspeople ['taunzpi:pl] *npl* Stadtbewohner *pl*.

towpath ['təupɑ:θ] *n* Leinpfad *m*.

towrope ['təurəup] *n* Abschleppseil *nt*.

tow truck (*US*) *n* Abschleppwagen *m*.

toxic ['tɔksɪk] *adj* giftig, toxisch.

toxin ['tɔksɪn] *n* Gift *nt*, Giftstoff *m*.

toy [tɔɪ] *n* Spielzeug *nt*.

▶ **toy with** *vt fus* (*object, idea*) spielen mit.

toyshop ['tɔɪ∫ɔp] *n* Spielzeugladen *m*.

trace [treɪs] *n* (*sign, small amount*) Spur *f* ♦ *vt* (*draw*) nachzeichnen; (*follow*) verfolgen; (*locate*) aufspüren; **without** ~ (*disappear*) spurlos; **there was no** ~ **of it** es war spurlos verschwunden.

trace element *n* Spurenelement *nt*.

tracer ['treɪsə'] n (MIL: also: ~ **bullet**) Leuchtspurgeschoss nt; (MED) Indikator m.

trachea [trə'kɪə] n Luftröhre f.

tracing paper ['treɪsɪŋ-] n Pauspapier nt.

track [træk] n Weg m; (of comet, SPORT) Bahn f; (of suspect, animal) Spur f; (RAIL) Gleis nt; (on tape, record) Stück nt, Track m ♦ vt (follow) verfolgen; **to keep ~ of sb/sth** (fig) jdn/etw im Auge behalten; **to be on the right ~** (fig) auf der richtigen Spur sein.

▶ **track down** vt aufspüren.

tracker dog ['trækə-] (BRIT) n Spürhund m.

track events npl Laufwettbewerbe f.

tracking station ['trækɪŋ-] n Bodenstation f.

track meet (US) n (SPORT) Leichtathletikwettkampf m.

track record n: **to have a good ~** (fig) gute Leistungen vorzuweisen haben.

tracksuit ['træksuːt] n Trainingsanzug m.

tract [trækt] n (GEOG) Gebiet nt; (pamphlet) Traktat m or nt; **respiratory ~** Atemwege pl.

traction ['trækʃən] n (power) Zugkraft f; (AUT: grip) Bodenhaftung f; (MED): **in ~** im Streckverband.

traction engine n Zugmaschine f.

tractor ['træktə'] n Traktor m.

trade [treɪd] n (activity) Handel m; (skill, job) Handwerk nt ♦ vi (do business) handeln ♦ vt: **to ~ sth (for sth)** etw (gegen etw) eintauschen; **foreign ~** Außenhandel m; **Department of T~ and Industry** (BRIT) ≈ Wirtschaftsministerium nt; **to ~ with** Handel treiben mit; **to ~ in** (merchandise) handeln in +dat.

▶ **trade in** vt in Zahlung geben.

trade barrier n Handelsschranke f.

trade deficit n Handelsdefizit nt.

Trade Descriptions Act (BRIT) n Gesetz über korrekte Warenbeschreibungen.

trade discount n Händlerrabatt m.

trade fair n Handelsmesse f.

trade figures npl Handelsziffern pl.

trade-in ['treɪdɪn] n: **to take sth as a ~** etw in Zahlung nehmen.

trade-in value n Gebrauchtwert m.

trademark ['treɪdmɑːk] n Warenzeichen nt.

trade mission n Handelsmission f.

trade name n Handelsname m.

trade-off ['treɪdɔf] n Handel m; **there's bound to be a ~ between speed and quality** es gibt entweder Einbußen bei der Schnelligkeit oder bei der Qualität.

trader ['treɪdə'] n Händler(in) m(f).

trade secret n (also fig) Betriebsgeheimnis nt.

tradesman ['treɪdzmən] (irreg: like man) n (shopkeeper) Händler m.

trade union n Gewerkschaft f.

trade unionist [-'juːnjənɪst] n Gewerkschaftler(in) m(f).

trade wind n Passat m.

trading ['treɪdɪŋ] n Handel m.

trading estate (BRIT) n Industriegelände nt.

trading stamp n Rabattmarke f.

tradition [trə'dɪʃən] n Tradition f.

traditional [trə'dɪʃənl] adj traditionell.

traditionally [trə'dɪʃnəlɪ] adv traditionell.

traffic ['træfɪk] n Verkehr m; (in drugs etc) Handel m ♦ vi: **to ~ in** handeln mit.

traffic calming n Verkehrsberuhigung f.

traffic circle (US) n Kreisverkehr m.

traffic island n Verkehrsinsel f.

traffic jam n Verkehrsstauung f, Stau m.

trafficker ['træfɪkə'] n Händler(in) m(f).

traffic lights npl Ampel f.

traffic offence (BRIT) n Verkehrsdelikt nt.

traffic sign n Verkehrszeichen nt.

traffic violation (US) n = **traffic offence**.

traffic warden n Verkehrspolizist für Parkvergehen; (woman) ≈ Politesse f.

tragedy ['trædʒədɪ] n Tragödie f.

tragic ['trædʒɪk] adj tragisch.

tragically ['trædʒɪkəlɪ] adv tragisch.

trail [treɪl] n (path) Weg m; (track) Spur f; (of smoke, dust) Wolke f ♦ vt (drag) schleifen; (follow) folgen +dat ♦ vi (hang loosely) schleifen; (in game, contest) zurückliegen; **to be on sb's ~** jdm auf der Spur sein.

▶ **trail away** vi (sound, voice) sich verlieren.

▶ **trail behind** vi hinterhertrotten.

▶ **trail off** vi = **trail away**.

trailer ['treɪlə'] n (AUT) Anhänger m; (US: caravan) Caravan m, Wohnwagen m; (CINE, TV) Trailer m.

trailer truck (US) n Sattelschlepper m.

train [treɪn] n (RAIL) Zug m; (of dress) Schleppe f ♦ vt (apprentice etc) ausbilden; (dog) abrichten; (athlete) trainieren; (mind) schulen; (plant) ziehen; (point: camera, gun etc): **to ~ on** richten auf +acc ♦ vi (learn a skill) ausgebildet werden; (SPORT) trainieren; **~ of thought** Gedankengang m; **to go by ~** mit dem Zug fahren; **~ of events** Ereignisfolge f; **to ~ sb to do sth** jdn dazu ausbilden, etw zu tun.

train attendant (US) n Schlafwagenschaffner m.

trained [treɪnd] adj (worker) gelernt; (teacher) ausgebildet; (animal) dressiert; (eye) geschult.

trainee [treɪ'niː] n Auszubildende(r) f(m).

trainer ['treɪnə'] n (SPORT: coach) Trainer(in) m(f); (: shoe) Trainingsschuh m; (of animals) Dresseur(in) m(f).

training ['treɪnɪŋ] n (for occupation) Ausbildung f; (SPORT) Training nt; **in ~** (SPORT) im Training.

training college (for teachers) ≈ pädagogische Hochschule f.

training course n Ausbildungskurs m.

traipse [treɪps] vi: **to ~ in/out** hinein-/herauslatschen.

trait [treɪt] n Zug m, Eigenschaft f.

traitor ['treɪtə'] n Verräter(in) m(f).

trajectory [trə'dʒɛktərɪ] n Flugbahn f.

tram [træm] (*BRIT*) *n* (*also*: ~**car**) Straßenbahn *f*.

tramline ['træmlaɪn] *n* Straßenbahnschiene *f*.

tramp [træmp] *n* Landstreicher *m*; (*pej*: *woman*) Flittchen *nt* ♦ *vi* stapfen ♦ *vt* (*walk through*: *town, streets*) latschen durch.

trample ['træmpl] *vt*: **to ~ (underfoot)** niedertrampeln ♦ *vi* (*also fig*): **to ~ on** herumtrampeln auf +*dat*.

trampoline ['træmpəliːn] *n* Trampolin *nt*.

trance [trɑːns] *n* Trance *f*; **to go into a ~** in Trance verfallen.

tranquil ['træŋkwɪl] *adj* ruhig, friedlich.

tranquillity, (*US*) **tranquility** [træŋ'kwɪlɪtɪ] *n* Ruhe *f*.

tranquillizer, (*US*) **tranquilizer** ['træŋkwɪlaɪzə*] *n* Beruhigungsmittel *nt*.

transact [træn'zækt] *vt* (*business*) abwickeln.

transaction [træn'zækʃən] *n* Geschäft *nt*; **cash ~** Bargeldtransaktion *f*.

transatlantic ['trænzət'læntɪk] *adj* transatlantisch; (*phone-call*) über den Atlantik.

transcend [træn'sɛnd] *vt* überschreiten.

transcendental [trænsɛn'dɛntl] *adj*: **~ meditation** transzendentale Meditation *f*.

transcribe [træn'skraɪb] *vt* transkribieren.

transcript ['trænskrɪpt] *n* Niederschrift *f*, Transkription *f*.

transcription [træn'skrɪpʃən] *n* Transkription *f*.

transept ['trænsɛpt] *n* Querschiff *nt*.

transfer ['trænsfə*] *n* (*of employees*) Versetzung *f*; (*of money*) Überweisung *f*; (*of power*) Übertragung *f*; (*SPORT*) Transfer *m*; (*picture, design*) Abziehbild *n* ♦ *vt* (*employees*) versetzen; (*money*) überweisen; (*power, ownership*) übertragen; **by bank ~** per Banküberweisung; **to ~ the charges** (*BRIT*: *TEL*) ein R-Gespräch führen.

transferable [træns'fɜːrəbl] *adj* übertragbar; **"not ~"** „nicht übertragbar".

transfix [træns'fɪks] *vt* aufspießen; **~ed with fear** (*fig*) starr vor Angst.

transform [træns'fɔːm] *vt* umwandeln.

transformation [trænsfə'meɪʃən] *n* Umwandlung *f*.

transformer [træns'fɔːmə*] *n* (*ELEC*) Transformator *m*.

transfusion [træns'fjuːʒən] *n* (*also*: **blood ~**) Bluttransfusion *f*.

transgress [træns'grɛs] *vt* (*go beyond*) überschreiten; (*violate*: *rules, law*) verletzen.

transient ['trænzɪənt] *adj* vorübergehend.

transistor [træn'zɪstə*] *n* (*ELEC*) Transistor *m*; (*also*: ~ **radio**) Transistorradio *nt*.

transit ['trænzɪt] *n*: **in ~** unterwegs.

transit camp *n* Durchgangslager *nt*.

transition [træn'zɪʃən] *n* Übergang *m*.

transitional [træn'zɪʃənl] *adj* (*period, stage*) Übergangs-.

transitive ['trænzɪtɪv] *adj* (*verb*) transitiv.

transit lounge *n* Transithalle *f*.

transitory ['trænzɪtərɪ] *adj* (*emotion, arrangement etc*) vorübergehend.

transit visa *n* Transitvisum *nt*.

translate [trænz'leɪt] *vt* übersetzen; **to ~ (from/into)** übersetzen (aus/in +*acc*).

translation [trænz'leɪʃən] *n* Übersetzung *f*; **in ~** als Übersetzung.

translator [trænz'leɪtə*] *n* Übersetzer(in) *m(f)*.

translucent [trænz'luːsnt] *adj* (*object*) lichtdurchlässig.

transmission [trænz'mɪʃən] *n* (*also TV*) Übertragung *f*; (*of information*) Übermittlung *f*; (*AUT*) Getriebe *nt*.

transmit [trænz'mɪt] *vt* (*also TV*) übertragen; (*message, signal*) übermitteln.

transmitter [trænz'mɪtə*] *n* (*TV, RADIO*) Sender *m*.

transparency [træns'pɛərnsɪ] *n* (*of glass etc*) Durchsichtigkeit *f*; (*BRIT*: *PHOT*) Dia *nt*.

transparent [træns'pærnt] *adj* durchsichtig; (*fig*: *obvious*) offensichtlich.

transpire [træns'paɪə*] *vi* (*turn out*) bekannt werden; (*happen*) passieren; **it finally ~d that ...** schließlich sickerte durch, dass ...

transplant [*vt* træns'plɑːnt, *n* 'trɑːnsplɑːnt] *vt* (*organ, seedlings*) verpflanzen ♦ *n* (*MED*) Transplantation *f*; **to have a heart ~** sich einer Herztransplantation unterziehen.

transport ['trænspɔːt] *n* Transport *m*, Beförderung *f* ♦ *vt* transportieren; **do you have your own ~?** haben Sie ein Auto?; **public ~** öffentliche Verkehrsmittel *pl*; **Department of T~** (*BRIT*) Verkehrsministerium *nt*.

transportation ['trænspɔː'teɪʃən] *n* Transport *m*, Beförderung *f*; (*means of transport*) Beförderungsmittel *nt*; **Department of T~** (*US*) Verkehrsministerium *nt*.

transport café (*BRIT*) *n* Fernfahrerlokal *nt*.

transpose [træns'pəʊz] *vt* versetzen.

transsexual [trænz'sɛksuəl] *adj* transsexuell ♦ *n* Transsexuelle(r) *f(m)*.

transverse ['trænzvɜːs] *adj* (*beam etc*) Quer-.

transvestite [trænz'vɛstaɪt] *n* Transvestit *m*.

trap [træp] *n* (*also fig*) Falle *f*; (*carriage*) zweirädriger Pferdewagen *m* ♦ *vt* (*animal*) (mit einer Falle) fangen; (*person*: *trick*) in die Falle locken; (: *confine*) gefangen halten; (*immobilize*) festsetzen; (*capture*: *energy*) stauen; **to set** *or* **lay a ~** eine Falle stellen; **to shut one's ~** (*inf*) die Klappe halten; **to ~ one's finger in the door** sich *dat* den Finger in der Tür einklemmen.

trap door *n* Falltür *f*.

trapeze [trə'piːz] *n* Trapez *nt*.

trapper ['træpə*] *n* Fallensteller *m*, Trapper *m*.

trappings ['træpɪŋz] *npl* äußere Zeichen *pl*; (*of power*) Insignien *pl*.

trash [træʃ] *n* (*rubbish*) Abfall *m*, Müll *m*; (*pej*: *nonsense*) Schund *m*, Mist *m*.

trash can (*US*) *n* Mülleimer *m*.

trashy ['træʃɪ] adj (goods) minderwertig, wertlos; (novel etc) Schund-.

trauma ['trɔːmə] n Trauma nt.

traumatic [trɔːˈmætɪk] adj traumatisch.

traumatize ['trɔːmətaɪz] vt traumatisieren.

travel ['trævl] n (travelling) Reisen nt ♦ vi reisen; (short distance) fahren; (move: car, aeroplane) sich bewegen; (sound etc) sich fortpflanzen; (news) sich verbreiten ♦ vt (distance) zurücklegen; **travels** npl (journeys) Reisen pl; **this wine doesn't ~ well** dieser Wein verträgt den Transport nicht.

travel agency n Reisebüro nt.

travel agent n Reisebürokaufmann m, Reisebürokauffrau f.

travel brochure n Reiseprospekt m.

traveling etc (US) = travelling etc.

traveller, (US) **traveler** ['trævlə*] n Reisende(r) f(m); (COMM) Vertreter(in) m(f).

traveller's cheque, (US) **traveler's check** n Reisescheck m.

travelling, (US) **traveling** ['trævlɪŋ] n Reisen nt ♦ cpd (circus, exhibition) Wander-; (bag, clock) Reise-; **~ expenses** Reisespesen pl.

travelling salesman n Vertreter m.

travelogue ['trævəlɒg] n Reisebericht m.

travel sickness n Reisekrankheit f.

traverse ['trævəs] vt durchqueren.

travesty ['trævəstɪ] n Travestie f.

trawler ['trɔːlə*] n Fischdampfer m.

tray [treɪ] n (for carrying) Tablett nt; (also: in-~/out-~: on desk) Ablage f für Eingänge/ Ausgänge.

treacherous ['tretʃərəs] adj (person, look) verräterisch; (ground, tide) tückisch; **road conditions are ~** die Straßen sind in gefährlichem Zustand.

treachery ['tretʃərɪ] n Verrat m.

treacle ['triːkl] n Sirup m.

tread [tred] (pt **trod**, pp **trodden**) n (of tyre) Profil nt; (footstep) Schritt m; (of stair) Stufe f ♦ vi gehen.

▶ **tread on** vt fus treten auf +acc.

treadle ['tredl] n Pedal nt.

treas. abbr = treasurer.

treason ['triːzn] n Verrat m.

treasure ['treʒə*] n (also fig) Schatz m ♦ vt schätzen; **treasures** npl (art treasures etc) Schätze pl, Kostbarkeiten pl.

treasure hunt n Schatzsuche f.

treasurer ['treʒərə*] n Schatzmeister(in) m(f).

treasury ['treʒərɪ] n: **the T~**, (US) **the T~ Department** das Finanzministerium.

treasury bill n kurzfristiger Schatzwechsel m.

treat [triːt] n (present) (besonderes) Vergnügen nt ♦ vt (also MED, TECH) behandeln; **it came as a ~** es war eine besondere Freude; **to ~ sth as a joke** etw als Witz ansehen; **to ~ sb to sth** jdm etw spendieren.

treatment ['triːtmənt] n Behandlung f; **to have**

~ for sth wegen etw in Behandlung sein.

treaty ['triːtɪ] n Vertrag m.

treble ['trebl] adj (triple) dreifach; (MUS: voice, part) (Knaben)sopran-; (instrument) Diskant- ♦ n (singer) (Knaben)sopran m; (on hi-fi, radio etc) Höhen pl ♦ vt verdreifachen ♦ vi sich verdreifachen; **to be ~ the amount/size of sth** dreimal so viel/so groß wie etw sein.

treble clef n Violinschlüssel m.

tree [triː] n Baum m.

tree-lined ['triːlaɪnd] adj baumbestanden.

treetop ['triːtɒp] n Baumkrone f.

tree trunk n Baumstamm m.

trek [trek] n Treck m; (tiring walk) Marsch m ♦ vi trecken.

trellis ['trelɪs] n Gitter nt.

tremble ['trembl] vi (voice, body, trees) zittern; (ground) beben.

trembling ['tremblɪŋ] n (of ground) Beben nt, Erschütterung f; (of trees) Zittern nt ♦ adj (hand, voice etc) zitternd.

tremendous [trɪˈmendəs] adj (amount, success etc) gewaltig, enorm; (holiday, view etc) fantastisch.

tremendously [trɪˈmendəslɪ] adv (difficult, exciting) ungeheuer; **he enjoyed it ~** es hat ihm ausgezeichnet gefallen.

tremor ['tremə*] n Zittern nt; (also: **earth ~**) Beben nt, Erschütterung f.

trench [trentʃ] n Graben m.

trench coat n Trenchcoat m.

trench warfare n Stellungskrieg m.

trend [trend] n Tendenz f; (fashion) Trend m; **a ~ towards/away from sth** eine Tendenz zu/ weg von etw; **to set a/the ~** richtungsweisend sein.

trendy ['trendɪ] adj modisch.

trepidation [trepɪˈdeɪʃən] n (apprehension) Beklommenheit f; **in ~** beklommen.

trespass ['trespəs] vi: **to ~ on** (private property) unbefugt betreten; **"no ~ing"** „Betreten verboten".

trespasser ['trespəsə*] n Unbefugte(r) f(m); **"~s will be prosecuted"** „widerrechtliches Betreten wird strafrechtlich verfolgt".

tress [tres] n (of hair) Locke f.

trestle ['tresl] n Bock m.

trestle table n Klapptisch m.

trial ['traɪəl] n (LAW) Prozess m; (test: of machine, drug etc) Versuch m; (worry) Plage f; **trials** npl (unpleasant experiences) Schwierigkeiten pl; **~ by jury** Schwurgerichtsverfahren nt; **to be sent for ~** vor Gericht gestellt werden; **to be/go on ~** (LAW) angeklagt sein/werden; **by ~ and error** durch Ausprobieren.

trial balance n Probebilanz f.

trial basis n: **on a ~** probeweise.

trial period n Probezeit f.

trial run n Versuch m.

triangle ['traɪæŋgl] n Dreieck nt; (US: set square) (Zeichen)dreieck nt; (MUS) Triangel

triangular [traɪˈæŋgjulə⁺] adj dreieckig.
triathlon [traɪˈæθlən] n Triathlon nt.
tribal [ˈtraɪbl] adj (warrior, warfare, dance)
Stammes-.
tribe [traɪb] n Stamm m.
tribesman [ˈtraɪbzmən] (irreg: like **man**) n
Stammesangehörige(r) m.
tribulations [trɪbjuˈleɪʃənz] npl Kümmernisse
pl.
tribunal [traɪˈbjuːnl] n Gericht nt.
tributary [ˈtrɪbjutərɪ] n (of river) Nebenfluss m.
tribute [ˈtrɪbjuːt] n Tribut m; **to pay ~ to**
Tribut zollen +dat.
trice [traɪs] n: **in a ~** im Handumdrehen.
trick [trɪk] n Trick m; (CARDS) Stich m ♦ vt
hereinlegen; **to play a ~ on sb** jdm einen
Streich spielen; **it's a ~ of the light** das
Licht täuscht; **that should do the ~** das
müsste hinhauen; **to ~ sb into doing sth** jdn
(mit einem Trick) dazu bringen, etw zu tun;
to ~ sb out of sth jdn um etw prellen.
trickery [ˈtrɪkərɪ] n Tricks pl, Betrügerei f.
trickle [ˈtrɪkl] n (of water etc) Rinnsal nt ♦ vi
(water, rain etc) rinnen; (people) sich
langsam bewegen.
trick photography n Trickfotografie f.
trick question n Fangfrage f.
trickster [ˈtrɪkstə⁺] n Betrüger(in) m(f).
tricky [ˈtrɪkɪ] adj (job, problem) schwierig.
tricycle [ˈtraɪsɪkl] n Dreirad nt.
trifle [ˈtraɪfl] n (detail) Kleinigkeit f; (CULIN)
Trifle nt ♦ adv: **a ~ long** ein bisschen lang
♦ vi: **to ~ with sb/sth** jdn/etw nicht ernst
nehmen; **he is not (someone) to be ~d with**
mit ihm ist nicht zu spaßen.
trifling [ˈtraɪflɪŋ] adj (detail) unbedeutend.
trigger [ˈtrɪgə⁺] n Abzug m.
▶ **trigger off** vt fus auslösen.
trigonometry [trɪgəˈnɔmətrɪ] n
Trigonometrie f.
trilby [ˈtrɪlbɪ] (BRIT) n (also: **~ hat**) Filzhut m.
trill [trɪl] n (MUS) Triller m; (of birds) Trillern
nt.
trilogy [ˈtrɪlədʒɪ] n Trilogie f.
trim [trɪm] adj (house, garden) gepflegt; (figure,
person) schlank ♦ n (haircut etc): **to have a ~**
sich dat die Haare nachschneiden lassen;
(on clothes, car) Besatz m ♦ vt (hair, beard)
nachschneiden; (decorate): **to ~ (with)**
besetzen (mit); (NAUT: a sail) trimmen mit;
to keep o.s. in (good) ~ (gut) in Form
bleiben.
trimmings [ˈtrɪmɪŋz] npl (CULIN): **with all the
~** mit allem Drum und Dran; (cuttings: of
pastry etc) Reste pl.
Trinidad and Tobago [ˈtrɪnɪdæd-] n Trinidad
und Tobago nt.
trinity [ˈtrɪnɪtɪ] n (REL) Dreieinigkeit f.
trinket [ˈtrɪŋkɪt] n (ornament)
Schmuckgegenstand m; (piece of jewellery)
Schmuckstück nt.

trio [ˈtriːəu] n Trio nt.
trip [trɪp] n (journey) Reise f; (outing) Ausflug
m ♦ vi (stumble) stolpern; (go lightly) trippeln;
on a ~ auf Reisen.
▶ **trip over** vt fus stolpern über +acc.
▶ **trip up** vi stolpern ♦ vt (person) zu Fall
bringen.
tripartite [traɪˈpɑːtaɪt] adj (agreement, talks)
dreiseitig.
tripe [traɪp] n (CULIN) Kaldaunen pl; (pej:
rubbish) Stuss m.
triple [ˈtrɪpl] adj dreifach ♦ adv: **~ the
distance/the speed** dreimal so weit/schnell;
~ the amount dreimal so viel.
triple jump n Dreisprung m.
triplets [ˈtrɪplɪts] npl Drillinge pl.
triplicate [ˈtrɪplɪkət] n: **in ~** in dreifacher
Ausfertigung.
tripod [ˈtraɪpɔd] n (PHOT) Stativ nt.
Tripoli [ˈtrɪpəlɪ] n Tripolis nt.
tripper [ˈtrɪpə⁺] (BRIT) n Ausflügler(in) m(f).
tripwire [ˈtrɪpwaɪə⁺] n Stolperdraht m.
trite [traɪt] (pej) adj (comment, idea etc) banal.
triumph [ˈtraɪʌmf] n Triumph m ♦ vi: **to
~ (over)** triumphieren (über +acc).
triumphal [traɪˈʌmfl] adj (return) triumphal.
triumphant [traɪˈʌmfənt] adj triumphal;
(victorious) siegreich.
triumphantly [traɪˈʌmfəntlɪ] adv
triumphierend.
trivia [ˈtrɪvɪə] (pej) npl Trivialitäten pl.
trivial [ˈtrɪvɪəl] adj trivial.
triviality [trɪvɪˈælɪtɪ] n Trivialität f.
trivialize [ˈtrɪvɪəlaɪz] vt trivialisieren.
trod [trɔd] pt of **tread**.
trodden [ˈtrɔdn] pp of **tread**.
trolley [ˈtrɔlɪ] n (for luggage) Kofferkuli m; (for
shopping) Einkaufswagen m; (table on
wheels) Teewagen m; (also: **~ bus**)
Oberleitungsomnibus m, Obus m.
trollop [ˈtrɔləp] (pej) n (woman) Schlampe f.
trombone [trɔmˈbəun] n Posaune f.
troop [truːp] n (of people, monkeys etc) Gruppe
f ♦ vi: **to ~ in/out** hinein-/hinausströmen;
troops npl (MIL) Truppen pl.
troop carrier n Truppentransporter m;
(NAUT: also: **troopship**)
Truppentransportschiff nt.
trooper [ˈtruːpə⁺] n (MIL) Kavallerist m; (US:
policeman) Polizist m.
trooping the colour [ˈtruːpɪŋ-] (BRIT) n
(ceremony) Fahnenparade f.
troopship [ˈtruːpʃɪp] n
Truppentransportschiff nt.
trophy [ˈtrəufɪ] n Trophäe f.
tropic [ˈtrɔpɪk] n Wendekreis m; **the tropics** npl
die Tropen pl; **T~ of Cancer/Capricorn**
Wendekreis des Krebses/Steinbocks.
tropical [ˈtrɔpɪkl] adj tropisch.
trot [trɔt] n (fast pace) Trott m; (of horse) Trab
m ♦ vi (horse) traben; (person) trotten; **on the
~** (BRIT, fig) hintereinander.

▶ **trot out** *vt* (*facts, excuse etc*) vorbringen.

trouble ['trʌbl] *n* Schwierigkeiten *pl*; (*bother, effort*) Umstände *pl*; (*unrest*) Unruhen *pl* ♦ *vt* (*worry*) beunruhigen; (*disturb: person*) belästigen ♦ *vi*: **to ~ to do sth** sich *dat* die Mühe machen, etw zu tun; **troubles** *npl* (*personal*) Probleme *pl*; (*POL etc*) Unruhen *pl*; **to be in ~** in Schwierigkeiten sein; **to have ~ doing sth** Schwierigkeiten *or* Probleme haben, etw zu tun; **to go to the ~ of doing sth** sich *dat* die Mühe machen, etw zu tun; **it's no ~!** das macht mir nichts aus!; **the ~ is ...** das Problem ist ...; **what's the ~?** wo fehlts?; **stomach** *etc* ~ Probleme mit dem Magen *etc*; **please don't ~ yourself** bitte bemühen Sie sich nicht.

troubled [trʌbld] *adj* (*person*) besorgt; (*country, life, era*) von Problemen geschüttelt.

trouble-free ['trʌblfriː] *adj* problemlos.

troublemaker ['trʌblmeɪkə*] *n* Unruhestifter(in) *m(f)*.

troubleshooter ['trʌblʃuːtə*] *n* Vermittler(in) *m(f)*.

troublesome ['trʌblsəm] *adj* (*child*) schwierig; (*cough etc*) lästig.

trouble spot *n* (*MIL*) Unruheherd *m*.

troubling ['trʌblɪŋ] *adj* (*question etc*) beunruhigend.

trough [trɒf] *n* (*also*: **drinking ~**) Wassertrog *m*; (*also*: **feeding ~**) Futtertrog *m*; (*channel*) Rinne *f*; (*low point*) Tief *nt*; **a ~ of low pressure** ein Tiefdruckkeil *m*.

trounce [traʊns] *vt* (*defeat*) vernichtend schlagen.

troupe [truːp] *n* Truppe *f*.

trouser press ['traʊzə-] *n* Hosenpresse *f*.

trousers ['traʊzəz] *npl* Hose *f*; **short ~** kurze Hose; **a pair of ~** eine Hose.

trouser suit (*BRIT*) *n* Hosenanzug *m*.

trousseau ['truːsəu] (*pl* **~x** *or* **~s**) *n* Aussteuer *f*.

trout [traʊt] *n inv* Forelle *f*.

trowel ['traʊəl] *n* (*garden tool*) Pflanzkelle *f*; (*builder's tool*) (Maurer)kelle *f*.

truant ['truːənt] (*BRIT*) *n*: **to play ~** die Schule schwänzen.

truce [truːs] *n* Waffenstillstand *m*.

truck [trʌk] *n* (*lorry*) Lastwagen *m*; (*RAIL*) Güterwagen *m*; (*for luggage*) Gepäckwagen *m*; **to have no ~ with sb** nichts mit jdm zu tun haben.

truck driver *n* Lkw-Fahrer(in) *m(f)*.

trucker ['trʌkə*] (*US*) *n* Lkw-Fahrer(in) *m(f)*.

truck farm (*US*) *n* Gemüsefarm *f*.

trucking ['trʌkɪŋ] (*US*) *n* Transport *m*.

trucking company (*US*) *n* Spedition *f*.

truculent ['trʌkjulənt] *adj* aufsässig.

trudge [trʌdʒ] *vi* (*also*: **~ along**) sich dahinschleppen.

true [truː] *adj* wahr; (*accurate*) genau; (*genuine*) echt; (*faithful: friend*) treu; (*wall, beam*) gerade; (*circle*) rund; **to come ~** wahr werden; **~ to life** lebensecht.

truffle ['trʌfl] *n* (*fungus, sweet*) Trüffel *f*.

truly ['truːlɪ] *adv* wahrhaft, wirklich; (*truthfully*) wirklich; **yours ~** (*in letter*) mit freundlichen Grüßen.

trump [trʌmp] *n* (*also*: ~ **card**, *also fig*) Trumpf *m*; **to turn up ~s** (*fig*) sich als Retter in der Not erweisen.

trumped-up *adj*: **a ~ charge** eine erfundene Anschuldigung.

trumpet ['trʌmpɪt] *n* Trompete *f*.

truncated [trʌŋ'keɪtɪd] *adj* (*message, object*) verstümmelt.

truncheon ['trʌntʃən] (*BRIT*) *n* Gummiknüppel *m*.

trundle ['trʌndl] *vt* (*trolley etc*) rollen ♦ *vi*: **to ~ along** (*person*) dahinschlendern; (*vehicle*) dahinrollen.

trunk [trʌŋk] *n* (*of tree*) Stamm *m*; (*of person*) Rumpf *m*; (*of elephant*) Rüssel *m*; (*case*) Schrankkoffer *m*; (*US: AUT*) Kofferraum *m*; **trunks** *npl* (*also*: **swimming ~s**) Badehose *f*.

trunk call (*BRIT*) *n* Ferngespräch *nt*.

trunk road (*BRIT*) *n* Fernstraße *f*.

truss [trʌs] *n* (*MED*) Bruchband *nt*.

▶ **truss (up)** *vt* (*CULIN*) dressieren; (*person*) fesseln.

trust [trʌst] *n* Vertrauen *nt*; (*COMM: for charity etc*) Stiftung *f* ♦ *vt* vertrauen +*dat*; **to take sth on ~** (*advice etc*) etw einfach glauben; **to be in ~** (*LAW*) treuhänderisch verwaltet werden; **to ~ (that)** (*hope*) hoffen(, dass).

trust company *n* Trust *m*.

trusted ['trʌstɪd] *adj* (*friend, servant*) treu.

trustee [trʌs'tiː] *n* (*LAW*) Treuhänder(in) *m(f)*; (*of school etc*) Aufsichtsratsmitglied *nt*.

trustful ['trʌstful] *adj* vertrauensvoll.

trust fund *n* Treuhandvermögen *nt*.

trusting ['trʌstɪŋ] *adj* vertrauensvoll.

trustworthy ['trʌstwɜːðɪ] *adj* (*person*) vertrauenswürdig.

trusty ['trʌstɪ] *adj* getreu.

truth [truːθ] (*pl* **~s**) *n*: **the ~** die Wahrheit *f*.

truthful ['truːθful] *adj* (*person*) ehrlich; (*answer etc*) wahrheitsgemäß.

truthfully ['truːθfəlɪs] *adv* (*answer*) wahrheitsgemäß.

truthfulness ['truːθfəlnɪs] *n* Ehrlichkeit *f*.

try [traɪ] *n* (*also RUGBY*) Versuch *m* ♦ *vt* (*attempt*) versuchen; (*test*) probieren; (*LAW*) vor Gericht stellen; (*strain: patience*) auf die Probe stellen ♦ *vi* es versuchen; **to have a ~** es versuchen, einen Versuch machen; **to ~ to do sth** versuchen, etw zu tun; **to ~ one's (very) best** *or* **hardest** sein Bestes versuchen *or* tun.

▶ **try on** *vt* (*clothes*) anprobieren; **she's ~ing it on** (*fig*) sie probiert, wie weit sie gehen kann.

▶ **try out** *vt* ausprobieren.

trying ['traɪɪŋ] *adj* (*person*) schwierig;

(*experience*) schwer.

tsar [zɑːʳ] *n* Zar *m*.

T-shirt ['tiːʃəːt] *n* T-Shirt *nt*.

T-square ['tiːskwɛəʳ] *n* (*TECH*) Reißschiene *f*.

TT *adj abbr* (*BRIT: inf*) = **teetotal** ♦ *abbr* (*US: POST: = Trust Territories*) der US-Verwaltungshoheit unterstellte Gebiete.

tub [tʌb] *n* (*container*) Kübel *m*; (*bath*) Wanne *f*.

tuba ['tjuːbə] *n* Tuba *f*.

tubby ['tʌbɪ] *adj* rundlich.

tube [tjuːb] *n* (*pipe*) Rohr *nt*; (*container*) Tube *f*; (*BRIT: underground*) U-Bahn *f*; (*US: inf*): **the ~** (*television*) die Röhre.

tubeless ['tjuːblɪs] *adj* (*tyre*) schlauchlos.

tuber ['tjuːbəʳ] *n* (*BOT*) Knolle *f*.

tuberculosis [tjubəːkjuˈləʊsɪs] *n* Tuberkulose *f*.

tube station (*BRIT*) *n* U-Bahn-Station *f*.

tubing ['tjuːbɪŋ] *n* Schlauch *m*; **a piece of ~** ein Schlauch.

tubular ['tjuːbjʊləʳ] *adj* röhrenförmig.

TUC (*BRIT*) *n abbr* (= *Trades Union Congress*) britischer Gewerkschafts-Dachverband.

tuck [tʌk] *vt* (*put*) stecken ♦ *n* (*SEWING*) Biese *f*.

▶ **tuck away** *vt* (*money*) wegstecken; **to be ~ed away** (*building*) versteckt liegen.

▶ **tuck in** *vt* (*clothing*) feststecken; (*child*) zudecken ♦ *vi* (*eat*) zulangen.

▶ **tuck up** *vt* (*invalid, child*) zudecken.

tuck shop *n* Süßwarenladen *m*.

Tue(s). *abbr* (= *Tuesday*) Di.

Tuesday ['tjuːzdɪ] *n* Dienstag *m*; **it is ~ 23rd March** heute ist Dienstag, der 23. März; **on ~** am Dienstag; **on ~s** dienstags; **every ~** jeden Dienstag; **every other ~** jeden zweiten Dienstag; **last/next ~** letzten/nächsten Dienstag; **the following ~** am Dienstag darauf; **~'s newspaper** die Zeitung von Dienstag; **a week/fortnight on ~** Dienstag in einer Woche/in vierzehn Tagen; **the ~ before last** der vorletzte Dienstag; **the ~ after next** der übernächste Dienstag; **~ morning/lunchtime/afternoon/evening** Dienstag Morgen/Mittag/Nachmittag/Abend; **~ night** (*overnight*) Dienstag Nacht.

tuft [tʌft] *n* Büschel *nt*.

tug [tʌg] *n* (*ship*) Schlepper *m* ♦ *vt* zerren.

tug of love *n* Tauziehen *nt* (*um das Sorgerecht für Kinder*).

tug-of-war [tʌgəvˈwɔːʳ] *n* (*also fig*) Tauziehen *nt*.

tuition [tjuːˈɪʃən] *n* (*BRIT*) Unterricht *m*; (*US: school fees*) Schulgeld *nt*.

tulip ['tjuːlɪp] *n* Tulpe *f*.

tumble ['tʌmbl] *n* (*fall*) Sturz *m* ♦ *vi* (*fall*) stürzen.

▶ **tumble to** (*inf*) *vt fus* kapieren.

tumbledown ['tʌmbldaun] *adj* (*building*) baufällig.

tumble dryer (*BRIT*) *n* Wäschetrockner *m*.

tumbler ['tʌmbləʳ] *n* (*glass*) Trinkglas *nt*.

tummy ['tʌmɪ] (*inf*) *n* Bauch *m*.

tumour, (*US*) **tumor** ['tjuːməʳ] *n* (*MED*) Tumor *m*, Geschwulst *f*.

tumult ['tjuːmʌlt] *n* Tumult *m*.

tumultuous [tjuːˈmʌltjuəs] *adj* (*welcome, applause etc*) stürmisch.

tuna ['tjuːnə] *n inv* (*also:* **~ fish**) T(h)unfisch *m*.

tune [tjuːn] *n* (*melody*) Melodie *f* ♦ *vt* (*MUS*) stimmen; (*RADIO, TV, AUT*) einstellen; **to be in/out of ~** (*instrument*) richtig gestimmt/verstimmt sein; (*singer*) richtig/falsch singen; **to be in/out of ~ with** (*fig*) in Einklang/nicht in Einklang stehen mit; **she was robbed to the ~ of 10,000 pounds** sie wurde um einen Betrag in Höhe von 10.000 Pfund beraubt.

▶ **tune in** *vi* (*RADIO, TV*) einschalten; **to ~ in to BBC1** BBC1 einschalten.

▶ **tune up** *vi* (*MUS*) (das Instrument/die Instrumente) stimmen.

tuneful ['tjuːnful] *adj* melodisch.

tuner ['tjuːnəʳ] *n*: **piano ~** Klavierstimmer(in) *m(f)*; (*radio set*) Tuner *m*.

tuner amplifier *n* Steuergerät *nt*.

tungsten ['tʌŋstən] *n* Wolfram *nt*.

tunic ['tjuːnɪk] *n* Hemdbluse *f*.

tuning fork ['tjuːnɪŋ-] *n* Stimmgabel *f*.

Tunis ['tjuːnɪs] *n* Tunis *nt*.

Tunisia [tjuːˈnɪzɪə] *n* Tunesien *nt*.

Tunisian [tjuːˈnɪzɪən] *adj* tunesisch ♦ *n* (*person*) Tunesier(in) *m(f)*.

tunnel ['tʌnl] *n* Tunnel *m*; (*in mine*) Stollen *m* ♦ *vi* einen Tunnel bauen.

tunnel vision *n* (*MED*) Gesichtsfeldeinengung *f*; (*fig*) Engstirnigkeit *f*.

tunny ['tʌnɪ] *n* T(h)unfisch *m*.

turban ['təːbən] *n* Turban *m*.

turbid ['təːbɪd] *adj* (*water*) trüb; (*air*) schmutzig.

turbine ['təːbaɪn] *n* Turbine *f*.

turbo ['təːbəʊ] *n* Turbo *m*; **~ engine** Turbomotor *m*.

turbojet [təːbəʊˈdʒɛt] *n* Düsenflugzeug *nt*.

turboprop [təːbəʊˈprɒp] *n* (*engine*) Turbo-Prop-Turbine *f*.

turbot ['təːbət] *n inv* Steinbutt *m*.

turbulence ['təːbjʊləns] *n* (*AVIAT*) Turbulenz *f*.

turbulent ['təːbjʊlənt] *adj* (*water, seas*) stürmisch; (*fig: career, period*) turbulent.

tureen [təˈriːn] *n* Terrine *f*.

turf [təːf] *n* (*grass*) Rasen *m*; (*clod*) Sode *f* ♦ *vt* (*area*) mit Grassoden bedecken; **the T~** (*horse-racing*) der Pferderennsport.

▶ **turf out** (*inf*) *vt* (*person*) rausschmeißen.

turf accountant (*BRIT*) *n* Buchmacher *m*.

turgid ['təːdʒɪd] *adj* geschwollen.

Turin ['tjuəˈrɪn] *n* Turin *nt*.

Turk [təːk] *n* Türke *m*, Türkin *f*.

Turkey ['təːkɪ] *n* die Türkei *f*.

turkey ['təːkɪ] *n* (*bird*) Truthahn *m*, Truthenne

f; (*meat*) Puter *m*.

Turkish ['tə:kɪʃ] *adj* türkisch ♦ *n* (*LING*) Türkisch *nt*.

Turkish bath *n* türkisches Bad *nt*.

Turkish delight *n* geleeartige Süßigkeit, mit Puderzucker oder Schokolade überzogen.

turmeric ['tə:mərɪk] *n* Kurkuma *f*.

turmoil ['tə:mɔɪl] *n* Aufruhr *m*; **in ~** in Aufruhr.

turn [tə:n] *n* (*change*) Wende *f*; (*in road*) Kurve *f*; (*rotation*) Drehung *f*; (*performance*) Nummer *f*; (*inf: MED*) Anfall *m* ♦ *vt* (*handle, key*) drehen; (*collar, steak*) wenden; (*page*) umblättern; (*shape: wood*) drechseln; (: *metal*) drehen ♦ *vi* (*object*) sich drehen; (*person*) sich umdrehen; (*change direction*) abbiegen; (*milk*) sauer werden; **to do sb a good ~** jdm einen guten Dienst erweisen; **a ~ of events** eine Wendung der Dinge; **it gave me quite a ~** (*inf*) das hat mir einen schönen Schrecken eingejagt; **"no left ~"** (*AUT*) „Linksabbiegen verboten"; **it's your ~** du bist dran; **in ~** der Reihe nach; **to take ~s (at)** sich abwechseln (bei); **at the ~ of the century/year** zur Jahrhundertwende/ Jahreswende; **to take a ~ for the worse** (*events*) sich zum Schlechten wenden; **his health** *or* **he has taken a ~ for the worse** sein Befinden *or* hat sich verschlechtert; **to ~ nasty/forty/grey** unangenehm/vierzig/ grau werden.

▶ **turn against** *vt fus* sich wenden gegen.

▶ **turn around** *vi* sich umdrehen; (*in car*) wenden.

▶ **turn away** *vi* sich abwenden ♦ *vt* (*applicants*) abweisen; (*business*) zurückweisen.

▶ **turn back** *vi* umkehren ♦ *vt* (*person, vehicle*) zurückweisen.

▶ **turn down** *vt* (*request*) ablehnen; (*heating*) kleiner stellen; (*radio etc*) leiser stellen; (*bedclothes*) aufschlagen.

▶ **turn in** *vi* (*inf: go to bed*) sich hinhauen ♦ *vt* (*to police*) anzeigen; **to ~ o.s. in** sich stellen.

▶ **turn into** *vt fus* (*change*) sich verwandeln in +*acc* ♦ *vt* machen zu.

▶ **turn off** *vi* (*from road*) abbiegen ♦ *vt* (*light, radio etc*) ausmachen; (*tap*) zudrehen; (*engine*) abstellen.

▶ **turn on** *vt* (*light, radio etc*) anmachen; (*tap*) aufdrehen; (*engine*) anstellen.

▶ **turn out** *vt* (*light*) ausmachen; (*gas*) abstellen ♦ *vi* (*appear, attend*) erscheinen; **to ~ out to be** (*prove to be*) sich erweisen als; **to ~ out well/badly** (*situation*) gut/schlecht enden.

▶ **turn over** *vi* (*person*) sich umdrehen ♦ *vt* (*object*) umdrehen, wenden; (*page*) umblättern; **to ~ sth over to sb** etw übertragen +*dat*; (*to sth*) etw verlagern zu.

▶ **turn round** *vi* sich umdrehen; (*vehicle*) wenden.

▶ **turn up** *vi* (*person*) erscheinen; (*lost object*) wieder auftauchen ♦ *vt* (*collar*) hochklappen; (*heater*) höher stellen; (*radio etc*) lauter stellen.

turnabout ['tə:nəbaut] *n* (*fig*) Kehrtwendung *f*.

turnaround ['tə:nəraund] *n* = **turnabout**.

turncoat ['tə:nkəut] *n* Überläufer(in) *m(f)*.

turned-up ['tə:ndʌp] *adj*: **~ nose** Stupsnase *f*.

turning ['tə:nɪŋ] *n* (*in road*) Abzweigung *f*; **the first ~ on the right** die erste Straße rechts.

turning circle (*BRIT*) *n* (*AUT*) Wendekreis *m*.

turning point *n* (*fig*) Wendepunkt *m*.

turning radius (*US*) *n* = **turning circle**.

turnip ['tə:nɪp] *n* Rübe *f*.

turnout ['tə:naut] *n* (*of voters etc*) Beteiligung *f*.

turnover ['tə:nəuvə*] *n* (*COMM: amount of money*) Umsatz *m*; (: *of staff*) Fluktuation *f*; (*CULIN*): **apple ~** Apfeltasche *f*; **there is a rapid ~ in staff** der Personalbestand wechselt ständig.

turnpike ['tə:npaɪk] (*US*) *n* gebührenpflichtige Autobahn *f*.

turnstile ['tə:nstaɪl] *n* Drehkreuz *nt*.

turntable ['tə:nteɪbl] *n* (*on record player*) Plattenteller *m*.

turn-up ['tə:nʌp] (*BRIT*) *n* (*on trousers*) Aufschlag *m*; **that's a ~ for the books!** (*inf*) das ist eine echte Überraschung!

turpentine ['tə:pəntaɪn] *n* (*also*: **turps**) Terpentin *nt*.

turquoise ['tə:kwɔɪz] *n* (*stone*) Türkis *m* ♦ *adj* (*colour*) türkis.

turret ['tʌrɪt] *n* Turm *m*.

turtle ['tə:tl] *n* Schildkröte *f*.

turtleneck (sweater) ['tə:tlnɛk(-)] *n* Pullover *m* mit rundem Kragen.

Tuscan ['tʌskən] *adj* toskanisch ♦ *n* (*person*) Toskaner(in) *m(f)*.

Tuscany ['tʌskənɪ] *n* die Toskana.

tusk [tʌsk] *n* (*of elephant*) Stoßzahn *m*.

tussle ['tʌsl] *n* Gerangel *nt*.

tutor ['tju:tə*] *n* Tutor(in) *m(f)*; (*private tutor*) Privatlehrer(in) *m(f)*.

tutorial [tju:'tɔ:rɪəl] *n* Kolloquium *nt*.

tuxedo [tʌk'si:dəu] (*US*) *n* Smoking *m*.

TV [ti:'vi:] *n abbr* (= *television*) TV *nt*.

TV dinner *n* Fertiggericht *nt*.

twaddle ['twɔdl] (*inf*) *n* dummes Zeug *nt*.

twang [twæŋ] *n* (*of instrument*) singender Ton *m*; (*of voice*) näselnder Ton *m* ♦ *vi* einen singenden Ton von sich geben ♦ *vt* (*guitar*) zupfen.

tweak [twi:k] *vt* kneifen.

tweed [twi:d] *n* Tweed *m* ♦ *adj* (*jacket, skirt*) Tweed-.

tweezers ['twi:zəz] *npl* Pinzette *f*.

twelfth [twɛlfθ] *num* zwölfte(r, s) ♦ *n* Zwölftel *nt*.

Twelfth Night *n* ≈ Dreikönige *nt*.

twelve [twɛlv] *num* zwölf; **at ~ (o'clock)** (*midday*) um zwölf Uhr (mittags); (*midnight*) um zwölf Uhr nachts.

twentieth ['twɛntɪɪθ] *num* zwanzigste(r, s).

twenty ['twɛntɪ] *num* zwanzig.

twerp [twɜːp] (*inf*) *n* Schwachkopf *m*.

twice [twaɪs] *adv* zweimal; ~ **as much** zweimal so viel; ~ **a week** zweimal die Woche; **she is** ~ **your age** sie ist doppelt so alt wie du.

twiddle ['twɪdl] *vt* drehen an +*dat* ♦ *vi*: **to** ~ **(with)** herumdrehen (an +*dat*); **to** ~ **one's thumbs** (*fig*) Däumchen drehen.

twig [twɪg] *n* Zweig *m* ♦ *vi, vt* (*BRIT: inf: realize*) kapieren.

twilight ['twaɪlaɪt] *n* Dämmerung *f*; **in the** ~ in der Dämmerung.

twill [twɪl] *n* (*cloth*) Köper *m*.

twin [twɪn] *adj* (*sister, brother*) Zwillings-; (*towers*) Doppel- ♦ *n* Zwilling *m*; (*room in hotel etc*) Zweibettzimmer *nt* ♦ *vt* (*towns etc*): **to be** ~**ned with ... ...** als Partnerstadt haben.

twin-bedded room ['twɪn'bɛdɪd-] *n* Zweibettzimmer *nt*.

twin beds *npl* zwei (gleiche) Einzelbetten *pl*.

twin-carburettor ['twɪnkɑ:bju'rɛtə*] *adj* Doppelvergaser-.

twine [twaɪn] *n* Bindfaden *m* ♦ *vi* sich winden.

twin-engined [twɪn'ɛndʒɪnd] *adj* zweimotorig.

twinge [twɪndʒ] *n* (*of pain*) Stechen *nt*; **a** ~ **of conscience** Gewissensbisse *pl*; **a** ~ **of fear/ guilt** ein Angst-/Schuldgefühl *nt*.

twinkle ['twɪŋkl] *vi* funkeln ♦ *n* Funkeln *nt*.

twin town *n* Partnerstadt *f*.

twirl [twɜːl] *vt* herumwirbeln ♦ *vi* wirbeln ♦ *n* Wirbel *m*.

twist [twɪst] *n* (*action*) Drehung *f*; (*in road*) Kurve; (*in coil, flex*) Biegung *f*; (*in story*) Wendung *f* ♦ *vt* (*turn*) drehen; (*injure: ankle etc*) verrenken; (*twine*) wickeln; (*fig: meaning etc*) verdrehen ♦ *vi* (*road, river*) sich winden; ~ **my arm!** (*inf*) überreden Sie mich einfach!

twisted ['twɪstɪd] *adj* (*wire, rope*) gedreht; (*ankle*) verrenkt; (*fig: logic, mind*) verdreht.

twit [twɪt] (*inf*) *n* Trottel *m*.

twitch [twɪtʃ] *n* (*jerky movement*) Zucken *nt* ♦ *vi* zucken.

two [tu:] *num* zwei; ~ **by** ~, **in** ~**s** zu zweit; **to put** ~ **and** ~ **together** (*fig*) zwei und zwei zusammenzählen.

two-bit [tu:'bɪt] (*inf*) *adj* (*worthless*) mies.

two-door [tu:'dɔ:*] *adj* zweitürig.

two-faced [tu:'feɪst] (*pej*) *adj* scheinheilig.

twofold ['tu:fəuld] *adv*: **to increase** ~ um das Doppelte ansteigen ♦ *adj* (*increase*) um das Doppelte; (*aim, value etc*) zweifach.

two-piece (suit) ['tu:pi:s-] *n* Zweiteiler *m*.

two-piece (swimsuit) *n* zweiteiliger Badeanzug *m*.

two-ply ['tu:plaɪ] *adj* (*wool*) zweifädig; (*tissues*) zweilagig.

two-seater ['tu:'si:tə*] *n* (*car*) Zweisitzer *m*.

twosome ['tu:səm] *n* (*people*) Paar *nt*.

two-stroke ['tu:strəuk] *n* (*also*: ~ **engine**) Zweitakter *m* ♦ *adj* (*engine*) Zweitakt-.

two-tone ['tu:'təun] *adj* (*in colour*) zweifarbig.

two-way ['tu:weɪ] *adj*: ~ **traffic** Verkehr *m* in beiden Richtungen; ~ **radio** Funksprechgerät *nt*.

TX (*US*) *abbr* (*POST*: = *Texas*).

tycoon [taɪ'ku:n] *n* Magnat *m*.

type [taɪp] *n* (*category, model, example*) Typ *m*; (*TYP*) Schrift *f* ♦ *vt* (*letter etc*) tippen, (mit der) Maschine schreiben; **a** ~ **of** eine Art von; **what** ~ **do you want?** welche Sorte möchten Sie?; **in bold/italic** ~ in Fett-/ Kursivdruck.

typecast ['taɪpkɑ:st] (*irreg: like* **cast**) *vt* (*actor*) (auf eine Rolle) festlegen.

typeface ['taɪpfeɪs] *n* Schrift *f*, Schriftbild *nt*.

typescript ['taɪpskrɪpt] *n* (maschinengeschriebenes) Manuskript *nt*.

typeset ['taɪpsɛt] (*irreg: like* **set**) *vt* setzen.

typesetter ['taɪpsɛtə*] *n* Setzer(in) *m(f)*.

typewriter ['taɪpraɪtə*] *n* Schreibmaschine *f*.

typewritten ['taɪprɪtn] *adj* maschine(n)geschrieben.

typhoid ['taɪfɔɪd] *n* Typhus *m*.

typhoon [taɪ'fu:n] *n* Taifun *m*.

typhus ['taɪfəs] *n* Fleckfieber *nt*.

typical ['tɪpɪkl] *adj* typisch; ~ (**of**) typisch (für); **that's** ~! das ist typisch!

typify ['tɪpɪfaɪ] *vt* typisch sein für.

typing ['taɪpɪŋ] *n* Maschine(n)schreiben *nt*.

typing error *n* Tippfehler *m*.

typing pool *n* Schreibzentrale *f*.

typist ['taɪpɪst] *n* Schreibkraft *f*.

typo ['taɪpəu] (*inf*) *n abbr* (= *typographical error*) Druckfehler *m*.

typography [tɪ'pɒgrəfɪ] *n* Typografie *f*.

tyranny ['tɪrənɪ] *n* Tyrannei *f*.

tyrant ['taɪərnt] *n* Tyrann(in) *m(f)*.

tyre, (*US*) **tire** ['taɪə*] *n* Reifen *m*.

tyre pressure *n* Reifendruck *m*.

Tyrol [tɪ'rəul] *n* Tirol *nt*.

Tyrolean [tɪrə'li:ən] *adj* Tiroler ♦ *n* (*person*) Tiroler(in) *m(f)*.

Tyrolese [tɪrə'li:z] = **Tyrolean**.

Tyrrhenian Sea [tɪ'ri:nɪən-] *n*: **the** ~ das Tyrrhenische Meer.

tzar [zɑ:*] *n* = **tsar**.

U, u

U¹, u [juː] n (letter) U nt, u nt; ~ **for Uncle** ≈ U wie Ulrich.

U² [juː] (BRIT) n abbr (CINE: = universal) Klassifikation für jugendfreie Filme.

UAW (US) n abbr (= United Automobile Workers) Automobilarbeitergewerkschaft.

UB40 (BRIT) n abbr (= unemployment benefit form 40) Arbeitslosenausweis m.

U-bend ['juːbɛnd] n (in pipe) U-Krümmung f.

ubiquitous [juːˈbɪkwɪtəs] adj allgegenwärtig.

UCCA [ˈʌkə] (BRIT) n abbr (= Universities Central Council on Admissions) akademische Zulassungsstelle, ≈ ZVS f.

UDA (BRIT) n abbr (= Ulster Defence Association) paramilitärische protestantische Organisation in Nordirland.

UDC (BRIT) n abbr (= Urban District Council) Stadtverwaltung f.

udder ['ʌdə⁺] n Euter nt.

UDI (BRIT) n abbr (POL: = unilateral declaration of independence) einseitige Unabhängigkeitserklärung f.

UDR (BRIT) n abbr (= Ulster Defence Regiment) Regiment aus Teilzeitsoldaten zur Unterstützung der britischen Armee und Polizei in Nordirland.

UEFA [juːˈeɪfə] n abbr (= Union of European Football Associations) UEFA f.

UFO [ˈjuːfəu] n abbr (= unidentified flying object) Ufo nt.

Uganda [juːˈgændə] n Uganda nt.

Ugandan [juːˈgændən] adj ugandisch ♦ n Ugander(in) m(f).

UGC (BRIT) n abbr (= University Grants Committee) Ausschuss zur Verteilung von Geldern an Universitäten.

ugh [ɔːh] excl igitt.

ugliness [ˈʌglɪnɪs] n Hässlichkeit f.

ugly [ˈʌglɪ] adj hässlich; (nasty) schlimm.

UHF abbr (= ultrahigh frequency) UHF.

UHT abbr (= ultra heat treated): ~ **milk** H-Milch f.

UK n abbr = **United Kingdom**.

Ukraine [juːˈkreɪn] n Ukraine f.

Ukrainian [juːˈkreɪnɪən] adj ukrainisch ♦ n Ukrainer(in) m(f); (LING) Ukrainisch nt.

ulcer [ˈʌlsə⁺] n (stomach ulcer etc) Geschwür nt; (also: **mouth** ~) Abszess m im Mund.

Ulster [ˈʌlstə⁺] n Ulster nt.

ulterior [ʌlˈtɪərɪə⁺] adj: ~ **motive** Hintergedanke m.

ultimata [ʌltɪˈmeɪtə] npl of **ultimatum**.

ultimate [ˈʌltɪmət] adj (final) letztendlich; (greatest) größte(r, s); (: deterrent) äußerste(r, s); (: authority) höchste(r, s) ♦ n: **the** ~ **in luxury** das Äußerste or Höchste an Luxus.

ultimately [ˈʌltɪmətlɪ] adv (in the end) schließlich, letzten Endes; (basically) im Grunde (genommen).

ultimatum [ʌltɪˈmeɪtəm] (pl ~**s** or **ultimata**) n Ultimatum nt.

ultrasonic [ʌltrəˈsɒnɪk] adj (sound) Ultraschall-.

ultrasound [ˈʌltrəsaund] n Ultraschall m.

ultraviolet [ˈʌltrəˈvaɪəlɪt] adj ultraviolett.

umbilical cord [ʌmˈbɪlɪkl-] n Nabelschnur f.

umbrage [ˈʌmbrɪdʒ] n: **to take** ~ **at** Anstoß nehmen an +dat.

umbrella [ʌmˈbrɛlə] n (for rain) (Regen)schirm m; (for sun) Sonnenschirm m; (fig): **under the** ~ **of** unter der Leitung von.

umlaut ['umlaut] n Umlaut m; (mark) Umlautzeichen nt.

umpire [ˈʌmpaɪə⁺] n Schiedsrichter(in) m(f) ♦ vt (game) als Schiedsrichter leiten.

umpteen [ʌmpˈtiːn] adj zig.

umpteenth [ʌmpˈtiːnθ] adj: **for the** ~ **time** zum x-ten Mal.

UMWA n abbr (= United Mineworkers of America) amerikanische Bergarbeitergewerkschaft.

UN n abbr (= United Nations) UNO f.

unabashed [ʌnəˈbæʃt] adj: **to be/seem** ~ unbeeindruckt sein/scheinen.

unabated [ʌnəˈbeɪtɪd] adj unvermindert ♦ adv: **to continue** ~ nicht nachlassen.

unable [ʌnˈeɪbl] adj: **to be** ~ **to do sth** etw nicht tun können.

unabridged [ʌnəˈbrɪdʒd] adj ungekürzt.

unacceptable [ʌnəkˈsɛptəbl] adj unannehmbar, nicht akzeptabel.

unaccompanied [ʌnəˈkʌmpənɪd] adj (child, song) ohne Begleitung; (luggage) unbegleitet.

unaccountably [ʌnəˈkauntəblɪ] adv unerklärlich.

unaccounted [ʌnəˈkauntɪd] adj: **to be** ~ **for** (passengers, money etc) (noch) fehlen.

unaccustomed [ʌnəˈkʌstəmd] adj: **to be** ~ **to** nicht gewöhnt sein an +acc.

unacquainted [ʌnəˈkweɪntɪd] adj: **to be** ~ **with** nicht vertraut sein mit.

unadulterated [ʌnəˈdʌltəreɪtɪd] adj rein.

unaffected [ʌnəˈfɛktɪd] adj (person, behaviour) natürlich, ungekünstelt; **to be** ~ **by sth** von etw nicht berührt werden.

unafraid [ʌnəˈfreɪd] adj: **to be** ~ keine Angst haben.

unaided [ʌnˈeɪdɪd] adv ohne fremde Hilfe.

unanimity [juːnəˈnɪmɪtɪ] n Einstimmigkeit f.

unanimous [juːˈnænɪməs] adj einstimmig.

unanimously [juːˈnænɪməslɪ] adv einstimmig.

unanswered [ʌnˈɑːnsəd] adj unbeantwortet.

unappetizing [ʌn'æpɪtaɪzɪŋ] *adj* (*food*) unappetitlich.

unappreciative [ʌnə'priːʃɪətɪv] *adj* (*person*) undankbar; (*audience*) verständnislos.

unarmed [ʌn'ɑːmd] *adj* unbewaffnet; ~ **combat** Nahkampf *m* ohne Waffen.

unashamed [ʌnə'ʃeɪmd] *adj* (*pleasure, greed etc*) unverhohlen.

unassisted [ʌnə'sɪstɪd] *adv* ohne fremde Hilfe.

unassuming [ʌnə'sjuːmɪŋ] *adj* bescheiden.

unattached [ʌnə'tætʃt] *adj* (*single: person*) ungebunden; (*unconnected*) ohne Verbindung.

unattended [ʌnə'tɛndɪd] *adj* (*car, luggage, child*) unbeaufsichtigt.

unattractive [ʌnə'træktɪv] *adj* unattraktiv.

unauthorized [ʌn'ɔːθəraɪzd] *adj* (*visit, use*) unbefugt; (*version*) nicht unautorisiert.

unavailable [ʌnə'veɪləbl] *adj* (*article, room*) nicht verfügbar; (*person*) nicht zu erreichen; ~ **for comment** nicht zu sprechen.

unavoidable [ʌnə'vɔɪdəbl] *adj* unvermeidlich.

unavoidably [ʌnə'vɔɪdəblɪ] *adv* (*delayed etc*) auf unvermeidliche Weise.

unaware [ʌnə'wɛə*] *adj*: **he was ~ of it** er war sich *dat* dessen nicht bewusst.

unawares [ʌnə'wɛəz] *adv* (*catch, take*) unerwartet.

unbalanced [ʌn'bælənst] *adj* (*report*) unausgewogen; **(mentally)** ~ geistig gestört.

unbearable [ʌn'bɛərəbl] *adj* unerträglich.

unbeatable [ʌn'biːtəbl] *adj* unschlagbar.

unbeaten [ʌn'biːtn] *adj* ungeschlagen.

unbecoming [ʌnbɪ'kʌmɪŋ] *adj* (*language, behaviour*) unpassend; (*garment*) unvorteilhaft.

unbeknown(st) [ʌnbɪ'nəun(st)] *adv*: ~ **to me/ Peter** ohne mein/Peters Wissen.

unbelief [ʌnbɪ'liːf] *n* Ungläubigkeit *f*.

unbelievable [ʌnbɪ'liːvəbl] *adj* unglaublich.

unbelievably [ʌnbɪ'liːvəblɪ] *adv* unglaublich.

unbend [ʌn'bɛnd] (*irreg: like* **bend**) *vi* (*relax*) aus sich herausgehen ♦ *vt* (*wire etc*) gerade biegen.

unbending [ʌn'bɛndɪŋ] *adj* (*person, attitude*) unnachgiebig.

unbias(s)ed [ʌn'baɪəst] *adj* unvoreingenommen.

unblemished [ʌn'blɛmɪʃt] *adj* (*also fig*) makellos.

unblock [ʌn'blɔk] *vt* (*pipe*) frei machen.

unborn [ʌn'bɔːn] *adj* ungeboren.

unbounded [ʌn'baundɪd] *adj* grenzenlos.

unbreakable [ʌn'breɪkəbl] *adj* (*object*) unzerbrechlich.

unbridled [ʌn'braɪdld] *adj* ungezügelt.

unbroken [ʌn'brəukən] *adj* (*seal*) unversehrt; (*silence*) ununterbrochen; (*record, series*) ungebrochen.

unbuckle [ʌn'bʌkl] *vt* aufschnallen.

unburden [ʌn'bəːdn] *vt*: **to ~ o.s. (to sb)** (jdm) sein Herz ausschütten.

unbusinesslike [ʌn'bɪznɪslaɪk] *adj* ungeschäftsmäßig.

unbutton [ʌn'bʌtn] *vt* aufknöpfen.

uncalled-for [ʌn'kɔːldfɔː*] *adj* (*remark etc*) unnötig.

uncanny [ʌn'kænɪ] *adj* unheimlich.

unceasing [ʌn'siːsɪŋ] *adj* (*search, flow etc*) unaufhörlich; (*loyalty*) unermüdlich.

unceremonious [ʌnsɛrɪ'məunɪəs] *adj* (*abrupt, rude*) brüsk, barsch.

uncertain [ʌn'səːtn] *adj* (*person*) unsicher; (*future, outcome*) ungewiss; **to be ~ about sth** unsicher über etw *acc* sein; **in no ~ terms** unzweideutig.

uncertainty [ʌn'səːtntɪ] *n* Ungewissheit *f*; **uncertainties** *npl* (*doubts*) Unsicherheiten *pl*.

unchallenged [ʌn'tʃælɪndʒd] *adj* unbestritten ♦ *adv* (*walk, enter*) ungehindert; **to go ~** unangefochten bleiben.

unchanged [ʌn'tʃeɪndʒd] *adj* unverändert.

uncharitable [ʌn'tʃærɪtəbl] *adj* (*remark, behaviour etc*) unfreundlich.

uncharted [ʌn'tʃɑːtɪd] *adj* (*land, sea*) unverzeichnet.

unchecked [ʌn'tʃɛkt] *adv* (*grow, continue*) ungehindert.

uncivil [ʌn'sɪvɪl] *adj* (*person*) grob.

uncivilized [ʌn'sɪvɪlaɪzd] *adj* unzivilisiert.

uncle ['ʌŋkl] *n* Onkel *m*.

unclear [ʌn'klɪə*] *adj* unklar; **I'm still ~ about what I'm supposed to do** mir ist immer noch nicht klar, was ich tun soll.

uncoil [ʌn'kɔɪl] *vt* (*rope, wire*) abwickeln ♦ *vi* (*snake*) sich strecken.

uncomfortable [ʌn'kʌmfətəbl] *adj* (*person, chair*) unbequem; (*room*) ungemütlich; (*nervous*) unbehaglich; (*unpleasant: situation, fact*) unerfreulich.

uncomfortably [ʌn'kʌmfətəblɪ] *adv* (*sit*) unbequem; (*smile*) unbehaglich.

uncommitted [ʌnkə'mɪtɪd] *adj* nicht engagiert; ~ **to** nicht festgelegt auf +*acc*.

uncommon [ʌn'kɔmən] *adj* ungewöhnlich.

uncommunicative [ʌnkə'mjuːnɪkətɪv] *adj* (*person*) schweigsam.

uncomplicated [ʌn'kɔmplɪkeɪtɪd] *adj* unkompliziert.

uncompromising [ʌn'kɔmprəmaɪzɪŋ] *adj* (*person, belief*) kompromisslos.

unconcerned [ʌnkən'səːnd] *adj* (*person*) unbekümmert; **to be ~ about sth** sich nicht um etw kümmern.

unconditional [ʌnkən'dɪʃənl] *adj* bedingungslos; (*acceptance*) vorbehaltlos.

uncongenial [ʌnkən'dʒiːnɪəl] *adj* (*surroundings*) unangenehm.

unconnected [ʌnkə'nɛktɪd] *adj* (*unrelated*) ohne Verbindung; **to be ~ with sth** nicht mit etw in Beziehung stehen.

unconscious [ʌn'kɔnʃəs] *adj* (*in faint*)

bewusstlos; (*unaware*): ~ **of** nicht bewusst
+*gen* ♦ *n:* **the** ~ das Unbewusste; **to knock sb**
~ jdn bewusstlos schlagen.
unconsciously [ʌn'kɔnʃəslɪ] *adv* unbewusst.
unconsciousness [ʌn'kɔnʃəsnɪs] *n*
Bewusstlosigkeit *f*.
unconstitutional ['ʌnkɔnstɪ'tjuːʃənl] *adj*
verfassungswidrig.
uncontested [ʌnkən'tɛstɪd] *adj* (POL: *seat,*
election) ohne Gegenkandidat; (*divorce*) ohne
Einwände der Gegenseite.
uncontrollable [ʌnkən'trəuləbl] *adj*
unkontrollierbar; (*laughter*) unbändig.
uncontrolled [ʌnkən'trəuld] *adj* (*behaviour*)
ungezähmt; (*price rises etc*) ungehindert.
unconventional [ʌnkən'vɛnʃənl] *adj*
unkonventionell.
unconvinced [ʌnkən'vɪnst] *adj:* **to be/remain**
~ nicht überzeugt sein/bleiben.
unconvincing [ʌnkən'vɪnsɪŋ] *adj* nicht
überzeugend.
uncork [ʌn'kɔːk] *vt* (*bottle*) entkorken.
uncorroborated [ʌnkə'rɔbəreɪtɪd] *adj*
(*evidence*) unbestätigt.
uncouth [ʌn'kuːθ] *adj* (*person, behaviour*)
ungehobelt.
uncover [ʌn'kʌvə*] *vt* aufdecken.
unctuous ['ʌŋktjuəs] (*form*) *adj* (*person,*
behaviour) salbungsvoll.
undamaged [ʌn'dæmɪdʒd] *adj* unbeschädigt.
undaunted [ʌn'dɔːntɪd] *adj* (*person*)
unverzagt; ~**, she struggled on** sie kämpfte
unverzagt weiter.
undecided [ʌndɪ'saɪdɪd] *adj* (*person*)
unentschlossen; (*question*) unentschieden.
undelivered [ʌndɪ'lɪvəd] *adj* (*goods*) nicht
geliefert; (*letters*) nicht zugestellt; **if**
~ **return to sender** (*on envelope*) falls
unzustellbar, zurück an Absender.
undeniable [ʌndɪ'naɪəbl] *adj* unbestreitbar.
undeniably [ʌndɪ'naɪəblɪ] *adv* (*true*) zweifellos;
(*handsome*) unbestreitbar.
under ['ʌndə*] *prep* (*position*) unter +*dat*;
(*motion*) unter +*acc*; (*according to: law etc*)
nach, gemäß +*dat* ♦ *adv* (*go, fly etc*) darunter;
to come from ~ **sth** unter etw *dat*
hervorkommen; ~ **there** darunter; **in** ~ **2**
hours in weniger als 2 Stunden; ~
~ **anaesthetic** unter Narkose; **to be**
~ **discussion** diskutiert werden; ~ **repair** in
Reparatur; ~ **the circumstances** unter den
Umständen.
under... ['ʌndə*] *pref* Unter-, unter-.
underage [ʌndər'eɪdʒ] *adj* (*person*)
minderjährig; ~ **drinking** Alkoholgenuss *m*
von Minderjährigen.
underarm ['ʌndərɑːm] *adv* (*bowl, throw*) von
unten ♦ *adj* (*throw, shot*) von unten;
(*deodorant*) Achselhöhlen-.
undercapitalized ['ʌndə'kæpɪtəlaɪzd] *adj*
unterkapitalisiert.
undercarriage ['ʌndəkærɪdʒ] *n* (AVIAT)

Fahrgestell *nt*.
undercharge [ʌndə'tʃɑːdʒ] *vt* zu wenig
berechnen +*dat*.
underclass ['ʌndəklɑːs] *n* Unterklasse *f*.
underclothes ['ʌndəkləuðz] *npl* Unterwäsche
f.
undercoat ['ʌndəkəut] *n* (*paint*) Grundierung
f.
undercover [ʌndə'kʌvə*] *adj* (*duty, agent*)
Geheim- ♦ *adv* (*work*) insgeheim.
undercurrent ['ʌndəkʌrnt] *n* (*also fig*)
Unterströmung *f*.
undercut [ʌndə'kʌt] (*irreg: like* **cut**) *vt* (*person,*
prices) unterbieten.
underdeveloped ['ʌndədɪ'vɛləpt] *adj*
unterentwickelt.
underdog ['ʌndədɔg] *n:* **the** ~ der/die
Benachteiligte.
underdone [ʌndə'dʌn] *adj* (*food*) nicht gar;
(: *meat*) nicht durchgebraten.
underemployment ['ʌndərɪm'plɔɪmənt] *n*
Unterbeschäftigung *f*.
underestimate ['ʌndər'ɛstɪmeɪt] *vt*
unterschätzen.
underexposed ['ʌndərɪks'pəuzd] *adj* (PHOT)
unterbelichtet.
underfed [ʌndə'fɛd] *adj* unterernährt.
underfoot [ʌndə'fut] *adv:* **to crush sth** ~ **etw**
am Boden zerdrücken; **to trample sth** ~ **auf**
etw *dat* herumtrampeln.
underfunded ['ʌndə'fʌndɪd] *adj*
unterfinanziert.
undergo [ʌndə'gəu] (*irreg: like* **go**) *vt* (*change*)
durchmachen; (*test, operation*) sich
unterziehen; **the car is** ~**ing repairs** das Auto
wird gerade repariert.
undergraduate [ʌndə'grædjuɪt] *n* Student(in)
m(f) ♦ *cpd:* ~ **courses** Kurse *pl* für
nichtgraduierte Studenten.
underground ['ʌndəgraund] *adj* unterirdisch;
(*POL: newspaper, activities*) Untergrund- ♦ *adv*
(*work*) unterirdisch; (: *miners*) unter Tage;
(*POL*): **to go** ~ untertauchen ♦ *n:* **the** ~
(BRIT) die U-Bahn; (*POL*) die
Untergrundbewegung; ~ **car park**
Tiefgarage *f*.
undergrowth ['ʌndəgrəuθ] *n* Unterholz *nt*.
underhand(ed) [ʌndə'hænd(ɪd)] *adj* (*fig:*
behaviour, person) hinterhältig.
underinsured [ʌndərɪn'ʃuəd] *adj*
unterversichert.
underlay [ʌndə'leɪ] *n* Unterlage *f*.
underlie [ʌndə'laɪ] (*irreg: like* **lie**) *vt* (*fig: be basis*
of) zugrunde *or* zu Grunde liegen +*dat*; **the**
underlying cause der eigentliche Grund.
underline [ʌndə'laɪn] *vt* unterstreichen; (*fig:*
emphasize) betonen.
underling ['ʌndəlɪŋ] (*pej*) *n*
Befehlsempfänger(in) *m(f)*.
undermanning [ʌndə'mænɪŋ] *n*
Personalmangel *m*.
undermentioned [ʌndə'mɛnʃənd] *adj* unten

genannt.

undermine [ʌndə'maın] vt unterminieren, unterhöhlen.

underneath [ʌndə'ni:θ] adv darunter ♦ prep (position) unter +dat; (motion) unter +acc.

undernourished [ʌndə'nʌrıʃt] adj unterernährt.

underpaid [ʌndə'peıd] adj unterbezahlt.

underpants ['ʌndəpænts] npl Unterhose f.

underpass ['ʌndəpɑːs] (BRIT) n Unterführung f.

underpin [ʌndə'pın] vt (argument) untermauern.

underplay [ʌndə'pleı] (BRIT) vt herunterspielen.

underpopulated [ʌndə'pɒpjuleıtıd] adj unterbevölkert.

underprice [ʌndə'praıs] vt (goods) zu billig anbieten.

underprivileged [ʌndə'prıvılıdʒd] adj unterprivilegiert.

underrate [ʌndə'reıt] vt unterschätzen.

underscore [ʌndə'skɔː'] vt unterstreichen.

underseal [ʌndə'siːl] (BRIT) vt (car) mit Unterbodenschutz versehen ♦ n (of car) Unterbodenschutz m.

undersecretary ['ʌndə'sekrətərı] n (POL) Staatssekretär(in) m(f).

undersell [ʌndə'sel] (irreg: like sell) vt (competitors) unterbieten.

undershirt ['ʌndəʃəːt] (US) n Unterhemd nt.

undershorts ['ʌndəʃɔːts] (US) npl Unterhose f.

underside ['ʌndəsaıd] n Unterseite f.

undersigned ['ʌndə'saınd] adj unterzeichnet ♦ n: the ~ der/die Unterzeichnete; we the ~ agree that ... wir, die Unterzeichneten, kommen überein, dass ...

underskirt ['ʌndəskəːt] (BRIT) n Unterrock m.

understaffed [ʌndə'stɑːft] adj unterbesetzt.

understand [ʌndə'stænd] (irreg: like stand) vt, vi verstehen; I ~ (that) you have ... (believe) soweit ich weiß, haben Sie ...; to make o.s. understood sich verständlich machen.

understandable [ʌndə'stændəbl] adj verständlich.

understanding [ʌndə'stændıŋ] adj verständnisvoll ♦ n Verständnis nt; to come to an ~ with sb mit jdm übereinkommen; on the ~ that ... unter der Voraussetzung, dass ...

understate [ʌndə'steıt] vt herunterspielen.

understatement ['ʌndəsteıtmənt] n Understatement nt, Untertreibung f; that's an ~! das ist untertrieben!

understood [ʌndə'stud] pt, pp of understand ♦ adj (agreed) abgemacht; (implied) impliziert.

understudy ['ʌndəstʌdı] n zweite Besetzung f.

undertake [ʌndə'teık] (irreg: like take) vt (task) übernehmen ♦ vi: to ~ to do sth es übernehmen, etw zu tun.

undertaker ['ʌndəteıkə'] n (Leichen)bestatter m.

undertaking ['ʌndəteıkıŋ] n (job) Unternehmen nt; (promise) Zusicherung f.

undertone ['ʌndətəun] n (of criticism etc) Unterton m; in an ~ mit gedämpfter Stimme.

undervalue [ʌndə'vælju:] vt (person, work etc) unterbewerten.

underwater [ʌndə'wɔːtə'] adv (swim etc) unter Wasser ♦ adj (exploration, camera etc) Unterwasser-.

underwear ['ʌndəweə'] n Unterwäsche f.

underweight [ʌndə'weıt] adj: to be ~ Untergewicht haben.

underworld ['ʌndəwəːld] n Unterwelt f.

underwrite [ʌndə'raıt] vt (FIN) garantieren; (INSURANCE) versichern.

underwriter ['ʌndəraıtə'] n (INSURANCE) Versicherer(in) m(f).

undeserved [ʌndı'zəːvd] adj unverdient.

undesirable [ʌndı'zaıərəbl] adj unerwünscht.

undeveloped [ʌndı'veləpt] adj (land) unentwickelt; (resources) ungenutzt.

undies ['ʌndız] (inf) npl Unterwäsche f.

undiluted ['ʌndaı'lu:tıd] adj (substance) unverdünnt; (emotion) unverfälscht.

undiplomatic ['ʌndıplə'mætık] adj undiplomatisch.

undischarged ['ʌndıs'tʃɑːdʒd] adj: ~ bankrupt nicht entlasteter Konkursschuldner m, nicht entlastete Konkursschuldnerin f.

undisciplined [ʌn'dısıplınd] adj undiszipliniert.

undiscovered ['ʌndıs'kʌvəd] adj unentdeckt.

undisguised ['ʌndıs'gaızd] adj (dislike, amusement etc) unverhohlen.

undisputed ['ʌndıs'pju:tıd] adj unbestritten.

undistinguished ['ʌndıs'tıŋgwıʃt] adj (career, person) mittelmäßig; (appearance) durchschnittlich.

undisturbed ['ʌndıs'təːbd] adj ungestört; to leave sth ~ etw unberührt lassen.

undivided [ʌndı'vaıdıd] adj: you have my ~ attention Sie haben meine ungeteilte Aufmerksamkeit.

undo [ʌn'du:] (irreg: like do) vt (unfasten) aufmachen; (spoil) zunichte machen.

undoing [ʌn'du:ıŋ] n Verderben nt.

undone [ʌn'dʌn] pp of undo ♦ adj: to come ~ (shoelaces etc) aufgehen.

undoubted [ʌn'dautıd] adj unzweifelhaft.

undoubtedly [ʌn'dautıdlı] adv zweifellos.

undress [ʌn'dres] vi sich ausziehen ♦ vt ausziehen.

undrinkable [ʌn'drıŋkəbl] adj (unpalatable) ungenießbar; (poisonous) nicht trinkbar.

undue [ʌn'dju:] adj (excessive) übertrieben.

undulating ['ʌndjuleıtıŋ] adj (movement) Wellen-; (hills) sanft.

unduly [ʌn'dju:lı] adv (excessively) übermäßig.

undying [ʌn'daıŋ] adj (love, loyalty etc) ewig.

unearned [ʌn'əːnd] adj (praise) unverdient;

~ **income** Kapitaleinkommen *nt*.

unearth [ʌn'ɔ:θ] *vt* (*skeleton etc*) ausgraben; (*fig: secrets etc*) ausfindig machen.

unearthly [ʌn'ɔ:θlɪ] *adj* (*eerie*) unheimlich; **at some ~ hour** zu nachtschlafender Zeit.

unease [ʌn'i:z] *n* Unbehagen *nt*.

uneasy [ʌn'i:zɪ] *adj* (*person*) unruhig; (*feeling*) unbehaglich; (*peace, truce*) unsicher; **to feel ~ about doing sth** ein ungutes Gefühl dabei haben, etw zu tun.

uneconomic ['ʌni:kə'nɒmɪk] *adj* unwirtschaftlich.

uneconomical ['ʌni:kə'nɒmɪkl] *adj* unwirtschaftlich.

uneducated [ʌn'ɛdjukeɪtɪd] *adj* ungebildet.

unemployed [ʌnɪm'plɔɪd] *adj* arbeitslos ♦ *npl*: **the ~** die Arbeitslosen *pl*.

unemployment [ʌnɪm'plɔɪmənt] *n* Arbeitslosigkeit *f*.

unemployment benefit (*BRIT*) *n* Arbeitslosenunterstützung *f*.

unemployment compensation (*US*) *n* = **unemployment benefit**.

unending [ʌn'ɛndɪŋ] *adj* endlos.

unenviable [ʌn'ɛnviəbl] *adj* (*task, conditions etc*) wenig beneidenswert.

unequal [ʌn'i:kwəl] *adj* ungleich; **to feel ~ to** sich nicht gewachsen fühlen +*dat*.

unequalled, (*US*) **unequaled** [ʌn'i:kwəld] *adj* unübertroffen.

unequivocal [ʌnɪ'kwɪvəkl] *adj* (*answer*) unzweideutig; **to be ~ about sth** eine klare Haltung zu etw haben.

unerring [ʌn'ɔ:rɪŋ] *adj* unfehlbar.

UNESCO [ju:'nɛskəu] *n abbr* (= *United Nations Educational, Scientific and Cultural Organization*) UNESCO *f*.

unethical [ʌn'ɛθɪkl] *adj* (*methods*) unlauter; (*doctor's behaviour*) unethisch.

uneven [ʌn'i:vn] *adj* (*teeth, road etc*) uneben; (*performance*) ungleichmäßig.

uneventful [ʌnɪ'vɛntful] *adj* ereignislos.

unexceptional [ʌnɪk'sɛpʃənl] *adj* durchschnittlich.

unexciting [ʌnɪk'saɪtɪŋ] *adj* (*film, news*) wenig aufregend.

unexpected [ʌnɪks'pɛktɪd] *adj* unerwartet.

unexpectedly [ʌnɪks'pɛktɪdlɪ] *adv* unerwartet.

unexplained [ʌnɪks'pleɪnd] *adj* (*mystery, failure*) ungeklärt.

unexploded [ʌnɪks'pləudɪd] *adj* nicht explodiert.

unfailing [ʌn'feɪlɪŋ] *adj* (*support, energy*) unerschöpflich.

unfair [ʌn'fɛə*] *adj* unfair, ungerecht; (*advantage*) ungerechtfertigt; ~ **to** unfair or ungerecht zu.

unfair dismissal *n* ungerechtfertigte Entlassung *f*.

unfairly [ʌn'fɛəlɪ] *adv* (*treat*) unfair, ungerecht; (*dismiss*) ungerechtfertigt.

unfaithful [ʌn'feɪθful] *adj* (*lover, spouse*) untreu.

unfamiliar [ʌnfə'mɪlɪə*] *adj* ungewohnt; (*person*) fremd; **to be ~ with sth** mit etw nicht vertraut sein.

unfashionable [ʌn'fæʃnəbl] *adj* (*clothes, ideas*) unmodern; (*place*) unbeliebt.

unfasten [ʌn'fɑ:sn] *vt* (*seat belt, strap*) lösen.

unfathomable [ʌn'fæðəməbl] *adj* unergründlich.

unfavourable, (*US*) **unfavorable** [ʌn'feɪvrəbl] *adj* (*circumstances, weather*) ungünstig; (*opinion, report*) negativ.

unfavourably, (*US*) **unfavorably** [ʌn'feɪvrəblɪ] *adv*: **to compare ~ (with sth)** im Vergleich (mit etw) ungünstig sein; **to compare ~ (with sb)** im Vergleich (mit jdm) schlechter abschneiden; **to look ~ on** (*suggestion etc*) ablehnend gegenüberstehen +*dat*.

unfeeling [ʌn'fi:lɪŋ] *adj* gefühllos.

unfinished [ʌn'fɪnɪʃt] *adj* unvollendet.

unfit [ʌn'fɪt] *adj* (*physically*) nicht fit; (*incompetent*) unfähig; ~ **for work** arbeitsunfähig; ~ **for human consumption** zum Verzehr ungeeignet.

unflagging [ʌn'flægɪŋ] *adj* (*attention, energy*) unermüdlich.

unflappable [ʌn'flæpəbl] *adj* unerschütterlich.

unflattering [ʌn'flætərɪŋ] *adj* (*dress, hairstyle*) unvorteilhaft; (*remark*) wenig schmeichelhaft.

unflinching [ʌn'flɪntʃɪŋ] *adj* unerschrocken.

unfold [ʌn'fəuld] *vt* (*sheets, map*) auseinander falten ♦ *vi* (*situation, story*) sich entfalten.

unforeseeable [ʌnfɔ:'si:əbl] *adj* unvorhersehbar.

unforeseen ['ʌnfɔ:'si:n] *adj* unvorhergesehen.

unforgettable [ʌnfə'gɛtəbl] *adj* unvergesslich.

unforgivable [ʌnfə'gɪvəbl] *adj* unverzeihlich.

unformatted [ʌn'fɔ:mætɪd] *adj* (*disk, text*) unformatiert.

unfortunate [ʌn'fɔ:tʃənət] *adj* (*unlucky*) unglücklich; (*regrettable*) bedauerlich; **it is ~ that ...** es ist bedauerlich, dass ...

unfortunately [ʌn'fɔ:tʃənətlɪ] *adv* leider.

unfounded [ʌn'faundɪd] *adj* (*allegations, fears*) unbegründet.

unfriendly [ʌn'frɛndlɪ] *adj* unfreundlich.

unfulfilled [ʌnful'fɪld] *adj* (*ambition, prophecy*) unerfüllt; (*person*) unausgefüllt.

unfurl [ʌn'fɔ:l] *vt* (*flag etc*) entrollen.

unfurnished [ʌn'fɔ:nɪʃt] *adj* unmöbliert.

ungainly [ʌn'geɪnlɪ] *adj* (*person*) unbeholfen.

ungodly [ʌn'gɒdlɪ] *adj* (*annoying*) heillos; **at some ~ hour** zu nachtschlafender Zeit.

ungrateful [ʌn'greɪtful] *adj* undankbar.

unguarded [ʌn'gɑ:dɪd] *adj*: **in an ~ moment** in einem unbedachten Augenblick.

unhappily [ʌn'hæpɪlɪ] *adv* (*miserably*) unglücklich; (*unfortunately*) leider.

unhappiness [ʌn'hæpɪnɪs] *n* Traurigkeit *f*.

unhappy [ʌnˈhæpɪ] adj unglücklich; ~ **about/ with** (dissatisfied) unzufrieden über $/ mit;+acc.

unharmed [ʌnˈhɑːmd] adj (person, animal) unversehrt.

UNHCR n abbr (= United Nations High Commission for Refugees) Flüchtlingskommission der Vereinten Nationen.

unhealthy [ʌnˈhɛlθɪ] adj (person) nicht gesund; (place) ungesund; (fig: interest) krankhaft.

unheard-of [ʌnˈhɜːdɔv] adj (unknown) unbekannt; (outrageous) unerhört.

unhelpful [ʌnˈhɛlpful] adj (person) nicht hilfreich; (advice) nutzlos.

unhesitating [ʌnˈhɛzɪteɪtɪŋ] adj (loyalty) bereitwillig; (reply, offer) prompt.

unholy [ʌnˈhəulɪ] (inf) adj (fig: alliance) übel; (: mess) heillos; (: row) furchtbar.

unhook [ʌnˈhuk] vt (unfasten) losmachen.

unhurt [ʌnˈhɜːt] adj unverletzt.

unhygienic [ˈʌnhaɪˈdʒiːnɪk] adj unhygienisch.

UNICEF [ˈjuːnɪsɛf] n abbr (= United Nations International Children's Emergency Fund) UNICEF f.

unicorn [ˈjuːnɪkɔːn] n Einhorn nt.

unidentified [ʌnaɪˈdɛntɪfaɪd] adj (unknown) unbekannt; (unnamed) ungenannt; see also UFO.

unification [juːnɪfɪˈkeɪʃən] n Vereinigung f.

uniform [ˈjuːnɪfɔːm] n Uniform f ♦ adj (length, width etc) einheitlich.

uniformity [juːnɪˈfɔːmɪtɪ] n Einheitlichkeit f.

unify [ˈjuːnɪfaɪ] vt vereinigen.

unilateral [juːnɪˈlætərəl] adj einseitig.

unimaginable [ʌnɪˈmædʒɪnəbl] adj unvorstellbar.

unimaginative [ʌnɪˈmædʒɪnətɪv] adj fantasielos.

unimpaired [ʌnɪmˈpɛəd] adj unbeeinträchtigt.

unimportant [ʌnɪmˈpɔːtənt] adj unwichtig.

unimpressed [ʌnɪmˈprɛst] adj unbeeindruckt.

uninhabited [ʌnɪnˈhæbɪtɪd] adj unbewohnt.

uninhibited [ʌnɪnˈhɪbɪtɪd] adj (person) ohne Hemmungen; (behaviour) hemmungslos.

uninjured [ʌnˈɪndʒəd] adj unverletzt.

uninspiring [ʌnɪnˈspaɪərɪŋ] adj wenig aufregend; (person) trocken, nüchtern.

unintelligent [ʌnɪnˈtɛlɪdʒənt] adj unintelligent.

unintentional [ʌnɪnˈtɛnʃənəl] adj unbeabsichtigt.

unintentionally [ʌnɪnˈtɛnʃnəlɪ] adv unabsichtlich.

uninvited [ʌnɪnˈvaɪtɪd] adj (guest) ungeladen.

uninviting [ʌnɪnˈvaɪtɪŋ] adj (food) unappetitlich; (place) wenig einladend.

union [ˈjuːnjən] n (unification) Vereinigung f; (also: **trade** ~) Gewerkschaft f ♦ cpd (activities, leader etc) Gewerkschafts-; **the U~** (US) die Vereinigten Staaten.

unionize [ˈjuːnjənaɪz] vt (employees) gewerkschaftlich organisieren.

Union Jack n Union Jack m.

union shop n gewerkschaftspflichtiger Betrieb m.

unique [juːˈniːk] adj (object etc) einmalig; (ability, skill) einzigartig; **to be ~ to** charakteristisch sein für.

unisex [ˈjuːnɪsɛks] adj (clothes) Unisex-; (hairdresser) für Damen und Herren.

UNISON [ˈjuːnɪsn] n Gewerkschaft der Angestellten im öffentlichen Dienst.

unison [ˈjuːnɪsn] n: **in ~** (say, sing) einstimmig; (act) in Übereinstimmung.

unit [ˈjuːnɪt] n Einheit f; **production ~** Produktionsabteilung f; **kitchen ~** Küchen-Einbauelement nt.

unitary [ˈjuːnɪtrɪ] adj (state, system etc) einheitlich.

unit cost n (COMM) Stückkosten pl.

unite [juːˈnaɪt] vt vereinigen ♦ vi sich zusammenschließen.

united [juːˈnaɪtɪd] adj (agreed) einig; (country, party) vereinigt.

United Arab Emirates npl: **the ~** die Vereinigten Arabischen Emirate pl.

United Kingdom n: **the ~** das Vereinigte Königreich.

United Nations npl: **the ~** die Vereinten Nationen pl.

United States (of America) n: **the ~** die Vereinigten Staaten pl (von Amerika).

unit price n (COMM) Einzelpreis m.

unit trust (BRIT) n (COMM) Investmenttrust m.

unity [ˈjuːnɪtɪ] n Einheit f.

Univ. abbr = university.

universal [juːnɪˈvɜːsl] adj allgemein.

universe [ˈjuːnɪvɜːs] n Universum nt.

university [juːnɪˈvɜːsɪtɪ] n Universität f ♦ cpd (student, professor) Universitäts-; (education, year) akademisch.

university degree n Universitätsabschluss m.

unjust [ʌnˈdʒʌst] adj ungerecht; (society) unfair.

unjustifiable [ˈʌndʒʌstɪˈfaɪəbl] adj nicht zu rechtfertigen.

unjustified [ʌnˈdʒʌstɪfaɪd] adj (belief, action) ungerechtfertigt; (text) nicht bündig.

unkempt [ʌnˈkɛmpt] adj ungepflegt.

unkind [ʌnˈkaɪnd] adj (person, comment etc) unfreundlich.

unkindly [ʌnˈkaɪndlɪ] adv unfreundlich.

unknown [ʌnˈnəun] adj unbekannt; **~ to me,** ... ohne dass ich es wusste, ...; **~ quantity** (fig) unbekannte Größe.

unladen [ʌnˈleɪdn] adj (ship) ohne Ladung; (weight) Leer-.

unlawful [ʌnˈlɔːful] adj gesetzwidrig.

unleaded [ʌnˈlɛdɪd] adj (petrol) bleifrei, unverbleit; **I use ~** ich fahre bleifrei.

unleash [ʌnˈliːʃ] *vt* (*fig: feeling, forces etc*) entfesseln.

unleavened [ʌnˈlɛvnd] *adj* (*bread*) ungesäuert.

unless [ʌnˈlɛs] *conj* es sei denn; ~ **he comes** wenn er nicht kommt; ~ **otherwise stated** wenn nicht anders angegeben; ~ **I am mistaken** wenn ich mich nicht irre; **there will be a strike** ~ ... es wird zum Streik kommen, es sei denn, ...

unlicensed [ʌnˈlaɪsnst] (*BRIT*) *adj* (*restaurant*) ohne Schankkonzession.

unlike [ʌnˈlaɪk] *adj* (*not alike*) unähnlich ♦ *prep* (*different from*) verschieden von; ~ **me, she is very tidy** im Gegensatz zu mir ist sie sehr ordentlich.

unlikelihood [ʌnˈlaɪklɪhud] *n* Unwahrscheinlichkeit *f*.

unlikely [ʌnˈlaɪklɪ] *adj* unwahrscheinlich; (*combination etc*) merkwürdig; **in the** ~ **event of/that** ... im unwahrscheinlichen Fall +*gen*/dass ...

unlimited [ʌnˈlɪmɪtɪd] *adj* unbeschränkt.

unlisted [ˈʌnˈlɪstɪd] *adj* (*STOCK EXCHANGE*) nicht notiert; (*US: TEL*): **to be** ~ nicht im Telefonbuch stehen.

unlit [ʌnˈlɪt] *adj* (*room etc*) unbeleuchtet.

unload [ʌnˈləud] *vt* (*box etc*) ausladen; (*car etc*) entladen.

unlock [ʌnˈlɒk] *vt* aufschließen.

unlucky [ʌnˈlʌkɪ] *adj* (*object*) Unglück bringend; (*number*) Unglücks-; **to be** ~ (*person*) Pech haben.

unmanageable [ʌnˈmænɪdʒəbl] *adj* (*tool, vehicle*) kaum zu handhaben; (*person, hair*) widerspenstig; (*situation*) unkontrollierbar.

unmanned [ʌnˈmænd] *adj* (*station, spacecraft etc*) unbemannt.

unmarked [ʌnˈmɑːkt] *adj* (*unstained*) fleckenlos; (*unscarred*) nicht gezeichnet; (*unblemished*) makellos; ~ **police car** nicht gekennzeichneter Streifenwagen *m*.

unmarried [ʌnˈmærɪd] *adj* unverheiratet.

unmarried mother *n* ledige Mutter *f*.

unmask [ʌnˈmɑːsk] *vt* (*reveal*) enthüllen.

unmatched [ʌnˈmætʃt] *adj* unübertroffen.

unmentionable [ʌnˈmɛnʃnəbl] *adj* (*topic, word*) Tabu-; **to be** ~ tabu sein.

unmerciful [ʌnˈməːsɪful] *adj* erbarmungslos.

unmistak(e)able [ʌnmɪsˈteɪkəbl] *adj* unverkennbar.

unmistak(e)ably [ʌnmɪsˈteɪkəblɪ] *adv* unverkennbar.

unmitigated [ʌnˈmɪtɪgeɪtɪd] *adj* (*disaster etc*) total.

unnamed [ʌnˈneɪmd] *adj* (*nameless*) namenlos; (*anonymous*) ungenannt.

unnatural [ʌnˈnætʃrəl] *adj* unnatürlich; (*against nature: habit*) widernatürlich.

unnecessarily [ʌnˈnɛsəsərɪlɪ] *adv* (*worry etc*) unnötigerweise; (*severe etc*) übertrieben.

unnecessary [ʌnˈnɛsəsərɪ] *adj* unnötig.

unnerve [ʌnˈnəːv] *vt* entnerven.

unnoticed [ʌnˈnəutɪst] *adj*: **to go** *or* **pass** ~ unbemerkt bleiben.

UNO [ˈjuːnəu] *n abbr* (= *United Nations Organization*) UNO *f*.

unobservant [ʌnəbˈzəːvənt] *adj* unaufmerksam.

unobtainable [ʌnəbˈteɪnəbl] *adj* (*item*) nicht erhältlich; **this number is** ~ (*TEL*) kein Anschluss unter dieser Nummer.

unobtrusive [ʌnəbˈtruːsɪv] *adj* unauffällig.

unoccupied [ʌnˈɒkjupaɪd] *adj* (*seat*) frei; (*house*) leer (stehend).

unofficial [ʌnəˈfɪʃl] *adj* inoffiziell.

unopened [ʌnˈəupənd] *adj* ungeöffnet.

unopposed [ʌnəˈpəuzd] *adj*: **to be** ~ (*suggestion*) nicht auf Widerstand treffen; (*motion, bill*) ohne Gegenstimmen angenommen werden.

unorthodox [ʌnˈɔːθədɒks] *adj* (*also REL*) unorthodox.

unpack [ʌnˈpæk] *vt*, *vi* auspacken.

unpaid [ʌnˈpeɪd] *adj* unbezahlt.

unpalatable [ʌnˈpælətəbl] *adj* (*meal*) ungenießbar; (*truth*) bitter.

unparalleled [ʌnˈpærəleld] *adj* beispiellos.

unpatriotic [ˈʌnpætrɪˈɒtɪk] *adj* unpatriotisch.

unplanned [ʌnˈplænd] *adj* ungeplant.

unpleasant [ʌnˈplɛznt] *adj* unangenehm; (*person, manner*) unfreundlich.

unplug [ʌnˈplʌg] *vt* (*iron, record player etc*) den Stecker herausziehen +*gen*.

unpolluted [ʌnpəˈluːtɪd] *adj* unverschmutzt.

unpopular [ʌnˈpɒpjulə*] *adj* unpopulär; **to make o.s.** ~ (**with**) sich unbeliebt machen (bei).

unprecedented [ʌnˈprɛsɪdəntɪd] *adj* noch nie da gewesen; (*decision*) einmalig.

unpredictable [ʌnprɪˈdɪktəbl] *adj* (*person, weather*) unberechenbar; (*reaction*) unvorhersehbar.

unprejudiced [ʌnˈprɛdʒudɪst] *adj* unvoreingenommen.

unprepared [ʌnprɪˈpɛəd] *adj* unvorbereitet.

unprepossessing [ˈʌnpriːpəˈzɛsɪŋ] *adj* (*person, place*) unattraktiv.

unpretentious [ʌnprɪˈtɛnʃəs] *adj* (*building, person*) schlicht.

unprincipled [ʌnˈprɪnsɪpld] *adj* (*person*) charakterlos.

unproductive [ʌnprəˈdʌktɪv] *adj* (*land*) unfruchtbar, ertragsarm; (*discussion*) unproduktiv.

unprofessional [ʌnprəˈfɛʃənl] *adj* unprofessionell.

unprofitable [ʌnˈprɒfɪtəbl] *adj* nicht profitabel, unrentabel.

UNPROFOR *n abbr* (= *United Nations Protection Force*) UNPROFOR *f*; ~ **troops** UNPROFOR-Truppen, UNO-Schutztruppen.

unprotected [ˈʌnprəˈtɛktɪd] *adj* ungeschützt.

unprovoked [ʌnprəˈvəukt] *adj* (*attack*) grundlos.

unpunished [ʌn'pʌnɪʃt] *adj*: **to go ~** straflos bleiben.

unqualified [ʌn'kwɔlɪfaɪd] *adj* unqualifiziert; (*disaster, success*) vollkommen.

unquestionably [ʌn'kwɛstʃənəblɪ] *adv* fraglos.

unquestioning [ʌn'kwɛstʃənɪŋ] *adj* bedingungslos.

unravel [ʌn'rævl] *vt* (*also fig*) entwirren.

unreal [ʌn'rɪəl] *adj* (*artificial*) unecht; (*peculiar*) unwirklich.

unrealistic ['ʌnrɪə'lɪstɪk] *adj* unrealistisch.

unreasonable [ʌn'riːznəbl] *adj* (*person, attitude*) unvernünftig; (*demand, length of time*) unzumutbar.

unrecognizable [ʌn'rɛkəgnaɪzəbl] *adj* nicht zu erkennen.

unrecognized [ʌn'rɛkəgnaɪzd] *adj* (*talent etc*) unerkannt; (*POL: regime*) nicht anerkannt.

unreconstructed ['ʌnriːkən'strʌktɪd] (*esp US*) *adj* (*unwilling to accept change*) unverbesserlich.

unrecorded [ʌnrə'kɔːdɪd] *adj* (*piece of music etc*) nicht aufgenommen; (*incident, statement*) nicht schriftlich festgehalten.

unrefined [ʌnrə'faɪnd] *adj* (*sugar, petroleum*) nicht raffiniert.

unrehearsed [ʌnrɪ'həːst] *adj* (*THEAT etc*) nicht geprobt; (*spontaneous*) spontan.

unrelated [ʌnrɪ'leɪtɪd] *adj* (*incidents*) ohne Beziehung; (*people*) nicht verwandt.

unrelenting [ʌnrɪ'lɛntɪŋ] *adj* (*person, behaviour etc*) unnachgiebig.

unreliable [ʌnrɪ'laɪəbl] *adj* unzuverlässig.

unrelieved [ʌnrɪ'liːvd] *adj* ungemindert.

unremitting [ʌnrɪ'mɪtɪŋ] *adj* (*efforts, attempts*) unermüdlich.

unrepeatable [ʌnrɪ'piːtəbl] *adj* (*offer*) einmalig; (*comment*) nicht wiederholbar.

unrepentant [ʌnrɪ'pɛntənt] *adj*: **to be ~ about sth** etw nicht bereuen; **he's an ~ Marxist** er bereut es nicht, nach wie vor Marxist zu sein.

unrepresentative ['ʌnrɛprɪ'zɛntətɪv] *adj*: **~ (of)** nicht repräsentativ (für).

unrepresented ['ʌnrɛprɪ'zɛntɪd] *adj* nicht vertreten.

unreserved [ʌnrɪ'zəːvd] *adj* (*seat*) unreserviert; (*approval etc*) uneingeschränkt, vorbehaltlos.

unreservedly [ʌnrɪ'zəːvɪdlɪ] *adv* ohne Vorbehalt.

unresponsive [ʌnrɪs'pɔnsɪv] *adj* unempfänglich.

unrest [ʌn'rɛst] *n* Unruhen *pl*.

unrestricted [ʌnrɪ'strɪktɪd] *adj* unbeschränkt; **to have ~ access to** ungehinderten Zugang haben zu.

unrewarded [ʌnrɪ'wɔːdɪd] *adj* unbelohnt.

unripe [ʌn'raɪp] *adj* unreif.

unrivalled, (*US*) **unrivaled** [ʌn'raɪvəld] *adj* unübertroffen.

unroll [ʌn'rəʊl] *vt* entrollen ♦ *vi* sich entrollen.

unruffled [ʌn'rʌfld] *adj* unbewegt; (*hair*) unzerzaust.

unruly [ʌn'ruːlɪ] *adj* (*child, behaviour*) ungebärdig; (*hair*) widerspenstig.

unsafe [ʌn'seɪf] *adj* unsicher; (*machine, bridge, car etc*) gefährlich; **~ to eat/drink** ungenießbar.

unsaid [ʌn'sɛd] *adj*: **to leave sth ~** etw ungesagt lassen.

unsaleable, (*US*) **unsalable** [ʌn'seɪləbl] *adj* unverkäuflich.

unsatisfactory ['ʌnsætɪs'fæktərɪ] *adj* unbefriedigend.

unsatisfied [ʌn'sætɪsfaɪd] *adj* unzufrieden.

unsavoury, (*US*) **unsavory** [ʌn'seɪvərɪ] *adj* (*fig: person, place*) widerwärtig.

unscathed [ʌn'skeɪðd] *adj* unversehrt.

unscientific ['ʌnsaɪən'tɪfɪk] *adj* unwissenschaftlich.

unscrew [ʌn'skruː] *vt* losschrauben.

unscrupulous [ʌn'skruːpjʊləs] *adj* skrupellos.

unseat [ʌn'siːt] *vt* (*rider*) abwerfen; (*from office*) aus dem Amt drängen.

unsecured ['ʌnsɪ'kjʊəd] *adj*: **~ creditor** nicht gesicherter Gläubiger *m*; **~ loan** Blankokredit *m*.

unseeded [ʌn'siːdɪd] *adj* (*player*) nicht gesetzt.

unseemly [ʌn'siːmlɪ] *adj* unschicklich.

unseen [ʌn'siːn] *adj* (*person, danger*) unsichtbar.

unselfish [ʌn'sɛlfɪʃ] *adj* selbstlos.

unsettled [ʌn'sɛtld] *adj* (*person*) unruhig; (*future*) unsicher; (*question*) ungeklärt; (*weather*) unbeständig.

unsettling [ʌn'sɛtlɪŋ] *adj* beunruhigend.

unshak(e)able [ʌn'ʃeɪkəbl] *adj* unerschütterlich.

unshaven [ʌn'ʃeɪvn] *adj* unrasiert.

unsightly [ʌn'saɪtlɪ] *adj* unansehnlich.

unskilled [ʌn'skɪld] *adj* (*work, worker*) ungelernt.

unsociable [ʌn'səʊʃəbl] *adj* ungesellig.

unsocial [ʌn'səʊʃl] *adj*: **to work ~ hours** außerhalb der normalen Arbeitszeit arbeiten.

unsold [ʌn'səʊld] *adj* unverkauft.

unsolicited [ʌnsə'lɪsɪtɪd] *adj* unerbeten.

unsophisticated [ʌnsə'fɪstɪkeɪtɪd] *adj* (*person*) anspruchslos; (*method, device*) simpel.

unsound [ʌn'saʊnd] *adj* (*floor, foundations*) unsicher; (*policy, advice*) unklug; **of ~ mind** unzurechnungsfähig.

unspeakable [ʌn'spiːkəbl] *adj* (*indescribable*) unsagbar; (*awful*) abscheulich.

unspoken [ʌn'spəʊkn] *adj* (*word*) unausgesprochen; (*agreement etc*) stillschweigend.

unstable [ʌn'steɪbl] *adj* (*piece of furniture*) nicht stabil; (*government*) instabil; (*person: mentally*) labil.

unsteady [ʌn'stɛdɪ] *adj* (*step, voice, legs*)

unsicher; (*ladder*) wack(e)lig.

unstinting [ʌn'stɪntɪŋ] *adj* (*support*) vorbehaltlos; (*generosity*) unbegrenzt.

unstuck [ʌn'stʌk] *adj*: **to come** ~ (*label etc*) sich lösen; (*fig: plan, idea etc*) versagen.

unsubstantiated ['ʌnsəb'stænʃɪeɪtɪd] *adj* (*rumour*) unbestätigt; (*accusation*) unbegründet.

unsuccessful [ʌnsək'sɛsful] *adj* erfolglos; (*marriage*) gescheitert; **to be** ~ keinen Erfolg haben.

unsuccessfully [ʌnsək'sɛsfəlɪ] *adv* ohne Erfolg, vergeblich.

unsuitable [ʌn'su:təbl] *adj* (*time*) unpassend; (*clothes, person*) ungeeignet.

unsuited [ʌn'su:tɪd] *adj*: **to be** ~ **for** *or* **to sth** für etw ungeeignet sein.

unsung ['ʌnsʌŋ] *adj*: **an** ~ **hero** ein unbesungener Held.

unsure [ʌn'ʃuə*] *adj* unsicher; **to be** ~ **of o.s.** unsicher sein.

unsuspecting [ʌnsəs'pɛktɪŋ] *adj* ahnungslos.

unsweetened [ʌn'swi:tnd] *adj* ungesüßt.

unswerving [ʌn'swɜ:vɪŋ] *adj* unerschütterlich.

unsympathetic ['ʌnsɪmpə'θɛtɪk] *adj* (*showing little understanding*) abweisend; (*unlikeable*) unsympathisch; **to be** ~ **to(wards) sth** einer Sache *dat* ablehnend gegenüberstehen.

untangle [ʌn'tæŋgl] *vt* entwirren.

untapped [ʌn'tæpt] *adj* (*resources*) ungenutzt.

untaxed [ʌn'tækst] *adj* (*goods, income*) steuerfrei.

unthinkable [ʌn'θɪŋkəbl] *adj* undenkbar.

unthinking [ʌn'θɪŋkɪŋ] *adj* (*uncritical*) bedenkenlos; (*thoughtless*) gedankenlos.

untidy [ʌn'taɪdɪ] *adj* unordentlich.

untie [ʌn'taɪ] *vt* (*knot, parcel*) aufschnüren; (*prisoner, dog*) losbinden.

until [ən'tɪl] *prep* bis +*acc*; (*after negative*) vor +*dat* ♦ *conj* bis jetzt; (*after negative*) bevor; ~ **now** bis jetzt; ~ **then** bis dann; **from morning** ~ **night** von morgens bis abends; ~ **he comes** bis er kommt.

untimely [ʌn'taɪmlɪ] *adj* (*moment*) unpassend; (*arrival*) ungelegen; (*death*) vorzeitig.

untold [ʌn'təuld] *adj* (*joy, suffering, wealth*) unermesslich; **the** ~ **story** die Hintergründe.

untouched [ʌn'tʌtʃt] *adj* unberührt; (*undamaged*) unversehrt; ~ **by** (*unaffected*) unberührt von.

untoward [ʌntə'wɔːd] *adj* (*events, effects etc*) ungünstig.

untrained ['ʌn'treɪnd] *adj* unausgebildet; (*eye, hands*) ungeschult.

untrammelled [ʌn'træmld] *adj* (*person*) ungebunden; (*behaviour*) unbeschränkt.

untranslatable [ʌntrænz'leɪtəbl] *adj* unübersetzbar.

untried [ʌn'traɪd] *adj* (*policy, remedy*) unerprobt; (*prisoner*) noch nicht vor Gericht gestellt.

untrue [ʌn'tru:] *adj* unwahr.

untrustworthy [ʌn'trʌstwɜ:ðɪ] *adj* unzuverlässig.

unusable [ʌn'ju:zəbl] *adj* (*object*) unbrauchbar; (*room*) nicht benutzbar.

unused[1] [ʌn'ju:zd] *adj* (*new*) unbenutzt.

unused[2] [ʌn'ju:st] *adj*: **to be** ~ **to sth** an etw *acc* nicht gewöhnt sein; **to be** ~ **to doing sth** nicht daran gewöhnt sein, etw zu tun.

unusual [ʌn'ju:ʒuəl] *adj* ungewöhnlich; (*exceptional*) außergewöhnlich.

unusually [ʌn'ju:ʒuəlɪ] *adv* (*large, high etc*) ungewöhnlich.

unveil [ʌn'veɪl] *vt* (*also fig*) enthüllen.

unwanted [ʌn'wɔntɪd] *adj* unerwünscht.

unwarranted [ʌn'wɔrəntɪd] *adj* ungerechtfertigt.

unwary [ʌn'wɛərɪ] *adj* unachtsam.

unwavering [ʌn'weɪvərɪŋ] *adj* (*faith, support*) unerschütterlich; (*gaze*) fest.

unwelcome [ʌn'wɛlkəm] *adj* (*guest*) unwillkommen; (*news*) unerfreulich; **to feel** ~ sich nicht willkommen fühlen.

unwell [ʌn'wɛl] *adj*: **to be** ~, **to feel** ~ sich nicht wohl fühlen.

unwieldy [ʌn'wi:ldɪ] *adj* (*object*) unhandlich; (*system*) schwerfällig.

unwilling [ʌn'wɪlɪŋ] *adj*: **to be** ~ **to do sth** etw nicht tun wollen.

unwillingly [ʌn'wɪlɪŋlɪ] *adv* widerwillig.

unwind [ʌn'waɪnd] (*irreg: like* **wind**) *vt* abwickeln ♦ *vi* sich abwickeln; (*relax*) sich entspannen.

unwise [ʌn'waɪz] *adj* unklug.

unwitting [ʌn'wɪtɪŋ] *adj* (*accomplice*) unwissentlich; (*victim*) ahnungslos.

unworkable [ʌn'wɜ:kəbl] *adj* (*plan*) undurchführbar.

unworthy [ʌn'wɜ:ðɪ] *adj* unwürdig; **to be** ~ **of sth** einer Sache *gen* nicht wert *or* würdig sein; **to be** ~ **to do sth** es nicht wert sein, etw zu tun; **that remark is** ~ **of you** diese Bemerkung ist unter deiner Würde.

unwrap [ʌn'ræp] *vt* auspacken.

unwritten [ʌn'rɪtn] *adj* (*law*) ungeschrieben; (*agreement*) stillschweigend.

unzip [ʌn'zɪp] *vt* aufmachen.

================================= *KEYWORD*

up [ʌp] *prep*: **to be** ~ **sth** (oben) auf etw *dat* sein; **to go** ~ **sth** (auf) etw *acc* hinaufgehen; **go** ~ **that road and turn left** gehen Sie die Straße hinauf und biegen Sie links ab ♦ *adv* **1** (*upwards, higher*) oben; **put it a bit higher** ~ stelle es etwas höher; ~ **there** dort oben; ~ **above** hoch oben.

2: **to be** ~ (*out of bed*) auf sein; (*prices, level*) gestiegen sein; (*building, tent*) stehen; **time's** ~ die Zeit ist um *or* vorbei.

3: ~ **to** (*as far as*) bis; ~ **to now** bis jetzt.

4: **to be** ~ **to** (*depending on*) abhängen von;

it's ~ **to you** das hängt von dir ab; **it's not** ~ **to me to decide** es liegt nicht bei mir, das zu entscheiden.

5: to be ~ **to** (*equal to*) gewachsen sein +*dat*; **he's not** ~ **to it** (*job, task etc*) er ist dem nicht gewachsen; **his work is not** ~ **to the required standard** seine Arbeit entspricht nicht dem gewünschten Niveau.

6: to be ~ **to** (*inf: be doing*) vorhaben; **what is he** ~ **to?** (*showing disapproval, suspicion*) was führt er im Schilde?

♦ *n*: ~**s and downs** (*in life, career*) Höhen und Tiefen *pl*

♦ *vi* (*inf*): **she** ~**ped and left** sie sprang auf und rannte davon

♦ *vt* (*inf: price*) heraufsetzen.

up-and-coming [ʌpənd'kʌmɪŋ] *adj* (*actor, company etc*) kommend.

upbeat ['ʌpbiːt] *n* (*MUS*) Auftakt *m*; (*in economy etc*) Aufschwung *m* ♦ *adj* (*optimistic*) optimistisch.

upbraid [ʌp'breɪd] *vt* tadeln.

upbringing ['ʌpbrɪŋɪŋ] *n* Erziehung *f*.

upcoming ['ʌpkʌmɪŋ] (*esp US*) *adj* kommend.

update [ʌp'deɪt] *vt* aktualisieren.

upend [ʌp'ɛnd] *vt* auf den Kopf stellen.

upfront [ʌp'frʌnt] *adj* (*person*) offen ♦ *adv*: **20%** ~ **20%** (als) Vorschuss, 20% im Voraus.

upgrade [ʌp'greɪd] *vt* (*house*) Verbesserungen durchführen in +*dat*; (*job*) verbessern; (*employee*) befördern; (*COMPUT*) nachrüsten.

upheaval [ʌp'hiːvl] *n* Unruhe *f*.

uphill ['ʌp'hɪl] *adj* bergaufwärts (führend); (*fig: task*) mühsam ♦ *adv* (*push, move*) bergaufwärts; (*go*) bergauf.

uphold [ʌp'həuld] (*irreg: like* hold) *vt* (*law, principle*) wahren; (*decision*) unterstützen.

upholstery [ʌp'həulstərɪ] *n* Polsterung *f*.

upkeep ['ʌpkiːp] *n* (*maintenance*) Instandhaltung *f*.

up-market [ʌp'maːkɪt] *adj* anspruchsvoll.

upon [ə'pɒn] *prep* (*position*) auf +*dat*; (*motion*) auf +*acc*.

upper ['ʌpə*] *adj* obere(r, s) ♦ *n* (*of shoe*) Oberleder *nt*.

upper class *n*: **the** ~ die Oberschicht.

upper-class ['ʌpə'klaːs] *adj* vornehm.

uppercut ['ʌpəkʌt] *n* Uppercut *m*.

upper hand *n*: **to have the** ~ die Oberhand haben.

Upper House *n* (*POL*) Oberhaus *nt*.

uppermost ['ʌpəməust] *adj* oberste(r, s); **what was** ~ **in my mind** woran ich in erster Linie dachte.

Upper Volta [-'vɔltə] *n* (*formerly*) Obervolta *nt*.

upright ['ʌpraɪt] *adj* (*vertical*) vertikal; (*fig: honest*) rechtschaffen ♦ *adv* (*sit, stand*) aufrecht ♦ *n* (*CONSTR*) Pfosten *m*.

uprising ['ʌpraɪzɪŋ] *n* Aufstand *m*.

uproar ['ʌprɔː*] *n* Aufruhr *m*.

uproarious [ʌp'rɔːrɪəs] *adj* (*laughter*) brüllend; (*joke*) brüllend komisch; (*mirth*) überwältigend.

uproot [ʌp'ruːt] *vt* (*tree*) entwurzeln; (*fig: people*) aus der gewohnten Umgebung reißen; (: *in war etc*) entwurzeln.

upset [*vt, adj* ʌp'sɛt, *n* 'ʌpsɛt] (*irreg: like* set) *vt* (*knock over*) umstoßen; (*person: offend, make unhappy*) verletzen; (*routine, plan*) durcheinander bringen ♦ *adj* (*unhappy*) aufgebracht; (*stomach*) verstimmt ♦ *n*: **to have/get a stomach** ~ (*BRIT*) eine Magenverstimmung haben/bekommen; **to get** ~ sich aufregen.

upset price ['ʌpsɛt-] (*US, SCOT*) *n* Mindestpreis *m*.

upsetting [ʌp'sɛtɪŋ] *adj* (*distressing*) erschütternd.

upshot ['ʌpʃɒt] *n* Ergebnis *nt*; **the** ~ **of it all was that** ... es lief schließlich darauf hinaus, dass ...

upside down ['ʌpsaɪd-] *adv* verkehrt herum; **to turn a room** ~ (*fig*) ein Zimmer auf den Kopf stellen.

upstage ['ʌp'steɪdʒ] *adv* (*THEAT*) im Bühnenhintergrund ♦ *vt*: **to** ~ **sb** (*fig*) jdn ausstechen, jdm die Schau stehlen (*inf*).

upstairs [ʌp'stɛəz] *adv* (*be*) oben; (*go*) nach oben ♦ *adj* (*room*) obere(r, s); (*window*) im oberen Stock ♦ *n* oberes Stockwerk *nt*; **there's no** ~ das Haus hat kein Obergeschoss.

upstart ['ʌpstaːt] (*pej*) *n* Emporkömmling *m*.

upstream [ʌp'striːm] *adv, adj* flussaufwärts.

upsurge ['ʌpsəːdʒ] *n* (*of enthusiasm etc*) Schwall *m*.

uptake ['ʌpteɪk] *n*: **to be quick on the** ~ schnell kapieren; **to be slow on the** ~ schwer von Begriff sein.

uptight [ʌp'taɪt] (*inf*) *adj* nervös.

up-to-date ['ʌptə'deɪt] *adj* (*modern*) modern; (*person*) up to date.

upturn ['ʌptəːn] *n* (*in economy*) Aufschwung *m*.

upturned ['ʌptəːnd] *adj*: ~ **nose** Stupsnase *f*.

upward ['ʌpwəd] *adj* (*movement*) Aufwärts-; (*glance*) nach oben gerichtet.

upwardly mobile ['ʌpwədlɪ-] *adj*: **to be** ~ ein Aufsteigertyp *m* sein.

upwards ['ʌpwədz] *adv* (*move*) aufwärts; (*glance*) nach oben; **upward(s) of** (*more than*) über +*acc*.

URA (*US*) *n abbr* (= *Urban Renewal Administration*) Stadtsanierungsbehörde *f*.

Ural Mountains ['juərəl-] *npl*: **the** ~ (*also*: **the Urals**) der Ural.

uranium [juə'reɪnɪəm] *n* Uran *nt*.

Uranus [juə'reɪnəs] *n* Uranus *m*.

urban ['əːbən] *adj* städtisch; (*unemployment*) in den Städten.

urbane [əː'beɪn] *adj* weltgewandt.

urbanization ['ɔːbənaɪ'zeɪʃən] *n*
Urbanisierung *f*, Verstädterung *f*.

urchin ['ɔːtʃɪn] *(pej) n* Gassenkind *nt*.

Urdu ['uəduː] *n* Urdu *nt*.

urge [ɜːdʒ] *n (need, desire)* Verlangen *nt* ♦ *vt*:
to ~ sb to do sth jdn eindringlich bitten,
etw zu tun; **to ~ caution** zur Vorsicht
mahnen.

▶ **urge on** *vt* antreiben.

urgency ['ɜːdʒənsɪ] *n* Dringlichkeit *f*.

urgent ['ɜːdʒənt] *adj* dringend; *(voice)*
eindringend.

urgently ['ɜːdʒəntlɪ] *adv* dringend.

urinal ['juərɪnl] *n (building)* Pissoir *nt*; *(vessel)*
Urinal *nt*.

urinate ['juərɪneɪt] *vi* urinieren.

urine ['juərɪn] *n* Urin *m*.

urn [ɜːn] *n* Urne *f*; *(also:* **tea ~**) Teekessel *m*.

Uruguay ['juərəgwaɪ] *n* Uruguay *nt*.

Uruguayan [juərə'gwaɪən] *adj* uruguayisch
♦ *n (person)* Uruguayer(in) *m(f)*.

US *n abbr (= United States)* USA *pl*.

us [ʌs] *pl pron* uns; *(emphatic)* wir; *see also* **me**.

USA *n abbr (= United States of America)* USA *f*;
(MIL: = United States Army) US-Armee *f*.

usable ['juːzəbl] *adj* brauchbar.

USAF *n abbr (= United States Air Force)* US-
Luftwaffe *f*.

usage ['juːzɪdʒ] *n (LING)* (Sprach)gebrauch *m*.

USB *abbr (= universal serial bus)* USB.

USCG *n abbr (= United States Coast Guard)*
Küstenwache der USA.

USDA *n abbr (= United States Department of
Agriculture)* US-
Landwirtschaftsministerium.

USDAW ['ʌzdɔː] *(BRIT) n abbr (= Union of Shop,
Distributive and Allied Workers)*
Einzelhandelsgewerkschaft.

USDI *n abbr (= United States Department of the
Interior)* US-Innenministerium.

use [*n* juːs, *vt* juːz] *n (using)* Gebrauch *m*,
Verwendung *f*; *(usefulness, purpose)* Nutzen
m ♦ *vt* benutzen, gebrauchen; *(phrase)*
verwenden; **in ~** in Gebrauch; **out of ~**
außer Gebrauch; **to be of ~** nützlich *or* von
Nutzen sein; **to make ~ of sth** Gebrauch
von etw machen; **it's no ~** es hat keinen
Zweck; **to have the ~ of sth** über etw *acc*
verfügen können; **what's this ~d for?** wofür
wird das gebraucht?; **to be ~d to sth** etw
gewohnt sein; **to get ~d to sth** sich an etw
acc gewöhnen; **she ~d to do it** sie hat es
früher gemacht.

▶ **use up** *vt (food, leftovers)* aufbrauchen;
(money) verbrauchen.

used [juːzd] *adj* gebraucht; *(car)* Gebraucht-.

useful ['juːsful] *adj* nützlich; **to come in ~** sich
als nützlich erweisen.

usefulness ['juːsfəlnɪs] *n* Nützlichkeit *f*.

useless ['juːslɪs] *adj* nutzlos; *(person: hopeless)*
hoffnungslos.

user ['juːzə*] *n* Benutzer(in) *m(f)*; *(of petrol, gas
etc)* Verbraucher(in) *m(f)*.

user-friendly ['juːzə'frendlɪ] *adj*
benutzerfreundlich.

usher [ʌʃə*] *n (at wedding)* Platzanweiser *m*
♦ *vt*: **to ~ sb in** jdn hineinführen.

usherette [ʌʃə'rɛt] *n* Platzanweiserin *f*.

USIA *n abbr (= United States Information
Agency)* US-Informations- und
Kulturinstitut.

USM *n abbr (= United States Mint)* US-
Münzanstalt; *(= United States Mail)* US-
Postbehörde.

USN *n abbr (= United States Navy)* US-Marine *f*.

USPHS *n abbr (= United States Public Health
Service)* US-Gesundheitsbehörde.

USPO *n abbr (= United States Post Office)* US-
Postbehörde.

USS *abbr (= United States Ship)* Namensteil
von Schiffen der Kriegsmarine.

USSR *n abbr (formerly: = Union of Soviet
Socialist Republics)* UdSSR *f*.

usu. *abbr* = **usually**.

usual ['juːʒuəl] *adj* üblich, gewöhnlich; **as ~**
wie gewöhnlich.

usually ['juːʒuəlɪ] *adv* gewöhnlich.

usurer ['juːʒərə*] *n* Wucherer *m*.

usurp [juː'zɜːp] *vt (title, position)* an sich *acc*
reißen.

usury ['juːʒurɪ] *n* Wucher *m*.

UT *(US) abbr (POST: = Utah)*.

utensil [juː'tɛnsl] *n* Gerät *nt*; **kitchen ~s**
Küchengeräte *pl*.

uterus ['juːtərəs] *n* Gebärmutter *f*, Uterus *m*.

utilitarian [juːtɪlɪ'tɛərɪən] *adj (building, object)*
praktisch; *(PHILOSOPHY)* utilitaristisch.

utility [juː'tɪlɪtɪ] *n (usefulness)* Nützlichkeit *f*;
(public utility) Versorgungsbetrieb *m*.

utility room *n* ≈ Hauswirtschaftsraum *m*.

utilization [juːtɪlaɪ'zeɪʃən] *n* Verwendung *f*.

utilize ['juːtɪlaɪz] *vt* verwenden.

utmost ['ʌtməust] *adj* äußerste(r, s) ♦ *n*: **to do
one's ~** sein Möglichstes tun; **of the
~ importance** von äußerster Wichtigkeit.

utter ['ʌtə*] *adj (amazement)* äußerste(r, s);
(rubbish, fool) total ♦ *vt (sounds, words)*
äußern.

utterance ['ʌtərəns] *n* Äußerung *f*.

utterly ['ʌtəlɪ] *adv (totally)* vollkommen.

U-turn ['juː'tɜːn] *n (also fig)* Kehrtwendung *f*.

Uzbekistan [ʌzbɛkɪ'stɑːn] *n* Usbekistan *nt*.

V, v

V¹, v [viː] n (letter) V nt, v nt; ~ **for Victor** ≈ V wie Viktor.
V² abbr (= volt) V.
v. abbr = **verse** (= versus) vs.; (= vide) s.
VA (US) abbr (POST: = Virginia).
vac [væk] (BRIT: inf) n abbr = **vacation**.
vacancy ['veɪkənsɪ] n (BRIT: job) freie Stelle f; (room in hotel etc) freies Zimmer nt; **"no vacancies"** „belegt"; **have you any vacancies?** (hotel) haben Sie Zimmer frei?; (office) haben Sie freie Stellen?
vacant ['veɪkənt] adj (room, seat, job) frei; (look) leer.
vacant lot (US) n unbebautes Grundstück nt.
vacate [və'keɪt] vt (house) räumen; (one's seat) frei machen; (job) aufgeben.
vacation [və'keɪʃən] (esp US) n (holiday) Urlaub m; (SCOL) Ferien pl; **to take a** ~ Urlaub machen; **on** ~ im Urlaub.
vacation course n Ferienkurs m.
vaccinate ['væksɪneɪt] vt: **to** ~ **sb (against sth)** jdn (gegen etw) impfen.
vaccination [væksɪ'neɪʃən] n Impfung f.
vaccine ['væksiːn] n Impfstoff m.
vacuum ['vækjum] n (empty space) Vakuum nt.
vacuum cleaner n Staubsauger m.
vacuum flask (BRIT) n Thermosflasche ® f.
vacuum-packed ['vækjum'pækt] adj vakuumverpackt.
vagabond ['vægəbɒnd] n Vagabund m.
vagary ['veɪgərɪ] n: **the vagaries of** die Launen +gen.
vagina [və'dʒaɪnə] n Scheide f, Vagina f.
vagrancy ['veɪgrənsɪ] n Landstreicherei f; (in towns, cities) Stadtstreicherei f.
vagrant ['veɪgrənt] n Landstreicher(in) m(f); (in town, city) Stadtstreicher(in) m(f).
vague [veɪg] adj (memory) vage; (outline) undeutlich; (look, idea, instructions) unbestimmt; (person: not precise) unsicher; (: evasive) unbestimmt; **to look** ~ (absent-minded) zerstreut aussehen; **I haven't the** ~**st idea** ich habe nicht die leiseste Ahnung.
vaguely ['veɪglɪ] adv (unclearly) vage, unbestimmt; (slightly) in etwa.
vagueness ['veɪgnɪs] n Unbestimmtheit f.
vain [veɪn] adj (person) eitel; (attempt, action) vergeblich; **in** ~ vergebens; **to die in** ~ umsonst sterben.
vainly ['veɪnlɪ] adv vergebens.
valance ['væləns] n (of bed) Volant m.
valedictorian [vælɪdɪk'tɔːrɪən] (US) n (SCOL)

Abschiedsredner(in) bei der Schulentlassungsfeier.
valedictory [vælɪ'dɪktərɪ] adj (speech) Abschieds-; (remarks) zum Abschied.
valentine ['væləntaɪn] n (also: ~ **card**) Valentinsgruß m; (person) Freund/Freundin, dem/der man am Valentinstag einen Gruß schickt.
valet ['vælɪt] n Kammerdiener m.
valet parking n Einparken nt (durch Hotelangestellte etc).
valet service n Reinigungsdienst m.
valiant ['vælɪənt] adj (effort) tapfer.
valid ['vælɪd] adj (ticket, document) gültig; (argument, reason) stichhaltig.
validate ['vælɪdeɪt] vt (contract, document) für gültig erklären; (argument, claim) bestätigen.
validity [və'lɪdɪtɪ] n (soundness) Gültigkeit f.
valise [və'liːz] n kleiner Koffer m.
valley ['vælɪ] n Tal nt.
valour, (US) **valor** ['vælə*] n Tapferkeit f.
valuable ['væljuəbl] adj wertvoll; (time) kostbar.
valuables ['væljuəblz] npl Wertsachen pl.
valuation [vælju'eɪʃən] n (of house etc) Schätzung f; (judgement of quality) Einschätzung f.
value ['væljuː] n Wert m; (usefulness) Nutzen m ♦ vt schätzen; **values** npl (principles, beliefs) Werte pl; **you get good** ~ **(for money) in that shop** in dem Laden bekommt man etwas für sein Geld; **to lose (in)** ~ an Wert verlieren; **to gain (in)** ~ im Wert steigen; **to be of great** ~ **(to sb)** (fig) von großem Wert (für jdn) sein.
value-added tax [væljuː'ædɪd-] (BRIT) n Mehrwertsteuer f.
valued ['væljuːd] adj (customer, advice) geschätzt.
valuer ['væljuə*] n Schätzer(in) m(f).
valve [vælv] n Ventil nt; (MED) Klappe f.
vampire ['væmpaɪə*] n Vampir m.
van [væn] n (AUT) Lieferwagen m; (BRIT: RAIL) Wa(g)gon m.
V and A (BRIT) n abbr (= Victoria and Albert Museum) Londoner Museum.
vandal ['vændl] n Rowdy m.
vandalism ['vændəlɪzəm] n Vandalismus m.
vandalize ['vændəlaɪz] vt mutwillig zerstören.
vanguard ['vænɡɑːd] n (fig): **in the** ~ **of** an der Spitze +gen.
vanilla [və'nɪlə] n Vanille f.
vanilla ice cream n Vanilleeis nt.
vanish ['vænɪʃ] vi verschwinden.
vanity ['vænɪtɪ] n (of person) Eitelkeit f.
vanity case n Kosmetikkoffer m.
vantage point ['vɑːntɪdʒ-] n Aussichtspunkt m; (fig): **from our** ~ aus unserer Sicht.
vaporize ['veɪpəraɪz] vt verdampfen ♦ vi verdunsten.
vapour, (US) **vapor** ['veɪpə*] n (gas, steam)

Dampf *m*; (*mist*) Dunst *m*.

vapour trail *n* (*AVIAT*) Kondensstreifen *m*.

variable ['vɛərɪəbl] *adj* (*likely to change: mood, quality, weather*) veränderlich, wechselhaft; (*able to be changed: temperature, height, speed*) variabel ♦ *n* veränderlicher Faktor *m*; (*MATH*) Variable *f*.

variance ['vɛərɪəns] *n*: **to be at ~ (with)** nicht übereinstimmen (mit).

variant ['vɛərɪənt] *n* Variante *f*.

variation [vɛərɪ'eɪʃən] *n* (*change*) Veränderung *f*; (*different form: of plot, theme etc*) Variation *f*.

varicose ['værɪkəus] *adj*: **~ veins** Krampfadern *pl*.

varied ['vɛərɪd] *adj* (*diverse*) unterschiedlich; (*full of changes*) abwechslungsreich.

variety [və'raɪətɪ] *n* (*diversity*) Vielfalt *f*; (*varied collection*) Auswahl *f*; (*type*) Sorte *f*; **a wide ~ of** ... eine Vielfalt an +*acc* ...; **for a ~ of reasons** aus verschiedenen Gründen.

variety show *n* Varietee- *or* Varietévorführung *f*.

various ['vɛərɪəs] *adj* (*reasons, people*) verschiedene; **at ~ times** (*different*) zu verschiedenen Zeiten; (*several*) mehrmals, mehrfach.

varnish ['vɑːnɪʃ] *n* Lack *m* ♦ *vt* (*wood, one's nails*) lackieren.

vary ['vɛərɪ] *vt* verändern ♦ *vi* (*be different*) variieren; **to ~ with** (*weather, season etc*) sich ändern mit.

varying ['vɛərɪɪŋ] *adj* unterschiedlich.

vase [vɑːz] *n* Vase *f*.

vasectomy [væ'sɛktəmɪ] *n* Vasektomie *f*.

Vaseline ® ['væsɪliːn] *n* Vaseline *f*.

vast [vɑːst] *adj* (*knowledge*) enorm; (*expense, area*) riesig.

vastly ['vɑːstlɪ] *adv* (*superior, improved*) erheblich.

vastness ['vɑːstnɪs] *n* ungeheure Größe *f*.

VAT [væt] (*BRIT*) *n abbr* (= *value-added tax*) MWSt *f*.

vat [væt] *n* Fass *nt*.

Vatican ['vætɪkən] *n*: **the ~** der Vatikan.

vatman ['vætmæn] (*inf: irreg: like* man*) n ≈* Fiskus *m* (*bezüglich Einbehaltung der Mehrwertsteuer*).

vaudeville ['vɔːdəvɪl] *n* Varietee *nt*, Varieté *nt*.

vault [vɔːlt] *n* (*of roof*) Gewölbe *nt*; (*tomb*) Gruft *f*; (*in bank*) Tresorraum *m*; (*jump*) Sprung *m* ♦ *vt* (*also*: **~ over**) überspringen.

vaunted ['vɔːntɪd] *adj*: **much-~** viel gepriesen.

VC *n abbr* = **vice-chairman**; (*BRIT*: = *Victoria Cross*) Viktoriakreuz *nt*, *höchste britische Tapferkeitsauszeichnung*.

VCR *n abbr* = **video cassette recorder**.

VD *n abbr* = **venereal disease**.

VDU *n abbr* (*COMPUT*) = **visual display unit**.

veal [viːl] *n* Kalbfleisch *nt*.

veer [vɪə*] *vi* (*wind*) sich drehen; (*vehicle*) ausscheren.

veg (*BRIT*: *inf*) *n abbr* = **vegetable(s)**.

vegan ['viːgən] *n* Veganer(in) *m(f)* ♦ *adj* radikal vegetarisch.

vegeburger ['vɛdʒɪbəːgə*] *n* vegetarischer Hamburger *m*.

vegetable ['vɛdʒtəbl] *n* (*plant*) Gemüse *nt*; (*plant life*) Pflanzen *pl* ♦ *cpd* (*oil etc*) Pflanzen-; (*garden, plot*) Gemüse-.

vegetarian [vɛdʒɪ'tɛərɪən] *n* Vegetarier(in) *m(f)* ♦ *adj* vegetarisch.

vegetate ['vɛdʒɪteɪt] *vi* (*fig: person*) dahinvegetieren.

vegetation [vɛdʒɪ'teɪʃən] *n* (*plants*) Vegetation *f*.

vegetative ['vɛdʒɪtətɪv] *adj* vegetativ.

veggieburger ['vɛdʒɪbəːgə*] *n* = **vegeburger**.

vehemence ['viːɪməns] *n* Vehemenz *f*, Heftigkeit *f*.

vehement ['viːɪmənt] *adj* heftig.

vehicle ['viːɪkl] *n* (*machine*) Fahrzeug *nt*; (*fig: means*) Mittel *nt*.

vehicular [vɪ'hɪkjulə*] *adj*: **"no ~ traffic"** „kein Fahrzeugverkehr".

veil [veɪl] *n* Schleier *m* ♦ *vt* (*also fig*) verschleiern; **under a ~ of secrecy** unter einem Schleier von Geheimnissen.

veiled [veɪld] *adj* (*also fig: threat*) verschleiert.

vein [veɪn] *n* Ader *f*; (*fig: mood, style*) Stimmung *f*.

Velcro ® ['vɛlkrəu] *n* (*also*: **~ fastener** *or* **fastening**) Klettverschluss *m*.

vellum ['vɛləm] *n* (*writing paper*) Pergament *nt*.

velocity [vɪ'lɔsɪtɪ] *n* Geschwindigkeit *f*.

velours *n* Velours *m*.

velvet ['vɛlvɪt] *n* Samt *m* ♦ *adj* (*skirt, jacket*) Samt-.

vendetta [vɛn'dɛtə] *n* Vendetta *f*; (*between families*) Blutrache *f*.

vending machine ['vɛndɪŋ-] *n* Automat *m*.

vendor ['vɛndə*] *n* Verkäufer(in) *m(f)*; **street ~** Straßenhändler(in) *m(f)*.

veneer [və'nɪə*] *n* (*on furniture*) Furnier *nt*; (*fig*) Anstrich *m*.

venerable ['vɛnərəbl] *adj* ehrwürdig; (*REL*) hochwürdig.

venereal [vɪ'nɪərɪəl] *adj*: **~ disease** Geschlechtskrankheit *f*.

Venetian [vɪ'niːʃən] *adj* (*GEOG*) venezianisch ♦ *n* (*person*) Venezianer(in) *m(f)*.

Venetian blind *n* Jalousie *f*.

Venezuela [vɛnɛ'zweɪlə] *n* Venezuela *nt*.

Venezuelan [vɛnɛ'zweɪlən] *adj* venezolanisch ♦ *n* (*person*) Venezolaner(in) *m(f)*.

vengeance ['vɛndʒəns] *n* Rache *f*; **with a ~** (*fig: fiercely*) gewaltig; **he broke the rules with a ~** er verstieß die Regeln - und nicht zu knapp.

vengeful ['vɛndʒful] *adj* rachsüchtig.

Venice ['vɛnɪs] *n* Venedig *nt*.

venison ['vɛnɪsn] *n* Rehfleisch *nt*.

venom ['vɛnəm] n (poison) Gift nt; (bitterness, anger) Gehässigkeit f.

venomous ['vɛnəməs] adj (snake, insect) giftig; (look) gehässig.

vent [vɛnt] n (also: **air ~**) Abzug m; (in jacket) Schlitz m ♦ vt (fig: feelings) abreagieren.

ventilate ['vɛntɪleɪt] vt (building) belüften; (room) lüften.

ventilation [vɛntɪ'leɪʃən] n Belüftung f.

ventilation shaft n Luftschacht m.

ventilator ['vɛntɪleɪtə*] n (TECH) Ventilator m; (MED) Beatmungsgerät nt.

ventriloquist [vɛn'trɪləkwɪst] n Bauchredner(in) m(f).

venture ['vɛntʃə*] n Unternehmung f ♦ vt (opinion) zu äußern wagen ♦ vi (dare to go) sich wagen; **a business ~** ein geschäftliches Unternehmen; **to ~ to do sth** es wagen, etw zu tun.

venture capital n Risikokapital nt.

venue ['vɛnju:] n (for meeting) Treffpunkt m; (for big events) Austragungsort m.

Venus ['vi:nəs] n Venus f.

veracity [və'ræsɪtɪ] n (of person) Aufrichtigkeit f; (of evidence etc) Richtigkeit f.

veranda(h) [və'rændə] n Veranda f.

verb [və:b] n Verb nt.

verbal ['və:bl] adj verbal; (skills) sprachlich; (translation) wörtlich.

verbally ['və:bəlɪ] adv (communicate etc) mündlich, verbal.

verbatim [və:'beɪtɪm] adj wörtlich ♦ adv Wort für Wort.

verbose [və:'bəus] adj (person) wortreich; (writing) weitschweifig.

verdict ['və:dɪkt] n (LAW, fig) Urteil nt; **~ of guilty/not guilty** Schuld-/Freispruch m.

verge [və:dʒ] (BRIT) n (of road) Rand m, Bankett nt; **"soft ~s"** (BRIT: AUT) „Seitenstreifen nicht befahrbar"; **to be on the ~ of doing sth** im Begriff sein, etw zu tun.

▶ **verge on** vt fus grenzen an +acc.

verger ['və:dʒə*] n (REL) Küster m.

verification [vɛrɪfɪ'keɪʃən] n (see vt) Bestätigung f; Überprüfung f.

verify ['vɛrɪfaɪ] vt (confirm) bestätigen; (check) überprüfen.

veritable ['vɛrɪtəbl] adj (real) wahr.

vermin ['və:mɪn] npl Ungeziefer nt.

vermouth ['və:məθ] n Wermut m.

vernacular [və'nækjulə*] n (of country) Landessprache f; (of region) Dialekt m.

versatile ['və:sətaɪl] adj vielseitig.

versatility [və:sə'tɪlɪtɪ] n Vielseitigkeit f.

verse [və:s] n (poetry) Poesie f; (stanza) Strophe f; (in bible) Vers m; **in ~** in Versform.

versed [və:st] adj: **(well-)~ in** (gut) bewandert in +dat.

version ['və:ʃən] n Version f.

versus ['və:səs] prep gegen.

vertebra ['və:tɪbrə] (pl **~e**) n Rückenwirbel m.

vertebrae ['və:tɪbri:] npl of **vertebra**.

vertebrate ['və:tɪbrɪt] n Wirbeltier nt.

vertical ['və:tɪkl] adj vertikal, senkrecht ♦ n Vertikale f.

vertically ['və:tɪklɪ] adv vertikal.

vertigo ['və:tɪgəu] n Schwindelgefühle pl; **to suffer from ~** leicht schwindlig werden.

verve [və:v] n Schwung m.

very ['vɛrɪ] adv sehr ♦ adj: **the ~ book which ...** genau das Buch, das ...; **the ~ last** der/die/ das Allerletzte; **at the ~ least** allerwenigstens; **~ well/little** sehr gut/ wenig; **~ much** sehr viel; (like, hope) sehr; **the ~ thought (of it) alarms me** der bloße Gedanke (daran) beunruhigt mich; **at the ~ end** ganz am Ende.

vespers ['vɛspəz] npl (REL) Vesper f.

vessel ['vɛsl] n Gefäß nt; (NAUT) Schiff nt; see **blood**.

vest [vɛst] n (BRIT: underwear) Unterhemd nt; (US: waistcoat) Weste f ♦ vt: **to ~ sb with sth, ~ sth in sb** jdm etw verleihen.

vested interest ['vɛstɪd-] n (COMM) finanzielles Interesse nt; **to have a ~ in doing sth** ein besonderes Interesse daran haben, etw zu tun.

vestibule ['vɛstɪbju:l] n Vorhalle f.

vestige ['vɛstɪdʒ] n Spur f.

vestment ['vɛstmənt] n (REL) Ornat nt.

vestry ['vɛstrɪ] n Sakristei f.

Vesuvius [vɪ'su:vɪəs] n Vesuv m.

vet [vɛt] (BRIT) n abbr = **veterinary surgeon** ♦ vt (examine) überprüfen.

veteran ['vɛtərn] n Veteran(in) m(f) ♦ adj: **she's a ~ campaigner for ...** sie ist eine altgediente Kämpferin für ...

veteran car n Oldtimer m (vor 1919 gebaut).

veterinarian [vɛtrɪ'nɛərɪən] (US) n = **veterinary surgeon**.

veterinary ['vɛtrɪnərɪ] adj (practice, medicine) Veterinär-; (care, training) tierärztlich.

veterinary surgeon (BRIT) n Tierarzt m, Tierärztin f.

veto ['vi:təu] (pl **~es**) n Veto nt ♦ vt ein Veto einlegen gegen; **to put a ~ on sth** gegen etw ein Veto einlegen.

vetting ['vɛtɪŋ] n Überprüfung f.

vex [vɛks] vt (irritate, upset) ärgern.

vexed [vɛkst] adj (upset) verärgert; (question) umstritten.

VFD (US) n abbr (= volunteer fire department) ≈ freiwillige Feuerwehr f.

VG (BRIT) n abbr (SCOL etc: = very good) ≈ „sehr gut".

VHF abbr (RADIO: = very high frequency) VHF.

VI (US) abbr (POST: = Virgin Islands).

via ['vaɪə] prep über +acc.

viability [vaɪə'bɪlɪtɪ] n (see adj) Durchführbarkeit f; Rentabilität f.

viable ['vaɪəbl] adj (project) durchführbar;

(*company*) rentabel.
viaduct ['vaɪədʌkt] n Viadukt m.
vial ['vaɪəl] n Fläschchen nt.
vibes [vaɪbz] npl (*MUS*) see **vibraphone** (*inf: vibrations*): **I get good/bad ~ from it/him** das/er macht mich an/nicht an.
vibrant ['vaɪbrnt] adj (*lively*) dynamisch; (*bright*) lebendig; (*full of emotion: voice*) volltönend.
vibraphone ['vaɪbrəfəun] n Vibrafon nt, Vibraphon nt.
vibrate [vaɪ'breɪt] vi (*house*) zittern, beben; (*machine, sound etc*) vibrieren.
vibration [vaɪ'breɪʃən] n (*act of vibrating*) Vibrieren nt; (*instance*) Vibration f.
vibrator [vaɪ'breɪtə˄] n Vibrator m.
vicar ['vɪkə˄] n Pfarrer m.
vicarage ['vɪkərɪdʒ] n Pfarrhaus nt.
vicarious [vɪ'kɛərɪəs] adj (*pleasure, experience*) indirekt.
vice [vaɪs] n (*moral fault*) Laster nt; (*TECH*) Schraubstock m.
vice- [vaɪs] pref Vize-.
vice-chairman [vaɪs'tʃɛəmən] n stellvertretender Vorsitzender m.
vice chancellor (*BRIT*) n (*of university*) ≈ Rektor m.
vice president n Vizepräsident(in) m(f).
viceroy ['vaɪsrɔɪ] n Vizekönig m.
vice squad n (*POLICE*) Sittendezernat nt.
vice versa ['vaɪsɪ'vɜːsə] adv umgekehrt.
vicinity [vɪ'sɪnɪtɪ] n: **in the ~ (of)** in der Nähe or Umgebung (+gen).
vicious ['vɪʃəs] adj (*attack, blow*) brutal; (*words, look*) gemein; (*horse, dog*) bösartig.
vicious circle n Teufelskreis m.
viciousness ['vɪʃəsnɪs] n Bösartigkeit f, Gemeinheit f.
vicissitudes [vɪ'sɪsɪtjuːdz] npl Wechselfälle pl.
victim ['vɪktɪm] n Opfer nt; **to be the ~ of an attack** einem Angriff zum Opfer fallen.
victimization ['vɪktɪmaɪ'zeɪʃən] n Schikanierung f.
victimize ['vɪktɪmaɪz] vt schikanieren.
victor ['vɪktə˄] n Sieger(in) m(f).
Victorian [vɪk'tɔːrɪən] adj viktorianisch.
victorious [vɪk'tɔːrɪəs] adj (*team*) siegreich; (*shout*) triumphierend.
victory ['vɪktərɪ] n Sieg m; **to win a ~ over sb** einen Sieg über jdn erringen.
video ['vɪdɪəu] n (*film, cassette, recorder*) Video nt ♦ vt **auf Video aufnehmen** ♦ cpd Video-.
video camera n Videokamera f.
video cassette n Videokassette f.
video cassette recorder n Videorekorder m.
videodisc, videodisk ['vɪdɪəudɪsk] n Bildplatte f.
video game n Videospiel nt, Telespiel nt.
video nasty n Video mit übertriebenen Gewaltszenen und/oder pornografischem Inhalt.
videophone ['vɪdɪəufəun] n Bildtelefon nt.

video recorder n Videorekorder m.
video recording n Videoaufnahme f.
video tape n Videoband nt.
vie [vaɪ] vi: **to ~ with sb/for sth** mit jdm/um etw wetteifern.
Vienna [vɪ'ɛnə] n Wien nt.
Viennese [vɪə'niːz] adj Wiener.
Vietnam ['vjɛt'næm] n Vietnam nt.
Viet Nam ['vjɛt'næm] n = **Vietnam.**
Vietnamese [vjɛtnə'miːz] adj vietnamesisch
♦ n inv (*person*) Vietnamese m, Vietnamesin f; (*LING*) Vietnamesisch nt.
view [vjuː] n (*from window etc*) Aussicht f; (*sight*) Blick m; (*outlook*) Sicht f; (*opinion*) Ansicht f ♦ vt betrachten; (*house*) besichtigen; **to be on ~** (*in museum etc*) ausgestellt sein; **in full ~ of** vor den Augen +gen; **to take the ~ that** ... der Ansicht sein, dass ...; **in ~ of the weather/the fact that** in Anbetracht des Wetters/der Tatsache, dass ...; **in my ~** meiner Ansicht nach; **an overall ~ of the situation** ein allgemeiner Überblick über die Lage; **with a ~ to doing sth** mit der Absicht, etw zu tun.
viewdata ® ['vjuːdeɪtə] (*BRIT*) n Bildschirmtext m.
viewer ['vjuːə˄] n (*person*) Zuschauer(in) m(f); (*viewfinder*) Sucher m.
viewfinder ['vjuːfaɪndə˄] n Sucher m.
viewpoint ['vjuːpɔɪnt] n (*attitude*) Standpunkt m; (*place*) Aussichtspunkt m.
vigil ['vɪdʒɪl] n Wache f; **to keep ~** Wache halten.
vigilance ['vɪdʒɪləns] n Wachsamkeit f.
vigilance committee (*US*) n Bürgerwehr f.
vigilant ['vɪdʒɪlənt] adj wachsam.
vigilante [vɪdʒɪ'læntɪ] n Mitglied einer Selbstschutzorganisation oder Bürgerwehr ♦ adj (*group, patrol*) Bürgerwehr-, Selbstschutz-.
vigorous ['vɪgərəs] adj (*action, campaign*) energisch, dynamisch; (*plant*) kräftig.
vigour, (*US*) **vigor** ['vɪgə˄] n (*of person, campaign*) Energie f, Dynamik f.
vile [vaɪl] adj abscheulich.
vilify ['vɪlɪfaɪ] vt diffamieren.
villa ['vɪlə] n Villa f.
village ['vɪlɪdʒ] n Dorf nt.
villager ['vɪlɪdʒə˄] n Dorfbewohner(in) m(f).
villain ['vɪlən] n (*scoundrel*) Schurke m; (*in novel etc*) Bösewicht m; (*BRIT: criminal*) Verbrecher(in) m(f).
VIN (*US*) n abbr (= *vehicle identification number*) amtliches Kennzeichen nt.
vinaigrette [vɪneɪ'grɛt] n Vinaigrette f.
vindicate ['vɪndɪkeɪt] vt (*person*) rehabilitieren; (*action*) rechtfertigen.
vindication [vɪndɪ'keɪʃən] n Rechtfertigung f.
vindictive [vɪn'dɪktɪv] adj (*person*) nachtragend; (*action*) aus Rache.
vine [vaɪn] n (*BOT: producing grapes*) Weinrebe f; (: *in jungle*) Rebengewächs nt.

vinegar ['vɪnɪgə*] n Essig m.
vine grower n Weinbauer m.
vine-growing ['vaɪngrəuɪŋ] adj (region)
Weinbau- ♦ n Weinbau m.
vineyard ['vɪnjɑːd] n Weinberg m.
vintage ['vɪntɪdʒ] n (of wine) Jahrgang m ♦ cpd
(classic) klassisch; **the 1980 ~** (of wine) der
Jahrgang 1980.
vintage car n Oldtimer m (zwischen 1919 und 1930
gebaut).
vintage wine n erlesener Wein m.
vinyl ['vaɪnl] n Vinyl nt; (records) Schallplatten
pl.
viola [vɪ'əulə] n Bratsche f.
violate ['vaɪəleɪt] vt (agreement) verletzen;
(peace) stören; (graveyard) schänden.
violation [vaɪə'leɪʃən] n (of agreement etc)
Verletzung f; **in ~ of** (rule, law) unter
Verletzung +gen.
violence ['vaɪələns] n Gewalt f; (strength)
Heftigkeit f.
violent ['vaɪələnt] adj (behaviour) gewalttätig;
(death) gewaltsam; (explosion, criticism,
emotion) heftig; **a ~ dislike of sb/sth** eine
heftige Abneigung gegen jdn/etw.
violently ['vaɪələntlɪ] adv heftig; (ill) schwer;
(angry) äußerst.
violet ['vaɪələt] adj violett ♦ n (colour) Violett
nt; (plant) Veilchen nt.
violin [vaɪə'lɪn] n Geige f, Violine f.
violinist [vaɪə'lɪnɪst] n Violinist(in) m(f),
Geiger(in) m(f).
VIP n abbr (= very important person) VIP m.
viper ['vaɪpə*] n Viper f.
viral ['vaɪərəl] adj (disease, infection) Virus-.
virgin ['vəːdʒɪn] n Jungfrau f ♦ adj (snow, forest
etc) unberührt; **she is a ~** sie ist Jungfrau;
the Blessed V~ die Heilige Jungfrau.
virgin birth n unbefleckte Empfängnis f;
(BIOL) Jungfernzeugung f.
virginity [vəː'dʒɪnɪtɪ] n (of person)
Jungfräulichkeit f.
Virgo ['vəːgəu] n (sign) Jungfrau f; **to be ~**
Jungfrau sein.
virile ['vɪraɪl] adj (person) männlich.
virility [vɪ'rɪlɪtɪ] n (masculine qualities)
Männlichkeit f.
virtual ['vəːtjuəl] adj (COMPUT, PHYS) virtuell;
it's a ~ impossibility es ist so gut wie
unmöglich; **to be the ~ leader** eigentlich or
praktisch der Führer sein.
virtually ['vəːtjuəlɪ] adv praktisch, nahezu; **it
is ~ impossible** es ist so gut wie unmöglich.
virtual reality n virtuelle Realität f.
virtue ['vəːtjuː] n Tugend f; (advantage)
Vorzug m; **by ~ of** aufgrund or auf Grund
+gen or von.
virtuosi [vəːtju'əuzɪ] npl of **virtuoso**.
virtuosity [vəːtju'ɒsɪtɪ] n Virtuosität f.
virtuoso [vəːtju'əuzəu] (pl ~s or **virtuosi**) n
Virtuose m.
virtuous ['vəːtjuəs] adj tugendhaft.

virulence ['vɪruləns] n (of disease)
Bösartigkeit f; (hatred) Feindseligkeit f.
virulent ['vɪrulənt] adj (disease) bösartig;
(actions, feelings) feindselig.
virus ['vaɪərəs] n (MED, COMPUT) Virus m or nt.
visa ['viːzə] n Visum nt.
vis-à-vis [viːzə'viː] prep gegenüber.
viscose ['vɪskəus] n (also CHEM) Viskose f.
viscount ['vaɪkaunt] n Viscount m.
viscous ['vɪskəs] adj zähflüssig.
vise [vaɪs] (US) n (TECH) = **vice**.
visibility [vɪzɪ'bɪlɪtɪ] n (range of vision)
Sicht(weite) f.
visible ['vɪzəbl] adj sichtbar; **~ exports/
imports** sichtbare Ausfuhren/Einfuhren.
visibly ['vɪzəblɪ] adv sichtlich.
vision ['vɪʒən] n (sight) Sicht f; (foresight)
Weitblick m; (in dream) Vision f.
visionary ['vɪʒənrɪ] adj (with foresight)
vorausblickend.
visit ['vɪzɪt] n Besuch m ♦ vt besuchen; **a
private/official ~** ein privater/offizieller
Besuch.
visiting ['vɪzɪtɪŋ] adj (speaker, team) Gast-.
visiting card n Visitenkarte f.
visiting hours npl Besuchszeiten pl.
visiting professor n Gastprofessor(in) m(f).
visitor ['vɪzɪtə*] n Besucher(in) m(f).
visitors' book ['vɪzɪtəz-] n Gästebuch nt.
visor ['vaɪzə*] n (of helmet etc) Visier nt.
VISTA ['vɪstə] (US) n abbr (= Volunteers in
Service to America) staatliches
Förderprogramm für strukturschwache
Gebiete.
vista ['vɪstə] n Aussicht f.
visual ['vɪzjuəl] adj (image etc) visuell; **the
~ arts** die darstellenden Künste.
visual aid n Anschauungsmaterial nt.
visual display unit n (Daten)sichtgerät nt.
visualize ['vɪzjuəlaɪz] vt sich dat vorstellen.
visually ['vɪzjuəlɪ] adv visuell; **~ appealing**
optisch ansprechend; **~ handicapped**
sehbehindert.
vital ['vaɪtl] adj (essential) unerlässlich; (organ)
lebenswichtig; (full of life) vital; **of
~ importance (to sb/sth)** von größter
Wichtigkeit (für jdn/etw).
vitality [vaɪ'tælɪtɪ] n (liveliness) Vitalität f.
vitally ['vaɪtəlɪ] adv: **~ important** äußerst
wichtig.
vital statistics npl (fig: of woman)
Körpermaße pl; (of population)
Bevölkerungsstatistik f.
vitamin ['vɪtəmɪn] n Vitamin nt ♦ cpd (pill,
deficiencies) Vitamin-.
vitiate ['vɪʃɪeɪt] vt (spoil) verunreinigen.
vitreous ['vɪtrɪəs] adj: **~ china** Porzellanemail
nt; **~ enamel** Glasemail nt.
vitriolic [vɪtrɪ'ɒlɪk] adj (fig: language, behaviour)
hasserfüllt.
viva ['vaɪvə] n (SCOL: also: **~ voce**) [-'vəutʃɪ]
mündliche Prüfung f.

vivacious [vɪ'veɪʃəs] *adj* lebhaft.
vivacity [vɪ'væsɪtɪ] *n* Lebendigkeit *f*.
vivid ['vɪvɪd] *adj* (*description*) lebendig; (*memory, imagination*) lebhaft; (*colour*) leuchtend; (*light*) hell.
vividly ['vɪvɪdlɪ] *adv* (*describe*) lebendig; (*remember*) lebhaft.
vivisection [vɪvɪ'sɛkʃən] *n* Vivisektion *f*.
vixen ['vɪksn] *n* (*ZOOL*) Füchsin *f*; (*pej: woman*) Drachen *m*.
viz [vɪz] *abbr* (= *videlicet*) nämlich.
VLF *abbr* (*RADIO:* = *very low frequency*) VLF.
V-neck ['viːnɛk] *n* (*also:* ~ **jumper** *or* **pullover**) Pullover *m* mit V-Ausschnitt.
VOA *n abbr* (= *Voice of America*) Stimme *f* Amerikas.
vocabulary [vəu'kæbjulərɪ] *n* (*words known*) Vokabular *nt*, Wortschatz *m*.
vocal ['vəukl] *adj* (*of the voice*) stimmlich; (*articulate*) lautstark.
vocal cords *npl* Stimmbänder *pl*.
vocalist ['vəukəlɪst] *n* Sänger(in) *m(f)*.
vocals ['vəuklz] *npl* (*MUS*) Gesang *m*.
vocation [vəu'keɪʃən] *n* (*calling*) Berufung *f*; (*profession*) Beruf *m*.
vocational [vəu'keɪʃənl] *adj* (*training, guidance etc*) Berufs-.
vociferous [və'sɪfərəs] *adj* (*protesters, demands*) lautstark.
vodka ['vɔdkə] *n* Wodka *m*.
vogue [vəug] *n* (*fashion*) Mode *f*; (*popularity*) Popularität *f*; **in** ~ in Mode.
voice [vɔɪs] *n* (*also fig*) Stimme *f* ♦ *vt* (*opinion*) zum Ausdruck bringen; **in a loud/soft** ~ mit lauter/leiser Stimme; **to give** ~ **to** Ausdruck verleihen +*dat*.
voice mail *n* (*COMPUT*) Voicemail *f*.
voice-over ['vɔɪsəuvə*] *n* (Film)kommentar *m*.
void [vɔɪd] *n* (*hole*) Loch *nt*; (*fig: emptiness*) Leere *f* ♦ *adj* (*invalid*) ungültig; ~ **of** (*empty*) ohne.
voile [vɔɪl] *n* Voile *m*.
vol. *abbr* (= *volume*) Bd.
volatile ['vɔlətaɪl] *adj* (*person*) impulsiv; (*situation*) unsicher; (*liquid etc*) flüchtig.
volcanic [vɔl'kænɪk] *adj* (*rock, eruption*) vulkanisch, Vulkan-.
volcano [vɔl'keɪnəu] *(pl* ~**es**) *n* Vulkan *m*.
volition [və'lɪʃən] *n:* **of one's own** ~ aus freiem Willen.
volley ['vɔlɪ] *n* (*of gunfire*) Salve *f*; (*of stones, questions*) Hagel *m*; (*TENNIS etc*) Volley *m*.
volleyball ['vɔlɪbɔːl] *n* Volleyball *m*.
volt [vəult] *n* Volt *nt*.
voltage ['vəultɪdʒ] *n* Spannung *f*; **high/low** ~ Hoch-/Niederspannung *f*.
volte-face ['vɔlt'fɑːs] *n* Kehrtwendung *f*.
voluble ['vɔljubl] *adj* (*person*) redselig; (*speech*) wortreich.
volume ['vɔljuːm] *n* (*space*) Volumen *nt*; (*amount*) Umfang *m*, Ausmaß *nt*; (*book*) Band *m*; (*sound level*) Lautstärke *f*; ~ **one/two** (*of*

book) Band eins/zwei; **his expression spoke** ~**s** sein Gesichtsausdruck sprach Bände.
volume control *n* (*RADIO, TV*) Lautstärkeregler *m*.
volume discount *n* (*COMM*) Mengenrabatt *m*.
voluminous [və'luːmɪnəs] *adj* (*clothes*) sehr weit; (*correspondence, notes*) umfangreich.
voluntarily ['vɔləntərɪlɪ] *adv* freiwillig.
voluntary ['vɔləntərɪ] *adj* freiwillig.
voluntary liquidation *n* freiwillige Liquidation *f*.
volunteer [vɔlən'tɪə*] *n* Freiwillige(r) *f(m)* ♦ *vt* (*information*) vorbringen ♦ *vi* (*for army etc*) sich freiwillig melden; **to** ~ **to do sth** sich anbieten, etw zu tun.
voluptuous [və'lʌptjuəs] *adj* sinnlich, wollüstig.
vomit ['vɔmɪt] *n* Erbrochene(s) *nt* ♦ *vt* erbrechen ♦ *vi* sich übergeben.
voracious [və'reɪʃəs] *adj* (*person*) gefräßig; ~ **appetite** Riesenappetit *m*.
vortal ['vɔːtl] *n* (*COMPUT*) Vortal *nt*.
vote [vəut] *n* Stimme *f*; (*votes cast*) Stimmen *pl*; (*right to vote*) Wahlrecht *nt*; (*ballot*) Abstimmung *f* ♦ *vt* (*elect*): **to be** ~**d chairman** *etc* zum Vorsitzenden *etc* gewählt werden; (*propose*): **to** ~ **that** vorschlagen, dass ♦ *vi* (*in election etc*) wählen; **to put sth to the** ~, **(take a)** ~ **on sth** über etw *acc* abstimmen; ~ **of censure** Tadelsantrag *m*; **to pass a** ~ **of confidence/no confidence** ein Vertrauens-/ Misstrauensvotum annehmen; **to** ~ **to do sth** dafür stimmen, etw zu tun; **to** ~ **yes/no** mit Ja/Nein stimmen; **to** ~ **Labour/Green** *etc* Labour/die Grünen *etc* wählen; **to** ~ **for** *or* **in favour of/against sth** für/gegen etw stimmen.
vote of thanks *n* Danksagung *f*.
voter ['vəutə*] *n* Wähler(in) *m(f)*.
voting ['vəutɪŋ] *n* Wahl *f*.
voting paper (*BRIT*) *n* Stimmzettel *m*.
voting right *n* Stimmrecht *nt*.
vouch [vautʃ]: **to** ~ **for** *vt fus* bürgen für.
voucher ['vautʃə*] *n* Gutschein *m*; (*receipt*) Beleg *m*; **gift** ~ Geschenkgutschein *m*; **luncheon** ~ Essensmarke *f*; **travel** ~ Reisegutschein *m*.
vow [vau] *n* Versprechen *nt* ♦ *vt:* **to** ~ **to do sth/that** geloben, etw zu tun/dass; **to take** *or* **make a** ~ **to do sth** geloben, etw zu tun.
vowel ['vauəl] *n* Vokal *m*.
voyage ['vɔɪɪdʒ] *n* Reise *f*.
voyeur [vwɑː'jɜː*] *n* Voyeur(in) *m(f)*.
voyeurism [vwɑː'jɜːrɪzəm] *n* Voyeurismus *m*.
VP *n abbr* = *vice president*.
vs *abbr* (= *versus*) vs.
V-sign ['viːsaɪn] (*BRIT*) *n:* **to give sb the** ~ ≈ jdm den Vogel zeigen.
VSO (*BRIT*) *n abbr* (= *Voluntary Service Overseas*) *britischer Entwicklungsdienst*.
VT (*US*) *abbr* (*POST:* = *Vermont*).

vulgar ['vʌlgə*] *adj* (*remarks, gestures*) vulgär; (*decor, ostentation*) geschmacklos.

vulgarity [vʌl'gærɪtɪ] *n* (*see adj*) Vulgarität *f*; Geschmacklosigkeit *f*.

vulnerability [vʌlnərə'bɪlɪtɪ] *n* Verletzlichkeit *f*.

vulnerable ['vʌlnərəbl] *adj* (*person, position*) verletzlich.

vulture ['vʌltʃə*] *n* (*also fig*) Geier *m*.

vulva ['vʌlvə] *n* Vulva *f*.

W, w

W¹, w ['dʌblju:] *n* (*letter*) W *nt*, w *nt*; **~ for William** ≈ W wie Wilhelm.

W² ['dʌblju:] *abbr* (*ELEC*: = watt) W; (= *west*) W.

WA *abbr* (*US*: *POST*: = Washington) (*AUSTRALIA*: = Western Australia).

wad [wɔd] *n* (*of cotton wool*) Bausch *m*; (*of paper, banknotes*) Bündel *nt*.

wadding ['wɔdɪŋ] *n* Füllmaterial *nt*.

waddle ['wɔdl] *vi* watscheln.

wade [weɪd] *vi*: **to ~ across** (*a river, stream*) waten durch; **to ~ through** (*fig*: *a book*) sich durchkämpfen durch.

wafer ['weɪfə*] *n* (*biscuit*) Waffel *f*.

wafer-thin ['weɪfə'θɪn] *adj* hauchdünn.

waffle ['wɔfl] *n* (*CULIN*) Waffel *f*; (*inf*: *empty talk*) Geschwafel *nt* ♦ *vi* (*in speech etc*) schwafeln.

waffle iron *n* Waffeleisen *nt*.

waft [wɔft] *vt, vi* wehen.

wag [wæg] *vt* (*tail*) wedeln mit; (*finger*) drohen mit ♦ *vi* (*tail*) wedeln; **the dog ~ged its tail** der Hund wedelte mit dem Schwanz.

wage [weɪdʒ] *n* (*also*: **~s**) Lohn *m* ♦ *vt*: **to ~ war** Krieg führen; **a day's ~s** ein Tageslohn.

wage claim *n* Lohnforderung *f*.

wage differential *n* Lohnunterschied *m*.

wage earner [-ə:nə*] *n* Lohnempfänger(in) *m(f)*.

wage freeze *n* Lohnstopp *m*.

wage packet *n* Lohntüte *f*.

wager ['weɪdʒə*] *n* Wette *f* ♦ *vt* wetten.

waggle ['wægl] *vt* (*ears etc*) wackeln mit ♦ *vi* wackeln.

wag(g)on ['wægən] *n* (*horse-drawn*) Fuhrwerk *nt*; (*BRIT*: *RAIL*) Wa(g)gon *m*.

wail [weɪl] *n* (*of person*) Jammern *nt*; (*of siren*) Heulen *nt* ♦ *vi* (*person*) jammern; (*siren*) heulen.

waist [weɪst] *n* (*ANAT, of clothing*) Taille *f*.

waistcoat ['weɪskəut] (*BRIT*) *n* Weste *f*.

waistline ['weɪstlaɪn] *n* Taille *f*.

wait [weɪt] *n* Wartezeit *f* ♦ *vi* warten; **to lie in ~ for sb** jdm auflauern; **to keep sb ~ing** jdn warten lassen; **I can't ~ to** ... (*fig*) ich kann es kaum erwarten, zu ...; **to ~ for sb/sth** auf jdn/etw warten; **~ a minute!** Moment mal!; **"repairs while you ~"** „Reparaturen sofort".

▶ **wait behind** *vi* zurückbleiben.

▶ **wait on** *vt fus* (*serve*) bedienen.

▶ **wait up** *vi* aufbleiben; **don't ~ up for me** warte nicht auf mich.

waiter ['weɪtə*] *n* Kellner *m*.

waiting ['weɪtɪŋ] *n*: **"no ~"** (*BRIT*: *AUT*) „Halten verboten".

waiting list *n* Warteliste *f*.

waiting room *n* (*in surgery*) Wartezimmer *nt*; (*in railway station*) Wartesaal *m*.

waitress ['weɪtrɪs] *n* Kellnerin *f*.

waive [weɪv] *vt* (*rule*) verzichten auf +*acc*.

waiver ['weɪvə*] *n* Verzicht *m*.

wake [weɪk] (*pt* **woke, waked,** *pp* **woken, waked**) *vt* (*also*: **~ up**) wecken ♦ *vi* (*also*: **~ up**) aufwachen ♦ *n* (*for dead person*) Totenwache *f*; (*NAUT*) Kielwasser *nt*; **to ~ up to** (*fig*) sich *dat* bewusst werden +*gen*; **in the ~ of** (*fig*) unmittelbar nach, im Gefolge +*gen*; **to follow in sb's ~** (*fig*) hinter jdm herziehen.

waken ['weɪkn] *vt* = **wake**.

Wales [weɪlz] *n* Wales *nt*; **the Prince of ~** der Prinz von Wales.

walk [wɔːk] *n* (*hike*) Wanderung *f*; (*shorter*) Spaziergang *m*; (*gait*) Gang *m*; (*path*) Weg *m*; (*in park, along coast etc*) (Spazier)weg *m* ♦ *vi* gehen; (*instead of driving*) zu Fuß gehen; (*for pleasure, exercise*) spazieren gehen ♦ *vt* (*distance*) gehen, laufen; (*dog*) ausführen; **it's 10 minutes' ~ from here** es ist 10 Minuten zu Fuß von hier; **to go for a ~** spazieren gehen; **to slow to a ~** im Schritttempo weitergehen; **people from all ~s of life** Leute aus allen Gesellschaftsschichten; **to ~ in one's sleep** schlafwandeln; **I'd rather ~ than take the bus** ich gehe lieber zu Fuß als mit dem Bus zu fahren; **I'll ~ you home** ich bringe dich nach Hause.

▶ **walk out** *vi* (*audience*) den Saal verlassen; (*workers*) in Streik treten.

▶ **walk out on** (*inf*) *vt fus* (*family etc*) verlassen.

walkabout ['wɔːkəbaut] *n*: **the Queen/president went on a ~** die Königin/der Präsident mischte sich unters Volk *or* nahm ein Bad in der Menge.

walker ['wɔːkə*] *n* (*person*) Spaziergänger(in) *m(f)*.

walkie-talkie ['wɔːkɪ'tɔːkɪ] *n* Walkie-Talkie *nt*.

walking ['wɔːkɪŋ] *n* Wandern *nt*; **it's within ~ distance** es ist zu Fuß erreichbar.

walking holiday *n* Wanderurlaub *m*.

walking shoes *npl* Wanderschuhe *pl*.

walking stick *n* Spazierstock *m*.

Walkman ® ['wɔːkmən] *n* Walkman ® *m*.

walk-on ['wɔːkɔn] *adj* (*THEAT*): ~ **part** Statistenrolle *f*.

walkout ['wɔːkaut] *n* (*of workers*) Streik *m*.

walkover ['wɔːkəuvə*] (*inf*) *n* (*competition, exam etc*) Kinderspiel *nt*.

walkway ['wɔːkweɪ] *n* Fußweg *m*.

wall [wɔːl] *n* Wand *f*; (*exterior, city wall etc*) Mauer *f*; **to go to the** ~ (*fig: firm etc*) kaputtgehen.

▶ **wall in** *vt* (*enclose*) ummauern.

wall cupboard *n* Wandschrank *m*.

walled [wɔːld] *adj* von Mauern umgeben.

wallet ['wɔlɪt] *n* Brieftasche *f*.

wallflower ['wɔːlflauə*] *n* (*BOT*) Goldlack *m*; **to be a** ~ (*fig*) ein Mauerblümchen sein.

wall hanging *n* Wandbehang *m*.

wallop ['wɔləp] (*BRIT: inf*) *vt* verprügeln.

wallow ['wɔləu] *vi* (*in mud, water*) sich wälzen; (*in guilt, grief*) schwelgen.

wallpaper ['wɔːlpeɪpə*] *n* Tapete *f* ♦ *vt* tapezieren.

wall-to-wall ['wɔːltə'wɔːl] *adj*: ~ **carpeting** Teppichboden *m*.

wally [wɔlɪ] (*inf*) *n* Trottel *m*.

walnut ['wɔːlnʌt] *n* (*nut*) Walnuss *f*; (*tree*) Walnussbaum *m*; (*wood*) Nussbaumholz *nt*.

walrus ['wɔːlrəs] (*pl* ~ *or* ~**es**) *n* Walross *nt*.

waltz [wɔːlts] *n* Walzer *m* ♦ *vi* Walzer tanzen.

wan [wɔn] *adj* bleich; (*smile*) matt.

wand [wɔnd] *n* (*also:* **magic** ~) Zauberstab *m*.

wander ['wɔndə*] *vi* (*person*) herumlaufen; (*mind, thoughts*) wandern ♦ *vt* (*the streets, the hills etc*) durchstreifen.

wanderer ['wɔndərə*] *n* Wandervogel *m*.

wandering ['wɔndrɪŋ] *adj* (*tribe*) umherziehend; (*minstrel, actor*) fahrend.

wane [weɪn] *vi* (*moon*) abnehmen; (*influence etc*) schwinden.

wangle ['wæŋgl] (*BRIT: inf*) *vt* sich *dat* verschaffen.

wanker ['wæŋkə*] (*infl*) *n* Wichser *m*.

wannabe(e) ['wɔnəbiː] (*inf*) *n* Möchtegern *m*; **James Bond** ~ Möchtegern-James-Bond *m*.

want [wɔnt] *vt* (*wish for*) wollen; (*need*) brauchen ♦ *n* (*lack*): **for** ~ **of** aus Mangel an +*dat*; **wants** *npl* (*needs*) Bedürfnisse *pl*; **to** ~ **to do sth** etw tun wollen; **to** ~ **sb to do sth** wollen, dass jd etw tut; **to** ~ **in/out** herein-/hinauswollen; **you're** ~**ed on the phone** Sie werden am Telefon verlangt; **he is** ~**ed by the police** er wird von der Polizei gesucht; **a** ~ **of foresight** ein Mangel *m* an Voraussicht.

want ads (*US*) *npl* Kaufgesuche *pl*.

wanted ['wɔntɪd] *adj* (*criminal etc*) gesucht; "**cook** ~" „Koch/Köchin gesucht".

wanting ['wɔntɪŋ] *adj*: **to be found** ~ sich als unzulänglich erweisen.

wanton ['wɔntn] *adj* (*violence*) mutwillig; (*promiscuous: woman*) schamlos.

WAP [wæp] *n abbr* (*COMPUT*: = *wireless application protocol*) WAP *nt*.

war [wɔː*] *n* Krieg *m*; **to go to** ~ (*start*) einen Krieg anfangen; **to be at** ~ (**with**) sich im Kriegszustand befinden (mit); **to make** ~ (**on**) Krieg führen (gegen); **a** ~ **on drugs/crime** ein Feldzug gegen Drogen/das Verbrechen.

warble ['wɔːbl] *n* Trällern *nt* ♦ *vi* trällern.

war cry *n* Kriegsruf *m*; (*fig: slogan*) Schlachtruf *m*.

ward [wɔːd] *n* (*in hospital*) Station *f*; (*POL*) Wahlbezirk *m*; (*LAW: also:* ~ **of court**) Mündel *nt* unter Amtsvormundschaft.

▶ **ward off** *vt* (*attack, enemy, illness*) abwehren.

warden ['wɔːdn] *n* (*of park etc*) Aufseher(in) *m(f)*; (*of jail*) Wärter(in) *m(f)*; (*BRIT: of youth hostel*) Herbergsvater *m*, Herbergsmutter *f*; (: *in university*) Wohnheimleiter(in) *m(f)*; (: *also:* **traffic** ~) Verkehrspolizist(in) *m(f)*.

warder ['wɔːdə*] (*BRIT*) *n* Gefängniswärter(in) *m(f)*.

wardrobe ['wɔːdrəub] *n* (*for clothes*) Kleiderschrank *m*; (*collection of clothes*) Garderobe *f*; (*CINE, THEAT*) Kostüme *pl*.

warehouse ['wɛəhaus] *n* Lager *nt*.

wares [wɛəz] *npl* Waren *pl*.

warfare ['wɔːfɛə*] *n* Krieg *m*.

war game *n* Kriegsspiel *nt*.

warhead ['wɔːhɛd] *n* Sprengkopf *m*.

warily ['wɛərɪlɪ] *adv* vorsichtig.

Warks (*BRIT*) *abbr* (*POST*: = *Warwickshire*).

warlike ['wɔːlaɪk] *adj* kriegerisch.

warm [wɔːm] *adj* warm; (*thanks, applause, welcome, person*) herzlich; **it's** ~ es ist warm; **I'm** ~ mir ist warm; **to keep sth** ~ etw warm halten; **with my** ~**est thanks/congratulations** mit meinem herzlichsten Dank/meinen herzlichsten Glückwünschen.

▶ **warm up** *vi* warm werden; (*athlete*) sich aufwärmen ♦ *vt* aufwärmen.

warm-blooded ['wɔːm'blʌdɪd] *adj* warmblütig.

war memorial *n* Kriegerdenkmal *nt*.

warm-hearted [wɔːm'hɑːtɪd] *adj* warmherzig.

warmly ['wɔːmlɪ] *adv* (*applaud, welcome*) herzlich; (*dress*) warm.

warmonger ['wɔːmʌŋgə*] (*pej*) *n* Kriegshetzer *m*.

warmongering ['wɔːmʌŋgrɪŋ] (*pej*) *n* Kriegshetze *f*.

warmth [wɔːmθ] *n* Wärme *f*; (*friendliness*) Herzlichkeit *f*.

warm-up ['wɔːmʌp] *n* Aufwärmen *nt*; ~ **exercise** Aufwärmübung *f*.

warn [wɔːn] *vt*: **to** ~ **sb that** ... jdn warnen, dass ...; **to** ~ **sb of sth** jdn vor etw *dat* warnen; **to** ~ **sb not to do sth** *or* **against doing sth** jdn davor warnen, etw zu tun.

warning ['wɔːnɪŋ] *n* Warnung *f*; **without (any)** ~ (*suddenly*) unerwartet; (*without notifying*) ohne Vorwarnung; **gale** ~ Sturmwarnung *f*.

warning light n Warnlicht nt.
warning triangle n (AUT) Warndreieck nt.
warp [wɔ:p] vi (wood etc) sich verziehen ♦ vt
(fig: character) entstellen ♦ n (TEXTILES)
Kette f.
warpath ['wɔ:pɑ:θ] n: **to be on the ~** auf dem
Kriegspfad sein.
warped [wɔ:pt] adj (wood) verzogen; (fig:
character, sense of humour etc) abartig.
warrant ['wɔrnt] n (LAW: for arrest) Haftbefehl
m; (: also: **search ~**) Durchsuchungsbefehl m
♦ vt (justify, merit) rechtfertigen.
warrant officer n (MIL) Dienstgrad zwischen
Offizier und Unteroffizier.
warranty ['wɔrəntɪ] n Garantie f; **under ~**
(COMM) unter Garantie.
warren ['wɔrən] n (of rabbits) Bau m; (fig: of
passages, streets) Labyrinth nt.
warring ['wɔ:rɪŋ] adj (nations) Krieg führend;
(interests) gegensätzlich; (factions)
verfeindet.
warrior ['wɔrɪə*] n Krieger m.
Warsaw ['wɔ:sɔ:] n Warschau nt.
warship ['wɔ:ʃɪp] n Kriegsschiff nt.
wart [wɔ:t] n Warze f.
wartime ['wɔ:taɪm] n: **in ~** im Krieg.
wary ['wɛərɪ] adj (person) vorsichtig; **to be
~ about** or **of doing sth** Bedenken haben,
etw zu tun.
was [wɔz] pt of **be**.
wash [wɔʃ] vt waschen; (dishes) spülen,
abwaschen; (remove grease, paint etc)
ausspülen ♦ vi (person) sich waschen ♦ n
(clothes etc) Wäsche f; (washing programme)
Waschgang m; (of ship) Kielwasser nt; **he
was ~ed overboard** er wurde über Bord
gespült; **to ~ over/against sth** (sea etc)
über/gegen etw acc spülen; **to have a ~** sich
waschen; **to give sth a ~** etw waschen.
▶ **wash away** vt wegspülen.
▶ **wash down** vt (wall, car) abwaschen; (food:
with wine etc) hinunterspülen.
▶ **wash off** vi sich herauswaschen ♦ vt
abwaschen.
▶ **wash out** vt (stain) herauswaschen.
▶ **wash up** vi (BRIT: wash dishes) spülen,
abwaschen; (US: have a wash) sich waschen.
Wash. (US) abbr (POST: = Washington).
washable ['wɔʃəbl] adj (fabric) waschbar;
(wallpaper) abwaschbar.
washbasin ['wɔʃbeɪsn], (US) **washbowl**
['wɔʃbəul] n Waschbecken nt.
washcloth ['wɔʃklɔθ] (US) n Waschlappen m.
washer ['wɔʃə*] n (on tap etc) Dichtungsring
m.
washing ['wɔʃɪŋ] n Wäsche f.
washing line (BRIT) n Wäscheleine f.
washing machine n Waschmaschine f.
washing powder (BRIT) n Waschpulver nt.
Washington ['wɔʃɪŋtən] n Washington nt.
washing-up [wɔʃɪŋ'ʌp] n Abwasch m; **to do
the ~** spülen, abwaschen.

washing-up liquid (BRIT) n
(Geschirr)spülmittel nt.
wash-out ['wɔʃaut] (inf) n (failed event)
Reinfall m.
washroom ['wɔʃrum] (US) n Waschraum m.
wasn't ['wɔznt] = **was not**.
WASP, Wasp [wɔsp] (US: inf) n abbr (= White
Anglo-Saxon Protestant) weißer
angelsächsischer Protestant m.
wasp [wɔsp] n Wespe f.
waspish ['wɔspɪʃ] adj giftig.
wastage ['weɪstɪdʒ] n Verlust m; **natural ~**
natürliche Personalreduzierung.
waste [weɪst] n Verschwendung f; (rubbish)
Abfall m ♦ adj (material) Abfall-; (left over:
paper etc) ungenutzt ♦ vt verschwenden;
(opportunity) vertun; **wastes** npl (area of land)
Wildnis f; **it's a ~ of money** das ist Geldver-
schwendung; **to go to ~** umkommen; **to lay
~** (area, town) verwüsten.
▶ **waste away** vi verkümmern.
wastebasket ['weɪstbɑ:skɪt] (US) n
= **wastepaper basket**.
waste disposal unit (BRIT) n Müllschlucker
m.
wasteful ['weɪstful] adj (person)
verschwenderisch; (process) aufwändig,
aufwendig.
waste ground (BRIT) n unbebautes
Grundstück nt.
wasteland ['weɪstlənd] n Ödland nt; (in town)
ödes Gebiet nt; (fig) Einöde f.
wastepaper basket ['weɪstpeɪpə-] (BRIT) n
Papierkorb m.
waste pipe n Abflussrohr nt.
waste products npl Abfallprodukte pl.
waster ['weɪstə*] n Verschwender(in) m(f);
(good-for-nothing) Taugenichts m.
watch [wɔtʃ] n (also: **wristwatch**)
(Armband)uhr f; (surveillance) Bewachung f;
(MIL, NAUT: group of guards)
Wachmannschaft f; (NAUT: spell of duty)
Wache f ♦ vt (look at) betrachten; (: match,
programme) sich dat ansehen; (spy on, guard)
beobachten; (be careful of) aufpassen auf
+acc ♦ vi (look) zusehen; **to be on ~** Wache
halten; **to keep a close ~ on sb/sth** jdn/etw
genau im Auge behalten; **to ~ TV**
fernsehen; **~ what you're doing!** pass auf!;
~ how you drive! fahr vorsichtig!
▶ **watch out** vi aufpassen; **~ out!** Vorsicht!
watchband ['wɔtʃbænd] (US) n = **watchstrap**.
watchdog ['wɔtʃdɔg] n (dog) Wachhund m;
(fig) Aufpasser(in) m(f).
watchful ['wɔtʃful] adj wachsam.
watchmaker ['wɔtʃmeɪkə*] n Uhrmacher m.
watchman ['wɔtʃmən] (irreg: like **man**) n see
night watchman.
watch stem (US) n (winder) Krone f,
Aufziehrädchen nt.
watchstrap ['wɔtʃstræp] n Uhrarmband nt.
watchword ['wɔtʃwɔ:d] n Parole f.

water ['wɔ:tə°] n Wasser nt ♦ vt (plant) gießen;
(garden) bewässern ♦ vi (eyes) tränen; **a
drink of** ~ ein Schluck Wasser; **in British** ~**s**
in britischen (Hoheits)gewässern; **to pass** ~
(urinate) Wasser lassen; **my mouth is** ~**ing**
mir läuft das Wasser im Mund zusammen;
to make sb's mouth ~ jdm den Mund
wässrig machen.
▶ **water down** vt (also fig) verwässern.
water biscuit n Kräcker m.
water cannon n Wasserwerfer m.
water closet (BRIT: old) n Wasserklosett nt.
watercolour, (US) **watercolor** ['wɔ:təkʌlə°] n
(picture) Aquarell nt; **watercolours** npl
(paints) Wasserfarben pl.
water-cooled ['wɔ:təku:ld] adj
wassergekühlt.
watercress ['wɔ:təkrɛs] n Brunnenkresse f.
waterfall ['wɔ:təfɔ:l] n Wasserfall m.
waterfront ['wɔ:təfrʌnt] n (at seaside) Ufer nt;
(at docks) Hafengegend f.
water heater n Heißwassergerät nt.
water hole n Wasserloch nt.
water ice n Fruchteis nt (auf Wasserbasis).
watering can ['wɔ:tərɪŋ-] n Gießkanne f.
water level n Wasserstand m; (of flood)
Pegelstand m.
water lily n Seerose f.
water line n Wasserlinie f.
waterlogged ['wɔ:təlɔgd] adj (ground) unter
Wasser.
water main n Hauptwasserleitung f.
watermark ['wɔ:təmɑ:k] n (on paper)
Wasserzeichen nt.
watermelon ['wɔ:təmɛlən] n Wassermelone f.
waterproof ['wɔ:təpru:f] adj (trousers, jacket
etc) wasserdicht.
water-repellent ['wɔ:tərɪ'pɛlnt] adj Wasser
abstoßend.
watershed ['wɔ:təʃɛd] n (GEOG)
Wasserscheide f; (fig) Wendepunkt m.
water-skiing ['wɔ:təski:ɪŋ] n Wasserski nt.
water softener n Wasserenthärter m.
water tank n Wassertank m.
watertight ['wɔ:tətaɪt] adj wasserdicht; (fig:
excuse, case, agreement etc) hieb- und
stichfest.
water vapour n Wasserdampf m.
waterway ['wɔ:təweɪ] n Wasserstraße f.
waterworks ['wɔ:təwɔ:ks] n Wasserwerk nt;
(inf, fig: bladder) Blase f.
watery ['wɔ:tərɪ] adj (coffee, soup etc) wässrig;
(eyes) tränend.
watt [wɔt] n Watt nt.
wattage ['wɔtɪdʒ] n Wattleistung f.
wattle ['wɔtl] n Flechtwerk nt.
wattle and daub n Lehmgeflecht nt.
wave [weɪv] n (also fig) Welle f; (of hand)
Winken nt ♦ vi (signal) winken; (branches)
sich hin und her bewegen; (grass) wogen;
(flag) wehen ♦ vt (hand, flag etc) winken mit;
(gun, stick) schwenken; (hair) wellen; **short/**
medium/long ~ (RADIO) Kurz-/Mittel-/
Langwelle f; **the new** ~ (CINE, MUS) die
neue Welle f; **he** ~**d us over to his table** er
winkte uns zu seinem Tisch hinüber; **to**
~ **goodbye to sb** jdm zum Abschied
winken.
▶ **wave aside** vt (fig: suggestion etc)
zurückweisen.
waveband ['weɪvbænd] n (RADIO)
Wellenbereich m.
wavelength ['weɪvlɛŋθ] n (RADIO)
Wellenlänge f; **on the same** ~ (fig) auf
derselben Wellenlänge.
waver ['weɪvə°] vi (voice) schwanken; (eyes)
zucken; (love, person) wanken.
wavy ['weɪvɪ] adj (line) wellenförmig; (hair)
wellig.
wax [wæks] n Wachs nt; (for sealing)
Siegellack m; (in ear) Ohrenschmalz nt ♦ vt
(floor) bohnern; (car, skis) wachsen ♦ vi
(moon) zunehmen.
waxed [wækst] adj (jacket) gewachst.
waxen [wæksn] adj (face) wachsbleich.
waxworks ['wækswɔ:ks] npl (models)
Wachsfiguren pl ♦ n (place)
Wachsfigurenkabinett nt.
way [weɪ] n Weg m; (distance) Strecke f;
(direction) Richtung f; (manner) Art f;
(method) Art und Weise f; (habit)
Gewohnheit f; **which** ~ **to ...?** wo geht es zu
...?; **this** ~**, please** hier entlang, bitte; **on the**
~ (en route) auf dem Weg, unterwegs; **to be**
on one's ~ auf dem Weg sein; **to fight one's**
~ **through a crowd** sich acc durch die
Menge kämpfen; **to lie one's** ~ **out of sth**
sich aus etw herauslügen; **to keep out of**
sb's ~ jdm aus dem Weg gehen; **it's a long**
~ **away** es ist weit entfernt; (event) das ist
noch lange hin; **the village is rather out of**
the ~ das Dorf ist recht abgelegen; **to go**
out of one's ~ **to do sth** sich sehr bemühen,
etw zu tun; **to be in the** ~ im Weg sein; **to**
lose one's ~ sich verirren; **under** ~ (project
etc) im Gang; **the** ~ **back** der Rückweg; **to**
make ~ (for sb/sth) (für jdn/etw) Platz
machen; **to get one's own** ~ seinen Willen
bekommen; **put it the right** ~ **up** (BRIT) stell
es richtig herum hin; **to be the wrong**
~ **round** verkehrt herum sein; **he's in a bad**
~ ihm geht es schlecht; **in a** ~ in gewisser
Weise; **in some** ~**s** in mancher Hinsicht; **no**
~! (inf) kommt nicht infrage or in Frage!;
by the ~ ... übrigens ...; "~ **in**" (BRIT)
„Eingang"; "~ **out**" (BRIT) „Ausgang";
"**give** ~" (BRIT: AUT) „Vorfahrt beachten";
~ **of life** Lebensstil m.
waybill ['weɪbɪl] n Frachtbrief m.
waylay [weɪ'leɪ] (irreg: like **lay**) vt auflauern
+dat; **to get waylaid** (fig) abgefangen werden.
wayside ['weɪsaɪd] adj am Straßenrand ♦ n
Straßenrand m; **to fall by the** ~ (fig) auf die
Strecke bleiben.

way station (*US*) *n* (*RAIL*) kleiner Bahnhof *m*; (*fig*) Zwischenstation *f*.

wayward ['weɪwəd] *adj* (*behaviour*) eigenwillig; (*child*) eigensinnig.

WC (*BRIT*) *n abbr* (= *water closet*) WC *nt*.

WCC *n abbr* (= *World Council of Churches*) Weltkirchenrat *m*.

we [wiː] *pl pron* wir; **here ~ are** (*arriving*) da sind wir; (*finding sth*) na bitte.

weak [wiːk] *adj* schwach; (*tea, coffee*) dünn; **to grow ~(er)** schwächer werden.

weaken ['wiːkn] *vi* (*resolve, person*) schwächer werden; (*influence, power*) nachlassen ♦ *vt* schwächen.

weak-kneed ['wiːk'niːd] *adj* (*fig*) schwächlich.

weakling ['wiːklɪŋ] *n* Schwächling *m*.

weakly ['wiːklɪ] *adv* schwach.

weakness ['wiːknɪs] *n* Schwäche *f*; **to have a ~ for** eine Schwäche haben für.

wealth [welθ] *n* Reichtum *m*; (*of details, knowledge etc*) Fülle *f*.

wealth tax *n* Vermögenssteuer *f*.

wealthy ['welθɪ] *adj* wohlhabend, reich.

wean [wiːn] *vt* (*also fig*) entwöhnen.

weapon ['wepən] *n* Waffe *f*; **~s of mass destruction** Massenvernichtungswaffen *pl*.

wear [weə*] (*pt* **wore**, *pp* **worn**) *vt* (*clothes, shoes, beard*) tragen; (*put on*) anziehen ♦ *vi* (*last*) halten; (*become old: carpet, jeans*) sich abnutzen ♦ *n* (*damage*) Verschleiß *m*; (*use*): **I got a lot of/very little ~ out of the coat** der Mantel hat lange/nicht sehr lange gehalten; **baby~** Babykleidung *f*; **sports~** Sportkleidung *f*; **evening ~** Kleidung für den Abend; **to ~ a hole in sth** (*coat etc*) etw durchsetzen.

▶ **wear away** *vt* verschleißen ♦ *vi* (*inscription etc*) verwittern.

▶ **wear down** *vt* (*heels*) abnutzen; (*person, strength*) zermürben.

▶ **wear off** *vi* (*pain etc*) nachlassen.

▶ **wear on** *vi* sich hinziehen.

▶ **wear out** *vt* (*shoes, clothing*) verschleißen; (*person, strength*) erschöpfen.

wearable ['weərəbl] *adj* tragbar.

wear and tear [-tɛə*] *n* Verschleiß *m*.

wearer ['weərə*] *n* Träger(in) *m(f)*.

wearily ['wɪərɪlɪ] *adv* (*say, sit*) lustlos, müde.

weariness ['wɪərɪnɪs] *n* (*tiredness*) Müdigkeit *f*.

wearisome ['wɪərɪsəm] *adj* (*boring*) langweilig; (*tiring*) ermüdend.

weary ['wɪərɪ] *adj* (*tired*) müde; (*dispirited*) lustlos ♦ *vi*: **to ~ of sb/sth** jds/etw *gen* überdrüssig werden.

weasel ['wiːzl] *n* Wiesel *nt*.

weather ['weðə*] *n* Wetter *nt* ♦ *vt* (*storm, crisis*) überstehen; (*rock, wood*) verwittern; **what's the ~ like?** wie ist das Wetter?; **under the ~** (*fig: ill*) angeschlagen.

weather-beaten ['weðəbiːtn] *adj* (*face*) vom Wetter gegerbt; (*building, stone*) verwittert.

weathercock ['weðəkɔk] *n* Wetterhahn *m*.

weather forecast *n* Wettervorhersage *f*.

weatherman ['weðəmæn] (*irreg: like* **man**) *n* Mann *m* vom Wetteramt, Wetterfrosch *m* (*hum inf*).

weatherproof ['weðəpruːf] *adj* wetterfest.

weather report *n* Wetterbericht *m*.

weather vane [-veɪn] *n* = **weathercock**.

weave [wiːv] (*pt* **wove**, *pp* **woven**) *vt* (*cloth*) weben; (*basket*) flechten ♦ *vi* (*fig: pt, pp* **weaved**: *move in and out*) sich schlängeln.

weaver ['wiːvə*] *n* Weber(in) *m(f)*.

weaving ['wiːvɪŋ] *n* Weberei *f*.

web [web] *n* (*also fig*) Netz *nt*; (*on duck's foot*) Schwimmhaut *f*.

webbed [webd] *adj* (*foot*) Schwimm-.

webbing ['webɪŋ] *n* (*on chair*) Gewebe *nt*.

website ['websaɪt] *n* (*COMPUT*) Website *f*, Webseite *f*.

wed [wed] (*pt, pp* **wedded**) *vt, vi* heiraten ♦ *n*: **the newly-~s** die Jungvermählten *pl*.

Wed. *abbr* (= *Wednesday*) Mi.

we'd [wiːd] = **we had**; = **we would**.

wedded ['wedɪd] *pt, pp of* **wed** ♦ *adj*: **to be ~ to sth** (*idea etc*) mit etw eng verbunden sein.

wedding ['wedɪŋ] *n* Hochzeit *f*; **silver/golden ~** silberne/goldene Hochzeit.

wedding day *n* Hochzeitstag *m*.

wedding dress *n* Hochzeitskleid *nt*.

wedding present *n* Hochzeitsgeschenk *nt*.

wedding ring *n* Trauring *m*.

wedge [wedʒ] *n* Keil *m*; (*of cake*) Stück *nt* ♦ *vt* (*fasten*) festklemmen; (*pack tightly*) einkeilen.

wedge-heeled shoes ['wedʒhiːld-] *npl* Schuhe *pl* mit Keilabsätzen.

wedlock ['wedlɔk] *n* Ehe *f*.

Wednesday ['wednzdɪ] *n* Mittwoch *m*; *see also* **Tuesday**.

wee [wiː] (*SCOT*) *adj* klein.

weed [wiːd] *n* (*BOT*) Unkraut *nt*; (*pej: person*) Schwächling *m* ♦ *vt* (*garden*) jäten.

▶ **weed out** *vt* (*fig*) aussondern.

weedkiller ['wiːdkɪlə*] *n* Unkrautvertilger *m*.

weedy ['wiːdɪ] *adj* (*person*) schwächlich.

week [wiːk] *n* Woche *f*; **once/twice a ~** einmal/zweimal die Woche; **in two ~s' time** in zwei Wochen; **a ~ today/on Friday** heute/Freitag in einer Woche.

weekday ['wiːkdeɪ] *n* Wochentag *m*; (*COMM: Monday to Saturday*) Werktag *m*; **on ~s** an Wochentagen/Werktagen.

weekend [wiːk'end] *n* Wochenende *nt*; **this/next/last ~** an diesem/am nächsten/am letzten Wochenende; **what are you doing at the ~?** was machen Sie am Wochenende?; **open at ~s** an Wochenenden geöffnet.

weekly ['wiːklɪ] *adv* wöchentlich ♦ *adj* (*newspaper*) Wochen- ♦ *n* (*newspaper*) Wochenzeitung *f*; (*magazine*) Wochenzeitschrift *f*.

weep [wiːp] (*pt, pp* **wept**) *vi* (*person*) weinen; (*wound*) nässen.

weeping willow ['wiːpɪŋ-] n (*tree*) Trauerweide f.

weepy ['wiːpɪ] adj (*person*) weinerlich; (*film*) rührselig ♦ n (*film etc*) Schmachtfetzen m.

weft [wɛft] n Schussfaden m.

weigh [weɪ] vt wiegen; (*fig: evidence, risks*) abwägen ♦ vi wiegen; **to ~ anchor** den Anker lichten.

▶ **weigh down** vt niederdrücken.

▶ **weigh out** vt (*goods*) auswiegen.

▶ **weigh up** vt (*person, offer, risk*) abschätzen.

weighbridge ['weɪbrɪdʒ] n Brückenwaage f.

weighing machine ['weɪɪŋ-] n Waage f.

weight [weɪt] n Gewicht nt ♦ vt (*fig*): **to be ~ed in favour of sb/sth** jdn/etw begünstigen; **to be sold by ~** nach Gewicht verkauft werden; **to lose ~** abnehmen; **to put on ~** zunehmen; **~s and measures** Maße und Gewichte.

weighting ['weɪtɪŋ] n (*allowance*) Zulage f.

weightlessness ['weɪtlɪsnɪs] n Schwerelosigkeit f.

weightlifter ['weɪtlɪftə*] n Gewichtheber m.

weight limit n Gewichtsbeschränkung f.

weight training n Krafttraining nt.

weighty ['weɪtɪ] adj schwer (*fig: important*) gewichtig.

weir [wɪə*] n (*in river*) Wehr nt.

weird [wɪəd] adj (*object, situation, effect*) komisch; (*person*) seltsam.

weirdo ['wɪədəu] (*inf*) n verrückter Typ m.

welcome ['wɛlkəm] adj willkommen ♦ n Willkommen nt ♦ vt begrüßen, willkommen heißen; **~ to London!** willkommen in London!; **to make sb ~** jdn freundlich aufnehmen; **you're ~ to try** du kannst es gern versuchen; **thank you - you're ~!** danke - nichts zu danken!

welcoming ['wɛlkəmɪŋ] adj (*smile, room*) einladend; (*person*) freundlich.

weld [wɛld] n Schweißnaht f ♦ vt schweißen.

welder ['wɛldə*] n (*person*) Schweißer(in) m(f).

welding ['wɛldɪŋ] n Schweißen nt.

welfare ['wɛlfɛə*] n (*well-being*) Wohl nt; (*social aid*) Sozialhilfe f.

welfare state n Wohlfahrtsstaat m.

welfare work n Fürsorgearbeit f.

well [wɛl] n (*for water*) Brunnen m; (*oil well*) Quelle f ♦ adv gut; (*for emphasis with adj*) durchaus ♦ adj: **to be ~** (*person*) gesund sein ♦ excl nun!, na!; **as ~** (*in addition*) ebenfalls; **you might as ~ tell me** sag es mir ruhig; **he did as ~ as he could** er machte es so gut er konnte; **pretty as ~ as rich** sowohl hübsch als auch reich; **~ done!** gut gemacht!; **to do ~** (*person*) gut vorankommen; (*business*) gut gehen; **~ before dawn** lange vor Tagesanbruch; **~ over 40** weit über 40; **I don't feel ~** ich fühle mich nicht gut or wohl; **get ~ soon!** gute Besserung!; **~, as I was saying ...** also, wie ich bereits sagte, ...

▶ **well up** vi (*tears, emotions*) aufsteigen.

we'll [wiːl] = **we will**, **we shall**.

well-behaved ['wɛlbɪ'heɪvd] adj wohlerzogen, wohl erzogen.

well-being ['wɛl'biːɪŋ] n Wohl(ergehen) nt.

well-bred ['wɛl'brɛd] adj (*person*) gut erzogen.

well-built ['wɛl'bɪlt] adj gut gebaut.

well-chosen ['wɛl'tʃəuzn] adj gut gewählt.

well-deserved ['wɛldɪ'zəːvd] adj wohlverdient.

well-developed ['wɛldɪ'vɛləpt] adj gut entwickelt.

well-disposed ['wɛl'dɪspəuzd] adj: **~ to(wards)** freundlich gesonnen +dat.

well-dressed ['wɛl'drɛst] adj gut gekleidet.

well-earned ['wɛl'əːnd] adj (*rest*) wohlverdient.

well-groomed ['wɛl'gruːmd] adj gepflegt.

well-heeled ['wɛl'hiːld] (*inf*) adj betucht.

well-informed ['wɛlɪn'fɔːmd] adj gut informiert.

Wellington ['wɛlɪŋtən] n (*GEOG*) Wellington nt.

wellingtons ['wɛlɪŋtənz] npl (also: **wellington boots**) Gummistiefel pl.

well-kept ['wɛl'kɛpt] adj (*house, grounds*) gepflegt; (*secret*) gut gehütet.

well-known ['wɛl'nəun] adj wohlbekannt, wohl bekannt.

well-mannered ['wɛl'mænəd] adj wohlerzogen, wohl erzogen.

well-meaning ['wɛl'miːnɪŋ] adj (*person*) wohlmeinend; (*offer etc*) gut gemeint.

well-nigh ['wɛl'naɪ] adv: **~ impossible** geradezu unmöglich.

well-off ['wɛl'ɔf] adj (*rich*) begütert.

well-read ['wɛl'rɛd] adj belesen.

well-spoken ['wɛl'spəukn] adj: **to be ~** sich gut or gewandt ausdrücken.

well-stocked ['wɛl'stɔkt] adj gut bestückt.

well-timed ['wɛl'taɪmd] adj gut abgepasst.

well-to-do ['wɛltə'duː] adj wohlhabend.

well-wisher ['wɛlwɪʃə*] n (*friend, admirer*) wohlmeinender Mensch m; **scores of ~s had gathered** eine große Gefolgschaft hatte sich versammelt; **letters from ~s** Briefe von Leuten, die es gut meinen.

well-woman clinic ['wɛlwumən-] n ≈ Frauensprechstunde f.

Welsh [wɛlʃ] adj walisisch ♦ n (*LING*) Walisisch nt; **the Welsh** npl die Waliser pl.

Welshman ['wɛlʃmən] (*irreg: like* **man**) n Waliser m.

Welsh rarebit n überbackenes Käsebrot nt.

Welshwoman ['wɛlʃwumən] (*irreg: like* **woman**) n Waliserin f.

welter ['wɛltə*] n: **a ~ of** eine Flut von.

went [wɛnt] pt of **go**.

wept [wɛpt] pt, pp of **weep**.

were [wəː*] pt of **be**.

we're [wɪə*] = **we are**.

weren't [wəːnt] = **were not**.

werewolf ['wɪəwulf] (*pl* **werewolves**) n

Werwolf m.

werewolves ['wɪəwulvz] npl of **werewolf**.

west [west] n Westen m ♦ adj (wind, side, coast) West-, westlich ♦ adv (to or towards the west) westwärts; **the W~** (POL) der Westen.

westbound ['westbaund] adj (traffic, carriageway) in Richtung Westen.

West Country (BRIT) n: **the ~** Südwestengland nt.

westerly ['westəlɪ] adj westlich.

western ['westən] adj westlich ♦ n (CINE) Western m.

westerner ['westənə'] n Abendländer(in) m(f).

westernized ['westənaɪzd] adj (society etc) verwestlicht.

West German adj westdeutsch ♦ n (person) Westdeutsche(r) f(m).

West Germany n (formerly) Bundesrepublik f Deutschland.

West Indian adj westindisch ♦ n (person) Westinder(in) m(f).

West Indies [-'ɪndɪz] npl: **the ~** Westindien nt.

Westminster ['westmɪnstə'] n Westminster nt; (parliament) das britische Parlament.

westward(s) ['westwəd(z)] adv westwärts.

wet [wet] adj nass ♦ n (BRIT: POL) Gemäßigte(r) f(m), Waschlappen m (pej); **to get ~** nass werden; **"~ paint"** „frisch gestrichen"; **to be a ~ blanket** (fig: pej: person) ein(e) Spielverderber(in) m(f) sein; **to ~ one's pants/o.s.** sich dat in die Hosen machen.

wetness ['wetnɪs] n Nässe f; (of climate) Feuchtigkeit f.

wet suit n Taucheranzug m.

we've [wiːv] = **we have**.

whack [wæk] vt schlagen.

whacked [wækt] (BRIT: inf) adj (exhausted) erschlagen.

whale [weɪl] n Wal m.

whaler ['weɪlə'] n Walfänger m.

whaling ['weɪlɪŋ] n Walfang m.

wharf [wɔːf] (pl **wharves**) n Kai m.

wharves [wɔːvz] npl of **wharf**.

══════════════ KEYWORD

what [wɔt] adj 1 (in direct/indirect questions) welche(r, s); **~ colour/shape is it?** welche Farbe/Form hat es?; **for ~ reason?** aus welchem Grund?

2 (in exclamations) was für ein(e); **~ a mess!** was für ein Durcheinander!; **~ a fool I am!** was bin ich doch (für) ein Idiot!

♦ pron (interrogative, relative) was; **~ are you doing?** was machst du?; **~ are you talking about?** wovon redest du?; **~ is it called?** wie heißt das?; **~ about me?** und ich?; **~ about a cup of tea?** wie wärs mit einer Tasse Tee?; **~ about going to the cinema?** sollen wir ins Kino gehen?; **I saw ~ you did/what was on the table** ich habe gesehen, was du getan hast/was auf dem Tisch war; **tell me**

~ you're thinking about sag mir, woran du denkst

♦ excl (disbelieving) was, wie; **~, no coffee!** was or wie, kein Kaffee?

──────────────

whatever [wɔt'evə'] adj: **~ book** welches Buch auch immer ♦ pron: **do ~ is necessary/ you want** tun Sie, was nötig ist/was immer Sie wollen; **~ happens** was auch passiert; **no reason ~ or whatsoever** überhaupt kein Grund; **nothing ~ or whatsoever** überhaupt nichts.

whatsoever [wɔtsəu'evə'] adj = **whatever**.

wheat [wiːt] n Weizen m.

wheatgerm ['wiːtdʒɜːm] n Weizenkeim m.

wheatmeal ['wiːtmiːl] n Weizenmehl nt.

wheedle ['wiːdl] vt: **to ~ sb into doing sth** jdn beschwatzen, etw zu tun; **to ~ sth out of sb** jdm etw abluchsen.

wheel [wiːl] n Rad nt; (also: **steering ~**) Lenkrad nt; (NAUT) Steuer nt ♦ vt (pram etc) schieben ♦ vi (birds) kreisen; (also: **~ round**: person) sich herumdrehen.

wheelbarrow ['wiːlbærəu] n Schubkarre f.

wheelbase ['wiːlbeɪs] n Radstand m.

wheelchair ['wiːltʃeə'] n Rollstuhl m.

wheel clamp n Parkkralle f.

wheeler-dealer ['wiːlə'diːlə'] (pej) n Geschäftemacher(in) m(f).

wheelie-bin ['wiːlɪbɪn] n Mülltonne f auf Rädern.

wheeling ['wiːlɪŋ] n: **~ and dealing** (pej) Geschäftemacherei f.

wheeze [wiːz] vi (person) keuchen ♦ n (idea, joke etc) Scherz m.

wheezy ['wiːzɪ] adj (person) mit pfeifendem Atem; (cough) keuchend; (breath) pfeifend; (laugh) asthmatisch.

══════════════ KEYWORD

when [wen] adv wann

♦ conj 1 (at, during, after the time that) wenn; **she was reading ~ I came in** als ich hereinkam, las sie gerade; **be careful ~ you cross the road** sei vorsichtig, wenn du die Straße überquerst.

2 (on, at which) als; **on the day ~ I met him** am Tag, als ich ihn traf.

3 (whereas) wo ... doch, obwohl; **why did you buy that ~ you can't afford it?** warum hast du das gekauft, obwohl du es dir nicht leisten kannst?

──────────────

whenever [wen'evə'] adv, conj (any time that) wann immer; (every time that) (jedes Mal,) wenn; **I go ~ I can** ich gehe, wann immer ich kann.

where [weə'] adv, conj wo; **this is ~ ...** hier ...; **~ possible** so weit möglich; **~ are you from?** woher kommen Sie?

whereabouts ['weərə'bauts] adv wo ♦ n: **nobody knows his ~** keiner weiß, wo er ist.

whereas [wɛər'æz] *conj* während.
whereby [wɛə'baɪ] (*form*) *adv* wonach.
whereupon [wɛərə'pɒn] *conj* worauf.
wherever [wɛər'ɛvə*] *conj* (*position*) wo (auch) immer; (*motion*) wohin (auch) immer ♦ *adv* (*surprise*) wo (um alles in der Welt); **sit ~ you like** nehmen Sie Platz, wo immer Sie wollen.
wherewithal ['wɛəwɪðɔːl] *n*: **the ~ (to do sth)** (*money*) das nötige Kleingeld(, um etw zu tun).
whet [wɛt] *vt* (*appetite*) anregen; (*tool*) schleifen.
whether ['wɛðə*] *conj* ob; **I don't know ~ to accept or not** ich weiß nicht, ob ich annehmen soll oder nicht; **~ you go or not** ob du gehst oder nicht; **it's doubtful ~ ...** es ist zweifelhaft, ob ...
whey ['weɪ] *n* Molke *f*.

===================== *KEYWORD*

which [wɪtʃ] *adj* **1** (*interrogative: direct, indirect*) welche(r, s); **~ picture?** welches Bild?; **~ books?** welche Bücher?; **~ one?** welche(r, s)?
2: in ~ case in diesem Fall; **by ~ time** zu dieser Zeit
♦ *pron* **1** (*interrogative*) welche(r, s); **~ of you are coming?** wer von Ihnen kommt?; **I don't mind ~** mir ist gleich, welche(r, s).
2 (*relative*) der/die/das; **the apple ~ you ate/ which is on the table** der Apfel, den du gegessen hast/der auf dem Tisch liegt; **the chair on ~ you are sitting** der Stuhl, auf dem Sie sitzen; **the book of ~ you spoke** das Buch, wovon *or* von dem Sie sprachen; **he said he saw her, ~ is true** er sagte, er habe sie gesehen, was auch stimmt; **after ~** wonach.

whichever [wɪtʃ'ɛvə*] *adj*: **take ~ book you want** nehmen Sie irgendein *or* ein beliebiges Buch; **~ book you take** welches Buch Sie auch nehmen.
whiff [wɪf] *n* (*of perfume*) Hauch *m*; (*of petrol, smoke*) Geruch *m*; **to catch a ~ of sth** den Geruch von etw wahrnehmen.
while [waɪl] *n* Weile *f* ♦ *conj* während; **for a ~** eine Weile (lang); **in a ~** gleich; **all the ~** die ganze Zeit (über); **I'll/we'll** *etc* **make it worth your ~** es wird sich für Sie lohnen.
► **while away** *vt* (*time*) sich *dat* vertreiben.
whilst [waɪlst] *conj* = **while**.
whim [wɪm] *n* Laune *f*.
whimper ['wɪmpə*] *n* (*cry, moan*) Wimmern *nt* ♦ *vi* wimmern.
whimsical ['wɪmzɪkəl] *adj* wunderlich, seltsam; (*story*) kurios.
whine [waɪn] *n* (*of pain*) Jammern *nt*; (*of engine, siren*) Heulen *nt* ♦ *vi* (*person*) jammern; (*dog*) jaulen; (*engine, siren*) heulen.
whip [wɪp] *n* Peitsche *f*; (*POL*) ≈

Fraktionsführer *m* ♦ *vt* (*person, animal*) peitschen; (*cream, eggs*) schlagen; (*move quickly*): **to ~ sth out/off** etw blitzschnell hervorholen/wegbringen.

WHIP

Der Ausdruck **whip** *bezieht sich in der Politik auf einen Abgeordneten, der für die Einhaltung der Parteidisziplin zuständig ist, besonders für die Anwesenheit und das Wahlverhalten der Abgeordneten im Unterhaus. Die* **whips** *fordern die Abgeordneten ihrer Partei schriftlich zur Anwesenheit auf und deuten die Wichtigkeit der Abstimmungen durch ein-, zwei-, oder dreimaliges Unterstreichen an, wobei dreimaliges Unterstreichen (3-line whip) strengsten Fraktionszwang bedeutet.*

► **whip up** *vt* (*cream*) schlagen; (*inf: meal*) hinzaubern; (*arouse: support*) anheizen; (*: people*) mitreißen.
whiplash ['wɪplæʃ] *n* Peitschenhieb *m*; (*MED: also*: **~ injury**) Schleudertrauma *nt*.
whipped cream [wɪpt-] *n* Schlagsahne *f*.
whipping boy ['wɪpɪŋ-] *n* (*fig*) Prügelknabe *m*.
whip-round ['wɪpraund] (*BRIT: inf*) *n* (Geld)sammlung *f*.
whirl [wəːl] *vt* (*arms, sword etc*) herumwirbeln ♦ *vi* wirbeln ♦ *n* (*of activity, pleasure*) Wirbel *m*; **to be in a ~** (*mind, person*) völlig verwirrt sein.
whirlpool ['wəːlpuːl] *n* (*lit*) Strudel *m*.
whirlwind ['wəːlwɪnd] *n* (*lit*) Wirbelwind *m*.
whirr [wəː*] *vi* (*motor etc*) surren.
whisk [wɪsk] *n* (*CULIN*) Schneebesen *m* ♦ *vt* (*cream, eggs*) schlagen; **to ~ sb away** *or* **off** jdn in Windeseile wegbringen.
whiskers ['wɪskəz] *npl* (*of animal*) Barthaare *pl*; (*of man*) Backenbart *m*.
whisky, (*US, Ireland*) **whiskey** ['wɪskɪ] *n* Whisky *m*.
whisper ['wɪspə*] *n* Flüstern *nt*; (*fig: of wind*) Wispern *nt* ♦ *vt, vi* flüstern; **to ~ sth to sb** jdm etw zuflüstern.
whispering ['wɪspərɪŋ] *n* Geflüster *nt*.
whist [wɪst] (*BRIT*) *n* Whist *nt*.
whistle ['wɪsl] *n* (*sound*) Pfiff *m*; (*object*) Pfeife *f* ♦ *vi* pfeifen ♦ *vt* **to ~ a tune** eine Melodie pfeifen.
whistle-stop ['wɪslstɒp] *adj*: **to make a ~ tour of** (*fig*) eine Rundreise machen durch; (*POL*) eine Wahlkampfreise machen durch.
Whit [wɪt] *n* = **Whitsun**.
white [waɪt] *adj* weiß ♦ *n* (*colour*) Weiß *nt*; (*person*) Weiße(r) *f(m)*; (*of egg, eye*) Weiße(s) *nt*; **to turn** *or* **go ~** (*person: with fear*) weiß *or* bleich werden; (*: with age*) weiße Haare bekommen; (*hair*) weiß werden; **the ~s** (*washing*) die Weißwäsche *f*; **tennis/cricket ~s** weiße Tennis-/Krickettrikots.
whitebait ['waɪtbeɪt] *n* essbare *Jungfische*

(*Heringe, Sprotten etc*).
white coffee (*BRIT*) *n* Kaffee *m* mit Milch.
white-collar worker ['waɪtkɒlə-] *n*
Schreibtischarbeiter(in) *m(f)*.
white elephant *n* (*fig: venture*)
Fehlinvestition *f*.
white goods *npl* (*appliances*) große
Haushaltsgeräte *pl*; (*linen etc*) Weißwaren *pl*.
white-hot [waɪt'hɒt] *adj* (*metal*) weiß glühend.

WHITE HOUSE

White House, *eine weiß gestrichene Villa in
Washington, ist der offizielle Wohnsitz des
amerikanischen Präsidenten. Im weiteren Sinne
bezieht sich dieser Begriff auf die Exekutive der
amerikanischen Regierung.*

---

white lie *n* Notlüge *f*.
whiteness ['waɪtnɪs] *n* Weiß *nt*.
white noise *n* weißes Rauschen *nt*.
whiteout ['waɪtaut] *n* starkes Schneegestöber
nt.
white paper *n* (*POL*) Weißbuch *nt*.
whitewash ['waɪtwɒʃ] *n* (*paint*) Tünche *f*; (*inf:
SPORT*) totale Niederlage *f* ♦ *vt* (*building*)
tünchen; (*fig: incident, reputation*)
reinwaschen.
white water *n*: **white-water rafting**
Wildwasserflößen *nt*.
whiting ['waɪtɪŋ] *n inv* (*fish*) Weißling *m*.
Whit Monday *n* Pfingstmontag *m*.
Whitsun ['wɪtsn] *n* Pfingsten *pl*.
whittle ['wɪtl] *vt*: **to ~ away** *or* **down** (*costs
etc*) verringern.
whizz [wɪz] *vi*: **to ~ past** *or* **by** vorbeisausen.
whizz kid (*inf*) *n* Senkrechtstarter(in) *m(f)*.
WHO *n abbr* (= *World Health Organization*)
Weltgesundheitsorganisation *f*, WHO *f*.

========================= KEYWORD

who [hu:] *pron* **1** (*interrogative*) wer; (: *acc*)
wen; (: *dat*) wem; **~ is it?, who's there?** wer
ist da?; **~ did you give it to?** wem hast du es
gegeben?
2 (*relative*) der/die/das; **the man/woman
~ spoke to me** der Mann, der/die Frau, die
mit mir gesprochen hat.

---

whodunit, whodunnit [hu:'dʌnɪt] (*inf*) *n*
Krimi *m*.
whoever [hu:'ɛvə*] *pron*: **~ finds it** wer (auch
immer) es findet; **ask ~ you like** fragen Sie,
wen Sie wollen; **~ he marries** ganz gleich *or*
egal, wen er heiratet; **~ told you that?** wer
um alles in der Welt hat dir das erzählt?
whole [həul] *adj* (*entire*) ganz; (*not broken*) heil
♦ *n* Ganze(s) *nt*; **the ~ lot (of it)** alles; **the
~ lot (of them)** alle; **the ~ (of the) time** die
ganze Zeit; **~ villages were destroyed** ganze
Dörfer wurden zerstört; **the ~ of** der/die/
das ganze; **the ~ of Glasgow/Europe** ganz

Glasgow/Europa; **the ~ of the town** die
ganze Stadt; **on the ~** im Ganzen (gesehen).
wholefood(s) ['həulfu:d(z)] *n(pl)* Vollwertkost
f.
wholefood shop *n* ≈ Reformhaus *nt*.
wholehearted [həul'hɑ:tɪd] *adj* (*agreement etc*)
rückhaltlos.
wholeheartedly [həul'hɑ:tɪdlɪ] *adv* (*agree etc*)
rückhaltlos.
wholemeal ['həulmi:l] (*BRIT*) *adj* (*bread, flour*)
Vollkorn-.
whole note (*US*) *n* ganze Note *f*.
wholesale ['həulseɪl] *n* (*business*) Großhandel
m ♦ *adj* (*price*) Großhandels-; (*destruction etc*)
umfassend ♦ *adv* (*buy, sell*) im Großhandel.
wholesaler ['həulseɪlə*] *n* Großhändler *m*.
wholesome ['həulsəm] *adj* (*food*) gesund;
(*effect*) zuträglich; (*attitude*) positiv.
wholewheat ['həulwi:t] *adj* = **wholemeal**.
wholly ['həulɪ] *adv* ganz und gar.

========================= KEYWORD

whom [hu:m] *pron* **1** (*interrogative: acc*) wen;
(: *dat*) wem; **~ did you see?** wen hast du
gesehen?; **to ~ did you give it?** wem hast du
es gegeben?
2 (*relative: acc*) den/die/das; (: *dat*) dem/der/
dem; **the man ~ I saw/to ~ I spoke** der
Mann, den ich gesehen habe/mit dem ich
gesprochen habe.

---

whooping cough ['hu:pɪŋ-] *n* Keuchhusten
m.
whoosh [wuʃ] *vi*: **to ~ along/past/down**
entlang-/vorbei-/hinuntersausen ♦ *n* Sausen
nt; **the skiers ~ed past, skiers came by with
a ~** die Skifahrer sausten vorbei.
whopper ['wɒpə*] (*inf*) *n* (*lie*) faustdicke Lüge
f; (*large thing*) Mordsding *nt*.
whopping ['wɒpɪŋ] (*inf*) *adj* Riesen-, riesig.
whore [hɔ:*] (*inf: pej*) *n* Hure *f*.

========================= KEYWORD

whose [hu:z] *adj* **1** (*possessive: interrogative*)
wessen; **~ book is this?, ~ is this book?**
wessen Buch ist das?, wem gehört das
Buch?; **I don't know ~ it is** ich weiß nicht,
wem es gehört.
2 (*possessive: relative*) dessen/deren/dessen;
the man ~ son you rescued der Mann,
dessen Sohn du gerettet hast; **the woman
~ car was stolen** die Frau, deren Auto
gestohlen worden war
♦ *pron* **~ is this?** wem gehört das?; **I know
~ it is** ich weiß, wem es gehört.

Who's Who ['hu:z'hu:] *n* (*book*) Who's who *nt*.

========================= KEYWORD

why [waɪ] *adv* warum; **~ not?** warum nicht?
♦ *conj* warum; **I wonder ~ he said that** ich
frage mich, warum er das gesagt hat; **that's**

not ~ **I'm here** ich bin nicht deswegen hier; **the reason** ~ der Grund, warum *or* weshalb ♦ *excl (expressing surprise, shock)* na so was; *(expressing annoyance)* ach; ~, **yes (of course)** aber ja doch; ~, **it's you!** na so was, du bists!

WI *n abbr (BRIT: = Women's Institute) britischer Frauenverband* ♦ *abbr* = **West Indies**; (*US: POST*: = *Wisconsin*).

wick [wɪk] *n* Docht *m*; **he gets on my** ~ (*BRIT: inf*) er geht mir auf den Geist.

wicked ['wɪkɪd] *adj (crime, person)* böse; *(smile, wit)* frech; *(inf: prices)* unverschämt; *(: weather)* schrecklich.

wicker ['wɪkə*] *adj (chair etc)* Korb-; *(basket)* Weiden-.

wickerwork ['wɪkə*wɜːk] *adj (chair etc)* Korb-; *(basket)* Weiden- ♦ *n (objects)* Korbwaren *pl.*

wicket ['wɪkɪt] *n (CRICKET: stumps)* Tor *nt*, Wicket *nt*; *(: grass area)* Spielbahn *f.*

wicket-keeper ['wɪkɪtkiːpə*] *n* Torwächter *m.*

wide [waɪd] *adj* breit; *(area)* weit; *(publicity)* umfassend ♦ *adv*: **to open sth** ~ etw weit öffnen; **it is 3 metres** ~ es ist 3 Meter breit; **to go** ~ vorbeigehen.

wide-angle lens ['waɪdæŋgl-] *n* Weitwinkelobjektiv *nt.*

wide-awake [waɪdə'weɪk] *adj* hellwach.

wide-eyed [waɪd'aɪd] *adj* mit großen Augen; *(fig)* unschuldig, naiv.

widely ['waɪdlɪ] *adv (differ, vary)* erheblich; *(travel)* ausgiebig, viel; *(spaced)* weit; *(believed, known)* allgemein; **to be** ~ **read** *(reader)* sehr belesen sein.

widen ['waɪdn] *vt (road, river)* verbreitern; *(one's experience)* erweitern ♦ *vi* sich verbreitern.

wideness ['waɪdnɪs] *n (of road, river, gap)* Breite *f.*

wide open *adj (window, eyes, mouth)* weit geöffnet.

wide-ranging [waɪd'reɪndʒɪŋ] *adj (effects)* weitreichend, weit reichend; *(interview, survey)* umfassend.

widespread ['waɪdsprɛd] *adj* weitverbreitet, weit verbreitet.

widow ['wɪdəu] *n* Witwe *f.*

widowed ['wɪdəud] *adj* verwitwet.

widower ['wɪdəuə*] *n* Witwer *m.*

width [wɪdθ] *n* Breite *f*; *(in swimming pool)* (Quer)bahn *f*; **it's 7 metres in** ~ es ist 7 Meter breit.

widthways ['wɪdθweɪz] *adv* der Breite nach.

wield [wiːld] *vt (sword)* schwingen; *(power)* ausüben.

wife [waɪf] *(pl* **wives)** *n* Frau *f.*

wig [wɪg] *n* Perücke *f.*

wigging ['wɪgɪŋ] *(BRIT: inf) n* Standpauke *f.*

wiggle ['wɪgl] *vt* wackeln mit.

wiggly ['wɪglɪ] *adj*: ~ **line** Schlangenlinie *f.*

wigwam ['wɪgwæm] *n* Wigwam *m.*

wild [waɪld] *adj* wild; *(weather)* rau, stürmisch; *(person, behaviour)* ungestüm; *(idea)* weit hergeholt; *(applause)* stürmisch ♦ *n*: **the** ~ *(natural surroundings)* die freie Natur *f*; **the wilds** *npl* die Wildnis; **I'm not** ~ **about it** ich bin nicht versessen *or* scharf darauf.

wild card *n (COMPUT)* Wildcard *f*, Ersatzzeichen *nt.*

wildcat ['waɪldkæt] *n* Wildkatze *f.*

wildcat strike *n* wilder Streik *m.*

wilderness ['wɪldənɪs] *n* Wildnis *f.*

wildfire ['waɪldfaɪə*] *n*: **to spread like** ~ sich wie ein Lauffeuer ausbreiten.

wild-goose chase [waɪld'guːs-] *n* aussichtslose Suche *f.*

wildlife ['waɪldlaɪf] *n (animals)* die Tierwelt *f.*

wildly ['waɪldlɪ] *adv* wild; *(very: romantic)* wild-; *(: inefficient)* furchtbar.

wiles [waɪlz] *npl* List *f.*

wilful, *(US)* **willful** ['wɪlful] *adj (obstinate)* eigensinnig; *(deliberate)* vorsätzlich.

═══════════════════════════ *KEYWORD*

will [wɪl] *(vt: pt, pp* **willed)** *aux vb* **1** *(forming future tense)*: **I** ~ **finish it tomorrow** ich werde es morgen fertig machen, ich mache es morgen fertig; ~ **you do it? - yes I** ~/**no I won't** machst du es? - ja/nein.
2 *(in conjectures, predictions)*: **that** ~ **be the postman** das ist bestimmt der Briefträger.
3 *(in commands, requests, offers)*: ~ **you sit down** *(politely)* bitte nehmen Sie Platz; *(angrily)* nun setz dich doch; ~ **you be quiet!** seid jetzt still!; ~ **you help me?** hilfst du mir?; ~ **you have a cup of tea?** möchten Sie eine Tasse Tee?; **I won't put up with it!** das lasse ich mir nicht gefallen!
♦ *vt*: **to** ~ **sb to do sth** jdn durch Willenskraft dazu bewegen, etw zu tun; **he** ~**ed himself to go on** er zwang sich dazu, weiterzumachen.
♦ *n (volition)* Wille *m*; *(testament)* Testament *nt*; **he did it against his** ~ er tat es gegen seinen Willen.

willful ['wɪlful] *(US) adj* = **wilful.**

willing ['wɪlɪŋ] *adj (having no objection)* gewillt; *(enthusiastic)* bereitwillig; **he's** ~ **to do it** er ist bereit, es zu tun; **to show** ~ guten Willen zeigen.

willingly ['wɪlɪŋlɪ] *adv* bereitwillig.

willingness ['wɪlɪŋnɪs] *n (readiness)* Bereitschaft *f*; *(enthusiasm)* Bereitwilligkeit *f.*

will-o'-the-wisp ['wɪlədð'wɪsp] *n* Irrlicht *nt*; *(fig)* Trugbild *nt.*

willow ['wɪləu] *n (tree)* Weide *f*; *(wood)* Weidenholz *nt.*

willpower ['wɪl'pauə*] *n* Willenskraft *f.*

willy-nilly ['wɪlɪ'nɪlɪ] *adv (willingly or not)* wohl oder übel.

wilt [wɪlt] *vi (plant)* welken.

Wilts [wɪlts] (*BRIT*) *abbr* (*POST*: = *Wiltshire*).
wily ['waɪlɪ] *adj* listig, raffiniert.
wimp [wɪmp] (*inf: pej*) *n* Waschlappen *m*.
wimpish ['wɪmpɪʃ] (*inf*) *adj* weichlich.
win [wɪn] (*pt, pp* **won**) *n* Sieg *m* ♦ *vt* gewinnen
♦ *vi* siegen, gewinnen.
► **win over** *vt* (*persuade*) gewinnen.
► **win round** (*BRIT*) *vt* = **win over.**
wince [wɪns] *vi* zusammenzucken.
winch [wɪntʃ] *n* Winde *f*.
Winchester disk ['wɪntʃɪstə-] *n*
Winchesterplatte *f*.
wind¹ [wɪnd] *n* (*air*) Wind *m*; (*MED*)
Blähungen *pl*; (*breath*) Atem *m* ♦ *vt* (*take
breath away from*) den Atem nehmen +*dat*;
the winds *npl* (*MUS*) die Bläser *pl*; **into** *or*
against the ~ gegen den Wind; **to get** ~ **of
sth** (*fig*) von etw Wind bekommen; **to break**
~ Darmwind entweichen lassen.
wind² [waɪnd] (*pt, pp* **wound**) *vt* (*thread, rope,
bandage*) wickeln; (*clock, toy*) aufziehen ♦ *vi*
(*road, river*) sich winden.
► **wind down** *vt* (*car window*)
herunterdrehen; (*fig: production*)
zurückschrauben.
► **wind up** *vt* (*clock, toy*) aufziehen; (*debate*)
abschließen.
windbreak ['wɪndbreɪk] *n* Windschutz *m*.
windbreaker ['wɪndbreɪkə'] (*US*) *n*
= **windcheater.**
windcheater ['wɪndtʃiːtə'] *n* Windjacke *f*.
winder ['waɪndə'] (*BRIT*) *n* (*on watch*) Krone *f*,
Aufziehrädchen *nt*.
windfall ['wɪndfɔːl] *n* (*money*) unverhoffter
Glücksfall *m*; (*apple*) Fallobst *nt*.
winding ['waɪndɪŋ] *adj* gewunden.
wind instrument ['wɪnd-] *n* Blasinstrument
nt.
windmill ['wɪndmɪl] *n* Windmühle *f*.
window ['wɪndəu] *n* (*also COMPUT*) Fenster *nt*;
(*in shop*) Schaufenster *nt*.
window box *n* Blumenkasten *m*.
window cleaner *n* Fensterputzer(in) *m(f)*.
window dresser *n*
Schaufensterdekorateur(in) *m(f)*.
window envelope *n* Fensterumschlag *m*.
window frame *n* Fensterrahmen *m*.
window ledge *n* Fenstersims *m*.
window pane *n* Fensterscheibe *f*.
window-shopping ['wɪndəuʃɔpɪŋ] *n*
Schaufensterbummel *m*; **to go** ~ einen
Schaufensterbummel machen.
windowsill ['wɪndəusɪl] *n* Fensterbank *f*.
windpipe ['wɪndpaɪp] *n* Luftröhre *f*.
wind power ['wɪnd-] *n* Windkraft *f*,
Windenergie *f*.
windscreen ['wɪndskriːn] *n*
Windschutzscheibe *f*.
windscreen washer *n*
Scheibenwaschanlage *f*.
windscreen wiper [-waɪpə'] *n*
Scheibenwischer *m*.

windshield ['wɪndʃiːld] (*US*) *n* = **windscreen.**
windsurfing ['wɪndsə:fɪŋ] *n* Windsurfen *nt*.
windswept ['wɪndswept] *adj* (*place*) vom Wind
gepeitscht; (*person*) vom Wind zerzaust.
wind tunnel ['wɪnd-] *n* Windkanal *m*.
windy ['wɪndɪ] *adj* windig; **it's** ~ es ist windig.
wine [waɪn] *n* Wein *m* ♦ *vt*: **to** ~ **and dine sb**
jdm zu einem guten Essen ausführen.
wine bar *n* Weinlokal *nt*.
wine cellar *n* Weinkeller *m*.
wine glass *n* Weinglas *nt*.
wine list *n* Weinkarte *f*.
wine merchant *n* Weinhändler(in) *m(f)*.
wine tasting [-teɪstɪŋ] *n* Weinprobe *f*.
wine waiter *n* Weinkellner *m*.
wing [wɪŋ] *n* (*of bird, insect, plane*) Flügel *m*; (*of
building*) Trakt *m*; (*of car*) Kotflügel *m*; **the
wings** *npl* (*THEAT*) die Kulissen *pl*.
winger ['wɪŋə'] *n* (*SPORT*) Flügelspieler(in)
m(f).
wing mirror (*BRIT*) *n* Seitenspiegel *m*.
wing nut *n* Flügelmutter *f*.
wingspan ['wɪŋspæn] *n* Flügelspannweite *f*.
wingspread ['wɪŋspred] *n* = **wingspan.**
wink [wɪŋk] *n* (*of eye*) Zwinkern *m* ♦ *vi* (*with
eye*) zwinkern; (*light etc*) blinken.
winkle [wɪŋkl] *n* Strandschnecke *f*.
winner ['wɪnə'] *n* (*of race, competition*)
Sieger(in) *m(f)*; (*of prize*) Gewinner(in) *m(f)*.
winning ['wɪnɪŋ] *adj* (*team, entry*) siegreich;
(*shot, goal*) entscheidend; (*smile*)
einnehmend; *see also* **winnings.**
winning post *n* (*lit*) Zielpfosten *m*; (*fig*) Ziel
nt.
winnings ['wɪnɪŋz] *npl* Gewinn *m*.
winsome ['wɪnsəm] *adj* (*expression*)
gewinnend; (*person*) reizend.
winter ['wɪntə'] *n* Winter *m* ♦ *vi* (*birds*)
überwintern; **in** ~ im Winter.
winter sports *npl* Wintersport *m*.
wintry ['wɪntrɪ] *adj* (*weather, day*) winterlich,
Winter-.
wipe [waɪp] *vt* wischen; (*dry*) abtrocknen;
(*clean*) abwischen; (*erase: tape*) löschen; **to**
~ **one's nose** sich *dat* die Nase putzen ♦ *n*: **to
give sth a** ~ etw abwischen.
► **wipe off** *vt* abwischen.
► **wipe out** *vt* (*destroy: city etc*) auslöschen.
► **wipe up** *vt* (*mess*) aufwischen.
wire ['waɪə'] *n* Draht *m*; (*US: telegram*)
Telegramm *nt* ♦ *vt* (*also*: ~ **up**: *electrical fitting*)
anschließen.
wire brush *n* Drahtbürste *f*.
wire cutters *npl* Drahtschere *f*.
wireless ['waɪəlɪs] (*BRIT: old*) *n* Funk *m*; (*set*)
Rundfunkgerät *nt*.
wire netting *n* Maschendraht *m*.
wire service (*US*) *n* Nachrichtenagentur *f*.
wire-tapping ['waɪə'tæpɪŋ] *n* Anzapfen *nt* von
Leitungen.
wiring ['waɪərɪŋ] *n* elektrische Leitungen *pl*.

wiry ['waɪərɪ] *adj* (*person*) drahtig; (*hair*) borstig.

Wis. (*US*) *abbr* (*POST*: = *Wisconsin*).

wisdom ['wɪzdəm] *n* (*of person*) Weisheit *f*; (*of action, remark*) Klugheit *f*.

wisdom tooth *n* Weisheitszahn *m*.

wise *adj* (*person*) weise; (*action, remark*) klug; **I'm none the ~r** ich bin genauso klug wie vorher.

▶ **wise up** (*inf*) *vi*: **to ~ up to sth** hinter etw *acc* kommen.

...wise [waɪz] *suff*: **timewise/moneywise** *etc* zeitmäßig/geldmäßig *etc*.

wisecrack ['waɪzkræk] *n* Witzelei *f*.

wisely ['waɪzlɪ] *adv* klug, weise.

wish [wɪʃ] *n* Wunsch *m* ♦ *vt* wünschen; **best ~es** (*for birthday etc*) herzliche Grüße, alle guten Wünsche; **with best ~es** (*in letter*) mit den besten Wünschen *or* Grüßen; **give her my best ~es** grüßen Sie sie herzlich von mir; **to make a ~** sich *dat* etw wünschen; **to ~ sb goodbye** jdm auf *or* Auf Wiedersehen sagen; **he ~ed me well** er wünschte mir alles Gute; **to ~ to do sth** etw tun wollen; **to ~ sth on sb** jdm etw wünschen; **to ~ for sth** sich *dat* etw wünschen.

wishbone ['wɪʃbəʊn] *n* Gabelbein *nt*.

wishful ['wɪʃful] *adj*: **it's ~ thinking** das ist reines Wunschdenken.

wishy-washy ['wɪʃɪ'wɒʃɪ] (*inf*) *adj* (*colour*) verwaschen; (*person*) farblos; (*ideas*) nichts sagend.

wisp [wɪsp] *n* (*of grass*) Büschel *nt*; (*of hair*) Strähne *f*; (*of smoke*) Fahne *f*.

wistful ['wɪstful] *adj* wehmütig.

wit [wɪt] *n* (*wittiness*) geistreiche Art *f*; (*person*) geistreicher Mensch *m*; (*presence of mind*) Verstand *m*; **wits** *npl* (*intelligence*) Verstand *m*; **to be at one's ~s' end** mit seinem Latein am Ende sein; **to have one's ~s about one** einen klaren Kopf haben; **to ~** (*namely*) und zwar.

witch [wɪtʃ] *n* Hexe *f*.

witchcraft ['wɪtʃkrɑːft] *n* Hexerei *f*.

witch doctor *n* Medizinmann *m*.

witch-hunt ['wɪtʃhʌnt] *n* (*fig*) Hexenjagd *f*.

════════════════════ KEYWORD

with [wɪð] *prep* **1** (*accompanying, in the company of*) mit; **we stayed ~ friends** wir wohnten bei Freunden; **I'll be ~ you in a minute** einen Augenblick, ich bin sofort da; **I'm ~ you** (*I understand*) ich verstehe; **to be ~ it** (*inf: up-to-date*) auf dem Laufenden sein; (: *alert*) da sein.
2 (*descriptive, indicating manner*) mit; **the man ~ the grey hat/blue eyes** der Mann mit dem grauen Hut/den blauen Augen; **~ tears in her eyes** mit Tränen in den Augen; **red ~ anger** rot vor Wut.

withdraw [wɪθ'drɔː] (*irreg: like draw*) *vt* (*object,*

offer) zurückziehen; (*remark*) zurücknehmen ♦ *vi* (*troops*) abziehen; (*person*) sich zurückziehen; **to ~ money** (*from bank*) Geld abheben; **to ~ into o.s.** sich in sich *acc* selbst zurückziehen.

withdrawal [wɪθ'drɔːəl] *n* (*of offer, remark*) Zurücknahme *f*; (*of troops*) Abzug *m*; (*of participation*) Ausstieg *m*; (*of services*) Streichung *f*; (*of money*) Abhebung *f*.

withdrawal symptoms *npl* Entzugserscheinungen *pl*.

withdrawn [wɪθ'drɔːn] *pp of* **withdraw** ♦ *adj* (*person*) verschlossen.

wither ['wɪðə*] *vi* (*plant*) verwelken.

withered ['wɪðəd] *adj* (*plant*) verwelkt; (*limb*) verkümmert.

withhold [wɪθ'həʊld] (*irreg: like* **hold**) *vt* vorenthalten.

within [wɪð'ɪn] *prep* (*place*) innerhalb +*gen*; (*time, distance*) innerhalb von ♦ *adv* innen; **~ reach** in Reichweite; **~ sight (of)** in Sichtweite (+*gen*); **~ the week** vor Ende der Woche; **~ a mile of** weniger als eine Meile entfernt von; **~ an hour** innerhalb einer Stunde; **~ the law** im Rahmen des Gesetzes.

without [wɪð'aʊt] *prep* ohne; **~ a coat** ohne Mantel; **~ speaking** ohne zu sprechen; **it goes ~ saying** das versteht sich von selbst; **~ anyone knowing** ohne dass jemand davon wusste.

withstand [wɪθ'stænd] (*irreg: like* **stand**) *vt* widerstehen +*dat*.

witness ['wɪtnɪs] *n* Zeuge *m*, Zeugin *f* ♦ *vt* (*event*) sehen, Zeuge/Zeugin sein +*gen*; (*fig*) miterleben; **to bear ~ to sth** Zeugnis für etw ablegen; **~ for the prosecution/defence** Zeuge/Zeugin der Anklage/Verteidigung; **to ~ to sth** etw bezeugen; **to ~ having seen sth** bezeugen, etw gesehen zu haben.

witness box *n* Zeugenstand *m*.

witness stand (*US*) *n* = **witness box**.

witticism ['wɪtɪsɪzəm] *n* geistreiche Bemerkung *f*.

witty ['wɪtɪ] *adj* geistreich.

wives [waɪvz] *npl of* **wife**.

wizard ['wɪzəd] *n* Zauberer *m*.

wizened ['wɪznd] *adj* (*person*) verhutzelt; (*fruit, vegetable*) verschrumpelt.

wk *abbr* = **week**.

Wm. *abbr* (= *William*).

WO *n abbr* (*MIL*) = **warrant officer**.

wobble ['wɒbl] *vi* wackeln; (*legs*) zittern.

wobbly ['wɒblɪ] *adj* (*hand, voice*) zitt(e)rig; (*table, chair*) wack(e)lig; **to feel ~** sich wack(e)lig fühlen.

woe [wəʊ] *n* (*sorrow*) Jammer *m*; (*misfortune*) Kummer *m*.

woeful ['wəʊful] *adj* traurig.

wok [wɒk] *n* Wok *m*.

woke [wəʊk] *pt of* **wake**.

woken ['wəʊkn] *pp of* **wake**.

wolf [wʊlf] (*pl* **wolves**) *n* Wolf *m*.

wolves [wulvz] *npl of* wolf.

woman ['wumən] (*pl* **women**) *n* Frau *f*;
~ **friend** Freundin *f*; ~ **teacher** Lehrerin *f*;
young ~ junge Frau; **women's page**
Frauenseite *f*.

woman doctor *n* Ärztin *f*.

womanize ['wumənaɪz] (*pej*) *vi* hinter Frauen
her sein.

womanly ['wumənlɪ] *adj* (*virtues etc*) weiblich.

womb [wu:m] *n* Mutterleib *m*; (*MED*)
Gebärmutter *f*.

women ['wɪmɪn] *npl of* **woman**.

women's lib ['wɪmɪnz-] (*inf*) *n*
Frauenbefreiung *f*.

Women's (Liberation) Movement *n*
Frauenbewegung *f*.

won [wʌn] *pt, pp of* **win**.

wonder ['wʌndə'] *n* (*miracle*) Wunder *nt*; (*awe*)
Verwunderung *f* ♦ *vi*: **to** ~ **whether/why** *etc*
sich fragen, ob/warum *etc*; **it's no** ~ **(that)** es
ist kein Wunder(, dass); **to** ~ **at** (*marvel at*)
staunen über +*acc*; **to** ~ **about** sich *dat*
Gedanken machen über +*acc*; **I** ~ **if you
could help me** könnten Sie mir vielleicht
helfen.

wonderful ['wʌndəful] *adj* wunderbar.

wonderfully ['wʌndəfəlɪ] *adv* wunderbar.

wonky ['wɔŋkɪ] (*BRIT: inf*) *adj* wack(e)lig.

wont [wəunt] *n*: **as is his** ~ wie er zu tun
pflegt.

won't [wəunt] = **will not**.

woo [wu:] *vt* (*woman, audience*) umwerben.

wood [wud] *n* (*timber*) Holz *nt*; (*forest*) Wald *m*
♦ *cpd* Holz-.

woodcarving ['wudkɑ:vɪŋ] *n* (*act, object*)
Holzschnitzerei *f*.

wooded ['wudɪd] *adj* bewaldet.

wooden ['wudn] *adj* (*also fig*) hölzern.

woodland ['wudlənd] *n* Waldland *nt*.

woodpecker ['wudpɛkə'] *n* Specht *m*.

wood pigeon *n* Ringeltaube *f*.

woodwind ['wudwɪnd] *adj* (*instrument*)
Holzblasinstrument *nt*; **the** ~ die Holzbläser
pl.

woodwork ['wudwə:k] *n* (*skill*) Holzarbeiten
pl.

woodworm ['wudwə:m] *n* Holzwurm *m*.

woof [wuf] *n* (*of dog*) Wau *nt* ♦ *vi* kläffen; ~,
~! wau, wau!

wool [wul] *n* Wolle *f*; **to pull the** ~ **over sb's
eyes** (*fig*) jdn hinters Licht führen.

woollen, (*US*) **woolen** ['wulən] *adj* (*hat*)
Woll-, wollen.

woollens ['wulənz] *npl* Wollsachen *pl*.

woolly, (*US*) **wooly** ['wulɪ] *adj* (*socks, hat etc*)
Woll-; (*fig: ideas*) schwammig; (*person*)
verworren ♦ *n* (*pullover*) Wollpullover *m*.

woozy ['wu:zɪ] (*inf*) *adj* duselig.

Worcs (*BRIT*) *abbr* (*POST:* = *Worcestershire*).

word [wə:d] *n* Wort *nt*; (*news*) Nachricht *f* ♦ *vt*
(*letter, message*) formulieren; ~ **for** ~ Wort
für Wort, (*wort*)wörtlich; **what's the** ~ **for**
"**pen**" **in German?** was heißt „pen" auf
Deutsch?; **to put sth into** ~**s** etw in Worte
fassen; **in other** ~**s** mit anderen Worten; **to
break/keep one's** ~ sein Wort brechen/
halten; **to have** ~**s with sb** eine
Auseinandersetzung mit jdm haben; **to
have a** ~ **with sb** mit jdm sprechen; **I'll take
your** ~ **for it** ich verlasse mich auf Sie; **to
send** ~ **of sth** etw verlauten lassen; **to leave**
~ **(with sb/for sb) that** ... (bei jdm/für jdn)
die Nachricht hinterlassen, dass ...; **by** ~ **of
mouth** durch mündliche Überlieferung.

wording ['wə:dɪŋ] *n* (*of message, contract etc*)
Wortlaut *m*, Formulierung *f*.

word-perfect ['wə:d'pə:fɪkt] *adj*: **to be** ~ den
Text perfekt beherrschen.

word processing *n* Textverarbeitung *f*.

word processor [-prəusɛsə'] *n*
Textverarbeitungssystem *nt*.

wordwrap ['wə:dræp] *n* (*COMPUT*)
(automatischer) Zeilenumbruch *m*.

wordy ['wə:dɪ] *adj* (*book*) langatmig; (*person*)
wortreich.

wore [wɔ:'] *pt of* **wear**.

work [wə:k] *n* Arbeit *f*; (*ART, LITER*) Werk *nt*
♦ *vi* arbeiten; (*mechanism*) funktionieren; (*be
successful: medicine etc*) wirken ♦ *vt* (*clay,
wood, land*) bearbeiten; (*mine*) arbeiten in;
(*machine*) bedienen; (*create: effect, miracle*)
bewirken; **to go to** ~ zur Arbeit gehen; **to
set to** ~, **to start** ~ sich an die Arbeit
machen; **to be at** ~ **(on sth)** (an etw *dat*)
arbeiten; **to be out of** ~ arbeitslos sein; **to
be in** ~ eine Stelle haben; **to** ~ **hard** hart
arbeiten; **to** ~ **loose** (*part, knot*) sich lösen;
to ~ **on the assumption that** ... von der
Annahme ausgehen, dass ...

▶ **work on** *vt fus* (*task*) arbeiten an +*dat*;
(*person: influence*) bearbeiten; **he's** ~**ing on
his car** er arbeitet an seinem Auto.

▶ **work out** *vi* (*plans etc*) klappen; (*SPORT*)
trainieren ♦ *vt* (*problem*) lösen; (*plan*)
ausarbeiten; **it** ~**s out at 100 pounds** es
ergibt 100 Pfund.

▶ **work up** *vt*: **to get** ~**ed up** sich aufregen.

workable ['wə:kəbl] *adj* (*system*)
durchführbar; (*solution*) brauchbar.

workaholic [wə:kə'hɔlɪk] *n* Arbeitstier *nt*.

workbench ['wə:kbɛntʃ] *n* Werkbank *f*.

worker ['wə:kə'] *n* Arbeiter(in) *m(f)*; **office** ~
Büroarbeiter(in) *m(f)*.

workforce ['wə:kfɔ:s] *n* Arbeiterschaft *f*.

work-in ['wə:kɪn] (*BRIT*) *n* Fabrikbesetzung *f*.

working ['wə:kɪŋ] *adj* (*day, conditions*)
Arbeits-; (*population*) arbeitend; (*mother*)
berufstätig; **a** ~ **knowledge of English**
(*adequate*) Grundkenntnisse in Englisch.

working capital *n* Betriebskapital *nt*.

working class *n* Arbeiterklasse *f*.

working-class ['wə:kɪŋ'klɑ:s] *adj* (*family, town*)
Arbeiter-.

working man *n* Arbeiter *m*.

working order n: in ~ in betriebsfähigem Zustand.

working party (BRIT) n Ausschuss m.

working relationship n Arbeitsbeziehung f.

working week n Arbeitswoche f.

work-in-progress ['wə:kɪn'prəugrɛs] n laufende Arbeiten pl.

workload ['wə:kləud] n Arbeitsbelastung f.

workman ['wə:kmən] (irreg: like man) n Arbeiter m.

workmanship ['wə:mənʃɪp] n Arbeitsqualität f.

workmate ['wə:kmeɪt] n Arbeitskollege m, Arbeitskollegin f.

workout ['wə:kaut] n Fitnesstraining nt.

work permit n Arbeitserlaubnis f.

works [wə:ks] (BRIT) n (factory) Fabrik f, Werk nt ♦ npl (of clock) Uhrwerk nt; (of machine) Getriebe nt.

work sheet n Arbeitsblatt nt.

workshop ['wə:kʃɔp] n (building) Werkstatt f; (practical session) Workshop nt.

work station n Arbeitsplatz m; (COMPUT) Workstation f.

work-study ['wə:kstʌdɪ] n Arbeitsstudie f.

worktop ['wə:ktɔp] n Arbeitsfläche f.

work-to-rule ['wə:ktə'ru:l] (BRIT) n Dienst m nach Vorschrift.

world [wə:ld] n Welt f ♦ cpd (champion, power, war) Welt-; **all over the** ~ auf der ganzen Welt; **to think the** ~ **of sb** große Stücke auf jdn halten; **what in the** ~ **is he doing?** was um alles in der Welt macht er?; **to do sb a** or **the** ~ **of good** jdm unwahrscheinlich gut tun; **W**~ **War One/Two** der Erste/Zweite Weltkrieg; **out of this** ~ fantastisch.

World Cup n: **the** ~ (FOOTBALL) die Fußballweltmeisterschaft f.

world-famous [wə:ld'feɪməs] adj weltberühmt.

worldly ['wə:ldlɪ] adj weltlich; (knowledgeable) weltgewandt.

world music n World Music f, Richtung der Popmusik, die musikalische Stilelemente der Dritten Welt verwendet.

World Series (US) n Endrunde der Baseball-Weltmeisterschaft zwischen den Tabellenführern der Spitzenligen.

worldwide ['wə:ld'waɪd] adj, adv weltweit.

worm [wə:m] n Wurm m.

▶ **worm out** vt: **to** ~ **sth out of sb** jdm etw entlocken.

worn [wɔ:n] pp of **wear** ♦ adj (carpet) abgenutzt; (shoe) abgetragen.

worn-out ['wɔ:naut] adj (object) abgenutzt; (person) erschöpft.

worried ['wʌrɪd] adj besorgt; **to be** ~ **about sth** sich wegen etw Sorgen machen.

worrier ['wʌrɪə*] n: **to be a** ~ sich ständig Sorgen machen.

worrisome ['wʌrɪsəm] adj Besorgnis erregend.

worry ['wʌrɪ] n Sorge f ♦ vt beunruhigen ♦ vi sich dat Sorgen machen; **to** ~ **about** or **over sth/sb** sich um etw/jdn Sorgen machen.

worrying ['wʌrɪɪŋ] adj beunruhigend.

worse [wə:s] adj schlechter, schlimmer ♦ adv schlechter ♦ n Schlechtere(s) nt, Schlimmere(s) nt; **to get** ~ (situation etc) sich verschlechtern or verschlimmern; **he is none the** ~ **for it** er hat keinen Schaden dabei erlitten; **so much the** ~ **for you!** um so schlimmer für dich!; **a change for the** ~ eine Wendung zum Schlechten.

worsen ['wə:sn] vt verschlimmern ♦ vi sich verschlechtern.

worse off adj (also fig) schlechter dran; **he is now** ~ **than before** er ist jetzt schlechter dran als zuvor.

worship ['wə:ʃɪp] n (act) Verehrung f ♦ vt (god) anbeten; (person, thing) verehren; **Your W**~ (BRIT: to mayor) verehrter Herr Bürgermeister; (: to judge) Euer Ehren.

worshipper ['wə:ʃɪpə*] n (in church etc) Kirchgänger(in) m(f); (fig) Anbeter(in) m(f), Verehrer(in) m(f).

worst [wə:st] adj schlechteste(r, s), schlimmste(r, s) ♦ adv am schlimmsten ♦ n Schlimmste(s) nt; **at** ~ schlimmstenfalls; **if the** ~ **comes to the** ~ wenn alle Stricke reißen.

worst-case scenario ['wə:stkeɪs-] n Schlimmstfallszenario nt.

worsted ['wustɪd] n Kammgarn nt.

worth [wə:θ] n Wert m ♦ adj: **to be** ~ wert sein; **£2** ~ **of apples** Äpfel für £ 2; **how much is it** ~? was or wie viel ist es wert?; **it's** ~ **it** (effort, time) es lohnt sich; **it's** ~ **every penny** es ist sein Geld wert.

worthless ['wə:θlɪs] adj wertlos.

worthwhile ['wə:θ'waɪl] adj lohnend.

worthy [wə:ðɪ] adj (person) würdig; (motive) ehrenwert; ~ **of** wert +gen.

========================= KEYWORD

would [wud] aux vb **1** (conditional tense): **if you asked him he** ~ **do it** wenn du ihn fragtest, würde er es tun; **if you had asked him he** ~ **have done it** wenn du ihn gefragt hättest, hätte er es getan.

2 (in offers, invitations, requests): ~ **you like a biscuit?** möchten Sie ein Plätzchen?; ~ **you ask him to come in?** würden Sie ihn bitten hereinzukommen?

3 (in indirect speech): **I said I** ~ **do it** ich sagte, ich würde es tun.

4 (emphatic): **it WOULD have to snow today!** ausgerechnet heute musste es schneien!

5 (insistence): **she** ~**n't behave** sie wollte sich partout nicht benehmen.

6 (conjecture): **it** ~ **have been midnight** es mochte etwa Mitternacht gewesen sein; **it** ~ **seem so** so scheint es wohl.

7 (indicating habit): **he** ~ **go there on**

Mondays er ging montags immer dorthin; he ~ spend every day on the beach er verbrachte jeden Tag am Strand.

would-be ['wudbiː] *adj* (*singer, writer*) Möchtegern-.

wouldn't ['wudnt] = **would not**.

wound[1] [waund] *pt, pp of* **wind**[2].

wound[2] [wuːnd] *n* Wunde *f* ♦ *vt* verwunden; ~ed in the leg am Bein verletzt.

wove [wəuv] *pt of* **weave**.

woven ['wəuvn] *pp of* **weave**.

WP *n abbr* = **word processing, word processor** ♦ *abbr* (*BRIT: inf.* = *weather permitting*) bei günstiger Witterung.

WPC (*BRIT*) *n abbr* (= *woman police constable*) Polizistin *f*.

wpm *abbr* (= *words per minute*) Worte pro Minute (*beim Maschineschreiben*).

WRAC (*BRIT*) *n abbr* (= *Women's Royal Army Corps*) Frauenkorps der Armee.

WRAF (*BRIT*) *n abbr* (= *Women's Royal Air Force*) Frauenkorps der Luftwaffe.

wrangle ['ræŋgl] *n* Gerangel *nt* ♦ *vi*: **to** ~ **with sb over sth** sich mit jdm um etw zanken.

wrap [ræp] *n* (*shawl*) Umhang *m*; (*cape*) Cape *nt* ♦ *vt* einwickeln; (*also:* ~ **up**: *pack*) einpacken; (*wind: tape etc*) wickeln; **under** ~**s** (*fig: plan*) geheim.

wrapper ['ræpə*] *n* (*on chocolate*) Papier *nt*; (*BRIT: of book*) Umschlag *m*.

wrapping paper ['ræpɪŋ-] *n* (*brown*) Packpapier *nt*; (*fancy*) Geschenkpapier *nt*.

wrath [rɔθ] *n* Zorn *m*.

wreak [riːk] *vt*: **to** ~ **havoc (on)** verheerenden Schaden anrichten (bei); **to** ~ **vengeance** *or* **revenge on sb** Rache an jdm üben.

wreath [riːθ] (*pl* ~**s**) *n* Kranz *m*.

wreck [rɛk] *n* Wrack *nt*; (*vehicle*) Schrotthaufen *m* ♦ *vt* kaputtmachen; (*car*) zu Schrott fahren; (*chances*) zerstören.

wreckage ['rɛkɪdʒ] *n* (*of car, plane, building*) Trümmer *pl*; (*of ship*) Wrackteile *pl*.

wrecker ['rɛkə*] (*US*) *n* (*breakdown van*) Abschleppwagen *m*.

Wren (*BRIT*) *n abbr* weibliches Mitglied der britischen Marine.

wren [rɛn] *n* (*ZOOL*) Zaunkönig *m*.

wrench [rɛntʃ] *n* (*TECH*) Schraubenschlüssel *m*; (*tug*) Ruck *m*; (*fig*) schmerzhaftes Erlebnis *nt* ♦ *vt* (*pull*) reißen; (*injure: arm, back*) verrenken; **to** ~ **sth from sb** jdm etw entreißen.

wrest [rɛst] *vt*: **to** ~ **sth from sb** jdm etw abringen.

wrestle ['rɛsl] *vi*: **to** ~ **(with sb)** (mit jdm) ringen; **to** ~ **with a problem** mit einem Problem kämpfen.

wrestler ['rɛslə*] *n* Ringer(in) *m(f)*.

wrestling ['rɛslɪŋ] *n* Ringen *nt*; (*also:* **all-in** ~) Freistilringen *nt*.

wrestling match *n* Ringkampf *m*.

wretch [rɛtʃ] *n*: **poor** ~ (*man*) armer Schlucker *m*; (*woman*) armes Ding *nt*; **little** ~! (*often humorous*) kleiner Schlingel!

wretched ['rɛtʃɪd] *adj* (*poor*) erbärmlich; (*unhappy*) unglücklich; (*inf: damned*) elend.

wriggle ['rɪgl] *vi* (*also:* ~ **about**: *person*) zappeln; (*fish*) sich winden; (*snake etc*) sich schlängeln ♦ *n* Zappeln *nt*.

wring [rɪŋ] (*pt, pp* **wrung**) *vt* (*wet clothes*) auswringen; (*hands*) wringen; (*neck*) umdrehen; **to** ~ **sth out of sth/sb** (*fig*) etw/jdm etw abringen.

wringer ['rɪŋə*] *n* Mangel *f*.

wringing ['rɪŋɪŋ] *adj* (*also:* ~ **wet**) tropfnass.

wrinkle ['rɪŋkl] *n* Falte *f* ♦ *vt* (*nose, forehead etc*) runzeln ♦ *vi* (*skin, paint etc*) sich runzeln.

wrinkled ['rɪŋkld] *adj* (*fabric, paper*) zerknittert; (*surface*) gekräuselt; (*skin*) runzlig.

wrinkly ['rɪŋklɪ] *adj* = **wrinkled**.

wrist [rɪst] *n* Handgelenk *nt*.

wristband ['rɪstbænd] (*BRIT*) *n* (*of shirt*) Manschette *f*; (*of watch*) Armband *nt*.

wristwatch ['rɪstwɔtʃ] *n* Armbanduhr *f*.

writ [rɪt] *n* (*LAW*) (gerichtliche) Verfügung *f*; **to issue a** ~ **against sb, serve a** ~ **on sb** eine Verfügung gegen jdn erlassen.

write [raɪt] (*pt* **wrote**, *pp* **written**) *vt* schreiben; (*cheque*) ausstellen ♦ *vi* schreiben; **to** ~ **to sb** jdm schreiben.

► **write away** *vi*: **to** ~ **away for sth** etw anfordern.

► **write down** *vt* aufschreiben.

► **write off** *vt* (*debt, project*) abschreiben; (*wreck: car etc*) zu Schrott fahren ♦ *vi* = **write away**.

► **write out** *vt* (*put in writing*) schreiben; (*cheque, receipt etc*) ausstellen.

► **write up** *vt* (*report etc*) schreiben.

write-off ['raɪtɔf] *n* (*AUT*) Totalschaden *m*.

write-protected ['raɪtprə'tɛktɪd] *adj* (*COMPUT*) schreibgeschützt.

writer ['raɪtə*] *n* (*author*) Schriftsteller(in) *m(f)*; (*of report, document etc*) Verfasser(in) *m(f)*.

write-up ['raɪtʌp] *n* (*review*) Kritik *f*.

writhe [raɪð] *vi* sich krümmen.

writing ['raɪtɪŋ] *n* Schrift *f*; (*of author*) Arbeiten *pl*; (*activity*) Schreiben *nt*; **in** ~ schriftlich; **in my own** ~ in meiner eigenen Handschrift.

writing case *n* Schreibmappe *f*.

writing desk *n* Schreibtisch *m*.

writing paper *n* Schreibpapier *nt*.

written ['rɪtn] *pp of* **write**.

WRNS (*BRIT*) *n abbr* (= *Women's Royal Naval Service*) Frauenkorps der Marine.

wrong [rɔŋ] *adj* (*morally bad*) unrecht; (*unfair*) ungerecht ♦ *adv* falsch ♦ *n* (*injustice*) Unrecht *nt*; (*evil*): **right and** ~ Gut und Böse ♦ *vt* (*treat unfairly*) unrecht *or* (ein) Unrecht tun +*dat*; **to be** ~ (*answer*) falsch sein; (*in*

doing, saying sth) Unrecht haben; **you are
~ to do it** es ist ein Fehler von dir, das zu
tun; **it's ~ to steal, stealing is ~** Stehlen ist
unrecht; **you are ~ about that, you've got it
~** da hast du Unrecht; **what's ~? wo** fehlts?;
there's nothing ~ es ist alles in Ordnung; **to
go ~** (*person*) einen Fehler machen; (*plan*)
schief gehen; (*machine*) versagen; **to be in
the ~** im Unrecht sein.
wrongdoer ['rɔŋduːə*] *n* Übeltäter(in) *m(f)*.
wrong-foot [rɔŋ'fut] *vt*: **to ~ sb** (*SPORT*) jdn
auf dem falschen Fuß erwischen; (*fig*) jdn
im falschen Moment erwischen.
wrongful ['rɔŋful] *adj* unrechtmäßig.
wrongly ['rɔŋlɪ] *adv* falsch; (*unjustly*) zu
Unrecht.
wrong number *n* (*TEL*): **you've got the ~** Sie
sind falsch verbunden.
wrong side *n*: **the ~** (*of material*) die linke
Seite.
wrote [rəut] *pt of* **write.**
wrought [rɔːt] *adj*: **~ iron** Schmiedeeisen *nt*.
wrung [rʌŋ] *pt, pp of* **wring.**
WRVS (*BRIT*) *n abbr* (= *Women's Royal
Voluntary Service*) *karitativer
Frauenverband.*
wry [raɪ] *adj* (*smile, humour*) trocken.
wt. *abbr* = **weight.**
WV (*US*) *abbr* (*POST*: = *West Virginia*).
W.Va. (*US*) *abbr* (*POST*: = *West Virginia*).
WWW *n abbr* (= *World Wide Web*) WWW *nt*.
WY, Wyo. (*US*) *abbr* (*POST*: = *Wyoming*).
WYSIWYG ['wɪzɪwɪg] *abbr* (*COMPUT*: = *what
you see is what you get*) WYSIWYG *nt*.

======= *X, x*

X, x [ɛks] *n* (*letter*) X *nt*, x *nt*; (*BRIT: CINE:
formerly*) *Klassifikation für nicht jugendfreie
Filme*; **~ for Xmas** ≈ X wie Xanthippe.
Xerox ® ['zɪərɔks] *n* (*also*: **~ machine**)
Xerokopierer *m*; (*photocopy*) Xerokopie *f*
♦ *vt* xerokopieren.
XL *abbr* (= *extra large*) XL.
Xmas ['ɛksməs] *n abbr* = **Christmas.**
XML *abbr* (*COMPUT*: = *extensible markup
language*) XML.
X-rated ['ɛks'reɪtɪd] (*US*) *adj* (*film*) nicht
jugendfrei.
X-ray ['ɛksreɪ] *n* Röntgenstrahl *m*; (*photo*)
Röntgenbild *nt* ♦ *vt* röntgen; **to have an ~**
sich röntgen lassen.
xylophone ['zaɪləfəun] *n* Xylofon *nt*,
Xylophon *nt*.

======= *Y, y*

Y, y [waɪ] *n* (*letter*) Y *nt*, y *nt*; **~ for Yellow,** (*US*)
~ for Yoke ≈ Y wie Ypsilon.
yacht [jɔt] *n* Jacht *f*.
yachting ['jɔtɪŋ] *n* Segeln *nt*.
yachtsman ['jɔtsmən] (*irreg: like* **man**) *n* Segler
m.
yam [jæm] *n* Jamswurzel *f*, Yamswurzel *f*.
Yank [jæŋk] (*pej*) *n* Ami *m*.
yank [jæŋk] *vt* reißen ♦ *n* Ruck *m*; **to give sth a
~** mit einem Ruck an etw *dat* ziehen.
Yankee ['jæŋkɪ] (*pej*) *n* = **Yank.**
yap [jæp] *vi* (*dog*) kläffen.
yard [jɑːd] *n* (*of house etc*) Hof *m*; (*US: garden*)
Garten *m*; (*measure*) Yard *nt* (= 0,91 m);
builder's ~ Bauhof *m*.
yardstick ['jɑːdstɪk] *n* (*fig*) Maßstab *m*.
yarn [jɑːn] *n* (*thread*) Garn *nt*; (*tale*)
Geschichte *f*.
yawn [jɔːn] *n* Gähnen *nt* ♦ *vi* gähnen.
yawning ['jɔːnɪŋ] *adj* (*gap*) gähnend.
yd *abbr* = **yard.**
yeah [jɛə] (*inf*) *adv* ja.
year [jɪə*] *n* Jahr *nt*; (*referring to wine*)
Jahrgang *m*; **every ~** jedes Jahr; **this ~**
dieses Jahr; **a** *or* **per ~** pro Jahr; **~ in, ~ out**
jahrein, jahraus; **to be 8 ~s old** 8 Jahre alt
sein; **an eight-~-old child** ein achtjähriges
Kind.
yearbook ['jɪəbuk] *n* Jahrbuch *nt*.
yearling ['jɪəlɪŋ] *n* (*horse*) Jährling *m*.
yearly ['jɪəlɪ] *adj, adv* (*once a year*) jährlich;
twice ~ zweimal jährlich *or* im Jahr.
yearn [jɜːn] *vi*: **to ~ for sth** sich nach etwas
sehnen; **to ~ to do sth** sich danach sehnen,
etw zu tun.
yearning ['jɜːnɪŋ] *n*: **to have a ~ for sth** ein
Verlangen nach etw haben; **to have a ~ to
do sth** ein Verlangen danach haben, etw zu
tun.
yeast [jiːst] *n* Hefe *f*.
yell [jɛl] *n* Schrei *m* ♦ *vi* schreien.
yellow ['jɛləu] *adj* gelb ♦ *n* Gelb *nt*.
yellow fever *n* Gelbfieber *nt*.
yellowish ['jɛləuɪʃ] *adj* gelblich.
Yellow Pages ® *npl*: **the ~** die gelben Seiten
pl, das Branchenverzeichnis.
Yellow Sea *n*: **the ~** das Gelbe Meer.
yelp [jɛlp] *n* Jaulen *nt* ♦ *vi* jaulen.
Yemen ['jɛmən] *n*: **(the) ~** (der) Jemen.
Yemeni ['jɛmənɪ] *adj* jemenitisch ♦ *n*
Jemenit(in) *m(f)*.
yen [jɛn] *n* (*currency*) Yen *m*; (*craving*): **to have**

a ~ **for** Lust auf etw haben; **to have a** ~ **to do sth** Lust darauf haben, etw zu tun.

yeoman ['jəumən] (*irreg: like* **man**) *n*: **Y**~ **of the Guard** (königlicher) Leibgardist *m*.

yes [jɛs] *adv* ja; (*in reply to negative*) doch ♦ *n* Ja *nt*; **to say** ~ ja *or* Ja sagen; **to answer** ~ mit Ja antworten.

yes-man ['jɛsmæn] (*irreg: like* **man**) (*pej*) *n* Jasager *m*.

yesterday ['jɛstədɪ] *adv* gestern ♦ *n* Gestern *nt*; ~ **morning/evening** gestern Morgen/Abend; ~**'s paper** die Zeitung von gestern; **the day before** ~ vorgestern; **all day** ~ gestern den ganzen Tag (lang).

yet [jɛt] *adv* noch ♦ *conj* jedoch; **it is not finished** ~ es ist noch nicht fertig; **must you go just** ~**?** musst du schon gehen?; **the best** ~ der/die/das bisher Beste; **as** ~ bisher; **it'll be a few days** ~ es wird noch ein paar Tage dauern; **not for a few days** ~ nicht in den nächsten paar Tagen; ~ **again** wiederum.

yew [ju:] *n* (*tree*) Eibe *f*; (*wood*) Eibenholz *nt*.

Y-fronts ® ['waɪfrʌnts] *npl* (Herren-)Slip *m* (*mit Y-förmiger Vorderseite*).

YHA (*BRIT*) *n abbr* (= *Youth Hostels Association*) britischer Jugendherbergsverband.

Yiddish ['jɪdɪʃ] *n* Jiddisch *nt*.

yield [ji:ld] *n* (*AGR*) Ertrag *m*; (*COMM*) Gewinn *m* ♦ *vt* (*surrender: control etc*) abtreten; (*produce: results, profit*) hervorbringen ♦ *vi* (*surrender, give way*) nachgeben; (*US: AUT*) die Vorfahrt achten; **a** ~ **of 5%** ein Ertrag *or* Gewinn von 5%.

YMCA *n abbr* (*organization*: = *Young Men's Christian Association*) CVJM *m*.

yob(bo) ['jɔb(əu)] (*BRIT: inf. pej*) *n* Rowdy *m*.

yodel ['jəudl] *vi* jodeln.

yoga ['jəugə] *n* Yoga *m or nt*.

yog(h)ourt ['jəugət] *n* Jog(h)urt *m or nt*.

yog(h)urt ['jəugət] *n* = **yog(h)ourt**.

yoke [jəuk] *n* (*also fig*) Joch *nt* ♦ *vt* (*also:* ~ **together**: *oxen*) einspannen.

yolk [jəuk] *n* (*of egg*) Dotter *m*, Eigelb *nt*.

yonder ['jɔndə*] *adv*: (*over*) ~ dort drüben ♦ *adj*: **from** ~ **house** von dem Haus dort drüben.

yonks [jɔŋks] (*inf*) *n*: **for** ~ seit einer Ewigkeit.

Yorks [jɔːks] (*BRIT*) *abbr* (*POST*: = *Yorkshire*).

═══════════════════════════════ *KEYWORD*

you [ju:] *pron* **1** (*subject: familiar: singular*) du; (: *plural*) ihr; (: *polite*) Sie; ~ **Germans enjoy your food** ihr Deutschen esst gern gut. **2** (*object: direct: familiar: singular*) dich; (: *plural*) euch; (: *polite*) Sie; (: *indirect: familiar: singular*) dir; (: *plural*) euch; (: *polite*) Ihnen; **I know** ~ ich kenne dich/euch/Sie; **I gave it to** ~ ich habe es dir/euch/Ihnen gegeben; **if I were** ~ **I would** ... an deiner/eurer/Ihrer Stelle würde ich ...

3 (*after prep, in comparisons*): **it's for** ~ es ist für dich/euch/Sie; **she's younger than** ~ sie ist jünger als du/ihr/Sie.

4 (*impersonal: one*) man; ~ **never know** man weiß nie.

you'd [ju:d] = **you had**; **you would**.

you'll [ju:l] = **you will**; **you shall**.

young [jʌŋ] *adj* jung; **the young** *npl* (*of animal*) die Jungen *pl*; (*people*) die jungen Leute *pl*; **a** ~ **man** ein junger Mann; **a** ~ **lady** eine junge Dame.

younger [jʌŋgə*] *adj* jünger; **the** ~ **generation** die jüngere Generation.

youngish ['jʌŋɪʃ] *adj* recht jung.

youngster ['jʌŋstə*] *n* Kind *nt*.

your [jɔː*] *adj* (*familiar: sing*) dein/deine/dein; (: *pl*) euer/eure/euer; (*polite*) Ihr/Ihre/Ihr; (*one's*) sein; **you mustn't eat with** ~ **fingers** man darf nicht mit den Fingern essen; *see also* **my**.

you're [juə*] = **you are**.

yours [jɔːz] *pron* (*familiar: sing*) deiner/deine/dein(e)s; (: *pl*) eurer/eure/eures; (*polite*) Ihrer/Ihre/Ihres; **a friend of** ~ ein Freund von dir/Ihnen; **is it** ~**?** gehört es dir/Ihnen?; ~ **sincerely/faithfully** mit freundlichen Grüßen; *see also* **mine[1]**.

yourself [jɔː'sɛlf] *pron* (*reflexive: familiar: sing: acc*) dich; (: *dat*) dir; (: *pl*) euch; (: *polite*) sich; (*emphatic*) selbst; **you** ~ **told me** das haben Sie mir selbst gesagt.

yourselves [jɔː'sɛlvz] *pl pron* (*reflexive: familiar*) euch; (: *polite*) sich; (*emphatic*) selbst; *see also* **oneself**.

youth [ju:θ] *n* Jugend *f*; (*young man: pl youths*) Jugendliche(r) *m*; **in my** ~ in meiner Jugend.

youth club *n* Jugendklub *m*.

youthful ['ju:θful] *adj* jugendlich.

youthfulness ['ju:θfəlnɪs] *n* Jugendlichkeit *f*.

youth hostel *n* Jugendherberge *f*.

youth movement *n* Jugendbewegung *f*.

you've [ju:v] = **you have**.

yowl [jaul] *n* (*of animal*) Jaulen *nt*; (*of person*) Heulen *nt*.

yr *abbr* (= *year*) J.

YT (*CANADA*) *abbr* (= *Yukon Territory*).

Yugoslav ['ju:gəuslɑːv] (*formerly*) *adj* jugoslawisch ♦ *n* Jugoslawe *m*, Jugoslawin *f*.

Yugoslavia ['ju:gəu'slɑːvɪə] (*formerly*) *n* Jugoslawien *nt*.

Yugoslavian ['ju:gəu'slɑːvɪən] (*formerly*) *adj* jugoslawisch.

Yule log [ju:l-] *n Biskuitrolle mit Überzug, die zu Weihnachten gegessen wird.*

yuppie ['jʌpɪ] (*inf*) *n* Yuppie *m* ♦ *adj* yuppiehaft; (*job, car*) Yuppie-.

YWCA *n abbr* (*organization*: = *Young Women's Christian Association*) CVJF *m*.

Z, z

Z, z [zɛdɢ, ɢ(*USG*) ziː] *n* (*letter*) Z *nt*, z *nt*; ~ **for Zebra** ≈ Z wie Zacharias.
Zaire [zɑːˈiːəˈ] *n* Zaire *nt*.
Zambia [ˈzæmbɪə] *n* Sambia *nt*.
Zambian [ˈzæmbɪən] *adj* sambisch ♦ *n* Sambier(in) *m(f)*.
zany [ˈzeɪnɪ] *adj* verrückt.
zap [zæp] *vt* (*COMPUT*: *delete*) löschen.
zeal [ziːl] *n* Eifer *m*.
zealot [ˈzɛlət] *n* Fanatiker(in) *m(f)*.
zealous [ˈzɛləs] *adj* eifrig.
zebra [ˈziːbrə] *n* Zebra *nt*.
zebra crossing (*BRIT*) *n* Zebrastreifen *m*.
zenith [ˈzɛnɪθ] *n* (*also fig*) Zenit *m*.
zero [ˈzɪərəʊ] *n* (*number*) Null *f* ♦ *vi*: **to ~ in on sth** (*target*) etw einkreisen; **5 degrees below ~** 5 Grad unter null.
zero hour *n* die Stunde X.
zero option *n* (*esp POL*) Nulllösung *f*.
zero-rated [ˈziːrəʊreɪtɪd] (*BRIT*) *adj* (*TAX*) mehrwertsteuerfrei.
zest [zɛst] *n* (*for life*) Begeisterung *f*; (*of orange*) Orangenschale *f*.
zigzag [ˈzɪgzæg] *n* Zickzack *m* ♦ *vi* sich im Zickzack bewegen.
Zimbabwe [zɪmˈbɑːbwɪ] *n* Zimbabwe *nt*.
Zimbabwean [zɪmˈbɑːbwɪən] *adj* zimbabwisch.
zimmer ® [ˈzɪməˈ] *n* (*also*: ~ **frame**) Laufgestell *nt*.
zinc [zɪŋk] *n* Zink *nt*.
Zionism [ˈzaɪənɪzəm] *n* Zionismus *m*.
Zionist [ˈzaɪənɪst] *adj* zionistisch ♦ *n* Zionist(in) *m(f)*.
zip [zɪp] *n* (*also*: ~ **fastener**) Reißverschluss *m* ♦ *vt* (*also*: ~ **up**: *dress etc*) den Reißverschluss zumachen an +*dat*.
zip code (*US*) *n* Postleitzahl *f*.
zipper [ˈzɪpəˈ] (*US*) *n* = **zip**.
zither [ˈzɪðəˈ] *n* Zither *f*.
zodiac [ˈzəʊdɪæk] *n* Tierkreis *m*.
zombie [ˈzɔmbɪ] *n* (*fig*) Schwachkopf *m*.
zone [zəʊn] *n* (*also MIL*) Zone *f*, Gebiet *nt*; (*in town*) Bezirk *m*.
zonked [zɔŋkt] (*inf*) *adj* (*tired*) total geschafft; (*high on drugs*) high; (*drunk*) voll.
zoo [zuː] *n* Zoo *m*.
zoological [zuəˈlɔdʒɪkl] *adj* zoologisch.
zoologist [zuˈɔlədʒɪst] *n* Zoologe *m*, Zoologin *f*.
zoology [zuːˈɔlədʒɪ] *n* Zoologie *f*.
zoom [zuːm] *vi*: **to ~ past** vorbeisausen; **to ~ in (on sth/sb)** (*PHOT, CINE*) (etw/jdn) näher heranholen.
zoom lens *n* Zoomobjektiv *nt*.
zucchini [zuːˈkiːnɪ] (*US*) *n(pl)* Zucchini *pl*.
Zulu [ˈzuːluː] *adj* (*tribe, culture*) Zulu- ♦ *n* (*person*) Zulu *m/f*; (*LING*) Zulu *nt*.
Zürich [ˈzjuərɪk] *n* Zürich *nt*.

Grammar
Grammatik

USING THE GRAMMAR

The Grammar section deals systematically and comprehensively with all the information you will need in order to communicate accurately in German. The user-friendly layout explains the grammar point on a left-hand page, leaving the facing page free for illustrative examples. The boxed numbers (→ ①) direct you to the relevant example in every case.

The Grammar section also provides invaluable guidance on the dangers of translating English structures by identical structures in German. Important sections, explaining the use of Numbers and Punctuation are covered towards the end of this section. Finally, the index lists the main words and grammatical terms in both English and German.

ABBREVIATIONS

acc	accusative	*gen*	genitive
ctd	continued	*masc*	masculine
dat	dative	*neut*	neuter
fem	feminine	*nom*	nominative
ff	and following pages	*p(p)*	page(s)

5

CONTENTS

◻ **Tense Formation**

Tenses are either **simple** or **compound**. Once you know how to form the past participle, compound tenses are similar for all verbs (see pp 22 to 29). To form simple tenses you need to know whether a verb is **weak**, **strong** or **mixed**.

Simple tenses

In German these are:

> Present indicative ➞ ☐1
> Imperfect indicative ➞ ☐2
> Present subjunctive ➞ ☐3
> Imperfect subjunctive ➞ ☐4

Subjunctive forms are widely used in German, especially for indirect or reported speech (see pp 66 and 67).

The simple tenses are formed by adding endings to a verb **stem**. The endings show the number, person and tense of the subject of the verb ➞ ☐5

The types of verb you need to know to form simple tenses are:

◆ **Strong verbs** (pp 12 to 15), those whose vowel usually changes in forming the imperfect indicative ➞ ☐6

◆ **Weak verbs** (pp 8 to 11), which are usually completely regular and have no vowel changes. Their endings differ from those of strong verbs ➞ ☐7

◆ **Mixed verbs** (pp 16 and 17), which have a vowel change like strong verbs, but the endings of weak verbs ➞ ☐8

Examples

Grammar

1	**ich hole**	I fetch
		I am fetching
		I do fetch
2	**ich holte**	I fetched
		I was fetching
		I used to fetch
3	**(dass) ich hole**	(that) I fetch/I fetched
4	**(dass) ich holte**	(that) I fetched
5	**ich hole**	I fetch
	wir holen	we fetch
	du holtest	you fetched
6	**singen**	to sing
	er singt	he sings
	er sang	he sang
7	**holen**	to fetch
	er holt	he fetches
	er holte	he fetched
8	**nennen**	to name
	er nennt	he names
	er nannte	he named

☐ Weak Verbs

Weak verbs are usually **regular** in conjugation. Their simple tenses are formed as follows:

◆ **Present** and **imperfect** tenses are formed by adding the endings shown below to the verb **stem**. This stem is formed by removing the **–en** ending of the infinitive (the form found in the dictionary) → **1**

◆ Where the infinitive of a weak verb ends in **–eln** or **–ern**, only the **–n** is removed to form the verb stem → **2**

◆ The endings are as follows:

	PRESENT INDICATIVE	PRESENT SUBJUNCTIVE	
1st singular	**-e**	**-e**	
2nd	**-st**	**-est**	
3rd	**-t**	**-e**	→ **3**
1st plural	**-en**	**-en**	
2nd	**-t**	**-et**	
3rd	**-en**	**-en**	

	IMPERFECT INDICATIVE	IMPERFECT SUBJUNCTIVE	
1st singular	**-te**	**-te**	
2nd	**-test**	**-test**	
3rd	**-te**	**-te**	→ **3**
1st plural	**-ten**	**-ten**	
2nd	**-tet**	**-tet**	
3rd	**-ten**	**-ten**	

Examples

1

INFINITIVE		STEM
holen	*to fetch*	**hol-**
machen	*to make*	**mach-**
kauen	*to chew*	**kau-**

2

INFINITIVE		STEM
wandern	*to roam*	**wander-**
handeln	*to trade,*	**handel-**
	to act	

3

holen   *to fetch*

PRESENT INDICATIVE	PRESENT SUBJUNCTIVE	
ich hol**e**	ich hol**e**	I fetch
du hol**st**	du hol**est**	you fetch
er/sie/es hol**t**	er/sie/es hol**e**	he/she/it fetches
wir hol**en**	wir hol**en**	we fetch
ihr hol**t**	ihr hol**et**	you (*plural*) fetch
sie/Sie hol**en**	sie/Sie hol**en**	they/you (*polite*) fetch

IMPERFECT INDICATIVE AND SUBJUNCTIVE
(*These tenses are identical for weak verbs*)

ich hol**te**	I fetched
du hol**test**	you fetched
er/sie/es hol**te**	he/she/it fetched
wir hol**ten**	we fetched
ihr hol**tet**	you (*plural*) fetched
sie/Sie hol**ten**	they/you (*polite*) fetched

☐ **Weak Verbs** (Continued)

◆ Where the stem of a weak verb ends in -**d** or -**t**, an extra -**e**- is inserted before those endings where this will ease pronunciation → 1

◆ Weak verbs whose stems end in -**m** or -**n** may take this extra -**e**-, or not, depending on whether its addition is necessary for pronunciation. If the -**m** or -**n** is preceded by a consonant *other than* **l**, **r** or **h**, the -**e**- is inserted → 2

◆ Weak (and strong) verbs whose stem ends in a sibilant sound (-**s**, -**z**, -**ss**, -**ß**) normally lose the -**s**- of the second person singular ending (the **du** form) in the present indicative → 3

⚠ NOTE: When this sibilant is -**sch**, the -**s**- of the ending remains → 4

Examples

Grammar

---

1 **reden** *to speak*

PRESENT	IMPERFECT
ich rede	ich redete
du redest	du redetest
er redet	er redete
wir reden	wir redeten
ihr redet	ihr redetet
sie reden	sie redeten

arbeiten *to work*

PRESENT	IMPERFECT
ich arbeite	ich arbeitete
du arbeitest	du arbeitetest
er arbeitet	er arbeitete
wir arbeiten	wir arbeiteten
ihr arbeitet	ihr arbeitetet
sie arbeiten	sie arbeiteten

2 **atmen** *to breathe*

PRESENT	IMPERFECT
ich atme	ich atmete
du atmest	du atmetest
er atmet	er atmete
wir atmen	wir atmeten
ihr atmet	ihr atmetet
sie atmen	sie atmeten

segnen *to bless*

PRESENT	IMPERFECT
ich segne	ich segnete
du segnest	du segnetest
er segnet	er segnete
wir segnen	wir segneten
ihr segnet	ihr segnetet
sie segnen	sie segneten

 BUT:

umarmen *to embrace*

PRESENT	IMPERFECT
ich umarme	ich umarmte
du umarmst	du umarmtest
er umarmt	er umarmte
wir umarmen	wir umarmten
ihr umarmt	ihr umarmtet
sie umarmen	sie umarmten

lernen *to learn*

PRESENT	IMPERFECT
ich lerne	ich lernte
du lernst	du lerntest
er lernt	er lernte
wir lernen	wir lernten
ihr lernt	ihr lerntet
sie lernen	sie lernten

3 **grüßen** *to greet*

PRESENT
ich grüße
du **grüßt**
er grüßt
wir grüßen
ihr grüßt
sie grüßen

4 **löschen** *to extinguish*

PRESENT
ich lösche
du löschst
er löscht
wir löschen
ihr löscht
sie löschen

❏ Strong Verbs

A table of the most useful strong verbs is given on pp 86 to 97.

◆ What differentiates strong verbs from weak ones is that when forming their **imperfect indicative** tense, strong verbs undergo a vowel change and have a different set of endings → ☐1

Their past participles are also formed differently (see p 24).

◆ To form the **imperfect subjunctive** of strong verbs, the endings from the appropriate table below are added to the stem of the imperfect indicative, but the vowel is modified by an umlaut where this is possible, i.e. **a ⟶ ä, o ⟶ ö, u ⟶ ü**. Exceptions to this are clearly shown in the table of strong verbs → ☐2

◆ The endings for the simple tenses of strong verbs are as follows:

	PRESENT INDICATIVE	PRESENT SUBJUNCTIVE	
1st singular	**-e**	**-e**	
2nd	**-st**	**-est**	
3rd	**-t**	**-e**	→ ☐3
1st plural	**-en**	**-en**	
2nd	**-t**	**-et**	
3rd	**-en**	**-en**	

	IMPERFECT INDICATIVE	IMPERFECT SUBJUNCTIVE	
1st singular	—	**-e**	
2nd	**-st**	**-(e)st**	
3rd	—	**-e**	→ ☐3
1st plural	**-en**	**-en**	
2nd	**-t**	**-(e)t**	
3rd	**-en**	**-en**	

Examples

---

1 | Compare:

	INFINITIVE	PRESENT	IMPERFECT
WEAK	**sagen** *to say*	**er sagt**	**er sagte**
STRONG	**rufen** *to shout*	**er ruft**	**er rief**

---

2 | | IMPERFECT INDICATIVE | IMPERFECT SUBJUNCTIVE |

⚠ BUT:

	IMPERFECT INDICATIVE	IMPERFECT SUBJUNCTIVE
	er gab *he gave*	**er gäbe** (*umlaut added*)
	er rief *he shouted*	**er riefe** (*no umlaut possible*)

---

3 | **singen** *to sing*

PRESENT INDICATIVE	PRESENT SUBJUNCTIVE
ich sing**e**	ich sing**e**
du sing**st**	du sing**est**
er sing**t**	er sing**e**
wir sing**en**	wir sing**en**
ihr sing**t**	ihr sing**et**
sie sing**en**	sie sing**en**
Sie sing**en**	Sie sing**en**

IMPERFECT INDICATIVE	IMPERFECT SUBJUNCTIVE
ich sang	ich säng**e**
du sang**st**	du säng**(e)st**
er sang	er säng**e**
wir sang**en**	wir säng**en**
ihr sang**t**	ihr säng**(e)t**
sie sang**en**	sie säng**en**
Sie sang**en**	Sie säng**en**

❑ **Strong Verbs** (Continued)

◆ In the present tense of strong verbs, the vowel also often changes for the second and third persons singular (the **du** and **er/sie/es** forms). The pattern of possible changes is as follows:

$$\begin{array}{rcl}
\text{long } \mathbf{e} & \longrightarrow & \mathbf{ie} \\
\text{short } \mathbf{e} & \longrightarrow & \mathbf{i} \\
\mathbf{a} & \longrightarrow & \mathbf{ä} \\
\mathbf{au} & \longrightarrow & \mathbf{äu} \\
\mathbf{o} & \longrightarrow & \mathbf{ö}
\end{array}$$

Verbs which undergo these changes are clearly shown in the table on p 86 ➞ 1

◆ Strong (and weak) verbs whose stem ends with a sibilant sound (**-s, -z, -ss, -ß**) normally lose the **-s-** of the second person singular ending (the **du** form) in the *present indicative*, unless the sibilant is **-sch**, when it remains ➞ 2

◆ In the second person singular of the *imperfect* tense of strong verbs whose stem ends in a sibilant sound (including **-sch**) the sibilant remains, and an **-e-** is inserted between it and the appropriate ending ➞ 3

Examples

1

sehen to see	**helfen** to help	**fahren** to drive
ich sehe	ich helfe	ich fahre
du siehst	du hilfst	du fährst
er/sie/es sieht	er/sie/es hilft	er fährt
wir sehen	wir helfen	wir fahren
ihr seht	ihr helft	ihr fahrt
sie sehen	sie helfen	sie fahren

saufen to booze	**stoßen** to push
ich saufe	ich stoße
du säufst	du stößt
er säuft	er stößt
wir saufen	wir stoßen
ihr sauft	ihr stoßt
sie saufen	sie stoßen

2

wachsen to grow	**waschen** to wash
ich wachse	ich wasche
du wächst	du wäschst
er wächst	er wäscht
wir wachsen	wir waschen
ihr wachst	ihr wascht
sie wachsen	sie waschen

3

lesen to read	**schließen** to close	**waschen** to wash
ich las	ich schloss	ich wusch
du lasest	du schlossest	du wuschest
er las	er schloss	er wusch
wir lasen	wir schlossen	wir wuschen
ihr last	ihr schlosst	ihr wuscht
sie lasen	sie schlossen	sie wuschen

☐ Mixed Verbs

There are nine **mixed** verbs in German, and, as their name implies, they are formed according to a mixture of the rules already outlined for weak and strong verbs.

The mixed verbs are:

brennen *to burn*	**kennen** *to know*	**senden** *to send*
bringen *to bring*	**nennen** *to name*	**wenden** *to turn*
denken *to think*	**rennen** *to run*	**wissen** *to know*

Full details of their principal parts are given in the verb table beginning on p 86.

- Mixed verbs form their **imperfect** tense by adding the weak verb endings to a stem whose vowel has been changed as for a strong verb → ①

  ⚠ NOTE: **Bringen** and **denken** have a consonant change too in their imperfect forms → ②

- The **imperfect subjunctive** forms of mixed verbs are unusual and should be noted → ③

- Other tenses of mixed verbs are formed as for strong verbs.

- The past participle of mixed verbs has characteristics of both weak and strong verbs, as shown on p 24.

Examples

Grammar

---

1   IMPERFECT INDICATIVE

kennen *to know*	**senden** *to send*	**wissen** *to know*
ich k**annte**	ich s**andte**	ich w**usste**
du k**anntest**	du s**andtest**	du w**usstest**
er k**annte**	er s**andte**	er w**usste**
wir k**annten**	wir s**andten**	wir w**ussten**
ihr k**anntet**	ihr s**andtet**	ihr w**usstet**
sie k**annten**	sie s**andten**	sie w**ussten**

---

2   IMPERFECT INDICATIVE

bringen *to bring*	**denken** *to think*
ich **brachte**	ich **dachte**
du **brachtest**	du **dachtest**
er **brachte**	er **dachte**
wir **brachten**	wir **dachten**
ihr **brachtet**	ihr **dachtet**
sie **brachten**	sie **dachten**

---

3   IMPERFECT SUBJUNCTIVE

brennen	**kennen**	**senden**
ich brennte	ich kennte	ich sendete
du brenntest	du kenntest	du sendetest
er brennte *etc*	er kennte *etc*	er sendete *etc*

bringen	**nennen**	**wenden**
ich brächte	ich nennte	ich wendete
du brächtest	du nenntest	du wendetest
er brächte *etc*	er nennte *etc*	er wendete *etc*

denken	**rennen**	**wissen**
ich dächte	ich rennte	ich wüsste
du dächtest	du renntest	du wüsstest
er dächte *etc*	er rennte *etc*	er wüsste *etc*

❐ The Imperative

Ths is the form of a verb used to give an order or a command, or to make a request:

Come here/stand up/please bring me a beer → **1**

◆ German has three main imperative forms. These go with the three ways of addressing people - **Sie**, **du** and **ihr** (see p 160)

	FORMATION	EXAMPLES	
SINGULAR	stem (+ **e**)	**hol(e)!**	*fetch!*
PLURAL	stem + **t**	**holt**	*fetch!*
POLITE (*sing* and *pl*)	stem + **en Sie**	**holen Sie!**	*fetch!*

◆ The **-e** of the singular form is often dropped, ⚠ BUT not where the verb stem ends in **-chn**, **-ckn**, **-dn**, **-fn**, **-gn** or **-tm** → **2**

◆ **Weak verbs** ending in **-eln** or **-ern** take the **-e** ending in the singular form, but the additional **-e-** within the stem may be dropped → **3**

◆ Any vowel change in the present tense of a **strong verb** (see p 14) occurs also in its singular imperative form and no **-e** is added → **4**

⚠ BUT: If the vowel modification in the present tense of a **strong verb** is the addition of an umlaut, this is not added in the singular form of the imperative → **5**

◆ In the imperative form of a **reflexive verb** (see p 30) the pronoun is placed immediately after the verb → **6**

◆ **Separable prefixes** (see p 72) are placed at the end of an imperative statement → **7**

Examples

Grammar

---

1 SINGULAR   **Komm mal her!**   Come here!
PLURAL   **Steht auf!**   Stand up!
POLITE   **Kommen Sie herein!**   Do come in

2 **Hör zu!**   Listen!
Hol es!   Fetch it!

⚠ BUT:
Öffne die Tür!   Open the door!

3 <u>**wandern**</u>   to walk   <u>**handeln**</u>   to act
wand(e)re!   walk!   **hand(e)le!**   act!

4 <u>**nehmen**</u>   to take   <u>**helfen**</u>   to help
du nimmst   you take   **du hilfst**   you help
nimm!   take!   **hilf!**   help!

⚠ BUT:
<u>**sehen**</u>   to see
sieh(e)!   see!

5 <u>**laufen**</u>   to run   <u>**stoßen**</u>   to push
du läufst   you run   **du stößt**   you push
lauf(e)!   run!   **stoß(e)!**   push!

6 <u>**sich setzen**</u>   to sit down
Setz dich!   Sit down!
Setzt euch!   Sit down!
Setzen Sie sich!   Do sit down!

7 <u>**zumachen**</u>   to close   <u>**aufhören**</u>   to stop
Mach die Tür zu!   **Hör aber endlich auf!**
Close the door!   Do stop it!

◻ **The Imperative** (Continued)

◆ Imperatives are followed in German by an exclamation mark, unless the imperative is not intended as a command → ☐1

◆ **Du** and **ihr**, though not normally present in imperative forms, may be included for emphasis → ☐2

◆ An imperative form also exists for the **wir** form of the verb. It consists of the normal present tense form, but with the pronoun **wir** *following* the verb. It is used for making suggestions → ☐3

◆ The imperative forms of **sein** (*to be*) are irregular → ☐4

◆ The particles **auch**, **nur**, **mal**, **doch** are frequently used with imperatives. They heighten or soften the imperative effect, or add a note of encouragement to a request or command. Often they have no direct equivalent in English and are therefore not always translated → ☐5

Some alternatives to the imperative in German

◆ Infinitives are often used instead of the imperative in written instructions or public announcements → ☐6

◆ The impersonal passive (see p 34) may be used → ☐7

◆ Nouns, adjectives or adverbs can also be used with imperative effect → ☐8
Some of these have become set expressions → ☐9

1   **Lass ihn in Ruhe!**
Leave him alone
Sagen Sie mir bitte, wie spät es ist
What's the time please?

2   **Geht ihr voran!**   You go on ahead
Sag du ihm, was los ist   You tell him what's wrong

3   **Nehmen wir an, dass ...**
Let's assume that ...
Sagen wir mal, es habe 2.000 Euros gekostet
Let's just say it cost 2,000 euros

4   <u>**sein**</u>   to be
sei!
seid!
seien wir!
Seien Sie!

5   **Geh doch!**   Go on!/Get going!
Sag mal, ...   Tell me ...
Versuchen Sie es mal!   Do give it a try!
Komm schon!   Do come/Please come
Mach es auch richtig!   Be sure to do it properly

6   **Einsteigen!**
All aboard!
Zwiebeln abziehen und in Ringe schneiden
Peel the onions and slice them

7   **Jetzt wird aufgeräumt!**
You're going to clear up now!

8   **Ruhe!**   Be quiet!/Silence!
Vorsicht!   Careful!/Look out!

9   **Achtung!**   Listen!/Attention!
Rauchen verboten!   No smoking

❐ Compound Tenses

The present and imperfect tenses in German are **simple** tenses, as described on pp 6 to 17.

All other tenses, called **compound tenses**, are formed for all types of verb by using the appropriate tense of an **auxiliary verb** plus a part of the main verb.

There are three auxiliary verbs:

haben	for past tenses
sein	also for past tenses
werden	for future and conditional tenses

The **compound past tenses** in German are:

Perfect indicative → 1
Perfect subjunctive → 2
Pluperfect indicative → 3
Pluperfect subjunctive → 4

These are dealt with on p 26 ff.

The **future** and **conditional tenses** in German are all compound tenses. They are:

Future indicative → 5
Future subjunctive → 6
Future perfect → 7
Conditional → 8
Conditional perfect → 9

These are dealt with on p 28 ff.

Examples

	WITH **haben**	WITH **sein**
1	**er hat geholt** he (has) fetched	**er ist gereist** he (has) travelled
2	**er habe geholt** he (has) fetched	**er sei gereist** he (has) travelled
3	**er hatte geholt** he had fetched	**er war gereist** he had travelled
4	**er hätte geholt** he had fetched	**er wäre gereist** he had travelled
5	**er wird holen** he will fetch	**er wird reisen** he will travel
6	**er werde holen** he will fetch	**er werde reisen** he will travel
7	**er wird geholt haben** he will have fetched	**er wird gereist sein** he will have travelled
8	**er würde holen** he would fetch	**er würde reisen** he would travel
9	**er würde geholt haben** he would have fetched	**er würde gereist sein** he would have travelled

◻ **Compound Past Tenses: Formation**

- Compound past tenses are normally formed by using the auxiliary verb **haben**, plus the past participle of the main verb (see below) ➞ ☐1

- Certain types of verb take **sein** instead of **haben**, and this is clearly indicated in the verb table starting on p 86. They fall into three main types:

  1. intransitive verbs (those that take no direct object, often showing a change of state or place) ➞ ☐2
  2. certain verbs meaning "to happen" ➞ ☐3
  3. miscellaneous others, including:
     begegnen to meet, **bleiben** to remain,
     gelingen to succeed, **sein** to be, **werden** to become ➞ ☐4

- In some cases the verb can be conjugated with either **haben** or **sein**, depending on whether it is used transitively (with a direct object) or intransitively (where no direct object is possible) ➞ ☐5

The past participle: formation (see also p 50)

- **Weak** verbs add the prefix **ge-** and suffix **-t** to the verb stem ➞ ☐6
  Verbs ending in **-ieren** or **-eien** omit the **ge-** ➞ ☐7

- **Strong** verbs add the prefix **ge-** and the suffix **-en** to the verb stem ➞ ☐8
  The vowel of the stem may be modified (see verb table, p 86) ➞ ☐9

- **Mixed** verbs add the prefix **ge-** and the "weak" suffix **-t** to the stem. The stem vowel is modified as for many strong verbs ➞ ☐10

Examples

Grammar

---

1   **Haben Sie gut geschlafen?**
Did you sleep well?
Die Kinder hatten fleißig gearbeitet
The children had worked hard

2   **Wir sind nach Bonn gefahren**
We went to Bonn
Er ist schnell eingeschlafen
He quickly fell asleep

3   **Was ist geschehen?**
What happened?

4   **Er ist zu Hause geblieben**   **Er ist krank gewesen**
He stayed at home   He has been ill
Es ist uns nicht gelungen   **Sie ist krank geworden**
We did not succeed   She became ill
Er ist einem Freund begegnet
He met a friend

5   **Er hat den Wagen nach Köln gefahren**
He drove the car to Cologne
Er ist nach Köln gefahren
He went to Cologne

6   **holen** to fetch   **9**   **singen** to sing
geholt fetched   **gesungen** sung

7   **studieren** to study   **10**   **senden** to send
studiert studied   **gesandt** sent
prophezeien to prophesy   **bringen** to bring
prophezeit prophesied   **gebracht** brought

8   **laufen** to run
gelaufen run

For a full list of strong and mixed verbs see p 86.

❏ **Compound Past Tenses: Formation** (Continued)

The formation of past participles for weak, strong and mixed verbs is described on p 24, and a comprehensive list of the principal parts of the most commonly used strong and mixed verbs is provided for reference on pp 86 to 97.

How to form the compound past tenses:

Perfect indicative   the present tense of **haben** or **sein** plus the past participle of the verb ➞ 1

Perfect subjunctive   (used in indirect or reported speech) the present subjunctive of **haben** or **sein** plus the past participle ➞ 2

Pluperfect indicative   imperfect indicative of **haben** or **sein** plus the past participle ➞ 3

Pluperfect subjunctive   (for indirect or reported speech) imperfect subjunctive of **haben** or **sein** plus the past participle ➞ 4

⚠ NOTE: The pluperfect subjunctive is a frequently used tense in German, since it can replace the much clumsier conditional perfect tense shown on p 28

Examples

	WITH **haben**	WITH **sein**

1 PERFECT INDICATIVE

WITH **haben**	WITH **sein**
ich habe geholt	ich bin gereist
du hast geholt	du bist gereist
er/sie/es hat geholt	er/sie/es ist gereist
wir haben geholt	wir sind gereist
ihr habt geholt	ihr seid gereist
sie/Sie haben geholt	sie/Sie sind gereist

2 PERFECT SUBJUNCTIVE

WITH **haben**	WITH **sein**
ich habe geholt	ich sei gereist
du habest geholt	du sei(e)st gereist
er/sie/es habe geholt	er/sie/es sei gereist
wir haben geholt	wir seien gereist
ihr habet geholt	ihr seiet gereist
sie/Sie haben geholt	sie/Sie seien gereist

3 PLUPERFECT INDICATIVE

WITH **haben**	WITH **sein**
ich hatte geholt	ich war gereist
du hattest geholt	du warst gereist
er/sie/es hatte geholt	er/sie/es war gereist
wir hatten geholt	wir waren gereist
ihr hattet geholt	ihr wart gereist
sie/Sie hatten geholt	sie/Sie waren gereist

4 PLUPERFECT SUBJUNCTIVE

WITH **haben**	WITH **sein**
ich hätte geholt	ich wäre gereist
du hättest geholt	du wär(e)st gereist
er/sie/es hätte geholt	er/sie/es wäre gereist
wir hätten geholt	wir wären gereist
ihr hättet geholt	ihr wär(e)t gereist
sie/Sie hätten geholt	sie/Sie wären gereist

☐ **Future and Conditional Tenses: Formation**

- The **future** and **conditional** tenses are formed in the same way for all verbs, whether weak, strong or mixed.

- The auxiliary **werden** is used for all verbs together with the infinitive of the main verb.

- The infinitive is usually placed at the end of the clause (see p 224).

How to form the future and conditional tenses:

Future indicative	present tense of **werden** plus the infinitive of the verb → **1**
Future subjunctive	present subjunctive of **werden** plus the infinitive → **2**
Future perfect	present indicative of **werden** plus the **perfect infinitive** (see below) → **3**
Conditional imperfect	subjunctive of **werden** plus the infinitive → **4**
Conditional perfect	imperfect subjunctive of **werden** plus the **perfect infinitive** (see below) → **5**

⚠ NOTE: The conditional perfect is often replaced by the pluperfect subjunctive.

- The **perfect infinitive** consists of the infinitive of **haben/sein** plus the past participle of the verb.

1️⃣ FUTURE INDICATIVE

ich werde holen
du wirst holen
er/sie/es wird holen

wir werden holen
ihr werdet holen
sie/Sie werden holen

2️⃣ FUTURE SUBJUNCTIVE

ich werde holen
du werdest holen
er/sie/es werde holen

wir werden holen
ihr werdet holen
sie/Sie werden holen

3️⃣ FUTURE PERFECT

ich werde geholt haben
du wirst geholt haben
er wird geholt haben

wir werden geholt haben
ihr werdet geholt haben
sie/Sie werden geholt haben

4️⃣ CONDITIONAL IMPERFECT

ich würde holen
du würdest holen
er/sie/es würde holen

wir würden holen
ihr würdet holen
sie/Sie würden holen

5️⃣ CONDITIONAL PERFECT [1]

ich würde geholt haben
du würdest geholt haben
er würde geholt haben

wir würden geholt haben
ihr würdet geholt haben
sie/Sie würden geholt haben

---

[1] ⚠ NOTE: The conditional perfect is often replaced by the pluperfect subjunctive (see p 26).

☐ **Reflexive Verbs**

A verb whose action is reflected back to its subject may be termed reflexive:

she washes *herself*

Reflexive verbs in German are recognized in the infinitive by the preceding reflexive pronoun **sich** → 1

German has many reflexive verbs, a great number of which are not reflexive in English → 1

- Reflexive verbs are composed of the verb and a reflexive pronoun (see p 170). This pronoun may be either the direct object (and therefore in the accusative case) or the indirect object (and therefore in the dative case) → 2

- Many verbs in German which are not essentially reflexive may become reflexive by the addition of a reflexive pronoun → 3
  When a verb with an indirect object is made reflexive (see p 170) the pronoun is usually dative → 4

- A direct object reflexive pronoun changes to the dative if another direct object is present → 5

- In a main clause the reflexive pronoun follows the verb → 6
  After inversion (see p 226), or in a subordinate clause, the reflexive pronoun must come after the subject if the subject is a personal pronoun → 7
  It may precede or follow a noun subject → 8

- Reflexive verbs are always conjugated with **haben** *except* where the pronoun is used to mean *each other*. Then the verb is normally conjugated with **sein**.

- The imperative forms are shown on p 19.

Examples

---

1   **sich beeilen**   **wir beeilen uns**
to hurry   we are hurrying

2   <u>**sich** (*accusative*) **erinnern**</u>   to remember
ich erinnere mich   **wir erinnern uns**
du erinnerst dich   **ihr erinnert euch**
er/sie/es erinnert sich   **sie/Sie erinnern sich**

     <u>**sich** (*dative*) **erlauben**</u>   to allow oneself
ich erlaube mir   **wir erlauben uns**
du erlaubst dir   **ihr erlaubt euch**
er/sie/es erlaubt sich   **sie/Sie erlauben sich**

3   <u>**etwas melden**</u>   to report something
sich melden   **Ich habe mich gemeldet**
to report/to volunteer   I volunteered

4   <u>**wehtun**</u>   to hurt
sich wehtun   **Hast du dir wehgetan?**
to get hurt   Have you hurt yourself?

     <u>**kaufen**</u>   to buy
Er kaufte ihr einen Mantel   **Er kaufte sich** (*dative*)
He bought her a coat   **einen neuen Mantel**
                             He bought himself a new coat

5   **Ich wasche mich**   **Ich wasche mir die Hände**
I am having a wash   I am washing my hands

6   **Er wird sich darüber freuen**
He'll be pleased about that

7   **Darüber wird er sich freuen**
He'll be pleased about that
Ich frage mich, ob er sich darüber freuen wird
I wonder if he'll be pleased about that

8   **Langsam drehten sich die Kinder um** OR:
Langsam drehten die Kinder sich um
The children slowly turned round

❏ **Reflexive Verbs** (Continued)

Some examples of verbs which can be used with a reflexive pronoun in the accusative case:

sich anziehen to get dressed → **1**
sich aufregen to get excited → **2**
sich beeilen to hurry → **3**
sich beschäftigen mit[1] to be occupied with → **4**
sich bewerben um[1] to apply for → **5**
sich erinnern an[1] to remember → **6**
sich freuen auf[1] to look forward to → **7**
sich interessieren für[1] to be interested in → **8**
sich irren to be wrong → **9**
sich melden to report (for duty *etc*)/to volunteer
sich rasieren to shave
sich (hin)setzen to sit down → **10**
sich trauen[2] to trust oneself
sich umsehen to look around → **11**

Some examples of verbs which can be used with a reflexive pronoun in the dative case:

sich abgewöhnen to give up (something) → **12**
sich aneignen to appropriate
sich ansehen to have a look at
sich einbilden to imagine (wrongly) → **13**
sich erlauben to allow oneself → **14**
sich leisten to treat oneself → **15**
sich nähern to get close to
sich vornehmen to plan to do → **16**
sich vorstellen to imagine → **17**
sich wünschen to want → **18**

---

[1] For verbs normally followed by a preposition, see p 76 ff.
[2] **trauen** when non-reflexive takes the dative case.

1. **Du sollst dich sofort anziehen**
You are to get dressed immediately
2. **Reg dich doch nicht so auf!**
Calm down!
3. **Wir müssen uns beeilen**
We must hurry
4. **Sie beschäftigen sich sehr mit den Kindern**
They spend a lot of time with the children
5. **Hast du dich um diese Stelle beworben?**
Have you applied for this post?
6. **Ich erinnere mich nicht daran**
I can't remember it
7. **Ich freue mich auf die Fahrt**
I am looking forward to the journey
8. **Interessierst du dich für Musik?**
Are you interested in music?
9. **Er hat sich geirrt**
He was wrong
10. **Bitte, setzt euch hin!**
Please sit down
11. **Die Kinder sahen sich erstaunt um**
The children looked around in amazement
12. **Eigentlich müsste man sich das Rauchen abgewöhnen**
One really ought to give up smoking
13. **Bilde dir doch nichts ein!**
Don't kid yourself!
14. **Eins könntest du dir doch erlauben**
You could surely allow yourself one
15. **Wenn ich mir nur einen Mercedes leisten könnte!**
If only I could afford a Mercedes!
16. **Du hast dir wieder zu viel vorgenommen!**
You've taken on too much again!
17. **So hatte ich es mir oft vorgestellt**
I had often imagined it like this
18. **Was wünscht ihr euch zu Weihnachten?**
What do you want for Christmas?

❑ The Passive

In active tenses, the subject of a verb carries out the action of the verb, but in passive tenses the subject of the verb has something done to it.

Compare the following:

> *Peter kicked the cat* (subject: *Peter*)
> *The cat was kicked by Peter* (subject: *the cat*)

◆ English uses the verb "to be" to form its passive tenses. German uses **werden** → 1

A sample verb is conjugated in the passive on pp 39 to 41.

◆ In English, the word "by" usually introduces the agent through which the action of a passive tense is performed. In German this agent is introduced by:

> **von** for the performer of the action
> **durch** for an inanimate cause → 2

◆ The passive can be used to add impersonality or distance to an event → 3

It may also be used where the identity of the cause of the deed is unknown or not important → 4

◆ In general, however, the passive is used less in German than in English. The following are common replacements for the passive:

> 1 an active tense with the impersonal pronoun **man** as subject (meaning *they/one*). This resembles the use of *on* in French, and **man** is not always translated as *one* or *they* → 5
>
> 2 **sich lassen** plus a verb in the infinitive → 6

[1] **Das Auto wurde gekauft**
The car was bought

[2] **Das ist von seinem Onkel geschickt worden**
It was sent by his uncle

Das Kind wurde von einem Hund gebissen
The child was bitten by a dog

Seine Bewerbung ist von der Firma abgelehnt worden
(*the firm is viewed as a human agent*)
His application was turned down by the firm

Die Tür wurde durch den Wind geöffnet
The door was opened by the wind

Das Getreide wurde durch den Sturm niedergeschlagen
The crop was flattened by the storm

[3] **Die Praxis ist von Dr. Disselkamp übernommen worden**
The practice has been taken over by Dr Disselkamp

Anfang 1993 wurde ein weiterer Anschlag auf sein Leben verübt
Another attempt was made on his life early in 1993

[4] **In letzter Zeit sind neue Gesetze eingeführt worden**
New laws have recently been introduced

[5] **Man hatte es schon verkauft**
It had already been sold

Man wird es verkauft haben
It will have been sold

[6] **Das lässt sich schnell herausfinden**
We'll/You'll/One will be able to find that out quickly

◻ **The Passive** (Continued)

◆ In English the indirect object of an active tense can become the subject of a passive statement e.g.

> Peter gave *him* a car (*him* = to him)
> *He* was given a car by Peter

This is not possible in German, where the indirect object (*him*) must remain in the dative case (see p 110). There are two ways of handling this in German:

> 1 with the direct object (*car*) as the subject of a passive verb → ☐
> 2 by means of an impersonal passive construction, with or without the impersonal subject **es** → ☐

These constructions would however normally be avoided in favour of an active tense, when the agent of the action is known → ☐2

◆ Verbs which are normally followed by the dative case in German and so have only an indirect object (see p 80) should therefore be especially noted, as they can only adopt the impersonal or **man**-forms of the passive → ☐3

◆ Some passive tenses are avoided in German, as they are inelegant (and difficult to use!). For instance, the future perfect passives should be replaced by an active tense or a construction using **man** → ☐4

The conditional perfect passives are also rarely used, past conditional being shown by the pluperfect subjunctives, either passive or active → ☐5

◆ English passive constructions such as

> *he was heard whistling/they were thought to be dying*

are not possible in German → ☐6

---

1 **Ein Auto wurde ihm von Peter geschenkt**
OR:
Es wurde ihm von Peter ein Auto geschenkt
OR:
Ihm wurde von Peter ein Auto geschenkt
He was given a car by Peter

2 **Peter schenkte ihm ein Auto**
Peter gave him a car

3 **helfen** (+ *dative*)   to help
Sie half mir   **Mir wurde von ihr geholfen**
She helped me   OR:
                         Es wurde mir von ihr geholfen
                         I was helped by her

4 **Er meint, es werde schon gesehen worden sein**
He thinks that it will already have been seen

   ✔ BETTER: **Er meint, man werde es schon gesehen haben**

5 **Es würde geholt worden sein / Man würde es geholt haben**
It would have been fetched

   ✔ BETTER: **Es wäre geholt worden / Man hätte es geholt**

6 **Man hörte ihn singen**
He was heard singing
Man sah sie ankommen
She was seen arriving
Man glaubte, er sei betrunken
He was thought to be drunk

❏ Passive Tenses: Conjugation

Simple tenses

Present passive indicative
e.g. *it is seen*

present indicative of **werden** +
past participle of the verb → 1

Present passive subjunctive

present subjunctive of **werden** +
past participle of the verb → 2

Imperfect passive indicative
e.g. *it was seen*

imperfect indicative of **werden** +
past participle of the verb → 3

Imperfect passive subjunctive

imperfect subjunctive of **werden**
+ past participle of the verb → 4

Compound tenses

Perfect passive indicative
e.g. *it has been seen*

present indicative of **sein** + past
participle of the verb + **worden**
→ 5

Perfect passive subjunctive

present subjunctive of **sein** + past
participle of the verb + **worden**
→ 6

Pluperfect passive indicative
e.g. *it had been seen*

imperfect indicative of **sein** + past
participle of the verb + **worden**
→ 7

1 PRESENT PASSIVE INDICATIVE

ich werde gesehen   **wir werden gesehen**
du wirst gesehen   **ihr werdet gesehen**
er/sie/es wird gesehen   **sie/Sie werden gesehen**
OR: **man sieht mich/man sieht dich** *etc*

2 PRESENT PASSIVE SUBJUNCTIVE

ich werde gesehen   **wir werden gesehen**
du werdest gesehen   **ihr werdet gesehen**
er/sie/es werde gesehen   **sie/Sie werden gesehen**
OR: **man sehe mich/man sehe dich** *etc*

3 IMPERFECT PASSIVE INDICATIVE

ich wurde gesehen/wir wurden gesehen *etc*
OR: **man sah mich/man sah uns** *etc*

4 IMPERFECT PASSIVE SUBJUNCTIVE

ich würde gesehen/wir würden gesehen *etc*
OR: **man sähe mich/man sähe uns** *etc*

5 PERFECT PASSIVE INDICATIVE

ich bin gesehen worden/wir sind gesehen worden *etc*
OR: **man hat mich/uns gesehen** *etc*

6 PERFECT PASSIVE SUBJUNCTIVE

ich sei gesehen worden/wir seien gesehen worden *etc*
OR: **man habe mich/uns gesehen** *etc*

7 PLUPERFECT PASSIVE INDICATIVE

ich war gesehen worden/wir waren gesehen worden *etc*
OR: **man hatte mich/uns gesehen** *etc*

❑ **Passive Tenses: Conjugation** (Continued)

Pluperfect passive subjunctive	imperfect subjunctive of **sein** + past participle of the verb + **worden** → ①
Present passive infinitive e.g. *to be seen*	infinitive of **werden** + past participle of the verb → ②
Future passive indicative e.g. *it will be seen*	present indicative of **werden** + present passive infinitive of the verb → ③
Future passive subjunctive	present subjunctive of **werden** + present passive infinitive of the verb → ④
Perfect passive infinitive e.g. *to have been seen*	past participle of the verb + **worden sein** → ⑤
Future perfect passive e.g. *it will have been seen*	present indicative of **werden** + perfect passive infinitive of the verb → ⑥
Conditional passive e.g. *it would be seen*	imperfect subjunctive of **werden** + present passive infinitive of the verb → ⑦
Conditional perfect passive e.g. *it would have been seen*	imperfect subjunctive of **werden** + perfect passive infinitive of the verb → ⑧

Grammar

---

1 PLUPERFECT PASSIVE SUBJUNCTIVE

ich wäre gesehen worden/wir wären gesehen worden *etc*
OR: **man hätte mich/uns gesehen** *etc*

2 PRESENT PASSIVE INFINITIVE

gesehen werden

3 FUTURE PASSIVE INDICATIVE

ich werde gesehen werden/wir werden gesehen werden *etc*
OR: **man wird mich/uns sehen** *etc*

4 FUTURE PASSIVE SUBJUNCTIVE

ich werde gesehen werden/wir werden gesehen werden *etc*
OR: **man werde mich/uns sehen** *etc*

5 PERFECT PASSIVE INFINITIVE

gesehen worden sein

6 FUTURE PERFECT PASSIVE

ich werde/wir werden gesehen worden sein *etc*
OR: **man wird mich/uns gesehen haben** *etc*

7 CONDITIONAL PASSIVE

ich würde gesehen werden/wir würden gesehen werden
OR: **man würde mich/uns sehen** *etc*

8 CONDITIONAL PERFECT PASSIVE

ich würde/wir würden gesehen worden sein *etc*
OR: **man würde mich/uns gesehen haben** *etc*
OR: pluperfect subjunctive: **man hätte mich/uns gesehen** *etc*

❏ Impersonal Verbs

These verbs are used only in the third person singular, usually with the subject **es** meaning *it* → 1

♦ Intransitive verbs (verbs with no direct object) are often made impersonal in the passive to describe activity of a general nature → 2

When the verb and subject are inverted (see p 226), the **es** is omitted → 3

Impersonal verbs in the passive can also be used as an imperative form (see p 20) → 4

♦ In certain expressions in the active, the impersonal pronoun **es** can be omitted. In this case, a personal pronoun object begins the clause → 5
In the following lists * indicates that **es** may be omitted in this way:

Some common impersonal verbs and expressions

es donnert	it's thundering
es fällt mir ein, dass/zu*	it occurs to me that/to → 6
es fragt sich, ob	one wonders whether → 7
es freut mich, dass/zu	I am glad that/to → 8
es friert	it is freezing → 9
es gefällt mir	I like it → 10
es geht mir gut/schlecht	I'm fine/not too good
es geht nicht	it's not possible
es geht um	it's about
es gelingt mir (zu)	I succeed (in) → 11
es geschieht	it happens → 12
es gießt	it's pouring
es handelt sich um	it's a question of

1	**Es regnet**	It's raining

2 **Es wurde viel gegessen und getrunken**
There was a lot of eating and drinking

3 **Auf der Hochzeit wurde viel gegessen und getrunken**
There was a lot of eating and drinking at the wedding

4	**Jetzt wird gearbeitet!**	Now you're/we're going to work
5	**Mir ist warm**	I'm warm

6 **Nachher fiel (es) mir ein, dass der Mann ziemlich komisch angezogen war**
Afterwards it occurred to me that the man was rather oddly dressed

7 **Es fragt sich, ob es sich lohnt, das zu machen**
One wonders if that's worth doing

8 **Es freut mich sehr, dass du gekommen bist**
I'm so pleased that you have come

9 **Heute Nacht hat es gefroren**
It was below freezing last night

10 **Ihm hat es gar nicht gefallen**
He didn't like it at all

11 **Es war ihnen gelungen, die letzten Karten zu kriegen**
They had succeeded in getting the last tickets

12 **Und so geschah es, dass ...**
And so it came about that ...

☐ **Impersonal Verbs and Expressions** (Continued)

es hängt davon ab	it depends
es hat keinen Zweck (zu)	there's no point (in) → 1
es interessiert mich, dass/zu*	I am interested that/to
es ist mir egal (ob)*	it's all the same to me (if) → 2
es ist möglich(, dass)	it's possible (that) → 3
es ist nötig	it's necessary → 4
es ist mir, als ob*	I feel as if
es ist mir gut/schlecht *etc* **zumute** *or* **zu Mute***	I feel good/bad *etc* → 5
es ist schade(, dass)	it's a pity (that)
es ist (mir) wichtig*	it's important (to me)
es ist mir warm/kalt*	I'm warm/cold
es ist warm/kalt	it's *or* the weather is warm/cold
es ist zu hoffen/bedauern *etc**	it is to be hoped/regretted *etc*
es klingelt	someone's ringing the bell → 6
es klopft	someone's knocking
es kommt darauf an(, ob)	it all depends (whether)
es kommt mir vor(, als ob)	it seems to me (as if)
es läutet	the bell is ringing → 7
es liegt an	it is because of → 8
es lohnt sich (nicht)	it's (not) worth it → 9
es macht nichts	it doesn't matter
es macht nichts aus	it makes no difference → 10
es macht mir (keinen) Spaß(, zu)	it's (no) fun (to) → 11
es passiert	it happens → 12
es regnet	it's raining → 13
es scheint mir, dass/als ob*	it seems to me that/as if
es schneit	it's snowing
es stellt sich heraus, dass	it turns out that
es stimmt (nicht), dass	it's (not) true that
es tut mir Leid(, dass)	I'm sorry (that)
wie geht es (dir)?	how are you? → 14
mir wird schlecht	I feel sick

1. **Es hat keinen Zweck, weiter darüber zu diskutieren**
   There's no point in discussing this any further

2. **Es ist mir egal, ob du kommst oder nicht**
   I don't care if you come or not

3. **Es ist doch möglich, dass der Zug Verspätung hat**
   It's always possible the train has been delayed

4. **Es wird nicht nötig sein, uns darüber zu informieren**
   It won't be necessary to inform us of it

5. **Mir ist heute seltsam zumute** *or* **zu Mute**
   I feel strange today

6. **Es hat gerade geklingelt**
   The bell just went/The phone just rang

7. **Es hat schon geläutet**
   The bell has gone

8. **Woran liegt es?**
   Why is that?

9. **Ich weiß nicht, ob es sich lohnt oder nicht**
   I don't know if it's worth it or not

10. **Mir macht es nichts aus**
    It makes no difference to me
    Macht es Ihnen etwas aus, wenn ...
    Would you mind if ...

11. **Hauptsache, es macht Spaß**
    The main thing is to enjoy yourself

12. **Ihm ist bestimmt etwas passiert**
    Something must have happened to him

13. **Es hat den ganzen Tag geregnet**
    It rained the whole day

14. **Wie gehts denn? — Danke, es geht**
    How are things? — All right, thank you

❏ The Infinitive

Forms

There are four forms of the infinitive → **1**. These forms are used in certain compound tenses (see p 28). The present active infinitive is the most widely used and is the form found in dictionaries.

Uses

- Preceded by **zu** (*to*)

  1 as in English, after other verbs ("I tried *to come*") → **2**
  2 as in English, after adjectives ("it was easy *to see*") → **3**
  3 where the English equivalent is not always an infinitive:
     - after nouns, where English may use an "-ing" form → **4**
     - after **sein**, where the English equivalent may be a passive tense → **5**

- Without **zu**, the infinitive is used after the following:

  modal verbs → **6**
  lassen → **7**
  heißen → **8**
  bleiben → **9**
  gehen → **10**
  verbs of perception → **11**

⚠ NOTE: Verbs of perception can also be followed by a subordinate clause beginning with **wie** or **dass**, especially if the sentence is long or involved → **12**

---

1 INFINITIVES:

PRESENT ACTIVE
holen
to fetch

PERFECT ACTIVE
geholt haben
to have fetched

PRESENT PASSIVE
geholt werden
to be fetched

PERFECT PASSIVE
geholt worden sein
to have been fetched

2 **Ich versuchte zu kommen** I tried to come

3 **Es war leicht zu sehen** It was easy to see

4 **Ich habe nur wenig Gelegenheit, Musik zu hören**
I have little opportunity to listen to music

5 **Er ist zu bedauern** He is to be pitied

6 **Er kann schwimmen** He can swim

7 **Sie ließen uns warten** They kept us waiting

8 **Er hieß ihn kommen** He bade him come

9 **Er blieb sitzen** He remained seated

10 **Sie ging einkaufen** She went shopping

11 **Ich sah ihn kommen**
Er hörte sie singen
I saw him coming
He heard her singing

12 **Er sah, wie sie langsam auf und ab schlenderte**
He watched her strolling slowly up and down

☐ **The Infinitive** (Continued)

Used as an imperative
◆ The infinitive can be used as an imperative (see p 20) → ☐1☐

Used as a noun
◆ The infinitive can be made into a noun by giving it a capital letter. Its gender is always neuter → ☐2☐

Used with modal verbs (see p 52)
◆ An infinitive used with a modal verb is always placed at the end of a clause (see p 56) → ☐3☐

◆ If the modal verb is in a compound tense, its auxiliary will follow the subject in a main clause in the normal way, and the modal participle comes after the infinitive.

⚠ BUT: In a subordinate clause, the auxiliary immediately precedes the infinitive and the modal participle, instead of coming at the end → ☐4☐

◆ An infinitive expressing change of place may be omitted entirely after a modal verb (see p 56) → ☐5☐

Used in infinitive phrases

Infinitive phrases can be formed with:

zu	ohne ... zu	
um ... zu	anstatt ... zu	→ ☐6☐

◆ The infinitive comes at the end of its phrase → ☐7☐

◆ In separable verbs, **zu** is inserted *between* the verb and its prefix in the present infinitive → ☐8☐

◆ A reflexive pronoun comes first, immediately following an introductory word if there is one → ☐9☐

1. **Einsteigen und Türen schließen!**
   All aboard! Close the doors!

2. **rauchen**   to smoke
   Er hat das Rauchen aufgegeben
   He's given up smoking

3. **Wir müssen morgen einkaufen gehen**
   We have to go shopping tomorrow

4. **Sie haben gestern aufräumen müssen**
   They had to tidy up yesterday
   ⚠ BUT:
   Da sie gestern haben aufräumen müssen, durften sie nicht kommen
   They couldn't come as they had to tidy up yesterday

5. **Er will jetzt nach Hause**
   He wants to go home now

6. **es zu tun**   to do it
   es getan zu haben   to have done it
   um es zu tun   in order to do it
   um es getan zu haben   in order to have done it
   ohne es zu tun   without doing it
   ohne es getan zu haben   without having done it
   anstatt es zu tun   instead of doing it
   anstatt es getan zu haben instead of having done it

7. **Ohne ein Wort zu sagen, verließ er das Haus**
   He left the house without saying a word
   Er ging nach Hause, ohne mit ihr gesprochen zu haben
   He went home without having spoken to her

8. **aufgeben**   to give up
   um es aufzugeben   in order to give it up

9. **Sie gingen weg, ohne sich zu verabschieden**
   They left without saying goodbye

❒ The Present Participle

◆ The present participle for all verbs is formed by adding **-d** to the infinitive form → 1

◆ The present participle may be used as an adjective. As with all adjectives, it is declined if used attributively (see p 140) → 2

◆ The present participle may also be used as an adjectival noun (see p 148) → 3

The past participle

◆ For weak verbs, the past participle is formed by prefixing **ge-** and adding **-t** to the verb stem → 4

◆ For strong verbs, the past participle is formed by adding the prefix **ge-** and the ending **-en** to the verb stem → 5
The vowel is often modified too → 6
(See table of strong and mixed verbs beginning on p 86)

◆ Mixed verbs form their past participle by adding the **ge-** and **-t** of weak verbs, but they change their vowel as for strong verbs. (See table on p 86) → 7

◆ The past participles of *separable* verbs are formed according to the above rules and are joined on to the separable prefix → 8

◆ For *inseparable* verbs, past participles are formed without the **ge-** prefix → 9

◆ Many past participles can also be used as adjectives and adjectival nouns → 10

Examples

1   **lachen**   to laugh   **singen**   to sing
     lachend   laughing   **singend**   singing

2   **ein lachendes Kind**   a laughing child
     mit klopfendem Herzen   with beating heart

3   **der Vorsitzende/ein Vorsitzender**   the/a chairman

4   **machen**   to do/make
     gemacht   done/made

5   **sehen**   to see
     gesehen   seen

6   **singen**   to sing
     gesungen   sung

7   **wissen**   to know
     gewusst   known

8   **aufstehen**   to get up   **nachmachen**   to copy/imitate
     aufgestanden   got up   **nachgemacht**   copied/imitated

9   **bestellen**   to order   **entscheiden**   to decide
     bestellt   ordered   **entschieden**   decided

10   **seine verlorene Brille**   his lost spectacles
     Wir aßen Gebratenes   We ate fried food

❐ Modal Auxiliary Verbs

Modal verbs, sometimes called modal auxiliaries, are used to *modify* other verbs (to show e.g. possibility, ability, willingness, permission, necessity) much as in English:

> he *can* swim
> *may* I come?
> we *shouldn't* go

- In German the modal auxiliary verbs are: **dürfen**, **können**, **mögen**, **müssen**, **sollen** and **wollen**.

- Modal verbs have some important differences in their uses and in their conjugation from other verbs, and these are clearly shown in the verb tables on pp 86 to 97.

- Modal verbs have the following meanings:

dürfen
  to be allowed to/may → 1
  used negatively: *must not/may not* → 2
  to show probability → 3
  also used in some polite expressions → 4

können
  to be able to/can → 5
  in its subjunctive forms:
  would be able to/could → 6
  as an informal alternative to **dürfen** with the meaning: *to be allowed to/can* → 7
  to show possibility → 8

mögen
  to like/to like to → 9
  most common in its imperfect subjunctive form which expresses polite inquiry or request: *should like to/would like to* → 10
  to show possibility or probability → 11

1. **Darfst du mit ins Kino kommen?**
   Are you allowed to/can you come with us to the cinema?
   Darf ich bitte mitkommen?
   May I come with you please?
   Ich dürfte schon, aber ich will nicht
   I could/would be allowed to, but I don't want to

2. **Hier darf man nicht rauchen**
   Smoking is prohibited here

3. **Das dürfte wohl das Beste sein**
   That's probably the best thing

4. **Was darf es sein?**
   Can I help you?/What would you like?

5. **Wir konnten es nicht schaffen**
   We couldn't/weren't able to do it

6. **Er könnte noch früher kommen**
   He could/would be able to come even earlier
   Er meinte, er könne noch früher kommen
   He though he could come earlier
   Wir könnten vielleicht morgen hinfahren?
   Perhaps we could go there tomorrow?

7. **Kann ich/darf ich ein Eis haben?**
   Can I/may I have an ice cream?

8. **Wer könnte es gewesen sein?**   **Das kann sein**
   Who could it have been?   That may be so

   ⚠ BUT: **Das kann nicht sein**
   That cannot be so

9. **Magst du Butter?**
   Do you like butter?

10. **Wir möchten bitte etwas trinken**
    We should like something to drink
    Möchtest du sie besuchen?
    Would you like to visit her?

11. **Wie alt mag sie sein?**
    How old might she be?

☐ **Modal Auxiliary Verbs** (Continued)

müssen   *to have to/must/need to* → **1**

certain idiomatic uses → **2**

⚠ NOTE: For *must have ...,* use the relevant tense of **müssen** + past participle of main verb + the auxiliary **haben** or **sein** → **3**

For *don't have to/need not,* a negative form of **brauchen** (*to need*) may be used instead of **müssen** → **4**

sollen   *ought to/should* → **5**

to be (supposed) to where the demand is not self-imposed → **6**

to be said to be → **7**

as a command, either direct or indirect → **8**

wollen   *to want/want to* → **9**

used as a less formal version of **mögen** to mean: *to want/wish* → **10**

to be willing to → **11**

to show previous intention → **12**

to claim or pretend → **13**

1. **Er hatte jeden Tag um sechs aufstehen müssen**
He had to get up at six o'clock every day
Man musste lachen
One had to laugh/One couldn't help laughing

2. **Muss das sein?** Is that really necessary?
Ein Millionär müsste man sein! Oh to be a millionaire!
Den Film muss man gesehen haben
That film is worth seeing

3. **Es muss geregnet haben** It must have been raining
Er meinte, es müsse am vorigen Abend passiert sein
He thought it must have happened the previous evening

4. **Das brauchtest du nicht zu sagen**
You didn't have to say that

5. **Man sollte immer die Wahrheit sagen**
One should always tell the truth
Er wusste nicht, was er tun sollte
He didn't know what to do (*what he should do*)

6. **Ich soll dir helfen**
I am to help you (*I have been told to help you*)
Du sollst sofort deine Frau anrufen
You are to phone your wife at once (*She has left a message asking you to ring*)

7. **Er soll sehr reich sein**
I've heard he's very rich/He is said to be very rich

8. **Es soll niemand sagen, dass die Schotten geizig sind!**
Let no-one say the Scots are mean!
Sie sagte mir, ich solle damit aufhören
She told me to stop it

9. **Das Kind will LKW-Fahrer werden**
The child wants to become a lorry driver

10. **Willst du eins?** Do you want one?
Willst du/möchtest du etwas trinken?
Do you want/would you like something to drink?

11. **Er wollte nichts sagen** He refused to say anything

12. **Ich wollte gerade anrufen** I was just about to phone

13. **Keiner will es gewesen sein** No-one admits to doing it

❑ **Modal Auxiliary Verbs** (Continued)

Conjugation and use

- Modal verbs have unusual present tenses → **1**

  Their principal parts are given in the verb tables on pp 86 to 97.

- Each modal verb has two past participles.

  The first, which is the more common, is the same as the infinitive form and is used where the modal is modifying a verb → **2**

  The second resembles a normal weak past participle and is used only where no verb is being modified (see the verb tables on p 86) → **3**

- The verb modified by the modal is placed in its infinitive form at the end of a clause → **4**

- Where the modal is used in a compound tense, its past participle in the form of the infinitive is also placed at the end of a clause, immediately after the modified verb → **5**

- If the modal verb is modifying a verb, and if the modal is used in a compound tense in a subordinate clause, then the normal word order for subordinate clauses (see p 228) does not apply. The auxiliary used to form the compound tense of the modal is not placed right at the end of the subordinate clause, but instead comes before both infinitives → **6**

  Such constructions are usually avoided in German, by using a simple tense in place of a compound. (For notes on the use of tenses in German, see p 58 ff) → **7**

- A modified verb which expresses motion may be omitted entirely if an adverb or adverbial phrase is present to indicate the movement or destination → **8**

Examples

---

1 **dürfen**
ich/er/sie/es darf
du darfst
wir/sie/Sie dürfen
ihr dürft

können
ich/er/sie/es kann
du kannst
wir/sie/Sie können
ihr könnt

mögen
ich/er/sie/es mag
du magst
wir/sie/Sie mögen
ihr mögt

müssen
ich/er/sie/es muss
du musst
wir/sie/Sie müssen
ihr müsst

sollen
ich/er/sie/es soll
du sollst
wir/sie/Sie sollen
ihr sollt

wollen
ich/er/sie/es will
du willst
wir/sie/Sie wollen
ihr wollt

2 **wollen**: Past participle **wollen**
Er hat kommen wollen
He wanted to come

3 **wollen**: Past participle **gewollt**
Hast du es gewollt?
Did you want it?

4 **Er kann gut schwimmen**
He can swim well

5 **Wir haben das Haus nicht kaufen wollen**
We didn't want to buy the house
Sie wird dich bald sehen wollen
She will want to see you soon

6 COMPARE:
Obwohl wir das Haus gekauft haben, ...
Although we bought the house ...
Obwohl wir das Haus haben kaufen wollen, ...
Although we wanted to buy the house ...

7 **Obwohl wir das Haus kaufen wollten ...**
Although we wanted to buy the house ...

8 **Ich muss nach Hause**
I must go home
Die Kinder sollen jetzt ins Bett
The children have to go to bed now

❐ Use of Tenses

Continuous forms

- Unlike English, the German verb does not distinguish between its simple and continuous forms → **1**
- To emphasize continuity, the following may be used:
  - simple tense plus an adverb or adverbial phrase → **2**
  - **am** or **beim** plus an infinitive used as a noun → **3**
  - **eben/gerade dabei sein zu** plus an infinitive → **4**

The present

- The present tense is used in German with **seit** or **seitdem** where English uses a past tense to show an action which began in the past and still continues → **5**

  If the action is finished, or does not continue, a past tense is used → **6**
- The present is commonly used with future meaning → **7**

The future

- The present is often used as a future tense → **7**
- The future tense is used however to:
  - emphasize the future → **8**
  - express doubt or supposition about the future → **9**
  - express future intention → **10**

The future perfect

- The future perfect is used as in English to mean *shall/will have done* → **11**
- It is used in German to express a supposition → **12**
- In conversation it is replaced by the perfect → **13**

The conditional

- The conditional may be used in place of the imperfect subjunctive to express improbable condition (see p 62) → **14**
- It is used in indirect statements or questions to replace the future subjunctive in conversation or where the subjunctive form is not distinctive → **15**

1	**ich tue** I do (*simple form*) OR: I am doing (*continuous*)
	er rauchte he smoked OR: he was smoking
	sie hat gelesen she has read OR: she has been reading
	es ist geschickt worden it is sent OR: it is being sent
2	**Er kochte gerade das Abendessen**
	He was cooking the supper
	Nun spricht sie mit ihm Now she's talking to him
3	**Ich bin am Bügeln** I am ironing
4	**Wir waren eben dabei, einige Briefe zu schreiben**
	We were just writing a few letters
5	**Ich wohne seit drei Jahren hier**
	I have been living here for three years
6	**Seit er krank ist, hat er uns nicht besucht**
	He hasn't visited us since he's been ill
	Seit seiner Verlobung habe ich ihn nicht geshen
	I haven't seen him since his engagement
7	**Wir fahren nächstes Jahr nach Griechenland**
	We're going to Greece next year
8	**Das werde ich erst nächstes Jahr machen können**
	I won't be able to do that until next year
9	**Wenn er zurückkommt, wird er mir bestimmt helfen**
	He's sure to help me when he returns
10	**Ich werde ihm helfen**
	I'm going to help him
11	**Bis Sonntag wird er es gelesen haben**
	He will have read it by Sunday
12	**Das wird Herr Keute gewesen sein**
	That must have been Herr Keute
13	**Bis du zurückkommst, haben wir alles aufgeräumt**
	We'll have tidied up by the time you get back
14	**Wenn ich eins hätte, würde ich es dir geben**
	If I had one I would give it to you
	Wenn er jetzt bloß kommen würde!
	If only he would get here!
15	**Er fragte, ob wir fahren würden**
	He asked if we were going to go

❏ **Use of Tenses** (Continued)

The conditional perfect

- May be used in place of the pluperfect subjunctive in a sentence containing a **wenn**-clause ➞ ⒈
- But the pluperfect subjunctive is preferred ➞ ⒉

The imperfect

- Is used in German with **seit** or **seitdem** where the pluperfect is used in English to show an action which began in the remote past and continued to a point in the more recent past ➞ ⒊
  For discontinued actions the pluperfect is used ➞ ⒋
- Is used to describe past actions which have no link with the present as far as the speaker is concerned ➞ ⒌
  Is used for narrative purposes ➞ ⒍
  Is used for repeated, habitual or prolonged past action ➞ ⒎
  See also the ⚠ NOTE on **The Perfect** (below).

The perfect

- Is used to translate the English perfect tense, eg:
  I have spoken, he has been reading ➞ ⒏
- Describes past actions or events which still have a link with the present or the speaker ➞ ⒐
- Is used in conversation and similar communication ➞ ⒑

  ⚠ NOTE: In practice however the perfect and imperfect are often interchangeable in German usage, and in spoken German a mixture of both is common.

The pluperfect

- Is used to translate *had done/had been doing*, except in conjunction with **seit/seitdem** (see **The Imperfect**) ➞ ⒒

The subjunctive

- For uses of the subjunctive tenses, see pp 62 to 67.

Examples

1 **Wenn du es gesehen hättest, würdest dus geglaubt haben**
You would have believed it if you'd seen it

2 **Hättest du es gesehen, so hättest du es geglaubt**
If you had seen it, you'd have believed it
Wenn ich das nur nicht gemacht hätte!
If only I hadn't done it!
Wäre ich nur da gewesen!
If I'd only been there

3 **Sie war seit ihrer Heirat als Lehrerin beschäftigt**
She had been working as a teacher since her marriage

4 **Ihren Sohn hatten sie seit zwölf Jahren nicht gesehen**
They hadn't seen their son for twelve years

5 **Er kam zu spät, um teilnehmen zu können**
He arrived too late to take part

6 **Das Mädchen stand auf, wusch sich das Gesicht und verließ das Haus**
The girl got up, washed her face and went out

7 **Wir machten jeden Tag einen kleinen Spaziergang**
We went/We used to go for a little walk every day

8 **Ich habe ihn heute nicht gesehen**
I haven't seen him today

9 **Ich habe ihr nichts davon erzählt**
I didn't tell her anything about it
Gestern sind wir in die Stadt gefahren und haben uns ein paar Sachen gekauft
Yesterday we went into town and bought ourselves a few things

10 **Hast du den Krimi gestern Abend im Fernsehen gesehen?**
Did you see the thriller on television last night?

11 **Sie waren schon weggefahren**
They had already left
Diese Bücher hatten sie schon gelesen
They had already read these books

❏ The Subjunctive: when to use it

The subjunctive form in English has almost died out, leaving only a few examples such as:

> if I *were* rich
> if only he *were* to come
> so *be* it

German however makes much wider use of subjunctive forms, especially in formal, educated or literary contexts. Although there is a growing tendency to use indicatives in spoken German, subjunctives are still very common.

- The indicative tenses in German display fact or certainty. The subjunctives show unreality, uncertainty, speculation about a situation or any doubt in the speaker's mind → **1**

  Subjunctives are also used in indirect speech, as shown on pp 66 and 67.

- For how to form all tenses of the subjunctive, the reader is referred to the relevant sections on Simple Tenses (pp 6 to 17) and Compound Tenses (pp 22 to 29). See also the Subjunctive in Reported Speech (p 66).

- The **imperfect subjunctive** is very common. It is important to note that the imperfect subjunctive form does not always represent actions performed in the past → **2**

Uses of the subjunctive in German

- To show improbable condition (e.g. if he *came*, he would ...).
  The *if*-clause (**wenn** in German) has a verb in the imperfect subjunctive and the main clause can have either an imperfect subjunctive or a conditional → **3**

☐1 INDICATIVE

Das stimmt   **Es ist eine Unverschämtheit**
That's true   It's a scandal

SUBJUNCTIVE

Es könnte doch war sein
It could well be true
Sie meint, es sei eine Unverschämtheit
She thinks it's a scandal
(*speaker not necessarily in agreement with her*)

☐2 *imperfect subjunctive expressing the future:*
Wenn ich morgen nur da sein könnte!
If only I could be there tomorrow!

expressing the present/immediate future:
Wenn er jetzt nur käme!
If only he would come now!

speaker's opinion, referring to present or future:
Sie wäre die Beste
She's the best

☐3 **Wenn du kämest, wäre ich froh**

OR:

Wenn du kämest, würde ich froh sein
I should be happy if you came

Wenn es mir nicht gefiele, würde ich es nicht bezahlen

OR:

Wenn es mir nicht gefiele, bezahlte ich es nicht
If I wasn't happy with it, I wouldn't pay for it
(*The second form is less likely, as the imperfect subjunctive and
imperfect indicative forms of* **bezahlen** *are identical*)

❒ **The Subjunctive: when to use it** (Continued)

◆ The imperfect of **sollen** or **wollen**, or a conditional tense might be used in the **wenn**-clause to replace an uncommon imperfect subjunctive, or a subjunctive which is not distinct from the same tense of the indicative ➞ ①

◆ To show unfulfilled condition (if he *had come*, he would have ...)

The **wenn**-clause requires a pluperfect subjunctive, the main clause a pluperfect subjunctive or conditional perfect ➞ ②

⚠ NOTE: The indicative is used to express a *probable* condition, as in English ➞ ③

◆ **Wenn** can be omitted from conditional clauses. The verb must then follow the subject and **dann** or **so** usually begins the main clause ➞ ④

◆ With **selbst wenn** (*even if/even though*) ➞ ⑤

◆ With **wenn ... nur** (*if only ...*) ➞ ⑥

◆ To speculate or make assumptions ➞ ⑦

◆ After **als** (*as if/as though*) ➞ ⑧

◆ Where there is uncertainty or doubt ➞ ⑨

◆ To make a polite enquiry ➞ ⑩

◆ To indicate theoretical possibility or unreality ➞ ⑪

◆ As an alternative to the conditional perfect ➞ ⑫

---

1   **Wenn er mich so sehen würde, würde er mich für verrückt halten!**   OR:

    Wenn er mich so sehen würde, hielte er mich für verrückt!
OR:

    Wenn er mich so sehen sollte, würde er mich für verrückt halten!

    If he saw me like this, he would think I was mad!

    (**Wenn er mich so sähe** *would sound rather stilted*)

2   **Wenn du pünktlich gekommen wärest, hättest du ihn gesehen**
OR:

    Wenn du pünktlich gekommen wärest, würdest du ihn gesehen haben

    If you had been on time, you would have seen him

3   **Wenn ich ihn sehe, gebe ich es ihm**

    If I see him I'll give him it

4   **Hättest du mich nicht gesehen, so wäre ich schon weg**

    If you hadn't seen me, I would have been gone by now

5   **Selbst wenn er etwas wüsste, würde er nichts sagen**

    Even if he knew about it, he wouldn't say anything

6   **Wenn wir nur erfolgreich wären!**

    If only we were successful!

7   **Und wenn er Recht hätte?**   What if he were right?

    Eine Frau, die das sagen würde (OR: **die das sagte**), **müsste Feministin sein!**

    Any woman who would say that must be a feminist!

8   **Er sah aus, als sei er krank**

    He looked as if he were ill

9   **Er wusste nicht, wie es ihr jetzt ginge**

    He didn't know how she was

10   **Wäre da sonst noch etwas?**   Will there be anything else?

11   **Er stellte sich vor, wie gut er in dem Anzug aussähe**

    He imagined how good he would look in the suit

12   **Ich hätte ihn gesehen** OR: **Ich würde ihn gesehen haben**

    I would have seen him

☐ The Subjunctive in Indirect Speech

What a person asks or thinks can be reported in one of two ways, either **directly**:

Tom said, "I have been on holiday"

OR **indirectly**:

Tom said (that) he had been on holiday

♦ In English, indirect (or reported) speech can be indicated by a change in tense of what has been reported:

He said, "*I know* your sister"
He said (that) *he knew* my sister

In German the change is not in tense, but from indicative to subjunctive → **1**

♦ There are two ways of introducing indirect speech in German, similar to the parallel English constructions:

1 The clause which reports what is said may be introduced by **dass** (*that*). The finite verb or auxiliary comes at the end of the clause → **2**

2 **dass** may be omitted. The verb in this case must stand in second position in the clause, instead of being placed at the end → **3**

Forms of the subjunctive in indirect speech

For conjugation of verbs in the subjunctive, see pp 8 to 15 and 26 to 31. In indirect (or reported) speech, wherever the present subjunctive is identical to the present indicative form, the imperfect subjunctive is used instead → **4**

Examples

---

1 **Er sagte: „Sie kennt deine Schwester"**
He said, "She knows your sister"

Er sagte, sie kenne meine Schwester
He said she knew my sister

„Habe ich zu viel gesagt?", fragte er
"Have I said too much?", he asked

Er fragte, ob er zu viel gesagt habe
He asked if he had said too much

2 **Er hat uns gesagt, dass er Italienisch spreche**
He told us that he spoke Italian

3 **Er hat uns gesagt, er spreche Italienisch**
He told us he spoke Italian

4 PRESENT SUBJUNCTIVE IN INDIRECT SPEECH

WEAK VERBS

holen to fetch

ich holte	**wir holten**
du holest	ihr holet
er hole	**sie holten**

STRONG VERBS

singen to sing

ich sänge	**wir sängen**
du singest	ihr singet
er singe	**sie sängen**

❏ **Verbs with Prefixes**

Many verbs in German begin with a prefix. A prefix is a word or part of a word which precedes the verb stem → 1

◆ Often the addition of a prefix changes the meaning of the basic verb → 2

◆ Prefixes may be found in strong, weak or mixed verbs. Adding a prefix may occasionally change the verb conjugation → 3

There are four kinds of prefix and each behaves in a slightly different way, as shown on the following pages. Prefixes may be inseparable, separable, double or variable (i.e. either separable or inseparable depending on the verb).

Inseparable prefixes

◆ The eight inseparable prefixes are:

be-	ent-	ge-	ver-	→ 4
emp-	er-	miss-	zer-	

◆ These exist only as prefixes, and cannot be words in their own right.

◆ They are never separated from the verb stem, whatever tense of the verb is used → 5

◆ Inseparable prefixes are always unstressed → 6

Examples

1 zu + geben   = **zugeben**
       an + ziehen   = **anziehen**

2 **nehmen**   to take
       zunehmen   to put on weight/to increase
       sich benehmen to behave

3 WEAK   STRONG
       suchen   to look for   **stehen**   to stand
       versuchen to try   **verstehen**   to understand
       besuchen to visit   **aufstehen**   to get up

       WEAK   WEAK
       löschen   to extinguish   **fehlen**   to be missing

       STRONG   STRONG
       erlöschen to go out   **empfehlen**   to recommend

4 **beschreiben**   to describe
       empfangen   to receive
       enttäuschen   to disappoint
       erhalten   to contain
       gehören   to belong
       misstrauen   to mistrust
       verlieren   to lose
       zerlegen   to dismantle

5 <u>**besuchen**</u> to visit
       Er besucht uns regelmäßig   He visits us regularly
       Er besuchte uns jeden Tag   He used to visit us every day
       Er hat uns jeden Tag besucht   He visited us every day
       Er wird uns morgen besuchen   He will visit us tomorrow
       Besuche sofort deine Tante!   Visit your aunt at once

6 er**lau**ben, ver**steh**en, emp**fang**en, ver**gess**en

◻ **Verbs with Prefixes** (Continued)

Separable prefixes

Some common examples are:

ab	fest	herunter	mit
an	frei	hervor	nach
auf	her	hin	nieder
aus	herab	hinab	vor
bei	heran	hinauf	vorbei
da(r)	herauf	hinaus	vorüber
davon	heraus	hindurch	weg
dazu	herbei	hinein	zu
ein	herein	hinüber	zurecht
empor	herüber	hinunter	zurück
entgegen	herum	los	zusammen

◆ Unlike inseparable prefixes, separable prefixes may be words in their
   own right. Indeed, nouns, adjectives and adverbs are often used as
   separable prefixes → **1**

◆ The past participle of a verb with a separable prefix is formed with **ge-**.
   It comes between the verb and the prefix → **2**

◆ In main clauses, the prefix is placed at the end of the clause if the verb
   is in a simple tense (i.e. present, imperfect or imperative form) → **3**

◆ In subordinate clauses, whatever the tense of the verb, the prefix is
   attached to the verb and the resulting whole placed at the end of the
   clause → **4**

◆ Where an infinitive construction requiring **zu** is used (see p 48), the **zu**
   is placed between the infinitive and prefix to form one word → **5**

1. *noun + verb*:   **teilnehmen**   to take part
   adjective + verb: **loswerden**   to get free of
   adverb + verb: **niederlegen**   to lay down

2. **Er hat nicht teilgenommen**
   He did not participate
   Wir sind an der Grenze zurückgewiesen worden
   We were turned back at the border

3. **wegbringen**   to take for repair/to take away
   PRESENT
   Wir bringen das Auto weg
   IMPERFECT
   Wir brachten das Auto weg
   IMPERATIVE
   Bringt das Auto weg!
   FUTURE
   Wir werden das Auto wegbringen
   CONDITIONAL
   Wir würden das Auto wegbringen
   PERFECT
   Wir haben das Auto weggebracht
   PERFECT PASSIVE
   Das Auto ist weggebracht worden
   PLUPERFECT SUBJUNCTIVE
   Wir hätten das Auto weggebracht

4. PRESENT
   Weil wir das Auto wegbringen, ...
   IMPERFECT
   Dass wir das Auto wegbrachten, ...
   PERFECT
   Nachdem wir das Auto weggebracht haben, ...
   PLUPERFECT SUBJUNCTIVE
   Wenn wir das Auto weggebracht hätten, ...
   FUTURE
   Obwohl wir das Auto wegbringen werden, ...

5. **Um das Auto rechtzeitig wegzubringen, müssen wir morgen früh aufstehen**
   In order to take the car in on time we shall have to get up early tomorrow

☐ **Verbs with Prefixes** (Continued)

Variable prefixes

These are:

durch	über	unter	wider
hinter	um	voll	wieder

- These can be separable or inseparable → **1**

- Often they are used separably and inseparably with the same verb. In such cases the verb and prefix will tend to retain their basic meanings if the prefix is used separably, but adopt figurative meanings when the prefix is used inseparably → **2**

- Variable prefixes behave as separable prefixes when used separably, and as inseparable prefixes when used inseparably → **3**

Double prefixes

These occur where a verb with an inseparable prefix is preceded by a separable prefix → **4**

- The separable prefix behaves as described on p 70, the verb plus inseparable prefix representing the basic verb to which the separable prefix is attached → **5**

- Unlike other separable verbs, however, verbs with double prefixes have no **ge-** in their past participles → **6**

Grammar

---

1. **unternehmen** (*inseparable*) to undertake, take on
   Wir haben in den Ferien vieles unternommen
   We did a great deal in the holidays
   Du unternimmst zu viel
   You take on too much

   untergehen (*separable*) to sink, go down
   Die Sonne geht unter
   The sun is going down/is setting
   Die Sonne ist untergangen
   The sun has gone down/has set

2. **etwas wiederholen** (*separable*) to retrieve something
   etwas wiederholen (*inseparable*) to repeat something

3. **Er holte ihr die Tasche wieder**
   He brought her back her bag
   Er wiederholte den Satz
   He repeated the sentence

4. **ausverkaufen** to sell off

5. **Er verkauft alles aus**
   He's selling everything off
   Um alles auszuverkaufen ...
   In order to sell everything off ...
   Er wird alles ausverkaufen
   He'll be selling everything off

6. **Aber er hat doch alles ausverkauft**
   But he's sold everything off

❑ **Verb Combinations**

◆ *Noun + verb* combinations are written separately → ①

⚠ BUT: Compound verbs which are almost exclusively used in the infinitive or as participles are written as one word → ②

◆ *Infinitive + verb* combinations are written separately → ③

◆ *Participle + verb* combinations are written separately → ④

◆ *Adjective/adverb + verb* combinations are written as one word if the first component of the compound is not a word in its own right → ⑤

Or if the first component of the compound cannot be qualified or compared → ⑥

◆ *Adjective + verb* combinations are written separately if the adjective can be qualified or compared (in this case, negation counts as a qualification) → ⑦

◆ *Adverb + verb* combinations are written separately if the adverb is a compound word → ⑧

◆ Verb combinations with **-ander** are written separately → ⑨

◆ Verb combinations with **-seits** and **-wärts** are written separately → ⑩

◆ Verb combinations with **sein** are written separately → ⑪

1. Ski fahren, Eis laufen, Halt machen

2. bergsteigen, brustschwimmen, kopfrechnen, sonnenbaden

3. kennen lernen, sitzen bleiben, spazieren gehen

4. gefangen nehmen, verloren gehen

5. fehlschlagen, kundgeben, weismachen

6. bereithalten, fernsehen, totschlagen

7. bekannt machen, genau nehmen, kurz treten, nahe bringen

8. abhanden kommen, beiseite legen, überhand nehmen, zunichte machen

9. aneinander legen, auseinander laufen, durcheinander reden

10. abseits stehen, abwärts gehen

11. auf sein, zu sein

❐ **Verbs followed by Prepositions**

- Some verbs in English usage require a preposition (*for/with/by* etc) for their completion.
  This also happens in German, though the prepositions used with German verbs may not be those expected from their English counterparts → ☐1

- The preposition used may significantly alter the meaning of a verb in German → ☐2

- Occasionally German verbs use a preposition where their English equivalents do not → ☐3

- Prepositions used with verbs behave as normal prepositions and affect the *case* of the following noun (see p198).

- A verb plus preposition may be followed by a clause containing another verb rather than by a noun or pronoun. This often corresponds to an *-ing* construction in English:

  Thank you for *coming*

  In German, this is dealt with in two ways:

  1 Where the "verb-plus-preposition" construction has the same subject as the following verb, the preposition is preceded by **da-** or **dar-** and the following verb becomes an infinitive used with **zu** → ☐4

  2 Where the subject of the "verb-plus-preposition" is not the same as for the following verb, a **dass** clause is used → ☐5

- Following clauses may also be introduced by interrogatives (**ob**, **wie** etc) if the meaning demands them → ☐6

1 COMPARE:

sich sehnen *nach*	to long *for*
warten *auf*	to wait *for*
bitten *um*	to ask *for*

2

bestehen	to pass (an examination/a test *etc*)
bestehen aus	to consist of
bestehen auf	to insist on
sich freuen auf	to look forward to
sich freuen über	to be pleased about

3

diskutieren über	to discuss

4 **Ich freue mich sehr darauf, mal wieder mit ihm zu arbeiten**

I am looking forward to working with him again

5 **Ich freue mich sehr darauf, dass du morgen kommst**

I am looking forward to your coming tomorrow

Er sorgte dafür, dass die Kinder immer gut gepflegt waren

He saw to it that the children were always well cared for

6 **Er dachte lange darüber nach, ob er es wirklich kaufen wollte**

He thought for ages about whether he really wanted to buy it

Sie freut sich darüber, wie schnell ihre Schüler gelernt haben

She is pleased at how quickly her students have learned

❐ Verbs followed by Prepositions (Continued)

COMMON VERBS FOLLOWED BY PREPOSITION <u>PLUS ACCUSATIVE CASE</u>:

achten auf	to pay attention to, keep an eye on → 1
sich amüsieren über	to laugh at, smile about
sich ärgern über	to get annoyed about/with
sich bewerben um	to apply for → 2
bitten um	to ask for → 3
denken an	to be thinking of → 4
denken über	to hold an opinion of, think about → 5
sich erinnern an	to remember
sich freuen auf	to look forward to
sich freuen über	to be pleased about → 6
sich gewöhnen an	to get used to → 7
sich interessieren für	to be interested in → 8
kämpfen um	to fight for
sich kümmern um	to take care of, see to
nachdenken über	to ponder, reflect on → 9
sich unterhalten über	to talk about
sich verlassen auf	to rely on, depend on → 10
warten auf	to wait for

COMMON VERBS FOLLOWED BY PREPOSITION <u>PLUS DATIVE CASE</u>:

abhängen von	to be dependent on → 11
sich beschäftigen mit	to occupy oneself with → 12
bestehen aus	to consist of → 13
leiden an/unter	to suffer from → 14
neigen zu	to be inclined to
riechen nach	to smell of → 15
schmecken nach	to taste of
sich sehnen nach	to long for
sterben an	to die of
teilnehmen an	to take part in → 16
träumen von	to dream of → 17
sich verabschieden von	to say goodbye to
sich verstehen mit	to get along with, get on with
zittern vor	to tremble with → 18

1. **Er musste auf die Kinder achten**
   He had to keep an eye on the children

2. **Sie hat sich um die Stelle als Sekretärin beworben**
   She applied for the post of secretary

3. **Die Kinder baten ihre Mutter um Plätzchen**
   The children asked their mother for some biscuits

4. **Woran denkst du?** What are you thinking about?
   Daran habe ich gar nicht mehr gedacht
   I'd forgotten about that

5. **Wie denkt ihr darüber?** What do you think about it?

6. **Ich freute mich sehr darüber, Johannes besucht zu haben**
   I was very glad I had visited Johannes

7. **Man gewöhnt sich an alles** One gets used to anything

8. **Sie interessiert sich sehr für Politik**
   She is very interested in politics

9. **Er hatte schon lange darüber nachgedacht**
   He had been thinking about it for a long time

10. **Er verlässt sich darauf, dass seine Frau alles tut**
    He relies on his wife to do everything

11. **Das hängt davon ab** It all depends

12. **Sie sind im Moment sehr damit beschäftigt, ihr neues Haus in Ordnung zu bringen**
    They are very busy sorting out their new house at the moment

13. **Dieser Kuchen besteht aus Eiern, Mehl und Zucker**
    This cake consists of eggs, flour and sugar

14. **Sie hat lange an dieser Krankheit gelitten**
    She suffered from this illness for a long time
    Alte Leute können sehr unter der Einsomkeit leiden
    Old people can suffer dreadful loneliness

15. **Der Kuchen roch nach Zimt**
    The cake smelled of cinnamon

16. **Sie hat an der Bonner Tagung teilnehmen müssen**
    She had to attend the Bonn conference

17. **Er hat von seinem Urlaub geträumt**
    He dreamt of his holiday

18. **Er zitterte vor Freude** He was trembling with joy

❐ Verbs followed by the Dative

Some verbs have a direct object and an indirect object. In the English sentence "*He gave me a book*", *a book* is the direct object of *gave* and would be in the accusative and *me* (= *to me*) is the indirect object and would appear in the dative case in German → 1

- In German, as in English, this type of verb is usually concerned with giving or telling something to someone, or with performing an action for someone → 2
- The normal word order after such verbs is for the direct object to follow the indirect, *except* where the direct object is a personal pronoun (see p 224) → 2
  This order may be reversed for emphasis → 3
- Some examples of verbs followed by the dative in this way:

anbieten	gönnen	schicken
bringen	kaufen	schreiben
beweisen	leihen	schulden → 4
erzählen	mitteilen	verkaufen
geben	schenken	zeigen

- Certain verbs in German however can be followed *only* by an indirect object in the dative case. These should be noted especially, since most of them are quite different from their English equivalents:

begegnen	gratulieren	schmeicheln
danken	helfen	trauen
fehlen	imponieren	trotzen
gefallen	misstrauen	vorangehen → 5
gehören	nachgehen	wehtun
gelingen	schaden	widersprechen
gleichen	schmecken	widerstehen

- For how to form the passive of such verbs, see p 36.

Examples

1   **Er gab mir ein Buch**   He gave me a book

2   **Er wusch dem Kind** (*indirect*) **das Gesicht** (*direct*)
He washed the child's face
Er erzählte ihm (*indirect*) **eine Geschichte** (*direct*)
He told him a story
⚠ BUT:
Er hat sie (*direct*) **meiner Mutter** (*indirect*) **gezeigt**
He showed it to my mother
Kaufst du es (*direct*) **mir** (*indirect*)**?**
Will you buy it for me?

3   **Er wollte das Buch** (*direct*) **seiner Mutter** (*indirect*) **geben**
(*This emphasises* **seiner Mutter**)
He wanted to give the book to his mother

4   **Er bot ihr die Arbeitsstelle an**   He offered her the job
Bringst du mir eins?   Will you bring me one?
Ich gönne dir das neue Kleid
I want you to have the new dress
Er hat ihr mitgeteilt, dass ...   He told her that ...
Ich schenke meiner Mutter Parfüm zum Geburtstag
I am giving my mother perfume for her birthday
Das schulde ich ihm   I owe him that
Zeig es mir!   Show me it!

5   **Er ist seinem Freund in der Stadt begegnet**
He bumped into his friend in town
Mir fehlt der Mut dazu   I don't have the courage
Es ist ihnen gelungen   They succeeded
Wem gehört dieses Buch?   Whose book is this?
Er wollte ihr nicht helfen   He refused to help her
Ich gratuliere dir!   Congratulations!
Rauchen schadet der Gesundheit
Smoking is bad for your health
Das Essen hat ihnen gut geschmeckt
They enjoyed the meal

❏ **There is/There are**

There are three ways of expressing this in German:

Es gibt

- This is always used in the singular form, and is followed by an accusative object which may be either singular or plural → ①

- **Es gibt** is used to refer to things of a general nature or location → ②

- It also has some idiomatic usages → ③

Es ist/es sind

- The **es** here merely introduces the real subject. The verb therefore becomes plural where the real subject is plural. The real subject is in the nominative case → ④

- The **es** is not required and is therefore omitted when the verb and real subject come together. This happens when inversion of subject and verb occurs (see p 226) and in subordinate clauses → ⑤

- **Es ist** or **es sind** are used to refer to:
  1. subjects with a specific and confined location.
     This location must always be mentioned either by name or by **da, darauf, darin** *etc* → ⑥
  2. temporary existence → ⑦
  3. as a beginning to a story → ⑧

The passive voice

Often *there is/there are* in English will be rendered by a verb in the passive voice in German → ⑨

1 **Es gibt zu viele Probleme dabei**
There are too many problems involved
Es gibt kein besseres Bier
There's no better beer

2 **Es gibt bestimmt Regen**
It's definitely going to rain
Ruhe hat es bei uns nie gegeben
There has never been any peace here

3 **Was gibts (= gibt es) zum Essen?**   What is there to eat?
Was gibts?   What's wrong?, What's up?
So was gibts doch nicht!   That's impossible!

4 **Es waren zwei ältere Leute unten im Hof**
There were two elderly people down in the yard
Es sind so viele Touristen da
There are so many tourists there

5 **Unten im Hof waren zwei ältere Leute**
Down in the yard were two elderly people
Wenn so viele Touristen da sind, ...
If there are so many tourists there, ...

6 **Es waren viele Flaschen Sekt im Keller**
There were a lot of bottles of champagne in the cellar
**Ein Brief lag auf dem Tisch. Es waren auch zwei
Bücher darauf**
A letter lay on the table. There were also two books on it

7 **Es war niemand da**
There was no-one there

8 **Es war einmal ein König ...**
Once upon a time there was a king ...

9 **Es wurde auf der Party viel getrunken**
There was a lot of drinking at the party

☐ Use of "es" as an Anticipatory Object

Many verbs can have as their object a **dass** clause or an infinitive with **zu**
→ **1**

- ◆ With some verbs **es** is used as an object to anticipate this clause or infinitive phrase → **2**

- ◆ When the clause or infinitive phrase begins the sentence, **es** is not used in the main clause but its place may be taken by an optional **das** → **3**

COMMON VERBS WHICH <u>USUALLY HAVE THE "ES" OBJECT</u>:

es ablehnen, zu	to refuse to
es aushalten, zu tun/dass	to stand doing → **4**
es ertragen, zu tun/dass	to endure doing
es leicht haben, zu	to find it easy to → **5**
es nötig haben, zu	to need to → **6**
es satt haben, zu	to have had enough of (doing)
es verstehen, zu	to know how to → **7**

COMMON VERBS WHICH <u>OFTEN HAVE THE "ES" OBJECT</u>:

es jemandem anhören/ansehen, dass	to tell by listening to/looking at someone that → **8**
es begreifen, dass/warum/wie	to understand that/why/how
es bereuen, zu tun/dass	to regret having done/that
es leugnen, dass	to deny that → **9**
es unternehmen, zu	to undertake to
es jemandem verbieten, zu	to forbid someone to
es jemandem vergeben, dass	to forgive someone for (doing)
es jemandem verschweigen, dass	not to tell someone that
es jemandem verzeihen, dass	to forgive someone for (doing)
es wagen zu	to dare to

1 **Er wusste, dass wir pünktlich kommen würden**
He knew that we would come on time
Sie fing an zu lachen
She began to laugh

2 **Er hatte es abgelehnt mitzufahren**
He had refused to come

3 **Dass es Wolfgang war, das haben wir ihr verschwiegen**
OR:
Dass es Wolfgang war, haben wir ihr verschwiegen
We didn't tell her that it was Wolfgang

4 **Ich halte es nicht mehr aus, bei ihnen zu arbeiten**
I can't stand working for them any longer

5 **Er hatte es nicht leicht, sie zu überreden**
He didn't have an easy job persuading them

6 **Ich habe es nicht nötig, mit dir darüber zu reden**
I don't have to talk to you about it

7 **Er versteht es, Autos zu reparieren**
He knows about repairing cars

8 **Man hörte es ihm sofort an, dass er kein Deutscher war**
OR:
Dass er kein Deutscher war, (das) hörte man ihm sofort an
One could tell immediately (from the way he spoke) that he wasn't German

Man sieht es ihm sofort an, dass er dein Bruder ist
OR:
Dass er dein Bruder ist, (das) sieht man ihm sofort an
One can tell at a glance that he's your brother

9 **Er hat es nie geleugnet, das Geld genommen zu haben**
He has never denied taking the money

☐ **Strong and Mixed Verbs - Principal Parts**

INFINITIVE	TRANSLATION	3RD PERSON PRESENT ⇒
backen	to bake	**er bäckt**
befehlen	to command	**er befiehlt**
beginnen	to begin	**er beginnt**
beißen	to bite	**er beißt**
bergen	to rescue	**er birgt**
bersten	to burst *intr*	**er birst**
betrügen	to deceive	**er betrügt**
biegen	to bend *tr*/to turn *intr*	**er biegt**
bieten	to offer	**er bietet**
binden	to tie	**er bindet**
bitten	to ask for	**er bittet**
blasen	to blow	**er bläst**
bleiben	to remain	**er bleibt**
braten	to fry	**er brät**
brechen	to break	**er bricht**
brennen	to burn	**er brennt**
bringen	to bring	**er bringt**
denken	to think	**er denkt**
dreschen	to thresh	**er drischt**
dringen	to penetrate	**er dringt**
dürfen	to be allowed to	**er darf**
empfehlen	to recommend	**er empfiehlt**
erlöschen	to go out (*fire, light*)	**er erlischt**
erschallen	to resound	**er erschallt**
erschrecken[1]	to be startled	**er erschrickt**
erwägen	to weigh up	**er erwägt**
essen	to eat	**er isst**
fahren	to travel	**er fährt**

[1]**erschrecken** meaning "to frighten" is weak:
 erschrecken, erschreckt, erschreckte, hat erschreckt

3RD PERSON IMPERFECT	PERFECT	IMPERFECT SUBJUNCTIVE
er backte	er hat gebacken	er backte
er befahl	er hat befohlen	er befähle
er begann	er hat begonnen	er begänne
er biss	er hat gebissen	er bisse
er barg	er hat geborgen	er bärge
er barst	er ist geborsten	er bärste
er betrog	er hat betrogen	er betröge
er bog	er hat/ist gebogen	er böge
er bot	er hat geboten	er böte
er band	er hat gebunden	er bände
er bat	er hat gebeten	er bäte
er blies	er hat geblasen	er bliese
er blieb	er ist geblieben	er bliebe
er briet	er hat gebraten	er briete
er brach	er hat/ist gebrochen	er bräche
er brannte	er hat gebrannt	er brennte
er brachte	er hat gebracht	er brächte
er dachte	er hat gedacht	er dächte
er drosch	er hat gedroschen	er drösche
er drang	er ist gedrungen	er dränge
er durfte	er hat gedurft/dürfen[1]	er dürfte
er empfahl	er hat empfohlen	er empfähle
er erlosch	er ist erloschen	er erlösche
er erschallte	er ist erschollen	er erschölle
er erschrak	er ist erschrocken	er erschräke
er erwog	er hat erwogen	er erwöge
er aß	er hat gegessen	er äße
er fuhr	er ist gefahren	er führe

[1] The second (infinitive) form is used when combined with an infinitive construction (see p 56).

☐ Strong and Mixed Verbs (Continued)

INFINITIVE	TRANSLATION	3RD PERSON PRESENT ➠
fallen	to fall	**er fällt**
fangen	to catch	**er fängt**
fechten	to fight	**er ficht**
finden	to find	**er findet**
fliegen	to fly	**er fliegt**
fliehen	to flee *tr/intr*	**er flieht**
fließen	to flow	**er fließt**
fressen	to eat (*of animals*)	**er frisst**
frieren	to be cold/to freeze over	**er friert**
gebären	to give birth to	**sie gebärt**
geben	to give	**er gibt**
gedeihen	to thrive	**er gedeiht**
gehen	to go	**er geht**
gelingen	to succeed	**es gelingt**
gelten	to be valid	**er gilt**
genesen	to get well	**er genest**
genießen	to enjoy	**er genießt**
geraten	to get into (*a state etc*)	**er gerät**
geschehen	to happen	**es geschieht**
gewinnen	to win	**er gewinnt**
gießen	to pour	**er gießt**
gleichen	to resemble/to equal	**er gleicht**
gleiten	to glide	**er gleitet**
glimmen	to glimmer	**er glimmt**
graben	to dig	**er gräbt**
greifen	to grip	**er greift**
haben	to have	**er hat**
halten	to hold/to stop	**er hält**
hängen[1]	to hang *intr*	**er hängt**
heben	to lift	**er hebt**
heißen	to be called	**er heißt**

[1] **hängen** is weak when used transitively.

3RD PERSON IMPERFECT	PERFECT	IMPERFECT SUBJUNCTIVE
er fiel	er ist gefallen	er fiele
er fing	er hat gefangen	er finge
er focht	er hat gefochten	er föchte
er fand	er hat gefunden	er fände
er flog	er hat/ist geflogen	er flöge
er floh	er hat/ist geflohen	er flöhe
er floss	er ist geflossen	er flösse
er fraß	er hat gefressen	er fräße
er fror	er hat/ist gefroren	er fröre
sie gebar	sie hat geboren	sie gebäre
er gab	er hat gegeben	er gäbe
er gedieh	er ist gediehen	er gediehe
er ging	er ist gegangen	er ginge
es gelang	es ist gelungen	es gelänge
er galt	er hat gegolten	er gälte
er genas	er ist genesen	er genäse
er genoss	er hat genossen	er genösse
er geriet	er ist geraten	er geriete
es geschah	es ist geschehen	es geschähe
er gewann	er hat gewonnen	er gewönne
er goss	er hat gegossen	er gösse
er glich	er hat geglichen	er gliche
er glitt	er ist geglitten	er glitte
er glomm	er hat geglommen	er glömme
er grub	er hat gegraben	er grübe
er griff	er hat gegriffen	er griffe
er hatte	er hat gehabt	er hätte
er hielt	er hat gehalten	er hielte
er hing	er hat gehangen	er hinge
er hob	er hat gehoben	er höbe
er hieß	er hat geheißen	er hieße

☐ **Strong and Mixed Verbs** (Continued)

INFINITIVE	TRANSLATION	3RD PERSON PRESENT ➠
helfen	to help	**er hilft**
kennen	to know (*someone etc*)	**er kennt**
klingen	to sound	**er klingt**
kommen	to come	**er kommt**
kneifen	to pinch	**er kneift**
können	to be able to	**er kann**
kriechen	to crawl	**er kriecht**
laden	to load	**er lädt**
lassen	to allow	**er lässt**
laufen	to walk/to run	**er läuft**
leiden	to suffer	**er leidet**
leihen	to lend	**er leiht**
lesen	to read	**er liest**
liegen	to lie	**er liegt**
lügen	to tell a lie	**er lügt**
mahlen	to grind	**er mahlt**
messen	to measure	**er misst**
misslingen	to fail	**es misslingt**
mögen	to like to	**er mag**
müssen	to have to	**er muss**
nehmen	to take	**er nimmt**
nennen	to call	**er nennt**
pfeifen	to whistle	**er pfeift**
preisen	to praise	**er preist**
quellen	to gush	**er quillt**
raten	to advise/to guess	**er rät**
reiben	to rub	**er reibt**
reißen	to tear *tr/intr*	**er reißt**
reiten	to ride *tr/intr*	**er reitet**

3RD PERSON IMPERFECT	PERFECT	IMPERFECT SUBJUNCTIVE
er half	er hat geholfen	er hülfe
er kannte	er hat gekannt	er kennte
er klang	er hat geklungen	er klänge
er kam	er ist gekommen	er käme
er kniff	er hat gekniffen	er kniffe
er konnte	er hat gekonnt/können[1]	er könnte
er kroch	er ist gekrochen	er kröche
er lud	er hat geladen	er lüde
er ließ	er hat gelassen	er ließe
er lief	er ist gelaufen	er liefe
er litt	er hat gelitten	er litte
er lieh	er hat geliehen	er liehe
er las	er hat gelesen	er läse
er lag	er hat gelegen	er läge
er log	er hat gelogen	er löge
er mahlte	er hat gemahlen	er mahlte
er maß	er hat gemessen	er mäße
es misslang	es ist misslungen	es misslänge
er mochte	er hat gemocht/mögen[1]	er möchte
er musste	er hat gemusst/müssen[1]	er müsste
er nahm	er hat genommen	er nähme
er nannte	er hat genannt	er nennte
er pfiff	er hat gepfiffen	er pfiffe
er pries	er hat gepriesen	er priese
er quoll	er ist gequollen	er quölle
er riet	er hat geraten	er riete
er rieb	er hat gerieben	er riebe
er riss	er hat/ist gerissen	er risse
er ritt	er hat/ist geritten	er ritte

[1] The second (infinitive) form is used when combined with an infinitive construction (see p 56).

☐ **Strong and Mixed Verbs** (Continued)

INFINITIVE	TRANSLATION	3RD PERSON PRESENT
rennen	to run	**er rennt**
riechen	to smell	**er riecht**
ringen	to wrestle	**er ringt**
rinnen	to flow	**er rinnt**
rufen	to shout	**er ruft**
salzen	to salt	**er salzt**
saufen	to booze/to drink	**er säuft**
saugen	to suck	**er saugt**
schaffen[1]	to create	**er schafft**
scheiden	to separate *tr/intr*	**er scheidet**
scheinen	to seem/to shine	**er scheint**
schelten	to scold	**er schilt**
scheren	to shear	**er schert**
schieben	to shove	**er schiebt**
schießen	to shoot	**er schießt**
schlafen	to sleep	**er schläft**
schlagen	to hit	**er schlägt**
schleichen	to creep	**er schleicht**
schleifen	to grind	**er schleift**
schließen	to close	**er schließt**
schlingen	to wind	**er schlingt**
schmeißen	to fling	**er schmeißt**
schmelzen	to melt *tr/intr*	**er schmilzt**
schneiden	to cut	**er schneidet**
schreiben	to write	**er schreibt**
schreien	to shout	**er schreit**
schreiten	to stride	**er schreitet**
schweigen	to be silent	**er schweigt**

[1] **schaffen** meaning "to work hard/to manage" is weak:
schaffen, schafft, schaffte, hat geschafft

VERB TABLE

3RD PERSON IMPERFECT	PERFECT	IMPERFECT SUBJUNCTIVE
er rannte	er ist gerannt	er rennte
er roch	er hat gerochen	er röche
er rang	er hat gerungen	er ränge
er rann	er ist geronnen	er ränne
er rief	er hat gerufen	er riefe
er salzte	er hat gesalzen	er salzte
er soff	er hat gesoffen	er söffe
er sog	er hat gesogen	er söge
er schuf	er hat geschaffen	er schüfe
er schied	er hat/ist geschieden	er schiede
er schien	er hat geschienen	er schiene
er schalt	er hat gescholten	er schölte
er schor	er hat geschoren	er schöre
er schob	er hat geschoben	er schöbe
er schoss	er hat geschossen	er schösse
er schlief	er hat geschlafen	er schliefe
er schlug	er hat geschlagen	er schlüge
er schlich	er ist geschlichen	er schliche
er schliff	er hat geschliffen	er schliffe
er schloss	er hat geschlossen	er schlösse
er schlang	er hat geschlungen	er schlänge
er schmiss	er hat geschmissen	er schmisse
er schmolz	er hat/ist geschmolzen	er schmölze
er schnitt	er hat geschnitten	er schnitte
er schrieb	er hat geschrieben	er schriebe
er schrie	er hat geschrie(e)n	er schriee
er schritt	er ist geschritten	er schritte
er schwieg	er hat geschwiegen	er schwiege

☐ **Strong and Mixed Verbs** (Continued)

INFINITIVE	TRANSLATION	3RD PERSON PRESENT ➠
schwellen[1]	to swell *intr*	**er schwillt**
schwimmen	to swim	**er schwimmt**
schwingen	to swing	**er schwingt**
schwören	to vow	**er schwört**
sehen	to see	**er sieht**
sein	to be	**er ist**
senden[2]	to send	**er sendet**
singen	to sing	**er singt**
sinken	to sink	**er sinkt**
sinnen	to ponder	**er sinnt**
sitzen	to sit	**er sitzt**
sollen	to be supposed to be	**er soll**
spalten	to split *tr/intr*	**er spaltet**
speien	to spew	**er speit**
spinnen	to spin	**er spinnt**
sprechen	to speak	**er spricht**
sprießen	to sprout	**er sprießt**
springen	to jump	**er springt**
stechen	to sting/to prick	**er sticht**
stehen	to stand	**er steht**
stehlen	to steal	**er stiehlt**
steigen	to climb	**er steigt**
sterben	to die	**er stirbt**
stinken	to stink	**er stinkt**
stoßen	to push	**er stößt**
streichen	to stroke/to wander	**er streicht**
streiten	to quarrel	**er streitet**

[1] **schwellen** is weak when used transitively:
schwellen, schwellt, schwellte, hat geschwellt
[2] **senden** meaning "to broadcast" is weak:
senden, sendet, sendete, hat gesendet

VERB TABLE

3RD PERSON IMPERFECT	PERFECT	IMPERFECT SUBJUNCTIVE
er schwoll	er ist geschwollen	er schwölle
er schwamm	er ist geschwommen	er schwömme
er schwang	er hat geschwungen	er schwänge
er schwor	er hat geschworen	er schwüre
er sah	er hat gesehen	er sähe
er war	er ist gewesen	er wäre
er sandte	er hat gesandt	er sendete
er sang	er hat gesungen	er sänge
er sank	er ist gesunken	er sänke
er sann	er hat gesonnen	er sänne
er saß	er hat gesessen	er säße
er sollte	er hat gesollt/sollen[1]	er sollte
er spaltete	er hat/ist gespalten	er spaltete
er spie	er hat gespie(e)n	er spiee
er spann	er hat gesponnen	er spönne
er sprach	er hat gesprochen	er spräche
er spross	er ist gesprossen	er sprösse
er sprang	er ist gesprungen	er spränge
er stach	er hat gestochen	er stäche
er stand	er hat gestanden	er stünde
er stahl	er hat gestohlen	er stähle
er stieg	er ist gestiegen	er stiege
er starb	er ist gestorben	er stürbe
er stank	er hat gestunken	er stänke
er stieß	er hat/ist gestoßen	er stieße
er strich	er hat/ist gestrichen	er striche
er stritt	er hat gestritten	er stritte

[1] The second (infinitive) form is used when combined with an infinitive construction (see p 56).

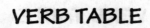

❐ **Strong and Mixed Verbs** (Continued)

INFINITIVE	TRANSLATION	3RD PERSON PRESENT ⏩
tragen	to carry/to wear	**er trägt**
treffen	to meet	**er trifft**
treiben	to drive/to engage in	**er treibt**
treten	to kick/step	**er tritt**
trinken	to drink	**er trinkt**
tun	to do	**er tut**
verderben	to spoil/to go bad	**er verdirbt**
verdrießen	to irritate	**er verdrießt**
vergessen	to forget	**er vergisst**
verlieren	to lose	**er verliert**
vermeiden	to avoid	**er vermeidet**
verschwinden	to disappear	**er verschwindet**
verzeihen	to pardon	**er verzeiht**
wachsen	to grow	**er wächst**
waschen	to wash	**er wäscht**
weichen	to yield	**er weicht**
weisen	to point	**er weist**
wenden	to turn	**er wendet**
werben	to recruit	**er wirbt**
werden	to become	**er wird**
werfen	to throw	**er wirft**
wiegen[1]	to weigh	**er wiegt**
winden	to wind	**er windet**
wissen	to know	**er weiß**
wollen	to want to	**er will**
ziehen	to pull	**er zieht**
zwingen	to force	**er zwingt**

[1]**wiegen** meaning "to rock" is weak.

3RD PERSON IMPERFECT	PERFECT	IMPERFECT SUBJUNCTIVE
er trug	er hat getragen	er trüge
er traf	er hat getroffen	er träfe
er trieb	er hat getrieben	er triebe
er trat	er hat/ist getreten	er träte
er trank	er hat getrunken	er tränke
er tat	er hat getan	er täte
er verdarb	er hat/ist verdorben	er verdürbe
er verdross	er hat verdrossen	er verdrösse
er vergaß	er hat vergessen	er vergäße
er verlor	er hat verloren	er verlöre
er vermied	er hat vermieden	er vermiede
er verschwand	er ist verschwunden	er verschwände
er verzieh	er hat verziehen	er verziehe
er wuchs	er ist gewachsen	er wüchse
er wusch	er hat gewaschen	er wüsche
er wich	er ist gewichen	er wiche
er wies	er hat gewiesen	er wiese
er wandte	er hat gewandt	er wendete
er warb	er hat geworben	er würbe
er wurde	er ist geworden	er würde
er warf	er hat geworfen	er würfe
er wog	er hat gewogen	er wöge
er wand	er hat gewunden	er wände
er wusste	er hat gewusst	er wüsste
er wollte	er hat gewollt/wollen[1]	er wollte
er zog	er hat gezogen	er zöge
er zwang	er hat gezwungen	er zwänge

[1] The second (infinitive) form is used when combined with an infinitive construction (see p 56).

☐ The Declension of Nouns

In German, all nouns may be declined. This means that they may change their form according to their:

> *gender* (i.e. masculine, feminine or neuter) → 1
>
> *case* (i.e. their function in the sentence) → 2
>
> *number* (i.e. singular or plural) → 3

♦ Nearly all *feminine* nouns change in the *plural* form by adding **-n** or **-en**. Many *masculine* and *neuter* nouns also change → 4

♦ *Masculine* and *neuter* nouns, with a few exceptions, add **-s** (**-s** or **-es** for nouns of one syllable) in the *genitive singular* (but see p 110) → 5

♦ All nouns end in **-n** or **-en** in the *dative plural*. This is added to the nominative plural form, where this does not already end in **-n** → 6

♦ A good dictionary will provide guidance on how to decline a noun:

The nominative singular form is given in full, followed by the gender of the noun, then the genitive singular and nominative plural endings are shown where appropriate → 7

♦ Adjectives used as nouns are declined as adjectives rather than nouns. Their declension endings are therefore dictated by the preceding article, as well as by number, case and gender (see p 140) → 8

Examples

1 **der Tisch** (*masculine*) the table
die Gabel (*feminine*) the fork
das Mädchen (*neuter*) the girl

2 **des Tisches** of the table
auf den Tischen on the tables

3 **die Tische** the tables
die Gabeln the forks
die Mädchen the girls

4

	NOM SING	NOM PLURAL
MASC	**der Apfel**	**die Äpfel**
FEM	**die Schule**	**die Schulen**
NEUT	**das Kind**	**die Kinder**

5

	NOM SING	GEN SING
MASC	**der Apfel**	**des Apfels**
FEM	**die Schule**	**der Schule**
NEUT	**das Kind**	**des Kind(e)s**

6

	DAT PLURAL
MASC	**den Äpfeln**
FEM	**den Schulen**
NEUT	**den Kindern**

7 <u>**Tiger** *m* **-s, -**</u>

NOM SING	**der Tiger**	the tiger
GEN SING	**des Tigers**	of the tiger, the tiger's
NOM PLURAL	**die Tiger**	the tigers

8 **der Angestellte** the employee
ein Angestellter an employee
(die) Angestellten (the) employees

◻ **The Gender of Nouns**

In German a noun may be masculine, feminine or neuter. Gender is relatively unpredictable and has to be learned for each noun. This is best done by learning each noun with its definite article, i.e.

> **der Teppich**
> **die Zeit**
> **das Bild**

The following are intended therefore only as guidelines in helping decide the gender of a word:

- Nouns denoting male people and animals are masculine → ☐1

- Nouns denoting the female of the species, as shown on p 104, are feminine → ☐2

- But nouns denoting an entire species can be of any gender → ☐3

- Makes of cars identify with **der Wagen** and so are usually masculine → ☐4

- Makes of aeroplane identify with **die Maschine** and so are usually feminine → ☐5

- Seasons, months, days of the week, weather features and points of the compass are masculine → ☐6

- Names of objects that perform an action are usually masculine → ☐7

- Foreign nouns ending in **-ant**, **-ast**, **-ismus**, **-or** are masculine → ☐8

- Nouns ending in **-ich**, **-ig**, **-ing**, **-ling** are masculine → ☐9

Examples

Grammar

1	**der Hörer**	(male) listener
	der Löwe	(male) lion
	der Onkel	uncle
	der Vetter	(male) cousin
2	**die Hörerin**	(female) listener
	die Löwin	lioness
	die Tante	aunt
	die Kusine	(female) cousin
3	**der Hund**	dog
	die Schlange	snake
	das Vieh	cattle
4	**der Mercedes**	Mercedes
	der VW	VW, Volkswagen
5	**die Boeing**	Boeing
	die Concorde	Concorde
6	**der Sommer**	summer
	der Winter	winter
	der August	August
	der Freitag	Friday
	der Wind	wind
	der Schnee	snow
	der Norden	north
	der Osten	east
7	**der Wecker**	alarm clock
	der Computer	computer
8	**der Ballast**	ballast
	der Chauvinismus	chauvinism
9	**der Essig**	vinegar
	der Schmetterling	butterfly

☐ **The Gender of Nouns** (Continued)

◆ Cardinal numbers are mostly feminine, but fractions are neuter → 1

◆ Most nouns ending in -**e** are feminine → 2

⚠ BUT: Male people or animals are masculine → 3
Nouns beginning with **Ge-** are normally neuter (*see below*)

◆ Nouns ending in -**heit**, -**keit**, -**schaft**, -**ung**, -**ei** are feminine → 4

◆ Foreign nouns ending in -**anz**, -**enz**, -**ie**, -**ik**, -**ion**, -**tät**, -**ur** are generally feminine → 5

◆ Nouns denoting the young of a species are neuter → 6

◆ Infinitives used as nouns are neuter → 7

◆ Most nouns beginning with **Ge-** are neuter → 8

◆ -**chen** or -**lein** may be added to many words to give a diminutive form. These words are then neuter → 9

⚠ NOTE: The vowel adds an umlaut where possible (i.e. on **a**, **o**, **u** or **au**) and a final -**e** is dropped before these endings → 10

◆ Nouns ending in -**nis** or -**tum** are neuter → 11

◆ Foreign nouns ending in -**at**, -**ett**, -**fon**, -**ma**, -**ment**, -**um**, -**ium** are mainly neuter → 12

◆ Adjectives and participles may be used as masculine, feminine or neuter nouns (see p 148) → 13

Examples

1	**Er hat eine Drei gekriegt**	He got a three (*mark*)
	ein Drittel davon	a third of it
2	**die Falte**	crease, wrinkle
	die Brücke	bridge
3	**der Löwe**	lion
	der Matrose	sailor
4	**die Eitelkeit**	vanity
	die Gewerkschaft	trade union
	die Scheidung	divorce
	die Druckerei	printing works
5	**die Distanz**	distance
	die Konkurrenz	rivalry
	die Theorie	theory
	die Panik	panic
	die Union	union
	die Elektrizität	electricity
	die Partitur	score (*musical*)
6	**das Baby**	baby
	das Kind	child
7	**das Schwimmen**	swimming
8	**das Geschirr**	crockery, dishes
	das Geschöpf	creature
	das Getreide	crop
9	**das Kindlein**	child
10	**das Bächlein** (*from* **der Bach**)	(small) stream
	das Kätzchen (*from* **die Katze**)	kitten
11	**das Ereignis**	event
	das Altertum	antiquity
12	**das Tablett**	tray
	das Telefon	telephone
	das Testament	will
	das Podium	platform, podium
13	**der Verwandte**	(male) relative
	die Verwandte	(female) relative
	das Gehackte	minced meat

❏ **The Gender of Nouns** (Continued)

The following are some common exceptions to the gender guidelines shown on pp 100 to 103:

das Weib	woman, wife
die Person	person
die Waise	orphan
das Mitglied	member
das Genie	genius
die Wache	sentry, guard
das Restaurant	restaurant

The formation of feminine nouns

As in English, male and female forms are sometimes shown by two completely different words e.g.

mother/father
uncle/aunt etc   ➞ **1**

Where such separate forms do not exist, however, German often differentiates between male and female forms in one of two ways:

◆   The masculine form may sometimes be made feminine by the addition of **-in** in the singular and **-innen** in the plural ➞ **2**

◆   An adjective may be used as a feminine noun (see p 148). It has feminine adjective endings which change according to the article which precedes it (see p 140) ➞ **3**

Examples

---

1 | **der Vater** | **die Mutter**
father | mother

der Bulle | **die Kuh**
bull | cow

der Mann | **die Frau**
man | woman

2 | **der Lehrer** | **die Lehrerin**
(male) teacher | (female) teacher

der König | **die Königin**
king | queen

der Hörer | **die Hörerin**
(male) listener | (female) listener

Liebe Hörer und Hörerinnen!
Dear listeners!

unsere Leser und Leserinnen
our readers

3 | **eine Deutsche**
a German woman
Er ist mit einer Deutschen verheiratet
He is married to a German

die Abgeordnete
the female MP
Nur Abgeordnete durften dabei sein
Only MPs were allowed in

❏ The Gender of Nouns: Miscellaneous Points

Compound nouns

Compound nouns, i.e. nouns composed of two or more nouns put together, are a regular feature of German.

◆ They normally take their gender and declension from the last noun of the compound word → **1**

◆ Exceptions to this are compounds ending in **-mut**, **-scheu** and **-wort**, which do not always have the same gender as the last word when it stands alone → **2**

Nouns with more than one gender

◆ A few nouns have two genders, one of which may only be used in certain regions → **3**

◆ Other nouns have two genders, each of which gives the noun a different meaning → **4**

Abbreviations

◆ These take the gender of their principal noun → **5**

Examples

1	**die Armbanduhr** (*from* **die Uhr**)	wristwatch
	der Tomatensalat (*from* **der Salat**)	tomato salad
	der Fußballspieler (*from* **der Spieler**)	footballer
2	**der Mut**	courage
	die Armut	poverty
	die Demut	humility
	die Scheu	fear, shyness, timidity
	der Abscheu	repugnance, abhorrence
	das Wort	word
	die Antwort	reply
3	**das/der Marzipan**	marzipan
	das/der Keks	biscuit
4	**der Band**	volume, book
	das Band	ribbon, band, tape, bond
	der See	lake
	die See	sea
	der Leiter	leader, manager
	die Leiter	ladder
	der Tau	dew
	das Tau	rope, hawser
5	**der DGB**	the Federation of German Trade Unions
	(*from* **der Deutsche Gewerkschaftsbund**)	
	die EG	the EC
	(*from* **die Europäische Gemeinschaft**)	
	das AKW	nuclear power station
	(*from* **das Atomkraftwerk**)	

❐ The Cases

There are four grammatical *cases* - nominative, accusative, genitive and dative - which are generally shown by the form of the article used before the noun (see p 118).

The nominative case

◆ The nominative singular is the form shown in full in dictionary entries.

The nominative plural is formed as described on p 98.

◆ The nominative case is used for:

- the subject of a verb ➝ ☐1

- the complement of **sein** or **werden** ➝ ☐2

The accusative case

◆ The noun in the accusative case usually has the same form as in the nominative ➝ ☐3

Exceptions to this are "weak" masculine nouns (see p 115) and adjectives used as nouns (see p 148).

◆ It is used:

- for the direct object of the verb ➝ ☐4

- after those prepositions which always take the accusative case (see p 206 ff) ➝ ☐5

- to show change of location after prepositions of place (see p 210) ➝ ☐6

- in many expressions of time and place which do not contain a preposition ➝ ☐7

- in certain fixed expressions ➝ ☐8

Grammar

1	**Das Mädchen singt**		The girl is singing
2	**Er ist ein guter Lehrer**		He's a good teacher
	Das wird ein Pullover		It's going to be a jumper
3	**das Lied**	the song	(*nominative*)
	das Lied	the song	(*accusative*)
	der Wagen	the car	(*nominative*)
	den Wagen	the car	(*accusative*)
	die Dose	the tin	(*nominative*)
	die Dose	the tin	(*accusative*)
4	**Er hat ein Lied gesungen**		He sang a song
5	**für seine Freundin**		for his girlfriend
	ohne diesen Wagen		without this car
	durch das Rauchen		through smoking
6	**in die Stadt** (*accusative*)		into town
	⚠ BUT:		
	in der Stadt (*dative*)		in town

7 **Das macht sie jeden Donnerstag**
She does that every Thursday
Die Schule ist einen Kilometer entfernt
The school is a kilometre away

8 **Guten Abend!** Good evening!
Vielen Dank! Thank you very much!

❏ **The Cases** (Continued)

The genitive case

◆ In the genitive singular, *masculine* and *neuter* nouns take endings as follows:

    1 **-s** is added to nouns ending in **-en**, **-el**, **-er** → ⟶ 1
    2 **-es** is added to nouns ending in **-tz**, **-sch**, **-st**, **-ss** or **-ß** ⟶ 2
    3 For nouns of one syllable, either **-s** or **-es** may be added ⟶ 3

◆ *Feminine singular* and all *plural* nouns have the same form as their nominative.

◆ The genitive is used:

  - to show possession ⟶ 3
  - after prepositions taking the genitive (see p 212) ⟶ 4
  - in expressions of time when the exact occasion is not specified ⟶ 5

The dative case

◆ Singular nouns in the dative have the same form as in the nominative ⟶ 6

◆ **-e** may be added to the dative singular of *masculine* and *neuter* nouns if the sentence rhythm needs it ⟶ 7

  This **-e** is always used in certain set phrases ⟶ 8

◆ Dative plural forms for all genders end in **-n** ⟶ 9

  The only exceptions to this are some nouns of foreign origin that end in **-s** in all plural forms, including the dative plural (see p 114) ⟶ 10

◆ The dative is used:

  - as the indirect object ⟶ 11
  - after verbs taking the dative (see p 80) ⟶ 12
  - after prepositions taking the dative (see p 202) ⟶ 13
  - in certain idiomatic expressions ⟶ 14
  - instead of the possessive adjective to refer to parts of the body and items of clothing (see p 122) ⟶ 15

1	**der Wagen** car	→	**des Wagens** of the car
	das Rauchen smoking	→	**des Rauchens** of smoking
	der Computer computer	→	**des Computers** of the computer
	der Reiter rider	→	**des Reiters** of the rider
2	**der Sitz** seat; residence	→	**des Sitzes** of the seat/residence
	der Arzt doctor	→	**des Arztes** of the doctor
	das Schloss castle	→	**des Schlosses** of the castle

3   <u>**das Kind** the child</u>

Die Zähne des Kindes waren faul geworden
The child's teeth had decayed

Der Name des Kinds war ihm unbekannt
The child's name was not known to him

4   **wegen seiner Krankheit**   because of his illness

      trotz ihrer Bemühungen   despite her efforts

5   **eines Tages**   one day

6   **dem Wagen**   to the car

      der Frau   to the woman

      dem Mädchen   to the girl

7   **zu welchem Zwecke?**   to what purpose?

8   **nach Hause**   home

      sich zu Tode trinken/arbeiten
to drink/work oneself to death

9   **mit den Anwälten**   with the lawyers

      nach den Kindern   after the children

10   SINGULAR   PLURAL

	SINGULAR	PLURAL
	das Auto	**die Autos**
	das Auto	**die Autos**
	des Autos	**der Autos**
	dem Auto	**den Autos**

11   **Er gab dem Mann das Buch**
He gave the man the book

12   **Sie half ihrer Mutter**   She helped her mother

13   **Nach dem Essen ...**   After eating ...

14   **Mir ist kalt**   I'm cold

15   **Ich habe mir die Hände gewaschen**
I've washed my hands

❏ The Formation of Plurals

The following pages show full noun declensions in all their singular and plural forms.

Those nouns shown represent the most common types of plural.

◆ Most feminine nouns add **-n**, **-en** or **-nen** to form their plurals:

	SINGULAR	PLURAL
NOM	**die Frau**	**die Frauen**
ACC	**die Frau**	**die Frauen**
GEN	**der Frau**	**der Frauen**
DAT	**der Frau**	**den Frauen**

◆ Many nouns have no plural ending.

These are mainly masculine or neuter nouns ending in **-en**, **-er**, **-el**.
An umlaut is sometimes added to the vowel in the plural forms:

	SINGULAR	PLURAL
NOM	**der Onkel**	**die Onkel**
ACC	**den Onkel**	**die Onkel**
GEN	**des Onkels**	**der Onkel**
DAT	**dem Onkel**	**den Onkeln**

	SINGULAR	PLURAL
NOM	**der Apfel**	**die Äpfel**
ACC	**den Apfel**	**die Äpfel**
GEN	**des Apfels**	**der Äpfel**
DAT	**dem Apfel**	**die Äpfeln**

❑ The Formation of Plurals (Continued)

◆ Many nouns form their plurals by adding ⸚**e**:

	SINGULAR	PLURAL
NOM	**der Stuhl**	**die Stühle**
ACC	**den Stuhl**	**die Stühle**
GEN	**des Stuhl(e)s**	**der Stühle**
DAT	**dem Stuhl**	**den Stühlen**

	SINGULAR	PLURAL
NOM	**die Angst**	**die Ängste**
ACC	**die Angst**	**die Ängste**
GEN	**der Angst**	**der Ängste**
DAT	**der Angst**	**den Ängsten**

◆ Masculine and neuter nouns often add **-e** in the plural:

	SINGULAR	PLURAL
NOM	**das Schicksal**	**die Schicksale**
ACC	**das Schicksal**	**die Schicksale**
GEN	**des Schicksals**	**der Schicksale**
DAT	**dem Schicksal**	**den Schicksalen**

◆ Masculine and neuter nouns sometimes add ⸚**er** or **-er**:

	SINGULAR	PLURAL
NOM	**das Dach**	**die Dächer**
ACC	**das Dach**	**die Dächer**
GEN	**des Dach(e)s**	**der Dächer**
DAT	**dem Dach**	**den Dächern**

❒ **The Formation of Plurals** (Continued)

Some unusual plurals

SINGULAR	TRANSLATION	PLURAL
das Ministerium	department	**die Ministerien**
das Prinzip	principle	**die Prinzipien**
das Thema	theme, topic, subject	**die Themen**
das Drama	drama	**die Dramen**
der Firma	firm	**die Firmen**
das Konto	bank account	**die Konten**
das Risiko	risk	**die Risiken**
das Komma	comma/decimal point	**die Kommas**
		or **Kommata**
das Baby	baby	**die Babys**
der Klub	club	**die Klubs**
der Streik	strike	**die Streiks**
der Park	park	**die Parks**
der Chef	boss, chief, head	**die Chefs**
der Israeli	Israeli	**die Israelis**
das Restaurant	restaurant	**die Restaurants**
das Bonbon	sweet	**die Bonbons**
das Hotel	hotel	**die Hotels**
das Niveau	standard, level	**die Niveaus**

German singular/English plural nouns

Some nouns are always plural in English, but singular in German.

◆ Some of the most common examples are:

eine Brille	glasses, spectacles
eine Schere	scissors
eine Hose	trousers

◆ They are only used in the plural in German to mean more than one pair, e.g. **zwei Hosen** *two pairs of trousers*

NOUNS

❏ The Declension of Nouns

"Weak" masculine nouns

Some masculine nouns have a weak declension, which means that in all cases apart from the nominative singular, they end in **-en** or, if the word ends in a vowel, in **-n**.

◆ The dictionary will often show such nouns as:
>**Junge** *m* **-n**, **-n** boy
>**Held** *m* **-en**, **-en** hero

◆ Weak masculine nouns are declined as follows:

	SINGULAR	PLURAL
NOM	**der Junge**	**die Jungen**
ACC	**den Jungen**	**die Jungen**
GEN	**des Jungen**	**der Jungen**
DAT	**dem Jungen**	**den Jungen**

◆ Masculine nouns falling into this category include:
- those ending in **-og(e)** referring to males:
  >**der Psychologe, der Geologe, der Astrologe**
- those ending in **-aph** (*in many cases now spelt* **-af**) or **-oph**:
  >**der Graph, der Paragraf, der Philosoph**
- those ending in **-nom** referring to males:
  >**der Astronom, der Gastronom**
- those ending in **-ant**:
  >**der Elefant, der Diamant**
- those ending in **-t** referring to males:
  >**der Astronaut, der Komponist, der Architekt**
- miscellaneous others:
  >**der Bauer, der Chirurg, der Franzose, der Katholik, der Kollege, der Mensch, der Ochse, der Spatz**

◆ **der Name** (*name*) has a different ending in the genitive singular, **-ns**: **des Namens**. Otherwise it is the same as **der Junge** shown above. Others in this category are: **der Buchstabe, der Funke, der Gedanke, der Glaube, der Haufe.**

❐ **The Declension of Proper Nouns**

◆ Names of people and places add **-s** in the genitive singular unless they are preceded by the definite article or a demonstrative → ☐1

◆ Where proper names end in a sibilant (**-s**, **-sch**, **-ss**, **-ß**, **-x**, **-z**, **-tz**) and this makes the genitive form with **-s** almost impossible to pronounce, they are best avoided altogether by using **von** followed by the dative case → ☐2

◆ Personal names can be given diminutive forms if desired. These may be used as a sign of affection as well as with diminutive meaning → ☐3

◆ **Herr** (*Mr*) is always declined where it occurs as part of a proper name → ☐4

◆ When articles or adjectives form part of a proper name (e.g. in the names of books, plays, hotels, restaurants etc), these are declined in the normal way (see p 118 and 140) → ☐5

◆ Surnames usually form their plurals by adding **-s**, unless they end in a sibilant, in which case they sometimes add **-ens**. They are often preceded by the definite article → ☐6

Nouns of measurement and quantity

◆ These usually remain singular, even if preceded by a plural number → ☐7

◆ The substance which they measure follows in the same case as the noun of quantity, and not in the genitive case as in English → ☐8

1. **Annas Buch**   Anna's book
   Klaras Mantel   Klara's coat
   die Werke Goethes   Goethe's works
   ⚠ BUT: **die Versenkung der Bismarck**
              the sinking of the Bismarck

2. **das Buch von Hans**   Hans' book
   die Werke von Marx   the works of Marx
   die Freundin von Klaus   Klaus's girlfriend

3. **von deinem Sabinchen**   from your Sabine
   Das kleine Kläuschen hat uns dann ein Lied gesungen
   Then little Klaus sang us a song

4. **an Herrn Schmidt**   to Mr Schmidt
   Sehr geehrte Herren   Dear Sirs

5. **im Weißen Schwan**   in the White Swan
   Er hat den „Zauberberg" schon gelesen
   He has already read "The Magic Mountain"
   nach Karl dem Großen   after Charlemagne

6. **Die Schmidts haben uns eingeladen**
   The Schmidts have invited us
   Die Zeißens haben uns eingeladen
   Mr and Mrs Zeiß have invited us

7. **Möchten Sie zwei Stück?**
   Would you like two?

8. **Er wollte zwei Kilo Kartoffeln**
   He wanted two kilos of potatoes
   Sie hat drei Tassen Kaffee getrunken
   She drank three cups of coffee
   Drei Glas Weißwein, bitte!
   Three glasses of white wine please

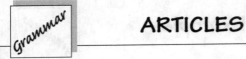

❑ **The Definite Article**

In English the definite article *the* always keeps the same form:

>   *the* book
>   *the* books
>   with *the* books

In German, however, the definite article has many forms:

- In its singular form it changes for masculine, feminine and neuter nouns → **1**

- In its plural forms it is the same for all genders → **2**

- The definite article is also used to show the function of the noun in the sentence by showing which case it is.

  There are four cases, as explained more fully on p 108:

  1   *nominative* for the subject or complement of the verb → **3**
  2   *accusative* for the object of the verb and after some prepositions → **4**
  3   *genitive* to show possession and after some prepositions → **5**
  4   *dative* for an indirect object (*to* or *for*) and after some prepositions and certain verbs → **6**

- The forms of the definite article are as follows:

	SINGULAR			PLURAL
	MASC	FEM	NEUT	ALL GENDERS
NOM	**der**	**die**	**das**	**die**
ACC	**den**	**die**	**das**	**die** → **7**
GEN	**des**	**der**	**des**	**der**
DAT	**dem**	**der**	**dem**	**den**

Examples

---

1   MASCULINE: **der Mann**   the man
                      der Wagen   the car
      FEMININE: **die Frau**   the wife/woman
                      die Blume   the flower
      NEUTER: **das Ding**   the thing
                      das Mädchen   the girl

2   **die Männer**   the men
     die Frauen   the women
     die Dinge   the things

3   **Der Mann ist jung**   The man is young
     Die Frau/das Kind ist jung   The woman/the child is young

4   **Ich kenne den Mann/die Frau/das Kind**
     I know the man/the woman/the child

5   **der Kopf des Mannes/der Frau/des Kindes**
     the man's/woman's/child's head
     wegen des Mannes/der Frau/des Kindes
     because of the man/the woman/the child

6   **Ich gab es dem Mann/der Frau/dem Kind**
     I gave it to the man/to the woman/to the child

7

SINGULAR

	MASC	FEM	NEUT
NOM	**der Mann**	**die Frau**	**das Kind**
ACC	**den Mann**	**die Frau**	**das Kind**
GEN	**des Mann(e)s**	**der Frau**	**des Kind(e)s**
DAT	**dem Mann**	**der Frau**	**dem Kind**

PLURAL

	MASC	FEM	NEUT
NOM	**die Männer**	**die Frauen**	**die Kinder**
ACC	**die Männer**	**die Frauen**	**die Kinder**
GEN	**der Männer**	**der Frauen**	**der Kinder**
DAT	**den Männern**	**den Frauen**	**den Kindern**

❐ Uses of the Definite Article

When to use and when not to use the definite article in German is one of the most difficult areas for the learner. The following guidelines show where German practice varies from English.

The definite article is used with:

- abstract and other nouns where something is being referred to as a whole or as a general idea → **1**

  Where these nouns are quantified or modified, the article is not used → **2**

- the genitive, unless the noun is a proper name or is acting as a proper name → **3**

- occasionally with proper names to make the sex or case clearer → **4**

- always with proper names preceded by an adjective → **5**

- sometimes with proper names in familiar contexts or for slight emphasis → **6**

- with masculine and feminine countries and districts → **7**

- with geographical names preceded by an adjective → **8**

- with names of seasons → **9**

- often with meals → **10**

- with the names of roads → **11**

Examples

1   **Das Leben ist schön**   Life is wonderful

2   **Es braucht Mut**   It needs (some) courage
Gibt es dort Leben?   Is there (any) life there?

3   **das Auto des Lehrers**   the teacher's car
Günters Auto   Günter's car
Muttis Auto   Mummy's car

4   **Er hat es Frau Lehmann gegeben**
Er hat es der Frau Lehmann gegeben
He gave it to Frau Lehmann

5   **Der alte Herr Brockhaus ist gestorben**
Old Mr Brockhaus has died

6   **Ich habe heute den Christoph gesehen**
I saw Christoph today
Du hast es aber nicht der Petra geschenkt!
You haven't given it to *Petra*!

7   **Deutschland is sehr schön**   Germany is very beautiful
Die Schweiz ist auch schön   Switzerland is also lovely

8   **im (= in dem) heutigen Deutschland**
in today's Germany

9   **Im (= in dem) Sommer gehen wir schwimmen**
We go swimming in summer
Der Winter kommt bald
Soon it will be winter

10   **Das Abendessen wird ab acht Uhr serviert**
Dinner is served from eight o'clock
Was gibts zum (= zu dem) Mittagessen?
What's for lunch?
⚠ BUT:
Um acht Uhr ist Frühstück
Breakfast is at eight o'clock

11   **Sie wohnt jetzt in der Geisener Straße**
She lives in Geisener Road now

☐ **Uses of the Definite Article** (Continued)

♦ with months of the year except after **seit/nach/vor** → ①

♦ instead of the possessive adjective to refer to parts of the body and items of clothing → ②
A reflexive pronoun or noun in the dative case is used if it is necessary to clarify to whom the parts of the body belong → ③

♦ in expressions of price, to mean *each/per/a* → ④

♦ with certain common expressions → ⑤

Other uses

♦ The definite article can be used with demonstrative meaning → ⑥

♦ After certain prepositions, forms of the definite article can be shortened (see p 198 ff).
Some of these forms are best used in informal situations → ⑦
Others are commonly and correctly used in formal contexts → ①
→ ⑤
→ ⑧

Omitting the definite article

The definite article may be omitted in German:

♦ in certain set expressions → ⑨

♦ in *preposition + adjective + noun* combinations → ⑩
For the declension of adjectives without the article see p 142.

Examples

1. **Wir fahren im (= in dem) September weg**
   We are going away in September
   Wir sind seit September hier
   We have been here since September

2. **Er legte den Hut auf den Tisch**
   He laid his hat on the table
   Ich drücke Ihnen die Daumen
   I'm keeping my fingers crossed for you

3. **Er hat sich die Hände schon gewaschen**
   He has already washed his hands
   Er hat dem Kind schon die Hände gewaschen
   He has already washed the child's hands

4. **Die kosten ...**   They cost ...
   ... fünf Mark das Pfund   ... five marks a pound
   ... sechs Mark das Stück   ... six marks each

5. **in die Stadt fahren**   to go into town
   zur (= zu der) Schule gehen to go to school
   mit der Post   by post
   mit dem Zug/Bus/Auto   by train/bus/car
   im (= in dem) Gefängnis   in prison

6. **Du willst *das* Buch lesen!**
   You want to read *that* book!

7. **für das → fürs   vor dem → vorm   um das → ums** *etc*

8. **an dem → am   zu dem → zum   zu der → zur** *etc*

9. **von Beruf**   by profession
   nach Wunsch   as desired
   Nachrichten hören   to listen to the news

10. **Mit gebeugtem Rücken ...**   Bending his back, ...

❏ The Indefinite Article

Like the definite article, the form of the indefinite article varies depending on the gender and case of the noun → ①

It has no plural forms → ②

The indefinite article is declined as follows:

	MASC	FEM	NEUT	
NOM	ein	eine	ein	
ACC	einen	eine	ein	→ ③
GEN	eines	einer	eines	
DAT	einem	einer	einem	

◆ The indefinite article is omitted in the following:

- descriptions of people by profession, religion, nationality etc → ④

- ⚠ BUT: Note that the article is included when an adjective precedes the noun → ⑤

- in certain fixed expressions → ⑥

- after **als** (*as a*) → ⑦

1 **Da ist ein Auto**   There's a car
   Er hat eine Wohnung   He has a flat
   Sie gab es einem Kind   She gave it to a child

2 **Autos sind in letzter Zeit teurer geworden**
   Cars have become more expensive recently

3
		SINGULAR	
	MASC	FEM	NEUT
NOM	**ein Mann**	**eine Frau**	**ein Kind**
ACC	**einen Mann**	**eine Frau**	**ein Kind**
GEN	**eines Mann(e)s**	**einer Frau**	**eines Kind(e)s**
DAT	**einem Mann**	**einer Frau**	**einem Kind**

4 **Sie ist Kinderärztin**   She's a paediatrician
   Sie ist Deutsche   She's (a) German

5 **Sie ist eine sehr geschickte Kinderärztin**
   She's a very clever paediatrician

6 **Es ist Geschmacksache**   It's a question of taste
   Tatsache ist ...   It's a fact ...

7 **Als Ausländer ist er hier nicht wahlberechtigt**
   As a foreigner he doesn't have the vote here

   ... und ich rede nun als Vater von vier Kindern
   ... and I'm talking now as a father of four

☐ **The Indefinite Article** (Continued)

In German, a separate negative form of the indefinite article exists. It is declined exactly like **ein** in the singular, and also has plural forms:

		SINGULAR		PLURAL
	MASC	FEM	NEUT	ALL GENDERS
NOM	**kein**	**keine**	**kein**	**keine**
ACC	**keinen**	**keine**	**kein**	**keine** → ①
GEN	**keines**	**keiner**	**keines**	**keiner**
DAT	**keinem**	**keiner**	**keinem**	**keinen**

◆ It has the meaning *no/not a/not one/not any* → ②

◆ It is used even where the equivalent *positive* phrase has no article → ③

◆ It is also used in many idiomatic expressions → ④

◆ **Nicht ein** may be used instead of **kein** where the **ein** is to be emphasized → ⑤

1

	SINGULAR		
	MASC	FEM	NEUT
NOM	**kein Mann**	**keine Frau**	**kein Kind**
ACC	**keinen Mann**	**keine Frau**	**kein Kind**
GEN	**keines Mann(e)s**	**keiner Frau**	**keines Kind(e)s**
DAT	**keinem Mann**	**keiner Frau**	**keinem Kind**

	PLURAL		
	MASC	FEM	NEUT
NOM	**keine Männer**	**keine Frauen**	**keine Kinder**
ACC	**keine Männer**	**keine Frauen**	**keine Kinder**
GEN	**keiner Männer**	**keiner Frauen**	**keiner Kinder**
DAT	**keinen Männern**	**keinen Frauen**	**keinen Kindern**

2

Er hatte keine Geschwister	He had no brothers or sisters
Ich sehe keinen Unterschied	I don't see any difference
Das ist keine richtige Antwort	That's no answer
Kein Mensch hat es gesehen	Not one person has seen it

3

Er hatte Angst davor	He was frightened
Er hatte keine Angst davor	He wasn't frightened

4

Er hatte kein Geld mehr   All his money was gone
Es waren keine drei Monate vergangen, als ...
It was less than three months later that ...
Es hat mich keine zehn Euro gekostet
It cost me less than ten Euro

5

Nicht ein Kind hat es singen können
Not *one* child could sing it

☐ Words declined like the Definite Article

The following have endings similar to those of the definite article shown on p 118:

aller, alle, alles	all, all of them
beide	both (*plural only*)
dieser, diese, dieses	this, this one, these
einiger, einige, einiges	some, a few, a little
irgendwelcher, -e, -es	some or other
jeder, jede, jedes	each, each one, every
jener, jene, jenes	that, that one, those
mancher, manche, manches	many a/some
sämtliche	all, entire (*usually plural*)
solcher, solche, solches	such/such a
welcher, welche, welches	which, which one

◆ These words can be used as:
  - articles → ☐1
  - pronouns → ☐2

◆ They have the following endings:

	SINGULAR			PLURAL
	MASC	FEM	NEUT	ALL GENDERS
NOM	**-er**	**-e**	**-es**	**-e**
ACC	**-en**	**-e**	**-es**	**-e**
GEN	**-es/-en**	**-er**	**-es/-en**	**-er**
DAT	**-em**	**-er**	**-em**	**-en**

Example declensions are shown on p 134 ff.

◆ **einiger** and **irgendwelcher** use the **-en** genitive ending before masculine or neuter nouns ending in **-s** → ☐3
  jeder, welcher, mancher and **solcher** may also do so → ☐4

1 **Dieser Mann kommt aus Südamerika**
   This man comes from South America

   Er geht jeden Tag ins Büro
   He goes to the office every day

   Manche Leute können das nicht
   A good many people can't do it

2 **Willst du diesen?**
   Do you want this one?

   In manchem hat er Recht
   He's right about some things

   Man kann ja nicht alles wissen
   You can't know everything

   Es gibt manche, die keinen Alkohol mögen
   There are some people who don't like alcohol

3 **wegen irgendwelchen Geredes**
   on account of some gossip

4 **der Besitz solchen Reichtums**
   the possession of such wealth

   trotz jeden Versuchs
   despite all attempts

◻ **Words declined like the Definite Article** (Continued)

◆ Adjectives following these words have the weak declension (see p 140) → ⒈

Exceptions are the plural forms of **einige**, which are followed by the strong declension (see p 142) → ⒉

Further points

◆ **Solcher, beide, sämtliche** may be used after another article or possessive adjective. They then take weak (see p 140) or mixed (see p 142) adjectival endings, as appropriate → ⒊

◆ Although **beide** generally has plural forms only, one singular form does exist. This is in the neuter nominative and accusative: **beides** → ⒋

◆ **Dies** often replaces the nominative and accusative **dieses** and **diese** when used as a pronoun → ⒌

◆ A fixed form **all** exists which is used together with other articles or possessive pronouns → ⒍

◆ **Ganz** can also be used to replace both the inflected form **aller/alle/alles** and the uninflected **all das/dieses/sein** *etc.*

It is declined as a normal adjective (see p 140) → ⒎

It must be used with collective nouns, in time phrases and geographical references → ⒏

Examples

1. **dieses alte Auto**
   this old car
   aus irgendwelchem dummen Grund
   for some stupid reason or other
   welche neuen Waren?
   which new goods?

2. **Dies sind einige gute Freunde von mir**
   These are some good friends of mine

3. **Ein solches Kleid habe ich früher auch getragen**
   I used to wear a dress like that too
   Diese beiden Männer haben es gesehen
   Both of these men have seen it

4. **Beides ist richtig**
   Both are right
   Sie hat beides genommen
   She took both

5. **Hast du dies schon gelesen?**
   Have you already read this?
   Dies sind meine neuen Sachen
   These are my new things

6. **All sein Mut war verschwunden**
   All his courage had vanished
   mit all diesem Geld
   with all this money

7. **mit dem ganzen Geld**
   with all the money

8. **die ganze Gesellschaft**
   the entire company
   Es hat den ganzen Tag geschneit
   It snowed the whole day long
   Im ganzen Land gab es keinen besseren Wein
   There wasn't a better wine in the whole country

❏ **Words declined like the Definite Article** (Continued)

● **derjenige/diejenige/dasjenige** (*the one, those*) is declined exactly as the definite article plus an adjective in the weak declension (see p 140) → **1**

● **derselbe/dieselbe/dasselbe** (*the same, the same one*) is declined in the same way as **derjenige** → **2**

After prepositions, however, the normal contracted forms of the definite article are used for the appropriate parts of **derselbe** → **3**

1 SINGULAR

MASC	FEM	NEUT
derjenige Mann	**die**jenige Frau	**das**jenige Kind
denjenigen Mann	**die**jenige Frau	**das**jenige Kind
desjenigen Mann(e)s	**der**jenigen Frau	**des**jenigen Kind(e)s
demjenigen Mann	**der**jenigen Frau	**dem**jenigen Kind

PLURAL

MASC	FEM	NEUT
diejenigen Männer	**die**jenigen Frauen	**die**jenigen Kinder
diejenigen Männer	**die**jenigen Frauen	**die**jenigen Kinder
derjenigen Männer	**der**jenigen Frauen	**der**jenigen Kinder
denjenigen Männern	**den**jenigen Frauen	**den**jenigen Kindern

2 SINGULAR

MASC	FEM	NEUT
derselbe Mann	**die**selbe Frau	**das**selbe Kind
denselben Mann	**die**selbe Frau	**das**selbe Kind
desselben Mann(e)s	**der**selben Frau	**des**selben Kind(e)s
demselben Mann	**der**selben Frau	**dem**selben Kind

PLURAL

MASC	FEM	NEUT
dieselben Männer	**die**selben Frauen	**die**selben Kinder
dieselben Männer	**die**selben Frauen	**die**selben Kinder
derselben Männer	**der**selben Frauen	**der**selben Kinder
denselben Männern	**den**selben Frauen	**den**selben Kindern

3 **zur selben (= zu derselben) Zeit**   at the same time
     im selben (= in demselben) Zimmer   in the same room

❑ **Words declined like the Definite Article** (Continued)

Sample declensions in full

◆ **dieser, diese, dieses** this, this one:

		SINGULAR	
	MASC	FEM	NEUT
NOM	dies**er** Mann	dies**e** Frau	dies**es** Kind
ACC	dies**en** Mann	dies**e** Frau	dies**es** Kind
GEN	dies**es** Mann(e)s	dies**er** Frau	dies**es** Kind(e)s
DAT	dies**em** Mann	dies**er** Frau	dies**em** Kind

		PLURAL	
	MASC	FEM	NEUT
NOM	dies**e** Männer	dies**e** Frauen	dies**e** Kinder
ACC	dies**e** Männer	dies**e** Frauen	dies**e** Kinder
GEN	dies**er** Männer	dies**er** Frauen	dies**er** Kinder
DAT	dies**en** Männern	dies**en** Frauen	dies**en** Kindern

◆ **jener, jene, jenes** that, that one:

		SINGULAR	
	MASC	FEM	NEUT
NOM	jen**er** Mann	jen**e** Frau	jen**es** Kind
ACC	jen**en** Mann	jen**e** Frau	jen**es** Kind
GEN	jen**es** Mann(e)s	jen**er** Frau	jen**es** Kind(e)s
DAT	jen**em** Mann	jen**er** Frau	jen**em** Kind

		PLURAL	
	MASC	FEM	NEUT
NOM	jen**e** Männer	jen**e** Frauen	jen**e** Kinder
ACC	jen**e** Männer	jen**e** Frauen	jen**e** Kinder
GEN	jen**er** Männer	jen**er** Frauen	jen**er** Kinder
DAT	jen**en** Männern	jen**en** Frauen	jen**en** Kindern

- **jeder, jede, jedes** each, every, everybody:

	MASC	SINGULAR FEM	NEUT
		SINGULAR	
	MASC	FEM	NEUT
NOM	jed**er** Wagen	jed**e** Minute	jed**es** Bild
ACC	jed**en** Wagen	jed**e** Minute	jed**es** Bild
GEN	jed**es** Wagens	jed**er** Minute	jed**es** Bild(e)s
	(jed**en** Wagens)		(jed**en** Bild(e)s)
DAT	jed**em** Wagen	jed**er** Minute	jed**em** Bild

- **welcher, welche, welches** which?, which:

	MASC	SINGULAR FEM	NEUT
		SINGULAR	
	MASC	FEM	NEUT
NOM	welch**er** Preis	welch**e** Sorte	welch**es** Mädchen
ACC	welch**en** Preis	welch**e** Sorte	welch**es** Mädchen
GEN	welch**es** Preises	welch**er** Sorte	welch**es** Mädchens
	(welch**en** Preises)		(welch**en** Mädchens)
DAT	welch**em** Preis	welch**er** Sorte	welch**em** Mädchen

	MASC	PLURAL FEM	NEUT
		PLURAL	
	MASC	FEM	NEUT
NOM	welch**e** Preise	welch**e** Sorten	welch**e** Mädchen
ACC	welch**e** Preise	welch**e** Sorten	welch**e** Mädchen
GEN	welch**er** Preise	welch**er** Sorten	welch**er** Mädchen
DAT	welch**en** Preisen	welch**en** Sorten	welch**en** Mädchen

☐ Words declined like the Indefinite Article

The following have the same declension pattern as the indefinite articles **ein** and **kein** (see pp 124 and 126):

The possessive adjectives

mein	my → 1
dein	your (*singular familiar*)
sein	his/its
ihr	her/its → 2
unser	our
euer	your (*plural familiar*)
ihr	their → 2
Ihr	your (*polite singular and plural*)

These words are declined as follows:

	SINGULAR			PLURAL
	MASC	FEM	NEUT	ALL GENDERS
NOM	—	**-e**	—	**-e**
ACC	**-en**	**-e**	—	**-e**
GEN	**-es**	**-er**	**-es**	**-er**
DAT	**-em**	**-er**	**-em**	**-en**

◆ Adjectives following these determiners have the mixed declension forms (see p 142), e.g.

sein altes Auto his old car

◆ **irgendein** (*some ... or other*) also follows this declension pattern in the singular.

Its plural form is **irgendwelche** (see p 128).

1 mein, meine, mein my:

	SINGULAR		
	MASC	FEM	NEUT
NOM	mein Bruder	meine Schwester	mein Kind
ACC	meinen Bruder	meine Schwester	mein Kind
GEN	meines Bruders	meiner Schwester	meines Kind(e)s
DAT	meinem Bruder	meiner Schwester	meinem Kind

	PLURAL		
	MASC	FEM	NEUT
NOM	meine Brüder	meine Schwestern	meine Kinder
ACC	meine Brüder	meine Schwestern	meine Kinder
GEN	meiner Brüder	meiner Schwestern	meiner Kinder
DAT	meinen Brüdern	meinen Schwestern	meinen Kindern

2 ihr, ihre, ihr her/its/their:

	SINGULAR		
	MASC	FEM	NEUT
NOM	ihr Bruder	ihre Schwester	ihr Kind
ACC	ihren Bruder	ihre Schwester	ihr Kind
GEN	ihres Bruders	ihrer Schwester	ihres Kind(e)s
DAT	ihrem Bruder	ihrer Schwester	ihrem Kind

	PLURAL		
	MASC	FEM	NEUT
NOM	ihre Brüder	ihre Schwestern	ihre Kinder
ACC	ihre Brüder	ihre Schwestern	ihre Kinder
GEN	ihrer Brüder	ihrer Schwestern	ihrer Kinder
DAT	ihren Brüdern	ihren Schwestern	ihren Kindern

◻ Indefinite Adjectives

These are adjectives used in place of, or together with, an article:

ander	other, different
mehrere (*plural only*)	several
viel	much, a lot, many
wenig	little, a little, few

- After the definite article and words declined like it (see p 128) these adjectives have weak declension endings → ☐1
  Adjectives following the indefinite adjectives are also weak → ☐2

- After **ein**, **kein**, **irgendein** or the possessive adjectives they have mixed declension endings → ☐3
  Adjectives following the indefinite adjectives are also mixed in declension → ☐4

- When used without a preceding article, **ander** and **mehrere** have strong declension endings → ☐5

- When used without a preceding article, **viel** and **wenig** may be declined as follows, though in the singular they are usually undeclined → ☐6

	SINGULAR			PLURAL
	MASC	FEM	NEUT	ALL GENDERS
NOM	viel	viel	viel	viele
ACC	viel	viel	viel	viele
GEN	vielen	vieler	vielen	vieler
DAT	viel(em)	vieler	viel(em)	vielen

- Any adjective following **viel** or **wenig** has strong endings → ☐7

1. **Die wenigen Kuchen, die übrig geblieben waren ...**
The few cakes which were left over ...

2. **Die vielen interessanten Ideen, die ans Licht kamen**
The many interesting ideas which came to light

3. **Ihr anderes Auto ist in der Werkstatt**
Their other car is in for repair

4. **Mehrere gute Freunde waren gekommen**
Several good friends had come

5. **Mehrere prominente Gäste sind eingeladen**
Various prominent guests are invited

Er war anderer Meinung
He was of a different opinion

6. **Es wurde viel Bier getrunken**
They drank a lot of beer

Sie essen nur wenig Obst
They don't eat a lot of fruit

7. **Er kaufte viele billige Sachen**
He bought a lot of cheap things

Es wurde viel gutes Bier getrunken
They drank a lot of good beer

Sie essen wenig frisches Obst
They don't eat a lot of fresh fruit

☐ The Declension of Adjectives

There are two ways of using adjectives:

1. They can be used **attributively**, where the adjective comes before the noun: *the new book*

2. They can be used **non-attributively**, where the adjective comes after the verb: *the book is new*

◆ In English the adjective does not change its form no matter how it is used.

In German, however, adjectives remain unchanged only when used non-attributively → 1

Used attributively, adjectives change to show the number, gender and case of the noun they precede → 2

The endings also depend on the nature of the article which precedes them → 3

There are three sets of endings:

1) The weak declension

These are the endings used after **der** and those words declined like it as shown on p 128 → 4

	SINGULAR			PLURAL
	MASC	FEM	NEUT	ALL GENDERS
NOM	-e	-e	-e	-en
ACC	-en	-e	-e	-en
GEN	-en	-en	-en	-en
DAT	-en	-en	-en	-en

1 **Das Buch ist neu**
The book is new
Der Vortrag war sehr langweilig
The lecture was very boring

2 **Das neue Buch ist da**
The new book has arrived
Während des langweiligen Vortrags sind wir alle eingeschlafen
We all fell asleep during the boring lecture

3 **der junge Rechtsanwalt**
the young lawyer
ein junger Rechtsanwalt
a young lawyer
manch junger Rechtsanwalt
many a young lawyer

4

		SINGULAR	
	MASC	FEM	NEUT
NOM	der alt**e** Mann	die alt**e** Frau	das alt**e** Haus
ACC	den alt**en** Mann	die alt**e** Frau	das alt**e** Haus
GEN	des alt**en** Mann(e)s	der alt**en** Frau	des alt**en** Hauses
DAT	dem alt**en** Mann	der alt**en** Frau	dem alt**en** Haus

		PLURAL	
	MASC	FEM	NEUT
NOM	die alt**en** Männer	die alt**en** Frauen	die alt**en** Häuser
ACC	die alt**en** Männer	die alt**en** Frauen	die alt**en** Häuser
GEN	der alt**en** Männer	der alt**en** Frauen	der alt**en** Häuser
DAT	den alt**en** Männern	den alt**en** Frauen	den alt**en** Häusern

☐ **The Declension of Adjectives** (Continued)

2) **The mixed declension**

These are the endings used after **ein**, **kein**, **irgendein** and the possessive adjectives (see p 136) → 1

	SINGULAR			PLURAL
	MASC	FEM	NEUT	ALL GENDERS
NOM	-er	-e	-es	-en
ACC	-en	-e	-es	-en
GEN	-en	-en	-en	-en
DAT	-en	-en	-en	-en

→ 2

3) **The strong declension**

Strong declension endings:

	SINGULAR			PLURAL
	MASC	FEM	NEUT	ALL GENDERS
NOM	-er	-e	-es	-e
ACC	-en	-e	-es	-e
GEN	-en	-er	-en	-er
DAT	-em	-er	-em	-en

→ 3

These endings are used where there is no preceding article. The article is omitted more frequently in German than in English, especially in *preposition + adjective + noun* combinations (see p 122).

These endings enable the adjective to do the work of the missing article by showing case, number and gender → 4

Examples

---

1 **Meine neue Stelle ist bei einer großen Druckerei**
My new job is with a large printing works
Ihre frühere Theorie ist jetzt bestätigt worden
Her earlier theory has now been proved true

2   SINGULAR

	MASC	FEM	NEUT
NOM	ein lang**er** Weg	eine lang**e** Reise	ein lang**es** Spiel
ACC	einen lang**en** Weg	eine lang**e** Reise	ein lang**es** Spiel
GEN	eines lang**en** Weg(e)s	einer lang**en** Reise	eines lang**en** Spiel(e)s
DAT	einem lang**en** Weg	einer lang**en** Reise	einem lang**en** Spiel

PLURAL

ALL GENDERS

NOM	ihre lang**en** Wege/Reisen/Spiele
ACC	ihre lang**en** Wege/Reisen/Spiele
GEN	ihrer lang**en** Wege/Reisen/Spiele
DAT	ihren lang**en** Wegen/Reisen/Spielen

3   SINGULAR

	MASC	FEM	NEUT
NOM	gut**er** Käse	gut**e** Marmelade	gut**es** Bier
ACC	gut**en** Käse	gut**e** Marmelade	gut**es** Bier
GEN	gut**en** Käses	gut**er** Marmelade	gut**en** Biers
DAT	gut**em** Käse	gut**er** Marmelade	gut**em** Bier

PLURAL

ALL GENDERS

NOM	gut**e** Käse/Marmeladen/Biere
ACC	gut**e** Käse/Marmeladen/Biere
GEN	gut**er** Käse/Marmeladen/Biere
DAT	gut**en** Käsen/Marmeladen/Bieren

4 **nach kurzer Fahrt**   after a short journey
mit gleichem Gehalt   with the same salary

☐ **The Declension of Adjectives** (Continued)

♦ Strong declension endings are also used after any of the following where they are not preceded by an article or other determiner:

ein bisschen	a little, a bit of
ein wenig	a little
ein paar	a few, a couple → 1
weniger	fewer, less
einige (*plural forms only*)	some
allerlei/allerhand	all kinds of, all sorts of
keinerlei	no … whatsoever, no … at all
mancherlei	various, a number of
etwas	some, any (*singular*) → 2
mehr	more
lauter	nothing but, sheer, pure
solch	such
vielerlei	various, all sorts of, many different
mehrerlei	several kinds of
was für	what, what kind of

(⚠ NOTE: **Was für ein** takes the mixed declension)

welcherlei	what kind of, what sort of
viel	much, many, a lot of
wievielerlei	how many kinds of
welch …!	what …! what a …! → 3
manch	many a
wenig	little, few, not much → 4
zweierlei/dreierlei *etc*	two/three *etc* kinds of
zwei, **drei** *etc*	two, three *etc* → 5

(⚠ NOTE: The mixed declension is used after **ein**)

♦ The strong declension is also required after possessives where no other word indicates the case, gender and number → 6

1. **ein paar gute Tipps** (*strong declension*)
   a couple of good tips

2. **Etwas starken Pfeffer zugeben** (*strong*)
   Add a little strong pepper

3. **Welch herrliches Wetter!** (*strong*)
   What splendid weather!

4. **Es gab damals nur wenig frisches Obst** (*strong*)
   At that time there was little fresh fruit

   ⚠ BUT:

   Das wenige frische Obst, das es damals gab ... (*weak*)
   The little fresh fruit that was then available ...

5. **Zwei große Jungen waren gekommen** (*strong*)
   Two big boys had come along

   ⚠ BUT:

   Die zwei großen Jungen, die gekommen waren (*weak*)
   The two big boys who had come along

   meine zwei großen Jungen (*mixed*)
   my two big sons

6. **Herberts altes Buch** (*strong*)
   Herbert's old book

   Muttis neues Auto (*strong*)
   Mum's new car

❏ **The Declension of Adjectives** (Continued)

Some spelling changes when adjectives are declined

- When the adjective **hoch** (*high*) is declined, its stem changes to **hoh-** → ①

- Adjectives ending in **-el** lose the **-e-** when inflected, i.e. when endings are added → ②

- Adjectives with an **-er** ending often lose the **-e-** when inflected → ③

The participles as adjectives

- The present participle can be used as an adjective with normal adjectival endings (pp 140 to 143) → ④

  The present participles of **sein** and **haben** cannot be used in this way.

- The past participle can also be used as an adjective → ⑤

Adjectives followed by the dative case

The *dative case* is required after many adjectives e.g.

ähnlich	similar to
bekannt	familiar to
dankbar	grateful to
fremd	alien to
gleich	all the same to/like → ⑥
leicht	easy for
nah	close to
peinlich	painful for
unbekannt	unknown to

1   **Das Gebäude ist hoch**   ⚠ BUT: **ein hohes Gebäude**
The building is high   a high building

2   **Das Zimmer ist dunkel**   ⚠ BUT: **in dem dunklen Zimmer**
The room is dark   in the dark room

3   **Das Auto war teuer**   ⚠ BUT: **Er kaufte ein teures Auto**
The car was expensive   He bought an expensive car

4   **die werdende Mutter**
the mother-to-be

    ein lachendes Kind
a laughing child

5   **meine verlorene Sachen**
my lost things

    die ausgebeuteten Arbeiter
the exploited workers

6   **Ist dir das bekannt?**
Do you know about it?

    Ich wäre Ihnen dankbar, wenn …
I should be grateful to you if …

    Diese Sache ist mir etwas peinlich
This matter is somewhat embarrassing for me

    Solche Gedanken waren ihm fremd
Such thoughts were alien to him

❐ Adjectives used as Nouns

All adjectives in German, and those participles used as adjectives, can also be used as nouns. These are often called **adjectival nouns**.

- Adjectives and participles used as nouns have:

  - a capital letter like other nouns → ⒈

  - declension endings like other adjectives, depending on the preceding article, if any (see below) → ⒉

Declension endings for adjectives used as nouns

- After **der**, **dieser** and words like it shown on p 128, the normal *weak* adjective endings apply (see p 140) → ⒊
  Der Junge (*the boy*) is an exception, and is declined like a weak masculine noun, as shown on p 115.

- After **ein**, **kein**, **irgendein** and the possessive adjectives shown on p 136, the *mixed* adjective endings apply (see p 142) → ⒋

- Where no article is present, or after those words shown on p 144, the *strong* adjective endings are used (see p 142) → ⒌

  When another adjective precedes the adjectival noun, the *strong* endings become *weak* in two instances:

  - in the *dative singular* → ⒍

  - in the *nominative and accusative plural* after a possessive, where the strong endings might cause confusion with the singular feminine form → ⒎

1 **der Angestellte**
the employee

2 **die Angestellte**
the (female) employee
das Neue daran ist ...
the new thing about it is ...
Es bleibt beim Alten
Things remain as they were
Er hat den ersten Besten genommen
He took the first that came to hand

3 **für den Angeklagten**
for the accused
mit dieser Bekannten
with this (*female*) friend

4 **Kein Angestellter darf hier rauchen**
No employee may smoke here
Sie machten einen Ausflug mit ihren Bekannten zusammen
They went on a trip with their friends

5 **Etwas Besonderes ist geschehen**
Something special has happened

6 **Ich hatte es Rudis jüngerem Verwandten versprochen**
I had promised it to Rudi's young relative

7 **Rudis jüngere Verwandten wollten es haben**
Rudi's young relatives wanted to have it

❒ Miscellaneous Points

Adjectives of nationality

◆ These are not spelt with a capital letter in German except in public or official names → ①

◆ However, when used as a noun to refer to the language, a capital letter is used → ②

◆ In German, for expressions like *he is English/he is German etc* a noun or adjectival noun is used instead of an adjective → ③

Adjectives derived from place names

◆ These are formed by adding **-er** to names of towns → ④

◆ They are never inflected → ⑤

◆ Adjectives from **die Schweiz** and from certain regions can also be formed in this way → ⑥

◆ Such adjectives may be used as nouns denoting the inhabitants of a town.
They are then declined as normal nouns (see p 98 ff) → ⑦
The feminine form is made by adding **-in** in the singular and **-innen** in the plural → ⑧

◆ Certain names ending in **-en** drop the **-e-** or the **-en** of their ending before adding **-er** → ⑨

◆ A second type of adjective formed from place names exists, ending in **-isch** and spelt with a small letter. It is inflected as a normal adjective (see p 140).
It is used mainly where the speaker is referring to the mood of, or something typical of, that place → ⑩

1 **die deutsche Sprache**   **das französische Volk**
the German language   the French people
⚠ BUT:
die Deutsche Bahn
the German railways

2 **Sie sprechen kein Englisch**
They don't speak English

3 **Er ist Deutscher**   **Sie ist Deutsche**
He is German   She is German

4 **Kölner, Frankfurter, Leipziger** *etc*

5 **der Kölner Dom**   **ein Frankfurter Würstchen**
Cologne cathedral   a frankfurter sausage

6 **Schweizer Käse**
Swiss cheese

7 **Die Sprache des Kölners heißt Kölsch**
von den Frankfurtern

8 **die Kölnerin, die Kölnerinnen**
die Londonerin, die Londonerinnen

9 **München ➤ der Münchner**
Bremen ➤ der Bremer
Göttingen ➤ der Göttinger

10 **ein echt frankfurterischer Ausdruck**
a real Frankfurt expression
Er spricht etwas münchnerisch
He has something of a Munich accent

❐ The Comparison of Adjectives

Adjectives have three basic forms of comparison:

1) A simple form used to describe something or someone

> e.g. a *little* house
> the house is *little*

♦ This form is fully dealt with on pp 140 to 147.

♦ Simple forms are used in *as ... as / not as ... as* comparisons → ☐1

2) A comparative form used to compare two things or persons

> e.g. he is *bigger* than his brother

♦ In German, comparatives are formed by adding **-er** to the simple form → ☐2

♦ *Than* in comparative statements is translated by **als** → ☐3

♦ Unlike English, the vast majority of German adjectives, including those of several syllables, form their comparatives in this way → ☐4

♦ Many adjectives modify the stem vowel when forming their comparatives → ☐5

1   **so ... wie**   as ... as
Er ist so gut wie sein Bruder
He is as good as his brother

   ebenso ... wie   just as ... as
Er war ebenso glücklich wie ich
He was just as happy as I was

   zwei-/dreimal *etc*   twice/three times etc
so ... wie   as ... as

   Er war zweimal so groß wie sein Bruder
He was twice as big as his brother

   nicht so ... wie   not as ... as
Er ist nicht so alt wie du
He is not as old as you

2   **klein/kleiner**   small/smaller
   schön/schöner   lovely/lovelier

3   **Er ist kleiner als seine Schwester**
He is smaller than his sister

4   **bequem/bequemer**   comfortable/more comfortable
   gebildet/gebildeter   educated/more educated
   effektiv/effektiver   effective/more effective

5   **alt/älter**   old/older
   stark/stärker   strong/stronger
   schwach/schwächer   weak/weaker
   scharf/schärfer   sharp/sharper
   lang/länger   long/longer
   kurz/kürzer   short/shorter
   warm/wärmer   warm/warmer
   kalt/kälter   cold/colder
   hart/härter   hard/harder
   groß/größer   big/bigger

❏ **The Comparison of Adjectives** (Continued)

◆ Adjectives whose simple form ends in **-el** lose the **-e-** before adding the comparative ending **-er** → ①

◆ Adjectives with a diphthong followed by **-er** in their simple forms also drop the **-e-** before adding **-er** → ②

◆ Adjectives whose simple form ends in **-en** or **-er** may drop the **-e-** of the simple form when adjectival endings are added to their comparative forms → ③

◆ With a few adjectives, comparative forms may be used not only for comparison, but also to render the idea of "-ish" or "rather ..." Some common examples are:

älter	elderly	**jünger**	youngish	
dünner	thinnish	**kleiner**	smallish	→ ④
dicker	fattish	**kürzer**	shortish	
größer	largish	**neuer**	newish	

◆ When used attributively (*before* the noun), comparative forms are declined in exactly the same way as simple adjectives (see pp 140 to 147)
→ ④
→ ⑤

3) **A superlative form used to compare three or more persons or things**

e.g. he is *the biggest/the best*

◆ Superlatives are formed by adding **-st** to the simple adjective. The vowel is modified, as for comparative forms, where applicable. Superlative forms are generally used with an article and take endings accordingly (see p 140) → ⑥

1. **eitel/eitler**   vain/vainer
   dunkel/dunkler   dark/darker

2. **sauer/saurer**   sour/more sour
   die saurere Zitrone
   the sourer lemon
   Der Wein ist saurer geworden
   The wine has grown more sour

   teuer/teurer   expensive/more expensive
   Das ist eine teurere Sorte
   That is a more expensive kind
   Die Neuen sind teurer
   The new ones are more expensive

3. **finster/finsterer**   dark/darker
   ein finstreres Gesicht
   OR:
   ein finstereres Gesicht
   a grimmer face

4. **ein älterer Herr**
   an elderly gentleman
   eine größere Summe
   a rather large sum
   von jüngerem Aussehen
   of youngish appearance

5. **Die jüngere Schwester ist größer als die ältere**
   The younger sister is bigger than the older one
   Mein kleinerer Bruder geht jetzt zur Schule
   My younger brother goes to school now

6. **Er ist der Jüngste**
   He is the youngest
   Ihr erfolgreichster Versuch war im Herbst 1998
   Her most successful attempt was in the autumn of 1998

☐ The Comparison of Adjectives (Continued)

◆ Many adjectives form their superlative forms by adding **-est** instead of **-st** where pronunciation would otherwise be difficult or unaesthetic → **1**

◆ The English superlative *"most"* meaning *"very"* can be shown in German by any of the following → **2**

> **äußerst**
>
> **sehr**
>
> **besonders**
>
> **außerordentlich**
>
> **höchst** (*not with monosyllabic words*)
>
> **furchtbar** (*conversational only*)
>
> **richtig** (*conversational only*)

Some irregular comparative and superlative forms

SIMPLE FORM	COMPARATIVE	SUPERLATIVE
gut	**besser**	**der beste**
hoch	**höher**	**der höchste**
viel	**mehr**	**der meiste**
nah	**näher**	**der nächste**

Grammar

1   **der/die/das schlechteste**
the worst

der/die/das schmerzhafteste
the most painful

der/die/das süßeste
the sweetest

der/die/das neueste
the newest

der/die/das stolzeste
the proudest

der/die/das frischeste
the freshest

2   **Er ist ein äußerst begabter Mensch**
He is a most gifted person

Das Essen war besonders schlecht
The food was really/most dreadful

Der Wein war furchtbar teuer!
The wine was dreadfully/most expensive!

Das sieht richtig komisch aus
That looks really/most funny

☐ Personal Pronouns

As in English, personal pronouns change their form depending on their function in the sentence:

> *I* saw *him*
> *He* saw *me* → 1 .
> *We* saw *her*

The personal pronouns are declined as follows:

NOMINATIVE		ACCUSATIVE		DATIVE	
ich	I	**mich**	me	**mir**	to/for me
du	you (*familiar*)	**dich**	you	**dir**	to/for you
er	he/it	**ihn**	him/it	**ihm**	to/for him/it
sie	she/it	**sie**	her/it	**ihr**	to/for her/it
es	it/he/she	**es**	it/him/her	**ihm**	to/for it/him/her
wir	we	**uns**	us	**uns**	to/for us
ihr	you (*plural*)	**euch**	you	**euch**	to/for you
sie	they	**sie**	them	**ihnen**	to/for them
Sie	you (*polite*)	**Sie**	you	**Ihnen**	to/for you
man	one	**einen**	one	**einem**	to/for one

→ 2

◆ As can be seen from the above table, there are three ways of addressing people in German, by **du**, **ihr** or **Sie**.

All three forms are illustrated on p 160.

◆ Personal pronouns in the dative require no preposition when acting as indirect object, i.e. *to* me, *to* him *etc* → 3

1 **Ich sah ihn**
I saw him

Er sah mich
He saw me

Wir sahen sie
We saw her

2 **Wir sind mit ihnen spazieren gegangen**
We went for a walk with them

Sie haben uns eine tolle Geschichte erzählt
They told us a great story

Soll ich Ihnen etwas mitbringen?
Shall I bring something back for you?

3 **Er hat es ihr gegeben**
He gave it to her

Ich habe ihm ein neues Buch gekauft
I bought a new book for him

OR:

I bought him a new book

◻ **Personal Pronouns** (Continued)

♦ **Du** is a singular form, used only when speaking to one person. It is used to talk to children, close friends and relatives, animals and objects of affection such as a toy, one's car etc.

When in doubt it is always best to use the more formal **Sie** form.

♦ **Ihr** is simply the plural form of **du** and is used in exactly the same situations wherever more than one person is to be addressed → ☐ 1

♦ The familiar forms and their possessives are written with a small letter → ☐ 2

♦ **Sie** is the polite, or formal, way of addressing people. It is written in all its declined forms with a capital letter, including the possessive → ☐ 3

Sie is used:

1 by children talking to adults outside their immediate family.

2 by adults talking to older children from mid-teens onwards. Teachers use it to their senior classes and bosses to their trainees etc.

3 among adult strangers meeting for the first time.

4 among colleagues, friends and acquaintances unless a suggestion has been formally made by one party and accepted by the other that the familiar forms should be used. Familiar forms must then continue to be used at all times, as a reversion to the formal might be considered insulting.

1. **Kinder, was wollt ihr essen?**

   Children, what do you want to eat?

2. **Er hat mir gesagt, du sollst deine Frau mitbringen**

   He told me you were to bring your wife

   Gestern bin ich deinem Bruder begegnet

   I met your brother yesterday

3. **Was haben Sie gesagt?**

   What did you say?

   Ich habe es Ihnen schon gegeben

   I have already given it to you

   Ja, Ihre Sachen sind jetzt fertig

   Yes, your things are ready now

❐ **Personal Pronouns** (Continued)

Er/sie/es

◆ All German nouns are masculine, feminine or neuter → **1**

◆ The personal pronoun must agree in number and in gender with the noun which it represents.

  Es is used only for neuter nouns, and not for all inanimate objects → **2**

  Inanimate objects which are masculine use the pronoun **er** → **3**

  Feminine inanimate objects use the pronoun **sie** → **4**

  Neuter nouns referring to people have the neuter pronoun **es** → **5**

  ⚠ NOTE: A common error for English speakers is to call all objects **es**.

Man

◆ This is used in much the same way as the pronoun **one** in English, but it is much more commonly used in German → **6**

◆ It is also used to make an alternative passive form (see p 34) → **7**

The genitive personal pronoun

◆ Genitive forms of the personal pronouns do exist → **8**

◆ In practice, however, these are rarely used. Wherever possible, alternative expressions are found which do not require the genitive personal pronoun.

◆ Special genitive forms exist for use with the prepositions **wegen** and **willen** → **9**

1   **der Tisch**   the table (*masculine*)
       die Gardine   the curtain (*feminine*)
       das Baby   the baby (*neuter*)

2   **Das Bild ist schön**   →   **Es ist schön**
       The picture is beautiful   →   It is beautiful

3   **Der Tisch ist groß**   →   **Er ist groß**
       The table is large   →   It is large

4   **Die Gardine ist weiß**   →   **Sie ist weiß**
       The curtain is white   →   It is white

5   **Das Kind stand auf**   →   **Es stand auf**
       The child stood up   →   He/she stood up

6   **Es tut einem gut**
       It does one good

7   **Man holt mich um sieben ab**
       I am being picked up at seven

8   **meiner**   of me   **unser**   of us
       deiner   of you   **euer**   of you (*plural*)
       seiner   of him/it   **ihrer**   of them
       ihrer   of her/it   **Ihrer**   of you (*polite*)

9   **meinetwegen**   because of me, on my account
       deinetwegen   because of you, on your account *etc*
       seinetwegen
       ihretwegen
       unsertwegen
       euretwegen
       Ihretwegen

       meinetwillen   for my sake, for me *etc*
       deinetwillen
       ihretwillen *etc*

☐ **Personal Pronouns** (Continued)

The use of pronouns after prepositions

- Personal pronouns used after prepositions and referring to a person are in the *case* required by the preposition in question (see p 198 ff) → ☐1

- When, however, a *thing* rather than a person is referred to, the construction

  preposition + pronoun

  becomes

  da- + *preposition* → ☐2

  Before a preposition beginning with a vowel, the form **dar-** + *preposition* is used → ☐3

This affects the following prepositions:

an	bei	in	neben	
auf	durch	mit	über	zwischen
aus	für	nach	unter	

- These contracted forms are used after verbs followed by a preposition (see p 76 ff) → ☐4

- After prepositions used to express motion the form with **da(r)-** is not felt to be sufficiently strong. Forms with **hin** and **her** are used as follows:

aus:	heraus/hinaus	
auf:	herauf/hinauf	→ ☐5
in:	herein/hinein	

Examples

1 **Ich bin mit ihm spazieren gegangen**
I went for a walk with him

2 **Klaus hatte ein Messer geholt und wollte damit den Kuchen schneiden**
Klaus had brought a knife and was about to cut the cake with it

3 **Lege es bitte darauf**
Put it there please

4 **Der Unterschied liegt darin, dass ...**
The difference is that ...

Ich erinnere mich nicht daran
I don't remember (it)

5 **Er sah eine Treppe und ging leise hinauf**
He saw some stairs and went up them quietly

Endlich fand er unser Zelt und kam herein
He finally found our tent and came in

Er öffnete den Koffer und legte das Hemd hinein
He opened his suitcase and put in his shirt

❐ Possessive Pronouns

meiner	mine
deiner	yours (*familiar*)
seiner	his/its
ihrer	hers/its
uns(e)rer	ours
eu(e)rer	yours (*plural*)
ihrer	theirs
Ihrer	yours (*polite*)

These have the same endings as **dieser**. Their declension is therefore the same as for possessive adjectives (see p 136) except in the masculine nominative singular and the neuter nominative and accusative singular:

		SINGULAR		PLURAL
	MASC	FEM	NEUT	ALL GENDERS
NOM	**-er**	**-e**	**-(e)s**	**-e**
ACC	**-en**	**-e**	**-(e)s**	**-e**
GEN	**-es**	**-er**	**-es**	**-er**
DAT	**-em**	**-er**	**-em**	**-en**

◆ The bracketed **(e)** is often omitted, especially in spoken German.

◆ Possessive pronouns must agree in number, gender and case with the noun they replace → **1**

◆ Note the translation of *of mine, of yours* etc → **2**

◆ **meiner** is declined in full opposite → **3**
  Deiner, **seiner** and **ihrer** are declined like **meiner**.
  Unserer and **euerer** are shown in full, since they have slightly different forms with an optional **-e-** → **4**

1. **Der Wagen da drüben ist meiner. Er ist kleiner als deiner**
   The car over there is mine. It is smaller than yours

2. **Er ist ein Bekannter von mir**
   He is an acquaintance of mine

3. **meiner** mine

| | SINGULAR | | | PLURAL |
	MASC	FEM	NEUT	ALL GENDERS
NOM	meiner	meine	mein(e)s	meine
ACC	meinen	meine	mein(e)s	meine
GEN	meines	meiner	meines	meiner
DAT	meinem	meiner	meinem	meinen

4. **uns(e)rer** ours

| | SINGULAR | | | PLURAL |
	MASC	FEM	NEUT	ALL GENDERS
NOM	uns(e)rer	uns(e)re	uns(e)res	uns(e)re
ACC	uns(e)ren	uns(e)re	uns(e)res	uns(e)re
GEN	uns(e)res	uns(e)rer	uns(e)res	uns(e)rer
DAT	uns(e)rem	uns(e)rer	uns(e)rem	uns(e)ren

eu(e)rer yours (*plural*)

| | SINGULAR | | | PLURAL |
	MASC	FEM	NEUT	ALL GENDERS
NOM	eu(e)rer	eu(e)re	eu(e)res	eu(e)re
ACC	eu(e)ren	eu(e)re	eu(e)res	eu(e)re
GEN	eu(e)res	eu(e)rer	eu(e)res	eu(e)rer
DAT	eu(e)rem	eu(e)rer	eu(e)rem	eu(e)ren

❐ **Possessive Pronouns** (Continued)

Alternative forms

There are two alternatives to the **meiner/deiner** *etc* forms shown on p 167:

der, die, das meinige *or* **Meinige**	mine
der, die, das deinige *or* **Deinige**	yours (*familiar*)
der, die, das seinige *or* **Seinige**	his/its
der, die, das ihrige *or* **Ihrige**	hers/its
der, die, das uns(e)rige *or* **Uns(e)rige**	ours
der, die, das eu(e)rige *or* **Eu(e)rige**	yours (*plural*)
der, die, das ihrige *or* **Ihrige**	theirs
der, die, das Ihrige	yours (*polite*)

◆ These are not as common as the **meiner/deiner** *etc* forms → ☐1

◆ These forms are declined as the definite article followed by a weak adjective (see p 140) → ☐2

◆ The bracketed **(e)** of the first and second person plural is often omitted in spoken German.

der, die, das meine *or* **Meine**	mine
der, die, das deine *or* **Deine**	yours (*familiar*)
der, die, das seine *or* **Seine**	his/its
der, die, das ihre *or* **Ihre**	hers/its
der, die, das uns(e)re *or* **Uns(e)re**	ours
der, die, das eu(e)re *or* **Eu(e)re**	yours (*plural*)
der, die, das ihre *or* **Ihre**	theirs
der, die, das Ihre	yours (*polite*)

◆ These forms are also less common than the **meiner/deiner** *etc* forms. They are declined as the definite article followed by a weak adjective (see p 140) → ☐3

---

1   **Ihr Auto ist aber neuer als das meinige** *or* **Meinige**
Your car is newer than mine
Paul hat seiner Freundin Blumen gekauft. Ich habe der
meinigen *or* **Meinigen Parfüm geschenkt**
Paul bought his girlfriend some flowers. I bought mine perfume

2   SINGULAR

	MASC	FEM	NEUT
NOM	der meinige	die meinige	das meinige
ACC	den meinigen	die meinige	das meinige
GEN	des meinigen	der meinigen	des meinigen
DAT	dem meinigen	der meinigen	dem meinigen

PLURAL
ALL GENDERS

NOM	die meinigen
ACC	die meinigen
GEN	der meinigen
DAT	den meinigen

3   SINGULAR

	MASC	FEM	NEUT
NOM	der meine	die meine	das meine
ACC	den meinen	die meine	das meine
GEN	des meinen	der meinen	des meinen
DAT	dem meinen	der meinen	dem meinen

PLURAL
ALL GENDERS

NOM	die meinen
ACC	die meinen
GEN	der meinen
DAT	den meinen

⚠ NOTE: **Der/die/das meinige** *etc* can also be spelt
der/die/das Meinige *etc* and **der/die/das meine** *etc* can also
be spelt **der/die/das Meine** *etc*

❏ **Reflexive Pronouns**

Reflexive pronouns, used to form reflexive verbs, have two forms, accusative and dative, as follows → ①

ACCUSATIVE	DATIVE	
mich	**mir**	myself
dich	**dir**	yourself (*familiar*)
sich	**sich**	himself/herself/itself/themselves
uns	**uns**	ourselves
euch	**euch**	yourselves (*plural*)
sich	**sich**	yourself/yourselves (*polite*)

◆ Unlike personal pronouns and possessives, the polite forms have no capital letter → ②

◆ For the position of reflexive pronouns within a sentence see p 30 (reflexive verbs) and pp 224 to 235 (sentence structure).

◆ Reflexive pronouns are also used after prepositions when the pronoun has the function of "reflecting back" to the subject of the sentence → ③

◆ A further use of reflexive pronouns in German is with transitive verbs where the action is performed for the benefit of the subject, as in the English phrase:

> I bought *myself* a new hat

The pronoun is not always translated in English → ④

Examples

1 **Er hat sich rasiert**

He had a shave

Du hast dich gebadet

You had a bath

Ich will es mir zuerst überlegen

I'll have to think about it first

2 **Setzen Sie sich bitte**

Please take a seat

3 **Er hatte nicht genug Geld bei sich** (⚠ NOT: **bei ihm**)

He didn't have enough money on him

4 **Ich hole mir ein Bier**

I'm going to get a beer (for myself)

Er hat sich einen neuen Anzug gekauft

He bought (himself) a new suit

☐ **Reflexive Pronouns** (Continued)

◆ Reflexive pronouns may be used for *reciprocal* actions, usually rendered by "each other" in English → **1**

Reciprocal actions may also be expressed by **einander**. This does not change in form → **2**

Einander is always used in place of the reflexive pronoun after prepositions. Note that the preposition and **einander** come together to form one word → **3**

Emphatic reflexive pronouns

In English, these have the same forms as the normal reflexive pronouns:

The queen *herself* had given the order

I haven't read it *myself*, but …

In German, this idea is expressed not by the reflexive pronouns, but by **selbst** or (in colloquial speech) **selber** placed at some point in the sentence after the noun or pronoun to which they refer → **4**

◆ **selbst/selber** do not change their form, regardless of number and gender of the noun to which they refer → **4**

◆ They are always stressed, regardless of their position in the sentence.

Examples

1 Wir sind uns letzte Woche begegnet

We met (each other) last week

Sie hatten sich auf einer Tagung kennen gelernt

They had got to know each other at a conference

2 Wir kennen uns schon

OR:

Wir kennen einander schon

We already know each other

Sie kennen sich schon

OR:

Sie kennen einander schon

They already know each other

3 Sie redeten miteinander

They were talking to each other

4 Die Königin selbst hat es befohlen

The queen herself has given the order

Ich selbst habe es nicht gelesen, aber ...

I haven't read it myself, but ...

❐ Relative Pronouns

These have the same forms as the definite article, except in the dative plural and genitive cases.

They are declined as follows:

		SINGULAR		PLURAL
	MASC	FEM	NEUT	ALL GENDERS
NOM	**der**	**die**	**das**	**die**
ACC	**den**	**die**	**das**	**die**
GEN	**dessen**	**deren**	**dessen**	**deren**
DAT	**dem**	**der**	**dem**	**denen**

- Relative pronouns must agree in gender and number with the noun to which they refer. They take their case however from the function they have in their own relative clause → ☐1

- The relative pronoun cannot be omitted in German as it sometimes is in English → ☐2

- The genitive forms are used in relative clauses in much the same way as in English → ☐3

  ⚠ NOTE, however, the translation of certain phrases → ☐4

- When a preposition introduces the relative clause, the relative pronoun may be replaced by **wo-** or **wor-** if the noun or pronoun it stands for refers to an inanimate object or abstract concept → ☐5
  The full form of relative pronoun plus preposition is however stylistically better.

- Relative clauses are always divided off by commas from the rest of the sentence → ☐1 - ☐5

1. **Der Mann, den ich gestern gesehen habe, kommt aus Hamburg**

   The man whom I saw yesterday comes from Hamburg

2. **Die Frau, mit der ich gestern gesprochen habe, kennt deine Mutter**

   The woman I spoke to yesterday knows your mother

3. **Das Kind, dessen Fahrrad gestohlen worden war, ...**

   The child whose bicycle had been stolen ...

4. **Die Kinder, von denen einige schon lesen konnten, ...**

   The children, some of whom could read, ...

   Meine Freunde, von denen einer ...

   My friends, one of whom ...

5. **Das Buch, woraus ich vorgelesen habe, ...**

   OR:

   Das Buch, aus dem ich vorgelesen habe, ...

   The book I read aloud from ...

🞏 **Relative Pronouns** (Continued)

Welcher

A second relative pronoun exists. This has the same forms as the interrogative adjective **welcher** without the genitive forms:

	SINGULAR			PLURAL
	MASC	FEM	NEUT	ALL GENDERS
NOM	**welcher**	**welche**	**welches**	**welche**
ACC	**welchen**	**welche**	**welches**	**welche**
GEN	—	—	—	—
DAT	**welchem**	**welcher**	**welchem**	**welchen**

◆ These forms are used only infrequently as relative pronouns, where sentence rhythm might benefit.

◆ They are also useful used as articles or adjectives to connect a noun in the relative clause with the contents of the main clause ➞ 1

Wer, was

These are normally used as interrogative pronouns meaning *who?*, *what?* and are declined as such on p 178.

◆ They may, however, also be used without interrogative meaning to replace both subject and relative pronoun in English:

> *he who*
> *a woman who*   ➞ 2
> *anyone who*
> *those who* etc

◆ **Was** is the relative pronoun used in set expressions with certain neuter forms ➞ 3

---

1. **Er glaubte, mit der Hausarbeit nicht helfen zu brauchen, mit welcher Idee seine Mutter nicht einverstanden war!**
He thought he didn't have to help in the house, an idea with which his mother was not in agreement!

2. **Wer das glaubt, ist verrückt**
Anyone who believes that is mad

   Was mich angeht, ...
   For my part, ...

   Was du gestern gekauft hast, steht dir ganz gut
   The things you bought yesterday suit you very well

3. | | |
   |---|---|
   | **alles, was ...** | everything which |
   | **allerlei, was ...** | all kinds of things that |
   | **das, was ...** | that which |
   | **dasjenige, was ...** | that which |
   | **dasselbe, was ...** | the same one that |
   | **einiges, was ...** | some that |
   | **Folgendes, was ...** | the following which |
   | **manches, was ...** | some which |
   | **nichts, was ...** | nothing that |
   | **vieles, was ...** | a lot that |
   | **wenig, was ...** | little that |

   Nichts, was er sagte, hat gestimmt
   Nothing that he said was right

   Das, was du jetzt machst, ist reiner Unsinn!
   What you are doing now is sheer nonsense!

   Mit allem, was du gesagt hast, sind wir einverstanden
   We agree with everything you said

❐ Interrogative Pronouns

These are the pronouns used to ask questions.

As in English, they have few forms, singular and plural being the same.

They are declined as follows:

	PERSONS	THINGS
NOM	**wer?**	**was?**
ACC	**wen?**	**was?**
GEN	**wessen?**	**wessen?**
DAT	**wem?**	—

- They are used in direct questions → **1**

  or in indirect questions → **2**

- When used as the subject of a sentence, they are always followed by a singular verb → **3**

  ⚠ BUT: When followed by a verb and taking a noun complement, the verb may be plural if the sense demands it → **4**

- The interrogative pronouns can be used in rhetorical questions or in exclamations → **5**

1   **Wer hat es gemacht?**

Who did it?

Mit wem bist du gekommen?

Who did you come with?

2   **Ich weiß nicht, wer es gemacht hat**

I don't know who did it

Er wollte wissen, mit wem er fahren sollte

He wanted to know who he was to travel with

3   **Wer kommt heute?**

Who's coming today?

4   **Wer sind diese Leute?**

Who are these people?

5   **Was haben wir gelacht!**

How we laughed!

❐ Interrogative Pronouns (Continued)

◆ When used with prepositions, **was** usually becomes **wo-** and is placed in front of the preposition to form one word ➞ 1

Where the preposition begins with a vowel, **wor-** is used instead ➞ 2

This construction is similar to **da(r)-** + *preposition* shown on p 164.

As with **da(r)-** + *preposition*, this construction is not used when the preposition is intended to convey movement.

Wohin (*where to*) and **woher** (*where from*) are used instead ➞ 3

Was für ein?, welcher?

◆ These are used to mean *what kind of one?* and *which one?*

◆ They are declined as shown on pp 124 and 128.

◆ They are used to form either direct or indirect questions ➞ 4

◆ They may refer either to persons or to things with the appropriate declension endings ➞ 5

1. **Wonach sehnst du dich?**

   What do you long for?

   Wodurch ist es zerstört worden?

   How was it destroyed?

2. **Worauf kann man sich heutzutage noch verlassen?**

   What is there left to rely on these days?

3. **Wohin fährst du?**

   Where are you going?

   Woher kommt das?

   Where has this come from?/How has this come about?

4. **Was für eins hat er?**

   What kind (of one) does he have?

   Welches hast du gewollt?

   Which one did you want?

5. **Für welchen hat sie sich entschieden?**

   Which one (*man/hat etc*) did she choose?

❏ Indefinite Pronouns

(Irgend)jemand someone, somebody

NOM	**(irgend)jemand**
ACC	**(irgend)jemanden, (irgend)jemand**
GEN	**(irgend)jemand(e)s**
DAT	**(irgend)jemandem, (irgend)jemand**

→ 1

Niemand no-one, nobody

NOM	**niemand**
ACC	**niemanden, niemand**
GEN	**niemand(e)s**
DAT	**niemandem, niemand**

→ 2

◆ The forms without endings are used in conversational German, but the inflected forms are preferred in literary and written styles.

◆ When **niemand** and **(irgend)jemand** are used with a following adjective, they are usually not declined, but the adjective takes a capital letter and is declined as follows:

NOM	**(irgend)jemand/niemand Neues**
ACC	**(irgend)jemand/niemand Neues**
GEN	**—**
DAT	**(irgend)jemand/niemand Neuem**

→ 3

◆ When **(irgend)jemand** and **niemand** are followed by **ander(e)s**, this is written with a small letter, e.g. **(irgend)jemand/niemand ander(e)s**.

1   **Ich habe es (irgend)jemandem** (*dat*) **gegeben**

I gave it to someone

(Irgend)jemand (*nom*) **hat es genommen**

Someone has stolen it

2   **Er hat niemanden** (*acc*) **gesehen**

He didn't see anyone

Er ist unterwegs niemandem (*dat*) **begegnet**

He encountered no-one on the way

3   **Diese Aufgabe erfordert (irgend)jemand Intelligentes**

Someone intelligent is needed for this task

❐ **Indefinite Pronouns** (Continued)

Keiner none

| | SINGULAR | | | PLURAL |
	MASC	FEM	NEUT	ALL GENDERS
NOM	**keiner**	**keine**	**keins**	**keine**
ACC	**keinen**	**keine**	**keins**	**keine**
GEN	**keines**	**keiner**	**keines**	**keiner**
DAT	**keinem**	**keiner**	**keinem**	**keinen**

- It is declined like the article **kein**, **keine**, **kein** (see p 126) except in the nominative masculine and nominative and accusative neuter forms → 1

- It may be used to refer to people or things → 1

Einer one

| | SINGULAR | | |
	MASC	FEM	NEUT
NOM	**einer**	**eine**	**ein(e)s**
ACC	**einen**	**eine**	**ein(e)s**
GEN	**eines**	**einer**	**eines**
DAT	**einem**	**einer**	**einem**

- This pronoun may be used to refer to either people or things → 2

- It exists only in the singular forms.

---

1   **Keiner von ihnen hat es tun können**

Not one of them was able to do it

Gibst du mir eine Zigarette? — Tut mir Leid, ich habe keine

Will you give me a cigarette? — Sorry, I haven't got any

2   **Sie ist mit einem meiner Verwandten verlobt**

She is engaged to one of my relatives

Wo sind die anderen Kinder? Ich sehe hier nur eins

Where are the rest of the children? I can only see one here

Gibst du mir einen? (e.g. *einen Whisky, einen Zehner* etc) OR:
Gibst du mir eine? (e.g. *eine Zigarette, eine Blume* etc) OR:
Gibst du mir eins? (e.g. *ein Buch, ein Butterbrot* etc)

Will you give me one?

❑ **Indefinite Pronouns** (Continued)

◆ Certain adjectives and articles can be used as pronouns.

◆ The following are all declined to agree in gender and number with the noun or pronoun they represent → ①

aller	all
ander	other
beide	both
derjenige	that one
derselbe	the same one
dieser	this one
einiger	some
irgendwelcher	someone or other/something or other
jeder	each (one), every one
jener	that one
mancher	some, quite a few
mehrere	several
sämtliche	all, the lot
solcher	such as that, such a one
welcher	which one

◆ The following do not change whatever the gender or number of the noun or pronoun they represent → ②

ein bisschen	a bit, a little
ein paar	a few
ein wenig	a little, a few
(irgend)etwas	some, something
mehr	more
nichts	nothing, none

◆ When an adjective follows **etwas** or **nichts**, it takes a capital letter and declension endings, e.g. **etwas/nichts Gutes**

1 **Andere machen es besser** (e.g. *Leute, Waschmaschinen* etc)
Others do it better

Mit einem solchen kommst du nicht bis nach Hause
(e.g. *Wagen* etc)
You won't make it home in one like that

Alles, was er ihr schenkte, schickte sie sofort zurück
Everything that he gave her she sent back at once

Er war mit beiden zufrieden (e.g. *Computern, Autos* etc)
He was satisfied with both

2 **Ich muss dir etwas sagen**
I must tell you something

(Irgend)etwas ist herausgefallen
Something fell out

Nichts ist geschehen
Nothing happened

Er ist mit nichts zufrieden
Nothing ever satisfies him

Gibst du mir bitte ein paar?
Will you give me a few?

Er hatte ein wenig bei sich
He had a little with him

Er braucht immer mehr um zu überleben
He needs more and more to survive

☐ **Use of Adverbs**

◆ Adverbs, or phrases which are used as adverbs, may:

1 modify a verb ➝ 1

2 modify an adjective ➝ 2

3 modify another adverb ➝ 3

4 modify a conjunction ➝ 4

5 ask a question ➝ 5

6 form verb prefixes (see p 72) ➝ 6

◆ Adverbs are also used, in much the same way as in English, to make the meaning of certain tenses more precise e.g.

1 with continuous tenses ➝ 7

2 to show a future meaning where the tense used is not future ➝ 8

1 **Er ging langsam über die Brücke**
He walked slowly over the bridge

2 **Er ist ein ziemlich großer Kerl**
He's quite a big chap

3 **Sie arbeitet heute besonders tüchtig**
She's working exceptionally well today

4 **Wenn er es nur aufgeben wollte!**
If only he would give it up!

5 **Wann kommt er an?**
When does he arrive?

6 **falsch spielen**
to cheat (*at cards*)

hintragen
to carry (*to a place*)

7 **Er liest gerade die Zeitung**
He's just reading the paper

8 **Er wollte gerade aufstehen, als ...**
He was just about to get up when ...

Wir fahren morgen nach Köln
We're driving to Cologne tomorrow

☐ The Formation of Adverbs

- Many German adverbs are simply adjectives used as adverbs. Used in this way, unlike adjectives, they are not declined → **1**

- Some adverbs are formed by adding **-weise** or **-sweise** to a noun → **2**

- Some adverbs are also formed by adding **-erweise** to an uninflected adjective.

  Such adverbs are used mainly to show the speaker's opinion → **3**

- There is also a class of adverbs which are not formed from other parts of speech e.g. **unten**, **oben**, **leider** → **4**

  and those shown in the paragraphs below.

- For the position of adverbs within a clause or sentence, see the section on sentence structure, pp 224 to 235.

- The following are some common adverbs of time:

endlich	finally
heute	today
immer	always
morgen	tomorrow
morgens	in the mornings
sofort	at once

  → **5** (after immer/morgen)

- The following are some common adverbs of degree:

äußerst	extremely
besonders	especially
beträchtlich	considerably
ziemlich	fairly

  → **6** (after besonders/beträchtlich)

1 **Habe ich das richtig gehört?**
Is it true what I've heard?

Sie war modern angezogen
She was fashionably dressed

2 | **beispielsweise** | for example |
beziehungsweise	or/or rather/that is to say
schrittweise	step by step
zeitweise	at times
zwangsweise	compulsorily

3 | **erstaunlicherweise** | astonishingly enough |
| **glücklicherweise** | fortunately |
| **komischerweise** | strangely enough |

4 **Unten wohnte Frau Schmidt**
Mrs Schmidt lived downstairs

Leider können wir nicht kommen
Unfortunately we cannot come

5 **Ich kann erst morgen kommen**
I can't come till tomorrow

Das Kind hat immer Hunger
The child is always hungry

6 **Das Paket war besonders schwer**
The parcel was unusually heavy

Diese Übung ist ziemlich leicht
This exercise is quite easy

☐ **Adverbs of place**

In certain respects German adverbs of place behave very differently from their English counterparts:

* Where no movement, or merely a movement within the same place, is involved, the adverb is used in its simple dictionary form → 1

* Movement *away from the speaker* is shown by the presence of **hin** → 2

  The following compound adverbs are therefore often used when movement away from the original position is concerned, even though a simple adverb would be used in English:

dahin	(to) there
dorthin	there
hierhin	here
irgendwohin	(to) somewhere or other
überallhin	everywhere
wohin?	where (to)?

  → 3

* Movement *towards the speaker* or central person is shown by the presence of **her**.

  The following compound adverbs are therefore often used to show movement towards a person:

daher	from there
hierher	here
irgendwoher	from somewhere or other
überallher	from all over
woher?	where from?

  → 4

1 **Wo ist er?**

Where is he?

Er ist nicht da

He isn't there

Hier darf man nicht parken

You can't park here

2 **Klaus und Ulli geben heute eine Party. Gehen wir hin?**

Klaus and Ulli are having a party today. Shall we go?

3 **Wohin fährst du?**

Where are you going?

Sie liefen überallhin

They ran everywhere

4 **Woher kommst du?**

Where do you come from?

Woher hast du das?

Where did you get that from?

Das habe ich irgendwoher gekriegt

I got that from somewhere or other

❑ Comparison of Adverbs

- The **comparative** form of the adverb is obtained in exactly the same way as that of adjectives, i.e. by adding **-er** → ①

- The **superlative** form is produced as follows:

    am + *adverb* + **-sten/-esten**

    It is not declined → ②

- Note the use of the comparative adverb with **immer** to show progression → ③

- *the more ... the more ...* is expressed in German by:

    je ... desto ... or **je ... umso ...** → ④

- Some adverbial superlatives are used to show the extent of a quality rather than a comparison with others. These are as follows:

bestens	very well/very warmly
höchstens	at the most/at best
meistens	mostly/most often
spätestens	at the latest
strengstens	strictly, absolutely
wenigstens	at least

    → ⑤

- Two irregular comparatives and superlatives:

    gern ➤ **lieber** ➤ **am liebsten** (used with **haben**)
    well ➤ better ➤ best

    → ⑥

    bald ➤ **eher** ➤ **am ehesten**
    soon ➤ sooner ➤ soonest

1. **Er läuft schneller als seine Schwester**
   He runs faster than his sister

   Ich sehe ihn seltener als früher
   I see him less often than before

2. **Wer von ihnen arbeitet am schnellsten?**
   Which of them works fastest?

   Er isst am meisten
   He eats most

3. **Die Mädchen sprachen immer lauter**
   The girls were talking more and more loudly

   Er fuhr immer langsamer
   He drove more and more slowly

4. **Je eher, desto besser**
   The sooner the better

5. **Er kommt meistens zu spät an**
   He usually arrives late

   Rauchen strengstens verboten!
   Smoking strictly prohibited

6. **Welches hast du am liebsten?**
   Which do you like best?

❐ Emphasizers

These are words commonly used in German, as indeed in English, especially in the spoken language, to emphasize or modify in some way the meaning of the sentence. The following are some of the most common:

Aber

Used to lend emphasis to a statement → ⃞1

Denn

As well as its uses as a conjunction (see p 214), **denn** is widely used to emphasize the meaning. It often cannot be directly translated → ⃞2

Doch

Used as a positive reply in order to correct negative assumptions or impressions → ⃞3

It can strengthen an imperative → ⃞4

It can make a question out of a statement → ⃞5

Mal

May be used with imperatives → ⃞6

It also has several idiomatic uses → ⃞7

Ja

Strengthens a statement → ⃞8

It also has several idiomatic uses → ⃞9

Schon

Is used familiarly with an imperative → ⃞10

It is also used in various idiomatic ways → ⃞11

Examples

---

1 **Das ist aber schön!**   **Aber ja!**
Oh that's pretty!   Yes indeed!

2 **Was ist denn hier los?**   **Wo denn?**
What's going on here then?   Where?

3 **Hat es dir nicht gefallen? — Doch!**
Didn't you like it? — Oh yes, I did!

4 **Lass ihn doch!**
Just leave him

5 **Das schaffst du doch?**
You'll manage it, won't you?

6 **Komm mal her!**   **Moment mal!**
Come here!   Just a minute!

7 **Mal sehen**   **Hören Sie mal ...**
We'll see   Look here now ...
Er soll es nur mal versuchen!
Just let him try it!

8 **Er sieht ja wie seine Mutter aus**
He looks like his mother
Das kann ja sein
That may well be

9 **Ja und?**   **Das ist ja lächerlich**
So what?/What then?   That's ridiculous
Das ist es ja
That's just it

10 **Mach schon!**
Get on with it!

11 **schon wieder**   **Schon gut**
again   Okay/Very well

In English, a preposition does not affect the word or phrase which it introduces, e.g.

| the women | a large meal | these events |
| *with* the women | *after* a large meal | *before* these events |

In German, however, the noun following a preposition must be put in a certain *case*:

accusative	→	1
dative	→	2
genitive	→	3

It is therefore important to learn each preposition with the case, or cases, it governs.

The following guidelines will help you:

- Prepositions which take the accusative or dative cases are much more common than those taking the genitive case.

- Certain prepositions may take a dative or accusative case, depending on whether *movement* is involved or not. This is explained further on p 202 ff → 4

- Prepositions are often used to complete the sense of certain verbs, as shown on p 76 ff → 5

- After many prepositions, a shortened or *contracted* form of the definite article may be merged with the preposition to form one word, e.g.

auf + **das**	→	**aufs**
bei + **dem**	→	**beim**
zu + **der**	→	**zur**

☐1   **Es ist für dich**

It's for you

     Wir sind durch die ganze Welt gereist

We travelled all over the world

☐2   **Er ist mit seiner Frau gekommen**

He came with his wife

☐3   **Es ist ihm trotz seiner Bemühungen nicht gelungen**

Despite his efforts, he still didn't succeed

☐4   **Es liegt auf dem Tisch**

It's on the table

(*dative*: no movement implied)

     Lege es bitte auf den Tisch

Please put it on the table

(*accusative*: movement *onto* the table)

☐5   **Ich warte auf meinen Mann**

I'm waiting for my husband

❐ Contracted forms

Contractions are possible with the following prepositions:

PREPOSITION	+ **das**	+ **den**	+ **dem**	+ **der**
an	ans		am	
auf	aufs*			
bei			beim	
durch	durchs*			
für	fürs*			
hinter	hinters*	hintern*	hinterm*	
in	ins		im	
über	übers*	übern*	überm*	
um	ums*			
unter	unters*	untern*	unterm*	
vor	vors*		vorm*	
von			vom	
zu			zum	zur

> * ⚠ NOTE: Those forms marked with an asterisk are suitable only for use in colloquial, spoken German.
> All other forms (not marked with an asterisk) may be safely used in any context, formal or informal → **1**

- Contracted forms are not used where the article is to be stressed → **2**

- Other contracted forms involving prepositions, as shown on pp 164 and 174, occur:

  1 in the introduction to relative clauses → **3**

  2 with personal pronouns representing inanimate objects → **4**

1 **Wir gehen heute Abend ins Theater**

We are going to the theatre this evening

Er geht zur Schule

He goes to school

Das kommt vom Trinken

That comes from drinking

2 **In dem Anzug kann ich mich nicht sehen lassen!**

I can't go out in that suit!

3 **Die Bank, worauf wir saßen, war etwas wackelig**

The bench we were sitting on was rather wobbly

4 **Er war damit zufrieden**

He was satisfied with that

Er hat es darauf gesetzt

He put it on it

☐ Prepositions followed by the Dative Case

Some of the most common prepositions taking the dative case are:

aus	gegenüber	seit
außer	mit	von
bei	nach	zu

Aus

- as a preposition meaning: *out of/from* → **1**
- as a separable verbal prefix (see p 72) → **2**

Außer

- as a preposition meaning: *out of* → **3**
  except → **4**

Bei

- as a preposition meaning: *at the home/shop/work etc of* → **5**
  near → **6**
  in the course of/during → **7**
- as a separable verbal prefix (see p 72) → **8**

Gegenüber

- as a preposition meaning: *opposite* → **9**
  to(wards) → **10**

  ⚠ NOTE: When used as a preposition, **gegenüber** is placed *after a pronoun*, but may be placed *before or after a noun*.

- as a separable verbal prefix → **11**

1. **Er trinkt aus der Flasche**
He is drinking out of the bottle
Er kommt aus Essen
He comes from Essen

2. **aushalten** to endure
Ich halte es nicht mehr aus
I can't stand it any longer

3. **außer Gefahr/Betrieb**
out of danger/order

4. **alle außer mir**
all except me

5. **bei uns in Schottland**
at home in Scotland
Er wohnt immer noch bei seinen Eltern
He still lives with his parents

6. **Er saß bei mir**
He was sitting next to me

7. **Ich singe immer beim Arbeiten**
I always sing when I'm working
Bei unserer Ankunft …
On our arrival …

8. **Er stand seinem Freund bei**
He stood by his friend

9. **Er wohnt uns gegenüber**
He lives opposite us

10. **Er ist mir gegenüber immer sehr freundlich gewesen**
He has always been very friendly towards me

11. **gegenüberstehen** to face/to have an attitude towards
Er steht ihnen kritisch gegenüber
He takes a critical view of them

❐ **Prepositions followed by the Dative Case** (Continued)

Mit

♦ as a preposition meaning: *with* → **1**

♦ as a separable verbal prefix (see p 72) → **2**

Nach

♦ as a preposition meaning: *after* → **3**
    to → **4**
    according to (it can be placed after the
    noun with this meaning) → **5**

♦ as a separable verbal prefix (see p 72) → **6**

Seit

♦ as a preposition meaning: *since* → **7**

    for (of time) → **8**

    ⚠ NOTE: Beware of the tense!

Von

♦ as a preposition meaning: *from* → **9**
    about → **10**

♦ as an alternative, often preferred, to the genitive case → **11**

♦ as a preposition meaning: *by* (to introduce the agent of a passive
    action, see p 34) → **12**

Zu

♦ as a preposition meaning: *to* → **13**
    for → **14**

♦ as a separable verbal prefix (see p 72) → **15**

1. **Er ging mit seinen Freunden spazieren**
   He went walking with his friends
2. **jemanden mitnehmen** to give someone a lift
   Nimmst du mich bitte mit?
   Will you give me a lift please?
3. **Nach zwei Stunden kam er wieder**
   He returned two hours later
4. **Er ist nach London gereist**
   He went to London
5. **Ihrer Sprache nach ist sie Süddeutsche**
   From the way she spoke I would say she is from southern Germany
6. **nachmachen** to copy
   Sie macht mir alles nach
   She copies everything I do
7. **Seit der Zeit …**
   Since then …
8. **Ich wohne seit zwei Jahren in Frankfurt**
   I've been living in Frankfurt for two years
9. **Von Frankfurt sind wir weiter nach München gefahren**
   From Frankfurt we went on to Munich
10. **Ich weiß nichts von ihm**
    I know nothing about him
11. **Die Mutter von diesen Mädchen …**
    The mother of these girls …
    Sie ist eine Freundin von Horst
    She is a friend of Horst's
12. **Er ist von unseren Argumenten überzeugt worden**
    He was convinced by our arguments
13. **Er ging zum Arzt**
    He went to the doctor's
14. **Wir sind zum Essen eingeladen**
    We're invited for dinner
15. **zumachen** to shut
    Mach die Tür zu!
    Shut the door!

❏ Prepositions followed by the Accusative Case

The most common of these are:

durch	für	ohne	wider
entlang	gegen	um	

Durch

- as a preposition meaning: *through* → $\boxed{1}$

- preceding the inanimate agent of a passive action (see p 34) → $\boxed{2}$

- as a separable verbal prefix

Entlang

- as a preposition meaning: *along* (it follows the noun with this meaning) → $\boxed{3}$

- as a separable verbal prefix → $\boxed{4}$

Für

- as a preposition meaning: *for* → $\boxed{5}$
  to → $\boxed{6}$

- in **was für/was für ein** *what kind of/what* (see p 144 and p 180) → $\boxed{7}$

Gegen

- as a preposition meaning: *against* → $\boxed{8}$
  towards/getting on for → $\boxed{9}$

- as a separable verbal prefix

Grammar

1. **durch das Fenster blicken**
   to look through the window

2. **Durch seine Bemühungen wurden alle gerettet**
   Everyone was saved through his efforts

3. **die Straße entlang**
   along the street

4. **Wir gingen die Straße entlang**
   We went along the street

5. **Ich habe es für dich getan**
   I did it for you

6. **Das ist für ihn sehr wichtig**
   That is very important to him

7. **Was für Äpfel sind das?**
   What kind of apples are they?

8. **Stelle es gegen die Mauer**
   Put it against the wall

   Haben Sie ein Mittel gegen Schnupfen?
   Have you something for colds?

   Ich habe nichts dagegen
   I've got nothing against it

9. **Wir sind gegen vier angekommen**
   We arrived at getting on for/around four o'clock

❐ **Prepositions followed by the Accusative Case**
(Continued)

Ohne

◆ as a preposition meaning: *without* → **1**

Um

◆ as a preposition meaning: *(a)round/round about* → **2**

at (in time expressions) → **3**

for (after certain verbs) → **4**

about (after certain verbs) → **5**

by (in expressions of quantity) → **6**

◆ as a variable verbal prefix (see p 74) → **7**

Wider

◆ as a preposition meaning: *contrary to/against* → **8**

◆ as a variable verbal prefix (see p 74) → **9**

1. **Ohne ihn gehts nicht**
   It won't work without him

2. **um die Ecke**
   (a)round the corner

3. **Es fängt um neun Uhr an**
   It begins at nine

4. **Sie baten ihre Mutter um Kekse**
   They asked their mother for some biscuits

5. **Es handelt sich um dein Benehmen**
   It's a question of your behaviour

6. **Es ist um zehn Euro billiger**
   It is cheaper by ten euros

7. **umarmen**   to embrace (*inseparable*)
   Er hat sie umarmt
   He gave her a hug

   umfallen   to fall over (*separable*)
   Er ist umgefallen
   He fell over

8. **Das geht mir wider die Natur**
   That's against my nature

9. **widersprechen**   to go against (*inseparable*)
   Das hat meinen Wünschen widersprochen
   That went against my wishes

   (sich) widerspiegeln   to reflect (*separable*)
   Der Baum spiegelt sich im Wasser wider
   The tree is reflected in the water

❏ Prepositions followed by the Accusative or the Dative Case

These prepositions are followed by:

    1 the **accusative** when *movement towards* a different place is involved.

    2 the **dative** when *position* is described as opposed to movement, or when the movement is *within* the same place.

◆ The most common prepositions in this category are:

an	*on/at/to*
auf	*on/in/to/at*
hinter	*behind*
in	*in/into/to* → 1
neben	*next to/beside*
über	*over/across/above*
unter	*under/among* → 2
vor	*in front of/before*
zwischen	*between* → 3

◆ These prepositions may also be used with figurative meanings as part of a *verb + preposition* construction (see p 76).

The case following **auf** or **an** is then not the same after all verbs → 4

It is therefore best to learn such constructions together with the case which follows them.

◆ Many of these prepositions are also used as verbal prefixes in the same way as the prepositions described on pp 202 to 209 → 5

1. **Er ging ins Zimmer** (*acc*)
He entered the room

   Im Zimmer (*dat*) **warteten viele Leute auf ihn**
A lot of people were waiting for him in the room

2. **Er stellte sich unter den Baum** (*acc*)
He (came and) stood under the tree

   Er lebte dort unter Freunden (*dat*)
There he lived among friends

3. **Er legte es zwischen die beiden Teller** (*acc*)
He put it between the two plates

   Das Dorf liegt zwischen den Bergen (*dat*)
The village lies between the mountains

4. **sich verlassen auf** (+*acc*) to depend on
   bestehen auf (+*dat*) to insist on

   glauben an (+*acc*) to believe in
   leiden an (+*dat*) to suffer from

5. <u>**anrechnen**</u> to charge for (*separable*)
   Das wird Ihnen später angerechnet
You'll be charged for that later

   <u>**aufsetzen**</u> to put on (*separable*)
   Sie setzte sich den Hut auf
She put her hat on

   <u>**überqueren**</u> to cross (*inseparable*)
   Sie hat die Straße überquert
She crossed the street

❒ Prepositions followed by the Genitive Case

The following are some of the more common prepositions which take the genitive case:

außerhalb	*outside*
beiderseits	*on both sides of*
diesseits	*on this side of*
... halber	*for ... sake/because of ...*
hinsichtlich	*with regard to*
infolge	*as a result of*
innerhalb	*within/inside* → 1
jenseits	*on the other side of* → 2
statt*	*instead of*
trotz*	*in spite of* → 3
um ... willen	*for ... sake/because of ...*
während*	*during* → 4
wegen*	*on account of* → 5

* ⚠ NOTE: Those prepositions marked with an asterisk may also be followed by the dative case → 6

⚠ NOTE: Special forms of the possessive and relative pronouns are used with **wegen**, **halber** and **willen** → 7

---

1 **innerhalb dieses Zeitraums**
within this period of time

2 **jenseits der Grenze**
on the other side of the frontier

3 **trotz seiner Befürchtungen**
despite his fears

4 **während der Vorstellung**
during the performance

5 **wegen der neuen Stelle**
because of the new job

6 **trotz allem**
in spite of everything

wegen mir
because of me

7 | | |
|---|---|
| **meinetwegen** | on my account, because of me |
| **deinetwegen** | on your account, because of you (*familiar*) |
| **seinetwegen** | on his account, because of him |
| **ihretwegen** | on her/their account, because of her/them |
| **unsertwegen** | on our account, because of us |
| **euertwegen** | on your account, because of you (*plural*) |
| **Ihretwegen** | on your account, because of you (*polite*) |
| **derentwegen** | for whose sake, for her/their/its sake |
| **dessentwegen** | for whose sake, for his/its sake |
| | |
| **meinethalben** *etc* | on my *etc* account |
| **derenthalben** | on whose account, on her/their/its account |
| **dessenthalben** | on whose account, on his/its account |
| | |
| **meinetwillen** *etc* | for my *etc* sake |
| **derentwillen** | for whose sake, for her/its/their sake |
| **dessentwillen** | for whose sake, for his/its sake |

❐ Co-ordinating Conjunctions

These are used to link words, phrases or clauses.

◆ These are the main co-ordinating conjunctions:

aber   *but* → 1

           however (with this meaning, **aber** is placed within the clause) → 2

denn   *for* → 3

oder   *or* → 4

sondern   *but* (after a negative construction) → 5

und   *and* → 6

◆ These do not cause the inversion of subject and verb, i.e. the verb follows the subject in the normal way (see p 224) → 1 - 6

◆ Inversion may however be caused by something other than the co-ordinating conjunction, e.g. **dann**, **trotzdem**, **montags** in the examples opposite → 7

Examples

Grammar

---

1 **Wir wollten ins Kino, aber wir hatten kein Geld**
We wanted to go to the cinema but we had no money

2 **Ich wollte ins Theater; er aber wollte nicht mit**
I wanted to go to the theatre; however he wouldn't come

3 **Wir wollten heute fahren, denn montags ist weniger Verkehr**
We wanted to travel today because the traffic is lighter on Mondays

4 **Er hatte noch nie Whisky oder Schnaps getrunken**
He had never drunk whisky or schnapps

Willst du eins oder hast du vielleicht keinen Hunger?
Do you want one or aren't you hungry?

5 **Er ist nicht alt, sondern jung**
He isn't old, but young

6 **Horst und Veronika**
Horst und Veronika

Er ging in die Stadt und kaufte sich ein neues Hemd
He went into town and bought himself a new shirt

7 **Er hat sie besucht und dann ist er wieder nach Hause gegangen**
He paid her a visit and then went home again

Wir wollten doch ins Kino, aber trotzdem sind wir zu Hause geblieben
We wanted to go to the cinema, but even so we stayed at home

Wir wollten heute fahren, denn montags ist der Verkehr geringer
We wanted to travel today because there is less traffic on Mondays

☐ Double Co-ordinating Conjunctions

These conjunctions consist of two separate elements, like their English counterparts, e.g.

> *not only ... but also ...*

The following are widely used:

> **sowohl .. als (auch)**
> *both ... and*

- This may link words or phrases → **1**

- The verb is usually plural, whether the subjects are singular or plural → **1**

> **weder ... noch**
> *neither ... nor*

- This may link words or phrases → **2**

- It may also link clauses, and inversion of subject and verb then takes place in both clauses → **3**

- The verb is plural unless both subjects are singular → **4**

1. **Sowohl sein Vater als auch seine Mutter haben sich darüber gefreut**

   Both his father and his mother were pleased about it

   Sowohl unser Lehrkörper also auch unsere Schüler haben teilgenommen

   Both our staff and our pupils took part

2. **Weder Georg noch sein Bruder kannte das Mädchen**

   Neither Georg nor his brother knew the girl

3. **Weder mag ich ihn noch respektiere ich ihn**

   I neither like nor respect him

4. **Weder die Befürworter noch die Gegner haben Recht**

   Neither the supporters nor the opponents are right

   Weder du noch ich würde es schaffen

   Neither you nor I would be able to do it

❏ **Double Co-ordinating Conjunctions** (Continued)

> **nicht nur ... sondern auch**
> *not only ... but also*

◆ This is used to link clauses as well as words and phrases → **1**

◆ The word order is: inversion of subject and verb in the first clause, and normal order in the second → **2**

 However, if **nicht nur** does not begin the clause, normal order prevails → **3**

◆ The verb agrees in number with the subject nearest to it → **4**

> **entweder ... oder**
> *either ... or*

◆ The verb agrees with the subject nearest it → **5**

◆ The normal word order is: inversion in the first clause, and normal order in the second → **6**

 However, it is possible to use normal order in the first clause, and this may lend a more threatening tone to the statement → **7**

> **teils ... teils**
> *partly ... partly*

◆ The verb is normally plural unless both subjects are singular → **8**

◆ Inversion of subject and verb takes place in both clauses → **9**

Examples

Grammar

1. **Er ist nicht nur geschickt, sondern auch intelligent** OR:
   Nicht nur ist er geschickt, sondern er ist auch intelligent
   He is not only skilful but also intelligent

2. **Nicht nur hat es die ganze Zeit geregnet, sondern ich habe mir auch noch das Bein gebrochen**
   Not only did it rain the whole time, but I also broke my leg

3. **Es hat nicht nur die ganze Zeit geregnet, sondern ich habe mir auch noch das Bein gebrochen**
   Not only did it rain the whole time, but I also broke my leg

4. **Nicht nur ich, sondern auch die Mädchen sind dafür verantwortlich**
   Not just me, but the girls are also responsible

   Nicht nur sie, sondern auch ich habe es gehört
   They weren't the only ones to hear it — I heard it too

5. **Entweder du oder Georg muss es getan haben**
   It must have been either you or Georg who did it

6. **Entweder komme ich morgen vorbei, oder ich rufe dich an**
   I'll either drop in tomorrow or I'll give you a ring

7. **Entweder du gibst das sofort auf, oder du kriegst kein Taschengeld mehr**
   Either you stop that immediately, or you get no more pocket money

8. **Die Studenten waren teils Deutsche, teils Ausländer**
   The students were partly German and partly from abroad

9. **Teils bin ich überzeugt, teils bleibe ich skeptisch**
   Part of me is convinced, and part remains sceptical

❒ Subordinating Conjunctions

These are used to link clauses in such a way as to make one clause dependent on another for its meaning. The dependent clause is called a **subordinate clause** and the other a **main clause**.

♦   The subordinate clause is always separated from the rest of the sentence by commas → **1**

♦   The subordinate clause may precede the main clause. When this happens, the verb and subject of the main clause are inverted, i.e. they swap places, as shown on p 226 → **2**

♦   The finite part of the verb (i.e. the conjugated part) is always at the end of a subordinate clause (see p 228) → **3**

♦   For compound tenses in subordinate clauses, it is the **auxiliary** (the main part of the verb) which comes last, after the participle or infinitive used to form the compound tense (see p 22 ff) → **4**

♦   Any **modal verb** (**mögen**, **können** etc, see p 52 ff) used in a subordinate clause is placed last in the clause → **5**

   ⚠ BUT: When the modal verb is in a compound tense, the order is as shown → **6**

1   MAIN CLAUSE   SUBORDINATE CLAUSE

Er ist zu Fuß gekommen, weil der Bus zu teuer ist
He came on foot because the bus is too dear

Ich trinke viel Bier, obwohl es nicht gesund ist
I drink a lot of beer although it isn't good for me

Wir haben weitergefeiert, nachdem sie gegangen waren
We carried on with the party after they went

2   SUBORDINATE CLAUSE   MAIN CLAUSE

Weil der Bus zu teuer ist, ist er zu Fuß gekommen

Obwohl es nicht gesund ist, trinke ich viel Bier

Nachdem sie gegangen waren, haben wir weitergefeiert

3   **Als er uns sah, ist er davongelaufen** OR:
Er ist davongelaufen, als er uns sah
He ran away when he saw us

4   **Nachdem er gegessen hatte, ging er hinaus**
He went out after he had eaten

5   **Da er nicht mit uns sprechen wollte, ist er
davongelaufen**
Since he didn't want to speak to us he ran away

6   **Da er nicht mit uns hat sprechen wollen, ist er
davongelaufen**
Since he didn't want to speak to us he ran away

❐ **Subordinating conjunctions** (Continued)

◆ Here are some common examples of subordinating conjunctions and their uses:

als	when → 1
als ob	as if, as though
bevor	before
bis	until → 2
da	as, since → 3
damit	so (that)
indem	while
inwiefern	to what extent
nachdem	after → 4
ob	whether, if
obwohl	although
wann	when (*interrogative*) → 5
während	while → 6
weil	because → 7
wenn	when, whenever/if → 8
wie	as, like
wo	where
wohin	to where
worauf	whereupon/on which
worin	in which
seitdem	since
so dass, sodass	such that, so that
sobald	as soon as
soweit	as far as

1 **Es regnete, als ich in Köln ankam** OR:
Als ich in Köln ankam, regnete es
It was raining when I arrived in Cologne

2 **Ich warte, bis du zurückkommst**
I'll wait till you get back

3 **Da er nicht kommen wollte, ...**
Since he didn't want to come ...

4 **Er wird uns Bescheid sagen können, nachdem er
angerufen hat** OR:
**Nachdem er angerufen hat, wird er uns Bescheid sagen
können**
He will be able to let us know for certain once he has phoned

5 **Er möchte wissen, wann der Zug ankommt**
He would like to know when the train is due to arrive

6 **Während seine Frau die Koffer auspackte, machte er
das Abendessen** OR:
**Er machte das Abendessen, während seine Frau die
Koffer auspackte**
He made the supper while his wife unpacked the cases

7 **Wir haben den Hund nicht mitgenommen, weil im
Auto nicht genug Platz war** OR:
**Weil im Auto nicht genug Platz war, haben wir den
Hund nicht mitgenommen**
We didn't take the dog because there wasn't enough room in
the car

8 **Wenn ich ins Kino gehe ...**
When(ever) I go to the cinema ...

Ich komme, wenn du willst
I'll come if you like

❐ Word Order: Main Clauses

◆ In a main clause the subject comes first and is followed by the verb, as in English:

His mother (*subject*) drinks (*verb*) whisky → **1**

◆ If the verb is in a compound or passive tense, the auxiliary follows the subject and the past participle or infinitive goes to the end of the clause → **2**

◆ The verb is the second concept in a main clause. The first concept may be a word, phrase or clause (see p 226) → **3**

◆ Any reflexive pronoun follows the main verb in simple tenses and the auxiliary in compound tenses → **4**

◆ The order for articles, adjectives and nouns is as in English: *article + adjective(s) + noun* → **5**

◆ A direct object usually follows an indirect, except where the direct object is a personal pronoun.

⚠ BUT: The indirect object can be placed last for emphasis, providing it is not a pronoun → **6**

◆ The position of adverbial expressions (see p 188) is not fixed. As a general rule they are placed close to the words to which they refer.

Adverbial items of *time* often come first in the clause, but this is flexible → **7**

Adverbial items of *place* can be placed at the beginning of a clause when emphasis is required → **8**

Adverbial items of *manner* are more likely to be within the clause, close to the word to which they refer → **9**

◆ Where there is more than one adverb, a useful rule of thumb is: "time, manner, place" → **10**

Examples

---

1 **Seine Mutter trinkt Whisky**
His mother drinks whisky

2 **Sie wird dir etwas sagen**   **Sie hat mir nichts gesagt**
She will tell you something   She told me nothing

   Es ist für ihn gekauft worden
It was bought for him

3
1ST CONCEPT	2ND CONCEPT	
Die neuen Waren	**kommen**	**morgen**
(The new goods are coming tomorrow)		
Was du gesagt hast,	**stimmt**	**nicht**
(What you said isn't true)		

4 **Er rasierte sich**   **Er hat sich rasiert**
He shaved   He (has) shaved

5 **ein alter Mann**   **diese alten Sachen**
an old man   these old things

6 **Ich gab dem Mann das Geld**
I gave the man the money

   Ich gab ihm das Geld   **Ich gab es ihm**
I gave him the money   I gave him it/I gave it to him

   Er gab das Geld seiner Schwester
He gave the money to his sister (*not his brother*)

7 **Gestern gingen wir ins Theater** OR:
   Wir gingen gestern ins Theater
We went to the theatre yesterday

8 **Dort haben sie Fußball gespielt** OR:
   Sie haben dort Fußball gespielt
They played football there

9 **Sie spielen gut Fußball**
They play football well

   Das war furchtbar teuer
It was terribly expensive

10 **Wir haben gestern gut hierhin gefunden**
We found our way here all right yesterday

☐ **Word Order: Main Clauses** (Continued)

- ◆ A pronoun object precedes all adverbs → **1**

- ◆ While the main verb must normally remain the second concept, the first concept need not always be the subject. Main clauses can begin with many things, including:

    an adverb → **2**
    a direct or indirect object → **3**
    an infinitive phrase → **4**
    a complement → **5**
    a past participle → **6**
    a prepositional phrase → **7**
    a clause acting as the object of the verb → **8**
    a subordinate clause → **9**

- ◆ If the subject does not begin a main clause, the verb and subject must be turned around or "inverted" → **2** - **9**

- ◆ Beginning a sentence with something other than the subject is frequent in German.
    It may however also be used for special effect to:

    highlight whatever is placed first in the clause → **10**
    emphasize the subject of the clause by forcing it from its initial position to the end of the clause → **11**

- ◆ After inversion, any reflexive pronoun precedes the subject, unless the subject is a pronoun → **12**

- ◆ The following do not cause inversion when placed at the beginning of a main clause, although inversion may be caused by something else placed after them:

    allein, denn, oder, sondern, und → **13**
    ja and **nein** → **14**
    certain exclamations: **ach, also, nun** *etc* → **15**
    words or phrases qualifying the subject: **auch, nur, sogar**, *etc*
    → **16**

---

1. **Sie haben es gestern sehr billig gekauft**
   They bought it very cheaply yesterday

2. **Gestern sind wir ins Theater gegangen**
   We went to the theatre yesterday

3. **So ein Kind habe ich noch nie gesehen!**
   I've never seen such a child!
   Seinen Freunden wollte er es nicht zeigen
   He wouldn't show it to his friends

4. **Seinen Freunden zu helfen, hat er nicht versucht**
   He didn't try to help his friends

5. **Deine Schwester war es**   It was your sister

6. **Geraucht hatte er nie**   He had never smoked

7. **In diesem Haus ist Mozart auf die Welt gekommen**
   Mozart was born in this house

8. **Was mit ihm los war, haben wir nicht herausgefunden**
   We never discovered what was wrong with him

9. **Nachdem ich ihn gesehen hatte, ging ich nach Hause**
   I went home after seeing him

10. **Dem würde ich nichts sagen!**
    I wouldn't tell *him* anything!

11. **An der Ecke stand eine riesengroße Fabrik**
    A huge factory stood on the corner

12. **Daran erinnerten sich die Zeugen nicht**
    The witnesses didn't remember that
    Daran erinnerten sie sich nicht
    They didn't remember that

13. **Peter ging nach Hause und Elsa blieb auf der Party**
    Peter went home and Elsa stayed at the party
    ⚠ BUT: **Peter ging nach Hause und unterwegs sah er Kurt**
    Peter went home and on the way he saw Kurt

14. **Nein, ich will nicht**   No, I don't want to
    ⚠ BUT: **Nein, das tue ich nicht**   No, I won't do that

15. **Also, wir fahren nach Hamburg**
    So we'll go to Hamburg
    ⚠ BUT: **Also, nach Hamburg wollt ihr fahren**
    So you want to go to Hamburg

16. **Sogar seine Mutter wollte es ihm nicht glauben**
    Even his mother wouldn't believe him
    ⚠ BUT: **Sogar mit dem Zug ginge es nicht schneller**
    It would be no faster even by train

❒ Word Order: Subordinate Clauses

◆ A subordinate clause may be introduced by:

1 a relative pronoun (see p 174) → ☐1

2 a subordinating conjunction (see p 222) → ☐2 - ☐3

◆ The subject follows the opening conjunction or relative pronoun - see **wir** and **er** → ☐1 - ☐3

◆ The main verb almost always goes to the end of a subordinate clause → ☐1 - ☐3

The exceptions to this are:

1 in a **wenn** clause where **wenn** is omitted (see p 64) → ☐4

2 in an indirect statement without **dass** (see p 64) → ☐5

◆ The order for articles, nouns, adjectives, adverbs, direct and indirect objects is the same as for main clauses (see p 224), but they are all placed between the subject of the clause and the verb → ☐6

◆ If the subject of a reflexive verb in a subordinate clause is a pronoun, the order is *subject pronoun + reflexive pronoun* → ☐7

If the subject is a noun, the reflexive pronoun may follow or precede it → ☐8

◆ Where one subordinate clause lies inside another, both still obey the order rule for subordinate clauses → ☐9

1. **Die Kinder, die wir gesehen haben ...**
The children whom we saw ...
2. **Da er nicht schwimmen wollte, ist er nicht mitgekommen**
As he didn't want to swim he didn't come
3. **Ich weiß, dass er zur Zeit in London wohnt**
I know he's living in London at the moment
Ich weiß nicht, ob er kommt
I don't know if he's coming
4. **Findest du meine Uhr, so ruf mich bitte an**
(= Wenn du meine Uhr findest, ruf mich bitte an)
If you find my watch, please give me a ring
5. **Er meint, er werde es innerhalb einer Stunde schaffen**
(= Er meint, dass er es innerhalb einer Stunde schaffen werde)
He thinks (that) he will manage it inside an hour
6. MAIN CLAUSE
Er ist gestern mit seiner Mutter in die Stadt gefahren
He went to town with his mother yesterday
SUBORDINATE CLAUSES
Da er gestern mit seiner Mutter in die Stadt gefahren ist, ...
Since he went to town with his mother yesterday ...
Der Junge, der gestern mit seiner Mutter in die Stadt gefahren ist, ...
The boy who went to town with his mother yesterday ...
Ich weiß, dass er gestern mit seiner Mutter in die Stadt gefahren ist
I know that he went to town with his mother yesterday
7. **Weil er sich nicht setzen wollte, ...**
Because he wouldn't sit down ...
8. **Weil das Kind sich nicht setzen wollte, ...** OR:
Weil sich das Kind nicht setzen wollte, ...
Because the child wouldn't sit down ...
9. **Er wusste, dass der Mann, mit dem er gesprochen hatte, bei einer Baufirma arbeitete**
He knew that the man he had been speaking to worked for a construction company

☐ Word Order

In the imperative

1   normal order → 1

2   with reflexive verbs → 2

3   with separable verbs → 3

4   with separable reflexive verbs → 4

In direct and indirect speech

- the verb of saying ("he replied/he said") must be inverted if it is placed within a quotation → 5

- the position of the verb in indirect speech depends on whether or not **dass** (see p 66) is used → 6

Verbs with separable prefixes (see pp 72 to 75)

- in main clauses the verb and prefix are separated in simple tenses and imperative forms → 7

- for compound tenses of main clauses and all tenses of subordinate clauses, the verb and its prefix are united at the end of the clause → 8

- in a present infinitive phrase (see p 46), the verb and prefix are joined together by **zu** and placed at the end of the phrase → 9

1. **Hol mir das Buch!** (*singular*)
   Holt mir das Buch! (*plural*) Fetch me that book!
   Holen Sie mir das Buch! (*polite*)

2. **Wasch dich sofort!** (*singular*)
   Wascht euch sofort! (*plural*) Wash yourself/yourselves
   Waschen Sie sich sofort! (*polite*) at once!

3. **Hör jetzt auf!** (*singular*)
   Hört jetzt auf! (*plural*) Stop it!
   Hören Sie jetzt auf! (*polite*)

4. **Dreh dich um!** (*singular*)
   Dreht euch um! (*plural*) Turn round!
   Drehen Sie sich um! (*polite*)

5. **„Meine Mutter" sagte er, „kommt erst morgen an"**
   "My mother", he said, "won't arrive till tomorrow"

6. **Er sagte, dass sie erst am nächsten Tag ankomme**
   He said that she would not arrive until the next day
   Er sagte, sie komme erst am nächsten Tag an
   He said she would not arrive until the next day

7. **Er machte die Tür zu**
   He closed the door
   Ich räume zuerst auf
   I'll clean up first
   Hol mich um 7 ab!
   Pick me up at 7!

8. **Er hat die Tür zugemacht**
   He closed the door
   Ich werde zuerst aufräumen
   I'll clean up first
   Er wurde um 7 abgeholt
   He was picked up at 7
   Wenn du mich um 7 abholst, ...
   If you pick me up at 7 ...
   Nachdem du mich abgeholt hast, ...
   After you've picked me up ...

9. **Um frühzeitig anzukommen, fuhren wir sofort ab**
   In order to arrive early we left immediately

☐ **Question Forms**

Direct questions

◆ In German, a direct question is formed by simply inverting the verb and subject → ☐1

◆ In compound tenses (see p 22 ff) the past participle or infinitive goes to the end of the clause → ☐2

◆ A statement can be made into a question by the addition of **nicht**, **nicht wahr** or **doch**, as with "isn't it" in English → ☐3

   Questions formed in this way normally expect the answer to be "yes".

◆ When a question is put in the negative, **doch** can be used to answer it more positively than **ja** → ☐4

Questions formed using interrogative words

◆ When questions are formed with **interrogative adverbs**, the subject and verb are inverted → ☐5

◆ When questions are formed with **interrogative pronouns** and **adjectives** (see pp 144 and 176 to 178), the word order is that of direct statements:

   1 as the subject of the verb at the beginning of the clause they do not cause inversion → ☐6
   2 if *not* the subject of the verb *and* at the beginning of the clause they do cause inversion → ☐7

Indirect questions

These are questions following verbs of asking and wondering etc. The verb comes at the end of an indirect question → ☐8

Examples

1 **Magst du ihn?**
Do you like him?

Gehst du ins Kino?
Do you go to the cinema? OR: Are you going to the cinema?

2 **Hast du ihn gesehen?**
Did you see him? OR: Have you seen him?

Wird sie mit ihm kommen?
Will she come with him?

3 **Das stimmt, nicht (wahr)?**
That's true, isn't it?

Das schaffst du doch?
You'll manage, won't you?

4 **Glaubst du mir nicht? — Doch!**
Don't you believe me? — Yes I do!

5 **Wann ist er gekommen?**
When did he come?

Wo willst du hin?
Where are you off to?

6 **Wer hat das gemacht?**
Who did this?

7 **Wem hast du es geschenkt?**
Who did you give it to?

8 **Er fragte, ob du mitkommen wolltest**
He asked if you wanted to come

Er möchte wissen, warum du nicht gekommen bist
He would like to know why you didn't come

❐ Negatives

A statement or question is made negative by adding:

nicht (*not*) or **nie** (*never*)

- The negative may be placed next to the phrase or word to which it refers. The negative meaning can be shifted from one element of the sentence to another in this way → 1

- **nie** can be placed at the beginning of a sentence for added emphasis, in which case the subject and verb are inverted → 2

- **nicht** comes at the end of a negative imperative, except when the verb is separable, in which case **nicht** *precedes* the separable prefix → 3

- The combination **nicht ein** is usually replaced by forms of **kein** (see p 126) → 4

- **doch** (see p 196) is used in place of **ja** to contradict a negative statement → 5

- Negative comparison is made with **nicht ... sondern** (*not ... but*).

  This construction is used to correct a previous false impression or idea → 6

---

1. **Mit ihr wollte er nicht sprechen**
   He didn't want to speak to *her*
   Er wollte nicht mit ihr sprechen
   He didn't *want* to speak to her

   Er will nicht morgen nach Hause
   OR: **Morgen will er nicht nach Hause**
   He doesn't want to go home *tomorrow*
   Er will morgen nicht nach Hause
   He doesn't want to go *home* tomorrow

   Wohnen Sie nicht in Dortmund?
   Don't you live in Dortmund?
   Warum ist er nicht mitgekommen?
   Why didn't he come with you?
   Waren Sie nie in Dortmund?
   Have you never been to Dortmund?

2. **Nie war sie glücklicher gewesen**
   She had never been happier

3. **Iss das nicht!**
   Don't eat that!
   Beeilen Sie sich nicht!
   Don't hurry!
   ⚠ BUT: **Geh nicht weg!**
   Don't go away!

4. **Gibt es keine Plätzchen?**
   Aren't there any biscuits?
   Kein einziges Kind hatte die Arbeit geschrieben
   Not a single child had done the work

5. **Du kommst nicht mit — Doch, ich komme mit**
   You're not coming — Yes I am

6. **Nicht Joachim, sondern sein Bruder war es**
   It wasn't Joachim, but his brother

Cardinal
(one, two etc)

Ordinal
(first, second etc)

null	0		
eins	1	**der erste** [2]	1.
zwei [1]	2	**der zweite** [1]	2.
drei	3	**der dritte**	3.
vier	4	**der vierte**	4.
fünf	5	**der fünfte**	5.
sechs	6	**der sechste**	6.
sieben	7	**der siebte**	7.
acht	8	**der achte**	8.
neun	9	**der neunte**	9.
zehn	10	**der zehnte**	10.
elf	11	**der elfte**	11.
zwölf	12	**der zwölfte**	12.
dreizehn	13	**der dreizehnte**	13.
vierzehn	14	**der vierzehnte**	14.
fünfzehn	15	**der fünfzehnte**	15.
sechzehn	16	**der sechzehnte**	16.
siebzehn	17	**der siebzehnte**	17.
achtzehn	18	**der achtzehnte**	18.
neunzehn	19	**der neunzehnte**	19.
zwanzig	20	**der zwanzigste**	20.
einundzwanzig	21	**der einundzwanzigste**	21.
zweiundzwanzig [1]	22	**der zweiundzwanzigste** [1]	22.
dreißig	30	**der dreißigste**	30.
vierzig	40	**der vierzigste**	40.
fünfzig	50	**der fünfzigste**	50.
sechzig	60	**der sechzigste**	60.

[1] **zwo** often replaces **zwei** in speech, to distinguish it clearly from **drei**: **zwo**, **zwoundzwanzig** *etc*.

[2] The ordinal number and the preceding definite article (and adjective if there is one) are declined, e.g.:

    bei seinem dritten Versuch *at his third attempt*

NUMBERS

siebzig	70	**der siebzigste**	70.
achtzig	80	**der achtzigste**	80.
neunzig	90	**der neunzigste**	90.
hundert	*a hundred*	**der hundertste**	100.
einhundert	*one hundred*		
hunderteins	101	**der hunderterste**	101.
hundertzwei	102	**der hundertzweite**	102.
hunderteinundzwanzig	121	**der hunderteinundzwanzigste**	121.
zweihundert	200	**der zweihundertste**	200.
tausend	*a thousand*	**der tausendste**	1000.
eintausend	*one thousand*		
tausendeins	1001	**der tausenderste**	1001.
zweitausend	2000	**der zweitausendste**	2000.
hunderttausend	100 000	**der hunderttausendste**	100 000.
eine Million	1 000 000	**der millionste**	1 000 000.

◆ With large numbers, spaces or full stops are used where English uses a comma, e.g.:

1.000.000 or 1 000 000 for 1,000,000 (*a million*)

◆ Decimals are written with a comma instead of a full stop, e.g.:

7,5 (**sieben Komma fünf**) for 7.5 (*seven point five*)

◆ When ordinal numbers are used as nouns, they are written with a capital letter, e.g.:

sie ist die Zehnte *she's the tenth*

Fractions

halb	**die Hälfte**	**eine halbe Stunde**
half (a)	half (the)	half an hour
das Drittel	**zwei Drittel**	**das Viertel**
third	two thirds	quarter
drei Viertel	**anderthalb, eineinhalb**	**zweieinhalb**
three quarters	one and a half	two and a half

Wie spät ist es? / Wie viel Uhr ist es?
What time is it?

Es ist ...
It's ...

00.00	**Mitternacht / null Uhr / vierundzwanzig Uhr / zwölf Uhr**
00.10	**zehn (Minuten) nach zwölf / null Uhr zehn**
00.15	**Viertel nach zwölf / null Uhr fünfzehn**
00.30	**halb eins / null Uhr dreißig**
00.40	**zwanzig (Minuten) vor eins / null Uhr vierzig**
00.45	**Viertel vor eins / drei viertel eins /**
	null Uhr fünfundvierzig
01.00	**ein Uhr**
01.10	**zehn (Minuten) nach eins / ein Uhr zehn**
01.15	**Viertel nach eins / ein Uhr fünfzehn**
01.30	**halb zwei /ein Uhr dreißig**
01.40	**zwanzig (Minuten) vor zwei / ein Uhr vierzig**
01.45	**Viertel vor zwei / drei viertel zwei /**
	ein Uhr fünfundvierzig
01.50	**zehn (Minuten) vor zwei / ein Uhr fünfzig**
12.00	**zwölf Uhr**
12.30	**halb eins / zwölf Uhr dreißig**
13.00	**ein Uhr / dreizehn Uhr**
16.30	**halb fünf / sechzehn Uhr dreißig**
22.00	**zehn Uhr / zweiundzwanzig Uhr / zwoundzwanzig Uhr**

morgen um halb drei
at half past two tomorrow

um drei Uhr (nachmittags)
at three (pm)

kurz vor zehn Uhr
just before ten o'clock

gegen vier Uhr (nachmittags)
towards four o'clock (in the afternoon)

erst um halb neun
not until half past eight

ab neun Uhr
from nine o'clock onwards

morgen früh/Abend
tomorrow morning/evening

Dates

Der Wievielte ist heute? / Welches Datum haben wir heute?
What's the date today?

Heute ist ...	It's ...
der zwanzigste März	the twentieth of March
der Zwanzigste	the twentieth

Heute haben wir ...	It's ...
den zwanzigsten März	the twentieth of March
den Zwanzigsten	the twentieth

Am Wievielten findet es statt?   When does it take place?

Es findet am ersten April statt ... ... on the first of April

Es findet am Ersten statt   ... on the first

Es findet (am) Montag, den ersten April statt OR:
Es findet Montag, den 1. April statt
It takes place on Monday, the first of April / April 1st

Years

Er wurde 1970 geboren	**(im Jahre) 1994**
He was born in 1970	in 1994

Other expressions

im Dezember/Januar *etc*	**im Winter/Sommer/Herbst/Frühling**
in December/January *etc*	in winter/summer/autumn/spring
nächstes Jahr	**Anfang September**
next year	at the beginning of September

❏ Punctuation

German punctuation differs from English in the following cases:

Commas

- Decimal places are always shown by a comma → ☐1

- Large numbers are separated off by means of a space or a full stop → ☐2

- Subordinate clauses are always marked off from the rest of the sentence by a comma → ☐3

  This applies to all types of subordinate clause, e.g.:

  1 clauses with an adverbial function → ☐3

  2 relative clauses → ☐4

  3 clauses containing indirect speech → ☐5

- A comma is not required between two main clauses linked by **und** or **oder** → ☐6

Exclamation marks

- Exclamation marks are used after imperative forms unless these are not intended as commands → ☐7

- An exclamation mark is occasionally used after the name at the beginning of a letter, but this tends to be rather old-fashioned → ☐8

1 **3,4 (drei Komma vier)**
3.4 (three point four)

2 **20 000**
OR: **20.000 (zwanzigtausend)**
20,000 (twenty thousand)

3 **Als er nach Hause kam, war sie schon weg**
She had already gone when he came home

Er bleibt gesund, obwohl er zu viel trinkt
He stays healthy, even though he drinks too much

4 **Der Mann, mit dem sie verheiratet ist, soll sehr reich sein**
The man she is married to is said to be very rich

5 **Er sagt, es gefällt ihm nicht**
He says he doesn't like it

6 **Wir gehen ins Kino oder wir bleiben zu Hause**
We'll go to the cinema or stay at home

7 **Steh auf!**
Get up!

Bitte nehmen Sie doch Platz
Do please sit down

8 **Liebe Elke! ...**
Dear Elke, ...

Sehr geehrter Herr Braun!...
Dear Mr Braun, ...

INDEX

The following index lists comprehensively both grammatical terms and *key words* in **German** and English contained in this book.

INDEX

INDEX

INDEX